THE
ENCYCLOPEDIA
OF
WORLD
AIRCRAFT

1/99

THE
ENCYCLOPEDIA
OF
WORLD
AIRCRAFT

General Editor: David Donald

BLITZ EDITIONS

REF
629.133
ENC

Copyright © 1997 Orbis Publishing Ltd
Copyright © 1997 Aerospace Publishing

All rights reserved. No part of this publication may be reproduced,
stored in a retrieval system, or transmitted in any form or by
any means, electronic, mechanical, photocopying, recording
or otherwise, without the prior written permission from the
publishers and the copyright holders.

This edition published in 1997 by Blitz Editions
an imprint of Bookmart Ltd
Registered Number 2372865
Trading as Bookmart Ltd
Desford Road
Enderby
Leicester LE9 5AD

Reprinted 1998

ISBN 1-85605-375-X

This material was previously published in 1990 as part of the
reference set *Airplane*

Produced by Brown Packaging Books Ltd
Bradley's Close
74-77 White Lion Street
London N1 9PF

Printed in Italy

100.00

Chronology of Flight

17 December 1903
At Kitty Hawk in North Carolina, Orville Wright makes the first controlled, powered flight in the *Wright Flyer*.

1 January 1914
In Florida, the world's first passenger air service begins operations between St Petersburg and Tampa Bay.

27 May 1919
A US Navy Curtiss flying boat, piloted by Lieutenant-Commander Albert Read, becomes the first aircraft to cross the Atlantic.

31 August 1924
Six US Army Air Service officers reach Labrador, having completed a circumnavigation of the globe, in nearly 175 days.

30 September 1929
German automobile manufacturer Fritz von Opel makes a 1.6-km (1-mile) flight in a rocket powered aircraft, the *Ente* (Duck).

24 May 1930
26-year-old Englishwoman Amy Johnson arrives in Darwin, Australia, after her epic 19-day flight from England.

21 May 1932
American Amelia Earhart becomes the first woman to make a non-stop solo crossing of the Atlantic, in 14 hrs 54 mins.

5 March 1936
Supermarine unveils the prototype Spitfire, destined to become one of the most famous and influential aircraft of all time.

27 August 1939
Heinkel test pilot Captain Erich Warsitz makes the maiden flight in the first turbojet powered aircraft, the He 178.

13 May, 1940
Russian-born Igor Sikorsky's VS-300 helicopter makes its first free flight.

14 October 1947
In a historic flight from Muroc Dry Lake in California Captain Charles "Chuck" Yeager flies faster than the speed of sound in a Bell X-1, nicknamed *Glamorous Glennis*.

2 March 1949
A Boeing B-50A bomber completes the first non-stop round-the-world flight. The *Lucky Lady II* makes the flight in 94 hours.

8 November 1950
In the first aerial combat between jet aircraft, Lieutenant Russell J. Brown in an F-80C Shooting Star brings down a Chinese MiG 15 over South Korea.

15 August 1951
Bill Bridgeman, flying the second Douglas D-558-II Skyrocket, sets a new world altitude record of 25,924 m (74,494 ft).

3 May 1952
The first Comet jet airliner goes into service on the London—South Africa route with BOAC. The staged journey takes nearly 24 hours.

24 May 1956
The Piper Comanche is launched.

21 December 1957
The first flight of the Boeing 707-120 takes place.

6 June 1967
The Boeing company deliver their thousandth jet airliner, a 707–323.

9 April 1969
The first Harrier jump-jets go into front-line service with the Royal Air Force.

21 January 1970
A Boeing 747 named *Clipper Young America* enters service with Pan Am, heralding a new era for commercial aviation.

1 September 1974
One of the USAF's highly secretive SR–71A Blackbird reconnaissance aircraft crosses the Atlantic in less than two hours.

21 January 1976
Air France and British Airways begin using Concorde airliners for scheduled passenger services.

11 August 1986
A Westland Lynx helicopter fitted with special composite rotor blades sets a new world speed record for helicopters. It averages 400.87 km/h (249.09 mph) over a 15-km (9.3-mile) course.

23 December 1986
Dick Rutan and co-pilot Jeanna Yeager land after their non-stop, unrefuelled flight around the world in the *Voyager* aircraft.

10 November 1988
The USAF unveils the Lockheed F–117A Nighthawk 'stealth' fighter. The aircraft, operational since 1983, is shrouded in secrecy.

17 July 1989
Northrop reveal the revolutionary B-2 Stealth bomber. The aircraft are expected to cost US$500 million each.

25 May 1995
Boeing–Sikorsky's new scout helicopter, the RAH–66 Comanche, is unveiled.

Introduction

It is difficult to underestimate the number and diversity of aircraft that have been designed, built and flown during the twentieth century, and fascinating to understand the myriad ways in which those aircraft have been used. We have only to look back over the last century to appreciate the astonishing progress that has taken place in the field of aircraft design. This comprehensive encyclopedia examines thousands of aircraft in-depth; from the wood, wire and fabric machines of the early pioneers such as Bleriot and Farnam, to the hugely complex 'stealth' aircraft that exploded onto the world stage during the Gulf War.

Air superiority is arguably the single most important aspect of modern warfare, and one that military tacticians can ill-afford to ignore. Military aircraft have undoubtedly been the single greatest influence on modern warfare and it has become accepted knowledge that 'he who rules the skies, rules the land'.

An awesome forty years

Aircraft design has advanced at a mind boggling pace – The Sopwith Camel and the Hawker Hunter are so radically different that it is difficult to believe that they are separated by only forty years. In hindsight, we can say that aircraft such as the Supermarine Spitfire, the P-51 Mustang, and the B-36 Flying Fortress changed the outcome of World War Two, and it is inconceivable that the coalition forces would have attempted to liberate Kuwait in 1991 without establishing air superiority. Also featured are machines such as the doomed BAC TSR2, the hugely ambitious North American Valkyrie, and the bizarre Bell X-22A – aircraft that never made it past the prototype stage but which were still hugely influential. This book is a detailed guide

Kitty Hawk, North Carolina, December 17 1903. Brothers Orville and Wilbur Wright make the historic first flight in a heavier-than-air craft, the Wright Flyer.

to the warplanes that have battled for the skies since World War One; their development history, specifications, combat role and service use and help to indicate the changing needs of modern air forces over the past ninety years.

Commercial aviation has made similarly impressive progress. In May 1919 a US Navy pilot made the first aerial crossing of the Atlantic ocean. The flight took some 53 hours, in an exposed cockpit, and he was forced to stop four times during the course of the crossing. Eighty years later this journey can be achieved by Concorde in just two hours, while 100 passengers dine in air-conditioned comfort on smoked salmon and champagne. The ascendancy of commercial airlines has been meteoric, bringing the four corners of the globe within of millions of people and creating a world were transcontinental flights have become routine. But the spirit of aeronautical adventurer is still thriving – in 1986 Dick Rutan and Jeana Yeager flew the Rutan Voyager aircraft non-stop around the globe on a single tank of fuel, maintaining a tradition that has been alive since the days of Orville and Wilbur Wright. It is this spirit that will carry aviation pioneers into the next century, the desire to fly faster, higher, longer, and further, whilst answering the increasing pressure for fuel economy, safety and environmental compatibility.

Aircraft have been applied to many uses – medical evacuation, firefighting, traffic control, weather research, even driving cattle across the Australian outback. Perhaps the ultimate realisation of

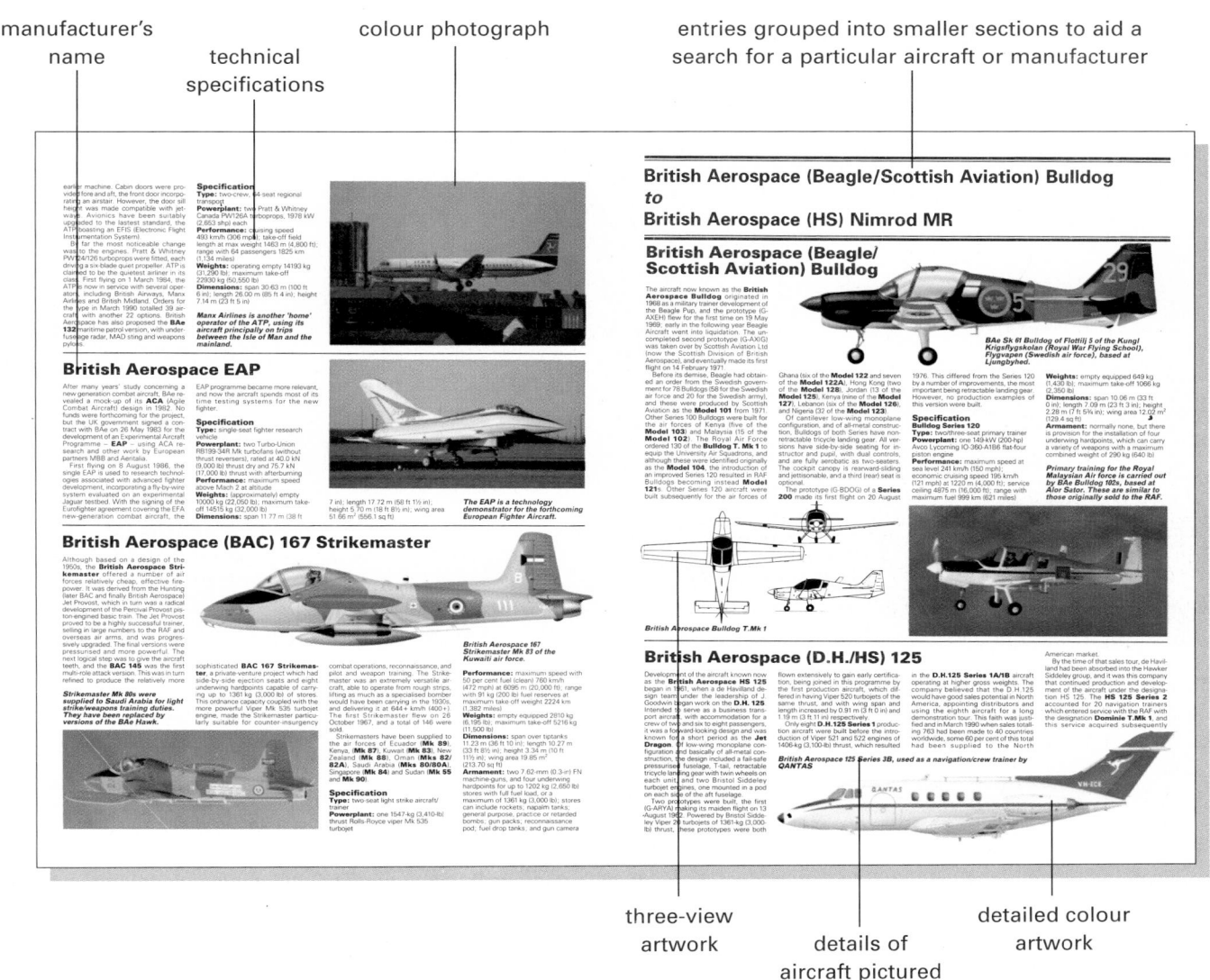

manufacturer's name

technical specifications

colour photograph

entries grouped into smaller sections to aid a search for a particular aircraft or manufacturer

three-view artwork

details of aircraft pictured

detailed colour artwork

'the flying machine' thus far has been the Space Shuttle, an major testimony to man's desire to conquer the skies. This book provides a comprehensive guide to the hundreds of manufacturers who have produced aircraft across the globe, from McDonnell-Douglas, Boeing, British Aerospace – the giants of the industry – to the smaller designers working with little more than their ingenuity. This is an invaluable guide to anyone with an interest in aviation.

How to use this book

Every page is packed with all the information you need. Full of photographs and illustrations, it's fascinating to browse through, yet designed in a way that makes it invaluable as a reference work.

Throughout the book the aircraft are listed alphabetically. The pages are grouped into small sections which open with a heading that gives the first and last entries of that section – a great help when leafing through the pages looking for a particular aircraft.

The information for each entry begins with a description of the aircraft and gives its background, history and the way it developed over the years. The text also lists any variants, indicated by bold type, that evolved from the original model.

Under the heading Specifications you'll find the facts and figures about each aircraft. It includes the type of aircraft and the technical information relevant to that model – its powerplant, its weight and dimensions, and its performance in terms of speed, climb rate, cruising speed, service ceiling, range and so on.

Many aircraft are illustrated with photographs or detailed side-profile artworks, each with its own caption. Many of the models are accompanied by line drawings showing the aircraft's outline.

As well as the alphabetical listing of the aircraft, a four-page index at the end of the book gives you an alternative way of finding the entry you need. The index lists all the aircraft by type – Commercial Airliners, Jet Fighters or Bombers, and so on.

AEG B, C, and J Series

The well-known German electrical company Allgemeine Elektrizitäts Gesellschaft (AEG) formed at an early date an aviation division that designed and built its first aircraft in 1910. By the time that World War I started in 1914, AEG had become established as an aircraft manufacturer, and was soon called upon to provide military aircraft for the German air service.

As a beginning, small numbers of an unarmed two-seat reconnaissance aircraft were acquired for service in 1914. Designated **B.I**, this was a three-bay biplane of unequal span, and introduced what was to become a standard form of construction for this company's aircraft. Almost the entire structure was welded steel tube, the wings each having two tubular steel spars with wooden ribs to provide the required aerofoil contours before being covered by fabric. The tail-skid landing gear included an unusual feature, namely a nosewheel unit mounted beneath the engine to protect the propeller from damage if the aircraft nosed-over during landing. The engine installation was almost unbelievably untidy, with most of the 100-hp (75-kW) Mercedes D.I. inline engine exposed above the streamlined nose cowling. Large cooling radiators for the engine were mounted on each side of the fuselage.

The **B.II** which followed in late 1914 represented an attempt to tidy up the design. This was a two-bay biplane of reduced span, and introduced the more powerful 89-kW (120-hp) Mercedes D.II engine, but no attempt had been made to improve the powerplant/radiator installation. It was followed in 1915 by a generally similar **B.III** that retained the same powerplant, but incorporated some detail improvements as the result of experience gained in service use. It was to be the last of AEG's unarmed reconnaissance types, for little time had been lost by the combatants in the introduction of weapons that could be used to attack and destroy an adversary's aircraft.

Little real development was necessary for the evolution of the **C.I** that was introduced in March 1915. It was virtually a B.II (the best of the B-series) with a 112-kW (150-hp) Benz Bz.III inline engine, and with a machine-gun for the observer on a flexible mount in the aft cockpit. With the emphasis changing gradually from a stable reconnaissance platform towards a more manoeuvrable aircraft that could evade enemy scouts and fight back, the **C.II** of October 1915 was a refined version of the C.I. More importantly its dimensions had been reduced to improve manoeuvrability and this, allied to a weight reduction of nearly 5 per cent, sharpened its performance.

An experimental **C.III** followed soon afterwards. This introduced a deep fuselage that filled the gap between the biplane wings, with a view to providing the crew with an unobstructed forward view over the upper wing and, by seating the pilot aft, to make it possible for the observer to fire his machine-gun forward, clear of the propeller disc. There must have been shortcomings, however, for despite the ingenuity of the idea, no production examples were built.

The most extensively constructed member of the C series was the **C.IV**, its development spurred by the German air service's growing appreciation of the importance of aerial reconnaissance. Generally similar in configuration to, but a little larger than the C.II, it introduced the more powerful Mercedes D.III engine, a fixed forward-firing machine-gun for the pilot, and a three-position variable-incidence tailplane that was adjustable on the ground. Production figures for the C.IV are not known precisely, but are estimated at 400.

The C series ended with experimental versions that included one **C.IV.N** night bomber, generally similar to the C.IV except that it had increased-span three-bay wings and a 150-hp (112-kW) Benz Bz.III engine; a **C.V** two-seat reconnaissance prototype, similar to the basic C.IV but with a 164-kW (220-hp) Mercedes engine; two **C.VIIIs** with single-bay wings and Mercedes D.III engine; one improved single-bay **C.VIII** with the same powerplant; and a **C.VIII.Dr** triplane version of the C.VIII.

In 1916 the German air service introduced *Infanterie-Flieger* units (infantry contact patrol units), which would now be regarded as close support or ground attack squadrons. Proving to be valuable when used on a small scale during the Battle of Verdun, such units were soon the subject of a high-priority programme of expansion and equipment. AEG's **J.I** was developed hurriedly to meet this requirement until a more suitable aircraft could be designed and developed for this specific role. The J.I was virtually a C.IV provided with a 200-hp (149-kW) Benz Bz.IV engine, plus 390 kg (860 lb) of armour plate to protect the crew and powerplant. Two LMG 08/15 machine-guns were mounted in the floor of the aft cockpit, pointing downward and forward at an angle of about 45°, so that they could be used for strafing enemy trenches or columns of infantry on the march. In addition, the observer had a Parabellum machine-gun on a ring mounting. The **J.II** of 1918 was generally similar, but introduced several refinements of controls and control surfaces. More than 600 J.I/J.II aircraft were built.

AEG C.IV of Fliegerabteilung (A) 224, Château Bellingkamps, spring 1917.

Specification
AEG C.IV
Type: two-seat armed reconnaissance aircraft
Powerplant: one 119-kW (160-hp) Mercedes D.III inline piston engine
Performance: maximum speed 158 km/h (98 mph); service ceiling 5000 m (16,400 ft); endurance 4 hours
Weights: empty 800 kg (1,764 lb); maximum take-off 1120 kg (2,469 lb)
Dimensions: span 13.45 m (44 ft 1½ in) length 7.15 m (23 ft 5½ in); height 3.35 m (10 ft 11¾ in); wing area 39.00 m² (419.81 sq ft)
Armament: one fixed forward-firing 7.92-mm (0.31-in) LMG 08/15 machine-gun, and one 7.92-mm (0.31-in) Parabellum machine-gun for observer on ring mounting

Aeritalia G91R

The Fiat G91 design was the winner of a NATO requirement for a light fighter/tactical support aircraft formulated in December 1953 and issued to European aircraft manufacturers early in 1954. Although the proposal that the G91 should become standard equipment in NATO air forces was not realised, the aircraft was subsequently built in substantial numbers in Italy and, under licence, in Germany, and equipped the air forces of three countries.

Externally resembling a scaled-down North American F-86K Sabre, the Fiat G91 was first flown on 9 August 1956 and during technical evaluation trials in France in 1957 the aircraft met all the requirements of the official specification, particularly regarding the ability to operate with or without external loads from semi-prepared grass airstrips.

The initial Fiat G91 production version was a ground-attack fighter. Deliveries commenced early in 1958, and the G91 became operational with the Italian air force in February 1959. After extensive trials the Fiat G91 was also adopted by the new Federal German air force in 1958 and a licence-production agreement between Fiat and Flugzeug Union Süd (Messerschmitt-Dornier-Heinkel) was signed on 11 March 1959.

The Fiat G91 is simple, light and easy to fly, and has generally proved itself in service. The basic aircraft was progressively made more versatile by various combinations of underwing stores and the evolution of new combat tactics. The importance of high-speed armed reconnaissance led to the development of a specialised photographic reconnaissance version of the basic G91 already by 1957. The initial variant, the **Fiat G91R/1**, first flown in 1959, is essentially a standard G91 ground-attack fighter equipped with three 70-mm focal length cameras in a shortened nose section for front and oblique photography; it is also possible to take vertical photographs from high altitudes. Adopted by the Italian air force, this modification also aroused interest in the USA and 10

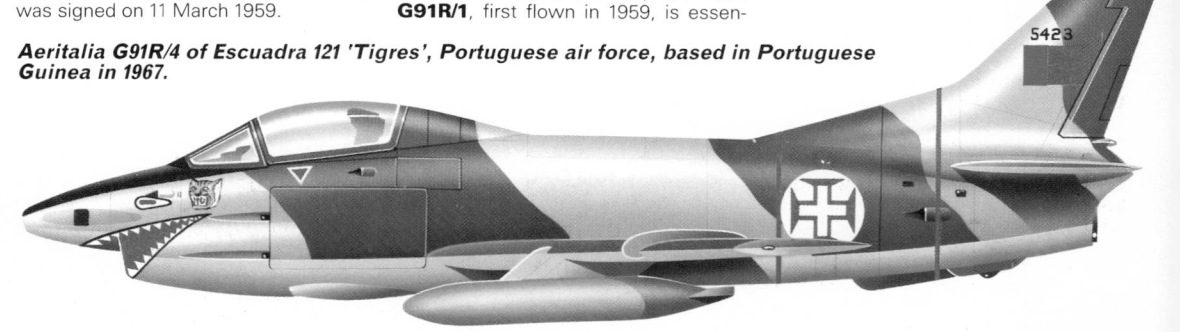

Aeritalia G91R/4 of Escuadra 121 'Tigres', Portuguese air force, based in Portuguese Guinea in 1967.

Part of the important Luftwaffe procurement of the G91R is seen in assembly by Dornier at Oberpfaffenhofen. These aircraft, intended for the 54th Reconnaissance Wing based at Oldenburg, are almost completed and this assembly paved the way for full licensed production of the G91.

G91R/1 aircraft were evaluated by the USAF during 1961-62.

The **G91R/1A** is similar, but features improved navigational aids as fitted to the **G91R/3** variant to make it independent of ground installations; the maximum under-wing ordnance has also been increased. A variant with reinforced structure, wheel brakes of increased capacity, tubeless tyres and some equipment changes is designated **G91R/1B** and also became operational with the Italian air force. This was followed by the G91R/3, which is similar to the G91R/1B, but built to West German specifications: it carries an armament of two 30-mm cannon instead of machine-guns. It also features certain equipment changes, including the installation of doppler radar and Position and Homing Indicator. The first Federal German air force unit equipped with G91R/3 was commissioned on 5 May 1962. This version was also subject to the first licence-production agreement between Fiat and FUS in Germany; of the total of 344 aircraft, 74 were built by Fiat (with 12 assembled by Dornier) and the remaining 270 in Germany, the first jet combat aircraft built in Germany since 1945.

The first Dornier-built G91R/3 was flown on 20 July 1965, the last in May 1966. Two Fiat G91R/3s were also evaluated by the US Army in the USA early in 1961.

The next variant, the **G91R/4**, is basically a G91R/3 with R/1 armament and some equipment changes. A total of 50 were procured by US authorities under the MAP scheme for Greece and Turkey but diverted instead to the Federal German air force; later the remaining 40 aircraft were transferred to the Portuguese air force.

Aeritalia G91R/1A of the 51° Aerobrigata, 14° Stormo, Italian air force. Note the four-gun armament.

Specification

Type: single-seat tactical strike/reconnaissance fighter
Powerplant: one 2268-kg (5000-lb) Fiat-built Bristol Siddeley Orpheus 803 turbojet
Performance: (at basic take-off weight) maximum speed at sea level 1075 km/h (668 mph); maximum level speed at 1520 m (5,000 ft) 1086 km/h (675 mph) or Mach 0.87; economical cruising speed 650 km/h (403 mph); initial rate of climb 1830 m (6,003 ft) per minute; service ceiling 13100 m (42,978 ft); combat radius (standard

fuel) 320 km (200 miles); ferry range 1850 km (1,150 miles)
Weights: empty 3100 kg (6,835 lb); basic operation take-off 5440 kg (11,995 lb); maximum take-off 5500 kg (12,125 lb)
Dimensions: wingspan 8.56 m (28 ft 1 in); length overall 10.30 m (33 ft 9¼ in); height overall 4.00 m (13 ft 1¼ in); wing area 16.42² (176.74 sq ft)
Armament: (G91R1) four 12.7-mm (0.50-in) Colt-Browning machine-guns (300 rpg) plus four underwing pylons (two inner) for two 227-kg (500-lb)

bombs, tactical nuclear weapons, Nord 5103 air-to-air guided missiles, clusters of six 76-mm (3-in) air-to-air rockets, honeycomb packs of 31 air-to-ground folding-fin rockets, pods containing one 12.7-mm (0.50-in) machine-gun with 250 rds; two outer for Nord 5103 missiles, 113-kg (250-lb) bombs, honeycomb packs of 19 folding-fin rockets, or gun pods as above; Photographic equipment: three 70-mm Vinten cameras
G91R/1A: as above, except for

improved navigational equipment
G91R/1B: as above, but with detailed improvements
G91R/3: two 30-mm DEFA cannon (125 rpg) instead of machine-guns; three 70-mm Vinten cameras; pylon loads similar
G91R/4: as G91R/3 but with four 12.7-mm (0.50-in) machine-guns; camera and pylon equipment same
G91R/6: an experimental variant with two 30-mm DEFA cannon and two AS.20 or AS.30 missiles on underwing pylons

Aeritalia G91T

The **Fiat G91T** two-seat version of the G91 ground-attack fighter was evolved during 1958 for advanced training at transonic speeds. Intentionally, the G91T was designed with minimum modifications to produce an aircraft that would be suitable for both training and combat tasks at short notice. The airframe is similar to the basic G91 except for a slightly longer fuselage with a new cockpit for two in tandem.

The first G91T was flown on 31 May 1960 powered by a Bristol Orpheus BOr.803-2 turbojet engine. A total of 76 was produced for the Italian air force under the designation **G91T/1**. The **Fiat G91T/3** differs only in equipment changes. Some 66 were produced for the Federal German air force (44 built by Fiat and 22 under licence in Germany). The last Dornier-built G91T/3 was delivered to the Federal German air force on 19 October 1972.

The **G91T/4** was a proposed G91T/1 variant with Lockheed F-104G Starfighter electronics, but it remained in the project stage.

Portugal is the last major user of the early G91 variants, its fleet containing a small number of G91Ts for training purposes.

Specification

Type: two seat transonic trainer
Powerplant: one 2268-kg (5,000-lb) Fiat-built Bristol Siddeley Orpheus 803 turbojet
Performance: (at basic take-off weight) maximum level speed at 1524 m (5,000 ft) 1030 km/h (640 mph); economical cruising speed of 650 km/h (403 mph); service ceiling 12200 m (40,000 ft); take-off to clear 15 m (50 ft) 1450 m (4,750 ft)

Below: This Waffenschule 50 G91T/3 has dayglo panels for high conspicuity during training missions.

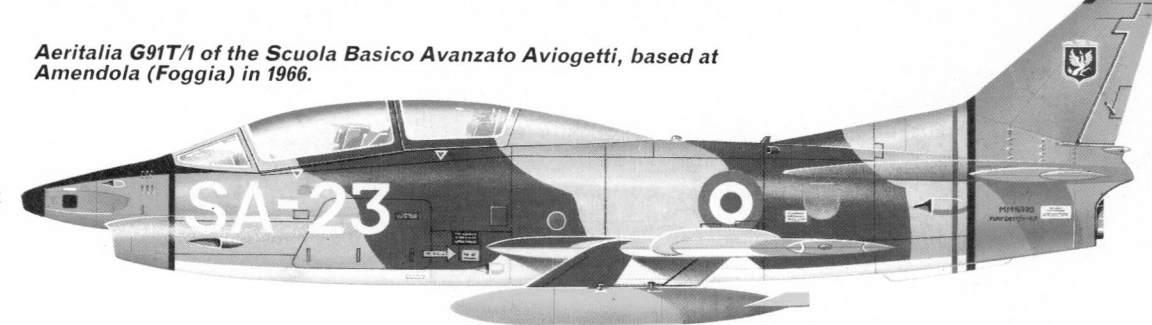

Aeritalia G91T/1 of the Scuola Basico Avanzato Aviogetti, based at Amendola (Foggia) in 1966.

Weights: basic operating 3865 kg (8,520 lb); basic take-off 5500 kg (12,125 lb); maximum take-off 6050 kg (13,340 lb)
Dimensions: wingspan 8.56 m (28 ft 1 in); length 11.67 m (38 ft 3½ in); height 4.45 m (14 ft 7¼ in); wing area 16.42 m^2 (176.74 sq ft)
Armament: two 12.7-mm (0.50-in) Colt-Browning machine-guns; two underwing pylons for light bombs, missiles, or extra fuel tanks

Aeritalia G91Y

The **Aeritalia (Fiat) G91Y** is essentially a twin-engined development of the G91. Project work in response to a specific Italian air force requirement for a light ground attack/fighter-reconnaissance aircraft began in 1965. The G91Y was based on the G91T airframe, the major change being the introduction of two General Electric J85-GE-13A turbojets in place of the single Bristol Siddeley Orpheus 803, giving a significant boost in power (over 60 per cent) at a minimum increase in powerplant weight. This improved power/weight ratio enables the new aircraft to carry considerably heavier military loads and/or more fuel, apart from the improved safety factor in combat and the ability to cruise with one engine stopped to extend the flight endurance.

The complete airframe structure has been extensively redesigned, incorporating the latest aerodynamic innovations and avionics, including an integrated nav/attack system.

Two prototypes of the G91Y were built, the first flying on 27 December 1966. The flight tests were generally successful and the new aircraft was accepted by the Italian air force. The pre-production batch comprises 20 aircraft, the first of which was flown in July 1968. At that time, plans were in hand for several variants of the basic G91Y, such as the **G91Y/T** basic/advanced trainer and the **G91Y/S** to meet Swiss specifications for a ground-attack aircraft, but none of these were built.

In the event, the pre-production series was followed by the initial 35 production G91Ys for the Italian air force.

The G91Y production version differs from the prototypes in having a slightly slimmer rear fuselage without the two ventral fins initially fitted.

The pilot is equipped with a zero-zero ejector seat and accommodated in an armoured, pressurised and air-conditioned cockpit.

Specification
Type: single-seat tactical strike/

The twin-engined G91Y has a more purposeful look to it compared with earlier variants. The powerplant and additional avionics made it a useful light strike platform.

reconnaissance fighter
Powerplant: two 1236-kg (2.725-lb) dry or 1850-kh (4,080-lb) with afterburning General Electric J85-GE-13A turbojets
Performance: (at maximum take-off weight) maximum speed at sea level Mach 0.93; maximum speed at 9145 m (30,000 ft) Mach 0.95; economical cruising speed at 10670 m (35,000 ft) Mach 0.75; maximum rate of climb at sea level (with afterburning) 5180 m (17,000 ft) per minute; service ceiling 12500 m (41,000 ft); take-off to 15 m (50 ft) 1100 m (3,610 ft); typical combat radius at sea level 600 km (372 miles); lo-lo-lo mission with 1320 kg (2,910 lb) load 385 km (240 miles); ferry range with maximum fuel 3500 km (2,175 miles)
Weights: basic empty 3682 kg (8,117 lb); normal take-off 7800 kg (17,196 lb); maximum overload 8700 kg (19,180 lb)
Dimensions: wingspan 9.01 m (29 ft 6½ in); length 11.67 m (38 ft 3½ in); height 4.43 m (14 ft 6½ in); wing area 18.13 m^2 (195.15 sq ft)
Armament: two 30-mm DEFA

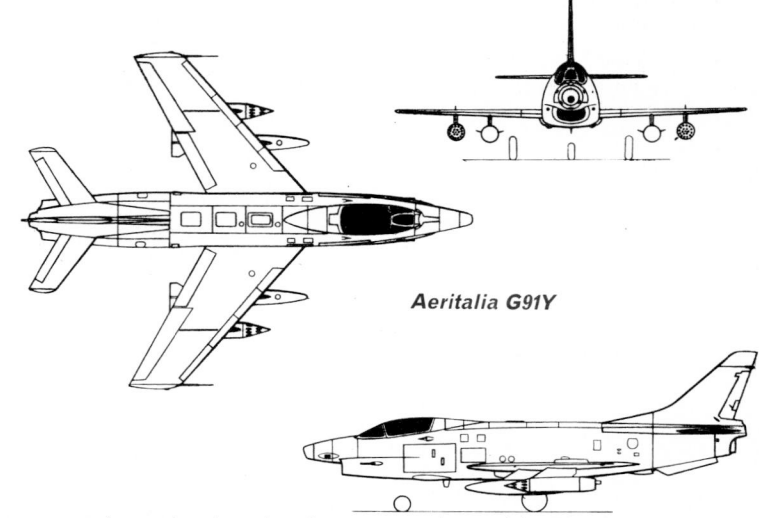

Aeritalia G91Y

cannon; four underwing pylons for 454-kg (1,000-lb) bombs, 340-kg (750-lb) napalm containers, rocket packs

each containing 70 or 28 50-mm (2-in) rockets or four 127-mm (5-in) rocket containers

Aeritalia G222

The initial **Aeritalia G222** originated with NBMR-4 (NATO Basic Military Requirement Four) formulated in 1962, resulting in several V/STOL tactical transport projects (using combined cruise turboprops and lift jets), none of which was realised. However, the research project contract for the G222 V/STOL transport awarded to Fiat by the Italian air force in 1963 was extended to cover the type's subsequent development in

more conventional form. An official contract for two military transport prototypes, originally designated G222TCM, and a static test airframe, was finally signed in 1968, the aircraft being considered a successor to the ageing Fairchild C-119 transports then in Italian service. Delays caused by changes in official policy, take-over of the parent company, and funding problems held up the completion of the first prototype, and it was not flown until 18 July 1970. The second prototype joined the flight-test programme on 21 July 1971. These

aircraft have 2283/2141-kW (3,060/2,870-shp) CT64-820 turboshaft engines and are unpressurised; the production model is pressurised, and fully air-conditioned and able to operate from semi-prepared airstrips.

The highly successful trials resulted in a firm Italian order for 44 production G222s in August 1972; by that time arrangements had been made to involve most of the Italian aircraft industry in the G222 programme.

The G222 airframe was redesigned once more to take the more powerful

General Electric T64-P4D turboprop engines and incorporate other detail improvements. The production prototype was flown on 23 December 1975, by which time Aeritalia had also obtained its first export order from Argentina.

The fuselage of the basic G222 transport version is an all-metal fail-safe structure, the underside of which forms a loading ramp. In standard troop-transport configuration the G222 carries 44 fully-equipped troops (32 sidewall seats and 12 folding seats), as a paratroop transport 32 (in side wall seats). As an

The G222 has superb performance for a transport aircraft, able to operate from very short, rough strips. The Italian air force is the major user, although examples have been exported.

ambulance, the G222 has space for 36 stretcher cases and two seated casualties, plus four medical attendants, while converted for cargo transport the aircraft has provision for a 1500-kg (3,305-lb) capacity cargo hoist and 135 tie-down points.

The basic G222 airframe is most suitable for adaptation to other military and civil roles, such as maritime patrol/anti-submarine warfare, surveillance and navaid/radar inspection. A prototype of the ECM version, designated **G222VS** *(Versione Speciale)* was flown on 9 March 1978 and has undergone protracted operational suitability trials. It is equipped with extensive electronic installations, and carries a flight crew of two, plus 10 systems operators.

A navaid/radar investigation/calibration version has also been completed, designated **G222RM** *(Radiomissura)* and used by the Italian air force. Exter-

nally similar to the standard transport version this modification has facilities to check VOR, ILS, TACAN and DME; it also has optional secondary survey capabilities for multiple control of approach and ground-control radars.

Another new version intended mainly for export to the Middle East and now in production is the G222 tactical transport powered by 3,400-shp (3536-kW) Rolls-Royce Tyne turboprop engines. Deliveries of the Tyne-powered **G222T** to Libya began in 1981. Other operators are Argentina, Somalia and Dubai.

In the civil field, successful trials have been carried out with a **G222 SAMA** fire-fighting modification (rebuilt second G222 prototype with 6300 litre/1,836-imperial gallon water tank), and projects exist for crop-spraying and aerial photogrammetry variants.

Specification
Type: twin-turboprop general-purpose transport
Powerplant: two 2536-kW (3,400-shp) Fiat-built General Electric T64-GE-P4D turboprops driving Hamilton Standard 63E60 three-blade variable-pitch propellers; provision in fuselage

for eight Aerojet General jet-assisted take-off rockets, delivering a total additional thrust of 3600kg (7,937 lb) for take-off in overload condition
Performance: (standard transport at maximum take-off weight) maximum speed at 4575 m (15,000 ft) 540 km/h (336 mph); cruising speed at 4500 m (14,750 ft) 360 km/h (224 mph); maximum rate of climb at sea-level 520 m (1,705 ft) per minute; time to 4500 m (14,750 ft) 8 minutes 35 seconds; service ceiling 7620 m (25,000 ft); take-off run 840 m (756 ft); range with maximum payload at optimum cruising speed at 6000 m (19,685 ft) 700 km (435 miles); range with 44 fully-equipped troops 2220 km (1,380 miles); ferry range with maximum fuel 4950 km (3,075 miles)
Weights: (standard transport) empty 14590 kg (32,165 lb); maximum payload 8500 kg (18,740 lb); normal take-off 24500 kg (54,013 lb); maximum take-off and landing 26500 kg (58,422 lb)
Dimensions: span 28.70 m (94 ft 2 in); length 22.70 m (74 ft 5½ in); height 9.80 m (32 ft 1¾ in); wing area 82.00 m² (882.6 sq ft)

Aermacchi M.B.326

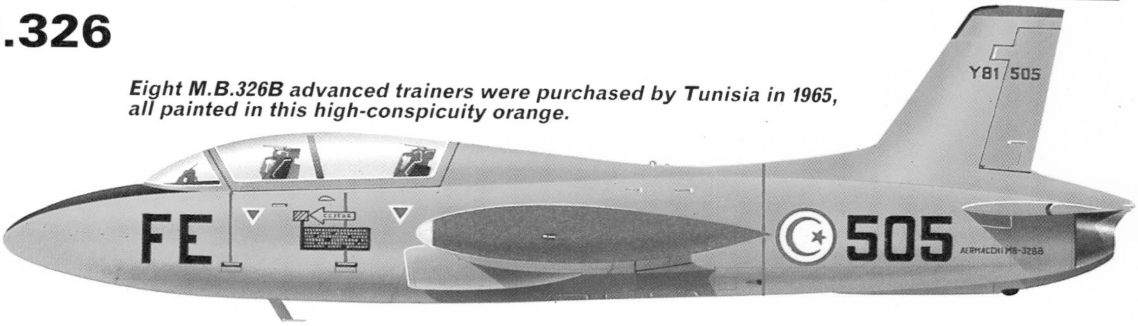

In an unbroken history dating back to before World War I, Aeronautica Macchi has produced more than 7,000 examples of aircraft of its own design; something like 10 per cent of that total are members of the **M.B.326** family of jet trainers and light attack aircraft. In company with the BAC Jet Provost and Fouga Magister, it is one of the classic types of its genre, having been in constant production for two decades.

Design began in 1954, and the first prototype made its initial flight on 10 December 1957, powered by a 794-kg (1,750-lb) static thrust Viper 8 turbojet. The second prototype, and 15 pre-production examples ordered by Italy's *Aeronautica Militare*, standardised on the 1134-kg (2,500-lb) Viper 11. The basic airframe, designed by Dr-Ing Ermanno Bazzocchi of Aermacchi, is simple, robust, stressed to g limits of +8 and −4, has full-equipped, pressurised tandem cockpits with twin ejection seats, and is intended for use in all stages of flying training from *ab initio* upwards. The first M.B.326s entered Italian service in February 1962, the AMI eventually receiving 85 of the initial model in addition to the 15 pre-production aircraft.

Ground-attack potential was first offered by Aermacchi on a proposed model known as the **M.B.326A**, to be equipped with six underwing attachments for alternative gun or rocket pods, bombs or other weapons. Such a version was not then required by the Italian air force, but similar armed models were ordered by Tunisia (eight **M.B.326B**s) and Ghana (nine **M.B.326F**s). Four examples of an unarmed **M.B.326D** were produced as airline pilot trainers for Alitalia. The **M.B.326H** for the Royal Australian Air Force (87) and Navy (10), had full armament provisions; they were assembled or licence-built in that country by CAC (Commonwealth Aircraft Corporation). **M.B.326M**s were produced, in two models, for the South African Air Force: 40 unarmed Italian-built aircraft for use in the training role, and about 125 assembled or licence-built in Transvaal by the Atlas Aircraft Corporation. The latter, known as the **Impala Mk 1**, have provision for externally-mounted armament.

All of the foregoing aircraft had the

Viper 11 as powerplant. Increased power was introduced in the spring of 1967, with the flight of the first Viper 540-powered **M.B.326G** prototype. Combined with some local reinforcement of the airframe, this can carry almost twice as heavy a weapons load as the Viper 11-engined models, and in production form is known as the **M.B.326GB**. This has been built in Italy for the Argentine navy (eight) and the air forces of Zaïre (17) and Zambia (20); a version with some features of the GB, but the Viper 11 engine, is the Italian air force's **M.B.326E**, six of which are newly-built and six converted from earlier M.B.326s. The largest overseas order to date has come from South America, where EMBRAER of Sao José dos Campos has completed the manufacture of 170 armed GCs (similar to the GB) under the designation **AT-26 Xavante** for the air forces of Brazil (167) and Togo (three).

Aermacchi's most recent two-seat version, the **M.B.326L**, is based upon the single-seat **M.B.326K** (see separate description) and likewise features a further increase in engine power by the use of a Viper 600 series engine. Two of the customers for the K model have also ordered the L type: Dubai (one) and Tunisia (four). Although fully equipped with dual controls for training, the M.B.326L retains the full attack/close-support potential of the K variant.

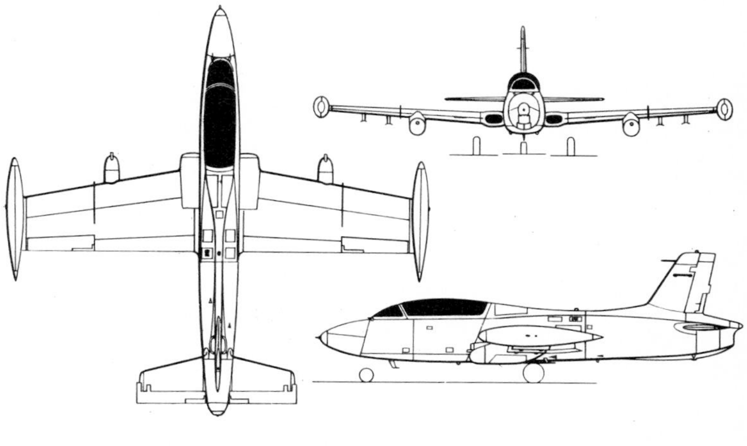

Specification
Type: two-seat basic/advanced trainer and light attack aircraft
Powerplant: one Rolls-Royce Viper turbojet 1134-kg (2,500-lb) static thrust Viper 11 in early models; 1547-kg (3,410-lb) static thrust Viper 20 Mk 540

Eight M.B.326B advanced trainers were purchased by Tunisia in 1965, all painted in this high-conspicuity orange.

Aermacchi M.B.326E, complete with four underwing hardpoints.

in GB, H and M; 1814-kg (4,000-lb) static thrust Viper 632-43 in L models
Performance: maximum speed (326) 806 km/h (501mph); (GB, clean) 867 km/h (539 mph); range on internal fuel (326) 1665 km (1,035 miles), (GB, clean) 1850 km (1,150 miles); combat radius (B, with armament) 460 km (290 miles), (GB, with armament) 648 km (403 miles); maximum rate of climb at sea level (B, with armament) 945 m (3,100 ft) per minute; (GB, with armament) 945 m (3,100 ft) per minute; service ceiling (326 clean) 12500 m (41,000 ft), (GB, clean) 14325 m (47,000 ft), (GB with armament) 11900 m (39,000 ft)
Weights: empty (326) 2237 kg (4,930 lb), (E) 2618 kg (5,772 lb); (GB, trainer) 2685 kg (5,920 lb); maximum take-off (326) 3765 kg (8,300 lb), (B) 4535 kg (10,000 lb), (GB, trainer)

4577 kg (10,090 lb), (GB, with armament) 5216 kg (11,500 lb)
Dimensions: span over tip-tanks (early models) 10.56 m (34 ft 8 in), (GB) 10.85 m (35 ft 7¼ in); length (early models) 10.65 m (34 ft 11¼ in), (GB) 10.67 m (35 ft 0¼ in); height 3.72 m (12 ft 2); wing area (early models) 19.00 m² (204.5 sq ft), (GB) 19.35 m² (208.3 sq ft)
Armament: two optional 7.7-mm (0.303-in) machine-guns in fuselage in early models, with six underwing points for machine-gun pods, rockets and/or bombs, or camera pod(s); maximum external load 907 kg (2,000 lb) on early models, 1814 kg (4,000 lb) on GB and L models

Aermacchi M.B.326K/Atlas Impala Mk 2

Aermacchi had proved at an early stage in its evolution that the basic two-seat MB.326 was an extremely manoeuvrable yet stable weapon-launching platform, and the early armed versions, the MB.326B and F, would normally be flown anyway with the second seat vacant in a ground-attack role. Nevertheless, the development of a genuine single-seat model offered attractive possibilities, especially with the introduction of a more powerful Rolls-Royce Viper engine.

Substitution of the Viper 540 for the original Viper 11 had allowed the weapon load to be effectively doubled from that of the early models, and with the still more powerful Series 600 engine available, the opportunity was taken to augment the offensive capability of the single-seat **MB.326K** by installing a pair of electrically operated cannons in the lower forward fuselage. Into the space normally occupied by the second cockpit are the ammunition drums for these guns, the avionics formerly housed in the nose, and an additional fuel tank. For the more demanding needs of low-level manoeuvring and weapon carriage/delivery, the airframe has been strengthened in selected areas, and servo assistance is provided for the ailerons. At first, Aermacchi felt that these changes were sufficient to justify the new designation MB.336, but decided later to retain the already-established basic one and call it the MB.326K.

Two prototypes of the MB.326K were completed, the first of these making its maiden flight on 22 August 1970, more than 12½ years after the debut of the original M.B.326, with a 1524-kg (3,360-lb) static thrust Viper 540. The intended powerplant, the higher-rated Viper 632-43, was installed in the second aircraft, which joined the flight test programme in 1971. Despite the widespread popularity of the earlier two-seat models, a first customer for the K did not emerge until 1974, when three examples were ordered for the Dubai Police Air Wing (together with one example of the K's two-seat counterpart the **MB.326L**). Later that year Aermac-

chi delivered seven MB.326Ks to South Africa, where Atlas Aircraft Corporation was soon due to end its licence production of the two-seat MB.326M (Impala 1). In 1975 these were followed by Italian-built KDCs (knock-down components) for 15 more single-seaters, and since assembling these locally Atlas has manufactured a version of the K under licence in South Africa as the **Impala 2**. Except for the installation of different avionics, the Impala 2 is similar to the standard MB.326K, but uses the lower-powered Viper 540 engine. These saw extensive action over Angola. In 1976 Italian-built Ks were ordered by the air forces of Ghana (six) and Tunisia (eight), two of the original customers for the early armed versions of the MB.326.

The presence of built-in guns, and the variety of underwing weapons available (see specification below), mean that the MB.326K is not necessarily confined to low-level ground-attack or close air support missions. It can carry a camera pod, for low- or medium-altitude tactical reconnaissance, without detriment to the attack weapon-carrying capacity of the remaining wing stations. Or, with twin cannon and heat-seeking dogfight missiles under the wing, it can perform in a visual interception role. Provision exists for a laser rangefinder and a bomb delivery computer to be installed.

Specification
Type: single-seat close air support or tactical reconnaissance aircraft, and limited air-to-air interceptor
Powerplant: one 1814-kg (4,000-lb) static thrust Rolls-Royce Viper 632-43 turbojet (MB.326K); 1524-kg (3,360-lb) static thrust Viper 540 (Impala Mk 2)

The M.B.326K was built under licence by Atlas as the Impala Mk II and is used by the South African Air Force in the light attack role, seeing extensive service in South Africa's involvement in the Angolan war.

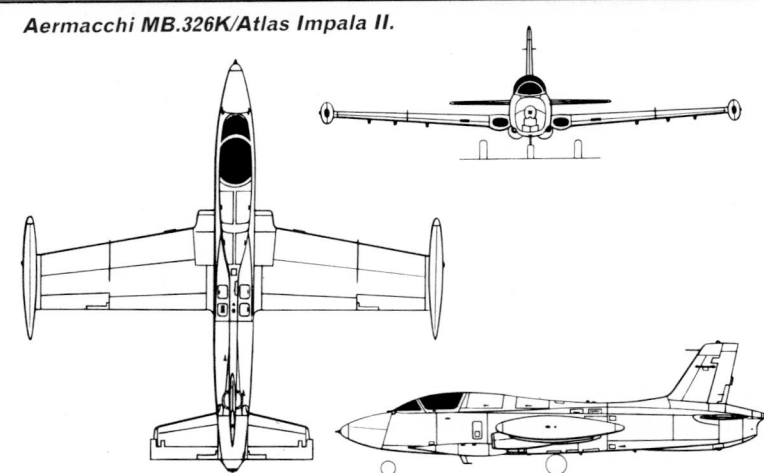

Aermacchi MB.326K/Atlas Impala II.

Performance: (M.B.326K) maximum speed, clean, at 1525 m (5,000 ft) 890 kmh (553 mph); maximum speed, with armament, at 9150 m (30,000 ft) 686 km/h (426 mph); typical combat radius, according to altitude and external load 268-1036 km (167-644 miles); ferry range with two drop-tanks more than 2130 km (1,323 miles); maximum rate of climb at sea level, clean, 1980 m (6,500 ft) per minute; maximum rate of climb at sea level, with armament 1143 m (3,750 ft) per minute
Weights: empty equipped 3123 kg (6,885 lb); take-off, clean, 4645 kg (10,240 lb); maximum take-off, with armament 5897 kg (13,000 lb)

Dimensions: span over tip-tanks 10.85 m (35 ft 7 in); length 10.67 m (35 ft 0¼ in); height 3.72 m (12 ft 2 in); wing area 19.35 m² (208.3 sq ft)
Armament: two 30-mm DEFA 553 cannon in lower fuselage, each with 125 rounds; and up to 1814 kg (4,000 lb) of external stores on six underwing stations, typical loads including four 1,000-lb bombs or two 750-lb and four 500-lb bombs, or six 7.62-mm (0.3-in) Minigun pods, or two AS.11 or AS.12 air-to-surface missiles, or two Matra 550 Magic air-to-air missiles, or various launchers for 37-mm, 68-mm, 100-mm, 2.75-in or 5-in rockets, or (on innermost port station) a four-camera reconnaissance pod

Aermacchi MB.339

Following the receipt of a study contract from the Italian air force in 1972, Aeronautica Macchi undertook no fewer than nine separate design studies in its efforts to evolve a second-generation jet trainer to succeed the MB.326 and Aeritalia (Fiat) G91T during the 1980s. Seven of these were variants of a design known as the **MB.338**, with numerous permutations of single or twin Viper, Larzac, Adour, RB.401 and TFE 731 turbo-

jets or turbofans. Not surprisingly, the single-Viper versions would have offered little advance in performance over the later models of the MB.326; neither, as it turned out, did the intermediately-powered models, which also would have been more expensive to produce than the MB.326; while the two most powerful versions, with a single Adour and twin Larzacs respectively, offered a marked increase in perform-

ance only at a considerably higher cost.
The most encouraging studies were the two proposed models of the **MB.339**, powered by either a single Larzac turbofan (MB.339L) or a single Viper 600 series turbojet (MB.339V). Moreover, a major part of the MB.339 airframe was common with that of the MB.326K, only the forward fuselage, with its modified cockpit and much superior all-round view, plus the enlarged vertical tail, being essentially different. In February 1975 the Italian air force decided to adopt the Viper-

powered version to meet its requirements, and the first of two prototypes made its initial flight at Venegono airfield on 12 August of the following year. Only comparatively minor modifications, to provide an anti-skid braking system for the main landing gear and a steerable nosewheel, plus improved air-conditioning in the cockpit, were introduced on the second prototype, which flew for the first time on 20 May 1977. (An amusing subliminal touch is Aermacchi's use of the word 'nine' in various languages in the registration of the development aircraft: I-NOVE for the first prototype, I-NINE for the second, and I-NEUF for the first production machine).

Redesign of the forward fuselage permits the rear (instructor's) seat to be elevated above that of his pupil in the now-fashionable manner, the elongated tandem canopy providing an all-round view much improved over that from the MB.326. Both occupants have Martin-Baker zero-zero ejection seats, fitted only in the E, K, and L models of the earlier MB.326. The avionics are suitably increased and updated to include Tacan, navigation computer, blind landing instrumentation, IFF (identification friend or foe), and both VHF and UHF radio. Fuselage and permanent wingtip tanks give a total 1413 litres (311 Imperial gallons) of usable fuel as standard, with a 340-litre (75-Imperial gallon) drop-tank able to be carried on the middle pylon under each wing.

Following the two prototypes (the second of which represents the production standard), the Italian air ministry ordered an initial batch of 15 MB.339s, of an expected total of 100. Although developed initially as an Italian air force trainer, the 339 retains the six wing hardpoints of its predecessor. Thus, Aermacchi has achieved a successor to the MB.326 with a compromise design. It may lack some sophistication and the performance 'edge' of the British Aerospace Hawk or Dassault-Breguet/Dornier Alpha Jet. However, these factors are more than offset by the lower unit cost, plus the commonality with an already well-proven airframe.

Italy received a total of 101 MB.339s, most of which are the **MB.339A** trainers which have a contingency close air support role in wartime. Four of the aircraft were converted to **MB.339RM** configuration for calibration duties, while others have been converted to **MB.339PAN** standard for use by the national aerobatic display team the *Frecce Tricolori*. Argentina, Dubai, Ghana, Malaysia, Nigeria and Peru are the export customers so far.

Yet to find a customer are the uprated versions. These are led by the **MB.339K** (previously Veltro II) single-

seat attack aircraft. First flying on 30 May 1980, the aircraft was a private venture featuring a new forward fuselage, internal cannon and greater fuel carriage. An uprated Viper Mk 680 turbojet develops 19.57-kN (4,400-lb) thrust. Also powered by this uprated engine are a pair of two-seat variants, the **MB.339B** which is similar to the trainer but with enhanced ground-attack capability, and the **MB.339C** which had advanced digital avionics for better capability in both trainer and close support roles. This model first flew on 17 December 1985. For the future, Aermacchi is developing the **MB.339D** which will be powered by a pair of Pratt & Whitney Canada JT15D turbofans mounted over the wings. This will be a possible candidate for future USAF trainer requirements.

Specification
Type: tandem two-seat basic/advanced jet trainer and close-support aircraft
Powerplant: one 1814-kg (4,000-lb) Piaggio-built Rolls-Royce Viper 632-43 turbojet
Performance: maximum limiting Mach number 0.86 (971 km/h/603 mph) equivalent airspeed); maximum speed at sea level 898 km/h (558 mph); maximum speed at 9150 m (30,000 ft)

917 km/h (508 mph) or Mach 0.77; maximum range on internal fuel 1760 km (1,093 miles); maximum range with two underwing drop-tanks 2110 km (1,310 miles); maximum rate of climb at sea level 2012 m (6,600 ft) per minute; service ceiling 14630 m (48,000 ft)
Weights: empty equipped (3215 kg (6,899 lb); take-off, clean 4400 kg (9,700 lb); maximum take-off, with underwing stores 5895 kg (13,000 lb)
Dimensions: span over tip-tanks 10.86 m (35 ft 7½ in); length 10.97 m (36 ft 0 in); height (3.99 m) (13 ft 1¼ in); wing area 19.30 m² (207.74 sq ft)
Armament: six underwing hardpoints, the outer pair each able to carry a 340 kg (750 lb) store and the others 454 kg (1,000 lb) each, subject to a maximum load of 1800 kg (3,968 lb).

The Aermacchi MB.339A is essentially a development of the MB.326 concept, with a more powerful engine, improved aerodynamics and a raised instructor's seat.

The two inboard points can carry 30-mm or multi-barrel 7.62-mm guns in a Macchi pod, and the two centre points are 'wet' for the carriage of drop-tanks. Wide variety of weapon loads including bombs, napalm, AS.11/AS.12 or Magic missiles, launchers for 50-mm, 68-mm or 2.75-in rockets, or a single four-camera reconnaissance pod

Carrying fuel, avionics and ammunition instead of a second cockpit, the MB.339K is a useful light attack type, but as yet has no orders.

Aermacchi AM.3C

The AM.3 was a joint venture by Aerfer Industrie Aerospaciali Meridionali SpA of Turin and Aermacchi of Varese. The first of two prototypes was built by Macchi and flew on 12 May 1967, to be followed by the Aerfer-built second prototype on 22 August 1968. Both aircraft were powered by a 254-kW (340-hp) Continental GTSIO-520-C engine. The AM.3C is a high-wing observation/liaison aircraft intended to replace the Cessna L-19s then serving with the Italian army.

The high wing is braced on each side by a single strut. The wing is of similar concept to that of the Aermacchi AL.60, with an all-metal D-spar torsion-box structure with piano-type ailerons and Fowler-type flaps. The AM.3 has a welded chrome-molybdenum steel-tube fuselage, covered forward with light alloy skinning, the cabin having glass-fibre reinforced plastic panels. The rear fuselage is a light alloy semi-monocoque. The wing is attached to the fuselage at three easily accessible points for swift removal. The cantilever all-metal tail unit has a variable camber tailplane and the rudder is fitted with a spring-tab.

Each leg of the fixed landing gear has a

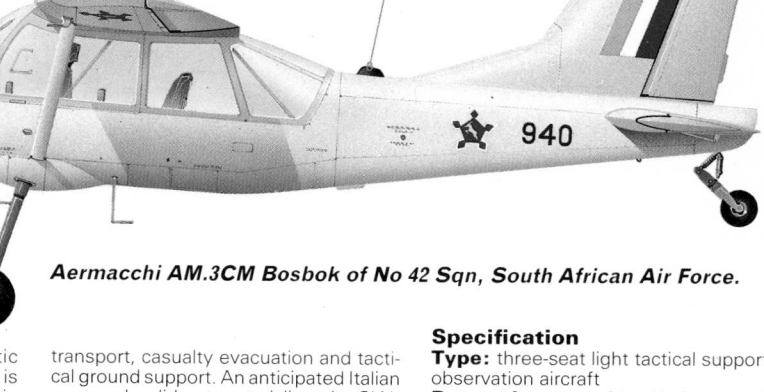

Aermacchi AM.3CM Bosbok of No 42 Sqn, South African Air Force.

tubular strut with an oleo-pneumatic shock absorber. The fixed tailwheel is steerable. The fully-glazed, raised cabin has two seats in tandem with dual controls. A third seat at the rear can be removed to accommodate a stretcher or freight, with access via three doors in the sides of the cabin.

The roles of the AM.3C production version include forward air control, observation, liaison, cargo or passenger

transport, casualty evacuation and tactical ground support. An anticipated Italian army order did not materialise, the SIAI-Marchetti SM.1019 being preferred, but 40 AM.3Cs were delivered to South Africa, the first aircraft of the order being delivered in May 1972. In SAAF service the aircraft is known as the **Bosbok**. Three were purchased by Rwanda.

Specification
Type: three-seat light tactical support/observation aircraft
Powerplant: one 254-kW (340-hp) Piaggio-Lycoming GSO-480-B1B6 six-cylinder horizontally-opposed air-cooled piston engine
Performance: maximum speed at 2440 m (8,005 ft) 278 km/h (173 mph); maximum cruising speed at 75 per cent power at 2440 m (8,005 ft) 246 km/h (153 mph); maximum range at

cruising speed 990 km (615 miles); service ceiling 8400 m (27,559 ft); take-off run 85 m (279 ft); landing run 66 m (217 ft)
Weights: empty 1080 kg (2,381 lb); maximum take-off (with underwing weaponry) 1700 kg (3,748 lb)
Dimensions: span 12.64 m (41 ft 5⅜ in); length 8.73 m (28 ft 7¾ in); height 2.72 m (8 ft 11 in); wing area 20.26 m² (219.2 sq ft)
Armament: carried on two underwing hardpoints; each can carry up to 170 kg (375 lb) of external stores. Alternative loads for each hardpoint are: a pod with two 7.62-mm (0.3-in) machine-guns; or a General Electric-Minigun with 1,500 rounds; a pod with six 70-mm (2.75-in) rockets; or a single AS.11 or AS.12 wire-guided missile; or a single 250-lb bomb

Aero A.10

Aero Tovarna Letadel Dr Kabes was formed in Prague during 1919, initially to manufacture accessories for the aircraft industry. In a very short time, however, the company began to build copies of the biplanes developed by Phönix Flugzeugwerft in Austria. These Phönix designs were themselves derived from the Hansa-Brandenburg series, originated by that company's talented chief designer, Ernst Heinkel. From the construction of these aeroplanes of foreign origin, it was a comparatively short step to the design and manufacture of a family of aircraft that, thanks to the good example set by the Heinkel designs, was to become known internationally.

The **Aero A.10** was one of this number, a six-seat biplane, transport that had the distinction of being the first commercial aircraft to be built in Czechoslovakia. Like many aircraft of its era it was not exactly a thing of beauty, with angular lines and a slab-sided fuselage. Primarily of wooden construction with fabric covering, the A.10 had its lower wing mounted at the base of the fuselage, the upper wing being supported above the fuselage by interplane and centre-section struts. Ailerons, on the upper wing

only, incorporated large horn balances.

The deep fuselage provided cabin accommodation for five passengers, with a baggage compartment behind the cabin, and the pilot in an open cockpit above the baggage compartment. The tail unit included a braced tailplane with horn-balanced elevators, and a horn-balanced rudder mounted directly onto the rear fuselage without a fin. Landing gear was of the fixed tailwheel type, the two mainwheels being carried on a stout, braced through-axle. The powerplant consisted of a Maybach six-cylinder inline engine, many of these being abandoned in Czechoslovakia by the Germans when World War I ended.

Construction of the prototype began during 1921, and this aircraft flew successfully in 1922. Four production A.10s followed, entering service with the Czech national airline Ceskoslovenské Aerolinie in 1924 for use on the Prague-Bratislava route.

Specification
Type: six-seat commercial transport
Powerplant: one 179-kW (240-hp) Maybach Mb IVa inline piston engine
Performance: maximum level speed

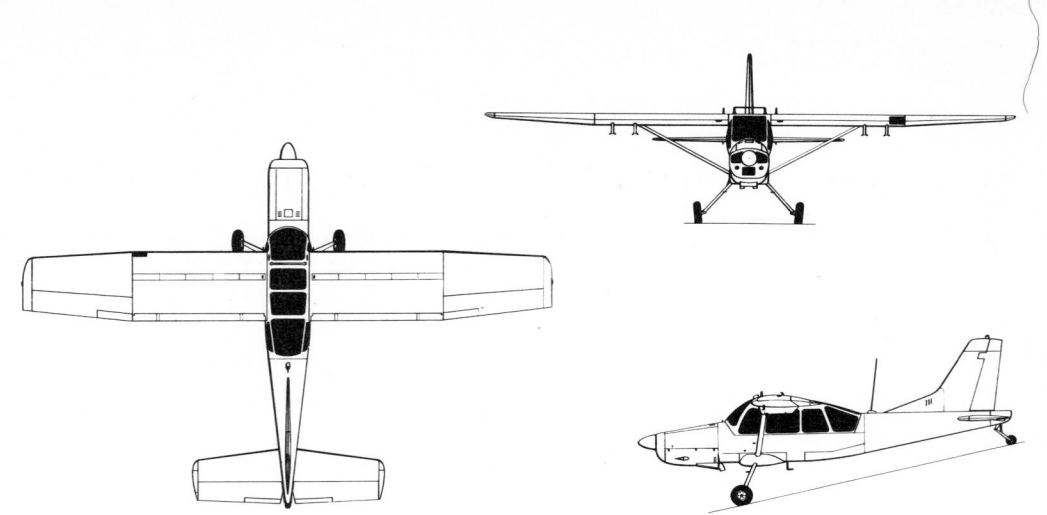

160 km/h (99 mph); cruising speed 130 km/h (81 mph); service ceiling 5800 m (19,030 ft); range 520 km (323 miles)
Weights: empty 1297 kg (2,860 lb); maximum take-off 2046 kg (4,510 lb)
Dimensions: span 14,20 m (46 ft 7 in); length 10.14 m (33 ft 3¼ in); wing area 51.00 m² (548.98 sq ft)

As the first commercial aircraft built in Czechoslovakia, the Aero A.10 went into service with the national airline CSA in the mid-1920s. Five passengers sat in the cabin while the pilot braved the elements from an open cockpit.

Aero A.18

A requirement of the Czech air force for a new single-seat fighter resulted in the development by Aero of a new biplane that was virtually a smaller version of the highly successful A.11. A single-bay biplane of unequal span, the **Aero A.18** was in construction similar to the A.11 except that the ailerons, mounted on the upper wing, were without horn balances. The landing gear, fuselage and tail unit all followed similar design and construction, though only a single cockpit was provided. In its initial A.18 version, of which 20 were supplied to the air force, power was provided by a 138-kW (185-hp) BMW IIIa engine, and armament comprised two forward-firing Vickers machine-guns, synchronised to fire through the disc of the two-blade wooden propeller.

In the early 1920s, the Czech Aero Club organised a national aircraft race, and to participate in the first event, flown in 1923, Aero entered a specially-prepared version of its little fighter. Designated **A.18B**, it differed from the standard air force version by having the wing span reduced to 5.70 m (18 ft 8½ in), giving a wing area of 9.84 m² (105.92

Aero A.18 of the 2nd air regiment, Czech air force. This unit was based at Olomouc in the mid-1920s.

sq ft). Although the A.18B won, the achievement was something of an anti-climax as the two contending aircraft both crashed during the race. Anticipating stronger opposition in 1924, Aero used a similar airframe to that of the

1923 winner, but installed a version of the Walter W-IV engine with a high compression ratio that enabled it to develop 224 kW (300 hp). Designated **A.18C**, this aircraft could demonstrate a maximum speed of 275 km/h (171 mph), a performance good enough to win the 1923 race at an average speed of 261 km/h (162 mph).

Specification
Type: single-seat biplane fighter
Powerplant: (A.18): one 138-kW

(185-hp) BMW IIIa inline piston engine
Performance: maximum level speed 229 km/h (142 mph); cruising speed 195 km/h (121 mph); service ceiling 9000 m (29,530 ft); range 400 km (249 miles)
Weights: empty 637 kg (1,404 lb); maximum take-off 862 kg (1,900 lb)
Dimensions: span 7.60 m (24 ft 11 ¼ in); length 5.90 m (19 ft 4 ¼ in); height 15.90 m² (171.15 sq ft)
Armament: two fixed forward-firing synchronised Vickers machine-guns

Aero L-29 Delfin
to
Aérospatiale (Fouga) CM.170 Magister/CM.175 Zéphyr

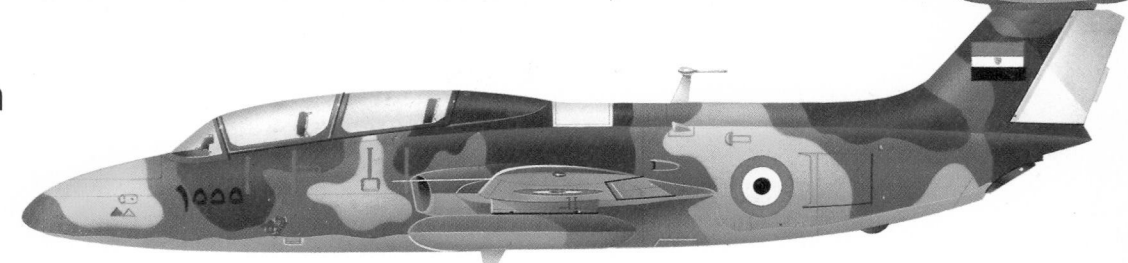

Aero L-29 Delfin

Even among the air forces of the Warsaw Pact nations, where large production contracts are common, manufacturing figures of over 3,000 of a single type of jet trainer indicate a particularly successful design. The first studies leading to the Czech **Aero L-29** were made in 1955 by a team under K. Tomas and Z. Rublic. Known as the XL-29, the prototype flew for the first time on 5 April 1959, powered by a Bristol Siddeley Viper turbojet. The second prototype which made its initial flight in July 1960, and a small pre-production batch of L-29s for service evaluation, had the Czech-designed M 701 turbojet.

A year later the Delfin (Dolphin), as the L-29 had been named, was subjected to competitive evaluation against the Yakovlev Yak-30 and PZL-Mielec TS-11 Iskra. As a result, all the Warsaw Pact countries except Poland, which continued supporting its own TS-11, decided to adopt the Delfin as their standard basic and advanced jet trainer. The first production Delfin was completed in April 1963, and approximately 3,500 had been built before the run ended some 12 years later. More than 2,000 of these were supplied to the Soviet air force, whose L-29s were assigned the reporting name 'Maya' by the NATO Air Standards Coordinating Committee, and about 400 to the Czech air force. Others were supplied to the air forces of Bulgaria, East Germany, Hungary and Romania. From its introduction the Delfin enabled these services to inaugurate 'all-through' training in jet aircraft, by replacing earlier piston-engined types. It was designed not only for basic pilot training but also for advanced and combat weapon training.

The L-29's concept is based upon a straightforward, easy-to-build design, simple to fly and uncomplicated to oper-

The L-29 Delfin was widely used by the Soviet Union and its client states, and a few remain in service. This aircraft wears the desert scheme of the Egyptian air force.

ate. Flight controls are manual, with generous flaps and a perforated airbrake on each side of the rear fuselage. The Delfin does not readily stall or spin, and its safety and reliability are said to be high. There is a manual backup for the landing gear, and both occupants are provided with ejection seats though, unlike modern trainers, the instructor's (rear) seat is no higher than the pupil's. Runway requirements are modest, and the L-29 can operate from grass, sand or waterlogged airstrips.

Aero also built a small batch of the single-seat **L-29A Delfin Akrobat** for aerobatic displays, but this did not go into large-scale production. Neither did an attack version, the **L-29R**, but the standard L-29 was supplied to a number of countries (including Egypt) with equipment to suit it for this role.

Variants
L-29: basic trainer used by Bulgaria, Czechoslovakia, East Germany, Egypt, Guinea, Hungary, Indonesia, Iraq, Nigeria, Romania, Syria, Uganda and USSR
L-29A: single-seat aerobatic version built only in small numbers
L-29R: attack version produced only in prototype form

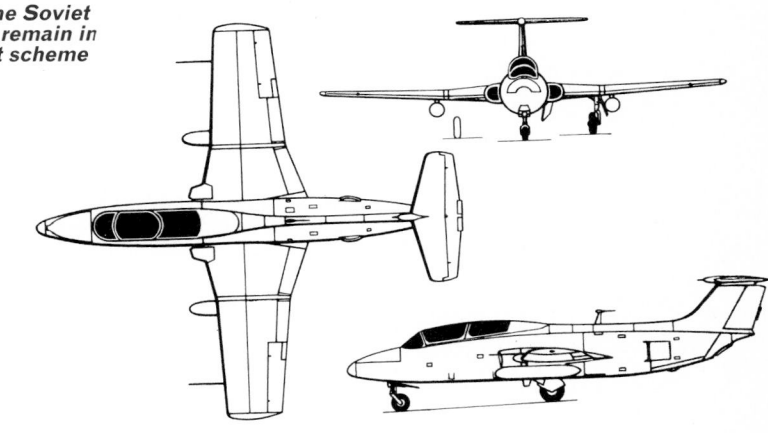

Aero L-29 Delfin basic trainer, with underwing drop tanks.

Specification
Aero L-29 Delfin
Type: tandem two-seat basic and advanced jet trainer
Powerplant: one 890-kg (1,960-lb) thrust Motorlet M 701 VC-150 or S-50 turbojet
Performance: maximum speed at 5000 m (16,400 ft) 655 km/h (407 mph); maximum speed at sea level 610 km/h (379 mph); maximum rate of climb at sea level 840 m (2,755 ft) per minute;

service ceiling 11000 m (36,100 ft); maximum range on internal fuel 640 km (397 miles); maximum range with two underwing drop tanks 895 km (555 miles)
Weights: empty 2280 kg (5,027 lb,); maximum take-off 3280 kg (7,231 lb)
Dimensions: span 10.29 m (33 ft 9 in); length 10.81 m (35 ft 5½ in); height 3.13 m (10 ft 3 in); wing area 19.80 m² (213.1 sq ft)

Aero L-39 Albatros

Designed before the Soviet armed intervention in Czechoslovakia in 1968, the **Aero L-39 Albatros** has now emulated its predecessor, the L-29 Delfin, as the standard jet trainer for Warsaw Pact (except Poland) and other air forces. Aero began with three prototypes, the middle one of which flew for the first time on 4 November 1968; the other two were subjected to structural and fatigue tests. Pilot for the first flight was Rudolf Duchon, who had also been responsible for the early test programme of the L-29 nine years before. The powerplant selected for the L-39 is the Soviet-designed Ivchenko Al-25 turbofan, and most of the early delays in the aircraft's development are thought to be the result of problems encountered in relating

Aero L-39 Albatros basic and advanced trainer of the Iraqi air force. This air arm also operates the L-39ZO single-seat version.

this to the L-39's airframe, so rendering it acceptable for licence production in Czechoslovakia. One of the chief problems seems to have been the supply of air to the engine: by late 1970, at which time five flying prototypes had been completed, modified intakes of greater

length and increased area were noticed on these development aircraft. During the following year, a pre-production batch of 10 L-39s was built to the modified configuration, and series production began in late 1972. By 1989, more than 2,000 had been ordered.

These are of three main versions. The basic **L-39C**, for elementary and advanced jet training, has been supplied in quantity to the Czech and Soviet air forces plus those of other Warsaw Pact nations as a successor to the L-29; it began to enter service in 1974. When equipped for weapons training, the two-seater is known as the **L-39ZA**. A single-seat armed variant, for use in the light close-support and ground-attack roles, is designated **L-39ZO**: Iraq is known to be among the operators of this last version.

Dipl.-Ing. Jan Vlcek, who led the Aero design team responsible for the L-39, has produced a physically attractive little aeroplane with a significant improvement in performance over its predecessor (Mach 0.83 top speed, compared with the L-29's Mach 0.75). Tandem seating (on zero-height ejection seats in the L-39C) is retained, but naturally with the rear (instructor's) seat elevated to improve his view forward. Simultaneously, this enables the lower-placed front cockpit to slope downward towards a finely-pointed nose that reduces drag and contributes to enhanced performance.

Construction is modular, the airframe being broken down into only three major sub-assemblies (wing, fuselage, and rear fuselage/tail unit) to facilitate major maintenance and overhaul. The entire wing, except for the moving surfaces, is in one piece, including the permanent tip tanks, and the swept fin is integral with the rear fuselage; the latter is removable to provide easy access to the engine for servicing. Including detachables such as nose-cone, control surfaces, landing gear and canopies, the entire L-39 airframe consists of little more than a couple of dozen basic components. This enables any one to be replaced quickly and easily; plenty of access panels are provided for reaching individual systems or installations.

A first-class all-round view is available from both pressurised cockpits, and dual controls are, of course, standard. The rear seat is removed in the L-39ZO, presumably providing space, if required, for avionics or an additional fuel tank. A small auxiliary power unit (APU), in the form of a compressed-air turbine and generator, makes the aircraft independent of ground power sources for engine starting, fuel flow or other services.

Variants
L-39C: basic two-seat trainer used by Afghanistan, Bulgaria, Czechoslovakia, East Germany, Hungary, Romania and USSR
L-39ZA: armed trainer
L-39ZO: single-seat version for light attack, used by Iraq and Libya
L-39MS: new advanced training version with more powerful engine and updated avionics

Specification
Aero L-39 Albatros
Type: tandem two-seat basic and advanced jet trainer (L-39C), weapons trainer (L-39Z) and single-seat light ground-attack aircraft (L-39ZO)
Powerplant: one 1720-kg (3,792-lb) thrust Walter Titan turbofan (Ivchenko AI-25-TL built under Czech licence by Motorlet)
Performance: maximum speed at sea level 700 km/h (435 mph); maximum speed (trainer, clean) at 6000 m (19,685 ft) 780 km/h (485 mph); (L-39ZO at same altitude with four rocket pods) 630 km/h (391 mph);

maximum rate of climb at sea level (trainer) 1320 m (4,330 ft) per minute, (L-39ZO) 960 m (3,150 ft) per minute; service ceiling (trainer) 11500 m (37,730 ft), (L-39ZO) 9000 m (29,525 ft); range on internal fuel (trainer) 850 km (528 miles), (L-39ZO with rocket pods) 780 km (485 miles); maximum range (trainer) with two drop tanks and no weapons 1600 km (994 miles), (L-39ZO) 1750 km (1,087 miles)
Weights: empty 3330 km (7,341 lb); normal take-off (trainer, clean and with tip tanks empty) 4570 kg (10,075 lb); maximum take-off (L-39ZO with four rocket pods) 5270 kg (11,618 lb)
Dimensions: span 9.46 m (31 ft 0½ in); length 12.32 m (40 ft 5 in); height 4.72 m (15 ft 5½ in); wing area 18.80 m² (202.4 sq ft)
Armament: (L-39ZO): up to 1100 kg (2,425 lb) of weapons on four underwing points, including bombs of up to 500-kg (1,102-lb) size, pods of 57- or 130-mm rockets, gun pods, a single five-camera reconnaissance pack, or two drop tanks; centreline point under fuselage for podded 23-mm GSh-23 23-mm twin-barrel cannon with 180 rounds

Simple servicing, viceless handling qualities and low operating costs were the determining features in the design of the Albatros trainer, which was then developed into an effective light attack warplane with gun pods, rocket launchers and light bombs. This is the standard trainer of the type acquired by the Soviet and Czechoslovak air forces.

Aerocar Aerocar

Moulton B. Taylor had long dreamed of developing a 'roadable aircraft', a vehicle that could be used as a family car and, when a journey by air was more practical, could be given quickly-attached wings, tail unit and propeller. The idea was not entirely new, for as early as 1921 René Tampier had exhibited an aeroplane of this type at the 1921 *Paris Salon*.

Soon after the end of World War II, Moulton Taylor established a company to begin the task of making his dream reality. By late 1949 the prototype of his **Aerocar** was flying and on 13 December 1956 the improved pre-production **Aerocar I** was awarded FAA certification. Four additional model Is were built, for demonstration and sale, and these six vehicles accumulated more than 200,000 miles (321890 km) of road travel, and in excess of 5,000 flight hours. Final version was the much-improved **Aerocar III**, converted from an earlier Aerocar I, and comprising a fairly conventional front-wheel drive motor car. Power was provided by an Avco Lycoming 0-320 aircraft engine, mounted in the rear end of the car, to drive the road wheels, or alternatively, the propeller via an extended drive shaft within the detachable tail boom: this

also mounted a tail unit of Y configuration. Braced monoplane wings could be attached in a high-wing configuration at the rear of the car, and unless the safety locks for wings and tailboom were all correctly engaged, it was not possible to start the engine for flight in the aeroplane mode. Conversion from air to road could be accomplished by one person in about five minutes. On arrival at an airfield the wings and tail assembly could be detached and towed behind the car, mounted on retractable wheels set in the leading-edge of the wing roots.

Moulton Taylor's dream was finally shattered by changing legislation for American automobiles. To meet the new requirements of the 1970s, the Autocar would have to become too heavy and expensive to be a practical proposition.

In Italy, Aerauto SA explored the roadable aircraft concept with a vehicle designated **PL.5C**. However, this relied upon the use of a rear-mounted engine and pusher propeller for both air and ground propulsion, and consequently would have had only limited application for road use if its development had been pursued.

Specification
Aerocar Aerocar III
Type: two-seat roadable aircraft
Powerplant: one 107-kW (143-hp) derated Avco Lycoming O-320-A1A flat-four piston engine
Performance: (A: aircraft; B: car) cruising speed A 201 km/h (125 mph) at 1525 m (5,000 ft), B 113 km/h (70 mph); service ceiling A 3660 m (12,000 ft); range A 805 km (500 miles), B 483 km (300 miles)
Weights: empty A 680 kg (1,500 lb), B 499 kg (1,100 lb); maximum take-off A 953 kg (2,100 lb)

Moulton Taylor's Aerocar has been the world's most successful attempt at a roadable aircraft, with detachable flying surfaces that could be attached to the roadable 'fuselage'.

Dimensions: span 10.36 m (34 ft 0 in); length A 7.01 m (23 ft 0 in), B 3.35 m (11 ft 0 in); B towing wings/tail assembly 8.08 m (26 ft 6 in); height A 2.13 m (7 ft 0 in), B 1.32 m (4 ft 4 in), B with trailer 2.44 m (8 ft 0 in); wing area 17.65² (190 sq ft)

Aeronca L-3 Grasshopper

The US Army Air Corps had been slow to appreciate the value of light aircraft for employment in an observation/liaison role, but information received from Europe in late 1940, where World War II was already more than a year old, high-lighted their usefulness. Consequently, in 1941 the US Army began its own evaluation of this category of aircraft, obtaining four commercial lightplanes from each of three established manufacturers, namely Aeronca, Piper and

Taylorcraft. For full field evaluation larger numbers of these aircraft were ordered shortly afterwards, to be deployed in the US Army's annual manoeuvres which were to be held later in the year. It took very little time for the service to appreciate that these lightweight aeroplanes had a great deal to offer, both for rapid communications and in support of

armed forces in the field.

The name Aeronca Aircraft Corporation had been adopted in 1941 by the company established in late 1928 as the Aeronautical Corporation of America. One of its most successful products was the **Model 65** high-wing monoplane, developed to meet commercial requirements for a reliable dual-control tandem two-seat trainer. The four of these aircraft supplied initially to the USAAC became designated **YO-56**, and these were followed by 50 **O-58**, 20 **O-58A** and 335 **O-58B** aircraft, serving with the USAAF (established on 20 June 1941). In the following year the O (Observation) designation was changed to L (Liaison), and the O-58, O-58A and O-58B designations became respectively **L-3**, **L-3A** and **L-3B**. An additional 540 aircraft were delivered as L-3Bs and 490 **L-3C**s were manufactured before production ended in 1944. The designations **L-3D/-3E/-3F/-3G/-3H/-3J** were applied to civil Model 65s with varying powerplant installations which were pressed into military service when the United States became involved in World War II.

Most L-3s were generally similar, with small changes in equipment representing the variation from one to another. All shared the welded steel-tube fuselage/tail unit with fabric covering, and wings with spruce spars, light alloy ribs and metal frame ailerons, all fabric-covered. Landing gear was of the non-retractable tailwheel type, with the main units divided and incorporating oleo-spring shock-absorbers in the side Vees.

With the requirement for a trainer suitable for glider pilots, Aeronca developed an unpowered version of the Model 65. This retained the wings, tail unit and aft fuselage of the L-3, but introduced a new front fuselage providing a third seat forward for an instructor, the original tandem seats being used by two pupils: all three occupants had similar flying controls and instruments. A total of 250 of these training gliders was supplied to the USAAF under the designation **TG-5**, and three supplied to the US Navy for evaluation were identified as **LNR**. Pro-

duction of Aeronca liaison aircraft continued after the war, with planes supplied to the USAF under the designation **L-16**.

Specification
Type: two-seat light liaison and observation monoplane
Powerplant: one 48-kW (65-hp) Continental O-170 flat-four piston engine
Performance: maximum speed 140 km/h (87 mph); cruising speed 74 km/h (46 mph); service ceiling 3050 m (10,000 ft); range 322 km (200 miles)
Weights: empty 379 kg (835 lb); maximum take-off 590 kg (1,300 lb)
Dimensions: span 10.67 m (35 ft 0 in); length 6.40 m (21 ft 0 in); height 2.34 m (7 ft 8 in); wing area 14.68 m² (158 sq ft)
Armament: none

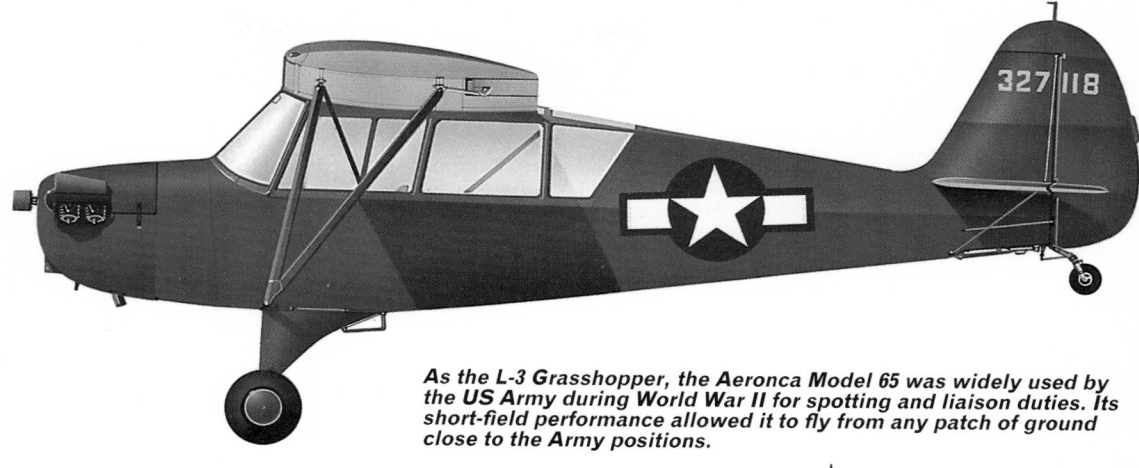

As the L-3 Grasshopper, the Aeronca Model 65 was widely used by the US Army during World War II for spotting and liaison duties. Its short-field performance allowed it to fly from any patch of ground close to the Army positions.

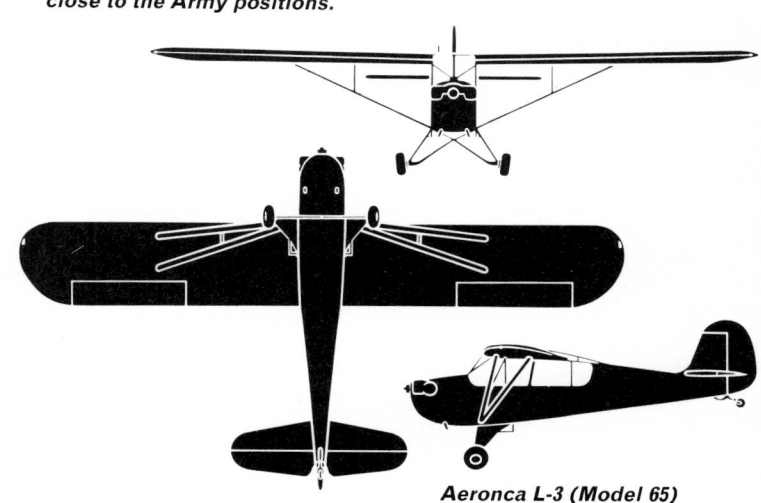

Aeronca L-3 (Model 65) Grasshopper.

Aeromarine 75

In the years immediately after World War I, Aeromarine designed and initiated modification of the model **75** 12-passenger commercial flying boat anticipating, like many other manufacturers in Europe and the USA, a considerable demand for civil air services. They were to discover, as did all other manufacturers with similar ambitious ideas, that they had anticipated such a requirement by a number of years.

Aeromarine's design for this early commercial flying boat was a conversion of the Curtiss F-5L, and accommodated its 12 passengers in two cabins, forward and aft of the unequal-span biplane wing, with the crew of two in an open cockpit in the hull, directly beneath the upper wing. Constructed of plywood, the hull incorporated very clean lines; the wings and braced tail unit were of wood, fabric-covered, with balancer floats mounted beneath the wingtips of the lower wing. Powerplant comprised two Liberty engines, each strut-mounted from the lower wing some distance outboard of the hull, and each driv-

ing a two-blade tractor propeller.

Two Aeromarine Model 75s were used on a Key West-Havana air service until 1923.

Specification
Type: commercial flying boat
Powerplant: two 261-kW (350-hp) Liberty 12 Vee piston engines
Performance: cruising speed 121 km/h (75 mph); range 1335 km (830 miles)
Weight: maximum take-off 6508 kg (14,348 lb)
Dimensions: span, upper 32.62 m (103 ft 9 in), lower 23.77 m (78 ft 0 in); length 15.04 m (49 ft 4 in); height 5.72 m (18 ft 9¼ in); wing area 129.78 m² (1,397 sq ft)

The Aeromarine 75 flying cruiser 'Mendoza' arrives in New York carrying 27 people, the largest number ever carried by a commercial flying boat in America at the time.

Aérospatiale (Fouga) CM.170 Magister/CM.175 Zéphyr

In its time one of the most widely used trainer/light attack aircraft, the **Aérospatiale CM.170 Magister** (first produced by Air Fouga and then by Potez) was designed to meet an Armée de l'Air requirement for a jet trainer (the first in the world). The prototype made its maiden flight on 23 July 1952, and a pre-production batch of 10 was ordered the following year. An initial order of 95 for the Armée de l'Air was placed in 1954 and the first production aircraft flew on 13 January 1954. Since then over 400 Magisters have been produced for the Armée de l'Air alone.

A specially-equipped naval version

was produced for the Aéronavale, designated **CM.175 Zéphyr**. Two prototypes and 30 production aircraft were built to this standard, and the Zéphyr provides naval pilots with their initial experience of operating from an aircraft-carrier.

In addition to French-manufactured Magisters offered for export, the trainer was manufactured under licence in West Germany by Flugzeug-Union-Sud for Luftwaffe training schools. However, with the transfer of most German flying training to the United States by the end of the 1960s, the Magister was phased out of service. Valmet OY in Finland built 62 Magisters under licence (in addition to 18 purchased from France) and Israel Aircraft Industries also acquired manufacturing rights for the type, building many for light-tactical use as well as training. Total production was 916 aircraft.

The Magister is all-metal. The mid-mounted wings have single-slotted flaps and airbrakes. The butterfly-type tail has surfaces separated by 110°.

Fuel is housed in two fuselage tanks of 255-litre (56-Imp gal) and 475-litre (104-Imp gal) capacity, with wingtip tanks each holding 125 litres (27.5 Imp gal).

The tandem cockpits are pressurised and air-conditioned, with individually regulated oxygen supplies. Ejection seats are not fitted. VHF, blind flying equipment and radio compass are standard in the trainer, while UHF, Tacan and IFF may be fitted to armed Magisters.

Armament combinations include two 7.5-mm (0.295-in) or 7.62-mm (0.3-in) machine-guns mounted in the nose, with 200 rounds of ammunition per gun. A gyro gunsight is fitted in both cockpits, the rear one having periscopic sighting. Underwing ordnance loads include two Matra Type 181 pods each with eighteen 37-mm rockets, two launchers each mounting seven 68-mm rockets, four 25-kg (55-lb) air-to-ground rockets, eight 88-mm rockets, two 50-kg (110-lb) bombs, or two Nord AS.11 air-to-surface guided missiles.

About 310 Magisters of the 437 originally procured remained in service with the Armée de l'Air until the mid-1980s. A 150-hour basic flying training course was provided for commissioned pupils at the *Ecole de l'Air* at Salon-de-Provence, and similar instruction was provided for other ranks at *Groupement Ecole* 315, Cognac. Magisters also served with *Groupement Ecole* 313 to provide instructor training for the Armée de l'Air and basic flying training for overseas students. The Force Aérienne Belge's Magisters at the *Ecole de Pilotage Avancé*, Brustem, were replaced by Dassault-Breguet/Dornier Alpha Jets in 1979. Finland's Magisters at the Central Flying School, Kauhava, were in the early 1980s replaced in service by the first of 50 British Aerospace Hawk trainers.

Israel is the foremost operator of the Magister as a light attack aircraft, some 80 remaining in service as both trainers and operational aircraft. The Magister was particularly successful during the Six-Day War of June 1967, flying ground attack sorties on both the Egyptian and Jordanian fronts. The Irish Army Air Corps also operates six **Super Magisters** in the dual light attack/training role, these being based at Baldonnel near Dublin. The Super Magister is an improved model with two 48-kg (1,058-lb) Marboré VI engines.

Specification
Aérospatiale CM.170 Magister
Type: two-seat jet trainer and light attack aircraft
Powerplant: two 400-kg (882-lb) Turboméca Marboré IIA turbojets
Performance: maximum speed 715 km/h (444 mph) at 9150 m (30,000 ft); initial climb rate 1020 m (3,345 ft) per minute; service ceiling 11000 m (36,090 ft; range 925 km) (575 miles)
Weights: empty equipped 2150 kg (4,740 lb); take-off with external tanks 3100 kg (6,835 lb); maximum take-off 3200 kg (7,055 lb)
Dimensions: span over tip tanks 12.12 m (39 ft 10 in); length 10.06 m (33 ft); height 2.80 m (9 ft 2 in); wing area 17.30 m² (186.1 sq ft)
Armament: two 7.5-mm (0.295-in) or 7.62-mm (0.3-in) machine-guns in the nose, plus underwing rockets, bombs or Nord AS.11 missiles

Variants
CM.170-1 Magister: initial production model with two Marboré IIA turbojets; three prototypes, 10 pre-production aircraft, 262 aircraft for France as well as export and licensed production for the Luftwaffe (250), Austria (18), Belgium (48), Cambodia (4), Congo/Léopoldville (6), Finland (82), Israel (52) and Lebanon (4)
CM.170-2 Magister: as CM.170-1 but with uprated Marboré VIC turbojets of 480 kg (1,058 lb) thrust; the last 130 aircraft for the Armée de l'Air and seven for Brazil were completed to this standard, and six CM.170-1 aircraft of the Irish Air Corps upgraded
CM.170-3 Super Magister: upgraded CM.170-2 with Martin-Baker ejection seats, modified canopy and increased fuel capacity
CM.171 Magister: single machine used as a test bed for the 1100-kg (2,425-lb) Turboméca Gabizo turbojet

CM.173 Super Magister: see CM.170-3
CM.175 Zéphyr: Aéronavale version with an arrester hook and other modifications; two prototypes (first flight 30 May 1959) and 30 production aircraft for service from the early 1960s
CM.191: four-seat 'bizjet' version developed by Heinkel and Potez with Marboré VI engines; only one prototype, first flown on 19 March 1962
Potez 94: planned production version of the Super Magister known as the P.94B, and the CM.173 prototype renamed as the P.94A
Fouga 90: improved descendant of the CM.170, first known as the FanJet 600, with two 700-kg (1,543-lb) Turboméca Astafan IIG turbofans and an enlarged cockpit of new design with modern avionics; only one prototype, this was first flown on 20 August 1978

Fouga CM.170 Magister of the French national aerobatic team, the 'Patrouille de France', in the colours used since 1972. Based at Salon-de-Provence, the team now uses the Alpha Jet.

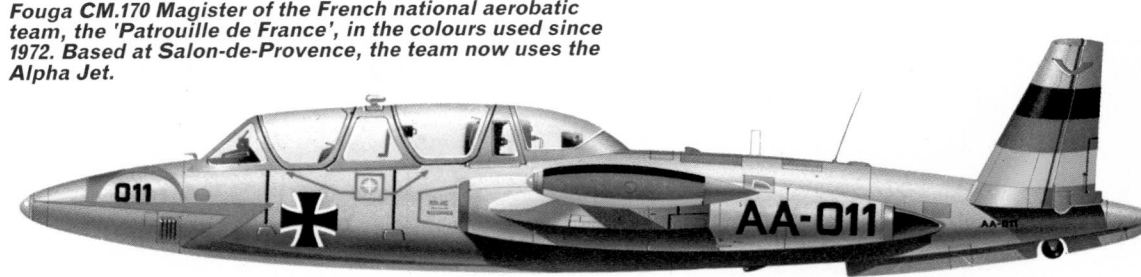

This Luftwaffe Fouga CM.170 was licence-built by Messerschmitt. It served with the demonstration team of Flugzeugführerschule A at Landsberg in 1962.

Previously operated by the Luftwaffe, this Messerschmitt-built CM.170 Magister was passed on to the Algerian air force, in whose colours it is depicted while based at Oran in 1975.

The main strength of the Irish Air Corps lies with a few Super Magisters, armed with 7.62-mm machine guns and rocket pods. Mostly used for training, the Irish Magisters have the more powerful Marboré VI engines.

Aero Spacelines Guppy Series
to
Aérospatiale SE 313B/SA 318C Alouette II

Aero Spacelines Guppy Series

Aero Spacelines, then based at Van Nuys, California, were quick to appreciate the potential of outsize cargo aircraft that would be able to airlift large booster rocket stages being employed in the American space programme, as well as for the transport of aircraft assemblies, oil drilling equipment, and other items too large to be carried by any then existing aircraft. Work started in 1961 on the conversion of a Boeing B-377 Stratocruiser to fulfil such a role: the fuselage was extended by 5.08 mm (16 ft 8 in) aft of the wing, and a new 'bubble' structure was added over the top of the fuselage to allow the loading of items up to 6.02 m (9 ft 9 in) in diameter. The resulting **B-377PG Pregnant Guppy** was flown for the first time on 19 September 1962, and was used from the summer of 1963, under contract to NASA, for the transport of space programme hardware.

An even larger **B-377SG Super Guppy** followed: this featured not only an outsize fuselage, with a cargo compartment measuring 33.17 m (108 ft 10 in) in overall length, 7.62 m (25 ft 0 in) in width, and 7.77 m (25 ft 6 in) in height, but also an increased wing span and four 5220-ekW (7,000-eshp) turboprop engines. This Super Guppy was also used in the American space programme, it being the only aircraft able to carry the third stage of a Saturn V launch vehicle, and the Lunar Module adapter.

To be seen in European skies are four Guppy-201s, acquired by Airbus Industrie for the transport of large Airbus assemblies from various construction points, these Guppy-201s being operated on the builder's behalf by a Union de Transports Aériens (UTA) subsidiary known as Aéromaritime. These are also conversions of Boeing B-377/C-97 airframes, with increased wingspan and Allison 501-D22C engines, the cargo compartment having a maximum length of 33.99 m (111 ft 6 in), with a height of 7.77 m (25 ft 6 in) and a width of 7.65 m (25 ft 1 in), and usable volume of 1104.4 m³ (39,000 cu ft). To facilitate loading and unloading, the forward fuse-

lage, including the flight deck, can be swung 110° to port, providing unrestricted access. The Guppy-201s have been in operation since 1972 and 1973.

Specification
Aero Spacelines Guppy 201
Type: heavy transport
Powerplant: four 3663-ekW (4,912-eshp) Allison 501-D22C turboprops
Performance: maximum cruising speed 463 km/h (288 mph) at 6100 m (20,000 ft); economic cruising speed 407 km/h (253 mph) at 6100 m (20,000 ft); certificated service ceiling 7620 m (25,000 ft); range with maximum payload and 45-min reserves 813 km (505 miles)
Weights: empty 45359 kh (100,000 lb); maximum take-off 77111 kg (170,000 lb)
Dimensions: span 47.63 m (156 ft 3 in); length 43.84 m (143 ft 10 in); height 14.78 m (48 ft 6 in); wing area 182.51 m² (1,964.6 sq ft)
Operator: Aéromaritime

The bulbous fuselage of the Guppy-201 allows the carriage of outsize cargo items. Aéromaritime operates this aircraft alongside four others on behalf of Airbus Industrie. They are used to transport components for the airliners from their respective factories to the central assembly plant at Toulouse.

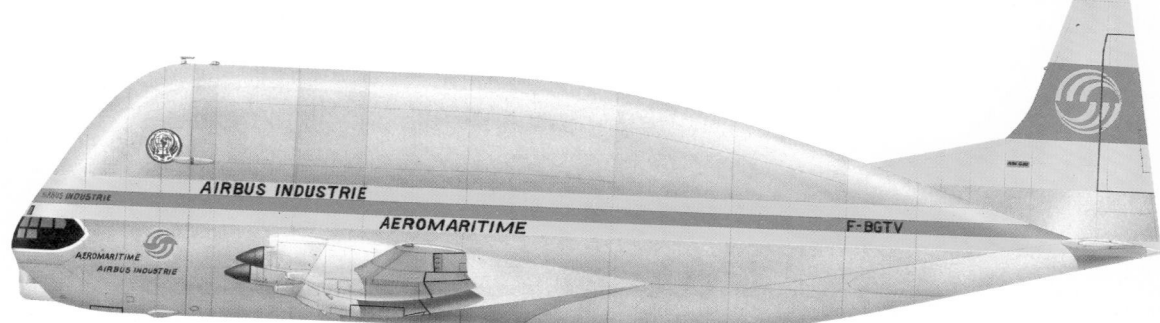

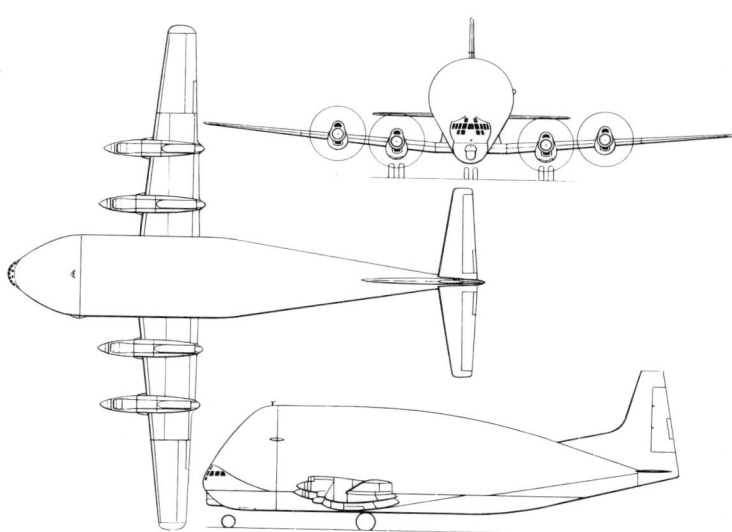
Aero Spacelines Guppy-201

Aérospatiale Epsilon

In September 1978 first details were given of the **Aérospatiale TB-30** piston-engined trainer, designed in collaboration with the Armée de l'Air to meet a new need for a light trainer able to weed out pupils before starting basic flying training on the jet Air Fouga-Potez Magister. Like several other air forces this move is a response to rising costs, and the TB-30, subsequently renamed **Epsilon**, is a simple and robust tandem

two-seater whose design has been steadily refined by the Aérospatiale aircraft division over a period of several years. Features include a metal airframe

The Aérospatiale Epsilon has been designed to meet an Armée de l'Air requirement for an efficient aerobatic basic trainer.

with a life in the military training role of not less than 10,000 hours, a cockpit resembling that of a jet combat aircraft, and equipment for full basic flying training, including aerobatic, instrument, night, formation, navigation, combat manoeuvres and VFR/IFR navigation. Later it is probable that liaison (four-seat) and tactical attack versions will be marketed. The first of two prototypes flew on 22 December 1977, but the programme was then delayed by the need to redesign the wingtips, lower the tailplane and add a ventral fin to cure high-speed pitch and yaw instability. The French air force requires between 100 and 150 Epsilons, deliveries beginning in 1982 from SOCATA, the Aérospatiale subsidiary at Tarbes. An order for 18 was received from the Portuguese air force, these being assembled locally by OGMA.

Specification
Type: primary trainer
Powerplant: one 224-kW (300-hp) Avco Lycoming AE10-540-K flat-six piston engine
Performance: maximum speed 355 km/h (221 mph) at sea level; initial climb rate 550 m (1,805 ft) per minute; service ceiling 6100 m (20,015 ft); range 1300 km (808 miles)
Weights: empty 870 kg (1,918 lb);

maximum take-off 1190 kg (2,623 lb)
Dimensions: span 7.90 m (25 ft 11 in); length 7.60 m (24 ft 11¼ in); height 2.70 m (8 ft 10¼ in); wing area 9.00 m² (96.88 sq ft)
Armament: four underwing hardpoints for up to 480-kg (1056-lb) of gun pods, bombs or rockets (not Armée l'Air machines)

Aérospatiale Caravelle

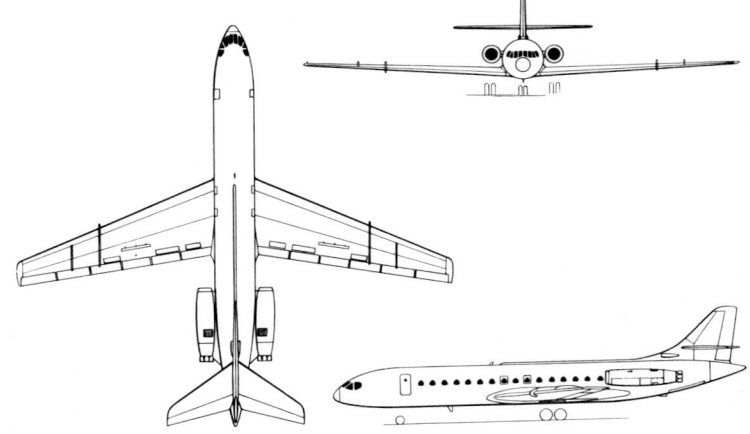

Aérospatiale (Sud) SE.210 Caravelle Super 12 of Sterling Airways, Denmark. Only a handful of Caravelles still remain in airline service.

The first French turbojet-powered airliner; the **Caravelle** had also the distinction of being the world's first short/medium-range turbojet airliner, and was then unique in having its powerplant pod-mounted on the rear fuselage. A French Ministry of Civil Aviation specification, of November 1951, called for the development in France of a turbine-powered airliner that could be marketed internationally, in competition with aircraft in this category already flown in Britain, and to be developed in the USA.

Design proposals were received from six national manufacturers, leading to selection of that from Sud-Est, from whom two prototypes were ordered by the Secrétariat d'Etat à l'Air in January 1953: the name of Caravelle for the new airliner was chosen a few weeks later. Sud-Est, or Société Nationale de Constructions Aéronautiques du Sud-Est (SNCASE) to give its full title, was merged with Sud-Ouest (SNCASO) on 1 March 1957 to form Sud-Aviation. This latter company was merged subsequently with Nord-Aviation and SEREB to form, on 1 January 1970, the Société Nationale Industrielle Aérospatiale.

In its initial form the Caravelle, which had the Sud-Est designation SE 210, had been intended to accommodate 52 passengers, and the first of the two prototypes, both of which were powered by two Rolls-Royce Avon RA.26 turbojets each of 4536-kg (10,000-lb) thrust, flew for the first time on 27 May 1955. However, the initial production **Caravelle I** had a fuselage lengthened by 1.41 m (4 ft 7½ in), providing standard accommodation for 64 passengers in a mixed-class seating arrangement.

The Caravelle was of low-wing monoplane configuration, and of all-metal construction. The swept wing included such features as hydraulically-powered ailerons, Fowler-type trailing-edge flaps, and air brakes on both upper and lower wing surfaces forward of the flaps. The tail unit also had powered control surfaces, the tailplane being mounted on the fin to keep it clear of the efflux of the powerplant, located in pods on the sides of the rear fuselage. This pioneering use of rear-mounted turbojets was intended primarily to ensure that the wing remained 'clean' (free from the aerodynamic interference caused by engines, engine mountings and nacelles) to provide optimum performance of the wing, but secondarily to reduce noise pollution of the cabin environment. In this latter respect those passengers seated furthest forward received the most benefit, and many who could later compare between the Caravelle, the Boeing 707 and the de Havilland Comet spoke glowingly of the Caravelle's 'quiet' cabin. Landing gear was of the hydraulically retractable tricycle type, with twin nosewheels, and a four-wheel bogie on each main unit. The powerplant of the Caravelle I (19 built) consisted of two 4763-kg (10,500-lb) Avon RA.29 Mk 522 engines, but the **Caravelle IA** which followed (13 built) had RA.29/1 Mk 526 engines.

A total of 78 **Caravelle III**s followed, these differing by the installation of 5307-kg (11,700-lb) thrust RA.29/3 engines. All but one of the Mk I and all 13 Mk IA Caravelles were subsequently converted to Mk III standard. Production of the **Caravelle VI** was to follow, the VI-N (53 built) and VI-R (56 built) differing in the following respect: the VI-N had

two 5534-kg (12,200-lb) thrust RA.29/6 Mk 531 turbojets, but the VI-R had 5715-kg (12,600-lb) 532R or Mk 533R engines which introduced thrust reversers to reduce the landing run. Other improvements incorporated in the VI-R included enlarged flight deck windows to improve fields of vision, more powerful brakes, and the provision of wing spoilers to serve as lift dumpers.

The next version to fly, on 3 March 1964, was the **Super Caravelle** (22 built), a considerably refined development of the basic Caravelle family, which introduced a number of aerodynamic improvements. These included a forward extension of the wing leading-edge, adjacent to the wing root, the introduction of double-slotted flaps and an extra 10° of flap travel, the provision of a bullet fairing at the intersection of the rudder and elevators, and an increase of 1.40 m (4 ft 7 in) in tailplane span. Other improvements included the installation of 6350-kg (14,000-lb) thrust Pratt & Whitney JT8D-7 turbofan engines; a fuselage 'stretch' of 1.00 m (3 ft 3½ in) to provide maximum tourist class accommodation for up to 104 passengers; introduction of an APU; updating of the electric and hydraulic systems; and provision of optional increased fuel capacity.

The Super Caravelle had been identified originally as the **Caravelle 10B**, and the model was followed by the **10R** (20 built), the first of which flew on 18 January 1965. This was basically a Caravelle VI airframe, with JT8D-7 engines, cascade thrust-reversers designed by Sud-Aviation, and airframe modification to increase the capacity of the lower cargo holds. The company developed subsequently the **Caravelle 11R**, to meet a requirement for increased cargo capacity on medium-range routes. The Caravelle 11R was thus a mixed passen-

The attractive Caravelle was among the first generation of jetliners, and was very successful, particularly in Europe. Air Inter had a sizeable fleet for services within France.

ger/cargo version with typical accommodation for 50 tourist-class passengers and 66.00 m² (2,331 cu ft) of cargo. This was achieved by a 'stretch' of 0.93 m (3 ft 0⅜ in) in the fuselage forward of the wing, the strengthening of the cabin floor and certain areas of the fuselage, the provision of a 3.32 by 1.84 m (10 ft 10¾ in by 6 ft 0¼ in) cargo door in the port side of the forward fuselage, and a moveable bulkhead to separate cargo and passengers. Only six of this version were built, however, the first of them flying on 21 April 1967.

Last of the Caravelle production aircraft was the **Mk 12**, developed from the Super Caravelle, and having a fuselage which was lengthened an additional 3.23 m (10 ft 7 in) to provide accommodation for a maximum of 140 passengers. Other changes included structural reinforcement to cater for the higher gross weight, and introduction of Pratt & Whitney JT8D-9 turbofans. First flown on 29 October 1970, production of the Caravelle 12 totalled 12, bringing total production to 280 aircraft, including prototypes. At the height of their utilisation, Caravelles served with some 35 airlines. A few remain in service in 1989, and a handful are deployed by small armed forces in a transport capacity.

Specification
Aérospatiale Caravelle 12
Type: short/medium-range transport
Powerplant: two 6577-kg (14,500-lb) thrust Pratt & Whitney JT8D-9 turbofans
Performance: maximum cruising speed, at AUW of 50000 kg (110,231 lb) 825 km/h (513 mph) at 7620 m (25,000 ft); range with maximum fuel, 11240 km (24,780 lb) payload, no fuel reserves 4040 km (2,510 miles); range with maximum payload of 13200 kg (29,101 lb), no fuel reserves 3465 km (2,153 miles)
Weights: empty 29500 kg (65,036 lb);

maximum take-off 58000 kg (127,868 lb)
Dimensions: span 34.29 m (112 ft 6 in); length 36.23 m (118 ft 10½ in); height 9.02 m (29 ft 7 in); wing area 146.70 m² (1,579.1 sq ft)

Aérospatiale SE 313B/SA 318C Alouette II

Of conventional configuration but sturdy design, the **Aérospatiale Alouette II** was one of the first true light multi-purpose helicopters and excelled in a variety of roles. This adaptability was facilitated by its reliable turboshaft engine, easy maintenance, and landing gear which could be either of wheel or skid type, or floats, with provision for emergency flotation gear.

The Alouette II originated as the **Sud-Est SE 3120 Alouette** (Lark), a three-seat light helicopter designed mainly for agricultural purposes. The first SE 3120 prototype was flown on 31 July 1952, powered by a 149-kW (200-hp) Salmson 9NH radial engine, and a year later established a new international helicopter closed-circuit duration record of 13 hours 56 minutes. The basic airframe was then completely redesigned to take the 269-kW (360-shp) Turboméca Artouste I turboshaft, and the first of two prototypes, designated **SE 3130**, was flown on 12 March 1955, followed by three pre-production aircraft in 1956. The Alouette II was granted a French Certificate of Airworthiness on 2 May 1956, and was soon in demand on the international market. In 1957 Sud-Est merged with Sud-Aviation, at which time the designation of the Alouette II was altered to **SE 313B**, remaining unchanged after Sud's take-over by Aérospatiale.

From the beginning, the Alouette II proved a most successful design and was found particularly suitable for operations in higher altitudes. Thus, during the period 9-13 June 1958, an Artouste-powered Alouette II set up a helicopter altitude record of 10981 m (36,027 ft) for all classes, and a height record of 9583 m (31,440 ft) in the 1000/1750-kg category. By September 1960 no fewer than 598 Alouette IIs had been ordered by customers in 22 different countries and the type was being assembled by Republic in the USA and Saab in Sweden. It also became the first French aircraft of any kind, and the first helicopter in the world, to be granted an American certification.

A development of the Alouette II with a 298-kW (400-shp) Turboméca Turmo II engine, with the designation **SE 3140**, was announced in May 1957 but did not reach the production stage. Another derivative, powered by the more economical Astazou IIA turboshaft engine and featuring a new centrifugal clutch, was far more successful. The first prototype, designated SA 3180, was flown on 31 January 1960 and after thorough trials an extension of the Alouette II French Certificate of Airworthiness was granted

on 18 February 1964. Production, as the **SA 318C**, commenced in the same year, with first deliveries taking place in 1965. Of generally similar appearance and versatility, the SA 318C had a slightly higher level speed, longer range and was capable of lifting heavier loads, but is less suitable for operations in higher altitudes. The success of the basic Alouette II design was reflected in the growing number of civil and military customers: by 1 June 1967 a total of 988 Alouette IIs (including those with Astazou engines) had been ordered (and 969 delivered); by 21 May 1970 the total had increased to 1,200 (923 with Artouste and 277 with Astazou engines); this total included 450 Alouette IIs delivered to the French air force, army and navy as well as private customers. By the spring of 1975, when the production of this helicopter was terminated, the number of Alouette IIs sold had reached 1,300, and it was used by 126 civil and military operators in 46 countries.

In the military role, both Alouette II versions can be fitted with a wide variety of rockets, missiles and guns.

Specification
Aérospatiale SE 313B Alouette II
Type: light general-purpose helicopter
Powerplant: one 395-kW (530-shp) Turboméca Artouste II C6 turboshaft, derated to 269 kW (360 shp)

The eminently successful Alouette II has proved popular in both the civil and military worlds, aircraft being widely used for utility transport, rescue work, liaison, observation and armed attack. This example was used for air-taxi operations from Innsbruck. The type is no longer in production, having been superseded by the Gazelle, but many soldier on with civil operators and some air arms.

Performance: (at maximum take-off weight) maximum speed at sea level 185 km/h (115 mph); maximum cruising speed at sea level 165 km/h (102 mph); rate of climb at sea level 252 m (925 ft) per minute; service ceiling 2150 m (7,050 ft); hovering ceiling in ground effect 1650 m (5,400 ft); hovering ceiling out of ground effect 920 m (3,000 ft); range with maximum fuel at sea level 565 km (350 miles); range with 545-kg (1,200-lb) payload at sea level 100 km (62 miles); range with 390-kg (860-lb) payload at sea level 300 km (186 miles); flight endurance with maximum fuel at sea level 4 hours 6 minutes
Weights: empty 895 kg (1,973 lb); maximum take-off 1600 kg (3,527 lb)
Dimensions: diameter of main rotor 10.20 m (33 ft 5⅝ in); diameter of tail rotor 1.81 m (5 ft 11 in); length (rotor blades folded) 9.70 m (31 ft 10 in); height 2.75 m (9 ft 0 in); main rotor disc area 81.7 m² (880 sq ft)

Aérospatiale SE 318C Alouette II Astazou
Type: light general-purpose helicopter

Powerplant: one 395-kW (530-shp) Turboméca Astazou IIA turboshaft
Performance: (at maximum military take-off weight) maximum speed at sea level 205 km/h (127 mph); maximum cruising speed at sea level 170 km/h (105 mph); rate of climb at sea level 400 m (1,312 ft) per minute; service ceiling 3300 m (10,800 ft); hovering ceiling in ground effect 1520 m (4,985 ft); hovering ceiling out of ground effect 900 m (2,950 ft); range with maximum fuel at sea level 720 km (447 miles); range with 600-kg (1,322-lb) payload 100 km (62 miles); range with 480-kg (1,058-lb) payload 300 km (186 miles); maximum flight endurance at sea level 5 hours 18 minutes
Weights: empty 890 kg (1,961 lb); maximum take-off (civil version) 1600 kg (3,527 lb)
Dimensions: diameter of main rotor 10.20 m (33 ft 5⅝ in); diameter of tail rotor 1.91 m (6 ft 3 in); length of fuselage (tail rotor turning) 9.75 m (31 ft 11¾ in); height 2.75 m (9 ft 0 in); main rotor disc area 81.7 m² (880 sq ft)

Aérospatiale SA 315B Lama
to
Aérospatiale SA 330 Puma

Aérospatiale SA 315B Lama

Initially evolved to meet an Indian armed forces requirement of 1968 and intended primarily for operations in 'hot-and-high' conditions, the basic design of the **Aérospatiale SA 315B Lama** combines a reinforced Alouette II airframe with SA 316B Alouette III dynamic components, including its Artouste powerplant and rotor system. The SA 315 prototype was first flown on 17 March 1969, received the French Certificate of Airworthiness on 30 September 1970, and the name Lama was bestowed by its manufacturers in July 1971.

From the outset the SA 315B excelled in load-to-altitude performance. During a series of demonstration flights in the Indian Himalayas during 1969 an SA 315B, carrying a crew of two and 120 kg (308 lb) of fuel, landed and took off at the highest altitude ever recorded: 7500 m (24,605 ft). On 21 June 1972, a Lama with only a pilot aboard established a helicopter absolute height record of 12442 m (40,820 ft). These achievements, and the high reputation for reliability established by its close relations, Alouette II and III, ensured a good reception on the market. Already in 1971 arrangements were completed for licence production of the SA 315B by HAL at Bangalore in India. The first Indian-assembled Lama flew on 6 October 1972, with deliveries commencing in December 1973. The HAL-produced Lama is renamed Chetak.

Similar to the Alouette series, the SA 315B Lama can be fitted out for various commercial roles, such as a light passenger transport or for agricultural tasks, while the military variants include conversions for liaison, observation, photography, air/sea rescue (hoist capacity 160 kg/352 lb), transport (maximum external load 1135 kg/2,502 lb), ambulance

(two stretchers and one medical attendant), and other tasks. Its altitude performance makes the SA 315B particularly suited for mountainous districts: the production Lama can transport underslung external loads of up to 1000 kg (2,205 lb) at an altitude of 2500 m (8,200 ft). Another important factor is its universal landing gear consisting of skids with removable wheels for ground handling, provision for floats for normal operations from water and emergency flotation gear, inflatable in the air.

In 1978 agreement was reached between Aérospatiale and Helibras in Brazil for the assembly of SA 315B Lama helicopters, leading to full licence production.

Specification
Aérospatiale SA 315B Lama
Type: five-seat general-purpose helicopter
Powerplant: one 649-kW (970-shp) Turboméca Artouste IIIB turboshaft, derated to 410 kW (550 shp)
Performance: (at 2300 kg/5,070 lb): maximum cruising speed 120 km/h (75 mph); maximum rate of climb at sea level 234 m (768 ft) per minute; service ceiling 3000 m (9,840 ft); hovering ceiling in ground effect 2950 m (9,675 ft); hovering ceiling out of ground effect 1550 m (5,085 ft)
Weights: empty 1021 kg (2,251 lb); normal take-off 1950 kg (4,300 lb); maximum take-off with externally-slung

The Aérospatiale SA 315B Lama combines the airframe of the Alouette II with the rotor system and Artouste powerplant of the Alouette III. This gives the type superb performance in 'hot-and-high' regimes, allowing the Lama to set an altitude record for helicopters.

cargo 2300 kg (5,070 lb)
Dimensions: main rotor diameter 11.02 m (36 ft 1¾ in); tail rotor diameter 1.91 m (6 ft 3¼ in); fuselage length 10.26 m (33 ft 8 in); height 3.09 m (10 ft 1¾ in); main rotor disc area 95.38 m² (1,026.5 sq ft)

Aérospatiale SA 316B/ SA 319B Alouette III

The **Aérospatiale Alouette III** is an enlarged and most successful development of the Alouette II, with increased cabin capacity, improved equipment, more powerful turbine engine and generally enhanced performance. The prototype, designated **SE 3160**, was first flown on 28 February 1959, followed by the first production series known as **SA 316A**. In June 1960 an Alouette III with seven people aboard demonstrated its extraordinary performance by making landings and take-offs at an altitude of 4810 m (15,780 ft) on Mont Blanc in the French Alps. Five months later the same Alouette III with two crew and a 250-kg (551-lb) payload made landings and take-offs at an altitude of 6004 m (19,698 ft) in

Aérospatiale Alouette III of No. 3 Squadron, Royal Malaysian Air Force. It is based at Kuala Lumpur for liaison and forward air control duties.

the Himalayas – both hitherto unprecedented achievements for a helicopter. The SA 316A was built for the domestic and export market and, in June 1962, became subject to a licence-production agreement with HAL in India. The first Indian-assembled Alouette III was flown on 11 June 1965.

Various experimental developments followed, including an all-weather variant which made its initial flight on 27 April 1964. The subsequent **SA 316B**, first flown on 27 June 1968, featured strengthened main and tail rotor transmissions and was generally slightly heavier, but could carry more payload. It became the principal production version, with first deliveries made in 1970, and was an immediate export success. The Alouette III prototypes and the first two

production series were powered by Turboméca Artouste IIIB turboshaft engines, replaced by the Artouste IIID on the **SA 316C**, built in limited numbers only.

The Alouette III's cabin is more enclosed than that of the Alouette II, and can accommodate up to seven. All passenger seats are easily removable to provide an unobstructed cargo space.

The Portuguese air force Alouette III deployed to Bissau Airport in 1971 for operations against 'liberation forces' in Portuguese Guinea. Note the large dust filter over the engine air intakes.

There is provision for an external sling for hauling loads up to 750 kg (1,653 lb) or, for the air/sea rescue role, a hoist of 175-kg (386-lb) capacity. Like most other light general-purpose helicopters the Alouette III can also be used for casualty evacuation, carrying two stretcher cases and two seated persons behind the pilot.

Experiments with the thermically more efficient and more economical Astazou turboshaft engine led to the **SA 319B Alouette III Astazou**, which is a direct development of the SA 316B. The first experimental SA 319B prototype was completed and flown in 1967, but full production did not start until 1973.

The Alouette III variants were even more successful on the international market than those of its predecessor, and by 1984 no less than 1,453 machines had been sold to 190 civil and military operators in 92 countries. In addition to licence-production by HAL at Bangalore in India (200) similar agreements were signed with ICA-Brasov in Romania (for 130) and Switzerland (for 60).

Specification
Aérospatiale SA 316B Alouette III
Type: general-purpose helicopter
Powerplant: one 649-kW (870-shp) Turboméca Artouste IIIB turboshaft, derated to 425 kW (570 shp)
Performance: (standard version, at maximum take-off weight) maximum speed at sea level 210 km/h (130 mph); maximum cruising speed at sea level 185 km/h (115 mph); maximum rate of climb at sea level 260 m (950 ft) per minute; service ceiling 3200 m

(10,500 ft); hovering ceiling in ground effect 2880 m (9,450 ft); hovering ceiling out of ground effect 1520 m (5,000 ft); range with maximum fuel at sea level 480 km (298 miles); range at optimum altitude 540 km (335 miles)
Weights: empty 1143 kg (2,520 lb); maximum take-off 2200 kg (4,950 lb)
Dimensions: diameter of main rotor 11.02 m (36 ft 1¾ in); diameter of tail rotor 1.91 m (6 ft 3¼ in); length overall (rotor blades folded) 10.03 m (32 ft 10¾ in); height 3.00 m (9 ft 10 in); main rotor disc area 95.38 m² (1,026 sq ft)

Aérospatiale SA 319C Alouette III Astazou
Type: general-purpose helicopter
Powerplant: one 649-kW (870-shp) Turboméca Astazou XIV turboshaft, derated to 448 kW (600 shp)
Performance: (at maximum take-off weight) maximum speed at sea level 220 km/h (136 mph); maximum cruising speed at sea level 197 km/h (122 mph); maximum rate of climb at sea level 270 m (885 ft) per minute; hovering ceiling in ground effect 3100 m (10,170 ft); hovering ceiling out of ground effect 1700 m (5,575 ft); range with six passengers (take-off at sea

The Alouette III was particularly successful in the Middle East, where its good performance makes it ideal for flying in the hot climate of the region. This desert-camouflaged example wears the markings of the Royal Jordanian Air Force.

level) 605 km (375 miles)
Weights: empty 1146 kg (2,527 lb); maximum take-off 2250 kg (4,960 lb)
Dimensions: diameter of main rotor 11.02 m (30 ft 1¾ in); diameter of tail rotor 1.91 m (6 ft 3¼ in); length (rotor blades folded) 10.03 m (32 ft 10¾ in); height 3.00 m (9 ft 10 in); main rotor disc area 95.38 m² (1,026.5 sq ft)

Aérospatiale SA 321 Super Frelon

The **SA 3200** Frelon (hornet) was built by Sud-Aviation as a medium transport helicopter and first flew on 10 June 1959. Powered by three Turboméca Turmo IIIB turboshaft engines driving a transmission system built in Italy by Fiat, the **SA 3200** was fitted with external fuel tanks to provide the volume for the accommodation of 28 troops in the hold. Two prototypes were built: the **SA 3210.01** (F-ZWWE) troop transport helicopter made its first flight on 7 December 1962 with the **SA 3210.02** (F-ZWWF) maritime version following on 28 May 1963.

The designation was changed to **SA 321** at the pre-production stage; the first production run consisted of 24 **SA 321G** helicopters for the Aéronavale. The **SA 321H** was the equivalent of the **SA 321G** for land-based operations. This was followed by the **SA 321F**, a passenger helicopter. The **SA 321J** civil helicopter could carry 27 passengers as a transport or 4000 kg (8,818 lb) of freight in the cabin or 5000 kg (11,023 lb) as an external load. This model was succeeded by the **SA 321Ja** with an increased operating weight; the People's Republic of China bought 16 examples of this model. Military export versions of this transport included the **SA 321K** (12 for Israel), the **SA 321L** (16 for South Africa) and the **SA 321M**

(nine for Libya). At the end of production in 1983, 99 Super Frelon helicopters had been built. China also undertook series production of the **SA 321** at the Changhe Aircraft Factory in Jiangxi Province as the **Z-8** (Zhishengji-8), of which the first example flew on 11 December 1985 with a powerplant of three Turmo turboshaft engines built in China with the designation Changzhou WZ-6. Delivery to the People's Liberation Army began in 1989.

Specification
Aérospatiale SA 321G Super Frelon
Type: anti-submarine helicopter with transport and anti-ship capabilities
Powerplant: three 1140-kW (1550-shp) Turboméca Turmo IIIC6 turboshafts
Performance: cruising speed 248 km/h (154 mph); initial climb rate 300 m (985 ft) per minute; service ceiling 3100 m (10,170 ft); hovering ceiling 1950 m (6,400 ft) in ground effect; endurance 4 hours 0

minutes for an anti-submarine patrol
Weights: empty 6,863 kg (15,130 lb); maximum take-off 13,000 kg (28,660 lb)
Dimensions: main rotor diameter 18.90 m (62 ft 0 in); length overall 23.03 m (75 ft 6.67 in) with rotors turning; height 6.76 m (22 ft 2.25 in); main rotor disc area 280.55 m² (3,019.91 sq ft)

This Super Frelon is seen in the course of a rescue operation using a winch-operated cage to lift the survivor.

23

Aérospatiale SA 330 Puma

In the early 1960s Sud-Aviation began the design and development of a twin turbine-powered helicopter that would not only meet a French army requirement for an all-weather tactical and logistic transport, but which would be suitable also for use by other armed forces. The first of two prototypes made its maiden flight on 15 April 1965, and the Anglo-French helicopter agreement (concluded on 2 April 1968) gave Westland Helicopters in the UK joint production of these aircraft. Intended initially for service with the French army and the Royal Air Force, the latter required this helicopter for deployment as a tactical transport.

The fuselage of the **SA 330 Puma**, as this aircraft has been named, is a conventional all-metal semi-monocoque structure, with the powerplant mounted externally on top of the fuselage shell and forward of the main rotor assembly. The rotor is driven via a main gearbox, with twin free-wheeling spur gears to combine the outputs of the two turboshaft engines to a single main drive shaft. In the event of an engine failure the remaining engine continues to drive the rotor, and should both engines fail the auto-rotating main rotor continues to drive the auxiliary take-offs for the shaft-driven tail rotor, alternator, dual hydraulic pumps, and ventilation fan. The tail boom, which carries the flapping-hinge five-blade tail rotor on the starboard side and a horizontal stabiliser on the port side, is a monocoque continuation of the aft fuselage. Early main rotor blades were of light alloy construction, but those fitted since 1976 are composite units of glassfibre, carbon fibre and honeycomb construction, with anti-abrasion leading edges of stainless steel. The landing gear is of the semi-retracting tricycle type, with twin wheels on each unit, all of which are partly exposed when retracted.

There have been a number of changes in powerplant: the first **SA 330B**s for the French army and air force, and the **SA 330E**s for the Royal Air Force, were powered by Turmo III C4 turboshaft engines with a take-off rating of 990 kW

This Aérospatiale SA 330E serves with the RAF's No.230 Squadron, based at RAF Odiham, with the designation Puma HC.Mk 1.

The Puma is used in many civilian roles, in particular offshore transport and support duties for the oil industry.

(1,328 shp); and the **SA 330C/H** military export versions, first flown in September 1968, had originally 1044-kW (1,400-shp) Turmo IVBs, but from the end of 1973 SA 330H aircraft were equipped with 1174-kW (1,575-shp) Turmo IVC engines which include anti-icing of the engine air intakes. The first **SA 330F/G** civil versions had Turmo IVA engines of 1070 kW (1,435 shp) as first flown on 26 September 1969 and delivered from the end of 1970; but like the SA 330H the SA

330G acquired Turmo IVC engines from the end of 1973; and this latter powerplant is installed also on the **SA 330J** (civil) and **SA 330L** (military) helicopters which were introduced in 1976.

Accommodation of the SA 330J provides for a standard crew of two on the flight deck, and the cabin can have 8, 9, or 12-seat VIP layouts, or can seat up to 20 passengers in a high-density configuration, with a toilet and baggage compartment at the rear of the cabin.

Equipped with thermal de-icing of the main rotor blades, thermal anti-icing of the tail rotor blades, special intakes and weather radar, the SA 330J can be flown in all weather conditions, including known icing conditions, since receiving certification in this form on 25 April 1978.

Aérospatiale AS 332 Super Puma and AS 532 Cougar

The Aérospatiale **AS 332 Super Puma** is a development of the **SA 330 Puma** with improved survivability features (including run-dry transmission, duplicated electrical and hydraulic systems, self-sealing fuel tanks and optional armour) for reduced vulnerability to ground fire, more powerful Turboméca Makila turboshafts, multi-purpose air intakes, an uprated transmission system, lightened Starflex rotor head, more survivable main rotor blades of composite construction with thermal de-icing and an advanced aerofoil section, single- rather than twin-wheeled main landing gear units of the high-impact type with greater track and an optional 'kneeling' capability to improve access to the cabin, a lengthened nose incorporating the black nose radome for the optional Bendix/King RDR-1400 or Honeywell Primus weather radar designed to enhance the all-weather flight capability inherited from the SA 330, a longer wheel base and, as a notable

distinguishing feature, a ventral fin.

Development of this improved model began in 1974, largely to meet the developing requirements of military operators of the SA 330 series, who had appreciated the overall capabilities of the type but now wanted more payload, better performance, and improved levels of crew and passenger survivability in the event of a crash landing. The first step was the revision of a single SA 330 to **AS 331** prototype standard with the powerplant of two Makila turboshafts driving an uprated transmission for a first flight on 5 September 1977. Series production of the new model started in August 1978, and the first **AS 332C** for the civil market was completed in 1981. The two-crew **AS 332 Super Puma** for civil applications has the same payload as the SA 330 (up to 19 passengers in a cabin 19 ft 10.5 in/6.05 m long, 5 ft 10.75 in/1.80 m wide and 5 ft 1 in/1.55 m high accessed by sliding doors) but in combination with better

overall performance (especially in range), reduced cabin noise and simpler maintenance. The **AS 332L** stretched version offers even greater capacity (22 passengers) and made its maiden flight on 10 October 1980. Compared with the original **AS 332 Super Puma** helicopter variants, the **AS 332L** has a 0.76 m lengthening of the cabin with an additional window on each side. The extra weight and drag had an adverse effect on range, however, and Aérospatiale therefore developed new blade tips which allowed a greater take-off weight and increased the range of the **AS 332L** to that of the **AS 332C**.

By 1995 more than 450 Super Puma and Cougar helicopters had been sold. Alternative designations for the Super Puma include HD.21 and HT.21 in Spain (SAR and troop transport respectively) and Hkp 10 in Sweden. IPTN in Indonesia assembles the Super Puma as the NAS-332 in both the C (Court, or short) and L (Longue, or long) versions.

Specification
Aérospatiale SA 332L2 Super Puma Mk II
Type: medium general-purpose helicopter
Powerplant: two 1356-kW (1,843-shp) Turboméca Makila 1A2 turboshafts
Performance: maximum speed 315 km/h (196 mph); normal cruising speed 276 km/h (171.5 mph); maximum climb rate 390 m (1,280 ft) per minute; service ceiling 3100 m (10,170 ft); hovering ceiling 2500 m (8,205 ft) in ground effect and 1585 m (5,200 ft) out of ground effect; range 371 km (231 miles) with 23 passengers
Weights: empty 4650 kg (10,251 lb); maximum take-off 9070 kg (19,996 lb)
Dimensions: main rotor diameter 16.20 m (53 ft 1.5 in); length overall 19.50 m (63 ft 11 in) with rotors turning; height 4.976 m (16 ft 4 in); main rotor disc area 206.00 m² (2,217.44 sq ft)

Aérospatiale SA 341/342
to
Agusta A 106

Aérospatiale SA 341/342 Gazelle

The **Aérospatiale SA 341 Gazelle** all-purpose lightweight helicopter originated as Aérospatiale project X 300 to meet a French army requirement for a light observation helicopter. The designation was changed to SA 340 soon afterwards. The finished design showed close affinity to the SA 318C Alouette II, and eventually used the same Astazou II powerplant and transmission system. Unlike the Alouette II, however, the new helicopter features a fully-enclosed fuselage structure and has two pilots side by side, with full dual controls. It also introduced two innovations: the *fenestron*, or shrouded tail rotor, and a rigid modified Bölkow-type main rotor. And it showed every sign of sharing its predecessor's sales success and popularity.

While still in the final design stages the SA 340 attracted British interest, leading to a joint development and production share-out agreement signed on 22 February 1967 and officially confirmed on 2 April 1968. The first prototype, designated **SA 340.001**, was flown on 7 April 1967, and the second on 12 April 1968. These were followed by four pre-production SA 341 Gazelles (first flown on 2 August 1968), of which the third was equipped to British Army requirements, assembled in France, and then re-assembled by Westland in the UK as the prototype Gazelle AH.1. It was first flown on 28 April 1970.

On 14 May 1970 the first Aérospatiale-built SA 341 pre-production aircraft, in slightly modified form, establishing three new speed records for helicopters of its class, arousing even more foreign interest.

The first French production Gazelle, **SA 341.1001**, was cleared for its initial test flight on 6 August 1971; it had a longer cabin than its predecessors, an enlarged tail unit and an uprated Astazou IIIA engine. The initial Westland-assembled Gazelles followed early in 1972 (first flown on 31 January 1972).

Variants

SA 341B Gazelle AH.1: British Army version; Astazou IIIN engine; Nightsun searchlight, Decca Doppler 80 radar and automatic chart display; first Westland-assembled example flown on 31 January 1972; entered operational

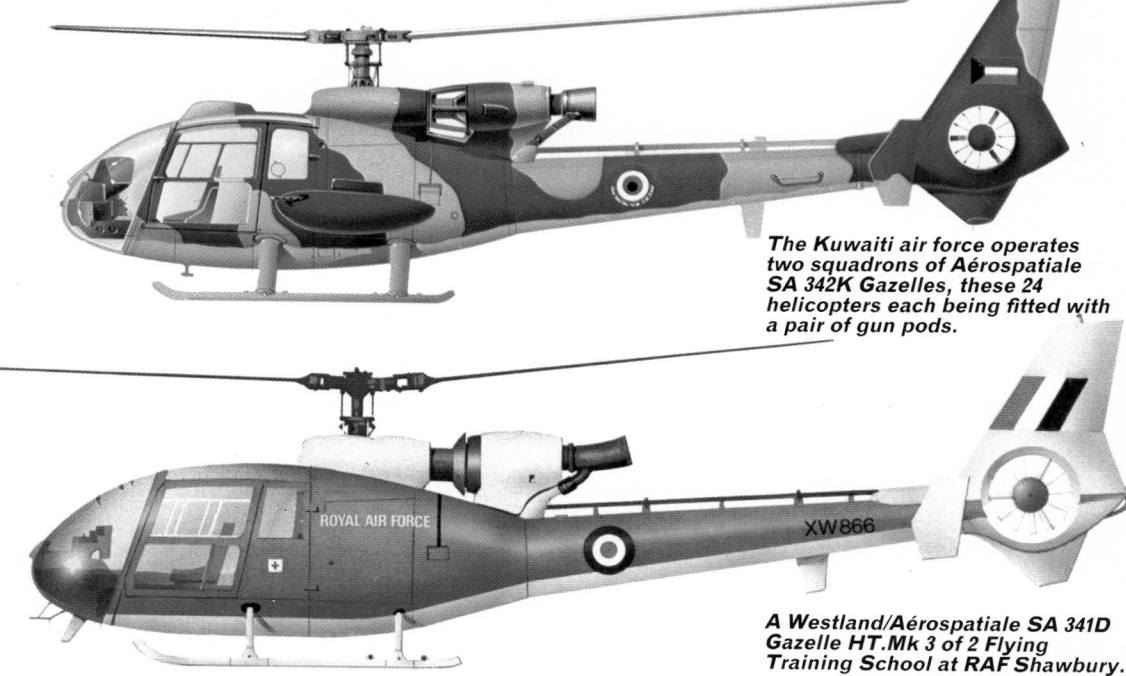

The Kuwaiti air force operates two squadrons of Aérospatiale SA 342K Gazelles, these 24 helicopters each being fitted with a pair of gun pods.

A Westland/Aérospatiale SA 341D Gazelle HT.Mk 3 of 2 Flying Training School at RAF Shawbury.

service on 6 July 1974 (total 158)
SA 341C Gazelle HT.2: Fleet Air Arm training versions; Astazou IIIN engine; stability-augmentation system and a hoist incorporated; first flown on 6 July 1972 and first entered service on 10 December 1974 (total 30)
SA 341D Gazelle HT.3: RAF training version; Astazou IIIN engine; stability-augmentation system; Schermuly flares installation; first deliveries to service on 16 July 1973 (total 14)
SA 341E Gazelle HCC.4: RAF communications version; Astazou IIIN engine (total 1)
SA 341F Gazelle: basic French army version; Astazou IIIC engine (total 166)
SA 341G Gazelle: civil commercial version; Astazou IIIA engine; officially certificated for passenger service on 7 June 1972; subsequently became the first helicopter to obtain US approval for operations under IFR Cat.1 conditions with a single pilot; also developed into a so-called 'Stretched Gazelle', with rear section of the cabin modified to provide additional 20-cm (8-

in) legroom for the rear passengers
SA 341H Gazelle: military export version; Astazou IIIB engine; subject to licence-production agreement signed on 1 October 1971 with SOKO in Yugoslavia (total 112)
SA 342J Gazelle: civil version of SA 342L; 649-kW (870-shp) Astazou XIV engine, improved *fenestron* tail rotor, increased take-off weight; approved for service on 24 April 1976; deliveries commenced in 1977
SA 342K Gazelle: military export version for 'hot and dry' areas; 649-kW (870-shp) Astazou XIVH engine with momentum-separation shrouds over air intakes; first flown on 11 May 1973; initial sales to Kuwait.
SA 342L Gazelle: military counterpart of SA 342J; 649-kW (870-shp) Astazou XIV engine; adaptable for wide range of armaments and equipment, including six Euromissile HOT anti-tank missiles
SA 342M Gazelle: French army anti-tank version with four Euromissile HOT missiles, SFIM APX M397 stabilised sight

Specification
Aérospatiale SA 341 Gazelle
Type: five-seat utility helicopter
Powerplant: one 440-kW (590-shp) Turboméca Astazou IIIA turboshaft
Performance: (SA 341 at maximum take-off weight) maximum permissible speed at sea level 310 km/h (193 mph); maximum cruising speed at sea level 264 km/h (164 mph); economical cruising speed at sea level 233 km/h (144 mph); maximum rate of climb at sea level 540 m (1,770 ft) per minute; service ceiling 5000 m (16,405 ft); hovering ceiling in ground effect 2850 m (9,350 ft); hovering ceiling out of ground effect 2000 m (6,560 ft); range at sea level with maximum fuel 670 km (416 miles); range with pilot and 500-kg (1,102-lb) payload 360 km (223 miles)
Weights: (SA 341G) empty 908 kg (2,002 lb); maximum take-off 1800 kg (3,970 lb)
Dimensions: diameter of main rotor 10.50 m (34 ft 5½ in); diameter of tail rotor 0.695 m (2 ft 3⅜ in); length overall 11.97 m (39 ft ⁵⁄₁₆ in); height 3.15 m (10 ft 2⅝ in); main rotor disc area 86.5 m² (931 sq ft)

Though designed principally for military applications, the Gazelle utility helicopter has also appeared in SA 341G and up-engined SA 342J civil variants. The latter also has an improved fenestron.

Aérospatiale SA 365 Dauphin

The **Aérospatiale Dauphin** is being developed in several versions, with single and twin engines, as a replacement for the Aérospatiale Alouette III. The first version to fly was the **SA 360**, with a single Astazou XVI turboshaft, on 2 June 1972. It was later re-engined with the Astazou XVIIIA and modifications were incorporated; in May 1973 this helicopter set up three speed records in its class. A second SA 360 prototype flew on 29 January 1973 and French Airworthiness Certification was awarded in December 1975. The first twin-engine Dauphin to fly was the **SA 365** prototype, on 24 January 1975. The basic designation was later changed to AS 365 while the military helicopters became AS 565. At the end of 1990 the 500th Dauphin was completed and more than 90 further examples had been ordered by the end of 1994.

Variants

SA 360: prototypes, the first flying on 2 June 1972 on the power of a 730-kW (980-shp) Turboméca Astazou XVI turboshaft; this initial helicopter was later re-engined with the 783-kW (1,050-shp) Astazou XVIIIA destined for the production version, and joined in the flight test programme by a second prototype; three class records were set by the first prototype

SA 360 Dauphin: initial production version; Astazou XVIIIA turboshaft; standard accommodation for a pilot and up to nine passengers, with an alternative of an internal or external payload of 1420 kg (3,130 lb) or 1300 kg (2,865 lb); performance includes maximum cruising speed 275 km/h (171 mph) at sea level, initial climb rate 540 m (1,770 ft) per minute, hovering ceiling in ground effect 3850 m (12,630 ft) and range 680 km (423 miles); empty weight 1580 kg (3,483 lb) and maximum take-off weight 3000 kg (6,613 lb); among the dimensions are main rotor diameter 11.50 m (37 ft 8 3/4 in), fuselage length 10.98 m (36 ft 0 in), height 3.50 m (11 ft 6 in) and main rotor disc area 103.87 m² (1.118 sq ft)

SA 361: experimental type based on the SA 360 with Starflex rotor head and powerplant of one 957-kW (1,300-shp) Astazou XX turboshaft; first flight on 12 July 1976 and then developed into the SA 361H

SA 361H: evolution of the SA 361 as a light combat and anti-tank helicopter with the powerplant of one Astazou XXB turboshaft developing 1044 kW (1,400 shp); this model could carry 13 fully equipped troops, or eight HOT anti-tank missiles controlled via a stabilised SFIM roof sight and a Vénus night sight mounted in the nose

SA 365 Dauphin 2: twin-engined development of the SA 360C with a powerplant of two Turboméca Arriel turboshafts each rated at 478 kW (650 shp); prototype had fixed landing gear and first flew on 24 January 1975, quickly followed by a second helicopter with retractable landing gear; entered production as the SA 365

SA 365C: first production version of the Dauphin 2 for commercial operations, with certification for single-pilot VFR and IFR flight in July and December 1978 respectively; deliveries began in December 1978, and the type was further developed as the SA 365C1 and SA 365C2; the Dauphin X380 was an experimental model with a five-blade Spheriflex rotor head and further improvements as well as a powerplant of two Arriel 1C1 turboshafts; with 660-kW (885-shp) Arriel 1X turboshafts, a new synchronised transmission system and aerodynamic improvements, this became the Dauphin Grande Vitesse (DGV) which set up a new speed record of 371 km/h (230.5 mph) at the beginning of 1992

SA 365F: naval version of the SA 365C with 515-kW (691-shp) Arriel 1M turboshafts; the first SA 365F off the production line flew on 2 July 1982, and the French navy and Ireland both acquired this version. The newer SA 365F1 version became the AS 565MA/SA Panther

SA 365K: based on the SA 365M Dauphin 2 prototype, this version was developed for military use, and was renamed as the Panther in 1986; the final prototype flew on 30 April 1986 powered by 558-kW (749-shp) Arriel 1M1 turboshafts, and the Brazilian army procured this variant that was renamed as the AS 565 in 1990

SA 365M: military prototype developed from the SA 361H for a first flight on 29 February 1984; able to carry 10-12 troops or alternatively eight HOT anti-tank missiles or 44 SNEB air-to-ground rockets, the SA 365M was overtaken by the SA 365K

SA 365N: SA 365C modified for civil use with between eight and 12 passengers; first flew on 31 March 1979 with a powerplant of two 492-kW (660-shp) Arriel 1C turboshafts, subject of a licence agreement with China for production as the Harbin Z-9; superseded by the AS 365N1 and AS 365N2 with 551-kW (739-shp) Arriel 1C2 turboshafts, and from 1993 the AS 365N3 with the five-blade Spheriflex rotor head proved in the Dauphin X380, an EFIS cockpit and a powerplant of two Arriel 2 turboshafts

SA 366: second Dauphin 2 prototype first flew on 28 January 1975 with a powerplant of two Lycoming LTS101 turboshafts and fixed landing gear but later adapted as the second SA 365 prototype with Arriel engines

SA 366G: subject of a 1979 requirement by the US Coast Guard (99 helicopters) for short-range SAR operations from ships as well as shore bases with the service designation HH-65A Dolphin; SA 366G prototype first flew on 23 July 1980 with a powerplant two 461-kW (618-shp) LTS101-750A1 turboshafts, and the helicopters were delivered between November 1984 and April 1989 to SA 366G1 upgraded standard with a 'fenestron' tail rotor; the HH-65A is fitted with American engines and much US-made equipment including a Rockwell Collins communications suite, a searchlight and a FLIR, the last being used for the detection of people in the water, from which they can be hauled to safety with the aid of a rescue winch

AS 565AA: military and armed Panther version resulting from the renaming of the SA 365K; also available in AS 565CA anti-tank and AS 565UA general-purpose variants

AS 565SA: armed naval version renamed from SA 365F1; also available as the unarmed AS 565MA

Z-9 Haitun: this is the AS 365N built under licence as the Zhishengji (vertical take-off) no. 9 by the Harbin Aircraft Manufacturing Company; the maiden flight of the first helicopter assembled in China (using French production parts) was made on 6 February 1982

The US Coast Guard service maintains a considerable fleet of Aérospatiale SA 366G Dauphins for sea patrol and rescue services with the local designation HH-65A Dolphin.

Aérospatiale SN 601 Corvette

In the late 1960s Aérospatiale initiated the design of a medium size multi-purpose aircraft with accommodation for up to 12 passengers in a high-density seating arrangement. The aircraft was designed for such roles as air-taxi, ambulance, executive transport, light freight, or training. An **SN 600** prototype, powered by two 998-kg (2,200-lb) thrust Pratt & Whitney Aircraft of Canada JT15D-1 turbofan engines, pod-mounted on each side of the rear fuselage, flew for the first time on 16 July 1970. Un-

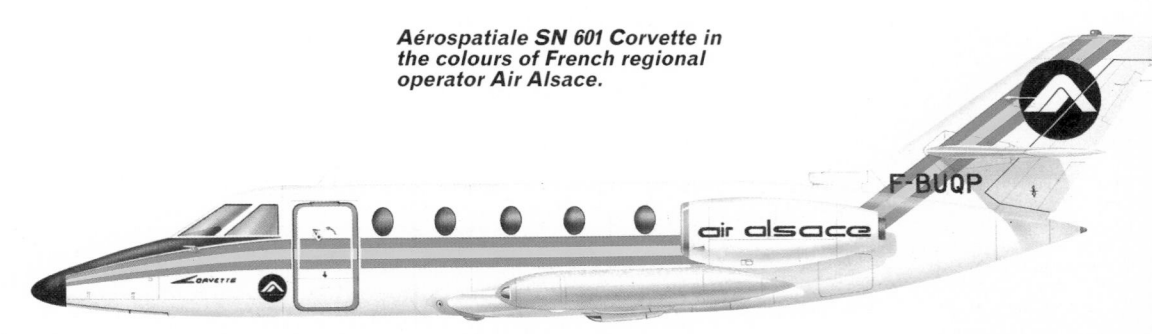

Aérospatiale SN 601 Corvette in the colours of French regional operator Air Alsace.

Despite its many attractions, strong competition made the SN 6012 Corvette a commercial failure, only 40 being manufactured (1974-1978).

fortunately, after completing more than 270 flight hours, this aircraft was destroyed in an accident on 23 March 1971, and it was not until 20 December 1972 that a production **SN 601**, by then named Corvette, was able to record its first flight.

In the interim period there had been some design changes, including a lengthened fuselage, increased capacity wingtip tanks, and the introduction of more powerful JT15D-4 engines. A low-wing monoplane of all-metal construction, the Corvette has wings with double-slotted trailing-edge flaps, three-section spoilers, and hydraulically actuated airbrakes above and below the wing surface. The tail unit is conventional, with the tailplane mounted on the fin to keep it clear of efflux from the turbine engines. The tricycle type retractable landing gear, with a single wheel on each unit, includes an anti-skid braking system. The lengthened fuselage allowed production aircraft to accommodate a maximum of 14 passengers and they, and the crew of two on a separate flight deck, enjoy a pressurised and air-conditioned environment. Blind flying instrumentation is standard, but avionics equipment was installed to the customer's specification.

Deliveries of production aircraft began in September 1974, but only 40 had been built when production was terminated in 1978 as a result of lack of orders, probably because of strong international competition in this particular category of aircraft.

Specification
Type: multi-purpose transport
Powerplant: two 2,500-lb (1134-kg) thrust Pratt & Whitney Aircraft of Canada JT15D-4 turbofans
Performance: maximum cruising speed 760 km/h (472 mph) at 9145 m (30,000 ft); economic cruising speed 566 km/h (352 mph); service ceiling 12500 m (41,000 ft); range with maximum fuel and 45-min reserves 2555 km (1,588 miles); range with 12 passengers and 45-min reserves 1555 km (966 miles)
Weights: empty 3510 kg (7,738 lb); maximum take-off 6600 kg (14,551 lb)
Dimensions: span 12.87 m (42 ft 2½ in); length 13.83 m (45 ft 4½ in); height 4.23 m (13 ft 10½ in); wing area 22.00 m² (236.81 sq ft)

Aérospatiale SN 601 Corvette.

Aérospatiale/British Aerospace Concorde

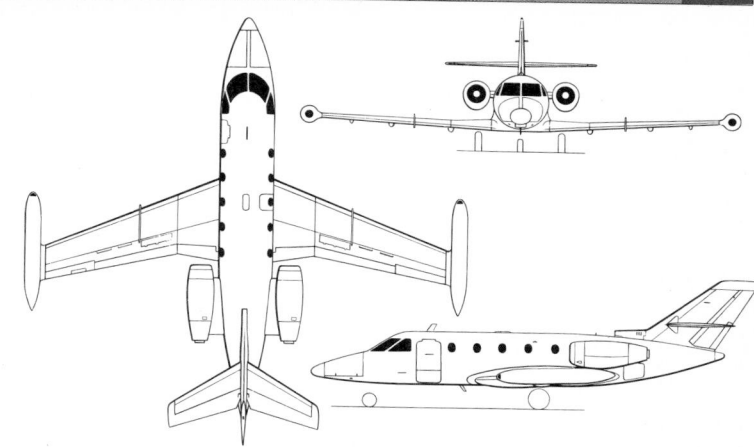

In the late 1950s both Bristol Aircraft Ltd in the UK (which in 1960 became a wholly-owned subsidiary of, and was ultimately absorbed into, the British Aircraft Corporation or BAC), and Sud-Aviation in France (which was merged with Nord-Aviation and SEREB in 1970 to form the Société Nationale Industrielle Aérospatiale) were each carrying out independent design studies for a practical supersonic transport. Both companies decided that the design and construction of such an aircraft was feasible, but that the cost of its development would be completely beyond the capability of any individual company. Indeed, it soon became clear that development costs were likely to exceed a figure which could be faced by either the British or French government alone. There thus followed discussions which resulted in the signature of agreements on 29 November 1962 to bring about international collaboration for the realisation of what was seen then as a highly desirable and readily marketable commodity. The governments of the UK and France agreed to provide the cash to finance development, and the British Aircraft Corporation and Rolls-Royce finalised agreements with Sud-Aviation and the Société Nationale d'Etude et de Construction de Moteurs d'Aviation (SNECMA) for collaboration to design and manufacture a joint supersonic transport (SST), this eventually becoming named appropriate **Concorde**, symbolising the determination of the two nations' manufacturing companies to produce a safe, reliable, world-beating aircraft.

Concorde's streamlined fuselage and ogival wing are designed for maximum efficiency at a cruising speed just above Mach 2. This aircraft is shown in the colours of Air France.

Design and development of the Concorde needed the solution to many complex technological problems if the collaborating companies were to attain their aim of manufacturing a safe and reliable SST. The first bridge to be crossed was a decision on maximum speed. If the intention was to cruise at a speed between Mach 2.5 and Mach 3.0, then there were problems to be faced from kinetic heating resulting from air friction which, during extended periods of high-speed cruising flight, would raise the temperature of certain areas of the aircraft's structure to a figure where conventional light alloys would be unable to maintain their structural integrity. Such speeds can, and have been, very considerably exceeded by manned research vehicles, and the world has a number of operational military aircraft capable of Mach 3 or over. Their structures, however, contain considerable amounts of heat-resistant metals such as titanium or stainless steel, but their use on a fairly large scale for a Mach 2.5 to Mach 3.0 Concorde would have very considerably increased structural costs. Instead, it was decided to put a limit of Mach 2.2 on the speed of the airliner.

Design, development and construction were shared between Aérospatiale and BAC, with the French partner responsible for wings and wing control surfaces; the rear cabin section; air conditioning, hydraulics, navigation and radio systems; and flying controls. BAC was responsible for the three forward fuselage sections; rear fuselage; vertical tail surfaces; engine nacelles and ducting; engine installation, fire warning and extinguishing systems; electrical, fuel and oxygen systems; and noise and thermal insulation. Construction of the first two prototypes began in February

1965, Concorde 001 being built by Aérospatiale at Toulouse, and 002 by BAC at Filton, Bristol. The first flight of 001 (F-WTSS) was made on 2 March 1969, and that of the British-assembled 002 (G-BSST) on 9 April 1969.

As early flight testing of these two aircraft showed no fundamental problems, 001 was used for a sales and demonstration tour which began on 4 September 1971. More or less simultaneously, 002 was giving demonstration flights to interested airlines, politicians and the press, and it was not until 2 June 1972 that it, too, carried out a sales tour of the Middle and Far East, this including visits to Australia and Japan. Despite the inherent problems of Concorde, posed by the fact that it was an SST, and including such items as engine noise, sonic boom, fuel consumption and cost, there was considerable interest in the aircraft and its earth-shrinking potential for business and VIP travel. Soon more than 70 aircraft had been ordered, and the prospects for a resounding commercial success then seemed quite within the bounds of possibility. This was not just wishful thinking, for with such customers on the order book as Air Canada, Air France, American Airlines, BOAC, Eastern Air Lines, Japan Air Lines, Lufthansa, Pan American, Qantas, Sabena, TWA and United Airlines, it was reasonable to assume that successful deployment by these companies would result in the generation of new orders.

Concorde's appearance is well known, for colourful photographs and illustrations have appeared regularly in both aviation and general press features which have extolled or denigrated this remarkable aeroplane. It is of cantilever low-wing configuration with a large-area delta wing, and a long, narrow fuselage with a maximum internal width of 2.63 m (8 ft 7½ in). The tail unit consists only of a vertical fin and rudder, for control in pitch and roll is provided by six elevons spaced across the trailing edge of the delta wing. The landing gear is of the hydraulically retractable tricycle type, with twin wheels on the nose unit and a four-wheel bogie on each main unit. Standard accommodation provides for a crew of three on the flight deck, with provision for a fourth seat behind the pilot, and there is a variety of four-abreast seating layouts to suit the requirements of individual airlines. The maximum possible seating capacity allows for the carriage of up to 144 passengers. Powerplant consists of four Rolls-Royce/SNECMA Olympus 593 Mk 610 turbojet engines, this particular version of the Olympus being developed specially to power Concorde.

Concorde has some particularly interesting design features which are the result of its configuration and usage. For example, the delta-wing planform requires that the aircraft is flown at a fairly

steep angle of attack at low subsonic speeds, which means that its flight crew would have a more restricted view of the ground during take-off, initial climb, approach and landing unless some special provision were made. This resulted in the design of a fuselage nose section which could be drooped to improve the forward view under the above conditions, and of a retractable visor, which is raised hydraulically, to fair in the windscreen during normal cruising flight.

Much of the Concorde's total fuel capacity of 119787 litres (26,350 Imperial gallons) is contained within the wing but a percentage is held in four fuselage tanks. The fuel is used for two other tasks in addition to the primary one of fuelling the engines: firstly, the large volume of fuel within the wing structure acts as a heat sink to reduce the wing temperature in prolonged supersonic flight; and secondly, fuel is transferred automatically throughout the network of storage tanks to maintain the aircraft's centre of gravity in cruising flight. In addition, a group of trim tanks maintains the correct relationship between the aircraft's CG and its aerodynamic centre of pressure, fuel being moved aft during acceleration, and forward as the aircraft returns to a subsonic flight regime.

Much of the efficiency and reliability of the powerplant result from the compu-

ter-controlled variable-area air intakes, which ensure the optimum air flow to each engine under all operating conditions. The Concorde's flight deck and cabin are air-conditioned and pressurised, and the advanced avionics include an automatic flight control system, and triplicated inertial navigation systems.

By the time that full passenger-carrying certification was awarded by the British and French authorities in late 1975, flight testing of prototype, pre-production, and the first production Concordes totalled 5,335 hours. SST scheduled services were inaugurated simultaneously by Air France and British Airways on 21 January 1976, but by then the escalating cost of these aircraft and the activity of anti-Concorde environmentalists had reduced the order book to the nine aircraft ordered by the above two airlines. There was, of course, a strong belief that the successful operation of these aircraft by Air France and British Airways would generate new orders, but this did not occur. A significant factor in this lack of sales has resulted from the large increases in the cost of fuel.

Concorde has probably generated more pride, and more noise and environmental pollution-hate, than any other civil airliner yet built. To whichever of these groups an individual belongs, there are few who will not agree that

British Airways uses its seven Concordes for North Atlantic operations and charter flights.

Concorde, one of the first fruits of international collaboration, has proved a supreme technological success.

Specification
Type: supersonic commercial transport
Powerplant: four Rolls-Royce/SNECMA Olympus 593 Mk 610 turbojet engines, each rated at 17259-kg (38,050-lb) thrust with 17 per cent afterburning
Performance: cruising speed for optimum range Mach 2.04 at 15635 m (51,300 ft), equivalent to 2179 km/h (1,354 mph); service ceiling 18290 m (60,000 ft); range with maximum fuel 6582 km (4,090 miles) with FAR fuel reserves and payload of 8845 kg (19,500 lb); range with maximum payload at Mach 2.02 cruise 6228 km (3,870 miles) with FAR fuel reserves
Weights: operating empy 78698 kg (173,500 lb); maximum take-off 185066 kg (408,000 lb)
Dimensions: span 25.55 m (83 ft 10 in); length 62.10 m (203 ft 9 in); height 11.40 m (37 ft 5 in); wing area 358.22 m² (3,856 sq ft)

Agusta A 106

One of Italy's oldest aviation companies, Agusta, was established in 1907, but entered the helicopter field in 1952 when a licence to build the Bell 47 was acquired. This was followed by a series of other licence agreements with both Bell and Sikorsky, but in more recent years Agusta has developed several of its own designs.

The smallest to come to fruition, even though only in a very modest way, the **Agusta A 106** was flown in prototype form in November 1965. A small production batch followed in the early 1970s and about five of these were operated by the air arm of the Italian navy (Marinavia) from 'Impavido' class ships in the anti-submarine warfare role, supplementing larger naval ASW helicopters such as the SH-3D, AB 204AS and AB 212ASW.

The A 106 had a two-blade main rotor and conventional tail rotor, and auxiliary flotation gear could be fitted to the skid framework, which had removable wheels for ground manoeuvring.

Operations in poor visibility were assisted by comprehensive instrumentation and electronics, and the Ferranti company developed an electronic three-axis stability augmentation system for the A 106, providing a stable firing platform and damping out external disturbances.

Specification
Type: shipboard single-seat anti-submarine helicopter
Powerplant: one 224-kW (300-shp) Turboméca-Agusta TAA 230 turboshaft, derated to 194 kW (260 shp)
Performance: (at take-off weight with two torpedoes) maximum speed at sea level 176 km/h (109 mph); cruising speed 167 km/h (104 mph); initial climb rate 372 m (1,220 ft) per minute; hovering ceiling in ground effect 3000 m (9,850 ft); hovering ceiling out of ground effect 1150 m (3,775 ft); range with maximum internal and external fuel 740 km (460 miles)

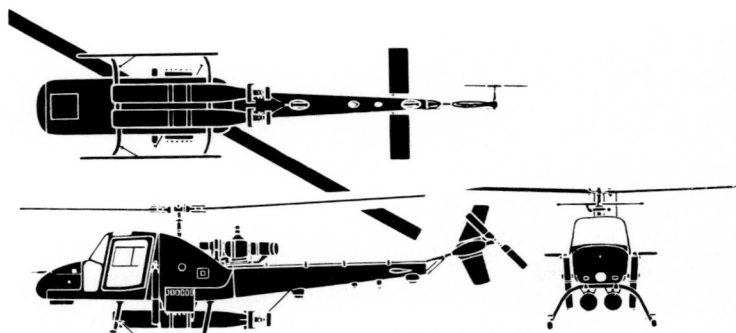

The diminutive Agusta A 106 was a powerful single-seat anti-submarine 'killer'. Two torpedoes (illustrated) or depth charges were carried under the fuselage.

Weights: empty 590 kg (1,300 lb); maximum take-off 1400 kg (3,086 lb)
Dimensions: main rotor diameter 9.50 m (31 ft 2 in); length, rotors turning 9.50 m (36 ft 0 in); height 2.50 m (8 ft 2 in); main rotor disc area 70.88 m² (763 sq ft)

Armament: two Mk 44 torpedoes, or 10 depth charges, or (ground attack) two 7.62-mm machine-guns and 10 80-mm rockets

Agusta A 109A
to
Aichi E11A

Agusta A 109A

Agusta A 109 of the Italian police.

The basic **Agusta A 109A** is notable as the first Agusta-designed helicopter to be built in large series, and is the end product of a special market analysis initiated in 1965. Initially envisaged for commercial use only, the A 109 was designed around a single 690-shp (515 kW) Turboméca Astazou XII turboshaft, but mainly for additional safety considerations, was redesigned in 1967 to take two 370-shp (276-kW) Allison 250-C14 turboshafts. The projected **A 109B** military utility model was abandoned in 1969 in favour of the eight-seat **A 109C Hirundo** (Swallow) civil version, the first of three prototypes flying on 4 August 1971. Protracted trials, minor alterations and other factors caused unforeseen delays and the first A 109 pre-production aircraft was not completed until April 1975. Delivery of production machines, designated A 109A, started in 1976.

In addition to its designated role as a light passenger transport, the A 109A can be adapted for freight-carrying, as an air ambulance or for search-and-rescue tasks. It has proved a great commercial success, especially since the uprated **A 109A Mk II** was introduced, this featuring uprated transmission and 298 kW (5400-shp) Allison 250-C20B turboshafts. First delivered in 1981, nearly 200 had been built by 1989, following on from the 150 or so of the original model. From 1985 the Mk II has been available in a 'wide-body' configuration with bulged fuselage sides for greater comfort.

Non-civil roles proposed for the A 109A Mk II include light attack with TOW missiles or rocket pods, aerial scout, troop carrier, electronic warfare, police work and naval missions. In addition, the helicopter can carry two Mirach RPV drones for battlefield surveillance.

More potent military versions are the **A 109 EOA** and **A 109K**. Both feature fixed undercarriage and a lengthened nose. The A 109 EOA has been ordered for the Italian army as an observation platform, powered by the Allison 250-C20R engine. The A 109K has two 538 kW (722 shp) Turboméca Arriel IK turboshafts for hot-and-high operations. This armed multi-role machine flew for the first time in April 1983, but only a few orders have been forthcoming.

Specification
Type: light general-purpose helicopter
Powerplant: two Allison 250-C20B turboshafts, each developing 313 kW (420 shp) for take-off, 287 kW (385 shp) continuous power, and derated to 258 kW (346 shp) for twin-engine operation
Performance: (at 2450 kg/5,400 lb) maximum permissible level speed 311 km/h (193 mph); maximum cruising speed 266 km/h (165 mph); optimum cruising speed at sea level 231 km/h (143 mph); maximum rate of climb at sea level 493 m (1,620 ft) per minute; service ceiling 4968 m (16,300 ft); hovering ceiling in ground effect 2987 m (9,800 ft); hovering ceiling out of ground effect 2042 m (6,700 ft); maximum range at sea level 565 km (351 miles); maximum endurance at sea level 3 hours 18 minutes
Weights: empty 1415 kg (3,120 lb); maximum take-off 2450 kg (5,402 lb)
Dimensions: main rotor diameter 11.00 m (36 ft 1 in); tail rotor diameter 2.03 m (6 ft 8 in); fuselage length 10.71 m (35 ft 1¾ in); height 3.30 m (10 ft 10 in); main rotor disc area 95.0 m² (1,022.6 sq ft)
Armament: (battlefield version) two 7.62-mm (0.3-in) flexibly-mounted machine guns and two XM157 rocket-launchers (each with seven 70-mm (2.75-in) rockets) basic; alternative weapons include four HOT or TOW missiles and an electrically operated 7.62-mm (0.3-in) Minigun on a flexible mount, or a fully automatic 7.62-mm (0.3-in) MG3 machine gun, or an XM-159C launcher for nineteen 70-mm (2.75-in) rockets, or an Agusta launcher for seven 81-mm (3.2-in) rockets, or an 200A-1 launcher for nineteen 70-mm (2.75-in) rockets
Armament: (naval version in ASW role) two homing torpedoes, six marine markers and optional MAD gear
Armament: (naval version in ASV role) high-performance long-range radar plus AS.12 or other wire-guided missiles; other naval equipment fitted according to mission

Variants
A 109: Agusta's first project for a high-performance helicopter with seven seats, maximum take-off weight of 2400 kg (5,291 lb) and the powerplant of one 515-kW (690-shp) Turboméca Astazou XII turboshaft; begun in 1965, the project did not proceed to series production
A 109B: 1967 project for a general-purpose military helicopter with fuselage similar to the Bell Model 205 and a powerplant of two 276-kW (370-shp) Allison 250-C14 turboshafts; not built
A 109C: reworked design of the initial A 109 with a powerplant of two Allison 250-C14 turboshafts and eight seats; it used the same fuselage design with tail boom and retractable tricycle landing gear with main units folding into exterior fairings
A 109 Hirundo: basic redesign of the A 109C carried out in 1969 with 313-kW (420-shp) Allison 250-C20 turbines, a more streamlined fuselage and angled front windscreen, flush fitting low-drag air intakes and main landing gear units retracting into the lower fuselage tub; the first of three prototypes flew on 4 August 1971, the other two following in January and May 1973; a pre-production series of 10 A 109 helicopters was built, and the model received its certification on 30 May 1975
A 109A: first full-production version with 313-kW Allison 250-C20B turboshafts; deliveries began early in 1976 and about 150 examples were built; five such helicopters went to the Italian army, of which three had TOW anti-tank missiles
A 109C: like the A 109A Mk II with 250-C20R/1 turboshafts, a transmission system upgraded to 596.5 kW, and maximum take-off weight of 2720 kg
A 109EOA: this Elicottero d'Osservazione Avanzata designation is used for 24 observation machines received by the Italian army in 1988 and typified by a lengthened nose, fixed landing gear, various weapon and equipment options including a SFIM M334-25 sight and CILAS laser rangefinder, and Allison 250-C20R/1 turboshafts
A 119 Koala: transport helicopter derivative of the A 109 with twin-skid landing gear and powerplant of one 747-kW Pratt & Whitney PT6B-37/1 turboshaft for a maximum take-off weight of 2710 kg, maximum speed of 278 km/h service ceiling of 5455 m, hovering ceiling of 3320 m in ground effect

The A 109 can operate in the armed scout/liaison role or for anti-armour work. This aircraft caries rocket pods on the weapons pylon; TOW missiles can be carried for use against tanks.

Agusta A 129 Mangusta

The **A 129** Mangusta (mongoose) was developed from 1972 in response to a Italian army requirement for a light observation and anti-tank helicopter. The release of a similar requirement by the Federal Republic of Germany led to this project being pursued jointly by Agusta and MBB, but after initial efforts Agusta proceeded alone with a design based on the **A109**. It was later recognised that the required performance meant a virtual total redesign, and this was concluded in 1980.

Five prototypes of the **A 129** were built, the first making its maiden flight on 11 September 1983 and the last on 1 March 1986. Series production of 60 helicopters then began in fulfilment of orders and options from the Italian army, and delivery began on 6 October 1990. Meanwhile as an experiment Agusta fitted the fifth prototype with Allison/Garrett LHTEC T800-LHT-800 turboshafts instead of the Rolls-Royce Gem turboshaft engines used in the actual Mangusta design.

The **A 129** is equipped with two seats arranged in tandem with the pilot located behind and above the co-pilot/gunner, who operates the Saab/ESCO HeliTOW weapon system with optical direct-vision sight, forward-looking infra-red sensor and laser rangefinder. The normal weapons load consists of eight TOW-2/2A wire-guided anti-tank missiles and options included two 7.62- or 12.7-mm (0.3- or 0.5-in) machine-gun pods, or two 20-mm cannon pods, or two seven-round rocket launchers on the inner hardpoints, and two 22-round rocket launchers on the outboard hardpoints for seven projectiles. Provision is made for the carriage of Hellfire or HOT anti-tank missiles in place of the TOW weapons, and the **A 129** can alternatively be armed with various air-to-ground and air-to-air missiles, and it may be equipped with a mast-mounted sight.

Making use of the high-powered system components of the **A 129**, Agusta designed a general-purpose and transport helicopter as an LBH (Light Battlefield Helicopter), this utility version being designated as the **A 139**. This version was to have a completely redesigned cabin fuselage, but the construction of prototypes has yet to take place.

Another unimplemented project based on the **A 129** was the TONAL. This was a light anti-tank helicopter that could also be configured for the reconnaissance role. CASA, Fokker and Westland as well as Agusta were involved in the definition phase of this battlefield helicopter.

Specification
Agusta A 129 Mangusta
Type: two-seat light anti-tank and scout helicopter
Powerplant: two 615-kW (825-shp) Rolls-Royce Gem 2 Mk 1004D turbo-shafts (licence-built by Piaggio)
Performance: maximum speed 250 km/h (155 mph) at sea level; maximum climb rate 618 m (2,028 ft) per minute; hovering ceiling 3140 m (10,300 ft) in ground effect and 1890 m (6,200 ft) out of ground effect; radius 100 km (62 miles) for a 90-minute battlefield loiter
Weights: empty 2529 kg (5,575 lb); maximum take-off capacity 4100 kg (9,039 lb)
Dimensions: main rotor diameter 11.90 m (39 ft 0.5 in); length overall 14.29 m (46 ft 10.5 in) with rotors turning; height 3.35 m (11 ft 0 in); main rotor disc area 112.22 m^2 (1,197.20 sq ft)
Armament: up to 1200 kg (2,645 lb) of disposable stores that include eight TOW 2, Hellfire or HOT anti-tank missiles, cannon/machine-gun pods and rocket launchers that are carried on four hardpoints under the stub wings; Sidewinder, Stinger, Javelin or Mistral air-to-air missiles can also be carried for self-defence or escort

Eight TOW anti-tank missiles represent the A 129's primary armament, with rocket launchers and machine/gun or cannon pods as secondary weapons.

Agusta-Bell AB 102

Under the designation **Agusta-Bell AB 102**, Agusta designed a 7/9-seat passenger transport helicopter which was intended for both civil and military applications. The name Agusta-Bell was applied because Agusta used in this aircraft a Bell two-blade main rotor system complete with stabilising bar below and at right angles to the rotor blades. In other respects it was of conventional pod and boom configuration, the tail pylon mounting a two-blade anti-torque rotor. Tubular skid landing gear was provided, and powerplant consisted of a Pratt & Whitney R-1340 radial engine mounted in the aft cabin. The forward cabin was furnished to accommodate a pilot and 7/9 passengers, but alternative configurations included an ambulance layout with four stretchers and seating for a medical attendant, and a combined passenger cargo interior. Up to 880 kg (1,950 lb) of freight could be carried internally in an all-cargo role. An electric hoist was also available optionally for use in SAR operations. Very limited production included two helicopters used for passenger services between Milan and Turin.

Specification
Type: general-purpose helicopter
Powerplant: one 447-kW (600-hp)

Pratt & Whitney R-1340-S1H4 radial piston engine
Performance: (at normal take-off weight) maximum level speed at sea level 177 km/h (110 mph); cruising speed at 1830 m (6,000 ft) 160 km/h (99 mph); service ceiling 3900 m (12,795 ft); range 400 km (249 miles)

Weights: empty 1810 kg (3,990 lb); normal take-off 2725 kg (6,008 lb); maximum take-off 3025 kg (6,669 lb)
Dimensions: main rotor diameter 14.50 m (47 ft 6¾ in); tail rotor diameter 2.59 m (8 ft 6 in); length 17.92 m (58 ft 9½ in); height 3.23 m (10 ft 7¼ in); main rotor disc area 165.13 m^2 (1,777.50 sq ft)

The AB 102 was designed to suit both civil and military markets based on a Bell two-blade rotor. Despite its operational flexibility it failed to satisfy potential customers and only a few were built.

Aichi B7A Ryusei

The requirement for a large torpedo/dive-bomber for operation from a new, larger class of aircraft carrier caused the Imperial Japanese navy to draw up in 1941 the specification of an aircraft to replace the Nakajima B6N and Yokosuka D4Y. As this specification called for an internal bombload of up to 500 kg (1,102 lb), or the carriage of a 800-kg (1,764-lb) torpedo externally, coupled with high maximum speed and long range, a powerful engine was essential. The navy selected what was virtually an experimental powerplant for this task: the Nakajima Homare 11 twin-row radial developing around 1342 kW (1,800 hp).

Aichi began work on this requirement, and its **AM-23** prototype flew in mid-1942. This large aircraft, then designated **Navy Experimental 16-Shi Carrier Attack Bomber (Aichi B7A1)**, was a mid-wing monoplane of inverted gull-wing configuration, a layout selected so that the main units of the retractable tail-wheel landing gear, mounted at the 'elbows' of each wing, would be as short as possible. A section of each outer wing panel folded for carrier stowage. The fuselage and tail unit were conventional, the former providing enclosed accommodation for a crew of two.

As might have been anticipated, the combination of problems from the airframe, coupled with the teething troubles of the new engine, meant that it was almost two years before the type was ordered into production as the **Navy Carrier Attack Bomber Ryusei** (Shooting Star), or **Aichi B7A2**. Apart from nine prototype B7A1s, only 80 examples were completed by Aichi before its factory was destroyed in the serious earthquake of May 1945: an additional 25 were built by the Naval Air Arsenal at Omura.

By the time these aircraft entered service, when they were allocated the Allied codename 'Grace', the Japanese navy no longer had any carriers from which they could operate, with the result that they saw only limited use from land bases.

Variants

Aichi B7A2 Experimental: single example of B7A2 powered by a 1491-kW (2,000hp) Nakajima Homare 23 radial engine
Aichi B7A3: projected version, to have been powered by one 1641-kW (2,200-hp) Mitsubishi MK9A radial engine

Specification
Aichi B7A2

Type: carrier-based torpedo-/dive-bomber
Powerplant: one 1361-kW (1,825-hp) Nakajima NK9C Homare 12 radial piston engine
Performance: maximum level speed at 6550m (21,490ft) 565km/h (351mph); climb to 4000m (13,125ft) in 6 minutes 55 seconds; service ceiling 11250m (36,910ft); maximum range 3040km (1,889 miles)

Weights: empty 3810kg (8,400lb); maximum take-off 5625kg (12,401lb)
Dimensions: span 14.40m (47ft 3in); length 11.49m (37ft 8¼in); height 4.075m (13ft 4½in); wing area 35.40m² (381.05sqft)
Armament: (late production B7A2) two wing-mounted 20-mm Type 99 Model 2 cannon and one 13-mm (0.5-in) Type 2 machine gun on flexible mount in aft position, plus either one 800-kg (1,764-lb) torpedo or a similar weight of bombs

Aichi B7A2 Ryusei 'Grace' of the Yokosuka Kokutai

The powerful and potent B7A could have made a significant impact in the Pacific war, but arrived in service too late for carrier operations.

Aichi D1A

Aichi Tokei Denki Kabushiki Kaisha, which was to become a significant aircraft design and construction company during World War II, had been established in Japan during 1899 as a manufacturer of electrical equipment and watches.

Like most Japanese companies that sought to expand their capabilities by turning initially to aircraft construction as a stepping stone to experience, that would lead eventually to the creation of indigenous designs, Aichi established a working relationship with Ernst Heinkel Flugzeugwerke in Germany. Wishing to contend in early 1931 for an Imperial Japanese navy requirement for a two-seat carrier-based dive-bomber, Aichi requested Heinkel to design and build an aircraft to meet the navy's specification. Required for operation with float or wheel landing gear, the resulting **Heinkel He 50** prototype flew in the summer of 1931 with twin floats. A second version, with wheel landing gear, was duly supplied to Aichi under the export designation **He 66**.

Basically, the He 66 was a two-bay biplane of metal construction with metal and fabric covering. The braced tail unit was conventional, and landing gear of fixed tailskid type. As supplied it was powered by a 365-kW (490-hp) Siemens SAM-22B (Jupiter VI) radial engine. Modifications carried out by Aichi included strengthening of the landing gear, and installation of a 418-kW (560-hp) Nakajima Kotobuki 2 Kai 1 radial engine. In this form the **Aichi Special Bomber** was successful in trials against competing prototypes from Nakajima and Yokosuka, and was ordered into production as the **Navy Type 94 Carrier Bomber (Aichi D1A1)**. The 162 production aircraft built, had the radial engine enclosed by a Townend ring, and other modifications included the introduction of slightly swept wings, and replacement of the tailskid by a non-castoring tailwheel. The last 44 had 433-kW (580-hp) Kotobuki 3 engines.

An improved **Aichi D1A2 (Navy Type 96 Carrier Bomber)** appeared in 1936-7, powered by a more powerful Nakajima Hikari 1 radial engine, and this model also introduced a NACA engine cowling, wheel spats, and improved windscreens. Production of this version totalled 428.

Only a small number of D1A1s remained in use with training units at the time of Japan's attack on Pearl Harbor, on 7 December 1941. About 70 DF1A2s were serving in second-line units, and these were duly allocated the Allied codename 'Susie'.

Specification
Aichi D1A2

Type: two-seat carrier-based dive-bomber
Powerplant: one 544-kW (730-hp) Nakajima Hikari 1 radial piston engine
Performance: maximum level speed at 3200m (10,500ft) 310km/h (193mph); cruising speed at 1000m (3,280ft) 220km/h (137mph); climb to 3000m (9,845ft) in 7 minutes 50 seconds; service ceiling 7000m (22,965ft); range 930km (578 miles)

Above: Aichi D1A2 'Susie'

The D1A saw widespread service in the Sino-Japanese war, but by the time of World War II it had been largely relegated to training duties.

Weights: empty 1516kg (3,342lb); maximum take-off 2610kg (5,754lb)
Dimensions: span 11.40m (37ft 4¾in); length 9.30m (30ft 6in); height 3.41m (11ft 2¼in); wing area 34.70m² (373.52sqft)

Armament: two fixed 7.7-mm (0.303-in) Type 92 machine-guns and one flexible 7.7-mm (0.303-in) Type 92 machine-gun, plus one 250-kg (550-lb) and two 30-kg (66-lb) bombs

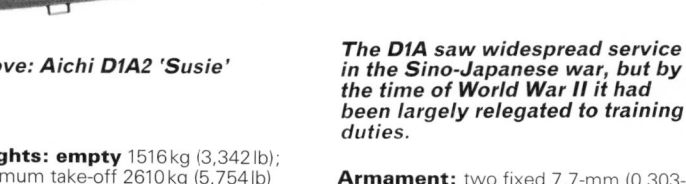

Aichi D3A

Designed to supersede the D1A, the **Aichi D3A** was to become far better known than its predecessor. Of low-wing monoplane configuration, the prototype had elliptical wings similar to those of the Heinkel He 70, a conventional tail unit, and a circular-section fuselage. Construction was basically all-metal. Non-retractable tailwheel landing gear incorporated main units with large speed fairings, and the prototype's powerplant was the 544-kW (730-hp) Hikari 1 radial that had powered the D1A2. Testing showed that the aircraft was underpowered, had a tendency to snap roll in tight turns, and had ineffective dive-brakes. The second prototype incorporated modifications to overcome these shortcomings, including increased wing span, changed outboard wing-section leading edges to overcome the roll problem, strengthened dive-brakes, and a 626-kW (840-hp) Mitsubishi Kinsei 3 radial engine. In this form it proved superior to Nakajima's contender for this requirement, and in December 1939 was ordered into production under the designation **Navy Type 99 Carrier Bomber Model 11 (Aichi D3A1)**.

Production aircraft differed from the second prototype by having a small decrease in wing span, and directional stability was improved by the addition of a long dorsal fin. Power was again increased, with the introduction of a 746-kW (1,000-hp) Mitsubishi Kinsei 43 engine on early production models. In this form the D3A1 completed carrier trials, and entered operational service with the navy in China and Indo-China. A total of 129 of these dive-bombers was carried by the task force that launched the attack on Pearl Harbor, and it was a force of D3A1s that sank the British aircraft carrier HMS *Hermes*, and the cruisers HMS *Cornwall* and HMS *Dorsetshire* in April 1942.

Identified by the Allies under the code-name *Val*, almost 1,500 D3As of different versions were built, about 201 of them by Showa, before production ended. Relegated to second-line duties

Above: Aichi D3A1 Model 11 Val *of the Yokosuka Kokutai in 1940.*

An effective type in the opening stages of World War II, the Aichi D3A was soon rendered obsolescent by its limited performance. Early successes included the attack on Pearl Harbor and the sinking of the Hermes.

during the second half of the Pacific war, the type nevertheless remained in service from beginning to end of this conflict, serving finally in *kamikaze* and training roles.

Variants

Aichi D3A2 Model 12: prototype of improved version with a 969-kW (1,300-hp) Mitsubishi Kinsei 54 engine, increased fuel tankage, modified rear canopy, and introducing a propeller spinner (total 1)
Aichi D3A2 Model 22: production version of the above; maximum level speed at 6200 m (20,340 ft) 430 km/h (267 mph); service ceiling 10500 m (34,450 ft), empty weight 2570 kg (5,666 lb) and maximum take-off weight 3800 kg (8,378 lb) (total 1,016)
Aichi D3A2-K: trainer version, produced by conversions of D3A1/2s

Specification
Aichi D3A (later production)
Type: two-seat carrier- or land-based dive-bomber
Powerplant: one 798-kW (1,070-hp) Mitsubishi Kinsei 44 radial piston engine
Performance: maximum level speed at 3000 m (9,840 ft) 385 km/h (239 mph); cruising speed at 3000 m (9,840 ft) 295 km/h (183 mph); climb to 3000 m (9,840 ft) in 6 minutes 25 seconds; service ceiling 9300 m (30,510 ft); range 1470 km (913 miles)

Weights: empty 2408 kg (5,309 lb); maximum take-off 3650 kg (8,047 lb)
Dimensions: span 14.365 m (47 ft 1½ in); length 10.195 m (33 ft 5¼ in); height 3.847 m (12 ft 7½ in); wing area 34.90 m² (375.67 sq ft)
Armament: two 7.7-mm (0.303-in) fixed forward-firing Type 97 machine guns and one 7.7-mm (0.303-in) Type 92 machine gun on flexible mount in rear cockpit, plus one 250-kg (551-lb) and two 60-kg (132-lb) bombs

Aichi E11A

The **Aichi E11A1** night reconnaissance flying boat, known to the Allies under the codename *Laura*, first flew in prototype form in June 1937. Competing against the Kawanishi E11K1, it proved to have superior performance, and was ordered into production as the **Navy Type 98 Night Reconnaissance Seaplane**.

Of biplane configuration, the two-step hull carried a braced tail unit, with the tailplane and elevator mounted almost halfway up the fin. Accommodation was provided for a crew of three, and there was an open bow position that could be used during on-water manoeuvres, such as making fast to a buoy, as well as mounting a defensive machine gun. To enhance stability on the water, balancer floats were mounted beneath each lower wing, close to the wingtip. Powerplant consisted of a Hiro Type 91 Model 22 inline engine, mounted at the centre-section of the upper wing, and driving a pusher propeller with spinner.

Production of E11A1s totalled only 17 aircraft, and these saw limited use in their intended role in the early stages of the Pacific war.

Specification
Type: night reconnaissance flying boat
Powerplant: one 462-kW (620-hp) Hiro Type 91 Model 22 inline piston

Aichi E11A Laura *reconnaissance flying boat*

engine
Performance: maximum level speed at 2400 m (7,875 ft) 215 km/h (134 mph); cruising speed 130 km/h (81 mph); climb to 3000 m (9,840 ft) in 18 minutes

30 seconds; service ceiling 4425 m (14,520 ft); range 1945 km (1,209 miles)
Weights: empty 1927 kg (4,248 lb); maximum take-off 3300 kg (7,275 lb)
Dimensions: span 14.50 m (47 ft

6¾ in); length 10.70 m (35 ft 1¼ in); height 5.50 m (18 ft 0½)
Armament: one 7.7-mm (0.303-in) Type 92 machine gun on flexible mount in bow cockpit

Aichi E13A
to
Airbus Industrie A330 and A340

Aichi E13A

Developed from a two-seat reconnaissance seaplane design (E12A), the **Aichi E13A** was designed to meet a 1937 Imperial Japanese navy requirement for a long-range reconnaissance floatplane that could serve as an escort to maritime convoys. The prototype of this three-seat aircraft was completed in the closing months of 1938, a low-wing monoplane with folding outboard wing panels, conventional tail unit, circular-section fuselage, and twin-float landing gear. Powered by a Kinsei 43 radial engine, the E13A proved superior to the competing Kawanishi E13K1 during service tests, and was ordered into production as the **Navy Type 0 Reconnaissance Seaplane Model 11 (Aichi E13A1)**. Aichi had built a total of 133 by 1942, when Watanabe (later Kyushu) became the prime contractor, building more than 1,100. About 50 were also built by the Hiro Naval Arsenal.

Identified by the Allies under the codename 'Jake', E13A1s entered service with the navy in late 1941, and flew reconnaissance patrols during the attack on Pearl Harbor. Serving throughout the Pacific war, they were operated from both ships and shore bases for roles which included air/sea rescue, long patrol sorties of up to 15 hours, shipping attacks, transport and, in the closing stages of the war, *kamikaze* operations.

Variants
Aichi E13A1a Model 11A: introduced in late 1944; featured improved float bracing struts, a propeller spinner and more advanced radio equipment
Aichi E13A1b Model 11B: based on the E13A1a but fitted with ASV radar.

Specification
Aichi E13A1a
Type: long-range reconnaissance floatplane

Aichi E13A 'Jake' reconnaissance floatplane of the Imperial Japanese navy.

Powerplant: one 805-kW (1,080-hp) Mitsubishi Kinsei 43 radial piston engine
Performance: maximum level speed at 2180 m (7,150 ft) 375 km/h (233 mph); cruising speed at 2000 m (6,560 ft) 220 km/h (137 mph); climb to 3000 m (9,845 ft) in 6 minutes 5 seconds; service ceiling 8730 m (28,640 ft); range 2090 km (1,299 miles)
Weights: empty 2642 kg (5,825 lb); maximum take-off 3640 kg (8,025 lb)
Dimensions: span 14.50 m (47 ft 6¾ in); length 11.30 m (37 ft 0¾ in); height 4.78 m (15 ft 8½ in); wing area 36.00 m² (387.51 sq ft)
Armament: one 7.7-mm (0.303-in) Type 92 machine gun on flexible mount in aft position, and up to 250 kg (551 lb) of bombs; a Type 99 20-mm cannon could be mounted on a ventral flexible mount for anti-ship strikes

Aichi E13A1.

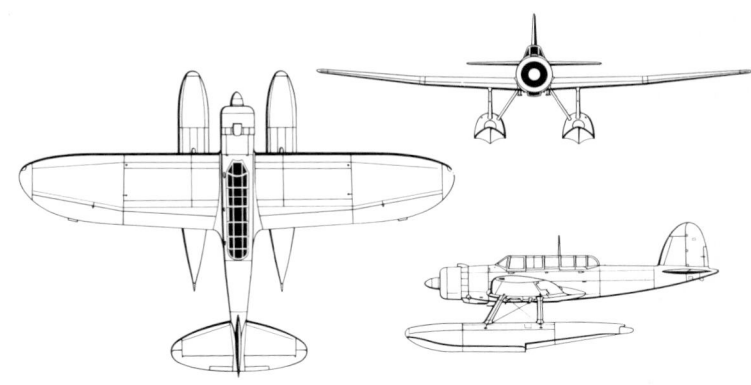

Air Tractor Model AT-301 Air Tractor

Leland Snow, now President of Air Tractor Inc., established the Snow Aeronautical Company in 1955 to manufacture and develop an agricultural aircraft of his own design. He was almost certainly better equipped than most to create a new and efficient 'agplane', for several years of experience as an agpilot had provided an acute appreciation of some of the shortcomings of existing aircraft within this category. The **Snow S-2A** and **S-2B** received certification on 2 April 1958 and 29 July 1959 respectively, and were followed by improved **S-2Cs** before this company was acquired by Rockwell Standard Corporation in 1965.

Subsequently, Leland Snow established Air Tractor Inc. to manufacture a new agricultural aircraft derived from the S-2B. Designated **Model AT-301 Air Tractor**, a prototype/pre-production example flew for the first time in September 1973. This cantilever low-wing monoplane is of all-metal construction, except that the conventional tail unit has fabric-covered control surfaces. The wing incorporates large Fowler-type trailing-edge flaps to simplify short-field operations, and extensive care has been taken to ensure that the fuselage structure is adequately sealed to prevent the ingress of corrosive chemicals. Similarly, the pilot's enclosed cabin is sealed, and uncontaminated fresh air ventilation provided. Fixed tailwheel landing gear includes rugged cantilever main units, and power is provided by an uncowled Pratt & Whitney R-1340 radial engine. Agricultural provisions comprise a 1211-litre (320-US gallon) chemical hopper and a 72-nozzle spraybar as standard. A spreader for dry chemicals is optional.

The Air Tractor is a classic 'ag plane' with such features as a sealed cockpit to prevent the ingestion of toxic chemicals, and a corrosion-resistant airframe structure.

Model AT-302 Air Tractor: a turboprop-powered version of the AT-301, first flown in June 1977; powerplant consists of one 447-kW (600-shp) Avco Lycoming LTP 101-600A1A; maximum level speed 274 km/h (170 mph); maximum cruising speed 266 km/h (165 mph), range with maximum fuel 644 km (400 miles); empty weight 1474 kg (3,250 lb) spray gear equipped; maximum take-off weight 2994 kg (6,600 lb); length 8.99 m (29 ft 6 in)

Model AT-302A Air Tractor: generally similar to the Model AT-302, but incorporating a 1514-litre (400-US gallon) chemical hopper to allow for economic dispersal of dry chemicals at high application rates; maximum take-off weight 3266 kg (7,200 lb)

Model AT-400 Air Tractor: a version of the Model 302A with a more powerful engine, consisting of a 507-kW (680-shp) Pratt & Whitney Aircraft of Canada PT6A-15AG turboprop

Specification
Air Tractor AT-301 Air Tractor
Type: single-seat agricultural aircraft
Powerplant: one 447-kW (600-hp) Pratt & Whitney R-1340 radial piston engine
Performance: maximum level speed 266 km/h (165 mph) at sea level; maximum cruising speed 241 km/h (150 mph) at 1830 m (6,000 ft); economic cruising speed 225 km/h (140 mph) at 2440 m (8,000 ft); range with maximum fuel 563 km (350 miles)
Weights: empty equipped 1656 kg (3,650 lb); maximum take-off 3130 kg (6,900 lb)
Dimensions: span 13.72 m (45 ft 0 in); length 8.23 m (27 ft 0 in); height 2.59 m (8 ft 6 in); wing area 25.08 m² (270 sq ft)

Airbus Industrie A300

At a similar time as Boeing in the USA was finalising the design of the world's first wide-body, the Model 747, discussions were starting in Europe to consider the production of a large capacity short-range European transport aircraft. During 1965-66, various alignments of European manufacturers studied different designs, the most promising being the HBN-100 developed by Hawker Siddeley, Breguet and Nord.

On 28 May 1969, France and West Germany decided to go ahead with the development of the European Airbus, as it had become, with Hawker Siddeley keeping alive the British interest despite the lack of government support. Construction of the **A300** began in September 1969, and in December 1970 Airbus Industrie was established to oversee the project. The General Electric CF6 turbofan was chosen as the main powerplant, but any engine in the same class could be substituted on production models according to customer wishes. The cylindrical fuselage could accommodate seating layouts from 220 to a maximum of 336 passengers, although most users would choose a multi-class layout to reflect the business nature of European operations. The advanced wing was a Hawker Siddeley design, with a full suite of high-lift devices.

The first two aircraft were designated **A300B1**, and the first (F-WUAB) made its inaugural flight on 28 October 1972, the second following on 5 February 1973. These were followed by the first pair of **A300B2s**, this considered the production model. The first four completed a lengthy flight test programme to allow European certification to be granted on 15 March 1974, US certification following on 30 May. This date also saw the first airline service, by Air France between Paris and London. At once the A300 impressed passengers with its comfort and quietness, the latter a factor appreciated by those living near the airports it visited.

Initial sales were slow, and there seemed little chance of breaking the US market until 6 April 1978, when Eastern Air Lines ordered the first of 38 A300s. These were the **A300B4** variant, with increased fuel capacity, Krüger leading edge flaps and increased gross weight for longer range. The British government also finally joined the consortium in 1978, taking a 20 per cent stake in the project. Aérospatiale and Deutsche Airbus remained the principal partners (37.9 per cent) with Spain's CASA having a 4.2 per cent stake. Two other companies became associates of the programme, the Dutch Fokker concern and the Belgian organisation Belairbus.

Since 1978 the A300 story has been one of gradual development. The **A300C4** was introduced as a convertible freighter version with a large cargo door in the port side. This and the passenger-only model have been superseded by a new series incorporating an extra row of seats, a new two-man forward-facing cockpit and a comprehensive list of small drag-reducing and weight-reducing items. The resultant **A300-600** first flew on 8 July 1983, and has been the major production version since, the last **A300B4** leaving the line in late 1984. Versions include the **A300-600R** with increased take-off weight and tailplane trim tank for long-range operations, and the **A300-600 Convertible** passenger/cargo version.

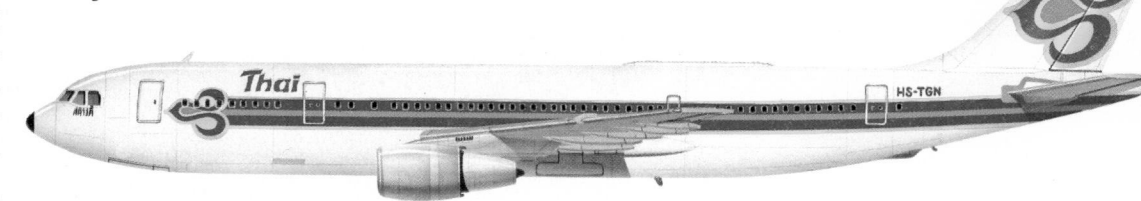

Airbus Industrie A300B4-203 of Thai Airways

Specification
Airbus A300-600
Type: large capacity short/medium-range commercial transport
Powerplant: two turbofans in the 249 kN (56,000 lb)-262.4 kN (59,000 lb) thrust class. These include Pratt & Whitney JT9D-7R4H1, PW4156 and General Electric CF6-80C2A1
Performance: maximum cruising speed at 7620 m (25,000 ft) 890 km/h (553 mph); long-range cruising speed at 9450 m (31,000 ft) 875 km/h (543 mph); range with 267 passengers and baggage, PW4156 engines 6968 km (4,330 miles); take-off run 2332 m (7,650 ft)
Weights: (with PW4156 engines) empty 78201 kg (172,403 lb); maximum take-off 165000 kg (363,765 lb)
Dimensions: span 44.84 m (147 ft 1 in); length 54.08 m (177 ft 5 in); height 16.62 m (54 ft 6½ in); wing area 260.0 m² (2,798.6 sq ft)

Eastern was the first major US airline to buy the A300. Pan Am and American have followed.

Airbus Industrie A310

One of the difficulties faced in the early days of the European Airbus development was the lack of clear guidance by airlines as to their exact capacity requirements, and at various stages up to 11 variants were proposed of differing lengths to suit the customers. While the A300 was under development, Airbus looked at a smaller capacity variant which was in much demand by many carriers. Thus was born the **A310**.

The fuselage was essentially the same as that of the A300, except it was considerably shorter. Much commonality allowed the development and manufacturing costs to be kept down considerably. The wing and horizontal tail surfaces were new, including a high technology wing from BAe of much reduced area and span. From the outset the cockpit was a forward-facing two-man area, with advanced digital avionics.

The A310 was officially launched in July 1978, offering a capacity between 210 to 250 passengers in mixed-class layouts. The prototype (F-WZLH) first flew on 3 April 1982 and on 11 March the following year received French and West German certification. In April the launch customers Lufthansa and Swissair began services. Since then sales have been healthy, including a major order from US carrier Pan Am.

The basic production version is designated the **A310-200**, and since May 1986 these have been delivered with drag-reducing wingtip fences. The **A310-200C** and **A310-200F** are convertible and all-cargo versions respectively. The first major variant was the **A310-300** with extended range. First flying on 8 July 1985, this variant has wingtip fences as standard, additional fuel in the tailplane and an optional central tank fitted in part of the cargo hold. Swissair was again the first customer, and in the hands of carriers such as Wardair these regularly make transatlantic crossings.

A feature of the long-range A310-300 from the outset was drag-reducing wingtip fences, although these are now standard on all models. Kenya Airways has three for its long-haul routes.

Specification
A310-300
Type: large-capacity medium-range commercial transport
Powerplant: two turbofans in 213.5 kN (48,000 lb) — 231.5 kN (52,000 lb) thrust class, including Pratt & Whitney JT9D-7R4D1, JT9D-7R4E1, PW4152 and General Electric CF6-80C2A2
Performance: long-range cruising speed at 10000 m (32,800 ft) Mach 0.8; range with 218 passengers and baggage, PW4152 engines 9175 km (5,700 miles); take-off run 2225 m (7,300 ft)
Weights: (with PW4152 engines) empty 70275 kg (154,930 lb); maximum take-off 157,000 kg (346,125 lb)
Dimensions: span 43.89 m (144 ft 0 in); length 46.66 m (153 ft 1 in); height 15.80 m (51 ft 10 in); wing area 219 m² (2,357.3 sq ft)

The A310-200 is the standard medium-range version, available in all-passenger, mixed cargo/passenger or all-freight versions. The Turkish national airline THY has seven of this model.

Airbus Industrie A320

Early Airbus proposals for a family of airliners centred around twin-aisle and single-aisle designs, and while the first two aircraft featured twin-aisles, the third member of the family introduced the single-aisle. Although it shared some aerodynamic similarities with its two larger cousins, the **A320** is essentially an all-new design, incorporating state-of-the-art airliner engineering features. Among the technological firsts are a full fly-by-wire control system with sidestick controllers, gust alleviation function for a smoother ride and greater fatigue life and a centralised fault display and warning system. Intended for the 737/MD-80 market, the A320 has seating for 150 to 179 passengers, these accommodated in a wider cabin than most single-aisle aircraft, allowing for far greater comfort

Braniff is the second US customer for the A320, and its sizeable order (40) highlights the high sales this type has achieved in a short time. Currently CFM56 and V2500 engines are available.

and the ability to take standard baggage containers.

Go-ahead for the programme was announced on 2 March 1984, and on 22 February 1987 the first aircraft (F-WWAI) took to the air from Toulouse with CFM56 engines. The first 21 aircraft were the basic **A320-100** version, but these have since been superseded by the definitive **A320-200**, this featuring an extra fuel tank and wingtip fences. Versions under consideration are a convertible passenger/freight model and an all-cargo freighter. In 1989 Airbus announced a stretched version, the **A321** with a 44.51 m (146 ft 0 in) long fuselage. With 186 passengers in a two-class layout, this will fill the capacity gap between the A320 and A310.

In service the A320 has proved extremely reliable and economical. These factors, together with the advanced technology, have made it the best-seller yet for the Airbus family. Air France took the first delivery on 28 March 1988, and the type was certificated in 1989 for operations with the IAE V2500 high technology engine. The type has achieved major sales in the United States with Northwest and Braniff.

Specification
A320-200
Type: medium capacity short/medium-range commercial transport
Powerplant: two 111.2-kN (25,000-lb) thrust CFM International CFM56-5-A1 or IAE V2500-A1 turbofans
Performance: typical cruising speed Mach 0.8; range with 150 passengers and baggage, V2500 engines 5263 km (3,270 miles); take-off run 2180 m (7,150 ft)
Weights: (V2500 engines) empty 40150 kg (88,515 lb); maximum take-off 73,500 kg (162,040 lb)
Dimensions: span 33.91 m (111 ft 3 in); length 37.57 m (123 ft 3 in); height 11.80 m (38 ft 8½ in); wing area 122.4 m² (1,317.5 sq ft)

Airbus Industrie A330 and A340

On the completion of a project study lasting several years, on 5 June 1987 Airbus Industrie began a programme for the full development, marketing and production of the **A330** and **A340** as advanced airliners able to compete of technical and cost terms with the latest American airliners such as the Boeing Models 767 and 777. Both of the new Airbus transport aircraft were optimised for airlines operating long-distance routes with high passenger volumes, and were the first airliners created with a 100% CAD (Computer-Aided Design) system. The **A330** and **A340** share the same fuselage, tail unit, landing gear, flight deck and wing geometry. For the best combination of range and useful load capacity with low operating costs, the **A330** was designed with a twin-engined powerplant for medium/long-range routes, while the **A340** was planned for very long range routes with a four-engined powerplant. The same basic wing is used by both types with the differences limited to insignificant changes to the structure and leading-edge slats.

Both models profited considerably from the flight control technology developed for earlier Airbus aircraft, for instance a fly-by-wire flight control system and the advanced two-man cockpit of the 'glass' type. The fuselage section matches that of the **A300** and the **A310**, allowing the use of the same cabin equipment and reducing design and development costs. As with all Airbus designs, the individual members of this European consortium are responsible for the development and manufacture of their respective parts of the **A330** and **A340**.

The **A340-300**, the longer of the two four-engined models planned from the outset, made its first flight at Toulouse on 25 October 1991. In the typical two-class layout the **A340-300** accommodates 375 passengers standard of 440 passengers optional, and the model entered service with Air France in March 1993. In similar three-class layout, the shorter-fuselage **A340-200** has accommodation for 263 passengers standard or 303 passengers optional, and entered service with Lufthansa in March 1993.

The first version of the **A330**, using the same fuselage, made its maiden flight on 2 November 1992 and entered service in January 1994 with Air Inter. The General Electric CF6-80E1 intended for the **A330** was fitted in the starboard nacelle of an **A300** test aeroplane and

was first run in flight on 14 February 1992.

Variants
A330-200: first flown on 13 August 1997 for service from April 1998, this is a longer-range version of the -300 with the fuselage shortened by 5.33 m (17 ft 6 in) and fitted with a strengthened wing derived from that of the A340-300 for the carriage of a maximum 380 passengers over a range of more than 10000 km (6,215 miles), or 253 passengers over a range of more than 12000 km (7,455 miles) after take-off at a maximum weight of 230000 kg (507,055 lb)
A330-300: basic version of this medium-range wide-body transport with accommodation for between 335 and 440 passengers, and a powerplant of two General Electric CF6-80E1 turbofans of 300.3 kN (67,500 lb st), or Pratt & Whitney PW4164/4168 turbofans of 302.5 kN (68,000 lb st) or Rolls-Royce Trent 768/772 turbofans of up to 316.3 kN (71,100 lb st)
A330-400X: proposed stretched version of the -300 with similar weights and powerplant for a two-class arrangement of 370 passengers in a fuselage lengthened by 6.35 m (20 ft 10 in) and offering a full-load range of 7300 km (4,535 miles)
A340-200: very-long-range widebody transport with a four-engined powerplant and a fuselage shortened by about two frames in comparison to the first version of the A340-300 to a figure of 59.39 m (194 ft 10 in); in a typical two-class layout room for 303 passengers changing to between 263 and 303 in a three-class layout; engine options as for the A340-300
A340-200 HGW (A340-8000): featuring increased fuel capacity in the rear of the cargo hold, greater weights and the same powerplant as the A340-300 HGW, this is a very-long-range model with 232-seat accommodation for a range of 14800 km (9,195 miles) after take-off at a maximum weight of 275000 kg (606,260 lb)
A340-300: first basic version of the four-engine stretched airliner with long fuselage; more seats but shorter range than the -200; originally fitted with four CFM International CFM56-5C2 turbofans of 154 kN (34,620 lb st), although options are the CFM56-5C2 of 141 kN (31,700 lb st) or the CFM56-5C3 of 147 kN (33,045 lb st)
A340-300 Combi: passenger and freight version of the -300 with large door to the main deck on the left side of the rear fuselage; a typical load is four freight containers and 221 passengers in three classes
A340-300 HGW: high gross weight variant of the -200 with a strengthened wing, additional fuel volume in the middle wing section increasing the range by 400 km (250 miles), and the uprated powerplant of four CFM International CFM56-5C4 turbofans of 154 kN (34,620 lb st) for a range of 13200 km (8,200 miles) after take-off at a maximum weight of 271000 kg (597,450 lb); entered service with Singapore Airlines in April 1966
A340-500: proposed longer-range version of the A340-300 with a wing enlarged by some 20% for a span of 63.6 m (208 ft 8 in) and carrying additional fuel, powerplant of four Rolls-Royce Trent 500 turbofans of 235 kN (52,830 lb st) and a range of 15335 km (9,530 miles) with 316 passengers after take-off at a maximum weight of 356000 kg (784,830 lb)
A340-600: proposed as the high-capacity (up to 550 seats) counterpart to the A340-500 with the fuselage lengthened by 7.54 m (24 ft 9 in) for the carriage of 372 passengers over a range of 13960 km (8,675 miles) after take-off at a maximum weight of 356000 kg (784,830 lb)
A340M: projected military variant of the A340-300 basic version for various roles such as personnel transport with 434 passengers, VIP service, mixed transport aircraft for personnel and matériel (for example 295 persons and 20 tons of freight) with similar design to the A340-300 Combi, pure freight flying, and inflight refuelling of other aircraft

This A340-300 with four CFM56 engines was the first member of this Airbus family to come into service. The shorter fuselage -200 with the same engines has considerably longer range.

Airco D.H. 2
to
Airspeed AS.57 Ambassador

Airco D.H.2

Airco D.H.2

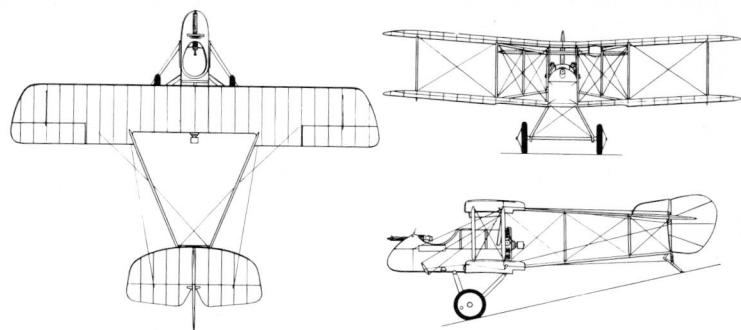

Geoffrey de Havilland's second design for Airco, the **D.H.2**, was basically a smaller version of the D.H.1. It retained the same pusher configuration as its predecessor, in order that a forward-firing gun could be used. This was necessary because by early 1915, when the prototype D.H.2 was first flown, no effective interrupter gear was available for use in British aircraft and, in fact, it was not until late 1916 that the Constantinesco hydraulically-actuated gear first entered service. Although in the D.H.2 the Lewis gun could not endanger the propeller, its initial installation provided plenty of problems for the would-be fighter pilot. A mounting was provided on each side of the central nacelle, and he was expected to set up the gun on whichever mount would provide the better opportunity of hitting his target. What with having to move the gun from one mount to the other, and changing its 47-round ammunition drums as they were expended, it was surprising that the pilot was able to retain adequate control of an aircraft that, until a fair amount of experience had been gained in handling it, was considered tricky to fly.

By comparison with its predecessor, the D.H.2 was considerably smaller, and differed by having a single-seat central nacelle, structural strengthening, design refinements to reduce drag, and a more powerful engine. The 'tricky to fly' criticism resulted from sensitive controls but, in fact, this made the D.H.2 a first-class fighter for its period when signifi-

cant numbers became operational in early 1916. When confronting the once-dreaded Fokker monoplanes, particularly during the 1st Battle of the Somme, they were able to regain air supremacy for the RFC. This was retained until the introduction of the Albatros D.I and D.II in late 1916.

The difficulty of handling the Lewis gun was eventually overcome, largely as a result of pressure from the pilots who flew these aircraft in battle, by mounting the gun centrally on the nacelle. Although it was possible to elevate or depress the muzzle, pilots preferred to use it as a fixed weapon, and soon learned how to aim the aircraft rather than the Lewis gun itself. By early 1917 the D.H.2 was outclassed on the Western Front, but continued to serve for some time in Macedonia and Palestine. However, none remained in RAF service in the autumn of 1918. A total of 400 was built.

Specification
Type: single-seat scout fighter
Powerplant: one 75-kW (100-hp) Gnome Monosoupape rotary piston engine; some late examples had one 82-kW (110-hp) Le Rhône rotary engine
Performance: (Gnome engine) maximum level speed at sea level 150 km/h (93 mph); climb to 1830 m (6,000 ft) in 11 minutes; service ceiling 4265 m (14,000 ft); endurance 2 hours 45 minutes
Weights: empty 428 kg (943 lb);

maximum take-off 654 kg (1,441 lb)
Dimensions: span 8.61 m (28 ft 3 in); length 7.68 m (25 ft 2½ in); height 2.91 m (9 ft 6½ in); wing area 23.13 m² (249 sq ft)
Armament: one forward-firing 7.7-mm (0.303-in) Lewis gun

A first-class fighter of its day, the D.H.2 was very manoeuvrable in capable hands, although it could catch the inexperienced. Major Lanoe Hawker was a well-known proponent, although he fell to Richthofen in November 1916.

Airco D.H.3

Under the designation **Airco D.H.3**, Geoffrey de Havilland designed a large two-bay biplane that was intended to fulfil a bombing role. The wide-span wings were made to fold in order to save hangar space, and were carried above a slender fuselage that terminated in a pleasingly curved rudder that was to become a feature of many subsequent de Havilland designs. Conventional tail-skid landing gear was complemented by two wheels beneath the fuselage nose,

which extended well forward of the main wheels, to prevent it from bumping on the ground. Two Beardmore engines were mounted between the wings, directly above the main landing gear, and each drove a pusher propeller mounted on an extension shaft to ensure that it cleared the trailing edge of the wing. Accommodation was provided for a crew of three, the pilot in an open cockpit just forward of the wings, and the two gunners in individual cockpits, one in the nose forward of the pilot, and the other just aft of the wings.

A second prototype was built with

more powerful Beardmore engines, each of 119 kW (160 hp), and with cutouts in the wing trailing edges in the area of the propellers so that the extended drive-shafts could be eliminated. This was designated **D.H.3A**, but neither of these aircraft was to enter production and both were reportedly scrapped within some 12 months without seeing service use.

Specification
Type: bomber
Powerplant: two 89-kW (120-hp) each Beardmore inline piston engines

Performance: maximum speed 153 km/h (95 mph) at sea level; climb to 1980 m (6,500 ft) in 23 minutes 30 seconds; endurance 8 hours
Weights: empty 1805 kg (3,980 lb); maximum take-off 2635 kg (5,810 lb)
Dimensions: span 18.54 m (60 ft 10 in); length 11.23 m (36 ft 10 in); height 4.42 m (14 ft 6 in); wing area 73.67 m² (793 sq ft)
Armament: two flexible 7.7-mm (0.303-in) Lewis guns, plus an unknown bomb load

Airco D.H.4

Regarded generally as the best day bomber to see service during World War I, the **Airco D.H.4** was intended originally to be powered by an uprated version of the Beardmore engine. There was nothing really remarkable about this powerplant, except that Frank Halford's skill enabled him to conjure 119 kW (160 hp) out of an engine that was rated at only 89 kW (120 hp). Equally, there was nothing very advanced about the airframe of this aircraft. It was a conventional two-bay biplane of wood and fabric structure, its forward fuselage given added strength by having plywood skins.

plane, to enable the pilot to trim the aircraft in flight, and landing gear was of fixed tailwheel type. The fuselage incorporated two open cockpits, the size of the structure making it possible to place them well apart; this was later found to be a serious disadvantage. What, then, made this such a memorable aeroplane?

During the period when design of the D.H.4 was being finalised, a new engine appeared on the scene. Designated B.H.P., it was designed and constructed by the combined talents of Sir William Beardmore, Frank Halford, and T.C. Pullinger. Rated at 172 kW (230 hp), the prototype engine was installed in the proto-

type D.H.4, and early testing in August 1916 progressed satisfactorily. Unfortunately, considerable delays occurred in getting the B.H.P. into production, but fortunately for the D.H.4 an alternative powerplant, rated at 186 kW (250 hp), became available from Rolls-Royce. This engine was to become known as the Eagle, and the D.H.4 was to be carried into aviation history by the splendid power and reliability of this unit. When the 280-kW (375-hp) Eagle VIII became available, D.H.4s with this engine were superior in performance to most of the contemporary fighter aircraft.

Equipping initially the RFC's No. 55

Squadron in early 1917, the D.H.4 was operating with no fewer than nine RAF and 13 American squadrons by the late spring of 1918. The type also served with the Royal Naval Air Service (combined with the RFC to form the RAF on 1 April 1918) for coastal patrol, and was used to equip home defence squadrons. The excellent performance of these aircraft meant that they were usually to be found at the forefront of any important actions and as a result, such diverse operations as the sinking of a U-boat, and an attack on the Mole at Zeebrugge, all formed a part of the colourful canvas of their history. One, piloted by Major E. Cadbury, with Captain R. Leckie as his gunner, destroyed the pride of the Imperial German Naval Airship Service, the Zeppelin L.70, on 5 August 1918. This vessel was commanded by Fregattenkapitän Peter Strasser, commander in chief of the airship operations, and his death marked a decline in the capability of this service.

Clearly, the D.H.4 was a most significant aircraft, superior to any other contemporary aeroplane of its class. A fundamental weakness, however, resulted from the spacing of the two cockpits. This layout had been adopted to ensure that the pilot had a good downward and forward view for bomb aiming, and the observer/gunner a maximum field of fire for his Lewis gun or guns. But lack of effective communication between the two-man crew made the D.H.4 extremely vulnerable when intercepted by enemy fighters and forced into combat.

Built under sub-contract by F.W. Berwick and Company, Glendower Aircraft Company, Palladium Autocars Ltd, The Vulcan Motor and Engineering Company, Waring & Gillow Ltd, and the Westland Aircraft Works, the combined output of these manufacturers and the parent company totalled 1,449. They also flew with a variety of engines, other than the Rolls-Royce III, IV or Eagle, including the 149-kW (200-hp) R.A.F.3a, 172-kW (230-hp) Siddeley Puma, and 194-kW (260-hp) Fiat. Experimental engine installations included a 224-kW (300-hp) Renault 12Fe, 239-kW (320-hp) Armstrong Siddeley Jaguar I, 263-kW (353-hp) Rolls-Royce 'G', 298-kW (400-hp) Sunbeam Matabele, and a Ricardo-Halford supercharged engine. Increasing engine powers required larger diameter propellers, steadily reducing clearance between the propeller tip and the ground, and resulted in the main landing gear units being extended sufficiently to cater for future growth.

Armament of the standard D.H.4s consisted of a fixed forward-firing Vickers machine-gun that was synchronised by a Constantinesco interrupter gear; the observer/gunner had one or two Lewis guns mounted on a Scarff ring. Underfuselage and underwing bomb racks had a maximum capacity of 209 kg (460 lb). Aircraft built by Westland Aircraft for the RNAS had twin Vickers machine-guns for the pilot, and the rear Lewis guns were on a pillar mounting. Two examples of the D.H.4 were modified to mount a Coventry Ordnance Works (C.O.W.) quick-firing gun, which fired a 0.68-kg (1.5-lb) shell. Mounted to fire almost vertically upward, this gun was intended for attacks on German Zeppelins; but by the time they were ready for service, Zeppelin raids on Britain had ended.

The D.H.4 also has the distinction of being the only early British aircraft to be built in large numbers in the USA, which

designated the type **DH-4**. It was the only US-built aircraft of British origin to be used operationally in France. By the end of World War I a total of 3,227 DH-4s, with Liberty engines, had been built by The Dayton-Wright Airplane Company, The Fisher Body Corporation, and Standard Aircraft Corporation. Of these, 1,885 were shipped to France for use by the American Expeditionary Forces; but only about one-third were used operationally.

The career of the D.H.4 was to continue long after the Armistice of 1918, war surplus examples going to the Belgian, Greek, Japanese, and Spanish air forces, with American-built machines continuing to serve with the United States Army Air Corps and with many Latin American countries. Large numbers of variants appeared in the USA during the early post-war years, these being conversions of ex-military aircraft, and many pioneering flights were made with them. As a single example, two USAAC **DH-4B**s were used in the first successful experiments that led to the important modern technique of inflight refuelling.

The D.H.4 was not limited to military applications in these early years of peace, and in the UK it was the earliest type to be used as a civil transport by Holt Thomas' Aircraft Transport & Travel Ltd for the first cross-Channel service between London and Paris. It was also used by Handley Page Transport Ltd and the Belgian airline SNETA. In the USA, a number, acquired by the US Post Office Department in 1919 and converted as mailplanes, remained in use until 1927. Canada, which received 12 of the aircraft as an 'Imperial Gift' from Britain, used them for spotting forest fires. It is a measure of the success of the aircraft that a descriptive entry of this nature is really inadequate to cover every facet of this remarkable machine. It emphasises the genius of Geoffrey de Havilland, and was to be followed by a succession of outstanding designs, including those that came from the de Havilland Aircraft Company which he founded in the early 1920s.

Westland-built D.H.4, of No. 5 (Naval) Squadron, Royal Naval Air Service, spring 1918. After the RNAS joined with the RFC, this unit became No. 205 Sqn, RAF.

Variants

Airco D.H.4A: designation of British post-war civil conversions with an enclosed two-seat passenger cabin formed from the aft cockpit
DH-4A: designation of US-built version with revised and increased-capacity fuel system
DH-4B/-4C/-4L/-4M/-4Amb/-4Ard: blanket designations covering a large number of US post-war variants; for examples, DH-4B variants included DH-4B, DH-4B-1, DH-4BD etc., to the extent of some 60 versions, many of them experimental
Airco D.H.4R: designation of a single racing version converted by clipping the lower wings and installing a 336-kW (450-hp) Napier Lion inline piston engine; maximum level speed 241 km/h (150 mph), empty weight 1129 kg (2,490 lb), maximum take-off weight 1447 kg (3,191 lb) and length 8.36 m (27 ft 5 in)

Specification
Airco D.H.4
Type: two-seat day bomber
Powerplant: one 280-kW (375-hp) Rolls-Royce Eagle VIII inline piston engine

Performance: maximum level speed 230 km/h (143 mph); climb to 1830 m (6,000 ft) in 4 minutes 50 seconds; service ceiling 6705 m (22,000 ft); endurance 3 hours 45 minutes
Weights: empty 1083 kg (2,387 lb); maximum take-off 1575 kg (3,472 lb)
Dimensions: span 12.92 m (42 ft 4½ in); length 9.35 m (30 ft 8 in); height 3.35 m (11 ft 0 in); wing area 40.32 m² (434 sq ft)
Armament: one (RFC) or two (RNAS) fixed forward-firing 7.7-mm (0.303-in) Vickers machine-guns and one or two 7.7-mm (0.303-in) Lewis guns in aft cockpit, plus up to 209 kg (460 lb) of bombs on underfuselage/wing racks; American-built DH-4s had two 7.62-mm (0.3-in) Marlin forward-firing machine-guns, but otherwise were as British production

The Airco D.H.4 was a magnificent bomber: with a variety of engines its performance was excellent and its armament (offensive and defensive) superior to that of most contemporary machines. Its one main disadvantage was the wide separation of the two cockpits.

Airco D.H.5

Whatever the shortcomings of the D.H.1 and D.H.2, their pusher configuration, adopted to permit the installation of a forward-firing weapon, had ensured that the pilots of these aircraft had an excellent field of view. When synchronising mechanisms made it possible for forward-firing guns to be mounted to fire through the propeller disc, this benefit was offset to some extent by the much inferior field of view for the pilot.

The **Airco D.H.5**, designed in 1916, was intended to replace the single-seat D.H.2, and was the first scout fighter of

de Havilland design to introduce a Constantinesco interrupter gear. While the tractor configuration promised far better performance, Geoffrey de Havilland was anxious to ensure that the pilot should not suffer by having a field of view that was much inferior to that of the D.H.2. This aim was responsible for the unusual configuration of the D.H.5, with considerable backward stagger of the biplane wings so that the pilot could be seated forward of the leading edge of the upper wing.

Apart from this feature, construction was conventional wood and fabric, land-

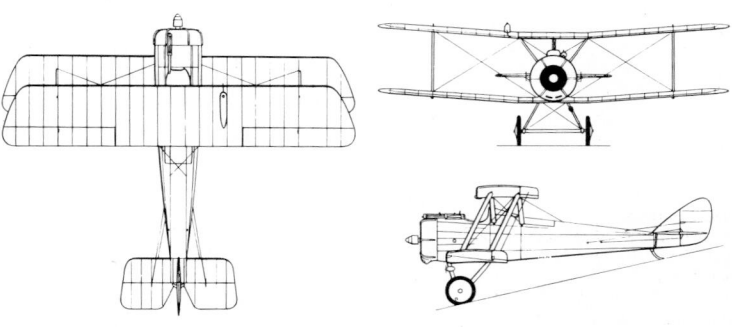

Airco D.H.5

Airco D.H.5 (continued)

ing gear of fixed tailskid skid type, and powerplant an 82-kW (110-hp) Le Rhône rotary engine. The D.H.5 entered service with the RFC's Nos 24 and 32 Squadrons in May 1917, and when flown by experienced pilots it proved to be a most useful weapon. But its handling characteristics and high altitude performance, inferior to those of many contemporary Allied and enemy aircraft, made it very vulnerable in inexperienced hands. After suffering fairly heavy losses in November 1917, the D.H.5 was used for ground-attack sorties until being replaced in

front-line service by the Royal Aircraft Factory S.E.5a in January 1918. It continued in use as an advanced trainer for only a short period.

Production of D.H.5s totalled about 550, built by Airco (200), and the balance sub-contracted to the British Caudron Company (50), The Darracq Motor Engineering Company (200), and March, Jones and Cribb (about 100). For experimental purposes a single example was powered by an 82-kW (110-hp) Clerget rotary engine.

Specification
Type: single-seat scout fighter
Powerplant: one 82-kW (110-hp) Le Rhône rotary piston engine
Performance: maximum level speed at 3050 m (10,000 ft) 164 km/h (102 mph); climb to 1980 m (6,500 ft) in 6 minutes 55 seconds; service ceiling 4875 m (16,000 ft); endurance 2 hours 45 minutes
Weights: empty 458 kg (1,010 lb); maximum take-off 677 kg (1,492 lb)

Dimensions: span 7.82 m (25 ft 8 in); length 6.71 m (22 ft 0 in); height 2.78 m (9 ft 1½ in); wing area 19.7 m² (212.1 sq ft)
Armament: one fixed forward-firing 7.7-mm (0.303-in) Vickers machine-gun, plus four 11.3-kg (25-lb) bombs on underwing racks; one aircraft was flown experimentally with a Vickers machine-gun firing upwards and forwards at an angle of about 45°

Airco D.H.9

When, as a result of daylight attacks on London by German bombers, it was decided in mid-1917 to increase the strength of the RFC, the Air Board directed that a large proportion of the new squadrons would be equipped with bomber aircraft. Large numbers of the excellent D.H.4 were ordered to serve with many of the squadrons, but it was appreciated that a new longer-range bomber would be needed if the area of bombing operations was to be extended. Understandably, there was some reluctance to scrap the facilities that had been developed for large-scale production of the D.H.4, and efforts were made to retain as much as possible of that structure in Airco's new design.

The prototype **Airco D.H.9** was produced by modification of a D.H.4. The D.H.9 retained the same wings, tail unit, and generally similar landing gear, but the fuselage was completely new, with a much improved, more streamlined nose, and the pilot's cockpit directly above the lower wing trailing edge; this put the pilot and observer/gunner close together so that communication presented no problem, thus eliminating the only serious shortcoming of the D.H.4. Powerplant was a 172-kW (230-hp) B.H.P., built by the Galloway Engineering Company, and referred to sometimes as the Galloway Adriatic. Early testing, which began in late July 1917, proceeded so well that existing D.H.4 contracts held by sub-contractors were amended to cover production of the D.H.9. Some of these early production aircraft had a Siddeley-built B.H.P. engine, but a new light-weight version of this engine, known as the Puma and developed by Siddeley-Deasy, was selected as the major production engine. Rated at 224 kW (300 hp) this was expected to give the D.H.9 outstanding performance, but when development problems meant that reliabil-

ity could only be assured by de-rating output to 172 kW (230 hp), the performance of the new bomber was inferior to that of the D.H.4 which it was intended to replace.

Despite this inadequacy, which, when the type was first introduced in April 1918, resulted in serious losses by the squadrons in France, something in excess of 3,200 were built in Britain by Airco and 12 sub-contractors. Thus the D.H.4 soldiered on, being supplemented, rather than replaced, by the D.H.9. In areas less active than the Western Front the D.H.9 did rather better, notably in Macedonia and Palestine, and the type was also to strengthen British coastal defence and anti-Zeppelin patrols. With the end of the war the D.H.9 soon faded from the RAF scene, eclipsed completely by the D.H.9A which replaced it.

War surplus D.H.9s served in Afghanistan, Australia, Belgium, Canada, Chile, Estonia, Greece, India, the Irish Free State, Latvia, the Netherlands, New Zealand, Poland and South Africa; and the type was built under licence by Hispano-Suiza for service with the Spanish air force, a figure in excess of 500 being quoted as the production figure, and at least 25 still being in service when the Spanish Civil War started in July 1936. Others were built by SABCA in Belgium; and the Netherlands Army Aircraft Factory also assembled 10 new D.H.9s, built by the de Havilland Aircraft Company in 1923, and in 1934 these were each given a Wright Whirlwind engine of 347 kW (465 hp). Despite this sort of demand, Britain's Aircraft Disposal Company still had large numbers of war surplus D.H.9s in stock in late 1930, and these were scrapped and burned during the following year.

In addition to standard powerplants mentioned, D.H.9s were also flown experimentally or as a result of conversion

with engines that included the 186-kW (250-hp) Fiat A-12, 216-kW (290-hp) Siddeley Puma high-compression engine, 224-kW (300-hp) A.D.C. Nimbus and Hispano-Suiza 8Fg, 321-kW (430-hp) Napier Lion, and 324-kW (435-hp) Liberty 12A. Conversions carried out by the South African Air Force, with the 149-kW (200-hp) Wolseley Viper, 336-kW (450-hp) Bristol Jupiter VI and 358-kW (480-hp) Bristol Jupiter VIII, were known respectively by the names of **Mantis, M'pala I** and **M'pala II**.

Variants
Airco D.H.9B: designation of aircraft converted for civil use, and carrying one passenger forward and one aft of the pilot
Airco D.H.9C: designation of aircraft converted for civil use, and carrying one passenger forward and two aft of the pilot
Airco D.H.9J: designation used for the SAAF M'pala I, and also for the D.H.9s modernised in the late 1920s for use by the de Havilland School of Flying. These latter aircraft had a strengthened forward fuselage structure; improved landing gear, aileron controls, and fuel system;

The D.H.9 moved the pilot and gunner/observer closer together, rectifying a main fault of the D.H.4.

introduced Handley Page leading-edge slots; and were powered by a 287-kW (385-hp) Armstrong Siddeley Jaguar III radial engine

Specification
Airco D.H.9 (standard RAF type)
Type: two-seat day bomber
Powerplant: one 172-kW (230-hp) Siddeley Puma inline piston engine
Performance: maximum level speed 178 km/h (110 mph) at 1980 m (6,500 ft); climb to 1980 m (6,500 ft) in 10 minutes 20 seconds; service ceiling 4725 m (15,500 ft); endurance 4 hours 30 minutes
Weights: empty 1012 kg (2,230 lb); maximum take-off 1508 kg (3,325 lb)
Dimensions: span 12.92 m (42 ft 4½ in); length 9.27 m (30 ft 5 in); height 3.44 m (11 ft 3½ in); wing area 40.32 m² (434 sq ft)
Armament: one fixed forward-firing 7.7-mm (0.303-in) Vickers machine-gun and one or two 7.7-mm (0.303-in) Lewis guns on Scarff ring in aft cockpit, plus up to 209 kg (460 lb) of bombs

Airco D.H.9A

The disappointing performance of the D.H.9 could clearly be overcome by the introduction of a more powerful and reliable engine. Could Rolls-Royce once again create success out of what was virtually a failure? Unfortunately, the answer was no. The demand for Rolls-Royce Eagle VIII engines considerably exceeded the supply.

To overcome this, Liberty 12 engines were ordered from the USA, and Airco, which was deeply involved with the new D.H.10, requested the Westland Aircraft Works at Yeovil, Somerset, to redesign the D.H.9 to accept the Liberty engine. Westland, which had built large numbers of both D.H.4 and D.H.9 aircraft

D.H.9A of 'B' Flight, No. 8 Squadron RAF, based at Hinaidi in Iraq during the early 1920s. Note the extra radiator located under the nose for desert use.

under sub-contract, did better than that, combining the best features of both with the US powerplant; and to ensure maximum benefit from the extra horsepower, strengthened the fuselage structure and introduced wings of increased span and chord. The prototype **Airco D.H.9A**, because no Liberty engines had been received, was flown initially with a 280-kW (375-hp) Eagle VIII engine. The first Liberty-engined aircraft was flown soon after, and the first deliveries were made to the RAF during June 1918.

Some 885 D.H.9A bombers were built by Westland and sub-contractors, and the type was to become regarded as the outstanding strategic bomber aircraft of World War I. Unlike that of most other wartime aircraft, production of the D.H.9A continued in the post-war years, serving the RAF reliably during air policing operations in Iraq and on the North-West Frontier of India. Carrying the nickname 'Nine-Ack', usually shortened to 'Ninak', several hundred were built by Westland and other British manufacturers, with Westland kept busy repairing and refurbishing these aircraft until they were finally withdrawn from RAF service in 1931. In addition to the air policing operations, the RAF's D.H.9As also equipped eight UK-based day bomber squadrons and six auxiliary squadrons, flown by Nos 30 and 47 Squadrons maintained the Cairo-Baghdad desert air mail service, served in Egypt and Palestine, and thrilled thousands of spectators at RAF Hendon Displays.

Variants
de Havilland D.H.9AJ Stag: designation of single prototype with improved main landing gear and powerplant of one 347-kW (465-hp) Bristol Jupiter VI radial engine
de Havilland D.H.9R: designation of a single racing version with sesquiplane wing, and powered by a 347-kW (465-hp) Napier Lion II inline engine
Engineering Division USD-9A: designation of nine generally similar US-built aircraft, each having its forward-firing 7.62-mm (0.3-in) Browning machine-gun on the starboard (instead of port) side, and a modified rudder
Engineering Division USD-9B: designation of one USD-9A following installation of a 313-kW (420-hp) Liberty 12A engine

Specification
Airco D.H.9A (standard RAF type)
Type: two-seat day bomber
Powerplant: one 298-kW (400-hp) Packard Liberty 12 inline piston engine
Performance: maximum level speed at sea level 198 km/h (123 mph); climb to 1980 m (6,500 ft) in 8 minutes 55 seconds; service ceiling 5105 m (16,750 ft); endurance 5 hours 15 minutes
Weights: empty 1270 kg (2,800 lb); maximum take-off 2107 kg (4,645 lb)
Dimensions: span 14.01 m (45 ft 11½ in); length 9.22 m (30 ft 3 in); height 3.45 m (11 ft 4 in); wing area 45.22 m² (486.7 sq ft)
Armament: one fixed forward-firing 7.7-mm (0.303-in) Vickers machine-gun and one or two 7.7-mm (0.303-in) Lewis guns on Scarff ring in aft cockpit, plus up to 299 kg (660 lb) of bombs

Airspeed AS.6 Envoy

The design of this Airspeed aircraft, which became designated **AS.6 Envoy**, began in late 1933 as a larger, twin-engined development of the AS.5 Courier. The prototype was flown for the first time on 26 June 1934 and for a British civil aircraft of that era was subsequently produced 'extensively', with 50 being built, this total including the prototype.

With standard accommodation for a pilot and eight passengers the Envoy, like the earlier Courier, was of conventional all-wood construction, with all control surfaces fabric-covered. Retractable tailwheel type landing gear and a variable-incidence tailplane were features of the design which, in the period 1934-9 when these aircraft were being produced, was to appear in three versions. The initial **Series I** (17 examples built) was without trailing-edge flaps; the **Series II** (13) introduced split flaps which extended from aileron to wing root on the trailing edge of each wing, and also from wing root to wing root beneath the centre-section; and the **Series III** (19) was generally similar, but had a number of detail improvements.

The most unstandard feature of the Envoys was their powerplant, and these included the **AS.6** with 149-kW (200-hp) Wolseley AR.9; the **AS.6A** with 179-kW (240-hp) Armstrong Siddeley Lynx IVC; the **AS.6D** with 261-kW (350-hp) Wright R-760-E2 Whirlwind 7; the **AS.6E** with 254-kW (340-hp) Walter Castor II; the **AS.6G** with 186-kW (250-hp) Wolseley Scorpio I; the **AS.6H** with 168-kW (225-hp) Wolseley Aries III; and the **AS.6J** and **AS.6JM/C** with 261-kW (350-hp) Armstrong Siddeley Cheetah IX.

Envoys were to fly in many different skies, being supplied to China, Czechoslovakia, France, India and Japan. For military service they were used by the RAF, Royal Navy and South African Air Force, and a number were used in the Spanish Civil War. The first Envoy Series II to be supplied to the RAF was of historical significance as this aircraft, initially G-AEXX and later L7270, was the founder member of the King's (now Queen's) Flight. The RAF also acquired two Envoys for communications service in India, and five for home service in a similar role, and at least one of these was used throughout World War II by the Fleet Air Arm. In addition, three impressed Envoys served with the RAF during the war. South Africa acquired seven Envoys in 1936: three of these were used by the SAAF and had an armament comprising a forward firing machine-gun and a dorsal gun turret. The four civil Envoys which made up the total, and which were for operation by South African Airways, were capable of quick conversion for use in a military role.

Specification
Type: seven-seat light transport aircraft
Powerplant: (AS.6J) two 261-kW (350-hp) each Armstrong Siddeley Cheetah IX radial piston engines
Performance: maximum speed 338 km/h (210 mph) at 2225 m (7,300 ft); cruising speed 290 km/h (180 mph) at 3050 m (10,000 ft); service ceiling 6860 m (22,500 ft); range 1046 km (650 miles)

One of three Airspeed AS.6JM(II) Envoys delivered to the South African Air Force in 1936. Four civil Envoys were also supplied to South African Airways, the military machines having provision for a dorsal gun turret.

Weights: empty 1840 kg (4,057 lb); maximum take-off 2858 kg (6,300 lb)
Dimensions: span 15.95 m (52 ft 4 in); length 10.52 m (34 ft 6 in); height 2.9 m (9 ft 6 in); wing area 31.49 m² (339 sq ft)

Airspeed AS.10 Oxford

Established in 1931, Airspeed had little prospect of obtaining a significant military contract in its early years. However, in 1936 the company was given the opportunity of submitting a proposal to meet Air Ministry Specification T.23/36, which called for a twin-engined trainer. Airspeed's design for this was based on the successful AS.6 Envoy, of which about 24 were already in civil use and earning a reputation for reliability which, possibly, may have helped the Air Ministry's decision to order an initial quantity of 136 **AS.10**s.

The prototype AS.10, by then bearing the name Oxford, made its first flight on 19 June 1937, and token deliveries began in November of that year, with four of the first six going to the RAF's Central Flying School, the other two to No. 11 Flying Training School. Very similar in overall proportions and configuration to the AS.6 Envoy, it shared also its wooden construction, tailwheel type retractable landing gear and basic airframe. The variations came in powerplant, internal layout and, in the **Oxford I**, provision of an Armstrong Whitworth gun turret with one machine-gun for the training of air gunners.

The Oxford was to be built in large numbers and used extensively for the Commonwealth Air Training Scheme when World War II began, and the considerable thought which Airspeed had put into its internal layout undoubtedly had a bearing on the demand for this aircraft. Normal accommodation was for a crew of three at any one time, but in addition to seats for a pilot/pupil and co-pilot/instructor, there were positions for the training of an air-gunner, bomb-

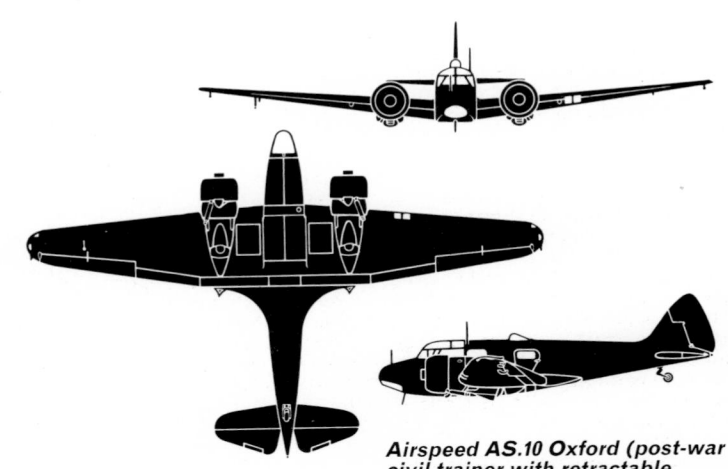

Airspeed AS.10 Oxford (post-war civil trainer with retractable wheel fairings).

aimer, camera operator, navigator, and radio operator. Dual controls were standard, making the Oxford suitable for use as a twin-engined trainer; with the dual-control set removed from the co-pilot's position, a bomb aimer could take up a prone position and drop practice smoke bombs which were carried in the centre-section well; or the seat could be slid back and a chart table, hinged to the fuselage side, erected for use by a trainee navigator; an aft-facing seat behind the co-pilot position was available for a radio operator; and, in the Oxford I, a turret was provided for an air-gunner's training. A hood was also available so that the Oxford could be used for instrument training.

Powerplants varied according to mark. The **Mk I**, a general-purpose, bombing and gunnery trainer, and the **Mk II** pilot, radio operator and navigator trainer, were both powered by two 280-kW (375-hp) Armstrong Siddeley Cheetah X radial engines, with fixed-pitch propellers. The **Mk V**, equipped for the same

role as the Mk II, had two 336-kW (450-hp) Pratt & Whitney R-985-AN6 radial engines, driving constant-speed propellers. The **Oxford Mk III**, of which only a single example was built, had two 318-kW (425-hp) Cheetah XV radials and Rotol constant-speed propellers; the **Mk IV** was a projected trainer version of the Mk III, but none was built. One example of a Mk II aircraft was fitted experimentally with two 186-kW (250-hp) de Havilland Gipsy Queen inline engines. Odd variants included an early Oxford I equipped with special McLaren landing gear, the main units of which could be offset to cater for a reasonable degree of crosswind at both take-off and landing, and one with a tail unit which included twin endplate fins and rudders, especially installed for a series of spin recovery tests.

As mentioned above, the outbreak of World War II created an enormous demand for these trainers, not only for use by the RAF, but also by those nations which were involved in the Com-

monwealth Air Training Scheme. These included Australia (nearly 400 Oxfords), Canada (200), New Zealand (300), Rhodesia (10), and South Africa (700). Examples went also to the Free French air force and, under reverse Lend-Lease, a number were used by USAAF units in Europe. In addition to their use for training purposes, a number were equipped to serve as air ambulances. Many served with anti-aircraft co-operation squadrons, these including Nos 282, 286, 289, 290, 567, 577, 598, 631, 667 and 691. The Fleet Air Arm also had one training unit, No. 758 Instrument Flying Squadron, equipped with Oxfords from June 1942.

The demand for Oxfords was beyond Airspeed's productive capacity, the company building a total of 4,411 at Portsmouth, Hants, and 550 at Christchurch, Hants. Other construction was by de Havilland at Hatfield (1,515), Percival Aircraft at Luton (1,360), and Standard Motors at Coventry (750), to give a grand total of 8,586. Airspeed built

its last example in July 1945, and the Oxford remained in service with the RAF at No. 10 Advanced Flying Training School, Pershore, until 1954. Many were supplied after the war to the Dutch air force.

Specification
Type: three-seat general-purpose trainer
Powerplant: (Mk V) two 336-kW (450-hp) each Pratt & Whitney R-985-AN6 Wasp Junior radial piston engines
Performance: maximum speed 325 km/h (202 mph) at 1250 m (4,100 ft); service ceiling 6400 m (21,000 ft); range 1127 km (700 miles)
Weights: empty 2572 kg (5,670 lb); maximum take-off 3269 kg (8,000 lb)
Dimensions: span 16.26 m (53 ft 4 in); length 10.52 m (34 ft 6 in); height 3.38 m (11 ft 1 in); wing area 32.33 m² (348 sq ft)
Armament: (Oxford I only) one 7.7-mm (0.303-in) machine-gun in dorsal turret

Airspeed Cambridge AS.45

Designed to satisfy Air Ministry Specification T.34/39 for an advanced trainer, the **Airspeed AS.45** design was conventional in appearance and in the same general mould as the Miles Master, being of low-wing monoplane layout, having retractable tailwheel type landing gear, and powered by a radial air-cooled engine. Following Air Ministry approval of the design, which was given the provisional name Cambridge, two prototypes were ordered, the first of these making a successful maiden flight on 19 February 1941.

Construction was fairly typical of that era, with wings and tail unit of wood with plywood skins, except for control surfaces which were fabric-covered. The trailing edge of each wing was shared almost equally by ailerons and flaps. The fuselage was integral with this to provide instructor and pupil with some pro-

tection in the event of an accident. Four doors were provided, two on each side, so that exit in emergency could be made on either side. The main units of the Dowty landing gear retracted inwards, the wheels lying flush in the undersurface of the wing centre-section. Instructor and trainee were seated in tandem beneath an extensively glazed canopy. Powerplant comprised a 544-kW (730-hp) Bristol Mercury VIII radial engine, driving a three-blade constant-speed propeller.

Flight testing of these two prototypes was to show that low-speed flight characteristics were poor, and speed was below that which had been estimated. Both of the aircraft were handed over to the RAF in July 1942, following a decision not to proceed with production. This may well have been because performance of the prototypes was disap-

pointing, but the official reason given at the time was that the design of the Cambridge had been initiated to fill an anticipated shortage of advanced trainers which had not materialised, due to an adequate supply of Masters and, via Lend-Lease, the excellent North American Harvard.

Specification
Type: two-seat advanced trainer
Powerplant: one 544-kW (730-hp) Bristol Mercury VIII radial piston engine

The fault-ridden Airspeed AS.45 Cambridge advanced trainer was cancelled in 1942.

Performance: maximum speed 381 km/h (237 mph) at 4875 m (16,000 ft); service ceiling 7560 m (24,800 ft); range 1094 km (680 miles)
Weights: no data available
Dimensions: span 12.8 m (42 ft 0 in); length 11 m (36 ft 1 in); height 3.51 m (11 ft 6 in); wing area 26.94 m² (280 sq ft)
Armament: none

Airspeed AS.57 Ambassador

Great Britain's wartime Brabazon Committee, set up to establish guidelines for post-war development of civil aircraft, included in its report of early 1943 a recommendation for the design and construction of a short/medium-range twin-engined transport with accommodation for about 30 passengers. This resulted in the **Airspeed AS.57 Ambassador**, designed by a team headed by Arthur Hagg, their work taking shape on the drawing-board while the UK was still at war.

The first flight of the prototype Ambassador (G-AGUA) was made on 10 July 1947, and just over a year later the first (and also the only) order for 20 aircraft was received from British European Airways. The Ambassador was a very attractive aircraft of cantilever high-wing monoplane configuration, of all-metal construction, with its fuselage stressed for cabin pressurisation. The distinctive three-finned tail unit was carried high on an upswept aft fuselage, and the retractable tricycle landing gear incorporated twin wheels on each unit. Accommodation was provided for a crew of three on the flight deck, with

maximum seating for 47 passengers in the cabin. Power was provided by two Bristol Centaurus sleeve-valve radial engines.

As a result of delays in development, it was not until 13 March 1952 that BEA was able to make its first scheduled service with the AS.57. So much time had been lost by then, that the Ambassador had been overtaken by more advanced aircraft, such as the Vickers Viscount turboprop-powered airliner, and no further sales interest was shown. Despite this, BEA's AS.57s, which were operated as the 'Elizabethan' class, proved a successful and well-liked interim type during their six years with the British airline.

The second AS.57 prototype (G-AKRD) was later used for development testing of the Bristol Proteus 705, Rolls-Royce Tyne and Rolls-Royce Dart turboprops, and was still airworthy in 1969, more than 20 years after its first flight. The third prototype (G-ALFR), was used for testing of the Napier Eland turboprop, but was later converted to airline standards and sold to Dan Air.

Specification
Type: twin-engine short/medium-range transport
Powerplant: two 1939-kW (2,600-hp) each Bristol Centaurus 661 two-row sleeve-valve radial piston engines
Performance: maximum cruising speed 438 km/h (272 mph); economic cruising speed 399 km/h (248 mph); range with maximum payload 1159 km (720 miles)
Weights: empty equipped 16230 kg (35,781 lb); maximum take-off 23814 kg (52,500 lb)

The Ambassador lived up to its name, showing grace and elegance in the air. Unfortunately the turboprop revolution, led by the Viscount, had swallowed it up due to development delays.

Dimensions: span 35.05 m (115 ft 0 in); length 24.69 m (81 ft 0 in); height 5.59 m (18 ft 4 in); wing area 111.48 m² (1,200 sq ft)

Albatros C.III
to
Albatros D.V. and D.Va

Albatros C.III

Most extensively built of the company's two-seaters, the **Albatros C.III** was generally similar in configuration and construction to the C.I from which it was developed. It differed in having biplane wings that were more equal in span, but the most distinctive new feature was a redesigned tail unit. Instead of the angular tailplane, elevators and rudder of the earlier aircraft, surfaces with rounded contours were adopted; these marked an interim stage towards a tailplane configuration that was to become a recognition feature of most late-war Albatros types.

C.IIIs entered service on the Western Front during late 1916, and it was soon discovered that a forward-firing synchronised machine-gun could be used, to supplement that operated by the rear gunner/observer, without any serious reduction in performance. So equipped, it was one of the first of the German C types with such armament, and a step nearer to the introduction of fighter scout aircraft. One other aggressive feature was the ability to carry a small bombload, carried internally in a stowage compartment between the two cockpits, but the lack of any means of aiming such weapons accurately represented a nuisance to the enemy, rather than a significant tactical capability.

The C.III was also built under licence by Ostdeutsche Albatros Werke, Deutsche Flugzeugwerke A.G. (D.F.W.), Hanseatische Flugzeugwerke (Hansa), Linke-Hofman Werke, Luft Verkehrs Gesellschaft (L.V.G.) and Siemens-Schuckert Werke.

Above: This Albatros C.III was flown by Leutnant Bruno Mass (hence the stylised insignia) of Fliegerabteilung 14 on the Eastern Front against Russia during January 1917.

Below: The C.III was the most widely-produced of the Albatros C-type two-seaters. It entered service in the late autumn of 1916, initially on the Western Front.

Specification
Type: two-seat general-purpose aircraft
Powerplant: one 112-kW (150-hp) Benz Bz.III or 119-kW (160-hp) Mercedes D.III inline piston engine
Performance: maximum level speed 140 km/h (87 mph); climb to 1000 m (3,280 ft) in 9 minutes; service ceiling 3350 m (11,000 ft); endurance 4 hours
Weights: empty 851 kg (1,876 lb); maximum take-off 1353 kg (2,983 lb)
Dimensions: span 11.69 m (38 ft 4¼ in); length 8 m (26 ft 3 in); height, Benz engine 3.07 m (10 ft 0¾ in), Mercedes engine 3.1 m (10 ft 2 in); wing area 36.91 m² (397.31 sq ft)
Armament: one 7.92-mm (0.31-in) Parabellum machine gun on flexible mount in rear cockpit and (on later aircraft) one 7.92-mm (0.31-in) LMG 08/15 fixed forward-firing machine gun, plus a small bombload

Albatros C.V

Continuing the development of its line of two-seat general-purpose aircraft, Albatros saw the new, more powerful Mercedes D.IV engines as representing the opportunity of producing a worthwhile successor to the C.III. However, this was a much bigger step than that involved in the C.I to C.III development, for the new engine, with eight rather than six cylinders inline, was longer and heavier than the D.III. The addition of a reduction gear added to both length and weight, but the resulting changed position of the propeller drive shaft made possible a much cleaner engine installation. The addition of a spinner on the two-blade propeller gave the new **Albatros C.V** an advanced, streamlined appearance, marred only by its so-called ear radiators, one on each side of the nose, just forward of the wing. The airframe was little changed from that of the C.III, except for an increase in wing span, a change in fin shape which produced what might be called the definitive Albatros tail unit, and the introduction of a balanced rudder.

When introduced into service in 1916, the C.V suffered from a variety of problems, proving to be very heavy on the controls, the ear radiators being inadequate for engine cooling, and the newly-introduced engine unreliable. To resolve this situation, efforts were made to improve flight characteristics: a new lower wing was introduced, together with balanced ailerons, elevators, and other refinements; and a new radiator was introduced into the upper-wing centre-section to replace the ear radiators. The two versions thus became identified as the **C.V/16** (of 1916) and the **C.V/17**. The engine was unchanged, and it was the continuing problems with crankshaft failure of the eight-cylinder engine that brought C.V production to an end, 424 C.Vs having been built.

Variant
Albatros C.V. experimental: designation of a single example of the C.V/16, with the standard interplane struts replaced by large I struts for evaluation purposes

Specification
Type: two-seat general-purpose aircraft
Powerplant: one 164-kW (220-hp) Mercedes D.IV inline piston engine

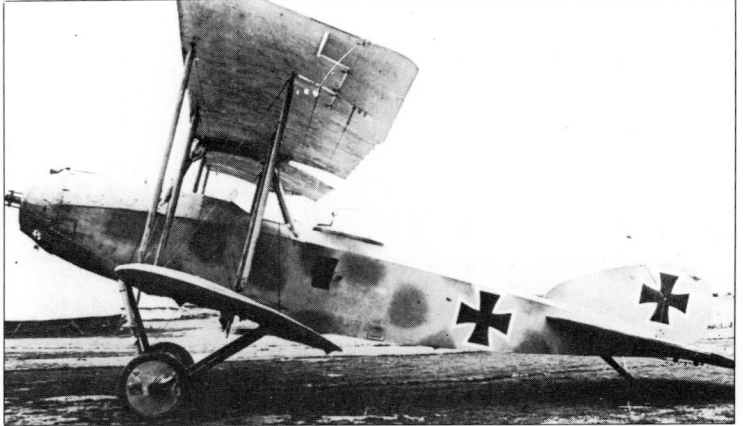

Performance: maximum level speed 170 km/h (106 mph); climb to 1000 m (3,280 ft) in 8 minutes; endurance 3 hours 15 minutes
Weights: empty 1069 kg (2,357 lb); maximum take-off 1585 kg (3,494 lb)
Dimensions: span, C.V/16 12.78 m (41 ft 11¼ in), C.V/17 12.62 m (41 ft 4¾ in); length 8.95 m (29 ft 4¼ in); height 4.5 m (14 ft 9¼ in); wing area 43.4 m² (467.17 sq ft)
Armament: one fixed forward-firing

A distinct aerodynamic improvement on its predecessors, the Albatros C.V might have proved a valuable weapon if only its powerplant had been more reliable.

7.92-mm (0.31-in) LMG 08/15 machine gun and one 7.92-mm (0.31-in) Parabellum machine gun on movable mount in aft cockpit

Albatros C.XII

Designed as a successor to the C.X, the **Albatros C.XII** two-seat reconnaissance/general-purpose aircraft was the first of the company's C series to introduce any significant change; it incorporated an elliptical-section fuselage of the type that had been developed for the company's single-seat fighter scouts. The overall fuselage contours were also enhanced by adoption of the large spinner first introduced on the C.V. Changes to the tail unit included a considerable reduction in tailplane area, and the addition of a triangular ventral fin to which the tailskid was mounted. In other respects the C.XII was similar to the C.X, retaining the wings, landing gear and powerplant of that aircraft with very little change.

Despite the use of this new fuselage, there was virtually no improvement in performance over that of the C.X, and almost certainly this was the result of inefficiency of the wing design. C.XIIs began to enter service in late 1917, and the type was used quite extensively until the end of the war.

Specification
Type: two-seat reconnaissance/general-purpose aircraft
Powerplant: one 194-kW (260-hp) Mercedes D.IVa inline piston engine
Performance: maximum level speed 175 km/h (109 mph); climb to 1000 m (3,280 ft) in 5 minutes; service ceiling 5000 m (16,405 ft); endurance 3 hours 15 minutes
Weights: empty 1021 kg (2,251 lb); maximum take-off 1639 kg (3,613 lb)
Dimensions: span 14.37 m (47 ft 1¾ in); length 8.85 m (29 ft 0½ in); height 3.25 m (10 ft 8 in); wing area 42.7 m^2 (459.63 sq ft)
Armament: one fixed forward-firing 7.92-mm (0.31-in) LMG 08/15 machine gun and one 7.92-mm (0.31-in) Parabellum machine gun on movable mount in aft cockpit, plus a light bombload carried on external racks

The difficulties in which Germany found itself from 1917 onwards were largely to blame for the widespread adoption of the Albatros C.XII, which offered no real performance or armament improvement on earlier C-types.

Albatros D.III

While the D.II was still in production, Robert Thelen initiated the design of an improved version, his particular aim being to achieve better manoeuvrability. This resulted in a changed wing configuration, comprising a narrower-chord lower wing, an increased-span upper wing with raked wingtips, the elimination of wing stagger, and the introduction of Vee interplane struts to improve wing rigidity. During production of these aircraft, engine power was raised from 127 to 130 kW (170 to 175 hp) by increasing the compression ratio, and the radiator in the upper wing centre-section was moved outboard to starboard. This was a result of combat experience, for many a pilot had lost his life when a bullet or shrapnel splinter had pierced the radiator directly over his head, the resulting stream of scalding water being thrown directly into his face by the slipstream.

D.IIIs began to enter service in the early months of 1917 and soon made their presence felt, retaining their superiority until Allied aircraft, including S.E.5s and Sopwith Camels, regained the upper hand in late 1917, and at which time almost 500 D.IIIs were in service.

Specification
Type: single-seat scout fighter
Powerplant: one 127/130-kW (170/175-hp) Mercedes D.IIIa inline piston engine
Performance: maximum level speed 175 km/h (109 mph) at 1000 m (3,280 ft); climb to 1000 m (3,280 ft) in 4 minutes; service ceiling 5500 m (18,040 ft); endurance 2 hours
Weights: empty 661 kg (1,457 lb); maximum take-off 886 kg (1,953 lb)
Dimensions: span 9.05 m (29 ft 8¼ in); length 7.33 m (24 ft 0½ in); height 2.98 m (9 ft 9¼ in); wing area 20.5 m^2 (220.67 sq ft)
Armament: two fixed 7.92-mm (0.31-in) LMG 08/15 machine guns

Introducing greater manoeuvrability to the Albatros fighter series but only at the expense of structural integrity of the wing cellule, the D.III nevertheless made an impact on the air war.

Albatros D.V and D.Va

In an attempt to contain the growing capability of Allied fighters, Albatros in 1917 initiated the development of an improved version of the D.III. The most radical change was in the construction of the fuselage, for a deeper elliptical cross section was realised to try to improve the streamlining of this structure and, consequently, to reduce drag. Other changes included a further reduction in the gap between the upper wing and fuselage, a redesigned rudder, revised aileron controls, the provision of an increased-diameter spinner, and the introduction of a pilot's headrest. As this last tended to restrict the pilot's rearward views, aircraft on active service were seen frequently with their headrests removed.

The **Albatros D.V** entered service in May 1917, but was soon supplemented by the **Albatros D.Va**, which differed by a reversion to the upper wing and aileron control system of the D.III. Both models proved to be inadequate for the task of reducing the activity of Allied fighters but, despite this, production continued on a large scale. At the peak of their utilisation in May 1918, well over 1,000 D.Vs and D.Vas were in service on the Western Front, in Italy and Palestine. Their use in such large numbers was an attempt to overcome the enemy by quantity rather than capability; they suffered heavy losses, not only from the enemy, but also as a result of structural failure of the lower wing.

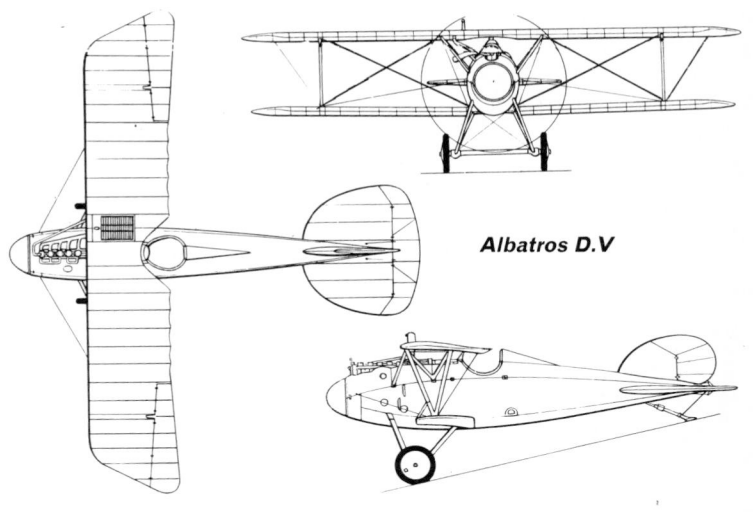

Albatros D.V

Variants

Albatros D.IV: designation of an experimental prototype, combining a D.II type wing and a D.Va fuselage, with an experimental 119-kW (160-hp) Mercedes D.III engine and reduction gear that allowed its installation completely within the fuselage contours; this provided no significant improvement in performance and, in consequence, no further examples were built

Albatros D.Va Experimental: designation of a single example with a 138-kW (185-hp) BMW IIIa engine; it was claimed that this aircraft climbed to an altitude of approximately 10500 m (34,450 ft)

Specification

Albatros D.V and D.Va
Type: single-seat scout fighter
Powerplant: one 134/149-kW (180/200-hp) Mercedes D.IIa inline piston engine (power varied according to compression ratio)
Performance: maximum level speed 186 km/h (116 mph); rate of climb 4 minutes to 1000 m (3,280 ft); service ceiling 5700 m (18,700 ft); endurance 2 hours

Weights: empty 687 kg (1,515 lb); maximum take-off 937 kg (2,066 lb)
Dimensions: span 9.05 m (29 ft 8¼ in); length 7.33 m (24 ft 0½ in); height 2.7 m (8 ft 10¼ in); wing area 21.2 m² (228.2 sq ft)
Armament: two fixed forward-firing 7.92-mm (0.31-in) LMG 08/15 machine guns

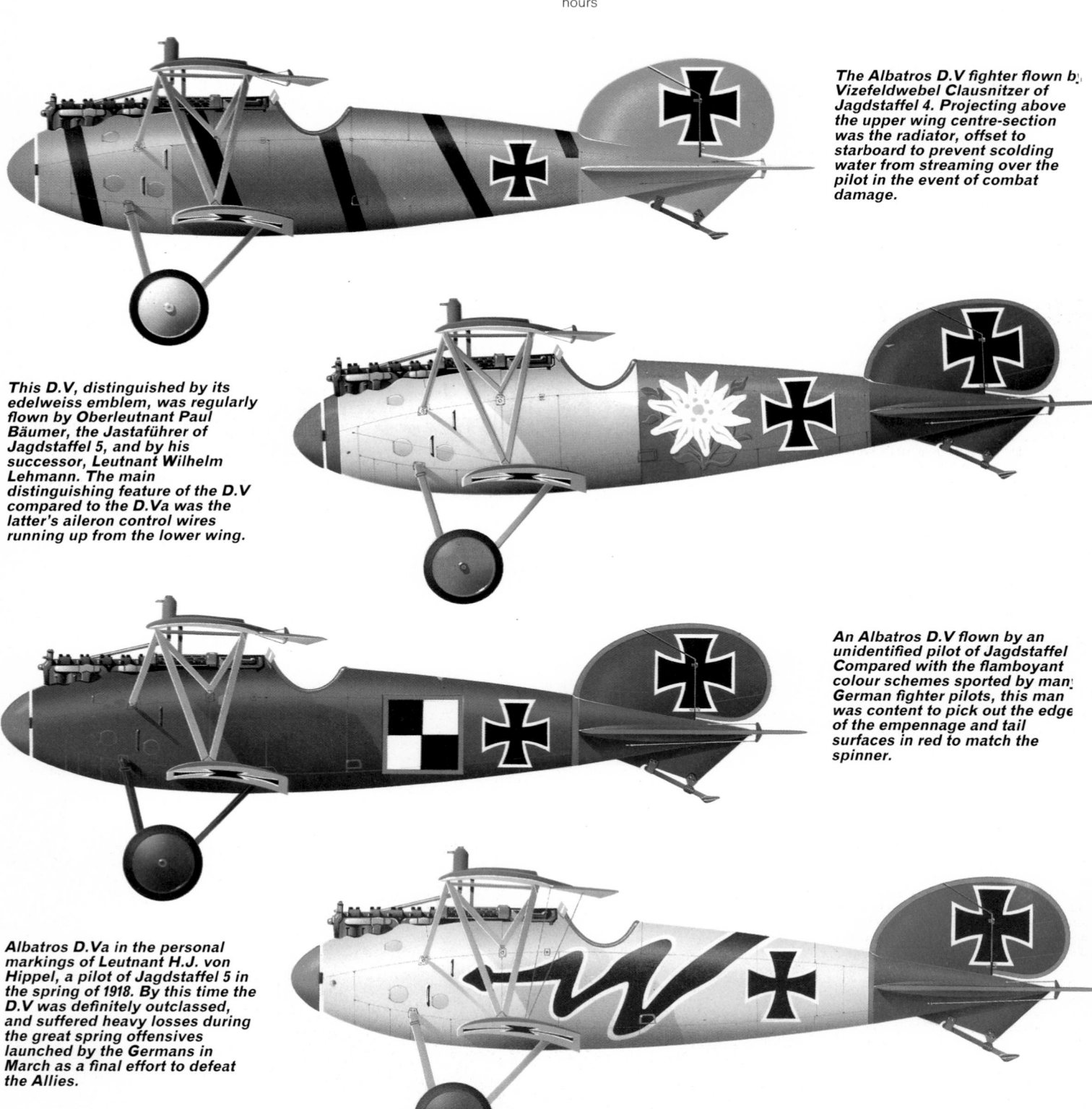

The Albatros D.V fighter flown by Vizefeldwebel Clausnitzer of Jagdstaffel 4. Projecting above the upper wing centre-section was the radiator, offset to starboard to prevent scolding water from streaming over the pilot in the event of combat damage.

This D.V, distinguished by its edelweiss emblem, was regularly flown by Oberleutnant Paul Bäumer, the Jastaführer of Jagdstaffel 5, and by his successor, Leutnant Wilhelm Lehmann. The main distinguishing feature of the D.V compared to the D.Va was the latter's aileron control wires running up from the lower wing.

An Albatros D.V flown by an unidentified pilot of Jagdstaffel Compared with the flamboyant colour schemes sported by many German fighter pilots, this man was content to pick out the edge of the empennage and tail surfaces in red to match the spinner.

Albatros D.Va in the personal markings of Leutnant H.J. von Hippel, a pilot of Jagdstaffel 5 in the spring of 1918. By this time the D.V was definitely outclassed, and suffered heavy losses during the great spring offensives launched by the Germans in March as a final effort to defeat the Allies.

Albatros L.72
to
Amiot 143

Albatros L.72

The **Albatros L.72** was a rather unusual transport aircraft designed to carry a pilot and four passengers, but could alternatively be used for the carriage of freight or newspapers. Of biplane configuration, the basic wing structure was of metal with fabric covering, while both the deep fuselage and braced tail unit were of welded steel tube with fabric covering. Landing gear was of typical Albatros tailskid type, and the B.M.W. engine, partially exposed in the fuselage nose, was otherwise very neatly cowled. The pilot was accommodated in an open cockpit aft of the engine, and the enclosed cabin could be furnished with seats for four passengers.

However, when used for the bulk delivery of newspapers the cabin was provided with two folding seats, and two chutes were mounted vertically, to extend through the lower surface of the fuselage. Each could contain 16 parcels of newspapers weighing 22 lb (10 kg) each, and these parcels could be dropped individually or collectively by means of a release control in the pilot's cockpit.

Specification
Type: light transport aircraft
Powerplant: one 224-kW (300-hp) B.M.W. IV inline piston engine
Performance: maximum level speed 160 km/h (99 mph); cruising speed 148 km/h (92 mph); service ceiling 3100 m (10,170 ft)

Weights: empty 1345 kg (2,965 lb); maximum take-off 2090 kg (4,608 lb)
Dimensions: span 13.00 m (42 ft 7¾ in); length 10.50 m (34 ft 5¼ in); height 3.60 m (11 ft 9¾ in); wing area 44.50 m² (479.01 sq ft)

The Albatros L.72 was an unusual machine, designed for the carriage of either four passengers or 16 packages of newspapers. The latter could be airdropped through a pair of chutes.

Albatros L.73

Designed for service with Deutsche Lufthansa, the **Albatros L.73** was a twin-engined civil transport intended specifically for night operation. A large impressive biplane of all-metal basic structure, with fabric and metal covering, it had a conventional braced tail unit, and a tailskid landing gear with wide-track main units. Two B.M.W. engines were mounted one each side of the fuselage, midway between the wings. The engine mountings shared attachment points with the interplane struts at the outboard ends of the wing centre-section, and the two powerplants projected well forward of the wing leading edges. The pilot and co-pilot were seated side-by-side in a compartment in

the fuselage nose: this was covered and had a windscreen, but the sides of this enclosure were left open. The pilots were provided with dual controls, radio equipment, and the sophistication of an early gyroscopic turn indicator that also indicated fore and aft levels. The enclosed cabin was both heated and ventilated, and had accommodation for eight passengers in comfortable seating; four of these seats could be converted easily to make two sleeping bunks.

It is believed that three or four of these aircraft entered service with Lufthansa in 1926, being used on night sectors of domestic and international routes until 1930.

Specification
Type: eight-passenger night transport
Powerplant: two 179-kW (240-hp)

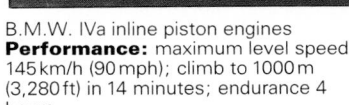

B.M.W. IVa inline piston engines
Performance: maximum level speed 145 km/h (90 mph); climb to 1000 m (3,280 ft) in 14 minutes; endurance 4 hours
Weights: empty 3024 kg (6,667 lb); maximum take-off 4610 kg (10,163 lb)
Dimensions: span 17.00 m (55 ft 9¼ in); length 14.60 m (47 ft 10¾ in);

The L.73 airliner had the unusual feature of a twin-crew cockpit with a windscreen and roof, but no protection from the elements at the sides. Only limited production was undertaken.

height 4.70 m (15 ft 5 in); wing area 92.00 m² (990.31 sq ft)

Albatros W.4

Frequent attacks on German air stations along the North Sea coastline, by British flying-boats and seaplanes, caused the German admiralty to order the development of a floatplane fighter that would be suitable for their defence. The requirement was considered to be urgent and, as a result, manufacturers took a short-cut by modifying existing scout fighter aircraft to incorporate a float landing gear.

In the case of Albatros Werke, it was decided to base this new aircraft on the D.I, and many writers have described the **Albatros W.4**, as it became designated, as a D.I on floats. This is not strictly correct, for in addition to being of greater overall dimensions, there were differences in the fuselage and tail unit. Most noticeable was deletion of the ventral fin, and a compensating increase in the area of the upper fin. Other changes included increased tailplane area; considerably increased wing gap, giving the pilot a good forward view beneath the upper wing; eared radiators on each side of the fuselage of early production examples, and upper wing centre-section radiators on later W.4s; and, of course, float instead of wheel landing gear. A fairly wide variety of single-step float designs was used throughout the production run, totalling some 117 aircraft, in attempts to arrive at the most

Exhibiting the lines of the Albatros landplane fighter series, the W.4 floatplane fighter was produced to try and halt the depredations of marauding Allied flying-boats.

efficient. Deliveries began in September 1916 and continued until December 1917.

The W.4 proved to be an effective base defence fighter, able to cope with most enemy aircraft with which it came into contact: the exception was British flying-boats which came into service in the summer of 1917. The W.4 began to be replaced by the more effective purpose-designed Hansa-Brandenburg W.12 two-seater from the end of 1917.

Specification
Type: single-seat floatplane base defence fighter

Powerplant: one 119-kW (160-hp) Mercedes D.III inline piston engine
Performance: maximum level speed 160 km/h (99 mph); climb to 1000 m (3,280 ft) in 5 minutes; service ceiling 3000 m (9,840 ft); endurance 3 hours
Weights: empty 790 kg (1,742 lb); maximum take-off 1070 kg (2,359 lb)

Dimensions: span 9.50 m (31 ft 2 in); length 8.50 m (27 ft 10¾ in); height 3.65 m (11 ft 11¾ in); wing area 31.60 m² (340.15 sq ft)
Armament: one or two fixed forward-firing 7.92-mm (0.31-in) LMG 08/15 machine-guns

Alon Model A-2 Aircoupe

The **Alon Model A-2 Aircoupe**, a classic American lightplane, has a long history, being designed by the Engineering and Research Corporation founded in 1930. The prototype of this company's **Ercoupe Model 415-C** was not flown until 1937, but it represented an advanced design for its era and was to be built subsequently in very large numbers.

A low-wing cantilever monoplane, it had wings of all-metal construction, with the exception of fabric-covered outer wing panels. The fuselage and tail unit were all-metal, the cantilever tailplane being mounted high on the fuselage and carrying twin endplate fins and rudders. The non-retractable tricycle landing gear had oleo-pneumatic shock-absorbers on all units, and power was provided by a Continental A65 flat-four engine.

The most unusual feature of the Ercoupe was its much-advertised 'easy-to-fly' two-control system, which eliminated rudder pedals unless an individual customer opted for a conventional set of controls. The Erco system linked ailerons, rudders and nosewheel so that turns in the air, or on the ground, were made by a control wheel, with elevator operation as normal.

Production of the Ercoupe ended with the outbreak of World War II, but was continued post-war with some 6,000 examples being built and marketed under the names of Aircoupe, Ercoupe, and Fornair. The company eventually ceased to operate, and all assets of Ercoupe were acquired by a new company, Alon Inc., incorporated on the last day of 1963. In due course an improved version of the Ercoupe was marketed as

the **Alon Model A-2 Aircoupe**, the first example making its initial flight on 24 October 1964. This differed from the original Ercoupe by having an all-metal structure, improved landing gear, a refined cockpit canopy, improved standards of equipment, and a more powerful engine. The two- or three-control system remained optional, and the Aircoupe continued in production as such until the company merged with Mooney Aircraft Inc. in 1967.

Specification
Type: two-seat light aircraft
Powerplant: one 67-kW (90-hp) Continental C90-16F flat-four piston engine
Performance: maximum level speed at sea level 208 km/h (129 mph); maximum cruising speed 200 km/h (124 mph); service ceiling 5275 m (17,300 ft); maximum range 732 km (455 miles)
Weights: empty 422 kg (930 lb); maximum take-off 658 kg (1,450 lb)
Dimensions: span 9.14 m (30 ft 0 in); length 6.20 m (20 ft 4 in); height 1.91 m (6 ft 3 in); wing area 13.25 m² (142.60 sq ft)

The Alon A-2 Aircoupe was evolved from the classic Erco Ercoupe, which was one of the first light aircraft to feature tricycle undercarriage. The type was very docile in all flight conditions, and featured rudders operated from the aileron controls to provide harmonised control at all times.

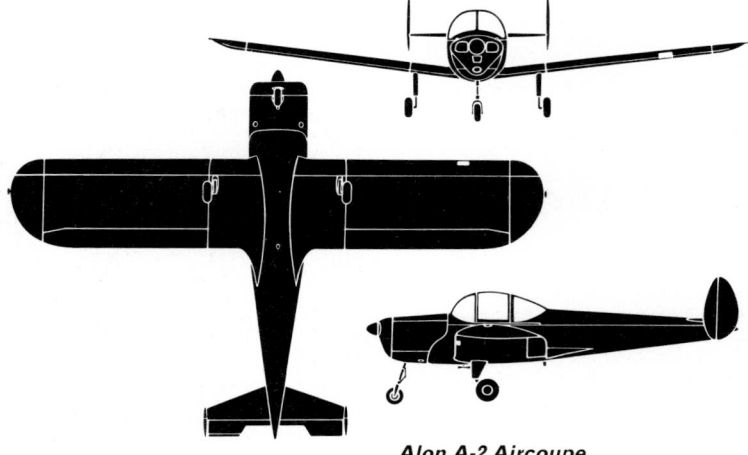

Alon A-2 Aircoupe

Ambrosini S.7

Sergio Stefanutti designed the **Ambrosini S.A.I.7** two-seat high-speed tourer monoplane between October 1938 and April 1939. The S.7 was undoubtedly one of the best looking aircraft ever, a sleek low-wing cantilever monoplane of wooden construction with fully retractable landing gear. The first two aircraft were specifically intended to take part in the prestigious IV Avio Raduno del Littorio contest for touring aircraft, and they flew within days of each other, only shortly before the competition opened at Rimini aerodrome on 15 July 1939. For the purpose of the contest, the culmination of which was a racing event, both aircraft had an additional streamlined glazed section added between the nose and the normal cabin enclosure.

Although the S.A.I.7s did not win the contest, due mainly to all too brief proving flights, their performance impressed the Italian authorities, especially after one machine captured an international speed record over the 100-km (62.1-mile) closed circuit on 27 August 1939. Nevertheless, little was heard of the S.7 during World War II, though the experimental **S.A.I.107**, **S.A.I.207** and **S.A.I.403** light fighters were developed from it,

and 10 of the S.A.I.7 militarised two-seat fighter trainer version appeared during 1943; but that was all until 1949, when S.A.I. Ambrosini placed it in full-scale production. The post-war version replaced the 209-kW (280-hp) Hirth HM.508D engine of the record-breakers and the 209-kW (280-hp) Isotta-Fraschini Beta RC.10 of the wartime version with an Alfa Romeo powerplant, but apart from improved constructional detail there were few major changes.

Most of the 145 post-war **Ambrosini S.7s**, some of them completed in single-seat configuration, formed the equipment of various flight training centres attached to the Aeronautica Militare zone headquarters. Apart from its military service, which terminated in 1956, the S.7 participated in numerous competitions with distinction. Leonardo Bonzi established international records over the 100-km (62.1-mile) and 1000-km (621.4-mile) distances on 21 December 1951, with average speeds of 367.36 km/h (228.27 mph) and 358.63 km/h (222.84 mph) respectively.

Variants
Ambrosini S.A.I.7: racing monoplane with 209-kW (280-hp) Hirth HM.508D; maximum speed 405 km/h (252 mph); range 3250 km (2,020

In its post-war form, the Ambrosini S.7 served with the Aeronautica Militare as an advanced trainer.

miles); empty weight 750 kg (1,653 lb) and maximum weight 1370 kg (3,020 lb); span 8.95 m (29 ft 4⅜ in) and length 7.25 m (23 ft 9½ in) (total 2)
Ambrosini S.A.I.7 Trainer: two-seat fighter trainer of 1941 with conventional cockpit enclosure and 209-kW (280-hp) Isotta-Fraschini Beta RC.10 inline; maximum speed 400 km/h (248 mph); maximum weight 1362 kg (3,003 lb); span 9.00 m (29 ft 6¼ in) and length 8.20 m (26 ft 11 in) (total 10)
Ambrosini S.A.I.107: experimental 1941 fighter with 403-kW (540-hp) Isotta-Fraschini Gamma inline;

maximum speed about 560 km/h (348 mph) and maximum weight 1000 kg (2,025 lb) (total 1)
Ambrosini S.A.I.207: developed version of the S.107 with 560-kW (750-hp) Isotta-Fraschini Delta RC.40 inverted Vee engine; maximum speed 640 km/h (398 mph); service ceiling 12000 m (39,370 ft); range 850 km (528 miles); empty weight 1750 kg (3,858 lb) and maximum weight 2415 kg

(5,324 lb), span 9.99 m (29 ft 6¼ in); length 8.02 m (26 ft 3¾ in); height 2.40 m (7 ft 10½ in); wing area 13.90 m² (149.62 sq ft) and armament of two 20-mm MG151/20 cannon and two 12.7-mm (0.5-in) Breda-SAFAT machine-guns (total of 15 out of an order for 2,000)

Ambrosini S.A.I.403 Dardo (Dart): developed version of the S.207 with 560-kW (750-hp) Isotta-Fraschini Delta RC.21/60; maximum speed 650 km/h (404 mph); service ceiling 10000 m (32,810 ft); range 1875 km (1,164 miles);

maximum weight 2640 kg (5,820 lb); span 9.80 m (32 ft 1¾ in); length 8.20 m (26 ft 10¾ in) and an armament of two 20-mm cannon and/or two 12.7-mm (0.5-in) machine-guns (total 1, out of an order for 3,000)

Ambrosini S.7: post-war version, designed as a single- or two-seat training/touring aircraft

Ambrosini Super S.7 Supersette: a more powerful version of the S.7, which first appeared in 1952; powered by a 261-kW (350-hp) de Havilland Gipsy Queen 70 inline and with

modified wing and increased overall dimensions; one was flown with a cut-down rear fuselage and 298-kW (400-hp) Alfa Romeo 121 RC engine, while another was fitted with a swept wing as part of the development programme for the Aerfer Sagittario light jet fighter; maximum speed 430 km/h (267 mph); span 9.30 m (30 ft 6 in) (total 10)

Specification
Ambrosini S.7 (post-war model)
Type: single- or two-seat training/touring aircraft

Powerplant: one 168-kW (225-hp) Alfa Romeo 115ter inline piston engine
Performance: maximum level speed 358 km/h (221 mph); economic cruising speed 264 km/h (164 mph); initial climb rate 335 m (1,100 ft) per minute; service ceiling 5250 m (17,225 ft); range 1000 km (621 miles)
Weights: empty 1105 kg (2,436 lb); maximum take-off 1317 kg (2,903 lb)
Dimensions: span 8.79 m (28 ft 10 in); length 8.17 m (26 ft 9¾ in); height 2.80 m (9 ft 2¼ in); wing area 12.80 m² (137.78 sq ft)

Ambrosini Sagittario

After tests with a 45° sweptback wing fitted to an otherwise standard Ambrosini S.7, thus nicknamed Freccia (Arrow), the designer Sergio Stefanutti designed the **Sagittario** (Archer) powered by a 400-kg (882-lb) thrust Turboméca Marboré turbojet. Intended mainly for aerodynamic research into transonic compressibility, the Sagittario was built largely of wood, and flew for the first time on 5 January 1953. From this initial prototype Stefanutti subsequently developed the **Sagittario II**, which made its maiden flight on 19 May 1956. Powered by a Rolls-Royce Derwent 9 turbojet, this more advanced aircraft was virtually a new design and of all-metal construction. The Sagittario II was the first aircraft of Italian design to exceed Mach unity when it reached Mach 1.1 in a dive on 4 December 1956.

Basically similar to the Sagittario II, the **Aerfer Ariete** (Battering Ram) was built by Industrie Aeronautiche Meridionali – Aerfer, and represented the next step towards the development of the finally abortive **Leone** (Lion) mixed-power light interceptor fighter, which was being worked upon with the financial support of the US government. The Ariete had a deeper rear fuselage and, in addition to the Derwent 9, had an 821-kg (1,810-lb) thrust Rolls-Royce Soar R.Sr 2

Built for research into the problems of transonic flight, the Sagittario's basic construction was of wood.

auxiliary turbojet, which improved overall performance. The Ariete prototype (MM 568) flew for the first time on 27 March 1958, but the entire project was later abandoned.

Specification
Ambrosini Sagittario II
Type: single-seat interceptor/tactical support aircraft
Powerplant: one 1633-kg (3,600-lb) thrust Rolls-Royce Derwent 9 turbojet

Performance: maximum level speed 1006 km/h (625 mph); service ceiling 14000 m (45,930 ft)
Weight: maximum take-off 3293 kg (7,260 lb)
Dimensions: span 7.50 m (24 ft 7¼ in); length 8.50 m (31 ft 2 in); height 2.02 m (6 ft 7½ in); wing area 14.73 m² (158.56 sq ft)
Armament: (proposed) two 30-mm forward-firing cannon, and provision for underwing weapons

The Ambrosini was an interim step towards the proposed Leone fighter, and featured an auxiliary turbojet in the upper rear fuselage. This was fed with air through a retractable dorsal inlet.

Ambrosini (Aerfer) Ariete

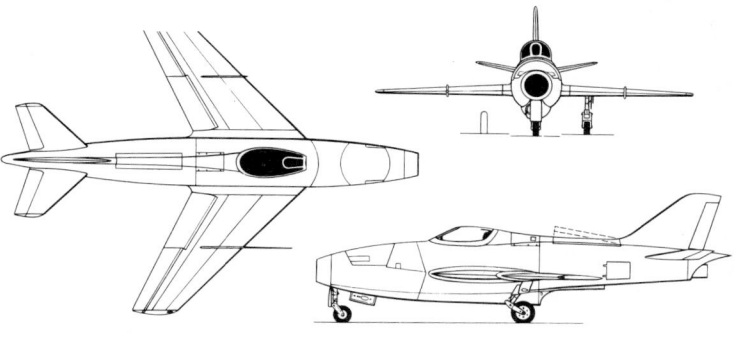

Ambrosini S.A.I.3

Designed as a two-seat light training and touring low-wing monoplane, the **Ambrosini S.A.I.3** was an extremely graceful aircraft, with long-span elliptical wings, a deep rear fuselage and, unfortunately for the type's looks, a fixed and

somewhat clumsy tailwheel type landing gear. The chosen powerplant was either a 63-kW (85-hp) Fiat A.50 radial or 97-kW (130-hp) Alfa Romeo A.110 inverted inline piston engine, the latter enclosed within a close cowling of nice pro-

portions. Small batches of the S.A.I.3 were built, some of them with an enclosed cabin in place of the more common tandem open cockpits. Not surprisingly, the more powerful Alfa Romeo-engined model had much superior performance, despite a maximum take-off weight increased by 40 kg (88 lb) to 830 kg (1,830 lb); maximum speed rose to 230 km/h (143 mph), service ceiling to 5200 m (17,060 ft) and range to 680 km (422 miles).

Ambrosini S.A.I.3S: version with
119-kW (160-hp) Bramo Sh.14 A-4
radial, and a wing of slightly decreased
chord; performance was generally
superior to that of the S.A.I.3 with
either powerplant alternative

Specification
Ambrosini S.A.I.3 (Fiat engine)
Type: two-seat light training and
touring monoplane
Powerplant: one 63-kW (85-hp) Fiat
A.50 radial piston engine
Performance: maximum speed
200 km/h (124 mph); cruising speed
170 km/h (106 mph); service ceiling
4000 m (13,120 ft); range 620 km (385
miles)

Weights: empty 550 kg (1,213 lb);
maximum take-off 790 kg (1,742 lb)
Dimensions: span 10.45 m (34 ft
3½ in); length 7.05 m (23 ft 1½ in);
height 2.80 m (9 ft 2¼ in); wing area
14.00 m² (150.7 sq ft)

*An elegant two-seater, the
Ambrosini S.A.I.3 also appeared
in a somewhat ungainly form
with a German radial engine and
open cockpits adding to the
unfortunate fixed landing gear.
This is the A.110-powered
version.*

Amiot 143

Avions Amiot, founded originally by Félix
Amiot as the Société d'Emboutissage et
de Constructions Mécaniques (SECM) in
1916, was one of four contenders for a
specification issued in 1928 by the
French *Service Technique de l'Aéronautique*. This called for a four-seat aircraft in
the so-called *multiplace de combat*
(multi-seat combat aircraft) category,
which was required to be suitable for
deployment in the day/night bomber,
long-range escort and reconnaissance
roles.

Although the French nation is renowned as a lover of beauty, this certainly did not extend to aircraft which
were designed to meet the *multiplace
de combat* requirements in the years between the wars. In fact, it was once suggested that the **Amiot 140** evolved to
satisfy this requirement of 1928 (in contention with the Blériot 137, Breguet 410
and SPCA 30) was selected for production because it was the ugliest of the
four. This is, without doubt, an apocry-
phal story and almost certainly of French
origin, but whether it be true or false,
Amiot's 140 prototype, which had flown
for the first time in April 1931, was
selected for production following service evaluation, 40 examples being
ordered for the Armée de l'Air in November 1933.

During the 31-month period between
the initial flight of the first prototype (two
were built) and receipt of a production
order, Amiot had been refining the design. This had led to the **Amiot 142**,
powered by two 641-kW (860-hp) Hispano-Suiza 12Ybrs inline Vee engines,
followed by the **Amiot 143** with two
supercharged Gnome-Rhône radial
engines, and it was this latter version
that was put into production. Of all-metal
construction, the Amiot 143 had some
unusual features, including a wide-chord
monoplane wing of such deep aerofoil
section that it provided access to the
engines in flight, and the main units of
the non-retractable tailwheel type landing gear had enormous speed fairings
some 2.13 m (7 ft) in length. The counter-
rotating engines of the **Amiot 143.01**
production prototype, which was first
flown in August 1934, were each rated at
597 kW (800 hp) for take-off, and fuel
was contained in six tanks, all of which
could be jettisoned. This latter feature
was discontinued in the 41st and subsequent production aircraft.

The ugliest part of the Amiot 143's
structure was undoubtedly the two-deck
fuselage. Three positions were provided
along the upper surface of the fuselage:
a nose turret, a pilot's cockpit above the
wing leading edge, and a dorsal turret at
its trailing edge. In the gondola-like lower

deck were housed the navigator/bomb-
aimer and bomb bay, while a fifth crew
member could be accommodated for
night bombing operation. A further gun
position was provided at the aft end of
the gondola. Armament consisted at
first of a Lewis gun in the nose turret,
plus two more in each of the other two
positions, but from the 41st production
aircraft this changed to a single 7.5-mm
(0.295-in) MAC machine-gun at each
position, plus one additional gun which
could be fired through a floor-hatch in the
front fuselage.

Initial deliveries of production Amiot
143s went to the Armée de l'Air in July
1935, equipping first the 3rd Group of the
22nd Bomber Squadron in the later summer, and eventually equipping the 14th
Independent Group and 21st, 22nd,
34th, 35th and 38th Bomber Squadrons.
At the outbreak of war in 1939, 60 of
these obsolete bombers remained in
operational service with some five
bomber groups, and until 10 May 1940
they were used only to bomb Germany
with futile propaganda leaflets. From
that date until the fall of France, they
were used almost exclusively for night
bombing attacks on enemy targets. The
one exception was a desperate and
heroic attempt by 13 aircraft of the 34th
and 38th Bomber Squadrons to destroy
the bridges over the Meuse at Sedan in a
daylight attack on 14 May: only one aircraft survived the raid.

Variants
Amiot 140: prototype (total 2)
Amiot 142: revised prototype (total 1)
Amiot 143: pre-production and
production model (total 138)
Amiot 142 (revised): based on third
prototype but with different engines
(total 1)
Amiot 144M: model with revised
wings and retractable landing gear
(total 1)
Amiot 150BE: reconnaissance/
torpedo bomber prototype; two
552-kW (740-hp) Gnome-Rhône radials;
interchangeable wheel/float landing
gear (total 1)

*Amiot 143M, the 78th production aircraft, of
the 3ᵉ Escadrille of GB II/35, based at
Pontarlier in September 1939 for night
reconnaissance.*

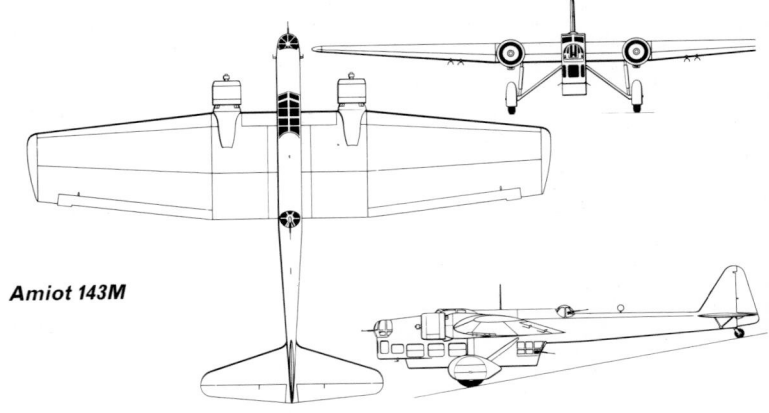

Amiot 143M

Specification
Amiot 143
Type: four/six seat two-engined
bomber/reconnaissance aircraft
Powerplant: (143M) two Gnome-
Rhône 14Kirs/Kjrs Mistral Major radial
piston engines, each rated at 649 kW
(870 hp) at 3215 m (10,550 ft), and at
671 kW (900 hp) at 4210 m (13,800 ft)
Performance: maximum speed
310 km/h (193 mph) at 4000 m
(13,120 ft); cruising speed 270 km/h
(168 mph) at 4000 m (13,120 ft); service
ceiling 7900 m (25,920 ft); range
1200 km (746 miles)
Weights: empty 6100 kg (13,448 lb);
maximum take-off 9700 kg (21,385 lb)

Dimensions: span 24.50 m (80 ft
4½ in); length 18.00 m (59 ft 0½ in);
height 5.50 m (18 ft 0½ in); wing area
100.00 m² (1,076.4 sq ft)
Armament: (from 41st production
aircraft) four 7.5-mm (0.295-in) MAC
machine-guns (one each in nose turret,
dorsal turret, ventral and under nose
positions), plus up to 800 kg (1,764 lb)
of bombs carried internally

*The Amiot 143M was undoubtedly
one of the ugliest aircraft
produced by the French in the
inter-war years.*

Amiot 350 Series
to
Antonov An-4

Amiot 350 Series

The 39th Amiot 354 delivered to the Armée de l'Air.

If the Amiot 143 were regarded, justly or unjustly, as the ugliest of the inter-war aircraft to be produced in France, the **Amiot 340.01** prototype bomber which flew for the first time on 6 December 1937 had the right to claim that it was the most elegant then designed by any nation. It had originated as a long-range mail transport (a single prototype being built under the designation **Amiot 341**), but before this had flown it was converted to a twin-engined bomber for operation by a crew of three. The powerplant comprised two Gnome-Rhône 14N 0/1 radial engines, each rated at 686 kW (920 hp) at 3700 m (12,140 ft). In this form redesignated **Amiot 340.01**, the prototype was flown for official acceptance trials at the end of March 1938.

As a result of these trials, the *Service Technique de l'Aéronautique* advised the Amiot company of the modifications required before a production order could be placed. These, together with development improvements introduced by the company, included the installation of 761-kW (1,020-hp) Gnome-Rhône 14N 20/21 engines; the provision of accommodation for a fourth crew member to man a new ventral gun position, firing through a floor hatch aft of the bomb bay; and the introduction of a new tail unit, the tailplane having a marked degree of dihedral and twin endplate fins and rudders. In this form the aircraft was redesignated **Amiot 351.01**, and was handed over for flight testing towards the end of January 1939.

These trials, conducted successfully, led to a number of variants, three of them being produced in prototype form; the remainder saw the light of day only on paper as projected designs. Production versions included the **Amiot 351** and **354**, these differing from the 351.01 prototype in having wing span reduced by 0.17 m (6½ in), length increased by 0.50 m (1 ft 7½ in), and a reduction in wing area of 0.50 m² (5.38 sq ft). The Amiot 351 retained the twin fin/rudder tail unit of the prototype, the vertical surfaces being increased in area, but the Amiot 354 reverted to the single-fin and rudder of the Amiot 340.01 prototype. In other respects their airframes were generally similar, comprising a high-set cantilever monoplane wing with wide-span ailerons and split trailing-edge flaps; the very clean tapered circular cross-section fuselage was a monocoque structure; and the main units of the tailwheel type landing gear retracted aft into the rear of the engine nacelles. Crew accommodation was provided for the bombardier/navigator in the fuselage nose, pilot almost in line with the propellers, a gunner in the dorsal turret, and radio operator/gunner in the lower fuselage aft of the bomb bay.

Engines differed between these two production aircraft, and accounted for most of the variants. Thus the **Amiot 350** was a project to re-engine the Amiot 340.01 with two Hispano-Suiza 12Y 28/29 engines; the production Amiot 351 had two Gnome-Rhône 14N 38/39 engines each developing 708 kW (950 hp) at 3700 m (12,140 ft); the **Amiot 352** was a project with two Hispano-Suiza 12Y 50/51 engines each rated at 820 kW (1,100 hp) at 3260 m (10,695 ft); and the **Amiot 353** was yet another project, with two Rolls-Royce Merlin III engines each developing 768 kW (1,030 hp) at 4950 m (16,250 ft). The production Amiot 354 had 865-kW (1,160-hp) Gnome-Rhône 14N 48/49 engines, and was followed by two prototypes and one project. The first of these was the **Amiot 355.01**, with two 895-kW (1,200-hp) Gnome-Rhône 14R 2/3 radials with two-speed superchargers; then came the **Amiot 356.01** with two 843-kW (1,130-hp) Rolls-Royce Merlin X engines; and finally there was the **Amiot 357**, intended as a high-altitude bomber with pressurised accommodation and two Hispano-Suiza 12Z turbocharged engines.

All of this activity would suggest a vast production programme but this, unfortunately, was not the case. So far as France was concerned in relation to international problems, the reorganisation of its aviation manufacturers into a nationalised industry could not have come at a worse time. Even those companies which opted out, and Amiot was one of them, were affected by the disruption to all branches of the industry. This meant that production examples of the very promising prototype which had first flown in December 1937 were not

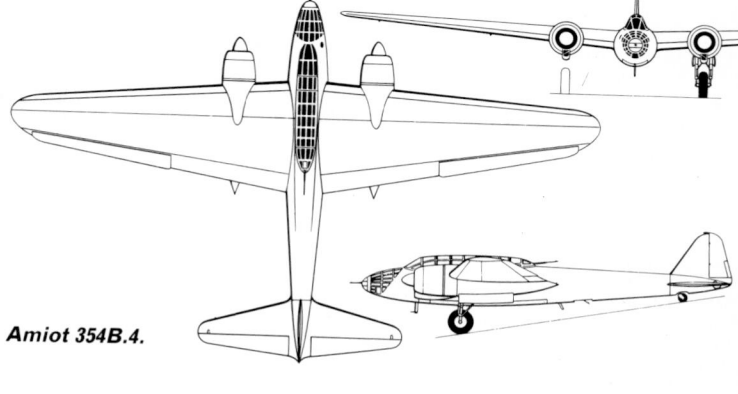

Amiot 354B.4.

entering service until it was too late for them to contribute any worthwhile support in the attempt to halt the relentless advance of the German divisions. The first two Amiot 354s, for example, had not been delivered to an operational unit until 7 April 1940, and of the total of about 62 which had been delivered before the fall of France in June 1940, hardly any were used operationally: they were short of armament and/or equipment, or were destroyed on the ground by German attacks.

A number were overhauled at a later date and, provided with additional fuel tanks in the bomb bay, were used by Air France for services between Vichy France and overseas territories. Four were seized by the Germans and used

by the Luftwaffe: one Amiot 354 was abandoned by them as their forces retreated into Germany and this survived to serve with the *Groupe de Liaisons Aériennes Ministérielles* from 1946.

Specification
Amiot 354
Type: four-seat medium bomber
Powerplant: two 790-kW (1,060-hp) Gnome-Rhône 14N 48/49 radial piston engines
Performance: maximum speed 480 km/h (298 mph) at 4000 m (13,125 ft); cruising speed 350 km/h (217 mph); service ceiling 10000 m (32,810 ft); range 2500 km (1,553 miles)
Weights: empty 4725 kg (10,417 lb); maximum take-off 11300 kg (24,912 lb)
Dimensions: span 22.83 m (74 ft 10¾ in); length 14.50 m (47 ft 6¾ in); height 4.08 m (13 ft 4½ in); wing area 67.00 m² (721.18 sq ft)
Armament: one 20-mm cannon in dorsal turret and two 7.5-mm (0.295-in) MAC machine-guns (one each in nose and ventral positions), plus up to 1200 kg (2,646 lb) of bombs

One of the best bombers available to the Armée de l'Air in 1939-40, the Amiot 354 was unfortunately built only in small numbers as a result of official delays to the ambitious development programme.

Andreasson BA-4B

The Swedish designer Björn Andreasson designed several light aircraft, their number including one identified as the **Andreasson BA-4**. To provide a good basic design for amateur construction by members of the Swedish Chapter of the Experimental Aircraft Association, he updated the BA-4, and a prototype of this revised design was built by apprentices of AB Malmö Flygindustri (MFI) under the designation **BA-4B**.

This small fully-aerobatic biplane is of all-metal construction and is entirely conventional, with fixed tailwheel landing gear. However, the design allows for the wings to be of alternative wooden basic structure. Powerplant of the prototype was a Rolls-Royce/Continental O-200, but the design was suitable for a variety of similarly powered engines, including a modified Volkswagen motor car engine. In addition to the plans available to the Swedish EAA, both plans and kits for several versions of the BA-4B were available in the UK from Crosby Aviation.

Specification
Andreasson BA-4B (prototype)
Type: single-seat light biplane for amateur construction
Powerplant: one 75-kW (100-hp) Rolls-Royce/Continental O-200 flat-four piston engine
Performance: maximum level speed 225 km/h (140 mph); minimum control speed 56 km/h (35 mph); range with standard fuel 282 km (175 miles)
Weight: maximum take-off 375 kg (827 lb)
Dimensions: span 5.34 m (17 ft 6¼ in); length 4.60 m (15 ft 1 in); wing area 8.30 m² (89.34 sq ft)

The Andreasson BA-4B light plane was typical of the small but pleasing aircraft designed by Andreasson with the demands and capabilities of homebuilders in mind.

A.N.F. Mureaux 113

André Brunet was appointed Chief Engineer of the Ateliers de Constructions du Nord et des Mureaux in 1926. Two years earlier the company had produced its first original design, the unsuccessful 'Express-Marin' fighter.

Brunet's first designs for the company were the models 3C.2 and 4C.2 fighters, followed by the Mureaux 130A.2 observation aircraft. These were all parasol-wing two-seat monoplanes embodying metal construction with sturdy wide-track landing gear. They were developed into the **Mureaux 110A.2** and **112GR** prototypes (six aircraft), which both flew in 1931. The French air ministry, impressed by the model 110, ordered a production version, subsequently designated **Mureaux 113R.2**. The 49 series aircraft retained the Brunet hallmark, with the pilot and observer in open tandem cockpits close together, but the rear cockpit was fitted with a distinctive oversize windscreen. The 485-kW (650-hp) Hispano-Suiza 12Ybrs engine had a prominent chin-type radiator.

Two **Mureaux 114CN.2** night-fighters were built, but a number of Mureaux 113s were adapted for the role with small underwing searchlights. Production developments included the **Mureaux 117R.2** with the more powerful 634-kW (850-hp) 12Ycrs engine, strengthened wing bracing and Chauvière wooden propeller in place of the Mureaux 113's Ratier metal type. The prototype flew in January 1935, and subsequently 115 series aircraft were built, 16 of them with the designation **Mureaux 117R.2B.2** (reconnaissance and bombing roles) and fitted with

The A.N.F. Mureaux 114CN.2 was a night-fighter derived from the basic Mureaux 113.

underwing racks for up to 400 kg (882 lb) of bombs. Final production version was the **Mureaux 115R.2**, which appeared in prototype form in 1935, flying on 6 March that year. Some of the 119 production aircraft were also adapted to the R.2B.2 role. The Mureaux 115 was distinguishable easily by the frontal radiator for its 12Ycrs engine.

The Mureaux parasols were very important to the Armée de l'Air in the late 1930s, 195 of all versions having been taken on charge by the beginning of 1937. By the outbreak of war 221 were in service with final Mureaux 115 deliveries due in September 1939.

Operating over the enemy lines during the first weeks of war, the Mureaux-equipped units suffered a number of losses. The first French aircraft shot down was a Mureaux 115 of GAO 553, which fell victim to German flak over

Karlsruhe while on a photographic mission on 8 September 1939. At the end of that month Mureaux were restricted to missions in close proximity to the front line. Strenuous efforts were made to replace the various obsolescent types, but when the German Blitzkrieg was launched on 10 May 1940, French observation units still had 119 Mureaux aircraft in service; most, however, were restricted to training and liaison duties. At the time of the 25 June 1940 Armistice all 53 Mureaux monoplanes left in the Unoccupied Zone of France were reduced to scrap.

It only remains to mention the special **Mureaux 113GR** no. 8, powered by a supercharged Hispano-Suiza 12Ybrs engine, which carried off the prized Coupe Bibesco, a 'point-to-point' air race between Romanian and French military aircraft, in July 1934, and the single prototype **Mureaux 200A.3** tested in the observation role in January 1936; compared with the model 115 it had a glazed canopy for the crew.

Specification
Mureaux 113
Type: two-seat reconnaissance aircraft or night-fighter
Powerplant: one 485-kW (650-hp) Hispano-Suiza 12Ybrs inline piston engine
Performance: maximum speed 290 km/h (180 mph) at 4000 m (13,125 ft); service ceiling 10400 m (34,120 ft); range 920 km (572 miles)
Weights: empty 1680 kg (3,704 lb); maximum take-off 2570 kg (5,666 lb)
Dimensions: span 15.40 m (50 ft 6¼ in); length 10.00 m (32 ft 9¾ in); height 3.81 m (12 ft 6 in); wing area 34.90 m² (375.67 sq ft)
Armament: two fixed synchronised 7.5-mm (0.295-in) MAC machine-guns and two flexible 7.5-mm (0.295-in) MAC machine-guns in rear cockpit, plus one 7.5-mm (0.295-in) MAC machine-gun firing through a trap in the underside of the fuselage

A.N.F. Mureaux 170C.1

A racy, gull-wing monoplane with non-retractable divided landing gear that incorporated wheel spats, the **Mureaux 170C.1** single-seat fighter prototype (Mureaux 170.01) flew initially on 19 November 1932. It was followed by a second machine (Mureaux 170.02) some 16 months later. These Mureaux fighters had many design innovations and featured remarkably light structures. The fuselage, for example, was covered with fine duralumin sheet and the

ailerons could also be used collectively to serve as flaps. Armament comprised two wing-mounted 7.5-mm (0.295-in) Chatellerault machine-guns. Powered by a 515-kW (690-hp) Hispano-Suiza HS 12Xbrs inline engine, it had a maximum level speed of 380 km/h (236 mph).

The aesthetically pleasing Mureaux 170C.1 did not enter production despite its performance.

Ansaldo A-1 Balilla

The prototype **Ansaldo A-1 Balilla** (Hunter) fighter scout flew for the first time in November 1917. It retained the basic fuselage design of the Ansaldo S.V.A. series, featuring a triangular cross-section, but had a wing braced by a pair of parallel vertical struts on each side in place of the W-form Warren-truss bracing of the earlier types. After exhaustive tests before a military commission, which included fighter aces Baracca and Ruffo, it was decided to adhere to a recent decision to employ the French SPAD S.7 in the Italian *squadriglie*, since the A-1 seemed less manoeuvrable than most of its contemporaries. In March 1918 the A-1 was demonstrated with an increased gap between the wings, which were also increased in area. The introduction of an S.P.A. 6A engine of greater efficiency, plus the modifications to the wing structure, resulted in an overall improvement in performance. A production order followed, and a total of 166 A-1s was delivered before the end of hostilities in November 1918; the first unit to re-equip

with the type was the 70 Squadriglia, but the A-1 saw only brief first-line service.

A number bought by Poland from Ansaldo fought with the renowned Kosciuszko Squadron during the Russo-Polish War of 1920. In the following year, however, 30 examples were delivered by Ansaldo to the Russians! And between 1921 and 1924 the Polish firm, Plage & Laskiewicz, completed some 70 A-1s under licence.

In the post-war years the A-1 appeared in a number of aeronautical displays and competitions. A lightweight, reduced-span racing version finished third in the 1920 Pulitzer Trophy competition. But efforts to sell the type in the USA were unsuccessful, and the type had only a short career.

Specification
Type: single-seat fighting scout
Powerplant: one 164-kW (220-hp) S.P.A. 6A inline piston engine
Performance: maximum speed 220 km/h (137 mph); service ceiling 5000 m (16,405 ft); range 550 km (342

miles)
Weights: empty 640 kg (1,411 lb); maximum take-off 885 kg (1,951 lb)
Dimensions: span 7.68 m (25 ft 2¼ in); length 6.60 m (21 ft 7¾ in); height 2.85 m (9 ft 4¼ in); wing area 21.30 m² (229.28 sq ft)
Armament: two fixed synchronised

Used only to a limited degree by the Italians, the Ansaldo A-1 Balilla was more profitably engaged on both sides in the Russo-Polish War of 1920.

7.7-mm (0.303-in) Vickers machine-guns

Ansaldo S.V.A.5 Primo

In the spring of 1916 the engineers U. Savoia and R. Verduzio, with the assistance of Celestino Rosatelli, began work on a project for a fighter biplane powered by the 164-kW (220-hp) S.P.A. 6A engine which was to be superior to any of its contemporaries. That autumn the Italian Ministry of War gave its backing, and the shipbuilding company Giovanni Ansaldo & Co. of Genoa was requested to build prototypes and obtain factory space for series production. The S.V. thus became the S.V.A., and the first prototype was tested at Grosseto airfield on 19 March 1917.

Particular features of the S.V.A. design were the diagonal wing bracing struts, and a rear fuselage of triangular section which permitted good downward visibility. The fuselage was plywood covered.

First **S.V.A.4** production aircraft, tested in the spring of 1917, proved fast, but insufficiently manoeuvrable to take on enemy fighters in dogfights. They were accordingly allocated to reconnaissance units. By the beginning of 1918 the S.V.A.4 was joined on the production lines by the **S.V.A.5**, the latter having provision for a bomb load and fuel for six hours of flight, while the S.V.A.4 had a duration of four hours and was equipped with a camera for photo-reconnaissance duties. As production built up at a number of factories, the **S.V.A.3** also went into service. This had reduced wingspan, and was put into service as an interceptor fighter. Performance was good and it demonstrated a greater degree of manoeuvrability than the S.V.A.4 and S.V.A.5.

A floatplane fighter version of the S.V.A. was designated **Idro-S.V.A.** Equipped with tubular-shaped twin floats, 50 were built, but were generally unsuccessful.

This was not the case with a pair of two-seat versions, the **S.V.A.9** and **S.V.A.10**, the former a dual-control trainer and the latter a two-seat bomber-reconnaissance machine. Tested at the

end of 1917, both types were accepted for service, and substantial deliveries of both versions began in early 1918.

S.V.A. biplanes became famous for long-distance flights against targets beyond the Alps, ranging as far away as Friedrichshafen on Lake Constance. The most famous formation flight took place on 9 August 1918 and was led by the great poet and flier Gabriele D'Annunzio. Eight aircraft from the 87 Squadriglia, renowned as the 'Serenissima', reached Vienna and spent 30 minutes photographing the enemy capital and dropping leaflets before returning safely to base.

Post-war several batches of S.V.A.5s and S.V.A.10s were built, some of the latter version being powered by the 186-kW (250-hp) Isotta-Fraschini V.6 engine. The S.V.A.s remained in service after the Regia Aeronautica was created in 1923 and took part in the conquest of Libya during the late 1920s.

Among several outstanding long-distance flights by S.V.A.s the most remarkable was a staged formation flight to Tokyo led by Lieutenant Arturo Ferrarin. Six aircraft left Rome on 26 February 1920, and two reached Tokyo after a journey of 15200 km (9,445 miles) on 21 May 1920.

Production ended finally in 1928, by which time over 2,000 S.V.A.s of all versions had been manufactured, about 100 of them for export to 11 different countries.

Specification
Ansaldo S.V.A.4 and S.V.A.5
Type: S.V.A.4, single-seat photographic reconnaissance aircraft (A), and S.V.A.5, single-seat reconnaissance bomber (B)
Powerplant: A and B one 198-kW (265-hp) S.P.A. 6A inline piston engine
Performance: maximum level speed A 226 km/h (140 mph), B 205 km/h (127 mph); climb to 3000 m (9,840 ft) A in 12 minutes, B in 10 minutes; service ceiling A 7000 m (22,965 ft), B 5400 m (17,715 ft); endurance A 3 hours 15

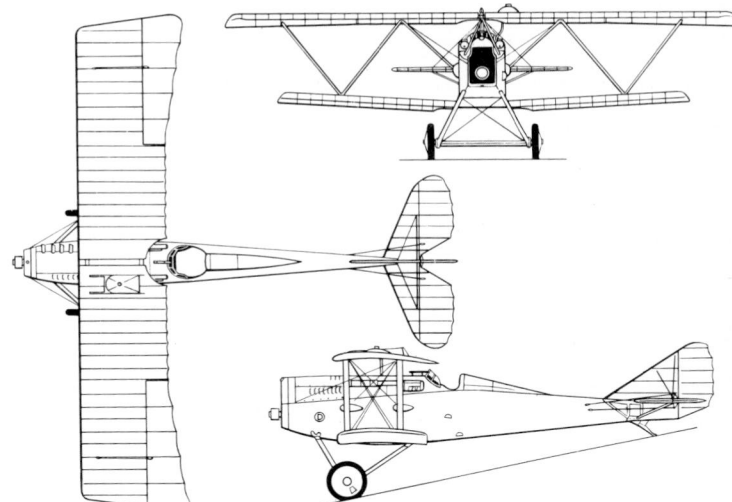

Ansaldo S.V.A.5.

minutes, B 3 hours
Weights: empty equipped A 690 kg (1,521 lb), B 700 kg (1,543 lb); maximum take-off A 940 kg (2,072 lb), B 1050 kg (2,315 lb)
Dimensions: (A and B) span 9.10 m (29 ft 10¼ in); length 8.10 m (26 ft 7 in); height 2.65 m (8 ft 8¼ in); wing area

The Ansaldo S.V.A.9 of Ferrarin is seen at Osaka after the classic Italian formation flight.

24.20 m² (260.50 sq ft)
Armament: one forward-firing synchronized 7.7-mm (0.303-in) Vickers machine-gun, B two Vickers guns

Antoinette Monoplanes

The Antoinette company's designer Leon Levavasseur produced several experimental designs before his first truly

successful machine, the **Antoinette IV**, flown for the first time on 9 October 1908. The definitive model IV tested the following February was a high-wing monoplane with angular wings of considerable surface area and a fuselage of very small, triangular cross-section, owing much to the designer's experience as a builder of racing motor boats. Wing-tip ailerons were fitted and the tail surfaces were of cruciform configuration.

On 19 February 1909 the Antoinette IV flew successfully from Mourmelon, covering 5 km (3.1 miles) before landing. By then an association had been formed between the Antoinette company and Hubert Latham, an English sportsman resident in France, which resulted in widespread fame for both parties. Twice Latham attempted to fly the English Channel. On 19 July 1909 he took off from Sangatte on the French coast in an Antoinette IV and covered some 11.2 km (7 miles) before coming down in the water due to engine failure.

Within a week Blériot had made his successful crossing, but undeterred Latham made a second attempt on 27 July 1909, flying the new **Antoinette VII**, which incorporated the then-conventional wing-warping controls in place of the Antoinette IV's ailerons. This second attempt was made on 27 July 1909, two days after Blériot had landed on the cliffs above Dover. This time Latham had clear sight of the English shore, only about 1.6 km (1 mile) away when again he had to come down in the sea. Undaunted, Latham took the duly repaired Antoinette VII to the Grande Semaine d'Aviation de la Champagne at Reims the following month, carrying off the height competition 155 m (509 ft) and coming second in the speed event (68.9 km/h/42.75 mph).

During the next two years Antoinette monoplanes were well to the fore at every aviation meeting, flown by Latham and other pioneers, but by 1912 *Jane's Aircraft* reported that 'the company has ceased to exist', and Levavasseur's graceful designs soon vanished from the scene.

Variants

Antoinette I: uncompleted project of 1907-8 for a canard monoplane with a pusher propeller
Gastambide-Mengin I: precursor of the classic Antoinette monoplane series, with a 37-kW (50-hp) Antoinette engine driving a tractor propeller; ungainly quadricycle landing gear; four flights (or rather hops) were made by the mechanic Boyer between 8 and 14 February 1908, the best being of 150 m (164 yards); span 10.50 m (34 ft 5½ in), wing area 24.00 m² (258.34 sq ft) and weight 350 kg (772 lb)
Antoinette II (or Gastambide-Mengin II): between February and August 1908 the Gastambide-Mengin I was rebuilt in this revised form, with triangular wingtip ailerons and other modifications; some three flights were made, the best being of 1 minute 36 seconds including the first circle flown by a monoplane (21 August 1908); and on 20 August Robert Gastambide became the first passenger to be carried by a monoplane
Antoinette III: alternative designation for the abortive Ferber IX after Capitaine Ferdinand Ferber joined the Société Antoinette for a short time

Antoinette IV: first truly successful Antoinette monoplane, with 37-kW (50-hp) Antoinette engine; flew between October 1908 and August 1909, making 50 flights in all including a best of 154.6 km (96.06 miles) in 2 hours 17 minutes 21 seconds as a world distance record on 26 August 1909; initially had wings of 30.00-m² (322.9 sq ft) area and weight of 460 kg (1,014 lb)
Antoinette V: similar to the Antoinette IV but with ailerons; it made some 20 flights between December 1908 and September 1909, the best being of 15 minutes
Antoinette VI: similar to the Antoinettes IV and V, but introduced wing-warping for lateral control; made some 15 flights between April and July 1909, the best being of 12 minutes
Antoinette VII: similar to the Antoinettes IV, V and VI but with wing-warping and powered by an uprated Antoinette engine delivering 45 kW (60 hp); it was used in July and August 1909, its best flight being of 70 km (43.5 miles) in 1 hour 1 minute 52 seconds on 23 August 1909
Antoinette VIII: similar to the Antoinettes IV. V. VI and VII, with wing-

Antoinette monoplanes were distinguished by the large wings and triangular cross-section fuselage.

warping and 37-kW (50-hp) Antoinette engine; its best flight was of 16 minutes
Antoinette (1909 general type): production model of 1909-11, at a price of £1,000; 37-kW (50-hp) Antoinette 8-cylinder inline engine, speed 70 km/h (43.5 mph), maximum take-off weight, 520 kg (1,146 lb), span 12.80 m (42 ft 0 in), length 11.50 m (37 ft 8¾ in) and wing area 50.00 m² (538.21 sq ft)

Specification
Antoinette IV and Antoinette VII
Type: single-seat monoplane
Powerplant: one 37-kW (50-hp) Antoinette inline engine in Antoinette IV, and one 45-kW (60-hp) Antoinette inline engine in Antoinette VII
Performance: maximum speed 70 km/h (43.5 mph)
Weight: maximum take-off 590 kg (1,301 lb)
Dimensions: span 12.80 m (42 ft 0 in); length 11.50 m (37 ft 8¾ in); height 3.00 m (9 ft 10 in); wing area 50.00 m² (538.21 sq ft)

Antonov An-2 'Colt'

With an interest in gliding that dated from his schooldays, Oleg Antonov was to become an established designer of gliders and sailplanes. During World War II he was concerned primarily with development and production of aircraft, but worked also as a designer within the Yakovlev organisation. Post-war he formed his own bureau to design and develop a new 'do anything – go anywhere' aeroplane, resulting in the **Antonov An-2 'Colt'**, identified briefly as the **SKh-1** (*Selskokhozyaistvennyi*-1, or 'agricultural-economic-1') before the Antonov designation was applied. It is a most appropriate designation, if for no other reason than the fact that the letters An begin the word anachronism, which is how an observer in the 1990s must regard this large biplane. First flown in prototype form on 31 August 1947, it still continues in production, although not by Antonov in the USSR since the late 1960s.

A single-bay sesquiplane, with a single streamline interplane strut on each side and dual flying- and landing wire bracing, the An-2 is almost entirely of all-metal construction. The exceptions are the wings, aft of the front spar, and tailplane, which are fabric-covered. The large capacity fuselage is a semi-monocoque structure, providing a comfortable heated and ventilated crew compart-

ment to accommodate two. The tailplane is strut braced, and the robust wide-track tailwheel type landing gear can be provided with low-pressure tyres, floats or skis, to cater for all surfaces.

Exceptional operating characteristics are provided by the wings: the upper wing includes electrically-actuated automatic leading-edge slots, trailing-edge slotted flaps, and ailerons which can be used conventionally for roll control, but can also be drooped collectively up to 20° to complement the flaps. The lower wing has only full-span slotted trailing-edge flaps. Powerplant of the prototype consisted of a 567-kW (760-hp) Shvetsov ASh-21 radial engine, but later production aircraft from Antonov had a 746-kW (1,000-hp) Shvetsov ASh-62IR engine.

Since 1960 production has been by WSK-PZL in Poland, and the An-2 has also been built under licence in China as the **Type 5 Transport Aeroplane**, and combined production from the three above sources is estimated at 15,000, of which about 60 per cent have been built in Poland.

An-2s are still used extensively, and also in a variety of roles not included among the above designations. They have served widely in a passenger transport capacity (carrying up to 12 adults and 2 children) with Aeroflot and airlines

of countries aligned with the East, but very few now remain in scheduled service: there is no doubt that many of these reliable aircraft are still used for passenger carrying, among other routine tasks.

Variants
(Russian-built)
An-2F: experimental artillery-observation model of 1948, with glazed fuselage mid-section, dorsal machine-gun position and twin vertical tail surfaces
An-2L: fire-fighting model equipped for the carriage of chemicals in glass containers under the wings and fuselage

Still an effective utility transport more than 40 years after its debut, the Antonov An-2 remains in Polish production in numerous forms, especially for the agricultural role.

An-2P (Passazhirskii): basic general-purpose model for up to 12 passengers or 1240 kg (2,733 lb) of freight
An-2P (Protivopozharnyi): fire-fighting model of the An-2V, developed in 1964 and able to uplift 1240 litres (271 Imp gal) of water in its floats
An-2S: agricultural model of the An-2 Passazhirskii, with spray equipment and long-stroke main landing gear legs

An-2V: twin-float model with shorter propeller blades

An-2ZA: high-altitude meteorological research model, with an extra cockpit forward of the fin for an observer to watch ice growth

Variants
(Polish-built)

An-2 Geofiz: geophysical survey model

An-2M: twin-float version of the An-2T, basically similar to the Russian An-2V

An-2P: passenger model, with better soundproofing than the Russian version, and fitted with an improved propeller

An-2PK: five-seat executive model

An-2P-Photo: special model equipped for photogrammetric operations

An-2PR: television relay model

An-2R: specialised agricultural model introduced in 1964, with hermetic sealing of the cockpit, revised tail surfaces of greater area, a more advanced propeller, and a fibreglass container for 1960 litres (421 Imp gal) of chemicals or 1350 kg (2,976 lb) of fertiliser dust

An-2S: ambulance model, with fittings for six litters and medical attendants

An-2T: basic general-purpose model

An-2TD: paratroop model with tip-up seats for 12

An-2TP: passenger/freight model based on the An-2TD

Lala-1: experimental model of 1972, with rear fuselage/empennage replaced by twin booms and revised tail, allowing installation of a turbofan in the stump fuselage as development for the M-15 Belphegor agricultural aircraft

Specification
Antonov (WSK-PZL) An-2P

Type: general-purpose biplane

Powerplant: one 746-kW (1,000-hp) Shvetsov ASh-62IR radial piston engine

Performance: maximum speed 258 km/h (160 mph) at 1750 m (5,740 ft); economic cruising speed 185 km/h (115 mph); service ceiling 4400 m (14,425 ft); range 901 km (560 miles) with 500-kg (1,102-lb) payload at optimum altitude

Weights: empty 3450 kg (7,605 lb); maximum take-off 5500 kg (12,125 lb)

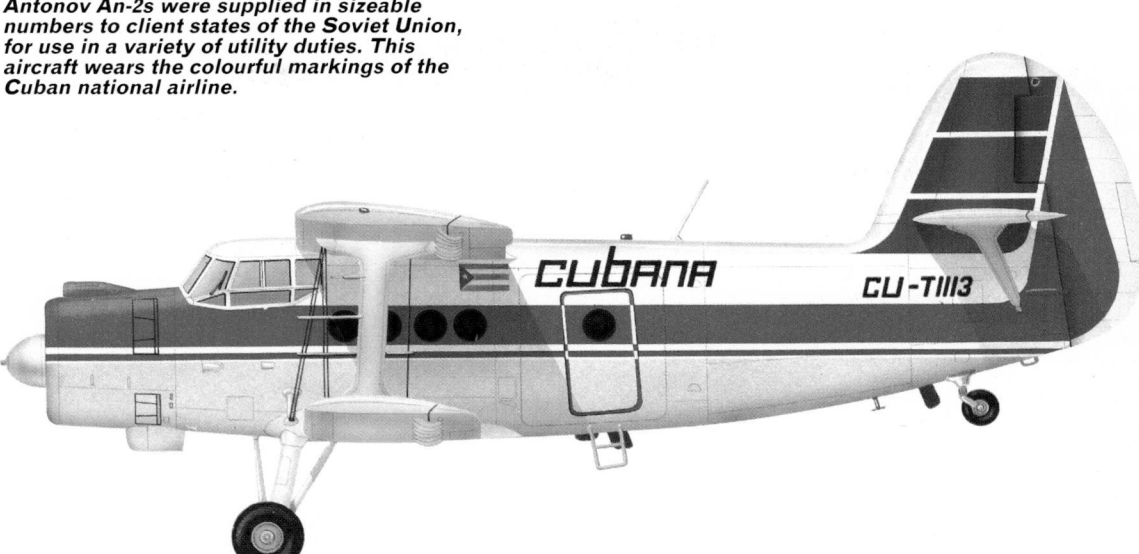

Antonov An-2s were supplied in sizeable numbers to client states of the Soviet Union, for use in a variety of utility duties. This aircraft wears the colourful markings of the Cuban national airline.

Since 1960 the An-2 has been built in Poland by WSK-PZL, and this company has produced several new variants, many adapted to agricultural needs. China also builds the type under licence.

Dimensions: span, upper 18.18 m (59 ft 7¾ in), lower 14.24 m (46 ft 8½ in); length 12.74 m (41 ft 9½ in); height 4.00 m (13 ft 1½ in); wing area, upper 43.60 m² (469.32 sq ft), lower 28.0 m² (301.4 sq ft)

Antonov An-3/4

Antonov An-4 is the design bureau designation for the An-227, a variant of the An-2 intended specifically for the role of high-altitude meterological research with a glazed position immediately in front of the tail fin for an observer. The ZA suffix stands for Zondirovanie Atmosfery, translatable as 'air sampling'.

The ASh-62IR engine has a TK super-charger mounted on the starboard side of the cowling. This arrangement enables the An-4 to maintain power up to an altitude of 1000 m (32,810 ft). The spinner of the An-2 standard model is deleted to aid engine cooling, and the original ailerons have been replaced by an unslotted variety.

The Antonov design office proposed a turboprop version of the An-2 as a new standard agricultural aeroplane for use mainly in the USSR and the countries of Eastern Europe. This model was the Soviet design bureau's response to the development in Poland of the WSK-PZL Mielec M-15 Belphegor agricultural aeroplane with a turbofan engine. The first plans for this turboprop-powered variant of the An-2 appeared in 1972, but the design became concrete only in 1979, when there appeared illustrations clearly revealing the existence of new An-3 prototypes. The only difference from the An-2 was the powerplant of one 701-kW (940-shp) Glushenkov TVD-10B turboprop.

The supplementary cabin in front of the An-4's otherwise standard unit was designed to accommodate a geo physical observer.

Antonov An-12 'Cub'
to
Antonov An-225 Mriya

Antonov An-12 'Cub'

Developed simultaneously with the An-10, the **An-12 'Cub'** was a generally similar transport for military service with the Soviet air force. The major difference was the provision of a completely new rear fuselage which was more sharply upswept to incorporate underfuselage loading doors which, when opened, allowed for the direct on-loading of vehicles. Also included was a gunner's position in the extreme tail position, the gunner being seated just below the trailing-edge of the rudder. The An-12 became a standard freight and paratroop transport in Soviet air force use. Over 100 remained in service in 1989 for this purpose, plus a small number of **An-12 'Cub-A'** and **'Cub-B'** electronic intelligence (Elint) and **An-12 'Cub-C'** electronic countermeasures aircraft. The 'Cub-A' has extra blade aerials, the 'Cub-B' has a variety of ventral radomes, while the 'Cub-C' has other radomes, including one in place of the twin 23-mm tail cannon of the 'Cub'. An-12s have been supplied also for service with the air forces of countries such as Algeria, Bangladesh, Egypt, India, Indonesia, Iraq, Poland, Sudan, Syria and Yugoslavia.

In 1965 a civil version of the An-12 was demonstrated at the Paris Air Salon. This had a differing arrangement of underfuselage doors which fold to permit the use of a detachable ramp for loading and unloading. Between the main aft cargo hold and the flight deck, a pressurised area was provided, allowing for the accommodation of 14 passengers. These mixed passenger/cargo An-12s began to enter service with Aeroflot in February 1966, and these have the tail gun position of the military freighter deleted and enclosed by a smooth fairing. Since that time civil An-12s have been supplied for similar mixed passenger/cargo services with several airlines.

Production ended in 1973 after some 850 An-12s had been produced for civil and military operators.

Specification
Type: mixed passenger/cargo transport
Powerplant: four 2983-ekW (4,000-ehp) Ivchenko AI-20K turboprops
Performance: maximum cruising speed 600 km/h (373 mph); normal cruising speed 550 km/h (342 mph) at 7620 m (25,000 ft); service ceiling 10200 m (33,465 ft); range 3400 km (2,113 miles) with 10000-kg (22,046-lb) payload and one hour fuel reserves
Weights: normal take-off 54000 kg (119,050 lb); maximum take-off 61000 kg (134,482 lb)
Dimensions: span 38.00 m (124 ft 8 in); length 33.10 m (108 ft 7¼ in); height 10.53 m (34 ft 6½ in); wing area 121.70 m² (1,310 sq ft)

Several An-12s serve with civil airlines, but most are in use with military forces. Included in the Soviet fleet are many configured for electronic duties, such as reconnaissance.

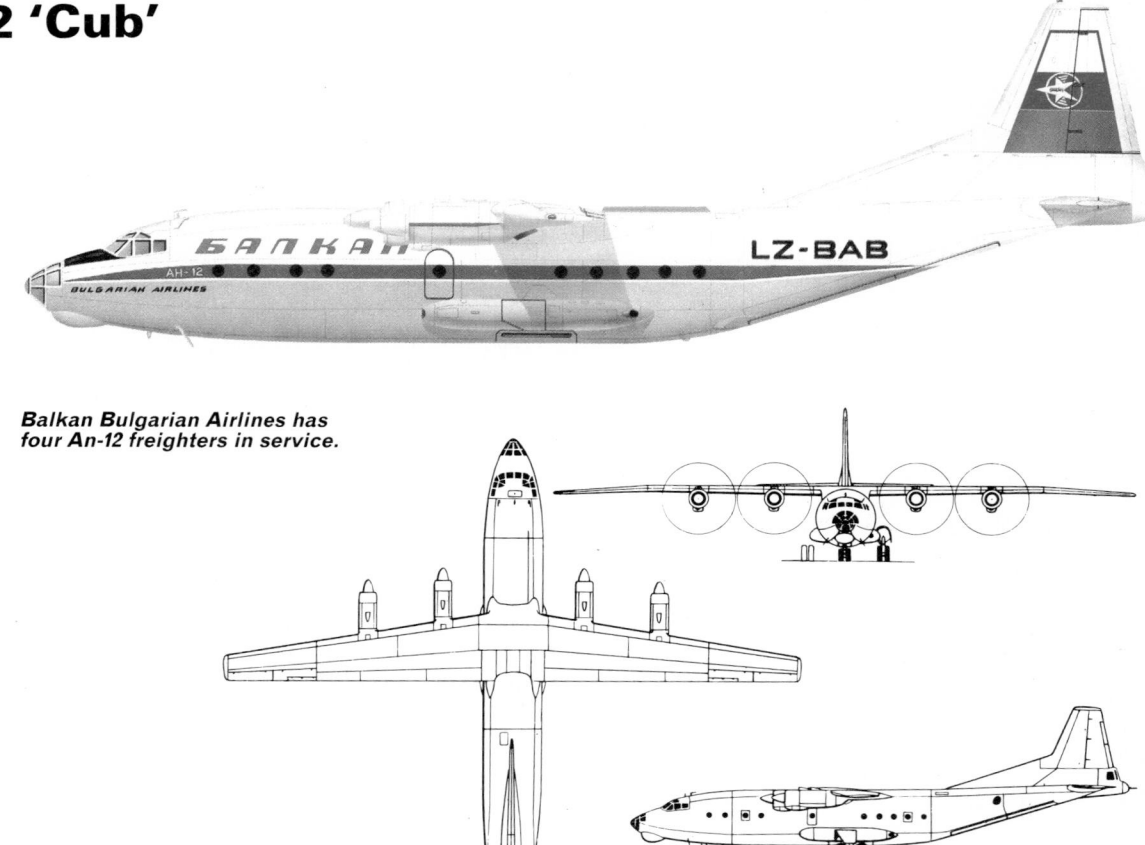

Balkan Bulgarian Airlines has four An-12 freighters in service.

Antonov An-12 'Cub'

Antonov An-14/-28

The **Antonov An-14 'Clod'** was designed in 1957 as a STOL (short-take-off-and-landing) freighter and feederliner, with handling characteristics which would enable it to be flown by inexperienced pilots. With its high-aspect-ratio braced wing and twin tailfins, it shows signs of inspiration from the French Hurel-Dubois transports of the early 1950s, the experimental designs which also led to the British Shorts Skyvan and 330.

The development of the An-14 was protracted, and it was not until 1965 that the type entered service. Production versions feature a very different tail design from the prototype, and the planform of the wing and the arrangement of the high-lift devices are also modified. The nose was slightly lengthened, and clamshell doors were fitted to the rear fuselage.

If the evolution of the An-14 has been slow, that of its turboprop development, the **An-28 'Cash'**, has been even less hurried. It was announced in 1967 that a turboprop version of the type was under development, and the first prototype, designated **An-14M**, flew at Kiev in September 1969. Powered by two

604-kW (810-shp) TVD-850 turboprops, the new version was stretched to accommodate up to 15 passengers, and weighed 5600 kg (12,500 lb) fully loaded. A production prototype of the aircraft was demonstrated in 1974, at which time the change in designation to An-28 was announced. Production is by PZL in Poland and the aircraft is in service with both civil and military users.

All variants of the An-14 and An-28 share the same pod-and-boom fuselage layout, permitting easy loading of cargo in the freight role. The high wing carries full-span double-slotted flaps and slats, ailerons being built into the outer flap sections.

Antonov An-14 'Clod' of the East German air force

Dimensions: span 22.0 m (72 ft 3 in); length 11.36 m (37 ft 3½ in); height 4.63 m (15 ft 2½ in); wing area 39.72 m² (422.8 sq ft)

Specification
Antonov An-14
Type: STOL light transport
Powerplant: two 224-kW (300-hp) Ivchenko AI-14RF radial piston engines
Performance: cruising speed 170-180 km/h (105-120 mph) at 2000 m (6,560 ft); maximum range with six passengers or 570-kg (1,200-lb) payload 650 km (400 miles); service ceiling 5000 m (16,400 ft); take-off run 100-110 m (330-360 ft); landing run 110 m (360 ft)
Weights: empty 2600 kg (5,700 lb); normal take-off 3450 kg (7,600 lb); maximum take-off 3630 kg (8,000 lb)

Antonov An-28
Type: STOL light transport
Powerplant: two 715-kW (960-shp) PZL-built Glushenkov TVD-10V turboprops
Performance: maximum cruising speed 350 km/h (217 mph); economical cruising speed 300 km/h (186 mph); range with 20 passengers 510 km (317 miles)
Weights: empty 3500 kg (7,716 lb); maximum take-off 6100 kg (13,448 lb)
Dimensions: span 22.06 m (72 ft 4½ in); length 12.98 m (42 ft 7 in); height 4.6 m (15 ft 1 in); wing area 40.28 m² (433.5 sq ft)

Antonov An-22

The Soviet Union has always been faced with the difficult problem of transporting cargo across its vast territories: this results not only from the very long distances involved, but also from a wide variety of terrain, and the need to provide a service of this nature into areas where little or no surface routes exist. Air transport has provided a solution to this problem, and explains why there has been considerable development and production of heavy cargo and cargo/passenger aircraft in the USSR.

Antonov's bureau was given the task in early 1962 of originating the design of an aircraft which would be able to carry heavy or large loads over long ranges and which would, in addition, be able to operate from and into a variety of unprepared fields. The resulting **Antonov An-22 Antei 'Cock'** prototype was flown for the first time on 27 February 1965, and was first seen by the Western aerospace industry when exhibited at the Paris Air Salon some four months later. Almost certainly this aircraft was the prototype, and it was then suggested that in addition to being available as a bulk cargo transporter, it was able to be made available in civil airliner form, with upper and lower deck cabins to accommodate a total of 724 passengers. Two years later, again at the Paris Salon, came the news that this latter proposal had been abandoned.

Antonov's design to meet the demanding requirements has resulted in a very large all-metal aircraft of high wing monoplane configuration, the wing including wide-span double-slotted trailing-edge flaps. The large-capacity fuselage includes an upswept rear section with a large loading-ramp door for direct onloading of vehicles, and to provide stability during such operations, retractable jacks can be extended at a point adjacent to the loading ramp hinges. Twin fins extend above and below the tailplane, with the rudders likewise in two halves. The landing gear is of the retractable tricycle type, but is designed to permit off-runway operation: the steerable nose unit carries twin wheels, but

each main unit consists of three twin-wheel levered-suspension units in tandem, so that on the ground the An-22 is supported on no fewer than 14 wheels. Tyre pressures of these wheels are adjustable in flight, or on the ground, to provide optimum performance for any particular airfield surface. It is reported that operation into and from water-sodden grass fields is possible.

Powerplant of production An-22s comprises four Kuznetsov turboprop engines, each of which drives a pair of contra-rotating four-blade propellers. Accommodation is provided for a crew of five or six, and in common with many Soviet transport aircraft, there is a small cabin area at the forward end of the fuselage, aft of the flight deck, with seating

for 28 or 29 passengers.

An-22s have established many payload-to-height and speed-with-payload records and are able to airlift the army's T-62 tank. Serving both with Aeroflot and the Soviet air force, the numbers remaining in service in 1989 were estimated at 20-30 and 55 respectively.

Specification
Type: long-range heavy transport
Powerplant: four 11186-kW (15,000-shp) Kuznetsov NK-12MA turboprops
Performance: maximum speed 740 km/h (460 mph); cruising speed 560-640 km/h (348-398 mph); range 5000 km (3,107 miles) with maximum payload; range 10950 km (6,804 miles)

For several years the world's largest aircraft, the An-22's giant turboprops enable it to lift outsize loads. Among the more interesting applications is the transport of complete An-124 wings carried 'piggy-back'.

with maximum fuel and 45000-kg (99,208-lb) payload
Weights: empty equipped 114000 kg (251,327 lb); maximum take-off 250000 kg (551,156 lb)
Dimensions: span 64.40 m (211 ft 3½ in); length 57.80 m (189 ft 7½ in); height 12.53 m (41 ft 1¼ in); wing area 345 m² (3,713.7 sq ft)

Antonov An-24

With the requirement for a turbine-engined short-range civil transport to replace the piston-engined Ilyushin Il-14 in Aeroflot service, the Antonov bureau initiated in late 1957 the design of a 32-40 seat aircraft which could be employed over short/medium-range routes. Its design had to include the ability to operate from small unpaved airfields, and also required that flight characteristics and powerplant should be such that it could be used between points with considerable variations in altitude and/or temperature. It was not until just over two years later, in April 1960, that the first of two prototypes had flown; the period between the beginning of the design and completion of the first prototype had been extended somewhat by a capacity change to 44-seat accommodation.

Typically 'Antonov' in its high-wing configuration, the **An-24 'Coke'** is fitted with a wing having wide-span Fowler-type trailing-edge flaps, these being double-slotted outboard of the engine nacelles, and single-slotted inboard. The tail unit is conventional, with the addition of a fairly large ventral fin on production aircraft, and the fuselage is a semi-monocoque structure introducing bonded/welded construction. The hydraulically retractable tricycle-type landing gear has twin wheels on each unit, a steerable and fully castoring nose unit, and includes the means of adjusting

tyre pressures in flight, or on the ground, to permit operation from a variety of different surfaces. The powerplant comprises two Ivchenko AI-24A turboprop engines, each driving a constant-speed and fully-feathering propeller.

Production aircraft began to enter service with Aeroflot in 1962 for crew training and proving flights, but it was not until September 1963 that the first 50-seat **An-24V** were used on the routes between Moscow, Voronezh and Saratov. Subsequent versions have included the **An-24V Srs II**, available with standard 50-passenger accommodation, but also with alternative mixed passenger/freight, convertible cargo/passenger, all-freight, or executive interiors; the **An-24RV**, similar to the foregoing, but with a 900-kg (1,985-lb) thrust auxiliary turbojet installed in the starboard engine nacelle and used for remote field engine starting, and operable also to improve take-off or airborne performance; the **An-24T**, equipped as a specialised freighter with the standard rear cabin passenger door deleted and replaced by an upward-opening ventral freight door, twin ventral fins outboard of the freight door to replace the single ventral fin, and with cargo hoist and conveyor installed; and the **An-24RT**, as the An-24T but with auxiliary turbojet installed. Also evaluated was an **An-24P**, equipped to airdrop parachute-equipped firefighters

to provide fast reaction to newly-reported forest fires.

Production of the An-24 series for civil and military operators totalled some 1,100 and the type continues in production and under development in China as the **Xian Y-7**.

Specification
Antonov An-24V
Type: short-range transport
Powerplant: two 1902-ekW (2,550-ehp) Ivchenko AI-24A turboprops
Performance: cruising speed 450 km/h (280 mph); service ceiling

China's Xian Aircraft Company is developing new and improved versions of the An-24 under the Y-7 designation.

8400 m (27,560 ft); range with maximum payload 550 km (342 miles); range with maximum fuel 2440 km (1,491 miles)
Weights: empty 13300 kg (29,321 lb); maximum take-off 21000 kg (49,297 lb)
Dimensions: span 29.20 m (95 ft 9½ in); length 23.53 m (77 ft 2½ in); height 8.32 m (27 ft 3½ in); wing area 74.98 m² (807.1 sq ft)

Antonov An-26, An-30 and An-32

Development of a military freighter based on the Antonov An-24 airliner was logical, especially in view of the increased performance available with the addition of the auxiliary engine introduced on the An-24RV.

As things turned out, three variations were developed on the theme of the An-24. The first of these was the **Antonov An-26 'Curl'**, which began to enter service in 1970, and is distinguishable by its more powerful 2103-ekW (2,820-ehp) Ivchenko AI-24T turboprops and redesigned rear fuselage. This latter includes a large downward-hinged rear ramp/door, which can be slid forward below the cabin floor to facilitate airdropping of freight or the direct loading of cargo (up to 5500 kg/12,125 lb) at truckbed height. Small vehicles can be driven straight into the hold, while other loads can be handled by inbuilt powered conveyors and winches. A large bulged observation window is fitted to the left side of the fuselage, just to the rear of the flight deck, for increased accuracy in para-dropping operations. The An-26 is in service as a light tactical transport (40 passengers or freight) with Warsaw Pact air arms, and considerable efforts have been made to export the type. It would appear to be a logical replacement for the Lisunov Li-2 and Ilyushin Il-14. The Chinese are developing their own version known as the **Xian Y-14.**

The second variation is the **Antonov An-30 'Clank'**, which first flew in 1974. This is a specialised aerial survey version of the An-26 with a raised flight deck and an extensively glazed nose, together with ventral ports for cameras and other survey equipment. It seems likely that the An-30's principal role is as

The An-26 is the standard transport of the Soviet Union and its client states. Shown is an East German machine.

part of the major geophysical effort to locate mineral resources within the USSR.

The third variation appeared in 1979, in the form of the **Antonov An-32 'Cline'**. This was designed specifically to offer better performance in 'hot and high' conditions, and is powered by two 3863-ekW (5,180-ehp) Ivchenko AI-20M turboprops, offering some 83 per cent more power than the AI-24s of the An-26. The AI-20M is an uprated version of the turboprop which powered the

much larger Antonov An-12, and requires a propeller of greater diameter than the AI-24 of the An-26. In order to avoid total redesign of the wing, therefore, in the An-32 the engines have been relocated to a position well above the wing. The propeller axes are thus above the widest point of the fuselage, with the advantage that asymmetric control problems are less than if the engines had been moved outwards rather than upwards. However, the destabilising effect of the larger cowlings and propellers has had to

be balanced by additional tail area (in the ventral fins); and the higher thrust line has necessitated an increase in outer-wing chord, resulting in a dog-tooth leading edge, and inverted slots on the tail-plane leading edge. No auxiliary turbojet is fitted, and production for civil and military operators began in 1980. The An-32 is readily capable of operations from airfields as high as 4600 m (15,000 ft), and has a maximum payload of 6000 kg (13,228 lb).

Specifications
Antonov An-26
Type: short-haul transport
Powerplant: two 2103-ekW (2,820-ehp) Ivchenko AI-24T turboprops
Performance: (at normal take-off weight) cruising speed at 6000 m (19,675 ft) 435 km/h (270 mph); initial climb rate 480 m (1,575 ft) per minute; service ceiling 8100 m (26,575 ft); range with 4500-kg (9,920-lb) payload 900 km (559 miles)
Weights: empty 15020 kg (33,133 lb); normal take-off 23000 kg (50,706 lb); maximum take-off 24000 kg (52,911 lb)
Dimensions: span 29.20 m (95 ft 9½ in); length 23.80 m (78 ft 1 in); height 8.575 m (28 ft 1½ in); wing area 74.98 m² (807.1 sq ft)

Antonov An-32
Type: short/medium-range transport
Powerplant: two 3862-ekW (5,180-ehp) Ivchenko AI-20M turboprops
Performance: normal cruising speed 510 km/h (317 mph); service ceiling 9500 m (31,150 ft); range with 6000-kg (13,228-lb) payload 800 km (497 miles)
Weight: maximum take-off 26000 kg (57,320 lb)
Dimensions: span 29.20 m (95 ft 9½ in); length 23.80 m (78 ft 1 in); height 8.575 m (28 ft 1½ in); wing area 74.98 m² (807.1 sq ft)

With an airframe similar to the An-26, the An-32 is intended for high performance operations.

Antonov An-72/-74

First flying on 22 December 1977, the **An-72** was designed principally as a replacement for the An-26 freighter, and the aircraft will form a basis for a sizeable family of variants similar to the earlier design. Bearing a similarity to the Boeing YC-14, the An-72 is a STOL freighter, with many advanced features suited to the main role. The high-wing mounts two large D-36 turbofans above the wing close to the fuselage, keeping them free from foreign object damage. These are set to be replaced by the more powerful Lotarev D-436.

Engine efflux is blown over the top surface of the wing. When the large multi-slotted flaps are deployed, the jet efflux is deflected downwards (the 'Coanda' effect) by 'sticking' to the flap surface, thereby increasing lift enormously. The An-72 is tailored to operations from unprepared fields, featuring multi-wheel, low pressure landing gear, and a rear loading ramp. The An-72 and its derivatives are in service with both Aeroflot and the Soviet air force. Production at the Kharkov plant numbers about 20 per year.

Variants
An-72 'Coaler-A': pre-production aircraft, numbering two flying prototypes, one static test airframe and eight pre-production machines
An-72A 'Coaler-C': main production version with increased fuselage length and wing span
An-72AT 'Coaler-C': specialist cargo-carrying version equipped to accommodate standard containers
An-72S 'Coaler-C': executive version with three cabins separated by bulkheads. In the front are toilet, galley and cloak facilities, the central section has work and rest areas while the rear contains 24 armchairs. Provision for cargo or vehicle carriage is made
An-74 'Coaler-B': arctic support

version identified by observation blisters on fuselage sides and enlarged radar in bulged radome. Able to be fitted with either wheels or skis, the An-74 also has increased fuel capacity
An-74 'Madcap': airborne early warning version with redesigned tail unit. The swept-forward fin has a large rotodome mounted on top housing the surveillance radar, while the horizontal tail surfaces have been moved to a conventional low-set position. The cabin contains operator stations and associated avionics

Specification
Antonov An-72A 'Coaler-C'
Type: STOL transport
Powerplant: two Lotarev D-36 turbofans each rated at 63.74 kN (14,330 lb) thrust, to be replaced by Lotarev D-436 turbofans of 73.6 kN (16,550 lb) thrust
Performance: maximum speed at 10000 m (32,800 ft) 705 km/h (438 mph); service ceiling 10700 m (35,105 ft); take-off run 930 m (3,050 ft); landing run 465 m (1,525 ft); range with maximum payload 800 km (497 miles); range with maximum fuel 3250 km

(2,020 miles)
Weights: maximum take-off from 1800 m (5,905 ft) runway 34500 kg (76,060 lb); maximum take-off from 1000 m (3,280 ft) runway 27500 kg (60,625 lb)
Dimensions: span 31.89 m (104 ft 7½ in); length 28.07 m (92 ft 1¼ in); height 8.65 m (28 ft 4½ in); wing area 98.62 m² (1062 sq ft)

This pre-production An-72 shows the unusual engine arrangement, chosen so that efflux blows back across the large flaps.

Antonov An-124

At the time of its first flight on 26 December 1982, the **An-124** was the largest aircraft in the world. Antonov's experience with the huge turboprop An-22 gave it a head start when design began on the new giant, as did knowledge of the slightly smaller Lockheed C-5 Galaxy. Indeed, apart from its low-set tailplane, the An-124 is very similar to the Lockheed product.

Four Lotarev D-18T turbofans power the giant, slung in pods under the large anhedralled wing. Full-span leading-edge slats and large flaps give the An-124 impressive short field capability, while its 20 main wheels allow the type to use rough fields. Two nose-wheel units each have a pair of wheels, and these can be retracted on the ground allowing the aircraft to 'kneel' to assist loading. Like the Galaxy, the An-124 has an upward-hingeing nose visor and rear clamshell/ramp doors to allow front or rear drive-on loading.

Accommodation on the flight deck caters for six crew (two pilots, two engineers, a navigator and a radio operator), and behind this is a rest area. Behind the wing on the upper deck is accommodation for up to 88 passengers. The 36 m (118 ft) long main cabin is pressurised and has two electric cranes in the roof, each lifting up to 20000 kg (44,100 lb). Two winches are fitted, able to pull loads through the cabin. Control of the aircraft is effected by a quadruple-redundant fly-by-wire system.

Following its first flight, with Vladimir Terski at the controls, the An-124 showed few problems, and production

aircraft appeared quickly. The second aircraft, named *Ruslan*, appeared at the 1985 Paris Air Salon. The aircraft entered service with Aeroflot in early 1986, and now serves principally on the Siberian run, carrying outsize items to the oil and mineral exploitation industries. In 1987 the An-124 began service with the air force. Production is reportedly eight to ten aircraft per year, and by 1989 over 25 had been completed. The An-124 was assigned the NATO reporting name 'Condor'.

Specification
Type: heavy transport
Powerplant: four Lotarev D-18T turbofans each rated at 229.5 kN (51,590 lb) thrust
Performance: maximum cruising speed 865 km/h (537 mph); approach speed 240 km/h (149 mph); take-off field length at maximum weight 3000 m (9,850 ft); landing run at max weight 800 m (2,625 ft); range with maximum payload 4500 km (2,795 miles); range with maximum fuel

16500 km (10,250 miles)
Weights: maximum take-off weight 405000 kg (892,872 lb); maximum fuel 230000 kg (507,063 lb); maximum payload 150000 kg (330,693 lb)
Dimensions: span 73.30 m (240 ft 5¾ in); length 69.10 m (226 ft 8½ in); height 20.78 m (68 ft 2¼ in); wing area 628.0 m² (6,760 sq ft)

In service with both Aeroflot and the Soviet air force, the An-124 'Condor' is also available to Western firms who wish to lease it.

Antonov An-225 Mriya

Currently the world's largest aircraft, the **An-225 Mriya** (dream) stemmed from the need to transport large items for the Soviet space programme. Previously a converted Myasishchev Mya-4 'Bison' bomber had been used to carry outsize items on its back, but this had a limited payload capacity, meaning many components had to be disassembled or not carried at all.

In mid-1985 Antonov was entrusted with the design of a new aircraft able to carry the *Buran* shuttle orbiter, large components of the *Energiya* launch vehicles and other outsize items for construction and mining industries. Construction of the An-124 provided the basis for the new aircraft, Antonov using many of the same components to keep cost and development effort down.

The fuselage and wings are similar to the An-124, the cabin retaining the same cross-sectional dimensions but with increased length. To save weight the rear loading ramp is removed, but the An-225 retains the nose visor. Standard An-124 wings are grafted on to a new centre section, thereby increasing the span while keeping the engine installations the same. An additional pair of D-36T turbofans is fitted to the new centre section, raising thrust to an amazing 1377 kN (309,540 lb). In order to support the increased weight, seven pairs of wheels are fitted to each side as opposed to five in the An-124.

The world's largest aircraft, the mighty six-engined An-225 was developed primarily as a transport for the Soviet space shuttle and rocket launcher components.

Outsize loads that cannot fit into the capacious cabin (including *Buran* and *Energiya* components) are carried 'piggyback', the load supported on two main attachments above the centre section. These supports and other smaller ones along the fuselage top are faired over when not in use. To avoid buffeting from the 'piggyback' load, the An-225 has twin vertical fins mounted on the end of a large tailplane.

The prototype made its first flight on 21 December 1988, and in March 1989 set up no fewer than 106 world and class

records in one flight from Kiev, at a maximum take-off weight in excess of 500000 kg (1,100,000 lb). Only two have been completed so far, and the first flew with *Buran* on 13 May 1989. This combination made a dramatic appearance in the West for the first time a month later at the Paris Air Salon.

Specification
Type: heavy transport
Powerplant: six Lotarev D-18T turbofans, each rated at 229.5 kN (51,590 lb) thrust

Performance: (estimated) cruising speed 800 km/h (497 mph); take-off run carrying *Buran* 2500 m (8,200 ft); turning radius about nosewheels 50 m (164 ft)
Weights: maximum take-off 600000 kg (1,322,750 lb); maximum payload (internal or external) 250000 kg (551,150 lb)
Dimensions: span 88.4 m (290 ft); length 84.0 m (275 ft 7 in); height 18.1 m (59 ft 4¾ in); tailplane span 32.65 m (107 ft 1½ in); length of freight hold 43 m (141 ft)

Arado Ar 64 and Ar 65
to
Arado Ar 234 Blitz

Arado Ar 64 and Ar 65

The **SD II** and **SD III** fighters, designed by Ing. Walter Rethel and developed in parallel, were used as the bases for the **Arado Ar 64**. The last was originally intended to be a replacement for the Fokker D XIII fighters then equipping the German flying training school at Lipezk in the Soviet Union. It retained the earlier types' mixed construction, with fabric-covered welded steel-tube fuselage and wooden wings, and the prototype **Ar 64a** of 1930 was powered by a 395-kW (530-hp) Jupiter VI radial engine, built under licence by Siemens, and driving a four-bladed wooden propeller. The **Ar 64c** introduced some structural changes, and the initial production version, the **Ar 64d**, featured modified landing gear and vertical tail surfaces of increased area. The final version was the **Ar 64e**, similar to the Ar 64d except for its two-bladed propeller, and armed, as in the case of earlier variants, with two 7.92-mm (0.31-in) machine-guns. Some 20 Ar 64s were included in the inventory of the Deutsche Verkehrsfliegerschule, at Schleissheim, where civil and military pilots were trained.

Variants
Ar 64b: the two prototype Ar 64b aircraft were powered by the 477-kW (640-hp) BMW VI 12-cylinder inline engine which, although not adopted for the production machines, powered the Ar 65 derivative
Ar 65: this was one of the first modern combat aircraft developed for Germany's emergent air arm, and was modelled closely on the Ar 64 apart from the substitution of the 560-kW (750-hp) BMW VI 7.3 Vee-12 engine for the earlier type's radial; early flight tests with the **Ar 65a** prototype indicated the need for further development

Ar 65d: 1932 development of the Ar 65a, with the engine thrust line and forward fuselage contours lowered, the rear fuselage deepened, and extra interplane struts added; despite an increase in maximum take-off weight from 1830 to 1920 kg (4,034 to 4,233 lb), performance and handling were improved
Ar 65E: production version of the Ar 65d; data include a maximum speed of 300 km/h (186 mph) at 1650 m (5,415 ft), cruising speed of 245 km/h (153 mph), climb to 1000 m (3,280 ft) in 1 minute 30 seconds, service ceiling of 7600 m (24,935 ft), empty weight of 1510 kg (3,329 lb) and maximum take-off weight of 1930 kg (4,255 lb), span of 11.20 m (36 ft 9 in), length of 8.40 m (27 ft 6¾ in), height of 3.42 m (11 ft 2¾ in), wing area 23.00 m² (322.917 sq ft) and an armament of two 7.92-mm (0.31-in) MG 17 machine-guns with 500 rounds

per gun; the type served for only a few months as a fighter before being supplemented and then replaced by the Heinkel He 51; the Ar 65E was then used as a fighter trainer until 1936
Ar 65F: production modification of the Ar 65E with superior equipment increasing weight by 40 kg (88 lb)

Specification
Arado Ar 64
Type: single-seat fighter
Powerplant: one 395-kW (530-hp) Siemens Jupiter VI radial piston engine
Performance: maximum speed 250 km/h (155 mph) at 5000 m (16,405 ft)
Weights: empty 1210 kg (2,667 lb); maximum take-off 1680 kg (3,704 lb)
Dimensions: span 9.90 m (32 ft 5¾ in); length 8.43 m (27 ft 8 in)
Armament: two fixed forward-firing 7.92-mm (0.31-in) machine-guns

Arado Ar 67 and Ar 68

In the closing months of 1933 Arado flew what proved to be the sole example of its **Ar 67**, somewhat smaller and lighter than the Ar 65, and powered by a 477-kW (640-hp) Rolls-Royce Kestrel VI engine which endowed it with a maximum speed of 340 km/h (211 mph). Like its antecedents, it was of mixed construction and was, similarly, to have carried two 7.92-mm (0.31-in) machine-guns.

Development was discontinued, however, in favour of the **Arado Ar 68**, which was to be the last biplane service to enter front-line service with the Luftwaffe. Reaching contemporary standards of aerodynamic efficiency, the aircraft had an oval-section fuselage of steel tube construction, with metal panels covering the rear decking and forward sections. The single-bay wings were of wood, with plywood and fabric covering. The distinctive fin, which was to be used almost without exception in subsequent single-engined Arado designs, was introduced on the Ar 68, which also featured spatted landing gear.

The prototype **Ar 68a** flew for the first time in 1934, powered by a BMW VId 12-cylinder Vee engine which provided a maximum continuous output of 410 kW (550 hp), resulting in disappointing performance. The problem was partially overcome in the **Ar 68b** second prototype, which was powered by a supercharged 455-kW (610-hp) Junkers Jumo 210 12-cylinder inverted-Vee engine, which both improved forward vision from the cockpit, and provided full power at higher altitudes. Even so, drag from the chin radiator depressed potential performance figures, and a redesigned unit was fitted to the **Ar 68c** third prototype which, flown in the summer of 1935, was the first to be fitted with the intended armament of two 7.92-mm (0.31-in) MG 17 machine-guns. The fourth and fifth prototypes, designated **Ar 68d** and **Ar 68e**, were powered respectively by the BMW VI

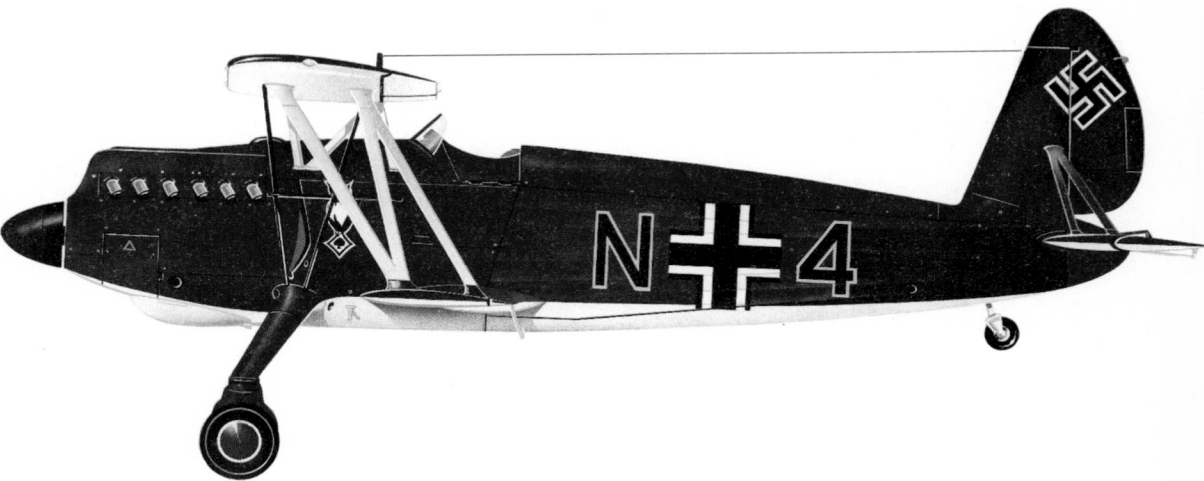

Arado Ar 68F night fighter of 10.(Nacht)/JG 53 based at Oedheim/Heilbron during September 1939. The Ar 68F was the first production version with the upright BMW VI. The better Ar 68E introduced an inverted Jumo 210 in a more streamlined cowl.

and Jumo 210 engines, and were regarded as pre-production aircraft.

Initial deliveries were made to the Luftwaffe in the late summer of 1936, commencing with I/JG134 'Horst Wessel'. By the outbreak of World War II, most surviving Ar 68s had been relegated to advanced fighter trainer status with the Jagdfliegerschulen (fighter pilot schools).

Variants
Ar 68E: the second production version, deliveries delayed until spring 1937 by inadequate supplies of Jumo 210 engines. An underfuselage rack could be fitted to carry six 10-kg (22-lb) bombs
Ar 68F: initial production version, with 570-kW (750-hp) BMW VI engine
Ar 68G: abortive version to have used a supercharged BMW engine
Ar 68H: prototype only, with 634-kW (850-hp) BMW 132 9-cylinder radial engine, which increased maximum speed by 65 km/h (40 mph); fitted with sliding cockpit canopy, and two additional MG 17 machine-guns located in the upper wing

Specification
Arado Ar 68E-1
Type: single-seat fighter
Powerplant: one 515-kW (690-hp) Junkers Jumo 210 Da inverted inline piston engine
Performance: maximum speed 305 km/h (190 mph) at sea level; service ceiling 8100 m (26,575 ft); range 415 km (258 miles)
Weights: empty 1840 kg (4,057 lb); maximum take-off 2475 kg (5,457 lb)
Dimensions: span 11.00 m (36 ft 1 in); length 9.50 m (31 ft 2 in); height 3.28 m (10 ft 9 in); wing area 27.30 m² (293.86 sq ft)
Armament: two fixed forward-firing 7.92-mm (0.31-in) MG 17 machine-guns

59

Arado Ar 79

Designed as an aerobatic two-seat training and touring aircraft, the **Arado Ar 79** first appeared in 1938, powered by a 78-kW (105-hp) Hirth HM 504A-2 engine. The forward fuselage was of welded steel-tube construction, the rear section being a monocoque structure. The wings were of single-spar wooden construction with plywood and fabric covering. The aircraft featured retractable tail-wheel landing gear, the main wheels retracting sideways and inwards into the wing centre section.

Ar 79s set a number of international class speed records during 1938, including solo 1000 km (621.4 miles) at 229.04 km/h (142.32 mph) on 15 July, and solo 2000 km (1,242.8 miles) at 227.029 km/h (141.07 mph) on 29 July. Later that year an Ar 79 was prepared for an attempt on the long-distance record, a jettisonable 106-litre (23.3-lmp gal) fuel tank being fitted under the fuselage and

a 520-litre (114.4-lmp gal) tank at the rear of the cabin. Pilots Oberleutnant Pulkowski and Leutnant Jennett ferried the aircraft from Brandenberg to Benghazi in Libya, the starting point for what was to be a 6303-km (3,917-mile) non-stop flight to Gaya, India, accomplished between 29 and 31 December at an average speed of 160 km/h (99 mph).

Specification
Type: two-seat training and touring aircraft
Powerplant: one 78-kW (105-hp) Hirth HM 504A-2 inverted inline piston engine
Performance: maximum speed 230 km/h (143 mph); cruising speed 205 km/h (127 mph); ceiling 5500 m (18,040 ft); range 1025 km (636 miles)

Arado Ar 79 in pre-war German civil markings.

Weights: empty 460 kg (1,014 lb); maximum take-off 760 kg (1,675 lb)
Dimensions: span 10.00 m (32 ft 9½ in); length 7.62 m (25 ft 0 in); height 1.87 m (6 ft 10½ in); wing area 14.00 m² (150.7 sq ft)

Arado Ar 95

Dipl. Ing. Walter Blume designed the **Arado Ar 95** in 1935 for service in the coastal patrol, reconnaissance and light attack roles. A two-seat twin-float seaplane, it was of all-metal construction, with parallel-chord wings which were attached to centre sections of unequal chord and thickness. This unusual feature was intended to provide easier access to the cockpits from the lower wing root, which was thicker and of wider chord, and improved upward visibility was to result from the thinner and narrower upper surface. The single-step floats were strut-braced to the fuselage and wing centre section. The twin cockpits were enclosed by a sliding canopy, the rear end being left open to permit the use of a 7.92-mm (0.31-in) machine-gun, supplementing the similar forward-firing weapon mounted in the upper fuselage.

In 1937 the first prototype was flown, powered by a 656-kW (880-hp) BMW 132De 9-cylinder engine. The second was fitted with the 515-kW (690-hp)

Junkers Jumo 210 12-cylinder engine, and both machines were evaluated competitively with two prototypes of the Focke-Wulf Fw 62 single-float seaplane. Although the BMW-powered version was adjudged worthy of further development, and a batch of six prototype and pre-production aircraft served a trial period with the Condor Legion during the Spanish Civil War, the Ar 95 was not immediately adopted for German military use.

Undaunted, Arado offered the design for export as the **Ar 95W** floatplane, ordered by Turkey in 1938, and as the **Ar 95L** with fixed, spatted landing gear, which was the subject of a Chilean order. The latter was fulfilled prior to the beginning of World War II, but the frustrated Turkish aircraft were instead diverted to the Luftwaffe under the designation **Ar 95A**, seeing wartime service as trainers with the Seeaufklärungsgruppen (coastal reconnaissance units).

Variant
Ar 195: Arado built three prototypes of the Ar 195 navalisd version which was first flown in 1937; main changes were the addition of an arrester hook and catapult spools and, in order to improve forward visibility for deck-landing, a cockpit canopy of increased height; data include maximum speed 280 km/h (174 mph), cruising speed 250 km/h (155 mph), service ceiling 6000 m (19,680 ft), range 650 km (404 miles), empty weight 2380 kg (5,248 lb) and maximum take-off weight 3745 kg (8,256 lb), span 12.50 m (41 ft 0 in), length 10.50 m (34 ft 5⅓ in), height 3.60 m (11 ft 9¾ in) and wing area 46.00 m² (495.14 sq ft)

Specification
Arado Ar 95A-1
Type: two-seat coastal patrol and light attack aircraft
Powerplant: one 656-kW (880-hp) BMW 132 De radial piston engine
Performance: maximum speed 310 km/h (193 mph) at 3000 m (9,840 ft); cruising speed 255 km/h (158 mph) at 1200 m (3,935 ft); service ceiling 7300 m (23,945 ft); range 1100 km (683 miles)
Weights: empty 2450 kg (5,402 lb); maximum take-off 3560 kg (7,870 lb)
Dimensions: span 12.50 m (41 ft 0⅛ in); length 11.10 m (36 ft 5 in); height 3.60 m (11 ft 9¾ in); wing area 45.40 m² (488.70 sq ft)
Armament: one fixed forward-firing 7.92-mm (0.31-in) MG 17 machine-gun and one flexible 7.92-mm (0.31-in) MG 15 in rear cockpit; an underfuselage rack accommodated a 800-kg (1,764-lb) torpedo or a 500-kg (1,102-lb) bomb

Arado Ar 96

With a total production run of more than 11,500 aircraft by the cessation of hostilities, the **Arado Ar 96** was the Luftwaffe's standard advanced trainer, designed by Walter Blume and first flown in 1938. Of all-metal light alloy construction, the prototype was powered by a 179-kW (240-hp) Argus As 10C 8-cylinder inline engine, and was fitted with main landing gear which retracted outwards into the wing. In order to widen the track, to make the aircraft easier for student pilots to handle, the legs were repositioned to retract inwards.

Reichsluftfahrtministerium trials were successfully completed and an initial production batch of the **Ar 96A** was manufactured in 1939, leading to large-scale orders for the more powerful **Ar 96B** which were placed in 1940. Manufacture was transferred to the Junkers subsidiary Ago Flugzeugwerke at Oschersleben/Bode and then, in mid-1941, to the Czech company Avia which was joined in the programme by the Prague-based Letov organisation in 1944. Czech production continued until 1948, supplying aircraft to the Czech air force under the designation **Avia C.2B**.

The Luftwaffe used the Ar 96 for

advanced, night and instrument flying duties with the pilot training schools, fighter training wings, fighter training and replacement units, and the officer cadet schools.

Variants
Ar 96B: the main production version; fuselage lengthened to permit increased fuel capacity, and engine of more power fitted; the **Ar 96B-1** subvariant was an unarmed pilot trainer and the **Ar 96B-2** carried a single 7.92-mm (0.31-in) MG 17 machine-gun or camera gun for gunnery training
Ar 96C: built only as a pre-production batch, for bomb-aiming training with a transparent panel in the cockpit floor; powered by a 358-kW (480-hp) Argus As 410C engine

Specification
Arado Ar 96B
Type: two-seat advanced trainer
Powerplant: one 347-kW (465-hp) Argus As 410A-1 inverted inline piston engine
Performance: maximum speed 330 kmh (205 mph) at sea level; cruising speed 295 km/h (183 mph);

climb to 3000 m (9,845 ft) in 6 minutes 50 seconds; service ceiling 7100 m (23,295 ft); range 990 km (615 miles)
Weights: empty 1295 kg (2,854 lb); maximum take-off 1700 kg (3,748 lb)
Dimensions: span 11.00 m (36 ft 1 in); length 9.10 m (29 ft 10¼ in); height 2.60 m (8 ft 6¾ in); wing area 17.1 m² (184.1 sq ft)
Armament: one fixed forward-firing 7.92-mm (0.31-in) MG 17 machine-gun

The Arado Ar 96 was widely built in two versions, the Ar 96A and the later Ar 96B (illustrated) with a lengthened fuselage to provide increased fuel capacity. A more powerful engine was also fitted. These were widely used as trainers, mostly for unarmed pilot training but some featuring a single gun and camera for basic gunnery training.

Arado Ar 196

In the autumn of 1936 the Reichsluft-fahrtministerium's Technische Amt (technical department) issued a specification for a catapult floatplane to replace the Heinkel He 50s then serving with the Bordfliegerstaffeln, the Luftwaffe units responsible for providing the Kriegsmarine with reconnaissance aircraft for its capital ships and other surface vessels. The requirement was for a two-seat single- or twin-float aircraft, to be powered by a single engine in the 597/671-kW (800/900-hp) range and, of the competing proposals, the Focke-Wulf Fw 62 biplane and **Arado Ar 196** monoplane were selected for development.

The Ar 196 was of all-metal construction, its rectangular-section steel-tube fuselage frame being faired to an oval section by the use of formers and stringers, with metal skinning forward and fabric covering aft. The wings were metal-skinned two-spar structures, hinged at the trailing edge to fold back along the fuselage sides once the outboard wing-to-float struts had been detached at the float end. Each of the twin floats housed a 300-litre (66-Imp gal) fuel tank.

Evaluation at Erprobungsstelle Travemünde in summer 1937 was undertaken by two prototypes of each design, but the clear superiority of the more advanced Arado aircraft quickly eliminated the Focke-Wulf contender. Powered by a 656-kW (880-hp) BMW 132 De radial piston engine, four prototype Ar 196s were ordered, the first two (as tested at Travemünde) with twin floats and designated **Ar 196A**, the third and fourth in single central/twin outboard stabilising float configuration and identified as **Ar 196B**s.

The fourth prototype was the first to be fitted with weapons, carrying two wing-mounted 20-mm MG FF cannon and a single 7.92-mm (0.31-in) MG 17 machine-gun in the starboard side of the forward fuselage. A fifth prototype, another Ar 196B, was powered by the more powerful 708-kW (950-hp) BMW 132K engine with a three-blade variable-pitch propeller in place of the two-blade, two-pitch unit fitted to the first four machines.

Comparative evaluation of the hydrodynamic qualities of the alternative float configurations was conducted by the Aerodynamischen Versuchsanstalt Göttingen, and at Travemünde. Although no distinct advantage could be discerned for either layout, the twin-float version

was preferred and 10 pre-production **Ar 196A-0**s were ordered.

Total production of the Ar 196 was well in excess of 500 aircraft, including those built in 1942-3 by the Société Nationale de Constructions Aéronautiques at St Nazaire, France, and by Fokker in Amsterdam between April and August 1943. Initial deliveries to the Luftwaffe were to Bordfliegerstaffeln 1./196 and 5./196, based at Wilhelmshaven and Kiel-Holtenau, these being under Kriegsmarine control. The first ship to take its **Ar 196A-1** to sea was the pocket battleship *Admiral Graf Spee*, scuttled off Montevideo in December 1939 after being trapped in the estuary of the River Plate by a British cruiser squadron under Commodore Henry Harwood.

The type was also used widely for coastal patrol, and a spectacular early success was the capture of the British submarines HMS *Seal* by two **Ar 196A-2**s of 1 Staffel/Küstenfliegergruppe 706, based at Aalborg, Denmark. Damaged by a mine and unable to submerge, the vessel was surrendered after the Arados had attacked with bombs and cannon fire. The Ar 196 served in most major battle zones (the Atlantic, North Sea, Baltic, eastern Mediterranean, Adriatic, Aegean and Black Seas). It also equipped the Bulgarian air force's 161st Coastal Squadron, and the 101st and 102nd Coastal Squadrons of the Rumanian air force.

Variants

Ar 196A-0: pre-production batch of 10 aircraft, fitted with bomb racks and rear cockpit-mounted MG 15 machine-gun only

Ar 196A-1: 20 aircraft with minor changes, built in 1939 and operated from major warships, including *Admiral Graf Spee, Deutschland, Scharnhorst, Gneisenau, Admiral Scheer* and *Prinz Eugen*; an example from the *Admiral Hipper* flight was captured in Norway and later evaluated at the Marine Aircraft Establishment, Helensburgh in 1940

Ar 196A-2: for coastal patrol duties; armament increased by the addition of two 20-mm MG FF wing cannon and a forward fuselage 7.92-mm (0.31-in) MG 17; empty weight 2075 kg (4,574 lb) and maximum take-off weight 3175 kg (7,000 lb)

Ar 196A-3: structurally strengthened version with additional radio equipment and new three-blade variable-pitch propeller; also built by SNCA and Fokker

Ar 196A-4: catapult version of the Ar 196A-3, 24 being ordered to replace A-1s with Bordfliegerstaffeln

Ar 196A-5: final production version with improved radio equipment and MG 81Z installation (twin 7.92-mm/0.31-in MG 81 machine-guns) in rear cockpit; last of 91 aircraft built by Fokker in August 1944

The Ar 196 was Germany's principal floatplane of World War II.

Ar 196B-0: pre-production batch of version with single main float and two stabilising floats, delivered for service evaluation in 1940-1

Ar 196C: project for an aerodynamically refined version, cancelled in 1941

Specification
Arado Ar 196A-3

Type: two-seat shipboard and coastal patrol floatplane

Powerplant: one 716-kW (960-hp) BMW 132K radial piston engine

Performance: maximum speed 310 km/h (193 mph) at 4000 m (13,120 ft); cruising speed 255 km/h (158 mph); service ceiling 7000 m (22,960 ft); range 1070 km (665 miles)

Weights: empty 2990 kg (6,593 lb); maximum take-off 3730 kg (8,223 lb)

Dimensions: span 12.40 m (40 ft 8¼ in); length 11.00 m (36 ft 1 in); height 4.45 m (14 ft 7¼ in); wing area 28.40 m² (305.71 sq ft)

Armament: two fixed forward-firing 20-mm MG FF cannon in wings, one fixed forward-firing 7.92-mm (0.31-in) MG 17 machine-gun in starboard forward fuselage and one flexible 7.92-mm (0.31-in) MG 15 machine-gun in rear cockpit, plus underwing racks for two 50-kg (110-lb) bombs

Arado Ar 232

Early in 1940, work began on the design of a transport aircraft to augment and ultimately replace the venerable and ubiquitous Junkers Ju 52/3m, of which more than 500 had been in service on 1 September 1939, when the German invasion of Poland precipitated World War II. A twin-engined design, the **Arado Ar 232** was to feature a pod and boom fuselage with a hydraulically operated rear loading door, and a novel arrangement of 11 pairs of small wheels used to support the fuselage during loading and unloading operations, the tricycle main landing gear having been partially raised by means of two hydraulic rams.

The first two prototypes, flown in 1941, were each powered by two 1193-kW (1,600-hp) BMW 801MA radial engines, but the insatiable demands of

the Focke-Wulf Fw 190 production lines necessitated a change of engine for subsequent aircraft. The selection of the lower-powered BMW-Bramo 323R-2

meant that four engines were needed, and the third aircraft introduced a 1.70 m (5 ft 7 in) increase in wing centre-section span to accommodate them. This was

The few production Ar 232 transports entered service in late 1943. Many flew with KG 200, the Luftwaffe's special operations unit.

the first of 20 **Ar 232B** models, some of which saw service with Luftwaffe units, initially on the Eastern Front and, later in the war, with the 'special missions'

61

Kampfgeschwader 200. A surviving aircraft from 3./KG 200 was flown from Flensburg to the Royal Aircraft Establishment at Farnborough after the capitulation. Others were used (during hostilities) for experimental purposes, including one with a boundary layer control system, one with four Gnome-Rhône 14M radial engines, and another with fixed landing gear and skis, for operations in Norway.

Specification
Type: heavy transport
Powerplant: four 895-kW (1,200-hp) BMW-Bramo 323R-2 radial piston engines
Performance: maximum speed 340 km/h (211 mph) at 4600 m (15,090 ft); cruising speed 290 km/h (180 mph) at 2000 m (6,560 ft); ceiling 8000 m (26,245 ft); range 1060 km (658 miles)
Weights: empty 12802 kg (28,224 lb); maximum take-off 21135 kg (46,595 lb)
Dimensions: span 33.50 m (109 ft 10¾ in); length 23.52 m (77 ft 2 in); height 5.69 m (18 ft 8 in); wing area 142.60 m² (1,535 sq ft)
Armament: one 13-mm (0.51-in) MG 131 machine-gun in the nose, one or two similar weapons at the rear of the fuselage pod and one 20-mm MG 151/20 cannon in a power-operated dorsal turret

Arado Ar 234 Blitz

Just as Messerschmitt's Me 262 was the world's first turbojet-powered fighter, so the **Arado Ar 234 Blitz** (Lightning) was the first jet-powered bomber, despite the fact that it was originally designed in response to a requirement of the Reichsluftfahrtministerium for a fast reconnaissance aircraft. Work on the Ar 234 began late in 1940 and, early in the following year, Arado's design team, led by Walter Blume and Hans Rebeski, completed a project study designated **E.370** which finally emerged in prototype form as the Ar 234 early in 1943. A shoulder-wing design, with its two engines underslung from the wings, the Ar 234 featured a narrow fuselage cross-section, so narrow that it could not accept conventional retractable landing gear, a problem for which the solution originally adopted was the provision of a jettisonable take-off trolley, and retractable skids on which the aircraft could return to earth.

Delays in the development of the Junkers turbojet engines meant that the first ship set of Jumo 004B-0 engines was not delivered to Warnemünde until February 1943, and the waiting prototype airframe was fitted with them so that taxiing trials could begin in March. By May two flight-cleared engines had been installed and the aircraft transferred to Rheine airfield, where the maiden flight took place on 15 June. The original take-off technique was to jettison the trolley on reaching a height of 60 m (195 ft), five braking parachutes being deployed to return the equipment safely to the ground for re-use. However, the parachute system proved troublesome, and after the first two trolleys had been destroyed it was decided that the wheels would be released immediately upon take-off.

The trolley-equipped version was designated **Ar 234A**, and the third prototype, which flew on 22 August 1943, was equipped with rocket-assisted take-off gear (RATOG) while the pressurised cockpit boasted an ejector seat. Prototypes four and five flew on 15 September and 20 December 1943 respectively. The next to fly was the eighth prototype, fitted with four 800-kg (1,764-lb) thrust BMW 003A-1 engines arranged in pairs. The same engines, in four separate nacelles, powered the sixth prototype, flown on 8 April 1944. By then the Junkers 004B engines had been uprated from 840-kg (1,852-lb) to 890-kg (1,962-lb) thrust, and two were installed in the seventh (and last of the A-series prototypes) which crashed after an engine fire, killing Arado chief test pilot Flugkapitän Selle.

The inability of the Ar 234 to be moved easily before the wheeled trolley had been fitted was clearly unacceptable in an operational environment. Thus the B-series was evolved, with a slightly widened fuselage to take conventional landing gear, albeit of relatively narrow track. The eighth prototype was the first of the new model and it flew on 10 March 1944. It was followed on 2 April by the tenth machine, which was without cabin pressurisation and ejector seat, but fitted with bomb racks beneath the engine nacelles and used to test the BZA (Bombenzielanlage für Sturzflug) bomb-aiming computer. Of the remaining B-series prototypes the most important was number 13, with two pairs of BMW 003A-1 engines, and numbers 15 and 17, each with two of the BMW engines, and used as test beds to hasten the solution to the turbojet's thrust control problems.

Despite their lack of mobility on the ground, in July 1944 the fifth and seventh prototypes were subjected to operational evaluation in the reconnaissance role by 1./Versuchsverband Oberbefehlshaber der Luftwaffe at Jivincourt, near Reims. Fitted with Walter RATO equipment, they defied interception during numerous sorties over Allied territory and were alter joined by a number of **Ar 234B-1** models which, in small numbers, equipped experimental reconnaissance units designated Sonderkommandos Götz, Hecht, Sperling and Sommer. Two other units, 1.(F)/33 and 1.(F)/100, were still operational at the war's end. The bomber version first became operational with the Stabsstaffel of KG 76. The Ar 234 was also flown by Kommando Bonow, an experimental night-fighter unit.

Variants
Ar 234B-0: 20 pre-production aircraft, the majority of which were delivered to Rechlin for intensive development; without ejector seats or cabin pressurisation
Ar 234B-1: reconnaissance version, which could be equipped with two Rb 50/30 or Rb 75/30 cameras, alternatively with an Rb 50/30 and an Rb 20/30
Ar 234B-2: bomber version, with maximum bombload of 2000 kg (4,409 lb) carried on ETC 503 bomb racks beneath engine nacelles

Ar 234C: production four-engined version with BMW 003A-1 engines; 19th prototype was to this standard and first flown on 30 September 1944
Ar 234C-1: four-engined equivalent of B-1, but with full cabin pressurisation and armed with two rearward-firing 20-mm MG 151/20 cannon
Ar 234C-2: four-engined equivalent of B-2
Ar 234C-3: multi-purpose version; 21st-25th prototypes completed with raised and redesigned cockpits; armed as C-1 but with two additional 20-mm MG 151/20 cannon beneath the nose; variable bomb load on three ETC 504 racks; empty weight 5200 kg (11,464 lb) and maximum take-off weight 11000 kg (24,250 lb), maximum speed 855 km/h (531 mph) at 6000 m (19,685 ft), ceiling 11000 m (36,090 ft) and maximum range 1230 km (765 miles)
Ar 234C-3/N: proposed two-seat night-fighter with two forward-firing 20-mm MG 151/20 and two 30-mm MK 108 cannon, using FuG 218 Neptun V radar
Ar 234C-4: armed reconnaissance version with two cameras and four 20-mm MG 151/20 cannon
Ar 234C-5: 28th prototype had side-by-side seating for pilot and bomb-aimer as development aircraft for this proposed version
Ar 234C-6: proposed two-seat reconnaissance aircraft; 29th prototype in this configuration
Ar 234C-7: night-fighter similar to C-3/N, but with crew side-by-side and enhanced FuG 245 Bremen 0 centimetric radar
Ar 234C-8: proposed single-seat bomber with two 1080-kg (2,381-lb) thrust Jumo 004D engines
Ar 234D: 31st-40th prototypes, which were being built at the war's end, were to have been representatives of this version, with a powerplant of two

In service the Ar 234B proved very difficult to catch in the reconnaissance or bombing role, although only a handful reached operations.

1300-kg (2,865-lb) thrust Heinkel-Hirth HeS 011A engines
Ar 234D-1: proposed Heinkel-Hirth HeS 011A-powered reconnaissance aircraft
Ar 234D-2: proposed Heinkel-Hirth HeS 011A-powered bomber
Ar 234P: projected night-fighter series
Ar 234P-1: two-seater with four BMW 003A-1 engines; one 20-mm MG 151/20 and one 30-mm MK 108 cannon
Ar 234P-2: also a two-seater, with redesigned cockpit protected by 13-mm (0.51-in) armour plate
Ar 234P-3: HeS 011A-powered P-2, but with two each MG 151/20 and MK 108 cannon
Ar 234P-4: as P-3 but with Jumo 004D engines
Ar 234P-5: three-seat version with HeS 011A engines, one 20-mm MG 151/20 and four MK 108 cannon

Specification
Arado Ar 234B-2
Type: twin-turbojet bomber
Powerplant: two 890-kg (1,962-lb) thrust Junkers Jumo 004B turbojets
Performance: maximum speed 740 km/h (460 mph) at 6000 m (19,685 ft); climb to 6000 m (19,685 ft) in 17 minutes 30 seconds with 1500-kg (3,307-lb) bombload; service ceiling 10000 m (32,810 ft); maximum range 1630 km (1,013 miles)
Weights: empty 5200 kg (11,464 lb); maximum take-off 9850 kg (21,715 lb)
Dimensions: span 14.10 m (46 ft 3½ in); length 12.64 m (41 ft 5½ in); height 4.30 m (14 ft 1½ in); wing area 26.40 m² (284.18 sq ft)

Armstrong Whitworth Argosy
to
Armstrong Whitworth A.W.41 Albemarle

Armstrong Whitworth Argosy

When in 1925 Imperial Airways adopted a policy of using only multi-engined aircraft to replace the 13 aircraft of four different types operated by its predecessor companies, the **Armstrong Whitworth Argosy** was one of the three types ordered.

Armstrong Whitworth produced the Argosy, a large biplane with fixed tailskid landing gear and its first airliner, to a 1922 specification for a three-engined aircraft with a 805-km (500-mile) range. The first example (G-EBLF) flew in March 1926, following receipt of an order from Imperial Airways for three aircraft. The second Argosy (G-EBLO) flew on 18 June 1926, and was the first to be delivered to the airline, which received it the following month.

Imperial lost no time in introducing its new airliner into service, G-EBLO making its first revenue flight between Croydon and Paris on 16 July 1926. Traffic figures showed an immediate upsurge while costs per ton/mile dropped substantially, and on 1 May 1927 the luxury 'Silver Wing' service was inaugurated on this route.

On standard services the Argosy carried 20 passengers in the cabin, with the captain and first officer in an open cockpit just behind the nose engine. To allow room for a steward to serve the gourmet meals for which the 'Silver Wing' service was famous, it was necessary to remove two passenger seats.

The Argosy was later used on such routes as those to Basle, Brussels and Cologne from Croydon, and Imperial

Despite its ungainly appearance, the Argosy served economically and faithfully on both European and Empire routes. This is a Mk 1 of Imperial Airways.

ordered a further three, later increased to four, which began to enter service in 1929.

The aircraft of the second batch were designated **Argosy II**, having 313-kW (420-hp) Armstrong Siddeley Jaguar IVA engines in place of the original Jaguar IIIs, and all-up weight increased from 8165 kg (18,000 lb) to 8709 kg (19,200 lb); after delivery of the Mk IIs, the original three Mk Is were re-engined with Jaguar IVAs.

The Argosy opened the first Empire air mail link with India on 30 March 1929, carrying the mail to Basle, where it was transferred by train to Genoa and then by air, via various stops, to Karachi. The fleet was gradually whittled down: in June 1931 an Argosy was lost in a forced landing near Aswan; two months previously another had burned out in a crash at Croydon during crew training. Fortunately no-one was injured in either incident. However, an unexplained fire in

the air over Belgium, in March 1933, resulted in a crash in which the crew of three and all 12 passengers were killed. The last Argosy in service was the sixth aircraft, which was used for joy-riding by United Airways at Blackpool during the second half of 1935; taken over by British Airways the following January, it was retired in December 1936.

Variants

Argosy Mk I: designation of original batch, at first with 287-kW (385-hp) Jaguar IIIA direct-drive radials, but later re-engined with Jaguar IVA radials; data as for Mk II except range 531 km (330 miles); empty weight 5443 kg (12,000 lb) and maximum take-off weight 8165 kg (18,000 lb), span 27.64 m (90 ft 8 in), length 20.07 m (65 ft 10 in), height 6.05 m (19 ft 10 in) and wing area 175.22 m² (1,886 sq ft)
Argosy Mk II: designation of second batch, powered by three 313-kW (420-

hp) Jaguar IVA radials; this variant also featured some slight refinements in control by the use of servo tabs on the lower wings

Specification
Armstrong Whitworth Argosy Mk II
Type: 20-passenger commercial transport
Powerplant: three 313-kW (420-hp) Armstrong Siddeley Jaguar IVA geared radial piston engines
Performance: maximum speed 177 km/h (110 mph); cruising speed 145-153 km/h (90-95 mph); climb to 915 m (3,000 ft) in 4 minutes 30 seconds; range 837 km (520 miles)
Weights: empty 5484 kg (12,090 lb); maximum take-off 8709 kg (19,200 lb)
Dimensions: span 27.53 m (90 ft 4 in); length 20.42 m (67 ft 0 in); height 6.10 m (20 ft 0 in); wing area 174.01 m² (1,873 sq ft)

Armstrong Whitworth Siskin

Originating in the **Siddeley Deasy S.R.2 Siskin**, produced by Armstrong Whitworth's parent company in 1919, the **Armstrong Whitworth Siskin** in its developed form was to become a mainstay of the RAF's fighter force from the mid-1920s.

The S.R.2 was designed for a 224-kW (300-hp) radial engine then being developed at Farnborough, and designated R.A.F.8. Further development of the engine was passed to Siddeley Deasy, but because of that company's involvement with the Puma engine, the R.A.F.8 was put on one side, and the S.R.2 first flew with the A.B.C. Dragonfly of 239 kW (320 hp). Although the aircraft's performance was good, the engine was a failure, and the design subsequently adopted the 242-kW (325-hp) Armstrong Siddeley Jaguar, the first of three Siskins, now under the Armstrong Siddeley name, flying in March 1921.

The Air Ministry's new policy of ordering only all-metal aircraft forced Armstrong Siddeley to redesign the Siskin, and after several composite wood and metal aircraft had been built, the first all-

metal **Siskin III** for the RAF, ordered in 1920, flew in May 1923; a production order for a batch of three followed, the first flying 10 months later.

Sales tours in Europe resulted in an

Armstrong Whitworth Siskin IIIA of No 43 Squadron, RAF, in 1929. This was the most prolific of the models developed as all-metal fighters for the RAF. It also achieved substantial foreign sales.

order for 65 aircraft from Romania, the first being flown in October 1924, with six others following by the end of the year. However, the order was cancelled following the crash of a Romanian Siskin

in which the pilot was killed.

The first RAF Siskin IIIs went to No. 41 Squadron at Northolt in May 1924, while No. 111 Squadron replaced its Sopwith Snipes with Siskins the following month.

Total Siskin III production reached 465, including some two-seaters. Estonia, the RCAF and Armstrong Whitworth's flying school each had two two-seaters; and the RAF also had some supplied new as two-seaters, while others were converted later.

Most prolific of the series was the **Siskin IIIA**, the prototype of which, converted from the prototype Siskin III, flew in October 1925.

An Armstrong Siddeley Jaguar IV supercharged engine gave considerably superior performance, and 387 were subsequently built for the RAF, the total including 47 dual-control trainers. All but 135 were built under sub-contract: 84 from Bristol, 74 from Gloster, 52 from Vickers and 42 from Blackburn.

The first squadron to be re-equipped was No. 111, in September 1926, and 10 other squadrons used the Siskin IIIA until No. 56s were replaced by Bristol Bulldogs in October 1932. It can be said that the art of formation aerobatics in the RAF was introduced and refined by the Siskin squadrons, particularly No. 43, well-known for its tied-together routines at the Hendon displays.

Following its evaluation of two Siskin IIIs, the RCAF ordered 12 IIIAs which

were delivered between 1926 and 1931, some new and others from the RAF. The Siskins with No. 1 (Fighter) Squadron, RCAF, were replaced by Hawker Hurricanes in 1939, and struck off charge from storage in 1947.

Variants
S.R.2 Siskin: original aircraft built by the Siddeley Deasy Motor Car Co (total 3)
Siskin II: civil prototype of 1923, flown in single- and two-seat configurations (total 1)
Siskin III: all-metal production version; powerplant one 242-kW (325-hp) Armstrong Siddeley Jaguar III radial piston engine, maximum speed 216 km/h (134 mph) at 1980 m (6,500 ft), climb to 1980 m (6,500 ft) in 5 minutes, service ceiling 6250 m (20,500 ft), endurance 3 hours, empty weight 830 kg (1,830 lb) and maximum take-off weight 1241 kg (2,735 lb), span 10.08 m (33 ft 1 in), length 7.01 m (23 ft 0 in), height 2.95 m (9 ft 9 in) and wing area 27.22 m² (293 sq ft) (total 64, all for RAF)
Siskin IIIA: main production variant (total 348: 340 for RAF and 8 for RCAF)
Siskin IIIB: prototype with

supercharged Jaguar VIII engine with reduction gear; climb to 4570 m (15,000 ft) was achieved in 11 minutes 30 seconds, some 2 minutes better than could be managed by the Siskin IIIA; at this altitude the Siskin IIIB was some 32 km/h (20 mph) faster than the Siskin IIIA, despite a maximum take-off weight increased by 104 kg (230 lb); however, Martlesham Heath pilots criticised the Siskin IIIB's handling and the full-throttle endurance of only 1 hour was wholly inadequate (total 1)
Siskin IIIDC: two-seat dual-control trainer derivative; served with the Central Flying School, the RAF College, Cranwell and Nos 3 and 5 Flying Training Schools; other examples were used by most Siskin fighter squadrons (total 53: 47 for the RAF, 2 for the RCAF, 2 for the AST and 2 for Estonia)
Siskin IV: civil version, developed for the 1925 King's Cup Race; based on the Siskin V with shorter-span wings (total 1)
Siskin V: civil version, developed for Romania but sole examples used for racing after cancellation of the Romanian order; metal and wood construction, with a two-spar lower wing; F.L. Barnard won the 1925 King's

Cup Race in a Siskin V at a speed of more than 243 km/h (151 mph); powerplant one 287-kW (385-hp) Jaguar, maximum speed 249 km/h (155 mph) at sea level, service ceiling 7620 m (25,000 ft), maximum take-off weight 1107 kg (2,400 lb), span 8.64 m (28 ft 4 in), length 6.50 m (21 ft 4 in) and wing area 23.78 m² (256 sq ft) (total 2)

Specification
Armstrong Siddeley Siskin IIIA
Type: single-seat fighter
Powerplant: one 313/336-kW (420/4500-hp) Armstrong Siddeley Jaguar IV radial piston engine
Performance: maximum speed 251 km/h (156 mph) at sea level; climb to 3050 m (10,000 ft) in 6 minutes 20 seconds; service ceiling 8230 m (27,000 ft); endurance at full throttle 1 hour 12 minutes
Weights: empty 935 kg (2,061 lb); maximum take-off 1366 kg (3,012 lb)
Dimensions: span 10.11 m (33 ft 2 in); length 7.72 m (25 ft 4 in); height 3.10 m (10 ft 2 in); wing area 27.22 m² (293 sq ft)
Armament: two fixed 7.7-mm (0.303-in) synchronised Vickers machine-guns in the forward fuselage, plus up to four 9-kg (20-lb) bombs on underwing racks

Armstrong Whitworth A.W.27 Ensign

In 1934 the British government decided that all first-class mail for the Empire would in future be sent by air, and Imperial Airways therefore needed larger aircraft on its South African and Australian routes. Although most of the requirements were to be met by Short flying boats, a new four-engine landplane was needed for European and Eastern routes.

A specification was issued in May 1934 by the airline to Armstrong Whitworth and the result was the **A.W.27 Ensign**, the first of which was ordered in September 1934 at a price of £70,000; delivery was to take place within two years and in May 1935 a further 11 were ordered at £37,000 each. The price differential was accounted for by design and initial manufacture changes for the first aircraft. A final two were ordered in January 1937, raising overall Ensign production to 14 aircraft.

As Armstrong Whitworth was busy with Whitley bomber production at its Coventry factory, the airliners were assembled in the Air Service Training workshops at Hamble. Constant detail changes in the design and construction periods were required by Imperial Airways (a pattern subsequently repeated post-war by BOAC with certain airliners), with a result that the first Ensign was almost two years late, making its first flight from Hamble on 24 January 1938.

Subsequent tests at Martlesham Heath in June 1938 showed that the aircraft was underpowered and a number of minor problems also occurred, but a certificate of airworthiness was issued. The following month the first aircraft flew a Croydon to Paris trip, but proper services did not begin on the route until October. Just prior to Christmas 1938, three more aircraft had joined the first and left the UK as relief aircraft, carrying Christmas mail to Australia. All three became unserviceable, one at Athens, one at Karachi and one in India. The type was subsequently withdrawn and returned

to the manufacturers for performance and reliability upgrading. A modest increase in performance was achieved by fitting the more powerful Armstrong Siddeley Tiger IXC engines to the sixth aircraft, and in spite of problems the Ensign fleet served the airline's European routes; 11 had been delivered by the outbreak of war. Two configurations were in use: four aircraft (named *Eddystone*, *Ettrick*, *Empyrean* and *Elysian*) were the European type with seats for 40 passengers, while the other seven (*Ensign*, *Egeria*, *Elsinore*, *Euterpe*, *Explorer*, *Euryalus* and *Echo*), intended for the Empire routes, carried 27 passengers in three cabins or, alternatively, sleeping berths for 20. The twelfth A.W.27 (*Endymion*) received its certificate of airworthiness in October 1939, and the fleet was evacuated to Bristol's Whitchurch airport along with a number of other airliners. Camouflage was hastily applied, and the A.W.27s operated a twice-daily service between Heston and Paris (Le Bourget).

When BOAC was formed in November 1939 by the merger of British Airways and Imperial Airways, ownership of the A.W.27s passed to the new company. Wartime service soon began to take its toll, and *Elysian* was destroyed on the ground at Merville on 23 May 1940. Others followed, *Ettrick* being abandoned at Le Bourget (it was subsequently repaired and used by the Germans with Daimler-Benz engines) and *Endymion* destroyed at Whitchurch in an air raid in November 1940.

A final two A.W.27s, on which construction had been halted, were subsequently completed in 1941. Named *Everest* and *Enterprise*, they were fitted with Wright Cyclone GR-1820 engines of 708 kW (950 hp) each, providing an extra 298 kW (400 hp) in all compared with the earlier Tigers, and in this form the type was designated **A.W.27 Ensign 2**. The remaining eight Mk 1s were also re-engined, and with the extra power were

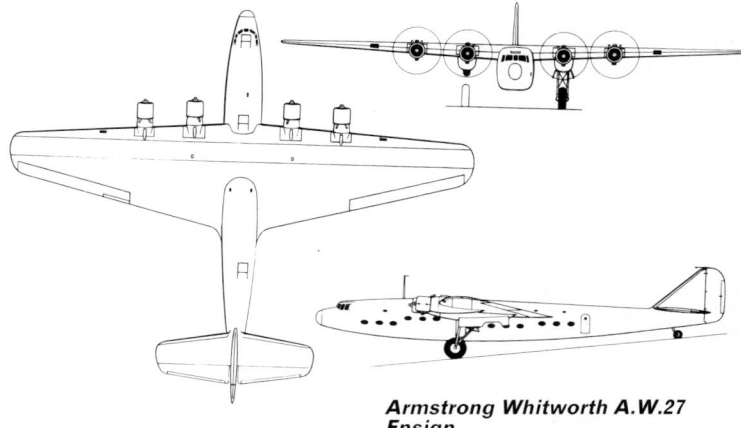

Armstrong Whitworth A.W.27 Ensign.

Although a useful and modern-looking airliner, the Ensign was hampered by a lack of power, especially in tropical conditions.

considered suitable for hot climates. Used between West and East Africa and Egypt, the A.W.27s were hard pushed, and since their American engines were out of production they were difficult to maintain.

In the face of mounting problems it was decided to bring the survivors home, and seven (*Egeria*, *Elsinore*, *Explorer*, *Eddystone*, *Empyrean*, *Echo* and *Everest*) were scrapped at Hamble in 1947. *Enterprise* had been abandoned in West Africa during 1942, was salvaged by the Vichy French and, like *Ettrick*, was eventually re-engined and flown by the Germans. The original *Ensign* had been damaged at Lagos in 1943 and was

scrapped in 1945, while *Euterpe* and *Euryalus*, damaged at Almaza and Lympne respectively, were cannibalised for spares.

Eddystone was the last flying A.W.27, returning from Cairo to Hurn in June 1946.

Variants
A.W.27 Ensign Mk 1: retrospective designation of the initial 12 aircraft fitted with Armstrong Siddeley Tiger radials
A.W.27 Ensign Mk 2: designation of the last two aircraft, built with four 707-kW (950-hp) Wright Cyclone GR-1820-G102A radial piston engines;

eight Mk 1 aircraft were subsequently upgraded to Mk 2 standard; maximum speed 338 km/h (210 mph), cruising speed 290 km/h (180 mph), service ceiling 7315 m (24,000 ft), range 2205 km (1,370 miles), empty weight 16595 kg (36,586 lb) and maximum take-off weight 25174 kg (55,500 lb)

Specification
Armstrong Whitworth A.W.27 Ensign Mk 1
Type: 40-seat commercial transport
Powerplant: four 634-kW (850-hp)

Armstrong Siddeley Tiger IXC radial piston engines
Performance: maximum speed 330 km/h (205 mph) at 2135 m (7,000 ft); maximum cruising speed 274 km/h (170 mph) at 2135 m (7,000 ft); service ceiling 5485 m (18,000 ft); range

with maximum fuel 1384 km (860 miles)
Weights: empty 14932 kg (32,920 lb); maximum take-off 2226 kg (49,000 lb)
Dimensions: span 37.49 m (123 ft 0 in); length 34.75 m (114 ft 0 in); height 7.01 m (23 ft 0 in); wing area 227.61 m² (2,450 sq ft)

Armstrong Whitworth A.W.38 Whitley

Designed to Air Ministry Specification B.3/34, which was circulated in July 1934, the **Armstrong Whitworth A.W.38 Whitley** was the most extensively built of the company's designs, production reaching a total of 1,814 aircraft. It also marked a departure from Armstrong Whitworth's traditional steel-tube construction, the Whitley's fuselage being a light alloy monocoque structure.

Production was authorised while the aircraft was still in the design stage, an order for 80 aircraft being placed in August 1935. Alan Campbell-Orde flew the first prototype at Whitley Abbey on 17 March 1936, the machine's two Armstrong Siddeley Tiger X engines turning the then-new three blade variable-pitch de Havilland propellers. A second prototype built to Specification B.21/35 had the more powerful Tiger XI engines and was flown by Charles Turner Hughes on 24 February 1937.

Trials at the Aircraft and Armament Experimental Establishment at Martlesham Heath were undertaken in the autumn of 1936, and the first production **Whitley Mk I**s were delivered early in 1937, including the second aircraft which was flown to RAF Dishforth on 9 March for No. 10 Squadron. Thirty-four Mk Is were built before the **Whitley Mk II** was introduced. This Mark had Tiger VIII engines with two-speed superchargers, the first fitted to an RAF aircraft; 46 Whitley Mk IIs completed the initial order for 80.

Mk I and Mk II Whitleys had Armstrong Whitworth manually-operated nose and tail turrets, each with a 7.7-mm (0.303-in) Vickers machine-gun, but in the **Whitley Mk III** the nose turret was replaced by a power-operated Nash and Thompson turret, and a retractable ventral turret with two 0.303-in Brownings was added. The 80 Whitley IIIs also had modified bomb bays to accommodate larger bombs.

By far the most numerous of the Whitley variants were those with Rolls-Royce

engines. A Whitley I was fitted with Merlin IIs and test-flown at Hucknall on 11 February 1938, although engine failure prematurely concluded the second flight. The programme was quickly resumed, however, and during April and May the aircraft carried out trials at Martlesham Heath.

Merlin IVs of 768 kW (1,030 hp) were installed in production **Whitley IV**s, the first of which flew on 5 April 1939. Other changes incorporated in this version included a power-operated Nash and Thompson tail turret with four 0.303-in Browning guns. A transparent panel was added in the lower nose to improve the view for the bomb-aimer, and two additional wing tanks were fitted to bring total capacity to 3205 litres (705 Imperial gallons). Production totalled 33, together with seven **IVA**s which had 854-kW (1,145-hp) Merlin X engines.

The same engines were retained for the **Whitley V**, which incorporated a number of improvements. The most noticeable of these were modified fins with straight leading edges and an extension of 0.38 m (1 ft 3 in) to the rear fuselage to provide a wider field of fire for the rear gunner. Rubber de-icer boots were fitted to the wing leading edges, and fuel capacity was increased to 3805 litres (837 Imperial gallons), or 4405 litres (969 Imperial gallons) if extra tanks were carried in the bomb bay. Production totalled 1,466 aircraft.

The **Whitley VI** was a projected version with Pratt & Whitney engines, studied as an insurance against short supply of Merlins. It was not built, however, and the ultimate production Whitley was the **Mk VII** which was essentially a Mk V with auxiliary fuel tanks in the bomb bay and in the rear fuselage to bring the total capacity to 5001 litres (1,100 Imperial gallons), increasing the range to 2701 km (2,300 miles) for maritime patrol duties. Externally the Mk VIIIs could be distinguished by the dorsal radar aerials of the ASV Mk II air-to-surface radar. Production reached 146, and

some Mk Vs were converted to the later standard.

As noted above, No. 10 Squadron at RAF Dishforth was the first to equip with the Whitley, which replaced the Handley Page Heyford in March 1937. Nos. 51 and 58 Squadrons at RAF Leconfield soon followed and, during the night of 3 September 1939, 10 Whitley IIIs from these two squadrons flew a leaflet raid over Bremen, Hamburg and the Ruhr. Just under a month later, during the night of 1 October, No. 10 Squadron flew a similar mission over Berlin. The first bombs were dropped on Berlin during the night of 25 August 1940, the attacking squadrons including Nos. 51 and 78 with Whitleys. To mark the entry of the Italians into the war, 36 Whitleys drawn from Nos. 10, 51, 58, 77 and 102 Squadrons were tasked to raid Genoa and Turin during the night of 11 June 1940, although only 13 actually reached their targets; weather and engine troubles taking their toll.

The Whitley was retired from Bomber Command in April 1942, the last operation being flown against Ostend during the night of 29 April, although some aircraft from operational training units were flown in the '1,000 Bomber' raid on Cologne on the night of 30 May 1942.

Coastal Command's association with the Whitley began in September 1939 when No. 58 Squadron was transferred to Boscombe Down to operate anti-submarine patrols over the English Channel. This lasted until February 1940, when the unit returned to Bomber Command, but during 1942 it took up patrol duties once again, flying over the Western Approaches from St Eval and Stornoway. Other units similarly occupied at that time included Nos 51 and 77 Squadrons, the latter operating in the Bay of Biscay area.

Mk V Whitleys replaced the Avro Ansons of No. 502 Squadron at RAF Aldergrove in the autumn of 1940 and a second Coastal Command Whitley unit, No. 612 Squadron, formed in May 1941.

The Mk Vs were replaced by the ASV Mk II-equipped Whitley VII, and an aircraft of No. 502 Squadron sank the type's first German submarine when it attacked *U-205* in the Bay of Biscay on 30 November 1941.

Whitleys were also used at No. 1 Parachute Training School at Ringway, Manchester, and were adapted for use as glider tugs, becoming attached to No. 21 Glider Conversion Unit at Brize Norton for the training of tug pilots. The paratroop raid on the German radar site at Bruneval used Whitleys of No. 51 Squadron, and the aircraft of special duty units at RAF Tempsford (Nos 138 and 161 Squadrons) flew numerous sorties, dropping agents into occupied territory and supplying Resistance groups with arms and equipment. Fifteen Whitley Vs were handed over to BOAC in May 1942 and, stripped of armament, but with additional fuel tanks in the bomb bays, flew regularly from Gibraltar to Malta carrying supplies for the beleaguered island.

Specification
Type: five-seat long-range night-bomber
Powerplant: (Mk V) two 854-kW (1,145-hp) Rolls-Royce Merlin X inline piston engines
Performance: maximum speed 370 km/h (230 mph) at 5000 m (16,400 ft); cruising speed 338 km/h (210 mph) at 4570 m (15,000 ft); service ceiling 7925 m (26,000 ft); range 2414 km (1,500 miles)
Weights: empty 8777 kg (19,350 lb); maximum take-off 15195 kg (33,500 lb)
Dimensions: span 25.60 m (84 ft 0 in); length 21.49 m (70 ft 6 in); height 4.57 m (15 ft 0 in); wing area 105.63 m² (1,137 sq ft)
Armament: four 7.7-mm (0.303-in) machine-guns in powered tail turret plus and one similar gun in nose turret; up to 3175 kg (7,000 lb) of bombs

Armstrong Whitworth Whitley Mk I of No. 10 Sqn, RAF. The unit was based at Dishforth during 1937.

This Whitley Mk V was converted to serve as a passenger carrier with British Overseas Airways Corporation.

Armstrong Whitworth
A.W.41 Albemarle

The Albemarle originated as a Bristol Aeroplane Company design to meet Air Ministry Specification P.9/38 for a twin-engined bomber, being allocated the company identification Type 155. With a change in the official specification, however, design responsibility was transferred to Armstrong Whitworth, under a team led by John Lloyd who was set the difficult task of taking over another company's creation and adapting it to meet Specification B.18/38 for a reconnaissance bomber. This duly became identified as the **Armstrong Whitworth A.W.41**, given the name Albemarle, which in detail and construction was very different from the original Bristol concept.

Designed for mixed composite steel and wood construction, the prototype flew in 1939, but was destroyed in a crash before the flight of the second prototype on 20 March 1940. The Albemarle's form of structure enabled wide use of sub-contracting, even to small companies outside the aircraft industry (one source mentions almost 1,000 sub-contractors), and an additional bonus came from conservation of light alloy and other strategic materials; the tricycle landing gear was of Lockheed design.

The first 32 aircraft were built as bombers, although not used as such, and there was considerable delay in establishing production lines. The first three production Albemarles left the factory in December 1941, by which time the decision had been made to adapt the aircraft as a glider tug and airborne forces transport.

Deliveries to the RAF began in January 1943 when No. 295 Squadron received its first aircraft; the type was blooded with Nos 296 and 297 Squadrons, part of No. 38 Wing operating from North Africa, in the invasion of Sicily in July 1943. On D-Day (6 June 1944) six No. 295 Squadron Albemarles, operating from Harwell, served as pathfinders for the 6th Airborne Division, dropping paratroops over Normandy.

In the glider tug role, four squadrons of Albemarles were used to tow Airspeed Horsas to France in support of ground operations, while in September 1944 two of No. 38 Group's squadrons participated in the ill-fated Arnhem operation, towing gliders carrying troops of the 1st Airborne Division.

Production of the Albemarle, apart from the prototypes, was undertaken by A.W. Hawksley Ltd, part of the Hawker Siddeley Group; production came to an end in December 1944 when 600 Albemarles had been built. Original orders had covered 1,080, but 478 from the second production batch were cancelled.

Deliveries to the RAF consisted of 380

The Albemarle was originally developed as a bomber, but only the first few aircraft were completed as such. Most were delivered for transport duties.

transport versions, (99 **Mk I**, 99 **Mk II**, 49 **Mk V** and 133 **Mk VI**) and 186 glider tugs (69 Mk I and 117 Mk VI). Additional to these were the original 32 bombers which were subsequently converted to transports. Ten Albemarles were delivered to the Russian air force from RAF stocks and were used as transports.

All Albemarles used the 1186-kW (1,590-hp) Bristol Hercules XI engine, apart from a single **Mk IV** prototype with Wright Double Cyclones, and differences in the marks were primarily in equipment. The original bomber versions were fitted with a four-gun Boulton Paul dorsal turret, but weight considerations dictated the removal of this in the transports and glider tugs which, instead, mounted twin Vickers 'K' hand-operated guns.

While the Albemarle was not a particularly significant aircraft, it did perform a useful role, releasing other types for more vital tasks. In addition, because of its method of construction and the materials used, production did not unduly disturb the flow of more important types at a time when these were vital to the UK's survival.

Specification
Type: four-seat transport and glider tug
Powerplant: two 1186-kW (1,590-hp)

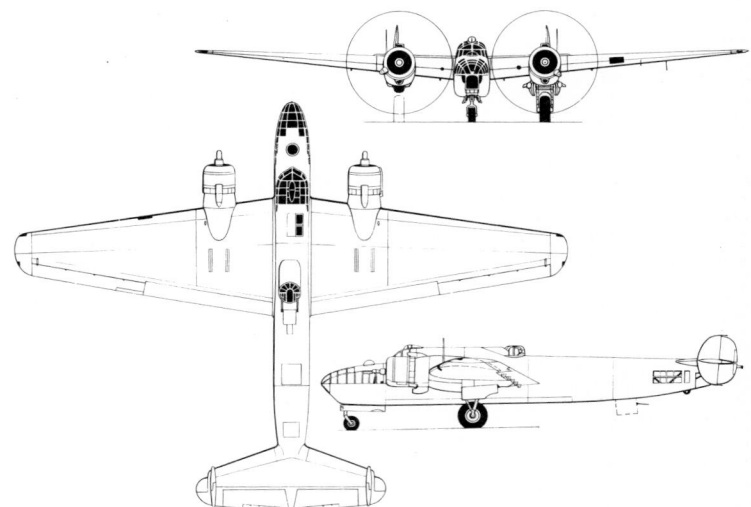

Armstrong Whitworth Albemarle Mk V.

Bristol Hercules XI radial piston engines
Performance: (glider tug) maximum speed 426 km/h (265 mph) at 3200 m (10,500 ft); cruising speed 274 km/h (170 mph); service ceiling 5485 m (18,000 ft); range 2092 km (1,300 miles)
Weight: maximum take-off 10251 kg (22,600 lb)

Dimensions: span 23.47 m (77 ft 0 in); length 18.26 m (59 ft 11 in); height 4.75 m (15 ft 7 in); wing area 74.65 m² (803.5 sq ft)
Armament: (glider tug and transport) twin 7.7-mm (0.303-in) Vickers 'K' machine-guns in dorsal position

Albemarle Mk V of No. 297 Sqn, RAF in July 1944. The squadron was based at Brize Norton for transport and glider tug duties, these tasks being of particular value during the Normandy landings.

Armstrong Whitworth Argosy
to
Atlas C4M Kudu

Armstrong Whitworth Argosy

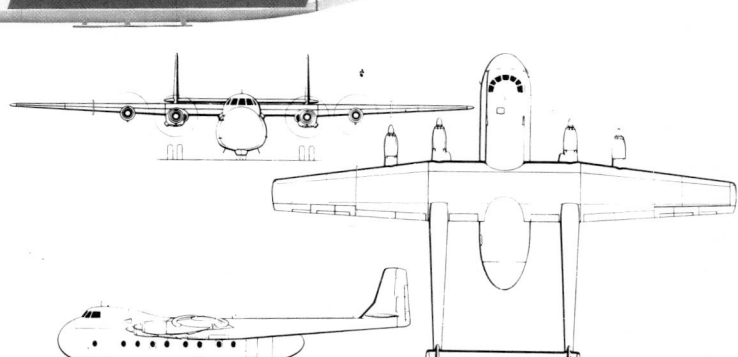

Armstrong Whitworth A.W.650 Argosy 100 of Air Bridge Carriers.

A British specification, issued in 1955 by the Air Ministry and calling for a medium-range freighter for military and civil application, was the first step towards the **AW.650 Argosy**. In that year Armstrong Whitworth began work on a design project with twin booms and two turboprops, but by 1956 the poor chances of getting military orders dictated that emphasis should be placed on a civil version.

In September the company decided to proceed with a revised design as a private venture. Designated AW.650, the new aircraft had a twin-boom, four-turboprop layout and was initially named Freightliner, but this was changed to Argosy in July 1958. The designation became **HS.650**, reflecting Armstrong Whitworth's membership of the Hawker Siddeley Group.

The first Argosy flew at Bitteswell on 8 January 1959, less than two years after the drawings had been issued, and before the end of 1959 a further five had flown. The first four aircraft participated in the certification programme and a restricted certificate of airworthiness was issued in May 1959; full British and US certification being achieved in December 1960. The fourth aircraft was the first to appear in public – at the 1959 Paris Air Show, while the following year this and the fifth Argosy appeared at the Farnborough Show.

European demonstration tours in October 1959, as a combined passenger/freighter priced fairly at £460,000, attracted interest but no orders. Riddle Airlines of Miami had been the first customer, ordering four (later increased to seven) Argosies in February 1959 to be used on bulky freight-carrying contracts for the US Air Force. On expiration of this contract, the seven Argosies were operated in the US by Capitol Airlines and Zantop Air Transport.

British European Airways took delivery of the first of three **Argosy 102**s in 1961 and operated its initial freight services in December of that year, replacing Douglas DC-3s and Avro Yorks. Ten Argosy Series 100 aircraft were built and all except one, the third aircraft, eventually found their way to USA. Operated by the companies mentioned above, at least four found their way back to the UK to operate with Sagittair, and later ABC, from East Midlands Airport. A batch of 56 **AW.660** aircraft, based on the civil Argosy 100, was built for the RAF, which designated the type as Argosy C.Mk 1.

The final Argosy variant was the **Series 222**, the first of which flew in March 1964. An enlarged freight hold and wider doors permitted the carriage of six 2.74-m (108-in) cargo pallets – the standard size then in use on international jets. A redesigned wing saved 181 kg

(400 lb) in weight and range was increased. With these improvements, BEA agreed to trade in its Series 102s in part-exchange for five 222s; these were delivered between January 1965 and June 1966, and freight services were increased in frequency. Loss of one aircraft at Milan, in July 1965, caused BEA to buy the last of seven production aircraft (the first remained with the manufacturers until being withdrawn from use in November 1965), but when another Argosy was burned out on the ground, in December 1967, no further replacement was made.

BEA's Argosy operations always lost money, and the corporation flew its last service with the type in April 1970. All four were subsequently sold to Transair at Winnipeg; later, two of these went to Australian freight operator IPEC, while the other two were sold to Safe Air in New Zealand. A few of the RAF aircraft eventually found their way to civil operators who were already using the Argosy, but one went to Philippine Air Lines.

Armstrong Whitworth A.W.650 Argosy 222.

Specification
Armstrong Whitworth AW.650 Argosy Series 100
Type: four-engine transport aircraft
Powerplant: four 1506-kW (2,020-shp) Rolls-Royce Dart 526 turboprops
Performance: average cruising speed 451 km/h (280 mph); service ceiling 6100 m (20,000 ft); range 3219 km (2,000 miles)
Weights: empty 20865 kg (46,000 lb); maximum take-off 39916 kg (88,000 lb)
Dimensions: span 35.05 m (115 ft 0 in); length 26.44 m (86 ft 9 in); height 8.23 m (27 ft 0 in); wing area 135.45 m² (1,458 sq ft)

One of the very few Argosy operators left is IPEC, which flies three on freight services in Australia.

Armstrong Whitworth F.K.8

As a replacement for the B.E.2c, Koolhoven designed the **Armstrong Whitworth F.K.8**, an aircraft of altogether more sturdy appearance, with a considerably larger fuselage to cope with the specialist equipment required for the type's army co-operation role. Produced at the same time as the Royal Aircraft Factory's R.E.8, which was intended for the same task, the F.K.8 was generally considerably superior, but no doubt politics were responsible for the much larger orders for the government-establishment machine.

First flown in May 1916, the F.K.8 was sent to the Central Flying School at Upavon for testing where, although its handling was satisfactory, it fell somewhat short of the specified performance. Nevertheless, substantial orders were placed. Armstrong Whitworth received contracts beginning in August 1916 for more than 700, while another 950 were built by Angus Sanderson in Newcastle. Production at the Armstrong Whitworth factory was between 80 and 100 F.K.8s per month by the end of 1917, and this continued until July 1918, when the com-

pany received contracts for Bristol Fighter production and handed over F.K.8 responsibility to Sanderson.

The F.K.8 served with several squadrons in France, the first to become fully equipped being No. 35, while other squadrons served overseas. Eight F.K.8s were civil-registered after the war, the two most noteworthy being used in Australia by Queensland and Northern Territory Aerial Services Ltd (later QANTAS), where they were part of a mixed fleet of hire aircraft.

Armstrong Whitworth F.K.8, one of a run of 200 aircraft ordered from Angus Sanderson & Co., Newcastle-upon-Tyne. Sandersons were the largest builder of the type.

Variants
Examples were flown with 112-kW (150-hp) Lorraine Dietrich and 112-kW (150-hp) R.A.F. 4A inline piston engines

Specification
Type: two-seat general-purpose aircraft
Powerplant: one 119-kW (160-hp) Beardmore inline piston engine
Performance: maximum speed 153 km/h (95 mph) at sea level; climb to

1980 m (6,500 ft) in 19 minutes; service ceiling 3960 m (13,000 ft); endurance three hours
Weights: empty 869 kg (1,916 lb); maximum take-off 1275 kg (2,811 lb)
Dimensions: span 13.26 m (43 ft 6 in); length 9.58 m (31 ft 5 in); height 3.33 m (10 ft 11 in); wing area 50.17 m² (540 sq ft)
Armament: one fixed 7.7-mm (0.303-in) synchronised Vickers machine-gun and one flexible 7.7-mm (0.303-in) Lewis machine-gun in the rear cockpit

---

Arrow Active

Arrow Aircraft Ltd, established in Leeds, Yorkshire, was primarily a manufacturer of aircraft components, but in 1931 built a single example of a single-seat aerobatic biplane which had been designed largely by A. C. Thornton. Of conventional biplane configuration, with a cut-out in the trailing edge of the upper wing and I-section interplane struts, this **Arrow Active I** had tailskid landing gear with divided axle main units. Powerplant comprised a Cirrus Hermes IIB inline engine. Although the manufacturer had hopes that there might be some military interest in the aircraft, this failed to materialise. The Active was used for sporting activities until destroyed by an accident in late 1935.

Specification
Arrow Active I
Type: single-seat aerobatic biplane
Powerplant: one 86-kW (115-hp) Cirrus Hermes IIB inline piston engine
Performance: maximum speed 225 km/h (140 mph); cruising speed 210 km/h (125 mph)
Weights: empty 387 kg (853 lb); maximum take-off 549 kg (1,210 lb)
Dimensions: span 7.32 m (24 ft 0 in); length 5.66 m (18 ft 7 in)

A favourite at air shows for many years, the sole Arrow Active II flew with the Tiger Club. Its small wings and powerful engine gave it fighter-like performance.

Variants
Arrow Active II: designation of one aircraft (G-ABVE), generally similar to that described above; it differed by introducing centre-section struts and

by the installation of an 89-kW (120-hp) de Havilland Gipsy III engine; rebuilt in 1957, it was then given a 108-kW (145-hp) de Havilland Gipsy Major, and in 1989 was still on the British register

Atlas C4M Kudu

Atlas Aircraft Corporation is the only South African manufacturer of military aircraft for the South African air force, and is best known for its production of single- and two-seat versions of the Italian Aermacchi M.B.326 under the name Impala. It has also built subassemblies for the Dassault Mirage F1 strike fighters ordered and operated by the SAAF. Atlas insists that it developed the **C4M Kudu** entirely in South Africa, but there is a clear design connection with an earlier Italian type, the Aeritalia/Aermacchi AM-3C, of which 40 were built for the SAAF for use on observation and light close-support duties, and the Kudu's Avco Lycoming engine is licence-built in Italy.

The Kudu, as the military C4M is known, is intended primarily as a general-purpose transport, having less cockpit glazing than the AM.3C, and accommodates a crew of two, and four to six troops or passengers in the cabin. Freight (up to a maximum load of 560 kg/1,235 lb) can be carried instead of passengers, loading being via a double door on the port side, and there is a sliding door for parachute-jumping on the starboard side. Other military applica-

tions include supply dropping and aerial survey, there being a 0.35 m² (3.77 sq ft) trap-door in the fuselage floor which can be used as a camera opening or for air-dropping; and doubtless the Kudu is also capable of use as an aeromedical transport. The first (civil) prototype of the C4M made its initial flight on 16 February 1974, followed by a military Kudu prototype on 18 June 1975. South African reticence where military matters are concerned makes genuine information on production difficult to come by, but it seems probable that more than 40 Kudus had been built when production ended in the early 1980s.

Specification
Type: six/eight-seat STOL utility light transport
Powerplant: one 340-hp Avco Lycoming GSO-480-B1B3 flat-six piston engine
Performance: maximum speed at 2440 m (8,000 ft) 259 km/h (161 mph); maximum cruising speed at 3050 m (10,000 ft) 233 km/h (145 mph); maximum rate of climb at sea level 244 m (800 ft) per minute; service ceiling 4270 m (14,000 ft); range with 400-kg (882-lb) payload (including

reserves) 740 km (460 miles); range with maximum fuel (including reserves) 1297 km (806 miles)
Weights: empty 1230 kg (2,711 lb); maximum take-off 2040 kg (4.497 lb)
Dimensions: span 13.075 m (42 ft 10¾ in); length 9.31 m (30 ft 6½ in); height 3.66 m (12 ft 0 in); wing area 20.97 m² (225.7 sq ft)

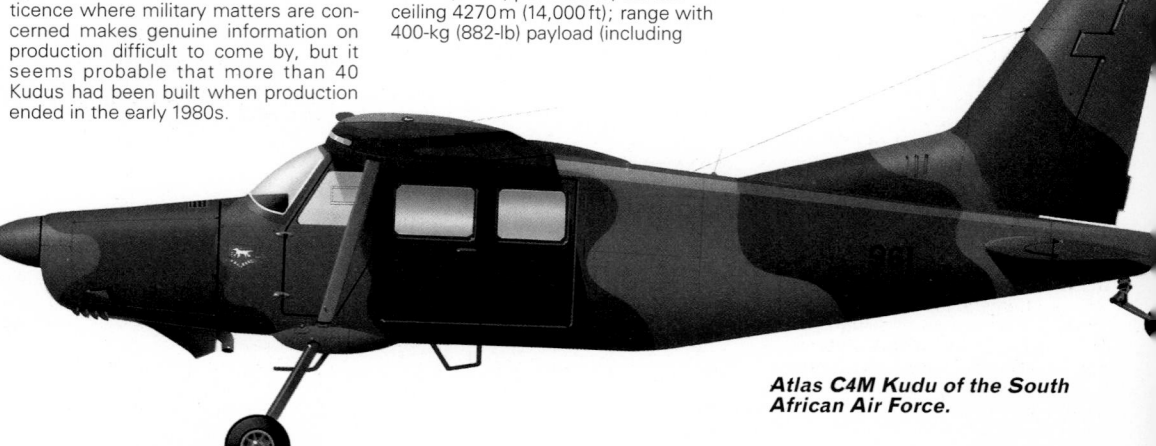

Atlas C4M Kudu of the South African Air Force.

Auster I-V Series

In 1936 the Taylorcraft Aviation Company was formed in the USA to design and manufacture light planes for private use. Most successful of the pre-war aircraft to emanate from this company were designated Models B, C, and D, and in November 1938 Taylorcraft Aeroplanes (England) Ltd was established at Thurmaston, Leicestershire, to build these aircraft under licence.

Six American-built Model As were imported into Britain, followed by one Model B, and these were typical of the aircraft to be built by the new company at Thurmaston. Of braced high-wing monoplane configuration, with a fabric-covered wing of composite wood and metal construction, the aircraft featured a fuselage and tail unit that were of welded steel tube with fabric covering. Accommodation within the enclosed cabin was for two persons, seated side by side, and landing gear was of basic non-retractable tailwheel type, with main unit shock-absorption by rubber bungee. Powerplant of the imported Model As consisted of one 30-kW (40-hp) Continental A-40 flat-four engine, and the Model B differed by having a 37-kW (50-hp) A-50 engine from the same manufacturer.

The British-built equivalent to the Model A was designated originally Model C, but this was soon to be redesignated **Auster Plus C**, reflecting the improved performance resulting from installation of a 41-kW (55-hp) Lycoming O-145-A2 engine. Including the prototype (G-AFNW), 23 Plus Cs were built. With a 67-kW (90-hp) Cirrus Minor 1 engine, the designation changed to **Plus D**, and nine civil aircraft were completed as such before the outbreak of World War II.

Of the 32 British-built aircraft mentioned above, 20 of the Plus Cs and four of the Plus Ds were impressed for service with the RAF. The Plus Cs, re-engined with the Cirrus Minor for RAF use, became redesignated **Plus C.2**. Most of these aircraft were used by No. 651 Squadron for evaluation of their suit-

ability for deployment in AOP and communications roles. This led to an initial order for 100 generally similar aircraft for military use under the designation **Auster I**.

Other than provision of split trailing-edge flaps to improve short-field performance, Austers were to change little throughout the war. During this time more than 1,600 were built for service use under the designations Auster I, III, IV and V – the Auster I entering service with No. 654 Squadron in August 1942. Only two **Auster II**s, with 97-kW (130-hp) Lycoming O-290 engines, were built because of a shortage of the American powerplant. This led to the **Auster III**, basically identical to the Auster I, but with a 97-kW (130-hp) Gipsy Major I engine. The 470 Auster IIIs were followed by 254 **Auster IV**s, which reverted to the Lycoming engine, and introduced a slightly larger cabin to provide space for a third seat. Major production version was the **Auster V**, of which approximately 800 were built, and this differed from the Auster IV by introducing blind-flying instrumentation.

At the height of their utilisation, Austers equipped Nos 652, 653, 657, 658, 659, 660, 661, 662, 664 and 665 Squadrons of the 2nd Tactical Air Force, and Nos 651, 654, 655, 656, 663, 666, 671, 672, and 673 Squadrons of the Desert Air Force. They were also used in small numbers by associated Canadian and Dutch squadrons. Their initial deployment in an operational role was during the invasion of Algeria, and they were to prove an indispensible tool in the Sicilian and Italian campaigns. Just three weeks after D-Day, these unarmed lightplanes were in the forefront of the action as the Allied armies advanced into France. Flown by British Army officers, who had been trained by the RAF for service with the AOP squadrons, the Austers not only spotted for the artillery, but a suitably equipped version also provided photographic evidence of the effectiveness of the artillery action.

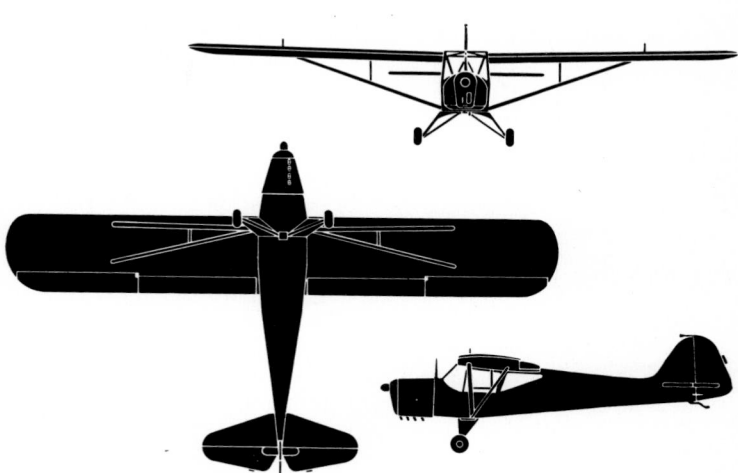

British Taylorcraft Suster I.

The Auster IV (illustrated) differed only in detail from the Auster V.

Specification
Type: light liaison/observation aircraft
Powerplant: (Auster V) one 97-kW (130-hp) Lycoming O-290-3 flat-four piston engine
Performance: maximum speed 209 km/h (130 mph) at sea level; cruising speed 180 km/h (112 mph);
normal range 402 km (250 miles)
Weights: empty 499 kg (1,100 lb); maximum take-off 839 kg (1,850 lb)
Dimensions: span 10.97 m (36 ft 0 in); length 6.83 m (22 ft 5 in); height 2.44 m (8 ft 0 in); wing area 15.51 m² (167.0 sq ft)
Armament: none

Auster A.O.P.6

The use of aircraft as air observation posts for the army had its origins in World War I, and in World War II a considerable number of American light aircraft types were pressed into service for this purpose. In the UK, developments of the pre-war US Taylorcraft design had resulted in a series of aircraft from that company which was re-named Auster Aircraft in 1946. Last of the type to serve was the Auster 5 with a 97-kW (130-hp) Avco Lycoming engine.

As the end of the war approached, it was decided to build a replacement for the Auster 5 using a British engine, and the **Auster A.O.P.6** appeared in 1945, with a strengthened rear fuselage, increased all-up weight and more power. The engine was a 108-kW (145-hp) de Havilland Gipsy Major 7, and lengthened landing gear struts were necessary to provide clearance for the larger-diameter

propeller. A significant difference in appearance resulted from the installation of external non-retractable aerofoil flaps. Of metal construction, these were mounted behind the wing to enhance the aircraft's take-off performance.

An initial production run of 296 A.O.P.6s was completed in 1949 but further production began in 1952 and the total built by the end of the run was around 400. Of these, 22 ex-British aircraft were delivered to the Belgian air force and two were transferred to the Royal Hong Kong Auxiliary Air Force, while new aircraft were supplied to the Royal Canadian Air Force (36), South African Air Force (5) and to the Arab Legion (4).

In his book *Soldiers in the Air*, Brigadier Peter Mead compared the A.O.P.6 with the Auster 5. He emphasised that it had no artificial horizon; that the aircraft, and therefore its controls, were heavier and clumsier, and that it had an inferior take-off performance. Indeed, the fact that its take-off run was noticeably longer than its landing run, Mead insisted, instilled doubts and apprehension in many pilots when lining up for

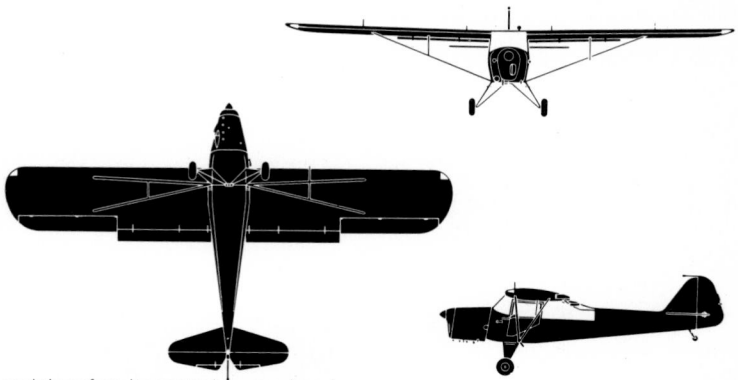

The A.O.P.6 was a follow-on to the Auster 5 in the observation role, serving briefly post-war until replaced by the more capable and better-performing A.O.P.9.

take-off from a new, small field.

However, the A.O.P.6 served for a number of years until it began to be replaced by the Auster A.O.P.9 in 1955, and as surplus A.O.P.6s began to appear, they were snapped up for conversion for civil use as the **Auster Mk 6A** and, later, the **Beagle Terrier**.

Variants
Auster Mk 6A Tugmaster: civil conversion intended primarily as a glider-tug, and powered by the 108-kW (145-hp) Gipsy Major 10 inline; a number converted for use in the UK, Finland and Sweden, while straightforward civil conversions were effected on at least 22 Canadian, 12 Belgian and two South African aircraft;

data include maximum speed 195 km/h (121 mph), cruising speed 169 km/h (105 mph), empty weight 671 kg (1,480 lb) and maximum take-off weight 998 kg (2,200 lb)
Auster Mk 6B/Beagle Terrier 1 and 2: at least 60 airframes converted by Beagle Aircraft into Terrier 1s and 2s; first production aircraft flew on 25 April 1962; powerplant as for Mk 6A Tugmaster; conversion otherwise included complete airframe and engine overhaul, new tail surfaces and ailerons, upholstering and soundproofing of the cabin; data include maximum speed 192 km/h (119 mph) at sea level, maximum cruising speed 172 km/h (107 mph) at 760 m (2,500 ft), range 451 km (280

miles), empty weight 726 kg (1,600 lb) and maximum take-off weight 1066 kg (2,350 lb)
Auster S: private-venture development of A.O.P.6 with a 134-kW (180-hp) Blackburn Cirrus Bombardier inline piston engine, retractable split trailing-edge flaps, bulletproof fuel tank and extra large mainwheels and tyres for soft-ground operation; one prototype only, written off in September 1955
Auster T.7: dual-control version of the A.O.P.6, quickly convertible to A.O.P. standard; over 80 built after conversion of the A.O.P.6 prototype as the T.7 prototype; overseas customers included RCAF (6), Burmese air force (3) and Arab Legion (2)

Specification
Auster A.O.P.6
Type: two-seat air observation post aircraft
Powerplant: one 108-kW (145-hp) de Havilland Gipsy Major 7 inline piston engine
Performance: maximum speed 200 km/h (124 mph) at 305 m (1,000 ft); cruising speed 174 km/h (108 mph); service ceiling 4265 m (14,000 ft); range 507 km (315 miles)
Weights: empty 641 kg (1,413 lb); maximum take-off 980 kg (2,160 lb)
Dimensions: span 10.97 m (36 ft 0 in); length 7.24 m (23 ft 9 in); height 2.55 m (8 ft 4½ in); wing area 17.09 m² (184 sq ft)

Auster A.O.P.9

A successor to the Auster 6 was required in the British Army's A.O.P. squadrons in the mid-1950s, and a completely new design was advanced as the **Auster A.O.P.9**. Of similar high-wing configuration to its predecessor, the A.O.P.9 was of slightly lower loaded weight, but had a considerably more powerful engine, the 134-kW (180-hp) Blackburn Cirrus Bombardier, giving greatly improved take-off and landing performance. It could operate from ploughed fields and muddy surfaces, thanks to robust landing gear with low-pressure tyres, and in addition to its A.O.P. role the aircraft could be used for light transport. The rear cockpit floor was easily detachable and replaced by a new floor, bringing within its scope such tasks as casualty evacuation, photographic work and cable-laying.

The prototype A.O.P.9 flew at the maker's airfield on 19 March 1954, and deliveries began in February 1955. The new aircraft was soon in action overseas, against terrorists in Malaya with No. 656 Squadron in Operation 'Firedog'. A leaflet-dropping sortie was the first operation for the A.O.P.9, and the type soon proved to be a valuable complement to the A.O.P.6 in that theatre. In September 1957 the Army Air Corps was formed, taking over responsibility for A.O.P. work from the RAF. By that time No. 656 Squadron had flown 143,000 sorties, more than any other unit in 'Firedog'.

With No. 653 Squadron in Aden, engine problems began to impair operations seriously; loss of power when operating from strips at between 1220 and 2135 m (4,000 and 7,000 ft) meant a

poor rate of climb, dangerous in view of hostile armed tribesmen. However, by this time the army was thinking seriously of helicopters for A.O.P. work, and funds were not available for Auster improvements. A total of 145 was built, and some were supplied to the Indian army, and the Indian and South African air forces.

Variants
Auster 9M: surplus army aircraft bought by Captain M. Somerton-Rayner in 1967; later fitted with a 134-kW (180-hp) Avco Lycoming O-360-A1D engine and civil registered
Auster A.O.P.11: three-seat STOL development of the A.O.P.9 with a 194-kW (260-hp) Rolls-Royce Continental IO-470-D engine, produced by Beagle Aircraft; one example only, also known as the **Beagle A.115** or **E.3**; the aircraft was restored to the civil register in 1971 in private

ownership; data as for A.O.P.9 except maximum speed 238 km/h (148 mph), empty weight 961 kg (2,119 lb) and maximum take-off weight 1157 kg (2,550 lb)

Specification
Auster A.O.P.9
Type: two/three-seat air observation and general-purpose aircraft
Powerplant: one 134-kW (180-hp) Blackburn Cirrus Bombardier 203 inline piston engine
Performance: maximum speed 204 km/h (127 mph); cruising speed 177 km/h (110 mph); initial climb 285 m (930 ft) per minute; service ceiling 5945 m (19,500 ft); range 389 km (242 miles)
Weights: empty 721 kg (1,590 lb); maximum take-off 1057 kg (2,330 lb)
Dimensions: span 11.10 m (36 ft 5 in); length 7.23 m (23 ft 8½ in); height 2.72 m (8 ft 11 in); wing area 18.35 m² (197.5 sq ft)

Avia B.534

The **Avia B.534** was the most important Czech aircraft of the period between the two world wars, with production totalling 566 — more than that of any other type. It was a classic single-seat fighter biplane, representing the penultimate stage in the evolution of this type. The final stage being provided by biplanes with retractable landing gear, such as the Soviet Polikarpov I-153 and the Grumman fighters for the US Navy.

Designer František Novotný had re-engined the unsuccessful Avia B.34/2 prototype with a Hispano-Suiza 12Ybrs engine, redesignating it **B.534/1**. It first flew in August 1933, piloted by Václav Koči, and showed great promise. The aircraft was an unequal-span staggered single-bay biplane, with splayed N-struts carrying the upper-wing centre section above the fuselage. Wing bracing was by N-struts and there were ailerons on both upper and lower wings. The two-spar riveted steel wing had fabric covering, while the carefully streamlined fuselage was a riveted and bolted steel-tube structure with detachable metal panels forward and fabric covering aft. The horizontal tailplane was strut-braced and the split-type landing gear, with half-axles hinged beneath the fuselage, was oleo-sprung. The second prototype (**B.534/2**) had an enclosed cockpit, an enlarged rudder and revised landing gear with mainwheel fairings. It established a Czech national speed record on 18 April 1934, reaching 365.74 km/h (227.27 mph).

Development was held up when both prototypes were damaged in crash landings during 1934, but the decision had

already been made to order the B.534 for the Czech air arm. The **Avia B.534-I**, the first production version, closely followed the design of the second prototype. The prototype's metal propeller was replaced by a wooden unit and, as on the first prototype, the pilot had an open cockpit. The main landing gear units were without spats.

Production of the B.534-I totalled 46. Armament comprised twin fuselage-mounted light machine-guns and two more in fairings on the lower wing. Production of the **Avia B.534-II** series reached 100. This version differed in having all four machine-guns mounted in the fuselage sides, with consequently enlarged fuselage side blister fairings to house them. Underwing racks for light bombs were fitted, since the new fighter was considered suitable also for ground attack. The 46 **B.534-III** aircraft ordered next had mainwheel fairings, and had the carburettor air intake moved forward under the nose. Six of this version were exported to Greece and 14 to Yugoslavia. The **B.534-IV** had an aft-sliding cockpit canopy and raised aft fuselage decking. Total Czech orders for this version were 253. The **Avia Bk.534** was a cannon-armed version, but otherwise similar to the Series IV aircraft. It was intended that its Hispano-Suiza 12Ycrs engine would have a 20-mm Oerlikon cannon mounted in the Vee of the engine cylinders, with its muzzle in the hollow propeller boss. However, as a result of a shortage of the Oerlikon weapons, many Bk.534s flew with three machine-guns, two mounted in the fuselage sides and one in place of the *moteur canon*. Some B.534-IV and Bk.534 fighters had the standard tail skid replaced by a castoring tailwheel.

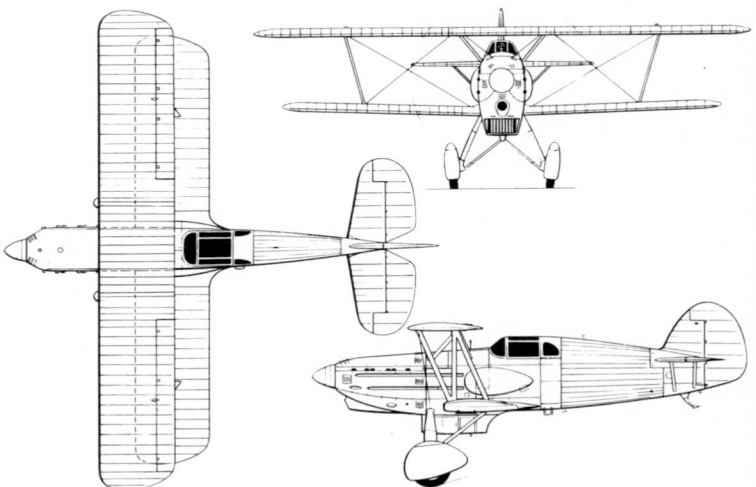

Above: Avia B.534-IV.

Below: This example of the sturdy Avia B.534-IV wears short skis for winter operations.

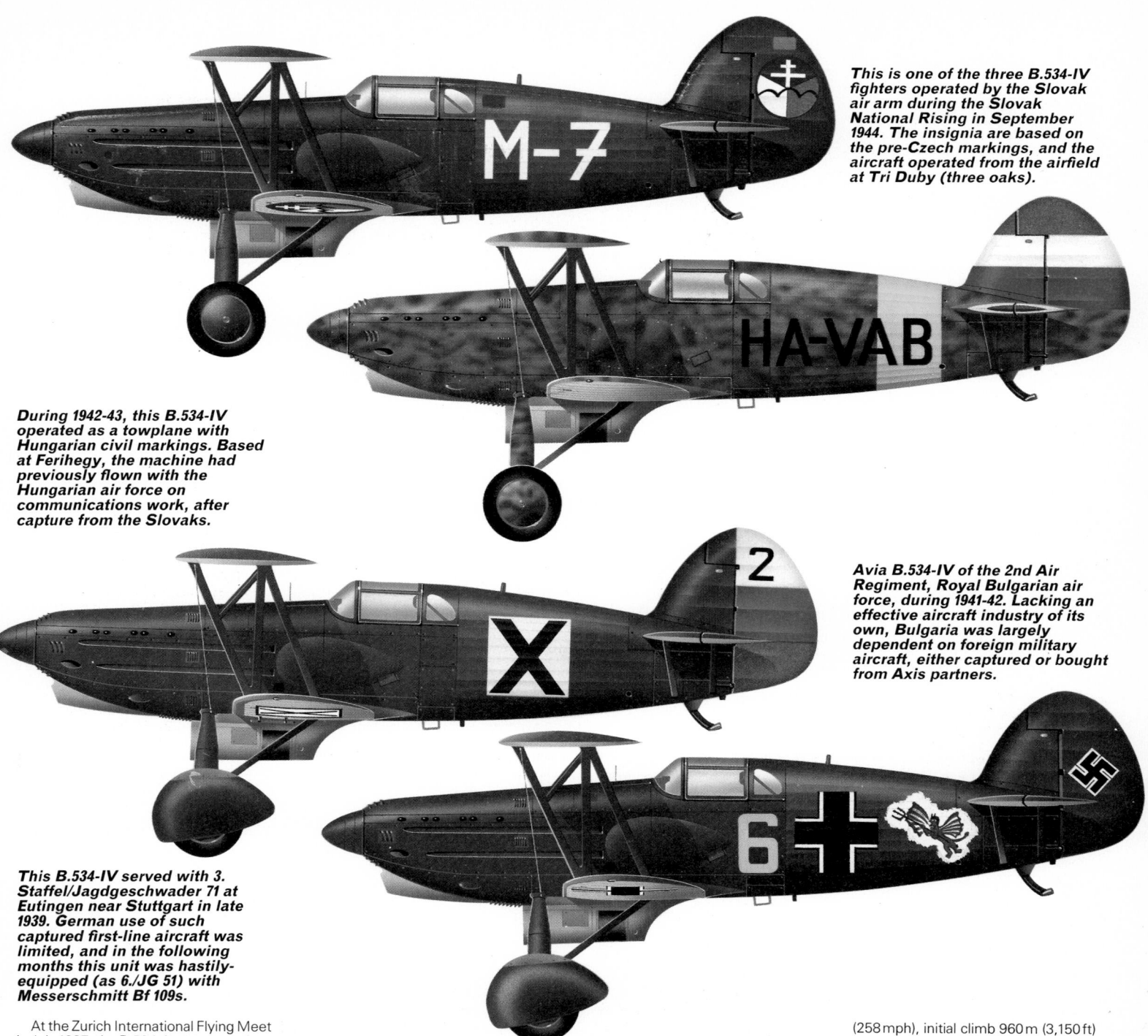

This is one of the three B.534-IV fighters operated by the Slovak air arm during the Slovak National Rising in September 1944. The insignia are based on the pre-Czech markings, and the aircraft operated from the airfield at Tri Duby (three oaks).

During 1942-43, this B.534-IV operated as a towplane with Hungarian civil markings. Based at Ferihegy, the machine had previously flown with the Hungarian air force on communications work, after capture from the Slovaks.

Avia B.534-IV of the 2nd Air Regiment, Royal Bulgarian air force, during 1941-42. Lacking an effective aircraft industry of its own, Bulgaria was largely dependent on foreign military aircraft, either captured or bought from Axis partners.

This B.534-IV served with 3. Staffel/Jagdgeschwader 71 at Eutingen near Stuttgart in late 1939. German use of such captured first-line aircraft was limited, and in the following months this unit was hastily-equipped (as 6./JG 51) with Messerschmitt Bf 109s.

At the Zurich International Flying Meet in July 1937, the B.534 demonstrated excellent manoeuvrability and good overall performance, proving itself in competition as the outstanding biplane fighter.

By the time of the Munich crisis in September 1938, B.534s formed the equipment of 21 first-line Czech fighter squadrons. After the occupation of the country by the Germans in March 1939, the puppet Slovak government used some B.534s in the brief border war with Hungary. Three Slovak squadrons subsequently took part in the invasion of the Soviet Union along the Ukrainian Front, but by mid-1942 all had been re-equipped and the type was relegated to training. During the winter of 1939-40, Bulgaria received 72 B.534s, which equipped five fighter squadrons. These were retained on Bulgarian territory and their only combat sorties were against Consolidated B-24 Liberator bombers returning from the disastrous 'Tidal Wave' bombing raid on Ploesti oilfields in Romania, on 1 August 1943. The B.534s were handicapped by their inadequate performance and soon afterwards were replaced by French-built Dewoitine D.520 monoplanes.

The Luftwaffe used other B.534s and Bk.534s as advanced trainers and as tow-planes for training gliders. Some were fitted with all-round-vision cockpit canopies and others, with arrester hooks, were used for deck landing trials and training in connection with the aircraft-carrier *Graf Zeppelin*, which was launched but never completed.

Finally, three Avias were used by the insurgents at Tri Duby airfield during the Slovak National Rising in the late summer of 1944. Two were lost on the ground during Luftwaffe raids and the third was burned to prevent it from falling into German hands.

The remarkable Avia B.534 is commemorated by a remarkably accurate full-scale replica, completed in 1975, and currently on proud display at the Air Force and Army Museum at Prague-Kbely.

Variants

Avia B.234: projected re-engined development of the B.34, but not built
Avia B.334: projected re-engined development of the B.34, but not built
Avia B.434: projected re-engined development of the B.34, but not built
Avia B.634: ordered as a 'cleaned up' development of the B.534 in 1935, the B.634 appeared as an aerodynamically refined aircraft, with carefully streamlined and spatted cantilever main landing gear legs; the upper wing had greater chord than that of the B.534, while that of the lower wing was reduced in comparison with that of the B.534, and the amount of wing stagger was also lessened; despite careful overall attention to streamlining, increased weight resulted in only marginal performance improvements; data include powerplant one Avia-built 634-kW (850-hp) Hispano-Suiza HS 12Ycrs inline engine, maximum speed 415 km/h

(258 mph), initial climb 960 m (3,150 ft) per minute, range 500 km (310 miles), empty weight 1710 kg (3,770 lb), span 9.40 m (30 ft 10 in) and length 8.35 m (27 ft 4¾ in)

Specification
Avia B.534-IV

Type: single-seat fighter
Powerplant: one 634-kW (850-hp) Hispano-Suiza HS 12Ydrs inline piston engine
Performance: maximum speed 394 km/h (245 mph) at 4400 m (14,435 ft); cruising speed 345 km/h (214 mph); initial climb 900 m (2,953 ft) per minute; service ceiling 10600 m (34,775 ft); range 580 km (360 miles)
Weights: empty 1460 kg (3,219 lb); maximum take-off 2120 kg (4,674 lb)
Dimensions: span 9.40 m (30 ft 10 in); length 8.20 m (26 ft 10¾ in); height (3.10 m (10 ft 2 in); wing area 23.56 m² (253.61 sq ft)
Armament: four fixed 7.7-mm (0.303-in) synchronised Model 30 machine-guns in the forward fuselage, plus up to six 20-kg (44-lb) bombs on underwing Pantof racks

Avia BH-9

The **Avia BH-9** was a low-wing strut-braced touring and sport monoplane derived directly from the BH-5. Powered by a 45-kW (60-hp) Walter NZ radial engine, it flew in prototype form during 1923. Army interest led to an order for 10 examples as liaison and primary training duties, and these aircraft had the military designation **B.9**.

B.9s made a number of notable flights for aircraft in their category, one example carrying off the 1925 Coppa d'Italia contest. A Lieutenant Jira flew B.9.11 (L-BONG) from Prague to Paris and back in the summer of 1926, the distance of 1800 km (1,118 miles) being covered at an average speed of 131.2 km/h (81.5 mph). In 1928 nine B.9s were in service with the Czech Army Flying School at Cheb, and in 1939 two examples were still flying with aero clubs.

Variants

Avia BH-10: single-seat aerobatic derivative of the BH-9; the first example appeared in 1924, and at least 20 were built, 10 of them as **B.10**s for the Czech air arm; data include powerplant one 45-kW (60-hp) Walter NZ radial piston engine, maximum speed 160 km/h (99 mph), empty weight 280 kg (619 lb) and maximum take-off weight 414 kg (913 lb), span 8.80 m (28 ft 10½ in), length 6.64 m (21 ft 9½ in) and wing area 9.80 m² (105.49 sq ft)

Avia BH-11: 1929 two-seater very similar to the BH-9; 15 were delivered to the Czech air arm under the designations **B.11**; in 1929 there appeared the **BH-11B** Antelope civil sport version, powered by a Walter Vega engine; produced in small numbers, the BH-11B was somewhat larger and heavier than the BH-11; data include powerplant one 63-kW (85-hp) Walter Vega radial piston engine, maximum speed 176 km/h (109 mph),

cruising speed 155 km/h (96 mph), service ceiling 3500 m (11,485 ft), range 700 km (435 miles), empty weight 379 kg (836 lb) and maximum take-off weight 627 kg (1,382 lb), span 10.40 m (34 ft 1½ in), length 6.82 m (22 ft 4½ in) and wing area 13.75 m² (148.01 sq ft)

BH-11C: had the same engine as the BH-11 (the 45-kW/60-hp Walter NZ) but a span of 11.10 m (36 ft 5 in)

Avia BH-12: another two-seat development of the BH-9, the BH-12 had a slightly modified wing profile but was otherwise very similar to the earlier aircraft; it appeared in 1924 in response to the need for a sport aircraft; the wings were easily folded for transport or stowage: they pivoted around the front spar and were then secured to the fuselage sides; thus folded the BH-12 could be towed by a car or moved by hand, the aircraft being very light

Specification
Avia BH-9

Type: two-seat sport and primary training monoplane
Powerplant: one 45-kW (60-hp) Walter NZ radial piston engine
Performance: maximum speed 158 km/h (98 mph); cruising speed 125 km/h (78 mph); service ceiling 4500 m (14,765 ft); range 470 km (292

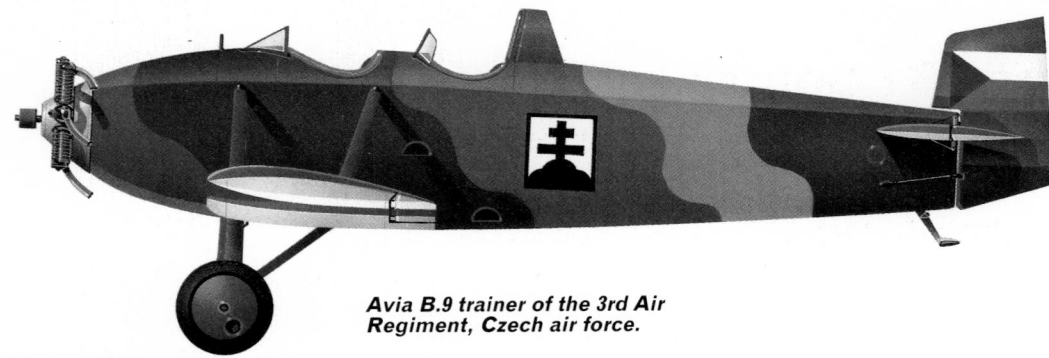
Avia B.9 trainer of the 3rd Air Regiment, Czech air force.

Six of the 15 Avia B.11s for the Czech air force line up for the camera. These were used as trainers, a straight military version of the BH-11 civilian aircraft, and provided sterling service through the mid-1920s.

miles)
Weights: empty 345 kg (761 lb); maximum take-off 550 kg (1,213 lb)
Dimensions: span 9.72 m (31 ft 10½ in); length 6.64 m (21 ft 9½ in); height 2.53 m (8 ft 3½ in); wing area 13.60 m² (146.39 sq ft)

Avia BH-21

Tested in January 1925, the **Avia BH-21** had been evolved by Benes and Hajn to overcome problems encountered in service with the earlier BH-17 single-seat fighter. The twin radiators for the Avia-built Hispano-Suiza 8Fb engine, which had been attached to the landing gear of the BH-17, were replaced by a single underfuselage radiator on the BH-21. Another problem with the BH-17 had been an obstruction of the pilot's view, caused by the faired pyramid between fuselage and upper wing. In the BH-21 this was replaced by conventional cabane struts. Finally, the I-struts of the BH-17 were replaced by single-bay conventional N-struts.

Adopted by the Czech air arm as the **B.21**, the new fighter proved robust and had a good performance. Some 137 were acquired for Czech service, and the type was successful in a competition held by the Belgian authorities in June 1925. This led to the purchase of one Czech-built aircraft, and the licence-manufacture of 44 more, 39 by SABCA and five by SEGA.

The B.21 saw widespread use in the Czech fighter squadrons until replaced by the Avia B.33 in the early 1930s. At air shows its paces as an aerobatic mount were demonstrated by service pilots such as Kapitán Malkovsky and this quality, plus the B-21's excellent turn of

Avia B.21 fighter of the 3rd Air Regiment of the Czech air force which bought some 137 of the type for service between 1925 and 1933.

speed, led to various developments mentioned below.

Variants

Avia BH-21J: standard BH-21 experimentally fitted with a Bristol Jupiter radial engine; the type proved successful and led to the development of the BH-33

Avia BH-21R: clipped-wing racing development of the BH-21 fighter, first flown in early 1925; power was provided by an uprated Hispano-Suiza 8Fb, developing 298 kW (400 hp) and

driving a specially developed Reed-Levavasseur propeller; wing area was reduced by 8.20 m² (88.27 sq ft); flown by a company pilot named Fritsch, the Avia BH-21R won the Czech national air races held in September 1925, covering the 200-km (124.27-mile) course at an average speed of 300.59 km/h (186.78 mph)

Specification

Type: single-seat fighter
Powerplant: one 231-kW (310-hp) Hispano-Suiza 8Fb inline piston engine

(licence-built by Avia)
Performance: maximum level speed 245 km/h (152 mph) at 3000 m (9,845 ft); climb to 5000 m (16,405 ft) in 13 minutes; service ceiling 5500 m (18,045 ft); range 550 km (342 miles)
Weights: empty 720 kg (1,587 lb); maximum take-off 1084 kg (2,390 lb)
Dimensions: span 8.90 m (29 ft 2½ in); length 6.87 m (22 ft 6½ in); height 2.74 m (8 ft 11¾ in); wing area 21.96 m² (236.38 sq ft)
Armament: two fixed 7.7-mm (0.303-in) synchronised Vickers machine-guns

Aviamilano P.19 Scricciolo

A side-by-side two-seater, the **Aviamilano P.19 Scricciolo** (Wren) was designed by Professor Ing. Ermenegildo Preti to meet the requirements of the Italian Aero Club. The prototype flew for the first time on 13 December 1959, and after receiving type approval in the following April, was delivered to the Milan Aero Club for evaluation.

An initial series of 25 aircraft was laid down at Aviamilano's factory at Bresso, Milan, and these had all been delivered by mid-1963 when work began on a similar batch. Three versions of the Scricciolo were offered. The first production batch, designated **P.19**, had a 75-kW (100-hp) Continental O-200-A engine with a two-blade fixed-pitch wooden propeller. Some were fitted with fixed tricycle landing gear in place of the nor-

mal tailwheel layout, and in this form were designated **P.19 trs**. The prototype was completed in 1965, but several of the earlier aircraft were retrofitted with the tricycle gear. Requirements for a glider tug led, in 1964, to the introduction of the **P.19R** with a 112-kW (150-hp) Lycoming O-320-A1A engine, which could use either a fixed-pitch or constant-speed propeller.

All versions of the Scricciolo had a welded steel-tube fuselage with fabric covering, while the wings and tail were of wooden construction, the wings with a glass-fibre reinforced plastic leading edge.

Specification
Type: two-seat light monoplane
Powerplant: one 75-kW (100-hp) Continental O-200-A flat-four piston engine
Performance: maximum speed 210 km/h (130 mph) at sea level; cruising speed 185 km/h (115 mph); service ceiling 3100 m (10,170 ft); range 644 km (400 miles)
Weights: empty 525 kg (1,157 lb); maximum take-off 785 kg (1,731 lb)
Dimensions: span 10.24 m (33 ft 7¼ in); length 7.03 m (23 ft 0¾ in); height 2.02 m (6 ft 7½ in); wing area 14.0 m² (150.7 sq ft)

Aviatik B.I and B.II

Automobil und Aviatik AG was established at Mulhausen, Alsace-Lorraine, during 1910, and began its aviation activities by building aircraft of French design. Experience so gained enabled the company to begin the design and construction of original aircraft, and with the outbreak of World War I it was able to develop quickly a two-seat reconnaissance machine. This was based upon

the design of a racing biplane of 1913, but differed by being of far more robust construction. Designated **Aviatik B.I**, a number of these aircraft appeared in service during 1914 in two-bay, and increased-span three-bay configuration. As with early B types from other manufacturers, the pilot was seated aft, since there was no weapon to be trained and fired by the observer. Landing gear was

of tailskid type, and the 75-kW (100-hp) Mercedes D.I inline engine was mounted in the nose, driving a tractor propeller.

By the time that the improved **B.II** entered service in 1915, Aviatik had moved from Mulhausen to Freiburg, deep in the homeland. While adhering to the same overall configuration as its predecessor, the B.II was of refined and lighter structure, and was provided with a more powerful Mercedes engine. No details are known of the number of B.I/B.IIs that

were constructed.

Specification
Aviatik B.II
Type: two-seat reconnaissance aircraft
Powerplant: one 89-kW (120-hp) Mercedes D.II inline piston engine
Dimensions: span 12.50 m (41 ft 0 in); length 7.10 m (23 ft 3½ in); height 00.00 m (00 ft 00 in); wing area 00.00 m² (000.0 sq ft)

Aviation Traders ATL.90 Accountant

In the early 1950s a number of companies explored the possibility of building a Douglas DC-3 replacement and even now, four decades later, the DC-3 flies on without a suitable successor.

The **ATL.90 Accountant**, a twin-engined 28-passenger light transport, was a brave attempt to fill this gap, particularly since Aviation Traders was not an aircraft manufacturing company. Success of the Rolls-Royce Dart turboprop in the Vickers Viscount dictated the choice of engines, and the Accountant made its first flight from the manufacturer's home airfield at Southend on 9 July 1957. Sufficient flying time, about 15 hours, was built up to enable the Accountant to appear in September at the SBAC Display, Farnborough. Early in January 1958 Airwork acquired the Aviation Traders group of companies, headed by Freddie Laker, and since

there were no immediate orders in prospect, development of the Accountant was abandoned. The prototype was the only example built, and this was duly cocooned at Southend, where it was eventually broken up in February 1960.

Specification
Type: medium-range airliner
Powerplant: two 1298-ekW (1,740-ehp) Rolls-Royce Dart R.Da.6 Mk 512 turboprops
Performance: maximum speed 475 km/h (295 mph) at 7620 m (25,000 ft); maximum cruising speed 470 km/h (292 mph) at 4570 m (15,000 ft); range with maximum fuel 3364 km (2,090 miles) at 7620 m (25,000 ft)
Weights: empty 7693 kg (16,961 lb); maximum take-off 12,928 kg (28,500 lb)
Dimensions: span 25.15 m (82 ft 6 in);

length 18.93 m (62 ft 1 in); height 7.70 m (25 ft 3 in); wing area 58.71 m² (632.0 sq ft)

The Accountant was an unsuccessful attempt to provide a 'DC-3 replacement'.

Aviation Traders ATL.98 Carvair

Aer Lingus, the Irish national airline, was among the customers which bought new Carvair conversions.

In the immediate years following the end of World War II, the Bristol Aeroplane Company produced Britain's first post-war civil transport, the Bristol Type 170. Most of those built (214 in all) were of the Series I Freighter version, able to accommodate in the Mk 32 configuration three motor cars in the forward hold and up to 20 passengers in the aft cabin. It was the Bristol Type 170 which, on 13 July 1948, was used to inaugurate with Silver City Airways the once-famous cross-Channel car/passenger air ferry between Lympne and Le Touquet.

The need to supplement, and eventually replace, the Mk 32 Freighter in this role led Aviation Traders Ltd to develop the **ATL.98**, which became named **Carvair** (a contraction of Car-via-air). In-

creased range and capacity was required, and Aviation Traders concluded that conversion of an existing aircraft would prove more economic than the development of a completely new design. Chosen for this role was the Douglas DC-4, robust and reliable, comparatively cheap to acquire from larger airlines that were updating their fleet and with a considerable spares backing. The conversion, planned with technical assistance from Douglas Aircraft, consisted basically of a new and longer forward fuselage, with the flight deck high above the new front hold, which had a sideways-hinged nose door through which vehicles could be loaded. Standard layout could accommodate five cars forward and 22 passengers in

The bulbous front fuselage of the Carvair demanded a taller tail compared to the DC-4 upon which it was based.

the rear cabin, but an alternative all-passenger layout could carry a maximum of 65 passengers. In addition to the fuselage conversion, a new vertical tail of increased height and area was provided.

First flown on 21 June 1961, the Carvair entered service with British United Air Ferries in March 1962. Some 21 conversions were completed, serving initially with Aer Lingus, Aviaco, Ansett-ANA, British United Air Ferries, and Inter-ocean Airways. They subsequently changed hands several times, and only a small number remain in service.

Specification
Type: air ferry transport
Powerplant: four 1081-kW (1,450-hp) Pratt & Whitney R-2000-7M2 Twin Wasp radial piston engines
Performance: maximum speed 402 km/h (250 mph); maximum cruising speed 343 km/h (213 mph); economic cruising speed 333 km/h (207 mph) at 3050 m (10,000 ft); service ceiling 5700 m (18,700 ft); range with maximum payload 3700 km (2,300 miles)
Weights: empty 18999 kg (41,885 lb); maximum take-off 33475 kg (73,800 lb)
Dimensions: span 35.81 m (117 ft 6 in); length 31.27 m (102 ft 7 in); height 9.09 m (29 ft 10 in); wing area 135.82 m² (1,462 sq ft)

Avions Fairey Fox

Development by the British Fairey Aviation Company of the Fox two-seat day bomber provided the RAF with an aircraft that was faster than any contemporary fighter. Interest in the type by Belgium's Aéronautique Militaire led to licence construction by Avions Fairey of an all-metal version designated **Fox IIM**, powered by a 358-kW (480-hp) engine. The first of 31 examples entered service with the Belgian air force in 1933, which was almost seven years after the type had first been used by the RAF. Appreciating the potential of this aircraft, Avions Fairey decided to develop an improved version. The resulting **Fox VI** incorporated an Hispano-Suiza 12Ydrs engine in place of the Kestrel, this providing an increase in power output of almost 80 per cent. Coupled with refinements that included an enclosed canopy for the cockpits and wheel speed fairings, this gave the Fox VI a maximum speed of 365 km/h (227 mph). A total of 94 was supplied to the Aéronautique Militaire, and construction figures totalled 195 of all marks when production ended in 1939.

Avions Fairey Fox VI of the 2e Régiment d'aéronautique of the Belgian air force. These reconnaissance fighters flew from La Zoute in May 1940.

Variants
Avions Fairey Fox III: production version of the Fox II prototype with 254-kW (340-hp) Armstrong Siddeley Serval radial, and used as a reconnaissance fighter (total 12)
Avions Fairey Fox IIIC: modified Fox II with enclosed cockpits and powered by one Kestrel V; a single example of the **Fox IIICS** dual-control sub-model was built (total 48)
Avions Fairey Fox IIIS: dual-control trainer (total 4)

Avions Fairey Fox V: prototype of the Fox VI produced by re-engining a Fox II with 485-kW (650-hp) Hispano-Suiza 12Ydrs inline
Avions Fairey Mono Fox VII: designation of a single-seat fighter development, also known as the Kangaroo because of the large ventral radiator installation; data included maximum speed 375 km/h (233 mph) and an armament of six machine-guns (two in the fuselage and two in each upper wing) (total 2 prototypes)
Avions Fairey Fox VIII: improved development of the Fox VI (total 12)

Still in limited service at the time of the German invasion in May 1940, the Mono Fox VII was a single-seat fighter variant. The underbelly radiator gave rise to the nickname 'Kangourou'.

Specification
Avions Fairey Fox VI
Type: two-seat reconnaissance fighter
Powerplant: one 641-kW (860-hp)
Hispano-Suiza 12Ydrs inline piston
engine

Performance: maximum speed
365 km/h (227 mph) at 4000 m
(13,125 ft); climb to 6000 m (19,685 ft) in
8 minutes 30 seconds; service ceiling
11200 m (36,745 ft); range 600 km (373
miles)

Weight: maximum takeoff 2245 kg
(4,950 lb)
Dimensions: span 11.58 m (38 ft 0 in);
length 9.17 m (30 ft 1 in); height 3.35 m
(11 ft 0 in)

Armament: one or two fixed 7.7-mm
(0.303-in) synchronised machine-guns
and one flexible 7.7-mm (0.303-in)
machine-gun, plus a light bombload

A.V. Roe Triplane III and IV

A.V. Roe's early ventures were triplanes. These were followed up by a more ambitious project of similar configuration. This was the **Avro Mercury**, a two-seater with plywood-covered fuselage, a 26-kW (35-hp) Green engine driving a two-blade tractor propeller (the earlier machines had featured four-blade propellers) and a sale price of £600. The *Mercury* had a span of 7.92 m (26 ft 0 in), a length of 7.47 m (24 ft 6 in), wing area of 22.85 m² (246.0 sq ft), empty weight of 204 kg (450 lb) and a maximum speed of 64 km/h (40 mph). Other sources show the span of the *Mercury* as 6.10 m (20 ft 0 in), it should be noted.

By this time Roe's ideas had been refined to accord with what was fast becoming the aerodynamic norm. The result was the **Avro Triplane No. 3 (Roe III)**, of which six were built in Manchester. Like the *Mercury* the Triplane No. 3 was a two-seater, and was powered by a 26-kW (35-hp) engine, either a Green or a J.A.P. And while the triplane layout for the wings and horizontal tail was retained, the Triplane No. 3 was more strongly built. Ailerons replaced wing-warping for lateral control, and longitudinal control was allocated to

conventional elevators rather than to the variable-incidence wings of earlier triplanes. The second and third Triplane No. 3, powered respectively by Green and J.A.P. engines, suffered an unusual fate: they were to have been used by Roe during the Blackpool Meeting of July and August 1910, but were both burned out when set on fire by sparks from the engine of the train on which they were being transported. Roe thus used the fourth example at Blackpool: this had been hurriedly built from spares in Manchester. The last two Triplane No. 3 were for the Harvard Aeronautical Society and Cecil Grace respectively.

The final triplane of the series was the **Avro Triplane No. 4 (Roe IV)**, which was also a product of 1910. This was a large single-seater powered by a 26-kW (35-hp) Green engine. The wings spanned 12.80 m (42 ft 0 in), and lateral control was effected by differential warping of the upper two wings. The fuselage, 9.14 m (30 ft 0 in) in length, terminated in a large single tailplane with substantial elevators. A single-seater weighing some 295 kg (650 lb) loaded, the Avro Triplane No. 4 was used for instructional purposes at Brooklands,

Surrey. The triangular-section fuselage configuration was retained, but the forward portion was clad in thin aluminium sheet.

Specification
Avro Triplane No. 3 (Roe III)
Type: two-seat triplane
Powerplant: one 26-kW (35-hp)
Green inline piston engine
Performance: maximum speed
64 km/h (40 mph)

*Alliott Verdon Roe perches
somewhat precariously in the
'cockpit' of his Roe III (Triplane
No. 3) during his trip to the
United States in September 1910.*

Weight: maximum take-off 249 kg
(550 lb)
Dimensions: span, upper and centre
9.45 m (31 ft 0 in); lower 6.10 m (20 ft
0 in); length 7.01 m (23 ft 0 in); height
2.74 m (9 ft 0 in); wing area 33.63 m²
(362.0 sq ft)

Avro Type D

The **Avro Type D** biplane marked the breakaway from A.V. Roe's three-year obsession with the triplane configuration, and although only six Type Ds were built all were different.

The first, flown on 1 April 1911 at Brooklands, was powered by a 26-kW (35-hp) Green engine and proved, according to various pilots, to be 'stable, vice-less and easy to fly'. Its first few weeks proved very busy with attempts on endurance records, taking part in a race, demonstrations for the Parliamentary Aerial Defence Committee, and so on. Bought for trials with the naval airship tender *Hermione*, the Type D was tested with floats and made the first British take-off from water on 18 November 1911.

A modified Type D, built to compete in the *Daily Mail* Circuit of Britain Race, had a 45-kW (60-hp) E.N.V. water-cooled engine but crashed before the race began.

An apparent total of six Type Ds was built, although the figure is unconfirmed. In addition to the engines already mentioned, the 34-kW (45-hp) Green, 26-kW (35-hp) Viale and 37-kW (50-hp) Isaacson were used. Three of the aircraft survived until withdrawn from use at Shoreham in May 1914.

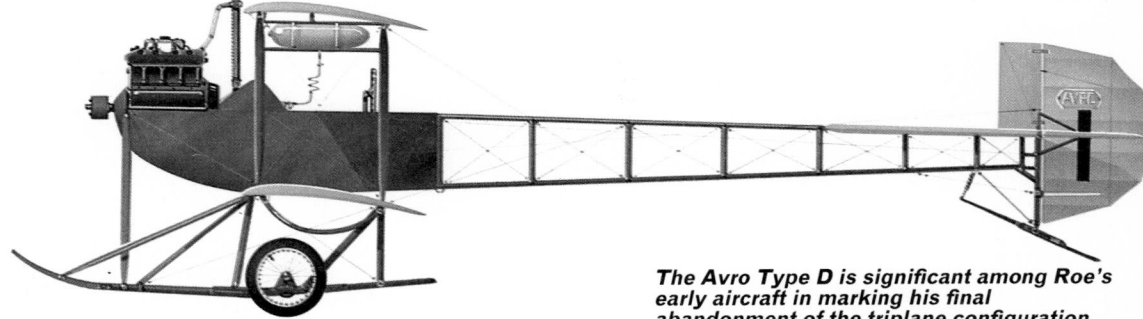

The Avro Type D is significant among Roe's early aircraft in marking his final abandonment of the triplane configuration.

Specification
Type: two-seat biplane
Powerplant: one 26-kW (35-hp)
Green inline piston engine
Performance: maximum speed
78 km/h (48.5 mph)
Weight: maximum take-off 227 kg
(500 lb)
Dimensions: span 9.45 m (31 ft 0 in);
length 8.53 m (28 ft 0 in); height 2.79 m

(9 ft 2 in); wing area 28.80 m²
(310.0 sq ft)

The Avro Type D has the distinction of being the first successful British seaplane. This float-equipped aircraft first flew on 18 November 1911.

Avro 504 Series

By any standards, the **Avro 504** was a remarkable aircraft; indeed it is one of the great aircraft worthy of being ranked alongside such names as Spitfire, Lancaster, Mosquito and Dakota. Its qualities were such that it is remembered with affection by thousands – as an aircraft on which many pilots were trained, or as a joy-riding biplane on which many members of the public were given their first flights.

The Avro 504's origins lay in the Avro 500, and the first Avro 504 flew at Brooklands in July 1913, powered by a 60-kW (80-hp) Gnome rotary engine. It took part in the Second Aerial Derby at Hendon in September, finishing in fourth place at an average speed of 107 km/h (66.5 mph).

A considerable amount of flying followed, and a War Office contract was placed for 12 for the RFC in the summer of 1913. A number of other Avro 504s were ordered by individuals, some with floats and other modifications, but it was in service use that the 504 was to achieve fame. It gained the dubious distinction of being the first British aeroplane to be brought down by the enemy, when a No. 5 Squadron aircraft was hit by infantry fire over Belgium, on 22 August 1914.

The Admiralty had also ordered Avro 504s, and its first four aircraft took part in the famous raid on the Friedrichshafen Zeppelin sheds on 21 November 1914, with the loss of one of their number. The Avro 504 did not, however, see much active service, being relegated to training, a task which it performed admirably.

Modifications to the basic design began with the **Avro 504A**, which had smaller ailerons and broader struts; 63 basic Avro 504s were produced, followed by 50 Avro 504As and by the end of the war in 1918 production had reached more than 8,000. A.V. Roe built 3,696, the balance coming from a number of other contractors, including Brush Electrical, Parnall, Saunders and Bleriot & Spad.

Early production 504s had used the 60-kW (80-hp) Gnome Monosoupape seven-cylinder engine in place of the prototype's nominal 60-kW (80-hp) Gnome, which in reality only gave about 46 kW (62 hp). Following the 504A came the **Avro 504B** for the RNAS with a larger fin and modified tailskid; the **Avro 504C**, a single-seat RNAS version for anti-Zeppelin patrols; and a similar single-seat conversion, the **Avro 504D**, for the RFC; all these laboured on with the 60-kW (80-hp) Gnome.

The overall designation 504K was given to Avro 504Js fitted with rotary engines surplus to other requirements, making the type an excellent trainer both during and after World War I.

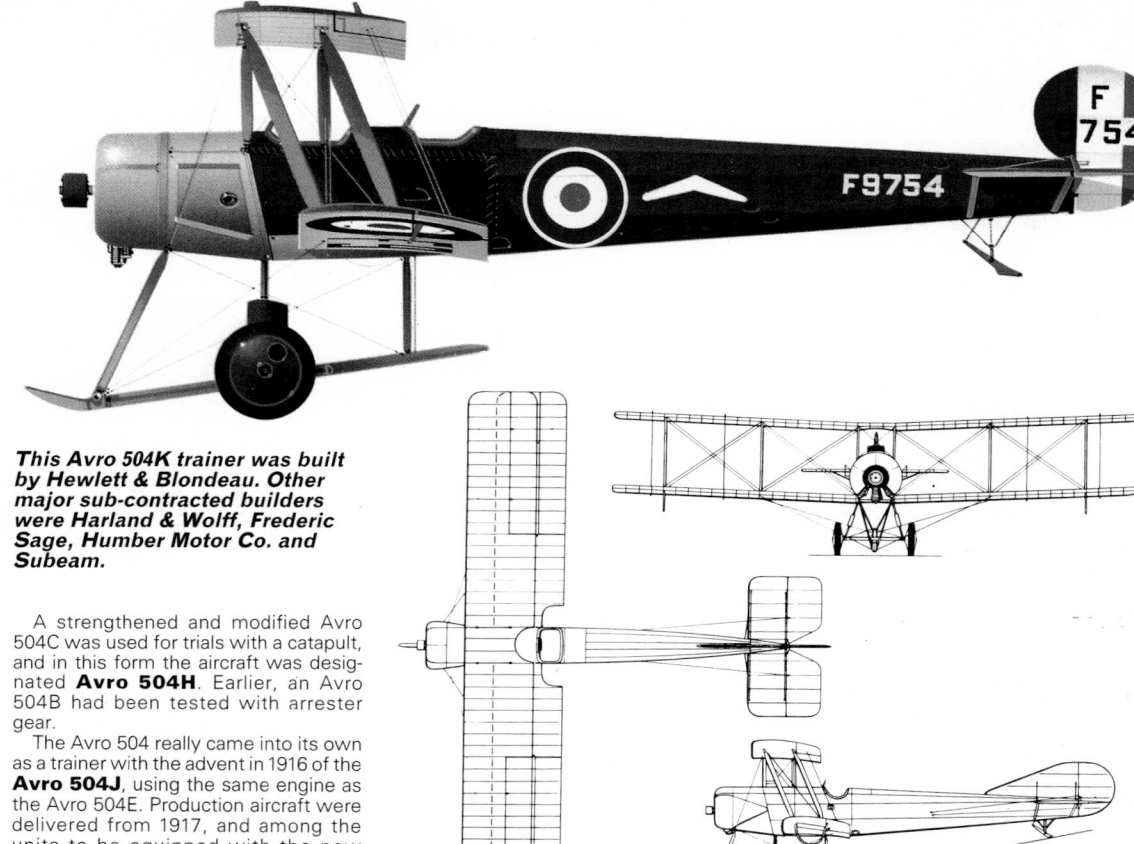

This Avro 504K trainer was built by Hewlett & Blondeau. Other major sub-contracted builders were Harland & Wolff, Frederic Sage, Humber Motor Co. and Subeam.

A strengthened and modified Avro 504C was used for trials with a catapult, and in this form the aircraft was designated **Avro 504H**. Earlier, an Avro 504B had been tested with arrester gear.

The Avro 504 really came into its own as a trainer with the advent in 1916 of the **Avro 504J**, using the same engine as the Avro 504E. Production aircraft were delivered from 1917, and among the units to be equipped with the new variant was the RFC's School of Special Flying at Gosport, commanded by the legendary Major R.R. Smith-Barry, who had developed a new instructional technique. This was remarkably successful and became the services' standard method. It was in this field that the Avro 504J excelled and large orders were placed.

Because of the Avro 504's early replacement as a front-line aircraft, orders for its Monosoupape engines had been allowed to run down, and engine manufacture was not keeping up with airframe production. To alleviate the situation, surplus rotary engines were recalled and fitted into the new airframes, so Avro 504Js were delivered with 97-kW (130-hp) Clergets, and with 82-kW (110-hp) or 60-kW (80-hp) Le Rhônes. The necessary modifications for making the airframe adaptable for the variety of engines was carried out by Avro, with the aircraft redesignated **Avro 504K**, regardless of engine type.

Post-war, the type continued in service as the standard trainer in the RAF, until it was replaced by the Avro 504N. A number of Avro 504Ks were used at RAE Farnborough for a wide variety of tests.

With the massive production pro-

Avro 504C

gramme undertaken in the UK, it was obvious that with the end of the war vast stocks of aircraft would be available for disposal. The Avro 504K was particularly suitable for civilian use and more than 300 were registered in Britain between 1919 and 1930. Training, pleasure flying and banner-towing were their main tasks, and the Avros continued flying well into the 1930s until de Havilland Moths and Avro Avians replaced them.

Many Avro 504Ks were sold abroad post-war to both civil and military customers; military users included Argentina, Australia, Belgium, Brazil, Canada, Chile, China, Denmark, Finland, Guatemala, Ireland, Japan, Mexico, the Netherlands Indies, New Zealand, Norway, Portugal, South Africa, Spain, Sweden and USA; civil customer countries were even more numerous. Licence production was undertaken in Australia, Belgium, Canada and Japan.

Two more variants of the 504 deserve mention before the 504N (described separately). The **Avro 504L**, the first post-war variant, was a seaplane; six were built as three-seaters, with the

112-kW (150-hp) Bentley B.R.1 rotary engine, and used for joy riding. Additionally, some Avro 504Ks with 97-kW (130-hp) Clerget engines were fitted with floats.

The **Avro 504M** was an attempt to provide a cabin biplane for two; a standard Avro 504K fuselage was built up and a plywood roof with portholes added. Powerplant was a nine-cylinder 75-kW (100-hp) Gnome Monosoupape engine, and the one and only Avro 504M enjoyed a busy spell of joy riding in the summer of 1919.

In an attempt to upgrade performance, the company produced the **Avro 504E** for the RNAS, using 75-kW (100-hp) Gnome Monosoupape engine. A number of changes were made, including reduction of wing stagger; 10 were built.

The Avro 504Q was a sole derivative produced for the 1924 Oxford University Arctic Expedition, powered by an Armstrong Siddeley Lynx with an internal cabin.

Variants
Avro 504J with a 60-kW (80-hp) Le Rhône or 75-kW (100-hp) Gnome Monosoupape
Avro 504K flew with a variety of engines including 67-kW (90-hp) R.A.F. 1A and Thulin, 75-kW (100-hp) Gnome Monosoupape, Curtiss K6 and

Sunbeam Dyak, 82-kW (110-hp) Le Rhône, 97-kW (130-hp) Clerget, 112-kW (150-hp) Bentley B.R.1, 127-kW (170-hp) A.B.C. Wasp 1, and 164-kW (220-hp) Hispano-Suiza

Specification
Type: two-seat basic trainer
Powerplant: one 82-kW (110-hp) Le Rhône rotary engine
Performance: maximum speed 145 km/h (90 mph); cruising speed 126 km/h (78 mph); climb to 1065 m (3,500 ft) in 5 minutes; service ceiling

4875 m (16,000 ft); range with maximum fuel 402 km (250 miles)
Weights: empty 558 kg (1,231 lb); maximum take-off 830 kg (1,829 lb)
Dimensions: span 10.97 m (36 ft 0 in); length 8.97 m (29 ft 5 in); height 3.17 m (10 ft 5 in); wing area 30.66 m² (330.0 sq ft)

Avro 504N

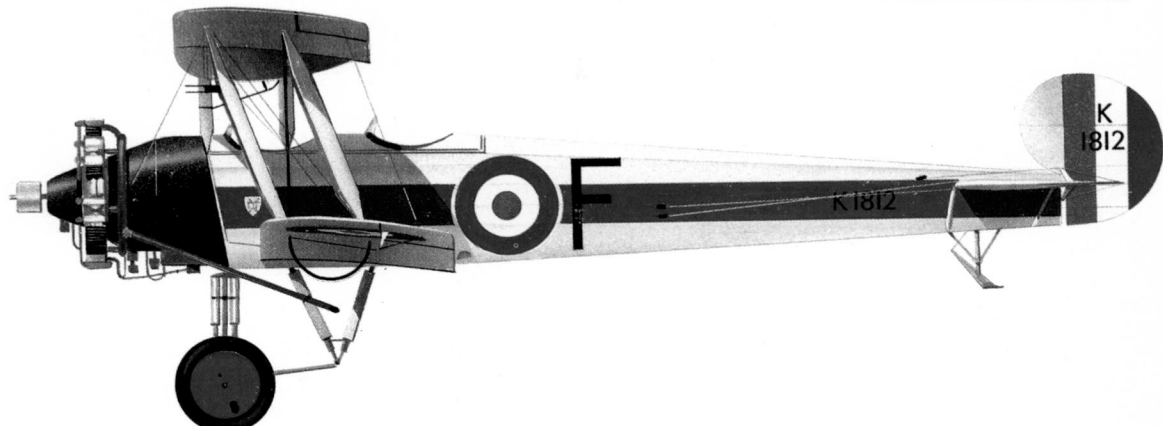

World War I left in its wake a considerable number of Avro 504s that were surplus to military requirements, and the number of subsequent conversions could literally fill a book.

In appearance the most noticeable difference between the **Avro 504N** and its predecessors was redesigned landing gear, which eliminated the ventral skid. At the same time, tapered ailerons were introduced. A number of individual conversions to partial 504N standard were made, but the first genuine 504Ns were two ordered by the Air Ministry in 1925, these using 1918-built but unused airframes. One had a 75-kW (100-hp) Bristol Lucifer engine, the other a 134-kW (180-hp) Armstrong Siddeley Lynx, and following comparative trials at Martlesham Heath, the latter engine was chosen for production aircraft, of which 598 were completed between 1925 and 1932.

Known as the Lynx-Avro, the 504N replaced the 504K in the RAF's five flying training schools – at Netheravon, Digby, Grantham, Sealand and in Egypt. Others served as communications aircraft, with Auxiliary Air Force squadrons, and in the University Air Squadrons. The first RAF instrument flying course began in September 1931 at Wittering, when six 504Ns were introduced with blind-flying hoods, turn indicators and a 1° reduction in dihedral to reduce inherent stability.

While early production aircraft had a wooden fuselage and tapered ailerons, later examples had a welded steel-tube fuselage and rectangular ailerons. Almost 80 early 504Ks were converted to 504N standard as an economy measure.

Exports of 504Ns included 17 to the Belgian air force, four to the Brazilian

naval air service, six to the Chilean naval air service (designated 5040), one to the Danish navy, six to the Royal Hellenic naval air service, 20 to the Royal Thai air force, and a number to the South African Air Force. Single examples were delivered to Japan and the Royal Swedish air force; the latter, as an evaluation aircraft, crashed a year after delivery. Additionally, licence manufacture was undertaken in Denmark (5), and in Belgium by SABCA (31). In Canada, some RCAF 504Ks were converted to 504Ns by Canadian Vickers, who also produced other 504Ns, including a single-float seaplane.

The single 504N supplied to Japan in January 1927, and an earlier 504K which had been navalised as the **Yokosuka K1Y1**, led to the **K2Y1** with a 97-kW (130-hp) Armstrong Siddeley Mongoose engine in 1928. By the following year the **K2Y2 Type 3** with the 97-kW (130-hp) Gasen Jimpu engine was in production.

Japanese-built 504 variants continued in production with various companies until 1940.

In 1932 the Avro Tutor was chosen as the RAF's 504N replacement, and by the following year the latter had been officially declared obsolete. A number came on to the civil market and were used for joy-riding and banner-towing and the type became well known throughout Britain.

A surprising extension of the 504N's military service came in 1940, when seven civilian aircraft were impressed into the RAF. Two were destroyed in a hangar fire in July 1940 before they could be used, and two others were scrapped. The remaining three were based with a Special Duty Flight at Christchurch, Hampshire, where they were used to tow wooden gliders out to sea so that trainee radar operators at Worth Matravers, Dorset, could attempt to track them at various altitudes.

The Avro 504N was a post-war adaptation of wartime Type 504 airframes to incorporate a new landing gear and the Armstrong Siddeley Lynx radial. It was widely used by the Royal Air Force.

Specification
Type: two-seat trainer
Powerplant: one 119-kW (160-hp) Armstrong Siddeley Lynx IV radial piston engine
Performance: maximum speed 161 km/h (100 mph); cruising speed 137 km/h (85 mph); service ceiling 4450 m (14,600 ft); range 402 km (250 miles)
Weights: empty 718 kg (1,584 lb); maximum take-off 1016 kg (2,240 lb)
Dimensions: span 10.97 m (36 ft 0 in); length 8.69 m (28 ft 6 in); height 3.33 m (10 ft 11 in); wing area 29.73 m² (320.0 sq ft)

Avro 531 Spider

With an eye to securing an Air Ministry order for a new single-seat fighter, Avro produced the **531 Spider** as a private venture. This flew at Hamble in April 1918, powered by a 82-kW (110-hp) Le Rhône rotary, it was later re-engined with a Clerget rotary. Use of a large number of 504K components helped open the possibility of rapid and economic manufacture, and rigging problems were simplified by the adoption of rigid welded steel-tube interplane bracing. Extensively tested, the Spider proved to be very manoeuvrable, with a good field of view for the pilot provided by a circular hole in the centre-section of the low-set upper wing. Unfortunately for Avro, the Sopwith Snipe had already been selected as the service's next fighter, and the single Spider prototype ended its days in the experimental role. A modified version, the **531A**, appears not to have been completed.

Variant
Avro 538: possibly built from parts earmarked for the Avro 531A, the Avro 538 was a considerably modified development of the basic Avro 531

design with equal-span wings, normal wing strutting and a larger upper wing/fuselage gap; intended as a racing aircraft, the 538 was never used as such because of a defective main spar; powered by a 112-kW (150-hp) Bentley B.R.2 rotary, it was instead employed by the Avro Transport Co. as a communication aircraft from May 1919 until September 1920; data similar to the Avro 531 except range 515 km (320 miles), empty weight 442 kg (975 lb) and maximum take-off weight 635 kg (1,400 lb), span 8.53 m (28 ft 0 in), height 2.59 m (8 ft 6 in) and wing area 19.51 m² (210.0 sq ft)

Specification
Avro 531
Type: single-seat fighter
Powerplant: one 97-kW (130-hp) Clerget rotary piston engine
Peformance: maximum speed 193 km/h (120 mph) at sea level; climb to 1525 m (5,000 ft) in four minutes; service ceiling 5970 m (19,000 ft); range about 402 km (250 miles)
Weights: empty 437 kg (963 lb); maximum take-off 688 kg (1,517 lb)

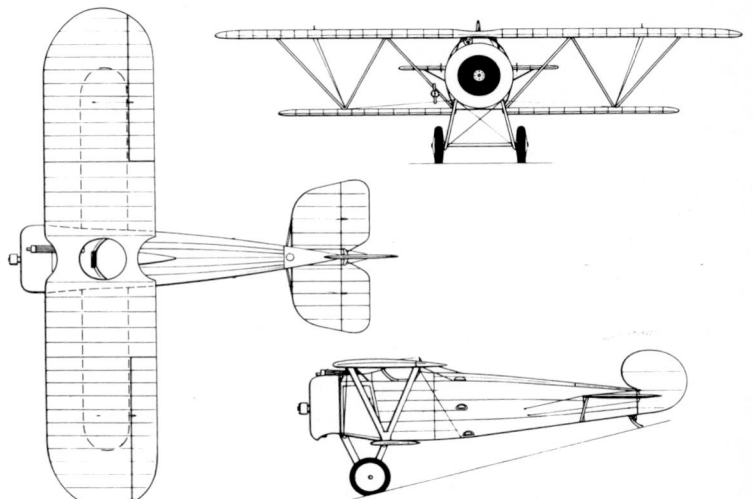

Avro 531 Spider

Dimensions: span 8.69 m (28 ft 6 in); length 6.25 m (20 ft 6 in); height 2.39 m (7 ft 10 in); wing area 17.56 m² (189.0 sq ft)

Armament: one fixed 7.7-mm (0.303-in) synchronised Vickers machine-gun in the forward fuselage

Avro 555 Bison

Avro entered naval aviation with the **Type 555 Bison**, a design to Specification 3/21 for a carrier-based fleet spotter and reconnaissance aircraft. Flown in 1921, the first prototype was soon joined by a second, built to the revised Specification 33/22, and this varied in a number of features, the main one being removal of the upper wing from its joint with the fuselage and raising it some 0.38 m (1 ft 3 in) above the fuselage on struts. A third prototype appeared in 1923, and was followed by a production batch of 12.

The production aircraft, to Specification 16/23, were based on the second prototype and became **Bison IA**s. This first batch of 12 was followed by orders for a further 18 in July 1924, 12 more in December of that year, and five in February 1927. All of these were designated **Bison II**s, with production completed in April 1927.

In spite of the fact that it was basically a naval aircraft, first Bison deliveries were made in 1922 to the RAF's No. 3 Squadron at Gosport, where they replaced Westland Walruses on coastal reconnaissance work. No. 423 Fleet Spotter Flight, also at Gosport, was the first naval unit to receive the Bison, and these aircraft subsequently embarked on HMS *Eagle* for a Mediterranean cruise. Several other flights in the same carrier, and in HMS *Furious*, were similarly

The Avro 444 Bison was the first of the company's naval aircraft. This example served aboard HMS Eagle during the late 1920s while the carrier was cruising in the Mediterranean.

equipped, and No. 448 Flight at Hal Far, Malta, served ashore with Bisons. All units subsequently received Fairey IIIFs in 1929 and the Bisons were retired.

An early production Bison was fitted with a central and two wing floats plus retractable wheels, but tests at the Maritime Aircraft Experimental Establishment at Felixstowe showed it to be unsatisfactory. Another early aircraft served for a year with the Engine Research Flight at RAE Farnborough on engine and radiator test work.

Variants
Bison I: two prototypes
Bison IA: initial production version
Bison II: later production version; data include range 579 km (360 miles), empty weight 1867 kg (4,116 lb) and maximum take-off weight 2781 kg (6,132 lb), height 4.32 m (14 ft 2 in) and wing area 58.53 m² (630.0 sq ft)

Specification
Avro 555 Bison IA
Type: three/four-seat fleet spotter reconnaissance biplane
Powerplant: one 336-kW (450-hp) Napier Lion II inline piston engine
Performance: maximum speed 177 km/h (110 mph); cruising speed 145 km/h (90 mph); service ceiling 4265 m (14,000 ft); range with maximum fuel 547 km (340 miles)
Weights: empty 1887 kg (4,160 lb); maximum take-off 2631 kg (5,800 lb)
Dimensions: span 14.02 m (46 ft 0 in); length 10.97 m (36 ft 0 in); height 4.22 m (13 ft 10 in); wing area 57.60 m² (620.0 sq ft)
Armament: one flexible 7.7-mm (0.303-in) Lewis machine-gun

Avro 594 Avian

The **Avro 594 Avian** was a contemporary of the de Havilland D.H. 60 Moth, but the prototype Moth flew in February 1925, more than a year before the Avian which was built for the *Daily Mail* two-seat light aeroplane trials at Lympne in September 1926. That vital lead was to have far-reaching effects, putting de Havilland in the forefront of light aeroplane design in Europe.

The Avian prototype, designated **Avro 581**, had a 56-kW (75-hp) Armstrong Siddeley Genet engine and, flown by Bert Hinkler, took second place in three of the six trials at Lympne, only to be eliminated finally with magneto problems. Modified subsequently as the **Avro 581E**, it flew with a 60-kW (80-hp) A.D.C. Cirrus engine and achieved some fame in racing and long-distance events, culminating in Hinkler's 15½-day flight from Croydon to Darwin. It is one of the few surviving Avians, being housed in Brisbane Museum.

Production aircraft bore the designation Type 594 and the first two, as **Avian Mk I**s, went to the RAE and Lancashire Aero Club. They were followed by nine **Avian Mk II**s, six of which had the same Cirrus engine but with some differences in the landing gear, while three for Australia had 56-kW (75-hp) Genet IIs.

The first **Avian Mk III**, with a 63-kW (85-hp) A.D.C. Cirrus II, flew in mid-1927; it differed from the Mk II only in having slimmer, tubular steel interplane and centre-section struts. A total of 33 Avian Mk IIIs were built, including one for the

RAF, before the **Avian Mk IIIA** was introduced. This originated when three earlier Avians were fitted with 67-kW (90-hp) Cirrus III engines to compete in the 1928 King's Cup Race; the Avian Mk IIIA production aircraft, of which 58 were built, were internally strengthened. At least two were operated on floats.

The final development of the wooden version was the **Avian Mk IV**, with modifications to the ailerons and landing gear. The standard engine was again the Cirrus III, but within the 90 production aircraft were versions with the 60-kW (80-hp) Genet II and 78-kW (105-hp) Cirrus Hermes I. Most of the Mk IVs were for export, customers including the Chinese National Air Service, the Norwegian Antarctic Expedition, and private owners in Argentina, Australia, Brazil, Canada, Mexico, South Africa and Spain.

At the outbreak of World War II, most of the surviving Avians were impressed as instructional airframes, but four survived to be restored to the British civil register and three are still extant but in storage.

Alongside the wooden Avians, the **Avro 616 Avian Mk IVM** with a steel-tube fuselage was produced in some numbers, following 1929 tests with the prototype powered by a 67-kW (90-hp) Cirrus III. The heavier constructions dictated the use of a larger engine, and early production Mk IVMs had either 78-kW (105-hp) Cirrus Hermes 1s or 75-kW (100-hp) Armstrong Siddeley Genet Major radials. Export aircraft went to Argentina, Australia, Estonia, Mexico, New

Zealand, Singapore, South Africa, Spain and Canada, where the Ottawa Car Manufacturing Co. built 18 for the RCAF powered by 101-kW (135-hp) Genet Majors. At least five were built in the USA by the Whittlesey Body Co.

A small batch of the **Avro 616 Sports Avian** was built, some with 78-kW (105-hp) Hermes engines, and others with de Havilland Gipsy engines of 75 kW to 89 kW (100 to 120 hp), and among the more unusual of this type were a pair of **Avro 625 Avian Monoplane**, one with a Genet Major and the other with a Hermes.

One **Avian Mk IVA** (named *Southern Cross Minor*) was built as a long-range single-seater for Sir Charles Kingsford-Smith, who later passed on a simi-

lar **Avian Mk V** to W. N. Lancaster for an attempt on the England-Cape Town record, which began in April 1933. No further news was heard until the remains of the aircraft were found in the Sahara in March 1962. They were subsequently returned to Britain and exhibited in 1979.

Variants
There were large numbers of sub-variants within each mark, so the list below can only describe the main variants
Avro 581 Avian: prototype, subsequently modified as the **Avro 581E**; data include maximum speed 113 km/h (70 mph); empty weight 340 kg (750 lb) and maximum take-off weight 717 kg (1,580 lb), span 9.75 m (32 ft 0 in), length 7.47 m (24 ft 6 in) and wing area 27.31 m² (294 sq ft) (total 1)
Avro 594 Avian I: pre-production

The Avian could not match de Havilland's Moth in the lightplane market although it was a sound design.

aircraft, with lower engine mounting and split axle (total 2)

Avro 594 Avian II: initial production model; data include maximum speed 158 km/h (98 mph), cruising speed 132 km/h (82 mph), service ceiling 4570 m (15,000 ft), range 523 km (325 miles), empty weight 411 kg (907 lb) and maximum take-off weight 665 kg (1,467 lb) (total 9)

Avro 594 Avian III: essentially a Mk II with tubular steel interplane and cabane struts (total 33)

Avro 594 Avian IIIA: production version with local strengthening (total 58)

Avro 594 Avian IV: improved development of the Mk IIIA with

revised ailerons and landing gear (total 90)

Avro 605 Avian: Avian floatplane (total 2 conversions from Mk IIIA)

Avro 616 Avian IVM: developed version with steel-tube fuselage; data include maximum speed 169 km/h (105 mph), cruising speed 145 km/h (90 mph), range 579 km (360 miles), empty weight 456 kg (1,005 lb) and maximum take-off weight 691 kg (1,523 lb) (total about 190)

Avro 616 Sports Avian: version largely for racing, with cut-down rear decking, through-axle and low-drag windscreens; data includes maximum speed 193 km/h (120 mph), cruising speed 169 km/h (105 mph) and

maximum take-off weight 726 kg (1,600 lb)

Avro 616 Avian IVA: modified version for Sir Charles Kingsford-Smith, with a 90-kW (120-hp) de Havilland Gipsy inline and extra fuel, giving a range of 2736 km (1,700 miles) (total 1)

Avro 616 Avian V: special version for Sir Charles Kingsford-Smith, as a long-range single-seater (total 1)

Avro 625 Avian Monoplane: braced low-wing monoplane development with faired main landing gear legs (total 2)

Specification
Avro 594 Avian Mk IIIA
Type: two-seat touring biplane
Powerplant: one 71-kW (95-hp) A.D.C. Cirrus III inline piston engine
Performance: maximum speed 164 km/h (102 mph); cruising speed 140 km/h (87 mph); service ceiling 5485 m (18,000 ft); range with maximum fuel 644 km (400 miles)
Weights: empty 424 kg (935 lb); maximum take-off 651 kg (1,435 lb)
Dimensions: span 8.53 m (28 ft 0 in); length 7.39 m (24 ft 3 in); height 2.59 m (8 ft 6 in); wing area 22.76 m² (245.0 sq ft)

Avro 621 Tutor/Sea Tutor

In the early 1930s it became necessary to replace the Avro 504N as the RAF's basic trainer and the logical choice as its successor was the **Avro 621**, later to become the **Tutor**.

Designed by Roy Chadwick in 1929, the Tutor employed welded steel-tube construction with fabric-covered surfaces. The civil registered prototype, powered by a 116-kW (155-hp) Armstrong Siddeley Mongoose IIIA radial engine went to the Aircraft and Armament Experimental Establishment, Martlesham Heath, for comparative trials in December 1929, making its first public appearance in the New Types Park at the RAF Display, Hendon, on 28 June 1930.

Following its service trials against other aircraft, the Tutor was selected by the RAF in 1930 and a trial batch of 21 was ordered to Specification 3/30, retaining the five-cylinder Mongoose engine. Virtually all the following production aircraft had the 179-kW (240-hp) Armstrong Siddeley Lynx IVC engine under a narrow chord Townend ring cowling, differing from the Mongoose-powered aircraft which had uncowled engines.

A number of civil 621s were built, plus others for foreign air forces, including three for the Irish Air Corps, seven for the Royal Canadian Air Force, two for the South African Air Force, 30 for the Greek air force, three for the Danish navy and five for the Kwangsi (Chinese) air force.

The biggest production orders came from the RAF, who had received 394 aircraft from the total of 795 built by the time Tutor production ceased in May 1936. The majority were built to Specification 18/31 but twin-float seaplane versions, known as **Sea Tutors**, were delivered against Specification 26/34. These were delivered between 1934 and 1936 for waterborne trials at Felixstowe and for use by the Seaplane Training School at Calshot. Sea Tutors had been withdrawn from service by April 1938.

Standard RAF Tutor deliveries began with a batch for the Central Flying School in 1933, and these were followed by deliveries to the RAF College, Cranwell, No. 5 Flying Training School, Sealand, and No. 3 FTS, Grantham. As the Tutors moved into the flying training schools to replace Avro 504Ns they became standard equipment; a number were also delivered to the university air squadrons and to station flights of the Auxiliary Air Force.

The Tutor's excellent handling qualities made it an ideal aircraft for aerobatic displays and the CFS Tutors first appeared in this role at the RAF Display, Hendon, on 26 June 1933, with the upper surfaces of both wings painted in

Avro 621 Tutor in typical RAF training yellow.

a red and white 'sunburst' pattern.

A licence was granted to permit Avro 621 production in South Africa, and 57 were built in that country.

With the impending re-equipment of RAF fighter squadrons in the late 1930s with the new Supermarine Spitfire and Hawker Hurricane, the RAF favoured monoplane trainers and the Tutors were phased out, to be replaced in the elementary training role by Miles Magisters.

Variants
Avro 621 Tutor II: single example with modified wing strut arrangement

P.W.S.18: Polish designation of 40 licence-built Tutors

Specification
Type: two-seat elementary trainer
Powerplant: (Tutor) one 179-kW (240-hp) Armstrong Siddeley Lynx IVC radial piston engine
Performance: maximum speed 196 km/h (122 mph); cruising speed 169 km/h (105 mph) at 305 m (1,000 ft) service ceiling 4940 m (16,200 ft); range 402 km (250 miles)
Weights: empty 839 kg (1844 lb); maximum take-off 1115 kg (2,458 lb)

Docile yet tractable, the Tutor served the RAF well as a basic trainer until the advent of the Miles Magister monoplane. 380 were deliverd to the service, most of which featured the cowled Armstrong Siddeley Lynx IVC radial engine.

Dimensions: span 10.36 m (34 ft 0 in); length 8.08 m (26 ft 6 in); height 2.92 m (9 ft 7 in); wing area 27.96 m² (301 sq ft)
Armament: none

Avro 652A Anson

The Avro Anson enjoyed one of the longest production runs of any British aircraft, this status being maintained from 1934 until 15 May 1952 when the last Anson T.21 completed its acceptance trials. Its origin lay in an Imperial Airways specification, sent to A.V. Roe in April 1933, which required that the resulting aircraft should be capable of transporting four passengers over 676-km (420-mile) sectors at a cruising speed in excess of 209 km/h (130 mph). Other requirements were that the stalling speed should not exceed 97 km/h (60 mph) and that the machine should be capable of maintaining 610 m (2,000 ft) on one engine.

In August 1933, a design team headed by Roy Chadwick produced a study, bearing the designation **Avro 652**, for a low-wing monoplane with retractable landing gear, to be powered by two Armstrong Siddeley Cheetah V engines, and with a design gross weight of 2948 kg (6,500 lb). A change in the Imperial Airways specification to enable the aircraft to fly the Karachi-Bombay-Colombo night mail service resulted in modifications which raised the gross weight to 3470 kg (7,650 lb).

An order for two Avro 652s was placed in April 1934, and the first flew on 7 January 1935. Type certification was awarded in March, and these two aircraft were delivered to Imperial Airways at Croydon on 11 March, to remain in service until sold to Air Service Training Ltd in 1938 for use as navigation trainers.

On 7 May 1934 the Director of Contracts at the Air Ministry notified A.V. Roe of a requirement for twin-engined landplanes for use as coastal reconnaissance aircraft, and requested information about the possibility of adapting existing designs. A new design study, based on the Imperial Airways machine, was designated **Avro 652A**.

The resulting Air Ministry contract called for delivery in March 1935, giving the company less than six months to complete detail design and prototype construction for the military version of an aircraft which had not then flown in civil form. External changes included rectangular rather than the round windows on the 652, and the addition of an Armstrong Whitworth dorsal turret with a single Lewis gun.

The prototype was flown on 24 March 1935 and delivered to Martlesham Heath for official trials in the following month. After minor modifications to tailplane and elevators, the machine was transferred to the Coastal Defence Development Unit at Gosport for a competitive fly-off with the D.H.89M. A fleet exercise provided a practical test of the capabilities of the contenders and the superior range and endurance of the Avro 652A enabled it to win the competition.

Specification 18/35 was written to cover production aircraft, designated **Anson Mk I**, and the first was flown on 31 December 1935. On 6 March 1936 No. 48 Squadron at Manston became the first operational RAF Anson unit; it also proved to be the last to use the type in front-line service, converting to the Lockheed Hudson in January 1942. Twenty-one Coastal Command squadrons used Ansons in general reconnaissance, and search and rescue roles.

Further RAF orders followed, together with export contracts which included aircraft for Australia, Egypt, Eire, Estonia, Finland and Greece, and almost 1,000 had been manufactured by the outbreak of war in September 1939. Some of

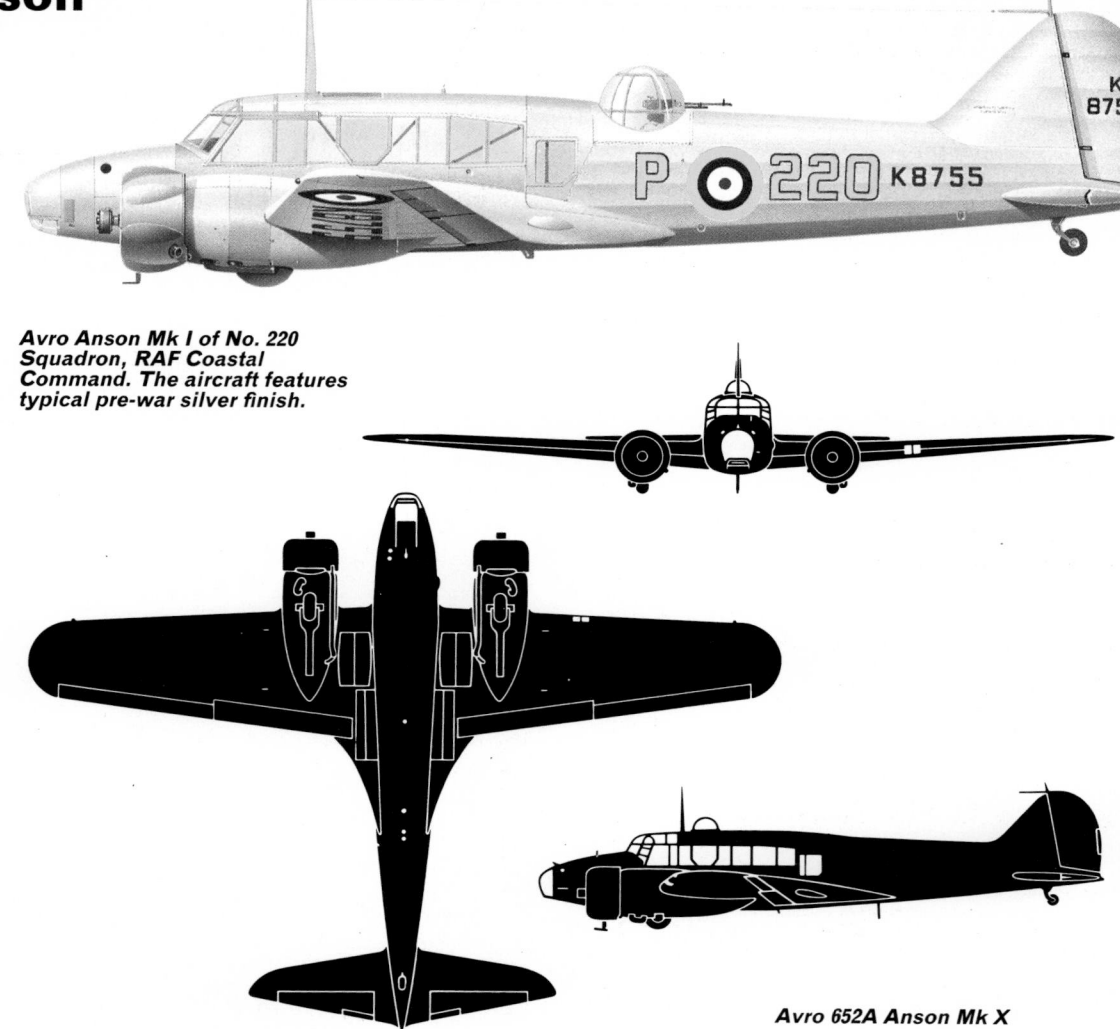

Avro Anson Mk I of No. 220 Squadron, RAF Coastal Command. The aircraft features typical pre-war silver finish.

Avro 652A Anson Mk X

these were training aircraft, and it was in this role that the Anson was to make its greatest contribution to the war effort. Although A.V. Roe had proposed a trainer version as early as November 1936, there was some delay before the first **Anson Trainers**, with dual controls and trailing-edge flaps, made their appearance. They were to serve in various forms with Operational Training Units, Pilots Advanced Flying Units, Schools of Air Navigation and Army Co-operation, Air Observer Schools and Air Gunnery Schools, the last using Ansons with Bristol B1 Mk VI power-operated turrets. Total Mk I production totalled 6,742, of which 3,935 were built at Woodford and the balance at Yeadon.

On 18 December 1939 the British Commonwealth Air Training Plan was instituted, and the Anson was selected as one of the standard training aircraft. The production contract was placed in Britain, engineless airframes being shipped to Canada from Woodford, to be fitted on arrival with either Jacobs L-6MB or Wright Whirlwind R-975-E3 radial engines. The former were designated **Anson III** and the latter **Anson IV**; Mk IIIs were later modified to incorporate Dowty hydraulically-actuated flaps and landing gear. Those British airframes which had turrets when delivered retained them, although most Ansons used in Canada did not have this equipment.

As the situation in Britain deteriorated, and after 223 airframes had been delivered, production was initiated in Canada, with Federal Aircraft Ltd set up to co-ordinate a multi-company manufacturing programme. The first version produced entirely in Canada was the **Anson Mk II**, with Jacobs engines, a moulded plywood nose, and hydraulically-actuated flaps and landing gear. The first of them was flown on 21 August 1941, and production totalled 1,832, 50 of which were supplied to the US Army air force as crew trainers under the designation **AT-20**.

The use of moulded plywood in the Mk II led to adoption of this material for the entire fuselage, in which the familiar 'glasshouse' or square window gave way to circular portholes. With standard Mk II components fitted to this new fuselage, the aircraft became the **Anson V**, powered by 336-kW (450-hp) Pratt & Whitney R-985-AN-12B engines, and accommodating five trainee crew members instead of three as in earlier versions. Mk V navigation trainers were built to the number of 1,050, and a single example of a gunner training version, with a Bristol B1 Mk VI dorsal turret, was produced in 1943. The designations **Anson VII, VIII** and **IX** were allocated for Canadian versions which were not built.

Subsequent marks were developed and manufactured in Britain, commenc-

ing with the **Anson X**, a Mk I with a strengthened cabin floor for freight/passenger use, and which saw service with the Air Transport Auxiliary as a communications aircraft for ferry pilots. It retained the 261-kW (350-hp) Cheetah IX engines of the later Mk Is and the manually-operated landing gear, but the fluted cowlings were replaced by smooth ones, as used on the two Avro 652s. Gross weight was increased to 4286 kg (9,450 lb), and 103 of this version were built at Yeadon.

The raising of the roofline, to provide more headroom in the cabin for passenger operations, led to the introduction of the **Anson XI** and **XII**, which had hydraulically-operated flaps and landing gear, and three large square windows on each side of the fuselage. The Anson XI was powered by 295-kW (395-hp) Cheetah XIXs, driving fixed-pitch Fairey-Reed metal propellers, and the Mk XII by 313-kW (420-hp) Cheetah XVs with variable-pitch Rotol propellers. Later Mk XIIs were designated Series 2, to denote the provision of an all-metal wing in place of the standard wooden assembly. Ambulance versions of both marks were produced, first flights having taken place on 30 July and 27 October 1944 respectively. Yeadon manufactured 91 Mk XIs and 254 Mk XIIs.

The **Ansons XIII** and **XIV** were to have been gunnery trainers, with Cheetah XI or XIX, and Cheetah XV engines respectively, but these, like the **Ansons XV** and **XVI** which were to have been navigation and bombing trainers, were not produced. The **Anson XVII** designation was not allocated. Early in 1945, with the end of the war in sight, the company produced a Mk XI airframe with five oval windows on each side of the fuselage and a furnished interior, meeting the requirements of the Brabazon Committee's civil transport Specification 19, and becoming the **Avro Nineteen**. It was operated over British internal routes, at that time administered by the Associated Airways Joint Committee, and then put into production as a civil feeder-liner.

The same aircraft in RAF service became the **Anson C.19**, and 264 of these were built between 1945 and 1947. Twenty were converted Mk XIIs, and 158 were Series 2 aircraft with metal wings and tailplanes. The production line at Woodford was reopened, producing three Series 1s and 167 Series 2s, while 137 Series 1s and 18 Series 2s were built at Yeadon. Developed from the Avro 19 were 12 specially equipped Ansons for police patrol, communications and aerial survey duties and this version, designated **Avro 18**, had been ordered by the Royal Afghan Air Force. In addition 13 **Anson 18C**s with Cheetah 15 engines were ordered by the Indian government for civil aircrew training, and all 25 of these aircraft were built at Woodford.

The **Anson T.20** was developed from the Anson 19 Series 2 to Speci-

fication T.24/46 for service as a bombing and navigation trainer in Southern Rhodesia. This was fitted with a transparent nose for the bomb aimer and with racks for 16 practice bombs under the fuselage and wings. The prototype flew on 5 August 1947 and a further 59 production T.20s were manufactured at Woodford. Specification T.25/46 covered the **Anson T.21** navigation trainer, which lacked the transparent nose and bomb racks of the T.20, but was otherwise similar. Following the maiden flight of the prototype on 6 February 1948, the Yeadon factory built 252 T.21s for Flying Training Command, the last finally closing the production line in May 1952. The T.21 was not the last variant produced, however, that distinction falling to the **T.22** which was developed to Specification T.26/46. Fifty-four of these radio trainers were built, the prototype having made its first flight on 21 June 1948.

The Anson's long service career, spanning 22 years, ended officially on 28 June 1958 when six aircraft of the Southern Communications Squadron carried out a formation fly-past at their Bovington, Hampshire, base.

Specification
Type: three/five-seat conversion, navigation, bombing, gunnery and radio trainer, or 8/11-seat communications aircraft
Powerplant: (Mk I) two 261-kW (350-hp) Armstrong-Siddeley Cheetah IX

radial piston engines
Performance: maximum speed 303 km/h (188 mph) at 2135 m (7,000 ft); cruising speed 254 km/h (158 mph); service ceiling 5790 m (19,000 ft); range 1271 km (790 miles)
Weights: empty 2438 kg (5,375 lb); maximum take-off 3629 kg (8,000 lb)
Dimensions: span 17.20 m (56 ft 5 in); length 12.88 m (42 ft 3 in); height 3.99 m (13 ft 1 in); wing area 38.09 m² (410 sq ft)
Armament: one 7.7-mm (0.303-in) fixed forward-firing machine-gun in port

The Anson T.Mk 20 was intended to serve as a bombing and navigation trainer in Rhodesia, with transparent aiming nose and bomb racks under the fuselage and wings.

side of nose and one 7.7-mm (0.303-in) gun in dorsal turret, plus up to 163 kg (360 lb) of bombs

Avro 679 Manchester

Seldom has the marriage between a new airframe and new engines been satisfactory, and the **Avro 679 Manchester** was no exception. Designed to specification P.13/36 as a twin-engined medium bomber with the new Rolls-Royce Vulture 24-cylinder engine, the Manchester would have been in competition with the Handley Page H.P.56. Plans for the latter were abandoned in 1937, however, leaving a clear field for the Avro design, while Handley Page concentrated its efforts on the four-engined Halifax, itself to become a rival to the Lancaster when the latter eventually replaced the Manchester.

The first of two Manchester prototypes flew on 25 July 1939, to be followed by the second on 26 May 1940. A production contract had been placed for 200 aircraft to meet another Air Ministry specification, 19/37, on 1 July 1937, and this was later increased to 400.

Following flight trials the wing span was increased by 3.05 m (10 feet) and a central fin was added to supplement the small twin fins and rudders. Later, after a number of Manchesters had been delivered as **Mk I**s, the central fin was deleted and the twin fins increased in area; in this form it became the **Mk IA**. The prototype and first two production aircraft were delivered to the Armament Experimental Establishment, Boscombe Down, for tests, while the second prototype went to the Royal Aircraft Establishment, Farnborough.

The first squadron delivery was to No. 207, which reformed at Waddington on 1 November 1940, and six Manchesters of the 18 on squadron strength carried out their first operational flight, to Brest, on the night of 24/25 February 1941.

As deliveries built up, so squadrons became equipped with the new bomber, and others to receive Manchesters included Nos 49, 50, 57, 61, 83, 97, 106,

Avro 679 Manchester Mk I of No. 207 Squadron, RAF Bomber Command in early 1941.

408 and 420, while No. 144 Squadron of Coastal Command received enough aircraft to form one flight.

The Manchester proved to be a failure mainly because of the unreliability of the Vulture engines, and the inability of these powerplants to deliver their designed power; there were also a number of airframe defects and it was with great relief that squadrons began to relinquish their Manchesters from mid-1942 as Lancasters began to replace them.

The last Bomber Command Manchester operation took place on 25/26 June 1942 against Bremen, and in the final tally it was found that the type had flown 1,269 sorties, dropping 1885 tonnes (1,826 tons) of HE, plus incendiaries. Some 202 aircraft were built, of which about 40 per cent were lost on operations and 25 per cent were written off in crashes.

However, on the credit side, the Manchester paved the way for the Lancaster, and without the earlier aircraft one must conjecture whether or not the RAF's finest bomber would have seen the light of day.

Avro 679 Manchester Mk IA (scrap views: tail unit of Manchester Mk I).

Specification
Type: seven-seat medium bomber
Powerplant: two 1312-kW (1,760-hp) Rolls-Royce Vulture inline piston engines
Performances: maximum speed 426 km/h (265 mph) at 5180 m (17,000 ft); cruising speed 298 km/h (185 mph) at 4570 m (15,000 ft); service ceiling 5850 m (19,200 ft); range 2623 km (1,630 miles) with 3674-kg (8,100-lb) bomb load

Weights: empty 13350 kg (29,432 lb); maximum take-off 25401 kg (56,000 lb)
Dimensions: span 27.46 m (90 ft 1 in); length 21.13 m (69 ft 4 in); height 5.94 n. (19 ft 6 in); wing area 105.63 m² (1,137 sq ft)
Armament: eight 7.7-mm (0.303-in) machine-guns (two each in nose and dorsal turrets, and four in tail turret), plus up to 4695 kg (10,350 lb) of bombs

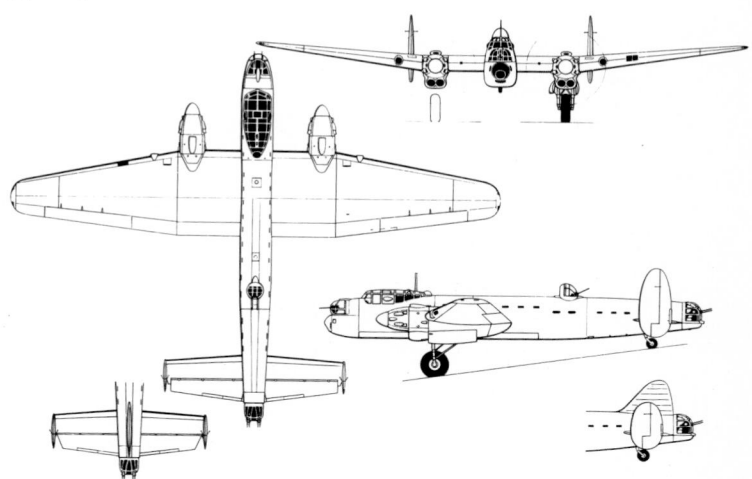

Avro 683 Lancaster
to
Avro 696 Shackleton

Avro 683 Lancaster

No-one would dispute the statement that the **Avro 683 Lancaster** was the finest British heavy bomber of World War II; few would even argue against the premise that it was the finest heavy bomber serving on either side during the conflict, and it is therefore strange to recall that it had its genesis in the unsuccessful twin-engined Manchester.

However, it is not entirely true to say that the Lancaster was virtually a four-engined Manchester; a four-engined installation in the basic airframe had been proposed before Manchester deliveries to the RAF began. But the prototype Lancaster was, in fact, a converted Manchester airframe with an enlarged wing centre section and four 854-kW (1,145-hp) Rolls-Royce Merlin Xs. This prototype initially retained the Manchester's triple tail assembly, but was later modified to the twin fin and rudder assembly which became standard on production Lancasters.

The prototype flew on 9 January 1941 and later that month went to the Aeroplane and Armament Experimental Establishment, Boscombe Down, to begin intensive flying trials. The second prototype, with some modifications and Merlin XX engines, flew on 13 May 1941, while by September of that year the first prototype had been delivered to No. 44 Squadron at Waddington for crew training and evaluation.

The new bomber was an immediate success, and large production orders were placed. Such was the speed of development in wartime that the first production Lancaster was flown in October 1941, a number of partially completed Manchester airframes being converted on the line to emerge as **Lancaster I**s (from 1942 redesignated **Lancaster B.1**s).

Avro's first contract was for 1,070 Lancasters, but others soon followed, and when it became obvious that the parent company's Chadderton and Yeadon production facilities would be unable to cope with the demand, other companies took on the task of building complete air-

The Lancaster became one of the main Allied weapons of World War II, blitzing German positions.

craft. They included Armstrong Whitworth at Coventry, Austin Morris at Birmingham, Metropolitan Vickers at Manchester and Vickers-Armstrong at Chester and Castle Bromwich.

Lancasters soon began to replace Manchesters, and such was the impetus of production that a shortage of Merlin engines was threatened. This was countered by licence-production by Packard in the USA of the Merlin not only for Lancasters but for other types. An additional insurance was effected in another way, the use of 1294-kW (1,735-hp) Bristol Hercules VI or XVI radial engines.

In this form, as the **Lancaster II**, a prototype was flown on 26 November 1941 and results were sufficiently encouraging to warrant this version going into production by Armstrong Whitworth at Coventry.

The first two Hercules-powered Lancasters were completed in September 1942 and went to the Aeroplane and Armament Experimental Establishment, where they were later joined by the third. Other Mk IIs from this first production batch were delivered to No. 61 Squadron at Syerston, Nottingham, the service trials unit for this version and a former Lancaster I squadron.

Gradually Lancaster B.IIs began to re-equip other squadrons, but the Mk II never achieved the success of the Merlin-engined Lancaster: it could not attain so high an altitude, was slightly slower, and had a bomb load 1814kg (4,000lb) less than the other marks. Production ceased after 301 had been built, and the Armstrong Whitworth factory changed over to Lancaster B.Is.

Meanwhile, the Merlin Lancasters were going from strength to strength. The prototype's engines gave way to

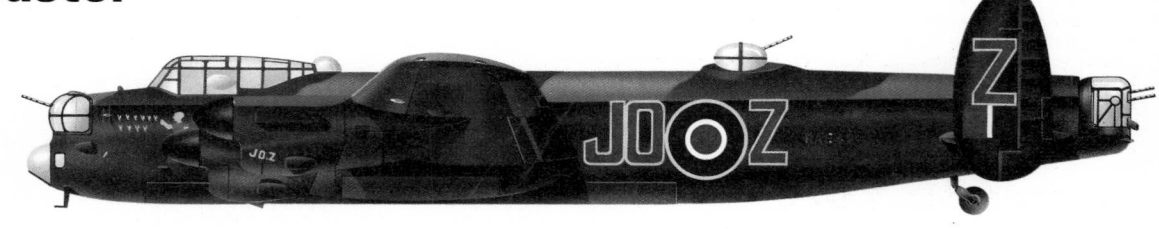

Lancaster Mk I of No. 463 Squadron, RAF, based at Waddington in spring 1945.

Avro 683 Lancaster Mk III

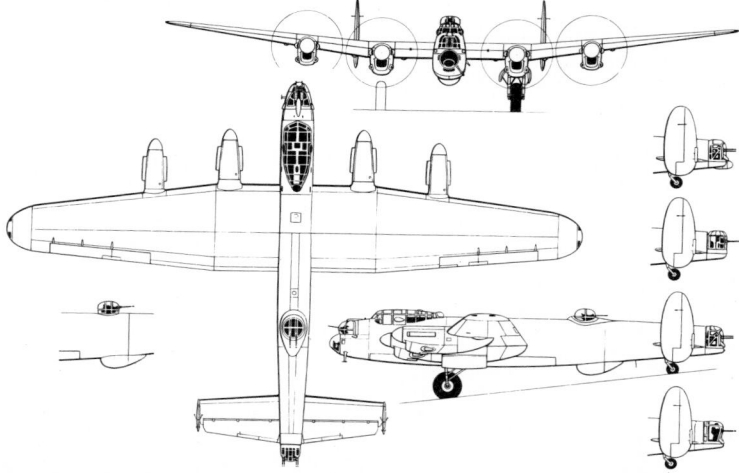

954-kW (1,280-hp) Merlin XXs and XXIIs, of 1208-kW (1,620-hp) Merlin XXIVs in production aircraft. Early thoughts of fitting a ventral turret were soon discarded, and the Lancaster B.I had three Frazer-Nash hydraulically-operated turrets with eight 7.7-mm (0.303-in) Browning machine-guns: two each in the nose and mid-upper dorsal positions and four in the tail turret. The bomb-bay, designed originally to carry 1814kg (4,000lb) of bombs, was enlarged progressively to carry bigger and bigger bombs: up to 3629 and 5443kg (8,000 and 12,000lb) and eventually to the enormous 9979-kg (22,000-lb) 'Grand Slam' – the heaviest bomb carried by any aircraft in World War II.

As Packard-built Merlins became available, so the **Lancaster B.III** appeared with these engines, although the B.I remained in production alongside the Packard-engined B.III. Externally the B.III was distinguishable by an enlarged bomb aimer's 'bubble' in the nose, but apart from this there were few differences other than in minor equipment changes.

To swell the UK production lines, Victory Aircraft in Canada was chosen in 1942 to build Lancasters, under the **Lancaster B.X** designation. Powered by Packard, Lancasters were delivered by air across the Atlantic and had their armament fitted on arrival from 6 August 1943, and 430 were built before production was completed.

Mention must be made of the **Lancaster B.VI**, production of which was proposed using Merlins, either 85s or 87s, of 1219 kW (1,635 hp). Nine airframes were converted by Rolls-Royce for comparative tests. No. 635 Squadron used several operationally on pathfinder work with nose and dorsal turret removed, and fitted with an improved H$_2$S radar bombing aid and early electronic countermeasures equipment, but although performance was superior to the earlier marks no production aircraft were built.

Final production version of the Lancaster was the **B.VII**, which had an American Martin dorsal turret with two 12.7-mm (0.50-in) guns in place of the normal Frazer-Nash turret; the new turret was also located further forward.

In spite of the other variants built from time to time, the Lancaster B.I (B.1 from

B.A.T. F.K.23 Bantam

When Frederick Koolhoven left Armstrong Whitworth in 1917, his first design for his new employers, the British Aerial Transport Co. Ltd (B.A.T.), was the **F.K.22** single-seat fighter. A two-bay biplane of wooden construction, with a monocoque fuselage, the F.K.22 was to have been powered by the 89-kW (120-hp) A.B.C. Mosquito radial engine, but the failure of this powerplant led to the installation of the 127-kW (170-hp) A.B.C. Wasp I in the first and third of a planned total of six development aircraft. The second machine, powered by a 75-kW (100-hp) Gnome Monosoupape rotary engine, was the first to fly and undertook development trials at Martlesham Heath in January 1918. It was later re-engined with a 82-kW (110-hp) Le Rhône 9J rotary.

The other three aircraft ordered under the original development contract were built under the designation **F.K.23 Bantam**, the second prototype F.K.22 then becoming known as the **Bantam II**. The prototype Bantam I retained the basic wooden structure but was of smaller size, the wing span being reduced from 7.52 m (24 ft 8 in) to 6.10 m (20 ft 0 in) and the length from 6.30 m (20 ft 8 in) to 5.61 m (18 ft 5 in). The A.B.C. Wasp engine was selected to power the Bantam I, and flight tests began in May 1918. Two further prototypes, of a slightly larger and modified design, were also completed; they were followed by at least nine of a development batch of 12. The first of these was flown to the Royal Aircraft Establishment at Farnborough on 26 July 1918. Two aircraft were sent overseas for evaluation, one to Villacoublay in France and one to Wright Field in the United States. The latter was given the US project number P.167, and was eventually placed in store on 30 September 1922.

The production Bantams incorporated a number of design changes, mainly to overcome the unsatisfactory spin characteristics of the prototypes. Wing span was increased, an enlarged tailplane and elevators were fitted, the fin was reduced in area and rudder area was increased. Continuing engine problems and the post-war contraction of the Royal Air Force were among factors which affected the future of the Bantam, although an attempt was made to overcome the first of these by re-engining the last production example with a 149-kW (200-hp) A.B.C. Wasp II. Following the closure of B.A.T., Koolhoven purchased this aircraft and took it to the Netherlands, where it was again re-engined, this time with a 149-kW (200-hp) Armstrong Siddeley Lynx radial. Several examples subsequently appeared on the British civil register, including one raced by B.A.T. test pilot Major Christopher Draper at Hendon on 21 June 1919. This featured a lower wing clipped to half its original length, the upper wing being supported by slanting struts in place of the outer set of interplane components.

B.A.T. F.K.23 Bantam, the fifth production machine, in racing trim as a civil aircraft. Number 5 identifies the aircraft as K-155, later G-EAFN.

Specification
B.A.T. F.K.23 Bantam
Type: single-seat fighter
Powerplant: one 127-kW (170-hp) A.B.C. Wasp I radial piston engine
Performance: maximum speed 206 km/h (128 mph) at 1980 m (6,500 ft); climb to 1980 m (6,500 ft) in 5 seconds; service ceiling 6100 m (20,000 ft); endurance 2 hours 30 minutes
Weights: empty 378 kg (833 lb); maximum take-off 599 kg (1,321 lb)
Dimensions: span 7.62 m (25 ft 0 in); length 5.61 m (18 ft 5 in); height 2.06 m (6 ft 9 in); wing area 17.19 m^2 (185.0 sq ft)
Armament: two fixed forward-firing 7.7-mm (0.303-in) Vickers machine-guns

A B.A.T. F.K.22 on trials at Martlesham Heath. Planned as a fighter, prolonged development and the contraction of the RAF brought about its demise.

Bachem Ba 349 Natter

The Luftwaffe's need for a weapon with which to combat Allied bomber streams more effectively led, early in 1944, to the Reichsluftfahrtministerium's issue of a requirement to Heinkel, Junkers, Messerschmitt and Bachem for what was, in effect, a piloted missile. The **Bachem BP 20 Natter** (Adder) project was selected for development and given the RLM designation **Ba 349**.

Bachem's design office, headed by Dipl. Ing. Erich Bachem and Herr H. Bethbeder, evolved a comparatively crude airframe, emphasis being placed on ease of manufacture by unskilled woodworkers, without the use of complex jigs. The short stubby wings had no ailerons, control about the roll axis being exercised by differential use of the elevators. The fuselage, with its small cockpit, housed a Walter 109-509A-2 sustainer rocket capable of producing 1700-kg (3,748-lb) thrust for 70 seconds at full power, but also able to run at outputs as low as 150 kg (331 lb) for increased endurance. The aircraft was to be launched vertically, and power for this purpose was provided by four Schmidding 109-533 solid-fuel rockets, two on each side of the fuselage, and each producing 1200-kg (2,646-lb) thrust for 10 seconds before being jettisoned.

The first of 15 Natters manufactured for the test programme became available in October 1944 and was used for unpowered handling trials, towed aloft behind a Heinkel He 111. Following further piloted gliding tests, in December 1944, the programme switched to unmanned flights using the booster rockets only. The first vertical launch with booster and sustainer rockets firing, still without a pilot, took place on 23 February 1945. Just a few days later, test pilot Lothar Siebert was killed when, in making the first and almost certainly the only piloted vertical launch, the cockpit cover became detached in flight and the aircraft dived into the ground from about 1525 m (5,000 ft).

Operational tactics evolved for the Natter involved a vertical launch on autopilot, the pilot assuming manual control when positioned above the approaching bombers. Placed in a shallow dive, the Natter would have been armed by jettisoning the nose cone to expose its battery of 24 Föhn 73-mm (2.87-in) rocket projectiles. Having fired these unguided missiles, the aircraft was flown clear of the battlezone, and the pilot would then prepare to bale out. After the pilot had released his straps, the entire nose section was to be jettisoned by uncoupling the control column, moving it forward to release the safety catches, and then releasing mechanical catches to separate the nose from the rest of the fuselage. The airflow having removed the forward fuselage the pilot was effectively ejected by the deceleration of the rear section as it streamed a braking and re-covery parachute, leaving him to descend on his own parachute. The rear fuselage was to be salvaged to facilitate re-use of the Walter rocket motor.

An expedient born of Germany's desperate straits in 1944, the Bachem Ba 349 Natter was a semi-expendable point interceptor.

Variants
Ba 349A: initial production version, 50 ordered for the Luftwaffe and 150 for SS; approximately 20 completed but not used operationally
Ba 349B: improved version with increased tail unit area and more powerful Walter 109-509C rocket which provided maximum thrust of 2000 kg (4,410 lb) and more effective throttle control down to 200 kg (441 lb)

Specification
Type: single-seat fighter
Powerplant: one 1700-kg (3,748-lb) thrust Walter 109-509A-2 rocket motor and four 1200-kg (2,640-lb) thrust Schmidding 109-533 booster rockets
Performance: maximum speed 800 km/h (497 mph) at sea level; initial climb rate 11100 m (36,415 ft) per minute; service ceiling 14000 m (45,920 ft); radius of action at 12000 m (39,360 ft) 40 km (24.8 miles)
Weight: maximum take-off 2200 kg (4,850 lb)
Dimensions: span 3.60 m (11 ft 9.75 in); length 6.10 m (20 ft 0 in); wing area 2.75 m^2 (29.60 sq ft)
Armament: 24 Föhn unguided missiles

Beagle B.121

The UK's pre-eminence in light aircraft design before World War II was unquestioned, and it was to be expected that an attempt to regain a foothold in this lucrative market would be made once the industry had readjusted to peacetime conditions. Miles made a brave try but eventually floundered, and it was with great hopes that Beagle launched its all-metal **Beagle B.121 Pup,** the two-seat prototype of which flew from the company's Shoreham factory on 8 April 1967, with a 75-kW (100-hp) Rolls-Royce Continental O-200-A engine.

The new aircraft proved to be a delight to fly and the next two examples, flown in October 1967 and January 1968, were prototypes for the **Pup Series 2** with an enlarged rudder and four seats. In this form the engine was changed to a 112-kW (150-hp) Avco Lycoming O-320-A2B, while the **Pup Series 3** had a 119-kW (160-hp) Avco Lycoming O-360-A. The Pup Series 1, 2 and 3 were more usually known as **Pup 100, Pup 150** and **Pup 160** respectively.

Following the Pup's first public appearance at the 1967 Paris Air Show, Beagle launched a sales drive and the orders began to come in. The first operator, not surprisingly, was the Shoreham School of Flying, which received the first of four Pups on 12 April 1968, but operated them for less than 18 months before re-equipping. It was said at the time that Beagle were so busy building aircraft they did not pay sufficient heed to the requirement for an efficient after-sales service, and spares were hard to get. But deliveries were mounting, to customers in the UK, Germany, Eire, Austria, Finland, Sweden, Denmark, the Netherlands, Luxembourg, Iraq, Australia, Malaysia, South Africa, Iran and USA.

Requirements for a military trainer version led to the re-engining of the prototype with a 149-kW (200-hp) Avco Lycoming engine in April 1969, and the definitive version, the **B.125 Bulldog,** flew the following month.

Speed of production can be gauged by the fact that the 100th Pup was handed over on 23 September 1969, only 17 months after the first production aircraft had flown. But Beagle were by this time in difficulties, and when the government withdrew its financial support the company was put into receivership, the last Pup flying on 12 January 1970.

It is ironic that 121 Pups had been delivered and a further 276 were on order when Beagle collapsed. It was said that production costs were outstripping sales values, since the Pup was not really suitable for mass production. When Beagle closed and further development of the Bulldog was taken over by Scottish Aviation at Prestwick, considerable redesign was needed to make production easier and more economical. More than 320 Bulldogs were built for military customers.

Specification
Beagle B.121 Pup 150
Type: four-seat light monoplane
Powerplant: one 112-kW (150-hp) Avco Lycoming O-320-A2B flat-four piston engine
Performance: maximum speed 222 km/h (138 mph) at sea level; cruising speed 211 km/h (131 mph) at 2285 m (7,500 ft); service ceiling 4480 m (14,700 ft); range 1019 km (633 miles)
Weights: empty 494 kg (1,090 lb); maximum take-off 873 kg (1,925 lb)
Dimensions: span 9.45 m (31 ft 0 in); length 7.06 m (23 ft 2 in); height 2.29 m (7 ft 6 in); wing area 11.10 m² (119.5 sq ft)

Although an excellent aircraft, the Pup suffered from overcomplication of construction, with corresponding weight and cost penalties.

Beagle B.206 Basset

Beagle's first completely original design was the attractive **Beagle B.206**, flown at Shoreham on 15 August 1961 as the **B.206X**, in which form it had five seats and was powered by two 194-kW (260-hp) Continental engines. Of all-metal construction, the new aircraft made its public debut at the Farnborough Air Show during the following month. Having second thoughts about the size, Beagle enlarged the design to a seven-seater, increased the span by 1.44 m (8 ft) and fitted geared Continental engines. This flew as the **B.206Y on 12 August 1962**.

First orders were, in fact, for a military version, designated **Beagle Basset CC.Mk 1**, of which 20 were delivered to the RAF from May 1965; two of the pre-production **B.206Z** model were supplied to Boscombe Down for evaluation.

The first production civil **B.206 Series 1**, built at the former Auster factory at Rearsby, flew on 17 July 1964, while the first delivery was made to Rolls-Royce on 13 May 1965. Eleven Series 1 aircraft were built for British customers, mostly companies; two were later converted to Series 2 standard, with supercharged engines and detail changes.

Total production of the **B.206 Series 2** amounted to 47 aircraft of which 28 were for UK customers and 19 for export. The latter included deliveries to Spain, Argentina, South Africa, Sudan, Zambia, USA, Nigeria, Brazil and the Royal Flying Doctor Service in Sydney, Australia. These two RFDS aircraft could carry two stretcher cases, a doctor and an attendant. The main difference between the B.206 Series 1 and Series 2 (in prototype form **B.206S**) was the latter's 254-kW (340-hp) supercharged Rolls-Royce Continental engines, though other refinements included an extra window and a 1.07 by 0.96 m (3 ft 6 in by 3 ft 2 in) freight door.

Other B.206s were found to be suitable for instrument flying training. Three aircraft, known as **B.206 Series 3**s, had a deeper rear fuselage and accommodation for 10 people, but this version was not developed further.

Production of the B.206 ended in 1969; 85 had been built, the majority for civil use, and when the Basset was declared surplus to RAF requirements in the late 1970s a number came on to the civil market.

Specification
Beagle B.206 Series 2
Type: five/eight-seat monoplane

A Beagle B.206 flies along the Sussex coast in formation with the prototype Pup. The B.206 is best-remembered in RAF colours as the Basset CC.Mk 1.

Powerplant: two 254-kW (340-hp) Rolls-Royce Continental GTSIO-520-C flat-six piston engines
Performance: maximum speed 415 km/h (258 mph) at 4875 m (16,000 ft); cruising speed 351 km/h (218 mph) at 2440 m (8,000 ft) and 3175 kg (7,000 lb) AUW; service ceiling 8260 m (27,100 ft); range 2575 km (1,600 miles)
Weights: empty 2177 kg (4,800 lb); maximum take-off 3401 kg (7,499 lb)
Dimensions: span 13.96 m (45 ft 6 9½ in); length 10.26 m (33 ft 8 in); height 3.45 m (11 ft 5 in); wing area 19.88 m² (214 sq ft)

Beech Model 17 Staggerwing

America's 'barnstorming' pilots of the early 1920s developed eye-catching razzle-dazzle routines that included aerobatics, wing-walking, trapeze acts, and rope-ladder transfers from one aircraft to another. Soon a crowd would gather to enjoy the show, and from them pilots would 'drum-up' a few passengers for a short flight around the meadow from which they were operating. Many were concerned only to scrape a living from this new and exciting field of aviation, using talents acquired during World War I; others wanted, more specifically, to make the nation air-minded. Far too many were to die in flying accidents, resulting from indifferent aircraft or poor standards of maintenance, but many survived to begin air-taxi operations. Some, like Walter Beech and Clive Cessna, became involved in the design and manufacture of aircraft that would be suitable for 'the man in the street' when the moment came for him to take to the air.

Together with Lloyd Stearman, Beech and Cessna formed the Travel Air Manufacturing Company during 1924, and six years later this was acquired by the Curtiss-Wright Corporation. Walter Beech then decided to plough his own furrow and, together with his wife Olive, established the Beech Aircraft Corporation during 1932. In late 1950 Walter Beech died but now, just on 50 years after the company's formation, Mrs. Olive Beech remains in office as chairman of the board of the success story that has built some 45,000 aircraft.

A key to that success was the **Beech Model 17**, but the high performance of the initial **Model 17R**, of which only two examples were built, meant that it was very much an experienced pilot's aeroplane, and unsuitable for the far wider market that was sought. First flown during November 1932, an exciting event witnessed by the company's staff of eight employees, the Model 17R was able to demonstrate a remarkable speed range of 97-322 km/h (60-200 mph). The most conspicuous feature of its configuration was the backward stagger of its biplane wings. Such an arrangement had

Beech's classic Model 17 featured back-staggered wings and retractable undercarriage. Together with the enclosed cabin these gave an air of speed and performance, which led to healthy sales to well-off, experienced pilots.

been selected to provide the pilot with a good field of view, to help structural integration, and because wind tunnel tests had shown that this particular layout offered a good combination of speed and stability. Basic structure was of welded steel tube, largely fabric-covered; the braced tail unit was conventional; but the narrow-track tailwheel landing gear, with a non-swivelling tailwheel, had an unusual feature. The main units were enclosed within large streamline fairings, but the wheels could be retracted some 0.15 m (6 in) in flight so that they were completely within the fairings. Enclosed cabin accommodation was provided for a pilot and three or four passengers, and the 313-kW (420-hp) Wright R-975-E2 radial engine was mounted within an unusual tunnel-type cowling.

The excellent performance of the 'Staggerwing', as the type became popularly known, meant that the company's efforts were concentrated upon making it easier to handle, especially on the ground, which led to a number of improvements, including wider-track main units. However, the real turning point to wider market acceptance came with the **Model B17L**, first flown in late February 1934. This introduced a new lower wing of deeper aerofoil section, allowing sufficient room for the main landing gear units to retract fully into it. This, coupled with a 168-kW (225-hp) Jacobs L-4 radial engine, gave much more docile handling characteristics, while retaining a speed range of 72-282 km/h (45-175 mph). With just a little more power, provided by the 213-kW (285-hp) Jacobs L-5, the Model 17 became the marketable commodity that was eventually to establish Beech as a

major aircraft manufacturer.

From that time a wide variety of Staggerwings were built for both civil and military use, being steadily improved, and incorporating over the years a number of different engines. The civil versions included **Model B17, C17, D17, E17** and **F17** variants before World War II, which were followed in the early postwar years by a much-improved **Model G17S**, of which only 20 were built to special order. Although the last of these was completed in 1949, it seems highly possible that at least some examples of Walter Beech's remarkable Staggerwing will still be in use at the end of this century.

When in 1939 the US Army Air Corps needed a small communications aircraft, the excellent performance of the Model 17 resulted in the procurement of three Model D17s for evaluation under the designation **YC-43**. However, it was not until expansion of the USAAF began during 1941-2 that an initial production order for 27 was received, this leading to a total procurement of 207 Beech 17s under the designation **UC-43**, these being powered by the 336-kW (450-hp) Pratt & Whitney R-985-AN-1 engine. After the United States became involved in World War II, an additional 118 civil Model 17s were impressed for military service, and comprising D17R, D17S, F17D, E17B, C17R, D17A, C17B, B17R, C17L, and D17W variants under the re-

spective designations of **UC-43A, UC-43B, UC-43C, UC-43D, UC-43E, UC-43F, UC-43G, UC-43H, UC-43J** and **UC-43K**.

The US Navy had acquired a single example of the Staggerwing as early as 1939. This was a civil C17R which became designated **JB-1**. The designation **GB-1** applied to 10 more, equivalent to the civil D17, acquired in 1939 and, later, to eight civil D17s impressed for military service. Wartime procurement totalled 342 **GB-2**s, of which 105 were supplied to the UK under Lend-Lease, used primarily by the Royal Navy which named them Traveller, a name adopted also by the US Navy.

Specification
Beech Model G17S
Type: four/five-seat cabin biplane
Powerplant: one 336-kW (450-hp) Pratt & Whitney R-985-AN-4 Wasp Junior radial piston engine
Performance: maximum speed 341 km/h (212 mph); economic cruising speed 298 km/h (185 mph) at 2895 m (9,500 ft); maximum range at economic cruising speed about 1609 km (1,000 miles)
Weights: empty 1270 kg (2,800 lb); maximum take-off 1928 kg (4,250 lb)
Dimensions: span 9.75 m (32 ft 0 in); length 8.15 m (26 ft 9 in); height 2.44 m (8 ft 0 in); wing area 27.65 m² (296.50 sq ft)

Beech Model 18

With the Model 17 well established, Beech began in 1935 the development of a six/eight-seat commercial transport identified as the **Beech Model 18**. This was a very different aeroplane from the Model 17, being a low-wing monoplane of all-metal construction, with a semi-monocoque fuselage of light alloy, a cantilever tail unit incorporating twin endplate fins and rudders, and electrically retractable tailwheel landing gear. Float or ski landing gear was to become optional. Standard accommodation provided for two crew and six passengers, and the initial powerplant installation comprised two 239-kW (320-hp) Wright R-760-E2 radial engines mounted in wing leading-edge nacelles.

The initial **Model 18A** was flown for the first time on 15 January 1937. Even

the most interested eyewitness of the event might have been little thrilled by the appearance of yet another twin-engined light commercial and, perhaps, would have expected it to gain only very limited marketing success. He could not have been more wrong, for the type was not only to remain in production for a record 32 years, but has since proved a popular choice for conversion by a number of American companies, with modifications intended to provide improved performance or greater capacity.

However, this glimpse at the future overlooks the early period when perhaps only Walter Beech was convinced that the Model 18 represented a worthwhile project. An improved **Model 18B** with lower-powered engines also sold in only penny-packet numbers, and the first

Beech Model 18 derivatives were widely used in World War II for training and communications duties. This is a trio of AT-11 Kansans, equipped with nose bombardier position.

sign that the company was on the right track came with the **Model 18D** of 1939. This had 246-kW (330-hp) Jacobs L-6 engines, providing improved performance and much the same economy of operation as the Model 18B. Only about 30 of these were sold in 1940, but the wartime demand for these aircraft was to total more than 4,000.

The first US Army Air Corps order, placed during 1940, was for the supply of 11 aircraft under the designation **C-45**, for use as staff transports, these being generally similar to the civil **Model B18S**. Subsequent procurement covered 20 **C-45A**s for use in a utility transport role, with interior and equipment changes being made in the 223 **C-45B**s that followed. Some of these aircraft were supplied to the UK under Lend-Lease, being designated **Expediter II**s in RAF service. The USAAF designations **C-45C**, **C-45D** and **C-45E** were applied respectively to two impressed B18S civil aircraft, two AT-7s completed for transport duties, and six AT-7Bs similarly modified. Major and final production version for the USAAF was the seven-seat **C-45F**, with a slightly longer nose and of which no fewer than 1,137 were built. Lend-Lease deliveries from the procurement served with the Royal Navy and RAF as **Expediter II**s, and with the Royal Canadian Air Force as **Expediter III**s. All of the foregoing C-45 designations were changed to a new **UC-45** category in January 1943.

In 1941, the **Beech AT-7 Navigator** was introduced to provide navigation training; this was equipped with three positions for trainee navigators, plus a dorsal astrodome. A total of 577 was built, being followed by six **AT-7A**s with float landing gear and a large ventral fin. Nine **AT-7B**s, basically winterized AT-7s were built to USAAF order: five were supplied to the UK, one being used by Prince Bernard of the Netherlands during his wartime exile. Final version of the Navigator was the **AT-7C** with a different powerplant, production totalling 549.

Another version of the Model 18 appeared in the AT (advanced trainer) category during 1941. This was the **AT-11 Kansan** (originally named Kansas), procured by the USAAF as a bombing and gunnery trainer. It incorporated a small bomb bay, had small circular portholes in place of the standard rectangular cabin windows, a redesigned nose to provide a bomb aiming position, and two 7.62-mm (0.3-in) machine-guns, one in the nose, the other in a dorsal turret. Production to USAAF orders totalled 1,582; of these 36 were converted for navigation training as **AT-11A**s. Twenty-four AT-11s ordered by the Netherlands for service in the Netherlands East Indies were, instead, taken on charge by the USAAF: they were delivered subsequently to the Royal Netherlands Military Flying School at Jackson, Mississippi, in early 1942.

Last of the US Army Air Force's wartime versions of the Beech Model 18 were photographic reconnaissance **F-2**s, 14 civil Model B18S being purchased and converted with cabin-mounted mapping cameras and oxygen equipment. They were supplemented later by 13 **F-2A**s with four cameras, converted from C-45As, and by 42 **F-2B**s, which were conversions from UC-45Fs: these had additional camera ports in both sides of the fuselage. In June 1948, under a general revision of the USAF designation system, all of the surviving F-2 photo/reconnaissance aircraft were redesignated **RC-45A**. Simi-

larly, AT-7, AT-7C and AT-11s dropped their A prefix: at the same time a small number of drone-directors converted from UC-45Fs and given the designation **CQ-3** became instead, **DC-45Fs**.

The US Navy and US Marine Corps also used the Model 18 extensively, to the extent of more than 1,500 examples. Initial procurement related to a version similar to the US Army's F-2, this being designated **JRB-1**, and followed by a **JRB-2** transport, and **JRB-3**s and **JRB-4**s equivalent to the C-45B and UC-45F respectively. The designations **SNB-1**, **SNB-2** and **SNB-3** were applied respectively to aircraft that were equivalent to the USAAF's AT-11, AT-7, and AT-7C. US Navy ambulance and photographic versions were the **SNB-2H** and **SNB-2P** respectively; the **SNB-3Q** was an electronic countermeasures trainer.

During 1951-2, in-service USAF UC-45E, T-7 and T-11 aircraft were remanufactured to zero-time condition and modernised, emerging with the new designations **C-45G** and **C-45H**. The former had an autopilot and R-985-AN-3 engines, the latter no autopilot and R-985-AN-14B engines. At the same time, US Navy SNB-2s, SNB-2Cs, and SNB-2Ps were remanufactured under the designations **SNB-5** and **SNB-5P**. Later, with introduction of the tri-service unified designation scheme in 1962, in-service SNB aircraft were redesignated **TC-45J** and **RC-45J** respectively in the training and photographic roles.

With a return to peace, Beech resumed manufacture of the civil Model 18, and in 1953 introduced a new larger and improved version of the D18S. Known as the **Super 18 (E18S)**, the prototype was flown for the first time on 10 December 1953. Structural improvements included external refinements to

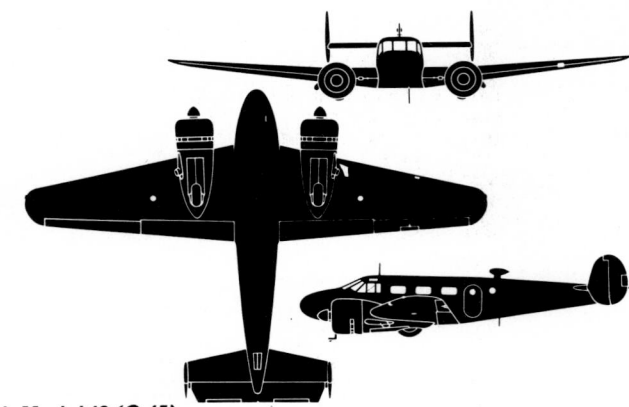

Beech Model 18 (C-45)

reduce drag, Geisse safety landing gear for cross-wind operations, the provision of a separate flight deck, and improved soundproofing. Progressive improvements continued throughout the production of 754 Super 18s, the last examples of the final **Model H18** version being built during 1969.

In September 1963 Beech introduced optional retractable tricycle landing gear which had been developed by Volpar Inc. of Los Angeles, California. This company also offered conversions of standard Beech 18s to **Volpar Turbo 18** standard, with tricycle landing gear and TPE331 turboprop engines, and also the lengthened turboprop-powered 15-passenger **Volpar Turboliner**. Conversions offered by other manufacturers have included the nine-passenger **Dumod I** and 15-passenger **Dumod Liner**, offered by Dumod Corporation; and Pacific Airmotive Corporation's 10-passenger **PAC Tradewind** and turboprop-powered **PAC Turbo Trade-**

wind. Still available from Hamilton Aviation in late 1981 were the **Hamilton Westwind II STD** and **Westwind III** turboprop-powered conversion of 17- and eight-passenger capacity respectively.

Specification
Beech Super H18
Type: Twin-engine light transport
Powerplant: two 336-kW (450-hp) Pratt & Whitney R-985-AN-14B radial piston engines
Performance: maximum cruising speed 354 km/h (220 mph) at 3050 m (10,000 ft); economic cruising speed 298 km/h (185 mph) at 3050 m (10,000 ft); service ceiling 6525 m (21,400 ft); maximum range 3060 km (1,530 miles)
Weights: empty 2651 kg (5,845 lb); maximum take-off 4491 kg (9,900 lb)
Dimensions: span 15.15 m (49 ft 8 in); length 10.73 m (35 ft 2½ in); height 2.84 m (9 ft 4 in); wing area 33.51 m² (360.70 sq ft)

Post-war, the Beech 18s saw much use as general transports, particularly in the Americas.

Beech Model H18 of Air Cortez, featuring tricycle undercarriage.

Beech Model 23
to
Beech Model 45 Mentor

Beech Model 23

Showing a general similarity to the earlier Bonanza/Debonair family, the prototype **Beech Model 23 Musketeer** was flown for the first time on 23 October 1961. Developed as a low-cost all-metal light business aircraft, it was of cantilever low-wing monoplane configuration, its fuselage providing enclosed cabin accommodation for a pilot and three passengers, and with non-retractable tricycle landing gear. Powerplant of the first production version, of which deliveries began in autumn 1962, was a 119-kW (160-hp) Avco Lycoming O-320-D2B flat-four engine.

Early popularity of the type resulted in a range of three Musketeers being marketed from late 1965. Identified as the **Musketeer Custom**, the two-seat (optional four-seat) **Musketeer Sport** and the **Musketeer Super**, they differed mainly by having 134-kW (180-hp), 112-kW (150-hp) and 149-kW (200-hp) Avco Lycoming engines respectively. Optional aerobatic kits were also available for the Musketeer Custom and Musketeer Sport when flown as two-seaters. A fourth version was introduced in late 1969: known as the **Musketeer Super R**, it was basically the same as the Musketeer Super but incorporated retractable tricycle landing gear.

A further change in marketing policy in 1971 was to mark the disappearance of the name Musketeer, and simultaneously production of the Musketeer Super was discontinued. The three remaining aircraft became known instead as the **Sundowner C23** (formerly Custom), **Sport B19** (Sport) and **Sierra A24R** (Super R). The designations were changed again in 1974 to indicate engine horsepower, the three types becoming respectively **Sundowner 180, Sport 150** and **Sierra 200**. Well over 4,400 Musketeers of all types had been built when production was suspended in 1984.

In addition to ordinary civil sales, Musketeers have been delivered for civil or military training use to Algeria, the Canadian Armed Forces, Indonesia and Mexico.

Specification
Beech Sierra 200
Type: four/six-seat cabin monoplane
Powerplant: one 149-kW (200-hp) Avco Lycoming IO-360-A1B6 flat-four piston engine
Performance: maximum speed at sea level 262 km/h (163 mph); economic cruising speed 213 km/h (132 mph) at 3050 m (10,000 ft); service ceiling 4690 m (15,385 ft); range with maximum fuel 1271 km (790 miles)
Weights: empty 772 kg (1,701 lb); maximum take-off 1247 kg (2,750 lb)
Dimensions: span 9.98 m (32 ft 9 in); length 7.85 m (25 ft 9 in); height 2.46 m (8 ft 1 in); wing area 13.56 m² (146.0 sq ft)

The Beech Sundowner was one of three lightplanes developed from the basic Musketeer series.

Beech Model 26

The rapid expansion of US training facilities in 1941 created a sudden need for trainer aircraft at a time when it seemed likely that raw materials, notably aluminium and magnesium alloys, would have to be conserved for first-line types. An engineering team led by Beech's T.A. Wells evolved the **Beech Model 26**, which was the first all-wood trainer to be accepted by the US Army Air Force. This was given the designation **AT-10 Wichita**. The design avoided, where possible, the use of compound curves and of hot moulding processes for the structure's sub-assemblies, allowing them to be sub-contracted to non-specialist wood-working firms: 85 per cent of the airframe was manufactured on this basis, with final assembly by Beech.

Metal airframe parts were limited to engine nacelles and cowlings, and panelling around the cockpit section. Perhaps the most interesting innovation was the use of wooden fuel tanks lined with synthetic rubber. For operation as a multi-engined conversion trainer, the Wichita was equipped with dual controls and an autopilot, and entry to the cockpit was via rearward-sliding side windows.

The AT-10 was powered by two 220-kW (295-hp) Lycoming R-680-9 engines, and by 1943 Beech had completed four contracts, for 150, 191, 18,080 and 350 aircraft respectively, bringing the total built at Wichita to 1,771. The last of these was delivered on 15 September 1943. Beech then supplied engineering and production data to the Globe Aircraft Corporation of Dallas, Texas, so that a further 600 could be manufactured.

Specification
Type: two-seat advanced trainer
Powerplant: two 220-kW (295-hp) Lycoming R-680 radial piston engines

Performance: maximum speed 319 km/h (198 mph); service ceiling 5150 m (16,900 ft); range 1239 km (770 miles)
Weights: empty 2155 kg (4,750 lb); maximum take-off 2781 kg (6,130 lb)
Dimensions: span 13.41 m (44 ft 0 in);

The AT-10 shows typical Beech design. It provided the USAAF with a simple and cheap trainer without using strategic materials.

length 10.46 m (34 ft 4 in); wing area 27.68 m² (298 sq ft)

Beech Model 28 Destroyer

The **Beech Model 28** merits brief mention as an unusual project for this manufacturer. Two examples of a twin-engined attack aircraft were ordered from Beech in 1943 under the designation **XA-38**, and the Model 28 was a large low-wing monoplane, with a fuselage accommodating a crew of three, and with a tail unit incorporating twin fins and rudders. Power was provided by two Wright R-3350-43 radial engines, and in addition to defensive armament, the Destroyer carried a 75-mm cannon for its attack role. Only the two aircraft were built, being delivered for evaluation in 1945.

Specification
Type: twin-engined attack aircraft
Powerplant: two 1715-kW (2,300-hp) Wright R-3350-43 Cyclone radial piston engines
Performance: maximum level speed 605 km/h (376 mph)
Weight: maximum take-off 15995 kg (35,264 lb)
Dimensions: span 20.52 m (67 ft 4 in); length 15.77 m (51 ft 9 in)

The most remarkable feature of the Model 28 was the 75-mm nose cannon. These were the only two aircraft built.

Beech Models 33, 35 and 36 Bonanza and Debonair

The **Beech Model 35 Bonanza** was the founder member of a remarkable family of aircraft, not only for the fact that production of Bonanzas of all types amounts to about 15,000, but also because the V-tail Bonanza extended over 35 years of production.

Flown for the first time on 22 December 1945, the prototype Model 35 Bonanza, distinguished easily by its V- (or butterfly-) tail, was to become another outstanding success in the mould of the Models 17 and 18. Unlike them, it got off the ground rather more quickly for when the company announced that full-scale production was to begin in March 1947, it already had a backlog of around 1,500 orders. It was a moment for the benefits of wartime experience to pay off, for about 1,000 deliveries had been made by the end of that year.

The general configuration of the Model 35 has remained virtually unchanged throughout the aircraft's history. A cantilever low-wing monoplane of all-metal construction, including the distinctive tail unit, the Model 35 has an enclosed cabin providing seating for a pilot and three or four passengers. From the outset the Model 35 has had retractable tricycle landing gear, but the original version had only a swivelling nosewheel: a steerable unit was introduced on the **Model A35** in 1949. An optional feature throughout the years has been a landing gear safety system of Beech design. Named 'Magic Hand', this ensures that the wheels cannot be retracted accidentally on the ground, or a landing made with the wheels up. As first flown, power was provided by a 138-kW (185-hp) Continental E-185-1 flat-six engine, but a variety of standard and optional powerplants have been installed during the long production run. These have included turbocharged units for the **V35 TC** and the **V35B TC**.

Despite the large demand for the V-tailed Model 35, there were many potential buyers who considered this tail unit to be something of a gimmick, one that might present problems. To meet the needs of such people, Beech introduced the **Model 33 Debonair**, following a first flight on 14 September 1959. Having a conventional tail unit, and with a slightly lower-powered engine, the Debonair accommodated a pilot and three passengers. It represented a lower-cost version of the Bonanza, and was built and marketed in parallel until production of the Debonair, as such, ended in 1966, by when almost 1,200 had been built. It was replaced in 1967 by the **Model E33 Bonanza**, a four/five-seat version that was virtually identical to the V-tail Model 35, except for the provision of a conventional tail unit with sweptback vertical surfaces. This version, in **F33A** standard and **F33C** aerobatic/utility versions, remained available in late 1989, by which time production of Model 33 Debonairs/Bonanzas was approaching a total of 3,000. Examples of these aircraft have been used for civil or military training by organisations that include the air force of Iran, Lufthansa, the Mexican navy, the Netherlands

The Beech 33 Debonair started life as essentially a conventionally-tailed Bonanza, and indeed developments of the type adopted the Bonanza name. Still in production is the Bonanza 36 with turbocharged engine.

The most interesting military use for the Bonanza series was the QU-22B Pave Eagle drone programme, used in Vietnam for relaying seismic sensor signals.

government, Pacific Southwest Airlines, and the Spanish air ministry/air force.

A third member of the Bonanza family was introduced in 1968, in the form of the **Model 36** six-seat utility aircraft. It is basically a slightly lengthened (0.25 m/10 in) version of the V35B, combining the tail unit of the Model 33, and the strengthened landing gear developed for the Beech Baron. It also has double doors on the starboard side of the fuselage, making it easier to load or unload cargo when used in a utility role. These cargo doors are available optionally for the Model 33/35 aircraft. A turbocharged version of the Model 36 has been available since 1979 under the designation **Model B36 TC Turbo Bonanza**. Production of Model 36 Bonanzas totalled some 3,390 by early 1989.

Since the introduction of each of these models, there has been steady improvement of the product, and a wide range of optional avionics and equipment is available for in-production versions.

Brief mention must be made of two military versions of the A36 Bonanza. Under the designation **QU-22B** a number were provided with special avionics equipment under the USAF's 'Pave Eagle' programme. With this they were deployed in Vietnam to pick up and relay to a ground station the data transmitted from acoustic sensors. Intended to keep track of enemy movements in the dense jungle, the sensors were air-dropped along known or suspected transport routes. To meet the requirements of the USAF's 'Pave Coin' competition, Beech developed a close-support two-seat armed version of the A36. Designated **Model PD 249**, this prototype was evaluated with a wide variety of weapons, carried on underwing racks that could accommodate loads of up to 535 kg (1,180 lb), but no production examples were built.

Specification
Beech Bonanza Model V35B
Type: four/five-seat cabin monoplane
Powerplant: one 213-kW (285-hp) Continental IO-520-BB flat-six piston engine
Performance: maximum speed at sea level 338 km/h (209 mph);

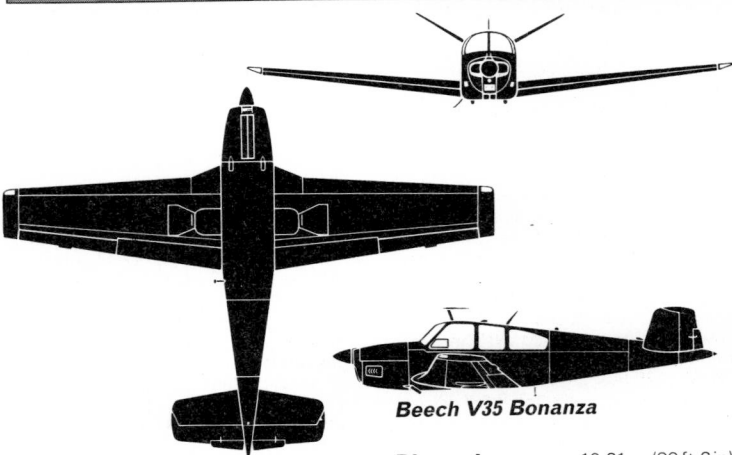

Beech V35 Bonanza

economic cruising speed 253 km/h (157 mph) at 2440 m (8,000 ft); service ceiling 5445 m (17,860 ft); range with maximum fuel at 2440 m (8,000 ft) 1648 km (1,023 miles)
Weights: empty 955 kg (2,106 lb); maximum take-off 1542 kg (3,400 lb)

Dimensions: span 10.21 m (33 ft 6 in); length 8.05 m (26 ft 5 in); height 2.31 m (7 ft 7 in); wing area 16.81 m² (181.0 sq ft)

The butterfly-tailed Bonanza was a classic among post-war US lightplanes, used for several class records.

Beech Model 45 Mentor

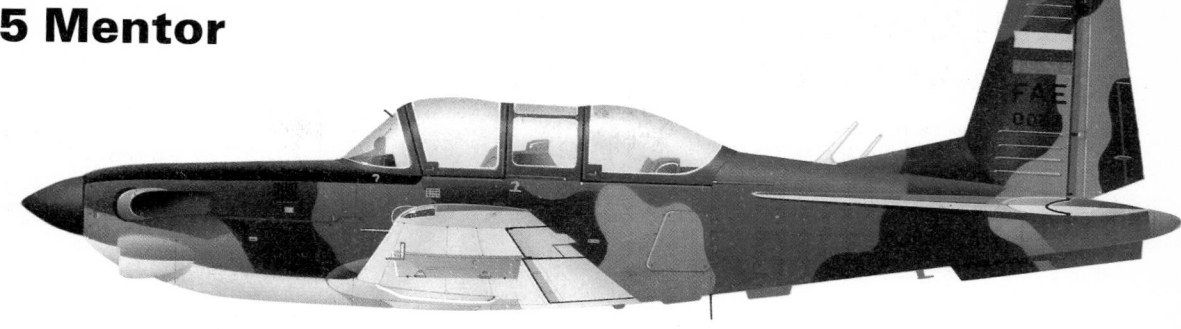

In 1948 Beech built as a private venture a two-seat trainer evolved from the V-tail civil Bonanza. It differed primarily by having tandem seating for pupil and instructor, and by the substitution of a conventional tail unit for the V-tail. This aircraft was designated **Beech Model 45 Mentor**, and flew for the first time on 2 December 1948.

At about this time the USAF, in common with many other air forces, was trying to make up its mind about the trend of future primary training. The problem facing them all was whether or not, as a result of the introduction into service of turbine engines, initial training should be on jet-powered aircraft. At the time it was a difficult question: an affirmative answer meant not only that the most ham-fisted of student pilots would have to cope from the outset with aircraft of much higher performance, but that at the same time they would be faced with the problem of handling a power unit which had not then been developed to a point of great reliability. On the credit side, however, they would work throughout their training with turbine engines and a constant handling technique: retention of piston-engine power for primary trainers would bring the need for a transition phase from piston- to turbine-engine at a later stage. USAF planners chose the latter as the more prudent course at that time. Among the various types evaluated were three examples of the Beech Model 45, two powered by the 153-kW (205-hp) Continental E-185-8 engine and one by the 168-kW (225-hp) Continental E-225-8; all three were designated **YT-34** by the USAF. These three aircraft made their first flights in May, June and July 1950, and were tested extensively during the competition period, being flown not only by evaluation pilots, but also in the primary training role with pupils and instructors. Almost three years later, on 4 March 1953, the USAF selected the Model 45 as its new primary trainer, under the designation **T-34A Mentor**, and ultimately 450 were built for that service, 350 by Beech and 100 by the Canadian Car & Foundry Company in Montreal, Canada. US Navy evaluation of the Model 45 began soon after the USAF had placed its initial contract with Beech, and on 17 June 1954 the Navy ordered 290 of these trainers, under the designation **T-34B**. A total of 423 was acquired eventually. In July 1951 one of the original prototypes was modified to mount two 7.62-mm (0.3-in) machine-guns in the wings, with provision additionally for underwing racks capable of

accepting six rockets or two 68-kg (150-lb) bombs; this was evaluated by the USAF as a potential light close-support aircraft, but no orders materialised.

Not surprisingly, in the jet age, most piston-engine trainers were gradually phased out of service, being replaced by sleeker, purpose-built jets which formed the first component of an all-jet training scheme, from *ab initio* to the moment when the pupil was considered fit for posting to an operational squadron.

The US Navy decided in 1973 to investigate the possibility of retaining the tried and trusted Mentor in service, with its piston engine replaced by turbine powerplant. Such a scheme offered a continuity of experience with the Mentor airframe and its excellent handling characteristics, and would provide the pupil pilot with an unbroken sequence of turbine-engine handling throughout his training. To evaluate this proposal, the USN instructed Beech to convert two T-34Bs to turbine power, under the designation **YT-34C**.

The powerplant chosen by Beech for the conversion was a Pratt & Whitney Aircraft of Canada PT6A-25. In this particular application it is provided with a torque limiter that restricts power output to some 56 per cent of maximum, ensuring constant performance over a wide range of altitude/temperature conditions, and also offering long engine life. The first YT-34C was flown on 21 September 1973, and following satisfactory evaluation of the two aircraft, Beech received contracts valued at approximately $72 million for the construction of 184 new aircraft. In addition to the installation of the new engine, the production aircraft were also given structural strengthening to ensure an airframe fatigue life of some 16,000 hours. The first **T-34C Turbo-Mentor** entered service with the USN's Naval Air Training Command in November 1977, and student training with the type began during the following January. Since then production has reached 353, with six being transferred to the US Army.

Beech T-34C-1 Turbo Mentor of the Ecuadorean air force

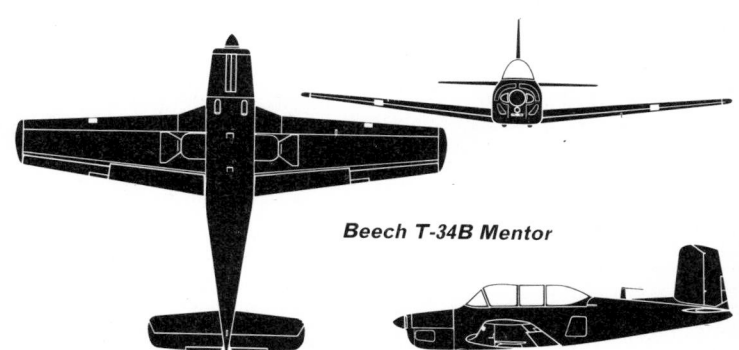

Beech T-34B Mentor

Subsequently, Beech developed a **T-34C-1** version for armaments system training, equipped with four underwing hardpoints having a total weapons capacity of 544 kg (1,200 lb). In addition to deployment in such a training role, the T-34C-1 is suitable also for forward air control and tactical strike training missions. Examples of this version have been supplied to the navies of Argentina, Ecuador, Peru and Uruguay, and to the

This is the civil version of the Turbo Mentor, seen in the colours of the Algerian pilot training school.

air forces of Ecuador, Indonesia and Morocco. An export civil version, known as the **Turbine Mentor 34C**, has also been delivered for use in Algeria's national pilot training school.

Specification
Beech Model 45 T-34C Turbo-Mentor
Type: two-seat primary trainer
Powerplant: one 533-kW (715-shp) Pratt & Whitney Aircraft of Canada PT6A-25 turboprop engine, torque-limited to a maximum output of 298 kW (400 shp)
Performance: maximum cruising speed 396 km/h (246 mph) at 5180 m (17,000 ft); service ceiling above 9145 m (30,000 ft); maximum range at 6095 m (20,000 ft) 1311 km (814 miles)
Weights: empty 1342 kg (2,960 lb); maximum take-off 1950 kg (4,300 lb)
Dimensions: span 10.16 m (33 ft 4 in); length 8.75 m (28 ft 8½ in); height 2.92 m (9 ft 7 in); wing area 16.68 m² (179.60 sq ft)

Since 1977 the T-34C Turbo Mentor has been the primary trainer for the US Navy, based in the south-eastern United States.

Beech Models 55, 56 and 58 Baron

The 'leap-year' **Beech Model 95-55 Baron**, first flown on 29 February 1960, was developed from the earlier Model 95 Travel Air. It differed primarily in having more powerful engines, but also in design refinements that included swept vertical tail surfaces, and improved all-weather capability. Deliveries began in November 1960, and ready acceptance of this new twin-engined four/five-seat aircraft resulted in further improvement and development of the type. The **Model B55**, introduced in 1963, had four-seat and optional five/six-seat accommodation, and in 1965 an additional **Model C55** was made available with more powerful 213-kW (285-hp) Continental IO-520-C engines. The Model C55 incorporated a number of other improvements, including increased tailplane span and an extended nose baggage compartment, and was developed later as a separate Baron model distinct from the B55.

A few months before the introduction of the C55, the US Army announced that the Model 95-B55 had been chosen for military service as an instrument trainer, which was ordered in an initial quantity of 55 under the designation **T-42A Cochise**. Ten more were procured for US Army service plus, in 1971, five for delivery to the Turkish army under the Military Assistance Program. By 1984, production of civil and military 95-B55 Barons was in excess of 2,400 and 1,201 examples of the **Model E55** (formerly C/D55) had been delivered when production ended.

In September 1967 deliveries began of a new **Model 56TC Baron**. This introduced turbocharged power, in the form of two 283-kW (380-hp) Avco Lycoming TIO-541-E1B4W engines, providing much improved performance. Air-conditioning was available as an option, Beech claiming this to be the first time that such a system had been offered on a lightweight twin. However, the higher cost of this version of the Baron attracted only 93 sales, and production ended in December 1971.

Before that date the range was extended when, in late 1969, Beech introduced the larger **Model 58 Baron**. First flown in June of that year, it had the fuselage lengthened by 0.25 m (10 in) to provide a more spacious cabin, and related to this was an extension of the wheelbase. Double doors on the starboard side of the fuselage gave easy access to baggage/cargo space behind the rear seats, and powerplant consisted of two engines as installed in the Model E55. Ready acceptance of this improved Baron, with delivery figures that have averaged about two per week for more than 12 years, resulted in the introduction of a pressurised **Model 58P**, with first deliveries in late 1975. It was something of a composite airframe, combining Model 95-B55 wings, Model 58 tail unit, a strengthened Model 58 fuselage to cater for pressurisation, and main landing gear units as developed for the Model 60 Duke. Power was provided by two Continental turbo-charged engines, currently TSIO-520-WB units with propeller synchrophasers as standard. The most recent addition to the range came

with initial deliveries in June 1976 of the **Model 58TC** which, apart from being unpressurised, is generally similar to its immediate predecessor, and retains its turbo-charged powerplant.

The Baron has proved to be a popular twin, and by January 1989 2,182 Model 58s had been delivered. In addition to these Beech production Barons, at least two turboprop conversions have been developed by other constructors. These include the **SFERMA Marquis**, produced in small numbers in France, and

combining Beech-built Baron airframes with 328-kW (440-shp) Turboméca Astazou engines; and the **American Jet Industries Turbo Star Baron** powered by two 298-kW (400-shp) Allison 250-B17 turboprops.

Specification
Beech Baron Model 58P
Type: four/six-seat cabin monoplane
Powerplant: two 242-kW (325-hp) Continental TSIO-520-WB turbocharged flat-six piston engines

Performance: maximum speed 483 km/h (300 mph); economic cruising speed 375 km/h (233 mph) at 7620 m (25,000 ft); service ceiling above 7620 m (25,000 ft); maximum range 2277 km (1,414 miles)
Weights: empty equipped 1822 kg (4,018 lb); maximum take-off 2,812 kg (6,200 lb)
Dimensions: span 11.53 m (37 ft 10 in); length 9.12 m (29 ft 11 in); height 2.79 m (9 ft 2 in); wing area 18.51 m² (199.2 sq ft)

Beech Model 95-E55 Baron.

The Baron 95-E55 introduced a larger tailplane and greater baggage volume. It was a popular version.

Below: The Baron B55 was selected for US Army navigation training duties, designated T-42A.

Beech Model 60 Duke

Beech entered the field of pressurised general aviation aircraft following a first flight of the **Beech Model 60 Duke** on 29 December 1966. Slightly larger than the members of the Baron family, the Duke was intended as a luxury four/six-seat aircraft, and was provided with an extensive range of equipment as standard. Overall configuration was similar to that of other Beech twin-engined models, but because it was intended for operation at a higher gross weight it had strengthened landing gear, and much more powerful Avco Lycoming TIO-541-E1C4 turbocharged engines. The pressurisation system installed in the then current production aircraft had an advanced controller which allowed selection of cabin altitude before take-off or landing, and the system was able to maintain a 3050-m cabin pressure altitude to a height of 7660 m.

Only two revised versions of the original Model 60 appeared during the production run, the **Model A60** and **Model B60** introduced in 1971 and 1974 respectively. The first provided a 23-kg (50-lb) increase in maximum take-off weight, the second a slightly larger cabin and increased fuel capacity. Such an aircraft was by no means cheap and, by American standards, was built in com-

paratively small numbers, with a total of 596 completed by the end of production in 1983.

Specification
Type: four/six-seat cabin monoplane
Powerplant: two 283-kW (380-hp) Avco Lycoming TIO-541-E1C4 turbocharged flat-six piston engines
Performance: maximum speed 455 km/h (283 mph) at 7010 m (23,000 ft); economic cruising speed 402 km/h (250 mph) at 7620 m (25,000 ft); service ceiling 9145 m (30,000 ft); maximum range 2165 km (1,344 miles)
Weights: empty equipped 2006 kg (4,423 lb); maximum take-off 3073 kg

The Duke was an attractive twin, fitting neatly in capacity between Baron and Queen Air/King Air.

(6,775 lb)
Dimensions: span 11.97 m (39 ft 3¼ in); length 10.31 m (33 ft 10 in); height 3.76 m (12 ft 4 in); wing area 19.78 m² (212.9 sq ft)

Beech Models 65, 70, 80 and 88 Queen Air

On 28 August 1958 Beech flew the prototype of the new **Beech Model 65 Queen Air** business aircraft. Designed to meet the requirements of what the company considered to be a growing market, this seven/nine-seat low-wing monoplane had retractable tricycle landing gear, and was powered by two 254-kW (340-hp) Avco Lycoming IGSO-480-A1B6 flat-six engines. Full IFR instrumentation was standard, and optionally available equipment, such as an autopilot, and navigation and weather-avoidance radar, could provide the Queen Air with the capability of a contemporary airliner. In the following January Beech flew the first of three Model 65s that were to be used by the US Army for evaluation. This resulted in orders totalling 71 of these aircraft, under the designation **L-23F Seminole**, an identification chosen because of the general similarity between the Twin Bonanza and Model 65 Queen Air, the latter differing primarily by its deeper section fuselage and more powerful engines. In 1962 the L-23F was redesignated **U-8F**, and some modified at a later date to provide improved interior accommodation became **U-8G**s. A number of commercial Queen Airs were

acquired by the Japan Maritime Self-Defence Force, for use in navigation trainer and transport roles, and others went to the air forces of Uruguay and Venezuela. An improved **Model A65 Queen Air**, introduced at a later date, had swept vertical tail surfaces and greater fuel capacity; and a version with a high-density seating arrangement for a crew of one or two, with 10 or nine passengers respectively, was known as the **Queen Airliner**. A Model 65 Queen Air was provided with two 373-kW (500-shp) Pratt & Whitney PT6A-6 turboprop engines. Identified initially by the company as the **Model 65-90T Queen Air**, this was evaluated by the US Army, from 17 March 1964, as the **NU-8F**.

Expansion of the Queen Air line came on 22 June 1961 with a first flight of the **Model 80 Queen Air**. This had more powerful engines (283-kW/380-hp), but the **Queen Air A80**, introduced in January 1964, had increased wing span that allowed for operation at a higher gross weight. Final version was the **Queen Air B80**, incorporating a number of design and equipment improvements, and 11-seat Queen Airliners were available for each of these basic versions. A pressurised version of the

Beech Model 80 Queen Air.

Model 80 was introduced in August 1965: generally similar to the Queen Air B80, it differed by having structural modification of the fuselage to cater for pressurisation, and by the incorporation of circular cabin windows. Identified as the **Model 88 Queen Air**, it was taken out of production during 1969 after 45 had been built.

A third member of the Queen Air family was introduced in 1968. Known as the **Model 70 Queen Air**, this was basically an A65 with the increased span

wing of the B80.

Manufacture of the Models 65 and 70 was terminated at the end of 1971, at which time production figures totalled 404 (including U-8Fs) and 42 respectively. Production of the Model 80 Queen Airs continued until the end of 1978, at which time approximately 510 had been built.

Specification
Beech Model B80 Queen Air
Type: six/eleven-seat business, commuter and utility aircraft
Powerplant: two 283-kW (380-hp) Avco Lycoming IGSO-540-A1D supercharged flat-six piston engines
Performance: maximum speed 400 km/h (248 mph) at 3505 m (11,500 ft); economic cruising speed 294 km/h (183 mph) at 4570 m (15,000 ft); service ceiling 8170 m (26,800 ft); maximum range 2441 km (1,517 miles)
Weights: empty equipped 2394 kg (5,277 lb); maximum take-off 3992 kg (8,800 lb)
Dimensions: span 15.32 m (50 ft 3 in); length 10.82 m (35 ft 6 in); height 4.33 m (14 ft 2½ in); wing area 27.3 m² (293.9 sq ft)

The B80 was the largest and most powerful of the Queen Air family. This aircraft wears Philippine registrations.

Beech Model 90 King Air

In early 1963 Beech had started flight tests of an aircraft, then identified as the **Beech Queen Air Model 65-80**, which was powered by two 373-kW (500-shp) Pratt & Whitney Aircraft of Canada turboprop engines. Then envisaged as a further extension of the Queen Air range, the type had been developed to satisfy a US Army requirement for a staff/utility transport. The above designation was a little confusing as there were Model 65 and Model 80 Queen Airs in production, so the aircraft became known temporarily as the **Model 65-90T** (T standing for turboprop). In due course, an even better job was made of clarifying the situation by renaming the turboprop-powered Queen Airs as King Airs. In effect, therefore, the Model 65-90T was the prototype for the **Beech Model 90 King Air** series, but more specifically became the prototype of the unpressurised military Kings Airs. Following the first flight of the Model 65-90T, a civil equivalent was produced in parallel with a pressurised cabin, and the first production prototype of this aircraft, designated Model 90 King Air, flew for the first time on 20 January 1964. These aircraft represented the beginning of the King Air series, which now represents an important area of Beech activities, and the 3,000th example of the King Air family was delivered to a customer on 17 April 1981.

US Army testing of the Model 65-90T, under the military designation **NU-8F**, had shown the aircraft to be suitable for the military requirement, so an initial order for 48 aircraft, under the designation **U-21A**, was placed. Beech distinguished its military King Airs from civil versions by identifying them as **Model 65-A90-1**, and began modification of the civil aircraft to provide a utility interior. This accommodates a crew of two and 10 troops, or six to eight command personnel, or three stretchers, and seating can be removed easily for the carriage of up to 1361 kg (3,000 lb) of cargo.

Initial deliveries of production U-21As, which were given the name Ute, began on 16 May 1967, and subsequent contracts resulted in more than 160 being built. These included U-21As and **RU-21A/RU-21D** variants all with 410-kW (550-shp) Pratt & Whitney PT6A-20 turboprops, and **RU-21B/RU-21C/RU-21E** variants with 462-kW (620-shp) PT6A-29s. The RU-21s were developed especially for operation in an electronic reconnaissance role in South-East Asia, sprouting a strange collection of aerials and sensors, and being equipped internally with related avionics' systems, plus nav/com systems suitable for all-weather operations. RU-21Bs and RU-21Cs had Beech designations **Model 65-A90-2** and **Model 65-A90-3** respectively, and the designation **U-21G** applied to 17 aircraft for the USAF that were similar to the U-21A.

Deliveries of the civil Model 90 King Air began in late 1964, this having cabin pressurisation, and accommodating a maximum of 10 persons, including the pilot. It was superseded in early 1966 by the **King Air A90**, which introduced the more powerful PT6A-20 engines, and one of these aircraft was supplied for military service under the designation **VC-6A**.

The King Air E90 was procured for the US Navy as the T-44A. These fly on multi-engined training duties. Similar machines serve the Japanese armed forces.

The A90 was followed by a **King Air B90** with detail improvements, and in September 1970 by the **King Air C90** which introduced a more advanced pressurisation and heating system for the cabin. The C90 remains the current production version in 1982, with a total close to 1,000 having been delivered by the end of the year. One of these, designated **VC-6B**, also serves with the USAF's 1,254th SAM Squadron. Since its introduction, the C90 has been the subject of steady improvement, and current powerplant is the PT6A-21. Ten examples of the C90 serve with the Spanish air force and civil aviation school for instrument training and liaison.

A first extension to the King Air 90 range came in the early summer of 1972 with the introduction of the **King Air E90**. Generally similar to its predecessor, it has more powerful PT6A-28 turboprops, flat-rated to 410 ekW (550 ehp), and this version remains in production in 1990. In 1976 Beech was awarded a contract from the US Navy for an advanced pilot-training aircraft that combined features of the C90 and E90, designated **T-44A**.

The most recent model in the King Air family was the **Model F90 Super King Air**, of which deliveries began in mid-1979. This combined the pressurised fuselage of the Model 90, with the wings and tail unit of the Models 100 King Air and 200 Super King Air respectively. Power was provided by two PT6A-135 engines, these driving slow-turning four-bladed propellers, that gave a much quieter cabin environment. While production of the F90 ended at 231 aircraft, the C90 continues in production, 1,415 of the low-tailplane variants having been delivered by early 1989.

Specification
Beech Model F90 Super King Air
Type: 7/10-seat business aircraft
Powerplant: two 559-kW (750-shp) Pratt & Whitney Aircraft of Canada PT6A-135 turboprops
Performance: maximum cruising speed 495 km/h (307 mph) at 3660 m (12,000 ft) with an AUW of 4309 kg (9,500 lb); service ceiling 9085 m (29,800 ft); maximum range 2920 km (1,814 miles)
Weights: empty 2971 kg (6,549 lb); maximum take-off 4966 kg (10,950 lb)
Dimensions: span 13.99 m (45 ft 10¾ in); length 12.13 m (39 ft 9½ in); height 4.6 m (15 ft 1¼ in); wing area 25.98 m² (279.7 sq ft)

Above: Equivalent to the King Air 90, the Beech U-21A however lacked pressurisation, as indicated by the rectangular windows. In addition to the regular liaison and light transport work, some were modified to serve as airborne intelligence gatherers, festooned with dipole aerials.

Below: The King Air F90 is the most capable of the short King Airs, combining the pressurised King Air 90 fuselage with the T-tail of the Model 200 and the wings of the 100. The four-blade propellers not only reduce cabin noise but also reduce external noise. Introduced in 1979, production amounted to 231 aircraft.

Beech Model 99 Airliner and Model 1900

During the early 1960s, the growing importance and increasing traffic of commuter airlines in the USA prompted Beech to embark on the design and construction of an aircraft to capture a share of this market. In 1965, therefore, the company became involved in the development of what was then the largest production aircraft manufactured by Beech, the prototype flying for the first time in July 1966. Identified as the **Beech Model 99 Airliner**, the new type had a general configuration similar to that of the contemporary Queen Airs, but a lengthened fuselage was designed to accommodate a crew of two and up to 15 passengers. Power was provided by two 410-kW (550-shp) Pratt & Whitney PT6A-20 turboprops, and options included a cargo door, and a movable bulkhead that gave considerable operational flexibility by allowing for the loading of various combinations of passengers and freight. The first production example was delivered to Commuter Airlines Inc. on 2 May 1968, by which time an alternative **Model 99 Executive** version was available optionally. Generally similar to the standard Model 99 Airliner, it had a variety of optional seating layouts and corporate interiors.

Improved **Airliner A99** and **Airliner B99** production versions followed, both available in the optional Executive variant, and these were powered by 507-kW (680-shp) PT6A-27 engines. By late 1976 demand for the Model 99 was falling, and production was terminated towards the end of 1977 after a total of 164 aircraft had been built and delivered to 64 operators, mostly in the USA.

However, on 7 May 1979, the company announced its intention to re-enter the commuter airliner market. To speed the certification programme an earlier production B99 aircraft, purchased from the Allegheny Commuter Consortium, was completely refurbished before being given a new powerplant of two flat-rated PT6A-34 engines. Designated **Commuter C99**, this was flown for the first time on 20 June 1980, and the manufacture of production aircraft began about three months later. Certification of the C99 was gained during the last week of July 1981, with initial de-

liveries to customers following within two or three days. This aircraft differs from the earlier B99 primarily in having more powerful engines, but there are a number of detail improvements.

Simultaneously with the announcement that the Commuter C99 was to be built, Beech gave details of a slightly larger pressurised version. Development of this aircraft, designated **Commuter 1900**, was deferred so that priority could be given to completion of the C99's certification programme. Intended to accommodate 19 passengers, and with power provided by two PT6A-65 turboprops, each flat-rated to 746-kW (1,000-shp), the first Commuter 1900 prototype flew in September 1982. It has established itself in the commuter market and has also seen military applications. Egypt uses the type for electronic surveillance, while the USAF Air National Guard uses the type for support duties as the **C-12J**.

Specification
Beech Model C99 Commuter
Type: commuter/cargo transport
Powerplant: two Pratt & Whitney Aircraft of Canada PT6A-36 turboprops, each flat-rated to 533 kW (715 shp)
Performance: maximum speed 496 km/h (308 mph) at 2440 m (8,000 ft); cruising speed 462 km/h (287 mph) at 2440 m (8,000 ft) at an AUW of 4536 kg (10,000 lb); service ceiling 8560 m (28,080 ft); range with maximum fuel 1687 km (1,048 miles)
Weights: basic operating 2946 kg (6,494 lb); maximum take-off 5126 kg (11,300 lb)
Dimensions: span 13.98 m (45 ft 10½ in); length 13.58 m (44 ft 6¾ in); height 4.38 m (14 ft 4¼ in); wing area 25.98 m² (279.7 sq ft)

Beech 99 Airliner of Mississippi Valley Airlines.

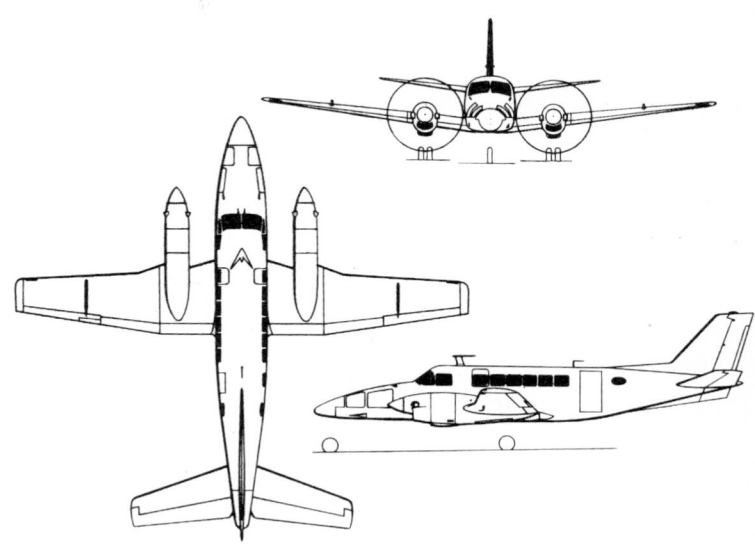

Beech 99 Airliner.

Below: The Beech 1900 has a strange fin arrangement, with an additional tailplane set low and small fins on the main tailplane.

Right: A military customer for the 1900 is the Egyptian air force, which uses its aircraft for electronic surveillance.

Beech Model 100 King Air

The **Beech Model 100 King Air** was added to the range of Beech corporate transports when initial deliveries were made in August 1969. It differed from the earlier King Airs in several respects: reduced wing span, a lengthened fuselage to provide accommodation for a maximum of 15 persons, increased elevator and rudder areas, twin-wheel main landing gear, and more powerful engines. The new wing was generally similar to that developed for the Model 99 Airliner.

In October 1971 Beech began deliveries of the improved **King Air A100**, this variant incorporating detail improvements, and the first five were supplied to the US Army under the designation **U-21F**. Examples have been procured by the Spanish air force, and a Universal Aircraft Com/Nav Evaluation (UNACE) configured version, for the rapid inspection and calibration of air navigation systems, has been supplied to countries that include Algeria, Belgium, Canada, Indonesia, Malaysia, Mexico, and the USA. Beech also produces specially modified camera-equipped versions of the King Air for aerial survey, and examples are in service in this role in Canada, Chile, France, Jamaica, Saudi Arabia, Thailand, and the USA.

In parallel with A100 production since late 1975, Beech has produced a complementary **King Air B100** offering higher performance. It differs by the installation of 533-kW (715-shp) Garrett TPE331-6-252B turboprop engines, and of equipment directly associated with the engine installation. Production of the King Air 100 ended in 1983.

Specification
Beech King Air A100
Type: light executive/freight/passenger transport
Powerplant: two 507-kW (680-ehp)

The lengthened King Air 100 has considerably increased payload capacity compared with the Model 90.

Pratt & Whitney Aircraft of Canada PT6A-28 turboprops
Performance: maximum cruising speed 459 km/h (285 mph) at 3050 m (10,000 ft) at an AUW of 4762 kg (10,500 lb); service ceiling 7575 m (24,850 ft); maximum range 2483 km (1,542 miles)
Weights: empty 3083 kg (6,797 lb); maximum take-off 5216 kg (11,500 lb)
Dimensions: span 14 m (45 ft 11 in); length 12.17 m (39 ft 11 in); height 4.7 m (15 ft 5 in)

Beech King Air 100

Beech Model 200 Super King Air

On 27 October 1972, Beech flew the prototype of a new and improved member of the King Air family which has become known as the **Beech Model 200 Super King Air**. It differs from King Air 100s by having greater wing span, the conventional tail unit replaced by a T-tail, and increased fuel capacity for more powerful Pratt & Whitney PT6A-41 turboprop engines. These changes make it possible for the improved version to operate at a higher gross weight.

First deliveries of Super King Airs were made in early 1974, and the better capability of this aircraft resulted in the company receiving contracts for the supply and support of 34 examples modified for service with the US Army. These are powered by 559-kW (750-shp) PT6A-38 turboprop engines, and were allocated the designation **C-12A**: subsequent military orders for the C-12A have to date included 27 and 30 for the US Army and USAF respectively. Other service variants are the **UC-12B** (66 ordered) for the US Navy/Marine Corps, powered by 634-kW (850-shp) PT6A-41 turboprops; the **C-12C** (14) for the US Army with

PT6A-41 engines; the generally similar **C-12D** (27) for the US Army, but with an added cargo door; and the special-mission **RU-21J** (three) bristling externally with antennae and equipped for the requirements of the US Army's 'Cefly Lancer' programme. More recent variants are the **RC-12D** 'Guardrail V' electronic reconnaissance platform, **C-12E** upgraded transport for the USAF, **C-12F** transport for USAF and **UC-12F** for the Navy, **RC-12H** reconnaissance variant and **UC-12M** utility transport.

The cargo door developed for the US Army's C-12D has been available as an option for civil production since 1979, and in April 1981 Beech introduced a new version, identified as the **Super King Air B200**. It differs by having PT6A-42 turboprop engines which offer improved cruising performance.

Three RU-21Js were procured for the US Army, equipped for electronic reconnaissance under the 'Cefly Lancer' programme. The similar RC-12D was procured in greater numbers.

Variants
Super King Air Model 200T: designation of two specially-equipped aircraft for the French Institut

Géographique National for high-altitude photographic and weather observation duties
Super King Air Maritime Patrol 200T: maritime patrol/multi-mission aircraft, with new outboard wing panels to provide for installation of

wingtip fuel tanks, strengthened landing gear, hatch for dropping survival equipment, bubble observation window in aft cabin, and search radar with a 360° scan underfuselage radome; orders include 13 for Japan Maritime Safety Agency, and one for Uruguayan navy.

Super King Air B200C: version of civil B200 with a cargo door as standard

Super King Air B200CT: version of civil B200 with a cargo door and removable wingtip fuel tank provisions as standard

Below: The soundness and success of the Beech King Air 200 design prompted Beech to explore a jet-powered version. This was the Fan Jet 400, fitted with a pair of JT15D turbofans in similar nacelles to the PT6A turboprops. Known as the Fan Jet 400, the jet-powered aircraft did not warrant production, and Beech later purchased the Mitsubishi Diamond design.

Beech Model 200 Super King Air of TI Industries, based in the UK.

Super King Air B200T: version of the civil B200 with removable wingtip fuel tank provisions as standard
Super King Air 300: improved version with PT6A-60A turboprops each rated at 783-kW (1,050-shp) and corresponding increase in take-off weight. The **300LW** is a lightened version optimised for European operations
1300 Commuter: King Air B200 version for commuter airlines. Accommodates up to 13 passengers with an optional belly luggage pack

Specification
Beech Super King Air B200
Type: executive/passenger light transport
Powerplant: two 634-kW (850-shp) Pratt & Whitney Aircraft of Canada PT6A-42 turboprops
Performance: maximum speed 545 km/h (339 mph) at 7620 m (25,000 ft); economic cruising speed 523 km/h (325 mph) at 7620 m (25,000 ft); service ceiling 10670 m (35,000 ft); maximum range 3756 km (2,334 miles)

Weights: empty 3419 kg (7,538 lb); maximum take-off 5670 kg (12,500 lb)
Dimensions: span 16.61 m (54 ft 6 in); length 13.34 m (43 ft 9 in); height 4.57 m (15 ft 0 in); wing area 28.15 m² (303 sq ft)

Many King Air 200s have been bought by US forces as communications, light transport and reconnaissance aircraft. Here a pair of C-12As formate for the camera; one for the US Army (background) and one for the USAF embassy support flights.

Beech Model 400 Beechjet

The Beech Aircraft Corporation acquired in December 1985 the **Diamond II** executive jet from Mitsubishi, and it is now marketed worldwide (except for Japan) as the **Model 400 Beechjet**. Initial Beech production centred on the completion of partially-built Mitsubishi airframes, but by June 1989 all production was being handled by Beech's Salina and Wichita plants.

The first Beech-assembled aircraft was rolled out on 19 May 1986 and deliveries began in June. By the beginning of 1989 46 Beechjets had been delivered. Beech is also providing support for previous Mitsubishi products, including the MU-2 and earlier Diamond versions.

In 1989, Beech announced the **Model 400A Beechjet**, featuring increases in payload and ceiling, greater cabin volume, a rear lavatory and improved soundproofing. A Collins Pro Line 4 EFIS is fitted as standard. Deliveries of this version began in early 1990.

The T-1A Jayhawk is a version of the Beechjet for the USAF, intended to train crews for tankers, transports and bombers.

To compete for the major USAF competition for a new Tanker-Transport Training System, Beech teamed with McDonnell Douglas and FlightSafety International to offer the Beechjet. The team was successful, with an eventual order for 211 aircraft likely. Expected to enter service in 1992, the aircraft will be known as the **T-1A Jayhawk**.

Specification
Beechjet 400A
Type: 10-seat executive jet or (T-1A) multi-engine trainer
Powerplant: two Pratt & Whitney Canada JT15D-5 turbofans, each rated at 12.9-kN (2,900-lb) thrust
Performance: maximum speed at

8840 m (29,000 ft); 854 km/h (531 mph); cruising speed at 11890 m (39,000 ft) 828 km/h (515 mph); ceiling 13715 m (45,000 ft); range 5375 km (2,222 miles) with four passengers
Weights: basic operating 4588 kg

(10,115 lb); maximum take-off 7303 kg (16,100 lb)
Dimensions: span 13.25 m (43 ft 6 in); length 14.75 m (48 ft 5 in); height 4.19 m (13 ft 9 in); wing area 22.43 m² (241.4 sq ft)

Beech Model 2000 Starship

To provide a new generation of corporate transports, Beech looked to Burt Rutan's Scaled Composites Inc. to design and produce the **SCAT 1**, an 85 per cent scale technology demonstrator of a canard-configured aircraft. Success in testing led to the construction of the **Model 2000 Starship 1**.

The Starship design has compound taper main wings, which mount the two pusher engines. Large endplate fins, known as tipsails, provide longitudinal stability, augmented by two small fins on the wing trailing edge. Additional keel area is provided by a ventral fin under the extreme rear of the slender fuselage. The large canard foreplanes are of variable-geometry, sweeping forward by 4°

for low-speed flight and 30° back in the cruise. Virtually the entire structure is made of Nomex honeycomb and graphite/epoxy composites, with titanium used in high-stress areas.

The first of three flying pre-production Starship 1s flew on 15 February 1986. Another three airframes were produced for static, damage tolerance and pressure testing. Basic FAA certification followed on 14 June 1988, and the first production machine flew on 25 April 1989.

This has been used for customer demonstration flights, resulting in 40 orders by June of that year.

Specification
Beech 2000 Starship 1
Type: 10-seat business aircraft
Powerplant: two Pratt & Whitney Canada PT6A-67A turboprops, each flat rated at 895 kW (1,200 shp) and driving a five-blade Hartzell fully-feathering and reversible-pitch propeller

Performance: maximum cruising speed at 7620 m (25,000 ft) 621 km/h (386 mph); maximum altitude 12495 m (41,000 ft); range at 10670 m (35,000 ft); 3132 km (1,946 miles)
Weights: empty equipped 4484 kg (9,887 lb); maximum take-off 6531 kg (14,000 lb)
Dimensions: span 16.60 m (54 ft 4¾ in); length 14.05 m (46 ft 1 in); height 3.96 m (13 ft 0 in); wing area 26.09 m² (280.9 sq ft)

The futuristic Starship is Beech's latest and hottest product, combining the proven turboprop reliability and efficiency with a aerodynamically-efficient airframe designed by Burt Rutan.

Bell P-39 Airacobra

Conventional in its external appearance, the **Bell P-39 Airacobra** was unique among US Army fighter aircraft of World War II in its powerplant installation, and was also the US Army's first single-seat fighter to be provided with tricycle type landing gear. These latter features were imposed by the desire to mount heavy armament in the nose, which reflects the general interest of all nations during the middle and late 1930s in developing fighter aircraft with good forward firepower.

In early 1935, executives of the Bell Aircraft Corporation had been present at a demonstration of the American Armament Corporation's T9 37-mm cannon. Impressed by what they had seen, they instigated the design of a fighter aircraft which would include a T9 cannon firing through the propeller hub, as well as two 12.7-mm (0.5-in) machine-guns mounted in the fuselage nose and synchronised to fire between the rotating propeller blades. The decision to locate the cannon to fire through the propeller hub meant that the engine had to be mounted within the fuselage, directly above the rear half of the low-set monoplane wing, with the propeller driven by an extension shaft which passed beneath the cockpit floor. In turn, this engine position, virtually over the aircraft's centre of gravity, highlighted the desirability of introducing a tricycle-type landing gear, an installation presenting few problems as there was adequate room in the fuselage nose to accommodate the nosewheel unit.

The concept was sufficiently attractive to the US Army Air Corps to win an order for a single **Bell XP-39 (Model 12)** prototype on 7 October 1937, and this flew for the first time on 6 April 1938. Twelve months later, following extensive evaluation by the US Army, 12 of the **YP-39** pre-production version were ordered for a wider service test, plus a single YP-39A without a turbocharger for the Allison V-1710 engine. Following service evaluation of the XP-39, the National Advisory Committee for Aeronautics (predecessor of the National Aeronautics and Space Administration) carried out a study of this prototype, recommending changes which included the provision of fairing doors for the mainwheel units; a lower-profile cockpit canopy; resiting of the engine air intake and coolant radiators; and deletion of the turbocharger. The original prototype, modified to this configuration under the

designation **XP-39B**, was test flown and demonstrated improved performance. As a result, a decision was made to delete the turbocharger from all future aircraft: the 13 pre-production prototypes were completed to XP-39B standard, provided with two additional 7.62-mm (0.3-in) machine-guns in the fuselage nose, and began service trials under the designation **YP-39**.

With the initial designation **P-45**, the new fighter was ordered into production on 10 August 1939, the first contract being for 80 aircraft; the designation reverted to P-39 before the first of these was delivered. The first 20, completed to XP-39B standard, were designated **P-39C (Model 13)**, but the remaining 60 each received two more 7.62-mm (0.3-in) machine-guns (all four then being mounted in the wings), introduced self-sealing fuel tanks, and had provision for a 227-kg (500-lb) bomb or a 284-litre (75-US gal) fuel drop tank to be carried beneath the fuselage: these changes resulted in the designation **P-39D (Model 15)**.

The first large order, for 369 P-39Ds, was placed in September 1940, and initial deliveries of these began about seven months later, the first export Airacobras ordered by a British Purchasing Commission beginning to come off the production line at about the same time. British orders totalled 675 **Model 14** aircraft similar to the P-39D, but with the 37-mm cannon replaced by one of 20-mm, and the six 7.62-mm (0.3-in) machine-guns replaced by an equal number of 7.7-mm (0.303-in) calibre.

Airacobras began to reach the UK in July 1941, and in September of that year No. 601 Squadron exchanged its Hawker Hurricanes for these new aircraft. Immediately they were introduced into service, the full implications of the decision to delete the turbocharger were appreciated for the first time, the aircraft

Bell Airacobra Mk I of No. 601 Squadron, the only operational RAF unit to fly the type, seen in October 1941.

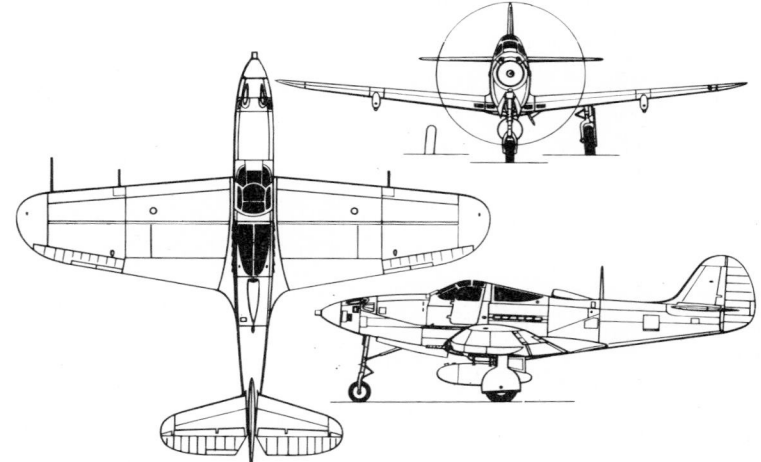

having an inadequate rate of climb and high-altitude performance unacceptable for deployment in the European theatre. Only about 80 of the total order entered service with the RAF, equipping only No. 601 Squadron, which exchanged them for Supermarine Spitfires in March 1942. Of the balance, more than 250 of the **Model 14A** were supplied to the Russian air force under a British aid scheme; about 200 in Britain were transferred to the 8th Air Force in late 1942, and about 200 were repossessed by the US Army Air Force in America after the USA entered World War II in December 1941. These ex-British Airacobras received the designation **P-400** in USAAF service.

Constructed in large numbers, a total of 9,558 Airacobras being built before production ended, there were no major design changes in the several variants which followed. The **P-39F**, of which 229 were built, succeeded the P-39D in

production. Generally similar, it differed by having an Aeroproducts hydraulically operated constant-speed propeller instead of the Curtiss type of the earlier models. The **P-39J**, of which 25 were built, had a different version of the Allison V-1710 engine, while the **P-39K** (210 built) and **P-39L** (250 built), both ordered initially under the designation **P-39G (Model 26)**, differed in detail equipment and by installation of the more powerful V-1710-63 engine; the former had an Aeroproducts, the latter a Curtiss propeller. The **P-39M** (240 built) had the lower-power V-1710-83 engine and an increased-diameter propeller. The final production versions, the **P-39N** and **P-39Q**, were built in large numbers for supply to the Russian air force under Lend-Lease. To improve performance the P-39N carried less fuel and armour, and the P-39Q could be identified easily by two underwing fairings, each housing a 12.7-mm (0.5-in)

The P-39 series lacked the agility for true air-to-air combat but was widely built for service as a close support fighter.

deployed widely in the Pacific theatre by the USAAF. Until 1944, when more potent fighters began to enter service, the P-39 together with the Curtiss P-40 represented the main first-line equipment of the USAAF's fighter squadrons. A small number of P-39s were used by the Portuguese air force, acquired after these aircraft had force-landed in Portugal, about 150 were supplied to Free French forces in the later stages of the war, and a similar number to the Italian co-belligerent air force.

Specification
Bell P-39M Airacobra
Type: single-seat monoplane fighter/fighter-bomber
Powerplant: one 895-kW (1,200-hp) Allison V-1710-83 inline piston engine
Performance: maximum speed 621 km/h (386 mph) at 2895 m (9,500 ft); cruising speed 322 km/h (200 mph); service ceiling 10970 m (36,000 ft); range 1046 km (650 miles)
Weights: empty 2545 kg (5,610 lb); maximum take-off 3810 kg (8,400 lb)
Dimensions: span 10.36 m (34 ft 0 in); length 9.19 m (30 ft 2 in); height 3.61 m (11 ft 10 in); wing area 19.79 m^2 (213 sq ft)
Armament: one 37-mm T9 cannon, two 12.7-mm (0.5-in) machine-guns and four 7.62-mm (0.3-in) machine-guns, plus provision for one 227-kg (500-lb) bomb

---

machine-gun in place of the four wing-mounted 7.62-mm (0.3-in) guns.

Total P-39 production was 9,558, of which 4,773 (primarily P-39D/-39N/-39Q) were supplied to Russia. Variants included three **XP-39E** experimental aircraft with laminar-flow wings, produced as prototypes for the abortive **P-76** powered by the Continental IV-1430-1, and small numbers of **TP-39F** and

RP-39Q two-seat trainers. Seven P-39s were supplied to the US Navy for use as target drones under the designation **F2L**. The US Navy had shown interest in the type for use as a ship-based fighter, and a single **XFL-1 Airabonita** was produced with tailwheel type landing gear, strengthened fuselage, and an arrester hook. First flown on 13 May 1940, it failed to enter production after

carrier trials had proved unsatisfactory. A radio-controlled target version was proposed under the designation **A-7**, but was not developed to the hardware stage.

Although deletion of the turbocharger had limited the Airacobra's potential as a fighter aircraft, it was used most successfully in North Africa in late 1942 in the ground-attack role, and was

---

Bell P-59 Airacomet

Details of development of the turbo-jet engine in the UK, stemming from the work of Frank (later Sir Frank) Whittle, were transferred as routine to the United States as part of an agreed interchange of technological progress, intended to speed the end of World War II. In the USA the General Electric Company, which had wide experience of the design development and construction of industrial turbines, dating back to before the start of the 20th century, was chosen initially to proceed with the development of national aircraft gas turbines based on the Whittle engine. Because of the Bell Aircraft Corporation's geographical location in relation to the General Electric plant, this company was chosen to design and build a fighter aircraft to be powered by the first American-built gas turbine.

Realising that early engines would develop only limited thrust, Bell elected for a twin-engine installation in its **Bell Model 27**, with one engine carried on

Bell XP-59A Airacomet, the third and last prototype of the design, in USAAF markings while undergoing evaluation at Muroc Dry Lake in summer 1943.

each side of the fuselage, beneath the wings. The configuration selected was that of a mid-wing monoplane, and wide-span main landing gear units were mounted under the wings, well outboard of the engines and retracting inward into the wing, the nose-wheel unit retracting aft into the fuselage nose. In other respects the design was conventional, with care taken to ensure a fairly high tailplane position so that it would be clear of the efflux from the turbojets.

The first **XP-59A**, powered by two 567-kg (1,250-lb) thrust General Electric Type I-A tubojets, was flown for the first time from Muroc Dry Lake on 1 October 1942. Two more XP-59As were built, followed by a batch of 13 of the pre-production **YP-59A** for test and evaluation.

The service Airacomets had a shorter fin than the prototypes, and incorporated the raised canopy of the YP-59s. This P-59B served with the USAF on drone control operations, fitted with nose armament and drop tanks, and having an open cockpit in the nose to seat a drone operator.

The majority of these latter aircraft, delivered during 1944, were each powered by two 748-kg (1,650-lb) thrust General Electric I-16 (later J31) turbojets. The 20 **P-59A** and 30 **P-59B Airacomets** which followed had J31-GE-3 and J31-GE-5 engines respectively, the P-59Bs also having increased fuel capacity.

Flown for test and evaluation by the USAAF's 412th Fighter Group, a specially formed trials unit, the P-59 was found to have inadequate performance

and proved an indifferent gun platform. As a result no further examples were built.

Specification
Bell P-59B Airacomet
Type: single-seat jet fighter
Powerplant: two 907-kg (2,000-lb) thrust General Electric J31-GE-5 turbojets
Performance: maximum speed 658 km/h (409 mph) at 10670 m

(35,000 ft); cruising speed 604 km/h (375 mph); service ceiling 14080 m (46,200 ft); range 644 km (400 miles)
Weights: empty 3704 kg (8,165 lb); maximum take-off 6214 kg (13,700 lb)
Dimensions: span 13.87 m (45 ft 6 in); length 11.62 m (38 ft 1½ in); height 3.66 m (12 ft 0 in); wing area 35.84 m^2 (385.8 sq ft)
Armament: one 37-mm M4 cannon and three 12.7-mm (0.5-in) machine-guns mounted in the nose

Bell P-63 Kingcobra
to
Bell Model 209 HueyCobra and SeaCobra

Bell P-63 Kingcobra

At a fairly early stage in the development of the Bell P-39 Airacobra, work had been carried out to enhance the performance of this aircraft by the introduction of aerodynamic improvements. Three experimental aircraft were built, each utilising the basic fuselage of the P-39D, to which were added a new laminar-flow wing with square wingtips and a revised tail unit. In fact, each of the three XP-39Es, as these aircraft were designated, had a different tail unit. It was planned originally to power the prototypes with the Continental Aviation and Engineering Corporation's IV-1430 12-cylinder inverted-vee piston-engine, which had demonstrated a power output in excess of 1491 kW (2,000 hp). However, Allison V-1710 engines of little more than half of that power output were installed, presumably because of unreliability of the Continental engine. Testing of the XP-39Es began in February 1942 and, proving satisfactory, the type was ordered into production under the designation P-76. Some 4,000 aircraft were to be built at Bell's Marietta, Ohio, facility but were cancelled only three months later.

It was decided, instead, to build a larger and more powerful version for utilisation in a close-support fighter/fighter-bomber role, and the research and design development which had been carried out for the XP-39E were used in finalising the design of what was to become known as the **Bell Model 33**, or **P-63 Kingcobra**. In its layout this latter aircraft was generally similar to the P-39, but apart from being larger and with the V-1710 engine more powerful than those installed in all but the P-39K and P-39L production aircraft, efforts had to be made to render this new development more suitable for the close-support role regarded as its primary mission.

Two prototypes were ordered by the US Army Air Corps in June 1941 under the designation XP-63, and these made their first flights on 7 December 1942 and 5 February 1943, both powered by

the 988-kW (1,325-hp) Allison V-1710-47 engine. Both aircraft were lost in an early stage of their test programme, resulting in the construction of a third prototype, the **XP-63A**, first flown on 26 April 1943 and powered by a V-1710-93 engine with a war emergency rating of 1119 kW (1,500 hp). It was planned subsequently to flight-test this prototype with a Packard-Merlin V-1650-5 engine installed, under the designation **XP-63B**, but this did not happen.

The performance of the XP-63A was found to be satisfactory, and the type was ordered into production in September 1942. Initial deliveries of the **P-63A** began in October 1943, and by the time production ended in 1945 more than 3,300 Kingcobras had been built in several versions. By far the majority, something in excess of 2,400, were supplied to the USSR under lend-lease, and about 300 went to the Free French Armée de l'Air. Very few of the total production of P-63 close-support fighters/fighter-bombers were delivered to the USAAF, and so far as is known no Kingcobras were used operationally by that service.

Equipment of production batches varied considerably, resulting in many sub-types. The first production **P-63A-1**s had V-1710-93 engines, a nose-mounted 37-mm M4 cannon and two 12.7-mm (0.5-in) machine-guns in underwing fairings; other sub-types had two additional 12.7-mm (0.5-in) guns mounted in the fuselage nose. P-63A-1s and **P63A-5**s could accommodate a 284-litre (75-US gal) or 662-litre (175-US gal) drop tank, or a 237-kg (522-lb) bomb beneath the wing centre-section; **P-63A-6**s had underwing racks for two similar bombs or additional fuel; and **P-63A-10**s could mount three air-to-surface rockets beneath each wing. The weight of defensive armour, intended primarily to give protection from ground weapons, increased progressively from 39.8 kg (87.7 lb) on the P-63A-1 to 107.2 kg (236.3 lb) on the P-63A-10.

The P-63A was succeeded on the pro-

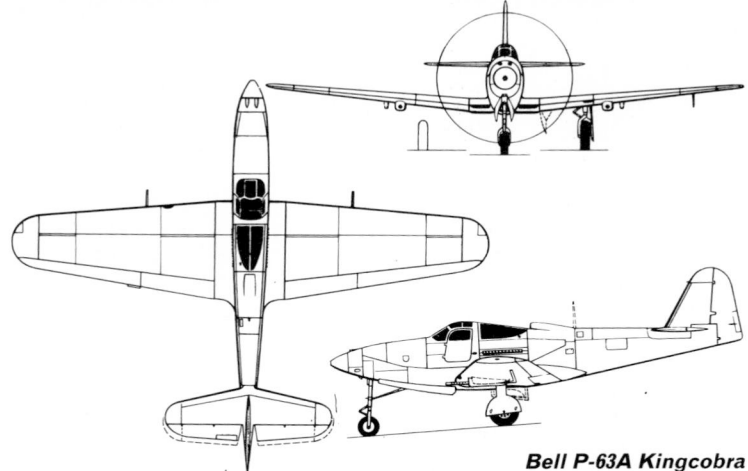

Bell P-63A Kingcobra

duction line by the **P-63C** with the V-1710-117 engine, this offering with water injection an emergency war rating of 1342 kW (1,800 hp). A distinctive identification feature of the P-63C was provided by the introduction of a small ventral fin. Other variants included a single **P-63D** with V-1710-109 engine, a bubble canopy, and increased wing span; 13 of the **P-63E** (or **Bell Model 41**), all that had been produced of 2,930 on order when contracts were cancelled at the war's end, and which were generally similar to the P-63D except for a reversion to the standard cockpit canopy; and two **P-63F**s, a version of the P-63E with a V-1710-135 engine and modified tail surfaces.

One other unusual version of the Kingcobra was built extensively (in excess of 300) for use by the USAAF in a training programme involving the use of live ammunition. Developed from the P-63A, all armour and armament was removed, and the external surface of the wings, fuselage and tail unit were protected externally by the addition of a duralumin alloy skin weighing some 680 kg (1,500 lb). Other protection included the installation of bulletproof glass in windscreen and cockpit side and upper windows, the provision of a steel grille over the engine air intake and steel guards for the exhaust stacks, and the use of a propeller with thick-walled hollow blades. All of these precautions were to make it possible for the aircraft to be flown as a target that could withstand, without significant damage, the impact of frangible bullets. When a hit was made by an attacking aircraft a red light blinked to confirm the accuracy of the weapon being fired against it.

The first five of these target aircraft were designated **RP-63A-11**; the 95 **RP-63A-12**s which followed had increased fuel tankage; the next production version, with the V-1710-117 engine, became designated **RP-63C** (200 built); and the final version was the **RP-63G** (32 built), this having the V-1710-135 engine. Although never flown as pilotless drone aircraft, the designations of these three versions were changed subsequently to **QF-63A, QF-63C** and **QF-63G** respectively.

Specification
Bell P-63A Kingcobra
Type: single-seat close-support fighter/fighter-bomber and target aircraft
Powerplant: one 988-kW (1,325-hp) Allison V-1710-93 inline piston engine
Performance: maximum speed 660 km/h (410 mph) at 7620 m (25,000 ft); cruising speed 608 km/h (378 mph); service ceiling 13110 m (43,000 ft); range with maximum weapon load and internal fuel 724 km (450 miles); ferry range with maximum internal and external fuel 3541 km (2,200 miles)
Weights: empty 2892 kg (6,375 lb); maximum take-off 4763 kg (10,500 lb)
Dimensions: span 11.68 m (38 ft 4 in); length 9.96 m (32 ft 8 in); height 3.84 m (12 ft 7 in); wing area 23.04 m² (248 sq ft)
Armament: one 37-mm M4 cannon, two wing-mounted and two nose-mounted 12.7-mm (0.5-in) machine-guns, plus up to three 237-kg (522-lb) bombs

The UH-1B was the main production version of the Model 204, featuring an enlarged cabin and broader rotor blades.

Bell Model 47

On 8 December 1945, Bell flew the prototype of a classic helicopter design, the **Bell Model 47**. On 8 March 1946 this was awarded the first Approved Type Certificate issued for a civil helicopter anywhere in the world. The type remained in continuous production by Bell into 1973, and was also built under licence by Agusta in Italy from 1954 to 1976. The Model 47 has been used on a large scale by armed forces all over the world, its simplicity and low cost more than outweighing its limited capabilities.

In 1947 the USAF (then USAAF) procured 28 of the improved **Model 47A**, powered by 117-kW (157-hp) Franklin O-335-1 piston engines, for service evaluation: 15 were designated **YR-13**, three **YR-13A**s were winterised for cold-weather trials in Alaska, and the balance of 10 went to the US Navy for evaluation as **HTL-1** trainers. Little time was lost by either service in deciding that the Model 47 was an excellent machine, and the orders began to flow in.

The US Army's first order was issued in 1948, 65 being accepted under the designation **H-13B**; all US Army versions were later named Sioux. Fifteen of these were converted in 1952 to carry external stretchers, with the designation **H-13C**. Two-seat **H-13D**s with skid landing gear, stretcher carriers, and Franklin O-335-5 engines followed, and generally similar three-seat dual control **H-13E**s. The **H-13G** differed by introducing a small elevator, and the **H-13H** introduced the 186-kW (250-hp) Lycoming VO-435 engine. Some of the H-13Hs were used also by the USAF, as were two **H-13J**s with 179-kW (240-hp) Lycoming VO-435s acquired for the use of the US President. Two H-13Hs converted for trial purposes, with an increased-diameter rotor and 168-kW (225-hp) Franklin 6VS-335 engine, were designated **H-13K**. In 1962 US Army H-13E, -G, -H and -K aircraft were redesignated with the prefix letter O, for observation. US Air Force H-13Hs and H-13Js were given the U prefix as utility helicopters. Later acquisitions were the three-seat **OH-13S** to supersede the OH-13H, and the **TH-13T** two-seat instrument trainer.

US Navy procurement began with 12 **HTL-2**s and nine **HTL-3**s, but the first major version was the **HTL-4**, followed by the **HTL-5** with an O-335-5 engine. **HTL-6** trainers incorporated the small movable elevator. The **HUL-1** was acquired for service on board ice-breaking ships, and the final **HTL-7** version for the US Navy was a two-seat dual-control instrument trainer with all-weather instrumentation. In 1962 the HTL-4, HTL-6, HTL-7 and HUL-1 were redesignated respectively **TH-13L, TH-13M, TH-13N** and **UH-13P**.

The Model 47 has been built under licence by Agusta in Italy, Kawasaki in Japan, and Westland in the UK (the 47G-2 for the British Army, with the name Sioux), and in various roles Model 47s have served with more than 30 armed services.

Experimental versions have been numerous. Perhaps the two most important were the **Bell Model 201** (service designation **XH-13F**) and the **Bell Model 207 Sioux Scout**. The Model 201 was powered by a Continental XT51-T-3 (licence-built Turboméca Artouste) turboshaft. The Model 207 was the first true armed helicopter: powered by the 194-kW (260-hp) turbocharged Avco Lycoming TVO-435-A1A piston engine, the Sioux Scout featured a revised cabin seating two in tandem, small stub wings containing additional fuel and helping to offload the main rotor in forward flight, and a remotely controlled chin barbette, containing two 7.62-mm (0.3-in) M60 machine-guns, and movable 200° in azimuth, with elevation from −45° to +15°.

In parallel with production of military aircraft, by both Bell and its licencees, there were civil versions for a wide variety of purposes. These have included the **Model 47B** (equivalent to the military YR-13/HTL-1), and the agricultural/utility **Model 47B-3** with open crew positions. The following **Model 47D** was the first to appear with a moulded 'goldfish bowl' canopy, and the **Model 47D-1** of 1949 introduced an openwork tailboom as on the H-13C.

A first important change came with introduction of the **Model 47G**, which combined the three-seat capacity of the Model 47D-1 with a 149-kW (200-hp) Franklin engine. Substitution of the similarly powered Avco Lycoming VO-435 resulted in the **Model 47G-2** (H-13H). A 179-kW (240-hp) VO-435 engine brought the changed designation **Model 47G-2A**, followed in 1963 by the wider cabin **Model 47G-2A-1** with improved rotor blades and increased fuel capacity. Other engine installations included a 168-kW (225-hp) supercharged Franklin 6VS-335-A (**Model 47G-3**); 209-kW (280-hp) turbocharged Avco Lycoming TVO-435 (**47G-3B**); and normally aspirated Avco Lycoming VO-540 and VO-435 engines in the three-seat utility **Model 47G-4** and **Model 47G-5** respectively. A two-seat agricultural version of the latter was known as the **Ag-5**, and a civil version of the USAF's H-13J VIP transport was marketed as the

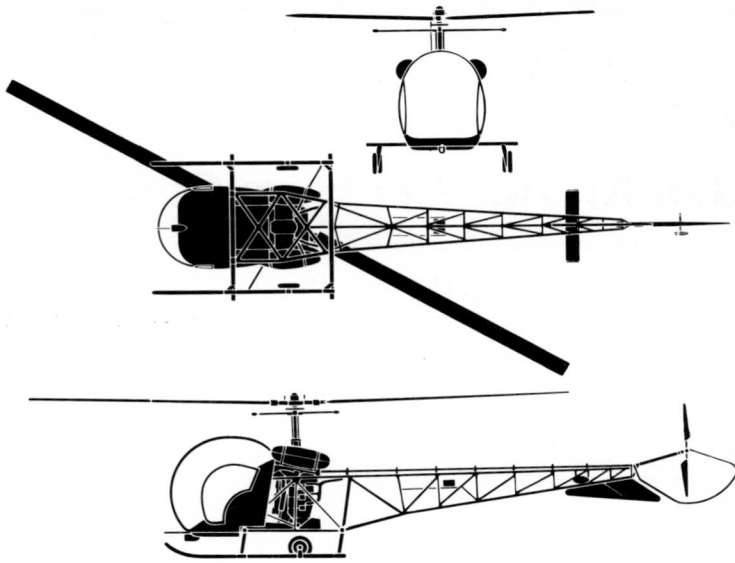

VO-435 engines in the three-seat utility **Model 47G-4** and **Model 47G-5** respectively. A two-seat agricultural version of the latter was known as the **Ag-5**, and a civil version of the USAF's H-13J VIP transport was marketed as the **Model 47J Ranger**. Bell's production of Model 47s eventually came to an end in late 1973, versions of the Model 47G-5 being the last to be built.

Agusta in Italy, and Kawasaki in Japan, both produced helicopters comparable to some of Bell's civil Model 47s, and added variants of their own. In addition there have been specialised conversions by at least two American companies, including a high-performance **Carson Super C-4**, and a number of **El Tomcat** agricultural aircraft developed by Continental Copters Inc. Turboshaft conversions of several models have been produced by Soloy in the USA.

Specification
Bell Model 47G-5A
Type: general utility helicopter

Bell Model 47G

Powerplant: one 198-kW (265-hp) Avco Lycoming VO-435-B1A flat-six piston engine

Performance: maximum speed at sea level 196 km/h (105 mph); cruising speed 137 km/h (85 mph) at 1525 m (5,000 ft); service ceiling 3200 m (10,500 ft); range with maximum fuel 412 km (256 miles)

Weights: empty equipped 786 kg (1,732 lb); maximum take-off 1293 kg (2,850 lb)

Dimensions: main rotor diameter 11.32 m (37 ft 1½ in); tail rotor diameter 1.78 m (5 ft 10 in); length, rotors turning 13.3 m (43 ft 7½ in); height 2.84 m (9 ft 3¾ in); main rotor disc area 100.61 m² (1,083 sq ft)

In both military and civil use, the Bell 47 has been a remarkably long-lived helicopter. Many have been re-engined with turbines to prolong their careers.

Bell Model 204

In 1955 the US Army initiated a design competition to speed the procurement of a new helicopter suitable for casualty evacuation, instrument training, and general utility duties. In June 1955 the US Army selected the Bell Helicopter Company's proposal, this having the company designation **Bell Model 204**. The new helicopter was known initially to the US Army as the **H-40**, changed to **HU-1** when it entered service, and given the name **Iroquois**. It was also the first of the 'Hueys', a nick-name evolved from the HU-1 designation which, in 1962, was altered to **UH-1** under the tri-service rationalisation scheme.

The US Army's first order was for three prototypes for testing, under the designation **XH-40**, the type having the H-40 designation allocated to it at that

time to identify it in the USAF helicopter category. The first of these prototypes made its first flight on 22 October 1956, and these were used by Bell for test and development. Just before the first flight, six examples of the pre-production **YH-40** were ordered, all being delivered by August 1958. One remained with Bell, but the remainder were distributed one each to Eglin AFB and Edwards AFB, and three to Fort Rucker, for trials. Duly ordered into production, nine of the definitive pre-production **HU-1A** were delivered on 30 June 1959, and were followed into service by 74 production examples, of which 14 went to the Army Aviation School at San Diego. The latter aircraft had dual controls and were used as instrument trainers. First major use overseas was with the 55th Aviation

Company in Korea, and HU-1As were among the first US Army helicopters to operate in Vietnam.

The Model 204 displayed its Bell parentage in the stabilising bar above and at right angles to the two blades of the main rotor, and also by the small elevator surfaces attached to the rear fuselage. Tubular skid-type landing gear was ideal for utility operations. Accommodation was provided for a crew of two and six passengers or two stretchers. Powerplant consisted of a 522-kW (700-shp) Avco Lycoming T53-L-1A turboshaft, and this made the Model 204 the first turbine-powered aircraft, rotary- or fixed-wing, to be ordered by the US Army.

The HU-1A was followed into service by the improved **HU-1B**, of which more than 700 were built, early production having the 716-kW (960-shp) Avco Lycoming T53-L-5 engine, and late pro-

duction models the 820-kW (1,100-shp) T53-L-11 engine. Other improvements in the HU-1B included redesigned main rotor blades, and an enlarged cabin to accommodate a crew of two, plus seven passengers or three stretchers. In the autumn of 1965 the UH-1B was superseded in production by the **UH-1C**, which had an improved 'door-hinge' rotor with wide-chord blades, this new main rotor conferring some increase in speed and improved manoeuvrability. A few UH-1As operating in Vietnam were equipped with rocket packs and two 7.62-mm (0.3-in) machine-guns for use in a close-support role, and the success of these resulted in many UH-1Bs serving in a similar capacity, armed mainly with four side-mounted 7.62-mm (0.3-in) machine-guns, or two similarly-mounted packs, each containing 24 rockets. Other military versions of the Model 204 include the **UH-1E** for the US Marine

The UH-1B was the main production version of the Model 204, featuring an enlarged cabin and broader rotor blades.

the T53-L-11 engine. Model 204Bs and UH-1s have been built by Fuji in Japan, under sub-licence from Mitsubishi, and in 1967 this company introduced the **Fuji-Bell 204B-2**, which differs from the Model 204B by having a more powerful engine and a tractor tail rotor. Agusta in Italy is another of Bell's licencees, and has built the Model 204B in large numbers for both civil and military use, many powered by Rolls-Royce Gnome turboshaft engines.

Specification
Fuji-Bell Model 204B-2
Type: general-purpose helicopter
Powerplant: one 1044-kW (1,400-shp) Avco Lycoming T5313B turboshaft
Performance: maximum speed 204 km/h (127 mph); hovering ceiling in ground effect 4635 m (15,200 ft); service ceiling 5790 m (19,000 ft); range at sea level 383 km (238 miles)
Weights: empty 2177 kg (4,800 lb); maximum take-off 3856 kg (8,500 lb)
Dimensions: main rotor diameter 14.63 m (48 ft 0 in); fuselage length 12.31 m (40 ft 4¾ in); height 3.77 m (12 ft 4½ in); main rotor disc area 168.1 m² (1,809.5 sq ft)

Corps (generally similar to the UH-1B, but equipped with a personnel hoist, rotor brake and special avionics). The first being delivered to the Marine Air Group 26 on 21 February 1964, and from October 1965 Bell's new 'door-hinge' rotor being fitted to production aircraft; the **UH-1F** for the USAF, generally similar to the UH-1B but with a 962-kW

(1,290-shp) General Electric T58-GE-3 turboshaft, increased-diameter rotor, and able to accommodate a pilot and 10 passengers; a similar **TH-1F** training version of the above for the USAF; the **HH-1K** SAR version for the US Navy, similar to the UH-1E but with 1044-kW (1,400-shp) T53-L-13 engine; **TH-1L** and **UH-1L** training and utility versions re-

spectively of the UH-1E with T53-L-13 engine; and three of the **UH-1M** with night sensor equipment for evaluation by the US Army.

The **Model 204B** was built in small numbers by Bell, for civil use and military export. Generally similar to the UH-1B, these were of 10-seat capacity, had the larger-diameter rotors of the UH-1F, and

Bell Model 205

The undoubted success of the Bell UH-1A/B Iroquois gave convincing proof that there was little wrong with the basic design of this utility helicopter. As detailed in the Model 204 entry, the UH-1A/B was developed continuously for differing roles and with progressively more powerful engines.

In early 1960 Bell proposed an improved version of the Model 204 design with a longer fuselage, plus additional cabin space resulting from relocation of the fuel cells, thus providing accommodation for a pilot and 14 troops, or space for six stretchers, or up to 1814 kg (4,000 lb) of freight. In July 1960, therefore, the US Army awarded Bell a contract for the supply of seven of these new helicopters for service tests, these having the US Army designation **YUH-1D** and being identified by the manufacturer as the **Bell Model 205**. The first of these flew on 16 August 1961, and following successful flight trials was ordered into production for the US Army, the first **UH-1D** being delivered to the 11th Air Assault Division at Fort Benning, Georgia, on 9 August 1963. The powerplant of these initial aircraft was the 820-kW (1,100-shp) Avco Lycoming T53-L-11 turboshaft, and the standard fuel storage of 832 litres (220 US gal) could be supplemented by two internal auxiliary fuel tanks to give a maximum overload capacity of 1968 litres (520 US gal) of fuel. Large-scale production of the UH-1D followed for the US Army, as well as for the armed forces of other nations, and 352 were built under licence by Dornier in West Germany for service with the German army and air force.

The UH-1D was followed into production by the more or less identical **UH-1H** which differed, however, in the use of the more powerful 1044-kW (1,400-shp) Avco Lycoming T53-L-13 turboshaft engine. Delivery of the UH-1H to the US Army began in September 1967, and this variant proved to be the final production version.

The UH-1H was built extensively for the US Army, nine were supplied to the RNZAF, and under the terms of licence agreement which was negotiated in 1969, the Republic of China (Taiwan) produced a total of 118 of these aircraft for service with the Nationalist Chinese army. Variants of the UH-1H include the **CH-118** (originally **CUH-1H**) built by Bell for the Canadian Armed Force's Mobile Command, with the first of 10 being delivered on 6 March 1968; and the **HH-1H** local base rescue helicopter of which 30 were ordered for the USAF on 4 November 1970, deliveries being completed during 1973.

The UH-1D/H was employed extensively on a very wide range of duties in South East Asia, and was regarded by many as the workhorse helicopter par excellence in Vietnam. In particular, the type played a major role in special warfare operations in Laos, Cambodia, and in some of the remote areas of South Vietnam, and USAF historians have commented that in this latter theatre of operations nearly all battlefield casualties were evacuated by UH-1 helicopters.

Since that time, a small number of UH-1Hs have been selected to fulfil an electronic counter-measures role under the designation **EH-1H**, and examples with advanced systems were being delivered from 1981. Under the US Army's Stand-Off Target Acquisition System (SOTAS) programme, four UH-1Hs were modified for evaluation. Their role was to obtain radar data of battlefield movements, relaying them to commanders on the ground and providing real-time information on the tactical situation.

However, the US Army intends to retain the basic UH-1H in large-scale service until the beginning of the 21st century, for deployment in roles that include command and control, electronic warfare, medical evacuation, minefield emplacement, resupply, and troop transport. In order to make this plan possible, the existing fleet of UH-1Hs is the sub-

Bell Model 205 (UH-1H)

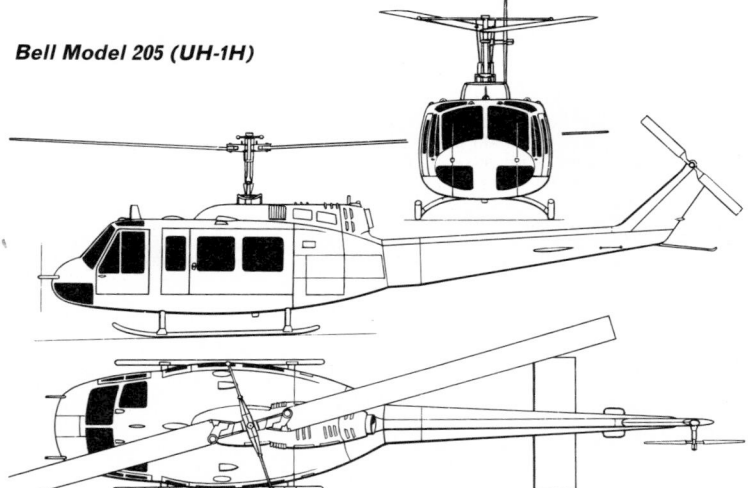

The UH-1H is still in widespread use with the US Army (and many other air arms), mainly used as an assault transport but also for rescue, liaison and other utility tasks.

The Model 205 introduced a longer cabin, and is easily distinguished from the 204 by having two large windows in the cabin door instead of one.

ject of a major product improvement programme which adds advanced avionics and equipment to give these helicopters the necessary capabilities and extended life.

Bell also produces a commercial version of the UH-1H under the designation **Model 205A-1**. It is powered by a 1044-kW (1,400-shp) Avco Lycoming T5813B turboshaft, derated to 932 kW (1,250 shp). Normal fuel capacity of the Model 205A-1 is 814 litres (215 US gal), with an optional fuel capacity of 1495 litres (395 US gal). Because it is intended for a wide range of users, special attention has been given to interior design to permit quick conversion for air freight, ambulance, executive, flying crane and search roles. Maximum accommodation is for a pilot and 14 passengers.

Agusta in Italy also builds the Model 205 under licence with the designation **AB.205A-1**, this being virtually the same as the Bell production model.

Customers have included the Italian armed forces, as well as those of several other countries. In Japan the **Fuji-Bell Model 205A-1** is available.

Specification
Bell Model 205/UH-1H
Type: civil/military utility helicopter
Powerplant: one 1044-kW (1,400-shp) Avco Lycoming T53-L-13 turboshaft
Performance: maximum speed 204 km/h (127 mph); hovering ceiling in ground effect 4145 m (13,600 ft); service ceiling 3840 m (12,600 ft); range with maximum fuel at sea level 511 km (318 miles)
Weights: empty equipped 2363 kg (5,210 lb); mission take-off 4100 kg (9,039 lb); maximum take-off 4309 kg (9,500 lb)
Dimensions: main rotor diameter 14.63 m (48 ft 0 in); tail rotor diameter 2.59 m (8 ft 6 in); length, rotors turning 17.62 m (57 ft 9¾ in); height, tail rotor turning 4.43 m (14 ft 5½ in); main rotor disc area 168.06 m² (1,809 sq ft)

Bell Model 206 JetRanger

In 1960 the US Army launched a design competition for a new aircraft which it identified as a Light Observation Helicopter (LOH). Perhaps, more truthfully, it was seeking two or three helicopters in just one all-purpose design, for the LOH was required to fulfil casualty evacuation, close support, observation, photoreconnaissance and transport missions. Previously no one aircraft had been able to embrace such a wide range of duties, and the specification called for four seats, a 181-kg (400-lb) payload and cruising speed of around 193 km/h (120 mph). Design proposals were put forward by 12 US helicopter manufacturers from whom Bell, Hiller and Hughes were each contracted to build five prototypes for competitive evaluation. From the tests which followed, the Hughes HO-6 (later OH-6A) was selected for production as the US Army's LOH.

If the US Army had some doubts about the capabilities of the **Bell HO-4** submission, the company did not share them, and after losing the competition it built a new prototype which it designated as the **Model 206A JetRanger**. This flew for the first time on 10 January 1966, and on 20 October 1966 this aircraft received FAA certification, after which it entered production for commercial customers, being built also by Agusta in Italy. The JetRanger was fundamentally the same as the **OH-4A** (formerly HO-4) prototypes, except for fuselage modifications to provide seating for five. It has been built in large numbers since 1966, and continues in production in 1989 in Canada under the designation **Model 206B JetRanger III**, having been the subject of progressive development and improvement programmes.

The US Army had expected to procure some 4,000 examples of the OH-6A, but became somewhat disenchanted with Hughes when the unit cost began to climb rather steeply, and the production rate to fall off. As a result, the US Army's LOH competition was reopened in 1967 and, on 8 March 1968, Bell's Model 206A was announced as the winner, with production under the designation **OH-58 Kiowa** starting without delay; some 2,200 of these aircraft were delivered by the end of 1973. The OH-58 differs from the commercial JetRanger by having a larger-diameter main rotor, with detail changes in internal layout and the provision of military avionics. Initial deliveries to the US Army began on 23 May 1969, and within something less than four months the Kiowa was deployed operationally in Vietnam.

Of the original 2,200 ordered for the US Army, 74 were withdrawn from the production line for delivery to the Canadian Armed Forces from December 1971 under the designation **COH-58A**, subsequently **CH-136**. An additional US Army contract for 74 aircraft was issued in January 1973 to replace those aircraft supplied to Canada.

In the early months of 1971, Bell began delivery of an improved **Model 206B JetRanger II**, and this subsequently replaced the Model 206A in production. It differed by having the more powerful 298-kW (400-shp) Allison 250-C20 turboshaft engine, the installation of which involved only minor airframe modification, so that it was possible also to provide kits for the upgrading of Model 206As to Model 206B standard. Australia acquired this version under the designation **Model 206B-1 Kiowa**, 12 being supplied by Bell and 44 produced under a co-production agreement. Commonwealth Aircraft Corporation in Australia was responsible for final assembly and only the powerplant and avionics came from the United States. Under a US Army development contract, a single OH-58A was equipped with a more powerful 313-kW (420-shp) Allison T63-A-720 turboshaft engine and an improved flat glass canopy. This modified aircraft has the designation **OH-58C**, and subsequently two additional OH-58A to OH-58C conversions were carried out to allow more extensive flight testing by Bell and the US Army. As a result of these tests, production modification of 275 OH-58As to a further-improved OH-58C configuration began in March 1978. Other versions include 12 **OH-58Bs**, similar to the OH-58A, supplied to the Austrian air force in 1976, and the US Navy has 40 **TH-57A SeaRangers**. These latter aircraft are dual-con-

trol trainers, which were ordered on 31 January 1968, to fulfil the requirement for a primary training helicopter for service with Naval Air Training Command at Pensacola, Florida. They are basically civil Model 206A JetRangers with US Navy avionics.

Production of the JetRanger II ended in the summer of 1977, when it was replaced by the **Model 206B JetRanger III**. This introduced a more powerful version of the Allison turboshaft engine, offering further improvement in performance, and was the current production version in late 1981. This engine is also available as an installation kit to upgrade JetRanger IIs to JetRanger III standard.

The capability and reliability of the JetRanger family resulted in Bell developing a medium-lift version under the designation **Model 206L LongRanger**. This had the powerplant of the JetRanger III, and a fuselage lengthened by 0.63 m (2 ft 1 in) to accommodate a total of five passengers. With a capacity of 2.35 m³ (83 cu ft), the LongRanger clearly had good freight-carrying capability, and to simplify the loading of bulky items a double door was incorporated in the port side of the fuselage. Other improvements included the use of an

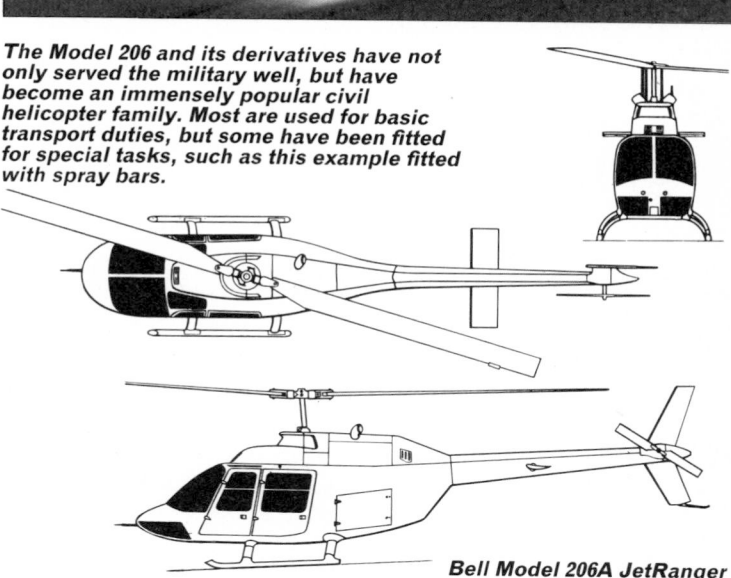

The Model 206 and its derivatives have not only served the military well, but have become an immensely popular civil helicopter family. Most are used for basic transport duties, but some have been fitted for special tasks, such as this example fitted with spray bars.

Bell Model 206A JetRanger

advanced main rotor, plus introduction of the company's patented Noda-Matic suspension system which gives much lower cabin vibration levels.

Deliveries of production LongRangers began in October 1975, but this was superseded by the **Model 206L LongRanger II** in mid-1978. The LongRanger II differs by having the more powerful Allison 250C-28B turboshaft with a maximum continuous rating of 365 kW (489 shp), a higher-rated transmission, and detail improvements. During 1981 the company developed the improved **LongRanger III** which has the 485-kW (650-shp) Allison 250-C30P engine and

numerous small changes. It is currently in production at Bell's plant at Mirabel in Canada.

Subsequently, Bell initiated development of a multi-role military variant of the commercial LongRanger under the designation **Model 206L TexasRanger**. The **Model 406** is a derivative using a new four-blade rotor, a conversion of OH-58As to provide the US Army with enhanced scout helicopters under the designation **OH-58D**. Featuring a mast-mounted sight, these have an Allison 250-C30R engine of 485 kW (650 shp) rating. The first conversion flew on 6 October 1983, and deliveries to the US

Army of 578 such aircraft is under way. Among these are some **AH-58D Warrior** armed examples.

In late 1989, overall production by Bell of members of the Model 206 family was considerably in excess of 7,000. Agusta, in Italy, has also produced JetRangers and LongRangers under licence from Bell, these being generally similar to their American counterparts.

Specification
Bell Model 206B JetRanger III
Type: general-purpose light helicopter

Powerplant: one 313-kW (420-shp) Allison 250-C20B turboshaft, flat-rated to 236 kW (317 shp)
Performance: maximum cruising speed 216 km/h (134 mph) at 1525 m (5,000 ft); service ceiling 4115 m (13,500 ft); range with maximum fuel and payload at 1525 m (5,000 ft) 608 km (378 miles)
Weights: empty 730 kg (1,610 lb); maximum take-off 1451 kg (3,200 lb)
Dimensions: main rotor diameter 10.16 m (33 ft 4 in); length, rotors turning 11.82 m (38 ft 9½ in); height 2.91 m (9 ft 6½ in); main rotor disc area 81.1 m² (837 sq ft)

Bell Model 209 HueyCobra & SeaCobra

In March 1965, Bell initiated company-funded development of the proven Model 204 (UH-1B/-1C Iroquois) to produce an armed helicopter suitable for close-support/attack roles. Intended to provide the US Army with an interim AAFSS (advanced aerial fire support system) helicopter, it combined a new narrow, low-profile, tandem-seat fuselage with the rotor/transmission system/ powerplant of the UH-1C. First flown in prototype form on 7 September 1965, the new **Bell Model 209** was evaluated by the US Army from December of that year, with orders for two pre-production and 110 production aircraft following during April 1966. Designated **AH-1G**, and named HueyCobra, the type was first delivered to the US Army in June 1967, and within two months the type was being used operationally in Vietnam. US Marine Corps interest in this helicopter resulted in 38 AH-1Gs being supplied from the US Army production line in 1969, pending initial deliveries of 49 of the **AH-1J SeaCobra** variant ordered by the US Marine Corps in May 1968. Examples generally similar to the US Army's AH-1G have been supplied to the Spanish navy (eight, designated **Z.14**) and Israel (six).

The HueyCobra has small stub-wings that serve the dual purpose of offloading the rotor in flight, and of carrying armament that, in the case of the AH-1G, can include folding-fin rockets or Minigun pods. Additionally, this version mounts beneath the nose an M-28 turret that can house two Miniguns, or two 40-mm grenade-launchers, or one of each. Armour protection is provided for the crew in the form of Noroc side panels and seats, with other vital areas of the helicopter protected by panels of the same material.

AH-1Q HueyCobra: designation of 93 AH-1Gs converted to launch TOW anti-tank missiles
AH-1R HueyCobra: version similar to AH-1G with a more powerful T53-L-703 turboshaft engine
AH-1S HueyCobra: overall designation under which existing US Army AH-1 aircraft were updated to have TOW capability and incorporated other improvements, and of new production aircraft to the same or higher standard; current designations include **Modified AH-1S**, which covers 197 AH-1Gs and the 93 AH-1Qs with upgraded gearbox, transmission, improved rotor, T53-L-703 engine, and TOW-capability; 100 generally similar **Production AH-1S**, being new production aircraft with advanced avionics, instrumentation, and systems; 98 **Up-Gun AH-1S**, generally as the Production AH-1S but with an improved turret and weapon management systems; and the **Modernised AH-1S** of which 126 new production aircraft have been ordered incorporating the improvements embodied in the other AH-1S aircraft, plus advanced nav/com, avionics, and protection systems. These are now known as **AH-1F** to avoid confusion with other variants
AH-1T Improved SeaCobra: generally improved version of the AH-1J, incorporating an uprated T400-WV-402 powerplant, the dynamic system of the Bell Model 214, and the fuselage lengthened by 1.09 m (3 ft 7 in); 57 built, and equipped for operation with TOW missiles
AH-1W SuperCobra: new USMC version with two GE T700-GE-700 engines, producing 1260-kW (1,690-shp) each. Better protection and avionics are incorporated. Conversion applied to AH-1T aircraft
Model 249: company designation of

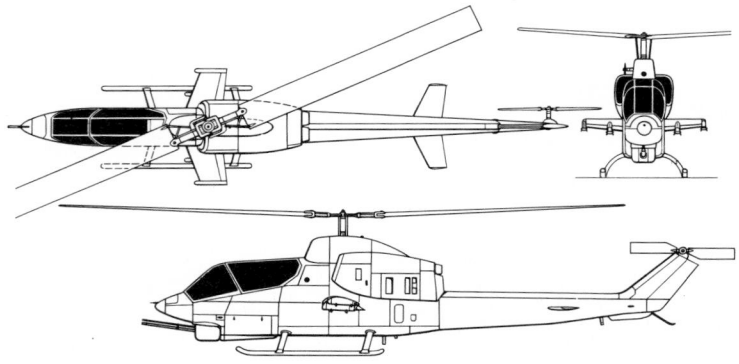

Bell Model 209 (AH-1T) Improved SeaCobra

a Modernised AH-1S which was equipped and tested with an advanced four-blade main rotor as developed for the Bell Model 412

Specification
Bell Model 209 AH-1J SeaCobra
Type: attack/close-support helicopter
Powerplant: one 1342-kW (1,800-shp) Pratt & Whitney Aircraft of Canada T400-CP-400 twin-engined turboshaft unit, flat-rated as detailed above
Performance: maximum speed at sea level 333 km/h (207 mph); hovering ceiling in ground effect 3795 m (12,450 ft); range with maximum fuel 577 km (359 miles)
Weights: empty operating 3294 kg (7,261 lb); maximum take-off 4535 kg (10,000 lb)
Dimensions: main rotor diameter 13.41 m (44 ft 0 in); tail rotor diameter

2.59 m (8 ft 6 in); length rotors turning 16.26 m (53 ft 4 in); height 4.15 m (13 ft 8 in); main rotor disc area 141.26 m² (1,520.53 sq ft)
Armament: one M-197 three-barrel 20-mm cannon in undernose turret, and up to 998 kg (2,200 lb) of weapons (XM-157 Minigun pods, XM-157 seven-tube or XM-159 19-tube 70-mm/2.75-in rocket pods) on four underwing racks

Until the advent of the McDonnell Douglas AH-64 Apache, the Bell AH-1 was the US Army's prime anti-armour helicopter, and large numbers are still in service. In addition to undernose armament, the Cobra is equipped to fire up to eight TOW anti-tank missiles from launchers under the stub wings. This is an AH-1S with flat-pane canopy to reduce glint; current aircraft have mostly been updated to AH-1F standard with 20-mm undernose cannon.

Variants
JAH-1G HueyCobra: one armament research aircraft which has been flown with the Hellfire air-launched missile, and multi-barrel cannon
TH-1G HueyCobra: designation of dual-control trainer conversions from AH-1G
AH-1J SeaCobra: initial US Marine Corps version powered by a twin-turboshaft T400-CP-400 powerplant; this power unit incorporates two turbine engines, flat-rated to 820 kW (1,100 shp) for continuous running, but with a take-off or emergency rating of 932 kW (1,250 shp); total of 69 delivered to USMC by early 1975, and 202 similar aircraft supplied to the Imperial Iranian Army Aviation from 1974

Bell Model 212 Twin Two-Twelve

On 1 May 1968 the Bell Helicopter Company announced that following negotiations with the Canadian government and Pratt & Whitney Aircraft of Canada, it had been agreed to proceed with the development of a new helicopter based upon the airframe of the Bell Model 205/UH-1H Iroquois, of which the first of 10 for the Canadian Armed Forces (CAF) had been delivered on 6 March 1968 under the designation CUH-1H. Powerplant of the UH/CUH-1 consisted of a 1044-kW (1,400-shp) Avco Lycoming T53-L-13 turboshaft engine. The CAF considered that the incorporation of twin turboshaft engines would provide a number of benefits, and this led to development of the initial military **Bell Model 212** and the Pratt & Whitney Aircraft of Canada (PWAC) PT6T powerplant for it. This programme was initiated as a joint venture, financed by Bell, the Canadian government and PWAC.

The revolutionary feature of this new helicopter was its powerplant, the PT6T Twin-Pac, designed and developed by PWAC, and consisting of two turboshaft engines mounted side-by-side and driving, via a combining gearbox, a single output shaft. This had an output in its initial production form of 2.83 shp per 1 lb of dry weight (4.66 kW/kg), compared with 2.55 shp/lb (4.19 kW/kg) for the already-developed Lycoming T53 turboshaft. There was another very considerable advantage: as installed in the Model 212 the PT6T-3 is limited to an output of 962-kW (1,290 shp) for take-off. In the event of a failure of one of the two turbines, sensing torquemeters in the combining gearbox signal the remaining turbine to develop a power output ranging from 764 kW (1,025 shp) to 596 kW (800 shp), for emergency and continuous operation respectively.

Initial deliveries of military Model 212s were made to the USAF in 1970, under the designation **UH-1N**, and deliveries of UH-1Ns for the US Navy and Marine Corps began in 1971. The first **CUH-1N** (later redesignated **CH-135**) for the CAF was handed over on 3 May 1971. Examples have been supplied also to the air forces of Argentina (eight) and Bangladesh (six). The airframe is generally similar to that of the UH-1H Iroquois, with an all-metal fuselage structure, skid landing gear, and rotor systems comprising a two-blade all-metal semi-rigid main rotor, and a two-blade tail rotor.

A 14-passenger commercial version known as the **Twin Two-Twelve** was developed more or less simultaneously, this differing from the military model primarily in its cabin furnishing and avionics equipment. The Twin Two-Twelve gained FAA Transport Type Category A certification on 30 June 1971, and the type has since gained certification for IFR operation, requiring a new avionics package, new instrument panel, and stabilisation controls for such use. In June 1977 it became the first helicopter to be certificated by the FAA for single-pilot IFR operation with fixed floats.

The enhanced safety offered by the Twin-Pac powerplant has resulted in many sales to operators who provide support to offshore gas/oil prospecting and production companies, as well as to air taxi organisations. Eight Model 212s were delivered to the Civil Air Authority of China during 1979, and were the first helicopters supplied to the People's Republic of China by a US manufacturer.

The Model 212 is also built under licence by Agusta in Italy as the **Agusta-Bell AB.212**, with initial deliveries made during 1971. These are generally similar to the American-built aircraft, but Agusta has developed an ASW version designated **AB.212ASW**. Structural strengthening took place, plus the provision of deck restraint gear, and the PWAC PT6T-6 Twin-Pac turboshaft rated at 1398 kW (1,875 shp) for take-off.

Specification
Type: civil/military utility helicopter
Powerplant: one Pratt & Whitney Aircraft of Canada PT6T-3 Turbo Twin-Pac coupled turboshaft, flat rated to 962 kW (1,290 shp) for take-off and to 843 kW (1,130 shp) for continuous operation
Performance: maximum cruising speed 230 km/h (143 mph) at sea level; service ceiling 4330 m (14,200 ft); range with standard fuel at sea level with no reserves 420 km (261 miles)
Weights: empty 2786 kg (6,143 lb); maximum take-off 5080 kg (11,200 lb)
Dimensions: main rotor diameter 14.69 m (48 ft 2¼ in); length overall, rotors turning 17.46 m (57 ft 3¼ in); height 4.53 m (14 ft 10¼ in); main rotor disc area 168.06 m² (1,809 sq ft)

Combining twin-engine capabilities with the proven features of the Bell Model 204 Series, the Model 212 is a versatile helicopter. Twin-engine safety has made it very attractive to offshore oil support operators.

Bell Model 214B BigLifter

As mentioned in the notes on the Bell Model 214ST, the company developed a Model 214A utility helicopter of which a total of 293 was delivered for service with Iranian Army Aviation, which gave them the name Isfahan. Subsequently, 39 generally similar aircraft, but with specific equipment for SAR operations, were delivered to the Iranian Air Force under the designation **Bell Model 214C**.

Testing of these military helicopters convinced Bell that there should be a significant market for a civil variant, for it would have a lifting capability better than any contemporary helicopter within the medium category range. Accordingly, the company announced in early 1974 its intention to develop such an aircraft under the designation **Bell Model 214B BigLifter**. Generally similar in configuration to the military helicopter, retaining the same airframe, rotor/transmission systems, and powerplant, the BigLifter differs by having emergency escape windows in the cargo doors, an engine fire extinguishing system; and avionics suited to civil rather than military operation.

Two versions were available, and the standard Model 214B was intended for a variety of purposes. They included operation as a 14-passenger transport with a crew of two; as a cargo lifter, with an external cargo hook certificated to carry a maximum load of 3629 kg (8,000 lb); in an agricultural role, carrying a very similar chemical load; or as a firefighter able to drop a total 2725 litres (720 US gal) of fire retardant, carried in cabin and underfuselage tanks. The alternative **Model 214B-1** was certificated to different standards that allowed for operation at a lower gross weight with an internal load.

The Model 214B was available to commercial operators from the receipt of certification on 27 January 1976 until production ceased in 1981.

Bell Model 214A Isfahan of the Imperial Iranian Army Aviation, lead customer for this advanced utility aircraft.

Specification
Bell Model 214B
Type: general-purpose civil helicopter
Powerplant: one 2185-kW (2,930-shp) Avco Lycoming T5508D
turboshaft, flat-rated to 1678 kW (2,250 shp) for take-off
Performance: cruising speed 259 km/h (161 mph)
Weights: maximum take-off, 214B with internal load 6260 kg (13,800 lb), 214B/214B-1 with external load 7257 kg (16,000 lb)
Dimensions: main rotor diameter 15.24 m (50 ft 0 in); tail rotor diameter 2.95 m (9 ft 8 in); main rotor disc area 182.41 m² (1,963.5 sq ft)

Bell Model 214ST

In late 1970 Bell Helicopters completed the construction of a prototype aircraft to which the identification **Bell Model 214 Huey Plus** was allocated. It was, in effect, an improved version of the well tried and proven UH-1H Iroquois, using the same airframe, but provided with increased power, some advanced features, and structural strengthening for operation at higher gross weights. From this helicopter was developed the **Bell Model 214A** 16-seat utility version with a 2185-kW (2,930-shp) Avco Lycoming LTC4B-8D turboshaft engine and, following its demonstration in Iran, the company received an order for 287 of these aircraft, to be acquired by Iran through the US government. Soon after this the government of Iran began negotiations with European and US helicopter manufacturers, with the intention of establishing an indigenous aircraft industry, and concluded an agreement with Bell Helicopters in 1975. This envisaged that the Iranian government and Bell would jointly create facilities in Iran for this purpose, with the Bell 214A as its initial project, to be followed by a new **Bell Model 214ST** developed especially for operation in Iran. The revolution of early 1979, and subsequent changed national policies in Iran, brought to an end these plans, but Bell decided to continue with independent development of the Model 214ST as a commercial transport with multi-mission capability.

A prototype of the Model 214ST was first flown in February 1977, and was followed by the construction of three pre-production aircraft, beginning in 1978, the first of these flying in the summer of that year. These aircraft were all used

Ideally tailored for offshore support, the Model 214ST can seat 19 passengers while also performing well in the rescue role.

in the development programme, with FAA certification for two-pilot IFR operation gained in 1982. By early 1989 a total of 96 had been delivered, the largest order being 45 to the Iraqi Air Force.

Features of the Model 214ST airframe include the large-capacity all-metal fuselage, which includes in its structure a roll-over protection ring, providing accommodation for a pilot and co-pilot, plus 16 or 17 passengers according to customer specification. The rotor system includes an advanced technology two-blade main rotor fabricated from glassfibre, its leading edges protected by a titanium abrasion strip and the blade tips each having a replaceable stainless steel cap. The rotor hub incorporates elastomeric bearings which require no lubrication, and the rotor system is mounted on a Bell-

developed nodal suspension beam from which the fuselage is suspended. This latter feature is based on the fact that a beam subjected to vertical vibrations will flex in wave form, with nodal points of no relative motion equidistant from the centre of the induced wave form. Bell suspends the helicopter fuselage from the nodal points of such a beam, resulting in a reduction of more than 70 per cent in rotor-induced vibration.

The other major change, by comparison with the Model 214A, is the replacement of the single Lycoming turboshaft by two General Electric turboshafts which, driving the rotor through a combining gearbox, give true single-engine flight capability. Multi-mission roles are catered for by the provision of easily-removable passenger seating to offer 8.95 m³ (316 cu ft) cargo capacity, full IFR avionics and instrumentation, emergency flotation gear, an external cargo

suspension system, and an internal rescue hoist.

Specification
Bell Model 214ST
Type: commercial transport helicopter
Powerplant: two 1212-kW (1,625-shp) General Electric CT7-2 turboshafts
Performance: maximum cruising speed 250 km/h (155 mph) at 1220 m (4,000 ft); normal cruising speed at sea level 256 km/h (159 mph); hovering ceiling in ground effect 3170 m (10,400 ft); range with standard fuel and no reserves 780 km (485 miles)
Weight: maximum take-off, internal or external load 7802 kg (17,200 lb)
Dimensions: main rotor diameter 15.85 m (52 ft 0 in); length overall, rotors turning 18.95 m (62 ft 2¼ in); height 4.84 m (15 ft 10½ in); main rotor disc area 197.32 m² (2,124 sq ft)

Bell Model 222

Bell Model 222 of Helikopter Service, Oslo, used to support oilrigs in the North Sea.

Bell Helicopters first announced in April 1974 the company's intention to develop a new commercial helicopter which would be the first light twin-turbine commercial helicopter to be built in the USA. This was no blind decision for, shrewdly, a mock-up of the company's design proposal had been exhibited at the annual convention of the Helicopter Association of America at the beginning of the year, giving potential customers an opportunity of making constructive suggestions for product improvement. The resulting interest was sufficient to warrant a decision to proceed with the construction of five prototypes, and the first of these flew on 13 August 1976.

Allocated the company designation **Bell Model 222**, these prototypes were used to complete the development and certification programme as quickly as possible, with FAA certification in VFR configuration being gained on 20 December 1979. The Model 222 benefits from new-technology features developed at an earlier date for both civil and military helicopters, and includes the nodal suspension system described for the Model 214ST, a no-lubricant elastomeric bearing main rotor hub, and glass-

fibre/stainless steel main rotor blades.

The airframe structure is primarily of light alloy, the fuselage having a short-span cantilever sponson mounted on each side. Of aerofoil section, these provide some lift in forward flight and thus supplement the main rotor; in addition, they provide a housing for the main units of the tricycle-type landing gear when retracted. The design includes more tail unit than seen on most helicopters, with both upper and lower sweptback fins and mounted further forward on the aft fuselage, a tailplane with endplate fins. Maximum high-density seating capacity is for 10 occupants, comprising one or two crew, and nine or eight passengers

respectively, but production aircraft are available in three versions. These comprise the basic Model 222 with a standard seating configuration for a pilot and seven passengers. Optionally there is the **Model 222 Executive**, fully equipped for IFR flight with a crew of one or two, and luxury accommodation for six or five passengers respectively; and the **Model 222UT** (Utility Twin) equipped for IFR operation with a crew of two, and with an emergency flotation system and auxiliary fuel tanks as standard while the wheeled undercarriage is replaced by tubular skids.

The twin turbine powerplant selected for the Model 222 consists of two Avco

Lycoming LTS 101-650C-2 turboshafts, their dry weight of only 110 kg (241 lb) each providing a maximum power/weight ratio of 4.58 kW/kg (2.80 shp/lb) at maximum rating. The current **Model 222B** production version introduced uprated LTS 101-750C-1 engines, with other minor improvements.

Initial deliveries of VFR certificated Model 222s were made to Petroleum Helicopters and Schiavone Construction in January 1980. A Model 222 delivered to Omniflight Helicopters, on 25 January 1981, was the 25,000th helicopter to be built by Bell. By January 1989, 176 Model 222s had been built.

Specification
Bell Model 222
Type: light commercial helicopter
Powerplant: two Avco Lycoming LTS 101-650C-2 turboshafts, each with a take-off rating of 503 kW (675 shp) and maximum continuous rating of 446 kW (598 shp)
Performance: maximum cruising speed 265 km/h (165 mph) at sea level; economic cruising speed 241 km/h (150 mph) at 2440 m (8,000 ft); service ceiling 6095 m (20,000 ft); range with maximum fuel 523 km (325 miles)
Weights: empty equipped 2204 kg (4,860 lb); maximum take-off 3650 kg (7,850 lb)
Dimensions: main rotor diameter 12.12 m (39 ft 9 in); length of fuselage 10.98 m (36 ft 0¼ in); height 3.51 m (11 ft 6 in); main rotor disc area 115.29 m² (1,241 sq ft)

An elegant helicopter, the Bell Model 222 is designed for eight occupants inlcuding the pilot, while the Model 222 Executive carries seven, and the 222 Offshore carries two pilots and five passengers.

Bell Model 412

Under the designation **Bell Model 412**, the company has developed a version of the Model 212 which introduces a new four-bladed main rotor of advanced design. Each blade is constructed of glass-fibre and Nomex honeycomb, incorporates a titanium abrasion strip on the leading edge, has lightning-protecting mesh included in the blade structure, and also has provisions for the inclusion of de-icing heater elements if required. The rotor hub is also of new design, being of steel and light alloy structure, with elastomeric bearings and dampers.

Two new Model 212s were modified for use in the development prgramme of this new helicopter, with both IFR and VFR certification gained by 13 February 1980. The initial delivery of a VFR certificated aircraft was made on 18 January 1981, and two were delivered to the Venezuelan Air Force later in the year.

The latest production version is the **Model 412SP**, with a 55 per cent increase in fuel capacity and other improvements. 100 of these are being built by IPTN in Indonesia, while Helikopter Services A/S is assembling 17 for the Royal Norwegian Air Force. By January 1989, 162 Model 412s had been delivered.

Agusta in Italy manufactures the type as the **AB 412SP**, and has delivered over 75. It has developed the **Griffon**, a strengthened version for military duties, the prototype flying in August 1982.

Specification
Bell Model 412
Type: civil/military utility helicopter
Powerplant: one 1342-kW (1,800-shp) Pratt & Whitney Aircraft of Canada PT6T-3B-1 Twin-Pac turboshaft engine, flat-rated to 975 kW (1,308 shp) for

take-off
Performance: maximum cruising speed at sea level 230 km/h (143 mph); service ceiling 4330 m (14,200 ft); maximum range at sea level 420 km (261 miles)
Weights: empty 2823 kg (6,223 lb); maximum take-off 5262 kg (11,600 lb)
Dimensions: main rotor diameter

Dispensing with the traditional Bell two-blade rotor, the Model 412 is based on the 212 but with a four-blade unit.

14.02 m (46 ft 0 in); length, rotors turning 17.07 m (56 ft 0 in); height, rotors turning (4.32 m (14 ft 2¼ in); main rotor disc area 154.39 m² (1,661.9 sq ft)

Bell X-1

The advent of the rocket motor and the turbojet engine enabled designers to contemplate seriously the development of aircraft capable of flying at speeds greater than that of sound. They then had to contend with the so-called 'heat-barrier', which necessitated the development of new materials capable of withstanding the friction-generated (kinetic) heat encountered in supersonic flight.

In February 1945, the United States Army Air Force and the National Advisory Committee for Aeronautics promoted and financed jointly the development of a series of research aircraft to investigate these problems. A contract for these aircraft was duly awarded to Bell. The bullet-shaped **Bell XS-1** (later **Bell X-1**) prototype was first air-launched for an unpowered flight on 19 January 1946, dropped from a specially modified Boeing B-29. The second prototype, flown by Chalmers Goodlin, made the first powered flight on 9 December of the same year, and on 14 October 1947 Captain Charles 'Chuck' Yeager piloted the aircraft through the 'sound barrier' for the first time, achieving 1078 km/h (670 mph) at 12800 m (42,000 ft), or Mach 1.05. Just a few days later this aircraft, which is now in the National Air and Space Museum in Washington, set an altitude record of 21372 m (70,119 ft). A third X-1 was built but was later destroyed in an accident at Edwards Air Force Base.

This is the second Bell X-1, the one used by 'Chuck' Yeager to break the sound barrier. All landings were made unpowered.

Variants
Bell X-1A: the first of three further X-1 airframes ordered in 1948, it featured a bulged cockpit in place of the almost flat canopy of the XS-1, a lengthened fuselage with increased fuel capacity, and turbo-driven fuel pumps in substitution for the original system which used nitrogen under pressure; on 12 December 1953, Yeager flew the aircraft at Mach 2.35,

and in June 1954 reached an altitude of more than 27430 m (90,000 ft)
Bell X-1B: used for thermal research, now preserved at the Alabama Space and Rocket Center at Huntsville
Bell X-1D: the third of the second batch, destroyed in August 1951 when jettisoned from its parent B-50 after an explosion
Bell X-1E: reworked prototype X-1, fitted with a new Stanley Aviation-manufactured wing with a 4 per cent thickness/chord ratio, and with a redesigned cockpit canopy; now located in front of the NASA offices at Edwards Air Force Base

Specification
Bell X-1 (with turbo-driven fuel pumps)
Type: rocket-propelled supersonic research aircraft
Powerplant: one 2722-kg (6,000-lb) thrust Reaction Motors rocket unit
Performance: maximum speed 2736 km/h (1,700 mph) at 18290 m (60,000 ft)
Weights: empty, including test equipment 2219 kg (4,892 lb); maximum launch 6078 kg (13,400 lb)
Dimensions: span 8.53 m (28 ft 0 in); length 9.45 m (31 ft 0 in); height 3.3 m (10 ft 10 in)

Bell X-2
to
Bell XP-83

Bell X-2

Bearing a superficial resemblance to the earlier X-1 series of research prototypes, the **Bell X-2** was designed to investigate the problems of flight at high altitude and high speed (up to Mach 3). Its stainless steel wing, and other parts of the airframe, were instrumented to gather information about the effect of heat on structural materials. Powered by a Curtiss Wright XLR25-CW-1 throttlable rocket motor, the X-2 was fitted with a conventional nosewheel, but the main landing gear was a retractable skid, supplemented by auxiliary underwing skids at mid-span. A ground-handling trolley was used to manoeuvre the X-2 into position beneath the launch aircraft, a specially adapted Boeing B-50 which was raised on hydraulic jacks to facilitate loading.

The test programme began in June 1952 with unpowered flights and, while

The Bell X-2 was a highly-swept research vehicle to explore the effects of high speed flight at high altitude. Note the belly skid.

undergoing tests on the pressure and rocket fuel systems in preparation for a powered flight, the prototype was blown from the B-50 by an explosion. Bell's chief test pilot was killed in the blast, and the aircraft fell 9145 m (30,000 ft) into Lake Ontario. The second X-2 made the first powered flight, on 18 November 1955, and on 7 September 1956 it achieved an altitude of 38405 m (126,000 ft). However, during a subsequent sortie, on 27 September 1956, having achieved a record speed of Mach 3.2 which was not bettered until 1961, it crashed and the pilot, Captain Milburn G. Apt, was killed.

Specification
Type: single-seat research aircraft
Powerplant: one 6804-kg (15,000-lb)

thrust Curtiss Wright XLR25-CW-1 rocket engine
Performance: maximum speed 3058 km/h (1,900 mph); service ceiling 38405 m (126,000 ft)
Dimensions: span 9.75 m (32 ft 0 in); length 13.41 m (44 ft 0 in); height 4.11 m (13 ft 6 in)

Bell X-5

When US forces occupied the German town of Oberammergau in April 1945, they discovered an experimental facility, the contents of which included the almost complete prototype of the Messerschmitt P.1101. With this single-seat jet research aircraft, its manufacturer had intended to investigate the effects of varied angles of wing sweep. Head of the investigating team sent in to evaluate the activities of the centre happened to be Bell's chief designer, Robert J. Woods. In the autumn of 1948, after the machine had been assessed at Wright Field, he succeeded in having it transferred to Bell as a test vehicle for his variable-sweep wing mechanism. Unfortunately, the P.1101 was damaged in transit, but in February 1949 Bell proposed the construction of two variable-geometry prototypes, and this was accepted.

Bearing a clear resemblance to the Messerschmitt design, and powered by an Allison J35-A-17 engine, the first **Bell X-5** carried out taxiing trials at Niagara Falls, New York, before being transferred to Edwards Air Force Base, where 'Skip' Ziegler flew it for the first time on 20 June 1951. The first sweep variation was attempted on the fifth flight, on 27 July 1951. The aircraft could operate at three possible angles of sweep, from a minimum of 20° to a maximum of 60°, and the wing moved fore and aft on rails

Derived from the P.1101, the X-5 was produced to research variable sweep wings.

as the wing angle changed.

The first prototype completed its variable sweep programme and was then retained at Edwards for use as a chase 'plane, but the second was destroyed in a crash on 13 October 1953, killing test pilot Major Raymond Popson. The survivor is part of the USAF Museum collection at Wright-Patterson Air Force Base, Dayton, Ohio.

Specification
Type: single-seat research aircraft
Powerplant: one 2223-kg (4,900-lb)

thrust Allison J35-A-17 turbojet
Performance: maximum level speed approximately 1046 km/h (650 mph)
Weight: maximum take-off 4536 kg (10,000 lb)
Dimensions: span, unswept 9.39 m (30 ft 9¾ in), swept 5.66 m (18 ft 7 in); length 10.16 m (33 ft 4 in); height 3.66 m (12 ft 0 in)

Bell X-22

Without doubt the most bizarre of the company's vertical lift airframes, the **Bell X-22A** was developed to a US Navy contract, placed in November 1962, for research into flight using tilting ducted propellers. The conventional fuselage had rear-mounted stub wings, each having a duct unit built onto its leading edge, and with an elevon control surface in the slipstream from the 2.13-m (7-ft) diameter Hamilton Standard three-bladed propeller. The foreplanes, mounted on each side of the fuselage

just aft of the flight deck, carried similar ducts and control surfaces. Power was provided by four General Electric YT58-GE-8D turboshaft engines, mounted in pairs at the root of each wing, and employing cross-shafting to ensure that, in the event of an engine failure, all ducts remained under power.

The first X-22A flew on 17 March 1966, achieving four vertical take-offs, to a height of 7.62 m (25 ft). STOL take-offs were also made, but hydraulic failure resulted in a heavy landing on 8 August 1966, the aircraft then being assessed as beyond economical repair. The second example flew for the first time on 26

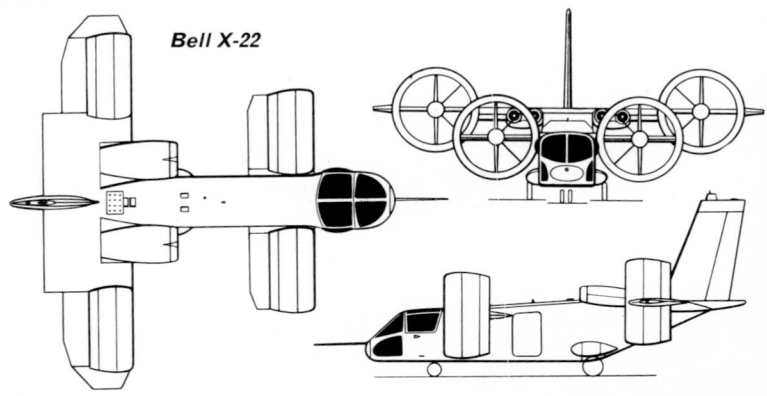

Bell X-22

January 1967, and successfully continued the programme to its end. When, on 19 May 1969, it was handed over for use in various tri-service, FAA and NASA V/STOL research projects, it had flown 110 hours. In this period it had recorded 185 full transitions, approximately 400 vertical take-offs and landings, and approximately 200 short take-offs and landings.

Specification
Type: tilting-duct V/STOL research aircraft
Powerplant: four 932-kW (1,250-shp) General Electric YT58-GE-8D turboshafts
Performance: maximum speed 509 km/h (316 mph) at sea level; cruising speed 343 km/h (213 mph) at 3355 m (11,000 ft); range 716 km (445 miles)
Weight: maximum take-off VTOL and STOL 8172 kg (18,016 lb)
Dimensions: span 11.96 m (39 ft 3 in); foreplane span 7.01 m (23 ft 0 in); length 12.06 m (39 ft 7 in); height 6.3 m (20 ft 8 in)

By any standards an extraordinary aircraft, the Bell X-22A combined VTOL and conventional flight by the use of four large ducted propulsors mounted at the 'corners' of the aircraft. Power to drive these fans came from turboshaft engines mounted on the rear wing, joined by cross-shafts to prevent any fan from failing.

Bell XP-77

During World War II, ever-growing fleets of bombers and fighters brought a real fear that there might be an acute shortage of the light alloys from which most were built. Bell's **Tri-4**, as known originally, was one of several projects intended to produce a fighter of so-called non-strategic materials. With a basic structure of wood, it was a cantilever low-wing monoplane with retractable tricycle landing gear, and power provided by a single Ranger inline engine.

After some negotiations and changes, Bell's proposal won an order for six **XP-77** prototypes. However, as a result of delays and rising costs, this was reduced to two, and the first of these made a maiden flight on 1 April 1944. Testing revealed a number of problems, and in December 1944, after the second

prototype had been destroyed in an accident two months earlier, the programme was terminated.

Specification
Type: single-seat lightweight fighter-bomber
Powerplant: one 388-kW (520-hp) Ranger XV-770-7 inline piston engine
Performance: maximum speed 531 km/h (330 mph); service ceiling 9175 m (30,100 ft); range 885 km (550 miles)
Weights: empty 1295 kg (2,855 lb); maximum take-off 1827 kg (4,028 lb)
Dimensions: span 8.38 m (27 ft 6 in); length 6.97 m (22 ft 10½ in); height 2.50 m (8 ft 2¼ in); wing area 9.29 m² (100.0 sq ft
Armament: two 12.7-mm (0.5-in)

The Bell XP-77 was designed as a lightweight fighter built largely of non-strategic materials. Its performance was not good.

machine-guns and one bomb not exceeding 136 kg (300 lb)

Bell XP-83

A rather frightening rate of fuel consumption was the primary shortcoming

of early turbojet-powered fighter aircraft. Bell's P-59 Airacomet, for example, had a range on internal fuel of only about 386 km (240 miles), and in 1944 the company began design of a longer-range fighter retaining the same general configuration. On 31 July 1944 Bell's proposal won a USAAF contract for two prototypes, under the designation **XP-83**, and the first made its maiden flight on 25 February 1945.

Like the P-59, the new type was a cantilever mid-wing monoplane with retractable tricycle landing gear, and two turbojet engines mounted one beneath each wing root. As increased range then had to rely on more fuel, rather than better engine technology, the fuselage of the XP-83 was deeper and wider to give greater internal fuel capacity. This

The portly lines of the XP-83 indicate its main raison d'être; to provide enough fuel for a decent range. However, performance was consequently compromised to an unsatisfactory level.

could be augmented if necessary by two underwing drop tanks. However, testing showed performance to be unsatisfactory and the project was abandoned.

Specification
Type: single-seat long-range fighter
Powerplant: two 1814-kg (4,000-lb) thrust General Electric J33-GE-5 turbojets
Performance: maximum speed 840 km/h (522 mph) at 4775 m (15,660 ft); service ceiling 13715 m (45,000 ft); range at 9145 m (30,000 ft) with drop tanks 2784 km (1,730 miles)
Weights: empty 6398 kg (14,105 lb); maximum take-off 10927 kg (24,090 lb)
Dimensions: span 16.15 m (53 ft 0 in); length 13.66 m (44 ft 10 in); height 4.65 m (15 ft 3 in); wing area 40.04 m² (431 sq ft)
Armament: six nose-mounted 12.7-mm (0.5-in) machine-guns

Bell/Boeing V-22 Osprey

Since the end of World War II, aircraft manufacturers in several parts of the world have sporadically tried to develop tiltrotor (proprotor) and convertible aircraft. The **Bell/Boeing V-22 Osprey** is the first result of a major effort to develop the tiltrotor concept for practical use, however, and to bring such an aeroplane into series production as a multi-role type. The **V-22** was based on Bell's XV-15 tiltrotor technology demonstrator combining the vertical take-off and landing capability of the helicopter and the high forward wingborne speed of the turboprop transport with the tilting proprotors in the horizontal and vertical planes respectively, and was designed to replace the traditional helicopter in the assault transport and rescue roles as well as the increasingly important task of inserting and recovering Special Forces troops.

The **Osprey** has a conventional cabin which is designed for a total of 24 troops with full combat equipment, and the crew consists of two pilots and a crew chief. The two halves of the shoulder-set wing are swept slightly forward and are equipped with usual control surfaces, while the upswept rear of the fuselage carries a rear ramp/door arrangement as well as the tail unit incorporating a low-aspect-ratio horizontal surface and endplate vertical surfaces, again with conventional moving surfaces controlled, like those on the wing, by the triplex fly-by-wire system.

The propulsion arrangement is based on a pair of Allison T406 turboshafts installed in wing-tip nacelles that can be

rotated through 97.5° between the forward horizontal position and an angle just to the rear of the vertical, and these engines drive three-blade contra-rotating proprotors via gearboxes that are interconnected for full synchronisation and continued two-proprotor drive in the event of a single engine failure. For stowage on aircraft carriers the whole wings swivels through 90° into alignment with the fuselage, and proprotor blades fold along the starboard side of the fuselage.

The first Bell-assembled **Osprey** prototype completed its maiden flight on 19 March 1989, while the first Boeing-assembled prototype was the fourth machine that flew on 21 December 1989. During the first flight of the fifth and final prototype machine on 11 June 1991, incorrect wiring within the avionics caused an accident without fatal results. In a later stage of the flight programme, the first

prototype crashed with the death of all persons on board.

The **Osprey** has been the subject of continuing budgetary argument and has also encountered severe political antipathy. As a result the EMD (Engineering and Manufacturing Development) stage was only just approved, leading to four more aircraft that entered flight test from a time late in 1996. The first deliveries to the US Marine Corps, initially planned for the end of 1991, are now to be expected no sooner than the early years of the 21st century.

Specification
Bell/Boeing CV-22A Osprey
Type: proprotor assault transport
Powerplant: two 4586-kW (6,150-shp) Allison T4066-AD-400 turboshafts
Performance: maximum cruising

speed 185 km/h (115 mph) in helicopter mode at sea level and 582 km/h (361 mph) in aeroplane mode at optimum altitude; initial climb rate 707 m (2,320 ft) per minute; service ceiling 7925 m (26,000 ft); range 935 km (592 miles) in the assault transport role or 3892 km (2,418 miles) in the ferry role after a short take-off
Weights: empty 15032 kg (33,140 lb); normal take-off 21545 kg (47,500 lb) for vertical take-off; maximum take-off 27442 kg (60,500 lb) for short take-off
Dimensions: proprotor diameter, each 11.58 m (38 ft 0 in); wing span 15.52 m (50 ft 11 in) including nacelles; overall width 25.55 m (83 ft 10 in) with proprotors turning; length 17.47 m (57 ft 4 in) excluding inflight-refuelling probe; height 6.63 m (21 ft 9 in) with nacelles vertical; rotor disc area, total 210.72 m² (2,268.23 sq ft); wing area 35.49 m² (382.00 sq ft) including centre section

Bellanca Citabria

Acquisition by Bellanca of the assets of Champion Aircraft Corporation, in September 1970, led to production of aircraft derived from that company's **Model 7AC Champ**, of which more than 7,000 had been built. The most enduring of these derivatives were the **Bellanca Citabria** ('airbatic' reversed) and **Bellanca Scout**, and before the suspension of production in 1980, three versions of the former were available.

The Citabria is of braced high-wing monoplane configuration, with wings of mixed construction, fuselage and tail unit with welded steel-tube basic structures, and all surfaces fabric-covered. Landing gear is of fixed tailwheel type, the main units of cantilever spring steel, with speed fairings on the two more advanced Citabria 150 versions. An enclosed cabin provides accommodation for two, and because of the aircraft's aerobatic capability (with g limits of +5 and −2), the cabin door is jettisonable in emergency.

The Bellanca Citabria combines a modest aerobatic facility with good cruising performance and a roomy cabin for the two occupants.

The three versions available until 1979 comprised the **Citabria Standard** with an Avco Lycoming O-235-K2C engine. The more advanced **Citabria 150** had a 112-kW (150-hp) Avco Lycoming O-320-A2D engine and higher standards of equipment, while the generally similar **Citabria 150S** differed in having an increased-span wing that incorporated trailing-edge flaps. When production ended in 1980, more than 5,000 of these aircraft had been built.

Specification
Type: two-seat cabin monoplane
Powerplant: (Standard) one 86-kW (115-hp) Avco Lycoming O-235-K2C flat-four piston engine

Performance: (A: Standard, B: 150S) maximum speed A 201 km/h (125 mph), B 209 km/h (130 mph); cruising speed A 189 km/h (117 mph), B 198 km/h (123 mph); service ceiling A 3660 m (12,000 ft), B 5180 m (17,000 ft); maximum range A 1154 km (717 miles), B 966 km (600 miles)

Weights: empty A 484 kg (1,067 lb), B 522 kg (1,150 lb); maximum take-off A and B 748 kg (1,650 lb)
Dimensions: span A 10.19 m (33 ft 5 in); B 10.49 m (34 ft 5 in); length A and B 6.92 m (22 ft 8½ in); height A and B 2.35 m (7 ft 8½ in); wing area A 15.33 m² (165 sq ft), B 15.79 m² (170 sq ft)

Bellanca Decathlon

The **Champion Model 8KCAB Decathlon** had been designed specifically as an aerobatic competition aircraft, and while in overall configuration it was generally similar to the Citabria, it introduced a reduced-span/wider-chord wing, and was structurally strengthened for loadings over the range of +6 to −5 g. Bellanca continued development and by 1979 three versions were available. These comprised the basic **Bellanca Decathlon**, virtually the same as the original Model 8KCAB and powered by a 112-kW (150-hp) Avco

Lycoming AEIO-320-E1B engine, driving a fixed-pitch propeller; the **Bellanca Decathlon CS** with a generally similar engine, but with a constant-speed propeller and a wider range of equipment as standard; and the **Bellanca Super Decathlon** which differed from the CS in having a more powerful Avco Lycoming AEIO-360-H1A flat-four engine with a constant-speed propeller. When production terminated in 1980, more than 550 of these aircraft had been built.

Specification
Bellanca Super Decathlon
Type: two-seat cabin monoplane
Powerplant: one 134-kW (180-hp) Avco Lycoming AEIO-360-H1A flat-four

Inheriting from the Citabria its basic design, the Bellanca Decathlon was provided with a lower aspect ratio wing for more exacting aerobatics.

piston engine
Performance: maximum speed 254 km/h (158 mph); cruising speed 241 km/h (150 mph); service ceiling 4875 m (16,000 ft); maximum range 1005 km (625 miles)
Weights: empty 596 kg (1,315 lb); maximum take-off 816 kg (1,800 lb)
Dimensions: span 9.75 m (32 ft 0 in); length 6.98 m (22 ft 10¾ in); height 2.36 m (7 ft 9 in); wing area 15.71 m² (169.1 sq ft)

Bellanca Cruisair

There is little doubt that the Bellanca company originated a number of basic designs that, like the old soldier, never died. The **Cruisair**, sometimes called the **Cruisair Senior**, can be numbered among these, having been built by Bellanca before and after World War II, by Downer Aircraft Industries from 1959, and finally by International Aircraft Manufacturing Inc.

The post-war version of **Bellanca Model 14-13-3** differed little from its predecessors, being a cantilever low-wing monoplane with wings of all-wooden construction, and incorporating simple trailing-edge flaps. The fuselage and wire-braced tail unit were of welded steel-tube framework, fabric-covered. An unusual and distinctive feature of the tail unit was provided by small endplate stabilising fins, which complemented the standard dorsally-mounted fin/rudder structure. Landing gear was of retractable tailwheel type, the main units retracting aft to leave the wheels partially exposed in the under-surfaces of the wing. Enclosed cabin accommodation was provided for four people, seated in two pairs, with a baggage compartment behind the rear seat, and power was provided by a Franklin flat-six engine. Not particularly exciting, but the continuity of Cruisair production was assured by the type's reputation as an easy-to-handle and reliable aeroplane

A classic lightplane, the Bellanca Model 14-13-3 Cruisair had a fuselage shaped basically like an aerofoil.

that could be economically operated and maintained.

The **Bellanca Model 14-13-3W** was basically similar but, intended for general utility use, had the cabin ply-wood-lined to prevent it from damage during the loading or unloading of cargo.

Space for freight was provided by easily removable rear seats, and a second cabin door was installed on the port side of the fuselage to give improved access.

Specification
Type: cabin monoplane
Powerplant: one 112-kW (150-hp) Franklin flat-six piston engine
Performance: maximum cruising

speed 266 km/h (165 mph) at 1980 m (6,500 ft); cruising speed 241 km/h (150 mph) at sea level; service ceiling 6705 m (22,000 ft)
Weights: empty 567 kg (1,250 lb); maximum take-off 975 kg (2,150 lb)
Dimensions: span 10.41 m (34 ft 2 in); length 6.5 m (21 ft 4 in); height 1.89 m (6 ft 2½ in); wing area 14.96 m² (161 sq ft)

Bellanca Cruisemaster/Viking

The **Bellanca Viking** is descended, through a number of differently named companies, from the original pre-war Model 14-9 Junior, via the early post-war Model 14-13-3 Cruisair and Model 14-19 Cruisemaster with a 172-kW (230-hp) Continental engine.

Bellanca Aircraft Corporation sold full rights and all tools and jigs for the **Model 14-19 Cruisemaster** to Northern Aircraft Inc., which became the Downer Aircraft Company Inc. in January 1959. More than 100 Cruisemasters were built before production changed over to the **Downer Bellanca 260**, a modified version of the earlier aircraft with tricycle landing gear and a 194-kW (260-hp) Continental engine. The prototype flew on 6 November 1958, and the first production model on 20 February 1959. Further changes in company structure resulted in Inter-Air (International Aircraft Manufacturing

Inc.) of Minnesota taking over manufacture, by which time the designation had changed to **Model 14-19-3A** in the early 1960s and the present shape of the Viking, with its distinctive swept fin and rudder, appeared.

By 1967, Inter-Air had become the Bellanca Sales Company (a subsidiary of Miller Flying Service) and had further developed the aircraft into the **Bellanca 260C Model 14-19-3C**, and at this time the **Viking 300** made its appearance, with a 224-kW (300-hp) Continental married to the 260C airframe. Production of the two aircraft continued at the rate of around 20 a month.

In 1970 the Bellanca Sales Company acquired the Champion Aircraft Corporation and the name was yet again changed, this time to Bellanca Aircraft Corporation. Early in 1980, financial problems caused the company to cease production. 1,670 Vikings had been built of

the three versions; the **Model 17-30A Super Viking 300A** with the 224-kW (300-hp) Continental IO-520-K engine; the **Model 17-31A Super Viking 300A** with the 224-kW (300-hp) Avco Lycoming IO-540-K1E5; and the **Model 17-31ATC Turbo Viking 300A** with the same Avco Lycoming engine plus two Rajay turbochargers.

Like other Bellanca designs, the Bellanca Viking proved to be long-lived, being built by six companies over a period of more than 40 years.

Specification
Bellanca Model 17-30A Super
Viking 300A
Type: four-seat light monoplane
Powerplant: one 224-kW (300-hp)

Continental IO-520-K flat-six piston
engine
Performance: maximum speed
364 km/h (226 mph); maximum cruising
speed 303 km/h (188 mph); service

ceiling 5180 m (17,000 ft); range
1366 km (849 miles)
Weights: empty 1006 kg (2,217 lb);
maximum take-off 1508 kg (3,325 lb)
Dimensions: span 10.41 m (34 ft 2 in);

length 8.03 m (26 ft 4 in); height 2.24 m
(7 ft 4 in); wing area 15 m² (161.5 sq ft)

Bellanca Skyrocket

Developed from the Pacemaker series,
the **Bellanca Skyrocket** was first
flown in 1930, and differed from the
earlier aircraft only in detail and in the
type of engine fitted – the 317-kW (425-
hp) Pratt & Whitney Wasp. Six seats
were fitted in the Skyrocket, and Edo
floats were available as an option to the
standard wheeled landing gear.

Rather surprisingly, the Skyrocket
was only 8 km/h (5 mph) faster than the
Pacemaker, but its initial rate of climb of
381 m (1,250 ft) per minute and ceiling of
6100 m (20,000 ft), compared with 274 m
(900 ft) per minute and 5485 m
(18,000 ft), showed the advantage of the
bigger engine. Very soon, the **De Luxe
Skyrocket** was offered with a 336-kW
(450-hp) Wasp giving a speed of
277 km/h (172 mph). This was known as
the **Bellanca Model D**, certificated in
April 1932, and production amounted to
only seven aircraft. It differed from its
predecessor, the **Bellanca CH-400**, in
having a new landing gear incorporating
spats and wheel brakes.

Three civil CH-400s were bought by
the US Navy in 1932. The first, desig-

*A sole example of the Bellanca
CH-400 was used as an aerial
ambulance by the US Marine
Corps under the designation
RE-3. Two similar aircraft, also
funded by the US Navy, were
employed as a radio research
aircraft and as a light transport.*

nated **Bellanca XRE-1**, was used for
radio research at NAS Anacostia; the
second, designated **Bellanca XRE-2**,
was a light transport; while the third,
Bellanca XRE-3, was a two-stretcher
ambulance version delivered to the US
Marine Corps.

By 1935, Bellanca was offering the
Model 31-42 Senior Skyrocket
with redesigned tail surfaces and a
410-kW (550-hp) Pratt & Whitney Wasp
S3H1 engine. The same accommodation
was provided, for pilot and five passengers; optionally, seven passenger seats
could be fitted, and this model was still in
production in 1939. A version known as
the **De Luxe Senior Skyrocket** also
appeared. This incorporated a number of
refinements, and also incorporated a

391-kW (525-hp) Pratt & Whitney Wasp
radial engine.

Post-war, a few Skyrockets were
licence-built in Canada by North-west Industries as the **Model 31-55A**.

Specification
Bellanca Model 31-42 Senior
Skyrocket
Type: six/eight-seat light transport
Powerplant: one 410-kW (550-hp)
Pratt & Whitney Wasp S3H1 radial

piston engine
Performance: maximum speed
306 km/h (190 mph); cruising speed
290 km/h (180 mph) at 3660 m
(12,000 ft); service ceiling 7620 m
(25,000 ft); range with maximum fuel
2060 km (1,280 miles)
Weights: empty 1560 kg (3,440 lb);
maximum take-off 2540 kg (5,600 lb)
Dimensions: span 15.39 m (50 ft 6 in);
length 8.51 m (27 ft 11 in); height 2.59 m
(8 ft 6 in); wing area 33.35 m² (359 sq ft)

Bensen Aircraft Corporation

Dr Igor Bensen, formerly chief research
engineer of helicopter-building Kaman
Aircraft Corporation, established his
own company at Raleigh, North Carolina,
in the early 1950s. Intending initially to
develop a series of lightweight commercial helicopters, he soon began to appreciate that the inherent safety of a rotary
wing would make a suitable aircraft of
this type very attractive to private pilots.

For such a market a low initial cost
was essential, so he developed an unpowered rotor-kite which could be
towed behind a motor car. Known as the
Bensen B-8 Gyro-Glider, this could
be flown without a pilot-licence in the
United States, and if costs had to be kept
to a minimum it could be built from
detailed plans and building instructions.
There was even a do-it-yourself flight instruction manual. An enthusiast with a
little more money in the kitty could
obtain from Igor Bensen a kit of easily-
assembled components: for the more
affluent the company produced completed aircraft.

The company's production of rotor
blades, and of kits for the home construction of rotor blades for the Gyro-
Glider and the powered **Bensen Gyro-
Copter**, continued until 1987. Aircraft

have been built in thousands over a
period of more than 25 years. Brief
details of other Bensen products that
were available are given below.

Variants
Model B-8HD: variant of the Model
B-8 Super Bug (below) which has a
hydraulic drive to turn the rotor during
all aspects of flight. This absorbs some
3 kW (4 hp) of the main engine output,
allowing shorter take-off runs and near-
vertical landings
Model B-8M Gyro-Copter: an
autogyro version of the Gyro-Glider,
powered by a McCulloch engine driving
a pusher propeller
Model B-8MH Hover-Gyro:
advanced version of the B-8M with
hovering capability, plus backwards and
sideways flight; achieved by two co-
axial rotors, the upper auto-rotating, the
lower powered by a separate engine
Model B-8MW Hydro-Copter:
versions of the B-8M with float landing
gear
Model B-8V Gyro-Copter:
designation of a version of the B-8M
with an alternative powerplant
comprising a modified Volkswagen
motor car engine

Model B-8 Super Bug: advanced
version of the B-8M with a twin-engine
installation; this allows the rotor to be
spun-up prior to take-off, and reduces
considerably the take-off run

Specification
Model B-8M (standard)
Type: single-seat light autogyro
Powerplant: one 54-kW (72-hp) or
67-kW (90-hp) McCulloch Model 4318
flat-four piston engine
Performance: maximum speed at
sea level 137 km/h (85 mph); economic
cruising speed 72 km/h (45 mph);

*Elaboration of the Bensen B-8
design philosophy resulted in the
B-9 Little Zipster helicopter, with
contra-rotating twin motors to
overcome torque reaction
problems.*

service ceiling 3810 m (12,500 ft);
normal range 161 km (100 miles)
Weights: empty 112 kg (247 lb);
maximum take-off 227 kg (500 lb)
Dimensions: rotor diameter 6.1 m
(20 ft 0 in); fuselage length 3.45 m (11 ft
4 in); height 1.19 m (6 ft 3 in); rotor disc
area 29.19 m² (314.16 sq ft)

*The Bensen autogyro was briefly
evaluated by the US Air Force
under the military designation
X-25B.*

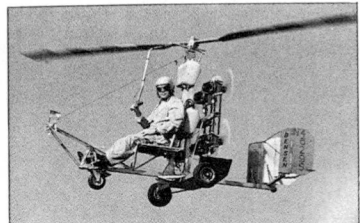

*This B-8 has two engines,
mounted one over the other. Note
the control column attached
directly to the rotor head.*

*Among the more unusual designs
originated by Igor Bensen was
the B-10 Flying Platform. This
was supported by two small
rotors, each driven by a 53.7-kW
(72-hp) McCulloch engine.*

*Powered by a pair of tip-mounted
ramjets, the Bensen Mid-Jet
weighed only 45 kg (100 lb) empty.
It is here seen with Betty
Skelton, a celebrated stunt pilot
of the early 1950s.*

Beriev Be-6 'Madge'

Development of a large maritime reconnaissance and bombing flying-boat was initiated by the Beriev design bureau in 1945, and the **Beriev LL-143** prototype flew for the first time in 1947. An all-metal high-wing monoplane, it was powered by two 1492-kW (2,000-hp) Shvetsov ASh-72 radial engines. Armament comprised twin NS-23 23-mm cannon in a tail turret (behind the twin fins and rudders) and similar provision in a remotely controlled dorsal barbette. A single NS-23 cannon was installed in the bow turret.

The LL-143 was developed into the **Beriev Be-6** production aircraft, the first example of which was flown by M.I. Tsepilov in 1949. It differed from the prototype by having more sophisticated equipment, which included a retractable radome aft of the second step, and a redesigned nose without cannon armament. At a later stage the tail gun position was replaced by MAD (magnetic anomaly detection) equipment. The Be-6, to which NATO allocated the codename 'Madge', carried a heavy offensive load comprising various combinations of mines, depth charges or torpedoes on underwing pylons outboard of the engines.

Be-6s operated patrol, maritime reconnaissance and anti-submarine duties until the early 1970s, and a few remained in service on transport or fishery patrol duties into the late 1970s.

Beriev Be-6 'Madge' of the Soviet navy, with a MAD 'stinger' aft of its tail.

Specification
Beriev Be-6
Type: maritime reconnaissance and bombing flying-boat
Powerplant: two 1715-kW (2,300-hp) Shvetsov ASh-73TK radial piston engines
Performance: maximum speed 415 km/h (258 mph) at 2400 m (7,875 ft); service ceiling 6100 m (20,015 ft); maximum range 4800 km (2,983 miles)
Weights: empty equipped 18827 kg (41,506 lb); normal take-off 23456 kg (51,711 lb)

Dimensions: span 33 m (108 ft 3¼ in); length 23.5 m (77 ft 1¼ in); height 7.45 m (24 ft 5¼ in); wing area 120 m² (1,291.71 sq ft)
Armament: five (later four) 23-mm NS-23 cannon, plus offensive load of mines, depth charges or torpedoes

The initial production version of the Beriev Be-6 had a retractable ventral radome (seen in the lowered position) and barbetted twin cannon in the tail.

Beriev Be-8 'Mole'

The **Beriev Be-8 'Mole'** of 1947 was an all-metal utility amphibian flying-boat, with the main units of the landing gear retracting into the sides of the hull just below the pilot's cabin. The wing was supported above the hull by a central pylon, together with a pair of parallel struts on each side. The passenger cabin accommodated six. A small batch of Be-8s was built, and examples were used in a variety of roles including flying ambulance, liaison, and training.

The Beriev Be-8 'Mole' was an attempt to produce a utility amphibian, but only limited production was undertaken.

Specification
Type: utility amphibian flying-boat
Powerplant: one 522-kW (700-hp) Shvetsov ASh-21 radial piston engine
Performance: maximum speed 266 km/h (165 mph) at 1800 m (5,905 ft); normal cruising speed 246 km/h (153 mph); service ceiling 5550 m

(18,210 ft); normal range 810 km (503 miles)
Weights: empty equipped 2815 kg (6,206 lb); normal loaded 3624 kg (7,990 lb)
Dimensions: span 19 m (62 ft 4 in); length 13 m (42 ft 7¾ in); wing area 40 m² (430.57 sq ft)

Beriev Be-10 'Mallow'

The **Beriev Be-10 'Mallow'** has the distinction of being the only turbojet-powered flying-boat in the world to have attained true production status. Developed from the **R-1**, it was first seen in public on the 1961 Soviet Aviation Day, when four of the type flew past in formation. During that summer, and under the designation **M-10**, the type established no fewer than 12 world class records. Outstanding among them were a speed record over a 15/25-km (9.3/15.5-mile) course of 912 km/h (566.7 mph), piloted by Nikolai Andrievskii; a speed of 875.86 km/h (544.24 mph) over a 1000-km (621.4-mile) closed circuit with a payload of 5000 kg (11,023 lb); and an altitude record of 12733 m (41,775 ft) with a 10000-kg (22,046-lb) payload, the latter two records attained with Georgi Buryanov at the controls.

The all-metal Be-10 was a high-wing monoplane with sharply sweptback wings; these had considerable anhedral, and incorporated two wing fences and a fixed wing-tip stabilising float on each wing. Armament comprised two 23-mm NS-23 cannon in the nose, plus two more operated under radar control in a tail barbette.

Specification
Type: maritime patrol/reconnaissance flying-boat
Powerplant: two 6500-kg (14,330-lb) thrust Lyul'ka AL-7PB turbojets
Performance: maximum speed 912 km/h (567 mph); absolute ceiling 14962 m (49,090 ft); range 4800 km (2,983 miles)
Weights: empty 24100 kg (53,131 lb); maximum take-off 46500 kg (102,515 lb)
Dimensions: span 22.3 m (73 ft 2 in); length 31.1 m (102 ft 0½ in); wing area

111.8 m² (1,203.44 sq ft)
Armament: four 23-mm NS-23 cannon, plus a weapons load of 2000 kg (4,409 lb) which could be carried over a distance of 2100 km (1,305 miles)

The only turbojet-powered flying-boat to have achieved true production status, the Beriev Be-10 'Mallow' was nevertheless built only in relatively small numbers.

Beriev Be-12 Tchaika 'Mail'

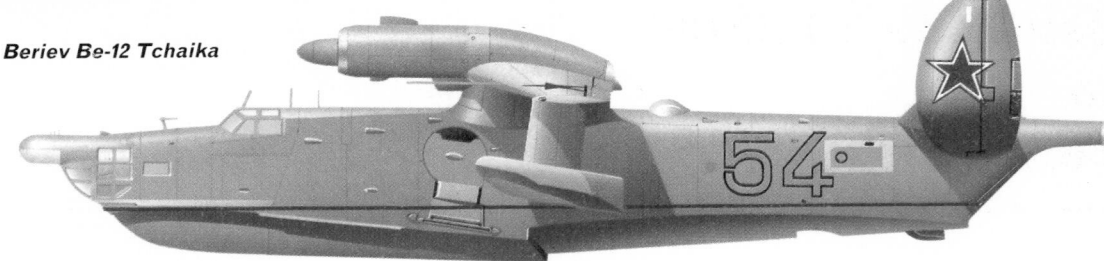
Beriev Be-12 Tchaika

Together with the Japanese Maritime Self-Defence Force, the AV-MF (Soviet Naval Aviation) is the last major service to operate fleets of combat flying-boats and amphibians. Elsewhere, the role of the patrol flying-boat was taken over by long-range landplanes in the 1950s. This process may continue, as no amphibious replacement for the **Beriev Be-12 Tchaika** (Seagull), codenamed 'Mail' by NATO, has been reported, and the AV-MF has introduced specialised land-planes for the anti-submarine role, the Ilyushin Il-38 'May' and the Tupolev Tu-142 'Bear-F'.

The Beriev design bureau, based at Taganrog on the Sea of Azov, has been the main supplier of marine aircraft to the Soviet Navy since 1945, most of its aircraft going to the Northern and Black Sea Fleets. The origins of the Be-12 go back to the LL-143 prototype of 1945, which led in 1949 to the Be-6 'Madge'. This latter twin-engined flying-boat served with success until 1967.

Following the Be-6, the Beriev team carried out a considerable amount of research into jet-powered flying-boats, producing the straight-winged Be-R-1 of 1952 and the swept-wing Be-10 of 1960-1. The latter, powered by two Lyul'ka AL-7RVs (unaugmented versions of the Su-7 powerplant), established a number of seaplane records in 1961, but only three or four are believed to have been built.

The lessons learned in the design of the Be-R-1 and Be-10, however, were incorporated in the design of a much improved flying-boat based loosely on the Be-6 and identified originally by NATO as a re-engined version of the older type. In fact, the Be-12, designated **M-12** in AV-MF service, bears little more than a general resemblance to the Be-6, sharing only the gull-wing layout and twin tail of its predecessor. The greater power and lighter weight of the turboprop engines have permitted a forward extension of the hull, with a new planing bottom similar to that of the Be-10. The prominent spray suppressor around the bows of the Be-10 is also a feature of the turboprop aircraft. The most significant change, however, was the addition of massive and sturdy rectractable landing gear, making the Be-12 amphibious and thus considerably more versatile than the earlier Beriev designs. The turreted gun armament of the Be-6 has been deleted, being replaced by MAD (magnetic anomaly detection) gear in the tail, above the tailwheel well, while the search radar is carried in a long nose housing instead of the ventral retractable dustbin radome of the Be-6. One of the drawbacks of the high-wing layout, the excessive height of the engines above the ground, has been mitigated by the design of engine cowling panels which drop down to form strong working platforms.

The considerable weight-lifting capability of the Be-12 was demonstrated in a series of class records for amphibians set up in 1964, 1968 and 1970, suggesting a normal weapons load as high as 5000 kg (11,023 lb). The Be-12 can load on the water through large side hatches in the rear fuselage, and stores can be dropped through a watertight hatch in the hull aft of the step. Unlike land-based ASW platforms, a marine aircraft can, in reasonably calm conditions, settle on the water, and search with its own sonar equipment, rather than relying exclusively on sonobuoys. This assumes that the Be-12 has this capability.

With the increasing use of the Mil

Mi-14 'Haze' ASW helicopter and the Ilyushin Il-38 'May', there would seem to be a diminishing ASW role for the Be-12, although the type will certainly remain in service as a high-speed search-and-rescue (SAR) vehicle. It is also believed to have been used for mapping, geophysical survey and utility transport. By Soviet standards the type was not built in large numbers, only 95 being reported in service in the late 1980s.

Specification
Type: maritime patrol amphibian
Powerplant: two 3125-kW (4,190-shp) lvchenko Al-20D turboprops
Performance: maximum speed

The gull wings and twin tail of the Beriev Be-6 were echoed in its turbine-powered successor, the Be-12 Tchaika ('Mail').

610 km/h (379 mph); economical patrol speed 320 km/h (199 mph); maximum range 4000 km (2,485 miles)
Weights: (estimated) empty 21700 kg (47,840 lb); maximum take-off 30000 kg (66,139 lb)
Dimensions: span 29.7 m (97 ft 5¼ in); length 30.2 m (99 ft 1 in); height on land 7 m (22 ft 11½ in)
Armament: bombs, rockets or guided ASMs on underwing pylons; depth charges and sonobuoys

Beriev A-40 Albatros 'Mermaid'

In 1983 Beriev began the design of a large amphibian flying boat with single-step hull as a successor to its Be-12 currently in the service of the Soviet navy, and this **Beriev A-40 Albatros** (NATO reporting name **'Mermaid'**) completed its maiden flight in December 1986 at Taganrog. On 20 August 1989 the flying boat made a public fly-past at the Aviation Day display at Tushino.

The **A-40** is an unusual design with a simple-stepped hull but with a variable-rise bottom for what is claimed by Beriev as exceptional stability and controllability on the water as well as a significant reduction in g forces during take-off and alighting. The landing gear is of the tricycle type with a nosewheel unit retracting into the underside of the bow and main units retracting into fairings under each wing root. Above the wing-root pods are the pylons that carry the nacelles for the two turbofan engines, which are located as high as possible to avoid water and spray ingestion; undernose strakes are also installed to minimise the amount of spray rising to the height of the engine inlets. A booster turbojet is also fitted in the rear of each engine pylon. At the rear of the hull is the tall and swept T-tail. Stabilising floats and ESM pods are mounted at the ends of the modestly

swept wings, the bow carries the radome for search radar with an inflight-refuelling probe above it, and there is also provision for sonobuoys.

The **A-40** is intended for coastguard and anti-submarine duties as successor to the Be-12 and Il-38, and an order was placed for 20 machines to equip units of the CIS Navy. The number of the examples built up to 1997, however, was limited to a mere two prototypes and the A-40's current production status is unknown in the light of the CIS's financial problems. The first prototype established no fewer than 128 class records for seaplanes.

Variants
A-40 Albatross 'Mermaid': basic version for maritime patrol, anti-submarine warfare and minelaying
Be-40P: projected passenger version for a total of 105 persons carried over a range of 4000 km (2,485 miles)
Be-40PT: projected mixed passenger/passenger transport with a payload of 10000 kg (22,046 lb) including up to 70 passengers carried over a range of 4200 km (2,610 miles)

Specification
Beriev A-40 Albatros 'Mermaid'
Type: eight-crew maritime patrol and anti-submarine amphibian flying boat

The prototype A-40, here making its fly-past at the 1990 Aviation Day display at Tushino, reveals the unusual configuration of this design.

Powerplant: two 117.70-kN (26,455-lb st) Aviadvigatel (Soloviev) D-30KPV turbofans and two 24.50-kN (5,510-lb st) RKBM (Novikov) RD-60K booster turbojets
Performance: maximum speed 760 km/h (472 mph) at 6000 m (19,685 ft); maximum cruising speed 720 km/h (447 mph) at 6000 m (19,685 ft); initial climb rate 1800 m (5,905 ft) per minute; service ceiling 9700 m (31,825 ft); range 5500 km (3,417 miles) with maximum fuel or 4100 km (2,547 miles) with maximum payload

Weight: maximum take-off 86000 kg (189,594 lb)
Dimension: span 41.62 m (136 ft 6.5 in); length 43.84 m (143 ft 10 in) including inflight-refuelling probe; height 11.07 m (36 ft 3.75 in); area 280.55 m² (3,109.91 sq ft)
Armament: torpedoes and/or mines carried in a weapons bay located in the bottom of the hull to the rear of the step

Beriev Be-30 'Cuff'
to
Bernard 20

Beriev Be-30 'Cuff'

The most unusual factor about the **Beriev Be-30** short-haul transport is the fact that it was the first land-plane to be designed and developed by the Beriev design bureau. Seen publicly for the first time at the Soviet Aviation Day display at Domodedovo in 1967, it appeared subsequently at the 1969 Paris Air Show. Designated Be-30, and allocated the NATO codename 'Cuff', it was reported to have flown for the first time on 3 March 1967. Of high-wing monoplane configuration, the Be-30 was of all-metal structure and introduced such features as metal bonding, spot welding, and the use of stiffened skin panels of light alloy honeycomb. Because of the high-wing configuration, the retractable tricycle landing gear incorporated very stalky main units, these retracting into the rear of the engine nacelles. Power-plant of the prototype consisted of two 552-kW (740-hp) Shvetsov ASh-21 radial piston engines, but two Glushenkov TVD-10 turboprops were used to power the very small number of production aircraft that followed. Accommodation was provided for a crew of two and 14 passengers, and advanced features included air-conditioning and blind-flying equipment that incorporated an autopilot and an automatic approach system.

It had been anticipated that the Be-30 would be built in large numbers for Aeroflot, but only a few were produced, presumably because of a decision to use the Czech Let L-410 Turbolet, of slightly larger capacity, as the standard short-haul type for service with Aeroflot.

Specification
Type: short-haul transport
Powerplant: two 708-kW (950-shp) Glushenkov TVD-10 turboprops
Performance: maximum cruising speed 480 km/h (298 mph) at 2000 m (6,560 ft); range with maximum fuel and 900-kg (1,984-lb) payload 1300 km (808 miles)
Weight: maximum take-off 5860 kg (12,919 lb)
Dimensions: span 17 m (55 ft 9¼ in); length 15.7 m (51 ft 6 in); height 5.46 m (17 ft 11 in); wing area 32 m² (344.46 sq ft)

The Beriev Be-30 was the bureau's first landplane design, and was of angular appearance as a result of its slab-sided fuselage and stalky main landing gear legs. Only small production was undertaken as Aeroflot decided to standardise on the Let L-410 feederliner.

Beriev KOR-2 (Be-4)

More or less in parallel with the construction and development of the KOR-1 floatplane, the Beriev bureau was working on the design of a small flying-boat. This was intended to fulfil the same requirement as the hastily developed KOR-1, but was intended to provide much enhanced performance.

First flown in 1940, this new and basically attractive flying-boat was of all-metal construction. The term 'basically attractive' is used judiciously, for without its wing-mounted powerplant this new aircraft had superb lines. The giant engine, however, rather like the disfigurement of a hunchback, dominated all else to spoil the aesthetic lines of Beriev's design. In configuration the **Beriev KOR-2**, as the new aircraft was designated, was a parasol-wing monoplane, the wing itself being pylon-mounted above the stepped flying-boat hull, and braced by two streamlined struts on each side. An unusual feature was the selection of an inverted gull wing, but almost certainly this was chosen to raise the wing-mounted engine as high as possible to provide adequate clearance for the three-bladed controllable-pitch propeller and, at the same time, to ensure that the mounting struts for the underwing stabilising floats could be kept as short as possible. The tail unit was similar in configuration to that of the KOR-1, except that the high-mounted tailplane was a strut-free cantilever structure.

Built in a factory at Taganrog, on the shore of the almost enclosed Sea of Azov, only a small number of these aircraft had been completed and delivered to the Soviet navy before the Taganrog area was over-run by the invading Germans in the autumn of 1941. Production

Beriev KOR-2 of the Soviet navy.

of the KOR-2, or **Beriev Be-4** as it had then been redesignated, was resumed at a Central Asian factory during 1942, but no records of the number constructed have so far been discovered.

Specification
Type: two-seat reconnaissance flying-boat
Powerplant: one 671-kW (900-hp) Shvetsov M-62 radial piston engine
Performance: maximum speed 360 km/h (223 mph); service ceiling 8100 m (26,575 ft); normal range 950 km (590 miles)
Weights: empty 2055 kg (4,530 lb); maximum take-off 2760 kg (6,085 lb)
Dimensions: span 12 m (39 ft 4½ in); length 10.5 m (34 ft 5¼ in); height 4.05 m (13 ft 3 in); wing area 25.5 m² (274.5 sq ft)
Armament: one 7.62-mm (0.3-in) machine-gun on flexible mount in aft cockpit, plus up to 300 kg (661 lb) of bombs or depth charges on underwing racks

Beriev MBR-2

Georgii Mikhailovich Beriev produced his first original design, Aircraft No. 25, at the Menschinsky plant in Moscow in 1932. Beriev had gained considerable expertise as an assistant to French designer, Paul-Aimé Richard, during the latter's stay in the Soviet Union from 1928 to 1930. The B.M.W. VIF-powered prototype was transported to Sevastopol on the Black Sea for flight tests, and these proving successful the new flying-boat went into production as the **MBR-2** (Morskoy Blizhnii Razvedchik, or naval short-range reconnaissance). In production form it was powered by a Soviet-built M-17B inline engine.

Deliveries of the **MBR-2M-17**, intended for use in the short-range bombing and maritime reconnaissance roles,

A short-range flying-boat, the Beriev MBR-2M-17 had its inline engine mounted above the wings on struts and driving a pusher propeller. Located in front of the engine was the large oval radiator.

began in 1934. It was a shoulder-wing cantilever monoplane, with its M-17B engine mounted on a pair of N-struts over the wing; it had a two-step wooden hull with plywood covering, and the pilot's cockpit located just in front of the wing. A strut-braced horizontal tailplane was set high on the single fin. Bow and midships gunners each had a single 7.62-mm (0.3-in) PV-1 machine-gun.

Variants
Beriev MBR-2AM-34: in 1935, with the first production version already in

service, Beriev carried out a radical redesign of the MBR-2; the pilot's

cockpit was fully enclosed, and the midships gunner's position protected

123

by a glazed cupola; the M-17B engine was replaced by the M-34NB (redesignated AM-34NB in 1937) of 619 kW (830 hp); an entirely new curved fin and rudder replaced the original angular vertical tailplane; and ShKAS machine-guns supplanted the obsolete PV-1s; the new version was soon placed in large-scale production, which continued until 1942, when some 1,300 of all variants had been built; maximum speed of the MBR-2AM-34 was 245 km/h (152 mph), a considerable improvement over the initial production version; range was 800 km (497 miles), and service ceiling was raised to 7150 m (23,460 ft); weight empty increased to 2718 kg (5,992 lb) and loaded weight was 4000 kg (8,818 lb); the MBR-2AM-34 served with all four main Soviet fleets and saw considerable service, first during the Winter War of 1939-40 with Finland, and then throughout the Great Patriotic War of 1941-5; it was tough, reliable and acquitted itself well; and it could be fitted with wheel or ski landing gear; post-war, the MBR-2 served for nearly a decade on fishery patrol duties; it received the NATO codename 'Mote'

Beriev MBR-2M-103: in 1937 a standard MBR-2AM-34 was modified to take a more powerful M-103 engine, but no production of this version was undertaken

Beriev MP-1: this was a civil passenger version of the MBR-2M-17; it carried six passengers in an enclosed cabin, or an equivalent weight of freight; used in some numbers by Soviet Civil Aviation

Beriev MP-1bis: a 1937 civil

Beriev MBR-2 with sea green streaking camouflage, flown by the Soviet navy.

development of the MBR-2AM-34, with similar capacity to that of the MP-1; one MP-1bis, piloted by Paulina Osipenka, established a number of women's world records; between 22 and 25 May 1937 she attained respectively 7605 m (24,950 ft) with a 500-kg (1,102-lb) payload and 7000 m (22,966 ft) with a 1000-kg (2,204-lb) payload; on 2 July the same year she made a non-stop flight of 2416 km (1,501 miles) between Novgorod and Archangelsk

Specification
Beriev MBR-2M-17
Type: short-range reconnaissance/bombing flying-boat
Powerplant: one 507-kW (680-hp) M-17B inline piston engine
Performance: maximum speed 200 km/h (124 mph); service ceiling

Beriev MBR-2

4400 m (14,435 ft); range 650 km (404 miles)
Weights: empty 2475 kg (5,456 lb); maximum take-off 4100 kg (9,039 lb)
Dimensions: span 19 m (62 ft 4 in);

length 13.5 m (44 ft 3½ in); wing area 55 m² (592.03 sq ft)
Armament: single 7.62-mm (0.3-in) ShKAS machine-guns on bow and midship ring mountings, plus up to 500 kg (1,102 lb) of bombs or depth charges on underwing racks

Berliner-Joyce OJ-2

To meet a US Bureau of Aeronautics design of 1930, which called for a lightweight observation biplane for use by the US Navy, the Berliner-Joyce Aircraft Corporation and Keystone Aircraft Corporation found themselves in competition. Each was to build a prototype, but it was the **XOJ-1** from Berliner-Joyce that won a Navy contract.

A conventional two-seat biplane, with ailerons on both wings, its fabric-covered fuselage incorporated two open cockpits, and mounted a strut-braced tailplane with elevators and a single fin and rudder. Landing gear was of non-retractable tailwheel type, and powerplant consisted of a Pratt & Whitney Wasp Junior radial engine. Special equipment included attachments to permit launch from the catapults of light cruisers.

A total of 39 was built for the US Navy under the designation **OJ-2**, the first of them entering service in 1933. Operated by Squadrons VS-5B and VS-6B until

they were withdrawn in 1935, they served in two-plane detachments on cruisers of the US fleet.

Berliner-Joyce OJ-2 of VS-6B, US Navy, in 1933.

Specification
Type: two-seat observation biplane
Powerplant: one 298-kW (400-hp) Pratt & Whitney R-985-A Wasp Junior radial piston engine
Performance: maximum speed

243 km/h (151 mph)
Weight: maximum take-off 1646 kg (3,629 lb)
Dimensions: span 10.26 m (33 ft 8 in); length 7.82 m (25 ft 8 in)

Berliner-Joyce P-16/PB-1

The Berliner-Joyce Aircraft Corporation was established on 4 February 1929, acquiring the assets of the former Berliner Aircraft Company Inc. The new company had intended to produce the Berliner Monoplane, but instead became involved in the design of a two-seat fighter to meet a USAAC specification. The prototype **Berliner-Joyce XP-16**, first flown in October 1929, had a basic structure of metal and was extensively fabric-covered. It was a single-bay biplane of unequal span, with the

Though it had good features such as excellent fields of vision for the two crew, the Berliner-Joyce P-16 suffered from lack of performance.

wings forward-staggered, and with the lower wing, mounted at the base of the fuselage, smaller than the upper in both span and chord. The upper wing was of gull-wing configuration, allowing the pilot a good forward view; the observer/gunner was accommodated in a cockpit

First member of the short-lived 'Pursuit, Biplace' designation series, the P-16/PB-1's most notable feature was the elegant gull-wing design.

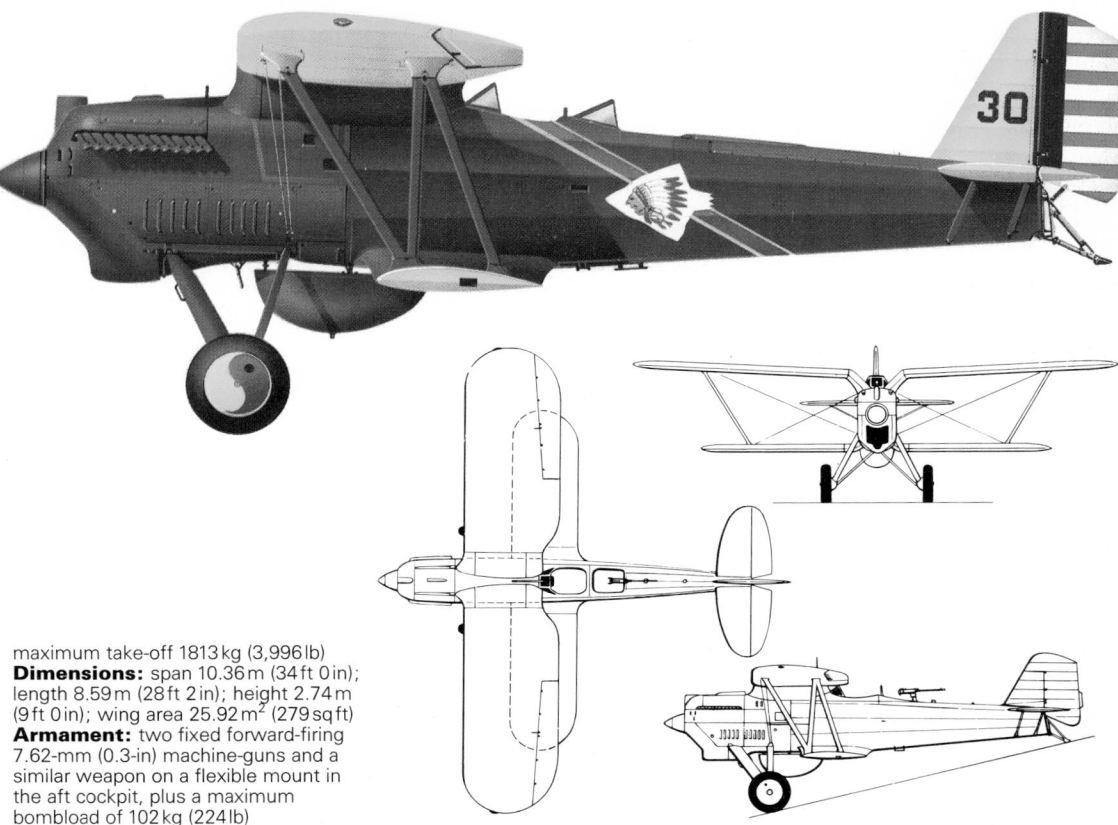

immediately aft of the pilot's position. A conventional braced tail unit, and tailskid landing gear with heavily-strutted main units, completed the basic airframe structure. Power for the prototype was provided by a 447-kW (600-hp) Curtiss V-1570A Conqueror supercharged inline piston engine.

Evaluation by the USAAC resulted in the award of two contracts, for 15 and 10 of the pre-production **Y1P-16** ordered in the 1931 fiscal year. Delivered in 1932, the production aircraft differed very little from the prototype, except for the installation of an unsupercharged version of the Conqueror engine. Later redesignated from **P16** to **PB-1** (Pursuit Biplace), they were found to be low on performance. This factor, coupled with a tendency to nose-over very easily, resulted in them being withdrawn from service in January 1934.

Specification
Berliner-Joyce P-16 (PB-1)
Type: two-seat fighter
Powerplant: one 447-kW (600-hp) Curtiss V-1570-25 Conqueror inline piston engine
Performance: maximum speed 282 km/h (175 mph) at sea level; cruising speed 243 km/h (151 mph); range 1046 km (650 miles)
Weights: empty 1271 kg (2,803 lb);

maximum take-off 1813 kg (3,996 lb)
Dimensions: span 10.36 m (34 ft 0 in); length 8.59 m (28 ft 2 in); height 2.74 m (9 ft 0 in); wing area 25.92 m² (279 sq ft)
Armament: two fixed forward-firing 7.62-mm (0.3-in) machine-guns and a similar weapon on a flexible mount in the aft cockpit, plus a maximum bombload of 102 kg (224 lb)

Bernard 20

A full-scale mock-up of the **Bernard 20** low-wing cantilever monoplane single-seat fighter was displayed at the Paris Salon de l'Aéronautique in 1928. Derived from the V.2 racer, the Bernard 20 was designed by Bechéreau to meet an official requirement for a lightweight interceptor. The mock-up had been used for wind-tunnel tests, recording some excellent figures. The sole prototype flew for the first time at Orly in July 1929, and with this aircraft test pilot Roger Baptiste attained a speed of 280 km/h (174 mph) at 4000 m (13,123 ft) during 1930. Unfortunately, at that time official circles did not regard the low-wing monoplane as suited to the fighter role, and after 18

Showing its derivation from its racing ancestors in its clean lines, the Bernard 20 was an attempt to break the French military's preference for biplane fighters.

months of tests development was abandoned.

Specification
Type: single-seat fighter
Powerplant: one 298-kW (400-hp) Hispano-Suiza 12Jb inline piston engine
Performance: maximum speed

280 km/h (174 mph)
Weights: empty equipped 1023 kg (2,255 lb); maximum take-off 1370 kg (3,020 lb)
Dimensions: span 10.8 m (35 ft

5¼ in); length 7.45 m (24 ft 5¼ in); height 2.5 m (8 ft 2½ in); wing area 16.7 m² (179.76 sq ft)
Armament: two fixed 7.7-mm (0.303-in) synchronised machine-guns

Bernard 190

The **Bernard 190T** was an enlarged and improved development of the **Bernard 18T**. Designed by Jean Galtier, the prototype (F-AIXX) made its first flight in Spring 1928 in the hands of Antoine Paillard. Total production amounted to eight aircraft, all operated by the CIDNA (Compagnie Internationale de Navigation Aérienne) on its various European services. Compared with the Bernard 18T, the Bernard 190T had a larger cabin, able to accommodate eight passengers, an enclosed crew cabin forward of the wing leading edge, and redesigned tail surfaces. It retained the wooden construction and cantilever high-wing configuration of its predecessor, but was powered by the 358-kW (480-hp) Gnome-Rhône 9Ady Jupiter radial engine.

Variants
Bernard 191 G. R. No. 1: flew for the first time in April 1928, and was essentially a long-range record-breaking development of the Bernard 190T, powered by a 447-kW (600-hp) Hispano-Suiza 12Lb inline; named *France* and painted overall in red, it had a tricolor diagonal band across the rear fuselage – the famous insignia of the Cicognes (Storks) Escadrille in World War I; the aircraft crashed on 7 July 1929 while attempting a North Atlantic crossing, the pilot (Capitaine Coudouret) being killed
Bernard 191 G. R. No. 2: flew for the first time on 5 August 1928; painted yellow overall, it was soon dubbed the *Oiseau Canari* (Canary Bird); in September 1928 the military pilot Jean Assollant used this aircraft in an attempt to cross the South Atlantic from east to west; the attempt came to grief with a forced landing at Casablanca, occasioned by an

Bernard 191 G.R. No. 2 'Oiseau Canari'. This aircraft is now preserved in the Musée de l'Air, Paris.

overheating engine; Assollant subsequently took the aircraft across the Atlantic by ship, and then made the first crossing of the North Atlantic by a French aircraft and crew: setting off from Old Orchard, Maine, on 13 June 1929, the *Oiseau Canari* landed after a flight of 29 hours 52 minutes on a beach near Santander in northern Spain; the *Oiseau Canari* is preserved in the Musée de l'Air, Paris; data includes maximum speed 245 km/h (152 mph), cruising speed 180 km/h (112 mph), range with 3760 litres (827 Imp gal) of fuel 5800 km (3,604 miles), empty weight 2420 kg (5,335 lb) and maximum take-off weight 5710 kg (12,588 lb)
Bernard 191 G.R. No. 3: piloted by Antoine Paillard, this established two world class records in November and December 1928 – the carriage of a 2000-kg (4,409-lb) payload over a 100-km (62.1-mile) course at an average speed of 223.546 km/h (138.9 mph), and a speed record for a payload of

1000 kg (2,205 lb) carried over a 1000-km (621.4-mile) course; this was the last Bernard 191 built and its career ended with a forced landing in January 1929
Bernard 192T: one-off transport built for Aéropostale; powered by a 358-kW (480-hp) Gnome-Rhône 9Kkx Jupiter, it had the disappointing maximum speed of 200 km/h (124 mph)
Bernard 193T: one-off transport version of the Bernard 197 G.R., powered by a 336-kW (450-hp) Lorraine 12Eb inline and possessing a maximum speed of 220 km/h (137 mph)
Bernard 197 G.R.: ordered by the Société des Moteurs Lorraine to demonstrate its engine in a sales tour of South America after a prestige crossing of the South Atlantic; the venture was abandoned because of technical difficulties, the aircraft instead being used for a pioneering flight to French Indo-China; piloted by Joseph Le Brix and Antoine Paillard, the Bernard 197 G.R. set off from

Istres in southern France on 18 February 1929 on the first leg of an anticipated 11000-km (6,835-mile) flight to Saigon; painted with the slogan *Marseilles-Saigon* and sporting an attractive blue and white colour scheme, the aircraft was forced down on the last leg of the flight, just after leaving Rangoon on 26 February

Specification
Bernard 190T
Type: passenger transport
Powerplant: one 313-kW (420-hp) Gnome-Rhône 9Ab Jupiter radial engine
Performance: maximum speed 216 km/h (134 mph); cruising speed 200 km/h (124 mph) at 2000 m (6,560 ft); service ceiling 3700 m (12,140 ft); range 1000 km (621 miles)
Weights: empty 1956 kg (4,312 lb); maximum take-off 3400 kg (7,496 lb)
Dimensions: span 17.3 m (56 ft 9 in); length 12.58 m (41 ft 3¼ in); height 3.59 m (11 ft 9¼ in); wing area 42.9 m² (461.79 sq ft)

Besson LB flying-boats

Pioneer designer Marcel Besson turned to marine aircraft in 1915, and produced a series of triplane flying-boats in conjunction with Georges Lévy. The **LB** designation showed this Lévy-Besson association, and development and production was carried out in the factory of Hydravions Georges Levallois et Levy.

Three distinct types were tested between 1917 and 1919, all with engines driving pusher propellers. First was a single-seat fighter triplane with I-type interplane struts, and powered by a 134-kW (180-hp) Hispano-Suiza engine. The three-seat deep-sea patrol type, like the single-seater, had the two upper wings of equal span, with a bottom wing of reduced span. It was powered by a 336-kW (450-hp) Renault engine. The third was the only one to be built in any number (a series of 12 machines). This was the coastal patrol type, powered by a lower-powered Renault engine. It could accommodate a crew of three, the

same as the deep-sea type, and like the larger machine had a bow gunner's cockpit. However, the upper and lower wings were of equal span, with the centre wing of greater span.

Specifications
Besson LB coastal patrol flying-boat
Powerplant: one 224-kW (300-hp) Renault 12Fe inline piston engine
Performance: maximum speed 170 km/h (106 mph) at 1500 m (4,920 ft); climb to 1000 m (3,280 ft) in 4 minutes; range 500 km (311 miles)
Weights: empty 840 kg (1,852 lb); maximum take-off 1570 kg (3,461 lb)
Dimensions: span 13 m (42 ft 7¾ in); length 9 m (29 ft 6¼ in); height 3.2 m (10 ft 6 in); wing area 47 m² (505.92 sq ft)
Armament: one 7.7-mm (0.303-in) machine-gun on ring mounting, plus racks for two 50-kg (110-lb) bombs

Besson LB deep-sea flying-boat
Powerplant: one 336-kW (450-hp) Renault inline piston engine
Performance: maximum speed 150 km/h (93 mph) at 1500 m (4,920 ft)
Weights: empty 2500 kg (5,512 lb); maximum take-off 4400 kg (9700 lb)
Dimensions: span 21 m (68 ft 10¾ in); length 16.5 m (54 ft 1½ in); height 4.8 m (15 ft 9 in); wing area 100 m² (1,076.43 sq ft)
Armament: two 7.7-mm (0.303-in) machine-guns, plus up to 400 kg (882 lb) of bombs

The Besson LB coastal patrol flying-boat was built only in small numbers, and was in reality an obsolescent design even before its debut into service.

Besson MB.410 and MB.411

The **Besson MB.410.01** flew for the first time during the Autumn of 1932. Developed by Marcel Besson from the MB.35, it was also capable of being assembled or dismantled rapidly for housing in a small hangar. Powered by a 101-kW (135-hp) Salmson radial engine, it had a large main float with twin wingtip stabilising floats. Tests continued during 1933, but the prototype was destroyed in a fatal crash.

Nevertheless, official interest in the type had been aroused, specifically to equip the *Surcouf*, the sole large ocean-going commerce-raiding submarine built in France. The MB.410 design was developed to produce the **Besson MB.411**, of which two were built in 1935-6. MB.411 No. 1 flew in June 1935, differing from the MB.410 mainly by having a more powerful Salmson engine, and in its redesigned tail-plane with twin auxiliary fins. Other improvements were made to the stabilising floats, fuselage shape and wing structure.

The first MB.411 was embarked on the *Surcouf* in September 1935. After being withdrawn for tests as a single-seater in early 1936, it was restored to two-seat configuration and returned to the *Surcouf*. The second MB.411 served for some time with Aéronavale Escadrille 7-S-4, based at Saint-Mandrier.

The MB.411 No. 1 was still aboard *Surcouf* in June 1940, when this vessel escaped from Brest and reached Plymouth. The diminutive seaplane made several flights off the south Devon and Dorset coasts, causing some confusion among aircraft spotters! As a result of damage sustained in an air raid, the seaplane did not accompany *Surcouf* on a mission to the West Indies which ended in tragedy, on 18 February 1942, when the submarine was rammed in darkness by an American freighter. Plans to operate the MB.411 from a British merchantman were never realised, and the ultimate fate of the aircraft is not known.

Salmson 9Nd radial piston engine
Performance: maximum speed 190 km/h (118 mph); service ceiling 5000 m (16,405 ft); range 400 km (249 miles)
Weights: empty equipped 760 kg (1,676 lb); maximum take-off 1140 kg (2,513 lb)
Dimensions: span 12 m (39 ft 4½ in); length 8.25 m (27 ft 0¾ in); height 2.85 m (9 ft 4¼ in); wing area 22 m^2 (236.81 sq ft)
Armament: none

Besson MB.411

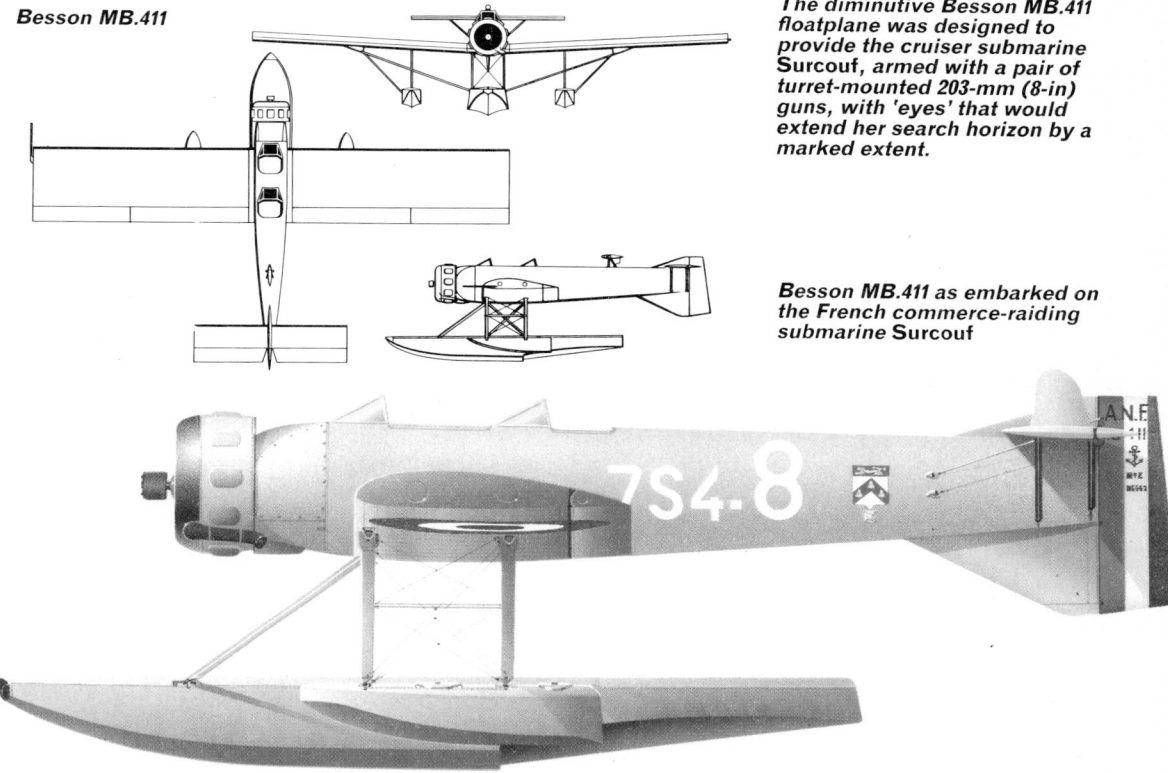

The diminutive Besson MB.411 floatplane was designed to provide the cruiser submarine Surcouf, armed with a pair of turret-mounted 203-mm (8-in) guns, with 'eyes' that would extend her search horizon by a marked extent.

Besson MB.411 as embarked on the French commerce-raiding submarine Surcouf

Specification
Besson MB.411
Powerplant: one 130-kW (175-hp)

Blackburn B-2

The success of its Bluebird series of two-seat side-by-side biplanes led Blackburn to develop a new type, the **Blackburn B-2**, which had the same basic layout but with a semi-monocoque all-metal fuselage. The wings were of steel and duralumin with fabric covering. The prototype B-2, with an 89-kW (120-hp) de Havilland Gipsy III engine, flew at Brough on 10 December 1931, appearing in public for the first time at the SBAC Display at Hendon in June 1932. It subsequently took part, with the first production B-2, in the King's Cup Air Race during the following month.

A demonstration tour in Portugal, in which the B-2, de Havilland Tiger Moth, and two foreign aircraft competed for a government order, was won by the Tiger Moth; apparently, the side-by-side seating of the B-2 was not favoured. Orders in the UK were also hard to achieve, in spite of numerous demonstrations, but Blackburn continued to build airframes in the hope that the situation would improve.

Various engine installations were

Developed from the Bluebird IV, the Blackburn B-2 was an attempt to produce a durable training and touring aircraft. The example illustrated was still flying in the 1950s on the power of a 112-kW (150-hp) Blackburn Cirrus Major 3.

tried; the second production B-2 had an 89-kW (120-hp) Cirrus Hermes IVA, and other airframes tried the 97-kW (130-hp) D. H. Gipsy Major 1, and the 101-kW (135-hp) Blackburn Cirrus Major 1. One of the only two examples to survive the war was fitted with a 112-kW (150-hp) Cirrus Major 3 in 1956.

A number of civil B-2s were built for Blackburn's flying schools at Hanworth in Middlesex, and at Brough in Yorkshire, these being operated by subsidiary companies. Considerable expansion was taking place in flying training in the mid-1930s, and Blackburn built a total of 42 B-2s. All were for civil use except the last three, bought by the Air Ministry in 1937 and issued to the Elementary and

Reserve Flying Training School at Brough. When World War II broke out in 1939, the Hanworth B-2s were moved to Brough and merged with that school's aircraft.

At that time the schools were still operated by Blackburn, but in February 1942 they were taken on RAF charge, and 24 of the surviving B-2s were presented to the Air Training Corps as instructional airframes; two were retained by Blackburn. These 26 aircraft survived

the war, but the eighth production example (G-ACLD) was destroyed in a crash in June 1951. The sole survivor in 1990 (G-AEBJ), the 30th production aircraft, is maintained in immaculate flying condition at Brough, now part of British Aerospace.

Specification
Type: two-seat primary trainer
Powerplant: one 97-kW (130-hp) de Havilland Gipsy Major 1 inline piston

engine
Performance: maximum speed
180 km/h (112 mph); cruising speed

153 km/h (95 mph); range with
maximum fuel 515 km (320 miles)
Weights: empty equipped 533 kg

(1,175 lb); maximum take-off 839 kg
(1,850 lb)
Dimensions: span 9.19 m (30 ft 2 in);

length 7.39 m (24 ft 3 in); height 2.74 m
(9 ft 0 in); wing area 22.85 m² (246 sq ft)

Blackburn B-5 Baffin

One might be forgiven for supposing that with the Ripon, Blackburn had succeeded in milking dry the basic design which had begun with the 1921 Swift, and proceeded via the Dart and Velos to the Ripon, production of which ended in 1932. However, as the design of radial engines improved, and their weight went down, Blackburn decided as a private venture to follow the lead of the Finns, who used a variety of radials in their licence-built Ripons. Two Fleet Air Arm Ripons were selected as test airframes, one with a 485-kW (650-hp) Armstrong Siddeley Tiger I, the other with a 406-kW (545-hp) Bristol Pegasus I.MS. The designation **T.5J Ripon V** was applied to both, which otherwise were known as the **Blackburn B-4** and **Blackburn B-5** respectively.

Following competitive trials the latter version was selected, to be powered by a Pegasus I.M3 engine developing 421 kW (565 hp), and two pre-production aircraft were ordered. Earlier Ripon IICs were converted on the production line to the new standard and the name **Blackburn Baffin** was approved, the first squadron to re-equip from Ripons being No. 812 aboard HMS *Glorious* in January 1934. Two other Baffin squadrons were No. 810 (HMS *Courageous*) and No. 811 (HMS *Furious*). In addition to the aircraft converted on the production lines, more than 60 Ripons were subsequently re-engined to Baffin standard; but since the type's performance proved little better than its predecessor it had a short life,

the last FAA aircraft being declared obsolete in 1937.

The Royal New Zealand Air Force took advantage of this situation to improve its Territorial Squadrons and bought 12 Baffins. These were followed by a further 17, and three squadrons were equipped, their Baffins being the only examples of the type to serve in World War II. Most of them had been withdrawn, and either scrapped or used as instructional airframes, by 1941.

Specification
Type: two-seat torpedo bomber
Powerplant: one 421-kW (565-hp)

Bristol Pegasus I.M3 radial piston engine
Performance: maximum speed 219 km/h (136 mph) at 1980 m (6,500 ft), and 206 km/h (128 mph) at 3050 m (10,000 ft); service ceiling 4570 m (15,000 ft); range with maximum fuel 869 km (450 miles)
Weights: empty equipped 1444 kg (3,184 lb); maximum take-off 3452 kg (7,610 lb)
Dimensions: span 13.88 m (45 ft 6½ in); length 11.68 m (38 ft 3¾ in); height 3.91 m (12 ft 10 in); wing area 63.45 m² (683 sq ft)
Armament: one forward-firing

7.7-mm (0.303-in) Vickers machine-gun and one 7.7-mm (0.303-in) Lewis gun on flexible mounting in rear cockpit, plus one torpedo or up to 907 kg (2,000 lb) of bombs

The Blackburn B-5 Baffin may be regarded as a revolutionary step between the Blackburn Ripon and Shark, the step being made possible by the pioneering use of a radial engine in the Ripons operated by Finland, which revealed the advantage of such a powerplant for a naval aircraft.

Blackburn B-6 Shark

Coming at the end of a distinguished line of Blackburn torpedo biplanes that had served with the Fleet Air Arm, the **Blackburn B-6 Shark** upheld the high reputations of its predecessors, the Dart, Ripon and Baffin.

Begun as a private venture to meet Specification S.15/33, the aircraft was based on the company's **M.1/30A** prototype, first flown on 24 February 1933. The Shark prototype, known as the B-6, flew on 24 August 1933 at Brough and was flown to the Aircraft and Armament Experimental Establishment at Martlesham Heath for testing on 26 November 1933. Deck landing trials aboard HMS *Courageous* early the following year were successful and a contract for 16 aircraft was placed for the Fleet Air Arm in August 1934.

The prototype was fitted with twin floats and flown at Brough the following April and successful sea trials took place from Felixstowe. Further contracts followed, and during the three-year production run Blackburn delivered 238 Sharks to the Fleet Air Arm, with which the Shark served in both seaplane and landplane configurations. Sharks from the first production batch went to No. 820 Squadron at Gosport early in 1935, replacing the squadron's Fairey Seals aboard HMS *Courageous*.

The **Shark I**, like the prototype, used the 522-kW (700-hp) Armstrong Siddeley Tiger IV engine, but the last aircraft in the first production batch was used for development flying with the uprated Tiger VI developing 567 kW (760 hp), 100 hours being flown by relays of pilots in

The Blackburn B-6 Shark over the carrier HMS Courageous, in company with a Fairey 3F. Designed as a torpedo-spotter-reconnaissance biplane, the Shark was still in limited service at the beginning of World War II.

just over seven days. This engine was used in the **Shark II**, production of which began in 1936, and an alternative engine was available for the next production variant, the **Shark III**, namely the 597-kW (800-hp) Bristol Pegasus III engine. Ninety-five Shark IIIs were delivered between April 1937 and the end of the year.

As Sharks were replaced by the Fairey Swordfish, they were relegated to second-line duties and a number were converted for target towing in various parts of the country.

Six **Shark IIA** floatplanes were purchased by the Portuguese Navy and delivered in March 1936; powered by 522-kW (700-hp) Armstrong Siddeley Tiger VIC engines, they served for several years on coastal defence duties.

The only other overseas customer for the Shark was Canada, and seven Shark IIs were bought for the Royal Canadian Air Force in 1936. Such was their success that Boeing Aircraft of Canada, a subsidiary of the American company, secured an agreement for licence pro-

duction at Vancouver and 17 Shark IIIs were built following delivery of two pattern aircraft from Blackburn. The Canadian Shark IIIs were fitted with the 626-kW (840-hp) Bristol Pegasus IX engine and served until 1944, when they were withdrawn. Five were transferred in June of that year to the British Air Observers' School at Trinidad.

Specification
Blackburn B-6 Shark II
Type: two/three-seat torpedo/reconnaissance biplane
Powerplant: one 567-kW (760-hp)

Armstrong Siddeley Tiger VI radial piston engine
Performance: (torpedo landplane) maximum speed 241 km/h (150 mph) at sea level; cruising speed 190 km/h (118 mph); service ceiling 4875 m (16,000 ft); range 1006 km (625 miles)
Weights: empty 1832 kg (4,039 lb); maximum take-off 3651 kg (8,050 lb)
Dimensions: span 14.02 m (46 ft 0 in); length 10.74 m (35 ft 3 in); height 3.68 m (12 ft 1 in); wing area 45.43 m² (489 sq ft)
Armament: one fixed forward-firing 7.7-mm (0.303-in) Vickers machine-gun and one 7.7-mm (0.303-in) Lewis or Vickers VGO gun on flexible mount in rear cockpit, plus one 680-kg (1,500-lb) torpedo or 907 kg (2,000 lb) of bombs

Blackburn B-24 Skua

Designed to Specification O.27/34, the all-metal **Blackburn B-24 Skua** broke away from the Royal Navy's tradition of biplanes with fabric covering: it was the UK's first naval dive-bomber and the country's first deck-landing aircraft to have flaps, retractable landing gear and a variable-pitch propeller.

The Skua competed with designs from Avro, Boulton Paul, Hawker and Vickers for the naval contract, and two prototypes were ordered in April 1935, the first of which flew at Brough on 9 February 1937, powered by a 626-kW (840-hp) Bristol Mercury IX.

After appearing in the New Types Park at the RAF Display, Hendon, on 26 June 1937 and the SBAC Display at Hatfield two days later, the prototype was sent to the Aircraft and Armament Experimental Establishment, Martlesham Heath, for the customary handling trials. Favourable reports were given on the Skua's qualities, and it subsequently carried out gunnery trials at Martlesham and, later, ditching experiments at Gosport.

Orders for 190 Skuas had been placed six months before the flight of the prototype, and some sub-contract work was awarded to speed up production. Because all Mercury engines were required for Bristol Blenheims, production Skuas were given the 664-kW (890-hp) Bristol Perseus XII sleeve-valve engine, under the designation **Skua II**.

The first production aircraft flew at Brough on 28 August 1938, and few modifications to the basic design were required apart from fitting upturned wingtips and a modified tailwheel oleo to

The Blackburn B-24 Skua was designed round a pair of mutually irreconcilable requirements. The aircraft illustrated belonged to No. 803 Sqn FAA.

cure juddering. The entire production run of 190 aircraft was delivered between October 1938 and March 1940, no mean feat at that period, although the programme was about a year behind schedule.

First Fleet Air Arm squadrons to receive Skuas in 1938 were Nos 800 and 803, for service on HMS *Ark Royal* where they replaced Hawker Nimrods and Ospreys. No. 801 Squadron aboard HMS *Furious* was re-equipped, and Skuas also joined No. 806 Squadron, then at Eastleigh, before the outbreak of World War II.

As a fighter, the Skua was already obsolete, but it made its mark in the dive-bombing role early in the war when 16 aircraft from Nos 800 and 803 Squadrons, flying from Hatston in the Orkneys, sank the German cruiser *Königsberg* in Bergen harbour at dawn on 10 April 1940. Although at the very limits of their range, all but one Skua returned from this long night flight. The squadrons suffered a severe setback 11 days later, however, losing most of their Skuas during an attack on Narvik.

Skuas from No. 801 Squadron flying from Detling covered the Dunkirk evacuation, but the type was withdrawn from operational service in 1941 when Nos 800 and 806 Squadrons re-equipped with Fairey Fulmars, while Nos 801 and 803 received Hawker Sea Hurricanes. The remaining Skuas ended their days comparatively peacefully as target tugs and on general training duties.

The burned-out remains of one Skua, recovered from a Norwegian lake, are preserved at the Fleet Air Arm Museum, Yeovilton.

Specification
Blackburn B-24 Skua II
Type: two-seat naval fighter/dive-bomber
Powerplant: one 664-kW (890-hp) Bristol Perseus XII radial piston engine
Performance: maximum speed 362 km/h (225 mph) at 1980 m (6,500 ft); cruising speed 266 km/h (165 mph) at 4570 m (15,000 ft); initial climb rate 482 m (1,580 ft) per minute; service ceiling 6160 m (20,200 ft); range 1223 km (760 miles)
Weights: empty 2490 kg (5,490 lb); maximum take-off 3732 kg (8,228 lb)
Dimensions: span 14.07 m (46 ft 2 in); length 10.85 m (35 ft 7 in); height 3.81 m (12 ft 6 in); wing area 28.98 m² (312 sq ft)
Armament: four fixed forward-firing 7.7-mm (0.303-in) Browning machine-guns in wings and one 7.7-mm (0.303-in) Lewis gun on flexible mount in rear cockpit, plus one 227-kg (500-lb) bomb beneath fuselage, and eight 14-kg (30-lb) practice bombs on underwing racks

Blackburn B-25 Roc

Developed from the Skua dive-bomber, the **Blackburn B-25 Roc** was the first Fleet Air Arm aircraft to have a power-driven gun turret. The idea was that the four guns would be brought to bear in broadside attacks on enemy bombers, but with a maximum speed of less than 322 km/h (200 mph) it is doubtful whether the Roc could have caught an enemy bomber and the idea was dropped.

Orders for 136 Rocs to Specification O.15/37 were received on 28 April 1937 and, because of Blackburn's involvement with the Skua programme, production was undertaken by Boulton Paul at Wolverhampton, the first aircraft flying on 23 December 1938. Following trials at Brough, the Roc went to the Aircraft and Armament Experimental Establishment, Martlesham Heath, in March 1939, and was joined there by the next two aircraft so that simultaneous handling and armament trials could be undertaken. As expected, the heavy turret penalised the Roc by comparison with the Skua, but the former could still be held steady in a steep dive with the use of dive-brakes. An enlarged propeller was fitted, and various other means of improving performance were tried, without much success.

Four Rocs were flown as seaplanes, fitted with Blackburn Shark floats, and these reduced the already low speed by another 48 km/h (30 mph), stability was rather poor, and low-altitude turns had to be avoided. One Roc floatplane was tested as a target tug, with a wind-driven winch in place of the turret, and was capable of streaming a target with 1830 m (6,000 ft) of cable at 3050 m (10,000 ft), and subsequently a number of landplane

Rocs were used as target tugs by Air Gunnery Schools.

After familiarisation with several Fleet Air Arm units, the first four Rocs to go into service were delivered to No. 806 Squadron at Eastleigh in February 1940 to serve alongside eight Skuas. Six Rocs went to join No. 801 Squadron's Skuas at Hatston, Orkney, four months later. No. 2 Anti-Aircraft Co-operation Unit at Gosport received 16 Rocs to replace its Blackburn Sharks and supplement its Skuas in June 1940, but perhaps the most unusual role for the Roc fell to four which had been damaged in a Junkers Ju 87 raid on Gosport, and were used subsequently as machine-gun posts with their turrets permanently manned.

Other Rocs were dispersed to various

locations in the UK and even to Bermuda, and the type gradually faded away until the last two aircraft were withdrawn from service in August 1943.

Specification
Type: two-seat naval fighter/target tug
Powerplant: one 675-kW (905-hp) Bristol Perseus XII radial piston engine
Performance: (landplane) maximum speed 359 km/h (223 mph) at 3050 m (10,000 ft); cruising speed 217 km/h (135 mph); service ceiling 5485 m (18,000 ft); range 1304 km (810 miles)
Weights: empty 2778 kg (6,124 lb); maximum take-off 3606 kg (7,950 lb)
Dimensions: span 14.02 m (46 ft 0 in); length 10.85 m (35 ft 7 in); height 3.68 m (12 ft 1 in); wing area 28.8 m² (310 sq ft)
Armament: four 7.7-mm (0.303-in) Browning machine-guns in electrically actuated Boulton Paul turret

The Blackburn B-25 Roc was designed to do for the Fleet Air Arm what the Boulton Paul Defiant did for the RAF, but both aircraft suffered the same failings: lack of performance, agility and basic firepower.

Blackburn B-26 Botha
to
Blackburn B.R.1 Iris

Blackburn B-26 Botha

When the Air Ministry issued Specification M.15/35 for a three-seat twin-engine reconnaissance bomber with ability to carry a torpedo, it attracted submissions from Blackburn and Bristol. Both envisaged 634-kW (850-hp) Bristol Perseus engines, but a change in the requirement increased the crew to four, leading to the new Specification 10/36, and both types were ordered, as the **B-26 Botha** and Beaufort respectively.

Because of the greater weight of the revised designs the Beaufort was given 843-kW (1,130-hp) Bristol Taurus radials, but these were in short supply and Blackburn was accordingly committed to using 656-kW (880-hp) Bristol Perseus X engines in the initial production version of the Botha.

Orders for 442 were received in 1936, and the first production aircraft flew at Brough on 28 December 1938. Trials at the Aircraft and Armament Experimental Establishment, Martlesham Heath, resulted in an increase in tailplane area and fitting of a horn-balanced elevator to provide better elevator control. Tests at the Torpedo Development Unit at Gosport began late in 1939 and production lines were established at Brough and Dumbarton. The first Botha to be delivered to the RAF was the third aircraft off the Dumbarton line which arrived at No. 5 Maintenance Unit, Kemble, on 12 December 1939.

A number of unexplained fatal accidents occurred in the first half of 1940 and the Botha came in for considerable criticism in view of its shortcomings and the fact that it was underpowered. Bristol managed to squeeze a little more power out of the Perseus engine, the Mk

The Blackburn B-26 Botha was drastically underpowered, and thus proved totally unsuited to its intended operational missions.

XA producing 694 kW (930 hp), and some other improvements were incorporated.

The fact that the Botha was underpowered and unfit for operational duties gave the Air Staff the idea that it could be relegated to training units where, not surprisingly, it continued to suffer fatal accidents. Probably the most appropriate, and certainly the safest Botha deliveries, came in late 1942 when some time-expired airframes went to RAF Schools of Technical Training. A few Bothas were fitted with winch gear and used by the Target Towing Unit at Abbotsinch as TT.1s.

A total of 580 Bothas was built, 380 at Brough and 200 at Dumbarton, and the type was finally withdrawn from service in September 1944.

Specification
Type: four-seat reconnaissance/torpedo-bomber/trainer
Powerplant: two 694-kW (930-hp) Bristol Perseus XA radial piston engines
Performance: maximum speed 401 km/h (249 mph) at 1675 m (5,500 ft); cruising speed 341 km/h (212 mph) at 4570 m (15,000 ft); service ceiling 5335 m (17,500 ft); range 2044 km (1,270 miles)
Weights: empty 5366 kg (11,830 lb); maximum take-off 8369 kg (18,450 lb)

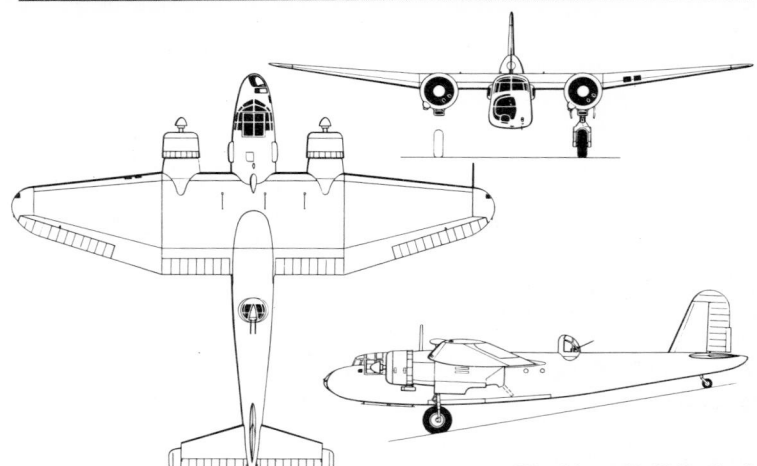

Blackburn B-26 Botha I

Dimensions: span 17.98 m (59 ft 0 in); length 15.58 m (51 ft 1½ in); height 4.46 m (14 ft 7½ in); wing area 48.12 m² (518 sq ft)
Armament: one fixed forward-firing

7.7-mm (0.303-in) machine-gun and two 7.7-mm (0.303-in) guns in dorsal turret, plus an internal torpedo, bombs or depth charges up to 907 kg (2,000 lb) in weight

Blackburn B-37 Firebrand

The origins of the **Blackburn B-37 Firebrand** lay in Naval Staff Requirement N.9/39, issued in December 1939, inviting submissions for a four-gun single-seat fleet fighter. In January 1941 three prototypes were ordered to Specification N.11/40, and the first of these was rolled out just a year later, making its first flight on 27 February 1942 in the hands of Flight Lieutenant Arthur Thompson. The second, armed with two 20-mm Hispano cannon in each wing and with racks for two 227-kg (500-lb) bombs, was flown on 15 July, and the third on 15 September. All three were powered by the 1719-kW (2,305-hp) Napier Sabre III engine, as were nine production **Firebrand F.I**s.

The second prototype undertook deck landing trials aboard HMS *Illustrious* in February 1943, operating from Machrihanish in Kintyre, and, following an accident, it was rebuilt as the prototype **Firebrand TF.II**, the centre-section of the wing being widened by 0.46 m (1ft 6 in) to allow a 839-kg (1,850-lb) torpedo

to be carried between the wheel bays. The first flight took place on 31 March 1943 and 12 production machines were completed. No. 708 Squadron at RNAS Lee-on-Solent flew TF.IIs as a trials unit, the only squadron to receive Firebrands during World War II.

Allocation of Sabre engine production for installation in the Hawker Typhoon

led to the substitution of the 1790-kW (2,400-hp) Bristol Centaurus VII in the **Firebrand TF.III**. The prototype was flown on 21 December 1943, followed by a second prototype and 27 production machines. These suffered some directional instability on take-off, the fault being remedied by the introduction of a fin and rudder of increased area on the

Firebrand TF.5 of No. 813 Sqn, with torpedo carrying MAT Mk IV directional stabilising tails.

Firebrand TF.4, which also had wing dive-brakes and a two-position torpedo carrier. The first of 102 Firebrand TF.4s flew on 17 May 1945 and the type entered service with No. 813 Squadron, reformed at RNAS Ford, on 1 September 1945.

The final production variants were the

A Blackburn Firebrand TF.4, designed as a high-performance torpedo-fighter that could launch its weapons at ships.

Derived conceptually from the Firebrand, the Blackburn B-48 strike fighter was designed round the Bristol Centaurus radial, and offered its pilot an excellent field of vision. The design eventually foundered with loss of official interest in piston-engined combat aircraft.

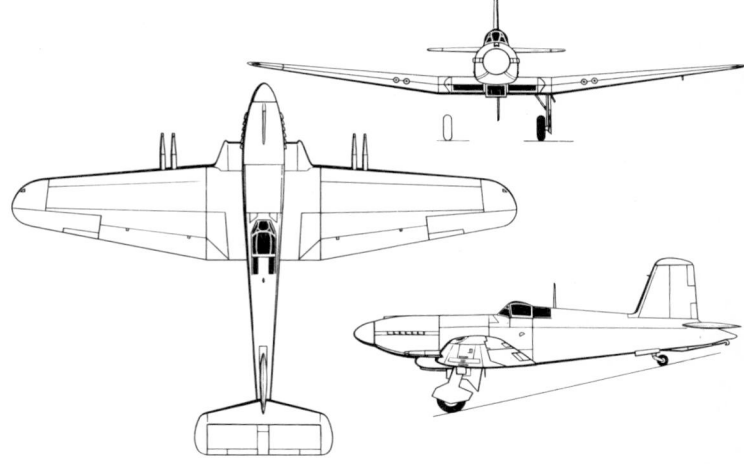

Firebrand TF.5 and **Firebrand TF.5A**, the latter having powered ailerons in addition to the horn-balanced rudder and elevators and the longer span aileron tabs common to all Mk 5s. Sixty-eight were manufactured and saw service with Nos 813 and 827 Squadrons.

Mention should be made of the **Blackburn B-48**, a potential successor to the Firebrand, powered by a 2047-kW (2,745-hp) Bristol Centaurus 59 radial engine. To give an improved view for the

pilot, the cockpit was raised and moved further forward, and a new inverted gull wing was incorporated to permit the use of shorter main landing gear units.

The first of two prototype B-48s (also designated **Y.A.1**) flew at Leconfield on 1 April 1947. The second prototype was not completed as such, but as a modification of the B-48 design, intended for research into power-boosted ailerons. The advent of the turboprop engine effectively killed development of the

B-48, but data was recorded that proved very useful in the B-54 strike aircraft.

Specification
Blackburn B-37 Firebrand TF.5
Type: single-seat carrier-based torpedo-strike fighter
Powerplant: one 1879-kW (2,520-hp) Bristol Centaurus IX radial piston engine
Performance: maximum speed 547 km/h (340 mph) at 3960 m

Blackburn B-37 Firebrand TF.1

(13,000 ft); cruising speed 412 km/h (256 mph); service ceiling 8685 m (28,500 ft); range 1191 km (740 miles)
Weights: empty 5368 kg (11,835 lb); maximum take-off 7938 kg (17,500 lb)
Dimensions: span 15.63 m (51 ft 3½ in); length 11.81 m (38 ft 9 in); height 4.04 m (13 ft 3 in); wing area 35.58 m² (383 sq ft)
Armament: four 20-mm cannon, plus one torpedo or 16 27-kg (60-lb) rockets

Blackburn B-54 and B-88

Specification GR.17/45 for a carrierborne anti-submarine aircraft attracted submissions from Fairey, Shorts and Blackburn, and it is fair to say that none of the aircraft would have won prizes for elegance.

Blackburn's first offering was the **B-54** (or **Y.A.5.**), a two-seat gull-wing monoplane with acute dihedral on the tailplane, and powered by a 1491-kW (2,000-hp) Rolls-Royce Griffon 56 piston engine driving contra-props; the original choice had been the Napier Double Naiad turboprop, but development of this had been stopped. The new engine brought a new SBAC designation (**Y.A.7**) and the aircraft flew for the first time at Brough on 20 September 1949, deck landings taking place the following February.

The Blackburn B-54 had a retractable ventral radome for its search radar, and an immense bomb trunk.

The second aircraft, known as the **Y.A.8**, was modified to carry a crew of three to meet new naval requirements and, with changes to the wings and tail, flew on 3 May 1950. Both the Y.A.7 and Y.A.8 were useful test aircraft paving the way for the third prototype, the turbine-powered **Y.B.1** which carried the Blackburn type number **B-88**. With an Armstrong Siddeley Double Mamba turboprop, driving contra-rotating propellers, it flew at Brough on 19 July 1950.

However, trials resulted in the production contract going to the Fairey entry,

later named Gannet, and the Y.B.1 became a test-bed with Armstrong Siddeley for the Double Mamba. The Y.A.7 and Y.A.8 served at RAE Farnborough for several years before being scrapped.

Specification
Blackburn B-88
Type: carrier-based anti-submarine aircraft
Powerplant: one 2200-ekW (2,950- ehp) Armstrong Siddeley Double Mamba turboprop
Performance: maximum speed 515 km/h (320 mph)
Weight: maximum take-off 5938 kg (13,091 lb)
Dimensions: span 13.46 m (44 ft 2 in); length 13 m (42 ft 8 in); height 5.11 m (16 ft 9 in)
Armament: (proposed) a wide variety of attack weapons in an internal bay, plus rockets or depth charges

Blackburn B-101 Beverley

Nearly 17 years separated Blackburn's two biggest aircraft, the Perth flying-boat of 1933 and the later **Blackburn B-101 Beverley**. The latter was, in fact, not of Blackburn design, originating with General Aircraft, builders of the Hamilcar glider.

Good looks, plus an ability to carry bulky and heavy loads in and out of short fields, seldom go hand in hand, and the **G.A.L. 60 Universal Freighter** provided confirmation of this fact. General Aircraft had made various studies for a large freight aircraft, and when Air Ministry Specification C.3/46 called for a medium-range tactical transport the G.A.L. 60 design was submitted. A contract was awarded for a prototype, and to power it a new version of the Bristol Hercules engine was developed.

In configuration the G.A.L. 60 was a simple unpressurised aircraft with fixed landing gear, and the prototype was built at the General Aircraft factory at Hanworth, Middlesex. General Aircraft merged with Blackburn on 1 January 1949, forming Blackburn and General Aircraft Ltd, and the G.A.L. 60 was taken by road to Brough for its first flight, made on 20 June 1950.

The flight test programme proceeded rapidly, but some changes were found to be desirable. These were incorporated in a second prototype with 2125-kW (2,850-hp) Bristol Centaurus engines; new techniques in parachuting stores demanded a change in design of the rear doors, and much larger removable doors

were fitted. The tail boom was enlarged to provide passenger accommodation, and the large single mainwheels were replaced by four-wheel bogies, more suited for operation from rough ground.

Designated **G.A.L.65** and **Blackburn B-100**, the second aircraft flew in June 1953, by which time 20 had been ordered for RAF Transport Command as the Blackburn B-101, subsequently named Beverley. The first two production aircraft flew in January and March 1955 respectively and remained with Blackburn for tests and modifications, while the next two went to the Aircraft and Armament Experimental Establishment, Boscombe Down, for acceptance trials. Hot weather trials in Tripoli were followed by cold trials in Canada, and the first squadron delivery was made to No. 47 at Abingdon on 12 March 1956. The Beverley was, at the time, the largest aircraft to be delivered to the RAF.

The Beverley's vast fuselage provided a main cabin or cargo hold measuring 10.97 m × 3.05 m × 4.72 m (36 ft × 10 ft × 15ft 6 in), and capable of accommodating an enormous variety of military equipment up to about 22.4 tonnes (22 tons) in weight. Tests with para-dropping loads culminated in the drop of a 18144 kg (40,000 lb) load beneath eight parachutes. As a transport, the Beverley could carry 94 troops or 70 paratroops, of whom 36 and 30 respectively were accommodated in the tail boom compartment.

In May 1954, an RAF order was placed

for a further 27 Beverleys, and the type served eventually with five squadrons (Nos 30, 34, 47, 53 and 84) in widely separated parts of the world including Africa, Brunei, the Middle East, Singapore, Vietnam and, of course, in the UK. The RAF finally retired its last Beverleys at the end of 1967, when they were replaced by the Lockheed Hercules.

There were several projects for civil versions of the design, including a cross-Channel car ferry with two decks, but none materialised. The two prototypes and first two production aircraft were allocated civil markings but, apart from one recorded instance, they do not appear to have been used. The fourth aircraft used its civil identity during late 1955 when it carried some heavy drilling equipment for the Iraq Petroleum Company.

Specification
Type: medium-range transport

An early example (late 1950s) of the Beverley shows off its bulk. Though limited in speed and range, the Beverley could accommodate a wide range of military equipment and a complement of 36 passengers.

Powerplant: four 2125-kW (2,850-hp) Bristol Centaurus 273 radial piston engines
Performance: maximum speed 383 km/h (238 mph) at 1735 m (5,700 ft); cruising speed 278 km/h (173 mph) at 2440 m (8,000 ft); service ceiling 4875 m (16,000 ft); maximum range 2092 km (1,300 miles)
Weights: empty 35940 kg (79,234 lb); maximum take-off 64864 kg (143,000 lb)
Dimensions: span 49.38 m (162 ft 0 in); length 30.3 m (99 ft 5 in); height 11.81 m (38 ft 9 in); wing area 270.9 m² (2,916 sq ft)

Blackburn B-103 Buccaneer

Blackburn Buccaneer S.2B of No. 16 Sqn based at RAF Laarbruch, West Germany.

Designed by a team under B.P. Laight, the **Blackburn B-103 Buccaneer** has proved to be a far better aeroplane than many believed. Developed to Royal Navy requirement NA.39 of the early 1950s, it was the world's first two-seat carrier-based low-level strike aircraft to be built for a high-speed under-the-radar means of penetrating enemy airspace. Design of the airframe incorporated a number of advanced features, including a full wing and tail boundary layer control system to give maximum lift; area-ruling of the bulky fuselage; a tailcone split vertically and hinged so that the two halves could be deployed as airbrakes; and a rotary bomb door carrying on its inner surface conventional or nuclear weapons. The bomb door is rotated to expose the weapons for delivery, avoiding the drag penalty of conventional bomb doors that open into a high-speed airstream.

Blackburn's B-103 design was chosen in 1955 to meet the NA.39 requirement, an order being placed in July of that year for an evaluation batch of 20 aircraft. Powerplant of the pre-production models, of which the first was flown on 30 April 1958, comprised two 3175-kg (7,000-lb) thrust de Havilland Gyron Junior DGJ.1 turbojets; the full naval 'kit' of folding wings and nose, arrester hook and catapult points, was introduced on the fourth example, which carried out the first carrier compatibility trials. An order for 40 examples of the production

Buccaneer S.1 version was placed in October 1959, these being powered by the Gyron Junior 101 of 3221-kg (7,100-lb) thrust. The first made its maiden flight on 23 January 1962, and on 17 July of that year No. 801 Squadron of the Fleet Air Arm was commissioned as the first operational Buccaneer squadron, embarking in HMS *Ark Royal* during the following January.

The Buccaneer S.1 was decidedly underpowered, and the Rolls-Royce Spey turbofan was selected as powerplant for the major production variant, the **Buccaneer S.2**, the first of 84 production examples making its initial flight on 5 June 1964. Buccaneer S.2s had a much greater range capability than the S.1s, for although the Spey engines provided some 30 per cent more power, they required less fuel, and the S.2s were also equipped for inflight-refuelling. They began to enter FAA service in October 1965, and eventually equipped Nos 800, 801, 803 and 809 Squadrons, operating from the aircraft-carriers HMS *Ark Royal, Eagle* and *Victorious*. Last to retire was No. 809 from HMS *Ark Royal,*

in 1979. Although scheduled for operation from shore bases, a fully 'navalised' **Buccaneer Mk 50** version of the Buccaneer was supplied to the South African Air Force in 1965. These aircraft were also fitted with a Bristol Siddeley BS.605 twin-chamber rocket motor in the rear of the fuselage, providing a 30-second boost of 3629-kg (8,000-lb) thrust to complement the standard

Blackburn Buccaneer S.2B

powerplant for take-off from 'hot and high' airfields.

Royal Navy Buccaneer S.2s were not retired when progressive depletion of the UK's carrier force brought their withdrawal from FAA service. From 1969 onwards they were transferred to the RAF, with No.12 Squadron the first to become operational with Buccaneer S.2s in July 1970. About 70 received modifications to internal systems and equipment to meet RAF requirements, being redesignated **Buccaneer S.2A**. From a subsequent modification/update programme they emerged as **Buccaneer S.2B**s, the primary difference being a capability to deliver the Martel anti-radar TV-guided missile, but a new bulged weapons bay door could accommodate an additional fuel tank. In addition to the foregoing, 43 new-production Buccaneer S.2Bs were ordered, the first making its initial flight on 8 January 1970. Before their retirement the remaining Royal Navy Buccaneers had undergone modifications comparable to those of the S.2Bs, becoming redesignated **Buccaneer S.2C** and **Buccaneer S.2D**, without and with Martel capability respectively.

Following the loss of an RAF Buccaneer on 7 February 1980, investigation revealed that this accident was the result of a wing fatigue problem. The RAF fleet was therefore grounded pending detailed inspection, and a return to normal operations was not resumed until late July of that year. Subsequently, No. 216 Squadron was disbanded, and in 1990 the type remains in service with No. 12 Squadron, No. 208 Squadron and No. 237 OCU at RAF Lossiemouth.

Specification
Buccaneer S.2B
Type: two-seat carrier- or land-based low-level strike aircraft
Powerplant: two 5105-kg (11,255-lb) thrust Rolls-Royce RB.168 Spey Mk 101 turbofans
Performance: maximum speed 1040 km/h (646 mph) at 61m (200 ft); service ceiling over 12190 m

(40,000 ft); typical range with weapons 3701 km (2,300 miles)
Weights: empty 13608 kg (30,000 lb); maximum take-off 28123 kg (62,000 lb)
Dimensions: span 13.41 m (44 ft 0 in); length 19.33 m (63 ft 5 in); height 4.97 m (16 ft 3 in); wing area 47.82 m² (514.7 sq ft)
Armament: four 454-kg (1,000-lb) bombs, fuel tank, or reconnaissance

Buccaneer S.2Bs of No. 15 Sqn, RAF Laarbruch, streak across the North Sea on a low-level attack mission. The main weapon load is housed in an internal bomb bay.

pack on inside of rotary bomb door, and up to 5443 kg (12,000 lb) of bombs and/or missiles on four underwing hardpoints

Blackburn R.B.1 Iris

Blackburn's first venture into flying-boats came in response to Air Ministry Specification R.14/24 calling for a large, long-range reconnaissance aircraft. The result was the **Blackburn R.B.1 Iris**, a three-engine biplane of wooden construction with accommodation for a crew of five. First flown on 19 June 1926, the big flying-boat undertook trials at the Marine Aircraft Experimental Establishment, Felixstowe, later that summer.

Blackburn had already decided to build a new metal hull, and the Iris was returned to the factory during the following year to have this incorporated along with other improvements. The original 485-kW (650-hp) Rolls-Royce Condor III engines were replaced by 503-kW (675-hp) Condor IIIAs, and in this new form the single Iris was redesignated **R.B.1A Iris II**.

Following RAF trials the Iris II undertook demonstration tours in the Mediterranean, Middle East, India and Scandinavia. As a result of its impressive showing, an Air Ministry order was placed for the **R.B.1B Iris III**, the first of three such boats flying in November 1929. With new duralumin construction, and other modifications, this version proved superior to its predecessor, and eventually the three aircraft were delivered to No. 209 Squadron, which had been re-formed at Mount Batten, Plymouth. Then the largest RAF aircraft, the Irises made a number of overseas tours, but in February 1931 one was lost in a fatal crash and a replacement ordered.

The **R.B.1C Iris IV** was the Iris II re-engined with three 597-kW (800-hp) Armstrong Siddeley Leopard III radials, the centre engine mounted as a pusher, the other two as tractor units. This version showed a tare weight saving of 649 kg (1,430 lb) and a sea level increase in speed to 209 km/h (130 mph).

The final variant, the **R.B.1D Iris V**, did not involve any further production, but the installation of a new powerplant in the three Iris IIIs, namely 615-kW (825-hp) Rolls-Royce Buzzard IIMS engines; the first of these conversions flew in

Blackburn Iris Mk III of No. 209 Squadron, RAF, based at Mount Batten in the early 1930s.

March 1932. The Iris Vs had a short service life, two being lost in January 1933, with the third returned to Brough for use as a flying test-bed for 537-kW (720-hp) Junkers Jumo IVC engines, built under licence by Napier as the Culverin Series 1.

Specification
Blackburn R.B.1B Iris III
Type: five-seat long-range reconnaissance flying-boat
Powerplant: three 503-kW (675-hp) Rolls-Royce Condor IIIB inline piston engines
Performance: maximum speed 190 km/h (118 mph) at sea level; maximum cruising speed 156 km/h (97 mph); service ceiling 3230 m

(10,600 ft); range with maximum fuel 1287 km (800 miles)
Weights: empty 8640 kg (19,048 lb); maximum take-off 13376 kg (29,489 lb)
Dimensions: span 29.57 m (97 ft 0 in); length 20.54 m (67 ft 4¾ in);

height 7.77 m (25 ft 6 in); wing area 207.07 m² (2,229 sq ft)
Armament: three 7.7-mm (0.303-in) Lewis guns (one each in nose, midships and tail positions) plus a bombload of up to 907 kg (2,000 lb)

The Blackburn R.B.1B Iris III was the last of the series with a 'conventional' tractor-propeller layout. The Iris IV introduced a combination of one pusher and two tractor units, and the surviving Iris IIIs were later modified to this standard under the designation Iris V.

Blackburn B.R.3A Perth
to
Blériot-SPAD S.33

Blackburn R.B.3A Perth

A development of the Iris, the **Blackburn R.B.3A Perth** was built to replace the earlier flying-boat in service with No. 209 Squadron at Plymouth, and differed from the Iris V primarily in having an enclosed cockpit, and a hull covered with corrosion-resistant material. An improvement in armament was the installation of a 37-mm gun in the bow position for anti-shipping work, but there was also an alternative rail-mounted 7.7-mm (0.303-in) machine-gun, as on the Iris.

The Perth's service introduction came in January 1934 when the second aircraft was delivered to Plymouth. At that time the first was still under test at Felixstowe, but by 31 May 1934 all three from the first contract had been delivered. A fourth Perth had been ordered subsequently and flew in April 1934, but this was retained at the MA&EE Felixstowe for experimental work.

Problems with the tail unit required the flying-boats to be modified at

Typical of the large biplane flying-boats operated by the RAF between the two world wars, the Blackburn R.B.3A Perth was, like the others, built only in small numbers, but had a formidable armament, centred on the provision of a 37-mm cannon in the nose.

Brough, keeping them out of service for several months. The first Perth was lost in heavy seas during September 1935, and two of the remaining three were eventually struck off charge in 1936. The last aircraft survived a further two years at Felixstowe.

Specification
Type: five-seat long-range reconnaissance flying-boat
Powerplant: three 615-kW (825-hp) Rolls-Royce Buzzard IIMS inline piston engines
Performance: maximum speed

212 km/h (132 mph) at sea level; economic cruising speed 175 km/h (109 mph); service ceiling 3505 m (11,500 ft); range with maximum fuel 2414 km (1,500 miles)
Weights: empty 9492 kg (20,927 lb); maximum take-off 17237 kg (38,000 lb)
Dimensions: span 29.57 m (97 ft 0 in); length 21.34 m (70 ft 0 in); height

8.06 m (26 ft 5½ in); wing area 233.27 m² (2,511 sq ft)
Armament: one Coventry Ordnance Works 37-mm gun and one 7.7-mm (0.303-in) Lewis gun in nose, one 7.7-mm (0.303-in) Lewis gun amidships and one 7.7-mm (0.303-in) Lewis in tail position, plus a bombload of up to 907 kg (2,000 lb)

Blackburn T.5 Ripon

Blackburn certainly believed in getting the most out of a basic design since the **Blackburn T.5 Ripon**, built to Air Ministry Specification 21/23, was a further development of the Swift/Dart/Velos family. The first of two prototypes flew as a landplane in April 1926; the second, completed as a floatplane, followed four months later. The Ripon was intended to replace the Dart in the Fleet Air Arm, and being a reconnaissance aircraft the Specification called for a 12-hour endurance.

The two prototype **Ripon I**s had 348-kW (467-hp) Napier Lion V engines, and as a result of competitive trials a contract was placed for one further prototype and an initial production batch of 20 of the improved **Ripon II**. This latter was considerably cleaned-up, and the performance improved by installation of a 425-kW (570-hp) Lion XI. Service entry began in July 1929, when Ripon IIs began to replace Darts on HMS *Furious* and *Glorious*.

Further modification resulted in the main production version, the **Ripon IIA**, of which 40 were ordered in early 1930. A variety of armament loads could be carried, including a torpedo. Final production version was the **Ripon IIC**, a variant which incorporated steel and duralumin to replace wood in the wing construction, but retained the Lion XI engine. Thirty-one examples of the Ripon IIC were built, production ending in 1932. A number of earlier aircraft were converted retrospectively to Ripon IIC standard, and some were also converted later to a radial powerplant, in which guise they became Blackburn Baffins. One prototype **Ripon III** was built, an

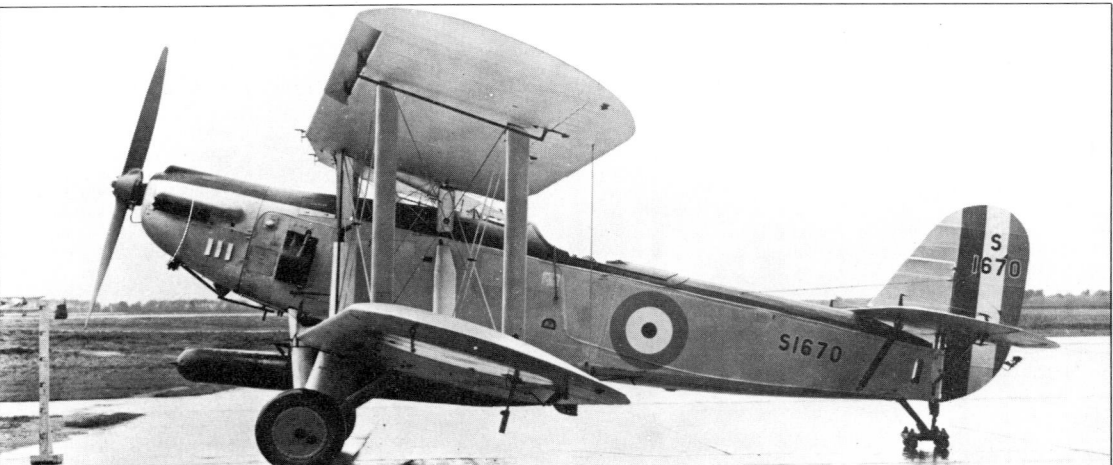

all-metal aircraft which progressed no further.

While the Ripon was offered for export with a wide variety of engines, Finland proved to be the only customer. A **Ripon IIF** with 395-kW (530-hp) Bristol Jupiter VIII radial engine and interchangeable wheel/float landing gear was bought by the Finnish government as a pattern aircraft, and licence production of 25 was undertaken at Tampere by the National Aircraft Factory. All had a radial powerplant: the first seven 358-kW (480-hp) Gnome-Rhône Jupiter VI engines, the next eight 399-kW (535-hp) Armstrong Siddeley Panther IIAs and the final 10 433-kW (580-hp) Bristol Pegasus

II.M3s. The last Finnish Ripon was not struck off charge until December 1944, and one survives in the Finnish air force historical collection.

Specification
Blackburn Ripon IIA
Type: two-seat carrier-based torpedo bomber
Powerplant: one 425-kW (570-hp) Napier Lion XIA inline piston engine
Performance: maximum speed 203 km/h (126 mph) at sea level; cruising speed 175 km/h (109 mph); service ceiling 3050 m (10,000 ft); range with maximum fuel 1706 km (1,060 miles)

Blackburn Ripon IIC of the Fleet Air Arm carrying its Mk 10 torpedo slung under its fuselage. The Ripon served with the FAA from 1929 till the late 1930s.

Weights: empty equipped 1930 kg (4,255 lb); maximum take-off 3359 kg (7,405 lb)
Dimensions: span 13.67 m (44 ft 10 in); length 11.2 m (36 ft 9 in); height 3.91 m (12 ft 10 in); wing area 63.45 m² (683 sq ft)
Armament: one fixed forward-firing 7.7-mm (0.303-in) Vickers gun and one 7.7-mm (0.303-in) Lewis gun in rear cockpit, plus one torpedo or up to 680 kg (1,500 lb) of bombs

Blériot XI

In 1906 Louis Blériot, then 34 years of age, ended his association with aviation pioneer Gabriel Voisin, and began to

build and fly aircraft of his own design.

Blériot decided that the future lay with the monoplane, and his first design of this configuration was the canard (tail-first) **Blériot V**, which flew, but soon crashed and was abandoned. The same

year he built the tandem-wing **Blériot VI** *Libellule* (Dragonfly), which made several short 'hops' at Issy-les-Moulineaux, near Paris, during the summer of 1907. These were all at an altitude of no more than 12 m (40 ft). Modified by the

installation of an Antoinette engine of 37 kW (50 hp), twice that of its predecessor, the machine was redesignated **Blériot VIbis**. Great progress was made with the **Blériot VII**, a tractor monoplane, followed by the fabric-covered

Blériot VIII, later rebuilt as the **Blériot VIIIbis** and **Blériot VIIIter** with flap-type and pivoting wingtip ailerons respectively. The much-improved **Blériot IX**, with paper-covered wings of reduced span, a fuselage largely fabric-covered, and powered by a 48-kW (65-hp) engine, was displayed at the December 1908 Paris Automobile Salon, but never flew. It was followed by the uncompleted **Blériot X** pusher biplane.

Blériot had gained only limited success with his monoplanes, while contemporary biplanes seemed to enjoy greater manoeuvrability. Then came the **Blériot XI**, the aircraft which has ensured its designer an important place in aviation history.

Its fuselage was built of ash with supporting struts and wire ties, and the shoulder-mounted wing was also of wooden construction, with wing-warping for lateral control. The tailplane comprised a central rudder, and elevators at each end of fixed horizontal tail surfaces. The main landing gear consisted of two large bicycle wheels, connected to a pair of steel tubes braced by wooden beams. The third component of the landing gear was a smaller wheel amidships, on a strut assembly below the rear fuselage.

The first Blériot XI was built at Neuilly (on the outskirts of Paris) at the end of 1908, and was displayed at the Exposition Internationale de la Locomotion Aérienne that December. It made its first flight at Issy-les-Moulineux on 23 January 1909, powered by a 21-kW (28-hp) R.E.P. engine. This first aircraft was distinguished by an auxiliary fixed vertical fin above the forward fuselage, but this was soon discarded as totally ineffective. The R.E.P. engine was replaced by an 18.7-kW (25-hp) Anzani driv-

The success of the Blériot XI in making the first heavier-than-air crossing of the English Channel also ensured the success of Blériot as an aircraft manufacturer. Widespread production of the Type XI followed, and the model was extensively used by the French military as a reconnaissance/spotter aircraft.

ing an effective Chauvière propeller before flying was resumed on 27 May 1909. On 26 June Blériot, using the **Blériot XI (mod)**, established a new European endurance record of 36 minutes 55 seconds, and on 13 July won a cross-country prize. With confidence thus gained, Blériot decided to enter for a £1,000 prize offered by the *Daily Mail* for the first cross-Channel flight. Among other things, Blériot needed to build up his finances, depleted by years spent on the design and construction of his aircraft.

At 4.41 in the morning of 25 July 1909, Blériot took off from a field near Calais and, maintaining an average altitude of 100 m (330 ft), landed on the cliffs by Dover Castle at 5.17. Louis Blériot at once became famous on both sides of the Channel, and soon a flood of orders for Blériot XI machines followed. Blériot began quantity production, but from the outset had to call on the aid of sub-contractors. Between 1909 and 1912, nearly every European aviation contest saw a Blériot XI among the winners, and the type was flown by most of the leading aviators throughout Europe. Among them was Alphonse Pégoud, famous for his multiple loops at Hendon aerodrome during 1913 and 1914. By the end of 1913

Blériot had delivered 800 aircraft of the total of 1,294 aircraft of all types built in France that year.

When France mobilised for war in July 1914, the Aéronautique Militaire had taken 25 Blériot XIs on charge. Two *escadrilles de cavalerie* were equipped with single-seat versions, while four other *escadrilles* had two-seat **Blériot XI-2** machines, powered by 52-kW (70-hp) Gnome engines, and with wings of increased area. The Blériot XI-2 could be armed with grenades or fléchettes (small darts).

The first military involvement of the Blériot XI had been with Italian units fighting the Turks in Cyrenaica and Libya during 1911 and 1912. Before the beginning of World War I the British RFC and RNAS had taken delivery of a number of Blériots, and at the outbreak of war five RFC squadrons had Blériot XIs on strength. In addition to imports from France, Britain and Italy had licence-built 104 and 70 respectively.

The **Blériot XI BG**, or Blériot-Gouin, parasol-wing two-seat variant was developed to give better visibility for reconnaissance and artillery observation duties. A number were used in the early stages of World War I by British units in France, and by three French *escadrilles*. Other military variants of the Blériot XI were the **Blériot XI-3**, a three-seater with an 89-kW (120-hp) engine; the **Blériot XI E1** single-seat trainer; the **Blériot XI-2 bis** a side-by-side two-seater with a tail reminiscent of German Taube designs; and the **Blériot XI R1** Pingouin (penguin), a 'rouleur' or ground trainer with clipped wings, used widely by the French and by American units in France. These were rendered incapable of take-off by the removal of large areas

The Blériot XI was one of history's more significant aircraft, which helps to explain why the type has proved relatively popular for replica-builders. Illustrated is a faithful copy based at Brienne in France.

of the canvas wing covering.

By early 1915 most Blériots had been withdrawn from operational service and redistributed among flying schools. One example was restored to flying condition in the early 1930s and used at flying displays by the 'Escadrille Blériot'.

Specification
Blériot XI-2
Type: two-seat touring, training or reconnaissance monoplane
Powerplant: one 52-kW (70-hp) Gnome 7B rotary piston engine
Performance: maximum speed 106 km/h (66 mph) at sea level; endurance 3 hours 30 minutes
Weights: empty 349 kg (769 lb); maximum take-off 625 kg (1,378 lb)
Dimensions: span 10.25 m (33ft 7½ in); length 8.45 m (27 ft 8¾ in); height 2.5 m (8 ft 2½ in); wing area 23 m² (247.58 sq ft)

Anzani-powered Blériot XI
Type: single-seat cross-Channel aircraft
Performance: maximum speed 74 km/h (46 mph)
Weight: maximum take-off 320 kg (705 lb)
Dimensions: span 7.81 m (25 ft 7½ in); length 7.05 m (23 ft 1½ in); height 2.52 m (8 ft 3¼ in); wing area 140 m² (150.7 sq ft)

Blériot-SPAD S.XX

Developed from Herbemont's unsuccessful cannon-armed **Blériot-SPAD S.XVIII**, the **Blériot-SPAD S.XX** was unusual in concept. Classified as a C.1 type (a single-seat fighter), it was intended to fight like a single-seater, being described as a 'monoplace protégé' or protected single-seater, the protection taking the form of a second crew member operating a single pivot-mounted Lewis gun in the rear cockpit. Its design bore what was to become the unmistakable stamp of André Herbemont: it was an unequal-span biplane, braced on each side by a single faired I-type strut. The upper wing had considerable sweepback, while the lower wing was straight and incorporated the ailerons; and the fuselage was a monocoque structure of wood.

The renowned test pilot Sadi Lecointe flew the prototype for the first time from Buc airfield on 7 August 1918. Service

tests were so successful that an order for 300 aircraft a month was placed by the Aéronautique Militaire. The end of World War I led to drastic curtailment of outstanding orders, and only 100 aircraft were built, 95 of them reaching French military units, initially the 2e Régiment d'Aviation at Strasbourg. Three S.XXs were exported to the Japanese Mitsubishi aircraft company and one was bought by the Bolivian government.

Between 1918 and 1922 numerous records and sporting events were carried off by the S.XX, including a world speed record with passenger of 230 km/h (143 mph) in 1918, and a world altitude record of 8900 m (29,199 ft) in July of the following year.

Variants
SPAD S.XXbis: one S.XX modified, with increased wing and fin area, and an unbalanced rudder: second aircraft

built and sold to Japan
SPAD S.20bis-1, bis-2 and bis-3: in a fierce contest with Nieuport-Délage racers to win speed records for France, Herbemont modified his S.XX design, converting it to a single-seater and progressively reducing the wing span and area; the S.20bis-1, bis-2 and bis-3, each showing reduced wing area compared with its predecessor, were all entered for the Prix Henry Deutsche

The Blériot-SPAD S.XX was an unusual fighter, designed to combine the agility and forward firepower of a single-seater with the extra protection and tactical flexibility bestowed by the carriage of a rear gunner. The type was also developed post-war as a racing aircraft of great renown.

de la Meurthe in September 1920; although a Nieuport-Délage eventually carried off the trophy, the S.20bis-3 attained an average speed of 252 km/h (156.59 mph) over the 190-km (118-mile) course
SPAD S.20bis-4: with wing span reduced to 6.6 m (21 ft 7¾ in), the S.20bis-4 achieved a world speed record of 283.864 km/h (176.38 mph) on 26 February 1920, flown by Jean Casale
SPAD S.20bis-5: entered for a new speed contest – the James Gordon Bennett Trophy – the S.20bis-5 had wing area reduced to 15 m² (161.46 sq ft) and cabane struts were eliminated, the top wing being connected directly to the fuselage; the contest took place at Etampes in September 1920, two S.20bis-5s competing, with one being disqualified

and the other taking second place
SPAD S.20bis-6: flown for the first time on 7 October 1920, the S.20bis-6 was powered by a special Hispano-Suiza engine developing 239 kW (320 hp), and had its upper wing braced by short cabane struts above the fuselage; flown by Bernard de Romanet, it established a world speed record of 309.012 km/h (192.01 mph) on 3 November 1920
SPAD S.26: powered by a 254-kW (340-hp) Hispano-Suiza, the S.26 was a twin-float seaplane with the lower wing of greater span than the upper. It was entered as aircraft No. 6 for the 1919 Schneider Trophy contest at Bournemouth, but a damaged float a few days beforehand led to its withdrawal; it subsequently participated in the 'Grand Meeting' at Monaco with S.XX wings of greater

span, being redesignated **S.26bis**; on 27 April 1920 it won the Roland Garros altitude trophy, climbing to 6500 m (21,325 ft) in 1 hour 16 minutes; temporarily converted back to its S.26 form it had won the Prix Guynemer speed event at an average 211.395 km/h (131.35 mph) four days earlier
SPAD S.31: intended to compete in the 1920 Schneider Trophy contest at Venice, this seaplane had an S.XX fuselage and a wing area of 31 m² (333.69 sq ft); it did not participate and was modified as the **S.31bis**
SPAD S.31bis: an experimental single-seat fighter seaplane; armed with twin synchronised machine-guns; it used the wing of the S.XX and was fitted with new Tellier-designed floats; sold to Japan during 1921

Specification
Blériot-SPAD S.XX
Type: two-seat fighter
Powerplant: one 224-kW (300-hp) Hispano-Suiza inline piston engine
Performance: maximum speed 217 km/h (135 mph) at 4000 m (13,125 ft); service ceiling 8000 m (26,245 ft); range 400 km (248 miles)
Weights: empty equipped 867 kg (1,911 lb); maximum take-off 1306 kg (2,879 lb)
Dimensions: span 9.72 m (31 ft 10¾ in); length 7.3 m (23 ft 11½ in); height 2.8 m (9 ft 2¼ in); wing area 30 m² (322.93 sq ft)
Armament: two synchronised forward-firing 7.7-mm (0.303-in) Vickers machine-guns and single or twin 7.7-mm (0.303-in) Lewis machine-guns on a ring mounting in the rear cockpit

Blériot-SPAD S.33

The prototype (F-CMAZ) of the **Blériot-SPAD S.33** first flew on 12 December 1920. This, and early production aircraft, were powered by a single 186-kW (250-hp) Salmson radial, but later machines had a 194-kW (260-hp) Salmson. Four passengers were accommodated in comfortable wicker armchairs in an enclosed forward cabin, and provided with a good view through three porthole windows on each side of the fuselage. Behind them in side-by-side open cockpits were the fifth passenger (to starboard) and the pilot.

The S.33 was a great success, with 41 examples being built. Fifteen flew with the Messageries Aériennes company, later incorporated in Air-Union; 20 were used on the routes between France and eastern Europe operated by the Compagnie Franco-Roumaine; and five were bought by the Belgian SNETA company, which was absorbed in the SABENA national airline in May 1923. S.33s became a familiar sight to passengers at most European commercial airports.

In 1925 the Franco-Roumaine company re-formed as the famous CIDNA (Compagnie Internationale De Navigation Aérienne), with Maurice Nogues as chief pilot. CIDNA's routes, which linked Paris with many east European capitals, were extended to Constantinople (now Istanbul), and the backbone of these services was the S.33. In May 1926 the Air-Union company inaugurated a direct service from Paris to Marseilles, utilising five S.33s and one S.56-3.

S.33 F-AICC was modified, by the incorporation of a larger wing and dual controls, for service as a blind-flying trainer for CIDNA pilots. The pupil pilot flew the aircraft from within the cabin, which had its windows blacked out!

The S.33 and its developments dominated the field of smaller European transport aircraft right through the 1930s.

Variants
SPAD S.46: to achieve improved performance, the basic S.33 design was modified to take a 276-kW (370-hp) Lorraine-Dietrich 12Da engine, and had its wing span extended by 0.94 m (3 ft 1 in); following the first flight of the prototype S.46 on 16 June 1921, the Compagnie Franco-Roumaine bought 38
SPAD S.48: designation of one S.33 fitted briefly with a 205-kW (275-hp) Lorraine engine
SPAD S.50: two prototypes of this version, differing mainly in having a

Blériot-SPAD S.56-5 passenger aircraft of the CIDNA company, circa 1930.

224-kW (300-hp) Hispano-Suiza 8Fb engine, were followed by conversions of three CMA S.33s; one prototype, with S.46 wings, was flown as a Ministerial transport
SPAD S.56: first example flown initially on 3 February 1923; this was a basic S.33 airframe fitted with metal wings spanning 13.08 m (42 ft 11 in) and powered by a 283-kW (380-hp) Gnome-Rhône Jupiter radial; cabin layout was altered, with two pairs of side-by-side seats, and a second access door provided; the prototype was followed by the sole **S.56/2** with a 298-kW (400-hp) Jupiter; the **S.56/3** with 283-kW (380-hp) Jupiter engine and improved divided landing gear (8 built); and then the **S.56/4**; this last version was altered radically, the pilot and 'open-air' passenger being accommodated in side-by-side cockpits immediately behind the 313-kW (420-hp) Jupiter engine, and with the cabin for six passengers (with four porthole windows each side) moved further aft; the upper wing was carried a little higher above the fuselage, and the lower wing acquired some dihedral; eight S.56/4s were joined by two uprated S.56/3s, five being operated by Air-Union and five by CIDNA; the **S.56/5** flew for the first time in 1928, and this had the cabin divided into forward and rear compartments for

four and two passengers respectively; the aft compartment could be converted easily for use as a freight hold; six existing S.56/3s of the CIDNA company were converted to S.56/5 standard; final version was the **S.56/6**, of which two were built; these were four-passenger aircraft, with the pilot restored to a cockpit at the rear of the cabin; they were produced specially for the Air-Publicité company, and intended for the towing of advertising banners
SPAD S.66: in 1925, when the CIDNA company was formed from the Compagnie Franco-Roumaine, the 34 S.46s then in service were given faired headrests for the pilot and the open-cockpit passenger, and redesignated S.66s; eight S.33s were modified extensively to bring them up to S.66 standard
SPAD S.116: SPAD S.66 No. 32 was converted as the sole S.116 in 1928, with a 336-kW (450-hp) Renault 12Ja engine in place of the original Lorraine-Dietrich
SPAD C.126: one only, converted from an S.66 in 1925 to a one-off **S.86** powered by a 336-kW (450-hp) Lorraine engine, it was again re-engined in 1929

The Blériot-SPAD S.33 transport. Of typical Herbemont design, with a sweptback upper wing, smaller and straight lower wing and simple interplane strutting, the S.33 had accommodation for four passengers. Note the extensive louvring in the cowl round the water-cooled Salmson radial engine.

with a Hispano-Suiza 12 Ha of 336-kW (450-hp), then being designated S.126

Specification
Blériot-SPAD S.33
Type: passenger transport
Powerplant: one 194-kW (260-hp) Salmson CM.9 radial piston engine
Performance: maximum speed 180 km/h (112 mph); economic cruising speed 160 km/h (99 mph); service ceiling 3800 m (12,470 ft); range 1080 km (671 miles)
Weights: empty operating 1050 kg (2,315 lb); maximum take-off 2062 kg (4,546 lb)
Dimensions: span 11.66 m (38 ft 3 in); length 9.08 m (29 ft 9½ in); height 3.2 m (10 ft 6 in); wing area 42.18 m² (454.04 sq ft)

Blériot 125
to
Bloch M.B.130 and M.B.131

Blériot 125

The **Blériot 125** was an unusual passenger aircraft, and attracted considerable attention when displayed on the Blériot stand at the 1930 Paris Salon de l'Aéronautique. Basically of wooden construction, it had a high wing supported by twin fuselages, each with a luxurious cabin for six passengers, a toilet and baggage compartment. Above the centre section was located an enclosed cabin for three crew members. A monoplane tailplane with four fins and rudders was mounted to the rear of the twin fuselages, and landing gear comprised tandem pairs of wheels partially enclosed in the bottom of the fuselages. Powerplant comprised two Hispano-Suiza engines mounted in tandem on the wing centre-section, and driving one tractor and one pusher propeller.

Léon Kirste's design was somewhat ahead of the state of the art, and the Blé-

The Blériot 125 was a twin-boom design, the passengers being accommodated in the booms, while the flight crew and engine were located in a central nacelle. One virtue of the design was its neat landing gear arrangement.

riot 125 demonstrated poor flight qualities when flown for the first time on 9 March 1931. Tests continued into 1933, but although allocated the civil registration F-ALZD, the Blériot 125 failed to gain an official flight certificate and was scrapped the following year.

Specification
Type: transport aircraft
Powerplant: two 410-kW (550-hp) Hispano-Suiza 12Hbr inline piston engines
Performance: maximum speed 220 km/h (137 mph); range 1000 km (621 miles)
Weights: empty 4440 kg (9,789 lb); maximum take-off 7260 kg (16,006 lb)
Dimensions: span 29.4 m (96 ft 5½ in); length (13.83 m (45 ft 4½ in); height 4 m (13 ft 1½ in); wing area 100 m² (1,076.43 sq ft)

Blériot 127

With a view to replacing the Caudron R-XI then in service with French *escadrilles de protection* (bomber-escort squadrons) Léon Kirste projected the **Blériot 107M** in 1922. This was developed into the **Blériot 117M,** which flew initially on 19 June 1924. The small twin fins and rudders of the tailplane proved ineffective, and flight characteristics were poor. However, Kirste persevered with the basic concept, replacing the 298-kW (400-hp) Lorraine 12Db engines with more powerful Hispano-Suiza 12Gb units, and designed a new tail unit with a large single fin and rudder. The single **Blériot 127** prototype flew on 7 May 1926. The modified **Blériot 127/2,** first flown on 10 January 1928, had more powerful Hispano-Suiza 12Hb engines, with radiators located under the wings to reduce drag. Pilot and copilot were located in open side-by-side cockpits with dual controls. After successful tests, this version was ordered to a total of 42 aircraft, built over a four-year period.

The Blériot 127 was a mid-wing monoplane, largely of wooden construction. Its unusual feature was provided by the gunner's positions: one was accommodated conventionally in the fuselage nose, but two additional positions were provided in wing trailing-edge extensions to the engine nacelles. Intended to provide a virtually unlimited field of fire to the rear, these latter positions could be reached from the fuselage during landing, via the deep-section wing. The Blériot 127 was in the M.4 category (four-seat multi-role aircraft) intended for bombing and reconnaissance, as well as fighter escort duties. Production aircraft equipped two *escadrilles de protection* of the 11e Régiment de Bombardement,

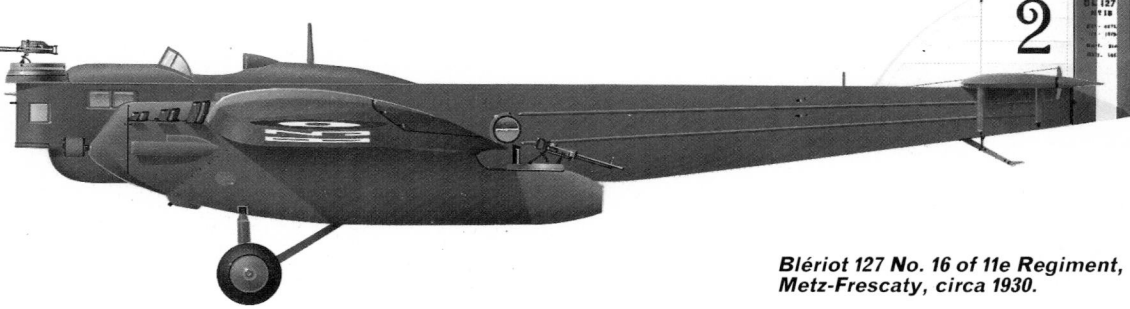

Blériot 127 No. 16 of 11e Regiment, Metz-Frescaty, circa 1930.

stationed at Metz, first deliveries being made in April 1929. The Blériot 127/2 proved cumbersome and ineffective in service, but was not withdrawn from first-line duties until the end of 1934.

The **Blériot 127/3** was a single night-bombing version; the **Blériot 127/4** was a Blériot 127/2 with standard dual-wheel main landing gear units converted to take large single wheels, initially with large 'trouser' type fairings.

Variants
Blériot 137: this was an all-metal high-wing development, with twin midships gunners' cockpits, side-by-side just behind a large cut-out in the wing trailing edge, replacing the Blériot 127's nacelle positions. Two Blériot 137s were built: the first, powered by Hispano-Suiza engines, was flown on 21 December 1930; the second, with Salmson engines, appeared a few months later. Of similar overall dimensions to its predecessor, though with more angular wing and tailplane outlines, the Blériot 137 had a maximum speed of 230 km/h (143 mph)

Specification
Blériot 127/2
Type: multi-purpose aircraft
Powerplant: two 410-kW (550-hp) Hispano-Suiza 12Hb inline piston engines
Performance: maximum speed 199 km/h (124 mph); service ceiling 6850 m (22,475 ft)
Weights: empty 3750 kg (8,267 lb); maximum take-off 4966 kg (10,948 lb)
Dimensions: span 23.2 m (76 ft 1¼ in); length 14.68 m (48 ft 2 in); height 3.41 m (11 ft 2¼ in); wing area 88 m² (947.26 sq ft)
Armament: six 7.7-mm (0.303-in)

One of a number of obsolescent designs to emerge from the French aircraft industry in the late 1920s, the Blériot 127 was a multi-role aircraft with the unusual feature of gunners' positions let into rearward extensions.

Lewis machine-guns, two each on mountings in nose cockpit and positions at rear of each extended engine nacelle, plus provision in fuselage bay for 250 kg (551 lb) of bombs

Blériot 165

Intended as a replacement for the Farman 'Goliath' airliners then in service, the **Blériot 165** was an equal-span two-

bay biplane with a rectangular fuselage and large single fin and rudder. The wide-spaced independent main legs of the landing gear each had twin-wheeled assemblies, and power was provided by two Gnome-Rhône Jupiter engines,

strut-mounted between the wings. Pilot and co-pilot were seated side by side in an open cockpit in the forward fuselage, and the cabin accommodated 16 passengers.

Blériot 165 No. 1 flew for the first time

on 27 October 1926. A second aircraft was powered by Renault engines and equipped for night flying. Designated **Blériot 175,** it was re-engined with Jupiters and became the second Blériot 165. Both examples flew on the Air-

Union 'Golden Ray' service between Paris and London, alongside the larger number of Lioré-et-Olivier 21s which had been built. No further Blériot 165s were built, as the Lioré-et-Olivier design was considered to be superior.

Plans to build a military variant as the **Blériot 123** three-seat bomber and a second Blériot 175 (intended for a long distance flight to Tokyo, piloted by Paul Codos) were abandoned.

Specification
Blériot 165
Type: passenger transport
Powerplant: two 313-kW (420-hp)

Fuel for the Blériot 165's two radial engines was carried in a pair of overwing slipper tanks. This example was named after a key figure in the early development of flying machines.

Gnome-Rhône 9Ab Jupiter radial piston engines
Performance: maximum speed 185 km/h (115 mph); practical ceiling 5000 m (16,405 ft); range 525 km (326 miles)
Weights: empty equipped 2919 kg

(6,435 lb); maximum take-off 5600 kg (12,36 lb)
Dimensions: span 23 m (75 ft 5½ in);

length 14.85 n (48 ft 8½ in; height 4.85 m (15 ft 11 in); wing area 119.1 m² (1,282.02 sq ft)

Blériot 195

The **Blériot 195** was a large low-wing cantilever monoplane powered by four engines in tandem pairs, carried above the wing by a complexity of struts. Intended originally as a mail-carrier for a

staged North Atlantic route, it was flown for the first time on 9 March 1929. At that time it was a landplane, designated **Blériot 195/2**, and utilised the landing gear of a standard production Blériot 127/2. With twin Blanchard-built floats it became the **Blériot 195/3** and was test-flown in September 1929. In March 1930

it was re-engined with four 172-kW (230-hp) Gnome-Rhône Titan engines and re-designated **Blériot 195/4**. It was hoped that it would meet an official requirement for a mail-carrying seaplane for the proposed Marseilles-Algiers route, but none of the competing designs was found suitable.

The Blériot was taken out of storage in April 1931.and given new landing gear, comprising large single-wheel main units, under the designation **Blériot 195/6**. It was tested as a cargo-carrier for the Air-Union company but, unfortunately, failed to gain a certificate of airworthiness in its new role.

Blériot-SPAD S.510

Developed from the experimental **SPAD S.91** to meet a French official requirement of 1930 for a new single-seat fighter, the **Blériot-SPAD S.510** was unique among the contenders built to meet the specification by being a biplane.

The prototype **S.510.01**, which made its first flight on 6 January 1933, had an oval section fuselage built up of duralumin and steel, the rear section being duralumin monocoque. The equal-span wings were of metal with fabric covering, and braced by typical Herbemont single faired I-type struts on each side. Sweepback was incorporated in the upper wing only, and ailerons were provided on both top and bottom wings. The Hispano-Suiza 12Xbrs Vee-type engine had a frontal radiator, and the legs of the independent main landing gear units were faired in, the main wheels also having spat-type fairings. An open pilot's cockpit was located immediately below a cut-out in the upper-wing trailing edge. Flight trials led to lengthening of the fuselage to improve directional and longitudinal stability, and modifications to the ailerons to improve lateral control.

The Dewoitine D.500 low-wing monoplane proved superior to the S.510 in speed and won the design competition. However, ace pilot Louis Massotte demonstrated an S.510 for the French Air Minister, General Dénain, showing off the biplane's unsurpassed manoeuvrability and rate of climb. As a result an order for 60 S.510s was placed in August 1935. Series aircraft began to reach the II/7 *Groupe de Chasse* of the Armée de l'Air in April 1937. Within three months the whole 7e *Escadre* had re-equipped with the type. Series S.510s had four Chatellerault 7.5-mm (0.295-in) machine-guns in small gondola-type fairings beneath the lower wings, in place of the twin synchronised guns of the prototype.

By the outbreak of World War II the S.510s had been relegated to flying schools and the *escadrilles régionales*, established for target defence of cities and industrial complexes well behind the

Blériot-SPAD S.510 of ERC 4/561, French air force, based at Havre-Octeville in October 1939.

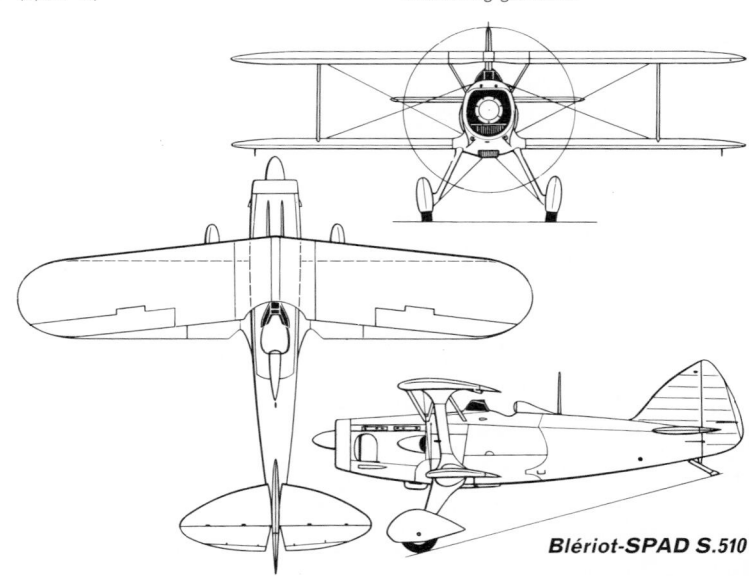

Blériot-SPAD S.510

front line. Little was heard of them in action. Rumours that a few Armée de l'Air machines were sent to the Republican side in the Spanish Civil War remain wholly unconfirmed.

The final SPAD fighter design was the **S.710,** a single prototype of which was built. This had many advanced design features, including a 'butterfly'-type tailplane, retractable landing gear, and an enclosed pilot's cockpit. However, it crashed on 15 June 1937, killing Louis Massotte. André Herbemont subsequently retired from aircraft design.

Specification
SPAD S.510 (series)
Type: single-seat fighter
Powerplant: one 515-kW (690-hp) Hispano-Suiza 12Xbrs inline piston engine
Performance: maximum speed 372 km/h (231 mph) at 4000 m (13,125 ft); climb to 4000 m (13,125 ft) in 4

minutes 31 seconds; service ceiling 10500 m (34,450 ft)
Weights: empty equipped 1250 kg (2,756 lb); maximum take-off 1677 kg (3,697 lb)

Dimensions: span 8.84 m (29 ft 0 in); length 7.46 m (24 ft 5¾ in); height 3.41 m (11 ft 2¼ in); wing area 22 m² (236.81 sq ft)
Armament: four 7.5-mm (0.295-in) Chatellerault machine-guns in underwing gondolas

Bloch M.B.81

Avions Marcel Bloch was formed in

1930, and its first designs were the **Bloch M.B.60** (later **M.B.61**) and **M.B.71** high-wing postal monoplanes, neither of which passed beyond the prototype stage. In 1932 the **Bloch M.B. 80** was designed for entry in a French air ministry contest for a purpose-built ambulance aircraft. The French authorities placed great stress on the importance of the 'avion sanitaire', following the appearance of an ambulance version of the Breguet 14T biplane in 1918. Bre

14Ts and Hanriot HD.14S biplanes had been used during the 1920s for casualty evacuation work in French colonial territories.

The M.B.80 prototype was an angular cantilever low-wing monoplane, powered by a single 89-kW (120-hp) Lorraine 5Pc engine, and with fixed wide-

Another example of the angularity seemingly favoured by French designers in the 1930s, the Bloch M.B.81 ambulance aircraft was fairly widely employed in France's far-reaching African empire.

track divided landing gear to facilitate operations from unprepared strips. Its pilot was seated forward in an open cockpit and behind him in the rear fuselage, under easily accessible panels, was accommodation for a single stretcher.

The M.B.80 was followed by the **M.B.81.01**, coded F.301, which made its initial flight in October 1932, powered by a Salmson 9Nc engine of 101 kW (135 hp). A production order followed, the first of 20 **M.B.81** production aircraft being delivered in 1935. The type found

considerable employment in Africa and the Middle East, a number surviving to operate during World War II. The fourth example flew with the RAF under serial AX677.

Specification
Bloch M.B.81
Type: ambulance aircraft
Powerplant: one 130-kW (175-hp) Salmson 9Nd radial piston engine
Performance: maximum speed 188 km/h (117 mph); economic cruising speed 161 km/h (100 mph) at 2500 m (8,200 ft); service ceiling 6400 m (20,995 ft); range 654 km (406 miles)
Weights: empty equipped 581 kg (1,281 lb); maximum take-off 880 kg (1,940 lb)
Dimensions: span 12.59 m (41 ft 3¾ in); length 8.4 m (27 ft 6¾ in); height 2.9 m (9 ft 6¼ in); wing area 17.8 m² (191.6 sq ft)

Bloch M.B.120

Selected by the French government from a number of competing designs for a transport suitable for colonial duties (passenger, mail and freight, transport and policing) in French overseas territories, the **Bloch M.B.120** was a cantilever high-wing monoplane of all-metal construction. The **M.B.120.01** prototype was, in fact, the re-worked M.B.71 monoplane. It was put into service in 1934 on the routes of Air Afrique, a new airline established by the French government, on 11 May 1934, to link various French African territories. Ten series aircraft followed the prototype, six of them for civil use and four in Armée de l'Air service; all served in French Africa. The Air Afrique civil aircraft made scheduled flights between Algiers, Niamey, Fort Lamy, and the French Congo. Two of them connected Tananarive, Madagascar with Broken Hill, South Africa. The four military M.B.120s were joined sub-

sequently by a fifth aircraft, formerly the civil F-APZV. One aircraft (F-ANTK, *Ville de Paris*) was reported to be in service as late as 1942.

Standard accommodation was for a crew of three and up to 10 passengers. More usually, however, the civil M.B.120s carried four passengers and a substantial load of mail. The general structure and layout of the three-engined M.B.120 was similar to that of the M.B.200 twin-engined bomber.

Specification
Type: colonial transport aircraft
Powerplant: three 224-kW (300-hp) Lorraine Algol 9Na radial piston engines
Performance: maximum speed 260 km/h (162 mph); economic cruising speed 230 km/h (143 mph); service ceiling 6300 m (20,670 ft)
Weights: empty equipped 3700 kg (8,157 LB); maximum take-off 6000 kg (13,228 lb)

Dimensions: span 20.54 m (67 ft 4¾ in); length 15.30 m (50 ft 2¼ in); wing area 61 m² (656.62 sq ft)

Designed for colonial use, the Bloch M.B.120 was intended to combine no more than adequate performance with great simplicity of construction and maintenance.

Bloch M.B.130 and M.B.131

Marcel Bloch's small factory at Courbevoie had been intended for the design and manufacture of lightplanes, but very shortly after settling into its premises the company had an opportunity of evolving a reconnaissance-bomber to satisfy the BCR requirement (Bombardement, Chasse, Reconnaissance) of the French air ministry.

First flown on 29 June 1934, the **Bloch M.B.130** prototype succeeded, despite indifferent performance, in gaining a contract for 40 production examples. There were, however, many problems to resolve if this aircraft were to attract more orders, and the company evolved instead an improved **M.B.131.** Details of its design and estimated performance were submitted to the French air ministry, and the contract for 40 M.B.130s was amended to cover the supply of M.B.131s. A prototype of this latter aircraft flew for the first time on 16 August 1936: it was an all-metal cantilever monoplane of low-wing configuration with a conventional fuselage and strut-braced tail unit, retractable tail-wheel type landing gear, and twin-engine powerplant.

The M.B.131 also had a performance envelope which left a great deal to be desired, so a second prototype was built and first flown on 8 May 1937. This differed by having increased-area wing and tail surfaces, and a new fuselage. In this

basic form it entered production towards the end of 1937. Construction was carried out by the new nationalised Société Nationale de Constructions Aéronautiques du Sud-Ouest (SNCASO), which consisted of the previous Bloch and Blériot concerns. The initial production version, of which 13 were built, had the designation **M.B.131 R.4**, this being a four-seat reconnaissance aircraft, and was followed by five **M.B.131 Ins** dual-control trainers. Major production version was the **M.B.131 RB.4**, a reconnaissance-bomber evolved from the R.4 and provided with an internal bomb bay and changes in equipment. A total of 119 of these was built, and other variants included one **M.B.133** prototype with a revised tail unit, and one **M.B.134** prototype with two 850-kW (1,140-hp) Gnome-Rhône 14N-48/49 engines.

Deliveries to the Armée de l'Air began in the autumn of 1938, and by the outbreak of World War II six reconnaissance *groupes* in France and one in North Africa had been equipped with M.B.131s. Almost immediately it was discovered that they were incapable of making daylight reconnaissance sorties without serious losses, even when virtually skirting German territory, and they were restricted to night operations only. At the time of the French collapse the only examples remaining in operational service were those which had been

deployed overseas, although a few were used subsequently by the Vichy French air force as target tugs.

Specification
Bloch M.B.131 RB.4
Type: four-seat reconnaissance-bomber
Powerplant: two 708-kW (950-hp) Gnome-Rhône 14N-10/11 radial piston engines
Performance: maximum speed 350 km/h (217 mph) at 3750 m (12,300 ft); cruising speed 270 km/h

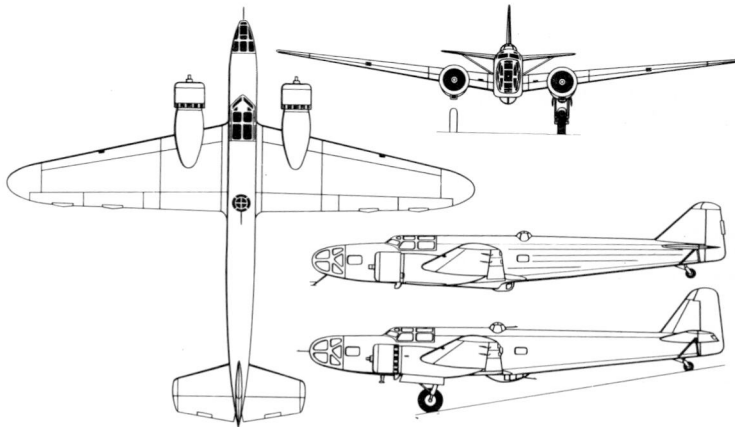

Bloch M.B.131 (upper side view: prototype)

(168 mph); service ceiling 7250 m (23,785 ft); range 1300 km (808 miles)
Weights: empty 4690 kg (10,340 lb); maximum take-off 8600 kg (18,960 lb)
Dimensions: span 20.3 m (66 ft 7¼ in); length 17.85 m (58 ft 6¾ in); height 4.1 m (13 ft 5½ in); wing area 54 m² (581.25 sq ft)
Armament: three 7.5-mm (0.295-in) machine-guns (one each in nose, dorsal turret and ventral cupola), plus up to 800 kg (1,764 lb) of bombs

Bloch M.B.151 and M.B.152
to
Bloch M.B.174

Bloch MB.151 and MB.152

In July 1934 Avions Marcel Bloch was a contender in a design competition which resulted from a French air ministry specification for a new fighter. Submissions were received also from Dewoitine, Loire, Morane-Saulnier and Nieuport, with Morane-Saulnier eventually selected as the winner. So far as Bloch was concerned, this was no close-drawn decision with its design team chewing its finger nails because it had been beaten to the pylon by the thickness of the paint skin on the propeller. True, it was biting its finger nails; but this was probably because its **Bloch M.B.150.01** prototype could not be induced to part company with the security of mother earth.

Nothing further happened for about nine months until, in early 1937, it was decided to force the 'ugly duckling' into the air. This was achieved in October 1937 after the provision of a strengthened wing of greater area, revised landing gear, and installation of a 701-kW (940-hp) Gnome-Rhône 14No radial engine with a three-blade constant-speed propeller. Handed over to the Centre d'Essais du Matériel Aérien (CEMA) for service trials, its performance proved sufficiently interesting to warrant further development. This brought, at the very beginning of 1938, a small increase in wing span and installation of a Gnome-Rhône 14N-7 engine. When trials were completed in the late spring of 1938, SNCASO was awarded an order for a pre-production batch of 25 of these aircraft.

Preparatory work before initiation of construction of the aircraft, in a new SNCASO factory, brought realisation that design of the M.B.150.01 was totally unsuited for mass production. The only solution was another redesign, during which wing area was reduced and the Gnome-Rhône 14N-11 engine selected for installation. It was in this form that a new prototype, redesignated **M.B.151.01**, flew for the first time on 18 August 1938. Construction of the balance of the pre-production order had already started by then, but despite the growing urgency of the situation only four of these aircraft had been delivered by April 1939.

Simultaneously, SNCASO's design team had been working on an improved version, but the only significant difference between this and the M.B.151.01 lay in the installation of a 768-kW (1,030-hp) Gnome-Rhône 14N-21 engine. First flown in December 1938 the new prototype, designated **M.B.152.01**, was provided with the slightly more powerful Gnome-Rhône 14N-25 before being handed over to the CEMA for flight testing in February 1939. The improved performance of this version created positive reaction, with a firm order being placed for 400 production aircraft, of which 340 were to be **M.B.152**s, the balance the earlier **M.B.151**s.

Unfortunately, equally positive action did not materialise on the production line, and by the out-break of World War II in September 1939 a combined total of 120 M.B.151 and M.B.152s had been delivered. Even more unfortunately, not one of these could be used in action, for all were without gunsights: 95 of them could not be used at all, for they had been delivered without propellers. This was the moment when pressure of circumstances should have eliminated all petty difficulties, but even by the end of November, at which time 358 had been delivered, 157 were still without propellers and there were serious problems with engine over-heating which needed attention.

Despite the problems, the Armée de l'Air did everything possible to speed introduction of what was potentially a valuable addition to its inventory. An experimental squadron was formed in September 1939, and initial deliveries to the fighter groupes began in the following month. Initial unit to convert to the type was Groupe de Chasse I/1, and by the end of 1939 newly equipped groupes included II/1 and II/10, III/9 and III/10, and the French navy's Escadrille AC-3. All were to discover that their M.B.151s and M.B.152s possessed the desirable attributes of a combat aircraft, and it was tragic that indifference and political intrigue forced so many courageous pilots of the Armée de l'Air to lose their lives in obsolete aircraft, instead of being able to contest the Luftwaffe on more equal terms with fighters such as the M.B.152.

When the German armoured Divisions swept through France in May 1940, Groupes I/8, II/8 and II/9 had also been equipped with these fighters and, just before this, nine M.B.151s had been supplied to the Greek air force. After the collapse of France and conclusion of the Franco-German Armistice, six groupes of the Vichy French air force retained M.B.151 and M.B.152 aircraft, namely I/1 and I/8; II/1, II/8 and II/9; and III/9, and when SNCASO production ended at the same time a total of more than 600 had been built. When, subsequently, three of these *groupes* were re-equipped with Dewoitine fighters, the M.B.151s and M.B.152s were handed over to the Romanian air force.

The only variant comprised one **M.B.153.01** prototype, an M.B.152 taken from the production line and re-engined with a 783-kW (1,050-hp) Pratt & Whitney R-1830-SC3-G Twin Wasp engine.

Bloch M.B.152 of the l' Escadrille, Groupe de Chasse I/1, based at Chantilly-les-Aigles (France) in May 1940.

Bloch M.B.152 of the 3e Escadrille, Group de Chasse II/9, based at Marseilles-Marignane (France) in May 1940.

Bloch M.B.152 (late series)

Specification
Bloch M.B.152
Type: single-seat fighter
Powerplant: one 805-kW (1,080-hp) Gnome-Rhône 14N-25, or 820-kW (1,100-hp) 14N-49 radial piston engine
Performance: maximum speed 515 km/h (320 mph) at 4000 m (13,125 ft); maximum cruising speed 450 km/h (280 mph); service ceiling 10000 m (32,810 ft); range 600 km (373 miles)
Weights: empty 2020 kg (4,453 lb); maximum take-off 2680 kg (5,908 lb)
Dimensions: span 10.55 m (34 ft 7¼ in); length 9.1 m (29 ft 10¼ in); height 3.95 m (12 ft 11½ in); wing area 15 m² (161.46 sq ft)
Armament: four 7.5-mm (0.295-in) machine-guns, or two 7.5-mm (0.295-in) guns and two 20-mm cannon

Bloch M.B.155

With production of the M.B.151 and M.B.152 in progress, SNCASO began the development of an improved version of this fighter, for both company and CEMA testing of the M.B.152 had left little doubt that the basic design had considerable potential. The aim was that of most design teams who sought to improve an existing fighter, namely to increase its speed, manoeuvrability and range.

Once again pressure of circumstance was to prevent any really significant improvement except in range, for the aim was to utilise most of the jigs and tooling of the M.B.152 so that production could begin without extensive delays, a factor of some importance in late 1939. A major problem, however, was how to provide additional internal fuel capacity, and this could only be achieved by extensive fuselage redesign to move the cockpit aft. In other respects the configuration remained unchanged, being that of a cantilever low-wing monoplane with conventional, but strut-braced, tail unit, and retractable tailwheel-type landing gear.

Other changes introduced in the new prototype (a converted M.B.152), included increased wing chord, and an improved lower-drag engine cowling. Following successful flight tests in early 1940, the type was put into production at the beginning of May under the designation **M.B.155**. Additional improvements on the production aircraft, which retained the Gnome-Rhône 14N-49 engine that powered many of the M.B.152s, included additional armour and an armoured windscreen. When production was initiated, time was already running out for the French nation, and the capitulation of 25 June came before any of the new fighters had been delivered. Subsequently, after ratification of the Franco-German Armistice, the M.B.155s (of which about 20 remained on the production line at Châteauroux-Déols) were completed and delivered to the Vichy French air force. When, in November 1942, the Vichy French forces were disbanded, all remaining examples of these aircraft were confiscated by the Germans.

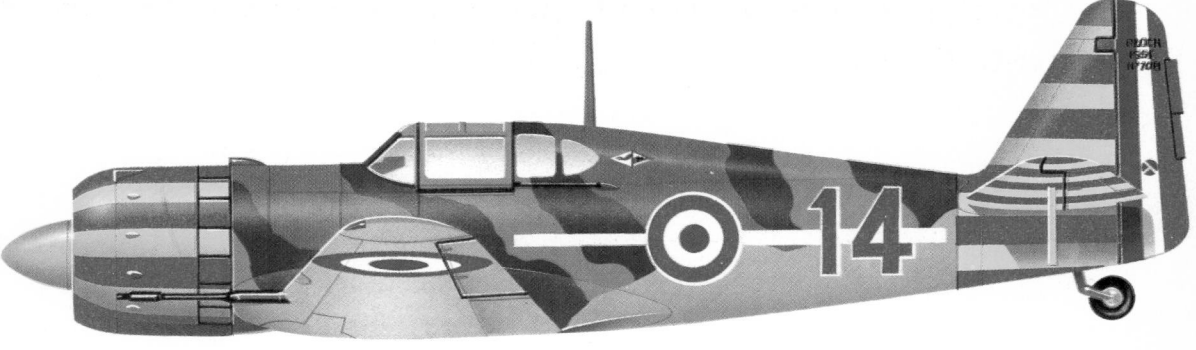

Bloch M.B.155 of the commander of Groupe de Chasse II/8, Vichy French air force, based at Marignane, France, July 1940.

Specification
Type: single-seat fighter
Powerplant: one 820-kW (1,100-hp) Gnome-Rhône 14N-49 radial piston engine
Performance: maximum speed 520 km/h (323 mph) at 5500 m (18,040 ft); service ceiling 10000 m (32,810 ft); range 1050 km (652 miles)
Weights: empty 2100 kg (4,630 lb); maximum take-off 2900 kg (6,393 lb)
Dimensions: span 10.55 m (34 ft 7¼ in); length 9.05 m (29 ft 8¼ in); height 3.95 m (12 ft 11½ in); wing area 17.3 m² (186.22 sq ft)
Armament: two 20-mm cannon and two or four 7.5-mm (0.295-in) machine-guns, or six 7.5-mm (0.295-in) machine-guns

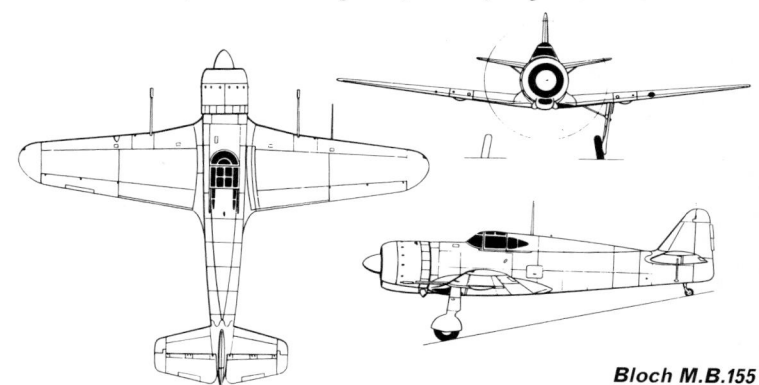

Bloch M.B.155

Bloch M.B.157

Representing the last of the fighter aircraft to be evolved from the M.B.150, which had declined to become airborne in 1936, the **Bloch M.B.157** resulted from an attempt to unite the airframe of the M.B.152 with a new and far more powerful Gnome-Rhône 14R, an air-cooled radial engine similar to those which powered the earlier Bloch fighters, but with a power output of 1186 kW (1,590 hp) for take-off, and having a supercharger that could provide a rating of 1268 kW (1,700 hp) at 8000 m (26,245 ft).

Such power suggested exciting possibilities for a high-altitude interceptor, but the increased size and weight of this engine brought realisation that it would not be practical to install it in the existing M.B.152 airframe. The conclusion that the full potential of the Gnome-Rhône 14R would be lost by attempting an adaptation of the airframe led to a decision to design a new fighter which would retain the same basic structural techniques.

Having postulated such a design philosophy, it was possible to formulate the details of the M.B.157 very rapidly, for the basic design already existed. The result of this was that within just over six months of design initiation, the components of the prototype were ready for

assembly but, once again, it was too late for France. With German forces closing in on Paris, the M.B.157 components were loaded to be taken to a place of security but, en route, this vehicle was intercepted by the Germans and ordered to proceed to an SNCASO establishment within the occupied zone.

Finally, in 1942, the M.B.157 was assembled and test flown under German supervision, demonstrating superb performance before being flown to Orly where the powerplant was removed for wind-tunnel testing. This was the most interesting feature so far as the Germans were concerned, and after tests had been completed the engine was transported to Germany. SNCASO's airframe, which had demonstrated in conjunction with Gnome-Rhône 14R engine a degree of performance that was not to be attained elsewhere until later in the war, was destroyed during an Allied air raid.

Specification
Type: single-seat fighter
Powerplant: one 1186-kW (1,580-hp) Gnome-Rhône 14R-4 radial piston engine
Performance: maximum speed 710 km/h (441 mph) at 7850 m (25,755 ft); cruising speed 400 km/h (248 mph); range 1095 km (680 miles)

Weights: empty 2390 kg (5,269 lb); maximum take-off 3250 kg (7,165 lb)
Dimensions: span 10.70 m (35 ft 1¼ in); length 9.7 m (31 ft 9¾ in); height 3.2 m (10 ft 6 in); wing area 19.4 m² (208.82 sq ft)
Armament: (intended) two 20-mm cannon and four 7.5-mm (0.295-in) machine-guns

Potentially the best fighter produced by France in World War II, the Bloch M.B.157 prototype offered sparkling combat performance and great reliability. The prototype was extensively tested by the Luftwaffe after its capture by the advancing German ground forces in June 1940.

Bloch M.B.161 Languedoc and M.B.162

It may seem strange that with France situated conveniently to deploy long-range strategic bombers against virtually any European target, as well as against many other targets in Africa, the Armée de l'Air was not equipped with such aircraft at the outbreak of World War II. This was not due to any reluctance on the part of the French air force to operate such a type, but rather for the same reason that the United States Army Air Corps was not well equipped with Boeing B-17s at

that time. Quite simply stated, any allocation of funds could procure more small aircraft than large aircraft, and for some peculiar reason governments of that era seemed more interested in quantity, rather than smaller numbers of carefully selected aircraft of special potential.

Following absorption of Bloch into the nationalised aviation industry as a component of SNCASO in 1936, the design team which had been brought together by Avions Marcel Bloch was involved

with a derivative of the earlier but unused 12-passenger **Bloch M.B.160**. The resulting **Bloch M.B.161.01** prototype (F-ARTV) was flown for the first time during September 1939, and a satisfactory result of early tests brought an order from Air France: it was to be almost seven years before the first was delivered. This was due primarily to delaying tactics of the French industry, anxious to ensure that none of the 20 ordered by Germany in 1942 should be

delivered. Consequently, it was not until 17 September 1945 that the redesignated **SE.161.1** was flown for the first time. Its configuration was that of a cantilever mid-wing monoplane of all-metal construction, having a high-mounted tailplane with endplate fins and rudders, retractable tailwheel landing gear, and power provided by four 858-kW (1,150-hp) Gnome-Rhône 14N-44/45 radial engines in wing leading-edge nacelles. Standard accommodation was provided for a crew of four and 33 passengers, but in 1951 Air France converted some of its SE.161s to a high-density seating

After World War II the M.B.161 design was revived to produce the Sud Est SE 161 Languedoc civil transport, one of a number of such developments.

arrangement for a maximum of 44 passengers.

Bloch 161.1s, by then named **Languedoc**, entered regular service on Air France's Paris-Algiers route on 28 May 1946, and on the Paris-Oran-Casablanca and Paris-Marseilles routes in June and July respectively. By October most had been withdrawn because, in addition to problems with their landing gear, they were unsuitable for winter operation. When they re-entered service, from March 1947, they had acquired Pratt & Whitney R-1830 engines, de-icing equipment, cabin heating and other modifications. They had also acquired the changed designation **SE.161.P7**.

When production ended a total of 100 Languedocs had been built and, despite landing gear problems that persisted for

almost four years, they saw extensive service, not only with Air France but also with the French air force and navy. In addition, five were supplied to the Polish national airline Polskie Linie Lotinicze (LOT).

Another derivative of the Bloch 160 was identified initially as the **Bloch M.B.162**. This promised excellent long-range performance which, coupled with good load-carrying capability, seemed to offer potential as a strategic bomber.

Preliminary design was initiated, and a mock-up to full-scale was built and exhibited at the Salon de l'Aéronautique held in Paris during November 1938. Considerable interest was created by this 'large' bomber, only slightly smaller than the B-17, and because of this it was decided to build a prototype. This, unfortunately for France, was delayed because production priority had been given to the commercial M.B.161, with the result that construction of the bomber was held up until the spring of 1940. Even then, it was completed in a

remarkably short time for such a large project, flying for the first time on 1 June 1940. Of cantilever low-wing monoplane configuration, the **M.B.162 B.5** was of all-metal construction, had a tail-plane with marked dihedral and twin endplate fins and rudders, retractable tailwheel type landing gear, and two engines mounted in nacelles at the leading-edge of each wing.

Flown from Villacoublay to Bordeaux-Mérignac, the M.B.162 was captured by the Germans. Its test programme was completed during 1942 under the supervision of the German Focke-Wulf company, subsequently entering service with the Luftwaffe for long-range clandestine operations.

Specification
Type: five-seat long-range strategic bomber
Powerplant: four 820-kW (1,100-hp) Gnome-Rhône 14N-48/49 radial piston engines
Performance: maximum speed

Converted from the M.B.162, the Bloch M.B.162 heavy bomber prototype arrived too late to do France any good in World War II. Had the type arrived sooner, production examples with heavy offensive and defensive armament might have proved a useful adjunct to French forces.

550 km/h (242 mph) at 5500 m (18,045 ft); range with 1600 kg (3,527 lb) of bombs 2400 km (1,491 miles)
Weights: empty 11865 kg (26,158 lb); maximum take-off 19000 kg (41,888 lb)
Dimensions: span 28.1 m (92 ft 2¼ in); length 21.9 m (71 ft 10¼ in); height 3.75 m (12 ft 3½ in); wing area 109 m² (1,173.27 sq ft)
Armament: one 7.5-mm (0.295-in) machine-gun in nose, one 20-mm cannon in dorsal position, and one 20-mm cannon and one 7.5-mm (0.295-in) gun in ventral position, plus up to 3600 kg (7,937 lb) of bombs

Bloch M.B.174

In late 1936 SNCASO initiated the design of a two/three-seat multi-role bomber which it identified as the **Bloch M.B.170**, and the **M.B.170.01** prototype flew for the first time on 15 February 1938. This was of cantilever low-wing monoplane configuration, and the wing and tail-plane both had marked dihedral, the latter carrying twin end plate fins and rudders. Landing gear was of the retractable tailwheel type, and the powerplant comprised two 708-kW (950-hp) Gnome-Rhône 14N-6/7 radial engines. The prototype featured an unusual cupola mounted beneath the fuselage, and intended to house a camera for use in the reconnaissance role, or alternatively to provide an additional position for a defensive gun. When the M.B.170.01 prototype was damaged as the result of a crash-landing, a second rather different **M.B.170.02** prototype continued the flight test programme. This was configured to serve essentially as a high-speed bomber: the under-fuselage cupola was deleted, the undersurface of the forward fuselage was extensively glazed, and the tail unit was provided with fins and rudders of increased area.

While this programme had been in progress, the design team had evolved a series of variants for differing roles, and allocated the identifications M.B.171, M.B.172, M.B.173 and M.B.174. It was this last proposal which aroused the interests of the French air ministry, leading

to construction of the **M.B.174.01** prototype, which flew for the first time on 5 January 1939. This differed yet again, with the crew accommodation and glazed canopy moved further aft, the fuselage nose extensively glazed, and powerplant comprising two 1,030-hp (768-kW) Gnome-Rhône 14N-20/21 engines. Six pre-production examples of this version were ordered before flight testing began, but there was no need for recriminations from the French Air Ministry, as the test programme proceeded smoothly, without any major problems. In consequence an order for an additional 50 production aircraft was placed.

The pre-production and production aircraft all had more powerful Gnome-Rhône 14N-48/49 engines, but early testing of the first pre-production aircraft showed that the cooling of these engines was only marginal, leading to a reduction in the diameter of the propeller spinners to allow an increased air-flow to the engine cylinders. Just before the first examples were delivered to units, it was decided to modify the defensive armament as a result of early combat experience with other types, and it was not until mid-March 1940 that the first

M.B.174 A.3 production aircraft were delivered to reconnaissance Groupe II/33, and used operationally for the first time on 29 March 1940.

Groupes I/33, I/52, and II/36 each received examples during the following month, and early operational experience with these aircraft proved them to be an excellent type for deployment in a reconnaissance role, sufficiently fast and manoeuvrable at altitude to be able to elude Luftwaffe interceptors. When the collapse of France was imminent, many of the M.B.174s in use with squadrons were destroyed to prevent their capture, but despite this a number remained in service with the Vichy French air force in Tunisia until after VE-Day. Additionally, isolated examples were used for development projects for two or three years after the war's end.

Specification
Type: three-seat reconnaissance/light bomber aircraft
Powerplant: two 820-kW (1,100-hp) Gnome-Rhône 14N-48/49 radial piston engine

Performance: maximum speed 530 km/h (329 mph) at 5200 m (17,060 ft); cruising speed 400 km/h (248 mph); service ceiling 11000 m (36,090 ft); range with 400 kg (882 lb) bombload 1290 km (802 miles); maximum range with internal fuel 1650 km (1,025 miles)
Weights: empty 5600 kg (12,346 lb); maximum take-off 7160 kg (15,784 lb)
Dimensions: span 17.90 m (58 ft 8¾ in); length 12.25 m (40 ft 2¼ in); height 3.55 m (11 ft 7¾ in); wing area 38.00 m² (409.03 sq ft)
Armament: two forward-firing 7.5-mm (0.295-in) machine-guns, two 7.5-mm (0.295) guns in dorsal position, and three 7.5-mm (0.295-in) guns on aft-firing ventral wobble mounts, plus a maximum bombload of 400 kg (882 lb)

Bloch M.B. 174 of Groupe de Reconnaissance II/33. The type served with this unit during the Battle of France on reconnaissance duties, some later seeing service in Tunisa with Vichy forces.

Bloch M.B.200
to
Blohm und Voss BV 142

Bloch M.B.200

When, in 1932, the French air ministry circulated its specification for a five-seat night bomber, there was so little demand for new military aircraft that no fewer than eight proposals were received from five companies. This was indicative of the anxiety to acquire manufacturing contracts, and both Bloch and Farman were successful on this occasion, although the resulting production aircraft were completed in differing bomber categories.

That of Bloch was finalised as a four-seat bomber, very similar in appearance and configuration to the contemporary Bristol Bombay and Handley Page Harrow built in the UK. A cantilever high-wing monoplane of all-metal construction, and with non-retractable tail-wheel type landing gear, the prototype **Bloch M.B.200.01** had a powerplant comprising two 567-kW (760-hp) Gnome-Rhône 14Krsd radial engines, and was first flown in July 1933. Subsequent flight testing resulted in an initial order for 25 aircraft, placed on 1 January 1934, despite the fact that the maximum speed of the prototype was some 18 per

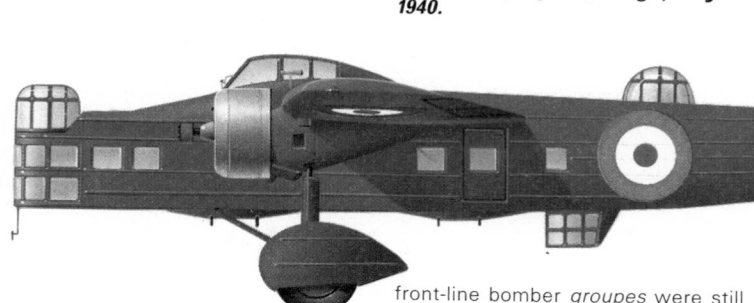

Bloch M.B.200 No. 77 of Section de Remorquage d'Otange, May 1940.

cent below estimate.

When the production **M.B.200** began to enter service towards the end of the year, it was found to be both reliable and viceless. The fact that it was slow, even though production aircraft had more powerful Gnome-Rhône engines, was not then terribly important, and 208 were eventually supplied to the Armée de l'Air, built by Bloch (4), Breguet (19), Hanriot (45), Loire (19), Potez (111) and SNCASO (10).

At the beginning of World War II seven front-line bomber *groupes* were still equipped with these obsolete aircraft, but at the time of the German offensive all had been relegated to a training role. The type had also been built under licence in Czechoslovakia by Aero and Avia, and these were seized by the Germans, serving as crew trainers and for general duties, as were those which had been captured in France. Many were passed on to German satellites.

Specification
Bloch M.B.200
Type: four-seat medium bomber

Powerplant: two 649-kW (870-hp) Gnome-Rhône 14Kirs/Kjrs radial piston engines
Performance: maximum speed 285 km/h (177 mph) at 4300 m (14,110 ft); service ceiling 8000 m (26,250 ft); range 1000 km (621 miles)
Weights: empty 4463 kg (9,840 lb); maximum take-off 7280 kg (16,049 lb)
Dimensions: span 22.45 m (73 ft 8 in); length 16 m (52 ft 6 in); height 3.9 m (12 ft 9½ in); wing area 67m² (721.18 sq ft)
Armament: three 7.5-mm (0.295-in) machine-guns (one each in nose, dorsal and ventral positions), plus up to 1200 kg (2,646 lb) of bombs

Bloch M.B.220

An all-metal cantilever low-wing monoplane, powered by two Gnome-Rhône radial engines and fitted with retractable landing gear, the **Bloch M.B.220** was an equivalent of the Douglas DC-2/DC-3/Dakota series, but was produced in only limited quantities. The prototype flew in December 1935, followed by 16 production aircraft. Normal crew comprised four, and there was comfortable accommodation for 16 passengers, with eight seats on each side of a central cabin aisle.

By mid-1938 10 M.B.220s had been delivered, and the type was utilised fully on Air France's European routes. The first service by the type on the Paris-London route was flown by the fifth aircraft (*Aunis*, F-AOHE) on 27 March 1938, with the scheduled time for the flight cut to 1 hour 15 minutes.

During World War II most M.B.220s were mobilised initially for service with

The Bloch M.B.220 transport was a later contemporary of the Douglas DC-3, but failed to offer its operators the same standard of operating economics and passenger appeal. The type nevertheless did well in the relatively parochial civil market prevalent in Europe before World War II.

Armée de l'Air military transport units. Later, examples of the M.B.220 operated under German, Free French and Vichy French colours in Europe, North Africa and the Middle East. At least five examples survived the war, being modified as **M.B.221**s with Wright Cyclone R-1820-97 engines. They flew short-range Air France European routes, but by 1949 four had been sold off to SANA (Société Auxiliaire de Navigation Aérienne), and within about a year all had been withdrawn from service.

Specification

Bloch M.B.220
Type: passenger transport aircraft
Powerplant: two 735-kW (985-hp) Gnome-Rhône 14N-16/17 piston engines
Performance: maximum speed 330 km/h (205 mph); economic cruising speed 280 km/h (174 mph); service

ceiling 7000 m (22,965 ft); range 1400 km (870 miles)
Weights: empty equipped 6807 kg (15,007 lb); maximum take-off 9500 kg (20,944 lb)
Dimensions: span 22.82 m (74 ft 10½ in); length 19.25 m (63 ft 1¾ in); wing area 75 m² (807.32 sq ft)

Blohm und Voss BV 40

Born of the necessity both to conserve strategic materials and to provide a gun platform of minimal frontal area, Dr Ing. Richard Vogt's **Blohm und Voss BV 40** was one of several designs submitted to the Reichsluftfahrtministerium in 1943. Experience had shown that attacks on the USAAF daylight bomber formations had resulted in mounting casualties, and the extensive frontal area of the Focke-Wulf Fw 190's radial engine, for example, presenting a very acceptable target for the Boeing B-17 gunners. The elimination of the engine, it was argued, would make an attacking fighter almost invisible from a head-on position, certainly until it was close enough to open fire.

The result, therefore, was a glider

fighter, armed with two 30-mm cannon, one in each wing root. The aircraft incorporated a heavily-armoured cockpit section; a metal centre fuselage; and wooden rear fuselage, wings and tail surfaces. The twin-wheel landing gear was jettisoned on take-off, a semi-re-

An interesting example of the strange lengths to which the Germans were compelled in their search for an effective counter to the USAAF's bomber fleets, the Blohm und Voss BV 40 glider fighter offered low frontal area and good pilot protection coupled with heavy gun armament. Illustrated is the BV 40 V1 first prototype.

tractable skid being provided for landing. The structure was comparatively simple, facilitating manufacture by craftsmen inexperienced in aircraft construction, and a further advantage was an apparent requirement for little more than glider training for the pilot.

The BV 40 was to be towed to altitude

by a Messerschmitt Bf 109G, singly or in pairs, to a position above and ahead of the approaching bomber stream which would be attacked in a head-on 20° dive, this initial cannon attack being followed by a secondary attack with a small explosive device suspended from the BV 40 on a wire cable. The use of the latter

Nineteen prototypes and 200 production BV 40s were ordered, and the first example made its maiden flight behind a Messerschmitt Bf 110 at the end of May 1944. Six prototypes took part in the test programme, which was almost complete when the project was abandoned in the autumn of 1944.

Specification
Blohm und Voss BV 40
Type: single-seat glider fighter
Powerplant: none
Performance: maximum diving speed 900 km/h (559 mph); maximum speed of Bf 109G towing one BV 40 555 km/h (344 mph) at 6000 m (19,685 ft)
Weights: empty 835 kg (1,841 lb);

maximum take-off about 950 kg (2,094 lb)
Dimensions: span 7.9 m (25 ft 11 in); length 5.7 m (18 ft 8½ in); height 1.63 m (5 ft 4½ in); wing area 8.7 m² (93.65 sq ft)
Armament: two 30-mm MK 108 cannon

Blohm und Voss BV 138

The first flying-boat design to be built by Hamburger Flugzeugbau GmbH, under the direction of chief engineer Dr Ing. Richard Vogt, was the **Ha 138**, which had been preceded by the **Ha 135** two-seat biplane, **Ha 136** single-seat mono-plane and **Ha 137** dive-bomber. Three prototypes of the original twin-engined design were each to have been powered by a different manufacturer's 746-kW (1,000-hp) engine for comparative evaluation, but development delays necessitated re-design to accept three 485-kW (650-hp) Junkers Jumo 205C engines. Almost two years after the completion of the mock-up, the first prototype (**Ha 138 V1**) took off on its maiden flight, the date being 15 July 1937. A second prototype (**Ha 138 V2**), with a modified hull design, joined the test programme at the Travemünde centre in November, but the aircraft were quickly proved to be un-stable, both hydrodynamically and aero-dynamically. Modifications to the vertical tail surfaces failed to improve the performance adequately and radical re-design was undertaken. The result was the **BV 138A**, adopting the designation system of the Blohm und Voss parent company. The hull was much enlarged, its planing surfaces were improved, and the revised tail surfaces were carried by more substantial booms. The prototype was followed by five more pre-series BV 138A aircraft, preceding production for the reconnaissance units of the Luftwaffe, with which it first saw action during the Norwegian campaign of 1940.

Blohm und Voss BV 138C-1 of 2/KüFlGr. 406, based in northern Norway in March 1942.

Blohm und Voss BV 138 MS of 6./MSGr.1, based at Grossenbrode in 1944-5.

Variants

BV 138A-1: the initial production version, first flown in April 1940, and built in small numbers; armament comprised one 20-mm cannon in the bow turret and two 7.92-mm (0.31-in) MG 15 machine-guns, one in each of two open positions, which were located behind the centre engine nacelle and at the rear of the hull (25 built)
BV 138B-1: structurally strengthened version developed following modification of the fourth pre-series BV 138A into the **BV 138B-0**; powered by three 656-kW (880-hp) Jumo 205D

engines and with revised armament which consisted of one 20-mm MG 151 cannon in the bow turret, and one in the rear hull position; beneath the starboard wing root a bombload of 150 kg (331 lb) could be carried (19 built)
BV 138C-1: further strengthening led to the introduction of this version (in March 1941) powered by the Jumo 205D engine; the centre engine was fitted with a four-blade propeller, the outer engines retaining three-blade units, albeit with broader blades; a 13-mm (0.51-in) MG 131 machine-gun was added, in the position behind the centre engine nacelle (227 BV 138C-1s were built out of total production of

279 BV 138s completed between 1938 and 1943).
BV 138 MS: mine-sweeping version converted from BV 138B-0 pre-production aircraft; armament deleted and degaussing loop of dural and field-generating equipment installed.

Specification
Blohm und Voss BV 138
Type: reconnaissance flying-boat
Powerplant: three 656-kW (880-hp) Junkers Jumo 105D inline piston engines
Performance: maximum speed 275 km/h (171 mph) at sea level; cruising speed 235 km/h (146 mph); service

ceiling 5000 m (16,405 ft); maximum range 5000 km (3,107 miles)
Weights: empty 8100 kg (17,857 lb); maximum take-off 14700 kg (32,408 lb)
Dimensions: span 27 m (88 ft 7 in); length 19.9 m (65 ft 3½ in); height 6.6 m (21 ft 8 in); wing area 112 m² (1,204.6 sq ft)
Armament: one 20-mm MG 151 cannon in the bow turret, one similar cannon in the rear hull position and one 13-mm (0.51-in) MG 131 machine-gun in the position at the rear of the centre engine nacelle, plus three 50-kg (110-lb) bombs under starboard wing root, or (BV 138C-1/U1) six 50-kg (110-lb) bombs or four 150-kg (331-lb) depth-charges

Blohm und Voss BV 139

For its newly-established transatlantic postal service, Lufthansa in 1935 issued a specification for a new marine aircraft. This was required to take off and land in rough water, to be suitable for catapult-launching, and to be capable of carrying a 500-kg (1,102-lb) minimum payload for at least 5000 km (3,107 miles) at a cruising speed of 250 km/h (155 mph). The Hamburger Flugzeugbau subsidiary of Blohm und Voss evolved a number of design studies, including the **P.15** project which later became the subject of an order for three prototypes. The selected powerplant was the specially-developed Junkers Jumo 205 diesel, offering a specific fuel consumption almost 25 per cent lower than comparable petrol engines.

The first prototype **Ha 139** made its maiden flight in the autumn of 1936, and by March 1937 the first two aircraft had been delivered to Lufthansa, to operate between Horta, in the Azores, and New York. During the period August-November 1937 they made seven crossings, operating in conjunction with the depot ships *Friesenland* and *Schwabenland*,

The Blohm und Voss Ha 139 was designed as a mailplane for Lufthansa's routes across the Atlantic, and was also stressed for catapult launches. Only three were built, and all served during World War II, two of them as transports and the V3 as a mine-sweeper.

both of which were equipped with cata-pults. Average speeds of 231 km/h (144 mph) and 250 km/h (155 mph) were achieved on east-west and west-east crossings respectively. Operations were suspended in November to facilitate modification, enlarged vertical tail sur-faces being fitted to improve directional stability, and to overcome cooling prob-lems underwing radiators were provided

for all four engines. The slightly enlarged and heavier third aircraft, designated **Ha 139B**, joined the programme in mid-1938 and completed 13 crossings on the Horta-New York route between 21 July and 19 October 1938. During that year the three Ha 139s amassed 597 flying hours, and the shortest recorded crossing times were 13 hours 40 minutes east-west and 11 hours 53 minutes west-east. The aircraft were then switched to the South Atlantic route, linking Bathurst and Natal/Recife.

Late in 1939 the Ha 139s and their crews were absorbed into the Luftwaffe, the third prototype being modified for reconnaissance duties. A lengthened glazed nose was fitted to accommodate an observer, and to compensate for this the vertical tail surfaces were again enlarged. Designated **Ha 139V3/U1**, this machine was subsequently modified for the mine-sweeping role, being equipped with a degaussing loop, energised by field-generating equipment located in the fuselage,

under the revised designation **Ha 139B/MS**. All three Ha 139s took part in the 1940 Norwegian campaign, the first two being used as troop transports.

Specification
Blohm und Voss BV 139
Type: long-range mail, mine-sweeping and reconnaissance floatplane
Powerplant: four 447-kW (600-hp) Junkers Jumo 205C diesel engines
Performance: maximum speed 315 km/h (196 mph); cruising speed

260 km/h (162 mph); service ceiling 3500 m (11,485 ft); maximum range 5300 km (3,293 miles)
Weights: empty 10360 kg (22,840 lb); maximum take-off 17500 kg (38,581 lb)
Dimensions: span 27 m (88 ft 7 in); length 19.5 m (63 ft 11¾ in); height 4.8 m (15 ft 9 in); wing area 117 m² (1,259.42 sq ft)
Armament: (Ha 139 V3/U1) four 7.92-mm (0.31-in) MG 17 machine-guns, mounted one each in nose, dorsal and twin beam positions

Blohm und Voss BV 141

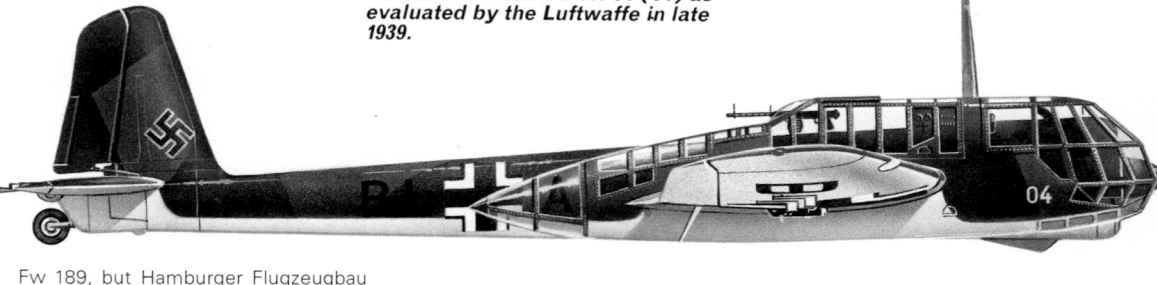

Blohm und Voss BV 141-04 (V7) as evaluated by the Luftwaffe in late 1939.

In 1937 the Reichsluftfahrtministerium issued a specification for a single-engined three-seat short-range reconnaissance and observation aircraft, the emphasis being placed on good all-round visibility. The requirement drew responses from Arado and Focke Wulf, in addition to the novel approach of Hamburger Flugzeugbau's Dr. Ing. Richard Vogt. This unorthodox design featured an asymmetric layout, the 645-kW (865-hp) B.M.W. 132N radial engine being installed at the forward end of a port-side tail boom, with the extensively-glazed crew nacelle mounted to starboard. Official preference was for the Focke Wulf

The BV 141 was an extremely unorthodox reconnaissance/army co-operation aircraft, its asymmetric configuration being designed to provide the crew with first-class fields of vision.

Fw 189, but Hamburger Flugzeugbau built a private-venture **BV 141** prototype which flew on 25 February 1938. Two further prototypes appeared in the autumn of 1938, both slightly larger than the first. The third aircraft, with wider-track landing gear, was armed with two fixed forward-firing 7.92-mm (0.31-in) MG 17 machine-guns, plus two MG 15s of similar calibre firing to the rear. It was also able to carry a camera and racks for

four 50-kg (110-lb) bombs, and was sufficiently successful in initial trials to extract from the RLM an order for five examples of the pre-production **BV 141A**.

Evaluation at the Erprobungstelle Rechlin was completed satisfactorily, but plans for production were terminated in April 1940 as the type was considered to be under-powered. Although five examples of a redesigned, strengthened and more powerful **BV 141B** were ordered, the second of which undertook service trials with the Luftwaffe's Aufklärungsschule 1 in the autumn of 1941, development was delayed and finally discontinued in 1943.

Variants

BV 141A: five pre-production aircraft with wing increased in span (15.45 m/50 ft 8¼ in) and area (42.86 m²/461.33 sq ft), and powered by a 746-kW (1,000-hp) B.M.W.-Bramo 323 radial engine
BV 141B: five pre-production aircraft, extensively redesigned; externally evident changes included the

introduction of equi-taper outer wing panels and asymmetric horizontal tail surfaces to improve the field of fire from the rear gun position in the glazed nacelle cone

Specification
BV 141B
Type: short-range reconnaissance and observation aircraft
Powerplant: one 1163-kW (1,560-hp) B.M.W. 801A radial piston engine
Performance: maximum speed 370 km/h (230 mph) at sea level; service ceiling 10000 m (32,810 ft); range 1200 km (746 miles)
Weights: empty 4700 kg (10,362 lb); maximum take-off 5700 kg (12,566 lb)
Dimensions: span 17.46 m (57 ft 3½ in); length 13.95 m (45 ft 9¼ in); height 3.6 m (11 ft 9¾ in); wing area 53 m² (570.51 sq ft)
Armament: two fixed forward-firing 7.92-mm (0.31-in) MG 17 machine-guns and two aft-firing flexibly-mounted 7.92-mm (0.31-in) MG 15 machine-guns, plus provision for four 50-kg (110-lb) bombs

Blohm und Voss BV 142

Designed for transatlantic mail services, and originally designated **Ha 142**, the **Blohm und Voss BV 142** was a direct derivative of the **Ha 139** floatplane, incorporating maximum structural commonality with its forebear. Based on the third prototype Ha 139, the new aircraft retained the inverted gull wing, but the original engines were replaced by four B.M.W. 132H radials, the outboard nacelles being elongated to accept the rearward-retracting main legs of the landing gear. The twin tailwheel assembly was also retractable.

The prototype Ha 142 flew for the first time on 11 October 1938, followed closely by the second machine, which carried the Blohm und Voss designation BV 142. Two further BV 142s joined the test and evaluation programme, including trials by Lufthansa, but no great interest was shown, and by the time that World War II began, all four were back with the manufacturer. A decision was taken to convert the first two prototypes for military use in a long-range maritime patrol/reconnaissance role. Principle

changes included the addition of a lengthened glazed nose, similar to that of the Ha 139 V3/U1, and of armament in nose, dorsal and ventral positions. Delivered to the Luftwaffe in the closing months of 1940, the aircraft served with 2/Aufklärungsgruppe Oberbefehlshaber der Luftwaffe, attached to Luftflotte III headquarters in France. The unmodified third and fourth prototypes were used as transports during the Norwegian invasion campaign, but all had been withdrawn from Luftwaffe service by 1942.

Specification
BV 142
Type: long-range transport/maritime reconnaissance aircraft
Powerplant: four 656-kW (880-hp) B.M.W. 132H radial piston engines

Performance: maximum speed 375 km/h (233 mph) at sea level; cruising speed 325 km/h (202 mph); service ceiling 9000 m (29,525 ft); maximum range 3900 km (2,423 miles)
Weights: empty 11000 kg (24,251 lb); maximum take-off 16500 kg (36,376 lb)
Dimensions: span 29.53 m (96 ft 10½ in); length 20.45 m (67 ft 1 in); height 4.44 m (14 ft 6¾ in); wing area 130 m² (1,399.35 sq ft)
Armament: one 7.92-mm (0.31-in) MG 15 machine-gun each in the nose, twin beam positions and ventral cupola, and power-operated dorsal turret

Derived from the Ha 139 transatlantic floatplane, the Blohm und Voss Ha 142 was intended as a land-based mailplane. The V1 prototype was evaluated under the civil registration D-AHFB, but later seems to have been adapted as a long-range reconnaissance aircraft for use by 2/Aufklärungsstaffel Oberbefehlshaber der Luftwaffe.

Blohm und Voss BV 222 Viking
to
Boeing Model 80

Blohm und Voss BV 222 Viking

The largest flying-boat to achieve operational status during World War II, the **Blohm und Voss BV 222** was designed originally by Dr Ing. Richard Vogt and Herr R. Schubert (chief of aerodynamics and hydrodynamics), to meet a 1937 Lufthansa requirement for a long-range passenger transport. This was required to operate between Berlin and New York in 20 hours with 16 passengers, or to accommodate up to 24 passengers on shorter routes.

Three aircraft, each powered by six 746-kW (1,000-hp) B.M.W.-Bramo Fafnir 323R radials, were ordered in September 1937, and work on the first began in January 1938. There were a number of notable features incorporated in the design, including an extensive unobstructed floor area, made possible by a beam of almost 3.05 m (10 ft) and an absence of intermediate bulkheads above floor level. The wing incorporated a tubular main spar that served also to contain fuel and oil tanks (a feature of Vogt designs), and the outboard stabilising floats each split into halves to retract sideways into the wing.

On 7 September 1940 Flugkapitän Helmut Rodig made the first flight with the prototype, which clearly had military potential. Indeed, soon afterwards it was fitted with enlarged doors for transport duties with the Luftwaffe, undertaking its first sortie on 10 July 1941. After

Blohm und Voss BV 222A-O (V5) of LTS 222, Petsamo, Finland, March 1943.

initial service in Norway it was transferred to the Mediterranean theatre, being used to carry supplies for German forces in North Africa.

Armament was introduced with the second and third prototypes, flown on 7 August and 28 November 1941 respectively. The third carried only a 7.92-mm (0.31-in) MG 81 machine-gun in the bow, but the second was fitted additionally with a similar weapon in each of four waist positions and in two upper turrets; plus a pair of 13-mm (0.51-in) MG 131 guns in two gondolas located beneath the centre section. The first prototype was retrospectively equipped with similar bow and waist armament, and with an MG 131 in each of the upper turrets. On 10 May 1942 it became the first BV 222 to be delivered to Luft-Transport-staffel (See) 222. It was joined by the

second prototype in August of that year, after the aircraft had been provided with a modified planing bottom to the hull to improve its hydro-dynamic qualities. This had been developed following trials at Erprobungstelle Travemünde.

At the end of 1942, a decision was taken to modify the BV 222 for a maritime reconnaissance role, for service with a redesignated Aufklärungsstaffel (See) 222 and, later, with 1.(Fern/See-Aufklärungsgruppe 129 at Biscarosse in France. For this task four aircraft of those already delivered to the Luftwaffe were modified to carry FuG 200 Hohentwiel search radar, plus revised armament which comprised three power-operated dorsal turrets, and two at quarter-span positions above the wings. Examples of the **BV 222C** production series also saw service in Norway. When the war ended, an example captured at Trondheim was flown to RAF Calshot, and then to the Marine Aircraft Experimental Establishment, Felixstowe, for evaluation; it later passed to No.201 Squadron.

Variants
BV 222A: additional prototypes in Luftwaffe service, carrying freight or up to 76 equipped troops (4 built)

The prototype BV 222 was rolled out in civil markings, and made its first flight in September 1940. It was later camouflaged and used by the Luftwaffe on transport tasks.

BV 222B: proposed version with Junkers Jumo 208 engines
BV 222C: production standard aircraft, five of which were completed and flown; the seventh prototype was the development aircraft, first flown on 1 April 1943 and powered by six 731-kW (980-hp) Junkers Jumo 207C diesel engines; additional machine-guns were fitted in the nose and the sides of the hull

Specification
BV 222C
Type: long-range transport/maritime reconnaissance and patrol aircraft
Powerplant: six 746-kW (1,000-hp) Junkers Jumo 207C inline diesel engines
Performance: maximum speed 390 km/h (242 mph) at 5000 m (16,405 ft); cruising speed 345 km/h (214 mph) at 5550 m (18,210 ft); service ceiling 7300 m (23,950 ft); range 6095 km (3,787 miles)
Weights: empty 30650 kg (67,572 lb); maximum take-off 49000 kg (108,027 lb)
Dimensions: span 46 m (150 ft 11 in); length 37 m (121 ft 4¾ in); height 10.90 m (35 ft 9 in); wing area 255 m² (2,744.89 sq ft)
Armament: (BV 222C-09) three 20-mm MG 151 cannon (one each in forward dorsal and two over-wing turrets) and five 13-mm (0.51-in) MG 131 machine-guns (one each in bow position and four beam hatches)

Blohm und Voss BV 238

In early 1940, and obviously with the belief then prevalent in Germany that war in Europe would very shortly come to an end, Dr Richard Vogt began work on the design of a very large long-range flying-boat for service with Lufthansa. However, this was shelved in early 1941 when the company received a request from the Reichsluftfahrtministerium to proceed with the design of a multi-purpose long-range flying-boat. The result was the **Blohm und Voss BV 238**, of which four prototypes were ordered, comprising three **BV 238A**s and a single **BV 238B**, each with six engines, but of liquid-cooled and air-cooled type respectively.

An interesting feature of this project resulted from the fact that the BV 238 was truly a giant, and would clearly involve an enormous capital expenditure. To ensure that as little financial risk as possible was involved, it was decided to

build a research replica of approximately quarter-scale, to be powered by six 15.7-kW (21-hp) engines. Built near Prague, the resulting **FGP 227** proved a complete financial loss, not flying until just a few months before the maiden flight of the one and only BV 238. The FGP 227's initial aerial effort ended in a forced landing, and the aircraft thus provided no data whatsoever for the BV 238 programme.

Although considerably larger than the BV 222 Wiking, the BV 238 was generally similar in configuration. It differed primarily by having a high- rather than shoulder-mounted wing, a modified tail unit, and one-piece (rather than split) retractable stabilising floats. Flown successfully in the spring of 1945 the **BV 238 V1**, the only prototype to be completed, was destroyed on Lake Schaal by strafing USAAF Mustangs a few days before the end of the war. Tests had

shown it to be suitable for service use, but this was not to be. The BV 238's claim to fame lay in the fact that it was the largest military flying-boat to be built and flown during World War II.

Specification
Blohm und Voss BV 238 V1
Type: long-range multi-role flying-boat
Powerplant: six 1305-kW (1,750-hp) Daimler-Benz DB 603V inline piston engines

Blohm und Voss BV 238 VI (lower side view and scrap view; BV 238B (V4) as envisaged with defensive armament).

Performance: maximum speed at AUW of 60000 kg (132,277 lb) 425 km/h (264 mph) at 6000 m (19,685 ft); range approximately 3900 km (2,423 miles) **Weights:** empty 50800 kg (111,995 lb); maximum take-off 80000 kg (176,370 lb) **Dimensions:** span 60.17 m (197 ft 4¾ in); length 43.5 m (142 ft 8½ in); height 13.4 m (43 ft 11½ in); wing area 365 m² (3,928.96 sq ft)

Boeing Model 1

Worthy of brief mention as the very first of the long line of Boeing aircraft, the **Model 1** was known also as the **B & W**. Its design was the result of a collaboration between William E. Boeing and a friend, Cdr G.C. Westervelt of the US Navy, and the B & W designation recognised this association. Of wood and fabric construction, extensively strutted and wire-braced, the Model 1 was an unequal-span biplane, with ailerons on the upper wings only. The fuselage, mounted directly on the lower wing, had two open cockpits in tandem, and carried at the rear a tail unit that was a typical braced structure of its period. Power was provided by a Hall-Scott engine mounted in the nose of the fuselage to drive a tractor propeller. Floatplane landing gear included two single-step floats, strut-mounted and braced

Boeing's first design was the Model 1, at the time called the B&W after its designers. This is a replica, faithfully built in 1966 to celebrate Boeing's diamond jubilee.

beneath the fuselage, plus a small float under the tail to prevent disaster in a tail-down landing.

The first of two Model 1s was flown initially on 29 June 1916, by which time Cdr Westervelt had been posted to the other side of the American continent. William Boeing decided, therefore, to establish a company to build these aircraft, and his Pacific Aero Products Company was founded on 15 July 1916. The first company to incorporate the Boeing name, the Boeing Airplane Company, was formed on 26 April 1917. The two Model 1s, construction numbers 1 and 2,

were sold to the New Zealand government.

Specification
Type: two-seat floatplane
Powerplant: one 93-kW (125-hp) Hall-Scott A-5 inline piston engine
Performance: maximum speed 121 km/h (75 mph); cruising speed 108 km/h (67 mph); range 515 km (320 miles)
Weights: empty 953 kg (2,100 lb); maximum take-off 1270 kg (2,800 lb)
Dimensions: span 15.85 m (52 ft 0 in); length 9.5 m (31 ft 2 in); wing area 53.88 m² (580 sq ft)

Boeing Model 15

With experience gained from sub-contract production of a variety of aircraft designed by other manufacturers, and in particular, the Thomas-Morse MB-3A, Boeing began the private-venture development of a single-seat fighter under the designation **Boeing Model 15**. First flown on 2 June 1923, it was a single-bay biplane with wings of unequal span, the lower wing also being of reduced span and chord. The wings were of wooden construction, fabric-covered, but the fuselage was of welded steel tube. The braced tail unit was also of wood, and incorporated a variable-incidence tailplane that could be adjusted in flight. Landing gear was of fixed tailskid type, with through-axle main units, and power was provided by a 324-kW (435-hp) Curtiss D-12 inline engine.

The US Army had become interested in the Model 15 before it was flown, and after early tests by Boeing it was evaluated by the US Army at McCook Field, under the designation **XPW-9**. There it was flown in competition against a Fokker XPW-7 and the Curtiss XPW-8A, its performance proving good enough to win an order for two extra XPW-9s for more extensive evaluation: these were delivered in May 1924. The third of the aircraft differed by having divided-axle instead of through-axle main landing gear units, and it was this type of landing gear that was chosen for the 30 examples of the production **PW-9** ordered in two batches (12 and 18) in September and December 1925.

The US Navy was as keen as the US Army to acquire examples of Boeing's new fighter, and the first of an order of 14 for service with the US Marine Corps, under the designation **FB-1**, was delivered on 1 December 1925. Only 10 were produced as FB-1s, these being virtually identical to the US Army's PW-9. The 11th and 12th aircraft on this order introduced the 380-kW (510-hp) Packard 1A-1500 inline engine, and were equipped with through-axle landing gear and an arrester hook for operation from aircraft-carriers. The change resulted in redesignation by the US Navy to **FB-2 (Boeing Model 53)**; the 13th aircraft was identical to the FB-2, except for twin float landing gear, and was designated **FB-3 (Boeing Model 55)**; and the

Boeing PW-9C of the 19th Pursuit Squadron at Hickam Field, Hawaii, in 1927.

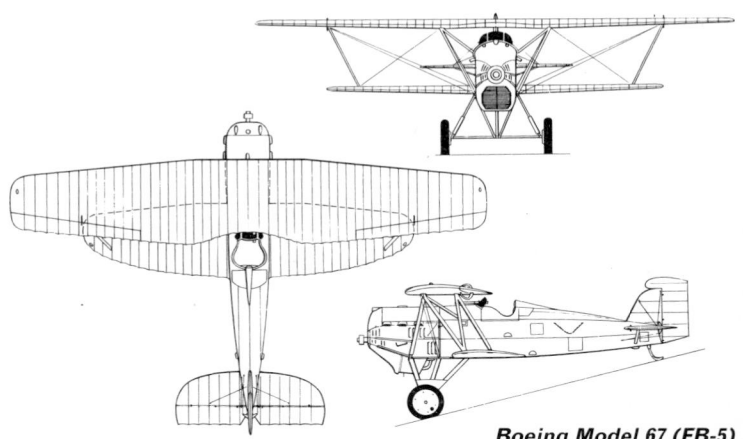

14th and last of the US Navy's initial order also had twin floats, but introduced a 336-kW (450-hp) Wright P-1 radial engine, becoming redesignated **FB-4 (Boeing Model 54)** or **FB-6** with the 298-kW (400-hp) Pratt & Whitney Wasp. These initial US Army and US Navy aircraft represented the first members of a family of similar aircraft, brief details of which are given below.

Variants
Boeing Model 15A: 24 of 25 ordered by the US Army under the designation **PW-9A**, with an improved D-12C similarly rated to the D-12, and with duplicated flying and landing wires
Boeing Model 15B: the 25th of the Army's PW-9As (above) incorporated detail improvements, and was intended to test the Curtiss D-12D engine; the changed US Army designation was **PW-9B**; 15 production examples were ordered but none was built as such
Boeing Model 15C: the 15 PW-9Bs (above) were built as **PW-9Cs**, with the D-12D engine and modified fittings for the flying and landing wires; an additional 25 were ordered in August 1926
Boeing Model 15D: the last of the 40 PW-9Cs was modified to incorporate changes to be introduced in a follow-on order for 16 **PW-9Ds**; these included an aerodynamically-balanced rudder of increased area, fitted retrospectively to most in-service PW-9s, and other detail improvements

Boeing Model 58: the 30th of the original PW-9s was completed as an experimental fighter under the designation **XP-4**; it differed from the PW-9 by having a super-charged engine and a lower wing of equal span and chord to that of the upper; no production examples were ordered
Boeing Model 67: Boeing's model number for the major production version of the Model 15 family built for the US Navy under the designation **FB-5**; this had a Packard 2A-1500 engine, and introduced redesigned landing gear structure and increased wing stagger; 27 built and all delivered by early 1926; the **Model 67A (FB-7)** with Pratt & Whitney Wasp engine failed to materialise
Boeing Model 68: under this model number the 24th PW-9A was converted to an experimental advanced trainer, its Curtiss engine replaced by a 134-kW (180-hp) Wright-Hispano Model E engine; designated **AT-3** by the US Army, its engine of less than half the output of the original powerplant gave much reduced performance and no production examples were built

Specification
Model 67 (FB-5)
Type: ship-based single-seat fighter
Powerplant: one 388-kW (520-hp) Packard 2A-1500 inline piston engine
Performance: maximum speed 283 km/h (176 mph) at sea level; cruising speed 241 km/h (150 mph); range 676 km (420 miles)
Weights: empty 1115 kg (2,458 lb); maximum take-off 1474 kg (3,249 lb)
Dimensions: span 9.75 m (32 ft 0 in); length 7.24 m (23 ft 9 in); height 2.87 m (9 ft 5 in); wing area 22.39 m² (241 sq ft)
Armament: two fixed forward-firing 7.62-mm (0.3-in) Browning machine-guns

Boeing Model 67 (FB-5)

147

Boeing Model 21

Having become recognised as a designer of military aircraft, following the supply of Model 15s to both the US Army (PW-9) and US Navy (FB-1), the company designed the **Boeing Model 21** to meet a US Navy requirement for a primary trainer. This was an equal-span biplane, incorporating an unusually wide wing centre-section, and introduced N-type interplane struts to eliminate wing incidence-bracing wires. The divided-axle main units of the tail-skid landing gear had rubber bungee shock absorbers, plus provision for easy conversion to operation with floats. The pilot and pupil were accommodated in tandem open cockpits. Power was provided by a Lawrance J-1 radial engine.

US Navy testing of the Model 21 was carried out with the prototype aircraft, under the designation **VNB-1**. From the potential operator's point of view, however, the type was unsuitable for the required role, being unspinnable and too easy to fly. On the understanding that modifications would be introduced to make the aircraft a little more demanding, and spinnable, 41 production aircraft were ordered under the designation **NB-1**. The first of these was delivered on 5 December 1924, and it was soon discovered that Boeing's spin modifications were too effective, since it was possible to get into a flat spin from which recovery was virtually impossible.

Further modifications produced an acceptable compromise. Some NB-1s had Lawrance J-2 or J-4 engines, and several aircraft had 164-kW (220-hp) Wright J-5 engines installed at a later date.

Following delivery of the NB-1s an additional 30 were ordered of the **NB-2** variant, this differing only by having war-surplus 134-kW (180-hp) Wright-Hispano E-4 engines, installed at the US Navy's request to utilise some of the very large number of these licence-built engines held in naval stores.

Variants

NB-3: in an attempt to improve still further the handling characteristics of the Model 21, the last two NB-1s were retained by Boeing for experimentation; the first of these became the **NB-3**, with a lengthened fuselage, tail unit modifications, and installation of a Wright-Hispano E-4 engine; testing in mid-1925 showed no significant improvement, and the NB-3 was reworked and delivered to NB-1 standard
NB-4: used for the same purpose as the NB-3, this aircraft had the same fuselage modifications, but incorporated the lighter-weight Lawrance engine; this, too, showed no improvement, and the NB-4 was reworked and delivered as an NB-1

Specification
Boeing Model 21 (NB-1)
Type: two-seat primary trainer
Powerplant: one 149-kW (200-hp) Lawrance J-1 radial piston engine
Performance: maximum speed 160 km/h (99 mph); cruising speed 145 km/h (90 mph); service ceiling 3110 m (10,200 ft); range 483 km (300 miles)
Weights: empty 969 kg (2,136 lb); maximum take-off 1287 kg (2,837 lb)
Dimensions: span 11.23 m (36 ft 10 in); length (floatplane) 8.76 m (28 ft

Boeing's Model 21 trainer was bought by the US Navy under the designation NB-1, some 41 examples being delivered in 1924 and 1925. Illustrated is a late-production example with Wright J-5 engine, fitted by the US Marine Corps with spraying equipment for mosquito control in the tropics.

9 in); height 3.56 m (11 ft 8 in); wing area 31.96 m² (344 sq ft)
Armament: (as gunner trainer) one 7.62-mm (0.3-in) machine-gun on flexible mount in rear cockpit

Boeing Model 40

To meet the requirements of the Air Mail Department of the US Post Office, which needed a new mailplane to replace its ageing DH-4s, Boeing designed in 1925 a large biplane transport under the designation **Boeing Model 40**. It was required to compete against the submissions of other manufacturers, and the Post Office specification had stipulated the use of a Liberty engine, plus an ability to carry 454 kg (1,000 lb) of air mail. A fairly conventional biplane of that period, with tailskid landing gear and a Liberty engine, the Model 40 had a mail compartment in the forward fuselage, with the pilot seated well aft in an open cockpit. First flown on 7 July 1925, the Model 40 was unsuccessful in the competition, the Douglas entry being declared winner. This was to result in Boeing's design gathering factory dust for some 18 months until, in early 1927, the US Post Office began the process of turning the government air mail service over to private enterprise.

Requiring an aircraft to operate on any of the routes for which it might bid, Boeing dusted off the Model 40, and began a process of redesign and conversion to make it suitable for the sort of operation the company had in mind. The resulting **Model 40A** had three major changes by comparison with the original Model 40 prototype: the Liberty engine was replaced by a Pratt & Whitney Wasp radial; its composite structure fuselage gave place to one of steel tube with fabric covering; and better use was made of fuselage capacity. The pilot's position remained unchanged, but an enclosed cabin for two passengers was provided more or less directly over the lower wing, with cargo/mail compartments between the pilot's cockpit and

the cabin, and between the cabin and the engine firewall.

Boeing was successful in its bid, being allocated the San Francisco-Chicago route, and was equally successful in gaining approval for its new aircraft. Following tests for certification, the Model 40A gained Approved Type Certificate No. 2, issued by the US Department of Commerce. A total of 25 was built, 24 for service with the new Boeing Air Transport Corporation, and one as an engine test-bed for Pratt & Whitney. The first example of the Model 40A was flown initially on 20 May 1927, and all 24 for Boeing Air Transport had been delivered in time for inauguration of the company's first air mail service on 1 July 1927.

Variants
Boeing Model 40B: this designation was applied to 19 Model 40As after the original Pratt & Whitney Wasp engine

had been replaced by a 391-kW (525-hp) Pratt & Whitney Hornet radial, giving improved performance
Boeing Model 40B-2: designation applied retrospectively to the Model 40Bs, to indicate seating for two passengers, following introduction of the four-passenger Model 40B-4
Model 40B-4: under this designation 38 new aircraft were built; these retained the Hornet powerplant, and introduced improvements that included seating for four passengers, openable cabin windows, a tailwheel replacing the tailskid, and shielding to improve radio communication
Model 40B-4A: one standard 40B-4 for service as an engine test-bed with Pratt & Whitney, and powered initially by a 503-kW (650-hp) R-1860 Hornet engine
Model 40C: designation of 10 aircraft, the first flown on 16 August 1928, with seating for four passengers, but retaining the Wasp engine of the Model 40A; all but one were later converted to Model 40B-4 standard
Model 40H-4: four standard 40B-4s

were built by Boeing-Canada, and this slight designation change was made to indicate their source of origin; two of them were exported to New Zealand
Model 40X: designation of one aircraft to special order; basically a Model 40C, it had an enclosed cabin for only two passengers, but a second open cockpit forward of the pilot
Model 40Y: designation of another aircraft to special order, generally similar to Model 40X, but with its Wasp engine replaced by the more powerful Hornet

Specification
Boeing Model 40A
Type: two-passenger cargo/mail aircraft
Powerplant: one 313-kW (420-hp) Pratt & Whitney Wasp radial piston engine
Performance: maximum speed 206 km/h (128 mph); cruising speed 169 km/h (105 mph); service ceiling 4420 m (14,500 ft); range 1046 km (650 miles)
Weights: empty 1602 kg (3,531 lb); maximum take-off 2722 kg (6,000 lb)
Dimensions: span 13.47 m (44 ft 2¼ in); length 10.12 m (33 ft 2¼ in); height 3.73 m (12 ft 3 in); wing area 50.82 m² (547 sq ft)

The radical superiority of the radial engine over inline units of the 1920s is nowhere better attested than in the better performance of the Boeing Model 40A over the original Model 40 with its Liberty inline: with only an extra 14.9 kW (20 hp), the Model 40A could carry two passengers as well as an extra 91 kg (200 lb) of mail, with maximum speed and range declining only marginally.

Boeing Model 69 (F2B)

In April 1925 the USAAC issued a specification for a single-seat fighter to be powered by a new 447-kW (600-hp) Packard engine of inverted layout.

Boeing's airframe for this requirement was generally similar to that of the Model 15 family, but recognisable easily by an unusual feature, namely the incorporation of a coolant radiator in the centre-section of the lower wing. Designated **XP-8 (Boeing Model 66)**, this failed to win a production contract.

US Navy evaluation of the FB-4 with a Wright P-1 radial engine, which gave a

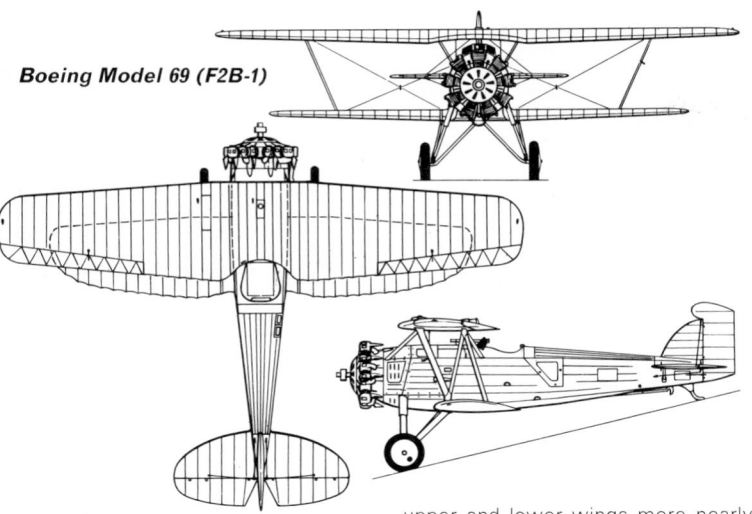

Boeing Model 69 (F2B-1)

first appreciation of the benefits of these air-cooled powerplants, led to this aircraft being re-engined with a Pratt & Whitney Wasp. Redesignated FB-6, it was flight-tested exhaustively, and demonstrated the clear superiority of the Wasp, leading to a decision to combine this engine with an airframe based on the Model 66. From this marriage of airframe and powerplant was produced the **Boeing Model 69**, designated **XF2B-1** by the US Navy, and first flown in prototype form on 3 November 1926. It differed mainly in having the span of upper and lower wings more nearly equal, and by the propeller having a large spinner.

Satisfactory testing of the prototype resulted in an order for 32 production aircraft under the designation **F2B-1**, with deliveries beginning on 30 January 1928, and these served with US Navy Squadrons VF-1B (fighter) and VB-2B (bomber) on board USS *Saratoga*. The F2B-1s differed from the prototype by deletion of the spinner, and introduction of a balanced rudder.

Variants

Boeing Model 69-B: under this designation two aircraft, generally similar to the US Navy's F2B-1s, were built for export, Brazil and Japan acquiring one each

Specification
Boeing Model 69 (F2B-1)
Type: single-seat carrier-based fighter
Powerplant: one 317-kW (425-hp) Pratt & Whitney R-1340-B Wasp radial piston engine
Performance: maximum speed 254 km/h (158 mph) at sea level; cruising speed 212 km/h (132 mph); initial climb rate 576 m (1,890 ft) per minute; service ceiling 6555 m (21,500 ft); range 507 km (315 miles)
Weights: empty 902 kg (1,989 lb);

Lieutenant Tomlinson, commander of the US Navy's VB-2B squadron, normally based aboard the carrier USS Saratoga, prepares to lead off his Boeing F2B-1s for an exhibition in the 1928 National Air Races, held at Los Angeles.

maximum take-off 1272 kg (2,805 lb)
Dimensions: span 9.17 m (30 ft 1 in); length 6.98 m (22 ft 11 in); height 2.81 m (9 ft 2¾ in); wing area 22.57 m² (243 sq ft)
Armament: two fixed forward-firing machine-guns, usually one 7.62-mm (0.3-in) and one 12.7-mm (0.5-in), and up to five 11.3-kg (25-lb) bombs on underfuselage/wing racks

Boeing/Stearman Model 75 Kaydet

The Stearman Aircraft Company, formed by Lloyd Stearman in 1927, became identified as the Wichita Division of the Boeing Airplane Company in 1939. In 1933 the company began design and construction of a new training biplane, derived from the earlier **Stearman Model C**; built as a private venture, this was first flown in December 1933 and, designated originally as the **Stearman X-70**, was submitted as a contender in 1934 to meet a US Air Corps requirement for a new primary trainer.

The first service to show positive interest in this aircraft was the US Navy which, in early 1935, contracted for the supply of 61 of the **Stearman Model 70** under the designation **NS-1** (Trainer, Stearman, 1). These, however, received a different powerplant from that installed originally, for the US Navy had in storage a quantity of 168-kW (225-hp) Wright J-5 (R-790-8) radial engines which were specified for installation in this initial order, the company changing the model number of aircraft so equipped to **Model 73**. The X-70 supplied for US Army evaluation was subjected to protracted testing and eventually, in early 1936, the USAAC contracted for the supply of 26 aircraft under the designation **PT-13** (Primary Trainer, 13). These, powered by 160-kW (215-hp) Lycoming R-680-5 engines, were the first of the **Stearman Model 75** series.

This cautious approach by the US Army should not be considered as a reflection upon the capability of the new trainer. The truth of the matter was that at that period the USAAC had little money to spend on new aircraft: not only had this service to be as certain as possible that it was procuring the best available, but even then was only able to procure small quantities. Soon, however, the fortunes of war were to bring Boeing contracts for thousands of the Stearman-designed trainers and although, officially, the aircraft were produced under the designation **Boeing Model 75** from 1939, they were persistently regarded as Stearman 75s throughout the war. The name Kaydet, bestowed later by Canada, and adopted generally in reference to these aircraft, was also unofficial except in Canada.

This attractive two-seat biplane was of mixed construction, the single-bay wings being basically of wood with fabric covering, the remainder of welded steel tube with mostly fabric covering. Landing gear was of non-retractable tailwheel type, the divided cantilever main units having cleanly faired oleo-spring shock absorbers. The powerplant varied considerably throughout a production

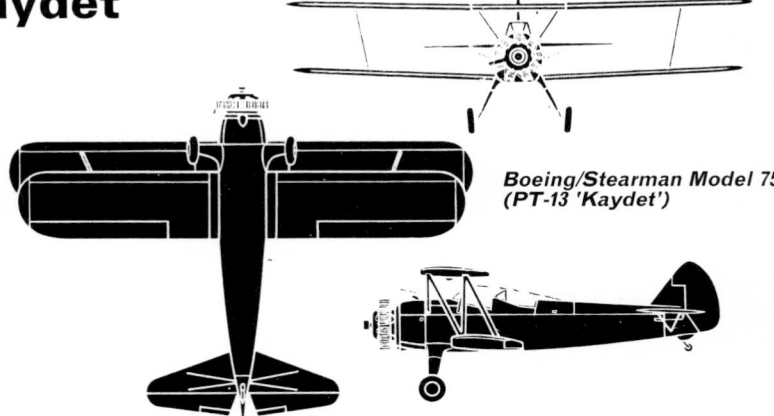

Boeing/Stearman Model 75 (PT-13 'Kaydet')

run which lasted until early 1945, and during which well over 10,000 examples were built.

USAAC procurement continued with the **PT-13A**, 92 of which were delivered from 1937, these having improved instrumentation and 164-kW (220-hp) R-680-7 engines, and by the end of 1941 the USAAF had received an additional 255 of the **PT-13B** with R-680-11 engine and only minor equipment changes. The designation **PT-13C** was allocated in 1941 to six PT-13As which were converted by the addition of equipment necessary to make them suitable for night or instrument flight. A change of

As the standard US wartime trainer, the Model 75 was used widely by both US Army Air Forces and Navy. This pair flew with the latter from NAS Anacostia near Washington.

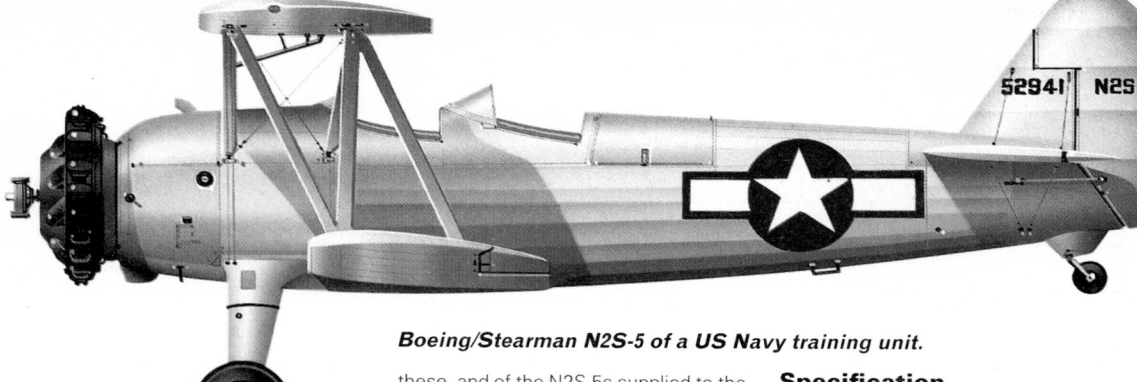

powerplant, the 164-kW (220-hp) Continental R-670-5 engine installed in a PT-13A type airframe, brought the designation **PT-17**, and 3,519 of these were built during 1940 to meet the enormous demand for training aircraft. Eighteen PT-17s were equipped with blind-flying instrumentation under the designation **PT-17A**, and three with agricultural spraying equipment for pest control had the designation **PT-17B**.

US Navy procurement during this same period included a first batch of 250 Model 75s with Continental R-670-14 engines, designated **N2S-1**, followed by 125 with Lycoming R-680-8 engines as **N2S-2**. The **N2S-3** model, totalling 1,875, had Continental R-670-4 engines, and 99 aircraft diverted from US Army PT-17 production plus 577 similar aircraft on US Navy contracts were designated **N2S-4**. For the first time both the US Army and US Navy had a common model in 1942, basically the PT-13A airframe with a Lycoming R-680-17 engine, and these had the respective designations **PT-13D** and **N2S-5**. These were the last major production variants for the US forces, the US Army receiving 318 and the US Navy 1,450. A shortage of

engines in 1940-1 had, however, produced two other designations: **PT-18** and **PT-18A**. The first related to 150 aircraft with the PT-13A type airframe and a 168-kW (225-hp) Jacobs R-755-7 engine, and the six PT-18As were six of the PT-18s converted subsequently with blind-flying instrumentation.

The designation **PT-27** applied to 300 aircraft procured by the US Army for supply under Lend-Lease to the Royal Canadian Air Force. A small number of

Boeing/Stearman N2S-5 of a US Navy training unit.

these, and of the N2S-5s supplied to the US Navy, had cockpit canopies, cockpit heating, full blind-flying instrumentation and a hood for instrument training.

In North America the Stearman Kaydet retains an aura of nostalgia which Britons equate with such aircraft as the Avro 504 and Tutor, and de Havilland Tiger Moth, or Germans with the Bücker trainers.

When declared surplus at the war's end many served with the air forces of other nations, and large numbers were converted for use as agricultural aircraft. Many remain in operation in this latter role in 1982, and the Kaydet is undoubtedly a collector's piece.

Specification
Boeing Model E-75 (N2S-5)
Type: two-seat primary trainer
Powerplant: one 164-kW (220-hp) Avco Lycoming R-680-17 radial piston engine
Performance: maximum speed 200 km/h (124 mph); cruising speed 171 km/h (106 mph); service ceiling 3415 m (11,200 ft); range 813 km (505 miles)
Weights: empty 878 kg (1,936 lb); maximum take-off 1232 kg (2,717 lb)
Dimensions: span 9.8 m (32 ft 2 in); length 7.63 m (25 ft 0¼ in); height 2.79 m (9 ft 2 in); wing area 27.59 m² (297 sq ft)

Boeing Model 77

In order to continue development of the Model 69 (F2B-1), Boeing produced an improved version of this aircraft as a private venture. Generally similar to the production F2B-1, the prototype differed by being completed for testing as a sea-

Boeing F3B-1 of Bomber Squadron VB-1B, based on board the US Navy aircraft-carrier Lexington. The photograph dates from early in the F3B-1's service career, for the US Navy soon devised a drag-reducing Townend-ring cowling for its Model 77s.

plane, and incorporated a single main float, plus wingtip balancer floats. Identified by the company as the **Boeing Model 74**, and tested by the US Navy under the designation **XF3B-1**, the type had a performance of insufficient improvement to make it worthy of production, and it was duly returned to Boeing.

Determined to gain further orders

from the US Navy, the company stripped down the Model 74 and began a major redesign and rebuild. The powerplant remained completely unchanged, and the fuselage differed only by being lengthened by some 0.61 m (2 ft), but virtually everything else was new. The increased-span wing gained some sweepback, the lower wing was of constant chord without sweepback, and new tail unit surfaces and main landing gear units were introduced. The resulting **Boeing Model 77** looked a far more workmanlike machine when first flown on 3 February 1928, and when tested by the US Navy was sufficiently impressive to win a contract for 74 of these aircraft (including the prototype) under the designation **F3B-1**. These began to enter service in August 1928, initially with Squadron VF-2B on board USS *Langley*.

Specification
Boeing Model 77 (F3B-1)
Type: single-seat carrier-based fighter
Powerplant: one 317-kW (425-hp) Pratt & Whitney R-1340-80 radial piston engine
Performance: maximum speed 253 km/h (157 mph) at sea level; cruising speed 211 km/h (131 mph); initial climb rate 616 m (2,020 ft) per minute; service ceiling 6566 m (21,500 ft); range 547 km (340 miles)
Weights: empty 988 kg (2,179 lb); maximum take-off 1336 kg (2,945 lb)
Dimensions: span 10.06 m (33 ft 0 in); length 7.57 m (24 ft 10 in); height 2.79 m (9 ft 2 in); wing area 25.55 m² (275 sq ft)
Armament: one 7.62-mm (0.3-in) and one 12.7-mm (0.5-in) machine-gun plus provision for five 11.3-kg (25-lb) bombs

Boeing Model 80

The growth of operations on Boeing Air Transport's San Francisco-Chicago route resulted in the design and development of a purpose-designed passenger transport, the **Boeing Model 80**, first flown during August 1928. A large unequal-span biplane, with the lower wing of reduced chord, the Model 80 had a wing structure of wood, fabric-covered, and a fuselage and tail unit of welded steel tube, also fabric-covered. Landing gear was of fixed tailwheel type, and power was provided by three 306-kW (410-hp) Pratt & Whitney Wasp radial engines. These were mounted in the classic tri-motor configuration, one in the fuselage nose, and one each side of the fuselage, between the biplane wings.

The main cabin of the Model 80 accommodated 12 passengers, plus a flight stewardess. This was very much an innovation, for although some European airlines had introduced male stewardesses at an earlier date, Boeing stewardesses, all registered nurses, represented the first of the air hostesses that are now an integral part of civil airline operations. Another feature of the Model 80 was the provision of a separate enclosed flight deck for the pilot and co-pilot/navigator, a development that was not accepted enthusiastically by all

flight crew. Four of these aircraft were built, entering service with Boeing Air Transport in the late summer of 1928.

The Model 80s were followed by 10 of the much improved **Model 80A**, this type having more powerful Pratt & Whitney Hornet engines, refinements to the wing, improved streamlining and, because of the increased power available, a cabin layout to accommodate a maximum of 18 passengers.

Variants
Model 80A-1: designation for the 10 Model 80As after a modification that introduced increased vertical tail area in the form of two auxiliary fins and rudders, mounted on the tailplane, one each side of the original fin and rudder assembly
Model 80B-1: the 12th aircraft off the Model 80A production line was completed with open accommodation for the flight crew, due to mixed feelings about the 'benefits' of the enclosed flight deck; following evaluation of this aircraft by the company's flight crews, it was subsequently converted to Model 80A-1 configuration, after it had been agreed that an enclosed flight deck made for more efficient operation

Model 226: designation of the 11th aircraft off the Model 80A production line, completed as an executive transport for the Standard Oil Company, and introducing the additional fins/rudders applied to the Model 80As

Specification
Boeing Model 80A-1
Type: 18-passenger commercial transport
Powerplant: three 391-kW (525-hp) Pratt & Whitney Hornet radial piston engines
Performance: maximum speed 222 km/h (138 mph); cruising speed 201 km/h (125 mph); service ceiling 4265 m (14,000 ft); range 740 km (460 miles)
Weights: empty 4800 kg (10,582 lb);

maximum take-off 7938 kg (17,500 lb)
Dimensions: span 24.38 m (80 ft 0 in); length 17.22 m (56 ft 6 in); height 4.65 m (15 ft 3 in); wing area 113.34 m² (1,220 sq ft)

The Boeing Model 80 was introduced as a result of Boeing Air Transport's experience with its airmail routes, which had shown that the extra revenue earned by passenger-carriage could be increased considerably by additional seating capacity. By comparison with the Model 40B-4, the Model 80 could carry three times the number of passengers at slightly lower speed and over marginally shorter stage lengths, but on only 2.3 times the installed horsepower.

Boeing 200

With continuing requirement for aircraft of the cargo/mail-carrying category, Boeing began the development of a far more advanced version in 1929, one which was intended to provide far superior performance. A cantilever low-wing monoplane of all-metal construction, the **Boeing Model 200 Monomail** had a performance that benefited from a number of new ideas. The cantilever wing eliminated drag-inducing struts and bracing wires; a semi-monocoque fuselage structure provided a more streamlined shape; semi-retractable tailwheel landing gear ensured that most of the main unit structure was retracted within the wing; and the Pratt & Whitney Hornet B radial engine was surrounded by an anti-drag cowling. It retained a couple of features from the earlier Model 40, namely an open cockpit for the pilot, seated well aft, and the forward cargo/mail compartments.

First flown on 6 May 1930, the Monomail was used for a number of tests and experimental flights before entering service on Boeing Air Transport's San Francisco-Chicago route in July 1931. The

The Boeing Model 200 Monomail was in every respect a pioneering aircraft, and was later converted into a passenger transport as the eight-seat Model 221A, as which it was also tested with a streamlined, fixed landing gear unit.

advanced design of this aircraft led to development of the Model 214 and Model 215 experimental bombers, and two variants of this basic civil design.

Variants
Boeing Model 221 Monomail: generally similar to the Model 200 Monomail, this single aircraft had a fuselage lengthened by 0.2 m (8 in) and cargo/mail capacity reduced from 1043 kg (2,300 lb) to 340 kg (750 lb), to provide accommodation for six passengers in an enclosed cabin; first flown on August 1930, and entered service with Boeing Air Transport
Boeing Model 221A: designation applied to the Models 200 and 221 following fuselage 'stretches' to provide accommodation for eight passengers; both saw service on the

Cheyenne-Chicago route of Boeing's newly-formed United Air Lines

Specification
Boeing Model 200
Type: single-seat cargo/mail transport
Powerplant: one 429-kW (575-hp) Pratt & Whitney Hornet B radial piston engine

Performance: maximum speed 254 km/h (158 mph); cruising speed 217 km/h (135 mph); service ceiling 4265 m (14,000 ft); range 853 km (550 miles)
Weights: empty 2158 kg (4,758 lb); maximum take-off 3629 kg (8,000 lb)
Dimensions: span 18.02 m (59 ft 1½ in); length 12.56 m (41 ft 2½ in)

Boeing Models 214, 215 and 246

In 1930 Boeing began the private-venture development of a bomber aircraft that, hopefully, would succeed in gaining a worthwhile military order. To achieve outstanding performance, it was decided to base its design on the revolutionary Model 200 Monomail and, in effect, the resulting prototypes and service evaluation bombers were scaled-up versions of this aircraft. They differed by having a twin-engined powerplant, installed in nacelles at the wing leading edge, and by adaptation of the slender fuselage to cater for the crew and weapons.

To provide the crew accommodation, the fuselage was extended well forward of the wing. A bomb-aimer/gunner was accommodated in the nose and immediately behind him, within the fuselage, was a radio operator's position. Aft of the radio operator were two cockpits in tandem, for pilot and co-pilot, with a fourth open cockpit, just aft of the wing trailing edge, for the rear gunner. A bombload totalling 1025 kg (2,260 lb) could be divided between an internal bomb bay and underwing racks.

First to fly was the **Boeing Model 215**, on 13 April 1931, powered by two

429-kW (575-hp) Pratt & Whitney R-1860-13 Hornet radials. This was tested by the USAAC under the initial designation **XB-901** (Experimental Bomber), and satisfactory conclusion of testing resulted in the procurement of this aircraft under the designation **YB-9**. At the same time the then incomplete **Boeing Model 214** was contracted under the designation **Y1B-9**, plus five additional service test aircraft with the designation **Y1B-9A (Model 246)**.

The Model 214, powered by 447-kW (600-hp) Curtiss V-1570-29 Conqueror in-line engines, was flown for the first time on 5 November 1931, and following further tests, the Model 214 was re-engined with a supercharged version of the Pratt & Whitney Hornet. This power-plant was chosen also for the Y1B-9As, the first of which was flown on 14 July 1932. This latter version differed exter-

nally from the earlier prototypes in having modified vertical tail surfaces, and had internally a number of equipment and structural changes to meet service requirements.

Subsequent testing, and evaluation against the Martin Model 123, resulted in the latter aircraft entering service as the B-10. This came as a great disappointment to the Boeing company, which had produced this first revolutionary bomber with performance superior to most contemporary fighter aircraft. However, this small B-9 family marked the very beginning of the company's specialisation in bomber design.

Specification
Boeing Model 246 (Y1B-9A)
Type: five-seat bomber
Powerplant: two 447-kW (600-hp) Pratt & Whitney SR-1860-11 supercharged radial piston engines
Performance: maximum speed 299 km/h (186 mph) at 1830 m (6,000 ft); cruising speed 266 km/h (165 mph); service ceiling 6325 m (20,750 ft); range 869 km (540 miles)
Weights: empty 4056 kg (8,941 lb); maximum take-off 6495 kg (14,320 lb)
Dimensions: span 23.42 m (76ft 10 in); length 15.77 m (51ft 9 in); height 3.66 m (12 ft 0 in); wing area 88.63 m² (954 sq ft)
Armament: two 7.62-mm (0.3-in) machine-guns (one each on a flexible mount in front and rear cockpits), plus up to 1025 kg (2,260 lb) of bombs

The Boeing Model 215 (and the similar Model 214) was an interim type which pioneered novel features (cantilever monoplane wing and retractable landing gear) but adhered to elderly practices (open cockpits, separated crew positions etc) in other respects. The single aircraft was tested as the XB-901 and then bought as the YB-9.

Boeing Model 234 series

Under the initial designations **Boeing Model 83** and **Boeing Model 89**, as a private venture the company developed two single-seat fighter prototypes for evaluation by the US Navy. Intended as replacements for the F2B and F3B in US Navy service, and hopefully for US

Army's PW-9, they retained the same Pratt & Whitney Wasp engine, and relied upon design refinements to offer improved performance. Both prototypes were of single-bay bi-plane configuration, with constant-chord unequal-span wings of wood and fabric construction, a

steel-tube fabric-covered fuselage, and a conventional braced tail unit. Landing gear of both prototypes was of fixed tail-skid type, but that of the Model 83 had main units that incorporated a spreader bar with Vee bracing struts to the mid-point of this bar, and also had arrester gear. The Model 89 had divided axle main landing gear, and an underfuselage attachment for a 249-kg (550-lb) bomb.

Both were evaluated by the US Navy during 1928 under the designation **XF4B-1**: the Model 89, flown at Navy Test Center Anacostia, Maryland, was also tested by US Army pilots operating from the same airfield.

As a result of US Navy evaluation, 27 aircraft were ordered under the designation **F4B-1**. These combined the arrester hook of the Model 83 with the Model

Boeing Model 100, painted in the markings of a P-12B of the 95th Attack Squadron of the 17th Attack Group. As delivered, the P-12 series originally had small streamlined fairings behind each cylinder head, but these were soon removed, and later a short-chord ring cowling was added.

The US Navy's equivalent to the US Army P-12C, the F4B-2 had the company designation Model 223, and was only slightly different from the F4B-1. The aircraft shown was on the strength of VF-6B Squadron based on board the carrier USS Saratoga. All F4B-2s were later retrofitted with the vertical tail unit developed for the F4B-4 series.

89 configuration as tested, and were built under the company identification of **Model 99**. The first production example was flown on 6 May 1929, and all were delivered within less than four months. Production of this family of aircraft eventually totalled 586 and, not surprisingly, there is an extended list of variants.

Variants
Model 99 (F4B-1A): designation of the fourth production F4B-1 following conversion as an executive aircraft for the Assistant Secretary of the US Navy
Model 100: company designation of four examples, similar to the F4B-1, that were built as commercial/export aircraft
Model 100A: one special two-seat aircraft, built originally for Howard Hughes
Model 100E: two aircraft, equivalent to the US Army P-12E (Model 234), supplied to Thailand
Model 100F: one aircraft, equivalent to the US Army's P-12F (Model 251), built as an engine test-bed for Pratt & Whitney
Model 101 (XP-12A): designation of the last of 10 P-12s (see below) incorporating modified ailerons and elevators, and landing gear with shortened main unit struts and a castoring tail skid
Model 102 (P-12): designation of the first nine of 10 aircraft, generally similar to the Model 89 (XF4B-1), ordered by the US Army as a result of testing of this aircraft at Anacostia
Model 102B (P-12B, XP-12G): the first large production order from the US Army covered 90 P-12Bs, incorporating the aileron/elevator improvements of the Model 101 (XP-12A); the first to be delivered was used by the US Army under the designation XP-12G, to test turbocharged versions of the Pratt & Whitney R-1340; later reverted to P-12B standard
Model 218: designation of a company aircraft with a semi-monocoque metal

The Boeing Model 251, which served with the US Army Air Corps as the P-12F, was the penultimate variant of the P-12/F4B series. The 25 P-12Fs were ordered as P-12Es, from which standard they differed only in having engines rated at a higher altitude.

fuselage structure, flown by the US Army and Navy as the prototype of the P-12E and F4B-3 respectively; subsequently sold to China
Model 222 (P-12C): designation of 95 aircraft for US Army, an improved P-12B incorporating an anti-drag ring cowl for its later model engine, and spreader-bar main landing gear similar to the Model 83; 131 aircraft were ordered originally, but the last 36 were completed as P-12Ds
Model 223 (F4B-2): designation of 46 of the US Navy version of Model 222 (P-12C) above, but fitted with a tailwheel
Model 227 (P-12D, XP-12H): designation of the last 36 P-12Cs which differed in small details; installation of an experimental engine in the 33rd P-12D resulted in the temporary designation XP-12H; reverted to P-12D after reconversion
Model 234 (P-12E): designation of 110 of 135 aircraft ordered in 1931; they were basically P-12Ds that incorporated the semi-monocoque fuselage first flown on the Model 218; examples of

The Boeing Model 235 entered service with the US Navy (70 aircraft) and with the US Marine Corps (22 aircraft) as the F4B-4. Illustrated is an F4B-4 of the VF-3B, one of the first two units to receive the type, and based on the carrier USS Langley. Most surviving F4B-4s were used up as radio-controlled target aircraft.

the P-12E were used for engine tests under the designation **XP-12E, P-12J, YP-12K** and **XP-12L**, but all reverted subsequently to P-12E designation
Model 235 (F4B-3, F4B-4): 21 F4B-3s for the US Navy were generally similar to the US Army's P-12Es except for installed equipment; 92 F4B-4s had a vertical fin of increased area, and the last 45 carried a life raft in the pilot's headrest; various P-12s, transferred from the US Army to the US Navy in 1940, were all designated **F4B-4A**
Model 251 (P-12F): designation applied to the last 25 aircraft of the original Model 234 (P-12E) order. They differed by having a later version of the Pratt & Whitney SR-1340 which maintained its rated power to a higher altitude; in addition, the 25th aircraft incorporated a cockpit enclosure for experimental purposes
Model 256: designation of 14 aircraft, similar to the US Navy's F4B-4s, supplied to Brazil in 1932; required for use as landplanes they had no arrester gear or flotation equipment
Model 267: designation of nine

Boeing P-12Es from the 27th Pursuit Squadron of the 1st Pursuit Group, stepped-up in right echelon.

additional aircraft supplied to Brazil; these combined P-12E wings with the rest of the F4B-3 airframe assembly

Specification
Boeing Model 235 (F4B-4)
Type: single-seat carrier-based fighter
Powerplant: one 410-kW (550-hp) Pratt & Whitney R-1340-16 radial engine
Performance: maximum speed 303 km/h (188 mph) at 1830 m (6,000 ft); climb to 1525 m (5,000 ft) in 2 minutes 42 seconds; service ceiling 8200 m (26,900 ft); range 595 km (370 miles)
Weights: empty 1068 kg (2,354 lb); maximum take-off 1638 kg (3,611 lb)
Dimensions: span 9.14 m (30ft 0 in); length 6.12 m (20ft 1 in); height 2.84 m (9 ft 4 in); wing area 21.13 m² (227.5 sq ft)
Armament: two 7.62-mm (0.3-in) fixed forward-firing machine-guns

Boeing Model 247

On 8 February 1933, Boeing flew the prototype of a new civil airliner which was identified by the company as the **Boeing Model 247**. This had derived via the design of the single-engined civil Model 200 Monomail and the twin-engined Model 215 (US Army designation B-9) bomber, each of which had a cantilever monoplane wing.

A revolutionary aircraft, the Boeing 247 has since become regarded as a prototype for the modern airliner, for it was a clean cantilever low-wing monoplane of all-metal construction with twin-engine powerplant, retractable landing gear, and accommodation for a pilot, co-pilot, stewardess and 10 passengers. With one engine inoperative it could climb and maintain altitude with a full load, and introduced a new feature for a civil transport aircraft by being equipped with pneumatic de-icing boots on wing, tailplane and fin leading edges to prevent ice accretion from reaching a dangerous level.

Sixty examples of the Model 247 were ordered 'off the drawing board' to re-equip the Boeing Air Transport System, shortly to become a major limb of United Air Lines, and another 15 were ordered subsequently for companies or individuals. That built for Roscoe Turner and Clyde Pangborn (to compete in the England-Australia 'MacRobertson' air race of 1934) was provided with fuselage fuel tanks instead of the standard airline cabin equipment, and introduced NACA engine cowlings (to reduce drag) and controllable-pitch propellers with optimum settings for take-off and cruising performance. These improvements were incorporated retrospectively on most airline Model 247s, thus elevating them to **Model 247D** standard.

When the USA became involved in World War II in late 1941, these Model 247Ds remained in airline use, and 27 of them were impressed for service with the USAAF under the designation **C-73**. It had been anticipated that they could be used for the carriage of cargo and troops, but it was discovered that the cabin doors were too small for this purpose. Instead, they were deployed to ferry aircrew and, later in the war, were used for training. In service they were provided with 447-kW (600-hp) Pratt & Whitney R-1340-AN-1 Wasp radials. When no longer required in late 1944, they were returned to civil airline service.

Variants
Model 247E: designation applied to the first Model 247, when used by Boeing to test improvements that were incorporated in the Model 247D, and retained after it entered airline service in Model 247D configuration
Model 247Y: after some service with United Air Lines, one Model 247D was converted under this designation as a private military aircraft; armed with two fixed forward-firing 12.7-mm (0.5-in)

machine-guns, plus one gun of similar calibre on a flexible mount in a dorsal position, it was delivered to a customer in China

Specification
Boeing Model 247D
Type: civil transport aircraft
Powerplant: two 410-kW (550-hp) Pratt & Whitney S1H-1G Wasp radial piston engines

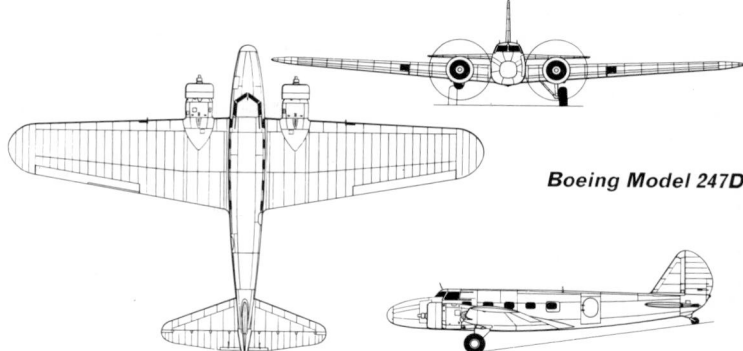

Boeing Model 247D

Performance: maximum speed 322 km/h (200 mph); cruising speed 304 km/h (189 mph) at 2440 m (8,000 ft); service ceiling 7740 m (25,400 ft); range 1199 m (745 miles)
Weights: empty 4148 kg (9,144 lb); maximum take-off 6192 kg (13,650 lb)
Dimensions: span 22.56 m (74 ft 0 in); length 15.72 m (51 ft 7 in); height 3.6 m (12 ft 1¾ in); wing area 77.68 m² (836.13 sq ft)

Boeing Model 266 (P-26)

Although Boeing's diminutive fighter had been retired from front-line service by the time the United States entered World War II, P-26s were among the aircraft ranged against the Japanese at Pearl Harbor, and machines of the Philippine Army Air Force's 6th Pursuit Squadron were in action as Japanese forces fought their way through the archipelago.

Work on the company-funded **Boeing Model 248** began in September 1931, although the US Army Air Corps contracted to supply engines and instruments for three trials aircraft which were designated **XP-936**. Destined to become the first all-metal production fighter and the first monoplane to serve with the USAAC in the pursuit role, the design retained an open cockpit and, despite Boeing's experience with retractable landing gear and cantilever wings, it had fixed landing gear and externally-braced wings. All of these deficiencies were remedied in the **Boeing Model 264** or **YP-29**, which was flown in 1934 as the **XP-940** but not put into production.

The first XP-936 was flown on 20 March 1932, and later completed an evaluation programme at Wright Field, where the second airframe had been delivered for static tests. On 25 April the third was sent to Selfridge Field, Michigan, for tests with operation squadrons. Boeing subsequently received a production order for 111 of the production **Model 266** version, which had the USAAC designation **P-26A**, later increased to 136, which were to incorporate some improvements, including a revised wing structure and the addition of flotation gear and radio; later aircraft also had higher headrests to protect the pilot in a roll-over crash. The first production P-26A made its maiden flight on 10 January 1934; the last of the 111 was delivered at the end of June 1934.

The need to reduce the landing speed

The Boeing Model 264 was one of several experimental monoplane fighters evolved by the company in the late 1920s and early 1930s. The Model 264 was built in several forms, and the first example was evaluated as the YP-29A after its original enclosed cockpit had been deleted. Novel features were the low-set cantilever wing and retractable landing gear.

of the P-26 resulted in the development of trailing-edge flaps, which were fitted retrospectively to aircraft already in service, and to those still on the production line. These included the additional order for 25 completed as the two **P-26B** (**Model 266A**) aircraft with fuel injection-equipped Pratt & Whitney Wasp R-1340-33 engines, and the 23 **P-26C** aircraft which had minor changes to the fuel system and carburation. Many were later converted to P-26B standard.

Production was completed by 12 ex-

port examples of the Boeing **Model 281**, comprising 11 for China and one for Spain.

Specification
Boeing Model 266 (P-26A)
Type: single-seat fighter
Powerplant: one 373-kW (500-hp) Pratt & Whitney R-1340-27 radial engine
Performance: maximum speed 377 km/h (234 mph) at 2285 m (7,500 ft); cruising speed 322 km/h (200 mph); initial climb rate 719 m

(2,360 ft) per minute; service ceiling 8350 m (24,400 ft); range 579 km (360 miles)
Weights: empty 997 kg (2,197 lb); maximum take-off 1340 kg (2,955 lb)
Dimensions: span 8.52 m (27 ft 11½ in); length 7.19 m (23ft 7¼ in); height 3.06 m (10 ft 0½ in); wing area 13.89 m² (149.5 sq ft)
Armament: two fixed forward-firing 12.7-mm (0.5-in), or one 12.7-mm (0.5-in) and one 7.62-mm (0.3-in) machine-guns, plus bombs

Boeing Model 294 (XB-15)

However determined the majority of Americans might have been in the 1930s to maintain the nation's long-established policy of isolation, there were still numbers of radicals, in both the United States government and services, who realised that almost certainly the day would dawn when, for one reason or another, the USA would have to become involved in warlike activities. Given such circumstances, one of the essential weapons would be an advanced strategic bomber, and in the US Army men like Colonels Hugh Knerr and C.W.

Howard were working steadily away in the 1930s to ensure, to the best of their capabilities, that when the moment came such a bomber would be available. This thinking had led to the introduction into service of such bombers as the Boeing B-9, and the Martin B-10 and B-12. While it was appreciated that these did not represent the ideal, they prepared the way for the procurement of a true strategic bomber.

In 1933 came the US Army's requirement for a design study of such an aircraft, then identified as the **XBLR-1** (Experimental Bomber Long Range): a range of 8046 km (5,000 miles) was included in the specification to provide long-range strategic capability. Both Boeing and Martin produced design studies, but it was the former company which received the US Army's contract for construction and development of its **Boeing Model 294**, under the designation **XB-15**. When this large monoplane flew for the first time, on 15 October 1937, it was then the largest aircraft to be built in the USA.

As might be expected, it introduced a number of original features, including internal passages within the wing to permit minor engine repairs or adjustments in flight; two auxiliary power units within the fuselage to provide a 110-volt DC electrical system; sleeping bunks to allow for 'two-watch' operation; and the introduction of a flight engineer into the crew to reduce the pilot's workload. In-

The Boeing Model 294 was a prodigious aircraft by the standards of the day, and failed largely for being ahead of its time: sufficiently powerful engines were not available. Nevertheless the XB-15 (designated XC-105 when it became a transport in World War II) has a place in history as the first 'modern' heavy bomber, introducing features such as clean design, turreted armament, four-engine powerplant and a comprehensive crew complement.

tended to be powered by engines of around 1491 kW (2,000 hp), which in fact did not materialise for some years, the actual powerplant comprised four 746-kW (1,000-hp) Pratt & Whitney Twin Wasp Senior radial engines, which meant that performance was far below that estimated. Purely an experimental aircraft, it was, however, provided with cargo doors and flown as a cargo transport during World War II under the designation **XC-105.**

Specification
Type: long-range bomber/transport
Powerplant: four 746-kW (1,000-hp) Pratt & Whitney R-1830-11 Twin Wasp Senior radial piston engines
Performance: maximum speed 314 km/h (195 mph); service ceiling 5760 m (18,900 ft); range 8256 km

(5,130 miles)
Weights: empty 17105 kg (37,709 lb); maximum take-off 41731 kg (92,000 lb)

Dimensions: span 45.42 m (149 ft 0 in); length 26.7 m (87 ft 7 in); height 5.51 m (18 ft 1 in); wing area 258.26 m²

Boeing Model 299 (B-17 Flying Fortress)

In May 1934 the US Army had issued its specification for an advanced multi-engine bomber, able to haul a bomb load of 907 kg (2,000 lb) over a range of between 1640 km (1,020 miles) and, optimistically, 3540 km (2,200 miles), at speeds of between 322 and 402 km/h (200 and 250 mph). So far as the US Army was concerned, 'multi' meant more than one engine but Boeing, invited to submit its proposal for this requirement, elected to use four engines to power its **Boeing Model 299**, on which design work was initiated in mid-June 1934.

On 28 July 1935 the Model 299 flew for the first time: just over three weeks later it was flown non-stop to Wright Field, Ohio, to be handed over for official test and evaluation. The 3380-km (2,100-mile) flight had been made at an average speed of 406 km/h (252 mph), a most impressive performance which augured well for the future. The elation of the Boeing company was understandable, especially with confirmation that initial trials were progressing well. On 30 October 1935 hopes were dashed with the news that the prototype had crashed on take-off. Subsequent investigation showed that the attempt to take off had been made with the controls locked, and in view of the satisfactory testing prior to this accident, the USAAC decided on the procurement of 13 YB-17s (later **Y1B-17**s), plus one example for static testing.

The prototype (X13372) which had crashed at Wright Field was powered by four 559-kW (750-hp) Pratt & Whitney R-1680-E Hornet radial engines. The cantilever monoplane wings were in a low-

wing configuration, the wing section at the root being so thick that it was equal to half the diameter of the circular-section fuselage; and wide span tailing-edge flaps were provided to help reduce take-off and landing speeds. Landing gear was of electrically retractable trail-wheel type. Armament comprised five machine-guns, and a maximum bomb load of 2177 kg (4,800 lb) could be carried in the fuselage bomb bay.

The initial Y1B-17 (36-149) flew for the first time on 2 December 1936, and differed from the prototype by having 694-kW (930-hp) Wright GR-1820-39 Cyclone radials, accommodation for a crew of nine, and minor changes in detail. Twelve were delivered between January and August 1937, equipping the USAAC's 2nd Bombardment Group at

Langley Field, Virginia. The thirteenth aircraft went to Wright Field for further tests, but after one of the Y1B-17s survived without damage the turbulence of a violent storm, it was decided that the static test example would, instead, be completed as an operational aircraft. Designated **Y1B-17A (Model 299F)**, this aircraft (37-369) was provided with 746-kW (1,000-hp) GR-1820-51 engines each fitted with a Moss/General Electric turbocharger (exhaust gas-driven supercharger). It flew for the first time on 29 April 1938, and subsequent testing by the USAAC gave convincing proof of the superiority of the turbocharged engine over those which were normally aspirated, and such engines became standard on all future versions of the Fortress.

Illustrating the shape of the early B-17s is this Y1B-17, one of the 13 built for evaluation. These served with the 2nd Bombardment Group during USAAC trials.

The order for Y1B-17s was followed by a contract for 39 of the **B-17B (Model 299E**, later **Model 299M)** variant more or less identical to the Y1B-17A prototype with turbo-charged engines. The

Boeing Fortress Mk IIA of No. 220 Squadron, RAF Coastal Command, in late 1942. The squadron flew long-range patrols from Ballykelly, Northern Ireland.

The B-17F was a major production version, 3,405 being built by Boeing-Seattle, Douglas-Long Beach and Lockheed-Vega. The 'F' introduced the moulded Plexiglas nose.

first of these flew on 27 June 1939, and all had been delivered by March 1940. In 1939 the **B-17C (Model 299H)** was ordered, the first of the 38 on contract making its initial flight on 21 July 1940. They differed by having 895-kW (1,200-hp) R-1820-65 engines, and by an increase from five to seven machine-guns.

The B-17C was the first version of this bomber to be supplied to the RAF in the UK, which designated the 20 examples received in early 1941 as **Fortress Is**. Equipping No. 90 Squadron, they were used operationally for the first time on 8 July 1941 when aircraft launched a high altitude (9145 m/30,000 ft) attack on Wilhelmshaven. In the 26 attacks made on German targets during the next two months the Fortress Is proved unsatisfactory, although there was American criticism of the way in which they had been deployed. Nonetheless, their use in daylight over German territory had proved that their operating altitude was an inadequate defence in itself, and that they needed more formidable defensive armament, for Messerschmitt Bf 109E and Bf 109F fighters had little difficulty in intercepting them at heights of up to 9750 m (32,000 ft). Until improvements in the Fortress were made, or means found of deploying them more effectively, they were withdrawn from operations over Europe.

With the end of 1941 drawing near, the USA was soon to become involved in World War II, initially in the Pacific theatre, but following the containment of Japan's initial explosive expansion it was decided that the Allies would first concentrate their efforts on bringing about a speedy conclusion of the war in Europe. Thus, large numbers of B-17s which otherwise would have found employment in the Far East were instead to equip the USAAF's 8th Air Force

in the UK. Those allocated to serve with the Anglo-American North-west African Air Forces later became part of the US 15th Air Force.

In 1940 Boeing received an order for 42 of the **B-17D**. These differed little from the B-17C and retained the same Boeing model number, but, as a result of early reports of combat conditions in Europe, were provided with self-sealing tanks and additional armour for protection of the crew, and these were delivered during 1941. The **B-17E**, **B-17F** and **B-17G** variants that followed (all **Model 299-O**), had redesigned and enlarged tail surfaces, and were easily recognisable from their predecessors by the large dorsal fin. The B-17Es and B-17Fs were the first of these bombers to serve with the 8th Air Force in Europe, and differed from each other primarily in armament and equipment. They were then the most advanced developments of the B-17, but in two major operations against German strategic targets, made on 17 August and 14 October 1943, a total of 120 aircraft was lost. Clearly the Fortresses could not mount an adequate defence, no matter how cleverly devised was the box formation in which they flew. The hard truth was that without adequate long-range fighter escort they were very vulnerable to attack during mass daylight operations. Many of the losses were attributed to head-on attack, and the final major production version was planned to offset this shortcoming.

Thus the B-17Gs had beneath the fuselage nose a 'chin' turret housing two

A pair of B-17Gs from the 381st Bomb Group, set out on a raid from their base at Ridgewell. This group suffered the heaviest losses during the first disastrous Schweinfurt raid.

12.7-mm (0.5-in) machine-guns, which meant that this version carried a total of 13 12.7-mm (0.5-in) guns. To increase the aircraft's operational ceiling, later production examples had an improved turbo-charger for their R-1820-97 engines. B-17G production totalled 8,680, built by Boeing (4,035), Douglas (2,395) and Lockheed Vega (2,250).

Although used most extensively in Europe and the Middle East, B-17s were operational in every area where US forces were fighting. In the Pacific theatre they offered invaluable service for maritime patrol, reconnaissance, and conventional and close-support bombing. A number of variants were also produced or converted for special purposes and operations, and details of these follow. Although almost 13,000 B-17s were built, only a few hundred B-17Gs were retained in USAAF service after the end of the war, and these were soon made redundant.

Variants

B-17H: small number of air-sea rescue aircraft with search radar and dropable lifeboat; later designated **SB-17G**
B-40: bomber escort, originating from **XB-40** converted from a B-17F; four **TB-40** trainers were built, and some **YB-40**s carried up to 30 guns; not operationally successful
BQ-7: pilotless flying-bomb, radio controlled, from which crew of two parachuted after setting it on course; inaccurate and little used
CB-17G and **VB-17G:** B-17Gs equipped as staff transports
DB-17P drone directors
F-9: photo-reconnaissance versions with different camera installations producing **F-9A**, **-9B** and **-9C** variants; other designations for PR aircraft included **FB-17** and **RB-17G**
Model 299-Z: identification of two B-17Gs, modified extensively to allow for the flight test of turboprop powerplant installed in the fuselage nose
Model 299AB: having run through

the alphabet on production aircraft and design studies, double letters followed the Model 299-Z; the Model 299AB was an executive transport conversion for Trans World Airlines, which used the aircraft for survey and liaison when establishing its post-war Near East routes
PB-1: designation applied to one B-17F and one B-17G used by the US Navy for various test projects
PB-1G: air-sea rescue aircraft for service with the US Coast Guard, and comprising 17 B-17Gs with similar conversions to those of the USAAF's B-17H
PB-1W: designation of 31 B-17Gs used by the US Navy in ASW and AEW roles, with APS-20 search radar and a radome mounted above or below the fuselage
QB-17L and **QB-17N:** target drones
TB-17G: special duty trainers
XB-38: one aircraft equipped experimentally with Allison V-710-89 inline engines
XC-108: transport conversion to accommodate 38 passengers
XC-108A: cargo transport with freight door on port side
XC-108B: experimental fuel tanker
YC-108: VIP transport

Specification
Boeing Model 299-O (B-17G)
Type: nine/10-seat long-range medium bomber/reconnaissance aircraft
Powerplant: four 895-kW (1,200-hp) Wright R-1820-97 Cyclone turbocharged radial piston engines
Performance: maximum speed 462 km/h (287 mph) at 7620 m (25,000 ft); cruising speed 293 km/h (182 mph); service ceiling 10850 m (35,800 ft); range with 2722-kg (6,000-lb) bombload 3219 km (2,000 miles)
Weights: empty 16391 kg (36,135 lb); maximum take-off 29710 kg (65,500 lb)
Dimensions: span 31.62 m (103 ft 9 in); length 22.66 m (74 ft 4 in); height 5.82 m (19 ft 1 in); wing area 131.92 m² (1,420 sq ft)
Armament: 13 12.7-mm (0.5-in) machine-guns, plus up to 7983 kg (17,600 lb) of bombs

The B-17H was a search and rescue conversion of the B-17G (later redesignated SB-17G). Radar was carried under the nose and an air-droppable lifeboat under the fuselage.

Boeing Model 307 Stratoliner
to
Boeing Model 400 (XF8B)

Boeing Model 307 Stratoliner

Boeing's Model 299, prototype for the military bomber aircraft which duly became the B-17 Flying Fortress, was developed in parallel with a civil version of the same aircraft which had the company designation **Boeing Model 300**. The basic plan was for both to have a common wing, tail unit and powerplant, but from the beginning a more spacious fuselage had been designed for the civil version. As the design progressed, however, it was decided to provide a circular-section fuselage with moderate pressurisation of 0.18 kg/cm^2 (2½ lb/sq in), providing a cabin altitude of 2440 m (8,000 ft) to a height of 4480 m (14,700 ft), and permitting the **Boeing Model 307**, as this final design was identified, to operate with passengers at 6095 m (20,000 ft), a height above much of the turbulent weather. When, in due course, the Model 307 entered airline service, this 'high-altitude' operational capability resulted in selection of the name Stratoliner.

Ten Model 307s were built, the first making its maiden flight on 31 December 1938. Unfortunately, this aircraft was

Boeing's Stratoliner introduced pressurisation, allowing the type to cruise above most of the weather. TWA and Pan Am were the main airline users, but only 10 were built.

lost before it could be delivered to Pan American. Of the nine which remained, three went to Pan Am (**S-307**), five to Transcontinental & Western Air (TWA) (**SA-307B**), and one modified aircraft to Howard Hughes (**SB-307B**).

Those which had been built for TWA were impressed into USAAF service in 1942, receiving the designation **C-75**. With accommodation for 33 passengers and with a crew of five, they were operated by TWA under contract to the USAAF's Air Transport Command, as VIP transports for the highest ranking civilian and military personnel. After two and a half years' service, during which these five aircraft accumulated between them approximately 3,000 transatlantic crossings, some 45,000 flight hours and travelled about 12 million km (7½ million miles), they were released from military

service and returned to Boeing for refurbishing and conversion back to airline standards. This was virtually a rebuild, involving among other work the incorporation of new wings, tail unit and the installation of more-powerful engines.

Specification
Boeing Model S-307
Type: long-range VIP transport
Powerplant: four 671-kW (900-hp) Wright GR-1820 Cyclone radial piston engines
Performance: maximum speed 396 km/h (246 mph); cruising speed 354 km/h (220 mph); service ceiling 7985 m (26,200 ft); range 3846 km (2,390 miles)
Weights: empty 13608 kg (30,000 lb); maximum take-off 19050 kg (42,000 lb)
Dimensions: span 32.61 m (107 ft 0 in); length 22.66 m (74 ft 4 in); height 6.34 m (20 ft 9½ in); wing area 138.05 m^2 (1,486 sq ft)

Boeing Model 314 Clipper

As early as January 1935, Pan American Airways had signified to the US Bureau of Air Commerce its wish to establish a transatlantic service and, despite its ownership of the large Martin M-130 and Sikorsky S-42 long-range four-engined flying-boats, the airline wanted a new aircraft for the route.

Boeing submitted a successful tender to the Pan American specification and a contract for six **Boeing Model 314** flying-boats was signed on 21 July 1936. The manufacturer used features of the earlier XB-15 heavy bomber, adapting the wing and horizontal tail surfaces for its 37421-kg (82,500-lb) gross weight flying-boat, which could accommodate up to 74 passengers in four separate cabins. The engines were not the 746-kW (1,000-hp) Pratt & Whitney R-1830 Twin Wasps of the XB-15, but 1119-kW (1,500-hp) Wright GR-2600 Double Cyclones which gave the

machine a maximum speed of 311 km/h (193 mph). The fuel capacity of 15898 litres (4,200 US gal) conferred a maximum range of 5633 km (3,500 miles); some of the fuel was stored in the stabilising sponsons, which also served as loading platforms.

The first Boeing 314 took off on its maiden flight on 7 June 1939, this original version having a single fin and rudder, later replaced by twin tail surfaces to improve directional stability. These proved to be inadequate, and the original centreline fin was restored, without a movable rudder. The aircraft was awarded Approved Type Certificate No. 704 and entered transatlantic airmail service on 20 May 1939, passenger service commencing on 28 June. At that time the Model 314 was the largest production airliner in regular passenger service.

Pan American ordered another six aircraft which were designated **Model 314A**, improved by the installation of 1193-kW (1,600-hp) Double Cyclones with larger-diameter propellers, and additional 4542 litres (1,200 US gal) of fuel capacity, and a revised interior. The first Model 314A flew on 20 March 1941 and delivery was complete by 20 January 1942. Five of the original order were retrospectively converted to Model 314A standard in 1942. Three of the repeat order were sold, before delivery, to BOAC for transatlantic service and operation on the Foynes-Lagos sector of the wartime 'Horseshoe Route'.

Of Pan American's nine Model 314/314As, four were requisitioned by Army Transport Command and given the military designation **C-98**. They were little used, however, and in November 1942 one was returned to the airline. The other three were transferred to the US Navy to join two acquired direct from Pan American; the airline provided crews for the US Navy's **B-314** opera-

tions and the aircraft were partially camouflaged but operated with civil registrations.

BOAC and Pan American terminated Boeing Model 314 services in 1946 and the surviving aircraft were sold to American charter airlines.

Specification
Boeing Model 314A
Type: long-range flying-boat transport
Powerplant: four 1193-kW (1,600-hp) Wright R-2600 Cyclone 14 radial piston engines
Performance: maximum speed 311 km/h (193 mph) at 3050 m (10,000 ft); cruising speed 295 km/h (183 mph); service ceiling 4085 m (13,400 ft); range 5633 km (3,500 miles)
Weights: empty 22801 kg (50,268 lb); maximum take-off 37421 kg (82,500 lb)
Dimensions: span 46.33 m (152 ft 0 in); length 32.31 m (106 ft 0 in); height 8.41 m (27 ft 7 in); wing area 266.34 m^2 (2,867 sq ft)

Undoubtedly the greatest passenger flying-boats to have operated in regular airline service, the Boeing Model 314 (six boats) and Model 314A (six boats) were partially the result of Boeing's useful policy of re-using what was good, in this instance the basic wing/powerplant arrangement of the Model 294/XB-15, in combination with a new hull and tail unit.

Boeing 345 Model (B-29 Superfortress)

The outbreak of war in Europe in 1939 made it essential that USAAC planners should at least talk about long-range bomber projects, and the initial identification of such was VHB (very heavy bomber). When it seemed likely that

such an aircraft might have to be deployed over the vast reaches of the Pacific Ocean the identification VLR (very long-range) seemed more apt, and it was the VLR project which General Henry H. ('Hap') Arnold, head of the

USAAC, got under way at the beginning of 1940.

Requests for proposals were sent to five US aircraft manufacturers on 29 January 1940: in due course design studies were submitted by Boeing, Con-

solidated, Douglas and Lockheed, these being allocated the respective designations **XB-29**, XB-32, XB-31 and XB-30. Douglas and Lockheed subsequently withdrew from the competition, and on 6 September 1940 contracts were awarded to Boeing and Consolidated (later Convair) for the construction and development of two (later three) proto-

B-29s inbound to Japan during the final months of World War II. Although best-known for the two atomic raids, the B-29 also did untold damage against Japan with conventional weapons.

types of their respective designs. Convair's XB-32 Dominator was the first to fly, on 7 September 1942, but extensive development delayed its entry into service.

Boeing, because of the company's foresight, was much further along the design road in 1940, and being able to convince the USAAC that it would have production aircraft available within two or three years, had received orders for more than 1,500 before a prototype was flown. The reason for the advanced design state of Boeing's proposal was due to the fact that as early as 1938 the company had offered to the USAAC its ideas for an improved B-17, with a pressurised cabin to make high-altitude operations less demanding on the crew. While there was then no requirement for such an aircraft, the US Army encouraged Boeing to keep the design updated to meet the changing conditions of war. This was reflected by designs identified as **Models 316, 322, 333, 334** and **341**. The design for the XB-29 was a development of the Model 341, designated **Model 345**, and the first of the prototypes made its maiden flight on 21 September 1942.

The USAAC's specification had called for a speed of 644 km/h (400 mph), so the XB-29 had a high aspect ratio cantilever monoplane wing mid-set on the circular-section fuselage. Because such a wing would entail a high landing speed, the wide-span trailing-edge flaps were of the Fowler type which effectively increased wing area by almost 20 per cent, thus allowing a landing to be made at lower speed. Electrically retractable tricycle landing gear was provided and, as originally proposed by Boeing, pressurised accommodation was included for

the flight crew. In addition, a second pressurised compartment just aft of the wing gave accommodation to crew members who, in the third XB-29 and production aircraft, sighted defensive gun turrets from adjacent blister windows. The crew and aft compartments were connected by a crawl-tunnel which passed over the fore and aft bomb bays. The tail gunner was accommodated in a pressurised compartment, but this was isolated from the other crew positions. The powerplant consisted of four Wright R-3350 Cyclone twin-row radial engines, each with two General Electric turbochargers mounted one in each side of the engine nacelle.

Prototype production was followed by 14 **YB-29** service test aircraft, the first of these flying on 26 June 1943. Deliveries of YB-29s began almost immediately to the 58th Very Heavy Bombardment Wing (VHBW), a unit which had been established on 1 June in advance of the first flight. B-29 production was the most diverse aircraft manufacturing project undertaken in the USA during World War II, with literally thousands of sub-contractors supplying components or assemblies to the four main production plants: Boeing at Renton and Wichita; Bell at Marietta, Georgia; and Martin at Omaha, Nebraska.

B-29 production totalled 1,644 from Boeing's Wichita plant, with 668 built by Bell and 536 by Martin. The Renton plant produced only the **B-29A** variant, with slightly increased span and changes in fuel capacity and armament: production continued until May 1946 and totalled 1,122 aircraft.

The designation **B-29B** related to 311 of the aircraft built by Bell. These were reduced in weight by removal of all

defensive armament except for the tail guns, which were then unmanned, being aimed and fired automatically by an AN/APG-15B radar fire-control system. The production total of nearly 4,000 B-29s of all versions must be regarded as very large, having regard to their size and cost, and it is not surprising that they saw a wide variety of employment in the post-war years, operating under several designations. A number of B-29s were used operationally during the Korean War.

Variants

RB-29/RB-29A: photo-reconnaissance versions of B-29 and B-29A aircraft, of which 118 were modified, originally under the designation **F-13**

SB-29: designation of B-29s converted for SAR missions, and carrying a lifeboat that could be dropped by parachute

B-29D: designation allocated originally to an improved version of the B-29 with Pratt & Whitney R-4360 engines; not built as such, but produced post-war as the B-50A

XB-29E: designation of a single B-29 converted and used for testing of fire-control systems

B-29F: six specially winterised aircraft were given this designation, and used for cold weather tests in Alaska; reconverted subsequently to standard B-29 configuration

XB-29G: one aircraft modified to flight test General Electric turbojet engines; one engine, carried within the bomb bay, could be lowered into the slipstream for testing

XB-29H: conversion of a B-29A for special armament tests

RB-29J: conversions of some YB-29Js (below) for use in a photo-reconnaissance role

YB-29J: under this designation a small number of B-29s (believed to be six) were given Wright R-3350-CA-2 fuel-injection engines.
improved nacelles

While itself one of the most innovative aircraft in aviation history, the B-29 also played a part in supersonic research, used as a launch platform for dropping rocket-powered research craft.

YKB-29J: designation of two YB-29Js converted subsequently as inflight-refuelling tankers

B-29K: one B-29 was operated as a cargo transport under this designation

B-29L: original designation of B-29s converted as inflight-refuelling tankers equipped with a British-developed hose system

B-29MR: designation of 79 B-29s equipped as inflight-refuelling receiver aircraft

KB-29M: under this designation 92 B-29s were converted to inflight-refuelling tankers using a hose system

KB-29P: under this designation 116 B-29s were converted to inflight-refuelling tankers, these being equipped with the Boeing-developed flying-boom system

YKB-29T: designation of one three-hose inflight-refuelling tanker, capable of dispensing fuel to three fighter aircraft simultaneously

XB-39: under this designation, one B-29 was converted as a testbed for newly-developed Allison V-3420 inline engines

XB-44: designation of one B-29A following conversion by Pratt & Whitney as a test-bed aircraft; its standard powerplant was replaced by four 28-cylinder R-4360 engines in new nacelles; this was the prototype conversion for the intended B-29D, but was used post-war for the B-50A

P2B-1S: designation of two B-29s used post-war by the US Navy for anti-submarine and research projects

P2B-2S: designation of two additional B-29s used by the US Navy as above

Washington I: designation allocated to 88 B-29s by the RAF, which received these aircraft on loan for a period of five years

Specification

Boeing B-29 Superfortress
Type: 10-seat long-range strategic bomber/reconnaissance aircraft
Powerplant: four 1641-kW (2,200-hp) Wright R-3350-23-23A/-41 Cyclone 18 turbocharged radial piston engines
Performance: maximum speed 576 km/h (358 mph) at 7620 m (25,000 ft); cruising speed 370 km/h (230 mph); service ceiling 9710 m (31,850 ft); range 5230 km (3,250 miles)
Weights: empty 31815 kg (70,140 lb); maximum take-off 56245 kg (124,000 lb)
Dimensions: span 43.05 m (141 ft 3 in); length 30.18 m (99 ft 0 in); height 9.02 m (29 ft 7 in); wing area 161.27 m² (1,736 sq ft)
Armament: two 12.7-mm (0.5-in) machine-guns in each of four remotely-controlled power-operated turrets, and three 12.7-mm (0.5-in) guns or two 12.7-mm (0.5-in) guns and one 20-mm cannon in the tail turret.

Boeing Model 345-2 (B-50)

Seeking enhanced capability for the B-29 Superfortress in 1944, Boeing took a standard B-29A and used it as the prototype for an improved **Model 345-2** which was given the provisional USAAF designation **B-29D**. Increased power was considered to be essential if the

new model was to have greater load-carrying capability and the chosen powerplant, comprising four 2610-kW (3,500-hp) Pratt & Whitney R-4360-45 radial engines, mounted in redesigned nacelles, was test flown in another B-29, given the USAAF designation **XB-44**.

While this area was being investigated Boeing got on with modification of the B-29A: this involved a new lighter-weight wing, strengthened but lighter-weight landing gear and, to retain good directional stability despite an increase of almost 60 per cent in power output, greater area for the vertical tail surfaces.

The use of a new 75-S light alloy for the wing structure, instead of the pre-

viously standard 24ST, brought a weight saving of 295 kg (650 lb), while providing a wing that was 16 per cent stronger than that of the production B-29s. Landing gear redesign made possible operation at higher gross weight, and the greater vertical tail surface area came from increasing the height of fin and rudder by about 1.52 m (5 ft). This would have made it impossible to put B-29Ds into standard hangars, making it necessary to provide for the fin and rudder to fold to starboard.

The USAAF ordered 200 of the new B-29Ds, but with the end of war in the Pacific, this was cut to only 60, and the considerable airframe and powerplant changes brought a decision to scrap the B-29D identity, resulting in the new aircraft being redesignated as the **B-50**. The initial production **B50A** (46-002) flew for the first time on 25 June 1947 and demonstrated not only improved performance but, by comparison with the B-29A, a gross weight increase of almost 20 per cent. Production of the B-50A eventually totalled 79 aircraft, and 57 of these were later converted to serve as inflight-refuelling tankers, and it was in this role that the type saw service in Vietnam before being retired in the latter half of the 1960s.

Variants
KB-50: cover-all designation of all B-50 conversions to initial inflight-refuelling tanker configuration, with three-point refuelling system (132 conversions)
WB-50: designation of B-50s modified for weather reconnaissance purposes
B-50A: designation of initial production model (59 built)
TB-50A: under this designation 11 B-50As were modified to trainers for Convair B-36s
B-50B: improved version, with maximum take-off weight increased by 590 kg (1,300 lb) to 77112 kg (170,000 lb) and numerous improvements (45 built)
EB-50B: B-50B retained by Boeing for experimental purposes, including at one time investigation of tracked landing gear
RB-50B: all 44 in-service B-50Bs were modified to this standard with a rear bomb bay capsule for photographic and

The KB-50J was the ultimate variant, with J47 turbojets in pods under the wings to boost speeds.

The B-50D was the most widely built variant of the B-50 series, its chief distinguishing feature being the two 2650-litre (700-US gal) underwing tanks.

electronic equipment and the extra crew necessary
YB-50C: designation of the 60th B-50A, taken in hand during construction for modification to improved standard with R-4360-51 turbo-compound engines to allow a maximum take-off weight of 93895 kg (207,000 lb); not completed
B-50D (Model 345-9-6): revised production version with nose cone moulded from single piece of perspex, take-off weight raised to 78473 kg (173,000 lb), provision for underwing fuel tanks, and (16th aircraft onwards) provision for inflight-refuelling (222 built)
DB-50D: B-50D modified as launch aircraft for the experimental GAM-63 Rascal stand-off missile
TB-50D: designation of 11 B-50Ss adapted as trainers for the Convair B-36
WB-50D: designation for B-50Ds modified as weather-reconnaissance aircraft
RB-50E: 14 RB-50Bs were modified under this revised designation for

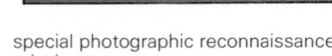

special photographic reconnaissance missions
RB-50F: 14 RB-50Bs were modified to this special-mission standard with SHORAN navigation radar
RB-50G: 15 RB-50Bs modified to a standard similar to the RB-50F but with extra radar and the nose section of the B-50D
TB-50H: 24 new-built aircraft for use as systems trainers for B-47 crews
WB-50H: conversion of some TB-50Hs as weather-reconnaissance aircraft
KB-50J: designation of 112 KB-50s modified to improved standard by Hayes Industries with extra fuel, three-point refuelling systems, no operational

equipment but a pair of podded 2359-kg (5,200-lb) thrust General Electric J47 jets under the wings to boost speed to 715 km/h (444 mph) for better compatibility with jet aircraft
KB-50K: modification of TB-50Hs to a standard identical with the KB-50J
B-54A: proposed production version of the YB-50C
RB-54A: proposed reconnaissance bomber version of the YB-50C

Specification
Boeing B-50A
Type: four-engined heavy bomber
Powerplant: four 2610-kW (3,500-hp) Pratt & Whitney R-4360-35 Wasp Major turbocharged radial piston engines
Performance: maximum level speed 620 km/h (385 mph); cruising speed 378 km/h (235 mph); service ceiling 11280 m (37,000 ft); range 7483 km (4,650 miles)
Weights: empty 36764 kg (81,050 lb); maximum take-off 76389 kg (168,408 lb)
Dimensions: span 43.05 m (141 ft 3 in); length 30.18 m (99 ft 0 in); height 9.96 m (32 ft 8 in); wing area 161.55 m² (1,739 sq ft)
Armament: twelve 12.7-mm (0.5-in) machine-guns, comprising two in each of three remotely-controlled turrets, four in a nose turret, and two plus one 20-mm cannon in tail turret, and up to 9072 kg (20,000 lb) of bombs

Boeing Model 367 (C/KC-97)

In early 1942 Boeing initiated a design study to examine the feasibility of producing a transport version of its B-29 Superfortress. In due course the company's proposal was submitted to the USAAF for consideration and, because at that time the long-range transport was a much-needed type of aircraft, a contract for three prototypes was awarded on 23 January 1943. Identified by the company as the **Boeing Model 367**, and designated **XC-97** by the US Army Air Force, the first made its maiden flight on 15 November 1944.

The XC-97 had much in common with the B-29, including the entire wing and engine layout. At first view the fuselage, of 'double-bubble' section, appeared to be entirely new, but in fact the lower 'bubble' was basically a B-29 structure, and so was the tail unit attached to the new (and larger) upper 'bubble'. On 6 July 1945, following brief evaluation of

The KC-97G introduced the ability to carry freight or passengers without any internal modification. Permanent underwing tanks were fitted, and in Air National Guard service these were often replaced by a pair of J47 turbojets to produce the KC-97L.

the prototypes, 10 service-test aircraft were ordered. These comprised six **YC-97** cargo transports, three **YC-97A** troop carriers, and a single **YC-97B** with 80 airline-type seats in its main cabin.

The first production contract, on 24 March 1947, for 27 **C-97A** aircraft with 2425-kW (3,250-hp) Pratt & Whitney

R-4360-27 engines, specified accommodation for 134 troops, or the ability to carry a 24040-kg (53,000-lb) payload. Two transport versions followed, under the designation **C-97C** and **VC-97D**, and following trials with three **KC-97A** aircraft equipped with additional tankage and a Boeing-developed flight-refuelling boom, **KC-97E** flight-refuelling tankers went into production in 1951. This version was powered by 2610-kW (3,500-

hp) R-4360-35C engines. The **KC-97F** variant which followed differed only in having R-4360-59B engines. Both the KC-97E and KC-97F were convertible tanker/transports, but for full transport capability the flight-refuelling equipment had to be removed. The most numerous variant, with 592 built, was the **KC-97G** which had full tanker or full transport capability without any on-unit equipment change.

When production ended in 1956 a total of 888 C-97s had been built, and many were converted later for other duties. The **KC-97L** variant had increased power by the installation of a 2359-kg (5,200-lb) thrust General Electric J47-GE-23 turbojet beneath each wing to improve rendezvous compatibility with Boeing B-47s. KC-97Gs converted to all-cargo configuration were redesignated **C-97G**, and in all-passenger configuration became **C-97K**. Search and rescue conversions were **HC-97G**, and three KC-97Ls went to the Spanish air force, being designated **TK-1** in that service. Several have served in many roles with Israel's air force.

Variants
C-97D: designation applied to the third YC-97A, the YC-97B, and two C-97As following conversion to a

standard passenger configuration; the three VC-97Ds were subsequently redesignated C-97D
KC-97H: designation applied to one KC-97F, following modification for service trials as a tanker using the probe-and-drogue flight-refuelling system developed in the UK
YC-97J: final designation of two KC-97Gs converted for USAF use as flying test-beds, each with four 4250-kW (5,700-shp) Pratt & Whitney YT43-P-5 turboprop engines

Specification
KC-97G
Type: long-range military transport or flight-refuelling tanker
Powerplant: four 2610-kW (3,500-hp) Pratt & Whitney R-4360-59B radial piston engines
Performance: maximum speed

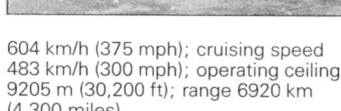 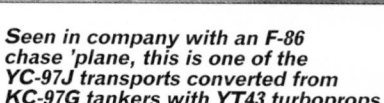

604 km/h (375 mph); cruising speed 483 km/h (300 mph); operating ceiling 9205 m (30,200 ft); range 6920 km (4,300 miles)
Weights: empty 37421 kg (82,500 lb); maximum take-off 79379 kg (175,000 lb)
Dimensions: span 43.05 m (141 ft

Seen in company with an F-86 chase 'plane, this is one of the YC-97J transports converted from KC-97G tankers with YT43 turboprops.

3 in); length 33.63 m (110 ft 4 in); height 11.66 m (38 ft 3 in); wing area 164.34 m² (1,769 sq ft)

Boeing Model 377 Stratocruiser

The **Boeing Model 377 Stratocruiser** was a commercial transport development of the Model 367 (military C-97), and based on the improved-structure YC-97A with Pratt & Whitney R-4360 engines. The first flight of the prototype **Model 377-10-19** was made on 8 July 1947, and it was delivered subsequently to Pan American World Airways, which was the biggest user of the Stratocruiser. There were a variety of interior configurations in the **Models 377-10-26, -28, -29, -30, -32** accommodating from 55 to 112 passengers or, if equipped as a 'sleeper', with 28 upper- and lower-berth units, plus five seats. The main cabin was in the upper lobe of the 'double-bubble' fuselage, with a luxury lounge or cocktail bar seating 14 on the lower deck, reached via a spiral staircase.

Caledonia was the first of only six Boeing Model 377-10-32 Stratocruisers ordered directly from Boeing by BOAC. The airline eventually acquired another 11 Stratocruisers from other airlines for its popular North Atlantic service and other routes.

Of the total of 55 that were built, Pan Am was operating 27 at one period. Of these, 10 were given additional fuel capacity to make them suitable for transatlantic operations, and were known as **Super Stratocruisers**. At a later date the entire fleet was equipped with General Electric CH-10 turbochargers, enabling each engine to develop an additional 37.3 kW (50 hp). British Overseas Airways Corporation also acquired a

fleet of 17: only six of these were original purchases from Boeing, the remainder acquired from other airlines. After just over nine years' service with BOAC, 10 were sold to Transocean Airlines in the USA during 1958. Of these, four were converted to 117-passenger high-density seating, the remainder each having an additional 12 seats added to their standard 63- and 84-seat layouts.

Before Stratocruisers disappeared

from service during 1963, a few had been modified to a cargo configuration, but by far the strangest conversion resulted from those airframes acquired by Aero Spacelines Inc. Under the designation **377-PG**, this company built an oversize cargo aircraft which it named 'Pregnant Guppy' and subsequently built other examples, using both Model 367 and 377 airframes, under variations of the Guppy name.

Specification
Boeing Model 377 (basic airline Stratocruiser)
Type: commercial transport
Powerplant: four 2610-kW (3,500-hp) Pratt & Whitney R-4360 Wasp Major radial piston engines
Performance: maximum speed 604 km/h (375 mph) at 7620 m (25,000 ft); maximum cruising speed 547 km/h (340 mph) at 7620 m (25,000 ft); service ceiling above 9755 m (32,000 ft); range with maximum fuel 6759 km (4,200 miles)
Weights: empty 37875 kg (83,500 lb); maximum take-off 66134 kg (145,800 lb)
Dimensions: span 43.05 m (141 ft 3 in); length 33.63 m (110 ft 4 in); height 11.66 m (38 ft 3 in); wing area 164.34 m² (1,769 sq ft)

Boeing Model 400 (XF8B)

US Navy carriers operating in the Pacific during World War II were, like similar vessels of any nation, very vulnerable to air attack. When the changing fortunes of war made it clear to the US Navy that a day could dawn when they would need to attack the Japanese home islands, concern was expressed at the need to deploy these vessels within easy range of large numbers of land-based aircraft.

If, however, the US Navy had available a long-range fighter/fighter-bomber, then it might be possible to engage the enemy without the need to bring the carriers within striking range of land-based defence aircraft.

The requirement for such a category of aircraft was communicated to Boeing, which immediately began its design under the designation **Boeing Model**

400. Submitted to the US Navy, Boeing's design study was sufficiently interesting to warrant the award of a contract for three **XF8B-1** prototypes on 4 May 1943. The first of these aircraft made its initial flight during November 1944, and was immediately seen to be the largest single-seat piston-engine fighter to be built in the USA. In fact, it subsequently proved to be one of the most powerful single-engine fighters to be developed by any nation involved in World War II, for its powerplant consisted of a Pratt & Whitney XR-4360-10 radial piston engine, which had four banks of seven cylinders, the 2237-kW (3,000-hp) power output being used to drive two three-blade contra-rotating metal propellers.

Boeing's Model 400 was the heaviest carrierborne aircraft of World War II, and would have been a formidable combat aircraft: the proposed F8B-1 version would have possessed high speed and long range, coupled to an offensive armament of six 20-mm cannon and a wide variety of external stores.

Only the first prototype was completed and flown before the end of World War II, but although the remaining two prototypes were completed and handed over after VJ-Day, the overriding interest in the development of turbine-engined aircraft meant that further test and evaluation of the XF8B-1s was abandoned.

Specification
Type: single-seat carrier-based long-range fighter/fighter-bomber
Powerplant: one 2237-kW (3,000-hp) Pratt & Whitney XR-4360-10 radial piston engine
Performance: maximum speed 695 km/h (432 mph) at 8200 m (26,900 ft); cruising speed 306 km/h (190 mph); service ceiling 11430 m (37,500 ft); range 4506 km (2,800 miles)
Weights: empty 6132 kg (13,519 lb); maximum take-off 9302 kg (20,508 lb)
Dimensions: span 16.46 m (54 ft 0 in); length 13.18 m (43 ft 3 in); height 4.95 m (16 ft 3 in); wing area 45.43 m² (489 sq ft)
Armament: six 12.7-mm (0.5-in) machine-guns or six 20-mm cannon, plus up to 1451 kg (3,200 lb) of bombs

Boeing Model 450 (B-47 Stratojet)
to
Boeing Model 707

Boeing Model 450 (B-47 Stratojet)

Following the development and introduction into service of the first turbojet-powered fighter aircraft, in the European theatre of operations during the closing stages of World War II, the USAAF realised that similarly powered bomber/reconnaissance aircraft would soon be essential. By early 1944 four companies were involved in the design of an aircraft to meet the specification drawn up by the USAAF, and Boeing's initial submission (**Model 424**) to meet this requirement failed to arouse any interest. A second submission (**Model 432**) was made in late 1944, with engines buried in the centre fuselage and a straight wing similar to that of the Model 424. This was awarded a contract covering design definition and the preparation of a mock-up, but during the progress of this stage of development, Boeing learned of German aerodynamic research data which were becoming available following the end of war in Europe. German investigation into the benefit of swept wings led to the adoption by Boeing of a sweptback configuration for its **Model 448** proposal, with a total of six engines housed within the fuselage. However, this proposed powerplant installation was not acceptable to the USAAF, which considered that it would create both maintenance and safety problems. It was to result in a fourth design proposal, the **Model 450**, retaining the swept wing, but with its six engines in underwing mountings. Boeing's mock-up was completed in this configuration, and official inspection in the spring of 1946 led to a contract for two **XB-47 (Model 450-3-3)** prototypes. These differed somewhat from the mock-up, incorporating changes that included increased wing span and modified landing gear.

The first of the two prototypes made its maiden flight on 17 December 1947, immediately creating an impression of speed and efficiency. The XB-47 had a high aspect ratio laminar-flow wing, set in a high-wing configuration, and the wing was so thin that it could not incorporate fuel storage. This thin structure also meant that the wings flexed, the wingtips moving as much as 1.52 m (5 ft) up or down from a datum position. The wing structure was responsible also for an unusual landing gear design, for there was no space in which wing-mounted main units could be housed. Instead, retractable twin wheel tandem units were mounted on the centreline of, and were housed within, the slender fuselage, and stability on the ground was provided by small outrigger wheels that retracted into the inboard engine nacelles. It was appreciated at an early stage that the well-spaced main units would make normal take-off rotation impossible and, as a result, the height of the two main units was designed so that the aircraft stood on the runway in an attitude at which it would take off when

Strategic reconnaissance for the US Air Force was handled by a fleet of RB-47H electronic surveillance aircraft, and three ERB-47Hs (illustrated) which performed similar work but of a more experimental nature.

flying speed was attained. Each wing also carried beneath it three podded engines, two paired inboard and the third a short distance in from the wingtips; in the case of the prototype these were General Electric J35s, each of 1701-kg (3,750-lb) thrust. The fuselage provided accommodation for a crew of three, comprising the pilot, co-pilot/gunner, and navigator/bomb-aimer; incorporated a large bomb bay to house the large and heavy thermonuclear bombs of that era, but one that could be modified to carry 9979-kg (22,000-lb) conventional bomb; had provisions for the installation of JATO (jet-assisted take-off) units; and was fitted with remotely-controlled defensive armament in the tail that could be operated manually by the co-pilot, or aimed and fired automatically by radar.

Evaluation of the XB-47 by what had then become the USAF resulted in a contract for 10 of the **B-47A (Model 450-10-9)** variant, which were required for wider-scale service testing and familiarisation. Generally similar to the prototypes, the B-47As differed by having more powerful J47-GE-11 turbojets, each of 2359-kg (5,200-lb) thrust, and were used largely for the evaluation of the best form of tail armament and fire control. The first of the B-47As made its maiden flight on 25 June 1950, a day that also marked the beginning of the Korean War, a conflict that speeded the demand for large numbers of the USAF's new bomber. So urgent was the requirement, in fact, that in addition to production by Boeing at Wichita, the World War II production association between Boeing, Douglas and Lockheed was re-

newed, with these two last named companies building B-47s at Tulsa and Marietta respectively.

The first true production version, of which 399 were built (381 by Boeing), was the **B-47B (Model 450-11-10)**. Douglas and Lockheed built 10 and eight respectively, these serving to get the new production lines established. This version differed from the B-47A by incorporating structural modifications to allow for operation at a higher gross weight, by being equipped for inflight-refuelling, and by having provision for underwing fuel tanks. Later production aircraft, beginning with the 88th, had 2631-kg (5,800-lb) thrust J47-GE-23 engines. The first of these flew on 26 April 1951, and they began to enter service with the USAF some two months later.

Major production version was the **B-47E (Model 450-157-35)**, of which more than 1,600 were built in bomber and reconnaissance versions. They incorporated a number of major changes, including strengthened landing gear for operation at higher weights, a modified nose section with inflight-refuelling receptacle and ejection seats for the crew, installation of a drag parachute to shorten landing runs, tail armament changed to two 20-mm cannon, the internal JATO system replaced by a jettisonable external rack to carry up to 33 454-kg (1,000-lb) thrust rockets, and the installation of J47-GE-25 engines, each developing 3266-kg (7,200-lb) thrust with water injection.

The first B-47E was flown on 30 January 1953, entering service with the

This was the first of 10 B-47As, procured primarily to provide service test and evaluation. These were similar to the second XB-47, but incorporated more powerful engines.

USAF's Strategic Air Command shortly after this. At the peak of B-47 utilisation, in 1957, 28 of SAC's medium bomber wings each had a combat strength of 45 B-47s, plus 300 deployed in other roles and 300 held in reserve, making a grand total of more than 1,800. It had been anticipated that the B-47 would be replaced by a more advanced aircraft by 1957, but it was soon appreciated that it would have to continue in service until well into the 1960s. This factor, plus a requirement to adopt a low-altitude 'under the radar' approach to a target, caused wing fatigue problems. Low-altitude attack required the use of a bomb-launching technique new for a bomber aircraft, involving delivery of the nuclear weapon by a toss-bombing method that had been developed earlier for fighter aircraft. This involved a fast low-level run to the target, a steep pull-up into a half loop (the weapon released just before the aircraft was in a vertical attitude), and a roll off the top of the loop. This latter part of the manoeuvre was the classic Immelmann turn, sending the B-47 streaking away from the target long before the bomb detonated. The B-47's wing had not been designed for such manoeuvres, or for the extended life that was being enforced upon it, with a result that massive sums of money were spent on wing structure revision and reinforcement. B-47Es so converted became redesignated **B-47E-II**. More-extensively modified B-47Bs, brought up to B-47E standard plus the wing structure modifications, were designated **B-47B-II**.

This programme, and others involving equipment updates, ensured that the B-47 saw 15 years of first-line service before being withdrawn in 1966. Even then, examples continued in use for weather reconnaissance, with Military Airlift Command, until the end of 1969. The B-47 represented a great technological achievement for Boeing, and has an honoured place in USAF history being its, and the world's first, swept-wing

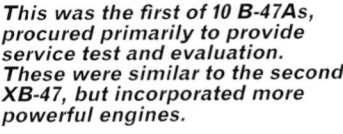

A specialist photo-reconnaissance version was the RB-47E, distinguished by a lengthened nose. This example flies in formation with an early B-47E, the principal bomber version.

turbojet bomber to be built on a large scale. And, because of this large volume of production, it is inevitable that a fairly large number of variants resulted.

Variants

B-47B-II: designation of B-47Bs after conversion to updated B-47E standard, see notes above

B-47B/CL-52: one B-47B was transferred to the RCAF, which loaned the aircraft to Canadair Ltd, this company using it as a test-bed for the Canadian-built Orenda Iroquois turbojet, pod-mounted on the starboard side of the rear fuselage

DB-47B: conversions of B-47Bs as control aircraft, primarily for GB-47Es (below), but also for other drones; tail armament removed and radio control equipment installed

RB-47B: designation of 24 B-47Bs converted for a reconnaissance role (some designated **YRB-47B**), carrying eight cameras and other equipment in a specially-heated compartment in the bomb bay

TB-47B: designation of 66 standard B-47Bs modified by the addition of a fourth (instructor's) crew position, and used for the conversion training of pilots and navigators

YDB-47B: one B-47B converted to carry, launch and control a Bell GAM-63 Rascal missile during initial dropping trials

XB-47D: under this designation two B-47Bs were converted to serve as test-beds for Wright YT49-W-1 turboprop engines; one of these 7241-ekW (9,710-eshp) powerplants was installed in lieu of the paired J47s on each side, with the single outboard J47 being retained on each wing

DB-47E: designation of two B-47E conversions, plus two generally similar **YDB-47E**s, also for launch and control trials with Bell GAM-63s

QB-47E: a total of 14 B-47Es was converted to radio-controlled drone configuration under this designation; used as targets, though not expendable because of their cost, and for tasks considered too hazardous for a human crew

RB-47E: major strategic photo-reconnaissance version of the B-47, 240 Boeing-built aircraft being completed to this configuration on the production line; bombing equipment deleted, and replaced by up to 11 cameras, and associated equipment for night photography

WB-47E: under this designation 24 B-47Es were converted to serve with MAC's Air Weather Service in a weather reconnaissance role

YB-47F: one B-47B, equipped with an inflight-refuelling probe, was used for probe-and-drogue refuelling tests under this designation

KB-47G: designation of one B-47B modified and equipped as a hose tanker for probe-and-drogue inflight-refuelling experiments with the YB-47F (above)

RB-47H: designation of 32 Boeing-built B-47s, completed in production for electronic reconnaissance missions, and equipped with nose, underfuselage and wing radomes, and with the bomb bay converted as a compartment to accommodate equipment and three specialist operators

ERB-47H: under this designation three B-47Es were converted for the same role as the RB-47H, but these accommodated a total crew of five only

YB-47J: designation of one standard bomber converted as a test-bed for a new radar bombing/navigation system (MA-2)

RB-47K: an additional 15 new RB-47Es were completed under this designation for use in photo/weather reconnaissance sorties at all altitudes

EB-47L: designation applied to 35 B-47Es following conversion during 1963 to serve as communications relay stations

Specification
Boeing B-47E-II Stratojet
Type: strategic medium bomber
Powerplant: six General Electric J47-GE-25 or -25A turbojets, each developing 3266-kg (7,200-lb) thrust with water injection
Performance: maximum speed 975 km/h (606 mph) at 4970 m (16,300 ft); cruising speed 896 km/h (557 mph) at 11735 m (38,500 ft); service ceiling 12345 m (40,500 ft); range 6437 km (4,000 miles)
Weights: empty 36630 kg (80,756 lb); maximum take-off 89893 kg (198,180 lb)
Dimensions: span 35.36 m (116 ft 0 in); length 33.48 m (109 ft 10 in); height 8.51 m (27 ft 11 in); wing area 132.66 m² (1,428 sq ft)
Armament: two 20-mm cannon in remotely-controlled tail turret, plus up to 9071 kg (20,000 lb) bombs carried internally

Boeing Model 464 (B-52 Stratofortress)

By normal standards long since rendered obsolete as a result of its unacceptable vulnerability to surface-to-air missiles, the mighty **Boeing B-52 Stratofortress** has seen two would-be successors fall by the wayside, and remains one of the three US strategic deterrents (the other two being the land- and sea-launched missiles). More than $1 billion has been spent on the 230 or so aircraft remaining in the front-line fleet to improve their safety, reliability, performance and weapon-delivery accuracy.

At Offutt Air Force Base, Nebraska, the headquarters of the US Air Force Strategic Air Command, an American journalist was told in 1976 that some of the B-52s would be operating into the next century. This claim was made at a time when the B-52's supersonic successor, the Rockwell B-1, was well into its flight-test programme and regarded as the linchpin of SAC's airborne might. If the B-52 does reach the year 2000 it will probably have had the longest career of any front-line combat type. By that time the youngest of these subsonic bombers will have been on the flight-line for 40 years.

What was to become SAC's 'long rifle' began life in 1948 as a turboprop successor to the piston-engined Boeing B-50, itself a development of the B-29 Superfortress, whose nuclear missions

against Japan brought World War II to a close in 1945. Designers were faced with a quandary: the B-50's successor was clearly going to have turbine engines, but how were such engines to be used? Ordinary jet engines of the period were so thirsty that a huge airframe would be needed to carry all the fuel. The answer was to harness them to large propellers, as the Soviet Union was to do later with its Tupolev Tu-95 'Bear'. Deciding on the right propulsion system was perhaps the biggest headache facing the early jet-bomber designers. Turboprops were the obvious answer, because they were more economical than pure jets, but on the other hand they were more complicated and less reliable.

Then, in 1949, Pratt & Whitney brought out the J57 turbojet engine. Far and away superior to any other US powerplant, it was to become over the next 30 years one of aviation's really great engines. Originally giving 3402-kg (7,500-lb) thrust, it helped to change the philosophy of both Boeing and the USAF.

Boeing and Convair, its rival in the big-bomber stakes, fought bitterly to get the contract for the new USAF bomber. Convair had already provided the mammoth B-36, and so had a wealth of experience with heavyweights. But its proposed YB-60, though cheaper than the com-

peting B-52, could not equal its performance, and Boeing won the day.

The prototype **XB-52 (Model 464-67)** took the air for the first time on 15 April 1952. Its technology was based on the medium-range B-47 that had flown five years previously. Thus it had a similar extremely thin, shoulder-mounted wing, with engines clustered in podded pairs, and with the same tandem main-wheel arrangement with wing-mounted outrigger wheels. The XB-52 was notable for its tandem seating of the pilots, a feature repeated in the **YB-52** second prototype.

The first three production aircraft were designated **B-52A (Model 464-201-0)** and spent their lives at Boeing as test and development aircraft, beginning an improvement programme that has gone on to this day. The first version to join the USAF was the **B-52B (Model 464-201-3)**, virtually identical to the B-52A but with a navigation/bombing system. Of the 50 built, 27 were converted as **RB-52B** reconnaissance versions.

The **B-52C (Model 464-201-6)** was substantially improved in performance and equipment, and was the first model (35 built) to have the white anti-radiation under-surface finish. It was succeeded by the **B-52D (Model 464-201-7)**, of which 170 were built with an improved fire-control system for the tail

armament of four 12.7-mm (0.5-in) machine-guns. As the B-52Ds were being turned out by Boeing's Wichita plant (the production line was progressively transferred there because of the huge build-up of KC-135 tanker construction at the Seattle factory), the USAF was thinking about the giant bomber's successor. This was to be the WS-110, later the North American B-70.

But the B-70 was years in the future, and B-52 improvement continued with the **B-52E (Model 464-259)**, whose 100 examples had a more advanced navigation and weapons system, and a new flight-deck layout to house the equipment displays. Continuing weight increases called for more power, especially at take-off, and the **B-52F (Model 464-260)**, of which 89 were built, had a later version of the J57 engine, fitted like earlier versions with water injection to boost take-off power.

The **B-52G (Model 464-253)**, which was planned initially as the final version pending arrival of the B-70, brought along a host of major improvements, and was the biggest single advance of any model. The airframe was substantially redesigned to save weight and to make it safer; integral wing-tanks greatly increased fuel capacity; the tail gunner was relocated in the crew compartment, this saving considerable weight; the fin was shortened; and provision was made for launching ECM decoys and stand-off missiles. The decoy was a small jet aeroplane known

161

as the Quail, designed to have a radar signature similar to that of the bomber to confuse missile radars. One hundred and ninety-three B-52Gs were built, the last in 1960. The missile to go with it was the AGM-28 Hound Dog, which had a range of 1207 km (750 miles). The B-52G, in fact, was to be less a bomber than the first stage of a missile.

Meanwhile, Boeing and the USAF were planning between them yet another version, the **B-52H (Model 464-261)**, which really was the final model. It was characterised by two major changes: the introduction of new Pratt & Whitney TF33 turbofan engines, which gave greater thrust allied to a considerably lower specific fuel consumption, and structural changes which permitted the aircraft to fly at low altitudes without excessive fatigue problems. It also exchanged the four 12.7-mm (0.5-in) tail guns for a single fast-firing 'Gatling' type gun. It was built to carry Skybolt ballistic missiles under the wings and Quail decoys in the bomb bay.

The final B-52H, the last of 744 B-52s, rolled out of Wichita in June 1962. The Skybolt missile, which had also been ordered by the RAF, was cancelled in December of that year, while the B-70 project had already been terminated. The B-52s were clearly going to have to soldier on for a long time while the USAF made up its mind what to do about a replacement.

In 1963 the B-52D was studied as a CBC (conventional bomb carrier) and the following year rebuilding of B-52Ds began at Wichita to permit the type to carry 105 'iron' bombs of 340-kg (750-lb) nominal weight, but actually weighing 374 kg (825 lb). In 1965 rebuilt CBC aircraft started to hammer suspected Communist hideouts in South Vietnam and the supply route from North Vietnam known as the Ho Chi Minh trail. The B-52s operated from Andersen AFB on Guam island, 4184 km (2,600 miles) away in the Pacific. Each mission lasted some 10 to 12 hours, with inflight-refuelling by means of Boeing KC-135 tankers.

With little sign of progress around the negotiating table, the B-52s were authorised in April 1966 to bomb North Vietnam. To cut the cost of what was turning out to be a very expensive war, and to provide quicker reaction, the big bombers were deployed to U Tapao air-

field in neighbouring Thailand, cutting the journey by three-quarters and dispensing with the need for inflight-refuelling.

Through the late 1960s and early 1970s the bombers continued to rain high-explosive bombs on Vietnam, aided by improved navigation and weapon-delivery techniques and to some extent protected by ever-increasingly sophisticated ECM devices. Used in an all-out attack on North Vietnam's capital and its harbour (Haiphong) during late 1972, they caused tremendous destruction, but the USAF lost 15 of these giant aircraft to enemy SAM defences. Soon afterwards, all US forces were withdrawn from that theatre.

Ten years earlier, the USAF had initiated defence studies that were to lead to the Advanced Manned Strategic Aircraft (AMSA) requirement of 1965. This was then envisaged as a low-altitude penetration bomber that would begin to replace SAC's B-52s by 1980. In mid-1970, North American Rockwell's Los Angeles Division was named as prime contractor for what was to become a politically controversial aircraft. Designated as the B-1, its production was cancelled by President Carter on 30 June 1977, his administration opting instead for development of the cruise missile. This decision was reversed in September 1981 by President Reagan, and the development and pro-

duction of 100 improved B-1Bs followed.

Clearly, the B-52 still has to shoulder a great deal of responsibility, and the 1976 forecast of B-52 deployment into the opening years of the 21st century would still seem to be very much on the cards. This means, of course, that the very large sums that have been spent on B-52 improvement programmes have not been wasted. The Offensive Avionics System (OAS) programme was implemented to update navigation and weapons delivery of B-52G and B-52H aircraft in USAF service. The first stage of this programme began with the first flight of an OAS-equipped B-52G on 3 September 1980. Following the completion of 12 months' flight testing, the B-52G fleet has been updated to this standard. Development of the B-52 as a cruise missile carrier was also pursued actively, with the modification of 173 B-52Gs each to carry 12 Boeing AGM-86B ALCMs (Air-Launched Cruise Missiles) on inboard underwing pylons. This is in addition to the eight Boeing AGM-69 SRAMs (short-range attack missiles), or optional weapons, carried in the internal weapons bay. All remaining B-52Hs were also converted to carry cruise missiles, adding eight weapons in the bomb bay.

Specification
Boeing B-52H Stratofortress
Type: six-seat long-range strategic

A Boeing B-52H Stratofortress in tactical camouflage. Evidence of the type's constantly-modified offensive and defensive avionics is provided by the wealth of bulges and antennae on and under the nose, and under the fuselage. Further modifications are inevitable as a result of the USAF's need to keep the venerable B-52 series in service, possibly into the early part of the 21st century.

bomber
Powerplant: eight 7711-kg (17,000-lb) thrust Pratt & Whitney TF33-P-3 turbofans
Performance: maximum speed at optimum altitude 958 km/h (595 mph); cruising speed at optimum altitude 819 km/h (509 mph); service ceiling 16765 m (55,000 ft); unrefuelled maximum range 16093 km (10,000 miles)
Weight: maximum take-off exceeds 221353 kg (488,000 lb)
Dimensions: span 56.39 m (185 ft 0 in); length 49.05 m (160 ft 11 in); height 12.40 m (40 ft 8 in); wing area 371.60 m² (4,000.0 sq ft)
Armament: one remotely-controlled 20-mm Vulcan cannon in tail turret, plus up to 20 AGM-86 ALCMs and nuclear free-fall bombs

Boeing Model 707

In the USA, The Boeing Company was first to appreciate the potential of the gas turbine engine to power a new generation of civil transport aircraft, and to take positive action to design and construct such a machine. The process began when the company initiated studies for a turbojet or turboprop-powered version of the military C-97 Stratofreighter, a heavy cargo/transport aircraft derived from the B-29 Superfortress. Little or no interest came in response to Boeing's proposals, and in August 1952 the company took the bold step of gambling some $16 million to build the prototype of a completely new turbojet-powered civil transport. To maintain a degree of secrecy for this project it was allocated the designation **Model 367-80**, known as 'Dash-80' to Boeing employees, although higher echelons of the company knew that it would be marketed as the **Model 707**.

Boeing were sufficiently realistic to appreciate from the very beginning that its large private-venture investment, even in 1952 dollars, was nowhere near

the amount that would be needed if large-scale production of a civil airliner was to become a reality. Shrewdly, they developed the initial design to serve as a high-speed military transport, or inflight-refuelling tanker, banking upon gaining a military contract which would underwrite the tooling costs and provide finance for the development of a first-class civil airliner.

The Model 367-80, which was rolled out on 14 May 1954, had clearly derived from the civil piston-engined Model 377 Stratocruiser and the military KC-97, but aerodynamically had a close relationship to the B-47 Stratojet which had entered service with the USAF in 1950. It retained the distinctive wing of the jet bomber, swept back 35° and the mounting of the inboard powerplant of the B-47, with two turbojets paired in side-by-side nacelles and carried on a cantilever underwing pylon, had received serious consideration for the 'Dash-80'. However, it was appreciated that under certain circumstances the failure of one unit of the pair could result in the need to

shut down the remaining operative engine, seriously compromising reserve power, and it was decided instead, as a safety measure, to install the engines in individual pylon-mounted pods which have become a characteristic feature of the Model 707/720 and later 747.

Flown for the first time on 15 July 1954, the 'Dash-80' was powered by four 4309-kg (9,500-lb) thrust Pratt & Whitney JT3P turbojets, and as originally flown was primarily a military demonstrator. At an early stage in its flight test programme the 'Dash-80' acquired a Boeing-designed inflight-refuelling boom, which had been developed to simplify the rapid transfer of fuel from tanker to receiver. With this combination of a high-performance large-capacity aircraft with inflight-refuelling capability, Boeing was able to demonstrate effectively to the USAF the potential of such a tanker for refuelling in-service and future bomber, fighter, reconnaissance, and

The first fan-engined version of the 707 was the Series 400, featuring the lengthened fuselage of the Series 300 mated to four Rolls-Royce Conway engines. BOAC was the major operator.

The Boeing Model 707's greatest claim to fame is as the airliner that truly opened the era of jet air travel, and the type's significance is shown by the fact that enormous numbers are still in service, including this Model 707-320 of Avianca, the Colombian flag-carrier, which has three Model 707s.

transport aircraft at or near their operational altitudes, and at speeds which would not present any real problems for either of the aircraft involved. In less than three months after the first flight of the Model 367-80 on 5 October 1954, Boeing received an initial contract for 29 KC-135A tanker/transports, and there must have been jubilation in the board room when it was realised that the gamble had paid off: in the long term the company was to build more than 800 military versions under basic Model 717 designations.

With military interest secured, the 'Dash-80' was equipped as a civil demonstrator offering, initially to US airlines, a turbojet aircraft that would soon make obsolete the existing piston-engine airliners operating US domestic transcontinental routes. The first contract came from pioneering Pan American, which on 13 October 1955 ordered six examples of the first production version, which had the designation **Model 707-120**. Just three months before that date, the USAF had given Boeing clearance to build civil developments of the 'Dash-80' simultaneously with the manufacture of military C/KC-135s, and no time was lost in establishing a production line for civil aircraft. Pan American's first Model 707-120 flew initially on 20 December 1957, was delivered to the airline in the following August, and on 26 October 1958 – despite being intended primarily for con-

The definitive 707 was the Series 320C, a convertible passenger/ freight version with JT3D turbofans.

tinental services – was used to inaugurate Pan Am's New York-London transatlantic jet airliner service. This move was, however, a flag-waving rather than a practical operation, and Pan Am's Model 707-120s soon reverted to the domestic routes for which they had been intended. It was not until this airline received its first true long-range versions of the 707, namely the Model 707-320 Intercontinental, that sustained scheduled transatlantic flights began on 10 October 1959.

Production of the Model 707 had virtually come to an end in 1990, with 999 aircraft built, including military derivatives, in a manufacturing programme of 30 years. In that time there have been a number of versions, and brief details of these are given under the heading of Variants below.

Final version in production was the Model 707-320C Convertible, a multi-purpose aircraft which in a typical layout accommodates 14 first-class and 133 coach-class passengers; it is, however, certificated to carry a maximum of 219 passengers in a high-density seating arrangement. Alternatively it can be operated in mixed passenger/cargo, or all-cargo roles, and in the latter configuration can accept up to 13 Type A containers in the main upper-deck cargo space, in addition to the 48.14 m (1,700 cu ft) of bulk cargo capacity on the lower, standard cargo deck. Throughout the 30 years that the 707 was in production, there had been continuing development to enhance performance, economy of operation, load-carrying capability, and range.

Not surprisingly, for an aircraft that has

a history which is contemperaneous with the development of the gas turbine engine, the Model 707 has had a variety of powerplants installed. The 4309-kg (9,500-lb) thrust JT3Ps, which first powered the 'Dash-80', were replaced by 6123-kg (13,500-lb) thrust JT3C-6s in the initial production version. Pratt & Whitney JT3D-1 or JT3D-3 turbofans of 7711-kg (17,000-lb) or 8165-kg (18,000-lb) thrust respectively were available for the Model 707-120B, and the highest powered turbojets for the first long-range Model 707-320 were JT4A-11s of 7938-kg (17,500-lb) thrust. The Rolls-Royce Conway Mk 508 turbofans which BOAC specified for installation in the 707-420 were of similar thrust. The late production Model 707-320Cs have Pratt & Whitney JT3D-7 turbofans, and the net result of this progession of engine powers is that the intercontinental Model 707-320C in all-cargo configuration has a maximum take-off weight almost 34 per cent greater than that of the domestic Model 707-220 of 1959.

These details of the Model 707 would be incomplete without a final mention of the 'Dash-80' which, in almost 18 years of service, was probably the most extensively modified aircraft in aviation history. In addition to changes which related to the continuing development programme of the Model 707, the 'Dash-80' was the subject of many major aerodynamic and structural changes, to test new ideas and advanced features of later Boeing jet transports. These included new wing planforms, aerofoil surfaces, powerplants, and an entirely new wing leading-edge and trailing-edge flaps. It was even flown with a fifth

engine in an aft mounted pod, to evaluate the proposed installation planned for the Model 727. Happily, it did not suffer final ignominous destruction at the hands of scrapyard breakers for, in May 1990, it returned to Seattle for display.

Variants

Model 707-120B: development of the initial production version with more powerful turbofan engines, plus wing and tail unit aerodynamic improvements introduced on the Model 720

Model 707-220: generally similar to original production version, but powered by Pratt & Whitney JT4A-3 engines

Model 707-320 Intercontinental: long-range transocean version, with wing span and fuselage length increased by 3.53 m (11 ft 7 in) and 2.03 m (6 ft 8 in) respectively, more powerful engines, and accommodation for 189 passengers

Model 707-320B Intercontinental: a developed version of the 707-320 with more powerful turbofan engines and aerodynamic refinements

Model 707-320C Convertible: passenger, mixed passenger/cargo, or cargo version of the 707-320B, with a cargo door and Boeing-developed cargo loading system; a maximum of 215 passengers can be carried in the all-passenger configuration

Model 707-320C Freighter: cargo version of the Model 707-320C, with all passenger facilities removed

Model 707-420 Intercontinental: generally similar to Model 707-320, but powered by Rolls-Royce Conway Mk 508 turbofan engines

VC-137B/-137C: designation of five VIP transports in USAF service; the first three were equivalent to Model 707-120s, but with special interiors and avionics, and were delivered as **VC-137A**s; were redesignated VC-137B after installation of turbofan engines; the two VC-137Cs, with accommodation for a crew of seven or eight and 49 passengers, are based on the Model 707-320B

Specification
Boeing Model 707-320C
Type: four-turbofan commercial transport
Powerplant: four 8618-kg (19,000-lb) thrust Pratt & Whitney JT3D-7 turbofans
Performance: maximum speed 1009 km/h (627 mph); maximum cruising speed 974 km/h (605 mph); economic cruising speed 885 km/h (550 mph); service ceiling 11890 m (39,000 ft); range with maximum fuel and 147 passengers, international fuel reserves, 9262 km (5,755 miles)
Weights: operating empty, passenger 66406 kg (146,400 lb), cargo 64002 kg (141,100 lb); maximum take-off 151318 kg (333,600 lb)
Dimensions: span 44.42 m (145 ft 9 in); length 46.61 m (152 ft 11 in); height 12.93 m (42 ft 5 in); wing area 283.35 m (3,050.0 sq ft)

Boeing (Model 707) E-3A Sentry
to
Boeing Model 720

Boeing (Model 707) E-3A Sentry

The requirement for an Airborne Warning And Control System (AWACS) aircraft was outlined by the US Air Force in 1963, at which time it was envisaged that a force of up to 64 of these specially-equipped aircraft would be needed. They were then considered essential to alert US air defences of approaching attack by manned or unmanned air vehicles of all classes, and to act as mobile control centres of unfixed geographical position, able to control all national air activities in both conventional or nuclear combat operations. However, since the origination of the concept, economic considerations have made it necessary to reduce considerably the number of aircraft to be acquired initially.

The resulting **Boeing E-3A Sentry** is essentially a flexible, jamming-resistant, mobile and survivable radar station, plus a command, communications and control centre, all contained within the well-proven airframe of a Boeing 707. In addition to its long-range high- or low-level surveillance capability, an AWACS aircraft can provide all-weather identification and tracking over all kinds of terrain, and the 22nd and subsequent aircraft also have a maritime surveillance capability. These aircraft can command and control the entire air effort of a nation, embracing interception, interdiction, reconnaissance and strike, plus the back-up roles of airlift and support.

Two main areas of use have been planned by the USAF, with the Tactical Air Command (TAC) using its AWACS aircraft for airborne surveillance, and as a command centre for the rapid deployment of TAC forces. A differing role is envisaged for the same aircraft by Aerospace Defense Command (ADC), who regard the AWACS aircraft was 'hard to find' command and control posts. (ADC has now become a component of TAC, but the two basic E-3A missions remain substantially unaltered.)

Boeing was the successful one of two contenders for the supply of an AWACS aircraft, being awarded a contract on 23 July 1970 to provide two prototypes under the designation **EC-137D**. The company's proposed AWACS was based on the airframe of the Boeing Model 707-320B commercial transport, and the prototypes were modified in the first place to carry out comparative trials between the prototype downward-looking surveillance radars designed by the Hughes Aircraft company and Westinghouse Electric Corporation. These tests continued into the autumn of 1972, and on 5 October the USAF announced that Westinghouse had been selected as prime contractor for the advanced radar that was to be the essential core of the AWACS. This has the difficult task of seeking and identifying low-flying targets at ranges as great as 370 km (230 miles), and in the case of high-altitude attack at even greater ranges.

The USAF had acquired an extensive knowledge of the operation and capabilities of the Boeing Model 707, especially in the form of the EC-135 variants which have served well and long. It was clear that with far more advanced equipment the same aircraft could provide the desired potential, thus ensuring that

equipment acquired for and experience derived from the EC-135 would offer an important and reliable contribution to the AWACS concept.

Very little modification of the basic 707-320B airframe was needed to make it suitable for the new role. Most important, and an external identification feature *par excellence*, is the large rotodome assembly carried on two wide-chord streamlined struts, which are secured to the upper rear fuselage. The remainder of the essential avionics antennae are housed within the wings, fuselage, fin and tailplane. New engine pylon fairings are provided for the more powerful turbofan engines of the pre-production EC-137Ds, and of the production aircraft which were designated E-3A and given the name Sentry. Internal modifications included strengthening of the cabin floor, provision of MPC (multi-purpose console) and other equipment bays, and addition of a crew rest area. Basic operations require a flight crew of four plus 13 AWACS specialist officers, but this number can vary for defence and tactical missions, and other personnel can be carried for systems management and radar maintenance.

Not surprisingly, the mass of avionics equipment needed for the E-3A to fulfil its AWACS role has required the installation of extensive cooling and wiring systems. The cooling and air-conditioning systems are complex to ensure an ideal working environment for crew and equipment. Thus, liquid cooling protects the radar transmitter, housed in the aft cargo hold, and a conventional air-cycle and ram-air environmental control system provides for crew comfort and the safe operation of other avionics equipment. There is also a large demand for electrical power, which is supplied by generators with a combined output of 600 kVA. The over-fuselage rotodome is 9.14 m (30 ft 0 in) in diameter and has a

maximum depth of 1.83 m (6 ft 0 in). This incorporates the AN/APY-1 surveillance radar and IFF/TADIL C antennae. During operational use the rotodome is driven hydraulically at 6 rpm, but in non-operational flight is rotated at one twenty-fourth of this speed to ensure that low temperatures do not cause the bearing lubricant to congeal and prevent normal operation when required.

The current Westinghouse radar, installed first in the 22nd Sentry, and scheduled to be updated in earlier aircraft, can function as a pulse and/or pulse-Doppler radar, and is operable in six different modes. The data processing capability of the first 23 E-3As is provided by an IBM 4 Pi CC-1 high-speed computer. It has a processing speed of some 740,000 operations per second, main memory capacity of 114,688 words, and a mass memory of 802,816 words. The IBM CC-2 computer, introduced on the 24th production aircraft, has a main

Based on the structure of the Model 707-320B, the Boeing E-3A Sentry AWACS aircraft offers the west a major advantage in air operations: its powerful radar and computer-controlled operations room allow the speedy co-ordination of American and allied aircraft for offensive and defensive tasks, even in face of electronic countermeasures.

memory capacity of 665,360 words. Also introduced on this aircraft is the newly-developed Joint Tactical Information Distribution System (JTIDS). This provides a high-speed secure communications channel for up to 98,000 users, and one that is less vulnerable to jamming.

The first production E-3A was delivered on 24 March 1977 to the USAF's 552nd Airborne Warning and Control

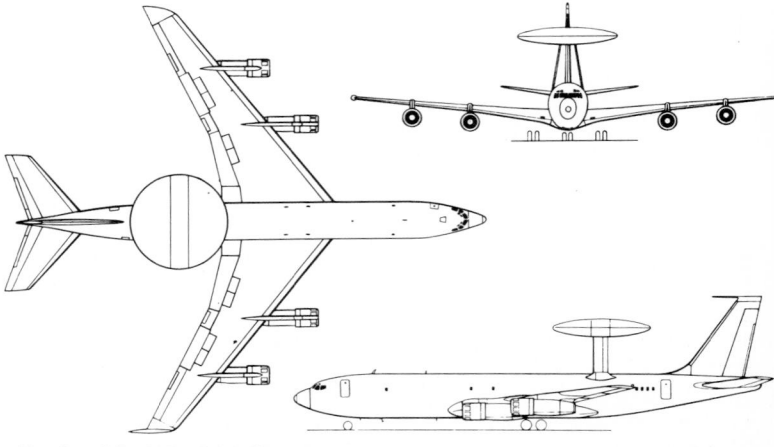

Boeing EC-137D (E-3A Sentry)

Sentry has also been sold to Saudi Arabia, France and the United Kingdom, all export aircraft being powered by CFM56 high bypass ratio turbofans.

Specification

Type: airborne early-warning and command post aircraft
Powerplant: four 9525-kg (21,000-lb) thrust Pratt & Whitney TF33-PW-100/100A turbofans
Performance: maximum speed 853 km/h (530 mph); service ceiling 8840 m (29,000 ft); endurance on station 1609 km (1,000 miles) from base 6 hours
Weight: maximum take-off 147418 kg (325,000 lb)
Dimensions: span 44.42 m (145 ft 9 in); length 46.61 m (152 ft 11 in); height 12.60 m (41 ft 4 in); wing area 283.35 m (3,050.0 sq ft)

Wing, based at Tinker AFB, Oklahoma. The current force of AWACS aircraft for service with the USAF is 34. In addition, a force of 18 generally similar aircraft was acquired by NATO. Initial deliveries of NATO's operational E-3As, which are based at Geilenkirchen, West Germany, were made during 1982. They differ from their USAF counterparts by comparatively minor changes in installed avionics to meet NATO communications requirements. They also introduced underwing hardpoints to carry self-defence weapons, but these mountings can be used optionally to carry ECM pods. The

Boeing (Model 707) E-6 Hermes

Boeing was awarded, in April 1983, a contract to develop a replacement for the US Navy's EC-130Q Hercules fleet, which was used for providing a communications link with the Trident nuclear submarine fleet. Under the mission acronym TACAMO (TAke Charge And Move Out), the new aircraft needed to be survivable and to have long mission endurance.

Boeing used the tried and trusted Model 707 airframe, fitting the communications gear and operator stations within the windowless capacious fuselage. For greater efficiency, the CFM International CFM56 (military designation F108) turbofan was fitted. Many of the systems were derived from those of the E-3A, but with the TACAMO gear added, this including a trailing wire VLF (Very Low Frequency) antenna and wingtip antenna pods.

Sixteen aircraft are required by the US Navy to replace the EC-130Q with squadrons VQ-3 and -4. Designated **E-6A Hermes**, the first prototype flew from Renton on 19 February 1987. Full systems flight trials began in June. The system is now fully operational.

Specification

Type: long range submarine communications platform
Powerplant: four CFM International F108 turbofans, each rated at 106.76 kN (24,000 lb) thrust
Performance: dash speed 981 km/h (610 mph); normal cruising speed

Again powered by CFM56 engines, the E-6A combines a large unobstructed interior, high dash speed and very long endurance, perfect attributes for its submarine support role.

842 km/h (523 mph); take-off run 1650 m (5,415 ft); service ceiling 12800 m (42,000 ft); normal patrol altitude 7620-9150 m (25,000-30,000 ft); unrefuelled mission range 11760 km (7,305 miles); on-station endurance 1850 km (1,150 miles) from base 10 hours 30 minutes unrefuelled or 28 hours 54 minutes with one refuelling
Weights: operating empty 78378 kg (172,795 lb); maximum take-off 155128 kg (342,000 lb)
Dimensions: span 45.16 m (148ft 2in); length 46.61 m (152ft 11in); height 12.93 m (42ft 5in); wing area 283.4 m² (3,050 sq ft)

Boeing (Model 707) E-8 J-STARS

To provide a stand-off battlefield reconnaissance capability, Grumman was awarded a $657 million contract in September 1985 to develop the USAF/US Army Joint Surveillance and Target Attack Radar System (J-STARS). The Norden radar system is designed to use synthetic aperture technology to provide high resolution information on enemy force dispositions at long oblique range, allowing the carrier platform to operate in friendly airspace well behind the front line.

Two Boeing 707-323C transports were modified by Boeing before delivery to Grumman which integrated the avionics package. The principal sensor is the radar which is housed in a 9.1 m (30ft) long canoe fairing under the forward fuselage. Originally designated

EC-18C, the two modified aircraft are now called **E-8A**. The **E-8B** is a proposed new-build aircraft powered by CFM International F018 turbofans, but the Air Force is currently proposing to modify existing 707 airframes if the programme is given the go-ahead.

The first aircraft flew with Boeing in April 1988, and in full J-STARS configuration with Grumman on 22 December 1988. Evaluation of the system has included limited deployments to Europe to test the system in an operational environment. With the change in the political climate, the J-STARS may be seen as an expensive luxury and consequently cancelled.

The first E-8A lifts off on a test mission, carrying the giant Norden J-STARS radar under its forward fuselage. Ground clearance is marginal.

Boeing Model 717 (C/KC-135 Stratolifter/Stratotanker)

In August 1954, the USAF announced that it intended to procure a number of tanker/transports developed from the prototype Boeing Model 387-80 which had first flown a few weeks earlier. These were allocated the designation **KC-135A**, and the first of them made its initial flight on 31 August 1956: 10 months later, on 28 June 1957, the first was delivered to Castle AFB, California. Since that time a family of variants has been produced in large numbers for service with the USAF, mainly as tankers (**Stratotankers**) or cargo transports (**Stratolifters**). Two modified KC-135As are used by the US Federal Aviation Administration (FAA) to check navigation aids throughout the United States.

This military version of the Model 367-80 is identified as the **Boeing Model 717**: it differs primarily from the later Model 707 by having a smaller-diameter fuselage, deletion of cabin windows, reduced size and weight, and accommodation for 80 passengers or an equivalent weight of cargo on the main deck. All equipment for the tanker role is carried on the lower deck, or normal cargo area, and includes the pivoted 'Flying Boom' refuelling gear. This was modified subsequently by the provision of an adaptor to allow for probe-and-drogue refuelling of Tactical Air Command and US Navy/Marine Corps aircraft. Power is provided by four 6123-kg (13,500-lb) thrust Pratt & Whitney J57-P-59W turbojets.

The Model 717 Stratolifter family differs from the foregoing by being equipped specifically to serve as long-range transports. These have the refuelling boom deleted, but there is a structural similarity between these two basic tanker/lifter types, with interior changes in the latter providing accommodation for up to 126 troops, or 44 stretchers plus 54 sitting casualties. Galley and toilet facilities are provided at the rear of the cabin, and provision is made for an alternative all-freight role. The initial version was the **C-135A** with turbojet engines, first flown on 19 May 1961, and delivered to MATS on 8 June 1961 to become the USAF's first strategic jet transport.

Now, almost 30 years later and with 820 delivered, it is inevitable that there are a number of variants, including specially-built versions and conversions, and brief details of these are given below. Recent modifications include structural strengthening and re-engining with CFM56 turbofans with increased thrust and reduced fuel consumption.

Boeing KC-135E Stratotanker of the 126th Air Refueling Wing, Illinois Air National Guard.

Variants

C-135B: redesignation of last 30 production C-135As as a result of an increase in tailplane span, and introduction of turbofan engines
C-135C: redesignation of WC-135B aircraft returning to transport role
C-135E: C-135A aircraft re-engined with TF33 turbofans
C-135F: 12 dual-purpose tanker/transports for French air force, with refuelling booms terminating in a drogue
C-135FR: C-135Fs re-engined with CFM56 turbofans
EC-135A: designation of KC-135As after adaptation as airborne command posts for back-up to EC-135C variants
EC-135B: TF33 powered aircraft with huge antenna in bulbous nose radome
EC-135C: later designation of KC-135B airborne command posts (below)
EC-135G: similar to EC-135A but with revised interior layout
EC-135H: designation of KC-135A command posts with more advanced equipment
EC-135J: turbofan-powered version of EC-135H
EC-135K: KC-135A with extra communication equipment, used for fighter deployment support
EC-135L: redesignation of KC-135As equipped to serve in dual role of communications relay stations and command posts
EC-135N: designation of eight C-135As modified to carry an outsize parabolic dish antenna (2.13m/7ft diameter) in nose for spacecraft tracking. Redesignated **EC-135E** when fitted with TF33 turbofans
EC-135P: designation of five KC-135As modified in the initial ABNCP programme leading to the Boeing E-4
EC-135Y: single command post modification
JKC-135A: designation of KC-135As used by Air Force Systems Command

The KC-135R has new-technology F108 turbofans to give increased safety, economy and reliability levels. For some degree of autonomous operation, an auxiliary power unit is added in the port rear fuselage, with a characteristic inlet and exhaust.

A trio of McDonnell Douglas F-4D Phantoms lines up to take on fuel from a Boeing KC-135 tanker before a strike into North Vietnam. The widespread use of the KC-135 fleet offers the USAF unrivalled tactical and strategic flexibility.

for special test purposes
KC-135B: designation of 17 airborne command posts with turbofan engines, and provided with inflight-refuelling capability to extend range or on-station endurance; redesignated subsequently as EC-135C
KC-135D: four RC-135As modified for tanker duties
KC-135E: KC-135A aircraft re-engined with TF33 turbofans
KC-135Q: designation of 56 KC-135As converted as special tankers for the Lockheed SR-71
KC-135R: designation of four KC-135As modified for special reconnaissance
KC-135R: major re-engining programme for mainstream tanker fleet which fits CFM56 turbofans, APU and updated avionics
NC-135A: three aircraft equipped to monitor nuclear weapon tests; used with special equipment to study a total solar eclipse during 1965
NKC-135A: designation of KC-135As used by Air Force Systems Command for special test purposes, and fitted with a wide variety of additional systems; also **NKC-135E** with TF33 engines
RC-135A: four KC-135As without inflight-refuelling booms and equipped for photo-reconnaissance and mapping; these have the Boeing identification of **Model 739**
RC-135B: 10 electronic reconnaissance aircraft based on the turbofan-powered C-135B; also identified by Boeing as Model 739
RC-135C: designation of aircraft RC-135B after modification by Martin with electronic reconnaissance equipment. Featured cheek fairings with many antennae
RC-135D: designation of KC-135As after equipping for electronic

reconnaissance role; refuelling boom deleted
RC-135E: designation of one C-135B after being equipped for electronic reconnaissance; refuelling boom deleted
RC-135M: designation of six fan-engined C-135Bs modified with a special radome in place of the refuelling boom, and a blister antenna on each side of the rear fuselage
RC-135S: designation of three aircraft similar to the RC-135Ms, but with additional rear-fuselage antennae and

The C-135B was the principal transport variant, featuring TF33 turbofans and a wider tailplane to handle the increased thrust. These were used heavily by MATS for a short while, flying nearly twice as fast as the C-118s and C-124s they augmented. They were soon put out of service by the introduction of the C-141 StarLifter.

dipole-like antennae on the top and sides of the forward fuselage. Large

Many C-135s have been grossly modified for special missions. This is an RC-135U, dripping with aerials for its strategic electronic reconnaissance role. Two serve alongside RC-135Vs and RC-135Ws with the 55th SRW.

transports

WC-135B: designation of 10 C-135Bs after conversion for long-range weather reconnaissance; one was later modified under the 'Speckled Trout' programme as an Air Force Systems Command avionics test-bed

Specification
Boeing C/KC-135B
Type: turbine-powered tanker/transport
Powerplant: four 8165-kg (18,000-lb) thrust Pratt & Whitney TF33-P-5 turbofans
Performance: maximum speed 966 km/h (600 mph); average cruising speed 853 km/h (530 mph) at 10670 m (35,000 ft)
Weights: operating empty 46403 kg (102,300 lb); maximum take-off 124965 kg (275,500 lb)
Dimensions: span 39.88 m (130 ft 10 in); length 41 m (134 ft 6 in); height 11.68 m (38 ft 4 in); wing area 226.03 m² (2,433 sq ft)

portholes and blacked wings for re-entry vehicle photography

RC-135T: designation of a single KC-135R modified with extra avionics and a thimble-shaped nose antenna radome

RC-135U: designation of three RC-135Cs further modified to carry additional highly specialised and secret avionics, including a chin radome, enlarged cheek fairings on the forward fuselage sides, and a mass of extra

antennae on the rear fuselage and tail surfaces

RC-135V: designation of seven RC-135Cs and one RC-135U after modification to combine features of the RC-135M and RC-135U, together with seven large blade aerials under the fuselage

RC-135W: designation of several RC-135Ms stripped of their refuelling booms but fitted with cheek fairings and extra antennae; similar to RC-135V

RC-135X: single TF33-powered aircraft for missile re-entry vehicle surveillance. Similar to RC-135S

TC-135S: single reconnaissance trainer. Similar to RC-135S but with reduced equipment

TC-135W: single trainer with reduced equipment for RC-135V/W fleet

VC-135A: VIP modification of J57-powered aircraft

VC-135B: designation of 11 C-135Bs with special interiors to serve as VIP

Boeing Model 720

The early success of the Boeing Model 707 led the company to proceed with the development of an intermediate-range version under the initial designation of **Boeing Model 707-020**. Externally very similar in appearance to the 707-120, it retained the same wing and tailplane span, and needed the discriminating eye of a teenage enthusiast to note the modified wing profile with increased sweepback and changes to the trailing edge at the wing roots. In fact, appearances were deceptive, for in terms of structure and weight the design was entirely new, resulting in the allocation of the designation **Model 720** to add emphasis to the point that it was not merely a re-engined 707.

Most significant of the aerodynamic changes introduced on this new aircraft were refinements to the wing leading edge, modifications that were later introduced to the Model 707 family on the Model 707-120B variant. The changes

After their US domestic service was over, many 720s went to second-line operators. Air Malta used five for service in Europe.

provided improved take-off performance and cruising speed. The length of the fuselage was reduced by 2.36 m (7 ft 9 in) by comparison with that of the Models 707-120 and 707-220, and reduction of the standard fuel load made it possible to lighten the structure. Typical accommodation was for 38 first-class and 74 tourist-class passengers, with facilities that included three galleys and three toilets.

The basic Model 720, powered by four 5670-kg (12,500-lb) thrust Pratt & Whitney JT3C-7 turbojet engines, flew for the first time on 23 November 1959, and entered service initially with United Airlines on 5 July 1960. It was followed by the improved **Model 720B** which introduced

Pratt & Whitney JT3D turbofan engines, initially JT3D-1s of 7711-kg (17,000-lb) thrust. These not only made it possible to operate from still shorter runways, but their greater efficiency allowed for some increase in range despite a higher payload. First flown on 6 October 1960, this version entered service with American Airlines on 12 March 1961. There was, however, only a limited demand for the smaller-capacity Models 720 and 720B, and production ended in 1969 after a total of 154 had been built and delivered.

Specification
Boeing Model 720B
Type: intermediate-range commercial transport
Powerplant: four 8165-kg (18,000-lb) thrust Pratt & Whitney JT3D-3 turbofans

Performance: maximum speed 1009 km/h (627 mph); maximum cruising speed 983 km/h (611 mph) at 7620 m (25,000 ft); economic cruising speed 896 km/h (557 mph) at 12190 m (40,000 ft); service ceiling 12800 m (42,000 ft); range with maximum payload and no reserves 6687 km (4,155 miles)
Weights: operating empty 51203 kg (112,883 lb); maximum take-off 106141 kg (234,000 lb)
Dimensions: span 39.88 m (130 ft 10 in); length 41.68 m (136 ft 9 in); height 12.66 m (41 ft 6½ in); wing area 234.2 m² (2,521 sq ft)

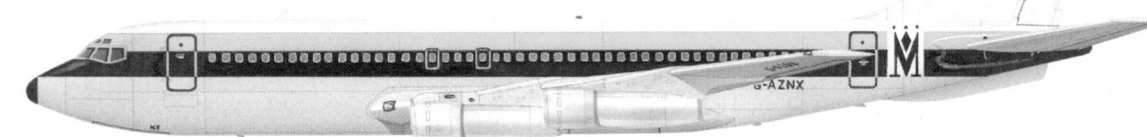

Boeing Model 720-051B of Monarch Airlines (UK).

Boeing Model 727
to
Boeing Model 747

Boeing Model 727

Even before the Boeing 707 was ready for service, the company had realised the desirability of complementing this aircraft with a new short/medium-range airliner, and in February 1956 began to study the market and its requirements. There were a number of important factors, some imposed by contemporary conditions, that played a significant part in the final design. For example, it was an era of rapid growth in air travel, when potential passengers were multiplying at a higher rate than aircraft seats to carry them: a short-term solution was to increase the seating density of existing airliners, or to lengthen the fuselage of suitable machines to provide greater accommodation. This could be done comparatively fast; airport runways to cater for such conversions, however, could only be lengthened and strengthened on a worldwide basis over a much longer period of time.

This gave a design starting point, for the new aircraft would need good takeoff and landing characteristics for the average runway length that was then general. Operation over 'short-haul' routes required an effective solution to a nasty problem: the provision of the highest possible cruising speed at the lowest possible altitude, whilst seat/mile costs were held to a minimum figure. Short-stage lengths meant also a higher proportion of landings in relation to flight hours, affecting not only the design of the landing gear, but also of servicing access to the airliner to cater for the increased number of 'turn-rounds', which are non-revenue periods. And with the capability of operating into and out of smaller airports, often nearer to city centres, the question of engine noise emission might prove a critical factor in determining final acceptance or rejection.

It is not surprising, therefore, that Boeing's Preliminary Design Group spent some three years in examining almost 70 different design proposals, before finalising the broad definition of the airliner which was considered most suitable for this particular portion of the contemporary air transport spectrum. Estimates suggested a potential market for 300 or more aircraft, and this factor also had some influence on design,

emphasising the economic desirability of using as many Model 707 and Model 720 components and systems as possible.

It was assumed that engines of suitable power would be available, irrespective of whether a two-, three-, or four-engined layout was selected, but engine position was not easy to define. The need to develop an efficient wing would be simplified if it did not have to serve also as a mounting for the powerplant, and this encouraged the investigation of rear-engine configurations. Several two- and four-engine wing-mounted arrangements were considered, as were rear-mounted podded engines similar to those selected for the Aérospatiale Caravelle (two) and BAC VC10 (four). A three-engine layout was finally selected: one in the tail of the fuselage, with its air intake forward of the fin, and a pod-mounted engine on each side of the aft fuselage. At an early stage the intention was to use an Allison version of the Rolls-Royce Spey to power this new design, but the Pratt & Whitney JT8D was selected at a later date, all three engines being fitted with thrust-reversers to help with short-field landing problems.

Of the utmost importance to the success of this project was the design of an advanced wing to provide the necessary broad range of performance: at the lower end this was required for short-field operation at comparatively low speeds, and at the other end of the wide speed range for economic high cruising speeds at the lower altitudes of short-haul operations. Consequently, the detail design and development of such a wing was started long before a decision was made to proceed with the new airliner, by then identified as the **Boeing Model 727**. As finalised it represented at the period of its design a fairly complex wing, and certainly one of the most advanced then projected for use on a civil airliner, resulting in extensive wind tunnel testing. The Model 707 'Dash-80' prototype became involved in the programme, not only completing almost a year of test flying to evaluate the new triple-slotted trailing-edge flaps, but posing also as a five-engined aircraft, with a pod-mounted rear-engine on the port side of the fuselage. In the long term this

was all very worthwhile, resulting in the development of a wing with the wide speed range and high lift that was considered essential, and there is little doubt that this structure has contributed significantly to the success of the Model 727.

The new fuselage utilised the upper lobe of that designed for the Model 707, offering additional economies, and the entirely new lower fuselage structure incorporated two features that gave the Model 727 an operational capability that was to help to make it attractive to operators working over very short-stage lengths. They consisted of an hydraulically actuated ventral air-stair, and an auxiliary power unit (APU) to provide compressed air and electrical power, thus making this aircraft capable of independent operation at small airports (or to speed turn-around). With engine self-start capability (from the APU), and able to put down or pick up passengers without the need for any airport ground service vehicles, the Model 727 was entirely capable of airbus cross-country services. A forward port passenger door was available for use with conventional airport equipment.

United Airlines had shown a great deal of enthusiasm in this aircraft from an early date, and the requirements of this operator had considerable influence on the final configuration of the Model 727. Eastern Air Lines was also a potential customer, and with these two companies expected to order 40 aircraft each, Boeing's management authorised a construction go-ahead in August 1960.

The first Model 727, a production aircraft in United insignia, made its maiden flight on 9 February 1963, some months behind schedule, and was followed by a Boeing demonstrator aircraft on 12 March and two more production aircraft very shortly after this. These four aircraft completed the FAA certification programme by the end of the year, making good the time that had been lost, and enabling the initial deliveries to Eastern and United to be made on the contract dates.

Airline services with the original **Model 727-100** were initiated by Eastern Air Lines on 1 February 1964, with United Airlines following only five days later. Both companies discovered very quickly that teething problems were minimal and, of even greater importance in the long term, that the Model 727's

economics were better than anticipated. United found the Model 727 cheaper to operate than its twin-engined Caravelles, even on the shortest stage lengths. Despite such encouragement orders for this aircraft totalled 127 in the early spring of 1962, and were unchanged by the end of the year. Clearly, if the hoped-for 300 or more sales were to be made, the airliner must prove attractive to a wider range of operators. This resulted in the certification of versions with higher gross weights and various fuel options, thus offering a greater operational flexibility. By the summer of 1964 total orders had crept slowly past the 200 mark, but there was still no clear indication that the Model 727 was likely to exceed by very much, if at all, the early sales estimates.

However, by late 1964 it had become clear to Boeing's management that there was a growing demand for a higher-capacity short-range transport, and the decision to develop a 'stretched' version of the Model 727, announced in August 1965, proved the turning point in the marketing of this aircraft. Designated **Model 727-200**, the new version had no significant differences from the earlier Model 727-100, except for the insertion of two 3.05-m (10-ft) fuselage plugs, one forward and one aft of the main landing gear wheel-well. Fuel tankage, gross weight and powerplant remained unchanged, leaving the individual airline to decide whether it needed maximum fuel and range with a smaller passenger load, or a maximum of up to 189 passengers with reduced fuel and range.

First airline to order this new version, shortly after the initial announcement, was Northeast Airlines (now merged with Delta), and following certification of the Model 727-200 on 29 November 1967, it was this operator which flew the first revenue service on 14 December 1967. By then Model 727 orders had climbed to more than 500, of which almost 130 were for the Model 727-200, and thus orders for the Model 727-100 versions were approaching the 400 mark. They increased to only a little over 500, however, before production of this version ended in late 1973. This emphasises the wisdom of the Boeing company in developing a stretched version, for Model 727 sales totalled 1,831 when production ended in the early 1980s, of which almost 1,300 were of the Model 727-200 and **Advanced Model 727-200** versions.

By the use of advanced technology, coupled with steady improvement and refinement of the aircraft's structure, Boeing's Model 727 took a lead in the sales of large commercial turbine-powered airliners recently surpassed by the Boeing 737. The company's decision in 1978 to develop the Model 757, a short/medium-range advanced technology aircraft based on the Model 727 fuselage, spelled the end for the tri-jet. However, the performance and efficiency of the large numbers of aircraft which are in service would suggest that

Six Boeing 727-270 Advanced airliners serve with the Iraqi national airline. These fly on services throughout the Middle East.

The US giant, Delta Air Lines, operates a vast fleet of airliners. The backbone of the fleet are the 130 or so Boeing 727s, which operate on domestic services.

enthusiasts at airports will still be logging the registrations and details of these machines for many years to come.

Variants

Model 727-100C: convertible version of the basic 727-100, incorporating strengthened flooring, and the cargo door and cargo handling system developed for the 707-320C; conversion from all-cargo to mixed passenger/cargo configuration (maximum 94 passengers), or vice-versa, in about two hours

Model 727-100QC: convertible version generally similar to 727-100C, but with quick-change (QC) palletised passenger facilities; conversion from one configuration to another achieved in about half an hour

Model 727-200: lengthened-fuselage version with structural modifications for operation at higher gross weights; standard and maximum passenger capacity 163 and 189 respectively; standard powerplant three Pratt & Whitney JT8D-9 turbofans each of 6577-kg (14,500-lb) thrust, with JT8D engines of up to 7031-kg (15,500-lb) thrust optional

Advanced Model 727-200: final production version, generally similar to Model 727-200, but with advanced features that included a performance data computer system to enhance economy and safety of operation, improved cabin interiors and equipment, and optional powerplants that included the JT8D-17R with automatic performance reserve (APR); if one of these engines has a significant loss in thrust during take-off

or initial climb, the thrust of the other two engines is increased automatically

Model 727RE: designation of a project which investigated the possibility of re-engining Model 727-200 aircraft with Pratt & Whitney PW2037 or Rolls-Royce RB.211-535 turbofans, to produce an aircraft with Model 757 capabilities at a fraction of the cost of the latter airliner

Specification
Boeing Advanced Model 727-200
Type: short/medium-range commercial transport
Powerplant: (standard) three 6577-kg (14,500-lb) thrust Pratt & Whitney JT8D-9A turbofans
Performance: (at maximum take-off weight) maximum speed 999 km/h (621 mph) at 6250 m (20,500 ft); economic cruising speed 917 km/h (570 mph) at 7530 m (24,700 ft); maximum range with maximum payload 4002 km (2,487 miles)
Weights: basic operating empty

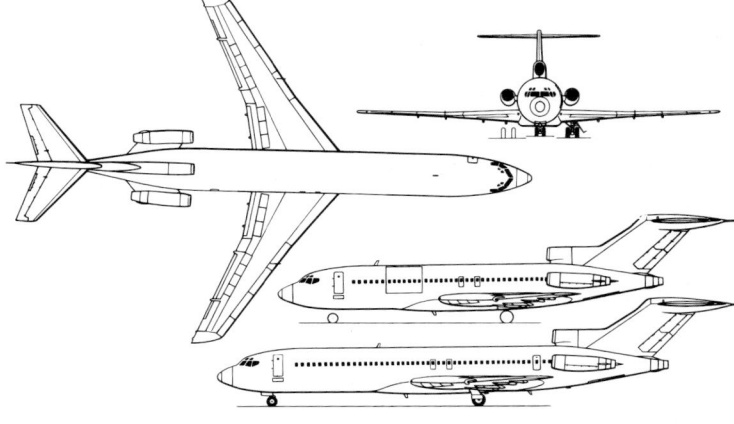

Boeing Model 727-200 (upper side view: Model 727-100C)

46675 kg (102,900 lb); maximum take-off 95027 kg (209,500 lb)
Dimensions: span 32.92 m (108 ft

0 in); length 46.69 m (153 ft 2 in); height 10.36 m (34 ft 0 in); wing area 157.93 m² (1,700 sq ft)

Boeing Model 737

To complete the 'family' of airliners initiated by the long-range Model 707, and short/medium-range Model 727, Boeing announced on 19 February 1965 the intention to build a complementary short-range twin-turbofan transport under the designation **Model 737**. A period of concentrated market research and design activity had preceded the company's decision, in November 1964, to develop this new aircraft, but no public announcement was made pending the receipt of an initial firm order, which in the event came from Lufthansa, the first non-US airline to be first on the order book for a new airliner of US origin. The West German national flag-carrier signed a contract for 21 Model 737s, and this was announced simultaneously with the Boeing production decision.

The 'family' likeness of the Model 737 to its larger sisters was plain to see, due largely to retention of what was basically a Model 727 fuselage and a tail unit which was of similar configuration to that of the Model 707. In fact, there was some 60 per cent commonality of structure and systems between the Models 727 and 737 but the latter, nevertheless, was a very different aircraft. As originally

Britannia Airways was the first British operator of the 737, receiving this aircraft in 1969. It has since built up a large fleet, numbering 33 in 1990. Series 300s were introduced to the inventory in 1984.

conceived, accommodation for 60 to 85 passengers was envisaged, but the negotiations leading to finalisation of Lufthansa's contract showed that this operator required seating capacity for 100 passengers, and the fuselage length was sized accordingly. The ventral airstair of the Model 727 was not retained, and passenger doors and airstairs were provided at the forward and aft ends of the cabin, both on the port side. With an internal cabin length of just over 19.9 m (62 ft), and the same maximum internal width as that of the Model 727, the accommodation appeared to be most spacious, and this undoubtedly contributed to the appeal of this transport.

The wing, like that of the Model 727, was required to provide good lift and

low-speed handling characteristics for short-field operations, coupled with economic high-speed performance at the comparatively low altitudes of short-range commuter services. It incorporates, therefore, much of the technology developed for the Model 727.

The major area of change concerned the powerplant, for the company's engineering studies had determined that only two engines would be required for

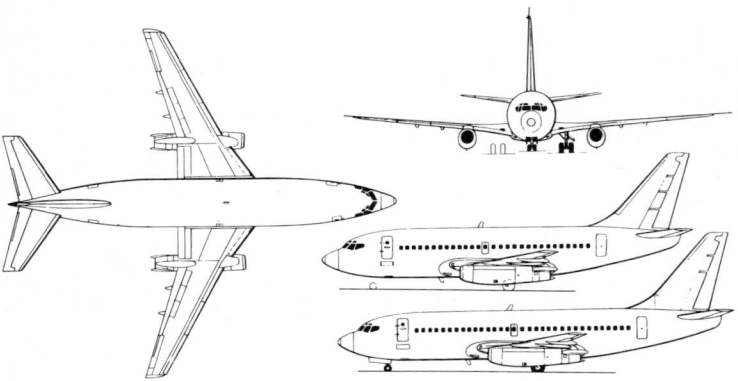

Boeing Model 737-200 (upper side view: Model 737-100)

the new aircraft. This virtually dictated a wing-mounted powerplant arrangement, avoiding any potential aerodynamic problems that might arise with a rear-engine/T-tail configuration. First choice was the Pratt & Whitney JT8D-1 turbofan of 6350-kg (14,000-lb) thrust, but by the time that the negotiations with Lufthansa had been completed the JT8D-7 turbofan had been substituted. Flat-rated to develop the same thrust at higher ambient temperatures than the JT8D-1, the Dash-7 became the basic standard powerplant for the **Model 737-100**, with JT8D-9s of 6577-kg (14,500-lb) thrust optional.

The first Model 737-100, a company demonstrator aircraft, made its maiden flight on 9 April 1967, and the first of Lufthansa's aircraft flew during the following month. FAA certification was gained on 15 December 1967, and Lufthansa inaugurated its first services with the type on 10 February 1968.

Less than two months after Boeing's announcement of the intention to develop and market the Model 737, the company disclosed that a larger-capacity variant was to be developed almost simultaneously. Identified as the **Model 737-200**, this became the standard model, the first of the type flying on 8 August 1967, gaining certification on 21 December, and entering revenue service with United Airlines on 29 April 1968. This lengthened-fuselage version (by 1.83 m/6 ft), accommodating a maximum of 130 passengers, was evolved to satisfy the requirements of operators who required greater seating capacity on 'local service' routes. The rapid growth in air travel, and consequently in seating capacity requirements, meant that there was virtually no demand for the 100/103-seat Model 737-100, which went out of production after a mere 30 had been built.

The comparatively short take-off and landing distances needed by the Model 737 meant that these aircraft were able to operate out of and into airfields with unpaved or gravel runways. This required that the aircraft and its engines should be protected against impact and ingestion damage respectively, and Boeing developed suitable protection in kit form. This proved sufficiently effective for the company to gain FAA certification for Model 737s so equipped to operate from and to airports with gravel or unpaved runways.

A small number of 737s has also been supplied to the US Air Force, for experience in Vietnam had shown that the USAF had inadequate facilities for the

Royal Brunei Airlines is typical of the many small national carriers that have adopted the 737 for short/medium range work.

training of navigators. A decision was made to procure an 'off the shelf' aircraft with a desirable specification to replace the Convair T-29 (a militarised version of the Convair-Liner) then in service. In May 1971 the USAF announced that the Model 737 had been selected to fulfil this role, and Boeing was awarded an $82.4 million contract for the supply of 19 aircraft under the designation **T-43A**. First flight was made on 10 April 1973, and all of these aircraft were delivered to Mather AFB, California, by the end of July 1974.

Although the general configuration of these training aircraft is the same as that of the commercial Model 737-200, there are a number of detail and interior changes to make the T-43As suitable for their specific role. These include a reduction in the number of doors and windows, strengthening of the cabin floor to accommodate avionics consoles, and installation of a 3027-litre (800-US gal) auxiliary fuel tank.

In addition to the standard flight crew, each of the T-43s accommodates 12 trainees, four advanced trainees, and three instructors. The aircraft are operated in conjunction with ground-based simulators to provide training over a wide range of missions, including high- and low-level flight by day or night, high-speed flight, and the requirements of airways navigation. On-board equipment is updated from time to time to ensure that it is the same as that in use with USAF operational aircraft.

New life was breathed into the 737 with the introduction of the **737-300** in 1984, this featuring a lengthened fuselage, revised systems and fuel-efficient CFM International CFM56 turbofans. A new family of variants was subsequently introduced, comprising different payload/range combinations.

These allowed the 737 to become the world's best-selling airliner, with 2,773

The second generation 737s have a distinctive look thanks to the CFM56 turbofans and additional fin fillet.

orders received by April 1990, of which 1,833 had been delivered.

Variants

Model 737-200C: convertible passenger/cargo version of the Model 737-200

Model 737-200QC: quick-change convertible passenger/cargo version of the Model 737-200, with palletised passenger facilities

Advanced Model 737-200: current standard production version, but aircraft with this designation first became available in 1971; maximum accommodation for 130 passengers; can operate at an optional maximum gross weight of 53070 kg (117,000 lb); optional engines include JT8D-15, JT8D-17 or JT8D-17Rs, each of 7031-, 7257- or 7711-kg (15,500-, 16,000- or 17,000-lb) thrust respectively

Advanced Model 737-200C/QC: convertible, or quick-change convertible versions of Advanced Model 737-200

Advanced Model 737-200 Executive Jet: generally similar to Advanced Model 737-200, but supplied in a form suitable for the installation of special business and executive luxury interiors to customer requirement

Advanced Model 737-200 High Gross Weight Structure: generally similar to Advanced 737-200, but with structural modifications including strengthened wing structure and landing gear; new tyres, wheels and brakes; and installation of an auxiliary fuel tank; two versions available, one with a maximum take-off weight of 58105 kg (128,000 lb)

Model 737-200 SLAMMR: three aircraft for service with the Indonesian air force, for use in a maritime

surveillance/transport role; to be equipped with side-looking airborne multi-mission radar (SLAMMR)

Model 737-300: generally similar to Advanced Model 737-200, but with a lengthened fuselage (2.64 m/8 ft 8 in) to accommodate a maximum of 148 passengers, and advanced CFM International CFM56-3 turbofan engines, each of 9072-kg (20,000-lb) thrust; much quieter and more economical than current Model 737; initial deliveries during 1984

Model 737-400: further lengthened variant for greater capacity, overall length being 36.45 m (119 ft 7 in); CFM56 engines; extended range model available

Model 737-500: short-body (31 m/101 ft 9 in) new generation version offering excellent range (over 5500 km/3417 miles with full load)

Specification
Boeing Advanced Model 737-200
Type: short-range civil transport
Powerplant: two 7031-kg (15,500-lb) thrust Pratt & Whitney JT8D-15 turbofans
Performance: maximum speed 943 km/h (586 mph) at 7165 m (23,500 ft); maximum cruising speed 927 km/h (576 mph) at 6890 m (22,600 ft); economic cruising speed Mach 0.73 at 9145 m (30,000 ft); range with maximum payload 4262 km (2,648 miles)
Weights: operating empty 27692 kg (61,050 lb); maximum take-off 53070 kg (117,000 lb)
Dimensions: span 28.35 m (93 ft 0 in); length 30.53 m (100 ft 2 in); height 11.28 m (37 ft 0 in); wing area 91.04 m² (980 sq ft)

Boeing Model 747

In 1963 the US Air Force began to study and define its requirements for a heavy logistics transport aircraft that would supplement the Lockheed C-141 StarLifters that were almost due to enter service. Identified originally as the CX-4 (Cargo, Experimental), this envisaged an aircraft with a gross weight of 272155 kg (600,000 lb), but this was increased in the following year when other factors had been taken into consideration, requiring the capability to airlift a payload of 56699 kg (125,000 lb) over a range of 12875 km (8,000 miles), to operate from the same length of paved or semi-prepared runway as the C-141, and to land on 1220 m (4,000 ft) semi-prepared runways in combat areas. Known as the CX-HLS (Cargo, Experimental-Heavy Logistics System) requirement at that stage, this led to a design competition initiated in May 1964. The result was that Boeing, Douglas and Lockheed were each awarded design development contracts. Lockheed was declared winner of the competition on 30 September 1965, a decision leading to that company becoming prime contractor for the USAF's C-5A Galaxy.

Boeing was keenly disappointed to lose this military contract. Perhaps it had been envisaged that, as with the Model 707, a military contract would prove a sound stepping stone to a civil variant, an idea then already in the background of the design team's thoughts. Market research had shown that a large-capacity airliner would become of interest to operators during the early 1970s, and even before the destination of the military contract was announced, Boeing had set a small design group working to outline the details of a civil transport.

With the C-5 contract awarded to Lockheed, Boeing was able to concentrate on the design of what was identified from the outset as the **Boeing Model 747**. Initial studies covered aircraft up to a gross weight of about 272155 kg (600,000 lb) and capable of accommodating as many as 430 passengers. A two-deck 'double-bubble' fuselage with each deck some 4.57 m (15 ft) wide featured in the initial proposals that were considered by a number of airlines. This failed to appeal to those operators who studied the Boeing preliminary design, and the project was reappraised. This led, in early 1966, to what was basically a 'big brother' of the Model 707, featuring a wing with advanced aerodynamic features, but set in the same low-wing configuration, with four podded wing-mounted engines, a somewhat similar conventional tail unit, and tricycle landing gear. The fuselage was of almost circular cross-section, the flight deck high on the forward fuselage within the now easily-recognisable 'hump' fairing, allowing the main passenger cabin to extend beneath it into the nose of the aircraft.

The most staggering feature of this fuselage was its size, providing a cabin 6.13 m (20 ft 1½ in) wide and 56.39 m (185 ft 0 in) long. Nine-abreast seating with two aisles dispelled immediately any hints of the claustrophobia-inducing interiors of many earlier airliners, and aft of the flight deck was an upper deck lounge with seating for up to 16 first-class passengers.

Early plans provided accommodation for 368 mixed-class passengers in a typical layout with a basic gross weight of 283495 kg (625,000 lb), which in turn meant that if the Model 747 was to operate from existing runways, it required landing gear that would support and distribute this 283-tonne (279-ton) load effectively without causing damage to

the runway. The resulting main units, four in total, each had a four-wheel bogie, and the nose unit had twin wheels. No firm conclusion had then been reached on powerplant: General Electric, Pratt & Whitney, and Rolls-Royce turbofan engines were all being considered.

It was with the design in this general form that Boeing began to seek prospective customers. Pan American was considered to be the most likely first buyer, but until there was positive airline interest it was not possible for the company to make a commitment to build the Model 747; with a price tag of more than $16.8 million (£6,000,000) each in 1966, it was too big a gamble for 'private venture' construction and development. Boeing's intuition proved to be correct, and on 13 April 1966 it was announced simultaneously that the company had designed and was to manufacture this new Model 747 long-range transport, and that Pan American had ordered no fewer than 25 of these giant aircraft. However, it was not until additional orders had been received from Japan Air Lines and Lufthansa that, on 25 July 1966, the decision was made to begin construction.

Pan Am's appraisal of Boeing's design had resulted in some changes being made, these increasing wing span, modifying landing gear layout, and raising the maximum take-off weight to 308443 kg (680,000 lb). Not surprisingly, the first press reports that followed Boeing's announcement were well laced with adjectives which implied magnitude: everything was on a giant scale, and very soon it was called a jumbo-sized aeroplane, leading to the name 'jumbo jet'

which is perhaps better known to large numbers of the world's population than the official Model 747 name.

No prototype of the Model 747 was built, the original production aircraft being intended as Boeing's demonstrator. This was rolled out on 30 September 1968 at Paine Field, Everett, where the company had established a completely new factory to house the Model 747 production line. The first flight was completed successfully on 9 February 1969, and with the participation of the next four production aircraft as they became available, the certification programme was completed by the five aircraft just before the end of 1969, FAA approval being granted on 30 December. On 22 January 1970 Pan American inaugurated its first service with the type, introducing it on the New York-London route.

The period between the beginning of construction and certification had not

A Boeing Model 747-256B of Iberia, the Spanish national flag-carrier, which operates four such aircraft. The Model 747-200B series (originally known as the Model 747B) uses an uprated powerplant permitting greatly increased take-off weights, with consequent gains in range and in payload.

been without its problems. Boeing's major difficulty had been to restrict weight growth, but in order to maintain the payload/range performance that had been specified, it was necessary to increase maximum take-off weight and this, in the case of the initial **Model 747-100**, rose to a figure of 322051 kg (710,000 lb).

The other major problem, one which was closely related to weight, concerned the powerplant. Pan American

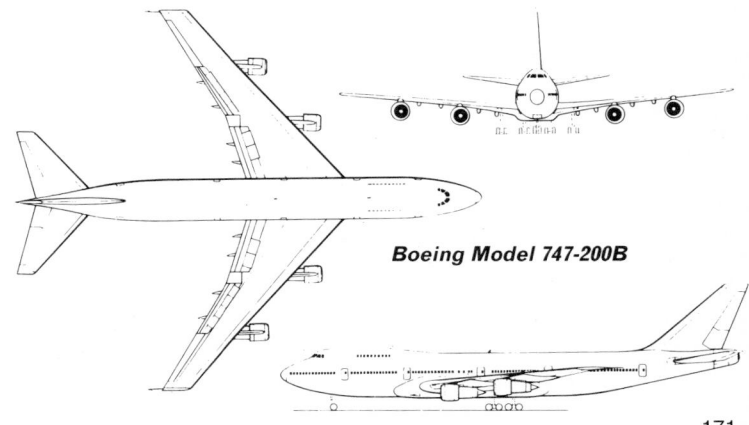

Boeing Model 747-200B

171

Packed with communications equipment, the E-4B is a national command post modification of the 747-200. Its task is to carry the President and his battle staff aloft in time of tension.

The 747SP is a radical modification to the basic design, featuring a reduced length fuselage and increased height fin. Enormous range is available, attractive to trans-Pacific operators such as CAAC.

had opted for Pratt & Whitney engines, and the JT9D was an entirely new project which had been proposed for this aircraft at an initial thrust of 18597 kg (41,000 lb). The engine not only suffered its own development problems, but as the gross weight of the airframe increased it also became essential that the engines should develop greater thrust. This accelerated evolution of the new turbofan engine created great difficulties for Pratt & Whitney, and although a JT9D-3 rated at 19731-kg (43,500-lb) thrust was readied for the production aircraft to be delivered for airline service, it suffered innumerable teething troubles. Only when similarly rated but modified JT9D-3A engines were introduced into service later in 1970 were the problems overcome.

The Model 747-100, which first entered service with Pan Am, had a maximum fuel capacity of 178703 litres (47,210 US gal), sufficient to enable a two-seat lightplane such as the Cessna 150, for example, to fly a distance in excess of 1.8 million km (1.1 million miles). The surprising thing is that the Model 747-100 could carry 385 passengers over a range of 9136 km (5,677 miles) and land with FAR specified reserves, which gave this turbofan-powered airliner about the same efficiency, but a cruising speed some six times greater, than that of the lightplane.

All flight controls of the Model 747 are powered, and an advanced automatic flight control system eases the pilots' workload, not only during long periods of cruising flight, but also in making automatic landings under suitable conditions. In fact, so well planned is the flight deck and equipment of these large airlines that they are handled without difficulty by a flight crew of three, compris-

Winglets identify the latest 747 variant, the Series 400. Increased range, aerodynamic refinements and a thorough systems modernisation are the principal improvements over the 300.

ing usually all pilots, or two pilots and a flight engineer. Navigation to great accuracy is catered for by standard avionics systems, plus inertial navigation systems (originally duplicated, but now triplicated).

By the time that the first Model 747s were entering service with Pan Am, Boeing had accumulated some 190 orders from 28 airlines. This looks like big money, but Boeing's investment was even bigger money, and at one point in the mid-1970s the company must have felt some qualms about the entire project. Airlines were then suffering a recession, and it seemed unlikely that marketing forecasts would ever be met. This situation changed, however, and by April 1990 orders for Model 747s of all types totalled 982, of which 777 had been delivered.

So far, however, only the basic Model 747-100 has been mentioned, but it was the company's intention from the outset to build a 'family' of Model 747s, and brief details of each of these are given under the Variants heading below. All are available optionally with powerplants by Pratt & Whitney, General Electric, or Rolls-Royce.

The introduction into service of the Model 747 caused few serious problems for their operators, for the company had done its utmost to ensure that it was fundamentally a large-size Model 727 that could be flown by a similar flight crew of three, and maintained easily by ground crews with experience of the other members of the Boeing 7X7 family. The advent of these wide-body jets, with their large seating capacity, was welcomed by air traffic controllers for, potentially, two Model 747 flights could replace from five to ten services by smaller aircraft. It was the airport operators who, initially, were caught on the hop. Unused to the arrival of an aircraft that could (but rarely did) accommodate up to 500 passengers, the passenger handling facilities were completely swamped when two or three Model 747s arrived almost simultaneously to

disgorge between 700 and 1,000 passengers. These conditions applied, of course, at the time of their early use, and since when airports have become accustomed to handling the Airbus, Boeing, Lockheed, and McDonnell Douglas wide-body jets which today carry such a major portion of the world's air travellers.

Variants

Model 747-100B: version of the Model 747-100 with strengthened fuselage, landing gear, and wing structure

Model 747-200B: generally similar to the Model 747-100B, but with different engines and increased fuel capacity, providing maximum take-off weights of up to 377842 kg (833,000 lb)

Model 747-200B Combi: version of the Model 747-200B with a port side cargo door as standard, allowing for use in an all-passenger or passenger/cargo configuration, with passengers and cargo separated by a movable or removable bulkhead

Model 747-200B Convertible: this version of the Model 747-200 is equipped for operation in all-passenger or all-cargo configurations, or in any one of five predetermined passenger/cargo variations

Model 747-200F Freighter: specialised all-cargo version of the Model 747-200, with the fuselage nose opening forward and upward to give clear loading access to the main deck, plus a cargo-loading system that can be operated by two men; fuselage side cargo door optional; maximum cargo payload 112491 kg (248,000 lb), which is almost 112.5 tonnes (111 tons)

Model 747SP: lighter-weight longer-range version; fuselage length is reduced by 14.35 m (47 ft 1 in), and a new tail unit incorporates increased surface areas; the Model 747SP has maximum high-density accommodation for 440 passengers, and can carry 331 passengers and baggage over a non-

stop range of 10841 km (6,736 miles)

Model 747SR: a short-range version of the Model 747-100B, incorporating structural modifications to allow for a much higher frequency of take-off and landing operations

Model 747SUD: stretched upper deck modification, available optionally on 747-100B/-200B/-200B Combi and 747SR, and providing economy-class seating for 69 passengers on the upper deck, plus an additional seven seats on the lower deck following deletion of the original circular staircase

Model 747-300: new-build version of 747SUD

Model 747-400: completely revised version with stretched upper deck, new technology engines, 'glass' two-man cockpit, lengthened wingtips and 1.83 m (6ft) drag-reducing winglets

Boeing E-4 Advanced Airborne Command Post: under the designation E-4, the USAF acquired a total of four Boeing 747s to serve as survivable airborne command posts, any one of which would be capable of controlling the USA's entire force of ICBMs, its manned bombers, and its nuclear-powered missile-carrying submarines; entering service were three of the **E-4A** version, provided with earlier-generation command and control equipment removed from the EC-135s that they replaced, plus one **E-4B** with advanced command and control equipment; the three E-4As have been upgraded to E-4B standard; all in-service E-4s are powered by General Electric CF6-50E turbofans, each of 24404-kg (52,500-lb) thrust

Boeing 747-123 Space Shuttle Carrier: designation of a single Model 747-100 acquired from American Airlines by NASA, and modified to make it suitable to carry a Space Shuttle Orbiter in 'piggy-back' mode; it was used originally for 13 flights with the Space Shuttle Orbiter *Enterprise.*

Specification
Boeing Model 747-200B

Type: long-range heavy transport
Powerplant: (365142 kg/805,000 lb gross weight version) four 22680-kg (50,000-lb) thrust Pratt & Whitney JT9D-7FW turbofans
Performance: maximum speed 969 km/h (602 mph) at 9145 m (30,000 ft; cruising ceiling 13715 m (45,000 ft); range with 442 passengers and baggage at maximum take-off weight 9624 km (5,980 miles)
Weights: operating empty 171004 kg (377,000 lb, maximum take-off 365142 kg (805,000 lb)
Dimensions: span 59.64 m (195 ft 8 in); length 70.51 m (231 ft 4 in); height 19.33 m (63 ft 5 in); wing area 510.95 m² (5,500 sq ft)

Boeing Model 757
to
Boeing Vertol Model 114 (CH-47)

Boeing Model 757

Increased-capacity versions of the highly successful Boeing Model 727 have been studied over the years, but despite several proposals none succeeded in attracting sufficient orders to warrant a production go-ahead. In the early months of 1978, however, the company announced that it proposed to develop a new family of advanced technology aircraft. Retaining the 7X7 designation formula, these three new designs carried the identifications **Model 757**, Model 767 and Model 777, the first of the three differing by retaining the same fuselage cross-section as the Model 727, whereas the Models 767 and 777 (assuming that this latter aircraft enters production) have a fuselage cross-section that is virtually mid-way between that of the Models 727 and 747.

A short/medium-range airliner, having a typical capacity of 178 mixed-class, or 196 tourist-class, or a maximum high-density seating arrangement for 224 passengers, the Model 757 provides its operators with new standards of fuel efficiency, now a vital area in the economics of airline operations. The Model 757 is one of the world's most economical turbofan-powered airliners in the short/medium-range category, showing a fuel saving of 45 per cent per passenger by comparison with earlier medium-range aircraft. This results from the combination of a new advanced-technology wing, high by-pass ratio turbofan engines, and avionics equipment that enables the aircraft to be operated at optimum efficiency.

The development programme of the Model 767 was some five months in advance of that of the Model 757, principally because the go-ahead for its construction was given some eight months before that of the Model 757. Initial orders for this latter aircraft, which has the designation **Model 757-200**, were announced on 31 August 1978, comprising 19 and 21 respectively for British Airways and Eastern Air Lines, and after contract finalisation in early 1979, the company announced a production go-ahead on 23 March 1979. The five-month

Boeing Model 757-225 of Eastern Air Lines (USA).

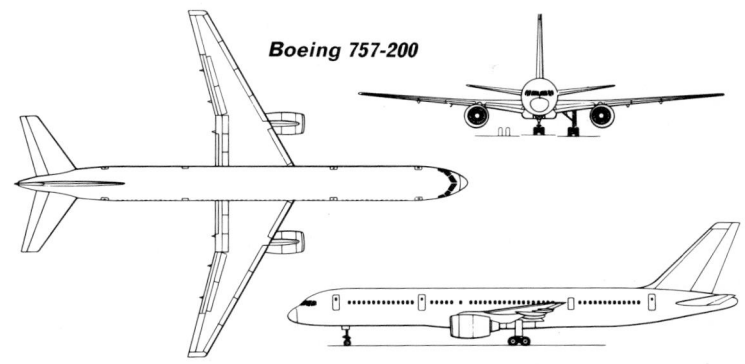

Boeing 757-200

gap between the programmes was essential for Boeing's management and control of the almost simultaneous development of two new major aircraft, but the Model 757 enjoyed the benefits of work already completed on its wide-body sister, for there is a considerable degree of commonality between the two aircraft. However, some 53 per cent, by value, of the Model 757 is being manufactured by outside companies, and major sub-contractors include Avco Aerostructures (wing centre section and fuselage keel), Fairchild Industries (overwing cabin section and wing leading-edge slats), Rockwell International (forward and aft fuselage sections) and Vought Corporation (fuselage tail cone, tailplane and fin).

Powerplant comprises two Rolls-Royce RB211-535C or Pratt & Whitney PW2037 turbofan engines, which are mounted in underwing pods, but the two launching airlines opted for Rolls-Royce engines, and this was the first time that Boeing had introduced a new airliner with a non-American powerplant. Follow-on engines (RB211-535E4 and PW2040) are now available with greater thrust. The new-technology wing has less sweep-back than that of the Model 727, and the Model 757's fuselage is 5.97 m (19ft 7 in) longer. Landing gear is of tricycle type, each main unit having a four-wheel bogie, with twin wheels on the nose gear. The Model 757 is operated by a flight crew of two, or three optionally, and the advanced avionics available to them include an inertial reference

system incorporating laser gyroscopes, a flight management computer system, and a digital air data computer. These integrate to provide optimum fuel efficiency when linked to automatic flight control and thrust management systems. This new generation avionics control is capable of handling an entire flight from shortly after take-off, including the landing if desirable, with the flight crew functioning as systems managers.

The first flight of a Model 757 took place in February 1982, and orders and options for 632 aircraft had been received by the end of March 1990. A **757-200M Combi** version is available, as is the **757-200PF** Package Freighter and a corporate version.

Specification
Boeing Model 757-200
Type: short/medium-range commercial transport
Powerplant: two 16964-kg (37,400-lb) thrust Rolls-Royce RB211-535C turbofans
Performance: cruising speed Mach 0.8; initial cruising height 11705 m (38,400 ft); maximum range 3985 km (2,476 miles)
Weights: operating empty 59430 kg (131,020 lb); maximum take-off 104326 kg (230,000 lb)
Dimensions: span 37.95 m (124 ft 6 in); length 47.32 m (155 ft 3 in); height 13.56 m (44 ft 6 in); wing area 181.25 m² (1,951 sq ft)

Boeing Model 767

Announced simultaneously with the Model 757, the **Boeing Model 767** introduced a completely new fuselage structure which is 1.24 m (4 ft 1 in) wider, providing seven- or eight-abreast seating with two aisles. Planned layouts cater for 211 mixed-class passengers, comprising 18 first-class in six-abreast accommodation, with the remaining 193 tourist-class seated seven-abreast; or 230 tourist-class in all seven-abreast seating; or a high-density eight-abreast configuration for a maximum of 289 passengers; but there are also other options. The go-ahead for the Model 767 programme was announced on 14 July 1978, following receipt of an order for 30 of these aircraft from United Airlines: in March 1990 orders and options totalled 483.

Computer Aided Design (CAD) was used to speed the preparation of drawings for much of the principal structure, their high accuracy being of great benefit when, as in this case, a large amount of the construction is being carried out by other companies. These include Aeritalia, Canadair, Grumman and Vought, plus a Japanese consortium, known as the Civil Transport Development Corporation, that comprises Fuji, Kawasaki and Mitsubishi. Together, 28 companies are manufacturing assemblies and components which, in terms of value, represent some 45 per cent of the total cost.

Wing design differs somewhat from that of the Model 757, and features increased sweepback, and greater span and wing chord, to provide approximately 53 per cent increase in wing area.

The tail unit and landing gear are similar in configuration, and the Model 767 shares with the Model 757 twin turbofan engines pod-mounted beneath the wings. These, however, are of greater thrust in the Model 767, with alternative Pratt & Whitney JT9D-7R4D and General Electric CF6-80A powerplants, each in the 21772-kg (48,000-lb) thrust class, being specified by early airlines. Later GE and PW engines are now on offer, along with the Rolls-Royce RB211.

Boeing planned initially to offer two versions: a **Model 767-100** with a shorter fuselage and accommodation for approximately 180 passengers, and the basic **Model 767-200** described above. It was then decided not to build the shorter-fuselaged Model 767-100, and instead the Model 767-200 is avail-

able at alternative gross weights. Thus the version which was ordered initially by United Airlines for US domestic service has a maximum take-off weight of 127913 kg (282,000 lb). That, with a gross weight of 140614 kg (310,000 lb), can carry 211 passengers over a range of up to 6013 km (3,736 miles), making it suitable for non-stop trans-continental services, and also for many international routes.

With an optional flight crew of two or three, provided with the same avionics equipment as described for the Model 757, this new airliner demonstrates seat-mile costs some 32 per cent below that of other wide-body tri-jets. The new fuselage also offers significant air freight capacity, with a cargo hold able to accept up to 22 LD-2 containers, or LD-3/-4/-8 containers to similar volume. With the inclusion of an optional forward cargo door measuring 1.75 m by 3.4 m (5 ft 9 in by 11 ft 2 in), Type 2 pallets can be loaded.

The first Model 767 was rolled out at Everett, Washington, on 4 August 1981, and made a 2 hour 4 minute maiden flight there on 26 September, which was a few days ahead of the target date set when the programme was launched in 1978.

In February 1983 Boeing announced the **767-300**, featuring a 6.42 m (21 ft 1 in) fuselage stretch to cater for additional capacity. Both -200 and -300 are offered in **ER** (Extended Range) variants, with increased fuel capacity and take-off weight for long-range operations.

Specification
Boeing Model 767-200 (basic version)
Type: medium-range commercial transport
Powerplant: two Pratt & Whitney JT9D-7R4D turbofans, each developing approximately 21772-kg (48,000-lb) thrust
Performance: normal cruising speed Mach 0.8; approach speed 248 km/h (154 mph); service ceiling 11885 m (39,000 ft); design range with 211 passengers 5152 km (3,201 miles)
Weights: operating empty 81230 kg (179,082 lb); maximum take-off 136078 kg (300,000 lb)
Dimensions: span 47.57 m (156 ft 1 in); length 48.51 m (159 ft 2 in); height 15.85 m (52 ft 0 in); wing area 283.35 m² (3,050 sq ft)

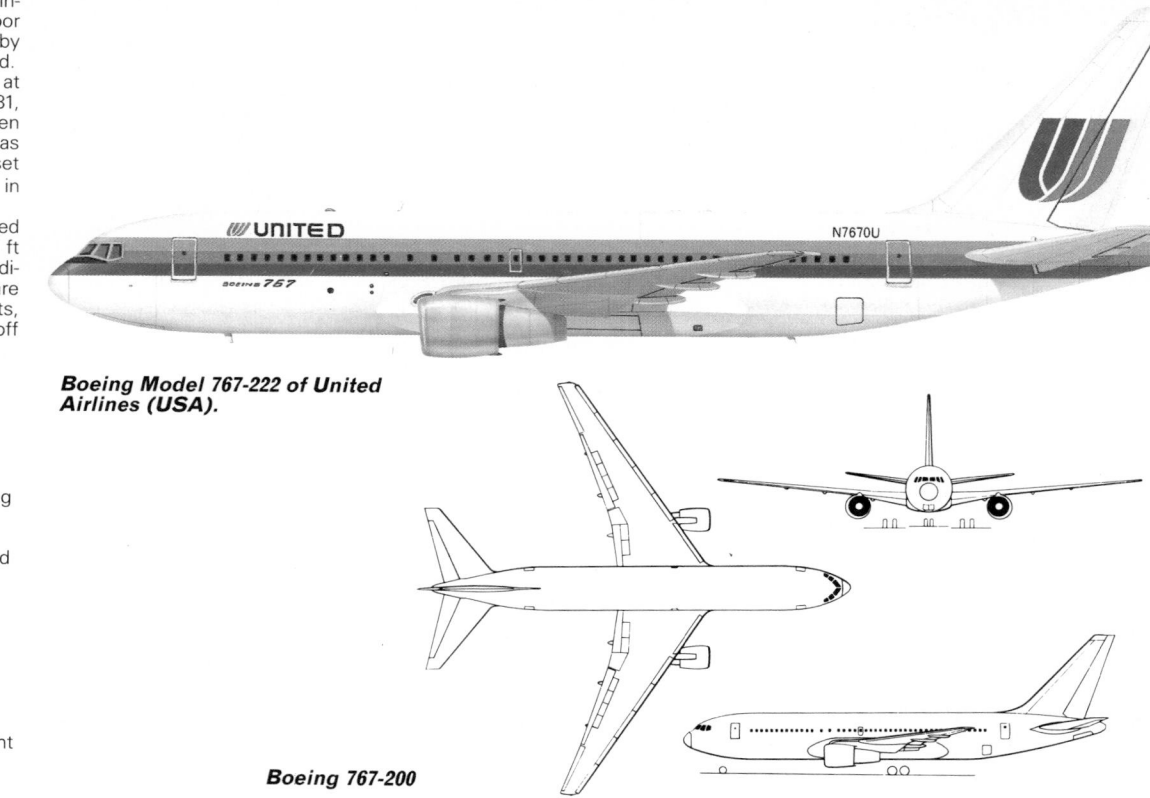

Boeing Model 767-222 of United Airlines (USA).

Boeing 767-200

Partnering the 757 in Boeing's assault on the airliner market, the 767 offers greater range and capacity in a wide-body airframe. The Series 300 aircraft are considerably longer than the Series 200 (illustrated), and both are available in Extended Range versions.

Boeing Model 777

The interest expressed by airlines in an airliner with a capacity between those of its Model 767-300 and Model 747-400 led Boeing at the end of 1986 to start the work of defining the type, which was seen as a rival to the Airbus A330 and A340 as well as another American type, the McDonnell Douglas MD-11. The project definition phase led to the launch of the **Model 777** on 29 October 1990.

The **Model 777** is a turbofan-powered long-haul airliner in which a major contribution comes from the Japanese aircraft industry, of which three companies have a risk-sharing partnership. New aluminium alloys and weight-saving composite materials are employed in many components. The two-man flight deck was designed to be similar to that of the Model 747-400 with all the basic flying information appearing on six flat liquid-crystal screens. As a result of the reliability of

the powerplant and on-board systems (including the company's first civil fly-by-wire control system) Boeing was able to achieve ETOPS (Extended-range Twin-engined OPerationS) certification for regular service: this demanded the ability to maintain level flight for three hours in single-engined configuration in order to reach a suitable landing site after suffering an inflight engine failure.

The **Model 777** is offered in two versions with the same trio of engine options. The **Model 777-200 A** Market (later just Model 777-200) has any of three maximum take-off weights between 229522 kg (506,000 lb) for a 375-passenger range of 7352 km (4,568 miles) and 242676 kg (535,000 lb) for a 375-passenger range of 8926 km (5,546 miles). The **Model 777-200 B** Market (later Model 777-200IGW, or Increased Gross Weight) is a heavier type offering greater fuel capacity, more powerful engines and

the option of three maximum take-off weights between 263088 kg (580,000 lb) for a 305-passenger range of 11168 km (6,939 miles) and 286902 kg (632,500 lb) for a 305-passenger range of 13667 km (8,493 miles).

The wing design of the **Model 777** depends on an aerofoil section in a structure possessing a quarter-chord sweep angle of 31.6°. The fuel is carried in the wings and in the central section of the fuselage. Some customers wanted the **Model 777** to possess the capability for using the taxiways and passenger gates developed for the DC-10 and aircraft of similar size, so Boeing offers wings in which the outer 6.48 m (21 ft 3 in) on each side can be folded up into the vertical position. The **Model 777** is offered with powerplant options that comprise turbofans from all three leading manufacturers in the forms of the Rolls-Royce Trent 800, General Electric GE90 and Pratt & Whitney PW4000 series engines. In the case of the basic **Model 777-200** these rated

at between 315.8 and 329.2 kN (71,000 and 70,000 lb st), and in the case of the **Model 777-200IGW** at between 364.7 and 378.1 kN (82,000 and 85,000 lb st) through the incorporation of new wide-blade fans and an increase in bypass ratio from 6:1 to 9:1.

Specification
Boeing Model 777-200 (United Airlines)
Type: long-range wide-body transport
Powerplant: two 329.17-kN (74,000-lb st) Pratt & Whitney PW4074 turbofans
Performance: cruising speed, maximum Mach 0.87 and cruising Mach 0.83; service ceiling 13135 m (43,100 ft); range 7785 km (4,840 miles) with 363 passengers in two classes
Weights: empty 135,581 kg (298,900 lb); maximum take-off 233,604 kg (515,000 lb)
Dimensions: span 60.93 m (199 ft 11 in); length 63.73 m (209 ft 1 in); height 18.51 m (60 ft 9 in); area 427.8 m² (4,605.00 sq ft)

Boeing Model 953 (YC-14)

In 1971 the USAF began to put together the specification of a new transport as a possible replacement for its fleet of Lockheed C-130 Hercules aircraft. The Hercules design had originated from a specification of just 20 years earlier, and in putting together its requirement for this new transport, the USAF planners had in mind the very important development in powerplants and aerodynamics which had taken place since 1951. In early 1972 requests for proposals were sent out to nine US manufacturers, and those of the Boeing Company and McDonnell Douglas Corporation were selected for competitive evaluation under the respective designations **YC-14** and **YC-15**.

Before the allocation of designations, the USAF specification had the identification AMST, signifying Advanced Military STOL Transport, and the emphasis required from the successful contenders was concerned primarily with STOL (short take-off and landing) capability. The **Boeing Model 953** design for STOL performance was based on the use of a supercritical wing, developed by NASA from the wind-tunnel research of

The unusual engine mountings of the YC-14 resulted from the use of the Coanda effect for short take-off/landing, whereby jet efflux is entrained down the large flap to give a vertical thrust component.

Dr Richard Whitcomb, which provides highly efficient performance from the wing at high subsonic speeds. To this wing Boeing added an advanced wing upper-surface blowing concept, mounting the twin engines above the wing so that their efflux was exhausted over the wing. With the wing's leading-edge and Coanda-type trailing-edge flaps extended, the high-speed airflow from the engines tended to cling to the upper surface of the wing/flap system, and was thus directed downwards to provide powered lift.

The YC-14 first flew on 9 August 1976, and soon proved to have admirable performance. Maximum payload was 150 troops or 36742 kg (81,000 lb) of freight in conventional operations, while for STOL operations from an airfield of less than 572 m (625 yards) the payload was still a useful 12247 kg (27,000 lb).

At the completion of testing, in the late summer of 1977, the YC-14 prototype was returned to Boeing for continuing development, if the company so wished, but no further government funding for development or procurement was forthcoming.

Specification
Type: advanced military STOL transport
Powerplant: two 23133-kg (51,000-lb) thrust General Electric CF6-50D turbofans

Performance: maximum speed 811 km/h (504 mph) at optimum altitude, or 649 km/h (403 mph) at sea level; service ceiling 13715 m (45,000 ft); operational radius 740 km (460 miles); ferry range 5133 km (3,190 miles)
Weights: operating empty 53297 kg (117,500 lb); maximum STOL take-off 77111 kg (170,000 lb); maximum take-off 107501 kg (237,000 lb)
Dimensions: span 39.32 m (129 ft 0 in); length 40.13 m (131 ft 8 in); height 14.73 m (48 ft 4 in); wing area 163.69 m² (1,762 sq ft)

Boeing Vertol Model 107 (H-46 Sea Knight)

Shortly after the formation of Vertol Aircraft Corporation in March 1956, the company initiated a design study for a twin-turbine commercial transport aircraft. In formulating the design, special attention was given to ensure that it would be suitable also for military use if the armed forces showed an interest in its procurement. As a result, the tandem rotor layout, which had been developed fully by Vertol, and by the Piasecki Helicopter Corporation before it, was adopted because of its known performance and reliability. Twin turbines were chosen to power this new helicopter for, despite the fact that they had not then acquired a long history of reliability and economy, there was no doubt that these engines offered a superb power/weight ratio, and were improving progressively all the time. To limit noise and provide maximum cabin space the engines were mounted above the fuselage, at the aft end of the cabin. To speed loading/unloading operations a large loading ramp formed the undersurface of the upswept rear fuselage, and this was sufficiently robust to allow straight-on loading of vehicles and/or bulky freight. A sealed and compartmented fuselage made it possible for this new helicopter to be operated from water, as well as land surfaces.

Allocated the designation **Vertol Model 107**, a prototype entered construction in May 1957, and the first flight of this aircraft was recorded on 22 April 1958. Company testing and development progressed well, and an extensive demonstration tour aroused considerable interest. First of the armed forces wishing to evaluate this new helicopter was the US Army which, in July 1958, ordered 10 slightly modified aircraft under the designation **YHC-1A**; the first of these flew for the first time on 27 August 1959. By that time the US Army had become more interested in a larger, more powerful helicopter which Vertol had developed from the Model 107 and, in consequence, reduced its order to only three YCH-1As. Subsequently, the company equipped the third of these with 783-kW (1,050-shp) General Electric T58-GE-6 turboshaft engines and rotors of increased diameter, and this derivative was fitted out with a commer-

cial interior as the **Model 107-II** prototype, which first flew on 25 October 1960. By that time Vertol had become a division of The Boeing Company.

When the US Marine Corps showed an interest in this aircraft, one was modified as the **Boeing Vertol Model 107M**, powered by T58-GE-8 engines, and this was successful in winning the USMC's design competition in February 1961, being ordered into production under the designation **HRB-1** (changed to **CH-46A** in 1962), and the name **Sea Knight**. Since that time Sea Knights have been used extensively by both the USMC and the US Navy. The former uses these helicopters for troop transport, the latter mainly in the vertical replenishment (VERTREP) role, carrying stores, ammunition and personnel from logistic support ships to combat ships at sea.

The first of the CH-46As flew on 16 October 1962, and testing continued into late 1964, with the first US Marine squadrons taking these aircraft into service in early 1965. Since then a number of versions have been built, these including the **CH-46D** for the USMC, generally similar to the CH-46A, but with 1044-kW (1,400-shp) T58-GE-10 turboshaft engines; the **CH-46F** for the USMC, generally similar to the CH-46D, but with additional avionics; the **UH-46A Sea Knight**, similar to CH-46A, procured by the US Navy for first deliveries to Utility Helicopter Squadron 1 in July 1964; and the **UH-46D** for the US Navy, virtually the same as the CH-46D. The US Marine Corps has updated 273 of its Sea Knights to **CH-46E** standard, with 1394-kW (1,870-shp) General Electric T58-GE-16 turboshafts and other improvements. Six utility models, almost identical to the CH-46A, were delivered to the RCAF in 1963-4 under the designation **CH-113 Labrador**, and 12 similar aircraft were built for the Canadian Army during 1964-5, these being designated **CH-113A Voyageur**. Under a Canadian Armed Forces' Search And Rescue Capability Upgrade Project (SARCUP), Boeing of Canada was contracted to modify six CH-113s and five CH-113As to an improved SAR standard by mid-1984. In 1962-3 Boeing Vertol supplied Model 107-IIs to Sweden for

service with the air force in the search and rescue role, and with the navy for ASW and minesweeping duties: both of these versions have the designation **HKP-4**.

In 1965, Kawasaki in Japan acquired from Boeing Vertol the worldwide sales rights for the Model 107-II, and in 1981 continued to produce these helicopters under the designation **KV-107/IIA**. A number of versions have been built and remain in production, and these are listed below.

Variants
KV-107/II-2: airline version, with accommodation for two flight crew, a stewardess and 25 passengers; 11 built; improved **KV-107/IIA-2** available currently
KV-107/II-3: mine counter-measures (MCM) version for JMSDF (two), plus seven of the uprated **KV-107/IIA-3** model
KV-107/II-4: tactical cargo/troop transport for JGSDF with strengthened cabin flooring; 42 supplied as such, with the last of 18 uprated **KV-107/IIA-4** versions delivered in late 1981
KV-107/II-5: designation of 13 long-range SAR helicopters for JASDF; 19 uprated, but otherwise similar aircraft, are designated **KV-107/IIA-5**, the last three being delivered during 1981; eight KV-107/II-5s supplied to Swedish navy without powerplant, these having Rolls-Royce Gnome H.1200 turboshafts installed in Sweden; Swedish navy designation **HKP-4C**

The Sea Knight is widely used by the US Marine Corps for assault transport, and also by the US Navy (illustrated) for transport and rescue work.

KV-107/II-7: designation of one six/eleven-seat VIP transport
KV-107/IIA-17: designation of single long-range transport for Tokyo Metropolitan Police Department; has a forward passenger compartment and aft cargo hold
KV-107/II-SM-1: designation of four helicopters equipped as firefighters
KV-107/IIA-SM-2: aeromedical and rescue version

Specification
Kawasaki KV-107/IIA-2
Type: twin-rotor transport helicopter
Powerplant: two 1044-kW (1,400-shp) General Electric CT58-140-1 or Ishikawajima-Harima CT58-IHI-110-1 turboshafts
Performance: maximum speed at sea level 254 km/h (158 mph); cruising speed 241 km/h (150 mph) at 1525 m (5,000 ft); service ceiling 5180 m (17,000 ft); range with maximum fuel 1097 km (682 miles)
Weights: empty equipped 5251 kg (11,576 lb); maximum take-off 9707 kg (21,400 lb)
Dimensions: rotor diameter, each 15.24 m (50 ft 0 in); length overall, rotors turning 25.4 m (83 ft 4 in); height 5.09 m (16 ft 8½ in); rotor disc area, each 182.41 m² (1,963.5 sq ft)

Boeing Vertol Model 114 (CH-47)

Following the evaluation of submissions by five US helicopter manufacturers, the US Army selected the **Boeing Vertol Model 114** as most nearly meeting its requirements for a battlefield mobility helicopter. This was expected to be suitably equipped for all-weather operations, to lift a load of 1814 kg (4,000 lb) internally or of 7257 kg (16,000 lb) suspended from an external sling, carry a maximum of 40 troops with full equipment, to have straight-in rear loading, be suitable for casualty evacuation roles, and be able to airlift any component of the Martin Marietta Pershing missile system. An initial contract for five **YHC-1B** pre-production examples was placed in June 1959, but soon after entering service these were redesignated **YCH-47A** and given the name **Chinook**.

The Model 114 was, in effect, a larger and more powerful version of the same company's Model 107 (CH-46 Sea Knight). The non-retractable landing gear is of quadricycle configuration, and the fuselage has sealed and compartmented fairing pods on each side of the lower fuselage, extending for almost three-quarters of the fuselage length to supplement the buoyancy of the sealed lower fuselage for water operations. The first YHC-1B made its initial flight on 21 September 1961, by which time the first production contract for **CH-47A** aircraft had been placed. These were powered initially by 1641-kW (2,200-shp) Lycoming T55-L-5 turboshafts (subsequently by 1976-kW/2,650-shp T55-L-7 turboshafts), and deliveries of CH-47As began in December 1972.

Since that time a number of versions have been built, including the **CH-47B**, a development with more powerful 2125-kW (2,850-shp) T55-L-7C turboshafts, redesigned rotor blades and other detail refinements, the first of two prototypes making its first flight during October 1966, with deliveries beginning on 10 May 1967. It was followed by the **CH-47C (Model 234)**, which is powered by two 2796-kW (3,750-shp) T55-L-11C turboshafts, has a strengthened transmission system, and incorporates increased fuel capacity. The first of these aircraft made its initial flight on 14 October 1967, and deliveries of pro-

Most CH-47 Chinooks are used as assault transports, transporting loads both internally and slung under hooks.

duction aircraft began in early 1968. Nine aircraft similar to the CH-47C have been built for the Canadian Armed Forces, under the designation **CH-147**; deliveries began in September 1974. The CH-147 has the latest safety features and an advanced flight-control system, with a maximum land take-off weight of 22680 kg (50,000 lb) and emergency water take-off weight of 20865 kg (46,000 lb). During the war in Vietnam, four of an **ACH-47A** derivative were built, similar in configuration to the CH-47A, but equipped with armour and armament which included a 40-mm grenade-launcher in the nose, a 20-mm forward-firing cannon and a 7.62-mm (0.3-in) machine-gun or a 19-round rocket pack mounted on a pylon, one on each side of the fuselage, plus five gun positions for air gunners stationed in the cabin, each having a 12.7-mm (0.5-in) or 7.62-mm (0.3-in) machine-gun on a flexible mounting. Three of these were evaluated in Vietnam, but no further examples were built.

Chinooks operated in South East Asia proved most valuable, not only for the transport of troops and supplies, and for casualty evacuation, but also for the recovery of disabled aircraft and the airlift of refugees. Chinooks are still considered an important component of the US Army's helicopter air logistic forces, and it is planned to modernise all surviving aircraft. Under a US Army development programme, one each of the models CH-47A, CH-47B, and CH-47C were stripped down to the basic airframe, and rebuilt to an improved standard to serve as **CH-47D** prototypes. These upgraded CH-47Ds have more-powerful turboshaft engines and higher-rated transmissions; a rede-

signed avionics; and many design refinements. They also introduce an auxiliary power unit and a triple hook cargo-suspension system. Following a successful conclusion to flight testing of these prototypes by the US Army, Boeing Vertol started a programme of remanufacturing CH-47As to CH-47D standard, and the first of these was delivered in 1982.

Under the designation **Chinook HC. Mk 1**, the Royal Air Force ordered 33 examples similar to the Canadian CH-147. They have British avionics and equipment, and a number of special provisions. The first was handed over in August 1980, and delivery of all 33 was completed during early 1982. Since 1970 Chinooks have been built in Italy for European and Middle East customers, following acquisition by Elicotteri Meridionali of co-production and marketing rights from Boeing Vertol. Agusta, SIAI-Marchetti, and other Italian manufacturers are also involved in this programme.

Production by Boeing Vertol of new military Chinooks is now limited to orders for the **Model 414**, which is an international export version and the **MH-47E**, a Special Forces variant of the CH-47D with night/low flying avionics and an inflight-refuelling probe. However, in the late summer of 1978 the company announced the development of a civil counterpart of the military Chinook, intended for commercial service. Two basic versions were planned, the long-range **Model 234LR** to serve in all-passenger, passenger/freight 'combi', or all-cargo civil roles; and the **Model 234UT** utility version for more specialised tasks such as resources exploration and development, logging, and general utility heavy construction work.

The Model 234LR programme was launched in November 1978, following the finalisation of a contract with British Airways Helicopters (BAH) for the initial supply of three of these aircraft required primarily by BAH to carry passengers and priority cargo from points in Scotland to and from North Sea platforms operated by the Esso and Shell petroleum companies.

To facilitate such operations, emphasis has been placed on the interior design so that it can be converted comparatively easily by the operator from all-passenger to 'combi' or all-cargo use. In full passenger configuration these Chinooks have the largest capacity of any commercial helicopter, with four-abreast seating for a maximum of 44 passengers. They enjoy a standard of interior design and comfort similar to that found in the Boeing Company's airliners, with roomy, comfortable seats; individual service units; complete lavatory facilities; overhead baggage compartments; ample windows, and pleasant lighting conditions; a food or beverage galley; and a stereo system. Access for passengers is via a door at the forward

end of the cabin on the port side, and the undersurface of the upswept rear fuselage is formed by an hydraulically-operated cargo-landing ramp.

In a typical 'combi' layout, 18 passengers can be accommodated in the forward area of the cabin, with 7258 kg (16,000 lb) of freight at the rear. In an all-cargo configuration up to 9072 kg (20,000 lb) can be carried internally, or a maximum of 12701 kg (28,000 lb) externally, suspended from a cargo hook or hooks.

The rotors of the civil Chinook are powered by two Avro Lycoming AL 5512 turboshaft engines, via a combining gearbox and interconnecting shafts which enable both rotors to be driven in emergency by either engine. To provide the essential range, large external fuel tanks are accommodated within the fairings which extend along both sides of the lower fuselage. These fairings serve a dual purpose, for they also provide a flotation capability that can ensure survival of the aircraft if forced down onto a sea surface with storm waves not exceeding 9.15 m (30 ft) in height. Overwater operation throughout the year demands a high standard of all-weather capability, and this is ensured by the provision of weather radar, duplicated full blind-flying instrumentation, and a dual four-axis automatic flight control system. Comprehensive de-icing provisions are embodied, though these are optional for service in less critical areas, and the glassfibre rotor blades incorporate an aluminium screen in their construction, to provide adequate protection against lightning strikes. Safety equipment includes two life-rafts, each of which is capable of accommodating up to 36 persons.

The first Model 234LR made its maiden flight on 19 August 1980, and two additional aircraft took part in the development programme. FAA and CAA certification were gained on 19 and 26 June 1981 respectively, and the first example entered service with BAH on 1 July 1981.

Specification
Boeing Vertol CH-47C Chinook
Type: twin-rotor medium transport helicopter
Powerplant: two 2796-kW (3,750-shp) Avco Lycoming T55-L-11A turboshafts
Performance: maximum speed at sea level 286 km/h (178 mph); cruising speed 257 km/h (160 mph); service ceiling 3290 m (10,800 ft); mission radius 185 km (115 miles)
Weights: empty 9736 kg (21,464 lb); maximum take-off 17463 kg (38,500 lb)
Dimensions: rotor diameter, each 18.29 m (60 ft 0 in); overall length, rotors turning 30.18 m (99 ft 0 in); height 5.68 m (18 ft 7¾ in); rotor disc area, each 262.67 m² (2,827.43 sq ft)

Boeing Vertol Model 234LR of British Airways Helicopters, used for supporting oil rigs.

Boeing Vertol Model 179

In 1971 the US Department of Defense issued a requirement for a new UTTAS (Utility Tactical Transport Aircraft System) helicopter to replace the Bell UH-1 in service with the US Army. The requirement called for much the same capacity as that available with the UH-1, but this payload had to be maintained up to much greater altitudes and at considerably higher ambient temperatures. The two leading contenders for UTTAS hardware were Sikorsky, with its S-70 ordered for evaluation as the YUH-60A, and Boeing Vertol, with the **Boeing Vertol Model 179 (YUH-61A)**.

The Model 179 was the first Boeing Vertol design with a single main rotor, and this profited from the company's licence-production of the MBB BO105 utility helicopter, for the Model 179 was designed round a similar type of hinge-less semi-rigid main rotor of composite construction. Powerplant was a pair of the specified General Electric YT700 turboshafts, located in two pods on the sides of the fuselage beside the shallow transmission unit above the rear of the

cabin. This latter could accommodate 11 troops (in addition to the three crew), or its area of 8.3m² (89.4 sq ft) could accommodate freight; alternatively, a slung load of 3175 kg (7,000 lb) could be lifted. The fuselage was of frame-and-stringer construction, a considerable quantity of glassfibre and honeycomb being used for strength and to reduce maintenance. The conventional pod-and-boom fuselage terminated in a four-blade glassfibre tail rotor and a large tail-plane with incidence varied automatically with airspeed for improved control. The landing gear was of fixed tricycle type, with single main wheels and a twin-wheel nose unit.

Three military prototypes were completed, the first flying on 29 November 1974. A competitive evaluation of the YUH-60A and YUH-61A was conducted

The Model 179 was test-flown as the YUH-61A in the US Army's UTTAS programme, but was beaten by the Sikorsky S.70 (YUH-60A) design.

from 1975, and the Sikorsky entrant was judged the winner. Boeing Vertol completed a fourth prototype as the Model 179 civil demonstrator, with accommodation for between 14 and 20 passengers. Subsequent development of both types was later abandoned.

Specification
Boeing Vertol Model 179 (YUH-61A)
Type: utility military helicopter
Powerplant: two 1146-kW (1,536-shp) General Electric YT700-GE-700

turboshafts
Performance: maximum speed 290 km/h (180 mph) at sea level; cruising speed 216 km/h (154 mph) at sea level; hovering ceiling out of ground effect 1722 m (5,650 ft); maximum range 964 km (598 miles) at 1525 m (5,000 ft)
Weights: empty 4302 kg (9,487 lb); maximum take-off 8481 kg (18,700 lb)
Dimensions: main rotor diameter 14.93 m (49 ft 0 in); length, rotors turning 18.13 m (59 ft 6 in); height 4.63 m (15 ft 2 in); main rotor disc area 175.19 m² (1,885.7 sq ft)

Boulton & Paul P.3 Bobolink

Although built only in prototype form, the **Boulton & Paul P.3 Bobolink** is worthy of mention as Boulton & Paul's first aeroplane. The company had manufactured wooden buildings at its Norwich factory, and during World War I built aircraft under sub-contract. Among the types produced were the Fe 2b and Camel, and the Bobolink was the result of a design competition to find a Camel replacement.

The winner of the competition was the Sopwith Snipe, so the Boulton & Paul aircraft did not enter production; three serial numbers were allocated for the prototypes, but records suggest that only one was built. An interesting feature made it possible for the Bobolink's pilot to jettison its main fuel tanks in the event of an in-flight fire.

As might have been expected, the Bobolink had a number of similarities to

The Bobolink was a good design beaten by a better one. The two-bay wing cellule was a distinct advantage, based on N-interplane struts to do away with the need for incidence bracing.

the Camel, and its performance was comparable with that of the Snipe, but the latter was considered to be more suitable for mass production.

Specification
Type: single-seat fighter
Powerplant: one 172-kW (230-hp) Bentley B.R.2 rotary piston engine
Performance: maximum speed 201 km/h (125 mph) at 3050 m (10,000 ft), and 175 km/h (109 mph) at 4570 m (15,000 ft); climb to 1980 m (6,500 ft) in 5 minutes 20 seconds; service ceiling 5945 m (19,500 ft);

endurance 3 hours 15 minutes
Weights: empty 557 kg (1,226 lb); maximum take-off 904 kg (1,992 lb)
Dimensions: span 8.84 m (29 ft 0 in); length 6.10 m (20 ft 0 in); height 2.54 m (8 ft 4 in); wing area 24.71 m²

(266.0 sq ft)
Armament: two forward-firing synchronised 7.7-mm (0.303-in) Vickers machine-guns on top of fuselage; provision for one 7.7-mm (0.303-in) Lewis gun above wing centre-section

Boulton & Paul P.29 Sidestrand

Following their experience with the Bourges and Bugle twin-engine biplane bomber prototypes, Boulton & Paul designed a new aircraft to meet Specification 9/24 for a three/four-seat medium day bomber. The first of two **Boulton & Paul P.29 Sidestrand Mk I** prototypes flew in 1926, and the company received an order for 18 production aircraft.

Deliveries to the newly re-formed No. 101 Squadron at Bircham Newton began in 1928, the first batch of six aircraft being of the **Sidestrand Mk II** version with ungeared Bristol Jupiter VI engines. These were followed by nine of the **Sidestrand Mk III** versions with geared Jupiter VIIIFs, and the final three production aircraft were replacement Mk IIs.

The Sidestrand inherited the good manoeuvrability of the Bourges, but despite proving to be an excellent aircraft for bombing and gunnery, only No. 101 Squadron was equipped. Three Sidestrand Mk IIIs were converted to **Sidestrand Mk V** configuration but were then renamed Overstrand; these began to replace their predecessors in December 1934.

Specification
Boulton & Paul Sidestrand Mk III
Type: three/four-seat medium bomber
Powerplant: two 343-kW (460-hp) Bristol Jupiter VIIIF radial piston engines
Performance: maximum speed 225 km/h (140 mph) at 3050 m

(10,000 ft); service ceiling 7315 m (24,000 ft); range 805 km (500 miles)
Weights: empty 2726 kg (6,010 lb); maximum take-off 4627 kg (10,200 lb)
Dimensions: span 21.92 m (71 ft 11 in); length 14.02 m (46 ft 0 in); height 4.52 m (14 ft 10 in); wing area 91.04 m² (980.0 sq ft)
Armament: three 7.7-mm (0.303-in) Lewis guns (one in nose and one each

The Boulton & Paul Sidestrand was the first RAF aircraft designated as a medium bomber, and was a remarkably agile aircraft. It could be looped, rolled and spun with ease, and was capable of flight on one engine.

in dorsal and ventral positions), plus a bomb load of up to 476 kg (1,050 lb)

Boulton & Paul P.31 Bittern

Air Ministry Specification 27/24 called for a single-seat night-fighter for use against formations of enemy bombers. In an era when single-engined single-seat biplanes generally dominated the RAF's fighter squadrons, Boulton & Paul's proposal for this requirement, a twin-engined monoplane, was so radical that unless it had exceptional performance and manoeuvrability it was almost certainly assured to fail.

Two prototypes were built under the designation **Boulton & Paul P.31** and given the name **Bittern**. The first (J7936) had shoulder-mounted wings with two mid-set Armstrong Siddeley Lynx radial engines at the wing leading edges. These were enclosed in cowlings that allowed the cylinder-heads to be exposed to the slipstream. The second prototype (J7937) differed in having a redesigned wing that was about 1.52 m (5 ft) greater in span and incorporated Handley Page leading-edge slots. The engines were mounted much lower on the wing, within Townend rings and without close cowling around the cylinders. The other major difference be-

Boulton & Paul B.31 Bittern (J7937, second prototype) with cowled lower-set engines and fuselage-mounted barbettes for the elevating armament.

tween the two prototypes lay in their armament: the first (J7936) had two fixed forward-firing Vickers machine-guns in the sides of the forward fuselage; and the second (J7937) had single Lewis guns on each side of the nose, in barbettes which could be elevated from 0° to 45°, and were interconnected with a ring-and-bead gunsight that was raised simultaneously and through the same range as the guns. This was intended to simplify the task of attacking a bomber

formation from below.

Despite the innovative ideas, both prototypes were seriously underpowered, which in retrospect seems strange when radial engines of almost double the power were then available. As a result when the prototypes were tested their performance was so poor that further development of the type was abandoned.

Specification
Boulton & Paul P.31 Bittern (1st prototype)

Type: single-seat twin-engined night-fighter
Powerplant: two 172-kW (230-hp) Armstrong Siddeley Lynx radial piston engines
Performance: maximum speed 233 km/h (145 mph)
Weight: maximum take-off 2041 kg (4,500 lb)
Dimensions: span 12.50 m (41 ft 0 in); length 9.75 m (32 ft)
Armament: two fixed forward-firing 7.7-mm (0.303-in) Vickers machine-guns

Boulton & Paul P.64 Mailplane and P.71A

In 1939 Boulton & Paul built a twin-engine all-metal biplane under a contract awarded by Imperial Airways. The airline had a requirement for a mailplane capable of carrying a 454-kg (1,000-lb) payload over a 1609 km (1,000 mile) range at reasonable speed, and the company considered its **Boulton & Paul P.64 Mailplane** to be the answer. Unfortunately it was both expensive and unsatisfactory. First flown at the company's airfield at Mousehold, Norwich, in March 1933, it lasted barely seven months before being destroyed in an unexplained fatal crash during trials at Martlesham Heath in October.

Development of the basic layout was continued, and the resulting **Boulton & Paul P.71A** was lighter, slimmer and longer. In place of the 414-kW (555-hp) Bristol Pegasus engines of the P.64, the P.71A had 365-kW (490-hp) Armstrong Siddeley Jaguar VIAs, and two aircraft were delivered to Imperial Airways at Croydon in February 1935.

By then, the airline had lost interest in the mail-carrying possibilities and the two aircraft, named *Boadicea* and *Brito-mart*, were converted for passenger carrying with 13 seats, which were easily removable if the aircraft were required for use as light freighters.

The P.71As were both lost within 19 months of delivery. The first of them

Boulton & Paul P.64 Mailplane

was damaged beyond repair in a landing accident at Brussels in October 1935; the second disappeared over the English Channel in September 1936.

Specification
Boulton & Paul P.71A
Type: twin-engine mailplane
Powerplant: two 365-kW (490-hp) Armstrong Siddeley Jaguar VIA radial piston engines
Performance: maximum speed 314 km/h (195 mph) at 1525 m (5,000 ft); cruising speed 267 km/h (166 mph) at 1525 m (5,000 ft); range 966 km (600 miles)
Weights: empty 2767 kg (6,100 lb);

maximum take-off 4309 kg (9,500 lb)
Dimensions: span 16.46 m (54 ft 0 in); length 13.46 m (44 ft 2 in); height 4.62 m (15 ft 2 in); wing area 66.75 m² (718.5 sq ft)

The Boulton & Paul P.71A was evolved from the disastrous P.64. Illustrated is G-ACOX Boadicea of Imperial Airways, which was later damaged beyond repair.

Boulton Paul P.75 Overstrand

A development of the Sidestrand, the **Boulton & Paul P.75 Overstrand** prototype which flew in 1933 was a conversion of the eighth production Sidestrand. Several other conversions followed, designated originally as Sidestrand Mk V, but the name Overstrand was adopted in March 1934.

By then the company name had changed to Boulton Paul Aircraft Ltd and construction of a new factory had begun at Wolverhampton. An order was placed for 24 production Overstrands to replace the Sidestrands in service with No. 101 Squadron, but the first aircraft to reach this unit in January 1935 was a Sidestrand conversion, to be followed by another conversion the following month. The first true production Overstrands

Depicted on a postcard optimistically entitled 'Britain Prepared', these Overstrands are seen in No. 101 Squadron service. The power-operated turret was the first in RAF service.

were not delivered until early the following year.

While the early conversions were powered by 414-kW (555-hp) Bristol Pegasus I engines, the production models had the Pegasus II of 433 kW (580 hp). Apart from having more powerful engines, the Overstrand differed from its predecessor by having an enclosed power-operated nose turret, the first in an RAF aircraft; this development led a contemporary annual to prophesy

Boulton Paul P.75 Overstrand of No. 101 Squadron, Royal Air Force, based at Bicester in Oxford during 1936-37.

equip with Bristol Blenheim Mk Is in June 1938. A few Overstrands lingered on as gunnery trainers until about 1941.

A proposed development, the **Super-strand** was to have had retractable landing gear and a generally cleaned-up airframe, but the advent of new mono-plane bombers killed this project.

Specification

Type: five-seat medium bomber
Powerplant: two 433-kW (580-hp) Bristol Pegasus IIM.3 radial piston engines
Performance: maximum speed 246 km/h (153 mph) at 1980 m (6,500 ft); service ceiling 6860 m (22,500 ft); range 877 km (545 miles)
Weights: empty 3600 kg (7,936 lb); maximum take-off 5443 kg (12,000 lb)
Dimensions: span 21.95 m (72 ft 0 in); length 14.02 m (46 ft 0 in); height 4.72 m (15 ft 6 in); wing area 91.04 m² (980.0 sq ft)
Armament: three 7.7-mm (0.303-in) Lewis guns (one in nose turret and one each in dorsal ventral positions), plus a bomb load of up to 726 kg (1,600 lb)

that 'it is likely to lead to a revolution in air tactics'. In addition to providing this luxury for the front gunner, the Over-strand had an enclosed cockpit with a movable windscreen for the pilot, and a controllable hot air supply for all crew positions was drawn from a new type of heater built into the engine exhaust system. Further evidence of the Over-strand's advanced design was the provi-sion of an auto-pilot, while Boulton Paul engine cowlings and exhaust collectors helped to reduce engine noise and mini-mise exhaust flame emissions respec-tively, both factors of benefit for night operation.

All Overstrands were built at Norwich, the last being delivered at the end of 1936, by which time the new factory at Wolverhampton was in use and the East Anglian premises closed down.

No. 101 Squadron, then based at Bic-ester, Oxon, was the main Overstrand user, but four aircraft were loaned to No. 144 Squadron which had been re-formed at Bicester in January 1937; their Over-strands were eventually replaced by Avro Ansons.

No. 101 Squadron phased out its Over-strands during 1937, and began to re-

Boulton Paul P.82 Defiant

A new tactical concept, first conceived in 1935, proposed the use in fighters of a power-operated multi-gun turret. This appeared to have more than one advan-tage: firstly, it relieved the fighter pilot of the dual task of flying the aircraft and concentrating on finding, holding and hit-ting a target; secondly, the weapons could be used offensively, or defen-sively, over a far greater field of fire than that possible for a fixed battery. The use of a power-operated turret was not en-tirely new, however, for a Hawker Demon biplane had been so equipped in 1934, but for a very different reason. This resulted from the fact that the high per-formance of this two-seat fighter made it almost impossible for the observer/gun-ner in the aft cockpit to sight and fire the single Lewis gun with sufficient accu-racy. A total of 59 Demons was manu-factured for Hawker by Boulton Paul Air-craft under sub-contract, and each had a Frazer-Nash hydraulically operated turret installed; in addition many Demons of Hawker manufacture were modified retrospectively.

Thus when the Air Ministry issued Specification F.9/35, calling for a two-seat fighter with a power-operated gun turret, both Boulton Paul and Hawker made submissions. The Hawker Hot-spur prototype was not, however, to compete against the two which were ordered from Boulton Paul, primarily because the Hawker factories had no productive capacity available, and con-sequently the Hotspur prototype was abandoned.

The first of the **Boulton Paul P.82 Defiant** prototypes made its initial flight on 11 August 1937. It was a low-wing cantilever monoplane of all-metal con-struction, provided with retractable tail-wheel type landing gear, and powered by a 768-kW (1,030-hp) Rolls-Royce Mer-lin I inline engine; the second prototype had a Merlin II engine. Both, of course, had the large and heavy four-gun turret mounted within the fuselage aft of the pilot's cockpit. Its weight, and the high degree of drag imposed by the protrud-ing section of the turret no matter how cleverly faired in, imposed severe limits on speed and manoeuvrability.

The first production **Defiant F.Mk I** day fighter was flown on 30 July 1939, and deliveries to No. 264 Squadron

Boulton Paul Defiant TT. Mk I of No. 286 Squadron, RAF, based at Colerne in 1943.

Boulton Paul Defiant TT. Mk I of an RAF fighter Operational Training Unit based in the Middle East in 1945. Black and yellow stripes were adopted for high conspicuity in the target-tug role.

began in December of that year. It was this squadron which first deployed the type operationally, on 12 May 1940 over the beaches of Dunkirk, achieving com-plete tactical surprise. Fighters making conventional attack on the tail of the Defiants were met with an un-precedented burst of fire from the four machine-guns: on one day they claimed 38 enemy aircraft destroyed, and a total of 65 by the end of May. It was, how-ever, only brief air superiority, for it took little time for Luftwaffe fighter pilots to discover that they could attack head-on, or against the belly of the Defiant, with complete impunity.

It was instead decided to use the Defiant in a night-fighter role, and the comparatively new and highly secret AI radar was installed in many of the Mk I aircraft, comprising either AI Mk IV or Mk VI, aircraft so fitted being designated **Defiant NF. Mk IA**. With this equip-

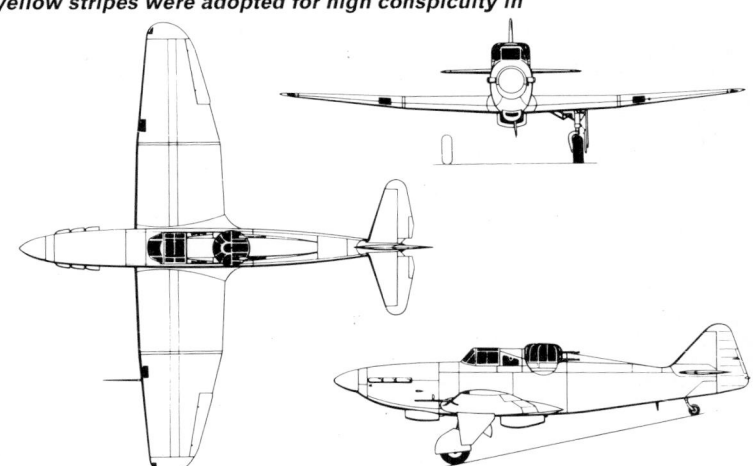

Boulton Paul P.82 Defiant Mk I with turret fairings

ment they proved a valuable addition to the UK's night defences in the winter of 1940-1, and during this period they recorded more 'kills' per interception than any other contemporary night-fighter.

In an attempt to improve the performance of the Defiant, two Mk Is served for conversion as prototypes of a new **Defiant Mk II** version. Apart from the installation of a more powerful Merlin XX engine, fuel capacity was increased, a rudder of greater area was provided, and there were modifications to the engine cooling and fuel systems. First flown on 20 June 1940, the Defiant Mk II was built to the number of 210 examples, of which many were later converted as **Defiant TT.Mk I** target tugs. In addition 150 Mk Is were converted to **Defiant TT.Mk III** tugs, and 140 new production TT Mk Is were built to bring total construction, including prototypes, to 1,065 when production ended in 1943.

At the peak of their deployment as night-fighters, Defiants equipped 13 RAF squadrons. They were used subse-quently at home, and in the Middle and Far East, as target-tugs, and in addition about 50 Mk Is were modified for use in an air/sea rescue role, serving with Nos 275, 276, 277, 280 and 281 Squadrons for this purpose.

Specification
Defiant Mk II
Type: two-seat night-fighter
Powerplant: one 954-kW (1,280-hp) Rolls-Royce Merlin XX inline piston engine
Performance: maximum speed 504 km/h (313 mph) at 5790 m (19,000 ft); cruising speed 418 km/h (260 mph); service ceiling 9250 m (30,350 ft); range 748 km (465 miles)
Weights: empty 2849 kg (6,282 lb); maximum take-off 3821 kg (8,424 lb)
Dimensions: span 11.99 m (39 ft 4 in); length 10.77 m (35 ft 4 in); height 3.45 m (11 ft 4 in); wing area 23.23 m² (250.0 sq ft)
Armament: four 7.7-mm (0.303-in) Browning machine-guns in power-operated dorsal turret

Boulton Paul Defiant F.Mk I day fighter of No.264 Squadron, Royal Air Force.

Boulton Paul P.108 Balliol

Air Ministry Specification T.7/45 called for a turboprop-powered three-seat advanced trainer, and to meet this requirement Boulton Paul designed the **Boulton Paul P.108 Balliol**. The airframe was ready before the engine, however, and the first flight was made on 30 May 1947 with an 611-kW (820-hp) Bristol Mercury radial piston engine. Ten months later a second prototype flew, powered by the chosen engine, an Armstrong Siddeley Mamba. It was the world's first single-turboprop aircraft to fly, and the first P.108 was similarly re-engined at a later date.

Having specified a three-seat turboprop, the Air Ministry had second thoughts and decided instead that it needed a two-seat piston-powered trainer. A new Specification T.14/47 was drawn up, with the Rolls-Royce Merlin defined as powerplant, and Boulton Paul received a contract for four prototypes having the same basic airframe as the earlier aircraft. Competing from Avro was the Athena which, like the P.108, had flown originally with a Mamba to Specification T.7/45, but Avro's production to these requirements amounted to three Athena T.Mk 1s (two with Mambas, one with a Rolls-Royce Dart), four Merlin-powered T.Mk 2 prototypes, and 15 similar production aircraft. Boulton Paul were more fortunate; they built the two turboprop P.108s, four prototypes of the Merlin-powered **Balliol T.Mk 2** and a pre-production batch of 17 before series production began.

In service trials the Balliol performed well, and sizeable contracts were awarded for Balliols to replace Harvards in RAF service. However, by 1951 the Air Ministry had again changed its mind, deciding instead to concentrate on all-through jet training, and orders were cut back. Sources differ on the number of Balliols constructed, but in addition to the prototype and pre-production aircraft

Boulton Paul Balliol T. Mk 2 of No. 7 Flying Training School, RAF, based at Cottesmore in the early 1950s.

The first prototype of the Boulton Paul P.108 Balliol was initially flown with a Bristol Mercury radial as the proposed Armstrong Siddeley Mamba turboprop was not ready. Production aircraft had the trusty Merlin.

it seems probable that 162 were built for the RAF, including a batch of 30 produced under subcontract by Blackburn. Some of the aircraft earmarked for the RAF were diverted to fulfil a contract for the Ceylon air force (variously reported as 9 or 12 aircraft), and Boulton Paul had a civil demonstrator between 1954 and 1956.

Pre-production Balliols went to the Central Flying School, while production models were delivered to No. 7 Flying Training School at Cottesmore, and served later at the RAF College, Cranwell until superseded by Vampire T.Mk 11s in 1956. A navalised version designated **Sea Balliol T.Mk 21** was ordered for the Fleet Air Arm, and the last of 30 aircraft was delivered in December 1954. The Sea Balliols differed from the RAF version in having a smaller-diameter propeller, strengthened landing gear, an arrester hook for deck landing, and some changes in

equipment. They equipped No. 781 Squadron at Lee-on-Solent and No. 1843 Squadron of the RNVR at Abbotsinch, Glasgow. One example survives in the RAF Aerospace Museum at Cosford, Wolverhampton.

Specification
Boulton Paul Balliol T.Mk 2
Type: two-seat advanced trainer
Powerplant: one 928-kW (1,245-hp) Rolls-Royce Merlin 35 inline piston engine
Performance: maximum speed 463 km/h (288 mph) at 2745 m (9,000 ft); service ceiling 9905 m (32,500 ft); range 1062 km (660 miles)
Weights: empty 3043 kg (6,730 lb); maximum take-off 3815 kg (8,410 lb)
Dimensions: span 11.99 m (30 ft 4 in); length 10.71 m (35 ft 1½ in); height 3.81 m (12 ft 6 in); wing area 23.23 m² (250.0 sq ft)
Armament: one 7.7-mm (0.303-in) Browning machine-gun in port wing, and provision for four 27-kg (60-lb) rockets

Boulton Paul P.111 and P.120

The **Boulton Paul P.111** and **P.120** delta wing research aircraft, built to Air Ministry Specification E.27/46 and E.27/49 respectively, were used to investigate high speed characteristics of the delta wing.

The P.111 flew in October 1950, powered by a Rolls-Royce Nene turbojet. Its delta wing had a leading-edge sweep of 45°, and detachable wingtips made it easy to carry out comparative tests with blunt and pointed tips. The fin tip was similarly detachable, and there was no tailplane.

After tests in its original form, the aircraft was fitted with a nose probe and four rectangular airbrakes around the front fuselage. Some internal modifications were also made and in this new form it received the designation **P.111A**, recommencing flight tests in July 1953. It could attain level speeds in the region of Mach 0.95-0.98, and become supersonic in a shallow dive. The P.111A survives in the Midland Air Museum at Coventry's Baginton Airport.

The **P.120**, flown on 6 August 1952, was similar in general layout to the P.111 but had an all-moving tailplane mounted on a squat fin. There was little chance

The P.111 was used for research of the transonic performance of delta wings. The pointed fin-tip was detachable.

to gain much information from the new aircraft as it was lost on 29 August, in an accident thought to have been caused by tail flutter.

Specification
Boulton Paul P.111A
Type: single-seat research aircraft
Powerplant: one 2313-kg (5,100-lb)

thrust Rolls-Royce Nene turbojet
Performance: maximum speed in level flight Mach 0.98
Weights: empty 2948 kg (6,500 lb); maximum take-off 4354 kg (9,600 lb)
Dimensions: (with wing and fin pointed tips) span 10.21 m (33 ft 0 in); length 7.95 m (26 ft 1 in); height 3.82 m

Similar to the P.111, the P.120 had revised tail surfaces with a T-tail. Flutter of the all-moving horizontal tail surfaces caused the loss of the aircraft in 1952.

(12 ft 6½ in); wing area 18.58 m² (200.0 sq ft)

Brantly-Hynes Model B-2

In 1943, N. P. Brantly began the design of a lightweight helicopter, built and flown in 1946 under the designation **Brantly B-1**. Like many contemporaries, Brantly used a co-axial twin-rotor configuration to overcome torque effects, but soon realised that his design was too heavy and complicated to appeal to the private pilot. An improved **Brantly B-2**, of single main rotor and anti-torque tail rotor configuration, was first flown on 21 February 1953, and a further improved second prototype flew on 14 August 1956. This was to enter production in 1958.

Changing fortunes have resulted in several different owners of the original Brantly interests, but this emphasises a wide appreciation of a good product, and of a steady demand for it. Michael K. Hynes is the present owner of the type

certificates, and he established Brantly-Hynes Helicopter Inc. on 1 January 1975, initially to provide product support for the large number of Brantly helicopters in use. He subsequently started up a production line for the B-2B, and also the larger Model 305.

The Model B-2B has a three-blade main rotor and two-blade rotor, an all-metal fuselage structure, and can oper-

ate with skid, wheel or float landing gear. Side-by-side two-seat accommodation is provided in an enclosed cabin, and dual controls are standard. The Avco Lycoming powerplant is mounted vertically in the fuselage, just aft of the cabin.

Specification
Model B-2B (skid landing gear)
Type: two-seat light helicopter
Powerplant: one 134-kW (180-hp) Avco Lycoming IVO-360-A1A flat-four piston engine

Performance: maximum speed at sea level 161 km/h (100 mph); maximum cruising speed 145 km/h (90 mph); service ceiling 3290 m (10,800 ft); range with maximum fuel 402 km (250 miles)
Weights: empty 463 kg (1,020 lb); maximum take-off 757 kg (1,670 lb)
Dimensions: main rotor diameter 7.24 m (23 ft 9 in); fuselage length 6.63 m (21 ft 9 in); height 2.06 m (6 ft 9 in); main rotor disc area 41.06 m² (442.0 sq ft)

In its B-2B form, the Brantly B-2 remained in production into the 1980s. The classic shape of the helicopter changed little during the long production run. The small wheels aided ground handling.

Brantly-Hynes Model 305

Basically a larger-scale version of the Model B-2B, the prototype of the original **Brantly Model 305** was flown for the first time during January 1964. Apart from its increased dimensions, it differs from its predecessor externally by having a small variable-incidence tailplane. Considerably more power is provided by an Avco Lycoming flat-six engine, and an enlarged cabin accommodates a total of five persons on two side-by-side forward seats, and an aft bench seat for three.

Specification
Type: five-seat light helicopter
Powerplant: one 227-kW (305-hp) Avco Lycoming IVO-540-A1A flat-six

Performance: maximum speed at sea level 193 km/h (120 mph); maximum cruising speed at sea level 177 km/h (110 mph); service ceiling 3660 m (12,000 ft); range with maximum fuel and payload 354 km (220 miles)
Weights: empty 816 kg (1,800 lb); maximum take-off 1315 kg (2,900 lb)
Dimensions: main rotor diameter 8.74 m (28 ft 8 in); fuselage length 7.44 m (24 ft 5 in); height 2.44 m (8 ft 0 in); main rotor disc area 59.96 m² (645.4 sq ft)

The five-seat Model 305 could be equipped with skis, floats (illustrated) or snow-skids for operations in all terrains.

Bratukhin Helicopters

In January 1940 a rotary-wing design bureau was established at the Moscow Aviation Institute, and in the spring of that year this became headed by Ivan P. Bratukhin. Impressed by the performance of Germany's Focke-Achgelis Fa 61, he decided to adopt a similar twin-rotor configuration for the first helicopter which he designed for the bureau. Whereas the twin rotors of the Fa 61 were powered by a single engine, Bratukhin decided that an individual powerplant for each rotor would prove to be less complicated and more efficient. The resulting prototype, designated **Omega**, had two 164-kW (220-hp) inline engines, one mounted at the end of each outrigger, and the design of the rotor-drive system was sufficiently sophisticated to allow rotor autorotation and, in the case of either engine failing, for both rotors to be driven by the remaining engine.

Early tests suffered from a variety of problems, and the German invasion in 1941 brought a break of some six months. During this period the design bureau was evacuated eastwards, and it was late 1942 before Omega was coaxed into the air. Unreliability of the powerplant eventually brought the tests to an end, but by that time it had been decided that the basic concept was promising and that further development would continue. Brief details of the related family of twin-rotors design that followed are given below.

Variants
Bratukhin Omega II: improved version of Omega, with 261-kW (350-hp) engines, structural strengthening and other improvements; one only; flown to altitude of 3000 m (9,845 ft) in January 1945, and used subsequently for pilot training
Bratukhin G-3: generally similar to Omega II, but powered by 336-kW (450-hp) Pratt & Whitney R-985 Wasp Juniors; two prototypes, followed by five production aircraft; of the latter, four were used for research and one for pilot training
Bratukhin G-4: very similar to original Omega, but powered by 373-kW (500-hp) AI-26GR engines which had been developed by A. Ivchenko for helicopter use; two prototypes and four production aircraft
Bratukhin B-5: improved and larger design initiated in 1945, powered by two improved AI-26 engines

The B-11 suffered from vibration and oscillation problems and its cancellation led ultimately to the dissolution of the design bureau. It was intended to serve as a communications helicopter.

Conceptually identical to the original Omega series of twin-rotor helicopters, the Bratukhin G-4 was designed round the specially-developed Ivchenko AI-26.

developing 410 kW (550 hp) for take-off; completed in 1947, but as a result of structural flexing and vibration only brief hops were made before this aircraft was abandoned
Bratukhin B-9: generally similar to B-5, except for having fuselage designed for use as air ambulance; failure of B-5 caused this to be abandoned also
Bratukhin B-10: following the same general configuration as the B-5 and B-9, had uprated AI-26 engines of 429 kW (575 hp); fuselage configured for use in an artillery observation role; although flown in 1947, development was abandoned as single-rotor helicopters were beginning to show greater promise
Bratukhin B-11: last of Bratukhin's twin-rotor helicopters before dissolution of his design bureau; generally similar to the B-5, and retaining its powerplant, but with an improved rotor system; two prototypes only, one lost in fatal accident on 13 December 1948; remaining prototype given uprated engines as fitted in B-10, but development abandoned for same reasons as for B-10

Specification
Bratukhin B-11
Type: transport helicopter prototype
Powerplant: two 429-kW (575-hp) Ivchenko AI-26GR(F) radial piston engines
Performance: maximum speed 155 km/h (96 mph) at 1500 m (4,920 ft); service ceiling 2550 m (8,365 ft); range 328 km (204 miles)
Weights: empty 3398 kg (7,491 lb); maximum take-off 4510 kg (9,149 lb)
Dimensions: rotor diameter, each 10 m (32 ft 9¾ in); fuselage length 9.76 m (32 ft 0¼ in); rotor disc area, each 74.71 m² (804.25 sq ft)

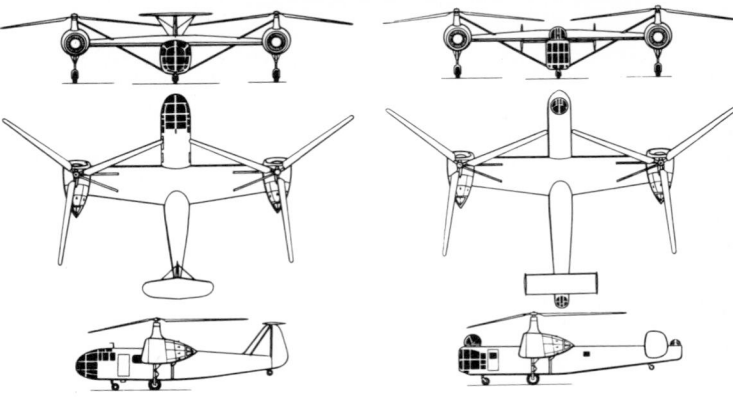

Bratukhin B-10   *Bratukhin B-11*

Breda Ba.27

The original concept for the **Breda Ba.27** was that of Cesare Pallavicino, his low-wing strut-braced single-seat fighter design being developed by Ing. Antonio Parano after Pallavicino had left Breda to take up a position with the Caproni-Bergamaschi company. Three prototypes were built, all flying during 1934. The first two featured a slab-sided fuselage, with the pilot's open cockpit located behind the trailing edge of the wing. Power was provided by a Bristol Jupiter IV radial engine, licence-built by Alfa Romeo. The third prototype retained the same basic steel-tube fuselage structure, married to wooden wings, but had rounded fuselage contours. The pilot's cockpit was moved further forward, his view being enhanced by cut-outs incorporated in the trailing edge of the wing roots, and en-

The Breda Ba.27, often known as the Metallico (Metal One), bore a striking resemblance to the Boeing P-26, but was a totally different aircraft, in reality inspired by the Travel Air Model R. One Chinese squadron was equipped with the type between 1935 and 1938.

larged fairings were provided for the independent wire-braced main landing gear units. A Mercury VI engine with a long-chord cowling replaced the Jupiter IV and Townend ring of the first two prototypes. This third prototype served briefly with the Italian 86ª Squadriglia d'Assalto during 1936.

The definitive Ba.27 was not accepted for production by the Italian authorities, but 18 were ordered by the Chinese government, which was anxious to obtain fighters to confront the Japanese invaders, but in fact only 11 were delivered during 1937, and little was heard of the type in action.

Specification
Type: single-seat fighter
Powerplant: one 481-kW (645-hp) Alfa Romeo (Bristol) Mercury VI radial

Breda Ba.27 of the Chinese Nationalist air force.

piston engine
Performance: maximum speed 380 km/h (236 mph) at 5000 m (16,405 ft); climb to 5000 m (16,405 ft) in 7 minutes 30 seconds; service ceiling 9000 m (29,530 ft); range 750 km (466 miles)

Weights: empty equipped 1260 kg (2,778 lb); maximum take-off 1790 kg (3,946 lb)
Dimensions: span 10.7 m (35 ft 1¼ in); length 7.6 m (24 ft 11¼ in); height 3.40 m (11 ft 1¾ in); wing area 18.85 m² (202.91 sq ft)
Armament: two fixed forward-firing 7.7-mm (0.303-in) Breda-SAFAT machine-guns

Breda Ba.39

A larger and heavier development of the Ba.33, the **Breda Ba.39** flew for the first time in September 1932, displaying even better flying qualities than its predecessor, which ensured that it was produced in some numbers. It achieved success in numerous sporting events and examples made several outstanding distance flights. Compared with the Ba.33, however, it had a lower maximum speed due to an increased all-up weight.

Civil production was augmented by 60 of the type ordered by the Italian air ministry for use in the liaison role. Of the 60, some 20 were specialised for use in the homeland as the **Ba.39 Met** (for *Metropolitano*) and 20 for overseas deployment as the **Ba.39 Col** (for *Coloniale*).

Specification
Breda Ba.39S: 1934 version with seating for three
Breda Ba.42: a small batch of this variant was built in 1934, one example being entered in that year's Challenge de Tourisme Internationale; power was provided by a 134-kW (180-hp) Fiat A.70S radial engine with a NACA cowling. The leading-edge slats were replaced by specially designed Breda-Mazzini wing-valve slots

Specification
Breda Ba.39

Scaled up from the Ba.33, the Breda Ba.39 was a more capable touring aircraft, its capabilities greatly enhanced by provision of leading-edge slots and trailing-edge flaps. The former opened automatically at high angles-of-attack, and permitted a reduction in landing speed from the 85 km/h (53 mph) of the Ba.33 to a mere 65 km/h (40 mph) despite greater weight.

Type: two-seat touring and liaison aircraft
Powerplant: one 97-kW (130-hp) Colombo S.63 inline piston engine
Performance: maximum speed 211 km/h (131 mph); service ceiling 5000 m (16,405 ft); endurance 3 hours 30 minutes; range 900 km (559 miles)
Weights: empty equipped 430 kg (948 lb); maximum take-off 730 kg (1,609 lb)
Dimensions: span 10.48 m (34 ft 4½ in); length 7.58 m (24 ft 10½ in); height 2.23 m (7 ft 3¾ in); wing area 15 m² (161.46 sq ft)

The Breda Ba.42 was evolved from the Ba.39 with a close-cowled radial engine and Breda-Mazzini wing-valve slots in place of the previous leading-edge slots. These valves can be seen in the open position just forward of the flap/aileron hinge lines in this photograph taken after World War II.

Breda Ba.65

Breda Ba.65 of No.5 (Fighter) Squadron, Iraqi air force, equipped with a Breda turret

Intended as an *aeroplano di combattimento*, capable of fulfilling the roles of interceptor fighter, light bomber, or reconnaissance/attack aircraft as required, the prototype **Breda Ba.65** (MM 325) made its initial flight in September 1935, piloted by Ambrogio Colombo. It was a cantilever low-wing monoplane with main landing gear units retracting rearwards into underwing fairings. Basic structure of the fuselage and wing was of chrome-molybdenum steel alloy tubing, covered overall with duralumin sheet, except for the trailing edges of the wing, which were fabric covered. The wing incorporated trailing-edge flaps and Handley Page leading-edge slats. A single fin and rudder tail assembly was strut- and wire-braced, and was of steel construction with light alloy skins.

An initial production order for 81 Ba.65s was placed in 1936, all being

powered by the French Gnome-Rhône K-14 engine of 522 kW (700 hp) as had been installed in the prototype. A batch of 13 aircraft from this production series equipped the 65ª Squadriglia of the Aviazione Legionaria, the Italian air contingent sent to support the Fascist cause in the Spanish Civil War. The unit took part in operations at Santander in August 1937, then at Teruel, and in the battles for the River Ebro. Like the prototype these were single-seat aircraft, with the pilot's cockpit fully enclosed by a glazed canopy which tapered to the rear.

Experience in Spain indicated that the Ba.65 was suited only to the attack role, and the type served thenceforth with most of the eight *squadriglie* attached to the two Regia Aeronautica assault Stormi (wings), the 5° and 50°. A second

series of 137 aircraft was built by Breda (80) and Caproni-Vizzola (57), before production ended in July 1939. They differed from the first production batch by having Fiat A.80 engines. Six Fiat-powered Ba.65s and four more of the Gnome-Rhône-powered version were sent to the Aviazione Legionaria in Spain in 1938.

Following Italy's entry into World War

II in June 1940, Ba.65s were involved in the fighting in North Africa against the British. They had a low serviceability rate in desert conditions and put up an unimpressive performance. The last serviceable aircraft were lost during the British offensive in Cyrenaica in February 1941.

A large number of the Ba.65s serving with Italian units were of two-seat configuration, with an observer/gunner in an open cockpit above the trailing edge of the wing. A smaller number of the type had a Breda L type turret, but in either case the observer/gunner operated a single 7.7-mm (0.303-in) machine-gun. While offensive armament could theoretically comprise up to 1000 kg (2,205 lb) of bombs, the load usually carried was up to 300 kg (661 lb) in the fuselage bomb bay or, alternatively, up to 200 kg (441 lb) on underwing racks.

Exports included 25 Fiat-powered Ba.65 two-seaters to Iraq in 1938, two of them dual-control trainers and the remainder with Breda L turrets; 20 Ba.65s with Piaggio P.XI C.40 engines to Chile later the same year, 17 of them single-seaters and three dual-control trainers; and 10 Fiat-powered two-seaters with Breda L turrets to Portugal in November 1939. A single Fiat-powered production aircraft was tested with an American Pratt & Whitney R-1830 engine in June 1937 in anticipation of an order from the Chinese Nationalist government, but this failed to materialise. The Iraqi Ba.65s saw limited action against the British during the 1941 insurrection in that country.

Specification
Breda 65/A.80 (single-seat version)
Type: ground-attack aircraft
Powerplant: one 746-kW (1,000-hp)

Breda Ba.65 of the 65a Squadriglia, Aviazione Legionaria, Spanish Civil War

Fiat A.80 RC.41 radial piston engine
Performance: maximum speed 430 km/h (267 mph); maximum speed, two-seat version 410 km/h (255 mph); service ceiling 6300 m (20,670 ft); range 550 km (342 miles)
Weights: empty equipped 2400 kg (5,291 lb); maximum take-off 2950 kg (6,504 lb)
Dimensions: span 12.1 m (39 ft 8½ in); length 9.3 m (30 ft 6¼ in); height 3.2 m (10 ft 6 in); wing area 23.5 m² (252.96 sq ft)
Armament: two 12.7-mm (0.5-in) and two 7.7-mm (0.303-in) Breda-SAFAT fixed forward-firing machine-guns in wings, plus up to 300 kg (661 lb) of bombs in fuselage bomb-bay and up to 200 kg (441 lb) of bombs on underwing racks

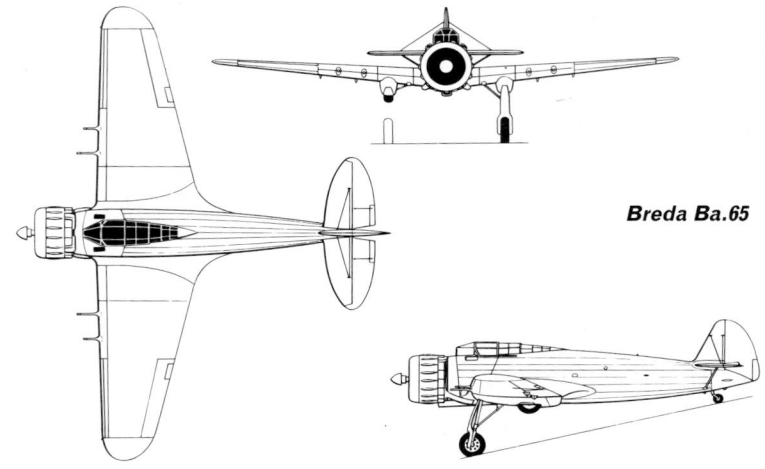

Breda Ba.65

The two-seat version of the Ba.65, generally designated Ba.65bis, was powered by a different engine, the Gnome-Rhône 14Kdrs built under licence as the Isotta-Fraschini K.14. This was identified by a different arrangement of rocker arm fairings on the cowling.

Breda Ba. 88 Lince

Breda Ba.88 Lince of the 7° Gruppo, 5° Stormo da Combattimento, Regia Aeronautica, based at Castel Benito [Libya] during 1940.

A propaganda triumph when its appearance was trumpeted by Mussolini's Fascist regime in 1936, the **Breda Ba.88 Lince** (Lynx), designed by Antonio Parano and Guiseppe Panzeri, was a sleek all-metal shoulder-wing monoplane with twin-engine powerplant. The prototype (MM 302), which had a single fin and rudder tail assembly, made its maiden flight during October 1936 flown by Furio Niclot, Breda's chief test pilot. In April 1937 Niclot established two world speed-over-distance records, averaging 321.25 mph (517 km/h) over a 62-mile (100-km) distance and 295.15 mph (475 km/h) over 621-mile (1000-km) circuit. In December of that year he raised these speeds to 344.24 mph (554 km/h) and 325.6 mph (524 km/h) respectively.

The prototype, which had retractable tailwheel landing gear, and powerplant comprising two 900-hp (671-kW) Gnome-Rhône K-14 radials, was then given a modified tail unit with twin fins and rudders. Regarded as an *aeroplano di combattimento*, suitable for attack, long-range reconnaissance or bombing operations, the Ba.88 then had its military equipment and weapons installed. Immediately, performance and flight characteristics fell off dramatically, but by then production orders were already being executed. The first batch of 80, plus eight dual-control trainers, was built by Breda between May and October 1939. Problems with the prototype led to a number of weight-saving modifications, and more power was provided by the installation of 1,000-hp (746-kW) Piaggio P.XI RC.40 radials.

On 16 June 1940, just after Italy's declaration of war on France and her

allies, the Ba.88 had its first taste of action. Twelve aircraft from the Regia Aeronautica's 19° Gruppo Autonomo made bombing and machine-gun attacks on the principal airfields of Corsica; three days later nine Ba.88s made a repeat attack. Analysis of these operations showed that the Ba.88 had only limited value, and any remaining doubts were settled when Ba.88s od the 7° Gruppo Autonomo joined action in Libya against the British. Fitted with sand filters the engines overheated and failed to deliver their designated power. Attacks on targets at Sidi Barrani had to be aborted in September 1940, the aircraft failing to gain sufficient altitude or maintain formation, and reaching a speed less than half that claimed by the manufacturers.

By mid-November 1940 most surviving Ba.88s had been stripped of useful equipment and were scattered around operational airfields as decoys for attacking British aircraft. During this time, however, further batches of Ba.88s were being delivered, comprising 19 built by Breda and 48 by I.M.A.M. (Meridionali). Most went straight to the scrapyard.

Three Ba.88s were modified by the Agusta plant in 1942 to serve as ground-

attack aircraft. Wing span was increased by 6 ft 6¾ in (2.00 m) to alleviate wing loading problems, their engines were placed by Fiat A.74s, nose armament was increased to four 12.7-mm (0.5-in) machine-guns, and dive-brakes were installed. These **Breda Ba.88Ms** were delivered to the 103° Gruppo Autonomo Tuffatori (independent dive-bombing group) at Lonate Pozzolo on 7 September 1943. They were flight-tested by Luftwaffe pilots, but that was the last to be heard of the Breda Ba.88s, which represented, perhaps, the most remarkable failure of any operational aircraft to see service in World War II.

Specification
Breda Ba.88 Lince
Type: fighter-bomber/reconnaissance aircraft
Powerplant: two 1,000-hp (746-kW) Piaggio P.XI RC.40 radial piston engines
Performance: maximum speed 304 mph (490 km/h); service ceiling 26,245 ft (8000 m); range 1,019 miles (1640 m)
Weights: empty equipped 10,251 lb (4650 kg); maximum take-off 14,881 lb (6750 kg)

Dimensions: span 51 ft 2¼ in (15.60 m); length 35 ft 4¾ in (10.79 m); height 10 ft 2 in (3.10 m); wing area 358.888 sq ft (33.34 m²)
Armament: three fixed forward-firing 12.7-mm (0.5-in) Breda-SAFAT machine-guns in nose and one 7.7-mm (0.303-in) Breda-SAFAT machine-gun on flexible mounting in rear cockpit, plus up to 2,204 lb (1000 kg) of bombs in fuselage bomb-bay or, alternatively, three 441-lb (200-kg) bombs carried semi-exposed in individual recesses in the fuselage belly

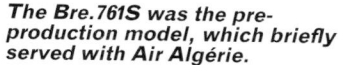

Breguet 763 Provence

The Bre.761S was the pre-production model, which briefly served with Air Algérie.

rie, but in the mid-1950s all three were used by the Armée de l'Air for service trials.

Air France had shown interest in the Br.761, and in 1951 ordered 12 examples of an improved version with the company designation **Br.763**. These introduced increased span, strengthened wings and a flight deck re-arranged for operation by a crew of three; the type also had more-powerful Pratt & Whitney engines. The first made its initial flight on 20 July 1951, and the type entered ser-

vice with Air France from August 1952 under the class name **Provence**. As then operated by Air France, the Br.763s had accommodation for 59 and 48 passengers on the upper and lower decks respectively, but a maximum of 135 could be carried in a high-density seating arrangement. Alternative layouts could allow for operation in mixed passenger/cargo, all-cargo, or air ferry roles.

During 1964 Air France transferred six of its Br.763s to the Armée de l'Air, these being given the military name **Sahara**. They were operated by the 64e Escadre de Transport, together with the original three Br.761S pre-production aircraft, plus four of the new variant which

incorporated removable cargo doors. These could accommodate up to 146 fully-equipped troops, 85 stretchers and medical attendants, or freight, vehicles and heavy equipment. They provided the Armée de l'Air with a valuable transport fleet, and it was not until late 1972 that the last of them was retired from service. Air France also continued to operate its six Br.763s, but in a freighter rather than passenger role under the name **Universal**. They remained in service until 1971.

Specification
Breguet Br.763
Type: short/medium-range utility

transport
Powerplant: four 1790-kW (2,400-hp) Pratt & Whitney R-2800-CA18 radial piston engines
Performance: maximum cruising speed 390 km/h (242 mph) at 3000 m (9,840 ft); economic cruising speed 335 km/h (208 mph) at 3000 m (9,840 ft); service ceiling 7300 m (23,950 ft); range with maximum payload 2165 km (1,345 miles)
Weights: empty 32535 kg (71,727 lb); maximum take-off 51600 kg (113,759 lb)
Dimensions: span 42.99 m (141 ft 0¼ in); length 28.94 m (94 ft 11½ in); height 9.55 m (31 ft 4 in); wing area 185.4 m² (1,995.7 sq ft)

Breguet 941

Breguet designed a four-engined STOL (short take-off and landing) transport that would be suitable for civil or military use. This **Breguet 941** relied upon the deflected-slipstream technique to generate additional lift. To provide this capability, the four engines were mounted in nacelles at the wing leading edges so that an optimum slipstream from their propellers was distributed over the entire span of the wing. Full-span double-slotted trailing edge flaps were provided, these also being within the slipstream when deployed to maximise their effect, and with no wing trailing edge available for ailerons to be installed for roll control, four hinged spoilers were provided on the upper surface of each wing.

Breguet's proposal appealed to the French air ministry, and a prototype was ordered on 22 February 1960. Like most large-volume transports, it was of cantilever high-wing configuration, with an upswept rear fuselage to incorporate a rear loading ramp. Its heavy-lift capability was highlighted by retractable tricycle landing gear that incorporated twin nosewheels, with tandem-wheel main units that retracted into fairings on each

The Br.941S STOL transport only served with l'Armée de l'Air. McDonnell attempted to market the type in the US.

side of the fuselage. Powerplant comprised four 895-kW (1,200-shp) Turboméca Turmo IIID turboprops, and the prototype was flown for the first time on 1 June 1961. Subsequent testing of the prototype resulted in Breguet receiving a contract from the French government for the supply of four production transports under the designation **Breguet 941S**.

The production aircraft differed from the prototype by having more powerful Turboméca Turmo engines, a longer nose to permit the installation of a large radome, and modification of the rear cargo door to allow for the airdrop of heavy loads. Operated by a crew of two, these aircraft could provide accommodation for up to 57 civil passengers, or 40 fully-equipped troops, or 24 stretchers. The first of the production Br.941S aircraft made its initial flight on 19 April 1967, and testing proved that with an all-up weight of 22000 kg (48,502 lb), which was in excess of an assault mission take-off weight, the Br.941S could become airborne in only 185 m (607 ft).

All four of the production aircraft entered service with the Armée de l'Air, but no additional examples were built. There had been hopes that, with assistance from the McDonnell Aircraft Corporation, orders might be generated in the USA, but despite a demonstration tour in America, no production orders were received.

Specification
Breguet Br.941S
Type: STOL transport
Powerplant: four 1119-kW (1,500-

shp) Turboméca Turmo IIID3 turboprops
Performance: maximum speed 450 km/h (280 mph) at sea level; economic cruising speed 400 km/h (249 mph) at 3000 m (9,840 ft); service ceiling 9500 m (31,170 ft); range with maximum payload 1000 km (621 miles)
Weights: empty equipped 13460 kg; maximum take-off 26500 kg (58,422 lb)
Dimensions: span 23.4 m (76 ft 9¼ in); length 23.75 m (77 ft 11 in); height 9.65 m (31 ft 8 in); wing area 83.8 m² (902.05 sq ft)

Breguet 1001 Taon

In response to a NATO requirement for a single-seat lightweight strike fighter, Breguet designed a small mid-wing monoplane with swept wings and tail surfaces. Retractable tricycle landing gear was provided, this being designed especially for operation on unprepared strips. The fuselage incorporated some area ruling, accommodated the pilot in an enclosed cockpit well forward, and housed its Bristol Orpheus BOr.3 turbojet. In competition with other proposals, Breguet's design won an order for three prototypes, the first of these making its

maiden flight on 26 July 1957. The second prototype incorporated minor aerodynamic improvements and had a slightly lengthened fuselage.

To enhance high-speed performance, improved area ruling was provided by the introduction of aerodynamic bulges at the wing roots, these serving also to house additional fuel. In this configuration the **Br.1001 Taon** (gadfly) set an international speed record for a 1000-km (621-4-mile) closed circuit, attaining a speed of 650.36 mph (1046.65 km/h) at 25,000 ft (7620 m) on 25 April 1958.

Three months later, on 23 July, the Taon raised this figure again for the same record to 667.98 mph (1075 km/h). Despite this high-speed performance, development was discontinued, and only the two prototypes were built.

Variants
Br.1002: designation applied to a proposed missile-carrying interceptor version of the Taon
Br.1003: advance designation allocated for production versions of the Taon, none of which were built; it was

planned that it would have a full area-ruled fuselage, and power provided by a Bristol Orpheus BOr.12 turbojet which would have developed 8,170-lb (3706-kg) thrust with reheat

Specification
Breguet 1001 Taon
Type: single-seat strike fighter
Powerplant: one 4,850-lb (2200-kg) thrust Bristol Orpheus BOr.3 turbojet
Performance: maximum speed 742 mph (1194 km/h) at sea level
Weights: approximate take-off 11,023 lb (5000 kg)
Dimensions: span 22 ft 3½ in (6.80 m); length 38 ft 3¾ in (11.68 m); height 12 ft 1¾ in (3.70 m)

Breguet 1050 Alizé

At a comparatively early stage of turbine engine development, before the introduction of more economical by-pass or ducted fan engines, a mixed powerplant concept was selected by a number of designers of military aircraft: this offered economical operation by the turboprop for long-range cruise, with the availability of a supplementary turbojet for take-off with heavy weapon loads or for high speed in combat. Breguet had chosen such a powerplant for the **Breguet 960 Vultur** naval strike aircraft, with an Armstrong Siddeley Mamba turboprop in the nose and a Hispano-Suiza Nene turbojet in the rear fuselage.

Experience with the Vultur, first flown on 3 August 1951, led the French navy to abandon the idea of such a powerplant for a strike aircraft. Instead, Breguet was contracted to develop a three-seat carrier-based anti-submarine aircraft from the Vultur. The second prototype was duly modified to serve as an aerodynamic test vehicle for the new design, the 731-kW (980-shp) Mamba in the nose being replaced by an uprated Mamba of 1230-kW (1,650-shp), the turbojet engine in the rear fuselage being removed to make room for a large retractable 'dustbin' radome, and dummy streamline nacelles being mounted beneath the monoplane wings: in a production version these would serve to house the main landing gear units and sonobuoy equipment. By the time this had been flown and tested, Breguet had received an order for two full prototypes and three pre-production aircraft, these being designated **Breguet 1050** and named **Alizé** (Tradewind). The first prototype made its maiden flight on 6 October 1956, and the first production example was handed over officially on 29 May 1959.

As finalised, the Breguet 1050 was a

Underneath the folding wings, the Alizé has pylons for depth charges, rockets or missiles. The retractable radar 'dustbin' can be seen under the rear fuselage.

cantilever low-wing monoplane with hydraulically-folding outer wing panels, retractable tricycle landing gear, arrester gear for carrier operations, and power provided by a Rolls-Royce Dart turboprop. The single-seat accommodation of the Vultur had been extensively modified to seat a pilot and two radar operators, and an underfuselage weapons bay housed a torpedo or depth charges, with a variety of stores being carried on underwing racks. Production totalled 75 for the French navy, equipping initially Flottilles 4F and 9F on board the carriers *Foch* and *Clémenceau*. An additional 12 were built for the Indian navy, which subsequently acquired further examples surplus to Aéronavale requirements.

Specification
Type: three-seat carrier-based anti-submarine aircraft
Powerplant: one 1,473-kW (1,975-shp) Rolls-Royce Dart R.Da7 Mk 21 turboprop
Performance: maximum speed 518 km/h (322 mph) at 3050 m (10,000 ft); patrol speed 240-370 km/h (149-230 mph); service ceiling 8000 m (26,245 ft); normal range 2500 km (1,553 miles); maximum endurance 7 hours 40 minutes
Weights: empty equipped 5700 kg (12,566 lb); maximum take-off 8200 kg (18,078 lb)
Dimensions: span 15.6 m (51 ft 2 in); length 13.86 m (45 ft 6 in); height 5 m (16 ft 4¾ in); wing area 36 m² (387.51 sq ft)

Below: The Breguet 690 Vultur was a mixed-powerplant design incorporating a turboprop in the nose and a turbojet in the rear. The jet provided additional thrust for combat performance and take-off.

Below: The Alizé has a large, tubby fuselage to accommodate three crew, search radar, sonobuoy launching equipment and an internal weapons bay. The type is still in use with the Aéronavale and the Indian navy.

Armament: underfuselage weapons bay accommodating one torpedo or three 160-kg (353-lb) depth charges; racks under inner wings for two 160-kg (353-lb) or 175-kg (386-lb) depth charges; racks beneath outer wings for six 12.7-cm (5-in) rockets or two Nord AS.12 air-to-surface missiles; and sonobuoys in underwing weapon/wheel nacelles

Brewster F2A

The first monoplane fighter to equip a squadron of the US Navy, the **Brewster F2A Buffalo** originated from a US Navy requirement of 1936 for a new generation of carrier-based fighters. In requesting proposals from US manufacturers for such an aircraft, the US Navy indicated requirements which included monoplane configuration, wing flaps, arrester gear, retractable landing gear and an enclosed cockpit. Clearly, this specification recognised the fact that the carrier-based biplane was nearing the end of its useful life.

Proposals were received from Brewster, allocated the designation **XF2A-1**, Grumman (XF4F-1) and Seversky (XFN-1), but of these the only significant aircraft in the long term was the Grumman design, which was initially of biplane configuration and given serious consideration by the US Navy as an insurance policy against the possible failure of new-fangled monoplanes.

A prototype of the Brewster XF2A-1 was ordered on 22 June 1936, and this flew for the first time in December 1937. While bearing a distinct family resemblance to the XSBA-1 of 1934, the new

Brewster F2A-2 of VF-2 'The Flying Chiefs', US Navy, aboard USS Lexington in March 1941.

fighter appeared to be tubbier and stubbier, but a comparison of dimensions showed this to be something of an illusion. Of mid-wing monoplane configuration, it was of all-metal construction, except for fabric-covered control surfaces. Hydraulically operated split flaps were provided, and the main units of the tail-wheel type landing gear retracted inward to be housed in fuselage wells. Powerplant consisted of a 708-kW (950-

hp) Wright XR-1820-22 Cyclone radial engine.

Service testing of the prototype began in January 1938, and on 11 June the US Navy contracted with Brewster for the supply of 54 of the **F2A-1** production model. Deliveries of these started 12 months later, nine aircraft going almost immediately to equip US Navy Squadron VF-3 aboard the USS *Saratoga*. The available balance of 44 aircraft was, sympath-

etically, declared surplus to requirements and, instead, supplied to Finland which was then fighting off the might of the Soviet Union. Later equipping the Finnish air force's HLeLv 24 and HLeLv 26 units, they remained successfully operational until mid-1944.

Some 43 of an improved version were ordered by the US Navy in early 1939, this having a more powerful engine, an improved propeller and built-in flotation gear. Designated **F2A-2**, this began to enter service in September 1940. It was

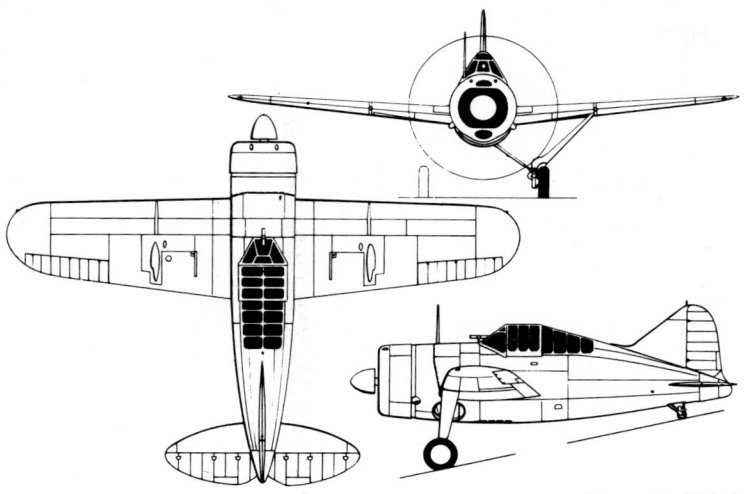

followed by 108 of the **F2A-3** variant with more armour and a bulletproof windscreen, and these two production versions equipped US Navy Squadrons VF-2 and VF-3, and US Marine Corps Squadron VFM-221. A number were used operationally in the Pacific but as

Brewster F2A-3

the type was overweight, unstable and of poor manoeuvrability, it was no match for opposing Japanese fighters.

Belgian and British purchasing missions ordered 40 **B-339** and 170 **B-339E** aircraft respectively, most of

the former going to the UK after Belgium had been overrun. These orders were for land-based versions, without arrester gear and other equipment specifically for shipboard operations, but were otherwise generally similar to the F2A-3s. Of those received from the Belgian order, a small number served with Nos 805 and 885 Squadrons of the Fleet Air Arm, the former squadron using them for support rather than combat duties during the defence of Crete.

Of those which were ordered for the RAF, which gave the type the name **Buffalo**, deliveries began in July 1940. No. 71 Squadron received the first of these for service trials in September, and it was realised immediately that the Buffalo's performance was totally inadequate for the type's deployment in the European theatre. Instead, they were sent to the Far East to equip the RAF's Nos 67, 146 and 243, the RAAF's Nos 21 and 453 Squadrons and the RNZAF's No. 488 Squadron to defend Singapore and Malaya. Completely unsuited to the task, the few which survived the Japanese invasion fought alongside the American Volunteer Group operating in Burma. Buffaloes with the most successful combat record were a

small number of almost 100 which had been ordered for the air arm of the Netherlands East Indies' army, which saw action in Java and Malaya. These had the Brewster model numbers **B-339D** and **B-439**. The former was similar to the B-339E, but the B-439 had an 8956-kW (1,200-hp) Wright GR-1820-G205A engine.

Specification
Brewster F2A-3
Type: single-seat land- or ship-based fighter
Powerplant: one 895-kW (1,200-hp) Wright R-1820-40 Cyclone radial piston engine
Performance: maximum speed 517 km/h (321 mph) at 5030 m (16,500 ft); cruising speed 415 km/h (258 mph); service ceiling 10120 m (33,200 ft); range 1553 km (965 miles)
Weights: empty 2146 kg (4,723 lb); maximum take-off 3247 kg (7,159 lb)
Dimensions: span 10.67m (35 ft 0 in); length 8.03 m (26 ft 4 in); height 3.68 m (12 ft 1 in); wing area 19.41 m² (208.9 sq ft)
Armament: four fixed forward-firing 12.7-mm (0.5-in) machine-guns, plus two 45-kg (100-lb) bombs

Brewster SBA/SBN

Naval Aircraft Factory (Brewster) SBN-1.

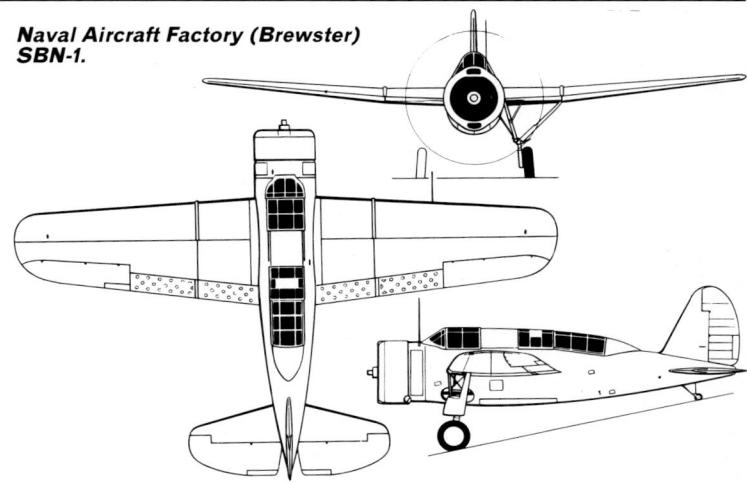

The Brewster Aeronautical Corporation was founded in the early 1930s, and for the first years of its existence concentrated on the manufacture of seaplane floats, wings and tail units under subcontract to other manufacturers. It was not until 1934 that the company became involved in the design and prototype construction of its first aircraft, a two-seat scout-bomber required by the US Navy for service aboard the carriers USS *Enterprise* and *Yorktown* which were scheduled for launch in 1936. Designated **Brewster XSBA-1**, this emerged as a clean-looking mid-wing monoplane of all-metal construction, except for its control surfaces which were fabric-covered. Trailing-edge flaps were provided to simplify ship-board operations. The powerplant of the prototype consisted of a single 559-kW (750-hp) Wright R-1820-4 Cyclone. The aircraft had a retractable tailwheel type landing gear, and internal stowage for bombs.

The XSBA-1 flew for the first time on 15 April 1936, but flight testing indicated that more power was necessary to provide satisfactory performance. In 1937, therefore, a 708-kW (950-hp) XR-1820-22 Cyclone engine was installed, and after tests the US Navy had no hesitation in ordering the type into production.

However, at that time Brewster had inadequate production facilities, and it was decided that the 30 aircraft which the US Navy required would be built by the Naval Aircraft Factory (NAF), which was located at Philadelphia, Pennsylvania.

First established in 1918, the NAF had built production runs of aircraft until 1922. It was not until the mid-1930s that manufacture was re-instated there, the NAF then becoming responsible for production of some 10 per cent of the US Navy's requirements for aircraft. This policy was introduced to keep some check on the costings of aircraft manufacturers who tendered for US Navy contracts, and also to keep up-to-date with production methods. From 1936 until the end of World War II, the NAF was again involved in aircraft production on a fairly large scale.

The Brewster-designed scout/bomber built by the NAF was given the designation **SBN-1**, and deliveries to the US Navy extended from November 1940 to March 1942. By that time more-advanced designs were becoming available, and production of SBNs came to an end. These aircraft were used by US Navy Squadron VB-3 when they first entered service, and most were employed for training at a later date. Squadron VT-8

used its SBN-1s for training on board the USS *Hornet*.

Specification
Brewster SBN-1
Type: two-seat carrier-based scout-bomber/trainer
Powerplant: one 708-kW (950-hp) Wright XR-1820-22 Cyclone radial piston engine
Performance: maximum speed 409 km/h (254 mph); service ceiling 8625 m

(28,300 ft); range 1633 km (1,015 miles)
Weights: empty 1851 kg (4,080 lb); maximum take-off 3066 kg (6,759 lb)
Dimensions: span 11.89 m (39 ft 0 in); length 8.43 m (27 ft 8 in); height 2.62 m (8 ft 7 in); wing area 24.06 m² (259 sq ft)
Armament: one fixed forward-firing 12.7-mm (0.5-in) machine-gun and one 7.62-mm (0.3-in) gun on flexible mount in rear cockpit, plus up to 227 kg (500 lb) of bombs in internal bay

Brewster SB2A Buccaneer

Brewster SB2A-4 Buccaneer

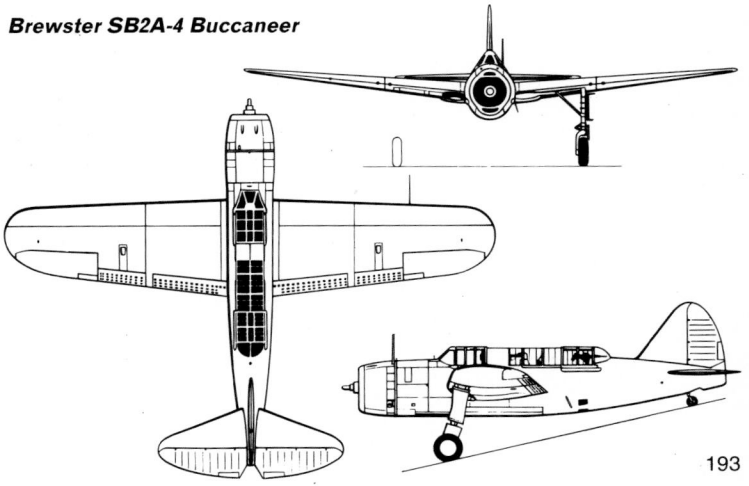

With its first design, the SBA, virtually off its hands and entering production with the Naval Aircraft Factory under the designation SBN, Brewster was able to turn to the design of an improved version. The aim was to produce a more effective scout-bomber with heavier armament, increased bomb load and higher performance; this dictated a slightly larger airframe and the installation of a more powerful engine.

In condfiguration the new aircraft was generally similar to the SBA; it differed primarily by having a larger bomb bay, and main landing gear units retracting inward into the undersurface of the wing, instead of into the fuselage. The only innovative proposal was the introduction of a power-operated gun turret in the rear cockpit (on the lines of the British Boulton Paul Defiant) but this did not materialise on production aircraft. Only the prototype was seen with such a turret and it, in fact, was only a mock-up.

A single prototype **Brewster XSB2A-1** was ordered by the US Navy on 4 April 1939 and this flew for the first time on 17 June 1941. By then the company had already received several production orders, comprising 140 for the US Navy, 162 for the Netherlands, and a total of 750 for the RAF, after a British purchasing mission of 1940 was convinced of the excellence of the design.

Procurement for the USAF was also intended and the designation **A-34** allocated, but the contract was cancelled before any production resulted.

The intention of providing heavier armament was realised without difficulty, the US Navy's **SB2A-1 Buccaneer** having eight 7.62-mm (0.3-in) machine-guns, six forward-firing and two on a flexible mounting in the aft cockpit. Unfortunately, performance was far below that anticipated and the larger, much heavier aircraft lacked manoeuvrability. Despite this, the US Navy continued to procure small numbers, acquiring 80 of the **SB2A-2** model with armament changes and 60 of the **SB2A-3** variant. These latter aircraft, intended for carrier operations, featured folding wings and an arrester hook. The 162 aircraft built for the Netherlands were also taken over by the US Navy, and these were given the designation **SB2A-4** and transferred to the US Marine Corps for use in a training role. They served a useful purpose in establishing the US Marines' first night-fighter

squadron, VFM (N)-531.

Deliveries of aircraft for the RAF began in July 1942; supplied under Lend-Lease, the type was identified as the **Bermuda** in RAF service, but its performance was such that the aircraft was completely unsuitable for combat operations. As a result, the majority were converted for target towing duties, and second-line deployment, so far as is known, was the fate of all the 771 aircraft produced by Brewster.

Specification
Brewster SB2A-2
Type: two-seat land- or carrier-based scout-bomber
Powerplant: one 1268-kW (1,700-hp) Wright R-2600-8 Cyclone radial piston engine
Performance: maximum speed 441 km/h (274 mph) at 3660 m (12,000 ft); cruising speed 259 km/h (161 mph); service ceiling 7590 m (24,900 ft); range without bomb load 2696 km (1,675 miles)
Weights: empty 4501 kg (9,924 lb);

maximum take-off 6481 kg (14,289 lb)
Dimensions: span 14.33 m (47 ft 0 in); length 11.94 m (39 ft 2 in); height 4.70 m (15 ft 5 in); wing area 35.21 m² (379 sq ft)
Armament: two 12.7-mm (0.5-in) fuselage-mounted machine-guns and four 7.62-mm (0.3-in) (two in wing and

Intended for the carrierborne bombing role, the Buccaneer was mostly used on second-line duties. In RAF service it was called the Bermuda.

two in aft cockpit on flexible mount), plus up to 454 kg (1,000 lb) of bombs

Bristol Boxkite

For exhibition at the 1910 Aero Show at Olympia, a Voisin-designed Zodiac biplane was imported from France by the newly-formed British and Colonial Aeroplane Company (Bristol). Powered by a 37-kW (50-hp) Darracq engine, it was never flown successfully and plans for the erection of a further five aircraft were abandoned in favour of a more refined version developed by Henri Farman. The **Bristol 'Boxkite'** (or **1910 Biplane**) incorporated a number of detailed improvements and different engines. The first example, originally with a 37-kW (50-hp) Gregoire 4-cylinder engine which proved to be unreliable and of inadequate output, was re-engined with a 37-kW (50-hp) Gnome rotary and flown successfully at Larkhill on 30 July 1910. The second was powered by a 37-kW (50-hp) E.N.V. 8-cylinder engine. They formed the initial equipment of the newly-established flying schools at Brooklands and Larkhill re-

spectively. Four others were shipped in pairs with air missions to Australia and India, arriving in December 1910, but the first overseas government order for the emerging British industry was one for eight Boxkites placed by Russia. Delivered to St Petersburg in April 1911, they were equipped with 52-kW (70-hp) Gnome engines, enlarged fuel tanks, wings of extended span, and three rudders. The initial War Office order, placed in March 1911, was for four aircraft: two with 37-kW (50-hp) Gnomes and two with 44.7-kW (60-hp) Renaults, to equip the Larkhill-based No. 2 (Aeroplane) Company of the British Army's Air Battalion, which was established on 1 April 1911. Two early Boxkites, one with a 52-kW (70-hp) Gnome, were used by the Royal Naval Air Service, and the Admiralty also ordered six for training duties at Eastchurch, Chingford and other naval air stations. Some 76 Boxkites were built, all but six at Filton; the

The Bristol Boxkite was a refined Henri Farman biplane. 76 were built, which was a large number for the period.

exceptions were the first aircraft to emerge from the Brislington works.

Specification
Type: two-seat trainer
Powerplant: one 37-kW (50-hp) Gnome rotary piston engine
Performance: maximum level speed

64 km/h (40 mph)
Weights: empty 408 kg (900 lb); maximum take-off 522 kg (1,150 lb)
Dimensions: span 14.17 m (46 ft 6 in); length 11.73 m (38 ft 6 in); height 3.61 m (11 ft 0 in); wing area 48.03 m² (517 sq ft)

Bristol Biplane Type 'T'

Built initially for the French pilot Maurice Tabuteau, the **Bristol Biplane Type T** was developed by the British and Colonial Aeroplane Company from the Boxkite. It differed by having an enclosed nacelle for the pilot, an extended skid structure forward of the main landing gear to prevent nosing-over, and a more powerful Gnome engine. In addition to that built for Tabuteau to fly in the 1911 Circuit de l'Europe, four more examples were built to compete in the *Daily Mail*-sponsored Circuit of Britain race in the same year, but none of these five aircraft achieved success in the contests. At least one of the four Circuit of Britain Type Ts was powered by a 45-kW (60-hp) Renault engine.

Variants
Bristol Challenge-England: Type T converted in 1911 by Gordon England to accommodate a 44.7-kW (60-hp) E.N.V. inline engine.

Specification
Type: single-seat sporting biplane
Powerplant: one 52-kW (70-hp) Gnome rotary piston engine
Performance: maximum speed 88 km/h (55 mph)
Weights: empty 295 kg (650 lb); maximum take-off 386 kg (850 lb)
Dimensions: span 10.67 m (24 ft 6 in); length 7.47 m (24 ft 6 in); wing area 32.52 m² (350 sq ft)

Seen here is the first of six Type Ts, no. 45, starting from Vincennes in the hands of Maurice Tabuteau during the Circuit de l'Europe race in 1911. The aircraft was one of only nine to complete the course.

Bristol Types 1-5 Scout

When the Italian contract for Henri Coanda's S.B.5 monoplane was cancelled in November 1913, the design was adapted by Frank Barnwell to become the **Scout A** biplane. The incomplete S.B.5 fuselage was finished and fitted with single-bay wings of 6.71 m (22 ft) span and with

redesigned tail surfaces. Powered by a 60-kW (80-hp) Gnome engine, the aircraft was taken to Larkhill for trials in February 1914, taking time out to appear at that year's Olympia Aero Show. At the end of April the Scout returned to Filton to be fitted with a new set of increased-

span wings which improved its low-speed performance. In June 1914 it was bought by Lord Carberry and re-engined with a 60-kW (80-hp) Le Rhône, surviving an accident during the London-Manchester Air Race on 20 June, only to run out of fuel on the second leg of the London-Paris-London Air Race on 7 July. Lord Carberry was rescued from the aircraft in the English Channel but the

Scout was lost.

Two more almost identical airframes were completed during the summer of 1914, retaining the same type of Gnome engine as fitted to the original machine. Given the designation **Scout B**, they were flown to Royal Flying Corps units in France in September, one to No.3 Squadron and one to No.5 Squadron. Locally-fitted armament consisted of two rifles in the former case and a rifle, a pistol and five rifle-grenades in the latter. Although subsequent production orders were placed, few of the Scouts had really effective armament. However, in March 1916 one aircraft, fitted with a Vickers machine-gun, was the first British machine equipped with a synchronised weapon to see service in France. Nevertheless, on 25 July 1915, Captain Lanoe G.Hawker, flying a **Scout C**, shot down two Aviatik C types and an Albatros (all two-seaters armed with machine-guns) winning the first Victoria Cross awarded for aerial combat.

Scouts served with the Royal Flying Corps and the Royal Naval Air Service, mostly in small numbers with squadrons equipped principally by other types. They acted as escorts for reconnaissance two-seaters or, in the case of RNAS aircraft, for anti-Zeppelin patrols, for which they were armed with Rankin darts.

Variants

Type 1 Scout C: 161 were built, 74 for the Admiralty and 87 for the War Office; the first production order was placed in November 1914 and the last example was delivered in March 1916; the 60-kW (80-hp) Gnome engine was originally specified and, indeed, fitted to all the RNAS aircraft because of its greater reliability, but shortages led to the installation of the 60-kW (80-hp) Le Rhône in the majority of those for the RFC

Types 2, 3, 4 and 5 Scout D: introduced in November 1915, this version featured revised fuel and oil tanks, and later examples were fitted with new wings with increased dihedral and shorter ailerons, and the underwing skids moved outboard from their original position beneath the interplane struts; some 130 Type 3s were delivered for the War Office, without engines, between February and September 1916; the first 50 retained the Scout C wings and the remainder were equipped with standardised gun mountings; 80 RNAS Scout Ds were delivered between April and December 1916, the first 60 (Type 4) with the 76-kW (100-hp) Gnome Monosoupape engine and a cut-away wing centre-section with a mounting for a flexible Lewis gun; the last 20 (Type 2) were powered by the 60-kW (80-hp) Gnome and served with RNAS training schools; three examples (Type 5) were provided with the 82-kW (110-hp) Clerget in response to RFC interest in a more powerful version

S.S.A.: Coanda-designed single-seat armoured biplane for French government; this aircraft had a bulletproof sheet-steel 'bath' protecting the pilot, petrol/oil tanks, engine and propeller hub; powered by a 59.7-kW (80-hp) Clerget rotary, the S.S.A. was capable of 171 km/h (106 mph), spanned 8.33 m (27 ft 4 in) and had a maximum take-off weight of 544 kg (1,200 lb); it first flew on 8 May 1914, and was handed over to the French on

3 July 1914
G.B.1: unrealised project for a single-seat racer with a 74.6 kW (100-hp) Gnome Monosoupape
S.2A: two-seater derivative of the Scout D intended to meet an Admiralty requirement for a two-seat fighter; powered by a 82.1-kW (110-hp) Le Clerget or 74.6-kW (100-hp) Gnome, two were eventually built for the War Office as side-by-side two-seat advanced trainers

Specification
Bristol Scout D
Type: single-seat scout

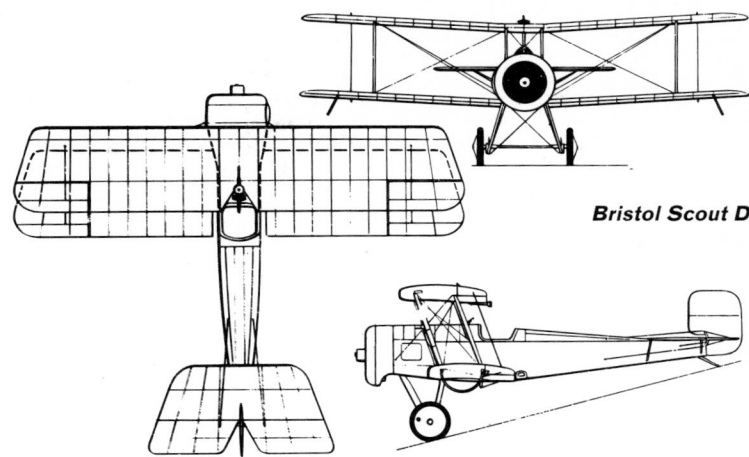

Bristol Scout D

Powerplant: one 59.7-kW (80-hp) Le Rhône rotary piston engine
Performance: maximum speed 161 km/h (100 mph) at sea level; 138 km/h (86 mph) at 3050 m (10,000 ft); climb to 3050 m (10,000 ft) in 18 minutes 30 seconds
Weights: empty 345 kg (760 lb); maximum take-off 567 kg (1,250 lb)
Dimensions: span 8.33 m (27 ft 4 in); length 6.02 m (19 ft 9 in); height 2.59 m (8 ft 6 in); wing area 18.59 m² (198 sq ft)
Armament: alternative arrangements of small arms and grenades, and later aircraft had one 7.7-mm (0.303-in) Lewis gun

Bristol Types 10, 11, 20 and 77 M.1A Monoplane Scout

The success of German Fokker E type monoplanes against the Royal Flying Corps' poorly-armed biplanes underlined the latter's need for a manoeuvrable, high-performance single-seater. Frank Barnwell's design, completed in mid-1916, was developed around a rotary engine in a closely-cowled installation with a large hemispherical spinner. This 82-kW (110-hp) Clerget installation was tested in the second production Scout D. With its practicality established, Barnwell evolved a streamlined fuselage based on a simple wire-braced box girder, built out with wooden longerons and spacers to a circular cross-section. The cockpit was located beneath a cabane formed by two half-hoops of steel tubing, to provide protection for the pilot in the event of the aircraft overturning, and also to locate the upper bracing wires for the monoplane wings; the lower flying wires were attached to the lower longerons.

The **M.1A (Type 10)** prototype was built as a private venture and its maiden flight, in the hands of F.P. Raynham, took place on 14 July 1916. Later that month the M.1A Monoplane Scout undertook trials at the Central Flying School at Upavon where it recorded a speed of 206 km/h (128 mph) at 1645 m (5,400 ft), and climbed to 3050 m (10,000 ft) in 8 minutes 30 seconds. On 9 October the War Office issued a contract for purchase of the M.1A and for the manufacture of four more aircraft. The latter, designated **M.1B (Type 11)**, incorporated a number of minor modifications, including a revised cabane which comprised four straight struts in a pyramid arrangement, a cut-out in the starboard wing root to provide limited downward vision from the cockpit, and a Vickers gun mounted on the port upper longeron. The first two M.1Bs, handed over in December 1916 and January 1917, were

Bristol Type 77 M.1D, winner of the 1922 Croydon Whitsun Handicap and Aerial Derby handicap races in 1922. This aircraft was a modified M.1B prototype equipped for racing.

fitted with 82-kW (110-hp) Clerget rotary engines but the third, taken on charge in February 1918, was powered by a 97-kW (130-hp) version of the engine and the fourth was delivered in March 1917 with a 112-kW (150-hp) Bentley A.R.1.

Trials at the Central Flying School revealed a landing speed of 79 km/h (49 mph), which was considered too high for the small airfields being used in France, so that the type never saw service on the Western Front. A production order was placed in August 1917, but fewer than 30 partially equipped a small number of units which included one Flight each of Nos 17 and 47 Squadrons in Macedonia (merged as No. 150 Squadron in April 1918), No. 111 Squadron in Palestine and No. 72 Squadron in Iraq. Others were issued to flying schools or used as personal aircraft by senior officers, and six were given to the Chilean government in 1917. Another six

were converted for civil use after the war, and one survives to this day, purchased from the Aircraft Disposals Board in July 1919 by Captain Harry Butler, who took it home to Australia. There it won the Australian Aerial Derby in September 1920 and, after being re-engined with an 89-kW (120-hp) de Havilland Gipsy III, won the Adelaide Aerial Derby in 1931 and 1932. It is now preserved at Minalton, near Adelaide, as the Harry Butler Memorial.

Variants

Type 20 M.1C: 125 production examples were ordered to this standard, powered by the 82-kW (110-hp) Le Rhône engine; the Vickers machine-gun was re-located to the fuselage centreline, in front of the pilot, and a cut-out provided in the port wing root
Type 77 M.1D: designation applied

to one of the four M.1B prototypes after it was rebuilt in 1922 with a 75-kW (100-hp) Bristol Lucifer radial engine

Specification
Bristol M.1C
Type: single-seat fighter
Powerplant: one 82-kW (110-hp) Le Rhône 9J rotary piston engine
Performance: maximum speed 209 km/h (130 mph) at sea level; service ceiling 6100 m (20,000 ft); endurance 1 hour 45 minutes
Weights: empty 406 kg (896 lb); maximum take-off 611 kg (1,348 lb)
Dimensions: span 9.37 m (30 ft 9 in); length 6.24 m (20 ft 5½ in); height 2.37 m (7 ft 9½ in); wing area 13.47 m² (145 sq ft)
Armament: one fixed forward-firing 7.7-mm (0.303-in) synchronised Vickers machine-gun

Bristol Types 12, 14-17 and 22 F.2 Fighter
to
Bristol Types 142M, 149, and 160 Blenheim

Bristol Types 12, 14-17 and 22 F.2 Fighter

In March 1916 Frank Barnwell completed the design of a two-seat reconnaissance aircraft which was intended to compete with the Royal Aircraft Factory R.E.8 as a replacement for the B.E.2. Designated **R.2A** (later **Type 9**), this was an equal-span two-bay biplane, powered by an 89-kW (120-hp) Beardmore engine. The later availability of a 112-kW (150-hp) Hispano-Suiza engine led to a second study, the **R.2B (Type 9A)**, which was a slightly smaller sesquiplane. The advent of the 142-kW (190-hp) Rolls-Royce Falcon resulted in fuselage redesign to accommodate this unit or the Hispano-Suiza. A prototype of each version was ordered on 28 August 1916, in a contract which also covered 50 production aircraft.

The first prototype, given the designation **F.2A (Type 12)** to denote its change to a fighter role, was flown on 9 September 1916 and the second on 25 October. Production F.2As were all powered by the Rolls-Royce Falcon and featured revised cowlings and wings of a modified planform. Unlike that of the prototypes, the pilot's seat was not armour-protected. Armament consisted of a Lewis gun mounted on a Scarff ring in the rear cockpit and a Vickers machine-gun mounted on the centreline beneath the engine cowling, its location necessitating the provision of a tunnel through the upper-fuselage fuel tank.

No. 48 was the first RFC squadron to re-equip with the F.2A, receiving its first aircraft in February 1917 and flying to France on 8 March. The unit became established at Bellevue and on 5 April six F.2As took off to make the squadron's first offensive patrol. From this only two returned, following an attack by an equal number of Albatros D.IIIs of Jagdstaffel 11 led by Freiherr Manfred von Richthofen. Similar disastrous encounters resulted from tactical errors, principally the use of the aircraft as a platform for the rear-gunner. As soon as pilots began to adopt single-seater tactics, using the forward-firing Vickers gun as the main offensive armament, the 'Brisfit' became one of the most effective fighters of World War I.

Post-war, the Bristol Fighter was used as an Army co-operation aircraft and as a trainer, remaining in RAF service overseas as late as 1932, when No. 6 Squadron re-equipped with the Fairey Gordon. Other operators included the air forces of Australia, Belgium, Canada, the Irish Free State, Greece, Mexico, New Zealand, Norway, Peru and Spain.

Production totalled 5,308 aircraft, built by Bristol at Filton and Brislington, and by sub-contractors which included Angus Sanderson, Armstrong Whitworth, Austin Motors, Gloucestershire Aircraft, Harris and Sheldon, Marshall and Sons, Standard Motors and Cunard Steamship (managing National Aircraft Factory No. 3 at Aintree).

Variants
Type 14 F.2B Fighter: the main production version, incorporating a number of modifications: the upper longerons were sloped downwards from just behind the cockpit, improving the pilot's view and making room for the installation of an enlarged fuel tank and a bigger ammunition box for the 7.7-mm (0.303-in) Vickers gun; in addition, the lower-wing anchorage frame, originally uncovered and uncambered, was given an aerofoil section and fabric covering; the first batch was powered by the 142-kW (190-hp) Rolls-Royce Falcon I, the second by the 164-kW (220-hp) Falcon II, and the majority by the 205-kW (275-hp) Falcon III; other engines, introduced when orders for the F.2B outstripped the supply of Falcons, included the 149-kW (200-hp) and 224-kW (300-hp) Hispano-Suizas (**Types 16** and **17** respectively), 149-kW (200-hp) Sunbeam Arab (**Type 15**), 149-kW (200-hp) R.A.F. 4d, 134-kW (180-hp) Wolseley Viper and 172-kW (230-hp) Siddeley Puma

Type 22 F.2C Fighter: among experimental re-enginings of the F.2B were installations of the 149-kW (200-hp) Salmson radial to produce the **Type 22 F.2C**, the 224-kW (300-hp) A.B.C. Dragonfly radial to produce the **Type 22A F.2C** and the 172-kW (230-hp) Bentley B.R.2 rotary to produce the **Type 22B F.2C**

Type 14 F.2B Mk II: first flown in December 1919 for Army co-operation duties, and fitted with desert equipment and a tropical cooling system; 435 were produced, some new manufacture and some reconditioned

Bristol F.2B Fighter of the Royal New Zealand Air Force in 1919.

Type 96 Fighter Mk III: structurally-strengthened version, 50 of which were delivered between October and December 1926, followed by 30 dual-control, unarmed aircraft between January and June 1927

O-1: the F.2B was one of the types chosen for production in the USA when America entered the war in 1917; 2,000 had been ordered from the Curtiss Aeroplane and Motor Company by December 1917, the first making its maiden flight on 5 March 1918 powered by a 298-kW (400-hp) Liberty 12 engine; this engine/airframe combination proved to be unsuitable and the contract was cancelled in July 1918 in favour of a version with an American-built 224-kW (300-hp) Hispano-Suiza, flown in June in the form of one of the two pattern airframes sent to the USA from Filton; the second of these was fitted with a 216-kW (290-hp) Liberty 8 but crashed before official evaluation could take place

Like other truly great warplanes, the Bristol Fighter at first seemed a failure, only emerging in its true form when the operator learned how to best use its capabilities. This aircraft was the first F.2B Mk II developed as an army co-operation platform for desert service.

Type 96A Fighter Mk IV: conversion of Mk III airframes with strengthened landing gear and fuselage longerons for operation at higher gross weight; also fitted with enlarged fin, horn-balanced rudder and Handley Page automatic slots

Specification
Bristol F.2B Fighter
Type: two-seat fighter and Army co-operation aircraft
Powerplant: one 205-kW (275-hp) Rolls-Royce Falcon III inline piston engine
Performance: maximum speed 198 km/h (123 mph) at 1525 m (5,000 ft); service ceiling 5485 m (18,000 ft); endurance 3 hours
Weights: empty 975 kg (2,150 lb); maximum take-off 1474 kg (3,250 lb)
Dimensions: span 11.96 m (39 ft 3 in); length 7.87 m (25 ft 10 in); height 2.97 m (9 ft 9 in); wing area 37.62 m^2 (405 sq ft)
Armament: one fixed forward-firing 7.7-mm (0.303-in) synchronised Vickers machine-gun and one or two flexible 7.7-mm (0.303-in) Lewis guns in rear cockpit, plus up to 12 9-kg (20-lb) bombs on underwing racks

This was the first Type 89A Advanced Trainer, distinguished from the Type 89 by a plywood-covered fuselage. This was the last derivative of the basic F.2B Fighter.

Bristol Type 105 Bulldog

With a need to re-equip the RAF's fighter squadrons, to enable them to cope with bomber aircraft with performance in the category of that of the Fairey Fox, the Air Ministry drew up Specification F.9/26. This called for a single-seat day/night fighter, to be powered by a radial air-cooled engine, and armed with two Vickers machine-guns. A number of competing types resulted, with the **Bristol Type 105 Bulldog** winning narrowly from the Hawker Hawfinch.

Bristol's **Bulldog Mk I** prototype flew for the first time on 17 May 1927, and was modified subsequently with large-span wings for an attempt on the altitude and climb-to-height records. The Mk I had been superseded for test purposes by a lengthened-fuselage **Bulldog Mk II** prototype, and it was the production version of this aircraft that entered service with the RAF's No. 3 Squadron at Upavon, Wiltshire, in June 1929. This was an unequal-span single-bay biplane, the basic structure of the airframe being all-metal with fabric covering. The tail unit incorporated a variable-incidence tailplane, and the tailskid landing gear had through-axle main units with rubber-in-compression shock absorption. Powerplant of this version comprised one Bristol Jupiter VII radial engine. Equipment included oxygen and a short-wave radio transmitter and receiver. The Bulldog was used widely in RAF service, a total of 312 of all versions equipping no fewer than 10 squadrons and remaining in use until 1937. In addition to the Bulldogs which served with the RAF, many were exported for the armed forces of Australia, Denmark, Estonia, Finland, Latvia, Siam, and Sweden.

Variants

Bulldog Mk IIA: major production version, generally similar to Mk II, but with a 365-kW (490-hp) Bristol Jupiter VIIF engine, strengthened structure for operation at a higher gross weight, and wider main landing gear; later Mk IIAs had the tailskid replaced by a tailwheel, and brakes incorporated in the main wheels

Bulldog Mk IIIA: designation of two interim aircraft with the 418-kW (560-hp) Bristol Mercury IVS.2 engine

Bulldog Mk IVA: final fighter production version with strengthened ailerons, and powered by the 477-kW (640-hp) Bristol Mercury VIS.2 engine

Bulldog TM: training version (TM: training machine) with a special removable rear fuselage incorporating a second cockpit, dual controls as standard, and no armament; the training rear fuselage could be replaced by a standard rear fuselage, and there was provision for the installation of machine-guns so that the TM could be converted to serve as a fighter

Specification

Type: single-seat day/night fighter
Powerplant: (Mk II) one 328-kW (440-hp) Bristol Jupiter VII radial piston engine
Performance: maximum speed 280 km/h (174 mph) at 3050 m (10,000 ft); service ceiling 8230 m (27,000 ft); range 443 km (275 miles)
Weights: empty 998 kg (2,200 lb); maximum take-off 1583 kg (3,490 lb)
Dimensions: span 10.34 m (33 ft 11 in); length 7.62 m (25 ft 0 in); height 3 m (9 ft 10 in); wing area 28.47 m² (306.6 sq ft)
Armament: two fixed forward-firing synchronised Vickers machine-guns, and four 9-kg (20-lb) bombs on underwing racks

Bristol Type 105A Bulldog Mk IIA of No. 17 Sqn, RAF, based at Kenley in 1935.

Bristol Type 105 Bulldog Mk IVA

The Bristol Type 105 Bulldog was one of the RAF's fighter mainstays during the inter-war years, the service opening its account for the type with 25 Type 105A Bulldog IIs, including J9576 illustrated. The success of the first Bulldogs in RAF squadrons soon attracted export orders.

Bristol Type 130

Designed to Air Ministry Specification C.26/31 as a replacement for the Vickers Valentia serving in the Middle East and India, the **Bristol Type 130 Bombay** was intended as a troop or cargo carrier. But it had also to be capable of self-defence and to double as a long-range bomber – one might almost say the UK's answer to the Junkers Ju 52/3m. A contract was awarded for one prototype in March 1933 and this made its first flight from Filton on 23 June 1935, flown by Cyril Uwins. It was at that time the largest aircraft built at Filton. Military trials at the Aircraft and Armament Experimental Establishment, Martlesham Heath, were undertaken by Flt Lt 'Bill' Pegg, later to join the company and become its chief test pilot. Development testing resulted in various improvements being made, including the installation of more-powerful engines: Bristol Pegasus XXIIs of 753-kW (1,010-hp) in place of the original 559-kW (750-hp) Pegasus IIIs.

A production contract for one batch of 50 was awarded to meet the revised Specification 47/36, but with Filton's production lines geared to the Bristol Blenheim, it was decided to undertake Bombay production in Belfast, by Short Brothers & Harland at a new government-owned factory.

The first production Bombay flew in March 1939, and the initial squadron to receive the type was No. 216 in Egypt during the following September. Other deliveries followed to Nos 117, 267 and 271 Squadrons, and Bombays fulfilled their dual transport and bomber roles during the Libyan campaign of 1940.

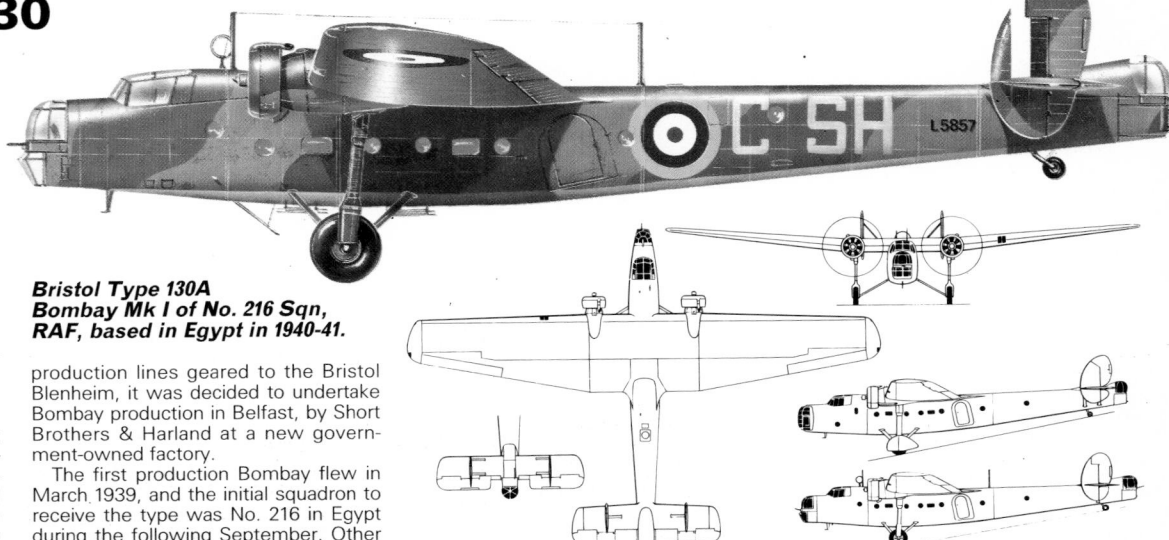

Bristol Type 130A Bombay Mk I of No. 216 Sqn, RAF, based in Egypt in 1940-41.

Bristol Type 130A Bombay (upper side view and scrap tail view: Type 130).

Although few in numbers, the Bombays were very active, and among their achievements was the evacuation of the Greek royal family from Crete to Egypt. A few UK-based aircraft ferried supplies across the English Channel before the collapse of France in 1940.

Bombays were eventually replaced by more modern types in the transport role as the bomber/transport concept be-came outdated, and the type passed quietly out of service in the mid-1940s, having achieved all and more than its de-signer had intended but having received little of the limelight.

Specification
Bristol Bombay
Type: bomber-transport with crew of 3 and up to 24 troops

Powerplant: two 753-kW (1,010-hp) Bristol Pegasus XXII radial piston engines
Performance: maximum speed 309 km/h (192 mph) at 1980 m (6,500 ft); cruising speed 257 km/h (160 mph) at 3050 m (10,000 ft); service ceiling 7620 m (25,000 ft); range 1416 km (880 miles) or 589 km (2,230 miles) with fuselage tanks

Weights: empty 6260 kg (13,800 lb); maximum take-off 9072 kg (20,000 lb)
Dimensions: span 29.18 m (95 ft 9 in); length 21.11 m (69 ft 3 in); height 5.94 m (19 ft 6 in); wing area 124.49 m² (1,340 sq ft)
Armament: two 7.7-mm (0.303-in) Vickers 'K' machine-guns (one each in nose and tail turrets), plus up to 907 kg (2,000 lb) of bombs

Bristol Type 138

On 11 April 1934 the Italian pilot Renato Donati, flying a Bristol Pegasus-engined Caproni biplane, broke Cyril Uwins' world altitude record, raising it from 13404 m (43,976 ft) to 14435 m (47,360 ft). Pressure then mounted for a British attempt to regain the record, and in June Bristol received an invitation to tender for two prototypes of a suitable aircraft. In November 1933 Frank Barnwell had proposed a single-seat high-altitude research aircraft, powered by a specially adapted Pegasus with a two-stage supercharger. This was revised to meet the new Specification 2/34, and given the company designation **Type 138A**.

The design was finalised in September as a low-wing monoplane of wooden construction in order to minimise weight. Simple, fixed landing gear was selected for the same reason. The pilot's cockpit was covered by a hinged plastic canopy, with hot-air demisting, and provision was made for a second crew position forward of the pilot's cockpit. Specially-developed pressurised flying suits and oxygen pressure helmets were available for the crew. The key to success lay in the Pegasus P.E.VIS engine which incorporated a mechanical super-charger, but which could also drive an auxiliary supercharger mounted on the firewall, via a flexible shaft and clutch.

The first aircraft was completed in early 1936 and Cyril Uwins made the maiden flight at Filton on 11 May. A standard Pegasus IV driving a three-bladed propeller was fitted for this and further flights on 22 May and 16 July. Following a visit to Farnborough in early August for trials with the oxygen equipment, the aircraft were returned to Filton on 15 August for installation of the special engine and its four-bladed propeller.

Squadron Leader F.R.D. Swain was selected as pilot for the attempt, and he collected the Bristol 138A from Filton on 5 September, returning to Farnborough. From that airfield he took off on 28 September to attain an FAI-homolo-gated record height of 15230 m (49,967 ft) before landing at Netheravon. Although the Italians regained the record in May 1937 with a flight to 15655 m (51,362 ft), minor improvements were made to the Type 138A to enable Flight Lieutenant M. J. Adam to raise it yet again, to 16440 m (53,937 ft) on 3 June 1937.

Variants
Type 138B: the second airframe was to have been powered by a 373-kW (500-hp) Rolls-Royce Kestrel supercharged engine for comparative tests, but although it was delivered to

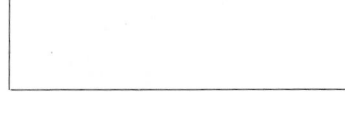

Farnborough in 1937 the engine installation was never completed

Specification
Type: high-altitude research aircraft
Powerplant: one 373-kW (500-hp) Bristol Pegasus P.E. VIS radial piston engine
Performance: maximum speed 285 km/h (177 mph) at 13715 m (45,000 ft); design ceiling 16459 m (54,000 ft); endurance 2 hours 15 minutes

The Bristol Type 138A is seen over Farnborough during its record-breaking flight of 30 June 1937, when an altitude of 16440 m (53,937 ft) was attained. The pilot wore a pressurised suit.

Weights: empty 1992 kg (4,391 lb); maximum take-off 2409 kg (5,310 lb)
Dimensions: span 20.12 m (66 ft 0 in); length 13.41 m (44 ft 0 in); height 3.12 m (10 ft 3 in); wing area 52.77 m² (568 sq ft)

Bristol Type 142M, 149 and 160 Blenheim

In 1934 Lord Rothermere, who was then proprietor of the *Daily Mail*, required for his personal use a fast and spacious private aeroplane, for this aviation-minded organisation had then appre-ciated the potential of what is today called the business or corporate aircraft. Lord Rothermere envisaged his require-ments as a fast aircraft that would accommodate a crew of two and six pas-sengers, and it just so happened that the Bristol Aeroplane Company had already drawn up the outline of a light transport in this category.

The brain-child of Frank Barnwell, the new aeroplane had been designed originally to be powered by two 373-kW (500-hp) Bristol Aquila I engines which were then under development. Lord Rothermere's interest in a high-speed transport resulted in Barnwell's proposal to mount a couple of 485-kW (650-hp) Bristol Mercury VIS engines in his embryo airframe and this resulted in the **Bristol Type 142**. First flown at Filton on 12 April 1935, it sparked off a hubbub of comment and excitement when during its initial trials it was found to be some 48 km/h (30 mph) faster than the prototype of the most-recently procured British fighter. Named *Britain First*, it was presented to the nation by Lord Rothermere after the Air Ministry had re-quested that it might retain it for a period of testing to evaluate its potential as a light bomber. This, then, was the sire of the **Bristol Blenheim**, which proved

an important interim weapon at the beginning of World War II. The Aquila-engined **Type 143** was similar, and first flew in January 1936. Only limited test-ing was undertaken, performance being severely curtailed by the non-availability of variable-pitch propellers.

Aware of Air Ministry interest in the Type 142, Bristol busied itself with homework to evolve a **Type 142M** mili-tary version of this aircraft, and in the Summer of 1935 the Air Ministry decided to accept the company's propo-sal, placing a first order for 150 aircraft to Specification 28/35 in September. The new aircraft was very similar to the Type 142, but there had of course been some changes to make it suitable for the mili-tary role, primarily to accommodate a bomb aimer's station, a bomb bay and a dorsal gun turret. Little time was lost by either the Bristol Company or the Air Ministry, for following the first flight of the prototype, on 25 June 1936, initial deliveries to RAF squadrons began in

Bristol Blenheim Mk I of the 1st Bomber Regiment, Royal Yugoslav air force, in April 1941.

March 1937, and in July 1937 the Air Ministry placed a follow-on order for 434 additional examples of the **Blenheim Mk I**, as the type had by then been named.

Of all-metal construction, except for fabric-covered control surfaces, the Blenheim Mk I was a cantilever mid-wing monoplane. The fuselage nose ex-tended only slightly forward of the engines, and both fuselage and tail unit were conventional light alloy structures. Landing gear was of the retractable tail-wheel type. Powerplant comprised two 626-kW (840-hp) Bristol Mercury VIII engines, mounted in nacelles on the wing leading edge. Accommodation was provided for a pilot, navigator/bomb-aimer, and air gunner/radio operator. A bomb bay in the wing centre-section could contain a maximum 454 kg (1,000 lb) of bombs, and standard arma-ment comprised a 7.7-mm (0.303-in) machine-gun in the port wing, plus a Vickers 'K' gun of the same calibre in the

dorsal turret.

The first RAF Squadron to receive Blenheim Mk Is was No. 114, then based at RAF Wyton, and it was this unit which first demonstrated the new type offi-cially to the public at the RAF's final Hen-don Display in the Summer of 1937. The Blenheims aroused excited comment with their high speed and modern appearance, being launched on their career in an aura of emotion created by the belief that, in an unsettled Europe, the RAF was armed with the world's most formidable bomber aircraft. Pro-duction contracts soared, necessitating the establishment of new construction lines by A. V. Roe at Chadderton and Rootes Securities at Speke, both these factories being in Lancashire. Between them the three lines built a total of 1,552 Blenheim Mk Is which, at their peak, equipped no fewer than 26 RAF squad-rons at home and overseas, the Blen-heim's first overseas deployments being with No. 30 Squadron in Iraq and No. 11 Squadron in India, in January and July 1938 respectively.

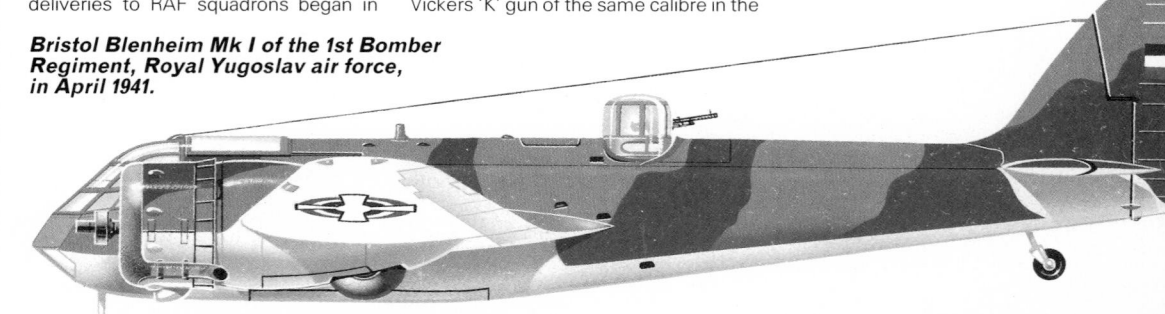

Blenheim Mk IVF of Esquadrilha ZE, Arma de Aeronautica (Portugal), based at Ota in 1943.

However, by the outbreak of World War II few Blenheim Mk Is remained in service with home-based bomber squadrons, having been superseded in the bombing role by the **Blenheim Mk IV**, which incorporated the lessons learned from the experience which squadrons had gained in operating the Mk.I. But the Mk I's usefulness was by no means ended, many continuing to serve as conversion trainers and, initially, as crew trainers in OTUs. More valuable by far were some 200 which were converted to serve as night-fighters, pioneering the newly conceived technique of AI (Airborne Interception) radar, carrying AI Mk III or Mk IV. The single forward-firing machine-gun was totally inadequate for this role, of course, and a special underfuselage pack to house four 7.7-mm (0.303-in) machine-guns was produced. So equipped, a **Blenheim Mk IF** scored the first AI success against an enemy aircraft on the night of 2-3 July 1940. The ultimate development of the basic Type 142M was the prototype **Blenheim Mk II**, a Mk I converted with extra tankage.

Export versions of the Blenheim Mk I were sold before the war to Finland, Turkey and Yugoslavia, and were also built under licence by these last two nations. In addition, a small number had been supplied to Romania as a diplomatic bribe in 1939, but this proved to be unsuccessful. The result, of course, was that Blenheim Mk Is fought for and against the Allies.

When, in August 1935, the Air Ministry had initiated Specification G.24/35 to find a successor to the Avro Anson for use in a coastal reconnaissance/light bomber role, Bristol had proposed its **Type 149**. Very similar to the Blenheim Mk I, this envisaged the use of Bristol Aquila engines to confer long range with the existing fuel capacity, but this was unacceptable to the Air Ministry. Subsequently renewed interest was shown

Blenheim Mk IVFs of No. 235 Sqn, RAF Coastal Command. Visible are the ventral machine-gun trays that turned them into 'fighters'.

in the Type 149 for use in a general-reconnaissance role, and a prototype was built, by conversion of an early Blenheim I, this retaining the Mercury VIII engines and being provided with increased fuel capacity. The fuselage nose was lengthened to provide additional accommodation for the navigator/observer and his equipment, and this was finalised as that which graced the Mk I's successor, the **Blenheim Mk IV**.

The Air Ministry then had misgivings about the Type 149, fearing that its introduction and manufacture would interfere with the production of urgently needed Blenheims. Instead, the Type 149 was adopted by the Royal Canadian Air Force for production in Canada as the **Bolingbroke Mk I**, the Bristol prototype being shipped to Canada to help in the establishment of a production line by Fairchild Aircraft at Longueuil, Quebec. The first Bolingbroke Mk Is had Mercury VIII engines, but after 18 of these had been built production changed to the definitive Canadian version, the **Bolingbroke Mk IV** with Mercury XV engines, and equipment from Canadian and US manufacturers. Later variants included a small number of **Bolingbroke Mk IV W**s with 895-kW (1,200-hp) Pratt & Whitney R-1830 Twin Wasp engines, and a number of **Bolingbroke Mk IV T** multi-purpose trainers.

Having blown hot and then cold over the Type 149, there was a sudden renewal of interest, primarily as an interim measure until the Type 152 torpedo-bomber, derived from the Blenheim, should become available. The decision was taken, therefore, to introduce the longer nose and stepped windscreen of the Bolingbroke, and to make provision for longer range by the introduction of increased wing fuel capacity. The Bristol designation Type 149 was retained for this changed configuration, the new RAF designation being **Blenheim Mk IV**. This change took place quietly on the production lines towards the end of 1938, although the first 68 Blenheim Mk IVs were built without the 'long-range wing'. The powerplant comprised two more powerful Mercury XV engines, and

these allowed gross weight to be increased eventually by 16 per cent. No. 90 Squadron was the initial unit to be equipped with Blenheim Mk IVs in March 1938, the first of more than 70 squadrons to operate these aircraft, and consisting of units from Army Co-operation, Bomber, Coastal, Far East Bomber, Fighter and Middle East Commands, both at home and overseas. Inevitably, such extensive use brought changes in armament and equipment, but especially the former, for the armament of the first Blenheim Mk IVs was unchanged from the initial two-gun armament of the Mk I. Protective armour was also increased, but while it was not possible to enlarge the capacity of the bomb bay, provision was made for an additional 145 kg (320 lb) of bombs to be carried externally for short-range missions.

With so many squadrons operating the type it was inevitable that Blenheims should notch up many wartime 'firsts' for the RAF. These included the first reconnaissance over German territory, made on 3 September 1939 by a Blenheim Mk IV of No. 139 Squadron; and the type was the first to drop bombs on German targets, on 4 September 1939, when 10 aircraft from Nos 107 and 110 Squadrons made an attack on the German fleet in the Schillig Roads, off Wilhelmshaven. From the beginning of the war, until replaced in home squadrons of Bomber Command by Douglas Bostons and de Havilland Mosquitoes in 1942, Blenheim Mk IVs were used extensively in the European theatre. Although vulnerable to fighter attack, they were frequently used for unescorted daylight operations and undoubtedly the skill of their crews and the aircraft's ability to absorb a great deal of punishment were the primary reasons for their survival, for high speed and heavy firepower were certainly not their forte. In the overseas squadrons Blenheims continued to serve long after their usefulness had ended in Europe, and except in Singapore, where they were no match for the Japanese fighters, they proved a valuable weapon. A total of 3,983 Blenheim Mk IVs and Bolingbrokes had been built

when production ended, and in addition to serving with the RAF had been used by the French Free and South African air forces, and used in small numbers by Finland and Greece. The **Blenheim Mk IVF** fighters were conversions analogous to the Mk IF.

Last of the direct developments of the Blenheim design was Bristol's **Type 160**, known briefly as the **Bisley**, which entered service in the Summer of 1942 as the **Blenheim Mk V**. Envisaged originally as a low-altitude close-support bomber, with a 'solid' nose housing four machine-guns, it was in fact built for deployment as a high-altitude bomber, powered by Mercury XV or XXV engines. Except for a changed nose, some alterations in detail and updated equipment, these aircraft were basically the same as their predecessors. Some 945 were built, all produced by Rootes at its Speke and Stoke-on-Trent factories, and the first unit to receive Blenheim Mk Vs was No. 18 Squadron. The type equipped six squadrons in the Middle East and four in the Far East, where they were used without distinction. This resulted from an increase in gross weight of over 17 per cent which, without the introduction of more-powerful engines, had brought about a serious fall of performance. It was only when the Blenheim Mk Vs were deployed in the Italian campaign, contending with the advanced fighters in service with the Luftwaffe, that losses rose to quite unacceptable proportions, and the type was withdrawn from service.

Specification
Bristol Blenheim Mk IV
Type: three-seat light bomber
Powerplant: two 675-kW (905-hp) Bristol Mercury XV radial piston engines
Performance: maximum speed 428 km/h (266 mph) at 3595 m (11,800 ft); cruising speed 319 km/h (198 mph); service ceiling 8310 m (27,260 ft); maximum range 2350 km (1,460 miles)
Weights: empty 4441 kg (9,790 lb); maximum take-off 6532 kg (14,400 lb)
Dimensions: span 17.17 m (56 ft 4 in); length 12.98 m (42 ft 7 in); height 3 m (9 ft 10 in); wing area 43.57 m² (469 sq ft)
Armament: five 7·7-mm (0.303-in) machine-guns (one forward-firing in port wing, two in power-operated dorsal turret, and two remotely controlled in mounting beneath nose and firing aft), plus up to 454 kg (1,000 lb) of bombs internally and 145 kg (320 lb) externally

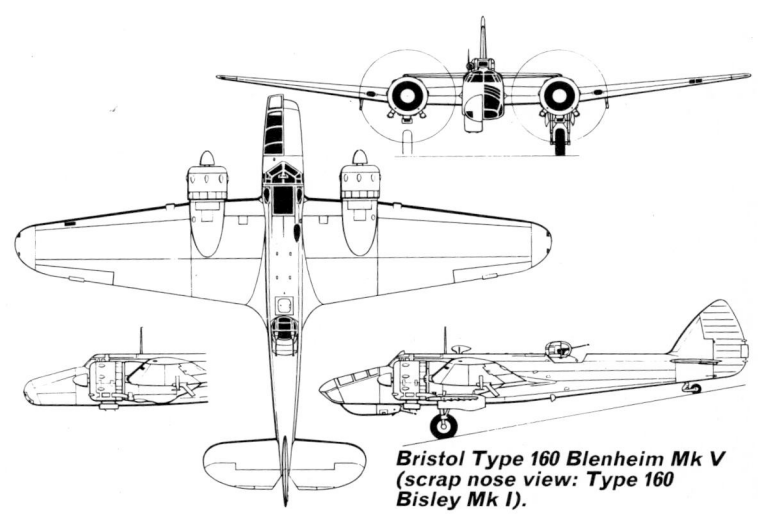

Bristol Type 160 Blenheim Mk V (scrap nose view: Type 160 Bisley Mk I).

199

Bristol Type 152 Beaufort
to
Bristol Type 166 Buckmaster

Bristol Type 152 Beaufort

In 1935 the Air Ministry had issued two Specifications, M.15/35 and G.24/35, which detailed requirements for a torpedo-bomber and a general reconnaissance/bomber respectively. The latter was required to replace the Avro Anson in service for this role, and as mentioned in the Bristol Blenheim entry, was met by the Bristol Type 149 which was built in Canada as the Bolingbroke. To meet the first requirement, for a torpedo-bomber, Bristol began by considering an adaptation of the Blenheim, identifying its design as the **Type 150**. This proposal, which was concerned primarily with a change in fuselage design to provide accommodation for a torpedo and the installation of more-powerful engines, was submitted to the Air Ministry in November 1935.

After sending off these details of the Type 150, the Bristol design team came to the conclusion that it would be possible to meet both of the Air Ministry's specifications by a single aircraft evolved from the Blenheim, and immediately prepared a new design outline, the **Type 152**. By comparison with the Blenheim Mk IV, the new design was increased slightly in length to allow for the carriage of a torpedo in a semi-exposed position, provided a navigation station, and seated pilot and navigator side-by-side; behind them were radio and camera positions which would be manned by a gunner/camera/radio operator. The Type 152 was more attractive to the Air Ministry, but it was considered that a crew of four was essential, and the accommodation was redesigned to this end. The resulting high roof line, which continued unbroken to the dorsal turret, became a distinguishing feature of this new aircraft, built to Air Ministry Specification 10/36, and subsequently named **Beaufort**.

Detail design was initiated immediately, but early analysis and estimates showed that the intended powerplant of two Bristol Perseus engines would provide insufficient power to cater for the increase of almost 25 per cent in gross weight without a serious loss of performance. Instead, the newly developed twin-row Taurus sleeve-valve engine was selected for the Beaufort, the only concern being whether it would be cleared for production in time to coincide with the construction of the new airframe. The initial contract, for 78 aircraft, was placed in August 1936, but the first prototype did not fly until just over two years later, on 15 October 1938. There had been a number of reasons for this long period of labour, partially overheating problems with the powerplant and also the need to disperse the Blenheim production line to shadow factories before the Beaufort could be built.

Test flying of the prototype revealed a number of shortcomings, leading to the provision of doors to enclose the main landing gear units when retracted, repositioning of the engine exhausts, and an increase to two machine-guns in the dorsal turret. These and other items, added to continuing teething problems with the new engine, delayed the entry into service of the **Beaufort Mk I**, which started to equip No. 22 Squadron

of Coastal Command in January 1940. It was this unit which, on the night of 15-16 April 1940, began the Beaufort's operational career by laying mines in enemy coastal waters, but in the following month all in-service aircraft were grounded until engine modifications could be carried out.

Earlier, the Australian government had shown interest in the Beaufort, and following the visit of a British Air Mission in early 1939, it was decided that railway and industrial workshops could be adapted to produce these aircraft, resulting in the establishment of two assembly plants (at Fishermen's Bend, Melbourne, and at Mascot, Sydney) with the production backing of railway workshops at Chullora, Islington and Newport. Twenty sets of airframe parts and the eighth production aircraft as a working sample were shipped out, but at an early stage the Australians decided they did not want the Taurus powerplant. Accordingly, they had obtained a licence from Pratt & Whitney to build the Twin Wasp, and this powered all Australian-built Beauforts, which eventually totalled 700.

Australian production began in 1940, the first Australian **Beaufort Mk V** making its initial flight in May 1941. Apart from the change in engines, these were generally similar to their British counterparts except for an increase in fin area to improve stability with the powerful Twin Wasp engine. In fact, engine and propeller changes accounted for most of the different variants produced by the Australian factories. These included the **Beaufort Mk V** (50) and **Beaufort Mk VA** (30), both with licence-built Twin Wasp S3C4-G engines; **Beaufort Mk VI** (60 with Curtiss propellers) and **Beaufort Mk VII** (40 with Hamilton propellers), all 100 being powered by imported S1C3-G Twin Wasps because of insufficient licence production; and the **Beaufort Mk VIII** with licence-built S3C4-Gs. This last mark was the definitive production version, of which 520 were built, and had additional fuel tankage, Loran navigation system and variations in armament, with production ending in August 1944. Some 46 of the last production batch were subsequently converted to serve as unarmed transports; designated **Beaufort Mk IX**, this variant had the dorsal turret removed and the resulting aperture faired in. The powerplant rating of all the Australian versions was 895 kW (1,200 hp). The Beaufort was used extensively by the Royal Australian Air Force in the Pacific theatre, serving from the Summer of 1942 until the end of World War II.

The early trials of the Australian Beaufort Mk V with Twin Wasp engines induced the Air Ministry to specify this powerplant for the next contract, and a prototype with these American engines was flown in November 1940. The first

A Bristol Type 152 Beaufort Mk I of No. 217 Sqn, RAF Coastal Command, shows off the aircraft's substantial forward fuselage section housing the crew, radio office, defensive armament and torpedo.

Bristol Type 152 Beaufort Mk I

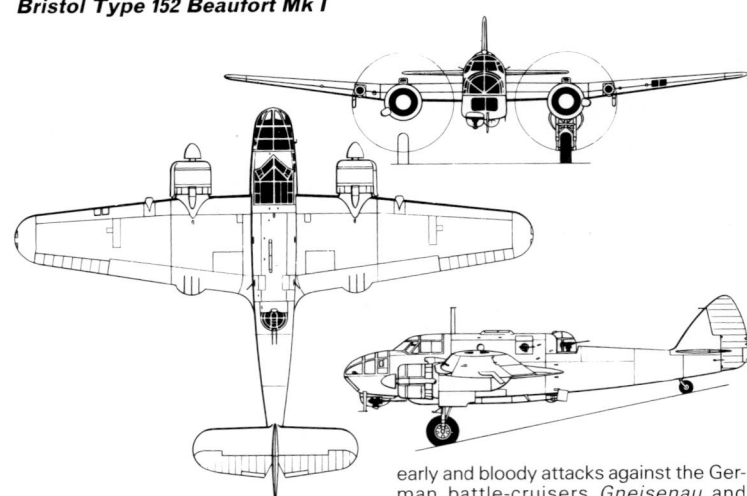

production **Beaufort Mk II** flew in September 1941, and by comparison with the Beaufort I revealed much improved take-off performance. However, because of a shortage of Twin Wasps in the UK, only 164 production Mk IIs were built before Mk Is with improved Taurus XII or XVI engines were re-introduced on the line. In addition to the powerplant change, this version had structural strengthening, a changed gun turret, and ASV radar with Yagi aerials. When production of this version ended in 1944, well over 1,200 Beauforts had been built in Britain.

The final two designations, **Beaufort Mk III** and **Beaufort Mk IV**, related respectively to a version with Rolls-Royce Merlin XX engines of which none was built, and a version with two 932-kW (1,250-hp) Taurus XX engines of which only a prototype was built.

Beauforts were the standard torpedo-bomber in service with Coastal Command during 1940-3, equipping Nos 22, 42, 86, 217, 415 and 489 Squadrons in home waters, and Nos 39, 47 and 213 in the Middle East. They acquitted themselves well until superseded by the Beaufighter, involved in many of the

early and bloody attacks against the German battle-cruisers *Gneisenau* and *Scharnhorst*, and the heavy cruiser *Prinz Eugen*, three vessels which often seemed to be invincible.

Specification
Bristol Beaufort Mk I
Type: four-seat torpedo-bomber
Powerplant: two 843-kW (1,130-hp) Bristol Taurus VI, XII, or XVI radial piston engines
Performance: maximum speed 418 km/h (260 mph) at 1830 m (6,000 ft); cruising speed 322 km/h (200 mph); service ceiling 5030 m (16,500 ft); normal range 1666 km (1,035 miles)
Weights: empty 5945 kg (13,107 lb); maximum take-off 9630 kg (21,230 lb)
Dimensions: span 17.63 m (57 ft 10 in); length 13.59 m (44 ft 7 in); height 3.78 m (12 ft 5 in); wing area 46.73 m² (503 sq ft)
Armament: four 7-7-mm (0.303-in) machine-guns (two each in nose and dorsal turrets) though some aircraft had three additional 7.7-mm (0.303-in) guns (one in blister beneath the nose and two in beam positions), plus up to 680 kg (1,500 lb) of bombs or mines, or one 728-kg (1,605-lb) torpedo

Bristol Type 156 Beaufighter

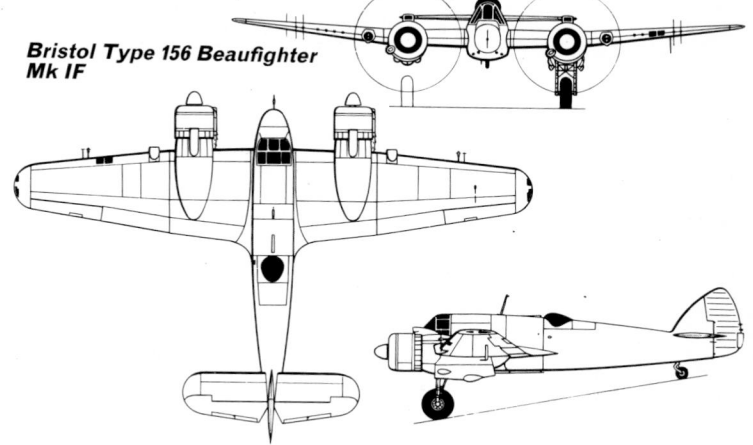

Bristol Beaufighter Mk X of Escuadrilha 8, Portuguese Forcas Aereas du Armada, Portela de Sacavem, 1945.

The **Bristol Type 156** design, which became known subsequently as the **Beaufighter**, was born of an improvisation forced upon the Bristol design staff, headed by Roy Fedden and Leslie Frise. This came in the wake of the Munich crisis of 1938, when the RAF was desperately short of modern fighters, and particularly of heavily armed aircraft for deployment in long-range escort or night-fighter roles. Bristol had then virtually completed design of the Beaufort torpedo-bomber, and the suggested improvisation was to involve major assemblies of this aircraft in a design that would produce a new long-range fighter in the shortest possible time. The proposal hinged upon use of the wings, tail unit and landing gear of the Beaufort, coupled with a powerplant comprising two of the company's Hercules sleeve-valve engines and requiring, in effect, only a new fuselage to unite these assemblies. A draft proposal, knocked together in a few days and submitted to the Air Ministry in October 1938, resulted in an order for four prototypes. On 17 July 1939 the first of these made its maiden flight, proving just what inspired improvisation can do.

A mid-wing cantilever monoplane of all-metal construction (except for fabric-covered control surfaces), the Beaufighter had conventional fuselage and tail unit structures, and its landing gear was of retractable tailwheel type. Powerplant consisted of two Hercules radial engines, the four prototypes experimenting with three different marks of this engine, the third and fourth both having Hercules IIs.

Factory and service testing revealed few airframe problems, although action was taken to incorporate a number of improvements considered to be desirable for future use. The area of concern centred upon the engines, for while the first prototype had been able to demonstrate its estimated speed of 539 km/h (335 mph) at 5120 m (16,800 ft), the second prototype was some 7½ per cent below this figure. What was even more disconcerting was the fact that the aircraft were then being flown without operational equipment, and it was realised by the company that introduction of the planned 1044-kW (1,400-hp) Hercules III would provide little, if any, improvement. The only alternative engine available at short notice was the 1119-kW (1,500-hp) Hercules XI, an uprated version of the Hercules III which used 100-octane fuel, and it was decided to use these engines for the unitial production versions.

The other vital factor to be settled, before the Beaufighter went into service, was the selection of suitable armament. This, of course, was to vary somewhat according to the basic role in which a particular version was intended to operate. The **Beaufighter Mk IF** was

visualised as a night-fighter as soon as it was appreciated that there was ample room within its fuselage to accommodate the then bulky AI radar, and this dictated a concentration of heavy fire to destroy or immediately disable an enemy aircraft after AI contact had brought the night-fighter to optimum range. Standard armament of the Mk IF was four 20-mm cannon in the fuselage nose, plus four 7.7-mm (0.303-in) machine-guns in the starboard wing and two more in the port wing, although early production aircraft off the Filton line had only the four cannon. Radar comprised AI Mk IV installed in the fuselage nose, and this became the standard equipment for Fighter Command Beaufighters.

Contracts for the Beaufighter having reached large proportions long before any of the type entered service, three production lines had been established. These were at the Bristol works at Filton, in a new Bristol factory at Weston-super-Mare, Somerset, and at the Fairey factory at Stockport in Lancashire. The first production Beaufighter Mk IF completed on this last production line made its initial flight on 7 February 1941; the first from Weston-super-Mare on 20 February 1941, but long before that, on 27 July 1940, the first Beaufighters were handed over to the RAF.

Nos 25 and 29 Squadrons each received their first example of the Beaufighter on 2 September 1940; by 17 September No. 29 Squadron was fully operational with the type, followed by No. 25 on 10 October; and Nos 219, 600 and 640 Squadrons were close behind. It was this last squadron which recorded the first Beaufighter victory with the AI Mk IV radar, on 19 November 1940, when a Junkers Ju 88 was mortally damaged over Oxfordshire and crashed before it could cross the English Channel. Unfortunately for the RAF, interception by AI Mk IV alone was inadequate, and it was not until the introduction of Ground Controlled Interception (GCI) in January 1941, which was able to put the night-fighter with AI contact range of its adversary, that the Beaufighter Mk IF was able to justify its promise.

An alternative employment for the Beaufighter Mk IF arose even while the initial night-fighter squadrons were being equipped in the autumn of 1940, for there was an urgent need for long-

range day fighters to operate around the Mediterranean and in the Western Desert. To meet this demand about 80 Beaufort Mk IFs were provided with desert equipment and their range extended by the temporary expedient of installing a 227-litre (50-Imp gal) fuel tank on the fuselage floor. At a later date additional tankage was provided in the wing outer panels, but this necessitated deletion of the wing guns.

The provision of special Coastal Command radio, plus navigational facilities, distinguishes the initial **Beaufighter Mk IC** (Coastal) which began to enter service with No. 143 Squadron in the spring of 1941. The aircraft of this mark proved a valuable weapon from the outset, becoming gradually more important as their capability was expanded.

A heavy demand for Hercules engines, which were also used to power the Short Stirling bomber, made it prudent to experiment with an alternative engine installation so that, in the event of a temporary or long-term interruption in the supply of these powerplants, Beaufort fighter production would not be penalised. Accordingly, two of three airframes supplied to Rolls-Royce at Hucknall were provided with 802-kW (1,075-hp) Merlin X inline engines, and these when test flown were found to give slightly improved performance, but had a slight change in the aircraft's centre of gravity. This manifested itself in some directional instability, which was resolved by the production of a tailplane with 12° dihedral, and this was adopted both retrospectively and as standard on all subsequent production aircraft. Merlin-engined Beaufighters were designated Mk II, and the first production **Beaufighter Mk IIF** with 954-kW (1,280-hp) Merlin XX engines made its initial flight on 22 March 1941. The Beaufighter Mk IIF was, in fact, the only Mer-

lin-engined version to be built, and the type served primarily as a home-defence night-fighter, but was used also by Nos 721, 723, 775, 779 and 789 Squadrons of the Fleet Air Arm.

The only other variant to fly among the early marks was a **Beaufighter Mk V**, armed with only two forward-firing 20-mm cannon, and the wing guns replaced by a Boulton Paul four-gun turret mounted in the fuselage just aft of the pilot. This, however, was found to erode performance so drastically that development of the project was abandoned.

Fortunately for both Bristol and the RAF, the feared shortage of Hercules engines did not materialise. On the contrary, production began to rise, and the more powerful Hercules VI, which had a rating of 1245 kW (1,670 hp) at 2285 m (7,500 ft), became available for installation in Beaufighters. Following tests of three aircraft provided with this powerplant, the Hercules IV or XVI was accepted as standard. Airframes so powered became designated **Beaufighter Mk VI**, supplanting both Mk Is and Mk IIs on the production lines towards the end of 1941, and the first Mk VIs began to enter service with Coastal and Fighter Command squadrons at the beginning of 1942.

These more powerful engines made possible a far wider variation in equipment and weapons, expanding the variety of roles which this superb aircraft was able to undertake. Wing guns could be replaced by a 227-litre (50-Imp gal) tank to starboard and a 109-litre (24-Imp gal) tank to port to confer longer range; two 1130kg (250-lb) bombs could be carried beneath the wings; eight 41-kg (90-lb) rocket projectiles could be carried in place of wing guns; and following experiments carried out in May 1942, it was made possible for the Beaufighter to carry and launch an American- or British-made standard marine torpedo. An initial batch of 16 **Beaufighter Mk VIC**s was similarly converted to equip No. 254 Squadron, and the resulting 'Torbeaus', as they were unofficially nicknamed, carried out a first successful operation against enemy shipping in early April 1943. This combination of

Bristol Type 156 Beaufighter Mk IF

A Beaufighter Mk IF of No. 29 Sqn, RAF Fighter Command, shows off its overall black finish used by night fighters in 1942. The tailplane had dihedral added to improve stability compared to early production aircraft.

Beaufighters proved themselves admirable anti-shipping weapons, armed either with rockets for small targets or torpedoes (illustrated) for larger vessels.

Beaufighter and torpedo represented a most formidable weapon in the air-sea war.

The **Beaufighter Mk VIF** was the first of the type to serve in the Burma-India theatre, used initially by No. 176 Squadron in the defence of Calcutta. Beaufighters of this mark were also used by four squadrons of the USAAF's 1st Tactical Air Command during operations in the Mediterranean theatre. Beaufighter Mk VICs which equipped Coastal Command were supplemented by an anti-shipping strike version designated **Beaufighter TF. Mk X**. These were powered by a modified version of the Hercules VI engine, designed to give peak output at low levels, and were also the first to standardise on AI Mk VIII radar mounted in a so-called 'thimble-nose', as this combination had been found to be particularly suitable for ASV use, as may be judged by the fact that Beaufighter TF. Mk Xs of Nos 236 and 254 Squadrons were to locate and destroy five German U-boats in the short space of 48 hours during March 1945. Other versions to serve with Coastal Command included 60 torpedo-carrying Mk VICs with Hercules XVI engines and eight underwing rockets in lieu of wing guns. These were designated **Beaufighter Mk VI (ITF)**, for Interim Torpedo Fighter, and were employed to

swell the ranks pending delivery of the Beaufighter TF. Mk Xs. These 60 were, in fact, subsequently converted to Mk X configuration. Final British production version was the **Beaufighter Mk XIC** for Coastal Command, this being generally similar to the Mk X but without the ability to carry a torpedo, and the 163 of this version brought total British construction to over 5,500 aircraft.

Of these, more than 50 had been supplied to Australia during 1941-2, and this country was to build under licence during 1944-5 a total of 364 aircraft, generally similar to the Beaufighter TF. Mk X, under the designation **Beaufighter Mk 21**. It was the Australian Beaufighters which, blasting Japanese

naval and merchant ships without pity, earned for this superb aeroplane the picturesque if grim name 'Whispering Death'. After the war, many of the RAF's Beaufighters were converted to serve as target tugs, under the designation **Beaufighter TT.10**, and the last example was withdrawn from service in 1960.

Specification
Bristol Beaufighter TF. Mk X
Type: two-seat anti-shipping strike fighter
Powerplant: two 1320-kW (1,770-hp) Hercules XVII radial piston engines
Performance: maximum speed 488 km/h (303 mph) at 395 m (1,300 ft);

maximum cruising speed 401 km/h (249 mph) at 1525 m (5,000 ft); service ceiling 4570 m (15,000 ft); range 2366 km (1,470 miles)
Weights: empty 7076 kg (15,600 lb); maximum take-off 11431 kg (25,200 lb)
Dimensions: span 17.63 m (57 ft 10 in); length 12.70 m (41 ft 8 in); height 4.83 m (15 ft 10 in); wing area 46.73 m² (503.0 sq ft)
Armament: four forward-firing 20-mm cannon, six fixed forward-firing 7.7-mm (0.303-in) machine-guns and one flexible 7.7-mm (0.303-in) Vickers 'K' gun in dorsal position, plus one torpedo and two 113-kg (250-lb) bombs or eight 41-kg (90-lb) air-to-surface rockets

Bristol Type 163 Buckingham

When design of a Bristol Blenheim replacement was begun, the Bristol team had no means of knowing that their new tactical day bomber, the **Type 163 Buckingham**, was to be rendered obsolete before it had flown by the superlative performance of a private venture wooden bomber. This was the de Havilland Mosquito, which could carry the same 1814-kg (4,000-lb) bombload at a speed of 80 km/h (50 mph) faster with a crew of two instead of four, although admittedly for a lesser distance.

Bristol's earlier project to Specification B.2/41, the **Type 162**, itself replacing a previous Bristol Beaufighter bomber scheme, the **Type 161 Beaumont**, was revised as a result of official delays in finalising requirements. It was further delayed by teething troubles with the new Bristol Centaurus engines, and it was not until 4 February 1943 that the prototype Buckingham flew, without armament. The second, armed, prototype followed shortly afterwards and was followed by two more, all with Centaurus IV engines with high-altitude rating, although production aircraft were to have medium-altitude Centaurus VIIs or XIs.

Minor control modifications were made before the first production Buckingham flew on 12 February 1944, but changes were made to the tail surfaces

after 10 had been completed to improve stability, particularly in single-engine performance.

Although outclassed by the Mosquito in European operations, it was felt that the Buckingham's superior range would prove a great asset against the Japanese. But by the time production aircraft were being delivered the end of the Far East war was in sight and the original order was cut from 400 to 119, plus the four prototypes.

With the end of their potential usefulness as bombers, it was decided to convert the Buckinghams to fast courier transports; the last batch of 65 on the line were completed as **Buckingham C. Mk 1** transports and it was intended that the earlier **Buckingham B. Mk 1** bombers would be retrospectively modified to the same standard. In this configuration (with extra tankage, seats for four passengers and a crew of three) the Buckingham had a range of 4828 km (3,000 miles) and was used on services to Malta and Egypt, although they were uneconomical with such a small passenger capacity. Two were adapted to accommodate seven passengers, but the modification proved too expensive and was not taken further.

Although the 54 bomber versions were returned to Filton for conversion, most were stored and eventually scrapped with very low hours, the last

surviving Buckingham being used as a ground testing rig until 1950.

Specification
Bristol Buckingham B. Mk 1
Type: four-seat tactical day bomber
Powerplant: two 1879-kW (2,520-hp) Centaurus VII or XI radial piston engines
Performance: maximum speed 531 km/h (330 mph) at 3660 m (12,000 ft); cruising speed 459 km/h (285 mph); service ceiling 7620 m (25,000 ft); range 5118 km (3,180 miles)

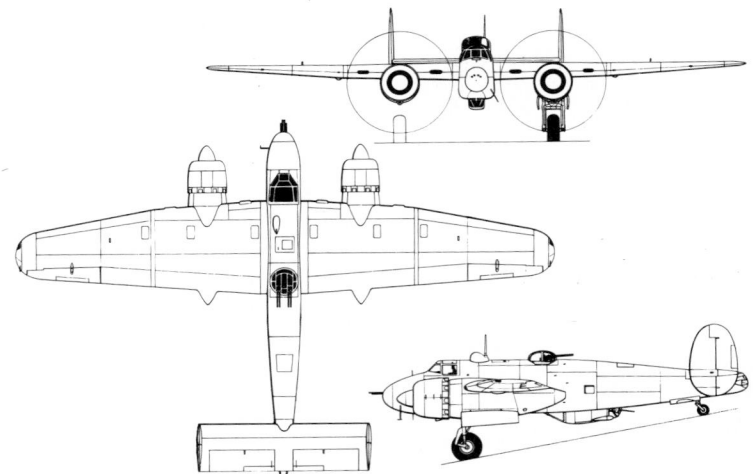

Bristol Type 163 Buckingham B.Mk 1

Weights: empty 10905 kg (24,042 lb); maximum take-off 17259 kg (38,050 lb)
Dimensions: span 21.89 m (71 ft 10 in); length 14.27 m (17 ft 6 in); height 5.33 m (17 ft 6 in); wing area 65.77 m² (708.0 sq ft)
Armament: 10 7.7-mm (0.303-in) machine-guns (four each in fixed forward position and ventral cupola, and two in dorsal turret), plus up to 1814 kg (4,000 lb) of bombs

Bristol Type 164 Brigand

Following the success of the Beaufighter as a torpedo-bomber, the Air Ministry issued Specification H.7/42 for a Coastal Command Beaufighter replacement. Bristol submitted the

Bristol Type 164, later to become the **Brigand**. Four prototypes were ordered in April 1943, the first flying on 4 December the following year, and production began using some jigs from the Buckingham.

The first 11 Brigand torpedo-bombers were delivered in 1946 to Nos 35 and 42 Squadrons and the Air/Sea Weapons Development Unit, Coastal Command, but by this time the requirement for coastal strike aircraft had ceased and the Brigands eventually returned to Filton for

conversion to fill a new RAF requirement: a light bomber for use in Burma and Malaya.

In their new role, under the designation **Brigand B.1**, the aircraft were delivered initially to No. 84 Squadron at Habbaniyah in Iraq in early 1949. Other Brigands went to No. 8 Squadron at Aden to replace that unit's Hawker Tem-

The Brigand B.Mk 1 light bomber was developed from the Brigand TF.Mk 1 torpedo fighter, but dispensed with the earlier variant's rear-defence gun. It was fitted with bomb and rocket racks for Far East service.

1949 a total of 147 Brigands had been built, including the four prototypes. Two Brigand B.1s went to Pakistan air force for evaluation in 1948; one crashed and the other returned, after major overhaul, to the RAF, where it received a new serial number; a new Brigand B.1 was built as an RAF replacement for the crashed aircraft.

Nine new radar trainer versions designated **Brigand T.4** were delivered to No. 228 Operational Conversion Unit at Leeming in 1950, and were used to train airborne interception (AI) radar operators for a year, the unit reforming at Colerne as No. 238 OCU in June 1952. In 1955 the **Brigand T.5** made its appearance, differing in the AI installation and this mark was a conversion from Brigand B.1s and Brigand T.4s.

The Brigand was phased out of service when No. 238 OCU, by then based at North Luffenham, was disbanded in March 1958.

About 600 radar navigators had been trained on the Brigand T.4 and T.5, and the Brigand was the RAF's last piston-engined attack aircraft, being replaced in this role by the English Electric Canberra.

pests, the unit thus changing from a fighter to a bomber squadron until December 1952, when de Havilland Vampires replaced the Brigands.

The RAF's last operational Beaufighters were serving with No. 45 Squadron in Ceylon, which began to receive Brigands in replacement in May 1949 shortly before moving to Malaya, and for the next five years these aircraft were in action against terrorists.

The Brigand B.1 had armour plating, a redesigned cockpit and a one-piece transparent canopy which could be jettisoned in emergency. Provision for the rear-firing gun was deleted, but the four 20-mm nose cannon remained in modified blast tubes.

Sixteen unarmed meteorological reconnaissance Brigands were delivered under the designation **Brigand Met.3** to No. 1301 Flight in Ceylon, and by the time production ended in the spring of

Specification
Bristol Brigand B.1

Type: three-seat ground-attack bomber

Powerplant: two 1842-kW (2,470-hp) Bristol Centaurus 57 radial piston engines

Performance: maximum speed 576 km/h (358 mph) at 4875 m (16,000 ft); cruising speed 501 km/h (311 mph); service ceiling 7925 m (26,000 ft); range 4506 km (2,800 miles) with drop tanks

Weights: empty 11611 kg (25,598 lb); maximum take-off 17690 kg (39,000 lb)

Dimensions: span 22.05 m (72 ft 4 in); length 14.15 m (46 ft 5 in); height 5.33 m (17 ft 6 in); wing area 66.70 m² (718.0 sq ft)

Armament: four fixed 20-mm nose cannon, plus underwing racks for rockets or up to 907 kg (2,000 lb) of bombs

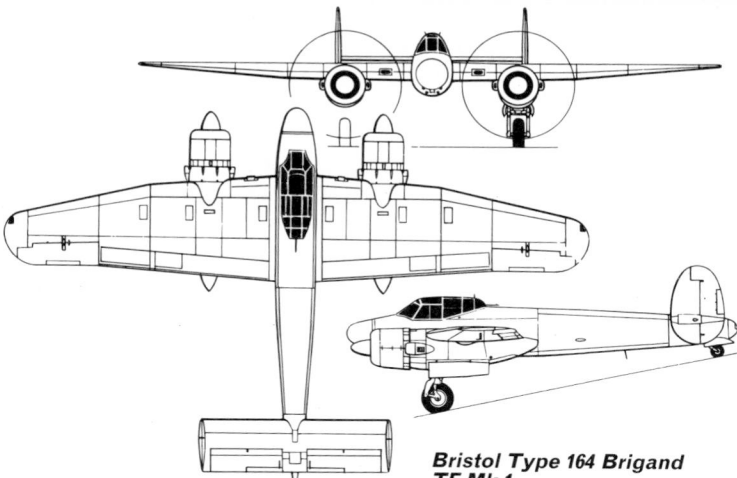

Bristol Type 164 Brigand TF.Mk 1

Bristol Type 166 Buckmaster

Derived from the Model 163 Buckingham as an advanced trainer, the **Bristol Type 166 Buckmaster** had considerable commonality with its predecessor, and in fact the last 110 Buckinghams were converted to Buckmasters by installation of dual controls and other modifications.

The prototype Buckmaster flew from Filton on 27 October 1944, and a second prototype followed, both aircraft being conversions from partly completed Buckinghams. One hundred and fifty additional sets of Buckingham components had already been manufacturered when the contract was cut back and these were used for the Buckmasters, the first of 100 production aircraft being completed in 1945 and the last the following year.

Although several Buckmasters served with No. 8 Squadron at Aden on communications duties, most were delivered to Operational Conversion Units

to train Brigand pilots, and the Buckmaster had the distinction of being one of the fastest and most powerful trainers to serve with the RAF when it was introduced. Blind-flying instruction and instrument training could be undertaken and the normal crew complement was pilot, instructor and air signaller.

The last Training Command Buckmasters served with No. 238 OCU at Colerne into the mid-1950s, while one or two were used on experimental work at Filton. One of these, probably the last survivor, was relegated to RAF Halton where it served as an instructional airframe until scrapped in 1958.

Specification
Bristol Buckmaster

Type: three-seat advanced trainer

Powerplant: two 1879-kW (2,520-hp) Bristol Centaurus VII radial piston engines

Performance: maximum speed 566 km/h (352 mph) at 3660 m (12,000 ft); service ceiling 9145 m (30,000 ft); range 3219 km (2,000 miles)

Weights: empty 10433 kg (23,000 lb); maximum take-off 15286 kg (33,700 lb)

Dimensions: span 21.89 m (71 ft 10 in); length 14.15 m (46 ft 5 in); height 5.33 m (17 ft 6 in); wing area 65.77 m² (708.0 sq ft)

Bristol Buckmaster T.Mk 1

Bristol Type 167 Brabazon
to
British Aerospace (BAC) 167 Strikemaster

Bristol Type 167 Brabazon

The post-war needs of civil aviation in the UK were the subject of a study undertaken by an Inter-Departmental Committee, chaired by Lord Brabazon of Tara. It recommended in early 1943 the development of five types of transport, including a transatlantic airliner with non-stop London-New York capability. On 11 March 1943 the Bristol Aeroplane Company was revealed as the manufacturer selected to design and develop this potentially prestigious trans-oceanic aircraft, which was designated the **Bristol Type 167 Brabazon I**, and which was intended to challenge the dominance of the United States in the transport field.

After much detailed discussion to determine the size, capacity and performance of the projected aircraft, it was defined by Specification 2/44 as a 50-passenger transport with a maximum take-off weight of 113858 kg (250,000 lb). The basic layout had been finalised by November 1944, featuring a fuselage with a maximum diameter of 5.11 m (16 ft 9 in), and a tricycle multi-wheel landing gear; power was to be supplied by four coupled pairs of Bristol Centaurus piston engines, driving contra-rotating propellers. The first drawings were released in April 1945 and manufacture of the first prototype began in October. The fuselage, wing centre section and tailplane assembly were built as an integral structure which moved into the final assembly shop on 4 October 1947. The completed aircraft was rolled out in December 1948 and Bristol chief test pilot A. J. ('Bill') Pegg made the first flight on 4 September 1949. A restricted certificate of airworthiness was issued on 14 June 1950 and on the following day the Brabazon I undertook a number of

demonstration flights at London Airport, the rear fuselage having been furnished with 30 seats for the occasion. Fatigue cracks in the propeller mounting structure were a factor in the Air Registration Board's refusal to grant unrestricted approval for commercial passenger-carrying flights, preventing trial operation in a 180-seat layout on the London-Nice route of British European Airways. After some £3 million had been spent on the UK's largest landplane, the project was cancelled and the prototype was broken up at Filton in October 1953, having flown fewer than 400 hours.

Variants
Brabazon II: designed to Specification 2/46, this version was to have carried 100 passengers and to

have been powered by four 5220-kW (7,000-hp) coupled pairs of Bristol Proteus 710 turboprop engines; structural changes were introduced, as were four-wheeled main landing gear bogies; the prototype, semi-complete when the programme was cancelled, was scrapped at Filton

Specification
Bristol Brabazon I
Type: long-range passenger transport
Powerplant: eight 1864-kW (2,500-hp) Bristol Centaurus radial piston engines
Performance: maximum speed 483 km/h (300 mph); cruising speed 402 km/h (250 mph); cruising altitude 7620 m (25,000 ft); range 8851 km (5,500 miles)

The thin 'nacelles' of the Brabazon Mk I indicate that they did not house the engines, but only the drive shafts for the contra-rotating propeller units, each driven by a pair of Bristol Centaurus radials buried in the wings. The definitive Brabazon Mk II was to have been powered by the Bristol Coupled-Proteus for an estimated top speed of 360 mph (579 km/h).

Weights: empty 65816 kg (145,100 lb); maximum take-off 131542 kg (290,000 lb)
Dimensions: span 70.1 m (230 ft 0 in); length 53.95 m (177 ft 0 in); height 15.24 m (50 ft 0 in); wing area 493.95 m² (5,317 sq ft)

Bristol Type 170 Freighter

One of the earliest post-World War II projects of the Bristol Aeroplane Company was the **Type 170** short-range utility transport. This had developed during the closing stages of the war, and its shape was determined largely by the British Army's needs, which included the ability to airlift the standard 3-ton truck. The design was finalised with a high-wing monoplane configuration, clam-shell nose doors, flight deck above the cargo hold/cabin, fixed landing gear, and two wing-mounted Bristol Hercules sleeve-valve engines. Two civil prototypes were financed by the Ministry of Supply as the need for military transports appeared to be nearing an end. But there was a condition to the MoS funding: the company was required to cover tooling costs and also to build two additional prototypes.

As a result, the opportunity was taken to construct the company examples as passenger/cargo variants. Thus, the MoS aircraft were of the variant known as the **Type 170 Mk I Freighter**, retaining nose loading doors; the company prototypes were built under the designation **Type 170 Mk II Wayfarer**, with a solid nose, side entrance/loading door, and with an optional reinforced freight floor. The Freighters were true cargo-

Bristol Type 170 Freighter Mk 31 of Safe Air Limited (New Zealand)

carriers, while the Wayfarers were available in several configurations, including one with a maximum of 32 passengers, with a galley and toilet.

First to fly was the Freighter prototype (G-AGPV) on 2 December 1945, followed by a Wayfarer (G-AGVB) in the 32-seat configuration on 30 April 1946. The first prototype was used for service trials at Boscombe Down, as a result of which the wing span was increased by 3.05 m (10 ft) to allow an increase in gross weight. This, in turn, required the instal-

lation of more powerful engines, and resulted in the version designated **Type 170 Freighter Mk 21**. The best known variant was the **Type 170 Freighter Mk 32**, with a fuselage lengthened by 1.52 m (5 ft 0 in): it was developed for Silver City Airways to provide increased passenger/car capacity for service on its Channel air bridge. Silver City's 'Super-freighters' could accommodate two or three cars and up to 23 passengers. Acquired later were 'Super-Wayfarers', that could carry a maximum of 60 passengers. In 1962, Air Charter and Silver City Airways were merged to form

British United Air Ferries, then operating a combined fleet of 24 Type 170s, increasing to 41 by 1970. When production ended in early 1958, a total of 214 of all variants had been built.

Variants
Type 170 Freighter Mk IA: mixed-traffic variant of Mk I with 16 passenger seats and toilet to rear of rear spar
Type 170 Freighter Mk IB: BEA version of Mk I
Type 170 Freighter Mk IC: BEA version of Mk IA

Type 170 Freighter Mk ID: BSAA version of Mk IA

Type 170 Wayfarer Mk IIA: version of Mk II with 32 seats, pantry and toilet

Type 170 Wayfarer Mk IIB: BEA version of Mk IIA, with two toilets

Type 170 Wayfarer Mk IIC: version of Mk II with 20 seats in front of rear spar, with baggage hold, and toilet

Type 170 Freighter Mk XI: version of Mk I with 32.92-m (108-ft) wing and extra tankage

Type 170 Freighter Mk XIA: mixed-traffic version of Mk XI

Type 170 Freighter Mk 21E: convertible version of Mk 21 with cabin heating, soundproofing and 32 removable seats

Type 170 Freighter Mk 31: version of Mk 21 with dorsal fin

Type 170 Freighter Mk 31E: convertible version of Mk 31

Type 170 Freighter Mk 31M: military version of Mk 31 with provision for supply dropping

Type 179 Freighter: project for a twin-boom version

Type 179A Freighter: project for a version with upswept tail and ramp-loading door

Type 216 Freighter: project for a car ferry with two Dart turboprops

Specification
Bristol Freighter Mk 32
Type: utility transport
Powerplant: two 1476-kW (1,980-hp) Bristol Hercules 734 radial piston engines
Performance: maximum speed 362 km/h (225 mph); cruising speed 262 km/h (163 mph); service ceiling 7470 m (24,500 ft); range 1320 km (820 miles)
Weights: empty 13404 kg (29,950 lb); maximum take-off 19958 kg (44,000 lb)

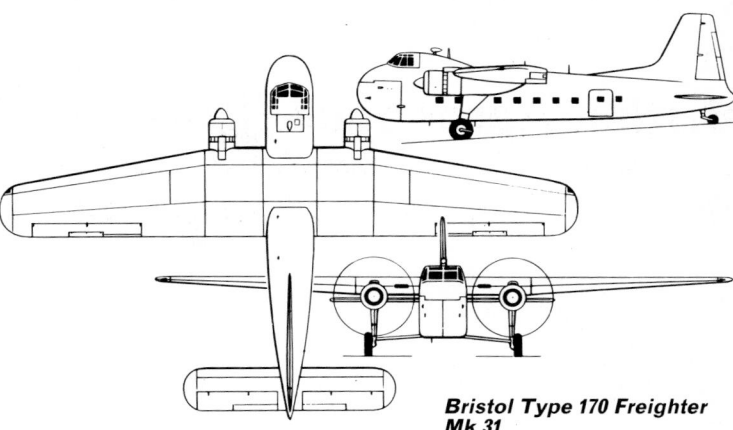

Bristol Type 170 Freighter Mk 31

Dimensions: span 32.92 m (108 ft 0 in); length 22.35 m (73 ft 4 in); height 7.62 m (25 ft 0 in); wing area 138.14 m² (1,487 sq ft)

Bristol Type 171 Sycamore

Late in 1944 the Bristol Aeroplane Company formed a Helicopter Department at Filton and recruited Raoul Hafner from the Airborne Forces Experimental Establishment, where he had been leading a British rotorcraft development team. Drawing on pre-war experience with his A.R.III Gyroplane, Hafner started work on a single-engined four-seat helicopter for both civil and military applications. The lack of sufficiently developed British engine of the required power led to selection of the widely-used 336-kW (450-hp) Pratt & Whitney Wasp Junior for the first two **Type 171 Mk 1** prototypes, developed to Ministry of Supply Specification E.20/45.

The design featured a light alloy cabin section and a stressed-skin tailboom attached to a central engine and gearbox mounting, the rotor head being fitted with three wooden monocoque blades. After extensive component testing, ground running of the completed airframe began on 9 May 1947, and the first flight was made by H. A. Marsh on 27 July. The second aircraft joined the test programme in February 1948 and on 25 April 1949, to facilitate its flight to the Paris Salon, it became the first British helicopter to be granted a civil certificate of airworthiness. An Alvis Leonides radial was installed in the third airframe which appeared in the static park at the 1948 SBAC exhibition at Farnborough.

The Bristol Sycamore HR.Mk 14 was the RAF multi-role version of the basic Type 171 design, and was in reality a universal machine incorporating the successful features of all previous Sycamore variants.

Designated **Type 171 Mk 2,** this helicopter made a successful first flight on 3 September 1949 although a second take-off attempt ended abruptly when the rotor disintegrated. With a strengthened rotor, development flying was resumed while work continued on the assembly of 15 production Mk 3s.

Variants
Type 171 Mk 3: airframe changes included a shortened nose and an 0.20-m (8-in) increase in cabin width to accommodate three passengers on the rear seat; in order to maintain essential systems in the event of engine failure, the accessory drive was transferred from engine to rotor gearbox; the initial production batch included one **Sycamore HC.10** and four **Sycamore HC.11** ambulance and communications machines for evaluation by the Army Air Corps, and four **Sycamore HR.12** helicopters for rescue duties with RAF Coastal Command; two **Mk 3A** helicopters, with a freight hold behind the engine bay, were built for British European Airways

Type 177 Mk 4: main production version, incorporating modifications evolved from Mk 3 experience, including taller landing gear, four cabin doors and the pilot's position moved from port to starboard; deliveries included three **Sycamore HR.50** and seven **Sycamore HC.51** helicopters for the Royal Australian Navy, three **Sycamore Mk 14** aircraft for Belgian air force use in the Congo, and 50 **Sycamore Mk 52s** for the Federal German Army and Navy; the Royal Air Force received two **Sycamore HR.13s** and more than 80 **Sycamore HR.14s**, equipped with winches for air-sea rescue duties, initially with No. 275 Squadron, Fighter Command,. which received its first helicopter on 13 April 1953; Sycamores also operated in the light assault and reconnaissance roles in Malaya, Cyprus and Borneo.

Specification
Sycamore HR.14
Type: five-seat communications/SAR/light troop carrying helicopter
Powerplant: one 410-kW (550-hp) Alvis Leonides 73 radial piston engine
Performance: maximum speed 204 km/h (127 mph) at sea level; cruising speed 169 km/h (105 mph); endurance 3 hours
Weights: empty 1728 kg (3,810 lb); maximum take-off 2540 kg (5,600 lb)
Dimensions: main rotor diameter 14.81 m (48 ft 7 in); length, rotors folded 14.07 m (46 ft 2 in); height 3.71 m (12 ft 2 in); main rotor disc area 172,22 m² (1,853.8 sq ft)

Bristol Types 173 & 192 Belvedere

The first British tandem-rotor helicopter, the **Bristol Type 173** combined two sets of Sycamore rotors and control systems, each powered by a 429-kW (575-hp) Alvis Leonides engine. These were each arranged to drive through a freewheel clutch so that, with both rotor gearboxes interconnected by a shaft, either engine could drive both rotors in the event of an engine failure.

The first of two prototypes, developed to Ministry of Supply Specification E.4/47, made its first hovering flight on 3 January 1952, flown by C. T. D. Hosegood, but ground resonance problems delayed further progress until July. The first flight from the airfield at Filton took place on 24 August, and this **Type 173 Mk 1** helicopter appeared at the SBAC Show in September. RAF evaluation followed and in 1953 naval trials were undertaken aboard the aircraft carrier HMS *Eagle*. The first prototype was sub-sequently given four-blade rotors, and a low-set tailplane without dihedral, but which incorporated small fins at the tips.

Two pairs of stub wings mounted fore and aft, and designed to offload the rotors in flight, characterised the second prototype, which also had castoring front wheels. Designated **Type 173 Mk 2**, this was first flown on 31 August 1953 and was transferred to the Royal Air Force in August 1954 for further naval trials, the stub wings having been removed and the rear set replaced by the upswept tailplane of the Mk 1. In August 1956 the helicopter was leased to British European Airways, but was withdrawn from use following an accident at Filton on 16 September. Three further prototypes, designated **Type 173 Mk 3**, were built for the Ministry of Supply, having 634-kW (850-hp) Leonides Major engines, four-blade metal rotors and a taller rear pylon. Only the first progressed beyond the ground-running stage, beginning hovering trials on 9 November 1956. The third had the shortened fuselage and long-stroke landing gear of the **Type 191** naval version, which in April 1956 secured an order (later cancelled) for three Leonides Major-powered prototypes and 65 production examples with Napier Gazelle turboshafts.

The Type 173 prototype (G-ALBN) suffered from ground resonance and flight stability problems.

The Type 192 Belvedere featured Gazelle turboshafts, and had downward-canted tailplanes to cure stability problems.

The cancellation of the naval variant was not the end of the story, however. The Royal Air Force had a requirement for a personnel and paratroop transport and casevac helicopter, capable also of lifting bulky loads on an external sling. An order for 22 of the **Type 192** versions was placed in April 1956, later increased to 26, all to be Gazelle-powered. The prototype, first flown at Weston-super-Mare on 5 July 1958, was joined in the development programme by nine pre-production aircraft. These originally had wooden rotor blades, and tailplanes with anhedral and end-plate fins; they were later brought up to production standard for delivery to the RAF. Modifications included the substitution of metal rotor blades and compound anhedral tailplanes; the provision of powered flying controls, sliding doors, improved air intakes and enlarged low-pressure wheels. The eleventh aircraft was completed as the first production **Belvedere HC.1**, delivered to No. 66 Squadron at RAF Odiham in August 1961. This unit was also the last to operate Belvederes, disbanding at RAF Seletar in March 1969. By the time No. 66 Squadron received its first Belvedere, Bristol's Helicopter Department had been acquired by Westland Aircraft Ltd, being known as that company's Bristol Helicopter Division. It was this division which continued production of the RAF's Belvederes, and maintained product support while they remained in service.

Specification
Bristol Belvedere HC.1
Type: short-range tactical transport
Powerplant: two 1092-kW (1,465-shp) Napier Gazelle N.Ga.2 turboshafts
Performance: maximum cruising speed 222 km/h (138 mph); service ceiling 5275 m (17,300 ft); range with payload of 2722 kg (6,000 lb) 75 miles; ferry range 750 km (460 miles)
Weights: empty 5277 kg (11,634 lb); maximum overload take-off 9072 kg (20,000 lb)
Dimensions: rotor diameter, each 14.91 m (48 ft 11 in); length, rotors turning 27.36 m (89 ft 9 in); height 5.26 m (17 ft 3 in); rotor disc area, total 349.30 m² (3,760.0 sq ft)

Bristol Type 175 Britannia

To meet early post-World War II requirements of the British Overseas Airways Corporation (BOAC) for a Medium-Range Empire (MRE) civil transport, Bristol Aircraft together with four other British manufacturers, submitted a total of eight designs to the specification which had been advised. Most nearly meeting the requirement was the **Bristol Type 175**, a pressurised low-wing monoplane with tricycle-type landing gear, to be powered by four Bristol Centaurus sleeve-valve piston engines, and providing accommodation for 32-36 passengers. These engines were, however, more powerful than required by the planned payload, and it was decided to amend the designs to accommodate 40-44 passengers, this being increased again at a later stage to seat 42-48. It was anticipated that BOAC would order this version, but it was, in fact, the UK's Ministry of Supply which ordered three prototypes on 5 July 1948.

More design changes followed, and when the first prototype (G-ALBO) made its maiden flight on 16 August 1952, it was of the same general configuration as the initial production **Series 100** aircraft which could accommodate a maximum of 90 tourist-class passengers. Powerplant of this prototype comprised four Bristol Proteus turboprop engines,

Bristol Britannia 253C of Gemini Air Transport (Ghana)

each of 2088-ekW (2,800-ehp), but the Series 100 production aircraft had the more developed Proteus 705 of 2819 ekW (3,780 ehp). Fifteen of this version were built for BOAC, these being designated **Britannia 102**, and they first entered service on 1 February 1957 on BOAC's South African routes.

A larger-capacity version followed under the designation **Britannia 300**, the prototype **Britannia 301** (G-ANCA) making its first flight on 31 July 1956. This had been evolved not only to provide increased capacity, its fuselage

The Britannia 253F was the civil designation of freighters originally built for the RAF as C.Mk 1 transports. This aircraft of Redcoat Air Cargo was one of the last in service.

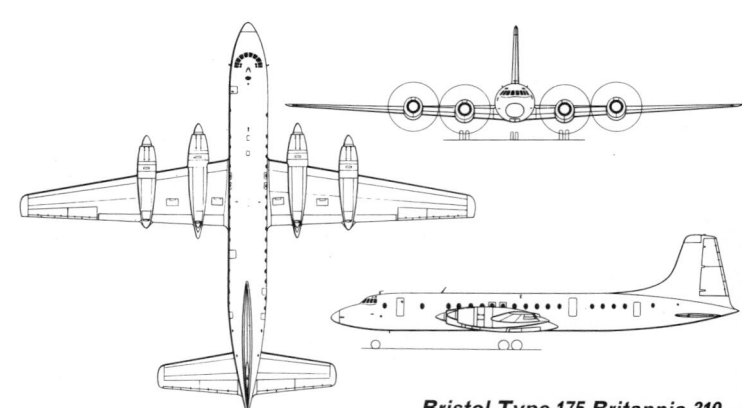

Bristol Type 175 Britannia 310

being lengthened by 3.12 m (10 ft 3 in) to accommodate up to 133 tourist-class passengers, but also to have nonstop transatlantic capability. Although seven were ordered by BOAC they did not serve with this airline, being delivered instead to Aeronaves de Mexico (two **Britannia 302**s), Transcontinental SA (two **Britannia 305**s), Air Charter (two **Britannia 307**s), and Ghana Airways (one **Britannia 309**).

BOAC transferred its order to **Series 300LR** (long-range) aircraft with increased fuel tankage, and initially with 3072-ekW (4,120-ehp) Proteus 755 turboprops, this designation changed subsequently to **Series 310**. The prototype **Britannia 311** (G-AOVA) flew first on 31 December 1956, and BOAC's first **Britannia 312** was delivered on 10 September 1957 and used for proving flights over the North Atlantic. This led to the inauguration of BOAC's London-New York service with Britannia 312s,

the first scheduled transatlantic passenger service to be flown by turbine-powered airliners, with G-AOVC making the first revenue flight on 19 December 1957. Final development produced the **Series 320**, which differed primarily by having 3318-ekW (4,450-ehp) Proteus 765 turboprops, but only two of these were built and leased to Canadian Pacific Air Lines (now CP Air).

It had seemed in the early days of Britannia production that this airliner might capture a significant bag of orders, but it was left behind in the wake of the new Boeing 707 and never recovered. Production of civil airliners totalled 60, and in addition a further 23 (three **Britannia 252** and 20 **Britannia 253** aircraft) were completed by Short Brothers and Harland at Belfast for service with the RAF's Transport Command as the **Britannia C. Mk 2** and **C. Mk 1** respectively. Basically similar to the Series 310, they incorporated a large cargo freight

door: the 22 remaining in service in 1975 were then retired, and were acquired by small airlines in Africa, Europe, and the Middle East. About 10 of these remained in service in early 1982.

The last of the Britannias to be delivered, at the end of November 1960, was the original prototype (G-ALBO) which, by then, had an unusual powerplant mixture. This comprised Proteus 705s in the two inboard positions, and one Proteus 755 and one 4101-ekW (5,500-ehp) Bristol Orion turboprop respectively in the starboard and port outer nacelles: it ended its days at RAF St Athan, serving as an instructional airframe. This, however, was not quite the end of the Britannia story, for a manufacturing licence had been granted to Canadiar Ltd in 1954. This company built inititally 33 **CL-28 Argus** maritime reconnaissance aircraft, derived from the Britannia, for service with the Royal Canadian Air Force. It was followed by

the construction of a transport version designated **CL-44**, for both military and civil use.

Specification
Bristol Type 175 Britannia Series 310
Type: four-turboprop commercial transport
Powerplant: four 3072-ekW (4,120-ehp) Bristol Proteus 755 turboprops
Performance: maximum speed 639 km/h (397 mph); cruising speed 575 km/h (375 mph); service ceiling 7315 m (24,000 ft); range with maximum payload 6869 km (4,268 miles)
Weights: empty 37438 kg (82,537 lb); maximum take-off 83915 kg (185,000 lb)
Dimensions: span 43.36 m (142 ft 3 in); length 37.87 m (124 ft 3 in); height 11.43 m (37 ft 6 in); wing area 192.77 m² (2,075.0 sq ft)

Bristol Type 188

The first Bristol turbojet design to progress to flight test, and beyond, the **Type 188** was developed in response to an invitation to tender to Specification ER.134, issued in February 1953. The requirement was for a research vehicle, capable of flight at twice the speed of sound, for investigation into the effects of kinetic heating on airframes. Manufactured from stainless steel, the Type 188 was to have been powered by two Rolls-Royce Avon RA.24R engines, but the de Havilland Gyron DGJ.10 was substituted. The original order was for six aircraft, later reduced to three, one of which was a structural test airframe transported to Farnborough in May 1960. The first flying prototype was rolled out on 26 April but technical snags, including engine intake design problems, delayed the maiden flight until 14 April 1962. Flown by chief test pilot Godfrey Auty,

The Type 188 was built mostly of stainless steel for experiments into steady-state kinetic heating at Mach 2.

the Type 188 took off from Filton to land after 23 minutes at the Aircraft and Armament Experimental Establishment at Boscombe Down. The second prototype flew for the first time on 29 April 1963. The Bristol 188's research career was unexpectedly short as, despite extensive fuselage tankage, fuel consumption was such that endurance in the required speed range was inadequate.

Specification
Type: single-seat high-speed research aircraft
Powerplant: two 6350-kg (14,020-lb) thrust de Havilland Gyron Junior DGJ.10 turbojets

Performance: maximum speed Mach 1.88
Weights: empty 12701 kg (28,000 lb); maximum take-off 17022 kg (37,527 lb)

Dimensions: span 10.69 m (35 ft 1 in); length 21.64 m (71 ft 0 in); height 4.06 m (13 ft 4 in); wing area 36.79 m² (396.0 sq ft)

British Aerospace 1000

With its successful 125 executive jet entering a new lease of life in the Series 800 version, British Aerospace began development of a larger variant to be produced concurrently, known as the **BAe 1000**. Using the tried and trusted 125 airframe as a basis, a 0.46 m (1 ft 6 in) plug was added forward of the wing and a 0.38 m (1 ft 3 in) plug aft, offering seating for up to 15 passengers in maximum density.

In order to considerably increase the range of the aircraft, the fairing under the centre-section was extended forward to accommodate extra fuel and fuel-efficient Pratt & Whitney Canada PW305 turbofans were fitted, each with reverse thrust for braking. Additional changes

concern a new-look cabin with increased headroom, external baggage hatch and revised avionics.

The prototype BAe 1000 first flew on 16 June 1990, with several orders already announced. It made its public debut on the 28th, and later appeared at the SBAC show at Farnborough.

Specification
Type: two-crew, 15-seat business transport
Powerplant: two Pratt & Whitney Canada PW305 turbofans, developing 23.23 kN (5,200 lb) thrust each
Performance: maximum speed with 867 km/h (539 mph) at 8840 m (29,000 ft); service ceiling 13100 m

(43,000 ft); take-off field length 1830 m (6,000 ft); range with maximum payload 6375 km (3,961 miles)
Weights: empty 7629 kg (16,820 lb); maximum take-off 14060 kg (31,000 lb)
Dimensions: span 15.66 m (51 ft 4½ in); length 16.42 m (53 ft 10½ in);

The first BAe 1000 made a public debut at the 1990 Farnborough show. Note the extended ventral fairing.

height 5.21 m (17 ft 1 in); wing area 34.75 m² (374.0 sq ft)

British Aerospace ATP

The 748 had been a steady seller for Avro, Hawker Siddeley and British Aerospace for many years, so it seemed natural the BAe should attempt to continue this line with a new and revised aircraft. On 1 March 1984, the company announced the intention to develop such an aircraft known as the **ATP** (Advanced TurboProp).

Using the 748 as a starting point, BAe retained the fuselage cross-section but made it much longer, resulting in an air-

British Midland use the ATP on domestic sectors within the UK. The type's very quiet operations make it one of the 'friendliest' airliners available.

craft able to carry 64 passengers in a standard one-class layout or up to 72 in high-density seating. The nose and tail profiles were revised to give the aircraft a thoroughly modern look, while the wings remain similar to those of the

earlier machine. Cabin doors were provided fore and aft, the front door incorporating an airstair. However, the door sill height was made compatible with jetways. Avionics have been suitably upgraded to the lastest standard, the ATP boasting an EFIS (Electronic Flight Instrumentation System).

By far the most noticeable change was to the engines. Pratt & Whitney PW124/126 turboprops were fitted, each driving a six-blade quiet propeller. ATP is claimed to be the quietest airliner in its class. First flying on 1 March 1984, the ATP is now in service with several operators, including British Airways, Manx Airlines and British Midland. Orders for the type in March 1990 totalled 39 aircraft, with another 22 options. British Aerospace has also proposed the **BAe 132** maritime patrol version, with underfuselage radar, MAD sting and weapons pylons.

Specification
Type: two-crew, 64-seat regional transport
Powerplant: two Pratt & Whitney Canada PW126A turboprops, 1978 kW (2,653 shp) each
Performance: cruising speed 493 km/h (306 mph); take-off field length at max weight 1463 m (4,800 ft); range with 64 passengers 1825 km (1,134 miles)
Weights: operating empty 14193 kg (31,290 lb); maximum take-off 22930 kg (50,550 lb)
Dimensions: span 30.63 m (100 ft 6 in); length 26.00 m (85 ft 4 in); height 7.14 m (23 ft 5 in)

Manx Airlines is another 'home' operator of the ATP, using its aircraft principally on trips between the Isle of Man and the mainland.

British Aerospace EAP

After many years' study concerning a new generation combat aircraft, BAe revealed a mock-up of its **ACA** (Agile Combat Aircraft) design in 1982. No funds were forthcoming for the project, but the UK government signed a contract with BAe on 26 May 1983 for the development of an Experimental Aircraft Programme – **EAP** – using ACA research and other work by European partners MBB and Aeritalia.

First flying on 8 August 1986, the single EAP is used to research technologies associated with advanced fighter development, incorporating a fly-by-wire system evaluated on an experimental Jaguar testbed. With the signing of the Eurofighter agreement covering the EFA new-generation combat aircraft, the

EAP programme became more relevant, and now the aircraft spends most of its time testing systems for the new fighter.

Specification
Type: single-seat fighter research vehicle
Powerplant: two Turbo-Union RB199-34R Mk turbofans (without thrust reversers), rated at 40.0 kN (9,000 lb) thrust dry and 75.7 kN (17,000 lb) thrust with afterburning
Performance: maximum speed above Mach 2 at altitude
Weights: (approximately) empty 10000 kg (22,050 lb); maximum take-off 14515 kg (32,000 lb)
Dimensions: span 11.77 m (38 ft

7 in); length 17.72 m (58 ft 1½ in); height 5.70 m (18 ft 8½ in); wing area 51.66 m² (556.1 sq ft)

The EAP is a technology demonstrator for the forthcoming European Fighter Aircraft.

British Aerospace (BAC) 167 Strikemaster

Although based on a design of the 1950s, the **British Aerospace Strikemaster** offered a number of air forces relatively cheap, effective firepower. It was derived from the Hunting (later BAC and finally British Aerospace) Jet Provost, which in turn was a radical development of the Percival Provost piston-engined basic train. The Jet Provost proved to be a highly successful trainer, selling in large numbers to the RAF and overseas air arms, and was progressively upgraded. The final versions were pressurised and more powerful. The next logical step was to give the aircraft teeth, and the **BAC 145** was the first multi-role attack version. This was in turn refined to produce the relatively more

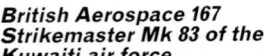

Strikemaster Mk 80s were supplied to Saudi Arabia for light strike/weapons training duties. They have been replaced by versions of the BAe Hawk.

sophisticated **BAC 167 Strikemaster**, a private-venture project which had side-by-side ejection seats and eight underwing hardpoints capable of carrying up to 1361 kg (3,000 lb) of stores. This ordnance capacity coupled with the more powerful Viper Mk 535 turbojet engine, made the Strikemaster particularly suitable for counter-insurgency

combat operations, reconnaissance, and pilot and weapon training. The Strikemaster was an extremely versatile aircraft, able to operate from rough strips, lifting as much as a specialised bomber would have been carrying in the 1930s, and delivering it at 644+ km/h (400+). The first Strikemaster flew on 26 October 1967, and a total of 146 were sold.

Strikemasters have been supplied to the air forces of Ecuador (**Mk 89**), Kenya, (**Mk 87**), Kuwait (**Mk 83**), New Zealand (**Mk 88**), Oman (**Mks 82/82A**), Saudi Arabia (**Mks 80/80A**), Singapore (**Mk 84**) and Sudan (**Mk 55** and **Mk 90**).

Specification
Type: two-seat light strike aircraft/trainer
Powerplant: one 1547-kg (3,410-lb) thrust Rolls-Royce viper Mk 535 turbojet

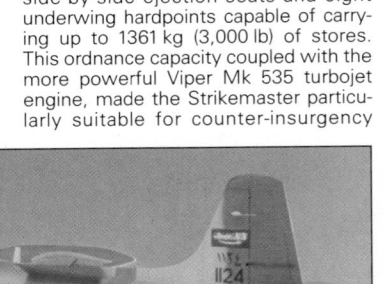

British Aerospace 167 Strikemaster Mk 83 of the Kuwaiti air force.

Performance: maximum speed with 50 per cent fuel (clean) 760 km/h (472 mph) at 6095 m (20,000 ft); range with 91 kg (200 lb) fuel reserves at maximum take-off weight 2224 km (1,382 miles)
Weights: empty equipped 2810 kg (6,195 lb); maximum take-off 5216 kg (11,500 lb)
Dimensions: span over tiptanks 11.23 m (36 ft 10 in); length 10.27 m (33 ft 8½ in); height 3.34 m (10 ft 11½ in); wing area 19.85 m² (213.70 sq ft)
Armament: two 7.62-mm (0.3-in) FN machine-guns, and four underwing hardpoints for up to 1202 kg (2,650 lb) stores with full fuel load, or a maximum of 1361 kg (3,000 lb); stores can include rockets; napalm tanks; general purpose, practice or retarded bombs; gun packs; reconnaissance pod; fuel drop tanks; and gun camera

British Aerospace (Beagle/Scottish Aviation) Bulldog

BAe Sk 61 Bulldog of Flottilj 5 of the Kungl Krigsflygskolan (Royal War Flying School), Flygvapen (Swedish air force), based at Ljungbyhed.

The aircraft now known as the **British Aerospace Bulldog** originated in 1968 as a military trainer development of the Beagle Pup, and the prototype (G-AXEH) flew for the first time on 19 May 1969; early in the following year Beagle Aircraft went into liquidation. The uncompleted second prototype (G-AXIG) was taken over by Scottish Aviation Ltd (now the Scottish Division of British Aerospace), and eventually made its first flight on 14 February 1971.

Before its demise, Beagle had obtained an order from the Swedish government for 78 Bulldogs (58 for the Swedish air force and 20 for the Swedish army), and these were produced by Scottish Aviation as the **Model 101** from 1971. Other Series 100 Bulldogs were built for the air forces of Kenya (five of the **Model 103**) and Malaysia (15 of the **Model 102**). The Royal Air Force ordered 130 of the **Bulldog T. Mk 1** to equip the University Air Squadrons, and although these were identified originally as the **Model 104**, the introduction of an improved Series 120 resulted in RAF Bulldogs becoming instead **Model 121**s. Other Series 120 aircraft were built subsequently for the air forces of

Ghana (six of the **Model 122** and seven of the **Model 122A**), Hong Kong (two of the **Model 128**), Jordan (13 of the **Model 125**), Kenya (nine of the **Model 127**), Lebanon (six of the **Model 126**), and Nigeria (32 of the **Model 123**).

Of cantilever low-wing monoplane configuration, and of all-metal construction, Bulldogs of both Series have non-retractable tricycle landing gear. All versions have side-by-side seating for instructor and pupil, with dual controls, and are fully aerobatic as two-seaters. The cockpit canopy is rearward-sliding and jettisonable, and a third (rear) seat is optional.

The prototype (G-BDOG) of a **Series 200** made its first flight on 20 August

1976. This differed from the Series 120 by a number of improvements, the most important being retractable landing gear. However, no production examples of this version were built.

Specification
Bulldog Series 120
Type: two/three-seat primary trainer
Powerplant: one 149-kW (200-hp) Avco Lycoming IO-360-A1B6 flat-four piston engine
Performance: maximum speed at sea level 241 km/h (150 mph); economic cruising speed 195 km/h (121 mph) at 1220 m (4,000 ft); service ceiling 4875 m (16,000 ft); range with maximum fuel 999 km (621 miles)

Weights: empty equipped 649 kg (1,430 lb); maximum take-off 1066 kg (2,350 lb)
Dimensions: span 10.06 m (33 ft 0 in); length 7.09 m (23 ft 3 in); height 2.28 m (7 ft 5¾ in); wing area 12.02 m² (129.4 sq ft)
Armament: normally none, but there is provision for the installation of four underwing hardpoints, which can carry a variety of weapons with a maximum combined weight of 290 kg (640 lb)

Primary training for the Royal Malaysian Air force is carried out by BAe Bulldog 102s, based at Alor Sator. These are similar to those originally sold to the RAF.

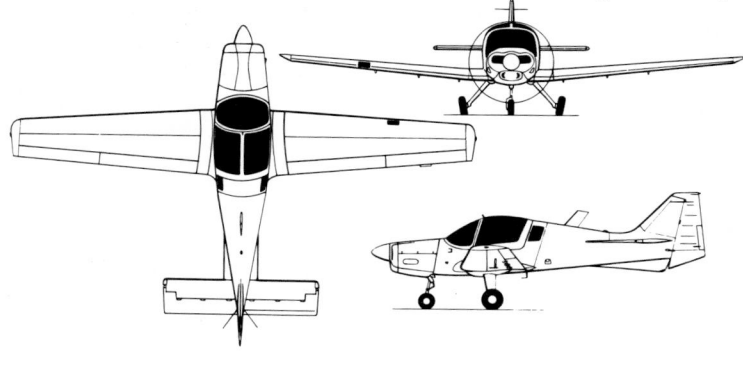

British Aerospace (D.H./HS) 125

Development of the aircraft known now as the **British Aerospace HS 125** began in 1961, when a de Havilland design team under the leadership of J. Goodwin began work on the **D.H. 125**. Intended to serve as a business transport aircraft, with accommodation for a crew of two and six to eight passengers, it was a forward-looking design and was known for a short period as the **Jet Dragon**. Of low-wing monoplane configuration and basically of all-metal construction, the design included a fail-safe pressurised fuselage, T-tail, retractable tricycle landing gear with twin wheels on each unit, and two Bristol Siddeley turbojet engines, one mounted in a pod on each side of the aft fuselage.

Two prototypes were built, the first (G-ARYA) making its maiden flight on 13 August 1962. Powered by Bristol Siddeley Viper 20 turbojets of 1361-kg (3,000-lb) thrust, these prototypes were both

flown extensively to gain early certification, being joined in this programme by the first production aircraft, which differed in having Viper 520 turbojets of the same thrust, and with wing span and length increased by 0.91 m (3 ft 0 in) and 1.19 m (3 ft 11 in) respectively.

Only eight **D.H.125 Series 1** production aircraft were built before the introduction of Viper 521 and 522 engines of 1406-kg (3,100-lb) thrust, which resulted

in the **D.H.125 Series 1A/1B** aircraft operating at higher gross weights. The company believed that the D.H.125 would have good sales potential in North America, appointing distributors and using the eighth aircraft for a long demonstration tour. This faith was justified and in March 1990 when sales totalling 763 had been made to 40 countries worldwide, some 60 per cent of this total had been supplied to the North

American market.

By the time of that sales tour, de Havilland had been absorbed into the Hawker Siddeley group, and it was this company that continued production and development of the aircraft under the designation HS 125. The **HS 125 Series 2** accounted for 20 navigation trainers which entered service with the RAF with the designation **Dominie T.Mk 1**, and this service acquired subsequently

British Aerospace 125 Series 3B, used as a navigation/crew trainer by QANTAS

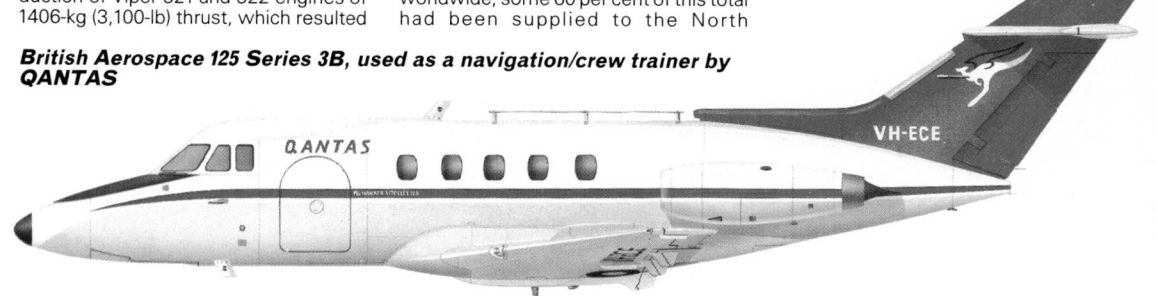

The Series 700 represented a major advance over earlier 125 variants. Drag-reducing external modifications were combined with low fuel consumption TFE731 turbofans to increase range.

122 CC.Mk 1, CC.Mk 2 and **CC.Mk 3** communications aircraft from later production series. **HS 125 Series 3** and **HS 125 Series 400** aircraft differed primarily by having more powerful variants of the Viper 522, but a major change was introduced on the **HS 125 Series 600** which had a fuselage lengthened by 0.94 m (3 ft 1 in) to provide accommodation for a maximum of 14 passengers in a high density layout.

The next production version was the **HS 125 Series 700**, first introduced in 1976, which benefited from the installation of Garrett turbofan engines that, by comparison with the Viper turbojets, are more efficient users of fuel. This version also had many detail improvements to provide optimum performance and comfort.

This was followed by the **Series 800**, which first flew on 26 May 1983. Featuring considerable upgrades, such as a curved windscreen, extended wings and a longer fin leading edge, the 800 is the current production model, of which 183 had been sold by March 1990. Six aircraft have been supplied to the US Air Force as **C-29A**s for navaid calibration work, with three similar aircraft ordered by Japan. In addition to the HS 125s that serve in a military capacity with the RAF,

small numbers have been supplied also to the Argentine navy, Brazilian air force, Royal Malaysian air force and the South African air force.

Variants

BAe HS 125 Protector: maritime surveillance version of the Series 700, for the surveillance role the Protector is equipped with specially-developed search radar, nav/com systems and cameras, and has a search endurance of approximately six hours

Specification

The 125 was procured by the Royal Air Force as the Dominie T.Mk 1, incorporating Decca Doppler radar for navigation training duties. These fly alongside Jetstreams and Jet Provosts with 6 FTS.

BAe HS 125 Series 700
Type: light civil transport or military aircraft
Powerplant: two 1678-kg (3,700-lb) thrust Garrett TFE 731-3-1H turbofans
Performance: maximum cruising speed 808 km/h (502 mph) at 7620 m (25,000 ft); economic cruising speed 723 km/h (449 mph) between 11280 and 12495 m (37,000 and 41,000 ft); service ceiling 12495 m (41,000 ft);

range with maximum fuel and payload with allowances and 45-min reserves 4482 km (2,785 miles)
Weights: empty 5826 kg (12,845 lb); maximum take-off 11567 kg (25,500 lb)
Dimensions: span 14.33 m (47 ft 0 in); length 15.46 m (50 ft 8½ in); height 5.36 m (17 ft 7 in); wing area 32.79 m² (353 sq ft)

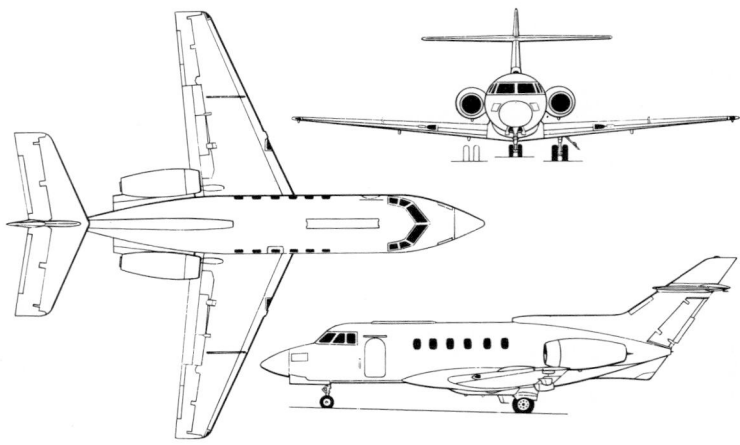

British Aerospace 125 Series 700

British Aerospace (Scottish Aviation) Jetstream

The name of Handley Page, once an integral part of the British aviation industry, disappeared from the active scene into aviation history in early 1970, following celebration of the company's diamond jubilee on 17 June 1969. The straw which finally broke the camel's back was the **Handley Page H.P.137** project for a twin-turboprop executive/feederliner transport, within the 12/20-seat capacity as orginally envisaged. When, in January 1966, the company decided to begin the construction of four prototypes, the launch costs were estimated at £3 million, but by the time the certification programme was well advanced, in August 1969, these had already exceeded £13 million, and on 8 August the company went into voluntary liquidation.

Following attempts to continue production with financial backing from the USA, as Handley Page Aircraft Ltd, and later by a newly formed Jetstream Aircraft Ltd which continued manufacture of the aircraft, it was finally Scottish Aviation Ltd which was to lose its identity as the Scottish Division of British Aerospace Aircraft Group on 1 January 1978.

Definitive civil version was the **Jetstream Series 200**, developed initially by Handley Page as a conventional low-wing monoplane of all-metal fail-safe

British Aerospace Jetstream T.Mk 1 multi-engine trainer of No. 6 Flying Training School, RAF Finningley.

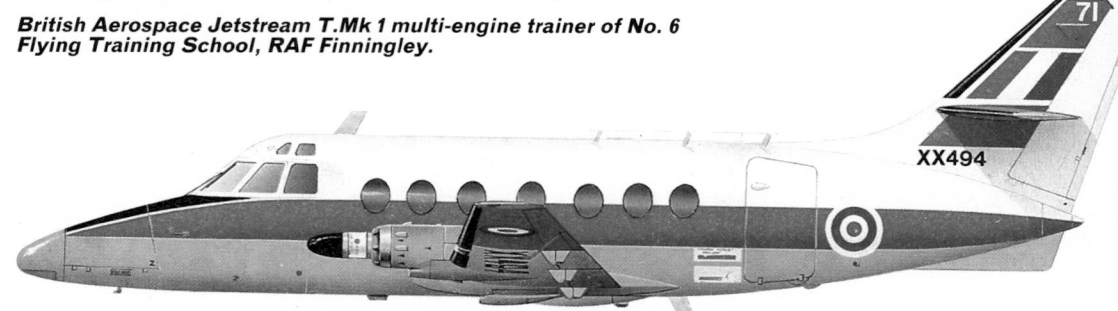

structure. Landing gear was of the hydraulically retractable tricycle type, and the pressurised cabin accommodated a crew of two on the flight deck, and a maximum of 18 passengers. Powerplant of civil Jetstream 200s comprised two Turboméca Astazou XVI turboprops, but earlier versions (**Jetstream 1**) completed by Handley Page and supplied to International Jetstream Corporation in the USA were powered by 626-ekW (840-ehp) Astazou XIV engines. Many were converted subsequently by Riley Aircraft of Carlsbad, California, to **Riley Jetstream** configuration with Astazou XVI engines. One, named *Life of Riley*, had two 584-ekW (783-ehp) Pratt & Whitney Aircraft of

British Aerospace Jetstream 31

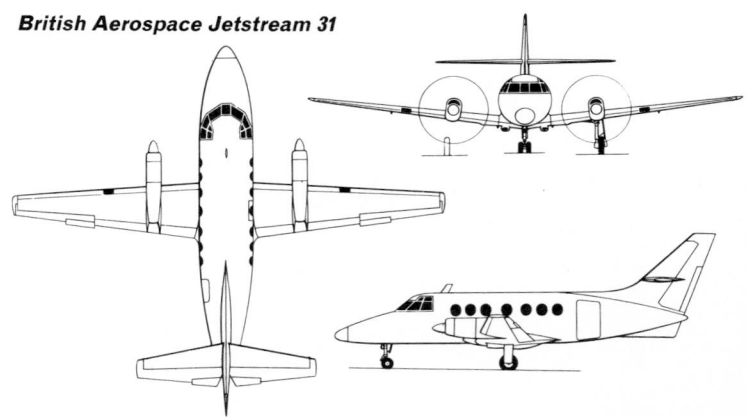

Canada PT6A-34 turboprops installed.

As early as 1967 there had been good prospects for military versions of the Jetstream, following the receipt of an order from the USAF. This was for 11 examples of the **Jetstream 3M**, which would have been designated **C-10A** in US Air Force service, plus options for 300 additional aircraft. This order was subsequently cancelled, but in February 1972 the RAF ordered 26 of the **Jetstream 201** variant. Similar to the civil Series 200, this model differs by having 743-ekW (996-ehp) Turboméca Astazou XVID turboprop engines, new 'eyebrow' windows above the flight deck, plus instrumentation and avionics to meet service requirements. The first of these (XX475) was flown on 13 April 1973, and all had been delivered by early 1976, but they were temporarily placed in storage pending a decision on their utilisation. In October of that year it was announced that eight were to be used by the RAF as **Jetstream T.Mk 1** multi-engine pilot trainers, and that 16 would be modified to serve with the Royal Navy as **Jetstream T.Mk 2** aircraft for observer training. The latter differed mainly from the RAF version by the installation of MEL E 190 weather and terrain-mapping radar in a nose radome. The **Jetstream**

T.Mk 3 featured radar in a ventral radome.

On 5 December 1978 British Aerospace announced its intention to develop a new version of this aircraft under the designation **Jetstream 31**. A development aircraft (G-JSSD), converted from a Jetstream 1, was flown for the first time on 28 March 1980, and the first production example (G-TALL) was rolled out on 25 January 1982. The contrived registration of this last aircraft was intended to highlight its superior cabin height by comparison with its direct competitors. It first flew on 18 March 1982 and received UK certification on 29 June. US approval followed on 30 November. Customers in the UK and Germany took the first deliveries in December. The Jetstream 31 is available

in four versions: a **Jetstream 31 Airliner**, designed to carry 18/19 passengers and baggage; a **Jetstream 31 Corporate** executive version seating 8/10 passengers; a **Jetstream Executive Shuttle** with 12-seat corporate interior; and a **Jetstream 31 Special**, which is intended for such roles as airfield calibration, cargo, casualty evacuation, military communications, multi-engine training, and resources survey and protection.

The Jetstream 31 and **Super 31** (featuring an increase in take-off weight) are to be joined by a stretched version, the **Jetstream 41** seating up to 29 passengers and intended for regional airlines. By March 1990 310 Jetstream 31s had been ordered.

Specification
BAe Jetstream 31
Type: light commuter/executive transport
Powerplant: two 671-kW (900-shp) Garrett TPE331-10 turboprops
Performance: (estimated) maximum cruising speed 488 km/h (303 mph); service ceiling 9630 m (31,600 ft); range with maximum payload and reserves 779 km (484 miles)
Weights: (estimated) manufacturer's empty 3450 kg (7,606 lb); maximum take-off 6600 kg (14,550 lb)
Dimensions: span 15.85 m (52 ft 0 in); length 14.36 m (47 ft 1½ in); height 5.32 m (17 ft 5½ in); wing area 25.08 m^2 (270 sq ft)

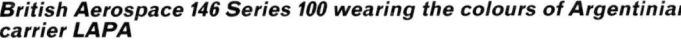

British Aerospace Jetstream I of Apollo Airways (USA)

British Aerospace (HS) 146

On 29 August 1973, Hawker Siddeley Aviation announced that the company was to receive support from the UK government to develop a new short-range transport aircraft which had been given the designation **Hawker Siddeley HS 146**. In its initial **HS 146 Series 100** version it was intended to provide accommodation for 71-88 passengers, to be capable of operation from short semi-prepared airstrips, and also to offer the benefits of comparatively low operating costs. The first flight of the first Series 100 pre-production aircraft was scheduled for December 1975.

This was not to be, for in the autumn of 1974 a worldwide recession resulted from the oil crisis of 1973-4, and in October Hawker Siddeley decided to suspend this programme. As it was a suspension, rather than a termination, minimal funds were allocated each year to keep the project alive, with design and research continuing on a restricted basis. Then, on 29 April 1977, Hawker Siddeley was absorbed into the newly-formed British Aerospace Corporation: the project continues now, with work

British Aerospace 146 Series 100 wearing the colours of Argentinian carrier LAPA

The 146 combines STOL capability, excellent load-carrying and extremely quiet operations.

being carried out at several factories of what is known as British Aerospace Aircraft Group. The decision to reinstate the HS 146 as an active programme was reached on 10 July 1978, following intensive research into potential markets.

Hawker Siddeley's HS 146 project had evolved through a series of designs embracing both high- and low-wing configurations, and with a variety of engine layouts. As the **BAe 146** it was finalised as a high-wing cantilever monoplane of light alloy construction, with a basically circular-section fuselage of 3.56 m (11 ft 8 in) diameter to provide comfortable five-abreast seating for 71 passengers in a pressurised, air-conditioned environment. Alternative six-abreast seating

accommodates a maximum of 93 passengers, and the **BAe 146 Series 200** with a fuselage lengthened by 2.39 m (7 ft 10 in) seats a maximum of 109 passengers.

The evaluation of suitable powerplants was extensive, but final choice was the Avco Lycoming ALF-502R-3 high-bypass-ratio turbofan, four of these being mounted in underwing pods. Designed for operation from surfaces which can include short semi-prepared airstrips, the retractable tricycle landing gear has twin wheels on each unit, and heavy-duty brakes, anti-skid units, lift-dumpers and airbrakes combine to provide the BAe 146 with exceptional short-field landing performance.

Risk-sharing partners include the Avco

Corporation in the USA (providing powerplant and wing boxes), and Saab-Scania in Sweden (tailplane and control surfaces). Short Brothers in the UK is a sub-contractor, manufacturing the pylon-mounted pods for the engines.

The Series 100 prototype (G-SSSH) made its maiden flight on 3 September 1981, followed by a second (G-SSHH) on 25 January 1982. The first Series 200 flew on 1 August 1982, and was followed on 1 May 1987 by the stretched **Series 300** offering seating for up to 128.

Among the variants on offer are a

British Aerospace 146 Series 100 (lower side view; Series 200)

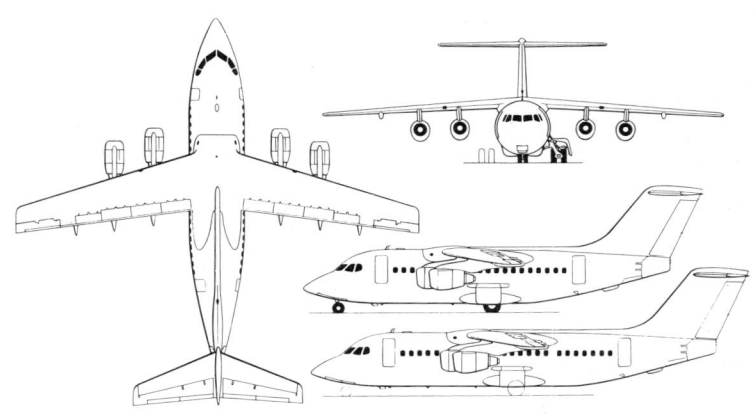

146QT (Quiet Trader) freighter version, **146QC** convertible passenger/freight transport, **Statesman** VIP/corporate transport and the **146STA** military side-loading transport based on the Series 100 with inflight-refuelling and para-dropping doors. A military rear-loader has been proposed, and a tanker version.

By May 1990, 186 146s of all versions had been ordered.

Specification
BAe 146-100
Type: short-range commercial transport

Powerplant: four 3039-kg (6,700-lb) thrust each Avco Lycoming ALF-502R-3 turbofans
Performance: (estimated) maximum cruising speed 776 km/h (428 mph) at 7925 m (26,000 ft); economic cruising speed 687 km/h (427 mph) at 9145 m (30,000 ft); range with maximum fuel,

including reserves 2872 km (1,785 miles)
Weights: (estimated) operating empty 20670 kg (45,570 lb); maximum take-off 36628 kg (80,750 lb)
Dimensions: span 26.34 m (86 ft 5 in); length 26.16 m (85 ft 10 in); height 8.61 m (28 ft 3 in); wing area 77.29 m² (832.0 sq ft)

British Aerospace (HS) Harrier

21 years after its entry into service the **BAe (HS) Harrier** is still, with the sole exception of the USSR's later but far less sophisticated Yakovlev Yak-36 'Forger', unique as the world's only operational V/STOL (vertical/short take-off and landing) combat aircraft. The origins of its design go back to 1957, when Sir Sydney Camm of Hawker Aircraft and Dr Stanley Hooker of Bristol Siddeley Engines got together to design a tactical aircraft around Bristol's radical new turbofan engine, then known as the BS.53. Evolved specifically to give jet-lift to vertical take-off fixed-wing aircraft, the BS.53's exhaust airflow was discharged through four nozzles, in fore-and-aft pairs, each of which could be pivoted through more than 90° to vector (direct) the exhaust thrust rearward, vertically downwards, or to any intermediate angle. Around the Pegasus, as the engine was eventually christened, Camm designed an essentially conventional all-metal shoulder-wing monoplane of compact dimensions, with anhedral on the wings and tailplane, a single-seat cockpit in the nose, and a large semi-circular fixed-geometry air intake on each side of the fuselage. The landing gear was less orthodox, comprising a single nosewheel and twin main wheels, mounted in tandem on the centreline, plus a small balancer wheel on a retractable outrigger leg at each wingtip.

With the complexities of operating the world's first operational V/STOL jet, the RAF required several two-seat trainers of the Harrier. This aircraft wears the markings of No. 4 Sqn from Gütersloh.

Known in its original form as the **Hawker P.1127**, the first of six prototypes made its initial hovering flight on 21 October 1960. Less than a year later, on 12 September 1961, the first complete transitions were made to and from vertical and horizontal flight. Vertical take-off was accomplished by vectoring the thrust from the engine downwards; after a safe height was reached, the four nozzles were rotated slowly rearward to provide forward thrust for the transition to horizontal flight. As soon as forward speed increased sufficiently for wing lift to support the aircraft, the nozzles were rotated fully aft. This sequence was reversed for vertical landing. To stabilise the aircraft during hovering and low-speed manoeuvres, small reaction control jets mounted in the nose, tail and each wingtip were activated; operated by the control column and rudder pedals, these utilised compressed air bled from the engine.

In-flight transitions soon became commonplace, and Hawker Siddeley was awarded a contract for nine more advanced pre-production aircraft to undergo evaluation in the fighter/ground-attack roles. These were known as the **Kestrel F(GA).1,** the first example making its maiden flight on 7 March 1964. Subsequently, a special three-nation squadron was formed in the UK, with pilots from the Royal Air Force, the Federal German Luftwaffe and all three US services. Between April and November 1965 this unit tested the Kestrel under various simulated operational conditions.

Before this, however, the British government had already ordered, in February 1965, another six development aircraft. These were the first to be given

the name **Harrier**, and the first made its initial flight on 31 August 1966. By that time the Mach 2 **Hawker Siddeley P.1154** multi-role V/STOL aircraft intended for the RAF and Royal Navy had been replaced by production Harriers for the RAF only. The single-seat **Harrier GR.1** was developed for ground-attack/reconnaissance, and the tandem two-seat **Harrier T.2** for combat readiness training. Total orders for the RAF subsequently rose to 132 single-seaters and 19 of the two-seat version, the first pro-

duction examples of each model making their maiden flights on 28 December 1967 and 24 April 1969 respectively.

The Harrier officially entered service with the Royal Air Force on 1 April 1969 – the service's 51st birthday – the first aircraft being used to equip an Operational Conversion Unit at RAF Wittering, Cambridgeshire. In the following year the first Harrier T.2s entered service, and both initial models were powered by Pegasus 101 turbofans of 8618-kg (19,000-lb) static thrust. They were later upgraded, being redesignated **Harrier GR.1A** and **Harrier T.2A** after refitting with 9072-kg (20,000-lb) Pegasus 102s; currently they are designated **Harrier GR.3** and **Harrier T.4**, powered by Pegasus 103s, and equipped one RAF squadron in the UK and three in West Germany. The RAF generally operated the Harrier GR.3 as a STOVL (short take-off and vertical landing) aircraft, since with a short take-off run it could carry a greater load of weapons than when taking off vertically. Equipment includes an inertial system, inflight-refuelling probe, head-up display and laser range-finder. Both the two-seater and the single-seater have the same nominal weapon-carrying capability, though the two-seater has a greater empty weight. A development of the Harrier is the Sea Harrier, which is in service with the Royal Navy.

At about the time that the Harrier entered RAF service, an initial buy of 12 was made by the US Marine Corps. This service, one of the first in the world to exploit the helicopter for tactical warfare in Korea and Vietnam, well appreciated the operational flexibility offered by VTOL. The prospect of allying this to the performance of a fixed-wing jet combat aircraft was too strong to resist, and the initial order was soon raised to 110, in-

British Aerospace Harrier GR.Mk 3 (lower side view: T.Mk 4)

cluding eight two-seaters. USMC Harriers, designated **AV-8A** and **TAV-8A** respectively, had Pegasus 103 engines, but lacked several of the navigation/attack systems of the RAF's Harrier GR.3. Instead they carried AIM-9 Sidewinder missiles for air-to-air combat. The USMC had one training and three operational squadrons equipped with the Harrier, and stated a requirement for 336 examples of the Advanced Harrier, the **BAe/McDonnell Douglas AV-8B**, which the RAF operates as the **Harrier GR.5**. In-service AV-8As were upgraded to AV-8C standard with a host of modifications to the airframe and systems.

The only other operator of the standard Harrier, equivalent to the USMC versions, is the Spanish navy, by whom the aircraft is known as the Matador. Nine **AV-8S** and two **TAV-8S Matador** aircraft now equip one Spanish squadron since augmented by AV-8Bs.

The Harrier GR.Mk 3 now serves only with the OCU (No. 233) and a flight in Belize (No. 1417), having been replaced by the GR.Mk 5 and 7 with front-line units. It provided over 20 years' operational VTOL experience.

Specification
BAe Harrier GR.Mk 3
Type: V/STOL close support and reconnaissance aircraft
Powerplant: one 9752-kg (21,500-lb) thrust Rolls-Royce Pegasus Mk 103 vectored-thrust turbofan
Performance: maximum speed at low altitude over 1186 km/h (737 mph); service ceiling over 15240 m (50,000 ft); range with one inflight-refuelling more than 5560 km (3,455 miles)
Weights: basic operating empty with pilot 5579 kg (12,300 lb); maximum take-off 11340 kg (25,000 lb)

Dimensions: span 7.7 m (25 ft 3 in); length 13.87 m (45 ft 6 in); height 3.45 m (11 ft 4 in); wing area 18.68 m² (201.1 sq ft)

Armament: up to a normal maximum of 2268 kg (5,000 lb) of stores on underfuselage and underwing hardpoints.

British Aerospace (HS) Hawk

The **British Aerospace Hawk,** originally known as the **Hawker Siddeley HS.1182,** replaced the Royal Air Force's Gnat and Hunter trainers.

The HS.1182 was selected for the RAF in 1971 in preference to a BAC design; five months later the Adour turbofan was chosen in place of the Rolls-Royce Viper turbojet. In March 1972 an order was placed for 176 **Hawk T.Mk 1**s. There was no prototype and only one pre-production aircraft, the first 10 production Hawks being allocated to the test programme. This saved considerable time, and the first two operational aircraft were handed over to the RAF in November 1976.

The Hawk is a tandem-seat transonic ground-attack and training aircraft of conventional layout, with a low-mounted wing. Its primary structure is designed for a safe fatigue life of 6,000 hours in the exacting conditions demanded by the RAF. Simplicity of design and manufacture are emphasised to ensure that

the aircraft has a high utilisation rate and is inexpensive to operate. One man can prepare the aircraft for its next flight in fewer than 20 minutes between sorties, and in the weapon-training role it can be re-armed by four men in fewer than 15 minutes.

Low operating costs are contributed to by the efficient Adour turbofan, which is an unaugmented version of that employed in the SEPECAT Jaguar. The Adour is of modular construction, so the spares holding is reduced. Any module can be changed without the need to re-balance the rotating assemblies, and large doors beneath the engine bay permit easy access and removal. An integral gas-turbine starter running off the aircraft's fuel supply makes the Hawk independent of external aids.

The Hawk had a remarkably trouble-free development programme, entering service only 27 months after its maiden flight. All performance objectives were met, and the top speed proved to be

higher than expected. The aircraft has reached Mach 1.15 in a dive and has a maximum level speed of Mach 0.88, allowing student pilots to experience transonic handling before they progress to true supersonic types.

The RAF operates the aircraft for weapon instruction (designation **Hawk T.Mk 1A**) as well as flying training, with three pylons. The centreline pylon is

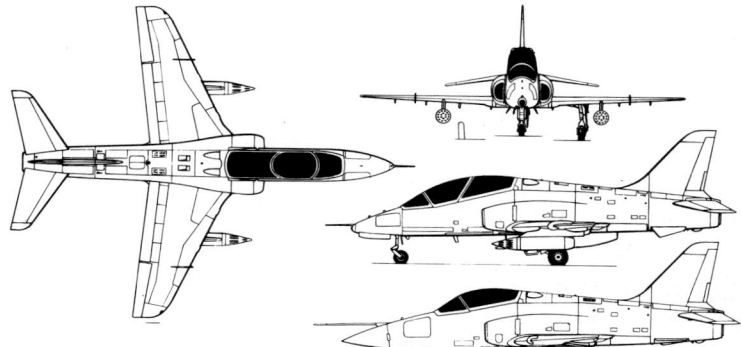

British Aerospace Hawk Mk 60 (lower side view: Hawk 200)

In addition to its advanced training role, the Hawk is a useful light attack/weapons training platform. The RAF uses it in the latter role in its T.Mk 1A version which serves with 1 (illustrated) and 2 TWUs.

normally occupied by an Aden cannon pod, with Matra rocket launchers or practice bombs beneath the wings. Potential export customers often demand heavier armament, however, and British Aerospace has tested the Hawk with about 40 combinations of air-to-surface and air-to-air weaponry. Two stations can be fitted beneath each wing, giving a total of five, and the use of multiple racks allows the aircraft to carry an exceptional 2954 kg (6,500 lb) of stores in the form of six 454-kg (1,000-lb) bombs plus the Aden gun-pack. Wingtip air-to-air missiles can also be carried following modification.

RAF Hawks serve with Nos 1 and 2 Tactical Weapon Units, at Brawdy, Wales, and Chivenor, Devon, respectively, No. 4 Flying Training School at RAF Valley, and with the CFS and Red Arrows aerobatic display team at RAF Scampton. Export Hawks include **Mk 50** aircraft with Adour 851 for Finland (who licence-built 46 of their 50 aircraft), Indonesia and Kenya. The **Mk 60** series with the uprated Adour 861 has been supplied to Abu Dhabi, Dubai, Kuwait, Saudi Arabia, South Korea, Switzerland and Zimbabwe.

A team comprising British Aerospace, together with McDonnell Douglas and Sperry in the USA, was selected by the US Navy on 19 November 1981 to continue programme development work on the Navy's VTX/TS requirement. This resulted in the **McDonnell Douglas/ BAe T-45A Goshawk**, suitably modified for carrier operations training with strong undercarriage and arrester hook, of which 302 are on order.

Two derivatives of the Mk 60 are concerned with combat disciplines. The **Hawk 100** has combat avionics such as a HUD, laser rangefinder and FLIR to exploit the weapons capability of the Hawk. Wingtip rails can carry air-to-air missiles. The more radical **Hawk 200** is a single-seat modification which can mount laser, FLIR or APG-66 radar in the nose. Customers for these variants so far are Brunei, Oman, South Korea and Saudi Arabia. In early 1990, total commitments for all Hawk variants had reached 689.

Specification
BAe Hawk T.Mk 1
Type: two-seat basic and advanced jet trainer
Powerplant: one 2359-kg (5,200-lb) thrust Rolls-Royce/Turboméca Adour Mk 151 turbofan
Performance: maximum speed 1038 km/h (645 mph); service ceiling 15240 m (50,000 ft); ferry range clean 2430 km (1,510 miles); endurance 4 hours
Weights: empty 3647 kg (8,040 lb); maximum take-off 7750 kg (17,085 lb)
Dimensions: span 9.39 m (30 ft 9¾ in); length, excluding probe 11.17 m (36 ft 7¾ in); height 3.99 m (13 ft 1¾ in); wing area 16.69 m² (179.64 sq ft)
Armament: underfuselage/wing hardpoints to accommodate 2567 kg (5,660 lb) of external stores.

British Aerospace (HS) Nimrod MR

Named after the 'mighty hunter' of the Book of Genesis, the **BAe Nimrod MR** derives from the de Havilland Comet, the world's first jet airliner. The Comet had been adopted as a military transport by the Royal Air Force in 1955, and when in early 1965 the RAF was seeking a new maritime patrol aircraft, the British government decided to see if this requirement could be met by adapting the basic airframe of the Comet 4. The outcome of that programme is now acknowledged as one of the finest overwater patrol and anti-submarine aircraft in current service.

Two **Hawker Siddeley HS 801** prototypes were modified from existing Comet 4C airframes, the first of them (XV148) being given Rolls-Royce Spey turbofan engines, while the second (XV147) retained its original Avon turbojets. Structural changes included a new shorter (by 1.98 m/6 ft 6 in) fuselage, with an unpressurised underfuselage pannier to accommodate operational equipment and a 14.78 m (48 ft 6 in) long weapons bay. Wings, horizontal tail surfaces and landing gear were generally similar to those of the Comet 4C, except that the landing gear units were strengthened for operation at higher gross

Wearing the current standard 'hemp' colour scheme, this Nimrod MR.Mk 2 is pictured before a considerable modification programme which added refuelling probe, wingtip ESM pods and tailplane blade aerials. Nimrods were highly active during the Falklands war and were deployed to the Gulf in response to the invasion of Kuwait.

weights. New structural features included a large dorsal fin, an electronic support measures (ESM) pod mounted on top of the fin, a magnetic anomaly detector (MAD) boom extending aft from the rear fuselage, a searchlight incorporated in the forward end of the starboard leading-edge fuel tank, and underwing pylons for air-to-surface missiles. The first (Spey-powered) HS 801 made its initial flight on 23 May 1967, the second (Avon-powered) following on 31 July 1967.

A contract for 38 production aircraft was placed, these being known under the designation **Nimrod MR.1**. The first of these flew on 28 June 1968, and deliveries began to No. 201 Squadron of RAF Strike Command in October of the following year. A further batch of eight Nimrod MR.1s was ordered in 1972, to permit the equipping of six RAF squadrons (Nos 42, 120, 201, 203, 206 and one other) with this version of the Nimrod. In the previous year, however, three examples of a different version, known as the **Nimrod R.1**, were received by No. 51 Squadron. These three aircraft each have a shorter, blunt tail cone and wing leading-edge pods of modified size and shape, and are especially equipped and used for electronic intelligence missions.

Primary Nimrod roles, for which the aircraft carries a standard crew of 12, are those of anti-submarine warfare, maritime surveillance and anti-shipping strike. The large weapons bay can accommodate a wide variety of ordnance, in addition to which there is ample storage space in the rear of the pressurised fuselage compartment for sonobuoys, marine markers and other

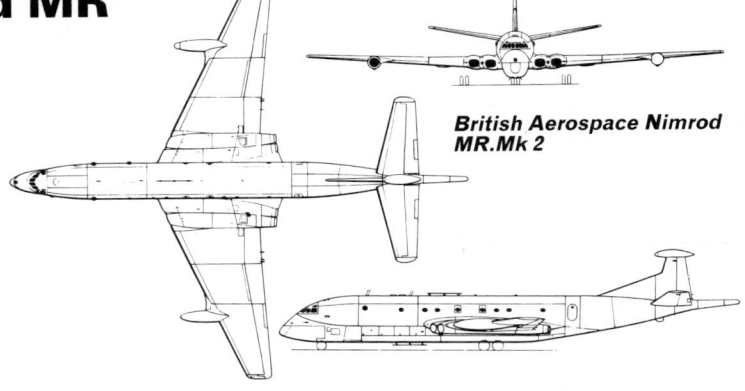

British Aerospace Nimrod MR.Mk 2

detection gear. Typical patrol endurance is 12 hours, and an on-station patrol of more than six hours can be maintained at a distance of 1850 km (1,150 miles) from shore base. This capability is made possible by cruising on only two engines, with the other pair shut down, and the Nimrod can, if necessary, cruise and climb on only one engine. Range can be extended still further by the installation of up to six auxiliary fuel tanks in the weapons bay. Search radar in the nose is an ASV.21D by EMI, and a Marconi computer-based system provides integrated navigation/weapon selection and delivery with appropriate operator displays in the tactical compartment. If required, the Nimrod can be used in a secondary transport role, with seats for up to 45 troops.

From 1975, 32 of the RAF's fleet of Nimrod MR.1s underwent a modernisation programme, with the first completely refitted aircraft, redesignated **Nimrod MR.2**, being redelivered to the RAF on 23 August 1979. Only five of the additional Nimrod MR.1s ordered in 1972 were delivered as such: one was used as the Nimrod MR.2 development aircraft, and the other two for development of the **Nimrod AEW.3**. Though a great deal of work is involved, the primary purpose of this Nimrod MR.2 conversion is to modernise and improve the operational equipment. Nimrods are expected to serve well into the 1990s, and in many respects the Nimrod MR.2 is superior to all other aircraft operated in a similar role.

Specification
BAe Nimrod MR.1
Type: maritime anti-shipping, anti-submarine, patrol and surveillance aircraft
Powerplant: four 5507-kg (12,140-lb) thrust each Rolls-Royce RB.168-20 Spey Mk 250 turbofans
Performance: maximum operational speed 925 km/h (575 mph); maximum cruising speed 880 km/h (547 mph); low-level patrol speed 370 km/h (230 mph); normal operational ceiling 12800 m (42,000 ft); typical ferry range 9262 km (5,755 miles); typical endurance 12 hours
Weights: typical empty 39009 kg (86,000 lb); maximum overload take-off 87090 kg (192,000 lb)
Dimensions: span 35 m (114 ft 10 in); length 38.63 m (126 ft 9 in); height 9.98 m (29 ft 8½ in); wing area 197.04 m² (2,121 sq ft)
Armament: wide variety of ASW weapons in weapons bay, though torpedoes and bombs are used primarily by the RAF; there is a second bay, for sonobuoys and launchers, in the rear of the pressurised fuselage; there is also a hardpoint beneath each wing for mine, gun- or rocket-pod, or air-to-surface missiles

British Aerospace Nimrod AEW.3
to
Britten-Norman BN-2A Mk III Trislander

British Aerospace Nimrod AEW.3

Detailed studies began in 1973 for an airborne early warning (AEW) version of the Nimrod, required to replace the RAF's Avro Shackletons in a role recognised as vital to the defence of the UK. The large capacity fuselage and ample reserve of power in the standard MR versions of the Nimrod offered considerable potential for the carriage of alternative equipment and the performance of other roles. After deliberating whether or not to participate in NATO plans to buy the Boeing E-3A, the British government decided in March 1977 to finance instead a developed version of the Nimrod.

Externally the resulting **BAe Nimrod AEW.3** version violated even further the original good looks of the Comet design. This was due mainly to the grotesquely swollen radomes mounted at each end of the fuselage, each housing a dual-frequency antenna. Because of their fore and aft location, the efficiency of these scanners was not reduced as a result of screening by other parts of the airframe, as is the case with the dorsally-mounted radar antenna of the Boeing E-3A or Grumman E-2C. The other outward sign of change in the Nimrod AEW.3 was the presence at each wingtip of a pod containing electronic support measures (ESM) equipment.

An onboard digital computer controlled the flow of data from the scanners (target range, speed, height and other data) and also correlated this information with a control station on the ground. The scanners, which were interfaced with the Nimrod's IFF (identification, friend or foe) system, were also part of a pulse-Doppler radar installation capable of ship surveillance as well as aircraft detection, and highly resistant to electronic jamming. Thus, despite its AEW designation, the Nimrod's function could have been defined more accurately by the AWACS (airborne warning and control system) description applied by the Americans to the Boeing E-3A.

Using the basic Nimrod airframe, the AEW.Mk 3 added giant radomes fore and aft to house the antennae for the radar.

The Nimrod's systems were intended to detect, track and classify aircraft, missiles or ships; control an interceptor fighter force; direct retaliatory strike aircraft; serve as an airborne air traffic control centre; or manage a search and rescue operation.

The first development aircraft, a converted Comet 4C (XW626), made its initial flight on 28 June 1977 carrying the nose radome only; and the first aerodynamically representative Nimrod AEW.3 (XZ286) made its initial flight on 16 July 1980. There was only a marginal change in directional stability resulting from the structural changes, compensated by an increase of 0.91 m (3 ft 0 in) in fin height. An initial quantity of 11 production Nimrod AEW.3s was ordered for service with the RAF, and it was anticipated that the first of these would begin to enter service with No. 8 Squadron at Waddington, Lincs, in early 1982. However, continuing problems with the technical capabilities of the system caused its eventual cancellation. The order passed to the Boeing E-3D Sentry, the first of seven aircraft arriving in No. 8 Squadron colours in July 1990.

Specification
Type: airborne early warning and control aircraft
Powerplant: four 5507-kg (12,140-lb) thrust each Rolls-Royce RB.168-20 Spey Mk 250 turbofans

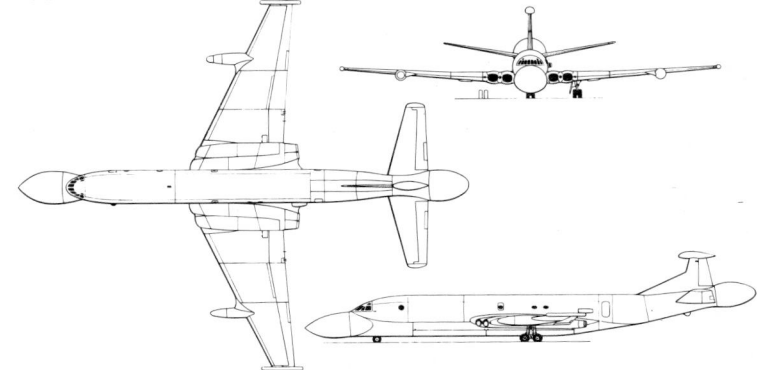

British Aerospace Nimrod AEW.Mk 3

Performance: data not available, but expected to be generally similar to that of Nimrod MR.2 versions
Weights: data not available
Dimensions: span over wingtip pods 35.08 m (115 ft 1 in); length 41.97 m (137 ft 8½ in); height 10.67 m (35 ft 0 in)

British Aerospace Sea Harrier

In 1969, watching a Harrier taking off vertically from the aft platform deck of the USS *Coronado*, a certain US admiral is reported to have said: 'You Brits gave us the angled deck, the mirror sight and the steam catapult – and now you've taken them all away!' The admiral had a point; conversely, it is fortunate for the Royal Navy, which over the past two decades, has seen its aircraft-carrier force eroded to nil by successive governments, that the UK has the Harrier. Not only has this unique warplane revolutionised land-based tactical combat techniques, but also its ability to operate from aft-platform warships, as well as conventional aircraft-carriers, has introduced a new factor into the tactics of surface vessel warfare.

Standard (i.e. land-based) Harriers have carried out innumerable trials and demonstrations from a wide variety of naval ships. With the Royal Navy and the US Marine Corps both keenly interested in an advanced version for their own use, it was hoped that such a variant could be evolved as a joint effort with McDonnell Douglas, Hawker Siddeley's American licensee. However, the British government decided in 1975 that there was not enough common ground between the two projected models, and that the UK would go it alone in developing an advanced Harrier for the Royal Navy. Nevertheless, it should not be supposed that the **BAe Sea Harrier FRS.Mk 1** is in any way a 'poor man's AV-8B', and in many ways it offers significant improvements in operational capability compared with the Harrier GR.Mk 3 of the Royal Air Force.

These improvements result from changes that include the introduction of a raised cockpit, a revision of operational avionics and, most importantly, the installation of Ferranti Blue Fox multi-mode radar. This is housed in a redesigned nose than can be folded to port for carrier stowage. The Sea Harrier can also carry the full range of weapons or surveillance equipment available for the land-based versions, but in addition can

British Aerospace Sea Harrier FRS.Mk 1

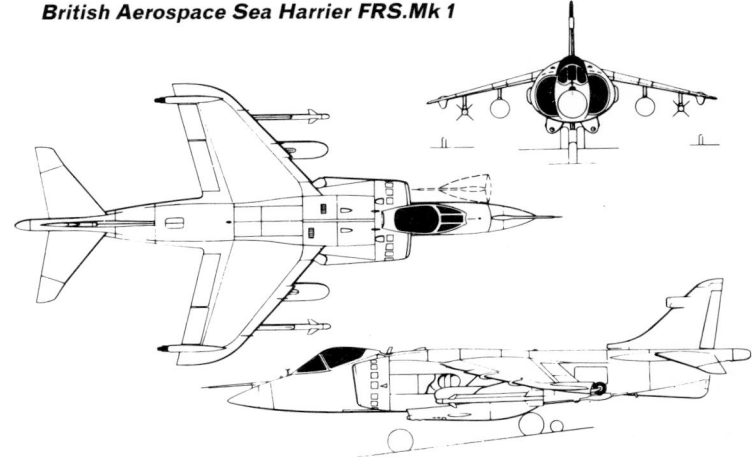

carry up to 4 heat-seeking Sidewinders, and has provision for two air-to-surface missiles of Sea Eagle or Harpoon type.

A total of 57 Sea Harriers has been ordered for service with the Royal Navy. In addition, the Royal Navy has acquired four standard **Harrier T.Mk 4N** two-seaters for land-based training. The Sea Harriers equip No. 899 HQ Squadron at RNAS Yeovilton, and Nos 800 and 801 Squadrons which operate from the anti-submarine cruisers HMS *Ark Royal*, *Illus-*

trious and *Invincible*. All three of these vessels are equipped with a 'ski-jump', a built-up ramp at the forward end of each ship's take-off area. These not only give the Sea Harriers extra payload capability, but also provide additional lift to overcome wind-over-deck problems. The ski-jump ramps of *Invincible* and *Illustrious* are set at an angle of 7°, that of *Ark Royal* at 12°. It has been demonstrated that a 20° ski-jump would allow a Sea Harrier to take-off with more than 1100 kg (2,425 lb) of additional weapons or fuel, by comparison with take-off from a flat deck. The Indian Navy has ordered six of the generally similar **Sea Harrier FRS.Mk 51** version, plus two **Sea Harrier T.Mk 60** two-seat land-based trainers. Delivery of the Sea Harriers, which serve on board the carrier INS *Vikrant*, began in 1983. They differ from their British counterparts in minor details, and by carrying Matra Magic instead of Sidewinder missiles.

In March 1990, a further 10 **Sea Harrier FRS.Mk 2**s were ordered, and the progressive upgrading of surviving FRS.Mk 1s. First flying in conversion form on 19 September 1988, the Mk 2

has a Blue Vixen pulse-Doppler radar with look-down/shoot-down capability. The capability to carry and fire up to four AIM-120 AMRAAM missiles is incorporated.

Specification
BAe Sea Harrier FRS.Mk 1
Type: V/STOL fighter, reconnaissance and strike aircraft
Powerplant: one 9752-kg (21,500-lb)

thrust Rolls-Royce Pegasus Mk 104 vectored-thrust turbofan
Performance: maximum speed 1184 km/h (736 mph); low-altitude cruising speed 650-834 km/h (404-518 mph); strike radius 463 km (288 miles)
Dimensions: span 7.7 m (25 ft 3 in); length 14.5 m (47 ft 7 in); height 3.71 m (12 ft 2 in); wing area 18.68 m² (201.1 sq ft)

The Sea Harrier is best remembered for its exploits in the Falklands War, where it was used to great effect against conventional aircraft.

Armament: up to a maximum of 3629 kg (8,000 lb) of weapons, including four Sidewinder missiles, on fuselage and underwing hardpoints

British Klemm L.25 Swallow

The reliability, safety and excellent low-power performance of the German Klemm L.25 two-seat lightplane resulted in it becoming an attractive proposition for private owners. The type was first flown in 1927, and British pilots had acquired 27 of these German-built aircraft by 1933, at which time the British Klemm Aeroplane Company was established at Hanworth, Middlesex, to build the type in the UK.

The British prototype (G-ACMK) was flown for the first time in November 1933, and this differed from the original Klemm by having some structural reinforcement to meet UK airworthiness standards. A cantilever low-wing monoplane of all-wood construction, except for fabric-covered control surfaces, it had wings that could be folded to simplify storage. Two open cockpits in tandem, non-retractable tailskid landing gear, and a reliable low-powered engine completes the basic description of this aircraft.

Irrespective of engine installation the

The Klemm L.25 was popular with UK pilots, and was built under licence. The revised British Aircraft Swallow 2 had more angular surfaces to facilitate production.

initial production version was designated **British Klemm L.25C 1A Swallow**, and the prototype (G-ACMK) and five other examples had a 56-kW (75-hp) British Salmson A.D.9 radial engine; all but one of the remainder had a 63-kW (85-hp) Pobjoy Cataract II radial. After 28 had been built the wings, tailplane, fin and rudder were given angular lines to speed production, the fuselage top decking losing its smooth curve for the same reason. At the same time the company name changed to the British Aircraft Manufacturing Company, with the result that the modified Swallow was redesignated **British Aircraft Swallow 2**. More than 100 were built, powered by 6.7 kW (90-hp) Pobjoy Cataract III or Blackburn Cirrus Minor 1

engines of similar rating. Some of these saw limited service during World War II as instructional airframes for the Air Training Corps and as unofficial 'hacks' for RAF station commanders.

Specification
B.K. Swallow 1A
Type: two-seat lightplane
Powerplant: one 63-kW (85-hp) Pobjoy Cataract II radial piston engine

Performance: maximum speed 167 km/h (104 mph); cruising speed 145 km/h (90 mph); service ceiling 5180 m (17,000 ft); range 676 km (420 miles)
Weights: empty 435 kg (960 lb); maximum take-off 680 kg (1,500 lb)
Dimensions: span 13 m (42 ft 7¾ in); length 8 m (26 ft 3 in); height 2.15 m (7 ft 0½ in); wing area 20 m² (215.29 sq ft)

Britten-Norman BN-2 Islander

Desmond Norman and the late John Britten had started their association in the development of crop-spraying equipment, and in 1964 began detail design work on a new lightweight feederline transport. Envisaged as a new-generation replacement for the ageing de Havilland Dragon Rapide and other aircraft in this class, the **Britten-Norman BN-2 Islander** soon attracted considerable interest, and construction of a prototype was initiated in September 1964. This aircraft (G-ATCT) flew for the first time on 13 June 1965, powered by two 157-kW (210-hp) Rolls-Royce/Continental IO-360-B engines, and with wings that spanned 13.72 m (45 ft 0 in). A number of changes resulted from flight testing, the most important being a 1.22 m (4 ft 0 in) increase in wing span, and the installation of 194-kW (260-hp) Avco Lycoming O-540-E engines, and this has remained the standard powerplant of the Islander, still being installed in production aircraft in its O-540-E4C5 version.

Initial production aircraft were BN-2 Islanders, of high-wing monoplane configuration with a functional rectangular-section fuselage, conventional tail unit, non-retractable tricycle-type landing gear with twin wheels on the main units, and accommodation for a pilot and nine passengers. This 'high-density' seating arrangement had been contrived in a cabin that was only 1.09 m (3 ft 7 in) wide at its maximum by installing 'wall-to-wall' seats, with access via two doors on the port side, and one on the starboard side, making an aisle unnecessary. Exit in emergency can be made by removing the door windows. The first production example of the BN-2 made its initial flight on 24 April 1967, and the first Islander entered service less than four months later, on 13 August. The BN-2 Islander was superseded in mid-1969 by the improved **BN-2A Islander**, which introduced detail aerodynamic and equipment improvements, in addition to a new side-loading baggage facility. Since 1978 the standard

production version has the designation **BN-2B Islander II**. This differs primarily by having an increased maximum landing weight, improved internal design, and smaller diameter propellers to reduce the cabin noise level.

Various items of alternative equipment have become available over the years to extend the usefulness of the Islanders. These include 224-kW (300-hp) Avco Lycoming IO-540-K1BS piston

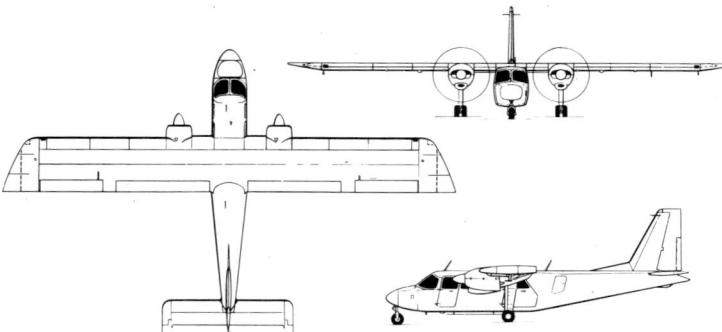

engines, or 239-kW (320-shp) Allison 250-B17C turboprop engines, and aircraft with this latter powerplant installation are designated **BN-2T Turbine Islander**. Other options include an extended nose to provide an additional 0.62 m³ (22 cu ft) of baggage space, raked wingtips containing auxiliary fuel tanks, and a Rajay turbocharger installation to enchance performance.

In addition to operation in a passenger-

Numerically the most important civil aircraft produced in the UK since World War II, the Islander has proved highly popular with small operators. This is the BN-2B with extended wingtips.

carrying capacity, the Islander can be used as a freighter with the passenger seats stored in the rear baggage bay, as an ambulance carrying three stretchers and two medical attendants, and for a variety of utility purposes when suitably equipped. **Defender** and **Maritime Defender** military versions are also available, and these can be adapted for casualty evacuation, patrol, transport, and search and rescue operations.

The success of this aircraft, which from the outset was intended to provide a low-cost reliable aircraft that could, if desired, be used in a number of differing roles, is highlighted by worldwide sales in approximately 120 countries, and

which in late 1989 were past the 1,100 mark. Of this total more than 300 had been built under licence in Romania, and 35 were assembled in the Philippines from components that had been manufactured by Britten-Norman.

Financial problems for Britten-Norman during the early 1970s led to the take-over by The Fairey Group in 1972. During the following year production of the Islander was transferred from Bembridge to Gosselies in Belgium. But in 1977 The Fairey Group itself went into receivership, and the Britten-Norman part of the Group was bought by Pilatus, and in the form of Pilatus Britten-Norman Ltd the company continues to com-

plete aircraft in the Isle of Wight after their basic manufacture in Romania.

Variants

Defender: military version for a variety of tasks (counter-insurgency, forward air control, casualty evacuation, patrol, light transport, etc); the main difference from civil Islanders is the provision of four underwing hardpoints able to carry a total stores weight of 1134 kg (2,500 lb), including machine-gun pods, rocket pods, bombs, missiles, flares or drop tanks. Several versions available, including AEW and ASTOR Defenders with large radars in a grossly enlarged nose

radome
Maritime Defender: version of the Islander intended for coastal patrol duties, SAR and fishery protection, with an endurance of 8 hours and Bendix RDR1400 search radar in a nose radome; the type can also carry rescue equipment (liferafts, etc) or underwing weapons.

Specification
Britten-Norman BN-2B Islander II
Type: feederline transport
Powerplant: two 194-kW (260-hp) each Avco Lycoming O-540-E4C5 horizontally-opposed piston engines
Performance: maximum cruising speed 257 km/h (160 mph) at 2135 m (7,000 ft); economic cruising speed 241 km/h (150 mph) at 3660 m (12,000 ft); service ceiling 4450 m (14,600 ft); range at economic cruising speed with full payload 1400 km (870 miles)
Weights: empty equipped 1638 kg (3,612 lb); maximum take-off 2994 kg (6,600 lb)
Dimensions: span 14.94 m (49 ft 0 in); length 10.86 m (35 ft 7¾in); height 4.18 m (13 ft 8¾in); wing area 30.19 m² (325 sq ft)

Britten-Norman BN-2A Mk III Trislander

The solution to the requirement for a 'stretched' version of the Britten-Norman Islander needed rather more than the insertion of a new piece of hardware in the fuselage. Enquiries had shown that at least a 50 per cent increase in capacity was required to meet the needs of interested customers, leading in 1970 to evolution of the three-engine **Britten-Norman BN-2A Mk III Trislander**. The incorporation of a third engine always raises problems to ensure that there is no asymmetry of thrust. Sometimes this can be resolved by installing an engine in the aircraft nose, or at the centre of the wing, but neither of these solutions was acceptable in the case of the Islander configuration. Instead, it was decided to take a leaf from the book of much larger sisters, such as the Boeing 727, and install the third engine in the tail.

In the Islander's case the size of the tail unit meant that the engine could not be 'buried' within its structure, and considerable modification of the tail was necessary to make it possible for the fin to serve also to carry the engine mounting. Other changes included the insertion of a 2.29 m (7 ft 6 in) fuselage section forward of the wing, strengthening of the rear fuselage structure, the installation of new main landing gear units with larger wheels and tyres, and provision of an interior furnished to accommodate 17 passengers. Because there

was no change in size of the fuselage cross-section, the same 'wall-to-wall' seating arrangement pioneered in the Islander was retained, but access to these in the Trislander was via two port and three starboard doors.

The prototype Trislander was converted from the second Islander prototype (G-ATWU), and the conversion flew for the first time on 11 September 1970. Later the same day it was flown to Farnborough to take part in the 1970 SBAC Display. The first production Trislander was flown on 6 March 1971: this incorporated the extended-span wings that had been an optional feature of the Islander, and additional fin area had been provided above the rear engine. Certification was granted by the ARB on 14 May 1971, and the first airline to receive a Trislander was Aurigny Air Services on 29 June 1971.

Designation of the first production version was BN-2A Mk III, which retained the standard nose of the Islander; this was followed by the **BN-2A Mk III-1 Trislander** grossing 4536 kg (10,000 lb). Later production versions include the **BN-2A Mk III-2 Trislander**, which differs by having as standard the optional extended nose of the Islander; the **BN-2A Mk III-3 Trislander** which incorporates a system to feather automatically the propeller of an engine which might fail on take-off; and the **BN-2A Mk III-4 Trislander** which has

Britten-Norman BN-2A Mk III-2 Trislander

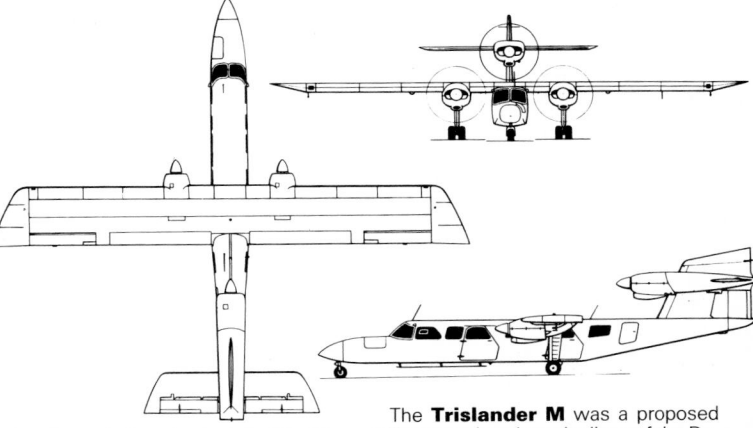

a standby rocket engine installed to provide extra thrust should there be an engine failure on take-off. Like that of the Islander, production of the Trislander was transferred to Belgium in 1973, but came back to the Isle of Wight in 1979. No production was undertaken in the 1980s, though a resurgence of interest could lead to a resumption.

The **Trislander M** was a proposed military version along the lines of the Defender, but no orders were received.

Specification
Britten-Norman BN-2A Mk III-2 Trislander
Type: feederline transport
Powerplant: three 194-kW (260-hp) each Avco Lycoming O-540-E4C5 horizontally-opposed piston engines
Performance: maximum cruising speed 267 km/h (166 mph) at 1980 m (6,500 ft); economic cruising speed 241 km/h (150 mph) at 3960 m (13,000 ft); service ceiling 4010 m (13,150 ft); maximum range at economic cruising speed 1609 km (1,000 miles)
Weights: empty equipped 2650 kg (5,843 lb); maximum take-off 4536 kg (10,000 lb)
Dimensions: span 16.15 m (53 ft 0 in); length 15.01 m (49 ft 3 in); height 4.32 m (14 ft 2 in); wing area 31.31 m² (337 sq ft)

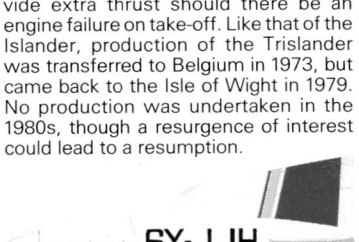

6Y-JJH

trans Jamaican

Britten-Norman BN-2A Mk III Trislander of Trans-Jamaican Airways.

Bücker Bü 131 Jungmann
to
CASA C-212 Aviocar

Bücker Bü 131 Jungmann

The first product of Bücker Flugzeugbau, established at Johannisthal, Germany, during 1932, was a two-seat light trainer known as the **Bücker Bü 131 Jungmann**. Designed by Anders Andersson, the company's Swedish chief engineer, it was a conventional single-bay biplane with fabric-covered wooden wings, a welded steel-tube fuselage that, with the exception of light alloy around the engine and cockpit, was also fabric-covered, and a wire-braced tail unit of similar construction to the fuselage. The tailwheel-type landing gear had rather stalky main units, and power for the prototype (D-3150), first flown on 27 April 1934, was provided by a 60-kW (80-hp) Hirth HM 60R inline engine.

The **Bü 131A**, as the initial production version was designated, proved to be very successful, manufactured not only for civil flying schools in Germany but also built extensively for the Luftwaffe, although production figures do not appear to have survived. Examples were exported also for service in some eight European countries with the largest numbers going to Hungary (100) and Romania (150), and in addition 75 were licence-built in Switzerland. The most

extensive licence-construction was in Japan, where 1,037 were built for the Japanese army as the **Type 4 Primary Trainer (Ki-86A)**. This followed the initiation of production on behalf of the Japanese navy for which it was licence-built by Watanabe (later Kyushu) as the **Navy Type 2 Primary Trainer Model 11 (K9W1)**. Production figures for the Japanese navy version differ according to source, varying from 217 to 339, but it seems reasonably certain that more than 200 were used at the navy's standard trainer.

Used throughout World War II by the Luftwaffe, the Bü 131A was later displaced by the improved Bücker Bü 181, and many saw service with auxiliary ground-attack squadrons. Carrying 1- and 2-kg (2.2- and 4.4-lb) bombs, they were used by night to maintain non-stop harassment over Soviet lines. Like other classic trainers, many Bü 131s survived the war, and were even built by Aero in Czechoslovakia during the 1950s under the designation **C4**.

Variants
Bücker Bü 131B: improved version with an uprated Hirth HM 504A-2

engine
Bücker Bü 131C: experimental version of which only a single example was built, powered by a 67-kW (90-hp) Cirrus Minor inline engine

Specification
Bücker Bü 131B
Type: two-seat primary trainer
Powerplant: one 78-kW (105-hp) Hirth HM 504A-2 inline piston engine
Performance: maximum speed at sea level 183 km/h (114 mph); cruising speed 170 km/h (106 mph); service ceiling 3000 m (9,840 ft); range 650 km

A great training aircraft on which many of Germany's ablest pilots cut their teeth, the Bücker Bü 131 Jungmann survives in some numbers, one example being this immaculately restored American machine.

(404 miles)
Weights: empty 390 kg (860 lb); maximum take-off 680 kg (1,499 lb)
Dimensions: span 7.4 m (24 ft 3¼ in); length 6.6 m (21 ft 8 in); height 2.25 m (7 ft 4½ in); wing area 13.5 m² (145.32 sq ft)

Bücker Bü 133 Jungmeister

Demand for the Bü 131 Jungmann had been such that Bücker's production facilities at Johannisthal were soon overwhelmed. A new factory was established at Rangsdorf and there, where it would be possible to expand production facilities, the company began development of a single-seat trainer based on the Bü 131 design. Generally similar in overall configuration and construction, it differed primarily by being of smaller dimensions, which meant that with a 101-kW (135-hp) Hirth HM 6 inline engine installed in the prototype (D-EVEO) had excellent aerobatic performance. Testing by the Luftwaffe resulted in production aircraft being ordered for use in an advanced training role, including the early instruction of fighter pilots, and the initial production examples were designated **Bü 133A** and named **Jungmeis-**

A chunky aerobatic derivative of the Jungmann, the Jungmeister is another popular aircraft with private owners today, whose numbers have been swelled in recent years by ex-Swiss and Spanish air force examples.

ter (Young Champion). No record of the number built for the Luftwaffe appears to have survived, but about 50 were manufactured by Dornier-Werke in Switzerland for the Swiss air force, plus a similar quantity by CASA in Spain.

Variants
Bücker Bü 133B: designation of licence-built versions with a 119-kW (160-hp) Hirth HM 506 inline engine
Bücker Bü 133C: designation of the major production version, powered by

a Siemens Sh 14A-4 radial engine

Specification
Bücker Bü 133C
Type: single-seat advanced trainer
Powerplant: one 119-kW (160-hp) Siemens Sh 14A-4 radial piston engine
Performance: maximum speed at sea level 220 km/h (137 mph); cruising

speed 200 km/h (124 mph); service ceiling 4500 m (14,765 ft); range 500 km (311 miles)
Weights: empty 425 kg (937 lb); maximum take-off 585 kg (1,290 lb)
Dimensions: span 6.6 m (21 ft 7¾ in); length 6 m (19 ft 8¼ in); height 2.2 m (7 ft 2½ in); wing area 12 m² (129.17 sq ft)

Bücker Bü 180 Student

Following design and the initiation of production of the Bü 133, the company turned its attention to the development of a two-seat cabin monoplane of high-wing configuration which carried the designation **Bücker Bü 134**. The single prototype of this aircraft (D-EGPA) proved to be unsuccessful when tested and its development was abandoned. Convinced that future trainers would need to be of monoplane configuration, the company persevered and designed another two-seat trainer of low-wing cantilever layout. Designated **Bücker Bü 180**, and later named **Student**, this was built in small numbers for civil use. The prototype (D-ELIO) was flown in the autumn of 1937, and was followed by

the production of a small number for civil use.

Specification
Type: two-seat sporting/training aircraft
Powerplant: one 45-kW (60-hp) Walter Mikron II inline piston engine
Performance: maximum speed 175 km/h (109 mph); cruising speed 160 km/h (99 mph); service ceiling 4500 m (14,765 ft); range 650 km (404 miles)

The Student was Bücker's first monoplane, and featured a metal fuselage and wooden flying surfaces.

Weights: empty 295 kg (650 lb); maximum take-off 540 kg (1,190 lb)
Dimensions: span 11.5 m (37 ft

8¾ in); length 7.1 m (23 ft 3½ in); height 1.85 m (6 ft 0¾ in); wing area 15 m² (161.46 sq ft)

Bücker Bü 181 Bestmann

Experience with the Bü 180 showed that even with an engine of small power output the two-seat monoplane could offer quite good performance. With this encouragement the company began the design of a new trainer, one that adopted the constructional techniques used in the Bü 180, but which introduced side-by-side seating in an enclosed cabin to provide ideal conditions for primary training. Identified as the **Bücker Bü 181**, and later named **Bestmann**, the new aircraft had wings of wooden basic construction with plywood and fabric covering, and a tail unit of similar structure, and a fuselage with steel-tube forward section and a wooden monocoque aft section. Landing gear was of tailwheel type, and power was provided by a Hirth HM 504 engine. The prototype (D-ERBV) was first flown in early 1939, and following testing by the Luftwaffe, production of the **Bü 181A** was ordered for service as a standard basic trainer. Details of the number constructed for the Luftwaffe are not accurately known, but it has been estimated that production must have run into many thousands. As they became available in large numbers they were

used also as communication aircraft and, in smaller numbers, as glider tugs.

In addition to production by Bücker, 708 were built by Fokker in the Netherlands during the war, and from 1944 to 1946 125 were built in Sweden for the nation's air force under the designation **Sk 25**. Wartime production had also started in Czechoslovakia, and continued there by Zlin after the war had ended, this company building the civil **Z.281** and **Z.381**, as well as the military **C.6** and **C.106** for the Czech air force. Under licence from Czechoslovakia, post-war production was undertaken by Heliopolis Aircraft Works in Egypt, which built a version similar to the Zlin Z.381 for several Arab states, and for the Egyptian air force, under the name **Gomhouria**.

Variant
Bücker Bü 181D: later production version with minor detail improvements

Specification
Bücker Bü 181A
Type: two-seat primary trainer

Powerplant: one 78-kW (105-hp) Hirth HM 504 inline piston engine
Performance: maximum speed at sea level 215 km/h (134 mph); cruising speed 195 km/h (121 mph); service ceiling 5000 m (16,405 ft); range 800 km (497 miles)
Weights: empty 480 kg (1,058 lb); maximum take-off 750 kg (1,653 lb)

With side-by-side seating, the Bestmann was adopted as the Luftwaffe's basic trainer to supplant earlier types.

Dimensions: span 10.6 m (34 ft 9¼ in); length 7.85 m (25 ft 9 in); height 2.05 m (6 ft 8¾ in); wing area 13.5 m² (145.32 sq ft)

Budd Conestoga

The **Budd Conestoga** was probably the first large aircraft of original design to be fabricated from stainless steel. It reflected another approach to the early World War II anxiety of ensuring that alternative materials could be found for aircraft construction, to replace the extensively-used aluminium alloys of which a shortage had been predicted.

Intended for use as a cargo carrier or troop transport, the Conestoga was developed by the Budd Manufacturing Company in collaboration with the US Navy Bureau of Aeronautics. The high-set monoplane wing was primarily of stainless steel stressed-skin construction, but the trailing edges of the wing outer panels and ailerons were fabric-covered. The tail unit was similar, but the fuselage was wholly of stressed-skin construction, the upswept rear fuselage incorporating an electrically-operated ramp which allowed military vehicles to be driven directly into the 2.44-m (8-ft) wide and 2.44-m (8-ft) high cargo hold. Because the flight deck was mounted high on the nose, the cargo compartment maintained the foregoing dimensions over a length of 7.62 m (25 ft). As an alternative to bulky cargo, 24 fully armed paratroops and equipment/supplies could be carried, or in a casualty evacuation role 24 stretchers and 16 sitting patients. Power was provided by two Pratt & Whitney Twin Wasp radial engines in wing-mounted nacelles, and landing gear was of semi-retractable tricycle-type.

In August 1942 the US Navy awarded a contract to the Budd company for 200 of these transports under the designation **RB-1**, and US Army Air Force interest brought a contract for an additional 600 aircraft under the designation **C-93**. The prototype flew for the first time on 31 October 1943, but production delays, cost overruns and a realisation that there was unlikely to be a shortage of conventional light alloys brought cancellation of the USAAF contract. Shortly after this the US Navy contract was reduced to only 25, and of these 17 were delivered before the war ended but were not used. Sold as war surplus items, 14 were acquired by Robert Presscott and used to start a freight airline known originally as National Skyway Freight Corporation. The line continued to operate until recently, known as the Flying Tiger Line.

Specification
Type: twin-engined cargo or troop transport
Powerplant: two 895-kW (1,200-hp) each Pratt & Whitney R-1830-92 Twin Wasp radial piston engines
Performance: maximum speed 317 km/h (197 mph) at 2285 m (7,500 ft); cruising speed 266 km/h (165 mph) at normal altitude; normal range with payload 1127 km (700 miles)
Weights: empty 9143 kg (20,156 lb); maximum take-off 15359 kg (33,860 lb)
Dimensions: span 30.48 m (100 ft 0 in); length 20.73 m (68 ft 0 in); height

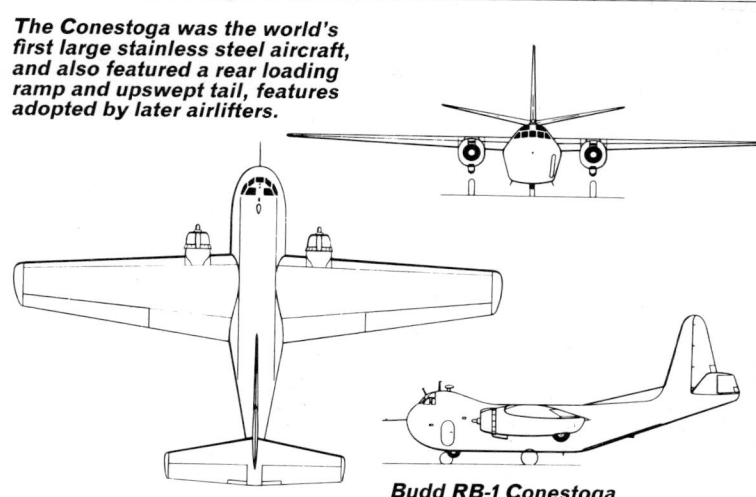

The Conestoga was the world's first large stainless steel aircraft, and also featured a rear loading ramp and upswept tail, features adopted by later airlifters.

Budd RB-1 Conestoga

9.68 m (31 ft 9 in); wing area 130.06 m² (1,400 sq ft)

CAMS 55

The prototype **CAMS 51** was a twin-engined bombing and reconnaissance biplane flying-boat (R.3 category) which made its maiden flight in January 1927. Power was provided by two 283-kW (380-hp) Gnome-Rhône Jupiter radial engines, mounted in tandem on a pair of N-struts over the hull and located just below the upper-wing centre-section. From this CAMS 51, and the long-range **CAMS 54 GR** which made an abortive attempt to cross the North Atlantic from east to west in 1928, was developed the **CAMS 55** bombing and reconnais-

sance flying-boat.

The prototype **CAMS 55.001**, powered by two tandem-mounted 447-kW (600-hp) Hispano-Suiza 12Lbr engines, made its maiden flight in 1928 piloted by its designer, Maurice Hurel. It was followed by four evaluation aircraft, two designated **CAMS 55J** and powered by Jupiter radials and two designated **CAMS 55H** with Hispano-Suiza in-line engines.

The CAMS 55 was of solid construction, particularly suited to its primary role of maritime reconnaissance. The struc-

ture was of wood, the two-step hull being ply-wood covered with the forward step reinforced by a sheath of galvanised steel sheet. The wooden-structure single-bay biplane wings were fabric covered, and incorporated dihedral on the lower wing only. The upper bow section of the hull, surrounding the forward gunner's cockpit, was widened to form a balcony with small windows set in the underside for downward observation; the open pilot's and co-pilot's cockpits were located side-by-side just forward of the wings, with the wireless operator's cabin immediately aft; and behind the wings was a midships gunner's cockpit.

The French Aéronautique Maritime was impressed by tests with the prototype and evaluation aircraft, and production orders for the **CAMS 55/1, 55/2** and **55/10** followed. At one time no fewer than 15 navy *escadrilles* had the type on strength, but the first unit to receive the type was Escadrille 3E1 at Berre. It flew the experimental CAMS 55H and CAMS 55J boats in 1930, and then fully re-equipped with the CAMS 55/2 which replaced the unsatisfactory Latham 47. With introduction into service of the Breguet Bizerte flying-boat from 1936 onwards, the CAMS 55 was relegated to coastal patrol duties. A number served during the early part of

World War II, the last operational boats flying with Escadrille 20S (formerly 8S5) from Tahiti in the French Pacific islands until scrapped in January 1941.

Variants

CAMS 55/1: first production version, powered by two 447-kW (600-hp) Hispano-Suiza 12Lbr inline engines; 43 built

CAMS 55/2: powered by two 358-kW (480-hp) Gnome-Rhône Jupiter 9Akx radial engines; 29 built in parallel with CAMS 55/1

CAMS 55/3: only a single prototype of this version was completed; it featured an all-metal hull and was built for a 1932 French navy contest for a new long-range flying-boat; built at Saint-Denis, it was assembled and test flown from the company's seaplane base at Sartrouville; after only limited testing the flying-boat crashed into the Seine on take-off, on 4 January 1932, killing the pilot, Antoine Brunel

CAMS 55/6: this one-off prototype had all-metal wing-tip floats and hull; it benefitted from the use of dural and vedal alloys so that the hull was 400 kg (882 lb) lighter than that of the earlier wooden structure; financial stringencies prevented quantity production

CAMS 55/10: this version appeared in 1934, powered by two Gnome-Rhône Mistral 9Kbr radial engines with reduction gear; like its predecessors it had folding wings, and additional fuel capacity was provided to give increased range; a total of 32 CAMS 55/10s was built, four of them modified for colonial use

CAMS 55/14: this 1934 variant, with Gnome-Rhône engines, metal hull and wooden wingtip float; did not go into production

Specification
CAMS 55/10

Type: maritime reconnaissance and bombing flying-boat

Powerplant: two 373-kW (500-hp) Gnome-Rhône 9Kbr radial piston engines

Performance: maximum speed at sea level 195 km/h (121 mph); cruising speed 150 km/h (93 mph); service ceiling 3400 m (11,155 ft); normal range 1280 km (795 miles); maximum range 1875 km (1,165 miles)

Weights: empty equipped 4590 kg (10,119 lb); maximum take-off 6900 kg

CAMS 55/2 of Escadrille 4S1, Aéronavale (French naval air force), based in North Africa during the 1930s.

(15,212 lb)

Dimensions: span 20.4 m (66 ft 11¼ in); length 15.03 m (49 ft 3¾ in); height 5.41 m (17 ft 9 in); wing area 113.45 m² (1,221.21 sq ft)

Armament: two pairs of 7.7-mm (0.303-in) Lewis machine-guns in bow and midships cockpits, plus two 75-kg (165-lb) Type G2 bombs on underwing racks

(CRDA) CANT Z.501 Gabbiano

CANT Z.501 of 2 Escuadrilla, grupo num, 62, Agrupacion Espanola (Spanish Nationalist air force) based in Majorca in 1939.

In 1931 Cantiere Navale Triestino was re-organised as Cantieri Riuniti dell'Adriatico (CRDA) and Marshal Italo Balbo, then Minister of Aviation in Italy, persuaded Ing. Filippo Zappata to return home from France to become the new company's chief engineer. His first design was the **CRDA CANT Z.501 Gabbiano** (Seagull), a long-range reconnaissance bomber flying-boat of wooden construction, with fabric covering on the upper hull, wing and tail surfaces. Power was supplied by a 671-kW (900-hp) Isotta-Fraschini Asso XI engine, driving a two-blade wooden or three-blade metal propeller, and its nacelle in the centre section was extended to include a cockpit for the flight engineer, who was responsible also for the operation of a 7.7-mm (0.303-in) machine-gun; two similar weapons were mounted in bow and dorsal positions. Racks were attached to the wing struts, inboard of the floats, and could carry a maximum load of 640 kg (1,411 lb) of bombs.

The prototype made its first flight on 7 February 1934, and in October of that year CANT's chief pilot, Mario Stoppani, flew the aircraft 4120 km (2,560 miles) from the company's base at Monfalcone, Trieste, to Massawa in Eritrea, a distance record for seaplanes. In July 1935, after France had taken the record, Stoppani regained it with a 4957-km (3,080-mile) flight to Berbera in British Somaliland.

The Z.501 entered squadron service with the Regia Aeronautica in 1937, and by the time Italy entered World War II on 10 June 1940 more than 200 formed the equipment of at least 17 squadrons and four flights. The Z.501's operational debut was with a unit of the Aviazione Legionaria, based in Majorca and operating in support of the Nationalist forces in the Spanish Civil War. A small number of Z.501s served as a coastal defence unit of the Romanian air force. A total of 454 was delivered before production ended in 1943.

Specification

Type: reconnaissance bomber flying-boat

Powerplant: one 671-kW (900-hp) Isotta-Fraschini Asso XI radial piston engine

Performance: maximum speed 275 km/h (171 mph) at 2500 m (8,200 ft); cruising speed 240 km/h (149 mph) at 2000 m (6,560 ft); cruising range with full payload 1000 km (621 miles); maximum range 2400 km (1,491 miles)

Weights: empty 3840 kg (8,466 lb); maximum take-off 7035 kg (15,510 lb)

Dimensions: span 22.5 m (73 ft 10 in); length 14.3 m (46 ft 11 in); height 4.42 m (14 ft 6 in); wing area 62 m² (667.38 sq ft)

Armament: three flexible 7.7-mm (0.303-in) machine-guns, plus up to 640 kg (1,411 lb) of bombs

(CRDA) CANT Z.506

In July 1935 there flew the prototype of a large wooden twin-float seaplane, powered by three 626-kW (840-hp) Isotta-Fraschini Asso XI inline engines. This was the **CRDA CANT Z.505**, which had been designed as a mailplane. On 19 August in the same year, Mario Stoppani conducted the first flight of the slightly smaller and lighter **Z.506**, a 12/14-passenger transport with three 455-kW (610-hp) Piaggio Stella IX radial engines. The type was put into production in 1936 as the **Z.506A**, and entered service with the Italian airline Ala Littoria during that year on routes around the Mediterranean. Powered by three 559-kW (750-hp) Alfa Romeo 126 RC 34 radial engines the Z.506A, flown mostly by Mario Stoppani, set several altitude,

The Z.509 was derived from the Z.506A to serve as a long range floatplane capable of crossing the South Atlantic. It broke several records but was abandoned at the outbreak of war.

distance and speed records during 1936-8, including speeds of 308.25 km/h (191.539 mph), 319.78 km/h (198.7 mph) and 322.06 km/h (200.118 mph) over distances of 5000 km (3,107 miles), 2000 km (1,243 miles) and 1000 km (621 miles) respectively. It carried a payload of 2000 kg (4,409 lb) to 7810 m (25,623 ft) and 5000 kg (11,023 lb) to 6917 m (22,693 ft) and later flew 5383.6 km (3,345.225 miles) over a closed circuit.

A military version, designated

Z.506B Airone (Heron), was shown at the October 1937 Milan Aeronautical Exhibition, and during the following month it set a load-to-height record of 10155 m (33,318 ft) with a 1000-kg (2,205-lb) pay-load and then flew 7020 km (4,362 miles) non-stop from Cadiz to Caravelas. This aircraft was fitted with 559-kW (750-hp) Alfa Romeo 127 RC 55 engines. Production of the Z.506B totalled 324, including two prototypes, which were supplied to the Regia Aeronautica and the Regia Marina; the latter service took over 29 aircraft, the balance of a Polish order for 30 which were not delivered due to the German invasion. Five were delivered to the Nationalist forces in the Spanish Civil War late in 1938. A number of aircraft, converted for air-sea rescue duties, remained in service until 1959.

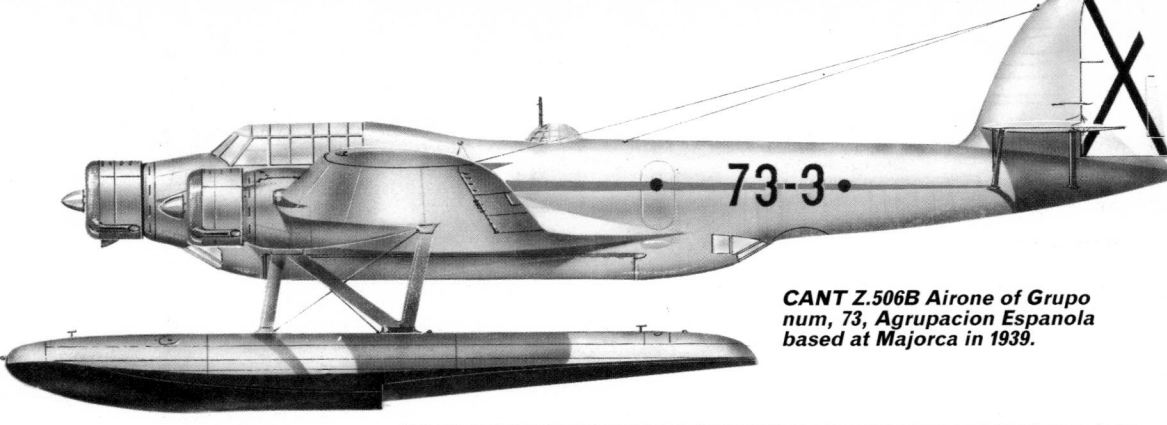

CANT Z.506B Airone of Grupo num, 73, Agrupacion Espanola based at Majorca in 1939.

Variants

Z.506B: this was a militarised version featuring a stepped, extensively glazed tandem two-seat cockpit and a ventral gondola which contained the bomb aimer's position and the bomb bay, immediately behind which was a gunner's position with a single 7.7-mm (0.303-in) Breda-SAFAT machine-gun; a 12.7-mm (0.5-in) gun was fitted in the Breda M.1 upper turret; the bomb bay could accommodate an 800-kg (1,764-lb) torpedo or a combination of smaller weapons to a similar total weight, while later versions were able to carry a bomb load of 1200 kg (2,645 lb) and were equipped with two 7.7-mm (0.303-in) Breda-SAFAT machine-guns in waist positions and a Caproni Lanciani Delta E turret replacing the Breda turret; the Z.506B was built at CANT's Monfalcone and Finale Ligure factories, and by Piaggio under licence
Z.506S: air-sea rescue version, including 20 Z.506Bs converted by Savoia-Marchetti in 1948
Z.506 landplane: one Z.506 was specially prepared for an endurance record attempt by Mario Stoppani, and was converted to landplane configuration with fixed, spatted landing gear; the flight was at first postponed and then cancelled as a

The Z.506B was the military version with a ventral gondola to accommodate a bomb aimer, the bomb load and a ventral gun position. A semi-retractable dorsal turret was added.

result of bad weather
Z.508: 1936 heavy bomber prototype, essentially a scaled-up version of the Z.501; data include powerplant three 627-kW (840-hp) Isotta-Fraschini Asso XI RC 40 engines, maximum speed 315 km/h (196 mph), span 30 m (98 ft 5 in) and length 21.45 m (70 ft 5 in); this sole example of the type set several records, including the carriage of a 1000-kg (22,046-lb) load to 2000 m (6,560 ft) and a speed of 248.25 km/h (154.26 mph) over a 2000-km (1,243-mile) course with a 5000-kg (11,023-lb) load
Z.509: three of this larger and heavier version of the Z.506A were built in 1937 for Ala Littoria's transatlantic postal service to South America, powered by three Fiat A.80 RC 41 radial engines and with a new wing of 28.32 m (92 ft 11 in) span and 100 m²

(1,076.43 sq ft) area to compensate for increased empty and maximum take-off weights of 9980 kg (22,000 lb) and 15965 kg (35,200 lb) respectively

Specification
CANT Z.506B Airone
Type: reconnaissance bomber and rescue floatplane
Powerplant: three 559-kW (750-hp) Alfa Romeo 126 RC 34 radial piston engines
Performance: maximum speed 365 km/h (227 mph); cruising speed

325 km/h (202 mph); service ceiling 8000 m (26,245 ft); maximum range 2745 km (1,705 miles)
Weights: empty 8300 kg (18,298 lb); maximum take-off 12300 kg (27,117 lb)
Dimensions: span 26.5 m (86 ft 11¼ in); length 19.25 m (63 ft 1¾ in); height 7.4 m (24 ft 3¼ in); wing area 87 m² (936.49 sq ft)
Armament: one or two 7.7-mm (0.303-in) machine-guns and one 12.7-mm (0.5-in) machine-gun, plus up to 1200 kg (2,645 lb) of bombs or a torpedo

(CRDA) CANT Z.1007

CANT Z.1007bis (MM24248) of Aviazione Nazionale Republicana, 1944.

Design studies which culminated in the **CRDA CANT Z.1007bis Alcione** (Kingfisher) began in 1935 and the prototype **Z.1007**, powered by three 615-kW (825-hp) Isotta-Fraschini Asso XI engines, made its first flight in March 1937. Changes made during initial flight test included the substitution of three-blade Piaggio metal propellers in place of the original two-blade wooden units, and modifications to the ventral radiators. Annular radiators identified an interim production version, 34 of which were built. Some were flown by the Regia Aeronautica's 221° Gruppo from 1939 but the aircraft were not used operationally.

In the meantime, Fillipo Zappata had completed work on a redesigned version powered by three 746-kW (1,000-hp) Piaggio P.XI R2C 40 radials. Early examples had the tailplane mounted lower on the fin than had been the case with the prototype, and later aircraft introduced revised horizontal tail surfaces with noticeable dihedral and oval endplate fins and rudders; this change was introduced to improve the field of fire from the dorsal turret. The first aircraft, in fact the 35th production airframe, was first flown in 1938 as the Z.1007bis, and after a total of eight pre-production examples had been completed for service trials at Guidonia, the type entered quantity production at CANT's Monfalcone factory, and was also built under licence by IMAM at Capodichino, Naples. Defensive armament comprised one Breda M or Caproni-Lanciani Delta E dorsal turret housing a 12.7-mm (0.5-in) Scotti or SAFAT machine-gun, a similar weapon in a ventral position behind the

bomb bay, and two 7.7-mm (0.303-in) SAFAT guns in beam positions. Production of all Z.1007 variants was 561.

Variants
Z.1007ter: improved Z.1007bis with three 858-kW (1,150-hp) Piaggio P.XIX radials and bombload reduced to 1000 kg (2,205 lb); maximum speed was 500 km/h (311 mph), range 2250 km (1,398 miles) and maximum take-off weight 10465 kg (23,071 lb)
Z.1015: prototype of military mailplane with three 1140-kW (1,500-hp) Piaggio P.XII RC 35 radials, maximum speed 560 km/h (348 mph), range 3000 km (1,864 miles) and maximum take-off weight 13600 kg (29,982 lb); intended for development as a bomber

Specification
CANT Z.1007bis Alcione
Type: medium bomber
Powerplant: three 746-kW (1,000-hp) each Piaggio P.XI R2C 40 radial piston engines
Performance: maximum speed 465 km/h (289 mph) at 4000 m (13,125 ft); service ceiling 8200 m (26,900 ft); range 1750 km (1,087 miles) at

380 km/h (236 mph) with maximum internal bombload
Weights: empty 9395 kg (20,712 lb); maximum take-off 13620 kg (30,027 lb)
Dimensions: span 24.8 m (81 ft 4¼ in); length 18.35 m (60 ft 2½ in); height 5.22 m (17 ft 1½ in); wing area 75 m² (807.32 sq ft)
Armament: two 12.7-mm (0.5-in) Scotti or SAFAT machine-guns (one

Z.1007bis bombers in both single- and twin-finned versions, serving with the 230 Squadriglia.

each in dorsal and ventral positions) and two beam-mounted 7.7-mm (0.303-in) SAFAT machine-guns, plus a maximum internal bomb load of 1200 kg (2,645 lb) or a maximum external bomb load of 1000 kg (2,205 lb)

CASA C-101 Aviojet

In 1972 Hispano Aviación SA merged with CASA and the two companies had built some 3,500 aircraft by mid-1978, including the HA.200 jet trainer. Work on this aircraft, the F-5 and the Hansa stood CASA in good stead when it was asked to design a replacement for the HA.200, and in September 1975 the company was awarded a development contract for a basic and advanced jet trainer. Six prototypes were covered, four for flight test and two for fatigue testing. The first prototype, by then wearing the designation **CASA C-101**, flew on 27 June 1977, followed in September by the second aircraft. The third and fourth followed on 26 January and 17 April 1978 respectively, and following manufacturer's trials they were handed over to the Spanish air force for service testing in late 1978, by which time the name **Aviojet** had been chosen. The military designation is **E.25**.

Assistance in the design stage came from MBB in West Germany, while the US Northrop Company helped with the jet inlet and wing section design. Imported components include the Dowty-built landing gear, Martin-Baker ejector seats, US-built air conditioning and pressurisation systems, Garrett-AiResearch turbofan and Sperry STARS integrated flight-control system.

Production of the initial batch of 10 **C-101EB** Aviojets began in early 1978 to meet orders for 60 for the Spanish air force as a replacement for the Hispano HA.200 and HA.220s, of which 80 or more were still in service. All these were replaced, and Spanish air force orders eventually totalled 92.

Deliveries began in 1980, and the Aviojet entered service with the training units in the following year.

Construction is on a modular basis for ease of maintenance and low cost, with ample internal space available for training equipment; there is a large bay behind the rear cockpit for quick-change equipment packages and a variety of underwing and underfuselage stores can be carried on hardpoints.

The twin Martin-Baker Mk 10E ejector seats are the zero-zero type, while the cockpit canopy is in two sections which open sideways; there is a separate internal windscreen for the rear cockpit, whose seat is elevated 0.325 m (1 ft 0¾ in) to give the occupant a clear view over the head of the man in front.

The Aviojet made its first public appearance outside Spain when the first and fourth prototypes accompanied two Aviocars to the 1978 Farnborough International Air Show in September; one took part in the flying programme while the other remained on static display surrounded by a variety of military ordnance. Light armed versions have followed, including the **C-101BB** for Chile (where it is known as the **T-36 Halcón**) and Honduras and the light attack **C-101CC** (**A-36 Halcón** in Chile where it is assembled by ENAER) with uprated TFE731-5-1J turbofan offering 20.91 kN (4,700 lb) thrust. Jordan operates the type as the **CC-04**. The **C-101DD** is an enhanced trainer version which first flew on 20 May 1985 – no orders have yet been announced.

Specification
Type: basic/advanced jet trainer and light strike aircraft
Powerplant: one 1588-kg (3,500-lb) thrust Garrett-AiResearch TFE731-2-25 turbofan
Performance: maximum speed Mach 0.69 at altitude, or 685 km/h

A useful trainer and light strike aircraft, the CASA 101 was developed with the aid of MBB and Northrop. This is the prototype, shown wearing mock Spanish air force markings, the air arm adopting the type as its advanced trainer.

(426 mph) at sea level; economical cruising speed Mach 0.56 at altitude; service ceiling 12500 m (41,010 ft); combat radius on a lo-lo-lo mission 185 km (115 miles); maximum range 3800 km (2,351 miles)
Weights: empty 3350 kg (7,385 lb); maximum take-off 5600 kg (12,346 lb)
Dimensions: span 10.6 m (34 ft 9 in); length 12.25 m (40 ft 2 in); height 4.25 m (13 ft 11 in); wing area 20 m² (215.3 sq ft)
Armament: one 30-mm DEFA cannon pod in bay below rear cockpit (which can alternatively accommodate cameras or ECM equipment), plus up to 2000 kg (4,410 lb) of disposable stores (rockets, missiles, bombs, napalm, etc) on six underwing hardpoints

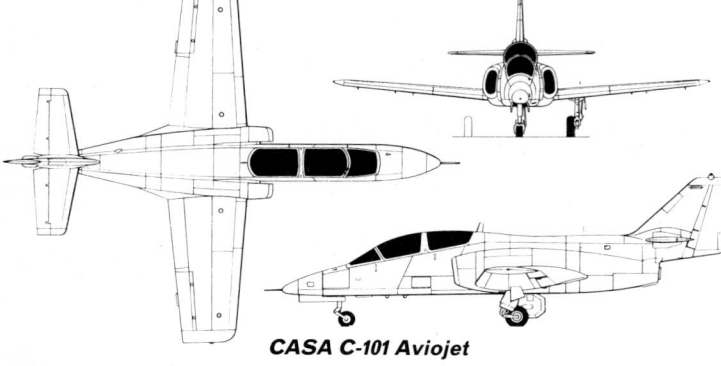

CASA C-101 Aviojet

CASA 202 Halcon

Designed primarily for use on Spain's internal air routes, the **CASA 202 Halcon** (Falcon) first flew in May 1953, and 20 were subsequently ordered. Generally similar to but slightly larger than the Alcotan, the Halcon differed in having tricycle landing gear and accommodation for a crew of three and 14 passengers in a heated and air-conditioned cabin. However, the production Halcons were delivered to the Spanish air force under the designation **T.6**. The aircraft served for several years before being replaced by the CASA 207 Azor, which also replaced some of the licence-built Ju 52/3ms.

Specification
CASA 202 Halcon

This is the sole CASA 202B Halcon, an improved version with a lengthened fuselage, reduced-span wings and R-1820-56 Cyclone engines.

Type: twin-engine transport
Powerplant: two 578-kW (775-hp) each Elizalde 9C-29-750 radial engines
Weights: empty equipped 5270 kg (11,618 lb); maximum take-off 7750 kg (17,086 lb)
Dimensions: span 21.55 m (70 ft 8½ in); length 16 m (52 ft 6 in); height 3.8 m (12 ft 5½ in); wing area 57.35 m² (617.33 sq ft)
Performance: maximum speed 345 km/h (214 mph) at 2840 m (9,315 ft); cruising speed 300 km/h (186 mph)

CASA C-207 Azor

The Spanish aircraft industry has produced four different types of twin-engined transport since the end of World War II, the first of these being the CASA 201 Alcotan, a dual military/civil type of modest size, and the second the somewhat similar CASA 202 Halcon; both were produced in small numbers only. Third, and to date the largest, the **CASA 207 Azor** is essentially a scaled-up development of the Halcon, and flew for the first time on 28 September 1955 as a contender originally for the domestic civil market. Here it found no takers, but the aircraft was rescued from obscurity by the Spanish government, which placed an initial order for 10 for the Ejército del Aire (Spanish air force).

Carrying a crew of four and having

A type virtually obsolete by the time of its appearance in 1958, the Azor was produced in only small numbers as the T.7 for the Spanish air force's transport arm.

cabin accommodation for up to 40 passengers, this first model received the Spanish air force designation **T.7A** and began to enter service in 1960; two of the 10 were fitted experimentally with Pratt & Whitney Double Wasp engines. The original batch were followed by a further 10 aircraft, configured for either paratroop transport or freight-carrying duties. Designated **CASA 207C** (military designation **T.7B**), they were distinguishable by large cargo-loading double doors at the rear of the fuselage,

and could transport up to 37 paratroops or 3350 kg (7,385 lb) of freight. The two CASA 207 prototypes, as well as the 20 production Azors, were used by the Spanish air force, which still had a few in service in the early 1980s with the 35th Wing of its Transport command at Madrid-Getafe. In 1973 CASA proposed a four-turboprop STOL design, known as the **CASA 401**, to replace the Azor, but this was eventually abandoned in favour of the smaller twin-turboprop CASA 212 Aviocar.

Specification
CASA 207 Azor
Type: short/medium-range troop and cargo transport
Powerplant: two 1522-kW (2,040-hp) each Bristol Hercules 730 radial piston engines
Performance: maximum speed 420 km/h (261 mph) at 1500 m (4,920 ft); maximum cruising speed 400 km/h (249 mph) at 3760 m (12,340 ft); service ceiling 8000 m (26,250 ft); range with 300-kg (6,614-lb) payload 2350 km (1,460 miles)
Weights: empty equipped (207A) 10600 kg (23,370 lb); maximum payload (207A) 3087 kg (6,806 lb); maximum payload (207C) 4000 kg (8,818 lb); maximum take-off (207A) 16000 kg (35,275 lb); maximum take-off (207C) 16500 kg (36,376 lb)
Dimensions: span 27.8 m (91 ft 2½ in); length 20.85 m (68 ft 5 in); height 7.75 m (25 ft 5 in); wing area 85.8 m² (923.5 sq ft)

CASA C-212 Aviocar

The Spanish air force's requirement to replace several of its elderly transport aircraft such as the DC-3, the licence-built Ju 52/3m and the CASA Azor led to CASA drawing up a specification for a twin-turboprop transport which would be a general-purpose aircraft and capable of adaptation for a number of roles. The possibility of civil orders was not overlooked.

The result was the **CASA C-212 Aviocar**, designed for a crew of two and up to 16 troops or, in a civil configuration, 19 passengers. The first prototype flew on 26 March 1971 and was demonstrated with verve at the Paris Air Salon only 10 weeks later; its STOL performance was well demonstrated, although the main spar suffered some damage apparently as a result of reverse thrust being applied while the aircraft was still several feet above the runway.

The second prototype flew in October 1971 and the test programme continued, being rewarded with an order from the Spanish air ministry for an initial batch of eight pre-production aircraft, which made their maiden flights between November 1972 and February 1974. The type was given the Spanish air force basic designation **T.12**, but there are a number of variants. The **C-212A (T.12B)** is a utility transport, and the first of 45 for the Spanish air force was delivered on 20 May 1974; the first squadron to be equipped with the new type was No. 461 at Gando in the Canary Islands.

Five examples of the **C-212AV** were ordered as VIP transports and the first arrived in May 1976. Of the eight pre-production Aviocars, six were completed to **C-212B (TR.12A)** standard as photographic survey aircraft with two Wild RC-10 aerial survey cameras and a darkroom, and the other two became **C-212E** navigation trainers. Following the delivery of these two aircraft, the Spanish air force ordered three more of the same type, to bring its total Aviocar orders to 61, later increased to 88. Other military export customers have included Chile, Indonesia, Jordan, Nicaragua and Portugal for the C-212A; Jordan for the C-212AV; and Portugal for the C-212B.

The basic commercial version is the **C-212C** (or **C-212-5**), of which three were ordered initially by Pertamina in Indonesia for operation by Pelita Air Service and Merpati Nusantara Air Lines, and the Turkish operator Bursa Hava Yollari has two.

As a result of the considerable sales interest in the Far East, CASA concluded an agreement under which Nurtanio Aircraft Industries Ltd would licence-build the Aviocar; production began in mid-1976 with the production rate established at one per month increasing to two a month by 1982. CASA and Nurtanio have received orders for Aviocars by early 1990 with production continuing.

In April 1978 CASA flew the prototype

of a higher powered and heavier Aviocar, the **C-212-10 (C-212-200)**. It was a conversion of the 138th production aircraft featuring a strengthened airframe and two 645-kW (865-hp) Garrett-AiResearch TPE331-10 turboprops. The more powerful engines enabled the maximum take-off weight to be increased by 1000 kg (2,205 lb) to 7450 kg (16,424 lb) and the maximum payload from 2000 kg (4,410 lb) to 3200 kg (7,054 lb).

In its troop-transport configuration the standard Aviocar can carry up to 18 fully-equipped troops or light vehicles; an underfuselage rear loading ramp can be used for airborne parachute troops and cargo drops. In the ambulance role 12 stretcher patients and two medical attendants can be carried. As a navigation trainer, desks for five pupils and an instructor can be fitted.

The VIP versions supplied to the Spanish and Jordanian air forces have 12 passenger seats and folding tables.

The current **Series 300** has enlarged, upturned wingtips and a lengthened, more pointed nose, offering better performance and increased capacity. By January 1990 207 civil and 227 military C-212s had been sold.

Specification
CASA C-212-200
Type: utility transport
Powerplant: two 671-kW (900-shp) each Garrett-AiResearch TPE331-10 turboprops
Performance: maximum cruising speed 385 km/h (239 mph) at 3050 m (10,000 ft); service ceiling 8500 m (27,885 ft); range with maximum payload (26 passengers) 760 km (472 miles); range with maximum fuel 1620 km (1,007 miles)
Weights: empty 3915 kg (8,631 lb); maximum take-off 7450 kg (16,424 lb)
Dimensions: span 19 m (62 ft 4 in); length 15.16 m (49 ft 9 in); height 6.68 m (21 ft 11 in); wing area 40 m² (430.56 sq ft)

The CASA 212 has proved popular with operators requiring short, rough field performance.

CASA C-212 Aviocar

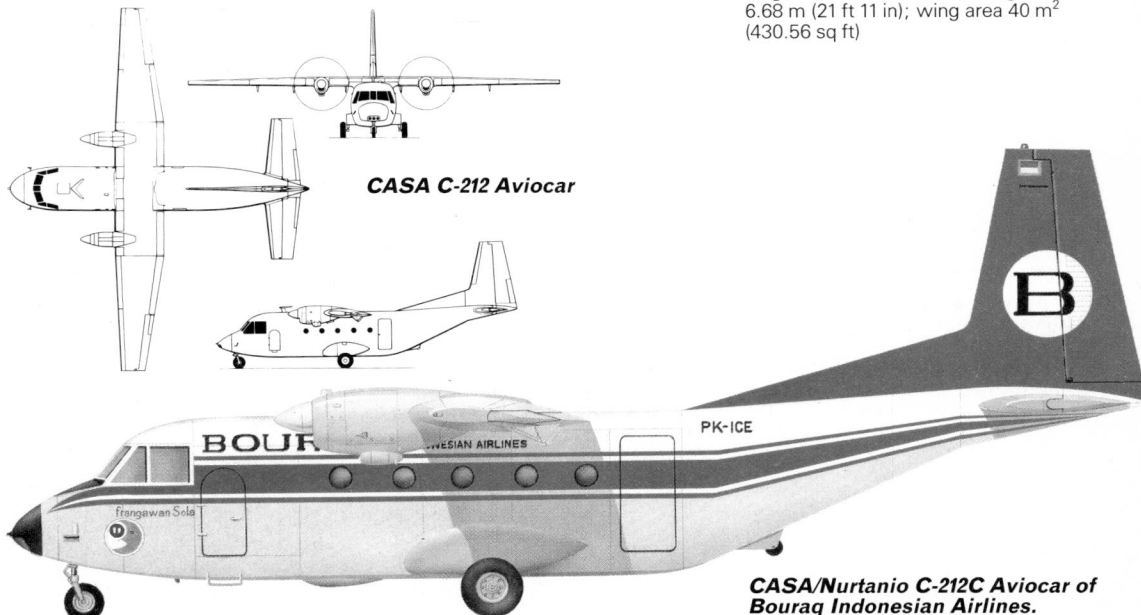

CASA/Nurtanio C-212C Aviocar of Bouraq Indonesian Airlines.

CASA (MBB) 223 Flamingo

The aircraft now known as the **CASA 223 Flamingo** spent so much of its development and production life undergoing changes of management that its relative obscurity is perhaps not surprising. Its origins go back to the German company SIAT (Siebelwerke-ATG) which was itself a successor to the famous prewar Klemm lightplane company. When aircraft design and production were again permitted in Germany in 1955, SIAT was one of the first to enter this field, with a four-seat sporting and touring monoplane known as the **SIAT 222**. SIAT's second design, the **SIAT 223 Flamingo**, won a government-sponsored design competition in the early 1960s for a fully-aerobatic club and training aircraft, and the first of four prototypes was flown on 1 March 1967. It was originally proposed in two versions, the basic aerobatic **223K** two-seater and the four-seat, extended-span **223N**, but after changes in requirements the two production versions emerged as the **223A1**, a 'two plus two' utility model, and the **223K1** single-seat aerobatic variant. In 1970, SIAT became a member of the MBB (Messerschmitt-Bölkow-Blohm) industrial group, with production of what became the **MBB 223** continuing until early 1972, when MBB transferred the whole Flamingo programme to Hispano Aviación of Spain. At that time German production had totalled 50, including 15 for the Turkish air force.

The first Spanish-built Flamingo was flown on 14 February 1972, but later in the same year Hispano was taken over by the Madrid-based Construcciones Aeronáuticas SA (CASA). A second series of 50 was built by Hispano/CASA, of which 30 were reportedly for the Syrian air force and three others for the Spanish air force.

Specification
Type: one/four-seat trainer and utility aircraft
Powerplant: one 149-kW (200-hp) Avco Lycoming IO-360-C1B flat-four piston engine
Performance: (two-seat) maximum speed 243 km/h (151 mph); cruising speed (75 per cent power) 216 km/h (134 mph); range (including reserves) 880 km (547 miles); maximum range 1150 km (715 miles); maximum rate of climb at sea level 258 m (846 ft) per minute; service ceiling 3750 m (12,300 ft)

Weights: (two-seat) empty equipped 685 kg (1,510 lb); maximum take-off 1050 kg (2,315 lb)

Dimensions: span 8.28 m (27 ft 2 in); length 7.43 m (24 ft 4½ in); height 2.7 m (8 ft 10¼ in); wing area 11.5 m² (123.8 sq ft)

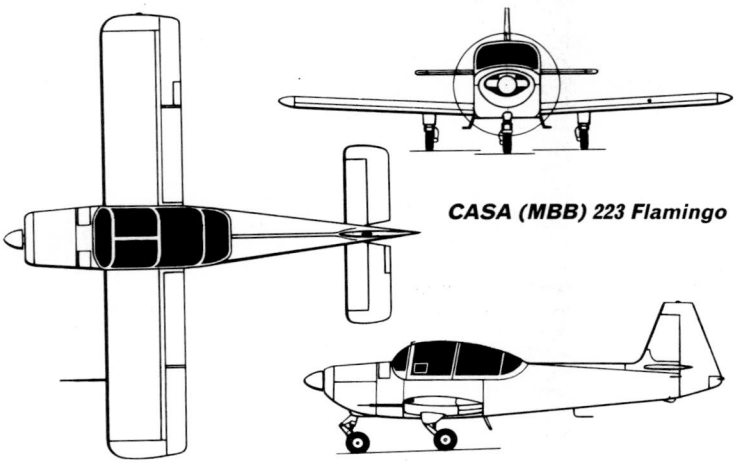

CASA (MBB) 223 Flamingo

Flamingos lined up outside the CASA factory in Spain. Most of these aircraft were delivered to the Syrian air force for primary training.

Flamingos lined up outside the CASA factory in Spain. Most of these aircraft where delivered to the Syrian air force for primary training.

Call-Air Model A

In the late 1930s members of the Call family of air-minded ranchers in Wyoming combined their talents to design a basic and robust utility aircraft for use by farmers and ranchers. Finalised as the **Model A**, it was ready for production in 1940, but with a major war raging in Europe there was no opportunity to proceed further at that time. Subsequently the Call Aircraft Company was formed at Afton, Wyoming, but although a prototype of the Model A was built, powered by a 60-kW (80-hp) Continental A-80 engine, it was not until 1946 that production of the **Model A-2** could begin. The designation **A-1** had been applied to the prototype when it was re-engined with a 75-kW (100-hp) Avco Lycoming O-235-A engine, and it was in this form that original type certification was gained on 26 July 1944. The production Model A-2 was a braced low-wing monoplane with wooden fabric-covered wings and fuselage and tail unit of welded steel tube with fabric covering. Landing gear was of fixed tailwheel type and powerplant of the A-2 was a 93-kW (125-hp) Avco Lycoming O-280-A. This model was followed by the **A-3** powered by a 93-kW (125-hp) Continental C-125-2, and then by the **A-4** with a 101-kW (135-hp) Avco Lycoming O-290-D2. Throughout the production of these three models there was little difference in basic design and changes, other than powerplant, were limited to refinements. The final versions to be developed by Call included the **A-4 Model 150, A-5,** and **A-6** as detailed in variants (below). The Call Air-

craft Company was acquired by Intermountain Manufacturing Company (IMCO) in 1962, and from the A-5 and A-6 a new agricultural aircraft was developed as the **IMCO CallAir A-9**. A scaled-up development of this appeared in 1966 as the **IMCO CallAir B-1**.

Many changes followed: the Aero Commander Division of Rockwell Standard Corporation acquired IMCO in December 1966, subsequently becoming the Aero Commader Division of the North American Rockwell Corporation. In 1971 Rockwell International Corporation entered into an agreement with Industrias Unidas SA of Mexico, and the resulting Aeronautica Agricola Mexicana SA continued production of one of these aircraft. The changing designations of these aircraft are listed below.

Variants
CallAir A-4 Model 150: two/three-seat cabin monoplane powered by a 112-kW (150-hp) Avco Lycoming O-320-A2A
CallAir A-5: agricultural duster/sprayer version of the A-4 Model 150 retaining the same powerplant
CallAir A-6: improved version of the A-5 with a 134-kW (180-hp) Avco

Lycoming O-360-A1A
IMCO CallAir A-9: improved agricultural aircraft developed from the A-5/A-6, powered by a 175-kW (235-hp) Avco Lycoming O-540-B2B5
IMCO CallAir B-1: scaled-up development of the CallAir design with increased span, greater hopper capacity and a 298-kW (400-hp) Avco Lycoming IO-720-A1A

Ag Commander A-9: designation of the IMCO A-9 as produced by Aero Commander
Ag Commander A-9 Super: version of the A-9 with increased hopper capacity and a 216-kW (290-hp) Avco Lycoming IO-540
Ag Commander B-1: designation of the IMCO B-1 as produced by Aero Commander

Two closely related aircraft are the Call-Air A-9 (background) and IMCO Call-Air B-1. The latter has a more powerful engine, allowing an increase in hopper size from 0.64 m³ (22.5 cu ft) to 1.13 m³ (40 cu ft).

Sparrow Commander: redesignation of Ag Commander A-9 by North American Rockwell

Quail Commander: redesignation of Ag Commander A-9 Super by North American Rockwell

Snipe Commander: redesignation of Ag Commander B-1 by North American Rockwell; production of this version ended when Rockwell International

came to an agreement with the Mexican company AAMSA

AAMSA A9B-M Quail: designation of production version of the Quail Commander; it incorporates a number of structural and aerodynamic refinements to improve maintenance and field performance

AAMSA Snipe: designation applied to Snipe Commander; production of this

version was terminated at the end of 1975

Specification
IMCO CallAir A-9
Type: single-seat agricultural aircraft
Powerplant: one 175-kW (235-hp) Avco Lycoming O-540-B2B5 flat-six piston engine
Performance: maximum speed

192 km/h (119 mph) at sea level; service ceiling 4265 m (14,000 ft)
Weights: empty 726 kg (1,600 lb); maximum take-off 1497 kg (3,300 lb)
Dimensions: span 10.67 m (35 ft 0 in); length 7.32 m (24 ft 0 in); height 2.31 m (7 ft 7 in); wing area 16.92 m² (182.1 sq ft)

Canadair CL-28 Argus

The **Canadair CL-28** (military designation **CP-107**) **Argus** was designed to meet a 1952 requirement for a maritime patrol and anti-submarine warfare (ASW) aircraft to succeed the Avro Lancaster Mk 10 and the Lockheed P2V Neptune in service with the Royal Canadian Air Force's Maritime Air Command. The aircraft was based on the Bristol Britannia airliner. The wings, tail and landing gear were virtually identical on both machines; the fuselage was redesigned to incorporate two weapons bays, and pressurisation was eliminated as it was not necessary at the low altitude customarily used by maritime reconnaissance aircraft.

The first **Argus Mk 1** first flew from Canadair's factory at Montreal, Quebec Province on 28 March 1957. It was followed by 12 further aircraft built to Mk 1 standard, fitted with American APS-20 radar in a chin-mounted radome. The 20 examples of the **Argus Mk 2** were fitted with British ASV-21 radar mounted in a smaller radome. Production ended in July 1960, with the completion of the RCAF's last Argus Mk 2.

The normal crew complement of the Argus was 15, comprising three pilots, two flight engineers, three navigators and seven ASW systems operators. This enabled the crew to work in shifts during a patrol which could last up to 20 hours, a crew rest area with bunks and a galley being provided.

The crew stations comprised an observer/bomb-aimer's position in the glazed nose; a flight deck with provision for pilot, co-pilot and flight engineer; behind them the routine navigator and radio operator's positions; and a rear compartment housed six or seven members of the ASW team under a tactical co-ordinator, with two beam lookout positions behind this compartment.

The ASW equipment carried by the Argus included search radar, magnetic anomaly detector, electronic counter-

The Argus was based on the Bristol Britannia airframe, but reverted to radial engines. Note the undernose search radar.

measures and a diesel exhaust detector. Sonobuoys, flares and marine markers were carried in an aft fuselage compartment and offensive weapons, which could include acoustic homing torpedoes and depth charges, were carried in the two internal weapon bays. In addition to ASW and maritime patrol, the Argus could be used also for minelaying and, in emergency, as a transport.

After grounding of the fleet of aircraft in 1972 because of landing gear problems, a specification was drawn up for a

Long-Range Patrol Aircraft to replace it in service as early as possible. This requirement was met by a special version of the Lockheed P-3 Orion designated the CP-140 Aurora, and by the end of 1981 all CP-107s had been withdrawn from service with the Canadian Armed Forces.

Specification
Type: long-range patrol aircraft
Powerplant: four 2535-kW (3,400-shp) each Wright R-3350-EA1 Cyclone turbo-compound radial piston engines
Performance: maximum speed 507 km/h (315 mph) at 3050 m (10,000 ft); service ceiling 7620 m

(25,000 ft) maximum range 9495 km (5,900 miles)
Weights: empty equipped 36741 kg (81,000 lb); maximum take-off 71214 kg (157,000 lb)
Dimensions: span 43.37 m (142 ft 3½ in); length 39.26 m (128 ft 9½ in); height 11.79 m (38 ft 8 in); wing area 192.77 m² (2,075 sq ft)
Armament: a maximum of 3629 kg (8,000 lb) of bombs, depth charges, homing torpedoes or mines in two internal weapons bays, plus up to 1724 kg (3,800 lb) of air-to-surface missiles or free-fall weapons on underwing hardpoints

Canadair CL-41 Tutor

The development programme for the **Canadair CL-41** was funded privately by the company because of the Canadian government's early lack of interest in this basic jet trainer. Two prototypes were built, each powered by a 1087-kg (2,400-lb) thrust Pratt & Whitney JT12A-5 turbojet, the first flying on 13 January 1960. In September 1961 the Canadian government ordered 190 examples of the **CL-41A** for the Royal Canadian Air Force (now the Canadian Forces) with the designation **CT-114 Tutor**. Features include side-by-side seats, an upward-opening canopy, lateral door-type airbrakes, a T-tail and a steerable nosewheel. These were

powered by the General Electric J85-CAN-40 turbojet of 1293-kg (2,850-lb) thrust. Delivery took place between 1963-6.

Further development resulted in the **CL-41G** armament trainer and light-attack aircraft. This has an uprated

engine and six underwing hardpoints; the landing gear is modified for soft-field operation, and 'zero level' automatic ejection seats are fitted. In March 1966 the Royal Malaysian Air Force ordered 20, these being named **Tebuan** (Wasp) in Malaysian service, and the first of these were delivered in 1967.

Main operator of the CT-114 Tutor in the Canadian Forces is Training Command's No. 2 Flying Training School at Moose Jaw, Saskatchewan. After primary training, pupils do some 200 hours on the CT-114 to gain their 'wings' before proceeding to specialised training for combat jets, multi-engined types or

Canadair CL-41G Tebuan of the Royal Malaysian air force

helicopters.

Ten Tutors were modified for the Golden Hawks (later Snowbirds) aerobatic team and the type also serves with the Flying Instructors' School. These units share the Moose Jaw base with No. 2 FTS. In 1976 the Canadian Forces began a 113-aircraft modification programme which included provision of external fuel tanks, upgrading of avionics, changes to the canopy electrical system and relocation of the engine ice-detector probe.

Specification
CL-41G Tebuan

Type: two-seat light-attack aircraft
Powerplant: one 1338-kg (2,950-lb) thrust General Electric J85-J4 turbojet
Performance: maximum speed 772 km/h (480 mph) at 8685 m (28,500 ft); service ceiling 12860 m (42,200 ft); range 2157 km (1,340 miles)
Weights: empty 2402 kg (5,296 lb);

maximum take-off 5120 kg (11,288 lb)
Dimensions: span 11.13 m (36 ft 6 in); length 9.75 m (32 ft 0 in); height 2.76 m (9 ft 0¾ in); wing area 20.44 m² (220 sq ft)
Armament: up to 1814 kg (4,000 lb) of weapons on underfuselage and underwing attachments

Canadair CL-44

Canadair CL-44-6 (CL-44D/CC-106 Yukon) of ANDES (Aerolineas Nacionales del Ecuador)

In March 1954 Canadair Ltd negotiated a manufacturing licence for the Bristol Britannia from the British company. This covered, initially, a maritime reconnaissance version of this airliner for service with the Royal Canadian Air Force, the first being delivered in the autumn of 1957 under the designation CL-28 Argus. It differed from its parent aircraft in having a redesigned and unpressurised fuselage to make possible the inclusion of weapon bays, and it had economical turbo-compound piston engines to give the long-range/endurance that is essential for a maritime role.

The RCAF had also a modest need for an aircraft which could be used in freight/troop-carrying roles, and to meet this requirement Canadair proposed another version of the Britannia. To provide for the large capacity/payload that was needed, Canadair's design included increased wing span and a lengthened fuselage, and alternative powerplant proposals included Bristol Orion, Pratt & Whitney T34, or Rolls-Royce Tyne turboprops, and Wright R-3350 radial piston engines. The first of these was selected by the RCAF, but when development of this engine came to an end in the UK the Rolls-Royce Tyne was chosen instead. The aircraft was designated **Canadair CL-44D** in this form, and 12 were built for the RCAF, with which they served as the **CC-106 Yukon**, the last of them being delivered in 1961.

These RCAF aircraft had what was then conventional side-loading, with large cargo doors in the fuselage, forward and aft of the wing. While the CL-44D was under development and construction, Canadair's design team proposed a then-revolutionary idea to simplify and speed cargo loading: the provision of a hinged aft fuselage section which would swing to one side, complete with tail unit, to permit straight-in loading or unloading of freight. This enabled large items of cargo, or palletised freight, to be transferred directly from trucks into the large cargo hold, and the **CL-44D-4**, as this version was de-

signated, became the world's first cargo aircraft to introduce this capability on the production line.

The concept appealed to large cargo operators, and Canadair soon received orders from The Flying Tiger Line, Seaboard World Airlines, and Slick Airways. The first CL-44D-4 flew on 16 November 1960, and FAA certification was gained seven months later. In July 1961 Flying Tiger and Seaboard flew the first services with these aircraft. A fourth customer was Loftleidir of Iceland, its initial order for three aircraft being completed as civil transports with seating accommodation for a maximum of 178 passengers. Used to provide low-cost transatlantic services, this fleet was supplemented by a fourth aircraft in 1966. It differed from the earlier trio by having a fuselage that was lengthened by 4.62 m (15 ft 1¾ in) to provide accommodation for a maximum of 214 passengers. Designated **CL-44J**, and known also as the **Canadair 400**, this flew for the first time on 8 November 1965, and after it had entered service the company's three 178-seat airliners were retrospectively converted to CL-44J standard.

One other variant resulted when the Conroy Aircraft Corporation in the USA purchased a CL-44D-4 from Flying Tiger for conversion as a large-cargo transporter. This company's founder, Jack Conroy, had developed the original Pregnant Guppy and its successors, and considered the CL-44 suitable for a similar exercise. In its completed form, designated **CL-44-O** and first flown on 26 November 1969, it had a maximum internal height of 3.45 m (11 ft 4 in), and a maximum width of 4.24 m (13 ft 11 in),

Canadair CL-44D-4

and retained the swing-tail loading capability.

Production of civil CL-44s totalled 27, and the RCAF's CC-106 Yukons eventually came on to the civil market. Many of these have changed hands several times and a few remain in service in 1990, including the sole CL-44-O with Heavylift Cargo Airlines in the UK.

Specification
Canadair CL-44D-4

Type: long-range cargo transport
Powerplant: four 4273-kW (5,730-hp) each Rolls-Royce Tyne 515/10 turboprops

Performance: cruising speed 621 km/h (386 mph) at 6095 m (20,000 ft) with typical payload; service ceiling 9145 m (30,000 ft); range with maximum payload 4627 km (2,875 miles); range with maximum fuel 8991 km (5,587 miles)
Weights: empty 40348 kg (88,952 lb); maximum take-off 95254 kg (210,000 lb)
Dimensions: span 43.37 m (142 ft 3½ in); length 41.73 m (136ft 10¾ in); height 11.79 m (38 ft 8 in); wing area 192.77 m² (2,075 sq ft)

Canadair CL-66 Cosmopolitan

With the advent of turboprop engines, a number of airliner manufacturers examined the possibility of re-engining airframes which had been designed for piston engines. Very few of these projects became actual hardware, but the Cosmopolitan was an exception.

Production of the Convair 440 was completed in 1958, by which time nearly 1,000 of the CV-240/340/440 transports had been built, of which almost half were delivered to the US military services. Convair was concentrating on development of the CV-880/990 series, but Pacific Airmotive Corporation undertook conversion of a number of CV-340/440 airframes to take Allison 501 turboprops for several airlines, the resulting aircraft being designated CV-580.

Meanwhile, the Royal Canadian Air Force was in the market for a twin-turbo-

prop transport, and under an agreement between Convair and Canadair the CV-440 jigs and tools were transferred to the latter company's factory at Cartierville, Montreal. In collaboration with the British aero-engine manufacturer Napier, Canadair proposed to use the Napier Eland turboprop married to newly-manufactured CV-440 airframes under the company designation **Canadair 540** (the **CL-66** in Canadair's own terminology). Two pre-production aircraft, actually re-engined

Built as a turboprop version of the CV-440, the Canadair CL-66 was used in small numbers by the RCAF/Canadian Forces as the CC-109 Cosmopolitan. In 1990 seven were still in use as VIP/liaison transports.

CV-440s, were used for demonstration purposes and Royal Canadian Air Force crew training; they were designated **Canadair 540C**, and were later bought by Quebecair in a 52-passenger configuration.

The first production 540 flew in January 1960 and 10 were built for the RCAF, which designated them **CC-109 Cosmopolitan**. As civil passenger transports the aircraft were offered with accommodation for 48 to 64, depending

on configuration, while the RCAF version was a convertible with a reinforced floor and 3,05 m (10 ft) cargo loading door; the payload was 6486 kg (14,300 lb).

In addition to its 10 Cosmopolitans, the RCAF eventually acquired the two Quebecair aircraft plus Canadair's demonstrator and all were re-engined subsequently with Allison 501 turboprobs. Seven remain in service in 1990.

Specification
Type: military transport

Powerplant: two 2610-kW (3,500-shp) each Napier Eland NE1.6 Mk 504A turboprops
Performance: maximum speed 547 km/h (340 mph); cruising speed 518 km/h (322 mph) at 6095 m (20,000 ft); range with 48 passengers 2002 km (1,244 miles)
Weights: empty 14666 kg (32,333 lb); maximum take-off 24131 kg (53,200 lb)
Dimensions: span 32.11 m (105 ft 4 in); length 24.84 m (81 ft 6 in); height 8.59 m (28 ft 2 in); wing area 89.54 m^2 (963.82 sq ft)

Canadair CL-84

Canadair's interest in V/STOL aircraft began in 1956, and in 1963 the company was joined by Canada's Department of Defence Production in the funding of a prototype of a tilt-wing research aircraft. Designated **Canadair CL-84**, the aircraft featured a conventional fuselage with crew positions for two and with internal capacity for test equipment, or seats for up to 12 troops for possible military evaluation. The wing could be tilted through an angle of 100°, effectively facilitating backward flight at 56 km/h (35 mph) in addition to forward and hovering flight. Krueger leading-edge flaps were fitted, together with full-span slotted trailing-edge flaps which could be operated differentially as ailerons. At tilt angles of up to 30° the tailplane and wing were inter-connected to adopt identical angles of incidence, but at higher angles the tailplane assumed a zero-incidence setting. At low speed, or in the hover, control in the pitch axis was maintained by the use of two small rotors mounted at the end of the fuselage.

The first hovering flight took place on 7 May 1965 and the aircraft embarked upon a test and development programme in which it had accumulated 145 hours before crashing on 12 September

One of the most advanced aircraft built in Canada, the CL-84 was a fascinating tilt-wing design. This example is seen in translational flight, and carries two external fuel tanks.

1967, an accident attributed to malfunction of the pitch control of the port propeller. In July, however, the Canadian Department of Defence had ordered three examples of the improved **CL-84-1** (Canadian Armed Forces designation **CX-84**) with 1119-kW (1,500-shp) Lycoming LTC1K-4A turboprop engines in place of the 1044-kW (1,400-shp) units which powered the prototype. Internal fuel capacity was also increased and two hardpoints were provided.

Maiden flight date for the first CX-84 was 19 February 1970, this event preceding a 150-hour manufacturer's test programme which included gun firing trials with a 7.62-mm (0.3-in) multi-barrel Mini-gun in a General Electric SUU 11A/A pod. In 1972-3 the second aircraft was used for a joint American/British/Canadian V/STOL Instrument Flight programme, flown from the US Naval Air Test Center at Patuxent River, Maryland. As a result of a demonstration to the US Navy in February 1972, during which it

made a number of landings on the Interim Sea Control Ship USS *Guam*, the first CX-84 was delivered to Patuxent River in July 1973 for an in-depth evaluation but crashed during that month. The programme was completed by the second aircraft and included sea trials aboard USS *Guadalcanal* in March 1974.

Specification
Type: V/STOL research aircraft
Powerplant: two 1119-kW (1,500-shp) each Lycoming LTC1K-4C turboprops

Performance: maximum speed 517 km/h (321 mph); maximum cruising speed 497 km/h (309 mph); range 547 km (340 miles)
Weights: empty 3827 kg (8,437 lb); maximum VTOL take-off 5715 kg (12,600 lb); maximum STOL take-off 6577 kg (14,500 lb)
Dimensions: span 10.16 m (33 ft 4 in); length 14.41 m (47 ft 3½ in); height with wing horizontal 4.34 m (14 ft 2¾ in); height with wing at 90° 5.22 m (17 ft 1½ in); wing area 21.65 m^2 (233 sq ft)

Canadair CL-215

The **Canadair CL-215** was designed to meet a requirement for a firefighting amphibian which could replace the miscellany of types used in the 'water bomber' role in the 1960s. The basic parameters of the CL-215 design emerged from a symposium on forest fire protection held in Ottawa in December 1963. Early in 1966 it was decided to put the type into production. The Canadian Province of Quebec and the French Protection Civile were the first customers, ordering 20 and 10 CL-215s respectively to undertake a primary role of forest fire detection and suppression. However, the robust and versatile amphibian was also available to military customers for the search and rescue and utility roles.

From the outset simplicity of design was a primary requirement, with ease of maintenance and reliability of equipment (achieved through the incorporation of already-proven systems wherever practicable) also receiving careful attention. Protection against salt-water corrosion was achieved through the use of corrosion-resistant materials and by carefully sealing components during assembly.

The CL-215 is an aircraft of substantial size. It has a single-step hull, and fixed stabilising floats are mounted just inboard of the wing-tips. The tricycle landing gear comprises a twin nosewheel and single mainwheels, the former retracting into the hull and the latter being raised to lie flat against the hull during operations from water.

The high-mounted wing and tailplane are single-piece structures, with ailerons and flaps occupying the entire wing trailing edge. All fuel is carried in flexible

Canadair CL-215 of the Royal Thai Navy, operating on search and rescue missions from Bangkok

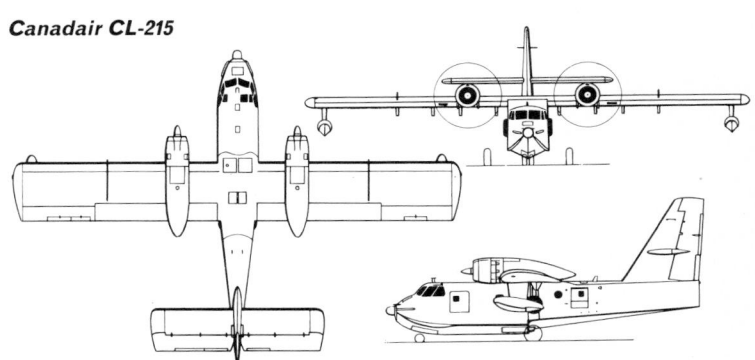

wing cells, and the engine nacelles are integral with the wing structure.

For its fire-fighting role the CL-215 can lift 5455 litres (1,200 Imp gal) of water or retardant fluid in two fuselage tanks. The water is scooped from a convenient lake or river through two retractable inlets mounted under the hull, while the CL-215 taxies across the surface. It then takes off and flies to the area of the fire where the load is jettisoned in under a second. The operation is repeated until the fire is under control. In most circumstances a load can be dropped at least every 10 minutes.

Configured for the search and rescue role, the CL-215 carries a crew of six. In addition to the pilot and co-pilot, a flight engineer is housed on the flight deck. The navigator's station is located further back in the forward fuselage, and two observers are carried in the rear fuse-

Canadair CL-215

lage. The basic avionics (typically HF, VHF and VHF/HM transceivers, ADF, VOR/ILS/glide slope and marker beacon) are augmented by an AVQ-21 weather and search radar in the nose, a radio altimeter, an UHF/VHF homer and DME. Maximum endurance is 12 hours.

First flight of the CL-215 was on 23

October 1967, and deliveries to France began in May 1969.

When production ceased in April 1990, 125 had been delivered to the Canadian Provinces and Territories of Alberta (4), Manitoba (5), Newfoundland (4), Northwest Territories (2), Ontario (9), Quebec (19), Saskatchewan (4) and Yukon (2): the governments of France (15), Greece (17), Italy (5), Spain (30), Thailand (2), Venezuela (2) and Yugoslavia (5), all equipped for firefighting. However, Spain has equipped eight for SAR and coastal patrol, and Thailand two; the

Venezuelan aircraft are operated by the government agency CVG Ferrominera Orinoco in passenger configuration.

In 1986 Canadair announced the go-ahead for a turboprop version of the CL-215 powered by two 1775-kW (2,380-shp) each Pratt & Whitney Canada PW123AF turbine engines and designated **CL-215T**. The first of two prototypes flew on 8 June 1989, quickly followed by the second on 20 September. Plans to build new airframes were abandoned in mid-1990, but retrofit kits have been ordered by the Quebec provincial

government (the launch customer for two) and Spain (15). CL-215T improvements include an upgraded and air conditioned flight deck, a new fuel system allowing both pressure and gravity refuelling, aerodynamic modifications including wingtip endplates and auxiliary fins on the tailplane, and a large capacity four-tank drop system for firefighting or aerial spraying.

Specification
Type: multi-purpose amphibian
Powerplant: two 1566-kW (2,100-hp)

each Pratt & Whitney R-2800-CA3 radial piston engines
Performance: cruising speed 291 km/h (181 mph) at 3050 m (10,000 ft); range with 1587-kg (3,500-lb) payload at long-range cruise power 2092 km (1,300 miles)
Weights: empty 12161 kg (26,810 lb); maximum take-off, land 19731 kg (43,500 lb); water 17100 kg (37,700 lb)
Dimensions: span 28.6 m (93 ft 10 in); length 19.82 m (65 ft 0½ in); height 8.92 m (29 ft 3 in); wing area 100.33 m² (1,080 sq ft)

Canadair CL-600 and CL-601 Challenger

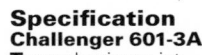

The Canadair CL-600 Challenger proved a popular executive transport. This aircraft wears Saudi colours

Originating from the drawing board of Bill Lear, designer of the Lear Jet, this executive aircraft was at first named **LearStar 600**. However, when Lear sold the exclusive production rights to Canadair in April 1976 it was redesignated **Canadair CL-600** and became known subsequently as the **Challenger 600**. Canadair's market research indicated a sales potential for some 1,000 business aircraft in this category. Believing it could capture some 40 per cent of this market, the company launched the Challenger development programme on 29 October 1976, at which time it had 53 firm orders and a Canadian government backing loan of Can$130 million.

Canadair introduced a number of changes in the basic design, the most noticeable being movement of the tailplane from a position near the bottom of the fuselage to the tip of the swept fin. A major selling point for the Challenger is a fuselage of large cross-section, with a width of 2.49 m (8 ft 2 in) and height of 1.85 m (6 ft 1 in), providing a 'walk about' cabin not shared by other purpose-built executive jets and providing comfortable accommodation for a maximum of 18 passengers. Powered by two 3402-kg (7,500-lb) each ALF 502L turbofans, three pre-production Challenger 600s were built, the first flying on 8 November 1978, and the first production aircraft flew on 21 September 1979. Canadian and FAA certification were gained during August 1980 and on 10 November 1980 respectively. Both imposed temporary restrictions, limiting gross weight to 14969 kg (33,000 lb) and speed to 587 km/h (365 mph), while flight into known icing conditions and the use of thrust reversers were prohibited.

To overcome these limitations Canadair carried out a weight and drag reduction programme which, at the same time, offered a considerable performance improvement.

Full certification of the CL-600 was gained in November 1980 and delivery of

production aircraft began early in 1981. When production ceased a total of 83 Challenger 600s had been built, and from 1983 their place on the production line was taken by the re-engined and significantly improved **Model 601**. In recent years 69 Model 600s have been retrofitted with winglets, which assist range/payload performance.

The improved Challenger, designated the **Model 601-1A**, and powered by General Electric CF34-1A turbofans, flew for the first time on 17 September 1982 and received FAA certification in March 1983. Customers for this version include the Canadian DND (4) for VIP use, Canadian DOT (2) for flight inspection, Luftwaffe (7), People's Republic of China (3) and the Malaysian Air Force (2).

In 1986 Canadair launched the **Challenger 600-3A** using more-powerful 9,220-lb Dash 3A engines giving better climb and high temperature take-off performance, an EFIS-equipped cockpit, power assisted passenger door, twin nose-mounted landing lights, and winglets. First flight was on 28 September 1986, certification followed in April 1987 and production deliveries began in May 1987. Total Challenger deliveries of all versions stood at around 220 by the end of 1990.

Variants
Challenger 601-3A/ER: a sub variant of the Model 3A offering extended range, the aircraft flew in November 1988 and received Canadian

certification in March 1989. Available as a new build aircraft or a modification kit applicable to Model 1A or 3A airframes, the option includes a new conformal fuel tank housed in an extended tail fairing which increases the fuselage length by 18 inches, and extends the Challenger 601 range to 3,600 miles.
Challenger 601-S: a lower-priced version of the Challenger business jet, the 601-S was launched in June 1989. With a reduced maximum weight reached by deleting auxiliary fuel tanks and some avionics together with a standard 12-seat cabin, the Model S is intended for transcontinental ranges rather than transoceanic, and the first examples were due for delivery before the end of 1990.

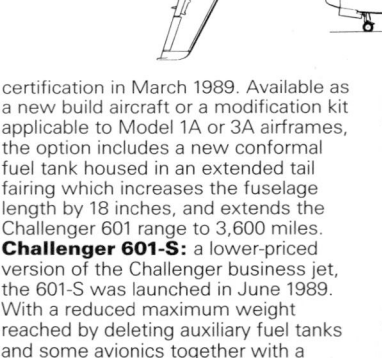

Canadair CL-600 Challenger

Specification
Challenger 601-3A
Type: business jet
Powerplant: two 3924-kg (8,650-lb) thrust each General Electric CF34-3A turbofans
Performance: maximum cruising speed 882 km/h (548 mph); long-range cruising speed 786 km/h (488 mph); maximum operating altitude 12500 m (41,000 ft); range with maximum fuel 6356 km (3,950 miles)
Weights: empty operating 11197 kg (24,685 lb); maximum take-off 19550 kg (43,100 lb)
Dimensions: span 19.61 m (64 ft 4 in); length 20.85 m (68 ft 5 in); height 6.3 m (20 ft 8 in); wing area 48.31 m² (520 sq ft)

Canadair Regional Jet

Following extensive studies lasting several years but with definitive design studies beginning in the autumn of 1987, the Canadair component of Bombardier Inc. officially launched the Regional Jet in March 1989 as a small airliner developed from its Challenger corporate transport. The decision to press ahead with the type was taken in the belief that there would be a demand for 500 or more small airliners, optimised for regional operations, in the period between 1992 and 2000, and Canadair expected that a large slice of this market could be captured by a high-performance type offering the comfort levels typical of larger airliners.

In its basic form the **Regional Jet** is a 50-passenger derivative of the Challenger 601 with the fuselage stretched by 5.92 m (19 ft 5 in) and other modifications incorporated to optimise the airframe. The **Regional Jet** is a low-wing monoplane of light alloy construction with tricycle landing gear, swept flying surfaces, a T-tail, and a powerplant of two fuel-economical turbofans pod-mounted on the sides of the rear fuselage. notable features are an advanced wing section for high transonic speed, and winglets for reduced drag at high speeds. The cabin is 14.76 m (48 ft 5 in) long with a maximum width of 2.49 m (8 ft 2 in), it

can accommodate a standard payload of 50 passengers in a four-abreast arrangement at a pitch of 0.79 m (31 in) with a central aisle; there is accommodation for a crew of up to four.

The first of three development aircraft was manufactured at Canadair's Dorval facility near Montreal, and lifted off on its first flight on 10 May 1991. The three development aircraft were used in the certification programme, which was completed first in the USA and then only one week later in Canada, and the first production aeroplane was completed in July 1992 and delivered to Lufthansa CityLine of Germany in October of the same year for the start of revenue-earning operations in the following month. By August 1997 the

manufacturer had received orders for 261 aircraft and made delivery of 159 machines after the production rate was increased from two to three aircraft in 1994 and to five aircraft per month during October 1995.

The current variants are the **Regional Jet Series 100** baseline model, the **Regional Jet Series 100ER** extended-range model with greater fuel capacity and a higher take-off weight for a range of 3000 km (1,864 miles), the **Regional Jet Series 100LR** long-range model with still further increases in fuel and take-off weight for a range of more than 3648 km (2,267 miles), the RegionalJet Series 200 with the powerplant of two CF34-3B1 turbofans with the same basic rating as the CF34-3A1 but maintained to higher ambient temperatures and offering greater climb and cruise power, the **Regional Jet Series 200ER** and **200LR** equivalent to their Series 100 counterparts, and the Corporate Jetliner company shuttle model with accommodation for between 18 and 30 corporate passengers.

Canadair is currently at work on the **Regional Jet Series 700** with span and length increased to 23.01 m (75 ft 6 in) and 32.41 m (106 ft 4 in) respectively, accommodation for 70 passengers, and the uprated powerplant of two 61.36-kN (13,795-lb st) CF34-8C1 turbofans. Other changes in this model, which was launched in January 1997 for a first flight in 1999 and a service entry in 2000, include a larger root plug, leading-edge

Lufthansa CityLine (formerly DLT) was the European lead customer for the Regional Jet, which it received from October 1992.

extensions and slats for improved field performance, and a larger tail unit. The launch order was placed by Brit Air of France, with another 67 ordered by other airlines up to August 1997.

Specification
Canadair Regional Jet Series 100
Type: 50-passenger regional airliner
Powerplant: two 41.01-kN (9,220-lb st) General Electric CF34-3A1 turbofans
Performance: cruising speed, maximum 851 km/h (529 mph) and normal 786 km/h (488 mph), in each

case at 11280 m (37,000 ft); maximum climb rate 1128 m (3,700 ft) at 460 m (1,500 ft); maximum operating altitude 12495 m (41,000 ft); range 1815 km (1,128 miles) with maximum payload

Weights: empty 13653 kg (30,100 lb); maximum take-off 21523 kg (47,450 lb)
Dimensions: span (69 ft 7 in 21.21 m); length 87 ft 10 in (26.77 m); height 20 ft 5 in (6.22 m); area 587.10 sq ft (54.54 m²) excluding winglets

---

Caproni Bergamaschi Ca 135

Caproni Bergamaschi Ca 135/P.XI of the Royal Hungarian air force, southern Russia, 1942

A medium bomber designed at Bergamo, the **Caproni Bergamaschi Ca 135** was not allocated a type number in the Caproni Bergamaschi Ca 300 series as it was to have been built at Caproni's main Taliedo factory. However, the project was retained at Ponte San Pietro and the prototype, completed in early 1935, was flown for the first time on 1 April. Powered by two 597-kW (800-hp) Isotta Fraschini Asso XI RC radial engines, the Ca 135 was of mixed construction, with a stressed skin forward fuselage and a wood and fabric-covered welded steel-tube rear section, the wing being a metal and wood structure with fabric and wood covering. Production Ca 135s had three-blade metal propellers instead of the two-blade wooden propellers of the prototype. Some aircraft, designated **Ca 135 Tipo Spagna** (Spanish type), were ordered by the Regia Aeronautica in 1936, these having 623-kW (836-hp) Asso XI RC 40 engines, and Breda turrets in nose, dorsal and ventral positions, the dorsal and ventral turrets being retractable. Maximum take-off weight had risen to 8390 kg (18,497 lb) from the prototype's 7360 kg (16,226 lb), but despite the increased power maximum speed dropped from 400 km/h (248 mph) to 365 km/h (227 mph). To restore overall

performance, in 1938 the Tipo Spagna aircraft had Fiat A.80 RC 41 or Piaggio P.XI RC 40 radials installed, each rated at 746 kW (1,000 hp). The Piaggio-engined version was the more successful and, redesignated **Ca 135 P.XI**, it was given revised engine cowlings, a refined nose section and a Caproni Lanciani dorsal turret. Unsuccessful in a May 1938 Imperial Japanese Army Air Force competition, in which the Fiat BR.20 was preferred, the Ca 135 P.XI was ordered by the Hungarian air force, which flew about 100 aircraft with the German Luftflotte IV against the Russians. The last example was retained by Caproni and fitted with a dihedral tailplane and 1044-kW (1,400-hp) Alfa Romeo 135 RC 32 Tornado radials which increased maximum speed of this **Ca 135bis Alfa** to more than 480 km/h (298 mph). Peru also pur-

chased the Ca 135, the initial order for six examples with 608-kW (815-hp) Asso XI RC 45 engines being followed by 32 aircraft designated **Ca 135 Tipo Peru** (Peruvian type) which had revised gun positions, modified cowlings and uprated 671-kW (900-hp) Asso XI RC 40 engines.

Variant
Ca 135 Raid: single example of special long-range version with extra fuel capacity and 736-kW (986-hp) Isotta-Fraschini Asso engines, built to order of the Brazilian pilot de Barros, who disappeared in the Ca 135 Raid over North Africa while attempting a 1937 flight from Italy to Brazil

Specification
Caproni Ca 135 P.XI

Type: medium bomber
Powerplant: two 746-kW (1,000-hp) each Piaggio P.XI RC 40 radial piston engines
Performance: maximum speed 440 km/h (273 mph) at 4800 m (15,750 ft); cruising speed 350 km/h (217 mph); service ceiling 6500 m (21,325 ft); maximum range 2000 km (1,243 miles)
Weights: empty 6050 kg (13,340 lb); maximum take-off 9550 kg (21,050 lb)
Dimensions: span 18.8 m (61 ft 8 in); length 14.4 m (47 ft 2¾ in); height 3.4 m (11 ft 1¾ in); wing area 60 m² (645.86 sq ft)
Armament: three 12.7 mm (0.5-in) machine-guns in nose, dorsal and ventral turrets, plus up to 1600 kg (3,527 lb) of bombs

---

Caproni Ca 1/Ca 3

In 1908 Count Gianni Caproni founded what was to become one of Italy's major aviation manufacturers, and his early designs included a biplane built in 1910 and a Blériot-like monoplane, powered by a 37-kW (50-hp) Gnome rotary, which flew in 1913. In October 1914, however, the company flew the **Caproni Ca 30** prototype of a three-engined bomber which had a central crew nacelle and twin booms to carry a triple-ruddered tail unit. The powerplant comprised a central engine mounted at the rear of the nacelle (a 75-kW/100-hp Gnome driving a pusher propeller) plus two wing-mounted 60-kW (80-hp) Gnomes each driving a tractor propeller. The definitive model, known to the firm as the **Ca 31**, was put into production as the **Ca 1**, and was powered by three 75-kW (100-hp) Fiat A.10 engines; the initial order was for 12 aircraft, although a further 150 were manufactured subsequently.

Variants
Ca.2: nine aircraft with the central engine replaced by a 112-kW (150-hp) Isotta-Fraschini V.4B

Specification
Caproni Ca 3

Type: heavy bomber
Powerplant: three 112-kW (150-hp) Isotta-Fraschini V.4B inline piston engines.
Performance: maximum speed 140 km/h (87 mph); service ceiling 4100 m (13,450 ft); range 450 km (280

miles)
Weights: empty 2300 kg (5,071 lb); maximum take-off 3312 kg (7,302 lb)
Dimensions: span 22.20 m (72 ft 10 in); length 10.90 m (35 ft 9¼ in); height 3.70 m (12 ft 1½ in)
Armament: two or four 7.7-mm (0.303-in) Revelli machine-guns, plus a bombload of 450 kg (992 lb)

Caproni Ca 31 of Escadrille CEP 115, Aéronautique Militaire (French air force), based on the Plateau de Malzéville during 1916

Caproni Ca 100

Based on the de Havilland D.H.60 Moth, but incorporating some minor differences in detail design, including an increased-span lower wing, the **Caproni Ca 100** was built in some numbers for civil and military use from 1929. Powered initially by the 63-kW (85-hp) de Havilland Gipsy engine, the Ca 100 was fitted also with a variety of engines of different output, including the 67-kW (90-hp) Blackburn Cirrus Minor, the 86-kW (115-hp) Isotta Fraschini Asso 80R, the 108-kW (145-hp) Colombo S.63 and the 63-kW (85-hp) Fiat A.50. A twin-float seaplane version, 30 of which were built by Macchi, was known as the **Ca 100 Idro** and in 1934 a light bombing trainer was built, powered by a 97-kW (130-hp) radial engine and able to carry four small bombs. In 1931 a Ca 100 Idro flown by Antonini and Trevisan established a seaplane altitude record of 5018 m (16,462 ft). In 1935 the Peruvian government signed a contract with Caproni which gave the company a 10-year

In effect a licence-built version of the de Havilland Moth, the Caproni Ca 100 featured several important differences. Most notable were the revised tail surfaces and longer lower wing.

monopoly for the manufacture and repair of military aircraft in that country. Several Ca 100s were supplied from Italy, and in May 1937 a factory was opened in Peru, charged with producing 25 Ca 100s within two years but actually building only 12 in that period, at an excessive cost. The type was also manufactured by a Caproni subsidiary in Bulgaria as the **KN-1**.

Specification
Type: two-seat trainer
Powerplant: one 63-kW (85-hp) de Havilland Gipsy inline piston engine
Performance: maximum speed 165 km/h (102 mph); cruising speed 140 km/h (87 mph); service ceiling 4000 m (13,125 ft); range 700 km (435 miles)
Weights: empty 400 kg (882 lb); maximum take-off 680 kg (1,499 lb)
Dimensions: span, upper 8.35 m (27 ft 4¾ in) and lower 10 m (32 ft 10 in); length 7.3 m (23 ft 11¼ in); height 2.75 m (9 ft 0¼ in); wing area 24.4 m² (262.65 sq ft)

Caproni Ca 101

A scaled-up Ca 97, the **Caproni Ca 101** appeared in 1927, initially as a civil transport powered by three 149-kW (200-hp) Armstrong Siddeley Lynx radial engines built under licence by Alfa Romeo. It was developed later as a bomber with 276-kW (370-hp) Piaggio Stella VII radials, equipping night bomber units of the Regia Aeronautica and later taking part in the campaign which followed the Italian invasion of Ethiopia on 3 October 1935. The Italian colonial administration in Italian East Africa used Ca 101s in a variety of roles, including reconnaissance and casualty evacuation, some of these aircraft being powered by 179-kW (240-hp) Walter Castor or 201-kW (270-hp) Alfa Romeo D2 radials.

Variants
Ca 102: similar to the Ca 101 but with two 373-kW (500-hp) each Bristol Jupiters replacing the three Piaggio Stella engines; used by the 62° Sperimentale Bombardieri Pesanti (experimental heavy bomber unit), the **Ca 102quater** was powered by two tandem pairs of engines
Ca 111: this was a single-engined version, powered originally by one 559-kW (750-hp) Fiat engine and with wing span increased to 23 m (75 ft 5½ in) and area to 855 m² (914.96 sq ft); in 1934 a new wing was developed and an Isotta Fraschini Asso

Caproni Ca 101 of the C./II Bombázó Osztály (2nd group of the 3rd bomber regiment), Magyar Királyi Légierő (Royal Hungarian air force), based at Papa, Hungary, early in 1941.

750RC substituted for the original Fiat engine. The prototype and four pre-production aircraft were followed by 148 Ca 111s, all of which were delivered to the Regia Aeronautica by 1936; 25 were completed as **Ca 111 Idro** twin-float seaplanes for use by long-range maritime reconnaissance units

Specification
Caproni Ca 111
Type: long-range reconnaissance aircraft
Powerplant: one 619-kW (830-hp) Isotta Fraschini Asso 750RC radial piston engine
Performance: maximum speed 290 km/h (180 mph); cruising speed

Although intended as a civil transport, the Ca 101 found a niche as a colonial bomber and military transport.

255 km/h (158 mph); service ceiling 6700 m (21,980 ft); range 1300 km (808 miles)
Weights: empty 3490 kg (7,694 lb); maximum take-off 5490 kg (12,103 lb)

The Ca 102quater was a heavy bomber project featuring two pairs of tandem radial engines.

Dimensions: span 19.65 m (64 ft 5½ in); length 15.3 m (50 ft 2½ in); wing area 61.5 m² (662 sq ft)

Caproni Ca 133

Designed by Ingeniere Rodolfo Verduzio, the **Caproni Ca 133** was an aerodynamically and structurally improved Ca 101. Of welded steel-tube construction with metal and fabric covering, the Ca 133 featured faired engine nacelles with NACA cowlings, main wheel spats, flaps and modified tail surfaces. The civil version, accommodating up to 16 passengers, was used by Ala Littoria, and

the military version saw wide service with the Regia Aeronautica, particularly in Italian East Africa. It could carry 18 fully-equipped troops and was armed with four 7.7-mm (0.303-in) machine-guns, one firing from the door on the port side and the others in dorsal turret and ventral positions.

Variants
Ca 133S: designation of bomber aircraft converted for use in an air ambulance role
Ca 133T: designation applied to a number of bomber aircraft deployed as military transports
Ca 148: introduced in 1938, a small number of this improved version of the Ca 133 served in East Africa and some flew with the post-war Italian air force: changes included moving the cockpit

forward by approximately 0.91 m (3 ft), relocation of the main cabin door from its original position below the port wing to a point to the rear of the trailing edge, and the introduction of strengthened landing gear

Specification
Caproni Ca 133
Type: passenger/troop transport
Powerplant: three 343-kW (460-hp) each Piaggio Stella P.VII C 16 radial piston engines

Performance: maximum speed 280 km/h (174 mph); cruising speed 230 km/h (143 mph); service ceiling 5500 m (18,045 ft); range 1350 km (839 miles)

Weights: empty 4000 kg (8,818 lb); maximum take-off 6565 kg (14,473 lb)

Dimensions: span 21.25 m (69 ft 8½ in); length 15.35 m (50 ft 4¼ in); height 4 m (13 ft 1½ in); wing area 65 m² (699.68 sq ft)

Armament: four 7.7 mm (0.303-in) machine-guns

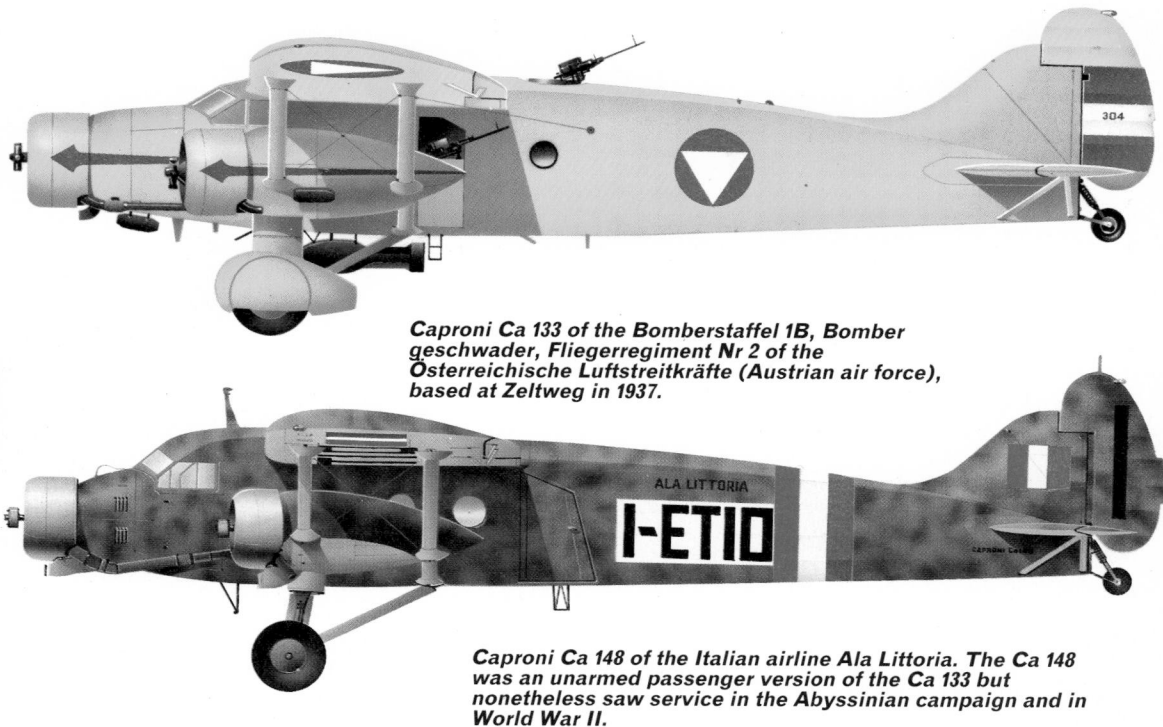

Caproni Ca 133 of the Bomberstaffel 1B, Bomber geschwader, Fliegerregiment Nr 2 of the Österreichische Luftstreitkräfte (Austrian air force), based at Zeltweg in 1937.

The Ca 133 was a modernised version of the Ca 101, cleaned up aerodynamically and given improved engines to prolong the type's career as an airliner and second-line bomber/transport into the early part of World War II. Seen here is an air ambulance version, complete with large fuselage cross for identification purposes.

Caproni Ca 148 of the Italian airline Ala Littoria. The Ca 148 was an unarmed passenger version of the Ca 133 but nonetheless saw service in the Abyssinian campaign and in World War II.

Caproni Ca 310 series

Developed in parallel with the Ghibli, the **Caproni Bergamaschi Ca 310 Libeccio** (south-west wind) was structurally similar to the earlier machine but was fitted with retractable landing gear and powered by two 350-kW (470-hp) Piaggio P.VII C.35 radial engines. The prototype, with 343-kW (460-hp) P.VII C.16 engines, flew for the first time on 20 February 1937. A total of 161 was delivered to the Regia Aeronautica between 1937 and 1939, including 10 originally destined for Romania; export deliveries went to Norway (4), Peru (16) and Yugoslavia (12). Sixteen were sent to Spain to serve with the Aviazione Legionaria. Thirty-six Ca 310s were supplied via the Regia Aeronautica to the Hungarian air force, between May and August 1939, but 33 of these were returned in 1940 in exchange for Caproni Ca 135bis bombers and were overhauled at Trento for operation by the Regia Aeronautica's 50° Stormo d'Assalto.

Variants

Ca 310 Idro: civil twin-float seaplane

Ca 310bis: a Ca 310 airframe built at Caproni's Taliedo factory was fitted with an unstepped extensively-glazed nose and redesignated Ca 310bis; 12 were supplied to Yugoslavia

Ca 311: the prototype Ca 310bis served as the development aircraft for the Ca 311, 320 of which were built for the Regia Aeronautica; the first flew on 1 April 1939 and most were later converted to **Ca 311M** standard with a stepped windscreen; of 15 ordered by Yugoslavia, five were delivered to the Royal Yugoslav air force in 1941 and 10 to the Croatian air force in 1942; defensive armament comprised a dorsal Caproni-Lanciani turret with a single 7.7-mm (0.303-in) machine-gun, complemented by two similar weapons, one forward-firing and mounted in the port wing root while the other fired aft through a ventral hatch

Caproni Ca 310M of the 8a Escuadrilla, Grupo num 18, Agrupacion Espanola (Spanish Nationalist air force) in Spain during late 1938.

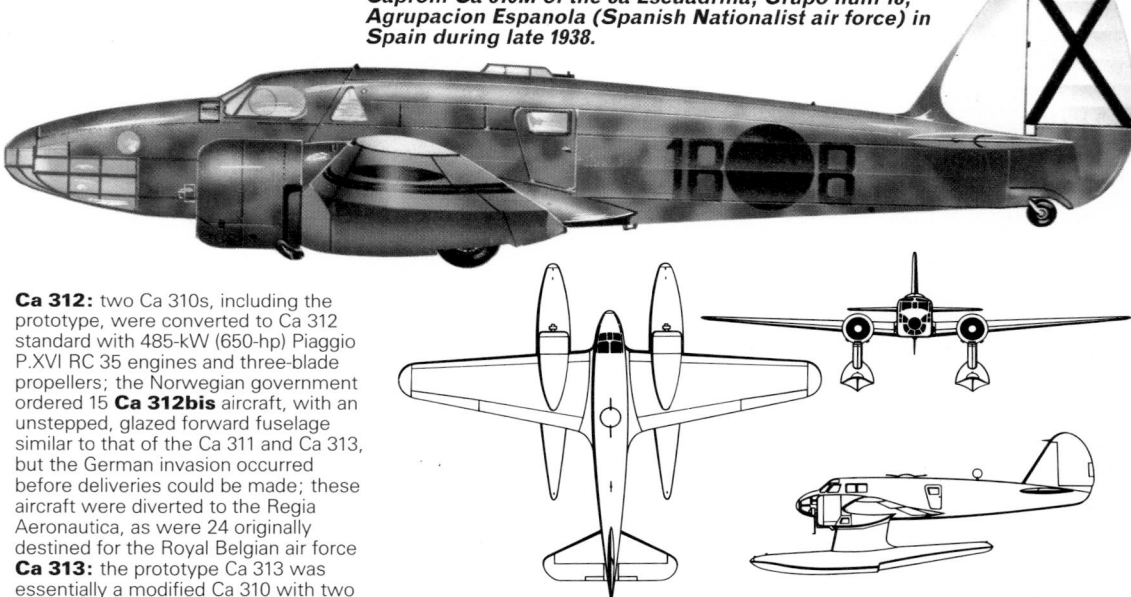

Ca 312: two Ca 310s, including the prototype, were converted to Ca 312 standard with 485-kW (650-hp) Piaggio P.XVI RC 35 engines and three-blade propellers; the Norwegian government ordered 15 **Ca 312bis** aircraft, with an unstepped, glazed forward fuselage similar to that of the Ca 311 and Ca 313, but the German invasion occurred before deliveries could be made; these aircraft were diverted to the Regia Aeronautica, as were 24 originally destined for the Royal Belgian air force

Ca 313: the prototype Ca 313 was essentially a modified Ca 310 with two Isotta-Fraschini Asso 120 IRCC 40 engines and it made its first flight on 22 December 1939; before this France had confirmed an order for 200 Ca 313s on 1 October, followed closely by British and Swedish orders for 300 and 64 aircraft respectively; Italy's entry into the war prevented delivery of any of the British machines and France received only five **Ca 313F** models, the rest being diverted to the Regia Aeronautica; Sweden received its first **Ca 313S** in November 1940 and

Caproni Ca 316

The Caproni Ca 316 was a floatplane version of which only a few prototypes were built. Intended as a maritime reconnaissance aircraft, it was capable of making catapult launches.

deliveries totalling 84 aircraft were completed in the early part of 1941, the Swedish designations **B.16, S.16, T.16** and **Tp.16S** identifying bomber, maritime reconnaissance, torpedo bomber and transport versions respectively; these initial production aircraft were basically Ca 311s with 544-kW (730-hp) Isotta-Fraschini Delta RC 35 I-DS engines and were designated **Ca 313 R.P.B.1**; a stepped cockpit was a feature of the **Ca 313 R.P.B.2** version, 122 of which were built for the Regia Aeronautica; and the **Ca 313G** was developed as a trainer and communications aircraft for the Luftwaffe, although only a small proportion of the order for 905 was completed; total Ca 313 production was 271

Ca 314: the first three production Ca 313 R.P.B.2s served as the prototypes for the **Ca 314A**, with revised armament which comprised one 12.7-mm (0.5-in) machine-gun in each wing root and a 7.7-mm (0.303-in) Breda-SAFAT machine-gun in the ventral position, plus two 100-kg (220-lb) or 160-kg (353-lb) bombs carried externally; the Ca 314A or **314-SC** (Scorta) was a convoy escort and maritime patrol aircraft whereas the **Ca 314B** or **314-RA** (Ricognizione-Aerosiluranti) was a torpedo-bomber with a 900-kg (1,984-lb) torpedo or a bomb load of one 500 kg (1,102 lb) or two 250-kg (551-lb) bombs; a ground-attack version was designated **Ca 314C**, with two additional 12.7-mm (0.5-in) Breda-SAFAT machine-guns beneath the wing roots; total Ca 314 production comprised

73 Ca 314As, 80 Ca 314Bs and 134 Ca 314Cs built at Taliedo, 60 Ca 314Cs built at Ponte San Pietro, and a further 60 Ca 314Cs manufactured by AVIS at Castellamare di Stabia.

Several versions of the Ca 314 were built, for tasks as diverse as air combat and convoy escort. It was the best variant of the series.

Specification
Caproni Ca 314A
Type: convoy escort and maritime patrol aircraft
Powerplant: two 544-kW (730-hp) each Isotta-Fraschini Delta RC 35 inline piston engines
Performance: maximum speed 395 km/h (245 mph) at 4000 m (13,125 ft); cruising speed 320 km/h (199 mph) at 4200 m (13,780 ft); service ceiling 6400 m (21,000 ft); maximum range 1690 km (1,050 miles)
Weights: empty 4560 kg (10,053 lb); maximum take-off 6620 kg (14,595 lb)
Dimensions: span 16.65 m (54 ft 7½ in); length 11.8 m (38 ft 8½ in); height 3.7 m (12 ft 1¾ in); wing area 39.2 m² (421.96 sq ft)
Armament: two 12.7-mm (0.5-in) machine-guns in the wing roots and one 7.7-mm (0.303-in) gun in a dorsal turret, plus a bombload of 500 kg (1,102 lb)

The Caproni Ca 310 was a useful light reconnaissance bomber, and enjoyed a brisk export career before World War II. Seen here is one of four Ca 310s received by Norway, wearing a complicated dappled camouflage.

Six Gruppi Osservazione Aerea were equipped with the Ca 311, pairs of units serving in Russia, Croatia and North Africa. Compared to the Ca 310, the Ca 311 had a completely redesigned nose and more glazing.

Caproni Vizzola F.4 and F.5

The Caproni Vizzola F.5 flew before the F.4, thanks to the ready availability of an Italian radial engine, whereas the F.5 had to wait for an imported Daimler-Benz DB 601A.

The **Caproni F.4** and **F.5** single-seat fighters were developed in parallel, having a common airframe. This was of cantilever low-wing monoplane configuration with a conventional tail unit, retractable tailwheel landing gear and single-seat accommodation. Planned powerplant for the F.4 was an Isotta-Fraschini Asso 121 RC 40 inline engine of 664 kW (890 hp), and that of the F.5 a 649-kW (870-hp) Fiat A.74 RC 38 radial. It was decided subsequently to power the F.4 by a more powerful German Daimler-Benz DB 601A, the delay caused by this change meaning that the prototype of the F.5 was the first to fly in early 1939. Testing resulted in an order for a pre-production batch of 14 aircraft, these differing from the prototype by having an enlarged fin and rudder and a non-retractable tailwheel. Despite plans to build several developments of the F.5, none materialised and only the 14 pre-production aircraft were completed. The F.4 was duly flown with its Daimler-Benz

engine during 1940, but no production aircraft followed as it was decided to produce a more-developed F.6.

The F.4 was the inline version, with a common airframe to the F.5. It did not enter production.

Specification
Caproni Vizzola F.5
Type: single-seat fighter
Powerplant: one 649-kW (870-hp) Fiat A.74 RC 38 radial piston engine
Performance: maximum speed 510 km/h (317 mph) at 3000 m (9,845 ft); climb to 6500 m (21,325 ft) in 6 minutes 30 seconds; service ceiling 9500 m (31,170 ft); range 770 km (478 miles)
Weights: empty 1850 kg (4,078 lb); maximum take-off 2350 kg (5,181 lb)
Dimensions: span 11.3 m (37 ft 1 in); length 7.9 m (25 ft 11 in); height 3 m (9 ft 10 in); wing area 17.6 m² (189.45 sq ft)
Armament: two 12.7-mm (0.5-in) forward-firing SAFAT machine-guns

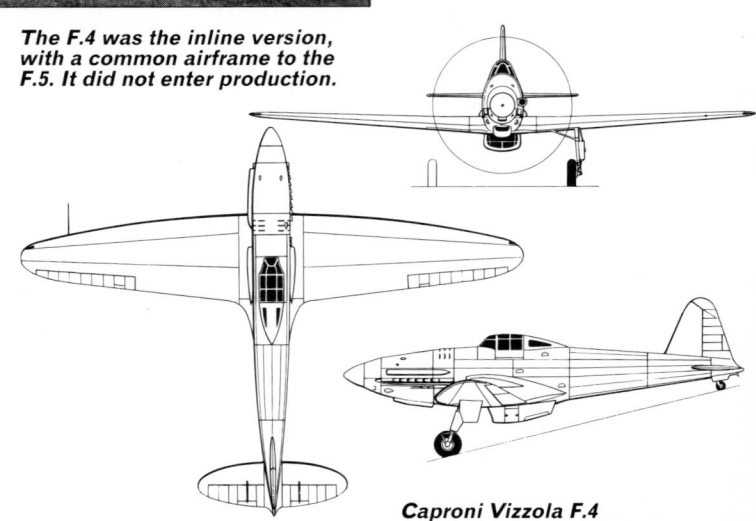

Caproni Vizzola F.4

Caproni Vizzola C22J

On 21 July 1980, the old-established Italian company of Caproni Vizzola Costruzioni Aeronautiche SpA flew the prototype (I-CAVJ) of a light-weight turbojet-powered basic training aircraft which has the designation **C22J**. Bearing some family resemblance to the company's family of Calif sailplanes designed by Carlo Ferrarin and Livio Sonzio, it shares with the Calif A-21SJ jet-powered sailplane that aircraft's Microturbo TRS powerplant.

A cantilever shoulder-wing monoplane, the C22J has a tadpole-shape fuselage structure designed as a liftingbody, a T-tail mounted on a slender tailboom, retractable tricycle landing gear and its twin-engine powerplant mounted in the fuselage behind the enclosed cabin, which provides side-by-side accommodation for pilot and pupil. Largely of metal construction, the C22J uses a certain amount of glassfibre for fairings or skins in unstressed areas.

Considered to be suitable for a wide range of roles in addition to that of a trainer, plans have been made by Agusta (which acquired a 50 per cent interest in the C22J programme during 1981) to develop a **C22R** prototype to evaluate its potential for forward air control, reconnaissance and tactical Elint operations.

Specification
Caproni Vizzola C22J
Type: two-seat basic trainer

Powerplant: two 100-kg (220-lb) thrust each Microturbo TRS 18-046 turbojets
Performance: maximum cruising speed 480 km/h (298 mph) at sea level; economic cruising speed 325 km/h (202 mph) at 3,000 m (9845 ft); service ceiling 7600 m (24,930 ft); range 740 km (460 miles)
Weights: empty 720 kg (1,587 lb);

maximum take-off 1135 kg (2,502 lb)
Dimensions: span 10 m (32 ft 9¾ in); length 6.19 m (20 ft 3¾ in); height 1.88 m (6 ft 2 in); wing area 8.75 m² (94.19 sq ft)
Armament: provision for two or four standard NATO underwing pylons able to accept a wide variety of stores up to a maximum load of 200 kg (441 lb)

Based on the A21SJ Calif sailplane, the Caproni Vizzola C22J twin-jet trainer offers adequate performance on two minute turbojets. SIAI-Marchetti joined the programme, which expanded to include reconnaissance versions.

Caudron G.3

The brothers René and Gaston Caudron had been designing aeroplanes for more than five years when the **Caudron G.3** (or **G.III**) made its first appearance in May 1914. It had been preceded by about 20 different designs and nearly 150 machines, and the new aircraft owed much to the earlier **Type B**.

The G.3 had been built at Rue and flown from the aerodrome at Le Crotoy, where the Caudron brothers had established a successful flying school. It was a sesquiplane and employed wing warping for lateral control. Only in late production aircraft was this system replaced by ailerons fitted to the upper wing. Observer and pilot were accommodated in tandem open cockpits in an abbreviated nacelle, in the nose of which was mounted a 60-kW (80-hp) Le Rhône rotary engine. Some aircraft were built with alternative rotaries (Gnome or Clerget) of the same power. The twin fin and rudder tail assembly was supported by four booms, the lower tail-booms acting as landing skids. The main landing gear comprised two pairs of wheels set wide apart and attached to the forward sections of the lower tail-booms.

The G.3 was developed from its immediate predecessor, the single-seat **G.2**, which had itself been built in some numbers and played a prominent role in air displays and meetings during 1913 and the early months of 1914. Designed with a military role in mind, the G.3 equipped Escadrille C.11 of the French Aviation Militaire when war broke out in August 1914. This *escadrille* was based at Montmédy and was attached to the 4th Army. Ordered into large-scale production, the G.3 was built by Caudron in new factories established at Lyons and Issy-les-Moulineux during the early part of World War I. In addition, the type was

built by several other contractors, this arrangement being made by the Caudron brothers without any provision for licence fee, an indication of their high degree of patriotism.

Production of the G.3 built up rapidly and the type was used widely in the first two years of World War I for corps reconnaissance and artillery observation duties. It proved tough and reliable, its qualities leading the French Ministry of War to declare in 1914 that it was to be retained in the first-line units at a time when all but four of the types then in service were either to be relegated to training or scrapped. The G.3 proved well suited to its allotted tasks, and, despite being unarmed, was popular with its crews. As the war progressed, however, and enemy aircraft became more threatening, the slow speed and vulnerability of the type began to tell against it. As a result, the French withdrew their G.3s from operational *escadrilles* in mid-1916.

Total French wartime production of the G.3 was 2,450. The Caudron factories alone constructed 1,423 machines, although some of them had been completed before the outbreak of war. In addition, the British Caudron company manufactured 233 machines and the A.E.R. company of Orbassano, near Turin, completed 166.

The Italian air arm used the G.3 on a wide scale for reconnaissance until March 1917. British aircraft were also used for the classic reconnaissance and observation roles, although the Royal Flying Corps is credited with employing a number of G.3s fitted with a machine-gun and carrying light bombs for strafing attacks on German troops and emplacements. Of the British-built G.3s, 124 went to the RFC and 109 to the Royal Naval Air Service. The RNAS used the type from the outset for training, but early in the war they were used for a

number of abortive sorties against marauding German airships. The RFC did not dispense with its last operational G.3s until August 1917.

The main versions of the G.3 to enter service during the war are best detailed by reference to the French High Command designation system. The standard artillery observation version, the **Cau 3 A.2**, was used by the Allies (including Belgian units) on the Western Front, in Russia and in the Middle East. The **Cau 3 D.2** was a dual-control trainer, while the **Cau 3 E.2** was the standard rotary-engined trainer. The number of G.3s used for training was greatly increased by the conversion of operational types as they were withdrawn from first-line service. Many thousands of Allied pilots received their primary training on the type, including members of the American Expeditionary Force in France, which received 192 French-built trainers during 1917 and 1918. One special type of trainer conversion was used only by the French and Americans. This was the **Cau 3 R.1**. The 'R' stood for *rouleur* (taxi aircraft), and the aircraft was a single-seater with the fabric stripped off large

The Caudron G.3 evolved from pre-war Caudron types such as the N.40 used by Frank Goodden for looping exhibitions. All that separates this aircraft from the G.3 is the engine, here a 45-kW (60-hp) uncowled Gnome.

areas of the wings so that it could not become airborne. It was used exclusively for ground training and could be seen running about training fields in the hands of embryo pilots. The final important version of the G.3 was the **Cau 3.12**, which replaced the 60-kW (80-hp) rotary powerplant with a 75-kW (100-hp) Anzani radial engine.

Post-war the G.3 was kept in the public eye by a number of remarkable flights. In January 1919 wartime ace Jules Vedrines landed his G.3 on the roof of the famous Galeries Lafayette department store, by the edge of the Seine in the heart of Paris, to the amazement and delight of the citizens, and in the same month a certain Madame de Laroche established a women's altitude record of 3900 m (12,795 ft) in her G.3. It was at that time, before the authorities tightened up the regulations, a popular exploit to fly under bridges. The G.3 achieved this distinction in September 1919 when a pilot named Maicon flew one beneath a bridge over the River Var at Nice.

Adrienne Bolland, a pioneering woman pilot, made a truly daring flight in a G.3, crossing the Andes from Tamarindos in Argentina to Santiago in Chile on 1 April 1921, reaching a maximum altitude of 4200 m (13,780 ft). The imagination of the French, however, was captured by Swiss pilot Francois Durafour, who landed a G.3 safely on the west slope of Mont Blanc on 31 July 1921, taking off from the mountainside successfully soon afterwards.

From 1919 onwards G.3s were sold to private owners, many of them ex-Aviation Militaire pilots. Other examples of the type were used by flying clubs for training and touring. One restored example of the G.3 is currently a star attraction at many air displays in France and several original aircraft are preserved, including one at the RAF Museum at Hendon in the UK.

Specification
Type: two-seat trainer or reconnaissance aircraft
Powerplant: one 60-kW (80-hp) Le Rhône rotary piston engine
Performance: maximum speed 108 km/h (67 mph); service ceiling 4000 m (13,125 ft); endurance 4 hours
Weights: empty equipped 420 kg (926 lb); maximum take-off 710 kg (1,565 lb)
Dimensions: span 13.4 m (43 ft 11½ in); length 6.4 m (21 ft 0 in); height 2.5 m (8 ft 2½ in); wing area 27 m² (290.64 sq ft)
Armament: usually none

Caudron G.4

The impossibility of installing effective defensive armament in the G.3 and its inability to lift a worthwhile bomb load led to the development of the twin-engined **Caudron G.4** (or **G.IV**), which first appeared in March 1915. Structurally similar to its immediate predecessor, the G.4 had increased wing span, a tailplane with four rudders instead of two, and twin engines mounted on struts between the wings. Power was provided by either 60-kW (80-hp) Le Rhône rotary engines with 'horse-shoe' or circular cowlings, or by uncowled 75-kW (100-hp) Anzani radials. The short crew nacelle had an observer/gunner's cockpit in the nose, though the field of fire was limited by the proximity of the engines. Locating the engines near the crew nacelle did, however, render the G.4 relatively easy to control in the event of an engine failure.

A good rate of climb, increased useful load and outstanding reliability promised increased operational capability compared with types currently in Allied service, and the G.4 was accordingly ordered into large-scale production. Two versions were built, the **Cau 4 B.2** day bomber and the **Cau 4 A.2** artillery observation and reconnaissance aircraft. Entering service with the French Aviation Militaire in November 1915, the G.4 was the first Allied twin-engined type to equip first-line units in any quantity. It played a leading role in bombing raids launched on targets behind the

The only feature distinguishing the Caudron G.6 from the G.4 was the former's conventional fuselage, which replaced the latter's apparently inadequate twin lattice booms for supporting the tailplane.

German lines as far distant as the Rhineland. However, increasing losses during the summer of 1916 led to withdrawal of French G.4 B.2s from first-line bomber units that autumn.

Production of the G.4 in France totalled 1,358. The British Royal Naval Air Service purchased 55 of the type, 43 imported and 12 built by the British Caudron Company. Flown by Nos 4 and 5 Wings, they were used in 1916 and early 1917 in attacks on German seaplane and airship bases in Belgium. One of the most important raids was made by No. 7 Sqn, RNAS, on the Bruges area in February 1917, but the RNAS G.4s were replaced by Handley-Page O/100s in the autumn of 1917.

The Italian Aeronautica Militare received imported G.4s and was also supplied with 51 examples built by the A.E.R. company at its factory near Turin. In May 1917 the 48ª Squadriglia was the first unit to re-equip with the G.4, to be followed by the 49ª and 50ª Squadriglie. Italian G.4s operated in the mountainous Alpine areas, demonstrating their good climb qualities and suitability for flying at altitude, often in poor weather conditions. During the war the type established several Italian altitude records. Numbers of Caudron G.4s were also supplied to the Imperial Russian Air Service, with which they flew in the reconnaissance role.

As well as a 7.7-mm (0.303-in) Lewis or Vickers machine-gun on a ring mounting in the front cockpit, some G.4s had a second Lewis gun mounted over the upper wing centre section for rear defence. Unfortunately, however, this second gun could only be operated with difficulty by the gunner standing at full stretch in his cockpit. An offensive load of 100 kg (220 lb) of bombs could be carried by the G.4 B.2 bomber version. A number of the G.4 A.2 version had wireless installed for reconnaissance or artillery spotting.

Towards the end of World War I G.4s were relegated to training duties, and 10 of the type were bought for that purpose by the United States Air Service in France in early 1918.

The G.4 gained a reputation for good flight characteristics, winning praise from such distinguished wartime pilots as the Italian ace Silvio Scaroni and the French ace of aces René Fonck. As a result it was used for a number of notable post-war flights and some hundreds were sold to private owners and flying clubs in France and Italy.

Specification
Type: two-seat bombing or reconnaissance biplane
Powerplant: two 60-kW (80-hp) each Le Rhône 9C rotary piston engines
Performance: maximum speed 132 km/h (82 mph) at sea level; service ceiling 4300 m (14,110 ft); endurance 3 hours 30 minutes
Weights: empty 500 kg (1,102 lb); maximum take-off 1330 kg (2,932 lb)
Dimensions: span 17.2 m (56 ft 5¼ in); length 7.2 m (23 ft 7½ in); height 2.6 m (8 ft 6¼ in); wing area 36.8 m² (396.12 sq ft)
Armament: one or two 7.7-mm (0.303-in) machine-guns, plus a bombload of 100 kg (220 lb) in B.2 version

Caudron R.4

The **Caudron R.4** appeared in prototype form in June 1915 and, for its time, was a remarkably clean and smooth-contoured aircraft. While the brothers Caudron had collaborated closely in aircraft design, the G.3 and G.4 had been credited largely to Gaston Caudron, while the R.4 was mostly the work of René Caudron.

The R.4 was a radical departure from its predecessors, with an attractive full-length fuselage and single fin and rudder. The unequal-span wings had three bays on each side, and there were ailerons on the upper wing only. As well as the twin-wheel main landing gear units and tailskid, there was a single nose-wheel intended to protect the propellers in the event of a rough landing. Power was provided by twin 97-kW (130-hp) Renault 12Db engines. The three-man crew included nose and midships gunners each provided with twin Lewis machine-guns.

The R.4 did well, defending itself brilliantly against enemy interceptors and building up a considerable score of victories. Intended originally as a bomber, it served mainly as an A.3 category three-seat reconnaissance aircraft, frequently engaged in photographic work. Its climb

rate was not impressive, and a few aircraft were built with more-powerful 112-kW (150-hp) Hispano-Suiza 8Aa engines in an attempt at improvement. The problem which emerged was that production aircraft began to reveal a certain structural weakness. Among the crashes that happened, the most disastrous for the Caudron firm occurred on 12 December 1915, when a series aircraft under test was destroyed and Gaston Caudron, who was piloting the aircraft, was killed.

In early use Escadrille C.46 had claimed 34 German aircraft brought down with its R.4s in an eight-week period, but it was soon clear that in addition to structural redesign, improved ceiling and greater manoeuvrability were highly desirable. The new Caudron chief designer, Paul Deville, accordingly set to work on a new improved development which was to emerge as the R.11. Production of the R.4 was terminated after 249 had been built. In the reconnaissance *escadrilles* it was replaced by the more-powerful Letord 1 during 1917.

Specification
Type: three-seat bomber or photographic reconnaissance biplane
Powerplant: two 97-kW (130-hp) each Renault 12Db inline piston engines

Performance: maximum speed 136 km/h (85 mph) at sea level; climb to 2000 m (6,560 ft) in 18 minutes; service ceiling 4600 m (15,090 ft); endurance 3 hours
Weights: empty 1710 kg (3,770 lb); maximum take-off 2330 kg (5,137 lb)
Dimensions: span 21.1 m (69 ft 2¾ in); length 11.8 m (38 ft 8½ in); wing area 70 m² (753.5 sq ft)
Armament: four 7.7-mm (0.303-in) Lewis machine-guns on two twin mountings, plus 100 kg (220 lb) of bombs

Designed as a bomber, the R.4 was chiefly employed as a reconnaissance platform, with three crew. In this role it proved successful, if underpowered, and its twin gun mountings were responsible for a high number of enemy aircraft. However, one of its worst moments was when a crash killed Gaston Caudron, one of the famous brothers who had inaugurated the company.

Caudron R.11

Alongside the abortive **O2** single-seat fighter and **R.5** and **R.10** bomber-reconnaissance prototypes designed by Paul Deville, there appeared in March 1917 the three-seat **Caudron R.11** which was soon to prove a great success.

Intended originally for the French A.3 three-seat Corps d'Armée reconnaissance category, the twin-engined R.11 biplane owed much to the earlier R.4. It differed in having a more pointed nose section, two bracing bays outboard of the engines instead of three, no nose-wheel, and a much enlarged tail fin. It had ailerons on the upper wing only, which had greater span than the lower, and was something of a structural achievement by being built in one piece. The 149-kW (200-hp) Hispano-Suiza 8Ba engines of the prototype were housed in streamlined nacelles located just above the lower wing.

Orders were placed for 1,000 R.11s to be built by Caudron, Régy Frères and a third company, Grémont. Production began in 1917, but the first aircraft were not completed until late in that year. Escadrille R.46, formerly designated C.46 and flying Letord L.1s, re-equipped with the R.11 in February 1918. Over the following five months it was followed by four more R.11 *escadrilles* (R.239, R.240, R.241 and R.242). Production had been slow, only 20 R.11s being operational by April 1918. The last *escadrille* to form with the R.11 was R.246 just weeks before the November 1918 Armistice. Production ended abruptly after 370 R.11s had been completed. The British RFC and the United States Air Service each acquired two R.11s for evaluation.

In service the R.11 was not used for reconnaissance but was deployed as a formidable escort fighter, armed with five Lewis machine-guns on twin nose and dorsal ring mountings, with the fifth weapon beneath the nose gunner's cockpit, firing downwards and to the rear. The R.11 *escadrilles* were used to protect formations of Breguet 14 B.2 day bombers of the 12e and 13e Escadres. On attacks well behind enemy lines the R.11 built up an impressive score at the expense of the German fighters. It was considered a formidable air weapon with good performance by the standards of its time.

The impact of the R.11 would have, no doubt, been much greater if more aircraft had been available by the spring of 1918, but difficulties with the geared Hispano-Suiza engines were never fully overcome and despite orders from the French GHQ Service Aéronautique that the R.11 was to be one of three aircraft types (the others being the Breguet 14 and the Salmson 2 A.2) to be given the utmost production priority, the projected production tempo was never attained.

The Caudron design team had given considerable thought to details of the R.11 design. The fuel supply system had been arranged in such a way as to ensure that both engines could be fed from either main fuel tank if necessary, and late production aircraft featured rear sections to the engine nacelles which could be jettisoned in flight along with the fuel tanks they contained. Many of these later aircraft had more-powerful 175-kW (235-hp) Hispano-Suiza 8Beb engines.

René Caudron and Paul Deville were well aware that a number of two- and multi-seat aircraft had been lost in action when the pilot had been hit, and they included among a number of extra features dual controls for the rear gunner's cockpit. This was no doubt a contributory factor to the high morale among Caudron-equipped *escadrilles*.

R.11 A.3s continued to form the equipment of what were by then known as the Escadrilles de Protection of the 11e and 12e Régiments d'Aviation in the post-war period. Surviving aircraft were withdrawn from service and scrapped in July 1922.

Variants

Caudron R.12: designation of an experimental 1918 version of the R.11 fitted with 224-kW (300-hp) Hispano-Suiza 8Fb engines in place of the 160-kW (215-hp) or 175-kW (235-hp) engines of the R.11; with the appearance of the more-promising R.14, development of the R.12 was terminated

Caudron R.14: an enlarged development of the R.11; the prototype appeared in August 1918, powered by the Hispano-Suiza 8Fb engines intended originally for the R.12; armament centred on a 37-mm Hotchkiss cannon supported by Lewis guns; detailed plans for quantity production were abandoned after the November 1918 Armistice

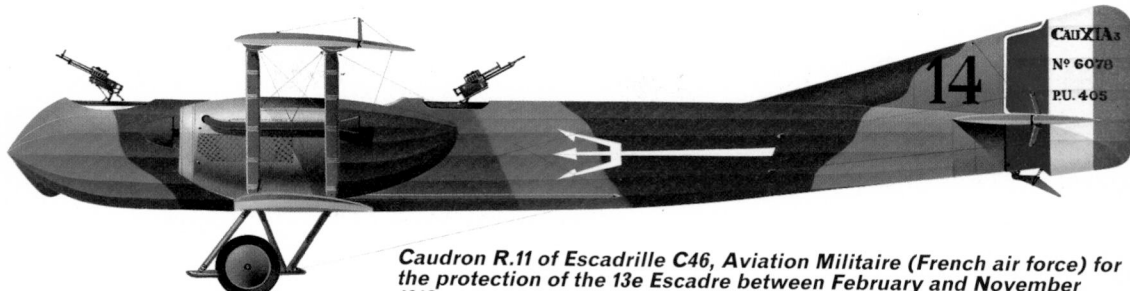

Caudron R.11 of Escadrille C46, Aviation Militaire (French air force) for the protection of the 13e Escadre between February and November 1918.

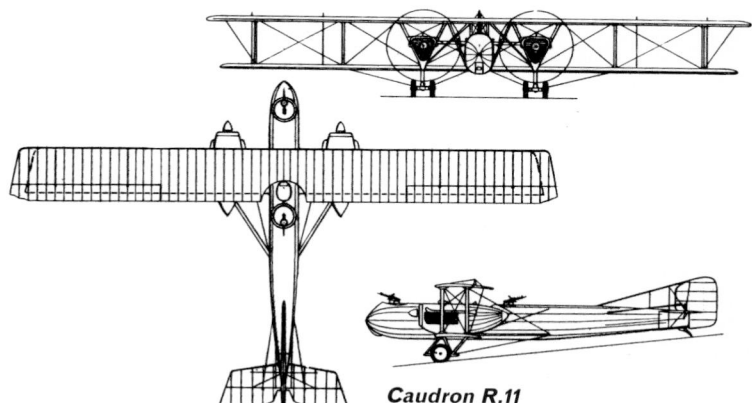

Caudron R.11

Specification
Caudron R.11
Type: three-seat escort fighter
Powerplant: two 160-kW (215-hp) each Hispano-Suiza 8Bba inline piston engines
Performance: maximum speed 183 km/h (114 mph) at 2000 m (6,560 ft); climb to 2000 m (6,560 ft) in 8 minutes 10 seconds; service ceiling 5950 m (19,520 ft); endurance 3 hours
Weights: empty equipped 1422 kg (3,135 lb); maximum take-off 2167 kg (4,777 lb)
Dimensions: span, upper 17.92 m (58 ft 9½ in); lower 16.97 m (55 ft 8 in); height 2.8 m (9 ft 2¼ in); wing area 54.25 m² (583.96 sq ft)
Armament: five 7.7-mm (0.303-in) Lewis machine-guns

Caudron C.59

Developed by Paul Deville assisted by René Talpin, the **Caudron C.59** intermediate trainer was a conventional unstaggered two-bay biplane of wooden construction with fabric covering. Ailerons were fitted to the upper wing only, which was also of slightly greater span than the lower, this latter surface incorporating dihedral. Power was provided by an Hispano-Suiza 8A engine with its Lamblin radiator located under the fuselage just forward of the cross-axle Vee-type fixed landing gear. The pupil was accommodated in an open cockpit under the centre-section of the upper wing, with the instructor's cockpit immediately behind it and located beneath a cut-out in the wing trailing edge. Dual controls were standard.

The prototype (F-ESAN) flew for the first time in August 1921. After extensive official tests had given evidence of robust construction, good flying qualities and reliable powerplant, the C.59 was ordered on a large scale by the French Aviation Militaire for service in the official Et.2 category (two-seat transitional trainer). A series of seven contracts received between 1922 and 1924 resulted in more than 1,000 C.59s being delivered to the French army, with smaller batches going to the Aéronautique Maritime. The type remained in French service for 15 years and on 1 January 1936 11 examples were still in use with the Armée de l'Air. Total production reached 1,800, and many C.59s went to French civil flying schools, while others were exported. C.59s were bought by Argentina, Brazil, Bulgaria, Finland, Manchuria, Portugal, Romania, Spain, Turkey and Venezuela.

Variant

Caudron C.59/2: only a single example built, powered by a 172-kW (230-hp) Lorraine 7Ma engine and incorporating redesigned wide-track landing gear

Specification
Type: two-seat intermediate trainer

Powerplant: one 134-kW (180-hp) Hispano-Suiza 8A inline piston engine
Performance: maximum speed 170 km/h (106 mph); endurance 3 hours 30 minutes
Weights: empty equipped 700 kg (1,543 lb); maximum take-off 988 kg (2,178 lb)
Dimensions: span, upper 10.24 m (33 ft 7¼ in), lower 9.52 m (31 ft 2¾ in); length 7.8 m (25 ft 7 in); height 2.9 m (9 ft 6¼ in); wing area 26 m² (279.87 sq ft)

A training biplane for French military pilots, the Caudron C.59 was typical of its era, with a well-tried Hispano-Suiza engine and a centrally-mounted Lamblin radiator. Large numbers were built, chiefly for the French services, although numbers were exported to nations as diverse as Argentina and Manchuria. In French service the type flew throughout most of the 1920s and 1930s.

Caudron C.61
to
Caudron C.714 Cyclone

Caudron C.61

The prototype (F-ESAE) of the **Caudron C.61** civil transport appeared in 1921. It was a three-bay biplane of wooden construction with fabric covering, powered by three 112-kW (150-hp) Hispano-Suiza engines. Pilot and co-pilot were seated in open side-by-side cockpits aft of the nose engine; behind them were the freight hold and, to the rear, a cabin for six passengers. Landing gear comprised two twin-wheel main units and a tail skid, plus a single wheel under the nose to prevent the aircraft from nosing-over on landing.

Twelve production C.61s were powered by Hispano-Suiza 8Ac engines and had an enlarged cabin for eight passengers. Six aircraft were purchased by the Compagnie Franco-Roumaine de Navigation Aérienne and operated a route between Bucharest and Belgrade from 1923 onwards. The remaining C.61s were flown by various French companies, one being lost in an accident when it came down at sea.

Variants
C.61bis: most of the C.61s were modified in 1924 to take two Salmson CM.9 radial engines, each of 194 kW (260 hp), in place of the outboard Hispano-Suizas; aircraft flown by CIDNA, successor to the Franco-

The C.61 was powered by inline engines, but as was common in the 1920s, provision was made for a radial-engined conversion, redesignated C.61bis.

Roumaine company, were fitted subsequently with twin nose-wheels, and loaded weight increased to 4834 kg (10,657 lb), but performance remained very similar except that range was reduced to 380 km (236 miles)
C.81: developed from C.61bis and powered by three Lorraine-Dietrich engines, the central unit rated at 201 kW (270 hp) and the two outboard units at 276 kW (370 hp) each; a small series for the Franco-Roumaine company followed; powered by a 298-kW (400-hp) Lorraine-Dietrich 12Db centre engine and two 194-kW (260-hp) Salmson CM.9 outboard engines, they were larger than the C.61 series, spanning 26.3 m (86 ft 3½ in), having a wing area of 145 m² (1,560.82 sq ft) and possessing a maximum take-off weight of 6370 kg (14,043 lb); despite the increased size they carried only seven passengers; the C.81 differed in several other respects from the C.61, the outboard engines being supported by an improved arrangement comprising a pair of Vee-struts, the pilot and co-pilot being located in open cockpits beneath the upper wing centre-section, and the fin and rudder

having a revised shape; apart from the prototype, four C.81s are known to have been built.
C.183: only one example built for the CIDNA company in 1925; it resembled closely the C.81, but was powered by one 298-kW (400-hp) Lorraine-Dietrich 12Db engine and two 194-kW (260-hp) Salmson CM.9s; it was identical in span to the C.81, but 1.1 m (3 ft 7¼ in) longer and with a maximum loaded weight 60 kg (132 lb) heavier; maximum speed at 2000 m (6,560 ft) was 139 km/h (86 mph), some 9 km/h (5 mph) faster than the C.81

Specification
Caudron C.61
Type: eight-passenger transport
Powerplant: three 134-kW (180-hp) Hispano-Suiza 8Ac inline piston engines
Performance: maximum speed 160 km/h (99 mph); service ceiling 4000 m (13,125 ft); range 640 km (398 miles)
Weights: empty 2200 kg (4,850 lb); maximum take-off 3480 kg (7,672 lb)
Dimensions: span, upper 24.14 m (79 ft 2½ in); lower 20.4 m (66 ft 11¼ in); length 14 m (45 ft 11¼ in); wing area 104 m² (1,119.48 sq ft)

Caudron C.230

The prototype **Caudron C.230** made its maiden flight in November 1930 piloted by Raymond Delmotte. Designed by Paul Deville, it was a two-seat light biplane with equal-span unstaggered single-bay wings. The upper wing centre-section was braced to the fuselage by four short vertical steel-tube struts; the outer panels, which could be folded, had a pair of vertical spruce interplane struts on each side. Ailerons were fitted on the lower wing only. The wooden fuselage structure was fabric-covered, and the cantilever tailplane had a wood frame and was plywood-covered. Each main unit of the wide-track fixed landing gear incorporated a vertical compression leg.

The C.230 was powered by a 71-kW (95-hp) Salmson radial engine and enjoyed some success in the French market for light touring and sports aircraft. Production totalled 15, to be followed by a number of variants. The C.230 series took part in practically every sporting air-

The C.232 was identical to the C.230 apart from having a Renault inline engine in place of the earlier type's Salmson radial. Both models enjoyed great interwar success.

craft rally or contest in France from 1931 onwards and the type appeared frequently elsewhere in Western Europe.

Variants
Caudron C.232: a total of 50 of this version was built; it was powered by a Renault 4Pb inline engine in place of the Salmson radial of the same horsepower; the fuselage had plywood covering
Caudron C.232/2: three built; same as C.232 but with wheel brakes
Caudron C.232/4: seven completed; identical to C.232/2 except improved equipment
Caudron C.233: single prototype to take unsuccessful Michel AM-16 engine; later fitted with Salmson

engine, thus becoming a C.230, registration F-ALBS
Caudron C.235: one airframe fitted with a German Argus As 8R 75-kW (100-hp) inline for French Air Ministry tests of this engine

Specification
Caudron C.232
Type: two-seat light sporting and touring biplane

Powerplant: one 71-kW (95-hp) Renault 4Pb inline piston engine
Performance: maximum speed 165 km/h (103 mph); service ceiling 4000 m (13,125 ft); endurance 4 hours
Weights: empty equipped 420 kg (926 lb); maximum take-off 700 kg (1,543 lb)
Dimensions: span 11 m (36 ft 1 in); length 7.87 m (25 ft 9¾ in); wing area 24 m² (258.34 sq ft)

Caudron C.270 Luciole

Developed from the C.230 series by Paul Deville, the first **Caudron C.270** appeared in 1931. It had less complicated wing folding, modified ailerons, rudder and elevators, and reverted to fabric covering for the fuselage. The landing gear was more refined compared with that of the C.230. Production of the basic C.270, powered by a 71-kW (95-hp) Salmson 7Ac seven-cylinder radial, totalled 82. Production of all versions of the Luciole totalled 725. After the outbreak of World War II many C.272/4s and C.275s were requisitioned for service use as liaison aircraft. In 1946 the surviving machines were used as glider tugs by the Ecole de l'Air at Salon-en-Provence.

Variants
Caudron C.270/1: powered by an improved Salmson 7Ac2 engine
Caudron C.271: had an 89-kW (120-hp) Lorraine 5Pc inline engine and a

Ratier metal propeller; only one built (F-AMBA)
Caudron C.271/2: powered by an 82-kW (110-hp) Lorraine 5Pb engine; five built
Caudron C.272: version with a Renault 4Pb engine; production totalled 52
Caudron C.272/2: powered by a Renault 4Pci engine; from the fifth example of the 22 C.272/2s completed the fin and rudder assembly was taller and more pointed, a shape which characterised all later Lucioles
Caudron C.272/3: total of 15 built,

powered by a Renault 4Pdi engine of 89 kW (120 hp) and fitted with Messier brakes
Caudron C.272/4: version with a 104-kW (140-hp) Renault 4Pei engine and Messier brakes; the luggage compartment forward of the cockpits was eliminated; total of 21 built
Caudron C.272/5: 80 examples of the C.272/5 were built, all powered by a 75-kW (100-hp) Renault 4Pgi engine
Caudron C.273: 14 of this version built, powered by the Michel 4 A-14 engine of 75 kW (100 hp) driving a Merville series 402 propeller

Caudron C.274: one example completed and displayed at the 1932 Paris Salon de l'Aéronautique; powered by the unsuccessful 101-kW (135-hp) Chaise 4Ba engine

Caudron C.275: this version was similar to the C.272/5, being powered by the same 75-kW (100-hp) Renault 4Pgi engine, but dispensed with wing folding; it was by far the most popular version of the Luciole, and like the other versions was sold to private owners in France and abroad, flew with the Caudron flying schools at Royan, Ambérieu and Guyancourt, and during the 1930s was seen regularly at aerial meetings and sporting contests; of the 433 C.275s built, 296 were ordered by the French government for the Aviation Populaire movement, which was intended to train would-be pilots who were unable to afford the fees charged by flying clubs

Caudron C.276: this version was powered by a 78-kW (105-hp) de Havilland Gipsy III engine, with brakes designed by the Charles company and a tailplane reminiscent of the earlier Lulcioles. One of these aircraft was used in the film *The Blue Max* to represent a German World War I fighter; the designation **C.276H** was given to two C.276s re-engined in 1956 with West German Hirth HM 504 A2 engines

Caudron C.277: nine of this version built, being identical with the C.272/4 except that the wings did not fold

Caudron C.277R: this was a solitary C.275 re-engined with a Renault 4Po 3 in 1949

Caudron C.278: one example built; this had new landing gear and a 101-kW (135-hp) Salmson 9Nc engine; participated in the Challenge Internationale de Tourisme competition with the contest code K-4

Specification
Caudron C.272
Type: two-seat sport and touring biplane
Powerplant: one 71-kW (95-hp) Renault 4Pb inline piston engine
Performance: maximum speed 158 km/h (98 mph) at sea level; cruising

speed 135 km/h (84 mph); service ceiling 4000 m (13,125 ft); range 500 km (311 miles)
Weights: empty 516 kg (1,138 lb); maximum take-off 780 kg (1,720 lb)
Dimensions: span 9.9 m (32 ft 5¾ in); length 7.67 m (25 ft 2 in); height 2.76 m (9 ft 0¾ in); wing area 24 m² (258.34 sq ft)

One of the many lightplane types to come from the Caudron stable in the inter-war years, the C.276 Luciole was the penultimate production version of the type. The glasshouse cockpit was not standard, being fitted later to this particular aircraft.

Caudron C.280 Phalène

The **Caudron C.280 Phalène** (Moth), conceived by Paul Deville as an air tourer, was a high-wing strut-braced cabin monoplane in a similar category to its British opposite number, the de Havilland Puss Moth.

The C.280 prototype made its maiden flight in March 1932 with the company's chief test pilot, Raymond Delmotte, at the controls. Its potential was obvious and it performed well; built to a total of over 240 in numerous versions it remained in production for some six years. Many examples were sold to private owners in a large number of European countries, as well as on the home market. Military versions, the **C.400** and **C.410**, served with the Armée de l'Air. Phalènes were selected for a number of long-distance staged flights and thus obtained considerable publicity in the aviation press of the time.

The original version was a three-seat aircraft with two seated side-by-side in the front of the cabin and the third occupant behind them. Hinged access doors on each side swung up when opened to clip to the under-surface of the wings. A baggage compartment was located aft of the cabin. Each panel of the fabric-covered wings of parallel chord and thickness and braced by a pair of streamlined duralumin struts. The entire wing trailing edge was hinged, the outer sections forming the ailerons and the inner sections folding upwards to enable the wings to be folded.

The rectangular-section fuselage was plywood-covered as far as the cabin, with fabric covering aft. Each main unit of the divided landing gear had an oleo-pneumatic strut, low-pressure tyres were standard and differential brakes fitted. The strut-braced horizontal tailplane, elevators and rudder were of spruce framework while the fin was of welded steel tube.

The prototype and the other four early examples bearing the main C.280 designation were each powered by a single 90-kW (120-hp) de Havilland Gipsy II four-cylinder inline engine.

Caudron made its mark in the inter-war years as a major manufacturer of lightplanes, many of them having a distinctly sporting character. The C.282 Phalène was the most numerous, appearing in many forms and in widespread service after World War I.

Variants
C.280/6: had rounded wingtips and revised, more pointed vertical tail surfaces (1 built)
C.280/9: fuselage 20 cm (8 in) longer than that of C.280 (3 built)
C.282: all C.282 series powered by Renault four-cylinder inline engines; this original version had Renault 4Pci (11 built)
C.282/2: the Phalène VI had a cabin with four seats; engine was Renault 4Pdi (21 built)
C.282/3: similar to C.282, but with reduced fuel capacity (1 built)
C.282/4: the first version to be named '**Super Phalène**', and provided with dual controls and automatic slots and flaps; a single conventional access door each side of cabin; wing span and fuselage length slightly reduced (9 built)
C.282/8: identical to C.282/2 except for fuselage lengthened by 13 cm (5.1 in), provision for more fuel and tailwheel replacing tailskid (89 built and 3 conversions)
C.282/10: earlier Merville series 496 propeller replaced by a Merville series 601 (11 built)
C.286: differed from C.282 in having the pilot's control column projecting downwards from cabin top and fin and rudder with revised contours; power provided (as with all C.286 series) by a de Havilland engine, in this case a Gipsy III (1 built)
C.286/2: as C.286 but with rounded wing tips; the **C.286/2 S.4** and **C.286/3 S.4** were special luxury

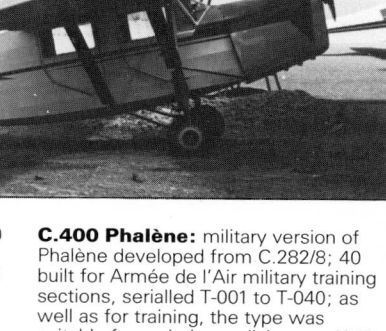

versions with Gipsy Major I engines (10 built)
C.286/4: fin and rudder as on C.280/6 (5 built)
C.286/5: Super Phalène, with Gipsy Major I engine, leading-edge slots, tail wheel, modified landing gear, sweepback on leading edge of tailplane (1 built)
C.286/6: Super Phalène, with Merville 501 propeller (5 built)
C.286/7: Super Phalène, with Ratier series 1175 variable-pitch propeller; fin and rudder same shape as C.286/4 and C.280/6 (8 built)
C.286/8: Super Phalène, with fuselage lengthened slightly as on the C.280/9; fin and rudder as on C.286 (4 built)
C.286/9: Super Phalène, with fuselage slightly shorter than that on C.286/8 (1 built)
C.289/2: powered by 112-kW (150-hp) Hispano-Suiza 5Q radial engine; same structure as C.286/9, except fin and rudder as C.286 (1 built)
C.289/9: same engine as C.289/2; fin and rudder as C.286 (5 built)
C.340 Micro Phalène: miniaturised Phalène, as a single-seater lightplane with single wing bracing strut on each side; 22-kW (30-hp) Chaise 4D engine; single example modified as **C.344** with 30-kW (40-hp) Chaise 4E
C.345 Phalène Junior: no dihedral on wings and 30-kW (40-hp) Train 4T engine, otherwise similar to C.340 (only prototype completed)

C.400 Phalène: military version of Phalène developed from C.282/8; 40 built for Armée de l'Air military training sections, serialled T-001 to T-040; as well as for training, the type was suitable for ambulance, liaison and VIP transport; a number were later converted for civil use; post-war, SCAN modified several C.400s for flying clubs and, redesignated **C.401**, a number remained in use until 1960; powered by 89-kW (120-hp) Renault 4Pdi engine
C.410: differed from C.400 in having 104-kW (140-hp) Renault 4Pei engine, baggage hold forward and air intake on port instead of starboard side of engine cowling (11 built)

Specification
Caudron C.282/8
Type: four-seat touring monoplane
Powerplant: one 108-kW (145-hp) Renault 4Pdi Bengali inline piston engine
Performance: maximum speed 185 km/h (115 mph); normal cruising speed 155 km/h (96 mph); ceiling 4500 m (14,765 ft); range 850 km (528 miles)
Weights: empty 550 kg (1,212 lb); maximum take-off 1100 kg (2,425 lb)
Dimensions: span 11.62 m (38 ft 1½ in); length 8.25 m (27 ft 0¾ in); height 2.05 m (6 ft 8¾ in); wing area 25.35 m² (272.87 sq ft)

Caudron C.440 Goéland

Developed by Marcel Riffard to meet the need for a fast, economical and comfortable transport to carry a limited number of passengers, the **Caudron C.440**

Goéland (Seagull) twin-engined low-wing cantilever monoplane made its appearance during 1934. Test flown by Raymond Delmotte, it proved its pedigree by combining economy with aero-

dynamic excellence. One of the most successful aircraft of its time, it was produced in greater numbers than any other transport in its category.

The two-spar wing was of spruce and

plywood with a plywood skin, and inboard of the inset ailerons the whole trailing edge of the wing was occupied by flaps which also extended beneath the fuselage. The fuselage was largely of wood and had plywood skinning except for the nose section and upper decking which had stressed sheet metal covering. The cantilever tail unit was also a wooden structure, its fixed surfaces plywood-covered and control surfaces fabric-covered. Streamlined nacelles for the 164-kW (220-hp) Bengali 6 engines extended below and to the rear of the wings; and the main landing gear units, each incorporating an oleo-sprung fork, retracted rearwards to lie wholly enclosed within the engine nacelles. The prototype had fairings attached to the front of each main leg to cover the wheel wells when the landing gear was retracted, but the next two C.440s had two wheel well doors attached to the underside of each nacelle, a feature of all future Goélands. A non-retracting steerable tailwheel was fitted.

In its basic passenger configuration the Goéland had comfortable cabin accommodation for six passengers. The pilot and co-pilot, who doubled as wireless operator, were seated side-by-side and had dual controls. Baggage holds were located fore and aft, and a toilet was situated at the rear of the cabin.

The Goéland remained in production in several versions up to World War II, the principal model being the **C.445**, also adopted by the Armée de l'Air as the **C.445M** and used for a variety of tasks, including military communications duties and crew training. Some C.445Ms were used by the Aéronavale. Civil users of the Goéland included Air France, Air Bleu and Régie Air Afrique. Air Bleu used one **C.444** and several C.445s on night mail routes from Paris to the Spanish border, and Régie Air Afrique operated the type on its North African routes. Other Goélands flew passenger services in French West Africa and Madagascar. The type was sold abroad to Aeroput of Yugoslavia, and to

Caudron C.440 Goéland, wearing the Free French Lorraine Cross markings during World War II.

Bulgaria and Spain. Two C.445Ms were supplied to the Belgian Aéronautique Militaire in 1940.

Production continued during World War II, and after the German occupation of France 44 C.445s and 10 C.445Ms were requisitioned, some flying on Lufthansa routes and others being operated by the Luftwaffe. Considerable numbers of the C.445M and **C.449** were built for the Germans at Renault's Billancourt and Caudron's Issy-les-Moulineaux factories. Production at Billancourt, however, was reduced to a trickle after a heavy RAF raid in 1943. The Germans used the Goéland as a pilot, radio and navigational trainer, for communications, and a small number had glazed noses for bomb-aimer training. In addition to the **C.447** specialised ambulance version, a few other Goélands were used for casualty transport.

Other Goélands served the French Vichy regime, while a number were scattered throughout France's overseas empire, most of them in North Africa. Several C.445s operated in the UK after June 1940.

In 1945 the Caudron plant was taken over by the French government as the Ateliers Aéronautiques d'Issy-les-Moulineaux. Here production of the C.445M and C.449 continued under the designation **AA.1**. Post-war Goélands continued in service with Air France. At the beginning of 1946 the company had 23 C.445s and 19 C.449s at its disposal; these flew domestic night mail services

for a time, but were employed for many years as crew trainers. Other civil operators included SABENA and two French companies, Aigle Azur and CAT (Compagnie Air Transport). Goélands continued to fly for a number of years on a wide range of duties with the Armée de l'Air.

Production of all versions of the Goéland totalled 1,702. A number of early aircraft were converted subsequently to later versions. The production listing below totals 1,446; it has not been possible to verify the sub-type designations of the remaining 256 Goélands.

Variants
C.440: prototype plus first two production aircraft
C.441: two 164-kW (220-hp) Renault 6Q-01 engines; 3° dihedral on outer wing sections (4 built)
C.444: first version to introduce counter-rotating engines and propellers (Renault 6Q-00 and 6Q-01) to overcome torque effects (17 built)
C.445: similar to C.444, but wing dihedral increased to 4° (114 C.445s, 2 C.445/1s and 3 C.445/2s) (40 built)
C.445M: militarised version; internal layout varied according to role (404 built)
C.445R: long-distance variant with additional fuel tanks in passenger cabin (1 built)
C.445/3: one of principal post-war

versions, with counter-rotating Renault 6Q-10 and 6Q-11 engines (510 completed)
C.446: Super Goéland (1 built)
C.447: air ambulance with accommodation for four stretchers, and additional side windows (31 built)
C.448: supercharged 6Q-02 and 6Q-03 engines, each of 179 kW (240 hp), and increased maximum take-off weight of 3700 kg (8,157 lb) (7 built)
C.449: final production model (349 built, many post-war: comprised 24 basic C.449s; 298 C.449/1s, /2s and /3s; and 27 C.449/4s and /5s, the C.449/4 being a specialised photographic aircraft)

Specification
Caudron C.445M Goéland
Type: military transport or trainer
Powerplant: two 164-kW (220-hp) each Renault 6Q-00/01 or 08/09 Bengali 6 inline piston engines
Performance: maximum speed 300 km/h (186 mph) at sea level; economic cruising speed 261 km/h (162 mph); service ceiling 7000 m (22,965 ft); range 1000 km (621 miles)
Weights: empty equipped 2292 kg (5,053 lb); maximum take-off 3500 kg (7,716 lb)
Dimensions: span 17.59 m (57 ft 8½ in); length 13.68 m (44 ft 10½ in); height 3.4 m (11 ft 1¾ in); wing area 42 m² (452.1 sq ft)

Caudron C.600 Aiglon

The **Caudron C.600 Aiglon** (Eaglet) light touring monoplane was the work of the outstanding French aircraft designer of the 1930s, Marcel Riffard. He had taken over the design department of the newly amalgamated Caudron and Renault combine at the end of 1933.

The first of two prototypes made its maiden flight at Issy-les-Moulineaux in March 1935. A low-wing cantilever monoplane with tandem open cockpits, it had the excellent aerodynamic qualities that became associated with all Riffard designs. The Aiglon proved itself with a number of outstanding flights. André Japy flew a single-seat **C.610** version from Paris to Saigon between 12 and 16 December 1935 at an average speed of 128 km/h (80 mph). The type was especially popular with French women fliers: Mesdames Dupeyron and Lion flew an Aiglon to establish new women's straight-line distance records in 1937 and 1938, while Suzanne Kohn flew her Aiglon from France to Madagascar in 1939.

Construction was entirely of wood, except for fabric covering of the rudder and elevators, the monoplane wing including wide-span trailing-edge flaps. The main units of the non-retractable tailwheel landing gear incorporated oleo-pneumatic struts, had differential brakes and housed the main wheels in speed

fairings. Two baggage compartments were located in front of the forward (passenger's) cockpit. There were variations in the shape of the fin and rudder, three distinct types being used.

Total production of the Aiglon was 203, some being fitted with continuous glazed canopies over the cockpits. The type was particularly popular with French private owners and flying clubs. A number were sold abroad, 14 being exported to Spain, two to Argentina and one to Japan. With the outbreak of war in 1939 many Aiglons were requisitioned by the French government and used as liaison aircraft by the Armée de l'Air. Some 178 of the basic C.600 Aiglon were completed, each powered by a 75-kW (100-hp) Renault 4Pgi Bengali Junior.

Variants
C.600G: powered by a de Havilland Gipsy Major engine with a Ratier metal propeller (5 built)
C.601 Aiglon Senior: version with the more powerful 104-kW (140-hp) Renault 4Pei engine (18 built)
C.610: special long-distance single-seat version with increased fuel capacity (2 built, registered F-ANSI and F-ANSK)

Specification

Caudron C.600
Type: two-seat light touring monoplane
Powerplant: one 75-kW (100-hp) Renault 4Pgi Bengali Junior inline piston engine
Performance: maximum speed 220 km/h (137 mph) at sea level; cruising speed 190 km/h (118 mph); service ceiling 4000 m (13,125 ft); range 700 km (435 miles)
Weights: empty 560 kg (1,235 lb); maximum take-off 880 kg (1,940 lb)
Dimensions: span 11.38 m (37 ft 4 in); length 7.64 m (25 ft 0¾ in); height 2.89 m (9 ft 5¾ in); wing area 14.51 m² (156.19 sq ft)

The chief difference between the Caudron C.600 and C.601 versions of the lightplane, named Aiglon, lay in the powerplant; the former (illustrated) had only 76 kW (100 hp) compared with the latter's 104 kW (140 hp). Both versions were produced with open or enclosed cockpits. Of the 200 or so built before the war, many were taken from their flying clubs and private owners and given to Armée de l'Air units to act as 'hacks' and liaison craft.

Caudron C.630 Simoun

An outstanding four-seat cabin touring monoplane of the 1930s with an excellent standard of reliability and comfort, the **Caudron C.630 Simoun** (Sandstorm) incorporated many technical features developed in designer Marcel Riffard's series of Coupe Deutsche de la Meurthe racers.

The experimental **C.500 Simoun IV** and **C.620 Simoun VI** were exhibited at the Paris Salon de l'Aéronautique in 1934. The C.620 was intended for the Challenge Internationale de Tourisme competition and its comfortable individual seats, deep windscreen and three large windows on each side of the cabin found g·eater favour than the more conventional layout and shallow windscreen and windows of the C.500. There was clearly a market for the Simoun with its new Renault six-cylinder engine and, apart from the one-off **C.520** and two long-range versions of the C.620 with extra fuel tanks in the cabin, the production **C.630** was the next version to appear.

The C.630 was an elegant low-wing cantilever monoplane of wooden construction, the wing covered by plywood plus fabric and incorporating flaps that occupied the entire trailing edge inboard of the ailerons. The slab-sided fuselage had light alloy covering for the carefully streamlined curved underside and roof. The non-retractable tailwheel landing gear had cantilever main legs with oleo-pneumatic shock absorbers, the legs, main wheels and castoring tailwheel all enclosed in streamlined fairings. Differential brakes were standard.

The prototype C.620 with a 127-kW (170-hp) Renault Bengali 6Pfi engine was flown for the first time in October 1934. Only a few months later, in mid-1935, deliveries began of the C.630 series with a 134-kW (180-hp) Renault 6Pri (or 6Q-07) driving a Ratier variable-pitch metal propeller. The new type found immediate favour, with orders for some 70 private tourers following. Commercially, 12 C.630s established France's first regular

air mail service, each in an elegant light blue finish with a silver arrow along the fuselage side; these belonged to Air Bleu, the air-mail subsidiary of Air France. Air Bleu's first flight from its Le Bourget base was on 10 July 1935. After somewhat erratic early progress, the criss-cross of domestic postal routes resumed in June 1937 and continued until May 1939, establishing a 95 per cent regularity record and carrying over 45 million letters. Other Simouns flew air mail routes in Madagascar.

A number of variants followed the C.630, but only the **C.635** with a 164-kW (220-hp) 6Q-09 or 6Q-15 Bengali engine was built in quantity. Five of the type in red livery equipped the French VIP Escadrille Ministerielle, while during 1935-6 the French services placed initial orders for the militarised **C.635M** version, 110 for the Armée de l'Air and 29 for the Aéronavale. Other military and naval orders followed, the Simoun being used widely for liaison, as a General Staff transport, and as a transition or navigation trainer. At the outbreak of World War II some 60 civil Simouns were requisitioned by the Armée de l'Air for the hastily formed Sections d'Avions Estafettes (air couriers) and Sections d'Avions Sanitaires (air ambulances). Of 103 Simouns captured by the Germans in November 1942, when they took over the Unoccupied Zone of France from the Vichy regime, 65 were used for training and liaison. Large numbers of Simouns flew with the French in North Africa, although the attrition rate was high. Several examples were reported in the UK during the war.

Many well-known French pilots of the 1930s used the Simoun in long distance attempts. Among those to gain success were Génin and Robert, who flew a C.635 (registered F-ANMA and named

Gody Radio) from Le Bourget on 18 December 1935, 57 hours 36 minutes later landing at Antananarivo in Madagascar, having covered a distance of 8665 km (5,384 miles). Marie Bastié flying solo took her C.635 *Jean Mermoz* from Orly on 12 December 1936, reached Dakar in West Africa on 19 December and then crossed the South Atlantic to Natal in Brazil, a distance of 3100 km (1,926 miles) averaging 264 km/h (164 mph). This beat the record held previously by Jean Batten of New Zealand. In another solo flight from France, in August 1937, Maryse Hilsz reached Saigon in less than four days.

Other more famous fliers were less fortunate. On a second attempt to reach Tokyo from Paris, Marcel Doret and his partner Micheletti made an emergency landing in Japan and were badly hurt. The great airman-poet Antoine de Saint Exupéry, attempting to reach Tierra del Fuego from New York in 1937, crashed on take-off at Guatemala City and was seriously injured. A number of Simouns remained in flying condition post-war. One was used (on the ground, alas) in the film entitled *The Little Prince*, appropriately enough a story written by Antoine de Saint Exupéry!

Variants

C.630: initial production version, with the 134-kW (180-hp) Renault Bengali 6Pri engine (20 built)

C.631: powered by 164-kW (220-hp)

Bengali 6Q-01 (3 built)

C.632: similar to C.631 (1 built)

C.633: modified fuselage and Bengali 6Q-07 engine (6 built)

C.634: modified wing, increased take-off weight and Bengali 6Q-01 or 6Q-09 engine (3 built)

C.635: improved cabin layout and Bengali 6Q-01 or 6Q-09 engine (46 built as C.635s and a number of earlier Simouns converted to C.635 standard)

C.635M: C.635 with military equipment, detailed modifications and Bengali 6Q-09 or 6Q-15 engine (436 built for Armée de l'Air, 52 for Aéronavale and one for US naval attaché in Paris)

Specification
Caudron C.635M Simoun
Type: four-seat military liaison, light transport or trainer aircraft

Powerplant: one 164-kW (220-hp) Renault Bengali 6Q-09 inline piston engine

Performance: maximum speed 300 km/h (186 mph) at sea level; economic cruising speed 260 km/h (162 mph); service ceiling 6000 m (19,685 ft); range 1500 km (932 miles)

Weights: empty equipped 755 kg (1,664 lb); maximum take-off 1380 kg (3,042 lb)

Dimensions: span 10.4 m (34 ft 1½ in); length 9.1 m (29 ft 10¼ in); height 2.3 m (7 ft 6½ in); wing area 16 m² (172.23 sq ft)

The bulky fuselage of the Simoun allowed the carriage of four passengers and a useful baggage load.

Caudron C.640 Typhon

Caudron C.640 Typhon no.5 Louis Blériot

Owing a great deal in concept to the British de Havilland D.H.88 Comet, of England to Australia Air Race fame, the **Caudron C.640 Typhon** was inspired by the French pioneer of long-range postal routes, the great Jean Mermoz. The C.640 was thus a high-speed long-range mail-carrier designed by Georges Otfinovsky in collaboration with Marcel Riffard.

The first C.640 made its debut in June 1935 with Raymond Delmotte at the controls. A twin-engined low-wing cantilever monoplane of wooden construction, it had narrow-chord ailerons inset from the wing-tips and split trailing-edge flaps, trim tabs fitted to all control surfaces and a variable-incidence tailplane adjustable in flight. Each main unit of the landing gear retracted rearwards to lie fully within engine nacelles that were carefully faired into the underside of the wing. The enclosed crew cabin accommodated two in tandem with dual controls and full wireless equipment. Seven C.640s were constructed, the fourth and seventh examples having an enlarged fin and rudder.

The Typhon established speed records over a 5000-km (3,107-mile) distance and participated in the celebrated

Istres-Damascus-Paris air race in August 1937. Unfortunately it was not particularly successful in operation as its wings were too flexible, resulting in buffeting problems of some severity.

Variants
C.641: two examples of this single-seat record-breaking version of the C.640 were built, the pilot seated beneath a raised canopy similar to that adopted for many fighters towards the end of World War II; fuel capacity was almost doubled to provide a range of up to 6700 km (4,163 miles); the second C.641 was sold to Romania

C.670: a prototype twin-engined high-speed bomber, or *avion de represailles* to use the contemporary description, flown in March 1937; it accommodated a crew of three comprising a bomb-aimer in the nose and the pilot and gunner under a raised glazed canopy; intended armament was two 20-mm cannon, one 7.5-mm (0.295-in) machine-gun and two bombs of either 100 kg (220 lb) or 250 kg (551 lb) depending on target distance; performance similar to C.640, dimensions and weights slightly increased; bore the provisional service serial FW-006, but soon abandoned

Specification
Caudron C.640 Typhon
Type: long-range high-speed mail-carrier

Powerplant: two 164-kW (220-hp) each Renault 6Q inline piston engines

Performance: maximum speed 400 km/h (249 mph); cruising speed 370 km/h (230 mph); service ceiling 7000 m (22,965 ft); range 3725 km (2,315 miles)

Weights: empty equipped 1630 kg (3,594 lb); maximum take-off 3400 kg (7,496 lb)

Dimensions: span 11.5 m (47 ft 6¾ in); length 10.95 m (35 ft 11 in); height 3 m (9 ft 10 in); wing area 28 m² (301.40 sq ft)

Caudron C.690M

With the same basic design characteristics as Marcel Riffard's lightweight all-wood low-wing cantilever monoplane racers, the **Caudron C.690** was designed as a trainer for pilots of single-seat fighters. It was similar to the earlier **C.720**, with a large rounded fin and rudder assembly and independent fixed cantilever main landing gear units with wheel spats, but had a 164-kW (220-hp) Renault 6Q-03 engine in place of a 104-kW (140-hp) Bengali Sport and was also heavier than the C.720. The first prototype flew in early 1936 and was followed by the second on 18 February 1936. This latter aircraft was demonstrated by the Caudron company's flight director Christian Sarton du Jonchay in several foreign countries, including Austria, Hungary, Romania and Yugoslavia. Soon afterwards the first C.690 was demonstrated to Japanese, Soviet and US air missions, resulting in one example of a Caudron single-seater being bought by the Soviet Union and one by Japan, although the exact types are unknown. It is thought they were basically C.690s, but may have had tailplanes of a more angular type as fitted to the earlier experimental **C.580**.

While undergoing official tests at Villacoublay on 10 May 1937, the first prototype crashed, killing Caudron's chief test pilot René Paulhan. Despite this disaster official interest continued to grow and a production series was ordered for the Armée de l'Air. These aircraft differed from the prototype in having a triangular shaped fin and rudder, longer landing gear legs and fixed leading-edge slots. Production was slow to get under way and the first **C.690M** did not begin flight tests until the beginning of April 1939. These military aircraft were unarmed but equipped with an OPL camera gun. Fifteen aircraft had been delivered by the end of May that year, being allocated to CICs (Centres d'Instruction à la Chasse, or Fighter Training Centres) at Salon, Dijon and Etampes, but none remained in flying condition after the French collapse in June 1940. One example (C.690 no. 9) was concealed from the occupying forces and restored to flying condition after the War, taking to the air on 12 April 1945. Repaired later after an accident, all trace of it was subsequently lost.

Specification
Caudron C.690M
Type: single-seat fighter trainer
Powerplant: one 164-kW (220-hp) Renault 6Q-05 inline piston engine
Performance: maximum speed 370 km/h (230 mph) at 2000 m (6,560 ft); economic cruising speed 320 km/h (199 mph); service ceiling 9700 m (31,825 ft); climb to 1000 m (3,280 ft) in 1 minute 30 seconds; range 1100 km (684 miles)
Weights: empty equipped 672 kg (1,482 lb); maximum take-off 1050 kg

Used as a fighter trainer, to familiarise pilots with the handling characteristics of fast monoplanes, the Caudron C.690 proved moderately useful, especially as its cost was considerably lower than any comparable type.

(2,315 lb)
Dimensions: span 7.7 m (25 ft 3¼ in); length 7.82 m (25 ft 7¾ in); height 2.6 m (8 ft 6¼ in); wing area 90 m² (96.88 sq ft)

Caudron C.714 Cyclone

Marcel Riffard, who joined the French company Société Anonyme des Avions Caudron as chief designer in 1932, became renowned during the next four years when well streamlined racing aircraft of his design won the Coupe Deutsch de la Meurthe contests in 1934, 1935 and 1936. The excellence of the basic design induced the company to develop a lightweight fighter aircraft that would benefit from the experience gained in construction and development of the Coupe Deutsch contenders, leading to the **Caudron C.710** prototype which flew for the first time on 18 July 1936.

The C.710, despite its small size and weight, soon showed its potential for development, for even with fixed landing gear and armed by two 20-mm cannon its 336 kW (450-hp) Renault 12Ro1 engine was sufficient to provide a maximum speed that exceeded that of many contemporary fighters. This led to the **C.713 Cyclone**, first flown in December

Caudron C.714 Cyclone of the Groupe de Chasse Polonaise (GC I/145) French air force, based at Lyon-Bron in May 1940.

The Caudron C.710.01 prototype lightweight fighter was notable for its performance on limited power, and the useful armament of two 20-mm cannon.

The C.760 was one of the last developments of the lightweight fighter concept in World War II. The Isotta-Fraschini Delta RC 40 was the engine used.

ber 1937, which was generally similar in overall design and powerplant, but which introduced retractable tailwheel type landing gear and redesigned vertical tail surfaces. Final evolution of Riffard's design was the **C.714.01** prototype, first flown in the summer of 1938, which differed by having some structural strengthening and a wing of improved profile.

The factory testing of this prototype confirmed Riffard's performance estimates, and it was handed over to the CEMA for trials in September 1938. In November there followed an order for 100 **C.714** production aircraft which were required to have four 7.5-mm (0.295-in) wing-mounted machine-guns. Of low-wing cantilever monoplane configuration, the C.714 was an all-wood construction, except that all control surfaces had light alloy framework and fabric covering. The wing section was so shallow that it was not possible to mount machine-guns conventionally, within the wing structure, and special streamlined pods were designed, these carrying a pair of guns beneath each wing.

Production began in the summer of 1939, and 50 of the aircraft which had been intended to serve with the Armée de l'Air were diverted to the assistance of Finland, but only six had been received by 12 March 1940, the balance being presumed to have been lost en route. It is believed that about 40 C.714s were delivered to the French air force, which, after some 90 had been built, cancelled production because of dissatisfaction with the type's rate of climb. They were used to equip an all-Polish

squadron which became known as the 'Warsaw Group' (GC I/145), this unit seeing action against the Germans between 2-13 June 1940. Following the collapse of France, a small number were used by the Vichy French air force, and about 20 were confiscated by the Germans for use by the Luftwaffe.

Variants
C.720: trainer version of the C.714, powered by a 164-kW (220-hp) Renault Bengali 6Q or by a 75-kW (100-hp) Renault 4Pei
C.760: prototype with 560-kW (750-hp) Isotta-Fraschini Delta RC 40
C.770: prototype with 597-kW (800-hp) Renault 626

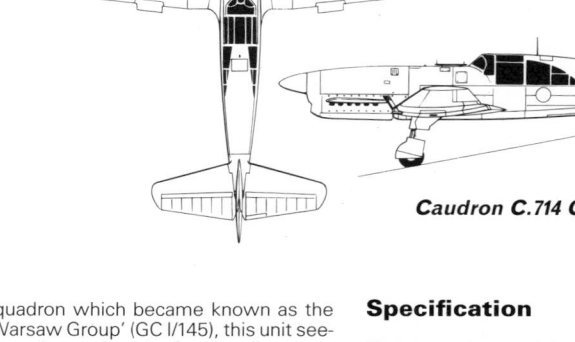

Caudron C.714 Cyclone

Specification

Type: single-seat lightweight fighter
Powerplant: one 336-kW (450-hp) Renault 12Ro1 inline piston engine
Performance: maximum speed 485 km/h (301 mph) at 4000 m (13,125 ft); cruising speed 320 km/h (199 mph); service ceiling 9100 m (29,855 ft); range 900 km (559 miles)
Weights: empty 1400 kg (3,086 lb); maximum take-off 1750 kg (3,858 lb)
Dimensions: span 8.97 m (29 ft 5 in); length 8.53 m (27 ft 11¾ in); height 2.87 m (9 ft 5 in); wing area 12.5 m² (134.55 sq ft)
Armament: four 7.5-mm (0.295-in) forward-firing machine-guns

Cavalier Mustang

The Cavalier Aircraft Corporation of Sarasota, Florida, the successor to Trans-Florida Aviation, acquired during the 1960s the type certificate to the North American F-51 Mustang. From the design, Cavalier developed a tandem two-seat business/sport conversion of the F-51 which it marketed under the designation **Cavalier 2000**. In addition to refinements to convert the Mustang from a military to an executive aircraft, the Cavalier 2000 gained two wingtip auxiliary fuel tanks. Power was provided by a 1189-kW (1,595-hp) Packard-built Rolls-Royce Merlin V-1650-7.

More importantly, however, Cavalier was awarded a contract by the US Air Force to manufacture a version of the **F-51D Mustang** for supply to air forces receiving MAP assistance from the USA. The result was a new production programme, aircraft being assembled from a combination of new parts and others taken from existing stocks; in addition, the new aircraft were delivered with many updated features, especially in the area of armament and avionics. While this programme was in progress, Cavalier developed as a private venture during 1967-68 an improved **Mustang II** specifically for use in the COIN (counter-insurgency) role. Reinforcement of the wings and fuselage, plus the installation of a more powerful Rolls-Royce Merlin engine developing 1312 kW (1,760 hp) made possible a higher take-off weight and the carriage of more armament.

At this stage the company decided to improve upon both the F-51D Mustang and the Mustang II by the development of an even more advanced version with turboprop powerplant. A prototype was built as the **Turbo Mustang III**, powered by a Rolls-Royce RDa.6 Dart Mk 510 turboprop, the overall length of the power unit requiring an extended cowling. Development continued with the installation of an Avco Lycoming T55-L-9 turboprop, which could be

accommodated within the standard engine bay, and design features of this new aircraft included provision of structural armour for cockpit and engine protection, the introduction of fire-suppressing reticulated foam in the fuel tanks and the planned installation of a zero-zero escape system for the pilot.

Shortly after this stage of development the programme was acquired by Piper Aircraft Corporation which flew the Lycoming-engined prototype for the first time on 29 April 1971. In September 1981 Piper received a USAF contract covering the design, development and testing of a lightweight turboprop-powered close-support aircraft based on the P-51. Designated the **PA-48 Enforcer**, two T55-L-9-powered prototypes were built, essentially improved Turbo Mustang IIIs, and the first flew on 9 April 1983. Following the completion in August 1984 of an extensive evaluation programme, the project did not proceed further and the two prototypes were placed in storage at Davis-Monthan AFB.

Specification
Cavalier Turbo Mustang III
Type: single-seat close-support fighter
Powerplant: one 1298-ekW (1,740-ehp) Rolls-Royce RDa.6 Dart Mk 510 turboprop
Performance: maximum cruising speed 869 km/h (540 mph); ferry range 3701 km (2,300 miles)
Weights: empty equipped 3037 kg (6,696 lb); maximum take-off 6350 kg (14,000 lb)
Dimensions: span 12.6 m (41 ft 4 in); length 10.41 m (24 ft 2 in); height 2.67 m (8 ft 9 in); wing area 22.76 m² (245 sq ft)

Based on the F-51D, the Turbo Mustang III was reworked to mount a Rolls-Royce Dart turboprop and numerous detail improvements to suit it for the close support role.

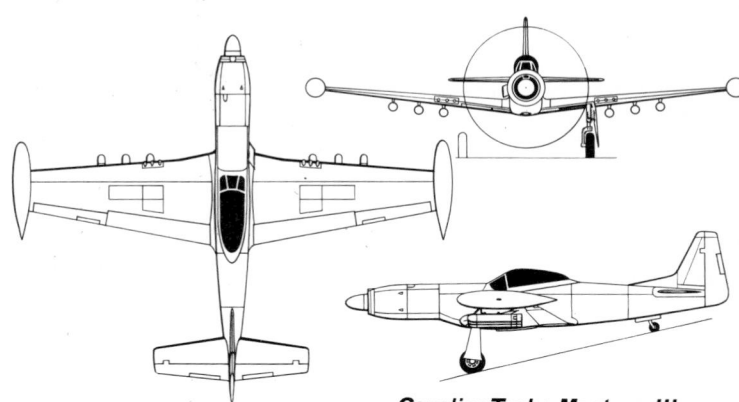

Cavalier Turbo Mustang III

Armament: six 12.7-mm (0.5-in) Browning M2 or M3 machine-guns, plus up to 2268 kg (5,000 lb) of stores (bombs, bomblet dispensers, fire-bombs, gunpods, grenade-launchers and rocket-launchers) on six hardpoints

Right: The Cavalier 2000 was a refurbished Mustang with tiptanks and the hood of the TP-51D to allow the carriage of a passenger.

Cessna early types

In 1911 Clyde V. Cessna built his first aircraft, a Blériot-type monoplane powered by a 45-kW (60-hp) Elbridge engine, and followed it with several more designs before he formed the Travel Air Manufacturing Company, with Walter Beech and Lloyd Stearman, in February 1925. Cessna soon withdrew from the Travel Air organisation and, with Victor Roos, set up the Cessna-Roos Aircraft Company in September 1927, founding the Cessna Aircraft Company Inc. in December 1927 following the departure of Roos.

The first Cessna design to enter series production was the **Cessna Model A**, the first of a long and immensely successful line of high-wing monoplanes which is perpetuated to this day in Cessna's single-engined range. A four-seater of mixed wood and steel-tube construction with fabric covering, the type was built in several versions with different engines: 14 of the **Model AA** were manufactured with an 89-kW (120-hp)

Lowest-powered of the Model A series was the Model AA, with a 89-kW (129-hp) Anzani radial. Note the port-side generator.

Anzani, one of the **Model AC** with a 97-kW (130-hp) Comet, three of the **Model AF** with a 112-kW (150-hp) Floco/Axelson, four of the **Model AS** with a 93-kW (125-hp) Siemens-Halske, and 48 of the **Model AW** powered by a 93-kW (125-hp) Warner Scarab. A three-seat version was known as the **Model BW**, of which 13 were built with a 164-kW (220-hp) Wright J-5 engine.

In November 1928 the **CW-6** was flown. A six-seater powered by a 164-kW (220-hp) Wright Whirlwind J-5 radial engine, it appeared at the 1929 Auto Show in Wichita. A scaled-down four-seat version, the **Model DC-6** with a 127-kW (170-hp) Curtiss Challenger engine, was rolled out in February 1929. This entered production in two versions, the **DC-6A** and **DC-6B** powered re-

The Model AW was the Warner Scarab-powered version of the Model A, the first product of the company in its present form.

Evolved from the Model A and its derivatives, the Model BW offered higher performance with four people instead of three.

Only the type of engine installed differentiated the Model DC-6A from the DC-6B. This is the Wright J-6 powered DC-6B.

A lightplane of remarkably clean lines for the period, the Cessna Model 34 was the precursor of the modern Cessna singles.

The Model C-37 differed from the C-34 in having a wider cabin for greater passenger comfort, and the installation of flaps.

The Model C-145 and C-165 Airmaster had different rated Warner Super Scarab radials.

spectively by the 224-kW (300-hp) Wright R-985 Whirlwind and the 168-kW (225-hp) Wright J-6, both versions gaining type certificates in September 1929. The depression which followed the Wall Street crash restricted production of the two models to around 24 of each, some of which were taken on charge by the USAAF in 1942 as the **UC-77** and **UC-77A** respectively. In an attempt to keep the factory going, Cessna designed and marketed the **CG-2** primary glider. Eldon Cessna, Clyde's son, designed the single-seat 19-kW (25-hp) Cleone-powered **EC-1** and two-seat **EC-2** with a 22-kW (30-hp) E-107A engine, both intended as low-cost, cheap-to-operate aircraft to meet the new economic conditions. Only the glider achieved produc-

tion status, however, before the company ceased operations, not to resume until January 1934.

In June 1935 the prototype **Model C-34** made its first flight, piloted by George Harte. Powered by a 108-kW (145-hp) Warner Super Scarab, this was a four-seater which demonstrated its aerodynamic efficiency by achieving a maximum speed of 261 km/h (162 mph), compared with 238 km/h (148 mph) for the much higher-powered DC-6B. Some 42 were built, two being impressed for USAAF under the designation **UC-77B**. The **Model C-37**, introduced during 1937, brought in minor improvements to the furnishing of the cabin, which was widened by 12.7 cm (5 in), and was fitted with electrically operated wing trailing-

edge flaps. Some 46 C-37s were built, and one impressed in 1942 was designated **UC-77C**. The 1938 **Model C-38** again featured minor improvements, with some of the previously optional equipment fitted as standard; airframe changes included the provision of wider track landing gear and a large under-fuselage flap which served as an air-brake to reduce landing speed. Production of the C-38 amounted to 16 aircraft. The final pre-war Cessna four-seat models were the **C-145** and **C-165 Airmaster**. By the time their manufacture ceased in 1941, production had comprised 42 C-145s, 34 C-165s and three of the **C-165D**, powered respectively by 108-kW (145-hp), 123-kW (165-hp) and 130-kW (175-hp) versions of the Warner

Super Scarab.

Specification
Cessna Model C-38
Type: four-seat tourer
Powerplant: one 108-kW (145-hp) Warner Super Scarab radial piston engine
Performance: maximum speed 261 km/h (162 mph); crusing speed 230 km/h (143 mph); service ceiling 5485 m (18,000 ft); cruising range 885 km (550 miles)
Weights: empty 621 kg (1,370 lb); maximum take-off 1066 kg (2,350 lb)
Dimensions: span 10.41 m (34 ft 2 in); length 7.52 m (24 ft 8 in); height 2.13 m (7 ft 0 in); wing area 16.81 m² (181.0 sq ft)

Cessna Model T-50

Cessna Aircraft's first twin-engined lightplane, built and flown in 1939, was a five-seat commercial transport typical of many very similar aircraft which became fairly common in the USA during the late 1930s. Designated **Cessna Model T-50** by the company, it was of low-wing cantilever monoplane configuration and of mixed construction. Wings and tail unit were of wood, the latter with fabric covering; the fuselage, however, was a welded steel-tube structure with fabric over lightweight wooden skinning. Retractable tailwheel type landing gear and wing trailing-edge flaps were both electrically actuated.

In 1940 the military potential of this aircraft, as a trainer suitable for the conversion of pilots from single-engine to twin-engine types, became apparent almost simultaneously to two North American nations. First was Canada, which re-

quired a machine of this type for the Commonwealth Joint Air Training Plan, and 550 aircraft were supplied under Lend-Lease, these being designated **Crane 1A**.

The second requirement was for the US Army Air Corps which, in late 1940, contracted for the supply of 33 T-50s for sevice evaluation, allocating to them the designation **AT-17**. These were powered by two 220-kW (295-hp) Jacobs R-680-9 radial engines, but service trials showed that these were unnecessarily powerful for use in a two-seat trainer, and when in 1941 the first real production contracts were placed, less powerful engines by the same manufacturer were specified. The initial production version, designated **AT-17**, was equipped with Jacobs R-755-9 engines driving wooden propellers. A total of 450 was built, and these aircraft were followed into produc-

tion by 223 of the generally similar AT-17A, which differed by having Hamilton-Standard constant-speed metal propellers. The later **AT-17B** (466 built) had some equipment changes, and the **AT-17C** (60 built) was provided with different radio for communications.

The original use of Cessna's T-50s had been in a light transport role, and in 1942 the USAAF decided that these aircraft would be valuable for liaison/communication purposes and as light personnel transports. Production of this variant totalled 1,287, the aircraft being named **Bobcat** and given the designation **C-78**, later changed to **UC-78**. In addition, a small number of commercial T-50s were impressed for service with the USAAF under the designation **UC-78A**.

The USAAF's requirement for the two-seat conversion trainers had been difficult to predict, and when it was discovered in late 1942 that procurement contracts very considerably exceeded

the training requirement, Cessna was requested to fulfil the outstanding balance of the AT-17B and **AT-17D** models as **UC-78B** and **UC-78C** Bobcats respectively. Both were virtually identical, but differed from the original UC-78s by having two-blade fixed-pitch wooden propellers and some minor changes of installed equipment. Production of these two versions amounted to 1,806 UC-78Bs and 327 UC-78Cs.

In the period 1942-3, the US Navy had a requirement for a lightweight transport aircraft to carry ferry pilots between delivery points and their home bases, as well as for the movement of US Navy flight crews. This led to the procurement of 67 aircraft, generally similar to the UC-78, which entered service under the designation **JRC-1**. Many examples of USAAF Bobcats remained in service for two or three years after the end of World War II.

Specification
Cessna UC-78
Type: five-seat light transport
Powerplant: two 183-kW (245-hp) Jacobs R-755-9 radial piston engines
Performance: maximum speed 314 km/h (195 mph); cruising speed 282 km/h (175 mph); service ceiling 6705 m (22,000 ft); range 1207 km (750 miles)
Weights: empty 1588 kg (3,500 lb); maximum take-off 2585 kg (5,700 lb)
Dimensions: span 12.78 m (41 ft 11 in); length 9.98 m (32 ft 9 in); height 3.02 m (9 ft 11 in); wing area 27.41 m (295.0 sq ft)

In military service the Cessna Bobcat was widely used for light transport and multi-engine training. Most served as UC-78s with the USAAF, but this example is a US Navy JRC-1.

Cessna Models 120 and 140

The **Cessna Model 120** prototype, first flown on 28 June 1945, represented the company's attempt to capture a share of the post-war market for personal lightplanes. A two-seat cabin monoplane with a strut-braced high-set

wing, it was the progenitor of derived models that ramained in production until the late 1980s. Structure was all-metal, except for fabric-covered wings, the landing gear was of fixed tailwheel type introducing cantilever spring steel main

units, and the enclosed cabin provided two seats side-by-side and dual controls as standard. Powerplant comprised an 63-kW (85-hp) Continental engine, and the higher power of this unit by comparison with competing types, plus a low price tag, ensured that Cessna gained an unexpectedly large measure of sales success.

The Model 120, a basic aircraft, was complemented by a 'de luxe' **Model 140** which provided as standard manually actuated trailing-edge flaps, extra cabin windows and a full electrical system. When production of the Models 120 and 140 ended in 1950 more than 2,200 Model 120s and 5,000 Model 140s had been built.

Specification
Cessna Model 140
Type: two-seat cabin monoplane
Powerplant: one 63-kW (85-hp) Continental C-85-12F flat-four piston

The Model 120 secured Cessna's post-war financial position, and paved the way for the development of a hugely successful lightplane family.

engine
Performance: maximum speed 193 km/h (120 mph); cruising speed 169 km/h (105 mph); service ceiling 4725 m (15,500 ft); range 724 km (450 miles)
Weights: empty 408 kg (900 lb); maximum take-off 680 kg (1, 500 lb)
Dimensions: span 10.01 m (32 ft 10 in); length 6.40 m (21 ft 0 in); height 1.91 m (6 ft 3 in); wing area 14.82 m (159.60 sq ft)

Cessna Models 150 and 152

When production of the Models 120 and 140 ended, Cessna concentrated upon the development of four-seat aircraft of similar configuration. It was not until the first flight of the **Cessna Model 150**, during September 1957, that the company re-entered the two-seat lightplane market. An all-metal braced high-wing monoplane, of similar configuration to the Model 140, this Model 150 differed primarily by the introduction of non-retractable tricycle landing gear, the installation of dual controls being optional, and by having a 75-kW (100-hp) Continental O-200 engine.

Production began in August 1958 and by the time it ended during 1977 a total of 23,836 had been built, this figure including 1,754 built in France by Reims Aviation under the designation **Reims F-150**. Just before the end of production the aircraft had been available in **Model 150 Standard, Commuter, Commuter II** and **Aerobat** versions. The differences between the first three represented varying standards of installed equipment, and there was also a wide range of optional avionics and equipment available. The aerobat embodied structural changes permitting a licence in the Aerobatic category for load factors of +6g and -3g at full gross weight, its aerobatic capability allowing such manoeuvres as aileron, barrel and snap rolls, chandelles, loops and vertical reverses.

In 1977 the Cessna 150 range was replaced on the production lines by the basically similar **Cessna Model 152**. Improvements included a more powerful Avco Lycoming 0-235 engine giving 80.5-kW (108-hp), plus installation and

The Model 152 designation reflected a change from the Continental powerplant of the 150 to an Avco Lycoming. Both aircraft were available in Aerobat versions.

cowling changes to reduce engine noise and vibration, together with a McCauley propeller of a modified blade section. Between 1977 and 1986 the aircraft was available in four versions; the standard Model 152, the slightly heavier Model 152 II with a package of factory installed avionics and omni-directional light beacon, the further improved Model 152 Trainer with other improvements including an intercom system and transponder, and the Model 152 Aerobat with the same aerobatic capabilities as the 150 Aerobat. When production ceased in 1986, 7,482 Model 152 and Aerobats had been produced including 640 built under licence in France by Reims Aviation.

Specification
Cessna Model 152 Standard
Type: two-seat cabin monoplane
Powerplant: one 80.5-kW (108-hp) Avco Lycoming O-235-N2C flat-four piston engine

Performance: maximum speed at sea level 202 km/h (125 mph); service ceiling 4480 m) (14,700 ft); maximum range 1158 km (719 miles)
Weights: empty 501 kg (1,104 lb);

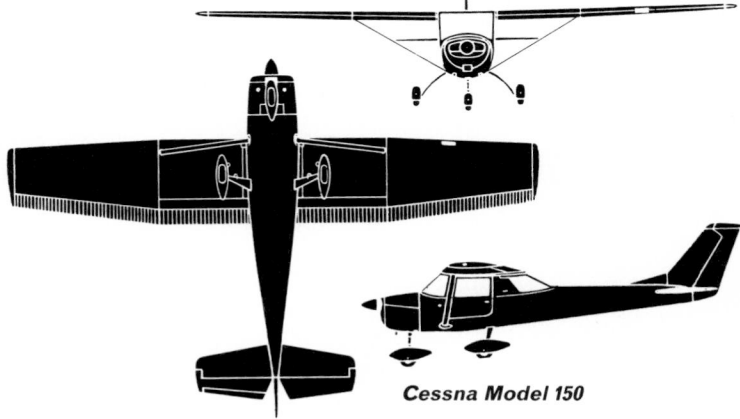
Cessna Model 150

maximum take-off 757 kg (1,670 lb)
Dimensions: span 9.97 m (32 ft 8½ in; length 7.34 m (24 ft 1 in); height 2.59 m (8 ft 6 in); wing area 14.59 m² (157.0 sq ft

Cessna Model 170/172/175/182/ Skylark/Skyhawk/Skylane/T-41

The **Cessna Model 170** and its immediate successors of the same family have the double distinction of being the best-selling series of lightplanes of all time, and also the most widely produced aircraft series yet developed, well over 30,000 examples having come off the production lines by the 1980s.

The origins of the series stretch back to 1948, when Cessna introduced the Model 170, itself little more than a four-

seat, re-engineered development of the earlier Model 120. The Model 170 proved popular, but the type's real success started in 1953 when Cessna introduced the **Model 170B**: this was powered, like its predecessor, by the 108-kW (145-hp) Continental C0145-2 air-cooled piston engine, but incorporated the slotted Fowler flaps pioneered for Cessna's Model 305. With these efficient flaps the field and low-speed performance of the

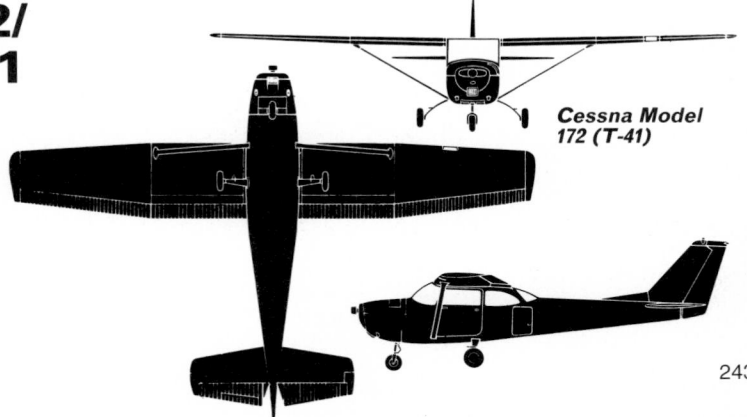
Cessna Model 172 (T-41)

The Skylane started life as the de luxe version of the 182, with factory-installed options to enhance customer appeal.

Model 170 were improved radically, and all subsequent Cessna aircraft of the type have been designed round similar flaps.

In 1955 the company developed the **Model 172**, which was essentially a Model 170B with detail improvements and the tailwheel landing gear replaced by a spatted tricycle unit. The improved ground safety of the new variant proved immediately attractive, and in 1956 some 1,170 Model 172s were sold, compared with a mere 174 of the Model 170B, whose production was terminated.

In 1958 Cessna brought into production the **Model 175**. This was in effect the latest version of the Model 172 with a number of improvements (free-blown windscreen, glassfibre speed fairings, etc) and a 131-kW (175-hp) GO-300-C geared engine driving a constant-speed propeller. In 1959 a de luxe version of the **Model 175A** was introduced as the **Skylark**, but the Model 175/Skylark type was dropped from production in 1963.

At the same time as the de luxe version of the Model 175 appeared as the Skylark, a similar de luxe version of the

Model 172 was introduced under the name **Skyhawk**. Further improvements were made in 1960, with the provision of a new rear fuselage (slimmer and with rear windows) and a stylish swept vertical tail. These modifications were also applied to the Skyhawk and the **Skyhawk II**, which featured yet more comprehensive equipment, adding sophisticated navigation and communication equipment to blind-flying instrumentation found in the Skyhawk. In March 1956 Cessna announced a new **Model 182**, which was an addition to the standard fixed-gear family, but powered by a 172-kW (230-hp) Continental O-470-S. It was available in **Standard**, **Skylane** and **Skylane II** versions.

Since that time there has been continuing development and several changes and versions available in 1982 included the Model 172 Skyhawk and **Skyhawk II**, the **Cutlass RG** and **Cutlass RG II** which is basically a

Initial training for USAF pilots is undertaken on the Cessna T-41 Mescalero, basically similar to the Model 172. These wear dual civil/military registrations.

Model 172 with retractable landing gear, the Model 182 Skylane/Skylane II which is available also in **Turbo Skylane** and **Turbo Skylane II** with a 175-kW (235-hp) Avco Lycoming O-540-L3C5D turbo-charged engine, and in **Skylane RG** and **Skylane RG II** and **Turbo Skylane RG** and **Turbo Skylane RG II** retractable landing gear equivalents.

The Model 172 also appealed to the US military and in July 1964 the US Air Force ordered 170 standard Cessna 172Ks powered by 134-kW (180-hp) Continental O-360 engines for the Air Academy, and these were designated T-41A. In August 1966, the US Army bought 255 Model R172Es fitted with the more powerful 157-kW (210-hp) IO-360D fuel injection engine, as the T-41B Mescalero. These were followed by similarly powered T-41Cs for the US Air Force, and export version, designated T-41D, for a number of other air forces under the Mutual Air Programme. Total production of the military T-41 series reached 864 built between 1963-83, and by the end of 1987 production of the 170, 172, 175 and 182 Models had reached over 60,000 including their civil and military derivatives.

Specification
Cessna Turbo Skylane RG
Type: four-seat cabin monoplane
Powerplant: one 175-kW (235-hp) Avco Lycoming O-540-L3C5D flat-six turbocharged piston engine
Performance: Maximum speed 346 km/h (215 mph) at 6095 m (20,000 ft); cruising speed at 6095 m (20,000 ft) 320 km/h (199); certified ceiling 6095 m (20,000 ft); range with maximum fuel at 3050 m (10,000 ft) 1909 km (1,186 miles)
Weights: empty 815 kg (1,797 lb); maximum take-off 1406 kg (3,100 lb
Dimensions: span 10.92 m (35 ft 10 in; length 8.72 m (28 ft 7½ in; height 2,72 m (8 ft 11 in; wing area 16.16 m² (174.0 sq ft)

Cessna Model 177/Cardinal/Cardinal Classic/Cardinal RG

Expanding its range of single-engined aircraft in an attempt to satisfy what then appeared to be an insatiable market for this class of aeroplane, the company introduced the **Cessna Model 177** at the end of September 1967. Generally similar in overall configuration to other members of the Cessna family of four-seaters, it was distinguished easily by a cantilever monoplane wing. Other 'advanced' features included weight-saving integral wing fuel tanks, an improved version of Cessna's Land-O-

Matic fixed tricycle landing gear, and what was regarded as an 'easy handling' control system. The Model 177 was, at the time of introduction, the designation of the basic model: a de luxe version, named **Cardinal**, included full blind-flying instrumentation, more extensive equipment, and luxury interior appointments as standard.

Powerplant of the initial version was a 112-kW (150-hp) Avco Lycoming O-320-E21D engine, but later versions had increased power and in late 1970 a third member of the family was added, the **Cardinal RG**, which introduced retractable landing gear actuated by an electrically powered hydraulic fuel injection engine. In 1971 **Cardinal II** and **Cardinal RG II** versions appeared, these differing by having more comprehensive equipment as standard. In 1976 the Model 177 was withdrawn, the Cardinal becoming regarded as the basic model of the remaining four versions. Two years later the Cardinal also disappeared, the Cardinal II being renamed

the **Cardinal Classic**, but at the end of 1978, at which time more than 4,000 of the Model 177 and Cardinal versions had been built, all Cardinal production was terminated.

Specification
Cessna Cardinal RG
Type: four-seat cabin monoplane
Powerplant: one 149-kW (200-hp) Avco Lycoming IO-360-A1B6D flat-four piston engine
Performance: maximum cruising speed 274 km/h (170 mph) at 2135 m (7,000 ft); economic cruising speed 224 km/h (139 mph) at 3050 m (10,000 ft); service ceiling 5210 m (17,100 ft); maximum range with maximum fuel at economic cruising speed 1658 km (1,030 miles)
Weights: empty 772 kg (1,703 lb); maximum take-off 1270 kg (2,800 lb)
Dimensions: span 10.82 m (35 ft 6 in); length 8.31 m (27 ft 3 in); height 2.62 m) 8 ft 7 in; wing area 16.16 m² 174.0 sq ft

The Cessna Model 177 was notable for its cantilever wing. Retractable undercarriage models appeared in 1971.

Cessna Model 180/185 Skywagon/AGcarryall/U-17

In 1953 Cessna introduced a more powerful partner for the Model 170: using the same wing and flap system as the Model 170B, the new **Cessna Model 180** featured a completely new fuselage and tail unit, plus an additional 60- kW (80 hp) delivered by the 168-kW (225-hp) Continental O-470-A flat-six engine. At the same time a fully adjustable tailplane was introduced, obviating the need for elevator trim tabs. Most significantly, the additional power available for the Model 180 permitted an increase in maximum take-off weight from 998 to 1157 kg (2,200 to 2,550 lb) with the same wing area of 16.16 m² (174 sq ft). In the late 1970s the Model 180 was available in two forms: the basic **Model 180**

Skywagon, and the improved **Model 180 Skywagon II** with a factory-installed avionics package. During 1981 production of the Model 180 ended after well over 6,000 had been built.

In July 1960 Cessna flew the prototype of the **Model 185 Skywagon**. This was in most respects similar to the Model 180 apart from the provision of extra power in the form of a 224-kW (300-hp) Continental IO-520 engine. Like its predecessor the Model 185 was a sixseater, and was made available in basic form as the Model 185 Skywagon, and in more advanced form as the **Model 185 Skywagon II**. Greater versatility is conferred on the two Model 185 versions by their ability to carry under the fuselage a

detachable glassfibre Cargo-Pack, capable of carrying some 136 kg (300 lb). The Model 185 Skywagons can also be fitted with Sorenson spray-gear for agricultural work, and like the Model 180 Skywagons can be fitted with alternative ski or float landing gears.

By February 1980, 4,000 Model 185 variants had been delivered and when production ceased, in mid-1985 4,356 Skywagons had been built, including 497 U-17A/B/C military versions.

In 1971 Cessna introduced an extremely versatile version of the Model 185 in the form of the **AGcarryall**. This was designed principally for the agricultural role in the widest possible sense, being able to demonstrate spraying pro-

cedures, ferry people and equipment, serve as an agricultural pilot trainer, and act as a backup spray aircraft in peak periods. It failed to attract sufficient sales and production ended in 1979 after 108 had been built.

During 1962 the USAF sought a suitable light utility aircraft for supply to countries eligible for MAP aid. Cessna's Model 185 was selected and ordered under the designation **U-17**, more than 450 being supplied. These comprised the **U-17A** with a 194-kW (260-hp) Continental IO-470-F flat-six engine, followed by the **U-17B** with a 224-kW (300-hp) Continental IO-520-D. The final **U-17C** production version had a Continental O-470-L engine which had a carburettor instead of fuel injection.

Specification
Cessna Model 185 (landplane)
Type: six-seat cabin monoplane
Powerplant: one 224-kW (300-hp) Continental IO-520-D flat-six piston engine
Performance: maximum speed at sea level 286 km/h (178 mph); cruising speed at 2135 m (7,000 ft) 274 km/h (170 mph); service ceiling 5455 m (17,900 ft); maximum range at 3050 m (10,000 ft) 1576 km (979 miles)
Weights: empty 769 kg (1,696 lb); maximum take-off 1520 kg (3,350 lb)
Dimensions: span 10.92 m (35 ft 10 in); length 7.81 m (25 ft 7½ in); height 2.36 m (7 ft 9 in); wing area 16.16 m² (174.0 sq ft

The Model 185 is a no-nonsense, go-anywhere utility transport, with performance and strength to match.

Cessna Model 188

Following an extensive survey into the requirements of agricultural aircraft operators, the company flew the prototype of the **Cessna Model 188 AGwagon** (later renamed **AG Wagon**) on 19 February 1965. A braced low-wing monoplane of all-metal construction, the new design had non-retractable tailwheel landing gear, with accommodation for the pilot in an enclosed cabin protected by a steel overturn structure. Power was provided by either a 172-kW (230-hp) Continental IO-470-R or a 224-kW (300-hp) Continental IO-520-D engine for the **AGwagon 230** or **AGwagon 300** respectively. Standard agricultural equipment included a 757-litre (200-US gal) or 816-kg (1,800-lb) capacity glassfibre hopper between the engine firewall and the cabin, and optional dusting or spraying equipment was available.

An increasing market for the AGwagon resulted in the introduction of a new model of this aircraft in late 1971, plus two additional versions designated as the **AGpickup** and **AGtruck**. The

AGpickup was the basic model, a new name applied to the Continental O-470-R version of the original AGwagon; the Continental IO-520-D AGwagon was renamed **AGwagon C** and introduced a number of detail refinements; and the AGtruck was generally similar to the AGwagon C, except for the provision of a 1060-litre (280-US gal) hopper plus a complete spray system and a wide range of equipment as standard. Of these three types the AGpickup was discontinued in 1976, and production of the

AGwagon ended during 1981, after 1,589 had been built.

In 1979 Cessna introduced the AG Husky, a turbocharged version of the AGtruck (later AG Truck) powered by a 231-kW (310-hp) TSIO-520-T engine giving all round improved performance. When production of both types ceased

The Model 188 was a hugely successful agricultural design, aimed at operators requiring a low-cost machine.

late in 1985, 386 AG Huskys had been delivered, alongside 1,949 AG Trucks.

Specification
Cessna AG Truck (with spray gear)
Type: single-seat agricultural monoplane
Powerplant: one 224-kW (300-hp) Continental IO-520-D flat-six piston engine
Performance: maximum speed at sea level 196 km/h (122 mph); cruising speed at 1980 m (6,500 ft 187 km/h (116 mph); service ceiling 2375 m (7,800 ft; range with allowances 466 km (290 miles)
Weights: empty 1012 kg (2,230 lb); maximum take-off 1905 kg (4,200 lb)
Dimensions: span 12.70 m (41 ft 8 in); length 7.90 m (25 ft 11 in; height 2.49 m (8 ft 2 in); wing area 19.05 m² (205.0 sq ft)

Cessna Model 190/195

The aircraft of the **Cessna Models 190** and **195** series were unique amongst postwar Cessna single-engined lightplanes in being powered by radial engines. The two types were produced in parallel between 1947 and 1954.

The Model 190, of which 233 were built, was powered by the 179-kW (240-hp) Continental R-670-23. The two version of the Model 195 were almost indistinguishable from the Model 190: the Model 195 was powered by the 224-kW (300-hp) Jacobs R-755-A2, while the **Model 195A** had the 183-kW (245-hp) Jacobs R-744-A2. Production of the Models 195 and 195A totalled 890, examples built in 1953 and 1954 being identifiable by their close-cowled engines, a small propeller spinner, and an increase of 50 per cent in the area of

The Model 190/195 were unique in being Cessna's only post-war radial-powered designs.

the flaps let into the undersurfaces of the high-set unbraced wings. The series is also notable for the fact that it introduced Cessna's now-celebrated spring-steel main landing gear legs.

Specification
Cessna Model 195A
Type: four/five-seat cabin monoplane
Powerplant: one 183-kW (245-hp) Jacobs R-744-A2 radial piston engine
Performance: maximum speed 278 km/h (173 mph); cruising speed 249 km/h (155 mph); service ceiling 4875 m (16,000 ft); range 1207 km (750 miles)
Weights: empty 921 kg (2,030 lb); maximum take-off 1520 kg (3,350 lb)
Dimensions: span 11.02 m (36 ft 2 in); length 8.33 m (27 ft 4 in); height 2.18 m (7 ft 2 in); wing area 20.26 m² (218.13 sq ft)

Cessna Model 205

The **Cessna Model 205**, introduced in 1962, was developed from the Model 182, although in appearance it was a fixed landing gear version of the Cessna 210. Indeed, FAA certification on 14 June 1962 was under the designation **Model 210-5**. Powered by a 194-kW (260-hp) Continental engine, the Model 205 was complementary to the tailwheel Model 185 Skywagon, having similar performance at slightly greater weight. Deliveries began in August 1962, and in December 1963 Cessna introduced the **Model 205A** with detail improvements. Around 600 of the Model 205/205A series were built before the type was superseded at the end of 1963.

The Model 205/205A series was available with agricultural equipment and could be flown, like most of the single-engine high-wing Cessna range, with floats, skis or various sizes of wheels.

Specification
Cessna Model 205A
Type: six-seat passenger/utility monoplane
Powerplant: one 194-kW (260-hp) Continental IO-460-S flat-six piston engine
Performance: maximum speed at sea level 278 km/h (173 mph); maximum cruising speed 261 km/h (162 mph) at 1980 m (6,500 ft); service ceiling 4905 m (16,100 ft); maximum range with standard fuel 1633 km (1,015 miles)
Weights: empty 794 kg (1,750 lb); maximum take-off 1497 kg (3,300 lb)
Dimensions: span 11.15 m (36 ft 7 in); length 8.46 m (27 ft 9 in); height 2.97 m (9 ft 9 in); wing area 16.30 m² (175.5 sq ft)

Many of Cessna's lightplanes are equally at home on floats or skis as on wheels. This is a Canadian-registered Model 205.

Cessna Model 206 Super Skywagon/Model 207 Skywagon/Stationair

Cessna's Model 185 had the civil name Skywagon and when an improved version was evolved this was designated **Cessna Model 206 Super Skywagon**. Changes included replacement of the tailwheel landing gear with one of tricycle type; introduction of conical-camber wingtips to reduce induced drag; enlargement of the tailplane and flaps; addition of double cargo doors measuring 1.22 by 0.91 m (4 by 3 by 3 ft); and a more powerful 213-kW (285-hp) Continental IO-520-A flat-six engine. Produc-

tion of the Model 206 ended in 1964, but examples remain in service with several armed forces.

On 3 January 1969 Cessna flew the first production example of the lengthened seven-seat **Model 207**, which reverted to the name **Skywagon**. This introduced a second access door on the starboard side; a 54-kg (120-lb) capacity baggage compartment, forward of the cabin; and the more powerful IO-520-J engine. Both the Models 206 and 207 can be flown with cargo doors removed

for the air-dropping of supplies, parachuting and photography. Both can carry a 136-kg (300-lb) glassfibre cargo pack beneath the fuselage, and ambulance kits comprising a stretcher, oxygen supply, and attendant seat are available. The Model 207 also serves with several armed services.

When production of the original Model 206 Super Skywagon ended in 1964, three new versions were introduced for 1965. Since that time there have been several changes in name and designation of both Model 206s and Model 207s and it is clearer to list them below as variants.

Replaced by the Model 208 Caravan, volume production of the 206 and 207 ended in 1985, although around 100 more airframes were produced and sold. By 31 December 1987, no less than 7,652 Model 206 Skywagon and Statio-

nairs had been delivered, including 643 Super Skylane luxury versions.

Variants
U206 Super Skywagon: standard utility version of the original Model 206, introduced in 1965, and retaining the double cargo loading doors
P206 Utility: introduced in 1965; generally similar to U206, but with passenger door at front of cabin on starboard side in lieu of cargo doors; this version was discontinued for 1968
P206 Super Skylane: introduced in 1965; a de luxe six-seat version of the Model 206; door at front and rear of cabin on the port side and at front of cabin on starboard side; discontinued in 1971
TU206 Super Skywagon: turbocharged version of the U206, introduced in 1966; similar to U206

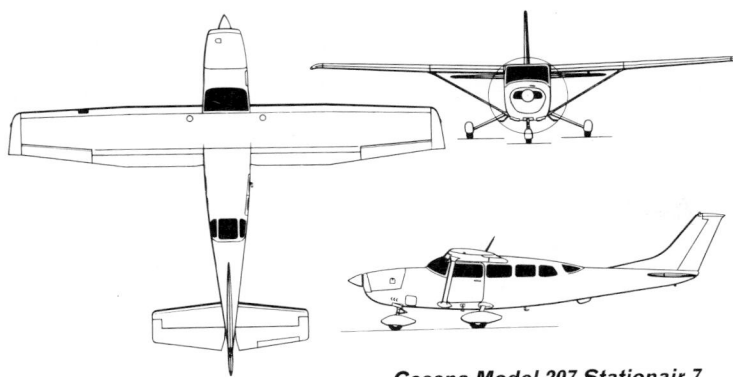

Cessna Model 207 Stationair 7

except for installation of a 13-kW (285-hp) Continental TSIO-520-C turbocharged engine

TP206 Super Skylane: turbocharged version of the P206 Super Skylane, introduced in 1966 with the same powerplant as for the TU206 above

TU206 Turbo-System Super Skywagon: new name for TU206 Super Skywagon applied for 1967

TP206 Turbo-System Super Skylane: new name for TP206 Super Skylane applied for 1967; discontinued for 1971

T207 Turbo-Skywagon: turbocharged version of the Model 207 Skywagon, both of which were introduced during 1969, and powered by a 224-kW

(300-hp) Continental TSIO-520-G and 224-kW (300-hp) IO-520-F respectively

Stationair: replaced the U206 Skywagon for 1971, combining the U206 airframe with a 224-kW (300-hp) Continental IO-520-F engine

Turbo-Stationair: name change of the TU206 Turbo-Skywagon introduced for 1971. Some serve with the USAF as the U-26A.

Stationair 6: new name allocated to Stationair for 1978

Turbo-Stationair 6: new name allocated to Turbo Stationair for 1978; this version was re-engined with a 231-kW (310-hp) Continental TSIO-520-M engine for 1977

Stationair 7: new name allocated to Model 207 for 1978, and powered by a 224-kW (300-hp) IO-520-F engine

Turbo-Stationair 7: new name allocated to T207 Turbo-Skywagon for 1978 and at the same time the 231-kW (310-hp) Continental TSIO-520-M turbocharged engine was introduced to this version

Stationair 8: new name allocated to Stationair 7 for 1980 following the in-

troduction of an extra seat to provide eight-seat capacity

Turbo-Stationair 8: new name allocated to Turbo-Stationair 7 for 1980 following seat change as for Stationair 8 above

Specification
Cessna Turbo-Stationair 8
Type: eight-seat utility aircraft
Powerplant: one 231-kW (310-hp) Continental TSIO-520-M flat-six piston engine
Performance: maximum speed 315 km/h (196 mph) at 5180 m (17,000 ft); cruising speed at 6095 m (20,000 ft) 298 km/h (185 mph); service ceiling 7925 m (26,000 ft); range with maximum fuel at economic cruising speed at 3050 m (10,000 ft) 1130 km (702 miles)
Weights: empty 1724 kg (2,183 lb); maximum take-off 1724 kg (3,800 lb)
Dimensions: span 10.92 m (35 ft 10 in); length 9.80 m (32 ft 2 in); height 2.92 m (9 ft 7 in); wing area 16.16 m² (174.0 sq ft)

Cessna Model 208 Caravan

Designed to replace extensive fleets of ageing utility aircraft still in wide service throughout the world such as the **DH Canada Beaver**, **Otter** and **Cessna 180**, **185** and **206** types, the **Model 208** was conceived in 1980/81 as the first all-new turboprop powered general aviation aircraft. The prototype **Cessna 208 Caravan I** flew for the first on 9 December 1982, and the first production aircraft rolled out in August 1984. FAA certification followed in October 1984 and the type is now in service with military air arms in Brazil, Liberia, Thailand and with the Royal Canadian Mounted Police as amphibians.

The higher gross weight **Model 208A**, ordered in December 1983 by the US small parcel airline Federal Express and called Cargomaster by them, is fitted with more comprehensive all-weather avionics and an underfuselage pannier, but has the fuselage windows deleted.

Following experience with the 208A, Federal Express ordered the **Model 208B Super Cargomaster** with the

fuselage stretched by four feet, also built without windows and equipped with a pannier. Flight testing began on 3 March 1986, followed by certification and first delivery to Federal Express, who have ordered 210, in October the same year.

By the end of 1989 more than 370 variants of the Model 208 had been delivered.

In 1985 Cessna released details of a quasi-military/special mission version of the **Caravan I** designated U-27A by the US Department of Defense and marketed as the Low Intensity Conflict Aircraft. Equipped with six hardpoints under the wing plus another on the fuselage centreline able to carry either a General Dynamics F-16 reconnaissance pod, or a cargo pannier, the LICA also has a electrically operated 'roll up' cargo door with slipstream deflector, openable in flight, and bubble windows for downward surveillance and observation. Cessna are also offering a similarly equipped version of the stretched Model 208B for special mission.

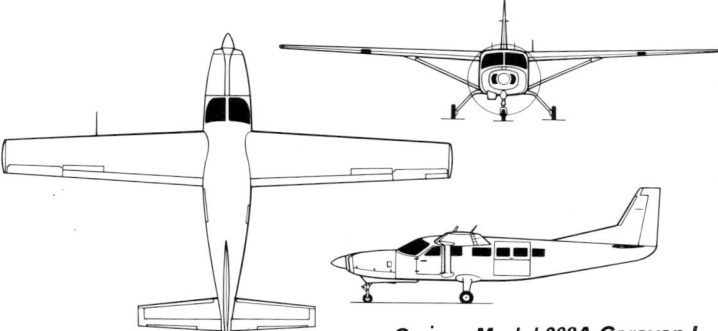

Cessna Model 208A Caravan I

Specification
Cessna Model 208 Caravan I
Type: single-engined utility monoplane
Powerplant: one 477-kW (600-hp) Pratt & Whitney Canada PT6A-114 turboprop engine
Performance: maximum cruising speed 341 km/h (212 mph); ceiling 8410 m (27,600 ft); range at economic cruising speed at 3050 m (10,000 ft) 1797 km (1,117 miles)
Weights: empty 1752 kg (3,862 lb);

maximum take-off 3629 kg (8,000 lb)
Dimensions: span 15.88 m (52 ft 1 in); length 11.46 m (37 ft 7 in); height 4.32 m (14 ft 2 in); wing area 25.96 m² (279.4 sq ft)

Taking over from the Beaver and Otter as the world's premier bushplane, the Caravan I has sold to many former DHC customers, including the Royal Canadian Mounted Police.

Cessna Model 210 Centurion/Turbo-Centurion/Pressurized Centurion

Flown for the first time in January 1957, the **Cessna Model 210** was the first of the company's high-wing range to feature retractable landing gear and swept vertical tail surfaces. The first production aircraft flew in December 1959 powered by a 194-kW (260-hp) Continental IO-470-E engine, and since that time progressive improvements were made each year.

The 1961 model introduced two more cabin windows, additional headroom and an improved heating and ventilating system, and by 1963 an autopilot was offered as an option. In January 1965 the **Model 210E Centurion** had supplanted earlier versions and was powered by a 213-kW (285-hp) Continental IO-520-A.

The **Model 210F** followed in 1966, and that year the first turbocharged model became available in the form of the **T210F Turbo-System Centurion** with a 213-kW (285-hp) Continental TSIO-520C; the extra power conferred a useful increase in performance, particularly in altitude. A new wing, first flown on a T210 in June 1965, was later introduced on production aircraft, and eliminated the need for external bracing struts.

By 1970 Cessna had dropped its suffix letter system from model numbers and in that year introduced two new versions, the **Centurion II** and **Turbo Centurion II** which incorporated a factory-installed package of avionics and equipment as standard, these being produced alongside the **Centurion** and

Turbo Centurion. By then the Centurions were of six-seat capacity and offered powerplant options of a 224-kW (300-hp) Continental IO-520-L for the Centurion and a 213-kW (285-hp) TSIO-520H for the Turbo Centurion.

In November 1977 a new pressurised version of the Model 210, the **Pressurized Centurion**, was announced. Generally similar to the standard Centurion, it differed by having a pressure cabin and a 231-kW (310-hp) Continental TSIO-520-P which incorporated a high-capacity turbocharger to support the pressurisation system, and like the earlier models was available in standard and **Pressurized Centurion II** versions.

All six versions remained available until 1986 when sales slowed down and at the end of 1987 when production ceased, a total of 8,453 Model 210s and Centurions had rolled off the line together with 851 Pressurized Centurions.

Turbocharged Centurions established several world records in their class: including time-to-height records, a round the world speed record of 204 km/h (127 mph), and an altitude record of 12905 m (42,344.16 ft) established as long ago as 13 May 1967.

Specification
Pressurized Centurion
Type: six-seat cabin monoplane
Powerplant: one 231-kW (310-hp)

The Pressurized Centurion offers retractable landing gear, pressurised cabin and underwing weather radar.

Continental TSIO-520-P flat-six turbocharged piston engine
Performance: maximum speed 357 km/h (221 mph) at 5180 m (17,000 ft); cruising speed at 3050 m (10,000 ft) 309 km/h (192 mph); certificated ceiling 7010 m (23,000 ft); range at economic cruising speed at 3050 m (10,000 ft) 1593 km (990 miles)
Dimensions: span 11.20 m (36 ft 9 in); length 8.50 m (28 ft 2 in); height 2.95 m (9 ft 8 in); wing area 16.26 m² (175.0 sq ft)

Cessna Model T303 Crusader

On 14 February 1978 Cessna flew the prototype (N303PD) of a new lightweight twin-engined aircraft which it then designated **Cessna Model 303 Clipper**. In this prototype form it was a four-seat aircraft of low-wing monoplane configuration with the wing incorporating a super-critical aerofoil section. Other features included retractable tricycle landing gear, swept vertical tail surfaces with a long dorsal fin, extensive use of bonded construction and powerplant comprising two 119-kW (160-hp) engines. Before the certification programme began it was superseded by a new **Model T303** which reverted to conventional construction, had six-seat accommodation, was powered by two turbocharged engines of increased output, and had acquired the new name **Crusader** because the earlier title of Clipper infringed a US trademark.

Cessna claimed the Crusader was the first lightweight twin of its class to have

full IFR avionics and equipment as standard, and that handling of the aircraft benefited from the high set tailplane, coupled with unusually, counter rotating engines, which minimise engine torque effect. Production model Crusaders were certificated in August 1981, and first deliveries followed in October. When production ceased in 1986 297 had been delivered.

Specification
Type: six-seat cabin monoplane
Powerplant: one Continental TSIO-520-AE and one LTSIO-520-AE turbocharged counter-rotating flat-six piston engine, each rated at 186 kW (250 hp)
Performance: maximum speed 400 km/h (248 mph) at 5485 m (18,000 ft); cruising speed at 6095 m (20,000 ft) 363 km/h (225 mph); certificated ceiling 7620 m (25,000 ft); maximum range, standard fuel with

reserves at 3050 m (10,000 ft) 1889 km (1,174 miles)
Weights: empty 1499 kg (3,305 lb); maximum take-off 2336 kg (5,150 lb)
Dimensions: span 11.90 m (39 ft 0½ in); length 9.27 m (30 ft 5 in);

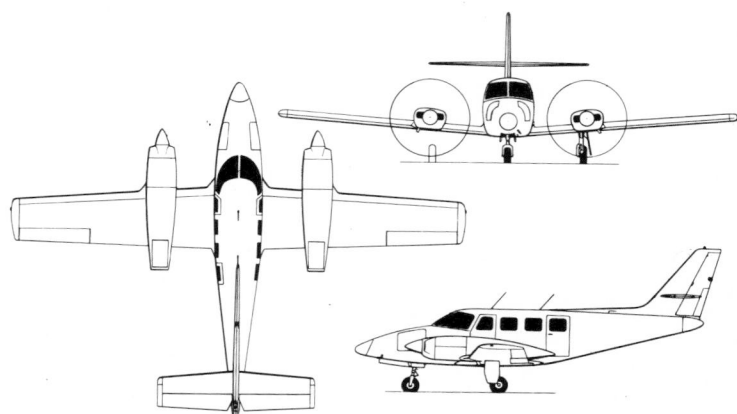

Cessna Model T303 Crusader

height 4.06 m (13¾ft 4 in); wing area 17.58 m² (189.20 sq ft.)

Cessna Model 305A/O-1 Bird Dog

In the late 1940s the US Army issued a specification for a two-seat liaison and

observation monoplane. From the submissions received from manufacturers

that of the Cessna Aircraft Company was declared the winner and in June

1950 an initial contract was awarded for 418 examples of the aircraft, which the company identified as the **Cessna Model 305A**.

Cessna's design was based upon the

successful Model 170, a light-weight strut-braced high-wing monoplane, powered by a 108-kW (145-hp) Continental flat-six engine, which provided accommodation for a pilot and three passengers. The Model 305A differed by having the aft fuselage redesigned to give a clear view to the rear and by the provision of transparent panels in the wing centre-section, which formed the cabin roof. A wider access door gave room to load a standard stretcher, for which support brackets were installed.

Deliveries of production aircraft began in December 1950, under the designation **L-19A** and with the name **Bird Dog**, and by October 1954, 2,486 had been delivered, of which 60 where diverted to the US Marine Corps which designated them **OE-1**. An **L-19A-IT** instrument trainer version was developed in 1953, **TL-19D** trainers with constant-speed propellers appeared in 1956 and improved **L-19E**, of higher gross weight, was the final version to bring total production of Bird Dogs to 3,431. With redesignation in 1962, the US Army's L-19A, TL-19E and L-19E aircraft became **O-1A**, **TO-1D** and **O-1E** respectively. The US Marines' OE-1 became **O-1B** and this service also acquired 25 of the higher-powered **O-1C**. US Army trainers, derived from standard production aircraft, had the designations **TO-1A** and **TO-1E**.

Bird Dogs were operated in small numbers during the Korean War, but the US Air Force acquired many of the US Army's O-1s for use by forward air controllers in Vietnam; former TO-1Ds and O-1As were redesignated **O-1F** and **O-1G** respectively when equipped for this role. In addition to being supplied to

Large numbers of O-1 Bird Dogs were used during the Vietnam War, both by US forces and, as here, the South Vietnamese. They were mostly used for forward air control work.

Cessna O-1A Bird Dog of a Royal Thai army air observation and liaison flight in 1957.

many nations, O-1s were also built under licence by Fuji in Japan.

Specification
Cessna O-1E

Type: liaison and observation aircraft
Powerplant: one 159-kW (213-hp) Continental O-470-11 flat-six piston engine
Performance: maximum speed 209 km/h (130 mph); range 853 km (530 miles)

Weights: empty 732 kg (1,614 lb); maximum take-off 1089 kg (2,400 lb)
Dimensions: span 10.97 m (36 ft 0 in); length, 7.85 m (25 ft 9 in); height 2.22 m (7 ft 3½ in); wing area 16.16 m² (174.0 sq ft)

Cessna Model 310/320/335/340/U-3

In 1952, Cessna initiated the design of a new five/six-seat twin-engined light monoplane designated **Cessna Model 310**. The prototype flew for the first time on 3 January 1953, proving in production form to be a popular twin. Of low-wing configuration and with tricycle landing gear, the prototype was powered by the 168-kW (225-hp) Continental O-470, an engine developed originally for military use under the designation E225. Its use to power the Cessna Model 310 was one of its first

civil applications, early production aircraft having the more powerful 194-kW (260-hp) IO-470. Good identification features of the design at that time were the two wingtip fuel tanks, then representing the entire fuel tankage.

Production deliveries began in 1954, with steady product improvement continuing year by year. A de luxe version with turbocharged engines, air-conditioning and an oxygen system as standard was introduced in 1966. This was then named the **Turbo-System**

Executive Skyknight, being known also for a short period as the **Model 320**, but later marketed as the **Turbo T310**. Final versions were the basic **Model 310** with 213-kW (285-hp) Continental IO-520-MB engines, the structurally identical **Model 310 II** which incorporated a factory installed avionics/equipment package, the Turbo T310 with TSIO-520-BB powerplants and the **Turbo T310 II** with the same additional equipment fit as the **Model 310 II**. In the mid-1950s, following competitive selection, a slightly modified version of the Model 310 was ordered for light cargo-liaison duties with the US Air Force under the designation **L-27A**, subsequently redesignated **U-3A**. A total of 160 were built followed by 36 **U-3Bs**, equipped for all-weather operation, and all were nicknamed 'Blue Canoes'. When production finished in 1981, 5,241 commercial examples of the Model 310 had been built, including a small number for the French air force, plus the 196 delivered to the USAF.

In December 1971 Cessna announced the introduction of the pressurised Model 340 developed from the Model 310. Powered by twin TSIO-520-NB engines each giving 213-kW (285-hp), the 340 incorporated the wing and tricycle landing gear developed for the Model 414, married to a new pressurised fuselage, but using the tail of the Model 310. This was followed in the mid-1970s by the **Model 340A** equipped with 231-kW (310-hp) engines and later by the similarly powered **Model 340A II** fitted with comprehensive factory-installed avionics allowing IFR operation. In 1978 Cessna introduced the **Model 340A III** equipped with an improved avionics package including colour weather radar and this version remained available until

The Model 340 pressurised twin business aircraft proved very popular. It was available with the usual Cessna range of avionics options and other equipment.

1985 when the type was taken out of production, by which time 1,287 had been delivered.

A lightweight unpressurised version of the Model 340 was offered to the market in 1979 as the **Model 335**, later available as the improved **Model 335 II** version, but production ended in 1980 after only 45 had been built.

Specification
Cessna Model 310
Type: five/six-seat cabin monoplane
Powerplant: two 213-kW (285-hp) Continental IO-520-MB flat-six piston engines
Performance: maximum speed at sea level 383km/h (238 mph); economic cruising speed 267 km/h (160 mph) at 3050 m (10,000 ft); service ceiling 6020 m (19,750 ft); range at economic cruising speed with maximum fuel at 3050 m (10,000 ft) 2840 km (1,765 miles)
Weights: empty 1523 kg (3,358 lb); maximum take-off 2495 kg (5,500 lb)
Dimensions: span 11.25 m (36 ft 11 in); length 9.74 m (31 ft 11½ in); height 3.25 m (10 ft 8 in); wing area 16.63 m^2 (179.0 sq ft)

Augmenting the straight-finned U-3A were 36 U-3B Blue Canoes for the USAF. These served on liaison and light freight duties.

Cessna Model 318/T-37/Model 318E/A-37 Dragonfly

Still in service training USAF pilots, the Cessna T-37 Tweet features side-by-side seating for closer co-ordination.

In the early 1950s the US Air Force was looking for a turbojet-powered trainer, and in 1953 Cessna was announced winner of this design competition, two prototypes being ordered under the designation **XT-37**. The company identified the type as the **Cessna Model 318**, and the first of these made its initial flight on 12 October 1954. It was a perfectly straightforward monoplane of all-metal construction, with pupil and instructor seated in what had long been considered to be an ideal side-by-side arrangement (contrary to the normal US tandem practice). Powerplant consisted of two Continental turbojets (Americanised versions of the French Turboméca Marboré) mounted within the wing roots on each side of the fuselage. The tailplane was mounted above the fuselage about one-third of the way up the fin to ensure that the airstream flowing past it was unaffected by the jet efflux.

The first production batch of 11 aircraft, which had the designation **T-37A**, was ordered during 1954, and the first of these flew on 27 September 1955. The T-37As, of which 534 were built under successive contracts, were slow in entering service as a result of the need for a number of changes and modifications before they were considered acceptable for training purposes.

When introduced into service, in 1957, the T-37s were used initially as basic trainers, the pupils transferring to these aircraft only after completing their primary training on Beech T-34 Mentors. In April 1961 all-through jet training was initiated, the pupil flying from the very beginning of his training on T-37 aircraft which had a speed range of 138-684 km/h (85-425 mph). No catastrophic accident resulted, as had been feared by many, but one point which had not been fully considered was the much higher training cost using jet aircraft. There is inevitably a varying pupil rejection rate at the end of primary training, and it was decided in 1964 to revert to light piston-engine trainers, which are much cheaper to operate, for this primary phase, so that T-37 pupils were those left after the first weeding-out.

The **T-37B** with more powerful engines and improved nav/com systems, was introduced into service in November 1959, and all surviving T-37As were converted retrospectively to this standard. Final version was the **T-37C** with provision for armament and wingtip fuel tanks. When production ended in 1977 a total of 1,268 T-37s had been built for the USAF and for export.

During 1962 two Cessna T-37B trainers were evaluated by the USAF's Special Air Warfare Center to consider their suitability for deployment in the counter-insurgency (COIN) role. These were first tested with their original powerplant of two 465-kg (1,025-lb) thrust Continental J69-T-25 turbojets, at a take-off weight of 3946 kg (8,700 lb), almost 33 per cent above the normal maximum take-off weight. Subsequently the airframes were modified to accept two 1089-kg (2,400-lb) thrust General Electric J85-GE-5 turbojets. This vast increase in power made it possible for the aircraft, then designated **YAT-37D**, to be flown at steadily increasing take-off weights until a safe upper limit of 6350 kg (14,000 lb) was reached. There was, clearly, plenty of scope for the carriage of a worthwhile load of weapons.

This exercise was academic, until the need of the war in Vietnam made the USAF take a closer look at this armed version of what had proved to be an excellent trainer. Accordingly, Cessna were requested to convert 39 T-37B trainers to a light-strike configuration, a contract being awarded in 1966: this related to the conversion of new T-37B aircraft taken from the production line. The new model was based on the earlier experiments with the two YAT-37Ds, and equipped with eight underwing hardpoints, provided with wingtip tanks to increase fuel capacity and powered by derated General Electric J85-GE-5 turbojets.

Delivery to the USAF began on 2 May 1967, and during the latter half of that year a squadron numbering 25 of these aircraft, designated **A-37A** and named **Dragonfly**, underwent a four-month operational evaluation in South Vietnam. Following this investigation they were transferred for operational duty with the 604th Air Commando Squadron at Bien Hoa; in 1970 they were assigned to the South Vietnamese air force.

During this period, Cessna had built the **Model 318E** prototype of a purpose-designated light-strike aircraft based on the T-37 and this flew for the first time in September 1967. Little time was lost in evaluation and the initial production batch of this **A-37B** was started quickly enough for the first deliveries to begin in May 1968.

The A-37B differed in construction from the prototype YAT-37D, its airframe stressed for 6g loading, maximum internal fuel capacity increased to 1920 litres (507 US gal) with the ability to carry four auxiliary tanks having a combined capacity of 1516 litres (400 US gal), and with provision for flight-refuelling.

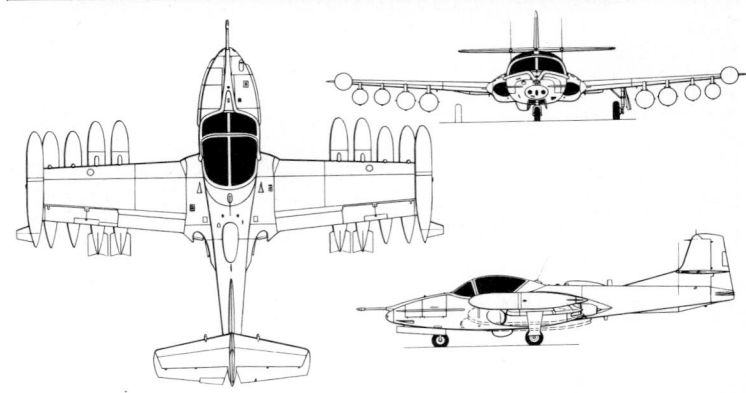

Powerplant was changed to two General Electric J85-GE-17A turbojets. A GAU-2B/A 7.62-mm (0.3-in) Minigun was installed, and the eight underwing hardpoints could carry in excess of 2268 kg (5,000 lb) of mixed stores. For the assessment of results both gun and strike cameras were carried, and some armour protection for the crew of two was provided by the inclusion of layered nylon flak-curtains installed around the cockpit.

By the time that production ended in 1967, a total of 577 A-37Bs has been built, and in addition to serving with the USAF the type was supplied in small numbers to friendly nations. Many were transferred to the US Air National Guard and to the South Vietnam air force.

Specification
Cessna A-37B
Type: two-seat light strike aircraft
Powerplant: two 1293-kg (2,850-lb) thrust General Electric J85-GE-17A turbojets
Performance: maximum speed at 4875 m (16,000 ft) 834 km/h (524 mph); maximum cruising speed at 7620 m (25,000 ft) 787 km/h (489 mph); range with maximum fuel at 7620 m (25,000 ft) with reserves 1629 km (1,012 miles); range with maximum payload, including 1860 kg (4,100 lb external weapons 740 km (460 miles)
Weights: empty equipped 2817 kg

Proving attractive to the US Air Force and many other nations as a light attack platform, the Cessna A-37 Dragonfly sold in large numbers. Carrying a useful weapons load, the A-37 is principally used for counterinsurgency work. Shown here is a South Vietnamese aircraft carrying fuel tanks and bombs.

(6,211 lb); maximum take-off 6350 kg (14,000 lb)
Dimensions: span 10.93 m (35 ft 10½ in); length 8.62 m (28 3¼ in); height 2.71 m (8 ft 10½ in); wing area

17.98 m² (183.9 sq ft)
Armament: can include bombs, incendiary bombs, cluster bombs, rocket pods and gun pods

Cessna Model 336/337 Skymaster/O-2/Reims F337/Milirole

The push-pull concept, with engines driving one tractor and one pusher propeller, was adopted by Cessna in the late 1950s for a light, low cost, easy-to-fly twin, and one obvious advantage over a normal twin layout was that, in the event of an engine failure, there would be no asymmetric thrust problems.

On 28 February 1961, the prototype **Cessna Model 336 Skymaster** flew and FAA certification followed 15 months later, with deliveries beginning in May 1963. Powered by two 157-kW (210-hp) Continental IO-360-A engines, the new aeroplane was a four-seater with fixed tricycle landing gear, although alternative seating arrangements for up to six were available. However, fixed landing gear on light twins was becoming passé, and after 195 Model 336s had been built the type was replaced on the production line in early 1965 by the **Model 337 Super Skymaster** with retractable landing gear. Additional baggage space was available in an optional glassfibre pack with a capacity of 136 kg

Augmenting the Bird Dog on forward air control duties was the O-2A, which could carry underwing gun pods for suppressive fire. Pods carried white phosphorus rockets for marking targets for strike aircraft.

(300 lb), which could be carried beneath the fuselage.

In 1969, Reims Aviation in France began licence assembly of the Model 337, with primary structures supplied by Cessna and Continental engines built in the UK under licence by Rolls-Royce. The US and French production lines continued in parallel, the French versions being classified **Reims F337**. The name **Milirole** was applied to the basic unpressurised F337 for a short time. Since 1974 Reims have developed a special unpressurised STOL version, designated **FTB337**, which can be provided with a wide range of equipment to make it suitable for such duties as maritime or overland patrol and rescue. Detail improvements continued each year, and a turbocharged version, the **Model 337 Turbo-System Super Skymaster**, was introduced in 1970, but the prototype of a pressurised **T337 Skymaster**, powered by 168-kW (225-hp) Continental TSIO-360 engines, flew in July 1971 (the word Super had then been dropped), and deliveries began the following May.

Military versions designated **O-2** were supplied to the US Air Force for various missions, including forward air control, for experience in Vietnam suggested that such sorties could be made more effective with FAC aircraft operated by a pilot and Forward Air Navigator

Baggage capacity of the Model 337 can be boosted by a ventral pannier, also available for other Cessna models.

(FAN), the latter being able to concentrate on the FAC mission without having to fly the aircraft.

Cessna's Model 337 was selected 'off the shelf' in late 1966 as being ideal for this role, and equipped with four underwing pylons to carry flares, rockets and light ordnance such as a 7.62-mm (0.3-in) Minigun pack. 501 were supplied to the USAF designated O-2A. In addition, a version equipped for psychological warfare missions entered USAF service under the designation **O-2B**. This carried a powerful air-to-ground broadcasting system using three 600-watt amplifiers and a battery of highly directional speakers. Total procurement of O-2B aircraft amounted to 31. Both versions carried advanced nav/com systems. Twelve O-2As were supplied to the Imperial Iranian air force in early 1970. A twin-turboprop **O-2T/O-2TT** did not proceed beyond USAF evaluation.

Production of the Model 337 series by Cessna ended in mid-1980 by which time 1,821 Model 337s, 313 pressurised Model 337s and 544 military O-2s had been delivered. French production by Reims Aviation totalled 66 Model F337s,

27 F337Ps and 61 FTB337s.

A military version of the T337, designated the Sentry O2-337, was marketed by Summit Aviation Inc. of Middletown, Delaware in 1980. These were commercial **Model T337s** built to zero-time status and equipped for a wide range of military missions. With four standard NATO pylons under the wings, each able to carry a 350-lb load, 10 O2-337s were supplied to the Royal Thai Navy between 1980 and 1983 and others were reported to be in service in Haiti, Honduras, Nicaragua and Senegal, all allegedly supplied by the CIA.

Specification
Cessna Model 337
Type: six-seat cabin monoplane
Powerplant: two 157-kW (210-hp) Continental IO-360-GB flat-six piston engines
Performance: maximum speed 332 km/h (206 mph) at sea level; maximum cruising speed 315 km/h (196 mph) at 1675 m (5,500 ft); service ceiling 5485 m (18,000 ft); range 2288 km (1,422 miles) at 3050 m (10,000 ft)
Weights: empty 1264 kg (2,787 lb); maximum take-off 2100 kg (4,630 lb)
Dimensions: span 11.63 m (38 ft 2 in); length, 9.07 m (29 ft 9 in); height, 2.79 m (9 ft 2 in); wing area 18.81 m²

Cessna Model 401/Utiliner/402/Businessliner/411

When flown for the first time on 18 July 1962, the **Cessna Model 411** then represented the company's largest business aircraft. Generally similar in configuration to the Model 310, it differed by having slightly increased wing span and area, a lengthened fuselage, more powerful 254-kW (340-hp) Continental GTSIO-520-C flat-six turbocharged engines and accommodation for a crew of two and four to six passengers. Production of the Model 411 was discontinued in June 1978, after the production of 400 examples, a small number of which were supplied to the French air force.

Cessna Model 402B of TAM Linha Aerea Regional, Brazil.

On 26 August 1965 Cessna flew the prototype of a generally similar aircraft which served for two new aircraft, the **Model 401** and **Model 402**, and when FAA certification of the Model 401 prototype was awarded on 20 September 1966 it covered also the Model 402. These two aircraft represented lower-cost versions of the Model 411, differing primarily by having two 2240-kW (300-hp) Continental TSIO-520-E flat-six engines and some reduction in basic installed equipment. The Model 401 accommodated a crew of two and four to six passengers, but the Model 402 had a cabin layout which permitted a quick change from nine-seat commuter use to an all-cargo configuration.

Production of the Model 401 was phased out in mid-1972, with development then being concentrated on the Model 402 which, in December 1971, had been named **Utiliner**. At the same time a new version of the Model 402 was introduced as the **Businessliner**.

Both versions, powered by 242-kW

(325-hp) TSIO-520-VB engines, were progressively improved and remained in production for some time, as the 10-seat **Utiliner II** small convertible passenger/cargo airliner and the **Businessliner II** executive transport able to carry 2-6 passengers. The final version was the **Businessliner III** corporate transport fitted with more sophisticated avionics, including weather radar. A downturn in sales led to production ceasing in 1986 by which time a total of 1,540 Cessna 402 variants had been built, including 12 delivered to the Royal Malaysian Air Force in 1975.

Specification
Cessna Model 402 Businessliner
Type: six/eight-seat business aircraft
Powerplant: two 242-kW (325-hp) Continental TSIO-520-VB flat-six turbocharged piston engines
Performance: maximum speed 428 km/h (266 mph) at 4875 m (16,000 ft); economic cruising speed 307 km/h (191 mph) at 6095 m

(20,000 ft); service ceiling 8200 m (26,900 ft); maximum range with maximum fuel at 3050 m (10,000 ft) 2359 km (1,466 miles)
Weights: empty 1845 kg (4,069 lb); maximum take-off 3107 kg (6,850 lb)
Dimensions: span 13.45 m (44 ft 1½ in); length 11.09 (36 ft 4½ in);

In addition to civil use, the Model 402B found favour with several military customers, such as Malaysia.

height 3.49 m (11 ft 5½ in); wing area 20.98 m² (225.80 sq ft)

Cessna Model 404 Titan

On 26 February 1975 Cessna flew the prototype of its new twin-engined **Cessna Model 404**, subsequently named **Titan**, of which initial deliveries began in October 1976. In appearance it is generally similar to the turboprop-powered Conquest, which flew later, and the two aircraft shared what was then a new feature for Cessna twins, a tailplane incorporating dihedral. Powered by two Continental GTSIO-520-M turbocharged engines, the Titan offered an increase of more than 30 per cent in ton/miles per gallon by comparison with the Cessna 402. Two versions were available initially, the **Titan Ambassador** passenger aircraft which offered an alternative executive interior, and the **Titan Courier**, a utility version for passengers or cargo, with seats for up to 10 passengers.

Until the spring of 1982, seven variants were available, comprising the standard Titan Ambassador, the **Titan Ambassador II** and **Titan Ambassador III**, the two latter having factory-installed avionic/equipment packages; the standard Titan Courier and **Titan Courier II** versions, the latter with the same avionic/equipment package as the Ambassador II; and the standard **Titan Freighter** and **Titan Freighter II** versions, both able to carry 1588 kg 3,500 lb) of cargo and equipped with factory-installed avionics and impact resis-

tant polycarbonate interiors to protect the fuselage from payload damage. When Titan production ceased in April 1982, 378 had been sold.

Specification
Cessna Titan Ambassador
Type: two/ten-seat passenger, executive or cargo transport
Powerplant: two 280-kW (375-hp) Continental GTSIO-520-M flat-six turbocharged piston engines
Performance: maximum speed 430 km/h (267 mph) at 4875 m (16,000 ft); economic cruising speed 303 km/h (188 mph) at 6095 m (20,000 ft); maximum range at economic cruising speed at 6095 m (20,000 ft) 3410 km (2,119 miles)

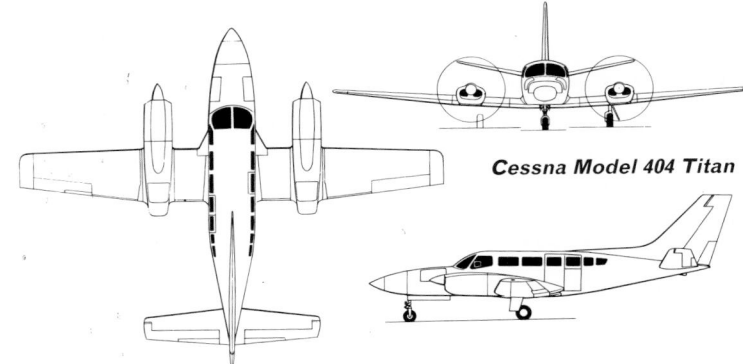

Cessna Model 404 Titan

Weights: empty 2192 km (4,834 lb); maximum take-off 3810 kg (8,400 lb)
Dimensions: span 14.12 m (46 ft

4 in); length 12.04 m (39 ft 6¼ in); height 4.04 m (13 ft 3 in); wing area 22.48 m² (242.0 sq ft)

The Titan was conceived as a versatile transport in three versions: the Ambassador passenger carrier, Courier convertible and Freighter cargo carrier.

Cessna Model 414 Chancellor

To provide a pressurised twin-engined transport which would serve as a 'step-up' aircraft for owners of light unpressurised twins, Cessna married the basic fuselage of the Model 421 with the wing developed for the Model 401. The resulting aircraft was designated **Cessna Model 414**, flown for the first time on 1 November 1968 and certificated during the following August. A number of optional seating layouts for up to seven passengers plus a wide range of cabin appointments were available to

customers, and new features introduced on the aircraft included engine cowlings with flush intakes to improve engine cooling and an accurate fuel monitoring system developed by Cessna to provide better fuel management.

From the time of its introduction until 1976, improvements introduced for the

The Model 414 can seat up to seven passengers. The circular windows denote a pressurised cabin.

Model 402 were reflected in the Model 414, and in that year the name **Chancellor** was adopted. It was available for 1976 in standard and **Model 414 II** versions, the latter incorporating a package of factory-installed avionics and equipment. For 1978, after 513 of the original Model 414s had been built, an improved version was introduced as the **Model 414A Chancellor**, major changes including a redesigned and increased-span

wing incorporating integral fuel tanks and more baggage capacity in an extended nose.

Versions available between 1978 and 1986, were the standard Model 414A Chancellor, the Chancellor II and later the Chancellor III, all with differing factory installed avionic/equipment packages. When Model 414/414A production ended in 1986 a total of 1,067 variants had been built.

Specification
Cessna Model 414A Chancellor
Type: six/eight-seat pressurised light transport
Powerplant: two 231-kW (310-hp) Continental TSIO-520-NB flat-six turbocharged piston engines
Performance: maximum speed 436 km/h (271 mph) at 6095 m (20,000 ft); economic cruising speed 340 km/h (211 mph) at 7620 m

(25,000 ft); service ceiling 9390 m (30,800 ft); maximum range at economic cruising speed at 3050 m (10,000 ft) 2459 km (1,528 miles)
Weights: empty 1994 kg (4,397 lb); maximum take-off 3062 kg (6,750 lb)
Dimensions: span 13.45 m (44 ft 1½ in); length 11.09 m (36 ft 4½ in); height 3.49 m (11 ft 5½ in); wing area 20.98 m² (225.80 sq ft)

Cessna Model 421 Golden Eagle

In October 1965 Cessna announced development of a new pressurised twin-engined business aircraft designated **Cessna Model 421**, the prototype of which had flown for the first time on 14 October 1965. Derived from the Model 401/411, the Model 421 differed primarily in its original configuration by having a fail-safe pressurised fuselage structure and an AiResearch air-conditioning and pressurisation system. Deliveries of initial production aircraft began in May 1967, following certification of the type on the fist day of that month.

Two new versions of the Model 421 were introduced for 1970, the **Model 421B Golden Eagle** and **Model 421B Executive Commuter**. Both had a number of improvements including lengthening of the nose to provide more avionics and baggage capacity, an increase in wing span, strengthening of the landing gear for operation at higher gross weights, and many detail refinements. The Executive Commuter was basically the same as the Golden Eagle, but the interior was laid out with lightweight easily-removable seating to provide alternative passenger/cargo config-

urations which could accommodate a maximum of 10 passengers. These two versions were replaced in 1976 by the **Model 421C Golden Eagle**, which introduced some important changes. These included a new wing that dispensed with the distinctive wingtip tanks, replaced by integral fuel tanks of the type introduced at a later date on the Model 414. Other changes provided increased area for the vertical tail surfaces and larger-capacity engine turbochargers. Four versions were available, the Model 421C Golden Eagle and **Model 421C Executive Commuter**, both produced in **Model 421C II**, versions with a factory-installed avionics/equipment package.

The Executive Commuter was discontinued for 1978, the Golden Eagle then being available in standard as well as Model 421C II and **Model 421C III** versions with differing avionics/equipment packages.

By late-1985 when production ceased, 1,909 Golden Eagles of all versions had been delivered, including three examples for the Royal New Zealand Air Force.

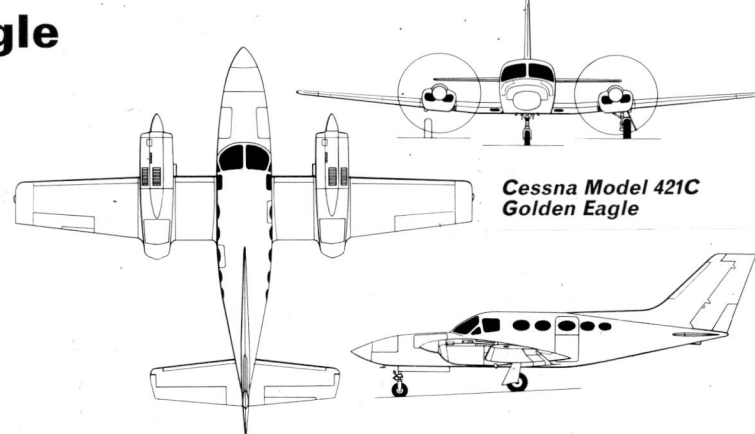

Cessna Model 421C Golden Eagle

Specification
Cessna Model 421C Golden Eagle
Type: six/eight-seat pressurised light transport
Powerplant: two 280-kW (375-hp) Continental GTSIO-520-N flat-six turbocharged piston engines
Performance: maximum speed 478km/h (297mph) at 6095m (20,000 ft); economic cruising speed

356 km/h (221 mph) at 7620 m (25,000 ft); service ceiling 9205 m (30,200 ft); maximum range at economic cruising speed at 3050 m (10,000 ft) 2752 km (1,710 miles)
Weights: empty 2129 kg (4,693 lb); maximum take-off 3379 kg (7,450 lb)
Dimensions: span 12.53 m (41 ft 1½ in); length 11.09 m (36 ft 4½ in); height 3.49 m (11 ft 5½ in); wing area 19.97 m² (215.0 sq ft)

Cessna Model 425 Corsair

In November 1977 Cessna began the design of a new pressurised light business aircraft and the prototype flew for the first time on 12 September 1978. The aircraft combined the airframe of the Model 421 Golden Eagle with two Pratt & Whitney of Canada PT6A turboprop engines. Other features included the dihedral tailplane of the Model 404, all endowing the new aircraft, introduced in 1980 as the Cessna **Model 425 Corsair**, with higher cruising speeds and operating altitudes. Like the Model 421, the Corsair offered six/eight seat accommodation in varying interior layouts and a wide range of cabin furnishings together with a high standard of avionics and equipment. **The Corsair** was certified in mid-1980 and first deliveries made in November the same year. Late in 1982 the aircraft was retrospectively designated and marketed as the **Corsair I** and 226 had been delivered when production terminated in 1986. The Garratt-engined **Corsair II** was built as the **Model 441**.

Specification
Type: six/eight-seat pressurised light transport
Powerplant: two Pratt & Whitney Aircraft of Canada PT6A-112 turboprops, each flat-rated at 335.5 kW (450 hp)
Performance: maximum cruising speed 489 km/h (304 mph) at 5400 m (17,700 ft); service ceiling 10180 m (33,400 ft); maximum range at economic cruising speed at 9145 m (30,000 ft) 2919 km (1,814 miles)
Weights: empty equipped 2229 kg

4,915 lb); maximum take-off 3901 kg (8,600 lb)
Dimensions: span 13.45 m (44 ft 1½ in); length 10.93 m (35 ft 10¼ in); height 3.84 m 12 ft 7¼ in); wing area 20.90 m² (224.98 sq ft)

The Cessna Model 421 was one of the company's most successful twin-engine designs, and it seemed a logical choice for conversion to turboprop powerplants. So was born the Model 425 Corsair, which combines the Model 421 airframe with Pratt & Whitney Canada PT6A turboprops to provide greater reliability, faster cruising speed and increased range. One major airframe difference was the incorporation of a dihedralled tailplane.

Cessna Model 441 Conquest II

On 15 November 1974, Cessna announced the development of a new turboprop-powered pressurised executive transport which is designated **Cessna Model 441**. The prototype was flown for the first time on 26 August 1975 and by the time that initial deliveries began in 1977 the type had been given the name **Conquest**. The aircraft was powered by two Garrett TPE331 turboprop engines which had been developed specially to provide the high-altitude/high-speed performance that Cessna required for this 11-seat transport.

Cessna had designed the Conquest in the hope that it would slot into the market between available powered business aircraft. However, marketing plans were delayed when problems arose in early 1978, one of the first production aircraft being involved in a crash; this resulted in the Conquest being grounded by Cessna. Modification of the tail unit was carried out before the type was recertificated, and as a result of this, aircraft that were already completed had to be provided with a new tailplane.

The Model 441 Conquest incorporated the wing and landing gear of the Model 404 Titan, with the span increased by the use of wingtip extensions. The pressurised and air-conditioned cabin could accommodate up to 10 passengers, although a four-seat de luxe version was offered for executive use. In 1983 the Model 441 was redesignated and marketed as the Conquest II and by 1986 when production ceased, 353 examples had been sold.

Cessna Model 441 Conquest in US civil markings

Specification
Type: five/eleven-seat pressurised executive transport
Powerplant: two Garrett TPE331-8-401S/402S turboprops, each flat rated at 474 kW (635.5 shp)
Performance: maximum speed 547 km/h (340 mph) at 4875 m (16,000 ft); service ceiling 10670 m (35,000 ft); maximum range at economic cruising speed with allowances at 10670 m (35,000 ft) 4245 km (2,638 miles)
Weights: empty 2631 kg (5,801 lb); maximum take-off 4468 kg (9,850 lb)
Dimensions: span 15.04 m (49 ft 4 in); length 11.89 m (39 ft 0¼ in); height 4.01 m (13 ft 1¾ in); wing area 23.56 m² (253.60 sq ft)

Cessna Model 500 Citation

The **Cessna Citation**, announced in 1968, was one of the first of the new generation of turbofan-powered business jets, a response to growing pressure from environmentalists for quieter engines and from operators for better fuel economy. Its development represented a very large investment for the company, but when the prototype **Fanjet 500** (as it was then named) flew for the first time on 15 September 1969, it posed a serious commercial threat to aircraft such as the D.H. 125, Falcon 20, Learjets and Sabreliner which had dominated the market to that time.

Renamed the **Model 500 Citation** shortly after the first flight, the eight-seat Model 500 has an overall configuration similar to that of earlier Cessna twins except for its powerplant installation. This featured two 9.8-kN (2,200-lb) Pratt & Whitney Canada JT15D-1 turbofans mounted in pods on each side of the rear fuselage just aft of the wing trailing edge. As a result of development flying, a number of important changes were made, and it was not until 1972 that initial deliveries were made. In 1976 deliveries began of an improved **Model 501 Citation I** with increased wing span and similarly rated but improved JT15D-1A engines. This was followed soon after by the **Citation 1/SP** version certificated for single-pilot operation. When production ceased in June 1985, 691 Citation 1s had been delivered.

Development of the Cessna business jet family continued with the **Model 550 Citation II**. Announced in September 1976, the prototype first flew on 31 January 1977. Powered by two 11.12-kN (2,500-lb) JT15D-4 engines, the 8-12-seat aircraft featured a lengthened fuselage, increased span wings and more fuel and baggage space. Certifica-

tion followed in March 1978, and the **Citation II/SP** cleared for single-pilot operation in July 1984. The Citation II was taken out of production in 1984 when 503 had been built, but resumed in 1987. By the end of 1989 667 plus 15 **T-47As** had been delivered, making the Model 550 the best selling business jet. In October 1983 the revised **Citation S/II** was announced and the first production aircraft made its initial flight on 14 February 1984, with deliveries following soon after. This version has the JT15D-4B engine giving more power at higher altitudes, a new aerofoil section wing, leading-edge extensions, modified engine pylons and increased cabin headroom and baggage capacity. A further modified version of the Citation S/II, the **Model 552**, was selected in May 1983 by the US Navy for training radar intercept operators and 15 examples designated T-47A are currently in service. These have shorter span wings and more powerful 12.89-kN (2,900-lb) JT15D-5 engines. The T-47A first flew on 15 February 1984.

The 8-11-seat **Model 650 Citation III** flew for the first time on 30 May 1979, was certificated in April 1982 and first deliveries made in the spring of 1983.

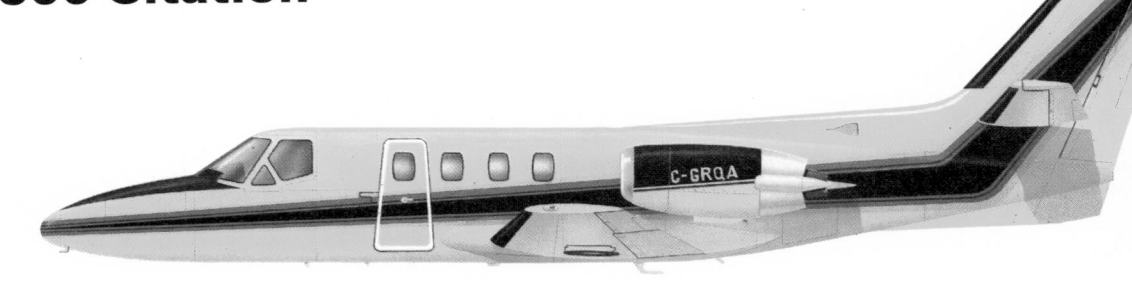

Cessna Model 500 Citation I in Canadian civil markings

Six cabin-side windows denote the lengthened fuselage of the Model 550 Citation II. This is the S/II advanced version with uprated JT15D-4B engines and a new section wing.

Powered by two 16.24-kN (3,650-lb) Garrett TFE 731-3-100S turbofans, the Citation III broke from tradition by having a T-tail, together with a stretched fuselage and increased span wing. By the end of 1989 174 had been delivered and the type continues in production.

The **Model 670 Citation IV** was revealed in 1989 as a 10-seat development of the III powered by 17.79-kN (4,000-lb) TFE 731-4 turbofans giving increased range and airfield performance. However, further development of the Model 670 was terminated by Cessna in May 1990 in favour of the **Citation VI** and **VII**.

In August 1987, Cessna flew an engineering prototype of the eight-seat **Model 560 Citation V**. This is essentially a development of the S/II equipped with 12.89-kN (2,900-lb) JT15D-5A engines, and a longer fuselage fitted with a seventh cabin window. The type was certificated on 9 December 1988, first delivery made the following April and by the end of 1989 the company had delivered 33 and claimed a full orderbook for the US $3.8m Citation V to the end of 1991.

The 8-10 seat Citation VI and VII were announced in May 1990, both based on the Citation III airframe but with factory-installed interior and avionics package. The 'simpler' and thus lower priced $8.6m Citation VI features a 'low speed' wing and a modified undercarriage bestowing the ability to operate from grass fields. Powered by two Garrett TFE 731-3B-100 turbofans, the Citation VI is designed to cruise at 874 km/h (543 mph) at 15544-m (51,000-ft). The first production aircraft is scheduled for delivery in April 1991.

The longer range Citation VII version of the III is high powered with 18.36-kN (4,080-lb) thrust TFE 731-4 turbofans offering improved performance. First models of the $8.6m midsize business jet are scheduled for delivery in January 1992.

Skipping the unused Citation VIII and IX designations, the company announced in May 1990 the development of a 'larger mid-size' long range ex-

ecutive transport. The aircraft, heavily promoted by Cessna as the world's fastest business jet, was publicly launched as the Model 750 Citation X at the NBAA Convention in New Orleans in October 1990. Five feet longer than the III, the X is powered by two GM/Allison GMA-3007A turbofans, each rated at 27 kN (6,000 lb), enabling the new aircraft to fly 6111 km (3,797 miles) at a cruising Mach number of 0.88 at 11278-m (37,000-ft). This gives the Citation X the capability to fly from Los Angeles to New York or New York to London non-stop. The prototype is due to fly in March 1993 and first customer

deliveries are scheduled for June 1995. The first ten aircraft are being offered to customers at approximately $14m each, completed.

Specification
Cessna Model 550 Citation II
Type: seven/ten-passenger executive transport
Powerplant: two 11.12-kN (2,500-lb) thrust each Pratt & Whitney Canada JT15D-4 turbofan engines
Performance: cruising speed 713 km/h (443 mph); certificated ceiling 13105 m (43,000 ft); range with six passengers plus allowances 3169 km

Swept wings and a T-tail were the major features introduced by the Citation III, together with a switch to Garrett TFE731 turbofan power. This variant provided the basis for subsequent developments, including the Citation IV, VI, VII and VIII.

(1,969 miles)
Weights: empty 3364 kg (7,416 lb); maximum take-off 6033 kg (13,300 lb)
Dimensions: span 15.9 m (52 ft 2 in); length 14.39 m (47 ft 2 in); height 4.57 m (15 ft 0 in); wing area 30 m² (322.9 sq ft)

Cessna Model 525 CitationJet

Cessna developed the **Model 525 CitationJet** with the aim of expanding its market share for business aircraft in the jet-powered sector. It was planned that the new type should make its mark through the exploitation of advanced technologies but, at an initial purchase price of approximately US $2.62 million for the standard model, the type was also directed at current operators of turboprop-powered business aircraft, and Cessna estimated the size of the potential market at up to 1,000 aircraft within a 10-year period.

In its design the **CitationJet** is new, although there is some constructional similarity with existing models, in particular through the use of the same nose cone, cockpit and fuselage diameter as those of the Citation II and IV. The six-seat cabin is equipped with adjustable armchair-type seats and provides 0.127 m (5 in) more headroom than the Citation I. The volume for luggage is 5.2 m³ (183.6 cu ft) in two external compartments and a compartment in the rear fuselage.

A key feature of this model is the powerplant of two Williams/Rolls-Royce FJ44 turbofans, whose simplicity, robustness, efficiency and

price gave the **CitationJet** the ability to compete with turboprop-powered aircraft. In addition wing design was carefully schemed on the basis of a supercritical aerofoil section with natural laminar flow for significantly reduced drag in cruising flight, the wing carrythrough structure was designed to pass under and behind the cabin so that no intrusion was made into passenger volume. The cockpit has modern avionics, including EFIS with two 0.127-m (5-in) screens, the Honeywell SPZ-5000 digital flight director/ autopilot.

Cessna secured an initial 50 orders at the 1989 NBAA Convention. **CitationJet** made its maiden flight on 29 April 1991, followed on 20 November 1991 by the initial flight of the second machine. The FAA certificated the model for single-pilot operation in October 1992, and the first delivery was effected on 30 March 1993.

The key features of the Cessna CitationJet are its natural laminar-flow wings, FJ44 turbofans and a six-seat cabin. N525CJ was the prototype, and flew for the first time in April 1991.

Specification
Cessna Model 525 CitationJet
Model: business jet
Powerplant: two 8.45-kN (1,900-lb st) Williams International/Rolls-Royce FJ44 turbofans
Performance: maximum cruising speed 709 km/h (441 mph) at 10060 m (33,000 ft); initial climb rate 1009 m (3,311 ft) per minute; certificated

ceiling 12495 m (41,000 ft); range 2696 km (1,675 miles) with one pilot, four passengers and 45-minute fuel reserves
Weights: empty 2823 kg (6,224 lb); 4717 kg (10,400 lb)
Measurements: span 14.26 m (46 ft 9.5 in); length 12.98 m (42 ft 7.25 in); height 4.18 m (13 ft 8.5 in); area 22.30 m² (240.00 sq ft)

Chance Vought V-166 (F4U Corsair)

Acknowledged universally to be the most outstanding carrier-based fighter of World War II, examples of the **Chance Vought Corsair** in service with the Royal Navy's Fleet Air Arm were the first to demonstrate the outstanding potential of this design. When used by the US Navy in the Pacific, from April 1944, the type was credited with no fewer than 2,140 victories against the Japanese for the loss of only 189 of its own number.

Development of the aircraft began in 1938, when the US Navy requested proposals for a single-seat carrier-based fighter. The Vought design team evolved the smallest possible airframe that could be tailored to fit the most powerful engine then available, the Pratt & Whitney XR-2800 Double Wasp. Identified initially by the company as the **V-166B**, its unusual wing configuration resulted from the choice of this engine, for the large-diameter propeller needed by the Double Wasp would require stalky landing gear, far from suitable for carrier operations. The highly-cranked inverted and folding gull-wing that was adopted allowed the retractable main landing gear units to be located at the 'pinion point' of the wing, keeping them as short as possible. The remainder of the airframe was conventional, of clean line and all-metal construction.

The **XF4U-1** prototype, ordered on 30 June 1938, was flown for the first time on 29 May 1940, but combat reports from Europe had shown a need to revise the armament. This delayed until February 1941 US Navy acceptance of the prototype, an initial production order for 585 **F4U-1** production aircraft being awarded on 30 June 1941. The first of these flew a year later, on 25 June 1942, and the first examples of these F4U-1 Corsairs were handed over to the US Navy on 31 July 1942. Carrier trials proved disappointing, the US Navy considering the Corsair unsuitable for carrier service, a fact which led to modification of the landing gear and raising of the cockpit to improve forward view. When these changes were introduced on the production line, after 688 F4U-1s had been built, subsequent aircraft became designated **F4U-1A**.

Initial US operational use of the Corsair was, therefore, with land-based units, the US Marine Corps' VMF-124 being the first squadron to take the type into action at Guadalcanal on 13 February 1943. The US Navy's first operational squadron, VF-17, was formed in April 1943 and this was the first unit to operate the modified F4U-1As. By that time Vought had received orders for very large numbers of Corsairs, resulting in production also by Brewster under the designation **F3A-1** and by Goodyear as the **FG-1**: this latter version had fixed

Chance Vought Corsair Mk IV (Goodyear FG-1) of No. 1850 Sqn, Fleet Air Arm, based aboard HMS Vengeance in August 1945.

wings. Corsairs saw extensive service with the Royal Navy's Fleet Air Arm from June 1943, and examples of the **F4U-1D** were supplied also to the RNZAF.

Production had been continuous for just over 10 years when the line at Dallas, Texas, was closed down in December 1952, a period in which 12,571 examples of this outstanding fighter had been built by Vought, Brewster and Goodyear.

Variants

F4U-1B: US designation of aircraft supplied to the UK under Lend-Lease
F4U-1C: version with four wing-mounted 20-mm cannon in place of standard six machine-gun armament
F4U-1D: version with R-2800-8W water-injection engine and revised armament (also built by Brewster and Goodyear as **F3A-1D** and **FG-1D** respectively)
F4U-1P: photo-reconnaissance variant of the F4U-1
F4U-2: night-fighter version, all conversions by Naval Aircraft Factory, with AI radar and reduced armament
F4U-3: designation allocated to a very-

high-altitude fighter; first prototype flown post-war, but the 13 Goodyear-built aircraft completed subsequently (under the designation **FG-3**) were used by the US Navy for high-altitude research flights
F4U-4: designation of second major production version with R-2800-18W or R-2800-42W engine
F4U-4C: variant with four 20-mm cannon in place of standard armament
F4U-4E: night-fighter version with APS-4 AI radar
F4U-4N: night-fighter version with APS-5 or APS-6 AI radar
F4U-4P: photo-reconnaissance variant
F4U-5: post-World War II fighter-bomber with R-2800-32W engine
F4U-5N: night-fighter version of F4U-5
F4U-5P: tactical reconnaissance variant of F4U-5
XF4U-6: prototype of low-altitude variant with R-2800-83W engine, additional armour protection and increased weapon-carrying capability; total of 110 built under designation **AU-1**
F4U-7: final production version, similar to AU-1 but with R-2800-18W; total of 90 built and supplied to French Aéronavale through MAP

Corsair Mk I: Fleet Air Arm designation of F4U-1
Corsair Mk II: Fleet Air Arm designation of F4U-1A
Corsair Mk III: Fleet Air Arm designation of F3A-1D
Corsair Mk IV: Fleet Air Arm designation of FG-1D

Specification
Chance Vought F4U-1A

Type: carrier-based single-seat fighter
Powerplant: one 1491-kW (2,000-hp) Pratt & Whitney R-2800-8 radial piston engine
Performance: maximum speed 671 km/h (417 mph) at 6065 m (19,900 ft) or 509 km/h (316 mph) at sea level; cruising speed 293 km/h (182 mph); initial climb rate 951 m (3,120 ft) per minute; service ceiling 11245 m (36,900 ft); range 1633 km (1,015 miles)
Weights: empty 4074 kg (8,982 lb); maximum take-off 6350 kg (14,000 lb)
Dimensions: span 12.5 m (41 ft 0 in); length 10.16 m (33 ft 4 in); height 4.9 m (16 ft 1 in); wing area 29.17 m² (314 sq ft)
Armament: six wing-mounted 12.7-mm (0.5-in) machine-guns

The Corsair was a potent fighter-bomber, capable of launching bombs, missiles and napalm. This is an F4U-1D, toting a pair of 454-kg (1,000-lb) bombs.

Chance Vought V-173 (XF5U-1)

Almost certainly the most unusual aircraft designed by the company, the **Chance Vought XF5U-1** was intended to produce a fighter aircraft which, in a fully-developed form, would have a speed range from 32 to 740 km/h

(20 to 460 mph). It had a wing of almost circular planform, which also comprised the primary structure of the aircraft. Control surfaces were confined to the rear of the wing, consisting of twin fins and rudders, with a swept tailplane on each

side. These latter surfaces each had an elevator which could be used collectively for control in pitch or differentially for roll control. Landing gear was of retractable tailwheel type. Power was provided by two Pratt & Whitney radial engines buried in the wing, one on each side for the fuselage and driving, via right-angle gearboxes, specially de-

veloped propellers, one at the forward extremity of each wing. Clutches and shafting were provided to ensure that, in emergency, both propellers could be driven by one engine.

To flight-test the concept a low-powered full-scale version was built as the **V-173**. Of wood and fabric construction, low-powered engines and fixed landing gear, this flew for the first time on 23 November 1942. Although the prototype XF5U-1 was completed and prepared for testing at Muroc Dry Lake (since renamed Edwards AFB), this aircraft was never flown.

The low-powered V-173 aerodynamic test vehicle fully validated the 'pancake' concept for the radical F5U fighter. Good handling and good speed range were among the characteristics.

Specification
Chance Vought XF5U-1
Type: experimental fighter aircraft
Powerplant: two 1007-kW (1,350-hp) each Pratt & Whitney R-2000 Twin Wasp radial piston engines
Performance: (estimated) maximum speed 684 km/h (425 mph); landing speed 64 km/h (40 mph); initial climb rate 1094 m (3,590 ft) per minute; service ceiling 10515 m (34,500 ft);

range 1143 km (710 miles)
Weights: empty 5945 kg (13,107 lb); maximum take-off 7585 kg (16,722 lb)
Dimensions: span, over 'ailevators' 9.91 m (32 ft 6 in); length 8.56 m (28 ft 1 in); height 5.08 m (16 ft 8 in); lifting surface area 44.13 m² (475 sq ft)
Armament: (proposed) six 12.7-mm (0.5-in) machine-guns or four 20-mm cannon, plus two 454-kg (1,000-lb) bombs

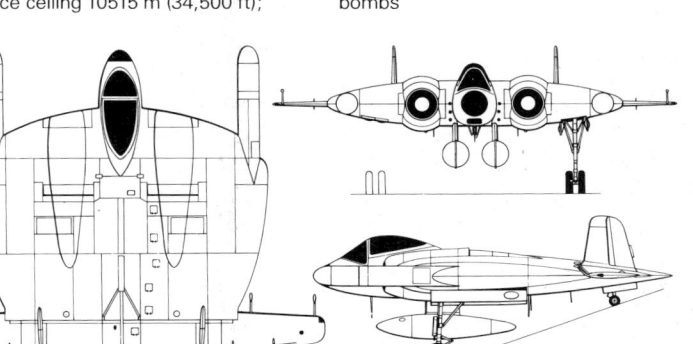

Chance Vought XF5U-1

The remarkable XF5U-1 never flew, a great disappointment for the aviation world. An immensely strong structure was a major feature.

Chance Vought V-340 (F6U Pirate)

Before World War II ended, Chance Vought was busy with the design of the **Chance Vought V-340** single-seat jet-propelled fighter for service with the US Navy. It was the first turbojet-powered aircraft to be designed by the company, but proved sufficiently attractive for the US Navy to award a contract for three **XF6U-1** prototypes on 29 December 1944.

Of low-wing monoplane configuration, the all-metal structure of the airframe had Metalite skins, patented by the company and comprising two sheets of high-strength light alloy bonded to a balsawood core. The tailplane was mounted on the fin, just above the fuselage, but production aircraft had two auxiliary fins, one towards the tip on each side of the tailplane. The Pirate had retractable tricycle landing gear, jettisonable auxiliary fuel tanks at each wingtip, and the pilot accommodated high on the fuselage, well forward of the wing.

The first of the three prototypes made its maiden flight at Muroc Dry Lake on 2 October 1946, powered by a 1361-kg (3,000-lb) thrust Westinghouse J34-WE-22 turbojet mounted in the aft fuselage. Production examples of the **F6U-1**, of which the first flew during July 1949, began to enter service with

the US Navy in the following month. A total of 65 had been ordered but after 30 had been delivered the remainder were cancelled.

Variant
F6U-1P: designation allocated to one of the production F6U-1s following the installation of cameras for evaluation in a reconnaissance role

Specification
Chance Vought F6U-1 Pirate
Type: single-seat naval fighter
Powerplant: one 1916-kg (4,225-lb) thrust Westinghouse J34-WE-30 afterburning turbojet
Performance: (estimated) maximum speed 908 km/h (564 mph) at 6095 m (20,000 ft); service ceiling 14110 m (46,300 ft); range 1851 km (1,150 miles)

Weights: empty 3320 kg (7,320 lb); maximum take-off 5702 kg (12,570 lb)
Dimensions: span, without tiptanks 10.01 m (32 ft 10 in); length 11.46 m (37 ft 7 in); height 3.94 m (12 ft 11 in); wing area 18.91 m² (203.5 sq ft)
Armament: four 20-mm cannon

The XF6U prototypes underwent numerous modifications. This is the second aircraft, seen fitted with a bullet fairing at the fin/tailplane joint.

Chance Vought V-346 (F7U Cutlass)

When first details of the aerodynamic research carried out in Germany during World War II began to reach the United States in late 1945, much of the information was of great help to manufacturers in the development of new aircraft of improved capability. Chance Vought became interested in Arado's work on tailless aircraft, this resulting in design and

development of the unconventional **F7U Cutlass** which dispensed with conventional tail surfaces. However unconventional, the F7U introduced new capability in a naval carrier-based fighter. It was the first aircraft to serve with the US Navy that was capable of being catapulted with an external stores load of nearly 2268 kg (5,000 lb) and its first pro-

duction aircraft to achieve supersonic flight. It also introduced such features as afterburners for its turbojet engines, powered controls with artificial 'feel' and an automatic stabilisation system.

After evaluation of Chance Vought's design proposals, embodied in the **Chance Vought V-346** designation, the US Navy ordered three **XF7U-1** pro-

totypes on 25 June 1946, the first of these flying on 29 September 1948. The short-span swept wings of the Cutlass mounted twin dorsal fins with rudders at about one-third span with large ventral fins beneath the wings. For control in pitch and roll wide-span trailing-edge elevons extended out-board of the fins to the wingtips. Other features of this advanced wing included airbrakes and full-span leading-edge slats. The retractable tricycle landing gear incorporated a

tall nose unit, giving the wing a high angle of attack on the deck, power was provided by two Westinghouse turbojets within the fuselage and the pilot, in an enclosed cockpit high on the nose, had an excellent all-round view.

Following initial evaluation of the prototypes, 14 **F7U-1** production aircraft were ordered for operational carrier trials, the first of them being flown on 1 March 1950. Production ended in December 1955, and details of Cutlass variants are given below.

Variants

F7U-2: proposed operational version of the F7U-1 with Westinghouse J34-WE-42 engines; difficulties with the development of this engine led to cancellation of the production contract
F7U-3: standard production version powered by two Westinghouse J46-WE-8A turbojets; introduced wing-folding and arrester gear for carrier operation, plus design refinements; first example flown 20 December 1951; 162 built
F7U-3M: version of the standard production aircraft equipped to carry four Sparrow I beam-riding missiles; 98 built
F7U-3P: designation of a photo-

reconnaissance version, of which 12 examples entered service

Specification
Chance Vought F7U-3
Type: single-seat carrier-based fighter
Powerplant: two 2767-kg (6,100-lb) thrust each Westinghouse J46-WE-8A afterburning turbojets
Performance: maximum speed 1094 km/h (680 mph) at 3050 m (10,000 ft); initial climb rate 3960 m (13,000 ft per minute); service ceiling 12190 m (40,000 ft); range 1062 km (660 miles)
Weights: empty 8267 kg (18,210 lb); maximum take-off 14365 kg (31,642 lb)
Dimensions: span 12.1 m (39 ft 8 in); length 13.5 m (44 ft 3 in); height 4.45 m (14 ft 7½ in); wing area 46.08 m² (496 sq ft)
Armament: four 20-mm cannon, plus underwing attachments for rockets or other stores

Chance Vought F4U-1 of the United States Navy display team, the Blue Angels.

A remarkable fighter for its time, the F7U dispensed with tailplanes. This is an F7U-3, exemplifying the main production variant.

Chetverikov MDR-6 (Che-2)

Marking a noteworthy advance in Soviet flying-boat design from both aerodynamic and hydrodynamic viewpoints, the **MDR-6** was a three-seat coastal reconnaissance aircraft of all-metal construction. The prototype, powered by 545-kW (730-hp) M-25E radials, was completed at Sebastopol in the Summer of 1937, undergoing state trials in December of that year. With M-63 radials of 821 kW (1,100 hp), the flying-boat was ordered into production at Taganrog during 1938 as the **MDR-6A** (this designation giving place to that of **Che-2** after 1941) and 50 were built during 1939-41.

Refinement of the basic design resulted in the **MDR-6B-1** with an improved planing bottom, a redesigned bow from which the swivelling turret was eliminated, and new tail surfaces, the braced single fin and rudder assembly giving place to oval endplate fins and rudders with a tailplane featuring marked dihedral. Completed in December 1940, the MDR-6B-1 was powered by two 783-kW (1,050-hp) M-105 liquid-cooled engines, and the **MDR-6B-2** which followed it in 1941 was essentially similar, both embodying retractable stabilising floats.

The **MDR-6B-3** differed in having M-105PF engines of 858 kW (1,150 hp) with revised engine nacelles incorporating frontal radiators, and redesigned retractable stabilising floats. But despite dramatic improvements in performance over the MDR-6A, these aircraft proved unacceptable to the Soviet navy on the score of their inadequate rough-sea hydrodynamic performance. In consequence, thoroughgoing hull redesign was undertaken by Chetverikov, resulting, in 1944, in the **MDR-6B-4**. Reverting to the fixed stabilising floats and retaining the M-105PF engines, the MDR-6B-4 had an appreciably deeper hull and added a central vertical fin to the tail assembly, lateral gun blisters also being introduced. Deliveries of PBY Catalinas under Lend-Lease motivated against production of the MDR-6B-4.

Despite the Soviet navy's refusal to accept for production the successive

B-series prototypes, Chetverikov persisted with development of the basic design and, in 1946, tested the **MDR-6B-5**, with 1268-kW (1,700-hp) VK-107 engines. Carrying a crew of four, this prototype featured a 20-mm B-20 cannon in the bow and a pair of similar weapons in an electrically operated dorsal turret. The MDR-6B-5 offered an excellent performance, including a maximum speed of 450 km/h (280 mph) at 6000 m (19,685 ft) and a range of 3000 km (1,864 miles), but this time the Soviet navy concluded that the Chetverikov flying-boat offered inadequate working space for crew members on long-duration patrols and further development was discontinued in consequence.

Specification
Chetverikov MDR-6A
Type: three-seat coastal reconnaissance flying-boat
Powerplant: two 821-kW (1,100-hp) each Klimov M-63 radial piston engines
Performance: maximum speed 360 km/h (224 mph) at 4000 m (13,125 ft); normal cruising speed 220 km/h (137 mph); climb to 5000 m (16,405 ft) in 12 minutes; service ceiling 9000 m (29,530 ft); maximum range 2650 km (1,647 miles)
Weights: empty 4100 kg (9,039 lb); normal loaded 6700 kg (14,771 lb); maximum take-off 7200 kg (15,873 lb)
Dimensions: span 19.4 m (63 ft 7¾ in); length 15.73 m (51 ft 7¼ in); height 4.3 m (14 ft 1¼ in); wing area 52.3 m² (562.97 sq ft)
Armament: one 7.62-mm (0.3-in) ShKAS machine-gun in bow turret and one 12.7-mm (0.5-in) UBT machine-gun in dorsal turret, plus a 1000-kg (2,205-lb) bombload

The MDR-6B-1 was the first of Chetverikov's flying-boats to feature retractable stabilisers. The small oval endplate fins were enlarged on later variants.

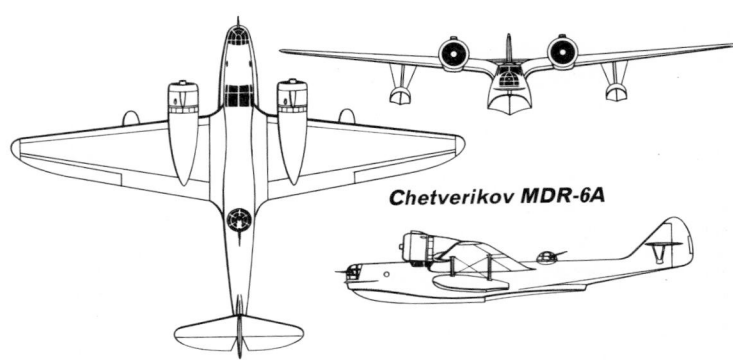

Chetverikov MDR-6A

Retaining little design commonality with preceding flying-boats in the series, the MDR-6B-5 did not enter flight test until 1946, and unsuccessfully competed with the Beriev Be-6.

Chetverikov TA-1

A small commercial utility amphibian in broadly the same category as the Grumman Albatross, the **TA-1** was an all-metal braced high-wing monoplane powered by two 700-hp (522 kW) ASh-21 radials. Three prototypes were built in 1947, the first of these commencing its flight test programme in July of that year. Although extensively tested, the TA-1 proved to possess poor handling characteristics. The wing of the second and third aircraft was marginally enlarged and structural weights were reduced, but the characteristics remained unacceptable and no production was undertaken.

Specification
Chetverikov TA-1 (third prototype)
Type: 10-seat light utility amphibian
Powerplant: two 700-hp (522-kW) Shvetsov ASh-21 radial piston engines

The last of Chetverikov's waterborne aircraft to be built was the TA-1 amphibian. Despite its attractive lines, it displayed poor handling characteristics which successive modifications made to the prototypes failed to improve sufficiently.

Performance: maximum speed 202 mph (330 km/h) at 5.575 ft (1700 m; service ceiling 19,355 ft (5900 m); normal range 435 miles (700 km); maximum range 746 miles (1200 km)

Weights: maximum take-off 12,694 lb (5758 kg)
Dimensions: span 58 ft 4¾ in (17.80 m); length 45 ft 11⅛ in (14.00 m); wing area 469.32 sq ft (43.6 m²)

Chilton D.W.1

Chilton Aircraft was formed at Hungerford, Berkshire during 1937 by A.H. Dalrymple and A.R. Ward, both former de Havilland Technical School students, to produce a single-seat lightplane of their own design. Designated **Chilton D.W.1**, this was a low-wing monoplane of all-wood basic construction with plywood skins and fabric-covered control surfaces. The landing gear was of fixed tailskid type, the main units being provided with 'trouser' fairings. Power for the prototype (G-AESZ), flown for the first time in April 1937, was a modified Carden/Ford motor car engine.

After only minor modifications three generally similar aircraft were built, G-AFGH, G-AFGI and G-AFSV, the latter powered by a 34-kW (45-hp) French-built Train 4T engine. Designated D.W.1S, it was flown for the first time in July 1939. All survived World War II and were popu-

lar as racers. Although the 41-kW (55-hp) Lycoming O-145 powered G-AFGH was badly damaged in May 1953, all four Chiltons still exist and are on long-term rebuilds at Coventry, Hungerford and White Waltham, two with Carden Ford engines and two with 46-kW (62-hp) Walter Mikrons.

Specification
Chilton D.W.1
Type: single-seat sporting aircraft
Powerplant: one 23.8 kW (32-hp) Carden/Ford modified motor car engine
Performance: maximum speed 180 km/h (112 mph); cruising speed 161 km/h (100 mph); range 805 km (500 miles)
Weights: empty 181 kg (398 lb); maximum take-off 318 kg (700 lb)

Dimensions: span 7.32 m (24 ft 0 in); length 5.49 m (18 ft 0 in); height 1.47 m (4 ft 10 in); wing area 7.15 m² (77.0 sq ft)

Completed in 1938, G-AFGH was the second Chilton D.W.1. It was seriously damaged in a forced landing during 1953, but restored with the aid of the half-completed fuselage of the D.W.2.

Chrislea Super Ace

In the years immediately after World War II, several smaller UK manufacturers applied themselves to the design of new light aircraft in an attempt to compete with the spate of surplus military trainers, such as Tiger Moths and Magisters, that were becoming available on the civil market. One such company was Chrislea Aircraft Ltd at Heston whose designer, R.C. Christophorides, produced the four-seat **Chrislea C.H.3 Ace**, a high-wing cabin monoplane with single fin and rudder. An innovation among British light aircraft at that time was its tricycle landing gear, and the powerplant was 93-kW (125-hp) Avco Lycoming, although it was intended that production models would use the new British Monaco engine of 75 kW (100 hp). The main difference, however, to established British practice was in the control system, where a single wheel on a universal joint replaced the conventional control column and rudder bar. The prototype Ace flew in September 1946, but within three weeks its single fin and rudder had been replaced by twin fins and rudders.

In 1947 the company moved to Exeter and the first **C.H.3 Series 2 Super**

Ace flew in February 1948 with the 108-kW (145-hp) de Havilland Gipsy Major 10 engine which had been chosen for production aircraft. Considerable criticism from flying instructors resulted in the unusual control system being replaced by a conventional 'stick and rudder bar' installation. A production batch was laid down, the sixth and seventh production models being exhibited at the 1948 SBAC Display at Farnborough. A number of Super Aces were sold abroad to customers in Argentina, Australasia, Brazil, France, Japan, Malaysia, New Zealand, Pakistan, Rhodesia and Switzerland. Some 27 Super Aces were laid down but only 21 were completed and flown. Construction of four was abandoned and two others were finished but did not fly; the assets of the company were bought by C.E. Harper Aircraft Ltd in 1952, when all partially assembled aircraft were scrapped.

In 1949 the prototype of the **C.H.3 Srs 4 Skyjeep** had been flown; this had a conventional control system, tailwheel landing gear and a 116-kW (155-hp) Blackburn Cirrus Major 3 engine. A removable top decking to the rear fuselage offered space for a stretcher or light

freight. Two further Skyjeeps were completed and sold to Argentina and Australia, while the prototype went subsequently to French Indo-China. Two others, uncompleted, were scrapped by Harper in 1952.

One Super Ace still flying, is the 14th production aircraft which spent nine years in Pakistan, before being restored to flying condition in 1982.

Specification
Chrislea C.H.3 Series 2 Super Ace
Type: four-seat light aircraft
Powerplant: one 108-kW (145-hp) de Havilland Gipsy Major 110 inline piston engine

The C.H.3 Skyjeep was typical of Chrislea design philosophy, and made its debut at the Royal Aeronautical Association's garden party at White Waltham in May 1950.

Performance: maximum speed 203 km/h (126 mph); cruising speed 180 km/h (112 mph); range with maximum fuel 644 km (400 nmiles)
Weights: empty equipped 612 kg (1,350 lb); maximum take-off 1066 kg (2,350 lb)
Dimensions: span 10.97 m (36 ft 0 in); length 6.55 m (21 ft 6 in); height 2.40 m (7 ft 7½ in); wing area 16.44 m² (177.0 sq ft)

Cierva autogyros
to
Conroy Aircraft Corporation

Cierva autogyros

Juan de la Cierva built his first autogyro, the **Cierva C.1**, at Madrid in 1920, using the fuselage of a French Deperdussin monoplane above which were mounted two four-blade contra-rotating rotors surmounted by a vertical surface to provide lateral control. Power was provided by a 45-kW (60-hp) Le Rhône engine but the machine would not fly; it was impossible to control and interference between the two rotors unbalanced the lift.

The following year Cierva tried again, this time with the **C.2**, a Hanriot biplane fuselage married to a three-blade rotor. The C.2 was damaged and rebuilt nine times before Cierva gave up and began work on the **C.3**, which was ready to fly early in 1922. Use of a rotor with five rigid blades improved the lateral control, but the C.3 had a tendency to fall over on its side and had to be rebuilt four times.

Experimenting with models, Cierva found that the secret of successful flight lay in flexible rotor blades, articulated to overcome imbalance between advancing and retreating blades. Based on this theory, the **C.4** was built in 1922 with a four-blade rotor articulated at the root. Initially it, too, was unsuccessful, but after some modifications it made a first flight on 9 January 1923, piloted by Teniente Alejandro Gomez Spencer from Madrid's Getafé aerodrome. Although this flight covered only 183 m (600 ft) it proved the concept, and at the end of that month the C.4, flying from Cuatro Vientos aerodrome near Madrid, achieved a 4-km (2.5-mile) closed circuit flight in four minutes at a height of about 30 m (100 ft). Power for the C.4 was provided by a 82-kW (110-hp) Le Rhône 9Ja engine. In July 1923 the similarly powered **C.5** was flown at Getafé with a three-blade rotor, and after this Cierva, who had previously financed his experiments from private sources, received subsidies from the Spanish government.

His next model, the **C.6**, was the beginning of a series of successful autogyros – a word coined by Cierva for his designs and which should only be used for his machines. However, it passed into the language to describe rotorcraft which derive their lift, or a substantial part of it, from an autorotating rotor system which has no direct power drive. This differs from a helicopter which, in vertical flight, obtains all its lift from a power-driven rotor.

The **C.6A**, using an Avro 504K fuselage and powered by a 82-kW (110-hp) Le Rhône 9Ja rotary engine flew in May 1924. Ailerons were mounted on outrigger spars and the four-blade 10.97-m (36-ft) diameter rotor had flapping hinges. By the use of a rope the rotor could be spun up to 60 rpm, shortening the take-off run, and when airborne rotational speed increased to 140 rpm. The first autogyro cross-country flight was made on 12 December 1924, between the two Madrid aerodromes of Cuatro Vientos and Getafé, a distance of 12 km (7.5 miles). A similarly-powered **C.6B** was also constructed.

Cierva brought the C.6A to England in October 1925 at the invitation of the Air Ministry's Director of Scientific Research and, following demonstrations at RAE Farnborough, the Ministry ordered several autogyros for evaluation by the RAF. The contract for their manufacture was given to A.V. Roe's Hamble factory, near Southampton. As a result of the British interest the Cierva Autogyro Company was formed in the UK to hold Cierva's patents and grant construction licences.

The designations **Avro Type 574** and **Type 575** were allocated to the Cierva **C.6C** and **C.6D** respectively; both were powered by the 97-kW (130-hp) Clerget engine, the first to fly being the C.6C on 19 June 1926, followed by the C.6D on 29 July. The C.6C was lost in a crash in January 1927, when a rotor blade detached at a height of 37 m (120 ft), but the pilot was only slightly hurt. The C.6D was the first two-seat autogyro, and in September it was flown in Berlin by Ernst Udet.

The number **C.7** was allocated to two Cierva-type autogyros built in Spain by Jorge Loring and flown at Cuatro Vientos in 1926. Powerplant was a 224-kW (300-hp) Hispano-Suiza and the C.7 was exhibited at the Madrid Air Show. Several **C.8** series, the most important up to that time, were built by Avro. The designation **C.8R (Avro Type 587)** was given to the C.6D after it had been modified with paddle-shaped rotor blades and

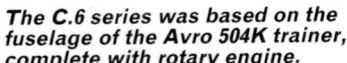

The C.6 series was based on the fuselage of the Avro 504K trainer, complete with rotary engine.

The fuselage of the Avro Avian IIIA is plainly recognisable as the basis for the C.17.

fitted with stub wings; it retained the 97-kW (130-hp) Clerget engine and in the course of development trials flew with both a three and a two-blade rotor. It was scrapped in 1929.

A two-seat Avro Type 552 fuselage with a 134-kW (180-hp) Wolseley Viper engine was fitted with a similar rotor system to the C.8R but had a dorsal fin; flown in 1926 it became the **C.8V (Avro Type 586)** and subsequent experiments took place with different landing gear configurations. It was rebuilt in 1930 as an Avro Type 552.

Favourable results from experiments persuaded the Air Ministry to order another prototype autogyro from Avro. Based on a Type 504N fuselage with a 134-kW (180-hp) Armstrong Siddeley Lynx engine, it became the **C.8L (Avro Type 611)** and piloted by H.J. Hinkler first flew at Hamble in 1927. Juan de la Cierva had then recently qualified as a

The most successful of the Cierva autogyros in commercial terms was the C.19, built by Avro as the Type 620.

pilot and Hinkler converted him on to a rotary-wing aircraft; thus Cierva was able to make the UK's first cross-country flight in this type of machine when he delivered the C.8L from the Hamble factory to RAE Farnborough on 30 September 1927. It spent almost three years there before crashing near Andover.

Air Commodore J.G. Weir, the Cierva company's chairman, ordered a civil **C.8L Mk II (Avro Type 617)** which not only differed in detail from the earlier model, but also introduced a short-span fixed wing and was powered by a Lynx IV engine. Flown at Hamble in May 1928, it subsequently took part in that year's King's Cup Air Race (surely the only autogyro ever to do so?) but retired when it ran short of fuel. A demonstration tour by this aircraft (G-EBYY) began when Cierva flew it to Paris in September 1928. It continued to Berlin via Brussels and returned via Amsterdam to Paris, where it remains now in the Musée de

The C.40 was a side-by-side two-seat trainer. It had the ability to spin the rotors on the ground at zero incidence allowing a vertical take-off.

The C.30 was based on the C.19 but used a new rotor control system with a hanging control column. The C.30P illustrated was built by Avro in 1934.

l'Air collection at Le Bourget airport. Orders were received for two C.8Ls – a **C.8L Mk III** for the Italian government, flown in September 1928, and a **C.8L Mk IV** (designated **C.8W**) for the US aircraft manufacturer Harold Pitcairn. This aircraft had a 168-kW (225-hp) Wright Whirlwind engine and made the first autogyro flight in the USA at Willow Grove in January 1929. Pitcairn bought the American rights and established the Pitcairn-Cierva Autogyro Co. in Pennsylvania; the C.8W is preserved in the Smithsonian Institution, Washington DC.

The next autogyro in the Cierva numerical sequence was the **C.9** this the first to exchange the pattern of using an existing fuselage. Two fuselages were built, a single-seater designated **Avro Type 576** and a two-seater **Avro Type 581**; the latter was used for the prototype of the famous Avian biplane. The C.9, powered by a 52-kW (70-hp) Armstrong Siddeley Genet engine, was flown at Hamble in September 1927 and was tested subsequently at RAW Farnborough with half-length untapered blade; it was presented to the Science Museum in 1930.

Parnall built two single-seat autogyros, neither of which was successful; the **C.10** of 1927 had a 52-kW (70-hp) Genet engine and stub wings; it crashed at RAE Farnborough during comparative trials against the Avro-built C.9. The Parnall **C.11** of 1928 was similar but powered by a 89-kW (120-hp) A.D.C. Airdisco engine. Cierva wrecked the machine at Yale during an attempt to take off before the rotor attained sufficient speed, but it was rebuilt with a simpler pylon and used later at Hamble as an instructional airframe.

The **C.12** built by Avro, was based on an Avian fuselage and flown in 1929. It was converted subsequently to single-seat configuration and mounted on Avian metal floats, becoming the first rotary-winged seaplane when it flew from Southampton Water in April 1930. Dubbed **Hydrogyro**, it was powered by a 75-kW (100-hp) Avro Alpha engine, but virtually nothing is known of its development or fate. In 1926 Short Brothers was given a specification 31/26, detailing a flying-boat autogyro designated **C.14**. This was to have had a metal hull and a 362-kW (485-hp) Bristol Jupiter engine, but tests in their seaplane tank showed problems with vibration and stability and the project was dropped.

The designations **C.15** and **C.16** are believed to have been projects, and the next Cierva number was the **C.17 (Avro Type 612)**, a smaller version of the C.8L Mk III with a 67-kW (90-hp) A.D.C. Cirrus III engine and based on the Avian IIIA fuselage. Flown by Cierva in October 1928 it was found to be underpowered and a second version, the **C.17 Mk II**, was built with a 75-kW (100-hp) Avro Alpha radial; this was equally unsuccessful and converted to an Avian in 1935.

The designation **C.18** was allocated to a two-seat cabin autogyro built in France by Weymann-Lepére in 1929. Powered by a 145-kW (195-hp) Salmson AC7 uncowled radial engine, the only example was imported into the UK by the Cierva Autogyro Company and registered to them in June 1929. It is believed to have been taken to the USA.

The most prolific of the early Cierva designs followed. This was the **C.19**, which was built in a number of variants, mainly by Avro. The first three of these, designated **Avro Type 620**, had been laid down as C.17 Mk IIs but were completed as **C.19 Mk I**. While Cierva had

developed the rotor systems for previous models, Avro's airframes had all been modified from existing fixed-wing types. The C.19 marked the beginning of the purpose-designed autogyro, and was the first to have automatic starting to get the rotor windmilling – a task undertaken previously with a length of rope! The three C.19 Mk Is had 60-kW (80-hp) Armstrong Siddeley Genet II engines. They were followed by three of the **C.19 Mk II**, one of the C.19 Mk IIA with an improved rotor head, six of the **C.19 Mk III**, 15 of the **C.19 Mk IVP** and one of the experimental **C.19 Mk V**; all had the 78-kW (105-hp) Genet Major 1 engine.

The British machines had varied careers; one Mk I and two Mk IIs were sold abroad, one of the latter going to the Pitcairn Autogyro Co. in December 1929. Two Mk IIIs went abroad, one to New Zealand, and two were delivered to the RAF. Mk IVPs were sold for use in Australia, Germany, Japan, Singapore, South Africa, Spain and Sweden.

A batch of C.19 Mk IVs licence-built by Focke-Wulf in Germany had 112-kW (150-hp) Siemens Sh.14B radial engines and carried the Cierva type number **C.20**; type **C.21** was allocated to a projected French C.19 Mk IV to be built by Lioré-et-Olivier; **C.22** and **C.23** are thought to have been projects only. The Cierva **C.24** two-seat autogyro was designed and built by the de Havilland Aircraft Co. with Cierva providing the rotor assemblies. Powered by a 89-kW (120-hp) de Havilland Gipsy III engine, the only example was first flown by Cierva in September 1931 with a three-blade rotor. Provided subsequently with a two-blade rotor, and thus becoming redesignated **C.26**, it completed a European tour in 1932; the aircraft has been preserved as a static exhibit.

The intervening **C.25** was one of the smallest autogyros, a single-seater built by Comper Aircraft and flown in early 1933. The fuselage appeared to be based on the Comper Swift airframe, with modified tail surface and low stub wings, and power was provided by a 63-kW (85-hp) Pobjoy Niagara R engine. Despite its high performance no orders were forthcoming.

In 1932 the French company Lioré-et-Olivier (LeO) acquired a Cierva licence and, basing their design on detailed studies of the C.19 Mk IV, built the **C.27**. Their designation was **CL.10**, referring to Cierva and the French designer, Georges Lepère. The C.27 was a two-seat cabin autogyro with no wings, powered by a 56-kW (75-hp) Pobjoy engine driving a three-blade cantilever

main rotor. Flown at Orly, it crashed after only a few flights.

Not strictly in chronological order, but convenient in the numbering sequence to mention at this point, is the **CL.20**, a two-seat cabin autogyro designed by Georges Lepère and built by Westland. This flew at Hanworth on 5 February 1935 with a 67-kW (90-hp) Pobjoy Niagara III radial engine mounted in an enclosed cowling. No further development took place by Westland, but it is interesting to note that in 1937 the Pitcairn Autogyro Co. in the USA proposed to build a version known as the **AC 35** with a 82-kW (110-hp) Pobjoy engine, while in 1956 Georges Lepère was said to be working on a private venture development of his 1934 design for the French Giravia Company. Designated **L.30**, it was to have three seats and a 108-kW (145-hp) Continental engine. Nothing is believed to have come of either project.

G. & J. Weir in Glasgow built a single-seat autogyro which flew in 1933. The Weir designation was **W-1** and, since it was built under a Cierva licence, the number **C.28** was allocated. Powered by a 30-kW (40-hp) Douglas Dryad engine, the autogyro had a two-blade rotor with mechanical spin-up. It flew in the early summer of 1933. Weir subsequently built other autogyros and the company's activities in this field were taken over by the Cierva company in 1943.

The idea of a larger than usual autogyro was tried by Westland with the **C.29** of 1934. A five-seat cabin aircraft with a 447-kW (600-hp) Armstrong Siddeley Panther II uncowled radial engine, it was designed by Westland with Cierva responsible for the rotor and its mechanism. Construction was of duralumin tubing, but ground resonance during tests prevented it from flying and Juan Cierva's death in an air crash (not an autogyro) caused the design to be abandoned.

The next designation in the sequence, **C.30**, is the best known, since production took place in several countries. Fol-

---

Cierva (Avro) Rota Mk I of No. 529 Squadron, RAF, operating on radar calibration duties during 1943-44.

The C.24 was built by de Havilland as a single example of the two-seat enclosed cockpit design. Here it is seen after modification to C.26 standard with a two-blade rotor.

lowing tests with a modified C.19 Mk V powered by a 75-kW (100-hp) Armstrong Siddeley Genet Major engine, and using a rotor head which could be tilted by use of a hanging control column, Avro commissioned National Flying Services to build a two-seat version which was designated **C.30**. It was flown in April 1933 and Avro obtained a manufacturing licence, subsequently allocating the designation **Type 671**. The prototype of an improved model, the **C.30P** with a 104-kW (140-hp) Genet Major, was built by Airwork at Heston in 1933 and featured folding rotor blades. Avro built three pre-production C.30Ps at Manchester (the Hamble factory had closed in 1932) and obtained a licence to build examples of the **C.30A** production model.

A batch of 12 was supplied to the RAF between August 1934 and May 1935, 10 of them serving initially with the School of Army Co-operation at Old Sarum under the service designation **Rota Mk 1**. Of the remaining two, one was tested with floats and the other was fitted experimentally with a Civet Major engine at RAE Farnborough. Civil C.30A production by Avro totalled 66, a number going to export customers but many to UK purchasers. When war came in 1939, 13 were impressed into service alongside the surviving RAF aircraft, eventually serving with No. 529 Squadron at Halton where their duties included radar calibration. A number survived the war to return to civil ownership after the war, and at least six have been preserved.

Other European countries which built the C.30A included France, where Lioré-et-Olivier produced 25 designated **LeO C301**; these had 130-kW (175-hp) Salmson 9Ne engines, and one survives in the

Musée de l'Air at Le Bourget Airport, Paris. Focke-Wulf built 40 C.30As with 112-kW (150-hp) Siemens Sh.14B engines.

Two Cierva projects came next in the sequence; the **C.31** of 1934 was to have been a two-seat coupé autogyro with retractable landing gear and powered by a 287-kW (385-hp) Napier Rapier IV engine to provide an estimated speed of 332 km/h (206 mph), while the similar **C.322** would have had a 149-kW (200-hp) de Havilland DH Gipsy Six engine and a speed of 290 km/h (180 mph). An Avro project, the **Type 665**, envisaged the combination of a four-seat Commodore biplane fuselage with a three-blade rotor, retaining the biplane's 179-kW (240-hp) Armstrong Siddeley Lynx IVC

engine; the designation **C.33** was allocated but the conversion was not completed.

The **C.34** of 1937 was built under licence by the Société Nationale de Constructions Aéronautiques du Sud Est (SNCASE) and had a 261-kW (350-hp) Gnome-Rhône K7 engine. The need for so much power in a two-seat autogyro was the result of a loaded weight of 2,300 kg (5,070 lb).

The **C.35**, **C.36** and **C.38** appear to have been projects, and the **C.37** was a twin-engine cabin autogyro, proposed by Avro as the **Type 668**, but which was not built. The **C.39** was a Cierva project for a 2/3-seat fleet spotter to Specification 22/38 for the Fleet Air Arm. This would have had a three-blade rotor

and a 447-kW (600-hp) Rolls-Royce Kestrel engine.

The last Cierva number was **C.40**; this was a two-seat side-by-side development of the C.30 with wooden fuselage and an internal metal structure. Powerplant was the 130-kW (175-hp) Salmson 9Ng uncowled radial engine, and nine C.40s were assembled by the British Aircraft Manufacturing Co. at Hanworth in 1938. An improved rotor head, which had been tried out on a C.30, enabled the autogyro to make a direct take-off. This was accomplished by speeding up the rotor beyond take-off revolutions with the blades at zero incidence, then putting them into positive pitch to create lift. Seven of the C.40s went to the RAF, the remaining two

being civil registered before they were impressed for military service.

Specification
Cierva C.30A
Type: utility autogyro
Powerplant: one 104-kW (140-hp) Armstrong Siddeley Genet Major IA radial piston engine
Performance: maximum speed 177 km/h (110 mph); cruising speed 153 km/h (95 mph); range 459 km (285 miles)
Weights empty 553 kg (1,220 lb); maximum take-off 816 kg (1,880 lb)
Dimensions: rotor diameter 11.28 m (37 ft 0 in); lenbgth 6.01 m (19 ft 8½ in); height 3.38 m (11 ft 1 in); rotor disc area 99.89 m² (1,075 sq ft)

Cierva W.11

The designation **W.10** was allocated to a project for a 4/5-seat single-engine helicopter, but the **W.11 Air Horse** was the largest helicopter in the world when it first flew on 7 December 1948. A single Rolls-Royce Merlin 24 engine of 1208 kW (1,620 hp) was mounted in the fuselage to drive three large three-blade rotors mounted on outriggers projecting from the square fuselage. Twin fins were carried at the end of a mid-mounted tailplane on the rear fuselage and there was accommodation for a crew of three.

As a passenger aircraft the W.11 would have carried 24, but other roles that were envisaged included air ambulance, aerial crane and crop sprayer. In September 1945 Pest Control Ltd had discussed the last possibility with Cierva and the W.11 design was modified to meet this role. As a result, Cierva received a development contract for one W.11 in July 1946, drafted to Specification E.19/46, and a second was ordered in early 1947. Cunliffe-Owen Aircraft Ltd were contracted to build the two aircraft at Southampton/Eastleigh Airport under the technical and financial control of the Cierva company.

With a payload of 3048 kg (6,720 lb) of insecticide the W.11 would have made an impressive sprayer, and following the first flight in December 1948 subsequent tests were promising. The Colonial Office made a grant of £45,000 to assist in the development costs since the type offered prospects of overseas use in the spraying role (total Ministry of Supply development costs were estimated at £350,000), but before the second W.11 had flown the first crashed on 13 June 1950, killing the three flight test crew members; the second W.11 never flew and was scrapped in 1960. The designation **W.11T** was allocated to a project for an enlarged W.11 with two 1208-kW (1,620-hp) Rolls-Royce Merlin 502 engines and the **W.12** was a projected freighter development with Rolls-Royce Dart turboprops. Neither of these materialised since by that time Cierva, not having used the number W.13, was involved in development of the **W.14** which became the Skeeter and was built by Saunders-Roe Ltd.

Specification
Type: single-engine three-rotor helicopter
Powerplant: one 1208-kW (1,620-hp) Rolls-Royce Merlin 24 inline piston engine

Performance: maximum speed 225 km/h (140 mph); cruising speed 153 km/h (140 mph); service ceiling 8535 m (28,000 ft); range with maximum fuel 531 km (330 miles)
Weights: empty equipped 5507 kg (12,140 lb); maximum take-off 7938 kg (17,500 lb)
Dimensions: rotor diameter (each) 14.33 m (47 ft 0 in); length, rotors

The W.11 was a design inherited by Cierva when it took over Weir in 1945. Seen here is the first prototype, which crashed fatally on 13 June 1950.

turning 27.00 m (88 ft 7 in); width overall, rotors turning 28.96 m (95 ft 0 in); height 5.41 m (17 ft 9 in); total rotor disc area 483.53 m² (5,205 sq ft)

Commonwealth Aircraft CA-1 Wirraway

The Commonwealth Aircraft Corporation Pty Ltd was formed in 1936 as the result of an Australian government scheme to establish an aircraft industry and make the country independent of outside suppliers. A number of wealthy industrial firms contributed to the financing of the company and, following a visit by an Air Board Technical Commission to the USA in 1936, negotiations were concluded for licence-manufacture of the North American NA-16 two-seat general-purpose monoplane and its Pratt & Whitney Wasp engine. Tugan Aircraft Ltd was taken over by Commonwealth and its chief designer, Wing Commander Lawrence Wackett, became general manager of the new company. An initial order was placed by the RAAF for 40 NA-33s, as the licence-built version was designated. The manufacturer's designation was **Commonwealth Aircraft CA-1**, being the first Commonwealth aircraft, and the name **Wirraway** was chosen.

The first Australian-built aircraft flew at Melbourne on 27 March 1939, and within four months the RAAF had accepted the first three aircraft. The outbreak of war in Europe led to increased orders for Wirraways, and the British government also financed the purchase

Commonwealth Aircraft CA-5 Wirraway of No. 4 Squadron, Royal Australian Air Force, based in New Guinea during December 1942.

of aircraft for the Empire Air Training Scheme in Australia. By June 1942 Commonwealth had built 620, and the type continued in limited production until the 755th and last aircraft was delivered in 1946. There were a number of Commonwealth designations for the Wirraway; these, together with the number built, were as follows: **CA-1** (40), **CA-3** (60), **CA-5** (32), **CA-7** (100), **CA-8** (200), **CA-9** (188) and **CA-16** (135). The **CA-10** was to have been a bomber version and the **CA-10A** a dive-bomber,

but both were cancelled. The designation **CA-20** was allocated to Wirraways converted for use by the Royal Australian Navy in the post-war training role.

Wirraways saw service on convoy patrol work from Darwin, in Malaya, New Britain and New Guinea before being replaced by more warlike equipment, and by mid-1943 most first-line Wirraway squadrons had re-equipped with CAC Boomerangs. As they were withdrawn from service almost 400 Wirraways were put into long-term storage;

eventually a number of these were used as the basis for the CA-28 Ceres agricultural aircraft.

Specification
Type: two-seat trainer and light bomber
Powerplant: one CAC-built 447-kW (600-hp) Pratt & Whitney Wasp R-1340 S1H1-G radial piston engine
Performance: maximum speed 354 km/h (220 mph) at 1525 m

(5,000 ft); maximum cruising speed 293 km/h (182 mph) at 1525 m (5,000 ft); service ceiling 7010 m (23,000 ft); range with maximum fuel 1159 km (720 miles)

Weights empty equipped 1811 kg (3,992 lb); maximum take-off 2991 kg (6,595 lb)
Dimensions: span 13.11 m (43 ft 0 in);

length 8.48 m (27 ft 10 in); height 2.66 m (8 ft 8¾ in); wing area 23.76 m² (255.7 sq ft)
Armament: two fixed forward-firing

7.7-mm (0.303-in) Vickers Mk V machine-guns and a similar weapon in the rear cockpit, plus up to 454 kg (1,000 lb) of bombs

Commonwealth Aircraft CA-12, CA-13, CA-14 and CA-19

Japan's entry into World War II found Australia ill-prepared, the only fighters on RAAF strength being a few obsolescent Brewster Buffaloes based in Malaya. However, the licence under which CAC built the Wirraway permitted modifications to the design and Lawrence Wackett used that aircraft's entire wing, landing gear and tail unit married to a new fuselage to produce a single-seat fighter, the **Commonwealth Aircraft CA-12**, later named **Boomerang Mk I**. An order was placed for 105 in February 1942, and because many Wirraway components were used the prototype was built in only three months, flying for the first time on 29 May.

Production of this first batch was completed in June 1943, and a second batch of 95 aircraft designated **CA-13 Boomerang Mk II** followed, these incorporating a number of minor modifications. A single **CA-14** was built with a General Electric turbocharger to improve high-altitude performance; it was modified later as the **CA-14A** to have a square fin and rudder, but availability of the faster Spitfire Mk VIIIs rendered these improvements unnecessary. The final production batch consisted of 49 designated **CA-19 Boomerang Mk II**, again with minor modifications, and the last of these was delivered in February 1945.

Boomerangs entered service in October 1942 when the RAAF's No. 2 Operational Training Unit at Mildura, Victoria, received its first aircraft. The Boomerang became operational with No. 84 Squadron, which was the first to receive the new fighters, in April 1943; initial contact with Japanese bombers was made during the following month when No. 85 Squadron equipped with Boomerangs. Other squadrons followed, including Nos 4 and 5, where Boomerangs replaced Wirraways in the army co-operation role. As higher-performance fighters became available, the Boomerangs were replaced, having proved to be extremely manoeuvrable, tough and blessed with a rapid rate of climb. They had acquitted themselves well in roles for which they were not designed and were remembered with affection by their pilots. Only one Boomerang, a CA-12, survives in a museum.

Specification
CAC CA-13 Boomerang Mk II
Type: single-seat fighter
Powerplant: one 895-kW (1,200-hp)

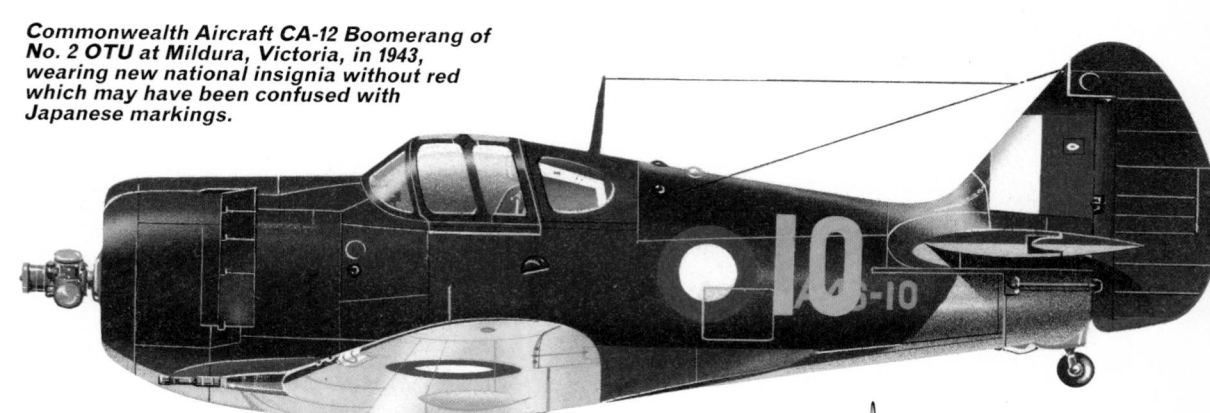

Commonwealth Aircraft CA-12 Boomerang of No. 2 Operational Training Unit, RAAF, based at Port Pirie, South Australia in October 1942.

A46-2

Commonwealth Aircraft CA-12 Boomerang of No. 2 OTU at Mildura, Victoria, in 1943, wearing new national insignia without red which may have been confused with Japanese markings.

10
A46-10

Pratt & Whitney R-1830-S3C4-G Twin Wasp radial piston engine
Performance: maximum speed 491 km/h (305 mph) at 4725 m (15,500 ft); initial climb rate 896 m (2,940 ft) per minute; service ceiling 10365 m (34,000 ft); range with maximum fuel 2575 km (1,600 miles)
Weights empty equipped 2437 kg (5,373 lb); maximum take-off 3742 kg (8,249 lb)
Dimensions: span 10.97 m (36 ft 0 in); length 7.77 m (25 ft 6 in); height 2.92 m (9 ft 7 in); wing area 20.90 m² (225.0 sq ft)
Armament: four 7.7-mm (0.303-in) Browning machine-guns and two 20-mm Hispano cannon in wings

Commonwealth Aircraft CA-14 Boomerang.

Comper C.L.A.7 Swift

In March 1929 the Comper Aircraft Company was formed by Flight Lieutenant Nicholas Comper, formerly of the RAF, to build an aircraft of his own design. Designated **Comper C.L.A.7** and named **Swift**, the prototype (G-AARX) made a first flight at Brooklands on 17 May 1930. A small and graceful single-seat aircraft for its period, the Swift was a braced high-wing monoplane of wooden construction, with fabric and plywood covering. The wing was mounted directly on top of the fuselage and the pilot, in an open cockpit immediately aft of its trailing edge, had a clear view forward. The

tail unit was a conventional braced structure and the landing gear of fixed tailskid type. Power for the prototype was provided by a 30-kW (40-hp) A.B.C. Scorpion piston engine.

Following successful testing of the prototype, seven more Swifts were completed during 1930, each powered by a 37-kW (50-hp) Salmson AD9 radial engine. A trial installation of a Pobjoy P prototype radial engine on the seventh of these production aircraft in preparation for an air race resulted in this unit being chosen as the standard engine, and most of the early construction

G-ABUS

The Swift was one of the UK's most delightful lightplanes, and it was widely raced. The Pobjoy engine was geared to reduce propeller revs.

Swifts were re-engined subsequently with the Pobjoy R. Production of the standard Swift ran to a total of 41, followed by three with de Havilland Gipsy engines prepared especially for air racing. Two had the 89-kW (120-hp) Gipsy III and one a 97-kW (130-hp) Gipsy Major.

Four Swifts remain on the British civil aircraft register but only two, both built in 1932, are airworthy, G-ABUU and G-ACTF, the latter currently on view at the Brooklands Museum.

Specification
Type: single-seat sporting aircraft

Powerplant: one 56-kW (75-hp) Pobjoy R radial piston engine
Performance: maximum speed 225 km/h (140 mph); cruising speed 193 km/h (120 mph); service ceiling 6705 m (22,000 ft); range 611 km (380 miles)
Weights: empty 245 kg (540 lb);

maximum take-off 447 kg (985 lb)
Dimensions: span 7.32 m (24 ft 0 in); length 5.40 m (17 ft 8½ in); height 1.61 m (5 ft 3½ in); wing area 8.36 m² (90.0 sq ft)

Comte AC-1

The Swiss company Flugzeugbau A Comte, established at Hargen, near Zurich, began aircraft production in the early 1920s by licence-construction of German designs. The company's first original venture was the **Comte AC-1**, developed privately to meet a Swiss Fliegertruppe requirement for a single-seat fighter. The prototype, flown for the first time on 2 April 1927, was of similar configuration to the French Dewoitine D.9, a braced high-wing monoplane with fixed tailskid type landing gear. Basic construction was of metal, with the wing and tail surfaces fabric-covered, but the fuselage had light alloy skins. Power was provided by a Gnome-Rhône radial engine.

Testing and evaluation by the Fliegertruppe resulted in the prototype being acquired, but no further production aircraft were ordered. Subsequently the AC-1 had its wing of Comte design replaced by one from a Dewoitine D.L. and in this configuration it was used to establish a Swiss altitude record on 19 November 1928.

Comte AC-1 of the Fliegertruppe (Swiss air arm) in 1927

Specification
Type: single-seat fighter
Powerplant: one 420-hp (313-kW) Gnome-Rhône Jupiter IX radial piston engine
Performance: maximum speed 152 mph (245 km/h); range 280 miles (450 km)
Weights: empty 2,028 lb (920 kg); maximum take-off 2,910 lb (1320 kg)

Dimensions: span 39 ft 4½ in (12 m); length 23 ft 4¾ in (7.13 m); height 10 ft 2¾ in (3.12 m); wing area 258.34 sq ft (24 m²)
Armament: (intended) two forward-firing machine-guns

Comte AC-4 Gentleman

Under the designation **Comte AC-4 Gentleman**, the company produced in 1927 the prototype of a two-seat cabin monoplane intended for sporting or training purposes. Of braced high-wing configuration it was of mixed construction, fabric-covered, with fixed tailskid type landing gear. Slightly staggered side-by-side seating for two was provided in an enclosed cabin, with dual controls optional, and power was provided by a 75-hp (56-kW) Cirrus II inline engine. Later production examples had the more powerful Cirrus Hermes or Genet Major.

Specification
Type: two-seat sport/training aircraft
Powerplant: one 115-hp (86-kW) Cirrus Hermes inline piston engine
Performance: maximum speed 109 mph (175 km/h); cruising speed 87 mph (140 km/h); service ceiling 13,125 ft (4000 m); range 435 miles (700 km)
Weights: empty 1,102 lb (500 kg); maximum take-off 1,764 lb (800 kg)
Dimensions: span 39 ft 9½ in (12.13 m); length 26 ft 5 in (8.05 m); height 9 ft 6 in (2.9 m); wing area 215.29 sq ft (20 m²)

The second series of Comte Gentleman light aircraft, numbering five in all, was designated AC-4B and could be differentiated from the earlier series by its Genet major radial engine. However, this was sometimes replaced by the Cirrus Hermes.

Conroy Aircraft Corporation

Founded by John M. Conroy, who had been responsible for development of the outsize Pregnant Guppy and its successor for Aero Spacelines Inc., the Conroy Aircraft Corporation intended to specialise in the development and conversion of existing aircraft. Its work has included the **Conroy/Douglas Turbo Three**, a convertion of the remarkable DC-3 to turboprop powerplant. This involved the installation of two 1193-kW (1,600-shp) Rolls-Royce RDa.6 Dart Mk 510 turboprops in new nacelles, each driving a Rotol four-blade propeller. The initial Turbo Three conversion was flown for the first time on 13 May 1969.

Work on the DC-3 was followed by a new large-capacity conversion of a Canadair CL-44 long-range freighter. To achieve this the upper half of the standard fuselage was removed, being replaced by a new pressurised structure

that provided a maximum internal height of 4.24 m (13 ft 11 in), almost doubling the volume of the cargo compartment. Designated **Conroy/Canadair CL-44-0**, the original conversion was flown for the first time on 26 November 1969 and since October 1982 has been operated by HeavyLift Cargo Airlines from their base at Stansted.

Turning to a very much smaller aircraft, Conroy then designed a turboprop conversion for the Cessna Model 337 Super Skymaster. This was a more extensive job, involving deletion of the Model 337's rear engine, the provision

of an aft fuselage extension virtually to double the volume of the cabin, and installation of a 429-kW (575-shp) Garrett TPE331-25A turboprop in the fuselage nose in place of the standard piston engine. At the same time the converted Cessna 337 was given STOL capability by incorporation of the high-lift system developed by the Robertson Aircraft Corporation for the Super Skymaster, accounting for the new name of **Stolifter** applied by Conroy to the converted aircraft.

Conroy also developed a turboprop conversion for the Grumman HU-16A Albatross amphibian called the Turbo Albatross, this involved the installation of two Rolls-Royce RDa.6 Dart Mk 510 turboprops complete with the cowling and engine mounting designed for the Vickers Viscount Series 500. First flown in its new form on 25 February 1970, the ensuing flight test programme showed that the lighter-weight but more powerful engines had improved performance of the aircraft by more than 25 per cent.

Conroy's most ambitious conversion was the single CL-44-0, which almost doubled the internal capacity. The swing-tail loading was retained, and it now serves with HeavyLift.

Consolidated biplane trainers
to
Consolidated P2Y

Consolidated biplane trainers

Consolidated Aircraft Corporation was formed at Buffalo, New York in 1923, the successor to the Dayton-Wright Airplane Company from which it acquired design rights, a production contract for the TW-3 side-by-side two-seat primary trainer and the services of chief engineer Colonel Virginius E. Clark. The TW-3 was developed as the **Consolidated PT-1** with tandem seating, revised tail surfaces and a 134-kW (180-hp) Wright E engine which was uncowled in all but the prototype. A total of 221 was built and one airframe, fitted with a Wright J-5 radial of 164 kW (220 hp), was designated **YPT-2**.

Variants

NY-1: US Navy interest in the PT-1 resulted in development of the NY-1, which incorporated structural changes, principally to permit the installation when required of a single under-fuselage float and wingtip stabilising floats; the fin and rudder were also increased in area for floatplane operations; power was supplied initially by a 149-kW (200-hp) J-4 series Wright Whirlwind, later aircraft being fitted with a 164-kW (220-hp) and with NY-2 wings under the designation **NY-1B; NY-1A** was the designation applied to NY-1s converted in service for use as gunnery trainers; an order for 40 NY-1s was placed early in 1926 and production eventually totalled 76

NY-2: in order to reduce the wing loading of the NY-1, Consolidated introduced wings increased in span from 10.52 m (34 ft 6 in) to 12.19 m (40 ft); the resulting weight penalty slightly reduced performance although the Wright J-5 was retained, but the aircraft was the subject of production contracts for 211 examples, 25 of which were **NY-2A** examples with fixed machine-gun mountings in the forward cockpit for pilot gunnery training and swivel-mounted weapons in the rear cockpit for observer training; in 1929 one NY-2 airframe was fitted with a Wright R-790-A radial to become the **N3Y-1**; the NY-2 was the **Consolidated Model 12**

NY-3: 20 aircraft similar to the NY-2 but each powered by a 179-kW (240-hp) Wright R-760-94 radial engine

PT-3: the Wright J-5 was retained for the PT-3, which featured further revision of the tail surfaces; production comprised 130 PT-3s and 120 of the

10 Y1PT-12 aircraft featured the uprated Wasp Junior engine, and were later redesignated BT-7 to reflect a change of role from primary to basic training.

slightly modified **PT-3A**; deliveries to the US Army Air Corps began in 1928, allowing the PT-1s to be transferred to National Guard units; the PT-3 was the first USAAC aircraft to be used for experiments with blind-flying hoods, and had the company designation **Model 12 Husky**

XPT-4: projected PT-3 with an experimental Fairchild-Caminez engine; not built

Consolidated Model 21-A (N4Y-1) of the US Coast Guard in 1933

XPT-5: one airframe fitted in 1929 with a 127-kW (170-hp) Curtiss Challenger six-cylinder radial engine; later converted back to PT-3 standard

O-17: developed in parallel with the PT-3, the O-17 featured increased fuel capacity, a more streamlined fuselage, balanced elevators and modified landing gear with oleo shock-absorbers and brakes; the rear cockpit had a detachable fairing to accept a Scarff gun ring, converting the aircraft from pilot trainer to observer trainer; 29 were built and the type was also offered on the civil market as the **Courier**

XPT-8: one airframe with a 168-kW (225-hp) Packard diesel engine was flown under this designation

PT-11: this was an aerodynamically cleaned-up development (**Consolidated Model 21**) of the PT-3 with, in particular, curved instead of angular tail surfaces; the first four aircraft, designated **YPT-11**, were powered by the 123-kW (165-hp)

Continental R-545-1 engine, but the last of them was later re-engined with a Curtiss Challenger R-600 to become the **PT-11A** and then with a 164-kW (220-hp) Avco Lycoming YR-680-1 under the designation **PT-11C**; the first two YPT-11s were converted to **PT-11D** standard with 149-kW (200-hp) R-680A engines, as were five of the **YPT-11B** model with Kinner YR-720-1 engines; new construction PT-11Ds totalled 21

PT-12: 10 aircraft similar to the PT-11 but with 224-kW (300-hp) Pratt & Whitney Wasp Junior R-985A radials

N4Y: single US Coast Guard PT-11, originally with a Wright J-6-5 engine, but converted later by the installation of a 164-kW (220-hp) Avco Lycoming R-680 which also powered three N4Ys purchased by the US Navy under the designation **N4Y-1**

BT-6: the third YPT-11 was

redesignated BT-6 when fitted with a 224-kW (300-hp) Wright R-975 engine

BT-7: later designation allocated to 10 examples of the **Y1PT-12** with 224-kW (300-hp) Pratt & Whitney Wasp Junior R-985A engines and minor equipment changes

Specification
Consolidated PT-11D

Type: two-seat primary trainer
Powerplant: one 149-kW (200-hp) Lycoming R-680A radial piston engine
Performance: maximum speed 190 km/h (118 mph); service ceiling 4175 m (13,700 ft); endurance 3 hours
Weights: empty 870 kg (1,918 lb); maximum take-off 1173 kg (2,585 lb)
Dimensions: span 9.63 m (31 ft 7 in); length 8.20 m (26 ft 11 in); height 2.95 m (9 ft 8 in); wing area 26.01 m^2 (280.0 sq ft)

Precursor of the Wasp Junior-engined BT-7 was this XBT-937 (Consolidated Model 21-C), which featured a notably clean installation for the 224-kW (300-hp) Pratt & Whitney radial.

Inspired by Curtiss practice before World War I, Consolidated favoured the single main float/twin balance float arrangement. Shown is an NY-2 of Training Squadron VN-15.

Consolidated (Model 32) B-24 Liberator

Readers with memories of World War II aircraft will recall the big, ugly, seemingly slow **Consolidated B-24 Liberator**. In the European theatre, of course, it was much over-shadowed by the Boeing B-17 Flying Fortress, and to those with no detailed knowledge of military aircraft it often comes as something of a shock to learn that not only was Consolidated's Liberator built in considerably greater numbers than the B-17, but it was the most extensively produced of the USA's wartime aircraft.

The origins of the Liberator stretch back to the early/mid-1930s, an era in which projects such as the Boeing XB-15 and Douglas XB-19, and development of the B-17, brought a far wider knowledge and appreciation of the 'big bomber'. The Liberator represents the next generation, its evolution spurred by the tense political situation in Europe and the growing threat of Japanese militancy. In January 1939 the US Army Air Corps invited Consolidated to prepare a design study for a heavy bomber with performance superior to that of the B-17.

Consolidated wasted little time in submitting a design proposal, identifying it as the **Consolidated Model 32** and, as long range was paramount, it was designed round the Davis wing, first introduced on the company's Model 31 flying-boat design, of which a prototype was then nearing completion. In reaching a decision to go ahead with prototype construction of the Model 32, the US Army almost matched the speed set by Consolidated, and in awarding the contract on 30 March 1939 they maintained the tempo, insisting that construction of the prototype, designated **XB-24**, must be completed by the end of the year. This was achieved by the company, with the first flight being made on 29 December 1939.

In size the XB-24 was marginally smaller than the Fortress except in span; in terms of wing area that of the XB-24 was approximately 26 per cent less, emphasising the high aspect ratio of the Davis wing. To ensure maximum capacity within the fuselage structure, the wing was high-mounted in shoulder-wing configuration, and to provide good low-speed handling characteristics and an acceptable landing speed, wide-span Fowler-type trailing-edge flaps were fitted. Construction of the fuselage was conventional, but deep in section to allow for installation of a bomb bay which could accommodate up to 3629 kg (8,000 lb) of bombs stowed vertically. The bay was divided into two sections by the fuselage keel beam, this being utilised to provide a catwalk for crew transition between the fore and aft sections of the fuselage. The most unusual feature of the bomb-bay was the provision of unique 'roller shutter' doors which retracted within the fuselage when opened for attack, causing less drag than conventional bomb-bay doors. The tail unit, with its easily recognisable oval-shaped endplate fins and rudders, was generally similar to that developed for the Model 31 flying-boat. Retractable tricycle landing gear and four wing-mounted 895-kW (1,200-hp) Pratt & Whitney R-1830-33 Twin Wasp engines completed the configuration.

Even before the prototype had flown, Consolidated had begun to receive orders for its new bomber. These included seven of the service test **YB-24** and 36 of the initial production **B-24A** models for the USAAC, and 120 aircraft 'off the drawing board' for a French pur-

chasing mission. Early flight tests proved successful, but to meet the USAAC specification some development was necessary to achieve higher speed; however, there was no doubt that the XB-24 was able to demonstrate excellent long-range capability. Furthermore, the large-volume fuselage lent itself to adaptation to fulfil other roles and it was this versatility combined with long range that was the key to success for the B-24.

The XB-24 was followed during 1940 by the seven YB-24s for service trials, and these differed from the prototype by the provision of pneumatic de-icing boots for the leading-edges of wings, tailplane and fins. By the time that the first production aircraft began to come off the line at San Diego, France had already capitulated, and the aircraft of the French order were completed to British requirements, as specified in an order for 164 which had been placed soon after that of 120 for France: the French order was later transferred to Britain.

The RAF allocated the name Liberator to its new bomber, this being adopted later by the USAAF, and the first of these (AM258) flew for the first time on 17 January 1941. They were, however, designated **LB-30A** by Consolidated, indicating Liberator to British specification, and the first six of these reached the UK during March 1941, flown directly across the North Atlantic. These initial aircraft were used as unarmed transports by BOAC, and later by RAF Ferry Command. The next batch, received in mid-1941, joined the RAF with the designation **Liberator Mk I** for service with Coastal Command and were modified in the UK to equip them with an early form of 'ASV' (Air-to-Surface Vessel) radar, and to increase the standard armament of five 7.72-mm (0.3-in) machine-guns to include an underfuselage gun pack, forward of the bomb bay, housing four 20-mm cannon. Liberator Mk Is began to equip No. 120 Squadron of Coastal Command in June 1941, and were the first RAF aircraft with the range and endurance to close the 'Atlantic Gap', that area of the ocean in which, until that time, sea convoys were beyond the range of air support from either North America or Great Britain.

In that same month, the USAAF began to receive its first B-24As and these, duplicating the role of the LB-30As in the UK, were allocated first to equip the Air Corps Ferrying Command, operating similar services across the North Atlantic as those of RAF Ferry Command. The first true operational bomber version, however, was the **Liberator Mk II (Consolidated LB-30)**, for which there was no USAAF equivalent. It differed from the Liberator Mk I primarily by having the fuselage nose extended 0.79 m (2 ft 7 in) by the insertion of a 'plug', by accommodating a maximum crew of 10 and by the installation of Boulton Paul power-operated turrets, each housing four 7.7-mm (0.303-in) machine-guns in mid-upper and rear fuselage positions. The RAF received 139 of this version and when Nos 159 and 160 Squadrons began operations with their Liberators in the Middle East in June 1942, they were the first to deploy these aircraft in a bombing role. One aircraft of

Marking a considerable advance, the XPB4Y-2 Privateer featured a large single fin in place of the Liberator's endplates.

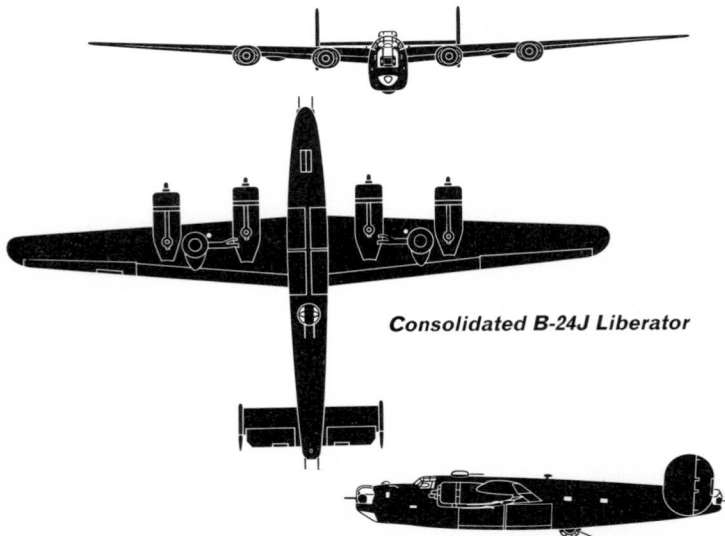

Consolidated B-24J Liberator

this batch (AL504) became the personal transport of Britain's prime minister, Winston Churchill, operated under the name *Commando*.

Meanwhile, the XB-24 prototype had been modified to a new **XB-24B** standard, introducing self-sealing fuel tanks and armour, but the most significant improvement was the installation of turbocharged R-1830-41 engines. This resulted in the second of the Liberator's easily identifiable features, oval-shaped nacelles, entailed by the relocation of the oil coolers in the sides of the front cowlings. With the introduction of these features, plus dorsal and tail turrets each with two 12.7-mm (0.5-in) machine-guns to supplement the original hand-held guns in beam and nose positions, nine aircraft were produced for the USAAF with the designation **B-24C**.

They were followed by the **B-24D**, the first major production variant and the first to be employed operationally by USAAF bomber squadrons. This differed initially by the installation of R-1830-43 engines, but subsequent production batches introduced progressive changes in armament, provision of auxiliary fuel in the outer wings and bomb bay, increases in gross weight and bomb-load, and in some late production examples external bomb racks below the inner wing for the carriage of two 1814-kg (4,000-lb) bombs. In RAF service the B-24D was designated **Liberator Mk III: Liberator Mk IIIA** identified

similar aircraft supplied under Lend-Lease with US armament and equipment. Most Liberator Mk III/IIIAs served with Coastal Command, eventually equipping 12 squadrons. A total of 122 was modified extensively in the UK, receiving ASV radar equipment including chin and retractable ventral radomes, a Leigh Light for the illumination of targets at night (especially surfaced U-boats), increased fuel capacity, but reduced armament, armour and weapon load. These were designated **Liberator GR. Mk V**. Some were provided with small stub wings on the forward fuselage to carry eight rocket projectiles. The USAAF also operated B-24Ds in an anti-submarine role, and in 1942 the US Navy began to receive small numbers of this version under the designation **PB4Y-1**. However, at the end of August 1943 the USAAF disbanded its Anti-Submarine Command, handing over its aircraft to the US Navy in exchange for an equivalent number of aircraft of bomber configuration to be produced against outstanding US Navy orders. These ex-USAAF B-24s, which were equipped with ASV radar, were also designated PB4Y-1 by the US Navy. This service later acquired the specially-developed **PB4Y-2 Privateer**, which introduced a new tail unit with a single tall fin and rudder, a lengthened forward fuselage, changes in the armament to provde a maximum of 12 12.7-mm (0.5-in) machine-guns, and the installation of

Pratt & Whitney R-1830-94 Twin Wasp engines without turbochargers.

The deployment of USAAF B-24Ds in the Middle East began in June 1942, one of the first operations being launched by 13 aircraft against the Romanian oilfields at Ploesti on 11/12 June 1942. All 13 aircraft completed what the USAAF described as 'an unsuccessful attack', its only success being to alert the defences of their vulnerability. Consequently, it was a very different story on 1 August 1943 when units of the 8th and 9th Air Forces sent 177 B-24s against the same target. Although rather more successful in terms of damage caused, of the force which set out from Benghazi 55 Liberators were lost, 53 damaged, and 440 crew killed or posted missing.

By that time, of course, B-24s were being built at an enormous rate, by Consolidated at San Diego and Fort Worth, Douglas at Tulsa, and Ford with a specially built new plant at Willow Run. In mid-1942 the first transport variants began to appear, with nose and tail gun positions deleted, a large cargo door installed in the port side of the fuselage, and accommodation provided for passengers or cargo. The USAAF acquired 276 under the designation **C-87** with accommodation for a crew of five and 20 passengers; 24 similar aircraft, but provided with side windows, served with RAF Transport Command as the **Liberator C. Mk VII** and examples flown by the US Navy were designated **RY-2**. Similar aircraft, but with R-1830-45 engines and equipped as VIP transports, were identified as **RY-1** and **C-87A** by the US Navy and USAAF respectively. The US Navy also acquired 46 of a transport variant designated **RY-3**, and 27 similar aircraft were delivered in early 1945 for use by RAF Transport Command. One special logistics version was the **C-109** fuel tanker, used to ferry 10977 litres (2,900 US gal) of aviation fuel per load over the Himalayan 'hump', to supply Boeing B-29 Superfortresses operating from forward bases in China. An **XF-7** prototype of a reconnaissance version was also produced in 1943, with bomb racks removed and extra fuel

tanks provided in the forward section of the bomb bay. This retained the normal defensive armament, and could also accommodate up to 11 cameras. F-7s were used extensively in the Pacific theatre, and later versions included the **F-7A** and **F-7B** with differing camera installations.

The first production aircraft to come from the Ford plant at Willow Run was the **B-24E**, generally similar to the B-24D except for different propellers and minor detail changes, and this version was built also by Consolidated and Douglas, some having R-1830-65 engines. There followed the **B-24G**, all but the first 25 of which introduced an upper nose turret and had the fuselage nose lengthened by 0.25 m (10 in). These came from a new production line operated by North American Aviation at Dallas, Texas. Similar aircraft produced by Consolidated at Fort Worth, by Douglas and by Ford were designated **B-24H**.

The major production variant was the **B-24J** (6,678 built), which came from all five production lines, and which differed from the B-24H in only minor details. B-24H and B-24Js supplied to the RAF under Lend-Lease were designated **Liberator GR. Mk VI** when equipped for ASW/maritime reconnaissance by Coastal Command, or **Liberator B. Mk VI** when used as a heavy bomber in the Middle East and Far East. Those used by the US Navy were identified as the PB4Y-1.

The final production versions were the **B-24L**, similar to the B-24D with the tail turret replaced by two manually controlled 12.7-mm (0.5-in) machine-guns, of which Consolidated San Diego built 417 and Ford 1,250; and the **B-24M** which differed from the B-24J in having a different tail turret. Convair built 916 of this latter version at San Diego and Ford another 1,677. Odd variants included a single B-24D provided with an experimental thermal de-icing system as the **XB-24F**; the **XB-24K** prototype of the single vertical tail version which it was intended should be produced in large numbers as the B-24N, although only the

XB-24N prototype and seven **YB-24N** service test aircraft were built before production ended on 31 March 1945; the single experimental **XB-41** bomber escort, armed with 14 12.7-mm (0.5-in) machine-guns and converted for flight engineer training under the designation **AT-22** (later **TB-24**). Most of the USAAF's Liberators were declared war surplus at the war's end, only a few remaining in service and the very last of these was disposed of in 1953.

From first to last more than 19,000 Liberators had been built. In addition to those supplied to the RAF, USAAF and US Navy, others had been operated by units of the Royal Australian Air Force, Royal Canadian Air Force and South African Air Force. Nowhere had they been of greater value than in the Pacific theatre, where their long range and versatility made them true 'maids of all work'.

Variant
Convair Model 39: this was an attempt to break into the post-war transport market, and took the form of the wings, powerplant and landing gear of the B-24, the tail unit of the PB4Y-2 and a new fuselage able to carry 45 passengers or 5443 kg (12,000 lb) of freight; the sole prototype was evaluated by the US Navy as the **R2Y**.

This is a B-24M, displaying its defensive armament of twin 12.7-mm (0.5-in) guns in nose, dorsal, ventral, waist and tail positions.

Specification
Consolidated B-24H/J
Type: long-range bomber/reconnaissance aircraft
Powerplant: four 895-kW (1,200-hp) Pratt & Whitney R-1830-65 Twin Wasp turbocharged radial piston engines
Performance: maximum speed 467 km/h (290 mph) at 7620 m (25,000 ft); cruising speed 346 km/h (215 mph); service ceiling 8535 m (28,000 ft); range 3380 km (2,100 miles)
Weights: empty 16556 kg (36,500 lb); maximum overload take-off 32296 kg (71,200 lb)
Dimensions: span 33.53 m (110 ft 0 in); length 20.47 m (67 ft 2 in); height 5.49 m (18 ft 0 in); wing area 97.36 m² (1,048.0 sq ft)
Armament: 10 12.7-mm (0.5-in) machine-guns (in nose, upper, ventral 'ball' and tail turrets, and beam positions), plus a maximum bomb load of 5806 kg (12,800 lb) or a normal bomb load of 2268 kg (5,000 lb)

Consolidated (Model 33) B-32 Dominator

For precisely the same requirement to which Boeing designed the B-29, Consolidated evolved a competing proposal, the **Consolidated Model 33**. Each company was awarded a contract to build three prototypes, those from Consolidated being allocated the designation **XB-32**.

The first prototype made its maiden flight on 7 September 1942, two weeks before the first XB-29. The second and third followed on 2 July 1943 and 9 November respectively. Like the XB-29 they featured pressurisation and remotely-controlled gun turrets, but each differed in some fairly major aspect of its configuration. The first had a rounded fuselage nose and twin fins and rudders based on those of the B-24 Liberator. The second retained this tail unit but had a modified fuselage nose with a stepped windscreen for the flight deck. The third prototype retained this fuselage design, but introduced a large single fin and rudder, and this was the basic configuration as finalised for production aircraft.

Somewhat smaller than the B-29, the B-32 was of cantilever high-wing monoplane configuration and powered by four Wright Cyclone 18 radial engines of the same series used for the B-29. Landing gear was of the retractable tricycle type

and two cavernous bomb bays could carry 9072 kg (20,000 lb) of bombs. Accommodation was provided for a standard crew of eight.

Consolidated experienced extensive problems in development of the **B-32**, to the extent that it was not possible to begin delivery of production examples until November 1944, almost eight months after XX Bomber Command B-29s had been deployed on forward bases in China. Even then, production aircraft (of which 115 were built) had the intended pressurisation system and remotely-controlled gun turrets deleted. In the final analysis, only 15 of these aircraft became operational before VJ-Day, equipping the USAAF's 386th Bombardment Squadron based on Okinawa. Some 40 of a version designated **TB-32** were also produced for training purposes, but with the end of the war all versions were soon withdrawn from service.

Specification
Type: long-range strategic bomber
Powerplant: four 1641-kW (2,200-hp) Wright R-3350-23 Cyclone radial piston engines
Performance: maximum speed 575 km/h (357 mph) at 7620 m

Consolidated B-32 Dominator

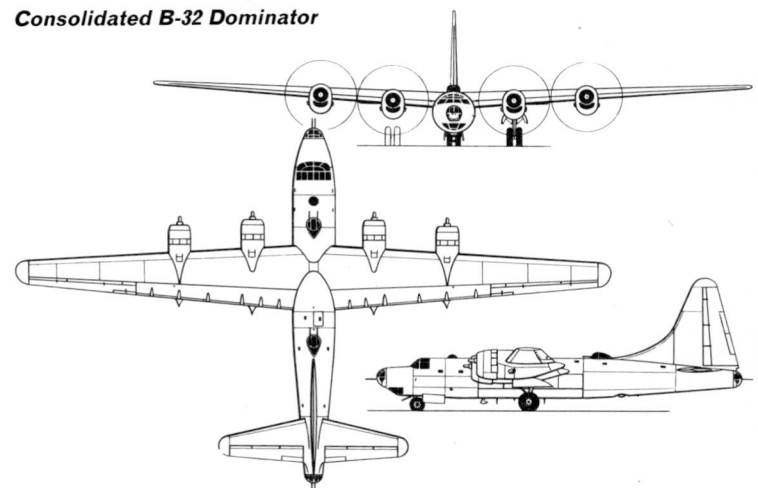

(25,000 ft); service ceiling 10670 m (35,000 ft); range with maximum bombload 1287 km (800 miles); maximum range 6115 km (3,800 miles)
Weights: empty 27339 kg (60,272 lb); maximum take-off 50576 kg (111,500 lb)
Dimensions: span 41.15 m

(135 ft 0 in); length 25.32 m (83 ft 1 in); height 10.06 m (33 ft 0 in); wing area 132.10 m² (1,422.0 sq ft)
Armament: two 20-mm cannon (one in nose and one in tail turret) and four 12.7-mm (0.5-in) machine-guns, plus up to 9072 kg (20,000 lb) of bombs

Consolidated P-30/PB-2

The Detroit Aircraft Corporation, of which Lockheed Aircraft Company was then a subsidiary, gave up its aviation activities during 1932. One of the company's designers joined Consolidated and there continued the development of a military aircraft based on the Lockheed Altair. This interested the US Army Air Corps sufficiently to gain a contract for two prototypes, one **Y1P-25** two-seat fighter and an attack version of the same aircraft designated **XA-11**. A cantilever low-wing monoplane of all-metal construction, except for fabric-covered tail control surfaces, the Y1P-25 had retractable tailwheel landing gear, a Curtiss V-1570-27 Conqueror turbocharged inline engine and accommodation for a crew of two in tandem.

First flown in late 1932, the Y1P-25 crashed on 13 January 1933, but in its short test life had shown sufficient promise for the USAAC to order four generally similar service test aircraft. They differed by having the V-1710-57 Conqueror turbocharged engine, simplified landing gear and revised cockpit canopies. Tested in the summer of 1934 under the designation **P-30**, their performance was good enough to gain a contract for 50 **P-30A** fighters in

Consolidated PB-2 (P-30) of the 94th Pursuit Squadron, US Army Air Corps in 1935

December 1934. These introduced the slightly more powerful V-1570-61 turbocharged engine and a variable-pitch propeller. Entering service in 1935, they had the distinction of being the only two-seat monoplane fighters to gain operational status with the US Army Air Corps during the between-wars years. Shortly after entering service the P-30As were redesignated **PB-2A**; simulataneously, surviving P-30s were reclassified as **PB-2**.

Development of the XA-11 continued

with the procurement of four service test **A-11** aircraft. These differed from the P-30s by having unsupercharged engines and two-blade propellers, but no production aircraft were ordered. One became the XA-11A flying test bed for the liquid-cooled Allison V-1710 engine.

Specification
Consolidated PB-2A

Type: two-seat monoplane fighter
Powerplant: one 522-kW (700-hp) Curtiss V-1570-61 inline piston engine

Performance: maximum speed 441 km/h (274 mph) at 7620 m (25,000 ft); cruising speed 346 km/h (215 mph); climb to 4570 m 15,000 ft) in 7 minutes 47 seconds; service ceiling 8535 m (28,000 ft); range 818 km (508 miles)
Weights: empty 1953 kg (4,306 lb); maximum take-off 2560 kg (5,643 lb)
Dimensions: span 13.39 m (43 ft 11 in); length 9.14 m (30 ft 0 in); height 2.51 m (8 ft 3 in); wing area 27.58 m² (297.0 sq ft)
Armament: two fixed forward-firing 7.62-,, (0.3-in) machine-guns, plus a similar gun on flexible mounting in rear cockpit

---

Consolidated P2Y

When the United States Navy requested proposals for its first monoplane patrol flying-boat, Consolidated responded with a project based on a hull design by Captain Dick Richardson, with overall design by Isaac M. Laddon who had joined the company in 1927 from the Army Air Service Engineering Division. A parasol monoplane with a fabric-covered wing and an aluminium-skinned hull, the prototype **Consolidated XPY-1** was the subject of a $150,000 US Navy contract awarded on 28 February 1928, and construction began during the following month. Named **Admiral** in honour of Rear Admiral William A. Moffett, Chief of the Bureau of Aeronautics, the XPY-1 was ready for its maiden flight towards the end of the year. By then, however, both Lake Erie and the Niagara River, near the company's headquarters at Buffalo, New York State, were ice-bound and the aircraft was transported to Anacostia NAS, Washington, DC. There it was reassembled and Lieutenant A. W. Gorton made the first flight on 10 January 1929. Two 336-kW (450-hp) Pratt & Whitney R-1340-38 Wasp engines were mounted on the parasol struts and, for a short time, a third engine was fitted experimentally above the wing in an unsuccessful attempt to raise the aircraft's speed. However, the production contract was opened to other manufacturers, being awarded to the Glenn L. Martin Company which, having borne none of the programme's development costs, was able to undercut Consolidated's bid. Nine were built under the designations **Martin P3M-1** and **P3M-2**. Undeterred, Consolidated turned to the promotion of a civil version, the Commodore, the improved **XP2Y-1**.

Variants

Model 16 Commodore: with a standard seating capacity of 22 and a crew of three, the Commodore commerical flying-boat was powered by two 429-kW (575-hp) Pratt &

Whitney Hornet radials; 14 were sold to the New York, Rio and Buenos Aires Line, a company set up by Captain Ralph O'Neill and Remington Rand's James Rand, backed by major investors who included Consolidated's Reuben Fleet, F. C. Munson of Munson Steamship, W. B. Mayo of Ford Motor Company, and L. Pearson of Irving Trust Company; the airline was formed to run services from Miami through the West Indies and along the east coast of South America to Rio de Janeiro and Buenos Aires, the first commercial Commodore service leaving Miami on 18 February 1930, providing the first through flight to Santiago, Chile; the airline was sold to Pan American on 15 September 1930 and some of the Commodores were still in use by Pan American after the end of World War II.
P2Y-1: under a US Navy contract awarded on 26 May 1931, Consolidated developed the XP2Y-1 improved version of the basic XPY-1, featuring an enclosed cockpit and a 13.79 m (45 ft 3 in) lower wing, the latter providing both additional lift and a mounting for stabilising floats, the upper wing and engine-bearing struts; power was supplied by three 429-kW (575-hp) Wright R-1820E Cyclone radial engines, and the first flight took place from the Niagara River on 26 March 1932; in

April 1932 the aircraft was delivered to Anacostia NAS for a test programme during which the third engine was removed; the first of 23 P2Y-1 production aircraft, ordered on 7 July 1931, was delivered to Patrol Squadron 10 (VP-10) at Norfolk, Virginia on 1 February 1933; all had been delivered by the end of 1933; on 7 September of that year six P2Y-1s of VP-5 left Norfolk en route to Coco Solo in the Panama Canal Zone, and a nonstop flying-boat record flight of 3314 km (2,059 miles) was accomplished in 25 hours 19 minutes; then VP-10 was assigned for duty in Hawaii and it was decided that, for the first time, the six aircraft would be delivered by air; they left Coco Solo on 7 October 1933, proceeding to San Diego to prepare for the Pacific crossing; the flight began on 9 January 1934, the squadron stopping overnight at Paradise Cove, San Francisco, before the formation set course of Oahu next day, arriving just after noon on 11 January in a flight time of just over 22 hours.
P2Y-2: the last of the P2Y-1s was fitted with more powerfulR-1820-88 engines, which were faired into the leading edges of the wing, to become the **XP2Y-2** prototypes; the P2Y-1s of VP-5 and VP-10 were converted to this P2Y-2 standard in 1936
P2Y-3: this was the production

The Consolidated P2Y-3 introduced a revised engine installation with two Wright R-1820s in the wing leading edge. This example was on the strength of Patrol Squadron VP-7.

version of the XP2Y-2, of which 23 were ordered on 27 December 1933; they were delivered during the first half of 1935 and entered service initially with VP-7.

Specification
Consolidated P2Y-3

Type: five-seat patrol flying-boat
Powerplant: two 559-kW (750-hp) Wright R-1820-90 radial piston engines
Performance: maximum speed 224 km/h (139 mph); cruising speed 188 km/h (117 mph); service ceiling 4905 m (16,100 ft); range 1899 km (1,180 miles)
Weights: empty 5792 kg (12,769 lb); maximum take-off 11460 kg (25,266 lb)
Dimensions: span 30.48 m (100 ft 0 in); length 18.82 m (61 ft 9 in); height 5.82 m (19 ft 1 in); wing area 140.65 m² (1,514.0 sq ft)
Armament: one flexible bow-mounted 7.62-mm (0.3-in) Browning machine-gun and two similar weapons in dorsal hatches, plus a 907-kg (2,000-lb) bombload

Consolidated (Model 28) PBY Catalina

With the requirement for a patrol flying-boat to offer greater range and load-carrying capability than the Consolidated P2Y or Martin P3M, which were in service in the early 1930s, the US Navy contracted Consolidated and Douglas in October 1933 to build competing prototypes, designated **Consolidated XP3Y-1** and Douglas XP3D-1. Only a single prototype of the Douglas design was built. Consolidated's XP3Y-1, however, was developed to become the most extensively-built flying-boat in aviation history.

Consolidated identified their design to meet the US Navy's requirements as the **Consolidated Model 28** and this, like the P2Y which preceded it, had a parasol-mounted wing. However, in the new design the introduction of internal bracing resulted in a wing which was virtually a cantilever, except for two small streamline struts between hull and wing centre-section on each side. Thus the Model 28 was free of the multiplicity of drag-producing struts and bracing wires which had limited the performance of earlier designs. Another innovation adding to aerodynamic efficiency was the provision of stabilising floats which, when retracted in flight, formed streamlined wingtips. The two-step hull design was very similar to that of the P2Y, but the Model 28 had a clean cruciform tail unit which was a cantilever structure. Powerplant of the prototype comprised two 615-kW (825-hp) Pratt & Whitney R-1830-54 Twin Wasp engines mounted on the wing leading-edges. Armament comprised four 7.62-mm (0.3-in) machine-guns and up to 907 kg (2,000 lb) of bombs.

First flown on 28 March 1935, the XP3Y-1 was soon transferred to the US Navy for service trials, which confirmed a significant improvement in performance over the patrol flying-boats in service. Its extended range and improved load-carrying capability caused the US Navy to request further development to bring this new aircraft into the category of a patrol-bomber, and in October 1935 the prototype was returned to Consolidated for the necessary work to be carried out, including installation of the 671-kW (900-hp) R-1830-64 engines which had been specified for the 60 examples of the **PBY-1** (a patrol-bomber designation) which had been ordered on 29 June 1935. At the same time redesigned vertical tail surfaces were introduced and the **XPBY-1**, as this prototype was redesignated, flew for the first time on 19 May 1936. After completing its trials this aircraft was delivered to US Navy Squadron VP-11F during October 1936, in which month the first of the PBY-1s began to reach the squadron.

Minor equipment changes brought the designation **PBY-2** for the second production order placed on 25 July 1936, while the **PBY-3** ordered on 27 November 1936 and **PBY-4** on 18 December 1937 had 746-kW (1,000-hp) R-1830-66 and 783-kW (1,050-hp) R-1830-72 Twin Wasp engines respectively. All but the first examples of the PBY-4 introduced large transport blisters over the waist gun positions, in place of sliding hatches,

and these became a characteristic feature of all subsequent production aircraft.

In April 1939 the last example of the PBY-4 production aircraft was returned to the company for the installation of wheeled landing gear so that these aircraft could operate as amphibians, thus making them far more versatile. This aircraft, when completed in November 1939, emerged with the designation **XPBY-5A**. Testing confirmed the very considerable advantages of the amphibian configuration and the 33 aircraft outstanding on US Navy contracts for the **PBY-5** variant were completed as **PBY-5A** amphibians; an additional 134 PBY-5As were contracted on 25 November 1940.

Extensive service use of the PBYs suggested that the hull would benefit from hydrodynamic improvement. The Naval Aircraft Factory carried out the necessary research and development work to achieve this end, receiving an order for 156 of these modified aircraft under the designation **PBN-1 Nomad**. This course was adopted in order that design changes would not interfere with the major production coming from Consolidated. However, when the final production version was built by Consolidated, between April 1944 and April 1945, the NAF's improvements and others were incorporated in a model designated **PBY-6A**.

From mid-1937 PBYs were introduced rapidly into service with the US Navy, and by the time that the USA became involved in World War II some 21 squadrons were equipped, 16 with PBY-5s, two with PBY-4s and three with PBY-3s.

Before this, however, interest shown by the Soviet Union resulted in an order for three aircraft and the negotiation of a licence to build the type in Russia. When these three machines were delivered they were accompanied by a team of Consolidated engineers who assisted in establishment of the Russian production facilities. Designated **GST**, these production aircraft were powered by Mikulin M-62 radial engines, a developed version of the M-25 (licence-built Wright Cyclone), which had a power rating of

Around 700 Catalinas were delivered to the Royal Air Force. This Catalina Mk II served briefly with No. 240 Sqn, flying from Killadeas and a detachment on Iceland.

671-746 kW (900-1,000 hp). The first of the GST's began to appear in late 1939 and an unspecified number certainly running into several hundreds, was built during the war for service with the Soviet navy.

European interest started with purchase by the British Air Ministry of a single aircraft for evaluation, this being identified by Consolidated as the **Model 28-5**. Flown across the Atlantic, the craft was allocated to the Marine Aircraft Experimental Establishment at Felixstowe, Suffolk in July 1939. The outbreak of war anticipated the termination of trials, but with little doubt of the excellence of the design a first batch of 50 was ordered under the designation **Catalina Mk I**.

Initial deliveries of the RAF's Catalinas began in early 1941, these entering service with Nos 209 and 240 Squadrons of Coastal Command. Catalinas subsequently equipped nine squadrons of Coastal Command, as well as an additional 12 squadrons serving overseas. The RAF received about 700 of these aircraft which, with the exception of 11 PBY-5As diverted to Britain from the US Navy order, were all non-amphibious flying-boats. They comprised 100 of the Catalina Mk I equivalent to the US Navy's PBY-5, 225 of the **Catalina Mk IB** (PBY-5B), 36 of the **Catalina Mk IIA**

(PBY-5), 11 of the **Catalina Mk III** (PBY-5A), 97 of the **Catalina Mk IVA** (PBY-5), 193 of the **Catalina Mk IVB**, which was built by Boeing Aircraft of Canada under the designation **PB2B-1** and was generally similar to the non-amphibious PBY-5, and 50 of the **Catalina Mk IV**, the Boeing-built **PB2B-2** which had the taller vertical surfaces first introduced on the NAF PBN-1. No Catalina Mk Vs served with the RAF, this designation being allocated for potential supplies of NAF PBN-1s, none of which was in the event sent to Great Britain.

Soon after receipt of the UK's first order for production aircraft, Consolidated received a French purchasing mission which, in early 1940, ordered 30 aircraft. Allocated the company's identification **Model 28-5MF**, none of these was delivered before the collapse of French resistance. Other foreign orders received at about the same time covered 18 aircraft for the Royal Australian Air Force, and 48 ordered by the Dutch government for use in the Netherlands East Indies.

Canada had its own close associations with the Catalina, both as manufacturer and customer. Under an agreement reached between the Canadian and US governments production lines were laid down in Canada, by Boeing Aircraft of Canada at Vancouver and by Canadian

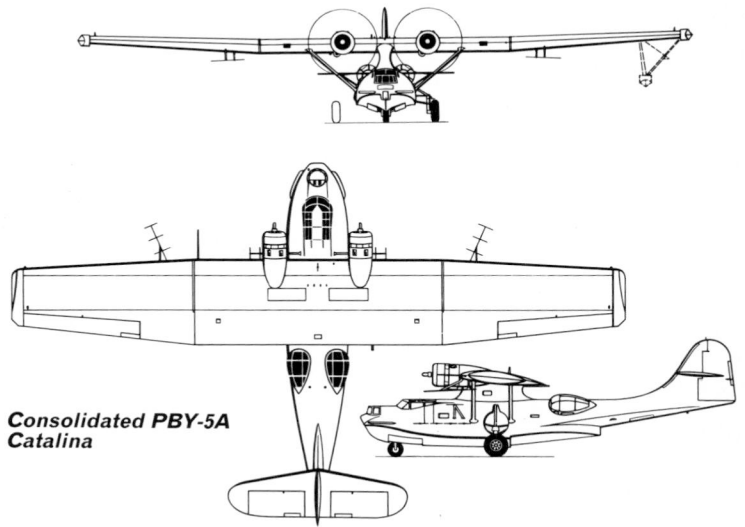

Consolidated PBY-5A Catalina

269

Vickers at Cartierville.

Boeing production totalled 362 aircraft, these comprising 240 PB2B-1s supplied to Australia, New Zealand and the UK; 50 PB2B-2s for the UK; 17 non-amphibious Catalinas for the RCAF, and 55 amphibians which, in Royal Canadian Air Force service, were designated **Canso**. Aircraft produced by Canadian Vickers totalled 379 equivalent to the PB2Y-5A, of which 149 were supplied to the RCAF. From the balance of 230 the US Navy planned to acquire 183 under the designation **PBV-1A**; in fact the US

Navy received none of these, all being supplied to the USAAF which had previously acquired 56 PBY-5As as a direct transfer from the US Navy and which it designated **OA-10**. These were used throughout World War II for search and rescue missions, some carrying an airdropped lifeboat beneath each wing. The 230 aircraft built by Canadian Vickers were designated **OA-10A** in USAAF service, and the final production aircraft to be received were 75 PBY-6As built by Consolidated, and which were designated **OA-10B**.

Specification
Consolidated PBY-5A
Type: seven/nine-seat long-range maritime patrol-bomber amphibian/flying-boat
Powerplant: two 895-kW (1,200-hp) Pratt & Whitney R-1830-92 Twin Wasp radial piston engines
Performance: maximum speed 288 km/h (179 mph) at 2135 m (7,000 ft); long-range cruising speed 188 km/h (117 mph); service ceiling 4480 m (14,700 ft); maximum range 4096 km (2,545 miles)

Weights: empty 9485 kg (20,910 lb); maximum take-off 16066 kg (35,420 lb)
Dimensions: span 31.70 m (104 ft 0 in); length 19.47 m (63 ft 10½ in); height 6.15 m (20 ft 2 in); wing area 130.06 m² (1,400.0 sq ft)
Armament: two 7.62-mm (0.3-in) machine-guns in bow, one 7.62-mm (0.3-in) machine-gun firing aft through a tunnel aft of the hull step and two 12.7-mm (0.5-in) machine-guns (one in each beam position), plus up to 1814 kg (4,000 lb) of bombs or depth charges

Consolidated (Model 29) PB2Y Coronado

Plans for the development of a maritime patrol-bomber larger than the PBY Catalina were drawn up by the US Navy very soon after the first flight of the Catalina's XP3Y-1 prototype. The aim was to procure a patrol flying-boat with increased performance and good weapon load capability, Consolidated and Sikorsky each receiving a contract for the construction of a prototype for evaluation. Sikorsky's XPBS-1 flew for the first time on 13 August 1937, but despite introducing a number of new features it was the **Consolidated Model 29** which, when evaluated as the **XPB2Y-1** following a first flight on 17 December 1937, was regarded as the more suitable for production. As at that time the US Navy had no funds for immediate procurement of any of these aircraft, Consolidated had almost 15 months in which to rectify the short-comings revealed by initial flight tests.

Most serious of the problems was lateral instability, which the company attempted to rectify by the addition of two oval-shaped fins, mounted one each side of the tailplane. This was a move in the right direction, but stability was still far from satisfactory and was resolved finally by the design of a new tail unit with endplate fins and rudders similar to those of the B-24 Liberator. The other problem concerned hydrodynamic performance of the flying-boat's hull; fortunately, the delayed procurement allowed time for redesign, the new hull being deeper than that of the prototype, with a much-changed nose profile.

Eventually, on 31 March 1939, the US Navy was able to order six of these aircraft under the designation **PB2Y-2** and the name **Coronado**, and delivery of these to US Navy Squadron VP-13 began on 31 December 1940. They were impressive aircraft, powered by four radial engines mounted on the high-set cantilever wing. Construction was all-metal, and interesting features included stabilising floats which retracted to form wingtips in flight, and bomb bays formed

in the deep-section wing. Accommodation was provided for a crew of 10.

These PB2Y-2s were used for service trials, leading to the procurement of the **PB2Y-3 Coronado**, following the conversion of one of the PB2Y-2s as a prototype **XPB2Y-3**. They differed by having increased armament and the provision of self-sealing tanks and armour. A total of 210 of this version was built, late production aircraft being equipped with ASV (Air to Surface Vessel) radar. Ten of the aircraft, designated **PB2Y-3B**, were supplied to the RAF and based initially at Beaumaris, Anglesey, intended for service with Coastal Command. Their stay there was only brief, for they were transferred to No. 231 Squadron of Transport Command and used from June 1944 to operate freight services.

Variants in US service, converted from PB2Y-3s, included 31 **PB2Y-3R** transports, fitted with single-stage supercharged R-1830-88 engines; one **XPB2Y-4** converted by the experimental installation of Wright R-2600 Cyclone engines; the **PB2Y-5** modified from PB2Y-3s with increased fuel capacity and R-1830-92 engines; and a number of **PB2Y-5H** casualty-evacuation aircraft which saw service in the Pacific theatre accommodating 25 stretchers.

Specification
Consolidated PB2Y-3
Type: long-range flying-boat bomber
Powerplant: four 895-kW (1,200-hp) Pratt & Whitney R-1830-88 Twin Wasp radial piston engines
Performance: maximum speed 359 km/h (223 mph) at 6095 m (20,000 ft); cruising speed 227 km/h (141 mph) at 460 m (1,500 ft); service ceiling 6250 m (20,500 ft); range with 3629-kg (8,000-lb) bomb load 2205 km (1,370 miles); maximum range 3814 km (2,370 miles)
Weights: empty 18568 kg (40,935 lb); maximum take-off 30844 kg (68,000 lb)
Dimensions: span 35.05 m (115 ft 0 in); length 24.16 m (79 ft 3 in); height

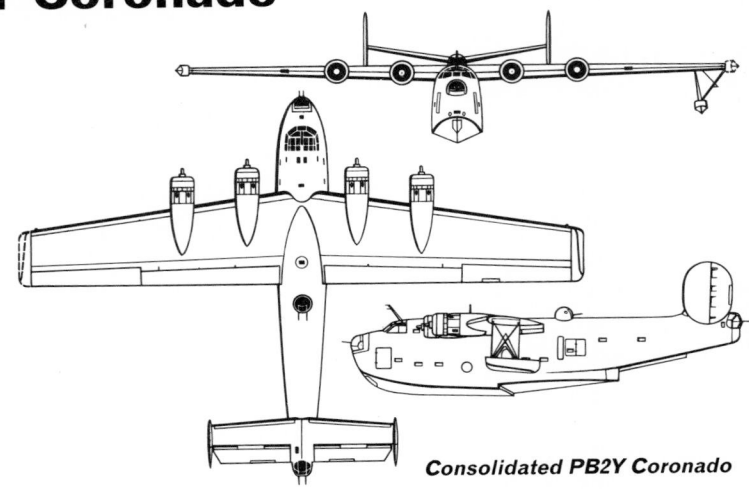

Consolidated PB2Y Coronado

8.38 m (27 ft 6 in); wing area 165.36 m² (1,780.0 sq ft)
Armament: two 12.7-mm (0.5-in) machine-guns each in bow, dorsal and tail turrets, and one 12.7-mm (0.5-in) gun in each two beam positions, plus up to 5443 kg (12,000 lb) of weapons

This PB2Y displays the characteristic deep hull pioneered by the PB2Y. Many Coronados had ASV radar fitted.

including bombs, depth charges, and torpedoes in bomb bays

Consolidated TBY-2 Sea Wolf

In April 1940 the American Chance Vought company received a US Navy contract for the prototype of a three-seat torpedo-bomber. Designated **XTBU-1**, this was a mid-wing cantilever monoplane with tailwheel landing gear, power provided by a Pratt & Whitney R-2800-22 radial engine, and the crew of three seated in tandem beneath a 'greenhouse' canopy. Successful testing was to result in the Navy placing a production contract with Chance Vought, but with the company lacking production capacity it was arranged instead that these should be built by Consolidated to the Chance Vought design.

Accordingly, a contract for 1,100 **TBY-2s** was placed with Consolidated in September 1943, these gaining the name **Sea Wolf**. They differed from the **TBY-1** (of which none were built, superseded by the TBY-2) by having a radar pod mounted beneath the starboard wing. Production was terminated after only 180 had been built, and none of these aircraft were used operationally, being confined to a training role. An improved **TBY-3** had been ordered (600), but this was cancelled simultaneously.

Consolidated TBY-2 Sea Wolf

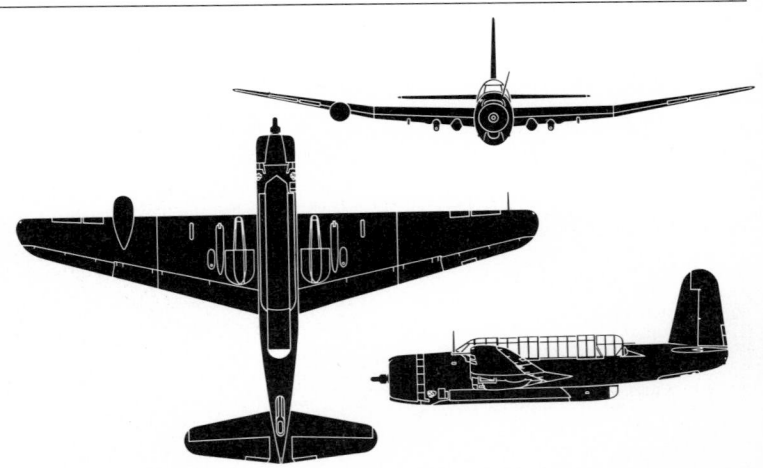

Specification
Type: three-seat torpedo bomber
Powerplant: one 1491-kW (2,000-hp)
Pratt & Whitney R-2800-22 radial piston engine
Performance: maximum level speed 501 km/h (311 mph) at 4480 m (14,700 ft)
Weights: maximum take-off 7370 kg (16,247 lb)
Dimensions: span 17.42 m (57 ft 2 in); length 11.89 m (39 ft 0 in)
Armament: two 12.7-mm (0.5-in) and one 7.62-mm (0.3-in) machine-guns, one torpedo and bombs on underwing racks

Convair (Model 36) B-36

The first intercontinental bomber, the **Convair B-36** originated from a specification issued on 11 April 1941 which called for an aircraft with ability to carry a maximum bombload of 32659 kg (72,000 lb) and, of even greater importance in view of the state of affairs at that time, to deliver 4536 kg (10,000 lb) of bombs on European targets from bases in the United States. An unrefuelled range of 16093 km (10,000 miles) was a prime requirement, with a maximum speed of 386-483 km/h (240-300 mph) and ceiling of 10670 m (35,000 ft). Selected from four competing designs, the **Consolidated Model 36** featured a pressurised fuselage, and 70.10-m (230-ft) span wings with a root thickness of 1.83 m (6 ft) to permit in-flight access to the six pusher engines. The aircraft was designed originally with twin fins and rudders, but by the time the **XB-36** prototype was ready to be rolled out at Fort Worth, on 8 September 1945, single vertical tail surfaces had been substituted.

First flown on 8 August 1946, the XB-36 had single 2.79-m (110-in) diameter main wheels, also a feature of the **YB-36** second prototype on which they were replaced later by the four-wheeled bogies adopted for production aircraft. In this form the aircraft was designated **YB-36A** and also differed from the first aircraft by introducing a raised cockpit roof. On 23 July 1943 100 aircraft were ordered but it was more than four years before the first of the 22 unarmed crew-trainer **B-36A** models took off on its maiden flight, on 28 August 1947. Production of the B-36 continued for almost seven years, the last example being delivered to Strategic Air Command on 14 August 1954, and the type was retired finally on 12 February 1959.

Variants

B-36B: 73 aircraft were built to this standard, each powered by six 2610-kW (3,500-hp) Pratt & Whitney R-4360-41 engines and operating at a maximum take-off weight of 148778 kg (328,000 lb); armament comprised six retractable and remotely controlled fuselage turrets (each with two 20-mm cannon) and two similar weapons in nose and tail turrets; the first example was flown on 8 July 1948
YB-36C: proposed version with R-4360-51 tractor engines
B-36D: first flown on 26 March 1949 as a B-36B conversion, this version was cleared to operate at a weight of 162386 kg (358,000 lb), permitting an increase in maximum bombload to 38102 kg (84,000 lb); in addition maximum speed was raised to 700 km/h (435 mph) and ceiling to more than 13715 m (45,000 ft); additional power for the 22 production B-36Ds and 64 B-36B conversions was provided in the form of two pairs of General Electric J47-GE-19 turbojet engines, mounted in pods outboard of

One of the most unusual aviation projects was FICON, whereby an RB-36 carried a Republic F-84 in a trapeze under its belly. Operational reconnaissance missions were launched using RF-84F Thunderflash aircraft.

the main engines; the first aircraft, mentioned above, had four Allison J35 turbojets; deliveries of the B-36D began on 19 August 1950 and the type first entered service with the 7th Bomb Wing at Carswell AFB
RB-36D: 17 new RB-36Ds and seven conversions from B-36Bs were built for strategic reconnaissance duties, deliveries starting on 3 June 1950; operating with a crew of 22, the RB-36D was equipped with 14 cameras installed in the space occupied normally by two of the bomber version's four bomb bays
RB-36E: the YB-36A and 21 B-36As were converted to a similar standard to that of the RB-36D, the first being flown on 18 December 1949
B-36F: similar to the B-36B but with uprated 2834-kW (3,800-hp) R-4360-53 engines, the B-36F was flown for the first time on 18 November 1950; production totalled 58, including 24 of the **RB-36F** with increased fuel capacity
GRB-36F: the USAF FICON (Fighter in Convair) parasite fighter programme, originally to have used the McDonnell XF-85, was continued with the Republic GRF-84F; following successful trials, involving test drops from a trapeze-equipped GRB-36F in May 1953, at least 12 aircraft were converted to this standard, and were used also as control aircraft for guided missile development
B-36H: first flown on 5 April 1952, the B-36H introduced improvements to the flight deck and 156 were built, including 73 of the **RB-36H**; one aircraft designated **NB-36H**, had a nuclear reactor installed for an experimental programme to study radiation shielding methods and the effects of radiation on airframe and equipment; first flight was made on 17 September 1955
B-36J: version with additional outer wing fuel tanks and strengthened landing gear for operation 185973 kg (410,000 lb), of which 33 were manufactured; the first example flew on 3 September 1953 and some aircraft were later modified by the deletion of all but the tail turret armament, reducing the crew complement to nine men
XC-99: designation allocated to a single transport variant (**Model 37**) of the B-36; retaining the same powerplant, tail unit and wings, it had a new two-deck fuselage which could accommodate 400 troops and their equipment, or 300 stretchers, or up to

45813 kg (101,000 lb) of cargo; first flown on 23 November 1947, it subsequently acquired bogie main wheel units and weather radar; it was used for special transport operations until withdrawn from service in 1957
YB-60: under the designation **XB-36G** a turbojet-powered version of the B-36 was proposed; a contract for two prototypes was awarded by the USAF on 15 March 1951, these being allocated the designation YB-60; they retained the basic fuselage of the B-36 with a modified nose and generally similar wing centre-section and landing gear; new swept outer wing panels, a new tail unit and powerplant comprising eight Pratt & Whitney J57 turbojets, pylon mounted in podded pairs forward of the wing leading-edge, distinguished the two YB-60s; the first was flown on 18 April 1952, but the type failed to gain a production contract, the USAF ordering instead the Boeing B-52
X-6: proposed nuclear-powered version

Specification
Convair B-36J

Type: long-range strategic/reconnaissance bomber

The prototype XB-36 did not have the raised canopy of subsequent aircraft. Here it is fitted with strange tracked undercarriage.

Powerplant: six 2834-kW (3,800-hp) Pratt & Whitney R-4360-53 radial piston engines and four 2359-kg (5,200-lb) thrust General Electric J47-GE-19 turbojets
Performance: maximum speed 661 km/h (411 mph) at 11095 m (36,400 ft); cruising speed 629 km/h (391 mph); service ceiling 12160 m (39,900 ft); range 10944 km (6,800 miles) with 4536-kg (10,000-lb) bombload
Weights: empty 77580 kg (171,035 lb); maximum take-off 185973 kg (410,000 lb)
Dimensions: span 70.10 m (230 ft 0 in); length 49.40 m (162 ft 1 in); height 14.22 m (46 ft 8 in); wing area 443.32 m² (4,772.0 sq ft)
Armament: six retractable and remotely controlled fuselage turrets, each with twin 20-mm M24A1 cannon, and similar weapons in nose and tail, plus a maximum bombload of 39009 kg (86,000 lb) with weight restrictions, or more normally up to 32659 kg (72,000 lb)

Bearing little resemblance to the B-36, the YB-60 was a jet-powered, swept-surface derivative intended to compete with the Boeing B-52.

Convair XB-46

Very shortly after the end of World War II Convair began the design of a turbojet-powered medium bomber, gaining a contract for three **XB-46** prototypes from the US Army Air Force. Of all-metal construction, the XB-46 was of high-wing cantilever monoplane configuration, had a slim oval-section fuselage, conventional tail unit, retractable tricycle landing gear and was designed to accommodate a crew of three. Powerplant consisted of four turbojet engines, these being mounted in pairs.

First flown on 2 April 1947, the XB-46 was handed over to the newly-formed US Air Force in late 1947, attaining an average speed of 858 km/h (533 mph) during its delivery flight to Wright Field at Daytona, Ohio. Despite this performance the XB-46 remained a one-off pro-

totype, the USAF ordering the Boeing B-47 Stratojet into production.

Specification
Type: medium bomber prototype
Powerplant: four 1814-kW (4,000-hp) thrust Allison-built General Electric TG-180 (J35) turbojets
Performance: (approximate) maximum speed 909 km/h (565 mph); service ceiling 13105 m (43,000 ft); range with 3629-kg (8,000-lb) of bombs 4023 km (2,500 miles)
Weights: maximum take-off 41277 kg (91,000 lb)
Dimensions: span 34.44 m (113 ft 0 in); length 32.31 m (106 ft 0 in); height 8.53 m (28 ft 0 in)
Armament: (intended) maximum bombload of 9072 kg (20,000 lb)

By putting four of the new General Electric TG-180 axial jets into a traditional-type airframe, Convair got the XB-46 bomber aloft in 1947.

Convair (Model 4) B-58 Hustler

In March 1949 the US Air Force's Air Research and Development Command (ARDC) invited proposals for a supersonic bomber, and after submissions had been reduced to two, from Boeing and Consolidated-Vultee's Fort Worth Division, the latter was selected in August 1952 to develop its **Convair Model 4** designed to the hardware stage under contract MX-1964. On 10 December 1952 the designation **B-58** was allocated and late in that year Convair received a contract for 18 aircraft, to be powered by a new J79 engine for which General Electric received a development contract at the same time. The performance requirement for the new aircraft demanded considerable advances in aerodynamics, structures and materials. The resulting design, one of the first to incorporate the NACA/Whitcomb-developed area-rule concept, was a delta-winged aircraft with four engines in underslung pods, a slim fuselage and, perhaps its most novel feature, a 18.90-m (62-ft) long under-fuselage pod to carry fuel and a nuclear weapon. The three-man crew, in individual tandem cockpits, were provided with jettisonable escape capsules.

In June 1954 the 18-aircraft order was reduced to two **XB-58** prototypes and 11 **YB-58A** pre-production examples, together with 31 pods. The first of these was rolled out at Fort Worth on 31 August 1956, making its first flight on 11 November piloted by B. A. Erikson. On 30 December, still without a pod, the XB-58 became the first bomber to exceed Mach 1. A further 17 YB-58As were ordered on 14 February 1958, together with 35 MB-1 bomb pods, to bring to 30 the number of aircraft available for the manufacturer's test programme and ARDC service trials with the 6592nd Test Squadron and the 3958th Opera-

Another impressive aircraft from Convair's adventurous designers, the Hustler strategic bomber carried fuel and nuclear weapons in its underfuselage pod, which was dropped over the target to permit high speed egress.

tional Test and Evaluation Squadron at Carswell AFB.

A total of 86 production **B-58A** Hustler bombers was ordered between September 1958 and 1960, supplemented by 10 YB-58As which were brought up to production standard to equip the 43rd Bomb Wing, initially at Carswell but later assigned to Little Rock AFB, Arkansas, and the 305th Bomb Wing at Bunker Hill AFB, Indiana. The first was handed over to the 65th Combat Crew Training Squadron at Carswell on 1 December 1959 and the 43rd Bomb Wing, activated as the first B-58 unit on 15 March 1960, became operational on 1 August 1960. The 116th and last B-58A was delivered on 26 October 1962 and the type was withdrawn from Strategic Air Command service on 31 January 1970.

With such outstanding performance it was clear that the B-58A had record-breaking potential. On 12 January 1961 Major Henry Deutschendorf and his crew secured the 2000-km (1,243-mile) closed-circuit record at 1708.8 km/h (1,061.8 mph) and on 14 January Major Harold E. Confer's aircraft raised the 1000-km (621-mile) record to 2067.57 km/h (1,284.73 mph). On 10 May Major Elmer Murphy won the trophy presented by Louis Blériot in 1930 for the first pilot to exceed 2000 km/h (1,242.75 mph) for a continuous period of 30 minutes. Sixteen days later Major William Payne and his crew flew from Carswell to Paris setting, en route,

record times of 3 hours 39 minutes 49 seconds from Washington and 3 hours 19 minutes 51 seconds from New York; sadly the Hustler crashed at the Paris Air Show on 3 June with the loss of the crew. Other flights included a supersonic endurance record of 8 hours 35 minutes from Haneda, Tokyo to London, on 16 October 1963.

Variants
TB-58A: eight aircraft converted from the pre-production YB-58As for pilot conversion duties, with dual controls, a raised seat in the second cockpit and extended glazing to provide forward vision for the instructor; the inflight-refuelling equipment was retained but the ASQ-42V bomb-navigation, ECM and defence systems were removed; the first TB-58A flew on 10 May 1960 and was delivered on 13 August
NB-58A: one aircraft converted as a test vehicle for the J93 engine, intended for the B-70 Valkyrie and

carried in a nacelle beneath the fuselage

Specification
Type: three-seat supersonic medium-range bomber
Powerplant: four 7076-kg (15,600-lb) afterburning thrust General Electric J79-GE-5A turbojets
Performance: maximum speed 2229 km/h (1,385 mph) or Mach 2.1 at 12190 m (40,000 ft); service ceiling 18290 m (60,000 ft); unrefuelled range 3219 km (2,000 miles)
Weights: maximum take-off 73936 kg (163,000 lb)
Dimensions: span 17.32 m (56 ft 10 in); length 29.49 m (96 ft 9 in); height 9.58 m (31 ft 5 in); wing area 143.25 m² (1,542.0 sq ft)
Armament: one 20-mm T171 Vulcan rotary cannon in radar-aimed tail barbette, plus nuclear or conventional weapons in disposable underfuselage pod

Convair CV-240, 340 and 440/C-131 Samaritan/T-29/R4Y

As elusive as the legendary 'crock of gold at the foot of the rainbow', but with similar promise of potential riches to an astute aircraft manufacturer, was the creation of an effective Douglas DC-3 replacement. One manufacturer who hoped to gain a success in this market was the Consolidated-Vultee Aircraft Corporation in the USA, which in the early 1950s began to identify its products as Convair types, and in 1954 became the Convair Division of General Dynamics Corporation. It is this division which now provides continuing product support for the Convair piston-engined air-

liner series and its derivatives.

In 1945, American Airlines issued its specification for an airliner to fulfil more effectively the operations being carried out by DC-3s. In due course this led to the construction of a prototpye, designated **Convair Model 110**, which was flown for the first time on 8 July 1946. A twin-engined aircraft, powered by two 1566-kW (2,100-hp) Pratt & Whitney R-2800-S1C3-G radial piston engines, it had accommodation for 30 passengers. Before it was flown, however, American Airlines had already decided that greater capacity had become necessary, and this led to

the development of the **Convair Model 240**, known later as the **Convairliner**. No prototype was built as such, all being completed to production standard, and the first aircraft made its maiden flight on 16 March 1947. While retaining the same powerplant and overall configuration of the Model 110, the new aircraft introduced a fuselage lengthened by 1.12 m (3 ft 8 in) to make possible a standard layout seating 40 passenger. Convair 240s entered service with American Airlines on 1 June 1948, and of the total built (176 for the civil airlines) a considerable number saw

military service.

With the requirement for a large 'flying classroom' type of trainer, for the instruction of navigators and radar operators, the USAF ordered two **XAT-29** prototypes from Convair, these being based on the Model 240. The first XAT-29 made it initial flight on 22 September 1949, and following the evaluation by the USAF a first production contract was placed for the **T-29A**, of which 46 were built. These differed from the Convair 240s on which they were based by being unpressurised, but most of the T-29s procured for the US Air Force, and

For third level operators such as Aero Leon of Mexico, the Convair 440 had great attractions as a result of its low capital cost and modest maintenance requirements. However, fuel has become expensive.

for the US Navy, were generally the same as their civil counterparts except for interior changes. Thus, the T-29A had positions for student navigators and four astrodomes in the upper fuselage. The **T-29B** was pressurised and provided for the simultaneous training of 10 navigators and four radar operators; the similar **T-29C** had more powerful engines. The **T-29D** was an advanced navigation/bombing trainer, with the 'K' system bombsight and camera scoring equipment.

Development of an improved civil version, known as the **Convair Model 340**, was initiated in early 1951. It differed by having R-2800-CB16 or -CB17 engines of 1864 kW (2,500 hp), and increased wing area to cater for a higher gross weight. A further 'stretch' of the fuselage, totalling 1.37 m (4 ft 6 in), increased standard accommodation to 44 passengers. The first example of this version flew first on 5 October 1951, and the initial delivery, to United Air Lines, was made on 28 March 1952.

Further refinement of this design led to the generally similar **Convair Model 440**, which incorporated aerodynamic and comfort improvements, plus a high-density seating arrangement to accommodate a maximum of 52 passengers. The first Convair 440 was produced by the conversion of a Convair 340, and it took to the air for its maiden flight on 6 October 1955; subsequently 155 civil airliners were built as new to this standard.

The first of the USAF's transport variants was the **C-131A Samaritan** for casualty evacuation. Based upon the Convair 240, this had large loading doors for stretchers or cargo, and was equipped to accommodate 27 stretchers or 37 sitting casualties. These were followed by 36 **C-131B** transport/electronic testbed aircraft; 33 **C-131D/VC-131D** transports of which 27 and six were to Convair. Model 340 and 440 standard respectively; and finally 15 **C-131E** ECM trainers delivered during 1956-7. The **RC-131F** designation was

applied to photo-survey conversions of C-131Es, and a single similarly-derived **RC-131G** was equipped to check airways navigational aids. Two aircraft re-engined with turboprops to provide handling experience with this type of powerplant, and four similarly-modified C-131Ds, were used as VIP transports under the designation **VC-131H**.

The US Navy received 36 **R4Y-1** (C-131F) cargo, personnel and evaluation transports; a single **R4Y-1Z** (VC-131F) VIP transport; and two **R4Y-2** (C-131G) transport versions of the Convair 440. It also operated a small number of T-29Bs

transferred from the USAF. The Canadian Armed Forces received eight aircraft similar to the USAF's VC-131Hs, designating them **CC-109 Metropolitan**. A number of ex-civil Convair 440s also entered service with the Bolivian, German, Italian and Spanish air forces.

Specification
Convair 440
Type: medium-range transport
Powerplant: two 1864-kW (2,500-hp) Pratt & Whitney R-2800-CB16 or -CB17 radial piston engines
Performance: maximum cruising

speed 483 km/h (300 mph) at 3960 m (13,000 ft); economic cruising speed 465 km/h (289 mph) at 6095 m (20,000 ft); service ceiling 7590 m (24,900 ft); range with maximum payload 756 km (470 miles)
Weights: operating empty 15111 kg (33,314 lb); maximum take-off 22226 kg (49,000 lb)
Dimensions: span 32.11 m (105 ft 4 in); length 24.13 m (79 ft 2 in); length with weather radar 24.84 m (81 ft 6 in); height 8.59 m (28 ft 2 in); wing area 85.47 m² (920.0 sq ft)

The Convair 110 was an early post-war attempt to break into the airline market. No production was undertaken as the type's payload was too small.

US forces bought a sizeable number of Convair twins, mostly for transport and training duties, although this C-131B was used as an electronics test-best.

A military variant of the CV-240, the T-29B was used for training navigators and radar operators. Note the underfuselage radome for bombing radar.

Convair CV-540, 580, 600 and 640

Convair CV-580 of Aspen Airways, USA

Many aircraft have had powerplant conversions to improve performance and/or economy, and the Convair 240/340/440 series is no exception to this exercise. The development of turboprop engines, which combine the light weight, smooth power, and reliability of the turbine with the reduction gear and propeller of a piston engine, offered an ideal replacement, but many early substitutions of turboprops for the piston engines of aircraft from an earlier era were not entirely successful. In the case of the Convairliners the reverse applied, for the robust, well-designed structures of these aircraft were able to accept the considerably more powerful turboprop engines without undue airframe stress, the result being a new lease of life for the series.

The first such conversions came in 1954, when D. Napier & Sons in the UK installed two of their 2282-ekW (3,060-ehp) Eland NE1.1 turboprop engines in a Convair 340, and this flew for the first time on 9 February 1955. This, and five similar aircraft entered service with

Allegheny Airlines in America, under the designation **Convair 540**. Subsequently, when development and production of the Eland came to an end in 1962, these particular aircraft reverted to piston-engine powerplant. Canadair, in Canada, converted three Convair 440s to Eland turboprops with the designation **Canadair 540**, and later built 10 new aircraft for service with the Royal Canadian Air Force under the designation **CL-66 Cosmopolitan**. They were re-engined with Allison

Model 501 turboprops.

In the USA, PacAero Engineering Corporation of Santa Monica, California, initiated a conversion programme for Convair 340 and 440 aircraft. This involved the installation of 2796-kW (3,750-shp) Allison 501-D13 turboprop engines, and the provision of greater area for the tail unit control surfaces. Designated **Convair 580**, and known sometimes as the **Super Convair**, all had accommodation for 52 passengers, as Convair 340 conversions included the installation of

the additional eight seats in the high-density arrangement. PacAero's first Model 580 made an initial flight on 19 January 1960, but it was not until June 1964 that the type began to enter airline service, with Frontier Airlines the first operator.

The last of these conversion programmes was that initiated by the original manufacturer, which selected the 2256-ekW (3,025-ehp) Rolls-Royce RDa.10/1 Dart 542 turboprop for installation in Model 240/340/440 aircraft. In

273

addition to the provision of these engines, the Model 240 was subjected also to airframe strengthening, and could be provided with a 48-seat interior arrangement, while the Model 340/440s could have a 56-seat layout. In their new form these aircraft were designated **Convair 240D, 340D,** and **440D** respectively, this being changed later to **Convair 600** for the Model 240D, and **Convair 640** for each of the other two. The first Model 600 entered service with Central Airlines on 30 November 1965, and the first Model 640 with Caribair on 22 December 1965.

Under the designations Convair 580/600/640 about 240 conversions were carried out, and a considerable number of these remain in service.

Specification
Convair 640
Type: medium-range transport
Powerplant: two 2256-ekW (3,025-ehp) Rolls-Royce RDa.10/1 Dart turboprops
Performance: cruising speed 483 km/h (300 mph); economic cruising speed 465 km/h (289 mph) at 6095 m (20,000 ft); range with maximum payload 1979 km (1,230 miles); range with maximum fuel 3138 km (1,950 miles)
Weights: operating empty 13733 kg (30,275 lb); maximum take-off 25855 kg (57,000 lb)
Dimensions: span 32.11 m (105 ft 4 in); length 24.84 m (81 ft 6 in); height 8.59 m (28 ft 2 in); wing area 85.47 m² (920.0 sq ft)

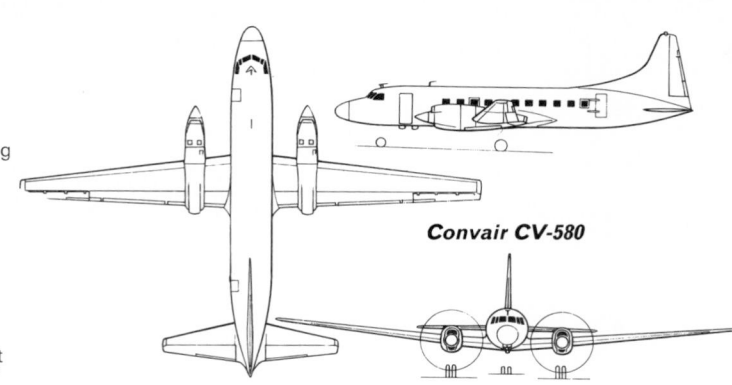

Convair CV-580

Convair CV-880 and 990

The news that Boeing and Douglas were building new-generation turbojet-powered airliners came as a challenge to Convair, who set out immediately to gain their share of this market. The company's interpretation of its market research led to a design that would carry fewer passengers than the competing Boeing 707 and Douglas DC-8, but which would have better high-speed performance.

In April 1956 Convair announced publicly its intention to build this new aircraft, simultaneously giving the news that Delta Air Lines and TWA had ordered respectively 10 and 30. Few aircraft can have had as many designations, beginning with the name **Convair Skylark,** later **Golden Arrow, Convair 600,** and finally **Convair 880** for the initial version, the prototype of which flew for the first time on 27 January 1959. In general appearance this was very similar to the Boeing 707, with a low-set monoplane wing that had an equivalent 35° of sweepback, swept conventional tail surfaces, and tricycle landing gear with four-wheel bogies on each main unit. Powerplant consisted of four 5080-kg (11,200-lb) thrust General Electric CJ805-3 turbojet engines, and these were also mounted similarly to those of the Boeing 707. The fuselage, however, was more slender than that of the production Boeing 707, limiting seating to a five-abreast layout that made provision for 88-110 passengers.

This original version of the Convair 880, known by the company as the **Model 22,** was intended for domestic use. Certification was gained on 1 May 1960, and Delta inaugurated its first service with the type exactly two weeks later. Despite a high cruising speed and range of close on 4828 km (3,000 miles) with full payload, its limited capacity by comparison with the competing Boeing and Douglas jet-powered airliners made the Convair 880 a far less attractive proposition to potential operators. By the time that production ended only 48 had been built. Even with the introduction of **Model 31** which, with increased fuel capacity and several other improvements, was intended for intercontinental services, restricted seating capacity meant it had little appeal to airline operators. Designated **Convair 880-M,** only 17 were built before production terminated.

Even before the Convair 880 prototype was flown the company had intended to build an increased-capacity higher-performance version known as the **Model 30.** It was, perhaps, unfortunate for Convair that an early order for this version from American Airlines sig-

Convair CV-990A of Spantax Transportes Aereos (Spain)

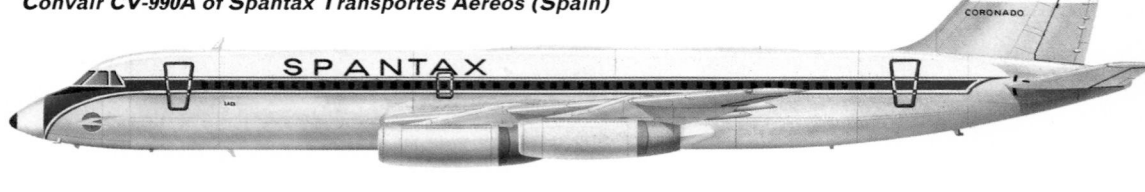

nalled a go-ahead for its production. Had there been more time in which to judge customer reaction to the Convair 880 a major redesign of the fuselage might have received consideration. Instead, the Model 30 was given a lengthened fuselage to increase capacity, but retained a fuselage width that was limited to the same five-abreast seating.

Other improvements were incorporated in the design of this aircraft, which was designated **Convair 990.** No prototype was built, and the first to fly on 24 January 1961 was one of those built for American Airlines. FAA certification was not gained until December of that year, and American was the recipient of the first aircraft for airline service on 7 January 1962. Swissair also received an initial aircraft at much the same time, and introduced yet another name, calling their aircraft **Coronado,** and made the first airline service with the type during the following month.

During the development flying that preceded certification, it was discovered that there were several aerodynamic shortcomings which eroded the planned performance of the Convair 990. Research and development to overcome these problems led to aerodynamic improvements that were introduced retrospectively to all 37 Convair 990s that were produced, aircraft as modified being redesignated **Convair 990A.**

Convair's 880 and 990 programme proved an extremely costly venture for the company and since that time the aviation divisions of General Dynamics

Corporation have confined their activities within the field of military aviation.

Specification
Convair 990A
Type: medium-range transport
Powerplant: four 7280-kg (16,050-lb) General Electric CJ805-23B turbofans
Performance: maximum level speed 990 km/h (615 mph) at 6095 m (20,000 ft); cruising speed 895 km/h (556 mph) at 10670 m (35,000 ft); service ceiling 12495 m (41,000 ft); range with maximum payload 6116 km (3,800 miles); range with maximum

Poorly conceived in terms of payload, operator options and cabin customer appeal, the CV-990 was nevertheless a good performer aerodynamically. Spantax amassed a large fleet.

fuel 8690 km (5,400 miles)
Weights: operating empty 54839 kg (120,900 lb); maximum take-off 114759 kg (253,000 lb)
Dimensions: span 36.58 m (120 ft 0 in); length 42.43 m (139 ft 2½ in); height 12.04 m (39 ft 6 in); wing area 209.03 m² (2,250.0 sq ft)

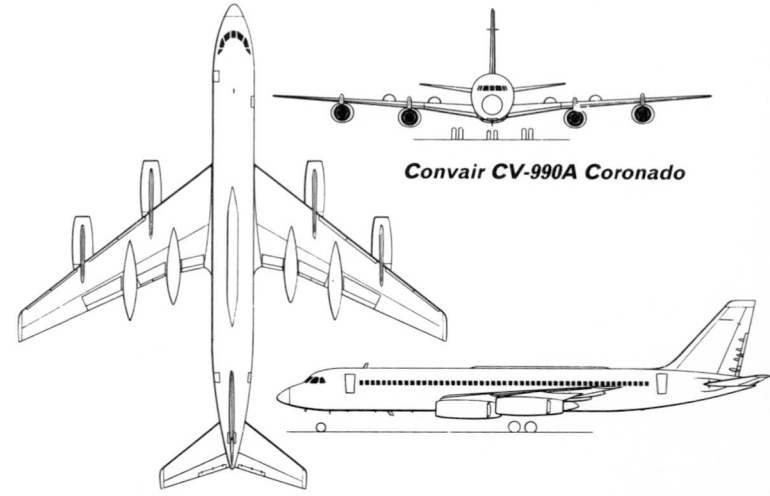

Convair CV-990A Coronado

Convair (Model 8) F-102 Delta Dagger

The **Convair F-102** was developed from the company's **XF-92A (Convair Model 7-002)** delta-wing research aircraft, which had been built under a USAF contract awarded on 16 May 1949. Germany's Dr Alexander Lippisch gave assistance in the design of this latter aircraft, which made its first flight on 18 September 1948. Only a single example was built, although the initial contract was for three aircraft, and in 1952 the USAF handed the XF-92A over to NACA (NASA's predecessor) after it had demonstrated a speed of 1014 km/h (630 mph) during tests with an Allison J33-A-29 turbojet engine.

Even before the contract for the XF-92A was awarded, the USAF had formulated an Advanced Development Objective (ADO) for an interceptor which would have performance considerably superior to that of Russian intercontinental jet bombers. However, this ADO was probably one of the most revolutionary in US Air Force history because, for the first time, it regarded this projected interceptor as a weapon system. It was realised that for far too long it had been customary to procure an airframe and its weapons as separate items; now the time had come to investigate the Weapon System concept, in which each of the differing units would integrate as a compatible system.

With these ideas in mind, requests for proposals were sent out on 18 June 1950 for a new interceptor, then identified as Project MX-1554. Four months later, Hughes Aircraft Company was awarded a contract for development of Project MX-1179, this being the Electronic Control System (ECS) with which the MX-1554 airframe would be compatible. In spite of an extended development period of the design concept, the MX-1179 failed to materialise within an acceptable time scale for this aircraft and was abandoned. Instead the Hughes E-9 (later designated MG-3) fire-control system was adopted, and finally replaced by the MG-10.

Six airframe manufacturers submitted proposals in January 1951, Convair, Lockheed and Republic being chosen to develop their designs to mock-up stage. However, it did not take the US Air Force long to realise that it could not afford three projects and on 11 September 1951 gave Convair a contract which authorised use of the Westinghouse J40 turbojet, pending availability of the more powerful Wright J67. A decision to proceed with production of the **Convair Model 8-80** was made on 24 November 1951, it being regarded as an interim project until an 'Ultimate Interceptor' should reach fruition. The first **YF-102** prototype made its first flight on 24 October 1953, but was lost in an accident only nine days later. By that time, however, it had demonstrated that performance was far below the required figures: this dismal forecast was confirmed by the second YF-102A when it flew on 11 January 1954.

It was not until a major redesign incorporated the area-ruled fuselage concept, which had emanated as a result carried out by Richard Whitcomb at NACA, that a new-looking wasp-waisted prototype flew on 19 December 1954. Powered by an advanced example of the Pratt & Whitney J57-P-23 turbojet engine that was to power production aircraft, this **YF-102A (Model 8-90)** prototype achieved a speed of Mach 1.22 and altitude of 16155 m (53,000 ft) during its first flight. The **F-102A (Model 8-10)** entered service with Air Defense Command's 327th Fighter-Interceptor Squadron at George AFB in April 1956, and procurement finally totalled 889. In addition, 111 **TF-102A (Model 8-12)** two-seat side-by-side trainers were built for the USAF, these retaining full operational armament and capability. To represent MiG-21s in aerial combat, six F-102As were converted, under a USAF contract awarded in April 1973, into two

Delta Daggers defended the far north of the United States. Those based in Alaska wore day-glo panels for high conspicuity.

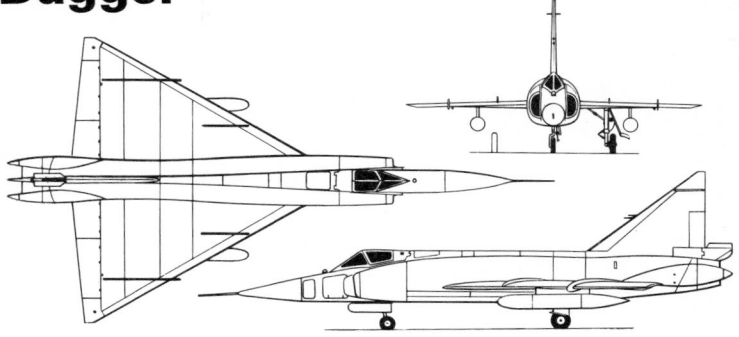

Convair F-102A Delta Dagger

QF-102A piloted and four **PQM-102A** unpiloted target drones under the 'Pave Deuce' programme, with further PQM-102As following. An improved **F-102B** was planned, but this materialised eventually as the F-106 Delta Dart.

Specification
Type: supersonic all-weather single-seat fighter-interceptor
Powerplant: one 7802-kg (17,200-lb) afterburning thrust Pratt & Whitney J57-P-23 or -25 turbojet
Performance: maximum speed 1328 km/h (825 mph) or Mach 1.25 at 10970 m (36,000 ft); initial climb rate 3960 m (13,000 ft) per minute; maximum range 2173 km (1,350 miles)
Weights: maximum take-off as point interceptor 12769 kg (28,150 lb); maximum take-off as area interceptor, with two 814-litre (215-US gal) drop tanks 14187 kg (31,276 lb)
Dimensions: span 11.62 m (38 ft 1½ in); length 20.84 m (68 ft 4½ in); height 6.46 m (21 ft 2½ in); wing area 61.45 m² (661.5 sq ft)
Armament: includes two AIM-26/26A Falcon missiles, or one AIM-26/26A plus two AIM-4A Falcons, or one AIM-26/26A plus two AIM-4C/Ds, or six AIM-4As, or six AIM-4C/Ds; aircraft not modified for interchangeable use of AIM-26 or AIM-4 missiles in the weapons bay could also carry 12 69.85-mm (2.75-in) folding-fin rockets

Convair (Model 8-24) F-106 Delta Dart

In the early 1950s it became clear that the 'Ultimate Interceptor' being developed by Convair would not be operational by its 1954 deadline. Faced with this problem the US Air Force decided to procure from Convair a less sophisticated interim interceptor. This emerged as the F-102A Delta Dagger, and the original 'Ultimate Interceptor' (Project MX-1554) was then designated **F-102B**. It is this latter project which eventually became the **Convair F-106 Delta Dart**.

It was fortunate that the USAF adopted such a policy, for the F-102A ran into serious development problems, and it was not until April 1956 that the first production examples of this 'interim' aircraft entered service. In the same period the F-102B was virtually at a standstill, starved of funds and still awaiting its powerplant and ECS. When the F-102A tests were seen to be successful the US Air Force contracted for 749 examples:

at the same time an order was placed for 17 F-102Bs. This was in November 1955, by which time the MX-1179 ECS had found a creator, the Hughes Aircraft Company, which designated it the Hughes MA-1 fire control system, and a mock up of the proposed cockpit with radically new equipment and cockpit displays was available for inspection in December 1955.

On 17 June 1956 the F-102B was redesignated officially as the F-106, reflecting the fact that the original requirement had now changed considerably. When the initial details became known, on 28 September 1956 it was clear that the USAF had raised its sights somewhat. Convair was now required to produce an aircraft capable of intercepting enemy vehicles in all weathers at altitudes up to 21335 m (70,000 ft) and within a radius of 692 km (430 miles). Armed with guided missiles, and/or rockets with atomic warheads,

the F-106 was expected also to carry out interceptions at speeds of up to Mach 2.0 at heights of up to 10670 m (35,000 ft), under automatic guidance from SAGE (semi-automatic ground environment) installations integrating with the MA-1 fire control system.

Two **F-106A (Convair Model 8-24)** prototypes made their first flights 26 December 1956 and 26 February

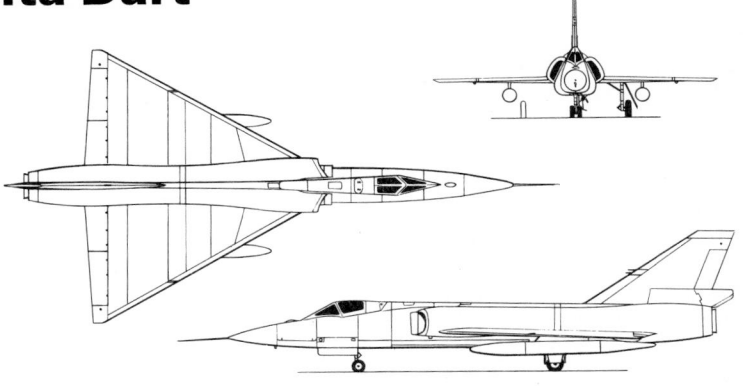

1957, but flight tests were disappointing, and it was painfully obvious that there were still many shortcomings. Maximum speed was some 15 per cent below the required figure, but causing greater concern was the slow rate of acceleration, and neither of these factors was helped by delays in the Pratt & Whitney J57-P-9 turbojet which had been substituted for the Wright J67 chosen originally. To aggravate the situation still further, the MA-1 ECS was not performing well, and a shortage of funds almost caused the USAF to scrap the entire F-106 programme.

To salvage something from this difficult situation, the USAF decided to reduce its planned procurement of 1,000 F-106s to 350. So much had already been spent on the programme that it seemed sensible to continue development so that the US Air Force would eventually acquire a smaller but high-quality force of interceptors. Engine intake modifications, and eradication of some of the bugs from engine and avionics, made it possible for the first deliveries of aircraft with an initial operational capability to be made to the 498th Fighter Interceptor Squadron at Geiger AFB, Washington, in October 1959. Production of 277 **F-106A** single-seat fighters and 63 **F-106B (Model 8-27)** two-seat combat trainers (which retained full combat capability) ended in December 1960. Improved **F-106C**, **F-106D** and **F-106X** variants were projected but none were built.

Late production F-106As differed from those which entered service in 1959, which meant that modification programmes to bring all aircraft to a common standard (**Model 8-31** for single-seaters and **Model 80-32** for two-seaters) were running concurrently with the production of new aircraft. Circumstances demanded that the F-106s remained in first-line service long beyond their originally anticipated life, which has meant that updating programmes have been almost continuous since that time. After more than 20 years' service with the USAF, F-106s were finally withdrawn from service in 1988.

Specification
Type: single-seat supersonic all-weather interceptor
Powerplant: one 11113-kg (24,500-lb) afterburning thrust Pratt & Whitney J75-P-17 turbojet
Performance: maximum speed 2454 km/h (1,525 mph) or Mach 2.31 at 12190 m (40,000 ft); service ceiling 17375 m (57,000 ft); combat radius with external fuel tanks 1173 km (729 miles)
Weights: empty 10728 kg (23,646 lb); maximum take-off for area interceptor mission 17554 kg (38,700 lb); maximum take-off 18975 kg (41,831 lb)
Dimensions: span 11.67 m (38 ft 3½ in); length 21.56 m (70 ft 8¾ in); height 6.18 m (20 ft 3¼ in); wing area 58.65 m² (631.3 sq ft)
Armament: one Douglas AIR-2A Genie or AIR-2B Super Genie rocket, and four Hughes AIM-4F or AIM-4G Super Falcon air-to-air missiles carried in internal weapons bay; many aircraft also have one 20-mm M61 Vulcan gun in place of Genie

Convair R3Y Tradewind

In March 1943, Reuben Fleet sold his interest in Consolidated Aircraft Corporation and the company was reorganised as Consolidated Vultee (Convair). Shortly after this the US Navy expressed interest in a new long-range multi-role flying-boat, and Convair's proposal for an aircraft powered by four turboprop engines, was the subject of a contract for two prototypes, awarded on 27 May 1946. Designated **XP5Y-1**, the new aircraft featured an unusually slim fuselage for an aircraft of this class with a length-to-beam ratio of 10 to 1. It was powered by four Allison T40-A4 turboprops, each driving two contra-rotating propellers through a common gearbox. The type's main role was anti-submarine warfare, and it was to have been fitted with advanced radar, ECM and MAD equipment in addition to carrying a heavy load of bombs, mines, rockets and torpedoes. The first aircraft was flown from San Diego on 18 April 1950, and in August the type set a turboprop endurance record of 8 hours 6 minutes. August was an eventful month for the XP5Y-1 as the US Navy decided to discontinue its development for maritime patrol, but to persevere with the basic design for use as a passenger and cargo aircraft.

Work continued, despite the loss of an XP5Y-1 in a non-fatal crash off San Diego in 15 July 1953 and the first **R3Y-1 Tradewind** flew on 25 February 1954.

This remarkable photo shows four Grumman Panthers refuelling simultaneously from an R3Y-2 Tradewind. The nose section was hinged.

Major changes included the deletion of all armament and of tailplane dihedral, the addition of a 3.05 m (10 ft) wide portside cargo hatch aft of the wing and the provision of redesigned engine nacelles to accept the improved T40-A-10 engines. Cabin sound-proofing and air-conditioning were installed and pressurised accommodation provided for up to 103 passengers or, in medevac configuration, for 72 stretcher cases and 12 attendants; cargo payload was 24.4 tonnes (24 tons).

The R3Y-1's performance was demonstrated on 24 February 1955 when one of the five aircraft built flew coast-to-coast at an average speed of 649 km/h (403 mph) on delivery to the Navy Test Center at Patuxent River, Maryland. Similarly, on 18 October a 6 hour 45 minute record flight at an average 579 m/h (360 mph) was accomplished between Honolulu and NAS Alameda, California. US Navy transport squadron VR-2 received the first of its mixed fleet of R3Y-1 and R3Y-2 flying-boats on 31 March 1956, but financial considerations and continuing problems with the engine/propeller combination, culminating in two in-flight separations of propell-

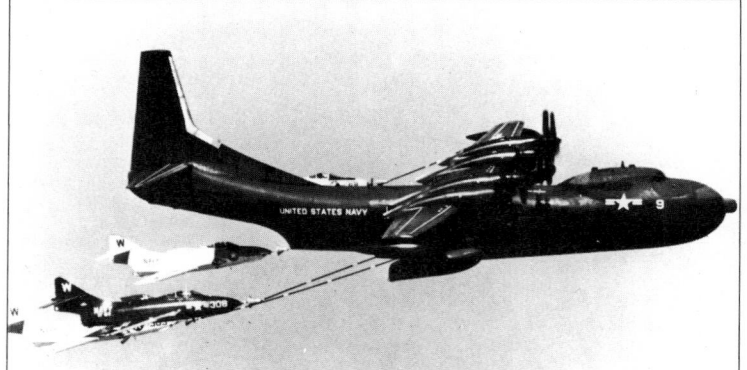

ers and gearbox from an engine (on 10 May 1957 and on 2 January 1958), led to a curtailment of Tradewind operations. Squadron strength was first cut to two R3Y-1s and two R3Y-2s and the unit was finally disbanded on 16 April 1958.

Variant
R3Y-2: six examples of this assault transport were built, featuring a hinged nose section which opened upward to provide an exit 2.03 m (6 ft 8 in) high and 2.54 m (8 ft 4 in) wide, through which men and equipment could be landed directly on to the beach using the aircraft's built-in ramp; the R3Y-2 made its first flight on 22 December 1954 and in September 1956 one example, equipped as a tanker, made

flight refuelling history by replenishing simultaneously four Grumman F9F-8 Cougar fighters.

Specification
Convair R3Y-1
Type: heavy transport flying-boat
Powerplant: four 4362-kW (5,850-shp) Allison T40-A-10 turboprops
Performance: maximum speed more than 579 km/h (360 mph); cruising speed 483 km/h (300 mph); maximum range 6437 km (4,000 miles)
Weights: normal take-off 74843 kg (165,000 lb); maximum take-off 79379 kg (175,000 lb)
Dimensions: span 44.42 m (145 ft 9 in); length 42.57 m (139 ft 8 in); height 13.67 m (44 ft 10 in)

Convair XFY-1

Contemporary with the Lockheed XFV-1, the **Convair XFY-1** was designed for the same US Navy competition. This was intended to investigate the potential of a small single-seat tail-sitting VTOL fighter aircraft for operation from and to small platforms on a variety of ships. The fuselage served to accommodate the pilot's cockpit and turboprop power-plant, and mounted externally the monoplane wings of modified delta planform and large dorsal and ventral tail surfaces in a cruciform arrangement. On the ground the XFY-1 rested on small castoring wheels at the tips of the horizontal and vertical surfaces.

Extensive tethered tests from a special rig were followed by a first vertical take-off and landing on 1 August 1954. Testing continued with a series of similar vertical flights before the first complete transition from vertical to horizontal flight and vice versa was accomplished on 2 November 1954. Although some 40 flight hours were accumulated by two prototypes of this experimental fighter, its development was abandoned as a result of major flight control problems.

Specification
Type: experimental VTOL fighter

Powerplant: one 4362-ekW (5,850-ehp) Allison YT40-A-6 turboprop driving large-diameter co-axial contra-rotating propellers
Performance: maximum speed 982 km/h (610 mph) at 4570 m (15,000 ft); initial climb rate 3200 m (10,500 ft) per minute; service ceiling 13320 m (43,700 ft)
Weights: empty 5345 kg (11,784 lb); maximum take-off 7371 kg (16,250 lb)
Dimensions: span 8.43 m (27 ft 7¾ in); tail span 6.98 m (22 ft 11 in); length 10.66 m (34 ft 11¾ in); wing area 32.98 m² (355.0 sq ft)
Armament: (proposed) four 20-mm cannon in wingtip pods, or 46 69.85-mm (2.75-in) unguided rockets

Landing and taking-off vertically, the XFY-1 had four bedstead-type wheels.

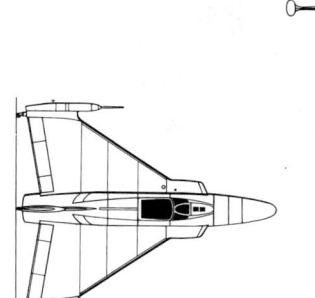

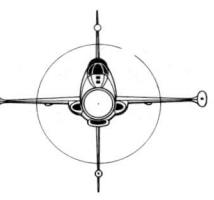

Convair XFY-1 'Pogo'

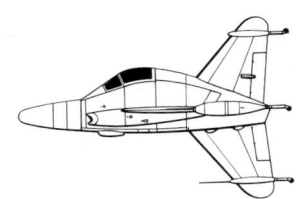

Convair (Model 2) XF2Y-1 Sea Dart

One of the most unusual single-seat fighters to be developed during the early years following World War II, the water-based **Convair Sea Dart** had a blended hull mounting delta wings and large vertical tail surfaces. For take-off and landing it had extendable hydro-skis; these produced sufficient hydrodynamic lift during the take-off run to raise the hull clear of the water, the Sea Dart then aquaplaning on the skis until flying speed was attained.

The concept embodied in the **Convair Model 2-2** proposal was sufficiently interesting to the US Navy to award a contract for a prototype **XF2Y-1** on 19 January 1951, followed by

an order for 12 production **F2Y-1** fighters on 28 August 1952; to this was added subsequently four **YF2Y-1** pre-production aircraft. First flown on 9 April 1953, the prototype offered performance much below expectations and this factor, coupled with serious vibration problems with the hydro-skis, led to the XF2Y-1 and the production F2Y-1s being cancelled. More power was needed than the 1542-kg (3,400-lb) thrust provided by each of the Westinghouse J34-WE-32 turbojets installed in the prototype and the first YF2Y-1. This latter aircraft was re-engined with two J34-WE-2s, the rear fuselage being modified to accommodate the engine

afterburners and the same powerplant was installed in the remaining three YF2Y-1s. On 3 August 1954 the YF2Y-1 exceeded a speed of Mach 1 in a shallow dive, the first seaplane to become supersonic, but only two of these aircraft were used in a limited test programme that was terminated finally during 1956.

Specification
Convair YF2Y-1
Type: experimental fighter seaplane
Powerplant: two 2722-kg (6,000-lb) thrust Westinghouse J46-WE-2 afterburning turbojets

Performance: (estimated) maximum speed 1118 km/h (695 mph) at 2440 m (8,000 ft); initial climb rate 9965 m (32,700 ft); service ceiling 16705 m (54,800 ft); range 826 km (513 miles)
Weights: empty 5739 kg (12,652 lb); maximum take-off 7495 kg (16,527 lb)
Dimensions: span 10.26 m (38 ft 8 in); length 16.03 m (52 ft 7 in); height on hydro-skis 6.32 m (20 ft 9 in); wing area 52.30 m² (563.0 sq ft)

Offering exceptional performance thanks to advanced aero- and hydro-dynamic research, the Sea Dart foundered as a programme due to severe vibration of the hydro-skis and lack of power.

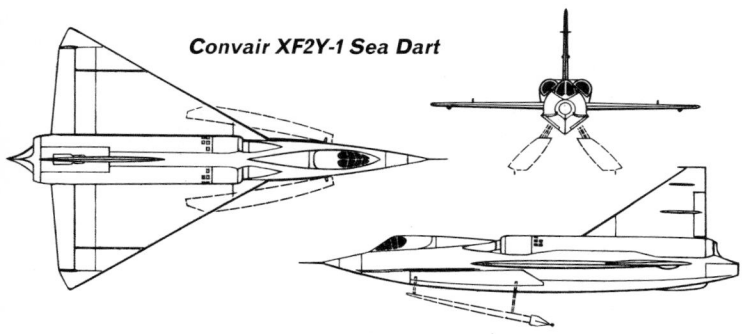

Convair XF2Y-1 Sea Dart

Curtiss early pushers

American Glenn Curtiss, like the Wright brothers, had a background as a cycle manufacturer. It was not long, however, before he designed and built an engine to power them, thus gaining a foothold in the motorcycle industry. The capability of his lightweight petrol engines led to their use to power a number of early airships, bringing an invitation to Curtiss from inventor Alexander Graham Bell to become a member of his Aerial Experiment Association, which was established formally on 1 October 1907. He contributed significantly to the design and development of four aircraft designated Aerodromes Nos 1, 2 3 and 4 and named respectively *Red Wing*, *White Wing*, *June Bug* and *Silver Dart*.

In 1909 Curtiss produced his first independent aeroplane, the **Curtiss No. 1**, known as the *Gold Bug* or *Golden Flyer*. It was followed by the **Reims Racer**, a slightly larger version of the *Gold Bug*, in which Curtiss won the 1909 Gordon Bennett Cup at Reims, France. In an attempt to win a $10,000 prize for a

flight routed over the River Hudson, between Albany and New York City, he modified one of his standard models, with the result that the **Hudson Flyer** was basically an amphibian, with

wheeled landing gear plus emergency flotation gear. It was good enough to achieve the 251-km (156-mile) flight and take the prize.

After building a one-off **Beachey Special** for exhibition pilot Lincoln Beachey, the Curtiss Aeroplane Company, established on 1 December 1910, got

This is one of eight Curtiss pushers bought for the US Navy between 1911 and 1913, the other seven being seaplanes. This aircraft was soon converted with floats. At the controls is Lieutenant Theodore G. Ellyson, Naval Aviator No. 1.

The Model D of 1911 was typical of the relatively obsolescent landplane types being built at the time in the United States, various powerplants were available, the most powerful being a 56-kW (75-hp) unit.

down to the serious business of designing, building and selling aircraft. Production included the single-seat **Model D**, available with 30-, 45- or 56-kW (40-, 60- or 75-hp) Curtiss engines driving two-blade pusher propellers; and the two-seat **Model E** with a similar range of engines.

Curtiss also devoted much energy to the development of seaplanes, both pusher and tractor, and these are covered in a separate entry.

Curtiss early seaplanes

Glenn Curtiss was the world's leading pioneer of flying-boat design before World War I, and a notable exponent of floatplanes too. The first time Curtiss had any dealings with waterplanes was in 1908, when the Aerial Experiment Association, of which Curtiss was a member, tried to coax its *Loon* (the Aerodrome No. 3 *June Bug*, fitted with cloth-covered wooden pontoons) off a lake. Though this trial was unsuccessful, some progress had been made by June 1910, when Curtiss made a satisfactory landing on Lake Keuka in a Curtiss Type III pusher biplane fitted with a canoe. The combination was quite unable to take off, however.

In 1911 Curtiss finally achieved moderately successful designs for seaplanes. The first of these was unnamed, being referred to by Curtiss merely as his **'hyroaeroplane'** or **'hydro'**: a pusher biplane with fore and aft elevators, the 'hydro' sat on a single main float, measuring 1.82 m (6 ft) in length and 1.52 m (5 ft) in width, under the wings and a smaller forward float and hydrofoil under the forward elevator. In this form the 'hydro' first flew on 26 January 1911, but the type was soon modified to single-float configuration. This one large unit was 3.65 m (12 ft) long, and 0.61 m (2 ft) wide and 0.305 m (1 ft) deep; small balancer floats were fitted under the wingtips.

Next appeared the **Tractor Hydro**, a modified Type III with a single main float. But Curtiss did not like the type as he had to sit in the slipstream and the engine fumes. He therefore went on to other machines: the **Triad** of February 1911 was the world's first successful amphibian, with a fixed nosewheel under the forward end of a 'hydro' float, and retractable mainwheels under the lower wings. Here followed several other floatplanes and flying-boats. In June 1911 Curtiss handed over to the US Navy an example of his Model E, revised to operate with the naval designation **A-1** (later **AH-1**) as a landplane, floatplane or amphibian; in the next three years the US Navy bought another 13 Curtiss pushers that could be used on floats.

Curtiss then turned his attention to the flying-boat as a basic type, logically starting with the **Flying-Boat No. 1**, which was an unsuccessful type with a large pontoon attached directly to the lower wings, and housing the 44.7-kW (60-hp) engine, which drove two wing-mounted tractor propellers by means of chain drives.

The basic configuration for the small single-engined biplane flying-boat was evolved by Curtiss in 1912, and remained fundamentally the same for the next 40 years. The **Curtiss Flying-Boat No. 2** incorporated for the first time the vital hydrodynamic step in the undersurface of the hull which was the secret of successful take-off from water. It was named *The Flying Fish*.

Thereafter a series of experimental aircraft appeared which culminated in the **Type F**. The US Navy bought five **Type C** flying-boats from Curtiss in 1913, but in reality each of these aircraft differed considerably from the next, and the **C-2** was identical to the early Type F except that the upper wing had increased span. The C-2 was used for experiments with a Sperry gyroscopic automatic pilot as early as August 1913! The **C-3** or **AB-3** carried out a number of spotting patrols over Vera Cruz harbour during United States action against Mexico in April 1914.

The definitive 1913 Model F was used by the US Army as well as the US Navy, and sold to several civil owners and a number were exported. Of wooden construction, the two-bay biplane had interplane ailerons on each side, fabric-covered wings and tail unit, and a carefully contoured single-step plywood-covered hull which accommodated two side-by-side in a cockpit location just forward of the wings. Power was provided by a 56-kW (75-hp) Curtiss O engine driving a pusher propeller, the engine being mounted on struts just below the upper wing centre-section.

The 1914 version of the Model F had rounded wingtips, a tougher hull and increased strut support for the engine to prevent it collapsing on the crew in the event of a crash. This basic design was ordered by the US Navy, and after the United States entered World War I on 6 April 1917 it was adapted as the service's standard primary training flying-boat, 144 more being ordered.

The 1917-18 version of the Model F eliminated the original shoulder-yoke type aileron control in favour of a more

Four examples of the Model L-2 triplane were built, three for the US Navy and one for the US Army.

conventional arrangement; and some aircraft had the ailerons transferred to the upper wing from the interplane position, span of the upper wing being extended. Several ambulance conversions flew with provision for a stretcher patient to be carried above the hull behind the cockpit. The more powerful Curtiss OXX-3 engine was fitted from 1917 onwards.

The Model F, particularly in its earlier versions, was sold to a number of foreign navies. Russia obtained a considerable number for operation in the Baltic and Black Seas. The Italians also flew the Model F and eight examples were licence-built by the Zari company at Bovisio.

Variants

Model MF: known under the Curtiss company's retrospectively applied numbering system as the **Model 18**, this was one of a number of experimental developments of the Model F but was the only one to be accepted for production; it was substantially improved structurally and incorporated sponsons on the side of the forward hull, and the MF designation implied 'Modernized Model F'; the type was fitted experimentally with engines in the 112-kW (150-hp) class; the 22 US Navy Model MFs delivered by Curtiss and the 80 additional aircraft built by the Naval Aircraft Factory retained the 75-kW (100-hp) Curtiss OXX-3 engine; during the early 1920s some ex-US Navy Model MFs were modified under the name *Seagull* for the civil market by Curtiss and Cox-Klemin, and others were built as new for private owners

Model 7 (Judson Triplane): produced late in 1916 or early in 1917, this was a slightly scaled-up version of the Model F built as a one-off for a Mr Judson; it was originally powered by a 112-kW (150-hp) Curtiss V-X engine, but was re-engined with a 298-kW (400-hp)

A Model F flying-boat of the US Navy in 1918. This was an early production model with interplane ailerons mounted on the outboard struts.

Curtiss K-12 for post-war exploratory flights in South America

Model K: 1915 larger development of Model F, which proved only moderarely successful in the USA but was widely exported; spanning 17.01 m (55 ft 10 in) and having a maximum take-off weight of 1769 kg (3,900 lb), the Model K was powered by a 112-kW (150-hp) V-X engine in pusher layout, and had a maximum speed of 113 km/h (70 mph)

Freak Boat: a small flying-boat of 1912, in which the pilot was seated on top of the shallow hull; extensively revised, the aircraft was sold to the US Navy as the **C-1**, later changed to **AB-1**; the C-1 was used for the first successful catapult launch of a flying-boat

Tadpole: like the Freak Boat a pusher biplane, the Tadpole was based on the use of an elongated hydro-float as the hull, an interesting feature being the built-up sides to cover the gap between the top of the float and the lower wing.

A-2: the US Navy's second aeroplane was the A-2, essentially a Model E landplane and modified in June 1912 as a seaplane; with a short hull, plus retractable wheels to give amphibious capability, this became redesignated initially **OWL** (Over Water and Land), subsequently **E-1** and finally **AX-1**; it was used experimentally from late 1912 until being destroyed in an accident in late November 1915; from these early basic designs, all of pusher configuration, was developed the Model F

Model M: one-off parasol-wing monoplane flying-boat for a Curtiss employee named Morris; appeared in 1913; powered by a 67-kW (90-hp) Curtiss O

Specification
Curtiss Model F (1917 version)
Powerplant: one 75-kW (100-hp) Curtiss OXX-3 inline piston engine
Performance: maximum speed 110 km/h (68 mph); service ceiling 1370 m (4,500 ft); endurance 5 hours 30 minutes
Weights: empty 844 kg (1,860 lb); maximum take-off 1116 kg (2,460 lb)
Dimensions: span 13.75 m (45 ft 1¼ in); length 8.48 m (27 ft 9¾ in); height 3.42 m (11 ft 2¾ in); wing area 35.95 m² (387.0 sq ft)

Curtiss NC
to
Curtiss Model 35/7, Model 64/67 (F11C) and Model 68

Curtiss NC

During 1917 the US Navy Bureau of Construction and Repair collaborated with Glenn Curtiss in an effort to produce a flying-boat that would be capable of crossing the Atlantic without difficulty. The intention was to ensure that such 'boats would be able to join operations in the war zone immediately after their arrival.

Preliminary designs, drawn up by naval team which included Commander Jerome Hunsaker, were developed by Curtiss and his engineers. The selected configuration was a wide-span biplane with three tractor engines, a short hull to accommodate a crew of five, and a biplane tail supported on booms projecting from the upper wing and the rear of the hull. Detail design was carried out by the Curtiss staff, except for the hull which was the work of US Navy Commander Holden Richardson. Soon afterwards Curtiss received an order for production of the **NC** 'boat as it had by then been designated (NC for Navy-Curtiss). Four aircraft were to be built by Curtiss, and it was decided that the Naval Aircraft Factory would build six more.

Existing factory space at the Curtiss Garden City, New York factory was greatly expanded with US Navy help for production of the NCs, which were to be taken by road in sections for final assembly at Rockaway Naval Air Station. When World War I ended only the **NC-1** had been completed and the original purpose of the design no longer existed. Although the NAF NCs were cancelled, the US Navy decided to go ahead with the four Curtiss 'boats which would be used in a transatlantic flight to the UK. It was felt that the publicity gained by such a flight would be of great value to the US Navy.

Three NC 'boats (NC-1, **NC-3** and **NC-4**) left Trepassey Bay, Newfoundland on 16 May 1919, NC-2 having already come to grief. Both the NC-1 and the NC-3 came down at sea short of Horta in the Azores, which was to be the first stop. Neither could take off again, the NC-1 being abandoned and its crew taken off by ship, but the NC-3 was able to taxi to Horta. Only the NC-4 completed the journey to Plymouth successfully, arriving on 31 May following stops at Horta, Ponta Delgada, Lisbon, and Ferrol del Caudillo. The total distance flown from take-off at Rockaway, New York on 8 May was 6317 km (3,925 miles), completed in 57 hours 16 minutes total flight time.

Variants
NC-1: powered by three 268-kW (360-hp) Liberty engines in tractor configuration; first flight on 4 October 1918 piloted by Commander Richardson, and lifted a record load of 51 passengers plus crew in November 1918; found to be unable to lift sufficient fuel for the transatlantic attempt, it was modified to take an additional Liberty engine: the centre engine was raised and nacelle fitted with additional engine at rear driving a pusher propeller.
NC-2: appeared in February 1919; centre of three engines was of pusher configuration; pilots were accommodated in the extended forward section of the nacelle for the pusher engine; the first modification involved relocation of the powerplant, four engines being installed in tandem pairs in the side nacelles. Finally the pilots' cockpits were relocated conventionally in the hull to produce what was then known as the **Type NC-T**; shortly afterwards NC-2 was wrecked in a storm, salvaged parts being used as spares for the remaining 'boats
NC-3: made debut April 1919; had four-engined NC-1 layout from start, and known as **NC-TA**; flagship of leader of Seaplane Division One, which made transatlantic attempt, under Captain John H. Towers
NC-4: appeared April 1919; also had revised NC-1 (NC-TA) configuration; after its successful transatlantic flight the hull was placed on display; in 1969 the whole machine was rebuilt and displayed in Washington DC to

Curtiss NC-4 of Lieutenant Commander A.C. Read, US Navy. In this aircraft he completed the first ever transatlantic flight in May 1919.

commemorate 50th anniversary of the flight; NC-4 now preserved at US Naval Aviation Museum at Pensacola, Florida.

Specification
Curtiss NC-4
Type: long-range flying-boat
Powerplant: four 298-kW (400-hp) Liberty 12A inline piston engines
Performance: maximum speed 137 km/h (85 mph); service ceiling 760 m (2,500 ft); endurance 14 hours 45 minutes at cruising speed

NC-4 is seen here taxiing in to Lisbon on 27 May after its momentous flight across the Atlantic. The flight left from Trepassey Bay in Newfoundland on 16 May.

Weights: empty 7257 kg (16,000 lb); maximum take-off 12701 kg (28,000 lb)
Dimensions: span 38.40 m (126 ft 0 in); length 20.80 m (68 ft 3 in); height 7.44 m (24 ft 5 in); wing area 226.77 m² (2,441.0 sq ft)

Curtiss JN-4

The **Curtiss JN-4** two-seat biplane soon acquired the nickname 'Jenny' which was used widely during the interwar years. It was one of the most significant American aircraft of its time. From April 1917 when the USA entered World War I it was built in large numbers and used to train some 95 per cent of all American and Canadian pilots. It achieved renewed fame from 1919 until the late 1920s, when thousands were flown in the barnstorming era, thrilling

spectators at travelling aerial pageants and shows throughout the United States.

The JN-4 was developed from the JN-2, via the interim **JN-3** which had featured unequal-span wings with ailerons on the upper wing only and introduced a wheel-type aileron control system. Redesigned vertical tail surfaces had a fin and rudder assembly with contours which were to be largely retained in the JN-4. The UK bought 91 JN-3s and the US Army two. Several JN-2s were converted subsequently to JN-3 standard by the incorporation of

JN-3 wings and vertical tail surfaces and by installation of the 75-kW (100-hp) Curtiss OXX engine. Total production was no more than 100, a dozen built at a newly-built Toronto factory.

The JN-4 in its original form closely resembled the JN-3, retaining the same unequal-span two-bay wing and cross-axle landing gear. It first appeared in July 1916 when 105 were sold to the UK and 21 to the US Army. Others were purchased by private owners and a number were operated by the Curtiss company's flying schools. As a result of British experience with the JN-3 and JN-4 the Cur-

tiss company developed the **JN-4A** (re-tro-designated **Model 1** in 1935), which incorporated a number of improvements (larger tailplane and engine downthrust). A total of 781 was completed, 87 of them at the Curtiss Canadian factory. The US Army bought 601, the US Navy five and the rest were exported to the UK. The **JN-4B (Model 1A)** appeared in late 1916, just before the JN-4A. It differed in several design details (it introduced the larger tailplane and used the OX-2 engine), and found a number of private purchasers and flying schools as customers, added to which the US Army bought 76 and the US Navy nine.

Two examples of the experimental **JN-4C** were followed by the very successful **JN-4 Can** and **JN-4D (Model 1C)**. The former had been developed from the JN-3 by the Curtiss company's Canadian associate, Canadian Aeroplanes Limited, and soon became known as the **Canuck**. Production totalled 1,260 of which 680 went to the US Army while the bulk of the remainder became the standard Canadian primary trainer. The JN-4 Can served with the Royal Canadian Air Force until 1924, while privately owned aircraft remained in use into the 1930s. John Ericson, chief engineer of Canadian Aeroplanes Ltd, assembled 127 aircraft in 1927, most of them reconditioned aircraft incorporating many parts which had been held in stock. Some had a third cockpit and were known under the designation **Ericson Special Three**.

The JN-4D appeared in June 1917 and went into large-scale production, 2,812 being built between November 1917 and January 1919. In view of the urgent need for efficient trainers in wartime conditions the production involved six other US manufacturers. As well as several new features, the JN-4D combined the more successful elements of both the JN-4 Can and JN-4A designs (stick control of the former, in place of the Deperdussin system, and the lines and engine downthrust of the latter). The end of World War I led to cancellation of contracts for 1,100 examples of a **JN-4D-2** version, which had a number of modifications requested by the US Army. In the event, only the prototype was delivered to the military authorities, although several were sold to civil operators in 1919.

In a bid to provide an advanced trainer to meet urgent wartime needs, the JN-4D was re-engined with the more powerful 112-kW (150-hp) Hispano-Suiza built by the Wright company. The resulting **JN-4H (Model 1E)** was in production from the end of 1917 to the November 1918 armistice, 929 being delivered to the US Army. The JN-4H was completed also in dual-control (**JN-4HT**), combing (**JN-4HB**) and gunnery trainer (**JN-4HG**) versions.

The one-off **JN-5H** advanced trainer was built to a US Army requirement, but was rejected in favour of the Vought VE-7. It was developed into the **JN-6H (Model 1F)** which had a strengthened aileron control structure. The US Army purchased 1,035 JN-6Hs, subsequently passing five examples to the US Navy. The aircraft delivered to the US Army were built in sub-variants specialised for various training functions. (**JN-6HB** single-control bomber trainer, **JN-6HG-1** dual-control trainer, **JN-6HG-2** single-control gunnery

trainer, **JN-6HO** single-control observation trainer and **JN-6HP** single-control pursuit [fighter] trainer).

As part of the post-war economy drive the US Army was forced to modernize the 'Jenny' rather than purchase new designs. This task was allocated to US Army Service Depots, which upgraded many of the earlier versions until 1926. The revised aircraft all used Wright-built 134-kW (180-hp) Hispano-Suiza engines and were redesignated **JNS** (standing for JN Standardized). Between 200 and 300 JNS trainers were completed.

The US Army used JN-4As, JN-4Ds and JN-4 Can primary trainers until 1919. The higher powered JN-4Hs and JN-6Hs remained in service until they were phased out in favour of new types in the mid-1920s, the last Jennies being withdrawn from US Army service in 1927.

Meanwhile, from 1919 onwards more and more Jennies had been sold to private owners, many of whom used their aircraft to earn a living as stunt pilots. Unhampered by regulations relating to their operation until the first restrictions were applied in 1927, Jennies became well known to a whole generation of citizens right across the United States. Operating on a travelling circus basis and flying from unprepared fields on the outskirts of thousands of American townships, the Jenny created thrills galore with exhibitions of wing walking, aerial trapeze work and low-level aerobatics, as well as providing joy-riding or pleasure flights. That there were badly maintained Jennies by the dozen cannot be denied, and it is true that there were many casualties, yet the barnstorming or 'Jenny' era helped to make America air-minded in a most remarkable manner. The Jenny also featured in many Hollywood films of the 1920s and early 1930s. A considerable number of Jennies survive in museums and several in private ownership are maintained in flying condition in the USA.

Variant
Twin JN: retrospectively designated **Model 1B**, the Twin JN appeared in

Curtiss JN-4 Can Canuck (built by Canadian Aeroplanes Ltd) of the School of Aerial Fighting in 1918.

Evolved from the JN-4 series, the Curtiss Twin JN was intended for observation duties. Seen here is the first production example, US Army serial no. 102.

April 1916 and was provisionally designated JN-5; it was an enlarged and twin-engined version of the JN-4 intended for observation; the standard wing cellule was used, though span was increased by 2.79 m (9 ft 2 in) by the use of a larger centre section; power was provided by two 67-kW (90-hp) OXX-2 engines mounted between the wings, and maximum speed was 129 km/h (80 mph); the vertical tail surfaces were derived from those of the R-4; total production was eight

Specification
Curtiss JN-4D
Type: two-seat primary trainer
Powerplant: one 67-kW (90-hp) Curtiss OX-5 inline piston engine

US Army serial no. 2900 was one of 1,400 Curtiss JN-4D trainers built by Curtiss in a contract valued at $4,417,337. Many of these fine aircraft survived World War I training duties and were used for barnstorming.

Performance: maximum speed 121 km/h (75 mph); cruising speed 97 km/h (60 mph); service ceiling 1980 m (6,500 ft)
Weights: empty 630 kg (1,390 lb); maximum take-off 871 kg (1,920 lb)
Dimensions: span 13.30 m (43 ft 7¾ in); length 8.33 m (27 ft 4 in); height 3.01 m (9 ft 10½ in); wing area 32.70 m² (352.0 sq ft)

Curtiss Model 2 (R-2)

At the beginning of 1915 there appeared the prototype **Curtiss Model R**, which was in 1935 given the retrospective designation **Model 2**, an enlarged version of the Model N with equal-span staggered wings. It was flown both as a landplane and float seaplane. Pilot and observer of this military reconnaissance biplane were housed in one long open cockpit and the Model R could be distinguished from the Model N by its interplane ailerons and lack of a fixed fin.

The R-2 introduced unequal-span wings with ailerons attached to the upper wing, a vertical tailplane which incorporated a fixed fin and horn-balanced

rudder and there were separate and widely spaced cockpits for the two crew members. The Curtiss V-X engine of the prototype was retained. The R-2 went into production at the end of 1915 and was built in some numbers, 12 going to the US Army and the latter making only limited use of the type. The US Army R-2s were flown in support of the expedition against the Mexican insurgent leader Pancho Villa, but although their serviceability was poor they flew a number of reconnaissance and liaison missions.

The one-off **R-2A** was an equal-span variant and established an American

domestic altitude record of 2740 m (8,105 ft), carrying pilot and three passengers, in August 1915. Two **R-3** seaplanes, resembling the R-2 but with increased wing span, were brought by the US Navy in 1916.

Variants
R-7: long-wing derivative of R-3, using same engine as the later R4; the sole example was bought by the *New York Times* for an attempted nonstop flight from Chicago to New York, which failed as a result of fuel leaks in November 1916 but set an American distance record of 727 km (452 miles)
Twin R: twin-engine experimental development of R-2, sole example flying in 1916

Pusher R: Curtiss attempt of 1916 to revive interest in the obsolescent pusher configuration, with a central nacelle for two crew and pusher engine/propeller, a new tailplane, and Model R (soon replaced by Model R-2) wings

Specification
Curtiss R-2
Type: reconnaissance biplane
Powerplant: one 119-kW (160-hp) Curtiss V-X inline piston engine
Performance: maximum speed 138 km/h (86 mph); endurance 6 hours 42 minutes
Weights: empty equipped 826 kg (1,822 lb); maximum take-off 1403 kg

(3,092 lb)

Dimensions: span 14.00 m (45 ft 11½ in); length 11.70 m (38 ft 4¾ in); wing area 46.90 m² (504.88 sq ft)

The US Navy's two Curtiss R-3 seaplanes were delivered in 1916, and were in reality a float-equipped version of the R-2 with wings of increased span to bear the extra weight of the floats. The anchor, painted in blue on the fin, was the first insignia of the US Navy.

Curtiss racers

Curtiss first became involved in the design and construction of racing aircraft in early 1920, when approached by millionaire S. Cox to produce two aircraft to take part in the James Gordon Bennett Trophy race being held in France in September of that year. Named *Texas Wildcat* and *Cactus Kitten*, the **Curtiss Model 22 Cox Racers** were originally braced high-wing monoplanes powered by the 318-kW (427-hp) Curtiss C-12 in-line piston engine. Only the *Texas Wildcat* was tested before being despatched to France where, again tested with its special thin racing wing, it was found to be unstable. A new biplane wing was designed hurriedly and installed, enabling the aircraft to take part in the race, but it was wrecked in a landing accident. The *Cactus Kitten* was returned to the USA without being flown, and was given a set of short-span triplane wings with which it gained second place in the 1921 Pulitzer Trophy Race.

This race was won, in fact, by another Curtiss racer, one of the company's **Model 23** biplanes built for the US Navy under the designation **CR-1** (contemporary designation **L-17-1**) and **CR-2** (**L-17-1**). The US Navy had intended to compete but withdrew, and Curtiss borrowed the CR-2 which was flown to success by the company's test pilot, Bert Acosta. Both the CR-1 and CR-2 were biplanes with tailskid landing gear, powered by Curtiss CD-12 inline engines, but differed in minor detail. They were converted subsequently to seaplanes (**Model 23A**, contemporary designation **L-17-3**) to compete in the 1928 Schneider Trophy Contest in the UK, under the designation **CR-3**. Apart from the changed landing gear they had new 347-kW (465-hp) Curtiss D-12 engines with Curtiss-Reed metal propellers, a significant combination which resulted in the two aircraft gaining first and second place in the Schneider contest.

With the usual US Army/US Navy rivalry, the US Army decided it must have racing aircraft, Curtiss building for them two examples of the **R-6** develop-

Curtiss R-6 flown into second place in the 1922 Pulitzer Trophy Race by Lieutenant Lester J. Maitland, US Army Air Corps.

Three R3C-1 racers were produced for the 1925 Pulitzer, this example being the one for the Army Air Corps. It won the race piloted by Lt Cyrus Bettis.

Both CR landplanes were converted to CR-3 floatplanes for the 1923 Schneider Trophy race. This aircraft came second; the other took the prize.

For the 1925 Schneider Trophy, the three R3C-1 landplanes were put on floats as R3C-2s. The USAAC's James Doolittle won the race in one.

ed from the US Navy's CR. The R-6s were considerably cleaner than their predecessors, and a major contribution to drag reduction was the introduction of wing surface radiators. With these aircraft the US Army gained first and second place in the 1922 Pulitzer race, and twice raised the world speed record, the second time to 380.74 km/h (236.587 mph). For 1923 the US Navy did its utmost to reverse this 1922 setback, ordering two examples of the new **R2C-1** (**Model 32**) from Curtiss. These were developed versions of the CR/R-6 family with more powerful (378-kW/507-

hp) Curtiss D-12A engines. They proved good enough for the Navy to take first and second places in the 1923 Pulitzer. One of these aircraft raised the world record to 429.02 km/h (266.59 mph), and it was sold subsequently to the US Army, which designated it **R-8**; it was destroyed in an accident on 2 September 1924. The US Navy had the other aircraft converted to float landing gear, this being redesignated **R2C-2** (**Model 32A**). Used as a trainer for the 1925 Schneider contest, it was destroyed in a flying accident during 1926.

Co-operation between the US Army and US Navy in 1925 resulted in an order for three new racers (this being the last for Curtiss racers). All three examples of the **Model 42**, designated **R3C-1**, were generally similar to the R2C-1s, differing by having a changed wing aerofoil section and more powerful Curtiss V-1400 engines. Two were entered in the 1925 Pulitzer race, with the US Army gaining first place and the US Navy second. All three were then given float landing gear for the 1925 Schneider Contest, being redesignated **R3C-2**

Lester Maitland poses by his Curtiss R-6 racer at about the time of the 1922 Pulitzer Trophy, in which he finished second.

Fitted with a set of cut-down Model 18-T triplane wings, the Curtiss Cactus Kitten was placed second in the 1921 Pulitzer.

The CR-2 won the 1921 Pulitzer, piloted by Curtiss employee Bert Acosta. The aircraft was borrowed from the US Navy.

Bought for $1 in 1923, the Navy's R2C-1 became the Army's R-8. Assigned serial 23-1235, it crashed in September 1924.

(**Model 42A**), but the US Navy withdrew and the race was won by the US Army's Lieutenant James H. Doolittle in R3C-2 A6979. With two consecutive wins in the Schneider contest the USA needed only one more win in 1926 to secure the Trophy permanently. Clearly an all-out effort was necessary but no large funds were available for new aircraft. One of the R3C-2s was given a new 522-kW (700-hp) Packard 2A-1500

inline engine by the Naval Aircraft Factory. With this the **R3C-3** demonstrated a speed of 410 km/h (255 mph). This was hopeful, as the 1925 Schneider had been won at an average 374.28 km/h (232.75 mph). Unfortunately this R3C-3 crashed during subsequent trials. A second R3C-2 was refurbished by Curtiss, being designated **R3C-4** after the work was completed, including the installation of a new 528-kW (708-hp) Cur-

tiss V-1550 engine. This aircraft was only a little luckier, for though it took part in the contest it was forced to retire in the last lap with petrol starvation. It remained for Lieutenant Christian Schilt of the US Marine Corps, flying the third R3C-2 as reserve, to take second place at a speed of 372.34 km/h (231.36 mph).

Specification
Curtiss R3C-2

Type: single-seat racing seaplane
Powerplant: one 421-kW (565-hp) Curtiss V-1400 inline piston engine
Performance: maximum speed 394 km/h (245 mph); range at full power 467 km/h (290 miles)
Weights: empty 968 kg (2,135 lb); maximum take-off 1242 kg (2,738 lb)
Dimensions: span and length 6.71 m (22 ft 0 in); height 3.15 m (10 ft 4 in); wing area 13.38 m² (144.0 sq ft)

Curtiss Model 33/34 (PW-8)

On its own initiative the Curtiss company began in 1922 the development of a new fighter design (**Curtiss L-18-1**, later designated **Model 33**) which owed much of its inspiration to the Curtiss racing biplanes. Drawing on this experience Curtiss built the first prototype **PW-8** at the end of 1922, the maiden flight being accomplished in January 1923. A two-bay biplane considerable wing stagger, the XPW-8 had a sleek well-streamlined fuselage and fixed tail-wheel landing gear. It employed the Curtiss wing surface radiators which had been developed for the racing biplanes and was powered by a 328-kW (440-hp) Curtiss D-12 engine.

The first prototype (officially redesignated **XPW-8** in March 1924) was bought by the US Army in April 1923, and was followed by two other prototypes. The first of these had improved streamlining and modified landing gear and its enhanced performance led to a production order for 24 PW-8s on 25 September 1923. Deliveries to the US Army pursuit squadrons took place over a 12-month period beginning in June 1924. On 23 June 1924, piloted by Lieutenant

Russell L. Maughan, an early production PW-8 made the first dawn-to-dusk crossing of the United States. The third prototype was modified to take newly designed single-bay wings and was then redesignated **XPW-8A** (company designation **Model 34**). It was tested with a new radiator which formed part of the centre-section of the upper wing, but this was soon replaced by a tunnel radiator under the nose. Delivered in September 1924, the XPW-8A gained third place in the 1924 Pulitzer Trophy race. Modified by the installation of new tapered wings, and redesignated **XPW-8B**, it formed the basis for the new Curtiss P-1 Hawk fighter.

The first prototype was modified temporarily as the **CO-X** two-seater in an unsuccessful attempt by Army engineers to carry off the 1923 Liberty Engine Builders Trophy contest for military two-seat aircraft. General protests led to its withdrawal from the race!

Specification
Curtiss PW-8
Type: single-seat biplane fighter
Powerplant: one 328-kW (440-hp) Curtiss D-12 inline piston engine
Performance: maximum speed

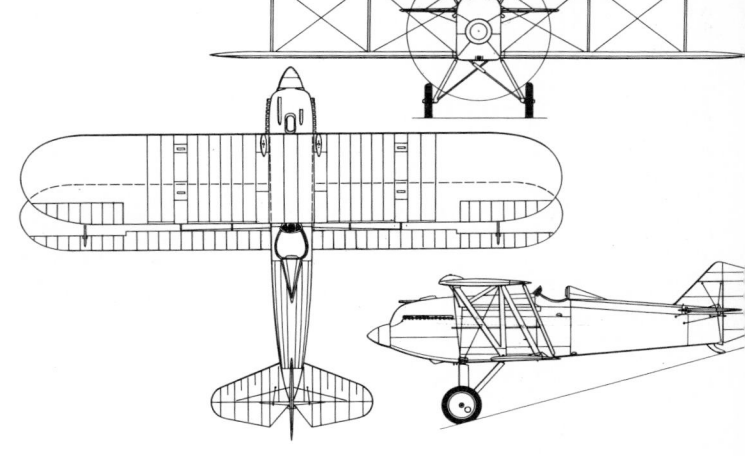

275 km/h (171 mph) at sea level; initial climb rate 558 m (1,830 ft) per minute; service ceiling 6205 m (20,350 ft); range 875 km (544 miles)
Weights: empty 991 kg (2,185 lb); maximum take-off 1431 kg (3,155 lb)
Dimensions: span 9.75 m (32 ft 0 in); length 7.03 m (23 ft 1 in); height 2.76 m (9 ft 1 in); wing area 25.94 m²

Curtiss PW-8

(279.3 sq ft)
Armament: two fixed fuselage-mounted synchronised 7.62-mm (0.3-in) machine-guns

Curtiss Model 34 (F6C Hawk)

In 1925 the US Navy ordered nine examples of the **Curtiss Model 34C** fighter under the designation **F6C-1 Hawk**. These were virtually identical to the US Army P-1 series, and were intended originally for shore use by the US Marine Corps. In fact only five aircraft were delivered as F6C-1s, the remaining four being completed as examples of the **F6C-2** (**Model 34D**), fitted with arrester hooks and strengthened for aircraft-carrier operations.

The US Navy obtained in 1927 35 **F6C-3s** (**Model 34E**), a modified version of the F6C-2. These were followed by 31 of the **F6C-4** (**Model 34H**), the first F6C-1 having been converted to take the 313-kW (420-hp) Pratt & Whitney Wasp radial engine and serving as the prototype **XF6C-4**. All of the US Navy's earlier F6C fighters had been powered by the Curtiss D-12 inline engine.

The F6C-1 formed part of the equipment of Marine Squadron VF-9M, while the F6C-2s operated with Squadron VF-2 on board the USS *Langley*. F6C-3s were flown from 1928 by Squadron VF-5S (which became VB-1B in July of that year in deference to the Hawk's intended fighter-bomber role) aboard the carrier USS *Lexington*. For a short period VB-1B operated its F6C-3s as twin-float seaplanes. Other F6C-3s served with the shore-based Marine Squadron VF-8M.

The US Navy decided that the maintenance of water-cooled engines aboard carriers presented insuperable prob-

lems, with the result that the radial-engined F6C-4s equipped VF-2B aboard the USS *Langley* until 1930.

Variants
XF6C-5: a conversion of the XF6C-4 (originally the first production F6C-1) to take the 6391-kW (525-hp) Pratt & Whitney R-1690 Hornet
F6C-6: a production F6C-3 adapted as a racing machine, with its radiator relocated inside the fuselage, the rear fuselage given a more streamlined configuration and low-drag landing gear replacing the standard pattern
XF6C-6: the F6C-3 which had won the 1930 Curtiss Marine Trophy was converted to parasol high-wing monoplane configuration and given wing surface radiators; the wing was braced to each side of the fuselage by a single strut and landing gear main units comprised single struts with large wheel 'spat' fairings; after achieving the fastest lap in the 1930 Thompson Trophy Race the XF6C-6 came to grief when its pilot was overcome by exhaust fumes
XF6C-7: designation of an F6C-4 converted temporarily in 1932 as a test-bed for an experimental 261-kW (350-hp) Ranger engine

An F6C-3 of Utility Squadron VJ-4 in 1952. Originally delivered with a tripod-type undercarriage, this was replaced by an F6C-4 style spreader-type gear.

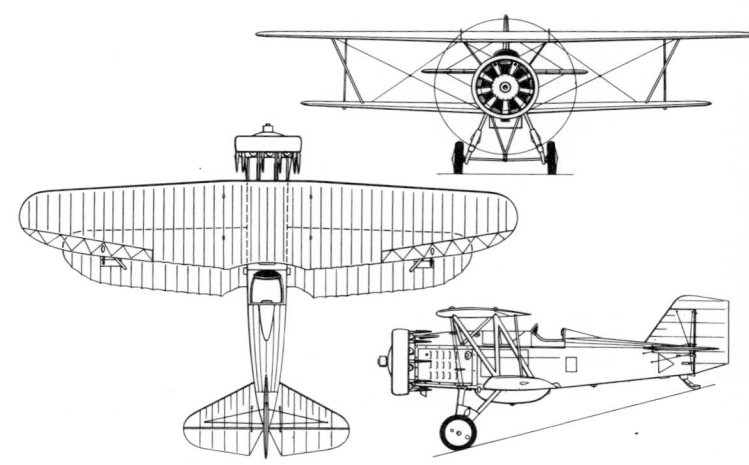

Curtiss F6C-4

Specification
Curtiss F6C-4
Type: single-seat carrier-based fighter
Powerplant: one 306-kW (410-hp)
Pratt & Whitney R-1340 Wasp radial
piston engine

Performance: maximum speed
249 km/h (155 mph) at sea level; climb
to 1525 m (5,000 ft) in 2 minutes 30
seconds; service ceiling 6980 m
(22,900 ft); range 547 km (340 miles)

Weights: empty equipped 898 kg
(1,980 lb); maximum take-off 1438 kg
(3,171 lb)
Dimensions: span 11.43 m (37 ft
6 in); length 6.86 m (22 ft 6 in); height
3.33 m (10 ft 11 in); wing area 23.41 m²

(252.00 sq ft)
Armament: two fixed synchronised
7.62-mm (0.3-in) machine-guns, plus
light bombs on underwing racks

Curtiss Model 34/35 (P-1 and P-6 Hawk)

Successful testing of the experimental XPW-8B, incorporating new tapered wings and a number of other modifications, led to an order for 15 production aircraft. Designated **P-1** under a new identification system then introduced by the US Army, 10 of these new single-seat fighters (**Curtiss Model 34A**) entered service with the 27th and 94th Pursuit Squadrons. A third unit, the 17th Pursuit Squadron, equipped with the Hawk following delivery of 25 examples of the **P-1A** (**Model 34G**), which retained the new wing and redesigned tailplane of the P-1 but included some detailed design improvements. An export version of the P-1A was offered for sale subsequently and eight were bought by Chile and a single example by Japan.

In late 1926 the US Army acquired 25 of the improved **P-1B** (**Model 34I**), powered by the 324-kW (435-hp) Curtiss V-1150-3 engine in place of the previously standard Curtiss D-12. The P-1B had larger diameter wheels and a more rounded radiator. Chile also obtained eight of this version. The **P-1C** (**Model 34O**) incorporated wheel brake and equipment changes which increased the overall weight; delivery of 33 P-1Cs to the US Army was completed by April 1929.

The first Hawk to bear the **P-6** designation was modified from one of the original P-1s. Powered by a Curtiss V-1570 Conqueror engine the **X-6** (**Model 34P**) took second place in the 1927 US National Air Races. A second conversion to compete in this contest was the **X-6A** (**Model 34K**), also powered by the Conqueror engine but with untapered wings similar to those of the PW-8 and wing surface radiators to reduce drag. The XP-6A took first place with a then remarkable speed of 323 km/h (201 mph).

The US Army was sufficiently impressed with the XP-6 to order an evaluation batch of 18 P-6s, the main difference between the two being improved fuselage contours and the deeper, more rounded nose of the latter. Nine of the 18, fitted with Prestone-cooled V-1570 engines, were designated **P-6A**. The **XP-6B**, which made a remarkable flight from the eastern United States to Alaska, was a P-1C converted to take the V-1570 engine. One P-6A became the sole **XP-6D** after conversion to take a turbocharged Conqueror engine. All the P-6As (except one) and all the P-6s were re-engined with the turbocharged Curtiss V-1570-C Conqueror in the spring of 1932, thereupon being redesignated **P-6D**.

Ordered in July 1931 under the designation **Y1P-22**, 46 examples of the **P-6E** were delivered in the winter of 1931-2. The most illustrious and impressive of the US Army's Hawk family, the P-6E (**Model 35**) showed excellent manoeuvrability, equipping the crack 17th and 33rd Pursuit Squadrons. It differed from the P-6D in having a slimmer forward fuselage with the engine radiator mounted just forward of the landing gear, the latter comprising single-strut main legs with spat-type

wheel fairings. One P-6E was powered by an unsupercharged V-1570F engine, being redesignated **XP-6G**, while a standard P-6E was tested as the **XP-6H** with four 7.62-mm (0.3-in) wing-mounted machine-guns.

Variants
XAT-4: one P-1A converted as an exerimental advanced trainer (**Model 34J**) by the installation of a 134-kW (180-hp) Wright-Hispano E engine in 1926
AT-4: in 1927 35 production versions of the XAT-4 were delivered, but they were soon afterwards converted to **P-1D** standard with D-12 engines
AT-5: five advanced trainers (**Model 34K**) fitted with the 164-kW (220-hp) Wright J-5 Whirlwind engine; ordered originally as AT-4s, they were converted later to **P-1E** standard with Curtiss D-12 engines
AT-5A: resembling closely the AT-5, the AT-5A (**Model 34M**) had a lengthened fuselage; 31 were delivered, being redesignated **P-1F** when later re-engined with Curtiss D-12s
P-2: five of the original P-1 order were completed under the designation P-2 (**Model 34B**) with 373-kW (500-hp) Curtiss V-1400 engines developed from the D-12; three were converted later to P-1As and another became the XP-6 prototype
P-3A: this was the designation for five service test aircraft (**Model 34N**) powered by the air-cooled Pratt & Whitney Wasp radial engine; one was redesignated **XP-3A** when used in connection with experiments to develop the NACA engine cowling, and a second aircraft designated XP-3A was a P-1A airframe powered by a 306-kW (410-hp) Pratt & Whitney R-1340-1 Wasp radial
P-5: five high-altitude evaluation Hawks (**Model 34L**) having D-12F engines with side-mounted turbochargers to raise service ceiling to 9660 m (31,700 ft)
P-11: this designation was given to three machines with P-6 airframes intended to be powered by the untried 447-kW (600-hp) Curtiss H-1640 Chieftain engine; with the failure of this powerplant two P-11s were completed as Conqueror-powered P-6s, the third becoming the **YP-20** powered by a Wright Cyclone radial; the YP-20 was later re-engined with a Curtiss Conqueror and with new landing gear and tailplane to become the sole **XP-6E**, prototype for the P-6E series; further modified, with supercharged engine and experimental enclosed pilot's cockpit, it became the **XP-6F**
XP-17: the first P-1 built was used as a test-bed for the experimental Wright V-1470 inverted-Vee air-cooled engine, becoming redesignated XP-17
XP-21: two conversions of XP-3As to test the 224-kW (300-hp) Pratt & Whitney R-985 Wasp Junior radial; one became **XP-21A** with the modified R-975 Wasp Junior and the other was converted to P-1F standard

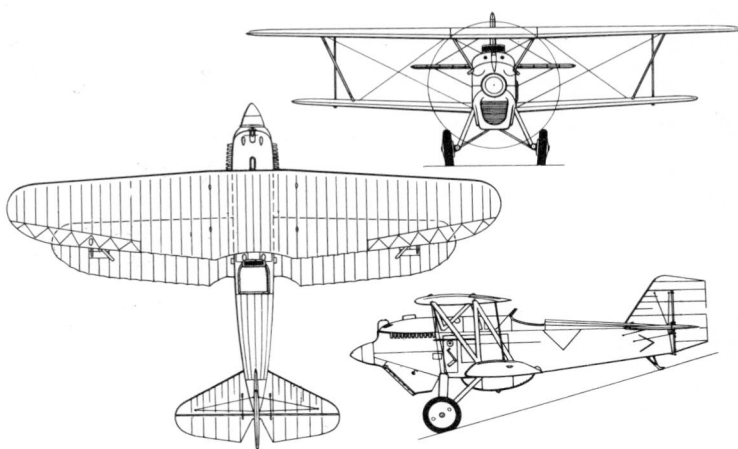

Curtiss P-1C Hawk. Note the large chin radiator and ventral tank. 33 were built for the US Army Air Corps.

XP-22: the temporary designation for a P-6A used to test the new radiator and air cooler installations for the V-1570-23 engine; reverted later to P-6A
XP-23: produced by conversion of the unfinished last P-6E, the XP-23 (**Model 63**) had a monocoque metal fuselage, improved tail, and turbocharged geared G1V-1570-C Conqueror; only high-altitude performance was better than standard P-6E; became **YP-23** with turbocharger removed
Hawk I: at first no Curtiss designation was given to various export versions of the P-6: eight developed P-6Ds with the Curtiss Conqueror engine were sold to the Netherlands East Indies government in 1930 and eight more of the type were built in the Netherlands; three **P-6S** fighters with 450-hp Pratt & Whitney Wasp radials were sold to Cuba and one to Japan in 1930: and the sole **Japan Hawk** of 1930 had a Conqueror inline, but may have been the same airframe as the Japanese

P-6S; from 1932 these export Hawks were retrospectively designated Hawk I

Specification
Curtiss P-6E
Type: single-seat pursuit (fighter) biplane
Powerplant: one 503.5-kW (675-hp) Curtiss V-1570-23 Conqueror inline piston engine
Performance: maximum speed 319 km/h (198 mph); initial climb rate 756 m (2,480 ft) per minute; service ceiling 7530 m (24,700 ft); range 917 km (570 miles)
Weights: empty equipped 1224 kg (2,699 lb); maximum take-off 1559 kg (3,436 lb)
Dimensions: span 9.60 m (31 ft 6 in); length 7.06 m (23 ft 2 in); height 2.72 m (8 ft 11 in); wing area 23.41 m² (252.00 sq ft)
Armament: two synchronised fuselage-mounted 7.62-mm (0.3-in) machine-guns

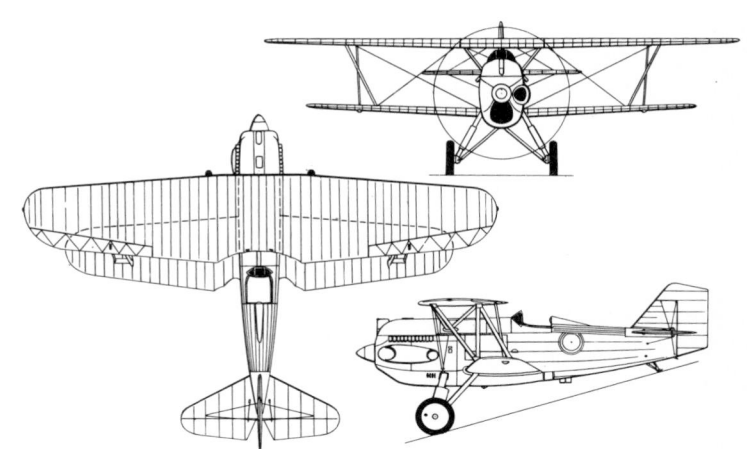

Curtiss P-6A Hawk. The Curtiss V-1570 Conqueror engine with Prestone cooling introduced a bulkier but smoother nose profile.

Curtiss Model 35/47 Hawk II, Model 64/67 (F11C) and Model 68 Hawk III

The **Curtiss Model 35 Hawk II** single-seat fighter was an unequal-span heavily staggered biplane largely of wooden construction. Developed from the original P-6E it was powered by a Wright Cyclone radial engine, and the main units of its tailwheel landing gear had single struts with the wheels partially enclosed by streamlined fairings.

Hawk II company-owned demonstrators were taken all over the world and secured considerable export orders for Curtiss. One aircraft (**Model 64A**) was bought by the US Navy as the **XF11C-2**. It was tested against **Model 64** (XF11C-1) that had been delivered in September 1932 and which differed mainly in having a 447-kW (600-hp) Wright R-1510-98 Whirlwind radial. The US Navy ordered 28 **F11C-2** production aircraft in October 1932; being required as fighter-bombers they were fitted with a special crutch under the fuselage for launching a 227-kW (500-lb) bomb in a dive and from 1933 the type equipped Squadron VF-1B aboard the USS *Saratoga*. In March 1934 a number of modifications were incorporated in these aircraft, including the introduction of a semi-enclosed cockpit, and the type was then redesignated **BFC-2** to indicate its fighter-bomber role. The BFC-2s flew with VF-1B (renumbered VB-2B and later VB-3B) until early 1938. They were sometimes called **Goshawk** although the name did not achieve popularity.

Hawk IIs were exported in some numbers. Purchasers included Bolivia (nine); Chile (four plus unknown quantity built under licence); China (50, used extensively against the Japanese); Colombia (26 examples of a twin-float version with additional ventral fin); Cuba (four); Germany (two aircraft bought at the behest of Ernst Udet to investigate dive-bombing techniques); Norway (single example slightly modified); Siam, now Thailand (12); and Turkey (19). Total exports were 127, all Model 35 variants, with the exception of the Norwegian aircraft, which was the sole **Model 47**.

Variants

BF2C-1: one aircraft from the US Navy F11C-2 contract was completed as the **XF11C-3**, soon redesignated **XBF2C-1** (**Curtiss Model 67**); it differed mainly in having manually operated retractable landing gear, the wheels retracting into the forward fuselage which was modified and deepened to accommodate them; deliveries of 27 examples of the production **BF2C-1** (**Model 67A**) to Navy Squadron VB-5B began in October 1934 but all had been withdrawn within a year as problems with landing gear operation and vibration in the wing structure could not be overcome

Hawk 1: perhaps the single most famous Hawk, this aircraft was built as a long-range demonstrator in 1929, with a Curtiss Conqueror inline and extra fuel tanks in the sides of the fuselage; rebuilt as the **Hawk 1A** after a crash it became the property of the Gulf Oil Company and then of Alford J. Williams, and was powered by a succession of radial engines (429-kW/575-hp Wright Cyclone, 429-kW/575-hp Bliss Jupiter, 530-kW/710-hp Wright R-1820F-3 Cyclone, and finally 448-kW/600-hp Pratt & Whitney Wasp); named *Gulfhawk* by Williams, the aircraft was retired to a

trade school in 1936, and rescued from there by Frank Tallman in 1958; the last flying example of the whole Hawk series, the aircraft is with the US Marine Corps Museum at Quantico, Virginia

Hawk III: designation of the export version of the BF2C-1; it retained the wooden wings of the Hawk II and did not suffer from the vibration problems which plagued the US Navy's BF2C-1s; apart from a single **Model 68A** demonstrator, 137 Hawk IIIs were exported: Siam, (Thailand) obtained 24 **Model 68B** aircraft during 1935-6, Argentina bought 10 Hawk IIIs in 1936, in 1935 a single Hawk III was sold to Turkey; and the largest customer was China, which received 102 examples of the **Model 68C** between March 1936 and June 1938 for use against the Japanese **Hawk IV**: this was the sole **Curtiss Model 79** and differed from the Hawk III mainly in having a fully enclosed cockpit; after use as a demonstrator it was purchased by the Argentine government in July 1936

Specification
Curtiss F11C-2
Type: single-seat fighter-bomber
Powerplant: one 521.6-kW (700-hp) Wright SR-1820-78 Cyclone radial piston engine

Performance: maximum speed 325 km/h (202 mph); initial climb rate 701 m (2,300 ft) per minute; service ceiling 7650 m (25,100 ft); range 840 km (522 miles)
Weights: empty equipped 1378 kg (3,037 lb); maximum take-off 1874 kg (4,132 lb)
Dimensions: span 9.60 m (31 ft 6 in);

length 6.88 m (22 ft 7 in); height 2.96 m (9 ft 8½ in); wing area 24.34 m² (262.00 sq ft)
Armament: two fuselage-mounted forward-firing 7.62-mm (0.3-in) synchronised machine-guns, plus one 227-kg (500-lb) bomb beneath the fuselage or four 51-kg (121-lb) bombs on underwing racks

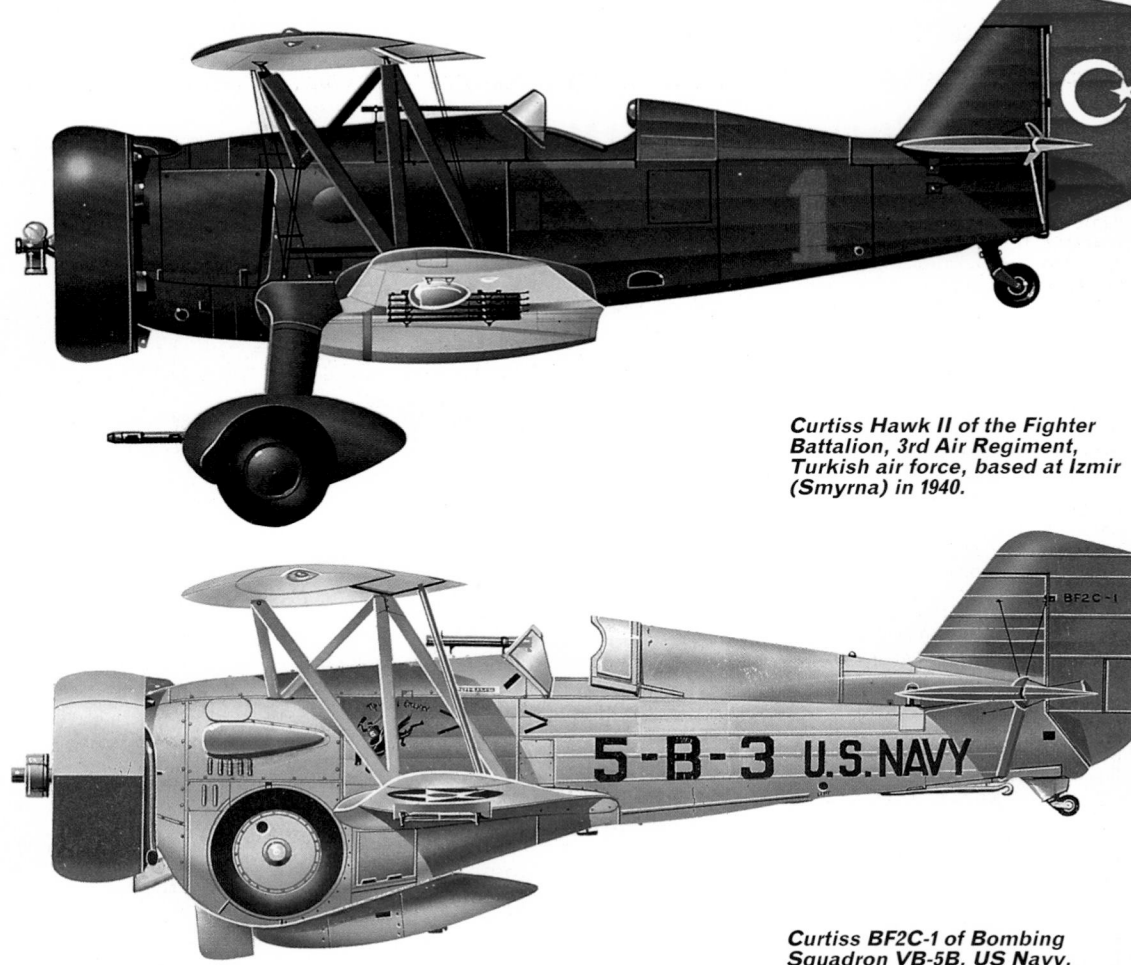

Curtiss Hawk II of the Fighter Battalion, 3rd Air Regiment, Turkish air force, based at Izmir (Smyrna) in 1940.

Curtiss BF2C-1 of Bombing Squadron VB-5B, US Navy, based aboard the USS Ranger *in 1934-35.*

Produced by conversion of a civil Hawk II, the XF11C-2 used the more powerful Wright R-1820 Cyclone and had a number of detail refinements. The F11C-2 was later redesignated BFC-2.

Curtiss Model 37/38/44 (O-1/F8C Falcon Series)

The first Curstiss biplane to bear the name **Falcon** was the Liberty-powered **Curtiss L-113** (**Model 37**) which appeared in 1924. It was unsuccessful when evaluated as the **XO-1** in competition with the Douglas XO-2 but was accepted for production the following year when re-engined with a 380-kW (510-hp) Packard 1A-1500. It was a conventional unequal-span biplane with a wing of wooden construction that incorporated considerable sweep-back on the outer panels of the upper wing. The fuselage showed innovation, being built up from aluminium tubing with steel tie-rod bracing, and the tail unit included a balanced rudder; the sturdy fixed divided landing gear was of tailskid type.

The new biplane went into production as the **O-1** (**Model 37A**) for observation duties with the US Army. The initial order was for 10 aircraft re-engined with a Curtiss D-12. One of these was completed later as the **O-1A** with a Liberty engine, and the first O-1 was converted to **O-1 Special** configuration as a VIP transport. Forty-five examples of the **O-1B** (**Model 37B**) were ordered in 1927, this first major production version incorporating such refinements as wheel brakes and an underbelly auxiliary fuel tank which could be jettisoned in flight. They were followed by four **O-1C** aircraft, part of the O-1B order, converted to serve as VIP transports by enlargement of the rear cockpit and the addition of a baggage compartment. (The designation O-1D was not used.)

In 1929 the US Army ordered 41 of the **O-1E** (**Model 37I**) with V-1150E engines developed from the original Curtiss D-12. A number of other improvements included the introduction of oleopneumatic shock-absorbers and horn balanced elevators. One O-1E was modified subsequently as a VIP transport becoming redesignated **O-1F** (**Model 37J**). The **XO-1G** replacing the twin Lewis guns on a Scarff mounting that equipped the earlier models by a single gun on a post mounting. Other modifications introduced redesigned horizontal tail surfaces and a steerable tailwheel. The XO-1G was originally an O-1E which had been modified previously to contend as a new US Army basic trainer under the designation **XBT-4** (**Model 46**). Successful tests led to construction of 30 series examples of the **O-1G**, bringing total O-1 production for the US Army to 127.

The O-1 Falcon and its variants saw a decade of service with the observation squadrons of the US Army Air Corps and ended their days with reserve National Guard units. The basic design was adapted also as the A-3 attack biplane which saw considerable use. There were also export versions and a number of commercial Falcons. The basic design proved tough and workmanlike, but its dedication to a variety of less glamorous military and civil roles prevented it from achieving the renown of the contemporary Hawk fighter family.

Variants

A-3: a straightforward conversion of the O-1B as an attack (light bomber)

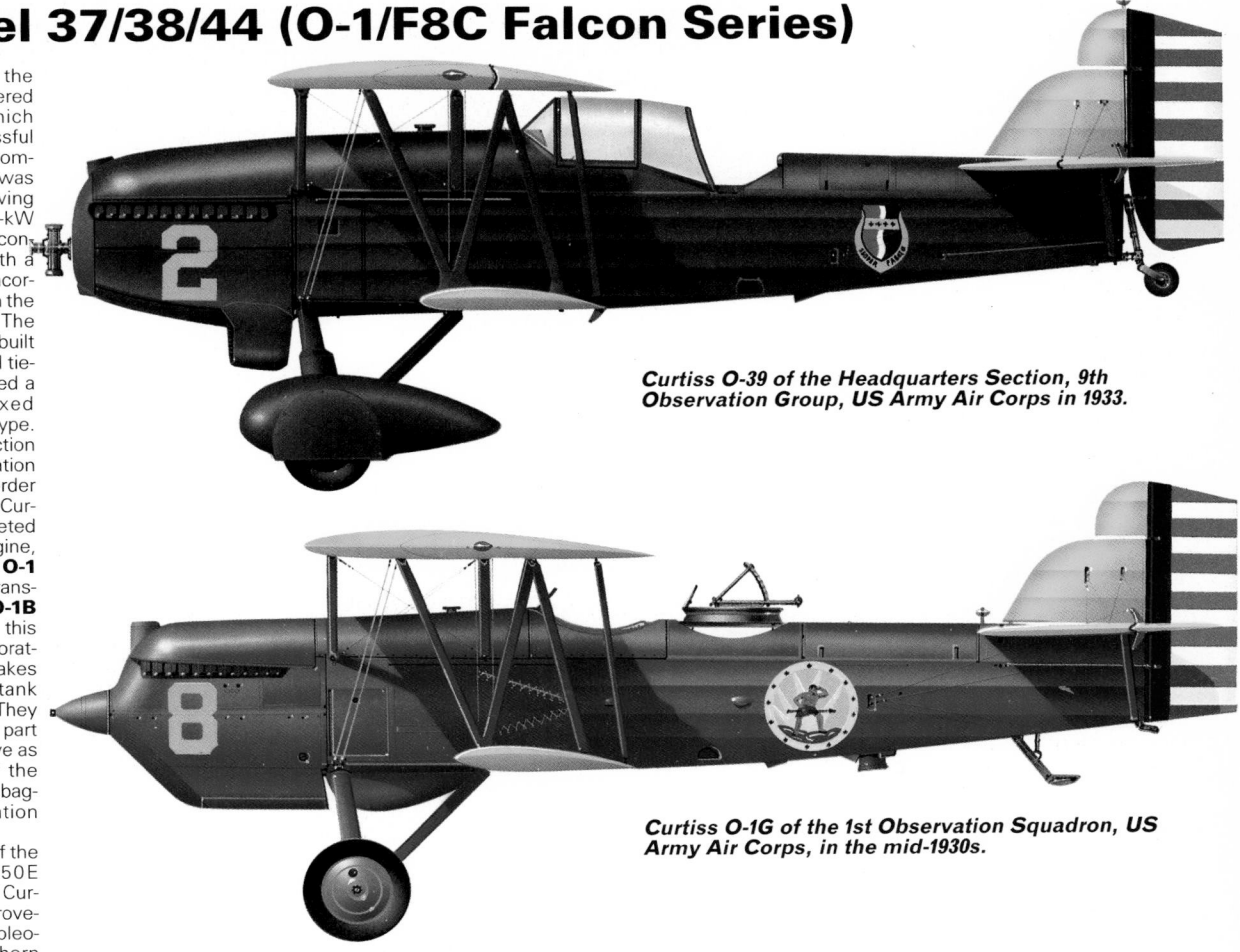

Curtiss O-39 of the Headquarters Section, 9th Observation Group, US Army Air Corps in 1933.

Curtiss O-1G of the 1st Observation Squadron, US Army Air Corps, in the mid-1930s.

aircraft; production for the US Army totalled 66 of this **Model 44** type; armament increased by adding two 7.62-mm (0.3-in) machine-guns in the lower wing and underwing racks for up to 91 kg (200 lb) of bombs; six were converted as **A-3A** dual-control transition trainers

A-3B: had the same airframe as the O-1E observation aircraft; total constructed of this **Model 37H** variant was 78; soldiered on in reserve units until 1937

XA-4: one A-3 converted by installation of a 328-kW (440-hp) Pratt & Whitney R-1340-1 Wasp radial

O-11: this was a version (**Model 37C**) of the O-1 intended for reserve (National Guard) units and powered by government-surplus Liberty engine; the **XO-11** was a conversion of an O-1 and was followed by 66 production O-11s; one O-11 used for test purposes became a second XO-11; another was fitted with modified tail surfaces, dual controls and other improvements, becoming designated **O-11A**; the final production O-11 became the **XO-12** with the new Pratt & Whitney R-1340 Wasp engine

XO-13: one O-1 was redesignated XO-13 when re-engined with the new Curtiss Conqueror engine, being entered for and competing successfully in the 1927 National Air Races; the

XO-13A was another conversion to compete in these races, this having wing surface radiators to reduce drag; one O-1C became the **O-13B** when powered by a Conqueror engine and tested for observation work, and three O-1Es were redesignated **YO-13C** (**Model 37K**) when similarly re-engined; the sole **YO-13D** was an O-11 with a supercharged Conqueror engine; it was converted later as an O-13C and finally as an O-1B

XO-16: an O-11 with a modified fuselage and Conqueror engine (company designation **Model 37G**)

XO-18: an O-1B used briefly to test the new Curtiss Chieftain engine

YO-26: an O-1E with a Conqueror engine and Prestone cooling requiring a smaller radiator (company designation **Model 37L**)

O-39: this was an O-1G airframe with the Curtiss V-1570-25 Conqueror engine; 10 of this **Model 38A** type were built in 1931, these having the same sized radiator as the P-6E Hawk fighter and all were fitted initially with wheel spats; in service the rudder was reduced in area, and a number of glazed canopies over the tandem cockpits

Civil Falcon: 20 civil aircraft were built; they included the **Conqueror Mailplane** and **D-12 Mailplane**, a **Lindbergh Special** aircraft sold to

Colonel Charles Lindbergh, and 14 of the **Liberty Mailplane** single-seat mailplanes with Liberty engines, used for night mail flights by National Air Transport; of the survivors sold off at a later date, at least two were used for smuggling spirits into the USA during the prohibition era

F8C-1: developed from the US Army experimental XO-12 biplane, two **XF8C-1** (**Model 37D**) aircraft for the US Navy were followed by four US Marine Corps F8C-1s in January 1928; intended as fighters or light bombers, the F8C-1s were redesignated **OC-1** during 1928, implying their relegation to the observation role

F8C-3: the US Navy took delivery of 21 F8C-3 aircraft (later redesignated **OC-2**) during 1928; like the F8C-1s these were powered by the 313-kW (420-hp) Pratt & Whitney R-1340 radial engine; as the OC-2 the type equipped US Marine Squadrons VO-8M and VO-10M

XOC-3: the second XF8C-1 was thus designated when fitted for evaluative purposes with a 448-kW (600-hp) Curtiss Chieftain engine

Export Falcon: 16 examples of a twin-float version of the D-12-powered O-1B were sold to Colombia under the designation

Model 37F: and 10 similar landplanes were exported to Peru; contemporary name for these aircraft was **South American D-12 Falcon**; Colombia later purchased 100 of the **Colombia Cyclone Falcon** powered by 531-kW (712-hp) Wright Cyclone radial engines; some were employed as landplanes, but most were operated at twin-float seaplanes during the war against Peru which broke out in 1932; both cockpits were protected by additional glazing and main wheels of the landing gear on the landplane version had open-sided speed fairings; a small batch of O-1E-type Falcons (**Chilean Falcon**) was built under licence in Chile and 10 were sold later to Brazil which used them against secessionists during 1932

The only factor differentiating the O-39 (illustrated) from the earlier O-16 was the use of the V-1570-25 Conqueror engine in a cowling resembling that of the P-6E. Note the enclosed cockpit.

Specification
Curtiss O-1E
Type: two-seat observation biplane
Powerplant: one 324-kW (435-hp) Curtiss V-1150E inline piston engine
Performance: maximum speed 227 km/h (141 mph); service ceiling 4665 m (15,300 ft); range 1014 km (630 miles)
Weights: empty equipped 1325 lb (2,922 lb); maximum take-off 1972 kg (4,347 lb)
Dimensions: span 11.58 m (38 ft 0 in); length 8.28 m (27 ft 2 in); height 3.20 m (10 ft 6 in); wing area 32.79 m² (353.00 sq ft)
Armament: one fixed forward-firing synchronised 7.62-mm (0.3-in) Lewis machine-guns on a Scarff mounting

Curtiss Model 49 (O2C-1 Helldiver)

Ordered by the US Navy at the same time as two XF8C-1 Falcon biplanes, the **Curtiss XF8C-2** was in fact an entirely new design (**Model 49**) produced specifically for dive-bombing. Externally it differed from the US Navy's Falcons by having its two forward-firing machine-guns moved from the lower to the upper wing and in having the upper wing reduced in area and span. The first XF8C-2 was destroyed when it crashed during a test dive in December 1928. It was replaced rapidly by Curtiss and followed by another prototype, the **XF8C-4** (**Model 49A**). The second XF8C-2 and the XF8C-4 had cowled Wasp engines and were capable of carrying a 227-kg (500-lb) bomb on a special rack which launched the weapon clear of the propeller arc during a dive-bombing attack.

The fuselage of the new machine, named **Helldiver**, was of welded steel tube and the wings were of wood. A total of 25 **F8C-4** (**Model 49B**) aircraft was built, these entering carrier service in 1930. The Helldivers were frequently in the spotlight and were used to obtain publicity for US naval aviation. Though tough and durable, their performance was not impressive and the last were withdrawn from reserve service just before World War II.

Variants
F8C-5: 63 of this version were delivered to US Marine Corps land-based observation units from 1931 on

wards; by then dive-bombing had become regarded as a secondary mission and the F8C-5s were soon redesignated **O2C-1**; like the F8C-4s, many of them were relegated to reserve units in 1934; two F8C-5s were fitted temporarily with leading-edge slots and wing flaps, and redesignated **XF8C-6**; the US Navy later obtained 30 more aircraft which were designated O2C-1 from the outset
Cyclone Helldiver: two civil-registered and company-owned aircraft, designated **Model 49C** and similar to the F8C-5s, were powered by Wright Cyclone engines and had glazed crew canopies; both had US Navy markings from the outset, although they were only bought by the US Navy after considerable use by Curtiss; one designate **XF8C-7** by the US Navy, then **X2C-2** and finally **O2C-2**, was used as a VIP transport; the second company machine, registered 938V, became the **XF8C-8**; two identical aircraft were bought by the US Navy and designated **O2C-2**
XS3C-1: this one-off variant (**Model 61**) was supplied to the US Navy to replace the XF8C-8 after it had crashed; modified extensively, it had a new tailplane, single-strut main landing gear legs and was powered by a 485-kW (650-hp) Wright Cyclone engine; it was considered for the two-seat fighter role and known officially as the **XF10C-1**

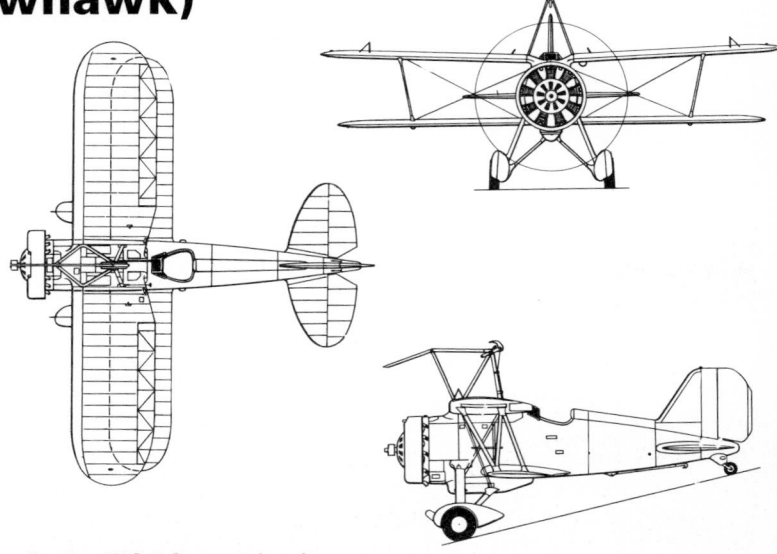

Specification
Curtiss F8C-5 (O2C-1)
Type: observation and dive-bombing biplane
Powerplant: one 336-kW (450-hp) Pratt & Whitney R-1340-4 Wasp radial piston engine
Performance: maximum speed 235 km/h (146 mph) at sea level; service ceiling 4955 m (16,250 ft); range 1159 km (720 miles)
Weights: empty equipped 1143 kg (2,520 lb); maximum take-off 1823 kg (4,020 lb)
Dimensions: span 9.75 m (32 ft 0 in);

The XF8C-4 prototype used features of the Falcon series and of the F7C-1. It had fuel tanks scabbed on to either side of the fuselage by the cockpit, a distinct tactical disadvantage.

length 7.82 m (25 ft 8 in); height 3.12 m (10 ft 3 in); wing area 28.61 m² (308.00 sq ft)
Armament: one 227-kt (500-lb) or two 52.6-kg (116-lb) underwing bombs, plus two fixed and one or two flexibly mounted 7.62-mm (0.3-in) machine-guns

Curtiss Model 58 (F9C Sparrowhawk)

In 1930 the US Navy called for a new single-seat fighter for operation from aircraft-carriers. To increase the aircraft complement of the carriers without having to resort to the introduction of folding wings the US Navy requirement specified aircraft of very small dimensions. After testing three contending prototypes, the Atlantic-Fokker XFA-1, the Berlinger-Joyce XFJ-1 and the **Curtiss XF9C-1** (company designation **Model 58**), the US Navy was not satisfied with any of them. All would have passed into oblivion if at that time there had not been another urgent problem requiring resolution: how to produce in a very short time a single-seat fighter able to operate from the US Navy's new giant rigid airship USS *Akron*. The *Akron* (ZRS-4) had a hangar within the envelope for four fighters to be launched and retrieved by means of a trapeze which could be lowered through doors in the belly of the airship. A hook mounted above the fuselage of the fighters could engage with the trapeze, allowing the

fighter to be drawn up inside the mother ship. The wings of the **XF9C-1** were small enough to pass through the hangar doors of the *Akron* and so the US Navy adapted it accordingly. It was tested with a trapeze fitted to the airship USS *Los Angeles* in the autumn of 1931. A second prototype, financed by the company as the **Model 58A** and tested as the **XF9C-2**, was flown with simplified landing gear which had single-strut main legs and wheel spats.

Six examples of the production version, the **F9C-2 Sparrowhawk**, were delivered in 1932. They differed from the prototypes in having an upper gull wing instead of the flat wing attached directly to the upper fuselage which had been a feature of the XF9C-1 and XF9C-2. Although it was intended that they should have the XF9C-2 landing gear, they went into service aboard the *Akron* in September 1932 with standard main units as incorporated on the XF9C-1.

There were no Sparrowhawks aboard the *Akron* when it came down at sea in

Curtiss F9C-2 Sparrowhawk

1933 and they went on to fly with her sister ship, the USS *Macon* (ZRS-5); when the *Macon* too was lost in 1935 she took four F9C-2s with her. During service aboard this latter airship the fighters had been launched and hooked on with the main units of the landing gear removed and replaced by a 114-litre (30-US gal) streamlined auxiliary fuel tank.

During their relatively brief career the racy Sparrowhawks with their colourful paint schemes and light-hearted unit insignia caught the imagination of the American people. They gained publicity out of all proportion to their small numbers, as a result of the unique and dramatic scenario of single-seat fighters operating from their huge lighter-than-air mother ship. One Sparrowhawk has been preserved and is the property of the Smithsonian Institution, Washington.

Specification
Curtiss F9C-2 Sparrowhawk
Type: airship-based single-seat fighter
Powerplant: one 327-kW (438-hp) Wright R-975-E Whirlwind radial piston engine
Performance: maximum speed 283 km/h (176 mph) at 1220 m (4,000 ft); initial climb rate 515 m (1,690 ft) per minute; service ceiling 5850 m (19,200 ft); range 478 km (297 miles)
Weights: empty equipped 948 kg (2,089 lb); maximum take-off 1261 kg (2,779 lb)
Dimensions: span 7.77 m (25 ft 6 in); length 6.13 m (20 ft 1½ in); height (with skyhook) 3.23 m (10 ft 7 in); wing area 16.05 m² (172.80 sq ft)
Armament: two fixed fuselage-mounted synchronised 7.62-mm (0.3-in) machine-guns

Curtiss Model 59/60 (A-8/A-10/A-12 Shrike)

The quest for speed led to the production of two competing monoplane prototypes to meet a US Army attack bomber requirement which was formulated in 1929. The Atlantic-Fokker XA-7 remained only a prototype, but the **Curtiss XA-8 Shrike** (**Model 59**) which made its maiden flight in June 1931 had a considerable impact on the US Army Air Corps. It was indeed an impressive aircraft for its time, the first Curtiss all-metal low-wing monoplane, with such advanced features as automatic leading-edge slots and trailing-edge flaps. The wing was strut-and wire-braced, and the main landing gear comprised two fully-enclosed trousered units, these fairings housing also two 7.62-mm (0.3-in) machine-guns. Pilot and observer-gunner were accommodated in widely separated cockpits, the former under a fully enclosed canopy and the latter protected by an extended windscreen. Power was provided by a 447-kW (600-hp) Curtiss V-1570C inline engine with a radiator beneath the nose, slightly forward of the wing leading edge.

Curtiss won a contract for five service test **YA-8** (**Model 59A**) aircraft on 29 September 1931, and these were followed by eight **Y1A-8** machines in the following year. Both YA-8s and Y1A-8s had open pilot's cockpits. All were later redesignated **A-8** except for one YA-8 which was reworked as the experimental **YA-10** (**Model 59B**) with a 466-kW (625-hp) radial engine and one **Y1A-8**

which became the **Y1A-8A** with a 503-kW (675-hp) V-1570-57 geared engine and a redesigned wing. The A-8s, powered by Prestone-cooled V-1570-31 engines each of 447 kW (600 hp), created something of a sensation in US aviation circles when they went into service with the 3rd Attack Group at Fort Crockett, Texas in April 1932. At that time all other standard equipment was of biplane configuration and the first US Army low-wing monoplane fighter, the Boeing P-26A 'Peashooter', did not enter squadron service until eight months later.

The US Army had ordered a further 46 Shrikes under the designation **A-8B**, but maintenance problems with the liquid-cooled engines of the A-8s led to the new aircraft being powered by Wright R-1820-21 radial air-cooled engines of 500 kW (670 hp), resulting in the new designation **A-12** (**Model 60**). These aircraft retained the open pilot's cockpit with faired headrest which had been introduced on the A-8 production batch, and carried the same machine-gun armament and bombload. In an attempt to improve co-operation between pilot and observer a major modification had been introduced, the rear cockpit being moved forward with its glazed covering forming a continuation of the fuselage decking immediately behind the pilot's cockpit.

After long service with the US Army's attack groups the Shrikes were rele-

gated to second-line units in 1939, but nine A-12s still remained in service in Hawaii when Pearl Harbor was attacked in December 1941. The Chinese nationalist government bought 20 of an export version of the A-12 in 1936; these saw some action against the Japanese in 1937-8.

Specification
Curtiss A-12
Type: two-seat attack (light bomber) aircraft
Powerplant: one 515-kW (690-hp) Wright R-1820-21 Cyclone radial piston engine
Performance: maximum speed 285 km/h (177 mph) at sea level; service ceiling 4620 m (15,150 ft); range 821 km (510 miles)

The A-8 brought a new and powerful dimension to the USAAC's attack capability, though the effect of the Shrike was greatly exaggerated.

Weights: empty equipped 1768 kg (3,898 lb); maximum take-off 2611 kg (5,756 kg)
Dimensions: span 13.41 m (44 ft 0 in); length 9,83 m (32 ft 3 in); height 2.84 m (9 ft 4 in); wing area 26.38 m² (284.00 sq ft)
Armament: five 7.62-mm (0.3-in) machine-guns, four with limited adjustment in landing gear fairings and one on a ring mounting operated by observer/gunner, plus provision for four 55-kg (122-lb) 10 13.6-kg (30-lb) bombs on underwing racks

Curtiss T-32 Condor II

The **Curtiss T-32 Condor II** (**Curtiss-Wright CW-4**) biplane transport of 1933 was even more of an anachronism than its namesake, the Condor 18 of four years earlier. Its only concession to the then current modernity was the landing gear, its main units retracting into the engine nacelles. A two-bay biplane of mixed construction, with a strut-braced single fin and rudder tail assembly, the T-32 prototype made its first flight on 30 January 1933. Layout for most of the production batch of 21 aircraft that followed was as a luxury 12-passenger night sleeper transport, and a number of T-32s

flew with Eastern Air Transport and American Airways during the following three years on regular night services.

Two modified T-32s were bought as transports for the US Army and operated until 1938 under the designation **YC-30**. One Condor was completed with extra fuel tanks as a long-range version for use by the 1933 Byrd Antarctic Expedition. Equipped to operate with either twin floats or skis, it was unique in having fixed landing gear.

Ten T-32s were ultimately converted to AT-32 standard (see below), being redesignated **T-32C**. Four T-32s were

being operated under British civil registrations at the outbreak of World War II; these were impressed and flown by the RAF.

Variants
Curtiss AT-32: this version differed from the original T-32 in detail and was provided with variable-pitch propellers for its Wright Cyclone engines; these had full NACA cowlings instead of the Townend rings of the T-32; the three **AT-32A** sub-variants had 529-kW (710-hp) Wright SCR-1820-23 Cyclones, the three **AT-32B** models 537-kW (720-hp) SCR-1820-F2s, the sole **AT-32C** SCR-1820-F2 engines and the four examples of the **AT-32D** SCR-1820-23 engines; all were convertible from night sleepers into comfortable 15-passenger day transports; the two **AT-32E** aircraft were built for the US Navy and operated under the designation **R4C-1** by the US Navy and US Marines as 12-passenger de luxe transports; both were used by the US Antarctic Survey, finally being abandoned in the Antarctic in 1941
BT-32: eight examples of this bomber development of the AT-32 were

completed; defensive armament comprised five machine-guns with single guns located in manually operated turrets in the nose and above the rear fuselage, the other guns being aimed through lateral ports and from an extensively glazed ventral position; the prototype BT-32 was sold to China, three aircraft with twin floats were exported to Colombia and four landplanes went to Peru
CT-32: this was a military cargo version with a large loading door in the starboard side of the fuselage; all three built went to Argentina

Specification
Curtiss BT-32
Type: heavy bomber
Powerplant: two 529-kW (710-hp) Wright SCR-1820-23 Cyclone radial piston engines
Performance: maximum speed 283 km/h (176 mph); service ceiling 6705 m (22,000 ft); range 1352 km (840 miles)
Weights: empty equipped 5095 kg (11,233 lb); maximum take-off 7938 kg (17,500 lb)
Dimensions: span 24.99 m (82 ft 0 in); length 15.09 m (49 ft 6 in); height 4.98 m (16 ft 4 in); wing area 118.54 m² (1,276.0 sq ft)
Armament: five flexible 7.62-mm (0.3-in) machine-guns, plus up to 762 kg (1,680 lb) of bombs

Swissair used the Curtiss Condor for its Zurich – Berlin service, the passengers tended to by Europe's first stewardess.

Curtiss Model 71 (SOC Seagull)

Last of the Curtiss biplanes to be used operationally by the US Navy, the **SOC Seagull** has a service history which very nearly duplicates that of the Royal Navy's Fairey Swordfish torpedo-bomber. Both originated in 1933, both should have become obsolescent during the early stages of World War II, both remained operational until the end of the war surviving, superbly, later designs intended to replace them.

The US Navy's requirement for a new scouting/observation aircraft was circulated to US manufacturers in early 1933, resulting in proposals from Curtiss, Douglas and Vought, but it was the **XO3C-1** prototype, company-designated **Curtiss Model 71**, ordered on 19 June 1933 and first flown in April 1934, which was ordered into production as the **SOC-1** (**Model 71A**). This changed official designation reflected the combination of scout and observation roles.

When first flown the prototype was equipped with amphibious landing gear, twin main wheels being incorporated in the central float. However, standard production aircraft were built as floatplanes, with non-retractable tailwheel landing gear optional; in any event they were easily convertible from one configuration to the other. Construction was mixed, with the foldable wings and tail unit of light alloy, a welded steel-tube fuselage structure, and a mixture of light alloy and fabric covering. The pilot and gunner/observer were accommodated in tandem cockpits, enclosed by a continuous transparent canopy with sliding sections for access. To provide a maximum field of fire for the flexibly-mounted gun in the rear cockpit, the turtleback could be retracted.

Deliveries of the first SOC-1 production aircraft began on 12 November 1935. These were powered by Pratt & Whitney R-1340 Wasp engines, and the first squadrons to become fully equipped with the type comprised Scouting Squadrons VS-5B/-6B/-9S/-10S/-11S. Production of 135 SOC-1s was followed by 40 examples of the SOC-2 (**Model 71B**) with wheeled landing gear, detail improvements and R-1340-22 Wasp engines. A total of 83 examples of the **SOC-3** (**Model 71E**) was built, these being generally similar to the SOC-1. SOC-2s and SOC-3s, after modification to install arrester gear during 1942, became redesignated **SOC-2A** and **SOC-3A** respectively. Curtiss also built three aircraft virtually the same as the SOC-3 for service with the US Coast Guard: these **SOC-4** (**Model 71F**) aircraft were acquired by the US Navy in 1942 and equipped with arrester gear to bring them up to SOC-3A standard. In addition to the SOC Seagulls built by Curtiss, 44 were produced by the Naval Aircraft Factory at Philadelphia, Pennsylvania. Basically the same as the Curtiss-built SOC-3, these were designated **SON-1** or, if fitted with arrester gear, **SON-1A**.

Following termination of SOC production in early 1938, Curtiss became involved in the development and manufacture of a successor, designated SO3C Seamew. However, when the operational performance of the Seamew proved unsatisfactory it was withdrawn from first-line service; all available SOCs then reverted to operational status, continuing to fulfil their appointed role until the end of the war.

Variants
XSO2C-1: under this designation a single **Model 71C** was evaluated as an improved SOC, but was not favoured with production orders

A Curtiss SOC-3 Seagull of the US Navy's Observation Squadron VO-2, seen after delivery in 1938. The full-span leading edge slats are seen in the open position, these improving lift at low speeds.

Specification
Curtiss SOC-1 (floatplane)
Type: two-seat scout/observation aircraft
Powerplant: one 447-kW (600-hp) Pratt & Whitney R-1340-18 Wasp radial piston engine
Performance: maximum speed 266 km/h (165 mph) at 1525 m (5,000 ft); cruising speed 214 km/h (133 mph); service ceiling 4540 m (14,900 ft); range 1086 km (675 miles)
Weights: empty 1718 kg (3,788 lb);
maximum take-off 2466 kg (5,437 lb)
Dimensions: span 10.97 m (36 ft 0 in); length 8.08 m (26 ft 6 in); height (floatplane) 4.50 m (14 ft 9 in); wing area 31.77 m² (342.0 sq ft)
Armament: two 7.62-mm (0.30-in) machine-guns, one forward-firing and one on flexible mount, plus external racks for up to 295 kg (650 lb) of bombs

Curtiss Model 79 (P-36)

In 1934 Curtiss decided to design and develop as a private venture a new monoplane pursuit (fighter) aircraft. Known as the **Curtiss Model 75**, it had such advanced features as retractable landing gear and an enclosed cockpit for the pilot, and the company believed that the US Army would be prepared to consider it as a replacement for the lower-performance Boeing P-26.

The Model 75 prototype, powered by a 671-kW (900-hp) Wright XR-1670-5 radial engine, was submitted to the US Army Air Corps in May 1935 for evaluation in a design competition for a single-seat pursuit aircraft. This failed to materialise because no competing designs were ready, and it was not until April 1936 that the contest began. By then the Model 75 had been re-engined with an 634-kW (850-hp) Wright R-1820 radial, being identified as the **Model 75B** with this powerplant.

The Seversky Aircraft Corporation won the USAAC's competition with a not-too-dissimilar aircraft, but Curtiss gained some slight compensation by being awarded a contract for just three examples of its design. Powered by a derated version of the 783-kW (1,050-hp) Pratt & Whitney R-1830-13 Twin Wasp radial engine, they were used for test and evaluation under the designation **Y1P-36** (**Model 75E**). By comparison with the original Model 75 prototype, these had cockpit modifications to improve fore and aft view, and introduced a retractable tailwheel.

Service testing of the Y1P-36s was considered so successful that a contract for 210 examples of the production **P-36A** (**Model 75L**) fighters was awarded on 7 July 1937, then the US Army's largest peacetime contract for pursuit aircraft. Delivery of these began in April 1938, but by late 1941 when the United States became involved in World War II they were already considered obsolete. Circumstances compelled limited use of P-36As in the opening stage of hostilities with Japan, but they were very soon relegated for use in a training role.

Variants included a single **P-36B** with a 746-kW (1,000-hp) Pratt & Whitney R-1830-25 engine, and the last 31 of the original production run were completed as **P-36C** fighters with a more powerful Twin Wasp engine and two wing-mounted guns. The designations **XP-36D, XP-36E** and **XP-36F** were applied to experimental examples with differing armament.

Examples of the **H75A** export model were supplied to the French Armée de L'Air as **H75-A1/-A2/-A3/-A4** fighters with different engines and armament, but the majority were transferred to the UK after the fall of France; being designated respectively **Mohawk Mks I/II/III/IV. H75A-5** was the designation of a model to be assembled in China by the Central Aircraft Manufacturing Company. After a few aircraft had been built

On the day Germany invaded Poland, 1 September 1939, these 27th Pursuit Squadron P-36Cs are seen lined up at the Cleveland National Air Races, wearing war game camouflage schemes.

in China, the company was transferred to India as Hindustan Aircraft Ltd, and its H75A-5s were accepted by the RAF as Mohawk Mk IVs. The type was supplied to Norway which ordered initially 24 of the **H75A-6** model, followed by 36 of the **H75A-8**. The latter were not delivered to Norway, six being handed over to Free Norwegian forces in Canada following German occupation of Norway and the remaining 30 requisitioned for service with the USAAC under the designation **P-36G**. The Netherlands ordered 20 of the **H75A-7** model, these being delivered to the Netherlands East Indies, and Persia (now Iran) ordered 10 examples of the **H75A-9**. Hawks also served, indirectly, with the air forces of Finland, India, Peru, Portugal, South Africa and Vichy France.

Variants
Model 75J: designation of Model 75A demonstrator fitted with a mechanical supercharger for its R-1830 engine

Model 75K: unrealised project for a version with the Pratt & Whitney R-2180 Twin Hornet, finally produced as the **Model 75R** by conversion of the Model 75A demonstrator

Specification
Curtiss P-36G
Type: single-seat fighter
Powerplant: one 895-kW (1,200-hp) Wright R-1820-G205A Cyclone radial piston engine
Performance: maximum speed 518 km/h (322 mph) at 4635 m (15,200 ft); cruising speed 420 km/h (261 mph); climb to 4570 m (15,000 ft) in 6 minutes; service ceiling 9860 m (32,359 ft); range 1046 km (650 miles)
Weights: empty 2121 kg (4,675 lb); maximum take-off 2667 kg (5,880 lb)
Dimensions: span 11.28 m (37 ft 0 in); length 8.69 m (28 ft 6 in); height 2.82 m (9 ft 3 in); wing area 21.92 m² (236.0 sq ft)
Armament: four wing-mounted 7.62-mm (0.3-in) machine-guns and two fuselage-mounted 12.7-mm (0.5-in) machine-guns

Curtiss Hawk 75-A3 of the 2e Escadrille, Groupe de Chasse I/4, Vichy French air force, based at Dakar (Senegal) in the summer of 1942.

Curtiss P-36C of the US Army Air Force in early 1942, painted in the standard wartime olive-drab colour scheme.

Curtiss Model 75 (Hawk 75)

The belief that there would be a market for a less sophisticated export version of the Curtiss Model 75 led to development in 1937 of such a version, known as the **Curtiss Hawk 75**. Two **Hawk 75H** demonstrators were built, these being generally similar in construction to the Y1P-36 but having a lower-powered Wright radial engine and fixed tailwheel type landing gear.

The original demonstration model was bought by the Chinese Nationalist government during 1937, and was followed in 1938 by an order for an additional 112 aircraft under the designation **Hawk 75M** to equip the new reorganised Chinese air force. In 1938 the delivery of 12 similar aircraft for the Royal Siamese air force began. Designated **Hawk 75N**, they differed by being armed with two additional machine-guns and were used briefly in combat during 1941. Production of the **Hawk 75O** for the Argentine, which had acquired the second demonstrator, totalled 29 aircraft. This nation also negotiated with Curtiss a licence to build the

type and 20 were produced from 1940 in a government aircraft factory at Cordoba. The **Hawk 75Q**, of which two were built, was another demonstrator model: one, converted with a retractable landing gear was given to Claire Chennault by Madame Chiang Kai-shek; the other had fixed landing gear and crashed in China during 1939.

Specification
Curtiss Hawk 75M
Type: single-seat fighter

Curtiss Hawk 75A-5 of the Chinese Nationalist air force, based at Kunming in 1942. These aircraft fought bravely alongside early P-40 variants against the Japanese until more modern equipment arrived.

Powerplant: one 652-kW (875-hp) Wright GR-1820-G3 radial piston engine
Performance: maximum speed 451 km/h (280 mph) at 3050 m (10,000 ft); cruising speed 386 mph (240 mph); service ceiling 9690 m (31,800 ft); range 877 km (545 miles)
Weights: empty 1803 kg (3,975 lb); maximum take-off 2406 kg (5,305 lb)

Dimensions: span 11.28 m (37 ft 0 in); length 8.71 m (28 ft 7 in); height 2.82 m (9 ft 3 in); wing area 21.92 m² (236.0 sq ft)
Armament: two wing-mounted 7.62-mm (0.3-in) machine-guns and two fuselage-mounted 7.62-mm (0.3-in) or 12.7-mm (0.5-in) machine-guns

Curtiss Model 77 (SBC Helldiver)

Requiring a new two-seat fighter, the US Navy ordered a prototype from Curtiss in 1932 under the designation **XF12C-1**. This **Curtiss Model 73** flew for the first time during 1933, in the form of a two-seat parasol-wing monoplane with retractable landing gear powered by a 466-kW (625-hp) Wright R-1510-92 Whirlwind 14 engine. When, at the end of the year, it was decided to use this aircraft in a scout capacity, its designation

was changed to **XS4C-1**. Following yet another change of heart, its role became that of a scout-bomber in January 1934 and a Wright R-1820 Cyclone engine was installed. Extensive trials followed, and during a dive test in September 1934 there was structural failure of the wing and the **XSBC-1**, as it had been designated, was damaged extensively.

The parasol wing was clearly unsuitable for the dive-bombing requirement,

and a new prototype was ordered as the **XSBC-2** (**Model 77**), this having biplane wings and a 522-kW (700-hp) Wright R-1510-12 Whirlwind 14 engine. When, in March 1936, this engine was replaced by a 522-kW (700-hp) Pratt & Whitney R-1535-82 Twin Wasp Junior engine, and the designation changed yet again to **XSBC-3**. The production **SBC-3** (**Model 77A**), of which the US Navy ordered 83 on 29 August 1936, was

generally similar and the first deliveries, to Navy Squadron VS-5, were made on 17 July 1937.

A late production SBC-3 was used as the prototype of an improved **XSBC-4** (**Model 77B**) with a more powerful Wright R-1820-22 engine. Following an initial contract of 5 January 1938, the first of 174 production examples of the **SBC-4** for the US Navy was delivered in March 1939. Because of the desperate situation in Europe in early 1940, the US Navy diverted 50 of its SBC-4s to France but these were received too late to be used in combat. Five were recovered for use by the RAF, and these were issued to RAF Little Rissington for allocation as ground trainers under the designation **Cleveland**. The US Navy's deficiency of 50 aircraft was made good by delivery of 50 out of the 90 aircraft which had been in production for France. Retaining the SBC-4 designation, these differed from standard in having self-sealing fuel tanks.

By the time the USA became involved in World War II, the SBC-3s had become obsolescent, but SBC-4s were then in service with US Navy Squadrons VB-8 and VS-8 on board the USS *Hornet* and with US Marine Squadron VMO-151.

Specification
Curtiss SBC-4
Type: two-seat carrier-based scout-bomber
Powerplant: one 671-kW (900-hp) Wright R-1820-34 Cyclone 9 radial piston engine
Performance: maximum speed 377 km/h (234 mph) at 4365 m

(15,200 ft); cruising speed 282 km/h (175 mph); service ceiling 7315 m (24,000 ft); range with 227-kg (500-lb) bomb 652 km (405 miles)
Weights: empty 2065 kg (4,552 lb); maximum take-off 3211 kg (7,080 lb)
Dimensions: span 10.36 m (34 ft

0 in); length 8.57 m (28 ft 1½ in); height 3.17 m (10 ft 5 in); wing area 29.45 m² (317.0 sq ft)
Armament: two 7.62-mm (0.3-in) machine-guns, one forward-firing and one on flexible mount, plus one 227-kg (500-lb) bomb

Curtiss SBC-3 Helldiver of VS-5, US Navy, based aboard the USS Yorktown in 1937.

Curtiss Model 81/87 (P-40 Warhawk)

Last of the famous Hawk line, the **Curtiss P-40 Warhawk** has always been something of an enigma. By no stretch of the imagination could it be numbered among the 'great' fighter aircraft of World War II. Yet, with the exceptions of the Republic P-47 and North American P-51, it was the most extensively built US fighter, with 15,000 delivered before production ended in December 1944.

Evolution towards the aircraft which the company designated the **Model 81** began in 1937, when the Model 75 prototype's airframe was modified to accept a 858-kW (1,150-hp) Allison V-1710-11 in-line. In this form the **Model 75I** became the first American fighter capable of a speed exceeding 483 km/h (300 mph). The Model 75I was evaluated by the USAAC as the **XP-37**: despite engine and supercharger difficulties, the potential of the design was clear, and the service ordered 13 of the **YP-37** service test model with the improved V-1710-21 engine and slightly longer fuselage. The new B-2 supercharger was also fitted, but all YP-37s continued to suffer problems with the powerplant installation.

A little later the tenth P-36A was re-engined by a 865-kW (1,160-hp) Allison V-1710-19 engine, instead of the 783-kW (1,050-hp) Pratt & Whitney R-1830-13 radial which was standard. In other respects it varied little from the P-36A when it was flown for the first time on 14 October 1938. In May 1939 this **Model 75P**, by then designated **XP-40**, was flown in competition against other pursuit prototypes and was selected for production as most closely meeting US Army Air Corps requirements. A total of 524 **P-40** production aircraft (Model 81) was ordered on 27 April 1939, this then representing the largest single order for fighters to originate from the US Army. Just over a year later, in May 1940, the first P-40s began to come off the production line, the initial three being used for service trials. These differed from the initial XP-40, with a less powerful supercharged Allison V-1710-33 engine installed and two 7.62-mm (0.3-in) machine-guns in the wings to supplement the two 12.7-mm (0.5-in) machine-guns mounted in the fuselage nose. By September 1940 a total of 200 of these aircraft had been delivered to the USAAC.

Before that, in April 1940, production

priority had been accorded to delivery of 185 generally similar **Hawk 81-A1** fighters ordered by France. None, however, left the assembly line before that nation's collapse and, instead, these aircraft were diverted to the UK where they were designated **Tomahawk Mk I**. Deliveries to England and to Takoradi in West Africa, began in late 1940, but the Tomahawk was unsuited for operational employment in Europe and the majority were relegated to training duties.

The next version for the RAF (**Hawk 81-A2**) was designated **Tomahawk Mk IIA** and this, basically the same as USAAC's **P-40B (Model 81-B)**, had self-sealing fuel tanks, armour, and was armed with two wing-mounted 7.7-mm (0.303-in) machine-guns. Unfortunately, the increased weight resulting from these improvements reduced performance, while improved self-sealing tanks and the addition of two more wing guns on the **P-40C** brought a further erosion of performance. A total of 930 of this version was built for the RAF (**Hawk 81-A3**), those which entered service being designated **Tomahawk Mk IIB**. These had US radio equipment but were armed with six 7.7-mm (0.303-in) machine-guns. A total of 100 of the allocation of Hawk 81-A3s for the RAF was diverted to China, 90 of these reaching the American Volunteer Group (AVG) operating from Kunming and Mingaladon; 49 shipped direct from the USA, plus 146 re-shipped from Great Britain, were supplied to the Soviet Union, and a small number went to the Turkish air force.

Some American P-40s were modified in 1941 to serve in a reconnaissance role, under the designation **RP-40**, but Curtiss had already begun redesign of the Hawk 81-A in an attempt to improve its performance and effectiveness. The

Curtiss Hawk 81-A2 of Henry Geselbracht, 2nd Squadron, American Volunteer Group, based at Toungoo (Burma) in February 1942.

Curtiss YP-37

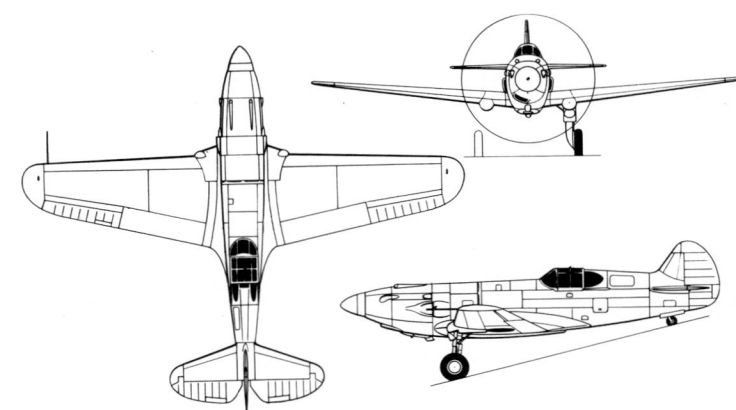

changes included installation of the 858-kW (1,150-hp) Allison V-1710-39, which could maintain this power output to an altitude of 3565 m (11,700 ft), and the addition of armour, provision of four 12.7-mm (0.5-in) wing-mounted machine-guns, and an underfuselage hardpoint for the carriage of a 227-kg (500-lb) bomb or 197-litre (52-US gal) fuel drop tank. First flown on 22 May 1941 as the **Kittyhawk Mk I**, having been ordered as such by the UK, it was identified as **Hawk 87-A2** by Curtiss, and as the **P-40D** by the USAAC, which had also ordered this version in September 1940. Only the first 22 aircraft delivered to the USAAF had the armament of four wing-mounted guns, subsequent deliveries having six guns and the designation **P-40E (Model 87-B2)**. A total of 1,500 of this version, identified as the **P-40E-1 (Hawk 87-A3** and **-A4)**, was procured by the USAAF for supply to Britain under Lend-Lease, the model being designated **Kittyhawk Mk IA** in RAF service; in addition large numbers of this version were supplied to British Commonwealth air forces. Other P-40Es were supplied to Brigadier General Claire Chennault's AVG in China where, deployed with considerable skill, the P-40 in several variants achieved notable success against Japanese aircraft. A few P-40Es were converted as two-seat trainers, losing their fuselage tank to provide space for the second cockpit.

Throughout the next three years Curtiss made tremendous efforts to improve the capability of the P-40, resulting in a number of variants (see below). Despite all the effort, which resulted in quite considerable improvement, it left performance of the Warhawk below that of contemporary Allied and Axis fighters and production ended in December 1944.

Variants
P-40A: retrospective designation of a single camera-carrying P-40 (serial 40-326)
XP-40F: designation of a single experimental aircraft (**Model 87-B3**) combining a P-40D airframe and a Rolls-Royce Merlin 28 inline engine
P-40F: production version resulting from above, powered by a 69-kW (1,300-hp) Packard-built V-1650-1 Merlin; more than 1,300 built
XP-40G: a single prototype (**Model 81-AG**) with armament and fuel tank changes
P-40G: 43 P-40s retrofitted with Tomahawk Mk IIA wings; 16 were sent to Russia in late 1941, and in October 1942 those in US service were redesignated RP-40G
P-40J: designation allocated to a version to be powered by a turbocharged Allison engine; not built
P-40K: virtually an improved version of the P-40E powered by an Allison V-1710-73 engine; 1,300 built, of which the RAF received 21, designating them **Kittyhawk Mk III**
P-40L: version generally similar to P-40F except for equipment changes; 700 built
P-40M: version generally similar to the P-40K but powered by an Allison V-1710-71 engine and with detail improvements; almost 400 supplied to the RAF which designated them Kittyhawk Mk III
P-40N: major and final production version of which 5,200 built (**Model 87V** and **Model 87W** variants); improved performance achieved by weight saving and by use of Allison V-1710-81 engine or, subsequently, similar powered -99 or -115 versions of that engine; lighter weight and improved equipment incorporated during production run; supplied also to

Australia, China, South Africa, UK (RAF designation **Kittyhawk Mk IV**) and Soviet Union
P-40P: designation initially allocated to 1,500 aircraft ordered with V-1650-1 engine but actually built as P-40Ns with V-1710-81 engines
XP-40Q: designation allocated to two P-40Ks and one P-40N modified extensively as **Model 87X**, including the installation of two-stage superchargers and bubble canopy, to achieve improved performance
P-40R: designation of P-40F and P-40L aircraft following conversion to trainers in 1944, with Allison engines replacing the original Packard Merlin engines
TP-40: designation given to some P-40s following conversion to two-seat pilot transition trainers
Twin-Engined P-40: proposed variant of 1942, a P-40C being mocked up with two Merlin powerplants (from P-40F/Kittyhawk Mk II aircraft) on the wings above the main landing gear
Kittyhawk Mk II: RAF designation for 330 P-40Fs and P-40Ls received under Lend-Lease; the first 230 are sometimes known under the designation **Kittyhawk Mk IIA**
Model 81-AC: 40 conversions of P-40Cs to British specification
Model 81-AG: conversions of P-40s to P-40G, plus one XP-40G prototype
Model 87: first batch of P-40Ds
Model 87-A1: unknown number ordered by France but not delivered
Model 87-A5: sub-variant of Model 87-A4 order

Specification

Curtiss Kittyhawk Mk III (P-40K-1) of No. 250 (Sudan) Squadron, RAF, based in southern Italy during late 1943.

Curtiss P-40N (Kittyhawk Mk IV)

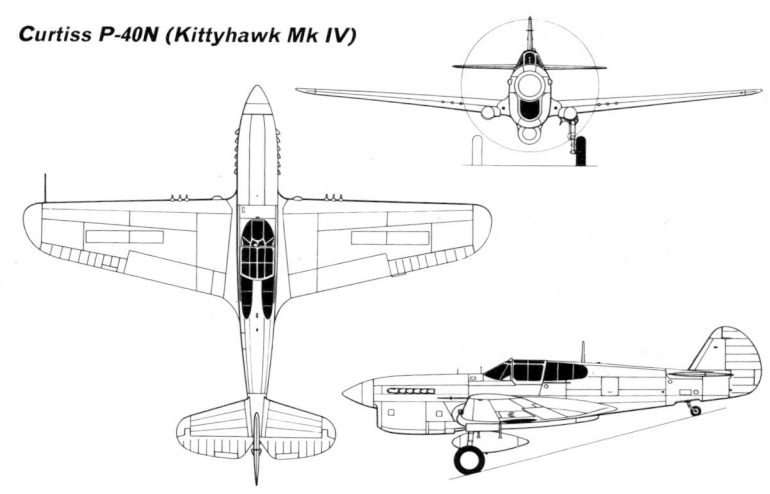

Curtiss P-40N
Type: single-seat fighter-bomber
Powerplant: one 895-kW (1,200-hp) Allison V-1710-81 inline piston engine
Performance: maximum speed 552 km/h (343 mph) at 4570 m (15,000 ft); climb to 4265 m (14,000 ft) in 6 minutes 42 seconds; service ceiling 9450 m (31,000 ft); range with auxiliary fuel at 3050 m (10,000 ft)

1738 km (1,080 miles)
Weights: empty 2812 kg (6,200 lb); maximum take-off 4014 kg (8,850 lb)
Dimensions: span 11.38 m (37 ft 4 in); length 10.16 m (33 ft 4 in); height 3.76 m (12 ft 4 in); wing area 21.92 m² (236.0 sq ft)
Armament: six 12.7-mm (0.5-in) machine-guns, plus up to 680 kg (1,500 lb) of bombs

Curtiss Model 82 (SO3C-2)

In 1937 the US Navy invited proposals for the design of a scout monoplane which would offer improved performance over the Curtiss SOC Seagull then in operational service. It was required for operation from either ships at sea or land bases, which meant that easily interchangeable float/wheel landing gear was essential. From the proposals received both Curtiss and Vought were awarded prototype contracts in May 1938 under the respective designation **XSO3C-1** and **XSO2U-1**. The latter prototype (1440), powered by a 410-kW (550-hp) Ranger XV-770-4 engine, was duly flown in competition, but it was the **Curtiss Model 82** design which was ordered into production. Despite this, the XSO3C-1 had serious instability problems. These were resolved finally by the introduction of upturned wingtips and increased tail surfaces, but the resulting aircraft in its landplane form was almost certainly the ugliest aircraft to be produced by the Curtiss company. Of all-metal construction, except for fabric-covered control surfaces, the XSO3C-1 had a crew of two accommodated in tan-

The SO3C-1 could operate as a floatplane or with simply-attached wheeled landing gear. The upturned wings were a response to stability problems.

dem enclosed cockpits. Floatplane landing gear comprised a large single-step central float and strut-mounted wingtip stabiliser floats and the wheeled landing gear was conspicuous by having large streamlined fairings. The prototype XSO3C-1 flew for the first time on 6 October 1939, and it and the **Model 82A** production **SO3C-1** initially named **Seagull**, were powered by a 388-kW (520-hp) Ranger V-770-6 engine.

SO3C-1 production aircraft began to enter service on board the USS *Cleveland* in July 1942, and 300 were built before production switched to the **SO3C-2**. This **Model 82B** differed in having equipment for carrier operations, including an arrester hook, plus an underfuselage rack on the landplane version to mount a 227-kg (500-lb) bomb. Production of this model totalled 456, of

which 250 were allocated to the UK under Lend-Lease, although British records would seem to suggest that only 100 were received. Designation of the version intended originally for the Royal Navy was **SO3C-1B (Model 82C)**, but those actually delivered were of the **SO3C-2C** variant with a more powerful engine, hydraulic brakes for aircraft with wheeled landing gear and other refinements. In British service these aircraft were designated **Seamew**, a name adopted subsequently by the US Navy,

but none were used operationally in Great Britain. Instead, they equipped Nos 744 and 745 Training Squadrons, based at Yarmouth, Canada and Worthy Downs, Hampshire respectively, for the instruction of air gunners/wireless operators.

The unsatisfactory performance of the SO3C-1 in the US Navy led to their withdrawal from first-line service. Many were converted for use as radio-controlled targets under the designation

SO3C-1K, 30 being assigned to the UK, by whom they were designated **Queen Seamew** and used to supplement the fleet of de Havilland Queen Bee target aircraft.

In an attempt to retrieve the situation, Curtiss introduced in late 1943 a lighter-weight variant equipped with the more powerful SGV-770-8 engine; designated **SO3C-3 (Model 82C)**, only 39 were built before production ended in January 1944. Plans to introduce an SO3C-3 variant with arrester gear, and production by the Ryan Aeronautical Corporation of SO3C-1s under the designation **SOR-1**, were cancelled.

Specification
Curtiss SO3C-2C (floatplane)
Type: two-seat scout/observation

increased fuel capacity; 970 built
Powerplant: one 447-kW (600-hp) Ranger SGV-770-8 inline piston engine
Performance: maximum speed 277 km/h (172 mph) at 2470 m (8,100 ft); cruising speed 201 km/h (125 mph); service ceiling 4815 m (15,800 ft); range 1851 km (1,150 miles)
Weights: empty 1943 kg (4,284 lb); maximum take-off 2599 kg (5,729 lb)
Dimensions: span 11.58 m (38 ft 0 in); length 11.23 m (36 ft 10 in); height 4.57 m (15 ft 0 in); wing area 26.94 m² (290.0 sq ft)
Armament: one 7.62-mm (0.3-in) forward-firing machine-gun and one 12.7-mm (0.5-in) machine-gun on flexible mount, plus two 45-kg (100-lb) bombs or 147-kg (325-lb) depth charges beneath wings

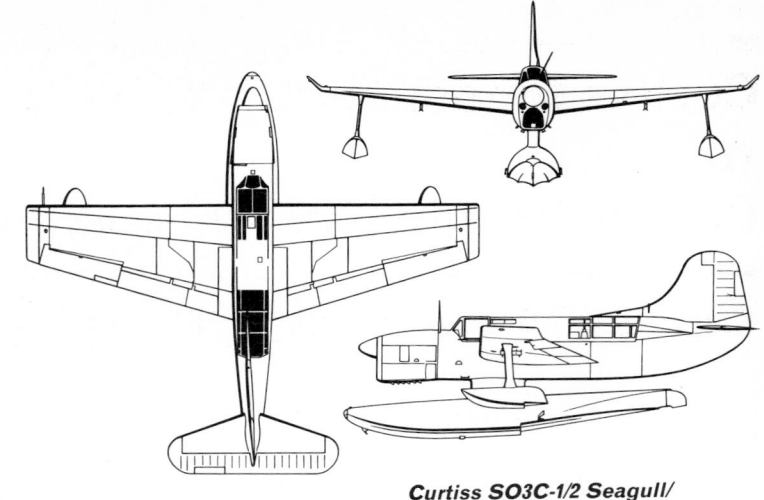

Curtiss SO3C-1/2 Seagull/ Seamew

Curtiss Model 84 (SB2C Helldiver)

First Curtiss-built US Navy aircraft to bear the name Helldiver was the F8C/O2C biplane of the early 1930s. Second in line was the SBC Helldiver of the late 1930s, the last combat biplane to be built for the US services. Last and most famous of the line was the **SB2C Helldiver** of the early 1940s: this was the final combat aeroplane built by Curtiss for the US Marine Corps/US Navy, and the most extensively built of all US Navy dive-bombers.

In 1938 the US Navy began the process of procuring a new scout-bomber, to replace the SBC Helldiver which was then still in production. From the proposals received, Brewster and Curtiss were awarded contracts for prototypes of their contenders, the former being designated XSB2A-1 and entering production as the SB2A Buccaneer. The **Curtiss Model 84** prototype, designated **XSB2C-1** (1758), flew for the first time on 18 December 1940, but was destroyed in a flying accident in early January 1941. Fortunately, the US Navy had great faith in this design (to the extent that large scale production had been authorised on 29 November 1940), but it was not until 18 months later, in June 1942, that the first production **SB2C-1** was flown. This extended development period resulted mainly from a US Army Air Corps order for 900 **A-25A Shrike** aircraft in April 1941. Generally similar to the SB2C-1, this **Model S84** caused delay as a result of the need to ensure compatability of design and equipment to satisfy both the US Navy and US Army. In the final analysis only a few of the A-25As entered US Army service; the majority were re-assigned to the US Marine Corps under the designation **SB2C-1A**.

Production SB2C-1s began to enter service with US Navy Squadron VS-9 in December 1942, but further protracted delays in finalising details of the best combat configuration prevented their initial operational employment until late 1943.

In configuration the SB2C was a low-wing cantilever monoplane largely of all-metal construction, the outer panels of the wings folding upwards for carrier stowage. The trailing-edge flaps were perforated and of split type so that they could be used also as dive-brakes, and wingtip leading-edge slats, of approximately the same span as the ailerons, were deployed automatically as the landing gear was lowered to ensure that the ailerons remained fully effective at low speeds. Retractable wide-track landing included a semi-retractable steerable tailwheel. Arrester gear and catapult

launching spools were standard, but this latter equipment and wing-folding capability was deleted from the A-25A version produced for the US Army. Powerplant of the prototype and SB2C-1s consisted of a 1268-kW (1,700-hp) Wright R-2600-8 Cyclone 14 twin-row radial engine. Armament comprised four wing-mounted 12.7-mm (0.5-in) machine-guns, two 7.62-mm (0.3-in) guns in the rear cockpit, and up to 454 kg (1,000 lb) of bombs carried in an underfuselage bomb bay.

It is not surprising that, with production totalling more than 7,000 examples, there were several variants of the basic design, details of which are given below. Only 26 of this total were used by any other service during World War II, for the type was of such great value in the Pacific theatre that the US Navy absorbed almost the entire production. Many continued in service with the US Navy in early postwar years, and some were eventually sold to other nations.

Variants
SB2C-1C: many of the SB2C-1s had their four wing-mounted machine-guns replaced by two 20-mm cannon, the suffix 'C' denoting cannon armament; company designation was **Model 84A**
XSB2C-2: experimental long-range seaplane prototype, one conversion (**Model 84C**) of an early production SB2C-1 with twin floats and specialised equipment
SB2C-3: second production version, the **Model 84E** of which 1,112 were built; more powerful R-2600-20 engine and detail improvements
SB2C-4: major production version, the **Model 84F** of which 1,985 were built; differed by having underwing racks for four 127-mm (5-in) rockets or a 227-kg (500-lb) bomb on each wing
SB2C-4E: designation of an unknown number of SB2C-4s equipped with radar for night operations
SB2C-5: final Curtiss production version (**Model 84G**) with increased fuel capacity; 970 built
XSB2C-6: two **Model 84H** prototypes with 1566-kW (2,100-hp) R-2600-22 engine, lengthened fuselage, square wingtips and increased fuel capacity; did not enter production
SBF-1: under SBF designations Fairchild Aircraft Corporation's Canadian division supplemented Curtiss production for the US Navy; equivalent to the SB2C-1C, and 50 built
SBF-3: total of 150 built, equivalent to SB2C-3
SBF-4E: total of 100 built, equivalent

A Curtiss SB2C-3 from an aircraft-carrier of Task Force 58, US Navy, on patrol in the Saipan area of the Marianas islands before the great invasion of August 1944.

Canadian Car and Foundry SBW-1B Helldiver (Curtiss SB2C-1)

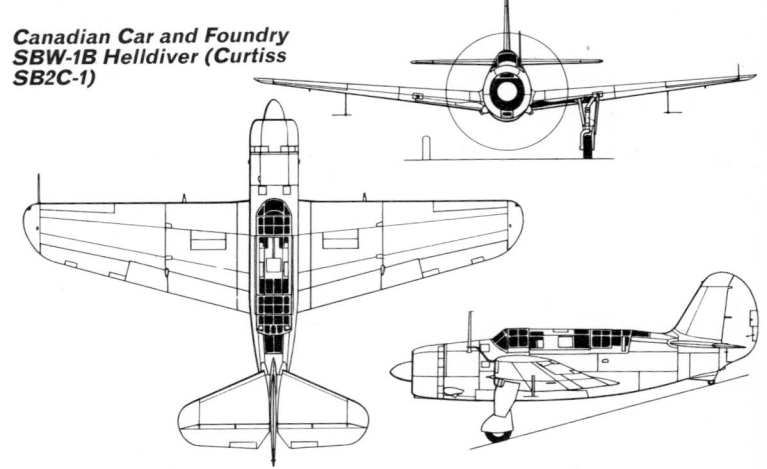

to SB2C-4E
SBW-1: under SBW designations the Canadian Car & Foundry Company supplemented Curtiss production; equivalent to SB2C-1C, 40 built
SBW-1B: designation of 450 SBW-1s for the Royal Navy, the 'B' suffix denoting British; only 26 built and supplied to Royal Navy as **Helldiver Mk I**, but did not become operational
SBW-3: total of 413 built, equivalent to SB2C-3
SBW-4E: total of 96 built as such, equivalent to SB2C-4E, plus 174 of the SBW-1B order completed instead as SBW-4E
SBW-5: total of 86 built, equivalent to SB2C-5

Specification
Curtiss SB2C-4

Type: two-seat carried based scout/bomber
Powerplant: one 1417-kW (1,900-hp) Wright R-2600-20 Cyclone 14 radial piston engine
Performance: maximum speed 475 km/h (295 mph) at 5090 m (16,700 ft); cruising speed 254 km/h (158 mph); service ceiling 8870 m (29,100 ft); range 1875 km (1,165 miles)
Weights: empty 4784 kg (10,547 lb); maximum take-off 7537 kg (16,616 lb)
Dimensions: span 15.16 m (49 ft 9 in); length 11.18 m (36 ft 8 in); height 4.01 m (13 ft 2 in); wing area 39.20 m² (422.0 sq ft)
Armament: two wing-mounted 20-mm cannon and two 7.62-mm (0.3-in) machine-guns in rear cockpit, plus up to 907 kg (2,000 lb) of bombs in fuselage bay and on underwing racks

Curtiss Model 90/95 (XP-60 series)
to
Curtiss-Wright CW-20 (C-46 Commando)

Curtiss Model 90/95 (XP-60 series)

From 1940, when the first P-40s had become established on the production line, Curtiss had sought to develop an improved version which would offer superior performance. The proposal which first aroused the interest of the US Army Air Corps involved a variation of the P-40 design with a modified wing, eight-gun armament and powerplant comprising a Continental XIV-1430-3 in-line inverted-Vee engine. This was designated **Model 88**.

Awarded a contract on 1 October 1940 for two prototypes under the designation **XP-53**, Curtiss had made little progress before the USAAC decided it would like to evaluate one of these airframes with a Rolls-Royce Merlin engine installed. The second XP-53 was cancelled, and a new contract awarded for the Merlin-engined version (**Model 90**) as the **XP-60**. Priority was given to this latter aircraft and, with a Merlin 28 engine installed, it flew for the first time on 18 September 1941. The original XP-53 prototype was converted subsequently to serve as a static airframe for the P-60 production version. As testing of the XP-60 progressed, it was realised that Packard-built Merlins were likely to be in short supply and a decision was made to use instead an Allison V-1710-75 with turbocharger. With this as the chosen powerplant, Curtiss received a USAAF contract for 1,950 **P-60A** fighters on 31 October 1941. It was the beginning of a fruitless saga which extended into 1944.

Curtiss estimated that the P-60A with the V-1710-75 engine would not meet the USAAF's performance specification, and this led to suspension of the P-60A contract. Instead, instructions were given on 2 January 1942 to build one example of each of three different prototypes designated **XP-60A, XP-60B** and **XP-60C (Model 95A, 95B** and **95C)** to be powered respectively by an Allison V-1710-75 with General Electric turbocharger, a V-1710-75 with a Wright turbocharger, and a Chrysler XIV-2220 inline engine. Knowing of problems with the last engine the company suggested as an alternative was so the Pratt & Whitney R-2800 Double Wasp with contra-rotating propellers. This was approved by the USAAF and official interest centred on this version. However, because it was not possible at the time to obtain an engine with suitable reduction gear and contra-rotating propellers, an R-2800-10 was installed with a single four-blade propeller, this aircraft then being redesignated **XP-60E (Model 95D)**. The **XP-60D** designation had been applied to the original XP-60 following installation of a Merlin 61 engine.

The XP-60C with an R-2800-53 engine and contra-rotating propellers was flown eventually on 27 January 1943, and at that time the XP-60E, delayed by engine installation modifications, had not flown at all. There was some consternation therefore when, towards the end of April 1943, the USAAF demanded that this latter aircraft must be available within

four days for service trials. It still had not made its first flight, so the XP-60C was hurriedly prepared and flown to Patterson Field where its performance was so disappointing that this virtually brought an end to all US Army interest. The only hope remaining lay on one **YP-60E** powered by a 1566-kW (2,100-hp) Pratt & Whitney R-2800-18 engine, first flown on 13 July 1944, but this was flown only twice before being abandoned.

Specification
Curtiss XP-60C
Type: single-seat interceptor fighter
Powerplant: one 1491-kW (2,000-hp) Pratt & Whitney R-2800-53 Double Wasp radial piston engine

The Curtiss XP-60E was powered by a R-2800 radial engine: earlier it had been fitted with a V-1710 inline as the XP-60A.

Performance: maximum speed 666 km/h (414 mph) at 6205 m (20,350 ft); climb to 9145 m (30,000 ft) in 6 minutes; service ceiling 11550 m (37,900 ft); range 507 km (315 miles)
Weights: empty 3945 kg (8,698 lb); maximum take-off 4892 kg (10,785 lb)
Dimensions: span 12.59 m (41 ft 3¾ in); length 10.34 m (33 ft 11 in); height 3.77 m (12 ft 4¼ in); wing area 25.56 m² (275.15 sq ft)
Armament: four wing-mounted 12.7-mm (0.5-in) machine-guns

Curtiss Model 96/98 (XBTC/XBT2C)

In late 1943 Curtiss received a US Navy order for two single-seat torpedo-bomber aircraft prototypes under the designation **XBTC-1**. A clean-looking low-wing monoplane with considerable dihedral on the outer wing panels, retractable tailwheel landing gear and a 2237-kW (3,000-hp) Pratt & Whitney R-4360-14 Wasp Major engine, the **Curtiss Model 96** promised performance that should assure a production order. Before the first flew, a slightly different version of the R-4360 engine was installed in each aircraft, bringing the redesignation **XBTC-2**. However, Curtiss was now in competition with Douglas, Fleetwings and Martin for this requirement, losing out to Douglas and Martin whose contenders were produced as the AD-1 Skyraider and AM Mauler respectively.

In March 1945 Curtiss gained a contract for 10 of the generally similar **XBT2C-1**. This **Model 98** differed by having a lower-powered Wright R-3350-24 engine, reduced armament,

A powerful torpedo-bomber of first-class performance and weapon-carrying ability, the XBTC-2 won no orders as competing Douglas and Martin designs were already in production.

accommodation for a crew of two and a search radar pod mounted beneath the starboard wing. Only nine of the 10 were built, and these were the last Curtiss-built aircraft for the US Navy.

Specification
Curtiss XBT2C-1
Type: one/two-seat torpedo-bomber aircraft
Powerplant: one 1864-kW (2,500-hp) Wright R-3350-24 radial piston engine
Performance: maximum speed 531 km/h (330 mph) at 5180 m (17,000 ft); service ceiling 8015 m (26,300 ft); range 2108 km (1,310 miles)
Weights: empty 5565 kg (12,268 lb);

maximum take-off 8618 kg (19,000 lb)
Dimensions: span 14.50 m (47 ft 7 in); length 11.94 m (39 ft 2 in); height 3.68 m (12 ft 1 in); wing area 38.65 m² (416.0 sq ft)
Armament: two 20-mm cannon, plus up to 907 kg (2,000 lb) of bombs or one torpedo

Curtiss Model 97 (SC Seahawk)

Development of the **Curtiss SC Seahawk** began in June 1942, when the US Navy requested the company to submit proposals for an advanced wheel/float scout aircraft. The easily convertible landing gear configuration was required so that the aircraft could be operated from aircraft carriers and land bases, or be catapulted from battleships, and the type was required to replace the rather similar Curtiss Seamew and Vought Kingfisher which stemmed from 1937

procurements to satisfy a similar role. The **Curtiss Model 97** design proposal was submitted on 1 August 1942 but it was not until 31 March 1943 that a contract for two **XSC-1 (Model 97A)** prototypes was issued.

An all-metal cantilever low-wing monoplane, the SC Seahawk had foldable wings with considerable dihedral on their outer panels and strut-mounted wingtip stabiliser floats. The central float, which could also accommodate some auxiliary fuel, and the main wheeled landing gear units shared common attachment points. Power was provided by a Wright R-1820-62 Cyclone 9 radial engine.

The first prototype made its maiden flight on 16 February 1944, and was followed by 500 production **SC-1 (Model 97B)** aircraft which had been contracted in June 1943. All were delivered as landplanes, the stabiliser floats and Edo central float being purchased separately and installed as and when required by the US Navy. Delivery of production aircraft began in October 1944, the first equipping units aboard the USS *Guam*. A second batch of 450 SC-1s was contracted, but of these only 66 had been delivered before contract cancellation at VJ-Day.

An improved version was developed, changes including the installation of a 1063-kW (1,425-hp) R-1820-76 engine, provision of a clear blown canopy, and a jump seat behind the pilot. The modified prototype, at first designated **XSC-1A** and then **XSC-2 (Model 97C)**, led to receipt of a contract for similar production **SC-2 (Model 97D)**, but only 10 had been delivered by the war's end.

Specification
Curtiss SC-1
Type: single-seat scout or ASW aircraft
Powerplant: one 1007-kW (1,350-hp)

Wright R-1820-62 Cyclone 9 radial piston engine
Performance: maximum speed 504 km/h (313 mph) at 8715 m (28,600 ft); cruising speed 201 km/h (125 mph); service ceiling 11370 m (37,300 ft); range 1006 km (625 miles)
Weights: empty 2867 kg (6,320 lb);

maximum take-off 4082 kg (9,000 lb)
Dimensions: span 12.50 m (41 ft 0 in); length 11.09 m (36 ft 4½ in); height 3.89 m (12 ft 9 in); wing area 26.01 m² (280.0 sq ft)
Armament: two 12.7-mm (0.5-in) machine-guns, plus two underwing bomb racks with a combined capacity

of 295 kg (650 lb)

This aircraft is the second of the initial series of 500 production Seahawks. The type was procured to replace Kingfishers and Seamews which were launched from battleships.

Curtiss-Wright CW-19/23

The **CW-19L Coupe** was designed by George Page as an advanced all-metal two-seat cantilever low-wing monoplane for the private owner. Built in 1935 and powered by a 67-kW (90-hp) Lambert engine, tests showed it to be manoeuvrable but underpowered. The **CW-19W** retained the side-by-side cabin layout of the earlier machine but replaced the Lambert engine with a 108-kW (145-hp) Warner Super Scarab. Another feature common to the whole CW-19 series was the streamlined 'trouser-type' fairing over each main unit of the fixed landing gear.

The militarised **CW-19R** was a radical redesign intended for the export market. The two-man crew was accommodated in tandem under a long sliding canopy

and there was provision for a forward-firing synchronised machine-gun plus another gun on a flexible mounting operated by the observer; light bombs could be carried on underwing racks and additional guns for ground attack could be attached to the landing gear fairings.

The Curtiss-Wright management believed the CW-19R would satisfy a need for a utility fighter, reconnaissance and ground attack aircraft. In the event sales were limited, comprising 20 aircraft purchased by China and three by Cuba. Power was greatly increased, the CW-19R having a 261-kW (350-hp) Wright R-760E2 (J-6-7), with the 336-kW (450-hp) Wright R-975E3 (J-6-9) as an alternative; the aircraft demonstrated good flight characteristics and had an

outstanding rate of climb.

An unarmed basic trainer version of the CW-19R was built as the **CW-A19R**. Flown in February 1937 it was tested by the US Army but no production orders followed. Three were completed, one being converted subsequently to a CW-22. The sole **CW-23** was developed from the CW-19R. It had a 447-kW (600-hp) Pratt & Whitney R-1340 Wasp engine, inward retracting landing gear and was intended as a basic combat trainer for the US Army. Flown in 1939, official testing led to its rejection for production.

Specification
Curtiss-Wright CW-19R
Type: two-seat light fighter and attack aircraft
Powerplant: one 261-kW (350-hp) Wright R-760E2 Whirlwind radial piston

engine
Performance: maximum speed 298 km/h (185 mph); initial climb rate 576 m (1,890 ft) per minute
Weights: empty 904 kg (1,992 lb); maximum take-off 1588 kg (3,500 lb)
Dimensions: span 10.67 m (35 ft 0 in); length 8.03 m (26 ft 4 in); height 2.49 m (8 ft 2 in); wing area 16.16 m² (174.00 sq ft)
Armament: two 7.7-mm (0.3-in) machine-guns and provision for two additional guns on the outer sides of the landing gear fairings, plus light bombs on underwing racks

A CW-19R utility aircraft of the Ecuadorean air force. Light bombs could be carried, and machine-guns added, including a single synchronised weapon in the fuselage.

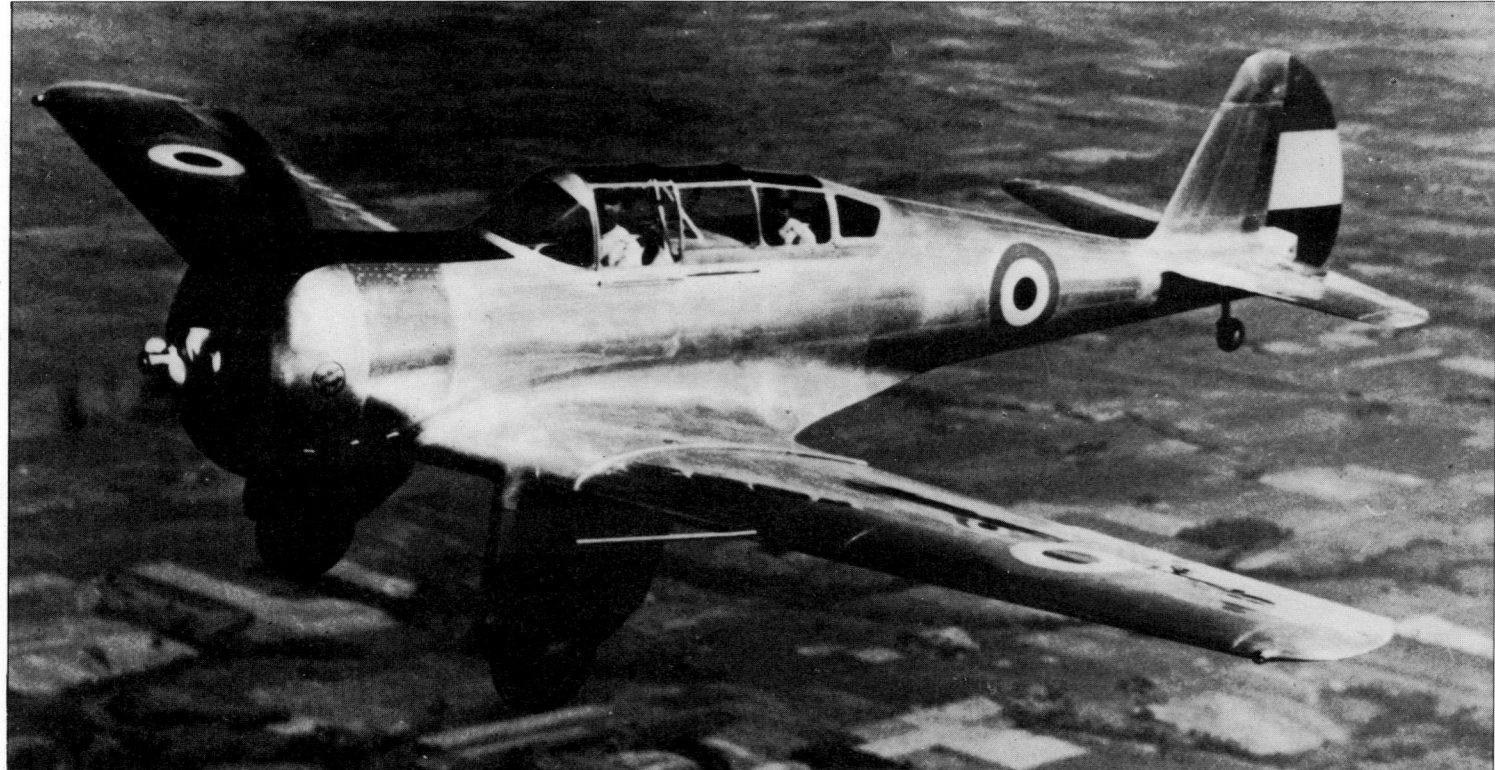

Curtiss-Wright CW-20 (C-46 Commando)

On 26 March 1940 Curtiss-Wright flew the prototype of a 36-seat commercial airliner which had the company designations **CW-20**. Its large capacity fuselage aroused US Army interest for cargo/transport, casualty evacuation, and a militarised version with 1491-kW (2,000-hp) Pratt & Whitney R-2800-43 engines was ordered into production under the designation **C-46** and named **Commando**. When the first of this **CW-20B** model entered service in July 1942 they were the largest and heaviest twin-engine aircraft to serve with the USAAF, and proved such a valuable transport in the Pacific theatre of operations that well over 3,000 Commandoes were built before production ended.

Apart from differing engines and few cabin windows, the original C-46s were generally similar to the CW-20 prototype. The C-46A which followed had a large cargo door on the port side of the rear fuselage, a strengthened cargo floor, and folding seats for 40 troops. Pratt & Whitney R-2800-51 engines of equivalent power replaced the R-2800-43s of the C-46, these having better performance at altitude. This proved of great importance and C-46As 'humping' vital supplies over the Himalayas to China from India, after the loss of the 'Burma Road', were found to have better performance than the C-47 at the altitudes involved. They made a vital contribution to the success of this airlift of essential war materials into China.

In the Pacific the Commando played a significant role in the island-hopping operations which culminated in Japanese surrender, and 160 **R5C-1** aircraft (similar to the USAAF C-46As) supplied to the US Marine Corps made an important contribution. Later versions for the USAAF included the **C-46D (CW-20B-2)** personnel version with an extra door on the starboard side (1,610 built), the **C-46E (CW-20B-3)** utility version with the door arrangement of the C-46A and the stepped windscreen of the XC-46B (17 built), the **C-46F (CW-20B-4)** cargo model with doors on both sides and square-cut wingtips, and a single **C-46G (CW-20B-5)** combining a stepped windscreen and square wingtips. Commandos remained in service with both the USAAF/USAF and USMC after World War II had ended. The USAF employed C-46s operationally during the Korean War, as well as in the early stages of hostilities in Vietnam, and a very small number remain in service with civilian operators, chiefly freight haulers in Central and South America.

Variants

CW-20T: original prototype with dihedralled tailplane, endplate vertical tail surfaces and 1268-kW (1,700-hp) Wright R-2600 Twin Cyclone radials
CW-20A: modification of the original prototype with straight tailplane, single fin and rudder assembly, and detail improvements; evaluated by the US Army as the **C-55**, it was then returned to Curtiss, who then sold it to BOAC
CW-20B-1: single conversion from a C-46A to evaluate a stepped windscreen design; powered by 1567-kW (2,100-hp) R-2800-34W radials and service designated **XC-46B**

CW-20E: project for an **AC-46K** version with 1865-kW (2,500-hp) Wright R-3350-BD radials
CW-20G: designation of the single C-46G when converted as a testbed for the General Electric TG-100 turboprop, which was installed in the starboard nacelle leaving the original R-2800-34W radial in the port nacelle; the service designation was originally **XC-46C** but was changed to **XC-113**
CW-20H: designation of three examples with Wright R-3350 radials delivered in 1945 under the service designation **XC-46L**

Specification
C-46A Commando
Type: troop and freight transport
Powerphant: two 1492-kW (2,000-hp) Pratt & Whitney R-2800-51 radial piston engines
Performance: maximum speed 435 km/h (270 mph) at 4570 m (15,000 ft); cruising speed 278 km/h (173 mph); service ceiling 7470 m (24,500 ft); range at 278 km/h (173 mph) 5069 km (3,150 miles)
Weights: empty 13608 kg (30,000 lb); maximum take-off 20412 kg (45,000 lb)
Dimensions: span 32.91 m (108 ft 0 in); length 23.26 m (76 ft 4 in); height 6.62 m (21 ft 9 in); wing area 126.34 m² (1,360 sq ft)

Below: Ex-military C-46s proved popular with freight operators, especially in Central and South America, where a handful are still in service. This is one of two flown today by Air Haiti.

Above: The C-46 Commando saw particularly heavy service in Burma and the Far East. Production stopped at the end of the Pacific War, but the type survived for many years after.

Below: Overshadowed in fame by the Douglas C-47, the C-46 nevertheless could carry a far greater load, and was instrumental in supplying forces in China over the 'Hump' route.

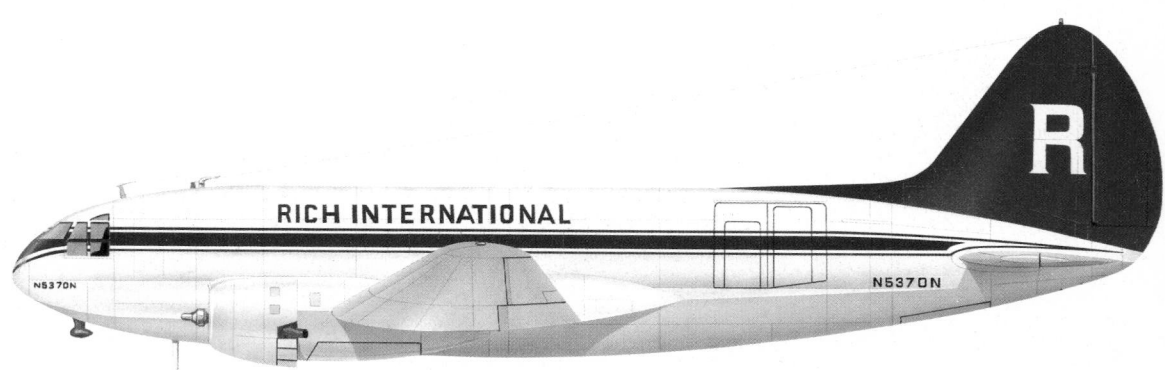

Curtiss C-46F freighter of Rich International Airways (USA).

Curtiss-Wright CW-22 (SNC Falcon)

The prototype **Curtiss Wright CW-22** two-seat low-wing general-purpose or advanced training monoplace was developed at the Curtiss-Wright St Louis factory in 1940. The two crew members were housed under a continuous glazed canopy, and the all-metal CW-22 showed its lineage by landing gear which had main units retracting rearward into underwing fairings as on the CW-21 single-seat interceptor. Powered by a 313-kW (420-hp) Wright R-975 Whirlwind radial, 36 CW-22s were exported to the Netherlands East Indies, but due to the Japanese advance in that region were delivered to the Dutch in northern Australia during March 1942.

A developed **CW-22B** version was sold to Turkey (50); the Netherlands East Indies (25); and various Latin American countries (totalling about 25). Several Dutch aircraft were later captured and flown by the Japanese. Both the CW-22 and CW-22B were armed with two machine-guns, one fixed and the other flexibly mounted.

After a demonstrator had been tested by the US Navy, a **CW-22N** advanced training version went into production. The US Navy applied the designation **SNC-1 Falcon** to the type, a total of 455 being purchased in three batches of 150, 150 and 155 respectively; the aircraft of the third batch had a modified, higher cockpit canopy. Many SNC-1s were sold to private owners in the USA after World War II.

Specification
Curtiss-Wright SNC-1
Type: two-seat advanced trainer
Powerplant: one 313-kW (420-hp) Wright R-975-28 Whirlwind piston engine
Performance: maximum speed 319 km/h (198 mph); service ceiling 6645 m (21,800 ft); range 1255 km (780 miles)

Weights: empty equipped 1241 kg (2,736 lb); maximum take-off 1718 kg (3,788 lb)
Dimensions: span 10.67 m (35 ft 0 in); length 8.23 m (27 ft 0 in); height 3.02 m (9 ft 11 in); wing area 16.14 m² (173.70 sq ft)

The US Navy received 455 CW-22s, designating the type SNC-1. These were used as scout trainers.

Armament: two 7.62-mm (0.3-in) machine-guns

Curtiss-Wright CW-24 (XP-55)

On 27 November 1939 the US Army Air Corps issued to interested manufacturers its specification for a single-seat interceptor fighter that was to be powered by a newly-developed Pratt & Whitney engine which had the designation X-1800-A3G. The USAAC also intimated that unconventional designs could be put forward providing they achieved the three desirable characteristics of low drag, exceptional pilot visibility and powerful armament.

Three manufacturers submitted design proposals in early 1940, all three receiving contracts to develop their design, with options for the contruction of prototypes. The **Curtiss-Wright CW-24** was, however, so advanced that the US Army soon lost interest. As a result, the company decided to produce at its own cost a full-scale flying mock-up which was identified as the **CW-24B**.

This aircraft had an all-wood wing, fabric-covered welded steel-tube fuselage structure, and was powered by a 205-kW (275-hp) Menasco C68 inline engine. Flight testing indicated some instability problems, but in the course of more than 160 flights these had been resolved by a series of modifications. On 10 July 1942 Curtiss-Wright was awarded a USAAF contract for the construction of three **XP-55** prototypes, to be powered by Allison V-1710 engines as the Pratt & Whitney X-1800 had failed to materialise.

The XP-55 was of tailless configuration, with a sharply-swept aft-mounted low-set cantilever monoplane wing. This incorporated ailerons, trailing-edge flaps and, near to the wingtips, vertical fins, and rudders which extended above and below the wing. The oval-section fuselage was of all-metal construction, and a small fixed horizontal surface with elevators hinged to its trailing edge was mounted at the fuselage nose. The XP-55s also marked the company's first use of retractable tricycle landing gear.

The first prototype made its maiden flight in July 1943, but was destroyed in an accident four months later, on 15 November, while stall tests were being carried out. The second prototype made its first flight on 9 January 1944, and its test programme was kept well clear of the stall area until the third prototype, incorporating modifications to overcome this shortcoming, was completed and flying. This event occurred on 25 April 1944, and with the second prototype similarly modified both were handed over to the USAAF for evaluation in September 1944. This showed that low-speed handling characteristics were poor, and while these aircraft were satis-

A radical design to produce a fast-climbing and heavily-armed interceptor, the XP-55 Ascender proved to have tricky control problems, especially in the stall region.

factory in level flight their performance fell below that of contemporary conventional fighters and their development was abandoned.

Specification
Type: single-seat interceptor fighter
Powerplant: one 951-kW (1,275-hp) Allison V-1710-95 inline piston engine driving a pusher propeller
Performance: maximum speed 628 km/h (390 mph) at 5885 m (19,300 ft); cruising speed 476 km/h

(296 mph); climb to 6095 m (20,000 ft) in 7 minutes 6 seconds; service ceiling 10545 m (34,600 ft); range 1022 km (635 miles)
Weights: empty 2882 kg (6,354 lb); maximum take-off 3579 kg (7,929 lb)
Dimensions: span 12.36 m (40 ft 7 in); length 9.02 m (29 ft 7 in); height 3.53 m (11 ft 7 in); wing area 19.41 m² (209.0 sq ft)
Armament: four nose-mounted 12.7-mm (0.5-in) machine-guns

Curtiss-Wright CW-25 (AT-9 Jeep)

In 1940, with Europe already at war, the US Army Air Corps knew that it was essential to begin preparations for the very real possibility that, in the not too distant future, the United States of America might become involved. As a part of this general thinking the US Army had already begun evaluation of the Cessna T-50 as an 'off-the-shelf' twin-engined trainer which would prove suitable for the transition of a pilot qualified on single-engined aircraft to a twin-engined aircraft and its very different handling technique. Procured as the AT-8, Cessna's T-50 was built in large numbers.

For the more specific transition to a 'high-performance' twin-engine bomber it was considered that something less stable than the T-50 was needed. However, Curtiss-Wright had anticipated this requirement with the design of the **Curtiss-Wright CW-25**, a twin-engined pilot transition trainer which had the take-off and landing characteristics of a light bomber aircraft. The CW-25 was of low-wing cantilever monoplane configuration, provided with retractable tail-wheel landing gear and powered by two Lycoming R-680-9 radial engines. The single prototype acquired for evaluation had a welded steel-tube fuselage structure with the wings, fuselage and tail unit fabric-covered.

Evaluation proving satisfactory, the type was ordered into production under the designation **AT-9**, and name **Jeep**. The production examples differing from the prototype by being of all-metal construction. A total of 491 AT-9s was produced and these were followed into service by 300 generally similar **AT-9A** aircraft. They remained in use for a comparatively short time, for the USA's involvement in World War II in late 1941 resulted in the early development of far more effective training aircraft.

Specification
Type: twin-engined advanced trainer
Powerplant: two 220-kW (295-hp)

Avco Lycoming R-680-9 radial piston engines
Performance: maximum speed 317 km/h (197 mph); cruising speed 282 km/h (175 mph); range 1207 km (750 miles)
Weights: empty 2087 kg (4,600 lb); maximum take-off 2722 kg (6,000 lb)
Dimensions: span 12.29 m (40 ft 4 in); length 9.65 m (31 ft 8 in); height 3.00 m (9 ft 10 in); wing area 21.65 m² (233.0 sq ft)

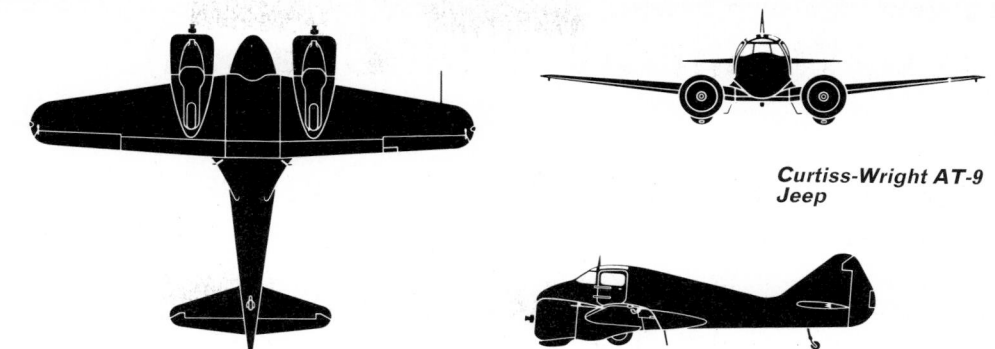

Curtiss-Wright AT-9 Jeep

DFS 228

The Deutsches Forschungsinstitut für Segelflug (German Gliding Research Institute, or DFS) had started its work in 1925, but with the outbreak of World War II became involved in more advanced programes. It was realised that research which had been carried out in relation to glider flight at high altitude could possibly be associated with rocket motor powerplant, leading to the development of a high-performance reconnaissance aircraft.

Under the designation **DFS 228**, work began on the realisation of such an aircraft, a cantilever midwing monoplane with skid landing gear. Primarily a wooden structure the design included a pressurised cabin of metal construction to allow the pilot to operate at heights of up to 2500 m (82,020 ft). In emergency, the pilot would have escaped from the aircraft by firing explosive bolts to sever the complete nose section; this would be lowered by parachute to a height at which he could be ejected from the cabin to complete a normal parachute descent to the ground. Intended powerplant was a Walter controllable rocket motor providing thrust of 300 to 1500 kg (661 to 3,307 lb).

However, unpowered trials with the DFS 228 carried above a Dornier Do

The DFS 228 V1 was experimentally launched from the back of the Dornier Do 217K V3 some 40 times, though the controllable rocket motor was never used to sustain the DFS 228's flight.

217K showed the pressure cabin to be unsuitable and gliding flight revealed limitations in the flight control systems. The project was abandoned without being flown under rocket power.

Specification
Type: rocket-powered reconnaissance aircraft
Powerplant: (intended) one 1500-kg (3,307-lb) thrust Walter 109-509A-1 rocket motor
Performance: (estimated) maximum speed 900 km/h (559 mph) at 10000 m (32,810 ft); absolute ceiling 25000 m (82,020 ft); range 1050 km (652 miles)
Weights: empty 1650 kg (3,638 lb); maximum take-off 4200 kg (9,259 lb)
Dimensions: span 17.56 m (57 ft 7½ in); length 10.58 m (34 ft 8½ in); wing area 30.00 m² (322.93 sq ft)

DFS 230

The DFS 230 design began life as the basis for a meteorological glider able to carry a useful load of instruments. It found fame, however, as a troop transport. This is the first production version, the DFS 230A-1.

Following military interest in a research glider developed by DFS, a contract was awarded for the construction of a prototype. Demonstrated successfully during 1937 it was ordered into limited production as the **DFS 230A**; these and subsequent versions totalling more than 1,000 aircraft were built by Gothaer Waggonfabrik. A braced high-wing monoplane of mixed construction, the DFS 230 provided accommodation for a crew of two and eight fully armed troops. Towable by a variety of Luftwaffe aircraft, the DFS 230 used jettisonable landing gear for take-off, and landing was accomplished on a central skid mounted beneath the fuselage.

The DFS 230 mounted the world's first operation by gliderborne troops when the Belgian fort of Eben-Emael was captured on 10 May 1940. DFS 230s were used also in the invasion of Crete and the surprise rescue of Benito Mus-

solini after he had been imprisoned, and also saw extensive service in supply missions on the Eastern Front.

Variants
DFS 230A-2: dual-contol version of DFS 230A-1
DFS 230B-1: generally similar to DFS 230A but fitted with braking parachute
DFS 230B-2: dual-control version of DFS 230B-1
DFS 230C-1: generally similar to DFS 230B-1, but with redesigned nose incorporating three braking rockets
DFS 230D-1: designation of one prototype converted to DFS 230C-1 configuration
DFS 230 V7: prototype of conversion

to carry 15 troops; no production examples built

Specification
Type: assault transport glider
Performance: maximum gliding speed 290 km/h (180 mph); normal towing speed 180 km/h (112 mph)
Weights: empty 860 kg (1,896 lb);

maximum take-off 2100 kg (4,630 lb)
Dimensions: span 21.98 m (72 ft 1¼ in); length 11.24 m (36 ft 10½ in); height 2.74 m (9 ft 0 in); wing area 41.30 m² (444.56 sq ft)

DINFIA IA 35 Huanquero

The Argentine aeronautical research and production organisation Dirección Nacional de Fabricaciones e Investigaciónes Aeronáuticas (DINFIA) was established in 1957. It evolved from the earlier Fabrica Militar de Aviones of 1927, Instituo Aerotécnico of 1943 and Industrias Aeronáuticas y Mecánicas of 1953. The **DINFIA IA 35 Huanquero**

was the organisation's first design to enter production. It was a twin-engine general-purpose aircraft which, except for fabric-covered ailerons, was of all-metal construction. Of low-wing cantilever monoplane configuration, the IA 35 had a high-mounted tailplane with twin fins and rudders, retractable tricycle landing gear and power provided by two

IA 19R El Indio radial engines which had also been designed and developed by the Institute Aerotécnico.

The first flight of the IA 35 prototype was made on 21 September 1953 and following test and evaluation it was planned to build an initial batch of 100 production aircraft. The first of these was flown on 29 March 1957 but construction was terminated in the mid-1960s after less than half of the planned number had been built. During

the production run the IA 35 was available to order in several variants as noted below.

Specification
IA 35 Type IA: powered by IA 19R El Indio engines and equipped for use as an advanced instrument or navigation trainer
IA 35 Type IU: powered by 559-kW (750-hp) IA 19SR1 El Indio engines and equipped for use as a bombing and

gunnery trainer

IA 35 Type II: light transport version with IA 19R El Indio engines and accommodation for a crew of three and seven passengers

IA 35 Type III: ambulance version with IA 19R El Indio engines and accommodating a crew of three, four stretchers and a medical attendant

IA 35 Type IV: photographic version with IA 19R El Indio engines, crew of three plus camera operator and survey cameras

Constancia II: projected version with Turboméca Bastan turboprops

Pandora: civil transport version with IA 19SR1 El Indio engines and accommodation for 10 passengers

Examples of the DINFIA IA 35 Huanquero in flight. The three aircraft with glazed noses are Huanquero Type IA crew trainers, while the fourth is a Huanquero Type II transport or Type III air ambulance.

Specification
DINFIA 35 Type IA
Type: advanced trainer
Powerplant: two 462-kW (629-hp) IA 19R El Indio radial piston engines
Performance: maximum speed 361 km/h (225 mph) at 3000 m (9,840 ft); economic cruising speed 320 km/h (199 mph) at 3000 m (9,840 ft); service ceiling 6400 m (21,000 ft); range with maximum fuel 1570 km (976 miles)

Weights: empty equipped 3500 kg (7,716 lb); maximum take-off 5700 kg (12,566 lb)

Dimensions: span 19.60 m (64 ft 3¾ in); length 13.98 m (45 ft 10¼ in); wing area 42.00 m² (452.10 sq ft)

DINFIA IA 50 Guarani II

A twin-engined light transport known as the **DINFIA Guaranu I** was developed from the IA 35 Huanquero, and this flew for the first time on 6 February 1962. Retaining some 20 per cent of the structure of the earlier transport, the Guarani I was basically a refined version with an all-metal wing, accommodation for a maximum of 15 passengers and with power provided by two 634-kW (850-shp) Turboméca Bastan IIIA turboprop engines.

On 23 April 1963 DINFIA flew the prototype of a more developed version of this light transport under the designation IA 50 Guarani II. This looked very different by having a tail unit incorporating a single swept fin and rudder and a shortened rear fuselage. It introduced de-icing equipment and more powerful Bastan VIA turboprops. Built for service with the Argentine air force, and 15 examples

of the Guarani II remain operational with the Fuerza Aerea Argentina.

Specification
DINFIA IA 50 Guarani II
Type: light transport
Powerplant: two 694-kW (930-shp) Turboméca Bastan VIA turboprops
Performance: maximum speed 500 km/h (311 mph); economic cruising speed 450 km/h (280 mph); service ceiling 12500 m (41,010 ft); range with maximum payload 1995 km (1,240 miles)
Weights: empty equipped 3924 kg (8,651 lb); maximum take-off 7120 kg (15,697 lb)
Dimensions: span 19.53 m (64 ft 1 in); length 14.86 m (48 ft 9 in); height 5.81 m (19 ft 0¾ in); wing area 41.80 m² (449.95 sq ft)

Stemming from the same basic design as the IA 35 Huanquero, the DINFIA IA 50 Guarani II introduced turboprop power and swept vertical tail surfaces. Some 24 were still in service at the beginning of the 1980s, I Brigada Aérea's aircraft being used for transport.

Dart Kitten

Following the Flittermouse, Dart Aircraft built in 1937 for the International Horseless Carriage Corporation of Brooklands a flying replica of Blériot's cross-Channel aircraft with an original 19-kW (25-hp) Anzani engine; the aircraft was involved subsequently in demonstration flying. However, the next and as it transpired the last type to emerge from Dart Aircraft was the **Dart Kitten**, another single-seat ultralight monoplane but this time with a low wing and no external bracing, and powered by a 20-kW (27-hp) Ava 4a-00 flat-four.

The designer was A. R. Weyl and the customer, again, Dr H. N. Bradbrooke at Witney. The **Kitten I** (G-AERP) first flew on 15 January 1937 and was sold to the doctor in August, but for reasons unknown he resold it to a private owner at Tollerton, Nottingham, the following month. Stored throughout World War II

G-AEXF was the sole Dart Kitten II. Built in 1937, it had four owners before crashing on 29 November 1964.

at Rearsby, the Kitten survived to fly again in 1949 at Broxbourne, where it was re-engined with an Aeronca-J.A.P. J-99; it was destroyed in a crash on 23 November 1952.

A second aircraft, the **Kitten II** (G-AEXT) was built with a J.A.P. J-99 from the outset and flew in the spring of 1937. It too survived the war, re-appearing at Southend, and was followed by a post-war built (1951) **Kitten III** (G-AMJP) which differed by having wheel brakes.

Specification
Dart Kitten II/III
Type: single-seat light monoplane
Powerplant: one 27-kW (36-hp) Aeronca J.A.P. J-99 flat-two piston

engine
Performance: maximum speed 153 km/h (95 mph); cruising speed 134 km/h (83 mph) at 610 m (2,000 ft); ceiling 6005 m (19,700 ft); range 547 km (340 miles)

Weights: empty 231 kg (510 lb); maximum take-off 341 kg (752 lb)
Dimensions: span 9.68 m (31 ft 9 in); length 6.5 m (21 ft 4 in); height 2.41 m (7 ft 11 in); wing area 11.98 m² (129 sq ft)

Dassault Etendard/Super Etendard

By the mid-1950s the growing complexity, cost and weight of attack fighters made the idea of a lightweight, low-cost aircraft that could fulfil such a role particularly attractive. It appealed especially to the NATO air forces and Dassault began the design and development of two funded and one private-venture prototype under the name **Dassault Etendard** (Standard).

The **Etendard II** was the first of these to fly, on 23 July 1956, and was

clearly derived from the earlier Mystère family, having swept wings/tail surfaces and tricycle landing gear. It was, however, smaller and powered by two Turboméca Gabizo turbojets, each developing 1100-kg (2,425-lb) thrust, but problems with this powerplant resulted in the Etendard II being abandoned after only limited flight tests. The second of the funded prototypes had the designation **Etendard VI**; basically similar to the Etendard II, it had powerplant comprising a single Bristol Siddeley Orpheus BOr. 3, developing 2200-kg (4,850-lb) thrust, and was first flown on 16 March 1957. It was planned that a production version would have an Orpheus BOr. 12 developing 3706-kg (8,170-lb) thrust with reheat, but when it was announced that the Fiat G.91 had been selected as winner of the NATO competition for a light tactical fighter, further development of the Etendard VI was abandoned.

The private-venture **Etendard IV**

was to have better prospects, for Dassault considered that the Etendards II and VI were restricted by the NATO specification. From the outset the company opted for a larger aircraft that would accommodate more fuel and more powerful engines, and thus be suitable for roles that included that of a carrier-based multi-role fighter. Dassault's design assumptions were correct, and following a first flight on 24 July 1956 France's Aéronavale began to show interest. This led to a contract for continued development of this aircraft under the designation **Etendard IVM** to meet

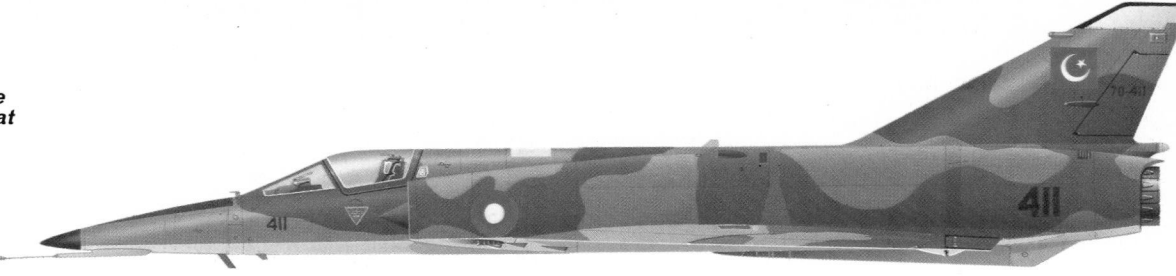

Dassault Mirage 5PA of the Pakistani air force, based at Masroor in the early 1980s.

an Atar 9C turbojet in a slightly longer fuselage. It was equipped with Cyrano II radar which, together with a Doppler radar and TACAN navigation, made possible low-level operations in all weathers and bestowed the ability to launch blind attacks without, however, any terrain-following capability. From the Mirage IIIE was derived the less sophisticated ground-attack fighter for operation under VFR conditions and intended for export. Designated as the **Mirage 5** and developed primarily to meet Israeli requirements, the first of this version was flown on 19 May 1967. It incorporates simplified avionics, has greater fuel capacity and increased stores-carrying capability. More sophisticated IFR/all-weather avionics and equipment can be installed optionally by the customer, but at the expense of fuel or weapons load. Delivery of the 50 aircraft ordered by Israel was stopped by General de Gaulle and these later served with the Armée de l'Air under the designation **Mirage 5F**.

Another development of the Mirage III/5 family, first flown in prototype form on 15 April 1979, is the **Mirage 50** multi-mission fighter. This is powered by the SNECMA Atar 9K-50 turbojet and can carry the entire range of armament, equipment and operational stores developed for the Mirage III/5 series, plus more advanced radar and a head-up display. Available also in reconnaissance and two-seat training versions, the first customer for the Mirage 50 was the air force of Chile. In addition to the considerable numbers of Mirage III/5 aircraft supplied to the Armée de l'Air, they have entered service with some 20 foreign nations.

When series production finished in 1989, over 1,400 Mirage III, Vs and 50s had been delivered, nearly 950 of them for export. About half the existing Mirage III operators have embarked on upgrade programmes to extend the lives of their aircraft, some of which are now 20-30 years old. These updates can include new navigation and weapon delivery systems, the integration of modern weapons such as runway denial submunitions, laser-guided bombs or missiles, anti-ship missiles, and more advanced AAMs. Other upgrade items are re-engining with the Atar 9K-50 giving a 20 per cent increase in thrust, installation of single point pressure refuelling or inflight-refuelling equipment, introduction of zero/zero ejection seats and more visibly, the addition of canard foreplanes to improve dogfighting qualities. Also available are liquid oxygen, a steerable nosewheel, a buddy flight-refuelling pod and other pods for ECM, laser designation, reconnaissance and infra-red imagery.

Variants
Mirage IIID: two-seat trainer version
Mirage IIIEX: A Mirage IIIE modified

The Mirage IIIB and IIID are two-seat versions for conversion and continuation training. Switzerland flies the Mirage III on interceptor duties.

with a Mirage F1 type nose, underfuselage strakes of the Mirage 5D; an inflight-refuelling probe offset to port ahead of the cockpit, and fixed canards. The Doppler fairing under the nose is deleted
Mirage IIIO: Australian licence-built version
Mirage IIIR: reconnaissance version with five cameras or an infra-red package
Mirage IIIS: Swiss licence-built version
Mirage IIIT: designation of one aircraft which served as a test-bed for the 9000-kg (19,482-lb) thrust SNECMA TF-106 turbofan engine
Mirage IIIX: announced in 1982, this is a version designed to keep the type

competitive (with the F-5G Tigershark and IAI-Kfir) by modifications including canard foreplanes, fly-by-wire control, Atar 9K-50 engine and updated electronics
Balzac V-001: conversion of a Mirage III airframe with eight Rolls-Royce RB.162 lift-jets and a SNECMA TF-104 turbofan for service as a VTOL research aircraft to develop the control system for the Mirage IIIV prototypes
Mirage IIIV: designation of two aircraft, each equipped with eight Rolls-Royce RB.162 lift-jets to evaluate VTOL fighter technology
Mirage 5D: two-seat trainer version of Mirage 5
Mirage 5R: reconnaissance version of Mirage 5
Mirage Milan: one prototype modified from a Mirage IIIE with an Atar 9K-50 turbojet, and retractable foreplanes in the fuselage nose; intended to alleviate problems associated with the tailless delta

configuration, the Milan was later abandoned

Specification
Dassault Mirage 50
Type: single-seat multi-mission fighter
Powerplant: one 7200-kg (15,873-lb) thrust SNECMA Atar 9K-50 turbojet
Performance: maximum speed at altitude Mach 2.2; service ceiling at Mach 2 18000 m (59,055 ft); combat radius with two 400-kg (882-lb) bombs 630 km (391 miles)
Weights: empty equipped 7150 kg (15,763 lb); maximum take-off 13700 kg (30,203 lb)
Dimensions: span 8.22 m (26 ft 11½ in); length 15.56 m (51 ft 0½ in); height 4.5 m (14 ft 9 in); wing area 35 m² (376.75 sq ft)
Armament: can include basic armament of two 30-mm DEFA cannon in fuselage, plus a wide variety of external stores on seven attachment points

The Mirage IIIE is a multi-role version capable of carrying air-to-ground loads and characterised by undernose Doppler and engine intakes in line with the rear of the canopy. This example from the CEAM (Centre d'Experimentations Aériennes Militaires) carries a MATRA Martel missile.

Dassault Mirage 5SDE of the Egyptian air force's Air Defence Command in 1975.

Dassault Mirage IV
to
Dassault Super Mystère B-2

Dassault Mirage IV

Renowned for highly nationalistic policies, the French decided in 1954 to create their own nuclear deterrent force. One of the first priorities was to develop a launch platform for the weapons, a project headed by Dassault in association with a number of other companies. With a requirement for a long-range high-speed mission to be met, Dassault looked initially at developments of the Vautour but later directed its attention to a twin-engined night-fighter design of 1956. Basically a scaled-up Mirage III, the project redesign considered many changes in size and powerplant as speed, load and range requirements were formulated, but the solution became clearer when it was decided to make extensive use of inflight-refuelling.

The first **Dassault Mirage IVA** prototype flew on 17 June 1959, then powered by two 6000-kg (13,228-lb) SNECMA Atar 09 augmented turbojets. On its 14th test flight during July 1959 it reached Mach 1.9, and attained Mach 2 on its 33rd flight. Three pre-production prototypes followed, the first of which flew on 12 October 1961. Powered by a pair of 6400-kg (14,110-lb) Atar 9Cs, this aircraft was larger and more representative of the production Mirage IVA, incorporating a large circular radome under the centre fuselage forward of the semi-recessed nuclear free-fall bomb.

The first of these pre-production aircraft was used for bombing trials and development at Colomb-Béchar; the second similar aircraft was used to develop the navigation and inflight-refuelling systems; and the third, a completely operational model with Atar 9Ks, full equipment including nose-probe for refuelling and armament, flew on 23 January 1963. Satisfied with the trials, the French air force ordered 50 production aircraft for delivery in 1964-5, with a repeat order for a further 12 placed later.

Although a heavy aircraft and fairly 'hot' to operate, the Mirage IVs of the French air force are maintained on an extremely quick alert. They can take-off directly from the hardened shelters in which they are housed with their engines running at full power, and have even been used from short unpaved strips with the aid of auxiliary take-off rockets, operating from surfaces which have been hardened by the application of fast-drying chemicals.

The last of nine Mirage IVA strategic bomber units disbanded in July 1988 with passing of the French nuclear deterrent to silo-based S-3 strategic missiles. However, two units still operate remaining **Mirage IVPs** (= Penetration) of 18 upgraded between May 1983 and December 1987 to carry the ASMP medium-range nuclear-tipped air-to-sur-

face missile. Mirage IVPs have Arcana pulse doppler radar, dual inertial navigation systems, a Thomson-CSF Barem self protection jamming pod, a BOZ-100 chaff/flare pod and Thomson-CSF Serval radar warning receivers. Eighteen unconverted Mirage IVAs remain in store.

Specification
Dassault Mirage IVA
Type: two-seat supersonic strategic bomber
Powerplant: two SNECMA Atar 9K turbojets, each developing 7000 kg (15,432 lb) thrust with reheat
Performance: maximum dash speed 2340 km/h (1,454 mph) or Mach 2.2 at 13125 m (40,060 ft); maximum

Dassault Mirage IVA

sustained speed 1966 km/h (1,222 mph) or Mach 1.7 at 19685 m (60,000 ft); tactical radius (dash to target, high-subsonic return) 1240 km (770 miles); ferry range 4000 km (2,485 miles)
Weights: empty equipped 14500 kg (31,967 lb); maximum take-off 33475 kg (73,800 lb)
Dimensions: span 11.85 m (38 ft 10½ in); length 23.49 m (77 ft 1 in); height 5.4 m (17 ft 8½ in); wing area 78 m² (839.61 sq ft)
Armament: one 60-kiloton free-fall bomb recessed in fuselage belly, or up to 7260 kg (16,005 lb) of weapons on wing and fuselage hardpoints, plus electronics countermeasures

Dassault Mirage F.1

The **Dassault Mirage F.1** is effectively a successor to the extremely successful Mirage III/5 series, although differing substantially from the design originally planned to replace this family. In 1964 Dassault was awarded a French government contract to build a prototype of the Mirage F.2 two-seat fighter, with a conventional wing and tailplane and powered by a SNECMA/Pratt & Whitney TF306 turbofan. This aircraft made its maiden flight in June 1966 but in December of that year was followed into the air by the first Mirage F.1, a smaller single-seat fighter which Dassault had designed as a private venture and sized to the smaller Atar turbojet.

The Mirage F.1 prototype crashed, but was regarded as a more attractive proposition and in September 1967 the French government ordered three pre-production Mirage F.1s plus a structural test airframe. The first of these new aircraft made its maiden flight in March 1969 and completed its initial series of flight trials some three months later. Despite being powered by a SNECMA Atar 9K-31, which produced less thrust than the Atar 9K-50 adopted later, the first pre-production Mirage F.1 notched up a series of impressive performances during this early period. These included a speed of Mach 2.12 or 2260 km/h (1,405 mph) at 11000 m (36,090 ft), and 1300 km/h (808 mph) at low level.

The Mirage F.1 has proved to be a more than adequate successor to the Mirage III as a multi-role aircraft, with emphasis on a large payload, easy handling at low altitude, and a high rate of

climb. Excellent short take-off and landing performance results from the high-lift system, comprising leading-edge droops and large flaps fitted to the sharply swept wing. At its average mission weight the Mirage F.1 can take-off and land within 500 to 800 m (1,640 to 2,625 ft). Although the Mirage III and Mirage F.1 have practically identical external dimensions (and in particular the same wetted area) the internal fuel capacity of the latter aircraft is 40 per cent more, achieved by eliminating bladder-type tanks and replacing them with integral fuel space.

A fast reaction time is necessary for an interceptor, and almost equally so for an attack aircraft, and the Mirage F.1 is acceptable on this score. The ground handling equipment is kept to a minimum, and that which is used is fully air-transportable. A self-starter is used, and the high-pressure refuelling system allows all internal tanks to be filled in about six minutes; this contributes to a turn-round time of 15 minutes between missions where identification of in-

Dassault Mirage F.1CG of the 114e Ptérix (wing), Elleniki Aeroporia (Hellenic air force) based at Tanagra in the late 1970s.

truders rather than interception is required.

The Mirage F.1's Thomson-CSF Cyrano IV monopulse radar has 80 per cent greater range than the Cyrano II in Mirage IIIs, and allows intruders to be intercepted at all altitudes, even if they are flying low in ground clutter. Once the target has been selected manually by the pilot, the radar continues to track it automatically. The weapons can be fired automatically by the fire-control computer, or manually with the computer supplying the pilot with clearance to engage the target.

A Mirage F.1 can be scrambled within two minutes thanks to the use of the GAMO self-propelled preparation truck. This supplies electrical power to preheat the navigation and weapon-system equipment, circulates a fluid to cool the radar and controls the cockpit air-conditioning, as well as carrying a sunshade

on a telescopic arm so that the pilot can sit at readiness for extended periods in the heat of the day. When the pilot is ordered to scramble and starts the engine, the sunshade is withdrawn automatically, the air-conditioning and radar-cooling systems are switched off and, as soon as the engine is running fast enough for the alternators to supply sufficient electrical power, the connector to GAMO is automatically ejected and the pilot can begin to taxi.

The variant in service with the French air force is the **Mirage F.1C** interceptor, the first production example of which made its maiden flight on 15 February 1973 and was delivered to the air force on 14 March 1973.

By 1990 over 770 Mirage F.1s had been ordered including 251 for the French air force, 18 for Ecuador, 40 for Greece, 113 for Iraq, 36 for Jordan, 33 for Kuwait, 38 for Libya, 50 for Morocco, 15 for Qatar, 48 for South Africa and 73 for Spain. Production ended in 1990 with a further batch of 16 for Iraq but these are reported to be in store in France.

Variants
Mirage F.1A: ground-attack and VFR fighter version with less sophisticated avionics and increased fuel capacity; built also under licence by Atlas Aircraft in South Africa
Mirage F.1B: designation of two-seat trainer which, with the radar screen and head-up display duplicated in the rear cockpit, can be used as a fully operational trainer

Mirage F.1C-200: designation of 25 French air force F.1Cs following permanent installation of inflight-refuelling probes
Mirage F.1CR: See F.1R
Mirage F.1D: Two-seat version of F.1E
Mirage F.1E: generally similar to F.1C but with a more comprehensive nav/attack system making it more suitable for all-weather operations; one F.1E was completed with a SNECMA M53 turbofan but its development was later abandoned
Mirage F.1R: reconnaissance version with conventional cameras;

electromagnetic, infra-red and optical sensors; and advanced inertial and radar navigation systems. French air force designation is F.1CR

Specification
Dassault Mirage F.1C
Type: single-seat multi-mission fighter/attack aircraft
Powerplant: one 7200 kg (15,873 lb) reheat thrust SNECMA Atar 9K-50 turbojet
Performance: maximum speed at high altitude 2350 km/h (1,460 mph) or Mach 2.2, and at low altitude Mach 1.2; initial climb rate 12780 m

(41,930 ft) per minute; service ceiling 20000 m (65,615 ft); range with maximum external load 900 km (560 miles)
Weights: empty 7400 kg (16,314 lb); maximum take-off 15200 kg (33,510 lb)
Dimensions: span 8.4 m (27 ft 6¾ in); length 15 m (49 ft 2¼ in); height 4.5 m (14 ft 9 in); wing area 25 m² (269.11 sq ft)
Armament: two 30-mm DEFA cannon, plus a maximum external combat load of 4000 kg (8,818 lb) which can include air-to-air and air-to-surface missiles, air-to-surface rockets, bombs, gun pods and napalm tanks

Dassault Mirage F.2

The **Dassault Mirage F.2** was intended originally to serve as a flying testbed for the SNECMA TF306 turbofan engine. Although retaining some features of the Mirage III, it was really a very different design, departing from the delta wing configuration. A high-wing monoplane with a swept wing and swept tail surfaces incorporating an all-moving tailplane, it was powered by a Pratt & Whitney TF30 turbofan engine when flown for the first time on 12 June 1966. Only a single Mirage F.2 prototype was built, but a scaled-down version of the wings designed for this aircraft were used in the Mirage F.1.

The Mirage F.2 also played a part in the development of the **Mirage G** prototype, a variable-geometry experimental fighter which had a generally-similar fuselage. This was flown for the first time on 18 November 1967; within a week it had been flown at the maximum wing sweep of 70°, and demonstrated a speed of Mach 2.1 powered by its 9300 kg (20,503 lb) reheat thrust SNECMA TF306E turbofan engine during January 1968. Subsequently, the French government ordered two prototypes of a twin-engined version of the

Mirage G for use as experimental variable-geometry combat aircraft. Both aircraft were designated **Mirage G8**, and the first to fly, on 8 May 1971, had tandem two-seat accommodation; the single-seat version did not fly until 13 July 1972. Having an overall similarity to the Mirage G, the Mirage G8s differed primarily by having two SNECMA Atar 9K-50 turbojet engines, each developing 7200 kg (15,873 lb) thrust with afterburning. Flown in an intensive test programme, these two aircraft provided valuable information, and on 13 July 1973 the single-seat model attained a speed of Mach 2.34 at an altitude of 15000 m (49,215 ft).

Following this research, a version known initially as the **Mirage G8A** (later **Super Mirage**) was projected to meet a French air force requirement for a so-called **ACF** (Avion de Combat Futur, or future combat aircraft). This resembled the single-seat version of the Mirage G8, but would have incorporated a fixed wing of 55° sweep which testing had shown to give optimum performance. This last was not built, however, but the Mirage F.2 and Mirage G programmes had considerable influence on

The Dassault Mirage F.2 was ordered in prototype form during 1964 as an advanced low-level penetration strike aircraft. Potentially a highly effective combat aircraft, it was axed in favour of the simpler and smaller Mirage F.1.

development of the Mirage 2000 and Super Mirage 4000.

Specification
Dassault Mirage F.2
Type: two-seat attack fighter prototype
Powerplant: one Pratt & Whitney TF30 turbofan in the 9072 kg (20,000 lb) thrust class

Performance: maximum speed 2333 km/h (1,450 mph) or Mach 2.2 at altitude; service ceiling 20000 m (65, 615 ft)
Weights: empty 9500 kg (20,944 lb); maximum take-off 18000 kg (39,683 lb)
Dimensions: span 10.5 m (34 ft 5½ in); length 17.6 m (57 ft 9 in); height 5.8 m (19 ft 0½ in)

Dassault Mystère-Falcon 10/100

The baby of the Dassault Mystère-Falcon family of business jets, the **Dassault Falcon 10** was known at first as the **Minifalcon** when announced at the end of the 1960s. Like the rest of the family it has rear-mounted turbofan engines and is basically a scaled-down version of the Mystère/Falcon 20, providing accommodation for a crew of two and up to seven passengers. A prototype (F-WFAL), powered originally by General Electric CJ610 turbojet engines, was flown for the first time on 1 December 1970. Six months later it set a 1000 km (621.4 mile) closed-circuit speed record for its class of 930.4 km/h (578.13 mph). A similar record over a 2000 km (1,243 mile) closed circuit was established by the third prototype in May 1973, a month after the first production aircraft had flown.

In addition to the normal executive transport role, the Mystère/Falcon 10 can be equipped for aerial photography, ambulance duties, liaison, navigation/attack system training and radio navigation aid calibration. Several of these aircraft are operated by the Aèronavale under the designation **Falcon 10MER**. They are used in general communications and liaison duties, as well as to give training to pilots of the Dassault Super Etendard carrier-based fighter. The Aéronavale's aircraft serve with ES3 at Hyeres and ES57 at Landivisiau. In this

last role the Falcon 10MER has been found to make a good mock intruder, used not only to train interceptor pilots but also ground control radar crews.

Introduced in 1985 to supersede the Falcon 10 and certificated in December

The smallest member of the Mystère/Falcon family, the Falcon 10 was intended for the comfortable and speedy transport of up to seven passengers. It has also found a military role with the Aéronavale.

1986, the **Series 100** featured increased weights (Ramp and Max. Take-off), a

fourth cabin window on the starboard side, bigger luggage compartment and a 'glass cockpit'. When production ceased in 1989 223 Falcon 10/100s had been delivered to customers in 24 countries.

Specification

Dassault Mystère-Falcon 10
Type: executive transport
Powerplant: two 1465 kg (3,230 lb) thrust each Garrett TFE731-2 turbofans
Performance: maximum cruising speed 912 km/h (566 mph) at 7620 m (25,000 ft); range with four passengers, with reserves 3560 km (2,212 miles)
Weights: empty equipped 4880 kg (10,760 lb); maximum take-off 8500 kg

(18,740 lb)
Dimensions: span 13.08 m (42 ft 11 in); length 13.86 m (45 ft 5¾ in); height 4.61 m (15 ft 1½ in); wing area 24.1 m² (259.42 sq ft)

Dassault Mystère-Falcon 20/200

Development of a light twin-turbojet executive transport was initiated by Dassault in conjunction with Aérospatiale (then Sud-Aviation), with construction of the prototype starting in January 1962. A cantilever low-wing monoplane with swept wings and tail surfaces, a circular-section fuselage and retractable tricycle landing gear, the prototype had a fuselage built by Dassault and wings and tail unit by Sud-Aviation. However, for production aircraft Dassault builds the wings and Aérospatiale the fuselages and tail units.

First flown on 4 May 1963, and at the time powered by two 1497 kg (3,300 lb) thrust Pratt & Whitney JTF12A-8 turbojets pod-mounted one on each side of the rear fuselage, the new aircraft was identified as the **Dassault Mystère-Falcon 20** (Mystère in France, and Falcon for export sales). It was re-engined subsequently with General Electric CF700 turbofans, which became the standard powerplant. Following certification the Business Jets Division of Pan American World Airways (now known as Falcon Jet Corporation) became interested in this aircraft for sale in North America, where they were marketed under the name **Fan Jet Falcon**. The Mystère-Falcon 20 found employment for both civil and military use with orders approaching 500.

The first production aircraft made its maiden flight on 1 January 1965 and this initial series became identified as the **Standard Falcon 20**. From this was developed a version with increased fuel capacity, available as the **Falcon 20C** with the same 1871 kg (4,125 lb) thrust General Electric CF700-2C powerplant as the Standard Falcon, or as the **Falcon 20D** with the more powerful CF700-2D with a thrust rating of 1928 kg (4,250 lb). The introduction of 2041 kg (4,500 lb) thrust CF700-2D-2 engines resulted in a version designated **Falcon 20E**, and the addition of high-lift devices to improve take-off and landing performance and a further increase in fuel capacity were identifying features of the **Falcon 20F**.

Development of an improved **Falcon 20G** was initiated and this was offered by Falcon Jet Corporation to meet a US Coast Guard requirement for a medium-range surveillance aircraft. A contract for 41 aircraft, designated **HU-25 Guardian**, was awarded in 1977. Basically similar to the Falcon 20F, they differed in having airframe modifications required to accommodate varying role equipment, plus the installation of 2512-kg

Dassault Falcon 20E of Federal Express (USA). The parcel carrier used the type for speedy carriage of high value cargo between US cities. With the boom in this business, FedEx now uses a huge fleet of 727s.

(5,538-lb) thrust Garrett ATF 3-6-2C turbofan engines. In USCG service the HU-25A is used in the search and rescue role, HU-25B is the pollution control version, and the FLIR-equipped HU-25C modified for the drug interdiction role using a Westinghouse APG-66 search radar.

Most recent development is the **Falcon 200** which replaced the Falcon 20F on the production line in 1983, after 473 Falcon 20s had been delivered. Originally designated **Falcon 20H**, the prototype 200, fitted with less powerful 2360-kg (5,200-lb) thrust ATF 3-6A-4C engines, bigger fuel tanks in the rear fuselage, some systems' changes and redesigned wingroot fairings, flew for the first time on 30 April 1980. Announced at the 1981 Paris Air Salon the Falcon 200 was certificated by the DGAC on 21 June 1981 and deliveries began in 1982. By 1989 35 had been delivered to 11 countries. The maritime patrol and enforcement version of the Falcon 200 is marketed as the Gardian 2,

and has a Thomson-CSF Varan search radar, two Exocet sea-skimming air to surface missiles mounted on underwing pylons, electronic surveillance and countermeasures equipment and target-towing capability. Five are in service with the French navy.

Variants
Falcon CC: one aircraft basically similar to Standard Falcon but with low-pressure tyres for grass-field operation
Falcon ST: designation of two Falcons used by the French air force as system trainers, equipped with combat radar and navigation systems as installed in the Mirage IIIE
Falcon 20FH: designation of development aircraft for Falcon 20H programme, with basic Falcon 20F fuselage and powerplant, plus new structural fuel tank; this aircraft was re-engined subsequently with Garrett ATF 3 turbofans and used for Falcon 20H certification

Specification
Dassault Mystère-Falcon 20F
Type: 8-12 passenger civil/military executive transport
Powerplant: two 2041 kg (4,500 lb) thrust each General Electric CF700-2D-2 turbofans
Performance: maximum cruising speed 863 km/h (536 mph) at 7620 m (25,000 ft); economic cruising speed 750 km/h (466 mph) at 12190 m (40,000 ft); absolute ceiling 12800 m (42,000 ft); range with eight passengers and maximum fuel 3300 km (2,050 miles)
Weights: empty equipped 7530 kg (16,601 lb); maximum take-off 13000 kg (28,660 lb)
Dimensions: span 16.3 m (53 ft 6 in); length 17.15 m (56 ft 3 in); height 5.32 m (17 ft 5 in); wing area 41 m² (441.33 sq ft)

The Falcon 20G Guardian was developed to meet a US Coast Guard order for a surveillance and smuggling interdiction platform. Known as HU-25 in service, the Guardian has extra large observation windows.

Dassault Mystère-Falcon 50

The requirement for an executive jet with transcontinental or transatlantic range led Dassault to study how best to increase the range of the Mystère-Falcon 20. The problem was solved by the introduction of a supercritical wing, by using three engines of lower power than the two of the earlier series and by the design of a structural fuel tank within the fuselage to provide a maximum internal fuel capacity of 8765 litres (2,315 US gal). In this way the **Dassault Mystère-**

Falcon 50 was evolved, using many basic components from the Falcon 20 but introducing three Garrett TFE731 turbofan engines, two pod-mounted on the sides of the rear fuselage and the third attached to two top mounts on the upper rear fuselage, forward of the fin and fitted with a thrust-reverser. Many basic components of the Falcon 20 were used and the same fuselage cross-section retained, providing standard accommodation for eight passengers but a

maximum of 12 in a high-density layout.
The Falcon 50 first prototype (F-WAMD) was flown for the first time on 7 November 1976, followed by the second during February 1978 and the pre-production model in June 1978. French certification was gained in February 1979 with the FAA following suit in the following month. The fourth aircraft, flown in March 1979, became the demonstration aircraft of the US distributor, Falcon Jet Corporation, which had secured 70 of the 100 orders recorded by the end of 1979. First delivery was made to a former Falcon 20 operator in July 1979. By early

1990 215 Falcon 50s had been delivered to operators in 35 countries and customers included the governments of France, Italy, Spain, Yugoslavia, Iraq, Jordan, Libya, Morocco and South Africa. An ambulance version was announced in 1980, providing accommodation for three stretcher cases and two medical attendants, and a maritime surveillance and patrol version with equipment similar to the Gardian 2 is available as the **Gardian 50**.

Specification
Dassault Mystère-Falcon
Type: long-range executive transport

Powerplant: three 1678 kg (3,700 lb) thrust each Garrett TFE731-3-1C turbofans
Performance: maximum cruising speed 880 km/h (546 mph); service ceiling 13800 m (45,275 ft); range 6300 km (3,915 miles)
Weights: empty 9150 kg (20,170 lb); maximum take-off 17600 kg (38,801 lb)
Dimensions: span 18.86 m (61 ft 10½ in); length 18.5 m (60 ft 8½ in); height 6.97 m (22 ft 10½ in); wing area 46.83 m² (504.09 sq ft)

Dassault Falcon 50. The upgrade of the Falcon series to include this tri-jet variant reflected the need for much greater range. The type has proved popular with corporate and VIP military users alike.

Dassault Falcon 900

Largest member of the Dassault family of business jets, the **Falcon 900** tri-jet was announced in May 1983, initially as the **Mystère-Falcon 900**, to compete with the Challenger and Gulfstream long-range corporate jets. Roll-out of the prototype took place in May 1984 and the first flight took place on 21 September 1984 from Bordeaux-Merignac airfield. DGAC and FAA certification followed in March 1986 and the first customer delivery made in December 1986. Eighty-three had been delivered by the beginning of 1990, all but two for export. The Falcon 900 is aimed at the top-end of the business jet market and the aircraft provides fast comfortable transport for 12-19 passengers in a wide-body cabin over transcontinental ranges. A number of governments have bought Falcon 900s for VIP use including France, Nigeria, Malaysia, Spain and Australia. In September 1987 the Japanese Maritime Safety Agency ordered two specially-adapted long-range maritime surveillance versions of the Falcon 900 fitted with an operations control station, special communications equipment, observation hatches and sonobuoy, marker and flare dropping chutes. The aircraft entered service in September 1989.

Specification
Dassault Falcon 900
Type: 12-19 passenger executive jet transport
Powerplant: two 2041-kg (4,500-lb) thrust each Garrett TFE731-5AR turbofans
Performance: maximum cruising speed 927 km/h (575 mph); service ceiling 15550 m (51,000 ft); range with 8 passengers 7840 km (4,235 miles)
Weights: empty 10240 kg (22,570 lb); maximum take-off 20640 kg (45,500 lb)
Dimensions: span 19.33 m (63 ft 5 in); length 20.21 m (66 ft 4 in); height 7.55 m (24 ft 9 in); wing area 49 m² (527.44 sq ft)

Based on the Falcon 50, the Falcon 900 introduces a 'wide-body' cabin offering much greater internal capacity. The type has found favour at the top end of the corporate market.

Dassault Super Mystère B-2

The **Dassault Super Mystère B-1** prototype, first flown on 2 March 1955, shortly afterwards exceeded the speed of sound in level flight, subsequently becoming the first European aircraft with a Mach 1-plus performance to enter full-scale service. Developed from Dassault's earlier Mystère IVA via an interim Rolls-Royce Avon-engined variant known as the Mystère IVB, the Super Mystère differed chiefly in having a new thinner-section wing with more marked sweepback, a flat oval air intake and a larger and more swept fin and rudder.

Production began in 1956, the first series-built **Super Mystère B-2** flying for the first time on 26 February 1957; deliveries to the Armée de l'Air began later that year. One hundred and eighty were produced (plus five pre-production examples) over the next two years, including 24 for the Israeli air force. Those in French service had, in addition to the armament listed, a capability to carry the AIM-9 Sidewinder air-to-air missile. In February 1958 Dassault flew a prototype **Super Mystère B-4**, powered by a 6000 kg (13,228 lb) Atar 9 afterburning turbojet, but this programme was overshadowed by the greater promise of the Mirage III, and the Super Mystère B-4 did not go into production.

By the late 1970s only a few Mystère B-2s remained in French service, most having been replaced by Mirage F.1s, but the type then still served with the Israeli air force, and Israel supplied Honduras with 12 examples of a version modified by Israel Aircraft Industries to take a 4218 kg (9,300 lb) thrust non-reheat Pratt & Whitney J52-P-8A turbojet. Despite the absence of an afterburner, this version is seen to have a considerably longer rear fuselage than the standard Super Mystère, and can carry a wider variety of external stores; it first appeared in the early 1970s and was used with some success in the Yom Kippur War of October 1973.

Specification
Dassault Super Mystère B-2
Type: single-seat fighter/fighter-bomber
Powerplant: one 4460 kg (9,833 lb) reheat thrust SNECMA Atar 101G-2/-3 turbojet
Performance: maximum speed 1040 km/h (646 mph) at sea level and 1195 km/h (743 mph) at 12000 m (39,370 ft); initial climb rate 5335 m (17,505 ft) per minute; service ceiling 17000 m (55,775 ft); normal range 870 km (540 miles)
Weights: empty equipped 6932 kg (15,282 lb); maximum take-off 10000 kg (22,046 lb)
Dimensions: span 10.52 m (34 ft 6 in); length 14.13 m (46 ft 4¼ in); height 4.55 m (14 ft 11 in); wing area 35 m² (376.75 sq ft)
Armament: two 30-mm DEFA cannon, plus rockets in retractable fuselage pack and up to 1000 kg (2,205 lb) of weapons on underwing hardpoints

The Super Mystère was the first European production aircraft to have a maximum speed above Mach 1. Compared with the similar Mystère IVA it featured increased wing sweep and revised inlet geometry.

Dassault MD.452 Super Mystère B-2

Dassault Mirage 2000
to
de Havilland D.H.53 Humming Bird

Dassault Mirage 2000

The French air force requirement of the early 1970s for an Avion de Combat Futur (ACF, or future combat aircraft), mentioned briefly under the Dassault Mirage F.2 entry, led to the ACF programme which was later cancelled by the French government. This came in 1975, roughly six month before Dassault's prototype for this requirement was due to fly, following continuing project evaluation by the Armée de l'Air. It came to the conclusion that a twin-engined aircraft based on the SNECMA M53-3 turbofan was too big. It wanted a smaller aircraft, with approximately the performance of the General Dynamics F-16 lightweight fighter.

On 18 December 1975 the French government gave a go-ahead for a new **Dassault Mirage 2000** programme, an aircraft which Dassault had made as small and as light as possible to provide a thrust:weight ratio of 1:1 at combat weights using the power of a single SNECMA M53-5 turbofan. The Mirage 2000 reverted to the delta-wing configuration of the Mirage III family, and to enhance manoeuvrability the aircraft has an electronic fly-by-wire flight control system which allows the aircraft's centre of gravity range to be extended further aft than on a conventional aircraft. This results in less basic stability, and is a concept applied previously in the General Dynamics F-16. Shortcomings experienced with the delta wing of the Mirage IIIs mean that the Mirage 2000 has a larger-area wing to reduce wing-loading and to provide better low-speed performance; it also permits greater turn rates at high altitude. Additionally, automatic leading-edge flaps used in conjunction with the elevons provide a variable-camber wing which enhances still further low-speed performance and controllability at such speeds. In other respects the Mirage 2000 is similar in overall configuration to its Mirage III predecessor.

Five prototypes were built, four under contract to the French air force and the other with company funds, the latter used to develop equipment and techniques applicable to future variants and export models. The first prototype made its maiden flight on 10 March 1978 and the fifth, a Mirage 2000B two-seat trainer version, flew on 11 October 1980. The first production Mirage 2000C flew on 20 November 1982; first deliveries made to the French air force in 1983 and the type declared operational in 1984. Deliveries of 136 firmly ordered are scheduled to continue until 1998. By 1990 more than 440 Mirage 2000s had been ordered by seven customers. Dassault claims that a Mirage 2000 can intercept a target flying at Mach 3 at 80,000 ft four minutes after a scramble take-off.

Dassault Mirage 2000 first prototype, wearing French air force markings.

Variants
Mirage 2000B: two-seat trainer version of Mirage 2000C retaining almost full operational capability. Fixed gun installation deleted but capability retained through external gunpods. The first production aircraft flew on 7 October 1983. French air force requirement is for 23 aircraft

Mirage 2000D: Originally allocated to two-seat versions of the Mirage 2000E, the 2000D designation is now applied to the former **2000N'**(= N Prime), and denotes (Diversified). The aircraft is basically a Mirage 2000N optimised for conventional attack and not equipped to carry ASMP. Enhanced stand-off capability is endowed by a laser-guided weapons delivery system. Thirty-nine 2000Ds firmly ordered by French air force are scheduled for delivery up to the year 2000.

Mirage 2000E: export versions of the Mirage 2000C for Abu Dhabi, Egypt, Greece, India (renamed Vajra), Jordan and Peru. First deliveries were made in September 1984 and 126 exported by 1990.

Mirage 2000N: first flown on 3 February 1983, the 2000N (N = nuclear penetration) two-seat all-weather low-level high speed delivery version is dedicated to long-range interdiction using either conventional or nuclear weapons. Although similar to the Mirage 2000B, the airframe has been strengthened to withstand low-level flight and the new weapon system includes the ESD ANTILOPE V terrain-following and navigation radar; SAGEM twin inertial navigation system; TRT radar altimeter, automatic pilot, OMERA vertical camera and Thomson-CSF and Dassault ECM equipment. Powered by a SNECMA M53-P2 engine, the first Mirage 2000N was delivered to the French air force in January 1987 and three squadrons are operational equipped with the 900-kg (1,990-lb) Air-Sol Moyenne Portee (ASMP) nuclear-tipped air-to-surface missiles. Deliveries of 75 2000Ns firmly ordered to date are scheduled to end in 1992 when production 2000Ds come on line.

Mirage 2000S: the 2000S (S= strike) two-seat export version of the 2000D, but fitted with a flight-refuelling probe to extend operating range.

Mirage 2000-5: projected multi-role 'stealth' version of the 1986 'Rafale cockpit' Mirage 2000-3 (which flew in prototype form in May 1988) fitted with a new Doppler radar. Thomson-CSF RDY look-down/shoot-down multi-target radar, matched with advanced Matra Mica air-to-air missiles and powered by the M53-P2 engine. Offered to the Swiss air force in 1990 in both single- and two-seat versions for delivery in 1993.

Specification
Dassault Mirage 2000C
Type: single-seat interceptor
Powerplant: one afterburning 9700-kg (21,385-lb) thrust SNECMA M53-P2 turbofan
Performance: maximum speed more than 2333 km/h (1,450 mph) or Mach 2.2 at altitude, and 1110 km/h (690 mph) at low altitude; service ceiling 17060 m (56,000 ft); range with auxiliary fuel 3335 km (2,073 miles)
Weights: empty 7500 kg (16,534 lb); maximum take-off 17000 kg (37,480 lb)
Dimensions: span 9.13 m (29 ft 11 in); length 14.36 m (47 ft 1 in); height 5.2 m (17 ft); wing area 41 m^2 (441.33 sq ft)
Armament: two 30-mm DEFA 554 cannon, plus five underfuselage and two underwing hardpoints for external stores that can include bombs, missiles, reconnaissance pods, rocket pods, cannon pods and fuel tanks up to a weight of 6300 kg (13,890 lb)

Continuing the delta theme of the Mirage III, the Mirage 2000 has a fly-by-wire control system for superb agility and high angle-of-attack performance, especially at low speeds. A variety of air-to-air and air-to-ground missions can be undertaken by the various versions of the aircraft.

Dassault Super Mirage 4000

Following cancellation of the Avion de Combat Futur (ACF) programme in 1975, Dassault continued the development of a so-called 'twenty-tonne' combat aircraft, virtually a scaled-up twin-turbofan version of the Mirage 2000 and which it initially named the **Dassault Super Mirage Delta**. The prototype, later re-designated the **Super Mirage 4000**, flew for the first time on 9 March 1979, and achieved Mach 2.2 by its sixth flight. Considerably larger than the Mirage 2000, it was basically of similar configuration but differed primarily by having small swept variable-incidence fore-planes (or canards) mounted at the forward end of each engine intake duct and having two SNECMA M53 engines in the 10000-kg (22,046-lb) thrust class mounted side-by-side in the fuselage.

Intended as a long-range interceptor, or for deep low-level penetration of enemy airspace, the prototype had the RDM multimode radar and weapon system of the Mirage 2000 air superiority fighter. It also had a similar computer-derived fly-by-wire control system, which allowed angles of attack up to 25 degrees to be demonstrated.

Dassault claimed that the Mirage 4000 performance, with a power-to-weight ratio better than 1:1, exceeded any known aircraft at the time and although exhibited regularly at the Paris and Farnborough air shows, no hard interest in the Mirage 4000 emerged. After a period of inactivity the aircraft was repainted in desert camouflage and resumed flying in 1986 in support of the Rafale programme, researching the behaviour of delta-canard aircraft in turbulence.

Specification

Type: single-seat long-range fighter or interdictor
Powerplant: two 10000-kg (22,046-lb) thrust SNECMA M53 afterburning turbofan engines
Performance: maximum speed 2333 km/h (1,450 mph) or Mach 2.3 at altitude; radius of action with fuel tanks and recce pod 1850 km (1,150 miles); rate of climb 18300 m (60,000 ft/min); service ceiling 20000 m (65,600 ft)
Dimensions: span 12 m (39 ft 4 in); length 18.7 m (61 ft 4 in); wing area 73 m² (786 sq ft)
Armament: two 30-mm DEFA cannon in lower air intakes plus two underfuselage and eight underwing hardpoints allowing carriage of bombs, Magic AAM or Exocet ASM missiles, buddy refuelling pod, rocket pods or fuel tanks

The Super Mirage 4000 was cancelled as a combat aircraft programme on cost grounds, but was used to provide data for the Rafale programme.

Dassault Rafale

Dassault designed the ACX (Avion de Combat Expérimental, or experimental combat aeroplane) as a technology demonstrator for a national rather than international warplane programme, the design already existed on paper when France left the multi-national European Fighter Aircraft programme in August 1985. The two potential operators, in the form of the French air force and more significantly the French navy, wanted a fighter lighter and smaller fighter than the EFA with a take-off weight of 17,637 lb (8000 kg). First came the **Rafale A** (Squall A) with an empty weight of 20,944 lb (9500 kg). The **Rafale A** flew for the first time on 4 July 1986 confirming the correctness of the aerodynamic concept, which was being schemed as the ACT (Avion de Combat Tactique). The same was true of the fly-by-wire flight control system and the airframe, which was constructed of composite materials, but not to the powerplant of two General Electric F404-400 turbofan engines each with a maximum rating of 16,000 lb st (71.17 kN) with afterburning. After test flights, the Rafale A's port engine was replaced by a SNECMA M88-2 turbofan then rated at 72.95 kN (16,400 lb st) with afterburning.

It was intended that the Rafale multi-role fighter would replace half a dozen of the Armée de l'Air's attack, defence and reconnaissance types such as the Mirage III and 5, Mirage F1 and Jaguar in the tactical- and operational-level roles, and probably the Mirage IVP in the strategic-level role. The design features of the ACX were indeed maintained in the **Rafale D** family designed for the Armée de l'Air, but this production model is a little smaller and lighter than the original demonstrator with a maximum take-off weight below 9000 kg (19,841 lb). Changes effected to reduce radar reflectivity included less acute leading edge/fuselage junctions, a canopy plated with gold on its inner surface, dark grey radar-absorbent paint, and a curved junction between the rear fuselage and fin.

After operational experience with Jaguar and Mirage 2000C aircraft in the Gulf War had revealed the enormous workload faced in combat by the pilots of single-seat warplanes, the Armée de l'Air changed the balance of its planned procurement of the **Rafale D** in favour of a greater number of two-seat machines. It was appreciated that the **Rafale B** would be up to 5 per cent more expensive than **the Rafale C**, as well as being 350 kg (772 lb) heavier.

Economic factors trimmed the procurement of the Rafale from the originally required 450 fighters planned for service from the 1990s to 390 and then 336 aircraft for service from about 2002 with a powerplant of two M88-3 turbofans each rated at 93.00 kN (20,907 lb st) with afterburning.

Variants

Rafale A: Rafale prototype classified as an advanced experimental aeroplane by Dassault, was the flying test bed for technology intended for production versions; slightly larger and heavier than the Rafale C/M, and powered by two 84.74-kN (16,000-lb st) F404-GE-400 turbofans pending development of the M88 turbofan
Rafale B: one development prototype ordered in July 1989 for the French air force completed as a two-seat trainer version of Rafale C, but retaining full operational capability; first flew in April 1993 and now under development as the primary operational model (140 aircraft) for service in about 2005 with a crew comprising either a pilot or a pilot and weapons system operator
Rafale C: two development prototypes ordered in April 1988 for the French air force, but revised to one example of this single-seat multi-role fighter originally scheduled to become the primary operational model; the aeroplane made its first flight in May 1991 known up to 1990 as the Rafale D; procurement plans now trimmed to 95 aircraft for service from the later part of the 21st century's first decade.
Rafale M: two development prototypes ordered for the French navy in December 1988 and July 1990 as M (Marine) navalised and therefore slightly heavier versions of the Rafale C for carrierborne operation with features such as arrester hook and nosewheel unit modified to incorporate a jump strut; achieved its maiden flight on 12 December 1991, and the type (86 required) should enter service in 2002 as successor to the Vought F-8E(FN) Crusader

Specification
Dassault Rafale C
Type: single-seat multi-role warplane
Powerplant: two 72.95-kN (16,400-lb st) SNECMA M88-2 afterburning turbofans
Performance: maximum speed 2126 km/h (1,321 mph) or Mach 2.0 at high altitude declining to 1390 km/h (864 mph) or Mach 1.135 at low altitude; service ceiling 19810 m (65,000 ft); range 1851 km (1,150 miles) in the air-to-air role with eight Mica AAMs and four drop tanks; radius 1093 km (679 miles) in the low-level penetration role with 250-kg (12 551-lb) bombs, four Mica AAMs and three drop tanks
Weights: empty 9060 kg (19,873 lb); maximum ramp 19500 kg (42,990 lb) Dimensions: span 10.90 m (35 ft 9.25 in); length 15.30 m (50 ft 2.5 in); height 5.34 m (17 ft 6.25 in); area 46.00 m² (495.16 sq ft)
Armament: one 30-mm cannon, plus up to 8000 kg (17,637 lb) of disposable stores on 14 hardpoints, and generally comprising AAMs, ASMs, anti-ship missiles, stand-off bombs, free-fall and/or laser-guided bombs, multiple rocket launchers, and reconnaissance, Elint and jammer pods

Dassault-Breguet/Dornier Alpha Jet

One of a number of international aircraft development and production programmes that have been initiated since the end of World War II, the **Dassault-Breguet/Dornier Alpha Jet** was announced as a design and development programme on 22 July 1969. Both France and West Germany required a new subsonic basic/advanced trainer and light-attack aircraft to replace in-service Lockheed T-33A, Fouga Magister and Dassault Mystère IVA trainers and Aeritalia (Fiat) G91 attack aircraft. Following a design submission by Dassault-Breguet and Dornier to meet this requirement, it was announced on 24 July 1970 that the Alpha Jet had been selected and French and West German government approval for a start to the programme was given in late 1972. Following evaluation of prototypes the go-ahead for production in quantity was given on 26 March 1975.

A cantilever shoulder-wing monoplane of all-metal construction, the Alpha Jet has a swept wing and tail surfaces, retractable tricycle landing gear, accommodation for two persons in tandem seated on ejection seats, and powerplant comprising two SNECMA/Turboméca Larzac turbofan engines. It is available in basically four versions: the Alpha Jet E(Ecole) advanced trainer for France; the Alpha Jet A(Appui) light-ground attack aircraft for Germany; the Alpha Jet 2, originally known as the MS-1 and MS-2 versions and latterly the NGEA (Nouvelle Generation d'Ecole et d'Ataque) incorporating new avionics, a head-up display, inertial navigation system and a laser rangefinder to provide optimum weapon delivery capability, and lastly, the Alpha Jet 3 ATS (Advanced Training System/Advanced Tactical Support) originally launched in the mid-1980s as the Lancier.

The Alpha Jet 2 has a fully integrated SAGEM Uliss 81 INS, TRT radar altimeter, SFIM gyro-magnetic compass, Thomson-CSF HUD and a TMV 630 laser/rangefinder mounted in the nose. More powerful Larzac 04-C20 engines delivering 1440 kg (3,175 lb) thrust each are also fitted. The Alpha Jet 2 first flew in April 1982 and delivery was made to Egypt (which ordered 45) in June 1983 with seven following for the Cameroon.

Evolved from the Alpha Jet 2, the Larzac 04-C20 powered Alpha Jet 3 ATS is effectively a flying simulator equipped to lead pilots into new advanced combat aircraft such as the Mirage 2000, Rafale,

Gripen and F-16 and other types expected to enter service between 1990-2010. The ATS is equipped with an advanced VEM 130 HUD, new types of sensors, day/night navigation and intercept radar such as Agave/Anemone, FLIR pod, a laser-designator pod, laser-guided stand-off weapons and electronic warfare systems.

The first of four Alpha Jet prototypes made its maiden flight on 26 October 1973; delivery of the Alpha Jet E for the French Armèe de l'Air began during the summer of 1978 and of the Alpha Jet A for the Federal German Luftwaffe in March 1979. The requirements of these two services, 200 and 176 respectively, were completed in early 1982 and orders for all versions of the Alpha Jet have reached just over the 500 mark. They include, in addition to the French and German requirements, examples for Belgium (33), Egypt (45), Ivory Coast (7), Morocco (24), Nigeria (24), Qatar (6), Cameroon (7) and Togo (5).

One Alpha Jet A was modified during 1980 to evaluate an experimental transonic wing of super-critical section which has been developed by Dornier. Other changes to this aircraft, first flown in its new form on 12 December 1980, include the incorporation of leading- and trailing-edge manoeuvring flaps.

Specification
Dassault-Breguet Alpha Jet E
Type: two-seat basic/advanced jet trainer

Two basic forms of Alpha Jet are produced, the Alpha Jet A attack aircraft with pointed nose, and the Alpha Jet E for training. This is one of the latter, serving with GE 314, the Armée de l'Air's principal advanced training unit.

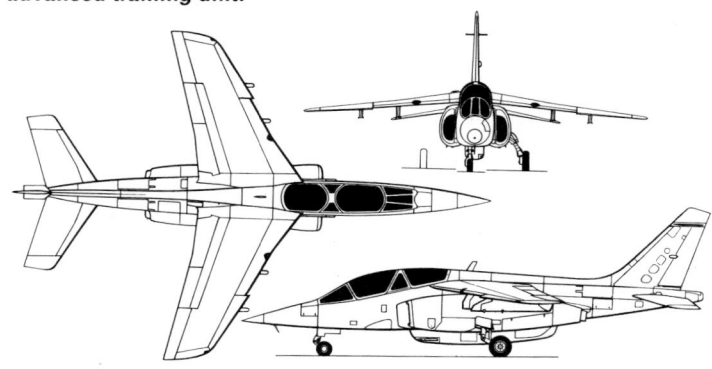

Dassault-Breguet/Dornier Alpha Jet A

Powerplant: two 1440 kg (3,175 lb) thrust each SNECMA/Turboméca Larzac 04-C6 turbofan engines
Performance: maximum speed 920 km/h (572 mph) or Mach 0.85 at 10000 m (32,810 ft), and 1000 km/h (621 mph) at sea level; service ceiling 14630 m (48,000 ft); high-altitude operational radius with maximum internal fuel 1230 km (764 miles)
Weights: empty equipped 3345 kg (7,374 lb); maximum take-off 7500 kg

(16,535 lb)
Dimensions: span 9.11 m (29 ft 10¾ in); length 12.29 m (40 ft 3¾ in); height 4.19 m (13 ft 9 in); wing area 17.5 m² (188.37 sq ft)
Armament: one underfuselage detachable pod containing a DEFA 30-mm cannon, plus provision for two hardpoints beneath each wing suitable for a variety of stores including rockets and air-to-air and air-to-surface missiles

Dassault-Breguet Atlantic

To meet a NATO requirement of early 1958 for a long-range maritime patrol aircraft, 24 designs were submitted by aircraft manufacturers in nine countries. From these the **Breguet Br.1150** design study was selected for production at the end of 1958, and was later named **Atlantic**. Responsibility for production was entrusted to SECBAT (Société d'Etudes et de Construction du Breguet Atlantic). The original members of this consortium, led by Breguet (later Dassault-Breguet), comprised Sud-Aviation (later part of Aérospatiale), the Belgian ABAP grouping (Fairey, FN and SABCA), Dornier in Germany and Fokker in the Netherlands. Italy joined the programme in 1968 with some of the work being allocated to Aeritalia. A similar multi-national organisation was set up to build the Tyne turboprop engines, designed by Rolls-Royce, other members including FN in Belgium, MAN in Germany and SNECMA in France. Thus, the Dassault-

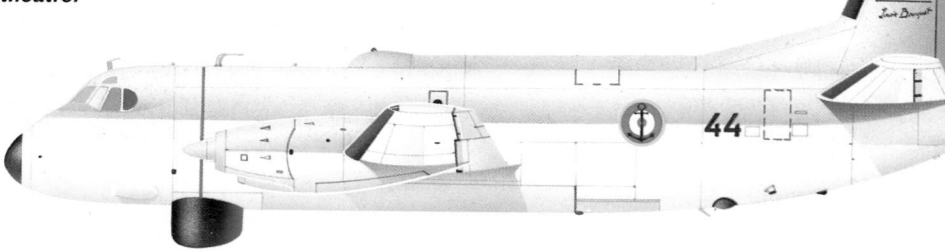

Dassault-Breguet Br.1150 Atlantic of the Aéronautique Navale (French naval air arm). The French fleet is split between bases at Nîmes-Garons for the Mediterranean region and Lann-Bihoué for the Atlantic theatre.

Breguet Atlantic had the distinction of being the first combat aircraft to be designed and built as a completely multi-national project.

A cantilever mid-wing monoplane of all-metal construction, the Atlantic incorporates a 'double-bubble' fuselage with a pressurised upper deck and a MAD tail boom, a conventional tail unit with an ECM pod at the tip of the fin, retractable

tricycle landing gear with twin wheels on each unit, and two Tyne turboprops in wing-mounted nacelles. Suitable for a variety of missions, including the anti-ship role, coastal reconnaissance, the direction of air-sea rescue, fleet escort, logistic support, freight and passenger transport and mine-laying, the Atlantic was designed primarily for the ASW role, a capacity for which it is equipped with sonobuoys and Thomson-CSF search radar which can detect a submarine's schnorkel at ranges of up to 75 km (47 miles). For attack the Atlantic carries in its 9 m (29 ft 6¼ in) weapons bay, in the unpressurised lower fuselage, bombs, depth charges and homing torpedoes; air-to-surface missiles or rockets can be carried on underwing attachments. The Atlantic's crew of 12 includes seven specialists to co-ordinate and direct the aircraft's operations.

The first prototype made its maiden flight on 21 October 1961 and the first of 40 aircraft for the French navy was delivered in July 1965, followed by 20 aircraft for the West German navy. A second production batch included nine for the Netherlands navy and 18 for the Italian air force and the last Mk.1 was delivered in 1974. Three of those supplied to the French navy were transferred subsequently to Pakistan. Several advanced versions of the Atlantic were proposed but it was not until July 1977 that the French government authorised design definition of an improved version to enter service in the period 1985-90. Originally designated **Atlantic ANG** (Atlantic Nouvelle Generation) and now known as the **Atlantique ATL 2**, the aircraft is derived directly from the earlier version. Programme go-ahead was received in September 1978 and work on the first two prototypes, modified from production Mk.1 airframes, began in January 1979. The first of these flew on 8 May 1981 followed by the second on 26 March 1982. Although existing operators monitored the development programme, only the French navy went ahead and ordered 19 examples of the ATL 2, the first batch of a 42-plane requirement to replace the entire Atlantic Mk.1 fleet. Production was authorised in May 1984 and the first aircraft delivered in October 1989. A normal 10-man crew consists of two pilots, a flight engineer, a tactical co-ordinator, a navigator/communications operator, an ESM/ECM/MAD systems operator, a radar oper-

ator, two acoustic equipment operators and a visual observer located in the nose.

Built by the same SECBAT airframe and engine consortia, the ATL differs by having improved structural integrity requiring less maintenance and a longer fatigue life through improved construction techniques. Enhanced operational capability comes with the installation of a retractable Thomson-CSF Iguane long-range search radar mounted under the nose, Arar 13 radar countermeasures suite and a Sadang sonobuoy data processor combined with other equipment including an on-board computer to co-ordinate communications between the systems components. Used as a secondary transport the ATL 2 can carry either 24 men, or a spare engine, propeller and APU mounted on a special pallet. The aircraft is also offered for the AEW and flight-refuelling roles.

Specification
Dassault-Breguet Atlantique ATL 2
Type: maritime patrol aircraft
Powerplant: two 4638-kW (6,220-ehp) each Rolls-Royce Tyne RTy.20 Mk 21 turboprops
Performance: maximum speed at optimum altitude 648 km/h (402 mph); normal patrol speed 315 km/h (195 mph); service ceiling 9145 m (30,000 ft); maximum endurance 18 hours
Weights: empty equipped 25600 kg (56,438 lb); maximum take-off 46200 kg (101,850 lb)
Dimensions: span 37.42 m (122 ft 9 in); length 33.63 m (110 ft 4 in); height 10.89 m (35 ft 8 in); wing area 120.3 m² (1,295 sq ft)
Armament: the 9 m (29 ft 6 in) long lower fuselage weapon bay can accommodate two AM-39 Exocet anti-shipping missiles, six bombs, 70 day/night markers, 60 flares, eight depth charges, eight Mk.46 homing torpedoes, 100 sonobuoys, six 250-kg mines or eight search and rescue kits. The four underwing hardpoints are capable of carrying four Armat anti-radiation missiles, rocket pods or four Magic AAMs for self-defence.

The Atlantique ATL 2 is a new-build version of the Atlantic (although the first two were rebuilds) which introduces a new avionics system with far better ASW capability. This is the first prototype, carrying anti-ship missiles on its wing pylons.

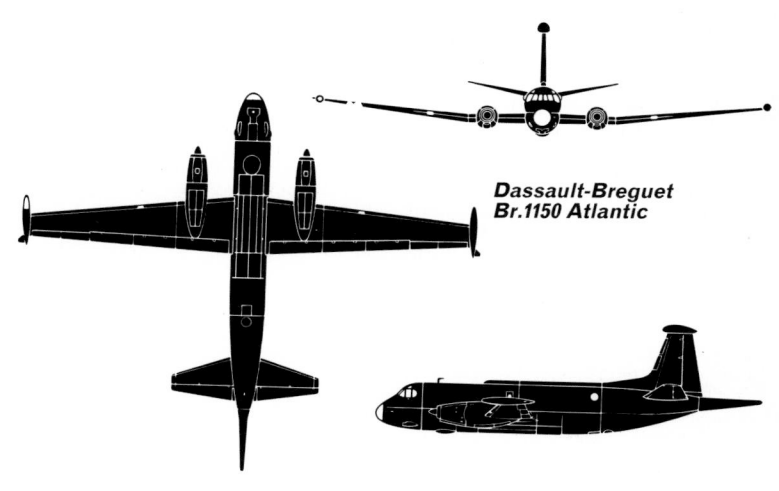

Dassault-Breguet Br.1150 Atlantic

---

de Havilland D.H.16

The end of World War I and the subsequent vast surplus of military aircraft was not a time for new civil designs to emerge. Instead, many conversions of military models were attempted, but the **de Havilland D.H.16** was a redesign of the D.H.9A with a wider fuselage for four passengers. Following its first flight at Hendon in March 1919, the D.H.16 was sold to Aircraft Transport and Travel Ltd (AT&T), who used it for pleasure flying before it inaugurated a London-Paris service on 25 August of that year.

Total D.H.16 production was nine aircraft, all but one being used by AT&T. The sole exception was sold to a customer in Buenos Aires, where it operated a service to Montevideo. The first six D.H.16s were powered by the 239-kW (320-hp) Rolls-Royce Eagle engine, while the last three had Napier Lions.

The derivation of the de Havilland D.H.16 from the wartime D.H.9A is unmistakeable, the main alteration being the widening of the rear fuselage to accommodate a glazed cabin. Four passengers were carried in addition to the pilot.

AT&T closed in December 1920 and its seven remaining D.H.16s (one had been lost in a crash) were stored. All were broken up in 1922 except for two sold for newspaper delivery flights; one of these was lost in a fatal crash in 1923, and the remaining aircraft was subsequently withdrawn and scrapped.

Specification
Type: four-seat commercial biplane
Powerplant: one 336-kW (450-hp) Napier Lion inline piston engine
Performance: maximum speed

219 km/h (136 mph); cruising speed 161 km/h (100 mph); service ceiling 6400 m (21,000 ft); range 684 km (425 miles)
Weights: empty 1431 kg (3,155 lb);

maximum take-off 2155 kg (4,750 lb)
Dimensions: span 14.17 m (46 ft 5¾ in); length 9.68 m (31 ft 9 in); height 3.45 m (11 ft 4 in); wing area 45.5 m² (489.75 sq ft)

---

de Havilland D.H.18

The designation **D.H.17** was allocated to a project for a twin-engined 16-passenger biplane which was not built. The next type number, **de Havilland D.H.18**, was allocated to a large single-engined biplane accommodating eight passengers in an enclosed cabin; the pilot was seated in an open cockpit

behind the wings. Built at Hendon, the D.H.18 first flew early in 1920 and was delivered to Aircraft Transport & Travel Ltd for use on the Croydon-Paris service. However, this D.H.18 had a short life, terminated by a forced landing near Croydon in August of the same year.

During 1920 the Aircraft Manufacturing Company, which had been building de Havilland designs, was re-formed as the de Havilland Aircraft Company Ltd. The new organisation built two modified aircraft designated **D.H.18A** for Instone Air Line, followed by a third. These were kept busy on Continental services until the first, having accumulated high flying hours, was withdrawn from use in September 1921; another was lost in a crash only two months after delivery. The third production D.H.18A, delivered to Instone in June 1921, was passed to Daimler Hire Ltd in April 1922, only to be destroyed over France a few days later in a mid-air collision with a Farman Goliath.

The last two aircraft were designated **D.H.18B**, and had plywood-covered fuselages and increased weights; they served with Instone for a short time before the second was dismantled in 1923. The first was used in Air Ministry flotation tests, being deliberately landed in the sea off Felixstowe in May 1924. Strangely, the last surviving D.H.18 was the first production aircraft which, following its withdrawal from Instone's use

in 1921, was delivered to RAE Farnborough for test purposes. It was finally scrapped in 1927.

Specification
de Havilland D.H.18A
Type: eight-seat commercial biplane
Powerplant: one 336-kW (450-hp) Napier Lion inline piston engine
Performance: maximum speed 206 km/h (128 mph); cruising speed 161 km/h (100 mph); service ceiling 4875 m (16,000 ft); range 644 km (400 miles)
Weights: empty 1833 kg (4,040 lb); maximum take-off 2956 kg (6,516 lb)
Dimensions: span 15.62 m (51 ft 3 in); length 11.89 m (39 ft 0 in); height 3.96 m (13 ft 0 in); wing area 57.71 m^2 (621.25 sq ft)

G-EARO was the second D.H.18 passenger transport, and was completed as the D.H.18A. It was first used by AT&T, and then passed to the Air Council which loaned the machine to Instone Air Line. It then went to the RAE at Farnborough.

de Havilland D.H.34

Building on commercial experience obtained with the D.H.18 and structural experience with the D.H.29, de Havilland began work on a new type, the **de Havilland D.H.32**, in 1921. Considerable progress had been made, and plans for construction of the first aircraft (with the 268-kW/360-hp Rolls-Royce Eagle engine as its powerplant) had been announced. The new design showed great promise, but since the main customers would be Instone and Daimler Hire, who were already using Napier Lion-powered D.H.18s, de Havilland bowed to their wishes and redesigned the aircraft to use that engine. The result was the **de Havilland D.H.34**, the company's most successful aircraft of the early post-war period.

The first of 11 aircraft flew in March 1922, and made an inaugural Croydon-Paris flight on 2 April. Daimler Hire eventually used six D.H.34s and Instone four, while one was sold to Dobrolet, the Russian airline. When Imperial Airways was formed in 1924 it took over seven D.H.34s and used them over the next two years before deciding to re-equip with larger aircraft.

There can be no doubt that the D.H.34s made an impressive mark on the air transport scene during the four

years or so in which they served. Some 8,000 hours were recorded by December 1922, less than nine months after the prototype's appearance, and over 160934 km (100,000 miles) flown without overhaul by the second Daimler aircraft. However, no fewer than six D.H.34s were lost in accidents, several

of them fatal. An early stalling crash led to extensions being added to the top wing to increase its area, giving rise to the designation **D.H.34B**. The last four D.H.34s in UK service were scrapped in 1926.

Specification
de Havilland D.H.34
Type: 10-seat commercial biplane
Powerplant: one 336-kW (450-hp)

Napier Lion inline piston engine
Performance: maximum speed 206 km/h (128 mph); cruising speed 169 km/h (105 mph); range 587 km (365 miles)
Weights: empty 2075 kg (4,574 lb); maximum take-off 3266 kg (7,200 lb)
Dimensions: span 15.65 m (51 ft 4 in); length 11.89 m (39 ft 0 in; height 3.66 m (12 ft 0 in); wing area 54.81 m^2 (590 sq ft)

de Havilland D.H.34, the aircraft with which Daimler Airways inaugurated their service.

de Havilland D.H.37

De Havilland's first venture into the field of private-owner aircraft was the **de Havilland D.H.37**, a two-seat biplane built to the specification of Alan Butler, a well-known aviator and DH director. The first of two aircraft flew in June 1922 and the second in 1924, the latter being sold to Australia. Butler's aircraft was used extensively over the next five years, and in 1927 its Rolls-Royce Falcon III engine was exchanged for a 224-kW (300-hp) A.D.C. Nimbus, the aircraft being converted to single-seat configuration for racing as the **D.H.37A**. However, in June that year it crashed while flying as a two-seater, killing the passenger and injuring the pilot.

The Australian D.H.37 had a longer life, being used initially by the Controller of Civil Aviation and later by the Guinea Gold Company in New Guinea, being the first aeroplane in that country. It crashed in New South Wales in March 1932.

Specification
de Havilland D.H.37
Type: two-seat touring biplane
Powerplant: one 205-kW (275-hp)

Rolls-Royce Falcon III inline piston engine
Performance: maximum speed

196 km/h (122 mph); service ceiling 6400 m (21,000 ft)
Weights: empty 961 kg (2,118 lb); maximum take-off 1505 kg (3,318 lb)

Dimensions: span 11.28 m (37 ft 0 in); length 8.53 m (28 ft 0 in); wing area 36.97 m^2 (398 sq ft)

The first of only two de Havilland D.H.37s built, subsequently re-engined and converted to a single-seat racing aircraft (and re-named Lois).

de Havilland D.H.50

Realising in 1922 that war-surplus D.H.9Cs could not be expected to serve much longer, de Havilland used the experience gained in its operation to design a replacement, the **de Havilland D.H.50**, which carried four passengers in an enclosed cabin between the wings, with the pilot to the rear in an open cockpit. The D.H.9C's Siddeley Puma engine was retained and the result was a reliable and economical light transport.

First flown in August 1923, the D.H.50 made an excellent start to its career when, four days later, it was flown by Alan Cobham to compete and win first prize in reliability trials which were being flown daily between Copenhagen and Gothenburg from 7–12 August. Cobham made several long-distance flights with the prototype before using the second aircraft, powered by a 287-kW (385-hp) Armstrong Siddeley Jaguar radial engine and redesignated **D.H.50J**, for a 25749-km (16,000-mile) flight from Croydon to Cape Town, carried out between 16 November 1925 and 17 February 1926. This was followed later in 1926 by a survey flight to Australia and back, for which twin floats were fitted.

A number of orders were placed for D.H.50s, and 16 production aircraft were built by de Havilland. Australian licence production was carried out by QANTAS, which built four **D.H.50A** and three D.H.50J aircraft; by West Australian Airways, which built three D.H.50As; and by the Larkin Aircraft Supply Company, which built a single D.H.50A. European licences were granted to SABCA for con-

De Havilland D.H.50J with Armstrong Siddeley Jaguar engine, as used by Alan Cobham for survey flights to South Africa and Australia.

struction of three D.H.50As at Brussels and to Aero at Prague for seven. The SABCA aircraft were used in the Belgian Congo.

Of the total de Havilland production (17 aircraft), only four were based in the UK, two of them with Imperial Airways. One went to the Czech government, 10 to Australia and one to New Zealand. The longest survivor was the 15th British production aircraft, delivered in 1928 to the Australian Controller of Civil Aviation and destroyed by enemy action in New Guinea during 1942.

A wide variety of engines was used in the D.H.50 family; in addition to those mentioned already there were the 224-kW (300-hp) A.D.C. Nimbus, 313-kW (420-hp) Bristol Jupiter IV, 336-kW (450-hp) Jupiter VI, 384-kW (515-hp) Jupiter XI, 336-kW (450-hp) Pratt & Whitney Wasp C and, in the Czech-built versions, the 179-kW (240-hp) Walter W-4.

Specification
de Havilland D.H.50
Type: four-passenger cabin biplane

Powerplant: one 172-kW (230-hp) Siddeley Puma inline piston engine
Performance: maximum speed 180 km/h (112 mph); cruising speed 153 km/h (95 mph); service ceiling 4450 m (14,600 ft); range 612 km (380 miles)
Weights: empty 1022 kg (2,352 lb); maximum take-off 1769 kg (3,900 lb)
Dimensions: span 13.03 m (42 ft 9 in); length 9.07 m (29 ft 9 in); height 3.35 m (11 ft 0 in); wing area 40.32 m² (434 sq ft)

de Havilland D.H.51

Following the D.H.37 two-seat tourer of 1922, de Havilland's next aircraft in this category was the **de Havilland D.H.51**. However, in this case economy of operation was a criterion and the design was developed around the 67-kW (90-hp) R.A.F.1A engine, of which war-surplus supplies were available at knockdown prices.

First flown in July 1924 by Geoffrey de Havilland, the D.H.51 proved to be satisfactory, but since the engine did not have dual ignition a Certificate of Airworthiness was refused. Ten hours of airborne testing would have been required with the single-ignition RAF1A, but de Havilland decided that the cost of this was not justified. As things turned out this was probably a major error of judgement, since once certificated the type might have gone on to achieve the fame which was to come later with the D.H.60, the first of the Moths.

After returning from Kenya in 1965, this D.H.51 was restored by the Shuttleworth Trust and continues to fly occasionally.

It was decided to re-engine the D.H.51 with an Airdisco engine and this move, although conferring considerably enhanced performance, took the aircraft well outside the economic operating bracket for which it was designed. As a result, only three were built; the first two enjoyed reasonably long and active lives, being written-off in 1931 and scrapped in 1933 respectively, but the third, built in 1925 and shipped to Kenya, became the first aircraft on that country's civil register. Dismantled during the war, it survived to fly again and now, after several rebuilds, is again back in the country of its birth, maintained by the Shuttleworth Trust at Old Warden as the

oldest airworthy design of the de Havilland Aircraft Company.

Specification
de Havilland D.H.51
Type: three-seat touring biplane
Powerplant: one 89-kW (120-hp) Airdisco inline piston engine

Performance: maximum speed 174 km/h (108 mph); service ceiling 4570 m (15,000 ft)
Weights: empty 609 kg (1,342 lb); maximum take-off 1016 kg (2,240 lb)
Dimensions: span 11.28 m (37 ft 0 in); length 8.08 m (26 ft 6 in); height 2.97 m (9 ft 9 in); wing area 30.19 m² (325 sq ft)

de Havilland D.H.53 Humming Bird

De Havilland entered the field of ultralight aircraft with the **de Havilland D.H.53 Humming Bird** which was built for the *Daily Mail* light aeroplane trials held at Lympne, Kent, in October 1923.

Two examples of the little monoplane were built, powered by 750-cc (45.77-cu in) Douglas motorcycle engines, and in spite of considerable problems with this powerplant both aircraft did well.

In an effort to make the type more reliable, a Blackburn Tomtit engine was installed and other detail changes made before the Humming Bird was flown to the Brussels Aero Show in 1923. It later took part in several air races together with the second aircraft, owned by a group of RAF officers who re-engined it

with a 26-kW (35-hp) A.B.C. Scorpion engine which proved unreliable.

Because of its economical performance, the first Humming Bird had secured for de Havilland an Air Ministry order for eight aircraft for communications and flying practice. Five others were built for civil customers, three going to Australia, one to Czechoslovakia and one to Russia.

The last two RAF Humming Birds were used in experiments which involved launching them from the airship R-33 and recovering them in the air. Following the disposal of all eight aircraft by the RAF in 1927, six were civil registered and flown for several years. One survives with the Shuttleworth Trust at Old Warden, having been rebuilt with a num-

This is a replica of the Humming Bird, powered by a Continental flat-twin engine in place of the original Tomtit. One genuine Humming Bird survives in England at Old Warden.

ber of new components post-war. It was flown on occasions, but following extensive damage is no longer airworthy and maintained as a static exhibit.

Specification
de Havilland D.H.53
Type: single-seat ultralight monoplane
Powerplant: one 19-kW (26-hp) Blackburn Tomtit two-cylinder vee piston engine
Performance: maximum speed

117 km/h (73 mph); cruising speed 97 km/h (60 mph); service ceiling 4570 m (15,000 ft); range 241 km (150 miles)
Weights: empty 148 kg (326 lb); maximum take-off 256 kg (565 lb)
Dimensions: span 9.17 m (30 ft 1 in); length 5.99 m (19 ft 8 in); height 2.21 m (7 ft 3 in); wing area 11.61 m² (125 sq ft)

de Havilland D.H.60 Moth
to
de Havilland D.H.88 Comet

de Havilland D.H.60 Moth

The idea of cheap flying for the man in the street has attracted aircraft manufacturers throughout the history of flight. One of the earliest examples of a design to this concept was the **de Havilland D.H.60 Moth**, the forerunner of a whole family of Moths which revolutionised the flying scene in the UK during the 1920s and 1930s.

First flown in February 1925, the D.H.60 prototype had a 45-kW (60-hp) Cirrus I engine, a new powerplant which was in fact half a 90-kW (120-hp) Airdisco engine on a new crankcase and weighing only 132 kg (290 lb). Such was the immediate success of the type that the Air Ministry was persuaded to subsidise five flying clubs equipped with Moths, and the first of these aircraft was delivered to the Lancashire Aero Club in July 1925, a bare five months after the flight of the prototype; 20 were built in that year. Orders flowed in, and 1926 production totalled 35; customers at home were joined by others in Australia and Japan, and military interest was evidenced by orders from the Air Ministry and the Irish Air Corps. Following the delivery by Alan Cobham of a floatplane Moth to the USA, an agreement was reached for production in that country (see below).

In 1926, the Cirrus engine was improved to give 63 kW (85 hp), in which form it became the Cirrus II and supplemented the earlier model. A one-off lightweight D.H.60 built for the 1926 Air Ministry light aeroplane trials at Lympne had a 56-kW (75-hp) Armstrong Siddeley Genet radial engine and was used subsequently for aerobatics.

The next year's model had further improvements, including a span increase of 0.3 m (1 ft) and carried the official designation, later dropped, of **D.H.60X**; it was referred to subsequently as the **Cirrus II Moth**.

Records were set, long-distance flights undertaken and the orders continued to roll in. The RAF's Central Flying School bought six Genet-engined models and the Irish Air Corps two. Cirrus II Moths were supplied also to Argentina, Canada, Finland, Germany, India, Italy, New Zealand, Singapore, South Africa, Spain, Sweden and the USA.

The designation D.H.60X was reintroduced for the next variant with the 67-kW (90-hp) A.D.C. Cirrus III engine, introduced in 1928. This model also pioneered a split-axle landing gear, and by the end of that year a total of 403 Moths had been built. Additionally, production licences had been agreed with

the General Aircraft Company in Australia and with two companies in Finland, the Government Aircraft Factory and Veljekset Karhumäki. Twenty-two Cirrus II Moths were supplied to the Finnish air force, some of these being re-engined subsequently with 78-kW (105-hp) Hermes engines. Quantity production of the D.H.60X was ended in September 1928 when newer models were introduced, but a few more were built to special order. One is preserved in flying condition by the Shuttleworth Trust at Old Warden.

Although the power of the D.H.60's engine had been increased by 50 per cent, from the original 45 kW (60 hp) to 67 kW (90 hp), the weight had also gone up considerably, if not quite to the same extent. To cope better with this increase, and to make up for the dwindling supplies of Cirrus engines, de Havilland decided to build its own engine. Major Frank Halford, who had designed the Cirrus engine for A.D.C., was in 1927 asked to design a Cirrus replacement. His answer was the 75-kW (100-hp) Gipsy, a design which was later developed through a whole range of engines bearing this famous name, one which paved the way for the entire Moth family.

Delivered in June 1928, the new engine was flown initially in a D.H.60X used by the company for test installations; it greatly improved the already good performance of the Moth and the re-engined design was designated **D.H.60G**, but forever after was called, obviously, **Gipsy Moth**. A prototype Gipsy engine was installed in one of the D.H.71 racers which was to compete in the 1927 King's Cup Air Race, but the aircraft was withdrawn and used subsequently for record-breaking flights.

The first production D.H.60G, flown by W.L. Hope, won the 1928 King's Cup Race at 169 km/h (105 mph) and several others set new records. In July 1928, for example, Geoffrey de Havilland established an altitude record of 6090 m (19,980 ft) and the following month Hubert Broad, in a D.H.60G with extra tankage, stayed airborne for 24 hours. In December, A.S. Butler and his wife set a new two-seater 100-km (62.1-mile) closed-circuit record at 192.86 km/h (119.84 mph). A reliability test, carried out over nine months beginning in late December 1928, involved a D.H.60G Moth flying for 600 hours with only routine servicing. It emerged from the test with flying colours having completed 82076 km (51,000 miles) of trouble-free flight.

With this remarkable proof of reliabil-

ity, the D.H.60G became a favourite mount for long-distance fliers. In this respect, Amy Johnson's 20-day epic solo flight between Croydon and Darwin in May 1930 in the famous D.H.60G *Jason* (preserved in the London Science Museum), and Francis Chichester's flight over a similar route in January of that year and his subsequent travels in the Pacific area, have become part of aviation history; but there were many others. Variants were legion and too many to record here, but among them were a pair of amphibians with one central float and underwing floats. One of these Moths had a Gipsy, the other a 78-kW (105-hp) Cirrus Hermes I engine. A few coupé versions were flown but were not popular.

Total D.H.60G production by de Havilland reached 595 before it ceased in 1934, but 40 were built in France by Morane-Saulnier where they were known as Morane Moths, 18 by the Moth Aircraft Corporation in USA and 32 by the Larkin Aircraft Supply Company Ltd in Australia.

While the wooden-structure D.H.60G was suitable for many countries there were others, particularly where aircraft had to operate in remote areas, which required a strengthened and more easily repaired version. To fill this requirement de Havilland produced in 1928 the **D.H.60M**, with welded steel fuselage and other modifications, but with the same engine as the D.H.60G. Production in the UK totalled 535, while 40 were assembled by de Havilland Aircraft of Canada, 10 in Norway and 161 by the Moth Aircraft Corporation in USA. A large number of D.H.60Ms went to service customers, in particular the RAF and the air forces of Canada, Iraq and Sweden, as well as to the Norwegian army and Danish naval air service.

Since de Havilland was now building its own engines it was logical that engine and airframe development went side-by-side. When the 89-kW (120-hp) Gipsy II engine appeared in 1931 with the ability

Undoubtedly one of the most popular, successful and historically important types designed by de Havilland, the D.H.60 Moth was produced in many variants.

to operate when inverted, as a result of internal modifications, it became the Gipsy III, offering improved pilot visibility and better streamlining to the forward fuselage. Installation in a new airframe and first flight in March 1932 saw the birth of another new series, the **D.H.60GIII** which, like its predecessors, attracted considerable interest and world-wide orders. Thirty were built before the 99-kW (133-hp) Gipsy Major IIIA engine was installed to produce the version named **Moth Major**; 87 of this model were built.

Final development of the D.H.60 series came when a modified D.H.60M appeared as the **D.H.60T Moth Trainer**, intended for military use and powered by the Gipsy II engine. It marked the beginning of development of the most famous Moth of all, the D.H.82 Tiger Moth. All the orders received were from overseas military customers, comprising Brazil (40), China (1), Egypt (6), Iraq (5) and Sweden (10), making a total of 64 including two sold during 1931 to an unspecified country.

Specification
de Havilland D.H.60G Gipsy Moth
Type: two-seat touring lightplane
Powerplant: one 74.6-kW (100-hp) de Havilland Gipsy I inline piston engine
Performance: maximum speed 164 km/h (102 mph); cruising speed 137 km/h (85 mph); service ceiling 4420 m (14,500 ft); range 515 km (320 miles)
Weights: empty 417 kg (920 lb); maximum take-off 748 kg (1,650 lb)
Dimensions: span 9.14 m (30 ft 0 in); length 7.29 m (23 ft 11 in); height 2.68 m (8 ft 9½ in); wing area 22.57 m² (243 sq ft)

de Havilland D.H.66 Hercules

The need of a replacement for the D.H.10s used on the RAF's air-mail service between Cairo and Baghdad, coupled with an agreement reached in 1925 for Imperial Airways to take over the service, led to a requirement being issued which was met by the **de Havilland D.H.66 Hercules**, a three-engined biplane with a 4.39-m³ (155-

cu ft) baggage compartment, space for seven passengers and 13.17 m³ (465 cu ft) of mail and a three-man crew.

The prototype flew on 30 September 1926 following receipt of an order for five aircraft from Imperial Airways. Such was the speed and comparative simplicity of procedures in those days that the prototype carried out acceptance flights, took

part in some crew training and was delivered to Cairo by mid-December. An inaugural flight between Croydon and India left the UK on 27 December and arrived in Delhi on 8 January 1927.

The fifth aircraft was delivered to Cairo in March 1927. The performance of these aircraft impressed West Australia Airways, then using D.H.50s. Four examples of the Hercules were ordered, the first flying in March 1929, and the type entered service with WAA on the

Perth-Adelaide route on 2 June. By then Imperial had ordered a sixth aircraft and its seventh and final aircraft followed in February 1930.

Imperial's sixth Hercules had an enclosed pilot's cabin, a modification which later became standard on the remaining aircraft. The airline's need for these last two Hercules followed the loss of three in crashes between September 1929 and April 1931, but only the first caused fatalities. Aircraft shortage led to the purchase by Imperial of two WAA Hercules in 1930-1; one of these crashed in Southern Rhodesia in November 1935 and Imperial eventually withdrew its last aircraft from service in December 1935, having sold three to the South African Air Force. Their eventual history is not known, but the longest surviving Hercules was probably one of the two former WAA aircraft, being used in New Guinea between Lae and Wau, and destroyed by enemy action in 1942.

Specification
de Havilland D.H.66 Hercules
Type: seven-passenger airliner

Built for service in the desert regions, the D.H.66 served ably, if slowly, for many years. This machine was one of four built for West Australian Airways with enclosed cockpit.

Powerplant: three 313-kW (420-hp) Bristol Jupiter VI radial piston engines
Performance: maximum speed 206 km/h (128 mph); cruising speed 177 km/h (110 mph); service ceiling 3960 m (13,000 ft); range 845 km (525 miles)
Weights: empty 4110 kg (9,060 lb); maximum take-off 7076 kg (15,600 lb)

Dimensions: span 24.23 m (79 ft 6 in); length 16.92 m (55 ft 6 in); height 5.56 m (18 ft 3 in); wing area 143.72 m² (1,547 sq ft)

de Havilland D.H.71 Tiger Moth

In order to carry out research on high-speed flight and to test replacement engines for the Cirrus, de Havilland built in 1927 two small single-seat monoplanes designated **de Havilland D.H.71 Tiger Moth**. Such was the degree of streamlining required that it was designed around test pilot Hubert Broad. The two aircraft were entered for the King's Cup Air Race, for it then seemed accepted that any new light aircraft of that time were required to thus prove themselves. However, one was scratched before the race; the other, powered by an A.D.C. Cirrus II engine, was withdrawn during the race due to bumpy conditions.

In August 1927 the first D.H.71, then with alternative wings of only 5.69 m (19 ft) span and a new 101-kW (135-hp) Gipsy engine, was flown by Broad to a

new 100-km (62.1-mile) closed circuit record for aircraft of its class of 300.09 km/h (186.47 mph). Five days later Broad attempted the world's altitude record for the category, but having no oxygen the limitation was on man and not machine. He reached 5849 m (19,191 ft) before having to give up, although the aircraft was still climbing at over 305 m (1,000 ft) per minute.

In 1930 the first D.H.71 was taken to Australia, but crashed during practice for an air race after suffering engine failure on take-off, killing the pilot. The second airframe, minus engine, was destroyed at Hatfield in an air raid during October 1940.

Specification
de Havilland D.H.71 Tiger Moth
(standard configuration)

Type: single-seat high-speed research monoplane
Powerplant: one 63-kW (85-hp) A.D.C. Cirrus II inline piston engine
Performance: maximum speed

267 km/h (166 mph)
Weights: empty 280 kg (618 lb); maximum take-off 411 kg (905 lb)
Dimensions: span 6.86 m (22 ft 6 in); length 5.66 m (18 ft 7 in); height 2.13 m (7 ft 0 in); wing area 7.11 m² (76.5 sq ft)

The first Tiger Moth was this trim racing and research monoplane. Two were built and used for testing new engines and wings, and for racing and record-breaking.

de Havilland D.H.80 Puss Moth

Developed to provide the growing numbers of affluent private pilots with cabin comfort, the prototype **de Havilland D.H.80** was first flown at Stag Lane on 9 September 1929. It introduced the inverted de Havilland Gipsy II engine, improving the pilot's view over the nose, and had a slab-sided plywood-covered fuselage accommodating the pilot (forward) and two passengers side-by-side at the rear of the cabin. Two doors were provided on the starboard side. Production aircraft began to appear in March 1930, designated **D.H.80A Puss Moth**, incorporating a new welded steel-tube and fabric-covered fuselage, the first de Havilland light aircraft to feature this method of construction. Notable were swivelling main landing gear shock-absorber fairings which could be turned broadside to the airflow to act as airbrakes. Other changes included single doors on each side of the fuselage, and installation of the improved 89-kW (120-hp) Gipsy III; later

examples were powered by the 97-kW (130-hp) Gipsy Major. A total of 259 aircraft was manufactured in the UK, the last leaving Stag Lane in March 1933, and many were used for pioneering flights. Another 25 aircraft were built by de Havilland Aircraft of Canada Ltd.

During July 1931 Amy Johnson used *Jason II* to fly from Lympne to Tokyo in 8 days 22 hours 35 minutes, and in 1932 Jim Mollison flew from Lympne to Cape Town in 4 days 17 hours 19 minutes. Mollison's second Puss, *The Heart's Content*, had a 727-litre (160-Imp gal) fuel tank installed in the front of the cabin and additional windows in the rear, its 5794-km (3,600-mile) range enabling him to make the first solo east-west North Atlantic crossing, leaving Portmarnock Strand, Dublin, on 18 August 1932 and arriving 31 hours 20 minutes later at Penfield Ridge, New Brunswick. On 6 February 1933, Mollison took off from Lympne en route to Natal, Brazil, and became the first man to make a solo cross-

ing of the South Atlantic.

Specification
de Havilland D.H.80 Puss Moth
Type: two/three-seat cabin
Powerplant: one 89-kW (120-hp) de Havilland Gipsy III inline piston engine
Performance: maximum speed 206 km/h (128 mph); cruising speed 174 km/h (108 mph); service ceiling 5335 m (17,500 ft); range 483 km (300

miles)
Weights: empty 574 kg (1,265 lb); maximum take-off 930 kg (2,050 lb)
Dimensions: span 11.2 m (36 ft 9 in); length 7.62 m (25 ft 0 in); height 2.13 m (7 ft 0 in); wing area 20.62 m² (222 sq ft)

The D.H.80 Puss Moth was an answer to the calls from touring lightplane owners for greater comfort. The high-wing monoplanes layout allowed an enclosed cabin to be provided.

de Havilland D.H.82 Tiger Moth

The success of the de Havilland Moth as a civil trainer led, inevitably, to the development of a military version known as the D.H.60T Moth Trainer. Compared with the earliest civil versions the D.H.60T was strengthened to allow it to operate at a higher all-up weight, and it could also carry four 9-kg (20-lb) practice bombs under the fuselage. It could also be fitted with a camera gun, or reconnaissance cameras, and was therefore suitable for various training roles. To aid escape from the front cockpit in emergency, the rear flying wires were angled

forward to the front wing root fitting, and the cockpit doors deepened. However, centre-section struts still surrounded the front cockpit, and in a new trainer which was developed to Specification 15/31 these were moved forward to provide improved egress. To offset the effect of resulting centre of gravity changes caused by staggering of the wings, the mainplanes were given a small amount of sweepback. An 89-kW (120-hp) Gipsy III inverted inline engine was installed, the sloping line of the engine cowling providing improved visibility from the

cockpit.

Eight pre-production aircraft were built, still designated D.H.60T, but bearing the name **Tiger Moth**. These were followed by a machine with increased lower wing dihedral and sweepback. This aircraft, designated **de Havilland D.H.82**, was first flown at Stag Lane on 26 October 1931. An order for 35 was placed to Specification T.23/31, and first deliveries were made to No. 3 Flying Training School at Grantham in November 1931. Others went to the Central Flying School in May 1932, and a team of

five CFS pilots displayed their skill and the inverted flying capability of this new trainer at the 1932 Hendon Display. Similar machines were supplied to the air forces of Brazil, Denmark, Persia, Portugal and Sweden and two, with twin floats supplied by Short Brothers, were built to Specification T.6/33 for RAF evaluation at Rochester and Felixstowe.

De Havilland then developed an improved version, with a 97-kW (130-hp) Gipsy Major engine, and plywood rear fuselage decking in place of the fabric covering of the initial production aircraft. This was designated **D.H.82A** and named **Tiger Moth II** by the RAF, which ordered 50 to Specification

T.26/33. Tiger Moth IIs had hoods which could be positioned over the rear cockpit for instrument flying instruction, and were delivered to Kenley between November 1934 and January 1935. Others were supplied to the Bristol Aeroplane Company, the de Havilland School of Flying, Brooklands Aviation Ltd, Phillips and Powis School of Flying, Reid and Sigrist Ltd, Airwork Ltd and Scottish Aviation Ltd for the Elementary and Reserve Flying Schools which these companies operated under the RAF expansion scheme. No fewer than 44 such schools were in operation in August 1939, although 20 of them closed when hostilities began.

Pre-war licence manufacture of the Tiger Moth included aircraft built in Norway, Portugal and Sweden, and by de Havilland Aircraft of Canada, whose pre-war output included 227 D.H.82As. The company later built 1,520 of a winterised version, designated **D.H.82C**, which had a 108-kW (145-hp) Gipsy Major engine with a revised cowling, sliding cockpit canopies, cockpit heating, wheel brakes and a tailwheel in place of the standard skid. Skis or floats could be fitted if required, and some examples were powered by a Menasco Pirate engine when Gipsy Majors came into short supply. A batch of 200 D.H.82Cs was ordered by the US Army Air Force, with the designation **PT-24**, although they were diverted for use by the Royal Canadian Air Force.

The outbreak of war saw civil machines impressed for RAF communications and training duties, and larger orders were placed. A further 795 were built at Hatfield before the factory was turned over to de Havilland Mosquito production, when the Tiger Moth line was re-established at the Cowley works of Morris Motors Ltd, where some 3,500 were manufactured. De Havilland Aircraft of New Zealand built a further 345, and in Australia de Havilland Aircraft Pty produced a total of 1,085.

On 17 September 1939, just two weeks after war had been declared, 'A' Flight of the British Expeditionary Force Communications Squadron (later No. 81 Squadron) was despatched to France. Throughout the winter and the following spring, the unit's Tiger Moths operated in northern France, providing valuable communications facilities until the Dunkirk evacuation, when surviving aircraft were flown back to Britain.

Preparations were also made for the Tiger Moth to be used in an offensive role, to combat the threatened German invasion. Racks designed to carry eight 9-kg (20-lb) bombs were fitted under the rear cockpit or, more suitably, beneath the wings. Although some 1,500 sets of racks were made and distributed to the Flying Schools, none were used operationally. Rather earlier, in December 1939, six coastal patrol squadrons were formed, five of them equipped with Tiger Moths. However futile this may seem, it was considered that despite an inability to attack, the sound of any engine might deter a U-boat commander from running on the surface and thus reduce his capacity to attack shipping.

In the Far East a small number of Tiger

Moths were converted for use as ambulance aircraft, the luggage locker lid being enlarged and a hinged lid cut into the rear fuselage decking, providing a compartment some 1.83 m (6 ft) long which could accommodate one casualty.

It was in a wartime trainer role, however, that the Tiger Moth made its greatest contribution. The type equipped no fewer than 28 Elementary Flying Training Schools in the UK, 25 in Canada (plus four Wireless Schools), 12 in Australia, four in Rhodesia (plus a Flying Instructors School), seven in South Africa, and two in India. After the war 22 Reserve Flying Schools and 18 University Air Squadrons flew Tiger Moths, most re-equipping with the de Havilland Chipmunk between 1950 and 1953.

Mention should be made also of the **D.H.82B Queen Bee** radio-controlled target aircraft, which was essentially a version of the Tiger Moth with a basic structure of wood: it had the Moth Major fuselage, Tiger Moth wings, Gipsy Major engine, a wind-driven generator to provide electrical power, and a larger-capacity fuel tank. The prototype was flown manually on 5 January 1935, and 380 were built subsequently.

More than 8,000 Tiger Moths had been built by the end of the war and, as can be imagined, there were large numbers to be disposed of as war-surplus. The RAF transferred many for civil and military use to Belgium, France and the Netherlands, but in the UK and elsewhere they became available in quantity on the civil market. In addition to obvious use as trainers, or for sport and pleasure, they found unexpected employment. Many gave valuable service in an agricultural duster/sprayer capacity, a role which proved to be of great importance to New Zealand.

A number were the subject of conversion schemes, usually to provide enclosed accommodation. The most ambitious was that carried out by the British company Jackaroo Aircraft Ltd, which involved widening the fuselage to seat four passengers in side-by-side pairs; open cockpit and enclosed cabin variants were included in the 19 **Thruxton Jackaroo** conversions completed by the company in the period 1957-9. It was once said that the initials D.H. stood for Durable and Hefficient, and that is

de Havilland D.H.82A Tiger Moth Mk II of an RAF Elementary and Reserve Flying Training School during 1940.

De Havilland D.H.82 Tiger Moth

In recent years the Tiger Moth has become a firm favourite with private owners and restorers. Still available in some numbers, the type offers open-cockpit flying with some aerobatic capability.

particularly true of the Tiger Moth. In 1991 large numbers remain in use worldwide, veritable treasures that are difficult to acquire and likely to appreciate in value and continue to provide pleasure for many years to come.

Specification
de Havilland D.H.82C
Type: two-seat trainer/sporting aircraft
Powerplant: one 108-kW (145-hp) de Havilland Gipsy Major 1C inline piston

engine
Performance: maximum speed 172 km/h (107 mph); cruising speed 145 km/h (90 mph); service ceiling 4450 m (14,600 ft); range 443 km (275 miles)
Weights: empty 506 kg (1,115 lb); maximum take-off 828 kg (1,825 lb)
Dimensions: span 8.94 m (29 ft 4 in); length 7.29 m (23 ft 11 in); height 2.69 m (8 ft 10 in); wing area 22.2 m^2 (239 sq ft)

de Havilland D.H.83 Fox Moth

De Havilland designer A. E. Hagg evolved the **de Havilland D.H.83 Fox Moth** in 1932 to meet a perceived need for a light transport aircraft with good performance, economical operations and low initial cost. To standard Tiger

Moth components (including wings, tail unit, landing gear and engine mounting) he added a new plywood-covered wooden fuselage, locating the pilot in an open cockpit behind an enclosed cabin which accommodated up to four pas-

sengers. The prototype, powered by an 89-kW (120-hp) de Havilland Gipsy III engine, was flown at Stag Lane in March 1932. It was later shipped to Canada for trials on floats and skis, undertaken in service with Canadian Airways Ltd. Eight of the 98 British-built Fox Moths were exported to Canada between 1932 and 1935, and two more examples were built

by de Havilland Aircraft of Australia. Many of these were powered by the Gipsy Major engine and some had sliding hoods over the cockpit. A single Japanese-built copy, powered by a 112 kW (150 hp) radial engine and known as the **Chidorigo**, was flown by the Japanese Aerial Transport Company. After the war, in 1946, de Havilland

This aircraft was one of the aircraft built in Canada after World War II as D.H.83Cs. These aircraft featured more powerful Gipsy Major 1C engines, enclosed pilot cockpit and an enlarged loading door. Four passengers could be carried.

Canada built 52 examples of the **D.H.83C**, which had a number of small improvements including trim tab on the elevators, an enlarged clear-view hood over the cockpit and the installation of a 108 kW (145 hp) Gipsy Major 1C engine. Another example of the D.H.83C (there were no **D.H.83A** or **D.H.83B** variants) was completed by Leavens Bros Ltd in 1948.

Specification
de Havilland D.H.83 Fox Moth
Type: light transport
Powerplant: one 97 kW (130 hp) de Havilland Gipsy Major inline piston engine
Performance: maximum speed 182 km/h (113 mph); cruising speed 154 km/h (96 mph); service ceiling 3870 m (12,700 ft); range 579 km (360 miles)
Weights: empty 499 kg (1,100 lb); maximum take-off 939 kg (2,070 lb)
Dimensions: span 9.41 m (30 ft 10½ in); length 7.85 m (25 ft 9 in); height 2.68 m (8 ft 9½ in); wing area 24.25 m² (261 sq ft)

de Havilland D.H.84 Dragon

The **de Havilland D.H.84 Dragon** was designed by Arthur Hagg in response to Fox Moth operator Edward Hillman's request for a twin-engined aircraft to be used on a proposed service from southern England to Paris. The slab-sided plywood box used successfully in the Fox Moth was adopted for the fuselage of the new design, a two-bay biplane with wings that could be folded outboard of the two de Havilland Gipsy Major engines. The pilot was provided with a separate compartment in the extreme nose and the main cabin could seat six passengers. The prototype made its maiden flight on 12 November 1932, at Stag Lane, Edgware. It was later delivered to Hillman's Airways at Maylands, Essex, together with three examples of the production **Dragon 1**, which facilitated inauguration of the Paris route in April 1933. British production totalled 115 aircraft built at Stag Lane and, from 1934, at Hatfield. A further 87 were built in Australia during World War

This is the prototype D.H.84 Dragon, after delivery to Hillman Airways on 12 November 1932. It later flew with Aberdeen Airways, crashing at Dunbeath in 1941.

II, the de Havilland Australian factory at Bankstown, Sydney, producing navigation trainers for the Royal Australian Air Force, the first of these flying on 29 September 1942.

Variants
Dragon 2: the 63rd aircraft was the first of an improved version with the glasshouse cabin windows replaced by individual framed transparencies, and with main landing gear fairings
D.H.84M: militarised version with a dorsal gun ring and a fin fillet; supplied to Denmark, Iraq and Portugal

Specification
de Havilland D.H.84 Dragon
Type: medium transport
Powerplant: two 97 kW (130 hp) de Havilland Gipsy Major inline piston engines
Performance: maximum speed 216 km/h (134 mph); cruising speed 183 km/h (114 mph); service ceiling 4420 m (14,500 ft); range 877 km (545 miles)
Weights: empty 1060 kg (2,336 lb); maximum take-off 2041 kg (4,500 lb)
Dimensions: span 14.43 m (47 ft 4 in); length 10.52 m (34 ft 6 in); height 3.3 m (10 ft 1 in); wing area 34.93 m² (376 sq ft)

de Havilland D.H.85 Leopard Moth

Introduced in 1933 as a successor to the Puss Moth, the **de Havilland D.H.85 Leopard Moth** bore a superficial resemblance to the earlier aircraft but incorporated a number of major changes,

not the least of which was revised fuselage construction. The steel-tube structure of the Puss Moth was replaced by the spruce and plywood box which was becoming a de Havilland standard, providing accommodation for the pilot, and for two passengers who were seated

The D.H.85 was the successor to the Puss Moth, with a lighter structure and reduced price. With slightly more power from its Gipsy Major, it could carry three people.

side-by-side in the rear of the cabin. New tapered and foldable wings with swept leading edges were fitted, and the main landing gear upper shock-absorber attachment points were relocated. The prototype made its first flight on 27 May 1933 at Stag Lane, and just two weeks later won that year's King's Cup Race at Hatfield; two similar aircraft finished third and sixth. This auspicious start ensured commercial success, and three years' production, initially at Stag Lane and then at Hatfield, totalled 132 examples.

Specification
de Havilland D.H.85 Leopard Moth
Type: three-seat touring aircraft
Powerplant: one 97 kW (130 hp) de Havilland Gipsy Major inline piston engine
Performance: maximum speed 220 km/h (137 mph); cruising speed 192 km/h (119 mph); service ceiling 6555 m (21,500 ft); range 1151 km (715 miles)
Weights: empty 637 kg (1,405 lb); maximum take-off 1009 kg (2,225 lb)
Dimensions: span 11.43 m (37 ft 6 in); length 7.47 m (24 ft 6 in); height 2.67 m (8 ft 9 in); wing area 19.14 m² (206 sq ft)

de Havilland D.H.86

Designed and built in response to an Australian government requirement for a multi-engined aircraft to be used by QANTAS for service across the Timor Sea, between Singapore and Australia, the **de Havilland D.H.86** was awarded its Certificate of Airworthiness on 30 January 1934, only four months after a start of work on the project. The aircraft was of wooden construction with fabric covering, and powered by four de Havilland Gipsy Six engines. The

first flight was made on 14 January 1934 at Stag Lane, in the hands of Hubert Broad, and certification trials were conducted at Martlesham. The prototype and two identical aircraft were equipped for single-pilot operation. The latter were used by Railway Air Services from 21 August 1934 on a new Croydon-Birmingham-Manchester-Belfast-Glasgow route. A second crew member (navigator/wireless operator) was carried, accommodated behind the pilot. However, QANTAS and Imperial Airways required that two pilots should be seated side-by-side, and in August 1934 the prototype re-emerged from the Stag Lane factory with a longer and wider nose to provide the necessary accommodation. The first of 29 production examples was one of four flown by Holyman Airways in Australia, and other operators comprised QANTAS (six), Imperial Airways (five), Jersey Airways (six), Misr Airwork, Egypt (four), Hillman's Airways (three) and Wrightways (one).

Variants

D.H.86A: introduced in late 1935, this version featured a modified windscreen, metal rudder, pneumatic landing gear legs, larger brakes and tailwheel; 20 were built, most converted to D.H.86B standard in 1937; production included four RAF aircraft including two for the RAF Radio School, Cranwell, and two for No. 24 Squadron at Hendon; others were impressed for wartime use
D.H.86B: conversions of D.H.86As with auxiliary endplate finlets, fitted following an accident in September 1936 which resulted in an investigation

at Martlesham and a subsequent report criticising rudder and aileron control; newly-built D.H.86Bs also had tailplanes with increased chord at the tips and higher gearing provided in the aileron circuit

Specification
de Havilland D.H.86B
Type: medium transport
Powerplant: four 149 kW (200 hp) de Havilland Gipsy Six inline piston engines
Performance: maximum speed 267 km/h (166 mph); cruising speed

229 km/h (142 mph); service ceiling 5305 m (17,400 ft); range 1287 km (800 miles)
Weights: empty 2943 kg (6,489 lb); maximum take-off 4649 kg (10,250 lb)
Dimensions: span 19.66 m (64 ft 6 in); length 14.05 m (46 ft 1 in); height 3.96 m (13 ft 0 in); wing area 59.55 m² (641 sq ft)

This D.H.86 was delivered to Imperial Airways for use on African services. It was later modified to D.H.86B standard with endplate fins.

de Havilland D.H.87 Hornet Moth

For biplane afficionados with a taste for additional comfort, the company designed the **de Havilland D.H.87 Hornet Moth**, an enclosed side-by-side two-seater structurally similar to the D.H.86. It had tapered wings and a spruce/plywood box fuselage with external longerons, stringers and fabric covering. The prototype, first flown at Hatfield on 9 May 1934, was joined in a year-long test programme by two similar aircraft, preparing for production deliveries which began in August 1935 under the designation **D.H.87A**. Rather more than 60 aircraft were manufactured to this standard with new wings of increased taper and span (9.93 m/32 ft 7 in), but in 1936 yet another set of wings was introduced, first fitted retrospectively to the second production Hornet Moth. These new mainplanes, virtually without taper and with almost square tips, were made available to existing owners on a trade-in basis and were fitted also to almost 100 new aircraft designated **D.H.87B**. Following development of a floatplane version by de

Havilland Aircraft of Canada Ltd, four examples were acquired by the Air Ministry in 1937 for evaluation as seaplane trainers at the Marine Aircraft Experimental Establishment at Felixstowe, Suffolk. Hornet Moth production, including the prototype, totalled 165 aircraft.

Specification
de Havilland D.H.87B Hornet Moth (landplane)
Type: two-seat touring aircraft
Powerplant: one 97 kW (130 hp) de Havilland Gipsy Major inline piston engine

Performance: maximum speed 200 km/h (124 mph); cruising speed 169 km/h (105 mph); service ceiling 4510 m (14,800 ft); range 998 km (620 miles)
Weights: empty 563 kg (1,214 lb); maximum take-off 885 kg (1,950 lb)
Dimensions: span 9.73 m (31 ft 11 in); length 7.61 m (24 ft 11½ in); height 2.01 m (6 ft 7 in); wing area 20.44 m² (220 sq ft)

This Canadian-registered Hornet Moth was a floatplane version developed by de Havilland Canada. Note the extended exhaust leading back under the rear fuselage.

de Havilland D.H.88 Comet

Designed specifically for the 1934 Victorian Centenary Air Race from Mildenhall to Melbourne, for which the prize money was donated by Sir MacPherson Robertson, the **de Havilland D.H.88 Comet** attracted three orders before the February 1934 deadline which had been stipulated by the manufacturer for guaranteed delivery before the Race in October. Purchasers were Mr A. O. Edwards, managing director of the Grosvenor House Hotel, Bernard Rubin, and Jim and Amy Mollison. The Comet was of wooden construction throughout, the front section of the fuselage containing three large fuel tanks behind which were two tandem seats for the pilot and copilot. Two high compression de Havilland Gipsy Six R engines were installed, driving Ratier two-position propellers which were set to fine pitch before each flight. These went into coarse pitch automatically at 241 km/h (150 mph), when a sealing disc in the spinner opened to release the unit's internal pressure and thus activate the control mechanism. Other notable features included the provision of manually retractable landing gear and split trailing-edge flaps.

Hubert Broad flew the first Comet, that intended for the Mollisons, at Hatfield on 8 September 1934. Its Certificate

of Airworthiness was issued on 9 October and certificates for the other two aircraft on 12 October, just eight days before the Race. Dawn on 20 October saw the departure of the first contestants, including the Mollisons' *Black Magic*, Owen Cathcart-Jones and Ken Waller's G-ACSR (owned by Rubin) and C. W. A. Scott and T. Campbell Black in *Grosvenor House*. *Black Magic* accomplished successfully the non-stop London-Baghdad leg but was forced to retire with engine trouble at Allahabad. Cathcart-Jones and Waller, after getting lost and being forced to land in Persia, struggled through to Melbourne to finish fourth in the speed section. They flew straight back, with mail and film, to set an out-and-return record of 13½ days. Scott and Black were the speed section winners, covering the course in 70 hours 54 minutes; *Grosvenor House* is now preserved by the Shuttleworth Trust at Old Warden, Bedfordshire. Two more Comets were built, one as a mailplane for the French government and the other for Mr Cyril Nicholson, who sponsored two unsuccessful attempts on the London-Cape record. During the second attempt the crew baled out over Sudan, on 22 September 1935.

Specification
de Havilland D.H.88 Comet
Type: two-seat racer/mailplane
Powerplant: two 172 kW (230 hp) de Havilland Gipsy Six R inline piston engines
Performance: maximum speed 381 km/h (237 mph); cruising speed 354 km/h (220 mph); service ceiling 5790 m (19,000 ft); range 4707 km (2,925 miles)
Weights: empty 1288 kg (2,840 lb);

maximum take-off 2413 kg (5,320 lb)
Dimensions: span 13.41 m (44 ft 0 in); length 8.84 m (29 ft 0 in); height 3.05 m (10 ft 0 in); wing area 19.69 m² (212 sq ft)

Bringing much useful publicity to de Havilland, the D.H.88 was triumphant in the 1934 MacRobertson race from London to Melbourne. This aircraft is now preserved at Old Warden.

de Havilland D.H.89 Dragon Rapide/Dominie
to
de Havilland D.H.106 Comet

de Havilland D.H.89 Dragon Rapide/Dominie

Designed in the light of experience gained from production and operation of the de Havilland D.H.84 Dragon and D.H.86 light transports, the prototype **de Havilland D.H.89 Dragon Six**, powered by two 149 kW (200 hp) de Havilland Gipsy Six engines, was flown at Stag Lane by Hubert Broad on 17 April 1934. Production aircraft, which were named **Dragon Rapide**, were delivered from July 1934, the first customers including Hillman's Airways Ltd, Railway Air Services and Olley Air Service Ltd. From March 1937 small trailing-edge flaps were fitted to the lower wings, outboard of the engine nacelles, the type then being redesignated **D.H.89A**. Civil Rapides were soon in wide-scale use with operators around the world, some even entering service in Canada on floats and skis. Their reliability and economy generated significant sales for the mid/late-1930s, and by the outbreak of war almost 200 had been delivered to civil operators.

A militarised version, designated **D.H.89M**, was developed to meet Air Ministry Specification G.18/35, which called for a general reconnaissance aircraft for service with Coastal Command. A forward-firing gun was mounted in the nose, to the right of the pilot's seat, and a gun mounting ring installed in the roof, aft of the cabin door. The Air Ministry contract was awarded to the Avro Anson, but two D.H.89Ms were built for Lithuania (now a constituent republic of the Soviet Union), and three with additional modifications were delivered to the Spanish government for service in Morocco. The latter aircraft had additional armament, an extra ventral gun to fire downwards through the floor, plus an underfuselage rack for 12 12 kg (26.5 lb) bombs.

Although the D.H.89M did not gain an Air Ministry contract as a reconnaissance aircraft, the Dragon Rapide was selected as a communications aircraft, a single example being purchased for use by the Air Council and operated by No. 24 Squadron at Hendon; two were delivered in November 1938. Civil Rapides were used to supply British forces in France in the spring and early summer of 1940, and many were impressed for communications duties, particularly with the Air Transport Auxiliary.

In 1939, three D.H.89s had been acquired as wireless trainers, to Air Ministry Specification T.29/38, followed by a further 14 for use by No. 2 Electrical and Wireless School. The first two D.H.89As, also for No. 2 E&WS, were delivered in September 1939. The trainer version was identified by the direction-finding loop in the cabin roof, later being designated **Dominie Mk I**, the communications version being the **Dominie Mk II**.

Of 728 Rapides built before production ended in July 1946, 521 were to British military contracts, mostly under the designation **D.H.89B**. Some 186 were built at Hatfield before pressure of work on other aircraft resulted in the transfer of production to Brush Coachworks Ltd at Loughborough, Leicestershire. The military D.H.89 figure includes 65 aircraft used by the Royal Navy, between 1940 and 1958, when the last was retired; some were impressed civil machines, some supplied new, and others transferred from the RAF.

Soon after hostilities had ended, several hundred war-surplus Dominies were supplied to such overseas air forces as those of Belgium and the Netherlands, or stripped of military equipment, were sold to civil buyers. In this way they became used in almost every country of the free world. Addi-

Built to RAF order as a Dominie, this Dragon Rapide was one of many which had a fruitful career after the war.

tionally, the last 100 production aircraft built by Brush Coachworks, but undelivered because of the war's end, were finished to the requirements of civil operators by de Havilland's repair unit at Witney. They became initial post-war equipment of airlines which included Iraqi Airways, Jersey Airways and KLM. At one period, during the 1950s, British European Airways operated a large fleet of Rapides on its services to the islands around Britain's coastline.

The Dragon Rapide has proved not only to be reliable but also enduring, with examples still flying in 1991.

Variants
D.H.89A Mk 4: conversion with Gipsy Queen 2 engines and constant speed propellers; prototype conversion was made in 1953, and many were modified subsequently to this standard, which allowed an increased take-off weight and gave improved performance
D.H.89A Mk 5: one-off conversion made by the company to one of its own communications aircraft, involving the installation of special Gipsy Queen

3 engines with manually operated variable-pitch propellers
D.H.89A Mk 6: designation of aircraft with standard engines but modified by addition of Fairey X5 fixed-pitch metal propellers

Specification
de Havilland D.H.89A Mk 4
Type: eight/10-seat light transport
Powerplant: two 149 kW (200 hp) de Havilland Gipsy Queen 2 inline piston engines
Performance: maximum speed 241 km/h (150 mph); cruising speed 225 km/h (140 mph); service ceiling 4875 m (16,000 ft); range 837 km (520 miles)
Weights: empty 1465 kg (3,230 lb); maximum take-off 2722 kg (6,000 lb)
Dimensions: span 14.63 m (48 ft 0 in); length 10.52 m (34 ft 6 in); height 3.12 m (10 ft 3 in); wing area 31.21 m² (336 sq ft)

de Havilland D.H.90 Dragonfly

The external similarity between the **de Havilland D.H.90 Dragonfly** and the D.H.89 Dragon Rapide belied its very different internal structure, the earlier design's spruce and plywood box fuselage being replaced by a pre-formed plywood monocoque shell strengthened with spruce stringers. The lower wing centre-section was strengthened, making possible deletion of the nacelle/wing root bracing struts and inner bay rigging wires, and so providing easy access to the cabin, with its accommodation for a pilot and four passengers. Powered by two de Havilland Gipsy Major engines, the prototype made its first flight at Hatfield on 12 August 1935 and the first **D.H.90A** production aircraft, with Gipsy Major II engines, flew in February

1936. Production totalled 66 Dragonflies, the type being popular initially with the prominent private owners of the time, both in the UK and abroad, but most were used eventually for commercial purposes. Military purchasers included Canada, Denmark and Sweden.

Specification
de Havilland D.H.90 Dragonfly
Type: light transport
Powerplant: two 97 kW (130 hp) de Havilland Gipsy Major inline piston engines
Performance: maximum speed 232 km/h (144 mph); cruising speed 201 km/h (125 mph); service ceiling 5515 m (18,100 ft); range 1006 km (625 miles)

Weights: empty 1134 kg (2,500 lb); maximum take-off 1814 kg (4,000 lb)
Dimensions: span 13.11 m (43 ft 0 in); length 9.65 m (31 ft 8 in); height 2.79 m (9 ft 2 in); wing area 23.78 m² (256 sq ft)

Intended for luxury touring, the D.H.90 Dragonfly was in effect a scaled-down Rapide. Due to its high purchase price (£2,650 in 1935) it found only a limited market.

de Havilland D.H.91 Albatross

Designed by A. E. Hagg to an Air Ministry specification for a transatlantic mailplane, the **de Havilland D.H.91 Albatross** was aerodynamically and aesthet-

ically one of the outstanding commercial aircraft of the pre-war era. Of wooden construction, it introduced the ply-balsa-ply sandwich fuselage structure later

used so successfully for the Mosquito, and had a one-piece wing similar to that of the Comet. Powerplant consisted of four de Havilland Gipsy Twelve engines driving constant-speed propellers, and the landing gear main units were electrically retractable. The prototype, initially

with twin fins mounted at mid-span on the tailplane, was flown for the first time at Hatfield on 20 May 1937. Flight test results indicated that the vertical tail surfaces were unsatisfactory, and the redesigned tail unit incorporated endplate fins with unbalanced rudders and trim tabs.

Problems with the landing gear retraction system resulted in a wheels-up landing for the first prototype on 31 March 1938, and a structural weakness in the rear fuselage was revealed when the second prototype broke into two a few months later when landing during overload trials. Effective modifications were soon evolved and the two prototypes were repaired and used experimentally by Imperial Airways. However, their range made them particularly useful for a shuttle service between the UK and Iceland, and they were impressed for RAF use with No. 271 Squadron in September 1940. Five Albatrosses, with reduced capacity, additional cabin windows and slotted flaps replacing the split trailing-edge flaps, were delivered to Imperial Airways between October 1938 and June 1939. Providing accommodation for 22 passengers and a crew of four, they saw wartime service on the Bristol-Lisbon and Bristol-Shannon routes until, with their numbers reduced to two by enemy action or accidents, the survivors were scrapped in September 1943.

Specification
de Havilland D.H.91 Albatross
(passenger version)
Type: passenger transport
Powerplant: four 391 kW (525 hp) de Havilland Gipsy Twelve piston engines
Performance: maximum speed 362 km/h (225 mph); cruising speed 338 km/h (210 mph); service ceiling 5455 m (17,900 ft); range 1674 km (1,040 miles)
Weights: empty 9630 kg (21,230 lb); maximum take-off 13381 kg (29,500 lb)
Dimensions: span 32 m (105 ft 0 in); length 21.79 m (71 ft 6 in); height 6.78 m (22 ft 3 in); wing area 100.15 m² (1,078 sq ft)

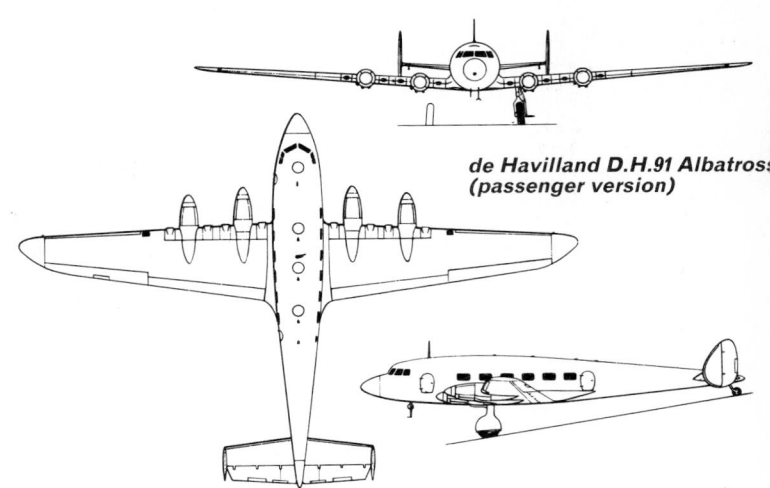

de Havilland D.H.91 Albatross (passenger version)

de Havilland D.H.93 Don

The de Havilland Gipsy Twelve engine installed originally in the D.H.91 Albatross was renamed Gipsy King for military use and selected to power a multi-role trainer designed to Air Ministry Specification T.6/36. This **de Havilland D.H.93 Don** was of wooden stressed-skin construction and was intended for use as a pilot, radio and gunnery trainer. The prototype was flown on 18 June 1937 and following manufacturer's initial trials, during the course of which small auxiliary fins were fitted beneath the tailplane, the aircraft was transferred to Martlesham Heath for official evaluation. Required modifications resulted in increased weight, and heavy equipment (including the turret) had to be removed. Of the original order for 250 Dons only 50 airframes were completed; of this total

The Don was a multi-role trainer, incorporating a rear turret for gunnery instruction. Note the clean engine installation.

20 were delivered as engineless airframes and the remainder converted for communications duties with No. 24 Squadron and a number of station Flights.

Specification
de Havilland D.H.93 Don
Type: communications aircraft
Powerplant: one 391 kW (525 hp) de Havilland Gipsy King 1 inline piston engine
Performance: maximum speed 304 km/h (189 mph) at 2665 m (8,750 ft); service ceiling 7100 m

(23,300 ft); range 1432 km (890 miles)
Weights: empty 2291 kg (5,050 lb); maximum take-off 3112 kg (6,860 lb)
Dimensions: span 14.48 m (47 ft 6 in); length 11.38 m (37 ft 4 in); height 2.87 m (9 ft 5 in); wing area 28.24 m² (304 sq ft)

de Havilland D.H.94 Moth Minor

On 24 August 1931 the company had flown the only example of the **de Havilland D.H.81 Swallow Moth**, a low-wing open-cockpit two-seater powered by a 60 kW (80 hp) Gipsy IV engine. With production capacity filled by orders for various models of the Moth the project was discontinued, to be resurrected some years later when advantage could be taken of some structural techniques used in the Comet and Albatross. Of wooden construction throughout, the prototype **D.H.94 Moth Minor** was first flown by Captain Geoffrey de Havilland at Hatfield on 22 June 1937. Production followed and by the outbreak of World War II some 71 examples had been completed, including nine **Moth Minor Coupé** aircraft with built-up rear fuselages and hinged cabin tops. Early in 1940, when Hatfield's production capacity was required urgently for aircraft more vital to the war effort, the Moth Minor drawings, jigs, components and finished but undelivered airframes were delivered to de Havilland Aircraft Pty Ltd at Bankstown, Sydney. More than 40 were supplied to the Royal Australian Air Force.

Specification
de Havilland D.H.94 Moth Minor
Type: two-seat tourer/trainer
Powerplant: one 67 kW (90 hp) de Havilland Gipsy Minor inline piston engine
Performance: maximum speed 190 km/h (118 mph); cruising speed 161 km/h (100 mph); service ceiling 5030 m (16,500 ft); range 483 km (300 miles)
Weights: empty 446 kg (983 lb);

maximum take-off 703 kg (1,550 lb)
Dimensions: span 11.15 m (36 ft 7 in); length 7.44 m (24 ft 5 in); height 1.93 m (6 ft 4 in); wing area 15.05 m² (162 sq ft)

The Moth Minor was an attempt to continue the earlier success of the D.H.60, but this was largely denied due to the outbreak of World War II.

de Havilland D.H.95 Flamingo

The company's first aircraft of all-metal stressed-skin construction, the **de Havilland D.H.95 Flamingo** was designed by R. E. Bishop as a medium-range passenger transport to carry 12-17 passengers and a crew of three. It featured hydraulically retractable landing gear, split trailing-edge flaps and was powered initially by two 664 kW (890 hp) Bristol Perseus XIIc radial engines. The prototype was first flown by de Havilland chief test pilot Geoffrey de Havilland Jr at Hatfield on 28 December 1938; during subsequent flight testing a third, central fin was fitted temporarily. In May 1939 this aircraft was delivered to Guernsey & Jersey Airways Ltd for route-proving trials, linking Heston and Southampton's Eastleigh Airport with the two principal Channel Islands.

The outbreak of war precluded commercial use on these services, but the Royal Air Force had ordered two Flamingoes for communications duties with No. 24 Squadron and one for The King's Flight, the last being delivered to RAF Benson on 7 September 1940. It was transferred to No. 24 Squadron in February 1941, the unit having acquired also the prototype, two aircraft ordered by civilian customers and the fifth airframe which had been used by the manufacturer for development of the Bristol Perseus XVI radial. This engine was fitted to all subsequent examples, including one used by the Royal Navy's No. 782 Squadron at Donibristle for communications flights to the Orkney and Shetland Islands and to Northern Ireland, and eight flown by BOAC on Middle East services, based at Cairo. The Royal Navy's Flamingo was the only aircraft to return to civil use after the war, seeing limited service with British Air Transport at Redhill where it was scrapped in 1954. Flamingo production totalled 16 aircraft.

Variant
Hertfordshire: this was to have been a fully militarised version, to

320

Specification 19/39, which could carry 22 paratroops. Only the prototype was completed.

Specification
de Havilland D.H.95 Flamingo
Type: medium transport
Powerplant: two 694 kW (930 hp) Bristol Perseus XVI radial piston engines
Performance: maximum speed 385 km/h (239 mph); cruising speed 296 km/h (184 mph); service ceiling 6370 m (20,900 ft); range 1947 km (1,210 miles)
Weights: empty 5137 kg (11,325 lb); maximum take-off 7983 kg (17,600 lb)
Dimensions: span 21.34 m (70 ft 0 in); length 15.72 m (51 ft 7 in); height 4.65 m (15 ft 3 in); wing area 59.36 m² (639 sq ft)

The D.H.95 represened de Havilland's first design, with an all-metal stressed-skin construction.

de Havilland D.H.98 Mosquito

de Havilland Mosquito B.Mk IV of No. 139 Squadron, Royal Air Force, based at Marham, Norfolk in 1942-43.

Designed and planned as a private venture by the de Havilland company in the autumn of 1938, the **de Havilland D.H.98 Mosquito** was intended for use as an unarmed bomber or reconnaissance aircraft, one that would fly so fast and high that defensive armament would be superfluous. The powerplant was to comprise two Rolls-Royce Merlins, and to save strategic materials all-wood construction was chosen. Although this may not now seem a very advanced aircraft, it was certainly far too much for the Air Ministry of that day to swallow and de Havilland's proposal was neatly filed in the 'pending' tray.

It was not until World War II had started that the Air Ministry gave serious thought to the possibility that light alloys might become in short supply. In such circumstances an all-wood aircraft might be a useful ace up the sleeve. Even then, the committal to proceed was only to the extent of authorising detail design and de Havilland's design team began work at the end of December 1939, resulting in an order on 1 March 1940 for 50 aircraft against Air Ministry Specification B.1/40. Even then the way ahead was not clear, for in the post-Dunkirk frenzy of concentration to build up stocks of standard in-production aircraft, de Havilland's new bomber was temporarily postponed.

In due course the programme was reinstated and eventually, on 25 November 1940, the prototype **Mosquito Mk I** was flown for the first time. There was little doubt from factory testing that this new bomber was capable of development into an outstanding aircraft, comfortably exceeding the performance margins of the Specification. When demonstrated to military and government officials shortly afterwards, these sceptical gentlemen discovered that the new bomber had the manoeuvrability of a fighter, a dashing high speed that was not far short of 644 km/h (400 mph), and were staggered to see it performing smooth climbing rolls on the power of one engine, the propeller of the second engine 'feathered' to prevent windmilling and to cut drag to a minimum.

Official trials followed immediately, beginning on 19 February 1941 and leading to the initiation of priority production by July of that year. Three prototypes were built and the last of these to fly, on 10 June 1941, was of a photo-reconnaissance (PR) version. The promised combination of high speed and high altitude had made the Mosquito a natural selection for such a role, and a PR version was the first of these exciting new aircraft to enter operational service. The initial sortie, a daylight reconnaissance over Brest, La Pallice and Bordeaux, was made on 20 September 1941, and immediately confirmed the concept of high speed and no armament as being correct, for during this initial deployment the lone **Mosquito PR.Mk I** was able easily to outpace three Messerschmitt Bf 109s which attempted to intercept.

Next into service was the bomber version, the first being designated **Mosquito B.Mk IV**. Deliveries to the RAF's No. 2 Group began in November 1941, the Mosquitoes going first to No. 105 Squadron, then based at Swanton Morley, Norfolk. The winter months were spent in familiarisation and working up, for the Mosquito was a very different aeroplane from the Bristol Blenheim which it had replaced. This pioneering squadron had not only to learn how to handle a very much faster and more manoeuvrable aircraft, but also how best to deploy it in attacks against the enemy. At that time there must have been some doubt among the crews who were to fly these aircraft of just how this 'plywood' bomber would withstand the enemy's defences. They soon discovered that the Mosquito had an enormous capacity to absorb punishment. By no means did it consist only of plywood, but the strength and flexibility of this material was exploited to the full in its construction. The cantilever wing, mounted in a mid-position, was a one-piece assembly, with plywood used for the spar webs and all skins. Tail unit structure was similar, but the fuselage was entirely different. This consisted of a plywood-balsa-plywood sandwich, built up onto spruce formers, and was constructed in two halves which were completely equipped individually with their appropriate control, pipe and wiring runs before the two halves were united. The retractable tailwheel type landing gear was unusual in that shock absorption dispensed with costly-to-build oleo-pneumatic struts, substituting rubber-in-compression springing. All versions had accommodation for a crew of two, seated side-by-side.

As noted above, the first of the three Mosquito prototypes was a bomber version, and the last intended for photo-reconnaissance. The second, first flown on 15 May 1941, was equipped as a night-fighter, and carrying initially Al Mk IV radar and a nose armament of four 20 mm cannon and four 7.7 mm (0.303 in) machine-guns. Designated **Mosquito NF.Mk II**, the type began to enter service first with No. 157 Squadron, which made its first operational sortie on the night of 27-28 April 1942. The type equipped No. 23 Squadron shortly afterwards, and this was the first unit to operate the type in the Mediterranean theatre when based at Luqa, Malta, from December 1942. These were deployed not only as night-fighters, but also in a day or night intruder role, making the first night intruder sortie on 30-31 December 1942.

The missing one in the versions detailed so far is the **Mosquito T.Mk III**, a dual-control trainer used for conversion to the type, and 343 were constructed. The story of the Mosquito's operational deployment is too extensive to be covered in an A-Z entry such as this; however, the list of variants that follows gives an appreciation of the wide role played by the Mosquito during World War II. The Mosquito was built not only in the UK, but also by the de Havilland factories in Australia and Canada; when production was finally terminated a total of 7,781 had been built.

Many examples of the Mosquito continued to give valuable service in the RAF during the immediate post-war years. Photographic-reconnaissance Mosquitoes were used extensively in the Middle and Far East, and No. 81 Squadron in Malaya was the last unit to use the type operationally, in late 1955. The bomber versions were displaced by English Electric Canberras in 1952-3, some then being used in a training role, with others converted for photo-reconnaissance or target-tug duties. In this latter role some remained in service until 1961. Fighter versions, however, disappeared in the early 1950s, their role taken over by the new-generation of turbine-powered fighters.

Variants
Mosquito PR.Mk IV: reconnaissance conversion from B.Mk IV with provision for up to four cameras
Mosquito B.Mk V: development of B.Mk IV with underwing hardpoints; single prototype only
Mosquito FB.Mk VI: most extensively built version, an intruder or fighter-bomber developed from the F.Mk II fighter prototype: had provision for internal and underwing bombs and, from 1944, for rocket projectiles
Mosquito B.Mk VII: a Canadian-built version based on the B.Mk V prototype
Mosquito PR.Mk VIII: reconnaissance version similar to B.Mk IV but powered by Merlins with two-

Identified by its fuselage codes as an aircraft of No. 487 Squadron, this is a Mosquito FB.Mk VI, complete with bomb on the underwing pylon.

stage superchargers

Mosquito PR.Mk IX: definitive reconnaissance version with two-stage engines and increased fuel capacity

Mosquito B.Mk IX: high-altitude bomber equivalent of PR.Mk IX; modified from 1944 with provision to carry one 1814 kg (4,000 lb) 'blockbuster' bomb

Mosquito NF.Mk X: proposed night-fighter with two-stage engines, not built

Mosquito FB.Mk XI: proposed fighter-bomber with two-stage engines, not built

Mosquito NF.Mk XII: redesignation of NF.Mk II conversions following installation of AI Mk VIII centimetric radar

Mosquito NF.Mk XIII: new production night-fighters, equivalent to the NF.Mk XII conversions

Mosquito NF.Mk XIV: proposed development of the NF.Mk XIII with two-stage engines, not built

Mosquito NF.Mk XV: high-altitude night-fighter with increased wing span, pressure cabin, AI Mk VIII radar and two-stage engines; conversions from B.Mk IV

Mosquito B.Mk XVI: development of the B.Mk IX with pressurised cabin and most with provision to carry a 1814 kg (4,000 lb) bomb

Mosquito PR.Mk XVI: reconnaissance variant of the B.Mk XVI, introducing small astrodome; first pressurised PR version

Mosquito NF.Mk XVII: redesignation of NF.Mk II conversions following installation of American-developed AI Mk X radar

Mosquito FB.Mk XVIII: development of the FB.Mk VI, equipped with 57 mm Molins anti-tank gun, rocket projectiles and increased armour protection; used primarily for attacks on enemy U-boats and shipping

Mosquito NF.Mk XIX: night-fighter development of NF.Mk XIII with 'universal' nose to accept American or British AI radar

Mosquito B.Mk XX: Canadian-built bomber equivalent of the B.Mk IV

Mosquito FB.Mk 21: Canadian-built equivalent of the FB.Mk VI

Mosquito T.Mk 22: Canadian-built equivalent of the T.Mk III

Mosquito B.Mk 23: designation allocated to Canadian equivalent of B.Mk IX, not built

Mosquito FB.Mk 24: designation allocated to a Canadian fighter-bomber with two-stage engines, not built

Mosquito B.Mk 25: Canadian-built development of B.Mk XX with Packard-Merlin engines

Mosquito FB.Mk 26: Canadian-built development of FB.Mk 21 with Packard-Merlin engines

Mosquito T.Mk 27: Canadian-built development of T.Mk 22 with Packard-Merlin engines (note: no 28 designation was used)

Mosquito T.Mk 29: designation allocated to some trainers converted from FB.Mk 26s

Mosquito NF.Mk 30: high-altitude night-fighter with two-stage Merlins and carrying some early ECM equipment

Mosquito NF.Mk 31: designation allocated to proposed version of NF.Mk 30 with Packard-Merlin engines, not built

Mosquito PR.Mk 32: high-altitude reconnaissance version, similar to NF.Mk XV

Mosquito TR.Mk 33: naval torpedo-reconnaissance fighter (Sea Mosquito) for carrier-based operations; similar to FB.Mk VI but including folding wings, arrester gear and detail changes

Mosquito PR.Mk 34: very-long-range reconnaissance version with additional fuel in the 'bulged' bomb bay; main PR type in post-war RAF service

Mosquito B.Mk 35: long-range/higher-altitude development of B.Mk XVI with pressurised cabin; post-war service only

Mosquito NF.Mk 36: generally similar to NF.Mk 30, but with Merlin engines rated for operation at higher altitudes

Mosquito TR.Mk 37: variant of TR.Mk 33, equipped with British-built radar

Mosquito NF.Mk 38: similar to NF.Mk 30, but equipped with British-built radar

Mosquito TT.Mk 39: redesignation of B.Mk XVIs following conversion to target-tugs for service with the Royal Navy

Mosquito FB.Mk 40: Australian-built version of the FB.Mk VI

Mosquito PR.Mk 40: designation of Australian reconnaissance conversions from FB.Mk 40s

Mosquito FB.Mk 41: designation allocated to Australian-built fighter-bomber prototype, similar to FB.Mk 40 but with two-stage engines

Mosquito PR.Mk 41: Australian-built reconnaissance aircraft, a development of the PR.Mk 40 but with two-stage engines

Mosquito FB.Mk 42: designation of single Australian conversion from FB.Mk 40 with Merlin 69 engines

Mosquito T.Mk 43: Australian-built trainer equivalent to T.Mk III

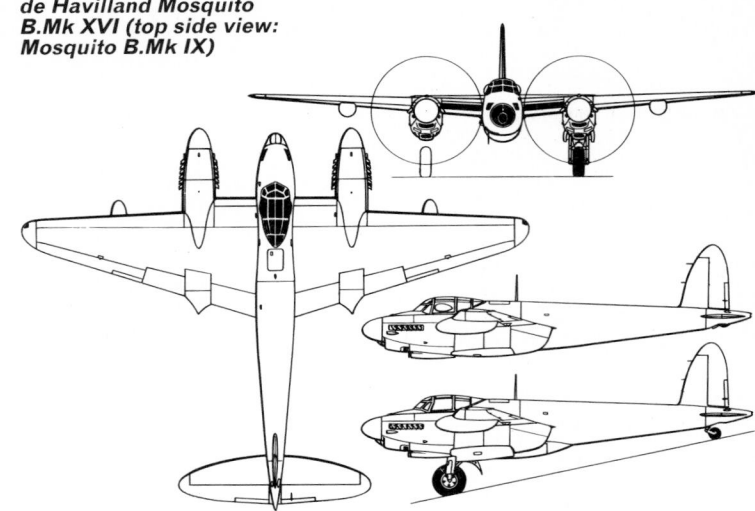

de Havilland Mosquito B.Mk XVI (top side view: Mosquito B.Mk IX)

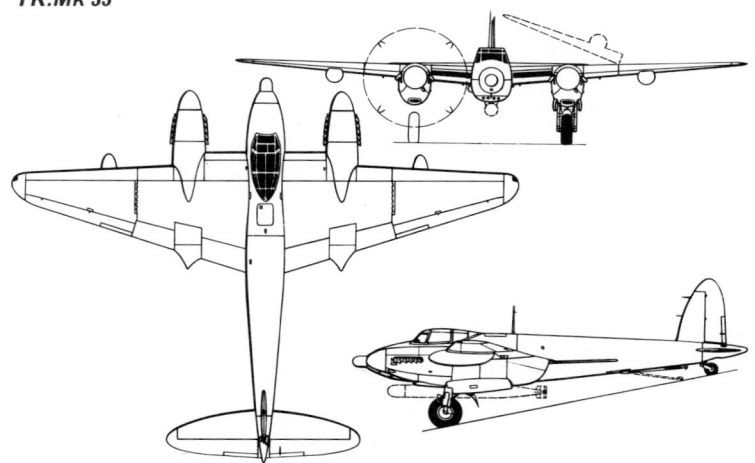

de Havilland Sea Mosquito TR.Mk 33

Specification
de Havilland Mosquito FB.Mk VI
Type: two-seat fighter-bomber
Powerplant: two 1208 kW (1,620 hp) Rolls-Royce Merlin 25 piston engines
Performance: maximum speed 583 km/h (362 mph) at 1675 m (5,500 ft); maximum cruising speed 523 km/h (325 mph) at 4570 m (15,000 ft); service ceiling 10060 m (33,000 ft); range with internal bomb load 2655 km (1,650 miles)
Weights: empty 6486 kg (14,300 lb); maximum take-off 10115 kg (22,300 lb)
Dimensions: span 16.51 m (54 ft 2 in); length 12.47 m (40 ft 10¾ in); height 4.65 m (15 ft 3 in); wing area 42.18 m² (454 sq ft)
Armament: four 20-mm cannon and four 7.7-mm (0.303-in) machine-guns in nose, plus 907 kg (2,000 lb) of bombs, or 454 kg (1,000 lb) of bombs and eight rocket projectiles

de Havilland D.H.100/113/115 Vampire

The **de Havilland D.H.100 Vampire** was the UK's first single-jet fighter, the prototype flying at Hatfield on 29 September 1943, piloted by Geoffrey de Havilland, only 16 months after the beginning of detail design. The type entered service with the RAF in 1946 as the **Vampire F.Mk 1** and a number of this early variant were used for experimental work.

Development led to the **Vampire F.Mk 3**, which eventually replaced the Vampire F.Mk 1s in RAF service, and the Vampire F.Mk 3 was the basis for a series of export Vampires, four going to Norway and 85 to Canada. Arrangements were made for production of the Vampire in Australia and 80 were built by de Havilland Aircraft Pty Ltd, powered by Australian-built Rolls-Royce Nene engines and designated **Vampire FB.Mk 30.** (Three Vampire F.Mk 1s fitted with Nene engines in the UK had been intended as prototypes of the proposed **Vampire F.Mk 2** series.)

A ground-attack version of the Vampire F.Mk 3, with strengthened wing and reduced span, entered production as the **Vampire F.Mk 5** and this attracted a number of export orders. Examples were supplied to Egypt, Finland, France, Iraq, Lebanon, New Zealand, Norway, Sweden and Venezuela. Some standard Vampire FB.Mk 5s were supplied to the Indian and South African air forces, and production licences were negotiated successfully with a number of countries. In Italy, Macchi built 80 **Vampire FB.Mk 52A**s, while Switzerland produced 178 **Vampire F.Mk 6** aircraft and France 67 Vampire FB.Mk 5s. The last were assembled by SNCASE from British-made components, but subsequently SNCASE built 183 Goblin-powered Vampire FB.Mk 5s and 250 **Vampire FB.Mk 53** aircraft with French-built Rolls-Royce Nene engines, in which form they were designated **Sud-Est SE 535 Mistral.** The naval version of the Vampire FB.Mk 5 was the **Sea Vampire F.Mk 20,** of which 30 were delivered to the Fleet Air Arm. The **Sea Vampire F.Mk 21,** of which six were produced, by conversion from Vampire F.Mk 3s, had strengthened bellies for trials with landings on flexible decks.

The last single-seat Vampire variant to see service with the RAF was the **Vampire FB.Mk 9,** a version of the Vampire FB.Mk 5 with cockpit air-conditioning; Vampire FB.Mk 9s were also delivered to Ceylon (Sri Lanka), Jordan and Rhodesia (Zimbabwe). Total UK production of single-seat Vampires amounted to more than 1,900 when the line closed in December 1953. The last single-seaters remaining in military service were about 20 Vampire FB.Mk 6s in Switzerland.

Brief mention must be made of the **D.H.113 Vampire NF.Mk 10,** a two-seat night-fighter development, of which 95 were built, mainly for the RAF A few were delivered to Italy under the designation **Vampire NF.Mk 54,** and 29 ex-RAF aircraft were sold to the Indian air force between 1954 and 1958. No Vampire night-fighters remain.

Experience with the wide side-by-side (Mosquito-type) seating of the Vampire NF.Mk 10 proved invaluable in the development of the **D.H. 115 Vampire Trainer**, flown on 15 November 1950 as a private venture with Martin-Baker ejection seats. The foresight of de Havilland was rewarded by production orders from the RAF and Royal Navy. First RAF deliveries were made in 1952 while those of the RN version, which was basically similar, began in 1954; the respective designations were **Vampire T.Mk 11** and **Sea Vampire T.Mk 22**. More than 530 went to the RAF and 73 to the RN from a total UK production of 804, completed in 1958. Export deliveries, as **Vampire T.Mk 55s**, were made to Austria (5), Burma (8), Ceylon/Sri Lanka (5), Chile (5), Egypt (12), Eire (6), Finland (5), India (5), Indonesia (8), Iraq (6), Lebanon (3), New Zealand (2), Norway (4), Portugal (2), South Africa (21), Sweden (57), Switzerland (39), Syria (2) and Venezuela (6). Ex-RAF Vampire T.Mk 11s were supplied to Jordan (2) and Rhodesia/Zimbabwe (4). Additionally, 109 were built in Australia under the designations **Vampire T.Mks 33, 34** and **35**, and 50 were assembled in India. 15 Vampire T.Mk 55s were still in service in Switzerland until 1990.

Vampire FB.Mk 9s of the RAF College put up a formation. The FB.Mk 9 was the last RAF single-seat version before Venoms took over. The type had air conditioning for the cockpit.

Specification
D.H.100 Vampire FB.Mk 6
Type: single-seat jet fighter-bomber
Powerplant: one 1520 kg (3,350 lb) thrust D.H. Goblin 3 turbojet
Performance: maximum speed 882 km/h (548 mph) at 9145 m (30,000 ft); service ceiling 13045 m (42,800 ft); range 1963 km (1,220 miles)

Weights: empty 3304 kg (7,283 lb); maximum take-off 5620 kg (12,390 lb)
Dimensions: span 11.58 m (38 ft 0 in); length 9.37 m (30 ft 9 in); height 2.69 m (8 ft 10 in); wing area 24.34 m² (262 sq ft)

Armament: four 20 mm cannon in nose, plus provision for underwing stores including eight 27.2 kg (60 lb) rockets, or two 454 kg (1,000 lb) bombs, or two drop-tanks

de Havilland D.H.103 Hornet/Sea Hornet

Designed as a scaled-down version of the Mosquito and retaining its ply/balsa/ply method of fuselage construction, but with a new wood-and-metal wing, the **de Havilland D.H.103 Hornet** was evolved as a long-range fighter, principally for use against the Japanese. Specification F.12/43 was written around the original private-venture design and work began in June 1943. The prototype flew for the first time at Hatfield on 28 July 1944, piloted by Geoffrey de Havilland Jnr: it was powered by a pair of Merlin 130/131 engines, which were of reduced frontal area, and each turned its four-bladed de Havilland Hydromatic propeller inward to overcome the normal tendency of an aircraft to swing during take-off or landing. Initial deliveries to the Royal Air Force were made in April 1945 and the first squadron, No. 64, was formed at RAF Horsham St Faith in May 1946. Although too late to see active service during World War II, the Hornet was used as a ground-attack aircraft during anti-terrorist operations in Malaysia, entering service with No. 33 Squadron in March 1951. The last RAF Hornet unit, No. 45 Squadron, re-equipped with Vampires in June 1955.

A naval version of the Hornet was included in early project planning and it became the first British single-seat twin-engined carrier-based fighter. Three **Sea Hornet** prototypes were converted from Hornet F.Mk 1 airframes, the first of these making its maiden flight on 19 April 1945. The first fully-navalised prototype (the last of the three) was engineered by Heston Aircraft Company Ltd to Specification N.5/44 and featured folding wings, arrester hook, tail-down accelerator gear and naval radio and radar. Revised main landing gear legs were fitted to absorb the high rates of descent inherent in deck operations. Operational trials were carried out with No. 703 Squadron and the first front-line squadron was No. 801, commissioned at RNAS Ford on 1 June 1947. Sea Hornets remained in service with Fleet Requirements Units as late as 1955.

Variants
Hornet F.Mk 1: initial production version, 60 built, of which the first was delivered to Boscombe Down on 28 February 1945
Hornet PR.Mk 2: a Mk 1 conversion with cameras mounted in the rear fuselage
Hornet F.Mk 3: the most prolific of the land-based Hornets with a dorsal fillet (later fitted retrospectively to earlier Marks) and internal fuel capacity increased: attachment points provided under each wing for a drop tank, alternative loads being a 1,000 lb bomb or rocket projectiles; 120 built, initially at Hatfield but at Chester from late 1948
Hornet FR.Mk 4: the last Hornet F.Mk 3s were completed to this standard, with rear fuselage fuel tank removed to accommodate a single F.52 camera
Sea Hornet F.Mk 20: 78 production aircraft with similar armament to that

carried by the Hornet F.Mk 3; the first was flown on 13 August 1946 and the last delivery was made on 12 June 1951
Sea Hornet NF.Mk 21: two-seat night-fighter version, used also as a strike formation lead aircraft; developed by Heston Aircraft Company, the first prototype was a Hornet F.Mk 1 conversion with non-folding wings, but with ASH radar nose and flame-damped exhausts; first flown on 9 July 1946, 79 were built, the last in November 1950
Sea Hornet PR.Mk 22: 43 aircraft similar to the Sea Hornet F.Mk 20, but with two F.52 cameras or one Fairchild K.19B camera, the latter for night photography

Specification
de Havilland Hornet F.Mk 3
Type: single-seat fighter
Powerplant: two 1544 kW (2,070 hp) Rolls-Royce Merlin 130/131 piston engines

Production Sea Hornet F.Mk 20s of No. 801 Squadron. The type served with this squadron from July 1947 to April 1951, augmented by camera-carrying PR.Mk 22s. Later the Fleet Air Arm received the two-seat NF.Mk 21 night fighter, which was appreciably slower.

Performance: maximum speed 760 km/h (472 mph) at 6705 m (22,000 ft); initial climb rate 1417 m (4,650 ft) per minute; service ceiling 10670 m (35,000 ft); range 4828 km (3,000 miles)
Weights: empty 5842 kg (12,880 lb); maximum take-off 9480 kg (20,900 lb)
Dimensions: span 13.72 m (45 ft 0 in); length 11.18 m (36 ft 8 in); height 4.32 m (14 ft 2 in); wing area 33.54 m² (361 sq ft)
Armament: four 20 mm guns in the nose plus up to 907 kg (2,000 lb) of bombs or rockets under the wings

de Havilland D.H.104 Dove

To provide a post-war replacement for the D.H.89 Dragon Rapide biplane transport, which had also seen extensive service with the Royal Air Force and Royal Navy as the Dominie, the de Havilland design team under R. E. Bishop's leadership in 1944 evolved a new low-wing monoplane which, with the exception of fabric-covered elevators and rudder, was of all-metal construction. Powerplant consisted of two de Havilland Gipsy Queen engines, and their constant-speed fully-feathering and reversible-pitch propellers made the **de Havilland D.H.104 Dove** the first British transport aircraft to use reversible-pitch propellers for braking assistance. Standard accommodation as a transport was for 8 to 11 passengers.

First flown on 25 September 1945, the prototype soon demonstrated that there was little wrong with the basic design. Apart from the addition of a dorsal fin at an early stage of development to improve stability with one engine out, much later of a redesigned elevator, and of a domed roof to give a little more headroom on the flight deck, production aircraft were generally similar to the original prototype.

The Dove production variants resulted from differing Gipsy Queen powerplants, these including the 246 kW (330 hp) Gipsy Queens 71 and 70-3 powering the prototype and the Dove 1/2 respectively; 254 kW (340 hp) Gipsy Queen 70-4 in the Dove 1B/2B; 283 kW (380 hp) Gipsy Queen 70-2 in the Dove 5/6, and 298 kW (400 hp) Gipsy Queen 70-3 in the Dove 7/8. A number of Dove

conversions carried out subsequently by Riley Aircraft in the USA as the **Riley Turbo Executive 400** introduced 298 kW (400 hp) Avco Lycoming IO-72-A1A flat-eight piston engines. A more ambitious conversion by Carstedt Inc. at Long Beach, California introduced two 451 kW (605 ehp) Garrett AirResearch TPE331 turboprop engines and a lengthened fuselage to accommodate 18 commuter passengers. Named **Carstedt Jet Liner 600**, the type was supplied primarily to Apache Airlines.

Like the Rapide, which it superseded and supplemented (replaced is an unsuitable word, for Rapides just went on flying), the Dove proved to be reliable and popular, and 542 were built before production ended in 1968. Of these just over 100 were supplied under the name Devon to many air forces, including the RAF, and a small number went to the Royal Navy with the name Sea Devon. In addition to the light transport role for which they were intended, many have served as business, executive, and VIP aircraft.

Variants

Dove 1: initial production version for up to 11 passengers
Dove 2: first executive version, with seating for six passengers
Dove 1B and **2B:** Mks 1 and 2

This de Havilland Dove was a Mk 8 used by British Aerospace as a corporate transport. A modest number still remain in service in this role.

retrofitted with uprated powerplant installation
Dove 3: projected high-altitude survey version
Dove 4: company designation for 39 examples of the RAF **Devon C. Mk.1**, 13 examples of the RN **Sea Devon C.Mk 20**, and others for export
Dove 5: uprated equivalent of Mk 1, with maximum take-off weight increased to 3992 kg (8,800 lb) and payload boosted by 20 per cent on 805 km (500 mile) stages
Dove 6: uprated equivalent of Mk 2, with same performance gains as Mk 5
Dove 6B: version of Mk 6 cleared to a maximum of 3856 kg (8,500 lb)
Dove 7: upengined version of Mk 1 series
Dove 8: upengined version of Mk 2 series

Dove 8A: version of Mk 8 for US market, for which it was designated **Custom Dove 600**

Specification
de Havilland Dove 7 and 8
Type: light transport
Powerplant: two 298 kW (400 hp) de Havilland Gipsy Queen 70-3 inline piston engines
Performance: maximum speed 378 km/h (235 mph); cruising speed 261 km/h (162 mph); service ceiling 6615 m (21,700 ft); range 1891 km (1,175 miles)
Weights: empty 2985 kg (6,580 lb); maximum take-off 4060 kg (8,950 lb)
Dimensions: span 17.37 m (57 ft 0 in); length 11.99 m (39 ft 4 in); height 4.06 m (13 ft 4 in); wing area 31.12 m² (335.00 sq ft)

de Havilland D.H.106 Comet

The Brabazon Committee's Specification IV for a post-war jet airliner met with an initial response from de Havilland in 1944, although it was to be 27 July 1949 before John Cunningham lifted the first prototype **de Havilland D.H.106 Comet** from the Hatfield runway on a 31-minute maiden flight. Of all-metal construction and powered by four of the newly certificated de Havilland Ghost 50 turbojet engines, the aircraft began an intensive programme of test flights, among which were a number of overseas trips. These included London-Castel Benito on 25 October 1949 and London-Rome, London-Copenhagen and London-Cairo in early 1950. Tropical tests were undertaken at Khartoum and high-altitude take-off tests at Nairobi. The second prototype was flown on 27 July 1950, and in April 1951 it was delivered to the BOAC Comet Unit at Hurn, with flights to Johannesburg, Delhi and Singapore contributing to a 500-hour programme of proving flights and crew training. BOAC's nine examples of the **Comet 1**, with multi-wheel bogies replacing the prototypes' single main wheels, were delivered between January 1951 and September 1952. After scheduled services to South Africa (with freight only) began in January 1952, following the issue of a certificate of airworthiness on 22 January, the world's first jet passenger service was inaugurated between London and Johannesburg on 2 May 1952. London-Tokyo became a Comet route on 3 April 1953.

Just a month later, on 2 May 1953, a Comet crashed in unexplained circumstances soon after take-off from Calcutta. Following two similar accidents, on 10 January and 8 April 1954, in which the aircraft crashed into the Mediterranean, the fleet was grounded. A subsequent investigation revealed the

cause to be structural failure of the pressure cabin, and although the Comets 2s being built for BOAC were modified for Royal Air Force service, more than four years elapsed before Comet 4s were able to resume commercial operations.

Variants

Comet 1A: basically as Comet 1 but with fuel capacity increased and with provision for water methanol injection; 10 aircraft were built, including two each for Canadian Pacific Airlines and the Royal Canadian Air Force, and three each for Air France and Union Aeromaritime de Transport
Comet 2X: one aircraft only, a Mk 1 airframe powered by Rolls-Royce Avon 502 engines and flown as a development aircraft for the Comet 2; first flight on 16 February 1952
Comet 2: incorporating a 0.91 m (3 ft) fuselage 'stretch' and increased fuel capacity to increase the range by some 563 km (350 miles), the 44-seat Comet 2 was powered by four 2948 kg (6,500 lb) thrust Rolls-Royce Avon 503 engines; the first of 12 ordered by BOAC was flown on 27 August 1953, but following the Mk 1 crashes the completed airframes were rebuilt with rounded cabin windows and heavier-gauge skinning; 10 were delivered to RAF Transport Command for use by No. 216 Squadron, comprising two **Comet T.Mk 2** crew trainers and eight **Comet C.Mk 2** transports; three more were fitted with specialised electronics and served with Nos 51 and 192 Squadrons of No. 90 Group; RAF Comet Mk 2s were withdrawn in April 1967
Comet 2E: two aircraft with Avon 504s in the inner nacelles and Avon 524s in the outer positions, and used by BOAC for proving flights during

1957-8 pending certification and delivery of the Comet 4
Comet 3: one aircraft only, first flown on 19 July 1954 and powered by Avon 523 engines; an 5.64 m (18 ft 6 in) increase in fuselage length allowed up to 78 passengers to be carried and additional fuel capacity was provided in the form of pinion tanks on the wings; it served later as development aircraft for the cropped-wing Comet
Comet 4: production version of the Mk 3 for North Atlantic operations, powered by 4763 kg (10,500 lb) thrust Avon 524 engines and seating up to 78 passengers; 19 Comet 4s were ordered by BOAC and the first made its maiden flight on 27 April 1958; eastbound and westbound services linking London and New York were inaugurated simultaneously on 4 October 1958; production totalled 27, including six for Aerolineas Argentinas and two for East African Airways
Comet 4B: designed for operation over shorter stage lengths; had a longer (35.97 m 118 ft) fuselage accommodating up to 99 passengers, a clipped wing of 32.87 m (107 ft 10 in) span, and no pinion tanks; the Comet 4B was built for British European Airways (14) and Olympic Airways (four), the first example flying on 27 June 1959
Comet 4C: final production version, combining the stretched fuselage of

G-ALZK was the second prototype Comet 1, seen wearing BOAC colours. The aircraft first flew on 27 July 1950.

the Comet 4B with the wing of the Comet 4; the first of three for Mexicana was used for certification and development flying and had its maiden flight on 31 October 1959; other customers comprised Aerolineas Argentinas (1), East African Airways (1), King Ibn Saud (1), Kuwait Airways (2), Middle East Airlines (4), Misrair (9), Royal Aircraft Establishment (1), Royal Air Force (5) and Sudan Airways (2); two additional aircraft were converted as prototypes for the Nimrod maritime patrol aircraft

Specification
de Havilland Comet 4
Type: long-range passenger transport
Powerplant: four 5216 kg (11,500 lb) thrust Rolls-Royce Avon 524 turbojets
Performance: cruising speed 809 km/h (503 mph); cruising altitude 12800 m (42,000 ft); range with full payload 5190 km (3,225 miles)
Weights: empty 34212 kg (75,424 lb); maximum take-off 73482 kg (162,000 lb)
Dimensions: span 35.00 m (114 ft 10 in); length 33.99 m (111 ft 6 in); height 8.99 m (29 ft 6 in); wing area 197.04 m² (2,121.00 sq ft)

de Havilland D.H.108
to
de Havilland Canada DHC-4 Caribou

de Havilland D.H.108

Built to Air Ministry Specification E.18/45, the **de Havilland D.H.108** was developed to conduct research into the characteristics of swept wings in support of the D.H.106 Comet and D.H.110 programmes. The first prototype, a standard Vampire fuselage mounting a mid-set wing with a sweep angle of 43°, and with elevons which acted as elevators and ailerons (there being no horizontal tail surfaces), was a low-speed test vehicle with a maximum speed of 451 km/h (280 mph). It had anti-spin parachutes in wing-tip containers and fixed Handley Page leading-edge slots, both precautions against loss of lateral control at low speeds, and was first flown by Geoffrey de Havilland Jnr on 15 May 1946 at Woodbridge, Suffolk. A modified 45° swept wing with powered flying controls and automatic slats was fitted to the second prototype, which was flown in June 1946 and was intended to explore the transonic area of the flight envelope. Sadly, the aircraft broke up in flight on 27 September and Geoffrey de Havilland Jnr was killed. A

The third D.H.108 could be identified from its predecessors by its more pointed nose and improved cockpit streamlining. It was the first British aircraft to break the sound barrier.

third D.H.108, powered by a 1701-kg (3,750-lb) thrust Goblin 4 engine, made its first flight at Hatfield on 24 July 1947 piloted by de Havilland's new chief test pilot, John Cunningham. Identified by its longer, pointed nose and more streamlined cockpit canopy, this aircraft became the first in Britain to exceed the speed of sound, flown by John Derry on 9 September 1948. Earlier, on 12 April 1948, the same pilot had flown it in a successful attempt on the 100-km (62.1-mile) closed-circuit speed record, raising this to 974.02 km/h (605.23 mph). It was destroyed in a fatal crash on 15 February 1950, as was the first prototype on 1 May.

Specification
de Havilland D.H.108 (second

prototype)
Type: single-seat research aircraft
Powerplant: one 1497-kg (3,300-lb) thrust de Havilland Goblin 3 turbojet
Performance: maximum speed 1030 km/h (640 mph)

Weight: maximum take-off 4064 kg (8,960 lb)
Dimensions: span 11.89 m (39 ft 0 in); length 7.47 m (24 ft 6 in); wing area 30.47 m² (328.0 sq ft)

de Havilland D.H.110 Sea Vixen

Designed originally as a land-based all-weather fighter for the Royal Air Force, in competition with the Gloster Javelin, the **de Havilland D.H.110** was flown in prototype form on 26 September 1951, a second aircraft joining the programme on 25 July 1952. In the autumn of 1954 the latter aircraft undertook 'touch-and-go' trials on HMS *Albion* and the first naval order was placed in January 1955. The de Havilland factory at Christchurch was entrusted with the **Sea Vixen** programme and a partially navalised prototype was first flown on 20 June 1955. It made the first full-stop arrested landing, aboard HMS *Ark Royal*, on 5 April 1956. The first of the initial production order for 45 **Sea Vixen FAW.Mk 1** aircraft introduced a hinged and pointed radome, power-folding wings and hydraulically steerable nosewheel; this aircraft flew for the first time on 20 March 1957. Following service trials with Y Flight of No. 700 Squadron in November 1958, aboard HMS *Victorious* and HMS *Centaur*, the type became operational with No. 892 Squadron which was formed at Yeovilton on 2 July 1959 and went to sea in HMS *Ark Royal* in March 1960. A total of 114 Sea Vixen FAW.Mk 1s was built at Christchurch and Chester.

Variants
Sea Vixen FAW.Mk 2: developed version with additional fuel capacity in the forward sections of the tail booms, which were extended forward of the wings, and provision for four Red Top missiles in place of the Firestreaks carried by the Mk 1; two development aircraft, converted from Mk 1s, were flown on 1 June and 17 August 1962 and later brought up to full Sea Vixen FAW.Mk 2 standard at Chester; 14 Mk 1s were completed as Mk 2s on the line, the first flying on 8 March 1963, and 15 were newly built; 67 conversions were made from Mk 1s; the Sea Vixen FAW.Mk 2 entered service in December 1963 with No. 899 Squadron, which embarked in HMS *Eagle* a year later, and which was a component of her air group when she was finally decommissioned in 1972.

Specification
de Havilland Sea Vixen
Type: two-seat all-weather strike fighter
Powerplant: two 5094-kg (11,230-lb) thrust Rolls-Royce Avon 208 turbojets
Performance: maximum speed 1110 km/h (690 mph) at sea level; climb to 3050 m (10,000 ft) in 1 minute 30

Easily identified by the tailboom extensions forward of the wing, the Sea Vixen FAW.Mk 2 had extra fuel and could carry Red Top missiles in place of the FAW.Mk 1's Firestreak.

seconds; service ceiling 21790 m (48,000 ft)
Weight: maximum take-off 18858 kg (41,575 lb)
Dimensions: span 15.54 m (51 ft 0 in); length 17.02 m (55 ft 7 in); height 3.28 m (10 ft 9 in); wing area 60.20 m² (648.0 sq ft)

Armament: four Red Top air-to-air missiles for two retractable fuselage containers each with 51-mm (14.2-in) rocket projectiles, plus four 227 kg (500 lb) bombs or Bullpup air-to-surface missiles on underwing racks

de Havilland D.H. 112 Venom

Developed from the Vampire, the **de Havilland D.H.112 Venom** single-seat fighter-bomber was intended to gain maximum performance benefit from the higher-thrust versions of the de Havilland Ghost turbojet. Known initially as the **Vampire FB.Mk 8,** it was redesignated subsequently as a result of extensive changes in the design and was identified easily from its predecessor by

one conspicuous feature, a new wing. This had a straight trailing edge instead of the tapered wings of the Vampire, was of thinner section and, to add to ease of identification, was equipped to carry jettisonable wingtip fuel tanks.

The first Venom prototype was flown at Hatfield on 2 September 1949, and the Venom FB.Mk 1 became operational with the RAF just under three years later,

in August 1952. The type saw service in Germany, the Near East and Far East, equipping 19 squadrons, as well as No. 14 Squadron, Royal New Zealand Air Force. Two-seat Venom NF.Mk 2 and NF.Mk 3 fighters served between 1953 and 1957, and the Royal Swedish air force flew the type until 1960. Foreign users of Venom fighter-bombers included Iraq and Venezuela.

Following successful manufacture and use of Vampire FB.Mk 6s, Switzerland made arrangements to build the

Venom under licence. Using the same consortium that had produced the Vampire, comprising the Federal Aircraft Factory (EFW) at Emmen, Pilatus at Stans and the Flug und Fahrzeugwerke at Altenrhein, work began in 1953 on a batch of 150 Venom Mk 50s completed to FB.Mk 1 standard. A further batch of 100, to FB.Mk 4 standard, was completed by 1957. They were replaced by F-5s in the mid-1980s. Few would disagree that the Venom gave remarkable service, and, operating from airfields in mountain valleys up to 1400 m (4,500 ft) above sea level, the aircraft's manoeuvrability proved a great asset. Modifications introduced by the Swiss included a redesigned nose housing UHF communications, strengthening of the inner wing sections to allow the use of rocket-launchers, and introduction of link collectors beneath the cannon.

Royal Navy evaluation of the Venom led to development of a two-seat carrier-based all-weather fighter, the initial production version being designated Sea Venom FAW.Mk 20. These had strengthening for catapult take-offs, power-operated folding wings, arrester gear and naval equipment. Equiping the Fleet Air Arm in 1954, the type saw service also with the Royal Australian Navy and French Aéronavale.

Variants

Venom FB.Mk 1: initial production version for RAF with a 2200-kg (4,850-lb) thrust de Havilland Ghost 103 engine
Venom NF.Mk 2: night-fighter version of Venom FB.Mk 1 incorporating a new fuselage; this was widened to accommodate pilot and radar operator side-by-side and had an extended nose to house AI radar
Venom NF.Mk 2A: redesignation of Venom NF.Mk 2s following incorporation of a clear-view canopy and tail unit modifications
Venom NF.Mk 3: improved version of Venom NF.Mk 2 with power-operated ailerons, tail unit modifications, powered jettison system for canopy and uprated Ghost 104 engine developing 3345 kg (4,950 lb) thrust
Venom FB.Mk 4: improved version of Venom FB.Mk1 with power-operated ailerons, redesigned tail unit and ejection seat
Venom FB.Mk 50: export version of the Venom FB.Mk 1, supplied to Iraq and Italy, and 150 built in Switzerland under licence for Swiss air force
Venom NF.Mk 51: version of Venom NF.MK 2 built for Royal Swedish air force (which designated them **J33**), and powered by Ghost engines built by Svenska Flygmotor in Sweden
Sea Venom FAW.Mk 20: initial version of Sea Venom
Sea Venom FAW.Mk 21: improved version of Sea Venom FAW.Mk 20 with power-operated ailerons, clear-view jettisonable canopy, uprated Ghost 104 engine, ejection seats and

This is a Sea Venom FAW.Mk 22, the navalised night fighter version. Cannon armament was augmented by two Firestreaks.

long-stroke landing gear
Sea Venom FAW.Mk 22: improved version of Sea Venom FAW.Mk 21 with uprated Ghost 105 engine, AAMs and ejection seats
Sea Venom Mk 52: UK designation of version built in France for the Aéronavale (see Aquilon below)
Sea Venom FAW.Mk 53: designation of Sea Venom for service with Royal Australian Navy; generally similar to Sea Venom FAW.Mk 21, with radar and equipment to RAN requirements
Aquilon 20: designation of four Sea Venom FAW.Mk 20s assembled in France and powered by Fiat-built Ghost 48 engines developing 2195 kg (4,840 lb) thrust
Aquilon 201: one-off French licence-built prototype with short-stroke landing gear and ejection seats
Aquilon 202: French licence-built production version with long-stroke landing gear
Aquilon 203: French licence-built production version with short-stroke landing gear, single-seat accommodation and fire-control radar
Aquilon 204: French licence-built two-seat trainer version

Specification
de Havilland Sea Venom FAW.Mk.22
Type: carrier-based all-weather fighter
Powerplant: one 2404-kg (5,300-lb) thrust de Havilland Ghost 105 turbojet
Performance: maximum speed 925 km/h (575 mph); initial climb rate 1753 m (5,750 ft) per minute; service ceiling 12190 m (40,000 ft); range 1135 km (705 miles)
Weight: maximum take-off 7167 kg (15,800 lb)
Dimensions: span 13.08 m (36 ft 7 in); length 11.15 m (36 ft 7 in); height 2.60 m (8 ft 1/4 in); wing area 25.99 m² (279.75 sq ft)
Armament: four 20-mm cannon, and provision for two Firestreak air-to-air missiles, or two 454-kg (1,000-lb) bombs, or eight rockets

One of the RAF's night fighter version was the Venom NF.Mk 3, which had an uprated engine and powered ailerons.

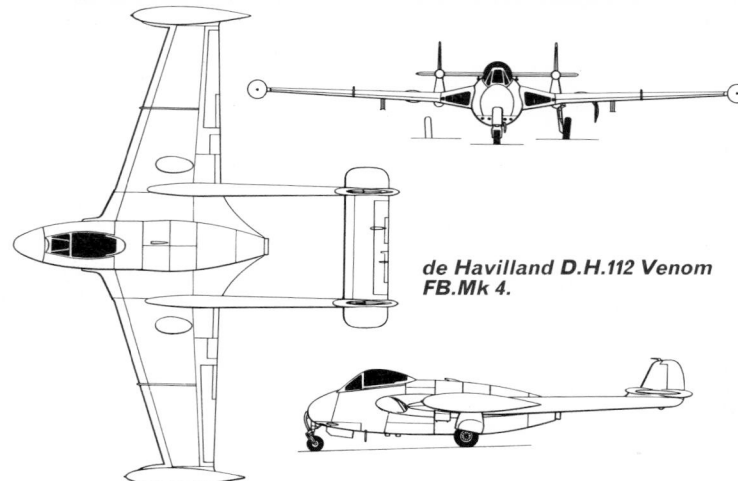

de Havilland D.H.112 Venom FB.Mk 4.

de Havilland D.H. 114 Heron

Adopting the same philosophy that had produced the highly successful four-engined D.H.86B after the D.H. 84 Dragon, de Havilland continued the success of the Dove by designing a scaled-up version designated **de Havilland D.H.114 Heron**. Simplicity and reliability were the keynotes for the new aircraft, which provided accommodation for a crew of two and 14 passengers (17 if no toilet was installed). Fixed tricycle landing gear eliminated the complications of a hydraulic system, and excellent short-field performance was assured by good wing design coupled with the use of variable-pitch propellers, driven by Gipsy Queen 30s which had a long operating period between overhauls. The prototype (G-ALZL) was flown for the first time on 10 May 1950.

The first production **Heron 1** was acquired by New Zealand National Airways, this and all subsequent aircraft

having a tailplane with considerable dihedral. The seventh production example served as the prototype for the **Heron 2**, incorporating retractable landing gear which gave an increase in speed and a reduction in fuel consumption. This proved to be the most popular version, representing almost 70 per cent of the 150 Herons built. Despite these relatively small production figures, the

Heron saw service in 30 countries, some with major airlines, many as luxury transports (including four operated by The Queen's Flight at RAF Benson), and about 25 of the total were used as communications aircraft by nine military services.

In their later years Herons were the subject of a number of modification programmes, the **Riley Turbo Skyliner**

Riley Turbo Skyliner (modified D.H.114 Heron 2) of Californian regional airline Baja Cortez Airlines.

produced by the Riley Turbostream Corporation in the USA being typical of re-engined aircraft. This replaced the standard powerplant by 216-kW (290-hp)

Avco Lycoming IO-540 engines, with or without turbochargers according to customer requirements. Far more ambitious was the conversion carried out by Saunders Aircraft Corporation of Gimli, Manitoba. Designated **Saunders ST-27**, this had a fuselage lengthened by 2.59 m (8 ft 6 in) to provide accommodation for a maximum of 23 passengers, the wing rebuilt to incorporate a redesigned main spar and the four Gipsy engines replaced by two 559-kW (750-shp) Pratt & Whitney Aircraft of Canada PT6A-34 turboprop engines. A total of 12 ST-27 conversions was completed and the prototype of an improved **ST-28** was built before Saunders went into receivership.

Variants
Heron 1B: version of Heron 1 certificated for operation at the higher take-off weight of 5897 kg (13,000 lb)

Heron 2A: designation of single Heron 2 sold in the USA
Heron 2B: version of Heron 2 operating at same take-off weight as Heron 1B
Heron 2C: redesignation of Heron 2Bs with optional fully-feathering propellers
Heron 2D: designation of aircraft with luxury interiors and certificated at take-off weight of 6123 kg (13,500 lb)
Heron 2E: designation of a custom-built aircraft with special VIP interior
Heron 3: two VIP aircraft for The Queen's Flight
Heron 4: one VIP aircraft for The Queen's Flight
Sea Heron C.Mk 20: Royal Navy designation of ex-civil Heron 2s (3) and 2Bs (2) acquired in 1961

Specification
de Havilland Heron 2D

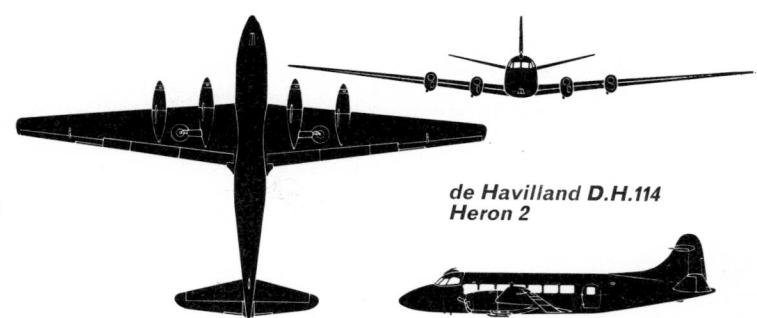

de Havilland D.H.114 Heron 2

Type: light transport
Powerplant: four 186-kW (250-hp) de Havilland Gipsy Queen 30-2 inline piston engines
Performance: cruising speed 295 km/h (183 mph); at 2438 m (8,000 ft); service ceiling 5640 m

(18,500 ft); range 1473 km (915 miles)
Weights: empty 3697 kg (8,150 lb); maximum take-off 6123 kg (13,500 lb)
Dimensions: span 21.79 m (71 ft 6 in); length 14.78 m (48 ft 6 in); height 4.75 m (15 ft 7 in); wing area 46.36 m² (499.0 sq ft)

de Havilland Australia DHA-3 Drover

Australia's famous Flying Doctor Service began in the late 1920s, with QANTAS using a D.H.50 to fly the world's first service of this type; in the first year the doctor made 50 flights, saw 250 patients and covered 32187 km (20,000 miles).

A series of other standard aircraft continued the service. Something larger was required after World War II, and the new **de Havilland Australia DHA-2 Drover** eight-seat light transport was chosen. The Drover was based broadly on the D.H.104 Dove, but had three 108-kW (145-hp) Gipsy Major 10 Mk 2 engines and tail-wheel landing gear. The prototype Drover flew on 23 January 1948 and versions were offered with variable- and fixed-pitch propellers as the **Drover 1** and **Drover 1F** respectively; the **Drover 2** had double-slotted flaps. Limited construction began in 1949 and 20 had been built when production ended in September 1953.

After fitment with Lycoming engines in place of the Gipsy majors, all six Drover 3s flew with Australia's Royal Flying Doctor Service.

Customers for the Drover included Qantas, Trans-Australian Airlines and Fiji Airways, the last being the only export customer. In Royal Flying Doctor Service the Drover carried two medical staff and two stretcher patients; all six aircraft were converted in 1960 to have Avco Lycoming O-360 engines under the revised designation **Drover 3**.

Specification
de Havilland Drover 3
Type: eight-seat utility transport
Powerplant: three 134-kW (180-hp) Avco Lycoming O-360-A1A flat-four piston engines
Performance: maximum speed

254 km/h (158 mph); cruising speed 225 km/h (140 mph); service ceiling 6095 m (20,000 ft); range 1448 km (900 miles)
Weights: empty 1860 kg (4,100 lb);

maximum take-off 2948 kg (6,500 lb)
Dimensions: span 17.37 m (57 ft 0 in); length 11.13 m (36 ft 6 in); height 3.28 m (10 ft 9 in); wing area 30.19 m² (325.0 sq ft)

de Havilland Canada DHC-1 Chipmunk

The **de Havilland Canada DHC-1 Chipmunk** was designed to succeed de Havilland's classic Tiger Moth biplane trainer. Flying for the first time at Downsview, Toronto on 22 May 1946, the tandem-seat stressed-skin monoplane was the first indigenous design of de Havilland Aircraft of Canada Ltd. The prototype, put through its paces by Pat Fillingham from the parent company at Hatfield, was powered by a 108-kW (145-hp) de Havilland Gipsy Major 1C.

Chipmunks built to the prototype's specification were designated DHC-1B-1, while those with a Gipsy Major 10-3 were designated DHC-1B-2. Most Canadian-built Chipmunks had a bubble canopy.

Downsview built 218 Chipmunks, the last in 1951. Two were evaluated by the Aeroplane and Armament Experimental Establishment at Boscombe Down. As a result, the fully-aerobatic Chipmunk was ordered from Hatfield and Chester to Specification 8/48 as an *ab initio* trainer for the RAF.

The RAF received 735 Chipmunks out of 1,014 manufactured in the UK. The first to wear RAF roundels were flown by the Oxford University Air Squadron from February 1950; thereafter, the type replaced the Tiger Moth with all 17 university air squadrons, as well as equipping many RAF Volunteer Reserve flying schools in the early 1950s. National ser-

vice pilots underwent their initial training on the 'Chip', which served intermittently at the RAF College, Cranwell.

A few Chipmunks of No. 114 Squadron were pressed into service in Cyprus on internal security flights during the troubles of 1958.

Under an agreement concluded between de Havilland and the General Aeronautical Material Workshops (OGMA) of Portugal 60 Chipmunks were licence-manufactured from 1955 for the Portuguese air force, and the type was still being operated by this service until replaced in 1989. Other users included Burma, Ceylon, Chile, Colombia, Denmark, Egypt, Eire, Iraq, Jordan, Lebanon, Malaya, Saudi Arabia, Syria, Thailand and Uruguay.

Variants
DHC-1A-1: Canadian-built with Gipsy Major 1C and only partially aerobatic; designated **Chipmunk T.Mk 1** by the RCAF
DHC-1A-2: Canadian-built with Gipsy Major 10 and only partially aerobatic
DHC-1B-1: Canadian-built with Gipsy Major 1C and fully aerobatic
DHC-1B-2: Canadian-built with Gipsy Major 10 and fully aerobatic
DHC-1B-2-S1: Canadian-built with Gipsy Major 10 for the Royal Egyptian air force
DHC-1B-2-S2: Canadian-built with

Gipsy Major 10 for the Royal Thai air force
DHC-1B-2-S3: Canadian-built with Gipsy Major 10 for RCAF refresher training by Royal Canadian Flying Clubs with the service designation **Chipmunk T.Mk 2**
DHC-1B-2-S4: Canadian-built for Chile
DHC-1B-2-S5: Canadian-built with Gipsy Major 10 for RCAF under the designation **Chipmunk T. Mk 10:** British-built with Gipsy Major 8 for RAF (735 completed)
Chipmunk Mk 20: British-built export version of Chipmunk T.Mk 10 but with Gipsy Major 10 Series 2 engine (217 completed)
Chipmunk Mk 21: British-built as Mk 20 but to civil requirements (28 completed)
Chipmunk Mk 22: conversions of Chipmunk T.Mk 10 aircraft to civil standard with Mk 20 powerplant

This Chipmunk T.Mk 10 was converted for crop-spraying duties with a single cockpit and Lycoming engine as a Chipmunk Mk 23.

Chipmunk Mk 22A: as Mk 22 but with extra fuel tankage
Chipmunk Mk 23: two single-seat conversions from Chipmunk T. Mk 10 standard with Mk 20 powerplant and agricultural spray equipment
Aerostructures Sundowner: single Australian-converted Chipmunk 134-kW (180-hp) Avco Lycoming O-360 engine, wingtip tanks, clear-view canopy and metal wing skinning; several Canadian aircraft were also fitted with Avco Lycoming engines
Masefield Variant: Bristol Aircraft variant possible on Chipmunks Mks 20, 21, 22 and 22A, and comprising blown canopy, luggage compartments in the wings, landing gear fairings and greater

fuel capacity

Sasin SA-29 Spraymaster: several Australian conversions similar to the British Chipmunk Mk 23

Super Chipmunk: specially converted aerobatic aircraft fitted with a 194-kW (260-hp) Avco Lycoming GO-435, revised flying surfaces and retractable landing gear; the sole example was flown in American colours for the 1970 world aerobatic championships

Turbo Chipmunk: In 1967-68 Hants & ssex Aviation converted, flew and tested a Chipmunk Mk 22A powered by a 86.42-kW (116-shp) Rover 90 turboprop engine

de Havilland Canada Chipmunk T.Mk 10 of the Royal Air Force. Still wearing these colours the type is in widespread use, flown by elementary training units of RAF, Army Air Corps and Royal Navy, and by Air Experience Flights providing cadets with flying experience.

Specification
de Havilland Chipmunk T.Mk 10
Type: tandem two-seat primary trainer
Powerplant: one 108-kW (145-hp) de Havilland Gipsy 8 inline piston engine

Performance: maximum speed at sea level 222 km/h (138 mph); cruising speed 187 km/h (116 mph); service ceiling 4815 m (15,800 ft); range

451 km (280 miles)
Weights: empty 646 kg (1,425 lb); maximum take-off 914 kg (2,014 lb)
Dimensions: span 10.46 m (34 ft

4 in); length 7.75 m (25 ft 5 in); height 2.13 m (7 ft 0 in); wing area 15.97 m² (172.0 sq ft)

de Havilland Canada DHC-2 Beaver

Design of the **de Havilland DHC-2 Beaver** light transport was started in Toronto during late 1946. The concept behind this first of de Havilland Canada's line of effective STOL transports was influenced by the specific requirements of the Ontario Department of Lands and Forests. The resulting aircraft also suited the exacting requirements of 'bush' pilots in North America and elsewhere for an effective, rugged and reliable STOL utility transport.

The prototype was flown for the first time on 16 August 1947 with Russ Bannock at the controls, and the type was certificated in Canada during March 1948. Large-scale production had already begun, and the **Beaver I** was soon in service, powered by the Pratt & Whitney R-985 radial. Of the 1,657 Beaver Is built, no fewer than 980 went to the US forces (**YL-20** service test, **L-20A** and **L-20B** production aircraft, redesignated **U-6** in 1962) and 46 to the British Army. There followed a single **Beaver II** with the Alvis Leonides radial and, in 1964, a few 10-passenger **Turbo-Beaver III** powered by the 431-ekW (578-ehp) United Aircraft of Canada Ltd (later Pratt & Whitney Aircraft of Canada) PT6A-6 or -20 turboprop. Most

of the Turbo-Beavers were used by civil operators. In New Zealand one Beaver had an AiResearch TPE331 turboprop engine installed. Production ended in the mid-1960s as de Havilland Canada concentrated on the development of more ambitious projects and products.

At the height of its career, the Beaver was to be found in some 50 countries, where it won universal acclaim for performance, ground stability conferred by wide-track tailwheel landing gear, and versatility. Basic accommodation was provided for a pilot and seven passengers, the latter replaceable by up to 680 kg (1,500 lb) of freight. Great flexibility was bestowed on the Beaver by its ability to operate on wheel, ski, float or amphibious float landing gears.

Airtech Canada of Peterborough, Ontario, has converted a number of Beavers to take the 447-kW (600-hp) Polish PZL-3S seven-cylinder air-cooled radial piston engine driving a PZL four-bladed propeller.

Specification
de Havilland Canada DHC-2

Beaver I
Type: light utility transport
Powerplant: one 336-kW (450-hp) Pratt & Whitney R-985 Wasp Junior radial piston engine
Performance: maximum speed at 1525 m (5,000 ft) 262 km/h (163 mph); cruising speed at 1525 m (5,000 ft) 230 km/h (143 mph); service ceiling 5485 m (18,000 ft); maximum range 1180 km (733 miles)
Weights: empty 1293 kg (2,850 lb); maximum take-off 2313 kg (5,100 lb)
Dimensions: span 14.63 m (48 ft 0 in); length 9.22 m (30 ft 3 in); height 2.74 m (9 ft 0 in); wing area 23.23 m² (250 sq ft)

Dependable and versatile on a variety of landing gears, the Beaver is the classic bushplane. Immense strength is married to superb STOL performance and ease of maintenance.

de Havilland Canada DHC-3 Otter

Success with the DHC-2 Beaver persuaded de Havilland Canada in the late 1940s that there was room in the STOL utility market for a larger version of the Beaver, with cabin space for some 14 passengers or a freight load of up to 1016 kg (2,240 lb). The company therefore developed the **de Havilland Canada DHC-3 Otter**, which was essentially a scaled-up Beaver, with an all-metal airframe and a 447-kW (600-hp) Pratt & Whitney R.1340 Wasp radial, and which was initially known as the **King Beaver**. The choice of a single engine for an aircraft designed to operate in Canada's harsh climate and sparsely populated hinterland regions may seem lacking in forethought. However, successful operations by the Beaver and other single-engined types had confirmed that the well-proven radials of the

Pratt & Whitney design were more than adequate for the task: they were universally familiar and, more importantly, were extremely reliable.

Notable for its parallel-chord wing with double-slotted flaps for good STOL performance, the Otter is an attractive high-wing monoplane with a single bracing strut on each side. The prototype first flew on 12 December 1951, and first deliveries were made in 1952. When production ceased in 1968, some 460 had been built, including 66 for the Royal Canadian Air Force and 227 for the US armed forces (223 of the **U-1A** for the US Army and four of the **UC-1** [changed to **U-1B** in 1962] for the US Navy). When released by military operators, many Otters joined those already on the civil market, where again the type had found ready acceptance for its versatility. Like

Building on the success of the Beaver, DHC introduced the larger Otter. This could haul far greater loads with only a slight decrease in STOL performance.

the Beaver, the Otter can operate on wheel, ski, float or amphibious float landing gears.

Despite its already impressive STOL peformance, the Otter was selected as the basis for a Canadian experiment in advanced STOL characteristics, a programme undertaken by the company in conjunction with the Defense Research Board. As part of this programme an Otter was fitted with extremely large flaps inboard of the strut/wing junction points; this also necessitated an enlargement of the tail surfaces, and ground stability was ensured by the replacement of the original tailwheel landing gear with a float chassis fitted with quadricycle wheels instead of the floats. The STOL modifications reduced the Otter's stalling speed by some 16 km/h (10 mph). The flaps were then removed, and a 1112-kg (2,450-lb) thrust General Electric J85-GE-7 turbojet installed, in the fuselage aft of the wings, with adjustable nozzles protruding one through each side of the fuselage. This arrangement permitted far greater control of speed, and allowed spot landings. Finally, the single Wasp radial was replaced by a pair of wing-mounted Pratt & Whitney Aircraft of Canada PT6 turboprops, whose slipstream was found beneficial to the controllability of the aircraft.

Under the designation **DHC-3-T Turbo-Otter**, one aircraft has been modified by Cox Air Resources to turbo-prop power, a 494-kW (662-hp) PT6A-27 replacing the standard Wasp. Empty weight is thus reduced to 1861 kg (4,100 lb), resulting in a useful payload increment.

Airtech Canada of Peterborough, Ontario, has recently converted a number of Otters to take either the 447-kW (600-hp) PZL-3S or 746-kW (1000-hp) Kalisz ASz-621R nine-cylinder aircooled radial engines manufactured in Poland, each driving a PZL four-bladed constant speed propeller. The re-engined aircraft offer increased climb rates and greater fuel economy at lower power settings. The first PZL-3S conversion flew in August 1983.

Specification
DHC-3 Otter (landplane)
Type: STOL utility transport
Powerplant: one 447-kW (600-hp) Pratt & Whitney R-1340-S1H1-G Wasp radial piston engine
Performance: maximum speed at sea level 246 km/h (153 mph); maximum cruising speed 212 km/h (132 mph); economical cruising speed 195 km/h (121 mph); service ceiling 5485 m (18,000 ft); range with 953-kg

de Havilland Canada DHC-3 Otter

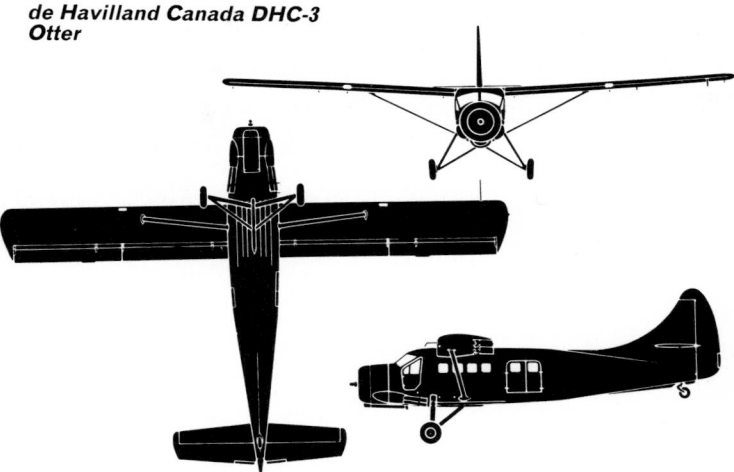

(2,100-lb) payload and reserves 1408 km (875 miles)
Weights: empty 2010 kg (4,431 lb); maximum take-off 3629 kg (8,000 lb)

Dimensions: span 17.68 m (58 ft 0 in); length 12.75 m (41 ft 10 in); height 3.84 m (12 ft 7 in); wing area 34.84 m² (375 sq ft)

de Havilland Canada DHC-4 Caribou

The decision to build the **de Havilland Canada DHC-4 Caribou** was taken in 1956, the object being to develop an aircraft combining the load-carrying capability of the Douglas DC-3 with the STOL performance of the Beaver and Otter. The Canadian army placed an order for two and the US Army followed with five, the US Secretary of Defense waiving a restriction which limited the US Army to fixed-wing aircraft with an empty weight less than 2268 kg (5,000 lb).

The prototype flew in July 1958, its high wing having a characteristic centre-section with marked anhedral. The rear door was designed as a ramp for items weighing up to 3048 kg (6,720 lb). In the trooping role up to 32 soldiers could be carried. The Caribou served with the RCAF as the **CC-108** and with the US Army as the **AC-1** (1962 designation **CV-2A**). As a result of its evaluation of the first five aircraft the US Army adopted the Caribou as standard equipment and placed orders for 159.

The second batch of aircraft was designated **CV-2B**. Following tension on the border between China and India, the US Army handed over two Caribous to the Indian Air Force in early 1963. In January 1967 the 134 Caribous still in service with the US Army were transferred to US Air Force charge as **C-7A** and **C-7B** transports. The aircraft was a general sales success and examples flew not only with air forces throughout the world, but also with civil operators. In Canadian service the Caribou was replaced by the DHC-5 Buffalo and surplus examples were sold to a number of nations including Colombia, Oman and Tanzania. Many of the Canadian aircraft had been loaned to the United Nations, seeing extensive international service. Production ended in 1973. The **DHC-4A** model supplanted the DHC-4 on the production line from aircraft no. 24: the two models are very similar apart from the later model's increase in weight, maximum take-off weight of the DHC-4 being 11793 kg (26,000 lb). Total production was 307.

de Havilland Canada DHC-4 Caribou of No. 5 Squadron, Royal Malaysian air force in 1970. The Caribou proved popular with the military with its no-nonsense operations, able to get into rough, small airstrips with heavy loads. It was widely used by the US and Vietnam during the South East Asia conflict.

Specification
DHC-4A Caribou
Type: STOL tactical transport
Powerplant: two 1081-kW (1,450-hp) Pratt & Whitney R-2000-7M2 Twin Wasp radial piston engines
Performance: maximum speed 348 km/h (216 mph) at 1980 m (6,500 ft); cruising speed 293 km/h (182 mph) at 2285 m (7,500 ft); service

ceiling 7560 m (24,800 ft); range with maximum payload and reserves 389 km (242 miles)
Weights: empty 8283 kg (18,260 lb); maximum take-off 12927 kg (28,500 lb)
Dimensions: span 29.15 m (95 ft 7½ in); length 22.12 m (72 ft 8 in); height 9.68 m (31 ft 9 in); wing area 84.72 m² (912 sq ft)

Relatively few DHC-4 Caribou aircraft reached the civil market, but one such transport comprised the sole equipment of Air Cargo America, which operated a once-daily round trip between Miami and Key West via Marathon. Other civil Caribous were flown in South East Asia during the war by the CIA-sponsored Air America.

de Havilland Canada DHC-5 Buffalo
to
Dewoitine D.500 Series

de Havilland Canada DHC-5 Buffalo

Developed from the DHC-4 Caribou, being an enlarged fuselage version of that aircraft, the **de Havilland Canada DHC-5 Buffalo** was known originally as the **Caribou II**. Four were ordered for evaluation by the US Army, their development cost shared by the US Army together with the Canadian government and de Havilland Canada; the first of these transports made its maiden flight on 9 April 1964. The DHC-5 had been developed to meet the requirements of the US Army for a transport that would be able to carry loads such as the Pershing missile, a 105-mm howitzer or ¾-ton truck.

No further orders resulted from US Army evaluation of the DHC-5 (designated originally **YAC-2** by the US Army, and later **C-8A**), but the Canadian Armed Forces acquired 15 of the **DHC-5A** which it designated **CC-115**: six were converted subsequently for deployment in a maritime patrol role. Following delivery of 24 to the Brazilian air force and 16 to the Peruvian air force, the production line was closed down. In 1974 the company realised there was a continuing demand for the Buffalo and production of an improved **DHC-5D** Buffalo was initiated. This had more powerful engines which permitted operation at higher gross weights, and offered improved all-round performance. Production of the Buffalo ended in 1982, but the last of 122 aircraft built was not delivered until April 1985. DHC-5Ds were bought by the armed forces of Abu Dhabi (5), Cameroun (3), Chile (1), Ecuador (3), Egypt (10), Kenya (8), Mauritania (1), Mexico (3), Sudan (4), Tanzania (6), Togo (2), Zaire (3) and Zambia (7). With some interest being shown by civil operators, DH Canada developed the **DHC-5E Transporter**, certificated in Canada in 1981. Generally similar to the military Buffalo, it could seat 44 passengers in a standard layout but with quick-change passenger/cargo and VIP/executive interior. Two were acquired by Ethiopian Airlines.

Variants
DHC-5B: designation of proposed version with General Electric CT64-P4C engines, not built

The DHC-5E Transporter was aimed at the resources support market, able to transport men and equipment in all types of climate and terrain.

DHC-5C: designation of proposed version with Rolls-Royce Dart RDa.12 engines, not built
NASA/DITC XC-8A: designation of C-8A following conversion for use as an augmentor wing research aircraft; extensively modified, it has clipped wings, fixed landing gear, two Rolls-Royce Spey engines with vectored nozzles complementing the augmentor wings
XC-8A ACLS: redesignation of C-8A following conversion for use as an Air-Cushion Landing System research aircraft; instead of conventional landing gear it has an inflatable but perforated rubber air cushion which permits operation from and to almost any type of surface, including ice, rough airfields, soft soils, snow, swamps and water
NASA/Boeing QSRA: redesignation of C-8A following conversion for use as a Quiet Short-haul Research Aircraft; this aircraft has a new wing incorporating upper-surface blowing and boundary-layer control; engines are four Avco Lycoming F102 turbofans

Specification
de Havilland Canada DHC-5D
Type: STOL utility transport
Powerplant: two General Electric CT64-820-4 turboprop engines each flat-rated at 2336 kW (3,133 shp)
Performance: maximum cruising speed for STOL transport mission 420 km/h (261 mph) at 3050 m (10,000 ft); normal maximum operating

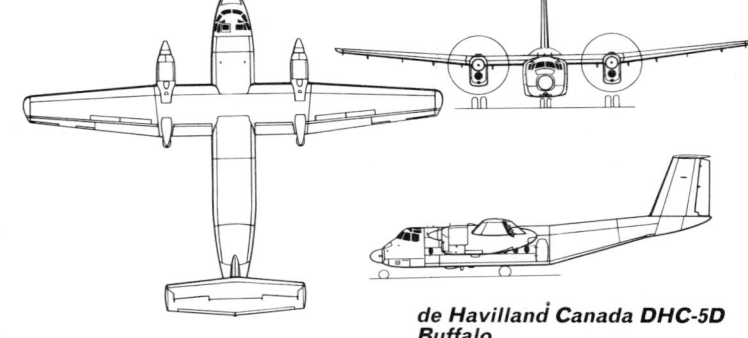

de Havilland Canada DHC-5D Buffalo

altitude 7620 m (25,000 ft); range with maximum payload 416 km (259 miles); maximum range with no payload 3280 km (2,038 miles)
Weights: empty operating 11412 kg (25,160 lb); maximum take-off 22317 kg (49,200 lb)
Dimensions: span 29.26 m (96 ft 0 in); length 24.08 m (79 ft 0 in); height 8.76 m (28 ft 9 in); wing area 87.79 m² (945 sq ft)

de Havilland Canada DHC-6 Twin Otter

In 1964 de Havilland Canada announced that it was developing a twin-turboprop high-wing monoplane with STOL capability to provide accommodation for 13 to 18 passengers. Identified as the **de Havilland Canada DHC-6 Twin Otter**, the first of an initial batch of five made its maiden flight on 20 May 1965.

Powerplant of the first three aircraft consisted of two 432-ekW (579-ehp) Pratt & Whitney Aircraft of Canada PT6A engines, but the fourth and subsequent examples of this first **Twin Otter Series 100** production version had PT6A-20 engines of similar output. Design of the aircraft's wing includes double-slotted trailing-edge flaps and ailerons which can be drooped simulta-

neously with the flaps to enhance STOL performance. Fixed tricycle landing gear can have optional float or ski installations, as well as the standard wheels.

Intended primarily for service with commuter or third-level airlines, the Twin Otter has nevertheless seen wide use with air forces and government agencies. Military operators include Argentina, Canada, Chile, Ecuador, Ethiopia, France, Haiti, Jamaica, Nepal, Norway, Panama, Paraguay, Peru, the USA and Venezuela.

The first Twin Otter Series 100 entered service in 1966, and, following manufacture of 115 of that version, production switched to the **Twin Otter Series 200**. It differed by having in-

creased baggage capacity in a lengthened fuselage nose and was certificated for operation at a higher gross weight. After 115 had been built the production **Twin Otter Series 300** was introduced, this having more powerful PT6A-27 engines which make possible an increase of almost 454 kg (1,000 lb) in maximum take-off weight. Later production aircraft had a 20-seat commuter interior as standard and all floatplane versions, irrespective of series, retain the shorter fuselage nose of the original Series 100. Specialised equipment that has been developed to enhance the capabilities of these popular aircraft includes a ventral pod to carry 272 kg (600 lb) of freight and an expendable fabric mem-

brane tank holding 1818 litres (400 Imp gal) of water for water-bombing firefighting operations.

In 1982 DH Canada offered two specialised military versions designated **Twin Otter Series 300M** basic military transport or COIN version armed with cabin-mounted machine-guns and underwing hardpoints, and the **300MR** maritime reconnaissance version equipped with search radar, comprehensive avionics and a wing-mounted searchlight. Although a prototype 300MR (C-GFJQ-X) was flown, the only buyer was Senegal with a single aircraft. When the last Twin Otter was delivered in December 1988 production had reached 844. Studies for a successor are designated DHC-9.

Variants

Twin Otter 300S: designation of six aircraft fitted with 11 seats, an improved high-capacity anti-skid braking system and wing spoilers, built for the 1973 experimental Air Transit service linking downtown STOL airports in Montreal and Ottawa
Twin Otter Series 400: proposed development to meet US FAR 36 noise regulations. Not built
UV-18A: two standard Series 300s delivered October 1976 onwards to the US Army Alaska National Guard, followed by four more in 1979 and 1982. Operating on wheels, floats or skis they are used for command, personnel or logistic flights within Alaska
UV-18B: two standard Series 300s delivered to the US Air Force Academy in 1977 and used for sporting parachuting activities

Specification
DHC-6 Twin Otter Series 300
(landplane)
Type: utility STOL transport
Powerplant: two 486-ekW (652-ehp) Pratt & Whitney Aircraft of Canada PT6A-27 turboprops
Performance: maximum cruising speed 338 km/h (210 mph) at 3050 m

de Havilland Canada DHC-6 Twin Otter Series 300 of NorOntair

(10,000 ft); service ceiling 8140 m (26,700 ft); range with 1134 kg (2,500 lb) payload 1297 km (806 miles); range with maximum payload 185 km (115 miles)
Weights: empty operating 3363 kg (7,415 lb); maximum take-off 5670 kg (12,500 lb)
Dimensions: span 19.81 m (65 ft 0 in); length 15.77 m (51 ft 9 in); height 5.94 m (19 ft 6 in); wing area 39.02 m² (420 sq ft)

The Twin Otter introduced a far greater level of passenger comfort compared to the Otter and Beaver.

de Havilland Canada DHC-7 Dash 7

The undoubted sales success of the Twin Otter led de Havilland Canada to initiate market research to estimate the interest in a large STOL aircraft which would incorporate the rugged reliability that had become associated with the products of the company. The intention was to develop a small airliner with advanced STOL capability, so that higher standards of comfort, comparable with much larger aircraft, would be available to those airlines which operate from runways about 915 m (3,000 ft) in length.

The necessary interest was forthcoming, and with backing from the Canadian government the construction of two pre-production **de Havilland Canada DHC-7** aircraft began in late 1972, the first of these (C-GNBX-X) making its initial flight on 27 March 1975. Of high-wing monoplane configuration, the DHC-7, which is named **Dash 7**, derives its essential STOL capability from wide-span double-slotted trailing-edge flaps that operate within the slipstream of the slow-turning propellers of the four wing-mounted turboprop engines. In addition, there are four spoilers in the upper surface of each wing. The inboard pair serve as spoilers or lift dumpers, the outboard pair as air spoilers which can also be operated differentially in conjunction with the ailerons to augment lateral control.

The fuselage is of fail-safe construction to permit pressurisation, and a very high T-tail places the tailplane and elevator well clear of the propeller slipstream. The landing gear is of the retractable tricycle type, with twin wheels on each unit, and the powerplant consists of four Pratt & Whitney Aircraft of Canada PT6A-50 turboprop engines. To reduce noise levels to a minimum, each drives a large-diameter 3.42 m (11 ft 3 in), slow-turning propeller.

Accommodation is provided for 50 passengers, with access to the main cabin via a single door, incorporating air-stairs, at the rear of the cabin on the port side. There are provisions for optional mixed passenger/cargo or all-cargo operations, and a large freight door can

de Havilland Canada DHC-7 Dash 7 of Air Pacific (USA)

be installed at the forward end of the cabin on the port side. In passenger service there is ample room within the cabin for a galley, toilet facilities, and one or two flight attendants. The flight crew of two is accommodated on a separate flight deck, and advanced avionics to enhance their efficiency include an auto-pilot/flight director system which incorporates flight and air data computers, and weather radar.

The first operator to receive the Dash 7 was Rocky Mountain Airways, on 3 February 1978.

When production finished in December 1988 113 had been delivered to 35 customers in 22 countries. Military use of the Dash 7 was restricted to two used as VIP/transports (designated **CC-132**) by the Canadian Armed Forces in Germany from August 1979 to April 1987, and a single aircraft delivered to the Venezuelan Navy in May 1982 used in the patrol and transport roles.

Variants
Dash 7 Series 100: standard passenger version seating 50 passengers
Dash 7 Series 101: all-cargo version of Series 100 able to accommodate five standard pallets
Dash 7 Series 150: developed passenger version introduced in 1978 with higher gross weight, increased fuel capacity and improved passenger

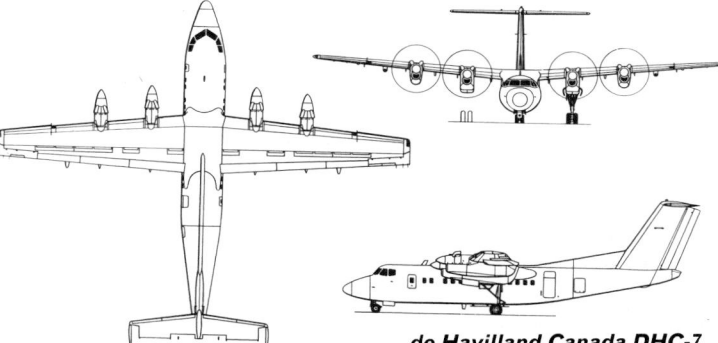

de Havilland Canada DHC-7 Dash 7

amenities
Dash 7 Series 151: all-cargo version of Series 150
Dash 7 IR: single special ice reconnaissance version of the Series 150 built for the Canadian government. Equipped with SLAR and computers to track ice formations and flow patterns, the aircraft was delivered in May 1986 and is operated by Bradley Air Services for the Department of Environment

Specification
de Havilland Canada DHC-7 Dash 7 Series 100
Type: short/medium-range quiet STOL transport
Powerplant: four Pratt & Whitney Aircraft of Canada PT6A-50 turboprops, each flat-rated to 835 kW (1,120 shp)
Performance: maximum cruising speed at 18597 kg (41,000 lb) at 2440 m (8,000 ft) 436 km/h (271 mph); service ceiling 6400 m (21,000 ft); range with 50 passengers, IFR reserves 1279 km (795 miles)
Weights: empty operating 12542 kg (27,650 lb); maximum take-off 19958 kg (44,000 lb)
Dimensions: span 28.35 m (93 ft 0 in); length 24.58 m (80 ft 7¾ in); height 7.98 m (26 ft 2 in); wing area 79.89 m² (860 sq ft)

de Havilland Canada DHC-8 Dash 8

To meet growing demands for a quiet short-range transport in the 30-40 seat category, DH Canada initiated the design and development of the **DHC-8 Dash 8** in 1980, and the aircraft is the company's first transport not optimised for short take-off and landing. The fuselage cargo-loading door is standard, and other features include a retractable tricycle landing gear with twin-wheel units, large-span T-tail, and a high-mounted wing carrying two fuel-efficient Pratt & Whitney PW120 advanced turboprop engines driving large-diameter slow-turning four-bladed propellers ensuring very low noise levels. These engines also have safety features which ensure that if one fails the other automatically increases its output to 1492 kW (2,000 shp).

The design has since grown into a family of aircraft offering between 36 and 70 seats and the prototype of the 36-seat **Series 100** flew for the first time on 20 June 1983. Certification followed in September 1984 and the type went into service with the Canadian airline NorOntair in the following December.

The **Series 300**, formally launched in March 1986, is stretched by 3.43 m (11 ft 3 in), to carry between 50 and 56 passengers depending on the cabin configuration. Wing span is also increased by tip extensions and the first aircraft flew on 15 May 1987. Certification followed in February 1989 and the Series 300 entered airline service with Time Air the same month. Also available is the increased payload **Series 300A** able to carry 6272 kg (13,800 lb).

In June 1987, by which time DH Canada had been acquired by Boeing, studies for a further stretched version were under way. Designated the **Series 400**, and intended to compete with the ATP and ATR72, the 650-km/h (400-mph) 25175-kg (55,000-lb) 66/70-seat airliner could be flying by 1993, and certificated and delivered before the end of 1994. Powerplants offered for the new variant are the 2948-kW (4,000-shp) free-turbine Allison GMA 2100 and the GE/Lycoming GLC38 advanced turboprops driving slow-turning six-bladed

de Havilland Canada DHC-8 Dash 8 of NorOntair (Ontario Northland Transportation Commission)

propellers. A tentative 1990 go-ahead has been suspended awaiting the outcome of the current Aérospatiale/Alenia consortium bid to take over Boeing Canada.

By January 1991 the Dash 8 orderbook stood at 361 aircraft, comprising 251 Series 100s and 110 Series 300s, with around 230 delivered.

Variants
CC-142: designation of two Series 100s bought by the Canadian Department of National Defence but operated since March 1987 by the Canadian Forces at Lahr, Germany. Used as passenger/cargo transports, the aircraft are equipped with long-range fuel tanks, rough field landing gear, high strength floors and a special-mission-related avionics fit
CT-142: designation of four Series 100s, acquired by the Canadian DND, and operated as specially configured navigation trainers by the Canadian Forces. Otherwise equipped similarly to the CC-142, the trainers are distinguished by their extended noses
Dash 8M-100: two specially-equipped Series 100s used by the Canadian Department of Transport to calibrate ILS, VOR and MLS systems at Canadian airports
Dash 8M-300ASW Triton: designation of a proposed maritime patrol or anti-submarine warfare version of the Series 300 equipped with Harpoon or Exocet-type anti-

shipping missiles mounted on lower side fuselage sponson hardpoints, and four underwing pylons, outboard of the engines, capable of carrying missiles, torpedoes, mines, sonobuoys or searchlights. With a full range of ASW sensors including FLIR, MAD and search radar operated by a six-man crew, maximum endurance is over 11 hours
E-9A: designation of two standard Series 100 aircraft acquired by the US Air Force in 1985 as airborne platforms to perform telemetry and data link duties in connection with drone and missile testing at Tyndall AFB, Florida. Modified by the Sierra Research division of LTV, the E-9A carries a large fuselage fairing containing a steerable phased-array antenna, underfuselage search radar and special avionics. Both aircraft were delivered in 1988

de Havilland Canada DHC-8 Dash 8

Specification
de Havilland Canada DHC-8 Dash 8 Series 100
Type: 36-passenger short-range transport
Powerplant: two 1491-kW (2,000-hp) Pratt & Whitney Canada PW120A turboprops
Performance: maximum cruising speed at 4575 m (15,000 ft) 497 km/h (308 mph); operating ceiling 7620 m (25,000 ft); range with full passenger load 2010 km (1,249 miles)
Weights: empty 9979 kg (22,000 lb); maximum take-off 15650 kg (34,500 lb)
Dimensions: span 25.91 m (85 ft 0 in); length 22.25 m (73 ft 0 in); height 7.49 m (24 ft 7 in); wing area 54.35 m² (585 sq ft)

Deperdussin aircraft

Wealthy French silk merchant Armand Deperdussin founded his aircraft-building company Société Pour les Appareils Deperdussin (SPAD) at Betheny, near Reims, in 1910. He was fortunate in employing Louis Bechereau to be responsible for the running of the company and later engaged a young engineering graduate named André Herbemont. These two brought undying fame to the original short-lived SPAD organisation, which went into liquidation in 1913 after Deperdussin had been arrested for embezzlement.

Bechereau designed a series of monoplanes of increasing capability, perfecting a monocoque form of fuselage construction that combined a desirable circular cross-section with light weight and strength. Typically, the Deperdussins were braced high-wing mono-

planes, two king-posts on the forward fuselage carrying a skein of wires to brace the slender wings. Lateral control was by wing warping. Landing gear was normally of fixed tailskid type, but seaplane versions had, for their day, a very neat float installation. Power was provided for most of the range by Gnome rotary engines of various power outputs.

A first major success came on 9 September 1912, when a Deperdussin powered by a 119-kW (160-hp) Gnome and piloted by Jules Védrines won the fourth James Gordon Bennett Aviation Cup race at Chicago, Illinois. Even greater were the achievements of 1913, Maurice Prévost winning the first Schneider Trophy race at Monaco on 16 April, the Gordon Bennett Cup at Reims, France, on 29 September, and setting a world absolute speed record of

The best-known Deperdussin aircraft was the Monocoque racer, which had exceptionally clean lines. In it Maurice Prévost set a world speed record in September 1913.

203.85 km/h (126.67 mph) on the same date. To complete the year's achievements, a Deperdussin piloted by Eugène Gilbert won the Henry Deutsch de la Meurthe air race around Paris on 27 October. Thus, in a few months, Bechereau and Herbemont had created for Deperdussin the world's fastest pre-war aeroplane: from this pinnacle of achievement came collapse of the Deperdussin company. It was taken over by Louis Blériot and renamed Société Pour L'Aviation et ses Dérives (also SPAD), which gained fame for its products during World War I.

Specification
Deperdussin 'Monocoque' racer (1913)
Type: single-seat racing aircraft
Powerplant: one 119-kW (160-hp) Gnome rotary piston engine
Performance: maximum speed 204 km/h (127 mph)
Weight: maximum take-off 450 kg (992 lb)
Dimensions: span 6.65 m (21 ft 9¾ in); length 6.1 m (20 ft 0⅛ in); height 2.3 m (7 ft 6½ in); wing area 9.66 m² (104 sq ft)

Desoutter aircraft

The Desoutter Aircraft Company was established at Croydon, Surrey, in 1929 to undertake licence production of the Koolhoven F.K.41, a three-seater with plywood fuselage and fabric-covered wooden wings, and powered by a Cirrus III engine. The second F.K.41 to be built

was flown to Desoutter's Croydon base where company modifications included new cowlings and horizontal tail surfaces lowered from the top of to a more conventional position at its base. In this form it appeared at the July 1929 Olympic Aero Show as the **Desoutter Dol-**

phin, although this name was not used for production aircraft.

Known simply as the **Desoutter** and powered by a 78-kW (105-hp) Cirrus Hermes I or 86-kW (115-hp) Hermes II engine, it was ordered by National Flying Services, which received 19 of the 28 aircraft built. An improved **Desoutter II** prototype was flown in June 1930, this introducing redesigned tail surfaces,

wheel brakes and a de Havilland Gipsy III engine. The original Desoutter was retrospectively redesignated **Desoutter I** with introduction of the Desoutter II, of which 12 were built, including six for export. One, sold to the Danish airline Det Dansk Lufffarrtselskab in June 1931, completed successfully the Mildenhall Melbourne course set for the MacRobertson Victorian Centenary Air

Race in 129 hours 47 minutes. Piloted by Lieutenant Michael Hansen it gained seventh place on handicap.

One Desoutter I had an inverted Cirrus IV engine installed before delivery to the Dutch East Indies in 1933. Another, with a Menasco C-4 Pirate engine, modified windscreen and Desoutter II tail surfaces was acquired by Richard Shuttleworth in 1935. It survives to this day, owned by the Shuttleworth Trust. Also preserved, in the airport terminal at Launceston, Tasmania, is a Desoutter II delivered to Ireland's Iona National Air Taxis in 1931. This was flown to Australia by H. Jefferson and H. Jenkins in 1932 and was later used by Captain L. McK. Johnson to fly a Launceston-Flinders Island route, thus accounting for its

The Desoutter I was a Koolhoven F.K.41 licence-built in Britain. The type achieved limited success in the inter-war period, this example surviving to be impressed for war work.

name *Miss Flinders*.

Specification
Desoutter II
Type: three-seat cabin monoplane
Powerplant: one 89-kW (120-hp) de Havilland Gipsy III inline piston engine
Performance: maximum speed 201 km/h (125 mph); cruising speed 161 km/h (100 mph); service ceiling 5180 m (17,000 ft); range 805 km (500 miles)

Weights: empty 535 kg (1,180 lb); maximum take-off 862 kg (1,900 lb)
Dimensions: span 10.88 m (35 ft 8½ in); length 7.92 m (26 ft 0 in); height 2.13 m (7 ft 0 in); wing area 17.00 m² (183.0 sq ft)

Dewoitine D.1

The first design by Frenchman Emile Dewoitine after establishing his own company in October 1920 was a high-wing single-seat fighter monoplane. This **Dewoitine D.1** was built in response to a requirement issued by the French Service Technique de l'Aéronautique. Development was somewhat protracted as a result of changes in official policy, but the first prototype flew eventually in November 1922. The machine was of advanced general concept, with a metal oval-section fuselage and metal strut-braced parasol wing, the former with dural sheet skinning and the latter fabric-covered. The **D.1.01** was powered by a 224-kW (300-hp) Hispano-Suiza 8Fb engine with twin Lamblin radiators under the nose. The **D.1bis** rejected the faired cabane strut arrangement of the prototype as a result of its adverse affect on pilot visibility and used instead conventional bracing: the **D.1ter** had reduced-span wings of increased chord and radiators attached to the forward legs of the fixed landing gear.

The D.1 was demonstrated in a number of countries by Dewoitine company pilot Marcel Doret and foreign sales soon followed, 79 aircraft being delivered to Yugoslavia, while Switzerland purchased two and Japan one. The Italian Ansaldo company bought a D.1 bis and then constructed 112 D.1ter fighters under licence for the Regia Aeronautica; they remained in first-line service until 1929, bearing the designation **Ansaldo A.C.2**. Although rejected eventually for service with the French Aviation Militaire, 30 D.1ter fighters were acquired by the Marine Nationale, 15 of them equipping Escadrille 7C1 operating from the carrier *Béarn*.

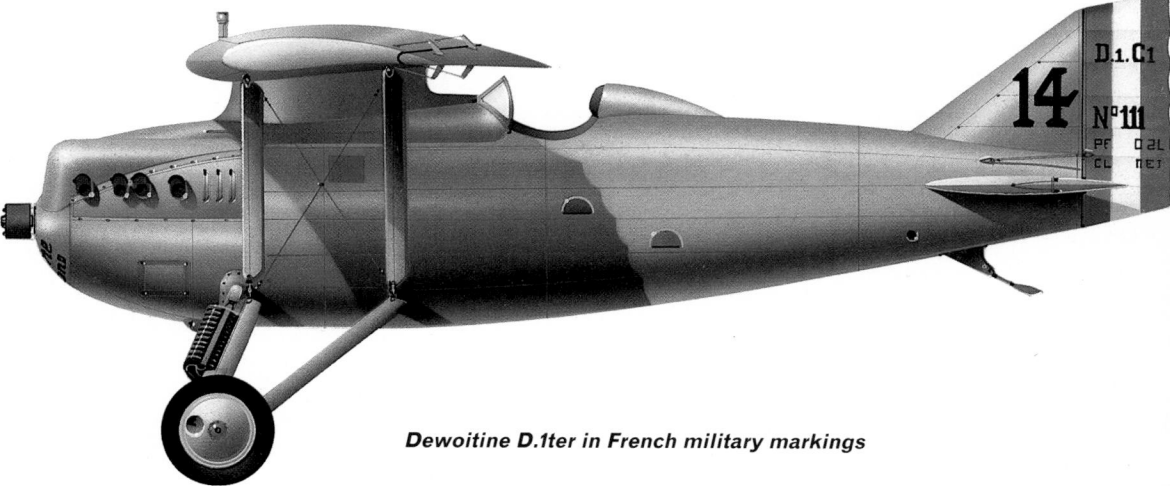

Dewoitine D.1ter in French military markings

Specification
Dewoitine D.1ter
Type: single-seat fighter
Powerplant: one 224-kW (300-hp) Hispano-Suiza 8Fb inline piston engine
Performance: maximum speed 255 km/h (158 mph); maximum climb rate 450 m (1,476 ft) per minute; service ceiling 8000 m (26,245 ft); range 400 km (249 miles)
Weights: empty 820 kg (1,808 lb); maximum take-off 1240 kg (2,734 lb)
Dimensions: span 11.50 m (37 ft 8¾ in); length 7.50 m (24 ft 7¼ in); height 2.75 m (9 ft 0 in); wing area 20.00 m² (215.29 sq ft)
Armament: two fuselage-mounted synchronised 7.7-mm (0.303-in) Vickers machine-guns

An advanced aircraft by the standards of the day, the D.1 received few domestic orders. Seen here is a D.1ter modified to two-seat configuration for use as a demonstration aircraft.

Dewoitine D.7

In the early 1920s Emile Dewoitine found time from development of his series of fighter designs to make a contribution to the then-current vogue, the production of a viable ultralight aircraft. The spate of French and British designs which appeared were an attempt to achieve a machine that was very light so that it could be quickly taken apart and conveyed along roads and over fields – if necessary by a couple of enthusiasts 'walking' it along. The true 'amateur' of flying could own such a machine, storing it in his garden when not in use. Dewoitine's design was the single-seat **Dewoitine D.7**, a shoulder-wing

monoplane weighing just 250 kg (551 lb) loaded. It had considerable span and a relatively short fuselage. The D.7 scored a notable success, winning a prize offered by *Le Matin* newspaper for a flight by an ultralight aircraft over the English Channel and back in 1923. Several D.7s were built, one being sold to the Japanese army for experimental purposes.

Specification
Type: ultralight single-seat sport monoplane
Powerplant: one 9-kW (12-hp) Salmson DA3 three-cylinder piston engine
Performance: maximum speed 90 km/h (56 mph); service ceiling

3000 m (9,840 ft); endurance 5 hours
Weights: maximum take-off 250 kg (551 lb)

Dimensions: span 12.60 m (41 ft 4 in); length 5.60 m (18 ft 4½ in); wing area 15.00 m² (161.46 sq ft)

Emile Dewoitine's solution to the problems of getting an ultralight aircraft into the air on only a small power output was a lightweight structure with considerable wing area. The D.7 was the result, produced in only small numbers.

Dewoitine D.9

The **Dewoitine D.9** single-seat fighter was of the same basic configuration as the D.1 but its wing, although of similar shape, had its span increased by 1.30 m (4 ft 3¼ in); it was powered by a Gnome-Rhône Jupiter radial in place of the D.1's inline engine.

Flown for the first time during 1924, the D.9 was (like the D.1) rejected by the French army, but it also achieved export sales. Belgium and Yugoslavia bought two and eight respectively, and the Swiss EKW factory assembled three from parts supplied by the Dewoitine workshops. Most important, however, was a Regia Aeronautica order for 150, delivered as **Ansaldo A.C.3** fighters by the Ansaldo company which built them under licence. After service with fighter *squadriglie*, the Italian A.C.3s survived into the 1930s as the equipment for the newly formed ground-attack 5° Stormo Assalt based at Ciampino.

The D.9 failed to receive any French military orders, but was built for the Swiss air force locally by Eidg. Konstruktions-Werkstätte.

Specification
Dewoitine D.9
Type: single-seat fighter
Powerplant: one 313-kW (420-hp) Gnome-Rhône 9Ab Jupiter radial piston engine
Performance: maximum speed 245 km/h (152 mph) at sea level; maximum climb rate 525 m (1,722 ft) per minute; service ceiling 8500 m (27,885 ft); range 400 km (249 miles)
Weights: empty 945 kg (2,083 lb); maximum take-off 1333 kg (2,939 lb)
Dimensions: span 12.80 m (42 ft 0 in); length 7.30 m (23 ft 11½ in); height 3.00 m (9 ft 10¼ in); wing area

25.00 m² (269.10 sq ft)
Armament: two fuselage-mounted synchronised 7.7-mm (0.303-in) Vickers

machine-guns and two wing-mounted 7.7-mm (0.303-in) Darne machine-guns (latter not always installed)

Dewoitine D.21

The prototype **Dewoitine D.21** flew in 1925. It followed the experimental **D.12** and the **D.19** (three sold to Switzerland, two of them for assembly in that country) which shared its parasol-wing configuration, and the **D.15**, the only biplane Dewoitine fighter. The D.21 was a development of the D.12, which in its turn evolved from the D.9, differing mainly in its inline Lorraine-Dietrich 12E engine with frontal radiator. The chosen engine for the D.21 was the reliable Hispano-Suiza 12Gb, and with its increased power the D.21 achieved considerable export sales, although once again the French authorities remained indifferent to the quality of Dewoitine designs, Argentina bought seven D.21s, all constructed at the EKW workshops at Thun, Switzerland, subsequently building under licence another 58, which were powered by the Lorraine-Dietrich engine. The Turkish government bought a batch of D.21s and 25 were licence-

built by Skoda in Czechoslovakia for that country's air arm. The Skoda fighters were powered by the Skoda L, a licensed version of the Hispano-Suiza 12Gb, and were designated **Skoda-Dewoitine D.1**.

Specification
Dewoitine D.21
Type: single-seat fighter
Powerplant: one 373-kW (500-hp) Hispano-Suiza 12Gb inline piston engine
Performance: maximum speed 270 km/h (168 mph); maximum climb rate 600 m (1,968 ft) per minute; range 400 km (249 miles)
Weights: empty 1090 kg (2,403 lb); maximum take-off 1580 kg (3,483 lb)
Dimensions: span 12.80 m (41 ft 0 in); length 7.64 m (25 ft 0¾ in); height 3.00 m (9 ft 10¼ in); wing area 24.80 m² (266.95 sq ft)
Armament: two fuselage-mounted

synchronised 7.7-mm (0.303-in) Vickers machine-guns and (optionally) two wing-mounted 7.5-mm (0.295-in) Darne machine-guns in the centre-section

The two D.21s assembled in Switzerland by the EKW had Chausson frontal radiators for their Hispano-Suiza 12Jb engines. Armament was a pair of 7.7-mm (0.303-in) machine-guns.

Dewoitine D.26

Ordered by the KTA (the Swiss Military Technical Service) at the same time as the D.27 series fighters, the **Dewoitine D.26** was a single-seat fighter trainer of similar construction to the D.27 but with a lower-powered Wright 9Qa uncowled radial engine. Nine D.26s were delivered in 1931, intended mainly for training in gunnery and formation flight. Shortly afterwards two more D.26s were purchased, powered by 224-kW (300-hp) Wright 9Qc engines; these were intended specifically for training in air-to-air combat and were fitted with wing-mounted camera guns.

These aircraft were noted for their longevity, nearly all of them flying with training schools until 1948, when they were handed over to the Swiss Aero Club which used them for many years as

Switzerland was perhaps the Dewoitine company's best customer for civil and military aircraft alike. This is a D.26.

glider tugs. The last machine (serial U-288) was not retired until 1970 and is now on display at Dübendorf.

Specification
Type: single-seat fighter trainer
Powerplant: one 186-kW (250-hp) Wright 9Qa radial piston engine
Performance: maximum speed 240 km/h (149 mph); service ceiling 7500 m (24,605 ft); range 500 km (311 miles)
Weights: empty 763 kg (1,682 lb); maximum take-off 1068 kg (2,355 lb)
Dimensions: span 10.30 m (33 ft

9½ in); length 6.72 m (22 ft 0½ in); height 2.78 m (9 ft 1½ in); wing area 17.55 m² (188.91 sq ft)

Armament: one or two synchronised 7.5-mm (0.295-in) machine-guns

---

Dewoitine D.27

The most famous of the Dewoitine parasol monoplane fighters, the **Dewoitine D.27** was developed in response to a French official requirement of 1926, but like the previous designs was rejected by the Aviation Militaire. The prototype D.27 was built by the EKW workshops in Switzerland and flew for the first time during 1928. Power was provided by the Hispano-Suiza 12Mb engine with a chin-

type radiator. The prototype was flown originally with the angular fin and rudder which had characterised earlier Dewoitine fighters, but this was soon replaced by an early redesigned and less angular tail assembly. The Swiss Fliegertruppe bought the prototype and then ordered five pre-production aircraft. Delivered in 1930, they were followed by two batches of 15 and 45 aircraft in 1931 and

1932 respectively. In 1932, 15 Swiss D.27s were provided with wheel spats and their HS 12Mb engines were replaced by the more powerful HS 12Mc. These engines were soon abandoned in favour of the original engines, but the wheel spats were retained. Swiss D.27s remained in first-line service until 1940, thereafter equipping flying schools until scrapped finally in 1944.

Emile Dewoitine discontinued aircraft manufacture in France in January 1927, but re-established himself in March 1928

with the Société Aéronautique Française-Avions Dewoitine. This new company built 20 more D.27s; four were bought by Yugoslavia for final assembly by the Zmaj factory, and three were obtained by Romania, but plans to produce the D.27 for the Yugoslav and Romanian air arms were abandoned. Eight D.27s were used for various experiments, including evaluation flights from the aircraft-carrier *Béarn*. Five D.27s had their wing structure strengthened and were thus redesignated **D.53**, being used for test programmes involving various engines: the **D.531** had a Hispano-Suiza engine of unknown type, the **D.532** had a Rolls-Royce Kestrel, and the **D.535** was fitted with an HS 12Xbrs. The **D.534** was used for parachute trials.

Specification
Dewoitine D.27
Type: single-seat fighter
Powerplant: one 373-kW (500-hp) Hispano-Suiza 12Mb inline piston engine
Performance: maximum speed 298 km/h (185 mph) at sea level; maximum climb rate 600 m (1,968 ft) per minute; service ceiling 8300 m (27,230 ft); range 425 km (264 miles)
Weights: empty 1038 kg (2,288 lb); maximum take-off 1415 kg (3,120 lb)
Dimensions: span 10.30 m (33 ft

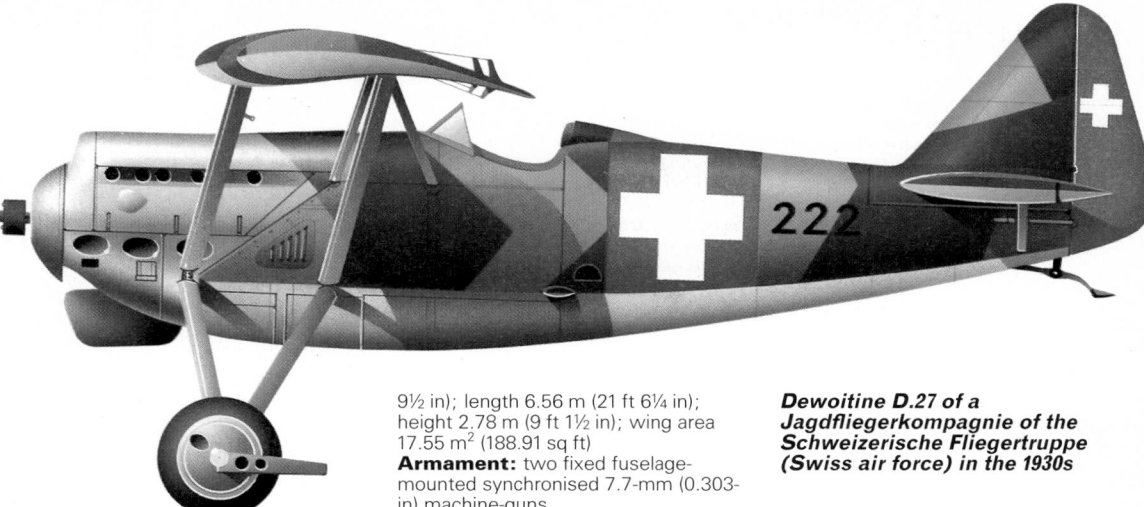

9½ in); length 6.56 m (21 ft 6¼ in); height 2.78 m (9 ft 1½ in); wing area 17.55 m² (188.91 sq ft)
Armament: two fixed fuselage-mounted synchronised 7.7-mm (0.303-in) machine-guns

Dewoitine D.27 of a Jagdfliegerkompagnie of the Schweizerische Fliegertruppe (Swiss air force) in the 1930s

Dewoitine D.37 Series

Developed at about the same time as the D.500, the **Dewoitine D.37** marked the culmination of the Dewoitine parasol monoplane fighter concept. Completed by the Lioré-et-Olivier company in August 1932, and powered by a 522-kW (700-hp) Gnome-Rhône 14Kds engine, the D.37 showed sufficient promise to merit further development and the revised **D.371** prototype, with an 597-kW (800-hp) Gnome-Rhône 14Kds radial, made its maiden flight in September 1934. It had an all-metal monocoque fuselage and fabric-covered metal wing. The main units of its wide-track landing gear formed a complex structure, braced to the fuselage and to the forward wing bracing struts. The Armée de l'Air ordered a batch of 28 D.371s in the spring of 1935. They differed from the prototype mainly by having close-cowled Gnome-Rhône 14Kfs radials. Armament comprised two wing-mounted Darne machine-guns and two fuselage-mounted synchronised Vickers guns.

Lithuania ordered 14 examples of the **D.372** export version but later accepted seven D.500s and seven cannon-armed D.501s. Ten D.371s were diverted from the Armée de l'Air order and these, together with the 14 D.372s, were delivered to the Spanish Republican government during 1936. Shortly after-

The French were innovative in the use of armament. This D.371 had two 20-mm Oerlikon cannon above the wings in addition to the synchronised fuselage guns.

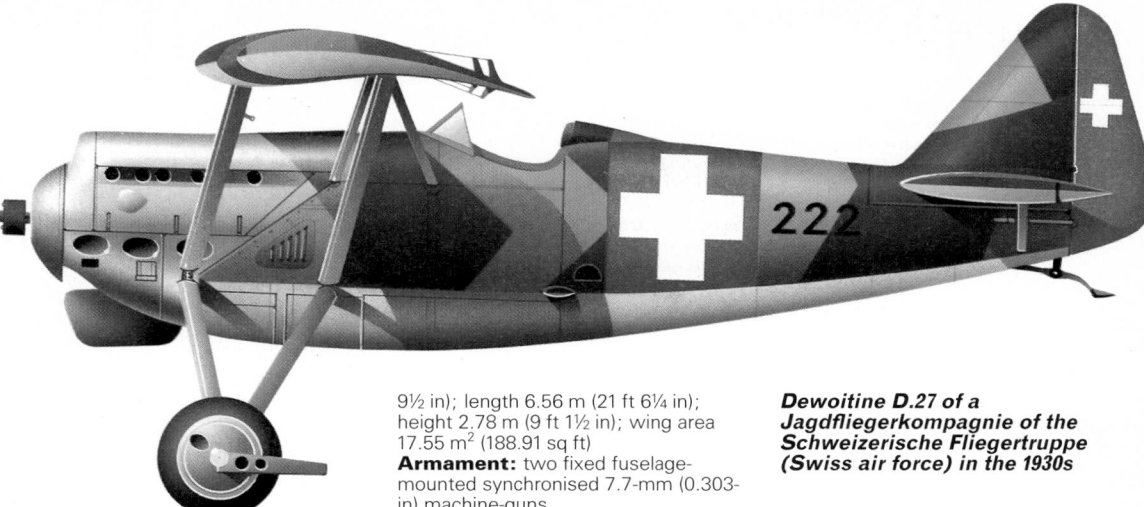

wards two more D.372s, ordered in the name of the Saudi Arabian government in order to avoid open French identification with the Spanish Republican cause, were delivered at Barcelona. All the Spanish aircraft were armed eventually with two 7.7-mm (0.303-in) Vickers machine-guns. They claimed 21 Nationalist aircraft destroyed in two months fighting during the early stages of the Spanish Civil War, but thereafter were relegated to coast protection or advanced training duties.

In November 1934, 40 examples of a navalised variant were ordered by the

Dewoitine D.372 of the Escuadra Espana, Aviacion Militar Republicana (Spanish Republican air force), based near Madrid in 1936

French Aéronautique Maritime. All were fitted with an arrester hook and flaps for operation from the aircraft-carrier *Béarn*. The basic version was designated **D.373** while a folding-wing variant, delivered in some numbers as part of the 40-plane order, was designated **D.376**. The D.373s and D.376s retained the four-gun armament of the D.371, although some aircraft were modified later to take a single 13.2-mm (0.52-in) Hotchkiss machine-gun in place of the two standard Vickers guns. D.373s and D.376s still formed the equipment of naval Escadrille AC1 at the outbreak of World War II.

Specification
Dewoitine D.371
Type: single-seat fighter

Powerplant: one 694-kW (930-hp) Gnome-Rhône 14Kfs radial piston engine
Performance: maximum speed 405 km/h (252 mph) at 4400 m (14,765 ft) in 5 minutes 12 seconds; absolute ceiling 11000 m (36,090 ft); range 900 km (559 miles)
Weights: empty equipped 1295 kg (2,855 lb); maximum take-off 1860 kg (4,100 lb)
Dimensions: span 11.80 m (38 ft 8½ in); length 7.44 m (24 ft 4¾ in); height 3.40 m (11 ft 1¾ in); wing area 17.80 m² (191.60 sq ft)
Armament: two synchronised fuselage-mounted 7.7-mm (0.303-in) Vickers machine-guns and two 7.5-mm (0.295-in) MAC machine-guns mounted in the wings to fire forward outside the propeller disc

Dewoitine D.371

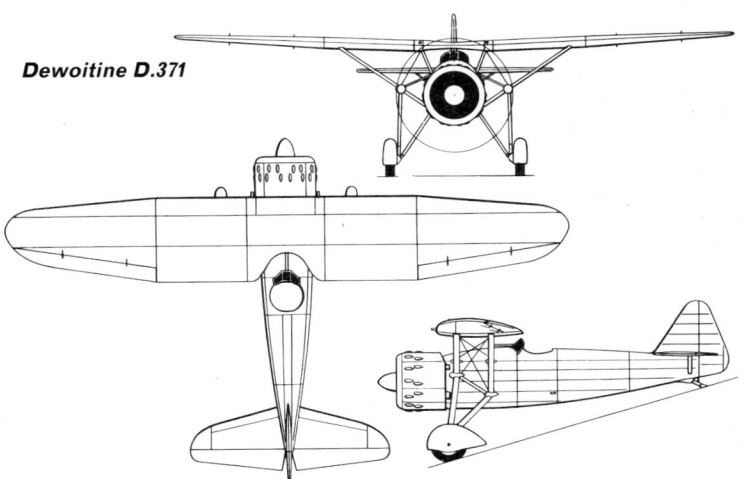

Dewoitine D.332

An all-metal cantilever low-wing monoplane, the **Dewoitine D.332** was an eight-passenger transport which was flown for the first time on 11 July 1933, piloted by Marcel Doret. The main landing gear legs had 'trouser'-type fairings, and the single vertical tail assembly was strut-braced and of typical Dewoitine appearance. Pilot and co-pilot were accommodated side-by-side in a cabin located forward of the wing leading edge, with the radio operator's post immediately behind them. The passenger cabin was roomy, well heated and ventilated, and had seats which could be folded down for night flying comfort. Power was provided by three Wright Cyclone radial engines licence-built by Hispano-Suiza.

Named *Emeraude* (Emerald), the new transport made a number of impressive demonstration flights to various European capitals. A world class record was gained on 7 September 1933 when a 1000-km (621-mile) course was flown with a useful load of 2000 kg (4,409 lb) at an average of 259.56 km/h (161.3 mph). Intended for use on Air France's proposed regular service to Saigon (French Indo-China, now Vietnam), the D.332 set off on a trail-blazing flight to that destination on 21 December 1933, reaching it on 28 December. When only some 400 km (249 miles) from Le Bourget airport on the return flight, the *Emeraude* struck a hill near Corbigny during a violent thunderstorm and all aboard were killed.

Variants

D.333: despite loss of the D.332, Air France ordered three D.333s, a heavier and strengthened development accommodating up to 10 passengers and weighing 1650 kg (3,637 lb) more when fully loaded: they were used to operate the Toulouse-Dakar (West Africa) sector of the Air France South American route for several years

D.338: following the first flight of a D.338 prototype in 1936, Air France bought 30 production aircraft: these had retractable landing gear, slightly increased span and a fuselage lengthened by 3.18 m (10 ft 5¼ in) by comparison with the D.332; on short- and medium-distance routes they had provision for 22 passengers, while aircraft on the Far Eastern service had 12 luxury-seats, six of which could be converted as sleeping berths; powered by three 485-kW (650-hp) Hispano-Suiza V16/17 radials, the D.338 had a maximum speed of 301 km/h (187 mph) and cruised at 260 km/h (161 mph); the D.338s achieved a high reputation for reliability, many of them flying passenger routes in French overseas possessions during World War II; nine aircraft which remained airworthy operated the post-war Paris-Nice service for several months.

D.343: one only, built in 1939; had improved lines, accommodated 24 passengers, and was powered by three 682-kW (915-hp) Gnome-Rhône 14N

radial engines; registered F-ARIZ, it was delivered to Air France during 1942

D.620: development of the D.338 with three supercharged 656-kW (880-hp) Gnome-Rhône 14Krsd radials and provision for 30 passengers; the only example built was never delivered for airline service and its ultimate fate is unknown

Specification
Dewoitine D.332
Type: eight-passenger transport
Powerplant: three 429-kW (575-hp) Hispano-Suiza 9V radial piston engines (Wright Cyclones built under licence)
Performance: maximum speed

The D.338 shared the same engine and airframe combination as the D.332, but was far more satisfactory. It was a mainstay of Air France operations.

300 km/h (186 mph); cruising speed 250 km/h (155 mph); service ceiling 6300 m (20,670 ft); range 2000 km (1,243 miles)
Weights: empty equipped 5280 kg (11,640 lb); maximum take-off 9350 kg (20,613 lb)
Dimensions: span 29.00 m (95 ft 1¾ in); length 18.95 m (62 ft 2 in); wing area 80.00 m² (861.14 sq ft)

Dewoitine D.500 Series

Designed to satisfy a French air ministry requirement for a single-seat fighter to replace the Nieuport 62/622, which had entered service during the period 1928-31, the **Dewoitine D.500** was a far more attractive aeroplane. Gone was the antiquated structure with the multiplicity of drag-inducing struts required by a sesquiplane, replaced by a clean cantilever monoplane wing set in low-wing configuration. Construction was all-metal, including the skinning, and construction of wing, fuselage and strut-braced tail unit entirely conventional. The fixed tailwheel landing gear was strongly reminiscent of the D.37 series. Powerplant of the prototype **D.500.01**, which flew for the first time on 19 June 1932, consisted of a 492-kW (660-hp) Hispano-Suiza 12Xbrs inline piston.

Launched with an order for 57 of the **D.501** production varient, placed on 23 November 1933, the D.500 series had many variations, especially in the armament and engines of the 380-odd aircraft which were built by Dewoitine, Loire-Nieuport, Lioré-et-Olivier, and SNCASE after nationalisation of the French aviation industry. The version most extensively in use at the outbreak of World War II was the **D.510**, which had the more powerful 641-kW (860-hp) Hispano-Suiza 12Ycrs engine, increased fuel capacity, a slightly lengthened fuselage nose and refined main landing gear units. Such aircraft equipped Groupes GC I/1, II/1 and I/8 in France in September 1939, and both D.501s and D.510s were in service with a number of overseas squadrons. Of those in France, most had been withdrawn from service or transferred to overseas squadrons before the German attack in May 1940, for the 400-km/h (249-mph) maximum speed of the obsolescent D.510 fighters gave them no chance of survival against the Luftwaffe's Messerschmitt Bf 109s.

Specification
Dewoitine D.501
Type: single-seat fighter
Powerplant: one 515-kW (690-hp) Hispano-Suiza 12Xcrs inline piston engine
Performance: maximum speed 335 km/h (208 mph) at 2,000 m (6,560 ft); cruising speed 225 km/h (140 mph); climb to 1000 m (3,280 ft) in 1 minute 20 seconds; service ceiling 10200 m (33,465 ft); range 870 km (541 miles)
Weights: empty 1287 kg (4,222 lb); normal take-off 1787 kg (5,863 lb)
Dimensions: span 12.09 m (24 ft 9¾ in); length 7.56 m (24 ft 9¾ in); height 2.70 m (8 ft 10¼ in); wing area 16.50 m² (177.61 sq ft)
Armament: one 20-mm HS S7 (Oerlikon) cannon firing through the propeller hub and two wing-mounted 7.5-mm (0.295-in) Darne machine-guns

Dewoitine D.510

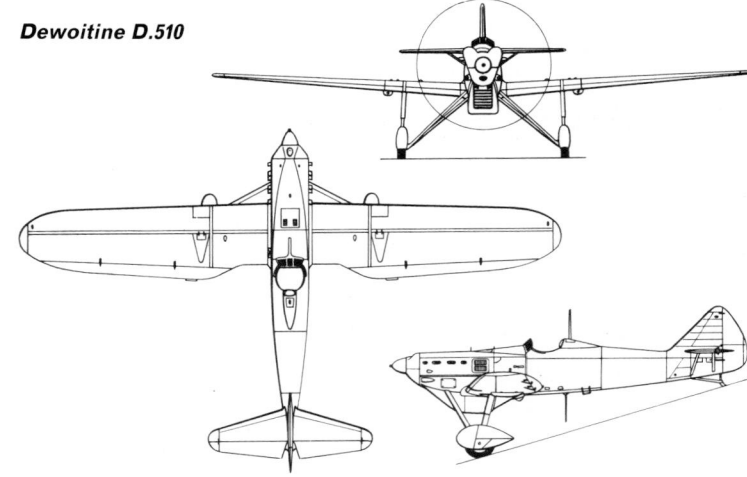

Dewoitine D.510 of the 1ᵉ Escadrille, Groupe de Chasse I/8, Armée de l'Air, based at Marignane in September 1938.

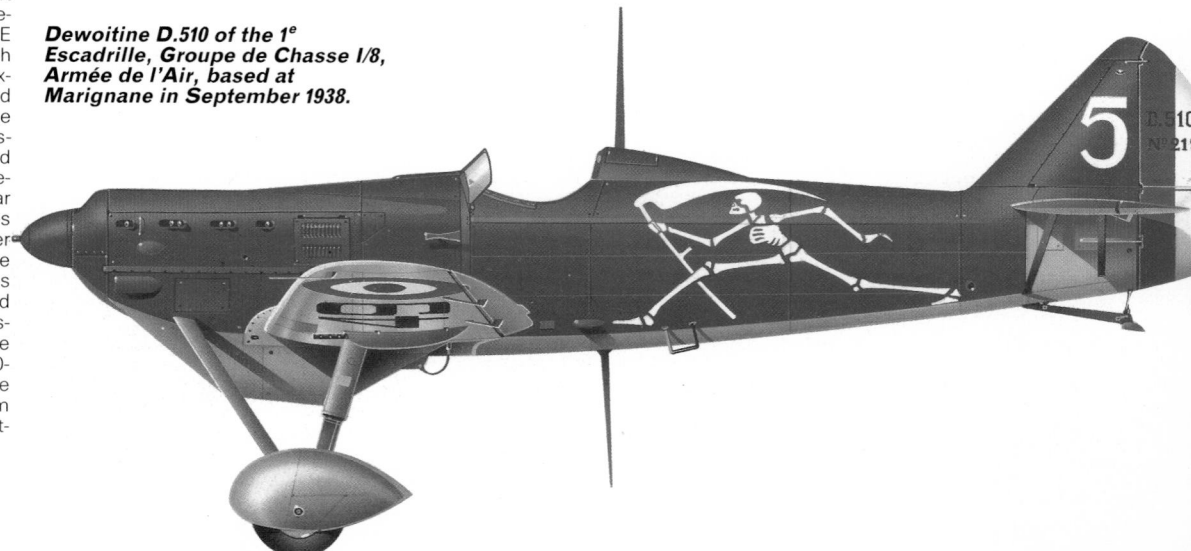

Dewoitine D.520
to
Dornier Do 27

Dewoitine D.520

With development of the D.513 at an end, the company used the lessons learned in the construction of these prototypes to produce the modern-looking **Dewoitine D.520**, the first of whose two prototypes made its maiden flight on 2 October 1938. A cantilever low-wing monoplane, the D.520 looked from the cockpit aft very similar to the D.513. Forward of the cockpit, however, was a wing of new planform with increased dihedral and a much cleaner engine installation. Before the last of three prototypes flew, on 5 May 1939, Dewoitine had already received an order for 200 D.520s and two months later this number had risen to 710.

By then the last details had been finalised for production aircraft, which were to be powered by the Hispano-Suiza 12Y 45 engine with a Szydlowski supercharger, and the first of these was flown on 31 October 1939. Without doubt the most capable fighter of French origin available to the Armée de l'Air in World War II, only about 300 D.520s had been delivered by mid-June 1940 and 403 taken on charge by the time of the armistice with Germany on 25 June 1940. Production of the D.520 was authorised in

Vichy, France, 478 being built before and after Germany occupied the whole of France. Captured aircraft plus production aircraft were delivered to Germany's allies, including Bulgaria, Italy and Romania, and were used also by the Luftwaffe as fighter trainers.

Variants
D.521: designation of a single D.520 following installation of a 768-kW (1,030-hp) Rolls-Royce Merlin III inline engine; production of this version had been planned but was subsequently cancelled; in any event the heavy Merlin engine proved unsatisfactory
D.524: designation allocated for the D.521 following removal of the Merlin engine and installation of a 895-kW (1,200-hp) Hispano-Suiza 12Z; its development was abandoned

Specification
Dewoitine D.520
Type: single-seat fighter
Powerplant: one 697-kW (935-hp) Hispano-Suiza 12Y 45 inline piston engine
Performance: maximum speed 534 km/h (332 mph) at 5500 m

(18,045 ft); climb to 4000 m (13,125 ft) in 5 minutes 48 seconds; service ceiling 10500 m (34,450 ft); range at cruising speed 1530 km (950 miles)
Weights: empty 2036 kg (4,489 lb); maximum take-off 2677 kg (5,902 lb)
Dimensions: span 10.20 m (33 ft

5½ in); length 8.60 m (28 ft 2½ in); height 2.57 m (8 ft 5¼ in); wing area 15.97 m² (171.91 sq ft)
Armament: one 20-mm engine-mounted HS 404 cannon and four wing-mounted 7.5-mm (0.295-in) MAC 34 M39 machine-guns

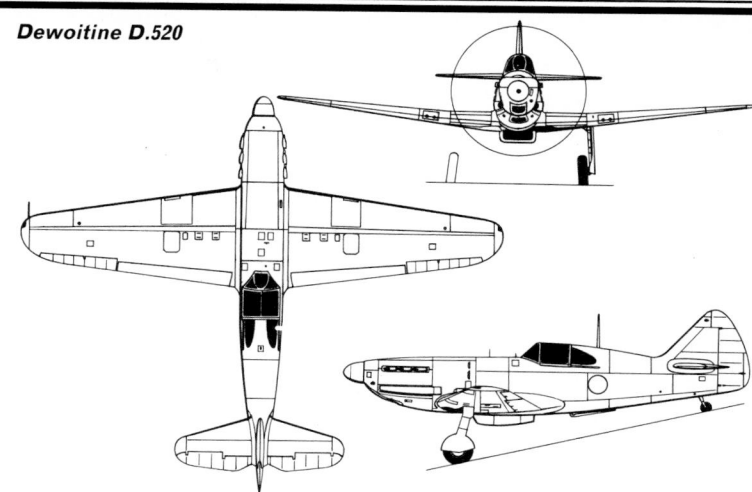

Dewoitine D.520

Dewoitine HD.730

To meet a French navy requirement of 1937 for a light observation/scout aircraft suitable for catapult launching, a team led by Emile Dewoitine designed the **Dewoitine HD.730** for the Société Nationale de Constructions Aéronautiques du Midi (SNCAM): this was the nationalised concern which had absorbed the original Dewoitine company.

Of all-metal construction, except for fabric-covered control surfaces, the HD.730 was a cantilever low-wing monoplane with wings that could be folded for shipboard stowage, twin-float landing gear, a tail unit incorporating endplate fins and rudders, and a fuselage providing accommodation for a crew of two in tandem beneath a long transparent canopy. Two prototypes were ordered in March 1938, powered initially by a Renault 6Q-03 inline engine, and the **HD.730.01** prototype flew for the first time from the Berre lake in February 1940. Testing of this aircraft, and of the **HD.730.02** which flew in May 1940, showed that more power was needed, so a 261 kW (350 hp) Bearn 6D engine was planned for production aircraft. Because of the French collapse no production was undertaken and development of the HD.730 prototypes temporarily came to an end.

Despite the capitulation, a redesigned third machine was developed under the designation **HD.731.01**. This was of reduced dimensions by comparison with the HD.730, and had the Bearn 6D powerplant that had been planned for production aircraft. In this form the aircraft was flown for the first time on 11 March 1941, but flight testing was interspersed with modifications until it was decided that increased wing area was

Dewoitine HD.730 first prototype under test in 1940.

essential, and further development was abandoned.

By then the original prototypes had been re-engined with Bearn 6D engines, but only the HD.730.2 was flown and, on a stop-start basis, this was modified and flown over a five-year period until interest in its development had evaporated.

Variant
HD.732: designation allocated to the prototype of a training version with a Renault 6Q engine; construction not completed

Specification
Dewoitine HD.730.01
Type: two-seat observation/scout floatplane prototype
Powerplant: one 164-kW (220-hp) Renault 6Q-03 inline piston engine
Performance: maximum speed

230 km/h (143 mph) at 2000 m (6,560 ft); cruising speed 225 km/h (140 mph) at 1500 m (4,920 ft); service ceiling 5120 m (16,800 ft); range without bombs 1350 km (839 miles)
Weights: empty 1173 kg (2,586 lb); maximum take-off 1870 kg (4,123 lb)
Dimensions: span 12.60 m (41 ft

4 in); length 9.75 m (32 ft 0 in); height 3.18 m (10 ft 5¼ in); wing area 20.00 m² (215.29 sq ft)
Armament: two 7.5-mm (0.295-in) Darne machine-guns (one forward-firing and the other on flexible mount for the observer/gunner), plus up to eight 10-kg (22-lb) bombs

The HD.730 was a potentially useful design wasted by protracted development with inadequate engines.

Donnet-Denhaut flying-boats

Donnet and Denhaut formed a new partnership in 1914 with workshops on the Isle de la Jatte. When the French navy was confronted with the U-boat menace at the outbreak of World War I there were a mere handful of seaplanes of assorted types in service. The French admiralty accordingly turned to established companies, including Donnet-Denhaut, to produce flying-boats in large numbers for coastal patrol work. When the first Donnet-Denhaut 'boats went into service during 1916 they represented a considerable advance over the early FBA types then operating at the naval air stations. Powered by 119-kW (160-hp) Salmson/Canton-Unné engines, they had an endurance of 4 hours 30 minutes and could carry two 35-kg (77-lb) or 52-kg (115-lb) bombs.

The construction and layout was typical of all Donnet-Denhaut flying-boats (of which over 1,100 were built up to 1922) with unequal-span wings and hull of wood, the former fabric-covered and the latter skinned with plywood. Denhaut's designs were unique among French flying-boats of the period in having the fin of the tail unit built integrally with the hull, and the rudder in two sections as a result of the tailplane being mounted halfway up the fin. Initial production aircraft, designated **HB.2** (*Hydravion de Bombardement 2-Places*, or two-seat bomber flying-boat), had the unequal-span wings typical of Denhaut designs, but these were only of single-bay construction; when production reached its peak two-bay wings were introduced. As with all contemporary single-engined flying-boats the pilot was seated in an open cockpit just forward of the wing leading edge, with the observer/gunner in a cockpit in the bow

Successor to the DD.2, the DD.8 was the company's most successful flying-boat. This example was attached to Brest naval air station. Note the rudder split in two by the elevators.

operating the sole defensive armament of one 7.7-mm (0.303-in) machine-gun. The engine was mounted between the wings, driving a two-blade pusher propeller.

The company's next offering was the **DD.2**, powered by a 112-kW (150-hp) Hispano-Suiza; it was followed by the **DD.8**, which went into production in May 1917. This had a more powerful Hispano-Suiza and considerable structural strengthening, including the introduction of a pair of diagonal bracing struts on the outer wing sections on each side. DD.2s and DD.8s not only saw widespread service with the French Aéronautique Maritime, from bases on the Channel and Atlantic coasts and in the Mediterranean, but were employed in considerable numbers by the US Navy, which flew them from eight bases in France during 1917 and 1918. A batch of DD.8s was also purchased by Portugal, some serving with the naval air arm until 1923.

After four Dunkirk-based FBA flying-boats had been forced down and captured by German floatplanes in May 1917, an accelerated programme was started to produce more heavily defended French 'boats. Denhaut designed the **DD.9**, with a three-man crew and twin machine-gun mountings in bow and midships cockpit. Approximately 100 were built. In appearance the DD.9 resembled an enlarged DD.8, but with

four-bay wing configuration and an enlarged rounded rudder, powered by the same 149-kW (200-hp) engine. The next development of the DD.8 was a three-bay biplane in the HB.3 three-seat category, powered by a 224-kW (300-hp) Hispano-Suiza 8Fd (and similarly-rated Salmson) engine, and this version was often known as the **'Donnet-Denhaut 300-hp'**. In fact, in the French navy most flying-boats of the period were known to personnel by the total horse-power of their powerplant; it at least avoided entanglement with rather complex manufacturers' designations!

Culmination of the Donnet-Denhaut designs was the twin-engine **DD.10**, which appeared in 1918. A three-bay biplane, its two 224-kW (300-hp) Hispano-Suiza engines were strut-mounted between the hull and upper wing centre section, arranged to drive a tractor and a pusher propeller. Armament comprised four machine-guns on twin bow and midships mountings. However, the November 1918 armistice prevented the DD.10s from flying operationally, and it is doubtful if all of the 30 aircraft on order were delivered.

After the war Donnet and Denhaut parted company, but Hydravions J. Donnet opened repair shops in Tunis to sup-

plement premises in France and continued production of the 224-kW (300-hp) model on a limited scale. In 1919 a number were converted for civil use and a route linking Antibes on the French Riviera and Ajaccio (Corsica) was inaugurated with Donnet 'boats in November 1921. The operating company, Aéronavale, retained a number of the type in service until the last examples were scrapped in 1927.

Specification
Donnet-Denhaut DD.8

Type: coastal reconnaissance and patrol flying-boat

Powerplant: one 149-kW (200-hp) Hispano-Suiza 8A V-8 piston engine

Performance: maximum speed 130 km/h (81 mph); range 500 km (311 miles)

Weights: empty equipped 950 kg (2,094 lb); maximum take-off 1800 kg (3,968 lb)

Dimensions: span 16.80 m (55 ft 1½ in); length 9.50 m (31 ft 2 in); height 3.00 m (9 ft 10 in); wing area 61.00 m² (656.62 sq ft)

Armament: one 7.7-mm (0.303-in) Lewis machine-gun, plus up to 104 kg (229 lb) of bombs

By the standards of the day the DD.9 was well-protected, with pairs of Lewis guns in the nose and dorsal positions. Between the turrets is the sturdy pylon arrangement for the engine.

The DD.10 was a pleasing four-bay flying-boat with elegant hull lines. Notable features are the tandem engine arrangement, strut connecting upper and lower ailerons and long dorsal fin.

Dorand AR.1/AR.2

During 1916 Colonel Dorand, then head of the French army's Section Technique de l'Aéronautique, designed a two-seat reconnaissance biplane. This was built in considerable numbers by the government's factory at Chalais-Meudon, as well as by Farman and Letord under subcontract. Of fairly conventional construction for its day, it was unusual in having back-staggered wings with the fuselage set well above the lower wing; both wings incorporated large cut-outs in their trailing edges. Robust fixed tailskid landing gear was provided for operation from rough airfields, and powerplant of

the first production version, the **Dorand AR.1**, was a Renault 8Gdy inline engine. The second production version, designated **AR.2**, was generally similar, but differed by having reduced wing span and was powered by a 142 kW (190-hp) Renault 8Ge engine.

Built in large numbers for the Aviation Militaire, which used them on the Italian and Western Fronts from the spring of 1917 until early 1918, the AR.1 and AR.2 were also acquired by the Air Service, American Expeditionary Force. A total of 22 AR.1s and 120 AR.2s was bought by the US, these being operated as trainers

Worthy but unexceptional, the AR.1 was notable mainly for its backward-staggered wings and its fuselage set in mid-gap between the upper and lower centre-sections.

and advanced trainers respectively. Dorand's first design had been the unsuccessful pre-war **DO.1**.

Specification
Dorant AR.1

Type: two-seat observation aircraft

Powerplant: one 149-kW (200-hp) Renault 8Gdy inline piston engine

Performance: maximum speed 148 km/h (92 mph) at 2000 m (6,560 ft)

Weight: maximum take-off 1315 kg (2,900 lb)

Dimensions: span 13.30 m (43 ft 7½ in); length 9.15 m (30 ft 0 in); wing area 50.17 m² (540.0 sq ft)

Armament: one fixed forward-firing synchronised 7.7-mm (0.303-in) Vickers machine-gun and one or two flexible 7.7-mm (0.303-in) Lewis machine-guns

Dornier Do 17/Do 215

In response to a Lufthansa specification of 1933 for a six-passenger mailplane, Dornier designed a shoulder-wing all-metal monoplane to be powered by two 492-kW (660-hp) BMW VI engines. Three prototypes of this **Dornier Do 17** were built in 1934, but although the airline carried out an evaluation programme early in the following year, the aircraft's slim fuselage provided such limited passenger accommodation that all three were returned to the manufacturer. The design had military potential, however, and a fourth prototype (**Do 17 V4**) with twin vertical tail surfacs and a shortened fuselage was flown in the summer of 1935. Among development prototypes, the fifth was powered by 641-kW (860-hp) Hispano-Suiza 12Ybrs engines, the seventh mounted a 7.92-mm (0.31-in) MG 15 machine-gun in a dorsal blister, and the tenth was fitted with 559-kW (750-hp) BMW VI engines. The initial production versions were the Do 17E-1 bomber and the Do 17F-1 reconnaissance aircraft, both of which made their operational debut in Spain during 1937.

Variants
Do 17E-1: developed from the ninth prototype; had a glazed, shortened nose and carried a 500-kg (1,102-lb) bombload

Do 17F-1: a photographic reconnaissance aircraft with two cameras and increased fuel capacity

Do 17K: developed for Yugoslavia, the Do 17K was similar to the Do 17M but powered by two 731-kW (980-hp) Gnome-Rhône 14N½ engines; the type was licence-built by the Drzavna Fabrika Aviona at Kraljevo; the three versions were the **Do 17Kb-1** bomber, and the **Do 17Ka-2** and **Do 17Ka-3** reconnaissance aircraft with secondary bombing and attack capability

Do 17L: two prototypes of a proposed pathfinder version, powered by two 671-kW (900-hp) Bramo 323A-1 engines

Do 17M: the thirteenth and

fourteenth prototypes, powered by Bramo 322A-1 engines, were used to develop the airframe/engine combination for the production **Do 17M-1**, which could carry a 1000-kg (2,205-lb) bombload and was armed with three 7.92-mm (0.31-in) MG 15 machine-guns, in dorsal and ventral positions and one firing through the starboard windscreen

Do 17R: two engine test-beds, one with 708-kW (950-hp) Daimler-Benz DB 600Gs and other with 746-kW (1,000-hp) Daimler-Benz DB 601As

Do 17P: the photographic-reconnaissance version of the Do 17M, which was powered by two 652-kW (875-hp) BMW 132N engines and fitted with Rb20/30 and Rb50/30, or Rb20/8 and Rb50/8 cameras in the **Do 17P-1** production series

Do 17S-0: three DB-600G-powered high-speed reconnaissance aircraft for trials with a prone gunner's posititon in the underside of the forward fuselage, housing an aft-firing MG 15 machine-gun; the nose was extensively glazed

Do 17U: 15 **Do 17U-0** and **Do 17U-1** aircraft were built to this standard as pathfinders, carrying two radio operators among the five-man crew

Do 17Z: the most numerous of the Do 17s, some 1,700 being built between 1939 and 1940, the Do 17Z appeared in several versions: the **Do 17Z-0** was similar to the Do 17S, with two 671-kW (900-hp) Bramo 323A-1 engines and armed with three MG 15 guns; the **Do 17Z-1** had an additional nose-mounted MG 15 but was under-powered and able to carry only a 500-kg (1,102-lb) bombload, the substitution of 746-kW (1,000-hp) Bramo 323P engines in the **Do 17Z-2**

restored the bombload to 1000 kg (2,205 lb) and up to eight MG 15s were fitted; 22 **Do 17Z-3** aircraft were built for reconnaissance duties, with Rb50/30 or Rb20/30 cameras; the **Do 17Z-4** was a dual-control conversion trainer and the **Do 17Z-5** was essentially a Do 17Z-2 with flotation bags in the fuselage and the rear of the engine bays; a single **Do 17Z-6 Kauz I** (Screech Owl I) long-range intruder and night-fighter was produced, incorporating a Junkers Ju 88C-2 nose carrying a 20-mm MG FF cannon and three MG 17 machine-guns; a new nose was developed for the nine **Do 17Z-10 Kauz II** aircraft, housing four 7.92-mm (0.31-in) MG 17s and four MG FF's; for night-fighter duties they were equipped with *Lichtenstein C1* radar and *Spanner-II-Anlage* infra-red detection apparatus

Do 215: developed originally as an export Do 17Z, the **Do 215A-1** (with 802-kW/1,075-hp Daimler-Benz DB 601-A engines) was ordered by Sweden in 1939 but the 18 aircraft were embargoed and delivered instead to the Luftwaffe as the **Do 215B-0** and **Do 215B-1**; two **Do 215B-3**

aircraft were delivered to the Soviet Union in 1940 and the **Do 215B-4** was a photographic reconnaissance aircraft with Rb20/30 and Rb50/30 cameras; a new nose similar to that of the Do 17Z-10 and with similar armament was fitted to the **Do 215B-5** night-fighter

Specification
Dornier Do 17Z-2
Type: four-seat medium bomber
Powerplant: two 746-kW (1,000-hp) Bramo 323P Fafnir radial piston engines
Performance: maximum speed 410 km/h (255 mph) at 1220 m (4,000 ft); cruising speed 300 km/h (186 mph) at 4000 m (13,125 ft); service ceiling 8200 m (26,905 ft); range 1160 km (721 miles)
Weights: empty 5210 kg (11,488 lb); maximum take-off 8590 kg (18,940 lb)
Dimensions: span 18.00 m (59 ft 1 in); length 15.80 m (51 ft 10 in); height 4.55 m (14 ft 11 in); wing area 55.00 m² (592.0 sq ft)
Armament: up to seven 7.92-mm (0.31-in) MG 15 machine-guns, plus 1000 kg (2,205 lb) of bombs

The Do 17E-1 was the first production example of this famous bomber. Ten 50-kg (110-lb) or four 100-kg (220-lb) bombs were standard loads.

The Do 215B-1 began life as the Do 215A-1 bomber for the Swedish air force, but was completed on the lines as a long-range reconnaissance aircraft for service with 3./Aufklärungsstaffel/ObdL.

Do 17Z-2 bombers of 15.(Kroat)/KG 53, a Croatian volunteer unit. The Z-2 introduced a greater bombload compared with the Z-1, but only with a drop in combat radius to just 330 km (205 miles).

Dornier Do 18

Successor to the very successful Wal flying-boats, the **Dornier Do 18** was developed as a transoceanic mail plane for Lufthansa in 1934. It retained the basic metal hull and stabilising sponsons which had characterised the earlier aircraft, but was aerodynamically more efficient. Powered by two 493-kW (540-hp) Junkers Jumo 5 diesel engines, the **Do 18a** prototype was first flown on 15 March 1935 and was followed by four of the **Do 18E** version with improved 447-kW (600-hp) Jumo 205C engines. Lufthansa's sixth aircraft was the sole **Do 18F**, first flown on 11 June 1937 and which between 27-29 March 1938 established a non-stop straightline seaplane distance record of 8391 km (5,214 miles) in 43 hours, flying from England to

Brazil. It later became the **Do 18L** when modified by the installation of 656-kW (880-hp) BMW 132N engines and made its first flight thus powered on 21 November 1839.

The Do 18 was adopted for Luftwaffe use with coastal reconnaissance units and entered service in September 1938. The second German aircraft to be brought down by British forces in World War II was a Dornier 18 of 2./Küstenfliegergruppe 506 which, on 26 September 1939, was forced down by Lieutenant B. S. McEwen of the Fleet Air Arm's No. 803 Squadron, operating from HMS *Ark Royal* in the North Sea. Production of just over 100 Do 18s was completed in 1940 and, following replacement by the Blohm und Voss Bv 138, the type had been relegated to air-sea rescue duties by 1942.

Variants
Do 18D-1: this was the first military production version, powered by Jumo 205C engines and armed with single 7.92-mm (0.31-in) MG 15 machine-guns

Built for the mailplane role, the Do 18 nevertheless proved a useful long-range reconnaissance platform in the first phases of World War II.

Dornier Do 18D of 3./Küstenfliegergruppe 406, based at List on the island of Sylt in August 1939.

in open bow and dorsal positions; equipment changes led to the **Do 18D-2** and **Do 18D-3** in 1938

Do 18G-1: an improved version of the Do 18D, with 656-kW (880-hp) Jumo 205D engines and with a 13-mm (0.51-in) MG 131 machine-gun in the bow and a 20-mm MG 151 cannon in a power-operated dorsal turret

Do 18H: this designation was applied to a small number of dual-control unarmed trainers

Do 18N-1: unarmed air-sea rescue aircraft converted from Do 18Gs

Specification
Dornier Do 18G-1
Type: four-seat coastal reconnaissance flying-boat
Powerplant: two 656-kW (880-hp) Junkers Jumo 205D diesel engines
Performance: maximum speed 260 km/h (162 mph); cruising speed 220 km/h (137 mph); service ceiling 4200 m (13,780 ft); maximum range 3500 km (2,175 miles)
Weights: empty 5850 kg (12,897 lb); maximum take-off 10000 kg (22,046 lb)
Dimensions: span 23.70 m (77 ft 9 in); length 19.25 m (63 ft 2 in); height 5.35 m (17 ft 6½ in); wing area 98.00 m² (1054.89 sq ft)
Armament: one 13-mm (0.51-in) MG 131 machine-gun in the bow position and one 20-mm MG 151 cannon in the dorsal turret, plus two 50-kg (110-lb) bombs under the starboard wing

Dornier Do 19

Potentially a useful long-range bomber, the Dornier Do 19 took to the air only in the form of the Do 19 V1 first prototype, and the project was cancelled after the death of General Wever. Note the lack of turreted armament.

The Luftwaffe's first Chief of Staff, Generalleutnant Walther Wever, was a keen advocate of the long-range strategic bomber and, largely as a result of his promptings, the RLM's Technische Amt issued a specification for a four-engined heavy bomber of this category. Both Dornier and Junkers completed preliminary studies for such an aircraft, and each received in late 1935 an order for three prototypes under the respective designations **Dornier Do 19** and Ju 89.

A mid-wing cantilever monoplane, largely of metal construction, the Do 19 had a rectangular-section fuselage; a tail unit with braced twin fins and rudders mounted on the upper surface of the tailplane, at approximately mid-span on each side; tailwheel landing gear, with all three units retracting; and powerplant comprising four Bramo 322H-2 radial engines, mounted in nacelles at the wing leading edges. Accommodation was provided for a crew of nine, consisting of pilot, co-pilot/navigator, bomb-aimer, radio operator and five gunners.

The **Do 19 V1** prototype flew for the

first time on 28 October 1936, but by then an event had occurred which was to bring development of the long-range strategic bombers to an end. On 3 June 1936 Generalleutnant Wever had lost his life in an aircraft crash and his successor, Generalleutnant Albert Kesselring, concluded that the Luftwaffe's more urgent requirements were increased numbers of fighters and tactical bombers of greater capability. The **Do 19 V2**, which was almost ready to fly, and the incomplete **Do 19 V3** were both scrapped; the Do 19 V1 saw limited use as a military transport following conversion for such a role during 1939.

Specification
Type: long-range strategic bomber
Powerplant: four 533-kW (715-hp) Bramo 322H-2 radial piston engines
Performance: maximum speed at sea level 315 km/h (196 mph); cruising speed 250 km/h (155 mph) at 2000 m (6,560 ft); service ceiling 5600 m (18,370 ft); range 1600 km (994 miles)
Weights: empty 11850 kg (25,125 lb); maximum take-off 18500 kg (40,786 lb)
Dimensions: span 35.00 m (114 ft 10 in); length 25.45 m (83 ft 6 in); height 5.77 m (18 ft 11 in); wing area 162.00 m² (1,743.81 sq ft)
Armament: (intended) two 7.92-mm (0.31-in) MG 15 machine-guns (one each in nose and tail positions) and two 20-mm cannon (one each in two-man operated ventral and dorsal turrets), plus up to 1600 kg (3,527 lb) of bombs in internal bays

Dornier Do 22

Development of the three-seat **Dornier Do 22** floatplane was the responsibility of Dornier's Altenrhein factory in Switzerland, where two prototypes were built. Of all-metal construction with fabric covering throughout, except for the metal-skinned forward fuselage, the Do 22 was powered by a Hispano-Suiza 12Ybrs engine driving a three-bladed propeller. The Do 22 carried a crew of three, the rear cockpit providing accommodation for a gunner, and a radio operator whose position in the front half of the cockpit was protected by a glazed canopy. Four 7.92-mm (0.31-in) MG 15 machine-guns were fitted, one in the forward fuselage above the engine, one in a ventral position and two in the rear cockpit. Although not ordered by the Luftwaffe, approximately 30 were built at Friedrichshafen in Germany and the first

production aircraft was flown on 15 July 1938. Do 22s were supplied to the Greek, Yugoslav and Latvian air forces as the **Do 22Kg**, **Do 22Kj** and **Do 22K1** respectively.

Variant
Do 22L: designation applied to a single landplane version, with fixed spatted landing gear, which was flown on 10 March 1939

Specification
Type: three-seat utility floatplane
Powerplant: one 641-kW (860-hp) Hispano-Suiza 12Ybrs inline piston engine
Performance: maximum speed 350 km/h (217 mph) at 3000 m (9,840 ft); service ceiling 9000 m (29,530 ft); range 2300 km (1,429 miles)
Weights: empty 2600 kg (5,734 lb); maximum take-off 4000 kg (8,820 lb)

Intended primarily for export, the Do 22 was built for Greece, Latvia and Yugoslavia (illustrated). Twelve Do 22Kj were delivered to Yugoslavia, eight escaping to Egypt in 1941.

Dimensions: span 16.20 m (53 ft 2 in); length 13.12 m (43 ft 0½ in); height 4.85 m (15 ft 11 in); wing area 45.00 m² (484.39 sq ft)
Armament: four 7.92-mm (0.31-in) MG 15 machine-guns (in nose and ventral positions and in the rear cockpit), plus one 800-kg (1,764-lb) torpedo or four 50-kg (100-lb) bombs

Dornier Do 24

The **Dornier Do 24** originated from a Dutch navy requirement of 1935 for a replacement for the Dornier Wals then being used in the Netherlands East Indies. An all-metal monoplane with a shallow, broad-beamed hull and stabilising sponsons, the Do 24 had a strut-mounted wing which carried three

engines. The first two prototypes, for possible German use, were powered by 447-kW (600-hp) Junkers Juno 205C diesel engines. The third prototype (which was the first to fly, on 3 July 1937) and the fourth were powered by 652-kW (875-hp) Wright R-1820-F52 Cyclones, in order to meet the Dutch desire to use the same engine as those fitted to their Martin 139 bombers; on successful completion of the test programme the

rest of the Dutch order was completed at Altenrhein under the designation **Do 24K-1**. Licence production of a further 48 **Do 24K-2** aircraft, with 746-kW (1,000-hp) R-1820-G102 engines, was undertaken by Aviolanda in Holland, de Schelde building the wings, but only 25 had been delivered before the German occupation in May 1940. Three completed aircraft and a number of partly built airframes were transferred to Ger-

many for evaluation in the air-sea rescue role and, as a result, the Dutch line was re-established under the control of the German company Weser Flugzeugbau, its production totalling 170 aircraft. A further 48 **Do 24T-1** aircraft were built for the Luftwaffe at the SNCA du Nord plant at Sartrouville in France between 1942 and August 1944, and 40 more were delivered to the French navy after the liberation. Twelve **Do 24T-3** aircraft were supplied to Spain under the designation **HR.5**, deliveries starting in June 1944, to provide search and rescue cover in the Mediterranean for aircrew of both sides. The type remained in Spanish service, based at Pollensa, Majorca, until well into the 1970s.

Variants

Do 24N-1: 11 Dutch-built Do 24K-2s were completed to this standard as air-sea rescue aircraft for the Luftwaffe, retaining the Wright R-1820-G012 engines; the first was delivered in August 1941

Do 24T: 159 Do 24T-1, Do 24T-2 and **Do 24T-3** aircraft, with minor equipment changes, were manufactured during the German occupation of Holland; they were powered by three 746-kW (1,000-hp) BMW-Bramo 323R-2 Fafnir engines and served principally with 1., 2. and 3./Seenotgruppe based at Biscarosse, near Bordeaux, and Beere near Marseilles

Do 24TT: flying in early 1983, a Do 24TT prototype was built with the TNT

advanced technology wing developed for the Do 228 commuter airliner and with three Pratt & Whitney of Canada PT6A-45 turboprop engines

Do 318: designation of a single prototype modified in 1944 by Weser with an Arado-designed boundary-layer control system; tests were very successful, but the aircraft was scuttled in Lake Constance in 1945

Specification
Dornier Do 24T

Type: maritime patrol-search and rescue flying-boat
Powerplant: three 746-kW (1,000-hp) BMW-Bramo 323R-2 radial piston engines
Performance: maximum speed 340 km/h (211 mph) at 3000 m (9,840 ft); cruising speed 295 km/h (183 mph); service ceiling 5900 m (19,355 ft); maximum range 2900 km (1,802 miles)
Weights: empty 9200 kg (20,286 lb); maximum take-off 18400 kg (40,565 lb)
Dimensions: span 27.00 m (88 ft 7 in); length 21.95 m (72 ft 0½ in);

height 5.75 m (18 ft 10¼ in); wing area 108.00 m² (1,162.5 sq ft)
Armament: one 7.92-mm (0.31-in) MG 15 machine-gun in each of the bow

and tail positions, and one 20-mm MG 151 cannon in a power-operated dorsal turret

Derived for German service from the Do 24K-2, the Do 24N-1 had a dorsal turret fitted with a 20-mm Hispano-Suiza HS 404 cannon, large stocks of which were captured in 1940.

Dornier Do 26

Aerodynamically the cleanest of the Dornier flying-boats, the all-metal **Dornier Do 26** was developed for transatlantic mail services, designed to carry a crew of four and 500 kg (1,102 lb) of mail between Lisbon and New York. The midspan stabilising floats retracted completely into the wings, and the rear pair of the two tandem pairs of Junkers Jumo 205 diesel engines could be given an upward tilt of 10° on take-off so that the three-bladed metal propellers were clear of the spray from the hull. Three Do 26s, stressed for catapult launching from support ships, were ordered by Deutsche Lufthansa in 1937, and the first of these was flown on 21 May 1938. Two of the three were completed before the outbreak of World War II and delivered to the airline under the designation **Do 26A**. They were never used as intended, across the North Atlantic, and

made just 18 crossings of the South Atlantic.

Variants

Do 26B: this designation was applied originally to the third aircraft which was to have been built with an enlarged cabin seating for passengers; it was completed as the first Do 26D

Do 26D: four aircraft built for the Luftwaffe, with 522-kW (700-hp) Jumo 205Ea engines and armed with three 7.92-mm (0.31-in) MG 15 machine-guns and a bow turret containing a 20-mm MG 151b cannon; by April 1940, together with the two Lufthansa aircraft, they were being used as transports in Norway capable of carrying up to 12 fully-equipped troops; the Do 26Ds served with the Transozean Staffel and later with Küstenfliegergruppe 406

Specification
Dornier Do 26A

Type: transatlantic mail or coastal patrol flying-boat
Powerplant: four 447-kW (600-hp) Junkers Jumo 205 diesel engines
Performance: maximum speed 335 km/h (208 mph); long-range cruising speed 265 km/h (165 mph); service ceiling 4800 m (15,750 ft); maximum range 9000 km (5,592 miles)
Weights: empty 10700 kg (23,589 lb);

A radical feature of the Do 26 (V4 fourth prototype illustrated) was the rear engines which angled upwards for take-off.

maximum take-off 20000 kg (44,092 lb)
Dimensions: span 30.00 m (98 ft 5 in); length 24.60 m (80 ft 8½ in); height 6.85 m (22 ft 6 in); wing area 120.00 m² (1,291.71 sq ft)

Dornier Do 27

The **Dornier Do 27** was the first aircraft to enter production in Germany after World War II. Claudius Dornier recommenced activities in Spain in 1949, his Oficinas Tecnicas Dornier working closely with the Spanish CASA. The initial fruits of this collaboration were evident with the first flight of the **Do 25** in June 1954. Prepared to meet a Spanish air ministry specification, the STOL transport was powered by a single 112-kW (150-hp) ENMA Tigre engine; 50 similar aircraft appeared subsequently under the designation **CASA C-127**.

Developed from this, the prototype Do 27 was flown on 8 April 1955. Production took place in Germany at Dornier-Werke, the first example flying in October 1956. With a large 'wraparound' windscreen and generous five-seat layout, the **Do 27A** proved popular. Deliveries began at 20 aircraft per month.

The main military Do 27A and dual-control **Do 27B** differed little. The strutless high wing provided ease of access for loading passengers or freight. Large flaps give an amazing STOL capability. More than 600 were built before production ended during 1965. By far the largest

user was the Federal German Republic, which received 428 Do 27As; another early customer was the Swiss Flugwaffe, whose initial seven aircraft had wheel-and-ski landing gear. Others were supplied to the Belgian, Congolese, Israeli, Nigerian, Portuguese, Swedish, South African and Turkish air forces.

Variants

Do 27H: civil or military version powered by 254-kW (240-hp) Avco Lycoming GSO-480 engine

Do 27Q-5: civil version, similar to Do 27A, but with provision for the installation of quick conversion kits for use in advanced training, ambulance, glider-towing and photographic survey roles

Do 27Q-5(R): restricted-category version of Q-5, equipped for operation by pilot only in agricultural or forest dusting/spraying roles

Do 27Q-6: basically similar to Q5, but completed to the certification requirements of the US civil aviation authority

Do 27S: designation of a twin floatplane version of which a single prototype was built

Do 27T: designation of a single prototype powered by Turboméca Astazou II turboprop engine

Specification
Dornier Do 27A

Type: general-purpose light transport
Powerplant: one 201-kW (270-hp) Avco Lycoming GO-480-B1A6 flat-six piston engine
Performance: maximum speed 227 km/h (141 mph) at 1000 m (3,280 ft); economic cruising speed 175 km/h (109 mph); service ceiling 3300 m (10,825 ft); range with maximum fuel 1100 km (684 miles)
Weights: empty equipped 1130 kg

Proving popular with civil and military customers alike, the Do 27 offered its occupants exceptional all-round visibility and its operators a high degree of reliability and economy.

(2,491 lb); maximum take-off 1850 kg (4,079 lb)
Dimensions: span 12.00 m (39 ft 4½ in); length 9.60 m (31 ft 6 in); height 2.80 m (9 ft 2¼ in); wing area 19.40 m² (208.83 sq ft)

Dornier Do 28
to
Dornier Do J Wal and Do Super Wal

Dornier Do 28

Following the success of the Do 27 it was decided to produce a basically similar twin-engined version designated **Dornier Do 28**, the prototype flying for the first time on 29 April 1959 powered by two 134-kW (180-hp) Avco Lycoming O-360-A1A engines. Although it bore a strong resemblance to its predecessor, the Do 28 was, however, a completely new aircraft with the engines mounted near the tips of short stub wings. Experience with the prototype led to an increase in wing span and area and the engines were replaced by 186-kW (250-hp) Avco Lycoming O-540s. In this form it went into production as the **Do 28A-1** and 60 were built. The next production model was the **Do 28B-1** with Avco Lycoming IO-540 engines and a number of improvements such as auxiliary wing-tip fuel tanks, and enlarged tailplane and electrically actuated flaps. The Do 28B-1 entered production in 1963 and 60 were built, these including a few of the **Do 28B-2** version with turbocharged engines.

In addition to those delivered for the home market, Do 28s were supplied to a number of companies around the world, including some in the UK, Canada, Denmark, Japan, Spain, Sweden and the USA. Interest in the Do 28 was shown also by the German military authorities, leading to development of the **Do 28D Skyservant** which retained the basic layout of the earlier design but was completely new in all other aspects and is described separately.

Variants
Do 28A-1-S: designation of a floatplane conversion of the Do 28A-1 by the Jobmaster Company of Seattle, Washington
Do 28B-1-S: designation applied to a projected floatplane conversion of the Do 28B-1 by the Jobmaster Company in the USA
Do 28C: designation allocated to proposed development of the Do 28B-1 with two 216-kW (530-shp) Turboméca Astazou II turboprop engines, pressurised accommodation and a redesigned flight deck

Specification
Dornier Do 28B-1

This view of a Do 28B-1 shows clearly the unorthodox engine mounting. Also visible is the dorsal fin added to the original Do 27 fin.

Type: eight-seat general-purpose transport
Powerplant: two 216-kW (290-hp) Avco Lycoming IO-540A flat-six piston engines
Performance: maximum speed 290 km/h (180 mph); economic cruising speed 240 km/h (149 mph); service ceiling 6300 m (20,670 ft); range with maximum payload and standard fuel 1235 km (767 miles)
Weights: empty equipped 1730 kg (3,814 lb); maximum take-off 2720 kg (5,997 lb)
Dimensions: span 13.8 m (45 ft 3¼ in); length 9 m (29 ft 6¼ in); height 2.8 m (9 ft 2¼ in); wing area 22.4 m² (241.12 sq ft)

Dornier Do 28D/Do 128

While the original Do 28 series had an advantage over the Do 27 by providing twin-engine safety and enhanced performance, it did not have any more internal space, the cabin dimensions being identical to those of its predecessor. Financial assistance provided by the German Ministry of Economics helped Dornier to develop the layout into a bulkier, higher-powered STOL transport which could carry up to 13 passengers and this redesigned version was designated **Dornier Do 28D**, later being named **Skyservant**. The redesign was so drastic that, apart from the layout and designation, the Do 28D bore little resemblance to the Do 28B. The prototype flew on 23 February 1966, receiving type approval a year later. Developed as the **Do 28D-1**, the type won FAA certification on 19 April 1968 and military type

approval in January 1970. Orders for 125 were placed for the German Luftwaffe and Bundesmarine, and other military deliveries have been made to Ethiopia, Morocco, Nigeria, Turkey and Zambia. More than 220 Skyservants are in operation world-wide.

A Do 28D-1 set several class records for piston-engined business aircraft in 1972, including an altitude of 8624 m (28,294 ft) with a 1000-kg (2,205-lb) payload, as well as several time-to-height records. It was followed by the **Do 28D-2**, which introduced a number of refinements, and in 1980, a Luftwaffe Do 28D-2 was re-engined with Avco Lycoming TIGO-540 turbocharged engines under a contract from the German Federal Ministry of Defence prior to upgrading that country's military Skyservants; the new designation was **Do 28D-2T**.

Further development of the basic Do 28D design continued under a new designation: **Do 128 Skyservant**. Two basic designs were offered, the **Do 128-2** and **Do 128-6**. Both 10-passenger models, the main difference was in powerplant, the Do 128-2 having two Avco Lycoming IGSO-540 piston engines and the Do 128-6 two 298-kW (400-shp) Pratt & Whitney PT6A-110 turboprops. The latter had first been seen in prototype form as the **Do 28D-5X** (D-IBUF), known then as the **TurboSky** and powered by two 447-kW (600-shp) Avco Lycoming LTP 101-600-1A turboprops flat-rated to 298 kW (400 shp). The Do 128-6 had, in addition, a new fuel tank, reinforcements to the underwing engine supports and other modifications. Orders and options for 30 Do 128-6s from African customers were announced, the first going to Lesotho Airways. A variant of the Do 128-6 was also delivered to

Cameroun for maritime patrol work, equipped with a 360° MEL Marec surveillance radar. Production ceased in the mid-1980s.

Specification
Dornier Do 128-2
Type: STOL utility transport
Powerplant: two 283-kW (380-hp) Avco Lycoming IGSO-540-A1E flat-six piston engines
Performance: maximum speed 325 km/h (202 mph) at 3050 m (10,000 ft); economic cruising speed 211 km/h (131 mph) at 3050 m (10,000 ft); service ceiling 7680 m (25,195 ft); range at maximum cruising speed 642 km (399 miles)
Weights: empty 2346 kg (5,172 lb); maximum take-off 3842 kg (8,470 lb)
Dimensions: span 15.55 m (51 ft 0¼ in); length 11.41 m (37 ft 5¼ in); height 3.9 m (12 ft 9½ in); wing area 29 m² (312.16 sq ft)

Right: The Do 28D was redesignated Do 128 in the 1980s, but retains its Skyservant role as a utility transport.

Below: Providing more power and greater efficiency is the TurboSky with Lycoming turboprops. STOL capability is outstanding.

Dornier Do 31/Do 231

During the 1960s much thought was being given to the problems of vertical take-off and landing (VTOL). The UK's P.1127 series had flown and there was talk of VTOL transports capable of supporting fighters in the field. Dornier flew the first of two **Dornier Do 31E** experimental V/STOL transports on 10 February 1967. Primary powerplant was the Rolls-Royce Bristol Pegasus vectored-thrust turbofan, one being mounted beneath each wing, while for direct lift a large pod at each wingtip contained four Rolls-Royce RB.162 jets.

The first Do 31E flew with only the Pegasus engines but the second, flown on 14 July 1967, had all 10 engines installed, making its first transition from vertical take-off to horizontal flight on 16 December 1967, transitioning the other way (horizontal flight to vertical landing) five days later. Although ungainly in appearance, the Do 31 was no slouch and established several new class records for jet lift aircraft on its way from Munich to the 1969 Paris Air Salon. In addition to the two flying aircraft, a third was completed for static tests. During 1969-70 the type was involved in an eval-

The ambitious Do 31E had good performance, but suffered from having to carry the deadweight of redundant lift engines when in conventional flight.

uation programme in the USA as a result of agreements concluded between Dornier, the Federal German government and NASA.

The German government considered a number of designs for a V/STOL civil jet transport and selected a Dornier project, the **Do 231**, for further consideration. Based broadly on the Do 31 layout, the new design would have had two 10886-kg (24,000-lb) thrust Rolls-Royce RB.220 turbofans beneath the wings for forward flight and 12 5942-kg (13,100-lb) thrust RB.202 lift fans, housed in the front and rear fuselage and two large pods in the outer wings. The civil version (**Do 231C**) would have accommodated 100 passengers, while the military model (**Do 231M**) would have had modified landing gear and a longer rear fuselage with rear-loading ramp. However, nothing further came of these interesting projects.

Specification
Dornier Do 31E
Type: V/STOL experimental jet transport
Powerplant: two 7031-kg (15,500-lb) Rolls-Royce Bristol Pegasus 5-2 vectored-thrust turbojets and eight 1996-kg (4,400-lb) thrust Rolls-Royce RB.162-4D turbojets
Performance: cruising speed

644 km/h (400 mph) at 6095 m (20,000 ft); service ceiling 10515 m (34,500 ft)
Weights: empty 22453 kg (49,500 lb); maximum take-off 27442 kg (60,500 lb)
Dimensions: span 18.06 m (59 ft 3 in); length 20.88 m (68 ft 6 in); height 8.53 m (28 ft 0 in); wing area 57.00 m² (613.56 sq ft)

Dornier Do 217

Essentially an enlarged Do 17, the **Dornier Do 217** was flown as a prototype in August 1938, powered by two 802-kW (1,075-hp) Daimler-Benz DB 601A engines. Although this aircraft crashed a few weeks later, the programme was continued by three prototypes powered by 708-kW (950-hp) Junkers Jumo 211A engines. The last of these (**Do 217 V4**) carried armament and, to improve stability, had enlarged vertical tail surfaces and modified dive brakes, whose four segments when closed formed the tail cone. A further three Jumo-engined aircraft were followed by two with 1156-kW (1,550-hp) BMW 139 radials in an attempt to improve performance; the improved BMW 801, introduced in late 1939, was adopted for the production **Do 217A** reconnaissance aircraft, which entered service with the Aufklärungsgruppe Oberbefehlshaber der Luftwaffe in 1940. The first major production version, however, was the **Do 217E** which appeared in 1940, with a deeper fuselage and enlarged bomb bay which could accept several bombs or a torpedo. The Do 217E became operational in the reconnaissance role with 3.(F)/11 in the closing months of 1940 and as a bomber with II./KG40 in the spring of 1941. Some 1,730 Do 217s were built.

Variants
Do 217A: eight **217A-0** reconnaissance aircraft were built, carrying two cameras and armed with three 7.92-mm (0.31-in) MG 15 machine-guns
Do 217C: five examples of this bomber version were built, the first (**Do 217C V1**) with Jumo 211A engines and the remainder (**Do 217C-0**) with DB 601As; all armed with one 15-mm (0.59-in) MG 151/15 cannon and five MG 15 machine-guns, plus a bombload of 3000 kg (6,614 lb)
Do 217E: the first series production variant, the **Do 217E-1** could carry a 3000-kg (6,614-lb) bombload and was armed with one 15-mm (0.59-in) MG 151 cannon and five 7.92-mm (0.31-in) MG 15 machine-guns; the **Do 217E-2** introduced a dorsal turret with a 13-mm (0.51-in) MG 131 gun, a similar gun

mounted ventrally, three 7.92-mm (0.31-in) MG 15s in the forward fuselage, and a 15-mm (0.59-in) MG 151 cannon in the nose; developed for anti-shipping operations over the Atlantic, the **Do 217E-3** carried additional armour plating to provide crew protection, two additional fuel tanks with a capacity of 750 litre (165 Imp gal) in the bomb bay, and seven MG 15s supplementing a single 20-mm (0.78-in) MG FF cannon in the nose; the **Do 217E-4** was the 1941 version of the Do 217E-2, with BMW 801C engines and cable-cutters in the leading edges of the wings; some 65 **Do 217E-5** aircraft were manufactured, these having underwing racks for the carriage of two Henschel Hs 293 missiles
Do 217H: designation of 21st Do 217E when fitted with turbocharged DB 601 engines for trial purposes
Do 217J: starting in 1942, 157 aircraft were built to **Do 217J-1** and **Do 217J-2** standard; the former was a fighter-bomber, with a nose similar to that of the Do 17Z-10, housing four 7.92-mm (0.31-in) MG 17 machine-guns and four 20-mm (0.78-in) MG FF cannon, in addition to the dorsal and ventral positions each with a pair of 13-mm (0.51-in) MG 131 guns; the Do 217J-2 was a night-fighter with 20-mm MG 151/20 cannon replacing the MG FF weapons of the Do 217J-1 and fitted with FuG 212 *Lichtenstein BC* radar
Do 217K: introduced in the autumn of 1942, the **Do 217K-1** bomber had a new glazed nose with an unstepped cockpit; two SD 1400 X (Fritz X) missiles were carried beneath the wings of the **Do 217K-2**, and FuG 203a and FuG 230a guidance equipment was installed in the fuselage; it was a missile launched by a Do 217K-2 of III/KG 100, operating from Marseilles, that sank the Italian battleship *Roma*; this missile or the Hs 293 could be carried by the **Do 217K-3**
Do 217L: two experimental developments of the Do 217K with modified cockpit and defensive dispositions
Do 217M: the **Do 217M-1** was essentially the Do 217K-1, but re-engined with Daimler-Benz DB 603As, the similar **Do 217M-5** being equipped with an under-fuselage rack for an Hs 293 missile; the

Above: Like other fast medium bombers, the Do 217 proved adaptable to the night fighter role. This is a Do 217N-2 before installation of the radar array.

Below: The Do 217E was the first production-series aircraft, this being an E-4 with cable cutters in the wing leading-edges. Note the tailcone divebrake.

Do 217M-3 was the DB 603A-engined equivalent of the Do 217K-3; the **Do 217M-11** was an extended-span missile carrier equivalent to the Do 217K-2
Do 217N: a nose similar to that of the Do 217J-2 was incorporated in the Do 217M airframe to produce the **Do 217N-1** night-fighter, which was quickly replaced in production by the **Do 217N-2**, identified by deletion of the dorsal turret

Specification
Dornier Do 217M-1
Type: four-seat medium bomber
Powerplant: two 1305-kW (1,750-hp) Daimler-Benz DB 603A inverted V-12 piston engines

Performance: maximum speed 560 km/h (348 mph) at 5700 m (18,700 ft); cruising speed 400 km/h (248 mph); service ceiling 9500 m (31,170 ft); maximum range 2150 km (1,336 miles)
Weights: empty 8840 kg (19,489 lb); maximum take-off 16700 kg (36,817 lb)
Dimensions: span 19.00 m (62 ft 4 in); length 16.90 m (55 ft 5¼ in); height 5.00 m (16 ft 4¾ in); wing area 57.00 m² (613.54 sq ft)
Armament: two 13-mm (0.51-in) MG 131 and up to six 7.92-mm (0.31-in) MG 81 machine-guns, plus up to 4000 kg (8,818 lb) of bombs

Dornier Do 228

In June 1979 Dornier flight tested a new high-technology wing intended for the proposed Do 228 series of commuter airliners. Using a modified Skyservant fuselage fitted with the so-called TNT wing and powered by 533-kW (715-shp) Garrett turboprop engines, the aircraft completed a 2½-year test programme during which seven different types of propeller were evaluated. The first definitive **Do 228-100** (D-IFNS), fitted with a new fuselage and tail plus the TNT wing, flew for the first time on 28 March 1981. German certification followed on 18 December the same year and the first production aircraft was delivered to the Norwegian commuter airline Norving early in 1982. Unfortunately the Do 228-100 prototype was lost in a fatal accident near Augsburg while undergoing tests for British certification in March 1982. About 35 Series 100s were built and customers included the German Alfred Wegener Institute which used three 'Polar' aircraft on research duties in

The Do 228 combines a rugged structure and useful internal capacity with an advanced technology wing and fuel-efficient truboprops.

Antarctica. Development of a 'stretched' version followed, designated the **Do 228-200**. Able to carry 19 passengers, the prototype (D-ICDO), made its first flight on 9 May 1981 and became the standard production version with around 175 sold by the end of 1990. More than 50 airlines have ordered the Series 200, with the most recent including Air Caledonie, Air Moorea, Air Tahiti, Air Guadeloupe, Air Maldives and Aerotuy of Venezuela. Other customers include the governments of Germany, Nigeria, Saudi Arabia, India, Niger, Malawi, Bolivia and Japan. In 1983 the Do 228 was selected by the Indian Government for licence production by Hindustan Aeronautics, which are to build around 150 aircraft in a technology transfer pro-

gramme. The first Indian-built aircraft flew in January 1986, and was delivered to the internal airline Vayadoot the following March.

Specification
Dornier Do 228-200
Type: 19-seat commuter airliner
Powerplant: two 578-kW (776-shp) Garrett TPE331-5 turboprops
Performance: maximum cruising speed 428 km/h (266 mph) at 3050 m

(10,000 ft); economic cruising speed 333 km/h (207 mph) at 3050 m (10,000 ft); service ceiling 9020 m (29,600 ft); range with maximum passenger load and 45-min reserves 1130 km (702 miles)
Weights: empty 3086 kg (6,803 lb); maximum take-off 5700 kg (12,566 lb)
Dimensions: span 16.97 m (55 ft 8 in); length 16.56 m (54 ft 4 in); height 4.86 m (15 ft 11 in); wing area 32 m² (344.3 sq ft)

Dornier Do 328

The success of its Do 228 encouraged Dornier to undertake from August 1988 development of a high-technology regional airliner derivative as the 30-passenger **Do 328**. The design preserved the Do 228's supercritical wing section but added an extended centre section for additional fuel tank and new flaps, and introduced a more modern powerplant. The slab-sided fuselage of the Do 228 was replaced by a circular-section fuselage with a maximum cabin width of 2.18 m (7 ft 2 in), an aisle height of 1.89 m (6 ft 2.5 in) and, importantly, cabin pressurisation.

Manufacture of the **Do 328** also involved Daewoo of South Korea (replaced by OGMA of Portugal), Aermacchi of Italy, Westland of the UK, and Daimler-Benz Aerospace Airbus of Germany. The first of three development aircraft made its maiden flight on 6 December 1991, during the test programme insignificant problems were found which were resolved by the beginning of 1993, the airworthiness certificate was granted at the end of 1993. The first production machine made its initial flight in January 1993, 60 orders were placed by the beginning

of 1994. The three initial variants are the basic **Do 328-100**, the **Do 328-110** with maximum take-off weight raised to 13990 kg (30,843 lb) and range to 1851 km (1,150 miles), and the **Do 328-120** with improved short-field capability and a number of performance enhancements. Dornier was working on a stretched 48-seat derivative, but Dornier was sold by its parent company, DASA, to Fairchild in 1996. Fairchild Dornier dropped the stretched **Do 328** in favour of a radically updated model, the **Do 328JET** with two 26.9-kN (6,050-lb st) Pratt & Whitney Canada PW306B turbofans for greater cruising speed and range. The first **Do 328JET** flew in 1998.

Specification
Dornier Do 328-100
Type: 33-passenger regional airliner
Powerplant: two 1625-kW (2,180-shp) Pratt & Whitney Canada PW119B turboprops
Performance: maximum cruising speed 620 km/h (388 mph) at 6095 m (20,000 ft); cruising altitude, normal 7620 m (25,000 ft) and optional 9450 m (31,000 ft); range with 30 passengers 1666 km (1,035 miles) at 7620 m (25,000 ft) or 1851 km (1,150 miles) at 9450 m (31,000 ft)
Weights: empty 8920 kg (19,665 lb); maximum take-off 13990 kg (30,842 lb)

Dornier Do 335 Pfeil (Arrow)

Following feasibility trials with the experimental **Göppingen Gö 9** research aircraft, designed by Ulrich Hütter and built by Schempp-Hirth in 1939, the unconventional tandem engine layout patented by Dr Claudius Dornier in 1937 was adopted by the Reichsluftfahrtministerium for a bomber under the project number **Do P.231**, despite the fact that Dornier's original design proposal was for a fighter! When work was at an advanced stage the project was cancelled, but an emerging need for a high-performance fighter resulted in the reactivation of Dornier's plans for an interceptor. Of all-metal construction and powered by two 1342-kW (1,800-hp) Daimler-Benz DB 603 engines, one buried in the rear fuselage and driving a three-bladed pusher propeller via an extension shaft, the first **Dornier Do 335** prototype made its maiden flight on 26 October 1943. The type was built in a number of versions, around forty, but the closest it came to service was with operational test unit Erprobungskommando 335 in the spring of 1945.

Three variants of the design were projected but failed to materialise. These included a **Do 435** two-seat night-fighter; the **Do 535** to be developed in conjunction with Heinkel, the rear piston engine to be replaced by a turbojet of Heinkel design; and a long-range reconnaissance **Do 635** which would have united two Do 335 airframes by means of a new wing centre-section.

Specification
Dornier Do 335A-1
Type: single-seat fighter-bomber
Powerplant: two 1305-kW (1,750-hp) Daimler-Benz DB 603A-2 inverted V-12 piston engines
Performance: maximum speed 770 km/h (478 mph) at 6400 m (21,000 ft); cruising speed 685 km/h (426 mph) at 7100 m (23,295 ft); climb to 8000 m (26,250 ft) in 14 minutes 30 seconds; service ceiling 11400 m (37,400 ft); range 1380 km (857 miles)
Weights: empty 7400 kg (16,314 lb); maximum take-off 9600 kg (21,164 lb)
Dimensions: span 13.80 m (45 ft

The Do 335A-0 pre-production fighter was armed with a hub-firing MK 108 30-mm cannon and two cowling-mounted MG 151 15-mm weapons. A few reached test units before the war's end.

3¼ in); length 13.85 m (45 ft 5¼ in); height 5.00 m (16 ft 4¾ in); wing area 38.50 m² (414.42 sq ft)
Armament: one 30-mm (1.17-in) MK 103 and two 15-mm (0.59-in) MG 151

cannon, plus one 500-kg (1,102-lb) or two 250-kg (551-lb) bombs internally and two 250-kg (551-lb) bombs externally

Dornier Do F, Do 11, Do 13 and Do 23

To overcome the restrictions of the Treaty of Versailles, which forbade the construction of large aircraft in Germany, Claudius Dornier established factories in Japan, Spain and Switzerland. An all-metal high-wing monoplane with an open cockpit, the **Do F** was built by the

Swiss Dornier company at Altenrhein and flown on 7 May 1932. Power was supplied by two engines. It was designed from the outset as a heavy bomber and featured retractable landing gear. In 1933 a new version was introduced, developed ostensibly as a

freighter but being in reality a bomber, this having fixed landing gear and being redesignated **Do 11**. Powered by two 410-kW (550-hp) Siemens Sh.22B radials (licence-built Jupiters), the **Do 11C** production aircraft was initially supplied to German state railways for cargo operations, a cover for the training of bomber

crews. It was later built openly as a military aircraft, capable of carrying a bomb-load of 1000 kg (2,205 lb) and armed with three MG 15 machine-guns (one each in open nose, dorsal and ventral positions). A number of **Do 11D** aircraft, with reduced-span wings, were delivered to form the equipment of the first Luftwaffe bomber squadrons, but structural deficiencies and unacceptable handling characteristics led to their premature withdrawal from production.

A new version, designated **Do 13**, was built in 1934 and also had fixed landing gear. Powered by two 559-kW (750-hp) BMW VI engines, the **Do 13c** was ordered into production as the **Do 13C**, Do 11 orders being switched to the new model. The type was further developed as the **Do 13e** with a strengthened airframe and Junkers trailing-edge auxiliary flying surfaces. This model was then re-designated **Do 23F** and entered production in March 1935; it was later superseded by the **Do 23G** with glycol-cooled BMW VIU engines. More than 200 Do 23s were built for the Luftwaffe, although the type was soon made obsolescent by the Do 17 which began to replace it in 1936.

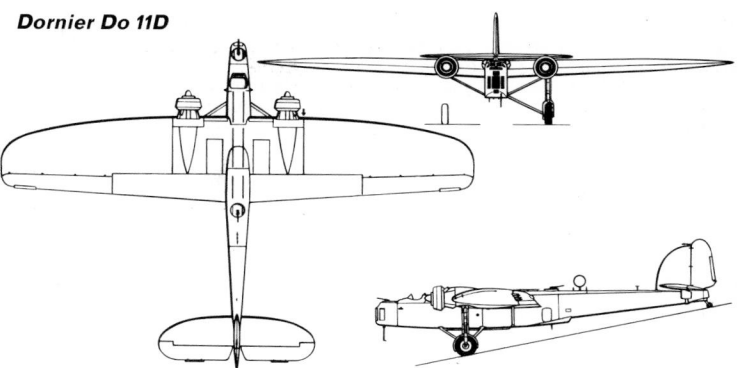

Dornier Do 11D

Final development of the Do F was the Do 23G. Although ungainly and unsprightly, it allowed the Luftwaffe to develop bombing tactics in the 1930s.

Specification
Dornier Do 23G
Type: four-seat heavy bomber
Powerplant: two 559-kW (750-hp) BMW VIU V-12 piston engines
Performance: maximum speed 260 km/h (161 mph); service ceiling 4200 m (13,780 ft); range 1500 km (932 miles)
Weights: empty 5600 kg (12,346 lb); maximum take-off 9200 kg (20,282 lb)
Dimensions: span 25.60 m (84 ft 0 in); length 18.80 m (61 ft 8 in); height 5.40 m (17 ft 8½ in); wing area 108.00 m² (1,162.54 sq ft)
Armament: three 7.92-mm (0.31-in) MG 15 machine-guns (in nose, mid-upper and ventral positions), plus up to 1000 kg (2,205 lb) of bombs carried internally

Dornier Do J Wal and Do Super Wal

The **Dornier Do J Wal** (Whale) was the most important of the aircraft designed by the Dornier company in the early 1920s, establishing a flying-boat configuration of classic lines that was to endure (albeit in refined form) for many years, and was almost certainly the most advanced and successful flying-boat of the 1920s and early 1930s. Its broad all-metal two-step hull incorporated aerofoil-section sponsons to give stability on the water, and carried above it a strut-braced untapered parasol wing; the rear end of the hull was upswept, mounting the braced conventional tail unit. Powerplant comprised two engines mounted in tandem above the wing centre-section, these driving a tractor and a pusher propeller. The large-capacity hull provided for a variety of accommodation according to the Wal's employment in civil or military service, with a pilot and co-pilot seated side-by-side in a forward compartment. Behind them were navigation and radio compartments, still leaving a volume of the hull that could be used for cargo, mail or passengers.

The prototype was flown for the first time on 6 November 1922, but because of the Allied ban which then prohibited aircraft of this class from being built in Germany, this aircraft and early production versions were built by the Società di Costruzioni Meccaniche di Pisa, which had been established in Italy by Dornier to manufacture these flying-boats. The 'boats soon proved a great commercial success, being used on European and international civil routes, and were built also in Japan, the Netherlands, Spain and Switzerland before indigenous production began at Friedrichshafen in 1933. The Italian company also produced during 1924-25 a number of Wals for the Spanish navy, these being powered by 268-kW (360-hp) Rolls-Royce Eagle IX engines.

The load-carrying capability of the Wal/Rolls-Royce Eagle combination was demonstrated conclusively during February 1925 when 20 world class records were established with payloads of 250 to 2000 kg (551 to 4,409 lb). In the same year two Wals were acquired by the Norwegian explorer Roald Amundsen for an expedition from Spitzbergen to the North Pole. One of these Wals (N-24) was lost in the pack ice, but following repair under the most difficult conditions the second (N-25) returned to

Spitzbergen in June 1926. It was subsequently overhauled and re-engined for a planned Atlantic crossing by a British pilot. When this failed to materialise the aircraft was acquired in 1928 by Wolfgang von Gronau for use in the German Commercial Flying School (DVS). Following overhaul and the installation of BMW VI engines, it became registered D-1422 and was used at the DVS for many long-distance over-water training flights. In this aircraft, on 18 August 1930, von Gronau and crew took off from List (on Sylt) en route for New York via the Faroes, Iceland, Greenland and Labrador. After 44 hours 25 minutes of flying time the Wal landed safely in New York harbour to mark a great achievement.

Wals featured in a round-the-world flight during 1932. By this time Luft Hansa, which was planning to establish an air mail service to South America, decided to unite the proven Wal with a specially-converted cargo vessel to serve as a mid-ocean refuelling base. The first of these vessels, the *Westfalen*, was equipped to take the Wal aboard, refuel it and then relaunch it into the air by steam catapult. After trial flights during 1933, the first scheduled flight from Germany to South America began on 3 February 1934, flown from Stuttgart to Buenos Aires via Seville, Bathurst (Banjul), and the *Westfalen* to Natal, the route completed in just under four days. The success of this operation can be judged from the fact that the planned fortnightly schedule was very soon converted into a regular weekly service.

About 300 Wals were built before production ended in the mid-1930s, but before that date the Wal had been supplemented by the **Do R Super Wal**,

produced at Friedrichshafen following the maiden flight of the first **Do R2** in September 1926. Of increased wing span and hull length, the Super Wal had two cabins to accommodate a total of 19 passengers and was operated by a crew of four. The Do R2 was of similar overall configuration to the contemporary Wal, with two 485-kW (650-hp) Rolls-Royce Condor engines mounted in tandem. However, the **Do R4** of 1927 benefitted from the power of four Siemens-built Jupiter engines, these being mounted in two tandem pairs and providing gross weight and speed increases of some 33 and 16 per cent respectively. In addition to production by Dornier, Super Wals were licence-built in several countries; they gave valuable service to a number of airlines including, of course, Deutsche Luft Hansa. In 1934 the Wal series was redesignated as the **Do 15**.

Specification
Dornier Do R4

Dornier Do J Wal of Grupo 1-G-70, Agrupacion Espanola (Spanish Nationalist air force) based in the Balearic Islands in the late 1930s.

Type: four-engined commercial flying-boat
Powerplant: four 391-kW (525-hp) Siemens-built Bristol Jupiter radial piston engines
Performance: maximum speed 210 km/h (130 mph); cruising speed 180 km/h (112 mph); range 2000 km (1,243 miles)
Weights: empty equipped 9850 kg (21,716 lb); maximum take-off 14000 kg (30,864 lb)
Dimensions: span 28.60 m (93 ft 10 in); length 24.60 m (80 ft 8½ in); height 6.00 m (19 ft 8 in); wing area 137.00 m² (1,474.70 sq ft)

Four Jupiter engines powered the Do R4 Super Wal, an Italian-registered aircraft seen here.

Dornier Do X
to
Douglas A2D Skyshark

Dornier Do X

Then the largest aeroplane in the world, the **Dornier Do X**, which made its first flight from the Bodensee on 12 July 1929, was the product of the Altenrhein-based Swiss Dornier company. Work on the design, which was the ultimate development of the Wal series, began in 1927, and the aircraft was intended to carry up to 100 passengers across the Atlantic in comfort comparable with that of ocean liners. Of all-metal construction and powered initially by six tandem pairs of 373-kW (500-hp) Siemens Jupiter engines, it had individual sleeping cabins, lounge, smoking room, bathroom, kitchen and dining room arranged on three decks in the 40-m (131-ft) hull. The flight-deck crew comprised two pilots, a navigator and a radio operator, but the throttles were the responsibility of the flight engineer, whose position was sufficiently far to the rear of the cockpit area to make power adjustments an interesting exercise in communications! The flight engineer was able also to inspect the powerplant in flight by using access tunnels in the very thick wing. The Siemens engines developed insufficient power and were replaced by 12 Curtiss Conquerors, but cooling problems continued to reduce the output of the rear engines. Nevertheless, proof of the aircraft's load-carrying capability was provided by a flight made on 31 October 1929 when stowaways increased the

In its definitive form, the Do X featured 12 Curtiss Conqueror engines, developing a total of 5729 kW (7,680 hp). It still suffered from poor performance.

number of persons on board to 170, 10 more than the planned maximum of 160 passengers and crew.

On 2 November 1930 the Do X left Friedrichshafen on the Bodensee for a flight to the United States, via Amsterdam, Calshot and Lisbon. The flight was not without incident. At Lisbon, fire in a fuel tank damaged one of the wings, necessitating a delay of a month for repairs. Then, when attempting a take-off at Las Palmas in the Canary Islands, the Do X suffered hull damage which resulted in a further delay of some three months. The aircraft was lightened by the removal of non-essential equipment and fittings, and operated with a reduced crew for its next attempt. Although still unable to reach normal operating altitude for much of the crossing, the modified Do X completed the next stage to Natal (Brazil) via Portuguese Guinea, the Cape Verde Islands and Fernando Noronha. The Do X then flew to Rio de Janeiro before turning back en route to the United States, reaching New York, via the West Indies and Miami, on 27 August 1931; the return flight began on 19 May 1932, the Do X returning to Germany on 24 May 1932 after a successful flight via Harbour Grace, Horta, Vigo and Calshot, landing on the Müggelsee in

Berlin. The aircraft was among those destroyed when the Berlin Museum was severely damaged by bombs during World War II. Two further examples were built, with Fiat engines, and were used experimentally by the Italian air force before being scrapped.

Specification
Type: transoceanic flying-boat
Powerplant: 12 477-kW (640-hp) Curtiss Conqueror V-12 piston engines

Performance: maximum speed 210 km/h (130 mph); cruising speed 175 km/h (109 mph); service ceiling 1250 m (4,100 ft); range 2200 km (1,367 miles)
Weights: empty equipped 32675 kg (72,036 lb); maximum take-off 56000 kg (123,459 lb)
Dimensions: span 48 m (157 ft 5¾ in); length 40.00 m (131 ft 4 in); height 10.10 m (33 ft 1½ in); wing area 450.0 m² (4,843.92 sq ft)

Dornier Komet and Merkur

Retaining a resemblance to earlier members of the family, the **Dornier Do C III Komet I** (Comet 1) was flown for the first time during 1921. It had a deep fuselage, fixed tailskid landing gear, conventional braced tail unit and a very large constant-chord braced wing. Powerplant of production Komet Is consisted of a BMW III or IIIa of 134 kW (180 hp) or 138 kW (185 hp) respectively, and accommodation was provided for four passengers in an enclosed cabin, with the pilot in an open cockpit on the upper surface of the fuselage, just to the rear of the wing trailing edge. Surviving records leave doubts about the number built, complicated by the fact that some were converted subsequently to Merkur configuration, but examples of the Komet I served initially with Deutsche Luft-Reederei, later with Deutscher Aero Lloyd and finally with Deutsche Luft Hansa (DLH) when it was formed in 1926.

The improved **Komet II**, first flown on 9 October 1922, was built in larger numbers and served with airline operators in Colombia, Spain, Switzerland, the Ukraine and the USSR, as well as with DLH in Germany. It differed by having a lengthened fuselage, seated the same number of passengers but accommodated a crew of two, and was powered by a 186-kW (250-hp) BMW IV engine. Final version was the **Komet III**, first flown on 7 December 1924. This was a refined and enlarged version, the braced wing carried above the fuselage on four short struts, and with power provided by a Rolls-Royce Eagle IX engine. It

provided accommodation for six passengers and the two-man crew was still in an open cockpit; this was resited beneath the wing, just below its leading edge and offset to port. Komet IIIs saw service with German airlines and in Denmark, Switzerland and the Ukraine, and a small number were licence-built in Japan.

The first generally similar **Dornier Do B Merkur I** (Mercury I) made its maiden flight on 10 February 1925. It differed from the Komet III by having slightly increased wing span, an unbraced tail unit incorporating vertical tail surfaces of greater area, and a more powerful BMW engine. In fact, power-plant determined the difference be-

Dornier Merkur I of Luft Hansa in the late 1920s.

A refined and enlarged version of the Komet II, the Komet III had typically low Dornier landing gear and was the equivalent of the Delphin III flying-boat.

tween the Merkur I and **Merkur II**, the former having a 447-kW (600-hp) BMW IV without reduction gear, the latter a 373-kW (500-hp) BMW VI with reduction gear. Both provided accommodation for a crew of two and six to eight passengers, but the Merkur II was certificated for operation at a higher gross weight.

The largest operator of the Merkur was undoubtedly DLH which, including converted Komet IIIs, may have had more than 30 in service at one period, but they were used also by China, Japan and Switzerland. In addition, Brazil and Colombia each had one Merkur in floatplane configuration.

Specification
Dornier Merkur II (landplane)
Type: civil transport
Powerplant: one 373-kW (500-hp) BMW VI V-12 piston engine
Performance: maximum speed 192 km/h (119 mph); service ceiling

4000 m (13,125 ft)
Weights: empty 2780 kg (6,129 lb); maximum take-off 4100 kg (9,039 lb)
Dimensions: span 19.60 m (64 ft 3¾ in); length 12.85 m (42 ft 2 in); height 3.56 m (11 ft 8¼ in); wing area 62.00 m² (667.38 sq ft)

Dornier Libelle

Throughout World War I Dr Claudius Dornier had been in charge of design and construction at the German company of Zeppelin-Werke Lindau at Friedrichshafen. Produced during the war was a series of aircraft (including the C I, C II, CS I, D I, Rs I, Rs II, Rs III, Rs IV and V 1), details of which will be found under the entry for Zeppelin-Lindau. After the war the works were transferred to Manzell, near Friedrichshafen, and renamed Dornier Metallbauten GmbH, where during the early 1920s Dr Dornier designed and developed a number of interesting civil aircraft.

First of these was the **Dornier Libelle I** (Dragonfly I), a two-seat sports/trainer flying-boat which was first flown on 16 August 1921. Of all-metal construction, except for fabric covering on part of the wings and all control surfaces, it was a parasol-wing monoplane with its constant-chord foldable wing strut-mounted above the hull. The flat-bottomed hull incorporated a conventional tail unit, and had sponsons of aerofoil section projecting from each side to

provide stability on the water. An open cockpit beneath the wing provided accommodation for a pilot and one passenger forward, with a second passenger seated behind. Dual controls were standard. Power was provided by a Siemens-Halske engine of up to 45 kW (60 hp) mounted in a neat nacelle on the upper surface of the wing centre section. A later **Libelle II**, of increased dimensions and powered by a similar engine of 52 to 60 kW (70 to 80 hp) was stated to have carried a pilot and four passengers without difficulty although only intended as a three-seater. It was also reported that the hull structure of the Libelle was so robust that take-offs and landings had been performed on ice-covered surfaces. The type was produced in some numbers.

Variant
Dornier Spatz (Sparrow): virtually a landplane version of the Libelle without the hull sponsons but with fixed tailskid landing gear; a 60-kW (80-hp) Siemens-Halske engine was standard, but a 75-kW (100-hp) engine and an open cockpit or enclosed cabin were optional

A great future was anticipated for light seaplanes in the inter-war years, as reflected by the development of types such as the Libelle I, a two-seat trainer and sport amphibian.

Specification
Dornier Libelle I
Type: sport/trainer flying-boat
Powerplant: one 37- to 45-kW (50 to 60-hp) Siemens-Halske radial piston engine
Performance: maximum speed

about 120 km/h (75 mph); service ceiling about 1600 m (5,250 ft)
Weights: empty 400 kg (882 lb); maximum take-off 650 kg (1,433 lb)
Dimensions: span 8.50 m (27 ft 10½ in); length 7.18 m (23 ft 6½ in); height 2.27 m (7 ft 5¼ in); wing area 14.00 m² (150.70 sq ft)

Douglas A-3 (A3D) Skywarrior

The largest and heaviest aircraft designed for operation from an aircraft-carrier when the Douglas El Segundo division's project design was completed in 1949, the **Douglas A3D Skywarrior** originated from a US Navy requirement of 1947. An attack bomber with strategic strike capability was envisaged, tailored to the giant new aircraft-carriers that were ultimately (after prolonged opposition from the USAF) to materialise as the 'Forrestal' class of four ships, as it was believed that the moment had come to exploit the potential of the rapidly-developing gas turbine engine.

The Douglas design was a high-wing monoplane, with retractable tricycle landing gear, two podded turbojets beneath the wing, and a large internal weapons bay to accommodate up to 5443 kg (12,000 lb) of varied weapons. The wings were swept back 36° and had high-aspect ratio for long range, all tail surfaces were swept, and the outer wing panels and vertical tail folded.

The first of two prototypes made its maiden flight on 28 October 1952, powered by 3175-kg (7,000-lb) Westinghouse XJ40-WE-3 engines, but the failure of this engine programme meant that the 4400-kg (9,700-lb) thrust Pratt & Whitney J57-P-6 powered the production **A3D-1**. The first of these A3D-1s flew on 16 September 1953, and deliveries to the US Navy's VAH-1 attack squadron began on 31 March 1956.

In 1962 the designation was changed to **A-3**, the initial three-seat production version becoming **A-3A**. Five of these were modified subsequently for ECM missions under the designation **EA-3A**. The **A-3B** (previously **A3D-2**) which entered service in 1957 had more powerful J57-P-10 engines and an inflight-refuelling probe. A reconnaissance variant

with cameras in the weapons bay was designated **RA-3B (A3D-2P)**, and **EA-3B (A3D-2Q)** identified ECM aircraft with a four-man crew in the weapons bay. Other designations include 12 **TA-3B (A3D-2T)** trainers for radar operators, one **VA-3B (A3D-2Z)** executive transport, and the final variants in front-line US Navy service were **KA-3B** inflight-refuelling tankers and 30 **EKA-3B** tanker/countermeasures/strike aircraft. Skywarrior variants still in service include TA-3B crew trainers, EKA-3B early-warning 'aggressor' trainers, and KA-3B tankers with Squadrons VAQ-33 at Key West and VAQ-34 at NAS Point Mugu, together with an NA-3B test aircraft operated by the Naval Weapons Test Center and NRA-3Bs with the Pacific Missile Test Center.

Designed for long-range nuclear strikes from US carrier decks, the A-3 Skywarrior was little used in the bomber role, but soldiered on for many years in secondary roles such as KA-3B tanker (illustrated), EA-3B and RA-3B reconnaissance platforms and EKA-3B ECM/tanker. ERA-3B jammers are still in service.

Specification
Douglas A-3B
Type: carrier-based attack bomber
Powerplant: two 4763-kg (10,500-lb) thrust Pratt & Whitney J57-P-10 turbojets
Performance: maximum speed 982 km/h (610 mph) at 3050 m (10,000 ft); cruising speed 837 km/h (520 mph); service ceiling 12495 m (41,000 ft); normal range 1690 km (1,050 miles)
Weights: empty 17876 kg (39,409 lb); maximum take-off 37195 kg (82,000 lb)
Dimensions: span 22.10 m (72 ft 6 in); length 23.27 m (76 ft 4 in); height 6.95 m (22 ft 9½ in); wing area 75.43 m² (812 sq ft)
Armament: two 20-mm cannon in radar-controlled rear turret, plus up to 5443 kg (12,000 lb) of assorted weapons in internal bay

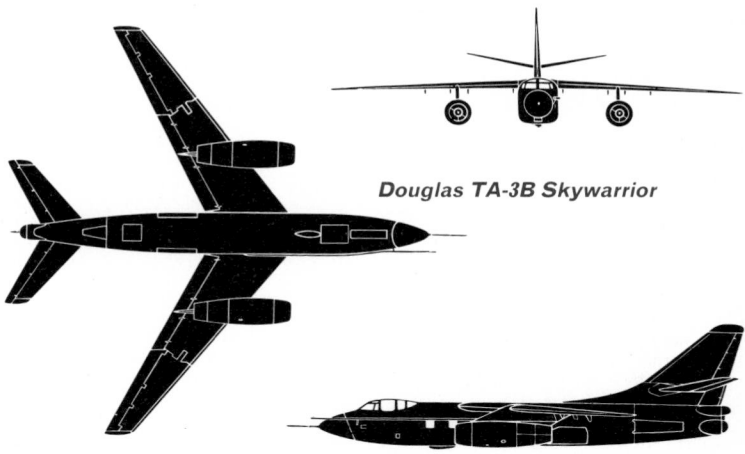

Douglas TA-3B Skywarrior

347

Douglas A-20/DB-7/Boston/Havoc series

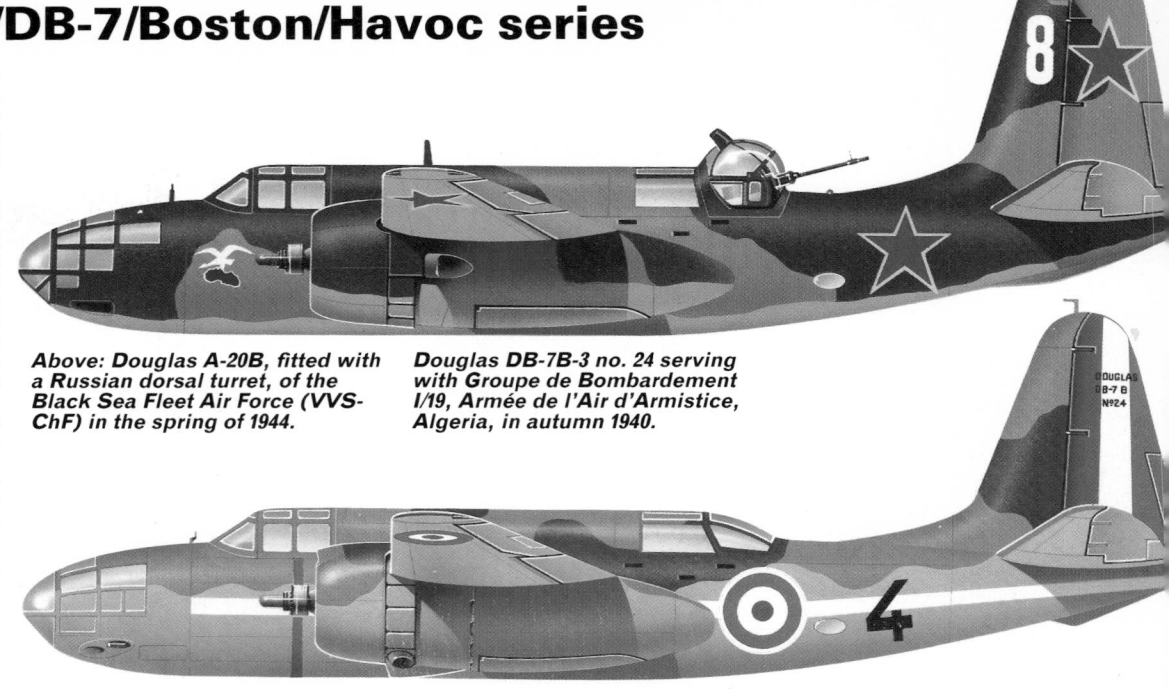

The **Douglas A-20** (company designation **DB-7**) was one of the most extensively built light bombers of World War II. It was a ubiquitous aeroplane, used in a variety of roles and performing well, no matter where it was deployed.

The basic design originated in 1936, when the Douglas Aircraft Company began to consider the creation of an attack aircraft that would be an effective replacement for the single-engined light bombers then in service. By discussion with engineering staff of the US Army Air Corps it became possible to outline a fairly advanced specification, leading to the company project identified as the **Model 7A**.

Redesign in 1938 produced the **Model 7B**, also of twin-engined configuration, but with the proposed 336-kW (450-hp) engines replaced by two 820-kW (1,100-hp) Pratt & Whitney R-1830 Twin Wasps. Of cantilever shoulder-wing configuration, the Model 7B had an upswept aft fuselage, mounting a conventional tail unit. Landing gear was of the then-radical tricycle type, but an unusual feature was the introduction of interchangeable fuselage nose sections that would make for easy production of either attack or bomber versions. First flown in this form on 26 October 1938, the Model 7B evinced the characteristics of a thoroughbred: it was fast, highly manoeuvrable and, in fact, could be regarded as a 'pilot's aeroplane'.

Immediately that the company realised its potential it offered the type for export, as the USAAC then had no requirement for such a machine. The first order, for 100 aircraft, came from a French purchasing mission in February 1939. Although impressed by the performance of the Model 7B, they required modifications to render the aircraft more suitable for deployment in Europe, where advanced aircraft in service with the Luftwaffe had demonstrated their potential in the recently ended Spanish Civil War.

So extensive were the modifications that even the basic configuration of the Model 7B was changed. The fuselage was deepened to increase internal bomb capacity and fuel tankage, and its cross-section was reduced; the wing was lowered from shoulder- to mid-wing position; a longer oleo-strut for the nose-wheel was introduced; armour protection for the crew and fuel tanks was provided; and uprated Twin Wasp engines developing 895 kW (1,200 hp) each were installed. In view of the foregoing changes, the resulting aircraft was redesignated **DB-7** (Douglas Bomber), and the production prototype was flown for the first time on 17 August 1939. Despite efforts made by Douglas to complete manufacture of the initial 100 DB-7s by the end of 1939, the French had only just over 60 in service at the time of the German attack in May 1940, and only 12 aircraft of the 2e Groupement de Bombardement were used operationally, on 31 May 1940, in low-level attacks against German armoured columns.

During the period when Douglas was developing the DB-7, a French order for an improved version was received. Required to operate at a gross weight some 24 per cent higher than that of the DB-7, as a result of additional equipment, it needed more powerful Wright Cyclone 14 radial engines in revised nacelles and changes in the engine installation; this version was designated **DB-7A**. Moreover, because the DB-7 had shown that directional stability was bordering on the marginal, increased fin and rudder area were provided to cater for the higher-power engines.

When it was clear that the collapse of

Above: Douglas A-20B, fitted with a Russian dorsal turret, of the Black Sea Fleet Air Force (VVS-ChF) in the spring of 1944.

Douglas DB-7B-3 no. 24 serving with Groupe de Bombardement I/19, Armée de l'Air d'Armistice, Algeria, in autumn 1940.

France was imminent, steps were taken to arrange for the UK to take over the balance of the French orders, plus a small quantity which had been ordered by Belgium. Thus some 15 to 20 DB-7s entered service with the RAF. These were allocated the name **Boston Mk I** and were used as conversion trainers. The next batch to be received, about 125 DB-7 aircraft, was allocated originally the designation **Boston Mk II**. However, their load-carrying capability and high speed confirmed a suitability for conversion to desperately needed night-fighters, and in the winter of 1940 these were provided with AI (Airborne Interception) radar, additional armour, eight 7.7-mm (0.303-in) machine-guns in the nose, flame-damping exhaust systems, and overall matt black finish. One unusual addition was the provision of basic dual flying controls in the gunner's position: as no crew member could get to the pilot's aid in emergency they provided a long-odds chance that the gunner might achieve a non-calamitous landing. First delivered to the RAF in December 1940 under the designation **Havoc Mk I**, the type became operational with No. 85 Squadron on 7 April 1941. A second batch of about 100 DB-7As was converted similarly, except for being armed with 12 nose-mounted machine-guns, and were designated **Havoc Mk II**. About 40 DB-7s were modified to serve as night intruders, retaining the bomb aimer's nose and able to accommodate up to 1089 kg (2,400 lb) of bombs; gun armament of four 7.7-mm (0.303-in) machine-guns was mounted beneath the nose. Named officially **Havoc Mk I (Intruder)**, the type also acquired such unofficial names as **Moonfighter, Ranger** and **Havoc Mk IV**. In order to enhance the somewhat limited capability of the AI radar installed in the Havoc Mk Is, 21 were each equipped with a Helmore/GEC searchlight of some 2,700-million candlepower intensity. Designated **Havoc Mk I (Turbinlite)**, the aircraft were used, with little success, to illuminate German aircraft after stalking to within contact distance, when escorting Hawker Hurricane fighters were intended to attack and destroy the well-lit target. Some 39 conversions of Havoc Mk IIs were also made, under the designation **Havoc Mk II (Turbinlite)**. The name Havoc was adopted subsequently by the USAAF as the general name for its A-20s of all versions.

The slim fuselage of the DB-7 family is shown to advantage by this BD-2 target tug of the US Navy. This model was in reality the USAAF's A-20B with all armament removed.

A few DB-7As were retained for use in a light bomber role under the designation **Boston Mk III**, but the UK had ordered an improved version, the **DB-7B**, with changed electric and hydraulic systems, and instrumentation which conformed to RAF requirements and layout. These were also designated Boston Mk III, and carried four 7.7-mm (0.303-in) guns in the nose, two on a high-speed mounting in the aft cockpit, and a seventh gun firing through a ventral tunnel, plus a bombload of up to 907 kg (2,000 lb). These Boston Mk IIIs were used extensively by squadrons of No. 2 Group, and served also in North Africa from early 1942, replacing Bristol Blenheims.

Initial USAAC contracts for the DB-7, placed in May 1939, produced 63 aircraft designated **A-20**, with turbocharged Wright R-2600-7 Cyclone 14 engines. Of these, three were converted to serve in a photo-reconnaissance role; the remainder became the **XP-70** prototype and 59 **P-70** production night-fighters, the prototype with unsupercharged R-2600-11 engines, and all with British-built AI radar and an armament of four

20-mm cannon mounted beneath the fuselage. These night-fighters were used primarily in a training role, so that USAAC crews could become conversant with the newly developed technique of radar interception.

The first bomber version to serve with the USAAC was the **A-20A**, generally similar to the A-20, but powered by unsupercharged R-2600-3 engines and with armament as for the DB-7B except that the machine-guns were of 7.62-mm (0.3-in) calibre. In addition, two remotely controlled aft-firing guns were mounted in the rear of each engine nacelle, and the bombload was 499 kg (1,100 lb). One **XA-20B** prototype was modified from a production A-20A and had changed armament (three remotely controlled turrets). This was not adopted for the production **A-20B**, which had two 12.7-mm (0.5-in) nose-mounted guns, and which was in most respects similar to the DB-7A.

Large-scale production dictated more standardisation, so that the RAF's Boston Mk III and USAAC **A-20C** were one and the same, equipped with R-2600-23 engines. To boost production, Douglas granted a licence to Boeing and this latter company produced 140 A-20Cs for supply to the RAF under Lend-Lease and **Boston Mk IIIA**: these aircraft differed in their electrical system, and in some changes to the ancillary equipment of the engines. DB-7s of this version were supplied also to the USSR under Lend-Lease during 1942. Boston Mk IIIs of the RAF's No. 226 Squadron provided training facilities for crews of the USAAF's 15th Bombardment Squadron, which arrived in the UK during May 1942 as the vanguard of the US 8th Air Force. Six crews of this squadron, together with six British crews, made the first mission by the 8th Air Force from England on 4 July 1942. The next major production variant was the **A-20G**, of which 2,850 aircraft were built by Douglas at Santa Monica. These also had R-2600-23 engines, and were some 20.32 cm (8 in) longer to provide a nose armament comprising two 12.7-mm (0.5-in) machine-guns and four 20-mm cannon, and either two 12.7-mm (0.5-in) guns or one 12.7-mm (0.5-in) and one 7.62-mm (0.3-in) gun in the rear cockpit. Most of the early production A-20Gs in this configuration were supplied to the USSR; the next A-20G variant had the 20-mm cannon replaced by 12.7-mm (0.5-in) machine-guns, and the final variant introduced a rear fuselage 15.24 cm (6 in) wider to accommodate an electrically operated dorsal turret with two 12.7-mm (0.5-in) guns, as well as having underwing bomb racks to accept an additional 907 kg (2,000 lb) of bombs, extra fuel tanks in the bomb bay, and provision for an underfuselage drop tank to provide a ferry range of more than 3219 km (2,000 miles). This was, of course, vital for the type's deployment in the Pacific theatre, where its arrival in 1942 came as something of a mixed blessing to Major General George C. Kenney's 5th Air Force, struggling to defeat the Japanese threat to New Guinea. As delivered, the aircraft were considered to be too lightly armed, so the basic armament was supplemented by four 12.7-mm (0.5-in) machine-guns, and as there were no bombs available as required for their employment in a close-support role, Kenney suggested the provision of 10-kg (23-lb) fragmentation bombs with small parachutes attached. With the A-20s each able to carry 40 of these 'para-frag' bombs, the aircraft played a vital role in dislodging the enemy from Buna.

Other improvements introduced gradually to A-20G Havocs included better armour, navigation and bomb-aiming equipment, and winterisation accessories for aircraft to be operated in low-temperature zones. Also produced were 412 of the **A-20H** model, with little change except for the installation of 1268-kW (1,700-hp) R-2600-29 engines. Neither the A-20 nor A-20H version served with the RAF, but the **A-20J** and **A-20K**, bomb-leader versions of the A-20G and A-20H respectively, were built for both the USAAF and RAF, with the respective designations **Boston Mk IV** and **Boston Mk V** in service with the latter air force. They differed only by having a frameless transparent nose to accommodate the bomb-aimer.

When production ended, on 20 September 1944, Douglas had built 7,385 DB-7s of all versions, and these had been used by the USAAF and its allies in the widest imaginable number of roles. They had been supplied also to Brazil, the Netherlands and the USSR, and small numbers from those received by the UK had been diverted to serve with the Royal Australian Air Force, Royal Canadian Air Force, Royal New Zealand Air Force and South African Air Force. In addition, one A-20A had been supplied to the US Navy for evaluation under the designation **BD-1**, and in 1942 eight A-20Bs were procured for use as target tugs under the designation **BD-2**.

Variants

A-20D: projected lightweight version with turbocharged R-2600-7 radials fed from larger fuel tanks of non-self-sealing design
A-20E: 17 A-20As with internal modifications of a minor nature
XA-20F: one A-20A modified to test two twin 12.7-mm (0.5-in) General Electric turrets (one above and the other below the fuselage); the aircraft was later modified again to incorporate a 37-mm cannon in the nose
XF-3: three prototype reconnaissance aircraft converted from A-20s
YF-3: two experimental reconnaissance aircraft, similar to the

XF-3s but fitted with R-2600-23 radials and a twin 12.7-mm (0.5-in) manned turret
F-3A: 46 reconnaissance aircraft converted from A-20J and A-20K standard
O-53: heavy observation variant equivalent to the A-20B; 1,489 were ordered in October 1940, but the contract was cancelled before a single aircraft had been completed
P-70A-1: 39 night-fighter conversions from A-20C standard, produced in 1943 with six 12.7-mm (0.5-in) guns in the nose and two pivoted at the rear, with improved radar
P-70A-2: 65 night-fighter conversions from A-20G standard, equivalent to the P-70A-1 but without rear guns
P-70B-1: single experimental conversion from A-20G standard with SCR-720 radar and six 12.7-mm (0.5-in) guns in three blisters on each side of the nose
P-70B-2: 105 night-fighter trainers produced by conversion of A-20G and A-20J aircraft with SCR-720 or SCR-729 radar and provision (not always taken up) for a nose/ventral installation of six or eight 12.7-mm (0.5-in) guns
Havoc Mk I (Pandora): about 20 Havoc Mk I (Intruder) aircraft modified to carry the Long Aerial Mine, an abortive parachute weapon for use against bomber streams
Havoc Mk III: original designation for

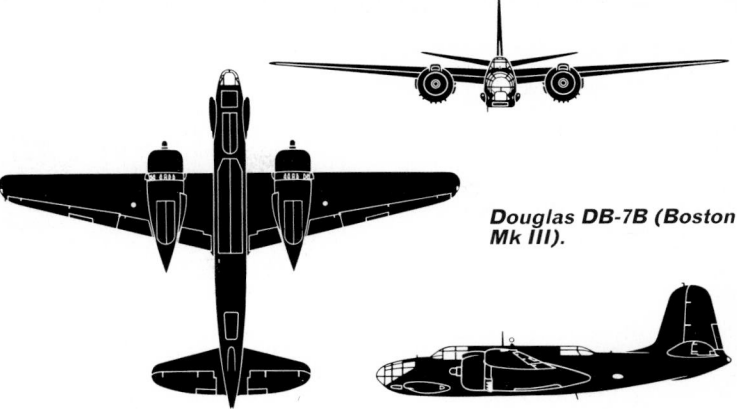

Douglas DB-7B (Boston Mk III).

Havoc Mk I (Pandora)
Boston Mk III (Intruder): designation of Boston Mk IIIs modified for intruder missions with a pack of four 20-mm cannon under the fuselage
Boston Mk III (Turbinlite): three conversions similar to the Havoc Mks I and II (Turbinlite)

Specification
Douglas A-20G
Type: three-seat light bomber
Powerplant: two 1193-kW (1,600-hp) Wright R-2600-23 Cyclone 14 radial piston engines
Performance: maximum speed 510 km/h (317 mph) at 3050 m (10,000 ft); cruising speed 370 km/h (230 mph); service ceiling 7620 m (25,000 ft); range with 2744 litres (725 US gal) of fuel and 907 kg (2,000 lb) of bombs 1650 km (1,025 miles)
Weights: empty 7250 kg (15,984 lb); maximum take-off 12338 kg (27,200 lb)
Dimensions: span 18.69 m (61 ft 4 in); length 14.63 m (48 ft 0 in); height 5.36 m (17 ft 7 in); wing area 43.20 m² (465.0 sq ft)
Armament: six 12.7-mm (0.5-in) forward-firing machine-guns, two 12.7-mm (0.5-in) guns in power-operated dorsal turret and one 12.7-mm (0.5-in) gun firing through ventral tunnel, plus up to 1814 kg (4,000 lb) of bombs

Douglas A-26/B-26 Invader

The USAAF issued a requirement for an attack aircraft in 1940, before it had information on World War II combat operations in Europe. Consequently, three prototypes were ordered in differing configurations: the **Douglas XA-26** attack bomber with a bomb-aimer's position; the **XA-26A** heavily-armed night-fighter; and the **XA-26B** attack aircraft with a 75-mm cannon. After flight testing and careful examination of reports from Europe and the Pacific, the **A-26B Invader** was ordered into production, and initial deliveries of the 1,355 built were made in April 1944.

The A-26B had six 12.7-mm (0.5-in) machine-guns in the nose, remotely controlled dorsal and ventral turrets each with two 12.7-mm (0.5-in) guns, and up to 10 more 12.7-mm (0.5-in) guns in underwing and underfuselage packs. Heavily armoured, and able to carry up to 1814 kg (4,000 lb) of bombs, the A-26B was potentially a formidable weapon. Moreover, its two 1491-kW (2,000-hp) Pratt & Whitney R-2800 engines conferred a maximum speed of 571 km/h (355 mph), making the A-26 the fastest US bomber of World War II. Invaders remained in USAF service until well into the 1970s.

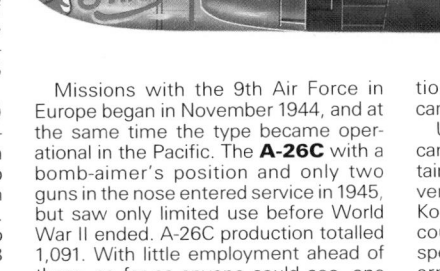

Douglas A-26B-15-DT (43-22369) 'Stinky' of the 552nd Bomb Squadron, 386th Bomb Group, US 9th Air Force, based at Beaumont-sur-Oise, France, in April 1945.

Missions with the 9th Air Force in Europe began in November 1944, and at the same time the type became operational in the Pacific. The **A-26C** with a bomb-aimer's position and only two guns in the nose entered service in 1945, but saw only limited use before World War II ended. A-26C production totalled 1,091. With little employment ahead of them, so far as anyone could see, one A-26B and one A-26C were converted to **XJD-1** configuration, this pair being followed by 150 A-26Cs converted as target tugs for the US Navy with the designation **JD-1**; some were converted later to launch and control missile test vehicles and drones, under the designa-

tion **JD-1D**. These designations became **UB-26J** and **DB-26J** in 1962.

USAF A-26B and A-26C aircraft became **B-26B** and **B-26C** in 1948, and retained this designation until 1962. Both versions saw extensive service in the Korean War, and were again used in a counter-insurgency role in Vietnam. A special COIN version with very heavy armament and extra power was developed by On Mark Engineering in 1963, a prototype being designated **YB-26K** and named **Counter Invader**. Subsequently about 70 B-26s were converted to **B-26K** standard, 40 later being redesignated **A-26A**. Some were deployed in Vietnam, and others

were supplied to friendly nations under the Military Assistance Program. B-26s were used also for training (**TB-26B** and **TB-26C**), transport (**CB-26B** freighter and **VB-26B** staff transport), RPV control (**DB-26C**), night reconnaissance (**FA-26C**, from 1948 redesignated **RB-26C**) and missile guidance research (**EB-26C**). After the war, many A-26s were converted to executive, survey, photographic and even fire-fighting aircraft. Brief details of the two semi-production marks are given in the variants list.

Variants

XA-26C: projected version with four 20-mm cannon in the nose; with the

abandonment of the project, the C-suffix was reallocated to the transparent-nose version of the Invader
XA-26D: single prototype powered by two 1567-kW (2,100-hp) Chevrolet-built R-2800-83 radials, the precursor of the proposed **A-26D** production series, of which 750 were cancelled after VJ-Day
XA-26E: single prototype powered by two 1567-kW (2,100-hp) R-2800-83 radials, the precursor of a planned production batch of 1,250 A-26E transparent-nose aircraft cancelled after VJ-Day
XA-26F: single prototype (later redesignated **XB-26F**) with two R-2800-83 radials and a 726-kg (1,600-hp) thrust General Electric J31 turbojet in the tail to boost performance; maximum speed was 700 km/h (435 mph) at 4570 m (15,000 ft), an insufficient performance gain to warrant production
A-26Z: Douglas designation for a proposed post-war model to have been built as the **A-26G** and **A-26H** with unglazed and glazed noses respectively; improvements included a raised pilot's canopy and wingtip drop tanks
Invader Mk I: RAF designation of 140

A large number of USAF A-26Cs were handed over to the US Navy as JD-1s for use in the target-tug and drone-directing roles. Some survived beyond 1962 to be redesignated UB-26J and DB-26J.

A-26Cs received under Lend-Lease
On Mark Marketeer: unpressurised version of the Marksman C
On Mark Marksman A: pressurised executive transport produced by On Mark Engineering on almost production-line basis; powered by 1567-kW (2,100-hp) R-2800-83AM3s
On Mark Marksman B: similar to the Marksman A apart from the provision of wingtip tanks and R-2800-83AM4A radials
On Mark Marksman C: similar to the Marksman A apart from extra fuel tankage in the wings and 1865-kW (2,500-hp) R-2800-CB-16/17 radials
Smith Biscayne 26: high-speed transport version developed by the L. B. Smith Company and able to seat up to 15 passengers
Smith Super 26: standard Invader airframe converted with wingtip tanks and an executive interior
Smith Tempo I: unpressurised executive conversion with R-2800 B-series engines

Smith Tempo II: pressurised executive conversion with a new fuselage 2.93 m (9 ft 7½ in) longer than the standard, able to seat up to 13 passengers

Specification
Douglas B-26B
Type: three-seat light bomber
Powerplant: two 1491-kW (2,000-hp) Pratt & Whitney R-2800-27 or -79 Double Wasp radial piston engines
Performance: maximum speed 571 km/h (355 mph) at 4570 m

(15,000 ft); cruising speed 457 km/h (284 mph); service ceiling 6735 m (22,100 ft); normal range 2253 km (1,400 miles)
Weights: empty 10365 kg (22,850 lb); maximum take-off 15876 kg (35,000 lb)
Dimensions: span 21.34 m (70 ft 0 in); length 15.24 m (50 ft 0 in); height 5.64 m (18 ft 6 in); wing area 50.17 m² (540 sq ft)
Armament: 10 12.7-mm (0.5-in) machine-guns and up to 1814 kg (4,000 lb) of bombs

Douglas XA-42/XB-42

Under the initial designation **Douglas XA-42** for an attack bomber, redesignated subsequently **XB-42** as a bomber, Douglas designed and built two prototypes and one static test airframe under a contract received from the US Army Air Force on 25 June 1943. Named **Mixmaster** by the company, this unusual aircraft had a mid-set cantilever monoplane wing, cruciform tail surfaces and tricycle landing gear, whose main units retracted aft to be housed in the sides of the fuselage. The broad and deep fuselage provided accommodation for a crew of three, consisting of a bomb-aimer/navigator in the nose, with the pilot and co-pilot in a side-by-side cockpit well forward on the fuselage, each beneath an individual canopy; the fuselage also incorporated a large internal bomb bay, as well as housing the twin-engine powerplant in a compartment immediately to the rear of the pilot's cockpit. The two Allison V-1710 engines were used to drive, via shafting and a reduction gearbox in the tailcone, two three-

The XB-42 was a bold attempt to combine all the best features of contemporary aerodynamic and piston-engine technology, but it failed as official faith had already been replaced in jets.

bladed contra-rotating pusher propellers to the rear of the tail unit.

Despite its unusual features, when first flown on 6 May 1944 the Mixmaster more than lived up to expectations. The second prototype was flown for the first time on 1 August 1944, soon afterwards being modified by the addition of a single canopy over the pilot/co-pilot cockpit. This prototype was destroyed in a crash during December of that year, but by that time the USAAF had decided not to proceed with production of this design, awaiting instead the development of higher-performance turbojet-powered bombers. As an interim step to allow evaluation of turbine power, the first prototype was given a mixed powerplant comprising

two 1025-kW (1,375 hp) Allison V-1710-133 piston engines to drive the propellers, plus two 726-kg (1,600-lb) thrust Westinghouse 19XB-2A turbojets mounted in underwing nacelles. Redesignated **XB-42A**, this aircraft was used for performance testing over several months before being retired at the end of June 1949.

Specification
Douglas XB-42
Type: three-seat bomber prototype
Powerplant: two 988-kW (1,325-hp) Allison V-1710-125 V-12 piston engines
Performance: maximum speed

660 km/h (410 mph) at 8960 m (29,400 ft); cruising speed 502 km/h (312 mph); service ceiling 8960 m (29,400 ft); standard range 2897 km (1,800 miles)
Weights: empty 9475 kg (20,888 lb); maximum take-off 16193 kg (35,700 lb)
Dimensions: span 21.49 m (70 ft 6 in); length 16.36 m (53 ft 8 in); height 5.74 m (18 ft 10 in); wing area 51.56 m² (555 sq ft)
Armament: two 12.7-mm (0.5-in) machine-guns in each of two remotely-controlled wing turrets, plus an internal bombload of 3629 kg (8,000 lb)

Douglas A2D Skyshark

Interest in the efficiency of the turbo-prop engine at the end of World War II resulted in Douglas receiving a contract for a prototype version of the AD-1 Skyraider with a turboprop replacing its piston-engine powerplant. This apparently simple conversion failed to materialise because the Allison XT40 turboprop had more than twice the power output of the piston engine it was intended to replace, requiring considerable airframe redesign.

Two prototypes were ordered under the designation **Douglas XA2D-1**, the first of them flying on 26 May 1950. These retained the same overall configuration of the AD-1, but had a new tail unit, modified and strengthened landing gear, and a fuselage redesigned to accommodate the Allison XT40 engine. This consisted of two separate turbines driving two co-axial contra-rotating propellers through the medium of a com-

A turboprop development of the Skyraider, the Skyshark was a massive machine with an impressive performance.

mon gearbox.

Early testing showed great promise, and 10 pre-production aircraft were ordered under the designation **A2D-1 Skyshark**. However, development problems with the powerplant and gearbox led to delays, and after two aircraft had been lost in accidents the programme was cancelled.

Specification
Type: single-seat carrier-based attack aircraft
Powerplant: one 3803-kW (5,100-shp) Allison XT40-A-2 turboprop, comprising two XT38 turbines driving through a common gearbox
Performance: maximum speed

805 km/h (500 mph) at 7620 m (25,000 ft); cruising speed 443 km/h (275 mph); service ceiling 14660 m (48,100 ft); range with standard fuel 1025 km (637 miles)
Weights: empty 5871 kg (12,944 lb); maximum take-off 10417 kg (22,966 lb)
Dimensions: span 15.24 m (50 ft

0 in); length 12.56 m (41 ft 2½ in); height 5.20 m (17 ft 0¾ in); wing area 37.16 m² (400 sq ft)
Armament: four fixed forward-firing 20-mm cannon, plus up to 2495 kg (5,500 lb) of mixed stores on hardpoints under the fuselage and wings

Douglas AD-1 (A-1) Skyraider
to
Douglas D-558-2 Skyrocket

Douglas AD-1 (A-1) Skyraider

Ed Heinemann, chief engineer at Douglas El Segundo, (who also created the Boston/Havoc, Invader, Skyknight, Skyray, Skywarrior, Skyrocket and Skyhawk) was so unimpressed by his XBTD-1 series, built to US Navy specification for a carrier-based dive-bomber/ torpedo-carrier, that he took it upon himself to design a simpler machine which he judged more useful. Designated **XBT2D-1** when flown on 18 March 1945, this aircraft became the **Douglas AD-1 Skyraider**, and enjoyed an amazingly long and varied career.

Crewed by a pilot only, the AD-1 was at the time the largest production single-seater. Of low-wing monoplane configuration, the design was based on the Wright R-3350 radial engine, smaller than the R-4360 of other competing prototypes. Although there was plenty of internal space this was not used for weapons; instead the folding wings were given no fewer than seven hardpoints on each side, and a robust structure gave the Skyraider great integrity. Wartime experience had shown that the most important characteristic for an aircraft in this category was the ability to deliver a wide range of weapons. Douglas ensured that the AD was capable of this, and its basic versatility was such that 3,180 had been built when production ended in 1957.

Just too late for World War II, the AD-1 proved a valuable weapon in the Korean War, when its heavy weapon load and up to 10-hour endurance contrasted sharply with payload/endurance performance of the jets. **AD-1** to **AD-4** versions differed in detail, but the **AD-5** had a wider cockpit seating two (side-by-side) and several early versions had APS-20A radar and a rear cabin for two/three operators for AEW missions. The AD-5 also introduced conversion kits for ambulance, freight, transport or target towing. The **AD-6** and **AD-7** were improved single-seaters. Large numbers of single-seat versions were used by the French Armée de l'Air in Algeria.

In 1962 Skyraiders were redesignated **A-1D** to **A-1J**, and in South Vietnam the USAF's 1st Air Commando Group of the Tactical Air Command used A-1E, A-1H and A-1J versions with great success, continuing to use them after the US Navy Skyraiders had been withdrawn from that theatre. Called 'Sandy' or 'The Spad', A-1 versions were among the most hardworked and versatile aircraft in that theatre.

Variants

XBT2D-1N: under this designation two of the 25 prototype and service-test XB2D-1 aircraft were modified as three-seat night-attack prototypes with two radar operators (in the fuselage behind the pilot), radar in a pod under the port wing and a searchlight in a pod under the starboard wing

XBT2D-1P: single XBT2D-1 converted as a photographic-reconnaissance prototype

XBT2D-1Q: single XBT2D-1 converted as a two-seat electronic counter-measures aircraft, with the electronics operator located within the fuselage, and

Something of an anachronism on the 1960s carrier deck, the A-1 Skyraider nevertheless played an important part during the first years in Vietnam. This is a VA-176 A-1H.

the radar and chaff pods under the port and starboard wings respectively

AD-1: initial production version, with the 1865-kW (2,500-hp) R-3350-24W radial and an armament of two cannon and 3629 kg (8,000 lb) of disposable stores (242 built)

AD-1Q: two-seat electronic countermeasures aircraft based on the XBT2D-1Q (35 built)

XAD-1W: single XBT2D-1 converted as a three-seat airborne early warning prototype, with two radar operators in the main cabin behind the pilot, and search radar in a bulky fairing under the fuselage

XAD-2: single XBT2D-1 converted as the prototype of an upgraded attack model; this was at first designated **BT2D-2**, and was powered by the 2014-kW (2,700-hp) R-3350-26W radial

AD-2: improved model, evaluated by means of an AD-1 modified with wheelwell covers, greater fuel capacity and other detail alterations (156 built)

AD-2D: unofficial designation for AD-2s used as remotely-controlled aircraft to gather radioactive material in the air after nuclear tests

AD-2Q: two-seat electronic countermeasures version of the AD-2 (21 built)

AD-2QU: AD-2Q fitted to tow an aerial target (one built)

AD-3: designation for a proposed turbine-powered version, for which were considered the General Electric TG-100, two Allison 500s, two Westinghouse 24Cs, two Westinghouse 19XBs or even suggested Douglas-designed twin turbine powerplants; this project was eventually redesignated A2D Skyshark

AD-3: this designation fell to an improved model of the AD-2 after the turbine-powered version became the A2D; compared with the AD-2 various improvements (longer-stroke landing gear, redesigned canopy, improved propeller etc) were worked in (125 built)

AD-3E and **AD-3S:** versions produced as the two components of an aerial anti-submarine team, with the AD-3E as the search aircraft and the AD-3S as the attack aircraft; two AD-3Ws were converted into the AD-3Es, and two AD-3Ns into the pair of AD-3Ss; though the feasibility of the system was proved, the later conversion of one AD-3S into a hunter-killer (with AN/APS-31 radar in a pod under the port wing, and useful capacity left for offensive stores) showed the way for later production models

AD-3N: three-seat night-attack version of the AD-3 (15 built)

AD-3QU: target-towing version of the AD-3, rendered superfluous by the success of the AD-2QU; the aircraft were thus delivered as **AD-3Q**

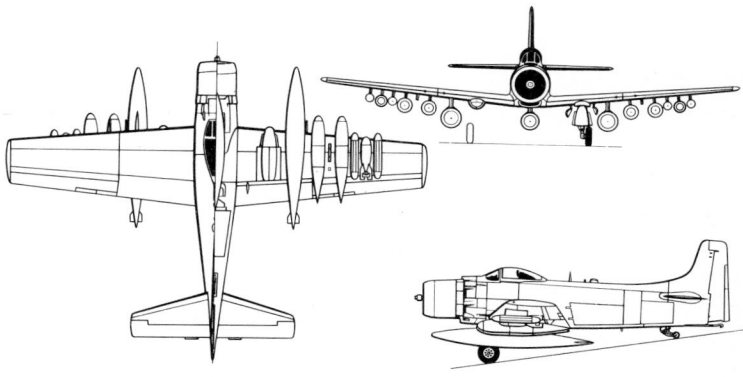

Douglas A-1J (AD-7) Skyraider.

electronic countermeasures machines, though provision for the Mk 22 target was retained (23 built)

AD-3W: three-seat airborne early warning version of the AD-3, with systems based on those of the XAD-1W (31 built)

AD-4: major production model of the Skyraider series; the type was fitted with the 2014-kW (2,700-hp) R-3350-26WA radial and an autopilot, and the canopy was further improved (372 built)

AD-4B: specialised AD-4 variant with the provision for a nuclear weapon, launched using the over-the-shoulder toss-bombing technique; wing armament was increased to four 20-mm cannon in this version (28 conversions from AD-4 standard and 165 built)

AD-4L: version of the AD-4 fitted with anti-icing and de-icing equipment for winter operations in Korea; wing armament also increased to four 20-mm cannon (63 conversions)

AD-4N: three-seat night-attack version of the AD-4, delivered or retrofitted with 'S' equipment to suit them for the submarine hunter/killer role (307 built)

AD-4NA: designation of 100 AD-4Ns stripped of night-attack equipment to permit heavier bombloads for Korean operations; fitted with four 20-mm cannon

AD-4NL: version of the AD-4N equivalent to the AD-4L (36 conversions)

AD-4Q: two-seat electronic countermeasures version of the AD-4 (39 built)

AD-4W: three-seat airborne early warning version of the AD-4; 50 were transferred to the Royal Navy under the designation **Skyraider AEW.Mk 1**, and the 118 remaining in US Navy

service were fitted for the 'E' search part of the anti-submarine mission (168 built)

AD-5: the initial AD-5 proposed by Douglas was a 1948 development with the R-3350 Turbo-Compound engine; but as this needed a considerable amount of fuselage redesign, the US Navy refused development funds, and the AD-5 designation thus went to a variant that combined within one airframe the hunter and killer roles for anti-submarine warfare, the two crew being seated side-by-side in a widened forward fuselage; at the same time the length of the fuselage was increased by 0.58 m (1 ft 11 in), the fuselage dive brakes were eliminated, and the vertical tail surfaces were increased in area; wing armament was again increased to four 20-mm cannon; the utility of the version was recognised at an early stage, and AD-5s were delivered with kits enabling the aircraft to be converted as casevac aircraft with accommodation for four litters, troop transport with seating for 12 on bench seats, staff/VIP transport with four rearward-facing seats, cargo transport for up to 907 kg (2,000 lb) of freight, target tug and photographic reconnaissance aircraft; and in 1953 Douglas developed an inflight-refuelling store to be carried externally (212 built)

AD-5N: four-seat night-attack version of the AD-5 (239 built)

AD-5Q: four-seat electronic countermeasures version of the AD-5N (54 conversions)

AD-5S: one experimental aircraft evaluated in the anti-submarine role with MAD gear

AD-5W: four-seat airborne early warning version of the AD-5 (218 built)

AD-6: essentially an improved version of the AD-4B single-seat attack aircraft, and provided with special equipment for accurate low-level bombing (713 built)

AD-7: the final production version of the Skyraider, the AD-7 differed from the AD-6 in having an R-3350-26WB engine instead of an R-3350-26WA, and local strengthening for the landing gear, engine mountings and outer wing panels (72 built)
A-1D: 1962 redesignation of the AD-4NA
A-1E: 1962 redesignation of the AD-5
EA-1E: 1962 redesignation of the

AD-5W
UA-1E: 1962 redesignation of the AD-5 in a utility role with conversion kits
EA-1F: 1962 redesignation of the AD-5Q
A-1G: 1962 redesignation of the AD-5N
A-1H: 1962 redesignation of the AD-6
A-1J: 1962 redesignation of the AD-7

Specification
Douglas AD-7 (A-1J)
Type: single-seat attack bomber
Powerplant: one 2088-kW (2,800-hp) Wright R-3350-26B radial piston engine
Performance: maximum speed 515 km/h (320 mph) at 5640 m (18,500 ft); cruising speed 306 km/h (190 mph) at 1830 m (6,000 ft); service ceiling 7740 m (25,400 ft); range 1448 km (900 miles)

Weights: empty 4785 kg (10,550 lb); maximum take-off 11340 kg (25,000 lb)
Dimensions: span 15.47 m (50 ft 9 in); length 11.84 m (38 ft 10 in); height 4.78 m (15 ft 8¼ in); wing area 37.16 m² (400 sq ft)
Armament: four 20-mm cannon, plus up to 3629 kg (8,000 lb) of weapons on 15 hardpoints, including bombs, depth charges, mines, napalm, rockets and torpedoes

Douglas B-7 and O-35

In the late 1920s the US War Department was taking note of developments in aircraft design, such as the technical revolution created by the appearance of all-metal cantilever monoplanes with retractable landing gear. It was decided initially to adopt such features in twin-engined aircraft that were intended for fast long-range reconnaissance, and the War Department ordered two Fokker XO-27 prototypes in this category. Fearing it might lose a valuable source of revenue, Douglas designed an aircraft incorporating such features and in March 1930 received an order for one example each of the **Douglas XO-35** and **Douglas XO-36**. They were intended to differ only in their engines, the former having geared Curtiss Conquerors and the latter a direct-drive version of the same engine.

In the event, the XO-36 was redesignated **XB-7** and built as a bomber. In a parallel development the second of the Fokker XO-27s was completed as the XB-8 bomber. Later, six YO-27s and six Y1O-27s were delivered to the US Army.

The Douglas XO-35 was test-flown in spring 1931, causing quite a stir among a public used to seeing the lumbering twin-engined biplanes used by the US Army. It was a slim monoplane with a gull wing set high on the fuselage, the main units of its landing gear retracting into streamlined engine nacelles leaving only the lower part of the wheels ex-

posed. The engine nacelles were attached to the wing undersurfaces and fuselage sides by complex strut assemblies, with the fuselage having corrugated metal sheet covering. There were open gunners' cockpits in the nose and amidships; the pilot's open cockpit was located immediately forward of the wing leading edge; and the fourth crew member, the radio-operator, had an enclosed cabin behind the pilot's position.

The XB-7 was almost identical, but had underfuselage racks for up to 544 kg (1,200 lb) of bombs. During the US Fiscal Year 1932 orders were placed for seven **Y1B-7** and five **Y1O-35** service-test aircraft. These differed from the prototypes mainly by having smooth metal sheet covering for the fuselages, and strut- rather than wire-braced horizontal tailplanes.

The Y1B-7s, later designated **B-7**, were attached to the two US Army bombardment squadrons based at March Field, California, while the **O-35** aircraft (previously Y1O-35s) flew with observation units. In February 1934 the five O-35s, six B-7s and XO-35 prototype were all assigned to the air mail route linking Wyoming with the west coast of the United States. Operations at night and in bad weather took their toll and in the four-month emergency period during which the US Army ran the nation's air mail service no fewer than four of the B-7s were lost in crashes. Soon afterwards the remaining B-7s and O-35s were relegated to second-line duties, an O-35 being the last to be grounded in February 1939.

Specification
Douglas B-7
Type: four-seat medium bomber
Powerplant: two 503-kW (675-hp) Curtiss V-1570-53 Conqueror V-12

Douglas Y1B-7 of the 31st Bomb Squadron, US Army Air Corps, in the markings carried for the 1933 USAAC anti-aircraft exercises.

piston engines
Performance: maximum speed 293 km/h (182 mph); cruising speed 254 km/h (158 mph); service ceiling 6220 m (20,400 ft); range 661 km (411 miles)
Weights: empty equipped 2503 kg (5,519 lb); maximum take-off 5070 kg (11,177 lb)
Dimensions: span 19.81 m (65 ft 0 in); length 14 m (45 ft 11 in); height 3.53 m (11 ft 7 in); wing area 57.71 m² (621.2 sq ft)
Armament: two 7.62-mm (0.3-in) machine-guns (one each on a ring mounting over the nose and mid-ship cockpits), plus up to 544 kg (1,200 lb) of bombs on underfuselage racks

Douglas B-18 Bolo

Faced with a US Army Air Corps requirement of early 1934 for a bomber with virtually double the bomb load and range capability of the Martin B-10, which was then the USAAC's standard bomber, Douglas had little doubt that it could draw upon engineering experience and design technology of the DC-2 commercial transport which was then on the point of making its first flight.

Private-venture prototypes to meet the US Army's requirements were evaluated at Wright Field, Ohio, in August 1935, these including the Boeing Model 299, **Douglas DB-1** and Martin 146. The first was built as the B-17 Flying Fortress, the last was produced as an export variant of the Martin B-10/B-12 series, and the Douglas DB-1 (**Douglas Bomber 1**) was ordered in January 1936 into immediate production under the designation **B-18**. Derived from the commercial DC-2, the DB-1 prototype retained a basically similar wing, tail unit and powerplant. There were, however, two differences in the wing: while retaining the same basic planform as the DC-2, that of the DB-1 had a 1.37-m (4-ft 6-in) increase in span and was mounted in a mid-wing instead of low-wing position on an entirely new fuselage, one that was deeper than that of the commercial transport to provide adequate accommodation for a crew of six, and to

The RCAF's Digby Mk I was similar to the USAAC's B-18A apart from British armament and numerous internal items of British or Canadian manufacture.

include nose and dorsal turrets, a bomb-aimer's position, and an internal bomb bay. There was, in addition, a third gunner's position, with a ventral gun discharging via a tunnel in the underfuselage structure. Powerplant comprised two 694-kW (930-hp) Wright R-1820-45 Cyclone 9 engines.

A total of 133 B-18s was covered by the first contract, this number including the single DB-1 which had served as a prototype. True production aircraft, which had the type name **Bolo**, had a number of equipment changes, producing an increase in the normal loaded weight, and more-powerful Wright R-1820-45 radials. The last B-18 to come off the production line differed by having a power-operated nose turret, and carried the company identification **DB-2**, but this feature did not become standard on subsequent production aircraft.

The next contracts, covering 217 **B-18A** aircraft, were placed in June 1937 (177) and mid-1938 (40). This version differed by having the bomb-aimer's position extended forward and over the nose-gunner's station, and the

installation of yet-more-powerful Wright R-1820-53 engines. Most of the USAAC's bomber squadrons were equipped with B-18s or B-18As in 1940, and the majority of the 33 B-18As which equipped the USAAC's 5th and 11th Bomb Groups, based on Hawaiian airfields, were destroyed when the Japanese launched their attack on Pearl Harbor.

When in 1942 B-18s were replaced in first-line service by B-17s, some 122 B-18As were equipped with search radar and magnetic anomaly detection (MAD) equipment for deployment in the Caribbean on anti-submarine patrols under the designation **B-18B**. The Royal Canadian Air Force also acquired 20 B-18As which, under the designation **Digby Mk I**, were employed on maritime patrol. The designation **B-18C** applied to two other aircraft reconfigured for ASW patrol. Another two air-

craft were converted for use in a transport role under the designation **C-58**, but many others were used similarly without conversion or redesignation.

Variants
B-18AM: 18 B-18As modified as trainers during World War II by the removal of bomb gear
B-18M: 22 B-18s modified as trainers in 1942 in the same way as the B-18AMs
B-22: projected development of B-18A with 1194-kW (1,600-hp) Wright R-2600-3 radials

Specification
Douglas B-18A
Type: medium bomber and ASW aircraft
Powerplant: two 746-kW (1,000-hp) Wright R-1820-53 Cyclone 9 radial piston engines

Performance: maximum speed
346 km/h (215 mph) at 3050 m
(10,000 ft); cruising speed 269 km/h
(167 mph); service ceiling 7285 m

(23,900 ft); range 1931 km (1,200 miles)
Weights: empty 7403 kg (16,321 lb);
maximum take-off 12552 kg (27,673 lb)
Dimensions: span 27.28 m (89 ft

6 in); length 17.63 m (57 ft 10 in);
height 4.62 m (15 ft 2 in); wing area
89.65 m² (965 sq ft)
Armament: three 7.62-mm (0.3-in)

machine-guns (in nose, ventral and
dorsal positions), plus up to 2948 kg
(6,500 lb) of bombs

Douglas B-23 Dragon

The Douglas B-18, which had been designed to meet a US Army Air Corps requirement of 1934 for a high-performance medium bomber, was clearly not in
the same league as the Boeing B-17 Flying Fortress, which had been built to the
same specification. Figures highlight the
facts: 350 B-18s were procured in total,
by comparison with almost 13,000
B-17s. In an attempt to rectify the shortcomings of their DB-1 design, Douglas
developed in 1938 an improved version
and the proposal seemed sufficiently
attractive for the US Army to award a
contract for 38 of these aircraft under the
designation **B-23** and with the name
Dragon.

Although the overall configuration
was similar to that of the earlier aircraft,
when examined in detail it was seen to
be virtually a new design. Wing span
was increased, the fuselage was entirely
different and of much improved aerodynamic form, and the tail unit had a
much higher vertical fin and rudder.
Landing gear was the same retractable
tailwheel type, but the engine nacelles
had been extended so that when the
main units were lowered in flight they
were faired by the nacelle extensions
and created far less drag. Greatly im-

proved performance was expected from
these refinements, plus the provision of
60 per cent more power by the use of
two Wright R-2600-3 Cyclone 14
engines. An innovation was the provision of a tail gun position, this being the
first US bomber to introduce such a
feature.

First flown on 27 July 1939, the B-23s
were all delivered to the US Army during
that year. Early evaluation had shown
that performance and flight characteristics were disappointing. Furthermore,
information received from the European
theatre during 1940 made it clear that development would be unlikely to result in
range, bombload and armament capabilities to compare with the bomber aircraft
then in service with the combatant
nations, or already beginning to emerge
in the USA. As a result these aircraft saw
only limited service in a patrol capacity
along the US Pacific coastline before
being relegated to training duties. During
1942 about 15 of these aircraft were converted to serve as utility transports
under the designation **UC-67**, and
some of the remainder were used for a
variety of purposes including engine
testbeds, glider towing experiments and
weapons evaluation.

Following the end of World War II
many surplus B-23s and UC-67s were
acquired by civil operators for conversion as corporate aircraft. The majority
were modified by Pan American's
Engineering Department, equipped to
accommodate a crew of two and 12 passengers. Some of them remained in civil
use for about 30 years.

Specification
Douglas B-23
Type: four/five-seat medium bomber
Powerplant: two 1193-kW (1,600-hp)
Wright R-2600-3 Cyclone 14 radial
piston engines
Performance: maximum speed
454 km/h (282 mph) at 3660 m
(12,000 ft); cruising speed 338 km/h
(210 mph); service ceiling 9630 m

*Bearing much the same kinship to
the DC-3 as did the B-18 to the
DC-2, the Douglas B-23 was little
more than an interim type pending
large-scale deliveries of the
Boeing B-17. Several were used on
civil transport duties after the war.*

(31,600 ft); range 2253 km (1,400 miles)
Weights: empty 8659 kg (19,089 lb);
maximum take-off 14696 kg (32,400 lb)
Dimensions: span 28.04 m (92 ft
0 in); length 17.8 m (58 ft 4¾ in); height
5.63 m (18 ft 5½ in); wing area
92.25 m² (993 sq ft)
Armament: one 12.7-mm (0.5-in)
machine-gun in tail position and three
7.62-mm (0.3-in) guns in nose, dorsal
and ventral positions, plus up to
1996 kg (4,400 lb) of bombs

Douglas XB-43

Anxious to speed the development of a
pure jet bomber, the US Army Air Force
contracted Douglas to produce two
Douglas XB-43 bomber prototypes
using the basic design of the XB-42. The
proposed conversion was comparatively
simple, replacing the XB-42's Allison piston engines with two turbojets and providing them with air inlets, incorporating
two extended tail pipes to discharge the
jet efflux at the tail, and replacing the cruciform tail unit with a conventional structure which, however, had a fin and rudder of increased height and area by
comparison with the XB-42.

To save time it was decided to modify
the XB-42 static test air-frame to produce the first XB-43. It was a short-cut
plan doomed to disappointment, with
seemingly endless delays resulting from
the war's end and the provision of the
turbojet powerplant. Eventually, the
XB-43 was flown for the first time on 17
May 1946. By that time, however, and
despite the prototype's good overall performance, the USAAF was already looking to much-more-capable turbojet-

*The XB-42 was a straightforward
conversion of the XB-42 static test
airframe, retaining the twin
canopies but dispensing with the
ventral fin. The second XB-43 had
a plywood nose as the glazed
version was prone to cracking.*

powered bombers. Thus this, the US
Army Air Force's first jet-bomber, was
used only for flight-test purposes. The
second prototype was completed and
delivered in May 1947, being used as an
engine testbed before it was retired in
late 1953.

Specification
Type: three-seat turbojet-powered
bomber prototype
Powerplant: two 1701-kg (3,750-lb)
thrust each General Electric J35-GE-3
turbojets
Performance: maximum speed at
sea level 829 km/h (515 mph); cruising
speed 676 km/h (420 mph); service
ceiling 11735 m (38,500 ft); range
1770 km (1,100 miles)

Weights: empty 9877 kg (21,775 lb);
maximum take-off 17932 kg (39,533 lb)
Dimensions: span 21.69 m (71 ft
2 in); length 15.6 m (51 ft 2 in); height
7.39 m (24 ft 3 in); wing area 52.3 m²
(563 sq ft)
Armament: (proposed bomber

variant) up to 2722 kg (6,000 lb) of
bombs or (proposed attack variant) 16
forward-firing 12.7-mm (0.5-in)
machine-guns and 16 127-mm (5-in)
rockets, plus (both versions) two
12.7-mm (0.5-in) machine-guns in a
remotely-controlled tail turret

Douglas B-66 Destroyer

US Air Force involvement in the Korean
War highlighted an urgent need for a
high performance day/night tactical
bomber. To speed the availability of such
an aircraft it was planned to procure a
land-based version of the A3D Skywarrior then being developed for the US
Navy. To this end Douglas was given a
contract for five pre-production
Douglas RB-66A all-weather/night
photo-reconnaissance aircraft, the first
of which was flown on 28 June 1954 at
the Long Beach plant.

Although retaining the basic overall

configuration of the A3D Skywarrior,
the USAF's **RB-66A Destroyer** dispensed
with the arrester gear, strengthened
landing gear and wing-folding of the
naval version; it introduced aerodynamic
changes in the wing design, revised
accommodation for the three-man crew
who were provided with ejection seats,
and detail changes in equipment, including a multiple-camera installation and the
provision of bombing and navigation
radar. Power for this initial version was
provided by two 4341-kg (9,570-lb)
thrust Allison YJ71-A-9 turbojets. Suc-

cessful testing of the RB-66As led to a
contract for the first production version,
the **RB-66B**, powered by 4627-kg
(10,200-lb) thrust Allison J71-A-11s or
J71-A-13s. The first of 145 RB-66Bs was
flown in March 1955 and deliveries to the
USAF began on 1 February 1956.

Production versions included also the
B-66B bomber (72 built), which had the
same powerplant as the RB-66B and
could carry up to 6804 kg (15,000 lb) of
bombs in place of reconnaissance equipment; the **RB-66C** (36 built), which was
an electronic reconnaissance and ECM
aircraft with J71-A-11 or J71-A-13 turbojets and a crew of seven including five
specialist radar operators, four of them

accommodated in what had initially been
the bomb bay; and the **WB-66D** (36
built) combat-area weather reconnaissance aircraft with J71-A-13 engines and
a crew of five (two plus equipment in the
bomb bay).

ECM versions of the B-66/RB-66
proved of great value during operations
in Vietnam, locating, classifying and jamming enemy radars, but withdrawal of
US forces from Southeast Asia brought
retirement of these aircraft.

Variants
EB-66B: ECM (radar-jamming) version
of which 13 were converted from
B-66Bs

NB-66B: two joint-services aircraft converted from B-66Bs for the high-altitude test paradropping of items such as Gemini and Apollo spacecraft
EB-66C: redesignation of RB-66Cs following installation of advanced ECM equipment
EB-66E: ECM version of which 52 were converted from RB-66Bs; equipped similarly to EB-66Bs
X-21A: under this designation two WB-66Ds were used by Northrop Corporation in a research programme; both were modified by the substitution of a new laminar-flow wing and to ensure that the aerodynamic characteristics of the wing were not compromised by wing-mounted engines, two 4305-kg (9,490-lb) thrust General Electric XJ79-GE-13 turbojets were pod-mounted one on each side of the rear fuselage

This photograph of an RB-66B reveals the type's pleasing lines and the radar-directed tail barbette, though here the 20-mm cannon are absent. The Destroyer saw action as an ECM platform in Vietnam, under various EB-66 designations.

Specification
Douglas RB-66B
Type: all-weather day/night reconnaissance aircraft
Powerplant: two 4627-kg (10,200-lb) thrust each Allison J71-A-11 or J71-A-13 turbojets
Performance: maximum speed 1015 km/h (631 mph) at 1830 m (6,000 ft); cruising speed 845 km/h (525 mph); service ceiling 11855 m (38,900 ft); combat radius 1489 km (925 miles)
Weights: empty 19720 kg (43,476 lb); maximum take-off 37648 kg (83,000 lb)
Dimensions: span 22.1 m (72 ft 6 in); length 22.9 m (75 ft 2 in); height 7.19 m (23 ft 7 in); wing area 72.46 m² (780 sq ft)
Armament: two 20-mm cannon in radar-controlled tail turret.

Douglas BT series

The excellent flight characteristics of the Douglas O-2 family led to the conversion of 40 O-2Ks in 1930 as basic trainers for the US Army. Dual controls were installed and armament was deleted, the modified aircraft then being designated **Douglas BT-1**. The only O-32 to be built was given dual controls, also in 1930, and became designated **BT-2**. Thirty O-32As were modified similarly to the O-2Ks; used by US Army and National Guard units for basic training these were redesignated **BT-2A**. Some 146 **BT-2B** aircraft were built as such, the first appearing in 1931. Powered by the 336-kW (450-hp) Pratt & Whitney R-1340-11 radial, they survived many years in basic training units.

Variants

BT-2B1: in 1932 58 BT-2Bs were provided with a folding blind-flying hood over the rear cockpit, and were thus redesignated BT-2B1
BT-2C: an order for 20 BT-2Cs was received by Douglas at the end of 1930; these differed from the BT-2B in having slightly shorter fuselages and revised landing gear; 13 of them were converted later to instrument trainers and redesignated as **BT-2C1**; in 1940

The BT-2B basic trainer was based on the O-38 airframe, but with a considerably less powerful engine. It was the first basic trainer ordered as such by the USAAC.

seven BT-2Cs were modified as control aircraft for Douglas A-4 aerial targets (see below) and redesignated as **BT-2CR**
A-4: in 1940 two BT-2B1s and 15 BT-2Bs had fixed tricycle landing gear installed and were modified as radio-controlled anti-aircraft gun targets, sporting a bright red fuselage; designated originally as **BT-2BG** and **BT-2BR**, they all subsequently received the definitive designation A-4

Specification
Douglas BT-2B
Type: two-seat dual-control basic trainer
Powerplant: one 336-kW (450-hp) Pratt & Whitney R-1340-11 radial piston engine
Performance: maximum speed 216 km/h (134 mph); cruising speed 188 km/h (117 mph); service ceiling 5850 m (19,200 ft); range 515 km (320 miles)
Weights: empty equipped 1324 kg (2,918 lb); maximum take-off 1845 kg (4,067 lb)
Dimensions: span 12.19 m (40 ft 0 in); length 9.5 m (31 ft 2 in); height 3.3 m; (10 ft 10 in); wing area 33.63 m² (362 sq ft)

Douglas BTD Destroyer

Early service use of the Douglas SBD Dauntless had convinced the US Navy of its capability as a dive-bomber: its later wartime record, in such actions as the Battle of the Coral Sea (May 1942) and the Battle of Midway (June 1942), merely provided confirmation. Long before that date, however, the US Navy had initiated the procurement of a more advanced dive-bomber, leading to the development by Douglas of a two-seat aircraft in this category, of which two prototypes were ordered by the US Navy in June 1941.

Designated **Douglas XSB2D-1 Destroyer**, the first prototype (03551) made its initial flight on 8 April 1943. But instead of being ordered into production, it was used as the basis of a new aircraft which the cut-and-thrust of war in the Pacific had shown to be more essential. As the XSB2D-1, the prototype was a clean and purposeful-looking two-seat dive-bomber, introducing an internal bomb bay and, for the first time in an aircraft to operate from an aircraft-carrier, retractable tricycle landing gear. The US Navy's new requirement was for a single-seat torpedo/dive-bomber, and the XSB2D-1 was modified for this new role by conversion to a single-seat cockpit, the addition of two wing-mounted 20-mm cannon, enlargement of the bomb bay and the provision of increased fuel capacity. Airbrakes were installed in each side of the fuselage, and the big Wright Cyclone 18 engine of the XSB2D-1 was retained to give the requisite high performance.

A contract on 31 August 1943 increased earlier orders for this aircraft, designated **BTD-1** and retaining the name **Destroyer**, to 358. Deliveries of production aircraft began in June 1944,

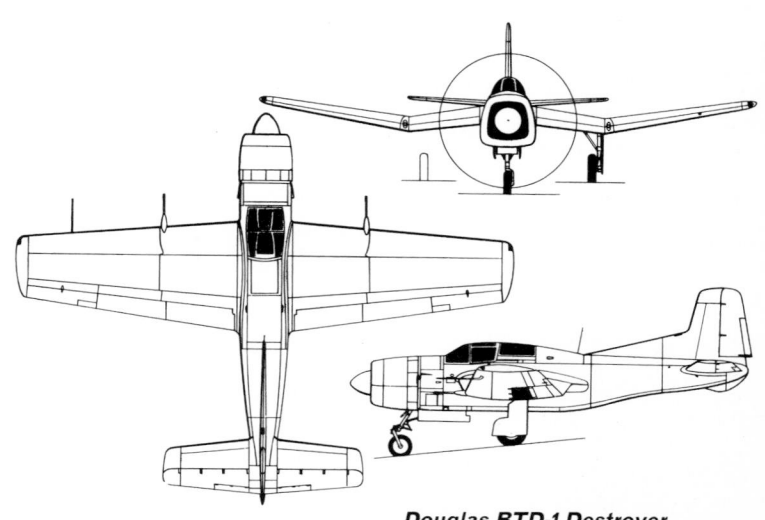

Douglas BTD-1 Destroyer.

but only 28 had been delivered before contract cancellation was initiated soon after VJ-Day. The Destroyer's performance was disappointing and, so far as is known, the type was not used operationally. Two aircraft were provided experimentally with a mixed powerplant, a 680-kg (1,500-lb) thrust Westinghouse WE-19XA turbojet being fitted in the rear fuselage and fed with air through a dorsal inlet aft of the cockpit. Thus desig-

nated **XBTD-2**, the aircraft were the first jet-powered machines of Douglas and the US Navy. A first flight was made in May 1945, but at speeds over 322 km/h (200 mph) the downward-angled turbojet could not be used. The project was cancelled in late 1945.

Specification
Douglas BTD-1
Type: single-seat torpedo/dive-bomber
Powerplant: one 1715-kW (2,300-hp) Wright R-3350-14 Cyclone 18 radial piston engine
Performance: maximum speed 554 km/h (344 mph) at 4905 m (16,100 ft); service ceiling 7195 m (23,600 ft); range 2382 km (1,480 miles)
Weights: empty 5244 kg (11,561 lb); maximum take-off 8618 kg (19,000 lb)
Dimensions: span 13.72 m (45 ft 0 in); length 11.76 m (38 ft 7 in); height 5.05 m (16 ft 7 in); wing area 34.65 m^2 (373 sq ft)
Armament: two 20-mm cannon in wing leading edges, plus one torpedo or up to 1451 kg (3,200 lb) of bombs in internal bay

Douglas C-74 Globemaster I/C-124 Globemaster II

Immediately after the United States became engaged in World War II, and particularly as a consequence of that nation's initial involvement against Japanese forces in the Pacific, it was clear that transport aircraft would be of vital importance. Because of the theatre of operations envisaged, such aircraft would require both long range and great load-carrying capability, and in early 1942 Douglas began development of an aircraft to meet this requirement.

Designated **Douglas C-74 Globemaster I**, the first example of which 50 had been ordered by the US Army Air Force did not fly until 5 September 1945. It was a cantilever low-wing monoplane of all-metal construction, with a conventional tail unit, retractable tricycle landing gear with twin wheels on each unit, and power provided by four wing-mounted 2237-kW (3,000-hp) Pratt & Whitney R-4360-27 radial engines. The C-74's large-capacity fuselage provided accommodation for the crew and 125 troops, or 115 stretchers with medical attendants, or up to 21840 kg (48,150 lb) of cargo.

The Globemaster I suffered typical contract cancellations after VJ-Day, and only 14 were completed. One, with 103 passengers and crew, flown from the USA to the UK on 18 November 1949, was the first aircraft to fly across the North Atlantic with more than 100 persons on board. There was little doubt of the load-carrying capability of the C-74 and when, in late 1947, the newly-formed US Air Force decided it needed a heavy strategic cargo transport, discussions between the USAF and Douglas resulted in development of the **C-124 Globemaster II**, based on the C-74.

In fact, the prototype **YC-124** was basically the fifth C-74 provided with a new, deeper fuselage and strengthened landing gear. Powered by 2610-kW (3,500-hp) R-4360-49 radial engines, it was flown for the first time on 27 November 1949. The type entered production as the **C-124A**, of which 204 were built, the first of them entering service with the USAF in May 1950. The next, and final, production version was the **C-124C**, with more-powerful R-4360 engines, weather radar in a distinctive nose radome and, equally useful recognition points, wingtip fairings housing combustion heaters to de-ice the

Seen here are C-124As brought up to C-124C standard with AN/APS-42 weather radar in the prominent nose radome and with heaters on the wingtips.

wing and tailplane leading edges and to heat the cabin. C-124C production totalled 243, the last machine being delivered during May 1955.

The fuselage of the Globemaster II had clamshell nose loading doors with an associated built-in loading ramp, an electric hoist amidships which was a carry-over from the C-74, and two overhead cranes (each with a capacity of 7257 kg (16,000 lb) which could traverse the entire length of the 23.47 m (77 ft)-long cargo hold. The flight deck, accommodating a crew of five, was mounted high in the nose, over the clamshell doors. When used in a transport role (with two decks installed), the Globemaster II could carry a maximum of 200 fully-equipped troops, or 123 stretcher cases plus 45 ambulatory patients and 15 medical attendants.

Serving with the USAF's Air Materiel Command, Far Eastern Air Force, Military Air Transport Service, Strategic Air Command and Tactical Air Command, and used in conjunction with Douglas C-133s, the Globemaster IIs remained in service until replaced by the Lockheed C-5A Galaxy during 1970.

When the Globemaster Is ended their useful service life, some were acquired by civil cargo operators.

Variants
DC-7: civil version of C-74; 26 for Pan Am 1944, later cancelled
YKC-124B: designation of single aircraft with 4139-ekW (5,550-eshp) Pratt & Whitney YT34-P-1 turboprop engines intended as the prototype of a tanker version
YC-124B: redesignation of YKC-124B when its development as a tanker was abandoned

Specification
Douglas C-124C Globemaster II
Type: heavy cargo transport
Powerplant: four 2834-kW (3,800-hp) Pratt & Whitney R-4360-63A radial piston engines
Performance: maximum speed at

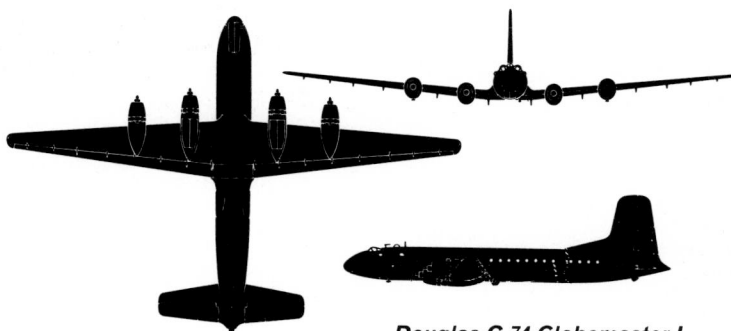

Douglas C-74 Globemaster I (original version).

sea level 436 km/h (271 mph); cruising speed 370 km/h (230 mph) at 3050 m (10,000 ft); service ceiling 5610 m (18,400 ft); range with 11963 kg (26,375 lb) of cargo 6486 km (4,030 miles)
Weights: empty 45888 kg

(101,165 lb); maximum take-off 88224 kg (194,500 lb)
Dimensions: span 53.07 m (174 ft 1½ in); length 39.75 m (130 ft 5 in); height 14.72 m (48 ft 3½ in); wing area 232.81 m^2 (2,506 sq ft)

Douglas C-133 Cargomaster

US Air Force procurement of such aircraft as the C-74 Globemaster I and C-124 Globemaster II gave evidence of awareness of the importance of aircraft in this category. The Berlin Airlift and Korean War added greater emphasis, and Douglas received from the USAF in the early 1950s development contracts for two new turboprop-powered transports: the **Douglas C-132** and **C-133**. The giant C-132, with a wing-span of 56.9 m (186 ft 8 in), did not progress

beyond the mock-up stage, but the smaller aircraft, which was designed to meet the requirements of the USAF's Logistic Carrier Supporting System SS402L, won an initial contract for 12 aircraft. No prototype was built, and the first production **C-133A**, later named **Cargomaster**, made its maiden flight on 23 April 1956.

The C-133A differed considerably from the C-74 and C-124 transports that had preceded it. A high-mounted wing,

and main landing gear units retracting into one external pod on each side of the fuselage, ensured that access to, and the volume of, the large cargo hold, were not compromised by these structures. The circular-section fuselage provided a cargo hold 27.43 m (90 ft) in length, this being pressurised, heated and ventilated. It was loaded via a two-section rear door, the lower section forming a ramp, or by a cargo door on the port side of the forward fuselage. It was possible for vehicles up to 3.66 m (12 ft) in height to be driven up the rear ramp direct into the cargo hold, and the C-133 was able to

accept practically every type of vehicle in service with the US Army.

The first C-133As were delivered to the Military Air Transport Service in August 1957. A total of 35 was built: early models were powered by 4474-ekW (6,000-eshp) Pratt & Whitney T34-P-3 turboprops, while later production aircraft had T34-P-7W engines which, with water injection, had a maximum power rating of 5294 ekW (7,100 eshp). The last three aircraft had clamshell rear loading doors which increased the hold length by 0.91 m (3 ft), making it possible to airlift completely assembled Titan missiles. These were followed by 15 **C-133B** aircraft that retained the clamshell doors and incorporated more-powerful T-34-P-9W engines.

The fleet of 50 aircraft proved itself invaluable during the US involvement in Vietnam, but fatigue problems led to their withdrawal from service during 1971; the aircraft were then placed in storage. A few machines were later released onto the civil market.

Specification
Douglas C-133B Cargomaster
Type: strategic heavy freighter
Powerplant: four 5593-ekW (7,500-eshp) Pratt & Whitney T34-P-9W turboprops
Performance: maximum speed 578 km/h (359 mph) at 2650 m

The Douglas C-133 Cargomaster was an advanced transport with multiwheel landing gear in side blisters and an inbuilt ramp for the straight-in loading of vehicles. It was used on the US-Vietnam air bridge.

(8,700 ft); cruising speed 520 km/h (323 mph); service ceiling 9130 m (29,950 ft); range with payload of 23587 kg (52,000 lb) more than 6437 km (4,000 miles)
Weights: empty 54550 kg (120,263 lb); maximum take-off 129727 kg (286,000 lb)
Dimensions: span 54.77 m (179 ft 7¾ in); length 48.02 m (157 ft 6½ in); height 14.71 m (48 ft 3 in); wing area 248.32 m² (2,673 sq ft)

Douglas D-558-1 Skystreak

First conceived in 1945, the **Douglas D-558-1 Skystreak** was designed to meet the requirements of the US Navy Bureau of Aeronautics and NACA (NASA's predecessor) for a high-speed research aircraft. It was required to accumulate air/load measurements in free flight at speeds from Mach 0.75 to 0.85 and at heights between sea level and 12190 m (40,000 ft), data which at that time were unobtainable from wind tunnels.

The design of the aircraft was kept as simple as possible, being a cantilever low-wing monoplane with a slender circular-section fuselage, and large-area vertical tail surfaces, with the horizontal surfaces mounted approximately one-third of the way up the fin. Retractable tricycle landing gear was provided and the fuselage, incorporating a single seat for the pilot, had mounted within it the powerplant comprising one Allison J35 turbo-jet. An unusual feature was the pilot's escape system, the entire nose section of the aircraft, from the rear of the pilot's seat forward, being jettisonable in emergency; it was intended that the pilot should bale out conventionally from this nose-section when it had

slowed sufficiently after separation. To gather the data for which the Skystreak was designed, an automatic pressure recording system was installed, with connections to 400 measuring points on the airframe; additionally, strain gauges were attached to selected positions on the wings and tail unit.

Three D-558-1s were built, the first of these flying in May 1947: on 20 August 1947 it established a new world speed record of 1031.04 km/h (640.66 mph), a figure raised five days later to

1047.36 km/h (650.8 mph). On 3 May 1948 the second Skystreak was lost in an accident when its engine compressor disintegrated just after take-off. The third aircraft completed successfully on 10 June 1953 a series of 82 flights, having been sustained in this programme by spares and components taken from the first prototype.

Specification
Type: single-seat jet-powered research aircraft
Powerplant: one 2268-kg (5,000-lb) thrust Allison J35-A-11 turbojet
Performance: maximum speed at

sea level 1048 km/h (651 mph)
Weight: maximum take-off 4584 kg (10,105 lb)
Dimensions: span 7.62 m (25 ft 0 in); length 10.88 m (35 ft 8½ in); height 3.7 m (12 ft 1¾ in); wing area 14 m² (150.7 sq ft)

In its initial form the D-558-1 Skystreak had a rounded windshield, but for high-speed flights the V-shaped screen illustrated was fitted. In this form the pilot had to wear a chamois cover over his helmet to avoid scratching the glazing.

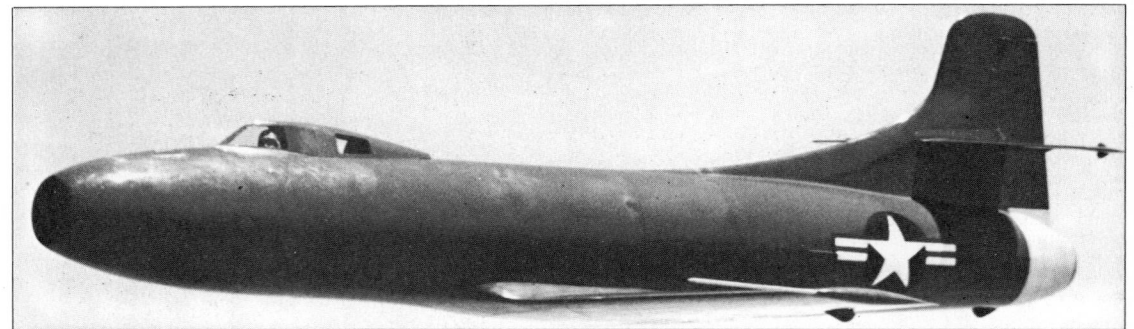

Douglas D-558-2 Skyrocket

To progress beyond the capability of the D-558-1 Skystreak programme it had been planned initially to modify the powerplant, replacing the turbojet by one of smaller dimensions and by adding a rocket motor. Before this stage was reached, however, it was decided additionally to investigate sweptback wings, and this led to Heinemann's new research aircraft, the **Douglas D-558-2 Skyrocket**.

To accommodate the mixed power-plant, a larger-diameter fuselage was designed, retaining the jettisonable nose-section of the Skystreak and its tricycle landing gear. Mid-set wings, swept at 35°, and a tail unit with swept horizontal and vertical surfaces replaced the more conventional surfaces of the earlier aircraft. Following evaluation of the design by the US Navy and NACA, three of these aircraft were ordered and the first was flown on 4 February 1948. In the course of a highly successful test programme one of them, in August 1951, attained a speed of 1992 km/h (1,238 mph) on rocket engine power alone following launch from a Boeing P2B-1S mother-plane. A few days later the same aircraft attained an altitude of 24230 m (79,494 ft), which is just over

24 km (15 miles). This was bettered on 31 August 1953 when the D-558-2 reached 25370 m (83,235 ft), and just less than three months later, on 20 November, a speed of Mach 2.05 was recorded, making the Skyrocket the first piloted aircraft in the world to be flown at twice the speed of sound. The Skyrocket programme ended in June 1953.

Variant
D-558-3: project by designer/ aerodynamicist Kermit E. Van Every for a hypersonic development with very thin, straight wings and rocket power alone; anticipated performance maxima were a speed of 9735 km/h (6,050 mph) or Mach 9 and an absolute altitude of 228600 m (750,000 ft) or 228.6 km (142 miles); this ambitious project was abandoned in favour of the multi-agency North American X-15

Specification
Type: swept-wing research aircraft
Powerplant: one 1361-kg (3,000-lb) thrust Westinghouse J34-WE-22 turbojet, plus one 2722-kg (6,000-lb) thrust Reaction Motors XLR-8 rocket motor
Performance: maximum speed

(turbojet only) 941 km/h (585 mph) at 6095 m (20,000 ft), or (mixed-power, conventional take-off) 1159 km/h (720 mph) at 12190 m (40,000 ft) or (rocket power only, air-launched) 2012 km/h (1,250 mph) at 20575 m (67,500 ft)
Weights: maximum take-off (turbojet only) 4795 kg (10,572 lb), or (mixed powerplant) 6925 kg (15,266 lb) or (rocket only) 7171 kg (15,787 lb)

Small wing area and very considerable loaded weight gave the Skyrocket sluggish take-off performance. Partly resolving the problem were jettisonable take-off rockets.

Dimensions: span 7.62 m (25 ft 0 in); length 13.79 m (45 ft 3 in); height 3.51 m (11 ft 6 in); wing area 16.26 m² (175.0 sq ft)

Douglas DC-1/DC-2
to
Douglas DC-3/C-47 Series

Douglas DC-1/DC-2

When TWA, faced with an urgent need to replace its Fokker airliners, found itself behind United Air Lines in the queue for Boeing's Model 247, the airline drew up a specification (for an all-metal three-engined airliner with seats for at least 12 passengers) which it issued to the US industry on 2 August 1932.

Donald W. Douglas responded within a fortnight to this specification and a contract was signed on 20 September, Douglas having convinced TWA technical adviser Charles Lindbergh that the required performance could be achieved safely on only two engines. The prototype, identified as the **Douglas DC-1** (Douglas Commercial), was rolled out on 22 June 1933 and, powered by two Wright R-1820 Cyclones, made its maiden flight on 1 July.

Despite initial carburettor problems, the test programme was completed successfully and the aircraft handed over to TWA at Los Angeles Municipal Airport in December. The DC-1 never entered service, however, being used instead for promotional purposes by TWA. These included a coast-to-coast record flight of 13 hours 4 minutes through the night of 18-19 February 1934. TWA signed an initial contract for 25 production aircraft; they differed from the DC-1 by having more-powerful engines and fuselage lengthened by 0.61 m (2 ft 0 in) to provide accommodation for 14 passengers. These structural changes brought redesignation to **DC-2**, and the type was soon adopted by other US operators including American Airlines, Eastern Air Lines, General Air Lines, Panagra and Pan American.

Few DC-2s survive, this being an aircraft painted in TWA colours as City of Santa Monica. The airline was the first operator of this important type.

DC-2s were also used in Europe by airlines which included KLM, Lineas Aéreas Postales Espanolas (LAPE) and Swissair. The most famous of these aircraft was KLM's *Uiver* (PH-AJU), which, flown by K. D. Parmentier and J. J. Moll, was winner in the transport division of the 1934 'MacRobertson' England-Australia Air Race. In fact, its flight time of 90 hours 13 minutes 36 seconds was beaten only by the winning de Havilland D.H.88 Comet flown by C. W. A. Scott and T. Campbell Black with no payload.

Such performance capability made the DC-2 worthy of military interest, the US Navy leading the way with a single **R2D** transport in 1934, supplemented later by four of the **R2D-1** model. The US Army Air Corps opened its purchases for Fiscal Year 1936 with a 16-seat DC-2, which was evaluated as the **XC-32**, and led to orders for two externally similar **YC-34** (later **C-34**) passenger transports and 18 **C-33** freight aircraft, the latter type with enlarged vertical tail surfaces and a cargo door. In 1937 a C-33 was fitted with a DC-3 tail unit and redesignated **C-33A** (later **C-38**); from it was developed the **C-39**, with other DC-3 components, which included the wing centre-section and landing gear, and 727-kW (975-hp) R-1820-55 engines.

Thirty-five were ordered for the US Army's transport groups, entering service in 1939.

The fourth and fifth C-39s were converted while still on the production line to **C-41** and **C-42** standard, respectively. The first was fitted with 895-kW (1,200-hp) Pratt & Whitney R-1830-21 Twin Wasps and cleared to operate at a gross weight of 11340 kg (25,000 lb) as the aircraft of the chief-of-staff, USAAC, while the second was powered by similarly rated Wright R-1820-53 Cyclones and cleared at 10716 kg (23,624 lb) as the aircraft of the commanding general, Air Force GHQ. Two more C-39s were converted later to C-42s.

The DC-2s in military service were used extensively in the early years of World War II, and are remembered especially for their role in carrying US survivors from the Philippines to Australia in December 1941. A number of DC-2s, acquired for wartime service by the RAF, were used by No. 31 Squadron in India. Total DC-2 production was 193 aircraft.

Variants

DC-2A: designation of two civil aircraft with Pratt & Whitney Hornet engines

DC-2B: designation of two aircraft acquired by the Polish airline LOT which were powered by 559-kW (750-hp) Bristol Pegasus VI radial engines

Douglas DC-2 of KLM (previously registered PH-ALE and named Edenvalk) based at Whitchurch near Bristol, England, throughout most of World War II.

C-32A: military designation applied to 24 civil DC-2s impressed by the USAAF in 1942: these transports were without cargo doors

Specification
Douglas DC-2
Type: 14-passenger civil transport
Powerplant: two 652-kW (875-hp) Wright SGR-1820-F52 Cyclone radial engines
Performance: maximum speed 338 km/h (210 mph) at 2440 m (8,000 ft); cruising speed 306 km/h (190 mph) at 2240 m (8,000 ft); service ceiling 6845 m (22,450 ft); range 1609 km (1,000 miles)
Weights: empty 5628 kg (12,408 lb); maximum take-off 8419 kg (18,560 lb)
Dimensions: span 25.91 m (85 ft 0 in); length 18.89 m (61 ft 11 ¾ in); height 4.97 m (16 ft 3¾ in); wing area 87.23 m² (939 sq ft)

The R2D-1 was the US Navy's equivalent of the DC-2 airliner, fitted out as a staff transport. USN procurement was five, all powered by R-1820-12 radials.

Douglas DC-3/C-47 series

Undoubtedly a classic airliner, and almost certainly as well known to travellers all over the world as to aviation enthusiasts, by the end of 1991 the **Douglas DC-3**, as a type, will have been in service continuously for 55 years. Few can have appreciated the potential longevity of this design when,

in 1934, the Douglas Company was requested by American Airlines to develop an enlarged version of the DC-2 to provide a 'sleeper' that could be used on US transcontinental flights.

This resulted in the **Douglas DST** (Douglas Sleeper Transport) with 16 sleeping berths, first flown on 17

December 1935. It was, however, the 24-seat day version of this airliner, designated DC-3, which became so important a part of aviation history. Before US involvement in World War II the DC-3 had gained a dominant position in the nation's airlines, and the type's rugged reliability also appealed to military planners as soon as the requirement for large numbers of transport aeroplanes was appreciated.

By the end of the war, 10,692 of these aircraft had been built in the USA, and a further 2,000 or so were also built under licence in the USSR with the designation **Lisunov Li-2**. The DC-3's robust construction meant that very large numbers of the type survived the war, and when these were disposed of as war surplus items, operators all over the world acquired them as fast as they could lay hands on them. Used in the passenger-

Arguably the most significant aircraft of all time, the DC-3/C-47 is here represented by a C-47B of the US Army Air Corps.

carrying and utility roles, DC-3s played a significant part in establishing many new airlines and new air services.

Of cantilever low-wing configuration, the DC-3 is of all-metal construction except for fabric-covered control surfaces. A feature of the wing is its multi-spar structure, derived from the DC-1, which has played a significant part in the long service life of these aircraft. The all-metal fuselage is almost circular in cross-section, and the landing gear is of the retractable tailwheel type, with a fully-castoring tailwheel, and the cantilever tail unit is of metal construction.

Civil DC-3s delivered to US airlines before the nation became involved in World War II played a most important part in the development of reliable national air routes. It has been recorded that in the period 1936-41 national passenger mileage in the USA increased by almost 600 per cent, a growth that was very largely due to the DC-3, which was the primary equipment of most US airlines in this period, whose safety record has become almost legendary. Civil models (including the DST) were built in five series, and the standard powerplant was either the Wright SGR-1820 or the Pratt & Whitney Twin Wasp, in ratings between 746 and 895 kW (1,000 and 1,200 hp) for various maximum take-off weights.

The capability of various DC-2 derivatives had convinced the US Army of their excellence of design and construction, and a study of the DC-3 enabled the US Army to outline to Douglas the modifications required for the DC-3's use as a military transport. These included more-powerful engines, strengthening of the rear fuselage and cabin floor, and the provision of large loading doors. The airline-type interior disappeared, replaced by utility seats lining the cabin walls; powerplant of the initial production version comprised two 895-kW (1,200-hp) Pratt & Whitney R-1830-92 radial engines. Ordered in large numbers in 1940, these aircraft became designated **C-47** and acquired the name **Skytrain**, and were the precursors of an enormous and diverse military series.

C-47s were notable glider tugs, being involved in actions in Sicily, Burma and Normandy. Many of those supplied to the UK under Lend-Lease were involved in the D-Day operations in Normandy, and these aircraft were named **Dakota** in British service. C-47s took part in the Berlin Airlift, were involved in the Korean War and, under the designation **AC-47D**, were deployed as well-armed gunships in Vietnam.

The US Navy and US Marine Corps have also used this aircraft under a number of designations, although the original and basic identification was **R4D**: in 1962 those still in service acquired the tri-service C-47 designations. Like the US Army, the USN and USMC used the R4D initially primarily for personnel or cargo transport. Later utilisation included, however, radar countermeasures, air-sea warfare training and, with skis, operations in the Antarctic.

Throughout the entire period of production there was little significant change in airframe design. The same was not true of powerplants, for as improved and/or more-powerful engines became available they were installed to provide enhanced performance or load-carrying capability. Manufacturer's lists show 13 variants of the Wright

Right: The civilian DC-3 and ex-military C-47s opened up the commercial market, proving reliable, economical and of extremely sound structure.

SGR-1820 Cyclone, with ratings from 686 to 895 kW (920 to 1,200 hp). There were also 11 civil and military Pratt & Whitney Twin Wasp engines installed in prewar and wartime production aircraft, these having ratings between 783 and 895 kW (1,050 and 1,200 hp).

When these DC-3/C-47 variants came onto the market after the war, there was such an acute shortage of aircraft suitable for the initiation of civil passenger and cargo services that many were operated without any alteration to the military interior. The majority, however, were subjected to modification schemes which brought internal furnishings and equipment up to an acceptable airline standard. Some were provided with executive and VIP interior layouts.

Continuing use and the popularity of DC-3s and their derivatives encouraged Douglas to evolve a suitable replacement. To save time and cost it was decided to modernise existing aircraft, and two second-hand DC-3s were acquired for this exercise. These had the fuselage extended and strengthened to provide a 30-seat interior, extra windows were added, and an airstair cabin door was installed. Some changes were made to aerofoil surfaces to improve handling and stability, and the retracted main wheel units were totally enclosed in near fairings. The powerplant of the first prototype comprised two 1100-kW (1,475-hp) Wright R-1820-C9HE Cyclones; the second had two 1081-kW (1,450-hp) Pratt & Whitney R-2000-D7 radials.

Designated **DC-35**, or **Super DC-3**, the first of these revised aircraft flew on 23 June 1949. Testing gave excellent results, demonstrating much improved performance over the basic DC-3. It was too late, however, because faster and more comfortable aircraft of more modern design were already in service, or about to begin operations, and the company's gamble failed to pay off.

In 1991 many DC-3/C-47 aircraft remain in service with airlines of varying sizes.

Variants
Douglas DST: original model with accommodation for 28 day or 14 night passengers, and powered by Wright Cyclone radials (21 built)
Douglas DST-A: similar to the DST but powered by Pratt & Whitney Twin Wasp radials (19 built)
Douglas DC-3: basic day passenger transport with accommodation for

between 21 and 28 passengers, and power provided by Cyclone radials (266 built)
Douglas DC-3A: basic day passenger transport similar to the DC-3 but powered by Twin Wasp radials (114 built)
Douglas DC-3B: convertible model with seat/berths in the forward cabin and seats in the aft cabin for 28 day passengers and fewer night passengers; recognisable by small extra windows on each side over the first and third main windows (10 built)
C-41A: initial military model, essentially a version of the DC-3A with military instrumentation, swivelling seats and R-1830-21 Twin Wasp radials, used as a command transport (1 built)
C-47: initial military production model, with 15.2 cm (6 in) greater span, revised fuel tankage, R-1830-92 radials, small astrodome, and accommodation for 2722 kg (6,000 lb) of freight, or 28 paratroops, or 14 casualties and three attendants (965 built)
C-47A: improved C-47 with 24- rather than 12-volt electrical system (5,253 built – 2,954 at Long Beach and 2,299 at Oklahoma City)
RC-47A: postwar modification used in Korea for limited reconnaissance missions and flare-dropping in support of tactical combat aircraft
SC-47A: postwar search and rescue variant, in 1962 redesignated **HC-47A**
VC-47A: postwar modification to produce staff transports with conventional seating
C-47B: version developed for operations 'over the hump' between India and China, with better heating and R-1830-90C radials with two-stage blowers; the type proved only marginally successful, and many were later converted to C-47D standard (3,232 built – 300 at Long Beach and

2,932 at Oklahoma City)
TC-47B: specialised navigation trainer model (133 built at Oklahoma City)
VC-47B: conversions of the C-47B to serve as staff transports
XC-47C: experimental model mounted on twin Edo Model 78 amphibious floats, each able to carry some 1136 litres (300 US gal) of fuel; no production was undertaken, but 150 sets of floats were delivered for field installation (1 built)
C-47D: designation of C-47Bs after the removal of the high blower
AC-47D: designation of 26 Airways Check versions operated by the Military Air Transport Service from 1953 to 1962, when they were redesignated **EC-47D**
AC-47D: 1965 designation for gunship conversions with three 7.62-mm (0.3-in) General Electric Miniguns firing through the fourth and fifth windows and from the open door on the port side of the fuselage
RC-47D: reconnaissance version
SC-47D: search and rescue variant, in 1962 redesignated **HC-47D**
TC-47D: trainer modification
VC-47D: staff transport conversion
C-47E: initially intended for C-47s modernised and fitted with 1100-kW (1,475-shp) Wright R-1820-80 radials, but used instead for eight aircraft modified for the USAAF by Pan American with 962-kW (1,290-hp) Pratt & Whitney R-2000-4 radials for use as Airways Check aircraft
YC-47F: a single Super DC-3 evaluated by the USAF, initially under the designation **YC-129**
C-47M: designation of C-47H and C-47J aircraft fitted with special electronic equipment for use in the Vietnam War
EC-47N: version of the C-47A specially fitted for electronic reconnaissance in Vietnam

EC-47P: version of the C-47D specially fitted for electronic reconnaissance in Vietnam

EC-47Q: version with R-2000-4 engines specially fitted for electronic reconnaissance in Vietnam

C-48: one DC-3A taken over from United Air Lines during construction

C-48A: three DC-3As taken over during construction

C-48B: 16 impressed aircraft

C-48C: seven DC-3As taken over from Pan American during construction, and nine impressed aircraft

C-49: six DC-3s taken over from TWA during construction

C-49A: one DC-3 taken over from Delta during construction

C-49B: three DC-3s taken over from Eastern during construction

C-49C: two DC-3 taken over from Delta during construction

C-49D: six DC-3s taken over from Eastern during construction, and five impressed aircraft

C-49E: 22 impressed aircraft

C-49F: nine impressed aircraft

C-49G: eight impressed aircraft

C-49H: 19 impressed aircraft

C-49J: 34 DC-3s taken over during construction

C-49K: 23 DC-3s taken over during construction

C-50: four DC-3s taken over from American during construction

C-50A: two DC-3s taken over from American during construction

C-50B: three DC-3s taken over from Braniff during construction

C-50C: one DC-3 taken over from Penn Central during construction

C-50D: four DC-3s taken over from Penn Central during construction

C-51: one DC-3 taken over from Canadian Colonial during construction

C-52: one DC-3A taken over from United during construction

C-52A: one DC-3A taken over from Western during construction

C-52B: two DC-3As taken over from United during construction

C-52C: one DC-3A taken over from Eastern during construction

C-52D: one impressed aircraft

C-53 Skytrooper: dedicated troop-transport version with 28 seats, glider-towing hook, no freight door and power provided by R-1830-92 radials (221 built at Santa Monica)

XC-53A: C-53 modified in 1942 with full-span slotted flaps and hot-air rather than pneumatic-boot de-icing

C-53B: eight C-53s modified in 1942 for Arctic operations with winterised equipment and extra fuel tankage

C-53C: 17 airline-ordered aircraft impressed during construction

C-53D: identical with the C-53 apart from having side seats rather than seats in rows (159 built at Santa Monica)

C-68: two impressed DC-3As

C-84: four impressed aircraft

C-117A: staff transports with 21 seats and generally similar to C-47Bs (17 built at Oklahoma City)

C-117B: 11 C-117As modified by the removal of the high blowers for their R-1830-90C radials

C-117C: designation of VC-47 models upgraded to C-117B standard

C-117D: designation from 1962 for R4D-8 aircraft

XCG-17: experimental troop-carrying glider conversion, produced by removing the engines and fairing over the nacelles of a C-47; surprisingly enough, the XCG-17 had excellent glide performance, but by the time tests were completed in 1944, only limited requirement for gliders was felt by the USAAF and no production followed

R4D-1: initial freight model for the US Navy, generally similar to the C-47 apart from the use of naval instrumentation (100 built at Long Beach)

R4D-2: two DC-3s taken over from Eastern during construction and used by the US Navy as staff transports; they were later designated **R4D-2F** and **R4D-2Z**

R4D-3: 20 C-53 personnel transports received from the USAF

R4D-4: 10 DC-3s taken over from Pan American during construction, and used by the US Navy as personnel transports; some were later modified for electronic countermeasures under the designation **R4D-4Q**

R4D-5: 238 C-47As received by the US Navy from USAAF contracts; surviving aircraft were redesignated **C-47H** in 1962

R4D-5E: R4D-5 aircraft modified for special electronic operations

R4D-5L: R4D-5 aircraft modified for operations in the Arctic and Antarctic; later designated **LC-47H**

R4D-5Q: R4D-5 aircraft modified for radar countermeasures; later redesignated **EC-47H**

R4D-5R: R4D-5 aircraft modified as personnel transports; later redesignated **TC-47H**

R4D-5S: R4D-5 aircraft modified for air-sea warfare training; later redesignated **SC-47H**

R4D-5T: R4D-5 aircraft modified for navigation training

R4D-5Z: R4D-5 aircraft modified as staff transports; later redesignated **VC-47H**

R4D-6: 150 C-47B aircraft received by

the US Navy from USAAF contracts; survivors were redesignated **C-47J** in 1962; versions equivalent to various R4D-5 variants were identified as **R4D-6E, R4D-6L (LC-47J), R4D-6Q (EC-47J), R4D-6R (TC-47J), R4D-6S (SC-47J), R4D-6T** and **R4D-6Z (VC-47J)**

R4D-7: 47 TC-47B aircraft received by the US Navy from USAAF contracts; in 1962 the surviving examples were redesignated **TC-47K**

Dakota Mk I: RAF equivalent of the C-47 (52 aircraft supplied under Lend-Lease and one built from spares)

Dakota Mk II: RAF equivalent of the C-53 (nine aircraft supplied under Lend-Lease)

Dakota Mk III: RAF equivalent of the C-47A (12 supplied by the USAAF and 950 supplied under Lend-Lease)

Dakota Mk IV: RAF equivalent of the C-47B (896 supplied under Lendlease)

Lisunov Li-2: Russian licence-built version, originally powered by 671-kW (900-hp) Shvetsov M-62 radials in the **PS-84** first version, but later fitted with uprated Shvetsov ASh-62 radials: production comprised a number of variants, some of them armed with turreted armament; the **Li-2G** freighter, **Li-2P** personnel transport, **Li-2PG** convertible model and the **Li-2V** high-altitude model are best known of the variants (2,000 or more built in Russia, and supplemented by 707 Lend-Lease aircraft)

Showa L2D: in 1938 Mitsui acquired a licence to produce the DC-3 in Japan and Manchukuo (Manchuria), and also bought 13 DC-3s and seven DC-3As; Mitsui subcontracted production of the DC-3 to Showa, which built 414 L2D transports for the Imperial Japanese Navy – **L2D2** personnel transports with 746-kW (1,000-hp) Kinsei 43 radials, **L2D3** personnel transports with 970-kW (1,300-hp) Kinsei 51s, **L2D3a** personnel transports with 970-kW

(1,300-hp) Kinsei 53s, **L2D3-1** freighters with Kinsei 51s, **L2D3-1a** freighters with Kinsei 53s, **L2D4** personnel transports with a 13.2-mm (0.52-in) machine-gun in a dorsal turret and powered by Kinsei 51s, **L2D4-1** freighter versions of the L2D4, and **L2D5** personnel transports based on the L3D4 but built partially of wood and steel, and powered by 1164-kW (1, 560-hp) Kinsei 62s; another 71 L2D2s were built by Nakajima

Super DC-3 (DC-35): improved post-war version, originally known as the **DC-3S** (2 built)

R4D-8X: US Navy designation for the prototype YC-129/YC-47F when evaluated for naval use

R4D-8: designation of 100 US Navy aircraft modified to Super DC-3 standard from R4D-5s, R4D-6s and R4D-7s; some aircraft were also modified for special roles as **R4D-8T (TC-117D)** trainers, **R4D-8Z (VC-117D)** staff transports and **R4D-8L (LC-117D)** winterised transports; after 1962 all surviving R4D-8s were designated in the C-117D series

Specification

Douglas C-47 (typical postwar conversion for civil use)

Type: short/medium-range transport

Powerplant: two 895-kW (1,200-hp) Pratt & Whitney R-1830-S1C3G Twin Wasp radial piston engines

Performance: maximum speed 370 km/h (230 mph) at 2590 m (8,500 ft); cruising speed 333 km/h (207 mph); service ceiling 7070 m (23, 200 ft); range with maximum fuel 3420 km (2,125 miles)

Weights: empty 7650 kg (16,865 lb); maximum take-off 11430 kg (25,200 lb)

Dimensions: span 28.96 m (95 ft 0 in); length 19.65 m (64 ft 5½ in); height 5.17 m (16 ft 11½ in); wing area 91.69 m² (987.00 sq ft)

Douglas DC-3

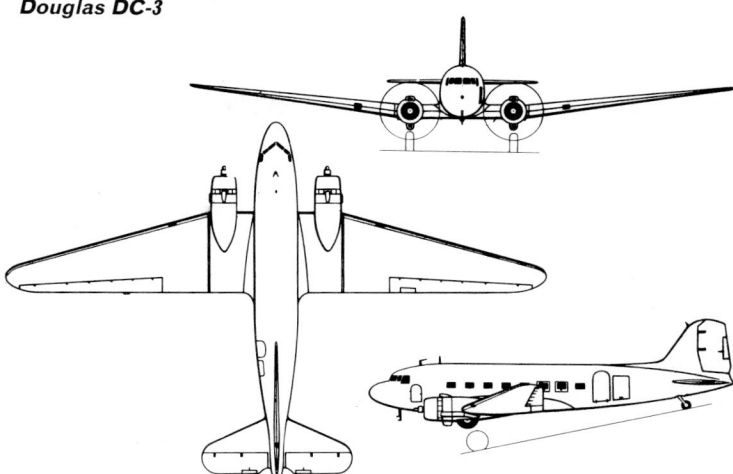

The R4D-8 (C-117D after 1962) was a US Navy variant converted from earlier machines with increased sweep-back wings, enlarged tail surfaces and fully-enclosed main wheels. This aircraft is from VT-29.

Long after the end of World War II, the DC-3/C-47 has much to offer civilian operators. Freighting, passenger transport and special missions are still undertaken by a sizeable number.

Douglas DC-4/C-54 Skymaster

Even before the DC-3 had flown, United Air Lines (UAL) and Douglas had started discussions regarding the development of a more advanced airliner of larger capacity, and by early 1936 had induced four other airlines to help finance the construction of a prototype. This was the **DC-4E**, orginally designated **DC-4.**

The new **Douglas DC-4** of 1939 was almost a different design, considerably lighter in construction, having a new high-aspect ratio wing, a conventional tail unit with a single fin and rudder, and landing gear of retractable tricycle type with the main units carrying twin wheels. Initial powerplant selection had been for four engines, each of around 746 kW (1,000 hp), but after discussion with interested airlines the type was put into production (without construction of a prototype) with four 1081-kW (1,450-hp) Pratt & Whitney R-2000-2SD1-G Twin Wasp radials.

Before the first aircraft had flown, the USA was embroiled in World War II. This meant that the aircraft on the production line were completed for the USAAF under the designation **C-54 Skymaster**, the first flying with military markings on 14 February 1942. These were virtually drab-painted civil airliners, but production contracts were soon drawn up for militarised versions capable of deployment for the transport of troops, cargo and casualties. First of these for the USAAF was the **C-54A** with strengthened floor, cargo door and handling equipment, followed by other military models, with development progressing along the line of maximum seating capacity (50) for short/medium-range operations and restricted seating (20) for long-range flights. As the **R5D**, the DC-4 was also built for the US Navy 'in many variants, total combined construction for these two services exceeding 1,000 aircraft.

At the end of military production Douglas built 79 civil DC-4s and these, together with large numbers of demilitarised C-54s, gave valuable service on long-range passenger and cargo routes until the new-generation airliners became available.

Specialised derivatives of the DC-4 included 24 aircraft with 1286-kW (1,725-hp) Rolls-Royce Merlin engines, developed by Canadair Ltd in Montreal for service with the RCAF, which allocated the aircraft the name **North Star**. There followed prduction of the **DC-4M** for civil operators. Another DC-4 derivative was the Aviation Traders Carvair. Both these types are covered in greater detail under their respective manufacturer entries.

Accommodation of these different DC-4s varied considerably. The basic version provided for a crew of four and 44 passengers with plenty of room between the seats, and this enabled some operators to introduce as many as 86 seats in high-density layouts; DC-4Ms carried up to 62 economy-class passengers.

Apart from many record-breaking flights, DC-4s are remembered in aviation history for their very considerable contribution to the Berlin Airlift of

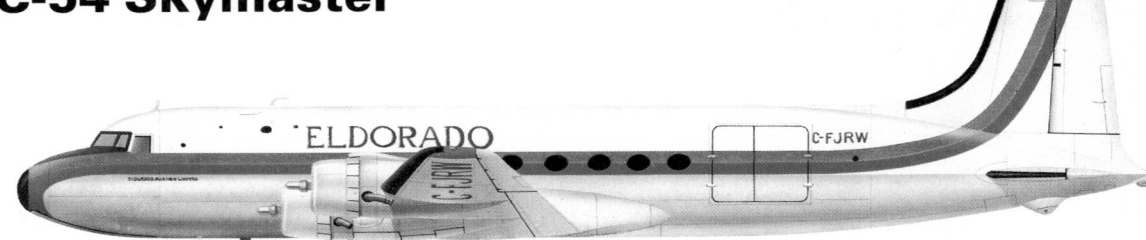

Douglas DC-4 of Eldorado Aviation (Canada).

1948-49. Their use by major airlines dwindled fairly rapidly as more advanced aircraft became available, but a small number still remain in service.

Variants

C-54: initial personnel transport with accommodation for 26 and powerplant comprising four 1007-kW (1,350-hp) Pratt & Whitney R-2000-3 radials (24 built)

C-54A: fully militarised version capable of lifting 50 troops or 14742 kg (32,500 lb) of freight on the power of four 1007-kW (1,350-hp) R-200-7 radials (252 built – 97 at Santa Monica and 155 at Chicago)

C-54B: version similar to the C-54A apart from the deletion of two auxiliary fuel tanks in the cabin in favour of integral tankage in the wings; early aircraft had R-2000-3s and later aircraft R-2000-7s (220 built – 100 at Santa Monica and 120 at Chicago)

VC-54C: one C-54A modified as the personal transport of President Franklin D. Roosevelt, and named *Sacred Cow*

C-54D: major Skymaster production version, basically similar to the C-54B but powered by four 1007-kW (1,350-hp) R-2000-11 radials (380 built at Chicago)

AC-54D: a small number of C-54Ds modified with special electronic and communication gear to check air routes

EC-54D: 1962 redesignation of AC-54Ds

HC-54D: 1962 redesignation of SC-54Ds

JC-54D: nine C-54Ds modified for operations concerned with missile nose-cone recovery

SC-54D: 38 aircraft modified by Convair for service with the MATS Air Rescue Service with special radar and observation blisters

TC-54D: C-54Ds modified to serve as multi-engine trainers

VC-54D: C-54Ds modified to serve as staff transports

C-54E: version of the C-54D with the final two cabin fuel tanks replaced by bag tanks in the inner wings; the cabin was specially designed to facilitate rapid conversion between roles (passenger with 50 seats, freighter for 14742 kg/32,500 lb and staff transport with 44 seats); by this time total fuel capacity had decreased from the 13703 litres (3,620 US gal) of the C-54 to the 13324 litres (3,520 US gal) of the C-54E (125 built at Santa Monica)

XC-54F: one C-54B experimentally

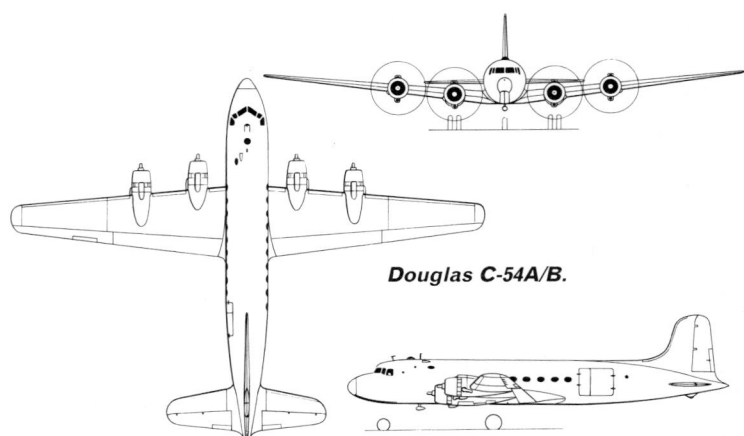

Douglas C-54A/B.

fitted with twin paratroop doors as the prototype of the proposed

C-54F: based on the airframe of the C-54D

C-54G: troop-carrier version based on the C-54E with R-2000-9 radials (162 built at Santa Monica)

VC-54G: C-54Gs converted as staff transports

C-54GM: designation of the DC-4 derivative produced by Canadair

C-54H: projected paratroop version with four R-2000-9 radials

C-54J: projected staff transport version based on the C-54G but without provision for freighting

XC-54K: one C-54E fitted experimentally with four 1063 kW (1,425 hp) Wright R-1820-HD Cyclone radials

C-54L: one C-54A modified with a revised fuel system

C-54M: designation of 38 C-54Es stripped out to serve as coal-carriers during the Berlin Airlift; payload was increased by 1134 kg (2,500 lb)

MC-54M: designation of 30 C-54Es fitted out as casevac aircraft with accommodation for 30 litters plus medical attendants, and used in the Korean War

EC-54U: post-1962 designation of R5D-4s modified with electronic countermeasures equipment for evaluation and training

XC-112: projected version with cabin pressurisation and power provided by four Pratt & Whitney R-2800-22W radials

XC-114: prototype based on the C-54E with a fuselage stretch of 2.06 m (6 ft 9 in) and powered by four 1209-kW (1,620-hp) Allison V-1710-131 V-12s

XC-115: proposed version based on the XC-114 with four 1231-kW (1,650-hp) Packard V-1650-209 V-12s

XC-116: one prototype similar to the XC-114 but having thermal rather than pneumatic-boot de-icing

R5D-1: designation of 56 C-54As transferred to the US Navy

R5C-1C: designation of R5D-1s modified in service with a fuel system based on that of the C-54B

R5D-1F: staff transport version of the R5D-1, after 1962 designated **VC-54N**

R5D-1Z: interim designation for the R5D-1F/VC-54N model

R5D-2: designation of 30 C-54Bs transferred to the US Navy

R5D-2F: staff transport version of the R5D-2, after 1962 designated **VC-54P**

R5D-2Z: interim designation of the R5D-2F/VC-54P model

R5D-3: designation of 86 C-54Ds transferred to the US Navy, after 1962 designated **C-54Q** (basic transport), **RC-54V** (photographic aircraft) and **VC-54Q** (staff transport), the last having served under the interim designation **R5D-3Z**

R5D-4: designation of 20 C-54Es transferred to the US Navy

R5D-4R: personnel transport version of the R5D-4, after 1962 designated **C-54R**

R5D-5: designation of 13 naval equivalents of the C-54G used mainly by the US Coast Guard, and after 1962 designated **C-54S**

R5D-5R: personnel transport version of the R5D-5, after 1962 designated **VC-54T**

R5D-5Z: staff transport version of the R5D-5, after 1962 designated **VC-54S**

R5D-6: projected model equivalent to the C-54J

DC-4-1009: postwar civil model intended for passenger operations with maximum accommodation for 44 passengers, later increased to 86
DC-4-1037: postwar civil model intended for freight operations, and so retaining the large door of the C-54 series

Skymaster Mk I: RAF designation of one C-54B and 22 C-54Ds received under Lend-Lease

Specification
Douglas DC-4-1009
Type: long-range transport
Powerplant: four 1081-kW (1,450-

shp) Pratt & Whitney R-2000-2SD-13G Twin Wasp radial piston engines
Performance: maximum speed 451 km/h (280 mph) at 4265 m (14,000 ft); cruising speed 365 km/h (227 mph) at 3050 m (10,000 ft); service ceiling 6800 m (22,300 ft); range 4023 km (2,500 miles) with

5189-kg (11,440-lb) payload
Weights: empty 19640 kg (43,300 lb); maximum take-off 33112 kg (73,000 lb)
Dimensions: span 35.81 m (117 ft 6 in); length 28.6 m (93 ft 10 in); height 8.38 m (27 ft 6 in); wing area 135.63 m² (1,460 sq ft)

Douglas DC-5

Designed at Douglas Aircraft Company's El Segundo facility, the **Douglas DC-5** was developed as a 16/22-passenger commercial transport for local service operations out of smaller airports. Interestingly, at a time when the low-wing configuration was in the ascendant, the DC-5 was a high-wing monoplane, although it also featured the then relatively novel tricycle-type landing gear. With a design gross weight of 8391 kg (18,500 lb), the DC-5 was offered with either Pratt & Whitney R-1690 or Wright Cyclone radial engines.

The prototype, powered by two 634-kW (850-hp) Wright GR-1820-F62 Cyclones, flew for the first time on 20 February 1939, piloted by Carl Cover. Orders were placed by KLM (four aircraft), Pennsylvania Central Airways (six) and SCADTA of Columbia (two), but the programme was overtaken by the war and only the KLM aircraft were delivered. Although intended for service in Europe, two went first to the Netherlands West Indies to link Curaçao and Surinam and the other two to Batavia in the Netherlands East Indies. All four were used to evacuate civilians from Java to Australia in 1942 and one,

damaged at Kemajoran Airport, Batavia, on 9 February 1942, was captured by the Japanese and extensively test-flown at Tachikawa Air Force Base. The three surviving DC-5s were operated in Australia by the Allied Directorate of Air Transport and were given the USAAF designation **C-110**.

The earliest DC-5 military operations, however, were by the US Navy which had ordered seven examples in 1939. Three were **R3D-1** 16-seat personnel transports, the first of which crashed before delivery, and four were **R3D-2** aircraft for the US Marine Corps with 746-kW (1,000-hp) R-1820-44 engines, a large sliding cargo door, and bucket seats for 22 paratroops. The prototype, after certification and development flying had been completed, was sold with a 16-seat executive interior to William E. Boeing, and was later impressed for US Navy use as the sole **R3D-3**.

Derived from the DB-7 bomber, the DC-5 was dramatically superior to Santa Monica's DC-3. Designer Ed Heinemann was told by General H. H. Arnold to cancel the programme because of the Army's selection of the C-47.

Specification
Douglas DC-5
Type: cargo and passenger/paratroop

Douglas DC-5.

transport
Powerplant: two 634-kW (850-hp) Wright GR-1820-F62 radial piston engines
Performance: maximum speed 356 km/h (221 mph) at 2345 m (7,700 ft); cruising speed 325 km/h (202 mph) at 3050 m (10,000 ft);

service ceiling 7225 m (23,700 ft); range 2575 km (1,600 miles)
Weights: empty 6202 kg (13,674 lb); maximum take-off 9072 kg (20,000 lb)
Dimensions: span 23.77 m (78 ft 0 in); length 19.05 m (62 ft 6 in); height 6.05 m (19 ft 10 in); wing area 76.55 m² (824 sq ft)

Douglas DC-6/C-118 Liftmaster

With major involvement in a war (1941-45) that was centred at the far side of the Pacific Ocean, USAAF interest in long-range landplanes was understandable. The DC-4/C-54 series proved to be a valuable tool, and a glowing tribute to its reliability is provided by a total of almost 80,000 wartime ocean crossings (Atlantic/Pacific) during which only three aircraft were lost. Such a record induced the USAAF to look for a larger-capacity transport from the same source, and the first of these to fly, on 15 February 1946, had the designation **Douglas XC-112A**. By then, of course, it was too late for participation in World War II, and the new type was developed instead for service with postwar airlines under the company identification **DC-6**.

By comparison with its predecessor, the DC-6 retained the same wing, but had a pressurised fuselage that was lengthened by 2.06 m (6 ft 9 in) to give increased passenger capacity. Seating for 48 to 52 was standard, but a high-density layout could accommodate 86. Powerplant of the initial DC-6 comprised four 1566-kW (2,100-hp) Pratt & Whitney R-2800-CA15 Double Wasp engines, and the first of 50 civil airliners ordered by American Airlines made its initial flight on 29 June 1946. The DC-6 began to enter service in April 1947, initially on the New York-Chicago route of American Airlines.

During 1948 the company began development of an increased-capacity version (with the fuselage lengthened by 1.52 m/5 ft 0 in) powered by 1790-kW (2,400-hp) Double Wasp engines. Offered initially in an all-cargo version as the **DC-6A**, with two freight doors on the port side (one forward and one aft of

the wing), no windows, and strengthened flooring, the DC-6A was followed by the generally similar **DC-6B** passenger transport. In early production examples the standard seating capacity was 54, but high-density layouts for up to 102 passengers were introduced subsequently.

Civil DC-6s were built alongside 166 aircraft for the US Air Force and Navy, partially to support operations of the Military Air Transport Service (MATS). Those which served with the USAF had the designation **C-118A** and could accommodate 74 passengers, or 12247 kg (27,000 lb) of cargo, or 60 stretcher cases. The 29th DC-6 was given a VIP interior for President Truman; this was the **VC-118** *The Independence*, which had a cabin for 24 passengers or night accommodation for 12, and an executive stateroom.

DC-6s in US Navy service included 61 **R6D-1** and four **R6D-1Z** aircraft, the latter with VIP interiors; these became **C-118B** and **VC-118B** in 1962. Other military services also acquired DC-6s, the majority of them ex-civil aircraft.

Last of the civil designations was **DC-6C**, this applying to a convertible cargo/passenger version that was generally similar to the DC-6A, but with standard cabin windows. Construction of DC-6 civil and XC-112A/C-118/C-118A/R6D military aircraft totalled 704. Among variants were two DC-6Bs modified by SABENA, these being given swing-tails to simplify the direct in-loading of bulky cargo. There were also a number of DC-6Bs provided with a 61356-litre (3,000-US gal) capacity underfuselage tank to carry fire-retardant chemicals, and these saw considerable service in

Like many DC-6s which have served in civilian colours, this aircraft was originally built as a C-118. It has been converted to freighter standard, with windowless cabin and port-side cargo door.

Douglas DC-6B.

Canada and the USA during periods of high fire risk in national timberlands.

The DC-6 came to be regarded as a worthy example of the reliable and

efficient piston-engined airliners that were soon to be displaced by first-generation turboprop- and turbojet-powered aircraft. As DC-6s became surplus to the

361

requirements of major users they were
eagerly sought by operators in the lower
echelons of air transport. They, too,
benefitted from the DC-6's excellence,
and about 50 remain in service.

Specification
Douglas DC-6B
Type: long-range transport
Powerplant: four 1865-kW (2,500-hp)
Pratt & Whitney R-2800-CB17 Double
Wasp radial piston engines

Performance: cruising speed
507 km/h (315 mph); service ceiling
7620 m (25,000 ft); range with
maximum payload 4836 km (3,005
miles); range with maximum fuel
7596 km (4,720 miles)

Weights: empty 25110 kg (55,357 lb);
max take-off 48534 kg (107,000 lb)
Dimensions: span 35.81 m (117 ft
6 in); length 32.18 m (105 ft 7 in);
height 8.74 m (28 ft 8 in); wing area
135.91 m² (1,463 sq ft)

Douglas DC-7

Design and development of the
Douglas DC-7 were prompted by
American Airlines, which was seeking
an aircraft superior in performance to the
Lockheed Super Constellation being
used by TWA. The Super 'Connie' benefitted from the use of new Wright Turbo-
Compound engines, each of which had
three exhaust-driven turbochargers
giving some 20 per cent more output
than the standard unit, and to meet the
requirement of American Airlines it was
decided to develop an improved version
of the DC-6B using this new powerplant.

The initial DC-7 was a direct development of the DC-6B, with the fuselage
lengthened by 1.02 m (3 ft 4 in) to allow
for the inclusion of an additional row of
seats. Installation of the 2424-kW
(3,250-hp) R-3350 Turbo-Compound
engines made possible an increase in
gross weight of 6895 kg (15,200 lb), and
required some strengthening of the
landing gear structure. There were also
some minor changes in detail, but externally the DC-7 appeared little different
from the DC-6B.

A total of 105 DC-7s was built, and the
112 **DC-7B** aircraft which followed
showed only minor changes. Most importantly, the engine nacelles were extended further aft to permit the installation of saddle tanks within the rear of the
nacelles (which were made of the new
metal titanium).

Not all operators opted for this additional fuel capacity, but those who did,
such as Pan American which inaugurated non-stop London-New York
services with the DC-7B on 13 June
1955, soon discovered that fuel capacity
was marginal for North Atlantic services.
In fact, with a full load and normal head-
winds, DC-7Bs which were used to
operate the east-to-west service frequently had to divert for a refuelling stop.
This was clearly unsatisfactory, and
potentially dangerous, and Douglas set
about the task of developing a version of
the DC-7B with greater range.

The third version was designated
DC-7C and had, therefore, increased
span to provide for greater fuel capacity.
This was achieved by inserting a new
parallel-chord wing section between the
fuselage and the inboard engine

*This aircraft was one of six
DC-7Bs built for Delta Air Lines.
After its airline career it was
rebuilt for fire-fighting with a
large ventral tank holding 9085
litres (2,400 US gal) of fire
retardant. The use of this large
aircraft for the role had been
validated as early as 1953 at Palm
Springs, where it produced a
mile-long deluge of water.*

nacelles, which had the added advantage of improving the cabin environment
by reducing engine noise. During the development of the DC-7C, Curtiss-Wright
was able to offer a further increase in
engine power and, as a result, the fuselage was lengthened by the insertion of a
1.02 m (3 ft 4 in) plug to provide accommodation for up to 105 passengers.

Production of DC-7Cs totalled 120,
and the alphanumeric suffix of this version became corrupted most appropriately to **Seven Seas**, for this aircraft
was able to take the oceans in its stride
without any problems. Not only were
they used on North Atlantic and Pacific
Ocean services, but they also made possible non-stop scheduled operations
across the continental USA, and were
used also by SAS to inaugurate a Europe-
to-Far East route over the North Pole. An
improved **DC-7D** was planned, to be
powered by four 4273-ekW (5,730-eshp)
Rolls-Royce Tyne turboprop engines,
but the emergence of the Boeing 707
and the Douglas Company's purpose-

built DC-8 jetliner meant that this remained only as an unfulfilled project.

Because the turbo-compound engine
increased operating costs, these fine airliners disappeared quickly from the
aviation scene when replaced by the first
turboprop- and turbojet-powered airliners.

Specification
Douglas DC-7C
Type: long-range transport
Powerplant: four 2535-kW (3,400-
hp) Wright R-3350-18EA-1 turbo-
compound radial piston engines

Performance: maximum speed
653 km/h (406 mph) at 6615 m
(21,700 ft); normal cruising speed
571 km/h (355 mph); service ceiling
6615 m (21,700 ft); range with
maximum payload 7411 km (4,605
miles)
Weights: empty 33005 kg (72,763 lb);
maximum take-off 64864 kg
(143,000 lb)
Dimensions: span 38.86 m (127 ft
6 in); length 34.21 m (112 ft 3 in); height
9.70 m (31 ft 10 in); wing area
152.08 m² (1,637 sq ft)

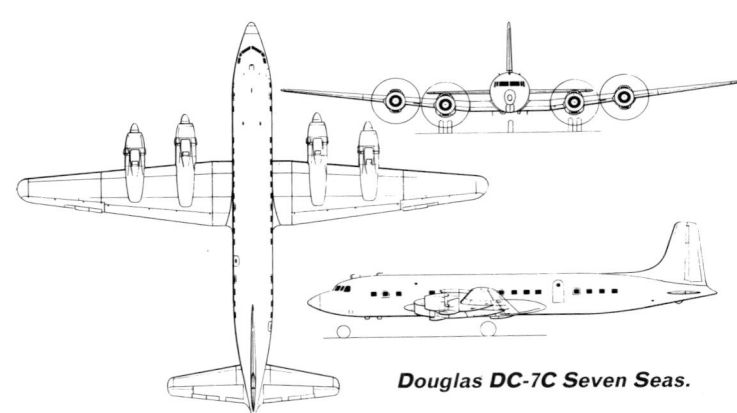

Douglas DC-7C Seven Seas.

Douglas DC-8

Aware that Boeing was well advanced
with its Model 707, and anxious to maintain a substantial share of the market for
civil transports, Douglas announced on 7
June 1955 its intention of developing a
turbojet-powered airliner to supersede
the DC-7, and design of the **Douglas
DC-8** went ahead without delay. One
prototype/demonstrator was built, and
when this first aircraft flew on 30 May
1958, it was seen to be very similar externally to the Boeing 707. It was of the
same basic configuration: a low-wing
monoplane with four pylon-mounted
turbojets, and a tail unit with all-swept
surfaces. The tricycle landing gear had a
steerable nose unit with twin wheels
and each main unit carried a four-wheel
bogie, the rear pair of wheels on each

being free-castoring to make possible
small-radius turns.

Nine aircraft took part in the certification programme, comprising three with
Pratt & Whitney JT3C turbojets, four
with JT4As and two with Rolls-Royce
Conways. This seems a lot of development aircraft but, conscious of Boeing's
lead, the Douglas company wanted to
gain FAA approval for the DC-8 at the
earliest possible date. This was awarded
on 31 August 1959, when Delta Airlines
and United Air Lines became the recipients of the first aircraft.

During the following nine years
Douglas built a total of 294 examples of
the transports, produced in five series
and all of the same overall dimensions.
They comprised the **DC-8 Series 10**,
the original domestic version powered
by four 6123-kg (13,500-lb) thrust Pratt &
Whitney JT3C-6 engines; a generally

similar **DC-8 Series 20**, but equipped
with more powerful engines for operation from hot and/or high airfields; the
long-range intercontinental **DC-8
Series 30** with, typically, 7620-kg
(16,800-lb) thrust JT4A-9 turbojets; a
basically similar intercontinental **DC-8
Series 40** with 7938-kg (17,500-lb)
thrust Rolls-Royce Conway 509 turbofans; and the **DC-8 Series 50** with
Pratt & Whitney JT3D turbofans and
with a rearranged cabin interior to provide accommodation for a maximum of
189 passengers. A major improvement
developed subsequently for these versions of the DC-8 was a new leading
edge; this changed the wing profile, reducing drag and improving both speed
and range. Standard on all late-production DC-8s, it has been fitted retrospectively to many early aircraft. Series 50 aircraft were available also as **DC-8F Jet**

Traders in AF (all-cargo) or CF (convertible passenger/cargo) versions.

The foregoing were followed in 1967
by three **DC-8 Super Sixty** variants, of
which 262 were built. These consisted
of the **DC-8 Super 61**, with a fuselage
extended by 11.18 m (36 ft 8 in) and able
to carry up to 259 passengers; the ultra-
long-range **DC-8 Super 62**, with span
increased by 1.83 m (6 ft 0 in) and with
standard seating for 189 passengers in a
fuselage lengthened by 2.03 m (6 ft
8 in); and the **DC-8 Super 63** combining
the long fuselage of the Super 61 with the
aerodynamic improvements of the Super
62. All versions of the Super Sixty series
were available in all-cargo or convertible
cargo/passenger configurations.

In 1979, with the Douglas Aircraft
Company by then a division of the
McDonnell Douglas Corporation, plans
were announced to re-engine Series 61,

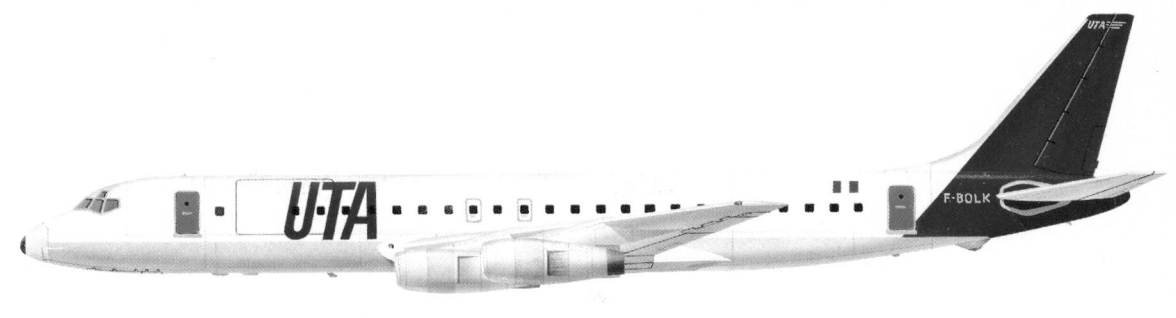

Douglas DC-8-55CF convertible passenger/freight version in the colours of French airline UTA.

62 and 63 aircraft with advanced-technology engines as the **DC-8 Super Seventy** series, numbered 71, 72 and 73 respectively. This involved installation of General Electric/SNECMA CFM56 advanced turbofans, and certification of the **DC-8 Super 71** with this powerplant was gained during April 1982. Similarly powered, the first **DC-8 Super 72** and **DC-8 Super 73** conversions made their initial flights on 5 December 1981 and 4 March 1982, respectively, gaining certification later in the year. Overall management of this re-engining programme was handled by Cammacorp of Los Angeles, California, and by mid-1982 almost 100 firm orders for conversions had been received. It is claimed that in addition to being considerably quieter than original DC-8s, the Super Seventy family demonstrates dramatic improvements in performance and operating costs.

Specification
Douglas DC-8-63
Type: long-range transport
Powerplant: four 8618-kg (19,000-lb) thrust Pratt & Whitney JT3D-7 turbofans
Performance: maximum cruising speed 966 km/h (600 mph) at 9145 m (30,000 ft); economic cruising speed 842 km/h (523 mph); range with maximum payload 7242 km (4,500 miles)
Weights: empty operating 69739 kg (153,749 lb); maximum take-off 158757 kg (350,000 lb)
Dimensions: span 45.24 m (148 ft

5 in); length 57.12 m (187 ft 5 in); height 12.93 m (42 ft 5 in); wing area 271.92 m² (2,927.0 sq ft)

Production of the specialised DC-8-63AF freighter amounted to just seven aircraft for Flying Tigers. Many Super 60s have been re-engined with the CFM56 to provide greater economy and capability.

Douglas DT

Following the failure of the Cloudster to complete its US coast-to-coast flight, David R. Davis lost interest in the Davis-Douglas Company and withdrew his financial support. Thus, after some difficulty in gaining backing, Donald Douglas established the Douglas Company (later Douglas Aircraft Company) in July 1921.

One of the reasons that this then little-known designer/engineer was able to gain the requisite backing to form the new company stemmed from his design of a torpedo-bomber, gaining a contract in April 1921 to build three evaluation prototypes for the US Navy under the designation **Douglas DT-1**. It was to prove an historic design: the first military aircraft to be produced by the new Douglas Company, and one of the US Navy's first successful torpedo-bombers.

Retaining in its wings and fuselage a family likeness to the earlier Cloudster, the single-seat DT-1 differed by being of composite construction: its foldable wings were of wood with fabric covering, fuselage of welded steel tube with light alloy covering forward and fabric covering aft, the vertical tail surfaces of wood and horizontal surfaces of steel tube, both fabric-covered. The fixed tail-skid landing gear had wide track main units suitable for wheels or floats, and power was provided by a 298-kW (400-hp) Liberty engine. The first DT-1 made its maiden flight at the beginning of November 1921 and completed its acceptance trials during the following month. However, the US Navy decided that two-seat accommodation would be more suitable for an aircraft in this category and instructed the company to so

modify the remaining two aircraft under the changed designation **DT-2**. Even before these were received, the DT-1 had shown itself to be superior to competing designs, resulting in further orders for Douglas. The company built 38 DT-2s, in addition to the two modified DT-1s, and 26 more were built by the Naval Aircraft Factory (6) and the LWF Engineering Company (20).

In addition to their torpedo-bombing role, in which capacity they proved valuable in the development of air-launched torpedoes, the DT-2s were used also for gunnery practice, observation and scouting. Before they were retired from service, during 1926, one float version was used in 1925 for early catapult launch tests from the USS *Langley*.

Variants
DT-3: designation of proposed improved version of DT-2; not built
DT-4: bomber conversion, four being modified from DT-2s by the Naval Aircraft Factory, re-engined with direct-drive 523-kW (650-hp) Wright T-2 V12 engines
DT-5: redesignation of two DT-4s following the installation of geared 523-kW (650-hp) Wright T-2B V12 engines
DT-6: designation of a single DT-2 following installation of a 336-kW (450-hp) Wright P-1 radial engine
DT-2B: under this designation one Liberty-engined DT-2 was supplied to the Norwegian government; seven similar aircraft were built under licence in Norway, and some remained in second-line service in 1940
DTB: designation of four aircraft with 523-kW (650-hp) Wright Typhoon V12 engines built for the Peruvian navy
SDW-1: redesignation of three DT-2s

modified by the Dayton-Wright company as long-range scout floatplanes; they had a deeper section centre fuselage accommodating additional fuel tanks

Specification
Douglas DT-2 (landplane)
Type: two-seat torpedo-bomber
Powerplant: one 336-kW (450-hp) Liberty V-12 piston engine
Performance: maximum speed 163 km/h (101 mph); service ceiling 2,375 m (7,800 ft); range 472 km (293 miles)

Two DT-2s of Torpedo Squadron VT-2 on patrol. The unit was the first to receive the type, starting in December 1922. It mostly used the aircraft on float undercarriage.

Weights: empty 1695 kg (3,737 lb); maximum take-off 2949 kg (6,502 lb)
Dimensions: span 15.24 m (50 ft 0 in); length 10.41 m (34 ft 2 in); height 4.14 m (13 ft 7 in); wing area 65.68 m² (707 sq ft)
Armament: one 832-kg (1,835-lb) torpedo

Douglas DWC
to
Douglas O-2 series

Douglas DWC

In early 1923 the United States Army Air Services became interested in the possibility of making a round-the-world flight using a small formation of aircraft. With official approval to plan such an expedition came the primary task of selecting a suitable aircraft for the purpose. It needed to be robust and reliable, have good range capability and be suitable for easy conversion from wheel to float landing gear and vice versa. Initial interest was shown in the Davis-Douglas Cloudster, but the Douglas Company proposed instead a version of the US Navy's DT-2, incorporating modifications that would provide a maximum extension of range.

The proposal was accepted by the US Army which ordered a **Douglas DWC** prototype in the late summer of 1923 and, because it was basically a DT-2 airframe, it was built and had completed its service trials (with both wheel and float landing gear) so quickly that a go-ahead for the flight was given on 19 November 1923. Four more DWCs were ordered, and the last of these was delivered in mid-March 1924. They differed from the DT-2 by having almost six times the fuel

Chicago seen over Asian waters during its round-the-world flight in 1924. Two of the World Cruisers completed the epic journey, the others being lost en route with no casualties.

capacity, which replaced the military equipment of the US Navy's aircraft, and by having a modification of the engine cooling system to allow an easy interchange of small- or large-capacity cooling radiators.

The four aircraft, numbered 1 to 4 and named respectively *Seattle, Chicago, Boston* and *New Orleans*, began their epic journey on 4 April 1924. Their round-the-world route was from east to west via Canada and Alaska, where the *Seattle* was destroyed in a crash. After suffering an engine failure the *Boston* sank off the Faroe Islands under tow, but the *Chicago* and *New Orleans* successfully completed their truly remarkable journey on 28 September 1924, having flown 46582 km (28,945 miles). In so doing they had also achieved the first staged crossing of the Pacific Ocean, a point which is not generally appreciated.

Variant
DOS: initial designation of six aircraft,

generally similar to the DWCs, ordered by the USAAS for service as observation seaplanes; later designated **Q-5**, they differed from the DWCs by having a standard fuel system and armament of twin machine-guns on a flexible mounting in the rear cockpit

Specification
Douglas DWC
Type: two-seat long-range aircraft
Powerplant: one 313-kW (420-hp)

Liberty V12 piston engine
Performance: (landplane) maximum speed 166 km/h (103 mph); low cruising speed 85 km/h (53 mph); service ceiling 3050 m (10,000 ft); range 3541 km (2,200 miles)
Weights: empty 1950 kg (4,300 lb); maximum take-off 3137 kg (6,915 lb)
Dimensions: span 15.24 m (50 ft 0 in); length 10.82 m (35 ft 6 in); height 4.14 m (13 ft 7 in); wing area 65.68 m^2 (707.0 sq ft)

Douglas Dolphin

The **Douglas Dolphin** high-wing cantilever monoplane amphibian flying-boat was developed from the **Sinbad**, a flying-boat powered by two 224-kW (300-hp) Wright J-5C Whirlwind engines and which had flown for the first time in July 1930. The only example of the Sinbad served with the US Coast Guard from 1931 to 1939.

The Dolphin and the Sinbad had the same engine layout: two radial engines driving tractor propellers and mounted (in the Dolphin) on a complex strut arrangement over the wing. The landing gear introduced on the Dolphin comprised main units attached to the hull by hinged Vee-struts and to the undersurfaces of the wings by oleo legs. While the Sinbad had a tail skid for use in conjunction with its detachable beaching gear, the Dolphin had a tail wheel, located at the rear of the second hull step. In flight or for operations from water, the main wheels were retracted above the waterline. The pilot and co-pilot were seated side-by-side in a fully enclosed position just forward of the wing leading edge, with the passenger cabin located immediately behind them.

The Dolphin was characterised by an auxiliary aerofoil surface, attached to the top of the engine nacelles, to overcome turbulence problems. Early examples also had a pair of auxiliary fins to provide additional directional stability. Construction was similar to that of the Sinbad, with an all-metal hull and ply-covered wooden wing, but the bow of the Dolphin's hull was redesigned.

Total Dolphin production was 58, but the type achieved a remarkable reputation for dependability, and several sea rescue successes by US Coast Guard and US Navy Dolphins caught the public's imagination. There were no fewer than 17 versions, differing mainly

Ten RD-4s were purchased by the US Coast Guard for search and rescue duties. Their service lasted from 1934 to 1943, performing with great distinction.

in engine installation and passenger cabin layout. The main design change came with the 14th aircraft built, the fin and rudder assembly being redesigned with greater area, thus permitting the deletion of the auxiliary fins. Wing area was also increased by 2.79 m^2 (30 sq ft) and hull length by 0.48 m (1 ft 7 in).

The first two Dolphins were built for the Wilmington-Catalina Airline, linking the Los Angeles area with Santa Catalina Island, a distance of just 32 km (20 miles). Powered by 224-kW (300-hp) Wright J-5C Whirlwind radials, these aircraft were known originally as **Model 1** aircraft, with accommodation for six passengers, pilot and co-pilot. They were modified later as **Model 1 Special** machines, with accommodation increased to eight passengers.

Production of the Dolphin continued into 1935, most examples going to the US Army, US Navy or US Coast Guard. Few survived World War II, and one example seen on the US west coast in the 1980s was reported to be in airworthy condition.

Variants
Y1C-21: eight ordered in 1931 for the US Army, and intended originally to escort bombardment units on over-sea flights, providing navigational and, if necessary, rescue assistance; the speed of the Martin B-10 and B-12 bombers coming into service rendered this policy impracticable and the aircraft, by then designated **C-21**, were used for staff transport duties in

coastal areas; later they were loaned to the US Treasury (temporarily designated **FP-1**) for anti-smuggling border patrols to enforce Prohibition; although later redesignated **OA-3** (Observation Amphibian), the aircraft were used towards the end of their US Army careers mainly as transports
Y1C-26: two delivered to the US Army in 1933; these were the first Dolphins to feature the enlarged fin/rudder and so dispensed with the auxiliary fins; they were later redesignated **OA-4**, also **FP-2** when temporarily used by US Treasury; later fitted with stainless steel wings and 298-kW (400-hp) Pratt & Whitney R-985-9s as **OA-4C**; eight **C-26A** aircraft, differing only slightly from the C-26, were delivered soon afterwards, and had the temporary US Treasury designation **FP-2A**; four were modernised on the same lines as the C-26s in 1936 and also redesignated OA-4C; four **C-26B** aircraft were delivered in 1933, powered by Pratt & Whitney R-985-9s and were later redesignated **OA-4B**; one was used for experiments with a fixed tricycle landing gear, while another was later converted to OA-4C standard
C-29: two built for US Army in 1933, powered by 410-kW (550-hp) Pratt &

Whitney R-1340-29 radials; when on loan to US Treasury the type was known as **FP-2B**
XRD-1: one only, delivered to the US Navy in August 1931; powered by two 324-kW (435-hp) Wright R-975E radials, used for seven years as a US Navy staff transport
RD: one civil Model 1 Special acquired for US Coast Guard patrol duties in August 1932; served until 1939
RD-2: four built; first, with 373-kW (500-hp) Pratt & Whitney R-1340-10s, for US Coast Guard to same basic design as C-26; three later aircraft were more similar to C-26A; one was used as five-passenger luxury transport for President Franklin D. Roosevelt from June 1933, powered initially by 307-kW (410-hp) Pratt & Whitney R-1340-1s, replaced later by 373-kW (500-hp) R-1340-10s, and relegated to other duties 1939; two others with 336-kW (450-hp) R-1340-29s were less luxurious and used as naval staff transports until March 1940
RD-3: six delivered to the US Navy in 1935-36 as utility transport versions of the RD-2
RD-4: 10 built, similar to the RD-3 but with 313-kW (420-hp) Pratt & Whitney Wasp C-1s; all for US Coast Guard and employed mainly on search and rescue

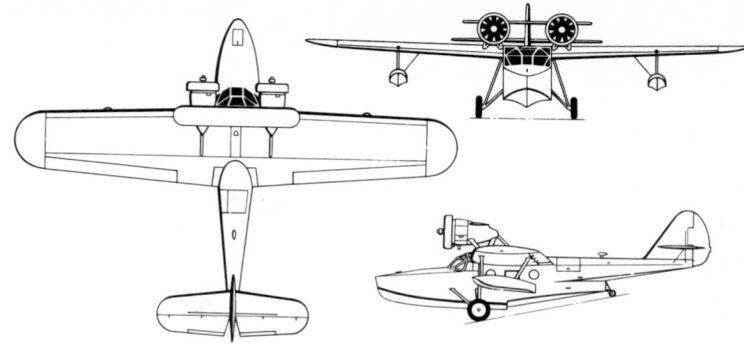

duties; four surviving aircraft were used for security coastal patrol when the US Coast Guard was taken over directly by the US Navy on American entry into World War II; all were withdrawn from active service by June 1943
Civil Dolphins: apart from the first two Dolphins delivered, 10 more civil Dolphins were built; the sole **Model 3** was a four-seat luxury aircraft built for an American millionaire in 1931; it was then sold to an Australian owner and later taken over by the Royal Australian Air Force for liaison work during 1942-45; the remaining civil machines resembled the US Coast Guard RD-4; one, with 410-kW (550-hp) Wasp S1D1 engines, was sold to a French owner,

while another six were all built to the individual order of wealthy Americans; one of them was bought by William E. Boeing, founder of The Boeing Company; another was used by the Los Angeles-Santa Catalina airline. The last two Dolphins went to the China National Aviation Corporation (a PanAm subsidiary) and operated between Shanghai and Canton for a number of years

Specification
Douglas C-21
Type: staff transport or observation amphibian
Powerplant: two 261-kW (350-hp) Wright R-975-3 radial piston engines
Performance: maximum speed

225 km/h (140 mph); cruising speed 192 km/h (119 mph); service ceiling 4330 m (14,200 ft); range 885 km (550 miles)
Weights: empty equipped 2659 kg (5,861 lb); maximum take-off 3893 kg

(8,583 lb)
Dimensions: span 18.29 m (60 ft 0 in); length 13.36 m (43 ft 10 in); height 4.29 m (14 ft 1 in); wing area 52.21 m² (562 sq ft)

Douglas F3D (F-10) Skyknight

A US Navy requirement for a turbojet-powered carrier-based night fighter resulted in Douglas receiving a contract for three prototype aircraft in this category under the designation **Douglas XF3D-1**.

The type emerged as a cantilever mid-wing monoplane of all-metal construction, the wings incorporating hydraulic folding for carrier stowage. The circular-section fuselage mounted hydraulically actuated speed-brakes, provided side-by-side pressurised accommodation for the pilot and radar operator, and carried at the rear a tail unit very similar to that of the D-558-1 Skystreak. An unusual feature was a crew escape tunnel, extending from the rear of the cabin to the underside of the fuselage. Landing gear was of retractable tricycle-type, and the powerplant of the prototypes comprised

two 1361-kg (3,000-lb) thrust Westinghouse J34-WE-24 turbojets, mounted on the lower edges of the forward fuselage, beneath the wing roots.

The first prototype made its maiden flight on 23 March 1948, but while company testing was still in progress an initial contract for the construction of 28 **F3D-1 Skyknight** production aircraft was received. The first of these was flown on 13 February 1950 and the type began to enter service in early 1951. The F3D-1 differed from the prototypes by having improved avionics and equipment and, as delivered initially, had 1361-kg (3,000-lb) thrust J34-WE-32 turbojets. These engines were uprated subsequently to 1474-kg (3,250-lb) thrust, becoming redesignated J34-WE-34.

Before delivery of the first F3D-1,

Douglas had received a contract for production of an improved **F3D-2**, which was to be the major and ultimate production version, with a total of 237 built. It was intended that the F3D-2 should be powered by 2087-kg (4,600-lb) thrust J46-WE-3 turbojets, but development of this engine was abandoned and, instead, they were all powered by J34-WE-36s. Improvements included the provision of an autopilot and updated systems and equipment. The first of these F3D-2s was flown on 14 February 1951 and all had been delivered just over a year later.

The Skyknight saw extensive use in Korea, this all-weather fighter accounting for the majority of all victories scored by the US Navy and US Marine Corps. The first combat victory came on 2 November 1952, being the first occasion that one jet aircraft had destroyed another (in this case a MiG-15) in a night interception. F3D-1s and F3D-2s were redesignated **F-10A** and **F-10B** respectively with introduction of the new US tri-service designation system in September 1962. Some Skyknights had been retired by 1965, but many ECM versions were operating in Vietnam until 1969.

Variants
F3D-1M (MF-10A): designation of

some 12 F3D-1s following modification as test vehicles for Sparrow guided missiles
F3D-2B: redesignation of one F3D-2 while used during 1952 for special armament tests
F3D-2M (MF-10B): redesignation of 16 F3D-2s following conversion to carry Sparrow missiles
F3D-2Q (EF-10B): redesignation of 35 F3D-2s following conversion for an ECM role
F3D-2T: under this designation five F3D-2s were converted for use as night-fighter trainers
F3D-2T2 (TF-10B): redesignation of 55 F3D-2s which served as radar-operator trainers and electronic-warfare aircraft
F3D-3: projected advanced version with swept wings

Specification
Douglas F3D-2
Type: carrier-based all-weather fighter
Powerplant: two 1542-kg (3,400-lb) thrust Westinghouse J34-WE-36/36A turbojets
Performance: maximum speed 909 km/h (565 mph) at 6095 m (20,000 ft); cruising speed 628 km/h (390 mph); initial climb rate 1220 m (4,000 ft) per minute; service ceiling 11645 m (38,200 ft); range 1931 km (1,200 miles)
Weights: empty 8237 kg (18,160 lb); maximum take-off 12179 kg (26,850 lb)
Dimensions: span 15.24 m (50 ft 0 in); length 13.97 m (45 ft 6 in); height 4.88 m (16 ft 0 in); wing area 37.16 m² (400 sq ft)
Armament: four fixed forward-firing 20-mm cannon

An F3D-2 Skyknight of VF-14 seen in landing configuration during carrier operations in November 1954. The US Marine Corps took this version into action in Korea, scoring notable victories at night.

Douglas F4D (F-6) Skyray

US Navy interest in German delta-wing research led, in 1947, to the design by Douglas of a carrier-based interceptor which embodied a variation of the pure delta wing. Approval of the Douglas design was signified by the award of a contract for two **Douglas XF4D-1** prototypes on 16 December 1948, the first making its maiden flight on 23 January 1951 powered by a 2268-kg (5,000-lb) thrust Allison J35-A-17 engine. This represented an emergency powerplant, resulting from delays in development of the Westinghouse J40 turbojet which had been the planned engine. Both prototypes were flown subsequently with the XJ40-WE-6 developing 3175-kg (7,000-lb) thrust and the XJ40-WE-8 which had a rating of 5262 kg (11,600 lb) with afterburning, but problems with this engine programme led to final selection of the Pratt & Whitney J57 engine

The F4D was notable for its exceptional rate of climb: in May 1958 five time-to-height records were captured by a USMC pilot. This aircraft is from VFAW-3, a US Navy squadron shore-based and assigned to NORAD.

for production aircraft.

The **F4D Skyray** was a cantilever mid-wing monoplane, the wing of modified delta configuration incorporating elevons to serve collectively as elevators or differentially as ailerons. The tail unit had only swept vertical surfaces, landing gear was of retractable tricycle-type and the pilot was accommodated well forward of the wing in an enclosed cockpit that provided excellent visibility.

The potential of the F4D was demonstrated effectively by the second prototype on 3 October 1953, then powered

by the XJ40-WE-8 turbojet, which set a new world speed record of 1211.746 km/h (752.9 mph). The first production **F4D-1** was flown on 5 June 1954, powered by a Pratt & Whitney J57-P-2 turbojet developing 6123-kg (13,500-

lb) thrust with afterburning, but it was not until 16 April 1956 that deliveries began, initially to US Navy Squadron VC-3. The 419th and last production aircraft was delivered on 22 December 1958, but in the intervening period a change had been made by installation of the higher-rated J57-P-8 engine. All aircraft retained the F4D-1 designation, the popular (derived) name being Ford.

At the peak of its utilisation, the Skyray equipped 11 US Navy, six US Marine and three reserve squadrons, but none was used operationally. The type survived in first-line service until the late 1960s, with two front-line squadrons not converting to the type until 1964. It was redesig-nated **F-6A** in September 1962.

Variant
F4D-2N: proposed development with improved all-weather capability, eventually built as the **F5D-1** Skylancer prototype

Specification
Type: single-seat carrier-based fighter
Powerplant: one Pratt & Whitney J57-P-8B turbojet developing 6577-kg (14,500-lb) thrust with afterburning
Performance: maximum speed 1162 km/h (722 mph) at sea level and 1118 km/h (695 mph) at 10975 m (36,000 ft); initial climb rate 5580 m (18,300 ft) per minute; service ceiling 16765 m (55,000 ft); range 1931 km (1,200 miles)
Weights: empty 7268 kg (16,024 lb); maximum take-off 11340 kg (25,000 lb)
Dimensions: span 10.21 m (33 ft 6 in); length 13.93 m (45 ft 8¼ in); height 3.96 m (13 ft 0 in); wing area 51.75 m² (557 sq ft)
Armament: four fixed forward-firing 20-mm cannon, plus up to 1814 kg (4,000 lb) of stores (including auxiliary fuel, bombs, rockets or missiles) on six underwing hardpoints

Douglas F5D-1 Skylancer

The **Douglas F5D** was envisaged originally as an improved all-weather development of the F4D (F-6) Skyray, and two prototypes were ordered in 1953 under the designation **F4D-2N**. However, substantial changes, including wings of much reduced thickness/chord ratio, a lengthened fuselage, revised vertical tail surfaces and the introduction of a new cockpit canopy brought the redesignation **F5D-1** (subsequently named **Skylancer**) before the first flight was recorded on 21 April 1956.

By then, nine preproduction and 51 production examples had been ordered, but following early flight testing the programme was cancelled except for two of the preproduction aircraft. This termination was not due to shortcomings in the aircraft, but rather to the realisation that the performance of the F5D was little better than that of the Chance Vought F8U-1 which was on the point of entering service. However, the four F5D-1s fulfilled a useful role, being used by the US Navy as flying testbeds for a variety of equipment before they were handed over to NASA for experimental use.

Specification
Type: single-seat carrier-based fighter
Powerplant: one 7257-kg (16,000-lb) afterburning thrust Pratt & Whitney J57-P-8 turbojet
Performance: maximum speed 1767 km/h (1,098 mph) at 3050 m (10,000 ft); cruising speed 1025 km/h (637 mph); service ceiling 17525 m (57,500 ft); range 2140 km (1,330 miles)
Weights: empty 7912 kg (17,444 lb); maximum take-off 12733 kg (28,072 lb)
Dimensions: span 10.21 m (33 ft 6 in); length 16.4 m (53 ft 9¾ in); height 4.52 m (14 ft 10 in); wing area 51.75 m² (557 sq ft)
Armament: (intended) Sidewinder or Sparrow air-to-air missiles or unguided rockets

Supersonic son of the Skyray, the F5D-1 offered good performance and adequate all-weather capability, but was cancelled in favour of the all-round excellence of the F8U.

Douglas M series

The US Post Office Department had been responsible for US internal air mail routes from 1918 onwards, and by 1925 the various types of DH-4 biplane which had been primary equipment since inception of the service were worn out. A decision was thus made to order a conversion of the Douglas O-2 observation biplane, which had been ordered into quantity production for the US Army.

The **Douglas DAM-1** (Douglas Air Mail-One), quickly shortened to **M-1**, was test flown during the spring of 1925. It had twice the payload of the DH-4, but made use of the same tried and tested Liberty engine, of which large numbers were in store and readily available. The M-1 was a straightforward conversion of the O-2, with the forward cockpit covered in sheet aluminium to form a reinforced mail compartment with access through two deck hatches, the pilot being located in what was formerly the rear (observer's) cockpit in the O-2. During tests, extended exhaust piping was installed to keep fumes away from the pilot. The M-1 was adjudged successful, but no production order was received by Douglas.

With the introduction of Contract Air Mail (CAM) routes, however, the newly formed Western Air Express Company (later Western Airlines) ordered six Douglas mailplanes. Designated **M-2**,

Modelled closely on the O-2 series, the M-2 had a large mail compartment forward of the pilot's cockpit. This machine was used on Western Air Express' CAM.4 route between Los Angeles and Salt Lake City.

they differed from the M-1 mainly by replacement of the original tunnel radiator with a frontal type. Provision was also made for quick conversion of the freight section to permit carriage of a passenger in place of mail.

A month before Western Air Express inaugurated its Los Angeles-Salt Lake City service in April 1926, the US Post Office ordered 50 of the **M-3** version for its major routes. The M-3s differed only in detail from the M-2s, sporting an overall aluminium finish with US Air Mail emblazoned in black on the fuselage sides and on the undersurfaces of the lower wing. Western's machines had a red and silver paint scheme.

The Douglas Company's chief engineer, J. H. 'Dutch' Kindelberger, then redesigned the M-3 with the aim of doubling its payload. The main change in this new **M-4** was an entirely new 'stretched' wing which spanned 1.47 m (4 ft 10 in) more than the 12.09 m (39 ft 8 in) of the earlier types, and lacked the cut-out in the trailing edge of the upper

wing inherited from the US Army O-2s. The Post Office was sufficiently impressed to arrange for 40 of the 50-plane M-3 order to be delivered in M-4 configuration. A single M-4 bought by Western Air Express was designated **M-4A** by Douglas to differentiate it from the Post Office order.

With the leasing of route CAM-3 (Chicago-Dallas) to National Air Transport (NAT) in October 1925, a need arose for more mailplanes. NAT at first used the Curtiss Carrier Pigeon and then, having acquired the important Chicago-New York route, bought at auction all 10 M-3s and eight M-4s from the Post Office when, during July 1926, that department relinquished all its routes to

private operators.

The Douglas mailplanes were introduced by NAT on 1 September 1927, and were phased out during 1930 in favour of three-engined Ford tri-motors. In their three years' service they performed admirably in all weathers and in the most difficult flying conditions. NAT had bought other M-4s from a variety of sources and at one stage had as many as 24 Douglas mailplanes in operation. Among them was a privately owned aircraft which had been confiscated by the US Treasury while illegally smuggling liquor from Cuba to Florida during Prohibition; it became known as the 'Booze Ship'. NAT M-3s were flown with new long-span wings from the spring of 1928 onwards; for economic reasons these had been designed and constructed by the company's own engineering department. One M-4 was converted by NAT to take a 391-kW (525-hp) Pratt & Whitney Hornet radial engine.

A total of 57 Douglas mailplanes was built, but with the advent of the Ford and other three-engined types they were soon withdrawn from air mail services. A few were sold to private owners but the majority were scrapped.

One long-wing M-4 which survived was restored to flying condition by Western Airlines (successor to Western Air Express) in the old authentic colours of red and silver to commemorate in 1956 the company's 30th anniversary.

Specification
Douglas M-4
Type: single-seat mailplane
Powerplant: one 298-kW (400-hp) Liberty 12 V-12 piston engine
Performance: maximum speed 225 km/h (140 mph); cruising speed 177 km/h (110 mph); service ceiling 5030 m (16,500 ft); range 1127 km (700 miles)
Weights: empty equipped 1544 kg (3,405 lb); maximum take-off 2223 kg (4,900 lb)
Dimensions: span 13.56 m (44 ft 6 in); length 8.81 m (28 ft 11 in); height 3.07 m (10 ft 1 in); wing area 38.18 m² (411.0 sq ft)

Douglas O-2 series

This important family of observation aircraft sprang from two **Douglas XO-2** prototypes, the first of which was powered by a 313-kW (420-hp) Liberty V-1650-1 engine and test-flown in the autumn of 1924. The second XO-2 was powered by a 380-kW (510-hp) Packard 1A-1500 engine, which proved an unreliable powerplant. The US Army ordered 45 production **O-2** aircraft in 1925, these retaining the XO-2's welded steel-tube fuselage, wooden wings and overall fabric covering, but introducing aluminium panels on the forward fuselage. The XO-2 had been flown with short-span and wide-span wings, but the latter gave improved handling and were specified for series aircraft. The landing gear was of the divided type, the horizontal tailplane strut-braced, and the engine cooled by a tunnel radiator. The O-2 proved to be a conventional but very reliable biplane which soon attracted orders for 25 more aircraft: 18 **O-2A** machines equipped for night flying and six **O-2B** dual-control command aircraft for the US Army, plus one civil **O-2BS** modified specially for James McKee, who made a remarkable solo trans-Canada flight in September 1926. In 1927 the O-2BS was adapted as a three-seater with a radial engine.

Douglas O-2H of the 91st Observation Squadron, US Army Air Corps, 1928. The blue and yellow was the standard USAAC colour scheme of the day.

Variants

O-2C: the success of the O-2s in US Army observation squadrons led to orders for 46 O-2C aircraft in 1926; these differed from the O-2 in having frontal radiators for their Liberty engine and modified oleo-strut landing gear; the US Army Air Corps (USAAC) took delivery of 19 aircraft, while the remaining 27 went to reserve National Guard units
O-2D: two unarmed staff transport versions of the O-2C
O-2E: a one-off machine which replaced the wire link between upper and lower wing ailerons of production aircraft by rigid struts
O-2H: realising that the basic O-2 design was nearing the end of its useful life, Douglas engineers in 1926 produced a radically revised aircraft in the O-2H; the fuselage was redesigned and a new tailplane fitted, while the wings, which were of unequal span with considerable stagger (as opposed to the equal-span, unstaggered structure of all previous models) incorporated the rigid-strut aileron interconnections of the O-2E; an improved split-axle landing gear was standard; between 1928 and 1930 the USAAC received 90 O-2Hs and the National Guard a further 50
O-2J: three unarmed O-2Hs for use as USAAC staff transports
O-2K: a slightly modified version of the O-2J for US Army staff transport and liaison duties; total production 57, comprising 37 for the USAAC and 20 for the National Guard
XO-6: five all-metal versions of the O-2, built in the mid-1920s by Thomas-Morse

XO-6B: radically altered (smaller and lighter) version of the XO-6, precursor of the Thomas-Morse O-19 series
O-7: three O-2 airframes with 380-kW (510-hp) Packard 1A-1500 direct-drive engines; later converted to O-2 (two) and O-2C (one) standard
O-8: only one built; when completed it had a 298-kW (400-hp) Curtiss R-1454 radial engine instead of the intended inverted Packard; later became an O-2A
O-9: single example built; it had a geared 373-kW (500-hp) Packard 1A-1500 engine; it resembled the O-7, but had a four-bladed instead of a two-bladed propeller; later became an O-2A.
XO-14: a one-off reduced-scale version of an O-2H and the first Douglas aircraft with wheel brakes
O-22: two built; it differed from the O-2H in having N-type wing struts, sweepback on upper wing, metal-covered vertical tail surfaces, and a 336-kW (450-hp) Pratt & Whitney R-1340-9 radial engine with a Townend ring; a tailwheel replaced the previous tailskid
O-25: an O-2H with a 447-kW (600-hp) Curtiss Conqueror V-1570-5 liquid-cooled engine; new type of machine-gun mounting fitted for the observer; later flown as the **XO-25A** with Prestone cooling system
O-25A: production version of O-25, powered by geared 447-kW (600-hp) Curtiss V-1570-7 Conqueror; incorporated tailwheel similar to that on the O-22; the USAAC received 50
O-25B: three unarmed examples of the O-25A with dual controls for use as staff transports
O-25C: developed from the XO-25A, with same Prestone-cooled geared Curtiss Conqueror engine; radiator located further back beneath the forward fuselage; the USAAC took delivery of 30 O-25Cs
O-29: one aircraft similar to the O-2K, but with Wright R-1750 air-cooled radial engine; originally designated **Y1O-29A** and finally **O-29A**
O-32: similar to final version of

experimental O-29, but had a 336-kW (450-hp) Pratt & Whitney R-1340-3 Wasp radial engine
O-32A: production version of O-32; 30 built for the USAAC
YO-34: similar to the O-22 but fitted with the Curtiss Conqueror engine; single example only
O-38: resembled the O-25, but with 391-kW (525-hp) Pratt & Whitney R-1690-3 radial engine and Townend ring; US National Guard received all 44 production aircraft
O-38A: single unarmed O-38 staff liaison machine for National Guard
O-38B: a version of the O-38 with a 391-kW (525-hp) Pratt & Whitney R-1690-5 radial engine; total production was 63, comprising 30 for USAAC observation squadrons and 33 for US National Guard
O-38C: single aircraft similar to the O-38B for use by US Coast Guard
O-38E: with widened and deepened fuselage on lines of private-venture O-38S, with a sliding canopy over cockpits; powered by 466-kW (625-hp) Pratt & Whitney R-1690-13 radial engine with metal propeller; could be operated on twin Edo floats; US National Guard took delivery of 37
O-38F: eight delivered to US National Guard in 1933; powered by R-1690-9 radial and with revised fully enclosed canopy; unarmed staff liaison machines
O-38S: private-venture development of the O-38 with a wider and deeper fuselage, crew canopy and smooth-cowled 429-kW (575-hp) Wright R-1820-E radial; in effect was the prototype of the O-38E
Export Observation Biplanes: eight examples of the O-2C were purchased by Mexico, and followed in 1929 by eight examples of the O-2M, a version of the O-32A but with the 391-kW (525-hp) Pratt & Whitney Hornet radial engine; six of the **O-38P**, a version of the O-38E which could have wheel or float landing gear, were delivered to Peru's naval air arm during 1932; Chinese orders were impressive, totalling 82 aircraft in a six-year period beginning in 1930 – 10 **O-2MC** aircraft,

closely resembling the O-38 except for their Hornet radials, were followed by 20 examples of the **O-2MC-2**, which had the cylinders of their Hornet engines surrounded by a Townend ring, by five of the **O-2MC-3** variant with an uprated 429-kW (575-hp) Hornet, by 12 **O-2MC-4** and by 12 **O-2MC-5** aircraft with the less powerful Pratt & Whitney Wasp C1 delivering 313 kW (420 hp), by 22 **O-2MC-6** machines with 429-kW (575-hp) Wright R-1820-E radials, and by a single **O-2MC-10** with a 500-kW (670-hp) Wright R-1820-F21 radial engine
XA-2: the 46th aircraft of the original O-2 contract was completed as an attack aircraft; it was powered by a 313-kW (420-hp) Liberty V-1410 inverted-Vee engine, and with a total of eight machine-guns (two in the engine cowling, two in the upper wing, two in the lower wing and twin guns on a ring-mounting operated by the observer) was remarkably well armed for its day; it competed against the Curtiss A-3 in 1926 but was not selected for production
OD-1: designation applied to two O-2Cs, ordered by the US Navy, which served with the US Marine Corps from 1929

Specification
Douglas O-2
Type: two-seat observation biplane
Powerplant: one 313-kW (420-hp) Liberty V-1650-1 V-12 piston engine
Performance: maximum speed 206 km/h (128 mph); service ceiling 4960 m (16,270 ft); range 579 km (360 miles)
Weights: empty equipped 1375 kg (3,032 lb); maximum take-off 2170 kg (4,785 lb)
Dimensions: span 12.09 m (39 ft 8 in); length 8.76 m (28 ft 9 in); height 3.20 m (10 ft 6 in); wing area 38.18 m² (411.0 sq ft)
Armament: one fuselage-mounted forward-firing synchronised 7.62-mm (0.3-in) machine-gun and one similar gun on a ring mounting in the rear cockpit, plus four racks each for a bomb of up to 45 kg (100 lb)

Douglas 0-31, 0-43 and 0-46
to
Enstrom F-28/280 Shark

Douglas O-31, O-43 and O-46

Anxious to retain its position as chief supplier of observation aircraft to the US Army Air Corps, the Douglas company developed a proposal for a high-wing monoplane to succeed the biplane types which in the late 1920s were nearing the end of their development potential. A contract was signed in January 1930 for two **Douglas XO-31** aircraft, the first of them being flown in December of that same year. A gull-wing monoplane, it had open tandem cockpits for the pilot and observer, a slim fuselage with a 447-kW (600-hp) Curtiss Conqueror V-1570-25 V-12 engine, and split-axle landing gear with provision for large wheel fairings. The wing was wire-braced above to a four-strut cabane over the fuselage, and below to the lower section of the fuselage itself. The all-metal aircraft had excellent lines, somewhat marred by the corrugated duralumin skinning which covered the fuselage aft of the engine cowling.

The XO-31 suffered from directional instability and experiments were made with various fin and rudder shapes, and with auxiliary tail fins in order to cure the problem. The second aircraft was completed as the **YO-31**, differing mainly in having a geared version of the Conqueror engine and an enlarged fin. Four **YO-31A** aircraft delivered during the first half of 1932 were modified radically, having elliptical wings, a new tail assembly, a semi-monocoque fuselage with smooth metal-sheet covering, and a canopy over the crew cockpits. They appeared with a variety of tail units, the

The YO-31A was the precursor of a distinguished line, but one of the features destined to disappear along the production run was the gull wing.

final version (when the machines were redesignated **O-31A**) featuring a very tall pointed fin with an inset rudder. The single **YO-31B** was an unarmed staff transport and the sole **YO-31C** had cantilever spatted landing gear and a ventral bulge in the fuselage, which enabled the observer to operate his single 7.62-mm (0.3-in) machine-gun more effectively from a standing position.

Five **Y10-31A** service-test aircraft were ordered in the summer of 1931, being delivered to the USAAC in the spring of 1933 under the designation **Y10-43**. They differed considerably from the final configuration of the O-31As, with wire-braced parasol wings and a revised tail unit with a new fin and rudder. They went into service under the designation **O-43**. An order for 23 **O-43A** aircraft was completed during 1934, this variant differing from the O-43s in having a deepened fuselage, which obviated the need for the ventral bulge under the gunner's position, together with an enlarged fin with inset rudder similar to that of the O-31A. The crew canopy was enlarged, and fully enclosed both cockpits. O-43s and O-43As served with US Army Air Corps observation squadrons for several years before being assigned to reserve National Guard units.

The 24th airframe of the O-43A contract was completed as the **XO-46** prototype, which differed from the O-43A in having its wing braced on each side by parallel streamlined struts, thus dispensing with the cabane-type wire bracing of all the earlier Douglas high-wing observation aircraft. And, for the first time, a radial engine (the Pratt & Whitney R-1535-7) replaced the previously favoured V-12 powerplant. The XO-46 passed its tests with flying colours and an order for 71 **O-46A** production aircraft was subsequently increased to 90 machines, delivered between May 1936 and April 1937. The O-46As differed externally from the XO-46 in having their crew canopies faired into the raised rear fuselage decking.

O-46As served with US Army Air Corps observation squadrons until 1940, when most were transferred to reserve National Guard units before being finally withdrawn for training duties in 1942. The last first-line USAAC unit to operate the O-46A was the 2nd Observation Squadron, which had several on charge when the Japanese attacked its base at

Nichols Field in the Philippines in December 1941.

Specification
Douglas O-46A
Type: two-seat observation monoplane
Powerplant: one 541-kW (725-hp) Pratt & Whitney R-1535-7 radial piston engine
Performance: maximum speed 322 km/h (200 mph); cruising speed 275 km/h (171 mph); service ceiling 7360 m (24,150 ft); range 700 km (435 miles)
Weights: empty equipped 2166 kg (4,776 lb); maximum take-off 3011 kg (6,639 lb)
Dimensions: span 13.94 m (45 ft 9 in); length 10.53 m (34 ft 6¾ in); height 3.25 m (10 ft 8 in); wing area 30.84 m² (332.0 sq ft)
Armament: one fixed forward-firing 7.62-mm (0.3-in) machine-gun in leading edge of starboard wing and one similar gun on ring mounting in the observer's cockpit

Douglas SBD Dauntless

Without any doubt the **Douglas SBD Dauntless** must be regarded as being the most successful dive-bomber produced by the American aviation industry during World War II. It was successful both in terms of achievement and longevity, blunting the might of the Japanese navy in actions in the Coral Sea, Midway and during the Solomons campaign, and continuing to offer a valuable contribution to US Navy and US Marine Corps actions until late 1944, long after contemporary creations had disappeared from the scene.

A product of John Northrop's influence on Douglas design philosophy, the Dauntless stemmed from the Northrop BT-1 which began to enter service with the US Navy in spring 1938. One of the production BT-1s served as the prototype for a new naval dive-bomber allocated the designation **XBT-2**; however, by the time that this entered production in 1940, Northrop had become a division of the Douglas Company, resulting in the **SBD** designation. The chief designer throughout was Ed Heinemann.

There had been structural and engine changes, and while the SBD retained a general family likeness to its progenitor, it was really a very different aeroplane. Of low-wing cantilever monoplane configuration, it was all-metal of construction except for fabric-covered control surfaces. Fuselage construction included a number of watertight compart-

ments, the tail unit was conventional, and the main units of the tailwheel-type landing gear retracted inward. Arrester gear was provided for shipboard operation. The two-man crew, in tandem cockpits, was accommodated beneath a continuous transparent canopy and provided with dual controls. Powerplant of the prototype was a 746-kW (1,000-hp) Wright XR-1820-32 Cyclone radial engine.

Testing of the prototype showed not only its superiority over the earlier Northrop BT-1, but also performance and flight characteristics that immediately singled it out as an exceptional aircraft. Initial production orders for 57 **SBD-1** and 87 **SBD-2** aircraft were placed on 8 April

1939, the SBD-2s differing by having increased fuel capacity and armament revisions. SBD-1s began to enter service with the US Marine Corps in late 1940, equipping Marine Squadron VMB-2, with deliveries to VMB-1 following in early 1941. The SBD-2s went to the US Navy, and by the end of 1941 were serving aboard the USS *Enterprise* with Squadrons VB-6 and VS-6, and with VB-2 on the USS *Lexington*.

An improved **SBD-3** version began to enter service in March 1941, introducing self-sealing tanks (and with increased fuel capacity), armour protection, a bullet-proof windscreen, a 746-kW (1,000-hp) Wright R-1820-52 engine, and armament changes that initiated the standard

Douglas SBD-5 Dauntless of Escuadron Aéreo de Pelea 200, Fuerza Aérea Mexicana (Mexican air force), based at Pie de la Cuesta in 1946.

of two 12.7-mm (0.5-in) and two 7.62-mm (0.3-in) machine-guns. The SBD-3 was followed into production by the **SBD-4**, which differed only in having a 24-volt instead of 12-volt electrical system. Production of these two versions totalled 1,364 units, making possible a wider distribution of these much-needed and important aircraft to US Navy and to many US Marine Corps squadrons. Some 16 SBD-4s were later fitted as reconnaissance aircraft with the designation **SBD-4P**.

Most extensively built was the **SBD-5**, produced in a new Douglas factory at Tulsa, Oklahoma. This differed from earlier versions in having a 895-kW (1,200-hp) R-1820-60 engine and increased ammunition capacity, and introduced illuminated gunsights for both the fixed forward-firing and rear cockpit flexibly-mounted machine-guns. A total of 2,409 was built for the US Navy before Douglas turned to the final production variant, the **SBD-6**, with an even more powerful R-1820-66 engine and increased fuel tankage. Also supplied to the US Navy in small numbers were photo-reconnaissance variants of the earlier production versions, with camera installations and related equipment, under the designations **SBD-1P**, **SBD-2P** and **SBD-3P**. Nine examples of the SBD-5 version were supplied for service with the Royal Navy's Fleet Air Arm in January 1945, these being designated **Dauntless DB.Mk I**, but none of them were used operationally. Another small quantity was supplied to Mexico. Although US Navy and US Marine Corps use of the Dauntless in a first-line capacity tailed off in late 1944, many late-version aircraft remained in use for some years after the end of World War II.

The success of the German Junkers Ju 87 as a dive-bomber, when Hitler's armoured columns raced over much of Europe in 1940, made the US Army conscious of the fact that it possessed no significant aircraft within this category. Accordingly, 168 of the US Navy's SBD-3 version were ordered from Douglas as a matter of some urgency, these being delivered in the summer of 1941 under the US Army designation **A-24**. They were virtually identical to the SBD-3 (in contracts the designation **SBD-3A** was used), except for the deletion of the arrester hook, and the provision of an inflated tailwheel tyre instead of the solid rubber favoured by the US Navy. About a third of these aircraft were despatched to the Philippines in November 1941 for service with the USAAF's 27th Bombardment Group, but as they were still at sea when Pearl Harbor was attacked they were diverted instead to Australia, equipping the 91st Bombardment Squadron in February 1942, and subsequently the 8th Bombardment Squadron. Both of these units found the A-24 lacking in performance and range for operational deployment in this theatre.

Despite these apparent shortcomings, the US Army continued to procure A-24s, during 1942 receiving first 170 **A-24A** aircraft equivalent to the US

Douglas SBD Dauntless

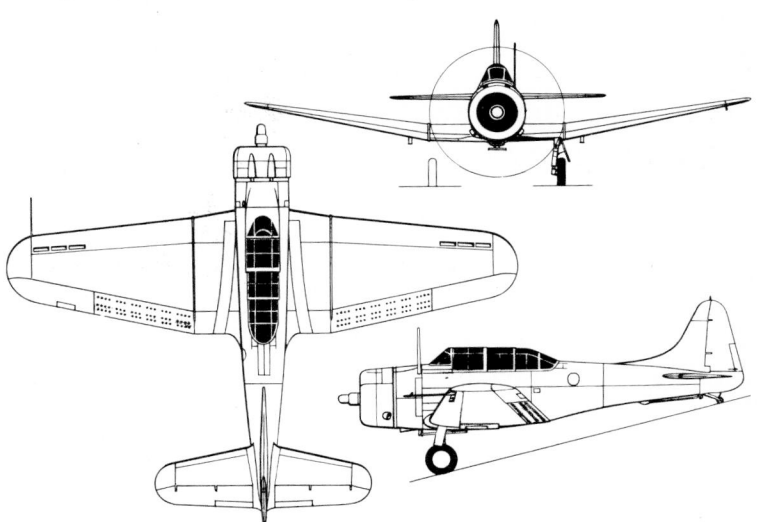

Navy's SBD-4 (and contractually designated **SBD-4A**), and finally 615 **A-24B (SBD-5A)** aircraft. These machines met with no significant success, confirming the experience of Ju 87 usage in Europe and Asia, that their role was strictly confined: within that limited role, of course, they were indeed the 'tool for the job'. Their failure in US Army service was due to the fact that there was no identical job for them to do. Despite this, a number remained in USAAF/USAF use for some years after World War II. One A-24A was converted into the sole **A-24A** radio-controlled drone, and when in 1948 all surviving A-24As were redesignated **F-24A** this aircraft became the **QF-24A**. At the same time the A-25Bs were redesignated **F-24B**, a single drone-director being the **DF-24B**.

Clearly visible under the fuselage of these SBDs is the crutch which swung forward to release the bomb clear of the propeller arc.

Specification
Douglas SBD-6
Type: two-seat scout/dive-bomber
Powerplant: one 1007-kW (1,350-hp) Wright R-1820-66 Cyclone 9 radial piston engine
Performance: maximum speed 410 km/h (255 mph) at 4265 m (14,000 ft); cruising speed 298 km/h (185 mph) at 4265 m (14,000 ft); service ceiling 7680 m (25,200 ft); range as a scout-bomber 1244 km (773 miles)
Weights: empty 2964 kg (6,535 lb); maximum take-off 4318 kg (9,519 lb)
Dimensions: span 12.65 m (41 ft 6 in); length 10.06 m (33 ft 0 in); height 3.94 m (12 ft 11 in); wing area 30.19 m² (325.0 sq ft)
Armament: two forward-firing 12.7-mm (0.5-in) machine-guns and two 7.62-mm (0.3-in) machine-guns on flexible mount, plus underfuselage mountings for up to 726 kg (1,600 lb) of bombs and up to a total of 295 kg (650 lb) carried beneath the wings

---

Douglas T2D

In July 1925 the US Navy Bureau of Aeronautics ordered three **Douglas XT2D-1** twin-engined torpedo-bomber/general-purpose biplanes. They were required to be suitable for use with wheel or float landing gear, and for operation from aircraft-carriers. Two months earlier a single XTN-1 aircraft, with similar general characteristics, had been ordered from the US Naval Aircraft Factory.

The first XT2D-1 prototype flew on 27 January 1927 as a landplane. Soon afterwards its 373-kW (500-hp) Wright P-2 radial engines were replaced by Wright R-1750s and the other two prototypes were similarly re-engined. The three aircraft participated successfully in trials with US Navy Torpedo Squadron VT-2 in spring 1927 and, in consequence, nine examples of the production **T2D-1** were purchased.

The basic configuration of the XT2D-1 prototypes was retained, the aircraft being characterised by their bluff noses with angled bomb- or torpedo-aiming panel, large single fin and rudder, wide-track divided landing gear capable of easy conversion to take twin floats, and two-bay equal-span wings with rounded tips. The fuselage of the T2D-1 was, however, 0.90 m (2 ft 11½ in) shorter

than that of the XT2D-1 and the engine nacelles were repositioned. A crew of four was carried, the pilot and co-pilot in tandem open cockpits, with gunner/bomb-aimer in the nose and radio-operator/gunner in the fourth cockpit amidships.

The T2D-1 performed satisfactorily in service, operating from aircraft-carriers (being the first twin-engined aircraft to do so) during the 1928 US Navy fleet exercises. However, its size precluded embarkation of the carrier's full aircraft complement and, as a result, the type was re-allocated to patrol squadrons. T2D-1s flew subsequently with VP-1 and VP-2 from Pearl Harbor, Hawaii, operating on wheels or twin floats as required until scrapped in 1933.

Variant
P2D-1: in June 1930 the Douglas company received an order for 18 aircraft based on the T2D-1, but intended specifically for over-sea patrol duties; these new **P2D-1** aircraft had twin fins and rudders to ensure better flight characteristics, particularly with one engine inoperative, and were powered by 429-kW (575-hp) Wright R-1820-E radial engines; deliveries were completed by the end of 1931 and the P2D-1s, almost always in twin-float configuration, flew with VP-3 of

the US Navy stationed in the Panama Canal Zone, until withdrawn from first-line service in 1937

Specification
Douglas T2D-1 (land plane)
Type: torpedo-bomber/general-purpose biplane
Powerplant: two 391-kW (525-hp) Wright R-1750 radial piston engines
Performance: maximum speed 201 km/h (125 mph); service ceiling 4215 m (13,830 ft); range 735 km (457 miles)
Weights: empty 2726 kg (6,011 lb);

Ordered under the designation T2D-2, the P2D-1 was redesignated to reflect the type's primary role of overwater patrol, here with squadron VP-3.

maximum take-off 4773 kg (10,523 lb)
Dimensions: span 17.37 m (57 ft 0 in); length 12.80 m (42 ft 0 in); height 4.85 m (15 ft 11 in); wing area 82.31 m² (886.0 sq ft)
Armament: two flexible 7.62-mm (0.3-in) machine-guns, plus one 734-kg (1,618-lb) torpedo or equivalent weight in bombs

Douglas XT3D

Designed and built to meet a US Navy requirement for a three-seat torpedo-bomber, the **Douglas XT3D-1** prototype was flown for the first time in early 1931. A large and ugly biplane, basically of metal construction with fabric covering, the XT3D-1 incorporated folding wings and arrester gear for carrier-based operations, had fixed tailwheel landing gear, and was powered initially by a Pratt & Whitney S2B1-C Hornet radial piston engine. Accommodation was provided for a crew of three in open cockpits, a bomb-aimer/gunner forward, the pilot in the centre cockpit, just aft of the wing trailing edge, and a second gunner to his rear.

Failing to meet requirements in its initial service trials, the XT3D-1 was returned to Douglas for modification, gaining a more powerful 597-kW (800-hp) Pratt & Whitney XR-1830-54 radial engine, wheel fairings for the main units and an enclosed canopy for the two rear-most cockpits. Redesignated **XT3D-2**, it was returned for further service testing but again failed to attract a production order. It was flown by the US Navy for about 10 years for general-purpose duties before being relegated for use as an instructional airframe in 1941.

Specification
Douglas XT3D-1
Type: three-seat torpedo-bomber prototype
Powerplant: one 429-kW (575-hp) Pratt & Whitney S2B1-G Hornet radial piston engine
Performance: maximum speed 206 km/h (128 mph) at 1830 m (6,000 ft); service ceiling 4265 m (14,000 ft); range 893 km (555 miles)
Weights: empty 1922 kg (4,238 lb); maximum take-off 3564 kg (7,857 lb)
Dimensions: span 15.24 m (50 ft 0 in); length 10.79 m (35 ft 5 in); height 4.03 m (13 ft 2½ in); wing area 57.97

m² (624.0 sq ft)
Armament: two 7.62-mm (0.3-in) machine-guns (on flexible mounts in front and rear cockpits), plus one 832-kg (1,835-lb) torpedo or an equivalent weight in bombs

The XT3D-2 was the XT3D-1 extensively modified to improve performance. An uprated powerplant was fitted, with a full NACA cowl instead of a Townend ring.

EH Industries EH.101

One of the most important helicopter programmes at present under way in Europe, the **EH.101** based on the Westland WG 34 design. Before even a prototype had been completed, however, the WG 34 project was cancelled in the expectation that this would pave the way for a revised design which would satisfy the needs of the Italian navy as well as the Royal Navy. Westland and Agusta began negotiations for a collaborative undertaking in November 1979, and the result was European Helicopter Industries Ltd. established in June 1980 to manage the overall programme which was approved in February 1984. Both governments agreed to the financing of nine experimental helicopters and later the full development of the **EH.101**.

Consideration was given to roles including transport and the utility task. Some of these roles can be implemented with the unchanged airframe of the baseline naval helicopter, while others require modification of the fuselage structure to permit the incorporation of features such as a ventral ramp/door arrangement in a fuselage adapted to the pod-and-boom type. The nine prototype helicopters ordered were assigned to particular functions, such as proving of the dynamic system, anti-submarine equipment, combat and transport/ supply features, general-purpose civilian aspects, and passenger capability for the **Heliliner** commercial model.

The **EH.101** is a three-engined helicopter with a main rotor comprising a composite rotor head carrying five composite-structure blades with BERP high-speed blade tips. Composite materials are used extensively in other parts of the structure although the fuselage is mainly of aluminium alloy construction. On-board systems and equipment vary in accordance with the helicopter's role and operator. For the Royal Navy, the **Merlin HAS.Mk 1** shipboard anti-submarine model has IBM as joint prime contractor with Westland for the provision and integration of the advanced mission equipment, and further avionics equipment includes GEC Ferranti Blue Kestrel search radar with 360° coverage, GEC Avionics AQS-950 acoustic data processing and display system, Racal 'Orange Reaper' ESM,

Ferranti-Thomson dipping sonar, and sonobuoys launched by two rotary dispensers. The Merlin's armament consists of four Marconi Sting Ray homing torpedoes. An alternative anti-ship missile armament of Exocet, Harpoon, Sea Eagle or Marte Mk 2 anti-ship guided missiles can also be carried.

The initial Royal Navy requirement for 50 Merlin helicopters for service on board 'Type 23' class frigates, 'Invincible' class aircraft carriers, ships of the Royal Fleet Auxiliary and land bases) was to 44 examples which are scheduled to enter service in 1998 with the powerplant of three 1724-kW (2,312-shp) Rolls-Royce/Turboméca RTM 322 turboshafts, the Italian navy wants to procure 24 helicopters with the powerplant of three 1278-kW (1,715-shp) General Electric T700-GE-T6A turboshafts assembled in Italy: the Italian prototypes have the CT7-6 civil version of this engine.

The **PP1** first prototype made its maiden flight at Yeovilton on 9 October 1987, and the similar **PP2** prototype flew in Italy on 26 November 1987. Next the **PP6** Italian ASW prototype flew in Italy on 26 April 1989, followed by its **PP4** British counterpart on 15 June of the same year. The **PP5 Merlin** prototype had its maiden flight on 24 October, the **PP3** and **PP8** prototypes were produced to the civil standard, and the **PP7** prototype of the military variant with rear ramp/door first flew on 18 December 1989 in Italy.

The lead customer for the general-purpose version was Canada, which ordered an initial 50 **EH.101** helicopters as 15 multi-role machines for the SAR role and 35 helicopters for the shipboard role in succession to the CH-124 version of the Sea King in fulfilment of its New Shipborne Aircraft requirement. These **EH.101**s were to have been assembled by IMP Group Ltd. in Canada with a powerplant of three 1454-kW (1,950-shp) CT7-6A1 turboshafts. The entire Canadian EH.101 programme was cancelled with the change of the Canadian government in 1993, and only in 1998 was it partially revived with an order for the Cormorant general-purpose helicopter based on the civil EH.101 with GEC-Marconi Cormorant dunking sonar.

Specification
European Helicopter Industries EH.101 Merlin HAS.Mk 1
Type: four-seat anti-submarine helicopter
Powerplant: three 1724-kW (2,312-shp) Rolls-Royce/Turboméca RTM 322-01 turboshafts
Performance: maximum speed 309 km/h (192 mph) at sea level; cruising speed, average 278 km/h (173 mph) at optimum altitude and economical 259 km/h (161 mph); service ceiling 4570 m (15,000 ft); hovering ceiling 721 m (2,365 ft) in ground effect and 370 m (1,215 ft) out of ground effect; range 1490 km (926 miles)
Weights: empty 10500 kg (23,149 lb); maximum take-off 13000 kg (28,660 lb)
Dimensions: main rotor diameter 18.59 m (61 ft 0 in); length overall 22.81 m (74 ft 10 in) with rotors turning; height 6.65 m (21 ft 10 in) with rotors turning; main rotor disc area 271.50 m2 (2,922.46 sq ft)
Armament: up to 960 kg (2,116 lb) of disposable weapons (see above)

The Merlin HAS.Mk 1 is the new-generation ASW helicopter for the Royal Navy, and designed to operated mainly from 'Type 23' class frigates.

EMBRAER EMB-110 AND EMB-111 Bandeirante

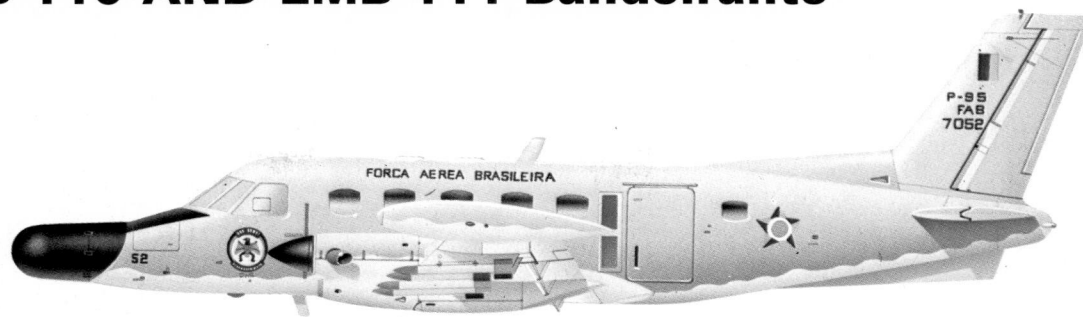

In the mid-1960s the Brazilian air force was still operating the Beech Super 18 for light transport but felt that a more modern type was needed. The Brazilian air ministry's Centro Técnico de Aeronáutica allocated the task to a team headed by Max Holste, the expatriate French designer, whose response was the PAR-6504 low-wing monoplane with semi-retractable tricycle landing gear and two 550-shp (410-kW) Pratt & Whitney Canada PT6A-20 turboprops. Prototype construction was allocated to the Instituto de Pesquisas e Desen-volvimento, and the first of three IPD-6504 (later EMB-100 and YC-95) prototypes flew on 26 October 1968. This nine-passenger type revealed a number of aerodynamic shortcomings and technical infelicities, but an improvement programme would clearly yield a type that was well suited to the needs of the Brazilian air force and also become a strong contender in the growing world market for third-level and commuter airliners.

Thus the nacelles were revised to allow for 680-shp (507-kW) PT6A-27 turboprops as well as fully retractable main landing gear units, the fuel capacity was increased, the rear fuselage was lengthened and fitted with an enlarged vertical tail surface, the forward fuselage was revised for improved streamlining, the central fuselage was modified with provision for an inbuilt airstair door and square windows in place of the original round units, and accommodation was provided for between 12 and 16 passengers.

By now the program had been taken over by EMBRAER, and the first **EMB-110** flew on 9 August 1972 before the baseline **EMB-110 Bandeirante** (pioneer) entered production for service with the Brazilian air force from February 1973 as the C-95 general-purpose transport with a payload of 12 passengers. Deliveries to the Brazilian air force totalled 58 aircraft at the start of a development and manufacturing effort that saw the delivery of 500

EMBRAER P-95 (EMB-111A/A) of the 7° Grupo de Aviaçao, Forca Aérea Brasileira's maritime command, based at Salvador.

The **EMB-110B** is the photo-survey version with a flight crew of two and accommodation for five (normally three) in the cabin, Doppler navigation, and a door over the ventral window for Zeiss vertical cameras. The Brazilian air force took six of the type with the designation **RC-95**. The **EMB-110B1** is the transport counterpart of the **EMB-110B** with quick-change accommodation for up to 14 passengers.

The **EMB-110C** is an improved transport with accommodation for 15 passengers or equivalent freight load. The variant was intended for the civil market, but five were delivered to the Uruguayan air force and a version sold to the Chilean navy (three aircraft for maritime patrol) is designated **EMB-110C(N)**. The **EMB-110E(J)** was produced for the executive transport market with seating for seven or eight passengers. The **EMB-110K1** is an improved freighter with two 559-kW (750-shp) PT6A-34 turboprops, the forward fuselage stretched by 0.85 m (2 ft 9.5 in) to permit the carriage of a payload of 1880 kg (4,125 lb) loaded and unloaded through a port-side rear cargo door, and a ventral fin added to offset the destabilising effect of the longer forward fuselage. The Brazilian

The Bandeirante found favour with a large number of regional airlines in several parts of the world and in particular the USA.

cabin; **EMB-110P1A** updated version of the **EMB-110P1** with a dihedralled tailplane and other improvements; **EMB-110P1K** military derivative of the **EMB-110P1**; **EMB-110P1SAR** for the SAR role with a pair of bulged observation windows on the rear sides of the cabin, a maximum take-off weight of 6000 kg (13,228 lb) with a cabin laid out for six litters plus seats for two observers, and provision for air-dropped inflatable dinghies and other SAR stores; **EMB-110P2** for 21 passengers; **EMB-110P2A** version of the **EMB-110P2** with the same updating features as the **EMB-110P1A**; and **EMB-110P/41** with the maximum take-off weight increased to 5900 kg (13,010 lb) and provided in **EMB-110P1/41**, **EMB-110P1A/41**, **EMB-110P2/41** and **EMB-110P2A /41** subvariants. A pressurised model, the **EMB-110P3**, did not enter production. The Brazilian air force took 31 **EMB-110P1Ks** as 29 **C-95B** transports and two **EC-95B** navaid calibration aircraft, five **EMB-110P1SARs** as **SC-95B** aircraft, and 10 **EMB-110P1As** as **C-95C** aircraft, while Colombia and Peru bought two and three examples respectively of the **EMB-110P1A**.

The **EMB-111A Bandeirante Patrulha** is the land-based maritime reconnaissance aeroplane that was derived from the **EMB-110** transport type to meet a requirement of the Brazilian air force's coastal command. After a first flight on 15 August 1977, the type entered service in April 1978 with the service designation **P-95**, and is visually distinguishable from the baseline transport model by its tip tanks and the large nose radome for the Eaton-AIL SPAR-1 (APS-128 Sea Patrol) surveillance radar; other electronic equipment includes the Thomson-CSF DR 2000A Mk II ESM system and the

Litton LN-33 INS. The type also has four underwing hardpoints for up to 1000 kg (2,205 lb) of disposable stores, generally comprising eight 127 mm (5 in) unguided rockets or four multiple launchers each carrying seven 70 mm (2.75 in) unguided rockets, and the **EMB-111A** also features a number of equipment differences including a ventral chute for smoke markers, target-illumination flares and, as an option in place one of the hardpoints, a 50 million-candlepower searchlight installed in the wing leading edge.

Specification
EMBRAER EMB-110P2A Bandeirante
Type: 21-passenger general-purpose transport
Powerplant: two 59-kW (750-shp5) Pratt & Whitney Canada PT6A-34 turboprops
Performance: maximum speed (460 km/h 286 mph) at 2440 m (8,000 ft); cruising speed, maximum 413 km/h (257 mph) at 2440 m (8,000 ft) and economical 335 km/h (208 mph) at 3050 m (10,000 ft); initial climb rate 545 m (1,788 ft) per minute; service ceiling 6860 m (22.500 ft); range 2001 km (1,244 miles) with reserves
Weight: empty 3516 kg (7,751 lb); maximum take-off 5670 kg (12,500 lb)
Dimensions: span 15.33 m (50 ft 3.5 in); length 5.10 m (49 ft 6.5 in1); height 4.92 m (16 ft 1.75 in); area 29.10 m² (313.23 sq ft)

aircraft before the end of production in 1990.

The **EMB-110A** is the navaid calibration version of the **EMB-110** with a flight crew of two and accommodation for six in the cabin. Two such aircraft were delivered to the Brazilian air force with the designation **EC-95**.

air force took 20 examples with the designation **C-95A**.

The **EMB-110P** is a development of the **EMB-110K1** with a flat rather than dihedralled tailplane, and was produced as the basic **EMB-110P** for between 18 and 20 passengers; **EMB-110P1** with a quick-change passenger/freight

EMBRAER EMB-110P1 Bandeirante (side views, from top to bottom: EMB-110B1, EMB-110S1, EMB-110K and EMB-110P1).

EMBRAER EMB-120 Brasilia

Encouraged by the successful penetration of the commuter airline market by the EMB-110 Bandeirante, EMBRAER initiated design studies for a completely new and pressurised twin-turboprop regional airliner in September 1979. Designated the **EMBRAER EMB-120 Brasilia,** the prototype flew for the first time on 27 July 1983 and certification was achieved by May 1985. Primary design objective was to carry a full 30-passenger payload for up to three 185-km (115-mile) sectors without refuelling. The fuselage has an interior diameter of 2.28 m (7 ft 5 in) and a cabin height of 1.76 m (5 ft 9 in), the aisle being offset by the two-and-one seating arrangement. In cargo configuration the Brasilia has a maximum available cabin volume of 31.1 m³ (1,098 cu ft) and is fitted with a cargo door in the starboard side of the rear fuselage.

Powered by advanced-technology Pratt & Whitney Canada PW118 turboprops driving four-bladed Hamilton

Standard 14RF-9 propellers, the engines can be ground-run without turning the propellers to facilitate speedier turn-rounds, thus obviating the need to shut down during loading or unloading. The starboard engine can act as an auxiliary power unit, to provide ground electrical power and cabin air-conditioning, but a conventional APU is optional.

By early 1991 EMBRAER had received 346 orders from over 30 operators around the world, and more than 200 had been delivered since entering service in October 1985, including four VIP transport versions for the Brazilian Air Force designated **VC-97**. Current production rate is six per month.

Specification
EMBRAER EMB-120
Type: 30-seat regional airliner and general transport
Powerplant: two Pratt & Whitney Aircraft of Canada PW118 turboprops each rated at 1342 kW (1,800 shp)

Performance: maximum cruising speed at 6100 m (20,000 ft) 552 km/h (343 mph); economic cruising speed at 7620 m (25,000 ft) 482 km/h (299 mph); service ceiling 9085 m (29,800 ft); range with 30 passengers 1750 km (1,088 miles)
Weights: empty equipped 7070 kg (15,586 lb); maximum take-off 11500 kg (23,353 lb)

A natural successor to the Bandeirante, the larger Brasilia is aimed specifically at third-level operators requiring excellent operating economics.

Dimensions: span 19.78 m (64 ft 10 in); length 20.00 m (65 ft 7 in); height 6.35 m (20 ft 10 in); wing area 39.43 m² (424.42 sq ft)

EMBRAER EMB-121 Xingu

Bearing a likeness to the Bandeirante, the pressurised **EMBRAER EMB-121 Xingu** featured a reduced-span version of the EMB-110P wing, a fuselage of circular cross-section similar to that of the Brasilia, and followed the same general configuration with twin turboprop engines and retractable tricycle landing gear, but differed by having a cantilever T-tail. It was, however, the smallest member of the family, providing accommodation for a crew of two and nine passengers.

The prototype **Xingu** (PP-ZXI) flew for the first time on 10 October 1976, followed by the first production aircraft just over six months later.

When production ceased at the end of 1987, a total of 111 had been built, including six for use by the special transport group of the Brazilian air force under the designation **VU-9**. Other users include the French navy and air force with 41 aircraft, and five others serve with the SABENA pilot training school.

The original version, designated **EMB-121A Xingu I,** was powered by two Pratt & Whitney Canada PT6A-28 turboprop engines. From this was developed the **EMB-121A1 Xingu II** with 559-kW (750-shp) PT6A-135 turboprops, these being available also as retrofits for the Xingu I. Thirty-two earlier machines were later reworked to this standard.

A prototype of the **EMB-121V Xingu III** was flown. It was generally similar to its predecessors except that it had the fuselage lengthened by 0.89 m (2 ft 11 in), and was powered by two 634-kW (850-shp) PT6A-42 engines. Seating the same number of passengers but in greater comfort, the Xingu III featured an optional 'club' layout for seven passengers, with folding tables and a galley.

Specification
EMBRAER EMB-121A Xingu I
Type: general-purpose transport/advanced training aircraft
Powerplant: two 507-kW (680-hp)

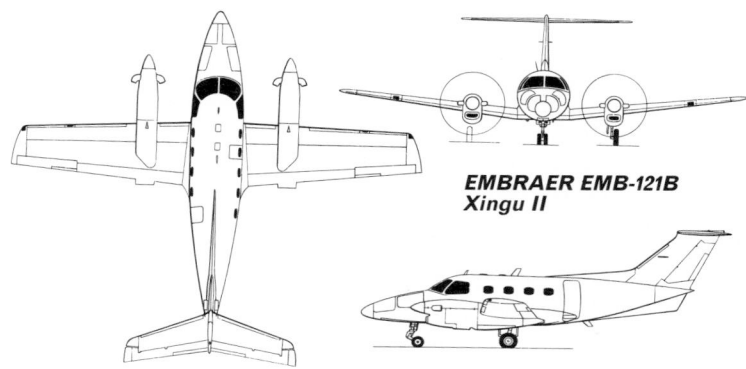

EMBRAER EMB-121B Xingu II

Pratt & Whitney Aircraft of Canada PT6A-28 turboprops
Performance: maximum cruising speed 450 km/h (280 mph); economic cruising speed 365 km/h (227 mph); service ceiling 7925 m (26,000 ft); range with 780-kg (1,720-lb) payload and fuel reserves 2270 km (1,411 miles)

Weights: empty equipped 3620 kg (7,981 lb); maximum take-off 5670 kg (12,500 lb)
Dimensions: span 14.45 m (47 ft 5 in); length 12.25 m (40 ft 2¼ in); height 4.74 m (15 ft 6½ in); wing area 27.5 m² (296.02 sq ft)

EMBRAER EMB-200/201 Ipanema

Design of an agricultural aircraft, to a specification laid down by the Brazilian Ministry of Agriculture, was initiated in May 1969 by the Departmento de Aeronaves of the nation's Centro Téchnico de Aeronáutica. Following the establishment of EMBRAER on 2 January 1970 to promote a Brazilian aircraft industry, responsibility for development of this new single-seat agricultural aircraft was transferred to EMBRAER and the prototype (PP-ZIP) was flown for the first time on 30 July 1970.

Designated originally **EMBRAER EMB-200 Ipanema**, the aircraft was a cantilever low-wing monoplane of all-metal construction with fixed tailwheel landing gear and power provided by a 194-kW (260-hp) Avco Lycoming O-540-H2B5D engine. Brazilian type certification was gained on 14 December 1971

The EMB-201A Ipanema is an improved version of the basic design, playing an important part in Brazil's food production cycle.

and initial production versions were the EMB-200 and **EMB-200A**, which differed by having fixed-pitch and variable-pitch propellers respectively. In 1974, after 73 EMB-200 series aircraft had been built, production of an improved **EMB-201** began; this latter differed by having a 224-kW (300-hp) IO-540 engine with a constant-speed propeller and detail improvements. A total of 200

EMB-201s was built. In 1977, the updated **EMB-201A**, first flown on 10 March, entered production. This introduced a new wing profile, improved systems and revisions in cockpit layout. Built since 1981 by Industria Aeronautica Neiva, an EMBRAER subsidiary, a total of 355 had been ordered by 1990, bringing total Ipanema sales to more than 630.

In 1988, by which time 600 had been delivered, a further improved Ipanema

was launched, but without a new designation, and options include a three-bladed Hartzell propeller.

Variant
EMBRAER EMB-201R: glider-towing version with the wing and tailplane reduced in span, agricultural equipment deleted and a towing hook added; three were supplied to the Brazilian air force academy gliding club under the

designation **U-19**

Specification
EMBRAER EMB-201A
Type: single-seat agricultural aircraft
Powerplant: one 224-kW (300-hp) Avco Lycoming IO-540-K1J5D flat-six piston engine
Performance: (agricultural) maximum speed 225 km/h (140 mph) at sea level; maximum cruising speed

204 km/h (127 mph) at 1830 m (6,000 ft); service ceiling 3470 m (11,395 ft); range 877 km (545 miles)
Weights: empty 1011 kg (2,229 lb); maximum take-off 1800 kg (3,968 lb)
Dimensions: span 11.20 m (36 ft 9 in); length 7.43 m (24 ft 4½ in); height 2.22 m (7 ft 3½ in); wing area 19.94 m² (214.64 sq ft)

EMBRAER EMB-312 Tucano

Work on the **EMBRAER EMB-312 Tucano** (toucan) trainer began in 1978 under the leadership of Joseph Kovacs, and was undertaken in response to the Brazilian air force's requirement for a successor to the **Cessna T-37** in the basic training role. Having made its first flight on 16 August 1980, the first **T-27 Tucano** was delivered in September 1983 to the Air Force Academy near São Paulo, an institution that operates the majority of the 133 such aircraft ordered by the Brazilian air force (including 10 and five examples ordered in 1990 and 1993 respectively), although some machines serve with a conversion unit and also with the Brazilian air force's aerobatic team. An option for a further 35 **T-27**s has been placed with EMBRAER but not yet exercised.

From the start the **Tucano** was intended to provide the performance and handling characteristics typical of current jet-powered aircraft, and for this reason was equipped with a single lever for engine throttling and propeller blade pitch control, as well as a cockpit with a tandem arrangement of vertically staggered ejection seats. The **Tucano** is also equipped for weapons training and light attack, having four hardpoints under the wings for loads of up to 1000 kg (2,205 lb) and including machine-gun pods, multiple rocket launchers and light bombs.

An export order for 134 **Tucanos** was received from Egypt in September 1983 and, with the exception of the first 10 machines, these were assembled at Helwan. The Egyptian air force itself flies only 54 of the aircraft, the other 80 being delivered to the Iraqi air force. Deliveries followed to the air forces of Argentina (30 from May 1987), Colombia (14 from December 1992), Honduras (12 from May 1984), Iran (25 from 1989), Paraguay (six from 1988), Peru (30 from April 1987) and Venezuela (31 from July 1986). One further large order was delivered from July 1994 and comprised 80 examples of the somewhat modified **EMB-312F** variant for France. Evaluated from July of the previous year in the form of two pre-production aircraft, this variant has an airframe optimised for a longer fatigue life, an air brake on the underside of the fuselage, propeller and canopy de-icing, repositioned refuelling and jacking points, and French avionics. The other 78 aircraft were delivered in

batches of 20, 28, 15 and 15 aircraft up to 1998.

The greatest export success occurred in March 1985, when the **Tucano** won the hotly-contested order from the UK for 130 aircraft to succeed the BAe (BAC/Hunting) Jet Provost in service with the Royal Air Force. In order to get this order, **EMBRAER** had implemented a number of significant changes including the replacement of the original engine by the considerably more powerful 820-kW (1,100-shp) AlliedSignal (Garrett) TPE331-12B turboprop and the extensive revision of the airframe and on-board systems in order to fulfil the taxing demands of the RAF. Shorts in Belfast is responsible for the licensed manufacture of the **Tucano**, and as well as the 130 **Tucano T.Mk 1** machines for the RAF it has also produced 12 and 16 examples to the basically same standard for the air forces of Kenya and Kuwait respectively. At the beginning of 1994, the list of firm orders amounted to 653 aircraft, of which almost 600 had been delivered.

In June 1991 **EMBRAER** announced the **EMB-312H** (later **EMB-314**) Super Tucano version with

the more powerful 932-kW (1,250-shp) Pratt & Whitney Canada PT6A-68/1 turboprop. To accommodate this engine and to preserve the aircraft's stability and centre of gravity, the fuselage had to be stretched by 1.37 m (4 ft 6 in) by the insert of 'plugs' ahead of and behind the cockpit. In co-operation with Northrop, **EMBRAER** entered the **EMB-312HJ** subvariant of this uprated model in the USAF/USN Joint Primary Aircraft Training System competition, but this became one of several types beaten to the large production order by the Raytheon Beech Mk II version of the Pilatus PC-9. The development cost was not wasted, however, for in August 1995 the Brazilian air force decided to take a development of this model to meet its AL-X requirement for a light attack model with higher-rated hardpoints and more advanced avionics including a head-up display, head-down displays, GPS-uprated inertial navigation system, mission computer and cockpit lighting compatible with night vision goggles. Intended for the Amazon surveillance role, the variant will be built in A-29 single-seat and AT-29 two-seat variants, the latter with a FLIR sensor providing night targeting capability.

Specification
EMBRAER EMB-312 Tucano
Type: two-seat basic trainer
Powerplant: one 559-kW (750-shp) Pratt & Whitney Canada PT6A-25C turboprop
Performance: maximum speed 448 km/h (278 mph) at 3050 m (10,000 ft); cruising speed, maximum 411 km/h (255 mph) and economical 319 km/h (198 mph), both at 3050 m (10,000 ft); initial climb rate 680 m (2,231 ft) per minute; service ceiling 9145 m (30,000 ft); range 3330 km (2,069 miles) with underwing tank and 1843 km (1,145 miles) with internal fuel
Weights: empty 1870 kg (4,123 lb); normal take-off 2550 kg (5,622 lb); maximum take-off 3175 kg (7,000 lb)
Dimensions: span 11.14 m (36 ft 6.5 in); length 9.86 m (32 ft 4.25 in); height 3.40 m (11 ft 1.75 in); area 19.40 m2 (208.82 sq ft)
Armament: up to 1000 kg (2,205 lb) of disposable stores (see above)

The Tucano has been especially successful in winning export sales in South America. Venezuela has received 31 Tucanos which are used for riot control (in camouflage) and training (in silver).

EMBRAER EMB-145 Jetliner

At the Paris Air Show in June 1989 EMBRAER announced the development of a 45/48-seat turbofan-powered regional airliner based on its turboprop-powered **EMB-120 Brasilia** transport. A minimum-change design process led initially to the **EMB-145 Amazon** in which a modified version of the **EMB-120**'s airframe (with a lengthened fuselage) was combined with the

revised powerplant of two 31.14-kN (7,000-lb st) Allison AE 3007 turbofans in nacelles located above the wing roots with their inlets slightly ahead of the wings' leading edge. This concept was adopted in an effort to keep the development costs, estimated at about US $200 million, as low as possible and to achieve operating costs comparable with those of large turboprop-powered

aircraft, and **EMBRAER** envisaged that the Amazon would have between 70 per cent and 75 per cent commonality with the Brasilia.

Wind-tunnel tests in the third quarter of 1990 revealed several shortcomings, so the design was reworked between October 1990 and March 1991 to implement changes to the wings, landing gear and powerplant installation. The CTA testing and research laboratory in São Jose dos Campos then carried out further tests,

which were subsequently verified in the Boeing wind tunnel in Seattle, and as a result a series of further changes was announced in April 1991: the previous straight wing planform was replaced by a shorter and stiffer wing of supercritical section and swept at 22.3°, the engines mounted on pylons under the wings, and the forward fuselage lengthened so that a longer nosewheel unit could be incorporated. Further changes were announced in October 1991 after the engine installation had been altered to nacelles pylon-mounted on the sides of the rear fuselage. Subsonic and transonic wind tunnel tests confirmed the sound nature of these changes and indicated significant improvement in performance, and the design was finally frozen in July 1992.

In February 1993 Parker-Hannifin of the USA and GAMESA of Spain came on board the programme as risk-sharing partners: the first was responsible for the control surfaces and provision of on-board systems, while the latter took on the development and construction of the wings and engine nacelles. Companies that later became involved in the programme included Sonaca of Belgium (centre and rear fuselage sections plus engine pylons), ENAER of Chile (tail unit), Norton of the USA (nose radome), and C & D Interiors of the USA (passenger cabin and baggage compartment interiors).

Specification
EMBRAER EMB-145
Type: 50-passenger regional airliner
Powerplant: two 31.32-kN (7,040-lb st) Allison AE 3007A turbofans
Performance: cruising speed, maximum 823 km/h (511 mph) at 11280 m (37,000 ft) and economical 680 km/h (423 mph) at 9755 m (32,000 ft); initial climb rate 725 m (2,379 ft) per minute; service ceiling 11280 m (37,000 ft); range 1569 km (975 miles) with maximum payload
Weights: empty 11690 kg (25,772 lb); maximum take-off 19200 kg (42,328 lb)
Dimensions: span 20.04 m (65 ft 9 in); length 29.87 m (98 ft 0 in); height 6.75 m (22 ft 1.75 in); area 51.18 m² (550.91 sq ft)

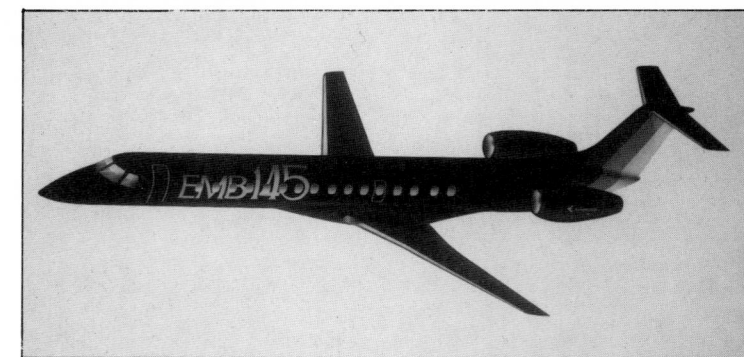

Both of EMBRAER's third-generation regional airliners are derived from the Brasilia. The turbofan-powered EMB-145 had a laborious birth with many changes of configuration, in particular with regard to the location of the engines.

EMBRAER/FMA CBA-123 Vector

For its third-generation turboprop airliner, EMBRAER relied on the experience it had gained with the highly successful **Bandeirante** and **Brasilia** programmes. Outlined in their most important features, the characteristics desired in the new type were accommodation for 19 passengers, lower fuel consumption, higher speed with full payload, higher cruising altitude, better rates of climb and descent for manoeuvring in the air within the context of high traffic densities, and better field performance (shorter take-off and landing distances).

The company took the design of the new aeroplane, announced as the **EMB-123**, into the marketplace during 1985. Subsequent negotiations with the Argentine Fábrica Militar de Aviones (FMA) led to the decision to enter into a technical, industrial and commercial collaboration programme, and in May 1987 the two partners signed a 70/30 agreement for co-operative development of what was now the **CBA-123 Vector**.

The structure of the **Vector** had approximately 60 per cent commonality with that of the **Brasilia**, although the conventional low-wing monoplane design featured a completely new propulsion concept with a T-tail above the carbonfibre nacelles that were carried on pylons extending up and out from the rear fuselage to carry not the otherwise standard pair of turbofans but rather two turboprops driving pusher propellers. This arrangement lowered cabin noise levels and at the same time allowed the creation of fuselage and nacelle designs of exceptionally clean aerodynamic form. The fuselage was in essence a shortened version of the Brasilia's

fuselage and was combined with completely redesigned wings of supercritical section with double-slotted Fowler flaps on their trailing edges. The powerplant comprised two electronically controlled Garrett TPF351-20 turboprops, derated to 969 kW (1,300 shp), driving a pair of Hartzell counter-rotating propellers that each comprised six scimitar-shaped auto-feathering and reversible-pitch blades.

Three prototypes were built, two of them in Brazil and the other in Argentina. The first prototype made its maiden flight on 18 July 1990, and the second followed in March 1991. Then in 1992 the straitened financial situation in which EMBRAER found itself let to an interruption in the further development of the Vector. Meanwhile

the Vector prototypes had accomplished a total of 975 test flights by June 1993. The decision to start series production at the beginning of 1994 depended on confirmation of the government orders from the Brazilian and Argentine authorities, whose air forces had expressed the desire for 40 and 20 aircraft respectively, but this confirmation was not forthcoming and the Vector programme fell into abeyance.

Specification
EMBRAER/FMA CBA-123 Vector
Type: 19-passenger regional and corporate transport
Powerplant: two 969-kW (1,300-shp) Garrett TPF531-20/20A turboprops
Performance: cruising speed, maximum 594 km/h (370 mph) at 7315 m (24,000 ft) and economical 569 km/h (354 mph) at 9145 m (30,000 ft); initial climb rate 716 m (2,350 ft) per minute; service ceiling 10670 m (35,000 ft); range 1851 km (1,150 miles) with 19 passengers and standard fuel or 3055 km (1,900 miles) with nine passengers and auxiliary fuel
Weights: empty 6230 kg (13,735 lb); maximum take-off 9500 kg (20,944 lb)
Dimensions: span 17.72 m (58 ft 1.5 in); length 18.09 m (59 ft 4.25 in); height 5.97 m (19 ft 7 in); area 27.20 m² (292.79 sq ft)

The Vector had a novel configuration with rear-mounted engines and pusher propellers. With a speed of almost 600 km/h (373 mph), it was one of the fastest aircraft of its type.

ENAER T-35 Pillán and T-35DT Aucán

In the early 1980s ENAER had assembled 27 **Piper PA-28 Dakota** aircraft for flying clubs and the Chilean air force. When the latter required a similar two-seat trainer with full aerobatic capability, Piper developed the **PA-28R-300** that was based on the **PA-32 Saratoga** but equipped with wings stressed for aerobatics, a new central fuselage section with tandem accommodation under a clear-view canopy, and a 224-kW (300-hp) Lycoming engine. The two prototypes built by Piper made their maiden flights on 6 March and 31 August 1981, and were followed by three machines

assembled by ENAER for a first flight on 30 January 1982. Known in Chile as the **T-35 Pillán** (devil), the new trainer then went into series production with changes that included the replacement of the original all-moving tailplane with a fixed but trimmable tailplane carrying a conventional elevator.

The **T-35** was intended for the basic flying training role by the domestic air forces, and from July 1985 60 **T-35A** basic trainers and 20 **T-35B** instrument flying trainers were delivered mainly to the air force college, otherwise known as the Escuela de Aviación 'Capitán Avalos' at El Bosque, Santiago,

although several of the aircraft are operated at Los Cerillos by another training unit, Grupo No 11 of the Brigada Aérea II.

ENAER has also produced 41 **T-35C** trainers for Spain, where they are assembled by CASA and operate with the air force designation E.26 Tamiz for use mainly in the basic training role although some are also with Ala 54 of the Mando de Materiel. The **T-35D** instrument trainer was acquired by the air forces of Panama (10 examples supplied 1988-89) and Paraguay (15).

Design studies for a turboprop-powered Pillán of the two-seat type

were completed in 1985, and in 1986 ENAER fitted a Pillán with an Allison 250-B17D turboprop to create the T-35TX Aucán (laughing warrior). After the maiden flight in February of the same year, the Aucán made about 500 test flights up to 1987, when the machine was returned to the manufacturer for further modifications. The Aucán soon returned to service after ENAER had installed a one-piece cockpit canopy hinged on the side. Further development by ENAER followed in 1990, and in that year the Soloy corporation of the USA was contracted to develop a kit, centred on the 250-B17D engine, to facilitate upgrade of the **T-35** to **T-35DT Turbo Pillán** standard. The first Pillán upgraded with such a kit flew in March 1991.

Specification
ENAER T-35A Pillán
Type: two-seat basic flying trainer
Powerplant: one 224-kW (300-hp) Textron Lycoming IO-540-K1K5 piston engine
Performance: maximum speed 311 km/h (193 mph) at sea level; cruising speed, maximum 266 mph (166 mph) at 2680 m (8,800 ft) and economical 255 km/h (159 mph) at 5120 m (16,800 ft); initial climb rate 465 m (1,525 ft) per minute; service ceiling 5840 m (19,160 ft); range 1362 km (846 miles)
Weights: empty 930 kg (2,050 lb);

normal take-off 1315 kg (2,900 lb); maximum take-off 1338 kg (2,950 lb)
Dimensions: span 8.84 m (29 ft 0 in); length 8.00 m (26 ft 3 in); height 2.64 m (8 ft 8 in); area 13.69 m² (147.34 sq ft)
Armament: up to 500 kg (1,102 lb) of disposable stores on two underwing hardpoints, and generally comprising two 227- or 113-kg (500- or 250-lb) bombs, or two machine-gun pods or two multiple rocket launchers

The Pillán is the Fuerza Aérea de Chile's basic and instrument flying trainer, it is available in T-35A basic flying trainer and T-35B instrument flying trainer forms.

Edgar Percival E.P.9

Edgar Percival's name was made in the 1930s when he designed the Gull series of light aircraft. His company went on to build the Prentice and Provost trainers after World War II, but was acquired in 1954 by the Hunting Group, and the airframe company became part of British Aircraft Corporation in 1960.

In 1954, the Australian-born designer founded a new company, Edgar Percival Aircraft Ltd, at Stapleford airfield and built as a private venture a high-wing utility aircraft known as the **Edgar Percival E.P.9**. Intended as a multi-role workhorse for crop-spraying and light transport, the prototype flew on 21 December 1955, and construction of a first batch of 20 began soon after this. An Australian demonstration tour by the fourth certificated aircraft earned orders for four E.P.9s from that country; two were delivered by air in September 1957 to SuperSpread Aviation (Pty) Ltd of Melbourne, and two others to Skyspread Ltd of Sydney followed in the next month.

Other overseas customers were found in Canada, France, New Zealand and Tasmania, and a number of British-

registered E.P.9s operated abroad on spraying and freight work. Two were bought by the British Army in March 1958 for evaluation, and served for several years before being put up for civil disposal.

Samlesbury Engineering Ltd acquired rights to the E.P.9 in 1958, and these included some assembled and partly assembled aircraft. The company was renamed Lancashire Aircraft Co. Ltd and it completed three aircraft with 220-kW (295-hp) Avco Lycoming GO-480-G1A6 engines, and in this form the designation **Lancashire Prospector E.P.9** was applied.

A further five aircraft were completed before production stopped with the 27th airframe. Mention should be made of a **Skyspread E.P.9** re-engined with a 280-kW (375-hp) Armstrong Siddeley Cheetah 10 radial engine in 1959; a similar engine was used on the last Lancashire-built Prospector in 1960. Three airframes remain in existence in the UK, all with the Museum of Army Flying at Middle Wallop for rebuilding into one flying aircraft.

Specification
Edgar Percival E.P.9
Type: light utility aircraft
Powerplant: one 201-kW (270-hp) Avco Lycoming GO-480-B1B flat-six piston engine
Performance: maximum speed 235 km/h (146 mph); cruising speed 206 km/h (128 mph); service ceiling 5335 m (17,500 ft); range 933 km (580 miles)
Weights: empty 912 kg (2,010 lb); maximum take-off 1610 kg (3,550 lb)

Dimensions: span 13.26 m (43 ft 6 in); length 8.99 m (29 ft 6 in); height 2.67 m (8 ft 9 in); wing area 21.14 m² (227.6 sq ft)

Lancashire Prospector E.P.9s were built with the Avco Lycoming GO-480 horizontally-opposed engine, but in 1959 the last Lancashire-built aircraft was fitted with a Cheetah 10 radial. The E.P.9 was used as a utility transport and crop-sprayer.

Edgley EA7 Optica

Combining the visibility of a helicopter with outstanding slow-flying capabilities, the original concept for the **Edgley EA7 Optica** was as a three-seat touring aircraft. Designer John Edgley, at that time a post-graduate student at the Imperial College of Science & Technology, London, began the final aerodynamic design in 1974 and a model was wind tunnel tested in 1975. Construction of a prototype began in 1976 in London, and final assembly was carried out at the College of Aeronautics, Cranfield. The first flight was made on 14 December 1979 with a 119-kW (160-hp) Avco Lycoming O-320 engine but this was later changed to a 134-kW (180-hp) IO-360. The engine drives a five-bladed fixed-pitch ducted fan, and the Optica is claimed to be the world's quietest powered aircraft.

Mounting the whole cockpit assembly ahead of the fan and engine gives the pilot and passengers 270° panoramic vision, plus almost vertical downward vision; the cockpit canopy design allows photography through the panels. The tricycle landing gear is fixed and unfaired, with maintenance-free solid suspension, and the airframe is of all-metal construction; its internal cabin width of 1.68 m (5 ft 6 in) permits three-abreast seating, while baggage space and positions for mounting specialised observa-

tion equipment are provided behind the seats and in the unrestricted floor area in front of the two passenger seats.

Roles for the Optica are virtually unlimited, from the obvious aerial photography and surveillance patrols to traffic reporting, powerline inspection etc, and it has the ability to perform much of a helicopter's work with fixed-wing economy and range. Considerable interest was shown in the Optica from the time of its first appearance, and at the 1981 Paris air show the announcement of a first production order was made – 25 for Australian distributor H. C. Sleigh Aviation Ltd.

With £2.3-million funding, Edgley bought Old Sarum airfield near Salisbury, and set up a production line in existing hangars. Initial plans covered the construction of 200 aircraft, beginning in mid-1983, with first production models to be available at the end of that year for approximately £55,000 each. However, the crash of an early production aircraft in 1985 led to the collapse of the company. In October 1985, Optica Industries was formed to continue activities, and by the end of 1986 15 aircraft had been produced. In January 1987 the factory was destroyed by arson along with all but one airworthy Optica. The company was reformed again as Brooklands Aircraft (later Aerospace), and the Optica

Scout, renamed the **Scoutmaster,** returned to production with a 194-kW (260-hp) Textron Lycoming O-540 engine. Six had been delivered to customers by the end of 1989. In March 1990, after building another five aircraft, all manufacturing was halted and a receiver called in. In July 1990 the Optica project was acquired by Lovaux Ltd at Hurn and a resumption of full-scale production and marketing is planned. Continuing optimism for the Optica concept is supported by market studies indicating that around 8,000 aircraft are used wholly or partly for observation work, ranging from expensive helicopters to simple single-engined fixed-wing types, but none specifically designed for the task, and a sales penetration of five or 10 per cent would bring substantial business.

Specification
Edgley EA7 Optica

The Optica is ideal for surveillance work due its bug-eyed canopy and slow speed.

Type: three-seat slow-flying observation aircraft
Powerplant: one 149-kW (200-hp) Avco Lycoming IO-360 or 156-kW (210-hp) TO-360 flat-four piston engine driving a ducted fan
Performance: maximum speed 203 km/h (126 mph); cruising speed 174 km/h (108 mph); observation speed 92 km/h (57 mph); service ceiling 4265 m (14,000 ft); range with normal reserves at 65 per cent power 1046 km (650 miles)
Weights: empty 850 kg (1,875 lb); maximum take-off 1236 kg (2,725 lb)
Dimensions: span 11.99 m (39 ft 4 in); length 8.15 m (26 ft 9 in); height 2.31 m (7 ft 7 in); wing area 15.84 m² (170.5 sq ft)

Enstrom F-28/280 Shark

Designed and built by Rudy J. Enstrom, the **Enstrom F-28** light helicopter was flown in experimental form on 12 November 1960 as a two-seat machine with a two-bladed main rotor and an un-skinned tubular rear fuselage. It was followed into the air, on 26 May 1962, by the first of two three-seat pre-production examples, and the production version appeared in the autumn of 1963. Powered by a 134-kW (180-hp) Avco Lycoming O-360-A1A engine, it had a three-bladed main rotor and a light alloy and glassfibre cabin section with an all-metal semi-monocoque tail boom.

Variants

F-28A: introduced in 1968, the F-28A was powered by a 153-kW (205-hp) Avco Lycoming HIO-360-C1A engine; production was discontinued in February 1970, when the R. J. Enstrom Corporation ceased operations, but restarted in 1971 when reformed as the Enstrom Helicopter Corporation

280 Shark: developed in 1973 as a luxury version of the F-28A, the Shark introduced a more streamlined cabin-section, dorsal and ventral vertical tail surfaces with small endplate fins at the ends of the small horizontal tailplanes; standard fuel capacity was increased to 151 litres (40 US gal); FAA certification was achieved in September 1974

F-28C/280C: improved versions, introduced in 1975, powered by the 153-kW (205-hp) Avco Lycoming HIO-360-E1AD engine with a Rajay 301-E-10-2 turbocharger; the tail rotor was moved to the port side of the fuselage and the direction of rotation reversed; the **F-28C-2** introduced a one-piece windscreen and a pedestal central instrument console for improved forward and downward vision. Production ceased in Novembr 1981.

F-28F Falcon/280F: FAA certificated in January 1981, the F-28F and 280F were powered by the turbocharged 168-kW (225-hp) Avco Lycoming HIO-360-F1AD engine

F-28F-P Sentinel: dedicated police version of Model 280F developed for Pasadena Police Department, and fitted with special equipment including a searchlight. First delivery in October 1986

280FX: updated version of the Model 280F fitted with faired landing gear, redesigned vertical and horizontal tail surfaces, covered tail rotor shaft and tail rotor guard. First flown in December 1983 and certificated in January 1985. Export customers include the Chilean army which bought 15

280L Hawk: work on a four-seat version of the 280C began in January 1978 and a prototype was first flown on 27 December 1978. The main rotor diameter was increased by 0.61 m (2 ft) and the fuselage lengthened by 0.91 m (3 ft). Powerplant of the F-28F/280F was retained and fuel capacity

increased to 170 litres (45 US gal). However, full development was postponed indefinitely in 1983 following a change in company ownership

Spitfire Mk 1: developed by the Spitfire Helicopter Company of Lynnfield, Massachusetts, from the basic Enstrom F-28A design, the Spitfire Mk 1 appeared in 1976, powered by a 313-kW (420-shp) Allison 250-C20B turboshaft

Specification
Enstrom F-28C
Type: three-seat light helicopter
Powerplant: one 153-kW (205-hp) Avco Lycoming HIO-360-E1BD piston

engine
Performance: maximum speed 180 km/h (112 mph); cruising speed 172 km/h (107 mph); service ceiling 3660 m (12,000 ft); range 435 km (270 miles)
Weights: empty 680 kg (1,500 lb); maximum take-off 1066 kg (2,350 lb)
Dimensions: main rotor diameter 9.75 m (32 ft 0 in); length 8.94 m (29 ft 4 in); height 2.79 m (9 ft 2 in); main rotor disc area 74.69 m² (804 sq ft)

The F-28A is a compact light helicopter. The height of the rotor mast allows occupants to leave the helicopter safely without having to crouch.

Enstrom 480 Eagle

The five-seat **Enstrom 480 Eagle** was developed mainly from the **280L Hawk** four-seat helicopter and is powered by one 313-kW (420-shp) Allison 250-C20W turboshaft derated to 212.5 kW (285 shp). The first flight of a re-engined **280FX** proof-of-concept vehicle took place in December 1988, and the genuine prototype of the definitive model followed on 7 October 1989 as what was in effect a **280FX** with a cabin widened from 1.50 m (4 ft 11 in) to 1.80 m (5 ft 10.25 in)

permitting the installation of a three-seat bench seat behind the two separate front seats.

Enstrom also planned a three-seat **TH-28** military version for the training and patrol tasks. This has a crashworthy fuel system and three crashworthy seats, and can be outfitted for the simultaneous training of two pupils in the alternative visual and instrument flight rules regimes. Enstrom offered the **TH-28** to the US Army for its NTH (New Training Heli-

copter) programme, but the US Army opted for the **TH-67 Creek** version of the Bell Model 206B-3 JetRanger III. Enstrom enjoyed greater success with the civil variant, a total of 40 from the first production run of the **480 Eagle** having already been sold to operators in more than seven countries.

Specification
Enstrom 480 Eagle
Type: four/five-seat light utility helicopter
Powerplant: one 313-kW (420-shp)

Allison 250-C20W turboshaft derated to 212.5 kW (285 shp)
Performance: maximum cruising speed 211 km/h (131 mph) at optimum altitude; service ceiling 3965 m (13,000 ft); hovering ceiling 4265 m (14,000 ft) in ground effect and 3660 m (12,000 ft) out of ground effect; range 707 km (439 miles)
Weights: empty 760 kg (1,675 lb); maximum take-off 1293 kg (2,850 lb)
Dimensions: main rotor diameter 9.75 m (32 ft 0 in); length overall 8.92 m (29 ft 3 in) with rotors stationary; height 2.92 m (9 ft 7 in) to top of rotor had; main rotor disc area 74.69 m² (804.00 sq ft)

Entwicklungsring Süd VJ 101C

The design departments of the firms Bölkow, Heinkel and Messerschmitt were amalgamated into the Entwick-lungsring Süd during 1959 for the purpose of designing and developing a Mach 2 interceptor with **VTOL** capability. Heinkel left the consortium in 1964, and the firm was reconstituted as Entwick-lungsring Süd GmbH, generally known just as EWR.

Two prototypes of the single-seat **EWR VJ 101C** VTOL experimental model were built. This was a high-wing monoplane of all-metal construction with retractable tricycle landing gear, a pressurised cockpit for the pilot on a Martin-Baker ejection seat, and powerplant of six 12.23-kN (2,750-lb st) RB.145 non-afterburning turbojets developed jointly by Rolls-Royce and MAN. Two of the engines were installed vertically in the fuselage behind the cockpit for vertical lift, and the other four were located as a superimposed pair in each of the wing-tip nacelles that could be swivelled hydraulically between the vertical and horizontal positions. This system allowed vertical take-off, after which the tip-mounted nacelles were swivelled forward to the horizontal

position, in the process accelerating the aeroplane into forward wing-borne flight and allowing the fuselage engines to be shut down.

The flight-control system had been tested with a hover platform powered by three Rolls-Royce RB.108 turbojets. The **VJ 101C X-1** prototype was tested for the first time in free flight on 10 April 1963 after the completion of ground tests starting in December 1962. This machine had made many flights before it was lost in an accident on 14 September 1964.

The **VJ 101C X-2** second proto-type differed from the first aeroplane only in having an uprated powerplant with afterburner units on the wing-tip engines to raise their thrust to 16.24 kN (3,650 lb st) each and thereby provide the capability for a level speed in excess of Mach 1. The **X-2** carried out its first successful hovering manoeuvre on 12 June 1965 and four months later,

on 22 October, achieved its initial complete transition from vertical to level flight and vice versa for the first time. VTOL capability would have been maintained through the use of a powerplant comprising five 24.47-kN (5,500-lb st) Rolls-Royce/Man RB.162-31 turbojets mounted vertically in the forward fuselage and two 30.47-kN (6,850-lb st) Rolls-Royce/MAN RB.153-61 vectored-thrust turbofans mounted horizontally in the rear fuselage.

Specification
Entwicklungsring Süd VJ 101

Type: single-seat VTOL experimental aeroplane
Powerplant: six Rolls-Royce/MAN RB.145 turbojets rated at 16.24 kN (3,650 lb st) each in the X-1 but with four rated at 16.24 kN (3,650 lb st) each in the X-2
Performance: maximum speed (X-1) Mach 1.08; minimum wing-borne flying speed 260 km/h (161.5 mph)
Weight: maximum take-off (X-1) 6000 kg (13,228 lb) or (X-2) 8000 kg (17,637 lb st)
Dimensions: span 6.61 m (21 ft 8.5 in); length 15.70 m (51 ft 6 in); height 4.13 m (13 ft 6.5 in) over tail

The VJ 101C used the comb-ination of forward and vertical thrust through a pair of engines in swivelling nacelles at the wing tips, and vertical thrust from a pair of engines in the fuselage.

Eurocopter (Aérospatiale) AS 532 Cougar

When the helicopter now known as the **Cougar** was proposed in 1974, it was intended as successor to the **SA 330 Puma** and bore the designation **AS 332 Super Puma**. The Puma's basic configuration was retained, but considerable improvement in overall performance was gained from glassfibre and carbonfibre rotor technology, and the type is easily recognised by its ventral fin and the nose radome for the optional Bendix/King RDR-1400 or Honeywell Primus 500 weather radar. The helicopter was initially produced for the civil market but had been schemed with military survivability features such as a gearbox which can operate for one hour without lubrication and also rotors which can be run for 40 hours even after hits from 12.7-mm (0.5-in) machine-gun rounds. The Turmo turboshafts of the Puma series were replaced by a pair of Makila 1A turboshafts each rated at 1327 kW (1,780 shp) and capable of accelerating from idle to maximum revolutions within a mere 1.5 seconds.

Specific components of the **Super Puma**, such as the Makila turboshaft and elements of the tail unit, are used in South Africa's comprehensive update of the **Puma**, the type that was originally known as the **Atlas Gemsbok** but now as the **Denel (Atlas) Oryx** with a revised airframe.

After its first flight on 13 September 1978 the **Super Puma** entered service in 1981 with the military and civil designations **AS 332B** and **AS 332C** respectively. Both the military and the civilian version have a cabin volume of 11.4 m³ (402.6 cu ft) and the same seating capacity as the **Puma**, with accommodation in the civil model for 21 passengers or in the military version for up to 15 fully-equipped soldiers. In the following year there began delivery of the **AS 332L** civil and **AS 332M** military 'stretched' variants with their fuselages lengthened by 0.76 m (2 ft 6 in) to permit the enlargement of the cabin to a volume of 13.3 m³ (469.7 cu ft).

In January 1990 the military variants of the **AS 332 Super Puma** received the revised designation **AS 532 Cougar**, and at the same time the different variants were identified by the following pairs of suffix letters indicating their basic roles: **AC** and **UC** for the short-fuselage military armed and unarmed versions; **AL** and **UL** for the long-fuselage military armed and unarmed versions; **MC** for the short-fuselage maritime version for SAR and surveillance; and **SC** for the short-fuselage maritime version for armed tasks such as anti-submarine and anti-ship warfare. The **AS 332L** is still in series production, and the improved version **AS 332L Tiger** was developed for the firm Bristow Helicopters, responsible for the support of the drilling platforms in North Sea.

Later examples of the **Cougar Mk I** are equipped with 1400-kW (1,877-shp)

Makila 1A1 turboshafts. Further development resulted in the Mk II model that entered service in 1992 as the **AS 332L2 Super Puma Mk II** with two 1573-kW (2,109-shp) Makila 1A2 turboshafts.

A specifically military version of the **AS 532 Cougar Mk II** was wanted by the French army for the carriage of a long-range battlefield surveillance radar with its antenna in a hinge-down installation on the pod/boom junction. The service initially evaluated the concept from 1986 in an **SA 330B Puma** conversion with the small Orchée radar, and then wanted 20 examples of the **AS 532 Cougar Mk II** with the considerably more capable Orchidée radar (data-linked to a ground station) and specialised ECM gear. A prototype was completed in June 1990. The prototype was used with considerable success in the course of 24 sorties during Operation 'Desert Storm', however, and this led to a revival of the programme in a smaller form with an order for just four **AS 532UL** helicopters with a battlefield surveillance system known as HORIZON (Hélicoptère d'Observation Radar et d'Investigation sur ZONe, or radar observation and zone surveillance helicopter). Eurocopter received a development order in October 1992 for two platforms for a full evaluation of the performance potential of the Orchidée combined with the flight time of the larger **AS 532UL**. The first flight with complete equipment occurred on 8 December 1992, and delivery of the first helicopter to French army aviation

was made in April 1994. In addition the French army is supplementing its original inventory of the **SA 330** helicopters with smaller numbers of **AS 532 Cougars**, the first of 22 examples reaching the Force d'Action Rapide at the end of 1991.

After manufacturing the standard **SA 330 Puma** under licence at the beginning of the 1980s, IPTN in Indonesia went on to produce the **AS 332C** and **AS 332L Super Puma**. Up to now the Indonesian navy has received 10 helicopters for transport and SAR services, the Ministry of Finance one for VIP transport, and the presidential flight three examples of the **AS 332L1**, all bearing the local designation **NAS-332**. More than 460 **Super Puma** and **Cougar** helicopters had been ordered by the beginning of 1995, more than two-thirds of them military variants. The operator base of this model is very numerous and includes Abu Dhabi, Argentina, Brazil, Cameroon, Chile, China, Ecuador, France, Gabon, Indonesia, Japan, Jordan, Kuwait, Malaysia, Mexico, Nepal, Nigeria, Oman, Panama, Qatar, Saudi Arabia, Singapore, South Korea, Spain, Sweden, Switzerland, Togo, Turkey, Venezuela and Zaire.

Specification
Eurocopter (Aérospatiale) AS 532UC Cougar
Type: multi-purpose 21-passenger military helicopter
Powerplant: two 1400-kW (1,877-shp) Turboméca Makila 1A1

turboshafts
Performance: cruising speed 262 km/h (163 mph) at sea level; initial climb rate 420 m (1,378 ft) per minute; service ceiling 4100 m (13,450 ft); hovering ceiling 2800 m (9,185 ft) in ground effect and 1650 m (5,415 ft) out of ground effect; range 618 km (384 miles) with standard fuel and 1017 km (632 miles) with two external tanks
Weights: empty 4330 kg (9,546 lb); normal take-off 9000 kg (19,841 lb) with internal load; maximum take-off 9350 kg (20,615 lb) with 4500 kg (9,921 lb) maximum external load
Dimensions: main rotor diameter 15.60 m (51 ft 2.25 in); length overall 18.70 m (61 ft 4.25 in) with rotors turning and fuselage 15.53 m (50 ft 11.5 in) including tail rotor; height 4.92 m (16 ft 1.75 in); main rotor disc area 191.13 m2 (2,057.42 sq ft)
Armament: (military) one 20-mm cannon, or two 7.62-mm (0.3-in) machine-guns or two multiple launchers with 68-mm (22 2.68-in) or 70-mm (19 2.75-in) rockets, or (naval) two AM.39 Exocet anti-ship missiles or two anti-submarine torpedoes

The AS 532 Cougar is easily distinguished from its predecessor the SA 330 Puma by its nose-mounted weather tradar and ventral fin. The Zaïrean air force has a single AS 532 for VIP transport.

Eurocopter (Aérospatiale) AS 350 Ecureuil and AS 550 Fennec

The four/five-seat **AS 350 Ecureuil** (squirrel) was planned as a multi-purpose helicopter to replace the Alouette, and made its maiden flight on 27 June 1974 as a prototype with a three-blade main rotor, a Starflex bearingless glassfibre main rotor head and a Textron Lycoming LTS101 turboshaft, but the second prototype that first flew on 14 February 1975 had a Turboméca Arriel powerplant. Power for the **AS 350B** initial civil model was provided by a 478-kW (641-shp) Arriel 1B, while the **AS 350C** AStar variant for North America had the 441-kW (592-shp) LTS101. Uprated engines were installed in the later **AS 350BA**, **AS 350B2** and **AS 350B3** as well as the **AS 350D** AStar for North America.

An armed version of the **Ecureuil** was later developed as the **AS 350L** with provision for a wide assortment of weapon types including the 20-mm M621 cannon, 7.62-mm (0.3-in) machine-gun pods, various types of multiple rocket launchers, and the Saab/Emerson Electric HeliTOW anti-tank system with four Hughes TOW missiles. Twelve of such helicopters were assigned the new designation **AS 550C2 Fennec** before their delivery to Denmark in 1990.

Further military variants had the designation **AS 550U2** (unarmed general-purpose helicopter), **AS 550A2** (armed with cannon or rockets), **AS 550C2** (armed with anti-tank missiles), **AS 550M2** (unarmed general-purpose naval helicopter) and **AS 550S2** (armed naval anti-ship helicopter), and 22 of the **AS 350M2** variant serve with the French navy in the liaison role.

The **Ecureuil** assembled by Helibras in Brazil is basically the **AS 350B**, and the Brazilian manufacturer's desig-nations for these Esquilo (squirrel) variants are **HB 350B** and **B1** for the unarmed models and **HB 350L1** for the armed model. Some 30 **HB 350B** and **B1** machines were delivered to the Brazilian air force as **CH-50** communications and **TH-50** training helicopters, and another nine to the Brazilian navy as **UH-12** utility helicopters for the use of the 1° Esquadrão de Helicopteros de Emprego Gerel, while 36 **HB 350L1** machines were built for the Brazilian army, which designates the variant as the **AH-1** for service with the 1st Aviation Battalion at Taubaté; as can the **UH-12**, the **AH-1** may be fitted with armament such as one 7.62 mm (0.3-in) machine-gun pintle-mounted in a cabin door as well as two 7.62 mm (0.3-in) twin machine-gun pods or two multiple launchers each carrying seven 70-mm (2.75-in) rockets.

Other military operators of the Esquilo include the forces of Argentina, Bolivia, Paraguay, and Venezuela, while the single-engined version of the **Ecureuil** serves with the forces of Abu Dhabi, Australia, Benin, Botswana, Central African Republic, Denmark, Ecuador and Peru. By the beginning of 1995 Eurocopter's orders for all versions of the Ecureuil stood at 1,850 helicopters, of which 1,816 had been delivered.

Specification
Eurocopter (Aérospatiale) AS 350B2 Ecureuil
Type: five/six-seat multi-purpose light helicopter
Powerplant: one 546-kW (732-shp) Turboméca Arriel 1D1 turboshaft
Performance: maximum cruising speed 246 km/h (153 mph) at sea level; initial climb rate 534 m (1,750 ft) per minute; service ceiling 4800 m (15,750 ft); hovering ceiling 2550 m (8,350 ft) out of ground effect; range 666 km (414 miles)
Weights: empty 1153 kg (2,542 lb); maximum take-off 2250 kg (4,960 lb)
Dimensions: main rotor diameter 10.69 m (35 ft 0.75 in); length overall 12.94 m (42 ft 5.5 in) with rotors turning and fuselage 10.93 m (35 ft 10.5 in); height 3.14 m (7 ft 1.5 in); main rotor disc area 89.75 m² (966.12 sq ft)

The Ecureuil has had an outstanding sales performance (particularly in the civilian field) and over 1,800 helicopters of this model have been delivered. The AS 350B illustrated earns its keep as a flying news gatherer for a TV organisation.

Eurocopter (Aérospatiale) AS 355 Ecureuil 2 and AS 555 Fennec

In mid-1978 Aérospatiale started on the development of a twin-engined version the **AS 350 Ecureuil**, and the first prototype made its maiden flight on 28 September 1979. This twin-engined development retained much of the original single-engined model's structure, and the main changes involved the powerplant (two engines of French design except for the TwinStar variant for the US market with two American engines), transmission system, fuel system and fuselage structure.

The first production version was the **AS 355E Ecureuil 2** with two 313-kW (420-shp) Allison 250-C20F turboshafts, followed by the **AS 355F** with broader rotor blades the current model is the **AS 355N** with the revised powerplant of two 357-kW (479-shp) Turboméca TM319 Arrius turboshafts.

The principal operator is the French air force, which has 52 examples. Eight of these are **AS 355F1** machines flown by the 67e Escadre d'Hélicoptères at Villacoublay and EHOM 68 in French Guyana; the helicopters of the latter unit are armed with a 20-mm M621 cannon on the starboard side of the fuselage. The remaining 44 are **AS 555AN Fennecs** supplied from 19 January 1990 with the Arrius powerplant and used for the training and anti-helicopter roles, the latter with a 20-mm M621 fixed forward-firing cannon under the fuselage and aimed by means of a T-100 sight. In February 1992 the French army took delivery of 10 **AS 555UN Fennecs** for instrument flying training.

In Brazil the Helibras company assembled the **AS 355F2** with the local designation **HB 355F2 Esquilo**. The Brazilian air force acquired a total of 13 examples for use as 11 CH-55 armed helicopters by the 1° Esquadrão of the 8° Grupo de Aviacão in Manaus, and two **VH-55 VIP** helicopters for the Grupo de Transports Especial in Brasilia.

Specification
Eurocopter (Aérospatiale) AS 555N Fennec
Type: five/six-seat multi-role naval light helicopter
Powerplant: two 357-kW (479-shp) Turboméca TM319 Arrius 1A turboshafts
Performance: maximum cruising speed 255 km/h (140 mph) at sea level; initial climb rate 408 m (1,340 ft) per minute; service ceiling 4000 m (13,125 ft); hovering ceiling 2600 m (8,530 ft) in ground effect and 1550 m (5,085 ft) out of ground effect; range 129 km (81 miles) on a SAR mission with two survivors
Weights: empty 1382 kg (3,046 lb); normal take-off 2540 kg (5,600 lb) with an internal load; maximum take-off 2600 kg (5,732 lb) with the maximum 1134-kg (2,500-lb) sling payload
Dimensions: main rotor diameter 10.69 m (35 ft 0.75 in); length overall 12.94 m (42 ft 5.5 in) with rotors turning and fuselage 10.93 m (35 ft 10.5 in); height 3.14 m (7 ft 1.5 in); main rotor disc area 89.75 m² (966.12 sq ft)
Armament: one 20-mm GIAT M621 cannon, or two 7.62 mm (0.3-in) machine-gun pods, or two multiple launchers for 68- or 70-mm (2.68- or 2.75-in) rockets, or one homing torpedo

The French air force operates two armed variants of the Fennec twin-engined armed helicopter. Some of the AS 355F1 machines, with 20-mm GIAT cannon, are stationed near Paris, while others are in French Guyana to protect the European Ariane space centre.

Eurocopter (Aérospatiale) AS 565 Panther

After development of the **SA 361H** for evaluation of the potential of the original single-engined model of the Dauphin helicopter in military tasks such as light transport and anti-tank warfare, Aérospatiale decided that real practicality in tasks as demanding as these demanded the use of a twin-engined powerplant, and therefore concentrated on the development of an improved multi-role version based on the twin-engined airframe of the **AS 365 Dauphin 2**. This made its maiden flight on 29 February 1984 as the **AS 365M** with a payload of 10 to 12 troops or an armament of eight HOT anti-tank missiles or two multiple launchers each carrying 68-mm (22 2.68-in) SNEB rockets. Evolutionary development of the basic concept then resulted in the **AS 365K Panther** that first flew in prototype form during April 1986.

The **Panther** is currently offered in several forms as the **AS 565AA** armed battlefield helicopter, **AS 565CA** anti-tank helicopter, **AS 565UA** unarmed general-purpose helicopter, **AS 565SA** armed naval helicopter, and **AS 565MA** unarmed helicopter for the SAR and other maritime roles. Helibras assembles the **AS 565** in Brazil as the **HB 565**, and the Brazilian army has 36 examples with the service designation HM-1.

A joint Aérospatiale and LTV programme offered the US Army an **AS 565** equipped with a pair of LHTEC T800-LHT-800 turboshafts as a replacement for the UH-1H. This prototype, designated Panther 800, completed its maiden flight in the United States on 12 June 1992.

Before the military/naval series of the **AS 365** had been renamed as the **AS 565 Panther**, Saudi Arabia had ordered 24 examples of the **AS 365F** naval model: four of these were completed in the **AS 565SC** configuration for the SAR role with ORB 32 search radar, while the other 20 were delivered in the **AS 565SA** configuration with Agrion 15 radar and four Aérospatiale AS.15TT anti-ship missiles. The French navy has three **AS 565MA** planeguard helicopters for Flottille 35 on board the helicopter carrier *Jeanne d'Arc* and the aircraft carriers *Clémenceau* and *Foch*. The service has a requirement for 40 such helicopters, and the first 15 of an additional batch are being delivered up to 1999. Five **AS 365N2** helicopters

were ordered by the Chinese Nationalist police in 1992 for SAR and patrol tasks in Taiwan, Abu Dhabi contracted for seven **AS 565MA** helicopters (with AS.15TT missiles) in 1995, and in April 1994 Israel ordered the first of a possible 20 **AS 565MA Panter** (sic) helicopters for its 'Saar 5' class corvettes.

Other customers of the **AS 565** include Ireland which bought two examples for fishery protection on board the corvette *L. E. Eithne*, which is equipped for the helicopters' harpoon-type down-haul system, and three further examples of the **AS 565MA** carry out SAR and transport tasks. All the Irish helicopter have Bendix/King RDR-1500 search radar, SFIM 155 autopilot, Sextant ONS 200A and Nadir Mk II navigation equipment, Cina B Doppler and Sextant ONS 200A long-range navigation systems, auto-stabilisation equipment, and a five-

screen EFIS cockpit. Angola has six cannon-armed **AS 565AA** machines for attack and reconnaissance duties as well as 10 **AS 565UA** transport helicopters. Chile has ordered four **AS 565SA** machines with provision for MU90 Impact torpedoes or AM.39 Exocet guided missiles.

Chinese production of the Dauphin **AS 365N Dauphin 2** began at Harbin in 1982 with the local name Haitun (dolphin). After 50 examples had been delivered by January 1992, work started on a second series of 30 helicopters. The **Z-9** and **Z-9A** (then **Z-9A-100** with a greater proportion of Chinese-made parts) correspond to the **AS 365N** and **AS 365N1** respectively, while the Chinese-manufactured Arriel 1C and Arriel 1C1 turboshafts are known as the **WZ-8** and **WZ-8A** respectively. Nine of the **Z-9A** machines were supplied to the Royal Thai navy.

Specification
Eurocopter (Aérospatiale) AS 565UA Panther
Type: 10-passenger multi-purpose light helicopter
Powerplant: two 584-kW (783-shp) Turboméca Arriel 1M1 turboshafts
Performance: maximum cruising speed 278 km/h (173 mph) at sea level; initial climb rate 420 m (1,378 ft) per minute; hovering ceiling 2600 m (8,530 ft) in ground effect and 1850 m (6,070 ft) out of ground effect; 875 km (range 544 miles)
Weights: empty 2255 kg (4,791 lb); maximum take-off 4250 kg (9,369 lb) with the maximum 1600-kg (3,527-lb) payload carried internally or externally
Dimensions: main rotor diameter 11.94 m (39 ft 2 in); length overall 13.68 m (44 ft 10.75 in) with rotors turning and fuselage 12.11 m (39 ft 8.75 in); height 3.98 m (13 ft 0.25 in); main rotor disc area 111.97 m² (1,205.26 sq ft)
Armament: see above

The Aéronavale has 1988 three AS 565MA helicopters for planeguard duties mainly on board aircraft carriers Foch and Clémenceau, and the current procurement for 15 more such helicopters may pave the way for an eventual total of 40 naval Panthers.

Eurocopter Tiger

The development of the **Eurocopter Tiger** can be traced to the issue of the German army's requirement for a **PAH-2** (Panzerabwehrhubschrauber Nr 2) new-generation anti-tank helicopter to replace the MBB BO105 in service as the **PAH-1** and, at much the same time, the French army's proposal for the procurement of a sophisticated modern helicopter of the same basic type as the **Hélicoptère Anti-Char (HAC)**. The governments of the two countries therefore signed an agreement in 1984 for the collaborative development of a new helicopter which would satisfy the national needs of both armed forces. The programme was temporarily stopped in mid-1986, however, so that the requirement could be completely reappraised in terms of its technical and financial implications. The programme was resumed during

March 1987 in a modified form to produce an anti-tank version common to both armies, and a **HAP (Hélicoptère d'Appui et de Protection)** escort and fire support version for the French Army.

Aérospatiale in France and MBB in Germany had already set up a common subsidiary, Eurocopter Tiger GmbH, in the course of September 1985, and since January 1992 all the helicopter projects of both manufacturers have been taken under the aegis of a new combined Eurocopter SA enterprise with Eurocopter Deutschland and Eurocopter France as its main elements. On 30 November 1989 **Eurocopter Tiger** received a contract for the completion of the design and the construction of five prototypes. These latter were to comprise three unarmed helicopters for the evaluation

of the new type's aerodynamics, structure and avionics, one **HAC-2 Tiger/HAC Tigre** anti-tank helicopter, and one HAP helicopter that originally received the name **Gerfaut** (gerfalcon).

In its final design the **Tiger** revealed a slim, low-drag fuselage with a vertically staggered tandem arrangement of seats for the pilot with the weapon systems operator behind and above him. Much use is made of composite materials in the construction of the core airframe, while the semi-rigid main rotor (with a titanium rotor head and tapered starplates carrying elastomeric bearings) has four blades produced almost wholly from composite materials; the three-blade tail rotor is based on the Aérospatiale Spheriflex type. The fixed tricycle landing gear has a single wheel on each unit, and was designed for high impact speeds. The primary weapon accommodation is provided by a stub

wing arrangement with anhedralled outer sections, and a cannon turret can be fitted under the nose.

In its **PAH-2/HAC** configuration the helicopter was designed for the carriage of up to eight **HOT 2** and/or Trigat anti-tank missiles or of four of these weapons together with Mistral or Stinger air-to-air missiles for the self-defence and escort tasks. Control all the weapons except the anti-tank missiles, which are reserved for the weapon systems operator, can be exercised by either of the two crew members using the their helmet-mounted sights drawing data from either the Osiris mast-mounted sight (TV, FLIR and laser rangefinder) above the main rotor in the case of the weapon systems operator or the nose-mounted FLIR in the case of the pilot.

The **PAC-2** variant was then abandoned in favour of a single multi-purpose version after the Germans had decided that the **PAH-1** would

The PT1 is seen in HAP configuration armed with a 30-mm cannon, Mistral air-to-air missiles and launchers for 22 air-to-surface rockets, and has a STRIX sight unit on top of the fuselage.

continue to be adequate for the anti-tank role in the lower-threat situation pertaining after the collapse of the USSR and the dissolution of the Warsaw Pact, but that the growing threat of low-intensity warfare now required a more versatile combat helicopter. Germany thus transferred its allegiance to the **UHU** (Unterstützungshubschrauber, or support helicopter), whose final design is not yet defined but which will be optimised for multiple roles including escort. This implies a stronger emphasis on air-to-air capability with the Stinger rather than Mistral AAM, and possibly the DAV millimetric-wavelength radar being developed by Dassault Electronique for the **Tigre**.

While the French **HAC Tigre** is armed and equipped similarly to the **PAH-2**, the **HAP** has a 30-mm GIAT cannon in an undernose turret and on the stub wing two multiple launchers each carrying 68-mm rockets and either four Mistral AAMs or two more multiple launchers each carrying 12 rockets. The weapon systems operator controls these weapons with the aid of a STRIX gyro-stabilised roof sight with direct-view optics.

As part of the **Tiger** development programme an Aérospatiale Panther was used to test the MTR 390 engines, making its first flight on 14 February 1991. Three other experimental machines (two Pumas and a Dauphin) were used for development of the mast-mounted sight, the pilot's night vision subsystem and the fire-control system. The first **PT1** prototype of the **Tiger** took off as planned for its maiden flight at Marignane on 29 April 1991 and later validated the aerodynamic shapes of the mast-mounted and roof-mounted sights. The **PT2** first

prototype of the **HAP** with all essential avionics and on-board systems was completed at Ottobrunn late in 1991 and flew for the first time on 22 April 1993. These two helicopters were first flown as aerodynamic and avionic test platforms, but by 1997 had received the complete equipment of the **HAC** and **HAP** respectively. The **PT3** first flew on 19 November 1993 with full core avionics and in 1997 was modified to **UHU** standard for development of this German variant. The **PT4** and **PT5** were completed in December 1994 and early in 1996 to full **HAP** and **UHU** standards (including armament) respectively.

The announced requirement initially consisted of 75 **HAP** and 140 **HAC** helicopters for France and 212 **PAH-2**

(later **UHU**) helicopters for Germany. France looks set to order 115 **HAP** and 100 **HAC** machines, while the intended German procurement was subject to recent examination, and in the 1995 budget resources were allocated for only 75 helicopters. It then began to appear that the full requirement might now be funded in an extended programme that would also be useful in spreading development costs, thus making the helicopter a more attractive proposition for a third European user.

Specification
Eurocopter HAC Tigre
Type: two-seat anti-tank and fire-support helicopter
Powerplant: two 958-kW (1,285-shp) MTU/Turboméca/Rolls-Royce

MTR 390 turboshafts
Performance: cruising speed, maximum 280 km/h (174 mph) at optimum altitude and economical 250 km/h (155 mph) at optimum altitude; initial climb rate more than 600 m (1,970 ft) per minute; service ceiling 4000 m (13,125 ft); range 670 km (416 miles)
Weights: 3300 kg (7,275 lb); normal take-off between 5300 and 5800 kg (11,685 and 12,787 lb) according to mission; maximum take-off 6000 kg (13,227 lb)
Dimensions: main rotor diameter 13.00 m (42 ft 7.75 in); fuselage length 14.00 m (45 ft 11.25 in); height 4 .32 m (14 ft 2 in); main rotor disc area 132.73 m² (1,428.74 sq ft)
Armament: see above

Eurofighter 2000

Following the successful tri-national programme for almost 1,000 Tornado warplanes, the same three countries (Germany, Italy and UK) were joined by Spain and in June 1986 formed the **Eurofighter** consortium. This organisation was to produce a multi-role fighter that would be available for service by the end of the 1990s. Other European nations, most notably France, had participated in early **EFA** investigations and meetings, but finally decided not to join this consortium, instead laying plans for the modernisation of current warplanes or in the case of France starting the alternative development of an indigenous warplane.

The essential aspects of the **EFA** concept include a canard configuration that is basically unstable but controlled by an active digital fly-by-wire flight control, complex avionics, multi-function cockpit displays, and an advanced structure making extensive use of carbonfibre composite materials as well as aluminium/lithium and titanium alloys. Much experience of all these was gained from the BAe Experimental Aircraft Programme (**EAP**) machine financed by industry and the British Ministry of Defence. Powered by two Rolls-Royce RB199 turbofans, the **EAP** was a technology

demonstrator produced by the British aircraft industry with some early Italian involvement. This prototype made its first flight on 8 August in 1986 and during 259 test flights generated an enormous amount of invaluable data before its retirement on 1 May 1991.

The finally requirement formulated for the **EFA** by the European Staff Requirement for Development, dated September 1987, called for a relatively light and sophisticated single-seat fighter optimised for air combat (air defence and air superiority) at anything between close and BVR (Beyond-Visual-Range) distances, but also possessing a secondary attack capability. Other elements of the requirement called for STOL capability as well as the ability to operate from austere airfields. In addition the warplane was to have a small radar cross-section and high supersonic performance as well as a high level of manoeuvrability and easy handling to assist the pilot in the combat arena. Germany and Italy required only the air-to-air capability, but accepted the common criteria of an empty weight of 9750 kg (21,500 lb), wing area of 50 m² (540 sq ft) and powerplant of two turbofans each rated at 90 kN (20,250 lb) with afterburning. The required engine was to be created and

manufactured by the Eurojet consortium (Rolls-Royce, MTU, Fiat Avio and SENER [now ITP]) as the EJ200 with about 30 per cent fewer components than the RB199 of the Tornado and a rating of about 60 kN (13,490 lb) dry.

On 23 November 1988 a development contract with a total value of £5.5 billion was signed, and this covered the construction and testing up to 1999 of eight development aircraft including a pair of two-seat aircraft, although this was later reduced to seven aircraft as two each in Germany, Italy and the UK as well as one in Spain. The shareholding in the programme was allocated on the basis of the participating nations' intended procurements, with BAe and MBB each allocated 33 per cent, Aeritalia (now Alenia) 21 per cent and CASA 13 per cent: this reflected the planned procurement of 765 EFA aircraft made up of 250 examples each for the RAF and the Luftwaffe, 165 machines for the Aeronautica Militare Italiana and 100 aircraft for the Ejercito del Aire.

After vehement discussion, the May 1990 decision about the all-important radar went in favour of the new **ECR-90** rather than a performance-enhanced version of the Hughes **APG-65** favoured by Germany, this European radar to be developed by GEC Ferranti in co-operation with FIAR in Italy and INISEL in Spain. The **ECR-**

90 is a multi-mode pulse-Doppler radar with several air-to-air and air-to-ground modes, a long acquisition range, and the ability to identify and track both single and multiple targets. The **ECR-90** is optimised for use with the Hughes AIM-120 AMRAAM missile but also provides the continuous-wave illumina-tion needed by missiles with semi-active radar guidance. Four AAMs can be carried semi-recessed into low-drag troughs in the fuselage, and the availability of nine hardpoints (one under the fuselage and eight under the wings), including three plumbed for drop tanks, allows for the carriage of additional air-to-air or air-to-surface weapons up to a total of 6500 kg (14,330 lb). There is also a 27-mm Mauser BK 27 cannon in the starboard side of the forward fuselage.

The **ECR-90** radar is complemented by the Eurofirst (FIAR, Thorn EMI Electronics and Eurotronica) IR search-and-track system with passive multi-target capability, and data from these sensors are displayed on up to three Smiths coloured head-down displays, a GEC-Marconi wide-angle head-up display, and a helmet-mounted sight. The pilot therefore has a mass of information available to him, although the ease of operating the aeroplane is ensured by the HOTAS (Hands On Throttle And Stick) design of the cockpit, a direct voice input command system, and the advanced computer

The DA1 is seen here at Manching. With DASA's chief test pilot at the controls, the aeroplane completed the Eurofighter 2000's first flight at the end of March 1994.

system. The contract for the integrated DASS (Defensive Aids Sub-Subsystem) was assigned to a Euro-DASS (Marconi Defence Systems and Elettronica) consortium, and the DASS includes radar warning, missile approach warning and laser warning receiver systems linked to active jammer pods on the wing tips, a towed decoy system, and chaff/flare dispensers: Germany and Spain opted out of the DASS system but will probably rejoin.

The **DA1** and **DA2** first and second prototypes built by DASA (successor to MBB) and BAe should have been ready for their maiden flights in Manching and Warton at the beginning of 1993 with intermediate RB199-22 engines. The Alenia-built **DA3** was the first machine completed with EJ200 turbofans, the BAe-built **DA4** was the first two-seat aeroplane and the first with full avionics, the DASA-built **DA5** was the first with the ECR-90 radar and intended for avionics and weapons trials, the CASA-built **DA6** was the second two-seater and intended for avionics development, and the Alenia-built **DA7** was a single-seater and intended for performance and weapons integration trials.

The decision regarding funding for series production was due at the beginning of 1993, but the **EFA** cost study of April 1992 set up by German defence minister, Volker Rühe, decided that the estimated unit price of DM 133.9 million was unacceptably high. It was thus against the background of German threats to leave the programme that decisive changes were suggested for the project. After seven different new EFA concepts were taken into consideration, in most cases based on a single-engined airframe, at the end of 1992 the four participating nations

accepted a slightly simplified and less highly specified version as the New **EFA** or **Eurofighter 2000**, with the possibility of more economical final equipment on a national basis, opening the possibility for Germany to look for a unit price in the order of DM 90 million through the adoption of 'off the peg' electronics such as the APG-65 radar and less capable defensive systems.

The first **EFA** flight was by the **DA1** at Manching on 27 March 1994. The British-built **DA2** was actually ready earlier, but BAe felt obliged to let the German partner take precedence and this machine took off from BAe's Warton airfield for a 50-minute maiden flight on 6 April 1994. Before the **DA1**s first flight DASA had introduced revised flight-control software after a tyre had burst during high-speed taxiing trials at the end of January 1994. This precautionary measure was undoubtedly influenced by the software

problems encountered during testing for the Saab JAS 39 Gripen, in which BAe was also involved.

While the Royal Air Force has adhered strongly to its initial number of 250 aircraft with deliveries beginning in the first part of the 21st century, the Luftwaffe trimmed its requirement to about 140 aircraft as equipment for eight 12/15-aircraft squadrons plus reserves, but may increase this total. The German government also postponed its decision on **Eurofighter 2000** production to 1995 with entry into service in 2002 or later, and only in the last stages of 1997 finally agreed to the start of the programme's production phase. Meanwhile the Aeronautica Militare Italiana also trimmed its requirement to only 130 **Eurofighter 2000** fighters (equipment for five squadrons and one OCU) but now requires 165 machines. The Ejercito del Aire cut its requirement to

72 **Eurofighter 2000** warplanes but now wants 100.

Specificiation
Eurofighter 2000
Type: single-seat multi-role fighter
Powerplant: two Eurojet EJ200 turbofans each rated at 60.00 kN (13,490 lb st) dry and 90.00 kN (20,235 lb st) with afterburning
Performance: maximum speed 2333 km/h (1,450 mph) or Mach 2.2 at high altitude; combat radius between 463 and 555 km (288 and 345 miles) depending on load and altitude
Weights: empty 10000 kg (22,046 lb); maximum take-off 21000 kg (46,297 lb)
Dimensions: span 10.95 m (35 ft 11 in) over tip-mounted pods; length 15.96 m (52 ft 4.25 in); height 5.28 m (17 ft 3.875 in); area 52.40 m² (564.05 sq ft) including canard foreplanes
Armament: see above

Extra 230 and 300

Designed to the specification of Swiss aero clubs, the single-seat **Extra 230** was planned as a high-performance type for competition aerobatics. Under the auspices of the Swiss enterprise Thommen, specialist in the production of precision and flying instruments, Walter Extra in Dinslaken built a prototype of this model, and this **Extra 230** is a mid-wing monoplane powered by the 149-kW (200-hp) Textron Lycoming AEIO-360-A1E four-cylinder horizontally opposed engine. The fuselage structure consists of a tubular steel frame covered largely with sheet aluminium, and the fabric-covered wings are based on an extremely strong wooden box girder. The second aeroplane made the first flight of this model on 14 July 1983, and followed shortly after this by the first machine. Since then the **Extra 230** has participated successfully in several aerobatic competitions, and during the European championship of 1985 an **Extra 230** took third place.

A prototype of the subsequent model, the **Extra 300**, first flew on 6 May 1988. This aeroplane is larger, equipped with tandem seats, and powered by the more potent 224-kW (300-hp) Textron Lycoming AEIO-540-L1B5 six-cylinder horizontally opposed engine. Another difference from the **Extra 230** was that the wing and tail

unit were now considerably stronger, being based on carbon composite spars covered in the case of the wings with carbon composite sandwich shells and in the case on the tail unit with glassfibre shells. In single- and two-seat forms the **Extra 300** can be stressed to ±10 *g* and ±8 *g*.

Series production of the **Extra 300** began at the end of 1988, and the type has found its main market in the civilian sector although it has also secured two military customers. Six machines were delivered in 1989-90 to Gruop de Aviación No. 11 of the Chilean air force in Santiago-Los Cerillos: the Chilean aerobatics team, the Escuadrilla de Alta Acróbacia, better known under the name 'Los Halcones', now flies these **Extra 300s** instead of its previous Pitts S-2A/S aircraft. The 'Equipe de Voltige' of the French air force at Salon de Provence has also acquired one **Extra 300** and one **Extra 300/S** for advanced aerobatic training. The quasi-military 'Falcons', the aerobatics team of Jordan, has also switched to the **Extra 300**. Delivered from March 1992, the **Extra 300/S** is a single-seat

The Extra 230 and 300 are high-performance aerobatic machines for competition. The third Extra 230 went to members of the national Swiss aerobatic teams.

derivative with the wings shortened by 0.50 m (1 ft 7.5 in) and fitted with more powerful ailerons, and the **Extra 300/L** is a further modified version delivered from November 1994.

Specification
Extra 300
Type: two-seat aerobatic aircraft
Powerplant: one 224-kW (300-hp) Textron Lycoming AEIO-540-L1B5 six-cylinder horizontally opposed piston engine
Performance: maximum level speed

343 km/h (213 mph) at optimum height and maximum manoeuvring speed 293 km/h (182 mph); initial climb rate 1005 m (3,300 ft) per minute; range 974 km (605 miles)
Weights: empty 630 kg (1,389 lb); normal take-off 820 kg (1,808 lb) for one-man aerobatics or 870 kg (1,918 lb) for two-man aerobatics; maximum take-off 950 kg (2,094 lb)
Dimensions: span 8.00 m (26 ft 3 in); length 7.12 m (23 ft 4.25 in); height 2.62 m (8 ft 7.25 in); area 10.70 m² (115.17 sq ft)
Armament: none

F + W C-3605

Development of the **Farner-Werke C-3605** two-seat target-tug can be traced back to the **Fabrique Fédérale C-3602**, two prototypes of which were built in 1939-40 for long-range reconnaissance and ground-attack. Following flight tests, modifications were made and an initial batch entered production as the **C-3603**. Ten were built, and after service evaluation a further 142 followed, serving with the Swiss air force between 1942 and 1952 in the combat role. Two others, designated **C-3603-1 TR**, were produced for training and parachute tests. In 1945 a C-3603-1 was converted for target-towing; after considerable flight testing a successful installation was evolved and fitted to 20 other aircraft within a year.

Further improvements followed, and in 1946 Farner-Werke at Grenchen converted a C-3603-1 into a more advanced target-tug. A long tube was fitted from the rear cockpit to eject the target sleeve above the tailplane and between the twin fins, with a cable-cutting device available to the pilot. Twenty C-3603s were converted to this standard.

Development of the basic airframe had meanwhile continued with the **C-3604**, a version using the 933-kW (1,250-hp) Saurer YS-2 engine in place of the 746-kW (1,000-hp) Hispano-Suiza used in earlier models. A prototype and 12 production C-3604s were built, the

type entering service in 1947-48. Spares produced for the C-3603 and not used enabled a further six C-3603-1s to be assembled in 1948.

During the early 1950s a requirement for an aircraft to tow illuminated targets at night was met with the conversion of a C-3603-1, and this machine remained in service until replaced by the C-3605 in 1972. Further conversions of 40 C-3603-1s to target-tugs began in 1953, while another aircraft was fitted beneath one wing with a winch built by ML Aviation in the UK for high-speed towing, and a ballast tank beneath the other wing. In the same year, 20 more C-3603-1s were converted by the military at Dübendorf for catastrophe relief using underwing supply containers.

The ultimate development of the C-3603 airframe came when the Hispano-Suiza engines of the 40 C-3603-1 conversions began to wear out. Various types of foreign aircraft were considered as replacements but all were rejected for various reasons and a proposal to re-engine the C-3603-1 with a Lycoming T53-L-7 turboprop was accepted. A prototype was converted and flown on 19 August 1968; it was handed over to the Swiss air force in December 1968 for acceptance trials, which proved satisfactory and, with a few modifications, a series of 23 aircraft was re-engined and given the new designation C-3605. A

third, central, fin was added and the lower weight of the turboprop necessitated a major 1.82 m (6 ft) increase in the length of the nose. The first C-3605s entered service in 1971 and the last was delivered in January 1973.

Specification
F + W C-3605
Type: two-seat target-tug
Powerplant: one 820-kW (1,100-shp) Avco Lycoming T53-L-7 turboprop
Performance: maximum speed 432 km/h (268 mph) at 3050 m (10,000 ft); economic cruising speed 350 km/h (217 mph) at 6095 m

(20,000 ft); service ceiling 10000 m (32,810 ft); range with maximum fuel and 10 per cent reserves 980 km (605 miles)
Weights: empty 2634 kg (5,806 lb); maximum take-off 3716 kg (8,192 lb)
Dimensions: span 13.74 m (45 ft 1 in); length 12.03 m (39 ft 5¾ in); height 4.05 m (13 ft 3½ in); wing area 28.70 m² (308.93 sq ft)

The remarkable C-3605 'Schlepp' usually wore yellow and black stripes for high conspicuity. The long nose offset the light weight of the turboprop.

F + W D-3802/D-3803

In an attempt to improve the performance obtained with the D-3801, Dornier-Werke AG (Doflug) at Altenrhein collaborated with Morane-Saulnier in the design of a new aircraft, the **D-3802**, which was based on the M.S.540. A new engine was also available, the 932-kW (1,250-hp) Saurer YS-2 built in Switzerland, and the prototype D-3802 flew in the autumn of 1944; a second airframe was built for structural testing.

Following Swiss air force evaluation of the D-3802, a batch of 12 was ordered, but in spite of various modifications the type was plagued with problems and never entered series production. One of the batch had another new engine installed, the 1119-kW (1,500-hp) Saurer YS-3, and incorporated a cut-down rear fuselage to enable a bubble canopy to be fitted; in this form it was designated **D-3803**. As a result of the problems the aircraft were relegated to other duties and replaced by North American P-51 Mustangs.

Specification
F + W D-3803
Type: single-seat fighter
Powerplant: one 1119-kW (1,500-hp) Saurer YS-3 12-cylinder Vee piston engine
Performance: maximum speed 680 km/h (422 mph) at 7000 m

(22,965 ft); service ceiling 12000 m (39,370 ft); range 650 km (404 miles)
Weights: empty 2945 kg (6,493 lb); maximum take-off 3905 kg (8,609 lb)
Dimensions: span 10.02 m (32 ft 10½ in); length 9.32 m (30 ft 7 in); height 3.33 m (10 ft 11 in); wing area 17.68 m² (190.4 sq ft)
Armament: one 20-mm Hispano

F + W D-3802A of Fliegerstaffel 17, Swiss air force, in 1949-50.

cannon in propeller shaft and two 20-mm cannon in the wings, plus 200 kg (441 lb) bombs or rockets beneath wings

F.B.A. flying-boats 1913-18

The moving spirit behind the Franco-British Aviation Company, registered at Charing Cross Road, London, in 1913, was Frenchman Louis Schreck, and it was in France that F.B.A. activities were centred. Schreck had taken over the French Tellier concern in 1911 and had built several interesting landplanes and seaplanes. He became manager of the F.B.A. workshops at Argenteuil and later opened new workshops at Vernon, also on the Seine. One of a small batch of flying-boats (**F.B.A.-Lévêque**) developed from the Donnet-Lévêque Model A was flown by the celebrated André Beaumont (pseudonym for Lieutenant de Vaisseau Conneau of the French navy) to

Brighton, where it was demonstrated from a seaplane station established on the seafront by Magnus Volk, whose light electric railway is still operating there!

These first production F.B.A. 'boats were powered by Gnome rotary engines of between 37-75 kW (50-100 hp). They were of straightforward construction with single-step wooden hulls, ply-covered, and two-bay unequal-span wooden wings, fabric covered; the engine was mounted between the wings to drive a pusher propeller. They were successful with various private owners, but the French navy took no interest in F.B.A. until the outbreak of

World War I. By early 1915 deliveries of the **F.B.A. Type B**, a much improved development of the F.B.A.-Lévêque, were being made to the British Royal Naval Air Service and the French navy. The Type B introduced folding wings, subsequently a standard F.B.A. feature, and was soon followed by a re-engined Type B with improved all-round performance, known as the **Type C**, which attracted export orders and was also built abroad.

The most successful wartime F.B.A. was the **Type H**, of which over 1,000 were supplied to the French navy and nearly as many were built under licence in Italy. The Type H was a three-seater

powered by a 112-kW (150-hp) engine, had an improved hull, redesigned wings and a new tailplane. Final wartime F.B.A. to go into service was the **Type S**, with re-designed hull, 149-kW (200-hp) engine, a triangular fin and a curved, balanced rudder. It remained in French naval service for five years after the war.

Experimental F.B.A. aircraft produced during this period included a modified Type C with two rotary engines; a Type C with a reshaped, strengthened bow and a 37-mm cannon mounted in the nose cockpit; and a single-seat *avion canon* cannon-armed aircraft with a hull-type fuselage and conventional wheeled landing gear. Amphibian versions of all the principal types were tested.

F.B.A. flying-boats made a major contribution during World War I to the Allied campaign against German U-boats.

Variants

F.B.A. Type A: first production F.B.A., powered by a 37-kW (50-hp) Gnome N1 rotary engine; as in subsequent designs, the biplane wings were supported above the hull on four short struts; pilot and passenger seated side-by-side forward of the lower wing in an open cockpit, protected by sharply raised wooden fairing immediately in front of windscreen; the Type A displayed at Paris Salon de l'Aéronautique in December 1913; a special version with a 75-kW (100-hp) Gnome was piloted by Swiss Ernest Burri to take second place in the Schneider Trophy Contest on 20 April 1914; the type was also known as the F.B.A.-Lévêque

F.B.A. Type B: hull strengthened by comparison with Type A; redesigned tailplane with new rudder and no fin; appeared early 1915; RNAS bought 36 from F.B.A., while Thompson and Gosport companies built further 80 under licence; very few F.B.A.s (British or French) were armed, the majority being used as trainers

F.B.A. Type C: simply the Type B re-engined with a 97-kW (130-hp) Clerget 9B rotary; Russia imported 30 examples and built a further 34 at Lebedev factory; Italy bought a number for use against the Austrians in the Adriatic; the Type C was the first F.B.A. 'boat used widely by the French; usual armament was a single 7.7-mm (0.303-in) machine-gun; the Type C remained popular post-war; three civil machines were used by the Swiss Ad Astra company on the Swiss lakes and others operated passenger services in Sweden and Uruguay; in 1923 F.B.A. brought out the **Type 11**, an *hydravion d'école 2-places* (HE.2), or 2-seat training flying-boat, virtually identical to the Type C but built specifically for elementary training; this was developed into the **Type 14** two-seat trainer, 20 of which were built and flew for several years alongside wartime survivors of the Type C variant as French navy trainers

F.B.A. Type H: the most numerous F.B.A. type; it was as popular in Italy, where 982 were built by the Savoia company and a group of smaller contractors, as in France; used widely by the Italians in the Adriatic; Italian version powered by a 112-kW (150-hp) Isotta-Fraschini V-4-B engine and armed with 7.5-mm (0.30-in) Fiat machine-gun; some still in service in Tripolitania in 1922; the Type H was used by French Aéronautique Maritime for anti-submarine patrols from bases on Atlantic, Channel and Mediterranean coasts; other examples flown by Belgium, USA (US Navy from French and Italian bases), and Yugoslavia (postwar); side-by-side cockpits in front of wings linked by passageway to bow gunner's cockpit

F.B.A. Type S: final wartime production F.B.A. 'boat; improved hull (incorporating redesigned planing bottom) and new tailplane; powered by 149-kW (200-hp) Hispano-Suiza 8Bb engine; appeared in November 1917 and used exclusively by French, who flew it from metropolitan bases; Type S 'boats remained in French service until 1923; an experimental version, with wings of reduced chord and a redesigned strut assembly, crashed into the Seine on test flight and development was abandoned

Specification
F.B.A. Type H

Type: 3-seat coastal patrol flying-boat
Powerplant: one 112-kW (150-hp) Hispano-Suiza 8Aa 8-cylinder piston engine
Performance: maximum speed 150 km/h (93 mph); service ceiling 4900 m (16,080 ft); range 450 km (280 miles)
Weights: empty equipped 984 kg (2,169 lb); maximum take-off 1420 kg (3,130 lb)
Dimensions: span 14.12 m (46 ft 4 in); length 9.92 m (32 ft 6½ in); height 3.10 m (10 ft 2 in); wing area 40.00 m² (430.57 sq ft)
Armament: one 7.7-mm (0.303-in) machine-gun plus two 35-kg (77-lb) Type F bombs

The Type B appeared in the spring of 1915, featuring a 97-kW (130-hp) Clerget rotary engine. The first 44 for the RNAS were bought as complete aircraft, but the last 20 were bought as hulls.

FFA P-16

In 1948 the Swiss air headquarters issued a specification for an interceptor/ground-support aircraft tailored to fit the country's operational requirements. Two factories were contracted to produce prototypes: the FFA at Altenrhein and EFW at Emmen, the latter's competitor being projected as the EFW N-20.

FFA (Flug- und Fahrzeugwerke) submitted a design for a straight-wing, single-seat jet and the prototype flew (as the **FFA P-16-01**) for the first time on 25 April 1955 with a 3629-kg (8,000-lb) thrust Armstrong Siddeley Sapphire axial-flow turbojet. As the EFW N-20 project had been abandoned in 1953, the P-16 had the field to itself, but the requirements of the specification were demanding. A high transonic performance with STOL ability for operation from high-altitude strips was needed, as well as good manoeuvrability, a rapid climb with combat load and the ability to use grass airfields. In fact, the P-16 could take off in just under 488 m (1,600 ft) and land with a braking parachute in less than 305 m (1,000 ft). Its remarkable performance was attributable to a very strong thin wing of low aspect ratio, with leading- and trailing-edge flaps; wingtip fuel tanks were a permanent fixture, and to assist in operations from grass twin mainwheels and nosewheels were fitted. Between 28 February and 12 March 1956 this aircraft was evaluated by the Swiss air force, but reports indicate that in spite of a number of good features the overall flight performance was unsatisfactory. However, the programme was proceeding well when, on the 22nd test flight, the prototype was lost following engine failure caused by a fractured fuel line; the pilot ejected successfully just before the aircraft crashed into Lake Constance.

Work on the second prototype had begun, but the programme suffered some delay before the **P-16-02** flew on 16 June 1956; it became supersonic in a dive for the first time on its 18th flight on 15 August 1956 following extensive trials which included weapon evaluations and spinning. A third aircraft, the **P-16-03**, flew on 4 April 1957 powered by the bigger Sapphire Sa.7 of 4990-kg (11,000-lb) thrust. As a result of the improvement in performance the Swiss government placed an order in March 1958 for 100 aircraft, known as the **P-16 Mk III**, but only a week later the P-16-03 was lost, also in Lake Constance, the pilot again ejecting successfully. Apparently a failure in the hydraulic-powered flight-control system on landing approach at low altitude prevented the pilot switching to manual control in time to save the aircraft. The production order was suspended immediately and two months later was cancelled. The Swiss government considered that the hydraulic system was faulty and the complete redesign necessary would cause too great a delay in the programme, but FFA and experts from the RAE Farnborough found that the system met British design requirements, an exactly opposite view to the official Swiss investigation team, whose findings were responsible for the cancellation of the order. The relatively simple modifications to the hydraulic system were made by FFA and two pre-series aircraft were built on the company's own initiative, the **P-16-04** flying on 8 July 1959 and the **P-16-05** in March 1960. The design was eventually proven to be sound, but the production order was not reinstated.

It was reported in 1965 that General Electric and FFA were co-operating on development of a subsonic ground-support aircraft designated **AJ-7**, based on the P-16, but nothing came of the project. It is thought that the P-16-04 and P-16-05 still survive (P-16-02 was scrapped) but the wing design lives on in a far better known aircraft (the Gates Learjet) as a result of a company set up in 1960 by William P. Lear, as the Swiss American Aviation Corporation, to manufacture a high speed twin-jet executive aircraft originally designated SAAC-23 but later Learjet 23. It was planned to complete the two prototypes at Altenrhein from parts sub-contracted to various European countries, but in the event the Swiss part of the planning did not come to fruition and the Lear Jet Corporation was established at Wichita, Kansas.

Specification
FFA P-16-01

Type: single-seat ground-support/combat aircraft
Powerplant: one 3629-kg (8,000-lb) Armstrong Siddeley Sapphire Sa.6 turbojet
Performance: maximum speed 1120 km/h (696 mph); service ceiling 14020 m (46,000 ft); range with auxiliary tanks 998 km (620 miles)
Weights: empty 7040 kg (15,520 lb); maximum take-off 11700 kg (25,795 lb)
Dimensions: span 11.15 m (36 ft 7 in); length 14.25 m (46 ft 9 in); height 4.09 m (13 ft 5 in); wing area 29.77 m² (320.44 sq ft)
Armament: two 30-mm Hispano-Suiza 825 cannon in nose, plus up to four 500-kg (1,102-lb) bombs on racks beneath wings, or rockets on racks, and a high-speed launcher for 44 68-mm (2.68-in) rockets in fuselage

The P-16 attack fighter was tailored expertly to the peculiar needs of the Swiss air force, this example being the fourth prototype, the first to the definitive P-16 Mk III standard. The programme was cancelled.

FFVS J22
to
Fairchild C-82 Packet/C-119 Flying Boxcar

FFVS J22

An aircraft forced on the Swedes due to the refusal to export aircraft from the US, the J22 featured adequate performance and handling, but suffered from poor visibility.

In October 1940 the United States government placed an export embargo on 292 fighter and fighter-bomber aircraft ordered by the Swedish authorities. This created an immediate crisis for the Flygvapen (Swedish air force) and an emergency programme was established to design and build a single-seat fighter relying upon domestic industry and talent. The design team was led by Bo Lundberg, and the Flygförvaltningens Verkstad (FFVS) or Air Board Workshop was established to oversee the whole programme from project stage to quantity delivery to the Flygvapen.

The production programme involved over 500 sub-contractors, hardly any with experience of aircraft construction. Lundberg had as a primary objective simplicity of manufacture and in this he succeeded. Powered by a Swedish version of the Pratt & Whitney Twin Wasp SC3-G radial engine, the **FFVS J22** was a cantilever mid-wing monoplane of mixed steel tube and wood construction. Its tubular-steel fuselage had a covering of moulded plywood panels

that were integral with the load-bearing structure of the machine. The landing gear main legs retracted into the fuselage and the tailwheel was also fully retractable.

The first of two J22 prototypes flew for the first time on 21 September 1942, from Bromma airport where the final assembly plant had been set up. Before that flight 60 series J22s had been ordered and eventually 198 production fighters were delivered, beginning in October 1943, the last example being received by the air arm in April 1946. J22s served principally with the F3 and F9 wings of the Swedish air arm, based at Malmslätt and Göteborg respectively. They proved popular with their pilots, demonstrating good performance and excellent manoeuvrability, the only criticism being the poor visibility which the pilot had for ground handling.

Two versions of the J22 were built, these differing only in armament: the

J22A had two 7.9-mm (0.31-in) machine-guns and two 13.2-mm (0.52-in) guns and the **J22B** four 13.2-mm (0.52-in) guns. Experience gained in building the J22 proved invaluable in establishing Sweden's postwar aviation industry.

Specification
FFVS J22B
Type: single-seat monoplane fighter
Powerplant: one 794-kW (1,065-hp) SFA STWC3-G 14-cylinder radial piston engine
Performance: maximum speed 575 km/h (357 mph) at 3500 m (11,485 ft); service ceiling 9300 m (30,510 ft); range 1270 km (789 miles)
Weights: empty equipped 2020 kg (4,453 lb); maximum take-off 2835 kg (6,250 lb)
Dimensions: span 10.00 m (32 ft 9¾ in); length 7.80 m (25 ft 7 in); height 2.60 m (8 ft 6¼ in); wing area 16.00 m² (172.23 sq ft)
Armament: four 13.2-mm (0.52-in) M/39A machine-guns

FMA I.Ae.27 Pulquí

Designed by Emile Dewoitine, well known in the French aviation industry before World War II, the **I.Ae.27 Pulquí** (Arrow) was not only the first single-seat fighter to be designed in Argentina; it was also the first turbojet-powered aircraft to be built and flown by the nation. A cantilever low-wing monoplane of all-metal construction, the Pulquí had a conventional tail unit, retractable tricycle landing gear, and accommodation for the pilot well forward on the fuselage beneath a jettisonable canopy. Power was provided by a Rolls-Royce Derwent turbojet mounted in the aft fuselage.

First flown on 9 August 1947, the Pulquí proved disappointing in tests, with

performance well below estimates, and further development was abandoned.

Specification
Type: single-seat fighter
Powerplant: one 1633-kg (3,600-lb) thrust Rolls-Royce Derwent 5 turbojet engine
Performance: maximum speed 720 km/h (447 mph); service ceiling 15500 m (50,855 ft); range 900 km (559 miles)
Weights: empty 2358 kg (5,198 lb); maximum take-off 3600 kg (7,937 lb)
Dimensions: span 11.25 m (36 ft 11 in); length 9.69 m (31 ft 9½ in); height 3.39 m (11 ft 1½ in); wing area 19.70 m² (212.06 sq ft)
Armament: (intended) four nose-mounted 20-mm cannon

Though an eminent prewar designer of piston-engined fighters, Emile Dewoitine did not take naturally to the transition to turbine power. The resultant Pulquí was very disappointing in every aspect of its performance.

FMA I.Ae.33 Pulquí II

Intended to replace the Gloster Meteor F.Mk 4s in service with the Argentine air force, the **I.Ae.33 Pulquí II** (Arrow II) was designed by a team headed by Germany's brilliant Dr Kurt Tank. Not surprisingly, it embodied some of the results of the advanced research carried out in Germany during World War II, incorporating a shoulder-mounted wing with 40° of sweep-back, and a T-tail with all-swept surfaces. Landing gear was of retractable tricycle-type and power provided by a Rolls-Royce Nene turbojet mounted in the rear fuselage. The pilot was accommodated on an ejection-seat in a pressurised cockpit, protected by armour and a bulletproof windscreen, and enclosed by a sliding canopy that could be jettisoned in emergency.

The first of four flying prototypes made its maiden flight on 27 June 1950 but it was not until 18 September 1959 that the last was flown. In the intervening period the first prototype had crashed and Dr Tank and his team had left Argentina. These factors, coupled with serious financial problems, meant that development came to an end.

Specification
Type: single-seat fighter
Powerplant: one 2268-kg (5,000-lb) thrust Rolls-Royce Nene 2 turbojet engine
Performance: maximum speed

1050 km/h (652 mph) at 5000 m (16,405 ft); service ceiling 15000 m (49,210 ft); endurance 2 hours 12 minutes
Weights: empty 3600 kg (7,937 lb); maximum take-off 5550 kg (12,236 lb)

Dimensions: span 10.60 m (34 ft 9¼ in); length 11.68 m (38 ft 3¾ in); height 3.50 m (11 ft 5¾ in); wing area 25.10 m² (270.18 sq ft)
Armament: four nose-mounted 20-mm cannon

The Pulquí II was intended as a replacement for the Meteor.

FMA IA 58 Pucará

Development of the **FMA IA 58 Pucará** ground-attack aircraft began in

August 1966 and led to the flight of an unpowered aerodynamic test vehicle on

26 December 1967. The first powered prototype, by then known as the **AX-2 Delfin**, and with two 674-kW (904-shp) Garrett TPE331I/U-303 turboprop engines installed, was flown for the first

time on 20 August 1969. Subsequent prototypes were powered by Turbomeca Astazou XVIG engines and fitted to all production aircraft. A cantilever low-wing monoplane of all-metal construc-

This Pucará is in typical COIN configuration, with light bombs under the fuselage and rocket pods under the wings. Six internal guns are fitted.

tion, the Pucará has what is virtually a T-tail, a retractable tricycle landing gear, and accommodation for a pilot and co-pilot in tandem on Martin-Baker ejection seats beneath a large transparent canopy. The initial production version, the **IA 58A**, flew for the first time on 8 November 1974 and first deliveries of 108 ordered for the Argentine air force began early in 1976 and continued until 1986. Six were also ordered for the air force of Uruguay. Forty improved **IA 58B Pucará Bravos** with advanced avionics and more powerful armament (30-mm instead of 20-mm cannon) were ordered for the Argentine air force in 1980 but were completed as IA 58As following the Falklands campaign. A single **IA 66**, a Pucará with more-powerful 746-kW (1,000-shp) Garrett TPE331 engines, began its flight test programme in 1980 but did not proceed any further.

Pucará production ended with a batch of 40 IA 58As built from 1986 onwards but no further sales were subsequently announced and they are believed to be in store as 'white tails'.

Specification
FMA IA 58A Pucará
Type: close-support counter-insurgency or reconnaissance aircraft
Powerplant: two 729-kW (978-shp) Turbomeca Astazou XVIG turboprops
Performance: maximum level speed 500 km/h (310 mph) at 3000 m (9,840 ft); economic cruising speed 430 km/h (267 mph); service ceiling 10000 m (31,800 ft); range with maximum fuel 3710 km (2,305 miles)
Weights: empty equipped 4020 kg (8,862 lb); maximum take-off 6800 kg (14,991 lb)

Dimensions: span 14.50 m (47 ft 6 in); length 14.25 m (46 ft 9 in); height 5.36 m (17 ft 7 in); wing area 30.30 m² (326.16 sq ft)
Armament: two 20-mm cannon and four 7.62-mm (0.3-in) machine-guns, all forward-firing, plus up to 1620 kg (3,307 lb) of mixed weapons on underfuselage and underwing racks

FMA IA 63 Pampa

Design of the **FMA IA 63 Pampa** basic jet trainer began in 1979, and a definitive configuration was selected in 1980 with technical assistance from Dornier. Construction of three flying prototypes was initiated in March 1981 and the first (EX-01) flew on 6 October 1984.

Basically a cantilever shoulder-wing monoplane, the fuselage incorporates a tricycle landing gear, a single turbofan engine and a pressurised cockpit with tandem seats for the pupil and instructor on zero/zero ejection seats. The Argentine air force ordered 100 Pampas and the first three aircraft were delivered in April 1988. In 1990, FMA teamed with LTV to offer a version of the IA 63, designated **Pampa 2000**, to compete for the Joint Services Primary Aircraft Train-

ing System (JPATS) search for a common US trainer.

Specification
Type: two-seat basic/advanced jet trainer
Powerplant: one 1588-kg (3,500-lb) thrust Garrett TFE 731-2-2N turbofan
Performance: maximum speed 755 km/h (469 mph) at 7000 m (22,965 ft); service ceiling 12900 m (42,325 ft); range at 556 km/h (345 mph) at 4000 m (13,125 ft) with maximum internal fuel 1500 km (932 miles)
Dimensions: span 9.69 m (31 ft 9 in); length 10.93 m (35 ft 9 in); height 4.29 m (14 ft 1 in); wing area 15.63 m² (168.25 sq ft)

The prototype Pampa shows the neat lines of the type. This entry into the jet trainer market has been earmarked for competition for the USAF's JPATS T-37 replacement programme.

FWA AS 202 Bravo and AS 32T Turbo Trainer

In the late 1960s, SIAI-Marchetti in Italy and Flug- und Fahrzeugwerke AG Altenrhein (FFA) of Switzerland agreed to develop jointly a two/three-seat lightweight touring/training aircraft. It was intended that it should be built in both countries, as the **SA 202 Bravo** in Italy and **AS 202 Bravo** in Switzerland, but it was decided subsequently that as a result of a shortage of production space in SIAI-Marchetti's factory it should be built exclusively in Switzerland. Since that time the aircraft division of the Swiss

FFA company has been re-named Flugzeugwerke Altenrhein AG (FWA), accounting for the current designation of this aircraft.

The Bravo is a fairly conventional lightplane, a cantilever low-wing monoplane with non-retractable tricycle landing gear and power provided by an Avco Lycoming piston engine. Side-by-side accommodation for two is provided in aerobatic versions, plus a rear seat or space for 100 kg (221 lb) of baggage in utility aircraft. The first Swiss-built prototype (HB-HEA) was flown on 7 March 1969, followed two months later, on 7 May, by the second prototype, the only example built by SIAI-Marchetti. Production versions include the **AS202/15** powered by a 112-kW (150-hp) O0-320-E2A, **AS202/18A** with an inverted flight oil system, and the single AS202/26A, powered by a 194-kW (260-hp) Lycoming O-540 engine fitted with a fuel and oil system for unlimited inverted flight.

About 215 Bravos had been built by 1990, the majority sold to military oper-

ators including the air forces of Indonesia (40), Iraq (48) (some of which were transferred to Jordan), and Morocco (10). Civil operators include Royal Air Maroc (5), the Royal Flight of Oman (4), the Uganda Central Flying School (8) and the British Aerospace Flying College (11) which renamed its Bravos the **Wren**.

In 1979 FWA proposed a turboprop Bravo development intended mainly as a military trainer. Designated the **AS 32T Turbo Trainer** and powered by a 268-kW (360-shp) Allison 250-B17C, the aircraft retained Bravo wings and tail unit but had a new fuselage seating two in tandem and a retractable tricycle under-

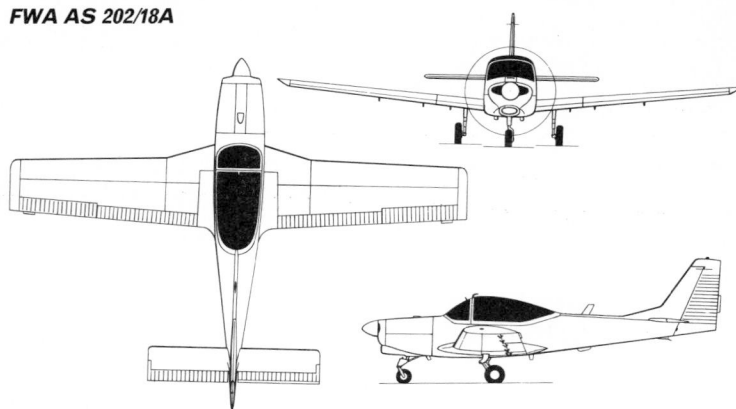

FWA AS 202/18A

Relatively high cost, coupled with good performance and agility, is the main reason the FWA AS 202 has sold better to military customers than to civil. The Bravo is available with several different power ratings.

carriage. In August 1980 a standard Bravo (HB-HEY), designated **AS202/32**, was fitted and flew with an Allison 250 turboprop powerplant as part of the AS 32T test programme, but in the absence of orders, development of the type did not proceed further.

Specification
FWA AS 202/18A Bravo
Type: two/three-seat light aircraft
Powerplant: one 134-kW (180-hp) Avco Lycoming AEIO-360-B1F flat-four piston engine
Performance: maximum cruising speed 226 km/h (140 mph) at 2440 m (8,000 ft); economic cruising speed 203 km/h (126 mph) at 3050 m

(10,000 ft); service ceiling 5485 m (18,000 ft); range with maximum fuel 965 km (600 miles)
Weights: empty equipped 700 kg (1,543 lb); maximum take-off, utility 1050 kg (2,315 lb)
Dimensions: span 9.75 m (31 ft 11¾ in); length 7.50 m (24 ft 7¼ in); height 2.81 m (9 ft 2¾ in); wing area 13.86 m² (149.19 sq ft)

Fairchild 24

The mounting sales of the Fairchild 22 Model C7A induced the company to produce what was basically an enclosed cabin version of that aircraft. To achieve this, the configuration was changed to that of a braced high-wing monoplane, the resulting cabin seating two side-by-side. Other changes included the introduction of a tailwheel, and the initial **Fairchild 24 Model C8** was powered by a 71-kW (95-hp) A.C.E. Cirrus (licence-built) Hi-Ace 4-cyclinder inverted inline engine. Most variants were available with optional float or ski landing gear. Certificated during April 1932, the basic Fairchild 24 Model C8 was produced to the extent of only 10 examples, but these modest numbers, like those of the initial Model C7, soon created interest and new orders.

Variants
Model C8A: generally similar to the Model C8, but introduced radial powerplant that changed fuselage lines; prototype flown with 82-kW (110-hp) Warner Scarab 7-cylinder engine,

The Fairchild 24 was produced with both radial and inline engines for wide customer appeal. This restored example is an Argus Mk III, as delivered under Lend-Lease to the RAF.

but production aircraft had a 93-kW (125-hp) version of this engine; about 25 built
Model C8B: two examples only, almost identical to original Model C8 version, but powered by a 93-kW (125-hp) Menasco Pirate 4-cylinder inline engine
Model C8C: while retaining the same general configuration, this version had slightly increased overall dimensions to provide three-seat accommodation; it was powered by a 108-kW (145-hp) Warner Super Scarab 7-cylinder radial engine, and was first certificated in April 1934; about 130 built
Model C8D: three-seat version, similar to Model C8C, but with the radial engine replaced by a 108-kW (145-hp) Ranger 6-390B 6-cylinder inverted inline engine; about 14 built
Model C8E: version of the Model C8C with improved equipment and refinements; about 50 built
Model C8F: version of the Model C8D with improved equipment and refinements; about 40 built
Model 24-G: similar to Model C8E but available in two versions: 3-seat de luxe and 4-seat utility; combined total of 100 built
Model 24-H: basically a de luxe version of the Model C8D, but with a 112-kW (150-hp) Ranger 6-390D-3 engine; about 25 built
Model 24-J: similar to the Model 24-G and available in de luxe and utility

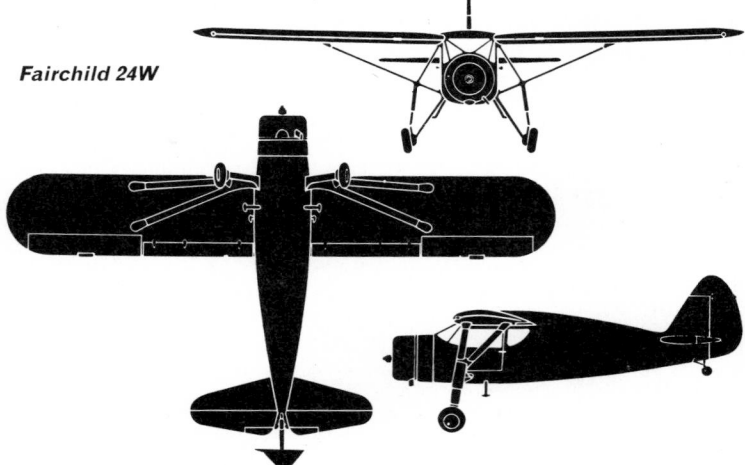

Fairchild 24W

versions, but both 4-seat capacity; about 40 built
Model 24-K: similar to Model 24-H, but available in de luxe and utility versions, both of 4-seat capacity, and with a 112-kW (150-hp) Ranger 6-410-B 6-cylinder inverted inline engine; about 34 built
Model 24R9: refined version of the Model 24-K, available in de luxe and utility versions, but with 123-kW (165-hp) Ranger 6-410-B1 engine; about 35 civil sales
Model 24R40: generally similar to the Model 24R9, but available only to order in de luxe version; about 25 built
Model 24W9: refined version of the Model 24-J, available in de luxe and utility versions; about 40 built
Model 24W40: similar to Model 24W9 but available only in utility version; about 75 built
Model 24W41: similar to the Model 24W40 but with Warner Super Scarab Series 50A; about 40 built
Model 24W41A: similar to the Model 24W41, but with 123-kW (165-hp) Warner Super Scarab 165D; about 10 civil sales
C-61 (later **UC-61**): USAF designation of military version of the Model 24W41 with 108-kW (145-hp) R-500-1 Super Scarab; 161 built, and two impressed civil aircraft also given this designation

C-61A (later **UC-61A**): USAAF designation of military version of Model 24W41A with radio and system revisions; 509 built, and three impressed civil aircraft also given this designation
GK-1: US Navy designation of 13 Model 24W40s impressed for military use
JK-1: US Navy designation of two Model 24-Hs impressed for military use
J2K-1: US Coast Guard designation of two Model 24Rs impressed for wartime use
J2K-2: US Coast Guard designation of two additional but slightly differing Model 24Rs impressed for wartime use
UC-61B to **UC-61J:** inclusive designations allocated to 14 civil aircraft impressed for military use
UC-61K Forwarder: final wartime production version, powered by 149-kW (200-hp) Ranger 1-440-7 6-cylinder inline engine; 306 built
UC-86: USAAF designation of nine civil Model 24R40s impressed for military use
Argus Mk I: RAF designation of UC-61s supplied under Lend-Lease
Argus Mk II: RAF designation of UC-61As supplied under Lend-Lease
Argus Mk III: RAF designation of UC-61Ks supplied under Lend-Lease

Specification
Fairchild 24-G
Type: three/four-seat cabin monoplane
Powerplant: one 108-kW (145-hp) Warner Super Scarab Series 50 7-cylinder radial piston engine
Performance: maximum speed 209 km/h (130 mph); cruising speed 190 km/h (118 mph); service ceiling 5030 m (16,500 ft); range 764 km (475 miles)
Weights: empty 669 kg (1,475 lb); maximum take-off 1089 kg (2,400 lb)
Dimensions: span 11.07 m (36 ft 4 in); length 7.26 m (23 ft 10 in); height 2.24 m (7 ft 4 in); wing area 16.09 m² (173.16 sq ft)

Fairchild 71

Basically an updated version of the Fairchild FC-2W2, the **Fairchild 71** incorporated many improvements that resulted from experience with the FC-2 and its variants. Providing comfortable seating for a pilot and six passengers, it was powered by a 313-kW (420-hp) Pratt & Whitney Wasp 9-cylinder radial engine. The Fairchild 71 was built in modest numbers from 1928 until 1930, when it was replaced in production by the **Fairchild 71A**. This differed primarily by having a few degrees of sweepback on the wings, and it introduced a number of refinements to the interior.

Though civil operators acquired most of the Fairchild 71s and 71As, the US Army acquired one Fairchild 71 for evaluation as a light transport under the designation **XC-8**; dedicated later for photographic work it was redesignated **XF-1**; eight service-test aircraft were ordered under the designation **YF-1**, and all nine of the foregoing were later redesignated **C-8**. Six production Fairchild 71As followed with the designation **F-1A**, later redesignated **C-8A**. The US Navy also acquired a single example for service test under the designation **XJ2Q-1**, later redesignated **R2Q-1**.

In 1930 a Canadian branch of the company was established at Longueuil, Quebec, as Fairchild Aircraft Ltd. In addition to providing support for something like 70 Fairchild aircraft operating in Canada, it began producing the Fairchild 71 for the Canadian Department of National Defence. These aircraft differed from standard by the removal of the features introduced for passenger comfort and were equipped specifically for aerial photography. A commercial **Fairchild 71-C** was built and marketed later and was available also as the **Fairchild 71-CM** with a metal-skinned fuselage.

With a view to meeting Canadian requirements for a freight carrier of greater capacity than the standard Fairchild 71, the **Fairchild Super 71** floatplane was developed in 1934. Of slightly greater span, it had also a longer and entirely new oval-section fuselage of light alloy construction. The pilot was given a cockpit on the upper surface of the fuselage, to the rear of the cabin, with a somewhat restricted forward view between the top of the fuselage and the undersurface of the wing. The cabin could accommodate eight passengers, but the seats were easily removable to create an uncluttered cargo space. Large cargo doors were inset in the port side of the cabin and a passenger door to starboard, the entire accommodation being heated and ventilated. Power was provided by a Pratt & Whitney Wasp radial engine enclosed completely in a low-drag cowling. Only two Super 71s were completed and supplied to the Canadian Department of National Defence.

Fittingly enough, given that Sherman Fairchild started in aviation as a means of using his advanced aerial cameras, this Fairchild 71 was used for the company's thriving aerial survey business.

Specification
Fairchild (Canada) Super 71 (landplane)
Type: eight-passenger or cargo transport
Powerplant: one 388-kW (520-hp) Pratt & Whitney Wasp 9-cylinder radial piston engine
Performance: maximum speed 249 km/h (155 mph); cruising speed 209 km/h (130 mph); range 1314 km (817 miles)
Weights: empty 1544 kg (3,405 lb); maximum take-off 3175 kg (7,000 lb)
Dimensions: span 17.68 m (58 ft 0 in); wing area 36.24 m² (392.0 sq ft)

Fairchild 82

In 1935-36 Fairchild Aircraft Ltd in Canada continued development of the Super 71, leading to the larger-capacity **Fairchild 82**. Following the same general lines as its predecessors, it was a braced high-wing monoplane of mixed construction with a braced tail unit, tailwheel landing gear (optionally replaceable by floats or skis) and power provided by a Pratt & Whitney Wasp radial engine. Like that of the Super 71, the fuselage of the Fairchild 82 incorporated a separate passenger cabin which, in this case, could seat a maximum of 10, and large doors were provided on each side to make easy the loading of cargo as an alternative. In the Super 71 the pilot was accommodated in a separate cockpit, behind and above the passenger cabin, a far from ideal situation. This was resolved in the Fairchild 82 by providing a flight deck forward of the cabin to seat two, side-by-side, with its windscreen on top of the fuselage, forward of the wing, providing an excellent forward view. Only about 12 Fairchild 82s were built, four being exported and the remainder operated by Canadian airlines.

Specification
Type: general-purpose light transport
Powerplant: one 410-kW (550-hp) Pratt & Whitney S3H1 Wasp 9-cylinder radial piston engine
Performance: maximum speed 249 km/h (155 mph) at 1525 m (5,000 ft); cruising speed 227 km/h (141 mph) at 1525 m (5,000 ft); service ceiling 5335 m (17,500 ft); range 1054 km (655 miles)
Weights: empty 1630 kg (3,593 lb); maximum take-off 2869 kg (6,325 lb)
Dimensions: span 15.54 m (51 ft 0 in); length 11.25 m (36 ft 10¾ in); wing area 31.86 m² (343.0 sq ft)

The Fairchild 82 was versatile enough for bush operations on wheels, floats or skis.

Fairchild AT-21 Gunner

The importance of heavy defensive/offensive armament for its bomber aircraft had not been appreciated by US Army Air Corps planners until early in World War II, when information on combat experience in Europe became available to them. This can be illustrated by the fact that the Boeing B-17B Fortress then carried only five machine-guns on separate mountings. Whilst additional weapons could be added to most aircraft, their crews needed training in the most effective deployment of these weapons.

The USAAC lost little time in ordering two specialised gunnery trainer prototypes from Fairchild. The first (**XAT-13**) was intended to provide team training for a bomber aircraft's entire crew, and this aircraft was powered by two Pratt & Whitney R-1340-AN1 Wasp 9-cylinder radial engines. The second prototype (**XAT-14**) was of similar layout and powered by two 388-kW (520-hp) Ranger V-770-6 inline engines. It was adapted subsequently as a specialised trainer for bomb-aimers, with its defensive guns removed, under the designation **XAT-14A**. Testing and evaluation of these aircraft resulted in the procurement of a specialised gunnery trainer under the designation **AT-21 Gunner**.

A cantilever mid-wing monoplane of mixed construction, the AT-21 had a deep oval-section fuselage, a tail unit incorporating twin fins and rudders and retractable tricycle landing gear, and was powered by two Ranger V-770 engines.

Accommodation was provided for a crew of five, including pilot, co-pilot/gunnery instructor and three pupils. Of the 175 AT-21s constructed, 106 were built by Fairchild and, to speed deliveries to the USAAF, 39 were built by Bellanca Aircraft Corporation and 30 by the McDonnell Aircraft Corporation at St Louis. Entering service with newly-established air gunnery schools, the AT-21s remained in service until 1944, when they were displaced by training examples of the operational aircraft in which the air gunners would eventually serve. Many of these surplus aircraft were then converted for use as target tugs.

The Fairchild AT-21 Gunner is seen as rolled out without nose cone or dorsal turret. The airframe was made by the company's Duramold process using preformed bonded veneer.

Variant
Fairchild XBQ-3: designation of one AT-21 following conversion for evaluation as a flying bomb; provided with a radio control system and carried a 1814-kg (4,000-lb) explosive charge

Specification
Fairchild AT-21 Gunner
Type: specialised gunnery trainer
Powerplant: two 388-kW (520-hp) Ranger V-770-11/-15 12-cylinder inverted Vee piston engines

Performance: maximum speed 362 km/h (225 mph) at 3660 m (12,000 ft); cruising speed 315 km/h (196 mph) at 3660 m (12,000 ft); service ceiling 6750 m (22,150 ft); range 1464 km (910 miles)

Weights: empty 3925 kg (8,654 lb); maximum take-off 5129 kg (11,288 lb)
Dimensions: span 16.05 m (52 ft 8 in); length 11.58 m (38 ft 0 in); height 4.00 m (13 ft 1½ in); wing area 35.12 m² (378.0 sq ft)

Fairchild C-82 Packet/C-119 Flying Boxcar

To meet a US Army requirement of 1941 for a specialised military freighter, Fairchild began work on the design of its **Fairchild F-78**. Following approval of the design and a mock-up in 1942, a contract for a single prototype was awarded and the designation **XC-82** allocated. First flown on 10 September 1944, the XC-82 was a cantilever high-wing monoplane of all-metal construction, the roomy fuselage incorporating a flight deck for a crew of five and a large-capacity cabin/cargo hold with clamshell doors at the rear to provide easy access for wheeled or tracked vehicles. The rear doors could be removed completely for the deployment of heavy loads by parachute-extraction techniques, and could accommodate 78 persons for emergency evacuation, 42 fully-equipped paratroopers or 34 stretches. The fuselage was supported on the ground by robust retractable tricycle landing gear and power provided by two 1566-kW (2,100-hp) Pratt & Whitney R-2800-34 Double Wasp 18-cylinder radial engines in wing-mounted nacelles. Extending aft from these nacelles were tail-booms carrying twin fins and rudders and united at the rear by the tailplane mounting a single elevator.

The US Army Air Force placed an initial contract for 100 **C-82A** aircraft, these being named **Packet**. The first were delivered for evaluation in 1945 and a contract for 100 more followed. Because of wartime demands a second production line was laid down by North American Aviation at Dallas, Texas, but from a contract for 792 **C-82N** only three were completed before the general rash of contract cancellations that followed VJ Day. Fairchild eventually built a total of 220 with deliveries ending in 1948. Although too late to operate during World War II, the Packet provided valuable service to the USAF's Tactical Air Command and Military Air Transport Service before it was retired in 1954.

An offensive role was bestowed on the C-119 in the form of the AC-119G/K gunship. This is the basic AC-119G, which was armed with four 7.62-mm Miniguns in the port side of the cabin.

Fairchild C-119G 'Jet-Pak' conversion for the Indian Air Force.

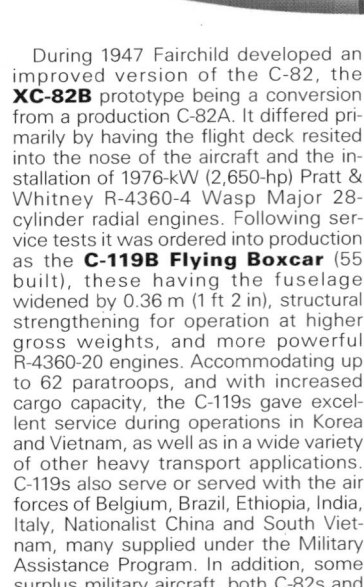

Fairchild C-119F/G Flying Boxcar

During 1947 Fairchild developed an improved version of the C-82, the **XC-82B** prototype being a conversion from a production C-82A. It differed primarily by having the flight deck resited into the nose of the aircraft and the installation of 1976-kW (2,650-hp) Pratt & Whitney R-4360-4 Wasp Major 28-cylinder radial engines. Following service tests it was ordered into production as the **C-119B Flying Boxcar** (55 built), these having the fuselage widened by 0.36 m (1 ft 2 in), structural strengthening for operation at higher gross weights, and more powerful R-4360-20 engines. Accommodating up to 62 paratroops, and with increased cargo capacity, the C-119s gave excellent service during operations in Korea and Vietnam, as well as in a wide variety of other heavy transport applications. C-119s also serve or served with the air forces of Belgium, Brazil, Ethiopia, India, Italy, Nationalist China and South Vietnam, many supplied under the Military Assistance Program. In addition, some surplus military aircraft, both C-82s and C-119s, were acquired by civil operators.

In 1961 Steward-Davis Inc. of Long Beach, California, developed a **Jet-Pak** conversion for C-119 aircraft. This involved the installation of a 1542-kg (3,400-lb) thrust Westinghouse J34-WE-36 turbojet engine in a specially-developed nacelle mounted on the upper surface of the wing centre-section. At least 26 Indian Air Force C-119s had a more powerful HAL-built Orpheus jet pod to enable them to operate with greater payloads under 'hot and high' conditions.

Variants
EC-82A: redesignation of one C-82A after being equipped with tracked landing gear units
XC-119A (later C-119A): designation of XC-82B after modification to intended production standards
EC-119A: redesignation of above aircraft after conversion to serve as an ECM testbed
C-119C: production version (303 built) with revised tail unit; last 41 assembled by Kaiser Manufacturing Company
YC-119F: one service-test aircraft with two 2610-kW (3,500-hp) Wright R-3350 Duplex Cyclone 18-cylinder radial engines
C-119F: production version (212 built, 141 by Fairchild, 71 by Kaiser) with further tail revision
C-119G: production version (480 built, 392 by Fairchild, 88 by Kaiser) with propeller and equipment changes
AC-119G: 26 gunship conversions of C-119G with four 7.62-mm (0.3-in) six-barrel Miniguns, armour protection and flare-launchers
YC-119H Skyvan: one conversion from a C-119C; increased wing and tailplane span, revised tail surfaces, underwing fuel tanks and two R-3350 engines
C-119J: redesignation of 62 C-119F/G aircraft following incorporation of in-flight openable door in rear fuselage
EC-119J: redesignation of C-119Js converted for satellite tracking; about six completed
YC-119K: redesignation of one C-119G following installation of two 2759-kW (3,700-hp) R-3350 radial engines and two underwing 1293-kg (2,850-lb) thrust General Electric J85-GE-17 turbojets
C-119K: redesignation of five C-119Gs after conversion to above (YC-119K)

standard plus incorporation of brake anti-skid units
AC-119K: designation of 26 C-119Gs converted originally to AC-119G gunship standard, but given later the addition of two 20-mm cannon, improved avionics and installation of two underwing J85-GE-17 turbojets
C-119L: redesignation of 22 C-119Gs following updating and installation of new propellers
R4Q-1: version of C-119C for US Marine Corps; 39 built
R4Q-2: version of C-119F for US Marine Corps; 58 built
XC-120 Packplane: conversion of one C-119B to meet USAF requirement for an experimental detachable-fuselage transport; C-119B wings and tail surfaces combined with new upper fuselage component with a flat surface; lower component with flat upper surface, and incorporating cargo compartment, could be mated with the Packplane; flight deck in upper component; the type could be flown with or without the pack and it was intended that various packs for different military operations would be provided; no production contract followed military evaluation

Specification
Fairchild C-119G Flying Boxcar
Type: cargo and troop transport
Powerplant: two 2610-kW (3,500-hp) Wright R-3350-85 Duplex Cyclone 18-cylinder radial piston engines
Performance: cruising speed 322 km/h (200 mph); range with standard fuel 3669 km (2,280 miles)
Weights: empty 18136 kg (39,982 lb); maximum take-off 33747 kg (74,000 lb)
Dimensions: span 33.30 m (109 ft 3 in); length 26.37 m (86 ft 6 in); height 8.00 m (26 ft 3 in); wing area 134.43 m² (1,447.0 sq ft)

Fairchild C-123 Provider
to
Fairey Albacore

Fairchild C-123 Provider

In 1943 the Chase Aircraft Company was founded to undertake the design, development and production of a heavy assault cargo glider for the US Army. Following successful demonstration of an **XCG-18A** cargo glider, five **YCG-18A** pre-production examples followed. One of these was converted to a **YC-122** light assault transport aircraft by the addition of two wing-mounted radial engines, and **YC-122A/B/C** aircraft followed for service trials, leading to construction of two prototypes of an even larger troop/cargo transport. Designed **XCG-20** (later **XG-20**) in glider form, one was redesignated **XC-123** when powered by two 1641-kW (2,200-hp) Pratt & Whitney R-2800-23 Double Wasp 18-cylinder radial engines; it was first flown on 14 October 1949. Chase received a contract in 1952 for five pre-production **C-123B Provider** transports which were built and flown in 1953. In that same year Kaiser-Frazer Corporation acquired a majority holding in the Chase Aircraft Company, and was awarded a USAF production contract for 300 C-123Bs. This was cancelled in mid-1953 and awarded instead to Fairchild, which then assumed responsibility for continued development and production of the C-123B.

A cantilever high-wing monoplane of all-metal construction, the C-123 had a large-capacity fuselage upswept at the rear and incorporating a loading door in the undersurface that could be lowered to serve as a ramp. Other features of the configuration were a conventional but tall tail unit, retractable tricycle landing gear, and power provided by two Pratt & Whitney Double Wasp radial engines. As an alternative to cargo, the main cabin could accommodate 60 fully-equipped troops, or 50 stretcher patients plus six sitting patients and six medical attendants. Fairchild's interest in develop-

A specialist role the Provider undertook in Vietnam was the spraying of defoliants to deny guerrillas jungle cover.

ment of this aircraft brought the introduction of a large dorsal fin to improve directional stability. The company's first production C-123B, powered by two Pratt & Whitney R-2800 Double Wasp radial engines, made its initial flight on 1 September 1954. Production by Fairchild totalled 302, including one static test airframe and 24 for delivery, to Saudi Arabia (6) and Venezuela (18). At a later date surplus USAF C-123Bs were supplied also to the Philippines, Taiwan and South Vietnam. At least one **C-123K** squadron was operating with the US Air Force Reserve as late as 1982.

Three experimental versions of this aircraft were built for USAF evaluation by the Stroukoff Aircraft Corporation whose president, Michael Stroukoff, had been the chief engineer of the Chase Aircraft Company. These include the **YC-123D**, similar to a C-123B but with a boundary-layer control system; a **YC-123E** with a revised fin and rudder and a Stroukoff 'Pantobase' landing system incorporating retractable land and water skis, wheels and wingtip floats for operation from a wide variety of surfaces; and one **YC-134A** incorporating both of the above systems.

Variants

HC-123B: designation applied sometimes to 11 C-123Bs transferred

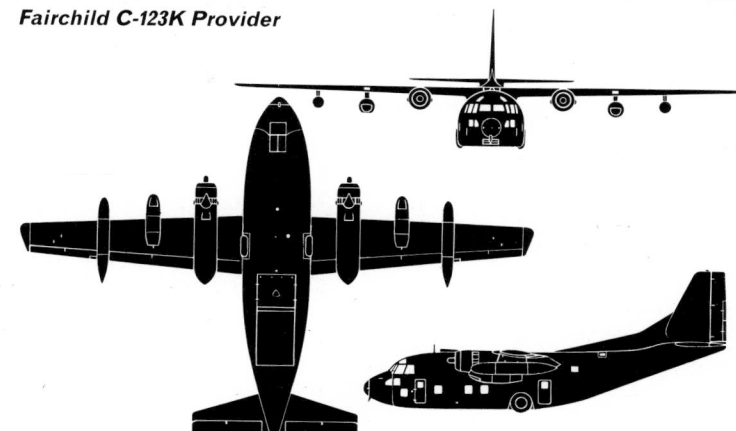

Fairchild C-123K Provider

to the US Coast Guard
UC-123B: designation of a small number of C-123Bs converted for use as crop destruction/forest defoliation aircraft in Vietnam
VC-123C: proposed command transport not built by Kaiser-Frazer
YC-123H: evaluation prototype with special wide-track landing gear; later tested with auxiliary power provided by two 1293-kg (2,850-lb) thrust General Electric J85-GE-17 turbojets in underwing pods
C-123J: redesignation of 10 C-123Bs for operation under Arctic conditions

following installation of Fairchild J44 auxiliary turbojets in wingtip pods
C-123K: redesignation of 183 C-123Bs following installation of two J85-GE-17 auxiliary turbojets in underwing pods, larger wheels and an anti-skid braking system
NC-123K: redesignation of two C-123Ks after conversion for armed night surveillance; sometimes known as **AC-123K**
UC-123K: designation of 34 C-123Ks converted for forest defoliation missions in Vietnam
VC-123K: designation of one C-123K following conversion as a VIP transport

Specification
Fairchild C-123B Provider
Type: tactical transport
Powerplant: two 1715-kW (2,300-hp) Pratt & Whitney R-2800-99W Double Wasp 18-cylinder radial piston engines
Performance: maximum speed 394 km/h (245 mph); cruising speed 330 km/h (205 mph); range 2366 km (1,470 miles)
Weights: empty 13562 kg (29,900 lb); maximum take-off 27216 kg (60,000 lb)
Dimensions: span 33.53 m (110 ft 0 in); length 23.09 m (75 ft 9 in); height 10.39 m (34 ft 1 in); wing area 113.62 m² (1,223.0 sq ft)

Fairchild FC-1/FC-2

In the early 1920s Sherman Fairchild was engaged actively in the business of aerial photography and survey. A variety of aircraft were used for this purpose, all with some shortcomings, so he designed what he considered to be an ideal aircraft for the purpose. Tenders for construction of a number of these aircraft appeared to be prohibitive, resulting in a decision to build them 'in house'. Thus Fairchild acquired premises at Farmingdale, Long Island, in which to begin aircraft manufacture, and the company's Fairchild Republic Division is still based at Farmingdale.

As first flown in mid-1926, the **Fairchild FC-1** was of braced high-wing monoplane configuration, with a wing that could be folded for storage, a braced tail unit, tailskid landing gear and power provided by a 67-kW (90-hp) Curtiss

OX-5 8-cylinder Vee engine. The fuselage provided enclosed-cabin accommodation for a pilot and one or two passengers, and there were ample

windows and ports for easy use of cameras. After extensive testing during 1926, the FC-1 was re-engined with a 149-kW (200-hp) Wright J-4 Whirlwind

The FC-2 was one of the original 'bushplanes', here exemplified by a FC-2W2. The civil registration is the old style for Canada.

9-cylinder radial engine, being redesignated **FC-1A** in this form. Further tests followed into 1927 before a decision was made to put the aircraft into production for general sales under the designation **FC-2**. This version differed by having increased cabin volume to seat a pilot plus four passengers, and a new Wright J-5 Whirlwind engine (standard) or Curtiss C-6 engine (optional). FC-2s were also available with float or ski landing gear in place of the standard main wheels. A total of 56 FC-2s were built over an eight-month period from 1 June 1927.

Variants

Fairchild FC-2W: generally similar to FC-2 but intended more specifically as a cargo carrier; modified windows, increased wing span and area, and more powerful 298-kW (400-hp) Pratt & Whitney Wasp 9-cylinder radial engine
Fairchild FC-2W2: similar to FC-2W, but with fuselage lengthened by 0.66 m (2 ft 2 in) and revised interior to accommodate a pilot and up to six passengers; seats easily removed for cargo carrying; most famous FC-2W2 was *Stars and Stripes*, used by the Byrd Antarctic Expedition of 1928
Fairchild FC-2C (Challenger): designation of small number of five-

seat FC-2s built for Curtiss Flying Service and powered by the 119-kW (160-hp) Curtiss C-6 Challenger 6-cylinder inline piston engine
C-96: designation allocated by the USAAF in 1942 to three FC-2W2s impressed for military service
XJQ-1: under this designation the US Navy acquired a single example of the FC-2 for evaluation; re-engined subsequently with a 336-kW (450-hp) Pratt & Whitney R-985 Wasp Junior 9-cylinder radial it became redesignated **XJQ-2,** later **XRQ-2**

Specification

Fairchild FC-2
Type: five-seat utility aircraft
Powerplant: one 149-kW (200-hp) Wright J-5 Whirlwind 9-cylinder radial piston engine
Performance: maximum speed 196 km/h (122 mph); cruising speed 169 km/h (105 mph); service ceiling 3505 m (11,500 ft); range 1127 km (700 miles)
Weights: empty 980 kg (2,160 lb); maximum take-off 1633 kg (3,600 lb)
Dimensions: span 13.41 m (44 ft 0 in); length 9.45 m (31 ft 0 in); height 2.74 m (9 ft 0 in); wing area 26.94 m² (290.0 sq ft)

Fairchild FH-227

In April 1956 Fokker in the Netherlands concluded an agreement with Fairchild for manufacture of the F27 Friendship then under development in Holland. Thus Fairchild became responsible for production and marketing in North America of the F27 series of aircraft that corresponded to some of those built by the Dutch company. However, when Fokker developed a 'stretched' version known as the F27 Mk 500, Fairchild decided to design its own version with a lengthened fuselage and this was identified as the **Fairchild Hiller FH-227**.

The FH-227 differed from the standard F27 by having a fuselage 'stretch' of 1.83 m (6 ft 0 in) to provide accommodation for a maximum of 52 passengers, with increased baggage and cargo space, and by the installation of 1678-ekW (2,250-eshp) Rolls-Royce Dart RDa.7 Mk 532-7 turboprop engines. The first of two FH-227 prototypes made its initial flight on 27 January 1966. Production of FH-227s and their variants had reached 79 when production ended. About 30 FH-227s of different marks remained in airline service in 1991.

Variants

FH-227B: certificated in June 1967, this version had structural strengthening for operation at a higher gross weight, uprated Dart RDa.7 Mk 532-7L engines, larger-diameter propellers and a redesigned windscreen
FH-227C: basically a standard FH-227

Identified by its lengthened fuselage, the FH-227 was a development of the Fokker F27. ACES Colombia had one on strength, and now operates two Fairchild-built F27s in its domestic fleet.

with the larger-diameter propeller of the FH-227B
FH-227D: introduced anti-skid braking units; an intermediate flap setting for take-off, and Dart RDa.7 Mk 532-7L engines
FH-227E: basically an FH-227C with the FH-227D improvements incorporated

Specification
Fairchild Hiller FH-227B
Type: passenger transport
Powerplant: two 1715-ekW (2,300-eshp) Rolls-Ryoce Dart RDa.7 Mk 532-7L turboprops
Performance: maximum cruising speed 473 km/h (294 mph) at 6095 m (20,000 ft); economic cruising speed 453 km/h (270 mph) at 7620 m (25,000 ft); service ceiling 8535 m (28,000 ft); range with maximum payload and fuel reserves 975 km (606 miles)
Weights: empty 10523 kg (23,200 lb); maximum take-off 20638 kg (45,000 lb)
Dimensions: span 29.01 m (95 ft 2 in); length 25.50 m (83 ft 8 in); height 8.41 m (27 ft 7 in); wing area 70.05 m² (754.0 sq ft)

Fairchild-Hiller FH-227B of Touraine Air Transport (France). The airline is now named Transport Aérien Transrégional, and still operates eight FH-227s with two Fairchild-built F27Js.

Fairchild M62

For many years it had been traditional to use light two-seat biplanes for primary flying training. This meant that the inexperienced pilot began his tuition in what was generally accepted to be the most easily mastered of all aeroplanes, slow, stable, and forgiving of errors and hard treatment. It was suggested, however, that this could breed over-confidence, making the next stage of training more difficult. Many experienced instructors believed that a monoplane with higher wing loading, which needed to be thoughtfully flown for more of the time, could ensure that the step to be climbed from primary to advanced training would not be quite so high.

This line of thought led to a break with tradition so far as the US Army Air Corps was concerned, and with a need for more primary training aircraft in 1939 the

USAAC carried out an evaluation of the **Fairchild M62** two-seat monoplane. By comparison with the US Army's most advanced biplane trainer then in service (the Stearman PT-13), maximum speed, rate of climb and service ceiling were very nearly the same. But the wing loading of the M62 was almost 43 per cent higher, which meant that its stalling speed was also higher and its low-speed handling characteristics just that little more critical. It seemed to be exactly what was needed, and in 1940 an initial order was placed for these trainers under the designation **PT-19**.

A cantilever low-wing monoplane of mixed construction, the M62 had a conventional tail unit, tailwheel landing gear and power provided by a 130-kW (175-hp) Ranger L-440-1 six-cylinder inline engine. Instructor and pupil were accommodated in tandem cockpits enclosed by a sliding transparent canopy.

Delivery of PT-19s began in 1940, and

Fairchild PT-26/Cornell

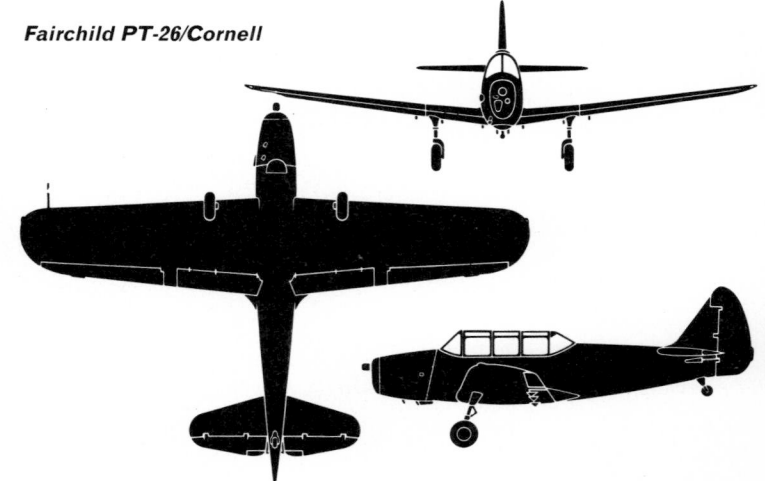

the aircraft soon proved that they were not lethal instruments of destruction in the hands of embryo pilots. With the expansion of flying training in 1941 Fairchild rapidly discovered it had contracts for more aeroplanes than could be built in its existing factory. Steps were taken to double its capacity, and arrangements made with Aeronca Aircraft Corporation at Middletown, Ohio, and St Louis Aircraft Corporation at St Louis, Missouri, to initiate production on Fairchild's behalf. At a later stage the Howard Aircraft Corporation of St Charles, Illinois, provided an additional source of production.

A total of 270 PT-19s was built before a new **PT-19A (M62A)** version was introduced on the production lines of Fairchild, Aeronca and St Louis, these companies turning out 3,182, 432 and 44 respectively. The only significant change in this version was the introduction of the slightly more powerful Ranger L-440-3 engine and some refinements in detail. The PT-19A, like the original version, had only basic instrumentation and so was unsuitable for blind-flying or instrument flight training. This shortcoming was rectified in the subsequent **PT-19B**, which had full blind-flying instrumentation and a hood to cover the pupil's front cockpit when such training was in progress. Production totalled 774 by Fairchild and 143 by Aeronca.

The combination of production contracts covering numbers far in excess of those which Fairchild had anticipated,

with the urgency of the US Army's requirements, resulted in 1942 in a famine of Ranger engines. To resolve the situation the company produced an **XPT-23** (M62A) prototype by the installation of an uncowled 164-kW (220-hp) Continental R-670-5 seven-cylinder radial engine and, after evaluation, this was put into production with the designation **PT-23**. A total of 869 was built by Fairchild (2), Aeronca (375), Howard (199), St Louis (200) with the R-670-11 engine, as well as 93 by Fleet Aircraft Ltd of Fort Erie, Ontario, for use in the Commonwealth Air Training Scheme which had been established in Canada. A version of the PT-23, with the blind-flying instrumentation and hood which had been introduced on the PT-19B, was built by Howard (150) and St Louis (106) under

the designation **PT-23A**. This was the last version to be built for the USAAF in America, with almost 6,000 delivered before the production lines closed down.

The PT-23s which Fleet in Canada had built for service under the Commonwealth Air Training Scheme had resulted in the request for a slightly more advanced version, and this reverted to use of the Ranger L-440-3 engine. Improvements included duplication of all controls and blind-flight and navigation instruments in each cockpit, plus the provision of cockpit heating. Construction of this **M62A-3** version totalled 1,727, with Fairchild in the USA building 670. These had the designation **PT-26** and were supplied under Lend-Lease to the RCAF, which named them **Cornell Mk I**. Fleet in Canada produced 807 **PT-26A** aircraft with 149-kW (200-hp)

Ranger L-440-7 engines, identified by the RCAF as **Cornell Mk II**, and 250 generally similar **PT-26B** aircraft which the RCAF used as **Cornell Mk III**.

Specification
Fairchild PT-26A
Powerplant: one 149-kW (200-hp) Ranger L-440-7 six-cylinder inverted piston engine
Performance: maximum speed 196 km/h (122 mph); cruising speed 163 km/h (101 mph); service ceiling 4025 m (13,200 ft); range 644 km (400 miles)
Weights: empty 917 kg (2,022 lb); maximum take-off 1241 kg (2,736 lb)
Dimensions: span 10.97 m (36 ft 0 in); length 8.45 m (27 ft 8½ in); height 2.32 m (7 ft 7½ in); wing area 18.58 m² (200 sq ft)

Fairchild Cornell of the Royal Norwegian air force, based at 'Little Norway' (Ontario airport) during late World War II.

Fairchild Republic A-10A Thunderbolt II

In 1967 the US Air Force initiated its A-X programme to procure a new close-support aircraft. As a result of design submissions Fairchild and Northrop were each contracted to build two prototypes of their design for competitive evaluation, Fairchild's design being allocated the designation **Fairchild Republic YA-10A**. The first of these prototypes (71-1369) was flown on 10 May 1972, and on 18 January 1973 it was announced that Fairchild had been selected as winner of the contest. An initial contract for six **A-10A** service test aircraft followed, the first of them flying on 15 February 1975, and the first production A-10A was flown on 21 October 1975. The procurement of 747 aircraft was planned by the USAF, but funding for the last 20 of this number was deleted from the US Fiscal Year 1983 budget.

A cantilever low-wing monoplane of all-metal construction, the A-10A incorporates a tail unit with twin fins and rudders, retractable tricycle landing gear, and two General Electric TF34-GE-100 turbofan engines enclosed in pods, these last being mounted on opposite

sides of the upper sides of the rear fuselage. An enclosed cockpit well forward of the wings accommodates the pilot on a zero-zero ejection seat and his protection against ground weapons includes a bullet-proof windscreen and an armoured 'bath-tub' structure of titanium which is designed to give protection against weapons of 23-mm calibre.

Intended to have the capability to operate from primitive or unprepared areas, so that it can offer short-term response against enemy vehicles, the A-10A has been especially designed for this task. A large-area wing gives low-speed manoeuvrability over the battlefield while carrying heavy loads of weapons. In addition to the armour protection of the pilot's 'office', survivability is optimised by the incorporation of armour-protected flight control systems; self-sealing fuel tanks are filled with reticulated foam and fuel lines to the engines have self-sealing protection; and redundancy for the powered flight controls is provided by duplicated hydraulic systems plus manual back-up.

Primary weapon of the A-10A is its

General Electric GAU-8/A Avenger 30-mm seven-barrel cannon, with a maximum firing rate of 4,200 rounds per minute. Its magazine contains 1,174 devastating armour-piercing rounds, each weighing 0.73 kg (1.6 lb). In addition, three underfuselage and eight underwing stores pylons have a combined external load capacity of 7257 kg (16,000 lb). Stores that can be carried include AGM-65 Maverick missiles; ALE-40 chaff/flare system; ALQ-119 ECM pods or other jammer pods; BLU-1 or BLU-27B incendiary bombs; CBU-52/71 dispenser weapons; Mk 82 LDGP bombs, laser-guided or retarded bombs; Mk 84 electro-optically-guided, laser-guided or general-purpose bombs; Rockeye II cluster bombs; SUU-23 gun pods; and SUU-25 flare-launchers.

The USAF's 354th Tactical Fighter Wing began to receive production A-10As in March 1977, and subsequently became the first combat-ready wing.

The first overseas deployment was made on 25 January 1979, to RAF stations Bentwaters and Woodbridge in the UK, and in early 1982 the first A-10As were stationed in South Korea. Also in 1982 deliveries of new A-10As began to the US Air National Guard and the US Air Force Reserve. The 600th Thunderbolt II was delivered during 1982, this total including 30 combat-ready two-seat trainers.

On 4 May 1979 Fairchild flew the prototype of a company-funded two-seat **Night/Adverse Weather A-10** allowing the carriage of a weapons system officer in the rear cockpit, and responsible for ECM, navigation, and target or

Still an important type in the USAF inventory, the A-10 is a dedicated battlefield aircraft, able to survive in an environment of intense ground fire and to cripple tanks, vehicles and artillery with its 30-mm cannon and Maverick missiles. It was a crucial weapon type in the war with Iraq.

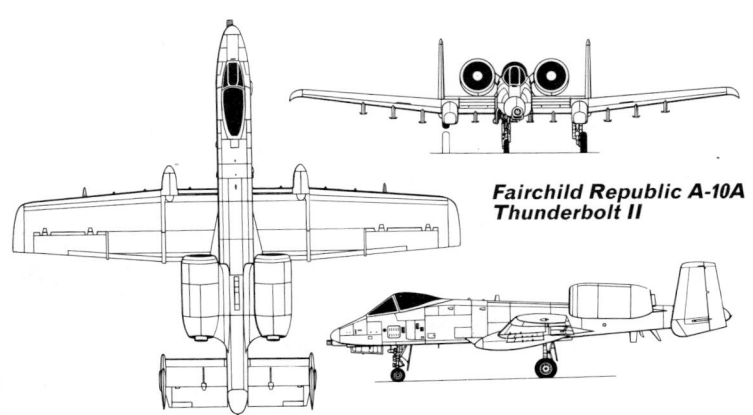

Fairchild Republic A-10A Thunderbolt II

threat acquisition and designation. This was intended to reduce the workload of the pilot, allowing him to concentrate on control of the aircraft during operations in adverse weather or darkness. However, no further development of this version followed service testing in 1980.

Specification
Fairchild A-10A Thunderbolt II
Type: single-seat close-support aircraft
Powerplant: two 4112-kg (9,065-lb)

The YA-10B was a company-funded two-seat night-attack version which was not procured.

thrust General Electric TF34-GE-100 turbofans
Performance: maximum speed (clean, at sea level) 706 km/h (439 mph); cruising speed 555 km/h (345 mph) at sea level; loiter endurance at 463 km (288 miles) from base 1 hour 40 minutes
Weights: empty operating 11321 kg (24,959 lb); maximum take-off 22680 kg (50,000 lb)
Dimensions: span 17.53 m (57 ft 6 in); length 16.26 m (53 ft 4 in); height 4.47 m (14 ft 8 in); wing area 47.01 m² (506 sq ft)
Armament: as detailed in text

Fairchild Swearingen Merlin II/III and Metro III

Swearingen Aviation Corporation became a wholly-owned subsidiary of Fairchild Industries in 1979, and from early 1981 has been known as Fairchild Swearingen Corporation. Ed J. Swearingen built up his business initially by building prototypes for other companies, and by designing and marketing improved versions of Beech Queen Air and Twin Bonanza aircraft. In 1964 Swearingen began the development of an aircraft known as the **Swearingen Merlin IIA**. This was a turboprop-powered eight-seat executive aircraft, which combined a new fuselage of Swearingen design with a modified Queen Air wing and Twin Bonanza landing gear. First flown on 13 April 1965, the Merlin IIA proved a tractable design and deliveries began in August 1966 shortly after the receipt of certification.

The Merlin IIA was powered by two 410-kW (550-shp) Pratt & Whitney (then

United Aircraft of Canada) PT6A-20 turboprops, but in June 1968 it was superseded by an improved **Merlin IIB** powered by two 496-kW (665-shp) Garrett TPE 331-1-151G turboprop engines. Shortly after this the new **Merlin III** was introduced, this having the fuselage lengthened by 0.62 m (2 ft 0½ in) and incorporating wings, tail unit and landing gear of Swearingen design plus two 626-kW (840-shp) TPE 331-303G turboprops. Developed more or less simultaneously with the Merlin III was the **SA 226TC Metro** 20-passenger commuter airliner with the same powerplant, and differing from it primarily by having a lengthened fuselage to provide the necessary accommodation. Introduced at the same time was the **Merlin IV**, a corporate version of the Metro which differed by accommodating only 12 passengers in a more luxurious interior.

The Merlin IIB was discontinued in

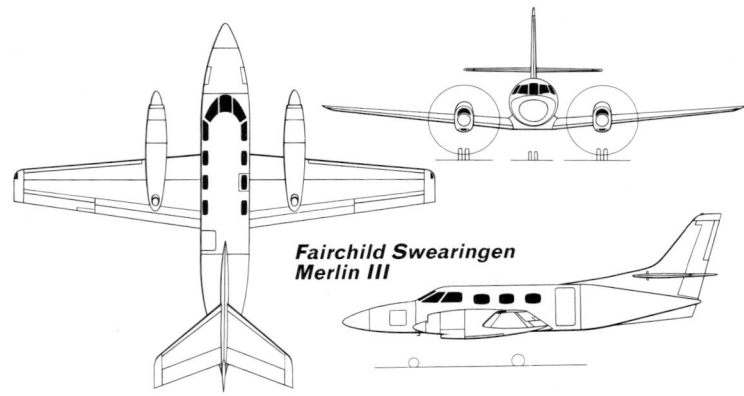

Fairchild Swearingen Merlin III

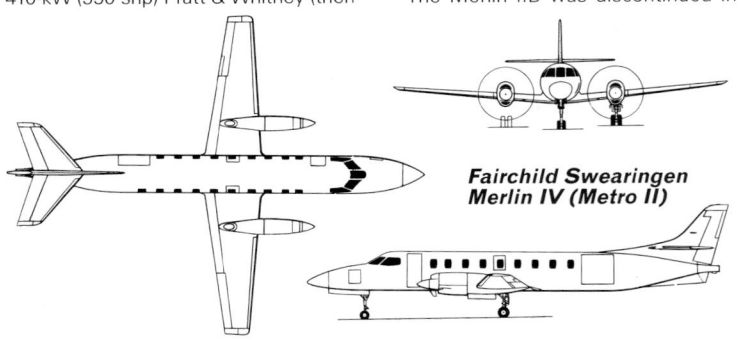

Fairchild Swearingen Merlin IV (Metro II)

1972, but development of the Merlin and Metro continued with the 8/11-seat **Merlin IIIC** executive transport with 671-kW (900-shp) TPE 331-10U-503G turboprops; the **Merlin** IVC 13/16-seat corporate aircraft, and the generally similar **Metro III** 19/20-passenger commuter transport. An alternative version, the **Metro IIIA**, was schemed with two PT6A-45R turboprops each flat-rated at 820 kW (1,100 shp), but did not proceed.

In 1988, Fairchild announced the TPE 331-12-powered 19-seat **Metro V**, along with an executive version designated the **Merlin IV**, but development of both types was terminated in 1989. An even higher-powered variant, the **Metro VI** fitted with Garrett TPE 331-14 engines was also abandoned.

Between February 1990 and the spring of 1991, Fairchild Aircraft (by then a subsidiary of GMF Investments) was in Chapter 11 receivership, but series production of Metro IIIs, especially for the US Air Force as the **C-26** command

transport continued.

Latest development of the basic airframe is the **Metro 25**, a Metro III able to carry 25 passengers, with a rearranged interior, deleted cargo door and extra windows in the fuselage. A Metro III (N2671V), modified to incorporate Metro 25 features, flew in September 1989 and a full go-ahead awaits the resolution of the company's financial situation.

Specification
Fairchild Swearingen Metro III
Type: 20-passenger commuter airliner
Powerplant: two 820-kW (1,100-shp)

Compared with the standard Metro, the Metro II has a number of internal refinements. Crossair of Switzerland was a major European customer, buying the type to establish its regional services in Switzerland, Germany and France.

Garrett TPE 331-11U-601G turboprops
Performance: maximum cruising speed 515 km/h (320 mph) at 4570 m (15,000 ft); service ceiling 8380 m (27,500 ft); range with 19 passengers and fuel reserves 1611 km (1,001 miles)
Weights: empty operating 3963 kg (8,737 lb); maximum take-off 6577 kg (14,500 lb)
Dimensions: span 17.37 m (57 ft 0 in); length 18.09 m (59 ft 1¼ in); height 5.08 m (16 ft 8 in); wing area 28.71 m² (309 sq ft)

An updated version of the successful Merlin III, the Merlin IIIB offers a good combination of flight performance and economy coupled with useful payload and a high degree of comfort. Most aircraft went to corporate customers.

Fairey III family

The fact that a Fairey IIIF was still in service in 1941 when the basic design originated in 1917 illustrates convincingly the soundness of what was possibly Fairey's most successful aircraft in terms of service usage.

In late 1917, the Fairey N.10 seaplane was modified to landplane configuration and designated **Fairey IIIA**. Fifty were ordered as carrier-based two-seat bombers to replace RNAS Sopwith 1½-Strutters, and the first production Fairey IIIA flew at Northolt in June 1918. The cessation of hostilities prevented the aircraft seeing much service, and the type was declared obsolete in 1919.

Another variant, the **Fairey IIIB**, using the same fuselage and tail with increased wing, fin and rudder areas, entered small-scale production as a floatplane and saw some service on mine-spotting patrols from coastal bases. Twenty-five were built, and the first flew at Hamble in August 1918; like the Fairey IIIA, the Fairey IIIB was powered by the 194-kW (260-hp) Sunbeam Maori engine. Sixty serial numbers had been allocated for Fairey IIIB production, and the last 30 plus a few from the previous batch were converted on the production line into **Fairey IIIC** aircraft.

This version was similar to the Fairey IIIB, but reverted to the equal span wings of the Fairey IIIA; however, a great improvement in performance resulted from the use of the 280-kW (375-hp) Rolls-Royce Eagle VIII engine.

First production deliveries were made in November 1918 to No. 229 Squadron at Great Yarmouth, and others went to No. 267 Squadron in Malta. The only aircraft to see active service did so with the North Russian Expeditionary Force in 1919, transported by the seaplane-carrier HMS *Pegasus*.

The reliability of the Eagle engine earned the Fairey IIIC a high reputation, but only 35 were built, beginning to replace the earlier type in RAF service from 1921. Several Fairey IIICs survived to enter civilian service; one, fitted with sliding canopies and long-range tanks, was shipped to Newfoundland in March 1920 for a projected transatlantic flight which never materialised. It had formerly been used as a civil two-seat seaplane demonstrator by Fairey, and following damage in Canada was returned to the makers for rebuild and resale.

Next derivative in the series was the **Fairey IIID**, a direct development of the Fairey IIIC, incorporating a number of technical and constructional improve-

ments as a result of experience with the earlier models. In its landplane form the Fairey IIID was the first aircraft to be fitted with an oleo-pneumatic landing gear, flying for the first time in August 1920 with a 280-kW (375-hp) Rolls-Royce Eagle VIII engine. Air Ministry contracts to Specification 38/22 were placed and total production for the RAF amounted to 207, of which 56 had Eagle engines and the remainder 336-kW (450-hp) Napier Lions of various marks.

The majority of the Fairey IIIDs served as floatplanes with the Fleet Air Arm, operating from shore stations or from catapults on warships. Nos 441 and 444 Flights were the first to receive Fairey IIIDs, in 1924, the former operating landplanes from HMS *Argus* and the latter seaplanes aboard HMS *Vindictive*. On 30 October 1925 one of these earned the distinction of being the first FAA seaplane to be catapulted from a ship at sea. The FAA Fairey IIIDs replaced Parnall Panthers and Supermarine Seagull amphibians, and eventually served with nine flights ranging from Leuchars in Scotland to the Far East. Naval Fairey IIIDs were normally three-seaters, but a number of two-seat trainers were built and another two-seater was used for target towing.

As a landplane, the Fairey IIID's major contribution to RAF history was in 1926, when four aircraft flew from Heliopolis to Cape Town, returning to England via Greece, Italy and France without any mechanical failures. They covered a distance of 22371 km (13,901 miles) and were converted to seaplanes at Aboukir for the flight home to Lee-on-Solent. Only one RAF squadron received Fairey IIIDs: No. 202, which had formerly been No. 481 Flight of the FAA.

The sterling qualities of the Fairey IIID attracted several export orders. One from Australia was for six Eagle-engined aircraft, the first of which was handed over at Hamble on 12 August 1921. The third Australian Fairey IIID flew round that country's coastline, a distance of 13789 km (8,568 miles) in 1924, earning the Britannia Trophy for its crew. Eleven Fairey IIIDs were supplied to the Portuguese government, the first four with Eagle engines and the others with Lions. Two were lost in long-distance flight attempts, but a third completed the journey begun by the others from Lisbon to Rio de Janeiro. Two Fairey IIIDs were sold to Sweden and four to the Royal Netherlands naval air service for operations in the Dutch East Indies. A civil Fairey IIID with an Eagle IX engine was

modified for ambulance work in British Guiana in 1924 and another civil aircraft was used in 1927 as a four-seat D.H.50J replacement on a service between Khartoum and Kisumu. It lasted barely a month, being damaged beyond repair during salvage operations following landing gear collapse.

The designation **Fairey IIIE** does not appear to have been allocated, although some sources ascribe it to the Ferret. The final, and most prolific of the series, was the **Fairey IIIF**, a mainstay of the RAF and FAA between the two world wars. Intended as a replacement for the Fairey IIID, the Fairey IIIF was built to Specification 19/24, which called for a land-based two-seat general-purpose aircraft for the RAF and a three-seat spotter-reconnaissance aircraft for the FAA. The prototype, which flew in March 1926, had wooden wings with a composite wood/metal fuselage; production aircraft had an all-metal fuselage and later versions had all-metal wings. Compared with the Fairey IIID, the new version was considerably cleaned up and streamlined, with revised landing gear, curved fin and a Fairey-Reed metal propeller.

The Fairey IIIF had four basic marks, but within those were a multiplicity of sub-marks denoting type of construction (composite or all-metal) and equipment fits. A pre-production batch of 10 followed the two prototypes, and the Fleet Air Arm received a total of 352 aircraft, of which the first 50 comprised the early batch plus 40 **Fairey IIIF Mk I** aircraft, all with Napier Lion VA engines, while the remainder consisted of 33 **Fairey IIIF Mk II** and 269 **Fairey IIIF Mk III** aircraft of various types, all with Lion XIAs. RAF aircraft totalled 243, all variants of the basic **Fairey IIIF Mk IV**.

Four Dutch Fairey IIIDs in seaplane configuration, with the nearest machine showing the Fairey Patent Camber Gear ailerons, which could be drooped symmetrically to enhance the lift developed by the wing surfaces.

The first Fairey IIIFs to enter service were RAF machines although from the FAA pre-production batch; six went to No.47 Squadron at Khartoum in 1927 to replace Bristol Fighters. The first aircraft actually built for the RAF were a batch of 43 Mk IV and **Fairey IIIF Mk IVCM** aircraft delivered in January 1928 to No. 207 Squadron at Eastchurch, replacing elderly D.H.9As. Other RAF squadrons to be equipped with Fairey IIIFs were Nos 8, 14, 24, 35, 45 and 202, this last based at Malta and using the seaplane version. A number of outstanding flights were made by RAF Fairey IIIFs and the type was replaced eventually by the Fairey Gordon, a radial engine development known originally as the **Fairey IIIF Mk V**.

The Fleet Air Arm took delivery of its first Fairey IIIFs in 1928, when No. 440 Flight received its aircraft to replace Fairey IIIDs. Eventually, 12 flights operated the Fairey IIIF, which also replaced Avro Bisons, and Blackburn Blackbirds and Ripons. The type served with every aircraft-carrier of the period and on every naval air station; others equipped battleships and cruisers as floatplanes.

Among the experiments carried out with various Fairey IIIFs, one of the more interesting was the modification of three aircraft to autopilot/radio control for use as gunnery targets, in which form the type was known as the **Queen IIIF**. The first two aircraft were launched by catapult from HMS *Valiant* in January and

Five Fairey IIIFs of No. 202 Sqn, RAF, based in Malta in 1935. The new streamlined fuselage is shown to good effect.

April 1932 but both crashed after flights of 18 and 25 seconds respectively. The third flew successfully in September and in January 1933 was launched for its first test as a target. The Queen survived but the fleet failed miserably in its attempts, which lasted for two hours and exhausted the ammunition! However, in May 1933 the Royal Navy had the last laugh when it was shot down near Malta after 20 minutes' flight at 2440 m (8,000 ft).

The floatplane Fairey IIIFs began to be replaced by Hawker Ospreys in November 1932 and re-equipment was complete by 1935. Other Fairey IIIFs were gradually replaced from 1933 by Fairey Seals, the FAA equivalent of the Gordon. Known export sales of the Fairey IIIF included three to the Irish Army Air Corps, six to Argentina, two to New Zealand, 10 to Greece and one to Chile.

Various other engine installations were used on Fairey IIIFs, including the 343-kW (460-hp) Armstrong Siddeley Jaguar VI radial and the 336-kW (450-hp) Lorraine Ed12 water-cooled engine which was specified for the Argentine aircraft. These were later re-engined by the customer with 410-kW (550-hp) Armstrong Siddeley Panther VI radials. Other engines fitted for experimental work included 474-kW (635-hp) Rolls-Royce Kestrel II, 391-kW (525-hp) Panther IIA, 388-kW (520-hp) Bristol Jupiter VIII and the Napier Culverin, a licence-built Junkers Jumo V205C diesel engine.

Several Fairey IIIFs were civil-registered, the first of which was a Mk IIIM used as a demonstrator by Fairey; it later competed in the 'MacRobertson' England to Australia race in 1934. It remained in Australia following re-registration and was last recorded in 1936 in New Guinea.

Two Mk IIIMs were bought new by Air Survey Co. Ltd in 1930, but one was lost that year, the other carried out aerial mapping until it was retired in 1934.

Specification
Fairchild IIIF Mk IIIM/B seaplane
Type: two/three-seat spotter/reconnaissance/general-purpose aircraft
Powerplant: one 425-kW (570-hp) Napier Lion XIA 12-cylinder Vee piston engine
Performance: maximum speed 209 km/h (130 mph); service ceiling 6095 m (20,000 ft); endurance 3 to 4 hours
Weights: empty 1779 kg (3,923 lb); maximum take-off 2858 kg (6,300 lb)
Dimensions: span 13.94 m (45 ft 9 in); length 10.82 m (35 ft 6 in); height 4.26 m (14 ft 0 in); wing area 41.20 m² (443.50 sq ft)
Armament: one fixed forward-firing 7.7-mm (0.303-in) Vickers gun and one 7.7-mm (0.303-in) Lewis gun on Fairey high-speed mounting in rear cockpit, plus up to 227 kg (500 lb) of bombs

Fairey Albacore

As a replacement for the antiquated Fairey Swordfish, the **Fairey Albacore** appeared to have everything going for it. Neat in appearance, and with an enclosed cabin providing such luxuries as heating, a windscreen wiper and automatic emergency dinghy ejection, the Albacore nevertheless failed to come up to expectations. Far from supplanting the Swordfish, it merely complemented the older biplane and, ironically, was outlived by the latter in service.

Designed to Specification S.41/36, the Albacore was ordered off the drawing board in May 1937, the Air Ministry placing a contract for two prototypes and 98 production aircraft. The first prototype flew on 12 December 1938 from Fairey's Great West Aerodrome (now part of London's Heathrow Airport), and production began in 1939. The prototype was tested on floats at Hamble in 1940, but the results did not justify further development along these lines.

Later in the same year the first production aircraft underwent tests at the Aeroplane and Armament Experimental Establishment at Martlesham Heath, and it was this source that first had some misgivings but, despite this rather unpromising background, Albacores began to roll off the production line after a hold-up caused by engine development problems: the 794-kW (1,065-hp) Bristol Taurus II installed in early aircraft was later replaced by the Taurus XII.

No. 826 Squadron was formed at Ford, Sussex, specially to fly the Albacore, and received 12 aircraft on 15 March 1940, first using them in action on 31 May, attacking E-boats off Zeebrugge and road and rail targets at Westende, Belgium. The squadron moved to Bircham Newton, Norfolk, the following month, operating under the direction of Coastal Command until November, making night attacks, laying mines and bombing shipping. Three more Albacore squadrons formed before the end of 1940: No. 829 at Lee-on-Solent, No. 828 at Ford and No. 827 at Yeovilton, the last moving to Stornoway for anti-submarine patrols.

Albacores finally went to sea when Nos 826 and 829 Squadrons joined HMS *Formidable* on 26 November 1940, for convoy escort duty to Cape Town. Aircraft from these squadrons took part in the Battle of Cape Matapan in March 1941, pressing home their torpedo attacks in true Swordfish tradition against the Italian battleship *Vittorio Veneto*, the first occasion on which they had used torpedoes in action.

Fairey Albacore TB.Mk 1 strike- and torpedo-bomber of No. 826 Squadron, Fleet Air Arm.

By mid-1942 some 15 Fleet Air Arm squadrons were equipped with Albacores, operating from the Arctic Circle on Russian convoys, to the Western Desert, the Mediterranean and the Indian Ocean, and in November of that year Albacores of Nos 817, 820, 822 and 832 Squadrons were in action during the Allied invasion of North Africa, flying anti-submarine patrols and bombing enemy coastal guns. The type had reached its zenith in 1942, and the next year Fairey Barracudas began to replace them in all squadrons except No. 832, which was to be equipped with Grumman Avengers. The last two squadrons to give up their Albacores were Nos 820 and 841 in November 1943, aircraft from the latter unit being passed to No. 415 Squadron, Royal Canadian Air Force, at Manston for use in English Channel operations on D-Day.

Total Albacore production between 1939 and 1943 amounted to 800 including two prototypes.

Specification
Type: three-seat torpedo-bomber
Powerplant: one 843-kW (1,130-hp) Bristol Taurus XII 14-cylinder radial piston engine
Performance: maximum speed 259 km/h (161 mph) at 1370 m (4,500 ft); cruising speed 187 km/h (116 mph) at 1830 m (6,000 ft); service ceiling 6310 m (20,700 ft); range 1497 km (930 miles) with 726-kg (1,600-lb) weapons load
Weights: empty 3289 kg (7,250 lb); maximum take-off 4745 kg (10,460 lb)
Dimensions: span 15.24 m (50 ft 0 in); length 12.14 m (39 ft 10 in); height 4.32 m (14 ft 2 in); wing area 57.88 m² (623 sq ft)
Armament: one forward-firing 7.7-mm (0.303-in) machine-gun in starboard wing and twin 7.7-mm (0.303-in) Vickers 'K' guns in rear cockpit, plus one 730-kg (1,610-lb) torpedo beneath the fuselage, or six 113-kg (250-lb) or four 227-kg (500-lb) bombs beneath the wings

Fairey Barracuda
to
Fairey Flycatcher

Fairey Barracuda

The **Fairey Barracuda** torpedo- and dive-bomber originated from Specification S.24/37 to which six companies tendered, Fairey gaining an order for two prototypes in July 1938. Original powerplant selected was the 895-kW (1,200-hp) Rolls-Royce 24-cylinder Exe engine, but when its development was halted in favour of Merlins, Peregrines and Vultures a decision was made to use the 969-kW (1,300-hp) Merlin 30 to power the **Barracuda Mk I**. When flown on 7 December 1940 the first prototype was seen to be a cantilever shoulder-wing monoplane of all-metal construction, the foldable wings incorporating Fairey-Youngman trailing-edge flaps that gave this aircraft a much improved performance capability over its predecessors. The fuselage accommodated a crew of three in tandem cockpits, enclosed by a long 'greenhouse' canopy, and housed the main units of the tailwheel landing gear when retracted. Flight testing revealed that the low-set tailplane was badly positioned and a strut-based horizontal surface mounted high on a taller and narrower fin was designed for the second prototype. Because of the priority afforded to construction of fighters and bombers, this aircraft did not fly until 29 June 1941, and it was not until February 1942 that service trials and evaluation were completed. These showed the need for airframe strengthening which, together with the addition of equipment not included in the original Specification, resulted in the Barracuda

The Barracuda suffered from being too heavy, but nevertheless gave a good account of itself, notably during the Tirpitz attack.

suffering a weight problem that persisted through its service life. It played havoc with take-off and climb performance and after 30 Barracuda Mk Is had been built, introduction of the 1223-kW (1,640-hp) Merlin 32 resulted in redesignation to **Barracuda Mk II**, which was the main production version. Other companies selected to build the type under sub-contract included Blackburn, Boulton Paul and Westland. However, the last company built only five Barracuda Mk Is and 13 Barracuda Mk IIs from a total of 250 ordered, its contract being cancelled to allow the company to concentrate on the manufacture of Supermarine Seafires.

Barracudas built by Blackburn and Boulton Paul began to enter service in spring 1943, and although additional orders were placed, some of these were cancelled with the end of the war in Europe. In all, 1,688 Barracuda Mk IIs were built, plus 30 Barracuda Mk Is and two prototypes.

The **Barracuda Mk III** was evolved to take a new ASV radar installation, with a blister radome beneath the rear fuselage. The prototype, converted from a Boulton Paul-built Barracuda Mk II, flew first in 1943. Following orders placed that year, production of this version began in early 1944, built alongside Barracuda Mk IIs, and 852 Barracuda Mk IIIs were manufactured by Boulton Paul and Fairey.

The final production variant was the **Barracuda Mk V** (the Mk IV being an unbuilt project), and this differed considerably in appearance although the basic structure was unchanged. The shortfall in power of the Merlins available in 1941 made the designers consider alternatives, and the decision was taken to use a Rolls-Royce Griffon. Initial development was slow and the first Griffon-powered aircraft, converted from a Fairey-built Barracuda Mk II, did not fly until 16 November 1944.

In its production form, the Barracuda Mk V had a longer, squarer wing than earlier versions, enlarged fin area to counteract the greater torque of the 1514-kW (2,030-hp) Griffon 37, and increased fuel capacity. However, this development had come too late, and of the 140 Barracuda Mk Vs ordered only 30 were delivered before the end of the war brought cancellation of the outstanding balance.

The Barracuda's operational service life began when No. 827 Squadron received 12 Barracuda Mk IIs on being reformed at Stretton, Cheshire, on 10

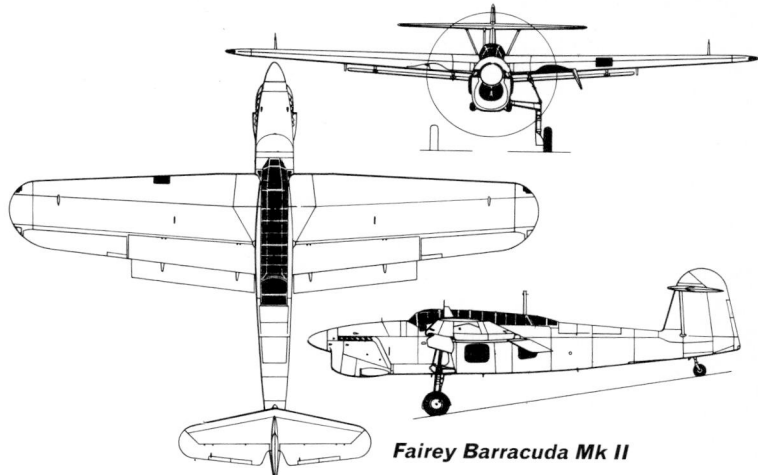

Fairey Barracuda Mk II

January 1943. A conspicuous action came when 42 aircraft dive-bombed the German battleship *Tirpitz* on 3 April 1944, inflicting heavy damage, and further attacks were made on the same target during the next four months.

The Barracuda squadrons of HMS *Illustrious*, Nos 810 and 847, introduced the type to the Pacific theatre in April 1944, supporting US Navy dive-bombers in an attack on Japanese installations in Sumatra. Barracudas flew from small escort carriers on anti-submarine patrols in European operations, using rocket-assisted take-off gear from the short decks. Most squadrons were disbanded soon after VJ-Day, or re-equipped with other aircraft, and after some shuffling within squadrons the last Barracudas in front-line service were replaced in 1953 by Grumman Avengers.

The Barracuda Mk Vs never entered front-line service, being used by Nos 705, 744 and 753 Squadrons for training until 1950.

Specification
Fairey Barracuda Mk II
Type: three-seat torpedo- and dive-bomber
Powerplant: one 1223-kW (1,640-hp) Rolls-Royce Merlin 32 12-cyliner Vee piston engine
Performance: maximum speed 367 km/h (228 mph) at 535 m (1,750 ft); maximum cruising speed 311 km/h (193 mph) at 1525 m (5,000 ft); service ceiling 5060 m (16,600 ft); range with torpedo 1101 km (684 miles)
Weights: empty 4241 kg (9,350 lb); maximum take-off 6396 kg (14,100 lb)
Dimensions: span 14.99 m (49 ft 2 in); length 12.12 m (39 ft 9 in); height 4.60 m (15 ft 1 in); wing area 34.09 m^2 (367.0 sq ft)
Armament: two 7.7-mm (0.303-in) Browning machine-guns in the rear cockpit, plus one 735-kg (1,620-lb) torpedo, or up to 726 kg (1,600 lb) of bombs, or six 113-kg (250-lb) depth charges, or 744 kg (1,640 lb) of mines

Fairey Battle

First flown on 10 March 1936, the prototype **Fairey Day Bomber**, as it was then known, originated as the company's submission to Specification P.27/32 for a two-seat single-engined monoplane bomber. This was required to carry 454 kg (1,000 lb) of bombs for 1609 km (1,000 miles) at a speed of 322 km/h (200 mph). In fact, this performance was exceeded by Fairey's aircraft which, contending against design proposals from Armstrong Whitworth, Bristol and Hawker, won the competition. However, a first production contract for 155 aircraft, to the revised Specification P.23/35, had been placed in 1935, before the prototype had flown. The first pro-

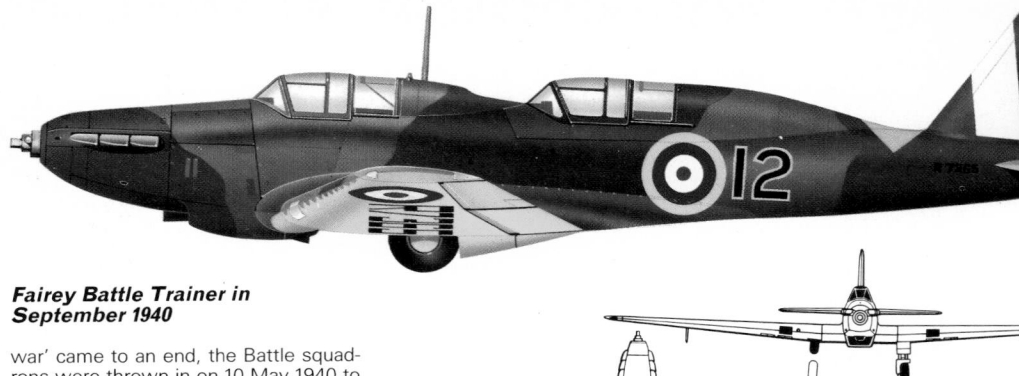

duction **Fairey Battle**, as the type was named, was built at Hayes, Middlesex, but the second and subsequent Fairey-built aircraft were manufactured at a new factory at Heaton Chapel, Stockport. It was to power the Battle that Rolls-Royce received the launching order for its famous 768-kW (1,030-hp) Merlin I engine, which powered the first 136 Fairey-built **Battle Mk I** aircraft. The introduction of Mk II to V versions of the Merlin engine identified equivalent **Battle Mk II** to **Battle Mk V** aircraft.

A cantilever low-wing monoplane of all-metal construction, except for some fabric-covered control surfaces, the Battle had a conventional tail unit, retractable tailwheel landing gear with the mainwheels partly exposed when retracted, and a fuselage incorporating a pilot's and a gunner's cockpit in tandem, both covered by a continuous transparent canopy. By the end of 1937 Fairey had completed 85 Battles, the first going to No. 63 Squadron at Upwood, Huntingdonshire, in May 1937. As new orders for Battles were placed, production sub-contracts were awarded to Austin Motors at Longbridge, Birmingham. Meantime, the last 19 Battles of the initial Fairey order for 155 were provided with Merlin II engines, and these were fitted also to the Austin-built aircraft. The first Battle from the Longbridge factory flew in July 1938, and 29 had been completed there by the end of the year. After 60 Austin-built Battles had been completed, the Merlin III engine was introduced on the production line.

By the outbreak of World War II more than 1,000 Battles had been delivered, and aircraft of No. 226 Squadron were the first to be sent to France as part of the Advanced Air Striking Force. It was here that the aircraft's inability to defend itself against enemy fighters became obvious. On armed daylight reconnaissance missions the type occasionally tangled with Messerschmitt Bf 109s, and although one of the latter was destroyed by a Battle's rear gunner in September 1940, the light bombers invariably suffered heavy casualties.

As the period of the so-called 'phoney

war' came to an end, the Battle squadrons were thrown in on 10 May 1940 to try to stop the advancing German ground forces. Without fighter escort, and attacking from a height of only 76 m (250 ft) with delayed-action bombs, they came under heavy ground fire, losing 13 of the 32 aircraft sent on the mission, all the others being damaged. The next day seven out of eight Battles were lost, and on 12 May five Battles of No. 12 Squadron, flown by volunteer crews, attacked two vital road bridges over the Albert Canal. In the face of extremely heavy ground fire the attack was pressed home and one bridge seriously damaged, but at a cost of all five aircraft. Further heavy losses came on 14 May, when 35 out of 63 Battles failed to return from attacks against bridges and troop concentrations. This marked the end of the aircraft's career as a day bomber, and although a few remained in front-line service until late 1940 the survivors were mostly diverted to other duties. The most important of these was for training, and 100 were built as dual-control trainers with separate cockpits, while 266 target-towing variants were also supplied.

The last production aircraft, Austin-built, was a **Battle TT.Mk 1** target tug (266 built and many others converted), and it was delivered on 2 September 1940. It brought total Battle production to 2,203 including the prototype, 1,156 being built by Fairey and 1,029 by Austin Motors.

Canada used a large number of Battles for training and target towing in the Commonwealth Air Training Plan, the first

Fairey Battle Trainer in September 1940

Fairey Battle Mk I

being supplied to the Royal Canadian Air Force at Camp Borden in August 1939. They were the vanguard of 739 of these aircraft, this total including seven airframes for instructional purposes. The Royal Australian Air Force received four British-built Battles and assembled 360 in Australia, including 30 target tugs, while other customers were Belgium (18 built under licence by Avions Fairey), Turkey (29), South Africa (190 or more) and Eire, where an RAF aircraft which landed at Waterford in 1941 was interned and later taken over by the Air Corps.

Several Battles were used as test-beds for such engines as the Napier Dagger and Sabre; Bristol Hercules and Taurus; Rolls-Royce Exe and Merlin XII; and Fairey Prince. Others were used for experiments with various types of propellers.

Specification
Fairey Battle Mk I
Type: three-seat light bomber
Powerplant: one 768-kW (1,030-hp) Rolls-Royce Merlin I 12-cylinder Vee piston engine
Performance: maximum speed 414 km/h (257 mph) at 6095 m (20,000 ft); cruising speed 338 km/h (210 mph); service ceiling 7620 m (25,000 ft); range 1609 km (1,000 miles)
Weights: empty 3015 kg (6,647 lb); maximum take-off 4895 kg (10,792 lb)
Dimensions: span 16.46 m (54 ft 0 in); length 12.90 m (42 ft 4 in); height 4.72 m (15 ft 6 in); wing area 39.20 m² (422.0 sq ft)
Armament: one 7.7-mm (0.303-in) machine-gun in starboard wing and one 7.7-mm (0.303-in) Vickers 'K' gun in rear cockpit, plus bomb load of 454 kg (1,000 lb)

Fairey F.D.2

Following the experiments with vertically-launched delta-wing models in 1947, Fairey was asked if these could be made to fly supersonically and, since this would not have been worthwhile unless a piloted supersonic aircraft was under consideration, the company anticipated that something might be in the wind and began studies.

In fact, the Ministry of Supply was interested in supersonic flight: Specification E.R.103 was issued for a research aircraft and accepted by Fairey and English Electric, who were to build two aircraft each. The latter eventually produced the P.1 which, in its developed form, became the Lightning; the former built the **Fairey F.D.2**, a needle-nose single-jet delta. The contract was signed in October 1950, but because the Gannet had priority programme the F.D.2 had to take second place, with manufacture beginning at the end of 1952.

The first aircraft flew at Boscombe Down in October 1954 and built up a

number of flights before it was damaged on landing, following loss of engine power and hydraulic power which prevented the landing gear from being lowered. The F.D.2 flew again in August 1955, becoming supersonic for the first time in October, and in subsequent flights the speed was gradually increased until, in November, Mach 1.56 (1654 km/h/1,028 mph) was reached at over 10975 m (36,000 ft). With this potential it was decided to go for the world's absolute speed record, then held by a North American Super Sabre at 1323 km/h (822 mph). A great deal of work had to be done on calibrating precisely the aircraft and cameras, but it was rewarded on 10 March 1956 by an average speed over two runs of a 15.6-km (9.7-mile) course of 1822 km/h (1,132 mph) at 11580 m (38,000 ft).

The second F.D.2 flew at Boscombe Down in February 1956 and both aircraft were used in a wide variety of research work; the first eventually went to the British Aircraft Corporation, and, as the **BAC.221**, was fitted with a completely new ogival wing to confirm wind-tunnel

This was the first of the F.D.2s, the first aircraft to take the absolute speed record over 1,000 mph. It was later remodelled as the BAC 221 for Concorde development work.

tests on the shape which was eventually to fly on Concorde. The F.D.2/BAC.221 had noses which could be lowered to improve visibility when landing and taking off, and this feature was incorporated in Concorde.

Both the research aircraft survived and are preserved.

Specification
Fairey F.D.2
Type: single-seat supersonic research aircraft
Powerplant: one 4536-kg (10,000-lb) thrust Rolls-Royce Avon 200 turbojet
Performance: maximum speed over 2092 km/h (1,300 mph) at 11580 m (38,000 ft); range 1336 km (830 miles)
Weights: empty 4990 kg (11,000 lb;) maximum take-off 6298 kg (13,884 lb)
Dimensions: span 8.18 m (26 ft 10 in); length 15.74 m (51ft 7½ in); height 3.35 m (11 ft 0 in); wing area 33.44 m² (360 sq ft)

Fairey Firefly

Designed to Admiralty Specification N.5/40, calling for a two-seat reconnais-

sance fighter, the **Fairey Firefly** represented a considerable advance over the company's earlier Fulmar. A cantilever low-wing monoplane of all-metal construction, it had a conventional tail unit,

retractable tailwheel landing gear and accommodation for the pilot and navigator/radio-operator in separate enclosed cockpits. Power was provided by a 1290-kW (1,730-hp) Rolls-Royce Griffon

IIB engine, but later production **Firefly F.Mk I** aircraft had the 1484-kW (1,990-hp) Griffon XII.

The first of four development aircraft was flown on 22 December 1941, and

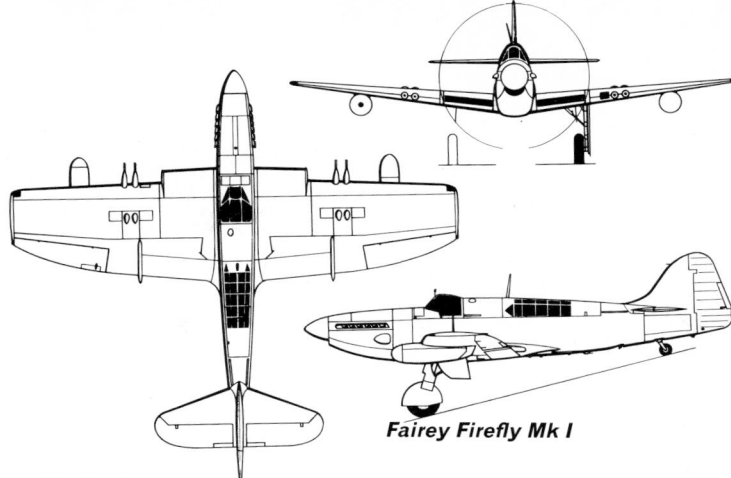

Fairey Firefly Mk I

The Royal Netherlands naval air service operated several Firefly variants, including these T.Mk 2 trainers (converted from F.Mk 1s).

the first production Firefly F.Mk I aircraft were delivered in March 1943. A total of 459 of this version was built, 327 by Fairey and 132 by General Aircraft under sub-contract. The addition of ASH radar beneath the engine identified the **Firefly FR.Mk I**, of which 236 were built, and a number of Firefly F.Mk Is modified to Firefly FR.Mk I standard had the designation **Firefly F.Mk 1A**. A **Firefly NF.Mk II** night-fighter version was developed, but when it was realised that its AI Mk 10 radar could be pod-mounted beneath the engine, as with the ASH radar of the Firefly FR.Mk I, the planned 328-aircraft programme was cancelled. Instead, 140 Firefly FR.Mk Is were modified on the production line to **Firefly NF.Mk I** configuration, the 37 Firefly NF.Mk IIs that had been built being converted back to Mk I standard. Post-war Mk I conversions included the unarmed dual-control **Firefly T.Mk I**

Performance of the Firefly was not great, but it was an agile and popular aircraft with delightful handling.

pilot trainer, the cannon-armed **Firefly T.Mk 2** operational trainer, and the **Firefly T.Mk 3** used for training in ASW operations. A few were also converted as **Firefly TT.Mk 1** target tugs.

Only a prototype of the **Firefly F.Mk III** with Griffon 61 engine was built, development being concentrated instead on the **Firefly F.Mk IV**. This had a 1566-kW (2,100-hp) Griffon 74 engine and new outer wing nacelles that could both carry fuel, or an ASH scanner (port) and fuel (starboard). About 160 were built, and the first **Firefly FR.Mk 4** delivered in July 1946; some were converted later to **Firefly TT.Mk 4** standard. The **Firefly Mk 5** and **Firefly Mk 6** were similar externally to the Mk 4, the first aircraft of each variant flying in December 1947 and March 1949 respectively. Some 352 Mk 5s were built in versions designated **Firefly FR.Mk 5**, **Firefly NF.Mk 5** and **Firefly AS.Mk 5**, the last with American sonobuoys and equipment that distinguished it from the British-equipped **Firefly AS.Mk 6** of which 133 were built. A few **Firefly T.Mk 5** trainers, and **Firefly TT.Mk 5**

and **Firefly TT.Mk 6** target tugs were converted in Australia from Firefly AS.Mk 5s.

The first production Griffon 59-powered **Firefly AS.Mk 7** was flown in October 1951, this reintroducing the beard radiator that had caused problems with the sole Mk III. Intended as an ASW aircraft accommodating two radar operators, few Firefly AS.Mk 7s were built as such, the majority being completed as **Firefly T.Mk 7** ASW trainers within a Mk 7 production of 151. Later conversions to pilotless target aircraft were carried out by Fairey, these including 34 **Firefly U.Mk 8** aircraft converted from Firefly T. Mk 7s, and 40 similar **Firefly U.Mk 9** conversions from Mk 4 and Mk 5 aircraft. They were used for missile development, and by the Royal Navy as targets for its Firestreak-armed fighters and Seaslug-carrying ships.

Fireflies entered service first with No. 1770 Squadron at Yeovilton, Somerset, on 1 October 1943. When embarked on HMS *Indefatigable*, they were active in operations against the German battleship *Tirpitz* in Norway during July 1944. They also saw action against Japanese oil refineries in Sumatra, in attacks on the Carolines and against shipping and ground targets in the Japanese home

islands. In 1950, after war broke out in Korea, Firefly Mk 5s were operated from Australian and British light fleet carriers, and in 1954 the type was in action in the ground-attack role in Malaya. Just over two years later the Firefly was retired after 13 years of valuable service.

Specification
Fairey Firefly AS.Mk 5
Type: two-seat carrier-based anti-submarine reconnaissance and strike aircraft
Powerplant: one 1678-kW (2,250-hp) Rolls-Royce Griffon 74 12-cylinder Vee piston engine
Performance: maximum speed 621 km/h (386 mph) at 4265 m (14,000 ft); cruising speed 354 km/h (220 mph); service ceiling 8655 m (28,400 ft); maximum range 2092 km (1,300 miles)
Weights: empty 4388 kg (9,674 lb); maximum take-off 7301 kg (16,096 lb)
Dimensions: span 12.55 m (41 ft 2 in); length 8.51 m (37 ft 11 in); height 4.37 m (14 ft 4 in); wing area 30.66 m² (330.0 sq ft)
Armament: four 20-mm cannon in wings, plus up to 16 27-kg (60-lb) rocket projectiles or two 454-kg (1,000-lb) bombs beneath the wings

Fairey Flycatcher

In 1922 Air Ministry Specification 6/22 called for a naval single-seat fighter to replace the Nieuport Nightjar in carrier-based operations. Alternative landplane/float-plane/amphibian configurations were required and the powerplant could be either the Bristol Jupiter or Armstrong Siddeley Jaguar engine.

Two designs were selected, the **Fairey Flycatcher** and the Parnall Plover each being ordered to the extent of three prototypes. Parnall later built 10 production Plovers, but although the aircraft was far superior in looks to the angular Flycatcher it was no match in other respects to the Fairey biplane and lasted barely a year in naval service.

The prototype Flycatcher, with a 298-kW (400-hp) Jaguar III engine, flew in November 1922 as a landplane and was subsequently re-engined with a Jupiter IV for the 1923 RAF Display. The second Jaguar II-engined prototype was a floatplane and flew from Hamble in May 1923, while the third was an amphibian.

Like most other Fairey aircraft, the Flycatcher had the camber-changing mechanism which gave an extremely short take-off, and an ability to fly onto

carrier decks without using arrester wires. Another advantage in carrier operations was the aircraft's short span, which enabled it to be taken down on the lift without need for wing folding. An unusual feature of the Flycatcher's construction was that the airframe was designed to be dismantled easily with no section more than 4.11 m (13 ft 6 in) long.

First unit to be equipped with production Flycatchers was No. 402 Flight of the Fleet Air Arm in 1923, and thereafter the Flycatcher continued to replace earlier types on all the aircraft-carriers

and as turret platform fighters in some capital ships serving in all parts of the world. Total production, including the three prototypes, amounted to 196. Flycatchers continued to serve with the fleet until 1934 when the last aircraft, floatplanes operating with No. 406 Flight attached to the East Indies Squadron, gave way to Hawker Ospreys.

Although angular in appearance, the Flycatcher was extremely popular with its pilots. It was very responsive and strong in spite of its mixed wood and metal construction with fabric covering, and could be dived vertically at full throttle – it was even aerobatic in floatplane form. No export sales of Flycatchers

were made, and no genuine aircraft survives, although a full-scale replica has been built and is currently flying in the UK, albeit with a non-standard engine.

Mention should be made of the **Flycatcher II**, a prototype built in 1927 to Specification N.21/26 for a new carrier fighter, intended eventually to replace the original Flycatcher, to which it bore no resemblance. First flown in October 1926 with an Armstrong Siddeley Jaguar VIII, followed by a 358-kW (480-hp) Mercury IIA. Problems with the Mercury and a cooling in official circles towards radial engines killed the project; the aircraft was destroyed in a take-off crash in May 1929.

Specification
Fairey Flycatcher I (landplane)
Type: single-seat fleet fighter
Powerplant: one 298-kW (400-hp) Armstrong Siddeley Jaguar III or IV 14-cylinder two-row piston engine
Performance: maximum speed 216 km/h (134 mph) at sea level; service ceiling 5790 m (19,000 ft); range 500 km (311 miles)
Weights: empty 924 kg (2,038 lb); maximum take-off 1372 kg (3,028 lb)
Dimensions: span 8.84 m (29 ft 0 in); length 7.01 m (23 ft 0 in); height 3.66 m (12 ft 0 in); wing area 26.76 m² (288.0 sq ft)
Armament: twin fixed forward-firing 7.7-mm (0.303-in) Vickers guns on fuselage, plus up to four 9-kg (20-lb) bombs beneath wings

Fairey Rotodyne
to
Farman F.60 Goliath

Fairey Rotodyne

The concept of a vertical take-off airliner has captured the imagination of designers and airlines virtually since passengers were first taken aloft in a balloon, almost exactly 200 years ago.

With the concept of the convertible helicopter proved on a small scale with the Jet Gyrodyne, the proposal put forward by Dr. J.A.J. Bennett and Captain A.G. Forsyth in 1947 for a large compound helicopter looked viable, and various designs were considered. In December 1951 British European Airways issued a specification for a 30-40 seat passenger aircraft for short/medium-haul routes and Fairey submitted a proposal along with other manufacturers; the layout corresponded roughly to Fairey's ideas and in 1953 the company received a Ministry of Supply research contract for a prototype.

Test rigs were established at White Waltham and Boscombe Down, where an elaborate installation eventually comprised the rotor assembly, both powerplants, stub wings, etc., with all controls in a hut where the aircraft's nose would have been. Extensive testing was carried out while the prototype was under construction, and the **Fairey Rotodyne** made its first flight as a helicopter on 6 November 1957; it was not until April 1958 that the first transition to normal flight was made.

Basic layout of the Rotodyne was a square-section fuselage with untapered stub wings on which were mounted two Eland turboprops for forward propulsion. The main wheels of the tricycle landing gear retracted forwards into the nacelles, and the nosewheel forwards below the cockpit. Twin fins and rudders, later joined by a central fin, were

An ambitious project but with great commercial promise, the Rotodyne was killed largely by political problems.

mounted on an untapered tailplane set on top of the rear fuselage. A large four-bladed rotor for vertical take-off and landing was driven by tip jets which received compressed air from the Eland engines via a compressor; each engine fed air to two opposing rotor blades to ensure that, in the event of an engine failure, there would be enough pressure in the remaining engine to keep two tip jets burning.

Following its success in establishing a speed record with the Gyrodyne, Fairey decided that the Rotodyne's performance would enable it to repeat the feat, and on 5 January 1959 it set a record in the convertiplane class with an average speed of 307.2 km/h (190.9 mph) over a 100-km (62.1-mile) closed circuit; this record stood until October 1961, when the Russians beat it with the Kamov Ka-22.

The Rotodyne's future looked bright;

during 1958 the Kaman Aircraft Corporation secured a licensing agreement for sales and service in the USA with a possibility of manufacture there. Okanagan Helicopters of Vancouver was interested in three and Japan Air Lines was considering the type for domestic routes. However, the biggest potential customer was New York Airways, which joined with Kaman in a letter of intent for five, plus options on 10, for delivery in 1964. These were to be the larger 54/65-seat versions with Rolls-Royce Tynes.

Fairey needed up to £10 million to develop this version and was offered 50 per cent of this by the government if BEA would place a firm order. The government contribution was to be a loan, repayable by a sales levy. In 1960 Fairey merged with Westland and although initially the Rotodyne project looked secure, it was not. In April 1960 Okanagan cancelled its order because of the long delivery dates, and five months later New York Airways expressed concern over the delay in production plans.

Westland was then involved in taking over Bristol's helicopter programme as well as with other work in hand. This, together with the ever-increasing weight of the Rotodyne, which reached a stage where the Eland could no longer be developed and the Tyne could not be afforded, led to withdrawal of government support, and the project was cancelled in February 1962.

Specification
Type: experimental compound helicopter
Powerplant: two 2088-kW (2,800-shp) Napier Eland NE1.7 turboprops
Performance: cruising speed 298 km/h (185 mph); range 724 km (450 miles)
Weight: maximum take-off 14969 kg (33,000 lb)
Dimensions: wing span 14.17 m (46 ft 6 in); rotor diameter 27.43 m (90 ft 0 in); length 17.88 m (58 ft 8 in); height 6.76 m (22 ft 2 in); rotor disc area 591.0 m² (6,361.7 sq ft)

Fairey Seafox

One of the less glamorous but necessary tasks performed by Fleet Air Arm aircraft in the interwar years was the fleet spotting and reconnaissance undertaken by aircraft catapulted from capital ships.

Specification S.11/32 for such an aircraft attracted a tender from Fairey for a biplane floatplane with a crew of two. The design was unusual in that the pilot sat in an open cockpit while the observer/gunner was in an enclosed rear cockpit, an arrangement designed to facilitate catapult launches and the subsequent recovery of the aircraft from the sea by crane. Construction was mixed, the fuselage being a metal monocoque, while the wings were fabric-covered. Fairey's bid was accepted, and a contract for 49 aircraft, to be named **Fairey Seafox**, was awarded in January 1936, with a follow-on contract for a further 15 in September the same year.

As originally designed the Seafox was to have had a 373-kW (500-hp) Bristol Aquila radial engine, but for some obscure reason the Napier Rapier 16-

cylinder 'H' air-cooled engine of only 295-kW (395-hp) was chosen, and the Seafox was consequently underpowered throughout its life. The first prototype flew at Hamble on 27 May 1936, while the second, with wheel landing gear, followed on 5 November 1936; this machine was later converted to floatplane configuration.

Production Seafoxes began to come off the line in 1937, the first delivered on 23 April. Catapult tests at the RAE with one of the prototypes in March 1937 were followed by trials on board HMS *Neptune* off Gibraltar, and as production aircraft became available, they were formed into catapult flights. Those equipped with Seafoxes were Nos 702, 713, 714, 716 and 718, and in January 1940 these flights were pooled to form No. 700 Squadron. The type also served with Nos 753 and 754 Squadrons in the training role. At the outbreak of World War II, Seafoxes equipped a number of cruisers, sharing their task with Walrus amphibians and Swordfish floatplanes, and it was not long before they were in action: against the German pocket battleship *Admiral Graf Spee* during the action in the River Plate in December

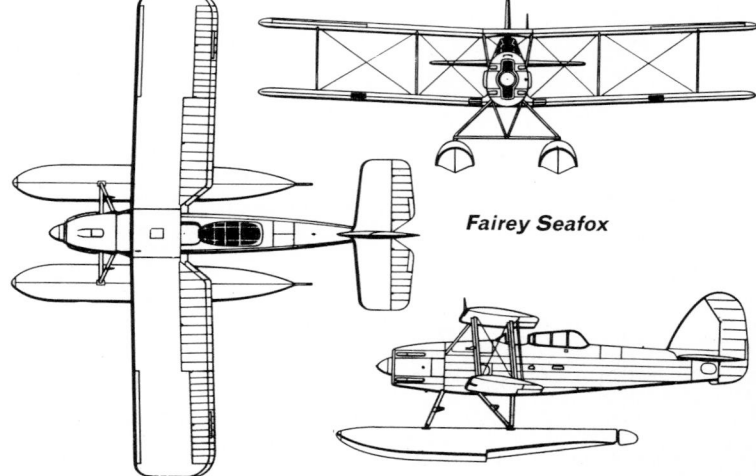

Fairey Seafox

1939. Pursued by the British cruisers HMS *Achilles*, *Ajax* and *Exeter*, the battleship had severely damaged the British ships and the two Walrus amphibians aboard *Exeter* had been put out of

action. One of the Seafoxes from HMS *Ajax* was catapulted and spotted for the guns, for the first time in the war.

Seafox production ended in 1938, but the type continued in front-line service

until about 1942, when it was replaced on ships' catapults by the Vought-Sikorsky Kingfisher. Even then, a few Seafoxes lingered on in the training role until July 1943.

Specification
Type: two-seat spotter

This was the 18th Seafox from the initial 49-aircraft contract, which was allocated to Fleet Air Arm catapult flights to provide aerial reconnaissance and spotting facilities for major surface warships. Note the enclosed observer's cockpit.

reconnaissance seaplane
Powerplant: one 295-kW (395-hp) Napier Rapier VI 16-cylinder 'H' piston engine
Performance: maximum speed 200 km/h (124 mph) at 1785 m (5,860 ft); cruising speed 171 km/h (106 mph); service ceiling 3350 m (11,000 ft); range 708 km (440 miles)
Weights: empty 1726 kg (3,805 lb); maximum take-off 2458 kg (5,420 lb)
Dimensions: span 12.19 m (40 ft 0 in); length 10.81 m (35 ft 5½ in); height 3.68 m (12 ft 1 in); wing area 40.32 m² (434.0 sq ft)
Armament: one rear-firing 7.7-mm (0.303-in) machine-gun

Fairey Swordfish

The **Fairey Swordfish** originated from the company's private-venture **T.S.R.1.** biplane, which was destroyed in an accident during September 1933. However, its early performance had proved sufficiently worthwhile to warrant further development and, when the Air Ministry issued Specification S.15/33 calling for a carrier-based torpedo-spotter-reconnaissance aircraft, Fairey submitted the design of its improved **T.S.R.2.** This became the prototype of the Swordfish (K4190), first flown on 17 April 1934.

The initial **Swordfish Mk I**, built to Air Ministry Specification S.38/34, was a two-bay biplane with a basic structure of metal, and was all fabric-covered except for some light alloy panels on the forward fuselage. Its wings were foldable for carrier stowage, the fuselage incorporated two open cockpits for the pilot (forward) and crew of one or two (aft), and mounted a conventional braced tail

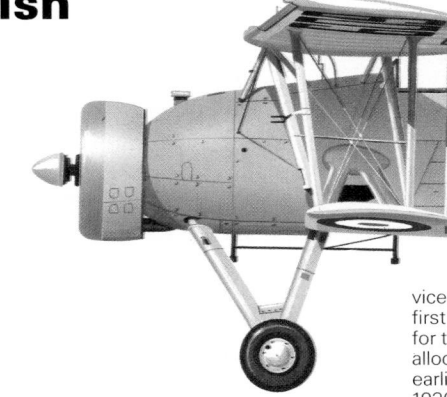

Fairey Swordfish of No. 822 Sqn, Fleet Air Arm, aboard HMS Courageous in 1939.

unit. Tailwheel landing gear was standard, with floats optional, and power was provided by a 515-kW (690-hp) Bristol Pegasus IIIM radial engine.

Swordfish Mk Is began to enter service with the FAA in July 1936, equipping first No. 825 Squadron as a replacement for the Fairey Seals which had first been allocated to squadrons some three years earlier. Next to go, before the end of 1936, were the Blackburn Baffins which had seen but little service with Nos 811 and 812 Squadrons before their replacement, and also the Seals of No. 823 Squadron. When, in 1938, the Blackburn Sharks of Nos 810, 820 and 821 Squadrons were superseded, having seen even less service than the Seals, the FAA's torpedo-bomber squadrons had become equipped exclusively with the Swordfish.

At the beginning of World War II the FAA had 13 operational Swordfish squadrons, 12 of them at sea aboard the carriers HMS *Ark Royal*, *Courageous*, *Eagle*, *Furious* and *Glorious*, but the 'phoney' start to the war meant that these aircraft had virtually no fighting until the beginning of the Norwegian campaign in 1940. This, of course, was beneficial rather than detrimental to the Swordfish cause, giving all squadrons ample time in which to work up to a state of perfection. It was to prove of immense value when on 11 April torpedo-carrying Swordfish went into action for the first time from the carrier *Furious*. Two days later a catapulted Swordfish from HMS *Warspite* sank submarine *U-64*, the first U-boat sinking of the war to be credited to the FAA.

Fairey's production commitments were such that the growing contracts for Swordfish were becoming a little embarrassing, so continued construction was left in the capable hands of Blackburn Aircraft at Brough, Yorkshire, a company which had been concerned primarily with the design and manufacture of naval aircraft from its earliest days. Only a single example was built by Blackburn in 1940, but in the following year 415 were produced.

Before 1940 had ended, however, Swordfish had become involved in a dif-

Swordfish were still active long after D-Day, used principally for attacks against enemy coastal shipping. These aircraft are seen diving in for a rocket attack.

ferent type of operation, under the guidance of RAF's Coastal Command. This involved them in mine-laying operations and bombing attacks on the German-occupied Channel ports, carrying a crew of two and with auxiliary fuel tanks mounted in the rear cockpit.

Also in 1940 came the supreme triumph of the Swordfish, the memorable attack on the Italian fleet at anchor in Taranto harbour, made after reconnaissance sorties had shown that six battleships, plus attendant cruisers and destroyers, were sheltering there. The attack, made by 21 Swordfish aircraft on the night of 11 November 1940, was launched in two waves, with an hour interval between them. Although initial debriefing suggested the entire operation to be a success, it needed reconnaissance confirmation to clarify the picture. When it came, the following day, it was realised that the Italian navy had been dealt a shattering blow: three battleships were damaged severely, two of them under water; a cruiser and two destroyers had been hit; and two auxiliary vessels had been sunk. In the short space of one hour the balance of naval power in the Mediterranean had been irrevocably changed.

The last of the great torpedo attacks made by these aircraft came in 1942, when a futile attempt was made to prevent the German battle-cruisers *Gneisenau* and *Scharnhorst*, accompanied by the heavy cruiser *Prinz Eugen*, from making good their escape eastwards through the English Channel. Almost as a last resort, six Swordfish from No. 825 Squadron, led by Lieutenant Commander Esmonde, were detailed to make a torpedo attack, but only a single Swordfish survived, and it was a miracle that five of the 18 crew members were rescued. All were subsequently decorated and the gallant leader, Esmonde, was posthumously awarded the Victoria Cross, the first to be given to a member of the FAA.

This experience gave confirmation, if any were needed, of the fact that it was no longer a practical proposition to deploy the Swordfish on torpedo attacks. Such operations called for a long, accurate approach if the weapon were to be launched successfully; such

Carriers were not the only ships from which Swordfish operated. This floatplane is being winched aboard HMS Malaya.

an approach also provided the enemy with an excellent opportunity of destroying its attacker. Thus came redeployment of the Swordfish in an anti-submarine warfare (ASW) role, using as its weapons against these underwater vessels conventional depth charges and, for on-surface attack, the newly-developed rocket projectiles.

This led to development of the **Swordfish Mk II**, which entered service in 1943, and differed from the earlier version by having the lower wing strengthened and metal skinned so that it could carry and launch rocket projectiles. Early production Swordfish Mk IIs retained the Pegasus IIIM engine, but later examples had the more powerful Pegasus XXX. The Swordfish Mk II was followed in the same year by what was to prove the final production version, the **Swordfish Mk III**, which mounted a radome carrying a scanner for its ASV Mk X radar between the landing gear main units; in other respects it was generally similar to the Swordfish Mk II. There were, in addition to the three main production versions, a few examples converted from Swordfish Mk IIs and provided with an enclosed cabin for operation in the much colder Canadian waters, these aircraft having the designation **Swordfish Mk IV**.

The advent of the rocket projectile into the armoury of the Fleet Air Arm had been the responsibility of the Swordfish, which carried out suitability trials before the weapon was accepted as standard. With rockets and mines, these aircraft achieved almost unbelievable success in

ASW operations, a highlight coming in September 1944 when Swordfish aboard the escort carrier HMS *Vindex*, then employed in escorting a convoy to the USSR, sank four U-boats in a single voyage.

Production ended in 1944, after Fairey had built 692 and Blackburn 1,699, for a grand total of 2,391. On 21 May 1945 No. 836 Squadron, the last first-line Swordfish squadron, was officially disbanded. Even then the Royal Navy was reluctant to lose such a doughty warrior, one which for five years of hard-fought war had served as a torpedo-bomber for the British fleet, as a shore-based minelayer, for convoy protection from escort car-

riers, as a night-flying flare-dropper, as a rocket-armed anti-shipping and ASW aircraft, as well as for training and general utility duties.

Specification
Fairey Swordfish Mk II
(landplane)
Type: two/three-seat torpedo-bomber-reconnaissance biplane
Powerplant: one 559-kW (750-hp) Bristol Pegasus XXX 9-cylinder radial piston engine
Performance: maximum speed 222 km/h (138 mph); cruising speed 193 km/h (120 mph); service ceiling 3260 m (10,700 ft); maximum range

1658 km (1,030 miles)
Weights: empty 2132 kg (4,700 lb); maximum take-off 3406 kg (7,510 lb)
Dimensions: span 13.87 m (45 ft 6 in); length 10.87 m (35 ft 8 in); height 3.76 m (12 ft 4 in); wing area 56.39 m² (607.0 sq ft)
Armament: one forward-firing synchronised 7.7-mm (0.303-in) Vickers machine-gun in fuselage and one 7.7-mm (0.303-in) Lewis or Vickers K gun on Fairey High-Speed Mounting in rear cockpit, plus a torpedo of 730 kg (1,610 lb), or depth charges, mines or bombs up to 680 kg (1,500 lb), or up to eight rocket projectiles on underwing racks

Farman F.40

The **Farman F.40** was a two-seat pusher biplane with unequal-span wings, representing an amalgam of the earlier Henry Farman (as typified by the H.F.22) and Maurice Farman (as exemplified by the M.F.11) design features. Its crew nacelle, located mid-way between the wings, had a smoother and more streamlined outline that that of the earlier biplanes. The upper pair of tail booms supported the angular horizontal tailplane and the large curved single fin was reminiscent of that used in the Henry Farman series.

The new type, known popularly as the **'Horace' Farman**, appeared at the end of 1915 and went into large-scale production; it served with more than 40 first-line Corps d'Armée (A.2 category) *escadrilles* of the French Aviation Militaire from early 1916. Versions of the F.40 were legion, and included the **F.40P** adapted to fire Le Prieur rockets; the **F.41** with shorter-span wings and a more angular crew nacelle; the **F.56**, similar to the F.41 but with a Renault engine of 127-kW (170-hp); the **F.60**, which combined the F.40 airframe with a 142-kW (190-hp) Renault; and the **F.61** with F.41 airframe and 142-kW (190-hp) engine.

'Horace' Farmans flew also with the

Farman F.40 of the Esquadrilha Expedicionaria a Mocambique, Portuguese air force, based in Mozambique, in 1917.

Royal Naval Air Service. Some of the 50 aircraft purchased from the Farman company operated with No. 5 Wing in France in 1916, and a small number were flown from British coastal stations, including Great Yarmouth. Other F.40s flew with the Belgian forces in France, alongside F.41s and F.56s, and the F.40 was also operated by the Russians.

French *escadrilles* relinquished their 'Horace' Farmans on the Western Front in early 1917, after just over a year's

operations. The type soldiered on with French units in Macedonia and Serbia and a few were adapted for night bombing, although their bomb load was very limited.

The Italian Savoia company built a version of the 'Horace' under licence, its normal powerplant being a 75-kW (100-hp) Colombo engine. Italian Farmans were used in police operations against rebel tribesmen in Libya up to 1922.

Specification
Farman F.40

Type: two-seat corps reconnaissance and observation biplane
Powerplant: one 101-kW (135-hp) Renault 12-cylinder Vee piston engine
Performance: maximum speed 135 km/h (84 mph) at 2000 m (6,560 ft); service ceiling 4000 m (13,125 ft); endurance 2 hours 20 minutes
Weights: empty equipped 748 kg (1,649 lb); maximum take-off 1120 kg (2,469 lb)
Dimensions: span 17.60 m (57 ft 9 in); length 9.25 m (30 ft 4¼ in); height 3.90 m (12 ft 9½ in); wing area 52.00 m² (559.74 sq ft)
Armament: one or two 7.7-mm (0.303-in) machine-guns in observer's cockpit, plus light bombs or 10 Le Prieur rockets

Farman F.60 Goliath

Numerically the most important twin-engined aircraft in the world during the decade following World War I, the **Farman F.60 Goliath** was built as an airliner, more than 60 examples being used on scheduled European and South American air routes, and as a night bomber or torpedo-carrier, some 300

military examples being built for France and for export.

The original **FF.60** (FF for Farman Frères) was designed in 1918 and was intended to serve in large numbers in the Allied campaigns planned for 1919. When fighting ceased in November

1918, the two prototypes nearing completion were converted to civil configuration, with cabins in the nose section and amidships accommodating four and eight passengers respectively. The first example was exhibited publicly in January 1919, its maiden flight taking

A decisive part was played in the early development of European airlines by the Farman F.60 Goliath, which was strong, reliable and comfortable.

place later that same month. On 8 February 1919 it was flown by Lieutenant Bossoutrot from Toussus-le-Noble to RAF Kenley, Surrey, with 11 military personnel as passengers. This remarkable achievement, so soon after the first test flight, has on occasion been claimed erroneously as the first scheduled international passenger flight.

While a bomber version was undergoing tests, the civil F.60 went into production. A number of impressive flights were made, including one during August 1919 of 2050 km (1,274 miles) from Paris to Casablanca in French Morocco. This aircraft, operated by a crew of six, had a total flying time of 18 hours 23 minutes. The civil F.60 went into service with the Compagnie des Grands Express Aériens between Le Bourget and Croydon on 29 March 1920, and less than four months later Lignes Farman, an associate of the Farman aircraft manufacturing company, inaugurated a Paris-Brussels route which by the end of 1921 had been extended via Amsterdam to Berlin. By that time, a second French operator, Compagnie des Messageries Aériennes, was using the Goliath on the London-Paris run. The fourth French company to employ the Goliath was the Compagnie Aériennes Française, while the Romanian LARES airline flew Goliaths with British Armstrong Siddeley Jaguar engines and SNETA (forerunner of the Belgian SABENA line) operated six. Other Goliaths were sold to South

Operated by two squadrons of the 1st Bomber Regiment of the Polish air force in 1925, the F.68 proved an ineffective bomber and was relegated to parachute training and crew familiarisation flights.

American operators.

In Czechoslovakia, Avia and Letov built a batch of Goliaths under licence, some with Bristol Jupiter radials manufactured under licence by the Walter company and others with Lorraine-Dietrich engines. Five were acquired by the Czech national airline CSA and a sixth aircraft was used by the Czech air arm as a VIP transport. An experimental Goliath ambulance was built with accommodation for 12 stretcher patients, a doctor and a nurse, but is not thought to have gone into service.

Bomber F.60s went into production in 1922 and the first were procured by the French Aéronautique Militaire, which took delivery of enough aircraft to equip six *escadrilles*. Later versions of the Goliath were built also for the French army and navy and, in addition, were exported in some numbers to equip pioneering night bombing units in Poland and the USSR. Examples were also purchased by Italy and Japan.

In basic configuration the Goliath underwent remarkably few changes throughout its decade of development. A classic equal-span biplane of its era, of wood construction with fabric covering, it had a wire-braced tail unit, fixed wide-track landing gear and a slab-sided fuselage which remained a feature of all Goliaths, although structural strengthening and improved aerodynamic shape were introduced in late production versions. However, nose configuration differed considerably to cater for the varied crew layouts of military aircraft. A variety of powerplants were also to be seen on the Goliaths, usually nacelle-mounted on each lower wing.

Among the best customers for the Goliath was the French navy, which operated a number of variants, all of which could be fitted either with a characteristic 'trousered' wheeled landing gear, or with large wooden twin floats supplemented by small auxiliary wingtip floats. Both French army and navy Goliaths saw action against the for-

midable Rif tribesmen in Morocco between 1925 and 1927.

Variants

FF.60: designation of prototypes, believed to be three, comprising two civil and one military, completed early 1919

F.60: designation for principal civil version; early production aircraft powered by two Salmson Z.9 radial engines, later aircraft had 194-kW (260-hp) Salmson CM.9s; over 60 civil Goliaths built, most of them F.60s; one civil F.60 was used by the French navy to carry out tests of a twin-float landing gear installation

F.60bis: designation of civil version as powered by two 224-kW (300-hp) Salmson 9Az engines

F.60 Bn.2: principal early bomber version with two Salmson 9Az engines; despite the Bn.2 (two-seat night bomber) suffix, it had a crew of three; armament of three 7.7-mm (0.303-in) machine-guns and up to 1040 kg (2,293 lb) of bombs; used by French army and navy; one supplied to Japan for experimental use by army

F.60 Torp: torpedo-carrying variant with float landing gear, redesigned nose section, open gunner's position with minimal glazing and two Gnome-Rhône Jupiter radial engines; 24 built

F.60M: blunt-nosed version of 1923 with 231-kW (310-hp) Renault 12Fy engines; pilot and co-pilot in side-by-side open cockpits with single windscreen; some F.60Ms had a glazed bomb-aiming panel projecting forward from lower part of nose; used by Aviation Militaire from 1926; one aircraft supplied to Japanese army

F.61: designation of civil version powered by 224-kW (300-hp) Renault 12Fe engines

F.62 BN.4: export version with 336-kW (450-hp) Lorraine-Dietrich V-12 engines, differing from F.60M by having nose balcony for forward gunner's position; acquired by USSR to equip two night bomber *eskadrilas* but saw little front-line service, being relegated to training role in 1926

F.63 BN.4: similar to export F.62 BN.4 but powered by 336-kW (450-hp) Gnome-Rhône Jupiter radial engines; Aviation Militaire acquired 42 but aircraft suffered from airframe defects

F.65: version of the Aéronautique Maritime with interchangeable float/wheel landing gear and blunt nose section similar to F.60 Torp and F.60M; about 100 delivered from 1925; five of them were used in conjunction with French army Goliaths to make bombing attacks against Rif insurgents in Morocco during 1925-7

F.66 BN.3: Jupiter-powered variant intended for Romania; at least one built

F.68 BN.4: designation of 32 Jupiter-powered bombers for Poland; used briefly as bombers but found ineffective and relegated to parachute training

F.4X: designation of one special Goliath with four Salmson radials in tandem pairs, built for the 1923 Grand Prix des Avions Transports

F.140 Super Goliath: a TGP (Très Gros Porteur) super-heavy bomber prototype powered by four 373-kW (500-hp) Farman engines in tandem pairs on the lower wings, and an armament of nose, amidships and ventral machine-gun positions plus up to 1500 kg (3,307 lb) of bombs; six production examples served with Aviation Militarie; the loss of one resulting from structural failure in August 1930 led to this version and all of the French army's F.60, F.63 and F.160 aircraft being scrapped

F.160: slightly developed version of F.60 in BN4 (four-seat strategic night bomber) category, with two 373-kW (500-hp) Farman engines; small number supplied to Aviation Militaire and one each to Italy and Japan; similar F.161 and F.165 not built

F.166: strengthened development of F.60 built for Aéronautique Maritime with optional wheel/float landing gear, redesigned fin and two 373-kW (500-hp) Gnome-Rhône radial engines; twin machine-guns in nose and midships positions, plus provision for a torpedo or bombs-on underfuselage racks; contemporary and generally-similar F.162 not developed beyond prototype stage

F.168: Jupiter-engined torpedo-bomber floatplane which, together with similar F.167, served with Aéronautique Maritime from 1928 to 1936; fuselage revisions to improve field of view for pilot/co-pilot; about 60 entered service

F.169: improved version of the Goliath transport which entered service with Lignes Farman in 1929; aerodynamic improvements and redesigned landing gear with independent single-wheel main units

Specification
Farman F.60
Type: passenger transport
Powerplant: two 194-kW (260-hp) Salmson CM.9 9-cylinder radial piston engines
Performance: maximum speed 140 km/h (87 mph); cruising speed 120 km/h (75 mph); service ceiling 4000 m (13,125 ft); range 400 km (249 miles)
Weights: empty equipped 2500 kg (5,512 lb); maximum take-off 4770 kg (10,516 lb)
Dimensions: span 26.50 m (86 ft 11¼ in); length 14.33 m (47 ft 0¼ in); height 4.91 m (16 ft 1¼ in); wing area 161.00 m² (1,733.05 sq ft)

The F.168 torpedo bomber served with a number of escadrilles of the Aéronautique Navale. The raised and curved upper decking gave the two pilots a much improved field of vision.

Farman F.190
to
Farman NC.223

Farman F.190

The most popular example of the high-wing cabin monoplane or air-taxi aircraft that was in vogue in France during the late 1920s and early 1930s, the **Farman F.190** was first flown in prototype form during 1928. An enclosed pilot's cockpit was located at the leading edge of the wing and behind him was a cabin seating up to four passengers, its round 'port-hole' windows, four on each side, providing a good recognition feature.

The original of the series, the Farman F.190 was powered by a five-cylinder radial fitted with an exhaust collector ring and a long pipe to duct the gases well down the fuselage. Note the Goliath in the background.

Access to the cabin was by a door on the right, immediately aft of the pilot's seat.

The wide-track divided landing gear main legs ensured successful operation of this robust monoplane from even low-grade flying fields, and the single fin and rudder tail assembly was of typically Farman design. With a basic structure of wood, and mixed fabric and plywood covering, more than 100 of all versions of the F.190 were built, over half of them comprising the original version with a single Gnome-Rhône 5Ba radial engine. An ambulance version known as the **F.197S** (Sanitaire) had provision for two stretcher cases and a medical attendant.

As well as private owners and air-taxi companies, a number of established airlines in France and abroad used aircraft of the F.190 series. Main operator was the Farman line with 14 aircraft, while Air Union had seven and other French oper-

ators included Air Orient and Air Afrique. Abroad, commercial operators included CIDNA in Prague and LARES in Bucharest. When Air France was formed in 1933 it took over 15 F.190s from the various companies it had absorbed.

The basic design appeared with a considerable variety of powerplants, each main variant bearing a different sub-type designation as follows: the **F.192** was powered by the 172-kW (230-hp) Salmson 9Ab radial, the **F.193** by the 172-kW (230-hp) Farman 9Ea, the **F.193** by the 186-kW (250-hp) Hispano-Suiza 6Mb, the **F.197** by the 179-kW (240-hp) Lor-

A popular cabin monoplane typical of its era, the F.190 series was offered in a wide variety of models using different engine types. Seen here is an F.192 powered by the Salmson 9Ab.

raine 7Me, the **F.198** by the 186-kW (250-hp) Renault 9A, and the **F.199** by the 242-kW (325-hp) Lorraine 9Na. Production ended in 1931.

Specification
Farman F.190
Type: five-seat light transport
Powerplant: one 172-kW (230-hp) Gnome-Rhône 5Ba 5-cylinder radial piston engine
Performance: maximum speed 185 km/h (115 mph); cruising speed 160 km/h (99 mph); service ceiling 5150 m (16,895 ft); range 850 km (528 miles)
Weights: empty 926 kg (2,041 lb); maximum take-off 1800 kg (3,968 lb)
Dimensions: span 14.40 m (47 ft 3 in); length 10.45 m (34 ft 3½); height 3.00 m (9 ft 10 in); wing area 40.20 m² (432.72 sq ft)

Farman F.220, F.221 and F.222

The **Farman F.211** and **F.212** prototypes established a configuration that was retained in a series of four-engined heavy bomber designs over the next decade: a typical Farman high-wing of considerable chord and thickness was

The F.220 prototype was conceived as a bomber, with the nose gunner in a forward-projecting balcony, but was later turned into a mailplane for the South Atlantic route.

united with an angular slab-sided fuselage; the powerplant comprised four engines, arranged in tandem pairs to drive two tractor and two pusher propellers, and mounted at the extremities of a pair of stub wings projecting from the lower fuselage. These prototypes were produced in response to an official requirement for a Bombardier Très Gros Porteur, a bomber capable of carrying heavy offensive loads over what were then regarded as medium and long ranges.

The F.211 and F.212 were developed into the **F.220.01** which flew on 26 May 1932. Powered by four 447-kW (600-hp) Hispano-Suiza 12 Lbr engines, the F.220 retained the basic concept of its predecessors, including the enclosed 'pilots' cabin, balcony nose gunner's position and fixed wide-track divided landing gear, but incorporated a number of detailed refinements. Later converted for civil use as *Le Centaure*, the sole F.220 was used as a pioneer long-range passenger-mail carrier over the South Atlantic route, making its first non-stop flight from Dakar (West Africa) to Natal (Brazil) on 3 June 1935.

Farman (centre) F.222.2

In May 1933, the **F.221.01** prototype took off on its maiden flight. It differed from the F.220 mainly in having a redesigned vertical tail, Gnome-Rhône Mistral Major radial engines, and the nose and ventral gunners' cockpits fully enclosed. A small production batch of F.221 bombers followed, with redesigned nose sections, including a manually operated gun turret and revised glazing for the bomb-aimer's station. The dorsal gun was housed under a domed hand-operated turret and the ventral position was semi-retractable. Whereas only the forward engines of the F.221.01 were cowled, the series aircraft

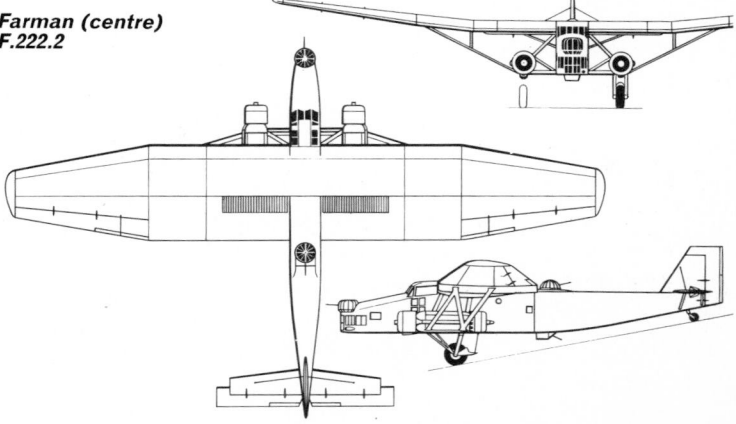

had long-chord cowlings on all four engines. Four civil variants, designated **F.2200**, appeared between 1936 and 1938 and were used by Air France on the South American service.

The prototype F.221.01 was modified as the **F.222.01** during the second half of 1935. The main change was the introduction of landing gear units which retracted forward into the engine nacelles. Series **F.222.1** aircraft were followed by two batches of **F.222.2** bombers with redesigned nose sections eliminating the balcony of the earlier Farmans and cut down to provide the pilot with improved visibility. The F.222.2 also featured dihedral on the outer wing sections. One civil F.222.1 was completed as the **F.2220** *Ville de Dakar* and delivered to Air France in October 1937.

The Farman bombers, all in the BN.5 (five-seat night bomber) category, were delivered to the 15ième de Bombardement, which was specifically formed for the purpose at Avord in July 1935. By 1 January 1938 18 F.221s and F.222.1s were in service, and two months earlier deliveries of the F.222.2s had started, the last of them delivered in July 1938. On 16 August 1939 the disposition of the Farman bombers included four machines in Indo-China, eight in France's African colonies and 30 in metropolitan France, including 20 in first-line service with the 15ième Escadre.

Between September 1939 and the beginning of May 1940, the F.221s and F.222s were engaged in leaflet-dropping night operations over Germany and Bohemia. During the *Blitzkrieg* on France in May and June 1940, the Farmans of the Armée de l'Air made 63 effective night sorties over western Germany and the occupied areas of northeast France. Three F.222.2s with additional fuel capacity were transferred to the French navy's newly formed Esca-

drille 10E, intended for long-range bombing and maritime patrol.

After the armistice between Germany and France Groupement 15, as the Farman-equipped unit was by then known, was re-formed as Groupe de Transport 15, comprising two *escadrilles* with a total of two F.221s, two F.222.1s and six F.222.2s. They served the French Vichy regime, playing an important part in the transfer of Armée de l'Air units to Syria during the fighting in that country.

Variants
F.221: 10 series aircraft delivered to Armée de l'Air between June 1936 and January 1937; they constituted the only effective four-engined bomber force in the world at that time except in the USSR, which fielded large numbers of

Tupolev TB-3s; single prototype built and flown in May 1933
F.222.1: known originally as F.222 but redesignated with appearance of F.222.2 version; it had increased fuel capacity; 11 series aircraft built, construction of first aircraft beginning in April 1936 and the last aircraft being completed October 1937; the prototype F.222 was conversion of original F.221 prototype

By 1939 the Farman F.221 bomber was totally obsolete by European standards, yet France was forced to use the type in service in the early part of the war.

Farman F.222.1 of the 2ième Escadrille, Groupement de Bombardement I/15, Armée de l'Air based at Reims-Courcy in May 1940. Most F.222s were made after Farman had been nationalised.

F.222.2: two batches built by Centre, first of eight and second of 16; redesigned nose section gave much improved fuselage contours compared with F.221 and F.222.1; no prototype built as such, aircraft No. 13 being the first F.222.2 completed

Specification
Farman (Centre) F.222.2
Type: heavy night bomber
Powerplant: four 868-kW (920-hp) Gnome-Rhône 14N 14-cylinder radial piston engines
Performance: maximum speed 360 km/h (224 mph) at 4000 m (13,125 ft); service ceiling 8000 m (26,245 ft); maximum range 2200 km (1,367 miles)
Weights: empty equipped 10800 kg (23,810 lb); maximum take-off 18700 kg (41,226 lb)
Dimensions: span 36.00 m (118 ft 1¼ in); length 21.45 m (70 ft 4½); height 5.20 m (17 ft 0⅓ in); wing area 186 m² (2,202 sq ft)
Armament: single 7.5-mm (0.295-in) MAC 1934 machine-gun in nose, dorsal and semi-retractable ventral turrets, plus up to 3900 kg (8,598 lb) of bombs; the F.221 and F.222.1 had Darne guns of same calibre, and the F.220.01 and F.221.01 had twin 7.7-mm (0.303-in) Lewis machine-guns in each of the three defensive positions

Farman M.F.7 'Longhorn'

Although Henry and Maurice Farman had established a collaborative business, each retained independent activities and ideas in respect of design. This accounts for designations prefixed by the differing H.F. and M.F. initials. Maurice began in 1909 by developing his own ideas for modification and improvement of the basic Voisin design, but when tested this proved to be unsatisfactory. However, experimentation during 1910 led to a successful biplane in 1911 that was the forerunner of the **Farman M.F.7**, which first appeared in 1913 and was often called a Type 1913.

An unequal-span biplane, with the multiplicity of struts and bracing wires that were then an essential component of an aircraft's structure, the M.F.7 had a central fuselage nacelle with open accommodation for a crew of two. Directly behind them was mounted the engine to drive a pusher propeller, its blades turning between four slender

The extension of the landing skids upwards into the supports for the forward elevator resulted in the M.F.7 gaining the nickname 'Longhorn'. The type performed creditably in operations early in World War I.

fuselage struts that served to mount the biplane tail unit. Landing gear was of tail-skid type, and extending forward from the main landing gear structure and braced from the wings were outriggers that carried the elevator, well forward of the nose of the fuselage nacelle. An excellent identification feature, these outriggers brought the nickname **'Longhorn'**, one that in many reference books has pre-eminence over the official M.F.7 designation. Original powerplant

was a 52-kW (70-hp) Renault engine, but many later had more powerful Renaults and a proportion of the considerable number licence-built in the UK during World War I had a 56-kW (75-hp) Rolls-Royce Hawk 6-cylinder inline engine.

Like many aircraft developed in the years 1912-14, the M.F.7 was adopted for use in communications and patrol duties when World War I began. But it was in the continuing role as an elementary trainer that the Longhorn became best known, large numbers of Allied pilots gaining their introduction to flight in it. Over 350 were built.

Specification
Farman M.F.7
Type: two-seat utility aircraft
Powerplant: one 52-kW (70-hp) Renault 8-cylinder Vee piston engine
Performance: maximum speed 95 km/h (59 mph); service ceiling 4000 m (13,125 ft); endurance 3 hours 15 minutes
Weights: empty 580 kg (1,279 lb); maximum take-off 855 kg (1,885 lb)
Dimensions: span 15.50 m (50 ft 10¼ in); length 12.00 m (39 ft 9¼); height 3.45 m (11 ft 4 in); wing area 60.00 m² (645.86 sq ft)

Farman M.F. 11

While retaining a similar basic configuration to the M.F.7, Maurice Farman's later

development introduced a number of refinements but had one major difference: it dispensed with the forward elevator. Instead, what would not be regarded as a conventional elevator was adopted, this being a hinged appendage of the monoplane tailplane; the twin rudders

were replaced by neat twin fins and rudders. Instead of being mounted on the lower wing, the fuselage nacelle was between the wings, and without the outriggers that had mounted the elevator on

the M.F.7, the new **Farman M.F.11** looked a more workmanlike aeroplane. It did, however, have a skid extending forward of the main wheels to reduce the

danger of nosing-over on rough surfaces and this, by comparison with the outriggers, was sufficient for the aircraft to gain the nickname **'Shorthorn'**. Power

The M.F.11 was obviously derived from the M.F.7, but the replacement of the forward elevator by a tail member resulted inevitably in the nickname 'Shorthorn'.

was provided usually by Renault engines of 52 or 75 kW (70 or 100 hp), but at least one was reported to have flown with a 97-kW (130-hp) Canton-Unné and it seems likely that other engines may have been used.

Available with wheeled or float landing gear, the M.F.11 was used more extensively than the M.F.7 for bombing, reconnaissance and training roles, and was built under licence for several manufacturers. The Royal Naval Air Service, for example, received about 90 M.F.11s, and many of them were used in a bombing role, able to carry a number of light bombs on underwing racks. In an attack launched against enemy guns near

Ostend, the Shorthorn recorded on 21 December 1914 the first operational night flight to be made by either side during World War I.

Specification
Farman M.F.11
Type: two-seat utility aircraft
Powerplant: one 70-hp Renault 8-cylinder Vee piston engine
Performance: maximum speed 100 km/h (62 mph); service ceiling 3800 m (12,470 ft); endurance 3 hours 45 minutes
Weights: empty 550 kg (1,213 lb); maximum take-off 840 kg (1,874 lb)
Dimensions: span 16.15 m (53 ft 0 in); length 9.50 m (31 ft 2 in); height 3.90 m (12 ft 9½ in); wing area 57.00 m² (613.56 sq ft)
Armament: up to 18 7.3-kg (16-lb) bombs on underwing racks, and (optionally) one machine-gun for the observer

Farman N.C.223

Retaining the engine layout of the earlier Farman four-engined bombers, but incorporating a new stressed-skin or metal wing of high aspect ratio, the **Farman F.223** was intended as an improved bomber. It had a more refined, though still angular fuselage, and a twin-fin-and-rudder tail assembly. However, the first example to fly, in June 1937, was a long-distance mail-carrier which was named subsequently *Laurent Guerrero* and flown on the South Atlantic route between West Africa and Brazil. This had the designation **NC.223.1** as the Farman company had by this time been merged, in March 1937, into the newly-formed nationalised company SNCAC. The NC.223.1 soon established a reputation by setting up a new world distance-with-payload record in October 1937.

The **NC.223.01** bomber prototype flew for the first time on 18 January 1938. It differed from the civil machine chiefly in its powerplant, which comprised four Hispano-Suiza radial engines in place of the engines of the civil transport, and in its military equipment and armament. The proposed **NC.223.2** BN-5 category (5-seat night bomber) aircraft with Gnome-Rhône 14N radials was not built.

Eight production **NC.223.3** BN.5 bombers were ordered and entered service with the Armée de l'Air in May and June 1940, at the time of the German *Blitzkrieg* on France. They were powered by four Hispano-Suiza 12Y-29 V-12 engines and armed with a nose-mounted 7.5-mm (0.295-in) MAC 1934 machine-gun, and single 20-mm Hispano-Suiza 404 cannon in power-operated dorsal and ventral turrets. Maximum bombload in four bays was

4200 kg (9,259 lb). The NC.223.3s flew alongside the earlier Farmans with the Groupement de Bombardement 15 before being withdrawn to North Africa. Three were converted subsequently as long-range mail and passenger aircraft, while the remaining survivors were flown with the Groupe de Transport I/15 in France's North Africa territories.

The **NC.223.4** was developed in parallel with the NC.223.3 and was intended from the outset as a high-speed mail-carrier. Three aircraft were built, the *Camille Flammarion*, *Jules Verne* and *Le Verrier*. Like the bomber, the NC.223.4 had a slim, tapering, high-aspect ratio wing with the engines supported on struts, but the nose incorporated considerable aerodynamic refinement and the twin fin and rudder tail assembly was of greater surface area.

Soon after the outbreak of war, in October 1939, the *Camille Flammarion* took part in the search for the German pocket battleship *Graf Spee* in the South Atlantic. Then, in May 1940, the French Aéronavale formed Escadrille B5 at Orly to operate the three NC.223.4s as long-range bombers and reconnaissance aircraft. In the event, only the *Jules Verne*

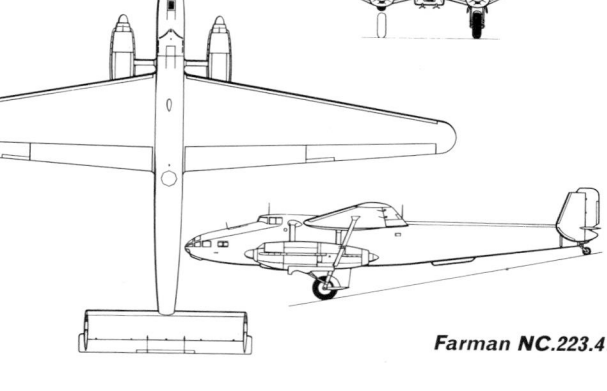

Farman NC.223.4

received military equipment, in the form of racks for up to eight 250-kg (551-lb) bombs and provision for a 7.5-mm (0.295-in) MAC machine-gun on a gimbal mount attached to the rear entry door. It carried out a number of night operations, the most remarkable being on the night of 7/8 June 1940 when Berlin was attacked by a long circuitous route over the North Sea and the Baltic. Later the three NC.223.4s made several attacks on Italian targets, but after the armistice with Germany they were returned to passenger and mail operations. *Le Ver-*

rier was shot down over the Mediterranean on 27 November 1940.

Specification
Farman NC.223.3
Type: four-engined night bomber
Powerplant: four 697-kW (910-hp) Hispano-Suiza 12Y-29 12-cylinder Vee piston engines
Performance: maximum speed 400 km/h (249 mph); cruising speed 280 km/h (174 mph); service ceiling 8000 m (26,245 ft); range 2400 km (1,491 miles)
Weights: empty equipped 10550 kg (23,259 lb); maximum take-off 19200 kg (43,329 lb)
Dimensions: span 33.58 m (110 ft 2 in); length 22.00 m (72 ft 2½ in); height 5.08 m (16 ft 8 in); wing area 132.40 m² (1425.19 sq ft)
Armament: one 7.5-mm (0.295-in) MAC 1934 machine-gun in nose, and one 20-mm HS 404 cannon in dorsal turret and semi-retractable ventral turret, plus a maximum bombload of 4190 kg (9,237 lb) in four internal bays

Though a masterpiece of aerodynamic refinement in comparison with earlier Farman bombers, the NC.223.3 was still a clumsy machine, the arrangement of engines, landing gear and struts adding considerably to the drag burden of the four engines. Eight were built for service with GB 15, and flew operations before the fall of France.

Farman NC.470
to
Fiat BR.20 Cicogna

Farman NC.470

Projected originally as the **F.470** in 1936, the **Farman NC.470** high-wing twin-engined crew trainer was flown in prototype form on 27 December 1937. At that time it had fixed wheeled landing gear although it was the intention to use it as a floatplane. Fitted with large twin floats of the type designed for the obsolete Farman F.168 biplanes, the prototype was tested as a seaplane in the spring of 1938.

The NC.470 was of typical angular Farman appearance, with a large cabin for the pilot and co-pilot forward of the wing, a blunt nose with glazed navigator's and bomb/torpedo-aimer's positions, low-set stub wings at the extremities of which were located the Gnome-Rhône radial engines, complex strut bracing for wings and floats, and tall single fin and rudder. Ten production NC.470s followed the prototype, the last being delivered in mid-1939. A single **NC.471** prototype differed only by having a different version of the Jupiter (Gnome-Rhône-licensed) engines.

Additional NC.470s were delivered after the outbreak of World War II; it is believed that 20 went into service with the French Aéronautique Maritime, which operated them on convoy escort and coastal reconnaissance duties with Escadrille 3S4 until the Armistice with Germany. Other NC.470s were on the strength of the aircrew training school at Hourtin.

Specification
Farman NC.470
Type: six-seat crew trainer or coastal reconnaissance floatplane
Powerplant: two 373-kW (500-hp) Gnome-Rhône 9Kgr 9-cylinder radial piston engines
Performance: maximum speed 230 km/h (143 mph); cruising speed 190 km/h (118 mph); service ceiling 6000 m (19,685 ft); range 1140 km (708 miles
Weights: empty equipped 3710 kg

(8,179 lb); maximum take-off 6000 kg (13,228 lb)
Dimensions: span 24.45 m (80 ft 2½ in); length 16.10 m (52 ft 10 in); height 4.85 m (15 ft 11 in); wing area 95.00 m² (1,022.60 sq ft)
Armament: one 7.5-mm (0.295-in)

Unmistakably Farman in origins, the NC.470 was a docile type well-suited to training seaplane crews.

Darne machine-gun in dorsal position, plus 200 kg (441 lb) of bombs

Felixstowe F.1 and F.2

Squadron Commander John Porte of the RNAS had been interested in aviation as early as 1909, joining Glenn Curtiss in America at the beginning of 1914 to participate in the design of a transatlantic flying-boat. Returning to the UK at the outbreak of World War I, Porte influenced the Admiralty in acquiring flying-boats of Curtiss design. During the first year of the war Porte gained operational experience with some of these 'boats and, when appointed to command the RNAS station at Felixstowe, Suffolk, in September 1915, he decided to devise modifications to these aircraft to improve their operational capability.

Hull modifications of the Curtiss biplane flying-boats in service met with mixed success, but the experience gained enabled Porte to design a completely new single-step hull which was to become known as the Porte I. With the wings and tail unit of a standard Curtiss H.4 flying-boat and with power provided by two Hispano-Suiza engines it was flown under the designation **Felix-**

The F.2A normally had a semi-enclosed cockpit, but this example has a completely open position for the pilots.

stowe F.1. Modifications made to the hull as a result of flight testing added two more steps and in this form the F.1 can be regarded as the prototype of the family of 'F' boats that were to follow.

The Curtiss H.4 had inadequate range and load capacity for North Sea patrols and Porte induced Glenn Curtiss to develop a larger aircraft. Known as the **H.8** or **Large America**, the first of 50 ordered by the Admiralty was delivered to Felixstowe in July 1916. Its installed 119-kW (160-hp) Curtiss engines proved to be too low powered, and Porte arranged for them to be replaced by two 186-kW (250-hp) Rolls-Royce Eagle Is, the resulting conversion redesignated **H.12**. Although the type's performance in the air was satisfactory, it was soon discovered that the original hull was unsuited for operations in the North Sea. Porte designed a new two-step hull based on that of the F.I and this, combined with a revised tail unit, H.12 wings and the Rolls-Royce Eagle engines, provided a much-improved flying-boat designated **Felixstowe F.2**. Testing showed that some slight modifications and more-powerful engines would make it an ideal patrol aircraft, and with Rolls-Royce Eagle VIIIs it entered production as the **F.2A**.

A single example of one variant appeared, this being designated **F.2C**. It had a modified hull of lighter construction and was powered initially by two 205-kW (275-hp) Rolls-Royce Eagle IIs. These were replaced subsequently by two 240-kW (322-hp) Eagle VIs, and although tests showed that in this form its performance was marginally better than that of the F.2A, the F.2C did not enter production. About 100 F.2As were built, the type remaining in operational use until the end of World War I.

Specification
Felixstowe F.2A
Type: fighter/reconnaissance flying-boat
Powerplant: two 257-kW (345-hp) Rolls-Royce Eagle VIII 12-cylinder Vee piston engines
Performance: maximum speed 153 km/h (95 mph) at 610 m (2,000 ft); service ceiling 2925 m (9,600 ft); endurance 6 hours
Weights: empty 3424 kg (7,549 lb); maximum take-off 4980 kg (10,978 lb)
Dimensions: span 29.15 m (95 ft 7½ in); length 14.10 m (46 ft 3 in); height 5.33 m (17 ft 6 in); wing area 105.26 m² (1,133.0 sq ft)
Armament: from four to seven free-mounted 7.7-mm (0.303-in) Lewis machine-guns, plus two 104-kg (230-lb) bombs on underwing racks

Felixstowe F.3

In February 1917 the prototype was flown of a new flying-boat developed from the F.2A. Generally similar in external appearance to its predecessor, the **Felixstowe F.3** differed primarily by having a slight increase in length and span, and was intended to offer more range and greater load-carrying capability. This was achieved, but as the F.3 had the same Rolls-Royce Eagle VIII powerplant as the F.2A the improvements were not gained without cost. Thus the F.3 was slower and less manoeuvrable than its predecessor and as a result was unable, unlike the F.2A, to engage enemy fighter seaplanes or Zeppelins. In consequence it was not popular with crews and because of its limitations was used mainly for anti-submarine patrols.

The prototype had flown originally with two 239-kW (320-hp) Sunbeam Cossack engines, probably because of

Based on the F.2, the F.3 sacrificed speed for offensive capability, much to the disquiet of its crews.

the general shortage of Rolls-Royce Eagles, but the Eagle VIII was installed in production F.3s. Orders for the aircraft, eventually totalling 263, considerably exceeded those for the higher-performance F.2A, probably because the type could carry double the bombload. However, only about 100 were completed by the end of the war, but some were completed subsequently as F.5s for delivery to the Royal Air Force.

Operational use of F.2As was confined to British home stations, and it is interesting to record that the F.3 was used extensively in the Mediterranean theatre. In fact so urgent was the requirement for these flying-boats in that area that 18 were built under sub-contract by the Dockyard Constructional Unit at Malta.

Specification
Type: anti-submarine patrol flying-boat
Powerplant: two 257-kW (345-hp) Rolls-Royce Eagle VIII 12-cylinder Vee piston engines
Performance: maximum speed 146 km/h (91 mph) at 610 m (2,000 ft); service ceiling 2440 m (8,000 ft); endurance 6 hours
Weights: empty 3610 kg (7,958 lb);

maximum take-off 6024 kg (13,281 lb)
Dimensions: span 31.09 m (102 ft 0 in); length 14.99 m (49 ft 2 in); height 5.69 m (18 ft 8 in); wing area 133.03 m² (1,432.0 sq ft)
Armament: four 7.7-mm (0.303-in) Lewis machine-guns on free mountings, plus four 104-kg (230-lb) bombs on underwing racks

Felixstowe F.5

First appearing in early 1918, the **Felixstowe F.5** was intended as a development of the F.3 that would incorporate the desirable improvements and refinements resulting from experience with the F.3 and its predecessor. Although externally similar to the F.3, the F.5 differed by having a slightly deeper hull with open cockpits for the crew plus an entirely new wing of greater span. Powerplant of the prototype was unchanged, but slightly uprated (261-kW/350-hp) Eagle VIIIs were installed. Flight testing of this prototype (N90) demonstrated much improved performance by comparison with the F.3; unfortunately, it was decided that economic considerations would not allow the introduction of this new type. Instead, the production F.5 introduced a hull that was similar to that of the prototype, but retained the F.3 wing and used in its construction as many F.3 components as possible. Flight tests with Eagle VIII engines showed that performance of the production F.5 was inferior to that of the F.3; not surprisingly, when powered by 242-kW (325-hp) Eagle VIIs (used when Eagle VIIIs were in short supply) its performance was distinctly disappointing.

Entering service too late to be used operationally during World War I, the F.5 became the RAF's standard post-war flying-boat until replaced by Supermarine Southamptons in August 1925. It should be noted that by the efforts of John Porte the F.5 had evolved from the Curtiss H.8 Large America. Thus arose the

Production of the Felixstowe F.5 series was diverse, and this example was built by the Gosport Aviation Company, one of five commercial manufacturers.

unusual situation in 1918 of Curtiss in the USA building a flying-boat that was an improved foreign version of one of its own designs. This resulted from the US Navy deciding to adopt the F.5 powered by the new Liberty engine. The type was produced for the Naval Flying Corps by Curtiss (60 built), Canadian Aeroplanes Ltd of Toronto (30) and the US Naval Aircraft Factory (138) under the designation **F-5L**, remaining the US Navy's standard patrol 'boat until the late 1920s.

Specification
Felixstowe F.5
Type: reconnaissance flying-boat
Powerplant: two 261-kW (350-hp) Rolls-Royce Eagle VIII 12-cylinder Vee piston engines

Performance: maximum speed 142 km/h (88 mph); service ceiling 2075 m (6,800 ft); endurance 7 hours
Weights: empty 4128 kg (9,100 lb); maximum take-off 5752 kg (12,682 lb)

Dimensions: span 31.60 m (103 ft 8 in); length 15.01 m (49 ft 3 in); height 5.72 m (18 ft 9 in); wing area 130.90 m² (1,409.0 sq ft)
Armament: four 7.7-mm (0.303-in) Lewis machine-guns, one in bow and three in midship positions, plus up to 417 kg (920 lb) of bombs on underwing racks

Felixstowe F.5 of the Royal Air Force.

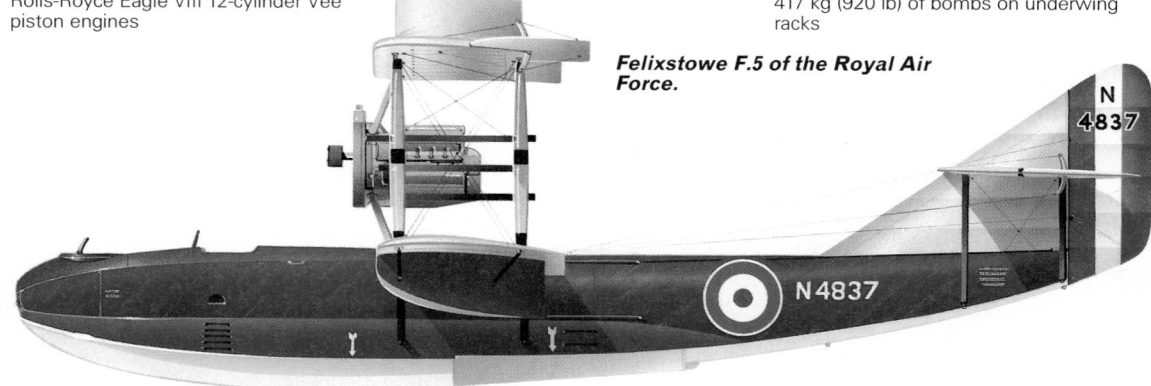

Fiat AS.1

Developed in a matter of weeks from the project stage, the prototype **Fiat AS.1** two-seat tourer flew in the summer of 1928. A very basic strut-braced high-wing monoplane, then powered by a 67-kW (90-hp) Czech Walter radial engine, the AS.1 had a typical Fiat tail unit and conventional cross-axle fixed landing gear. Its wings could be folded for towing or storage. Construction was mixed, with plywood and fabric covering, except for metal sheet panelling immediately behind the engine. Standard powerplant adopted for production AS.1s was the Fiat A.50.

The two crew members had dual controls and were seated in tandem open cockpits, each protected by small windscreens. They had additional protection from a larger windscreen built integral with the forward struts of the cabane and this, from some angles, gave the AS.1 the appearance of a fully-enclosed cabin aircraft.

The **AS.2** of 1929 had a strengthened structure and the 75-kW (100-hp) Fiat A.50S engine. Later versions of both the AS.1 and AS.2 were built with fully-enclosed crew accommodation. A twin-float seaplane version, **AS.1 Idro**, and the **AS.1 Sci** with skis, were introduced in 1930.

AS.1s made headlines throughout 1929 and 1930. In August 1929 eight of them won the cup for the Challenge Internationale de Tourisme team event. Donati and Capannini flew their AS.1 in January 1930 to establish world distance and endurance records for touring aircraft of 2746 km (1,706.29 miles) and 29 hours 4 minutes respectively. During the same month they set the world tourer height record at 6782 m (22,250 ft). In February Francis Lombardi flew from Rome to Mogadishu (East Africa), a distance of over 8047 km (5,000 miles) in seven days, but perhaps the most famous achievement of the AS.1 was a flight from Vercelli to Toyko by way of Siberia by Lombardi and Capannini, between 13 and 22 July 1930.

These achievements did not end the AS.1's career as a record breaker. On 28 December 1932 a Fiat AS.1 Idro reached an altitude of 7363 m (24,157 ft), powered by a CNA C7 engine, to establish a world record for tourer seaplanes. Two days later the same aircraft, with the CNA engine and wheel landing gear,

attained 9282 m (30,453 ft) to set a world landplane tourer record.

During 1929 the AS.1 production programme accelerated rapidly, for as well as achieving great popularity among private owners the AS.1 was used by the Regia Aeronautica as a liaison and courier aircraft and for training reserve pilots. It appears that at least 500 AS.1s were built, plus some 50 AS.2s, Italian air ministry orders alone totalling 276 AS.1s and 36 AS.2s.

Variant
TR.1: of similar configuration to the AS.1, but with a fully enclosed cabin faired into the rear upper fuselage decking and wide-track landing gear, the TR.1 was flown for the first time in 1930; basic structure was of metal

with fabric covering; the TR.1 won a number of sporting events in 1931, including the team event in the Giro Aereo d'Italia.

Specification
Fiat AS.1
Type: two-seat tourer and trainer
Powerplant: one 67-kW (90-hp) Fiat A.50 7-cylinder radial piston engine
Performance: maximum speed 158 km/h (98 mph); service ceiling 6800 m (22,310 ft); range 1000 km (621 miles)
Weights: empty equipped 450 kg (992 lb); max take-off 690 kg (1,521 lb)
Dimensions: span 10.40 m (34 ft 1½ in); length 6.10 m (20 ft 0¼ in); height 2.53 m (8 ft 3½ in); wing area 17.50 m² (188.37 sq ft)

The Fiat AS.1 was a remarkable lightplane, as indicated by the string of world records secured by the type.

Fiat BR, BR.1, BR.2, BR.3 and BR.4

In 1918 Engineer Celestino Rosatelli began work in the design bureau of the Societa Italiana Aviazione, the aircraft manufacturing section of the giant Fiat complex. His initial task was development of the S.I.A.9 reconnaissance biplane on which great hopes had been set, but which had proved structurally unsound.

The new design was that of a light bomber biplane, the **BR** (standing for Bombardiere Rosatelli); this appeared in 1919, by which time the S.I.A. had reverted to the name Fiat. In April 1919 the BR established a number of world records, lifting three passengers (although only a two-seat aircraft) to an altitude of 7240 m (23,753 ft) and attaining a maximum speed of 270 km/h (167.77 mph) with one passenger.

The BR completed its service trials successfully at the Montecello test centre in 1922 and went into production for the Aeronautica Militare, reorganised under the 1923 Fascist regime as the Regia Aeronautica.

Compared with the S.I.A.9, the BR had improved lines and a more robust structure. While retaining the two-bay

configuration of its predecessor, wing construction of the BR was revised and strengthened considerably, and a tailplane of new design was introduced, with a fin and rudder outline which was to characterise Rosatelli designs for the next decade. Landing gear was of conventional cross-axle type. The pilot's open cockpit was located immediately below a cut-out in the upper wing trailing edge, with the observer/gunner's cockpit immediately behind. Power for the BR was provided by the 522-kW (700-hp) Fiat A.14 V-12 engine.

The BR was a pleasing aircraft which showed signs of the great care lavished on it by Rosatelli to achieve good aerodynamic lines. Two examples were sold to Sweden, where they were given the service designation **B 1**.

Variants
BR.1: Rosatelli set about improving the BR design in 1923, the resulting BR.1 going into production and Regia Aeronautica service in the following year; differing mainly in having Warren-type W-form interplane bracing struts, a characteristic feature of all

subsequent Rosatelli biplanes, the BR.1 had a new wide-track landing gear with independent main units; the A.14 engine was retained but its frontal radiator was replaced by one of more advanced type; the new bomber demonstrated improved performance and an increased bombload by comparison with the BR; it also established a new world record, lifting a 1500-kg (3,307-lb) payload to an altitude of 5516 m (18,097 ft); the BR.1 became involved in tests with a new revolving cylinder-type bomb rack and was used also for torpedo dropping experiments; some 150 BR.1s were built; almost all of them going into service with the Regia Aeronautica; the Swedish air arm bought two examples which were designated **B 2** in Flygvapen service.

BR.2: the first flight of the prototype BR.2 took place in 1925; it had a more powerful Fiat A.25 engine, and other improvements included a strengthened structure, greater instrumentation and increased fuel capacity to ensure longer range; the landing gear was also redesigned and improved; in 1930 some 15 Regia Aeronautica light-bomber *squadriglie* were equipped with the BR.2, but by then the type had become obsolescent

BR.3: the last single-engined Fiat light bomber biplane to enter Regia Aeronautica service, the BR.3 was largely an update of the BR.2, appearing in 1930, and some 100 examples were built for Italian light bomber *squadriglie*; Hungary obtained a single example; in outward appearance the BR.3 differed little from the BR.2 which had gone into service

The BR.3 of 1930 gave ample proof of its Rosatelli design origins by its extreme robustness and Warren-type interplane bracing. The BR series was an excellent example of how a well-designed aircraft is capable of great development.

some five years before; the same Fiat A.25 engine was retained, but in a more developed version, the landing gear was again modified, simplified and strengthened, and equipment fitted for the first time included a radio transmitter-receiver and a panoramic camera; later production aircraft had Handley Page leading-edge slats; a BR.3 was entered for the October 1931 Coupe Bibesco military aircraft contest, and covered 1140 km (708 miles) at an average of 252 km/h (156.6 mph); in the mid-1930s BR.3s were relegated to training units, with which a number of examples were still serving in 1940

BR.4: last of Rosatelli's single-engined biplane bombers, the BR.4 made its maiden flight in 1934; a complete redesign, it had a chin-type tunnel radiator similar to that of the CR.30 and CR.32 fighters, the Fiat A.25 engine was retained and the divided landing gear had large, streamlined spat-type fairings; despite considerable aerodynamic refinement the BR.4 was too slow to compete with the new generation of light twin-engined low-wing monoplanes under development and only a single prototype was built.

Specification
Fiat BR.2
Type: two-seat bomber biplane
Powerplant: one 813-kW (1,090-hp) Fiat A.25 12-cylinder Vee piston engine
Performance: maximum speed 240 km/h (149 mph); service ceiling 6250 m (20,505 ft); range 1000 km (621 miles)
Weights: empty equipped 2646 kg (5,833 lb); maximum take-off 4195 kg (9,248 lb)
Dimensions: span 17.30 m (56 ft 9 in); length 10.66 m (34 ft 11¾ in); height 3.91 m (12 ft 10 in); wing area 70.22 m² (755.87 sq ft)
Armament: two 7.7-mm (0.303-in) machine-guns (one fixed forward-firing and one on pivoted mount over rear cockpit), plus up to 720 kg (1,587 lb) of bombs

Fiat BR.20

Flown for the first time from the Fiat company airfield in Turin by Enrico Rolandi on 10 February 1936, the prototype (MM.274) of the **Fiat BR.20 Cicogna** (Stork) immediately made a favourable impression. Before long this medium bomber was being publicised throughout the aeronautical world by the efficient propaganda machine of Mussolini's Fascist government.

The BR.20 was a cantilever low-wing monoplane, its slab-sided fuselage having a mixed covering of dural sheet and fabric. The wing had sheet metal covering and the fabric-covered tail assembly included twin fins and rudders. The main units of the landing gear retracted rearward into the engine nacelles, leaving the wheels partially exposed, and the fixed tailwheel had a streamlined protective fairing. The nose included a manually operated gun turret and below it was a glazed section for the bomb-aimer/navigator. The pilot and co-pilot were seated side-by-side in an enclosed cabin forward of the wing leading edge, the wireless operator's compartment being just in front of the main access door which was on the port side of the fuselage, behind the wing trailing edge. The bomb-bay, capable of carrying a weapon load of up to 1600 kg (3,527 lb), was located in the forward fuselage between the pilot's cabin and the wireless

operator's compartment. A retractable type DR dorsal turret (replaced by an MI turret from the 21st production BR.20 onwards) and a ventral gun position completed the defensive armament.

In the spring of 1937 two special **BR.20A** long-range civil aircraft appeared. They had rounded noses, were stripped of all military equipment and had no break in the fuselage underside as with the bomber. They were built especially to take part in the prestigious Istres-Damascus air race, in which they were able to gain only sixth and seventh places. One other civilianised BR.20 was built, the **BR.20L** *Santo Francesco*, first flown in early 1939. It had an elongated streamlined nose section and additional fuel tanks, enabling it to make a non-stop flight from Rome to Addis Ababa on 6 March 1939, the three-man crew led by Maner Lualdi achieving an average speed of 404 km/h (251 mph).

The first unit to equip with the BR.20 bomber was the 13° Stormo BT at Lonate Pozzolo, in the autumn of 1936. The original BR.20 remained in production until February 1940, a total of 233 being completed. Of these a single example went to Venezuela and 85 were sold to Japan. The Japanese BR.20s, known as the **Type I**, were based at first on the Chinese coastal areas and used to attack inland cities still in Chinese hands. Later they were used in the bomber fighting against the Russians at Nomanhan. According to reports the Imperial Japanese Army Air Force did not find their BR.20s particularly effective and, as soon as the long-awaited Mitsubishi Ki-21 (Type 97 Bomber) was available, surviving Fiats were quickly grounded.

A number of BR.20s operated with the Italian Aviazione Legionaria supporting the Franco-led Nationalists in Spain. Arriving from the summer of 1937 they

took part in day and night raids over the Teruel and Ebro fronts, frequently attacking troop and vehicle concentrations, as well as government-held cities. Nine BR.20s survived to take part in the Nationalist Aviation victory parade at Madrid-Barajas on 12 May 1939. When the Italian personnel left for home, the BR.20s were handed over to Spain.

When Italy entered World War II on 10 June 1940, a new version of the basic design, the **BR.20M** (M for Modificato) had been in production for some six months. It differed from the original BR.20 by having a nose section of entirely new design and smoother outline. In all, 264 examples of the BR.20M were constructed, production ending in the spring of 1942.

To be continued

Fiat BR.20M Cicogna of 4ª Squadriglia, 11° Gruppo, 13° Stormo, attached to the Corpo Aereo Italiano for operations against the UK from Belgium in late 1940.

Fiat BR.20 Cicogna (continued)

Regia Aeronautica BR.20s in service in June 1940 totalled 172 with a further 47 in reserve or under repair. The Fiat bombers took part in the brief campaign against France until 23 June 1940 and then 80 factory-fresh BR.20Ms were allocated to the 13° and 43° Stormi and sent to Belgian bases to participate in the Italian effort against the UK as part of the Corpo Aereo Italiano, which supported the Luftwaffe in the later stages of the Battle of Britain. They were involved in day and night raids against the ports of Harwich and Ramsgate and the industrial centre of Ipswich, between October and December 1940, when survivors were withdrawn.

BR.20s participated subsequently in the campaigns in North Africa, Greece and Yugoslavia, and in the attacks against Malta. Some missions were flown in the long-range reconnaissance role and this type of operation became more usual as the war progressed, the BR.20s carrying out many such missions against partisan areas in the Balkans.

At the time of the Armistice signed between Italy and the Allies in September 1943, 81 BR.20s were still with first-line operational units in Italy, Yugoslavia, Albania and Greece, but by that time most surviving aircraft were attached to bomber training schools. During the final war years a very few BR.20s remained in flying condition as trainers or transports.

Experimental versions tested included the **BR.20C** with a powerful 37-mm cannon in the nose section and another BR.20 flown with tricycle landing gear.

Final version to go into production was the **BR.20bis**, a complete redesign, with a rounded fully glazed nose, more graceful fuselage contours, a retractable tailwheel and pointed vertical tail surfaces. Main improvements, however, were in engine power and defensive armament. Between March and July 1943 15 BR.20bis aircraft were built, but there is no record of their operational use. Their two 932-kW (1,250-hp) Fiat A.82 RC 42 radial engines gave a maximum speed of 460 km/h (286 mph) and a service ceiling of 9200 m (30,185 ft). Dimensions were slightly increased compared with the BR.20M and maximum take-off weight rose to 11500 kg (25,353 lb). Defensive nose and ventral

Fiat BR.20M Cicogna of 56a Squadriglia, 86° Gruppo at Castelventrano, April 1942.

positions retained single 7.7-mm (0.303-in) machine-guns, there were additional weapons of the same calibre firing through ports on each side of the fuselage and a 12.7-mm (0.5-in) gun mounted in a Breda Type V dorsal turret.

Specification
Fiat BR.20
Type: twin-engined medium bomber
Powerplant: two 746-kW (1,000-hp) Fiat A.80 RC 41 18-cylinder radial piston engines

Performance: maximum speed 432 km/h (268 mph) at 5000 m (16,405 ft); service ceiling 9000 m (29,530 ft); range 3000 km (1,864 miles)
Weights: empty equipped 6400 kg (14,110 lb); maximum take-off 9900 kg (21,826 lb)
Dimensions: span 21.56 m (70 ft 8¾ in); length 16.10 m (52 ft 9¾ in); height 4.30 m (14 ft 1¼ in); wing area 74.22 m² (796.5 sq ft)
Armament: one 12.7-mm (0.5-in)

Serving with the Aviazione Legionaria, the BR.20 mounted successful operations in the Spanish Civil War.

machine-gun and two 7.7-mm (0.303-in) machine-guns (the prototype and first 20 production BR.20s had a DR twin 7.7-mm/0.303-in gun dorsal turret in place of a single 12.7-mm/0.5-in gun in MI turret on all later BR.20s and BR.20Ms), plus a bomb load of up to 1600 kg (3,527 lb)

Fiat CR.1

Two single-seat fighter prototypes, serialled MM.1 and MM.2 under the newly-formed Regia Aeronautica's numbering system, were built and tested in 1923. Designated **Fiat CR**, and designed under the leadership of Celestino Rosatelli, they were compact biplanes of inverted-sesquiplane configuration, the lower wing having greater span than the upper. Of mainly wooden construction, the CR had rigid Warren-type W-form wing bracing and a conventional cross-axle landing gear. The two prototypes differed in tail configuration, one having a rounded balanced rudder, and in the shape of the cowling for the Hispano-Suiza engine.

The decision was made to build the CR in quantity for the Regia Aeronautica, since it was shown to surpass its nearest rival, the SIAI S.52 biplane, in manoeuvrability and speed; however, the S.52 had the edge in rate of climb. Production aircraft were designated **CR.1**, but considerable care was taken in developing the type for service with the *squadriglie*, two further prototypes being tested under the CR.1 designation. These were followed by three production batches: the first, comprising 109 machines, was built by Fiat; the second, of 40 aircraft, was produced by O.F.M. (later IMAM-Meridionali) of Naples; and the last, of 100 fighters, came from SIAI (Savoia-Marchetti).

In total, 240 CR.1s went into Regia Aeronautica service, the first deliveries

taking place in 1925. The type soon equipped the 76ª, 77ª, 78ª, 79ª, 85ª, 86ª, 87ª and 88ª Squadriglie. They served well and faithfully, although they were never engaged in combat.

During the 1930s a number of CR.1s were modified to take the 328-kW (440-hp) Isotta Fraschini Asso Caccia engine. These were quite successful and showed a greatly improved performance. The Asso-powered CR.1 formed the equipment of the 163ª Squadriglia based at Rhodes in the Aegean and was only withdrawn from service in 1937.

A single CR.1 was purchased for the Belgian air arm and, after rejection of the type as squadron equipment, this was used by the 1ᵉʳ Escadrille de Chasse. Another example was tested by the Polish authorities, but the only export

production order was received from Latvia for nine Fiat-built machines which equipped the naval fighter unit based at Leipaja. They were not withdrawn from service until 1936.

Variants of the CR.1 which were tested included one powered by a Fiat A.20 engine cooled by two Lamblin radiators, and another with an Alfa Romeo Jupiter radial; reportedly they were designated **CR.10** and **CR.5**, respectively. In 1928 the **CR.2** was flight tested with a 149-kW (200-hp) Armstrong Siddeley Lynx radial engine.

Specification
Fiat CR.1
Type: single-seat fighter biplane
Powerplant: one 224-kW (300-hp) Hispano-Suiza 42 8-cylinder Vee piston

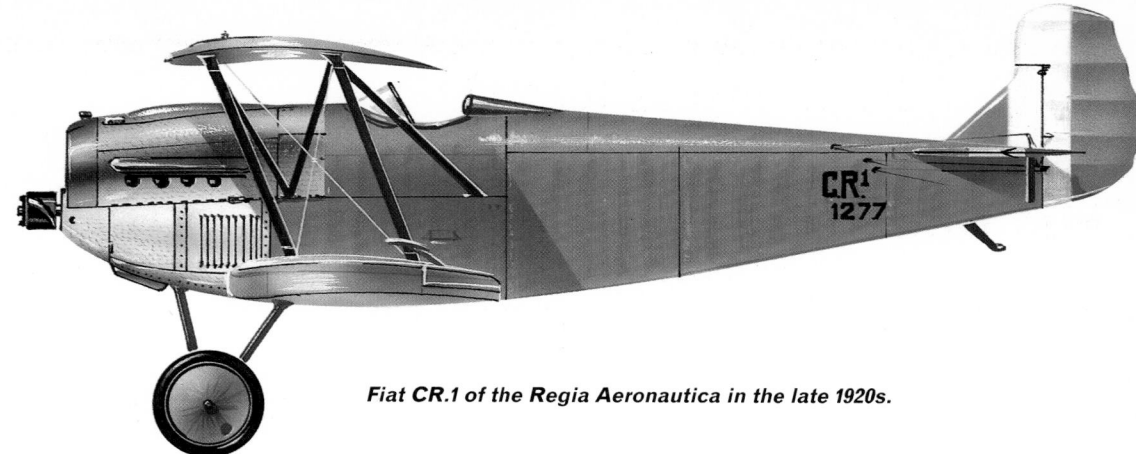

engine
Performance: maximum speed 272 km/h (169 mph); climb to 5000 m (16,405 ft) in 16 minutes 27 seconds; service ceiling 7450 m (24,440 ft); endurance 2 hours 35 minutes
Weights: empty equipped 839 kg (1,850 lb); maximum take-off 1154 kg (2,544 lb)
Dimensions: span 8.95 m (29 ft 4¼ in); length 6.16 m (20 ft 2½ in); height 2.40 m (7 ft 10½ in); wing area 23.00 m² (247.58 sq ft)
Armament: two forward-firing synchronised 7.7-mm (0.303-in) Vickers machine-guns

Fiat CR.1 of the Regia Aeronautica in the late 1920s.

Fiat CR.20

The Fiat CR.20 single-seat fighter was produced in considerable numbers for its time. It formed the equipment of the famous Regia Aeronautica aerobatic team and took part in the final stages of the Italian conquest of Libya, then in the campaign against the Emperor Haile Selassie in Abyssinia which ended in Italian victory in 1936. As there was no air opposition, the CR.20 was used for ground-attack duties in both campaigns. The various versions of the CR.20 ended their days in training units in the late 1930s.

This classic biplane had unequal-span wings and a carefully contoured fuselage. It was largely of metal construction with varnished fabric covering, except for metal panels over the forward fuselage. It was designed for the new Fiat A.20 engine and four prototypes were built and tested, the first flight being made at Turin on 19 June 1926. The following autumn the new fighter made a considerable impression at the Paris Salon de l'Aéronautique, recognisably Fiat by the W-type interplane struts and distinctive tail unit designed by Celestino Rosatelli. The nose was distinguished by a saddle-type radiator for its water-cooled engine. Publicity referred to an armament of four machine-guns, but in the event the CR.20 had the twin-gun arrangement typical of the inter-war period.

The fighter entered production in 1927, and when the last examples of the basic design were completed in 1932 some 250 aircraft had been manufactured. Apart from 46 twin-float seaplanes designated **CR.20 Idro**, built in equal numbers by the Macchi and CMASA concerns, all the remaining aircraft were constructed by Fiat and were handicapped by a rather crude conven-

Production of the CR.20 Idro floatplane fighter was undertaken by CMASA and Macchi. The type was not popular in service, the provision of floats bestowing some vicious handling characteristics such as falling out of a loop.

tional cross-axle landing gear with compressed rubber shock absorbers. As a result the **CR.20bis** appeared in 1930 with an entirely new divided landing gear with oleo-pneumatic shock absorbers and wheel brakes. Of the 235 CR.20bis aircraft completed by 1932, when production ended at the Fiat factories, a number with the A.20AQ engine, which gave an improved rate of climb and better high-altitude performance, had the designation **CR.20bisAQ**.

The final production version was the **CR.Asso**, a CR.20bis airframe married to the Isotta Fraschini Asso Caccia engine of 336 kW (450 hp), an air-cooled powerplant which was housed in a distinctive and elegant cowling. The only major structural modification was a redesigned tailplane with increased horizontal surface area. A total of 204 examples of the CR.Asso were produced between 1931 and 1933, Macchi building 104 aircraft and CMASA the remaining 100. The CR.Asso proved popular with the *squadriglie di caccia* (fighter squadrons) and replaced the CR.20bis in the aerobatic teams. The CR.20 family was also used in a variety of experimental roles, including the testing of a Handley Page leading-edge slat. One other version not so far mentioned was the **CR.20B**, a two-seat variant of the CR.20 and CR.20bis, used as a trainer and liaison aircraft with Italian fighter units. It is understood that the production figures quoted include limited numbers of these two-seaters.

The CR.20 family was also successful

on the export market. Lithuania purchased 15 CR.20s in 1928, and Hungary obtained one single-seat aircraft and one CR.20B for its clandestine air arm. Some mystery surrounds a single CR.20 reported as sold to the Soviet Union and four aircraft apparently used by Poland in the August 1929 fighter competition held between that country and others of the 'Little Entente' powers (Romania, Czechoslovakia and Yugoslavia). Certainly there were no further reports of the Polish CR.20s after the contest.

In 1932 12 CR.20bis fighters went to equip the Hungarian fighter units, where they remained in service until replaced by CR.32s in 1936. Deliveries to Austria, also in secret, totalled 16 CR.20bis, 16 CR.20bisAQ and four CR.20B machines. After the *Anschluss*, which annexed Austria to Germany, a number of the surviving aircraft were painted in Luftwaffe markings and used briefly at German training schools. Another customer for the CR.20bis was Paraguay, which flew six aircraft in the Gran Chaco War against Bolivia between 1932 and 1935.

It was in the Regia Aeronautica, how-

ever, that the CR.20 played a dominant role. For a number of years virtually all the fighter *squadriglie* were equipped with various versions of the type and, in addition, the CR.20 Idro formed the strength of the uniquely Italian seaplane fighter units, the *squadriglie di caccia marittima*.

Specification
Fiat CR.20bis
Type: single-seat fighter biplane
Powerplant: one 306-kW (410-hp) Fiat A.20 12-cylinder Vee piston engine
Performance: maximum speed 260 km/h (161 mph); service ceiling 8500 m (27,885 ft); endurance 2 hours 30 minutes
Weights: empty equipped 970 kg (2,138 lb); maximum take-off 1390 kg (3,064 lb)
Dimensions: span 9.80 m (32 ft 1¾ in); length 6.71 m (22 ft 0¼ in); height 2.79 m (9 ft 1¾ in); wing area 25.50 m² (274.5 sq ft)
Armament: two synchronised forward-firing 7.7-mm (0.303-in) Vickers machine-guns

Fiat CR.30

Rosatelli produced in the **Fiat CR.30** a completely new design for a single-seat fighter. The first (MM.164) of four prototypes was flown for the first time in March 1932 piloted by the famous Brack Papa. The rounded wingtips and tail surfaces, together with its carefully cowled Fiat A.30 RA engine and wide-track divided landing gear with wheel spats, all gave the CR.30 a distinctive and workmanlike appearance. The CR.30 retained the W-form interplane bracing which had characterised Rosatelli's earlier designs. Two of the prototypes participated in the Zurich international meeting in July 1932, creating widespread interest when they carried off the speed circuit contest at average speeds of 340 km/h (211.3 mph) and 330 km/h (205.0 mph).

The CR.30 was an entirely new design, rather than being derived from the CR.1. This is the first prototype with a concave leading edge to the fin and with different headrest and windscreen.

This success and others led to Regia Aeronautica orders, apart from the prototypes, and 121 CR.30s went to the *squadriglie di caccia*. Production lasted from 1932 to 1935, the last first-line CR.30s being retired from the 2º Stormo serving in Libya in 1938.

Successful conversion of two prototypes (MM.165 and MM.166) to two-seat configuration proved a great success and a large number of the single-seat aircraft were converted subsequently as **CR.30B** two-seat 'refresher' trainers and station hacks. That they

filled an important gap is shown by the CANSA works receiving a wartime order for 20 CR.30Bs to replace losses.

Two CR.30s were converted to seaplanes by fitting twin floats and these were flown as trainers at the Scuola

d'Alta Velocita at Desenzano under the designation **CR.30 Idro**.

Principal foreign operator of the CR.30 was the Hungarian air arm, which received two single-seat machines in the summer of 1936, followed by an ex-Regia Aeronautica aircraft in 1938 plus 10 CR.30B two-seaters; finally, the Luft-waffe passed two ex-Austrian CR.30s to Hungary after the annexation of the former country by Germany. Austria had received three CR.30s and three CR.30Bs in 1936. Two CR.30s were sent to the Spanish Nationalists in 1938, but before that two had served with the Chinese 3rd Air Corps from 1934, and

Paraguay had purchased two in 1937 as aerobatic trainers. A single CR.30 was handed over to Venezuela at the beginning of 1938 by an Italian aeronautical mission visiting that country. Total production of all versions was 176.

Specification
Fiat CR.30
Type: single-seat fighter biplane

Powerplant: one 447-kW (600-hp) Fiat A.30 RA 12-cylinder Vee piston engine
Performance: maximum speed 351 km/h (218 mph) at 3000 m (9,845 ft); climb to 4000 m (13,125 ft) in 6 minutes 40 seconds; service ceiling 8350 m (27,845 ft); range 850 km (528 miles)
Weights: empty equipped 1345 kg

(2,965 lb); maximum take-off 1895 kg (4,178 lb)
Dimensions: span 10.50 m (34 ft 5½ in); length 7.88 m (25 ft 10¼ in); height 2.78 m (9 ft 1½ in); wing area 27.05 m² (291.17 sq ft)
Armament: two synchronised forward-firing SAFAT 7.7-mm (0.303-in) machine-guns (prototypes had twin 12.7-mm [0.5-in] SAFAT guns)

Fiat CR.32

Not content with the excellent agility displayed by the CR.30 and determined to achieve an overall improvement in performance, Celestino Rosatelli and his design team produced a new fighter closely resembling the CR.30 but somewhat refined and with reduced overall dimensions. Manoeuvrability was enhanced by a judicious redistribution of loading, achieved mainly through relocation of fuel tanks. The resulting **Fiat CR.32** prototype (MM.201) took to the air for the first time on 28 April 1933. It was an instant success, the first production order being received in March 1934, and the type soon equipped the 1°, 3° and 4° Stormi of the Regia Aeronautica. Series aircraft had variable-pitch propellers and could be equipped with a radio transmitter-receiver, panoramic camera or bomb racks. Modified versions for the Regia Aeronautica were built up to 1939, each designed to reduce all-up weight and improve performance. In addition, the CR.32 was demonstrated widely abroad and attracted considerable export orders.

The CR.32 was used extensively in operations supporting the Nationalists in the Spanish Civil War, soon gaining a reputation as one of the outstanding fighter biplanes of all time. At least 380 took part in the air battles fought over Spain, proving formidable adversaries to the Soviet Polikarpov I-15 biplanes and Polikarpov I-16 monoplanes which formed the backbone of the Republican fighter arm.

Like the earlier CR.30, the CR.32s were used for numerous aerobatic displays, many of them in Italy. On the occasion of visits by foreign statesmen the 4° Stormo, based at Rome, invariably put on impressive shows with formations of five or 10 aircraft. During 1936 displays were given in other European capitals and major cities, and in 1937 throughout South America. The team's return to Europe culminated in a brilliant display at Berlin.

The remarkable aerobatic characteristics of the CR.32 and its undoubted success in Spain misled the Italian air ministry, which formed the view that a fighter biplane still had potential as a weapon of war, with the result that the CR.42, developed from the CR.32, was already an outdated concept before the prototype made its first flight.

The CR.32 itself soldiered on into World War II and when Italy declared war, in June 1940, 324 were still in first-line service, although by then hopelessly outclassed. Some were adapted as night-fighters, while those operated by units in Libya were used largely in the ground-attack role against British troops. The greatest wartime successes achieved by CR.32s were in Italian East Africa, aircraft of the 410ª and 411ª Squadriglia destroying a number of British and South African aircraft before the final Italian surrender.

The first customer for the CR.32 was China, which ordered 16 aircraft in 1933 and these aircraft, armed with twin Vick-

ers machine-guns, gave a good account of themselves against the invading Japanese. They were regarded as superior to the Curtiss Hawk biplanes which equipped most Chinese fighter units in the period 1934-36.

The Hungarian air arm received 76 CR.32s in 1935-36. These were used largely as fighter-trainers, but fired their guns in anger when Hungary moved against the German puppet regime in March 1939, ultimately annexing the territory of Ruthenia.

The Hungarians experimented with a CR.32 powered by a 559-kW (750-hp) Gnome-Rhône 14Mars radial engine. The modified aircraft achieved an impressive maximum speed of 420 km/h (261 mph) at 4000 m (13,120 ft), but the Hungarian government's inability to obtain more Gnome-Rhône engines thwarted the plan to re-engine all available CR.32s.

Austria ordered 45 **CR.32bis** fighters in the spring of 1936 to equip Jagdgeschwader II at Wiener Neustadt. In March 1938 the Austrian units were absorbed into Luftwaffe fighter groups, but after a brief period the 36 remaining aircraft were handed over to Hungary.

When the Spanish Civil War ended in the spring of 1939, survivors of the CR.32s operated by the Italian Aviazione Legionaria were handed over to Spain, joining 60 **CR.32ter** aircraft supplied direct to Spain in 1937 and 27 **CR.32quater** fighters received by Franco in 1938. In addition, Spain acquired a manufacturing licence in 1938 and by the end of 1942 Hispano Aviacion of Seville had completed 100 machines under the designation **HA-132-L Chirri**. Some of these remained in service as **C.1** aerobatic trainers up to 1953.

The aerobatic displays in South America also brought results, Paraguay ordering 10 CR.32s in 1937, although not all were delivered, and Venezuela obtained 10 CR.32quater aircraft.

Variants
CR.32: original version; supplied to Regia Aeronautica (291, including prototypes), Hungary (76) and China (16)
CR.32bis: produced from 1935; had provision for two forward-firing 7.7-mm (0.303-in) SAFAT machine-guns in lower wings in addition to two fuselage weapons of either 12.7-mm (0.5-in) or 7.7-mm (0.303-in) calibre; total production was 328, the Regia Aeronautica receiving 283 and Austria 45; the extra weight of the wing-mounted weapons often led to them being discarded
CR.32ter: this version had two fuselage-mounted weapons only, these being SAFAT 12.7-mm (0.5-in) machine-guns; total of 103 built and all serving in Spain, 60 of them with the Spanish air arm
CR.32quater: this was lighter than any version, other than the original CR.32 series; same armament as CR.32ter; 398 built, of which 105 served with the Italian Aviazione Legionaria in Spain; 27 went direct to Spain, 10 to Venezuela and (estimated) four to Paraguay; the balance was delivered to the Regia Aeronautica; this brought total Italian production to 1,212 aircraft
CR.33: version of the CR.32 with the 522-kW (700-hp) Fiat A.33 RC 35 engine; first prototype (MM.296) flown in 1935 and two others in 1937, but no production aircraft built
CR.40: short-nosed prototype (MM.202) powered by a 391-kW (525-hp) Bristol Mercury IV radial engine; built in parallel with the CR.32 prototype and test-flown in 1934; the upper wing was gulled and attached directly to the top of the fuselage, this arrangement giving the pilot a good forward and upward view
CR.40bis: designation of one prototype (MM.275) with the same

The most important biplane fighter of the 1930s, the CR.32 was still in service during the early part of World War II. Here Benito Mussolini and Marshal Balbo inspect Regia Aeronautica warplanes in Libya in June 1940, with CR.32 fighters to the fore and Savoia-Marchetti S.M.81 bomber/transports in the background.

wing configuration as the CR.40, but powered by a 522-kW (700-hp) Fiat A.59R radial engine; a disappointing maximum speed of 350 km/h (217 mph) ensured no production examples were built
CR.41: similar to the CR.40 in general appearance, the CR.41 (MM.207) was powered by a 671-kW (900-hp) 14-cylinder Gnome-Rhône 14Kfs; modified vertical tail surfaces of increased area were used to maintain directional stability; maximum speed 381 km/h (237 mph) at 5000 m (16,405 ft); tested during 1936 and 1937, the CR.41 was abandoned in favour of the later CR.42

Specification
Fiat CR.32
Type: single-seat fighter biplane
Powerplant: one 447-kW (600-hp) Fiat A.30 RA bis 12-cylinder Vee piston engine
Performance: maximum speed 375 km/h (233 mph) at 3000 m (9,840 ft); service ceiling 8800 m (28,870 ft); range 680 km (422 miles)
Weights: empty equipped 1325 kg (2,921 lb); maximum take-off 1850 kg (4,079 lb)
Dimensions: span 9.50 m (31 ft 2 in); length 7.45 m (24 ft 5¼ in); height 2.63 m (8 ft 7½ in); wing area 22.10 m² (237.89 sq ft)
Armament: two synchronised 7.7-mm (0.303-in) Breda-SAFAT machine-guns

Fieseler Fi 103R Reichenberg
to
Fletcher FU-24 Utility

Fieseler Fi 103R Reichenberg

Development of the **Fieseler Fi 103** flying-bomb, better known as the **V-1** reprisal weapon, is well recorded in aviation history. A small fixed-wing pilotless aircraft, it was powered by a pulse-jet engine mounted above the rear fuselage, incorporated a simple flight control system to guide it to its target, an air log device to make it dive to the ground after travelling a preset distance, and a warhead packed with high-explosive. The first of these weapons landed in the London area in the early hours of 13 June 1944.

Long before that, in late 1943, German officials were considering the use of piloted missiles to make precision attacks on high-priority targets, a policy that developed quite independently of the Japanese Kamikaze attacks. With a deteriorating war situation, Adolf Hitler gave a go-ahead for such a project in March 1944, and the Fi 103 was adopted

The Fi 103R-IV was intended as the operational version. It is hard to see how the pilot could have possibly escaped due to the canopy's poor mechanism and location just under the pulse jet's inlet.

for this programme, which was designated **Fi 103R** (Reichenberg). Four versions were planned initially: an unpowered **Fi 103R-I** for early flight tests; powered **Fi 103R-II** and **Fi 103R-III** aircraft to serve as basic and advanced two-seat trainers respectively; and the operational **Fi 103R-IV**. The last of these differed from the V-1 by having a cockpit for the pilot and conventional controls/control surfaces, and it was intended that after launch from a motherplane, the pilot would aim his R-IV at the target and then bale out, descending by

parachute. About 175 of these weapons were produced, but their continued development and planned use was abandoned in late 1944. Hanna Reitsch was test pilot.

Specification
Fieseler Fi 103R-IV

Type: piloted missile
Powerplant: one 350-kg (772-lb) thrust Argus 109-014 pulse-jet engine
Performance: maximum speed approximately 650 km/h (404 mph)
Dimensions: span 5.72 m (18 ft 9¼ in); length 8.00 m (26 ft 3 in)

Fieseler Fi 156 Storch

Best-known of all the Fieseler designs because of its extensive use during World War II, the **Fieseler Fi 156 Storch** (Stork) was a remarkable STOL (short take-off and landing) aircraft that was first flown during the early months of 1936. A braced high-wing monoplane of mixed construction, with a conventional braced tail unit and fixed tailskid landing gear with long-stroke main units, the Fi 156 was powered by an Argus inverted Vee piston engine, and its extensively glazed cabin provided an excellent view for its three-man crew. As with the Fi 97, the key to the success of this aircraft was its wing incorporating the company's high-lift devices and comprising, in the initial production series, a fixed slat extending over the entire span of the wing leading edge, and with slotted ailerons and slotted camber-changing flaps occupying the entire trailing edge. Flight testing of the first three prototypes (**Fi 156 V1, V2** and **V3**) showed that the capability of this aircraft more than exceeded its STOL expectations for, with little more than a light breeze blowing, it needed a take-off run of only about 60 m (200 ft) and could land in about a third of that distance.

Built to compete against fixed-wing submissions from Messerschmitt and Siebel and an autogyro from Focke-Wulf, the three prototypes were followed by the ski-equipped **Fi 156 V4** for winter trials, a pre-production **Fi 156 V5** and, in early 1937, by 10 **Fi 156A-0** aircraft for service evaluation. One of these was demonstrated publicly for the first time at an international flying meeting at the end of July 1937, by which time the general-purpose **Fi 156A-1** was in production. Service tests confirmed that Germany's armed forces had acquired a 'go-anywhere' aircraft, and for the remainder of World War II the Storch was found virtually wherever German forces were operating, production of all variants totalling almost 2,900 aircraft.

Because of their capability, Fi 156s were used in some remarkable exploits. Best known is the rescue of Benito Mussolini from imprisonment in an hotel

amid the Apennine mountains, on 12 September 1943, and the flight made by Hanna Reitsch into the ruins of Berlin on 26 April 1945, carrying General Ritter von Greim to be appointed by Adolf Hitler as his new Commander of the Luftwaffe.

During the war the Fi 156 had been built for the Luftwaffe by Morane-Saulnier in France and by Mraz in Czechoslovakia. These two companies continued production after the war, Morane-Saulnier producing **M.S.500** variants and Mraz the **K-65 Cap.**

Variants
Fi 156B: projected variant with movable leading-edge slats; not built
Fi 156C-0: pre-production version of an improved Fi 156A-1 with raised rear-cabin glazing to allow installation of a rear-firing 7.92-mm (0.31-in) machine-gun
Fi 156C-1: liaison and staff transport version
Fi 156C-2: reconnaissance version with one camera and two-man crew; some later examples equipped to carry one stretcher for casualty evacuation
Fi 156C-3: general-purpose version, some with improved Argus As 10P engine

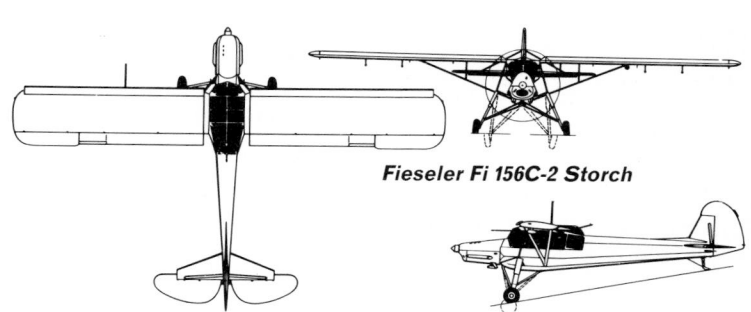

Fieseler Fi 156C Storch of the Kurierstaffel Oberkommando der Luftwaffe (Luftwaffe high command liaison squadron), operating on the Don section of the Eastern Front in August 1942 (the codes are those of the Geschwaderstab, Lehrgeschwader 2).

Fieseler Fi 156C-2 Storch

Fi 156C-3/Trop: tropicalised version of the Fi 156C-3 with engine dust/sand filters
Fi 156C-5: similar to 156C-3 but with Argus As 10P engine as standard and provision to carry an underfuselage drop tank or camera installation
Fi 156C-5/Trop: tropicalised version of the C-5
Fi 156D-0: pre-production ambulance version with improved accommodation for one stretcher and an enlarged loading/unloading hatch; powered by Argus As 10C engine

Fi 156D-1: production version of the D-0 with Argus As 10P engine as standard
Fi 156E-0: designation of 10 pre-production aircraft with a form of tracked landing gear, the main units each with two wheels in tandem linked by pneumatic rubber track; no further production
Fi 256: two examples only of larger capacity (5-seat) civil version, built at Morane-Saulnier factory at Puteaux, France, during 1943-44

Specification
Fieseler Fi 156C-2
Type: two-seat army co-operation/
reconnaissance aircraft
Powerplant: one 179-kW (240-hp)

Argus As 10C-3 8-cylinder inverted Vee
piston engine
Performance: maximum speed 175
km/h (109 mph) at sea level;
economical cruising speed 130 km/h

(81 mph); service ceiling 4600 m
(15,090 ft); range 385 km (239 miles)
Weights: empty 930 kg (2,050 lb);
maximum take-off 1325 kg (2,921 lb)
Dimensions: span 14.25 m (46 ft

9 in); length 9.90 m (32 ft 5¾ in);
height 3.05 m (10 ft 0 in); wing area
26.00 m² (279.87 sq ft)
Armament: one rear-firing 7.92-mm
(0.31-in) machine-gun on pivoted mount

Fieseler Fi 167

To meet a requirement for a ship-based
two-seat torpedo-bomber/reconnais-
sance aircraft, both Arado and Fieseler
submitted proposals to the RLM. Prototypes of both aircraft were built, but testing in late 1938 soon showed that Arado's Ar 195 could not meet the
requirements, whereas the **Fieseler Fi
167 V1** could not only meet but considerably exceed the specification. In
configuration the Fieseler design was a
two-bay foldable-wing biplane, primarily
of metal construction but with some
fabric covering, fixed tailwheel landing
gear with tall jettisonable main units, a
conventional braced tail unit and a Daimler-Benz DB 601 engine. The two-man
crew was accommodated in tandem,
beneath a long canopy that was designed to allow for operation at the rear
of a machine-gun on a pivoted mount.

As with the Fi 156, Fieseler's new aircraft had exceptional low speed characteristics, achieved in this case by both
wings incorporating ailerons and full-
span automatic leading-edge slats, and
the lower wing having large-area trailing-
edge flaps. Their effect, allied with the
lift of the biplane wings, made it possible
for the aircraft to sink slowly and almost
vertically under complete control.

The Fi 167 was intended for service
aboard the German aircraft-carrier *Graf
Zeppelin*, launched on 8 December
1938, and following the completion of a
second prototype (**Fi 167 V2**) a pre-pro-

*Fieseler Fi 167A-0 of Erprobungsstaffel 167, based in the
Netherlands during 1940-42.*

duction batch of 12 **Fi 167A-0** aircraft
was built. These differed little from the
prototypes, but incorporated some refinements considered desirable after
service testing, including the addition of
a two-man dinghy. When construction of
the *Graf Zeppelin* was stopped, in 1940,
the role for which the Fi 167 had been designed no longer existed. However, it
was expected that when construction
was resumed, manufacture of the Fi 167
would also go ahead; this was not to be
the case, for when in 1942 orders were

given for construction of the aircraft-carrier to be restarted, it was decided that a
version of the Ju 87 would amply meet
requirements and no further examples
of the Fi 167 were built. After being used
for a range of tests in the Netherlands,
nine of the Fi 167s were sold to Romania.

Specification
Fieseler Fi 167A-0
Type: ship-based torpedo-bomber/
reconnaissance aircraft
Powerplant: one 820-kW (1,100-hp)
Daimler-Benz 601B 12-cylinder inverted
Vee piston engine
Performance: (reconnaissance)
maximum speed 325 km/h (202 mph);

cruising speed 270 km/h (168 mph);
service ceiling 8200 m (26,905 ft);
range 1500 km (932 miles)
Weights: empty 2800 kg (6,173 lb);
maximum take-off 4850 kg (10,692 lb)
Dimensions: span 13.50 m (44 ft
3½ in); length 11.40 m (37 ft 4¾ in);
height 4.80 m (15 ft 9 in); wing area
45.50 m² (489.77 sq ft)
Armament: one fixed forward-firing
7.92-mm (0.31-in) MG17 machine-gun
and one 7.92-mm (0.31-in) MG15
machine-gun on pivoted mounting in
aft position, plus maximum load of one
1000-kg (2,204-lb) bomb or one 765-kg
(1,687-lb) torpedo

Fisher P-75A Eagle

In 1942, when the US Army Air Force
was desperately in need of a single-seat
fighter with a high rate of climb, the
Fisher Body Division of the General
Motors Corporation came up with an
unusual proposal. Evolved by the company's design team, under the leadership of Don Berlin, formerly chief
engineer of the Curtiss Airplane Division
of Curtiss-Wright, the proposal from
Fisher Body was that assemblies of aircraft already in large-scale production
could be combined with the most
powerful engine then available to produce a new high-performance fighter.
As a result approval was given for the
construction of two **Fisher XP-75** prototypes with a new fuselage and wing
centre-section that would unite North
American P-51 Mustang outer wing
panels, a Douglas A-24 tail unit and
Vought F4U retractable tailwheel landing
gear to form the airframe. It was decided
subsequently to use instead the outer
wing panels of the Curtiss P-40. Power
was provided by a 1939-kW (2,600-hp)
Allison V-3420-19 engine mounted
within the fuselage, aft of the cockpit,

*Among the unusual features of
the Fisher XP-75A was a 10-gun
armament, with four of the guns
ranged around the nose. The
mid-mounted engine drove a
contra-rotating propeller.*

and driving two contra-rotating propellers via an extended shaft and reduction
gearbox in the nose.

Before the first prototype (43-46950)
was flown on 17 November 1943, it had
already been decided that the requirement emphasis had shifted and that
long-range escort fighters were more
urgently needed than interceptors. This
brought a new contract for six long-
range **XP-75A** aircraft, plus a condi-
tional order for 2,500 production
examples of the **P-75A Eagle**, this
latter order being subject to the prototype aircraft meeting all requirements.
The XP-75As introduced a number of
changes brought about by the revised
role and as a result of tests with the
XP-75 prototype. They included a new
cockpit canopy, a redesigned tail unit
and the installation of a different mark of

the V-3420 engine. However, by the
time the first production P-75A was
ready for testing, in September 1944, the
requirement for this aircraft no longer
existed and only five were completed
and used subsequently for test purposes.

Specification
Fisher P-75A Eagle
Type: single-seat long-range escort
fighter
Powerplant: one 2151-kW (2,885-hp)
Allison V-3420-23 24-cylinder double-
banked Vee piston engine
Performance: (approximate)

maximum speed 644 km/h (400 mph);
cruising speed 499 km/h (310 mph);
service ceiling 10975 m (36,000 ft);
range with maximum fuel 4828 km
(3,000 miles)
Weights: empty 5214 kg (11,495 lb);
maximum take-off 8260 kg (18,210 lb)
Dimensions: span 15.04 m (49 ft
4 in); length 12.32 m (40 ft 5 in); height
4.72 m (15 ft 6 in); wing area 32.24 m²
(347.0 sq ft)
Armament: 10 12.7-mm (0.5-in)
forward-firing Browning machine-guns
(six in wings and four in fuselage), plus
two 227-kg (500-lb) bombs on racks
beneath the wing centre-section

Fleet 1, 2 and 7

The Consolidated PT-3, which was being
delivered to the US Army Air Corps in
1928, clearly had sales potential in a
rapidly expanding civil market that came
in the wake of Charles Lindbergh's solo
transatlantic flight of 1927. Retaining the
same general lines as the PT-3, the new

civil version was designated **Consolidated Model 14** and was named the
Husky Junior. Almost before the first
example was completed, Consolidated
reached a decision that it did not want to
become involved in the civil market. This
induced the company's president, Major

Reuben H. Fleet, to acquire rights for the
Husky Junior design from the company,
establishing Fleet Aircraft Inc. at Buffalo,
New York, to build and market it. Within
about six months Consolidated had a
change of heart, buying up Fleet Aircraft
Inc. to continue production in the USA,
and in 1930 established a Canadian
manufacturing/sales outlet by forming
Fleet Aircraft of Canada Ltd at Fort Erie,

Ontario.

With a new start it was decided not to
retain the name of Husky Junior and the
designation **Fleet 1** was adopted instead. This aircraft differed little from its
predecessor, having the same 82-kW
(110-hp) Warner Scarab 7-cylinder radial
engine and, basically similar airframe.
The only major change was in accommodation, the single elongated cockpit of

the Husky Junior (containing two individual seats) being replaced by two separate cockpits in tandem. It was followed by the generally similar **Fleet 2**, with detail improvements and power provided by a 75-kW (100-hp) Kinner K5 5-cylinder radial engine, but only a small number were built before the designation was changed to **Fleet 7** with installation of the more powerful Kinner B5 engine. This variant was known as the **Fleet 7B** in Canada, and examples in service with the Royal Canadian Air Force had the designation **Fawn Mk I**.

The Fleet 2 was the first version to be produced in Canada, the start of production being assisted by the receipt of at least three fuselage frames built in the US factory. As in the US, only small numbers of Fleet 2s were built before production of the Fleet 7 was initiated. They were seen in service, especially in Canada, with float and ski installations, and with more than one type of cockpit enclosure. Their robust construction has ensured that several restored aircraft remain in flying condition.

Variants
Fleet 3: two examples completed with 123-kW (165-hp) Wright J6 5-cylinder radial engines

Fleet 4: one test aircraft with a 127-kW (170-hp) Curtiss Challenger 6-cylinder radial engine
Fleet 5: one test aircraft with a 67-kW (90-hp) Brownback C-400 6-cylinder two-row radial engine
Fleet 6: configuration uncertain; believed to be a Fleet 2 with a trapeze above the upper wing for 'hook-on' experiments with military dirigibles
Fleet 7C: designation of versions powered by a 107-kW (140-hp) Armstrong Siddeley Civet I 7-cylinder radial engine; RCAF designation **Fawn Mk II**
Fleet 7G: redesignation of one RCAF Fleet 7B following installation of an 89-kW (120-hp) de Havilland Gipsy III 4-cylinder inline engine; reverted subsequently to Fleet 7B configuration
XPT-6: under this designation the US Army Air Corps acquired one Model 7 for service test, powered by a 75-kW (100-hp) Kinner R-370-1 (Kinner K5) engine
YPT-6: designation of 10 aircraft virtually identical to XPT-6 for more extensive service evaluation
YPT-6A: modified version of Model 7 with enlarged cockpit for service evaluation

Specification
Fleet 7/7B/Fawn Mk I
Type: two-seat sporting/training biplane
Powerplant: one 93-kW (125-hp) Kinner B5 5-cylinder radial piston engine
Performance: maximum speed 185 km/h (115 mph); cruising speed 140 km/h (87 mph); service ceiling 4265 m (14,000 ft); range 480 km (298 miles)
Weights: empty 520 kg (1,146 lb); maximum take-off 790 kg (1,742 lb)
Dimensions: span 8.53 m (28 ft 0 in);

This Fleet 7B served with the Royal Canadian Air Force until 1947, its great strength encouraging pilots to get the most out of their aircraft with manoeuvres such as the negative-g outside loop. In RCAF service the much-loved aircraft was known as the Fawn.

length 6.55 m (21 ft 6 in); height 2.44 m (8 ft 0 in); wing area 18.12 m² (195.0 sq ft)

Fleet 10 and 16

Towards the end of 1934, and by which time Consolidated had absorbed the US Fleet Aircraft Inc. operation as a cost-saving exercise, an order was received from China for a number of aircraft of Fleet 7 type, and these were built by the Canadian company. By then a number of refinements had been incorporated in the design, including tailwheel landing gear with wheel brakes, a revised tail unit and a number of detail improvements to bring the revised designation **Fleet 10**.

A total of 36 aircraft was built for China and despatched in mid-1935, these comprising six **Fleet 10A** (US designation **Fleet 5**) and 30 **Fleet 10D** (US **Fleet 10**) aircraft, together with components and materials for the assembly in China of an additional 20 aircraft. There were a number of Fleet 10 variants, listed below, the majority resulting from different powerplant installations, and export aircraft were supplied to Argentina, the Dominican Republic, Iraq, Mexico, Nicaragua, Portugal, Venezuela and Yugoslavia in addition to those already delivered to China.

In September 1938, following evaluation of a Model 10D by the Royal Canadian Air Force, the company was re-

quested to develop a trainer that would be suitable for aerobatics carrying full military equipment. This resulted in production of the **Fleet 16** which retained the same basic configuration as the Fleet 10, but had structural strengthening for the aerobatic role. More than 400 of these aircraft were supplied to the RCAF between 1939 and 1941 for use by the RCAF and in the British Commonwealth Air Training Plan under the designations **Finch Mk I** and **Finch Mk II**. Post-war many of these surplus aircraft came on the civil market, the majority acquired by buyers in Canada and the USA. A number remain airworthy.

Variants
Fleet 10A: basic version with a 75-kW (100-hp) Kinner K5 5-cylinder radial engine
Fleet 10B: as Fleet 10A but with a 93-kW (125-hp) Kinner B5 5-cylinder radial engine
Fleet 10D: as Fleet 10A but with a 119-kW (160-hp) Kinner R5 5-cylinder radial engine
Fleet 10-32D: generally as Fleet 10D, but with wing span increased by 1.22 m (4 ft 0 in)
Fleet 10E: generally as Fleet 10A but with a 93-kW (125-hp) Warner Scarab 7-cylinder radial engine
Fleet 10F: generally as Fleet 10A but

with a 108-kW (145-hp) Warner Super Scarab 7-cylinder radial engine
Fleet 10G: generally as Fleet 10A but with a 97-kW (130-hp) de Havilland Gipsy Major 4-cylinder inverted inline engine
Fleet 16B: (RCAF **Finch Mk II**): structurally strengthened version of the Fleet 10A, powered by a Kinner B5 engine
Fleet 16D: as Fleet 16B, but with a Kinner R5 engine
Fleet 16F: generally as Fleet 16B, but powered by a Warner Super Scarab engine
Fleet 16R (RCAF **Finch Mk I**): designation of version of Fleet 16D built specifically for RCAF use

Specification
Fleet 16B

Enclosed cabins, as demonstrated by this Fleet Finch Mk II, were particularly suitable in Canada to allow year-round training for the war effort.

Type: two-seat trainer
Powerplant: one 93-kW (125-hp) Kinner B5 5-cylinder radial piston engine
Performance: maximum speed 167 km/h (104 mph); cruising speed 137 km/h (85 mph); service ceiling 3200 m (10,500 ft)
Weights: empty 509 kg (1,122 lb); maximum take-off 907 kg (2,000 lb)
Dimensions: span 8.53 m (28 ft 0 in); length 6.60 m (21 ft 8 in); height 2.36 m (7 ft 9 in); wing area 18.06 m² (194.40 sq ft)

Fleet 60 Fort

Forsaking the biplane configuration, Fleet Aircraft of Canada designed as a private venture in 1938 a completely new two-seat trainer. Of all-metal construction, except for some fabric covering, the **Fleet 60** was a braced low-wing monoplane with a conventional tail unit, fixed tailwheel landing gear and instructor and pupil in separate tandem cockpits, each enclosed by a transparent canopy. Forward-looking was the inclusion of a raised rear cockpit, and unusual features included a reinforced fin that could support the aircraft if it were overturned, and retractable fairings on the fixed landing gear that were intended to get the pupil used to a retraction operation. If he failed to lower the fairings

before landing no damage would be caused.

First flown on 22 March 1940, the prototype was used for evaluation by the RCAF and an order for 200 **Fleet 60K** production aircraft, plus the prototype, followed under the designation **Fort Mk I**. The first two were delivered in the spring of 1941, but by then the RCAF had decided to reduce the order by 100, and the 101st Fort was delivered in mid-1942. In early 1942 it was decided that instead of using the Forts as intermediate trainers they would be re-equipped for use as wireless trainers and had the landing gear fairings removed. Then redesignated **Fort Mk II**, all but one were retired from service use in 1945.

Variants
Fleet 60L: unrealised version with 168-kW (225-hp) Jacobs L-4MB radial for use as a primary trainer
Fleet 60: unrealised project for an advanced trainer with 269-kW (360-hp) Jacobs L-7 radial

This aircraft was the last Fort built for the RCAF, the machine being delivered as a Mk I in June 1942, but modified to Mk II standard with the rear cockpit accommodating an aft-facing radio operator trainee.

Specification
Fleet 60K Fort Mk I
Type: two-seat intermediate trainer
Powerplant: one 246-kW (330-hp)

Jacobs L-6MB 7-cylinder radial piston engine
Performance: maximum speed 261 km/h (162 mph); cruising speed 217

km/h (135 mph); service ceiling 4570 m (15,000 ft); range 966 km (600 miles)
Weights: empty operating 1148 kg (2,530 lb); maximum take-off 1588 kg

(3,500 lb)
Dimensions: span 10.97 m (36 ft 0 in); length 8.18 m (26 ft 10 in); height 2.51 m (8 ft 3 in); wing area 20.07 m²

Fleet 80 Canuck

The last aircraft to be produced by Fleet Aircraft before it ran into early post-war financial problems was the **Fleet 80** two-seat lightplane. This originated from the **Noury N-75** prototype designed and first flown by Noury Aircraft Ltd of Stoney Creek, Ontario, during 1944. Design and manufacturing rights were acquired by Fleet Aircraft, the company flying the prototype in modified pre-production form on 26 September 1945. The required changes had been few; the most important introduced a redesigned fin and rudder, and in this form the aircraft was designated Fleet 80 and given the name **Canuck**. It was available with wheeled, float or ski landing gear. A three-seat **Fleet 81** was developed, baggage compartment space being used to accommodate a third person, but only a single example was built.

Looking externally like a Piper Cub or Taylorcraft Tandem, the Model 80 was built in reasonable numbers, including 24 exported to Argentina (19), Brazil (3), Portugal (1) and United States (1), before Fleet found itself in serious financial difficulties. As a result the design and production rights were sold to a company known as Leavens Brothers in Toronto, which built 26 more Canucks, largely from Fleet components.

Specification
Fleet 80 Canuck
Type: two-seat sport/touring aircraft
Powerplant: one 63-kW (85-hp) Continental C85-12J flat-four piston engine
Performance: maximum speed 180 km/h (112 mph) at 915 m (3,000 ft); economic cruising speed 130 km/h (81

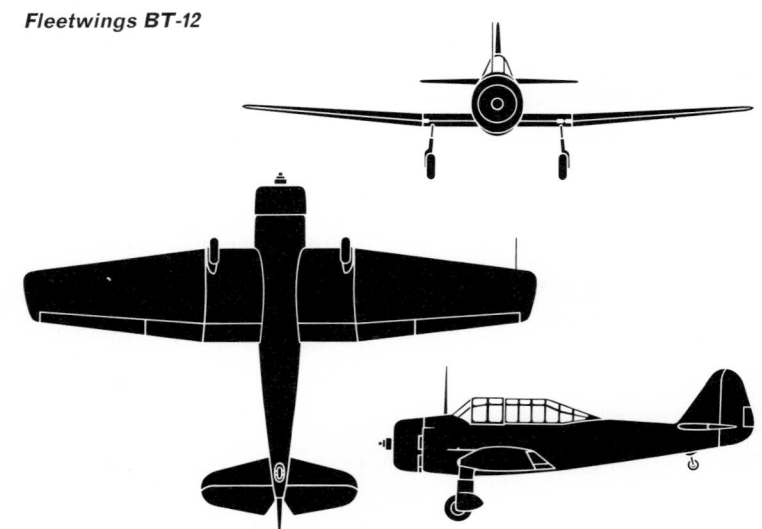

mph) at 915 m (3,000 ft); service ceiling 3660 m (12,000 ft); range 480 km (298 miles)
Weights: empty 390 kg (859 lb); maximum take-off 645 kg (1,422 lb)
Dimensions: span 10.35 m (34 ft 0 in); length 6.83 m (22 ft 5 in); height 2.16 m (7 ft 1 in); wing area 16.12 m² (173.50 sq ft)

The Fleet 80 Canuck was one of Canada's most successful lightplane designs, but led to the manufacturer's eventual demise. The type could be operated as a floatplane – note the wire connections between the base of the air rudder and the floats just forward of the water rudders.

Fleetwings Model 23/BT-12

Fleetwings BT-12

The Japanese attack on Pearl Harbor in December 1941 found the US Army Air Force largely unprepared for a major war. The desperate need for more and yet more aircraft resulted in unexpected manufacturers producing aircraft in equally unexpected materials. One of these manufacturers was Fleetwings, and because the company was a specialist fabricator in sheet stainless steel, the **Fleetwings Model 23** basic trainer, of which a prototype was ordered by the USAAF under the designation **XBT-12**, had a structure that incorporated a large percentage of this material.

Of cantilever low-wing monoplane configuration, the Model 23 had a conventional tail unit, fixed tailwheel landing gear and a Pratt & Whitney Wasp Junior engine. Accommodation was provided for instructor and pupil in separate fully-duplicated cockpits with a single continuous canopy covering both. Following

evaluation of the XBT-12 prototype (39-719), a contract for an additional 200 **BT-12** aircraft was awarded, 24 of these being completed and delivered in the period 1942-43 before the balance of the contract was cancelled.

Specification
Fleetwings Model 23/BT-12
Type: two-seat military basic trainer
Powerplant: one 336-kW (450-hp) Pratt & Whitney R-985-AN-1 Wasp Junior 9-cylinder radial piston engine
Performance: maximum speed 314 km/h (195 mph); cruising speed 282 km/h (175 mph); service ceiling 7255 m (23,800 ft); range 885 km (550 miles)
Weights: empty 1439 kg (3,173 lb); maximum take-off 2000 kg (4,410 lb)
Dimensions: span 12.19 m (40 ft 0 in); length 8.89 m (29 ft 2 in); height 2.64 m (8 ft 8 in); wing area 22.33 m² (240.40 sq ft)

Fletcher FU-24 Utility

In July 1954 Fletcher flew its **Fletcher FU-24** prototype, a single-seat utility aircraft which the company had designed primarily for agricultural use. A cantilever low-wing monoplane of all-metal construction, it had a tail unit incorporating an all-moving tailplane, fixed tricycle landing gear and an enclosed cockpit for the pilot. Power was provided by a 168-kW (225-hp) Continental O-470-8 flat-six engine.

The FU-24 must be regarded as the company's only real success in the field of aircraft design and construction, the first significant event being an agreement with Air Parts (NZ) Ltd of New Zealand to assemble 100 aircraft for use in top-dressing operations in that country. Fletcher developed subsequently the prototype of a six-seat passenger/cargo version under the designation **FU-24A**. However, in 1964 Fletcher sold all manufacturing and sales rights of the FU-24 to the New Zealand company, which continued its development and production. When, in early 1973, Air Parts merged with Aero Engine Services Ltd to form New Zealand Aerospace Industries Ltd,

it was decided to expand production of the FU-24 as much as possible and the improved **FU-24-954** was available in two-seat agricultural and eight-seat utility models. This resulted in a strange reversal, with FU-24-954s being manufactured in New Zealand and supplied in assembly/component form to Frontier-Aerospace Inc. of Long Beach, California, for assembly and marketing in the USA under the name **TaskMaster**. Frontier-Aerospace also developed a utility military version of the FU-24 which it named **Pegasus I**.

By mid-1979 Aerospace Industries had built a total of 272 FU-24s, including

the original 100, of which about 20 per cent had been exported to Australia, Bangladesh, Dubai, Iraq, Pakistan, Thailand, Uruguay and the USA. However, by early 1982 the company was in serious financial difficulties. Subsequently reformed as Pacific Aerospace Corporation, the company intended to continue support and manufacture of the FU-24-954.

Specification
Aerospace Fletcher FU-24-954 (agricultural)
Type: two-seat agricultural aircraft
Powerplant: one 298-kW (400-hp) Avco Lycoming IO-720-A1A or -A1B flat-eight piston engine
Performance: maximum speed 233

km/h (145 mph) at sea level; spraying speed 167-212 km/h (104-132 mph); service ceiling 4875 m (16,000 ft); range 710 km (441 miles)
Weights: empty equipped 1188 kg (2,620 lb); maximum take-off 2463 kg (5,430 lb)
Dimensions: span 12.80 m (42 ft 0 in); length 9.70 m (31 ft 10 in); height 2.84 m (9 ft 4 in); wing area 27.31 m² (294.0 sq ft)

Designed specifically for agricultural work, the FU-24 exhibited a capacious fuselage, wide-span wings for maximum swathe width, tough landing gear and a good field of vision for the pilot.

Fletcher FD-25B Defender

Undaunted by the failure of the FL-23, Fletcher designed and built the prototype of a single-seat light ground-attack aircraft under the designation **FD-25B Defender.** A cantilever low-wing monoplane of all-metal construction, the FD-25B had a conventional tail unit, fixed tailwheel landing gear, the pilot's cockpit enclosed by an acrylic canopy and power provided by a Continental E225 engine. For ground-attack two forward-firing machine-guns were mounted in the wings, and underwing racks were provided for the carriage of weapons that included bombs, napalm tanks and folding-fin rockets.

Specification
Type: single-seat ground-attack aircraft
Powerplant: one 168-kW (225-hp)

The basic concept of the FU-24 was retained in the Defender, but tailored for the counter-insurgency mission.

Continental E225-8 flat-six piston engine
Performance: maximum speed 301 km/h (187 mph) at sea level; cruising speed 261 km/h (162 mph) at sea level; service ceiling 5030 m (16,500 ft); range 1014 km (630 miles)
Weights: empty 557 kg (1,228 lb); maximum take-off 1134 kg (2,500 lb)
Dimensions: span 9.14 m (30 ft 0 in); length 6.38 m (20 ft 11 in); height 1.91 m (6 ft 3 in); wing area 13.94 m^2 (150.0 sq ft)
Armament: two 7.62-mm (0.3-in) forward-firing machine-guns, plus underwing racks for two 151-litre

(40-US gal) napalm tanks, or two 113-kg (250-lb) HE or fragmentation bombs, or

up to 40 70-mm (2.75-in) or 127-mm (5-in) folding-fin rockets

Flettner Fl 265

The pioneering work carried out in the field of rotary-wing aircraft by a German, Anton Flettner, is often overlooked and, perhaps for that reason, is particularly interesting. Seeking a way to overcome the torque induced when a rotor is driven from an airframe-mounted power source, Flettner explored the idea of putting a small engine and tractor propeller on each blade of a two-bladed rotor. This prototype helicopter made a successful tethered flight in 1932, but was destroyed shortly after on the ground when it overturned during a gale.

Flettner then built a two-seat **Flettner Fl 184** autogyro with a three-bladed auto-rotating rotor and power provided by a 104-kW (140-hp) Siemens-Halske Sh 14 radial engine driving a tractor propeller. This, too, was destroyed before it could be evaluated and the prototype **Fl 185** followed, this being a combined autogyro/helicopter. Its Siemens-Halske engine, mounted at the fuselage nose, could be used to drive two variable-pitch propellers mounted on outriggers, one on each side of the fuselage, but the main rotor was powered only when required for operation in a helicopter mode. When flown as an autogyro the propellers on the out-

The Fl 265 V1 had only a short career before its loss, so the bulk of the service trials were performed by this, the Fl 265 V2. The type was evaluated by the navy from small ships in the Baltic and Mediterranean.

riggers were both set to act as pushers and the main rotor auto-rotated. For helicopter flight the main rotor was powered from the engine and the outrigger propellers set so that one acted as a tractor and the other as a pusher to offset rotor torque.

The Fl 185 was only flown a few times before Flettner began construction, in 1937, of his **Fl 265 V1** prototype (D-EFLV), first flown in May 1939. This was of similar airframe configuration to the Fl 185, but dispensed with the outriggers and propellers, and introduced two two-bladed counter-rotating inter-meshing

and synchronised main rotors which, because they were rotating in opposite directions, each cancelled the effects of the other's torque. To simplify control problems a tail unit incorporated an adjustable tailplane for trimming purposes, and for steering a large fin and rudder to augment the use of differential collective-pitch change on the two rotors. The aircraft was lost in an accident some three months later when the counter-rotating blades struck each other, but the **Fl 265 V2** was used successfully for a variety of military trials. In all, six prototypes were built under contract to the German navy before, in 1940, an order was placed for quantity production. By then, however, Flettner had de-

signed a more advanced two-seat helicopter and it was decided instead to proceed with the development and manufacture of this improved aircraft.

Specification
Flettner Fl 265
Type: single-seat helicopter
Powerplant: one 119-kW (160-hp) Bramo Sh 14A 7-cylinder radial piston engine
Performance: maximum speed 160 km/h (99 mph)
Weights: empty 800 kg (1,764 lb); maximum take-off 1000 kg (2,205 lb)
Dimensions: diameter of each rotor 12.30 m (40 ft 4¼ in); total rotor disc area 237.65 m^2 (2,558 sq ft)

Flettner Fl 282 Kolibri

Flettner's improved helicopter was the two-seat **Fl 282 Kolibri** (Hummingbird), and to speed the development of an aircraft that could prove valuable for naval use, a total of 30 prototypes and 15 pre-production examples were ordered in early 1940. Although the basic fuselage configuration was similar to that of its predecessor, the Fl 282 differed in one important respect. Its Bramo Sh 14A

engine was mounted in the centre fuselage and the pilot was accommodated in the nose with enclosed, semi-enclosed and open cockpits provided in variety over the 24 prototypes that were built. Not all of these were two-seaters, but those that were accommodated an observer in a position aft of the main rotor pylon, seated so that his view was to the rear of the aircraft.

In 1942 the German navy began its trials of the Fl 282, finding the type extremely manoeuvrable, stable in poor weather conditions, and so reliable that in 1943 about 20 of the 24 prototypes were operating from warships in the Aegean and Mediterranean for convoy protection duties. It was discovered that as pilots gained experience the Fl 282s could be flown in really bad weather, leading to an order for 1,000 production aircraft. These were not built as a result of Allied bombing attacks on the BMW

and Flettner works, and only three of the prototypes survived at VE-Day, the remainder being destroyed to prevent them being captured.

Specification
Flettner Fl 282 V21
Type: single-seat open-cockpit helicopter
Powerplant: one 119-kW (160-hp) Bramo Sh 14A 7-cylinder radial piston engine

Performance: maximum speed 150 km/h (93 mph) at sea level; service ceiling 3300 m (10,825 ft); range 170 km (106 miles)
Weights: empty 760 kg (1,676 lb); maximum take-off 1000 kg (2,205 lb)
Dimensions: diameter of each rotor 11.96 m (39 ft 2¾ in); length of fuselage 6.56 m (21 ft 6¼ in); height 2.20 m (7 ft 2½ in); total rotor disc area 224.69 m² (2,418.6 sq ft)

Flettner Fl 282 V21 (Fl 282B) while undergoing evaluation in 1943, one of 24 prototypes built. The type was compact and eminently serviceable, but ambitious production plans were thwarted by Allied bombing.

Focke-Achgelis Fa 223 Drache

The outrigger-mounted twin-rotor layout of the Fa 61 was retained by Heinrich Focke for a scaled-up six-passenger version designated **Focke-Achgelis Fa 266 Hornisse** (Hornet), developed under contract from Deutsche Lufthansa. The prototype completed its ground running and tethered hovering programme during the summer of 1940 and the first free flight took place in August of that year. By then, however,

the project had acquired military importance and development continued under the designation **Fa 223 Drache** (Kite), 39 of them being ordered by the Reichsluftfahrt-ministerium for evaluation in a variety of roles, including those of training, transport, rescue and anti-submarine patrol. Equipment varied according to role and included an MG 15 machine-gun and two 250-kg (551-lb) bombs, a rescue winch and cradle, a re-

connaissance camera and a jettisonable 300-litre (66-Imp gal) auxiliary fuel tank. Ten of the 30 pre-production Fa 223s were completed at the Bremen factory before it was bombed, and a further seven were built at the company's new factory at Laupheim, near Stuttgart; another plant (in Berlin) had completed just one example by the time the war ended. Only a small number of Fa 223s were actually flown, and two were acquired by US forces during May 1945 at Ainring, Austria, where they had been in service with Lufttransportstaffel 40. In September one of them, flown by its German crew, became the first helicopter to cross the English Channel, en route to the Airborne Forces Experimental Establishment at RAF Beaulieu for

evaluation; in October it was destroyed in a crash, the result of mechanical failure. After the war two Fa 223s were built in Czechoslovakia from German-manufactured components and development was also continued in France under the designation **Sud Est SE 3000**, the first of which was flown on 23 October 1948.

Specification
Type: transport/rescue/reconnaissance helicopter
Powerplant: one 746-kW (1,000-hp) BMW 301R 9-cylinder radial piston engine
Performance: maximum speed 175 km/h (109 mph); cruising speed 120 km/h (75 mph); service ceiling 2010 m (6,595 ft); range with auxiliary fuel tank 700 km (435 miles)
Weights: empty 3175 kg (7,000 lb); maximum take-off 4310 kg (9,502 lb)
Dimensions: rotor diameter, each 12.00 m (39 ft 4½ in); span over rotors 24.50 m (80 ft 4¾ in); length 12.25 m (40 ft 2¼ in); height 4.35 m (14 ft 3¼ in); rotor disc area, total 226.19 m² (2,434.8 sq ft)

Though cumbersome in appearance, the Fa 223 was an effective helicopter, here epitomised by the V2 second prototype. Naval roles such as anti-submarine warfare and rescue were envisaged.

Focke-Wulf Fw 44 Stieglitz

Second only to the Fw 190 fighter as the most prolific Folke-Wulf design, the **Focke-Wulf A 44 (Fw 44) Stieglitz** (Goldfinch) trainer appeared in 1932, the prototype making its first flight in the late summer of that year in the hands of Gerd Achgelis. Powered by a 104-kW (140-hp) Siemens Sh. 14a radial, the aircraft was a single-bay biplane with a fabric-covered welded steel-tube fuselage and wooden wings with fabric and plywood covering. In its original form it had a number of unacceptable flight characteristics, but these were eradicated following an extensive test programme undertaken by Kurt Tank, who had joined the company in November 1931 from BFW and headed the design and flight test departments of Focke-Wulf when Heinrich

Focke became pre-occupied with his rotary-wing activities. The Stieglitz became an outstanding aerobatic mount, particularly in the hands of Achgelis, Emil Kropf and Ernst Udet, and it won export orders from Bolivia, Chile, China, Czechoslovakia, Finland, Romania, Switzerland and Turkey; licence production was

undertaken in Argentina, Austria, Brazil, Bulgaria and Sweden. The Stieglitz was also built in substantial numbers for the Luftwaffe, serving as a trainer until the end of World War II, and was used also by the pre-war Deutsche Verkehrsfliegerschule and the Deutsche Luftsportverband.

The Focke-Wulf Fw 44C was widely used for civil and military training in Germany and elsewhere, and had its reputation much enhanced by the aerobatic displays flown in the type by Germany's leading pilots.

Variants
Fw 44B/E: two further prototypes were fitted with the 101-kW (135-hp) Argus As 8 inline engine and small numbers were delivered to the Luftwaffe
Fw 44C/D/F: major production versions, with minor equipment changes, all powered by the Siemens Sh.14a
Fw 44J: final production version, also powered by the Siemens Sh.14a

Specification
Focke-Wulf Fw 44C
Type: two-seat trainer
Powerplant: one 112-kW (150-hp) Siemens Sh.14a 7-cylinder radial piston engine
Performance: maximum speed 184 km/h (115 mph); cruising speed 172 km/h (107 mph); service ceiling 3900 m (12,795 ft); range 675 km (419 miles)
Weights: empty 525 kg (1,157 lb); maximum take-off 900 kg (1,985 lb)
Dimensions: span 9.00 m (29 ft 6½ in); length 7.30 m (23 ft 11½ in); height 2.70 m (8 ft 10¼ in); wing area 20.00 m² (215.29 sq ft)

Focke-Wulf Fw 47

Developed to meet the requirements of the German meteorological service, the

prototype **Focke-Wulf A 47** weather reconnaissance aircraft was first flown

in June 1931, the pilot being Cornelius Edzard. Powered by a 164-kW (220-hp) Argus As 10 engine, the A 47 was a parasol-wing monoplane with a wing of wood construction and a fabric-covered

steel-tube fuselage. It was tested extensively by the Reichsverband der Deutschen Luftfahrtindustrie (predecessor of the present BDLI, or Federation of the German Aerospace Industries) and then evaluated operationally at the Hamburg weather centre, beginning in December 1932. Successful completion of the programme led to production orders for more than a score of aircraft, delivered between 1934 and 1936, and used by the meteorological service all over Germany.

Variants
Fw 47C: initial production version with radio, modified rear cockpit with a windscreen and powered by an Argus As 10c engine
Fw 47D: at least 11 aircraft, built between January and April 1938, powered by the Argus As 10e engine; at least one was fitted with skis

Designed to meet specific meteorological needs, the Fw 47 featured a distinctive large-area parasol wing.

Specification
Focke-Wulf Fw 47C
Type: two-seat meteorological aircraft
Powerplant: one 179-kW (240-hp) Argus As 10C 8-cylinder inverted Vee piston engine
Performance: maximum speed 190 km/h (118 mph); service ceiling 5600 m (18,375 ft); range 640 km (398 miles)
Weights: empty 1065 kg (2,348 lb); maximum take-off 1580 kg (3,484 lb)
Dimensions: span 17.75 m (58 ft 3 in); length 10.55 m (34 ft 7¼ in); height 3.04 m (9 ft 11¾ in)

Focke-Wulf Fw 56 Stösser

The first Focke-Wulf design for which Kurt Tank had responsibility from its beginning, the **Focke-Wulf Fw 56 Stösser** was evolved to meet a Reichsluftfahrministerium specification for an advanced trainer powered by the Argus As 10C engine. Tank's design incorporated a steel-tube fuselage with metal panels forward and fabric covering aft, and a wing of wooden construction with plywood covering back to the rear spar and fabric to the trailing edge. The first **Fw 56a** prototype was flown in November 1933 and, after initial testing had revealed landing gear deficiencies, the **Fw 56 V2** second machine had new main landing gear units. It also featured an all-metal wing and was without the original faired headrest behind the cockpit. The **Fw 56 V3** third aircraft, flown in February 1934, introduced further modified landing gear and had a wooden wing similar to that of the first.

The Stösser was evaluated competitively at Rechlin in the summer of 1935 and was selected, in preference to the Arado Ar 76 and Heinkel He 74, for use as a Luftwaffe advanced trainer. It also played a part in the development of Ernst Udet's ideas on the techniques of dive-bombing, later used so effectively by Junkers Ju 87 Stuka units. In late 1936 Udet flew the second prototype at Berlin-Johannisthal, and at his instigation it was fitted with a bomb rack beneath each wing, each carrying three 1-kg (2.2-lb) smoke bombs. It was flown to great effect by Flugkapitän Wolfgang Stein and substantial production orders were placed to equip the fighter and dive-bomber pilot schools of the Luftwaffe. Austria and Hungary also ordered

the Stösser, and a small number was delivered to civil pilots, including Gerd Achgelis. Total production was approximately 1,000 aircraft.

Variants
Fw 56A-0: three pre-production aircraft were built under this designation with minor wing and engine cowling modifications; the first two carried 7.92-mm (0.31-in) MG 17 machine-guns in the upper fuselage

decking and had a rack for three 10-kg (22-lb) practice bombs; the third had a single MG 17 gun
Fw 56A-1: major production version, with provision for one or two MG 17 machine-guns

Specification
Focke-Wulf Fw 56A-1
Type: single-seat advanced trainer
Powerplant: one 179-kW (240-hp) Argus As 10C 8-cylinder inverted Vee piston engine
Performance: maximum speed 278 km/h (173 mph) at sea level; service

ceiling 6200 m (20,340 ft); range 400 km (249 miles)
Weights: empty 695 kg (1,532 lb); maximum take-off 995 kg (2,194 lb)
Dimensions: span 10.50 m (34 ft 5½ in); length 7.70 m (25 ft 3 in); height 3.55 m (11 ft 7¾ in); wing area 14.00 m² (150.7 sq ft)
Armament: two 7.92-mm (0.31-in) MG 17 machine-guns

A Focke-Wulf Fw 56A-1 Stösser of the Royal Hungarian air force, which used 18 of these aircraft for advanced training of fighter pilots.

Focke-Wulf Fw 58 Weihe

Destined to see extensive service with the Luftwaffe as a crew trainer, light transport and communications aircraft, the **Focke-Wulf Fw 58 Weihe** (Kite) had a welded steel-tube fuselage with mixed metal and fabric covering, and a low-set braced monoplane wing of metal construction, with fabric covering aft of the main spar. Two Argus As 10C engines were mounted beneath the wing roots, one on each side of the fuselage, the main landing gear units retracting into the rear of their nacelles. The **Fw 58 V1** first prototype was flown in the summer of 1935, as a six-seat transport, and the **Fw 58 V2** second prototype had two open gunners' positions, each with a single 7.92-mm (0.31-in) MG 15 machine-gun, in the nose and behind the cockpit. The **Fw 58 V4** fourth prototype

had an aerodynamically cleaner fuselage with a glazed nose housing a single MG 15, and was the forerunner of the **Fw 58B** initial production version. Foreign operators of the Weihe included Argentina, Bulgaria, China, Hungary, the Netherlands, Romania and Sweden. Production totalled about 1,350 aircraft.

Variants
Fw 58B-1: production aircraft for the Luftwaffe, used in training, communications and casualty evacuation roles
Fw 58B-2: version with glazed nose and 7.92-mm (0.31-in) MG 15 for

Focke-Wulf Fw 58B of Bomberstaffel 1/B of the Bombergeschwader of Fliegerregiment 2, Österreichische Luftstreitkräfte (Austrian air force) in 1938.

gunnery training; 25 were built under licence by Fabrica de Galleao in Brazil
Fw 58C: major production version

introduced in 1938 and powered either by Argus As 10C or 194-kW (260-hp) Hirth HM508D engines. Production included four of each model built for Deutsche Lufthansa in 1938-39

Fw 58W: twin-float seaplane version

Specification
Focke-Wulf Fw 58B-1
Type: light transport/gunnery trainer
Powerplant: two 179-kW (240-hp) Argus As 10C 8-cylinder inverted Vee piston engines
Dimensions: span 21.00 m (68 ft 11 in); length 14.00 m (45 ft 11 in); height 3.90 m (12 ft 9½ in); wing area 47.00 m² (505.92 sq ft)
Performance: maximum speed 270 km/h (168 mph); service ceiling 5600 m (18,375 ft); range 800 km (497 miles)
Weights: empty 2400 kg (5,291 lb); maximum take-off 3600 kg (7,936 lb)
Armament: one 7.92-mm (0.31-in) MG 15 machine-gun

Focke-Wulf Fw 61/Fa 61

Heinrich Focke's rotary-wing experience was gained initially from licence production of Cierva C.19 and C.30 autogyros, leading to development of the **Focke-Wulf Fw 61** helicopter. The fuselage was similar to that of a light fixed-wing aircraft with a 119-kW (160-hp) Bramo Sh. 14A radial engine mounted in the nose, the primary purpose of this powerplant being to drive two outrigger-mounted three-bladed counter-rotating rotors; it also turned a small-diameter conventional propeller for engine cooling purposes. The rotors were fully articulated and control was achieved by the use of cyclic pitch, differential pitch and differential collective pitch in the longitudinal, directional and lateral axes respectively. Vertical control was achieved by varying rotor revolutions through the use of the throttle, in contrast to the present method of maintaining reasonably constant rotor speed and altering the pitch of the blades.

Following a maiden flight on 26 June 1936, one that is usually reported as lasting for 28 seconds, but which is recorded in Heinrich Focke's log book as 45 seconds, the Fw 61 prototype completed its initial development programme and then established a number of world rotorcraft records. On 25 June 1937 Ewald Rohlfs flew it to a height of 2440 m (8,000 ft) and remained airborne for 1 hour 20 minutes 49 seconds. Next day he set a straight-line distance record of 16.40 km (10.19 miles), a closed-circuit speed record of 122.55 km/h (76.15 mph)

and a closed-circuit distance record of 80.6 km (50.09 miles). Perhaps the most publicised flight was that made by Hanna Reitsch in the Deutschlandhalle during February 1938. Such achievements encouraged Deutsche Lufthansa to order a passenger-carrying development of this helicopter, leading to the Fa 223 and Fa 266. By then Heinrich Focke had formed the new company Focke-Achgelis & Co. GmbH to concentrate on his interest in rotary-wing aircraft, this explaining the redesignation of the Fw 61 as the **Fa 61**.

Specification
Focke-Wulf Fw 61 (as fully developed)
Type: single-seat experimental helicopter
Powerplant: one 119-kW (160-hp) Bramo Sh.14A 7-cylinder radial piston engine
Performance: maximum speed 112 km/h (70 mph) at sea level; cruising speed 100 km/h (62 mph); service ceiling 2620 m (8,600 ft); range 230 km (143 miles)
Weights: empty 800 kg (1,764 lb); maximum take-off 950 kg (2,094 lb)
Dimensions: rotor diameter, each 7.00 m (22 ft 11½ in); length 7.30 m (23 ft 11½ in); height 2.65 m (8 ft 8¼ in); rotor disc area, total 76.97 m² (828.51 sq ft)

The Fw 61 V1 had the look of an autogyro, but the small propeller was in fact a cooling aid for the radial engine, each of the two opposite-rotating rotors being driven by a shaft running up the central of the three tubes originating in the fuselage.

Focke-Wulf Fw 187 Falke

Kurt Tank's **Focke-Wulf Fw 187 Falke** (Falcon) single-seat fighter proposal was evolved originally in 1936 as a private venture, based on two Daimler-Benz DB 600 engines which were then under development. The Reichsluftfahrtministerium was persuaded to sanction the manufacture of the aircraft and detail design was entrusted to Tank's assistant, Obering R. Blaser. Of all-metal construction, the Fw 187 had an exceptionally slim fuselage with a cockpit so small that some instruments had to be located on the inboard sections of the engine cowlings where they could be seen by the pilot.

The specified DB 600 engines were in short supply and RLM approval for construction had been given on condition that the Jumo 210 would be substituted. Thus powered, the **Fw 187 V1** first prototype made its maiden flight during late spring 1937, in the hands of Flugkapitän Hans Sander. The 507 kW (680 hp) provided by each of the Jumo 210 Da engines was considerably below the power of the DB 600 but the aircraft nevertheless achieved a very creditable 523 km/h (325 mph), compared with the projected 560 km/h (348 mph) of the original powerplant. Changes were made during initial tests: VDM propellers were introduced in place of the original Junkers-Hamilton variable-pitch units, and twin wheels were installed on each main gear leg; a 7.92-mm (0.31-in) MG 17 machine-gun was mounted subsequently on each side of the cockpit. The **Fw 187 V2** second prototype, flown in the summer of 1937, was similar but with Jumo 210G engines and a reduced-chord rudder.

The **Fw 187 V3** third aircraft was completed, at Udet's request, as a two-seat interdictor, necessitating fuselage

Focke-Wulf Fw 187A-0 of the Industrie-Schutzstaffel in the winter of 1940-41.

redesign, longer engine bearers and revised engine nacelles. Armed with two 20-mm MG FF cannon, it was flown in the spring of 1938, followed by two similar aircraft in the summer and autumn. All three had full-span flaps. Despite the loss of the first prototype on 14 May 1938, the programme continued and a pair of 746-kW (1,000-hp) DB 600A engines was supplied to Focke-Wulf for installation in the **Fw 187 V6** sixth prototype which achieved a maximum speed of 636 km/h (395 mph). Three **Fw 187A-0** pre-production examples were built, armed with four MG 17s and two MG FFs, and these were used to defend Focke-Wulf's factory at Bremen during the summer of 1940. During the winter they served (unofficially) with 13.(Zerstörer) Staffel of JG77 in Norway.

Specification
Focke-Wulf Fw 187A-0
Type: single-seat day fighter
Powerplant: two 522-kW (700-hp) Junkers Jumo 210G 12-cylinder inverted Vee piston engines
Performance: maximum speed 529 km/h (329 mph) at 1000 m (3,280 ft); service ceiling 10000 m (32,810 ft)
Weights: empty 3700 kg (8,157 lb); maximum take-off 5000 kg (11,023 lb)
Dimensions: span 15.30 m (50 ft 2¼ in); length 11.10 m (36 ft 5 in); height 3.85 m (12 ft 7½ in); wing area 30.40 m² (327.23 sq ft)
Armament: four 7.92-mm (0.31-in) MG 17 machine-guns and two 20-mm MG FF cannon

The Fw 187A-0 aircraft were given service markings and camouflage for genuine operational as well as propaganda purposes, and the aircraft gave convincing proof that the design had been unduly neglected. Note the gun troughs just beneath the cockpit.

Focke-Wulf Fw 189 Uhu

In February 1937 a Reichsluftfahrtminis-terium specification for a short-range re-connaissance aircraft was issued to Arado, Hamburger Flugzeugbau and Focke-Wulf. Kurt Tank responded with the **Focke-Wulf Fw 189 Uhu** (Eagle Owl), an all-metal stressed-skin low-wing monoplane that had an extensively glazed fuselage pod, and twin booms carrying the tail surfaces. The main-wheels retracted to the rear, into the booms. The crew nacelle provided accommodation for pilot, navigator/radio operator, and engineer/gunner, and power for the prototype was supplied by two 321-kW (430-hp) Argus As 410 engines. Construction of this aircraft began in April 1937 and designer Tank performed the first flight in July 1938. The **Fw 189 V2** second prototype, flown in August, was armed with one 7.92-mm (0.31-in) MG 15 machine-gun in each of nose, dorsal and rear positions, two fixed MG 17 weapons in the wing roots, and four underwing racks each carrying a 50-kg (110-lb) bomb. A third, unarmed prototype was flown in Sep-tember, this **Fw 189 V3**'s engines driv-ing Argus-designed air-pressure-actuated variable-pitch propellers.

The award of a development contract was followed by the first flight of a fourth prototype, forerunner of the production **Fw 189A**, which was powered by two Argus As 410A-1 engines and armed with only two MG 15 guns. The fifth pro-totype was representative of the pro-posed **Fw 189B** dual-control trainer, its redesigned fuselage nacelle having a stepped cockpit and much reduced glaz-ing. An even more fundamental redesign was applied to the first prototype, which flew again in the spring of 1939 as the

Surpassing all expectations in operational service, the Uhu proved popular with its crew, largely on account of its agility and excellent all-round view.

Fw 189A-2 of 3/1 Ungarische Nahaufklärungsstaffel (Hungarian Short-range Reconnaissance Squadron) attached to Luftflotte IV, based at Zamocz in eastern Poland in March 1944.

Fw 189A-2 of 1.(H) Staffel, Aufklärungsgruppe 32, based on the Eastern Front in 1943.

Fw 189 V1b with the crew nacelle re-placed by a minute two-seat cockpit mounted on the centre-section and manufactured almost entirely from armour plating; its proposed role was ground attack. Total production of the Fw 189 amounted to 864 aircraft, includ-ing a number built between 1940 and 1943 at the Aero factory in Prague and by SNCASO at Bordeaux-Mérignac.

Variants
Fw 189A-0: 10 pre-production aircraft built at Bremen in 1940, some delivered to 9.(H)/LG 2 for operational trials
Fw 189A-1: initial production version, with single flexible MG 15 machine-guns in dorsal and rear positions, an MG 17 in each wing root and four underwing bomb racks, and carrying an Rb 20/30 or Rb 50/30 camera; further developments included the **Fw 189A-1/Trop** with desert survival equipment, and the **Fw 189A-1/U2**

and **Fw 189A-1/U3** VIP transports used by Kesselring and Jeschonnek
Fw 189A-2: developed from the ninth prototype, with the flexible MG 15s replaced by twin 7.92-mm (0.31-in) MG 81Zs, introduced in 1942
Fw 189A-3: two-seat dual-control trainer, built in limited numbers
Fw 189A-4: introduced in late 1942, this light ground-attack version featured 20-mm MG 151/20 cannon mounted in the wing roots, and armour plate protection for the underside of the fuselage, engines and fuel tanks
Fw 189B: developed from the fifth prototype; three **Fw 189B-0** and 10 **Fw 189B-1** five-seat crew trainers preceded the Fw 189As, and some were used as conversion trainers by 9.(H)/LS 2 during the spring and summer of 1940
Fw 189C: proposed close-support version, based on the modified first prototype and the sixth prototype; development abandoned in favour of the Henschel Hs 129

Fw 189D: proposed twin-float trainer; the seventh prototype, intended as the development aircraft, was completed instead as an Fw 189B-0
Fw 189E: proposed version with two 522-kW (700-hp) Gnome-Rhône 14M radial engines; one French-built Fw 189A-1 airframe modified, using drawings supplied by SNCASO at Chatillon-sur-Seine, but the aircraft crashed near Nancy in north-eastern France when being transferred to Germany for evaluation
Fw 189F: produced in **Fw 189F-1** and **Fw 189F-2** versions, the former being basically a re-engined Fw 189A-2 and the latter introducing electrically operated landing gear, increased fuel capacity and additional armour plating; both versions were powered by two 433-kW (580-hp) Argus As 411MA-1 engines

Specification
Focke-Wulf Fw 189A-1
Type: two-seat short-range reconnaissance aircraft
Powerplant: two 347-kW (465-hp) Argus As 410A-1 12-cylinder inverted Vee piston engines
Performance: maximum speed 335 km/h (208 mph); cruising speed 315 km/h (196 mph); service ceiling 7000 m (22,965 ft); range 670 km (416 miles)
Weights: empty 2805 kg (6,185 lb); maximum take-off 3950 kg (8,708 lb)
Dimensions: span 18.40 m (60 ft 4½ in); length 12.03 m (39 ft 5½ in); height 3.10 m (10 ft 2 in); wing area 38.00 m² (409.04 sq ft)
Armament: two flexible 7.92-mm (0.31-in) MG 15 machine-guns, two 7.92-mm (0.31-in) MG 17 machine-guns and four 50-kg (110-lb) bombs

Focke-Wulf Fw 190

Acknowledged generally by pilots to be a superior aircraft to the Luftwaffe's other main World War II fighter, the Mes-serschmitt Bf 109, the **Focke-Wulf Fw 190** was developed under a contract placed by the Reichsluftfahrtministe-rium in the autumn of 1937. Kurt Tank submitted two proposals, one powered by a liquid-cooled Daimler Benz DB 601 and the other by the then-new air-cooled BMW 139 radial. The radial was selected and detail design work began in the sum-mer of 1938 under the leadership of Obering. R. Blaser. A cantilever low-wing monoplane of stressed-skin con-struction, the prototype **Fw 190 V1** was rolled out in May 1939 and the first flight took place on 1 June 1939 at Bremen in the hands of Flugkapitän Hans Sander. A second aircraft, the **Fw 190 V2**, flew in October 1939, armed with two 13-mm (0.51-in) MG 131 and two 7.92-mm (0.31-in) MG 17 machine-guns. Both machines were fitted with large ducted spinners to reduce drag, but overheating problems were experienced and an NACA cowling was substituted. Before the first proto-

type had flown, however, a decision had been taken to replace the BMW 139 by the more powerful but longer and heavier BMW 801. This necessitated a number of major changes including structural strengthening and relocation of the cockpit further aft: the latter change solved a centre of gravity prob-lem and, as a bonus, alleviated pilot dis-comfort from fumes and overheating caused by proximity of engine to cockpit with the BMW 139 installation. The third and fourth prototypes were abandoned, and the **Fw 190 V5** with the new engine was completed in early 1940. Later in the year the aircraft was fitted with a wing of increased span, 1.00 m (3 ft 3½ in) greater than the original 9.50 m (31 ft 2 in), and although some 10 km (6 mph) slower, this **Fw 190 V5g** was both more manoeuvrable and superior in climb performance to the short-span version now designated **Fw 190 V5k**. Of a pre-production batch of **Fw 190-A-0** aircraft, the first seven had the original wing, the remainder being of greater span. During February 1941 the first aircraft were delivered to Erprobungskommando 190 at Rechlin-Roggenthin for service evaluation, and in March Jagdgeschwader 26 began to prepare for the new fighter's introduction into Luftwaffe service. The first operational unit, 6./JG 26 at Le Bourget, was equipped with the type in August 1941 and when the first clashes between Fw 190s and Supermarine Spitfires came soon afterwards, the superiority of the German aircraft over the Spitfire was immediately apparent. This was the beginning of a truly impressive service career which was to involve almost 20,000 aircraft, built in many versions by Focke-Wulf at Tutow/ Mecklenburg, Marienburg, Cottbus, Sorau/Silesia, Neubrandenburg and Schwerin and by Ago at Oschersleben, Arado at Brandenburg and Warnemünde, Fieseler at Kassel, Dornier at Wismar and by Weserflugzeugbau. Sixty-four Fw 190A-8s were also built as the NC.900 by SNCAC in France in 1945.

Variants

Fw 190A-1: 100 were ordered originally, powered by the 1238-kW (1,660-hp) BMW 801C-1 radial and equipped with long-span wings and FuG 7a radio; armament comprised four 7.92-mm (0.31-in) MG 17 machineguns which proved inadequate
Fw 190A-2: following a prototype installation of two MG 17s mounted above the engine and two 20-mm MG FF cannon in the wing roots, this version was introduced with similar armament, often augmented by two MG 17s in the outer wing panels; power was supplied by the improved BMW 801C-2 engine
Fw 190A-3: in this version the MG FF cannon were removed to the outer wing panels, being replaced by faster-firing MG 151 weapons in the original locations; introduced in autumn of 1941, the Fw 190 A-3 was powered by the 1342-kW (1,800-hp) BMW 801Dg engine; conversions included the **Fw 190 A-3/U1** and **Fw 190A-3/U3** close-support aircraft and the **Fw 190A-3/U4** reconnaissance fighter; these conversions usually involved removal of the outboard MG FF cannon and the addition of Rb 12 cameras or ETC 500 bomb racks
Fw 190A-4: deliveries of this version began in the summer of 1942; it had FuG 16Z radio with a fin-mounted radio mast, and its BMW 801D-2 engine had provision for MW-50 water-methanol fuel injection to boost output to 1566 kW (2,100 hp) for short periods, raising

Fw 190A-4/U8 long-range fighter-bombers on the flight line. One of the several armament/drop tank options available with this sub-type was a pair of 300-litre (66-Imp gal) tanks under the wings (as seen here) with a 250-kg (551-lb) bomb on the centreline. In this configuration only the wing-root cannon were retained.

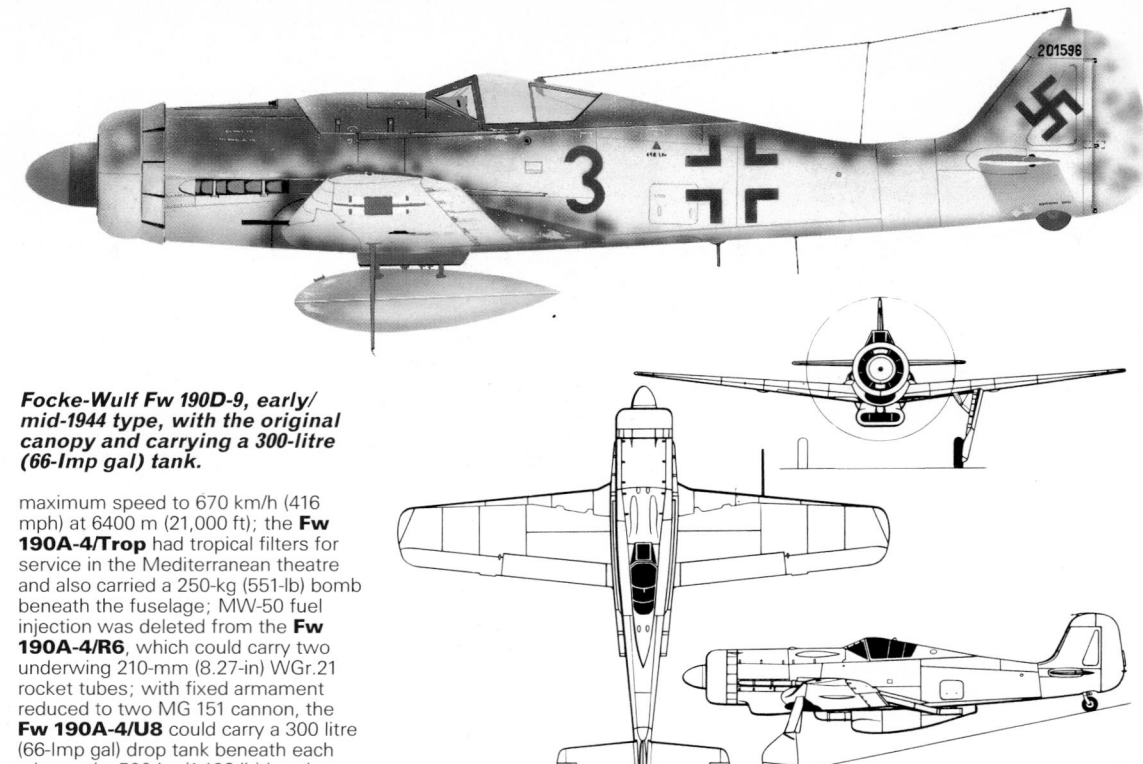

Focke-Wulf Fw 190D-9, early/mid-1944 type, with the original canopy and carrying a 300-litre (66-Imp gal) tank.

maximum speed to 670 km/h (416 mph) at 6400 m (21,000 ft); the **Fw 190A-4/Trop** had tropical filters for service in the Mediterranean theatre and also carried a 250-kg (551-lb) bomb beneath the fuselage; MW-50 fuel injection was deleted from the **Fw 190A-4/R6**, which could carry two underwing 210-mm (8.27-in) WGr.21 rocket tubes; with fixed armament reduced to two MG 151 cannon, the **Fw 190A-4/U8** could carry a 300 litre (66-Imp gal) drop tank beneath each wing and a 500-kg (1,102-lb) bomb under the fuselage
Fw 190A-5: introduced in early 1943, this version featured a new engine mounting which positioned the engine almost 15 cm (6 in) further forward; used for a variety of roles, versions of the Fw 190A-5 included the **Fw 190A-5/U2** with flame-damping equipment for night operations, two MG 151/20 cannon, an underfuselage ETC 501 bomb rack and two 300-litre (66-Imp gal) drop tanks; the similar **Fw 190A-5/U3** could carry a 500-kg (1,102-lb) bomb beneath the fuselage and two 115-kg (254-lb) bombs under the wings; and the **Fw 190A-5/U4** had two Rb 12 cameras for reconnaissance duties; fighter-bomber versions included the **Fw 190A-5/U6** and the long-range **Fw 190A-5/U8** while the **Fw 190A-5/U11** close-support aircraft carried a 30-mm MK 103 under each wing; the **Fw 190A-5/U12** featured fixed armament of two MG 151/20 cannon and two MG 17s, supplemented by two WB 151A pods, each with a pair of MG 151/20; torpedo-carriers able to mount an LT F5b and LT 950 torpedo were designated respectively **Fw 190A-5/U14** and **Fw 190A-5/U15**; a 30-mm

MK 108 cannon in the outboard wing position was standard for the **Fw 190A-5/U16**
Fw 190A-6: appearing in June 1943 and derived from the experimental **Fw 190A-5/U10**, this version introduced a new lighter wing which could accommodate four 20-mm MG 151/20 cannon; the **Fw 190A-6/R1** had six 20-mm MG 151/20 cannon, the **Fw 190A-6/R2** a 30-mm MK 108 in the outboard wing position, and the **Fw 190A-6/R3** two MK 103s under the wings; the **Fw 190A-6/R6** carried WGr.21 rocket tubes
Fw 190A-7: this version entered production in December 1943 and was similar to the **Fw 190A-6**, but with the engine-mounted 7.92-mm (0.31-in) MG 17s replaced by 13-mm (0.51-in) MG 131s
Fw 190A-8: in this basic model internal fuel was increased by 114 litres (25 Imp gal) and versions were similar to those produced under the **Fw 190A-6** designation; also produced were the **Fw 190A-8/R7** with an armoured cockpit and the **Fw 190A-8/**

Focke-Wulf Fw 190C

R11 all-weather fighter with heated canopy and PKS 12 radio navigation equipment; first flown on 23 January 1944, the **Fw 190A-8/U1** was a two-seat conversion trainer, while the **Fw 190A-8/U3** was the director component of the Fw 190/Ta 154 Mistel composite aircraft
Fw 190B: as part of the programme to improve high-altitude performance, three Fw 190A-1s were modified in various ways; the first (**Fw 190 V13**) was given a wing of increased area and had a pressurised cockpit, and its BMW 801D-2 engine had a GM-1 power boost system; the other two (**Fw 190 V16** and **Fw 190 V18**) were similar but had the standard wing and were armed with two MG 17 machine-guns and two MG 151/20 cannon; the Daimler Benz DB 603 V-12 engine with annular radiator was then substituted for the radial, and further development of the type was concentrated on the similar Fw 190C
Fw 190C: a small number of development aircraft were built with 1304-kW (1,750-hp) Daimler Benz DB

Two Fw 190A-5s were U12 Zerstörers with a pair of MG 151 20-mm cannon in a tray under each wing. In this version the outer wing MG FF cannon were removed.

603 engines with DVL-developed TK 11 or Hirth 2281 turbochargers in large ventral fairings which gave rise to the nickname Kanguruh; development was discontinued in favour of the Fw 190D

Fw 190D-9: late in 1943 several Fw 190A-7s were modified with Junkers Jumo 213A engines as prototypes for the Fw 190D-9, the use of this engine necessitating the inclusion of a 0.5-m (1-ft 7¾-in) rear fuselage plug to compensate for 0.6 m (2 ft) extra on the nose; the fin was increased in area for the same reason; known popularly as the 'long-nose 190' or 'Dora 9', the Fw 190D-9 was armed with two wing-mounted MG 151/20 cannon and two MG 131 guns above its engine, and had MW 50 water-methanol fuel injection to boost emergency power output to 1670 kW (2,240 hp). A 300-litre (66-lmp gal) drop tank or a 250-kg (551-lb) bomb could also be carried on each underwing rack; later aircraft were fitted with bubble canopies, as introduced earlier on the Fw 190F

Fw 190D-10: two Fw 190D-9 airframes were converted to this standard, with the Jumo 213C engine; a 30-mm MK 108 cannon firing through the spinner replaced the two MG 131 machine-guns

Fw 190D-11: seven prototypes with Jumo 213F engines, two MG 151/20 cannon in the wing roots and two outboard MK 108s

Fw 190D-12: this was essentially a ground-attack version, with the engine-mounted MK 108 and two MG 151/20s in the wings, with additional armour protection for the engine

Fw 190D-13: similar to the D-12 but with an MG 151/20 in place of the MK 108 cannon

Fw 190E: proposed reconnaissance fighter, development abandoned

Fw 190F-1: preceding the Fw 190D and developed as a specialised ground-attack variant which was introduced in early 1943; the Fw 190F-1 was based on the Fw 190A-4, with the engine and cockpit given additional armour protection, the outboard 20-mm cannon removed and an ETC 501 bomb rack beneath the fuselage

Fw 190F-2: this was based similarly on the Fw 190A-5 but introduced a cockpit bubble canopy

Fw 190F-3: developed from the Fw 190A-6 airframe, this variant could carry a 300-litre (66-lmp gal) drop tank or a 250-kg (551-lb) bomb beneath the fuselage and, in the **Fw 190F-3/R1** and **Fw 190F-3/R3** versions, four ETC 50 underwing bomb racks or two similarly located 30-mm MK 103 cannon respectively

Fw 190F-8: based on the Fw 190A-8, with two engine-mounted 13-mm (0.51-in) MG 131s and four ETC 50 bomb racks; the **Fw 190F-8/U2** and **Fw 190F-8/U3** were fitted with the TSA bomb sight for anti-shipping strikes with, respectively, a 700-kg (1,543-lb) BT 700 or a 1400-kg (3,086-lb) BT 1400 weapon

Fw 190F-9: similar to the Fw 190F-8

but powered by the BMW 801 TS/TH engine; this version introduced in mid-1944

Fw 190G-1: a fighter-bomber derived from the Fw 190A-5, the Fw 190G-1 could carry a 1800-kg (3,968-lb) bomb which required strengthened landing gear; wing-mounted armament was reduced to two MG 151/20 cannon; the Junkers-designed wing racks accommodated two 300-litre (66-lmp gal) drop tanks

Fw 190G-2: similar to the Fw 190G-1 but with Messerschmitt drop tank racks

Fw 190G-3: this version was introduced in late summer 1943 fitted with Focke-Wulf racks and PKS 11 autopilot

Fw 190G-8: final G-series production version incorporating Fw 190A-8 modifications and powered by a 1342-kW (1,800-hp) BMW 801D-2 engine

Specification
Focke-Wulf Fw 190D-9
Type: single-seat fighter/fighter-bomber
Powerplant: one 1324-kW (1,776-hp) Junkers Jumo 213A-1 12-cylinder inverted Vee piston engine
Performance: maximum speed 685 km/h (426 mph) at 6600 m (21,655 ft); climb to 6000 m (19,685 ft) in 7 minutes 6 seconds; service ceiling 12000 m (39,370 ft); range 835 km (519 miles)
Weights: empty 3490 kg (7,694 lb); maximum take-off 4840 kg (10,670 lb)
Dimensions: span 10.50 m (34 ft 5½ in); length 10.20 m (33 ft 5½ in); height 3.35 m (11 ft 0 in); wing area 18.30 m² (196.99 sq ft)
Armament: two 13-mm (0.51-in) MG 131 machine-guns and two 20-mm MG 151 cannon, plus one 500-kg (1,102-lb) SC500 bomb

The Fw 190A-8/U1 was a two-seat conversion trainer, produced by adaptation of standard single-seat fighters pending the definitive Fw 190S trainer which, in the event, did not materialise.

Focke-Wulf Fw 191

In the autumn of 1939 the Reichsluftfahrtministerium issued a technically demanding specification for a new twin-engined medium bomber which was to have a pressurised crew compartment, remotely-controlled armament, dive-bombing capability and the ability to carry a bomb load of 4000 kg (8,818 lb); power was to be provided by one of the 24-cylinder engines then being developed, principally the Daimler Benz DB 604 and the Junkers Jumo 222. The four competing designs were the Arado Ar 340, the Dornier Do 317, the Junkers Ju 288 and the **Focke-Wulf Fw 191**, the last an all-metal stressed-skin shoulder-wing monoplane intended to have Jumo 222 engines. The 1193-kW (1,600-hp) BMW 801MA radial was selected as an interim engine for the **Fw 191 V1** first

prototype, which flew in early 1942, but it produced insufficient power for the 20400 kg (44,974 lb) gross weight of the completed aircraft. It was overweight primarily because Focke-Wulf had been instructed to use electric motors to actuate all systems, despite the manufacturer's concern about the vulnerability of the single generator, and their use gave the Fw 191 its nickname of the 'flying power station'.

The prototype had a combined flap/dive-brake designed by Hans Multhopp, and this generated serious flutter when extended. Shortly after a second prototype (**Fw 191 V2**) joined the programme, test flying was suspended and major changes, including the replacement of the electrically operated systems by more conventional hydraulic systems, resulted in cessation of work on the third, fourth and fifth aircraft. The **Fw 191 V6** sixth machine, flown by Flugkapitän Hans Sander in December

1942, incorporated the required modifications and was powered by two 1641-kW (2,200-hp) Jumo 222 engines. Although various engines were proposed for further prototypes, no more aircraft were completed and the programme was cancelled at the end of 1943.

Specification
Focke-Wulf Fw 191B (estimated for production model)
Type: five-seat medium bomber
Powerplant: two 2013-kW (2,700-hp) Daimler Benz DB 606 24-cylinder inverted double-Vee piston engines
Performance: maximum speed 565 km/h (351 mph) at 4000 m (13,125 ft); service ceiling about 8200 m (26,900 ft); range 3850 km (2,390 miles)
Weight: maximum take-off 25300 kg (55,775 lb)
Dimensions: span 26.00 m (85 ft 3½ in); length 19.60 m (64 ft 3¾ in); height 5.60 m (18 ft 4½ in); wing area 70.50 m² (758.88 sq ft)
Armament: up to six 20-mm cannon plus a bombload of up to 4000 kg (8,818 lb)

An extremely ambitious project, the Fw 191 suffered from heaviness, complexity and the vulnerability of its electrically powered systems.

Focke-Wulf Fw 200 Condor
to
Fokker D.II D.III and D.V

Focke-Wulf Fw 200 Condor

Kurt Tank's ideas for a new transport aircraft for Deutsche Lufthansa were submitted to directors of the airline on 16 July 1936, with a promise that the first example would fly within a year. In fact, the **Focke-Wulf Fw 200 V1**, first of three prototypes, on which work had started in the autumn of 1936, flew on 27 July 1937, which was still a very creditable performance. An all-metal low-wing monoplane, the Fw 200 was powered initially by four 652-kW (875-hp) Pratt & Whitney Hornet radial engines and was designed to provide accommodation for up to 26 passengers in two cabins. Two further prototypes, the second of which became Adolf Hitler's personal transport, were each powered by four 537-kW (720-hp) BMW 132G-1 radials. The second prototype and four examples of the initial production **Fw 200A Condor** were delivered to Lufthansa, two Fw 200As to DDL Danish Air Lines and two to Lufthansa's Brazilian associate Syndicato Condor.

The prototype, redesignated **Fw 200S-1** and named *Brandenburg*, made a number of record flights in the latter half of 1938, beginning on 10 August when Lufthansa's Alfred Henke flew non-stop from Berlin to New York in a time of 24 hours 56 minutes, returning on 13 August in 19 hours 55 minutes. Departing on 28 November the Fw 200S-1 set a 46-hour 18-minute record for the journey from Berlin, via Basra, Karachi and Hanoi, to Tokyo. Further aircraft were supplied to Lufthansa before the outbreak of World War II and on 14 April 1945 a survivor flew the airline's last scheduled service before the cessation of hostilities, from Barcelona to Berlin.

The prototype's flight to Tokyo had resulted in an order for five airliners from Dai Nippon KK and a single maritime reconnaissance aircraft for the Japanese navy. Neither version was delivered to Japan, but the **Fw 200 V10** military prototype which was built had increased fuel capacity and armament comprising a 7.92-mm (0.31-in) MG 15 machine-gun

in a dorsal turret and fore- and aft-firing single MG 15s in a ventral gondola. From this model was developed the **Fw 200C**, which first entered service as a transport with KGrzbV 104 during the Norwegian campaign. The Condor soon became the scourge of Allied shipping as a long-range reconnaissance aircraft following its operational debut with Oberstleutnant Edgar Petersen's Fernaufklärungsstaffel (later 1./KG 40) on 8 April 1940. Operations in this role were discontinued finally in the autumn of 1944 and the Condors used during the closing stages of World War II were flown by transport units, including Transportstaffeln 5 and 200 and the Führerkürierstaffel. The last's inventory included the **Fw 200C-4/U1** allocated to Heinrich Himmler and equipped with an armour-plated seat for Himmler's use. It was captured intact at Achmer in 1945 and flown to Farnborough. Approximately 280 Condors were built.

Variants
Fw 200B-1: one aircraft built for Lufthansa and powered by four 634-kW (850-hp) BMW 132DC radial engines

Fw 200B-2: five ordered by Dai Nippon KK and two by Aero OY of Finland, powered by 619-kW (830-hp) BMW 132H radials; three were completed and diverted to Lufthansa, passing to KGrzbV 105 at Kiel-Holtenau in April 1940, together with the single Fw 200B-1

Fw 200C-0: 10 ordered in September 1939 as four unarmed aircraft (which served with KGrzbV 105) and six with armament which comprised one 7.92-mm (0.31-in) MG 15 machine-gun in each of forward and aft dorsal turrets and a third weapon firing through a ventral hatch

Fw 200C-1: initial production reconnaissance version with one 20-mm MG FF cannon in the nose, one MG15 in a ventral gondola, a similar weapon in a forward dorsal position and a third in a rear dorsal position;

offensive armament also included four 250-kg (551-lb) bombs on underwing racks

Fw 200C-2: similar to the Fw 200C-1 but with the rear of the outboard engine nacelles cut away and provided with streamlined bomb racks

Fw 200C-3: introduced in 1941, this was a structurally strengthened version powered by Bramo 323R-2 radial engines; the **Fw 200C-3/U1** version had a 15-mm MG 151 cannon in a revised forward turret and an MG 151/20 to replace the ventral MG FF weapon; in the **Fw 200C-3/U2**, the ventral MG 151/20 was replaced by a 13-mm (0.51-in) MG 131 machine-gun to permit installation of the Lofte 7D bomb sight, and the **Fw 200C-3/U3** carried an MG 131 in each of the front and rear dorsal positions; the final **Fw 200C-3/U4** version carried an extra gunner and two additional beam-mounted MG 131s

Fw 200C-4: entering production in 1942, the Fw 200C-4 was fitted with FuG *Rostock* search radar (later FuG 200 *Hohentwiel* equipment) and armed with an MG 151 cannon in the forward dorsal turret, a ventral MG 151/20 or

The first Condor was completed as an airliner, intended for service with Deutsche Lufthansa and for export.

(with Lofte 7D bomb sight) an MG 131 and MG 15s at the other stations; single examples of the **Fw 200C-4/U1** and **Fw 200C-4/U2** transports were also built

Fw 200C-6: a number of Fw 200C-3/U1s and Fw 200C-3/U2s were modified as interim missile carriers with two underwing Henschel Hs 293A rocket-propelled guided bombs and FuG 203b Kehl missile control equipment; this version entered service with III/KG 40 in November 1943

Fw 200C-8: definitive version of Fw 200C-6 with *Hohentwiel* search radar

Specification
Focke-Wulf Fw 200C-3/U4
Type: long-range reconnaissance bomber
Powerplant: four 895-kW (1,200-hp) Bramo 323R 9-cylinder radial piston engines
Performance: maximum speed 360 km/h (224 mph); cruising speed 335 km/h (208 mph); service ceiling 6000 m (19,685 ft); range 3560 km (2,212 miles); endurance 14 hours
Weights: empty 17005 kg (37,490 lb); maximum take-off 24520 kg (50,057 lb)
Dimensions: span 32.85 m (107 ft 9¼ in); length 23.45 m (76 ft 11¼ in); height 3.30 m (20 ft 8 in); wing area 119.85 m² (1,290.10 sq ft)
Armament: four 13-mm (0.51-in) MG 131 machine-guns in dorsal and beam positions, and one MG 131 or one 20-mm MG 151 in a ventral gondola, plus four 250-kg (551-lb) bombs
The Condor found fame in World War II as a long-distance maritime patroller.

Focke-Wulf Ta 152 and Ta 153

Further improvements to the Fw 190D series airframe to provide even better performance at high altitude led to the introduction of the **Focke-Wulf Ta 152** and **Ta 153**. The latter was built only as a development prototype, powered by a

Daimler Benz DB 603 engine, and introduced an entirely new high aspect ratio wing of increased span, together with revision of the fuselage structure, tail surfaces and internal systems. It was abandoned to avoid disruption of existing production facilities for the Fw 190.

The Ta 152 as conceived originally was structurally closer to the Fw 190D, except that the flap and landing gear systems were hydraulically and not electrically actuated. In the autumn of 1944 a prototype appeared with a Junkers Jumo 213E engine and high aspect ratio long-span wings, and although it crashed

on 8 October its replacement in the **Ta 152H** test programme had the Jumo engine but standard Fw 190 wings. The first of 20 pre-production **Ta 152H-0** aircraft, built at Focke-Wulf's Cottbus factory, flew in October 1944. Service trials were undertaken by Erprobungskommando 152 at Rechlin before the type's operational debut with JG 301. This unit was tasked with the protection of bases used by the Messerschmitt Me 262 jet fighter, which was particularly vulnerable during take-off and landing.

Variants
Ta 152C: the 1566-kW (2,100-hp) Daimler Benz DB 603LA-engined development prototype for the Ta 152C flew on 19 November 1944, the extra length of this engine requiring a compensating rear fuselage plug and enlarged tail surfaces; wing span was increased to 11.00 m (36 ft 1 in); armament for the **Ta 152C-1** and **Ta 153C-2** (the latter had improved radio) was an engine-mounted 30-mm MK 108 and four 20-mm MG 151/20 cannon; in the **Ta 152C-3**, the MK 108 was replaced by an MK 103
Ta 152E: photographic reconnaissance version of the Ta 152C with the standard wing in **Ta 152E-1** form, the **Ta 152E-2** being a high-altitude aircraft with the H-series wing; engine was the Jumo 213E
Ta 152H: high-altitude fighter with

The Focke-Wulf Fw 190 V32 began life as a prototype for the Fw 190C, but was developed as the prototype for the Ta 153 high-altitude fighter, the DB 603-powered parallel of the Jumo-engined Ta 152.

pressurised cabin and a long-span wing, increased to 14.50 m (47 ft 6¾ in) span. The **Ta 152H-0** pre-production aircraft were mostly rebuilt from Fw 190A-1 airframes and had a Jumo 213E engine with MW-50 water-methanol fuel injection; the production **Ta 152H-1** began to leave the Cottbus lines in November 1944, armed with one engine-mounted 30-mm MK 108 and two 20-mm MG 151/20 cannon in the wing roots

Specification
Focke-Wulf Ta 152H-1
Type: high-altitude fighter
Powerplant: one 1305-kW (1,750-hp) Junkers Jumo 213E 12-cylinder inverted Vee piston engine

Performance: maximum speed 760 km/h (472 mph) at 12500 m (41,010 ft) with MW-50 water-methanol fuel injection and GM-1 power boost; initial climb rate 1050 m (3,445 ft) per minute with MW-50; service ceiling 14800 m (48,555 ft); range 1200 km (746 miles)

Weights: empty 3920 kg (8,643 lb); maximum take-off 4750 kg (10,472 lb)
Dimensions: span 14.50 m (47 ft 6¾ in); length 10.80 m (35 ft 5½ in); height 4.00 m (13 ft 1½ in); wing area 23.50 m² (252.96 sq ft)
Armament: one 30-mm MK 108 and two 20-mm MG 151/20 cannon

Focke-Wulf Ta 154

In order to combat the RAF's nightly bombing raids against German urban and industrial centres, the Reichsluftfahrtministerium ordered the development of a specialised two-seat night-fighter, outlined in a specification issued in August 1942. The resulting contenders were the all-metal Heinkel He 219 and Tank's **Focke-Wulf Ta 154**, the latter a twin-engined shoulder-wing monoplane of wooden construction throughout in order to utilise the skills of trained woodworkers. Powered by two 1119-kW (1,590-hp) Jumo 211N engines, the **Ta 154 V1** first prototype was flown by Kurt Tank at Hannover/Langenhagen on 1 July 1943, joined soon after by the similarly-powered **Ta 154 V2** second prototype in handling and performance trials. The **Ta 154 V3** third prototype, flown on 25 November 1943 and powered by Jumo 211R engines, introduced FuG 202 *Lichtenstein BC-1* radar as the forerunner of the pre-production **Ta 154A-0**, armed with single forward-firing 20-mm MG 151/20 and 30-mm MK 108 cannons on each side of the fuselage below the cockpit. Four further prototypes were flown at Langenhagen be-

tween January and March 1944 and the remaining eight aircraft of the original RLM order were assembled at Erfurt under the designation Ta 154A-0. In armed and radar-equipped configuration the Ta 154As had a top speed of more than 644 km/h (400 mph), but the programme was cancelled in late 1944 following structural failure of two early production aircraft on 28 and 30 June 1944, the result of reaction between adhesive and plywood. The prototype and pre-production aircraft had used Tego-Film

adhesive, but when the factory which produced it at Wuppertal was bombed the alternative adhesive which was substituted brought disastrous results.

Variants
Ta 154A-1: 10 were built before production was cancelled; a small number with FuG 218 *Neptun* radar

Potentially a decisive night fighter, the Ta 154 failed to get into large-scale production. This example was the V15, otherwise the eighth Ta 154A-0 pre-production machine.

were used for a short period by 1./NJG 3 at Stade
Ta 154A-2/U3: six Mistel composite conversions of the Ta 154A-0 pre-production aircraft with a 2000-kg (4,409-lb) warhead in the nose and supports for the Fw 190 upper component whose pilot controlled the combination

Specification
Focke-Wulf Ta 154A-1
Type: two-seat night-fighter
Powerplant: two 1119-kW (1,500-hp) Jumo 211R 12-cylinder inverted Vee piston engines
Performance: maximum speed 650 km/h (404 mph); climb to 8000 m (26,250 ft) in 14 minutes 30 seconds; service ceiling 10900 m (35,760 ft); range 1365 km (848 miles)
Weights: empty 6405 kg (14,121 lb); maximum take-off 8930 kg (19,687 lb)
Dimensions: span 16.00 m (52 ft 6 in); length 12.10 m (39 ft 8½ in); height 3.50 m (11 ft 5¾ in); wing area 32.40 m² (348.76 sq ft)
Armament: two nose-mounted 20-mm MG 151/20 and two 30-mm MK 108 cannon, and one Mk 108 in the rear fuselage firing upward and forward at an angle of 45°

Fokker C-2

Following successful demonstration of the Fokker F.VIIA/3m transport in the United States, the Fokker-owned Atlantic Aircraft Corporation of New Jersey built a version of the F.VIIB/3m under the company designation **Fokker F.9**. This proved a commercial success, and three examples were ordered by the US Army under the designation **C-2**.

The first aircraft, intended for long-distance flights, had additional fuel tanks and a special wing of 21.70 m (71 ft 2 in) span built at the Netherlands Fokker factory. All three machines had Wright J-5 engines instead of the J-4s originally installed, a redesigned pilot's cockpit and an enlarged fuselage with a new internal layout. The long-range C-2 *Bird of Paradise*, piloted by USAAC Lieutenants Lester J. Maitland and Albert Hegenberger, was flown from Oakland, California, to Honolulu, Hawaii, on an epoch-making nonstop flight of some 3862 km (2,400 miles) on 1 June 1927.

The C-2s were followed by eight

The start of things to come: the Fokker C-2A Question Mark prepares to take on fuel from its Douglas C-1 tanker during the record-breaking endurance flight of 150 hours in 1929.

C-2A aircraft which had a wing of even greater span than that fitted to the C-2 record-breaker. One C-2A, named *Question Mark*, established an endurance record with the aid of air-to-air refuelling from a converted US Army Douglas C-1 biplane transport, staying aloft for 150 hours in January 1929.

Variants
XC-7: one C-2A converted to take three 246-kW (330-hp) Wright R-975 (J-6-9) radials
C-7A: six production developments of XC-7; they differed in having a bigger wing, new fins and fuselages resembling closely that of the commercial F.10A
XLB-2: one built (26-210) as an experimental light bomber developed from the C-7 and powered by two Pratt

& Whitney R-1340 radials each developing 306 kW (410 hp)

TA-1: designation for the US Navy version of the C-2; three bought in

1927 and 1928 and used by US Marines; later redesignated **RA-1** to avoid confusion with torpedo aircraft

RA-2: designated originally as **TA-2**, these three US Navy aircraft were equivalent to the US Army C-2As

The Fokker RA-2 was the US Navy's equivalent of the US Army's C-2 type. One of the three RA-2s is seen here with a replacement wing (strapped under the fuselage) for a US Marine Corps aircraft damaged during policing operations in Nicaragua in 1929.

RA-3: one built, originally **TA-3**, powered by Wright J-6 radials; both RA-1s and RA-2s were later re-engined with Wright J-6s and all were then known as RA-3s despite considerable differences, including variations in wing span

Specification
Fokker C-2A
Type: 10-passenger military transport
Powerplant: three 164-kW (220-hp) Wright J-5 (R-790) 7-cylinder radial piston engines
Performance: maximum speed 182 km/h (113 mph); normal cruising speed 145 km/h (90 mph); range 476 km (296 miles)
Weights: empty equipped 2951 kg (6,507 lb); maximum take-off 4715 kg (10,394 lb)
Dimensions: span 22.61 m (74 ft 2¼ in); length 14.73 m (48 ft 4 in); height 4.11 m (13 ft 6 in); wing area 66.70 m² (718.0 sq ft)

Fokker C.I

The **Fokker C.I**, a compact unequal-span two-seat reconnaissance biplane of mixed construction, was in effect an enlarged Fokker D.VII. Tested as the **V 38** at Schwerin in 1918, it was placed in production immediately, but World War I ended before any deliveries could be made to the German air arm. Fokker arranged to have all the German-built C.Is transferred to the Netherlands, where production continued and, in total, over 250 examples were built. Initial powerplant was the 138-kW (185-hp) BMW IIIa, but other installations included the 164-kW (220-hp) BMW IV, 119-kW (160-hp) Oberursel, 194-kW (260-hp) Mercedes and 149-kW (200-hp) Armstrong Siddeley Lynx. The C.I was recognisable easily by a fuel tank mounted on the landing gear axle, where it was protected by a streamlined fairing which was claimed by the manufacturers to provide additional lift.

The USSR purchased 42 C.Is, frequently operated on skis; Denmark acquired two and built three more under licence, and one Danish C.I was still flying as a trainer in 1940. The Dutch military air corps (LVA) procured a total of 62 C.Is which proved very reliable and were transferred eventually from first-line reconnaissance units to training units where, fitted with dual controls and rear cockpit folding hoods, they were often used as blind-flying trainers. Dutch naval

Fokker C.I of the Soviet air force in the 1920s.

aviation (MLD) obtained 16 C.Is, the last one remaining in operation as a trainer until 1938.

Variants

C.Ia: designation of modernised version of 1929 with 149-kW (200-hp) Armstrong Siddeley Lynx radial engine and redesigned vertical tail surfaces; 21 Dutch army air corps C.Is were modified to this standard
C.I-W: a twin-float experimental version flown by the Fokker company

at Schwerin in 1919 and test-flown in Germany; intended for naval reconnaissance and advanced training
C.II: a three-seat passenger-carrying version of the C.I; it retained the BMW IIIa engine but had a revised oval-fronted cowling; behind the pilot's open cockpit were two more cockpits enclosed in a glazed canopy; built in small numbers in 1919-20 and sold in Canada, the Netherlands, South America and the USA; some C.IIs were converted to take the 171-kW (230-hp) Armstrong Siddeley Puma engine
C.III: designation of an advanced trainer version of C.I sold to Spain; it resembled the C.I except that power was provided by a 164-kW (220-hp) Hispano-Suiza engine

Specification
Fokker C.I
Type: two-seat reconnaissance aircraft
Powerplant: one 138-kW (185-hp) BMW IIIa 6-cylinder inline piston engine
Performance: maximum speed 175 km/h (109 mph); service ceiling 4000 m (13,125 ft); range 620 km (385 miles)
Weights: empty equipped 855 kg (1,885 lb); maximum take-off 1255 kg (2,767 lb)
Dimensions: span 10.50 m (34 ft 5½ in); length 7.23 m (23 ft 8¾ in); height 2.87 m (9 ft 5 in); wing area 26.25 m² (282.56 sq ft)
Armament: one fixed forward-firing 7.7-mm (0.303-in) machine-gun and one gun of the same calibre on ring mounting over the rear cockpit, plus underwing racks for four 12.5-kg (27.5-lb) bombs

Fokker C.IV

At a time when sales of military aircraft were at a low ebb world-wide the **Fokker C.IV** proved a remarkable commercial success. The first example flew in 1923 and production deliveries began in 1924. Developed from the C.I, it was a larger and more robust machine. The Napier Lion engine which powered the 30 aircraft supplied to the LVA (Dutch army air corps) and the 10 flown by the LA (Dutch East Indies army), had twin retractable side radiators attached to the forward fuselage. By comparison with those of the C.I, the fuselage and the track of the cross-axle landing gear were both wider.

Total of C.IVs produced was 159, 20 of them being licence-built in Spain by the Jorge Loring firm. The Spanish C.IVs operated with the Spanish army of Africa in action against the Riff tribesmen in Morocco. Other customers included the USSR, which bought 55 machines, Argentina and the US Army Air Service. At least one example was tested in Italy.

Like many other Fokker designs the C.IV was renowned for its longevity. After a number of years as reconnaissance aircraft, C.IVs were operated as

trainers well into the 1930s in several parts of the world.

Variants

C.IVA: version with reduced span of 12.50 m (41 ft 0 in) and reduced maximum take-off weight of 2016 kg (4,444 lb); it was this version which was flown in the Dutch East Indies (10 aircraft)
C.IVB: same span as the original C.IV, but powered either by the Rolls-Royce

Eagle engine of 268-kW (360-hp) or the 313-kW (420-hp) American Liberty; some used by the Dutch army
C.IVC: long-range reconnaissance version with wings spanning 14.27 m (46 ft 9¾ in) and retaining the Napier Lion engine; some used by the Dutch army
C.IV-W: twin-float seaplane version with the Lion engine and increased wing span of the C.IVC; **C.IVH** (*Ciudad de Buenos Aires*) piloted by the

Argentine Major Zanni was flown from Amsterdam to Tokyo in 1924
CO-4: official designation of the US Army version; three experimental **XCO-4** aircraft were followed by five **CO-4A** machines, all powered by 313-kW (420-hp) Liberty 12A engines; the CO-4A had twin side radiators, and the fuselage lengthened by 0.24 m (9½ in); both XCO-4s and CO-4As were extensively tested by the USAAS at McCook Field

Specification
Fokker C.IV
Type: two-seat reconnaissance aircraft
Powerplant: one 336-kW (450-hp) Napier Lion 12-cylinder 'arrow' piston engine
Performance: maximum speed 214 km/h (133 mph); service ceiling 5500 m (18,045 ft); range 1200 km (746 miles)

Apart from its outstanding sales success, the Fokker C.IV also made a remarkable flight from Amsterdam to Tokyo in the hands of Major Zanni, an Argentinian pilot, during 1924.

Weights: empty equipped 1450 kg (3,197 lb); maximum take-off 2270 kg (5,004 lb)

Dimensions: span 12.90 m (42 ft 3¾ in); length 9.20 m (30 ft 2¼ in); height 3.40 m (11 ft 1¾ in); wing area 39.20 m² (421.96 sq ft)

Armament: one or two fixed forward-firing 7.7-mm (0.303-in) machine-guns, and twin guns of same calibre on a ring mounting over the rear cockpit

---

Fokker C.V Family

Fokker C.V of the 3. Eskadrille of the Danish army aviation during the mid-1930s.

There can be little doubt that the **Fokker C.V** series was one of the world's most successful military aircraft of the 1920s and 1930s. Originating with the C.V prototype which flew in May 1924, the series proliferated with the possibility of different engines and five types of wing. The **C.V-A, C.V-B** and **C.V-C** had parallel-chord wings possessing areas of 37.5 m² (403.66 sq ft), 40.80 m² (439.18 sq ft) and 46.10 m² (496.23 sq ft) respectively; the **C.V-D** and **C.V-E** had tapered sesquiplane wings, those of the C.V-D having an area of 28.8 m² (310.01 sq ft) and those of the C.V-E having N-struts and an area of 39.30 m² (423.04 sq ft). All C.Vs were of mixed construction, with a steel-tube fuselage and wooden wings; the five different types of wing above were available, each identified by a suffix to the designation (only the C.V-D and C.V-E were available after January 1926), and the type won early recognition as an outstanding multi-purpose aircraft. It was claimed that wings and engines could be changed in an hour, and a wide range of engines from 261- to 544-kW (350- to 730-hp) could be installed.

Early customers for the C.V-E included the Dutch naval air service and Bolivia; the former also received 10 **C.V-W** floatplanes which were converted later to C.V-C standard as landplanes. These early versions of the C.V were usually powered by 336-kW (450-hp) Hispano-Suiza engines, although a few had the 298-kW (400-hp) Lorraine-Dietrich.

Mass production centred on the C.V-D and C.V-E, which had the later tapered wings; the C.V-D with short-span wings was a fighter/army co-operation version, while the long-span C.V-E was intended as a reconnaissance bomber. Most Netherlands air force C.V-Ds had either 261- or 336-kW (350- or 450-hp) Hispano-Suiza engines, but some had 336-kW (450-hp) Armstrong Siddeley Jaguar radials.

Export aircraft included a batch for Denmark, one of which had a 544-kW (730-hp) Bristol Pegasus engine, resulting in the purchase of another 13 and

licence-production of 36 of this version. Some of these Danish aircraft, later captured by the Germans, were used by the Luftwaffe for night operations on the Eastern Front during the summer of 1944. Norway built a batch of C.V-Es, some of which remained in service until 1940; Sweden bought eight C.V-Es from Fokker and licence-built another 46 powered by Pegasus engines. Finland used 19 C.V-Ds and C.V-Es, some acquired as new, plus three C.V-Es from Sweden and two Norwegian C.V-Ds that were interned. The Swiss air force bought six new C.V-Es and built 49 under licence between 1932 and 1936, but Italy was probably the largest licence-producer of two versions known as the **Meridionali Ro.1**, with a 313-kW (420-hp) Bristol Jupiter or the **Ro.1bis** with 410-kW (550-hp) Piaggio-built Jupiter VIII.

Manfred Weiss in Hungary bought three C.Vs from Fokker and subsequently licence-built at least 100 under the name **WM Budapest 9** (Bristol Jupiter engine) and **Budapest 11** or **Budapest 14** with Hungarian-built 649-kW (870-hp) WM K-14 (Gnome-Rhône 14K) engines. A modified Weiss version, known as the **WM 21 Sólyom**, saw service in World War II.

A few other C.V versions also saw service during that conflict, in Finland and in the Netherlands, where 28 C.Vs were available on 10 May 1940 when the

Germans attacked. Many were destroyed on the ground but the survivors were used for ground-attack until resistance came to an end five days later. The longest surviving Fokkers were the C.V-Es of neutral Switzerland, the last aircraft used as target tugs being withdrawn from service only in 1954. A C.V-E is preserved at the Swiss air force museum at Dübendorf, near Zürich, while a Dutch-built aircraft can be seen at the Aviodome Museum at Amsterdam/Schiphol.

Variant

Fokker C.VI: 26 C.V-Ds converted with 261-kW (350-hp) Hispano-Suiza or 336-kW (450-hp) Armstrong Siddeley Jaguar engines

Specification
Fokker C.V-D
Type: two-seat reconnaissance/

bomber aircraft

Powerplant: one 336-kW (450-hp) Hispano-Suiza 12-cylinder Vee piston engine

Performance: maximum speed 225 km/h (140 mph) at 4000 m (13,125 ft); cruising speed 185 km/h (115 mph); service ceiling 5500 m (18,045 ft); range 770 km (478 miles)

Weights: empty 1250 kg (2,756 lb); maximum take-off 1850 kg (4,079 lb)

Dimensions: span 12.50 m (41 ft 0 in); length 9.50 m (31 ft 2 in); height 3.50 m (11 ft 5¾ in); wing area 28.80 m² (310.0 sq ft)

Armament: one or two 7.9-mm (0.31-in) forward-firing machine-guns, one or two similar guns in rear cockpit and (occasionally) one similar gun in a ventral position, plus up to 200 kg (441 lb) of bombs or mines

Among the Fokker biplanes delivered to the Dutch air arm was this C.V-D.

Fokker C.X

Fokker C.X of TLeLV 12, Suomen Ilmavoimat (Finnish air force) based at Suur-Merijoki in the winter of 1939-40.

Following the outstanding success of its C.V series, Fokker initiated in 1933 the design of a successor. The first **Fokker C.X,** powered by a Hispano-Suiza engine, made its initial flight in 1934 and was presented at that year's Paris Air Show. Of basically similar layout to its predecessor, the C.X had considerably higher performance in production form by virtue of having a Rolls-Royce Kestrel engine some 149 kW (200 hp) more powerful than the engine in the standard C.V-E.

A production line was laid down in 1935, the first customer being the Netherlands East Indies army air service, which had ordered 10. Deliveries began in 1937, by which time 20 had been ordered for the Royal Netherlands air force. While the earlier army aircraft had open cockpits and tailskids, the last 15 for the air force had cockpit covers and tailwheels. Dutch production totalled 36 aircraft.

An order for four C.Xs was received

from the Finnish air force in 1936, but these differed from earlier models by having a Bristol Pegasus XXI radial engine which gave a slight performance improvement. The type proved so suc-

cessful that a licence production agreement was negotiated, under which the Finnish State Aircraft Factory built 30 of this version of the C.X in 1936-37, and a further five in 1942. The Dutch-built aircraft were known as **C.X Srs I** aircraft, the four sold to Finland were **C.X Srs II**, and the subsequent two Finnish-built batches were **C.X Srs III** and **C.X Srs IV** respectively.

At the outbreak of World War II C.Xs

were serving with three Finnish air force squadrons. At least one survived the war and flew until it crashed in 1958.

When Germany attacked the Netherlands on 10 May 1940, 10 C.Xs were in action but they were completely outclassed by the Luftwaffe's modern aircraft. Even so, one C.X achieved a minor 'first' on the last day of the Netherlands' resistance when two Dutchmen flew it to England to become the first members of the Free Dutch forces.

429

Fokker C.X (Finnish-built)
Type: two-seat reconnaissance/
bomber aircraft
Powerplant: one 623-kW (835-hp)
Bristol Pegasus XII or XXI 9-cylinder

radial piston engine
Performance: maximum speed
335 km/h (208 mph) at 1850 m
(6,070 ft); cruising speed 275 km/h
(171 mph) at 1750 m (5,740 ft); service
ceiling 8100 m (26,575 ft); range

900 km (559 miles)
Weights: empty 1550 kg (3,417 lb);
maximum take-off 2900 kg (6,393 lb)
Dimensions: span 12.00 m (39 ft
4½ in); length 9.20 m (30 ft 2¼ in);
height 3.30 m (10 ft 10 in); wing area

31.70 m² (341.23 sq ft)
Armament: one 7.62-mm (0.3-in)
forward-firing machine-gun and one
similar gun in rear cockpit, plus up to
400 kg (882 lb) of bombs

Fokker C.XIV-W

Slightly smaller and lower powered than
the C.XI-W, the **Fokker C.XIV-W** first
appeared in 1937 and was used for training. Twenty-four were built for the
Netherlands navy, 11 of them earmarked
for the Netherlands East Indies.

The 12 aircraft which were still serviceable after the German invasion of
the Netherlands in May 1940 formed
part of the group of 26 Fokker floatplanes which escaped to England on 22
May (see entry for Fokker C.VIII-W).
Like the single C.XI-W, the 12 C.XIV-Ws were
crated and shipped to the Netherlands
navy in Surabaya, where they were subsequently destroyed during the
Japanese invasion.

Specification

*This was the 19th of 24 Fokker
C.XIV-W trainer floatplanes
delivered to the Dutch navy. Note
that the pilot had an enclosed
cockpit, but not the gunner.*

Type: two-seat training/
reconnaissance floatplane
Powerplant: one 336-kW (450-hp)
Wright Whirlwind R-975-E3 9-cylinder
radial piston engine
Performance: maximum speed
230 km/h (143 mph); cruising speed
195 km/h (121 mph); service ceiling
4800 m (15,750 ft); range 950 km (590
miles)
Weights: empty 2,903 lb (1315 kg);
maximum take-off 1945 kg)4,288 lb
Dimensions: span 12.05 m (39 ft

6½ in); length 9.55 m ()31 ft 4 in; height
4.25 m (13 ft 11¾ in); wing area
31.70 m² (341.23 sq ft)

Armament: one forward-firing
7.9-mm (0.31-in) machine-gun and one
similar gun on mount in rear cockpit

Fokker D.I and D.IV

The Fokker M.18z was in effect the prototype of the **D.I** fighter/scout. A single-
seat biplane of mixed construction, with
a conventional tail unit, tailskid landing
gear and power provided by an 89-kW
(120-hp) Mercedes D.II engine, the D.I
was built in small numbers from the
summer of 1916. It was soon discovered
that the type was very much underpowered and that in service on the

*A certain amount of development
work was undertaken with D.I
fighters, including this
modification with a fixed fin
supplementing the comma-shape
balanced rudder, and with
ailerons in place of wing-
warping.*

Western Front was unable to compete
with the French Nieuports. As a result it
was soon relegated to the less-demand-
ing Eastern Front or used on a non-operational role.

In an attempt to extend the use of the
basic design for a little longer, a slightly
modified and enlarged version was built
as the **Fokker D.IV** with a more power-

ful Mercedes engine. It needed little
first-line use to show that the marginal
increase in performance was inadequate, and remaining D.Is and D.IVs
were soon found only with training units.
Production of both versions totalled
about 60 aircraft.

Specification
Fokker D.IV
Type: single-seat fighter/scout
Powerplant: one 119-kW (160-hp)

Mercedes D.III 6-cylinder inline piston
engine
Performance: maximum speed
160 km/h (99 mph); climb to 1000 m
(3,280 ft) in 3 minutes; service ceiling
5000 m (16,405 ft); endurance 1 hour
30 minutes
Weights: empty 606 kg (1,336 lb);
maximum take-off 840 kg (1,852 lb)
Dimensions: span 9.70 m (31 ft 9 in);
length 6.30 m (20 ft 8 in); height
2.45 m (8 ft 0½ in); wing area 21.00 m²
(226.05 sq ft)
Armament: one or two fixed
forward-firing 7.92-mm (0.31-in) LMG
08/15 machine-guns

*There was little to distinguish the
D.IV from the D.I apart from
slightly larger dimensions, a
twin-gun armament and a 119-kW
(160-hp) Mercedes D.III engine in
place of the 90-kW (120-hp) D.II.*

Fokker D.II, D.III and D.V

Of slightly reduced wing span but with a
fuselage of greater length and improved
contours, the **Fokker D.II** derived from
the M.17z prototype. Of similar construction and overall configuration to the
D.I, the D.II was powered by a 100-hp
(75-kW) Oberursel U.I rotary engine over
which was mounted the single forward-
firing LMG 08/15 'Spandau' machine-
gun. D.IIs began to enter service during

*The D.III was evolved to adapt
the D.I airframe to a more
powerful engine and twin-gun
armament. The result was not
that successful, and only a small
production run was completed.*

the spring of 1916, when it was soon discovered that their performance was not
good enough to match new aircraft
entering service with the Allies. The
D.III represented an attempt to improve
performance by installing the far more
powerful Oberursel U.III twin-row rotary
engine in a strengthened fuselage structure of D.II design; at the same time the
increased-span wing of the D.I was
adopted and twin 'Spandau' machine-
guns installed.

Although these changes gave the D.III
much better load-carrying capability,
there was little improvement in performance and virtually none in manoeuvrability. Not only was the D.III inferior to

its Allied counterparts, it was also
already outclassed by the new Albatros
and Halberstadt scouts that were beginning to equip the German air force. A
combined total of nearly 300 D.II and
D.III scouts was built. Of those which
survived their few brief months at the
front, some were assigned to the Austro-Hungarian air force, but the majority
were transferred to training establishments.

The **Fokker D.V** represented a developed and refined version of the D.III,
and was powered by a 100-hp (75-kW)
Oberursel U.I rotary engine. This powerplant meant that when the D.V became
available in late 1916 there was little
doubt that its performance would be inadequate for service on the Western
Front, and most of the more than 200
built were used to train fighter pilots.

Specification
Fokker D.III
Type: single-seat fighter/scout
Powerplant: one 160-hp (119-kW)

*Martin Kreutzer's last design was
the D.V, which introduced sweep
to the upper wings, a greater
degree of stagger and ailerons as
the only means of lateral control.
The type served usefully as a
home-front interceptor.*

*As conceived, the D.II had single-
bay unstaggered wings, but by
the time the type got into
production this had been altered
to a staggered cellule with two
bays. Examples for Austria-
Hungary retained the single bay.*

Oberursel U.III 14-cylinder rotary piston
engine
Performance: maximum speed
99 mph (160 km/h); climb to 13,215 ft
(4000 m) in 20 minutes; service ceiling
15,420 ft (4700 m); endurance 1 hour
30 minutes
Weights: empty 996 lb (452 kg);
maximum take-off 1,565 lb (710 kg)
Dimensions: span 29 ft 8¼ in
(9.05 m); length 20 ft 8 in (6.30 m);
height 7 ft 4½ in (2.25 m); wing area
215.29 sq ft (20.00 m²)
Armament: one or two fixed
forward-firing 7.92-mm (0.31-in) LMG
08/15 machine-guns

Fokker D.VI
to
Fokker E.V/D.VIII

Fokker D.VI

Two single-seat fighter prototypes were built by Fokker during the winter of 1917-18, these combining the fuselage, tail unit and landing gear of the Dr.I with a reduced-span version of the wing which had been developed for the D.VII. The two prototypes differed in their power-plant, the **V 13/1** having a 145-hp (108-kW) Oberursel U.III and the **V 13/2** a 160-hp (119-kW) Siemens-Halske Sh.III. Testing and evaluation resulted in the type being ordered into production in early 1918 under the designation **D.VI**, but as the engines of the prototypes had both proved troublesome the Oberursel U.II was specified for series aircraft.

Built alongside the Fokker D.VII, the D.VI triplane was produced compara-tively slowly as the D.VII had priority. When, in August 1918, its manufacture

The advent of Reinhold Platz as chief designer was immediately apparent in more workmanlike designs. The D.VI combined the Dr.I's fuselage with D.VII wings.

was terminated so that all efforts could be concentrated on construction of the highly successful D.VII, D.VI production totalled about 60 aircraft. Of these, the majority were used as advanced trainers for potential fighter pilots.

Specification
Type: single-seat fighter
Powerplant: one 110-hp (82-kW) Oberursel U.II 9-cylinder rotary piston engine
Performance: maximum speed 122 mph (196 km/h); climb to 16,405 ft (5000 m) in 19 minutes; service ceiling 19,685 ft (6000 m); endurance 1 hour

30 minutes
Weights: empty 866 lb (393 kg); maximum take-off 1,290 lb (585 kg)
Dimensions: span 25 ft 1¼ in (7.65 m); length 20 ft 6 in (6.25 m); height 8 ft 4½ in (2.55 m); wing area

190.53 sq ft (17.70 m²)
Armament: two fixed forward-firing 7.92-mm (0.31-in) LMG 08/15 machine-guns

Fokker D.VII

To compete in Germany's first single-seat fighter competition of 1918, Rein-hold Platz developed a new prototype, the **VII**, which incorporated much of the design of the successful Dr.I. Its fuse-lage was similar in profile and construc-tion, the tail unit was revised but the landing gear was virtually unchanged. The intention to use a more powerful and heavier engine to attain a new level of performance meant that by compari-son with the D.VI, biplane wings of greater span/area would be necessary. Their construction was similar to that adopted for the cantilever wings de-signed for the Dr.I but, being consider-ably larger, were of two-spar instead of single-spar construction. Powerplant of the prototype and early production air-craft was a 160-hp (119-kW) Mercedes D.III engine, but later series-built machines had the more powerful B.M.W. III which gave improved per-formance.

As a result of the January 1918 fighter competition, the **Fokker D.VII** was ordered into immediate production, its overall capability being so much better than that of the Albatros D.V series that Albatros Werke GmbH was ordered to build it under sub-contract at both of its factories. Within three months of the competition the D.VII was in operational use, its performance matched only by the British Sopwith Snipe and the French Spad XIII. By the time of the Armistice on 11 November 1918, more than 700 D.VIIs had been delivered. Such was the poten-tial of this aircraft that the Peace Treaty specified that all machines of this type must be handed over to the Allies, the D.VII and Zeppelin airships being the only German aircraft singled out for con-fiscation.

Fokker managed to smuggle a num-ber of D.VIIs and components for these aircraft out of Germany and into his native Holland, where he set up a new aircraft factory. Production of the D.VII continued for several years after the war, new or ex-German aircraft serving with the air forces of many European nations.

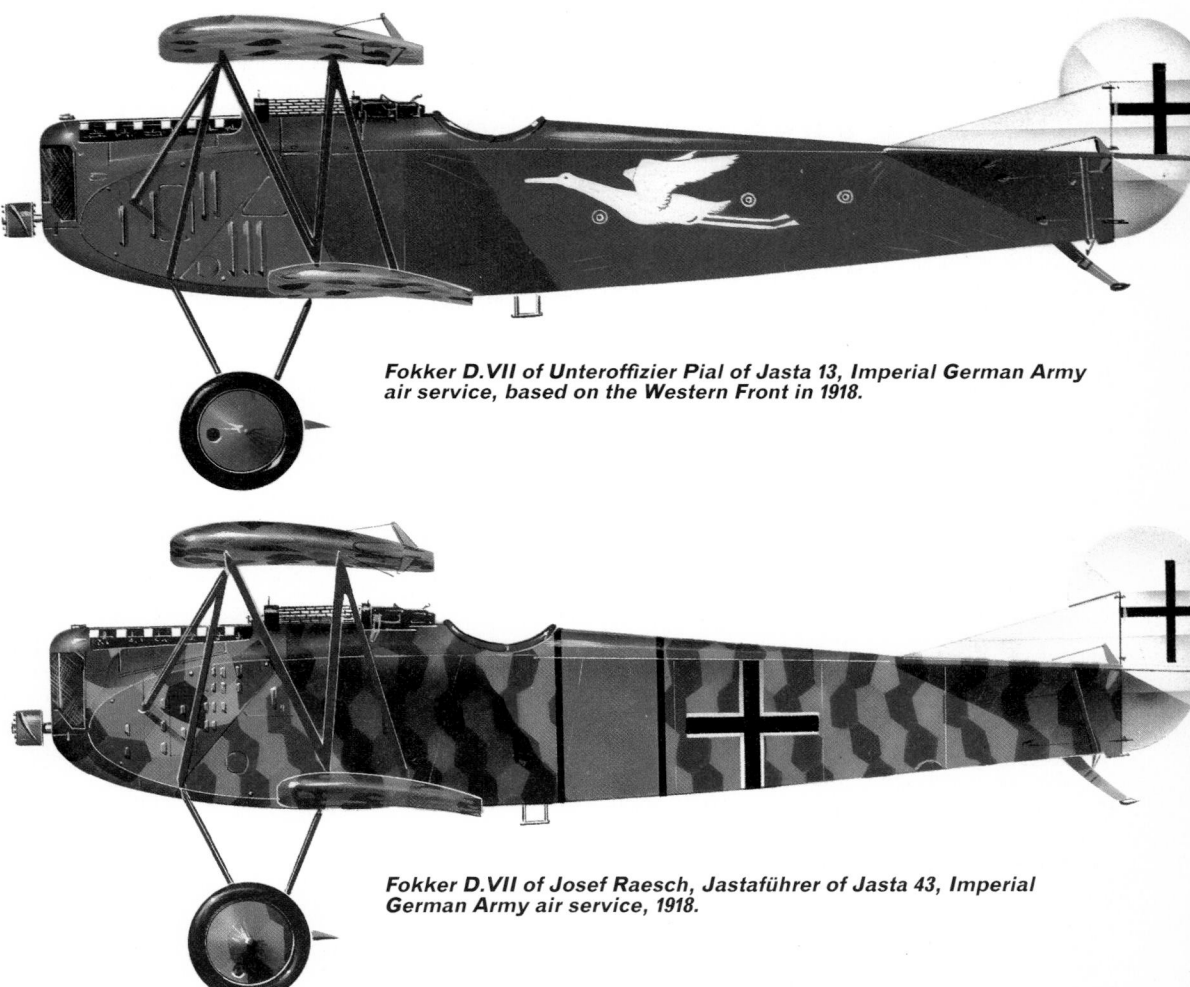

Fokker D.VII of Unteroffizier Pial of Jasta 13, Imperial German Army air service, based on the Western Front in 1918.

Fokker D.VII of Josef Raesch, Jastaführer of Jasta 43, Imperial German Army air service, 1918.

Variants
V 18: interim step between the V 11 and the D.VII, notably the addition of a fixed fin
V 21: variant of the D.VII with tapered wings and 160-hp (119-kW) Mercedes D.III engine; flown in the second

D-type competition
V 22: pre-production prototype of the D.VII, combining all the best features of the V 11, V 18 and V 21, and powered by the 160-hp (119-kW) Mercedes D.III
V 24: D.VII experimentally fitted with the 200-hp (149-kW) Benz engine

V 29: experimental parasol-wing monoplane version of the D.VII, and resembling a scaled-up V 27 apart from the use of the 185-hp (138-kW) BMW IIIa engine; took part in the third D-type competition
V 31: standard D.VII fitted with a hook

to tow the V 30

V 34: D.VII fitted with a V 33-type empennage and with its BMW engine in a neater cowling

V 36: of the two aircraft built, the first was similar to the V 34 but reverted to the D.VII-type empennage, and the second had no cut-out in the upper-wing trailing edge and was fitted with a fuel tank in the axle fairing

V 38: derivative of the D.VII formula to a larger scale, and intended as the prototype of the C.I, of which 70 sets of components were secretly smuggled to the Netherlands by Fokker at the end of World War I.

Specification

Type: single-seat fighter/scout
Powerplant: one 185-hp (138-kW) B.M.W. III 6-cylinder inline piston engine
Performance: maximum speed 124 mph (200 km/h) at 3,280 ft (1000 m); climb to 16,405 ft (5000 m) in 16 minutes; service ceiling 22,965 ft (7000 m); endurance 1 hour 30 minutes

Weights: empty 1,620 lb (735 kg); maximum take-off 1,940 lb (880 kg)
Dimensions: span 29 ft 2½ in (8.90 m); length 22 ft 9½ in (6.95 m); height 9 ft ¼ in (2.75 m); wing area 220.67 sq ft (20.50 m²)
Armament: two fixed forward-firing 7.92-mm (0.31-in) LMG 08/15 machine-guns

Fokker D.XI

A true sesquiplane, with the lower wing of much smaller dimensions than the upper, the sleek **Fokker D.XI** single-seat fighter designed by Reinhold Platz attracted considerable attention when it first flew on 5 May 1923. No Dutch orders were forthcoming as a result of financial stringencies, but in total 117 D.XIs were built for export. The D.XI was developed throughout its production life and versions built for different countries varied in design detail. All versions of the D.XI, however, shared the single-bay V-strut wing bracing so typical of Platz. All were powered by the 300-hp (224-kW) Hispano-Suiza engine, its twin radiators mounted on the sides of the nose to provide a well-streamlined appearance. Both upper and lower wings were tapered on the leading edge.

The principal customer for the D.XI was the USSR, which flew the type in its first-line fighter units until 1929. Others

Three of the D.XI were evaluated by the US Army Air Service under the designation PW-7. Seen here is the first of these, which retained the original V-struts and plywood-skinned wings (the other two having N-struts and fabric wings).

included Romania and Spain, whose original orders were cut back to small batches; Argentina which obtained six for its naval aviation fighter squadron; and the United States Army which operated three under the designation **PW-7** with 440-hp (328-kW) Curtiss D-12 V-12s. Plans to use the D.XI for the clandestine German air arm were abandoned and a provisional order for 50 cancelled.

Specification
Type: single-seat fighter
Powerplant: one 300-hp (224-kW) Hispano-Suiza 8 Fb 8-cylinder Vee piston engine
Performance: maximum speed 140 mph (225 km/h); service ceiling 22,965 ft (7000 m); range 273 miles (440 km)
Weights: empty equipped 1,907 lb (865 kg); maximum take-off 2,756 lb (1250 kg)
Dimensions: span 38 ft 3½ in (11.67 m); length 24 ft 7¼ in (7.50 m); height 10 ft 6 in (3.20 m); wing area 234.66 sq ft (21.80 m²)
Armament: two fixed forward-firing 0.303-in (7.7-mm) machine-guns

Fokker D.XIII

Following the unsuccessful **D.XII** single-seat fighter biplane intended for the US Army and tested with a Curtiss D-12 engine, the **Fokker D.XIII** prototype was flown for the first time on 12 September 1924. A developed version of the D.XI, powered by a Napier Lion engine, it had good lines and outstanding performance for its time.

One of the first of the 50 production D.XIIIs was flown on 16 July 1925 in a series of successful attempts on various world speed and load records. The series machines were all delivered by a circuitous route to the training centre established with great secrecy by the German army at Lipetsk in the Soviet Union. When the Germans withdrew from this base in 1933 they handed over some 20 D.XIIIs to the Russian air arm. By the time the D.XIII had entered pro-

duction, the experimental **D.XIV** semi-cantilever low-wing monoplane single-seat fighter had flown for the first time, on 28 March 1925. Loss of the sole example in a crash led Fokker to abandon the design and development of low-wing monoplane fighters until a decade later.

Specification
Type: single-seat fighter
Powerplant: one 570-hp (425-kW) Napier Lion XI 12-cylinder 'arrow' piston engine
Performance: maximum speed 168 mph (270 km/h); service ceiling 26,245 ft (8000 m); range 373 miles (600 km)
Weights: empty equipped 2,690 lb (1220 kg); maximum take-off 3,638 lb (1650 kg)
Dimensions: span 36 ft 1 in (11.00 m); length 25 ft 11 in (7.90 m);

height 9 ft 6 in (2.90 m); wing area 231.11 sq ft (21.47 m²)
Armament: two fixed forward-firing 0.303-in (7.7-mm) machine-guns

The D.XIII was a capable fighter for its period, and its importance lies mainly in the fact that it was used by the clandestine German air force training in the USSR.

Fokker D.XVII

Modified from the D.XVI, the **Fokker D.XVII** single-seat biplane fighter was intended originally to meet a Netherlands East Indies army specification, but when it appeared in 1932 this force had no funds. The prototype was instead evaluated by the Netherlands air force, which subsequently ordered 11. Despite this small number, at least three different types of engine were involved: the 690-hp (515-kW) Hispano-Suiza 12Xbrs, the 790-hp (589-kW) Lorraine-Dietrich Petrel and, most commonly, the Rolls-Royce Kestrel IIS; the prototype had used a Curtiss V-1570 Conqueror engine. In spite of this powerplant miscellany, the D.XVII was well liked by its pilots. Construction included a fabric-covered steel-tube fuselage, with ply-wood and fabric-covered wings. Had it not been for the success of the D.XXI monoplane, the D.XVII would have been modified to incorporate an enclosed

cockpit, but this idea was abandoned at the design stage.

Six D.XVIIs were based at the Netherlands air force flying school on the island of Texel when the Netherlands was attacked on 10 May 1940, but in the desperate situation which then existed the aircraft were used as fighter escorts to the C.Vs and C.Xs which were making attacks on German armoured columns.

Specification
Type: single-seat biplane fighter
Powerplant: one 595-hp (444-kW) Rolls-Royce Kestrel IIS 12-cylinder Vee piston engine
Performance: maximum speed 217 mph (350 km/h) at 13,125 ft (4000 m); cruising speed 180 mph (290 km/h) at 13,125 ft (4000 m); service ceiling 28,705 ft (8750 m); range 528 miles (850 km)
Weights: empty 2,425 lb (1100 kg); maximum take-off 3,263 lb (1480 kg)
Dimensions: span 31 ft 6 in (9.60 m); length 23 ft 7½ in (7.20 m); height 9 ft

10¼ in (3.00 m); wing area 215.29 sq ft (20.00 m²)
Armament: two 0.31-in (7.9-mm) forward-firing machine-guns in fuselage

An attractive single-bay biplane fighter, the D.XVII served up to 1940, and were used briefly in the campaign to defend the Netherlands.

Fokker D.XXI

The **Fokker D.XXI** represented a complete breakaway from previous Fokker biplane and high-wing monoplane designs, being a low-wing monoplane with fixed, spatted landing gear.

The Netherlands army air division contracted for a prototype in 1935 to evaluate the type's potential for use in the Netherlands East Indies, and although it was planned originally to use a 650-hp (485-kW) Rolls-Royce Kestrel IV engine, the prototype flew on 27 February 1936 at Eindhoven with a 645-hp (481-kW) Bristol Mercury VI-S radial. At this time the Netherlands government was inclined more towards bombers than fighters for home use, but a change in policy in the summer of 1937 led to an order for 36 D.XXIs to be powered by Bristol Mercury VII or VIII radial engines.

In the same year seven Mercury VIII-powered D.XXIs were ordered for the Finnish air force, and a licence-production arrangement was concluded under which the Finnish State Aircraft Factory at Tampere built 93 D.XXIs between 1938 and 1944. Of these, the first 38 Mercury-powered aircraft were completed by 1938, but a further 50 built in 1941 were modified to take the 825-hp (615-kW) Pratt & Whitney Twin Wasp Junior SB4-C/-G engine, 80 of which had been bought in 1940. Finnish D.XXIs had all four guns mounted in the wings, instead of two in the fuselage and two in the wings. A final batch of five Bristol Pegasus-powered D.XXIs appeared in 1944.

Dutch-built aircraft were delivered to Denmark and a further 10 were built in the Royal Army Aircraft Factory, Copenhagen; they had Mercury VI-S engines and one 20-mm Madsen cannon in a fairing beneath each wing. Licence production of the D.XXI in Spain by the Republican government was begun, but the

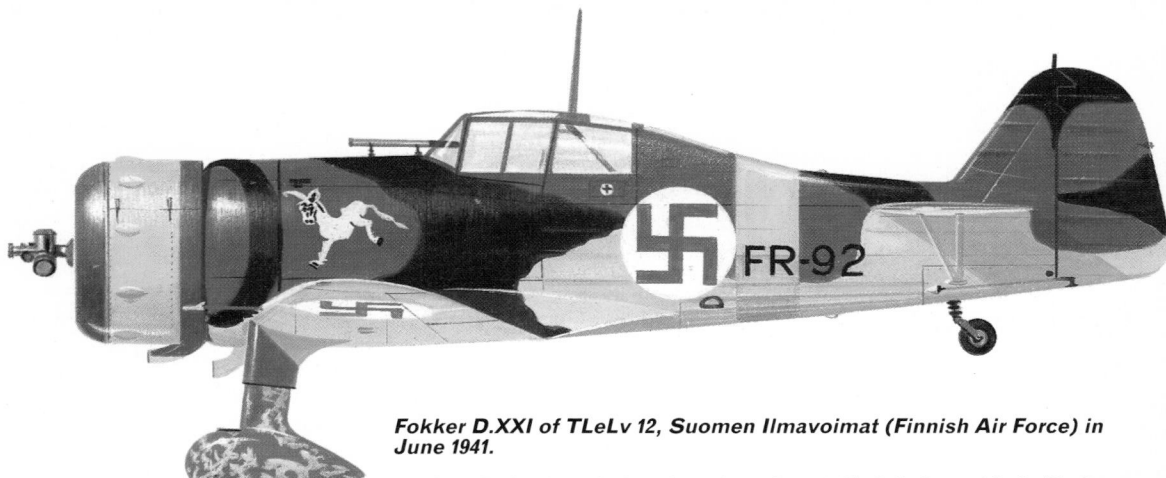

Fokker D.XXI of TLeLv 12, Suomen Ilmavoimat (Finnish Air Force) in June 1941.

assembly lines were captured by the Nationalists and it is thought that no D.XXIs were completed. Meanwhile, in Holland the first D.XXI for the Netherlands air force flew on 20 July 1938, and the last of 36 production aircraft was handed over on 8 September 1939.

At the time of Germany's invasion of the Netherlands on 10 May 1940, 28 D.XXIs were operational. The manoeuvrability of the Dutch fighters stood them in good stead during the five days before the Netherlands capitulated, although eventually they were overwhelmed by sheer weight of numbers and only eight remained airworthy. Their greatest victory came on 10 May, when D.XXIs destroyed 37 out of a formation of 55 Junkers Ju 52/3ms which crossed the Dutch border in the early morning.

When Finland capitulated to the Russians, on 12 March 1940, 29 D.XXIs were still on strength. It was decided subsequently to build another 50 aircraft, so the Finnish air force had a number available when hostilities with the USSR restarted in June 1941. Some of the D.XXIs began to be replaced by the relatively unsuccessful IVL Myrsky in August that year, although a few lingered on long after the end of the war until finally withdrawn from service in 1948.

Most of the Finnish D.XXIs operated with 'snowshoe' landing gear during the winter; one Twin Wasp-powered aircraft was modified to have retractable landing gear, but its performance was not improved sufficiently to warrant conversion of the other in-service aircraft.

A number of pre-war Dutch D.XXIs served as testbeds for engines such as the Rolls-Royce Kestrel V and Hispano-Suiza 12Y, and projects were in hand for versions with the Bristol Hercules (**Pro-**ject 150), Rolls-Royce Merlin (**Project 151**) and Daimler-Benz DB600H (**Project 152**), all with retractable landing gear and aerodynamic improvements to the design.

Specification
Type: single-seat fighter
Powerplant: one 830-hp (619-kW) Bristol Mercury VIII 9-cylinder radial piston engine
Performance: maximum speed 286 mph (460 km/h) at 14,500 ft (4420 m); cruising speed 239 mph (385 km/h); service ceiling 36,090 ft (11000 m); range 590 miles (950 km)
Weights: empty 3,197 lb (1450 kg); maximum take-off 4,519 lb (2050 kg)
Dimensions: span 36 ft 1 in (11.00 m); length 26 ft 10¾ in (8.20 m); height 9 ft 8 in (2.95 m); wing area 174.38 sq ft (16.20 m²)
Armament: four 0.31-in (7.9-mm) machine-guns, two in upper cowling and two in wings

---

Fokker D.XXIII

The **Fokker D.XXIII** prototype aroused considerable foreign interest when it appeared in 1939, not least because of its unusual layout. To take advantage of centre line thrust its designer, Ing. Marius Beeling, devised a short nacelle of metal construction with a tractor engine at the front and a pusher engine at the rear. The pilot was accommodated in an enclosed cockpit in the nacelle. The low-set cantilever wooden wing supported two booms which terminated in twin fins and rudders, these vertical tail surfaces being connected by a long horizontal tailplane. Fully retractable tricycle landing gear was installed.

Power was provided by two low-powered Walter Sagitta I-SR liquid-cooled engines. Fokker hoped for Dutch production orders and possible exports. To deal with the relatively modest performance achieved by the prototype, versions with Rolls-Royce or Daimler-Benz engines were projected. To meet complaints about pilot safety from the possibly lethal pusher propeller behind the cockpit, Beeling was studying a design for an ejector seat, but nothing came of this.

The D.XXIII made its maiden flight on 30 May 1939, but serious cooling problems were encountered with the rear engine. As a result only a few flying hours had been achieved by the time Germany invaded the Netherlands in May 1940 and nothing more was heard of the remarkable D.XXIII.

Specification
Type: single-seat fighter
Powerplant: two 530-hp (395-kW) Walter Sagitta I-SR 12-cylinder inverted Vee piston engines
Performance: (estimated) maximum speed 326 mph (525 km/h); service ceiling 29,530 ft (9000 m); range 522 miles (840 km)

Weights: empty equipped 4,806 lb (2180 kg); maximum take-off 6,504 lb (2950 kg)
Dimensions: span 37 ft 8¾ in (11.50 m); length 33 ft 5½ in (10.20 m); height 12 ft 5½ in (3.80 m); wing area 199.1 sq ft (18.50 m²)
Armament: (intended) two 0.31-in (7.9-mm) and two 0.52-in (13.2-mm) machine-guns

An interesting effort to overcome the problems of single-engine asymmetry in a twin-engined fighter, the D.XXIII proved to be difficult to bale out of without the pilot striking the rear propeller.

Fokker Dr.I

German pilots serving on the Western Front were quick to appreciate the high rate of climb and remarkable manoeuvrability of the Sopwith Triplane which RNAS squadrons were operating in the spring of 1917. When reports of their capability were transmitted to Germany, the nation's manufacturers lost little time in developing experimental aircraft of this category.

Fokker's chief designer, Martin Kreutzer, had been killed on 27 June 1916 while testing a D.I. He was replaced by Reinhold Platz, and it was the latter who was responsible for design and development of the company's new triplane. His first **V 3** prototype had three small cantilever wings, free of interplane struts, mounted to a typically Fokker fuselage, tailskid landing gear and vertical tail surfaces. Completely new was an aerofoil-section fairing enclosing the through axle of the main landing gear and a large tailplane with swept leading edges. However, when this aircraft was flown the wings were found to vibrate badly, leading to an improved version, the **V 4**, with lightweight hollow struts to overcome the problem. A number of other aerodynamic improvements were incorporated at the same time and, when testing proved satisfactory, this version was put into production in the early summer of 1917 under the initial designation **F.I**, quickly changed to the official military **Fokker Dr.I** (Dr for dreidecker, or triplane). Power was provided by a Thulin licence-built Le Rhône rotary or by an Oberursel engine that was virtually a copy of this powerplant.

The Dr.I soon gained an exaggerated reputation of capability, probably because it was a mount used by the legendary 'Red Baron', Manfred von Richthofen, who favoured the type for its superb manoeuvrability and high rate of climb. So far as maximum speed was concerned, the Dr.I was inferior to contemporary Allied fighter/scouts and a number were lost as a result of wing structural failure. At one period, in late 1917, the type was grounded while wing strengthening modifications were carried out. When production ended in May 1918 more than 300 had been built, and the Dr.I remained in service until the summer of 1918.

Variants
V 5: airframe of a Dr.I fitted with the 160-hp (119-kW) Goebel Goe.III rotary for trials purposes in the first D-type competition
V 6: development of the Dr.I with increased-span wings and a longer

fuselage, first flown in the summer of 1917 with the 120-hp (90-kW) Mercedes D.II inline engine; components later used for the extraordinary **V 8,** which had triplane wings at the extreme nose, biplane wings just aft of the cockpit, and a standard Dr.I tail unit

V 7: standard Dr.I fitted with the 160-hp (119-kW) Siemens-Halske Sh.III geared rotary and four-bladed propeller

V 9: experimental biplane of autumn 1917 using mostly Dr.I components and with its upper-wing centre-section supported on pairs of tripod cabane struts on each side; power was provided by the 80-hp (60-kW) Oberursel U.0 rotary

V 10: standard Dr.I fitted with the 145-hp (108-kW) Oberursel Ur.III and possessing the phenomenal ceiling of 31,170 ft (9500 m)

Specification
Type: single-seat fighter/scout
Powerplant: one 110-hp (82-kW) Thulin-built Le Rhône or Oberursel Ur.II 9-cylinder rotary piston engine
Performance: maximum speed 103 mph (165 km/h) at 13,125 ft (4000 m); climb to 3,280 ft (1000 m) in 2 minutes 54 seconds; service ceiling 20,000 ft (6095 m); endurance 1 hour 30 minutes
Weights: empty 895 lb (406 kg); maximum take-off 1,290 lb (585 kg)
Dimensions: span 23 ft 7½ in (7.20 m); length 18 ft 11¼ in (5.77 m); height 9 ft 8¼ in (2.95 m); wing area 201.29 sq ft (18.70 m²)
Armament: two fixed forward-firing 7.92-mm (0.31-in) LMG 08/15 machine-guns

This replica of Richthofen's Dr.I displays the keys to the type's agility. The overall compact proportions are allied to large control surfaces, and all the heavy items such as engine, fuel, guns, ammunition and pilot are grouped close to the centre of gravity.

Fokker E series

On 19 April 1915 a French Morane-Saulnier Type L was forced down behind the German lines after being hit by anti-aircraft fire. This event was significant in the development of fighter aircraft and their weapons for its pilot, Frenchman Roland Garros, had devised a scheme that allowed his single Hotchkiss machine-gun to be fired forward through the propeller disc: wedge-shaped steel plates attached to the rear of the propeller blades deflected any bullets that might endanger them.

German officers examining the damaged Type L saw immediately the significance of a fixed forward-firing machine-gun that could be aimed easily by the pilot. It resulted in Fokker being approached to develop a more sophisticated means of arriving at the same result, leading to the interrupter gear that 'timed' the bullets to pass harmlessly

between the spinning propeller blades. Early tests of this device were carried out on the Fokker M.5k/MG, production versions of this aircraft with an interrupter gear for its Maxim-type LMG 08/15 'Spandau' machine-gun having the designation **Fokker E.I** (E for Eindecker, or monoplane).

Of braced mid-wing configuration, the single-seat E.I had tailskid landing gear, a conventional tail unit and was powered by an 80-hp (60-kW) Oberursel U.0 rotary engine. The E.I was superseded by the generally similar but refined and strengthened **E.II** (company designation **M.14**) with a more powerful engine, and the **E.III** (company designation M.14 also) which only differed in detail from the E.II. Final production version was the heavier but less successful **E.IV** (company designation **M.15**), which was basically an E.III with a 160-hp (119-kW)

Oberursel U.III engine and two machine-guns. Production of all four versions is believed to have totalled about 300 aircraft.

It was early Fokker E-types that brought the so-called 'Fokker Scourge' when, from the autumn of 1915 to the spring of 1916, they played havoc with the B.E.2c units of the Royal Flying Corps.

Specification
Type: single-seat escort fighter/scout
Powerplant: one 100-hp (75-kW) Oberursel U.I 9-cylinder rotary piston engine
Performance: maximum speed 87 mph (140 km/h); climb to 9,845 ft (3000 m) in 30 minutes; service ceiling 11,480 ft (3500 m); endurance 1 hour 30 minutes
Weights: empty 880 lb (399 kg); maximum take-off 1,345 lb (610 kg)
Dimensions: span 31 ft 2¾ in (9.50 m); length 23 ft 7½ in (7.20 m);

Though in itself not an outstanding aircraft, the E.I achieved results out of all proportion to its numbers by means of its unique feature: the synchronised machine-gun firing through the propeller disc.

height 7 ft 10½ in (2.40 m); wing area 172.23 sq ft (16.00 m²)
Armament: one fixed forward-firing 7.92-mm (0.31-in) LMG 08/15 machine-gun

Fokker E.V/D.VIII

The **Fokker E.V,** designed to participate in the second German fighter aircraft competition held in June 1918, combined several features of earlier aircraft. The fuselage with single-seat accommodation was similar to that of the D.VII and had generally similar landing gear and vertical tail surfaces; the tailplane and powerplant were the same as those of the Dr.I. The E.V differed by having a cantilever monoplane wing strut-mounted in a parasol-wing configuration. The **V 26** performed well in the fighter trials, its manoeuvrability, take-off and climb performance being so good that the type was ordered into immediate production with the intention that it should eventually supersede the D.VII.

Early use by combat units revealed problems with engine lubrication and wing structural failure, leading to a temporary suspension of production and of operational use. However, remedial action was taken very quickly and production resumed under the new designation **D.VIII,** but the Armistice came shortly after and comparatively few D.VIIIs saw operational service. It had been planned to produce developments of the aircraft and prototype versions had flown with 140-hp (104-kW) Oberursel and 160-hp (119-kW) Goebel and Siemens-Halske engines, but none of these became production aircraft.

Fokker D.VIII under test at McCook Field in 1919 with US Army Air Service markings.

Variants
V 27: a competitor in the second fighter competition, the V 27 was essentially a V 26 modified with the 195-hp (145-kW) Benz IIIb Vee-8 engine; the aircraft was later modified into the sole **V 38,** with sheet armour protection for the pilot, engine and fuel tanks with a view to proposed trench-fighter aircraft
V 28: also flown in the second D-type competition, the V 28 was powered by either the 145-hp (108-kW) Oberursel

Ur.III or 640-hp (104-kW) Goebel Goe.III 11-cylinder rotary engines; for the third D-type competition the aircraft was re-engined with the Siemens-Halske Sh.III rotary
V 30: conversion of a V 26 into a glider, with the pilot seated in the extreme nose for centre-of-gravity reasons – the sole example was exhibited at the 1921 Paris Salon

Specification
Type: single-seat fighter/scout
Powerplant: one 110-hp (82-kW)

Oberursel U.II 9-cylinder rotary piston engine
Performance: maximum speed 127 mph (204 km/h) at sea level; service ceiling 19,685 ft (6000 m); endurance 1 hour 30 minutes
Weights: empty 893 lb (405 kg); maximum take-off 1,334 lb (605 kg)
Dimensions: span 27 ft 4¾ in (8.35 m); length 19 ft 2¼ in (5.85 m); height 9 ft 2¼ in (2.80 m); wing area 115.18 sq ft (10.70 m²)
Armament: two fixed forward-firing Spandau machine-guns

Fokker F.1 and F.II
to
Fokker T.VIII-W

Fokker F.I and F.II

The first commercial design by Reinhold Platz was the **Fokker F.I**, a parasol monoplane with open cockpits for pilot and passengers. Realising the need for better passenger accommodation, Platz abandoned development of the F.I and designed instead the **F.II** prototype. Like the F.I (**V 44**), the F.I (**V 45**) was built at the Fokker works at Schwerin in Germany, making its first flight in October 1919 and receiving the German civil registration D-57. The decision having been made by Fokker to transfer his activities to the Netherlands, the F.II prototype was flown out of Germany illegally by Bernard de Waal on 20 March 1920.

The F.II proved to be one of the first practical passenger transport aircraft in the world and some 30 were built, most being constructed under licence by Grulich in Germany, but several being produced at Netherlands Aircraft Factories in north Amsterdam and at Fokker's new Veere factory. It is believed also that three series machines were completed at Schwerin.

The thick-section cantilever wooden wing, intended originally for the F.I, was bolted to the top of the F.II's fuselage, which was of rectangular section and tapered in width to the strut-braced horizontal tailplane. There was no fixed fin and the rudder was of relatively small dimensions. Four passengers were accommodated in a cabin beneath the wing, while the pilot and a fifth passen-

Offering no frills, the F.II was a fully practical transport and was successful in a field where there were many failures.

ger were located in an open cockpit immediately forward of the cabin. The landing gear of the F.II was of cross-axle type with rubber-cord shock absorbers.

The **Fokker-Grulich F.II**, of which at least 19 were built, had an improved cockpit layout, redesigned cabin windows and strengthened landing gear. Ing Karl Grulich was technical manager of Deutsche Aero Lloyd (D.A.L.) and his version of the F.II was flown by that airline. The wings of the Grulich F.II were built by Albatros and the fuselages by D.A.L., who also carried out final assembly work.

Veere- and Schwerin-built F.IIs had BMW IIIa engines, but the Grulich ver-

sions had 186-kW (250-hp) BMW IVs. Most of the Grulich aircraft were re-engined subsequently with the 239-kW (320-hp) BMW Va and given the new designation **F.IIb**.

The three Schwerin-built F.II series aircraft were registered in the Free City of Danzig and used by the Deutsche Luftreederei airline. Dutch-built F.IIs flew from 1920 to 1927 with the national airline KLM and two were sold to the Belgian airline SABENA for a service between Brussels and Antwerp. One Dutch-built F.II had a 179-kW (240-hp) Armstrong Siddeley Puma engine and one was flown briefly with a BMW IV.

Longest-lived were the Fokker-Grulich F.IIbs. Taken over with some F.IIs by the newly-formed Deutsche Lufthansa in 1926, 10 still remained in service on

feeder routes linking Cologne with Aachen, Essen, Krefeld and Mülheim in the Ruhr in 1934.

Specification
Fokker F.II
Type: five-passenger transport
Powerplant: one 138-kW (185-hp) BMW IIIa 6-cylinder inline piston engine
Performance: maximum speed 150 km/h (93 mph); cruising speed 120 km/h (75 mph); range 1200 km (745 miles)
Weights: empty 1200 kg (2,646 lb); maximum take-off 1900 kg (4,189 lb)
Dimensions: span 16.10 m (52 ft 9¾ in); length 11.65 m (38 ft 2¾ in); height 3.20 m (10 ft 6 in); wing area 38.20 m² (411.19 sq ft)

Fokker F.III

Developed from the F.II, the **Fokker F.III** had a fuselage of reduced length and increased width, with a cabin accommodating five passengers in upholstered comfort. The pilot was seated in an open cockpit offset to starboard, its rear recessed into the wing leading edge. The thick-section monoplane wing was cantilevered, the fixed cross-axle landing gear had single-wheel units and, by comparison with the F.II, the rudder was of increased height.

The prototype, powered by a 138-kW (185-hp) BMW IIIa engine, was flown at Schwerin at the beginning of April 1921 and on 14 April inaugurated KLM flights for the year. The type was also exhibited at the 1921 Paris Salon de l'Aéronautique where it met with a mixed reception as a result of Fokker's association with the German cause during World War I. Later, however, the F.III became one of the most important European aircraft of the mid-1920s.

Of 31 F.IIIs built by Fokker, 12 were supplied to KLM and these were powered by the 179-kW (240-hp) Armstrong Siddeley Puma engine. They were used heavily from 1921 onwards on routes linking Amsterdam, Rotterdam and Croydon, and also on the route from the Netherlands to Bremen and Hamburg. Other customers were the German Deutsche Luftreederei, which used

Revealed as a product of the Platz design philosophy by its cantilevered thick-section wing, overhanging ailerons and robust landing gear, the F.III was for its time an effective transport.

a Danzig-registered machine with a BMW IIa engine; and the Hungarian MALERT company which operated four F.IIIs with BMW IIIas and two with 172-kW (230-hp) Hiero engines, these being used on routes from Budapest to Vienna and Graz. One F.III was demonstrated in North America, but with limited success, only two aircraft being sold there.

Later Fokker-built F.IIIs, powered by 268-kW (360-hp) Rolls-Royce Eagle engines, had the pilot's cockpit offset to port and some were completed as strut-braced parasol-wing monoplanes. The Deruluft airline, owned jointly by the USSR and Germany, acquired 10 of these Eagle-powered F.IIIs, and two were taken into service by KLM in 1922. The latter were re-engined with 298-kW (400-hp) Gnome-Rhône Jupiter VI radial engines in 1925 and used on the Amsterdam-Paris route. In 1926 five surviving F.IIIs were sold to the Swiss Balair company and made a formation delivery flight to Basle on 28 April.

In 1923 production of the F.III began in Germany, at the Staaken works, the Deutsche Aero Lloyd airline acquiring at least 20 of these so-called **Fokker-**

Grulich F.III aircraft. Some were powered by 186-kW (250-hp) BMW IV engines, while others had Armstrong Siddeley Pumas. Several were re-engined subsequently with 239-kW (320-hp) BMW Va engines, leading to the revised designation **F.IIIc.**

When Deutsche Lufthansa was formed in 1926 it took over 16 F.IIIs then operating services between Hamburg and Amsterdam, and transferred them to short routes linking north German coastal resorts; they were later used on internal freight services.

Two F.IIIs were sold to British Air Lines Ltd in 1929, a company then based at Croydon Airport.

Variants
Grulich V 1: although the German-built F.IIIs had various minor modifications they were indistinguishable externally from Dutch F.IIIs, apart from powerplant; the Grulich V 1, however, had a redesigned

fuselage, tailplane and landing gear; powered initially by a Rolls-Royce Eagle VIII engine, it later had an uncowled Gnome-Rhône radial, being then redesignated **V 1a**; used by Deruluft airline
Grulich V 2: similar to V 1, but with F.III landing gear; believed powered by a BMW IV engine

Specification
Fokker F.III
Type: five-passenger transport
Powerplant: one 179-kW (240-hp) Armstrong Siddeley Puma 6-cylinder inline piston engine
Performance: maximum speed 150 km/h (93 mph); cruising speed 135 km/h (84 mph); endurance 5 hours
Weights: empty 1200 kg (2,645 lb); maximum take-off 2000 kg (4,409 lb)
Dimensions: span 17.62 m (57 ft 9¾ in); length 11.07 m (36 ft 3¾ in); height 3.66 m (12 ft 0 in); wing area 39.10 m² (420.88 sq ft)

Fokker F.VIIA

Developed from the successful Fokker F.VII, five of which were built in 1924-25, the **Fokker F.VIIA** flew on 12 March 1925 with a 298-kW (400-hp) Packard Liberty engine. Following a demonstration tour of the United States, a number of orders were secured and further orders came from European operators. Almost 50 single-engined F.VIIAs were built, some of which were converted later to **F.VIIA-3m** standard with three engines. This variant, together with the slightly larger-span **F.VIIB-3m**, formed the backbone of many European airline operations in the early 1930s, with licence-production also being undertaken in Belgium, Italy, Poland and the UK.

Although two F.VIIAs were supplied to the Royal Netherlands air force and one to the RAF, the only example known to have been used by the military in World War II was the 12th production F.VIIA which, after a chequered career in the Netherlands and Denmark, was presented to the Finnish Red Cross and operated in military markings in the Continuation War which began in 1941. Those operated by the Netherlands and Polish air forces were destroyed at an early stage of the German invasion of these two nations.

Variant
Fokker F.VIIA-3m/M: conversion of an F.VIIA/3m into an Armstrong Siddeley Lynx-powered bomber prototype with bomb racks under the fuselage

Specification
Fokker F.VIIA
Type: 10-seat transport
Powerplant: one 298-kW (400-hp) Gnome-Rhône Jupiter 9-cylinder radial piston engine
Performance: maximum speed 185 km/h (115 mph); cruising speed 155 km/h (96 mph); service ceiling 2600 m (8,530 ft); range 1160 km (721 miles)
Weights: empty 1950 kg (4,299 lb); maximum take-off 3650 kg (8,047 lb)
Dimensions: span 19.30 m (63 ft 3¾ in); length 14.35 m (47 ft 1 in); height 3.90 m (12 ft 9½ in); wing area 58.50 m² (629.71 sq ft)

G-EBYI was the personal aircraft of the Belgian financier Albert Loewenstein, this F.VIIA-3m being one of only three on the British register. It was badly damaged in a crash in July 1929 in Sudan.

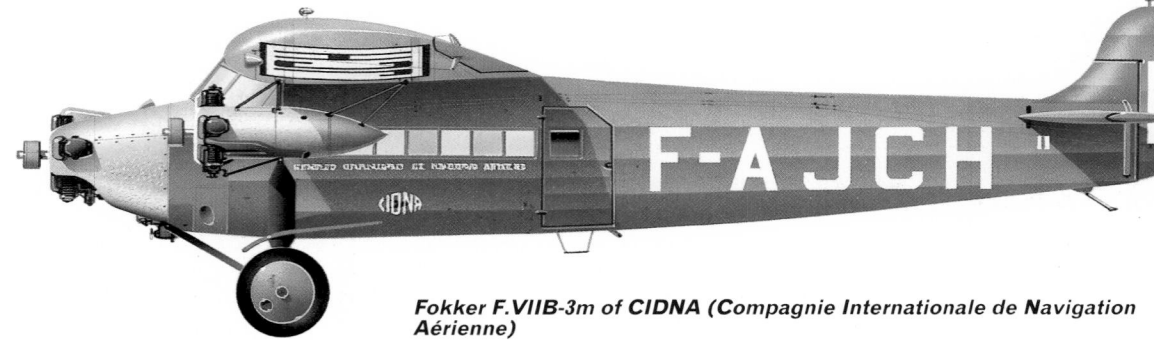

Fokker F.VIIB-3m of CIDNA (Compagnie Internationale de Navigation Aérienne)

Fokker F.VIII

Designed to meet a KLM (Royal Dutch Airlines) requirement for a larger aircraft than the F.VII single-engined series, the **Fokker F.VIII** flew in prototype form on 12 March 1927. While of similar general layout to its predecessors, the new aircraft had a wider fuselage capable of carrying 15 passengers and a crew of two. The nose contained a hinged baggage compartment, and the two 358-kW (480-hp) Gnome-Rhône Jupiter VI engines were slung beneath the wings.

The prototype and six production F.VIIIs were delivered to KLM in 1927-28; another was delivered to the Hungarian airline MALERT in 1928, and Manfred Weiss in Budapest built two more for MALERT under licence.

The KLM aircraft were subsequently re-engined, various aircraft being powered by 515-kW (690-hp) Wright R-1820 Cyclone or 373-kW (500-hp) Pratt & Whitney Wasp engines.

The only F.VIII to see service in military markings was the last Dutch production aircraft, sold by KLM to British Airways in 1936. It went to Sweden in 1939, and was subsequently donated to the Finnish air force, with whom it served in the Continuation War from 1941.

Specification
Type: commercial transport
Powerplant: two 358-kW (480-hp) Gnome-Rhône Jupiter VI 9-cylinder radial piston engines
Performance: maximum speed 200 km/h (124 mph); cruising speed 170 km/h (106 mph); service ceiling 5500 m (18,045 ft); range 1045 km (649 miles)
Weights: empty 3685 kg (8,124 lb); maximum take-off 5700 kg (12,566 lb)
Dimensions: span 23.00 m (75 ft 5½ in); length 16.75 m (54 ft 11½ in); height 4.20 m (13 ft 9¼ in); wing area 83.00 m² (893.43 sq ft)

The only two British-registered F.VIII airliners were bought from KLM in 1937 for cross-Channel services. G-AEPT had only a short career, being withdrawn in 1938.

Fokker F.XII

Another development of the F.VII/3m, but smaller than the F.IX, the **Fokker F.XII** prototype (PH-AFL) made its maiden flight at the beginning of 1930 and entered service on the KLM route to Batavia in March 1931. Ten more were built by Fokker, all for operation by KLM and its Far Eastern subsidiary KNILM, except for the final machine which was sold to Sweden and operated by AB Aerotransport as the *Värmland*.

The Dutch-operated F.XIIs maintained the routes to the Far East for two years, and were then switched to the European services connecting Amsterdam with London, Paris, Berlin and other principal cities. On the European runs the F.XIIs

An updated version of the famous F.VII series, the F.XII was powered by three Pratt & Whitney Wasp C radials, all of which were easily replaceable. However, this means of installation had considerable drag penalties.

carried a crew of two and 16 passengers, but on the Far East route only four passengers were carried in a fair degree of comfort on fully reclining seats.

The Danish Orlogsvaerftet built two F.XIIs under licence for the national airline DDL to operate on the Copenhagen-Berlin route. The second, delivered in May 1935, was designated **F.XIIM** and had some aerodynamic refinements resulting in improved performance.

Six Dutch F.XIIs were later sold to British operators, and in turn four of the British machines were re-sold to the Spanish government, which had already bought the last KLM-operated aircraft. All were flown in the Spanish Civil War and were lost during the course of the conflict.

Last survivors were the Swedish aircraft and the Danish F.XIIM, the first scrapped in 1946 and the second a year later.

Specification
Type: 16-passenger transport
Powerplant: three 317-kW (425-hp) Pratt & Whitney Wasp C 9-cylinder radial piston engines
Performance: maximum speed 230 km/h (143 mph); normal cruising speed 205 km/h (127 mph); service ceiling 3400 m (11,155 ft); range 1300 km (808 miles)
Weights: empty 4350 kg (9,590 lb); maximum take-off 7250 kg (15,984 lb)

Dimensions: span 23.02 m (75 ft 6¼ in); length 17.80 m (58 ft 4¾ in); height 4.72 m (15 ft 6 in); wing area 83.00 m² (893.43 sq ft)

Fokker F.XIV

The **Fokker F.XIV** of 1929 was built at the New Jersey factory as a seven/nine-passenger transport. Fuselage and wings were of normal Fokker design, although the upper fuselage decking was of corrugated duralumin. The major differences between this and other Fokker transports was that it had a parasol-type wing carried on struts above the fuselage, and a pilot's open cockpit behind the passenger cabin and beneath a cut-out in the wing trailing edge.

Variants
F.XIV: civil development with a 429-kW (575-hp) Pratt & Whitney Hornet radial engine
Y1C-XIV: designation of 20 examples of a military transport version of F-XIV procured by the US Army in 1931; powered by same engine as F-XIV; as

The high-set wing of the Fokker Y1C-14 made the type an ideal platform for tasks such as the training of aircrew in the techniques of parachuting.

with later versions described, in due course dropped Y1 prefix from designation and became simply **C-XIV**
Y1C-XIVA: designation of last aircraft delivered out of batch of 20, which was powered by a 429-kW (575-hp) Wright R-1820-7 Cyclone engine
Y1C-XIVB: redesignation following installation of a 391-kW (525-hp) Pratt & Whitney R-1690-5 Hornet engine
Y1C-15: conversion of ninth Y1C-XIV as an air ambulance able to transport four stretcher cases and medical attendant
Y1C-15A: redesignation of Y1C-15-air ambulance following installation of a 429-kW (575-hp) Wright R-1820 Cyclone engine

Specification
Fokker F.XIV
Type: seven/nine-passenger transport
Powerplant: one 391-kW (525-hp) Wright R-1750-3 9-cylinder radial piston engine
Performance: maximum speed 220 km/h (137 mph); normal cruising speed 187 km/h (116 mph); service ceiling 4420 m (14,500 ft); range 1110 km (690 miles)
Weights: empty 1971 kg (4,346 lb); maximum take-off 3266 kg (7,200 lb)
Dimensions: span 18.11 m (59 ft 5 in); length 13.18 m (43 ft 3 in); height 3.76 m (12 ft 4 in); wing area 51.19 m² (551.0 sq ft)

Fokker F.XVIII

A developed and enlarged version of the F.XII, the **Fokker F.XVIII** retained the same basic design with metal fuselage structure and a high-set cantilever wooden wing. The F.XVIII had rather better lines and a number of detail design improvements compared with earlier Fokker tri-motors.

Five F.XVIIIs were built in 1932 and all were put into service on the route from Amsterdam to Batavia in the Dutch East Indies. On this route to the East four passengers were accommodated in the main cabin in seats which converted for sleeping; the cabin also provided accommodation for the wireless operator and the navigator.

Several notable flights were made by F.XVIIIs over these routes. For example, PH-AIP *Pelikaan* (Pelican) carried the Christmas mail from Amsterdam to Batavia in December 1933 in a flying time of 73 hours 34 minutes; and in the

following year between 15 and 22 December PH-AIS *Snip* (Snipe), re-engined with Pratt & Whitney Wasp T1D1 radials, covered 10300 km (6,400 miles) from Amsterdam to Curaçao in a flight time of 55 hours 58 minutes carrying 100 kg (220 lb) of mail. The F.XVIIIs were withdrawn from the long-distance routes in 1935. PH-AIS was joined in the West Indies by PH-AIO *Oriol* and both remained in service until 1946. The *Oriol* was converted for military use during the war period and carried a defensive machine-gun.

Two F.XVIIIs were sold to the Czech national line CSA and operated the route from Prague to Berlin and Vienna, normally carrying 13 passengers. Another of the type was sold to a Palestine freight operator and the famous *Pelikaan* was bought in October 1936 by Air Tropic, a French company acting for the Spanish government, and it is believed that the *Pelikaan* ended its days on military liaison and transport duties during the Spanish Civil War.

Specification
Type: passenger transport
Powerplant: three 313-kW (420-hp) Pratt & Whitney Wasp C 9-cylinder radial piston engines
Performance: maximum speed 240 km/h (149 mph); normal cruising speed 210 km/h (130 mph); service ceiling 4800 m (15,750 ft); range 1820 km (1,131 miles)
Weights: empty 4623 kg (10,192 lb);

Built to the Platz pattern of steel-tube fuselage and wooden cantilever wing, the tri-motor F.XVIII was a descendent of the F.XII with a number of detail improvements.

maximum take-off 7850 kg (17,306 lb)
Dimensions: span 24.50 m (80 ft 4½ in); length 18.50 m (60 ft 8¼ in); wing area 84.00 m² (904.20 sq ft)

Fokker F.XX

The **Fokker F.XX** 12-passenger transport had an elliptical-section fuselage instead of the rectangular form of previous Fokker transports. The cantilever high wing was of wooden construction and the fuselage a steel-tube structure. Power was provided by three Wright Cyclone R-1820-F radial engines, one mounted in the nose and the other two carried on strut assemblies under the wings. The main landing gear units retracted rearwards into the engine nacelles. The F.XX was the first Fokker transport aircraft to have retractable landing gear, and the whole design showed much greater attention to aerodynamic refinement. Named *Zilvermeeuw* (Silver Gull) and registered PH-

AIZ, it was flown for the first time in 1933 and handed over to KLM for operation on services from Amsterdam to London and Berlin.

The F.XX was much more modern in design than previous Fokker high-wing monoplane transports, but the advent of the low-wing twin-engined Douglas DC-2 and DC-3 airliners soon rendered it obsolete and only a single example was built. It was later sold via Air Tropic to the Spanish Republican government and was used to maintain liaison between Madrid and Paris during 1937. Its ultimate fate is unknown.

Specification
Type: 12-passenger transport
Powerplant: three 477-kW (640-hp) Wright Cyclone R-1820-F 9-cylinder radial piston engines

Performance: maximum speed 305 km/h (190 mph); normal cruising speed 250 km/h (155 mph); service ceiling 6200 m (20,340 ft); range 1410 km (876 miles)
Weights: empty 6455 kg (14,231 lb); maximum take-off 9400 kg (20,723 lb)
Dimensions: span 25.70 m (84 ft 3¾ in); length 16.70 m (54 ft 9½ in);

A true mixture of old and new, the F.XX adhered to the traditional tri-motor configuration and thick-section wing, though combined with improved features for lower drag.

height 4.80 m (15 ft 9 in); wing area 96.00 m² (1,033.37 sq ft)

Fokker F.XXII and F.XXXVI

The first of these designs to appear bore the later designation, the sole **Fokker F.XXXVI** (PH-AJA) making its first

flight on 22 June 1934. Largest of the Fokker transports, it was a high-wing cantilever monoplane with fixed landing gear and powered by four 559-kW (750-hp) Wright Cyclone radial engines mounted forward of the leading edge. Of typical Fokker construction, the F.XXXVI provided accommodation for a crew of four, and 32 passengers in four eight-

seat cabins. As an alternative 16 passengers could be carried in sleeping accommodation. Operated on European routes by KLM from March 1935, it was sold in 1939 to Scottish Aviation of Prestwick and was flown from there as a crew and navigational trainer (registered G-AFZR) until scrapped in 1940.

The **F.XXII** closely resembled the F.XXXVI but was somewhat smaller, accommodating 22 passengers. The prototype (PH-AJP) flew in early 1935 and was followed by two production machines. All three were delivered to KLM, the prototype in March and the other two in May 1935. One aircraft crashed on 14 July 1935, but the other two operated European routes until they were sold in the UK, PH-AJR becoming G-AFXR in August 1939 on joining British American Air Services, and PH-AJP being re-registered G-AFZP in the follow-

ing month when it was acquired by Scottish Aviation. Impressed for RAF service as HM159 and HM160 in October 1941, the two aircraft were used for transport and crew training. HM159 caught fire in the air and was lost in the Highlands, but HM160 was returned to Scottish Aviation post-war under its previous civil registration. It flew between Prestwick

and Belfast for a time before being grounded finally at the end of 1947.

A fourth F.XXII was built for Swedish AB Aerotransport and delivered in March 1935. Named *Lappland*, it flew a regular schedule between Malmö and Amsterdam until destroyed in an accident at Malmö in June 1936.

Specification
Fokker F.XXII
Type: 22-passenger transport
Powerplant: four 373-kW (500-hp) Pratt & Whitney Wasp T1D1 9-cylinder radial piston engines
Performance: maximum speed

285 km/h (177 mph); normal cruising speed 215 km/h (134 mph); service ceiling 4900 m (16,075 ft); range 1350 km (839 miles)
Weights: empty 8100 kg (17,857 lb); maximum take-off 13000 kg (28,660 lb)
Dimensions: span 30.00 m (98 ft 5 in); length 21.52 m (70 ft 7¼ in); height 4.60 m (15 ft 1¼ in); wing area 30.00 m² (1,339.35 sq ft)

The smaller brother of the F.XXXVI, the F.XXII was better matched to European requirements, but still outmoded in concept and structure.

Appearing at about the same time as the Douglas DC series, the F.XXXVI had good payload capability, but was structurally and aerodynamically inferior to the new American airliners.

Fokker G.I

In November 1936 the prototype **Fokker G.I** heavy fighter caused a sensation when exhibited at the Paris Air Show, which in those days did not have a flying display but only a static exhibition in the Grand Palais. The concept of a twin-boom twin-engined fighter, later adopted for the Lockheed P-38 Lightning, was revolutionary at the time, and the new aircraft was the centre of much critical appraisal.

After the Show, the G.I was taken to Eindhoven/Welschap airfield, from where its first flight was made on 16 March 1937. The G.I was then powered by two 559-kW (750-hp) Hispano-Suiza 80-82 counter-rotating radial engines, but problems with these prototype units resulted in a change to similarly rated Pratt & Whitney SB4-G Twin Wasp Juniors during reconstruction, after the G.I suffered brake failure and rammed a hangar at Schiphol on 4 July 1937.

Demonstrations had already been given to the Netherlands army air corps at Soesterberg, and considerable interest was shown, resulting at the end of the year in an order for 36 aircraft to be designated **G.IA.** In order to ease the spares situation, it was stipulated that these must have Bristol Mercury VIII engines, which were also to power the T.V bomber and D.XXI fighter already on order for the air corps.

This decision brought delay because although G.IA production began immediately there was a hold-up in the supply of engines. Thus the first production aircraft to fly, actually the second of the batch, became airborne only on 11 April 1939. It remained with the makers for production testing and modifications, and the first aircraft was delivered to Soesterberg on 10 July 1939.

Possibilities of export orders followed the aircraft's debut at Paris and a number of foreign pilots came to Fokker to fly and evaluate the **G.IB** export version. Orders were placed by Finland (26), Estonia (9), Sweden (18) and Republican Spain (12), while a licence-production agreement was in negotiation with Denmark and another with Manfred Weiss in Hungary. The Dutch embargo on weapons exports before World War II

killed the Spanish order, but the Finnish batch was under construction when war broke out and a ban was then placed on its export. After lengthy negotiations a contract was drawn up to permit the G.IB's export on 17 April 1940, by which time 12 had been completed, apart from armament.

When Germany attacked the Netherlands on 10 May 1940, 23 G.Is were in service: 12 with the 4th Fighter Group at Alkmaar and 11 with the 3rd Fighter Group at Rotterdam/Waalhaven. The G.Is were successful in destroying several Junkers Ju 52/3ms during the early stages of the German invasion, but by the fifth day, when Dutch resistance ended, only a single example remained airworthy.

The Germans occupied the Fokker factory, ordering completion of the 12

G.Is intended for Finland, and these were used subsequently by the Luftwaffe as fighter trainers. Test flights from the factory were made under German supervision, but on 5 May 1941 two Dutch pilots succeeded in evading an escorting German-flown G.I and escaped to England. Their G.IB was taken to the Royal Aircraft Establishment, Farnborough, for examination, and used subsequently by Phillips and Powis (Miles Aircraft) at Reading for research into wooden construction.

A total of 62 G.Is is believed to have been built, and none survived the war.

Specification
Fokker G.IA
Type: two/three-seat heavy fighter/close-support aircraft
Powerplant: two 619-kW (830-hp)

Bristol Mercury VIII 9-cylinder radial piston engines
Performance: maximum speed 475 km/h (295 mph) at 2750 m (9,020 ft); cruising speed 355 km/h (221 mph) at 2750 m (9,020 ft); climb to 5000 m (16,405 ft) in 8 minutes 0 seconds; service ceiling 9300 m (30,500 ft); range 1400 km (870 miles)
Weights: empty 3360 kg (7,410 lb); maximum take-off 4800 kg (10,582 lb)
Dimensions: span 17.15 m (56 ft 3¼ in); length 11.50 m (37 ft 9 in); height 3.40 m (11 ft 2 in); wing area 38.30 m² (412.26 sq ft)
Armament: eight 7.9-mm (0.31-in) forward-firing machine-guns in nose and one similar gun on pivoted mount in tail cone, plus up to 400 kg (882 lb) of bombs

Fokker G.IB of the Luchtvaartafdeling (Dutch air force) in May 1940.

Fokker G.IA of the 3e or 4e Ja.V.A. (3rd or 4th Fighter Squadron), Luchtvaartafdeling, based at Waalhaven or Bergen in May 1940 (dashed line: lower edge of port boom, removed to show detail of gondola).

Fokker S.11 Instructor

Although the Fokker factory at Amsterdam was practically destroyed in World War II, its technical staff was maintained virtually intact. The factory was rebuilt in the space of a year after the end of hostilities and a simple low-wing trainer, the **Fokker S.11 Instructor**, was selected as the company's first post-war product. The S.11 prototype made its maiden flight during 1947. A cantilever low-wing monoplane, basically of metal construction but with some fabric covering, it had a braced tail unit, fixed tailwheel landing gear and power provided by an Avco Lycoming O-435-A engine.

The Royal Netherlands air force bought 40, Israel 41 and Italy's Macchi company built 150 under licence, designated **Macchi 416** in Italian air force service. Meanwhile, Fokker Industria Aeronautica SA was established at Rio de Janeiro's Galeao Airport in 1954. The first Brazilian-produced S.11 was accepted by the Brazilian air force on 29 December 1955 and a total of 100 was built.

The **S.12** with tricycle landing gear was also manufactured in Brazil, 50 being delivered. Little modification was needed to accommodate the new wheel arrangement as the wing had been stressed to support the gear in either position.

The 40 Instructors of the Royal Netherlands air force provided elementary flying training with No. 5 Instruction Squadron at Gilze-Rijen. With the introduction of more modern primary trainers in the 1970s, many S.11s were released to the civil market.

Specification
Fokker S.11
Type: two/three-seat primary trainer
Powerplant: one 142-kW (190-hp) Avco Lycoming O-435-A flat-six piston engine
Performance: maximum speed 210 km/h (130 mph) at sea level; cruising speed 165 km/h (103 mph); service ceiling 4000 m (13,125 ft); range 695 km (432 miles)
Weights: empty 810 kg (1,786 lb); maximum take-off 1100 kg (2,425 lb)
Dimensions: span 11.00 m (36 ft 1 in); length 8.15 m (26 ft 8¾ in); height 2.40 m (7 ft 10½ in); wing area 18.50 m² (199.14 sq ft)

A Fokker Instructor of the Dutch air force practising formation flying. The large cockpit enclosure permitted the installation of a 'jump seat' behind the two front seats.

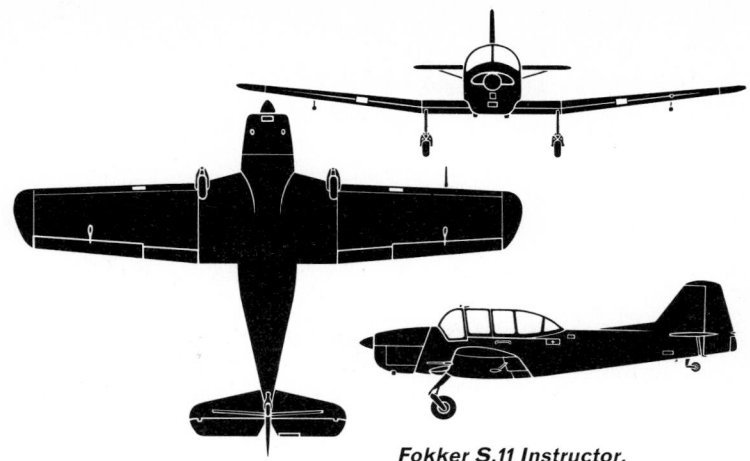

Fokker S.11 Instructor.

Fokker S.14 Mach-Trainer

The **Fokker S.14 Mach-Trainer** secured its place in aviation history by being the first Fokker-designed jet aircraft, the first jet-propelled trainer designed as such, and the first aircraft of its type to enter production.

The low-wing all-metal S.14 was powered by a Rolls-Royce Derwent turbojet with a bifurcated inlet in the nose. The outlet was in the extreme tail, aft of the horizontal tail surfaces, which were set somewhat aft of the fin and rudder. The nosewheel of the tricycle landing gear retracted forwards into the underside of the nose while the main units retracted inwards into the undersides of the wings. Pupil and instructor were seated side-by-side under a short, broad raised canopy set well forward on the circular-section fuselage. Martin-Baker ejector seats were standard.

Test pilot Gerben Sonderman made the first test flight on 19 May 1951. On a second flight during the same day the landing gear failed and the prototype was damaged in the subsequent belly-landing. However, the aircraft was repaired and displayed at the 1951 Paris Salon in June of that year.

A series of 20 S.14s was ordered by the Royal Dutch air arm, the Koninklike Luchtmacht, the first being flown initially on 15 January 1955. The prototype bore the serial K-1 and was powered by a Derwent V engine, while the production machines were serialled from L-1 to L-20 and had Derwent VIIIs. The S.14s served at four air stations: Twenthe, Ypenburg, Gilze-Rijen and Soesterberg. Aircraft L-4 was demonstrated in the USA during 1955, but crashed on 20 October that year at Hagerstown, Maryland, killing Gerben Sonderman. Aircraft L-8 took part in the London-Paris air race, known as the Arch to Arc since it started at Marble Arch and ended at the Arc de Triomphe. The last two S.14s were withdrawn from Dutch service on 29 March 1965. Serialled L-17 and L-19, they are preserved at the Museums at Schiphol and Soesterberg respectively.

The original K-1 prototype was re-engined with a 2313-kg (5,100-lb) thrust Rolls-Royce Nene 3 engine in 1953 and given the specially selected civil registration PH-XIV on 24 October 1960. It was then used by the Lucht en Ruuimtevaart Laboratorium (Dutch National Aeronautical and Space Laboratory) until scrapped on 4 March 1966.

Specification
Type: two-seat advanced jet trainer
Powerplant: one 1575-kg (3,472-lb) thrust Rolls-Royce Derwent VIII turbojet
Performance: maximum speed 730 km/h (454 mph); normal cruising speed 570 km/h (354 mph); service ceiling 11200 m (36,745 ft); range 965 km (600 miles)
Weights: empty equipped 3765 kg (8,300 lb); maximum take-off 5350 kg (11,795 lb)
Dimensions: span 12.00 m (39 ft 4½ in); length 13.30 m (43 ft 7½ in); height 4.70 m (15 ft 5 in); wing area 31.80 m² (342.30 sq ft)

The second and third production examples of the Fokker S.14 Mach-Trainer show off the type's unexceptional but highly practical lines.

Fokker S.IX

Designed as a replacement for the S.IV basic trainer, the **Fokker S.IX** was suitable also for aerobatic training. The S.IX was built in two versions. The first, designated **S.IX/1**, was powered by an Armstrong Siddeley Genet Major radial engine. First flown in 1937, the type was used by the Netherlands army air force from 1938 to 1940 as a standard basic trainer, and a number of S.IX/1s were built by the Dutch manufacturer Kromhout. The second version, designated **S.IX/2**, was powered by a 125-kW (168-hp) Menasco Buccaneer inline engine. A total of 27 S.IX/2s was ordered for the Netherlands navy air force, but only 15 had been delivered when production was terminated by the German invasion. Army orders for the S.IX/1 totalled 24, but there is some uncertainty about whether or not all of these were built and delivered, for, according to Fokker records, only 20 were completed.

Like many lightplanes used in service training schools, in the desperate circumstances which existed at the time of the German invasion the S.IXs were called upon to carry out roles for which they had never been intended, and S.IXs of both services were in use for liaison and evacuation duties until the end of Dutch resistance.

Fokker built three S.IX/1s after World War II had ended, these being powered by Kromhout-built Genet Major engines.

Specification
Fokker S.IX/1
Type: two-seat primary trainer
Powerplant: one 123-kW (165-hp) Armstrong Siddeley Genet Major 5-cylinder radial piston engine
Performance: maximum speed 185 km/h (115 mph); cruising speed 150 km/h (93 mph); service ceiling 4300 m (14,110 ft); range 710 km (441 miles)
Weights: empty 695 kg (1,532 lb); maximum take-off 975 kg (2,150 lb)

Dimensions: span 9.55 m (31 ft 4 in); length 7.65 m (25 ft 1 in); height 2.90 m (9 ft 6 in); wing area 23.00 m² (247.58 sq ft)

Undistinguished but useful, the S.IX/1 was used in small numbers by the Dutch air force between 1938 and 1940, mainly as a primary trainer but also for limited aerobatics.

Fokker T.IVA

One of the ugliest Fokker designs, the **Fokker T.IVA** twin-engined torpedo-bomber/reconnaissance floatplane was a progressive development of the 1927 **T.IV**, of which 18 had been built for service at home and in the Netherlands East Indies. Portugal also acquired three of these aircraft.

The T.IVA differed from its predecessor mainly in powerplant, having Wright Cyclone SR-1820-F2 radial engines in place of the T.IV's 336-kW (450-hp) Lorraine-Dietrich W-type engines. The more-powerful units required a strengthened airframe; at the same time an enclosed cockpit, as well as bow, dorsal and ventral gun positions, were installed. Twelve of these new aircraft were ordered for the Netherlands East Indies naval air force, and in 1936 the surviving T.IVs were brought up to T.IVA standard.

Coastal and sea reconnaissance operations in the Netherlands East Indies were still being flown when the Japanese invasion began in 1942, and the T.IVA was also used for air-sea rescue work, proving to be reliable and seaworthy.

Specification
Fokker T.IVA
Type: four-seat torpedo-bomber/reconnaissance aircraft
Powerplant: two 559-kW (750-hp) Wright Cyclone SR-1820-F2 9-cylinder radial piston engines
Performance: maximum speed 260 km/h (162 mph) at 800 m (2,625 ft); cruising speed 215 km/h (134 mph); service ceiling 5900 m (19,355 ft); range 1560 km (969 miles)
Weights: empty 4665 kg (10,285 lb); maximum take-off 7200 kg (15,873 lb)
Dimensions: span 26.20 m (85 ft 11½ in); length 17.60 m (57 ft 8¾ in); height 6.00 m (19 ft 8¼ in); wing area 97.80 m² (1,052.74 sq ft)
Armament: single 7.9-mm (0.31-in) machine-guns in nose, dorsal and ventral positions, plus up to 800 kg (1,764 lb) of bombs internally or one torpedo externally beneath the fuselage

The T.IV was a reliable and long-lived reconnaissance, bombing and torpedo-dropping platform. It served with some distinction in the Dutch East Indies.

Fokker T.V

The Netherlands possessed only one type of medium bomber when the Germans attacked on 10 May 1940: the **Fokker T.V.** Consideration had already been given to its replacement by the T.IX, but only the prototype of the latter had been completed. No T.V prototype was built, the first to fly on 16 October 1937 being one of a batch of 16 ordered for the Netherlands air force earlier that year. The rather ungainly looking aircraft went into service the following year, with the only Dutch bomber squadron, having rather poor stability and proving something of a handful to fly. The type was reasonably well protected by machine-guns and its bombload was carried internally.

All 16 aircraft had been delivered before the outbreak of hostilities, but on the day of the German invasion only nine were serviceable. Nevertheless they fought valiantly, destroying almost 30 German aircraft on the ground at Waalhaven airfield and making heavy attacks on the bridges over the Maas before being destroyed (two were shot down by Dutch gunners), and only one T.V survived at the time of the Dutch surrender.

Specification
Type: five-seat medium bomber
Powerplant: two 690-kW (925-hp) Bristol Pegasus XXVI 9-cylinder radial piston engines
Performance: maximum speed 415 km/h (258 mph) at 3050 m (10,000 ft); cruising speed 320 km/h (199 mph); service ceiling 7700 m (25,260 ft); range 1630 km (1,013 miles)
Weights: empty 4640 kg (10,229 lb); maximum take-off 7235 kg (15,950 lb)
Dimensions: span 21.00 m (68 ft 10¾ in); length 16.00 m (52 ft 6 in); height 5.00 m (16 ft 5 in); wing area 66.20 m² (712.59 sq ft)
Armament: twin 7.9-mm (0.31-in) machine-guns in nose and similar single guns in dorsal, ventral, lateral and tail positions, plus up to 1000 kg (2,205 lb) of bombs

The T.V was the best bomber available to the Dutch in 1940. It sported the odd feature of the co-pilot doubling as the dorsal gunner.

Fokker T.VIII-W

Designed to Netherlands naval air service specifications for a torpedo-bomber/reconnaissance aircraft suitable for home and the Netherlands East Indies service, the **Fokker T.VIII-W** floatplane was built in three versions: the **T.VIII-Wg** of mixed wood and metal construction, the **T.VIII-Wm** which was all metal and the **T.VIII-Wc**, a larger version of mixed construction.

An initial order for five aircraft was placed, and all were completed by June 1939, when a further batch of 26 was ordered, most of them intended as replacements for T.IVs in the East Indies, but none was delivered there. A total of 36 T.VIII-Ws was built, these comprising 19 T.VIII-Wgs, five T.VIII-Wcs and 12 T.VIII-Wms, the difference of five being accounted for by a Finnish order which was not delivered. These were of the T.VIII-Wc variant which had a 1.83 m (6 ft) longer fuselage, 2.01 m (6 ft 7 in) increase in wing span, an additional 8.00 m² (86.11 sq ft) of wing area, and power provided by 664-kW (890-hp) Bristol Mercury XI engines. In the event, the Fokker factory was overrun by the Germans before completion of this order, but the aircraft were finished and subsequently delivered to Germany along with 20 ex-Netherlands navy aircraft. A one-off landplane variant, the **T.VIII-L** built for Finland, was also seized by the Germans.

Meanwhile, eight T.VIII-Ws had been flown to England along with other Dutch floatplanes on 14 May 1940, and on 1 June 1940 No. 320 (Dutch) Squadron RAF was formed at Pembroke Dock, to operate the T.VIII-Ws on convoy escort work. These aircraft carried RAF markings, plus a small Dutch triangle badge. Three of the aircraft were lost, and with no spares available the remaining aircraft were flown to Felixstowe for storage. They were joined by another in May 1941, when four Dutchmen escaped from Amsterdam and brought their T.VIII-W down on the sea near Broadstairs.

German navy operations with their group of T.VIII-Ws were confined mostly to patrol work in the Mediterranean.

Specification
Fokker T.VIII-Wg
Type: three-seat torpedo-bomber/reconnaissance floatplane
Powerplant: two 336-kW (450-hp) Wright Whirlwind R-975-E3 9-cylinder radial piston engines
Performance: maximum speed 285 km/h (177 mph); cruising speed 220 km/h (137 mph); service ceiling 6800 m (22,310 ft); range 2750 km (1,709 miles)
Weights: empty 3100 kg (6,834 lb); maximum take-off 5000 kg (11,023 lb)
Dimensions: span 18.00 m (59 ft 0½ in); length 13.00 m (42 ft 8 in); height 5.00 m (16 ft 5 in); wing area 44.00 m² (473.63 sq ft)
Armament: one 7.9-mm (0.31-in) forward-firing machine-gun on port side of fuselage and one similar single gun on pivoted mount in rear cockpit, plus up to 605 kg (1,334 lb) of bombs, or one torpedo

Fokker T.VIII-Wg of Groep Vliegtuigen 4, Netherlands air force, operating from the Westeindermeer.

Fokker F27 Friendship
to
Found FBA-2/100 Centenniel

Fokker F27 Friendship

Fokker had produced some excellent airliners during the 'between wars' years, and with the end of World War II lost little time in formulating the design of a new medium-range aircraft in this category. The company's design study of 1950 was for a 32-seat transport to be powered by two Rolls-Royce Dart turboprop engines. Known as the **P.275** project, it was enlarged slightly and modified to incorporate a circular-section pressurised fuselage by 1952, when Dutch government backing was sought for its construction and development.

The type was then designated **Fokker F27**, and the first of two prototypes (PH-NIV) made its maiden flight on 24 November 1955, powered by two Dart 507 turboprops. Of high-wing monoplane configuration, the F27 has a pressurised fuselage, retractable tricycle landing gear and accommodation for 28 passengers. The second prototype, with Dart Mk 511 engines and its fuselage lengthened by 0.91 m (3 ft) to seat 32 passengers, was flown on 31 January 1957. Between the initial flights of these two prototypes, Fokker concluded an agreement with the Fairchild Engine and Airplane Corporation for the latter to manufacture and market the F27 in North America, where it was known as the **Fairchild F-27**.

Fokker's first **F27 Friendship** entered service with Aer Lingus in December 1958, but Fairchild had been a little quicker off the mark, its F-27 entering service with West Coast Airlines three months earlier. The American company had modified the interior layout to seat 40, increased the fuel capacity and made provision for weather

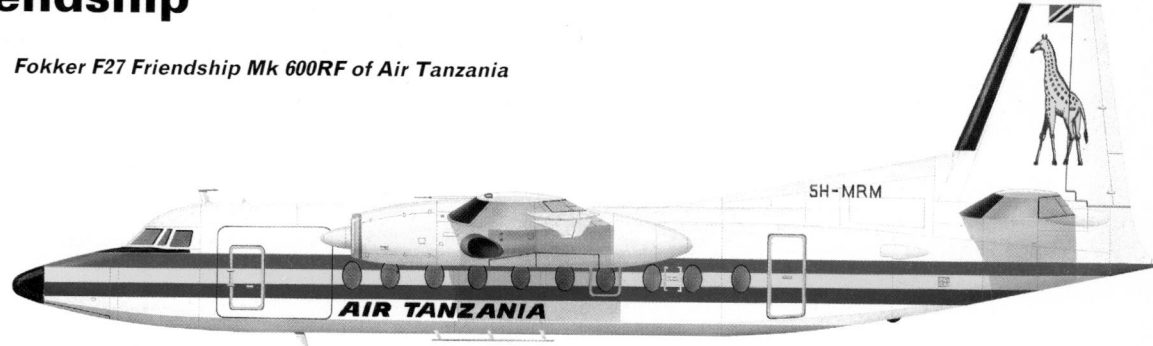

Fokker F27 Friendship Mk 600RF of Air Tanzania

radar in a lengthened nose; Fokker adopted similar improvements at a later date. The initial Dutch production version was designated **F27 Mk 100** (Fairchild F-27), and was powered by two 1279-kW (1,715-shp) Rolls-Royce Dart RDa.6 Mk 514-7 turboprops. It was followed by the similar **F27 Mk 200 (Fairchild F-27A)** with 1529-kW (2,050-shp) Dart RDa.7 Mk 532-7 engines. Both airliners had standard accommodation for 40 passengers, but a high-density arrangement made it possible to seat 52. An executive version of the Mk 200 was available with the interior design to customer requirements.

Subsequent versions include the **F27 Mk 300 Combiplane (Fairchild F-27B)**, a passenger/cargo aircraft with Mk 100 powerplant, a reinforced cabin floor, cargo tie-down rings and a large cargo door forward of the wing on the port side. A similar Combiplane version of the Mk 200 had the designation **F27 Mk 400**, but no equivalent version was

produced by Fairchild in America. Fokker next developed a lengthened fuselage (by 1.50 m/4 ft 11 in) variant of the Mk 200. Designated **F27 Mk 500**, this failed to appeal initially to airline operators, but 15 were acquired by the French government for service with the nation's Postale de Nuit. Friendship Mk 500s now in service with airlines have standard accommodation for 52 passengers, with high-density seating for 60. Fairchild in America produced its own stretched variant, the **FH-227**.

The last production version was the **F27 Mk 600**, combining the Mk 200 fuselage without the reinforced cabin floor but with the cargo door of the Mk 300/400 Combiplanes. The **F27 Mk 600** introduced an optional roller-track quick-change interior so that the type could be used for passenger/cargo services. Other versions included the **F27 Mk 400M** and **F27 Mk 500M** military aircraft, an F27 Mk 400M aerial-survey version and an **F27 Maritime** suitable for coastal patrol, fishery protection, and search and rescue. Late production aircraft had an updated flight deck and cabin interior. Manufacture was shared by Dassault-Breguet (France), MBB (Germany) and SABCA (Belgium). When production was terminated in 1986 in favour of the Fokker 50, the company had sold 581 F27s along-

In addition to the large number of Friendships in service with airlines, many serve with air arms in a staff and VIP transport role. This aircraft wears the colours of the Côte d'Ivoire air force.

side 205 Fairchild-built F-27/FH-227 variants. In mid-1991 Fokker stated that around 450 F27s were still in service and that the highest-time aircraft had made some 80,000 flights.

Specification
Fokker F27 Mk 200
Type: short/medium-range transport
Powerplant: two Rolls-Royce Dart Mk 536-7R turboprops, each with a maximum take-off rating of 1730 ekW (2,320 eshp)
Performance: normal cruising speed 480 km/h (298 mph) at 6095 m (20,000 ft); service ceiling 8990 m (29,500 ft); range with 44 passengers and fuel reserves 1926 km (1,197 miles)
Weights: empty operating 12148 kg (26,781 lb); maximum take-off 20410 kg (44,996 lb)
Dimensions: span 29 m (95 ft 1¾ in); length 23.56 m (77 ft 3½ in); height 8.5 m (27 ft 10½ in); wing area 70 m² (753.5 sq ft)

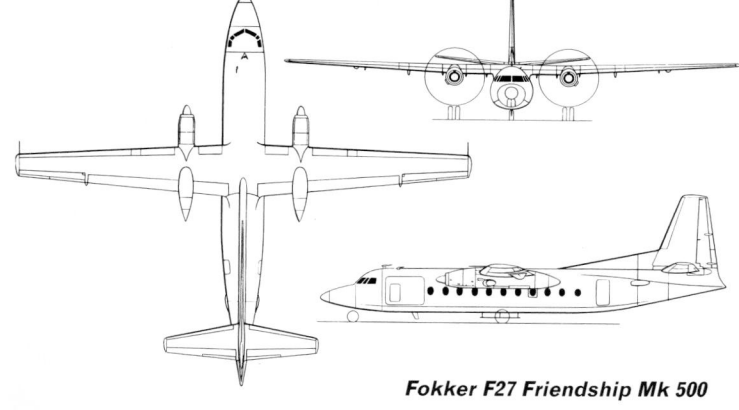

Fokker F27 Friendship Mk 500

Fokker F28 Fellowship

Fokker's experience with the F27 showed a requirement for a higher-performance airliner of slightly greater capacity, and in 1960 the company began design studies for such an aircraft. First details of the new **Fokker F28 Fellowship** were released in April 1962, and, with financial backing from the Netherlands government and risk-sharing support from MBB in West Germany and Shorts in the UK, a decision was made in 1964 to begin development and production of this new airliner.

Of cantilever low/mid-wing monoplane configuration with a circular-section fuselage, a T-tail unit with swept surfaces and retractable tricycle landing gear, the F28 was designed for a power-plant comprising two Rolls-Royce RB183 turbofan engines. The first of three prototypes (PH-JHG) made its maiden flight on 9 May 1967, and certification and delivery of the first production aircraft was achieved on 24 February 1969. This initial **F28 Mk 1000** short-fuselage version could seat 55 to 65 passengers and was powered by two 4468-kg (9,850-lb) thrust RB183-2 Mk 555-15 turbofans. It was available optionally as the **F28 Mk 1000C** for all-cargo or mixed passenger/

cargo operations with a large cargo door incorporated in the port side of the forward fuselage, aft of the standard passenger door.

The generally similar **F28 Mk 2000** differed only in having the fuselage lengthened by 2.21 m (7 ft 3 in) to accommodate a maximum of 79 passengers. Later production versions were the **F28 Mk 3000** and **F28 Mk 4000** with the fuselage lengths of the Mks 1000 and 2000 respectively.

The F28 Mk 3000 was offered with a 15-seat executive interior, and the F28 Mk 4000 has maximum seating capacity for 85 passengers. Sales reached 241 before the Fellowship gave way to the Fokker 100 on the production line in 1987. In mid-1991 Fokker stated that over 200 F28s were still in service and at least half of these were expected to be hush-kitted to Category 3 standard beginning in 1994, enabling them to continue in service for another 15 years.

Variants
F28 Mk 5000: proposed version combining F28 Mk 3000 fuselage with increased-span slatted wings; not built
F28 Mk 6000: version combining lengthened fuselage of F28 Mk 2000 with increased-span slatted wings; two examples only, one a conversion of the first F28 prototype
F28 Mk 6600: proposed version of F28 Mk 6000 with a 2.21-m (7-ft 3-in) fuselage 'stretch' to accommodate up to 100 passengers; not built

Specification
Fokker F28 Mk 3000
Type: short/medium-range airliner
Powerplant: two 4491-kg (9,900-lb) thrust Rolls-Royce RB183-2 Mk 555-15P turbofans

Fokker F28 Fellowship Mk 1000 of AeroPeru (Empresa de Transporte Aero del Peru)

Performance: maximum cruising speed 843 km/h (524 mph) at 7000 m (22,965 ft); economic cruising speed 678 km/h (421 mph) at 9150 m (30,020 ft); maximum cruising altitude 10670 m (35,005 ft); range with maximum fuel reserves and 65 passengers 2743 km (1,704 miles)
Weights: empty operating 16780 kg (36,994 lb); maximum take-off 33110 kg (72,995 lb)
Dimensions: span 25.07 m (82 ft 3 in); length 27.4 m (89 ft 10¾ in); height 8.47 m (27 ft 9½ in); wing area 79 m² (850.38 sq ft)

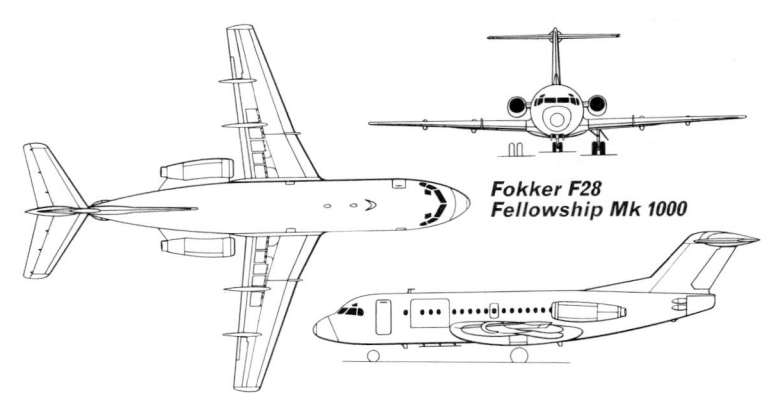

Fokker F28 Fellowship Mk 1000

Fokker 50

During celebrations held in November 1983 to mark the 25th anniversary of the F27 entering airline service, Fokker announced the launch of a 50-seat follow-on to be known as the **Fokker 50**. Based on the proven F27 airframe, but fitted with more fuel-efficient engines, six-bladed 'quiet' propellers, improved aerodynamics, a redesigned cockpit incorporating digital avionics and a new cabin interior, the external differences include extra windows, twin-nosewheel landing gear and upturned wingtips. Much use is made of lighter composite materials, and F50 commonality with the F27 is only 20 per cent. Production is shared with Dassault, Fuji Heavy Industries, Deutsche Airbus, SABCA, Dowty

Rotol and Pratt & Whitney Canada with final assembly, systems integration and flight test carried out by Fokker at Schiphol. The first two prototypes were conversions of F27 airframes, with the first (PH-OSO), flying on 28 December 1985 followed by (PH-OSI) on 30 April 1986. The first production aircraft (PH-DMO) flew on 13 February 1987 and first delivery made (to DLT), on 7 August 1987. By mid-1991 Fokker held firm orders from 18 customers for 132 Fokker 50s, and had delivered 116. The standard production variant is the 46/50-seat **Fokker 50-100** and the current build rate is 30 aircraft per year.

Variants
Fokker 50-200: proposed 68-seat version with fuselage stretched by 3 m (9 ft 9 in) ahead of the wing and 1.5 m

(4 ft 11 in) to the rear, making it the biggest turboprop airliner available or planned; originally offered with two PW130 engines, and with further improvements now developed into Series 400
Fokker 50-300: basically a Series 100 but fitted with PW127A engines offering better performance in hot and high conditions
Fokker 50-400: evolved from stretched Series 200, but currently offered with uprated PW127B engines; first aircraft could be available in 1994; all three versions (100/300/400) can be fitted with three or four passenger and cargo doors; a freight door 1.3 m (51 in) wide by 1.65 m (65 in) high installed on the port side fuselage aft of the wing is also available; no sales to date

Fokker Maritime Enforcer Mk 2: based on the Fokker 50-100 and powered with PW125B engines; offered as a cost-effective anti-submarine and anti-surface-unit warfare, and maritime patrol aircraft; equipped with sophisticated avionics including search radar, infra-red detection system, plus MAD, ESM and acoustic processing systems; could be armed with sonobuoys, torpedoes, depth charges and anti-shipping missiles such as Harpoon; endurance is 10 hours with a medium fuel and weapons load; no sales to date

Specification
Fokker 50-100
Type: 46-58 seat regional airliner
Powerplant: two Pratt & Whitney Canada PW125B turboprops, each with a maximum rating of 1864 kW (2,500 eshp)
Performance: normal cruising speed 522 km/h (325 mph); service ceiling 7620 m (25,000 ft); range with 50 passengers 2631 km (1,635 miles)
Weights: empty 12570 kg (27,710 lb); maximum take-off 18990 kg (41,865 lb)
Dimensions: span 29 m (95 ft 2 in); length 25.2 m (82 ft 10 in); height 8.3 m (27 ft 3 in); wing area 70 m² (753.5 sq ft)

The Fokker 50 is a follow-on to the hugely successful F27, representing a thorough re-working of the basic design using modern technology throughout. The most important change is the adoption of the PW125 turboprop with six-bladed propeller for quiet, efficient operation.

Fokker 100

When Fokker announced a successor to the F27 in November 1983, they also launched a similar follow-on to the Fellowship jet airliner. Derived from the proven F28 Mk 4000 airframe, the new aircraft was designated the Fokker 100 roughly reflecting the number of passenger seats offered. Re-engined with new-

technology fuel-efficient Rolls-Royce Tay turbofans and with a longer fuselage and redesigned and extended wings, other features include modernised systems incorporating a 'glass cockpit' and a revised cabin interior. Production is shared with Deutsche Airbus, Shorts, Grumman, Rolls-Royce and Dowty Rotol, with assembly and flight testing carried out by Fokker at Schiphol. IPTN of Indonesia also supply components.

The F100 flight test programme involved two prototypes, the first (PH-MKH) making its maiden flight on 30 November 1986 followed by the second (PH-MKC) on 25 February 1987. Certification of the Tay 620-15 powered version was achieved in November 1987 and first customer delivery was made to Swissair in February 1988. The uprated Tay 650 version, ordered by US Air was certificated in July 1989 and delivered to the

airline the same month. By mid-1991 Fokker had received orders for 232 F100s and had delivered 70. Options available on Tay 650 aircraft from 1993 include a higher gross weight of 45810 kg (101,000 lb) and an integral wing centre-section fuel tank giving improvements in range between 160 and 450 km (100 and 280 miles). Another option available from 1994 will be a quick-change version equipped with a cargo door 3.4 by 1.9 m (134 by 76 in) installed on the port side of the fuselage ahead of the wing, together with a specially designed cabin interior. Conversion time (by three men) is claimed to be 20 minutes, enabling 88 passengers to be carried by day and an 11,500 kg (25,000 lb) payload by night over 2800 km (1,500 miles).

Specification
Fokker 100
Type: 107-seat regional jet airliner
Powerplant: two 6849 kg (15,100 lb) Rolls-Royce Tay 650-15 turbofans
Performance: normal cruising speed 837 km/h (520 mph); service ceiling 10670 m (35,000 ft); range with 107 passengers 2956 km (1,836 miles)
Weights: empty 24375 kg (53,740 lb); maximum take-off 43090 kg (95,000 lb)
Dimensions: span 28 m (92 ft 1 in); length 35.5 m (116 ft 6 in); height 8.5 m (27 ft 10 in); wing area 93.5 m² (1,006.4 sq ft)

Fokker's reworking of the F28 into the Fokker 100 was more radical than the change from F27 to Fokker 50, involving a considerable fuselage stretch and uprated engines. The type has achieved outstanding sales, including a batch of six for Iran.

Folland 43/37

Folland Aircraft Ltd had its foundations in February 1936 at Hamble, Hampshire, when British Marine Aircraft Ltd was formed with the intention of producing the Sikorsky S-42A flying-boat under licence. This scheme came to nothing and in May 1937 the company underwent a complete reorganisation and change of name. H. P. Folland, formerly chief designer of the Gloster Aircraft Company, became managing director, and the firm initially undertook sub-contract work.

A series of projects beginning with Fo.101 remained paper designs only, and the firm's first real aircraft was the **Folland Fo.108**, designed to meet Specification 43/37 for an engine testbed. Percival and General Aircraft also tendered, but Folland won the contract for a batch of 12, surely the first aircraft designed specifically for engine testing.

A large, single-engined, low-wing monoplane with fixed landing gear, the **Folland 43/37** was as big as a Bristol Beaufort and considerably taller. Resembling a scaled-up Hurricane, it accommodated a pilot and two observers in a large cabin with complete instrumentation for monitoring engine performance in flight. Construction was mixed, the semi-monocoque fuselage of light alloy while the wings and tail were plywood-covered. Split trailing-edge flaps and automatic wingtip slots were fitted.

Testbed aircraft lack the glamour of operational types, but the Folland 43/37 accomplished a wealth of interesting test programmes. Engine installations included differing versions of the Napier Sabre, Bristol Hercules and Centaurus, and Rolls-Royce Griffon. The fifth aircraft was used later by de Havilland for propeller tests.

The first was delivered in 1940, and the first recorded loss was on 28 April 1944 when the eighth aircraft crashed on take-off from Heston during Bristol Centaurus IV tests. Centaurus Is and IVs rapidly disposed of three more Folland 43/37s in only three weeks, the third, first and second aircraft being lost on 28 August and 14 and 18 September 1944 respectively. The sixth aircraft was also lost on 14 September while fitted with a Sabre I. The only other recorded fates are two struck off charge in 1945: the eleventh on 5 March after testing the Hercules XI and the fifth on 27 March after Rolls-Royce Griffon tests.

Because of the variety of engines,

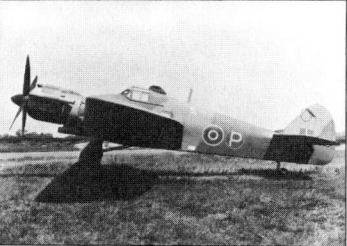

The strange Folland 43/37 was the first aircraft designed specifically as an engine testbed. Here it has a Centaurus.

Another radial often fitted to the 43/37 was the Bristol Hercules. Inline engines included the Sabre and Griffon.

weights and performance would have been variable and the only recorded details are noted below.

Specification
Type: flying testbed
Powerplant: various (see text)
Performance:
(Sabre I) maximum speed 428 km/h (266 mph) at 4755 m (15,600 ft); cruising speed 394 km/h (245 mph) at 1220 m (4,000 ft)
(Hercules) maximum speed 407 km/h (253 mph) at 3355 m (11,000 ft);

cruising speed 381 km/h (237 mph) at 4265 m (14,000 ft)
(Centaurus) maximum speed 470 km/h (292 mph) at 4570 m (15,000 ft); cruising speed 430 km/h (267 mph) at 3960 m (13,000 ft)
Weight: varying with engine installation, average maximum take-off 6804 kg (15,000 lb)
Dimensions: span 17.68 m (58 ft 0 in); length, varying with engine installation, approximately 13.21 m (43 ft 4 in); height 4.95 m (16 ft 3 in); wing area 54.63 m² (588 sq ft)

Folland Fo.139 Midge

As fighter design began to get more complex and the resulting aircraft heavier, W. E. W. Petter concluded that the new small jet engines then being developed would make a lightweight fighter possible. He therefore began design in 1951 of the **Folland Fo.141 Gnat Mk 1** around the 1724-kg (3,800-lb) thrust Bristol Saturn turbojet, but termination of the engine's development resulted in substitution of the 2050-kg (4,520-lb) thrust Bristol Orpheus.

To prove the concept a prototype, designated **Folland Fo.139 Midge**, was built with a 744-kg (1,640-lb) thrust Armstrong Siddeley Viper turbojet, and this was first flown at Boscombe Down, Wiltshire, on 11 August 1954. Extensive flight testing (nine hours in the first 13 days) included a supersonic dive, quite an achievement considering the low power of its engine, and was a tribute to clean lines.

Overseas pilots who flew the Midge came from the Royal Canadian Navy, Royal New Zealand Air Force, Indian Air Force, US Air Force and Jordanian air force, and the aircraft was praised for its ease of handling and simplicity of design. A total of 220 flights amassing 110 hours 33 minutes had been made before the Midge was destroyed in a fatal crash at Chilbolton on 26 September 1955 while being flown by a Swiss pilot. Examination of the wreckage showed no fault with the aircraft.

By the time of the crash, however, the lightweight concept had been proved and the first Orpheus-powered Gnat F.Mk 1 had flown. Although not adopted by the RAF as a fighter, Gnats were exported to Finland (13) and Yugoslavia (2), the latter really for a technology evaluation. India also adopted the single-seat Gnat; Hindustan Aeronautics developed the type into the Ajeet fighter and ultimately built 215 under licence between 1962-74, more recently converting some into two-seat Ajeet Trainer prototypes. In the UK the design was developed into the two-seat Fo.144 Gnat T.Mk 1 and adopted by the RAF as its advanced jet trainer.

Specification
Folland Midge
Type: single-seat lightweight fighter prototype
Powerplant: one 744-kg (1,640-lb) thrust Armstrong Siddeley Viper 101 turbojet
Performance: maximum speed 966 km/h (600 mph); absolute ceiling 12190 m (40,000 ft)
Weight: maximum take-off 2041 kg (4,500 lb)

Dimensions: span 6.3 m (20 ft 8 in); length 8.76 m (28 ft 9 in); height 2.82 m (9 ft 3 in); wing area 11.61 m² (125 sq ft)

The Folland Midge fully showed what could be achieved in the way of performance by a low-powered but lightweight design of clean lines. Despite the results of flight tests, the RAF favoured the 'heavy' approach.

Folland Gnat

Perhaps the most widely known of the RAF's jet trainers as a result of its outstanding performances in the hands of the pilots of the Red Arrows aerobatic team, the diminutive **Folland Fo.141 Gnat** was designed originally as a light fighter, as recounted in the entry for the Midge. The private-venture prototype Gnat, piloted by Folland's chief test pilot, Squadron Leader E. A. Tennant, flew at the Airplane & Armament Experimental Establishment at Boscombe Down on 18 July 1955. The aircraft's newly developed 1490-kg (3,285-lb) thrust Bristol Orpheus turbojet was also airborne for the first time and a more powerful version, rated at 1814-kg (4,000-lb) thrust, was installed on 30 August in readiness for the Gnat's debut at that year's SBAC flying display and exhibition at Farnborough. Six development aircraft were ordered by the Ministry of Supply in August 1955, the first flying on 26 May 1956, and these were used for a variety of trials at Boscombe Down, including firing of the 30-mm ADEN cannon, one of which was fitted in the lip of each intake. Evaluation in the ground-attack role was undertaken in Aden, in competition with a modified Hawker Hunter which was ordered subsequently as the Hunter FGA.Mk 9. Although the Royal Air Force had lost interest in the Gnat as a fighter, the Finnish air force took delivery of 13 aircraft in 1958-59 and these remained in service until 1972 when they were replaced by Saab Drakens. Two of the Finnish aircraft were fitted with camera noses for fighter reconnaissance duties. The Yugoslav government also bought two but the major export order was from India: 40 airframes in various stages of completion were supplied from the UK, and licence-production was undertaken by Hindustan Aeronautics Ltd at Bangalore, local production accounting for 175 aircraft. The Gnat entered Indian Air Force service in the spring of 1958, when the Gnat Handling Flight was first formed, and ultimately eight squadrons were equipped.

Although the RAF had not selected the Gnat for service in a front-line role, it did have a requirement for an unarmed, two-seat advanced trainer to replace the de Havilland Vampire T.Mk 11 and to follow the Hunting Jet Provost sections of the all-through jet training programme. Folland undertook a private-venture investigation of the changes necessary to install a second seat and to bring the landing speed down to less than 185 km/h (115 mph). The most significant of these changes was a new wing, increased in area by 3.72 m² (40 sq ft) and with additional fuel capacity, which reduced the fuel storage requirement in the fuselage, making room for additional equipment. The forward fuselage was increased slightly in length, the tail surfaces enlarged, and outboard ailerons and conventional inboard flaps replaced the inboard ailerons of the fighter version. Power was to be supplied by a 1919-kg (4,230-lb) thrust Orpheus 100. A Ministry of Supply design study contract was awarded in the autumn of 1956 and in August 1957 a batch of 14 pre-production **Fo.144 Gnat Trainer** aircraft was ordered, the first flying on 31 August 1959. It became clear, however, that no production order would be placed while Folland remained outside the major manufacturing groupings which the government favoured; thus the company was taken over by Hawker Siddeley Aviation, becoming its Hamble Division. Contracts for 30, 20 and 41 aircraft were awarded in February 1960, July 1961 and March 1962 respectively. The last production **Gnat T.Mk 1** flew on 9 April 1965 and was delivered to the RAF on 14 May, in the all-red scheme of the Red Arrows team. The Central Flying School, then at Little Rissington, first introduced the type in February 1962 but the major operator was No. 4 Flying Training School at Valley, which took its first aircraft on strength in November 1962 and which, in 1964, introduced the Gnat to the formation aerobatic scene, operating five all-yellow Gnats known as the Yellowjacks. The team reformed as the Red Arrows in 1965, under the control of the Central Flying School, and its Gnats were withdrawn finally at the end of the 1979 display season, to be replaced in 1980 by the British Aerospace Hawk T.Mk 1. No. 4 FTS retired its Gnats on 24 November 1978.

Specification
Folland (Hawker Siddeley) Gnat T.Mk 1
Type: two-seat advanced trainer
Powerplant: one 1919-kg (4,230-lb) thrust Bristol Siddeley Orpheus 100 turbojet
Performance: maximum speed 1024 km/h (636 mph) at 9450 m (31,000 ft); service ceiling 14630 m (48,000 ft); maximum range with two 300-litre (66-Imp gal) underwing tanks 1852 km (1,151 miles)
Weights: empty 2331 kg (5,140 lb); maximum take-off 3915 kg (8,630 lb)
Dimensions: span 7.32 m (24 ft 0 in); length 9.68 m (31 ft 9 in); height 2.93 m (9 ft 7½ in); wing area 16.26 m² (175 sq ft)

Operated by HavLlv 21 of the Ilmavoimat (Finnish air force) from Jyvaskyla air base north of Helsinki, the 13 Folland Gnats needed no special modifications to cope with the severe climatic conditions, which often meant operating at −30°C.

Ford Tri-Motor

For many years aviation enthusiasts have argued whether William B. Stout was the designer of the historic **Ford Tri-Motor**. There is, of course, no doubt that he designed the 2-AT Pullman which the Stout Metal Airplane Company was producing in early 1925. In August of that year Stout's organisation was acquired by the Ford Motor Company of which it became a division, and almost immediately development of a three-engined version of the Pullman was initiated under the designation **Ford 3-AT**. This particular tri-motor was clearly derived directly from the Pullman: a cantilever high-wing monoplane of all-metal construction, it incorporated the corrugated metal skin used on the 2-AT and which was a feature of the Ford Tri-Motor series. However, whereas the 2-AT with its single Liberty engine had been a good-looking aeroplane, the one-off 3-AT, with three uncowled radial engines mounted one on each wing and one low on a modified nose, must be numbered among the category of ugly air transports. Not surprisingly, no more were built.

The following **Ford 4-AT** differed very considerably, though its derivation from the Pullman was still discernible in the retention of the 2-AT's unusually-shaped cabin windows. First flown on 11 June 1926, the 4-AT was of the same basic airframe configuration, with a braced tail unit and fixed tailskid landing gear that introduced much refined main units. Accommodation was provided for a crew of two in an open cockpit forward of the wing, with eight passengers in an enclosed cabin. One of the three 149-kW (200-hp) Wright J-4 Whirlwind radial engines was mounted neatly in the nose of the fuselage, the other two in strut-braced nacelles, one beneath each wing.

The US Army Air Service's Ford C-4A tri-motor transport was the military equivalent of the Model 5-AT-D civil aircraft, and the four examples of the type were powered by R-1340-11 radials.

This configuration remained virtually unchanged until production ended in 1933, but a considerable number of variants were produced in the two main production versions, the 4-AT and the larger-capacity **5-AT** introduced in 1928.

Dubbed the 'Tin Goose', the Ford Tri-Motor appeared also with a variety of official and unofficial modifications, and the type was operated with wheel, float or ski landing gear. They also served with the US Army under the designations **XC-3, C-3, C-3A, C-4, C-4A, C-4B** and **C-9** (a total of 13 aircraft) and the US Navy/Marine Corps as **XJR-1, JR-2, JR-3, RR-1, RR-2, RR-3, RR-4** and **RR-5** (total of 9 aircraft). If proof of the Tri-Motor's longevity were needed, it is sufficient to remember that Scenic Airlines of Las Vegas is still operating a Ford 5-AT-C in 1991. The aircraft, still essentially in its original condition, has earned its keep since it was built in 1929 and is not a restoration.

Variants
Ford 4-AT-A: original production version; 14 built
Ford 4-AT-B: 1927 version with 177-kW (220-hp) Wright J-5 Whirlwind engines and seats for up to 12 passengers; 39 built
Ford 4-AT-C: as 4-AT-B but with nose engine replaced by one 298-kW (400-hp) Pratt & Whitney Wasp radial; 1 built
Ford 4-AT-D: designation of three aircraft similar to 4-AT-B but each with different engines and minor modifications
Ford 4-AT-E: generally as 4-AT-B, but with three 224-kW (300-hp) Wright J-6-9 Whirlwind engines; 24 built
Ford 4-AT-F: one aircraft differing from the 4-AT-E by incorporating aerodynamic refinements
Ford 5-AT-A: production version introduced in 1928; wing span increased by 1.17 m (3 ft 10 in); seating for 13 passengers; power provided by three 313-kW (420-hp) Pratt & Whitney Wasp radials; 3 built
Ford 5-AT-B: similar to 5-AT-A but with seats for 15 passengers; 41 built
Ford 5-AT-C: similar to 5-AT-A but with seats for 17 passengers; 51 built
Ford 5-AT-CS: seaplane version (Edo floats) of 5-AT-C; 1 built
Ford 5-AT-D: introduced a major change from the 5-AT-C by having the wing mounted 0.2 m (8 in) higher to increase cabin headroom but otherwise generally similar; 20 built
Ford 5-AT-DS: seaplane version (Edo floats) of 5-AT-D; 1 built
Ford 5-AT-E: proposed version with outboard engines relocated to the wing leading edges
Ford 6-AT-A: equivalent to 5-AT-C except for having three 224-kW (300-hp) Wright J-6-9 engines; 3 built
Ford 6-AT-AS: seaplane version (Edo floats) of 6-AT-A; 1 built
Ford 7-AT-A: redesignation of one 6-AT-A following installation of a 313-kW (420-hp) Pratt & Whitney Wasp engine in the nose; later converted to 5-AT-C configuration
Ford 8-AT: freighter conversion of one 5-AT-C with the two outer engines removed
Ford 9-AT: redesignation of one 4-AT-B following installation of three 224-kW (300-hp) Pratt & Whitney Wasp

Junior engines

Ford 11-AT: redesignation of one 4-AT-E following installation of three 168-kW (225-hp) Packard diesel engines; later converted to 4-AT-B configuration

Ford 13-A: redesignation of one 5-AT-D following installation of one 429-kW (575-hp) Wright Cyclone in the nose position and two 224-kW (300-hp) Junior engines

Wright J-6-9s; restored subsequently to 5-AT-D standard

Ford 14-A: started life as four-engined **Ford 10-A** with single engine, but redesignated when fitted with one 821-kW (1,100-hp) and two 533-kW (715-hp) Hispano-Suiza engines; accommodation for 40 passengers; built but not flown

XB-906: designation of a single 5-AT-C modified as a bomber; crashed during manufacturer's trials

Specification
Ford 5-AT-D
Type: commercial transport
Powerplant: three 313-kW (420-hp) Pratt & Whitney C-1 or SC-1 Wasp 9-cylinder radial piston engines
Performance: maximum speed 241 km/h (150 mph); cruising speed 196 km/h (122 mph); service ceiling 5640 m (18,500 ft); range 885 km (550 miles)
Weights: empty 3556 kg (7,840 lb); maximum take-off 6123 kg (13,500 lb)
Dimensions: span 23.72 m (77 ft 10 in); length 15.32 m (50 ft 3 in); height 3.86 m (12 ft 8 in); wing area 77.57 m² (835 sq ft)

Fouga CM.10/100/101

The French company Etablissements Fouga et Cie, formed in 1936 for the design and construction of sailplanes, developed in the late 1940s a large transport glider designated **Fouga CM.10** that was suitable for the airlifting of military cargo, paratroops, troops or equipment. The CM.10 was a cantilever high-wing monoplane of mixed construction with a conventional tail unit and fixed tricycle landing gear. The flight compartment for a crew of two was in the nose, and the nose section (complete with flightdeck) hinged to swing to starboard to allow direct loading of freight into the main cabin.

With virtually no demand for this class of aircraft, Fouga built the prototype of a light transport which retained the CM.10 airframe unchanged, including its folding nose. Two Renault 12S engines were installed in wing-mounted nacelles and the cabin could be arranged to carry up to 15 passengers or be equipped for cargo-carrying. Flown in this form as the **CM.100**, the type was also planned in a later version with retractable tricycle landing gear as the **CM.101R**; in addition it would have had two 110-kg (242-lb) thrust Turboméca Piméné turbojets mounted in the rear of the engine nacelles to provide a source of auxiliary power for overload or emergency use.

Specification
Fouga CM.100
Type: twin-engined light transport
Powerplant: two 433-kW (580-hp) Renault 12S 12-cylinder inverted Vee piston engines
Performance: cruising speed 245 km/h (152 mph) at 1500 m (4,920 ft); range 500 km (311 miles)
Weights: empty 4540 kg (10,009 lb); maximum take-off 7300 kg (16,094 lb)
Dimensions: span 26.7 m (87 ft 7¼ in); length 17.9 m (58 ft 8¾ in); wing area 71.9 m² (773.95 sq ft)

Abov: By the time the CM10 appeared in the late 1940s, the need for a heavy military transport glider had disappeared.

Below: The CM.100 differed from the CM.10 only in the provision of the twin engines and associated fuel system.

Fouga CM.8 family

The first aircraft in the CM.8 family was the **CM.8R-13**, named Sylphe. Powered by a 180-kW (242-hp) Turboméca Piméné engine, it flew on 14 July 1949 – the first flight of any Turboméca engine. A refined version was the **CM.8R-9.8**, the **Cyclope**, flown on 31 January 1951. Many Cyclope versions were built, including the **Cyclope II** and **Cyclope III** with 261-kW (350-hp) Palas engines. Then came an important development: the **CM.8R-8.3**, known as the **Midjet**, was a competition and aerobatic aircraft, of which 12 models were built.

To provide a quickly-built aircraft to service as a testbed for a number of Turboméca engines, Fouga decided to combine two CM.8R-9.8 airframes. Using a port and starboard outer wing, the airframes were united forward by a new wing centre-section and at the rear by the inboard section of the 'butterfly' tail units.

The type was flown as the **Fouga CM.88-R Gemeaux I** on 6 March 1951, power being provided by two 100-kg (220-lb) thrust Turboméca Piméné turbojets, giving this version a maximum level speed of 285 km/h (177 mph). The other four variants, differing only in installed powerplant, are listed below. Development is believed to have ended soon after the Gemeaux V version had finished its series of tests.

Variants

Gemeaux II: designation when powered by one 275-kg (606-lb) thrust Turboméca Marboré I turbojet; first flown 16 June 1951

Gemeaux III: designation when powered by one Turboméca Marboré II turbojet; flown on 24 August 1951 with prototype developing 350-kg (772-lb) thrust, and on 2 January 1952 with production engine developing 400-kg (882-lb) thrust

Gemeaux IV: designation when powered by one 200-kg (441-lb) thrust Turboméca Aspin I turbofan; first flown on 6 November 1951

Gemeaux V: final designation as powered by one 360-kg (794-lb) thrust Turboméca Aspin II turbofan; first flown on 21 June 1952

Specification
Fouga CM.88-R Gemeaux III
Type: engine test-bed aircraft
Powerplant: one 400-kg (882-lb) thrust Turboméca Marboré II turbojet
Performance: maximum speed 400 km/h (249 mph) at sea level; cruising speed 300 km/h (186 mph); service ceiling 10000 m (32,810 ft); endurance 1 hour
Weights: empty 890 kg (1,962 lb); maximum take-off 1170 kg (2,579 lb)
Dimensions: span 10.76 m (35 ft 3½ in); length 6.66 m (21 ft 10¼ in); height 1.93 m (6 ft 4 in); wing area 12.8 m² (137.78 sq ft)

The CM.88 Gemeaux was basically two CM.8 airframes joined by a common wing. A pair of small turbojets provided power.

Found FBA-2/100 Centennial

Found Brothers Aviation was formed at Malton, Ontario, during 1948 to produce the **Found FBA-1A** four-seat cabin monoplane designed by Captain S. R. Found. Powered by a 104-kW (140-hp) de Havilland Gipsy Major engine, the FBA-1A was flown for the first time on 13 July 1949. At a much later date it was developed into the all-metal four/five-seat **FBA-2** which, when flown in prototype form on 11 August 1960, had the fixed tricycle landing gear intended as standard for the production **FBA-2B**. However, it was with conventional tailwheel landing gear that the redesignated **FBA-2C** production version was first flown on 9 May 1962. Available with optional float or ski landing gear, the FBA-2C introduced a more powerful Avco Lycoming O-540-A1D engine, a slight increase in cabin length and enlarged rear cabin doors to simplify the handling of cargo. When production ended in favour of an improved version known as the **Found Centennial 100**, a total of 34 had been built.

Detail design work on the Centennial 100 began in October 1966 and the prototype, powered by a 216-kW (290-hp) Avco Lycoming IO-540-G1D5 engine was flown for the first time on 7 April 1967. Three prototypes and two production Centennials took part in the flight test programme, but shortly after award of certification in July 1968 the Found company went out of business.

Specification
Found FBA-2C
Type: four/five-seat cabin monoplane
Powerplant: one 186-kW (250-hp) Avco Lycoming O-540-A1D flat-six piston engine
Performance: maximum speed 237 km/h (147 mph) at 1525 m (5,000 ft); cruising speed 229 km/h (142 mph); service ceiling 4875 m (16,000 ft); range 966 km (600 miles)
Weights: empty 703 kg (1,550 lb); maximum take-off 1338 kg (2,950 lb)
Dimensions: span 10.97 m (36 ft

The Centennial 10 was an improved FBA-2, but could not compete in a market dominated by US designs.

0 in); length 7.77 m (25 ft 6 in); height 2.37 m (7 ft 9½ in); wing area 16.72 m² (180 sq ft)

Fournier RF4
to
General Dynamics F-16 Fighting Falcon

Fournier RF4

René Fournier designed and built in 1960 a single-seat ultralight aircraft which he designated **Fournier RF01**. The intention was to combine the characteristics of a light sporting aircraft with those of a sailplane, and the RF01 was of extremely clean design and powered by an 18.5-kW (25-hp) Volkswagen modified flat-four motorcar engine. Successful testing of the prototype brought French government support for the establishment of a production line. A second RF01 prototype and two pre-production **RF2** aircraft were followed by the first **RF3** production aircraft flown in March 1963. This gained certification in June and production deliveries began in November 1963.

Prior to that, René Fournier had entered into partnership with Alpavia SA, which became responsible for manufacture of the RF3. Some 95 RF3s were built before development of an improved **RF4D** superseded. A further

Combining features of the ultralight and sailplane, the RF4D offers low but adequate performance with low costs.

production change came in 1966 when Sportavia-Putzer was formed in Germany to take over production of RF designs. A total of 160 RF4Ds was built and several achieved notable flights. In May 1969 Miro Slovak flew one across the North Atlantic in 175 hours 42 minutes 7.11 seconds. It won an *Evening News* prize of £1,000 for the best performance by an aircraft of under 2268 kg (5,000 lb) weight in the *Daily Mail*'s transatlantic air race.

Late developments of the basic RF4 design include a 'stretched' **RF5** two-seater and the **Sportavia SFS 31 Milan** which combined the RF-4 fuselage and tail unit with the 15.00-m (49-ft 2½-in) span wing of the Scheibe SF-27M sailplane.

Specification
Fournier RF4D

Type: single-seat lightplane
Powerplant: one 30-kW (40-hp) Volkswagen modified flat-four motorcar engine
Performance: maximum cruising speed 180 km/h (112 mph); economic cruising speed 160 km/h (99 mph); service ceiling 6000 m (19,685 ft);

range 670 km (416 miles)
Weights: empty 265 kg (584 lb); maximum take-off 390 kg (860 lb)
Dimensions: span 11.26 m (36 ft 11¼ in); length 6.05 m (19 ft 10¼ in); height 1.57 m (5 ft 1¾ in); wing area 11.30 m² (121.64 sq ft)

Fournier RF6B

In December 1970 René Fournier began the design of a side-by-side two-seat lightplane under the designation **Fournier RF6**; this was developed subsequently into the **Sportavia RS 180 Sportsman**. In the early 1970s, Fournier established Avions Fournier at Nitray, near Montlouis, developing there a slightly smaller version with a less powerful engine, although still seating two side-by-side, which he designated the **RF6B Club**. The prototype was flown for the first time on 12 March 1974, then powered by a 67-kW (90-hp) Rolls-Royce Continental O-200-E engine. Intended role for the RF6B was training, including aerobatics, and its structure was stressed to limits of +6g and −3g. The first of five pre-production aircraft flew for the first time on 4 March 1976, its Rolls-Royce Continental O-200-A engine being adopted for all subsequent **RF6B-100** aircraft produced by Avions Fournier. Production ended in 1980 after 45 aircraft had been built, one additional airframe being used as an **RF6B-120** development aircraft, powered by an 88-kW (118-hp) Avco Lycoming O-235-L2A engine, and first flown on 14 August 1980.

Subsequently Slingsby Engineering Ltd in the UK (long known as a designer and builder of sailplanes and becoming

The T67A is the production model of the British licence-built version of the RF6B-120 trainer. Notable is the large cockpit which offers an excellent field of vision.

renamed Slingsby Aviation Ltd on 5 July 1982) gained a manufacturing and marketing licence from Avions Fournier. The new company, concentrating on further development of the RF6B-120 under the designation **T67**, flew its first aircraft (G-BIOW) on 15 May 1981. This was a T67A, powered by a 119-kW (160-hp) Lycoming O-235-L2A engine. By 1990 around 100 civil and military variants of the T67 had been sold. Slingsby developments of the RF-6 are listed below.

Variants
Slingsby T67B Firefly: generally as

T67A but with glass-reinforced plastic (GRP) structure replacing the wood of the T67A
Slingsby T67C Firefly 160: as T67B but powered by a 119-kW (160-hp) Lycoming AEIO-320-D1B flat-four engine
Slingsby T67D Firefly: as T67C but with optional fuel tanks in the wing, one- or two-piece canopy and constant-speed propeller
Slingsby T67M Firefly II: military basic trainer version of the T67C
Slingsby T67M-200: T67M with a 149-kW (200-hp) Lycoming AEIO-360-A1E engine driving a Hoffman three-bladed variable-pitch propeller

Specification
Fournier RF6B-100
Type: two-seat trainer/tourer aircraft

As indicated by the numerical suffix to the designation on the vertical tail, the RF6B was powered in its production form by a 75-kW (100-hp) Rolls-Royce Continental engine.

Powerplant: one 75-kW (100-hp) Rolls-Royce Continental O-200-A flat-four piston engine
Performance: maximum speed 200 km/h (124 mph) at sea level; cruising speed 180 km/h (112 mph) at sea level; service ceiling 4000 m (13,125 ft); range 650 km (404 miles)
Weights: empty 500 kg (1,102 lb); maximum take-off 750 kg (1,653 lb)
Dimensions: span 10.50 m (34 ft 5½ in); length 7.00 m (22 ft 11¾ in); height 2.52 m (8 ft 3 in); wing area 13.00 m² (139.94 sq ft)

Friedrichshafen FF 33/39/49/59

Derived from the two-seat FF 29 patrol/reconnaissance floatplane, the initial **Friedrichshafen FF 33** was flown towards the end of 1914. Generally similar in construction and configuration to its predecessor, except for revised floats, the FF 33 shared also the 89-kW (120-hp) Mercedes D.II powerplant. As in the FF 29, the pilot occupied the rear cockpit. Only six FF 33s were built for the German navy, being followed by five **FF 33b** aircraft which incorporated a number of changes. In this version the

pilot's and observer's positions were reversed, the latter also being provided with a machine-gun on a pivoted mount; two-step floats were introduced; and the Mercedes D.II was replaced by the more powerful 119-kW (160-hp) Maybach inline engine.

Most extensively-built version was the **FF 33e**, which introduced the Benz Bz.III inline engine, longer twin floats which allowed the undertail central float to be deleted and replaced by a ventral fin, and a radio transmitter at the expense of armament. Almost 190 FF 33es are believed to have been built, the final production batch delivered from late 1917 being equipped with dual controls. It was followed by the **FF 33j**, which incorporated a number of aerodynamic refinements and the provision of a radio transmitter and receiver, and the last of the reconnaissance FF 33s was the dual-control **FF 33s** trainer. One FF 33e was operated as a scouting aircraft by the German auxiliary cruiser *Wolf*. The forward reconnaissance capability and

radio transmitter of this aircraft, named *Wölfchen*, enabled the *Wolf* to gain some notable success against Allied shipping.

The FF 33 was developed also for scout/fighter patrols, the initial **FF 33f** being basically an FF 33e of reduced span and length but with a machine-gun on a pivoted mount for the observer. Only five were built before production switched to the **FF 33h** (about 50 built) with aerodynamic refinement and the duplication of some inboard wing-bay bracing cables as a safeguard if the observer were compelled to fire his machine-gun forward between the wings. Major production version was the **FF 33I** (about 130 built) which had some further dimensional reductions to improve manoeuvrability, plus additional refinements to increase performance. One example of the FF 33I was completed with wheeled landing gear for evaluation as a general-purpose biplane under the designation **C.I**.

Continued development of the patrol/reconnaissance two-seaters followed with the **FF 39** (14 built), which was basically a refined version of the FF 33e with its 112-kW (150-hp) powerplant replaced by a 149-kW (200-hp) Benz Bz.IV engine. The performance offered by this higher-powered unit resulted in production of the further improved **FF 49c** with the same Bz.IV engine, a strengthened structure, balanced controls, a radio receiver and transmitter, and a machine-gun for the observer. Introduced in mid-1917, the FF 49c proved so effective that it remained in service until the end of the war with between 200 and 250

built by the company and two other sub-contractors. Twenty-five examples of an **FF 49b** bomber variant were built, which differed in having the crew positions reversed, deletion of the observer's machine-gun, and provision for carrying a light bombload.

Final development of the FF 33 family came with the **FF 59c** introduced in mid-1918. This was basically a version of the FF 39 with a modified tail unit, the wing interplane struts placed further apart, and the inner-bay bracing wires deleted to make it less hazardous for the observer to fire his machine-gun forwards between the wings. The FF 59c had been preceded by single examples of the **FF 59a** and **FF 59b** development aircraft with differing tail units.

Specification
Friedrichshafen FF 49c
Type: two-seat patrol/reconnaissance floatplane
Powerplant: one 149-kW (200-hp)

Benz Bz.IV 6-cylinder inline piston engine
Performance: maximum speed 140 km/h (87 mph); climb to 1000 m (3,280 ft) in 8 minutes 0 seconds; endurance 5 hours 30 minutes
Weights: empty 1515 kg (3,340 lb); maximum take-off 2145 kg (4,729 lb)
Dimensions: span 17.15 m (56 ft 3¼ in); length 11.65 m (38 ft 2¾ in); height 4.50 m (14 ft 9¼ in); wing area

71.40 m² (768.57 sq ft)
Armament: one fixed forward-firing 7.92-mm (0.31-in) LMG 08/15 machine-gun and one 7.92-mm (0.31-in) Parabellum machine-gun on pivoted mount in rear cockpit

This is a Friedrichshafen FF 33h, an aerodynamically-refined version of the FF 33e.

Friedrichshafen G series

Although recognised primarily as a designer and constructor of floatplanes for the German navy, Friedrichshafen also designed and built a series of landplane bombers under G designations. Development began with the **Friedrichshafen G.I** prototype of 1915, a large three-bay biplane with accommodation for a crew of three. Power was provided by two 112-kW (150-hp) Benz Bz.III engines driving pusher propellers, one mounted between the wings on each side of the fuselage. It seems possible that this G.I prototype may have derived from the **FF 35** prototype built in February 1915 and intended as a torpedo-bomber for the German navy. Apart from having float instead of wheeled landing gear and a different tail unit, the FF 35 was in general configuration and dimensions similar to the G.I. From the single G.I prototype was developed an improved **G.II** that was produced in small numbers and entered service in late 1916. This version had reduced-span two-bay wings, a conventional tail unit replacing the biplane tail of the G.I, more-powerful 149-kW (200-hp) Benz Bz.IV engines and a defensive

armament of two machine-guns, one each in nose and rear cockpits. However, the G.II carried a bombload of only 450 kg (992 lb).

From these two early bomber types was developed the G.III which served from early 1917 until the end of the war, used in conjunction with the Gotha G.V to form Germany's main bomber force on the Western Front. The G.III reverted to the greater-span three-bay wing and was of mixed construction, retaining a monoplane tail unit which was of revised planform. The main units of the tailskid landing gear each had two wheels, mounted below the lower wing and directly beneath the engines, and a large single wheel was provided beneath the forward fuselage to prevent the aircraft from nosing over on rough surfaces. More-powerful Mercedes D.IVa engines were installed, these allowing an average bombload of 1500 kg (3,307 lb) to be carried, though this figure varied according to the range over which operations were launched. Variants included the generally similar **G.IIIa**, which differed primarily by reverting to the biplane tail unit; and the **G.IV** with a shortened

fuselage nose, biplane tail unit and the engines mounted in tractor configuration.

Accurate production figures for all versions of the Friedrichshafen Gs are not known, but about 340 were built by sub-contractors.

Specification
Friedrichshafen G.III
Type: twin-engined bomber
Powerplant: two 194-kW (260-hp) Mercedes D.IVa 6-cylinder inline piston engines
Performance: maximum speed 135 km/h (84 mph); endurance 5 hours

The G.III and G.IIIa (illustrated) were effective tactical bombers, partnering the Gotha G.V up to the end of World War I on the Western Front.

Weights: empty 2596 kg (5,941 lb); maximum take-off 3930 kg (8,664 lb)
Dimensions: span 23.70 m (77 ft 9 in); length 12.80 m (42 ft 0 in); wing area 95.00 m² (1,022.60 sq ft)
Armament: two or three 7.92-mm (0.31-in) Parabellum machine-guns on pivoted mounts in nose and rear cockpits, plus an average bombload of 1500 kg (3,307 lb)

Fuji FA-200 Aero Subaru

In 1964 Fuji began the design and development of a four-seat light aircraft designated **Fuji FA-200 Aero Subaru**. A cantilever low-wing monoplane of metal construction, the FA-200 has a conventional tail unit, fixed tricycle landing gear and seats four in two pairs in a heated and ventilated cabin. First flown in prototype form on 21 August 1965, the FA-200 has been produced in three main versions. The first basic production

model was the **FA-200-160**, powered by a 119-kW (160-hp) Avco Lycoming O-320-D2A engine. Introduction of a 134-kW (180-hp) IO-360 engine with a constant-speed propeller resulted in the **FA-200-180** or the **FA-200-180AO** with a fixed-pitch propeller. All three were certificated in Normal, Utility and Aerobatic (two-seat) categories.

Production began in March 1968 and a total of 274 had been delivered when

production ended in 1986, most of them for export.

Variant
Fuji FA-203S: under this designation a single short take-off and landing (STOL) version of the FA-200 was developed for the National Aerospace Laboratory; basically similar to FA-200-180, it incorporated leading-edge slats, full-span trailing-edge 'flaperons' and a boundary layer control (BLC) system

Specification
Fuji FA-200-180 (Normal category)
Type: four-seat cabin monoplane
Powerplant: one 134-kW (180-hp) Avco Lycoming IO-360-B1B flat-four

piston engine
Performance: maximum speed 233 km/h (145 mph) at sea level; economic cruising speed 167 km/h (104 mph) at 1525 m (5,000 ft); service ceiling 4175 m (13,700 ft); range 1344 km (835 miles)
Weights: empty 650 kg (1,433 lb); maximum take-off 1150 kg (2,535 lb)
Dimensions: span 9.42 m (30 ft 11 in); length 8.17 m (26 ft 9½ in); height 2.59 m (8 ft 6 in); wing area 14.00 m² (150.70 sq ft)

Though it has no frills, the FA-200 secured useful sales thanks to its price and reputation for reliability.

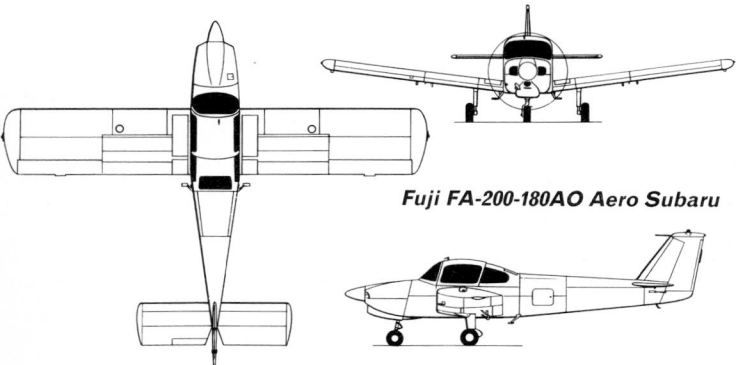

Fuji FA-200-180AO Aero Subaru

Fuji KM/LM

With the end of World War II aircraft development and manufacture in Japan was prohibited under the surrender terms, and it was not until April 1952 that approval was given for revival of the nation's aircraft industry. In July 1953 Fuji Heavy Industries was established as successor to the well-known Nakajima company, its aviation division being initiated by licence-construction of the Beech Model 45 Mentor. From the Mentor the company developed the **Fuji LM-1** liaison/general-purpose aircraft, which differed primarily by the removal of military equipment and the provision of a four/five-seat interior and increased fuel capacity. The LM-1 was powered by a 168-kW (225-hp) Continental O-470-13 engine, but introduction of the more powerful 254-kW (340-hp) Avco Lycoming IGSO-480 brought the designation **LM-2**. Both LM-1 and LM-2 served with the Japan Ground Self-Defence Force, the last aircraft being retired during 1981-82.

Contemporary with the LM-1 was the generally similar four-seat civil **Fuji KM**, which differed by having a version of the 254-kW (340-hp) Avco-Lycoming IGSO-480 engine that was introduced in the LM-2. A number of KMs were supplied to the Japanese government for use in its civil pilot training programme. Development for military use followed with the first flight of the **Fuji KM-2** on 16 July 1962. A two-seat (side-by-side) primary trainer, powered by a 254-kW (340-hp) Avco Lycoming IGSO-480 engine, the type began to enter service with the Japan Maritime Self-Defence

Force in September 1962. A total of 20 remained in use with this Force in 1991. Two examples were ordered by the Japan Ground Self-Defence Force under the designation **TL-1**, both of them delivered during 1981.

A further modification of the KM-2 design, combining the airframe/powerplant of the Japanese aircraft with the tandem two-seat cockpit layout of the Beech T-34A Mentor, led to the **KM-2B** primary trainer. A civil prototype was flown on 26 September 1974, and the first of six pre-production aircraft on 17 January 1978. It was selected by the Japan Air Self-Defence Force as a primary trainer to replace its Beech T-34As. Designated **T-3** in JASDF service, the last of 50 was delivered on 19 February 1982.

Specification
Fuji KM-2B
Type: two-seat primary trainer
Powerplant: one 254-kW (340-hp) Avco Lycoming IGSO-480-A1F6 flat-six piston engine
Performance: maximum speed 367 km/h (228 mph) at 2440 m (8,000 ft); economic cruising speed 254 km/h (158 mph) at 2440 m (8,000 ft); service ceiling 8170 m (26,800 ft); range 966 km (600 miles)
Weights: empty 1120 kg (2,469 lb); maximum take-off 1542 kg (3,400 lb)
Dimensions: span 10.01 m (32 ft 10 in); length 8.03 m (26 ft 4¼ in); height 3.02 m (9 ft 11 in); wing area 16.50 m² (177.61 sq ft)

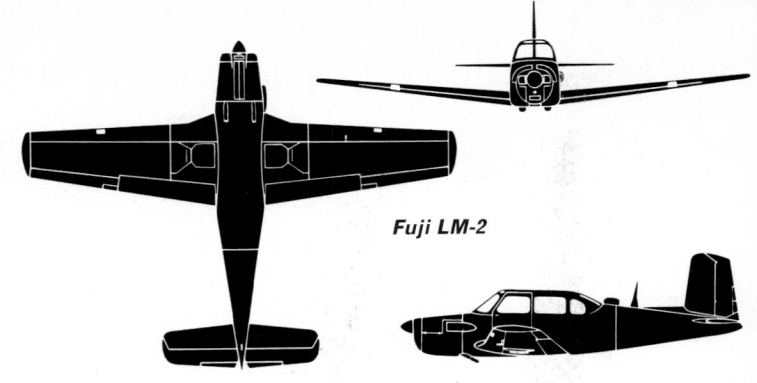

Fuji LM-2

The KM-2B primary trainer combines the airframe of the KM-2 lightplane with the tandem cockpit of the Beech T-34 Mentor, so bringing the design wheel full circle.

Fuji KM-2Kai

The **KM-2Kai** was devised in response to a 1986 JGSDF requirement for an aircraft to replace its ageing fleet of 32 KM-2 primary trainers. In March 1987 Fuji received an initial contract to rebuild KM-2s into a developed version of the turboprop KM-2D with changes in equip-

ment, a revised cabin structure with a rearward-sliding canopy, and upturned wingtips. Designated **T-5** by the JGSDF, the first aircraft flew on 27 April 1988. Deliveries began in August 1988 and out of 15 funded to date, 10 were in service by 1991, most with No. 201 Squadron at Ozuki. Although procured as a trainer, the JGSDF also uses some T-5s for liaison duties. Thus, the (A) aerobatic/

trainer version fitted with dual controls, seats an instructor and pupil side-by-side, while the (U) utility/liaison version seats a pilot and three passengers in two pairs.

Specification
Fuji KM-2kai/T-5
Type: primary trainer/liaison aircraft
Powerplant: one 261-kW (350-shp) Allison 250-B17D turboprop

Performance: maximum speed 357 km/h (222 mph); economic cruising speed 287 km/h (178 mph); service ceiling 7620 m (25,000 ft); range (U) 945 km (587 miles)
Weights: empty 1082 kg (2,385 lb); maximum take-off 1805 kg (3,980 lb)
Dimensions: span 10.0 m (32 ft 11 in); length 8.4 m (27 ft 8 in); height 3.0 m (9 ft 9 in); wing area 16.50 m²

Fuji T1F

Working to a Japanese Defence Agency requirement for a two-seat jet trainer to replace the North American T-6 trainers then in service, Fuji was successful in gaining an initial contract for prototype construction. It had been intended to power the first **Fuji T1F1** version with an Ishikawajima-Harima J3 turbojet engine, but delay in development of this powerplant led to a Bristol Siddeley (later Rolls-Royce) Orpheus turbojet being used to power the first **T1F2** prototype to fly on 8 January 1958. A cantilever low-wing monoplane of all-metal construction, the T1F has a conventional tail unit, retractable tricycle landing gear and the crew of two seated on tandem ejection seats in a pressurised and air-conditioned cabin. A total of 40 T1F2s with Orpheus powerplant was built for the Japan Air Self-Defence Force, all of which had been delivered by July 1962 and were allocated the JASDF designation **T-1A**.

Before delivery of the T-1As had been completed, the prototype of the T1F1 with a 1200-kg (2,646-lb) thrust J3-IHI-3 turbojet engine was flown on 17 May 1960. Although this engine is of lower power than the Orpheus engine of the T1F2, flight testing showed satisfactory performance and a batch of 20 T1F1s was ordered under the JASDF designation **T-1B**, delivery being completed by June 1963. In April 1965 a **T1F3** proto-

type was flown, powered by a developed version of the Ishikawajima-Harima turbojet, the J3-IHI-7 with a 1400-kg (3,086-lb) thrust rating. It was proposed to convert all T1F1s to this new powerplant under the designation **T-1C**, but after three had been completed the programme was abandoned. The majority of the T-1s remain in service in 1990, with No. 13 Air Training Wing at Ashiya, but they are scheduled for replacement by the Kawasaki T-4 twin-turbofan jet trainer by the mid-1990s.

Specification
Fuji T1F2/T-1A
Type: intermediate jet trainer

Powerplant: one 1814-kg (4,000-lb) thrust Rolls-Royce Orpheus 805 turbojet
Performance: maximum speed 925 km/h (575 mph) at 6095 m (20,000 ft); cruising speed 620 km/h (385 mph) at 9145 m (30,000 ft); service ceiling 15850 m (52,000 ft); maximum range with internal fuel 1300 km (808 miles)
Weights: empty 2420 kg (5,335 lb); maximum take-off 4150 kg (9,149 lb)
Dimensions: span 10.50 m (34 ft 5½ in); length 12.12 m (39 ft 9 in); height 4.08 m (13 ft 4½ in); wing area 22.22 m² (239.18 sq ft)
Armament: one 12.7-mm (0.5-in)

machine-gun in nose; if underwing fuel tanks are not carried each underwing rack can accommodate a gun pod, or Sidewinder air-to-air missile, or 340-kg (750-lb) bomb, or napalm tank, or cluster of 70-mm (2.75-in) folding-fin rockets

Japan's first post-war jet aircraft was the Fuji T1F. Illustrated is a T-1A (T1F2) initial production model, which was powered by the Rolls-Royce (Bristol) Orpheus engine. T-1As still serve today with 13 Wing, JASDF, at Ashiya, although they are being replaced by the Kawasaki T-4.

Fuji/Rockwell Commander 700/710

In collaboration with Fuji Heavy Industries in Japan, Rockwell International's General Aviation Division was involved in the development of a twin-engined six/eight-seat light transport aircraft. Design began in Japan in 1971, the aircraft then having the designation **FA-300**, and on 28 June 1974, Fuji and Rockwell signed an agreement covering its development as a joint venture, with Rockwell designating the aircraft **Commander 700** for marketing in North America.

Of cantilever low-wing monoplane configuration, the Commander 700 had a fuselage constructed for pressurisation, the tail unit being conventional with swept surfaces and the landing gear of retractable tricycle type. Powerplant comprised two Avco Lycoming turbocharged engines, these being wing-mounted in well streamlined nacelles. Standard accommodation was for a pilot and co-pilot plus four passengers, all in a pressurised, air-conditioned, heated and ventilated environment. The first of five prototypes made its initial flight in Japan on 13 November 1975, and the second, which was assembled by Rockwell, flew on 25 February 1976. Japanese JCAB certification was gained on 19 May 1977, and US FAA certification on 31 October.

Development of a generally similar aircraft, designated **Commander 710**, was proceeding simultaneously. This differed mainly by the installation of more powerful (335-kW/450-hp) engines. The first of two prototypes was flown in Japan on 22 December 1976, and JCAB certification was gained in early 1979. Later in the year it was reported that development was being continued, the Model 710 then being flown with winglets installed at the wingtips.

Rockwell's decision in late 1979 to sell off its General Aviation Division to the Gulfstream American Corporation brought termination of the collaboration agreement with Fuji. At that time Rockwell had delivered 25 Commander 700s and under the termination agreement Fuji acquired worldwide manufacturing and marketing rights for these aircraft. It was then believed that if production were initiated by the Japanese company efforts would be concentrated on the Commander 710, but no announcement of its intention to follow such a course has since been made by Fuji.

Specification
Fuji/Rockwell Commander 700
Type: six/eight-seat light transport
Powerplant: two 254-kW (340-hp) Avco Lycoming TIO-549-R2AD flat-six piston engines
Performance: maximum speed 409 km/h (254 mph) at weight of 2880 kg (6,350 lb) at 5180 m (17,000 ft); cruising speed 393 km/h (244 mph) at weight of 2880 kg (6,530 lb) at 6555 m (21,500 ft); service ceiling 8350 m (27,400 ft); maximum range with maximum fuel, allowances and 45-min reserves 2227 km (1,384 miles)
Weights: empty 2134 kg (4,704 lb); maximum take-off 3151 kg (6,947 lb)
Dimensions: span 12.94 m (42 ft 5½ in); length 12.03 m (39 ft 5¾ in); height 4.05 m (13 ft 3½ in); wing area 18.60 m² (200.2 sq ft)

Designed as the Fuji FA-300, this trim piston-engined twin was marketed in the USA under the designation Rockwell Commander 700 until 1979, when US production was terminated.

GAF Nomad

Australia's Government Aircraft Factory was established in July 1939 to produce aircraft mainly for the armed forces. After building Beauforts, Beaufighters, Lincolns, Canberras and Mirage IIIs under licence, a decision was made in the late 1960s to produce a civil type to lessen the organisation's reliance on military programmes, and so began the development of a light twin-engined turboprop STOL transport. This emerged as the GAF N2 Nomad and the first of two prototypes (VH-SUP) made its first flight on 23 July 1971. Of braced high-wing monoplane configuration, the N2 had its STOL performance provided by full-span double-slotted flaps and drooping ailerons. The semi-monocoque fuselage was basically of rectangular cross-section, the tail unit conventional, and landing gear of the retractable tricycle type. The powerplants are two Allison turboprop engines, each driving a constant speed three-bladed propeller with reverse pitch capability to enhance short-field landing performance.

Versions of the aircraft include the initial production model N22, seating up to 12 passengers, and the stretched N24 with fuselage lengthened by 1.14 m (3 ft 9 in). Major production versions included the 13-passenger N22B, and 17-seat N24A. The N22 Missionmaster was produced for the Australian Army along with the N22B civil version. The N22C cargo version was an improved and recertificated N22B with a higher maximum take-off weight. The twin-float N22F Floatmaster was certificated in the USA during 1979, followed by an amphibious version in 1980. Developments of the Missionmaster short-fuselage military versions were built as the basic coastal-patrol N22SB Searchmaster B, and the more sophisticated N22SL Searchmaster L. All these shared a common multi-role capability. Following a slow start, sales of Nomads had reached 170 by 1984 when production ended, 95 for military customers and 75 for civil users. In December 1986 GAF was reorganised into a private enterprise venture under the new name Aerospace Technologies of Australia (ASTA), although remaining wholly government owned.

One of the largest operators of the GAF Nomad is the Australian Army Aviation Corps, which flies them from its base at Oakey, Queensland, on light transport duties.

Specification
GAF N22B Nomad
Type: STOL utility aircraft
Powerplant: two 313-kW (420-shp) Allison 250-B17C turboprops
Performance: normal cruising speed 311 km/h (193 mph); service ceiling 6400 m (21,000 ft); range with standard fuel and reserves 1352 km (840 miles) at 3050 m (10,000 ft)
Weights: empty operating 2150 kg (4,740 lb); maximum take-off 3856 kg (8,500 lb)
Dimensions: span 16.52 m (54 ft 2½ in); length 12.56 m (41 ft 2½ in); height 5.52 m (18 ft 1¼ in); wing area 30.10 m² (324.0 sq ft)

Government Aircraft Factories N24A Nomad.

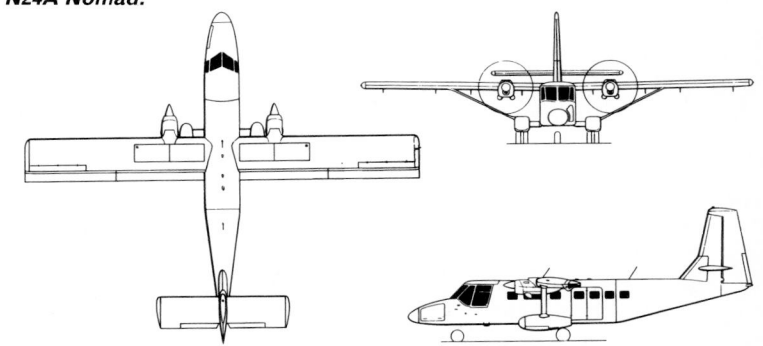

General Aircraft G.A.L.38 Fleet Shadower

Working to meet the same Admiralty requirement that resulted in the Airspeed A.S.39 Fleet Shadower, for a carrier-based aircraft that could remain in contact with an enemy naval force by night,

General Aircraft was no more successful than Airspeed, and only a single prototype **General Aircraft G.A.L.38 Fleet Shadower** was built.

General Aircraft adopted a sesqui-plane configuration, the lower wing having about one-third the span of the upper. Of all-wooden construction, the G.A.L.38 had a conventional tail unit with a tall fin and rudder, fixed tricycle landing gear and four Pobjoy Niagara V engines mounted in nacelles on the leading edge of the foldable upper wing. The fuselage accommodated the pilot in an enclosed cockpit on top of the fuselage, forward of the wing; an observer in the nose of the aircraft; and a radio operator below and behind the pilot.

Both contending companies used similar blown-flap techniques (by propeller slipstream) to attain the desired minimum control speed and, in addition, the G.A.L.38 had full-span split trailing-edge flaps on the lower wing. However, flight testing proved disappointing and only the single prototype was built.

Strange specs breed strange aircraft, and S.23/37 produced the G.A.L.38 Fleet Shadower. Only the prototype of this slow-speed maritime patroller was built.

Specification
Type: carrier-based patrol aircraft
Powerplant: four 97-kW (130-hp) Pobjoy Niagara V 7-cylinder radial piston engines
Performance: maximum speed 185 km/h (115 mph); minimum control speed 63 km/h (39 mph); service ceiling 1830 m (6,000 ft); endurance 11 hours
Weights: empty 2791 kg (6,153 lb); maximum take-off 4290 kg (9,458 lb)
Dimensions: span 17.02 m (55 ft 10 in); length 11.00 m (36 ft 1 in); height 3.86 m (12 ft 8 in); wing area 43.85 m² (472.0 sq ft)

General Aircraft G.A.L.42 Cygnet II

When C.W. Aircraft (Chronander and Waddington) collapsed for lack of finance in 1938, General Aircraft acquired all rights to the C.W. Cygnet two-seat light monoplane, the first all-metal stressed-skin light-plane to be built and flown in the UK.

A conventional cantilever low-wing monoplane with tailwheel landing gear, the **General Aircraft G.A.L.42 Cygnet II** was the company's modified version of the C.W. Aircraft prototype (G-AEMA) with twin fins and rudders and, later, fixed tricycle landing gear. Production of the Cygnet II began in 1939, but plans to build the type in large numbers were frustrated by the outbreak of World War II. Only about 10 were completed, five of them being impressed for service with the RAF to provide familiarisation with tricycle landing gear.

Specification
Type: two-seat trainer/sporting aircraft
Powerplant: one 112-kW (150-hp) Blackburn Cirrus Major II 4-cylinder inverted inline piston engine
Performance: maximum speed 217 km/h (135 mph); cruising speed 185 km/h (115 mph); service ceiling 4265 m (14,000 ft); range 716 km (445 miles)
Weights: empty 669 kg (1,475 lb); maximum take-off 998 kg (2,200 lb)
Dimensions: span 10.52 m (34 ft 6 in); length 7.09 m (23 ft 3 in); height 2.13 m (7 ft 0 in); wing area 16.63 m² (179.01 sq ft)

G-AFVR was the first G.A.L.42 Cygnet II, and was impressed during World War II as a hack with the RAF. It returned to the civil register in 1946, and survived until a crash in 1969.

General Aircraft G.A.L.48 Hotspur

The **General Aircraft G.A.L.48** design was drawn up to meet the requirements of Air Ministry Specification X 10/40. This required the provision of an assault glider that would be able to carry a pilot and seven passengers for a distance of 161 km (100 miles) following release from its tug at a height of 6095 m (20,000 ft). A cantilever mid-wing monoplane of wood construction, the resultant **Hotspur Mk I** was first flown in November 1940, and flight trials showed that it could not meet the specified performance. Thus only 24 examples were built. The type was, however, ordered into production as the **Hotspur Mk II** and **Hotspur Mk III** training versions for use by the UK military glider training schools.

The Hotspur Mk II differed from the initial version by having a wing with modified ailerons and trailing-edge flaps, and which was also reduced in span by 4.88 m (16 ft 0 in), a revised cockpit

Seen during a training exercise, troops move off in penny packets towards Hotspur Mk II training gliders.

canopy and entrance door, and the provision of dual controls. The Hotspur Mk III which followed differed by having an externally braced tail assembly and some changes in equipment. The prototype of a **Twin Hotspur** was also built which united two standard fuselages with a new wing centre-section and tail unit, and which was intended to accommodate a total of 16 airborne troops.

Becoming the primary training glider used by British forces during World War II, 1,012 Hotspur Mk IIs and Mk IIIs were built, mostly by the furniture manufacturer Harris Lebus of Tottenham, London.

Specification
General Aircraft Hotspur Mk II
Type: training glider
Performance: towing speed 209 km/h (130 mph); gliding speed 145 km/h (90 mph); landing speed 90 km/h (56 mph)
Weights: empty 753 kg (1,661 lb);
maximum tow-off weight 1632 kg (3,598 lb)
Dimensions: span 13.99 m (45 ft 10¾ in); length 11.98 m (39 ft 3½ in); height 3.30 m (10 ft 10 in)

General Aircraft G.A.L.49/G.A.L.58 Hamilcar

The **General Aircraft G.A.L.49 Hamilcar Mk I** was designed to meet an Air Ministry specification for a transport glider to carry the heavy support equipment needed by airborne troops. General Aircraft was successful in gaining the contract and more than 400 Hamilcar Mk Is were built, the majority under subcontract, providing the Allies with their largest glider to see service during World War II.

Germany had also developed a large transport glider, the Messerschmitt Me 321, and subsequently decided to power it. General Aircraft made similar plans for the Hamilcar, so that it could operate as a

The Hamilcar had jettisonable landing gears, a hinged nose to admit a Tetrarch tank and two pilots in tandem. The usual tug was the Halifax Mk I or Mk VII.

conventional aircraft with less than half its normal payload, or use its engine to assist take-off at overload weights. Of cantilever high-wing monoplane configuration and having a structure of wood, with mixed plywood and fabric covering, the powered **G.A.L.58 Hamilcar Mk X** differed only by having structural strengthening, the provision of essential

systems and the installation of two Bristol Mercury engines in nacelles at the wing leading edges. It was planned to build the type in quantity for use against Japanese forces in the Pacific theatre, but only 22 had been produced by conversion of Hamilcar Mk I airframes when the war ended, and Hamilcar Mk Xs were not used in action.

Specification
General Aircraft Hamilcar Mk X
(untowed)
Type: powered heavy transport glider
Powerplant: two 720-kW (965-hp) Bristol Mercury 31 9-cylinder radial piston engines
Performance: cruising speed 193 km/h (120 mph); service ceiling

3960 m (13,000 ft)
Weights: empty 11571 kg (25,510 lb); maximum take-off 14742 kg (32,500 lb)
Dimensions: span 33.53 m (110 ft 0 in); length 20.73 m (68 ft 0 in); height 6.17 m (20 ft 3 in); wing area 153.98 m² (1,657.50 sq ft)

General Aircraft ST-3 to ST-12

General Aircraft Ltd was formed in 1934 to take over the assets of the Monospar Wing Co. Ltd. The main asset, the Monospar wing, determined the course of the new company's early history, which began with design and construction of the four-seat **General Aircraft ST-4**. Before that an experimental Monospar wing had been built for Air Ministry testing under the designation **ST-1**, followed by a second structure **(ST-2)**, fabricated by the Gloster Aircraft Company, for flight testing on the Ministry's Fokker F.VIIB-3m. The first light aircraft designed specifically to use the wing was the three-seat **Experimental Monospar ST-3**, also built by the Gloster company. A small fabric-covered lowwing monoplane, powered by two 37-kW (50-hp) Salmson radial engines, the ST-3 was tested extensively and successfully, leading to the decision to set up General Aircraft Ltd to build aircraft based on this wing structure. Designed by a Swiss engineer, H. J. Steiger, this strong and light single spar (hence Monospar) wing was able to resist bending and had a pyramidal wire bracing

system to take the torsional loads.
General Aircraft's four-seat **ST-4** prototype (G-ABUZ) was an attractive monoplane with fixed tailwheel landing gear, powered by two 63-kW (85-hp) Pobjoy R radial engines. An initial batch of five ST-4 production aircraft was followed by a larger number – about 30 – of **ST-4 II** aircraft with marginal differences. In 1933 there appeared a generally similar **ST-6** prototype which differed by having manually retractable main landing gear units. One other production ST-6 was built and there were also two conversions from ST-4 IIs. In early 1934 came the next development of the type, the externally-similar **ST-10** which introduced 67-kW (90-hp) Pobjoy Niagara engines, a revised fuel system and aerodynamic refinements. This combination proved good enough for the ST-10 prototype (G-ACTS) to win the 1934 King's Cup Race. Despite this achievement only one more ST-10 was built, followed by two generally-similar **ST-11** aircraft with Gipsy Major engines and manually retractable tailwheel landing gear. Development of this early

family of General Aircraft Monosparwinged aircraft ended with the production of 10 **ST-12** machines, which differed from the ST-11s only by having fixed landing gear.

Specification
General Aircraft ST-12
Type: four-seat cabin monoplane
Powerplant: two 97-kW (130-hp) de Havilland Gipsy Major 4-cylinder inverted inline piston engines
Performance: maximum speed

254 km/h (158 mph); cruising speed 229 km/h (142 mph); service ceiling 6400 m (21,000 ft); range 660 km (410 miles)
Weights: empty 835 kg (1,840 lb); maximum take-off 1304 kg (2,875 lb)
Dimensions: span 12.24 m (40 ft 2 in); length 8.03 m (26 ft 4 in); height 2.39 m (7 ft 10 in); wing area 20.16 m² (217.0 sq ft)

The ST-4 was a result of Monospar's work, as evidenced by the single tubular spar exiting the wings just inboard of the engine nacelles.

General Aircraft ST-25

In 1935 General Aircraft flew the prototype (G-ADIV) of a new aircraft which carried the designation **General Aircraft ST-25**, this advanced type number and the name **Jubilee** being allocated to mark the Silver Jubilee of King George V's reign. The ST-25 was, to all intents and purposes, an updated version of the ST-10 which had won the King's Cup Race in the previous year. It differed by having a folding seat at the rear to accommodate a fifth passenger when required, cabin windows extended further aft, and Mk II versions of the Pobjoy Niagara engine.

The ST-25 was a popular aircraft and production continued until 1939. During that time there were few changes in the basic design until late 1936 when, to improve directional stability in an engine-out situation, the standard tail unit was replaced by one of new design incorporating twin endplate fins and rudders. No change was made in the type number as a result, but new aircraft to this configuration had the name **Universal** and also introduced more-powerful Niagara III engines. Production totalled 59, comprising 30 Jubilees and 29 Universals. An ambulance version of the ST-25 was de-

veloped, incorporating a large door on the starboard side to ease the loading of a stretcher patient, and a seat was provided for a medical attendant. As well as a number of **Ambulance** versions produced for export, five **Freighter** aircraft, retaining the large starboard door but otherwise to standard, were sold to a Canadian customer.

Variants
ST-25 De Luxe: designation of one aircraft (G-AEDY) of Jubilee configuration with controllable trim tabs, an enlarged fin and Niagara III engines with electric starters; converted subsequently to Universal standard
G.A.L.26: designation of one ST-25 Jubilee while being flown experimentally with two 67-kW (90-hp) Blackburn Cirrus Minor 4-cylinder inverted inline engines
G.A.L.41: designation of one ST-25 flown with an experimental pressurised cabin that utilised a 20-kW (27-hp) Douglas Sprite engine with a supercharger fan to provide pressurisation air
T42: identification of one ST-25

The most successful of the Monospar designs, the General Aircraft ST-25 Jubilee first flew in 1935. G-AEDY was the 20th to be registered, and crashed in 1940.

Universal while being flown experimentally during 1937 with tricycle landing gear

Specification
General Aircraft ST-25
Type: four/five-seat cabin monoplane
Powerplant: two 71-kW (95-hp) Pobjoy Niagara III 7-cylinder radial piston engines
Performance: maximum speed

211 km/h (131 mph); cruising speed 185 km/h (115 mph); service ceiling 4665 m (15,300 ft); range 676 km (420 miles)
Weights: empty 825 kg (1,818 lb); maximum take-off 1304 kg (2,875 lb)
Dimensions: span 12.24 m (40 ft 2 in); length 7.72 m (25 ft 4 in); height 2.39 m (7 ft 10 in); wing area 20.16 m² (217.0 sq ft)

General Avia F.20 Pegaso/Condor

In January 1970 Dott. Ing. Stelio Frati, renowned as a freelance designer of a series of successful light aircraft built by manufacturers such as Ambrosini, Aviamilano, Caproni, Pasotti, Procaer and SIAI Marchetti, established the Costruzioni Aeronautiche General Avia to construct prototypes of his designs. The first new type to be developed at the

Milan workshops was the **General Avia F.20 Pegaso**, a six-seat twin-engined light executive transport. Work on the first prototype began in September 1970, this aircraft flying on 21 October 1971; a second prototype, slightly larger and heavier than the first, flew on 11 August 1972.

At about the same time that General

Avia was being established, publisher Dr Gianni Mazzocchi was setting up Italair SpA to provide development, manufacturing and marketing facilities for light single- and twin-engined aircraft, and this organisation took over the two prototypes to conduct the certification programme in anticipation of production. Type approval was granted by the RAI on

19 November 1974, and by the FAA on 14 May 1975. By agreement production was handed back to General Avia, and the first aircraft flew on 17 December 1979, incorporating a number of minor changes which included improved cabin heating and sound-proofing, and the substitution of three-bladed Hartzell propellers for the original two-bladed units.

A prototype of a turboprop-powered military version of the Pegaso designated F.20TP Condor was built and made its first flight on 7 May 1983. Intended for use in the anti-armour, light ground attack, maritime surveillance, search and rescue, multi-engine and weapon trainer roles, further development was postponed in 1985 in favour of design work on the Jet Squalus also designed by Frati.

Specification
General Avia F.20TP Condor
Type: light utility military aircraft
Powerplant: two 298-kW (400-shp) Allison 250-B17B turboprops
Performance: maximum speed at sea level 460 km/h (286 mph); economic cruising speed at 3050 m

(10,000 ft) 389 km/h (242 mph); service ceiling 8500 m (27,900 ft); range with auxiliary fuel 3100 km (1,926 miles)
Weights: empty equipped 1400 kg (3,086 lb); maximum take-off 2700 kg (5,952 lb)
Dimensions: span 10.34 m (33 ft 11 in); length 8.92 m (29 ft 3 in); height

3.50 m (11 ft 5 in); wing area 16.02 m² (172.4 sq ft)
Armament: two hardpoints under each wing can carry gun or rocket pods, sensor pods, or fuel tanks (on the outer pylons)

General Dynamics F-16 Fighting Falcon

Design of the General Dynamics F-16 was initiated during 1971 to meet a US Air Force requirement for a new highly-manoeuvrable lightweight fighter (LWF). Five US companies submitted proposals on 28 February 1972 and less than two months later General Dynamics and Northrop were each contracted to build two prototypes. Required for competitive evaluation, the rival designs were allocated the respective designations YF-16 and YF-17, and the first **YF-16** flew on 2 February 1974. On 13 January 1975 it was announced that the YF-16 had won and full-scale engineering development authorised under the designation **F-16A**, together with the **F-16B** two-seat fighter/trainer. On 7 June 1975 came confirmation that four NATO allies, Belgium, Denmark, the Netherlands and Norway, had also selected the F-16 to meet the requirements of their air forces. Thus was initiated a massive production programme, with some 67 major and almost 4,000 other sub-contractors supplying avionics, components and equipment to the General Dynamics plant at Fort Worth, Texas. In Europe there were 33 major and nearly 400 additional sub-contractors keeping the production lines supplied in Belgium and the Netherlands.

The first production F-16A was flown on 7 August 1978 and was handed over formally to the US Air Force 10 days later. The first European F-16s were delivered to the air forces of Belgium on 26 January 1979, the Netherlands on 6 June 1979, Norway on 25 January 1980 and Denmark on 28 January 1980. The first F-16 for Israel, a two-seat F-16B, was handed over officially at Fort Worth, Texas, on 31 January 1980, and initial deliveries to Egypt began early in 1982.

The current order book for the F-16, officially named **Fighting Falcon** in 1980, shows that the USAF plans to acquire a total of 2,261, with the US Navy operating 26 Falcons, comprising 22 **F-16Ns** and four **TF-16N** two-seaters, all converted from **F-16C/D** models. Other users include Bahrain (12), Belgium (160), Denmark (70), Egypt (128), Greece (40), Indonesia (12), Israel (210), South Korea (164), Netherlands (213), Norway (74), Pakistan (111), Portugal (20), Singapore (8), Thailand (18), Turkey (160) and Venezuela (24). Iranian plans to buy 160 F-16s were cancelled in January 1979.

By August 1990 more than 2,600 F-16s had been delivered out of 3,530 ordered and were in service with 17 customers in 16 countries, with Portugal scheduled to join the Fighting Falcon club in 1993. Some of the latest technology can be seen in the structure and avionics systems of the F-16. For example, the wings are 'blended' into the fuselage, which not only helps to save weight, but also increases the overall lift at high angles of attack and reduces drag in the transonic speed range. Movable leading-and trailing-edge flaps, controlled automatically by the aircraft's speed and attitude, enable the wing to assume an optimum configuration for lift under all conditions of flight. The highly-swept

strakes that lead forward alongside the nose provide further lift: they also prevent wing-root stall, reduce buffeting and improve directional stability and roll control. All flying controls are operated by a 'fly-by-wire' electrical system, replacing mechanical linkages throughout the airframe, and enabling the aircraft to respond faster and more accurately to pilot commands. Advanced avionics include communications with a secure voice system, inertial and TACAN navigation, pulse-Doppler ranging and angle track radar, radar warning system, flight control computer, and central air data and fire control computers. Development continues by the company, as well as the US Air Force under programmes such as the Multi-national Staged Improvement Program (MSIP). This was intended to ensure that throughout production the necessary steps were taken to make possible the easy incorporation of systems then under development. As an example, aircraft delivered from November 1981 onwards had structural and wiring provisions to allow precision strike, night attack and beyond-visual-range interception missions when the equipment became available. Brief details of some of these developments are given below.

Production F-16A and B models were powered by 10800-kg (23,770-lb) thrust Pratt & Whitney F100 turbofans, but following a US government directive to double-source engine supplies, F-16Cs and Ds built after July 1986 can also be fitted with General Electric F110 turbofan powerplants giving 13150-kg (28,984-lb) thrust.

Variants

F-16(ADF): designation given to 270 F-16A/Bs modified to Air Defense Fighters to replace F-4s and F-106s used in 11 Air National Guard squadrons. Modifications include upgraded AN/APG-66 radar, improved ECCM and IFF, night identification light, voice message unit, and low altitude warning system, together with enhanced AAM capability allowing the carriage of two AIM-7 Sparrows, six AIM-120 AMRAAMs or six AIM-9 Sidewinders, or combinations of all three. Ordered in October 1986, the first F-16(ADF) was delivered on 1

March 1989 and the last early in 1991
F-16C: designation allocated to improved single-seat version of F-16A incorporating MSIP features outlined above and including ground-attack capability plus Low-Altitude Navigation, Targeting, Infra-Red for Night (LANTIRN) and Airborne-Self-Protection Jamming (ASPJ) systems. First deliveries made in October 1986 to 86th TFW at Ramstein, Germany
F-16D: two-seat version of F-16C with similar capabilities
F-16N: 22 single-seaters and four two-seaters (**TF-16Ns**) modified for the US Navy from F-16C and D models. Used as supersonic adversary aircraft with Top Gun Fighter Weapons School, and Squadrons VF-43, VF-45 and VF-126
F-16XL: GD designation of the company-funded advanced F-16 development featuring a new highly-swept 'cranked-arrow' wing, developed jointly by GD and NASA, having an area more than 120 per cent greater than standard; lengthened fuselage to increase internal fuel capacity by 82 per cent, and underwing hardpoints doubling the standard weapons load; the single-seat prototype (allocated **F-16E**) was flown for the first time on 3 July 1982 followed by the F110-powered two-seater (the **F-16F**) on 29 October 1982. Selection of the F-15E in February 1984 terminated USAF interest and both aircraft were leased to NASA and further modified in connection with other experiments
F-16/79: designation of an F-16A re-engined with a cheaper and lower-powered General Electric J79-GE-119 afterburning turbojet giving 8165-kg (18,000-lb) thrust. Intended as a reduced-cost version for export, the sole F-16/79 first flew on 29 October 1980 but no further interest has materialised
F-16/101: designation given to an early development aircraft loaned from the USAF, and fitted with a General Electric F110 turbofan engine (the Rockwell B-1 powerplant) for evaluation leading to double-sourcing F-16 engines. First flown on 19 December 1980, the feasibility programme was completed in May 1981
AFTI/F-16: single F-16A modified by General Dynamics under USAF

Arguably the world's most important current fighter, the F-16 is in widespread service around the world. The vast majority serve with US forces, including this F-16C of the Luke-based 944th TFG/AFRes.

contract to explore new fighter technology. Dubbed the Advanced Fighter Technology Integration (AFTI) programme, it was essentially an advanced control-configured vehicle (CCV) fitted with a unique digital flight control system which made it the first operationally-equipped fighter aircraft capable of executing flat, unbanked turns with weapons firing, and brought completely new dimensions to aerial combat. First flown on 10 July 1982, the AFTI has since been used to test a number of other advanced technologies, including the operation of certain essential functions by pilot's voice command

Specification
General Dynamics F-16A Fighting Falcon
Type: single-seat air combat and ground-attack fighter
Powerplant: either one 10800-kg (23,770-lb) Pratt & Whitney F100-PW-220 or one 13150-kg (28,984-lb) General Electric F110-GE-100 afterburning turbofan
Performance: maximum level speed more than 2142 km/h (1,320 mph) or Mach 2.0 at 12190 m (40,000 ft); service ceiling above 15240 m (50,000 ft); operational radius 925 km (575 miles)
Weights: empty 7070 kg (15,586 lb); maximum take-off 16057 kg (35,400 lb)
Dimensions: span 9.45 m (31 ft 0 in); length 15.09 m (49 ft 6 in); height 5.09 m (16 ft 8 in); wing area 27.87 m² (300.0 sq ft)
Armament: one General Electric M61A1 20-mm multi-barrelled cannon, a wingtip missile station on each wing plus one underfuselage and six underwing hardpoints enabling the carriage of a 9276-kg (20,450-lb) warload of air-to-air or air-to-surface missiles, ECM, reconnaissance or rocket pods, iron or 'smart' bombs or fuel tanks

General Dynamics F-111
to
Gloster Javelin

General Dynamics F-111

The major advantages offered by variable-geometry aircraft are a high supersonic performance with the wings swept back; economical subsonic cruising speed with the wings fully spread; a long operational or ferry range; and relatively short take-off and landing runs at very high weights. So when in 1960 the US Air Force's Tactical Air Command was seeking a strike aircraft to replace the Republic F-105 Thunderchief, it was very interested in the results of experiments with variable-geometry wing configurations that had been conducted by NASA's Langley Research Center at Hampton, Virginia. At the same time the US Navy was looking for a new fleet air-defence fighter to succeed the McDonnell Douglas F-4 Phantom, and eventually the Department of Defense decreed that the two requirements should be combined in a single programme known as TFX, or Tactical Fighter, Experimental.

The Defense Secretary, Robert McNamara, stuck to this decision despite strong objections from both services, and on 24 November 1962 a development contract for 23 aircraft was awarded to General Dynamics. Of these, 18 were to be basic tactical General Dynamics **F-111A** aircraft for the USAF and five **F-111B** aircraft developed primarily by Grumman for the US Navy.

The F-111B began to run into trouble almost immediately; despite a long and intensive flight development programme the type was cancelled in July 1968. The aircraft had consistently proved overweight and unable to meet the performance required, and only seven were completed: the five development machines, plus two of the 231 production F-111Bs which the US Navy had planned to order.

The F-111A, on which all subsequent models were based, had an almost equally unhappy early history after its first flight on 21 December 1964, but eventually it was cleared for service and deliveries of 141 production examples began in October 1967, to the 474th Tactical Fighter Wing at Nellis AFB, Nevada. On 15 March 1968 the 428th Tactical Fighter Squadron detached six of its F-111As to Thailand for operational deployment over Vietnam, losing three of them in four weeks. Groundings and modifications followed, and when 48 more F-111As were sent to Vietnam in 1972-73, they flew more than 4,000 combat sorties in seven months for the loss of only six aircraft. This latter deployment demonstrated adequately the potential of the F-111, and details of subsequent variants are given below.

Production totalled 563 aircraft, including 24 supplied to the Royal Australian Air Force. The majority remain in service with the USAF and RAAF, and it is expected that the type will continue to be important elements of these air forces for many more years. USAF

The most potent model of 'Aardvark' is the F-111F, renowned for its sterling work during the Gulf war. Laser-guided bombs (as carried here) are self-designated by the underfuselage 'Pave Tack' pod.

F-111Fs serving in the UK are equipped with AN/AVQ-26 'Pave Tack' thermal imaging/laser target acquisition, designation and tracking system, and RAAF **F-111Cs** have this same system.

Variants
F-111A: initial production version, a two-seat tactical fighter-bomber, with 8391-kg (18,500-lb) thrust Pratt & Whitney TF30-P-3 turbofan engines; 158 built, 18 of them development/service evaluation aircraft; first production example flown in June 1967

EF-111A Raven: ECM tactical jamming version; produced by Grumman as conversion from F-111As

FB-111A: two-seat strategic bomber version for USAF Strategic Air Command with a 2.13-m (7-ft) increase in wing span, strengthened landing gear, increased fuel tankage and 9185-kg (20,150-lb) thrust TF30-P-7 engines; 76 built

RF-111A: reconnaissance conversion of one development F-111A with a removable sensor pallet; tested successfully but did not enter production

YF-111A: redesignation of two F-111Ks almost completed for RAF when order cancelled; completed and allocated to the USAF for its research, development, test and evaluation programme

F-111B: carrier-based fleet defence aircraft for US Navy; seven built before development and production terminated

F-111C: designation of 24 strike aircraft ordered by RAAF in 1963 but of which delivery did not begin until 1973; increased span wings as on FB-111A, strengthened landing gear and TF30-P-3 engines; four F-111As, virtually to F-111C standard, have been delivered to the RAAF ex-USAF to replace cumulative losses of four F-111Cs

F-111D: similar ro F-111E but with 8890-kg (19,600-lb) thrust TF30-P-9 engines, advanced avionics to enhance air-to-air weapon deployment and navigational capability; 96 built

RF-111D: designation allocated for a sophisticated reconnaissance aircraft; not built for lack of funds

F-111E: superseded the F-111A on the production line from 160th aircraft; has modified air intakes for its TF30-P-3 engines; 94 built

F-111F: introduced improved avionics, including a combination of F-111D and FB-111A navigational and digital computer systems, improved wing structure and landing gear, and much more powerful TF30-P-100 engines; 106 built

F-111G: designation given to FB-111As displaced from Strategic Air Command in 1988 and converted to tactical role

FB-111H: proposed manned penetration bomber with two 13608-kg (30,000-lb) thrust General Electric F101-GE-100 turbofan engines, advanced avionics and increased weapon capacity; not built

F-111K: designation of 50 aircraft ordered for RAF but cancelled in 1968

Specification
General Dynamics F-111F
Type: two-seat multi-purpose attack aircraft

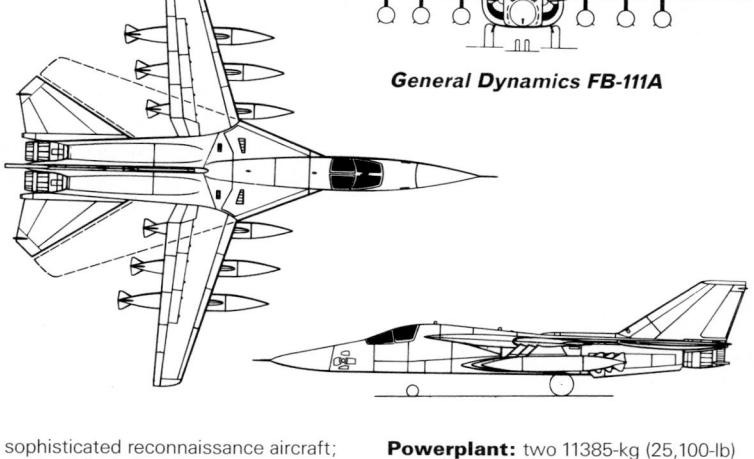

General Dynamics FB-111A

Powerplant: two 11385-kg (25,100-lb) thrust Pratt & Whitney TF-30-P-100 augmented turbofans

Performance: maximum speed at optimum altitude 2655 km/h (1,650 mph) or Mach 2.5; maximum speed at sea level 1473 km/h (915 mph) or Mach 1.2; service ceiling more than 17985 m (59,000 ft); range with maximum internal fuel 4707 km (2,925 miles)

Weights: empty 21398 kg (47,175 lb); maximum take-off 45359 kg (100,000 lb)

Dimensions: span unswept 19.20 m (63 ft 0 in); swept 9.74 m (31 ft 11½ in); length 22.40 m (73 ft 6 in); height 5.22 m (17 ft 1½ in)

Armament: one 20-mm multi-barrelled M61A-1 cannon and one 340-kg (750-lb) B43 bomb, or two B43 bombs in internal weapons bay; three underwing hardpoints on each outer wing panel, the inner four pivoting to keep stores aligned as wings sweep

Globe GC-1 Swift

Shortly before World War II Globe aircraft designed and developed a two-seat light cabin monoplane designated the **Swift Model GC-1**. Its production was frustrated not only by disappointing performance as a result of low power but also, of course, by US involvement in World War II. A cantilever low-wing monoplane, the Model GC-1 incorporated Duraloid bonded plywood in its wing and tail structure, but had a welded steel-tube fuselage with fabric covering. Retractable tail-wheel landing gear was standard, and power for the prototype was provided initially by a 48-kW (65-hp) Continental A65 engine. First flown in early 1941, the Model GC-1 was found to be seriously underpowered, leading to installation of a 60-kW (80-hp) Continental A80. It was with this latter powerplant that the aircraft was certificated in early 1942. Engines of 67 to 75 kW (90 to 100 hp) were to be offered as optional for definitive aircraft, but no production followed and it was not until 1946 that the programme was revived.

While of the same general configuration, the post-war **Swift Model GC-1A** was of all-metal construction and of much improved overall design.

Unfortunately, Globe started on the wrong foot by giving the almost 20 per cent heavier GC-1A a 63-kW (85-hp) Continental C85 engine. Despite docile performance, almost 400 were built before installation of a more powerful engine in the **Model GC-1B** produced a really sporty aircraft, which was built in large numbers by Globe and under sub-contract by Temco (Texas Engineering & Manufacturing Co.), this latter company acquiring production and sales rights when Globe ran into financial difficulties in 1947. Production as the **Temco Swift** continued until 1951, and many examples remain in service worldwide. In 1987 LeRoy LoPresti modified a 1946 Model Swift into the prototype LoPresti Piper Swiftfire (later renamed Swiftfury). Fitted with a 425-shp Allison 250 turbo-prop engine, it flew for the first time on 23 March 1989.

Specification
Temco Swift Model GC-1B
Type: two-seat cabin monoplane
Powerplant: one 93-kW (125-hp) Continental C125 flat-six piston engine
Performance: maximum speed 241 km/h (150 mph); cruising speed 225 km/h (140 mph); service ceiling 4875 m (16,000 ft); range 313 km (420 miles)
Weights: empty 517 kg (1,139 lb); maximum take-off 776 kg (1,710 lb)
Dimensions: span 8.94 m (29 ft 4 in); length 6.37 m (20 ft 10¾ in); height 1.79 m (5 ft 10½ in); wing area 12.23 m² (131.63 sq ft)

Definitive production development of the Globe GC-1, the Temco GC-1B Swift combined attractive lines with sturdy structure and sporting performance on a relatively low-powered engine. The design was briefly but unsuccessfully revived in 1990 as the LoPresti Piper Swiftfury.

Gloster I/II

The Gloucester Aircraft Company was established in mid-1917, its name being changed to Gloster Aircraft Company in late 1926; this came because of concern about the peculiarities of English pronunciation and the effect the original name might have on export sales. It may now seem a trivial reason for changing an established name, but such was the shortage of orders in that first post-World War I decade that anything which might deter an enquiry or order was best eliminated.

This same scarcity of orders also resulted in a conclusion that conspicuous success in competitive events might convince the Air Ministry that Gloster was the only worthwhile source for high-speed fighter aircraft. Thus was born the **Gloster Mars I** single-seat racer, nick-named **Bamel**, in which no efforts were spared by Henry Folland to achieve a genuine high-performance aircraft. The nickname is reputedly derived from a comment of Henry Folland while the Mars was under construction, that it was "half-bare, half-Camel". True or false, the Bamel was a remarkably clean biplane, with single I-type interplane struts and minimal wire bracing, powered by a 336-kW (450-hp) Napier Lion engine in an unusually neat installation. An odd feature was a faired cabane

structure to house the fuel and water header tanks, preventing direct forward view. First flown on 20 June 1921, the Bamel won the annual Aerial Derby during the following month, and modified and improved progressively established a British speed record of 316.1 km/h (196.4 mph) on 12 December 1921 before winning the Aerial Derby again in 1922.

During early 1923 the Mars I was given extensively modified wings, had the fuel and water header tanks transferred within the fuselage to lose the view-limiting cabane structure, and had a more powerful Lion engine installed, being redesignated **Gloster I**. After winning the Aerial Derby of 1923 it was acquired by the RAF and, with float landing gear, used by the RAF's High Speed Flight at Felixstowe for training purposes.

Gloster's policy of developing high-performance aircraft brought an order from the Air Ministry in early 1924 for two **Gloster II** aircraft to compete in the 1924 Schneider Trophy contest. Similar to the Gloster I, but with increased wing stagger, the Gloster II was powered by a 436-kW (585-hp) Napier Lion VA driving a Fairey Reed metal propeller, and featured remarkably clean floats and extensive fairing to improve aerodynamic efficiency. The first aircraft (J7504) was taken to RAF Felixstowe for flight testing on 12 September 1924. About a week later, while the aircraft was being flown

by Hubert Broad, a forward float strut collapsed as the machine touched down on roughish water. Almost immediately the aircraft sank and was a complete loss but, fortunately, Broad escaped without injury. Shortly after this event the 1924 Schneider Trophy contest was cancelled and the second Gloster II was completed with wheeled landing gear for high-speed flight development. It, too, was wrecked in a landing accident in mid-1925 and no further examples were built.

Specification
Gloster I (landplane)
Type: single-seat racing biplane
Powerplant: one 395-kW (530-hp)

A typical floatplane racer of its time, the Gloster II was notable for the attempt it represented to pack maximum engine into minimum airframe with scant regard for handling. Both examples were written off.

Napier Lion 12-cylinder 'arrow' piston engine
Performance: maximum speed at sea level 354 km/h (220 mph)
Weights: empty 894 kg (1,970 lb); maximum take-off 1202 kg (2,650 lb)
Dimensions: span 6.10 m (20 ft 0 in); length 7.01 m (23 ft 0 in); height 2.84 m (9 ft 4 in); wing area 15.33 m² (165.0 sq ft)

Gloster III

In February 1925 the Gloster company received an order from the Air Ministry for two examples of a new racing biplane, designated **Gloster III**, to compete in the 1925 Schneider Trophy contest. The new machine was derived from the Gloster II, and Henry Folland had spared no efforts to achieve a clean and small frontal area; he had also adopted a monocoque fuselage structure with plywood skinning for strength and light weight. The wings were of wood, fabric covered, and the twin floats were mounted on streamlined and wire-braced struts. The 522-kW (700-hp) Napier Lion VII engine was adopted for the Gloster III, making it then the smallest British aircraft to have such a high-

powered engine. Flight testing of aircraft serial N194 showed there was some directional instability and with little time for modifications to be introduced the wings were re-rigged and the area of the dorsal and ventral fins was increased. With these changes the aircraft was re-designated **Gloster IIIA**.

Flown by Hubert Broad, the Gloster IIIA gained second place in the Schneider Trophy contest at Baltimore, USA; the Gloster III (N195) was less fortunate, being damaged in practice before the race. After its return to the UK the Gloster IIIA was transferred to RAF Felixstowe, but the Gloster III was repaired and modified simultaneously, gaining wing surface radiators, a new tail unit and several other small changes. In this form it was redesignated **Gloster IIIB** and was also delivered to RAF Felix-

The Gloster III suffered from a lack of directional stability. It was intended to have surface radiators on the lower wings, but instead featured Lamblin radiators on the lower leading edges.

stowe, where both were used as trainers for pilots of the RAF's High Speed Flight.

Specification
Gloster IIIB
Type: single-seat racing float biplane
Powerplant: one 522-kW (700-hp) Napier Lion VII 12-cylinder 'arrow' piston engine
Performance: maximum speed 405 km/h (252 mph) at sea level
Weights: empty 1033 kg (2,278 lb); maximum take-off 1343 kg (2,962 lb)
Dimensions: span 6.10 m (20 ft 0 in), length 8.18 m (26 ft 10 in); height 2.95 m (9 ft 8 in); wing area 14.12 m² (152.0 sq ft)

Gloster IV

The Gloster company produced no contender for the 1926 Schneider Trophy contest, also held in the United States but won by Italy with the Macchi M.39, which meant that the next contest would be held in Italy. However, in early 1926 Henry Folland and his team were already working on the design of a successor to the the Gloster III, adhering to the biplane configuration which, in Folland's opinion, provided the ideal combination of light weight and structural integrity. To gain the desired increase in performance for this new **Gloster IV** a still more powerful version of the Napier Lion engine was chosen, and every possible aerodynamic refinement was incorporated to reduce drag to the absolute minimum. Wing surface radiators were used for engine cooling and, for the first time, the company designed and built its own floats for the three aircraft that were built; these floats also had cooling radiators included on their upper surfaces. The dissipation of heat from the powerful engines that were then being developed brought problems to all designers of competing aircraft, and in order to keep the lubricating oil at an

The Gloster IVA featured the W-form of the cylinder banks of the Napier Lion VIIIA faired beautifully into the dorsal strake and the wing leading edges. It did not get to race in the Schneider Trophy.

effective temperature the Gloster IVs acquired a combined oil tank/cooler in the undersurface of the nose and additional cooling surfaces on the fuselage sides. The aircraft's wings and all bracing struts were carefully blended at the fuselage/wing structure interface to such effect that, by comparison with the Gloster III, drag was reduced by a figure of approximately 40 per cent.

The three aircraft comprised the Gloster IV (N224) with a 671-kW (900-hp) direct-drive Napier Lion VIIA engine; the **Gloster IVA** (N222) with reduced wing span, a cruciform tail unit and the same powerplant; and the **Gloster IVB** (N223) which was the same as the Gloster IVA except for the installation of a Napier Lion VIIB engine incorporating a reduction gear.

It was the last which was chosen to compete in the contest as the third member of the British team. Unfortunately, the Gloster IVB had to retire

during the sixth lap. The team included two Supermarine S.5s, powered by Lion VIIA and VIIB engines, which gained first and second places respectively. Subsequently the Gloster IV was sold, but N222 and N223 continued to be used by the RAF for high-speed flight research.

Specification
Gloster IVB
Type: single-seat racing float biplane
Powerplant: one 660-kW (885-hp) Napier Lion VIIB 12-cylinder 'arrow' piston engine
Performance: maximum speed 475 km/h (295 mph) at sea level
Weights: empty 1185 kg (2,613 lb); maximum take-off 1499 kg (3,305 lb)
Dimensions: span 6.90 m (22 ft 7½ in); length 8.03 m (26 ft 4 in); height 2.79 m (9 ft 2 in); wing area 12.91 m² (139.0 sq ft)

Gloster VI

Development of a Gloster V had been projected, but this type failed to materialise, and it was not until early 1928 that Folland and his team began the design of a new monoplane contender to compete in the Schneider Trophy contest of 1929. A low-wing wire braced monoplane, the **Gloster VI** had a wing of wooden construction, a fuselage of light alloy, and a cantilever tail unit of similar construction to the wings. The floats were also of light alloy, both serving as fuel tanks with their contents pumped to a small header tank in the fuselage. The wing surfaces were almost entirely covered by coolers for the liquid-cooling system of the Napier Lion VIID engine; surface oil coolers conforming to the fuselage contours, to the rear of the cockpit, could be supplemented if needed by auxiliary oil coolers on the upper surface of the floats.

Two examples of the Gloster VI were

built, N249 and N250, but when tested at Calshot in August 1929 their highly-boosted and supercharged Lion VIID engines proved to be too temperamental and they were withdrawn from the contest. Both ended their days at RAF Felixstowe, but extensive work to resolve their engine problems was unsuccessful with the result that they saw little use.

Specification
Type: single-seat racing float monoplane
Powerplant: one 984-kW (1,320-hp) Napier Lion VIID 12-cylinder supercharged 'arrow' piston engine
Performance: maximum recorded speed 565 km/h (351 mph)
Weights: empty 1036 kg (2,284 lb); maximum take-off 1669 kg (3,680 lb)
Dimensions: span 7.92 m (26 ft 0 in); length 8.23 m (27 ft 0 in); height 3.29 m (10 ft 9½ in); wing area 9.85 m² (106.0 sq ft)

The Gloster VI was plagued throughout its life by problems with the Lion engine, which by the late 1920s had reached too high a degree of development for reliability.

Gloster E.28/39

The W.1 gas turbine designed by Frank Whittle, and built by Power Jets Ltd under an Air Ministry contract awarded in March 1938, needed an airframe, and specification E.28/39 was issued to Gloster on 3 February 1940. The design was to be based on fighter requirements, with provision for the weight and space that would be needed by four Browning 7.7-mm (0.303-in) machineguns, although these would not be fitted in the test aircraft. Two **Gloster**

Though it was fitted with provision for armament, the E.28/39 was nothing more than a highly important research aircraft, being the United Kingdom's first jet.

E.28/39 prototypes were covered by the contract, these aircraft being required to have tricycle landing gear with a steerable nosewheel.

Within just over a year the first prototype was ready for taxiing tests, undertaken at Gloster's Hucclecote airfield by the chief test pilot, P. E. G. Sayer, on 7 April 1941. The following day the aircraft made a few short hops, following which a new nose landing gear unit was fitted before the aircraft was dismantled and taken by road to Cranwell for flight tests,

as it was felt that the longer runways there would be an advantage. In fact, the E.28/39 was airborne in about 550 m (1,800 ft), with a thrust of 390 kg (860 lb) from the Power Jets W.1 engine installed for initial flight tests, becoming Britain's first jet-powered aircraft.

The first flight, made on 15 May 1941,

lasted for 17 minutes and was completely successful. A further 10 hours of flying was achieved in the following 13 days before the prototype was returned to the factory to await the new and more powerful 526-kg (1,160-lb) thrust W.1A engine.

A new series of tests began on 4 February 1942 at Edgehill, Warwickshire, but problems with the engine developed and the aircraft was slightly damaged. Pilots of the Royal Aircraft Establishment, Farnborough, also flew

the aircraft and during one of these flights, on 30 July with the first prototype, then powered by a new Rover W.2B engine of 692 kg (1,526 lb) thrust, the ailerons jammed at 11275 m (37,000 ft) putting the aircraft into an inverted spin: Squadron Leader Davie managed to bale out at 10060 m (33,000 ft) but the E.28/39 was lost.

The second prototype had been re-engined with a Power Jets W.2/500 engine of 771 kg (1,700 lb) thrust and testing continued, concluding with more

flying at the RAE to obtain aerodynamic data. By this time an improved Power Jets W.2/500 had been fitted, giving 798 kg (1,760 lb) thrust. At the conclusion of its test programme this aircraft was placed in the Science Museum, South Kensington, for permanent exhibition.

Specification
Type: single-seat turbojet-powered research aircraft
Powerplant: one 798-kg (1,760-lb)

thrust Power Jets W.2/500 turbojet engine
Performance: maximum speed 750 km/h (466 mph) at 3050 m (10,000 ft); service ceiling 9755 m (32,000 ft)
Weights: empty 1309 kg (2,886 lb); maximum take-off 1700 kg (3,748 lb)
Dimensions: span 8.84 m (29 ft 0 in); length 7.72 m (25 ft 3¾ in); height 2.82 m (9 ft 3 in); wing area 13.61 m² (146.5 sq ft)
Armament: none

Gloster Gambet

Requiring a replacement for its Sparrowhawk fighters, in early 1926 the Imperial Japanese Navy requested Aichi, Mitsubishi and Nakajima to submit designs for a new single-seat ship-based fighter. Nakajima was sufficiently astute to request Gloster to design a suitable aircraft, the result being the **Gloster Gambet** which Henry Folland was already developing as a private venture. An unequal-span single-bay biplane, largely of wooden construction, this single-seat fighter prototype had fixed tailskid landing gear, arrester hooks and flotation gear, and was armed with two Vickers machine-guns. The aircraft was acquired by Nakajima during July 1927, together with production rights, and a design team led by Engineer Takao Yoshida introduced modifications that would enable it to meet specifically the requirements of the navy and, at the

Based loosely on the Gamecock, the Gambet was designed to the requirements of the Imperial Japanese Navy and, flown with the registration J-AAMB, prevailed over Aichi and Mitsubishi designs.

same time, make it more suitable for production in Japan. A total of 150 was built by Nakajima in two versions as the **A1N1** (50) and **A1N2** (100), or **Type 3 Carrier-Based Fighter**.

Specification
Gloster Gambet
Type: single-seat carrier-based fighter prototype
Powerplant: one 313-kW (420-hp) Bristol Jupiter VI radial piston engine
Performance: maximum speed 245 km/h (152 mph) at 1525 m

(5,000 ft); service ceiling 7070 m (23,200 ft); endurance at 4570 m (15,000 ft) 3 hours 45 minutes
Weights: empty 912 kg (2,010 lb); maximum take-off 1395 kg (3,075 lb)
Dimensions: span 9.70 m (31 ft 0 in); length 6.49 m (21 ft 3½ in); height

3.25 m (10 ft 8 in); wing area 26.38 m² (284.0 sq ft)
Armament: two fixed forward-firing 7.7-mm (0.303-in) Vickers machine-guns, plus underwing racks to mount four 9-kg (20-lb) bombs

Gloster Gamecock

The **Gloster Gamecock**, built to Air Ministry Specification 27/23 calling for a single-seat fighter, was another development of the successful Gloster Grouse/Grebe family. It differed primarily by having a Bristol Jupiter engine to replace the Armstrong Siddeley Jaguar, which had caused problems by its unreliability. Other changes included improved ailerons, refined fuselage contours and internal mounting of the two machine-guns. First flown during February 1925, the Gamecock moved rapidly to service tests which resulted in modification of the tail unit. With such modifications this first of the three prototypes proved good enough to win an order for 30 production **Gamecock Mk I** fighters, the first of which entered service with No. 23 Squadron in May 1926, remaining operational until July 1931.

A total of almost 100 Gamecocks was acquired by the RAF, this number including three late-development **Gamecock Mk II** aircraft with a revised wing centre-section and other improvements. In addition to Gamecocks for the RAF, Gloster supplied three Gamecock Mk IIs to Finland, this nation building during 1929-30 a total of 15 more under licence. Named **Kikko**, these were in first-line service with the Finnish air force from 1929 to 1935 and subsequently used as trainers until the last was retired in 1941.

Variant
Gamecock Mk III: redesignation of one RAF Gamecock Mk II used for spinning trials following modifications to reduce tendency to spin

Specification
Gamecock Mk I
Type: single-seat fighter
Powerplant: one 317-kW (425-hp) Bristol Jupiter VI 9-cylinder radial piston

Gloster Gamecock Mk I of No. 32 Squadron, RAF, based at Kenley between September 1926 and April 1928.

engine
Performance: maximum speed 249 km/h (155 mph) at 1525 m (5,000 ft); climb to 3050 m (10,000 ft) in 7 minutes 35 seconds; service ceiling 6705 m (22,000 ft); endurance 2 hours
Weights: empty 875 kg (1,930 lb); maximum take-off 1299 kg (2,863 lb)
Dimensions: span 9.08 m (29 ft 9½ in); length 5.99 m (19 ft 8 in); height 2.95 m (9 ft 8 in); wing area 24.53 m² (264.0 sq ft)
Armament: two fixed forward-firing 7.7-mm (0.303-in) Vickers Mk I machine-guns

The Gamecock was little different from World War I fighters except for power, but gave the Royal Air Force sterling service. Seen here are the 12 Gamecock Mk I fighters of No. 23 Sqn at Kenley.

Gloster Gannet

The British Light Aeroplane Trials of 1923, organised by the *Daily Mail*, resulted in a variety of unusual small aircraft being submitted by the nation's aircraft manufacturers. The aim, of course, was to promote a lightplane which was cheap to buy, easy to maintain and easy to fly, and which could thus be acquired by the so-called 'man in the street'. The diminutive **Gloster Gannet** was a single-bay foldable-wing biplane of wooden construction with fabric covering. It had a conventional tail unit, fixed tailskid landing gear, and an open cockpit for the pilot beneath the upper wing, requiring it to incorporate a folding centre-section trailing edge so that the pilot could get in and out of the cockpit. Power was provided by a specially-developed Carden two-stroke engine, but the temperamental behaviour of this powerplant prevented the Gannet from being flown in the Light Aeroplane Trials.

During 1924 the Carden was replaced by a 5.2-kW (7-hp) Blackburn Tomtit engine, with which the aircraft was powered until last flown in 1929.

Specification
Type: ultra-light biplane
Powerplant: one 45.77-cu in (750-cc) Carden 2-cylinder inline piston engine
Performance: maximum speed 105 km/h (65 mph) at sea level; landing speed 56 km/h (35 mph); range 225 km (140 miles)
Weights: empty 128 kg (283 lb); maximum take-off 186 kg (410 lb)
Dimensions: span 5.49 m (18 ft 0 in); length 5.03 m (16 ft 6 in); height 1.83 m (6 ft 0 in); wing area 9.57 m² (103.0 sq ft)

Typical of the lightplane designs produced in the early 1920s to meet the expected boom in private owner flying, the Gloster Gannet was unremarkable, and for practical purposes hopelessly underpowered. The folding wings were intended to allow the machine to be kept at home in a garage.

Gloster Gauntlet

The **Gloster Gauntlet**, which in 1937 equipped no fewer than 14 squadrons of RAF Fighter Command, stemmed from the Air Ministry Specification F.9/26 against which the company had originally but unsuccessfully submitted its Goldfinch design. With this failure Gloster made an effort to produce a new aircraft to meet the specification, but before this was completed the new Specification F.20/27 was drawn up for a single-seat high-altitude interceptor fighter. Gloster's submission to this was the **SS.18** equal-span two-bay biplane prototype (J9125), with an all-metal basic structure having mixed fabric and metal covering. Landing gear was of fixed tailskid type and power provided by the unreliable 336-kW (450-hp) Bristol Mercury IIA radial engine, but despite having this powerplant the SS.18 was only narrowly beaten during service trials. Encouraged by this capability, development of J9125 continued by installation of a 358-kW (480-hp) Bristol Jupiter VIIF radial, resulting in the revised designation **SS.18A**, and the aircraft was flown later with a 418-kW (560-hp) Armstrong Siddeley Panther III (**SS.18B**). This heavy twin-row radial engine brought some handling problems and reversion to the Jupiter engine as the **SS.19**. During 1931 the SS.19 gained spats for the mainwheels and a spatted tailwheel, becoming redesignated **SS.19A**. The installation of a 400-kW (536-hp) Bristol Mercury VIS radial in October 1932 brought redesignation of J9125 as the **SS.19B**.

Eventually, in 1934, the type was ordered into production with a contract for 24 **Gauntlet Mk I** fighters powered by the Mercury VIS2 engine: initial deliveries to the RAF's No. 19 (Fighter) Squadron were made on 25 May 1935. Hawker Aircraft Ltd had taken over the Gloster company during 1934, with the result that the major production version, the **Gauntlet Mk II** (204 built), embodied Hawker construction techniques in the fuselage structure, but was otherwise generally similar. In addition to those aircraft produced for the RAF, which were the last open-cockpit biplane fighters used by this service, 17 were built under licence in Denmark and, at a later date, ex-RAF Gauntlet IIs were supplied to the Royal Australian Air Force (6), Finland (25), Rhodesia (3) and South Africa (6).

Specification
Gloster Gauntlet Mk II
Type: single-seat day/night fighter
Powerplant: one 477-kW (640-hp) Bristol Mercury VIS2 9-cylinder radial piston engine
Performance: maximum speed 370 km/h (230 mph) at 4815 m (15,800 ft); service ceiling 10210 m (33,500 ft); range 740 km (460 miles)
Weights: empty 1256 kg (2,770 lb); maximum take-off 1801 kg (3,970 lb)
Dimensions: span 9.99 m (32 ft 9½ in); length 8.05 m (26 ft 5 in); height 3.12 m (10 ft 3 in); wing area 29.26 m² (315.0 sq ft)
Armament: two fixed 7.7-mm (0.303-in) Vickers machine-guns

J9125 was the Gauntlet prototype, seen here in its SS.19 form with Jupiter single-row radial engine. Spats and tailwheel were added later to make it the SS.19A.

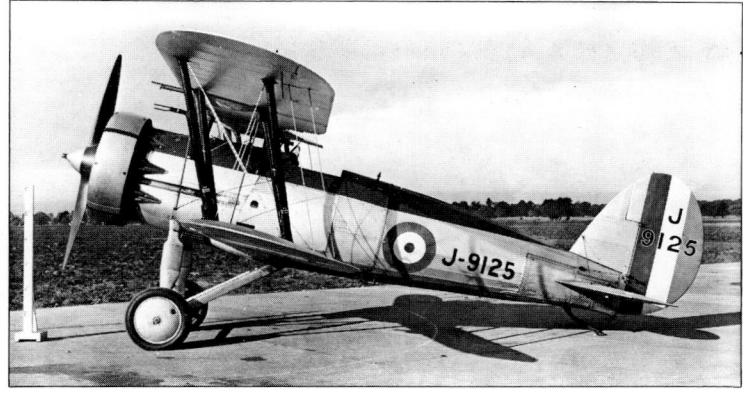

Gloster SS.37 Gladiator

The inability of British manufacturers to produce by the mid-1930s a Bristol Bulldog replacement led to further orders for Gloster Gauntlets to equip additional squadrons proposed under the 1935 RAF expansion scheme. Although design studies for monoplane fighters were showing considerable promise, Gloster designer H. P. Folland conducted a detailed examination of the Gauntlet design to define the extent to which performance might be improved; the wings were redesigned as single-bay units and the landing gear introduced Dowty internally-sprung wheels mounted on cantilever struts. Both changes reduced drag, promising a 16-24 km/h (10-15 mph) increase in maximum speed.

A prototype was built as a private venture, with the designation **Gloster SS.37**, and was first flown on 12 September 1934 by the company's chief test pilot, Flight Lieutenant P. E. G. Sayer. With a Mercury IV engine installed a maximum speed of 380 km/h (236 mph) was recorded, and this was increased to 389 km/h (242 mph) after the fitting of a 481-kW (645-hp) Mercury VIS in November 1934. With the Gauntlet's two fuselage-mounted Vickers Mk III guns supplemented by two underwing Lewis guns, the SS.37 met Air Ministry armament requirements, and it was flown to Martlesham Heath in early 1935 for official evaluation.

Gloster's design was submitted to the Air Ministry in June 1935 and Specification F.14/35 written around it; an order for 23 aircraft followed, the name **Gladiator** being announced on 1 July. The 626-kW (840-hp) Mercury IX was specified, and other changes included an enclosed cockpit, minor landing gear modifications, a revised tail unit, and the fitting of improved Vickers MK V guns.

The first production batch of 23 **Gladiator Mk I** fighters, delivered in February and March 1937, carried Lewis guns under the wings, as did the first 37 of the second order, for 100 aircraft. All of this second batch were fitted with a universal armament mounting under each wing, capable of accepting any Vickers or Lewis gun or, indeed, the licence-built Colt-Browning which was installed in fuselage and wing positions in the majority of aircraft delivered in 1938. A third order, for 28 machines, brought the RAF's Gladiator Mk I procurement to 231 aircraft, some of which were converted later to **Gladiator Mk II** standard.

The Royal Air Force later received 252 new Gladiator Mk IIs, built to Specification F.36/37, with an 619-kW (830-hp) Mercury VIIIA engine fitted with automatic mixture control, electric starter and a Vokes air filter in the carburettor intake. Thirty-eight Gladiator Mk IIs were fitted with arrester hooks and transferred to the Fleet Air Arm in December 1938, these being an interim replacement for Hawker Nimrods and Ospreys until the delivery of 60 fully-navalised **Sea Gladiator** fighters. These latter aircraft had an arrester hook, catapult points and a ventral dinghy stowage fairing. Gladiator production totalled 746, with orders from Belgium, China, Eire, Greece, Latvia, Lithuania, Norway and Sweden covering 147 Gladiator Mk Is and 18 Mk IIs.

Gladiators were first issued in February 1937 to No. 72 Squadron at Church Fenton, and although most of the squadrons that received the type had been re-equipped with Hawker Hurricanes or Supermarine Spitfires by September 1939, some of their aircraft had been reissued to home-based auxiliary units, four of which were fully operational when war broke out. Two of them, Nos 607 and 615 Squadrons, were posted to France in November 1939 as part of the Advanced Air Striking Force. No. 263 Squadron, together with No. 804 Squadron, Fleet Air Arm, participated in the Norwegian campaign; and the handful of aircraft of Hal Far Fighter Flight and of No. 261 Squadron, took part in the defence of Malta between April and June 1940. In the Middle East Gladiators saw service during the war with Nos 6, 33, 80, 94, 112 and 127 Squadrons and with No. 3 Squadron, Royal Austra-

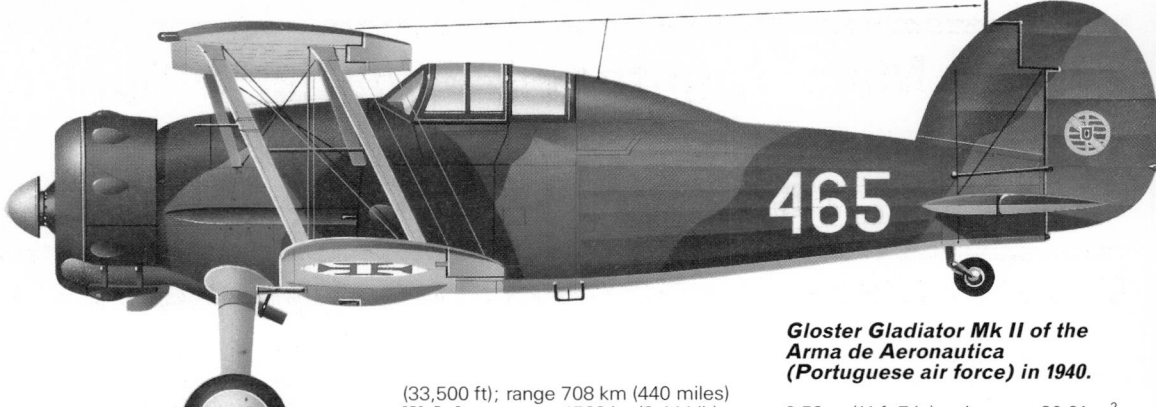

lian Air Force. In addition to No. 804 Squadron, Fleet Air Arm Sea Gladiator units included Nos. 769, 801, 802, 805, 813 and 855 Squadrons. After withdrawal from first-line service, the Gladiator continued in RAF use for communications, liaison and meteorological reconnaissance until 1944.

Specification
Gloster Gladiator Mk II
Type: single-seat biplane fighter
Powerplant: one 619-kW (830-hp) Bristol Mercury IX 9-cylinder radial piston engine
Performance: maximum speed 414 km/h (257 mph) at 4450 m (14,600 ft); service ceiling 10210 m

(33,500 ft); range 708 km (440 miles)
Weights: empty 1562 kg (3,444 lb); maximum take-off 2206 kg (4,864 lb)
Dimensions: span 9.83 m (32 ft 3 in); length 8.36 m (27 ft 5 in); height

Gloster Gladiator Mk II of the Arma de Aeronautica (Portuguese air force) in 1940.

3.53 m (11 ft 7 in); wing area 30.01 m² (323.0 sq ft)
Armament: four forward-firing 7.7-mm (0.303-in) machine-guns

Gloster Grebe

The **Gloster Grebe** single-seat fighter, which, together with the Woodcock and Siskin, was the first new fighter to be selected for re-equipment of the Royal Air Force in the between-wars years, was derived from the Gloster Grouse research biplane. Air Ministry interest in the company's tests of the Grouse led to service evaluation which proved so successful that three prototypes were ordered, the first of them becoming the Grebe prototype (subsequently designated **Grebe Mk I**) which was powered by a 242-kW (325-hp) Armstrong Siddeley Jaguar III radial engine. Service trials of this aircraft at RAF Martlesham Heath resulted in a production order for the **Grebe Mk II** incorporating a number of improvements. These included more advanced landing gear with a steerable tailskid and installation of the more powerful Jaguar IV engine.

The RAF received about 120 Grebe Mk IIs, a number of them two-seat **Grebe (Dual)** trainers with dual controls, the first entering service in October 1923. The Grebe remained in front-line use with the RAF for almost five years, during which time some took part in a number of unusual flight test programmes. One of these resulted in the Grebe II being the first RAF fighter to notch up a successful 386-km/h (240-mph) terminal velocity dive, and two of these aircraft with special attachments on the upper wings were used for air-launching experiments from the British airship *R33*. During 1928 three Grebes were acquired by New Zealand for service with the nation's air force.

Specification
Gloster Grebe Mk II
Type: single-seat fighter
Powerplant: one 298-kW (400-hp) Armstrong Siddeley Jaguar IV 14-cylinder radial piston engine

Performance: maximum speed 243 km/h (151 mph) at sea level; climb to 6095 m (20,000 ft) in 23 minutes; service ceiling 7010 m (23,000 ft); endurance 2 hours 45 minutes
Weights: empty 780 kg (1,720 lb); maximum take-off 1189 kg (2,622 lb)
Dimensions: span 8.94 m (29 ft 4 in); length 6.17 m (20 ft 3 in); height 2.82 m (9 ft 3 in); wing area 23.60 m²

Although it showed little advance over the designs of World War I, the Grebe Mk II was nevertheless one of the most delightful fighters to serve with the RAF.

(254.0 sq ft)
Armament: two fixed forward-firing 7.7-mm (0.303-in) Vickers machine-guns

Gloster Javelin

When production **Gloster Javelin** fighters began to enter service with No. 46 Squadron in February 1956, they were the first delta-winged aircraft to be operated by the RAF. It was also an advanced aircraft, the service's first all-weather fighter to be designed as such from the outset. Developed to meet the requirements of Air Ministry Specification F.4/48, Gloster's **GA.5** was of all-metal construction, its lightly-loaded large-area delta wing ensuring good high-altitude performance. Most delta-winged aircraft are devoid of conventional tail surfaces, resulting in a very high angle of attack for approach and landing, and this was considered to be hazardous for all-weather/night operations. As a result its design incorporated a T-tail with all swept surfaces which, in conjunction with wing trailing-edge flaps, allowed landings to be made at almost normal angles of attack. Retractable tricycle landing gear, two Armstrong Siddeley ASSa.6 turbojets, a fuselage seating a crew of two in tandem pressurised accommodation, and massive airborne interception radar in the fuselage nose completed the basic configuration of this aircraft.

The first of seven prototypes (WD804) was flown on 26 November 1951, and on 7 July 1952 it was ordered into production under the designation **Javelin F(AW).Mk 1**. The first production

No. 11 Squadron, RAF, flew the Javelin FAW.Mk 4 for two years from 1960, based at Geilenkirchen in Germany. It flew the updated FAW.Mk 9 until early 1966.

example (XA544) was flown on 22 July 1954, and there was a protracted development period before, on 29 February 1956, the first three Javelins were delivered to No. 46 Squadron at RAF Odiham, Hampshire. The type was finally withdrawn from RAF service in June 1967.

Variants
Javelin F(AW).Mk 1: initial production version with British AI.Mk 17 radar; 40 built
Javelin F(AW).Mk 2: differed primarily in having US-built APQ-43 radar; 30 built, the first of which was flown on 25 April 1956
Javelin T.Mk 3: dual-control trainer version, with a 1.12-m (3-ft 8-in) insert in the forward fuselage to offset the aft CG movement caused by removal of the AI radar equipment; 23 built, the first flown on 20 August 1956
Javelin F(AW).Mk 4: introduced a fully-powered all-moving tailplane; 50

built, the first example flown on 19 September 1955
Javelin F(AW).Mk 5: incorporated a modified wing with increased internal fuel capacity, and with provision to carry four de Havilland and Firestreak AAMs on underwing pylons; 64 built, the first flown on 26 July 1956
Javelin F(AW).Mk 6: similar to the Javelin F(AW).Mk 2 1/F(AW).Mk 5 relationship, differed from the Javelin F(AW).Mk 5 by having US APQ-43 radar; 33 built, the first flying on 14 December 1956
Javelin F(AW).Mk 7: major production version, 142 built, the first flown on 9 November 1956; differed by introduction of 4880-kg (11,000-lb) thrust Sapphire ASSa.7s, modified flying-control system, and revised armament comprising two 30-mm ADEN cannon and four Firestreak AAMs
Javelin F(AW).Mk 8: final production version, 47 built, the first flown on 9 May 1958; introduced Sapphire ASSa.7R engines, with limited re-heat capability providing

5579 kg (12,300 lb) thrust above 6095 m (20,000 ft), US APQ-43 radar, and a Sperry autopilot
Javelin F(AW).Mk 9: redesignation of 76 F(AW).Mk 7s following updating to F(AW).Mk 8 standard; additionally, 22 of these aircraft were provided with an inflight-refuelling probe

Specification
Gloster Javelin F(AW).Mk 1
Type: two-seat all-weather fighter
Powerplant: two 3629-kg (8,000-lb) thrust Armstrong Siddeley Sapphire ASSa.6 turbojets
Performance: maximum speed 1141 km/h (709 mph) at sea level; service ceiling 16000 m (52,500 ft);
Weights: maximum take-off 14324 kg (31,580 lb); overload take-off 16642 kg (36,690 lb)
Dimensions: span 15.85 m (52 ft 0 in); length 17.15 m (56 ft 3 in); height 4.88 m (16 ft 0 in); wing area 86.12 m² (927.0 sq ft)
Armament: two 30-mm ADEN cannon in each wing

Gloster Mars, Nighthawk, Nightjar & Sparrowhawk
to
Gotha Go 145

Gloster Mars, Nighthawk, Nightjar and Sparrowhawk

Gloster's Mars I/Bamel, which had led to the Gloster I and II, derived from the Nieuport Nighthawk designed by Harry Folland. From this same basic design came a further family of early Gloster aircraft, beginning with the **Gloster Mars Mk II**, which was developed as a single-seat fighter for the Imperial Japanese navy following the visit to Japan of a British Air Mission in January 1921. Advice given to the British mission on the desirable equipment with which to develop an air arm brought an order for 50 aircraft based on the Nighthawk.

A neat-looking equal-span biplane with a structure of wood, fabric-covered, the Mars Mk II had a tail unit incorporating dorsal and ventral fins, and fixed tailskid landing gear; it was powered by a 172-kW (230-hp) Bentley B.R.2 rotary engine. Production of Mars Mk IIs

This Nighthawk and one other machine were later converted into Mars Mk X aircraft for carrierborne operations.

totalled 30, and was followed by that of the generally similar **Mars Mk III** (10 built) that differed by having two open cockpits in tandem with dual control for use as trainers. The **Mars Mk IV** (10 built) had arrester gear, flotation bags and strut-mounted paravanes forward of the main landing gear (to reduce the danger of the aircraft over-turning if an emergency landing was made on water) and were for use as shipbased fighters. These aircraft were later redesignated **Sparrowhawk Mk I, Sparrowhawk Mk II** and **Sparrowhawk Mk III** respectively. All proved highly successful with the Japanese navy, remaining in service until 1928. In addition to the 10 Mars Mk III/Sparrowhawk Mk IIs for Japan, Gloster built a single example for use as a company demonstrator.

Under the designation **Mars Mk VI Nighthawk**, Gloster produced a small number of single-seat fighters for experimental use by the Royal Air Force. These were basically a Nieuport Nighthawk airframe re-engined with the 242-kW (325-hp) Armstrong Siddeley Jaguar II or

Bristol Jupiter III radial, or one 287-kW (385-hp) Bristol Jupiter IV. In addition to those supplied to the RAF, 25 powered by the Jaguar engine were supplied to the Greek army air force. With that nation they remained in first-line service until 1938, when they were relegated to training duties.

Final derivative of the Nieuport Nighthawk airframe was the **Gloster Mars Mk X Nightjar**, a single-seat naval fighter for service with the Fleet Air Arm. This was basically a navalised version of the RAF's Nighthawk with a reversion to the Bentley B.R.2 engine that powered Japan's Sparrowhawks. In addition they had new wide-track longer-stroke landing gear and arrester 'jaws' to engage fore and aft wings on a carrier's deck. From a holding of 22 Nightjars the RAF kept 12 in Fleet Air Arm service for a period of two years from July 1922, when they were replaced by Fairey Flycatchers.

Specification
Gloster Mars Mk X Nightjar
Type: single-seat naval fighter
Powerplant: one 172-kW (230-hp) Bentley B.R.2 9-cylinder rotary piston engine
Performance: maximum speed 193 km/h (120 mph) at sea level; climb to 4570 m (15,000 ft) in 20 minutes; service ceiling 4570 m (15,000 ft); endurance 2 hours
Weights: empty 801 kg (1,765 lb); maximum take-off 982 kg (2,165 lb)
Dimensions: span 8.53 m (28 ft 0 in); length 5.59 m (18 ft 4 in); height 2.74 m (9 ft 0 in); wing area 25.08 m² (270.0 sq ft)
Armament: two fixed forward-firing 7.7-mm (0.303-in) Vickers machine-guns

The Mars VI Nighthawk was a development with the Jupiter. Greece was the only customer for a radial-engined development.

Gloster G.41 Meteor

The only Allied turbojet-powered aircraft to see action during World War II, the **Gloster Meteor** was designed by George Carter, whose preliminary study gained Air Ministry approval in November 1940 under Specification F.9/40. Its twin-engine layout was determined by the low thrust produced by the turbojet engines then available. On 7 February 1941 an order was placed for 12 prototypes, although only eight were built. The first was fitted with Rover W.2B engines, each of 454 kg (1,000 lb) thrust, and taxiing trials began at Newmarket Heath in July 1942. Delays in the production of flight-standard engines meant that the fifth airframe, with alternative de Havilland-developed Halford H.1 engines of 680-kg (1,500-lb) thrust, was the first to fly, this event taking place at Cranwell on 5 March 1943.

Modified W.2B/23 engines then became available and were installed in the first and fourth prototypes, first flight dates being 12 June and 24 July respectively. On 13 November the third prototype made its maiden flight at Farnborough, powered by two Metrovick F.2 engines in underslung nacelles, and in the same month the second aircraft flew,

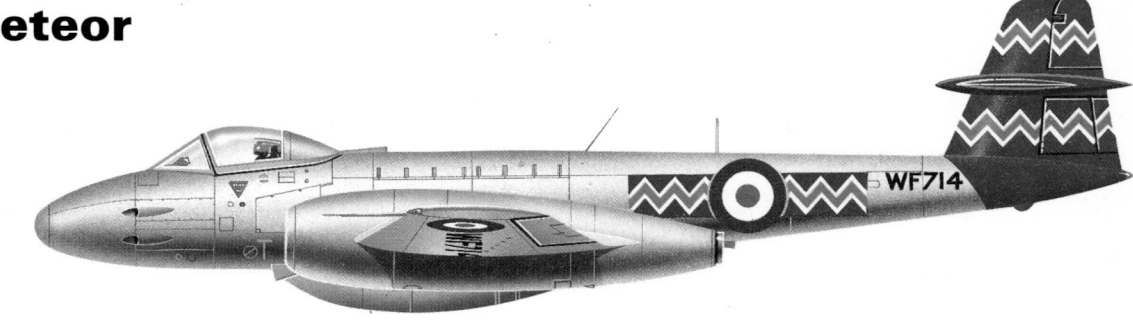

Gloster Meteor F.Mk 8 of Squadron Leader Desmond de Villiers, commanding No. 500 Squadron, Royal Auxiliary Air Force, based at West Malling (UK) in 1954.

Gloster Meteor T.Mk 7 of No. 203 Advanced Flying School, RAF, based at Driffield (UK) in the early 1950s.

initially with Power Jets W.2/500 turbojets. The sixth aircraft later became the prototype **Meteor F.Mk II**, with two 1225-kg (2,700-lb) thrust de Havilland Goblin engines, and was flown on 24 July 1945. It had been preceded by the seventh, used for trials with a modified fin, rudder, and dive brakes, and flown on 20 January 1944. The eighth, with Rolls-Royce W.2B/37 Derwent 1s, was flown on 18 April 1944.

Twenty **Gloster G.41A Meteor F.Mk I** fighters comprised the first production batch, these being powered by W.2B/23C Wellands and incorporating minor airframe improvements, including a clear-view canopy. After a first flight on 12 January 1944 the first Meteor Mk I was delivered to the United States in February, in exchange for a Bell YP-59A Airacomet, the first American jet aircraft. Others were used for airframe and engine development, and the 18th later became the **Trent-Meteor**, the world's first turboprop-powered aircraft, which was flown on 20 September 1945. The Trent was basically a Derwent engine provided with reduction gearing and a drive shaft that turned a five-bladed Rotol propeller of 2.41 m (7 ft 11 in) diameter, necessitating the introduction of longer-stroke landing gear to provide tip clearance. Each engine delivered 559 kW (750 shp) with a residual thrust of 454 kW (1,000 lb).

The first operational jet fighter squadron was No. 616, based at Culmhead, Somerset, equipped with Spitfire F.Mk VIIs when its first two Meteor F.Mk Is arrived on 12 July 1944. On 21 July the squadron moved to Manston, Kent, receiving more Meteors on 23 July to form a detached flight of seven. The first operational sorties were flown on 27 July, and on 4 August, near Tonbridge, Flying Officer Dean destroyed the first V1 flying bomb to be claimed by a jet fighter, using the Meteor's wingtip to tip it over into a spin after the aircraft's four 20-mm cannon had jammed. On the same day, Flying Officer Roger shot down a second V1 near Tenterden.

Conversion to Meteors was completed towards the end of August, and the autumn was spent preparing for operations on the continent. Between 10 and 17 October, however, four Meteors were detached to Debden, to take part in an exercise with the USAAF 2nd Bombardment Division and 65th Fighter Wing, to enable defensive tactics against the Luftwaffe's Messerschmitt Me 163 and Me 262 fighters to be devised. The first **Meteor F.Mk III** aircraft were delivered to Manston on 18

December, and on 17 January the squadron moved to Colerne, Wiltshire, where the remaining Meteor F.Mk Is were replaced. On 20 January 1945 one flight of No. 616's Meteors joined No. 84 Group, 2nd Tactical Air Force in Belgium, and in March No. 504 became the second Meteor F.Mk III unit to operate on the other side of the English Channel.

The Meteor F.Mk III, the second and last mark to see operational service during World War II, had increased fuel capacity and a sliding bubble canopy in place of the sideways-opening hood of the Meteor Mk.I. Fifteen F.Mk IIIs were completed with Welland engines and 195 with Derwents, some in lengthened engine nacelles. Derwents also powered the **Meteor F.Mk IV** (subsequently **Meteor F.Mk 4**), later examples of which were modified by a 1.78-m (5-ft 10-in) reduction in wingspan. Of 657 built, 465 were supplied to the RAF, enabling Meteor F.Mk IIIs to be passed to auxiliary units.

A 0.76-m (2-ft 6-in) fuselage extension, to accommodate a second cockpit in the Meteor F.Mk IV airframe, was a feature of Gloster's private-venture **Meteor Trainer**, first flown on 19 March 1948. Unarmed and with dual controls, the aircraft was ordered for RAF use as the **Meteor T.Mk 7**, 712 of which were built, including aircraft for the Royal Navy and overseas air forces.

The most prolific variant, however, was the **Meteor F.Mk 8** which had a lengthed fuselage, a redesigned tail unit, an additional 432-litre (95-Imp gal) fuel tank, and a bubble cockpit canopy. Extra equipment included a gyro gunsight and a Martin-Baker ejection seat. Derwent 8 turbojets of 1633 kg (3,600 lb) thrust were installed, to confer a top speed of almost 966 km/h (600 mph). The first of 1,183 Meteor F.Mk 8s was flown on 12 October 1948. For low-level tactical reconnaissance the Meteor **FR.Mk 9** was developed from the Meteor F.Mk 8, carrying a camera nose and retaining the nose armament. The first of 126 examples was flown on 22 March 1950. They were followed by an unarmed high-altitude version, designated **Meteor PR.Mk 10**. These were hybrids, with the F.Mk 3 wing, F.Mk 4 tail unit, and FR.Mk 9 fuselage. The first of 58 made its initial flight on 29 March 1950.

Development of a night-fighter version to Specification F.24/48 was assigned to Armstrong Whitworth Aircraft in 1949. The T.Mk 7 cockpit section, with an extended forward fuselage to accommodate SCR-720 AI Mk 10 radar, was mated to an F.Mk 8 rear fuselage

and tail unit, and a wing similar to that of the F.Mk I, but redesigned to house the four 20-mm cannon displaced from the nose. The definitive **Meteor NF. Mk 11** prototype flew on 31 May 1950. A tropicalised version, the **Meteor NF.Mk 13**, was first flown on 23 December 1952, and used only by two Middle East squadrons. The **Meteor NF.Mk 12**, flown for the first time on 21 April 1953, had a higher limiting Mach number than its predecessors, American-built APS-21 radar and fin leading-edge fairings. A revised clear-view canopy and some minor aerodynamic and equipment changes identified the final night-fighter variant, the **Meteor NF.Mk 14**.

Conversions included the **Meteor U.Mk 15** and **Meteor U.Mk 16** pilotless target aircraft, from F.Mk IV and F.Mk 8 airframes respectively. The **Meteor U.Mk 21** was a similar F.Mk 8 conversion for use at the Woomera range in Australia. NF.Mk 11s equipped for target towing duties with the Royal Navy were designated **Meteor TT.Mk 20**.

Specification
Gloster Meteor F.Mk I
Type: single-seat day fighter
Powerplant: two 771-kg (1,700-lb) thrust Rolls-Royce W.2B/23C Welland turbojets
Performance: maximum speed 668 km/h (415 mph) at 3050 m (10,000 ft); service ceiling 12190 m (40,000 ft)
Weights: empty 2692 kg (8,140 lb); maximum take-off 6257 kg (13,795 lb)
Dimensions: span 13.11 m (43 ft 0 in); length 12.57 m (41 ft 3 in); height 3.96 m (13 ft 0 in); wing area 34.74 m² (374.0 sq ft)
Armament: four 20-mm cannon

The Trent-Meteor was the world's first turboprop-powered aircraft, and was converted from the 18th Meteor F.Mk I fighter. Additional fin area was required.

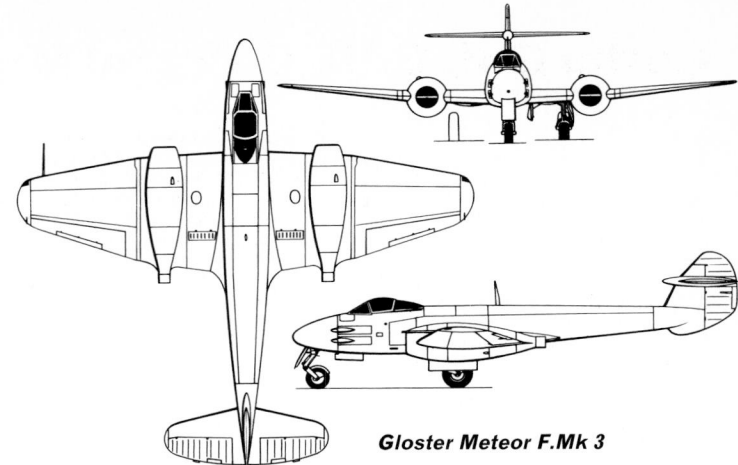

Gloster Meteor F.Mk 3

Goodyear GA-2 Duck

Shortly before the end of World War II, Goodyear Aircraft Corporation at Akron, Ohio, began the design of a small amphibious aircraft. First to fly, in September 1944, was the **Goodyear GA-1** prototype which had two-seat accommodation. Of cantilever high-wing monoplane configuration with underwing stabilising floats, the GA-1 had an all-metal fabric-covered wing, all-metal single-step hull, cruciform tail unit and retractable tail-wheel landing gear. Power was provided by an engine of 84 kW (113 hp), pylon-mounted above the fuselage to drive a pusher propeller. Successful testing of the prototype led to the construction of about 20 demonstration aircraft, none of which was offered for sale. Generally similar to the prototype, they differed by having accommodation for a pilot and two passengers. About 15 were built

under the designation **Goodyear GA-2**, powered by a 108-kW (145-hp) Franklin 6A4-145-A3 engine, while the balance, designated **GA-2B**, had a more powerful engine.

By the time that the test programme had been completed, and the demonstration aircraft evaluated on a worldwide scale, costs had escalated to a point where it would not be possible to market this aircraft to the private pilot for which it had been intended, and the project was abandoned.

Specification
Goodyear GA-2B
Type: three-seat light amphibian
Powerplant: one 123-kW (165-hp) Franklin 6A4-165-B3 flat-six piston engine
Performance: maximum speed

201 km/h (125 mph) at 305 m (1,000 ft); cruising speed 180 km/h (112 mph) at 305 m (1,000 ft); service ceiling 4570 m (15,000 ft); range 483 km (400 miles)
Weights: empty 726 kg (1,600 lb); maximum take-off 1043 kg (2,300 lb)
Dimensions: span 10.97 m (36 ft 0 in); length 7.92 m (26 ft 0 in); height,

Though superficially attractive for the private buyer, the Goodyear GA-32 Duck amphibian was too expensive for the market at which it was aimed.

on wheels 2.90 m (9 ft 6 in); wing area 16.55 m² (178.20 sq ft)

Gotha G.II, G.III, G.IV and G.V

During 1917 and 1918 British people generally, and those who lived in London particularly, came to dread air attacks by the 'Gothas', a name which they applied indiscriminately to all German bombers making day or night raids. Development by Gotha of aircraft in this class had started during 1915, and the first of these twin-engined bombers were the **Gotha G.II** and **G.III** of 1916. Built in only small numbers they were generally similar, differing only in internal detail, but early experience of these aircraft operating in Europe brought development during 1916 of the longer-range **G.IV**. Of mixed wood and steel construction, with plywood and fabric covering, the G.IV was of three-bay biplane configuration with a basically square-section fuselage, braced tail unit and tailskid landing gear incorporating twin-wheel main units. The twin-engined powerplant, comprising two Mercedes D.IVa inlines strutmounted between the wings, directly above the main landing gear, was arranged to drive pusher propellers, a large cut-out provided in the trailing edge of the upper wing to give the necessary propeller clearance. The G.IV was followed by an improved **G.V** that was basically the same, but introduced improved equipment and a number of refinements, including cleaner, more streamlined engine nacelles.

Daylight raids on England began on 25 May 1917 with a mass attack by 21 Gothas on Folkestone and Shorncliffe in Kent, followed by a first daylight raid on London on 13 June 1917. In this first attack on the capital a total of 162 people were killed and more than 400 injured, the largest number of fatalities of any World War I raid on the UK. It, and subsequent attacks during June and July, made without any significant opposition, brought a public outcry, which resulted in formation of the Royal Air Force as a completely independent service, unshackled by the British Army or Royal Navy. Interim measures taken to combat the Gothas included the withdrawal of

The G.VII's nose gun and gunner's position were removed, permitting the close location of the twin Mercedes D.IVa inlines, with consequent improvements in asymmetric handling.

some operational fighter squadrons from the Western Front, these proving sufficiently effective to make daylight raids too costly and compelling Bombengeschwader 3, which had responsibility for these attacks, to shift to night operations: these continued until May 1918. In the course of the 22 attacks made on the UK, the Gothas had dropped a total of more than 83 tons of bombs, no mean achievement for bomber aircraft of that era.

A number of Gotha G series aircraft followed the G.V, mostly built in ones or twos. They included the unusual **G.VI**, but with the fuselage offset to port and mounting one of two 194-kW (260-hp) Mercedes D.IVa engines in its nose, the other installed in a nacelle to starboard. The following **G.VII** was a twin-engined biplane, the prototype beautifully streamlined for its period, also powered by Mercedes D.IVas. Intended for a long-range reconnaissance role, the three or four production examples built were very considerably changed and lost the sleek lines. The **G.VIII** appears to have been little more than an increased-span version of the G.VII, but with 183-kW (245-hp) Maybach Mb.IV engines, and the **G.IX** was a similarly-powered twin, built by Luft-Verkehrs Gesellschaft, of which virtually nothing has been recorded. Last of the G series twins was the **G.X**, a smaller and lighter-weight reconnaissance aircraft powered by two 134-kW(180-hp) BMW IIIa engines.

Variant
Gotha Vb: version of standard Gotha V with a pair of auxiliary wheels mounted forward of each main landing

gear unit to reduce the danger of nosing-over during night operation

Specification
Gotha G.V
Type: three-seat long-range bomber
Powerplant: two 194-kW (260-hp) Mercedes D.IVa 6-cylinder inline piston engines
Performance: maximum speed 140 km/h (87 mph); service ceiling 6500 m (21,325 ft); range 500 km (311 miles)
Weights: empty 2740 kg (6,041 lb); maximum take-off 3975 kg (8,763 lb)
Dimensions: span 23.70 m (77 ft

The Gotha G.II bomber was built in small numbers in 1916, and was used mainly over the Western Front. The principal user was Bogohl III based at Ghent.

9 in); length 11.86 m (38 ft 11 in); height 4.30 m (14 ft 1¼ in); wing area 89.50 m² (963.40 sq ft)
Armament: two 7.92-mm (0.31-in) Parabellum machine-guns on pivoted mounts in nose and dorsal positions, and a bombload of 300 to 500 kg (661 to 1,102 lb) according to range of mission

---

Gotha Go 145

The Gotha company, having been closed down in 1919 under the terms of the Versailles Treaty, was reformed on 2 October 1933. Its first product was the **Gotha Go 145** trainer, a single-bay biplane of wooden construction with fabric covering, powered by an Argus As 10C engine. The prototype was first flown in February 1934 and the type entered service with the Luftwaffe in the following year. Although used originally as a pilot training aircraft, the Go 145 served also with the Störkampfstaffeln which were set up in December 1942, when the Luftwaffe decided to emulate the Russians' use of the Polikarpov Po-2 as a 'nuisance raider' during the hours of darkness. In October 1943 these units

were redesignated Nachtschlachtgruppen, and remained operational on the Eastern Front until the end of the war. Rather less than 10,000 Go 145s were built by Gotha, Ago, BFW and Focke-Wulf in Germany; the type was licence-built in Spain as the **CASA 1145-L**, and also in Turkey.

Variants
Go 145A: initial production dual-control trainer
Go 145B: produced from 1935, this model introduced an enclosed cockpit and landing gear spats
Go 145C: gunnery trainer with a 7.92-mm (0.31-in) MG 15 machine-gun on a pivoted mounting in the rear cockpit

Specification
Specification
Type: two-seat basic/gunnery trainer
Powerplant: one 179-kW (240-hp) Argus As 10C inverted-Vee piston engine
Performance: maximum speed 212 km/h (132 mph) at sea level;

cruising speed 180 km/h (112 mph); service ceiling 3700 m (12,140 ft); range 630 km (391 miles)
Weights: empty 880 kg (1,940 lb); maximum take-off 1380 kg (3,043 lb)
Dimensions: span 9.00 m (29 ft 6¼ in); length 8.70 m (28 ft 6½ in); height 2.90 m (9 ft 6 in); wing area 21.75 m² (234.12 sq ft)
Armament: Go 145C only, as noted under Variants

Wholly conventional in concept and structure, the Go 145 found the right combination of factors to become one of the most widely built aircraft of its era. The Luftwaffe used it mainly for basic training.

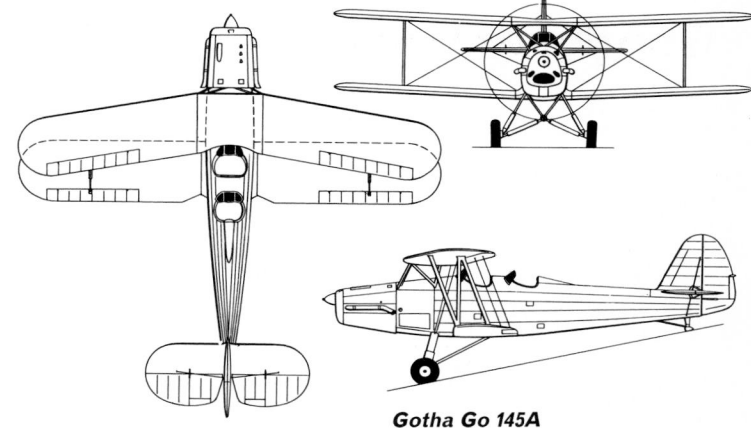

Gotha Go 145A

Gotha Go 242/244
to
Gourdou-Leseurre LGL-32 C.1

Gotha Go 242/244

The work of Dipl. Ing Albert Kalkert, the **Gotha Go 242** assault glider was developed with the approval of the Reichsluftfahrtministerium since it offered almost three times the troop-carrying capacity of the DFS 230 then in use. The fuselage pod was of steel tubular construction with fabric covering, and carried jettisonable landing gear and two retractable skids; the wings were made of wood with fabric and plywood covering. The aircraft could carry 21 fully-equipped troops, or equivalent weight in military loads, such as a Kübelwagen utility vehicle, loaded through the hinged rear fuselage. Two prototypes were flown in 1941 and production followed without delay, permitting entry into service in 1942. The type's operational debut was made in the Mediterranean and Aegean theatres, Go 242 units being based in Greece, Sicily and North Africa. Heinkel He 111 tugs were usually employed and rocket-assisted take-off equipment could be fitted, the variety of propulsion units including four 500-kg (1,102-lb) Rheinmetall-Borsig RI-502 solid fuel rockets. Production totalled 1,528 aircraft.

After the fall of France the French Gnome-Rhône 14M radial engine became available to the Germans in large numbers, and the Go 242 was modified to serve as the Go 244 twin-engined transport, each of the twin booms being extended forward of the leading edge of the wing to mount one of these engines; at the same time fixed tricycle landing gear was installed. A total of 133 conversions was made from the five Go 242B variants and these were designated correspondingly Go 244B-1 to B-5. First deliveries were made in March 1942 to the Greek-based KGrzbV 104 and to KGrzbV 106 in Crete, but they proved to be relatively easy targets for Allied fighter aircraft, one of the early withdrawn by November 1942. Some Go 244s had 492-kW (660-hp) BMW 132Z or captured Russian Shvetsov M-25As each of 559 kW (750 hp).

Variants
Go 242A: initial production version with deepened booms and, although essentially a cargo glider, the Go 242A-1 could be armed with up to four 7.92-mm (0.31-in) MG 15 machine-guns; the **Go 242A-2** was the troop-carrying equivalent

Gotha Go 244B-1 of a Luftwaffe transport unit

Go 242B: introduced in 1942, with jettisonable nosewheel landing gear, the two initial versions were the **Go 242B-1** and **Go 242B-2** which differed principally in the design of the main landing gear; troop-carrying equivalents were the **Go 242B-3** and **Go 242B-4**, both with double rear doors; the **Go 242B-5** incorporated dual controls for pilot training
Go 242C-1: specially developed for attacks on marine targets, in particular for a raid on the British fleet anchorage at Scapa Flow, this version had a planing hull and underwing stabilising floats; it was to have carried a small assault boat with an explosive charge but the type was not used operationally, although a number were delivered to 6./KG 200 in 1944

Specification
Gotha Go 244B-2
Type: assault/troop transport
Powerplant: two 522-kW (700-hp) Gnome-Rhône 14M 14-cylinder radial piston engines
Performance: maximum speed 290 km/h (180 mph); service ceiling 7500 m (24,605 ft); range 600 km (373 miles)
Weights: empty 5100 kg (11,243 lb); maximum take-off 7800 kg (17,196 lb)
Dimensions: span 24.50 m (80 ft 4½ in); length 15.80 m (51 ft 10 in); height 4.70 m (15 ft 5 in); wing area 64.40 m² (693.22 sq ft)
Armament: four 7.92-mm (0.31-in) MG 15 machine-guns optional

The Go 242A-1 was the initial production version of the assault glider. It could have an armament of four 7.92-mm (0.31-in) MG 15 machine-guns.

Gotha WD series

In parallel with its LD series of landplanes, Gotha developed simultaneously a family of floatplanes under WD designations. Initially the relationship was apparent, but whereas the reconnaissance landplanes faded out after the first two years of World War I, the floatplanes continued to be developed, the final version built being the truly giant WD 27 of 1918.

The series started with the pre-war **Gotha WD 1** and **WD 1a**, two-seat open-cockpit biplanes of wood and fabric construction, with twin-float landing gear and a small float beneath the tail unit. Powered by the 76-kW (100-hp)

Gnome rotary engine, a few were used by the German navy for coastal patrol duties during the opening stages of World War I. The **WD 2** which followed was a slightly larger floatplane of generally similar configuration, but without the small float beneath the tail unit. Powered by the 112-kW (150-hp) Benz Bz.III inline engine, it was built for the German navy and for Turkey, those that were exported having a single machine-gun on the top surface of the upper-wing centre-section. One WD 2, modified by a reduction in wing span and the installation of a 119-kW (160-hp) Mercedes D III engine, was redesignated **WD 5**. From

this one-off WD 5 aircraft was developed the **WD 9**, which differed primarily by having a single machine-gun on a pivoted mounting in the rear cockpit. Only one example was supplied to the German navy, but several were built for Turkey, these having the Benz Bz.III engine of the WD 2s delivered earlier.

When pure observation/reconnaissance aircraft began to give way to scout or fighter aircraft, one of the early solutions to provide an effective means of mounting a forward-firing weapon was the introduction of a central nacelle incorporating a rear-mounted engine with pusher propeller. This configuration was adopted by Gotha for the **WD 3**, the central nacelle being enclosed by twin booms, each carrying a single fin and

rudder, and united at the rear by a tailplane and elevator. Power was provided by a 119-kW (160-hp) Mercedes D.III mounted in the rear of the nacelle to drive a pusher propeller, and a single machine-gun was installed on a pivoted mount in the nose. After this single unorthodox design, Gotha reverted to a development of the WD 9 to produce the slightly larger one-off and unarmed **WD 12** supplied to the German navy; it was also built for Turkey, the machines delivered to that nation being the first it had received with Mercedes engines. A similar armed patrol floatplane, developed from the WD 9, was built for Turkey under the designation **WD 13**, and these reverted to use of the Benz Bz.III powerplant. The last of these single-engined

gear, the main units extensively faired, the Model R had a barrel-shaped fuselage dictated by the diameter of the radial-engined powerplant selected. Two were built, the **Model R-1** with a 597-kW (800-hp) Pratt & Whitney Wasp and the **Model R-2** with, initially, greater fuel capacity and a 410-kW (550-hp) Wasp Junior engine. Both were entered for the 1933 Bendix Trophy, the Model R-1 then with a 671-kW (900-hp) Hornet engine and the Model R-2 with the Wasp that had been installed previously in the Model R-1.

The legendary 'Jimmy' Doolittle had flown a Gee Bee to win the Thomson Trophy of 1932, and on 3 September 1932 he set a world landplane speed record of 476.83 km/h (296.287 mph) in the Model R-1. However, within a year both the Model R-1 and the Model R-2 had crashed (the remnants being used for a hybrid, the **Model R-1/R-2**, that was raced under the highly appropriate name *Intestinal Fortitude*) and in 1934 the eldest of the five brothers, Zantford (nicknamed 'Granny') was killed in another accident and, with the driving force missing, Granville Brothers slipped into bankruptcy.

There had been an attempt to sell a less potent version of the design to the sportsman pilot, stemming from the one-off **Model X Sportster** (82-kW/110-hp American Cirrus engine) of 1930, and leading to the design of a basic single-seat airframe that could be adapted easily to mount a variety of engines. Thus resulted the Sportster range, built in only very small numbers, but including the **Model B** with an 82-kW (110-hp) Cirrus Ensign engine, the **Model C** with a 71-kW (95-hp) Menasco B-4 Pirate, **Model D** with a 93-kW (125-hp) Menasco C-4 Pirate and, the only variant with a radial engine, the **Model E** with a 82-kW (110-hp) Warner Scarab. The **Model Y Senior Sportster** was an expansion of the Model X philosophy to provide two-seat accommodation, and two were built. The **Model Z**, precursor of the Model R, was a one-off racer evolved from the Models X and Y, and was powered by the 399-kW (535-hp) Wasp Junior and had a maximum speed of 435 km/h (270 mph). For an attempt on the world landplane speed record a 560-kW (750-hp) Wasp was fitted, but on 5 December 1931 the overstressed aircraft started to disintegrate in the air, the aircraft rolling into the ground with fatal results for the pilot after one wing folded back. Another Granville type of the same basic layout was the **Q.E.D.** of 1934; this was a long-range two-seater with the Pratt & Whitney Hornet radial. The type was plagued by mechanical problems, but in 1939 achieved a non-stop flight from Mexico City to New York. On the return flight the machine crashed, killing the pilot.

Specification
Gee Bee Sportster Model E
Type: single-seat sporting aircraft
Powerplant: one 82-kW (110-hp) Warner Scarab 7-cylinder radial piston engine
Performance: maximum speed 238 km/h (148 mph); cruising speed 204 km/h (127 mph); service ceiling 5790 m (19,000 ft); range 885 km (550 miles)

Best remembered for its exploits in air racing, the Gee Bee 'Sportster' Model E often appeared in a two-tone colour scheme with a scalloped design. Here NC46V warms up before rounding the pylons in another race.

Weights: empty 414 kg (912 lb); maximum take-off 636 kg (1,400 lb)
Dimensions: span 7.62 m (25 ft 0 in); length 5.11 m (16 ft 9 in); height 1.83 m (6 ft 0 in); wing area 8.83 m² (95.0 sq ft)

Great Lakes 2-T-1

The Great Lakes Aircraft Corporation, established in late 1928, began by building two examples of an eight-seat commercial aircraft designated **Miss Great Lakes**. This design was derived from the Martin T4M-1, but failing to gain little more than a flicker of interest for its transport, the company concentrated on the development of a two-seat sports/trainer biplane designated **Great Lakes 2-T-1**. The prototype, first flown in March 1929, was a single-bay biplane of fabric-covered mixed construction, and with fixed tailskid landing gear. Power was provided by a 63-kW (85-hp) Cirrus Mk III engine, and two open cockpits in tandem were provided for the pilot and passenger/pupil. Flight testing revealed that the aircraft was excessively tail heavy and, after three more had been built, the upper wing was given sweepback to overcome this problem.

It is believed that about 40 were built before production shifted to a generally similar **2-T-1A**, which introduced a 67-kW (90-hp) American-built Cirrus engine, slightly enlarged tail surfaces and a number of refinements. The 2-T-1A was ordered in very large numbers before the financial recession of late 1929 brought large-scale cancellations, but about 200 are thought to have been built. Final version, in production until 1933, was the **2-T-1E**, which introduced a new version of the American-built Cirrus engine and some slight refinement in lines. Only about a dozen were built, but many examples of the Great Lakes 2-T-1 have survived the years and are treasured possessions in the 1990s.

Specification
Great Lakes 2-T-1E
Type: two-seat sporting/training aircraft
Powerplant: one 71-kW (95-hp) American-built Cirrus 4-cylinder inverted inline piston engine
Performance: maximum speed 177 km/h (110 mph); cruising speed 153 km/h (95 mph); service ceiling 3660 m (12,000 ft); range 604 km (375 miles)
Weights: empty 459 kg (1,012 lb); maximum take-off 717 kg (1,580 lb)
Dimensions: span 8.13 m (26 ft 8 in); length 6.40 m (21 ft 0 in); height 2.39 m (7 ft 10 in); wing area 17.43 m² (187.60 sq ft)

Despite the financial crash of 1929, the 2-T-1A was a commercial success, with survivors being lovingly cherished up to the present day.

Great Lakes BG-1

With a requirement in 1932 for a new two-seat carrier-based dive-bomber, able to carry a 454-kg (1,000-lb) bomb beneath the fuselage, the US Navy contracted with Consolidated Aircraft Corporation and Great Lakes Aircraft Corporation to build competitive prototypes. The resulting **Great Lakes XBG-1** was an unequal-span biplane with tapered wings, fixed tailwheel landing gear and open cockpits in tandem for the pilot and observer/gunner. Power was provided by a 620-kW (750-hp) Pratt & Whitney R-1535-64 Twin Wasp Junior. Following its completion in mid-1933, the XBG-1 was tested by the US Navy and, when flown in competition against the XB2Y-1 from Consolidated, was found to be the superior aircraft. It was, therefore, ordered into production during November 1933 as the **BG-1**, this differing from the prototype in having an elongated canopy to enclose the two cockpits. Production totalled 61, including the prototype, and initial aircraft entered service with operational units in the autumn of 1934.

Experience gained with the TG-2 torpedo-bomber was applied to the design of the BG-1 dive-bomber. This aircraft served with VB-4M, one of three USMC units to operate the type.

The type remained in first-line service with the US Navy until 1938, then continued in use as a general-purpose aircraft for several years. About half of the production aircraft were allocated to the US Marine Corps, remaining operational with some units until 1940.

Variant
Great Lakes XB2G-1: a single example of a more developed version of the BG-1 was built for evaluation purposes but failed to gain a production contract; it differed from standard by having retractable main landing gear units and a deeper section fuselage to provide an internal bay for a 454-kg (1,000-lb) bomb

Specification
Great Lakes BG-1
Type: carrier-based dive-bomber
Powerplant: one 560-kW (750-hp) Pratt & Whitney R-1435-82 Twin Wasp Junior 14-cylinder radial piston engine
Performance: maximum speed 303 km/h (188 mph) at 2715 m (8,900 ft); service ceiling 6125 m (20,100 ft); range with maximum payload 869 km (540 miles)

Weights: empty 1770 kg (3,903 lb); maximum take-off 2880 kg (6,350 lb)
Dimensions: span 10.97 m (36 ft 0 in); length 8.76 m (28 ft 9 in); height 3.35 m (11 ft 0 in); wing area 35.67 m² (384.0 sq ft)
Armament: one forward-firing 7.62-mm (0.3-in) machine-gun and one similar weapon on pivoted mount in rear cockpit, plus one 454-kg (1,000-lb) bomb beneath the fuselage

Grigorovich I-2 and I-2bis

Unsatisfactory flight characteristics displayed by his **I-1** single-seat fighter biplane when it was tested in the spring of 1924 led Dmitri P. Grigorovich, head of a design team located at GAZ-1 (State Aircraft Factory No. 1) at Khodinka aerodrome, Moscow, to develop an improved version designated the **Grigorovich I-2**. This retained the wooden structure of its predecessor and was powered by the same 298-kW (400-hp) Liberty engine, but the fuselage was an oval monocoque and the parallel interplane struts were replaced by single I-type aerofoil-section struts. The engine cowling was modified to improve visibility, but the ventral radiator which was adopted finally for the I-1 was retained.

The I-2 prototype flew for the first time in the autumn of 1924, piloted by A. I. Zhukov. Although the I-2 was considered to be suitable for production it was realised that the cockpit, which was cramped even for the slightly-built test pilot, would have to be enlarged. This led

The Grigorovich I-2 was a clean design with I-type interplane struts and the ability to operate from wheel or ski landing gear.

to a revision of the central section of the fuselage and raising of the pilot's seat, but it was decided to make radical design improvements at the same time, these including the introduction of a welded steel-tube frame which also carried the bearers for the engine, which was to be a 313-kW (420-hp) M-5 12-cylinder unit, in fact a Soviet-built development of the American Liberty engine. Quantity production began in 1926 and ended in 1929. During that period GAZ-1 built 164 of the type, designated **I-2bis** in its definitive form, and GAZ-23 completed a further 47.

The I-2bis had the distinction of being the first Soviet-designed fighter to go into service in numbers with the Red Air Fleet. It was, however, a rather complex aircraft and the structure, although strong, was heavier than its designer had originally intended. Varying production standards led to quite marked differences in performance between different aircraft and, in addition, cooling prob-

Compared with the I-2, the I-2bis had modified struts, engine bearers and a larger upper wing centre-section fuel tank.

lems remained unsolved. A small number of a version with twin Lamblin-type radiators mounted between the landing-gear legs appeared under the designation **I-2prim**, and although engine cooling was improved as a result, there was a slight loss in overall performance.

The only other biplane fighter designed by Grigorovich was the two-seat **DI-3**, a two-seat single-bay aircraft of mixed construction, distinguished by its tail assembly (with twin vertical surfaces), which was intended to provide the gunner with a greater field of fire for his flexibly-mounted machine-gun. Powered by a 544-kW (730-hp) BMW VI engine, the DI-3 was test-flown in the summer of 1931 but was not accepted for quantity production.

Grigorovich I-1

Specification
Grigorovich I-2bis
Type: single-seat fighter
Powerplant: one 313-kW (420-hp) M-5 12-cylinder vee piston engine
Performance: maximum speed 235 km/h (146 mph) at sea level; service ceiling 5400 m (17,715 ft); range 600 km (373 miles)
Weights: empty equipped 1152 kg (2,540 lb); maximum take-off 1575 kg (3,472 lb)
Dimensions: span 10.80 m (35 ft 5¼ in); length 7.32 m (24 ft 0¼ in); height 3.00 m (9 ft 10 in); wing area 23.46 m² (252.53 sq ft)
Armament: two synchronised 7.62-mm (0.3-in) PV-1 machine-guns mounted in the upper engine cowling

Grigorovich IP-1 and IP-4

Developed during 1934 under the Grigorovich design bureau designation **DG-52**, the **Grigorovich IP-1** was a cantilever low-wing all-metal monoplane, the prototype flying for the first time in early 1935. A single-seat cannon fighter, its pilot was seated in an open cockpit over the wing and had a faired headrest. Power was provided by a 477-kW (640-hp) Wright Cyclone radial, and the design incorporated landing gear with main units which retracted rearward into bathtub-type underwing fairings.

Like the earlier I-Z, the IP-4 was developed to use the large-calibre recoilless Kurchevsky cannon, two 76.2-mm (3-in) APK-4 weapons being mounted under the wings. Each of these cannon could fire five rounds. The additional armament of two 7.62-mm (0.3-in) machine-guns was intended to assist the pilot in aiming the heavy cannon.

The IP-1 was ordered into production, but the series version was much modified, the Kurchevsky cannon being abandoned and replaced by two 20-mm ShVAK cannon in the wing roots. These were supplemented by six 7.62-mm

(0.3-in) ShKAS machine-guns, mounted three each in trays under the wings. A large dorsal fin was added to improve lateral stability and this was extended forward to blend into the fairing of the pilot's headrest. Some 90 IP-1s were completed between 1936 and 1937, but they were overshadowed by the Polikarpov I-16 which met all the needs of the VVS (Soviet air force) at that time. This led to the temporary eclipse of single-seat fighters of all-metal construction in favour of the wooden Polikarpov designs. Series IP-1s were powered by the Soviet M-25 radial engine.

The **IP-4** development appeared at the end of 1934. It had four of the new Kurchevsky APK-11 45-mm (1.77-in) cannon plus two light machine-guns. Like the IP-1 prototype it was powered

by a Wright Cyclone engine. Bureau designation of the IP-4 was then **DG-53**.

Although the IP-1 was the last of his designs to be built in quantity, Grigorovich produced several other notable aircraft before he became seriously ill in 1937. One of these was the **IP-2** (or **DG-54**), powered by a 619-kW (830-hp) Hispano-Suiza Xbrs engine, and armed with an engine-mounted ShVAK cannon plus no fewer than 10 wing-mounted ShKAS machine-guns. The IP-2 was almost complete when development was abandoned in 1936.

Other designs included the **DG-55** or **E-2**, a smooth-contoured two-seat low-wing cabin monoplane powered by two 89-kW (120-hp) Cirrus Hermes engines and intended as a long-range racing aircraft. The sole example built was used

from 1935 onwards as a long-range mail and courier aircraft, demonstrating a maximum speed of 296 km/h (184 mph) and range of 2200 km (1,367 miles).

The remaining projects were the **DG-56** or **LK-3** (LK for light cruiser) of 1936, a three-seat long-range escort fighter with two Hispano-Suiza 12Ybrs engines, and the **DG-58** or **PB-1** of 1937, a low-wing two-seat dive-bomber powered by a single M-85 (Soviet version of the Gnome-Rhône 14K radial). The developed **DG-58bis** or **DG-58R** version was intended for the 'Ivanov' reconnaissance aircraft competition.

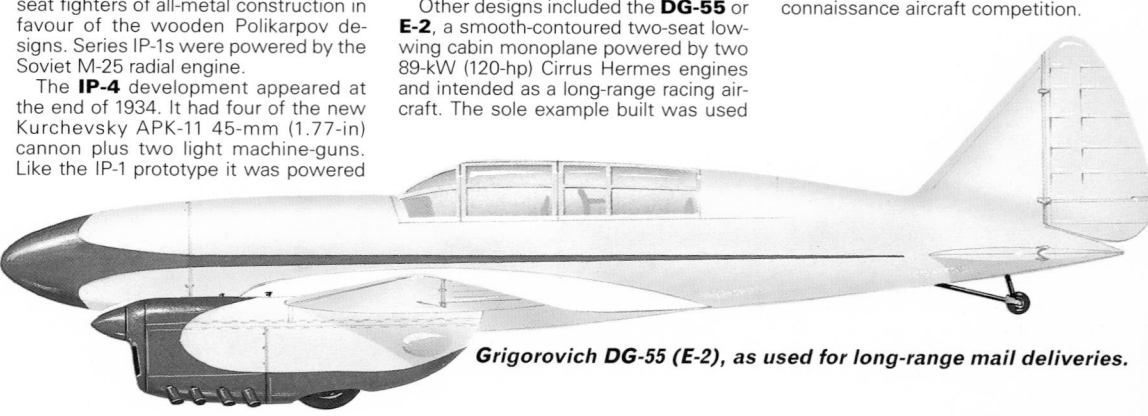

Grigorovich DG-55 (E-2), as used for long-range mail deliveries.

Grigorovich I-Z

Programme 'Z' was initiated in mid-1930 with the objective of developing a fighter which would be a vehicle for the new 76.2-mm (3-in) Kurchevsky recoilless cannon. The OMOS design team nominated for this task was led by Dmitri P. Grigorovich and, quite naturally, he drew heavily on features of the I-5 biplane single-seat fighter on which he had worked in collaboration with Nikolai Polikarpov. The forward fuselage and the engine installation, including the helmeted cylinder head cowlings, were identical with those of the second I-5 prototype. The remainder of the fuselage was a dural monocoque, Grigorovich adopting a low-wing single-seat configuration with the fabric-covered metal wing braced to the cross-axle type landing gear by steel-tube Vee struts. The large vertical fin had a curved leading edge, and the braced horizontal tail surfaces were mounted high on the fin so as to avoid any interference from the exhaust gases of the large-bore cannon. These two DRP weapons were mounted below the wings, outboard of the landing gear, and were single-shot cannon. They were complemented by a single light machine-gun, mounted in the fuselage, which was used for aiming the cannon.

The I-Z had a high-set tailplane to keep it clear of gases from the recoilless cannon, one of which can be seen under the port wing. The helmeted cowling was a legacy of the I-5 fighter, developed for Polikarpov.

Two prototypes of the new fighter were built the first, designated **Grigorovich I-Z**, flying for the first time in the summer of 1931; the second, slightly modified, strengthened and designated **I-Zbis**, appeared at the beginning of 1932. Both were powered by the 391-kW (525-hp) Gnome-Rhône Jupiter VI radial engine. The design bureau designation of the type was **TsKB-7**.

An order for 21 evaluation aircraft, powered by the Soviet 358-kW (480-hp) M-22 enclosed by a Townend ring, was received in 1933. The metal wings of the prototypes were rejected in favour of wooden structures. Later, 50 more I-Z fighters were built, but flight characteristics were not good and the heavy-calibre one-shot cannon was not a success. As a result, most of the aircraft were used for flight testing and experimental work. One example was used in the Vakhmistrov Zveno-7 parasite fighter trials. Series aircraft had a maximum

speed 40 km/h (25 mph) lower than the prototypes.

Specification
Grigorovich I-Z (series version)
Type: single-seat cannon fighter
Powerplant: one 358-kW (480-hp) M-22 (licence-built Jupiter) 9-cylinder radial piston engine
Performance: maximum speed 260 km/h (161 mph) at sea level;

service ceiling 7000 m (22,965 ft); range 600 km (373 miles)
Weights: empty equipped 1180 kg (2,601 lb); maximum take-off 1648 kg (3,633 lb)
Dimensions: span 11.50 m (37 ft 8¾ in); length 7.65 m (25 ft 1¼ in); wing area 19.50 m² (209.90 sq ft)
Armament: two 76.2-mm (3-in) Kurchevsky DRP-cannon, plus one 7.62-mm (0.3-in) PV-1 machine-gun

Grigorovich M-5

Dmitri Petrovich Grigorovich began his distinguished design career with the Shchetinin company in St Petersburg (formerly Leningrad). His **M-1** two-seat flying-boat powered by a 37-kW (50-hp) Gnome rotary engine in a pusher configuration appeared in 1913 when he was 30 years old, to be followed by the 59-kW (80-hp) Clerget-powered **M-2** the next year and the **M-3** with a 74-kW (100-hp) Gnome-Monosoupape in 1914.

The first successful flying-boat was the **M-4** (or **Shch-4**), four of which were built in 1914, two going into service with the Baltic Fleet and two in the Black Sea. It was soon followed by the **Grigorovich M-5** (alternative designation **ShchM-5**) in 1915. A two-bay unequal-span biplane flying-boat with a single-step hull, the M-5 was of wooden construction, the hull being ply-covered while the wings and tailplane were fabric-covered. Aft of the step the hull tapered sharply into little more than a boom, supporting a characteristic single fin and rudder tail unit, which was braced by means of a complexity of struts and wires. The Gnome-Monosoupape engine was mounted as a pusher between the wings. Pilot and observer were accommodated side-by-side in a

large cockpit forward of the wings, the observer provided with a single 7.62-mm (0.3-in) Vickers machine-gun on a pivoted mounting.

Some 300 M-5s were built, most serving in the Black Sea or Baltic, initially with the Imperial Russian naval air arm and then with both sides in the Russian Civil War. A few were still in flying condition with the Red Air Fleet in the mid-1920s. They proved tough and effective, frequently riding out rough weather and withstanding heavy seas.

Variants
M-10: with the same Gnome-Monosoupape engine and similar hull to the M-5, the M-10 which appeared in 1916 had wings of much reduced span, the upper wing having only slightly greater dimensions that the lower; span was 9.20 m (30 ft 2¼ in) and length 8.60 m (28 ft 2½ in); maximum speed increased to 125 km/h (78 mph)
M-20: powered by an 89-kW (120-hp) Le Rhône engine, this 1916 development of the M-5 which was built in limited numbers had exactly the same wings, but a hull shortened by 0.40 m (1 ft 3¾ in); it had a maximum speed of 115 km/h (71 mph)

Specification
Grigorovich M-5
Type: single-engined reconnaissance or training flying-boat
Powerplant: one 75-kW (100-hp) Gnome-Monosoupape rotary piston engine
Performance: maximum speed 105 km/h (65 mph); service ceiling 3300 m (10,825 ft); endurance 4 hours
Weights: empty equipped 660 kg (1,455 lb); maximum take-off 960 kg

By the standards of the day the Grigorovich M-5 was a successful and widely-produced flying-boat, with production exceeding 300 aircraft.

(2,116 lb)
Dimensions: span 13.62 m (44 ft 8¼ in); length 8.60 m (28 ft 2½ in); wing area 37.90 m² (407.9 sq ft)
Armament: one 7.62-mm (0.3-in) machine-gun

Grigorovich M-24 and M-24bis

Work on the design of the **Grigorovich M-24** reconnaissance flying-boat was begun at State Factory No. 3 (GAZ-3) in Petrograd in April 1922 at the request of the Soviet Directorate of Naval Aviation. Developed from the earlier M-9 and M-15, the M-24 had improved hull and wing design, with ailerons fitted to both upper and lower wings of this two-bay unequal-span biplane. The tailplane was of typical Grigorovich design but the powerplant, a 164-kW (220-hp) Renault water-cooled engine, was contained in a carefully streamlined nacelle which included a frontal radiator, and was faired into the upper wing. Pilot and observer sat side-by-side in an open cockpit located beneath the leading edge of the

wing, and were protected from the slip-stream by a single large windscreen. There was also a bow cockpit with a single machine-gun on a ring mounting.

Tested in the spring of 1923, the M-24 was placed in production in 1924, 40 examples being ordered. Performance was somewhat disappointing, the maximum speed being only 130 km/h (81 mph) and service ceiling 3500 m (11,480 ft). Complaints about the M-24 led to the **M-24bis**, of which 20 examples were built. They had detail design improvements and were powered by the 194-kW (260-hp) Renault engine. Loaded weight showed an increase of 50 kg (110 lb) by comparison with the 1750 kg (3,637 lb) of the M-24.

The M-24 and M-24bis were the last Grigorovich seaplane designs to be built in quantity. In the summer of 1925 Grigorovich became head of the OMOS design collective in Leningrad, which was to specialise in seaplanes. The collective met with a signal lack of success, despite a string of designs that included the Liberty-engined **MRL-1** and the three-bay **MUR-1** trainer, powered by a Le Rhône engine and developed from the original M-5. The design team, which included a number of engineers who were later to become designers in their own right, was moved to Moscow in November 1927 and reorganised as OPO-3. The previous October the **MR-2**, a variant of the MRL-1 with a

336-kW (450-hp) Lorraine-Dietrich engine, had crashed under test because of centre-of-gravity problems.

In 1927 Grigorovich produced the more ambitious long-range design, the **ROM-1**, a sesquiplane flying-boat with two tandem Lorraine Dietrich engines. This was developed into the **ROM-2** or **MDR-1** of 1929, which had its two engines mounted conventionally in the leading edge of the upper wing. Although the ROM-2 was improved as the **ROM-2bis** it did not enter production. Later single-engined biplanes included the neat **MU-2** single-bay trainer boat of 1928; the **MUR-2**, a greatly modified MUR-1 with shorter-span two-bay wings and improved hull design; and the **MR-3** with an all-metal hull and powerplant comprising a 507-kW (680-hp) BMW VI engine. When the MR-3 was test flown in the summer of 1929, first from the Moscow River and then from Sevastopol, it was found to have poor take-off performance.

The failure of all these aircraft cast a shadow over Grigorovich, ending his long association with marine aircraft design and contributing to his period of detention with the TsKB (Central Design Bureau), where he designed landplanes. Work on the MR-3 design was continued by Chetverikov, who built the **MR-3bis** with various hulls, mostly of wooden construction. The basic design was known later as the **MR-5** or **Type 0**, but by 1931 was outmoded. After a monoplane variant, the **MR-5bis**, all development of the basic Grigorovich flying-boat family was abandoned.

The lack of success enjoyed by Soviet flying-boats in the period 1925-1932 led to large-scale use of imported aircraft, including the German Dornier Wal, and Heinkel HD-55 flying-boats, together with the Italian Savoia-Marchetti S.16, S.55 and S.62bis. The S.62bis was known as the **MBR-4** in Soviet service, and the shipborne **HD-55** as the **KR-1**.

Specification
Grigorovich M-24bis
Type: two-seat coastal reconnaissance flying-boat
Powerplant: one 194-kW (260-hp) Renault V-8 piston engine
Performance: maximum speed 140 km/h (87 mph); service ceiling 4000 m (13,125 ft)
Weights: empty equipped 1200 kg (2,646 lb); maximum take-off 1700 kg (3,748 lb)
Dimensions: span 16.00 m (52 ft 6 in); length 9.00 m (29 ft 6¼ in); wing area 55.00 m² (592.03 sq ft)

Armament: one 7.62-mm (0.3-in) machine-gun on pivoted mounting in bow cockpit, plus up to 100 kg (220 lb) of bombs

The last Grigorovich flying-boat to be built in quantity was the M-24, an indifferent aircraft which suffered from a lack of advance in design.

Grumman A-6 Intruder/EA-6B Prowler

During the Korean War the US services flew more attack missions than any other type, in the case of the US Navy and US Marine Corps mostly with elderly piston-engined aircraft. This experience showed the need for a specially-designed jet attack aircraft that could operate effectively in the worst weather. In 1957 eight companies submitted 11 designs in a US Navy competition for a new long-range, low-level tactical strike aircraft. The **Grumman G-128**, selected on the last day of the year, was to fulfil that requirement admirably, becoming a major combat type in the later war in South East Asia, and leading to a family of later versions.

Eight development **YA-6A** (designated originally **A2F-1**) aircraft were ordered in March 1959, a full-scale mock-up was completed and accepted some six months later, and the first flight was made on 19 April 1960. The jet-pipes of the two 3856-kg (8,500-lb) static thrust Pratt & Whitney J52-P-6 engines were designed to swivel downwards, to provide an additional component of lift during take-off, but this feature was incorporated in only the first four development aircraft. All others have jet-pipes with a permanent slight downward deflection. The first production **A-6A Intruder** aircraft were delivered to US Navy Attack Squadron VA-42 in February 1963, and the first unit to fly on combat duties in Vietnam was VA-75, whose A-6As began operating from the USS *Independence* in March 1965; from then onwards Intruders of various models became heavily involved in the fighting in South East Asia. Their DIANE (Digital Integrated Attack Navigation Equipment) gave them a first-class operating ability and efficiency in the worst of the humid, stormy weather offered by the local climate, and with a maximum ordnance load of more than 7711 kg (17,000 lb) they were a potent addition to the US arsenal in South East Asia.

Production of the basic A-6A ran until December 1969 and totalled 482 aircraft, plus another 21 built as **EA-6A** variants, retaining a partial strike capability but developed primarily to provide ECM (electronic countermeasures) support for the A-6As in Vietnam and to act as Elint (electronic intelligence) gatherers. The first EA-6A was flown in 1963; the three YA-6As and three A-6As were also converted to EA-6A configuration.

The next three variants of the Intruder were also produced by the conversion of existing A-6As. First of these (19 converted) was the **A-6B**, issued to one USN squadron and differing from the initial model primarily in its ability to carry the US Navy's AGM-78 Standard ARM (anti-radiation missile) instead of the AGM-12B Bullpup. For indentifying and acquiring targets not discernible by the aircraft's standard radar, Grumman then modified 12 other A-6As into **A-6C** aircraft, giving them an improved capability for night attack by installing FLIR (forward-looking infra-red) and low light level TV equipment in a turret under the fuselage. A prototype conversion of an A-6A to **KA-6D** inflight-refuelling tanker was flown on 23 May 1966, and production contracts for the tanker version were placed. These were subsequently cancelled, but 78 A-6As were converted to KA-6D configuration, equipped with TACAN (tactical air navigation) intrumentation and mounting a hose-reel unit in the rear fuselage to refuel other A-6s and other carrier aircraft. The KA-6D can also operate as a day bomber, or as an air/sea rescue control aircraft, and after withdrawal of the EKA-3B from sea-going duty became the standard carrier-based tanker.

On 27 February 1970, Grumman flew the first example of the **A-6E**, an advanced, upgraded development of the A-6A, which the A-6E succeeded in production. Procurement of this version was planned for USN and USMC squadrons, of which some 120 were new-build and 240 converted from A-6As. The basis of the A-6E, which retains upgraded forms of the airframe and powerplant of the earlier models, is a new avionics fit, founded on the addition of a Norden AN/APQ-148 multi-mode navigation radar, an IBM/Fairchild AN/ASQ-133 computerised navigation/attack system, Conrac armament control unit, and an RCA video-tape recorder for assessing the damage caused during a strike mission.

Following the first flight of a test aircraft on 22 March 1974, all US Navy and US Marine Corps Intruders were progressively updated still further under a programme known as TRAM (Target Recognition Attack Multisensor). To the standard A-6E Intruder, this added a Hughes turreted electro-optical package of FLIR and laser detection equipment, integrated with the Norden radar; added CAINS (Carrier Airborne Inertial Naviga-

The EA-6B has an extended fuselage housing a four-man cockpit. Receivers for the sophisticated electronic suite are carried in the fin-tip radome.

tion System) to provide the capability for automatic landings on carrier decks; and incorporated provisions for automatic-homing and laser-guided air-to-surface weapons. The first US Navy squadron to be equipped with this **A-6E/TRAM** version was VA-165, which was deployed aboard the USS *Constellation* in 1977. All A-6Es were scheduled for conversion to TRAM standard and, in addition, a separate programme equipped 50 A-6Es each to carry six Harpoon anti-shipping missiles.

Early experience with EA-6A ECM escort aircraft led to the development of a more advanced version known as the **EA-6B Prowler**. Externally it is similar to the basic A-6A, but it differs by having a nose section which has been extended by 1.37 m (4 ft 6 in), and a distinctive fin pod to house passive receivers. Other changes include structural strengthening for operation at a higher gross weight, the provision of accommodation for two additional crew members to operate the more advanced ECM equipment, increased fuel capacity and more powerful Pratt & Whitney J52-P-408 engines. Deliveries of production aircraft began in January 1971. The Prowler's advanced ECM is based upon the ALQ-99 tactical noise jamming system and up to 10 jamming transmitters can be carried. Improved jamming ability and capacity results from the introduction since 1978 of ICAP (Increased Capability) modifications. More advanced ICAP-2 modifications which attained service status in 1982 are also being introduced retrospectively.

In 1984 Grumman received the go-ahead to develop an improved A-6 designated the **A-6F Intruder II**. This incorporated a new radar, stand-off weapons delivery system, 'glass' cockpit and a new engine, a non-afterburning version of the General Electric F404 turbofan. The first of five prototypes flew on 25 August 1987 but the programme was terminated in 1989 after

three had flown. Grumman then proposed a cheaper alternative, the **A-6G**, with most of the improvements but retaining the original J52 engine, but after evaluation by the US Navy this too was cancelled (in January 1989) in favour of the Systems Weapons Improvement Program, later applied to the bulk of the Intruder fleet.

When the last A-6 variant left the production line at the end of 1990 more than 660 of these expensive but versatile combat aircraft had been built and delivered to the US Navy and Marine Corps.

Variants
YEA-6A: prototype of the EA-6A, a conversion of one of the YA-6A development aircraft
NA-6A: redesignation of three YA-6As and three A-6As modified for use in special test roles
NEA-6A: single aircraft modified from a EA-6A for special test purposes
NEA-6B: redesignation of the two EA-6B prototypes after modification for special test purposes

Specification
Grumman A-6E Intruder
Type: two-seat carrier- or shore-based all-weather attack aircraft
Powerplant: two 4218-kg (9,300-lb) thrust Pratt & Whitney J52-P-8B turbojets
Performance: maximum speed 1036 km/h (644 mph) at sea level; cruising speed 763 km/h (474 mph); service ceiling 12,925 m (42,400 ft); range with maximum military load 1627 km (1,011 miles)
Weights: empty 12093 kg (26,660 lb); maximum take-off, catapult 26581 kg (58,600 lb), field 27397 kg (60,400 lb)
Dimensions: span 16.15 m (53 ft 0 in); length 16.69 m (54 ft 9 in); height 4.93 m (16 ft 2 in); wing area 49.13 m² (528.9 sq ft)
Armament: one underfuselage and four underwing attachment points for maximum external load of 8165 kg (18,000 lb).

Grumman Albatross
to
Grumman F4F Wildcat

Gruman Albatross

Experience with the Grumman Goose, which served throughout World War II with great reliability, prompted the US Navy to procure a somewhat larger amphibian with greater range capability. In 1944 the company initiated design of its **Grumman G-64** aircraft, which was to be named **Albatross**, and which saw service with the US Air Force, US Coast Guard and US Navy. The prototype was flown first on 24 October 1947, and was of generally similar configuration to its predecessor. Fixed underwing floats were retained, but these and the entire structure had been considerably refined to reduce drag. Other changes included the provision of a cantilever, instead of strut-braced, tailplane; tricycle type retractable landing gear; and pylons beneath the wing, outboard of the engines, which could carry weapons, or drop-tanks to increase range. Additional fuel could also be carried in the underwing floats. Accommodation was provided for a crew of four and the cabin could accommodate 10 passengers, stretchers, or cargo, according to requirements.

The prototype ordered by the US Navy for service as a utility aircraft had the designation **XJR2F-1**, and flew for the first time on 24 October 1947. Initial production was of the **UF-1** model, and a modified version introduced in 1955 was the **UF-2**. This latter aircraft had increased span, a cambered wing leading edge, ailerons and tail surfaces of increased area, and more effective de-icing boots for all aerofoil leading edges. In the tri-service rationalisation of designations in 1962, these aircraft became **HU-16C** and **HU-16D** respectively. Winterised aircraft for Antarctic service were designated **UF-1L** (later **LU-16C**), and five **UF-1T** dual-control trainers were redesignated **TU-16C**.

Although it was popular with military operators, the Albatross was not economical enough to attract much civil interest. This was largely due to the type being somewhat overpowered.

The USAF found the G-64 attractive for rescue operations, the majority of the 305 ordered serving with the MATS Air Rescue Service under the designation **SA-16A**. An improved version, equivalent to the US Navy's UF-2, entered service in 1957 as the **SA-16B**: in 1962 these became **HU-16A** and **HU-16B** respectively. **HU-16E** was the designation (originally **UF-1G**) of Albatross aircraft operated by the US Coast Guard, and 10 supplied to Canada were designated **CSR-110**. An anti-submarine version with nose radome, retractable MAD gear, ECM radome and searchlight was introduced in 1961, and was equipped to carry a small number of depth charges. The versatile Albatross continues in service with a few air forces and navies, but its powerful and fuel-hungry engines have meant that surplus aircraft which became available for use were not a particularly attractive proposition to airline operators, and in consequence few were adapted for such a role.

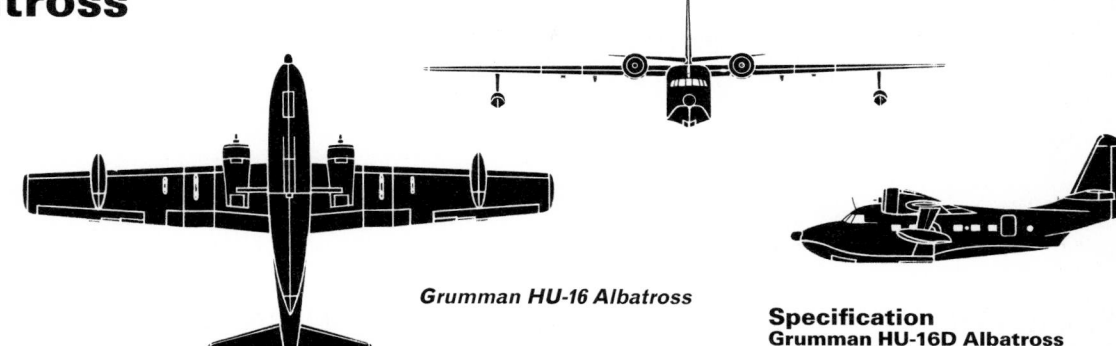

Grumman HU-16 Albatross

Specification
Grumman HU-16D Albatross
Type: general-purpose amphibian
Powerplant: two 1063-kW (1,425-hp) Wright R-1820-76A or -76B Cyclone 9-cylinder radial piston engines
Performance: maximum speed 380 km/h (236 mph); cruising speed 241 km/h (150 mph); service ceiling 6555 m (21,500 ft); range with maximum internal and external fuel 4587 km (2,850 miles)
Weights: empty 10380 kg (22,883 lb); maximum take-off 16193 kg (35,700 lb)
Dimensions: span 29.46 m (96 ft 8 in); length 18.67 m (61 ft 3 in); height 7.87 m (25 ft 10 in); wing area 96.15 m² (1,035 sq ft)

Grumman AF-2 Guardian

Despite the success achieved by the Grumman TBF/TBM Avenger, thoughts on its replacement began to crystallise during 1943 and emerged initially as the TB2F design to be powered by two Pratt & Whitney R-2800-22 radials, be heavily armed and carry a 3629-kg (8,000-lb) offensive payload over 3669 km (2,280 miles). However, the gross weight of 20412 kg (45,000 lb) was considered excessive for carrier operation and the project was abandoned in favour of the TSF, a derivative of the F7F Tigercat. This, in its turn, was cancelled, and in February 1945 the US Navy's Bureau of Aeronautics placed an order for three prototypes of the **Grumman G-70**. This was a mid-wing monoplane with side-by-side seating for the two-man crew, and intended to carry a 1814-kg (4,000-lb) load of bombs, depth charges or torpedoes in an internal weapons bay; two 20-mm

The Guardian operated in hunter-killer pairs against submarines. The near aircraft is an AF-2W with search radar; behind is an AF-2S with weapons.

(0.79-in) cannon were to complete the offensive armament. It was to rely on speed to escape if attacked, and for this purpose the main nose-mounted radial engine was to be supplemented by a Westinghouse turbojet, buried in the rear fuselage and supplied with air through oval intakes in the leading edges of the wings.

Three prototypes were planned, comprising two **XTB3F-1** aircraft with the 1715-kW (2,300-hp) Pratt & Whitney R-2800-34W and the 726-kg (1600-lb) thrust Westinghouse 19XB-2B, and one **XTB3F-2** with a Wright R-3350 and a Westinghouse 24C-4B. Grumman test

pilot Pat Gallo flew the first of these on 18 December 1946, with the jet intakes blanked off because of intake problems experienced during ground running. In fact, the jet engine was never used in flight and was soon removed. Just five days after the maiden flight the US Navy halted work on the TB3F, following a reappraisal of requirements, and it was dropped in its original role as a torpedo-bomber. However, the programme was reinstated to meet a new need for anti-submarine warfare aircraft, and the two prototypes still under construction were modified as a hunter/killer combination.

The third prototype, then designated **XTB3F-1S**, was completed without the Westinghouse jet engine, the space released being used to house electronic equipment and provide a third crew position for a radar operator. The former bomb bay was equipped with AN/APS-20 search radar and a large ventral radome. This aircraft flew in November 1948, followed by the four-seat second prototype, designated **XTB3F-2S**, on 12 January 1949. Both aircraft undertook service trials at Naval Air Test Center Patuxent River in February. By then production orders had been placed for the two machines, as the **AF-2S Guardian** strike aircraft with the **AF-2W Guardian** operating in a search role. Both were powered by the Pratt & Whitney R-2800-48W radial. The first production AF-2S flew on 17 November 1949 and

between May 1950 and November 1951 five of each model were flown on armament evaluation tests with Air Development Squadron 1 at Key West. Carrier qualification flying was conducted aboard USS *Wright* in November 1950, on USS *Palau* in December and USS *Monterey* in September 1951. VS-25 at NAS North Island accepted its first aircraft on 18 October 1950. The front-line service of the AF-2 Guardian was limited, however, for on 30 June 1950 the US Navy issued the requirement to which the S2F Tracker was developed and this new aircraft finally displaced the Guardian with VS-37 at NAS North Island on 31 August 1955. During the Guardian's operational life, however, a number of squadrons (including three Reserve units) flew combat missions in Korean waters between March 1951 and May 1953.

Variants

AF-2S: 193 examples of this weapon-carrying component of the hunter-killer combination were built; up to 1814 kg (4,000 lb) of stores were carried internally and six underwing pylons could accept HVAR rockets or 113-kg (250-lb) depth charges; AN/APS-31 radar was carried beneath the starboard wing and an AN/AVQ-2 high-intensity searchlight under the port wing; sonobuoys were dropped from pods mounted under the wing centre-section

AF-2W: production of this four-man search version totalled 153; unarmed, it was identified easily by the ventral radome for the AN/APS-20 radar which was supplemented by extensive avionics

AF-3S: 40 aircraft delivered between February 1952 and November 1953, similar to the AF-2S, but with additional ASW equipment including magnetic

anomaly detector boom on the starboard side of the fuselage

Specification
Grumman AF-2S
Type: two-seat anti-submarine aircraft
Powerplant: one 1780-kW (2,400-hp) Pratt & Whitney R-2800-48W 18-cylinder radial piston engine
Performance: maximum speed 510 km/h (317 mph) at 4875 m (16,000 ft); service ceiling 9905 m (32,500 ft); range 2414 km (1,500 miles)
Weights: empty 6613 kg (14,580 lb); maximum take-off 11567 kg (25,500 lb)
Dimensions: span 18.49 m (60 ft 8 in); length 13.21 m (43 ft 4 in); height 4.93 m (16 ft 2 in); wing area 52.02 m² (560.0 sq ft)
Armament: one 907-kg (2,000-lb) torpedo, or two 907-kg (2,000-lb) bombs, or two 726-kg (1,600-lb) depth charges

Grumman E-2 Hawkeye/TE-2/C-2 Greyhound

The original concept of AEW (airborne early warning) was developed during World War II, when it was realised that an airborne surveillance radar could overcome the range limitations imposed by the curvature of the Earth on land- or ship-based radar detectors. Early attempts to provide a radar 'eye in the sky' were not particularly successful, but over the next three decades both the equipment and the AEW concept have been developed to a considerable extent.

Grumman has been associated with AEW from its beginning, and claims with some justification that its **Grumman G-89** design was the first, and remains the only, aircraft in service today that was designed from the outset as an AEW/tactical airborne command and control aircraft. On 5 March 1957 it was named the winner of a US Navy competition to provide a radar-carrying aircraft that would form part of an overall Naval Tactical Data System. Grumman's design covered a twin turboprop-powered aircraft carrying a crew of five (two pilots, radar operator, air control officer and a combat information centre officer), and mounted a General Electric AN/APS-96 surveillance radar in a 7.32-m (24-ft) discus-shaped revolving radome on a pylon above the fuselage. To offset the effects of this structure on stability, a wide-span dihedral tailplane was incorporated, bearing four fins and twin rudders.

Known originally as the **W2F-1**, the first prototype made its initial flight on 21 October 1960, powered by two Allison T56-A-8 turboprops. This was an aerodynamic prototype only, the full avionics system being installed in the second prototype which was flown first on 19 April 1961. In 1962 the designation was changed to **E-2A Hawkeye**, and the first of 59 examples of this version (including prototypes) was delivered to US Navy Squadron VAW-11 on 19 January 1964. Two remained in USN service as **TE-2A** trainers and two others were converted to **E-2C** prototypes. In 1969, after a prototype conversion had flown on 20 February, all operational E-2As were modified to **E-2B** standard providing an improved computer and provision for inflight-refuelling. They are normally operated in teams of two or more aircraft, flying at altitudes of some 9145 m (30,000 ft) to provide long-range early warning of potential threats from hostile surface vessels and all kinds of aircraft.

The current E-2C variant can be distinguished from the earlier E-2A and B by the large intake above the fuselage forward of the centre-section.

In the summer of 1971, following the first flight of a prototype on 20 January, Grumman began production of the **E-2C Hawkeye**. This heralded a significant improvement in operational capability, with a major upgrading of the principal avionics, and E-2Cs entered service in November 1973 with VAW-123. Initial procurement for the US Navy was for 11 aircraft, but Grumman ultimately received orders for a total of 164 E-2Cs; around 140 of these have been delivered to date, including two **TE-2C** trainers. E-2Cs have been supplied to Israel (four), Japan (13), Egypt (six) and Singapore (four). Six converted E-2Bs are also in service with Taiwan as the E-2T.

The E-2C's APS-125 radar, developed jointly by General Electric and Grumman, is capable of detecting airborne targets in a 'land clutter' environment at ranges up to 370 km (230 miles). It provides automatic detection and tracking over land or water, with simultaneous surveillance of air as well as surface traffic. The onboard data processing equipment can track, automatically and simultaneously, more than 250 targets; it can also control over 30 airborne interceptions. As an addition to its radar system, the E-2C carries a passive detection system (PDS) which detects automatically the presence, direction and identity of any traffic in a 'high signal density' environment. The PDS can also alert its operators to the presence of electronic emitters at distances up to almost 805 km (500 miles), establish the location of the emission and identify the threat. At the same time, the E-2C's own radar system incorporates ECCM (electronic counter-countermeasures) to help ensure its own continued effectiveness in the face of hostile jamming.

With the Hawkeye operating successfully from and to aircraft-carriers at sea, it was logical that the US Navy should look favourably on a carrier onboard delivery (COD) version of this aircraft when it was proposed by Grumman in 1962. Three were ordered initially (one for static testing) under the designation **C-2A Greyhound**, and the first of these made its initial flight on 18 November 1964, being accepted by the US Navy in the following

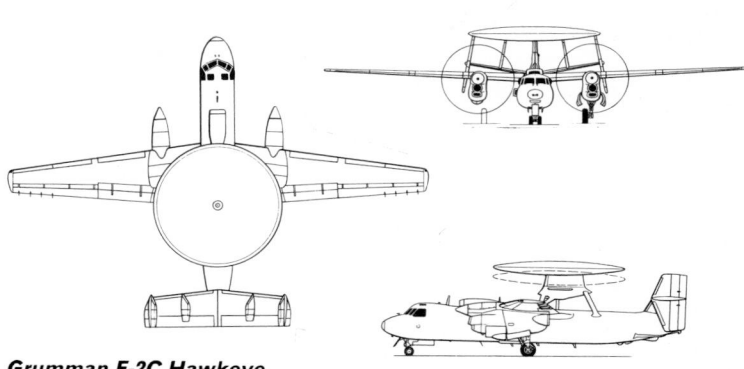

Grumman E-2C Hawkeye

month. The first batch comprised 19 aircraft generally similar to the E-2 except for the obvious deletion of the rotating overfuselage radome, the elimination of tailplane dihedral and provision of a new larger-capacity fuselage. In addition to being wider and deeper, the Greyhound fuselage incorporates an aft-loading cargo door which forms the undersurface of the upswept rear fuselage. Internal changes include strengthened cargo flooring to cater for heavier loads, and this is provided with flush tracks for the attachment of cargo tie-down fittings. As an alternative to palletised loads, the C-2A can accommodate 39 troops, or 20 stretchers and four nursing staff.

Early in 1982 Grumman received a new order from the US Navy covering a second batch of 39 C-2As based on the E-2C airframe; the first of these was delivered in 1985. All 19 of the original batch were withdrawn from service by 1987,

and the new aircraft differed from the earlier aircraft by having uprated engines, better passenger accommodation and improved avionics.

Specification
Grumman E-2C Hawkeye
Type: airborne early warning and control aircraft
Powerplant: two 3661-kW (4,910-eshp) Allison T56-A-425 turboprops
Performance: maximum speed 602 km/h (374 mph); long-range cruising speed 499 km/h (310 mph); service ceiling 9390 m (30,800 ft); endurance with maximum fuel 6 hours 6 minutes
Weights: empty 17211 kg (37,945 lb); maximum take-off 23503 kg (51,817 lb)
Dimensions: span 24.56 m (80 ft 7 in); length 17.54 m (57 ft 6¾ in); height 5.58 m (18 ft 3 in); wing area 65.03 m² (700.0 sq ft)

Grumman FF, SF and Goblin

On 28 March 1931 the US Navy placed its first contract with the Grumman Aircraft Engineering Corporation, beginning an association with the manufacturer which continues to this day. The subject of the contract was the prototype **Grumman XFF-1** two-seat biplane fighter which was the US Navy's first with retractable landing gear. Grumman had earlier produced a float incorporating such gear for use on Vought Corsair biplanes, and had expressed a wish to design a new aircraft thus fitted rather than instal its equipment in existing US Navy fighters. The XFF-1 was of all-metal construction and armed with two 7.62-mm (0.3-in) Browning machine-guns mounted in the forward fuselage top decking, and a similar weapon in the rear cockpit, attached to the gunner's seat so that gun and seat moved together in a gimballed mounting as the target was tracked. Construction of the prototype, powered by a 459-kW (616-hp) Wright R-1820E radial engine, was initiated at Grumman's Baldwin, Long Island, workshop. However, in November 1931 the company moved 13 km (eight miles) to Curtiss Field, from where the aircraft was flown on 29 December, piloted by NACA test pilot Bill McAvoy. Initial manufacturer's trials were completed quickly and in January 1932 the prototype was flown to the US Navy's test centre at NAS Anacostia for official evaluation. In the course of this programme the aircraft demonstrated a top speed of 314 km/h (195 mph) at sea level, faster than the single-seat Boeing F4B-4 which was then the US Navy's standard fighter. In November 1932 Grumman moved again, to larger premises at Farmingdale, and in the following month the company received its first production order, for 27 **FF-1 (G-5)**

Grumman SF-1 of VS-3B, based aboard the USS Lexington in the mid-1930s.

fighters which were delivered between 24 April and 1 November 1933. US Navy Squadron VF-5B began to receive the first aircraft on 21 June 1933, later going to sea aboard USS Lexington.

Variants
FF-2: 25 of the original 27 FF-1s were later converted by Naval Aircraft Factory for use as fighter trainers, fitted with dual controls
SF-1 (G-6): on 9 June 1931 the US Navy ordered one prototype of a scout version, with fuel capacity increased by 170 litres (45 US gal) at the expense of one of the forward-firing Brownings, and powered by a 522-kW (700-hp) R-1820-78 engine; it was flown in August 1932 and the 33 ordered by the US Navy in that month were delivered between 15 February and 12 July 1934; US Navy Squadron VS-3B began to receive its SF-1s on 30 March 1934, serving aboard USS Lexington
G-23 Goblin: this was the FF-1 as

built under licence by Canadian Car and Foundry Company for the Royal Canadian Air Force, which received 15 aircraft; when No. 1 (F) Squadron's Hurricanes left Canada for England in June 1940, No. 118 (F) Squadron was re-formed with Goblins and these comprised Canada's air defence capability until they were replaced in November 1941 by Curtiss Kittyhawks; 40 were ordered by Turkey in 1937 and delivered via Barcelona where they found their way into the hands of Spanish Republican forces; one aircraft each was delivered to Japan and Nicaragua
XSF-2: one aircraft only, delivered to the US Navy on 12 March 1934, the XSF-2 was an SF-1 airframe with a 485-kW (650-hp) Pratt & Whitney R-1535-72 engine driving a Hamilton Standard propeller
XSBF-1: the XSF-2 airframe was modified by the incorporation of a triangular frame, beneath the engine

mounting, to carry one 227-kg (500-lb) or two 45-kg (100-lb) bombs; it was first flown on 18 February 1936

Specification
Grumman FF-2/SF-1
Type: two-seat shipboard scout
Powerplant: one 522-kW (700-hp) Wright R-1820-78 9-cylinder radial piston engine
Performance: maximum speed 333 km/h (207 mph) at 1220 m (4,000 ft); service ceiling 6400 m (21,000 ft); range 1428 km (921 miles)
Weights: empty 1474 kg (3,250 lb); maximum take-off 2190 kg (4,828 lb)
Dimensions: span 10.52 m (34 ft 6 in); length 7.47 m (24 ft 6 in); height 3.38 m (11 ft 1 in); wing area 28.80 m² (310.0 sq ft)
Armament: one forward-firing and two pivoted rear 7.62-mm (0.3-in) Browning machine-guns

Grumman F2F

This F2F-1 was embarked with VF-5 in USS Wasp and remained in service until 1939. After 1940 the type continued to give good service as a trainer or hack.

The outstanding performance of the FF-1 two-seat fighter naturally turned the Grumman design team's thoughts to the even greater potential of a single-seat version, and the **Grumman G-8** proposal was submitted to the US Navy in June 1932. The **XF2F-1** prototype, ordered on 2 November 1932, was slightly smaller than its predecessor, with a metal semi-monocoque fuselage and fabric-covered metal wings with ailerons on the upper surfacs only. Power was supplied by a 466-kW (625-hp) XR-1535-44 Twin Wasp Junior engine and armament comprised two 7.62-mm (0.3-in) Browning machine-guns in the upper decking of the forward fuselage; racks could be fitted under the wings to carry two 53-kg (116-lb) bombs. The aircraft was rolled out for its first flight on 18 October 1933, Jimmy Collins being the pilot. Following manufacturer's trials it was handed over to the US Navy's test pilots for a six-month evaluation, during which it demon-

strated a maximum speed of 369 km/h (229 mph) at 2560 m (8,400 ft) and an initial rate of climb of 939 m (3,080 ft) per minute; on the debit side, the short, corpulent fuselage gave rise to some directional instability, and the aircraft tightened up in the spin. Minor changes were introduced, including an enlarged cockpit canopy, a 0.15-m (6-in) increase in span of the upper wings, and the replacement of the original smooth NACA cowling by one of smaller diameter with rocker arm blisters. On 17 May 1934 the US Navy placed a production order for 54 **F2F-1** fighters, the first of which was delivered on 28 January 1935 and the last exactly 10 months later. One crashed on its delivery flight on 16 March and a replacement was ordered on 29 June. Replacement of the Boeing F4B-2s of VF-2B ('Fighting Two') assigned to USS Lexington began on 19 February 1935,

and the type remained in service with this unit until 30 September 1940, when the 18-aircraft complement was flown to NAS Pensacola for use in the advanced trainer role.

Specification
Grumman F2F-1
Type: single-seat shipboard fighter
Powerplant: one 485-kW (650-hp) Pratt & Whitney R-1535-72 Twin Wasp Junior radial piston engine

Performance: maximum speed 383 km/h (238 mph); cruising speed 225 km/h (140 mph); range 1585 km (985 miles)
Weights: empty 1221 kg (2,691 lb); maximum take-off 1745 kg (3,847 lb)
Dimensions: span 8.69 m (28 ft 6 in); length 6.53 m (21 ft 5 in); height 2.77 m (9 ft 1 in); wing area 21.37 m² (230.0 sq ft)
Armament: two 7.62-mm (0.3-in) Browning machine-guns

Grumman F3F

Although the US Navy had accepted the shortcomings of the F2F, Grumman was determined to improve the directional stability, spinning characteristics and general manoeuvrability of its product. Built under a US Navy contract dated 15 October 1934 (placed three months before the first F2F-1 was delivered), the prototype **Grumman XF3F-1** retained the R-1535-72 engine of its predecessor but the fuselage was increased in length

by 0.56 m (1 ft 10 in), the wings were increased in overall span by 1.07 m (3 ft 6 in) and other minor aerodynamic improvements were introduced. Test pilot Jimmy Collins made the first flight at Farmingdale on 20 March 1935, but two days later he was killed when the wings and engine became detached during a test dive which was to demonstrate a 9-g recovery. Design limits had been exceeded, but the second aircraft was built with strengthened lower wing root fittings and engine mountings. It was first flown on 9 May and then delivered to

NAS Anacostia for US Navy test and evaluation, during which it was being flown by Grumman test pilot Lee Gehlbach when, on 17 May, it entered a flat spin from which recovery was impossible and the pilot baled out. Incredibly, the machine was not completely destroyed and was rebuilt within three weeks, test pilot Bill McAvoy completing the manufacturer's trials so that it could be returned to Anacostia on 20 June. The rebuilt aircraft was given a small ventral fillet beneath the tailcone, added after tests with a model in the

spin tunnel at NACA's Langley Field facility. A total of 54 production **F3F-1** fighters was ordered on 24 August and, following initial deliveries in January 1936, the type entered service with VF-5B aboard USS Ranger in April and VF-6B on USS Saratoga in June. Marine Squadron VMF-211 was the last operational unit with F3Fs, retiring them on 10 October 1941, and more than 100 aircraft then served with training units. The last was struck off charge in November 1943 and relegated to ground instruction airframe status.

Variants

F3F-1(G-77): 54 were built for the US Navy, similar to the XF3F-1 prototype but powered by an R-1535-84 Twin Wasp Junior with a hydraulic controllable-pitch Hamilton Standard two-bladed propeller; armament comprised a 7.62-mm (0.3-in) Browning machine-gun in the port side forward fuselage top decking and a 12.7-mm (0.5-in) Browning machine-gun to starboard; deliveries were made between 29 January and 18 September 1936

F3F-2 (G-19): the last production F3F-1 was converted to XF3F-2 standard with a supercharged 634-kW (850-hp) Wright XR-1820-22 Cyclone radial engine driving a three-bladed controllable-pitch propeller; fuel capacity was increased to 492 litres (130 US gal); though the aircraft was delivered to Anacostia on 27 July 1936, carburetion problems delayed the start of the test programme until January 1937; in March, however, 81 were ordered by the US Navy, the first entering service with VF-6 on 1 December; deliveries were made between 27 July 1937 and 11 May 1938

F3F-3: a production F3F-2 was returned to Grumman for conversion to XF3F-3 standard with minor drag-reducing modifications to the airframe, revised cowling and forward fuselage decking; 27 were built and delivered between 16 December 1938 and 10 May 1939

Specification
Grumman F3F-3

Type: single-seat shipboard fighter
Powerplant: one 708-kW (950-hp) Wright R-1820-22 9-cylinder radial piston engine
Performance: maximum speed 425 km/h (264 mph); cruising speed 241 km/h (150 mph); service ceiling 10120 m (33,200 ft); range 1577 km (980 miles)
Weights: empty 1490 kg (3,285 lb); maximum take-off 2175 kg (4,795 lb)
Dimensions: span 9.75 m (32 ft 0 in); length 7.06 m (23 ft 2 in); height 2.84 m (9 ft 4 in); wing area 24.15 m² (260.0 sq ft)

The F3F was an improved version of the F2F, serving on board US Navy carriers in the late 1930s. These aircraft are F3F-1s from VF-4 in Ranger.

Armament: two 7.62-mm (0.3-in) Browning machine-guns

Grumman F4F Wildcat

The US Navy's requirement of 1936 for a new carrier-based fighter resulted in the Brewster Aeronautical Corporation receiving an order for a prototype of its Model 39 under the designation XF2A-1. This became the US Navy's first monoplane fighter in squadron service, but so tentative was the US Navy in its decision to order this aircraft that it ordered also a prototype of Grumman's competing biplane design under the designation **XF4F-1**. However, a more careful study of the performance potential of Brewster's design, plus the fact that Grumman's earlier F3F biplane was beginning to demonstrate good performance, brought second thoughts. This led to cancellation of the biplane prototype and the initiation of an alternative **Grumman G-18** monoplane design. Following evaluation of this new proposal, the US Navy ordered a single prototype on 28 July 1936 under the designation **XF4F-2**.

Flown for the first time on 2 September 1937, the XF4F-2 was powered by a 783-kW (1,050-hp) Pratt & Whitney R-1830-66 Twin Wasp engine, and was able to demonstrate a maximum speed of 467 km/h (290 mph). Of all-metal construction, with its cantilever monoplane wing set in a mid-position on the fuselage, and provided with retractable tail-wheel landing gear, it proved to be marginally faster than the Brewster prototype when flown during competitive evaluation in the early months of 1938. Speed, however, was its major credit: in several other respects it was decidedly inferior, with the result that Brewster's XF2A-1 was ordered into production on 11 June 1938.

Clearly the US Navy believed the XF4F-2 had hidden potential, for it was returned to Grumman in October 1938, together with a new contract for its further development. The company adopted major changes before this **G-36** prototype flew again in March 1939 under the designation **XF4F-3**. These included the installation of a more powerful version of the Twin Wasp (the XR-1830-76 with a two-stage supercharger), increased wing span and area, redesigned tail surfaces, and a modified machine-gun installation. When tested in this new form the XF4F-3 was found to have considerably improved performance. A second prototype was completed and introduced into the test programme, this aircraft differing in having a redesigned tail unit in which the tailplane

A flight of Grumman F4F-4 Wildcats in the insignia (red border to the national markings) used only between July and September 1943. Modelled closely on the F4F-3, the F4F-4 differed mainly in having manually-folding wings.

was moved higher up the fin, and the profile of the vertical tail was changed again. In this final form the XF4F-3 was found to have good handling characteristics and manoeuvrability, and a maximum speed of 539 km/h (335 mph) at 6490 m (21,300 ft). Faced with such performance, the US Navy had no hesitation in ordering 78 **F4F-3** production aircraft on 8 August 1939.

With war seemingly imminent in Europe, Grumman offered the new **G-36A** design for export, receiving orders for 81 and 30 aircraft from the French and Greek governments respectively. The first of those, intended for the French navy, powered by a 746-kW (1,000-hp) Wright R-1820 Cyclone radial engine, flew on 27 July 1940 but by then, of course, France had already fallen. Instead, the British Purchasing Commission agreed to take these aircraft, increasing the order to 90, and the first began to reach the UK in July 1940 (after the first five off the line had been supplied to Canada), becoming designated **Martlet Mk I**. They first equipped No. 804 Squadron of the Fleet Air Arm, and two of the aircraft flown by this squadron were the first American-built fighters to destroy a German aircraft during World War II, in December 1940.

Subsequent Grumman-built versions to serve with the FAA included the Twin Wasp-powered folding-wing **Martlet Mk II**; 10 F4F-4As and the Greek contract G-36A aircraft as **Martlet Mk III**; and Lend-Lease F4F-4Bs with Wright GR-1820 Cyclone engines as **Martlet Mk IV**. In January 1944 they were all redesignated as **Wildcats**, but retained their distinguishing mark numbers.

The first **F4F-3** for the US Navy was flown on 20 August 1940, and at the beginning of December the type began to equip Navy Squadrons VF-7 and VF-41. Some 95 **F4F-3A** aircraft were ordered by the US Navy, these being powered by the R-1830-90 engine with single-stage supercharger, and deliveries began in 1941. An **XF4F-4** prototype was flown in May 1941, this incorporating refinements which resulted from Martlet combat experience in the UK, including six-gun armament, armour, self-sealing tanks, and wing-folding. Delivery of production **F4F-4 Wildcat** fighters, as the type had then been named, began in November 1941, and by the time that the Japanese launched their attacks on Pearl Harbor a number of US Navy and US Marine Corps squadrons had been equipped. As additional Wildcats entered service they equipped increasing numbers of US Marine and US Navy squadrons. In particular they served with the carriers USS *Enterprise*, *Hornet* and *Saratoga*, being involved with conspicuous success in the battles of the Coral Sea and Midway, and the operations in Guadalcanal. They were at the centre of all significant action in the Pacific until superseded by more advanced aircraft in 1943, and also saw action with the US Navy in North Africa during late 1942.

The final production variant built by Grumman was the long-range reconnaissance **F4F-7** with increased fuel capacity, camera installations in the lower fuselage and armament deleted. Only 20 were built, but Grumman also produced an additional 100 F4F-3s and two **XF4F-8** prototypes. With an urgent need to concentrate on development and production of the more advanced F6F Hellcat, Grumman negotiated with General Motors to continue production of the F4F-4 Wildcat under the designation **FM-1**. Production by General Motors' Eastern Aircraft Division began after finalisation of a contract on 18 April 1942, and the first of this company's FM-1s was flown on 31 August 1942. Production totalled 1,151, of which 312 were supplied to the UK under the designation **Martlet Mk V** (later **Wildcat Mk V**).

At the same time, General Motors was working on the development of an improved version, designated **FM-2**, which was the production version of the two Grumman XF4F-8 prototypes. Its major change was the installation of a 1007-kW (1,350-hp) Wright R-1820-56 Cyclone 9 radial engine, but a larger vertical tail was introduced to maintain good directional stability with this more powerful engine, and airframe weight was reduced to the minimum. A total of 4,777 FM-2s was built by General Motors, 370 of them supplied to the UK, these entering service with the FAA and designated **Wildcat Mk VI** from the outset.

Specification
Grumman F4F-4

Type: single-seat carrier-based fighter-bomber
Powerplant: one 895-kW (1,200-hp) Pratt & Whitney R-1830-36 Twin Wasp 14-cylinder radial piston engine
Performance: maximum speed 512 km/h (318 mph) at 5915 m (19,400 ft); cruising speed 249 km/h (155 mph); initial climb rate 594 m (1,950 ft) per minute; service ceiling 12010 m (39,400 ft); range 1239 km (770 miles)
Weights: empty 2612 kg (5,758 lb); maximum take-off 3607 kg (7,952 lb)
Dimensions: span 11.58 m (38 ft 0 in); length 8.76 m (28 ft 9 in); height 2.81 m (9 ft 2½ in); wing area 24.15 m² (260.0 sq ft)
Armament: six fixed 12.7-mm (0.5-in) Browning machine-guns, plus two 45-kg (100-lb) bombs

Grumman XF5F-1 and XP-50 Skyrocket
to
Grumman F11F Tiger

Grumman XF5F-1 and XP-50 Skyrocket

The **Grumman G-34** proposal of 1938 for a single-seat twin-engined shipboard fighter anticipated the realisation of an operational production example of such a type by quite a few years. In fact, the proposal was then considered to be so advanced that it bordered on the revolutionary; yet only four years later, on 18 April 1942, 16 North American B-25 twin-engined bombers were flown off the USS *Hornet* to attack Tokyo.

Not only was the G-34 an advanced concept, in its original form it was a most unusual-looking aircraft, with the leading edge of its low-set monoplane wing forward of the fuselage nose. The tail unit had twin endplate fins and rudders, and the landing gear was of the retractable tailwheel type, with the main units retracting aft into the wing-mounted engine nacelles. Powerplant comprised two Wright R-1820 Cyclones, each with a three-bladed propeller, these being geared to counter-rotate to offset the effects of propeller torque.

The US Navy was first to order a prototype, the **XF5F-1**, on 30 June 1938, which was flown for the first time on 1 April 1940. A number of modifications were introduced subsequently, the most noticeable being an extension of the fuselage nose so that it terminated forward of the wing. Although failing to win a production order, the XF5F-1 soldiered on until withdrawn from use in

December 1944, having done some useful work as a development prototype for the more advanced Grumman F7F. A land-based version of Grumman's design interested the US Army Air Force, which ordered a single **XP-50** prototype. Although generally similar to the naval version, it differed by having a lengthened nose to accommodate the nosewheel of the tricycle landing gear and had as powerplant two Wright R-1820-67/-69 turbocharged engines. First flown on 14 May 1941, the XP-50 was plagued with engine overheating

problems and was eventually written off after suffering serious damage when a turbocharger exploded. No further examples of the XP-50 were built.

Specification
Grumman XF5F-1
Type: single-seat carrier-based fighter prototype
Powerplant: two 895-kW (1,200-hp) Wright XR-1820-40/-42 Cyclone 9-cylinder radial piston engines
Performance: maximum speed 616 km/h (383 mph); cruising speed 338 km/h (210 mph); service ceiling 10060 m (33,000 ft); range 1931 km (1,200 miles)
Weights: empty 3677 kg (8,107 lb); maximum take-off 4599 kg (10,138 lb)
Dimensions: span 12.80 m (42 ft 0 in); length 8.75 m (28 ft 8½ in); height 3.45 m (11 ft 4 in); wing area 28.20 m² (303.5 sq ft)
Armament: provision for two 23-mm Madsen cannon

In its original form the XF5F had a truncated nose ending behind the wing leading edge. The nose was subsequently lengthened to a more orthodox shape.

Grumman F6F Hellcat

Developed from a project started by the company to evolve a successor to the F4F Wildcat, the **Grumman F6F Hellcat** benefitted in the design stage from early operational experience of US Navy pilots in the Pacific theatre, and from a feedback of information from the European Allies who had then been involved in war against the Axis for some 18 months. This project was an advanced development of the F4F, the family resemblance unmistakable, but with one major change: the mid-wing configuration of the Wildcat gave place to a new low-wing layout that made it possible for the main landing gear units to retract into the wing centre-section instead of the fuselage. This allowed the main gear units to be mounted further outboard from the fuselage, providing a much more stable wide-track landing gear. Other improvements that resulted from combat feedback included the provision of armour for the pilot, and increased ammunition capacity.

An evaluation by the US Navy of Grumman's design proposal resulted in an order, dated 30 June 1941, covering four prototypes, each with a different engine installation to permit competitive evaluation of the flight envelope. These prototypes were the **XF6F-1** with a two-stage turbocharged 1268-kW (1,700-hp) Wright R-2600-10 Cyclone 14; the **XF6F-2** with a turbocharged R-2600-16; the **XF6F-3** with a two-stage turbocharged 1491-kW (2,000-hp) Pratt & Whitney R-2800-10 Double Wasp; and the **XF6F-4** with the R-2800-27 and two-speed turbocharger.

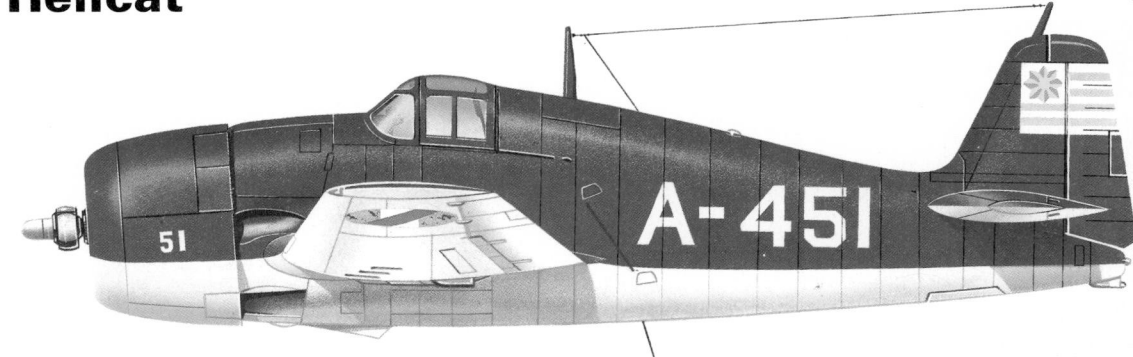

Grumman F6F-5 Hellcat of the Aviacion Naval Uruguaya during the 1950s.

On 26 June 1942, just under a year from order date, the XF6F-1 flew for the first time. By then there was great urgency to reinforce the Wildcats in service, resulting in a decision to install the most powerful engine then available, the Pratt & Whitney R-2800-10, into the first airframe; this made its second 'first flight' as the XF6F-3 on 30 July 1942. But even before the first prototype flight, the Grumman design had been ordered into production as the **F6F-3 Hellcat**, and from that moment the design similarity of the F4Fs and F6Fs paid immense dividends in terms of production. The first production F6F-3 flew for the first time on 4 October 1942; US Navy Squadron VF-9 on board USS *Essex* began to equip on 16 January 1943; and on 31 August 1943 Squadron VF-5 on board USS *Yorktown* became the first Hellcats to join combat with the Japanese.

Of all-metal construction with flush-riveted skins, the Hellcat's wings had outer panels which folded for carrier stowage. Standard armament comprised six 12.7-mm (0.5-in) machine-guns mounted in the leading edges of the wings. The fuselage and tail unit were conventional in structure and differed little, except in size, from those of the F4F. All three units of the landing gear were retracted hydraulically and a retractable arrester hook was standard. The pilot was accommodated in a capacious cockpit high above the wing.

Hellcat production was superb, with well over 2,500 delivered during 1943, making it possible to re-equip F4F squadrons rapidly with this more potent fighter, and the type remained in first-line service with the US Navy for the remainder of World War II. Even when the more advanced Vought F4U Corsair

joined the fleet in mid-1944 the Hellcat was not displaced. Instead, the two fighters worked side-by-side as a team that was extremely low in Japanese popularity ratings: the Hellcat finally credited with 4,947 enemy aircraft destroyed in air-to-air combat, the Corsair with a ratio of kills to losses of 11:1.

F6F-3 Hellcats also began to arrive in the UK during 1943, in the form of 252 designated originally **Gannet Mk I** (later **Hellcat Mk I**) and equipping first the Fleet Air Arm's No. 800 Squadron.

By the time F6F-3 production ended in mid-1944, a total of 4,423 Hellcats had been built. Their numbers included 18 **F6F-3E** night-fighters with APS-4 radar mounted in a pod beneath the starboard wing, and 205 generally similar **F6F-3N** night-fighters with APS-6 radar.

During the F6F-3 production run, Grumman developed an improved version, which was ordered into production as the **F6F-5**. This had aerodynamic improvements, including a redesigned engine cowling, new ailerons and strengthened tail surfaces. The same powerplant as that used in the F6F-3s was retained, but these had the designation R-2800-10W, the final letter 'W' of the designation indicating a water injection system which provided an additional 10 per cent of power for limited periods during take-off and combat. It also meant that take-off could be made at a higher gross weight, which gave scope to increase both armour and armament without any danger of penalising performance.

First flown on 4 April 1944, F6F-5s began to enter service with the US Navy very shortly after this date, and 930 were supplied to the UK under Lend-Lease, the type being designated **Hellcat Mk II** in FAA service. Of this number, some 70 were equivalent to the US Navy's **F6F-5N** model, equipped to serve in a night-fighter role, and were identified easily by the addition of a small radome on the starboard wing.

By far the majority of the FAA's Hellcats equipped the squadrons which served with the British Pacific Fleet in the Far East. The 70-odd night-fighter variants supplied to the UK were designated **Hellcat NF.Mk II**.

When production ended in November 1945, a total of 12,275 Hellcats had been built, this number including several variants as listed below.

Variants
XF6F-1: projected prototype flown initially with 1268-kW (1,700-hp) Wright R-2600-10 Cyclone 14, but later re-engined with a 1491-kW (2,000-hp) Pratt & Whitney R-2800-10 Double Wasp as an XF6F-3 prototype
XF6F-2: projected prototype with Wright R-2600-16 engine, but completed instead as a second XF6F-3
XF6F-3N: conversion of a production F6F-3 to serve as prototype of the F6F-3N night fighter with APS-6 radar in a pod beneath the starboard wing
XF6F-4: prototype conversion from an F6F-3 for evaluation of the 1566-kW (2,100-hp) Pratt & Whitney R-2800-27 engine
F6F-5K: designation of a number of F6F-5/5Ns converted for use as radio-controlled target drones
F6F-5P: under this designation a few F6F-5s were converted for reconnaissance duties with a camera installed in the rear fuselage
XF6F-6: two prototypes, converted from production F6F-5s, each with a 1566-kW (2,100-hp) Pratt & Whitney R-2800-18W engine and four-bladed propeller

Specification
Grumman F6F-5
Type: single-seat carrier-based fighter/fighter-bomber
Powerplant: one 1491-kW (2,000-hp) Pratt & Whitney R-2800-10W Double Wasp 18-cylinder radial piston engine
Performance: maximum speed 612 km/h (380 mph) at 7130 m (23,400 ft); cruising speed 270 km/h (168 mph); initial climb rate 908 m (2,980 ft) per minute; service ceiling 11370 m (37,300 ft); range with a 568-litre (150-US gal) drop-tank 2462 km (1,530 miles)
Weights: empty 4152 kg (9,153 lb); maximum take-off 6991 kg (15,413 lb)
Dimensions: span 13.06 m (42 ft 10 in); length 10.24 m (33 ft 7 in); height 4.11 m (13 ft 6 in); wing area 31.03 m^2 (334.0 sq ft)
Armament: six 12.7-mm (0.5-in) machine-guns (some late models had two machine-guns replaced by 20-mm cannon), plus two 454-kg (1,000-lb) bombs or six 127-mm (5-in) rocket projectiles

Grumman F7F Tigercat

Grumman's XF5F-1 twin-engined carrier-based fighter prototype failed to gain a production contract, but in the process of its evolution the company gained a far wider appreciation of the problems involved in the creation of such a machine. In early 1941 work was initiated on the design of a new twin-engined fighter for operation from the planned larger carriers in the 'Midway' class. Identified by the company as the **Grumman G-51 Tigercat**, there was little resemblance to its predecessor, for the US Navy by then wanted to procure a high-performance fighter with unprecedented fire-power.

Grumman's proposal resulted in the award of a contract for two **XF7F-1** prototypes on 30 June 1941, the first of them flown during December 1943. Of all-metal construction, the Tigercat was of cantilever shoulder-wing monoplane configuration, the outer panels of the wings folding for carrier stowage. Fuselage and tailplane were conventional, but the retractable landing gear was of tricycle type. A retractable deck arrester hook was mounted in the aft fuselage. Powerplant comprised two Pratt & Whitney R-2800-22W Double Wasp engines, installed in large underwing nacelles.

Before the first flight of the prototype, Grumman had received a contract for 500 production aircraft under the designation **F7F-1** for supply to the US Marine Corps which, by then, was already engaged in landing operations on Japanese-held islands in the Pacific. Operated from land bases, these aircraft would have provided the US Marines with their own close support but, in fact, the Tigercat materialised too late to see operational service with the USMC before the end of World War II.

The first production F7F-1 was generally similar to the prototypes, as were the 33 aircraft which followed, and delivery of these began in April 1944. The 35th aircraft on the production line was modified for use in a night-fighter role, under the designation **XF7F-2N**, and 30 production examples followed under the designation **F7F-2N** during 1944. These differed from the F7F-1 by deletion of the aft fuselage fuel tank (to provide space for the radar operator's cockpit) and removal of the nose armament. There followed production of a new single-seat version, the **F7F-3** Tigercat, of which 189 were built. This differed from the F7F-1 in having R-2800-34 engines to provide increased power at altitude, slightly increased vertical tail surface areas to cater for this, and a seven-per cent increase in fuel capacity. These aircraft terminated production of the original contract, with the balance cancelled after VJ-Day.

Post-war production included 60 **F7F-3N** and 13 **F7F-4N** night-fighters, both with a lengthened nose housing advanced radar, the latter 13 aircraft being the only examples with strengthening, arrester hook, and specialised equipment for carrier-based operation. A small number of F7F-3s were modified after delivery for use in electronic (**F7F-3E**) and photo-reconnaissance (**F7F-3P**) roles. Some squadrons remained in service with the US Marines in the immediate post-war years, but were soon displaced by higher-performance turbine-powered aircraft.

Specification
Grumman F7F-3
Type: twin-engined carrier-based fighter-bomber
Powerplant: two 1566-kW (2,100-hp) Pratt & Whitney R-2800-34W Double Wasp 18-cylinder radial piston engines
Performance: maximum speed 700 km/h (435 mph) at 6765 m (22,200 ft); cruising speed 357 km/h (222 mph); initial climb rate 1380 m (4,530 ft) per minute; service ceiling

One of the ultimate developments of piston-engined fighter technology, the F7F Tigercat was operated only by the US Marine Corps, one of whose machines is seen at MCAS Cherry Point.

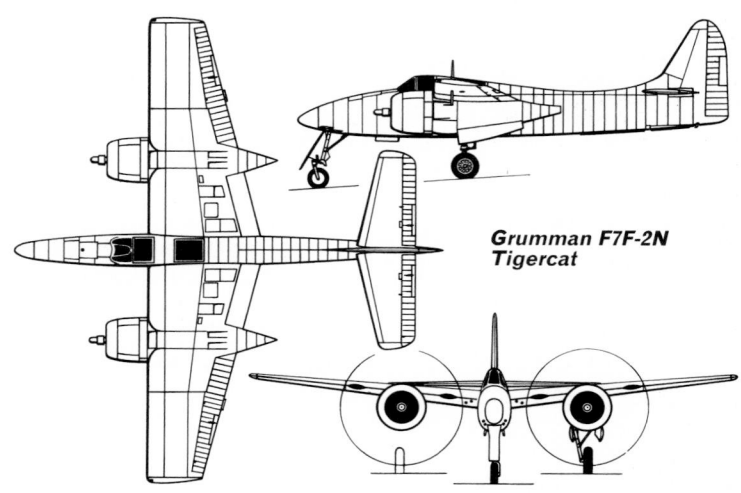

Grumman F7F-2N Tigercat

12405 m (40,700 ft); normal range 1931 km (1,200 miles)
Weights: empty 7380 kg (16,270 lb); maximum take-off 11666 kg (25,720 lb)
Dimensions: span 15.70 m (51 ft 6 in); length 13.83 m (45 ft 4½ in); height 5.05 m (16 ft 7 in); wing area 42.27 m^2 (455.0 sq ft)
Armament: four 20-mm (0.79-in) cannon in wing roots and four 12.7-mm (0.5-in) machine-guns in nose, plus one torpedo beneath the fuselage and up to 454 kg (1,000 lb) of bombs under each wing

Grumman F8F Bearcat

Last of the line of piston-engined carrier-based fighters which Grumman initiated with the FF of 1931, the **Grumman F8F Bearcat** was designed to be capable of operation from aircraft-carriers of all sizes and to serve primarily as an interceptor fighter, a role which demanded excellent manoeuvrability, good low-level performance and a high rate of climb. To achieve these capabilities for the two **XF8F-1** prototypes ordered on 27 November 1943, Grumman adopted the big R-2800 Double Wasp that had been used to power the F6F and F7F, but ensured that the smallest and lightest possible airframe was designed to accommodate the specified armament, armour and fuel.

First flown on 21 August 1944, the XF8F-1 was not only smaller than the US Navy's superb Hellcat, but was also some 20 per cent lighter, resulting in a rate of climb about 30 per cent greater than that of its predecessor. Grumman had more than achieved the specification requirements, but also crowned this by starting delivery of production aircraft in February 1945, only six months after the first flight of the prototype.

A cantilever low-wing monoplane of all-metal construction, the initial **F8F-1** had wings which folded at about two-thirds span for carrier stowage, retractable tailwheel landing gear, armour, self-sealing fuel tanks and, by comparison with prototypes, a very small dorsal fin had been added. Powerplant of these production aircraft was the Pratt & Whitney R-2800-34W and armament comprised four 12.7-mm (0.5-in) machineguns.

Shortly after initiation of the prototype's test programme in 1944, the US Navy placed a contract for 2,023 production F8F-1s, and the first of these began to equip US Navy Squadron VF-19 on 21 May 1945. This squadron, and other early recipients of Bearcats, were still in the process of familiarisation with their new fighters when VJ-Day put an end to World War II. It also cut 1,258 aircraft from Grumman's contract and brought complete cancellation of an additional 1,876 **F8M-1 Bearcat** fighters contracted from General Motors.

When production ended in May 1949, Grumman had built 1,266 Bearcats: 765 of the F8F-1; 100 of the **F8F-1B**, which differed by having the four standard machine-guns replaced by 20-mm cannon; 36 of the **F8F-1N** variant equipped as night-fighters; 293 of the **F8F-2** with redesigned engine cowling, taller fin and rudder, plus some changes in detail design, and adoption of the 20-mm cannon as standard armament; 12 of the night-fighter **F8F-2N**; and 60

The Grumman F8F Bearcat has become popular with competitors in the Reno air races and warbird restorers, these two immaculate veterans being presented in US Navy and Royal Thai Air Force colours.

photo-reconnaissance **F8F-2P** aircraft, this last version carrying only two 20-mm cannon. In late post-war service, some aircraft were modified to serve in a drone control capacity under the designations **F8F-1D** or **F8F-2D**.

By the time production ended, Bearcats were serving with some 24 US Navy squadrons, but all had been withdrawn by late 1952. Some of these, with a modified fuel system, were supplied to the French Armée de l'Air for service in Indo-China under the designation F8F-1D. One-hundred similar F8F-1Ds

and 29 F8F-1Bs were also supplied to the Thai air force.

Specification
Grumman F8F-1B
Type: single-seat carrier-based interceptor fighter
Powerplant: one 1566-kW (2,100-hp) Pratt & Whitney R-2800-34W Double Wasp 18-cylinder radial piston engine
Performance: maximum speed 678 km/h (421 mph) at 6005 m (19,700 ft); cruising speed 262 km/h (163 mph); initial climb rate 1395 m

(4,570 ft) per minute; service ceiling 11795 m (38,700 ft); range 1778 km (1,105 miles)
Weights: empty 3207 kg (7,070 lb); maximum take-off 5873 kg (12,947 lb)
Dimensions: span 10.92 m (35 ft 10 in); length 8.61 m (28 ft 3 in); height 4.22 m (13 ft 10 in); wing area 22.67 m² (244.0 sq ft)
Armament: four 20-mm cannon, plus underwing hardpoints for two 454-kg (1,000-lb) bombs, or four 127-mm (5-in) rocket projectiles, or two 568-litre (150-US-gal) drop-tanks

Grumman F9F Panther

The **Grumman F9F Panther**, the US Navy's most extensively used fighter during the Korean conflict, was developed from Grumman design study **G-79D** submitted to the Bureau of Aeronautics in June 1946. Three prototypes were ordered in September 1946 under the designation **XF9F-2**, to be powered by the British Rolls-Royce Nene engine, and their construction began in February 1947. The Nene was the subject of a licence agreement between Rolls-Royce and Pratt & Whitney, and the first engines were delivered to Bethpage in July 1947. The first and second prototypes were thus powered, but the third aircraft was completed as the **XF9F-3**, with a 2087-kg (4,600-lb) thrust Allison J33.

Powered by its 2268-kg (5,000-lb) thrust Nene, the first prototype began taxiing trials on 20 November and test pilot C. H. 'Corky' Meyer made the first flight four days later. As a precaution the Panther made its first landing on the much longer runway at Idlewild Airport, but then flew straight back to Bethpage. In February 1948 it was equipped with 454-litre (120-US gal) wingtip fuel tanks, later adopted as standard, and on 18 March the commanding officer of the Naval Air Test Center at Patuxent River became the first US Navy pilot to fly the aircraft. The second XF9F-2 arrived at NATC in October 1948 to undertake initial carrier compatibility trials but it

suffered a fuel system problem and crashed on 28 October. Its place in the programme was taken by an **F9F-2**, from the initial production batch of 30 which had been ordered prior to the first flight, and full carrier trials were carried out aboard USS *Franklin D. Roosevelt*, beginning in March 1949. Initial deliveries to a squadron began on 8 May 1949 and the recipient unit, VF-51, flew the first carrier jet fighter sortie of the Korean War, operating as a component of Carrier Air Group 5 aboard USS *Valley Forge* on 3 July 1950.

Variants
F9F-2: 567 production Panthers with Pratt & Whitney J42-P-6 (licence-built Nene) engines; the **F9F-2B** was a modified ground-attack version with hardpoints for underwing stores
F9F-3: 54 aircraft were built originally with Allison J33-A-8 engines but converted from February 1950 to F9F-2s when this engine proved unreliable
F9F-4: the prototype **XF9F-4**, with a water-injected 3152-kg (6,950-lb) thrust Allison J33-A-16 engine, flew on 6 July 1950, some months later than intended as the result of engine problems; planned production was 73, some of which were delivered to the US Marine Corps, but most were completed as F9F-5s
F9F-5: the most numerous of the

Panthers, the F9F-5 was similar to the F9F-4 but initially powered by the Pratt & Whitney J48-P-2 derivative of the Rolls-Royce Tay; the prototype flew on 21 December 1949 and 616 were built, delivered between 5 November 1950 and 13 January 1953
F9F-5P: 36 unarmed photo-reconnaissance aircraft with cameras in the nose, delivered between 25 October 1951 and 11 August 1952
F9F-5KD: when withdrawn from operational service, a number of F9F-5s were used as target drones or drone control aircraft under this designation, which was changed to **DF-9E** in 1962

Specification
Grumman F9F-5
Type: single-seat shipboard fighter
Powerplant: one 2835-kg (6,250-lb) Pratt & Whitney J48-P-6A turbojet engine

BuAer No. 126279 was one of 36 Panthers completed as F9F-5P photo-reconnaissance platforms. No hardpoints were fitted, and the 20-mm cannon were removed to make way for cameras in the nose.

Performance: maximum speed 932 km/h (579 mph); cruising speed 774 km/h (481 mph); initial climb rate 1550 m (5,090 ft) per minute; service ceiling 13045 m (42,800 ft); range 2092 km (1,300 miles)
Weights: empty 4603 kg (10,147 lb); maximum take-off 8492 kg (18,721 lb)
Dimensions: span 11.58 m (38 ft 0 in); length 11.84 m (38 ft 10 in); height 3.73 m (12 ft 3 in); wing area 23.23 m² (250.0 sq ft)
Armament: four 20-mm cannon, plus two 454-kg (1,000-lb) bombs or six 127-mm (5-in) HVAR rockets

Grumman F9F Cougar

Soon after the Grumman F9F Panther entered service, the company began development of a swept-wing variant under a US Navy contract dated 2 March 1951, and the prototype **Grumman XF9F-6** flew for the first time on 20 September 1951. Although the F9F portion of the designation was the same as

that of the Panther, confirming that it was a variant of the original design, the new name **Cougar** indicated that it was a rather different aeroplane.

A more powerful turbojet engine was installed, but the main difference lay in the wing and the structural changes needed by it. Thus, the Cougar's wing

had sweep-back of 35°, spoilers replacing ailerons, larger trailing-edge flaps, leading-edge slats and wing fences. In this form, the **F9F-6 Cougar** (subsequently redesignated **F-9F**) entered service with US Navy Squadron VF-32 in November 1952. They were followed by the generally similar **F9F-7 (F-9H)**, the **F9F-8 (F-9J)** with a longer fuselage and broad-chord wing, and the **F9F-8T** trainer with a still longer fuselage with

stepped tandem cockpits and only two guns. In 1962 the F9F-8Ts were redesignated **TF-9J**, many of them being flown operationally in Vietnam for various missions.

Variants
F9F-6D: drone director conversion of the F9F-6 (later **DF-9F**)
F9F-6K: target drone director conversion of the F9F-6 (later **QF-9F**)

F9F-6K2: improved version of F9F-6K (later **QF-9G**)
F9F-6P: photo-reconnaissance version of the F9F-6
F9F-6PD: redesignation of F9F-6P converted as drone directors
YF9F-8B: prototype conversion of F9F-8 for close support (later **YAF-9J**)
F9F-8B: production conversions of F9F-8s to YF9F-8B configuration (later **AF-9J**)
YF9F-8T: prototype trainer conversion of F9F-8 (later **YTF-9J**)
NTF-9J: designation of two TF-9Js used for special test duties

Specification
Grumman TF-9J
Type: carrier-based trainer
Powerplant: one 3266-kg (7,200-lb) thrust Pratt & Whitney J48-P-8A turbojet
Performance: maximum speed 1135 km/h (705 mph) at sea level;

service ceiling 15240 m (50,000 ft); range 966 km (600 miles)
Weight: maximum take-off 9344 kg (20,600 lb)
Dimensions: span 10.52 m (34 ft

6 in); length 13.54 m (44 ft 5 in); height 3.73 m (12 ft 3 in)
Armament: two 20-mm (0.79-in) cannon, plus up to 907 kg (2,000 lb) of weapons on underwing hardpoints

The Cougar was the swept-wing derivative of the Panther. This example is an F9F-8P with a bulged nose housing reconnaissance cameras.

Grumman F10F Jaguar

Although not the first American aircraft to employ a variable-sweep wing, that distinction falling to the US Air Force-funded Bell X-5, the **Grumman XF10F Jaguar** was the first to have been developed with production and operational service in mind. The design was born of the US Navy's Bureau of Aeronautics' concern about the increasing probability of approach and stalling speeds of its heavy swept-wing fighters becoming incompatible with operation from the aircraft-carriers then in service. The original XF10F project, two prototypes of which were ordered on 4 March 1948, was for a fixed swept-wing fighter to be powered by a Pratt & Whitney J42 (Rolls-Royce Nene) engine. However, this design became subjected to numerous alterations and major changes, and introduction of the variable-sweep wing was proposed by Grumman on 7 July 1949. The final configuration was established in the closing months of 1950 and the revised contract for two prototypes was issued on 14 December. The Jaguar was large and heavy, fitted with wings which could be swept hydraulically from 13.5° to 42.5° and which had high-lift devices in the form of full-span leading-edge slats,

The F10F Jaguar was not a success in its own right, but it did provide useful data on variable-geometry wings. Only one aircraft achieved flight status.

and Fowler flaps which occupied 80 per cent of the trailing edge. It was to be armed with four 20-mm cannon and carry bombs or rockets externally. The specified engine was the Westinghouse XJ40-WE-8 with a normal thrust rating of 3357 kg (7,400 lb), which was to be boosted to 4944 kg (10,900 lb) thrust by afterburning. In fact, a lower-rated 3084-kg (6,800-lb) thrust J40-WE-6 powered the only prototype to fly and the reheat system was never installed.

The first aircraft was completed in March 1952, and after some low-speed taxi runs at Bethpage was dismantled for transit by Douglas C-124 Globemaster to Edwards Air Force Base at Muroc Dry Lake on 16 April. Grumman test pilot C. H. 'Corky' Meyer flew it throughout the test programme, beginning with an eventful 16-minute maiden flight on 19 May. Control and systems problems were experienced, setting the pattern for almost the entire 32-flight pro-

gramme which ended on 25 April 1953. Much valuable experience had been gained and the wing-sweep mechanism proved a success, but grounding of the J40 engine in March 1953 was the final straw and, following the cancellation of orders for 100 production aircraft on 1 April and of that for the remaining 12 pre-production examples on 13 June, the project was abandoned. The two prototypes, one 90 per cent complete, were transferred to the Naval Air Materiel Center at Philadelphia for use in crash barrier tests, and the static test airframe became a gunnery target at the Aberdeen Proving Ground.

Specification
Type: single-seat shipboard fighter prototype

Powerplant: one 4944-kg (10,900-lb) thrust Westinghouse XJ40-WE-8 turbojet with afterburner
Performance: (estimated) maximum speed 1143 km/h (710 mph) at sea level; combat speed 1017 km/h (632 mph) at 10670 m (35,000 ft); service ceiling 13960 m (45,800 ft)
Weights: empty 9265 kg (20,426 lb); maximum take-off 16080 kg (35,450 lb)
Dimensions: span, extended 15.42 m (50 ft 7 in), swept 11.18 m (36 ft 8 in); length 16.59 m (54 ft 5 in); height 4.95 m (16 ft 3 in); wing area, maximum 41.81 m² (450.0 sq ft)
Armament: four 20-mm (0.79-in) cannon in the nose, plus two 907-kg (2,000-lb) bombs, or 48 70-mm (2.75-in) FFAR, or 12 127-mm (5-in) HVAR rockets beneath the wings

Grumman F11F Tiger

The last of an unbroken line of US Navy fighters which had begun with the 1931 Grumman FF-1, the **Grumman F11F Tiger** was designated originally **F9F-9**, to reflect its Panther/Cougar ancestry, although it was really an entirely new aircraft. Given the Grumman type number **G-98**, the design ordered by the US Navy on 27 April 1953 was certainly a single-seat fighter but no visible trace of the earlier aircraft remained. The fuselage was area-ruled to reduce drag, the tailplane and elevators were relocated to the rear fuselage and the main landing gear was fuselage-mounted, as were the intakes for the 3538-kg (7,800-lb) thrust Wright J65-W-6 turbojet engine, which with afterburning was rated at 4763 kg (10,500 lb) thrust. The thin wing introduced a new structural technique in that the outer skins, which enclosed a box beam, were milled from solid aluminium slabs. The first prototype **YF9F-9** was flown by 'Corky' Meyer on 30 July 1954, powered by a J65-W-7 without afterburning; the second, which flew in October, had its intended afterburner in-

stalled in January 1955. Redesignated **F11F-1** in April 1955, the Tiger was produced with a derated J65-W-18 engine following problems with the intended W-6 version. US Navy orders for two batches, of 42 and 157 aircraft, were delivered between 15 November 1954 and 23 January 1959. The Tiger first entered service (with VA-156) in March 1957, but the type's operational life was relatively short and it was quickly superseded by the Vought F-8 Crusader. Tigers were relegated to an advanced training role during 1959 but continued to equip the US Navy's 'Blue Angels' aerobatic team. The F11F-1 was re-designated **F-11A** in the joint USAF/USN system introduced in September 1962.

Variant
F11F-1F: two aircraft only, with the 4354 kg (9,600 lb) thrust General Electric XJ79-GE-3 engine, were modified from production F11F-1 airframes; they were fitted with a new wing and enlarged intakes, and the first was flown during June 1956; during

later trials, one was flown by US Navy Lieutenant Commander George Watkins to establish a world altitude record of 23449 m (76,932 ft)

Specification
Grumman F11F-1
Type: single-seat fighter
Powerplant: one 3379-kg (7,450-lb) thrust Wright J65-W-18 turbojet
Performance: maximum speed 1207 km/h (750 mph) at sea level; cruising speed 929 km/h (577 mph) at 11580 m (38,000 ft); initial climb rate 1565 m (5,130 ft) per minute; service ceiling 12770 m (41,900 ft); range

The F11F-1 was the Navy's first operational supersonic aircraft, featuring area-ruling and an afterburning turbojet. This aircraft served with VF-33.

2044 km (1,270 miles)
Weights: empty 6091 kg (13,428 lb); maximum take-off 10052 kg (22,160 lb)
Dimensions: span 9.64 m (31 ft 7½ in); length 14.31 m (46 ft 11¼ in); height 4.03 m (13 ft 2¾ in); wing area 23.23 m² (250.0 sq ft)
Armament: four 20-mm (0.79-in) cannon and four underwing Sidewinder air-to-air missiles

Grumman F-14 Tomcat
to
Grumman TBF Avenger

Grumman F-14 Tomcat

Unquestionably one of the finest warplanes in the world today, the **Grumman F-14 Tomcat** is fulfilling the role that, in the mid-1960s, it was hoped would be undertaken by the naval version of the General Dynamics F-111 variable-geometry strike aircraft. By the time that the F-111B programme was eventually cancelled in the summer of 1968, Grumman (also responsible for developing the F-111B version) had already reached an advanced stage in designing a new swing-wing carrier fighter, following a US Navy competition in which four other designs were in contention. From these, the US Navy selected the **Grumman G-303** proposal in January 1969, and following US Navy inspection of a mock-up four months later, initial contracts were placed for 12 development aircraft. The first of these made its maiden flight on 21 December 1970, but was lost nine days later after a complete hydraulic system failure, although both crew members were able to eject safely. Despite this setback, the development programme proceeded without further serious mishap after the second aircraft made its first flight on 24 May 1971.

Designed to later technology than the pioneering F-111, the **F-14A** was intended from the outset for operation from the US Navy fleet carriers, and is unique among variable-geometry aircraft so far developed in having, in addition to variable-sweep outer wings, smaller movable foreplanes which Grumman calls glove vanes. As the main wings pivot backwards, the glove vanes are extended automatically at supersonic speeds to regulate any alterations in the centre of pressure and prevent the aircraft from pitching. By deploying its variable-sweep wings to the best advantage, the Tomcat is able to vary its flying configuration to the different aerodynamic and performance requirements needed when taking off from (or landing on) a carrier, taking part in an air-to-air dogfight, or carrying out a low-level attack mission against a surface target. Wing sweep is maintained at optimum by a Mach sweep programmer, relieving the pilot of this task and enabling him to concentrate on his mission. With additional control surfaces which include full-span trailing-edge flaps, spoilers, leading-edge slats and all-moving horizontal tail surfaces, the Tomcat is a superbly manoeuvrable warplane; longitudinal stability is assured by the use of twin outboard-canted fins and rudders. The Tomcat is also very strong structurally, many of the airframe components being manufactured of titanium, and boron-epoxy or other composites.

The primary role of the Tomcat is to provide long-range air defence of the US fleet, and the two-man crew are seated in tandem on zero-zero ejection seats under a single upward-opening canopy. Armament for the air defence role includes air-to-air missiles such as the medium-range Sparrow and close-range AIM-9 Sidewinders, and for unexpected dogfights a Gatling-type multi-barrelled cannon. Primary interception armament consists of six Hughes Phoenix air-to-air missiles, currently the longest-range air-to-air missile in use anywhere in the

world (more than 200 km/124 miles). Its use in conjunction with the extremely powerful Hughes AWG-9 radar mounted in the nose provides the Tomcat with the ability to detect and attack an airborne target while it is still 160 km (100 miles) away. The F-14A also has a secondary capability in the low-level attack role, in which event the air-to-air missiles can be replaced by up to 6577 kg (14,500 lb) of externally-mounted bombs or other weapons.

The initial F-14A version of the Tomcat has been in service with the US Navy since October 1972, when the first deliveries were made to US Navy Squadrons VF-1 and VF-2. Subsequently, a number of powerplant problems were experienced, but these have been largely resolved by an increase in available thrust with the afterburners on. In 1979 the Naval Air Test Center at Patuxent River, Maryland, began development of a tactical air reconnaissance pod system (TARPS) to extend the versatility of the F-14A. About 50 F-14As are equipped to carry TARPS, the resulting **F-14/TARPS** being regarded as an important tactical reconnaissance vehicle until the development of advanced aircraft for this specific role.

By the time production ended in March 1987, 554 F-14As had been built, including the 12 development aircraft. Thirty-two were subsequently reworked to **F-14A (Plus)** standard, 18 to **F-14D(R)** and 79 others were exported to the Imperial Iranian Air Force in the mid-1970s. Cost escalation curtailed development of the original **F-14B** and later **F-14C** for the US Navy. Two prototypes of the F-14B were produced by installing 12741-kg (28,090-lb) thrust Pratt & Whitney F401-P-400 turbofans, the first flying on 12 September 1973, but the second was never completed. Development of the F-14C with TF30-P-414A engines and advanced avionics was also stopped.

In 1984 development began of an interim improved version of the Tomcat,

VF-1 'Wolf Pack' was the first fleet user of the Tomcat, receiving its aircraft in time to take them on a combat cruise in April/May 1975.

the F-14A (Plus). Re-engined with 12247-kg (27,000-lb) thrust General Electric F110-GE-400 afterburning turbofans, the first of 32 conversions (one of the F-14B prototypes) flew on 29 September 1986, followed by the first production aircraft on 14 November 1987. First deliveries were made to Squadron VF-101 in April 1988 and the last (163411) in May 1990. In 1991 the F-14A (Plus) was redesignated the **F-14B**.

In 1981, Grumman completed a short flight test programme of a Tomcat powered by two GE F101-DFE (Derivative Fighter Engines) later used in the F-16. Although there were no plans to use this powerplant in the F-14 the knowledge gained helped Grumman formulate ideas about Super Tomcat technology.

In the mid-1980s, funds were made available to develop a much improved Tomcat, the **F-14D**, with the AN/APG-71 radar, enhanced missile capability and a new ejector seat system (NACES). By 1988 37 had been funded out of a requirement for 127 but the programme was cancelled in 1989, resurrected in 1990, cancelled again in February 1991 and partially restored once again in April 1991. Present plans call for 37 new

F-14Ds to be built and **18 F-14D(R)**s to be converted from earlier Tomcats.

The first of three development conversions flew on 24 November 1987, and first delivery was made to Squadron VX-4 in May 1990. The first F-14D(R) was delivered to VF-124, the Tomcat training squadron, in June 1990 and the aircraft were fully accepted for service in November 1990.

Further proposed developments include the 'Quickstrike' programme which could add ground-attack capability to F-14Ds; the **Super Tomcat-21**, a company-funded study for a new multi-role fighter (and cheaper competitor to the naval version of the Advanced Tactical Fighter); the **ASF-14** Grumman pro-

The principal air-to-air weapon of the Tomcat is the massive AIM-54 Phoenix, seen here being launched during a trial by an F-14A of the Pacific Missile Test Center at Point Mugu, California.

posal for an alternative to the naval ATF but using avionics and powerplants developed for that aircraft; and the **AST-21 (Attack Super Tomcat-21)**, an interim replacement for the cancelled A-12 Avenger programme.

Specification
Grumman F-14A
Type: two-seat carrier-based multi-role fighter
Powerplant: two 9480-kg (20,900-lb) thrust Pratt & Whitney TF30-P-412A afterburning turbofans
Performance: maximum speed at altitude Mach 2.34 or 2517 km/h (1,564 mph); cruising speed 741 to 1019 km/h (460 to 633 mph); service ceiling over 15240 m (50,000 ft); range,

interceptor with external fuel, about 3219 km (2,000 miles)
Weights: empty 18036 kg (39,762 lb); normal take-off with six Phoenix missiles 31945 kg (70,426 lb); maximum take-off 33724 kg (74,348 lb)
Dimensions: span, unswept 19.54 m (64 ft 1½ in), swept 11.65 m (38 ft 2½ in); length 19.10 m (62 ft 8 in); height 4.88 m (16 ft 0 in); wing area 52.49 m² (565.0 sq ft)
Armament: one General Electric M61A-1 20-mm (0.79-in) multi-barrelled Vulcan cannon in forward fuselage; various combinations of bombs or missiles, the latter including Phoenix, Sidewinder and Sparrow, tactical reconnaissance pod, or ECM equipment

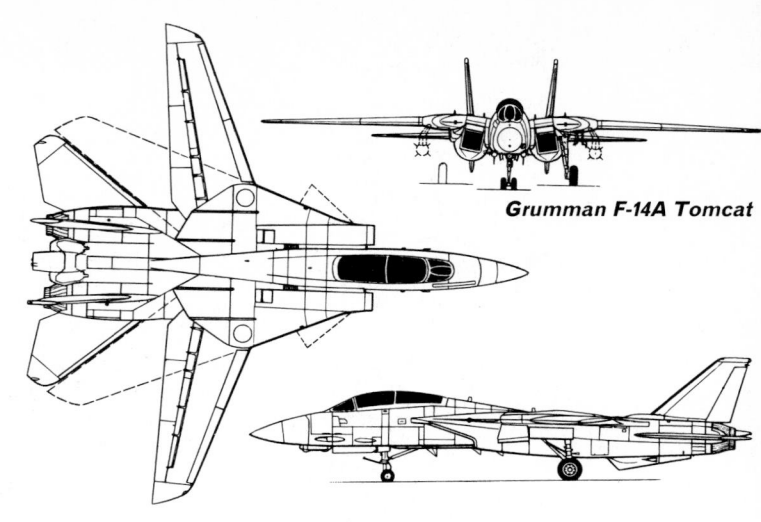

Grumman F-14A Tomcat

Grumman G-21 Goose

In 1937 the company produced a twin-engined amphibian flying-boat known as the **Grumman G-21 Goose.** Powered by two 336-kW (450-hp) Pratt & Whitney R-985 radial engines, it was of high-wing monoplane configuration, the wing serving also to mount the engines and carry underwing stabilising floats. The deep two-step hull was of conventional construction, and the tail unit included a braced tailplane. Amphibious capability was provided by tailwheel-type landing gear, all three units of which retracted into the hull. Built pre-war for commercial use as the **G-21A**, which had accommodation for up to seven passengers, the Goose continued in production during World War II for service with the USAAF, US Coast Guard and US Navy, some of this last service's aircraft serving also with the US Marine Corps.

Surviving commercial and war-surplus aircraft which came on to the market were to prove of value for certain post-war air services, and McKinnon Enterprises in the USA began to specialise in Goose refurbishment and the development of improved versions. These have included an early modification which replaced the two R-985s with four 254-kW (340-hp) Avco-Lycoming engines, but the majority of conversions have been to the **G-21C** and **G-21D Turbo-Goose** standard with two Pratt & Whitney Aircraft of Canada PT6A turboprops in place of the original radials. A number of improvements were incorporated during this conversion, including the introduction of retractable wingtip floats and the provision of larger cabin windows. A **G-21G Turbo-Goose** was available, this being a generally similar conversion but with a somewhat higher standard of equipment and some cabin improvements, as well as a **Turboprop Goose** having only the change to turboprop power without any of the airframe improvements of earlier conversions.

The G-21G Turbo-Goose and Turboprop Goose conversions were available until 1980, most recently from McKinnon-Viking Enterprises which was estab-

lished at Sidney, British Columbia, in 1978 to supersede the American McKinnon Enterprises Inc.

Specification
Grumman/McKinnon G-21G Turbo-Goose
Type: light amphibious transport
Powerplant: two 507-kW (680-shp) Pratt & Whitney Aircraft of Canada PT6A-27 turboprop engines
Performance: maximum speed 391 km/h (243 mph); service ceiling 6095 m (20,000 ft); range with standard fuel 2575 km (1,600 miles)
Weights: empty equipped 3039 kg (6,700 lb); maximum take-off 5670 kg (12,500 lb)
Dimensions: span 15.49 m (50 ft 10 in); length 12.06 m (39 ft 7 in); wing area 35.08 m² (377.64 sq ft)

The Goose appealed to many customers, and considerable numbers were subsequently updated with modern engines.

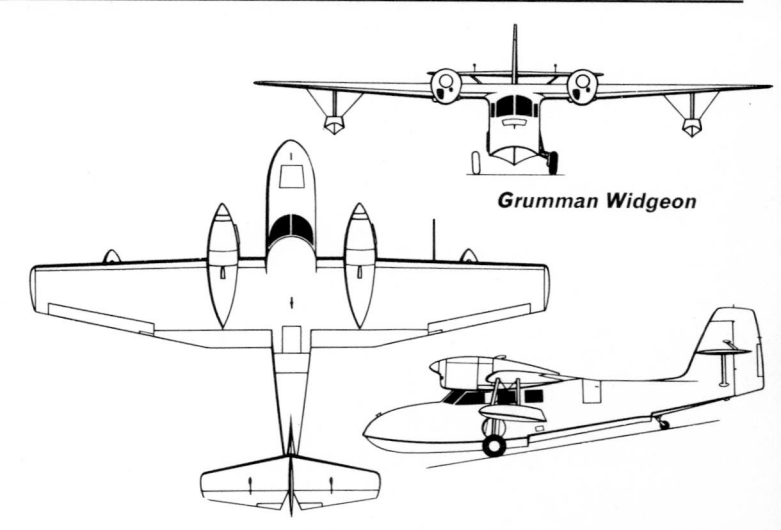

Grumman G-44 Widgeon

The success of the Grumman Goose eight-seat commercial amphibian, and the obvious market for a smaller and cheaper version, led directly to development of the five-seat **Grumman G-44 Widgeon**, powered by two 149-kW (200-hp) Ranger L-440C-5 engines. The prototype Widgeon was test-flown by Roy Grumman and Bud Gillies at Bethpage on 28 June 1940, and 10 examples had been sold to civil buyers before the first production aircraft was delivered on 21 February 1941. The initial production batch of 44 Widgeons was intended for the civil market, although 11 which had been built to fulfil a Portuguese contract, plus four other examples, were impressed for service with the USAF under the designation **OA-14**.

The second production run, of 25 aircraft, was earmarked for the US Coast Guard and, designated **J4F-1**, these were delivered between 7 July 1941 and 29 June 1942. In August 1942, a Widgeon of Coast Guard Squadron 212, based at Houma, Louisiana, sank the U-boat *U-166* off the Passes of the Mississippi, scoring the first US Coast Guard kill of an enemy submarine. Grumman built a total of 131 **J4F-2** aircraft for the US Navy, these being delivered between 13 July 1942 and 26 February 1945. Operated by a crew of two and with up to three passengers in the utility transport role, the J4F-2 was used also for coastal patrol and anti-submarine duties. Fifteen J4F-2s were supplied under Lend-Lease to the Royal Navy and

Grumman Widgeon

used for communications, principally in the West Indies where (at Piarco, Trinidad, for example) observer training schools were maintained. Royal Navy J4F-2s were known initially under the name **Gosling**, later **Widgeon**.

An improved **G-44A** was introduced by Grumman in 1944, flying first on 8 August. It had a revised hull with a deeper keel and incorporated hydrodynamic improvements. A total of 76 was built, the last being delivered on 13 January 1949, and some of these were later re-engined with Continental W-670s or Avco Lycoming 90-435As. During 1948-49 some 41 G-44As were built under licence by Société de Construction Aero-Navale (SCAN) at La Rochelle, France, as the **SCAN 30**. Subsequently, McKinnon Enterprises at Sandy, Oregon, initiated a conversion scheme for the Widgeon. The resulting **Super Widgeon**, of which more than 70 conversions were completed, introducing 201-kW (270-hp) Avco Lycoming GO-480-B1D engines, improvements to the hull and interior, and the provision of increased fuel capacity.

Specification
Grumman J4F-2
Type: five-seat light transport or coastal/anti-submarine patrol aircraft
Powerplant: two 149-kW (200-hp) Ranger L-440C-5 6-cylinder inline piston engines

Performance: maximum speed 246 km/h (153 mph); cruising speed 222 km/h (138 mph); service ceiling 4450 m (14,600 ft); maximum range 1481 km (920 miles)
Weights: empty 1447 kg (3,189 lb); maximum take-off 2041 kg (4,500 lb)
Dimensions: span 12.19 m (40 ft 0 in); length 9.47 m (31 ft 1 in); height 3.48 m (11 ft 5 in); wing area 22.76 m² (245.0 sq ft)
Armament: none

Grumman G-73 Mallard

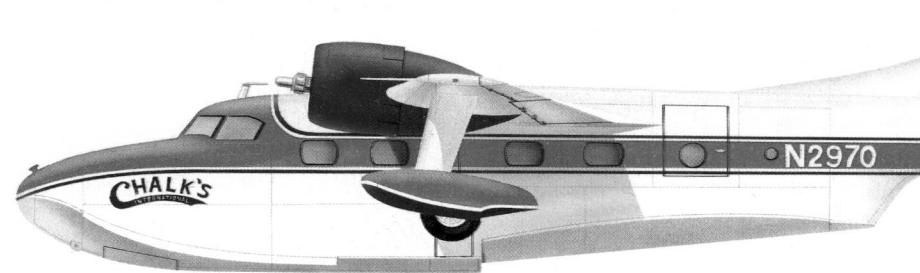

The Mallard was the second largest of the Grumman family of twin-engined amphibians developed during and after the war. Relatively few were built for civil operations. Chalk's International was a major operator for many years, flying the type between Miami and the Bahamas. Today the airline has four re-engined with turboprops.

In the early years following World War II Grumman developed, under the company designation **Grumman G-73** and the name **Mallard**, a twin-engined commercial amphibian that benefitted from the company's extensive experience of the design of military aircraft in this category. A high-wing cantilever monoplane of all-metal construction, with a stressed-skin two-step hull, the G-73 had an upswept tail unit, and retractable tricycle landing gear to provide amphibious capability. Balancer floats were mounted beneath the wings to provide stability on the water, and these could double also as auxiliary fuel tanks. Powerplant comprised two Pratt & Whitney Wasp radial piston engines, wing-mounted in 'clean' streamlined nacelles.

The hull provided air-conditioned, heated, and sound-proofed accommodation for up to 10 passengers in two compartments, with the crew of two situated on a separate flight deck. Interior furnishings and equipment were to a high standard but some VIP examples, such as that equipped specially for the personal use of King Farouk of Egypt, were finished with the most luxurious appointments. Fifty-nine were built.

Specification
Type: twin-engined amphibious flying-boat
Powerplant: two 447-kW (600-hp) Pratt & Whitney R-1340-S3H1 Wasp 9-cylinder radial piston engines
Performance: maximum speed 346 km/h (215 mph) at 1830 m (6,000 ft); cruising speed 290 km/h (180 mph) at 2440 m (8,000 ft); service ceiling 7010 m (23,000 ft); range with maximum fuel 2221 km (1,380 miles)
Weights: empty 4241 kg (9,350 lb); maximum take-off 5783 kg (12,750 lb)
Dimensions: span 20.32 m (66 ft 8 in); length 14.73 m (48 ft 4 in); height, on landing gear 5.72 m (18 ft 9 in); wing area 41.25 m² (444.0 sq ft)

Grumman JF/J2F Duck

Grumman's FF-1 and F2F carrier-based fighters for the US Navy, the company's first production aircraft, had introduced some new ideas, including retractable tailwheel landing gear, making them the first of their kind to enter US Navy service. The FF-1 was also the fastest fighter operational with the US Navy, but because of the limited procurement that was possible in the 'between wars' years, it was acquired in only small numbers.

With the FF-1 nearing production, Grumman began the development of a new utility amphibian which would combine the better features of the FF-1 and the Loening OLs then in service and in late 1932 submitted its proposal for review by the US Navy. This resulted in the award of a contract for the supply of a **Grumman XJF-1** prototype, which flew for the first time on 4 May 1933. Flight testing found no serious problems, and an uncomplicated evaluation by the US Navy resulted in an initial production order for 27 **JF-1** aircraft, the first of these being delivered in late 1934.

Intended to fulfil a general utility role, the type was used first to replace ageing Loening OL-9 and general-purpose aircraft in US Navy service, and it was not until 1936 that they began to reach squadrons. Their performance by comparison with the similarly configured Loenings was quite staggering, with maximum speed, rate of climb and service ceiling increased by more than 40 per cent, 50 per cent and 65 per cent respectively, but there were significant aerodynamic improvements in the design. The equal span biplane wings had a basic structure of light alloy with fabric covering, the fuselage was a conventional stressed-skin/light-alloy structure, and the large monocoque central float housed the main wheel units when retracted. Stabiliser floats were strut-mounted beneath each lower wing, and a crew of two or three could be carried in the tandem cockpits, pilot forward and observer aft as standard, but a radio operator could also be accommodated in the observer's cockpit. Powerplant of the prototype and the first batch of JF-1 production aircraft consisted of a 522-kW (700-hp) Pratt & Whitney R-1830 Twin Wasp engine.

The second production contract was for 14 **JF-2 (Grumman G-4)** aircraft for the US Coast Guard, these having equipment changes and 559-kW (750-hp) Wright R-1820 Cyclone engines. Four were transferred subsequently to the US Navy, which service also acquired five new aircraft with similar powerplant under the designation **JF-3**. There were few major changes in later production examples: the 20 **J2F-1** machines of 1937 and the later 21 **J2F-2**, 20 **J2F-3** and 32 **J2F-4** types differing in only minor detail. Nine **J2F-2A** floatplanes for Marine Squadron VMS-3 were armed with machine-guns and carried underwing bomb racks.

The last version to be built by Grumman was ordered in 1940, and comprised 144 of the **J2F-5** model, which was the first to carry the name **Duck** officially. Generally similar to previous utility models, this was powered by the 634-kW (850-hp) Wright R-1820-50 engine. Final production version, the **J2F-6**, was built by Columbia Aircraft Corporation of Long Island, New York, from which company the US Navy ordered 330 after the USA had become involved in World War II. These were generally similar to the Grumman-built Ducks except for the installation of a more powerful R-1820-54 engine.

Most of the JF/J2F Ducks remained in service throughout the war, operated both from carriers and land bases in a variety of roles, including patrol, photo-survey, rescue and target towing.

Specification
Grumman J2F-6
Type: two/three-seat utility amphibian
Powerplant: one 671-kW (900-hp) Wright R-1820-54 Cyclone 9-cylinder radial piston engine
Performance: maximum speed 306 km/h (190 mph); cruising speed 249 km/h (155 mph); service ceiling 7620 m (25,000 ft); range 1207 km (750 miles)

The main external distinguishing feature of the Grumman J2F compared with the original JF series was the later aircraft's lack of a strut linking the ailerons on the upper and lower wings. The retractable tailwheel landing gear was a particularly neat feature, the main wheels being housed in open wells in the side of the single central float.

Weights: empty 1996 kg (4,400 lb); maximum take-off 3493 kg (7,700 lb)
Dimensions: span 11.89 m (39 ft 0 in); length 10.36 m (34 ft 0 in); height 4.24 m (13 ft 11 in); wing area 38.00 m² (409.0 sq ft)
Armament: normally none, but provision for two 147-kg (325-lb) depth bombs

Grumman OV-1 Mohawk

In the mid-1950s both the US Army and US Marine Corps drew up specifications for a battlefield surveillance aircraft. Their requirements were generally similar: to carry a variety of reconnaissance equipment; to have rough-field capability; and to be able to operate on a STOL basis. It proved possible for both services to agree on a common design and in 1957 the US Navy, acting as programme manager for both the US Army and the US Marine Corps, ordered nine examples of the **Grumman G-134** design for test and evaluation. These were designated initially **YAO-1A**, subsequently **YOV-1A,** and the first of these aircraft was flown initially on 14 April 1959.

Early evaluation left little doubt of the excellence of the design, but even before the prototype had made its first flight the US Marine Corps had withdrawn from the initial contract, and no examples of that service's **OF-1** variant were built. Instead, the flight-test programme was speeded up, and before the end of 1959 the US Army had placed production contracts for **OV-1A** and **OV-1B** aircraft, the basic OV-1 acquiring the name **Mohawk**.

First turboprop-powered aircraft to enter service with the US Army, the OV-1 is comparatively slow but highly manoeuvrable, and to help offset its vulnerability as a result of its speed and role, has a well-armoured cockpit, a 0.64-cm (0.25-in) thick aluminium-alloy floor, flak curtains on both fore and aft bulkheads, and bullet-resistant windscreens. Although the OV-1 is conventional in its basic configuration, detail design has produced an easily identified and unusual-looking aircraft. Recognition features include its turboprop engines, one mounted high on each wing with its

centre-line canted outward and upward; a tail unit with three sets of fins and rudders, and sufficient tailplane dihedral for the endplate fins to be inward canted; bulged cockpit sides to provide the two-man crew with the best possible downward view; and as a final dash of the eccentric, in the OV-1B version the side-looking airborne radar (SLAR) is housed in a 5.49-m (18-ft) glass-fibre container carried on pylons below the fuselage and offset to starboard.

However, beautiful or not, the Mohawk was designed to carry out tactical observation and battlefield surveillance roles in direct support of army operations, a role which it soon demonstrated it could perform successfully. Normal deployment of Mohawk aircraft was four to each army division, and although these aircraft were capable of being armed, it was DoD policy from 1965 that US Army fixed-wing aircraft should not carry weapons, to avoid conflict and confusion with USAF close-support aircraft. However, like many other US aircraft, a number were deployed in Vietnam with underwing arms, a **JOV-1A** with four 227-kg (500-lb) capacity pylons having demonstrated suitability for the armed reconnaissance role.

The basic version was the OV-1A, equipped for day and night reconnaissance, and provided with dual controls. The OV-1B which followed had increased wing span, SLAR and an internal camera with inflight processor; the dual controls were deleted. Next came the **OV-1C**, similar to late production

The OV-1D is the major current variant in US Army use, combining both the SLAR (illustrated) and infra-red reconnaissance options.

OV-1As but equipped with the AN/AAS-24 infra-red (IR) surveillance system. Final production version was the **OV-1D** with side loading doors able to accept a pallet with SLAR, IR, or other sensors; in addition to new-build aircraft, many OV-1Bs and OV-1Cs were converted to OV-1D standard, and the designations **RV-1C** and **RV-1D** apply respectively to OV-1C and OV-1D aircraft that are modified permanently for electronic reconnaissance missions. Two Mohawks were rumoured to have gone to Israel in the 1970s and these were reported variously as either OV-1Ds or more mysteriously, **EV-1E** versions modified for Elint missions.

Specification
Grumman OV-1D

Type: two-seat multi-sensor observation aircraft
Powerplant: two 1044-kW (1,400-shp) Avco Lycoming T53-L-701 turboprops
Performance: maximum speed, SLAR mission 465 km/h (289 mph) at 3050 m (10,000 ft), IR mission 491 km/h (305 mph); maximum range with maximum fuel, SLAR mission 1519 km (944 miles), IR mission 1627 km (1,011 miles)
Weights: empty equipped 5468 kg (12,054 lb); maximum take-off, SLAR mission 8214 kg (18,109 lb), IR mission 8125 kg (17,912 lb)
Dimensions: span 14.63 m (48 ft 0 in); length 12.50 m (41 ft 0 in); height 3.86 m (12 ft 8 in); wing area 33.44 m² (360.0 sq ft)

Grumman S-2 Tracker/E-1 Tracer/C-1 Trader

In the years immediately following World War II, the US Navy's carrier-based ASW effort depended upon the use of twin-aircraft hunter/killer teams, one being a radar-equipped search aircraft that located the submarine for the suitably armed twin to attack. There were clearly snags to such a twin-aircraft attack: for example, the malfunction of one for something as simple as radio communication meant that both were virtually useless. The situation became further complicated by the growing capability of nuclear-powered submarines which were faster, deeper-diving and quieter. More complex avionics were needed to enhance search capability and provide an advanced weapon control system, as well as additional space for more weapons, more fuel to give longer patrol times, and better accommodation for the crew involved on extended search missions.

In the late 1940s the US Navy finalised its ideas on the kind of single hunter/killer aircraft which it needed to fulfill this role, and Grumman designed a fairly large twin-engined high-wing monoplane, designated **Grumman G-89**, to meet this requirement. The high-wing configuration maximised the cabin space to provide room for on-board equipment, and additional stowage space for expendable sonobuoys was provided in the rear of the engine nacelles. Other features include a large weapons bay, retractable search radar in the rear fuselage, MAD boom in a retractable fairing, searchlight beneath the starboard wing, plus folding wings and arrester hook for carrier operations.

On 30 June 1950 Grumman was awarded a contract to build for evaluation a single prototype of the G-89, the US Navy designation for this aircraft being **XS2F-1**, and this aircraft flew for the first time on 4 December 1952. **S2F Tracker**, **WF Tracer** and **TF Trader** versions appeared in due course, and under the 1962 tri-service rationalisation of designations these became respectively **S-2**, **E-1** and **C-1** series aircraft. The **S-2A**, the first production version of the Tracker, began to enter service with the US Navy's Anti-Submarine Squadron VS-26 in February 1954. In addition to the 500-plus examples built for the US Navy, more than 100 S-2As were exported to friendly nations. A number of these aircraft were used in a training role under the designation **TS-2A**.

The designation **S-2B** applied to S-2A aircraft which had been modified to carry AQA-3 Jezebel passive long-range acoustic search equipment, working in conjunction with Julie active acoustic echo-ranging by explosive charge. **S-2C** was the designation of the next production version, which had an enlarged weapons bay with an offset extension on the port side, and these also had a larger tail to compensate for a higher gross weight. Many S-2A/B/C aircraft were converted subsequently for utility use, such as target towing and light transports, under the designations **US-2A/B/C** respectively. A small number of S-2Cs were also modified to serve in a photo-reconnaissance role under the designation **RS-2C**.

The second major production version was the **S-2D**, of which the initial

example flew for the first time on 21 May 1959. This had a wing of increased span, still larger tail surfaces, plus greater fuel capacity and stowage for double the number of sonobuoys in each engine nacelle, for a combined total of 32. In addition, the forward fuselage was lengthened and widened to improve accommodation for the four-man crew. S-2Ds began to enter service in May 1961, and eventually equipped at least 15 US Navy squadrons. Those modified later to carry more advanced search equipment had the designation **S-2E**, and production of these ended in 1968 with a batch of 14 for the Royal Australian Navy. **S-2F** was the designation of S-2Bs retrofitted with the same advanced search equipment as that installed in the S-2Es. The de Havilland Aircraft of Canada company built 100 Trackers for the Royal Canadian Navy, the first 43 as **CS2F-1** and the remainder with improved equipment as **CS2F-2** aircraft, later redesignated **CP-121**.

In addition to these Tracker variants, 87 **TF-1 Trader** aircraft were built as nine-seat transports for COD (carrier on-board delivery), plus 88 **E-1B Tracer** aircraft with an overfuselage radome housing APS-82 search radar for AEW missions.

The final version of the Tracker was designated **S-2G**, and is similar to the S-2E, but with advanced equipment which enabled the type to serve on the US Navy's CVS-class aircraft-carriers until the Lockheed S-3A Viking entered service.

With the gradual replacement of Trackers by more advanced ASW types, and the ready availability of surplus airframes, life extension programmes and new roles are emerging for the sturdy twin.

In 1986, Grumman received a contract for $260 million to cover the supply of

The Tracker (here an S-2E of VS-31) became the US Navy's standard carrierborne anti-submarine warfare platform.

two **S-2T Turbo Trackers** to Taiwan, followed by kits allowing the completion (in Taiwan) of another 30. This involved replacing the existing powerplants with Garrett TPE331-15AW turboprops driving four-bladed propellers, and completely updating the avionics and ASW equipment. Performance is significantly improved and includes an increase in warload of over 500 kg (1,700 lb). The S-2T conversion is planned to remain in service for at least 20 years.

Also in the US, the Marsh Aviation Company of Mesa, Arizona, is offering two Tracker conversions, the **S-2ET** for military use and the **S-2AT** firefighter, both having their existing piston engines replaced with Garrett TPE331 turboprops. The S-2AT can accommodate the installation of a 3028-litre (666-Imp gal) or 830-litre (3773-Imp gal) retardant tank, dependent on whether the Dash 14 or higher-powered Dash 15 variant of the TPE331 is fitted. The S-2ET ASW and maritime patrol version includes aircraft-carrier re-qualification of the turboprop version and first deliveries of seven ordered by undisclosed customers were scheduled for late 1991. The prototype **Marsh S-2 Turbo Tracker** conversion flew for the first time on 24 November 1986.

In Israel, Bedek Aviation has proposed a complete upgrade of the Tracker and at least one conversion, designated **S-2UP**, is under way for an undisclosed customer. Due for delivery in 1992, this involves re-engining the aircraft with turboprops and the installation of advanced avionics and role equipment allowing credible ASW, EW, ESM and ECM operations to continue for many years.

In Canada, Conair of Abbotsford, operators of the largest fleet of firefighting aircraft in the world, has, since 1987, undertaken 36 conversions of Trackers into single-seat **Firecat** or **Turbo Firecat** water bombers. The simpler Firecat conversion involves modifying a standard S-2A or DHC-built CS2F Tracker to accommodate a 3296-litre (725-Imp gal) tank of fire retardant in the fuselage, fitting bigger wheels and low pressure tyres for soft field operations, rebuilding the cockpit instrument panels and rewiring the aircraft. The Turbo Firecat involves replacing the piston engines with P&W Canada PT6A-67AF turboprops and installing a single-point refuelling system together with a slightly larger retardant tank containing 3455 litres (760 Imp gal). Following a first flight on 7 August 1988, five Turbo Firecat conversions had been delivered to the French Sécurité Civile by 1991, with a sixth underway for use as a demonstrator.

Specification
Grumman S-2E
Type: naval anti-submarine carrier-based aircraft
Powerplant: two 1137-kW (1,525-hp) Wright R-1820-82WA Cyclone 9-cylinder radial piston engines
Performance: maximum speed at sea level 426 km/h (265 mph); patrol speed 241 km/h (150 mph) at 455 m (1,500 ft); ferry range 2092 km (1,300 miles); endurance with maximum fuel and 10 per cent reserves 9 hours
Weights: empty 8505 kg (18,750 lb); maximum take-off 13222 kg (29,150 lb)
Dimensions: span 22.12 m (72 ft 7 in); length 13.26 m (43 ft 6 in); height 5.05 m (16 ft 7 in); wing area 46.08 m^2 (496.0 sq ft)
Armament: one Mk 57 or Mk 101 nuclear depth bomb or similar store in weapons bay, 60 echo-sounding depth charges in fuselage, 32 sonobuoys in engine nacelles plus a variety of bombs, rockets, torpedoes on six underwing hardpoints

Grumman TBF Avenger

The TBF originated in early 1940 when the US Navy initiated a contest to procure a more modern torpedo-bomber, ordering two **XTBF-1** prototypes from Grumman on 8 April 1940, and two competing XTBU-1 prototypes from Vought a couple of weeks later. This latter aircraft was to enter production with Consolidated as the TBY Sea Wolf, but only about 180 were built. The XTBF-1 represented something of a challenge for the Grumman design team headed by Bill Schwendler, for although the company had produced a number of successful carrier-based fighters, this was the first attempt to develop a torpedo-bomber.

First flown on 1 August 1941, the prototype was seen to be a hefty mid-wing monoplane of all-metal construction, except for fabric-covered control surfaces, and for carrier stowage the outer wing panels could be folded. The fuselage and tail unit were of conventional construction, the retractable landing gear of tailwheel type. Attachment points for catapult launch, and an electrically actuated arrester hook, were standard. Later versions had RATO (rocket assisted take-off) provision. Powerplant consisted of a 1268-kW (1,700-hp) Wright R-2600-8 Cyclone 14 radial engine, driving a three-bladed constant-speed propeller. Accommodation was for a crew of three (pilot, bomb-aimer and radio operator/gunner) with a long transparent canopy covering all positions.

Flight testing of the prototype by Grumman was followed by US Navy evaluation which ended satisfactorily in December 1941. But 12 months before this the US Navy had placed its first production order for 286 **TBF-1** aircraft, and the first of these entered service on 30 January 1942. Despite the inauspicious start to the Avenger's career at Midway, the US Navy procured this aircraft in large numbers, and between first delivery at the end of January 1942 and December 1943, Grumman were to build a total of 2,293. These included **TBF-1**s, basically the same as the prototypes, and **TBF-1C** aircraft which differed by having two additional 12.7-mm (0.5-in) machine-guns mounted in the wings, and provision for the carriage of drop-tanks. Grumman also built **XTBF-2** and **XTBF-3** prototypes with XR-2600-10 and R-2600-20 engines respectively.

Of the above the Royal Navy received 402 aircraft under Lend-Lease, mostly procured under the designation **TBF-1B** for this purpose, with the Fleet Air Arm's No. 832 Squadron the first to be equipped, on 1 January 1943. These aircraft were designated initially as **Tarpon Mk I** in British service, but were redesignated **Avenger Mk I** in January 1944. The Royal New Zealand Air Force also acquired 63 examples of the TBF-1 version.

With the demand for Avengers exceeding Grumman's productive capacity, the Eastern Division of General Motors was contracted as a second source of supply. Avengers with the designations **TBM-1** and **TBM-1C** (equivalent to TBF-1 and TBF-1C respectively) were built from September 1942. A total of 7,546 of these and subsequent versions had been delivered when this company's production lines closed down in June 1945. Of these early versions from General Motors, the Royal Navy received 334 TBM-1s which were designated **Avenger Mk II**.

General Motors produced an **XTBM-3** prototype with an R-2600-20 engine, similar to Grumman's XTBF-3, but it differed by having strengthened wires to allow the carriage of mixed stores on underwing racks. Many were also supplied without the heavy power-operated dorsal turret. Designated **TBM-3**, delivery of this version began in April 1944, the Royal Navy acquiring 222 which were identified as the **Avenger Mk III**. General Motors also built the prototype **XTBM-4**, which differed primarily by having a strengthened fuselage, but contract cancellations that followed VJ-Day meant that no production examples were built.

However, the cancellation of production at the end of World War II did not also bring an end to the Avenger's career. In US Navy service they fulfilled a valuable role in the search and location of submarines until specialised aircraft were developed for this purpose. Other tasks for which conversions were developed included versions for all-weather and night operations, electronic countermeasures, carrier on-board delivery and target towing. The Royal Navy's wartime Avengers remained operational until 3 June 1946, but from 1953 this service began to acquire ASW versions under the Mutual Defense Assistance Program (MDAP) which it operated under the designations **Avenger AS.Mk 4** or **Avenger AS.Mk 5** until introduction of the Fairey Gannet in 1955. Avenger variants were also supplied post-war under MDAP to the French Aéronavale, Japanese Maritime Self-Defense Force, Royal Canadian Navy, and the Royal Netherlands Navy.

Variants
TBF-1D/TBF-1CD: conversions of TBF-1/TBF-1Cs with centrimetric radar
TBF-1E: TBF-1 conversion carrying additional avionics
TBF-1J: redesignation of TBF-1 when re-equipped for all-weather operation
TBF-1L: TBF-1 conversion with retractable searchlight in bomb bay
TBF-1P/TBF-1CP: photo-reconnaissance conversions of TBF-1/TBF-1C
TBM-1E/TBM-1J/TBM-1L/TBM-1P: General Motors equivalents to TBF-1E/TBF-1J/TBF-1L and TBF-1P respectively
TBM-3D: conversion of TBM-3 with centrimetric radar
TBM-3E: conversion of TBM-3 with additional avionics
TBM-3H: conversion of TBM-3 with ASV radar
TBM-3J: redesignation of TBM-3 when re-equipped for all-weather operation
TBM-3L: conversion of TBM-3 with retractable searchlight in bomb bay
TBM-3M/TBM-3M2: missile launcher conversions of TBM-3
TBM-3N: post-war night-attack conversion of TBM-3

TBM-3P: conversion of TBM-3 for photo-reconnaissance
TBM-3Q: conversion of TBM-3 for electronic countermeasures
TBM-3R: conversion of TBM-3 to provide seven-passenger/cargo capacity for carrier on-board delivery
TBM-3S/TBM-3S2: conversions of TBM-3 for anti-submarine strike
TBM-3U: utility/target-towing conversion of TBM-3
TBM-3W/TBM-3W2: conversions of TBM-3 for anti-submarine search; operated in conjunction with TBM-3S/TBM-3S2s to provide ASW hunter/killer team

Specification
Grumman/General Motors TBM-3
Type: three-seat carrier-based torpedo-bomber
Powerplant: one 1305-kW (1,750-hp) Wright R-2600-20 Cyclone 14 14-cylinder radial engine
Performance: maximum speed 430 km/h (267 mph) at 4570 m (15,000 ft); cruising speed 237 km/h (147 mph); service ceiling 7130 m (23,400 ft); range 1819 km (1,130 miles)
Weights: empty 4853 kg (10,700 lb); maximum take-off 8278 kg (18,250 lb)
Dimensions: span 16.51 m (54 ft 2 in); length 12.19 m (40 ft 0 in); height 5.00 m (16 ft 5 in); wing area 45.52 m^2 (490.0 sq ft)
Armament: two forward-firing 12.7-mm (0.5-in) machine-guns, one gun of same calibre in dorsal turret and one 7.62-mm (0.3-in) gun in ventral position, plus up to 907 kg (2,000 lb) of weapons in bomb bay, and provision for rocket projectiles, drop-tanks or radar pod under wing

Grumman (General Motors) TBM-3 from USS Randolph, part of Task Force 58 in January 1945.

Grumman X-29A

Designed to explore hitherto theoretical aerodynamic virtues of forward swept wings which promised improved agility, spin-proof flying characteristics, good low-speed handling and reduced stalling speeds, the **Grumman Model 712**, designated **X-29A** by the US Air Force, was a single-seat jet aircraft fitted with a wing mounted at the rear of the fuselage, swept forward at 35°, and having shoulder-mounted canards just behind the cockpit. Powered by a single GE F404 turbofan, the aircraft used major components of other aircraft to keep costs down, including an F-5A forward fuselage and nose landing gear, and F-16 main landing gear and control surface actuators. Two prototypes were ordered in 1981 under an $80 million contract. The first aircraft flew on 14 December 1984 but was grounded on 6 December 1988 after its 242nd flight. The second X-29A, flown for the first time on 23 May

The strange shape of the X-29 is a result of its intended role as a pure research aircraft for forward-swept wings.

1989, completed its flight test programme in October 1991. Between them the two aircraft completed 374 flights (more than any other X-craft) and demonstrated angles of attack up to 67° (the target was 80). They also flew at Mach numbers up tp 1.52 and reached altitudes up to 12200 m (40,000 ft). Both aircraft are now in store at the Ames-Dryden Flight Research Facility of NASA at Edwards AFB, California.

Specification
Type: single-seat experimental technology demonstrator
Powerplant: one 7257-kg (16,000-lb) thrust General Electric F404-GE-400 turbofan engine

Performance: maximum level speed approx. Mach 1.5; service ceiling 12200 m (40,000 ft)
Weights: empty 6260 kg (13,800 lb); maximum take-off 8074 kg (17,800 lb)

Dimensions: span 8.29 m (27 ft 2 in); length 16.44 m (53 ft 11 in); height 4.36 m (14 ft 3 in); wing area 17.54 m² (188.84 sq ft)

Grumman/General Dynamics EF-111A

Grumman, nominally a sub-contractor but fundamentally a component of the General Dynamics team that designed and developed the variable-geometry F-111, was awarded a contract in 1975 to complete two prototype conversions of General Dynamics F-111As to a new **Grumman/General Dynamics EF-111A** ECM tactical jamming configuration.

The major structural changes involve the installation of a canoe-shaped radome over the aircraft's weapons bay, and a fin-tip pod that is of similar shape to that introduced on the EA-6B Prowler. The weapons bay serves to house the jamming transmitters of the AN/ALQ-99E tactical jamming system, an improved and more capable version of the AN/ALQ-99 that is carried by the EA-6B. Claimed to be the most powerful airborne ECM system, its use allows the EF-111A to penetrate the most dense electronic defences and it is so

advanced that it can be pre-programmed with all known radar defences within the area of an operation, allowing the crew member known as the electronic warfare officer to concentrate upon new and more urgent threat radars.

Early prototype flights began on 15 December 1975 with an aircraft having the weapons bay radome installed. A fully aerodynamic prototype was flown on 10 March 1977 followed by the second on 17 May. Nearly 500 hours of manufacturer and US Air Force testing proved the capability and reliability of the system. Grumman then converted 40 F-111As into EF-111A Ravens, and the type entered service in November 1981.

A development EF-111A displays the main characteristics of the conversion, namely the 'canoe' fairing housing the jammers and the fin-tip 'football' for the receivers.

In the continental US, Tactical Air Command includes the 390th Electronic Combat Squadron of the 366th Tactical Fighter Wing based at Mountain Home AFB, Idaho, while in the UK Ravens serve with the 42nd ECS based at RAF Upper Heyford in Oxfordshire.

Specification
Type: ECM tactical jamming aircraft
Powerplant: two Pratt & Whitney TF30-P-3 turbofan engines, each rated at 8391-kg (18,500-lb) thrust with afterburning
Performance: maximum speed at combat weight 2216 km/h (1,377 mph); average operational speed in combat area 940 km/h (584 mph); service ceiling 13715 m (45,000 ft); combat radius 1495 km (929 miles)
Weights: empty 25072 kg (55,275 lb); combat take-off weight 31751 kg (70,000 lb); maximum take-off weight 40370 kg (89,000 lb)
Dimensions: span, wings spread 19.20 m (63 ft 0 in); wings swept 9.74 m (31 ft 11½ in); length 23.16 m (76 ft 0 in); height 6.10 m (20 ft 0 in); wing area 48.77 m² (525.0 sq ft)

Gulfstream Aerospace Gulfstream I/I-C

Grumman Aerospace Corporation began design in the mid-1950s of a twin-turboprop executive transport which was intended for a crew of two and 10-14 passengers in typical corporate versions: an alternative high-density layout could seat a maximum of 24 passengers. Designated **Grumman G-159 Gulfstream I**, this was a conventional low-wing monoplane with pressurised accommodation, retractable tricycle landing gear, and powered by two Rolls-Royce Dart turboprops. The prototype was flown for the first time on 14 August 1958.

In addition to the production of civil Gulfstream Is, Grumman also supplied nine **TC-4C** aircraft to the US Navy. Required for the training of crews to serve with Grumman A-6A Intruder squadrons, they are easily distinguished from standard Gulfstreams by having a bulbous nose radome. Two other Gulf-

stream Is were acquired by the US Coast Guard under the designation **VC-4A**, these being used as VIP transports.

Most of the 200 Gulfstream Is that were built went to customers in North America, but a number of these are now being converted to **Gulfstream I-C** configuration. This programme was initiated by Gulfstream American Corporation (now Gulfstream Aerospace Corporation) following the acquisition of Grumman's Gulfstream division. The conversion entails a fuselage 'stretch' of 3.25 m (10 ft 8 in) to provide seating for a maximum 37 passengers, but is otherwise little different from the original Gulfstream I.

Specification
Gulfstream Aerospace Gulfstream I-C
Type: commuter transport
Powerplant: two 1484-ekW (1,990-

ehp) Rolls-Royce Dart Mk 529-8X turboprops
Performance: maximum cruising speed at mid-cruise weight 571 km/h (355 mph); certificated altitude 9145 m (30,000 ft); range with maximum payload and IFR reserves 805 km (500 miles)
Weights: empty 10747 kg (23,693 lb); maximum take-off 16329 kg (36,000 lb)

Dimensions: span 23.88 m (78 ft 4 in); length 22.96 m (75 ft 4 in); height 7.01 m (23 ft 0 in); wing area 56.70 m² (610.30 sq ft)

The Gulfstream I combined high power and low operating cost with a capacious fuselage and good fuel tankage, resulting in a remarkable long-range corporate or VIP transport.

Gulfstream Aerospace Gulfstream II/II-B

Encouraged by pressure from existing Gulfstream I operators, in early 1965 Grumman began preliminary studies for a turbofan-engined version of its very successful corporate turboprop. Market research indicated a requirement for an aircraft with the cabin volume of the Gulfstream I with high-speed trans-oceanic capability, but also capable of good short-field performance. By the time the planned full-scale mock-up had been completed, Grumman had received 30 firm orders, resulting in a programme go-ahead on 5 May 1965. There was no prototype as such, the first aircraft making its maiden flight on 2 October 1966.

With two Rolls-Royce Spey Mk 511-8 engines, each producing 5171-kg (11,400-lb) thrust in an airframe some 65 per cent of the weight of a similarly powered aircrach such as the BAe (BAC) One-Eleven and Fokker F28, the **Grumman Gulfstream II** met the short-field performance with ease and had a maximum-fuel range of more than 6115 km (3,800-miles).

All Gulfstream IIs were fitted with avionics and custom interiors at distrib-

utors, and in December 1967 the fifth aircraft was handed over to AiResearch Inc. for completion before becoming the first to reach a customer, in this case National Distillers and Chemical Corporation of New York. It became the first executive jet to fly non-stop across the North Atlantic in both directions, flying from Teterboro, New Jersey, to London Gatwick in 6 hours 55 minutes on 5 May 1968, and back to Burlington, Vermont, on 12 May in 7 hours 10 minutes.

Manufacture and improvement continued until December 1979, when the last of 258 production aircraft was delivered. By then Gulfstream American (now Gulfstream Aerospace) had superseded it in production by the more advanced Gulfstream III, and the advanced wing developed for this aircraft has become available as a retrofit for the Gulfstream II, the resulting conversion designated **Gulfstream II-B**. Gulfstream Aerospace now has an active conversion programme in progress, the new wing increasing the range of the Gulfstream II and, at the same time, giving a significant improvement in fuel efficiency.

Specification
Gulfstream Aerospace Gulfstream II-B
Type: twin-turbofan executive transport
Powerplant: two 5171-kg (11,400-lb) thrust Rolls-Royce Spey Mk 511-8 turbofans
Performance: maximum cruising speed Mach 0.85 at 9145 m (30,000 ft); long-range cruising speed Mach 0.77; certificated ceiling 13715 m (45,000 ft); range with 8 passengers, NBAA IFR

The Gulfstream II, unlike its predecessor, adopted swept flying surfaces, a T-tail and two large turbofan engines.

reserves 6579 km (4,088 miles)
Weights: empty operating 17735 kg (39,100 lb); maximimum take-off 30935 kg (66,200 lb)
Dimensions: span 23.72 m (77 ft 10 in); length 24.36 m (79 ft 11 in); height 7.47 m (24 ft 6 in); wing area 86.82 m² (934.6 sq ft)

Gulfstream Aerospace Gulfstream III

Grumman announced in November 1976 the company's intention to develop the **Grumman Gulfstream III**. However, this programme was suspended temporarily in early 1977; it was resumed in 1978 and development continued under contract to Gulfstream American (now Gulfstream Aerospace) which had acquired the assets of Grumman's American Aviation Corporation.

By comparison with the Gulfstream II, fuselage length was increased by 1.19 m (3 ft 11 in); this allowed for the incorporation of a redesigned nose with improved windows on the flight deck, giving a better field of view, and also provided a longer cabin to seat a maximum of 19 passengers. Key to the improved performance of this aircraft was its new

supercritical wing incorporating NASA Whitcomb wingtip winglets, and its 2.74 m (9 ft) increase in span provided integral fuel tankage of 16655 litres (4,400 US gal). The first aircraft was converted from Gulfstream II airframe number 249, taken from the production line. After rollout, on 21 September 1979, this machine was flown for the first time on 2 December 1979, a second aircraft joining the flight test programme on 24 December.

The Gulfstream III is suitable for multimission operations, equally capable of being used for navaid checking, aeromedical/casevac, priority cargo and administrative transport roles. A dedicated **Gulfstream III Maritime** version is also available with sea surveillance radar and an inertial navigation

system. Three examples are in service with the Royal Danish air force which operates them primarily for fishery patrol, but they are equipped so that they can be used for airdrop, medevac, SAR, tactical air transport and other duties.

Specification
Gulfstream Aerospace Gulfstream III
Type: twin-turbofan executive transport
Powerplant: two 5171-kg (11,400-lb) thrust Rolls-Royce Spey Mk 511-8 turbofans
Performance: maximum cruising speed Mach 0.85; long-range cruising speed Mach 0.77; certificated ceiling 13715 m (45,000 ft); range with NBAA

IFR reserves 6759 km (4,200 miles)
Weights: empty operating 17237 kg (38,000 lb); maximum take-off 30935 kg (68,200 lb)
Dimensions: span 23.72 m (77 ft 10 in); length 25.32 m (83 ft 1 in); height 7.43 m (24 ft 4½ in); wing area 86.82 m² (934.6 sq ft)

Evolved from the Gulfstream II, the Gulfstream II introduced a fuselage stretch and a supercritical wing with winglets to squeeze the maximum range out of the increased fuel tankage.

Gulfstream Aerospace Gulfstream IV

With nearly 260 GIIs and over 200 GIIIs built and delivered, and with the Challenger the only real competitor in the top-of-the-range market, Gulfstream began the development of the **GIV** in 1983. Construction of four development

prototypes began in 1984. The first of these flew on 19 September 1985 from the factory at Savannah International Airport, Georgia. The aircraft was certificated in April 1987 following a 1,400-hour flight-test programme, and by the end of

1991 more than 185 GIVs had been delivered. Planned production rate is 30 aircraft per year, ensuring delivery not more than 12 months after placing an order.

Main differences from the GIII are a

structurally redesigned but lighter wing, a 54-in fuselage stretch incorporating a sixth window, increased tailplane span, EFIS flight deck and digital avionics plus the improved, fuel-efficient TAY 611-8 engine variant.

A special missions version of the Gulfstream IV designated the **SRA-4** has been flying since 1988. Equipped with a

1.6 × 2.1 m (5 × 7 ft) cargo door on the starboard side ahead of the wing, a search radar and tail-mounted MAD equipment, this version is offered for electronic warfare support, electronic surveillance and reconnaissance, medical evacuation, priority cargo transport and maritime patrol including ASW. For this last role the SRA-4, equipped with sonobuoys and torpedoes housed in a weapons' bay under the forward fuselage, and air-to-surface missiles under the wings, can loiter for over four hours on station using a hi-lo-hi mission profile.

Specification
Type: twin-turbofan 8-passenger/3-crew long-range executive transport
Powerplant: two 6295-kg (13,850-lb)

thrust Rolls-Royce Tay Mk 611-8 turbofans
Performance: maximum cruising speed Mach 0.88; long-range cruising speed Mach 0.80; ceiling 13716 m (45,000 ft); range with NBAA IFR reserves 7820 km (4,220 miles)
Weights: empty 16136 kg (35,500 lb); maximum take-off 33273 kg (73,200 lb)
Dimensions: span 23.7 m (77 ft 10 in); length 26.9 m (88 ft 4 in); height 7.6 m (24 ft 10 in); wing area 88.3 m² (950.4 sq ft)

Marking the ultimate in corporate transport, the Gulfstream IV introduced a further fuselage stretch and numerous other refinements.

Gulfstream American AA-1/T-Cat/Lynx

The Bede BD-1 was designed by Jim Bede as a low-cost two-seat sporting aircraft with a structure that made extensive use of aluminium honeycomb construction and metal-to-metal bonding. Design definition began in June 1962 and construction of a prototype began in October, the first flight following on 11 July 1963. Bede Aviation Corporation was formed at Cleveland, Ohio, in 1964, being re-named American Aviation Corporation in September 1967, to assume responsibility for the development, certification and manufacture of the aircraft as the **AA-1 Yankee**. An FAA type certificate for the production AA-1 was granted on 16 July 1968, the first example having flown on 30 May 1968.

Development of a training version was started in October 1969 and the prototype, on which work had begun on 1 February 1970, made its first flight on 25 March of that year. Designated **AA-1A**, it retained the 81-kW (108-hp) Avco Lycoming O-235-C2C engine of the AA-1, but incorporated a modified wing, minor equipment changes, and dual controls as standard. The first production AA-1A flew on 6 November 1970 and type certification was awarded on 14 January 1971.

The Grumman Corporation acquired American Aviation in 1972 and minor design and equipment changes introduced in 1974 resulted in redesignation as the **AA-1B**, further updating in 1977 producing the **AA-1C**. Dual-purpose touring/training variants of the AA-1B and AA-1C, with enhanced equipment and interiors, were manufactured as the **Tr 2** and **T-Cat**, respectively; a de luxe version was produced as the **Lynx**. In 1978, American Jet Industries acquired Grumman's American Aviation Corporation, renaming the company Gulfstream American Corporation. Production of the AA-1, T-Cat and Lynx family was terminated at the end of 1978.

Specification
Gulfstream American AA-1
Type: two-seat touring and training monoplane
Powerplant: one 81-kW (108-hp) Avco Lycoming O-235-C2C flat-four piston engine
Performance: maximum speed 232 km/h (144 mph) at sea level; cruising speed 217 km/h (135 mph) at 2440 m (8,000 ft); service ceiling 3415 m (11,200 ft); range with maximum fuel 824 km (512 miles)

Weights: empty 426 kg (940 lb); maximum take-off 680 kg (1,500 lb)
Dimensions: span 7.45m (24 ft 5½ in); length 5.86 m (19 ft 2¾ in); height 1.97 m (6 ft 5¾ in); wing area 9.11 m² (98.11 sq ft)

A Gulfstream American T-Cat (background) formates on a Lynx, the latter being the de luxe version of the series. These were refinements of the original AA-1 design.

Gulfstream American AA-5A/Cheetah and AA-5B/Tiger

In June 1970 American Aviation began work on an enlarged four-seat version of the AA-1, designated **AA-5 Traveler**. Wing span was increased by 2.13 m (7 ft 0 in); tail surfaces were increased in area, and the fuselage was lengthened by 0.84 m (2 ft 9 in) to accommodate two more seats. Power was increased by installation of an Avco Lycoming O-320-E2G engine. The prototype was flown on 21 August 1970 and certification was gained on 12 November 1971.

In 1974 changes included introduction of a new fin, extended rear cabin windows and an enlarged baggage compartment; two years later an enlarged tailplane and minor improvements brought

re-designation as the **AA-5A**. A de luxe version of the same aircraft was designated **Cheetah**. Versions equivalent to the AA-5A and Cheetah, but with the more powerful 134-kW (180-hp) Avco Lycoming O-360-A4K engine installed, were added to the range with the respective designations **AA-5B** and **Tiger**.

Specification
Gulfstream American AA-5A
Type: four-seat cabin monoplane
Powerplant: one 112-kW (150-hp) Avco Lycoming O-320-E2G flat-four piston engine
Performance: maximum speed

The AA-5 Traveler was a growth development of the AA-1 which raised seating to four and power to 112 kW (150 hp). The AA-5B Tiger (illustrated) differed from the baseline AA-5A Cheetah by having a 134-kW (180-hp) engine and increased tankage.

253 km/h (157 mph) at sea level; economic cruising speed 219 km/h (136 mph) at 2590 m (8,500 ft); service ceiling 3830 m (12,560 ft); maximum range with standard fuel 1041 km (647 miles)

Weights: empty 591 kg (1,303 lb); maximum take-off 998 kg (2,200 lb)
Dimensions: span 9.60 m (31 ft 6 in); length 6.71 m (22 ft 0 in); height 2.29 m (7 ft 6 in); wing area 12.98 m² (139.70 sq ft)

Gulfstream American GA-7/Cougar

The discerned need for an economical lightweight four-seat twin to equip flying schools offering multi-engine conversion courses, and to meet the requirements of private pilots looking for natural progression from high-performance single-engine aircraft, led Grumman American to develop the **GA-7**. The pro-

totype made its first flight on 20 December 1974, powered by two 119-kW (160-hp) Avco Lycoming O-320-D1D engines, and a production-standard trials aircraft flew on 14 January 1977. Deliveries began in February 1978, continuing until late 1979 when Gulfstream American suspended production of the GA-7 and

also of the single-engine range.
Basic production model was the GA-7, but a de luxe version was also available under the name **Cougar.** This incorporated as standard dual controls, communication and navigation avionics, full blind-flying instrumentation and additional electrical equipment.

Specification
Gulfstream American GA-7
Type: four-seat cabin monoplane
Powerplant: two 119-kW (160-hp) Avco Lycoming O-320-D1D flat-four piston engines
Performance: maximum speed 311 km/h (193 mph) at sea level;

economic cruising speed 211 km/h (131 mph) at 2590 m (8,500 ft); service ceiling 5580 m (18,300 ft); range with maximum fuel at 2590 m (8,500 ft) 2150 km (1,336 miles)
Weights: empty 1141 kg (2,515 lb); maximum take-off 1724 kg (3,800 lb)
Dimensions: span 11.23 m (36 ft 10¼ in); length 9.09 m (29 ft 10 in); height 3.16 m (10 ft 4¼ in); wing area 17.09 m² (184.0 sq ft)

Designed to compete with the highly successful Piper Twin Comanche series, the Gulfstream American GA-7 Cougar was a thoroughly workmanlike design, but failed to break into this highly competitive but also partisan market. The design was in production for less than two years.

Gulfstream Commander Jetprop

Gulfstream Commander Jetprop 840

When at the end of 1980 Gulfstream American acquired the Commander line of aircraft from Rockwell International's General Aviation Division, it was decided to continue to produce and develop the two aircraft known formerly as the **Rockwell Jetprop Commander 840** and **Jetprop Commander 980**. These were redesignated as the **Gulfstream Commander Jetprop 840** and **Commander Jetprop 980** respectively, and since then the company has introduced new versions known as the **Commander Jetprop 900** and **Commander Jetprop 1000**.

Developed from the Rockwell Turbo Commander 690B, the Commander Jetprop 840 is generally similar in overall configuration: a cantilever high-wing monoplane with conventional swept tail surfaces, retractable tricycle landing gear and two wing-mounted turboprop engines. It differs from the Model 690B by an increase in wing span and the introduction of a shallow winglet at each wingtip. Power is provided by two 626-kW (840-shp) Garrett TPE331-5-254K turboprops which, in this application, are each flat-rated to 522 kW (700 shp). First flown on 17 May 1979, the Jetprop 840 gained FAA certification on 7 September 1979, and deliveries began shortly afterwards. The Commander Jetprop 980 shares the same heritage, differing primarily in the powerplant installation and by increased fuel capacity. The engines are 730-kW (980-shp) Garrett TPE331-10-501K turboprops, which in this case are flat-rated to 533 kW (715 shp). A first flight on 14 June 1979 was

followed by certification on 1 November 1979.

The Commander Jetprop 1000, first flown in prototype form on 12 May 1980, is in the same mould. It has increased cabin space resulting from a rearward shift of the aft bulkhead, increasing cabin volume by some 25 per cent but reducing the baggage space. The cabin pressurisation differential was increased so that certification could be gained for operation at a higher altitude, and at increased gross weight so that greater economy of operation could be obtained from the installed powerplant. FAA certification was gained on 30 April 1981, with the service ceiling increased by 1220 m (4,000 ft) and gross weight by 227 kg (500 lb). The Commander Jetprop 980, which was introduced in 1982, combined the powerplant of the Jetprop 840 with the airframe of the Jetprop 1000.

All four Commander Jetprops pro-

vided maximum accommodation for a pilot and 10 passengers, but were generally used to carry six or seven passengers in a very comfortable and well-appointed cabin. This was pressurised, air-conditioned, heated and ventilated. A full de-icing system was standard and a very wide range of avionics equipment was available.

Further developments were the more powerful Jetprop 1200, fastest of the Commander twins. A prototype was flown in August 1983 but the type did not proceed any further. The extensively redesigned piston-engined Commander 800 was intended to replace the successful 500S. However, only one flew before production of all variants ceased in 1985. Gulfstream American took until December 1989 to find a buyer, namely Precision Airmotive of Arlington, Washington, (since renamed the Twin Commander Aircraft Corporation) which intends to resume production, but had

not done so by the end of 1991.

Specification
Jetprop 980
Type: twin-turboprop light transport
Powerplant: two 731-kW (980-shp) Garrett TPE331-10-501K turboprop engines, each flat-rated to 533 kW (715 shp)
Performance: maximum cruising speed 573 km/h (356 mph) at 6705 m (22,000 ft); economic cruising speed 462 km/h (287 mph) at 9450 m (31,000 ft); certificated ceiling 9450 m (31,000 ft); range with maximum payload and 45 minutes reserves 1514 km (941 miles)
Weights: empty 3051 kg (6,727 lb); maximum take-off 4853 kg (10,700 lb)
Dimensions: span 15.89 m (52 ft 1½ in); length 13.10 m (42 ft 11¾ in); height 4.56 m (14 ft 11½ in); wing area 25.95 m² (279.37 sq ft)

Häfeli DH-2 and DH-3

The **Häfeli DH-2** design for K+W was a conventional two-bay biplane, of wooden construction with fabric covering, and built for reconnaissance duties. Six aircraft were manufactured in 1916, five of them powered by the 89-kW (120-hp) Argus As/II water-cooled inline engine which required large flat radiators, these being mounted beside the front cockpit; the first had been equipped with a similarly-cooled 75-kW (100-hp) Mercedes D.I. Performance was disappointing and no production order was placed, but the DH-2s continued in use to train pilots and observers until withdrawn finally in 1922.

In early 1917 K+W received an order for 30 examples of the **DH-3**, an improved version of the DH-2 with an essentially similar airframe, although the upper wing had a semi-circular cut-out to provide an improved field of fire for the pivoted machine-gun mounted in the observer's cockpit. The landing gear proved troublesome and there were engine cooling problems until an improved system was fitted. A total of 24 was built with the Argus As II engine, and the type was withdrawn from use in 1923 when a structural strength test, conducted on an airframe which had amassed 600 hours, produced unsatisfactory results. In the meantime, a DH-3 inaugurated the first Swiss air mail service, between Zürich's Dübendorf airfield and Berne, on 8 January 1919.

Variants
DH-3a: four aircraft were built in 1918, three of the four with Hispano-Suiza HS-41 8Aa engines which had been acquired by the Swiss military authorities to provide improved performance; these aircraft were scrapped in 1922; a second series of 30 aircraft, essentially similar but with the Hispano-Suiza engines built under licence by Adolph Saurer AG at Arbon, was ordered in 1919, and a third order for 49 aircraft was placed in 1925; this last included six primary trainers with dual controls and a trials aircraft with a 134-kW (180-hp) HS-41 8Ab engine; this was evaluated by the Swiss air force between October 1929 and April 1930; following a prototype installation of Handley Page leading-edge slats, carried out on an aircraft flown to

Cricklewood for the purpose, a further 55 surviving DH-3a aircraft were modified similarly at Thun in 1932; at the same time they were subjected to modifications to allow pilot and observer to wear parachutes, necessitating changes to the seats and the replacement of the inner-bay rear bracing wires by struts to ease the pilot's exit from the front cockpit; a 600-hour airframe test was passed in December 1934 and these modified aircraft remained in service until 1939
DH-3b: three DH-3b aircraft were used for trials with the indigenous 112-kW (150-hp) LFW O engine, developed by the Swiss Locomotive and Machine Works at Winterthur; built in 1918, they were withdrawn in 1922; armament comprised two fixed machine-guns, mounted above the

engine, in addition to the observer's weapon

Specification
Häfeli DH-3a
Type: two-seat reconnaissance aircraft
Powerplant: one 112-kW (150-hp) Hispano-Suiza HS-41 8Aa 8-cylinder Vee piston engine
Performance: maximum speed 145 km/h (90 mph); service ceiling 4500 m (14,765 ft); range 400 km (249 miles)
Weights: empty 720 kg (1,587 lb); maximum take-off 1110 kg (2,447 lb)
Dimensions: span 12.50 m (41 ft 0 in); length 7.95 m (26 ft 1 in); height 3.10 m (10 ft 2 in); wing area 38.00 m² (409.04 sq ft)
Armament: one pivoted machine-gun in the rear cockpit

Totally unremarkable in its design and service career, the Häfeli DH-3 was designed as a reconnaissance aircraft but was generally used as a trainer.

Häfeli DH-5

In the autumn of 1918 K+W Thun was engaged in the construction of the prototype **Häfeli DH-5**, a wood and fabric single-bay biplane which was to be powered by a 134-kW (180-hp) LFW I engine produced by the Swiss Locomotive and Machine Works at Winterhur. Test flying commenced in March 1919, and Swiss military evaluation began in May 1920; after this the prototype was used for structural strength tests. Thirty-nine were ordered, the first entering service in 1922. In March 1929 one aircraft was civil-registered for a flight to England, where Handley Page leading-edge slats were fitted; another 23 aircraft were similarly modified at Thun in 1930. A second series of 20 was intro-

duced in 1924, powered by the 149-kW (200-hp) LFW II engine. DH-5s and DH-5As were finally withdrawn from use in 1940.

Variants
DH-5X: this trials' aircraft appeared in November 1924, powered by a 224-kW (300-hp) Hispano-Suiza HS-42 8Fb engine imported from France; production orders would have followed Swiss military evaluation, but further supplies of the engine were not available: the DH-5X crashed on the Weissflujoch on 31 January 1933, with the loss of the pilot
DH-5A: 20 aircraft, powered by the LFW III engine, were ordered and delivered in 1929; they were modified in 1930 by the installation of Handley Page slats and new seats to accept

Fully comparable with the reconnaissance aircraft being evolved in World War I, the DH-5 suffered from a protracted development period and only entered service in 1922.

back-type parachutes for pilot and observer; this version was used also for target towing

Specification
Häfeli DH-5A
Type: two-seat reconnaissance aircraft
Powerplant: one 164-kW (220-hp) LFW III Vee piston engine
Performance: maximum speed 180 km/h (112 mph); service ceiling 5600 m (18,375 ft); range 480 km (298 miles)

Weights: empty 859 kg (1,894 lb); maximum take-off 1271 kg (2,802 lb)
Dimensions: span 12.00 m (39 ft 4½ in); length 7.60 m (24 ft 11¼ in); height 3.10 m (10 ft 2 in); wing area 31.40 m² (338.0 sq ft)
Armament: one fixed forward-firing machine-gun and a pivoted machine-gun in the rear cockpit

Hafner rotary-wing aircraft

Austrian Raoul Hafner began preliminary work on helicopter models in the mid-1920s, and in 1928 began the design of his first aircraft, the **Hafner R.I** helicopter. Financed by the Scottish cotton millionaire, Major J. A. Coats, this had a comparatively short fuselage and a large diameter (9.14 m/30 ft) three-bladed main rotor; power was provided by a 22.4-kW (30-hp) ABC Scorpion flat-twin piston engine. When tested at Vienna in 1930 it was soon found that the gyroscopic action of this rotor was too great and, as a result, only a few brief hops were made. An improved **R.II** of similar configuration was built, but differed by having an increased vertical surface to offset the turning moment of the rotor, and by having a 30-kW (40-hp) Salmson lightweight radial piston engine.

In 1932 Raoul Hafner transferred his activities to England, continuing development of the R.II at Heston, Middlesex, but within two years had established the AR.III Construction (Hafner Gyroplane) Company to develop an autogyro of similar basic layout to the Cierva autogyros. Only one example (G-ADMV) was built and this flew successfully during 1937 and 1938. Of similar layout to Cierva autogyros, Hafner's **AR.III Gyroplane** carried the three-bladed auto-rotating rotor on a strutted pylon

One of the many experiments undertaken in World War II to increase battlefield mobility by the provision of rotary wings for men and vehicles, the Hafner Rotabuggy was intended as a stepping-stone to a flying Valentine tank.

above a fairly conventional fuselage. This mounted a Pobjoy Niagara radial engine in the nose to drive a two-bladed propeller, had fixed tailwheel landing gear and provided single-seat accommodation. An unusual feature was the rear fuselage, which incorporated a long dorsal fin that tapered to rudder thickness, providing ample vertical surface area. The special design feature was the Gyroplane's rotor control system, giving both cyclic and collective pitch control to the blades, which was to become standard for the dynamic system of helicopters.

Two- and three-seat autogyros, designated respectively **AR.IV** and **AR.V**, were planned, but although construction had been initiated the outbreak of World War II brought an end to these projects. Raoul Hafner's wartime work included the design and development of the **Rotachute**, a man-carrying glider with a rotating wing. Towed by an aircraft to heights of some 1220 m (4,000 ft), it

could be piloted in any direction after release. This was seen as a stage in the development of a man-carrying 'parachute' with a rotating wing that would allow such vehicles to be carried in an aircraft in a folded state and would deploy automatically when used in an emergency. Other wartime work was concentrated on the development of a **Rotabuggy**, basically a 'jeep'-type general-purpose military truck with an easily attached/detached rotary wing that would allow such vehicles to be towed and deployed behind enemy lines. A prototype was flown extensively during 1943-44, but did not become operational. In the post-war years, Raoul Hafner's great experience of rotating

wings proved of value to the Bristol and Westland aircraft companies.

Specification
Hafner AR.III Gyroplane
Type: single-seat autogyro
Powerplant: one 67-kW (90-hp) Pobjoy Niagara 7-cylinder radial
Performance: maximum speed 193 km/h (120 mph); cruising speed 177 km/h (110 mph)
Weights: empty 290 kg (640 lb); maximum take-off 408 kg (900 lb)
Dimensions: rotor diameter 10.00 m (32 ft 10 in); length 5.44 m (17 ft 10 in); rotor disc area 78.54 m² (845.43 sq ft)

Halberstadt CL.II and CL.IV
to
Handley Page H.P.52 Hampden

Halberstadt CL.II and CL.IV

Developed to a new specification for a two-seat fighter, required to act as escorts for the earlier and heavier C-type reconnaissance aircraft, the **Halberstadt CL.II** appeared in 1917 and soon entered service with the *Schutzstaffeln* (protection flights) of the Imperial German Aviation Service. A single-bay biplane with a plywood-covered wooden fuselage and fabric-covered wings with plywood leading edges, it was powered by a Mercedes D.III engine. The single cockpit had tandem accommodation for pilot and observer, the latter being provided with an elevated gun ring which allowed him to fire his Parabellum machine-gun both upwards and forwards over the upper wing. Trays were fitted on each side of the fuselage for the carriage of small anti-personnel grenades, or of four or five 10-kg (22-lb) bombs, which gave the type formidable capability in the close-support role. The CL.II soon demonstrated its value to the German high command when, on 6 September 1917, 24 aircraft attacked with great effect British troops crossing the bridges over the Somme at Bray and St Christ. The escort units were then rede-

A very useful escort and light ground-attack machine, the Halberstadt CL.IV featured a communal cockpit with an elevated gun ring.

signated as *Schlachtstaffeln* (battle flights) for close-support duties and were used extensively during the closing months of 1917, particularly at the Battle of Cambrai on 30 November when the Germans launched a successful counter-offensive. In addition to the output of the designing company, CL.IIs were also built under sub-contract by Bayerische Flugzeugwerke GmbH.

Variants
CL.IIa: designation of a small number of aircraft which were powered by the 138-kW (185-hp) BMW IIIa engine
CL.IV: essentially an improved CL.II with the same Mercedes D.III engine, the CL.IV introduced redesigned horizontal and vertical tail surfaces and had a fuselage some 0.76 m (2 ft 6 in) shorter than that of its predecessor; it went into service with the *Schlachtstaffeln* in time for the March

1918 German offensive; sub-contract production was undertaken by Luftfahrtzeug GmbH (Roland)

Specification
Halberstadt CL.II
Type: two-seat ground support aircraft and escort fighter
Powerplant: one 119-kW (160-hp) Mercedes D.III 6-cylinder inline piston engine
Performance: maximum speed 165 km/h (103 mph) at 5000 m

(16,504 ft); service ceiling 5100 m (16,730 ft); endurance 3 hours
Weights: empty 772 kg (1,701 lb); maximum take-off 1130 kg (2.493 lb)
Dimensions: span 10.77 m (35 ft 4 in); length 7.30 m (23 ft 11½ in); height 2.75 m (9 ft 0¼ in); wing area 27.50 m² (296.02 sq ft)
Armament: one or two fixed forward-firing 7.92-mm (0.31-in) LMG 08/15 machine-guns and one pivoted 7.92-mm (0.31-in) Parabellum machine-gun, plus four or five 10-kg (22-lb) bombs and grenades

Halberstadt D.I to D.IV

Developed by Dipl. Ing. Karl Theis from the Halberstadt B.II two-seat reconnaissance aircraft, the **Halberstadt D.I** single-seat fighter appeared in late 1915, and was powered initially by a 75-kW (100-hp) Mercedes D.I engine. It had some structural strengthening by comparison with the earlier two-seater and carried a fixed forward-firing LMG 08/15 (Spandau) machine-gun forward of the cockpit. It was later re-engined with an 89-kW (120-hp) Argus As.II engine and on 21 March 1916 an order was received for 12 production aircraft. These incorporated a number of modifications and were powered by the Mercedes D.II engine.

Redesignated **D.II** in this form, the aircraft had a revised cooling arrangement, the original frontal radiator replaced by a wing-mounted unit. It entered service in June 1916, originally as an escort fighter, but was then issued to the new *Jagdstaffeln*. The D.II's front-line service was limited to a matter of months, it being replaced by the Albatros D.III in early 1917. In addition to the aircraft built by Halberstadt, another 60 examples were produced by Automobil und Aviatik AG and by Hannoversche Waggonfabrik AG, each of which built 30 aircraft under licence.

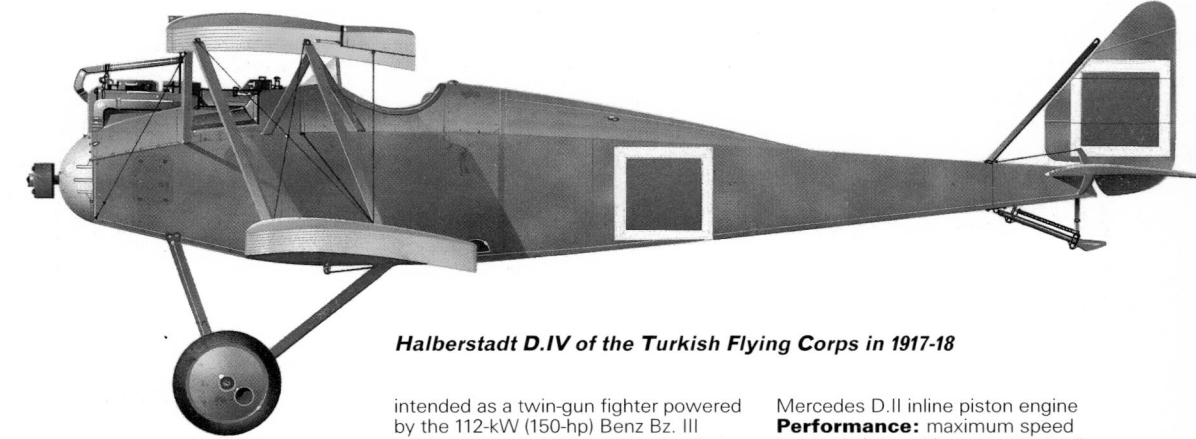

Halberstadt D.IV of the Turkish Flying Corps in 1917-18

Variants
D.III: powered by the 89-kW (120-hp) Argus AS.II engine, the D.III introduced further minor improvements, including enlarged horn-balanced ailerons and vertical centre-section supporting struts in place of the triangular cabane of the D.II
D.IV: developed under a contract awarded in March 1916, the D.IV was

intended as a twin-gun fighter powered by the 112-kW (150-hp) Benz Bz. III engine; a small number was supplied to Turkey
D.V: introduced in early 1917, the D.V had a streamlined ply-covered fuselage and a neatly-cowled Argus As.II engine, driving a propeller with spinner

Specification
Halberstadt D.II
Type: single-seat fighter
Powerplant: one 89-kW (120-hp)

Mercedes D.II inline piston engine
Performance: maximum speed 150 km/h (93 mph); range 250 km/h (155 miles)
Weights: empty 520 kg (1,147 lb); maximum take-off 730 kg (1,610 lb)
Dimensions: span 8.80 m (29 ft 10½ in); length 7.30 m (23 ft 11½ in); height 2.67 m (8 ft 9¼ in); wing area 23.6 m² (254.04 sq ft)
Armament: one fixed forward-firing 7.92-mm (0.31-in) LMG 08/15 machine-gun

Handley Page O/100 and O/400 (H.P.11 and H.P.12)

To meet an Admiralty specification of December 1914 for a large twin-engined patrol bomber, Handley Page lost little time in designing an aircraft to meet this requirement. Identified originally as the **Handley Page Type O**, it was later designated **O/100**, the figure 100 indicating its wing span in feet. Clearly, this was very much bigger than anything else that

had been built by the Handley Page company; in fact, when the prototype was completed, it was the largest aeroplane that had then been built in the UK.

The O/100 was of biplane configuration, with folding unequal-span constant-chord wings that had straight leading and trailing edges; these were mounted on a square-section cross-braced fuse-

lage that terminated in a biplane tail unit. The tailskid landing gear had twin wheels on each main unit and the two 198-kW (266-hp) Rolls-Royce Eagle II engines, in armoured nacelles, were mounted between the wings just outboard of the fuselage. Accommodation in the first prototype (serial number 1455) was in a glazed cockpit enclosure,

the floor and sides of the cockpit being protected by armour plate. Flown for the first time on 18 December 1915, the O/100 was found to be inadequate in performance, and the second prototype had a revised open cockpit for a crew of two (with provision for a gunner's position forward), the cockpit armour plating and most of that incorporated in the engine nacelles was deleted, and new radiators were introduced for the water-cooled engines. When the machine was first tested in April 1916 there was a marked improvement in performance, to an extent that in early May it was flown with 20 Handley Page employees aboard to a height of just over 2135 m (7,000 ft).

Formation of the first 'Handley Page Squadron', as it was then known, began in August 1916 and this unit became operational in France in late October or early November; its first recorded bombing attack was made on the night of 16-17 March 1917 against an enemy-held railway junction. In addition to their use as night bombers on the Western Front, O/100s also equipped the first bomber squadron of the RAF's Independent Force following its establishment on 5 June 1918.

Production deliveries of the **O/400** began in early 1918, this being an improved version of the O/100 which differed primarily by having more-powerful Rolls-Royce Eagle engines, a revised fuel system and radiators, and the introduction of a compressed-air engine starting system. Although production of O/100s totalled only 46 aircraft, substantial numbers of O/400s became operational before the end of the war and, for example, on the night of 14-15 September 1918 a force of 40 O/400s attacked targets in the Saar. It was also at about

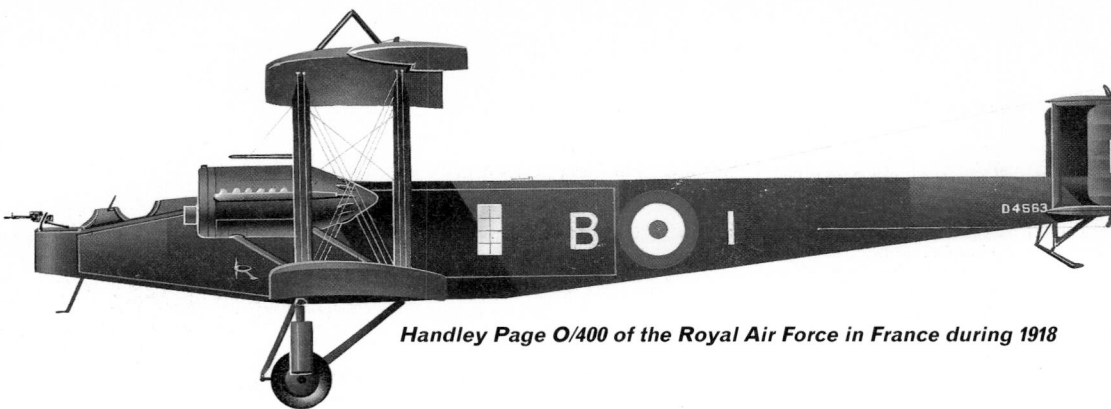

Handley Page O/400 of the Royal Air Force in France during 1918

this same time that these aircraft began to deploy 748-kg (1,650-lb) bombs, the heaviest used by British services during World War I.

More than 400 O/400s were delivered for service with the RAF before the Armistice of November 1918, these equipping Nos 58, 97, 115, 207, 214, 215 and 216 Squadrons. The type remained in service in reduced numbers until late 1919, when it was replaced by the Vickers Vimy. Eight O/400s were used by No. 86 (Communications) Wing, formed at Hendon in December 1918 to provide government and military VIP transport between London and Paris, and No. 214 Squadron used the type for military airmail services.

It had been planned to build the type in quantity in the United States, but only 107 Liberty-engined aircraft were completed by the Standard Aircraft Corporation before the Armistice brought contract cancellation of the balance of 1,500 that were on order. Post-war, a small number of British-built aircraft was supplied to China under the designation **O/7**, and three or four of these aircraft were used in India by Handley Page Indo-Burmese Transport Ltd. In addition, about 10 O/400s were converted from military to a civil configuration and used by Handley Page Transport Ltd in the UK with the designations **O/10** and **O/11**. In 1924, the O/100 became the **H.P.11** and the O/400 the **H.P.12**.

Specification
Handley Page O/400
Type: heavy bomber
Powerplant: two 268-kW (360-hp) Rolls-Royce Eagle VIII 12-cylinder Vee piston engines
Performance: maximum speed 156 km/h (97 mph); service ceiling 2590 m (8,500 ft); endurance 8 hours
Weights: empty 3719 kg (8,200 lb); maximum take-off 6350 kg (14,000 lb)
Dimensions: span 30.48 m (100 ft 0 in); length 19.16 m (62 ft 10¼ in); height 6.71 m (22 ft 0 in); wing area 153.10 m² (1,648.0 sq ft)
Armament: up to five 7.7-mm (0.303-in) Lewis gun on pivoted mounts, plus a maximum bombload of 907 kg (2,000 lb)

Handley Page V/1500 (H.P.15)

Designed and developed to make it possible for the RAF to mount attacks on German targets from bases in the UK, the **Handley Page V/1500** must be regarded as the first practical strategic bomber. Larger in size than the O/100s and O/400s that had preceded it, the V/1500 was powered by four Rolls-Royce engines, these mounted in tandem pairs between the wings, outboard of the fuselage, but was in other respects similar in overall configuration to the earlier bombers. The initial contract was placed with Harland and Wolff of Belfast, but orders eventually totalled more than 200, of which the majority were cancelled at the end of World War I. The prototype, assembled by Handley Page from components manufactured by Harland and Wolff, was flown for the first time during May 1918. This differed primarily from production aircraft by having a single large cooling radiator to serve all four engines, the standard installation becoming one hexagonal radiator forward of each pair of engines. This larger aircraft provided accommodation for a crew of five to seven.

When the Armistice was signed, only three V/1500s were ready for operational use, these standing by with No. 166

The Handley Page V/1500 was too late for World War I and too large for the post-war RAF, and was consequently built in only small numbers.

Squadron at Bircham Newton, Norfolk, where they had been frustrated by bad weather from attacking targets in Germany. The type saw only limited post-war service with the RAF, being replaced by the Vickers Vimy. One was used to record the first through flight from England to India: taking off on 13 December 1918, the aircraft flew via Rome, Malta, Cairo and Baghdad to Karachi, which it reached on 30 December. This aircraft was used in May 1919 to make a bomb attack on Kabul during the problems in Afghanistan. Another V/1500 was shipped to Newfoundland with the object of making a first west-east flight over the North Atlantic, but this project was abandoned when Alcock and Brown achieved the first crossing in a Vickers Vimy. The post-1924 designation was **H.P.15**.

Specification
Type: long-range heavy bomber
Powerplant: four 280-kW (375-hp)

Rolls-Royce Eagle VIII 12-cylinder Vee piston engines
Performance: maximum speed 159 km/h (99 mph) at 1980 m (6,500 ft); service ceiling 3355 m (11,000 ft); range 2092 km (1,300 miles)
Weights: empty 7983 kg (17,600 lb); maximum take-off 13608 kg (30,000 lb)

Dimensions: span 38.40 m (126 ft 0 in); length 19.51 m (64 ft 0 in); height 7.01 m (23 ft 0 in); wing area 278.70 m² (3,000 sq ft)
Armament: single or twin 7.7-mm (0.303-in) Lewis guns in nose, dorsal, ventral and tail positions, plus up to 3402 kg (7,500 lb) of bombs

Handley Page W.8, W.9 and W.10 (H.P.18/26, H.P.27 and H.P.30)

The internal bracing of the fuselage of the O/400 military bomber made it unsuitable for long-term use as a civil transport, leading to redesign and the development of an aircraft identified originally as the **Handley Page W/400 (H.P.16** in the 1924 designation system). This combined a fuselage of different construction, that would allow for up to eight pairs of forward-facing seats with a central gangway, with V/1500-type reduced-span wings,

V/1500 landing gear and power provided by two Rolls-Royce Eagle VIII engines. In this form the aircraft was flown for the first time on 22 August 1919. Testing confirmed that the basic design was sound, but it was decided to incorporate refinements and more-powerful engines in the production version, leading to the W.8 prototype (**H.P.18** in the 1924 system). Powered by two 336-kW (450-hp) Napier Lion IB engines, the W.8 had a further reduction in wing span (from 25.91 to 22.86 m/85 to 75 ft) and some revision of the tail unit, and was flown for the first time on 4 December 1919. It was

flown on 4 May 1920 with a payload of 1674 kg (3,690 lb) to a height of 4276 m (14,030 ft), which then qualified as a British record.

The W.8 was followed by four production **W.8b** aircraft, which had accommodation for 12 passengers in a well-glazed cabin, the pilot and co-pilot being seated in an open cockpit in the nose. Because of difficulty in the supply of Napier Lions these aircraft reverted to the Rolls-Royce Eagle VIII powerplant, the lower-powered engines accounting for certification to carry only 12 passengers. Three of the aircraft were used by Handley

Page Transport and one was supplied to the Belgian airline SABENA; subsequently, three more W.8b transports were licence-built for SABENA by SABCA in Belgium. The **W.8c** was a 1923 version with Eagle IX engines.

Subsequent versions of the same basic design included the **W.8e (H.P.26)** which introduced a third engine mounted in the nose of the fuselage, the three-engine powerplant then comprising one 268-kW (360-hp) Rolls-Royce Eagle IX and two 172-kW (230-hp) Siddeley Pumas. One was built for SABENA by Handley Page and eight more were licence-built for that airline by SABCA. A similarly-powered **W.8f Hamilton** was completed for service with Imperial Airways, this version having also a modified fin, and two more W.8f transports were later built by SABCA for service with SABENA. The **W.8g** was a Hamilton rebuilt in 1929 with two Rolls-Royce F.XIIA engines.

Other variants of this basic design included one **H.P.27 W.9a Hampstead** for Imperial Airways, powered initially by three 287-kW (385-hp) Armstrong Siddeley Jaguar radial engines and later by three 336-kW (450-hp) Bristol Jupiter VI radials, and this had accommodation for 14 passengers. Final civil version was the **H.P.30 W.10**, four of which were

G-EAPJ was the first W.8, flying in December 1919. The aircraft was written off after a crash landing near Poix in northern France in July 1923.

built in 1926 by Handley Page for Imperial Airways, and the last of these was not retired from service until 1933. They reverted to twin-engine powerplant, comprising two 336-kW (450-hp) Napier Lion IIB engines.

Specification
Handley Page W.9a Hampstead
Type: civil transport
Powerplant: three 287-kW (385-hp) Siddeley Jaguar 14-cylinder radial

piston engines
Performance: maximum speed 183 km/h (114 mph); service ceiling 4115 m (13,500 ft); range 644 km (400 miles)

Weights: empty 3794 kg (8,364 lb); maximum take-off 6577 kg (14,500 lb)
Dimensions: span 24.08 m (79 ft 0 in); length 18.39 m (60 ft 4 in); wing area 145.30 m² (1,564.0 sq ft)

Handley Page H.P.24 Hyderabad, H.P.33/36 Hinaidi and H.P.35 Clive

To meet the requirements of Air Ministry Specification 31/22, Handley Page developed from the W.8 airliners a twin-engined heavy night bomber which entered service with the RAF as the **Handley Page Hyderabad**. The prototype, then identified as the **W.8d** (later **H.P.24**), was flown for the first time during October 1923, its powerplant comprising two 336-kW (450-hp) Napier Lion IIB engines. Service trials proved it superior in performance to the competing Vickers Virginia Mk III, and production for the RAF eventually totalled 45 aircraft. The type entered service first with No. 99 Squadron in December 1925, remaining in first-line service until 1930, and then continued in use with the Auxiliary Air Force until the end of 1933.

An improved version was developed from the Hyderabad to meet the requirement of Air Ministry Specification 13/29. Known as the **Hinaidi Mk I**, this **H.P.33** differed primarily by having as powerplant two 328-kW (440-hp) Bristol Jupiter VIII radial engines. The initial prototype was a Hyderabad conversion, but was followed by two additional prototypes built as new by Handley Page, the second of these incorporating a W.10 fuselage for evaluation as a troop transport. Six production Hinaidi Mk Is followed, the last three completed with an

all-metal basic fuselage structure, and leading to the construction of one prototype **H.P.36** and 33 production **Hinaidi Mk II** aircraft with the same all-metal basic structure. In addition to the new-manufacture aircraft, seven RAF Hyderabads were converted to Hinaidi Mk I configuration. Like the Hyderabad before it, the Hinaidi entered service first with No. 99 Squadron, remaining in first-line use until replaced by the Handley Page Heyford from November 1933.

The second Hinaidi Mk I prototype, which was of all-wood construction and incorporated the W.10 fuselage, was later redesignated **Clive Mk I**. This **H.P.35** provided accommodation for 23 troops and was followed into service by two production **Clive Mk II** transports,

which had all-metal basic structure but were otherwise similar. The Clive Mk IIs were based at Lahore in India, serving for a number of years with the RAF Heavy Transport Flight. The Clive Mk I was converted subsequently to W.10 standard to meet an Air Council requirement, becoming redesignated **Clive Mk III**, but when this failed to materialise it was sold to Sir Alan Cobham who used it in his National Aviation Day Displays and for inflight-refuelling experiments.

Specification
Handley Page Hinaidi Mk II
Type: heavy night bomber
Powerplant: two 328-kW (440-hp) Bristol Jupiter VIII 9-cylinder radial piston engines
Performance: maximum speed

Handley Page Clive Mk I prototype as delivered against Air Ministry contract and before re-registration to Sir Alan Cobham as a Clive Mk III (G-ABYX) in 1933.

196 km/h (122 mph) at sea level; cruising speed 121 km/h (75 mph); service ceiling 4420 m (14,500 ft); range 1368 km (850 miles)
Weights: empty 3647 kg (8,040 lb); maximum take-off 6577 kg (14,500 lb)
Dimensions: span 22.86 m (75 ft 0 in); length 18.03 m (59 ft 2 in); height 5.18 m (17 ft 0 in); wing area 136.66 m² (1,471.0 sq ft)
Armament: three 7.7-mm (0.303-in) Lewis guns in nose, dorsal and ventral positions, plus up to 657 lb (1,448 lb) of bombs

Handley Page H.P.42 and H.P.45

In early 1928 Imperial Airways issued specifications of aircraft required to inaugurate new routes to link the British Empire by air, and Handley Page was delighted to receive contracts for four **Handley Page H.P.42E** (Eastern) and four **H.P.42W** (Western) airliners for use on Imperial Airways' long-range routes and European destinations respectively. It was some years before it was discovered that the real Handley Page designation for the H.P.42W was **H.P.45**.

Large unequal-span biplanes of all-metal construction, except for fabric covering of aerofoil surfaces and the rear fuselage, these aircraft had wings braced by massive Warren girder struts, a biplane tail unit incorporating three fins and rudders, substantial tailwheel landing gear, and a powerplant of four Bristol Jupiter radial engines. These comprised four 365-kW (490-hp) Jupiter XIFs for the H.P.42Es and four supercharged Jupiter XFBMs for the H.P.42Ws, mounted two on the upper wing and one on each side of the fuselage on the lower wing. New

ground was broken by the flight crew being accommodated in an enclosed flight deck, high in the fuselage nose. Passenger accommodation was in two cabins, forward and aft of the wing, but varied according to intended use. The H.P.42Es, for use on the Indian and South African routes, each seated six (later 12) forward and 12 aft; the H.P.42Ws for European routes each had seats for 18 forward and 20 aft, but reduced baggage capacity.

Although a number of short hops had been made during taxiing trials, the first true flight was recorded on 17 November 1930 by an H.P.42E, named subsequently *Hannibal*. The first for European routes, named *Heracles*, was delivered in September 1931, and the names of the remainder of this family of large airliners were *Horsa*, *Hanno* and *Hadrian* (H.P.42Es) and *Horatius*, *Hengist* and *Helena* (H.P.42Ws).

Many people still living have nostalgic memories of these fine aircraft; slow they may have been, once described by Anthony Fokker as incorporating built-in

head-winds, but they had an unmistakable aura of grace and safety. The latter characteristic was supreme, for when the H.P.42s were finally withdrawn from service on 1 September 1939 they had recorded almost a decade of service without causing a single fatal accident.

Specification
Handley Page H.P.42W (H.P.45)
Type: civil transport aircraft
Powerplant: four 414-kW (555-hp)

Bristol Jupiter XFBM 9-cylinder supercharged piston engines
Performance: maximum speed 204 km/h (125 mph); cruising speed 153 to 169 km/h (95 to 105 mph); range 805 km (500 miles)
Weights: empty 8047 kg (17,740 lb); maximum take-off 12701 kg (28,000 lb)
Dimensions: span 39.62 m (130 ft

Only four of the true H.P.42 were built, serving on Imperial Airways' long-haul services. Four similar H.P.45s served the European network.

Handley Page H.P.50 Heyford

In retrospect, the **Handley Page H.P.50 Heyford** had the appearance of something that only a mother (or perhaps designer) could love, its heavy-looking biplane structure and spatted main landing gear units suggesting low speed or inefficiency. This impression was heightened by the fact that the fuselage was mounted to the upper wing, strut bracing filling a large gap between the fuselage and lower wing. This layout had a purpose, of course, the lower wing centre-section being of almost double the normal aerofoil thickness to allow bombs to be stowed internally, and brought close to the ground to speed the business of re-arming after a bombing sortie. Other features of the configuration included wings of basic metal structure with fabric covering, a fuselage which was half metal- and half fabric-covered, accommodation for a crew of four, robust tailwheel landing gear, and a braced tailplane carrying twin fins and rudders. Power was provided by two Rolls-Royce Kestrel engines, mounted in nacelles beneath the upper wing, outboard of the fuselage and directly above the main landing gear units. The armament had one more unusual feature to add to the appearance of the Heyford,

Handley Page Heyford Mk IA of No. 10(B) Sqn, RAF, based at Boscombe Down during 1935.

one of its three defensive machine-guns being mounted in a ventral 'dustbin' turret that could be lowered beneath the fuselage, aft of the wing.

The prototype **H.P.38** was flown for the first time during June 1930, and successful service testing resulted in the type being ordered, initially as the **Heyford Mk I**. A total of 124 had been supplied to the RAF by the time that production ended in July 1936, these comprising 15 Heyford Mk I, 23 **Heyford Mk IA**, 16 **Heyford Mk II** and 70 **Heyford Mk III** aircraft; they differed

primarily in installed powerplant. Entering service first with No. 99 Squadron at Upper Heyford, Oxon, they eventually equipped also Nos 7, 9, 10, 38, 78, 97, 102, 148, 149 and 166 Squadrons until the last of them were displaced by Vickers Wellingtons in 1939. However, they continued in use for some time, especially in training units, until finally declared obsolete in July 1941 as the last biplane bombers to serve with the RAF.

Specification
Handley Page Heyford Mk IA

Type: heavy night bomber
Powerplant: two 429-kW (575-hp) Rolls-Royce Kestrel IIIS or IIIS-5 12-cylinder Vee piston engines
Performance: maximum speed 229 km/h (142 mph) at 3960 m (13,000 ft); service ceiling 6400 m (21,000 ft); range with 726-kg (1,600-lb) bombload 1481 km (920 miles)
Weights: empty 4173 kg (9,200 lb); maximum take-off 7666 kg (16,900 lb)
Dimensions: span 22.86 m (75 ft 0 in); length 17.68 m (58 ft 0 in); height 5.33 m (17 ft 6 in); wing area 136.56 m² (1,470.0 sq ft)
Armament: three 7.7-mm (0.303-in) Lewis guns in nose, dorsal and ventral 'dustbin' positions, plus up to 1588 kg (3,500 lb) of bombs

Handley Page H.P.52 Hampden

In September 1932 the Air Ministry issued Specification B.9/32 for a twin-engined bomber for which both Handley Page and Vickers tendered. Each was awarded a contract and the resulting prototypes, the **Handley Page H.P.52** and the Vickers 271, flew within a week of one another, the former on 21 June 1936 and the 271, known later as the Wellington, on 15 June.

Considering they shared the same specification, the two types could hardly have been more different, Handley Page going for an extremely slim fuselage with three manually-operated gun positions, Vickers adopting a portly fuselage with power-operated turrets and manual beam guns.

In spite of an antiquated appearance the **Hampden**, as the bomber was subsequently named, had several remarkable characteristics. With the use of Handley Page leading-edge slats it was able to land at only 117 km/h (73 mph), while its maximum speed of 409 km/h (254 mph) was higher than that of either the Wellington or the Armstrong Whitworth Whitley, and it could carry 1814 kg (4,000 lb) of bombs for 1931 km (1,200 miles), compared with the Wellington's 2041 kg (4,500 lb) bombload over the same distance.

Following an order for 180 Hampdens placed on 15 August 1936, to a new Specification B.30/36, the production prototype flew in 1937. Simultaneously with the first contract another was placed for 100 aircraft with Napier Dagger engines, these being produced under the name **Hereford**. In May 1938 the first production **Hampden Mk I** aircraft from the Handley Page line was flown at Radlett, and on 24 June the type was christened officially by the Viscountess Hampden.

Build up of the RAF was then in full swing and on 6 August 1938 other orders were placed: English Electric at Preston was contracted to build 75, and in Canada a British mission negotiated for 80 more to be constructed by a consortium named Canadian Associated Aircraft Ltd. These sub-contracted Hampdens began to come off the production lines during 1940.

Following trials at the Aircraft and

Armament Experimental Establishment, Martlesham Heath, and at the Central Flying School at Upavon, deliveries to the RAF began in September 1938, with the first batch of Hampdens going to No. 49 Squadron at Scampton, Lincolnshire. No 49 Squadron was part of No. 5 Group, which eventually was equipped completely with Hampdens. When World War II broke out 10 squadrons were using the type: Nos 7 and 76 at Finningley; Nos 44 and 50 at Waddington; Nos 49 and 83 at Scampton; Nos 61 and 144 at Hemswell; with Nos 106 and 185 in reserve.

Early operations in the daylight reconnaissance role were uneventful, but on 29 September the Hampden's shortcomings were highlighted vividly when five out of 11 aircraft in two formations were destroyed by German fighters when within sight of the German coast. Not long after this it was decided to operate in future under cover of darkness, and some leaflet-dropping missions were carried out.

By the winter of 1939-40 the Hampden had found its most useful role as a minelayer. Aircraft from five squadrons sowed mines in German waters on the night of 13-14 April 1940, just after the German invasion of Norway, and by the end of the year No. 5 Group's Hampden squadrons had flown 1,209 mine-laying sorties and delivered 703 mines, losing 21 aircraft in the operations, the loss rate of less than 1.8 per cent being considered acceptable.

The Norwegian campaign, however, once again showed the Hampden's

'Achilles heel': because of its inadequate defensive armament it suffered heavily at the hands of German fighters when used as a day bomber.

On the night of 25-26 August 1940, Hampdens and Armstrong Whitworth Whitleys took part in the RAF's first raid on Berlin, and the Hampden continued to support the night bombing offensive until late 1942 when, on the night of 15-16 September, aircraft of the RCAF's No. 408 Squadron attacked Wilhelmshaven in the Hampden's final sorties with Bomber Command.

From April 1942 Hampdens had begun to transfer to Coastal Command for torpedo-bombing operations, the 157 conversions to this role having the designation **Hampden TB.Mk I**. The first two squadrons in this role were Nos 144 and 455, the latter an RAAF unit, and detachments from both squadrons went to the northern USSR for convoy protection operations. Thirty-two Hampdens from the two squadrons left Sumburgh, in the Shetlands, on 4 September 1942, but nine were lost in the crossing, including two which crashed in Norway and one which crashed on landing in the USSR. The squadrons subsequently handed over their Hampdens to the Soviets before leaving for the UK on 23 October. No. 455 was also the last operational Hampden squadron, based at Sumburgh, and sinking a U-boat on 4 April 1943, before re-equipping with Bristol Beaufighters at the end of the year.

Thus the Hampden passed out of service. In spite of inadequacies it had its good points: among them were pleasant

Handley Page Hampden TB.Mk I of an RAF Operational Training Unit in Scotland during 1942.

handling characteristics and the excellent view for the pilot. On the debit side accommodation was very cramped, individual crew members being able to change places only with extreme difficulty, which posed great problems in the case of injuries. In all, 1,432 Hampdens were built, 502 of them by Handley Page, 770 by English Electric and 160 in Canada.

Variant
Hampden Mk II: designation of two aircraft experimentally re-engined with two 821-kW (1,100-hp) Wright R-1820 Cyclone radials under the company designation **H.P.62**

Specification
Type: four-seat medium bomber
Powerplant: two 746-kW (1,000-hp) Bristol Pegasus XVII 9-cylinder radial piston engines
Performance: maximum speed 409 km/h (254 mph) at 4205 m (13,800 ft); cruising speed 269 km/h (167 mph); service ceiling 5790 m (19,000 ft); range 3034 km (1,885 miles) with 907 kg (2,000 lb) of bombs
Weights: empty 5343 kg (11,780 lb); maximum take-off 8508 kg (18,756 lb)
Dimensions: span 21.08 m (69 ft 2 in); length 16.33 m (53 ft 7 in); height 4.55 m (14 ft 11 in); wing area 62.06 m² (668.0 sq ft)
Armament: two forward-firing 7.7-mm (0.303-in) machine-guns, and twin installations of similar guns in dorsal and ventral positions, plus up to 1814 kg (4,000 lb) of bombs

Handley Page H.P.53 Hereford

Like the Avro Manchester, the **Handley Page H.P.53 Hereford** was basically a good airframe with a bad engine. The **H.P.53** prototype, converted from the prototype of a Swedish patrol version of the Hampden, was flown on 1 July 1937 with two 712-kW (955-hp) Napier Dagger VIII H-type engines, and Short Brothers and Harland was contracted to build an initial batch of 100 aircraft, a number later increased to 152. The first of these production aircraft from the Belfast line flew on 17 May 1939.

Tests at the Aircraft and Armament Experimental Establishment, Martlesham Heath, showed the Hereford's performance to be almost the same as that of the Hampden, but there the similarity ended. The engines were unreliable, overheating on the ground and cooling too rapidly when airborne, while the very high pitched exhaust note proved uncomfortable for the crews.

One or two Herefords served alongside Hampdens in operational squadrons for a very short time, but were soon relegated to a training role, primarily with No. 16 Operational Training Unit (OTU) at Upper Heyford, Oxon, where first deliveries were made on 7 May 1940. Another Hereford unit was No. 14 OTU at Cottesmore, which had begun to operate the type as No. 185 Squadron; it was retitled No. 14 OTU in April 1940. One Hereford was used by the Torpedo Development Unit at Gosport, and at least 19 were subsequently re-engined and converted to Hampden standard.

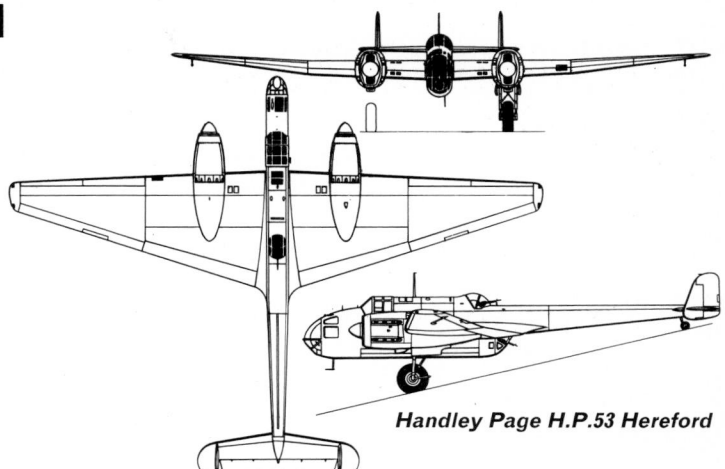

Handley Page H.P.53 Hereford

Specification
Type: four-seat medium bomber
Powerplant: two 746-kW (1,000-hp) Napier Dagger VIII 24-cylinder 'H' water-cooled piston engines
Performance: maximum speed 426 km/h (265 mph) at 4725 m (15,500 ft); cruising speed 277 km/h (172 mph); service ceiling 5790 m (19,000 ft); range 1931 km (1,200 miles) with 18714 kg (4,000 lb) of bombs
Weights: empty 5307 kg (11,700 lb); maximum take-off 8074 kg (17,800 lb)
Dimensions: span 21.08 m (69 ft 2 in); length 16.33 m (53 ft 7 in); height 4.55 m (14 ft 11 in); wing area 62.06 m² (668.0 sq ft)
Armament: two forward-firing 7.7-mm (0.303-in) machine-guns and single installations of similar weapons in dorsal and ventral positions, plus up to 1814 kg (4,000 lb) of bombs

Handley Page H.P.54 Harrow

Specification B.3/34 ushered in the era of the monoplane bomber for the Royal Air Force by asking, as it did, for modern twin-engine designs to replace the Handley Page Heyford and the lumbering Vickers Virginia.

Two companies were awarded contracts to the specification, one being Armstrong Whitworth who submitted the Whitley and the other Handley Page, whose **Handley Page H.P.54** was somewhat less original in concept, featuring a high wing and fixed landing gear. It should be acknowledged, however, that although the two designs were to the same basic specification, the Handley Page H.P.54, subsequently named **Harrow**, was intended for initial use as an interim bomber/trainer and later, when more advanced bombers were in quantity production, as a transport aircraft. One hundred Harrows were ordered to a new specification, B.29/35, before the prototype flew on 10 October 1936. This new aircraft was based largely on the **H.P.51** prototype troop-carrier, which had flown in May of the previous year.

Handley Page had initiated a new method of production for the Harrow, which enabled components to be manufactured by small firms under sub-contract, offering advantages both in construction and repair. The first 39 production aircraft were designated **Harrow Mk I** with 634-kW (850-hp) Bristol Pegasus X engines, which conferred a top speed of 306 km/h (190 mph), but the following 61 aircraft were **Harrow Mk II** aircraft with Pegasus XX engines of 690 kW (925 hp), giving an extra 16 km/h (10 mph). Power-operated gun turrets in the nose, tail and mid-upper positions were an advance over then current service types; although the Harrow Mk Is did not have them when delivered, they were fitted later.

No. 214 Squadron at Feltwell was the first unit to receive Harrows, in January 1937, when the type began to replace Virginias, and by the end of that year four other squadrons had re-equipped with the new bomber: Nos 37 (Feltwell), 75 (Driffield), 115 (Marham) and 215 (Driffield). No. 115 had been disbanded in 1919, and was re-formed in June 1937 to receive trhe Harrow, while No. 37 was also re-formed in April of that year from a nucleus of No. 214 Squadron.

Harrow production terminated with the 100th example in December 1937, but aircraft remained in service until the late stages of World War II.

A novel use of the Harrow was as an aerial minelayer when, in October 1940, No. 420 Flight was formed at Middle Wallop to carry out experiments under the code-name 'Pandora'. These aircraft carried 'Long Aerial Mines' (LAMs), which consisted of many small explosive charges suspended from parachutes with a 610-m (2,000-ft) length of piano wire trailing below. It was intended they should be launched in the path of a bomber stream, and if one of these aircraft flew into the wires it was expected to release one or more of the charges, which then slid down the wires to explode on contacting the enemy bomber. Three months of trial proved the idea to be impractical, although four or five 'kills' were achieved.

No. 271 Squadron formed at Doncaster on 1 May 1940 to operate in the transport role, equipped with Harrows, Bristol Bombays and some impressed civil aircraft, and although most of the other types had been replaced by 1944 a flight of Harrows was retained. These aircraft found employment in support of Allied forces operating in North West Europe, two of them evacuating casualties from the Arnhem operation in September 1944, and they remained in service until the flight re-equipped with Douglas Dakotas in May 1945.

Specification
Type: four/five-seat bomber or 20-seat

During the mid-1930s bomber construction changed from fabric-covered biplanes to all-metal monoplanes, the H.P.54 Harrow being a classic early example. It was swiftly relegated to the transport role.

transport
Powerplant: two 690-kW (925-hp) Bristol Pegasus XX 9-cylinder radial piston engines
Performance: maximum speed 322 km/h (200 mph) at 3050 m (10,000 ft); cruising speed 262 km/h (163 mph) at 4570 m (15,000 ft); service ceiling 6950 m (22,800 ft); range 2012 km (1,250 miles)
Weights: empty 6169 kg (13,600 lb); maximum take-off 10433 kg (23,000 lb)
Dimensions: span 26.95 m (88 ft 5 in); length 25.04 m (82 ft 2 in); height 5.92 m (19 ft 5 in); wing area 101.26 m² (1,090 sq ft)
Armament: four 7.7-mm (0.303-in) machine-guns, one each in nose and dorsal turrets and two in tail turret, plus provision for up to 1361 kg (3,000 lb) of bombs

Handley Page H.P.57 Halifax

Second of the four-engined heavy bombers to enter service with the RAF, in November 1940, the **Handley Page H.P.57 Halifax** was one of the famous triad comprised of the Halifax, Avro Lancaster and Short Stirling which mounted Bomber Command's night-bombing offensive against Germany. In conjunction with the daylight attacks for which the USAAF had accepted responsibility, this round-the-clock battering of German targets reached its peak in 1944, causing almost unbelievable devastation. But although it entered service more than a year ahead of the Lancaster, the Halifax was always somewhat over-shadowed in the bombing role by the achievement of the superb Lancaster. The Halifax, however, scored over the Lancaster in its multi-role capability, for in addition to its deployment as a heavy night-bomber, it was equally at home when employed as an ambulance, freighter, glider tug, personnel transport and maritime reconnaissance aircraft.

The origin of the Halifax stemmed back to an Air Ministry requirement of 1935 for a twin-engined bomber, to which Handley Page submitted a design identified as the **H.P.55**. This proved to be unsuccessful, but about a year later the Air Ministry issued a new specification, P.13/36, which called for a medium/heavy bomber to be powered by a 24-cylinder engine known as the Vulture which Rolls-Royce then had under development. Handley Page's **H.P.56** proposal was selected for prototype construction, but the company had doubts that the Vulture engine would emerge as a reliable production powerplant, and set about the task of redesigning the H.P.56 to take four Rolls-Royce Merlins instead. The overall configuration was not greatly changed, but the H.P.57 design, which was submitted to the Air Ministry for approval, was for a considerably larger and heavier aeroplane.

On 3 September 1937 Handley Page was awarded a contract for the manufacture of two prototypes of the H.P.57, with construction beginning in early 1938. When the first of these was nearing completion, it was realised that the company's airfield at Radlett, Hertfordshire, was too restricted for the first flight of such a large aircraft, and it was decided instead to use the nearest non-operational RAF airfield, which was at Bicester in Oxfordshire. Thus, final assembly was carried out at Bicester and it was from there that the first flight was made on 25 October 1939.

As then flown the H.P.57 was a mid-wing cantilever monoplane of all-metal construction, the wing incorporating automatic leading-edge slats, but these were deleted on production aircraft as the Air Ministry required that the wing leading edges should be armoured and provided with barrage balloon cable cutters. The tail unit comprised a large high-mounted tailplane and rudder assembly with twin endplate fins and rudders, and the fuselage was a deep, slab-sided all-metal structure with considerable internal volume; it was this feature which was to provide the later versions with multi-role capability. Accommodation was provided for a crew of seven, including three gunners to man nose, beam and tail positions. Landing gear was of retractable tailwheel type, and the powerplant comprised four Merlin engines. For its primary role as a bomber, a variety of weapons could be carried in a 6.71-m (22-ft) long bomb bay in the lower fuselage, supplemented by two bomb compartments in the wing centre-section, one on each side of the fuselage.

The second prototype made its first flight on 17 August 1940, followed just under two months later by the first production example, by then designated **Halifax Mk I**, and this was powered by 954-kW (1,280-hp) Rolls-Royce Merlin X engines. Armament of these early production aircraft consisted of two and four 7.7-mm (0.303-in) machine-guns in nose and tail turrets, respectively. Full designation of the first production version was **Halifax B.Mk I Series I**, and these began to equip the RAF's No. 35 Squadron during November 1940. It was this unit that, in early March 1941, was the first to use the Halifax operationally, in an attack on Le Havre, and a few days later the Halifax became the first of the RAF's four-engined bombers to make a night attack against a German target, when bombs were dropped on Hamburg. The Halifax was used for the first time in a daylight attack against Kiel on 30 June 1941, but it did not take long to discover that the aircraft's defensive armament was inadequate for daylight use, and by the end of 1941 the Halifaxes were used only by night in the bombing role. This resulted in the provision of better armament for later versions.

Early deployment of the Halifax had confirmed that this new four-engined bomber had much to offer, but although contracts for large-scale construction very quickly exceeded the productive capacity of the Handley Page factories at Cricklewood and Radlett, pre-war plans had been made for alternative sources of supply. The establishment of four new production lines was made easier by the unit method of construction which had been adopted for the Halifax, and the first of these sub-contract aircraft to fly, on 15 August 1941, came from the English Electric Company, which had earlier been involved in the manufacture of Handley Page's Hampden medium-bomber. The other three lines were those of Fairey at Stockport, Rootes Securities at Speke and the London Aircraft Production Group.

From their first introduction into operational service, Halifax bombers were in continuous use by Bomber Command, equipping at their peak usage no fewer than 34 squadrons in the European theatre, and four more in the Middle East. Two flights were in early use in the Far East, and following VE-Day a number of squadrons operating with the Halifax B.Mk VI flew their aircraft out for co-operation with the Allied forces fighting in the Pacific theatre. The Halifax was involved in the first Pathfinder operations in August 1942; was the first RAF aircraft to be equipped with the highly secret H_2S blind bombing radar equipment; was involved extensively in daylight attacks on German V-1 sites; and between 1941 and 1945 flew 75,532 sorties during which 231252 tonnes (227,610 tons) of bombs were dropped on European targets.

The Halifax was also operated by nine squadrons of the RAF's Coastal Command for anti-submarine, meteorological and shipping patrols, the aircraft being converted from standard bombers and specially equipped, taking the designations **Halifax GR.Mk II, GR.Mk V** or **GR.Mk VI** according to the bomber version from which they were derived. Similarly, RAF Transport Command acquired **Halifax C.Mk III, C.Mk VI** and **C.Mk VII** aircraft as casualty, freight and personnel transports. Little known in wartime was the work of Nos 138 and 161 (Special Duties) Squadrons, which had the task of dropping special agents and/or supplies by parachute into enemy territory.

One other vital use of the Halifax was by the Airborne Forces, for under the designations **Halifax A.Mk III, A.Mk V** and **A.Mk VII**, equivalent bomber versions were converted to serve for the deployment of paratroops or as glider tugs. The Halifax was, in fact, the only aircraft capable of towing the large General Aircraft Hamilcar glider, a capability first proven in February 1942. Soon after that date the Halifax tug made its operational debut when two Airspeed Horsas were hauled across the North Sea to attack the German heavy-water plant in south Norway.

The Halifax Mk I was followed into service by the **Halifax B.Mk II Srs I,** which introduced a Boulton Paul twin-gun dorsal turret, and an increase of 15 per cent in standard fuel capacity; the powerplant, initially Merlin XXs, was changed later to Merlin 22s of equal power output. These changes, plus others introduced after the prototypes had made their first flights, resulted in a steady increase in gross weight. As there had been no surplus engine power from the outset, the result was that operational performance was being eroded by enhanced capability. This can be accepted during wartime conditions provided the rate of attrition remains fairly constant, but in the case of the Halifax Mk II the dorsal turret represented 'the last straw', and steps were taken immediately to improve the performance of these aircraft.

The resulting **Halifax B.Mk II Srs IA** (company designation **H.P.59**) had a performance increase of some 10 per cent in both maximum and cruising speeds, which was achieved by efforts to reduce both weight and drag. The nose turret was deleted, the nose acquiring a streamlined fairing; the dorsal turret was removed. Later production switched to the B.Mk II Series IA, which introduced a Perspex nose fairing and Defiant-type four-gun dorsal turret.

A later change, introduced retrospectively to all aircraft then in service, involved replacement of the triangular fins by larger units of rectangular shape. This came after extensive testing, following some inexplicable losses of fully loaded aircraft had shown that it was possible for the Halifax to enter an inverted and uncontrollable spin. The last major production version was the **Halifax B.Mk III** (company designation **H.P.61**), the first of the bombers to introduce Bristol Hercules VI or XVI radial engines, which offered 1204 kW (1,615 hp) for take-off.

Although withdrawn from Bomber Command immediately after VJ-Day, the Halifax GR.Mk VI continued to serve with Coastal Command after the war, as did the Halifax A.Mk VII with transport squadrons at home and overseas. Post-war versions included the **Halifax C.Mk VIII** (company designation **H.P.70**), which could accommodate a 3629-kg (8,000-lb) capacity detachable pannier beneath the fuselage, and the **Halifax A.Mk IX** (company designation **H.P.71**) troop-carrier and supply-dropper for use by airborne forces. When production of these two versions ended, amounting to some 230 aircraft, a total of 6,178 Halifaxes had been built, and examples remained in RAF service until late 1947.

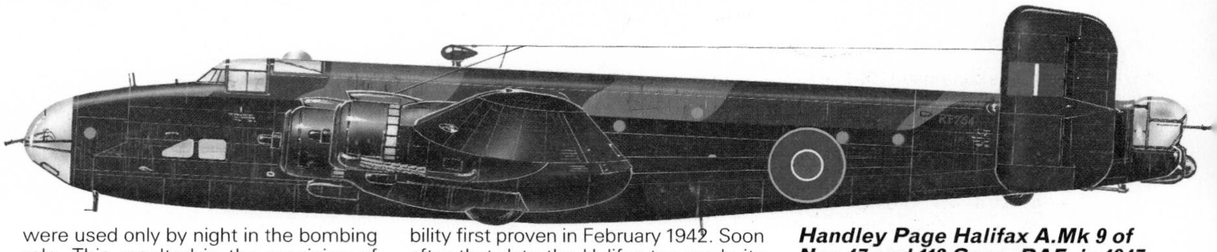

Handley Page Halifax A.Mk 9 of Nos 47 and 113 Sqns, RAF, in 1947.

When Transport Command Halifax C.Mk VIIIs became surplus to military requirements, 10 were converted by Short Bros and Harland as 10-seat **Halton Mk I (H.P.70)** civil transports for service with BOAC. Subsequently about 80 other civil conversions, some to near Halton standard, were carried out by a variety of contractors.

Variants

Halifax B.Mk I Srs II: generally similar to B.Mk I Srs I, but stressed for operation at a higher gross weight
Halifax B.Mk I Srs III: version of B.Mk I Srs I with increased fuel capacity; late production examples introduced Merlin XX engines
Halifax B.Mk II Srs I (Special): redesignation of B.Mk II Srs Is which incorporated in-service modification of as many as possible of the improvements of the B.Mk II Srs IA
Halifax B.Mk V Srs IA: as B.Mk II Srs IA, except for introduction of Dowty landing gear; the company designation was **H.P.63**
Halifax B.Mk V Srs I(Special): as B.Mk II Srs I(Special), except for introduction of Dowty landing gear and hydraulics
Halifax B.Mk VI: generally as B.Mk III, but with 1249-kW (1,675-hp) Bristol Hercules engines which developed 1342 kW (1,800 hp) at 3050 m (10,000 ft); company designation H.P.61
Halifax B.Mk VII: as B.Mk VI, but reverting to use of Bristol Hercules XVI radials as a result of shortage of Hercules 100s; company designation H.P.61

Specification

Handley Page Halifax B.Mk III
Type: seven-seat long-range heavy bomber
Powerplant: four 1204-kW (1,615-hp) Bristol Hercules XVI 14-cylinder radial piston engines
Performance: maximum speed 454 km/h (282 mph) at 4115 m (13,500 ft); long-range cruising speed 346 km/h (215 mph) at 6095 m (20,000 ft); service ceiling 7315 m (24,000 ft); range with maximum bombload 1658 km (1,030 miles)
Weights: empty 17345 kg (38,240 lb); maximum take-off 29484 kg (65,000 lb)
Dimensions: span 31.75 m (104 ft 2 in); length 21.82 m (71 ft 7 in); height 6.32 m (20 ft 9 in); wing area 118.45 m^2 (1,275 sq ft)
Armament: one 7.7-mm (0.303-in) machine-gun on pivoted mount in nose and four similar guns in each of dorsal and tail turrets, plus up to 5897 kg (13,000 lb) of bombs

Handley Page H.P.67 Hastings

Designed to meet the requirements of Air Ministry Specification C.3/4, the **Handley Page H.P.67 Hastings** was a long-range general-purpose transport that served with both the RAF and Royal New Zealand Air Force. A cantilever low-wing monoplane with a tubby circular-section fuselage, its configuration included a conventional tail unit and retractable tailwheel landing gear, and it had power provided by four Bristol Hercules 101 radial engines in the first Hastings prototype (TE580). This aircraft was flown for the first time on 7 May 1946, a second prototype following on 30 December 1946, and the initial **Hastings C.Mk 1** production version began to enter service with the RAF's No. 47 Squadron of Transport Command in October 1948. Production aircraft were operated by a crew of five and could accommodate 30 paratroops with supplies, or 32 stretchers plus 28 sitting casualties, or 50 fully-equipped troops, or freight. The aircraft of No. 47 Squadron, and also of No. 297 Squadron, saw extensive service throughout the Berlin Airlift.

A total of 147 Hastings aircraft was built for the RAF (including the two pro-

covered with dural panels.

The HD.1 was unfortunate in relying on the low-powered 82-kW (110-hp) Le Rhône 9J rotary engine and in being a contemporary of the SPAD S.VII, which performed well, had a more powerful engine and was soon ordered into quantity production for the French Aéronautique Militaire. However, the Belgians, fighting alongside the French but starved of new equipment, and the Italians newly entered into the war, were looking for a single-seat fighter and both decided on the HD.1.

As a result of recommendations of the Italian military mission in Paris, a limited number of HD.1s were exported to Italy, where the Macchi concern began licence manufacture of the type in November 1916. It is believed that the Italian air arm received about 100 French-built aircraft, while Macchi delivered a total of 901, 70 of them after the conclusion of hostilities. Meanwhile the Belgians had taken delivery of 125 French-built HD.1s from August 1917. French sources indicate that total HD.1 construction was 1,145.

After World War I the Swiss Fliegertruppe, impressed by flight tests with an Italian HD.1 which had force-landed in Switzerland, purchased 16 Italian war-surplus machines. Other HD.1s found their way to various Latin American countries.

The HD.1 performed well and showed outstanding manoeuvrability. Dissatisfaction was expressed with the armament and the limited power provided by

the engine. Later HD.1s were powered by the 89-kW (120-hp) Le Rhône 9Jb or 97-kW (130-hp) Le Rhône 9Jby rotaries, but HD.1 no. 301 was tested with a 112-kW (150-hp) Gnome Monosoupape in late 1917, while there were reports of another experimental aircraft fitted with a 127-kW (170-hp) Le Rhône. As for the armament, the Vickers gun was repositioned centrally on the forward decking with beneficial results. Experiments with heavier calibre guns or twin machine-guns were confined to single aircraft and it was found that loss in performance outweighed improvement in firepower.

The Aviation Militaire Belge re-equipped its 1ere Escadrille with the HD.1 in the late summer of 1917. Its pilots were reluctant to adopt an untried design in place of their highly esteemed Nieuport scouts, but Lieutenant Willy Coppens, the first to fly the new machine, was so impressed that his enthusiasm spread to his colleagues. Soon other escadrilles re-equipped with the type, which remained in service until 1926, when the 7ième Escadrille at Nivelles finally gave up its Hanriots.

By August 1917 several HD.1s were flying with the Italian 76ª Squadriglia. By the war's end another 12 squadriglie facing the Austrians had the HD.1 on strength and the type was also operational in Macedonia and Albania. As late as 1925 six first-line Regia Aeronautica squadriglie de caccia still flew the type.

In France a small number of an HD.1 variant with the 97-kW (130-hp) Clerget

flew with the Aviation Maritime. Most of these machines had redesigned vertical tail surfaces. They were operated in defence of Dunkerque naval air station and in late 1918 one was flown from a gun-turret platform on the battleship *Paris*.

Variant
HD.7: this single-seat fighter was evolved from the HD.1 and flew for the first time in 1918; powered by a 224-kW (300-hp) Hispano-Suiza 8Fb engine it attained a maximum speed of 214 km/h (133 mph); its development was abandoned after the end of World War I

Specification
Type: single-seat fighter scout
Powerplant: one 89-kW (120-hp) Le

Extremely nimble and well-harmonised in the controls, the Hanriot HD.1 was not well armed, but found favour with many pilots.

Rhône 9Jb 9-cylinder rotary piston engine
Performance: maximum speed 184 km/h (114 mph); climb to 3000 m (9,845 ft) in 11 minutes; service ceiling 6000 m (19,685 ft); endurance 2 hours 30 minutes
Weights: empty equipped 400 kg (882 lb); maximum take-off 605 kg (1,334 lb)
Dimensions: span 8.70 m (28 ft 6½ in); length 5.85 m (19 ft 2¼ in); height 2.94 m (9 ft 7¾ in); wing area 18.20 m² (195.91 sq ft)
Armament: one fixed forward-firing 7.7-mm (0.303-in) Vickers machine-gun

Hanriot HD.2

Developed as a replacement for the British Sopwith Baby, the first prototype of the **Hanriot HD.2** was a converted HD.1 with two short main floats and a third beneath the tailplane. The second prototype dispensed with the third float, having two elongated main floats, and also had the vertical tail surfaces enlarged to improve stability. The production version closely resembled the second prototype and was intended not only as an interceptor, but also as an escort for the slow French reconnaissance flying-boats, which had suffered heavy losses at the hands of relatively fast and powerful Hansa-Brandenburg two-seat floatplanes.

Beginning in January 1918, limited numbers of HD.2s were issued to Dunkerque and other bases, their armament of twin Vickers guns proving effective against enemy aircraft. The HD.2 attracted the attention of US Navy personnel stationed in France, and as a result 10 were ordered by that service in 1918. Delivered to Langley Field, they were converted as landplanes under the designation **HD.2C.** One of them, US Navy serial A-5624, was used for experimental short take-offs from a platform built over the forward turret of the battleship *Mississippi*, in a similar way to the

HD.1 aircraft flown from the French battleship *Paris*.

Variants
HD.12: fitted with wheeled landing gear and powered by a 127-kW (170-hp) Le Rhône rotary engine, this aircraft closely resembled the HD.2; development of the one aircraft built was abandoned in 1922
HD.27: powered by a 134-kW (180-hp) Hispano-Suiza 8Ac engine this one-off fighter was intended, like the HD.12, as a short-take-off shipborne fighter; it was test-flown from a platform built over the bow of the sloop *Bapaume* in 1923
H.29: two examples built in the ET.1 (single-seat trainer) category; the first workable French ship-board catapult was not available until 1926 and the French admiralty was anxious to find a way of launching aircraft from ships; the H.29 of 1924 used the most bizarre method of all, three metal rails being built out horizontally from the tripod mast of the battleship *Lorraine* for two pulley wheels attached to the wing upper surfaces of the H.29 and a third attached to the top of the fin, the aircraft then being launched along the rails under full power from its 134-kW (180-hp) Hispano-Suiza 8Ab engine; as might be anticipated the H.29 ended in the water, fortunately without loss of

life; the experiments were thereafter discontinued

Specification
Type: single-seat floatplane fighter
Powerplant: one 97-kW (130-hp) Clerget 9B 9-cylinder rotary piston engine
Performance: maximum speed 182 km/h (113 mph); service ceiling 4800 m (15,750 ft); range 300 km (186 miles)
Weights: empty equipped 495 kg (1,092 lb); maximum take-off 700 kg

There was little to distinguish the HD.2 from the preceding HD.1 apart from the larger vertical tail and floats of this useful maritime fighter.

(1,543 lb)
Dimensions: span 8.51 m (27 ft 11 in); length 7.00 m (22 ft 11½ in); height 3.10 m (10 ft 2 in); wing area 18.40 m² (198.06 sq ft)
Armament: twin fixed forward-firing 7.7-mm (0.303-in) Vickers machine-guns

Hanriot HD.3

Emile Dupont designed the **Hanriot HD.3** two-seat fighter which was built during 1917, the prototype flying towards the end of the year. It demonstrated good handling qualities and gave every indication of being an excellent fighting aircraft, with pilot and gunner close together in tandem cockpits. The Salmson 9Za radial was reliable, and every effort had been made to achieve

good aerodynamic characteristics.

The French authorities ordered 300 HD.3s, intending them to serve with both army and navy units for the great Allied offensive planned for 1919. In the event production was curtailed, but 75 HD.3s were delivered to the Aéronautique Militaire, fully equipping Escadrille HD.174 from October 1918, as well as being distributed among various other escadrilles. A small number of HD.3s went to the Aviation Maritime; one was used for flotation tests at RAF station

Isle of Grain in the autumn of 1918; and one was reported to have taken part in landing tests on the French aircraft-carrier *Béarn*. HD.3 no. 2000 was converted with twin floats and enlarged vertical tail surfaces as the prototype for the proposed **HD.4** two-seat fighter seaplane and tested in the summer of 1918, but its development was abandoned after the end of World War I. A CN.2 night-fighter version of the basic design, the **HD.3bis** with enlarged balanced ailerons, and rudder and wings of thicker

section, was tested in late 1918 and then abandoned.

Variants
HD.5: single example of a two-seat fighter powered by a 224-kW (300-hp) Hispano-Suiza 8Fb engine; flown briefly in 1918
HD.6: single example of a much larger machine than either the HD.3 or HD.5, this two-seat fighter had a 395-kW (530-hp) Salmson 18Z radial engine; it spanned 13.60 m (44 ft 7½ in) and

maximum level speed was an impressive 225 km/h (140 mph), but it was not flown until 1919, by which time there was no further need of the type

HD.9: although intended as a two-seater, this was in category AP.2 and intended for specialised photo-reconnaissance duties; powered by the same Salmson engine as the HD.3, the type was ordered as an evaluation batch of 10 machines in 1918, but it is not certain that all were completed

Specification
Hanriot HD.3
Type: two-seat fighter biplane
Powerplant: one 194-kW (260-hp) Salmson 9Za 9-cylinder radial piston engine

Performance: maximum speed 192 km/h (119 mph) at 2000 m (6,600 ft); climb to 3000 m (9,845 ft) in 12 minutes 15 seconds; service ceiling 5700 m (18,700 ft); endurance 2 hours
Weights: empty equipped 760 kg (1,675 lb); maximum take-off 1180 kg (2,601 lb)
Dimensions: span 9.00 m (29 ft 6¼ in); length 6.95 m (22 ft 9½ in); height 3.00 m (9 ft 10 in); wing area 25.50 m² (274.49 sq ft)
Armament: two fixed forward-firing 7.7-mm (0.303-in) Vickers machineguns, and two 7.7-mm (0.303-in) Lewis guns on a ring mounting over the observer's cockpit

The HD.9 was designed as a specialist photo-reconnaissance machine, and was powered by the excellent Salmson radial.

Hansa-Brandenburg C.I

One of the earliest designs of Ernst Heinkel for the Hansa und Brandenburgishe Flugzeug-Werke GmbH, the **Hansa-Brandenburg C.I** was built extensively for its era, being constructed not only by Brandenburg but also under licence by Phönix and Ufag in Austria. A conventional two-bay biplane of wood and fabric construction, it had a slender fuselage with the powerplant mounted in the nose, provided a combined open cockpit for the pilot and observer/gunner, and mounted a braced tail unit at the rear. Landing gear was of tailskid type.

Entering service in 1916, C.Is saw wide-scale use by the Austrian forces and some examples continued in service until the end of World War I. In the long period of time over which they were operational, C.Is were seen with powerplants ranging from 119 to 172 kW (160 to 230 hp) and with a variety of armaments. Basically this comprised a single machine-gun on a pivot mount at the rear of the cockpit, but later versions also had a single forward-firing machine-gun mounted in different positions. Some were used for light bombing missions

Hansa-Brandeburg C.I (Phönix-built with Hiero engine) of the Luftfahrttruppen (Austro-Hungarian air force) in 1918.

and were equipped to carry up to 100 kg (220 lb) of light fragmentation or incendiary bombs on racks beneath the fuselage or lower wing.

Specification
Ufag-built C.I Srs 169
Type: two-seat armed reconnaissance aircraft
Powerplant: one 164-kW (220-hp) Benz Bz.IVa 6-cylinder inline piston engine
Performance: maximum speed

158 km/h (98 mph); service ceiling 6000 m (19,685 ft)
Weights: empty 820 kg (1,808 lb); maximum take-off 1320 kg (2,910 lb)
Dimensions: span 12.25 m (40 ft 2¼ in); length 8.45 m (27 ft 8¾ in); height 3.33 m (10 ft 11 in)
Armament: (standard) one Schwarzlöse 8-mm (0.315-in) machine-gun on pivoted mount over rear of combined cockpit

Hansa-Brandenburg KDW

Designed by Ernst Heinkel, the **Hansa-Brandenburg KD** single-seat scout landplane was built under licence in Austria by the Phönix and Ufag companies under the designation **Hansa-Brandenburg D.I** with the 149-kW (200-hp) Hiero inline. From this design Heinkel developed subsequently the **KDW** single-seat fighter-scout seaplane to fulfil the German requirement for a fighter aircraft to be used in the defence of seaplane bases.

Like its predecessor, the KDW was a conventional biplane of wood and fabric construction. Fabric-covered wings were braced by V-struts in an unusual 'star'

arrangement, the robust fuselage was plywood covered, and the tail unit incorporated a large tailplane but a very small fin and rudder. Single-step wooden floats were mounted on N-type struts, and power for the prototype and early production aircraft consisted of 112-kW (150-hp) Benz Bz.III inline engine. Only about 60 were built, and all suffered from directional instability as a result of the small-area vertical tail surfaces.

Variants
Brandenburg W.11: two examples of this slightly larger development of the KDW were built and powered by the 149-kW (200-hp) Benz Bz.IV engine
Brandenburg W.25: further development of KDW/W.11; slightly greater span, conventional interplane struts and 112-kW (150-hp) Benz Bz.III engine
Phönix D.II: designation of the 1917 strutted landplane fighter evolved by

The W.25 was a development of the KDW which appeared in prototype form only. Noticeable is the very small fin and rudder area.

Phönix around the 149-kW (200-hp) Austro-Daimler inline; ailerons on upper wing only
Phönix D.III: variant with 172-kW (230-hp) Hiero inline and ailerons on upper and lower wings; appeared in 1918

Specification
Hansa-Brandenburg KDW (late production)
Type: single-seat fighter/scout seaplane
Powerplant: one 119-kW (160-hp) Maybach Mb.III 6-cylinder inline piston engine
Performance: maximum speed 170 km/h (106 mph) at sea level; climb to 3000 m (9,845 ft) in 21 minutes; endurance 2 hours 30 minutes
Weights: empty 940 kg (2,072 lb); maximum take-off 1210 kg (2,668 lb)
Dimensions: span 9.25 m (30 ft 4¼ in); length 8.00 m (26 ft 3 in); height 3.35 m (11 ft 0 in); wing area 20.00 m² (215.29 sq ft)
Armament: two fixed forward-firing 7.92-mm (0.31-in) LMG 08/15 machine-guns

Hansa-Brandenburg W.12

Defence fighters for seaplane bases, such as the Hansa-Brandenburg KDW and similar aircraft from other manu-facturers, were found to be of considerable value but had a common weakness: they were highly vulnerable to an attack from the rear. The **Hansa-Brandenburg W.12** represented Ernst Heinkel's solution to the problem, being a two-seat fighter seaplane with an observer/gunner in the rear open cockpit and armed with a machine-gun on a pivoted mounting.

Of wood and fabric construction, the W.12 was a conventional single-bay biplane mounted on twin wooden single-step floats. By comparison with the KDW it was larger in overall dimensions, had a wing structure that was sufficiently robust to be braced by two interplane struts towards each wingtip and dispensed with flying and landing bracing wires. Its most unusual feature was the tail unit, designed specifically to provide a maximum uninterrupted field of fire for the rear gun. Thus there was no fin, the fuselage tapering to a knife-edge to mount a rudder that extended below the fuselage; the tailplane, free from vulnerable bracing struts, was mounted atop the upswept rear fuselage.

The prototype was flown in early 1917 and with service tests proving satisfactory the type was soon deployed at German seaplane bases. The W.12 proved effective against Allied seaplanes and a total of 146 was built. Powerplant of early and late production aircraft was the Mercedes D.III, but just over half of the number that were constructed were powered by the 112-kW (150-hp) Benz Bz.III. One of the W.12s based at Zeebrugge gained distinction for destroying the British non-rigid airship *C.27* during December 1917.

Variants
Brandenburg W.19: scaled-up version of the W.12 to provide a fighting patrol seaplane with extended range; powered by 194-kW (260-hp) Maybach Mb.IV engine and with increased fuel capacity that, by comparison with the W.12, gave the W.19 some 50 per cent increase in endurance
Brandenburg W.27: single example of a developed version of the W.12 which differed primarily by having I-type interplane and centre-section struts and a 145-kW (195-hp) Benz Bz.IIIb engine
Brandenburg W.32: further developed version of the W.12/W.27, and basically a W.27 with a 119-kW (160-hp) Mercedes D.III engine; two or three built

Specification
Brandenburg W.12 (early version)
Type: two-seat fighter seaplane
Powerplant: one 119-kW (160-hp)

Hansa-Brandeburg W.12 (112-kW/150-hp Benz Bz.III) flown from Zeebrugge by Leutnant Becht of the Imperial German German Navy air service in early 1918.

Mercedes D.III 6-cylinder inline piston engine
Performance: maximum speed 160 km/h (99 mph); service ceiling 5000 m (16,405 ft); endurance 3 hours 30 minutes
Weights: empty 997 kg (2,198 lb); maximum take-off 1454 kg (3,206 lb)
Dimensions: span 11.20 m (36 ft 9 in); length 9.60 m (31 ft 6 in); height 3.30 m (10 ft 10 in); wing area 35.30 m² (379.98 sq ft)
Armament: one or two fixed forward-firing 7.92-mm (0.31-in) LMG 08/15 machine-guns, and one 7.92-mm (0.31-in) Parabellum machine-gun on pivoted mount in rear cockpit

Hansa-Brandenburg W.29

Ernst Heinkel's **Hansa-Brandenburg W.29** resulted from the need to endow the fighter seaplanes used by the German naval flying service with improved performance. The resulting design was basically a monoplane version of the W.12, retaining the same construction techniques, and a fuselage, tail unit and floats that were little changed. The braced monoplane wing was set low on the fuselage and was of wooden basic structure with fabric covering; its proportions in respect of span and wing chord were determined by the need to retain approximately the same wing area as provided by the biplane surfaces of the W.12. Powerplant for the majority of the 78 examples that were built consisted of the Benz Bz.III, but a few late-production examples had the more powerful 138-kW (185-hp) Benz Bz.IIIa engine.

Service testing proved to be satisfactory and the W.29s began to enter service in the spring of 1918, their slightly increased speed and improved manoeuvrability making them one of the most successful fighter seaplanes in use by the German naval flying units.

Variant
Brandenburg W.33: a scaled-up, but otherwise basically similar version of the W.29 produced in the summer and autumn of 1918; total of 26 built, all powered by the 183-kW (245-hp) version of the Maybach Mb.IV engine

Specification
Hansa-Brandenburg W.29 (early production)
Type: two-seat fighter seaplane

Hansa-Brandeburg W.33 (licence-built by the state factory IVL near Helsinki) of the No. 1 Detached Maritime Flying Squadron, Suomen Ilmavoimat (Finnish air force), based at Viipuri in the late 1920s. The skis were for winter operations from ice.

Powerplant: one 112-kW (150-hp) Benz Bz.III 6-cylinder inline piston engine
Performance: maximum speed 175 km/h (109 mph); climb to 3000 m (9,845 ft) in 23 minutes; service ceiling 5000 m (16,405 ft); endurance 4 hours
Weights: empty 1000 kg (2,205 lb); maximum take-off 1495 kg (3,296 lb)

Dimensions: span 13.50 m (44 ft 3½ in); length 9.36 m (30 ft 8½ in); height 3.00 m (9 ft 10 in); wing area 32.20 m² (346.61 sq ft)
Armament: one or two fixed forward-firing 7.92-mm (0.31-in) LMG 08/15 machine-guns and one 7.92-mm (0.31-in) Parabellum machine-gun on pivoted mount in rear cockpit

Harlow PJC-1 and PJC-2

Designed by Max B. Harlow, Professor of Aeronautics at the Pasadena Junior College, the two/four-seat **Harlow PJC-1** (the source of these initials obvious) was laid out and built as a class project by students at the college. A cantilever low-wing monoplane of all-metal construction, the PJC-1 possessed a fuselage structure which provided enclosed accommodation for a pilot and up to three passengers. The tail unit was entirely conventional, the landing gear of retractable tailwheel type, and the powerplant comprised a neatly-cowled Warner Super Scarab radial engine.

First flown on 14 September 1937, the PJC-1 progressed satisfactorily through its certification programme until, almost at the point of gaining an Approved Type Certificate, it crashed during a spin test. Investigation showed this had been caused by a control reversal and precautions were taken to ensure there would be no repetition of this fault in the **PJC-2** that followed. This aircraft gained certification on 26 August 1938 and about 10 were built and marketed by the Harlow Aircraft Company that had been established for this purpose. Further production was frustrated by the outbreak of World War II and there was no demand for this aircraft in the post-war scene.

Specification
Harlow PJC-2
Type: two/four-seat cabin monoplane
Powerplant: one 108-kW (145-hp) Warner Super Scarab Series 50 7-cylinder radial piston engine
Performance: maximum speed 257 km/h (160 mph); cruising speed 225 km/h (140 mph); service ceiling 4725 m (15,000 ft); range 788 km (490 miles)
Weights: empty 753 kg (1,661 lb); maximum take-off 1179 kg (2,600 lb)
Dimensions: span 10.92 m (35 ft 10 in); length 7.11 m (23 ft 4 in); height 2.21 m (7 ft 3 in); wing area 17.19 m² (185.0 sq ft)

One of the most advanced lightplanes to appear before World War II, the Harlow PJC-2 was unlucky financially and built in only small numbers.

Harbin SH-5

To replace its venerable Soviet-supplied Beriev flying boats, the PLA Naval Air Force selected the **SH-5** large, four-engined, amphibious flying-boat/bomber developed by the Harbin factory in Manchuria and the national Seaplane Design Institute. The prototype Shuishang Hongzhaji 5 (Maritime Bomber 5), although completed in December 1973, did not fly until 3 April 1976. After a protracted period of development, the type entered service in September 1986, since when four or five further examples have been built and delivered. The unpressurised turboprop-powered amphibian is tasked with carrying out anti-submarine and anti-surface shipping warfare, patrol and surveillance, mine-laying, search and rescue and cargo-carrying. A water-bombing version has also been tested. Normal eight-man SH-5 crew comprises pilot, co-pilot, navigator, flight engineer, radio operator and three systems/equipment operators. Western designation of the aircraft is **PS-5**.

Specification
Type: long-range maritime patrol amphibian
Powerplant: four 2349-kW (3,150-shp) Dongan WJ-5A turboprops
Performance: maximum speed 555 km/h (345 mph); patrol speed 230 km/h (143 mph); service ceiling 7000 m (22,965 ft); range with maximum fuel 4750 km (2,951 miles)

Weights: empty 26500 kg (58,422 lb); maximum take-off 45000 kg (99,208 lb)
Dimensions: span 36 m (118 ft 1 in); length 38.9 m (127 ft 7 in); height 9.79 m (32 ft 1 in); wing area 144 m² (1,550 sq ft)
Armament: two-gun dorsal turret plus four underwing hardpoints able to carry anti-shipping missiles or torpedoes (three on each pylon); an

The SH-5 was developed as a long-range maritime patroller for both surface search and anti-submarine operations. A water bomber version is under test.

internal weapons bay in the rear hull can carry a 6000-kg (13,228-lb) maximum load of depth charges, mines, bombs, sonobuoys and SAR equipment

Harbin Y-12

The Y-12 is a light feederliner in the class of the DHC-6 Twin Otter.

Derived from the 1975 nine-seat piston-engined Y-11 light transport, the **Y-12** or **Yun-12-I** (*Yunshuji* means transport aircraft) featured 272-kW (500-shp) PT6A-11 turboprop engines, a stretched fuselage and wing of increased span, and accommodated two crew and up to 17 passengers. The prototype **Y-12-I** flew on 14 July 1982 and was followed by around 30 production aircraft. The improved **Y-12-II** fitted with 507-kW (680-shp) PT6A-27 engines assembled in China, flew first on 16 August 1984, and received domestic certification in December 1985 and UK CAA approval on 20 June 1990. Around 50 had been ordered by the end of 1990 and about 30 delivered to China Southwest Airlines, China Feilong Airlines and Flying Dragon Air Services. Others have been exported

to Lao Aviation and the Sri Lankan air force. Planned developments include a further fuselage stretch, a pressurised version and re-engining with the 507-kW (680-shp) Chinese-designed WJ9 turboprop currently under development.

Specification
Harbin Y-12-II
Type: short-range turboprop feederliner
Powerplant: two 507-kW (680-shp) thrust Pratt & Whitney Canada PT6A-27 turboprops
Performance: cruising speed 250 km/h (155 mph); service ceiling 7000 m (22,960 ft); range with maximum payload 1340 km (832 miles)
Weights: empty 3000 kg (6,614 lb);

maximum take-off 5300 kg (11,684 lb)
Dimensions: span 17.2 m (56 ft 6 in); length 14.8 m (48 ft 9 in); height 5.5 m

(18 ft 3 in); wing area 34.2 m² (368.8 sq ft)

Hawker Audax

To meet Air Ministry Specification 7/31, which called for an army co-operation aircraft, Hawker was to propose yet another derivative of its Hart. Required to replace the Armstrong Whitworth Atlas, which had been the RAF's first army co-operation type when it entered service in October 1927, an early series-built Hart was used to evaluate the potential of this aircraft to meet the 7/31 requirement. It was, of course, eminently suitable for the task, and the first production **Hawker Audax**, as this new type was named, made its maiden flight on 29 December 1931.

The army co-operation Audax, which first entered service with No. 4 Squadron in February 1932, differed little from the Hart except in equipment. The most valuable distinguishing feature for the amateur spotter was the long exhaust pipe which extended to mid-fuselage just aft of the rear cockpit. This had been introduced to ensure that glare from the

standard ejector exhausts, as fitted to the Hart, would not impair the pilot's view when flying close to the ground. The other external feature to serve as a recognition aid was the long message pick-up hook beneath the fuselage, which pivoted from the landing gear spreader bar.

Production for the RAF totalled 624 by the time construction ended in 1937, but examples had also been built for Iraq, Persia and the Straits Settlements. Because of the numbers involved, many of the RAF aircraft had been sub-contracted, with examples being manufactured by Bristol (141), Gloster (25), A. V. Roe (244), and Westland (43), the balance coming from Hawker's production.

The Audax was used to equip home-based co-operation squadrons from the time it entered service in 1932 until being replaced in 1937-38 and relegated to advanced training, communications and glider tug duties. In these latter roles the Audax remained in home service well into the war years, and in the East African campaign No. 237 (Rhodesia)

K3055 was the first aircraft of the second production batch (91 aircraft) of Audax Mk I army co-operation aircraft, and first flew on 19 May 1933.

Squadron was operating during 1940 against the Italians in Eritrea and Somaliland. Others, based at Habbaniyah, were in action during the Iraqi revolt in May 1941.

Specification
Type: two-seat army co-operation aircraft
Powerplant: one 395-kW (530-hp) Rolls-Royce Kestrel IB 12-cylinder Vee

piston engine
Performance: maximum speed 274 km/h (170 mph) at 730 m (2,400 ft); service ceiling 6555 m (21,500 ft); endurance 3 hours 30 minutes

Weights: empty 1333 kg (2,938 lb); maximum take-off 1989 kg (4,386 lb)
Dimensions: span 11.35 m (37 ft 3 in); length 9.02 m (29 ft 7 in); height 3.17 m (10 ft 5 in); wing area 32.33 m²

(348.0 sq ft)
Armament: one 7.7-mm (0.303-in) forward-firing machine-gun and one 7.7-mm (0.303-in) Lewis gun on pivoted mount in rear cockpit, plus four 9-kg (20-

lb) or two 51-kg (112-lb) supply containers on underwing racks

Hawker Cygnet

In response to the Air Ministry's announcement of a Light Aeroplane Competition, to be held at Lympne, Kent, in September 1924, the H. G. Hawker Engineering Company designed and built two examples of a remarkable lightweight aircraft which it named the **Hawker Cygnet**. Of wood and fabric construction, the Cygnets were of unequal-span biplane configuration (the upper wing incorporating full span drooping ailerons), with a conventional tail unit and tailskid landing gear. One (G-EBMB) was powered by a 25-kW (34-hp) British Anzani engine, the other (G-

EBJH) by a 25-kW (34-hp) ABC Scorpion. Although only gaining places in the 1924 competition, when re-engined with Bristol Cherub III engines G-EBMB won the 1926 competition, taking the *Daily Mail* £3,000 prize, and G-EBJH was first in the Lympne Open Handicap Race.

Specification
Type: two-seat ultralight sporting aircraft
Powerplant: one 25-kW (34-hp) Bristol Cherub III flat-twin piston engine
Performance: maximum speed 132 km/h (82 mph) at sea level; absolute ceiling 2715 m (8,900 ft)
Weights: empty 169 kg (373 lb);

maximum take-off 431 kg (950 lb)
Dimensions: span 8.53 m (28 ft 0 in); length 6.22 m (20 ft 5 in); height 1.78 m (5 ft 10 in); wing area 15.33 m² (165.0 sq ft)

The first Cygnet is seen in 1924, flying on the power of a Bristol Cherub III engine. In this guise it won the 1926 Light Aeroplane competition.

Hawker Fury I/II

Design of the **Hawker Fury** biplane fighter reached back to 1927, when Air Ministry Specification F.20/27 was raised to detail the requirement for an interceptor fighter. Although Hawker's **F.20/27** prototype was powered as required by the specification with a radial engine, a 336-kW (450-hp) Bristol Jupiter, this prototype failed to gain a production contract. However, the experience with this aircraft proved valuable when entry into service of the Hart day bomber accelerated design and development of a new private-venture prototype which Hawker called the **Hornet**. In this aircraft Sydney Camm had decided to forget about the Air Ministry's interest in radial-engined powerplant and had installed instead a Rolls-Royce F.XIS. This aircraft was, in effect, the Fury prototype, duly acquired by the Air Ministry but redesignated **Fury** to conform to then-current RAF nomenclature. An attractive aircraft, with very clean lines, the Fury was the RAF's first fighter able to exceed a speed of 322 km/h (200 mph) when it entered service with No. 43 (Fighter) Squadron in May 1931. It was an unequal-span single-bay biplane with a basic structure of metal, fabric covered except for metal panels on the forward fuselage, and with tailskid landing gear and power provided by a 391-kW (525-hp) Rolls-Royce Kestrel IIS.

Like the Hart, however, the Fury appeared with a variety of powerplants, either for test purposes or specified by foreign purchasers, and these engines included the Armstrong Siddeley Panther, Bristol Mercury, Hispano-Suiza 12NB and 12X, Lorraine Petrel, and Pratt & Whitney S21B-G Hornet. Initial production of **Fury Mk I** fighters totalled about 160 aircraft, and these were followed by

Hawker Fury Mk I of No. 1(F) Squadron, based at RAF Tangmere in 1936-37.

two different but related private-venture aircraft, the **Intermediate Fury** and **High-Speed Fury**. They represented development aircraft to meet the requirements of Air Ministry Specifications F.7/30 and F.14/32 respectively, and led to conversion of an early Fury Mk I by installation of a more powerful Kestrel VI engine and the introduction of wheel spats. This was ordered into production as the **Fury Mk II** to Specification 6/35, the first of these aircraft entering service with No. 25 (Fighter) Squadron in early 1937. Although the Fury Mk II was able to demonstrate an increase of some 10 per cent in maximum speed by comparison with the Fury Mk I, it had not been achieved without cost, for in spite of the increased fuel capacity there was a reduction of 10 per cent in range.

Both versions appeared attractive to other nations, and Furies were built for

the air arms of Norway, Persia (Iran), Portugal, South Africa, Spain and Yugoslavia.

The Fury Mk IIs which were manufactured for the RAF, totalling 98, were used to equip six squadrons pending entry into service of the Hawker Hurricane which, in 1937, was under development. Furies remained in first-line service until replaced by Hurricanes in 1939, and after the outbreak of war some Fury Mk IIs continued to operate in a training role. Three squadrons of these fighters were used by the South African Air Force in East Africa during the early stages of World War II, and Yugoslav Furies were in combat during the German invasion of that country in April 1941.

Specification
Hawker Fury Mk II
Type: single-seat biplane fighter
Powerplant: one 477-kW (640-hp) Rolls-Royce Kestrel VI 12-cylinder Vee piston engine
Performance: maximum speed 359 km/h (223 mph) at 5030 m (16,500 ft); service ceiling 8990 m

(29,500 ft); range 435 km (270 miles)
Weights: empty 1240 kg (2,734 lb); maximum take-off 1637 kg (3,609 lb)
Dimensions: span 9.14 m (30 ft 0 in); length 8.15 m (26 ft 9 in); height 3.10 m (10 ft 2 in); wing area 23.41 m² (252.0 sq ft)
Armament: two forward-firing 7.7-mm (0.303-in) machine-guns

K2048 was a Hawker Fury Mk I, and the mount of the commander of No.1(F) Squadron. The Fury Mk I represented the RAF's front-line fighter force in the mid-1930s, serving with Nos 1 and 43 Squadrons at Tangmere, and with No. 25 at Hawkinge.

Hawker Fury/Sea Fury

Intended originally as a smaller, lightweight version of the Hawker Tempest, to meet the requirements of Specification F.6/42, the **Hawker Fury** fighter was developed to the joint Air Ministry/ Admiralty requirements of Specifications F.2/43 and N.7/43. Hawker was to design and develop the land-based version and Boulton Paul to undertake conversion of the naval aircraft.

By December 1943, six prototypes

had been ordered: one was to be powered by a Bristol Centaurus XII, two with the Centaurus XXII, and two with the Rolls-Royce Griffon; the sixth was to be a test airframe. The first to fly was the Centaurus XII-powered aircraft, which made its maiden flight on 1 September 1944, followed by the Griffon 85-engined second prototype on 27 November; the latter was later re-engined with a Napier Sabre VII.

Although production contracts had been placed in April 1944 for 200 aircraft designated **Hawker Fury** for the Royal Air Force, and a similar number of **Sea Fury** fighters for the Fleet Air Arm, including 100 to be built by Boulton Paul, the RAF order was cancelled at the war's end. Development of the Sea Fury continued, however, the first prototype having flown on 21 February 1945, powered by a Centaurus XII. This aircraft was fitted with an arrester hook, but retained non-folding wings; the first fully-navalised aircraft was the Centaurus XV-

powered second prototype, which first flew on 12 October 1947.

The Boulton Paul contract had been cancelled in January 1945 and, of the 100 Sea Furies that remained on order, the first 50 were completed as **Sea Fury Mk X** fighters. The first of these was flown on 7 September 1946, and the third undertook trials aboard HMS *Victorious* during the winter of 1946-47, as a prelude to the type's entry into service.

In May 1948 No. 802 Squadron was the first to receive the **Sea Fury FB.Mk 11**, of which 615 were built to British

503

contracts, including 31 and 35 aircraft for the Royal Australian and Royal Canadian Navies respectively. Sea Furies operated very successfully in the ground-attack role during the early stages of the Korean conflict in 1950, flying from HMS *Glory*, HMS *Ocean*, HMAS *Sydney*, and HMS *Theseus*. The Royal Navy also received 60 two-seat **Sea Fury T.Mk 20** trainers, 10 of which were converted later as target tugs to a German order.

Other overseas customers included the Netherlands with 22 **Sea Fury F.Mk 50** and **FB.Mk 50** aircraft; Pakistan with 93 **Sea Fury Mk.60** and five **T.Mk 61** aircraft; Egypt with 12 single-seaters; Burma with 18 ex-RN FB.Mk 11s (three adapted as target tugs) and three T.Mk 20s; Cuba with 15 FB.Mk 11s and two T.Mk 20s; and Iraq with 55 land-plane Furies and five Fury trainers with

With an 18-cylinder Centaurus and a top speed of well over 644 km/h (400 mph), the Sea Fury represented the pinnacle of piston-engine fighter design.

tandem canopies.

Specification
Hawker Sea Fury FB.Mk 11
Type: single-seat carrier-based fighter-bomber
Powerplant: one 1849-kW (2,480-hp) Bristol Centaurus 18 18-cylinder radial piston engine
Performance: maximum speed 700 km/h (435 mph) at 7470 m (24,500 ft); service ceiling 10455 m (34,300 ft); range 1094 km (680 miles) with internal fuel
Weights: empty 4191 kg (9,240 lb);

maximum take-off 5670 kg (12,500 lb)
Dimensions: span 11.7 m (38 ft 4¾ in); length 10.57 m (34 ft 8 in); height 4.84 m (15 ft 10½ in); wing area

26.01 m² (280 sq ft)
Armament: four 20-mm cannon in wings, plus underwing racks for eight 27-kg (60-lb) rockets or two bombs

---

Hawker Hardy

Basically an adaptation of the Hart/Audax design, the **Hawker Hardy** was developed in response to Air Ministry Specification G.23/33, which called for an aircraft suitable as a replacement for the Westland Wapiti that was serving with the RAF's No. 30 Squadron on air policing duties in Iraq. The Hardy was fundamentally a Hart with special equipment, the prototype being a standard production Hart day-bomber which was provided with a tropical radiator to enhance engine cooling and, like the Audax, had the extended engine exhaust system and message pick-up hook. To cater for a forced landing in the desert, a tropical survival kit and water containers were added.

First flown in this form on 7 September 1934, the Hardy began RAF trials very shortly after this date. The Hardy then entered service with No. 303 Squadron at Mosul, Iraq, during 1935, and Gloster Aircraft was to build all 47

production machines under sub-contract.

In 1938, when No. 30 Squadron was re-equipped with Bristol Blenheims, the Hardys were transferred to No. 6 Squadron, where they were quickly involved in operations, providing close support for the British 16th Infantry Brigade during the trouble in Palestine. Finally, all surviving Hardys in the Middle East were handed over to No. 237 (Rhodesian) Squadron, where they operated alongside the squadron's Hawker Audax aircraft. With this squadron they saw action at the beginning of World War II, deployed against the Italians in East Africa during 1940, and at least one aircraft is known to have survived as late as June 1941, being used for communications duties.

Specification
Type: two-seat general-purpose biplane
Powerplant: one 395-kW (530-hp) Rolls-Royce Kestrel IB or 436-kW (585-hp) Kestrel X 12-cylinder Vee piston

engine
Performance: maximum speed 259 km/h (161 mph) at sea level; service ceiling 5180 m (17,000 ft); endurance 3 hours
Weights: empty 1450 kg (3,196 lb); maximum take-off 2270 kg (5,005 lb)
Dimensions: span 11.35 m (37 ft 3 in); length 9.02 m (29 ft 7 in); height 3.23 m (10 ft 7 in); wing area 32.33 m²

(348 sq ft)
Armament: one 7.7-mm (0.303-in) forward-firing machine-gun and one 7.7-mm (0.303-in) Lewis gun on pivoted mount in rear cockpit, plus underwing racks and attachments for water containers, flares, or bombs

The Hardy was used overseas on general policing duties.

Hawker Hart/Demon

The **Hawker Hart** day-bomber, which first entered service with No. 33 Squadron of the RAF at Eastchurch in January 1930, was originated to meet Air Ministry Specification 12/26. This called for design and development of a day-bomber which was required to have an unprecedented maximum speed of 257 km/h (160 mph), a performance requirement that was comfortably exceeded thanks to a combination of excellent airframe design and the adoption of the Rolls-Royce F.XIB V-12 engine for the prototype, which was first flown in June 1928.

The Hart's introduction into service created immense problems for the Air Ministry, for not only was it very considerably faster than contemporary bombers, in some cases by as much as 124 km/h (80 mph), but could also show a 'clean pair of heels' to any fighters then in service. Among the many uses for which Harts were adopted, one must mention their temporary deployment as fighters with No. 23 (Fighter) Squadron. In the annual air exercises of 1931, Hart bombers were able to make their attacks on selected targets with virtually complete immunity from interception by the defending fighters. Only when No. 23 Squadron was brought into action was it possible to prevent them from gaining their target.

Such a state of affairs was, of course, to the ultimate benefit of the country and

Hawker Demon Mk II of the Royal Australian Air Force.

the RAF, for strenuous efforts were made to develop new fighter aircraft of much improved performance. The Hart was also included in this exercise, for following No. 23 (F) Squadron's experience with the **Hart Two-Seat Fighter**, attempts were made to improve and develop a specialised fighter version. This materialised as the **Hawker Demon**, which differed from the Hart primarily by having a different version of the Kestrel engine, a revised rear cockpit to improve the field of fire for the rear gun, installation of a radio transmitter and receiver and, in some late production aircraft, replacement of the tailskid by a tailwheel. In addition to 234 Demons built for the RAF, Hawker built 54 for the RAAF. Ten dual-control trainers, with provisions for target towing, were also built for the RAAF which designated them **Demon Mk II**.

In late 1934 a Demon was flown with the prototype of a Frazer-Nash power-operated gun turret in the rear position, this incorporating a 'lobster-back' shield to provide the gunner with some protection from the slipstream. A number were built with this as standard equipment, and many in-service aircraft were modi-

fied retrospectively, the type becoming known as the **Turret Demon**.

The Hart, however, was a highly successful venture, for more Harts or aircraft of Hart origin were built in the UK during the inter-war period than any other basic design. In addition to the standard Hart day-bomber they included six Hart Two-Seat Fighters for No. 23 (F) Squadron, 507 dual-control **Hart Trainer** machines, a number of aircraft without bomb gear and armament as **Hart Communications** aircraft for No. 24 Squadron, and tropicalised versions known as **Hart (India)** and **Hart (Special)**. When, in 1936, Harts began to be replaced by Hawker Hinds in operational units, the Air Ministry allowed a considerable number of Harts to be made available to the South African Air

Force, deliveries beginning towards the end of 1936. Other Harts to be operated abroad included eight for Estonia, with interchangeable wheel and float landing gear, which were delivered in late 1932. Sweden also found the Hart attractive and after four had been built and delivered in 1934, an additional 42 were built under licence by the State Aircraft Factory at Tröllhattan. Produced during 1935-36, they were powered by licence-built versions of the Bristol Pegasus radial engine.

This untypical engine installation reminds one that Harts saw extensive use as engine testbeds and, in addition to the standard Kestrel IB or XDR, they were flown with the Rolls-Royce Kestrel IS, IIB, IIS, IIIMS, V, VIS, XFP, XVI, P.V.2 and Merlin C and E; Armstrong Siddeley Panther; Bristol Jupiter, Pegasus, Perseus and Mercury; Hispano-Suiza 12Xbrs; Lorraine Petrèl Hfrs; and Napier Dagger.

Total production, including those built under licence in Sweden, exceeded 1,000, which was an impressive figure for an aircraft of the 1930s. Hart bombers had been withdrawn from front-line service in the UK in 1938, but at the outbreak of World War II continued to be operational in the Middle East until replaced gradually by more modern types, such as the Bristol Blenheim. In service with the South African Air Force, Harts were used in a communications role until 1943.

Specification
Hawker Hart (RAF)
Type: two-seat day-bomber
Powerplant: one 391-kW (525-hp) Rolls-Royce Kestrel IB or 380-kW (510-hp) Kestrel XDR 12-cylinder Vee piston engine
Performance: maximum speed 296 km/h (184 mph) at 1525 m (5,000 ft); service ceiling 6510 m (21,350 ft); range 756 km (470 miles)
Weights: empty 1148 kg (2,530 lb); maximum take-off 2066 kg (4,554 lb)
Dimensions: span 11.35 m (37 ft 3 in); length 8.94 m (29 ft 4 in); height 3.17 m (10 ft 5 in); wing area 32.33 m² (348 sq ft)
Armament: one 7.7-mm (0.303-in) forward-firing machine-gun and one 7.7-mm (0.303-in) Lewis gun on ring mounting in aft cockpit, plus up to 236 kg (520 lb) of bombs

Hawker Hartbees

Developed from the Hart and Audax series specially for service with the South African Air Force, the **Hawker Hartbees** (sometimes recorded as Hartbee or Hartebeeste) was built only in token numbers in the UK, to serve initially as construction examples to assist with licence-production in South Africa. The negotiations for a licence to build a version of the Audax had started in 1934, to meet an SAAF requirement for a ground support aircraft, and the Audax was generally agreed to most nearly satisfy this air force's need without an excess of modifications.

Four examples were built by Hawker, the first two being essentially the same as the RAF's Audax, except that the extended exhaust system was deleted and the Kestrel IB engine was replaced by the 453-kW (608-hp) Kestrel VFP. These first two aircraft were flown initially in the UK on 28 June 1935, before being despatched to South Africa in October 1935. The third and fourth examples were basically the same, differing only by having armour protection for the crew.

South African production was carried out at the Roberts Heights factory in Pretoria, the first examples being completed in the spring of 1937, and passing their acceptance tests successfully in July of that same year. Construction of production aircraft followed, 65 being built and supplied to two squadrons of the SAAF. A total of 53 of these remained in service at the outbreak of World War II and these were deployed in Kenya together with a number of ex-RAF Harts.

The Hartbees saw considerable action against the Italians during operations on the Kenya-Ethiopia border in mid-1940, their most significant operation being an attack in strength carried out on 11 June 1940. Not long after this the Hartbees were withdrawn from front-line use, then relegated to training and communication roles, some remaining in service until 1946.

Specification
Type: two-seat general-purpose/ground-support aircraft
Powerplant: one 453-kW (608-hp) Rolls-Royce Kestrel VFP 12-cylinder Vee piston engine
Performance: maximum speed 283 km/h (176 mph) at 1830 m (6,000 ft); service ceiling 6705 m (22,000 ft); endurance 3 hours 10 minutes
Weights: empty 1429 kg (3,150 lb); maximum take-off 2171 kg (4,787 lb)
Dimensions: span 11.35 m (37 ft 3 in); length 9.02 m (29 ft 7 in); height

Developed from the Audax, the Hartbees was produced under licence in South Africa after the supply of pattern aircraft.

3.17 m (10 ft 5 in); wing area 32.33 m² (348 sq ft)
Armament: one 7.7-mm (0.303-in) forward-firing machine-gun and one 7.7-mm (0.303-in) Lewis gun on pivoted mount in rear cockpit, plus underwing racks to carry light bombs, smoke-laying equipment, supply canisters or water containers

Hawker Hector

Last of the many variants of the Hart to remain in first-line service with the RAF, the **Hawker Hector** was designed as a replacement for the Audax. The requirement was for an Army co-operation aircraft of improved performance, and it was decided to use the Napier Dagger engine which had first been fitted experimentally to a Hart bomber in 1933. While basically a Hart, the Hector differed considerably in appearance. This was due, of course, primarily to the engine installation which, because of its increased height, changed completely the characteristic pointed nose of the Hart family. In addition, the alteration caused to the aircraft's centre of gravity by installation of this heavier engine was corrected by using an upper wing with a straight leading edge, instead of the swept-back upper wing of the earlier members of the family. In all other respects, equipment and layout were generally similar to that of the Audax.

The first of the production Hectors made its initial flight on 14 February 1936, and orders for this aircraft totalled 178 by May 1936, when a decision was made that these should be built under sub-contract by Westland at Yeovil, Somerset. The first Westland-built production aircraft was delivered in February 1937, and all had been constructed and handed over to the RAF before the end of that year.

Hectors first entered service with No. 4 Squadron in February 1937, equipping eventually seven RAF squadrons on home bases. When, in 1938-39, these units began to receive the new Westland Lysander as a replacement aircraft, the Hectors were used to equip Auxiliary Air Force Squadrons Nos 601, 612, 613, 614 and 615, and many remained in service with these units at the outbreak of World War II.

Hectors were used operationally by No. 613 Squadron, which despatched six of its aircraft to attack German troops near Calais, but the loss of two aircraft on this operation highlighted the fact that the Hector could no longer be deployed in first-line service. Relegated to the role of glider tug, the Hector was to continue in use for another two years.

Specification
Type: two-seat army co-operation aircraft
Powerplant: one 600-kW (805-hp) Napier Dagger III MS 'H' piston engine
Performance: maximum speed 301 km/h (187 mph) at 1980 m (6,500 ft); service ceiling 7315 m (24,000 ft); endurance 2 hours 25 minutes
Weights: empty 1537 kg (3,389 lb); maximum take-off 2227 kg (4,910 lb)
Dimensions: span 11.26 m (36 ft 11½ in); length 9.09 m (29 ft 9¾ in); height 3.17 m (10 ft 5 in); wing area 32.14 m² (346 sq ft)

The four-bank Napier Dagger gave the Hector a completely different look from the other Hawker biplanes. It did not differ in other respects much from the Audax which it replaced.

Armament: one 7.7-mm (0.303-in) forward-firing machine-gun and one 7.7-mm (0.303-in) Lewis gun in rear cockpit, plus underwing racks for supply containers or two 51-kg (112-lb) bombs

Hawker Henley

Air Ministry Specification P.4/34, issued in February 1934, detailed the requirement for a light-bomber that could be deployed also in a close-support role. High performance was required, with a maximum speed of around 483 km/h (300 mph).

With high performance paramount, and with only a modest requirement in respect of bombload, it seemed logical to the Hawker design team to evolve an aircraft somewhat similar in size to the Hurricane. This latter aeroplane was then in an advanced design stage, but, if at least some assemblies could be common to both, there would not only be some economies, but also certain production advantages. Thus the **Hawker Henley,** as this aircraft was to become known, had its tailplane and outer wing panels built from identical jigs to those of the Hurricane; the only difference was that the Henley wing did not incorporate four machine-guns in each outer panel. Despite the difference in size between Hurricane and Henley, the Merlin engine selected for the fighter was adopted also for the light-bomber. Configuration was that of a cantilever mid-wing monoplane, the space under the wing being used for a 454-kg (1,000-lb) bomb bay. Another major difference was in accommodation, the Henley providing for an observer/gunner.

Construction of a prototype began in mid-1935, but, with priority going to the Hurricane, it was not until 10 March 1937 that the Henley prototype was flown for the first time, then powered by a Merlin 'F' engine. This aircraft was provided subsequently with light-alloy, stressed-

Although designed as a light bomber, the Henley went into service as a target tug. This is the second prototype.

skin wings and a Merlin I engine, and tests that followed confirmed the excellence of its overall performance. It was at this point that the Air Ministry decided it no longer had a requirement for a light-bomber; instead, the Henley was ordered into production as a target tug, with 200 to be built under sub-contract by Gloster Aircraft. A second prototype was modified for this revised role and was flown on 26 May 1938; it differed primarily by having a propeller-driven winch to haul in the drogue cable after air-to-air firing sorties.

Designated **Henley Mk III**, produc-tion aircraft entered service with Nos 1, 5 and 10 Bombing and Gunnery Schools, as well as with the Air Gunnery Schools at Barrow, Millom and Squires Gate. It was then discovered that unless towing operations were restricted to an unreal-istically low speed, the rate of engine failure was unacceptably high. The Hen-leys were withdrawn from this role and deployed, instead, in an even less suit-able task, that of towing larger drogue targets with anti-aircraft co-operation units and squadrons. Not surprisingly, the number of engine failures increased and several Henleys were lost in acci-dents. The situation was resolved finally in mid-1942 when the Henleys were withdrawn from service, replaced by Boulton Paul Defiants adapted for this role and by purpose-built Miles Marti-nets.

Specification
Type: two-seat target tug
Powerplant: one 768-kW (1,030-hp) Rolls-Royce Merlin II or III 12-cylinder Vee piston engine
Performance: maximum speed with air-to-air target 438 km/h (272 mph), and with ground-to-air target 322 km/h (200 mph); service ceiling 8230 m (27,000 ft); range 1529 km (950 miles)
Weights: empty 2726 kg (6,010 lb); maximum take-off 3846 kg (8,480 lb)
Dimensions: span 14.59 m (47 ft 10½ in); length 11.1 m (36 ft 5 in); height 4.46 m (14 ft 7½ in); wing area 31.77 m² (342 sq ft)

Hawker Hind

With the beginning of RAF expansion in 1934, the Air Ministry issued Specifica-tion G.7/34, which called for a light-bomber that was required to serve as an interim replacement for the Hart bomber. This was considered a desir-able course of action to bridge the gap until new-generation aircraft, such as the Bristol Blenheim and Fairey Battle, began to enter service.

Hawker's proposal to meet this re-quirement was a new derivative of the Hart, differing primarily by installation of the more powerful Kestrel V engine, but with changes which included modifica-tion of the aft cockpit to improve con-ditions, field of fire and prone bombing position, and with a tailwheel replacing the Hart's tail-skid.

Named **Hawker Hind**, the prototype of this new aircraft flew for the first time on 12 September 1934, and just under a year later, on 4 September 1935, the first production Hind was flown. The first squadron to receive Hinds was No. 21, then at Bircham Newton, Norfolk, which was allocated sufficient aircraft to equip one flight, and at the same time one flight of Nos 18 and 34 Squadrons were similarly equipped. Subsequent produc-tion aircraft were delivered to these squadrons until each was at full strength, after which Nos 12 and 142

Squadrons were equipped. Such was the rate of production that by the spring of 1937 Bomber Command had received 338 Hinds, and a further 114 were in ser-vice with seven Auxiliary Air Force squadrons. Small numbers were also supplied to the air forces of India, New Zealand and South Africa.

Like the Hart, the Hind attracted con-siderable export interest, and was built for Afghanistan, Latvia, Persia (Iran), Por-tugal, Switzerland and Yugoslavia. As a result Hinds were to be seen with a variety of powerplants, including the Bristol Mercury VIII or IX, Gnome-Rhône Mistral K-9, or Rolls-Royce Kestrel VDR or XVI, in addition to the standard Kestrel V.

Peak utilisation of Hinds by the RAF came in 1937, when Battles and Blen-heims were entering service, and with a requirement for a bomber trainer for operation by the Volunteer Reserve FTS, it was decided to adapt the Hinds for this role. Changes included deletion of the rear cockpit gun mounting and modifica-tion of that cockpit to accommodate an instructor, with dual controls and full in-strumentation; the forward-firing gun was also deleted from most of these Hart trainers. In 1938, all were equipped with blind-flying hoods for instrument training.

At the outbreak of World War II, most Hinds were operating in the training role, but some were retained by squadrons

for use as communications aircraft, and six were supplied to Ireland during 1939-40 for use as trainers by the Irish Air Corps. Many were modified subse-quently to serve as glider tugs, remain-ing in use for this purpose until the type was phased out in 1942, remembered as the last bi-plane light-bomber in RAF ser-vice.

Specification
Type: two-seat light-bomber/trainer
Powerplant: one 477-kW (640-hp) Rolls-Royce Kestrel V12-cylinder Vee piston engine
Performance: maximum speed 299 km/h (186 mph) at 5000 m (16,400 ft); service ceiling 8045 m

Most of the Hawker biplanes had the familiar nose-shape of the Kestrel engine, but many for export featured radials for ease of maintenance. This was a Mercury-engined Hind for Persia.

(26,400 ft); range 692 km (430 miles)
Weights: empty 1475 kg (3,251 lb); maximum take-off 2403 kg (5,298 lb)
Dimensions: span 11.35 m (37 ft 3 in); length 9.02 m (29 ft 7 in); height 3.23 m (10 ft 7 in); wing area 32.33 m² (348 sq ft)
Armament: one 7.7-mm (0.303-in) forward-firing machine-gun and one 7.7-mm (0.303-in) Lewis gun in rear cockpit, plus up to 227 kg (500 lb) of bombs on underwing racks

Hawker Horsley

In response to Air Ministry Specification 26/23 for a two-seat medium-day-bomber, Hawker Engineering designed and built the prototype of a large two-bay biplane to fulfil this role. With unequal-span slightly-swept wings, a conven-tional braced tail unit, tailskid landing gear and power provided by a Rolls-Royce Condor III, the prototype **Hawker Horsley** was flown for the first time during 1925. Service testing re-sulted in a contract for 20 aircraft, these being the last aircraft of all-wood con-struction to be built by the company. The subsequent **Horsley Mk II** was mixed wood and metal construction and the final **Horsley Mk III** (a Hawker, not offi-cial designation), which began to enter service in 1929, was of all-metal basic structure.

The Horsley served initially with No. 11 (Bomber) Squadron and by early 1928 four squadrons had been equipped; it was during this year that the type be-came operational also as a torpedo-bomber. During 1931-33 a small number of Horsley torpedo-bombers of all-metal construction were converted for use as target tugs. Total production for the RAF was to exceed 120 aircraft of all versions and the type remained in home service until 1934 and into the following year with No. 36 Squadron based in Singa-pore. In addition to production for the RAF, six composite-construction Hor-

sley Mk IIs were built for the Greek naval air service, and two with 597-kW (800-hp) Armstrong Siddeley Leopard II radial engines were supplied to Denmark under the name **Dantorp**, these being three-seat torpedo-bombers. Licence-production in Denmark was planned but did not materialise.

In addition to their military use, a num-ber of Horsleys provided valuable ser-vice from 1926 to 1937 in an engine test-bed role, their endurance and flight characteristics making them ideal for such a purpose.

Hawker Horsely Mk II of No. 33(B) Squadron, RAF, based at Netheravon and Eastchurch in the early 1930s.

Specification
Hawker Horsley Mk II
Type: two-seat day-bomber
Powerplant: one 496-kW (665-hp) Rolls-Royce Condor IIIA 12-cylinder Vee piston engine
Performance: maximum speed 201 km/h (125 mph) at 1830 m (6,000 ft); service ceiling 4265 m (14,000 ft); endurance 10 hours
Weights: empty 2159 kg (4,760 lb);

maximum take-off 3538 kg (7,800 lb)
Dimensions: span 17.21 m (56 ft 5¾ in); length 11.84 m (38 ft 10 in); height 4.17 m (13 ft 8 in); wing area 64.38 m² (693 sq ft)
Armament: one fixed forward-firing 7.7-mm (0.303-in) Vickers machine-gun and one 7.7-mm (0.303-in) Lewis gun in observer's position, plus up to 680 kg (1,500 lb) of bombs or one 18-in torpedo carried externally

Hawker Hunter

Continuing the tradition of the Camm-designed fighters, the **Hawker Hunter** was the UK's most successful post-war military aircraft. A total of 1,972 was built, including 445 manufactured under licence in Belgium and the Netherlands. Not only an extremely capable warplane, the Hunter is remembered by its pilots as a sheer delight to fly. It has served with 22 air arms around the world, is still operational with about 10, and a survey suggests that, at nearly 40 years since first flight date, some 20 per cent of all Hunters ever built are still flying.

The vast majority of variants are powered by the Rolls-Royce Avon turbojet, but an Armstrong Siddeley Sapphire was installed in the Mks 2 and 5. The **P.1067** prototype was flown first on 20 July 1951, the first production Hunter F.Mk 1 on 16 May 1953 and the type began to enter RAF service in July 1954. Almost exactly a year later the **P.1101** two-seat trainer prototype was flown, entering service as the **Hunter T.Mk 7** in 1958. Deliveries of new production aircraft continued until 1966, during which time the breed was continually being improved. All versions of the aircraft were supersonic in a shallow dive, and power, armament and fuel capacity were increased progressively, reaching a peak in the **Hunter FGA.Mk 9**. This variant, embodying all the lessons to come from the earlier marks, is powered by the Rolls-Royce Avon Mk 207; it packs a greater punch in the form of heavier underwing weapon capacity and is generally strengthened to capitalise on its improved potency in the ground-attack role. The Hunter FGA.Mk 9 represented so great an improvement that although none of this version was built as new, the manufacturer was kept busy over the years with a steady flow of refurbishing and remanufacturing to this standard. Major operators of the considerable numbers of Hunters still in service are the Royal Air Force and Royal

A quartet of Hunters from Hawker's test fleet is led by a T.Mk 7 (which later served with the Empire Test Pilot School). Following are F.Mk 6s testing wingtip tanks and the Fairey Fireflash beam-riding air-to-air missile. Following is an F.Mk 6 which was later sold to India.

Navy, with a combined total of about 20 aircraft used in a training role, while the Swiss air force still retains about 150 in an operational attack role, following an update with radar-warning equipment and provision to carry the Hughes AGM-65 Maverick air-to-surface missile.

Variants

Hunter F.Mk 2: based on F.Mk 1 but with Armstrong Siddeley Sapphire Mk 101 turbojet
Hunter Mk 3: designation of P.1067 prototype with afterburning Avon R.A.7R turbojet; set a world speed record of 1171 km/h (727.6 mph) on 7 September 1953
Hunter F.Mk 4: with an Avon Mk 115/121 engine and increased fuel capacity; late versions had four underwing pylons and provision to carry rocket projectiles
Hunter F.Mk 5: generally similar to F.Mk 4 but with a Sapphire Mk 101 engine
Hunter F.Mk 6: with an Avon Mk 203/207 engine, 1773-litre (390-Imp gal) fuel capacity and late F.Mk 4-type armament; most given dogtooth leading edge
Hunter T.Mk 8: Royal Navy 'hooked' trainer version
Hunter FR.Mk 10: reconnaissance version of the FGA.Mk 9 for the RAF
Hunter GA.Mk 11: Royal Navy single-seat attack trainer
Hunter PR.Mk 11: Royal Navy equivalent of the RAF FR.Mk 10
Hunter Mk 50: version of F.Mk 4 (Sweden)
Hunter Mk 51: similar to F.Mk 4 (Denmark)
Hunter Mk 52: similar to F.Mk 4 (Peru)
Hunter T.Mk 53: version of T.Mk 7 (Denmark)
Hunter Mk 56: similar to F.Mk 6 (India)
Hunter FGA.Mk 56A: similar to FGA.Mk 9 (India)
Hunter FGA.Mk 57: similar to FGA. Mk 9 (Kuwait)
Hunter Mk 58 and Mk 58A: similar to F.Mk 6 (Switzerland)
Hunter FGA.Mk 59 and Mk 59A: similar to FGA.Mk 9 (Iraq)
Hunter FR.Mk 59B: similar to FR.Mk 10 (Iraq)
Hunter T.Mk 62: similar to T.Mk 7 (Peru)

The most successful of post-war British fighers, the Hunter is still in front-line service with some air arms today. This box-four is from No. 43 Sqn, which flew these F.Mk 4s from Leuchars from March to December 1956.

Hunter T.Mk 66, 66D and 66E: two-seat trainer versions for India with 200-series Avon
Hunter T.Mk 66B: similar to T.Mk 66 (Jordan)
Hunter T.Mk 66C: similar to T.Mk 66 (Lebanon)
Hunter T.Mk 67: similar to T.Mk 66 (Kuwait)
Hunter T.Mk 68: similar to T.Mk 66 (Switzerland)
Hunter T.Mk 69: similar to T.Mk 66 (Iraq)
Hunter FGA.Mk 70 and 70A: similar to FGA.Mk 9 (Lebanon)
Hunter FGA.Mk 71: similar to FGA.Mk 9 (Chile)
Hunter FR.Mk 71A: similar to FR.Mk 10 (Chile)
Hunter T.Mk 72: similar to T.Mk 66 (Chile)
Hunter FGA.Mk 73. 73A and 73B: similar to FGA.Mk 9 (Jordan)
Hunter FGA.Mk 74 and 74B: similar to FGA.Mk 9 (Singapore)
Hunter FR.Mk 74A: similar to FR.Mk 10 (Singapore)
Hunter T.Mk 75 and 75A: similar to T.Mk 66 (Singapore)
Hunter FGA.Mk 76: similar to

FGA.Mk 9 (Abu Dhabi)
Hunter FR.Mk 76A: similar to FR.Mk 10 (Abu Dhabi)
Hunter T.Mk 77: similar to T.Mk 7 (Abu Dhabi)
Hunter FGA.Mk 78: similar to FGA.Mk 9 (Qatar)
Hunter T.Mk 79: similar to T.Mk 7 (Qatar)
Hunter FGA.Mk 80: similar to FGA.Mk 9 (Kenya)
Hunter T.Mk 81: similar to T.Mk 66 (Kenya)

Specification
Hawker Siddeley Hunter F.Mk 6
Type: single-seat interceptor
Powerplant: one 4604-kg (10,150-lb) thrust Rolls-Royce Avon Mk 207 turbojet
Performance: maximum speed 1125 km/h (699 mph) at sea level; service ceiling 15695 m (51,500 ft); combat radius, clean 370 km (230 miles)
Weights: empty 6406 kg (14,122 lb); maximum take-off 10796 kg (23,800 lb)
Dimensions: span 10.25 m (33 ft 8 in); length 13.98 m (45 ft 10½ in); height 4.02 m (13 ft 2 in); wing area 32.42 m² (349 sq ft)
Armament: four 30-mm Aden cannon, plus four underwing pylons carrying 454-kg (1,000-lb) bombs inboard and 227-kg (500-lb) bombs outboard, with provision for up to 24 76-mm (3-in) rocket projectiles, or fuel drop-tanks outboard

Hawker Hurricane
to
Hawker Siddeley/Avro/British Aerospace 748/Andover

Hawker Hurricane

Few members of the British public could have been aware that a significant new fighter aircraft had joined the ranks of the RAF when, in December 1937, the first production examples of the **Hawker Hurricane Mk I** were delivered to No. 111 Squadron at RAF Northolt. It was not until two months later, during February 1938, that this news became common, and exciting, knowledge when banner headlines announced, on 11 February, that one of these new Hurricane fighters had more than lived up to its name on the previous afternoon. Piloted by Squadron Leader J. W. Gillan, Commanding Officer of No. 111 Squadron, this aircraft had been flown from Turnhouse, Scotland, to Northolt, a distance of 526 km (327 miles), in 48 minutes at an average speed of almost 658 km/h (409 mph).

The subject of all this excitement, the Hurricane, reached back as far as 1933, when Hawker's chief designer, Sydney Camm, decided to design a monoplane fighter based on the Fury biplane, using as its powerplant the Rolls-Royce Goshawk engine. As development progressed, the Goshawk was supplanted by the Rolls-Royce P.V.12 Merlin, and Hawker began construction of a prototype around which the Air Ministry Specification F.36/34 had been drawn up. As first flown, on 6 November 1935, this prototype had retractable landing gear, a strut-braced tailplane, conventional Hawker-structure fuselage with fabric covering, a new two-spar monoplane wing covered with fabric, and a power-plant comprising a 738-kW (990-hp) Rolls-Royce Merlin 'C' engine.

Official trials began in February 1936, when the most optimistic high-speed performance predictions were comfortably exceeded, and on 3 June 1936 an initial order for 600 production aircraft was issued to Hawker. At the end of the month the new fighter was named the Hurricane. Hawker had in fact anticipated the production contract, and plans for the construction of 1,000 examples had already been initiated when the Air Ministry order was received. This, however, called for introduction of the Merlin II engine, causing some delay for installation redesign, but Hawker's advance preparations made possible the first flight of a production Hurricane Mk I on 12 October 1937.

No. 111 Squadron at Northolt had one flight operational in December 1937 and was completely re-equipped by the end of the following month. Soon afterwards, Nos 3 and 56 Squadrons were equipped, and by the end of 1938 about 200 Hurricanes had been delivered to the RAF's Fighter Command. The early production aircraft differed little from the prototype, except for the installation of the 768-kW (1,030-hp) Merlin II engine.

No doubts existed that the Hurricane was anything but an important and essential aircraft to reinforce the expansion of the RAF, and plans were made in late 1938 for additional construction to be undertaken by Gloster Aircraft at Hucclecote, Gloucestershire. This latter

company's first production aircraft made its initial flight on 27 October 1939, and in little over 12 months Gloster had completed 1,000 Hurricanes, a figure that was to reach 1,850, plus 1,924 by Hawker, before later versions superseded the Hurricane Mk I in production. Before that happened, however, the fabric-covered wing had been replaced by one with metal stressed skin, and other progressively introduced improvements had included the Merlin III engine, a bulletproof windscreen, and armour protection for the pilot.

Despite the pressure of its production programme for the RAF, Hawker had found time and space to cope with modest production orders covering 24 aircraft and a production licence for Yugoslavia, followed by aircraft for Belgium, Iran, Poland, Romania and Turkey: Belgium also negotiated a production licence for construction to be carried out by Avions Fairey, but only two Belgium-built Hurricanes had been completed and flown before the German invasion. Arrangements were also completed for Hurricanes to be built in Canada by the Canadian Car and Foundry Co., the first production aircraft flying on 9 January 1940. Canadian aircraft were at first generally similar to the British-built Hurricane Mk I, but differed later by having the Packard-built Merlin engine.

At the outbreak of World War II, 19 RAF squadrons were fully equipped with Hurricanes, and within a short time Nos 1, 73, 85 and 87 Squadrons had been despatched to bases in France, but during the 'phoney' period of the war that followed these squadrons had comparatively little to do until the German push westward in May 1940. Immediately, six more Hurricane squadrons were flown to France, followed shortly after by two more squadrons, but these were an inadequate number to stem the flood of German arms, armour and aircraft. Post-Dunkirk accounting showed that almost 200 Hurricanes had been lost, destroyed or so severely damaged that they had to be abandoned. It represented a major disaster for the RAF, for this number of aircraft amounted to about a quarter of its total strength in first-line fighters.

Fortunately for the UK, and for the RAF, the anticipated invasion of the British Isles by Germany failed to mat-

erialise, and there was a breathing space during which the squadrons of Fighter Command were able to reinforce their numbers. On 8 August 1940, which is regarded officially as the opening date of the Battle of Britain, the RAF could call upon 32 squadrons of Hurricanes and 19 squadrons of Supermarine Spitfires. But despite the débâcle at Dunkirk and the resulting fighter famine in the UK, three Hurricane squadrons were transferred overseas. These comprised No. 261 Squadron sent to support the island of Malta, and Nos 73 and 274 Squadrons which, suitably 'tropicalised', began operations in the Western Desert.

Development of the type began with the introduction of a Merlin XX engine in a Hurricane Mk I airframe, this being re-designated **Hurricane Mk IIA Srs 1**. Generally similar, except for a slightly lengthened fuselage, was the **Hurricane Mk IIA Srs 2**, representing an interim change on the production lines to make possible the installation of newly-developed and interchangeable wings. Thus, with a wing housing no fewer than 12 7.7-mm (0.303-in) machine-guns and with provision for the carriage of two 113-kg (250-lb) or two 227-kg (500-lb)

Hawker Hurricane Mk IIB of Esquadrilha RV, Arma da Aeronautica (Portuguese air force), based at Espinho near Oporto in 1948.

bombs beneath the wings, the designation became **Hurricane Mk IIB**. The **Hurricane Mk IIC** was generally similar, but with the machine-guns replaced by four 20-mm cannon. When the Hurricane's life as a fighter had virtually come to an end, in 1942, the introduction of yet another wing was to rejuvenate this remarkable aircraft as the **Hurricane Mk IID**. The new wing carried two 40-mm Rolls-Royce B.F. or Vickers Type S anti-tank guns, plus one harmonised 7.7-mm (0.303-in) machine-gun for each anti-armour weapon to assist in aiming. The Hurricane Mk IID 'tank buster' proved a potent weapon, highly effective against German armour in North Africa and when opposing more lightly armoured Japanese fighting vehicles in Burma.

The success of these wing variations led to the final production version, the **Hurricane Mk IV** (early examples of this version were designated **Hurricane Mk IIE**), which introduced the 1208-kW (1,620-hp) Merlin 24 or 27 engine, and a 'universal wing' to make

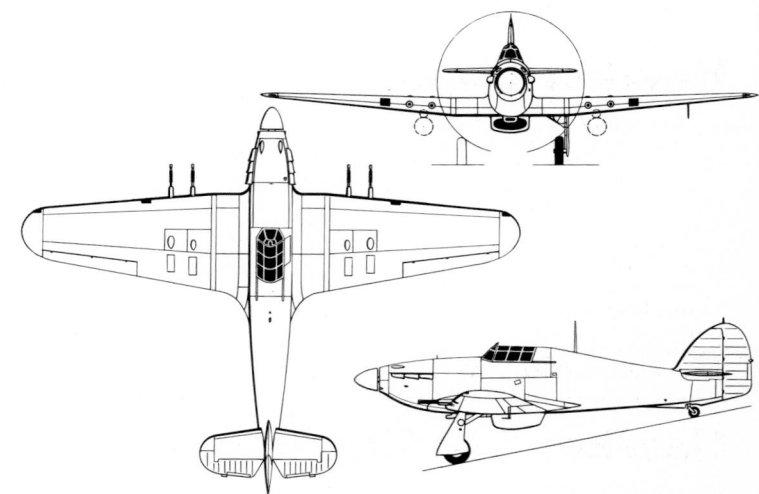

Hawker Hurricane Mk IIC (dashed lines: optional underwing bombs or tanks)

508

the Mk IV a highly-specialised ground-attack aircraft. This wing carried two 7.7-mm (0.303-in) machine-guns to assist in sighting other weapons, which could include two 40-mm (2.3-in) anti-tank guns, two 113-kg (250-lb) or 227-kg (500-lb) bombs, or smoke curtain installations, ferry- or drop-tanks, or eight rocket projectiles with 27-kg (60-lb) warheads. This last weapon, first proposed in late 1941, had been tested on a Hurricane in February 1942. When used operationally on the Hurricane IV, it was the first Allied aircraft to deploy air-to-ground rockets, and these weapons made the little Hurricane a giant in capability, extending its operational life beyond the end of World War II, for it was not until January 1947 that the RAF's last Hurricane squadron, No. 6, received replacement aircraft.

Hurricane production in Canada had grown considerably in proportions from the initial line of Hurricane Mk Is. The introduction of the 969-kW (1,300-hp) Packard-built Merlin 28 brought a designation change to **Hurricane Mk X**. This model was generally similar to the British-built Mk IIB with the 12-gun wing, and while small numbers were

supplied to the UK, the majority was retained for use by the Royal Canadian Air Force. The **Hurricane Mk XI** which followed was developed specifically for RCAF requirements, but differed from the Mk X primarily in having RCAF military equipment. Major production version was the **Hurricane Mk XII**, introducing the 696-kW (1,300-hp) Packard-built Merlin 29. Initially, this was provided with the 12-gun wing; subsequently, the four-cannon and 'universal' wings became available. The final land-based version to emanate from Canada was the **Hurricane Mk XIIA**, identical to the Mk XII except for having an eight-gun wing.

In addition to the Hurricanes which went to other countries before the war, wartime production supplied 2,952 of these aircraft to the USSR, although as a result of convoy shipping losses not all reached their destination. Other wartime deliveries, most made at a time when it was difficult to spare a single aircraft, went to Egypt (20), Finland (12), India (300), Irish Air Corps (12), Persia (1) and Turkey (14), and total production in the UK and Canada amounted to 14,231.

Undoubtedly one of the great fighter

aircraft of World War II, it is difficult to overstate the capabilities of this remarkable aircraft. In the Battle of Britain Hurricanes destroyed more enemy aircraft than all other defences, air or ground, combined. This statement must be put in perspective, as it resulted from Supermarine Spitfires taking on the Messerschmitt Bf 109s, allowing the slower Hurricanes to battle against the German bombers. 'Hurribombers' fought from Malta, carried out anti-shipping operations in the English Channel, and caused havoc to Axis columns in the Western Desert. 'Tank Busting' Hurricanes ranged far and wide in practically every operational theatre. One fighter, flown by Flight Lieutenant J. B. Nicholson of No. 249 (Fighter) Squadron, during that eventful late summer of 1940, helped earn for its gallant pilot the only Victoria Cross to be awarded to a member of Fighter Command. This occurred on 17 August when, his Hurricane badly damaged and wreathed in flames, the wounded and severely burnt Nicholson succeeded in destroying the attacking Messerschmitt Bf 110 before baling out, to be rescued and survive.

It is not really surprising, therefore,

that for many years after the end of World War II, a lone Hurricane had the honour of leading the RAF fly-past over London, flown each year to commemorate victory in the Battle of Britain.

Specification
Hawker Hurricane Mk IIB
Type: single-seat fighter/fighter-bomber
Powerplant: one 954-kW (1,280-hp) Rolls-Royce Merlin XX 12-cylinder Vee piston engine
Performance: maximum speed 550 km/h (342 mph) at 6705 m (22,000 ft); maximum cruising speed 476 km/h (296 mph) at 6095 m (20,000 ft); service ceiling 11125 m (36,500 ft); range with internal fuel 772 km (480 miles)
Weights: empty 2495 kg (5,500 lb); maximum take-off 3311 kg (7,300 lb)
Dimensions: span 12.19 m (40 ft 0 in); length 9.82 m (32 ft 2½ in); height 3.99 m (13 ft 1 in); wing area 23.92 m² (257.5 sq ft)
Armament: 12 7.7-mm (0.303-in) forward-firing machine-guns, plus two 113-kg (250-lb) or 227-kg (500-lb) bombs

Hawker Nimrod

From 1924 to 1932 the Fairey Flycatcher, with its apparently 'cocked-up' aft fuselage, had the distinction of being the only fleet fighter in service with the Fleet Air Arm. However, given the Flycatcher's speed of only 214 km/h (133 mph) at sea level, a performance which deteriorated with altitude, it was realised that steps needed to be taken to procure a fighter of improved capability. As early as 1926 an Air Ministry Specification had outlined the requirement, and Hawker Engineering offered as its contender a radial-engined biplane named the Hoopoe. This was not acceptable, but from it, out of the Fury, came a clean-looking biplane known unofficially at first as the **Norn.**

This became the **Hawker Nimrod**, generally similar in appearance to the RAF's Fury, the first production example of which was flown on 14 October 1931. During 1932 **Nimrod Mk I** fighters replaced Flycatchers in FAA Flights Nos 402, 408 and 409. Subsequently, in 1933, these aircraft came into the possession of No. 800 Squadron on board HMS *Courageous*, and of Nos 801 and 802 Squadrons (HMS *Furious* and *Glorious* respectively). Production of an improved **Nimrod Mk II** began in Sep-

tember 1933, with initial deliveries to the FAA being made in March 1934: these had arrester gear and, progressively, more powerful engines and tail surfaces of increased area. Many of the 57 Nimrod Mk Is were later modified to Mk II standard. It is interesting to note that the first three Nimrod Mk IIs had a basic structure of stainless steel, but the remaining 27 production examples reverted to Hawker's conventional structure of light alloy and steel.

Hawker was not successful in drumming up any significant export orders for the Nimrod. One was supplied to Japan, one to Portugal and two to Denmark, in which country they were known as **Nimrodderne.** The Royal Danish Naval Dockyard planned to licence-build an additional 10 examples of this aircraft, but there appears to be no conclusive evidence that this took place.

The FAA's Nimrods had been relegated to training and communications duties at the outbreak of World War II, but continued in service until declared obsolete in July 1941. The Danish Nimrodderne remained in service until the time of the German invasion in April 1940.

Specification
Hawker Nimrod Mk II
Type: single-seat carrier-based fighter
Powerplant: one 453-kW (608-hp) Rolls-Royce Kestrel VFP 12-cylinder Vee piston engine
Performance: maximum speed 311 km/h (193 mph) at 4265 m (14,000 ft); cruising speed 185 km/h (115 mph); service ceiling 8535 m (28,000 ft); endurance 1 hour 40 minutes at 3050 m (10,000 ft)
Weights: empty 1413 kg (3,115 lb); maximum take-off 1841 kg (4,059 lb)

A Hawker Nimrod Mk I of No. 800 Sqn, Fleet Air Arm, shows the wheeled landing gear of this navalised Fury derivative.

Dimensions: span 10.23 m (26 ft 6½ in); length 8.09 m (26 ft 6½ in); height 3.00 m (9 ft 10 in); wing area 27.96 m² (301.0 sq ft)
Armament: two forward-firing synchronised 7.7-mm (0.303-in) machine-guns, plus provision for four 9-kg (20-lb) bombs to be carried beneath the wings

Hawker Osprey

Best described as a navalised version of the RAF's Hart, the **Hawker Osprey** was designed as a two-seat fleet spotter reconnaissance aircraft. The prototype, a conversion of the Hart prototype with folding wings, strengthened fuselage for catapult launch and easily interchanged wheel/float landing gear, was flown first in the summer of 1930. The initial **Osprey Mk I** production version began to enter service in November 1932. The **Osprey Mk II** differed in its float installation and the **Osprey Mk III** intro-

duced a dinghy stowed in the starboard upper wing. All three versions were powered by the 470-kW (630-hp) Rolls-Royce Kestrel II, but the final production **Osprey Mk IV** had a 477-kW (640-hp) Kestrel V. Ospreys were in first-line service until 1938, and continued in secondary roles until 1940. About 130 were built and supplied also to Portugal (2), Spain (1) and Sweden (4).

Specification
Hawker Osprey Mk III (land-plane)

Type: two-seat fleet spotter and reconnaissance aircraft
Powerplant: one 470-kW (630-hp) Rolls-Royce Kestrel II 12-cylinder Vee piston engine
Performance: maximum speed 270 km/h (168 mph) at 1525 m (5,000 ft); service ceiling 7165 m (23,500 ft)
Weights: empty 1545 kg (3,405 lb); maximum take-off 2245 kg (4,950 lb)
Dimensions: span 11.28 m (37 ft 0 in); length 8.94 m (29 ft 4 in); height 3.17 m (10 ft 5 in); wing area 31.5 m² (339.0 sq ft)

There was little to distinguish the Osprey from the Hart apart from navalised gear and the ability to accept wheeled or float undercarriage.

Hawker Sea Hurricane

The early success of the Hawker Hurricane fighter in RAF service meant that the Royal Navy was keen to acquire

numbers of these aircraft to help in the Battle of the Atlantic which, in early 1940, was depicted statistically by a

steeply rising graph of shipping losses. A large proportion of such losses resulted far from shore, in areas where land-based aircraft could not provide air cover for Allied convoys. Thus German long-range patrol aircraft were able to range

freely, spotting convoys far out at sea, and calling in and directing U-boat packs to attack them.

An interim measure gave birth to the **'Hurricat'**, a converted Hurricane carried by CAM-ships (Catapult Armed Merchantmen). Mounted on and launched from a catapult at the ship's bows, the Hurricane was flown off on what was usually a one-way flight: after providing defence for the convoy there was no-where for the FAA or RAF pilot to land, which meant he was obliged to bale out, or ditch his aircraft as near as possible to the convoy, hoping to be picked up. The provision of long-range drop-tanks beneath the wings, introduced in August 1941 after the CAM-ships had been pro-vided with more powerful catapults for the higher gross weight, improved the situation a little. At best it was a desper-ate rather than a practical measure, but despite this six enemy aircraft were des-troyed in the last five months of 1941, the first success coming on 3 August 1941, when Lieutenant R. W. H. Everett inter-cepted and destroyed a Focke-Wulf Fw 200 Condor.

Hurricanes converted for the above role needed only the addition of catapult spools, and 50 Hurricane Mk I land-planes so modified were designated **Sea Hurricane Mk IA**. They were fol-lowed by about 300 Mk Is converted to **Sea Hurricane Mk IB** configuration, these having catapult spools plus a V-frame arrester hook: in addition 25 Mk IIA Srs 2 aircraft were similarly modified as **Sea Hurricane IB** or **Hooked Hur-ricane II** fighters. Their initial role was a considerable improvement on CAM-ship

deployment, for from October 1941 they began to go to sea aboard MAC-ships, these being large merchantships fitted with a small flight deck. They carried on deck (for there was no hangar accommo-dation) a small number of fighter and ASW aircraft, which were able to oper-ate from and to the mini-carriers. **Sea Hurricane Mk IC** fighters, introduced in February 1942 were, once again, con-ventional Mk I conversions with catapult spools and arrester hook; they had, how-ever, the four-cannon wing of the land-based Hurricane Mk IIC. Last of the Sea Hurricanes from British sources was the **Sea Hurricane Mk IIC**, intended for conventional carrier operations and, con-sequently, without catapult spools. They introduced also to navy service the Mer-lin XX engine, and carried FAA radio equipment. Last of the Sea Hurricane variants was the **Sea Hurricane Mk XIIA**, of which a small number were converted from Canadian-built Mk XIIs, and these were used operationally in the North Atlantic.

The Sea Hurricane's most famous action was fought during the late sum-mer of 1942, when aircraft serving with Nos 801, 802 and 885 Squadrons aboard the carriers HMS *Indomitable*, *Eagle* and *Victorious* respectively, joined with Fai-rey Fulmars and Grumman Martlets to protect a vital convoy to Malta. During three days of almost continuous attack

by an Axis force of bombers, torpedo-bombers and escorting fighters, 39 enemy aircraft were destroyed for the loss of eight naval fighters.

Specification
Hawker Sea Hurricane Mk IIC
Type: single-seat carrier-based fighter
Powerplant: one 954-kW (1,280-hp) Rolls-Royce Merlin XX 12-cylinder Vee piston engine
Performance: maximum speed 550 km/h (342 mph) at 6705 m

The Sea Hurricane Mk IA was an unhooked landplane conversion.

(22,000 ft); service ceiling 10850 m (35,600 ft); range with internal fuel 740 km (460 miles)
Weights: empty 2667 kg (5,880 lb); maximum take-off 3674 kg (8,100 lb)
Dimensions: span 12.19 m (40 ft 0 in); length 9.83 m (32 ft 3 in); height 3.99 m (13 ft 1 in); wing area 23.92 m² (257.5 sq ft)
Armament: four 20-mm cannon

Hawker Tempest

Hawker Tempest Mk II of No. 54 Squadron, Royal Air Force, based at Chilbolton in 1946.

The Hawker Typhoon proved a disap-pointment in its intended role as an inter-ceptor, but distinguished itself later as a fighter-bomber, particularly when armed with rocket projectiles. Its rate of climb and performance at altitude were rela-tively poor, and in 1941 it was suggested that remedial action might be taken in the form of a new, thinner wing, elliptical in planform. The radiator was to be moved from beneath the engine to the wing leading edges, and the Napier Sabre EC.107C was specified. As the new wing would be thinner than that of the Typhoon, the inclusion of an addi-tional fuselage fuel tank was needed to replace the lost wing-tank capacity.

The design study, known originally as the **Typhoon Mk II**, was submitted to the Air Ministry, and on 18 November 1941 two prototypes were ordered to Specification F.10/41. There were major changes, however, compared with the earlier aircraft, resulting in the name change to **Hawker Tempest** in early 1942. After cancellation of the Hawker Tornado programme, the alternative engine installations planned for that air-craft were, instead, applied to the Tem-pest. Thus the two original prototypes became the **Tempest Mk I** with Sabre IV and **Tempest Mk V** with Sabre II, and four more were ordered. Two **Tem-pest Mk II** aircraft were to have the 1879-kW (2,520-hp) Bristol Centaurus, and two **Tempest Mk III** aircraft with the Rolls-Royce Griffon IIB, becoming **Tempest Mk IV** when re-engined with the Griffon 61. Only one Griffon-engined aircraft was completed, in fact, as one of the prototype Hawker Furies.

Before any of the prototypes had flown the Air Ministry placed contracts for 400 Tempest Mk Is, although these orders were transferred later to other versions. The prototype Tempest Mk I, its lines not spoiled by the beard radiator of the Typhoon, was flown on 24 February 1943, and later achieved a maximum speed of 750 km/h (466 mph) at 7470 m (24,500 ft). However, the

engine programme suffered from tech-nical problems and delays, and the Tem-pest Mk I was dropped.

The first of the Tempest prototypes to fly had been the Tempest Mk V, during September 1942. Retaining the Typhoon's chin radiator it had originally a standard Typhoon tail unit, but this was modified subsequently. The first of 805 Tempest Mk Vs was flown from Langley on 21 June 1943, one of the initial pro-duction batch of 100 **Tempest Mk V Series 1** aircraft which had four 20-mm British Hispano Mk II cannon, their bar-rels protruding from the leading edges of the wings; the remaining Tempest Mk Vs had short-barrelled Mk V cannon, completely contained in the wings. In 1945, one Tempest Mk V was fitted with a 40-mm 'P' gun under each wing, simi-lar to the 40-mm cannon installation of the Hawker Hurricane Mk IID. After the war had ended some were converted for use as **Tempest TT.Mk 5** target tugs.

An order for 500 Centaurus-powered Tempest Mk IIs was placed in October 1942, before the first flight of the proto-type. This took place on 28 June 1943, the aircraft being powered by a Mk IV engine, superseded by the 1879-kW (2,520-hp) Mk V in production aircraft. These were to have been built by the Bristol Aeroplane Company, the first Bristol-built aircraft being flown on 4 October 1944, but only 36 were com-pleted before production was trans-ferred back to Hawker. The parent com-pany manufactured a further 100

Tempest F.Mk II fighters and 314 **Tempest FB.Mk II** fighter-bombers with underwing racks for bombs or rockets. In 1947 India ordered 89 tropicalised Tempest Mk IIs from RAF stocks, and in the following year Pakis-tan ordered 24 similar aircraft. Third and last production version of the Tempest was the **Tempest F.Mk VI** with the 1745-kW (2,340-hp) Napier Sabre V engine, first flown on 9 May 1944. In-tended for service in the Middle East, 142 tropicalised Tempest Mk VIs were built. As in the case of the Mk V, some were converted later as **Tempest TT.Mk 6** target tugs.

RAF service began in April 1944, when Tempest Mk Vs were delivered to New-church, Kent, where the first Tempest Wing was formed within No. 85 Group. The wing was active during the build-up to the Normandy invasion, but on 13 June the first V-1 flying-bomb fell at Swanscombe in Kent, and the Tempests were among aircraft tasked to combat the menace. Their success can be measured by the fact that of 1,847 bombs destroyed by fighters between June 1944 and March 1945, 481½ were accredited to the Tempest Wing.

Until the end of war in Europe, Tem-pest Mk Vs flew 'cab rank' patrols in sup-port of ground forces, moving up to air-fields in France and Belgium as the Germans fell back. In addition, they en-gaged in combat the Luftwaffe's Mes-serschmitt Me 262 jet fighters, 20 of which were destroyed before VE-Day.

Although plans were made for 50 Tempest Mk IIs to be sent to the Far East in May 1945, to operate with Tiger Force against the Japanese, the war in the Pacific ended before these aircraft were ready for service. They equipped No. 54 Squadron at Chilbolton in November 1945, this being the only post-war home-based Tempest Mk II unit, the others serving in Germany, Hong Kong, India and Malaysia. The Tempest Mk VI was also too late to see wartime service, although this mark was flown later by squadrons in Germany and the Middle East.

Specification
Hawker Tempest Mk V
Type: single-seat fighter/fighter-bomber
Powerplant: one 1626-kW (2,180-hp) Napier Sabre IIA 24-cylinder 'H' piston engine
Performance: maximum speed 686 km/h (426 mph) at 5640 m (18,500 ft); service ceiling 11125 m (36,500 ft); normal range 1191 km (740 miles)
Weights: empty 4082 kg (9,000 lb); maximum take-off 6142 kg (13,540 lb)
Dimensions: span 12.50 m (41 ft 0 in); length 10.26 m (33 ft 8 in); height 4.90 m (16 ft 1 in); wing area 28.06 m² (302.0 sq ft)
Armament: four 20-mm cannon, plus two 227-kg (500-lb) or two 454-kg (1,000-lb) bombs, or eight 27-kg (60-lb) rocket projectiles

Hawker Tomtit

When, in 1927, the Air Ministry was seeking an elementary trainer to replace the long-serving Avro 504, Sydney Camm designed a neat equal-span single-bay biplane to meet this requirement. Of conventional configuration, with instructor and pupil in tandem open cockpit, tailskid landing gear, and power provided by an Armstrong Siddeley Mongoose radial engine, the prototype **Hawker Tomtit** was flown for the first time during November 1928. The Tomtit had a basic structure of metal with fabric covering, and the introduction of Reid and Sigrist blind-flying instrumentation in this aircraft made it a significant trainer. Within three months of the first flight a first production batch was ordered for the RAF, which eventually acquired 25 (including the prototype) for service with the Central Flying School and No. 3 FTS. In addition to the military trainers built for the RAF, two were supplied to the Canadian Department of National Defence and four for the New Zealand Permanent Air Force.

The Tomtits entered RAF service in 1930 but were replaced by Avro Tutors

Hawker Tomtit Mk I of an RAF Flying Training School in the early 1930s.

from 1932, then distributed to various units for use as communications aircraft. The majority were disposed of as being surplus to requirements in late 1935. One is still flying.

Specification
Type: two-seat military trainer
Powerplant: one 112-kW (150-hp) Armstrong Siddeley Mongoose IIIC 5-cylinder radial piston engine
Performance: maximum speed

200 km/h (124 mph) at sea level; service ceiling 5945 m (19,500 ft)
Weights: empty 499 kg (1,100 lb); maximum take-off 794 kg (1,750 lb)
Dimensions: span 8.71 m (28 ft 6¾ in); length 7.21 m (23 ft 8 in); height 2.54 m (8 ft 4 in); wing area 22.09 m² (237.80 sq ft)

Hawker Typhoon

In response to Specification F.18/37, design of the **Hawker Typhoon** was initiated by Sydney Camm in 1937. The Specification required a Rolls-Royce Vulture or Napier Sabre engine, so two prototypes were built initially, that with the Vulture known as the Hawker Tornado. The Sabre-engined version, designated Hawker Typhoon, also encountered powerplant problems. However, these were overcome because the Napier company could devote more time and effort to development of the Sabre, whereas Rolls-Royce was too concerned with the Merlin to devote adequate resources to improving the troublesome Vulture.

Irrespective of trouble with the engine, when the Typhoon prototype was first flown, on 24 February 1940, it was soon discovered that the airframe had structural problems, which persisted even after the type had entered service. The original prototype had a 12-gun wing, and in production form, first flown on 27 May 1941, was designated **Typhoon Mk IA**. It, and virtually all production Typhoons, eventually totalling 3,330, were built by the Gloster Aircraft Company. A second prototype, flown on 3 May 1941, had a wing incorporating four 20-mm cannon, and in production form was designated **Typhoon Mk IB**.

The first production aircraft were supplied to the RAF in September 1941, initially to No. 56 (F) Squadron, and service use demonstrated only too quickly that the airframe problems had not been eradicated. Several pilots lost their lives and the Air Ministry discussed whether the type should be withdrawn from service. Fortunately, Hawker was able to discover the reason for an alarming number of aircraft losing the complete tail unit, but it was almost the end of 1942 before all engine and airframe bugs had been resolved.

Even then, the Typhoon had a poor rate of climb, but a forte for high speed at low altitude that was first put to effective use in November 1941. No. 609 Squadron, then operating from Manston in Kent, destroyed four Focke-Wulf Fw 190s making hit-and-run attacks. By the end of 1942, powered by the improved Sabre IIA engine, armed with four 20-mm cannon and able to carry bombs on underwing racks, the Typhoon had become a significant fighter-bomber. Thereafter Typhoon squadrons ranged over France and the Low Countries, playing havoc with German communications, but their full potential was realised in late 1943 when the type was equipped to carry rocket projectiles. So equipped, the Typhoon proved effective against German coastal shipping, and the type's almost continuous day and night low-level attacks on German communications made a major contribution to success on D-Day.

There was little change made to the Typhoon in the closing stages of the war, except for installation of more-powerful Sabre IIB and IIC engines, and variants comprised a single **Typhoon NF.Mk IB** night-fighter and a small number of tactical reconnaissance **Typhoon FR.Mk IB** aircraft. Some production aircraft were allocated to RCAF and RNZAF units operating in Europe. Initially so unreliable that it had almost been withdrawn, at peak utilisation the Typhoon was used by no fewer than 26 squadrons of 2nd Tactical Air Force, but few saw service after VE-Day.

Specification
Hawker Typhoon Mk IB
Type: single-seat fighter-bomber
Powerplant: one 1626-kW (2,180-hp) Napier Sabre IIA 24-cylinder 'H' piston

engine
Performance: maximum speed 652 km/h (405 mph) at 5485 m (18,000 ft); service ceiling 10365 m (34,000 ft); range with maximum weapon load 821 km (510 miles)
Weights: empty 3992 kg (8,800 lb); maximum take-off 5171 kg (11,400 lb)
Dimensions: span 12.67 m (41 ft 7 in); length 9.74 m (31 ft 11½ in); height 4.67 m (15 ft 4 in); wing area 25.92 m² (279.0 sq ft)
Armament: four 20-mm cannon in wings, plus up to eight 27-kg (60-lb) rocket projectiles or two 454-kg (1,000-lb) bombs on underwing racks

An early production Typhoon Mk IB with the restricted vision canopy displays the four 20-mm cannon with large barrel fairings. Typhoons were rarely encountered at such altitudes, finding their forte in low-level ground-attack work with cannon, rockets and bombs.

Hawker Woodcock

The **Hawker Woodcock** was designed to meet the requirement of Air Ministry Specification 25/22 for a single-seat night-fighter. Of wood and fabric construction, the original Woodcock prototype, later designated **Woodcock Mk I**, had two-bay biplane wings, a conventional braced tail unit, tailskid landing gear and was powered by a 267-kW (358-hp) Armstrong Siddeley Jaguar II

radial engine. When flown in 1923 its flight characteristics were found to be more than disappointing, resulting in a new **Woodcock Mk II** prototype with single-bay wings and power provided by a Bristol Jupiter IV radial. Testing of this version proved to be satisfactory and after modification to the tail unit it was ordered into production for the RAF. Initial examples, without night-flying

equipment, began to enter service for evaluation and familiarisation, but the first operational Woodcock Mk IIs were delivered to No. 3 (Fighter) Squadron in May 1925.

Production totalled 61 Woodcock Mk IIs for the RAF, the type remaining operational until 1928, although some examples were still finding occasional use as late as 1936. The company also built three slightly modified examples of the Woodcock, powered by the 287-kW (385-hp) Armstrong Siddeley Jaguar IV

engine, for use by the Danish army air service. These had the name **Danecock**, but a further 12 built under licence in Denmark in 1927 had the designation **L.B.II Dankok**. They remained in service until 1937.

Specification
Hawker Woodcock Mk II
Type: single-seat night-fighter
Powerplant: one 283-kW (380-hp) Bristol Jupiter IV 9-cylinder radial piston engine

Performance: maximum speed 227 km/h (141 mph) at sea level; cruising speed 166 km/h (103 mph); service ceiling 6860 m (22,500 ft); endurance 2 hours 45 minutes **Weights:** empty 914 kg (2,014 lb); maximum take-off 1351 kg (2,979 lb)

Dimensions: span 9.91 m (32 ft 6 in); length 7.98 m (26 ft 2 in); height 3.02 m (9 ft 11 in); wing area 32.14 m² (346 sq ft) **Armament:** two fixed forward-firing 7.7-mm (0.303-in) Vickers machine-guns

The dumpy Woodcock was one of the aircraft which equipped the RAF fighter squadrons during the mid-1920s. The double black zig-zag lines either side of the fuselage roundel identify this Mk II as from No. 17(F) Squadron.

Hawker Siddeley/Armstrong Whitworth Sea Hawk

Aesthetically one of the most appealing of Sydney Camm's early jet fighters, the prototypes of the **Hawker Sea Hawk** were completed to Specification No. 7/46, and the first of three, then identified as the **Hawker P.1040**, was flown on 2 September 1947. Hawker subsequently built 35 **Sea Hawk F.Mk 1** fighters before transferring all future development and production to Armstrong Whitworth. A further 60 F.Mk 1 and **Sea Hawk F.Mk 2** fighters were produced by that company, which then introduced the **Sea Hawk FB.Mk 3** fighter-bomber, with a stronger wing able to carry external stores. Production of 116 FB.Mk 3s was followed by 97 **Sea Hawk FGA.Mk 4** fighter/ground-attack aircraft, all models up to this point having a 2268-kg (5,000-lb) Nene 101 engine with twin nozzles, allowing fuel to be carried in the rear fuselage. Conversion of some Mk 3s to the Nene 103 produced the **Sea Hawk FB.Mk 5**, and production for the Royal Navy ended with 86 **Sea Hawk FGA.Mk 6** aircraft, with the Nene 103 but otherwise similar to the Mk 4. The Sea Hawk served with the Royal Navy until the end of 1960, and 22 export **Sea Hawk Mk 50** aircraft with the Royal Netherlands Navy until

the end of 1964. The other major export versions were the **Sea Hawk Mk 100** and all-weather **Sea Hawk Mk 101** ordered by the West German Marine-flieger. These were similar to the Sea Hawk FGA.Mk 6 but for a taller fin and rudder and, on the Mk 101, an Ekco Type 34 search radar in a pod under the starboard wing. Operated from shore bases, they were replaced by Lockheed F-104G Starfighters in the mid-1960s.

The last remaining operator of the Sea Hawk today was the Indian navy, which in the autumn of 1959 ordered 24 aircraft similar to the Mk 6. Some of these were new-built (although the production line had closed some three years earlier), the rest being refurbished ex-RN Mk 6s. They equipped No. 300 Squadron in the aircraft-carrier INS *Vikrant* and were joined later by 12 more ex-RN Mk 4s and Mk 6s, plus 28 Mk 100/101s from Germany. They were replaced by the Sea Harrier FRS.Mk 51, the first of which was handed over in an official ceremony on 27 January 1983.

Specification
Hawker Sea Hawk FGA.Mk 6
Type: single-seat shipboard fighter/attack aircraft

Four Sea Hawk FB.Mk 3s from No. 801 Sqn, Fleet Air Arm, from HMS Bulwark. The FB.Mk 3 was built by Armstrong Whitworth and was based on the F.Mk 2 but had provision for bombs or mines.

Powerplant: one 2449-kg (5,400-lb) thrust Rolls-Royce Nene Mk 103 turbojet
Performance: maximum speed 969 km/h (602 mph) at sea level; service ceiling 13565 m (44,500 ft); combat radius (clean) 370 km (230 miles)
Weights: empty 4409 kg (9,720 lb); maximum take-off 7348 kg (16,200 lb)
Dimensions: span 11.89 m (39 ft

0 in); length 12.09 m (39 ft 8 in); height 2.64 m (8 ft 8 in); wing area 25.83 m² (278.0 sq ft)
Armament: four 20-mm Hispano cannon in nose, plus underwing hardpoints for four 227-kg (500-lb) bombs, or two 227-kg (500-lb) bombs and 20 76-mm (3-in) or 16 127-mm (5-in) rockets, or two AIM-9 Sidewinder air-to-air missiles, or four 409-litre (90 Imp gal) drop tanks

Hawker Siddeley/Avro/British Aerospace 748/Andover

Starting life as an A. V. Roe project in 1958, the original **Type 748** was planned as a 20-seat short/medium-range feeder airliner. When no interest was shown in the design, it was scaled up in size and the Hawker Siddeley Group, of which Avro was a component company, decided to put the aircraft into production.

The first flight of the prototype (G-APZV) took place at Woodford on 24 June 1960. The first production aircraft, capable of seating a maximum of 48 passengers, was designated **Avro 748 Series 1**. It first flew on 31 August 1961, powered by two 1298-kW (1,740-ehp) Rolls-Royce Dart 514 turboprops.

Redesignated **HS.748** in 1963, later versions included the **Series 2** and **Series 2A** (1967) civil transports; **Andover CC.Mk 1** and **CC.Mk 2** for the RAF, the former being two specially equipped examples for The Queen's Flight; the Coastguarder variant was also developed, optimised for maritime patrol, flying in 1977. The improved **Series 2B**, by now called the **BAe 748**, flew in June 1979 and a further update, the **Super 748**, made its debut in 1984. Also produced was the Civil Transport with a large cargo door, and the similar Military Transport with additional fittings for a variety of roles. More than 50 military transports were sold to foreign armed services. Production of all versions, including assembly in India by Hindustan Aircraft, totalled 380 aircraft.

Specification
Hawker Siddeley HS 748 Series 2B
Type: short/medium-range passenger transport
Powerplant: two 1700-ekW (2,280-

Hawker Siddeley Andover C.Mk 1 of No. 46 Squadron, RAF Transport Command, based at Abingdon in the late 1960s.

ehp) Rolls-Royce Dart Mk 555 turboprops
Performance: cruising speed 452 km/h (281 mph); service ceiling 7620 m (25,000 ft); range with maximum payload and fuel reserves 1307 km (812 miles)
Weights: empty 11644 kg (25,671 lb); maximum take-off 23133 kg (51,000 lb)
Dimensions: span 31.23 m (102 ft 5½ in); length 20.42 m (67 ft 0 in); height 7.57 m (24 ft 10 in); wing area 77.00 m² (828.87 sq ft)

The HS.748 sold in small numbers over a long production period. Among the customers were many in the less-developed nations who valued the type's simplicity and reliability.

Hawker Siddeley/de Havilland Trident
to
Heinkel He 115

Hawker Siddeley/de Havilland Trident

The **Trident** originated as the **de Havilland D.H.121** proposal of 1956 to meet a British European Airways requirement for a fast short- and medium-range transport to accommodate about 100 passengers. It was ordered into production in August 1959, selected from design submissions by Avro, Bristol and de Havilland. Plans were made for the aircraft to be manufactured by a consortium comprising de Havilland, Fairey and Hunting, but when de Havilland became a component of the Hawker Siddeley Group in late 1959, Hawker Siddeley became responsible for continued development and manufacture of the Trident under the designation **HS.121**.

The D.H.121 was sized to 140 passengers, and powered by 6350-kg (14,000-lb) thrust Rolls-Royce RB.141 Medway turbofans. At a late stage, with the engine and aircraft in manufacture, BEA insisted that it should be cut down in size, and the D.H.121 was re-sized to 88-95 seats, with 4468-kg (9,850-lb) RB.163 Spey engines. This destroyed the hope of large export sales.

The first production **Trident 1C** (G-ARPA) was flown for the first time on 9 January 1962. The 103-passenger Trident 1 failed to interest other airlines, leading to development of the **Trident 1E**, first flown in September 1965. This had standard seating for 115 passengers, but up to 139 could be accommodated in a high-density seating arrangement. However, limited foreign sales came from the further-developed **Trident 2E**, for in addition to 15 for BEA, two were

supplied to Cyprus Airways and 33 to CAAC, the national airline of the People's Republic of China. From the outset it had been intended that the Trident, operating in the often unpredictable European weather conditions, should have equipment that would ensure high utilisation. This included Smiths Autoland system and the Trident 1/1E had been certificated for automatic landing in Category II weather conditions. However, the Trident 2Es for BEA were delivered with Smiths Autoland at full triplex level, and these airliners were the first in the world to have full all-weather operational instrumentation of this nature.

The last major production version, the **Trident 3B**, was basically a high-capacity short-range version of the Trident 1E, its fuselage 'stretched' by 5.00 m (16 ft 5 in) to seat a maximum of 180 pas-

sengers. Power for take-off was enhanced by installation of a 2381-kg (5,250-lb) thrust Rolls-Royce RB.162-86 turbojet in the aircraft's tail, below the rudder, and the first take-off of a Trident 3B with all four engines operative was recorded on 22 March 1970. The Trident 3B was also equipped with Smiths Autoland and in December 1971 this version was certificated for operation in full Category IIa weather conditions. When production ended in 1975 a total of 117 had been built, the last two being **Trident Super 3B** aircraft for CAAC. They differed from the standard Trident 3B by carrying additional fuel and having seats for 152 passengers.

Specification
Hawker Siddeley Trident 2E
Type: short/medium-range transport
Powerplant: three 5425-kg (11,960-

BAe (Hawker Siddeley) Trident 3B of the Civil Aviation Administration of China (CAAC).

lb) thrust Rolls-Royce Spey RB.163-25 Mk 512-5W turbofans
Performance: cruising speed 974 km/h (605 mph) at 7620 m (25,000 ft); economic cruising speed 959 km/h (596 mph) at 9145 m (30,000 ft); range with typical payload 3965 km (2,464 miles)
Weights: empty operating 33203 kg (73,200 lb); maximum take-off 65318 kg (144,000 lb)
Dimensions: span 29.87 m (98 ft 0 in); length 34.98 m (114 ft 9 in); height 8.23 m (27 ft 0 in); wing area 135.26 m² (1,456.0 sq ft)

Heinkel He 4, He 5, He 8 and He 31

Essentially similar to the He 2, with the same 268-kW (360-hp) Rolls-Royce Eagle IX engine, the **Heinkel He 4**, which appeared in 1926, was an interim aircraft leading to the more powerful **He 5** with a 336-kW (450-hp) Napier Lion. Competition honours included first place in the July 1926 German seaplane event at Warnemünde and a world seaplane

record for a climb to 4492 m (14,738 ft) with a 1000-kg (2,205-lb) payload. Introduced in 1927, the **He 8** was powered by a 336-kW (450-hp) Armstrong Siddeley Jaguar engine; 22 were purchased by Denmark for the naval flying corps, 16 of them built under licence by the Orlogsvaerftet (Naval Shipyards). A number were still in service in April 1940, the last

having been completed in 1938. The **He 31** was essentially an He 8 with a 597-kW (800-hp) Packard engine.

The main operator of the He 8 was the Danish navy, which found the type a reliable and effective coastal reconnaissance floatplane with a crew of three.

Heinkel He 46

Luftwaffe needs for an army co-operation and reconnaissance aircraft were met in 1931 by the **Heinkel He 46**, flown originally in **He 46a** prototype form as an unequal-span biplane. The lower wing reduced the observer's field of view and was removed, changing the configuration to a parasol-wing monoplane. Power was provided by a licence-built Bristol Jupiter engine for the **He 46b** second prototype flown in 1932, but this aircraft was later re-engined with the 485-kW (650-hp) Siemens SAM 22B which was adopted for production aircraft. The Luftwaffe's reconnaissance squadrons had been equipped by 1936, and production was to total 478 He 46s, these being based on the third development aircraft, the **He 46c**, armed with a 7.92-mm (0.31-in) machine-gun in the rear cockpit. Although replaced progressively by the Henschel Hs 126 from

1938, He 46s remained in service in training and utility roles, and from 1943 were used also by the *Storkampfstaffeln* (later *Nachtschlachtgruppen*).

Variants
He 46C-1: initial production version with a camera or 20 10-kg (22-lb) bombs; 20 sent to Spain in 1938 for use by Nationalist forces
He 46C-2: 18 aircraft for Bulgaria; had NACA engine cowlings
He 46D: six pre-production **He 46D-0** aircraft were built, incorporating improvements
He 46E: built in **He 46E-1**, **He 46E-2** and **He 46E-3** versions, often flown without their NACA engine cowlings to facilitate routine maintenance
He 46F: trials with a 418-kW (560-hp) Armstrong Siddeley Panther led to 14 **He 46F-1** and **He 46F-2** unarmed observer training aircraft with this engine

An He 46E-2 observation platform gets airborne. The engine cowling was often left off to ease maintenance problems.

Heinkel He 49 and He 51

Forerunner of the Luftwaffe's first fighter, the **Heinkel He 49a** single-seat biplane flown in November 1932 was ostensibly a civilian advanced trainer. Two more prototypes, the **He 49b** with a lengthened fuselage and **He 49c** with faired landing gear, led to the first **He 51A-0** pre-production aircraft flown in May 1933; eight more unarmed aircraft were built to this standard. Deliveries of the initial armed production version began in July 1934. In April 1935 some equipped the Luftwaffe's first squadron, Jagdgeschwader 'Richthofen'; He 51s flew with the Legion Condor during the Spanish Civil War, and were used also by the Nationalist forces. The type was later relegated to a training role, remaining in service until 1942-43.

Variants

He 51A: initial production **He 51A-1**; 75 built in 1935
He 51B: structurally strengthened **He 51B-0** landplanes (12 built) replaced He 51As on the production line in January 1936; the **He 51B-2** (38 built) was a float-plane fighter version equipped for catapult launching, but sometimes had

Heinkel He 51B-2 of 2./JG 132 'Richthofen' based at Döberitz in 1937.

racks for up to six 10-kg (22-lb) bombs; a long-span high-altitude version was designated **He 51B-3**
He 51C: designation of aircraft modified to carry four 50-kg (110-lb) bombs in basic **He 51C-1** and, with

improved radio, **He 51C-2** versions; used by Legion Condor and Spanish Nationalist units in the Civil War

Specification
Heinkel He 51B-1
Type: single-seat fighter
Powerplant: one 559-kW (750-hp)

BMW VI 7,3Z 12-cylinder Vee piston engine
Performance: maximum speed 330 km/h (205 mph) at sea level; service ceiling 7700 m (25,260 ft); range 570 km (354 miles)
Weights: empty 1460 kg (3,219 lb); maximum take-off 1895 kg (4,178 lb)
Dimensions: span 11.00 m (36 ft 1 in); length 8.40 m (27 ft 6¾ in); height 3.20 m (10 ft 6 in); wing area 27.20 m² (292.79 sq ft)
Armament: two fixed forward-firing 7.92-mm (0.31-in) MG 17 machine-guns

Heinkel He 59

Designed as a reconnaissance bomber, the **Heinkel He 59b** second prototype with faired wheeled landing gear first flew in September 1931. The **He 59a** first prototype, flown in January 1932, had twin single-step floats and all production aircraft, the majority built under sub-contract by Arado, were in marine configuration and powered by two 492-kW (660-hp) BMW VI 6,0ZU engines. Entering service in 1933, some were operated by the Legion Condor in Spain in 1936, and at the outbreak of World War II the type was in service with coastal reconnaissance units, being used as a multi-role trainer, for air-sea rescue, and as a minelayer.

Variants

He 59A: small evaluation batch of unarmed aircraft similar to He 59a prototype
He 59B: 16 pre-production **He 59B-1** aircraft with minor equipment changes and one 7.92-mm (0.31-in) MG 15 machine-gun in the nose; **He 59B-2** had an all-metal nose with glazed

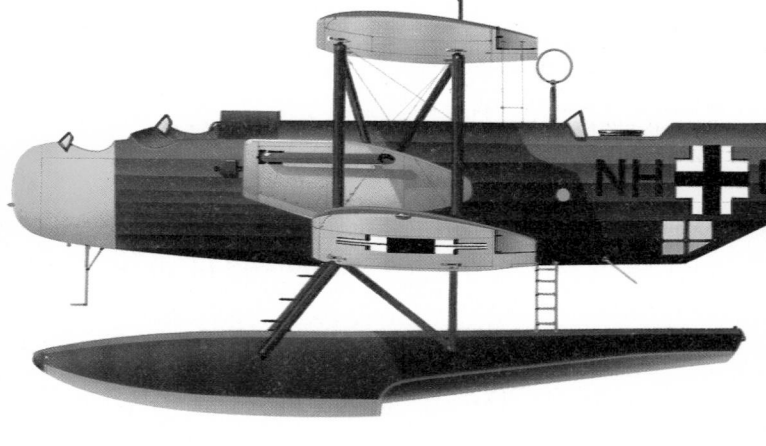

Heinkel He 59D-1 of the Luftwaffe in 1940.

panels for bomb-aimer and extra MG 15 in glazed ventral gun position; He 59B-2s used by Legion Condor for anti-shipping patrols carried a 20-mm MG FF cannon in nose; nose armament

deleted in **He 59B-3** reconnaissance version and auxiliary fuel tanks introduced in fuselage to supplement standard fuel in floats
He 59C: **He 59C-1** was stripped-

down long-range reconnaissance version; the unarmed **He 59C-2** carried six dinghies for air-sea rescue operations
He 59D: similar to He 59C-2, the **He 59D-1** was used as a crew trainer
He 59E: the **He 59E-1** was similar to He 59D-1 but used for training in torpedo launching; the long-range reconnaissance **He 59E-2** (six built) carried three cameras
He 59N: advanced navigation trainers converted from He 59D-1s

Heinkel He 60

Developed for catapult operation from larger German warships, the **Heinkel He 60a** prototype was flown in 1933. Its 492-kW (660-hp) BMW VI engine was replaced in the **He 60b** second prototype by a 559-kW (750-hp) version of the same engine; this offered no significant improvement and was not adopted for subsequent aircraft. The **He 60c** third prototype, equipped for catapult launching, was used for trials which confirmed its suitability for shipboard use. Unarmed aircraft entered service with training units in 1933, and operational versions served subsequently aboard German battle-cruisers and cruisers. Relegated to training duties in northern

Europe fairly early in World War II, the He 60 remained in service as a maritime reconnaissance aircraft with units based in Greece and Crete.

Variants

He 60A: 14 pre-production aircraft used in Kriegsmarine training schools
He 60B: initial production version; one aircraft designated **He 60B-3** evaluated with 671-kW (900-hp) Daimler-Benz DB 600 engine
He 60C: improved version of He 60B introduced in 1934
He 60D: unarmed trainer version

The He 60 was quickly relegated from its intended role as a catapult-launched spotter to coastal patrols and training.

Heinkel He 70, He 170 and He 270

Designed to a Deutsche Lufthansa specification issued in February 1932, for an aircraft to compete with Swissair's Lock-

heed Orions, the **Heinkel He 70** was developed as a fast, four-passenger mail aircraft. The original 285-km/h (177-mph)

maximum speed requirement was increased to 300 km/h (186 mph), the Günter brothers producing an aerodynamically efficient airframe with an elevated cockpit offset to port for the pilot, a navigator/radio operator's position below and behind, and a passenger cabin with four seats in facing pairs. Power was supplied by a closely-cowled 470-kW

Heinkel He 70F of a Luftwaffe Kurierstaffel in 1940/41.

(630-hp) BMW VI 6,0Z engine; this was cooled by ethylene-glycol, which required a smaller radiator and thus reduced drag.

The prototype, with fixed landing gear and faired-over wheel wells, was flown from Travemünde by Flugkapitän Werner Junck on 1 December 1932. In early 1933 this aircraft achieved a level speed of 376 km/h (234 mph) and in March and April the second prototype was used by Lufthansa's Flugkapitän R. Untucht to set eight world speed records. Production **He 70A** aircraft entered service with Lufthansa in June 1934; introduction of a 559-kW (750-hp) BMW VI 7,3 engine produced the **He 70D** military

communications and the civil counterpart was the lengthened-fuselage **He 70G**, which was crewed only by a pilot who sat in a cockpit relocated on the fuselage centreline. One **He 70G-1** was supplied to Rolls-Royce Ltd in 1935, powered initially by a 604-kW (810-hp) Kestrel engine and later used extensively as an engine test-bed. In addition to the He 70D communications aircraft, other military models comprised the **He 70E** with a crew of two, a 7.92-mm (0.31-in) MG 17 machine-gun in the rear cockpit and able to carry a 300-kg (661-lb) bombload, and the **He 70F**. The latter was produced in two versions, the **He 70F-1** long-range reconnaissance

variant and the generally similar **He 70F-2**, 18 of which were sent to the Legion Condor in Spain in the autumn of 1936, serving with the A/88 reconnaissance unit.

For export to Hungary in 1937, Heinkel developed the **He 170** which differed primarily in having a 679-kW (910-hp) Gnome-Rhône 14K Mistral-Major engine. Approximately 20 were delivered and served with the 1st Independent Long-Range Reconnaissance Group, remaining in service until July 1941. The last of the He 70 line was the **He 270**, built only as a prototype and flown in 1938. Its 876-kW (1,175-hp) Daimler-Benz DB 601A engine gave it a

maximum speed of 460 km/h (286 mph). Armed with one forward-firing MG 17 and two rearward-firing MG 15 machine-guns and capable of carrying the same 300-kg (661-lb) bombload as the He 70E, the He 270 was intended to combine the light bomber and reconnaissance roles, but was not adopted by the Luftwaffe.

Specification
Heinkel He 70D
Type: communications aircraft
Powerplant: one 559-kW (750-hp) BMW VI 7,3 12-cylinder Vee piston engine
Performance: maximum speed 360 km/h (223 mph); service ceiling 5485 m (18,000 ft); range 1250 km (776 miles)
Weights: empty 2530 kg (5,579 lb); maximum take-off 3640 kg (7,629 lb)
Dimensions: span 14.80 m (48 ft 6¾ in); length 11.70 m (38 ft 4½ in); height 3.25 m (10 ft 8 in); wing area 36.51 m² (393.0 sq ft)

Heinkel He 72 Kadett

An elementary trainer of 1933, the **Heinkel He 72 Kadett** (cadet) biplane was powered initially by a 104-kW (140-hp) Argus As 8B engine. The type equipped a number of National Socialist Flying Corps training schools before becoming a standard pilot trainer of the Luftwaffe.

Variants
He 72A: initial production version with Argus 8B engine; later aircraft had 112-kW (150-hp) Argus As 8R
He 72B: **He 72B-1** was major production version with Siemens Sh 14A engine; built also as **He 72B-3 Edelkadett** civil tourer/trainers, and **He 72BW** twin-float seaplanes
He 172: one improved He 72B prototype built 1934

Unglamorous but most effective, the Heinkel He 72B Kadett was used in large numbers by civilian and Luftwaffe schools. It was of great use to the war effort, training many military pilots.

Specification
Heinkel He 72B
Type: two-seat primary trainer
Powerplant: one 119-kW (160-hp) Siemens Sh 14A engine
Performance: maximum speed 185 km/h (115 mph); service ceiling 3500 m (11,485 ft); range 475 km (295 miles)
Weights: empty 540 kg (1,191 lb); maximum take-off 865 kg (1,907 lb)

Dimensions: span 9.00 m (29 ft 6¼ in); length 7.50 m (24 ft 7¼ in); height 2.70 m (8 ft 10¼ in); wing area 20.70 m² (222.82 sq ft)

Heinkel He 100

Although Messerschmitt's Bf 109 had been adopted as the Luftwaffe's standard monoplane fighter in preference to Heinkel's He 112 submission, Heinrich Hertel and Siegfried Günter designed a new high-speed fighter with a design maximum speed of 700 km/h (435 mph). It was also engineered for ease of production with few curves and the minimum number of parts and components. The resulting **Heinkel He 100a** prototype made its first flight on 22 January 1938, powered by a Daimler-Benz DB 601 engine with a special pressurised evaporative cooling system. A second prototype, with a DB 601M engine, captured the 100-km (62-mile) closed-circuit landplane record on 6 June 1938, piloted by Ernst Udet. The aircraft was referred to officially as an **He 112U**, to boost the reputation of the He 112B sold to Japan and Spain. The third prototype, built for an attempt on the world absolute speed record, had reduced wing span, a more streamlined cockpit canopy and a boosted DB 601 engine, but it crashed in September and was replaced by the similar eighth prototype. In this aircraft Hans Dieterle raised the record to 746.61 km/h (463.92 mph) at Oranienburg on 30 March 1939. The fourth and fifth aircraft were designated **He 100B,** prototypes six, seven and

Heinkel He 100D-1 in spurious Luftwaffe markings.

nine were completed to **He 100C** standard; the third of these was the first He 100 to be armed, carrying two 20-mm MG FF cannon and four 7.92-mm (0.31-in) MG 17 machine-guns.

Handling deficiencies revealed during service evaluation at Erprobungsstelle Rechlin resulted in introduction of the **He 100D** with enlarged tail surfaces and with a conventional, semi-retractable ventral radiator in place of the earlier enclosed system. It was armed with a 20-mm MG FF cannon in the nose and two 7.92-mm (0.31-in) MG 17 machine-guns in the wings. Fifteen He 100Ds were built, comprising three **He 100D-0** pre-production examples and 12 **He 100D-1** production aircraft, the latter being retained at Heinkel's Rostock-Marienehe factory and flown by

An altogether exceptional fighter, the He 100D fell foul of political factors and shortages of the DB 601 engine, and was therefore not placed into the widespread production its merits deserved.

Heinkel staff pilots as a local defence unit. As DB 601 engines had been earmarked for Bf 109 production, the He 100 was not adopted for Luftwaffe use and the company was authorised to offer it for foreign licence-manufacture. In October 1939 Japanese and Soviet teams visited Marienehe and, as a result, three He 100D-0 aircraft were sold to Japan and six of the prototypes to the USSR. Proposed Japanese production did not materialise.

Specification
Heinkel He 100D-1
Type: single-seat fighter
Powerplant: one 876-kW (1,175-hp) Daimler-Benz DB 601M 12-cylinder Vee piston engine
Performance: maximum speed 670 km/h (416 mph); service ceiling 9890 m (32,450 ft); range 1005 km (625 miles)
Weights: empty 2070 kg (4,563 lb);
maximum take-off 2500 kg (5,512 lb)
Dimensions: span 9.42 m (30 ft 10¾ in); length 8.19 m (26 ft 10¼ in); height 2.50 m (8 ft 2½ in); wing area 14.50 m² (156.08 sq ft)
Armament: one 20-mm MG FF cannon and two 7.92-mm (0.31-in) MG 17 machine-guns

Heinkel He 111

Although the **Heinkel He 111** was designed ostensibly as a civil airliner, its military potential was of greater importance. The **He 111 V1** first prototype, an enlarged development of the Heinkel He 70 with two 492-kW (660-hp) BMW VI 6,0Z engines, was flown on 24 February 1935. Shorter-span wings were introduced on the second and third prototypes (**He 111 V2** and **He 111 V3**), the second being a civil transport accommodating 10 passengers and mail, and the third the true bomber prototype. The **He 111 V4** (civil) prototype was demonstrated publicly on 10 January 1936, and six **He 111C** series aircraft derived from this prototype, entered service with Lufthansa in the same year with various engines including BMW 132 radials.

Development of the military version continued, but the 270-km/h (168-mph) cruising speed that resulted from too much military equipment and too little power proved disappointing. Thus the **He 111 V5**, prototype of the military **He 111B** series flown in early 1936, had two 746-kW (1,000-hp) Daimler-Benz DB 600A engines. Its improved performance brought substantial orders, requiring new production facilities that were completed in May 1937. Initial deliveries to an operational squadron, 1./KG 154 at Fassberg, were made in late 1936, and in February 1937 30 **He 111B-1** bombers were delivered to the Legion Condor bomber unit K/88 in Spain. The He 111 bore the brunt of the Luftwaffe's bombing effort in early World War II: Poland in the autumn of 1939, Norway and Denmark in April 1940, France and the Low Countries in May and British targets during the Battle of Britain. Large-scale introduction of the Junkers Ju 88, and the He 111's vulnerability to British fighters, resulted in the Heinkel bomber being transferred to night operations and a variety of specialised roles, including missile-carrier, torpedo-bomber, pathfinder and glider-tug. Transport duties were also undertaken, including operations to supply the beleaguered German army at Stalingrad between November 1942 and February 1943, and by the end of the war He 111s were virtually flown in a transport role only. Production of more than 7,300 for the Luftwaffe was completed in the autumn of 1944; in addition some 236 **He 111Hs** were built by CASA in Spain during and after the war as the **CASA 2.111**, about 130 with Jumo 211F-2 engines, the remainder with Rolls-Royce Merlin 500-29s; some were converted later for transport and training duties.

Variants
He 111A: following unsatisfactory tests of 10 pre-production **He 111A-0** bombers, all were sold to China
He 111B: testing of the fifth prototype with 746-kW (1,000-hp) DB 600A engines led in 1936 to the production **He 111B-1** with 656-kW (880-hp) DB 600C engines, followed by the **He 111B-2** with the 708-kW (950-hp) DB 600CG
He 111C: six 10-passenger airliners for Lufthansa

Heinkel He 111H-3 of 2./KGr 100 based at Vannes, Brittany in 1940/41, equipped with X-Gerät for the pathfinder role.

He 111D: improved version with DB 600Ga engines and auxiliary wing radiators deleted; production discontinued in favour of the He 111E
He 111E: shortage of DB 600 engines brought installation of 746-kW (1,000-hp) Junkers Jumo 211A-1 engines in an He 111D-0 airframe; the resulting **He 111E-0** pre-production prototype had increased bombload; production **He 111E-1** bombers were delivered in 1938, followed by the **He 111E-3** and **He 111E-4** with further increase in bombload and **He 111E-5** with fuselage auxiliary fuel tank
He 111F: the new wing of the He 111G and Jumo 211A-3 engines characterised the 24 **He 111F-1** bombers supplied to Turkey; the Luftwaffe received 40 similar **He 111F-4** aircraft in 1938
He 111G: first version with the new straight-taper wing which, incorporated on the He 111C, brought redesignation **He 111G-1**; the **He 111G-3** had 656-kW (880-hp) BMW 132Dc engines, the **He 111G-4** 671-kW (900-hp) DB 600Gs, and four **He 111G-5** aircraft for Turkey had DB 600Ga engines
He 111H: developed in parallel with the He 111P series, the **He 111H-0** and **He 111H-1** were basically He 111P-2s with 753-kW (1,100-hp) Jumo 211A engines; the **He 111H-2** of 1939 had improved armament; the **He 111H-3** introduced armour protection and a 20-mm cannon; the **He 111H-4** had Jumo 211D engines and two external racks for bombs or torpedoes, and the generally similar **He 111H-5** had increased fuel capacity; the **He 111H-6** introduced Jumo 211F-1 engines and machine-gun in the tailcone; **He 111H-8** was the redesignation of He 111H-3s and He 111H-5s following installation of fenders for balloon cables, most of them being converted later to **He 111H-8/R2** glider tugs; the **He 111H-10** for night bombing of UK targets had additional armour, reduced armament and wing leading-edge balloon cable-cutters; the **He 111H-11** and **He 111H-11/R1** had revised armament, the last becoming **He 111H-11/R2** when converted later as a glider tug; the **He 111H-12** and **He 111H-15** were missile-launchers, the **He 111H-14** a pathfinder version and the **He 111H-14/R2** a glider tug; introduced in 1942, the **He 111H-16**

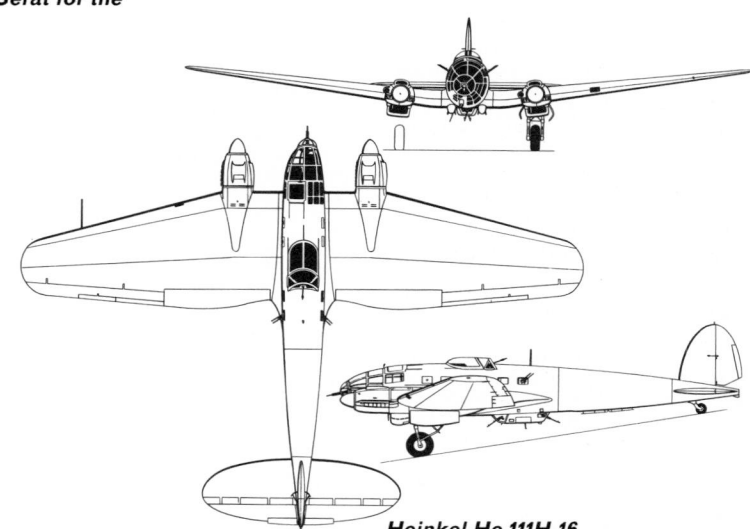

Heinkel He 111H-16

During the early part of World War II, the He 111 was the Luftwaffe's principal bomber, partaking in many campaigns.

was a major production variant similar to the He 111H-11 but able to carry a 3250-kg (7,165-lb) bombload with the use of rocket-assisted take-off gear; the **He 111H-16/R1** had a revolving dorsal turret, the **He 111H-16/R2** was for rigid-bar towing of gliders and the **He 111H-16/R3** was a pathfinder version, as was the **He 111H-18** with exhaust flame-dampers; four versions of the **He 111H-20** comprised the **He** 111H-20/R1 carrying 16 paratroops, the **He 111H-20/R2** night bomber/glider tug, the **He 111H-20/R3** with increased armour protection and the generally similar **He 111H-20/R4** which introduced GM-1 power boost equipment; a version of the He 111H-20/R3 with 1305-kW (1,750-hp) Jumo 213E-1 engines and two-stage superchargers was designated **He 111H-21**; the **He 111H-22** was

a missile-carrier; and the **He 111H-23** was a paratroop transport with 1324-kW (1,776-hp) Jumo 213A-1 engines
He 111J: torpedo-bomber version of the He 111F series, the **He 111J-0** and **He 111J-1** both had 708-kW (950-hp) DB 600CG engines
He 111L: alternative designation for He 111G-3 civil transport
He 111P: in 1939 the He 111P series introduced a major fuselage redesign, the stepped cockpit being replaced by an asymmetric glazed cockpit and nose; the **He 111P-0** introduced a prone position ventral gondola and was powered by two 858-kW (1,150-hp) DB 601Aa engines; first deliveries of the **He 111P-1** began in late 1939; the **He 111P-2** was similar but for radio revisions; the **He 111P-3** had dual controls; the five-crew **He 111P-4** had more armour and armament; the **He 111P-6** had 876-kW (1,175-hp) DB 601 N engines and its 2000-kg (4,409-lb) bombload

stowed vertically in the fuselage; when later converted as a glider tug the He 111P-6 became the **He 111P-6/R2**
He 111R: single prototype of proposed high-altitude bomber
He 111Z: the He 111Z (Zwilling, or twin) combined two He 111H-6 airframes, joined by a new wing centre-section to mount a fifth Jumo 211F-2 engine; designed to tow the Messerschmitt Me 321 Gigant transport glider; two prototypes and 10 **He 111Z-1** production aircraft were built

Specification
Heinkel He 111H-16
Type: medium bomber
Powerplant: two 1007-kW (1,350-hp) Jumo 211F-2 12-cylinder inverted-Vee piston engines
Performance: maximum speed 365 km/h (227 mph) at sea level; service ceiling 6700 m (21,980 ft); range 1950 km (1,212 miles)

Weights: empty 8680 kg (19,136 lb); maximum take-off 14000 kg (30,865 lb)
Dimensions: span 22.60 m (74 ft 1¾ in); length 16.40 m (53 ft 9½ in); height 4.00 m (13 ft 1¼ in); wing area 86.50 m² (931.11 sq ft)
Armament: one 20-mm MG FF cannon, one 13-mm (0.51-in) MG 131 machine-gun and three 7.92-mm (0.31-

One of World War II's great oddities was the He 111Z: two He 111Hs joined by a common centre-section mounting a fifth engine.

in) MG 81Z machine-guns, plus a normal internal bombload of 1000 kg (2,205 lb)

Heinkel He 112

Seeking a replacement for the Heinkel He 51 and Arado Ar 68 biplane fighters, the Reichsluftfahrtministerium issued in 1933 a specification for a monoplane, drawing submissions from Arado, Focke-Wulf, Heinkel and Messerschmitt. The prototype **Heinkel He 112** was evaluated competitively with the three other designs at Travemünde in October 1935 and both it and Messerschmitt's Bf 109 received orders for 10 aircraft. Powered by a 518-kW (695-hp) Rolls-Royce Kestrel V engine, the prototype was followed by two further aircraft with reduced-span wings and 447-kW (600-hp) Jumo 210C engines. The fourth prototype, with a new elliptical wing, was evaluated operationally with the Legion Condor in Spain in 1936, and was shown at the July 1937 Zürich International Flying Meeting. The proposed **He 112A** production aircraft was not adopted by the Luftwaffe, which re-

Heinkel He 112B-0 temporarily on the strength of III/JG 132 and based at Fürstenwalde during the Sudeten Crisis of August 1938.

ceived the Bf 109 instead, but work continued on the structurally-redesigned **He 112B**, the 507-kW (680-hp) Jumo 210Ea-powered production prototype which flew in July 1937. Twelve of 30 aircraft ordered by Japan were delivered in the spring of 1938, but the next 12 were im-

pressed for Luftwaffe use, although 11 of these and the final six were supplied later to the Spanish Nationalist air force in November 1938. Thirteen **He 112B-0** and 11 **He 112B-1** aircraft were delivered to the Romanian air force, the order being completed in September

1939, and three He 112B-1s were acquired by the Hungarian air force in the spring of 1939. Armament of the He 112B series was two wing-mounted 20-mm MG FF cannon and two 7.92-mm (0.31-in) MG 17 machine-guns in the upper engine cowling.

Heinkel He 114

Intended to replace Heinkel's own He 60, the **Heinkel He 114** was developed originally as a private venture. Five prototypes, flown in 1936 and 1937, were powered by a variety of engines, including the 716-kW (960-hp) Daimler-Benz DB 600, the 477-kW (640-hp) Junkers Jumo 210, the 656-kW (880-hp) BMW 132Dc and the 716-kW (960-hp) BMW 132K. Ten pre-production **He 114A-0**

aircraft were built, with the BMW 132Dc engine, which was adopted also for the 33 **He 114A-1** trainers. A development aircraft with a BMW 132K engine, flown on 16 February 1937, preceded the similarly-powered **He 114A-2** which was the first operational version, armed with a fixed forward-firing 7.92-mm (0.31-in) MG 17 machine-gun and an identical weapon mounted in the observer's cockpit. Export orders comprised 14 He 114A-2s for Sweden as the **He 114B-1**, and six **He 114B-2** aircraft for Romania

An He 114C-1 of 1. Staffel, Seeaufklärungsgruppe 125 in flight during 1941. This unit saw service in the eastern Mediterranean during 1941/42.

(three with DB 600 engines and three with Jumo 210s). Romania also bought 12 He 114B-2s with BMW 132K engines. Fourteen **He 114C-1** aircraft, with an additional fixed MG 17, were supplied to the Luftwaffe. The type saw limited wartime service, although production

ceased in 1939, and some were armed with up to four 50-kg (110-lb) bombs.

Heinkel He 115

Developed to replace the He 59, the **Heinkel He 115** floatplane prototype was flown during 1936. Its two machine-guns were then removed, their positions faired over, and on 30 March 1938 the aircraft set eight payload/speed records. The second prototype was similar, the third introduced the 'glasshouse' canopy which became standard, and the fourth was the production prototype with float/fuselage bracing wires replaced by struts. The He 115s were used by coastal reconnaissance squadrons of the Luftwaffe, and after the outbreak of World War II were deployed to drop parachute mines in British waters. Four reached the UK from Norway, three being modified later for clandestine operations to Norway and the Mediterranean.

An He 115B-1 built under licence by Weser Flugzeugbau is seen in mint condition while under test in the spring of 1940.

Variants
He 115A: 10 pre-production **He 115A-0** aircraft of 1937 had a single machine-gun; the **He 115A-1** added a nose-mounted machine-gun and the similar **He 115A-2** was exported to Norway and Sweden; the Luftwaffe's first **He 115A-3** production version had a modified bomb bay and radio changes
He 115B: the **He 115B-1** had increased fuel capacity, and the **He 115B-2** reinforced floats for operation from snow or ice; He 115B series aircraft, able to trade fuel and bombload, were able to carry a 1000-kg (2,205-lb) magnetic mine

He 115C: introduced in 1941, the **He 115C-1** had additional armament; the **He 115C-2** had reinforced floats like those of the He 115B-2; and the **He 115C-3** and **He 115C-4** were minelaying and torpedo-carrying versions respectively

He 115D: designation of one He 115A-1 airframe with two 1193-kW (1,600-hp) BMW 801C engines
He 115E: the production line was reopened in 1941, the new **He 115E-1** being similar to the He 115C but with armament revisions

Heinkel He 116
to
Helwan HA-300

Heinkel He 116

In reality little more than an experimental aircraft, the He 116B-0 was used for survey work only over German-occupied territory.

Developed in 1936 as a mailplane for Deutsche Lufthansa, the **Heinkel He 116** made use of design features of the He 70 and He 111, particularly the elliptical wing and tail surfaces. The aircraft was to have been powered originally by four 373-kW (500-hp) Hirth engines, but these were not available in time and the 179-kW (240-hp) Hirth HM 508 engine was substituted. Eight civil aircraft were built with the designation **He 116A-0**, the first making its maiden flight in the

summer of 1937. Two of them were purchased by Manchurian Air Transport and made their 15337-km (9,530-mile) delivery flights from Berlin to Tokyo between 23 and 29 April 1938, in a time of 54 hours 17 minutes. Another was modified for record-breaking, with 179-kW (240-hp) Hirth HM 508H engines, a wing of increased span and area and provision

for rocket-assisted take-off equipment. Designated **He 116R**, it set a distance record of 10,000 km (6,214 miles) in 48 hours 18 minutes, beginning on 30 June

1938. An **He 116B** long-range reconnaissance version was also developed, the last two civil aircraft serving as prototypes, and a total of six was built.

Heinkel He 119

Intended as a high-speed reconnaissance bomber, the single-engined **Heinkel He 119** developed in 1936 was notable for the unusual completely glazed nose in which two of the three-man crew sat on each side of a long propeller shaft. This was driven by two Daimler-Benz DB 601 engines, joined as a close-coupled unit under the designation DB 606. Four prototypes were built with retractable landing gear, the last of

them making a world class record flight on 22 November 1937, in which it achieved 620 km/h (385 mph) over 1609 km (1,000 miles) with a payload of 1000 kg (2,205 lb). A fifth prototype was completed as a twin float seaplane and evaluated by the German naval seaplane training school at Travemünde; it was scrapped at Marienehe in 1942.

Designed for maximum aerodynamic efficiency, the He 119 programme was plagued with technical problems. This is the V5.

Heinkel He 162 Salamander

The prototype of the **Heinkel He 162** turbojet-engined interceptor was flown for the first time on 6 December 1944, only 38 days after detail drawings had been issued to the factory. This prototype was lost in a fatal flying accident on 10 December, but the programme was continued and revealed some aerodynamic problems, these being remedied in the third and fourth prototypes, both flown on 16 January 1945; first deliveries of aircraft for operational evaluation and service trials were also made during January 1945.

On 4 May 1945 one *Gruppe* of three squadrons, with a total of 50 aircraft, was formed at Leck in Schleswig-Hol-

stein, but British forces occupied the airfield on 8 May and accepted the unit's surrender. A total of 116 He 162s was built, and more than 800 were in various stages of assembly when the underground production centres were captured.

Variant
He 162A: the 10 prototypes were also designated **He 162A-0** as pre-production aircraft; initial production **He 162A-1** fighters were followed by the more extensively-built **He 162A-2** which introduced further aerodynamic changes to enhance stability

Specification
Type: single-seat fighter
Powerplant: one 800-kg (1,764-lb) thrust BMW 003A-1 turbojet
Performance: maximum speed 840 km/h (522 mph) at 6000 m (19,685 ft); service ceiling 12040 m (39,500 ft); endurance 57 minutes at 10970 m (35,990 ft)
Weights: empty 2050 kg (4,520 lb); maximum take-off 2695 kg (5,941 lb)
Dimensions: span 7.20 m (23 ft 7½ in); length 9.05 m (29 ft 8¼ in); height 2.55 m (8 ft 4½ in); wing area 11.20 m^2 (120.56 sq ft)
Armament: two 20-mm MG 151/20 cannon

An attractive and potentially useful fighter, the He 162 was too hastily developed, and suffered many problems. Shown here is an He 162A-2 of JG 1.

Heinkel He 162A-2 of 3./JG 1, based at Leck in Schleswig-Holstein during May 1945.

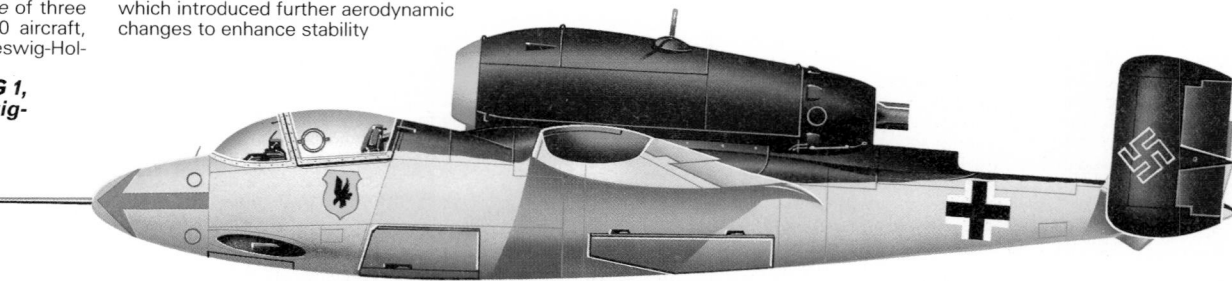

Heinkel He 177 Greif

Developed from Heinkel's **P.1041** project for a long-range bomber, the prototype of the resulting **Heinkel He 177 Greif** (griffon) was flown for the first time on 19 November 1939. With no engine in the 1492-kW (2,000-hp) class available, Daimler-Benz close-coupled two DB 601s to produce the 1939-kW (2,600-hp) DB 606, and two of these units were used to power the He 177. The design's other unusual feature was twin main landing gear units on each side, these retracting sideways into the wing, inboard and outboard of each

engine nacelle. There were many early teething problems, at least three prototypes being lost in accidents resulting from wing structural weakness or engine fires. The structural problems were soon rectified, but overheating of the coupled engine units, which occasionally caused engine fires, was never completely resolved.

Early production **He 177A-1**s were delivered in July 1942, these still having structural problems, and it was not until late 1942 that the more reliable **He 177A-3** began to enter service. French-

and German-based He 177s took part in operations against targets in the UK during Operation Steinbock and saw service on the Eastern Front, but a variety of problems and a need for the German industry to concentrate their efforts on more vital fighter aircraft meant that the He 177s had been virtually withdrawn from service by the end of 1944. One noteworthy but uncompleted aircraft was a single example under modification in Prague to accommodate the planned German atomic bomb.

Variants
He 177A-0: 35 pre-production aircraft used for development trials and

The He 177A-5/R2 had a ventral and two underwing racks for the carriage of Fritz X or Hs 293 anti-ship weapons.

conversion training
He 177A-1: 130 built by Arado in four versions, designated **He 177A-1/R1** to

He 177A-1/R4, each with minor variations; introduced in March 1942
He 177A-3: 170 built by Heinkel, the first 15 **He 177A-3/R1** bombers with DB 606A/B engines and the remainder with DB 610 engines; the **He 177A-3/R2** had improved armament; the **He 177A-3/R3** carried three Henschel Hs 293 missiles; the **He 177A-3/R4** had a gondola containing FuG 203 missile-control equipment; the **He 177A-3/R5** was armed with a 75-mm cannon in a ventral gondola; and three **He 177A-3/R7** aircraft were each equipped to carry two torpedoes
He 177A-4: proposed high-altitude version
He 177A-5: version with structural

modifications, primarily strengthened wing for heavier underwing loads; the **He 177A-5/R1** to **He 177A-5/R4** had minor armament changes; the **He 177A-5/R5** had a remotely-controlled barbette to the rear of the bomb bays, the first two of which were deleted in the **He 177A-5/R6**; the **He 177A-5/R7** had a pressurised cockpit; and the **He 177A-5/R8** had barbettes in chin and rear positions; five He 177A-5s had the bomb bay area modified to house an array of 33 rocket tubes, the weapons being fired upwards at a forward angle of 60°
He 177A-6/R1: six **He 177A-6/R1** aircraft were built as development examples of proposed version with

extra armament, and armour protection for the crew compartment and fuel tanks; one development aircraft was flown with new forward fuselage and heavier armament intended for **He 177A-6/R2**
He 177A-7: six He 177A-5 airframes were modified with a 36 m (118 ft 1½ in) wing intended for the production He 177A-7, and with DB 610 engines instead of the intended 2685-kW (3,600-hp) DB 613s

Specification
Heinkel He 177A-5/R2
Type: heavy-bomber
Powerplant: two 2200-kW (2,950-hp) Daimler-Benz DB 610A/B 24-cylinder

double inverted-Vee piston engines
Performance: maximum speed 490 km/h (304 mph) at 6000 m (19,685 ft); service ceiling 8000 m (26,245 ft); range 5500 km (3,417 miles) with two H5 293 missiles
Weights: empty 16800 kg (37,038 lb); maximum take-off 31000 kg (68,343 lb)
Dimensions: span 31.44 m (103 ft 1¾ in); length 20.40 m (66 ft 11¼ in); height 6.39 m (20 ft 11¾ in); wing area 102.00 m² (1,097.95 sq ft)
Armament: three 7.92-mm (0.31-in) MG 81, three 13-mm (0.51-in) MG 131 machine-guns and two 20-mm MG 151/20 cannon, plus 1000 kg (2,205 lb) of bombs internally and two Henschel Hs 293 missiles under the wings

---

Heinkel He 178

At the same time that work was in progress on the He 176 rocket aircraft, Heinkel was busily developing the turbojet-powered **Heinkel He 178** which featured the company's HeS 3b engine, with an effective rating of some 340-kg

(750-lb) thrust. It became the world's first turbojet aircraft to fly when, on 27 August 1939, Flugkapitän Erich Warsitz made a circuit of the factory airfield at Rostock-Marienehe. Development was very much on a private-venture basis and it was not until 28 October 1939 that official observers, in the persons of Milch, Udet and Lucht of the Reichsluftfahrts-

ministerium, were to see the aircraft in flight. The project attracted little interest at the time and work was discontinued in favour of the He 280.

Purely experimental, the He 178 was the world's first turbojet-powered aircraft, flying nearly two years before the E.28/39.

Heinkel He 219 Uhu

Potentially one of the Luftwaffe's most effective night-fighters, the **Heinkel He 219 Uhu** (owl) was another aircraft which suffered from misjudgements by senior members of the government and Luftwaffe high command. It derived from Heinkel's private-venture **P.1060** fighter-bomber proposal, which received little encouragement until 1941 when it was seen to have promise as a night-fighter. An all-metal shoulder-wing monoplane, the He 219 seated the pilot and navigator back-to-back, was the first operational aircraft in the world to introduce ejection seats, and was also the Luftwaffe's first operational aircraft with tricycle landing gear.

The first prototype was flown on 15 November 1942, powered by two 1305-kW (1,750-hp) Daimler-Benz DB 603A engines; the second prototype, flown in December, had a different armament installation. Following evaluation of one of the prototypes in mock combat against a Dornier Do 217N and a Junkers Ju 88S, an 'off the drawing board' order for 100 aircraft was increased to 300; further prototypes were used in the aircraft's development programme. From April 1943 a small number of **He 219A-0** pre-production aircraft flew with 1.NJG 1 at Venlo in the Netherlands, and on the night of 11 June 1943 Major Werner Streib shot down five Avro Lancasters in a single sortie. The first six operational sorties flown by

the unit resulted in claims for 20 RAF aircraft, including six de Havilland Mosquitoes. Despite cancellation of the programme in May 1944, production deliveries of a number of versions were made, principally to 1./NJG 1 and NJGr 10.

Variants
He 219A-2: the **He 219A-1** reconnaissance bomber having been abandoned at the project stage, the **He 219A-2/R1** night-fighter was the first production version; armed with two 30-mm MK 108 cannon in a ventral tray and two 20-mm MG 151/20s in the wing roots; the *schräge Musik* installation of two MK 108 cannon behind the cockpit, firing obliquely upwards and forwards, was a retrospective installation
He 219A-5: first major production version, generally similar to He 219A-1; the **He 219A-5/R1** had 1342-kW

(1,800-hp) DB 603A engines and increased fuel capacity; and the **He 219A-5/R4**, which differed by carrying a third crew member, had a stepped cockpit with a pivoted 13-mm (0.51-in) machine-gun
He 219A-6: stripped-down version of the He 219A-2/R1 with 1305-kW (1,750-hp) DB 603L engines and four MG 151/20s; developed specifically to combat RAF Mosquitoes
He 219A-7: similar to the He 219A-5 but with improved supercharger intakes for its DB 603G engines; in addition to the standard *schräge Musik* installation, the **He 219A-7/R1** had two wing root-mounted MK 108s, and two MG 151s and two 30-mm MK 103s in the ventral tray; the **He 219A-7/R2** had MK 108s in place of the ventral MK 103s, and the **He 219A-7/R3** had the wing root MK 108s replaced by MG 151s and the ventral tray of the He 219A-7/R2; the **He 219A-7/R4** had tail warning radar and just four MG 151s; six **He 219A-7/R5** night-fighters were effectively He 219A-7/R3s with 1417-kW (1,900-hp) Junkers Jumo 213E engines and a water-methanol injection system; the single **He 219A-7/R6** had

two 1864-kW (2,500-hp) Jumo 222A/B engines

Specification
Heinkel He 219A-7/R1
Type: two-seat night-fighter
Powerplant: two 1417-kW (1,900-hp) Daimler-Benz DB 603G piston engines
Performance: maximum speed 670 km/h (416 mph); cruising speed 630 km/h (391 mph); service ceiling 12200 m (40,025 ft); range 2000 km (1,243 miles)
Weights: empty 11200 kg (24,692 lb); maximum take-off 15300 kg (33,730 lb)
Dimensions: span 18.50 m (60 ft 8¼ in); length 15.54 m (50 ft 11¾ in); height 4.10 m (13 ft 5¼ in); wing area 44.50 m² (479.01 sq ft)
Armament: four 30-mm MK 108, two 20-mm MG 151/20 and two 30-mm MK 103 cannon

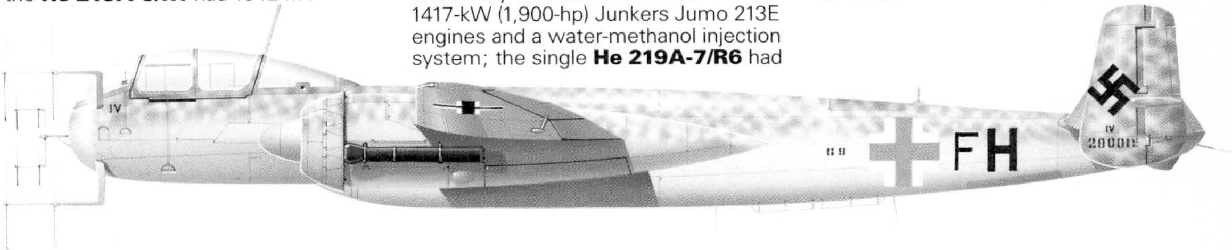

Heinkel He 219A-5/R1 of NJG 1, based at Munster in the autumn of 1944.

Heinkel He 274

Developed in substitution for the planned He 177A-4 high-altitude bomber, the **Heinkel He 274** was the detail design responsibility of Société Anonyme des Usines Farman's Suresnes factory in occupied France. Fitted with a pressure cabin, the aircraft was powered by four 1305-kW (1,750-hp) Daimler-Benz DB 603A-2 engines and featured a lengthened version of the He 177A-3 fuselage, with a new high-aspect-ratio wing and twin fins and rudders. Two prototypes were ordered in May 1943, together with four **He 274A-0** pre-production examples, which were to have 1417-kW (1,900-hp)

DB 603G engines. Despite an unsuccessful German attempt to destroy the almost-complete first prototype when they retreated from Paris in July 1944, the aircraft was finished by the French after the liberation and flown from Orleans-Bricy in December 1945 as the **AAS 01A**. It was used later to test-fly models of such aircraft as the Aerocentre NC 270 and the Sud-Ouest SO 4000.

The sole prototype of the He 274 to be completed was evaluated in France, where it was finished after the liberation.

Heinkel He 277

In an effort to overcome the problems being experienced with the coupled DB 606 engines of the He 177, Heinkel suggested in 1940 that four separate DB 603s should be substituted. Although the Reichsluftfahrtsministerium rejected the plan, work continued unofficially under the designation **He 177B** and the design was resurrected in response to Hitler's May 1943 demand for a heavy bomber to facilitate effective strikes on London. Converted from an He

The He 277V1 differed mainly from the He 177 by introducing a genuine four-engine powerplant which reduced the fire problem.

177A-3/R2 airframe, with four DB 603A engines, the first **Heinkel He 277** prototype flew at Vienna-Schwechat in the closing months of 1943, followed by the second aircraft on 28 February 1944. Directional instability resulted in the fitting of a twin fin and rudder tail unit to the

third prototype. Eight 1305-kW (1,750-hp) DB 603A-powered **He 277B-5/R2** production models were completed

before the priority given to fighter production in July 1944 brought the programme to an end.

Heinkel He 280

Conceptually less advanced than the rival Me 262, the He 280 suffered from wholly inadequate power.

When work on the He 178 was discontinued in the autumn of 1939, effort was transferred to a more advanced twin-engined design which was to be powered by pairs of two new Heinkel turbojets, the HeS 8 and HeS 30. Neither engine was ready for flight when the **Heinkel He 280** prototype airframe was itself complete and first trial flights, which began on 22 September 1940, were unpowered, the aircraft being towed to release height behind a Heinkel He 111. A pair of the HeS 8 engines was

installed in March 1941 and Fritz Schäfer made the first powered flight on 2 April. The engines were producing little more than 500 kg (1,102 lb) thrust, however, and although available thrust had risen to some 600 kg (1,323 lb) by early 1943 when the second and third prototypes were flown, in April of that year BMW 109-003 engines were adopted. Six further prototypes were built, the eighth

with a V-tail, but the rival Messerschmitt Me 262 was selected for production and

the He 280s were regarded only as useful research aids.

Helio Courier/Super Courier

Helio Aircraft Corporation (later Company) designed and built the original **Helio Courier** prototype in 1953. Of cantilever high-wing monoplane configuration, its development and production continued through the 4-seat **H-391B Courier** of 1954, 4/5-seat **H-395/H-395A** of 1958/1959, and 6-seat **H-250** of 1964. The subsequent **Model H-295 Super Courier** was flown in prototype form on 24 February 1965, a comfortable and well-equipped six-seat cabin monoplane. Full-span leading-edge slats, upper surface spoilers, Frise ailerons and 74-per cent span slotted trailing-edge flaps meant the Super Courier had excellent STOL performance. This attracted the attention of the US military and one civil H-391B was evaluated by the US Army as the **YL-24**. Orders were later received for three H-395/**L-28A/U-10A**s, 26 H-395A/U-10As, 57 H-295/U-10Bs (some with tricycle landing gear) and 36 **U-10D**s

(U-10Bs with higher gross weight). Volume production ended in December 1974, and the number of piston-engined Couriers built is reliably estimated at around 500. The type achieved notoriety in that the CIA almost certainly manufactured a further number clandestinely using spare parts, an endeavour that was later the subject of a legal dispute with the builders.

In the early 1980s the design rights and tooling were sold to a number of companies and 18 **Courier 700/800** variants were built before production ceased in 1984. These rights are currently held by the Aircraft Acquisition Corporation and the type is once again available from the Helio Aircraft Corporation of Morgantown, West Virginia, as the Helio Courier 5/6-seat STOL utility aircraft offered with four engine ratings. These are the **600** with a 186.4-kW (250-hp) Textron Lycoming 0-540, the **700** (224-kW/300-hp) Teledyne Continental

Voyager, the **800** (261-kW/350-hp) Textron TIO-540 and the **900** with a 298-kW (400-hp) Textron IO-720-A1B. Conventional or tricycle landing gear is optional, as are seaplane or amphibious floats.

Specification
Helio U-10D
Type: six-seat STOL utility and communications aircraft
Powerplant: one 220-kW (295-hp) Textron Lycoming GO-480-G1D6 flat-six piston engine
Performance: maximum speed 269 km/h (167 mph) at sea level;

The Courier's STOL performance was attractive to the USAF, which bought the type as the U-10A. It served in Vietnam.

cruising speed 265 km/h (165 mph) at 2590 m (8,500 ft); range 2220 km (1,380 miles)
Weights: empty 943 kg (2,080 lb); maximum take-off 1542 kg (3,400 lb)
Dimensions: span 11.89 m (39 ft 0 in); length 9.45 m (31 ft 0 in); height 2.69 m (8 ft 10 in); wing area 21.46 m^2 (231.0 sq ft)

Helio H-550A Stallion

The excellent STOL capability of the Courier led to development of the slightly larger and turboprop-powered **Helio HST-550 Stallion** prototype, first flown on 5 June 1964. Certification of the production version, the **H-550A Stallion**, was gained in August 1969 but, costing more than $100,000, it had little appeal to civilian buyers. The US Air Force acquired 15 as **AU-24A** aircraft with hardpoints beneath wing/fuselage

The USAF was the main purchaser of the Stallion, a number of AU-24 light gunships being procured but not seeing service.

and a cabin mounting for such roles as armed reconnaissance, close air support, forward air control and general transport. All but one were transferred to the Khmer Air Force. Powered by a

507-kW (680-shp) Pratt & Whitney Aircraft of Canada PT6A-27 turboprop, the AU-24A could be armed with a 20-mm

cannon, CBU-14A/A bomb dispensers and a 227-kg (500-lb) HE bomb for counter-insurgency (COIN) operations.

Helwan HA-300

First jet fighter to be built in Egypt, the **Helwan HA-300** originated from the Hispano HA-300 designed in Spain by a team headed by Professor Willy Messerschmitt. Intended for service with the Ejército del Aire, the project was abandoned in 1960, the programme being taken over by the United Arab Republic and transferred to the Helwan factory. Designed to be powered by the Bristol Orpheus BOr.12 afterburning turbojet,

the airframe was modified instead for the E-300, an Egyptian turbojet designed under the direction of Dr Brandner. Three prototypes were built, the first two being flown on 7 March 1964 and 22 July 1965 powered by the 2200-kg (4,850-lb) thrust Orpheus Mk 703-S-10. The third prototype, with E-300 engine, completed taxiing trials only, before the programme was abandoned in late 1969.

A trim tailed delta design, the HA-300 had a fascinating multi-national design history but foundered through a lack of power.

Henschel Hs 123

Designed to a 1933 dive-bomber requirement, the first of three **Henschel Hs 123** sesquiplane prototypes was flown in 1938 on the power of a 485-kW (650-hp) BMW 132A-3 radial engine. The first three aircraft were tested at Rechlin in August 1935, two of them being destroyed in dives because of wing structural failure. Successful testing of a fourth prototype incorporating changes to overcome this shortcoming led to a production order. The **Hs 123A-1** entered service with 1./StG 162 in the autumn of 1936, but the type's front-line career was short-lived, it being replaced by the Junkers Ju 87A in 1937. Five Hs 123As were supplied to the Condor Legion in Spain during December 1936, and the type saw operational service in Poland in 1939 and in France and Belgium in 1940. It was overworked in the Soviet Union in 1943, when few were left.

Variant
Hs 123 V5 and **V6:** designation of two 1938 prototypes with 716-kW (960-hp) BMW 132K engines and revised armament as development aircraft for proposed improved **Hs 123B** version; no production aircraft

Henschel Hs 123A-1 of 7./Stukageschwader 165 'Immelmann', based at Fürstenfeldbruck in October 1937.

Specification
Henschel Hs 123A-1
Type: dive-bomber/close-support aircraft
Powerplant: one 656-kW (880-hp)

BMW 132Dc 9-cylinder radial piston engine
Performance: maximum speed 340 km/h (211 mph) at 1200 m (3,935 ft); cruising speed 315 km/h (196 mph) at 2000 m (6,560 ft); service ceiling 9000 m (29,530 ft); range 855 km (531 miles)
Weights: empty 1500 kg (3,307 lb); maximum take-off 2215 kg (4,884 lb)
Dimensions: span, upper 10.50 m (34 ft 5½ in) and lower 8.00 m (26 ft 3 in); length 8.33 m (27 ft 4 in); height 3.20 m (10 ft 6 in); wing area 24.85 m² (267.49 sq ft)
Armament: two forward-firing 7.92-mm (0.31-in) MG 17 machine-guns, plus provision for up to 450 kg (992 lb) of bombs

Henschel Hs 126

From the earlier parasol-wing Hs 122, the company derived the **Henschel Hs 126** two-seat reconnaissance aircraft which incorporated a new wing, cantilever main landing gear and a canopy over the pilot's cockpit. An Hs 122A airframe was converted to produce the 455-kW (610-hp) Junkers Jumo 210-powered prototype, which was first flown in the autumn of 1936. This was followed by two development aircraft, each with a 619-kW (830-hp) Bramo Fafnir 323A-1 engine. During 1937 Henschel built 10 pre-production **Hs 126A-0** aircraft based on the third prototype, some being used for operational evaluation by the Luftwaffe. Production **Hs 126A-1** aircraft entered service first with Aufklärungsgruppe 35, and by the outbreak of World War II the re-equipment of reconnaissance units was well under way. Withdrawn progressively from service during 1942, Hs 126s were replaced by the Focke-Wulf Fw 189. More than 600 were built, including six used by the Condor Legion in Spain, later transferred to the Spanish air force, and 16 for the Greek air force.

Variant
Hs 126B-1: introduced during summer 1939, this version was powered by the Bramo 323A-1 or the 671-kW (900-hp) 323A-2, and equipped with FuG 17 radio

Specification
Henschel Hs 126B-1
Type: two-seat short-range reconnaissance aircraft
Powerplant: one 634-kW (850-hp) Bramo 323A-1 radial engine
Performance: maximum speed 310 km/h (193 mph) at sea level; service ceiling 8300 m (27,230 ft); maximum range 720 km (447 miles)
Weights: empty 2030 kg (4,476 lb);

Henschel Hs 126B-1 of 2. (H)/Aufklärungsgruppe 31, operating on the eastern Front in 1941/42.

maximum take-off 3090 kg (6,813 lb)
Dimensions: span 14.50 m (47 ft 6¾ in); length 10.85 m (35 ft 7¼ in); height 3.75 m (12 ft 3½ in); wing area 31.60 m² (340.15 sq ft)
Armament: two 7.92-mm (0.31-in) machine-guns, plus one 50-kg (110-lb) or five 10-kg (22-lb) bombs

Henschel Hs 129

Designed to meet an RLM requirement for a twin-engined ground-attack aircraft, carrying at least two 20-mm cannon and extensive armour protection, the prototype **Henschel Hs 129** was flown in the spring of 1939. Its triangular-section fuselage had a cramped cockpit with restricted view, a windscreen of 75-mm (2.95-in) armoured glass, and the nose constructed of armour plating. Luftwaffe testing of the three prototypes, each powered by two 347-kW (465-hp) Argus

As 410 engines, showed the cockpit to be unacceptable and the aircraft sluggish in performance. Eight pre-production aircraft were ordered for continued test and evaluation, but the planned production **He 129A-1** was considered unacceptable and was replaced by the **Hs 129B-1**, introducing several improvements and more powerful Gnome-Rhône 14M 4/5 engines. Hs 129Bs entered service first with 4./SchG 1 in April 1942, becoming operational on

the Eastern Front where the type was most widely used. Hs 129s served also in North Africa, Italy and in France after the D-Day landings. Production, including prototypes, totalled 879.

Variants
Hs 129B-0: 10 pre-production aircraft, similar to production Hs 129B-1s and delivered for Luftwaffe evaluation from December 1941
Hs 129B-1/R1: version of production aircraft carrying additionally two 50-kg (110-lb) bombs or 96 anti-personnel bombs

Hs 129B-1/R2: as production aircraft, but with an underfuselage 30-mm MK 101 cannon
Hs 129B-1/R3: as production aircraft but with four extra MG 17 machine-guns
Hs 129B-1/R4: version replacing the Hs 129B-1/R1's bombs with one 250-kg (551-lb) bomb
Hs 129B-1/R5: as production aircraft but incorporating an Rb 50/30 camera for reconnaissance duties
Hs 129B-2/R1: first of versions introduced in early 1943 with heavier weapons for anti-tank operations,

armed with two 20-mm MG 151/20 cannon and two 13-mm (0.51-in) MG 131 machine-guns

Hs 129B-2/R2: as Hs 129B-2/R1 but with additional 30-mm MK 103 underfuselage cannon

Hs 129B-2/R3: as Hs 129B-2/R2 but with MK 103 cannon replaced by 37-mm BK 3.7 gun and the MG 131s deleted

Hs 129B-2/R4: carried a 75-mm PaK 40 gun in an underfuselage pod

Hs 129B-3: developed from the Hs 129B-2/R4, the PaK 40 gun being replaced by an electro-pneumatically operated 75-mm BK 7.5 gun

Specification
Henschel Hs 129B-1/R2
Type: single-seat ground-attack aircraft

Henschel Hs 129B-1 of 4./Schlachtgeschwader 2, operating in Libya during November 1942.

Powerplant: two 522-kW (700-hp) Gnome-Rhône 14M 4/5 14-cylinder radial piston engines
Performance: maximum speed 407 km/h (253 mph) at 3830 m (12,565 ft); service ceiling 9000 m

(29,525 ft); range 560 km (348 miles)
Weights: empty 3810 kg (8,400 lb); maximum take-off 5110 kg (11,266 lb)
Dimensions: span 14.20 m (46 ft 7 in); length 9.75 m (31 ft 11¾ in); height 3.25 m (10 ft 8 in); wing area

29.00 m² (312.16 sq ft)
Armament: two 20-mm MG 151/20 cannon, two 7.92-mm (0.31-in) MG 17 machine-guns and one 30-mm MK 101 cannon

Hiller Model 360, UH-12 and OH-23 Raven

Hiller Helicopters Inc. was formed in 1942 for the development and production of rotary-wing aircraft. Early work on the **Hiller Model XH-44, UH-4 Commuter** and the **UH-5**, which introduced a newly-developed 'Rotor-Matic' rotor control system, led to the **Hiller Model 360** prototype. The company's first production helicopter followed and this, known as the **Hiller UH-12** as Hiller had become part of United Helicopters, was of simple construction, incorporating a two-bladed main rotor and a two-bladed tail rotor on an upswept boom. The design was highly successful, being built extensively in two- and three-seat configurations for both civil and military use, and an early Model 12 was the first commercial helicopter to record a transcontinental flight across the United States. More than 2,000 were built before production ended in 1965, some 300 of this total being exported, and throughout this period the power and capability of the helicopter was steadily improved.

The commercial **UH-12A** to **UH-12D** became the **OH-23A** to **OH-23D Raven** respectively for service with the US Army, and the US Navy acquired UH-12As as **HTE-1** and **HTE-2**. The **UH-12E** was basically a three-seat dual

control version of the OH-23D and was built also as the military **OH-23G**. A lengthened-fuselage four-seat civil **UH-12E4** was produced as the military **OH-23F**, and late civil versions with uprated powerplant included the UH-12E variants suffixed **L3, L4, SL3** and **SL4**. OH-23s were exported to Argentina, Bolivia, Colombia, Chile, Cuba, Dominica, Guatemala, Guyana, Mexico, Morocco, the Netherlands, Paraguay, Switzerland, Thailand and Uruguay. The Canadian army acquired OH-23Gs which it operated with the designation **CH-112 Nomad**, and the Royal Navy used a number of ex-US Navy HTE-2s under the designation **Hiller HT.Mk 2**.

At the height of UH-12/OH-23 production Hiller was taken over by the Fairchild Corporation, but in 1973 a new company, Hiller Aviation, acquired design rights and production tooling for the UH-12E, and for some years provided support for the world-wide fleet of UH-12 variants. In April 1984 Hiller became a subsidiary of Rogerson Aircraft of Port Angeles, Washington. Renamed Hiller Helicopters and later Rogerson Helicopters, the company, now known as Rogerson Hiller, relaunched the piston-engined UH-12E in 1991 as the Hauler, and a num-

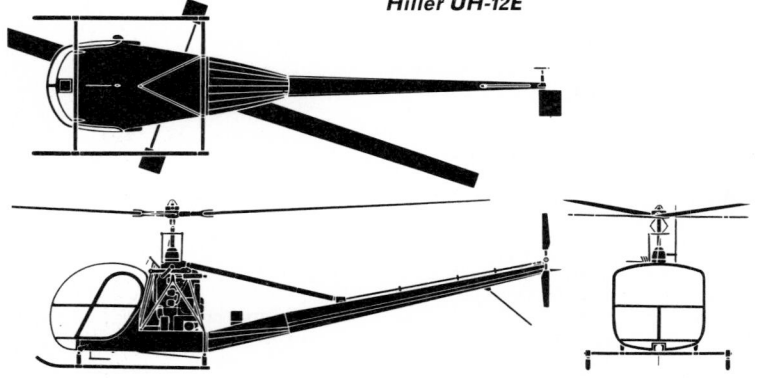

Hiller UH-12E

ber have been exported. The company is also proposing the Allison turbine-powered **UH-12ET** development for the US Army's NHT (New Training Helicopter) requirement.

Specification
Hiller OH-23D Raven
Type: three-seat military helicopter
Powerplant: one 241-kW (323-hp) Avco Lycoming VO-540-A1B flat-six

piston engine
Performance: maximum speed 153 km/h (95 mph); cruising speed 132 km/h (82 mph); service ceiling 4025 m (13,200 ft); range 330 km (205 miles)
Weights: empty 824 kg (1,816 lb); maximum take-off 1225 kg (2,700 lb)
Dimensions: main rotor diameter 10.82 m (35 ft 6 in); length 8.53 m (28 ft 0 in); height 2.97 m (9 ft 9 in); main rotor disc area 92.47 m² (995.38 sq ft)

Hiller FH-1100 (OH-5A)

The US Army's LOH (light observation helicopter) design competition of 1961 was finalised between the prototypes built as the Bell OH-4A, **Hiller OH-5A** and Hughes OH-6A, but it was the last which won the production order. Hiller decided to develop its design as a civil helicopter, resulting in the **FH-1100** of which the first production examples were delivered in the summer of 1966. Available in five-seat utility or four-seat executive versions, a total of 246 had been built when production ended in 1974. A total of about 30 FH-1100s was supplied to the armed services of Argentina, Brazil, Chile, Cyprus, Ecuador, Panama, the Philippines and Salvador. Hiller Aviation, formed in 1973 to acquire the UH-12 programme, became a subsidiary of Rogerson Aircraft of Port

Angeles, Washington. Subsequently renamed Hiller Helicopters and Rogerson Helicopters, the company now operates as Rogerson Hiller and, since 1984, has built and marketed updated versions of the original FH-1100. These are the **RH-1100A Pegasus** civil helicopter and the **RH-1100M Hornet** military rotorcraft, the latter capable of carrying the latest battlefield avionics and armed with guns, rocket pods and ATM and AAM missiles.

Specification
Hiller FH-1100A Pegasus
Type: five-seat utility helicopter
Powerplant: one 313-kW (420-shp) Allison 250-C20B turboshaft
Performance: economical cruising speed 196 km/h (122 mph); service

ceiling 6550 m (21,500 ft); range 692 km (430 miles)
Weights: empty 680 kg (1,500 lb); maximum take-off 1,247 kg (2,750 lb)
Dimensions: main rotor diameter 10.80 m (35 ft 5 in); fuselage length 9.08 m (29 ft 9½ in); height 2.83 m (9 ft

The OH-5A failed to win any US Army orders, but went on to a moderately successful sales career with civil operators.

3½ in); main rotor disc area 91.0 m² (979.0 sq ft)

Hindustan Ajeet and Ajeet Trainer

The Folland Gnat was licence-built by Hindustan Aeronautics Ltd (HAL, formed in 1963 by the amalgamation of Hindustan Aircraft with Aeronautics Ltd)

for the Indian air force, and when production ended in January 1974 a total of 213 had been constructed. Hindustan then developed an improved version which it

named **HAL Ajeet** (invincible), the last two Gnats off the production line being modified to serve as prototypes. They have a redesigned fuel system (with in-

tegral wing tanks) enabling them to dispense with drop-tanks, thus increasing underwing weapon capacity, and more advanced nav/com systems. A total of 80 have been built as new and 10 Gnats were converted to Ajeet configuration. One development is a tandem two-seat

Ajeet Trainer, the prototype being flown for the first time on 20 September 1982; further development was cancelled in mid-1983.

HAL Gnat of an Indian Air Force operational training unit.

Hindustan HF-24 Marut

Design of the **HAL HF-24 Marut** (wind spirit) single-seat supersonic fighter for the Indian air force was started in 1956 under a team headed by the renowned German designer Kurt Tank. With swept wings and tail surfaces, and having some resemblance to the Hawker Hunter, the prototype was flown for the first time on 17 June 1961. Powerplant of the prototype comprised two Rolls-Royce Bristol Orpheus 703 turbojets, but the 129 production **HF-24 Marut Mk 1** aircraft had a licence-built version of this powerplant produced by Hindustan's engine division. The prototype of a tandem two-seat trainer, the **Marut Mk 1T**, was first flown on 30 April 1970, and 18 had been built when production ended in 1977. Hindustan's Marut was

the first supersonic fighter aircraft designed by an Asian country, excluding the Soviet Union. Experience showed the need for more powerful engines, but the realisation proved impractical, except by major fuselage redesign at prohibitive cost. The type was replaced in the mid-1980s by Jaguars.

Specification
Hindustan Marut Mk 1
Type: single-seat ground-attack fighter
Powerplant: two 2200-kg (4,850-lb) thrust HAL/Rolls-Royce Orpheus Mk 703 turbojets
Performance: maximum speed Mach 1.02 at 12000 m (39,370 ft); combat radius 396 km (246 miles) at 12000 m (39,370 ft)

Weights: empty 6195 kg (13,658 lb); maximum take-off 10908 kg (24,048 lb)
Dimensions: span 9.00 m (29 ft 6¼ in); length 15.87 m (52 ft 0¾ in); height 3.60 m (11 ft 9¾ in); wing area 28.00 m² (301.40 sq ft)
Armament: four 30-mm ADEN cannon, plus a retractable pack of 50

The HAL Marut was Asia's first supersonic production aircraft. It failed to live up to its true potential owing to lack of power.

68-mm (2.68-in) SNEB rockets in the belly and four underwing hardpoints for a variety of weapons

Hindustan HJT-16 Kiran

Designed to meet Indian air force needs for a basic jet trainer, the **HAL HJT-16 Kiran** (ray of light) powered by a Rolls-Royce Viper Mk 11 turbojet engine, was flown for the first time on 4 September 1964. The first six of a pre-production batch of **Kiran I** aircraft was delivered in March 1968, but late production aircraft, with a hardpoint beneath each wing to enable the Kiran to be used for weapon training, have the designation **Kiran IA**. A total of 190 has been built for the Indian air force and navy. The improved **Kiran II** with a 1542-kg (3,400-lb) thrust Rolls-Royce Orpheus Mk 701-01 turbojet and greater weapon-carrying capability entered Indian air force service in April

1984 and the last of 61 built was delivered in March 1989.

Specification
Hindustan HJT-16 Kiran I/IA
Type: two-seat basic jet trainer
Powerplant: one 1134-kg (2,500-lb) thrust Rolls-Royce Viper Mk 11 turbojet
Performance: maximum speed 695 km/h (432 mph) at sea level; service ceiling 9145 m (30,000 ft); endurance on internal fuel 1 hour 45 minutes
Weights: empty 2560 kg (5,644 lb); maximum take-off 4235 kg (9,336 lb)
Dimensions: span 10.70 m (35 ft 1¼ in); length 10.60 m (34 ft 9 in);

height 3.63 m (11 ft 11 in); wing area 19.00 m² (204.52 sq ft)
Armament: two 227-kg (500-lb) bombs, or two pods each containing seven 68-mm (2.68-in) SNEB rockets, or two pods each with twin 7.62-mm

The Kiran I showed a conceptual affinity with the Hunting Jet Provost.

(0.3-in) machine-guns, or two 226-litre (50-Imp gal) drop-tanks

Hispano HA-100, HA-200 and HA-220

The **Hispano HA-100 Triana** two-seat advanced trainer, designed under the direction of Professor Willy Messerschmitt, was first flown in **HA-100-E1** prototype form on 10 December 1954. Two HA-100-E1 prototypes were built, powered by 563-kW (755-hp) ENMA Beta B-4 engines, plus two **HA-100-F1** prototypes with 597-kW (800-hp) Wright Cyclone engines, but it was the HA-100-E1 version that was ordered into production. Entering service with the Spanish air force during 1958, under the designation **E.12**, a total of 40 was built and used as armament trainers.

Major HA-100 components were used in the **HA-200 Saeta** (Arrow) which was also developed under the guidance of Willy Messerschmitt. The first Spanish turbojet aircraft, the prototype was flown on 12 August 1955 and the first production aircraft on 11 October 1962. The HA-200 entered service shortly after this, being designated **E.14** by the Spanish air force. A single-seat attack version of the Saeta, the **HA-220**, began to enter service in 1971-7 under the Spanish air force designation **C.10**. In addition to the accommodation change it had more powerful

engines and provision to carry rocket pods. When production ended a total of 110 HA-200 and HA-220s had been built for the Spanish air force; the type was replaced by the CASA C.101 from 1980 onwards.

Variants
HA-200A: initial production version, 30 built for the Spanish air force
HA-200B: designation of 10 pre-production aircraft with Turboméca Marboré IIA turbojets built for Egypt before licence production by Helwan Air Works as the **Al-Kahira**; Helwan duly initiated production of 90 aircraft
HA-200D: improved version for service with the Spanish air force; 55 built with more-modern systems and heavier armament
HA-200E Super Saeta: redesignation of 40 HA-200Ds after updating with Marboré VI turbojets, advanced avionics and provisions for air-to-ground rockets

A C.10-C ground attack/trainer aircraft of the Spanish air force, carrying a variety of underwing stores. These aircraft were in service until the mid-1980s.

HA-220: single-seat ground-attack version of HA-200E for Spanish air force: total of 25 built

Specification
Hispano HA-200E Super Saeta
Type: two-seat advanced trainer
Powerplant: two 480-kg (1,058-lb) thrust Turboméca Marboré VI turbojets
Performance: maximum speed 690 km/h (429 mph) at 3000 m (22,965 ft); service ceiling 13000 m (42,650 ft); range 1500 km (932 miles)
Weights: empty operating 2020 kg (4,453 lb); maximum take-off 3600 kg (7,937 lb)
Dimensions: span 10.41 m (34 ft

The HA-100 Triana was only used by the Spanish air force, which procured 40 for use as trainers. Major parts of this aircraft were used in the construction of the jet-powered Saeta.

1¾ in); length 8.97 m (29 ft 5 in); height 2.85 m (9 ft 4¼ in); wing area 17.40 m² (187.30 sq ft)
Armament: underwing hardpoints for a range of weapons; provision for one 20-mm cannon in fuselage

Horten tailless aircraft

The German brothers Reimar and Walter Horten were exponents of tailless aircraft design, resulting initially in a series of sailplanes dating from 1931. These included the **Horten Ho I, Ho II** and **Ho III**, followed by a more sophisticated **Ho IV** in 1941. This had high aspect ratio swept wings, while the more developed **Ho IVB** incorporated a laminar-flow wing. The **Ho V** was powered by two 60-kW (80-hp) Hirth HM 60R engines driving pusher propellers, and this aircraft was tested during 1943. The **Ho VI**

was of even higher aspect ratio than the Ho IV and found to be impractical, and was followed by the powered **Ho VII** with two 179-kW (240-hp) Argus As 10C engines, although it is not known whether this flew. A commercial/military transport to seat some 60 passengers was planned under the designation **Ho VIII**, construction of a prototype initiated but not completed by the end of World War II. Even more ambitious was the **Ho IX** fighter which was intended to be powered by turbojet engines, the **Ho IX**

VI prototype being flown as a glider during 1944. A second prototype was completed with two 900-kg (1,984-lb) thrust turbojets, but the failure of one of these engines in flight resulted in the aircraft being destroyed after only very limited testing. A production version of this fighter was planned, prototypes being built by Gotha under the designa-

tion **Go 229**, and the first of these had been completed (but not flown) when the Gotha workshops were captured by American forces. A single-engined turbojet-powered fighter had also been planned under the designation **Ho X**, but the prototype of this was incomplete when World War II ended.

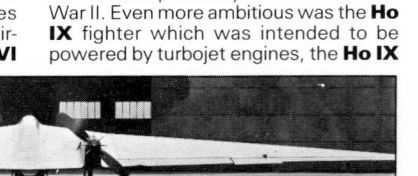

Intended as a two-seat trainer for later fighters, the Ho VII gave valuable experimental service. Only two were delivered to the RLM.

The Ho IX V2 was the first jet-powered Horten aircraft. After only two hours' flying time the aircraft crashed in flames after an engine cut.

Howard aircraft

Ben Howard, who designed and built his first aeroplane, the **Howard DGA-1** (Damned Good Airplane 1) in 1933, established Howard Aircraft Corporation in 1937 to build and market his designs. A series of successful racers includes the **DGA-3** *Pete*, **DGA-4** *Ike* and **DGA-5** *Mike*, culminating in the **DGA-6** *Mister Mulligan*, a four-seat cabin monoplane which won all three of the major American air races in 1935. From the DGA-6 was developed a commercial **DGA-8** in 1936, a generally similar **DGA-9** in 1937 which differed in its powerplant, and leading through **DGA-11** and **DGA-12** aircraft with other engine installations to the **DGA-15** four/five-seat cabin monoplane. Versions of this aircraft with different powerplant comprised the **DGA-15J** with 224-kW (300-hp) Jacobs L-6, **DGA-15W** with 261-kW (350-hp)

The NH-1 was basically a naval version of the DGA-15P. 205 were built, the green band around the fuselage denoting use as an instrument trainer.

Wright R-760-E2, and the **DGA-15P** with 336-kW (450-hp) Pratt & Whitney Wasp Junior.

The last version proved of interest to the US Navy, and in 1941 it was ordered initially as the **GH-1** transport, of which 31 were built and three impressed from civil sources. It was followed by 131 **GH-2** ambulance aircraft, 115 **GH-3** transports which differed in equipment from the GH-1, and 205 **NH-1** instrument trainers. The US Army Air Force impressed a total of 19 from civil sources for use in a light transport/communications role, these having the designations **UC-70** (DGA-15P), **UC-70A** (DGA-12),

UC-70B (DGA-15J), **UC-70C** (DGA-8) and **UC-70D** (DGA-9). These robust and reliable aircraft remained in service with the US Army and US Navy for a number of years.

In addition to these military aircraft, Howard also supplied about 60 trainers for use in the US Civil Pilot Training Pro-

gram. A cantilever low-wing monoplane, with instructor and pupil accommodated in tandem open cockpits, the type was designated **DGA-18W** with the Warner Super Scarab engine, **DGA-18K** with the Kinner engine, and **DGA-125** with a lower-powered 93-kW (125-hp) Warner Scarab engine.

Hughes H-4 Hercules

Designed under the direction of Howard Hughes, the 180-ton aircraft, sometimes called the **HK-1** and popularly nicknamed the 'Spruce Goose', was the largest flying-boat ever built. Piloted by the eccentric millionaire with D. Grant as co-pilot, the **Hercules** made only one flight. This was in a straight line measuring about one mile over Los Angeles Harbor on 2 November 1947. After a long

period of storage, the aircraft was presented to the Aero Club of Southern California and is now a star attraction preserved in its own circular building alongside the former ocean liner *Queen Mary* at Long Beach, California.

Specification
Type: flying-boat freighter
Powerplant: eight 2236-kW (3,000-hp)

In its time, the H-4 was the largest aircraft in the world. Its intended role was to ferry vast amounts of troops and cargo across the Pacific.

Pratt & Whitney R4360-4A piston engines
Performance: maximum speed at sea level 378 km/h (235 mph); cruising speed 225 km/h (140 mph); service ceiling (est) 6400 m (21,000 ft); range 2535 km (1,575 miles)
Dimensions: span 97.5 m (319 ft

11 in); length 66.6 m (218 ft 8 in); height 24.1 m (79 ft 4 in); wing area 1061.8 m² (11,430 sq ft)

Hughes XF-11

The **Hughes XF-11** long-range photographic reconnaissance aircraft was designed and assembled during World War II, but did not fly until 1946. The sleek twin-boom design was related to the experimental wooden Hughes D-2 twin-engined high-performance aircraft first flown in July 1943 from Harper's Dry Lake, but later destroyed in a hangar fire. The prototype XF-11 (44-70155) made its first flight on 15 April 1946 from Culver City Field but crashed in flames onto Beverly Hills on 7 July, severely injuring the pilot, Howard Hughes. A second prototype (44-70156) flew in 1947 but further development was abandoned. A cantilever high-wing twin boom two-

seat monoplane with twin fins and rudders, the XF-11 was powered by two 3,000-hp Pratt & Whitney R4360-31 engines.

Whereas the first XF-11 featured contra-rotating propellers, the second had a conventional four-bladed unit. Ninety-eight were ordered for the USAF reconnaissance role, but this was cancelled at the end of World War II, as was the rival Republic XF-12.

Hughes Model 269/200/300 and TH-55A
to
IAI Kfir

Hughes Model 269/200/300 and TH-55A

Design and development of the **Hughes Model 269** two-seat helicopter began in September 1955, and the first of two prototypes was flown during October 1956. A simple fuselage structure carried on two skids accommodated the crew, housed the powerplant, mounted the rotor pylon and three-bladed main rotor, plus a light alloy tubular tailboom to carry the two-bladed tail rotor. Five **Model 269A** pre-production helicopters were acquired by the US Army for evaluation in command and observation roles under the designation **YHO-2HU**. Production of the Model 269A for civil use began in October 1961, and subsequent developments of the type are listed below.

Sole manufacturing rights to the **Series 300** were acquired from Hughes by the Schweizer Aircraft Corporation of Elmira, New York, in July 1983 and the whole **Model 300C** programme bought from McDonnell Douglas Helicopters in November 1986. Schweizer flew first Series 300C in June 1984 and by the end of 1991 the company was to have delivered around 450 new machines in addition to 2,800 built by Hughes. Current production models are the **TH-300C** military trainer and **300C Sky Knight** police helicopter.

Variants
Hughes Model 200 Utility: a refined version of the original 269A with a 134-kW (180-hp) Avco Lycoming HIO-360-B1A engine; derived from this design under the Hughes engineering designation **Model 269A-1** was the US Army's **TH-55A Osage** light helicopter primary trainer, of which 792 were built; this last version was also built by Kawasaki in Japan as the **TH-55J** for the JGSDF

Hughes Model 200 Deluxe: generally similar to the Model 200 Utility, but with engineering refinements and high quality interior furnishing

Hughes Model 300: three-seat version derived from the **Model 269B** engineering design; a quiet tail rotor was introduced in 1967 and was available retrospectively for earlier versions

Hughes Model 300C: developed version of Model 300 with Avco Lycoming HIO-360-D1A engine; also built under licence in Italy by Breda

Nardi as the **NH-300C**

Hughes Model 300CQ: a version of the Model 300C incorporating noise-reducing modifications; it is some 75 per cent quieter than earlier versions, which can be modified to CQ standard

Sky Knight: police patrol version of the Model 300C with special equipment

Specification
Hughes Model 300C
Type: two/three-seat light helicopter
Powerplant: one 142-kW (190-hp) Avco Lycoming HIO-360-D1A flat-six piston engine
Performance: maximum cruising speed 153 km/h (95 mph) at 1220 m (4,000 ft); service ceiling 3110 m (10,200 ft); range at 1220 m (4,000 ft) with allowances and reserves 370 km (230 miles)
Weights: empty 476 kg (1,050 lb); maximum take-off 930 kg (2,050 lb)
Dimensions: main rotor diameter 8.18 m (26 ft 10 in); length, rotors turning 9.40 m (30 ft 10 in); height 2.67 m (8 ft 9 in); main rotor disc area 52.53 m² (565.5 sq ft)

The Model 300 has seen much service with civil operators since its first flight in 1956. This example was used by a Canadian radio station to give traffic reports, one of many civilian roles for the type.

Hughes Model 369/OH-6 Cayuse

Designed to a US Army requirement of 1960 for a Light Observation Helicopter (LOH), the **Hughes Model 369** was evaluated against submissions from Bell and Hiller under the designation **HO-6** (later **OH-6**). The Hughes design was ordered into production, but after 1,434 had been delivered from a total requirement of some 4,000, the Hughes contract was terminated. This resulted from falling production and rising costs, an unfortunate situation, for the **OH-6A Cayuse** was a superb light helicopter which, flown by service and civilian pilots, set a series of international helicopter records. Accommodation is for a crew of two, with two folding seats in the rear cabin which, when folded, provide sufficient space on the floor for four fully-equipped troops or a worthwhile load of cargo.

OH-6As began to enter US Army service in September 1966, all 1,434 being delivered by August 1970. The majority

Popularly called the 'Loach', the OH-6 Cayuse was built in large numbers for the US Army and saw valuable service in Vietnam. Many small weapons can be carried, including machine-guns and grenade launchers.

remain in service, the Cayuse being employed for a wide range of duties, including offensive operations when equipped with a kit which mounts a machine-gun or grenade-launcher on the port side of the fuselage.

In January 1984, Hughes Helicopters became a subsidiary of the McDonnell Douglas Corporation and the Model 269/300 sold to Schweizer. Development of military and civil versions of the 500 continued but the improved **Series 500E**

and **530F Lifter** (optimised for load-carrying) are the current production aircraft, along with earlier **Model 500Ds** built under licence in Italy (by Agusta), Argentina (by RACA), Japan (by Kawasaki) and South Korea (by Korean Air). Following the construction and flight-testing of a NOTAR (NO TAil Rotor) testbed, certificated versions are now produced of the **MD520N** (a NOTAR MD500) and the **MD530N** (a NOTAR 530F) and output is already sold out to

1994. Also available are military versions of the 500 and 530 designated **AH-6, MH-6, Nightfox** and **Defender**.

Specification
Hughes OH-6A Cayuse
Type: light observation helicopter
Powerplant: one 263-kW (317-shp) derated Allison T63-A-5A turboshaft
Performance: maximum cruising speed 230 km/h (143 mph) at sea level; normal range 665 km (413 miles) at

1525 m (5,000 ft)
Weights: empty equipped 524 kg (1,156 lb); maximum take-off 1225 kg (2,700 lb)
Dimensions: main rotor diameter 8.03 m (26 ft 4 in); length, rotors turning 9.24 m (30 ft 3¾ in); height 2.48 m (8 ft 1½ in); main rotor disc area 50.60 m² (544.63 sq ft)
Armament: XM27 7.62-mm (0.3-in) machine-gun or XM-75 grenade-launcher

Hunting (Percival) P.56 Provost

Designed by Percival Aircraft before it became part of the Hunting Group in 1954, the **Hunting P.56 Provost** was accepted as the RAF's standard basic trainer in 1953, superseding the Percival Prentice in Flying Training Command. A cantilever low-wing monoplane with fixed tailwheel landing gear and powered by an Alvis Leonides 126 engine, it provided side-by-side seating for instructor and pupil. Three prototypes were built, two powered initially by the Armstrong Siddeley Cheetah 18, the other by an Alvis Leonides, the first Cheetah-engined prototype flying on 23 February 1950. Entering service under the designation **Provost T.Mk 1**, the aircraft were delivered first to the Basic Training Squadron of the CFS at South Cerney. When production ended in 1959 a total of 461 had been built.

Variants
Provost T.Mk 51: unarmed version for the Irish Air Corps
Provost T.Mk 52: armed version for

Hunting (Percival) Provost T.Mk 1 of No. 6 FTS based at Ternhill.

the Royal Rhodesian Air Force
Provost T.Mk 53: armed version for the Irish Air Corps, and the air forces of Burma, Iraq and Sudan

Specification
Type: two-seat basic trainer
Powerplant: one 410-kW (550-hp) Alvis Leonides 126 radial piston engine
Performance: maximum speed 322 km/h (200 mph) at 700 m (2,300 ft); service ceiling 6860 m (22,500 ft); endurance 4 hours

Weights: empty equipped 1520 kg (3,350 lb); maximum take-off 1996 kg (4,400 lb)
Dimensions: span 10.72 m (35 ft 2 in); length 8.74 m (28 ft 8 in); height 3.72 m (12 ft 2½ in); wing area 19.88 m² (214.0 sq ft)

Hunting (Percival) P.66 Pembroke, President and Sea Prince

The **Percival P.50 Prince**, flown in 1948, had potential for development and resulted in the 10-seat **P.66 Pembroke** communications/light transport aircraft flown on 21 November 1952. A total of 44 was built for the RAF as the **Pembroke C.Mk 1**, differing from the civil Prince by increased wing span, a re-inforced cabin floor, strengthened landing gear and rear-facing seats for the passengers. An additional six were supplied with fuselage-mounted cameras for photo-reconnaissance under the designation **Pembroke C(PR).Mk 1**. Export versions were built for the air forces of Belgium, Denmark, Finland, West Germany, Sweden and Sudan. The Royal Navy acquired four similar aircraft as the **Sea Prince C.Mk 1**, followed by 42 **Sea Prince T.Mk 1** aircraft

Hunting (Percival) Pembroke C.Mk 1 of No. 60 Squadron, based in Germany.

equipped as 'flying classrooms' for training in navigation and ASW. Last of the variants for the Royal Navy was the **Sea Prince C.Mk 2**, a communications version of the T.Mk 1 of which three were built. A civil **President** was also de-

veloped, three being ordered by a Spanish airline but never delivered.

Hunting (Percival) P.84 Jet Provost

Royal Air Force use of the piston-engined Provost and turbine-engined de Havilland Vampire in its training sequence seemed illogical to Hunting, who proceeded with the private-venture design of a turbojet-powered version of the Provost to provide a pupil with all-through jet training. This retained the wings and tail unit of the Provost, but introduced a new fuselage housing the turbine engine and retractable tricycle landing gear. Ten of these aircraft were ordered for the RAF as the **Hunting Jet Provost T.Mk 1** in March 1953, the first of them being flown on 16 June 1954, and these were used by the RAF during 1955 for comparative trials, the first pupil making a solo flight in the type

Hunting (Percival) Jet Provost T.Mk 5A, wearing the blue fuselage stripe of the RAF College, Cranwell.

I.M.A.M. Ro.41

The prototype **I.M.A.M. Ro.41** made its first flight on 16 June 1934. Intended as a light single-seat fighter or aerobatic trainer, it performed well, but then failed to attract any attention. It was two years later that the Regia Aeronautica ordered this compact, gull-winged biplane into large-scale production as a basic trainer, in both single- and two-seat versions. In fact, 480 single-seat and 230 two-seat dual-control Ro.41s were built by I.M.A.M., Agusta and AVIS between 1936 and 1943.

Service flying schools used a high proportion of both single- and two-seaters, the single-seaters often being used for aerobatic training. The Spanish Civil War brought a considerable drain on Regia Aeronautica first-line aircraft, and many single-seat Ro.41s were attached to first-line fighter *squadriglie* bases to make up deficiencies in complement. Although lacking many of the fighting qualities of the Fiat C.R.32, the Ro.41 did

in fact possess a rate of climb superior to that of its famous contemporary. The Spanish Nationalists received 25 Ro.41s from Italy, which were used as fighter trainers, and nine were exported to Hungary.

On 31 July 1943, 443 Ro.41s were still in Regia Aeronautica service, a small number surviving into the post-war period. In 1949 Agusta built 13 two-seat and 12 single-seat Ro.41s, which were used as military trainers and liaison aircraft for several years.

Specification
I.M.A.M. Ro.41 (single-seat)
Type: basic and aerobatic trainer
Powerplant: one 291-kW (390-hp) Piaggio P.VII radial piston engine
Performance: maximum speed 322 km/h (200 mph) at 5000 m (16,405 ft); service ceiling 7750 m (25,425 ft); range 568 km (353 miles)
Weights: empty equipped 1010 kg

Like many Italian military aircraft of that period the Ro.41 saw service during the Spanish Civil War, usually as a trainer.

(2,227 lb); maximum take-off 1265 kg (2,789 lb)
Dimensions: span 8.81 m (28 ft 10¾ in); length 6.90 m (22 ft 7¾ in);

height 2.68 m (8 ft 9½ in); wing area 19.50 m² (209.90 sq ft)
Armament: two fixed synchronised 7.7-mm (0.303-in) machine-guns

---

Ikarus IK-2

After producing Potez 25 reconnaissance biplanes and Avia BH-33E fighters under licence, the Ikarus factory built the **IK-L1**, a prototype gull-wing monoplane fighter powered by a 641-kW (860-hp) Hispano-Suiza 12Ycrs engine, and first flown on 22 April 1935. After this crashed a second **IK-02** prototype was built, followed by a series of 12 **Ikarus IK-2** fighters delivered in early 1939. Generally similar to the earlier prototypes, the IK-2s flew with 107 Eskadrila against the invading Germans in April 1941. Armament comprised one Hispano-Suiza 404 20-mm cannon and two synchronised 7.7-mm (0.303-in)

Twelve Ikarus IK-2s were built for the Yugoslav Air Force and eight survived to fight the German invasion in 1941. It was followed by the IK-3 prototype, which resembled a Hurricane.

machine-guns. The wings spanned 11.40 m (37 ft 4¾ in), maximum take-off weight was 1857 kg (4,094 lb), and maximum speed was 435 km/h (270 mph).

Last new Ikarus design to fly in 1940 before the German occupation was the **Orkan** twin-engined attack bomber. An all-metal shoulder wing monoplane with retractable landing gear and twin fins and rudders, the Orkan had heavy cannon and machine-gun armament and

an effective bomb load. Estimated maximum speed was 550 km/h (342 mph)

with two 627-kW (840-hp) Fiat A.74 RC 38 radials.

Ilyushin DB-3

The **TsKB-26** long-range bomber prototype appeared in 1935, a twin-engined metal low-wing monoplane powered by 597-kW (800-hp) Gnome-Rhône K-14 radials. Demonstrated by test pilot Vladimir Kokkinaki on May Day 1936, the prototype went on to establish two world altitude records during July 1936. A second prototype, the **TsKB-30**, had an enclosed instead of open position for the pilot, Soviet M-85 engines and a metal rear fuselage. The TsKB-30 also broke records and then attracted world interest by flying from Moscow to Canada, where pilot Kokkinaki had to make a wheels-up landing on 28 April 1939 after covering a distance of 8000 km (4,971 miles).

By then the bomber had been in production for the Soviet air arm for more than two years. Under the military designation **DB-3** it served widely with the ADD (Long-Range Aviation) and the

V-MF (Naval Aviation), remaining operational well into the war with Germany, DB-3s being credited with some of the earliest attacks on Berlin.

The DB-3 served also with the Finnish air arm between 1940 and 1945, five captured aircraft being augmented by six purchased from German war booty supplies. DB-3 production terminated in 1940 with the 1,528th machine.

Variants
DB-3M: this refined version entered production in 1939, powered by two M-87 engines
DB-3T: specialised torpedo-bomber version which carried the Type 45-12-AN aerial torpedo
DB-3PT: designation of a twin-float seaplane torpedo-bomber variant

Specification
Ilyushin DB-3M
Type: twin-engined long-range medium bomber
Powerplant: two 708-kW (950-hp)

M-87B radial piston engines
Performance: maximum speed 445 km/h (277 mph); service ceiling 9700 m (31,825 ft); range 3800 km (2,361 miles)
Weights: empty equipped 5270 kg (11,618 lb); maximum take-off 7660 kg (16,887 lb)
Dimensions: span 21.44 m (70 ft 4 in); length 14.22 m (46 ft 7¾ in);

This DB-3B long-range bomber was captured and then operated by the Finnish air force.

height 4.19 m (13 ft 9 in); wing area 65.60 m² (706.14 sq ft)
Armament: three 7.62-mm (0.3-in) ShKAS machine-guns, plus a maximum short-range bombload of 2500 kg (5,512 lb)

Ilyushin Il-2 Shturmovik

One of the most formidable military aircraft of World War II, the **Ilyushin Il-2** was produced in vast numbers, Soviet sources giving the total figure as 36,163 aircraft. It began as the **TsKB-55** developed by Sergei Ilyushin and his team, who formed in 1938 part of the Central Design Bureau (TsKB).

The special feature of the two-seat TsKB-55 or **BSh-2** was the armoured shell which formed an integral part of the fuselage structure and protected the crew, engine, radiators and fuel tank.

The resulting aircraft was well suited to its designated low-level ground-attack role, but was rejected in favour of a lighter single-seat development, the **TsKB-57**, which had a 1268-kW (1,700-hp) AM-38 engine, a raised, faired canopy for the pilot, substituted 20-mm cannon for two of the four wing-mounted machine-guns, and had provision for underwing rocket-launchers. The first prototype flew on 12 October 1940.

Official trials ended just three months

before the German invasion in June 1941. By then, large-scale production of the **Il-2**, as the type was designated, had been started, the first unit receiving its aircraft in May 1941. By the end of June, 249 Il-2s had been taken on charge by the Soviet air force (the V-VS). Production aircraft were generally similar to the TsKB-57 prototypes, but some modifications had been introduced, principally to the pilot's accommodation to give improved protection, including a modified windscreen and a shorter fairing aft of the cockpit.

The single-seat Il-2 was used on a vast scale and proved itself a potent weapon

against German transport and armour. Losses were heavy, however, and during 1941-42 fighter cover was often not available. In February 1942 it was decided to introduce a two-seat Il-2 in line with Ilyushin's original concept. The resulting **Il-2M** had provision for a rear gunner under an extended canopy. Two conversions were flight-tested in March 1942, and production aircraft appeared from September 1942; other aircraft were converted to two-seaters in the field.

Other changes introduced on the production lines included the installation of the more powerful AM-38F engine, re-

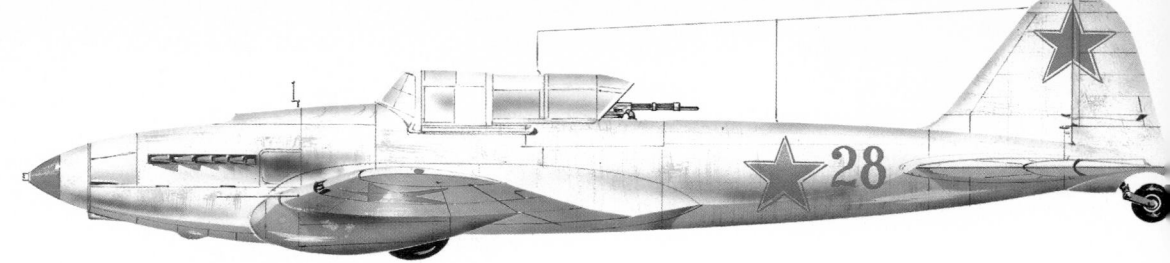

placement of the two 20-mm ShVAK cannon with more effective 23-mm VYa weapons, various aerodynamic refinements to improve performance and to compensate for the increased weight of the gunner and revised armament, the enforced introduction of wooden outer wing panels (replacing metal), and increased fuel capacity.

A new version, the **Il-2 Type 3** (or **Il-2m3**) made its first appearance at Stalingrad in early 1943. Tested during 1942, it had redesigned wings with 15° sweepback on the outer panels. Performance and flying qualities were much improved and the Type 3 went on to become the most important and numerous version of the Il-2.

The Il-2s became renowned in the Soviet Union, used with much increased tactical effect in 1944-45 after their mode of operation had been studied carefully and fighter cover provided on a large scale. Improvement in armament included cassettes containing 200 PTAB hollow-charge anti-tank bombs, the use of a DAG-10 anti-aircraft grenade-launcher, and the introduction of a limited number of **Il-2 Type 3M** aircraft with a pair of 37-mm NS-11 or P-37 cannon mounted in fairings outboard of the landing gear.

Il-2s were used by the Soviet navy for anti-shipping duties, and the specialised **Il-2T** torpedo-bomber was also developed. On land the type was used on occasion for reconnaissance and laying smoke-screens. In the last year of World War II Il-2s were used by Polish and Czechoslovak units flying with the Soviets, and the type continued in service for several years post-war with the V-VS and for a slightly longer period with

Ilyushin Il-2m3 of an unidentified Red Air Force close support regiment operating in temporary winter camouflage over the Stalingrad front in February 1943.

other East European regimes.

Between September 1941 and April 1942 an experimental Il-2 powered by an M-82 radial engine was tested extensively, but no production was undertaken. Trainer versions of the Il-2 were known variously as the **U-Il-2** or **Il-2U**.

Specification
Ilyushin Il-2 Type 3
Type: two-seat ground-attack aircraft
Powerplant: one 1282-kW (1,720-hp) Mikulin AM-38F piston engine
Performance: maximum speed 410 km/h (255 mph) at 1500 m (4,920 ft); service ceiling 4525 m (14,845 ft); range 765 km (475 miles)
Weights: empty equipped 4525 kg (9,976 lb); maximum take-off 6360 kg (14,021 lb)
Dimensions: span 14.60 m (47 ft 10¾ in); length 11.65 m (38 ft 2½ in); height 4.17 m (13 ft 8 in); wing area 38.50 m² (414.42 sq ft)
Armament: two 23-mm VYa cannon and two 7.62-mm (0.3-in) ShKAS machine-guns (all wing-mounted) and one 12.7-mm (0.5-in) UBT machine-gun

Ilyushin Il-2 (single-seat early model)

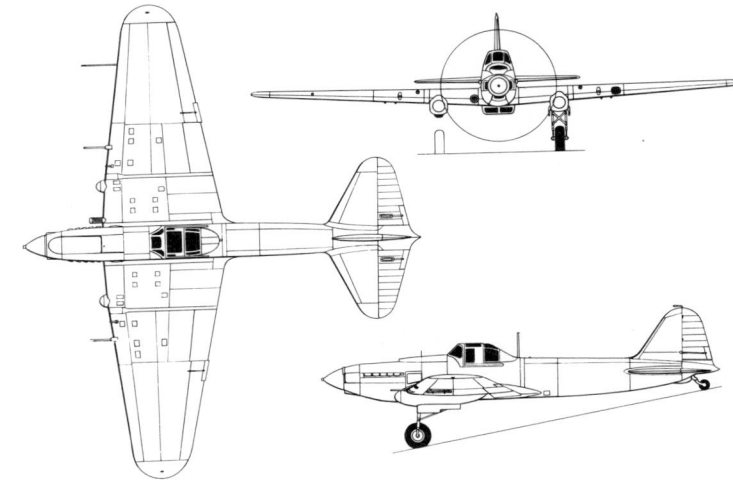

for the gunner, plus 100-kg (220-lb) bombs (four carried internally and two under the fuselage), or two 250-kg

(551-lb) bombs (under fuselage), eight RS-82 rockets or four RS-132 rockets under outer wing panels

Ilyushin Il-4

In 1938 a version of the DB-3 was developed with a totally new, easily-built airframe. As a result the appearance of the design was completely changed, the nose being slim, streamlined and with a large glazed area, with the nose turret of the DB-3 replaced by a swivel gun-mounting. State acceptance trials were completed successfully in June 1939 and by the end of that year the type was readied for quantity production. This new version was known as the **Ilyushin DB-3F**, later redesignated **Il-4** when delivered in quantity to the bomber regiments of the long-range air arm, the ADD. A small number had the same type of dorsal turret as the DB-3, but this was soon replaced by a more effective design. Additionally, the ventral machine-gun ring was replaced by a more complex semi-retractable mount.

The Il-4 remained in large-scale production until 1944, the number built being 5,256. The original M-87A engine was replaced by the more powerful M-88B with a two-speed supercharger in 1942. Most aircraft built in 1942 were completed with wooden wing spars as a result of shortage of light alloys, but metal components were reintroduced in late production machines.

In addition to its use for long-range bombing raids, the Il-4s of the ADD's various long-range bomber corps were

Ilyushin Il-4 (DB-3F) of a Red Air Force bombardirovoishchnaya aviatsionnyi polk (bomber regiment) operating over the Eastern front in 1944.

used frequently in attacks on tactical targets immediately behind enemy lines, carrying their maximum bombload. The Il-4 also came to be used widely by the mine/torpedo bomber regiments attached to the Baltic, Black Sea and Northern Fleets; when deployed in a torpedo-carrying role the Il-4 was armed with a 940-kg (2,072-lb) 45-36-AN (low-level) or 45-36-AV (high-level) torpedo. There was also provision for an auxiliary external fuel tank mounted under the rear fuselage.

The Il-4 was a robust and successful aircraft, a number surviving into the post-war period for use in a variety of support roles. It had sufficient longevity to earn the NATO codename '**Bob**'. Four Il-4s

purchased from German war booty stores were used by the Finns against the Soviet forces from 1943 to 1945.

In 1943 design work began on the **Il-6**, an advanced bomber with pressurised crew accommodation for high-level operations, considerable sweepback on the wing leading edge, and power provided by two 1119-kW (1,500-hp) Charomsky ACh-30B diesel engines, but development was abandoned before the prototype had flown.

Specification
Ilyushin Il-4
Type: three-seat long-range bomber
Powerplant: two 820-kW (1,100-hp) M-88B radial piston engines

Performance: maximum speed 430 km/h (267 mph) at 6700 m (21,980 ft); service ceiling 9700 m (31,825 ft); range 3800 km (2,361 miles)
Weights: empty equipped 5800 kg (12,787 lb); maximum take-off 11300 kg (24,912 lb)
Dimensions: span 21.44 m (70 ft 4¼ in); length 14.80 m (48 ft 6¾ in); height 4.10 m (13 ft 5½ in); wing area 66.70 m² (717.98 sq ft)
Armament: one 12.7-mm (0.5-in) and two 7.62-mm (0.3-in) machine-guns, plus an internal bombload of 1000 kg (2,205 lb) or a maximum bombload (internal and external) of 2500 kg (5,512 lb)

Ilyushin Il-10

To provide a replacement for the Il-2 *shturmovik* (ground-attack aircraft), the Ilyushin design bureau developed two different prototypes in 1943. The **Il-8**

bore a close resemblance to the Il-2, but was powered by a more powerful AM-42 engine, and had new wings, horizontal tail surfaces and landing gear married to a late-production Il-2 fuselage. Test-flown in April 1944, the Il-8 was rejected in favour of the contemporary

Ilyushin Il-10, which began its test flight programme in that month.

The Il-10 was a completely new design of all-metal construction and improved aerodynamic form. It provided better crew accommodation, the gunner seated with his back to the pilot in an en-

larged cockpit, and both crew members were located within the protective armoured shell. Revised main landing gear units retracted within the wing, eliminating the large landing gear fairings of the Il-2 and requiring only small fairings over the pivoting mechanism.

Early favourable reports of the proto-type test programme led to a batch of pre-series machines, quantity production being initiated in August 1944, with evaluation in operational regiments starting two months later. The type was used first in operations in February 1945 and by that spring output reached a peak. Many regiments re-equipped with the Il-10 before the German surrender, and a considerable number took part in the brief but large-scale operations against the Japanese in Manchuria and Korea during August 1945.

Production of the Il-10 continued into the post-war period, with Soviet factories building 4,966 machines, the last leaving the production lines in 1955. Additionally, Il-10s were also built at the Czech Avia factory, under the designations **B-33** and **CB-33**, the latter being the equivalent of the **Il-10U** trainer variant. Czech production finished in 1954 when over 1,200 examples had been completed. From 1951 onwards Soviet production had concentrated on the **Il-10M**, which featured an entirely new wing of revised planform and deeper aerofoil section, a slightly lengthened fuselage, modified landing gear with increased track, and increased fuel capacity.

The Il-10 formed the sole equipment

Ilyushin Il-10 of a 1951 Polish air force assault regiment.

of Soviet assault units for a number of years and was also used widely by Warsaw Pact countries. Other Communist countries to employ the type included North Korea in the opening stages of the Korean War in 1950. Losses were heavy and the type was clearly obsolete but, nevertheless, Il-10s remained in service with the Soviet V-VS until 1956 and with various satellite air arms for several years longer. For some time after that they were flown as gunnery trainers but most had been scrapped by the mid-1960s.

The Il-10 had been tested with a ZhRD-1 auxiliary rocket engine in the rear fuselage to provide short-term perform-ance boost, but this modification was not adopted. The Ilyushin bureau strove to develop later *shturmovik* designs, including the Il-20 single-seater and the Il-40 with twin turbojets, but official encouragement was minimal, the Soviet authorities having accepted the Western concept of the tactical strike fighter.

Specification
Ilyushin Il-10
Type: two-seat ground-attack aircraft
Powerplant: one 1492-kW (2,000-hp) Mikulin AM-42 piston engine
Performance: maximum speed 530 km/h (329 mph) at 2400 m (7,875 ft); service ceiling 7250 m

(23,785 ft); range 800 km (497 miles)
Weights: empty equipped 4680 kg (10,317 lb); maximum take-off 6535 kg (14,407 lb)
Dimensions: span 13.40 m (43 ft 11½ in); length 11.06 m (36 ft 3½ in); height 4.18 m (13 ft 8½ in); wing area 30.00 m² (322.9 sq ft)
Armament: two 7.62-mm (0.3-in) ShKAS machine-guns, and either two 23-mm VYa-23 cannon or two 23-mm NS-23 cannon (mounted in the wings) and one 20-mm UB-20 cannon or 12.7-mm (0.5-in) UBT machine-gun in dorsal position, plus up to 500 kg (1,102 lb) of bombs plus four RS-82 or RS-132 rockets

Ilyushin Il-12

Design of the **Ilyushin Il-12** twin-engined transport began in 1943, but wartime commitments delayed the building of prototypes and the first flight took place in early 1946. An all-metal low-wing monoplane powered by two ASh-82FNV radial engines, the Il-12 had a flight crew of four and cabin accommodation for up to 27 passengers. The air force (V-VS) version had additional double-entry cargo doors in the port side fuselage, plus provision for machine-guns firing from cabin windows. Service deliveries began in 1947, while Aeroflot received its first aircraft during 1948. Later examples went to the Czech,

Polish and Chinese national airlines.

A dorsal fin was soon added and passenger seating increased to 32, though Aeroflot limited seating to 16 or 18, an uneconomical load.

Total production is reported to have exceeded 2,000 by the time the Il-12, which had the NATO Codename **'Coach'**, was phased out in 1953 in favour of the Il-14.

Specification
Type: passenger and cargo transport

The Ilyushin Il-12 displayed slightly more than a passing resemblance to the Douglas DC-3 (Lisonov Li-2) it replaced in civil and military service.

Powerplant: two 1365-kW (1,830-hp) Shvetsov ASh-82FNV piston engines
Performance: maximum speed 407 km/h (253 mph) at 2500 m (8,200 ft); service ceiling 6700 m (21,980 ft); range 2000 km (1,243 miles)

Weights: empty equipped 9000 kg (19,842 lb); maximum take-off 17250 kg (38,030 lb)
Dimensions: span 31.70 m (104 ft 0 in); length 21.31 m (69 ft 11 in); wing area 100.00 m² (1,076.43 sq ft)

Ilyushin Il-14

The post-war **Ilyushin Il-14** transport was a logical development of the earlier Il-12. It had improved aerodynamic qualities, a greatly modified and refined structure and greater power. Externally the greatest differences lay in the redesigned wing and crew cabin, and the enlarged angular vertical tail.

The Il-14 flew in prototype form in 1952 and over 3,500 were built in the Soviet Union in a variety of versions for passenger transport, and in military variants for trooping or cargo transport. The military Il-14s had strengthened floors, large double doors for freight loading in the port side rear fuselage, and observation blisters for use by the controller during employment as a paratroop transport. The NATO reporting name for the type is **'Crate'**.

East Germany and Czechoslovakia built the Il-14 under licence from 1956 and when Soviet production terminated in 1958, Czechoslovak development and production continued into the 1960s. Il-14s served with the airlines of the Soviet bloc and with those of other countries, while it formed the military equipment of all the Soviet Union's allies plus Algeria, Egypt, India and Yugoslavia. The type is still used widely in the Soviet Union for freight transport.

Variants
Il-14P: original commercial version for 18-26 passengers
Il-14M: lengthened-fuselage version accommodating 24-28 passengers; widely used
Il-14T: designation for freight conversions of passenger aircraft for Aeroflot
Avia 14/Avia 14P: Czechoslovak-built Il-14s and Il-14Ps
Avia 14-32: Czechoslovak-built Il-14M in 32-seat configuration
Avia 14T: freighter version of Il-14M built in Czechoslovakia, with single very

large freight door in port side fuselage
Avia 14FG: aerial survey version
Avia 14-42: pressurised and enlarged version with porthole-type windows; flown in 1960
'Crate-C': military electronic warfare version, first seen in 1979

Specification
Ilyushin Il-14M
Type: passenger transport
Powerplant: two 1417-kW (1,900-hp) Shvetsov ASh-82T radial piston engines
Performance: maximum speed 417 km/h (259 mph); service ceiling

A long-obsolete design, only a few Ilyushin Il-14 'Crates' survive today in either civilian or military service, notably in Poland and Cuba.

7400 m (24,280 ft); range with full payload 1305 km (811 miles)
Weights: empty equipped 12600 kg (27,778 lb); maximum take-off 18000 kg (39,683 lb)
Dimensions: span 31.70 m (104 ft 0 in); length 22.30 m (73 ft 2 in); height 7.90 m (25 ft 11 in); wing area 99.70 m² (1,073 sq ft)

Ilyushin Il-18 and Il-38

The **Ilyushin Il-18** was developed in the mid-1950s to meet an Aeroflot requirement for a medium-range 75/100-seat transport, and the first prototype flew on 4 July 1957. Aeroflot inaugurated use of the type on its Moscow-Adler and Moscow-Alma Ata routes on 20 April 1959, and eventually something more than 700 of these aircraft were built. It is believed that about 100 remain in service with Aeroflot, probably in a freighter role, and perhaps another 150 are in use worldwide. Of the total built only small numbers entered military service, primarily for VIP transport.

As Il-18s have been retired from civil use, some have been converted into the ECM or electronic intelligence (Elint) Il-20s, and these have the NATO reporting name **'Coot-A'**. It seems likely that the numbers of these aircraft will increase as the turboprop-powered Il-18s are retired from Aeroflot use when replaced by turbofan-powered airliners. In addition to the 'Coot-A' there is another military version, the maritime reconnaissance/ASW **Il-38 'May'** developed from the Il-18 airliner. This differs from the standard Il-18 by having a lengthened fuselage, MAD (magnetic anomaly detection) tail 'sting', weapon-carrying capability, and the wing located much further forward on the fuselage to offset the change in centre of gravity resulting from the introduction of more equipment and stores. About 60 are believed to be in use by the Soviet naval air force and one squadron in India.

Variants
Ilyushin Il-18: original production version with 75-passenger capacity and powerplant of four 2983-ekW (4,000-eshp) Kuznetsov NK-4 turboprops; Ivchenko AI-20 turboprops optional, but standard from 21st aircraft
Ilyushin Il-18B: generally similar to Il-18, but with seating rearranged for a maximum of 84 passengers
Ilyushin Il-18V: improved production version of 1961 with seating for 90 to 100 passengers; some repositioning of cabin windows
Ilyushin Il-18I: designation of development aircraft with more powerful AI-20M engines, increased fuel capacity, lengthened cabin seating 122 passengers (summer) or 110 (winter) when increased cloakroom space is needed
Ilyushin Il-18D: production version of the Il-18I
Ilyushin Il-18E: production version of the Il-18I without the increased fuel capacity
Ilyushin Il-18T: designation of Aeroflot aircraft converted for use as cargo transports

Specification
Ilyushin Il-18D
Type: long-range transport
Powerplant: four 3169-ekW (4,250-eshp) Ivchenko AI-20M turboprops

Performance: maximum cruising speed 675 km/h (419 mph); operating altitude 8000 to 10000 m (25,250 to 32,810 ft); range with maximum payload and fuel reserves 3700 km (2,299 miles)
Weights: empty equipped (90 seats) 35000 kg (77,162 lb); maximum take-off 64000 kg (141,096 lb)
Dimensions: span 37.40 m (122 ft 8½ in); length 35.90 m (117 ft 9¼ in); height 10.17 m (33 ft 4¼ in); wing area 140.00 m² (1,507.0 sq ft)

The Il-38 'May' was the Soviet Union's first long-range maritime reconnaissance aircraft and was a familiar sight the world over, shadowing NATO warships.

The Il-18 provided Eastern European airlines with a reliable and long-lived transport that still survives today, if in dwindling numbers, as a cargo aircraft.

Ilyushin Il-28

The first of three prototypes of the **Ilyushin Il-28** tactical bomber (NATO reporting name **'Beagle'**) flew on 8 August 1948. Just over a year earlier the **Il-22** with four Lyulka TR-1 jets had begun flight testing but proved unsuccessful.

The Il-28 is an all-metal shoulder-wing monoplane with a straight wing and swept tail surfaces, and retractable tricycle landing gear, and is powered by two 2270-kg (5,002-lb) thrust Klimov RD-45F turbojets (derived from the Rolls-Royce Nene). The pilot is located under a raised, carefully faired canopy, the navigator's nose station is fully glazed and the rear gunner (who doubles as radio operator) operates a twin-cannon Il-K6 turret in the tail.

A formation of 25 pre-production Il-28s took part in the 1950 May Day Moscow flypast, by which time large-scale production had been initiated at several factories. Series aircraft, which entered service with a large number of V-VS bomber regiments, incorporated aerodynamic refinements, Klimov VK-1 turbojets in place of the RD-45s, and had

provision for detachable wingtip fuel tanks.

The Il-28 proved reliable and adaptable and in the early 1950s was supplied to China (which received over 500 and licence-built others), Czechoslovakia and Poland; it was eventually exported to more than 20 countries and remained in first-line Soviet service for many years.

Ilyushin's bureau produced several other bomber prototypes during this period, but none was accepted for production. These included two twin-jet swept-wing tactical bombers, the **Il-30** of 1951 and the **Il-54** of 1954, and the considerably larger **Il-46** of 1952 which had a maximum take-off weight of 42000 kg (92,594 lb).

Variants
Il-28T: naval torpedo-bomber version
Il-28U: operational trainer version, with solid nose and second cockpit for pupil located ahead of and below standard cockpit
Il-28R: for tactical reconnaissance, has optical or electronic sensors in weapons bay; some have an underfuselage radome
Il-20: civil version used by Aeroflot from early 1956 on Moscow-

Sverdlovsk-Novosibirsk route; intended as proving aircraft for jet airliners; also carried matrices for national newspapers intended for simultaneous publication throughout Soviet Union

Specification
Ilyushin Il-28

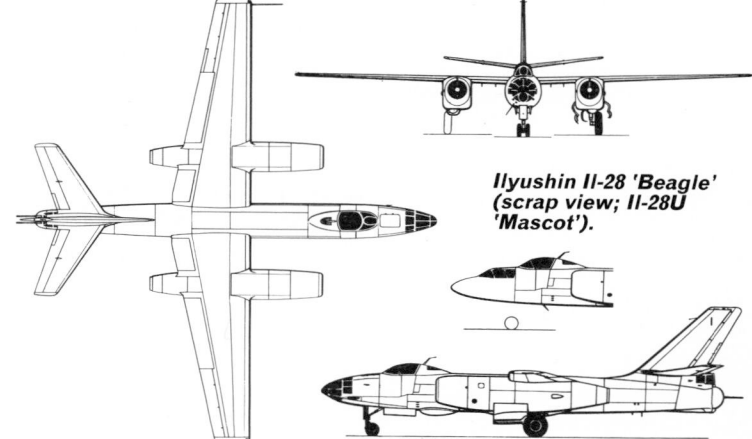

Ilyushin Il-28 'Beagle' (scrap view; Il-28U 'Mascot').

Type: tactical day bomber
Powerplant: two 2700-kg (5,952-lb) thrust Klimov VK-1 turbojets
Performance: maximum speed 900 km/h (559 mph) at 4500 m (14,765 ft); service ceiling 12300 m (40,355 ft); range 2180 km (1,355 miles)

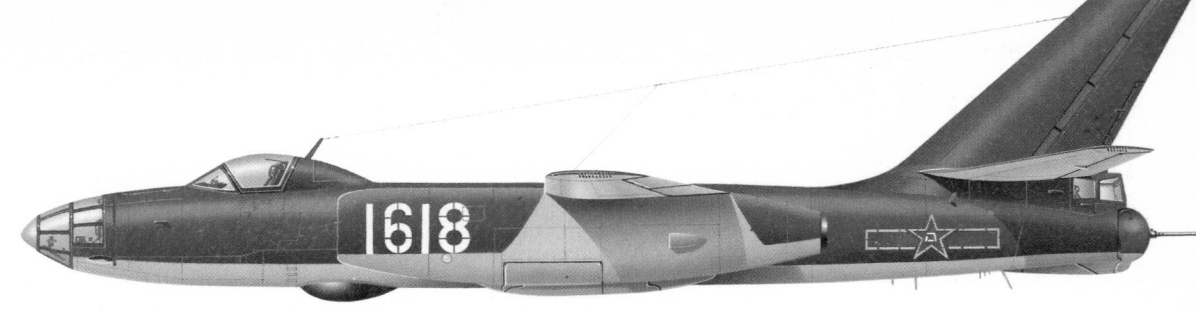

Weights: empty equipped 12890 kg (28,418 lb); maximum take-off 21000 kg (46,297 lb)
Dimensions: span 21.45 m (70 ft 4½ in); length 17.65 m (57 ft 10¾ in); wing area 60.80 m² (654.47 sq ft)
Armament: two fixed forward-firing 23-mm NS-23 cannon in nose and two NS-23 cannon in tail turret, plus a normal internal bombload of 1000 kg (2,205 lb) or a maximum bombload of 3000 kg (6,614 lb)

Soviet-built Ilyushin Il-28 of the Chinese People's Liberation Air Force.

Ilyushin Il-62

Ilyushin Il-62 of the Czech national airline CSA, powered by four Kuznetsov NK-8-4 engines.

First flown in January 1963, the **Ilyushin Il-62** was designed to complement and partially to replace the Tupolev Tu-114 on Aeroflot's long-range domestic and intercontinental routes. A cantilever low-wing monoplane with swept wings, a T-tail with all swept surfaces, retractable tricycle landing gear and four engines mounted in pairs on each side of the rear fuselage, the Il-62 entered service during 1967. Initial operations had been on cargo services, but on 10 March passenger/mail services were inaugurated on the Moscow-Khabarovsk and Moscow-Novosibirsk routes. When, on 15 September 1967, Aeroflot introduced the type on its Moscow-Montreal route, the Il-62 represented the Soviet Union's first long-range four-engined intercontinental jet transport. The Il-62 has the NATO reporting name **'Classic'** and it is believed that more than 210 have been built, some 200 remaining in airline service.

Variants
Il-62: initial production version, accommodating a crew of five and a maximum of 186 passengers
Il-62M: more powerful Soloviev D-30K engines, increased fuel capacity, a containerised baggage and freight system, and other improvements
Il-62MK: version with strengthened

The Il-62 was the Soviet Union's first and is still its 'best' long-range airliner. Today, rapidly becoming an anachronism, most operators are abandoning it.

wings and landing gear for operation at higher gross weights and with seating for a maximum of 195 passengers

Specification
Ilyushin Il-62M
Type: long-range transport
Powerplant: four 11000-kg (24,250-lb) thrust Soloviev D-30KU turbofans
Performance: cruising speed 900 km/h (559 mph) at optimum altitude; range with maximum payload and fuel reserves 7800 km (4,847 miles)
Weights: empty operating 69400 kg (153,001 lb); maximum take-off 165000 kg (363,763 lb)
Dimensions: span 43.20 m (141 ft 8¾ in); length 53.12 m (174 ft 3¼ in); height 12.35 m (40 ft 6¼ in); wing area 282.20 m² (3,037.67 sq ft)

Ilyushin Il-76

Designed as a heavy transport for use in the Siberian regions of the Soviet Union, the **Ilyushin Il-76,** codenamed **'Candid'** by NATO, is a large-capacity turbofan-powered jet freighter designed to operate from short, unprepared airstrips. The prototype flew on 25 March 1971 and test flying continued until 1975 when the type was put into production at the Tashkent factory. During the same year the Il-76 established 25 international records for speed and altitude with payload.

The production **Il-76T 'Candid A'**, with greater cargo capacity and higher gross weights, went into service with Aeroflot on domestic routes early in 1978, and the Moscow-Japan international route in April the same year. Around 50 are estimated to be in service with Aeroflot and about 100 have been exported to civil users including Libyan Arab Airlines, Syrianair and, more recently, Cubana, while military customers include the Czech, Polish, Algerian, Iraqi and Indian air forces, this last operating the type as the **Gajaraj**. The military

transport version, intended for the deployment of paratroops and troops, together with strategic heavy freighting, differs primarily by having military, rather than civil, avionics and equipment. The Soviet air force, with about 450 'Candids' in service, also use the aircraft for firefighting (the **Il-76DMP**), able to carry over 40 tons of water or retardant; as an engine testbed (the **Il-76LL**); for flight refuelling (as the **Il-78 'Midas'**); airborne early warning (as the **A-50 'Mainstay'** in the USSR, and the **'Adnan 1'** in Iraq) and for Antarctic support flights and cosmonaut training providing simulated weightlessness. By early 1991 total production had reached about 680 aircraft.

Specification
Ilyushin Il-76T 'Candid A'
Type: medium/long-range jet freighter
Powerplant: four 12000-kg (26,455-lb) thrust Soloviev D-30KP turbofans
Performance: maximum level speed 850 km/h (528 mph); cruising speed 800 km/h (497 mph); ceiling 15500 m (50,850 ft); range with maximum

payload 3650 km (2,265 miles)
Weights: maximum payload 40000 kg (88,185 lb); maximum take-off 170000 kg (374,785 lb)
Dimensions: span 50.5 m (165 ft 8 in); length 46.5 m (152 ft 10 in); height 14.7 m (48 ft 5 in); wing area 300.0 m² (3,229.2 sq ft)

Pseudo-military Ilyushin Il-76 'Candid' of Iraqi Airways

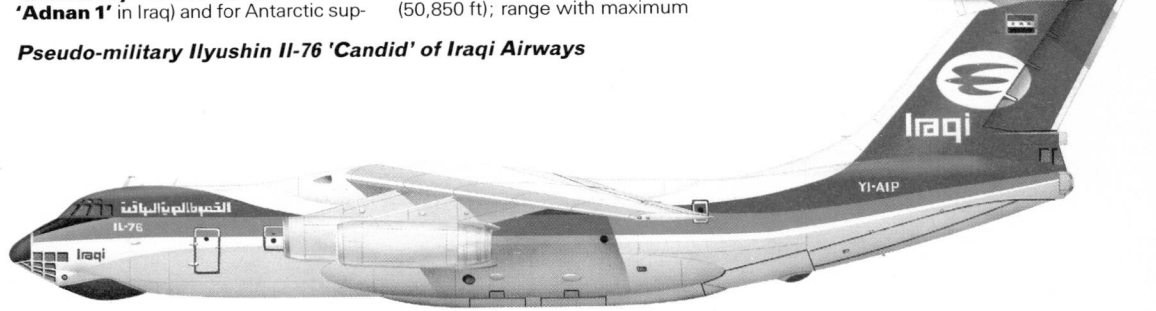

Ilyushin Il-86

The **Ilyushin Il-86**, which has the NATO reporting name **'Camber'**, is the Soviet Union's first wide-body civil transport. Of low/mid-wing monoplane configuration, it has a circular-section pressurised fuselage with a maximum internal width of 5.70 m (18 ft 8½ in), and is powered by four Kuznetsov NK-86 turbofan engines pylon-mounted beneath the wings. Accommodation is provided for a crew of three or four on the flight deck, and there is seating for a maximum of 350 passengers, distributed between three cabins which are separated by wardrobes. Access to this aircraft is unique, being via three lower-deck airstair-type doors which allow the aircraft to be operated without conventional airport loading/unloading bridges. The airstairs reach down to ground level and, after boarding, passengers can deposit their baggage in lower-deck stowage positions before climbing an internal fixed staircase to the passenger cabin.

Prototype of Ilyushin's less than spectacular Il-86 'Camber' airliner.

The Polish PZL factory at Mielec is involved in the manufacture of parts for the Il-86.

Construction of two prototypes began in 1974 and the first flew on 22 December 1976. The Il-86 was subjected to rigorous testing and the first production aircraft flew in October 1977. Deliveries to Aeroflot began in September 1979, since when between 80 and 85 have entered service out of an order for 100. Although most former Eastern Bloc airlines, and particularly CSA and LOT, were mentioned as potential export customers, no orders have materialised and the type remains peculiar to Aeroflot. Domestic operations began on 26 December 1980 followed by international services in July 1981. Poor performance, particularly in terms of payload/range, has led to the suggested re-engining of the Il-86 with Soloviev PS90 or CFM56 engines.

Specification
Type: short/medium-range wide-body airliner
Powerplant: four 13000-kg (28,660-lb) thrust Kuznetsov NK-86 turbofans
Performance: cruising speed 950 km/h (590 mph) at 11000 m (36,000 ft); range with maximum payload 3600 km (2,235 miles)
Weights: maximum take-off 208000 kg (458,560 lb)
Dimensions: span 48.0 m (157 ft 8 in); length 59.4 m (195 ft 4 in); height 15.8 m (51 ft 10 in); wing area 320.0 m² (3,444 sq ft)

Ilyushin Il-96

The **Il-96** was, in effect, a redesign of the Il-86 and, although superficially similar, really a new design. Construction of five airframes, three flying prototypes and two static test specimens, began in 1986/87 and the first aircraft (SSSR-96000) flew on 28 September 1988 from the Khodinka factory, followed by the second in November 1989. The production version, designated **Il-96-300,** was scheduled for certification in 1991 but early in 1992 the programme was running about nine months late, partly due to avionics unreliability. The two upper-fuselage cabins can accommodate 234 and 66 passengers respectively, with cargo holds under the floor. Passenger boarding has reverted to three conventional doors in the fuselage rather than the walk-in lower-deck entrances of the Il-86. PZL Mielec is subcontracted to build the fin, tailplane, engine pylons and wing slats for the Il-96-300.

Variants
Il-96MK: designated **Il-96-350** until 1990; projected export version of the Il-96-300 fitted with Pratt & Whitney PW2037 turbofan engines and Rockwell Collins avionics; fuselage stretched by 9.0 m (29 ft 6 in) to accommodate 312-375 passengers, cabin crew plus 2/3-man flight-deck crew; first flight scheduled for 1993 and certification (to FAR 25) planned for 1995
Il-96MD: projected twin-engined version of Il-96-300; two 27200/31750-kg (60,000/70,000-lb) thrust engines required and first examples would fly with Lotarev D-18 turbofans, with PW2337 and RR Trent versions also under study
Il-96-550: projected 550-passenger development of Il-96-300 requiring four ultra-high bypass engines giving between 18000/22000-kg (39,700/48,500-lb) thrust; the two-deck double-bubble fuselage could accommodate 190 and 360 passengers in the upper and lower cabins respectively

Specification
Ilyushin Il-96-300
Type: long-range wide-body jet airliner
Powerplant: four 16000-kg (35,275-lb) thrust Soloviev PS-90A turbofans
Performance: (estimated) normal cruising speed at 12100 m (39,700 ft) 900 km/h (559 mph); range with maximum payload 7500 km (4,660 miles)
Weights: maximum payload 40000 kg (88,185 lb); basic operating 117000 kg

(257,940 lb); maximum take-off 216000 kg (476,200 lb)
Dimensions: span 60.1 m (197 ft 2 in); length 55.3 m (181 ft 7 in); height 17.5 m (57 ft 7 in); wing area 391.6 m² (4,215 sq ft)

Originally intended to become the flagship of Aeroflot's international routes, the Il-96 now faces a very uncertain future, with the prospect of Western assistance its only hope.

Ilyushin Il-114

Development of the **Il-114**, designed to replace the widely-used Antonov An-24, began in 1984/85. The first of three flying prototypes (SSSR-54000) flew for the first time on 29 March 1990 from the Zhokovsky test centre and the second was scheduled to fly in August 1991. Full-scale production was expected to begin by the end of 1991 and certification is planned for 1993 with first deliveries to Aeroflot following in 1994. Planned production rate is 100 aircraft per year from the Tashkent factory, and Aeroflot are expected to require around 500 Il-114s. The aircraft, a British Aerospace ATP 'lookalike', is of conventional twin-engined layout with a low-set straight wing and a tall single fin and rudder. Each engine drives a six-bladed low-noise propeller, and the tricycle undercarriage is designed for rough field operation. The Il-114 can carry up to 60 passengers plus two pilots and a cabin attendant, and, although claimed to be a freighter, is not equipped with a cargo door.

Specification
Type: twin turboprop short-range passenger airliner and freighter
Powerplant: two 1865-kg (2,500-shp) thrust Klimov TV7-117 turboprop engines
Performance: (estimated) cruising speed 500 km/h (310 mph); range with 60 passengers 1000 km (621 miles)
Weights: maximum payload 6000 kg (13,227 lb); empty operating 13700 kg (30,200 lb); maximum take-off 21000 kg (46,300 lb)
Dimensions: span 30.0 m (98 ft 5 in); length 26.3 m (86 ft 4 in); height 9.32 m (30 ft 7 in)

The Il-114 has, hopefully, a brighter future than some of the other current Russian transport designs. There is a need for the type both within the former Soviet Union and abroad.

Junkers early aircraft

In 1910 the German engineer Dr Hugo Junkers patented a flying-wing aircraft; it was never built, but the thick-section cantilever wing that he designed for it was used in the first Junkers aeroplane to fly, the **Junkers J 1**, on 12 December 1915. Of advanced appearance for its day, a mid-wing cantilever monoplane with fixed tailskid landing gear and powered by an 89-kW (120-hp) Mercedes D.II engine, the J1 was covered by thin sheet iron, gaining it the nickname 'Tin Donkey'.

Impressed by Junkers constructional techniques, the German air ministry asked for the design and development of an armoured biplane. This was the **Junkers J 4**, which entered service as a two-seat close-support aircraft towards the end of 1917 under the military designation **J.I**. An unequal-span biplane with fixed tailskid landing gear and powered by a 149-kW (200-hp) Benz Bz.IV engine, the J.I was covered by the corrugated light-alloy skins that soon became a feature of Junkers aircraft. Powerplant and crew were enclosed in

an armoured capsule, the protection which this provided against small-arms fire from the ground making the J.I popular with its crews. Production totalled 227, these aircraft being armed with two fixed forward-firing LMG 08/15 machine-guns, plus one Parabellum gun on a trainable mount in the rear cockpit.

With the J 4 in production, Junkers turned to a new series of cantilever low-wing monoplanes, the single-seat **J 7** of 1917 introducing originally swivelling wingtips of ailerons for lateral control. The J 7 served as prototype for the slightly longer **J 9** single-seat fighter which, powered by the 138-kW (185-hp) B.M.W. engine and armed with twin forward-firing LMG 08/15 machine-guns, was built in small numbers under the military designation **D.I**.

An enlarged two-seat version of the J 7, for evaluation as an escort and close-support aircraft, had the company designation **J 8** and led to development of the **Junkers J 10** powered by a 134-kW (180-hp) Mercedes D.IIIa engine. About 50 examples of this were built before the

The unsuccessful Junkers canard monoplane of 1909 featured the familiar corrugated construction.

Armistice of 1918, entering service as the **Junkers CL.I** and carrying the same armament as the D.I. Three examples of a floatplane version of this aircraft, the **Junkers J 11**, entered service with the German navy during 1918 under the designation **Junkers CLS.I**.

Specification
Junkers J.I
Type: two-seat close-support aircraft
Powerplant: one 149-kW (200-hp) Benz Bz.IV six-cylinder inline piston engine
Performance: maximum speed

155 km/h (97 mph); endurance 2 hours
Weights: empty 1766 kg (3,885 lb); maximum take-off 2176 kg (4,787 lb)
Dimensions: span 16.0 m (52 ft 6 in); length 9.10 m (29 ft 10½ in); height 3.40 m (11 ft 1¾ in); wing area 49.40 m² (533.52 sq ft)
Armament: two fixed forward-firing 7.92-mm (0.31-in) LMG 08/15 machine-guns and one trainable 7.92-mm (0.31-in) Parabellum machine-gun

Junkers aircraft of the 1920s

Derived from the World War I Junkers J 10 (CL.I), the **Junkers F 13** was the world's first purpose-built all-metal commercial monoplane to enter service. In its original form, as first flown on 25 June 1919, the two-man crew was accommodated in a forward open cockpit, with the four passengers in an enclosed cabin to its rear; at a later date the crew also had enclosed accommodation. The first F 13 was powered by the 119-kW (160-hp) Mercedes D.IIIa engine, but this was superseded in early production aircraft by a 138-kW (185-hp) B.M.W. IIIa engine. Production continued until 1932, and by far the majority (of more than 320 built in some 60 variants) were powered by the 156-kW (210-hp) Junkers L-5 engine. Between 40 and 50 were supplied to Deutsche Luft-Hansa, the remainder being used for both civil and military service on a world-wide basis.

The F 13's success was certainly not matched by the **K 16**, a three-seat cabin monoplane of 1922 of which only a few examples were built. It was followed by the sleek **A 20** low-wing monoplane, first flown in 1923, which had seats for a crew of two in tandem open cockpits. Intended for use as a freight or mail-carrier, the A 20 entered production, after approval by the Allied control commission, in both **A 20L** landplane and **A 20W** float-plane forms, built in Germany and at the Junkers factory in Sweden. These were powered by the Mercedes D.IIIa or 164-kW (220-hp) Junkers L-2 engine respectively, and a developed version with the 231-kW (310-hp) Junkers L-5 engine had the designation **A 35**. A military version of this last aircraft, armed with two forward-firing and two rear-mounted machine-guns, was developed in Sweden under the designation **R 53**.

Civil development continued with the **G 23**, which entered service in 1925, and was then the world's first three-engined all-metal commercial transport monoplane. Operated by a crew of three, it accommodated nine passengers, and was flown with a variety of powerplants. The designation **G 24** applied to the major production version, usually powered by three 231-kW (310-hp) Junkers L-5 engines, but a number of **F 24** aircraft which appeared in 1928 had a single-engine powerplant (the outer wing-mounted engines being removed) but were otherwise generally similar. A

12/15-passenger version designated **G 31**, of which 15 were built, had three Gnome-Rhône Jupiter or B.M.W.-built Pratt & Whitney Hornet engines. There was also a military bomber version of the G 24, which had the designation **K 30**; it introduced three gunners' positions and carried bombs on racks beneath the wings; this model was built in the USSR, Sweden and Turkey under the designation **R 42**. The first post-World War I design intended for military use was the **Junkers H 21**, a two-seat armed reconnaissance aircraft of parasol-wing monoplane configuration, powered by the 138-kW (185-hp) B.M.W. IIIa engine. About 100 H 21s were built by the Junkers factory at Fili, near Moscow, all of them entering service with the Soviet air force; the first was delivered in 1924.

Developments at the Junkers Swedish factory included the **K 37**, a three-seat general-purpose military aircraft derived from the **S 36** twin-engined transport of 1927, and one example supplied to Japan was developed as the **Mitsubishi Ki-2**; the **K 39** three-seat bomber/reconnaissance aircraft appeared only in prototype form; a few examples of the **K 47**, a two-seat fighter, were built in 1928 for export to China; the type was also built in civil form as the **A 48**.

The last Junkers aircraft to be designed and built before the company adopted the Ju series of designations was the giant **G 38**, of which only two were built. Powered by four 559-kW (750-hp) Junkers Jumo 204 engines mounted at the leading edge of the 44-m (144-ft 4-in) span wing, the G 38 accommodated 26 passengers in the main fuselage cabins, two in the fuselage nose, and three in each of two wing-root cabins. The first example to fly, on 6 November 1929, was named *Deutschland*, serving with Deutsche Luft-Hansa until it crashed during 1936. The second, *Generalfeldmarschall von Hindenburg*, remained in use with Deutsche Luft-Hansa until destroyed in an RAF bombing attack during 1940. Six similar aircraft were licence-built in Japan under the designation **Mitsubishi Ki-20**, and were intended to serve as heavy bombers with the Japanese army.

The **Junkers Ju 46** floatplane, of which five were built for Deutsche Luft-Hansa in 1932 as freight- and mail-car-

riers, was a two-seat monoplane powered by the 488-kW (650-hp) B.M.W.132 engine. Next, in numerical designation, was the single-engined **Ju 52** commercial freight transport of which six were built, the first flying on 13 October 1930. The designation **Ju 60** was allocated to a six-passenger aircraft of 1932, of which only four were built, but the improved **Ju 160** of 1934 was far more successful, with almost 50 produced and more than half of them serving with Deutsche Luft-Hansa. Under the designation **Ju 252** Junkers developed for Deutsche Luft-Hansa a 35-passenger three-engined transport which incorporated an hydraulically-operated ventral loading door; although intended to supersede the Ju 52/3m, only 15 were built. A generally similar **Ju**

352 Herkules, of which 33 production examples were built, replaced the light-alloy construction of the Ju 252 by mixed wood and steel with fabric covering to save short-supply aluminium alloys for the production of fighter aircraft. Finally, mention must be made of the **Ju 287**, a four-engined turbojet-powered heavy-bomber with a forward-swept wing, of which only an aerodynamic testbed prototype was flown; two production prototypes were incomplete when World War II ended.

For a design completed in 1919 the Junkers F 13 was a very advanced aircraft, both in construction and appearance. This is a relatively late-production example.

Identifiable from its registration D-2000, this is the initial Junkers G 38 (the G 38a 'Deutschland'). The windows in the leading edge of the wing roots indicate the size of the passenger cabins inside the wings.

Junkers Ju 52/3m
to
Kaman H-2 Seasprite

Junkers Ju 52/3m

A decision to evaluate the single-engined Ju 52 as a three-engined transport led to the seventh airframe on the production line being converted as the prototype **Junkers Ju 52/3m**, powered by three 410-kW (550-hp) Pratt & Whitney Hornet engines. When tested in April 1931, the performance of this **Ju 52/3mce** was so markedly improved by comparison with that of the single-engined version that production of the single-engined Ju 52 was terminated. The first customer was Lloyd Aero Boliviano, which received seven aircraft from 1932.

The type was available with float, ski or wheel landing gear, and Aero O/Y (Finland) and AB Aerotransport (Sweden) acquired the floatplane version, but the Ju 52/3mce aircraft supplied to Deutsche Luft-Hansa had wheel landing gear. In this last airline's service the type quickly made a name for itself; by the end of 1935 97 were in airline use, including 51 with Luft-Hansa.

Evaluation of the Ju 52/3m's military potential by the clandestine Luftwaffe led to an interim bomber version, the **Ju 52/3mge** and a later improved **Ju 52/3mg3e**. They first saw action in the Spanish Civil War, initially as troop transports ferrying some 10,000 Moorish troops from Morocco to Spain. However, by the time the war ended in 1939 Ju 52s had amassed some 13,000 operational hours and had dropped more than 6,000 tons of bombs. Civil production continued in parallel, more than 230 being registered to Luft-Hansa in the mid-1930s, although some of these were no doubt passed on to the Luftwaffe, which received 450 from Junkers during 1934-35, and 593 during 1939; another 59 were commandeered from Luft-Hansa at the outbreak of World War II.

The versatility of the Ju 52/3m meant that the type was used extensively by the Luftwaffe throughout the war, and replacements for attrition were met by laying down a new production line at the Amiot factory in Colombes, France, the first aircraft from this source being accepted in June 1942. Assembly of 26 Ju 52/3ms from German-built components was carried out by PIRT in Budapest, all but four from this source being

supplied to the Hungarian air force. When production ended in mid-1944, a total approaching 5,000 had been built in France and Germany. Post-World War II, the French built more than 400 for Air France and air force, the latter designating the type **AAC.1 Toucan**. CASA, in Spain, built 170 for the Spanish air force under the designation **CASA 352**.

Developments of the Ju 52/3m included the Ju 252 and the redesigned version, the Ju 352, both previously described.

It is interesting to record that three Ju 52/mg4e transport aircraft delivered to the Swiss air force in the late-1930s were not retired from service until 1981, and still fly regularly giving joyrides around Europe.

Variants
Ju 52/3mg3e: military version with three 541-kW (725-hp) B.M.W. 132-A3 engines, improved radio and bomb-release mechanism
Ju 52/3mg4e: military version; internal equipment changes from Ju 52/3mg3e and tailskid replaced by tailwheel
Ju 52/3mg5e: military version; three 619-kW (830-hp) B.M.W. 132T engines, exhaust heat for de-icing, interchangeable float/ski/wheel landing gear and improved radio
Ju 52/3mg6e: as Ju 52/3mg5e but with simplified radio; basically land-based
Ju 52/3mg7e: as Ju 52/3mg6e but with autopilot and large loading hatch
Ju 52/3mg8e: as Ju 52/3mg7e but extra cabin roof hatch; late production

had improved B.M.W. 132Z engines
Ju 52/3mg9e: as Ju 52/3mg8e late production but with strengthened landing gear; glider towing gear standard
Ju 52/3mg10e: similar to Ju 52/3mg9e but suitable for float or wheeled operations
Ju 52/3mg11e: no details known
Ju 52/3mg12e: as Ju 52/3mg10e but with three B.M.W. 132L engines; some went to Luft-Hansa as **Ju 52/3m12**
Ju 52/3mg13e: no details known
Ju 52/3mg14e: last production version; as Ju 52/3mg9e but improved armour protection for pilot and heavier defensive armament

Specification
Junkers Ju 52/3mg3e
Type: medium bomber and troop

Junkers Ju 52/3mg4e of Grupo de Bombardeo Nocturno 2-6-22 of the Spanish Nationalist air force.

While still a tri-motor, the Ju 252 V1 had a smooth stressed skin quite unlike the corrugated finish of its predecessor.

transport
Powerplant: three 541-kW (725-hp) B.M.W. 132A-3 radial piston engines
Performance: maximum speed 275 km/h (171 mph) at 900 m (2,955 ft); service ceiling 5900 m (19,360 ft); range with auxiliary fuel 1300 km (808 miles)
Weights: empty 5720 kg (12,610 lb); maximum take-off 10500 kg (23,149 lb)
Dimensions: span 29.25 m (95 ft 11½ in); length 18.90 m (62 ft 0 in); height 5.55 m (18 ft 2½ in); wing area 110.50 m² (1,189.45 sq ft)
Armament: two 7.92-mm (0.31-in) MG 15 machine-guns, plus up to 500 kg (1,102 lb) of bombs

Junkers Ju 86

The **Junkers Ju 86**, developed as a 10-passenger airliner and four-seat bomber, was designed around the Junkers Jumo 205 diesel engine. The first of five prototypes was flown during 1934, its performance proving disappointing but, nevertheless, the type entered production as both airliner and bomber in late 1935. Initial deliveries of **Ju 86A-1** pre-production bombers were made in February 1936 and the first **Ju 86B** pre-production transport for Swissair was delivered in April 1936.

Five **Ju 86D-1** bombers with improved Jumo 205C engines served with the Legion Condor during the Spanish Civil War, but the powerplant did not stand up well to combat conditions and

HB-IXI was the second Ju-86B-0 and was delivered to Swissair in April 1936. It was used on the carrier's night mail runs between Zurich and Frankfurt-am-Main.

the aircraft proved markedly inferior to the Heinkel He 111. Military export orders included the **Ju 86K-1** for South Africa and Sweden, where Saab subsequently licence-built the type; the **Ju 86K-2** for Hungary, which built 66; and the **Ju 86K-6** for Chile and Portugal.

Luftwaffe dissatisfaction with the capability of the Ju 86D led to the far more reliable **Ju 86E-1** with B.M.W. 132F radial engines and the **Ju 86E-2** with B.M.W. 132Ns; improvements introduced during production brought re-designation of the last 40 Ju 86Es on the production line as **Ju 86G-1** aircraft,

with round glazed noses; production ended in 1938. However, in 1939 two Ju 86D airframes were used for conversion as the Jumo 207A-engined prototypes of a high-altitude version with a two-seat pressurised cabin. Successful trials led

to two initial production versions, the **Ju 86P-1** bomber and **Ju 86P-2** reconnaissance aircraft. The latter had a ceiling of about 12800 m (42,000 ft), and in an effort to gain more altitude a high aspect ratio wing spanning 32.00 m

(104 ft 11¾ in) was introduced to produce the **Ju 86R-1** reconnaissance aircraft and **Ju 86R-2** bomber. Only a few reached service, but one demonstrated a ceiling of 14400 m (47,250 ft). Development of the **Ju 86R-3** with supercharged Jumo 208 engines and of the proposed **Ju 186** four-engined high-altitude bomber based on the Ju 86 were abandoned. A six-engined **Ju 286** high-altitude bomber did not progress beyond the initial planning stage.

Variants

Ju 86abl: first prototype; bomber, powered originally by Siemens SAM 9 radials
Ju 86bal: second prototype; transport, with Jumo 205C diesel engines
Ju 86cb: third prototype; bomber, as Ju 86abl, powered later by Jumo 205C engines

Ju 86 V4: production prototype for commercial Ju 86B
Ju 86 V5: production prototype for Ju 86A bomber
Ju 86A-0: 13 pre-production bombers
Ju 86B-0: seven pre-production transports
Ju 86C-1: six Luft-Hansa transports with Jumo 205C diesels
Ju 86E-1: Luftwaffe bombers with B.M.W. 132F radials
Ju 86E-2: uprated version of Ju 86E-1
Ju 86K-4: as Ju 86K-1 but with Bristol Pegasus III radial engines for Sweden (**B 3A**)

Ju 86K-5: as Ju 86K-4 but with Swedish-built Pegasus XII engines (**B 3B**)
Ju 86K-13: Swedish-built bombers with Swedish- and Polish-built Pegasus engines

Specification
Junkers Ju 86D-1
Type: four-seat medium bomber
Powerplant: two 447-kW (600-hp) Junkers Jumo 205C-4 diesel engines
Performance: maximum speed 325 km/h (202 mph) at 3000 m (9,840 ft); service ceiling 5900 m

Junkers Ju-86D-1 medium bomber of 5/Kampfgeschwader 254, based at Eschwege in September 1937.

(19,360 ft); maximum range 1500 km (932 miles)
Weights: empty 5150 kg (11,354 lb); maximum take-off 8200 kg (18,078 lb)
Dimensions: span 22.50 m (73 ft 9¾ in); length 17.87 m (58 ft 7½ in); height 5.06 m (16 ft 7¼ in); wing area 82.00 m² (882.67 sq ft)
Armament: three 7.92-mm (0.31-in) machine-guns, plus a bombload of up to 800 kg (1,764 lb) carried internally

---

Junkers Ju 87

Junkers Ju 87D of 4/Stukageschwader 3

The reputation of the **Junkers Ju 87 Stuka** (*Sturzkampfflugzeug*, or dive-bomber) was made during the Polish campaign in close-support operations across Europe. The Luftwaffe believed it to be virtually invincible, but this was true only after air superiority had been gained, as demonstrated during the Battle of Britain when the Stukas were mauled so severely by the RAF that they were later withdrawn from operations over western Europe.

Three prototypes were started in 1934, the first with twin vertical tail surfaces and powered by a Rolls-Royce Kestrel engine. During dive tests in 1935 the tail unit of this aircraft collapsed and the aircraft was destroyed. The second prototype introduced a single fin and rudder and was powered by a 455-kW (610-hp) Junkers Jumo 210A, and official evaluation of this aircraft and a further improved third prototype led to a pre-production batch of 10 **Ju 87A-0** aircraft with the 477-kW (640-hp) Jumo 210Ca engine. The initial **Ju 87A-1** production version began to replace Hs 123 biplanes in the spring of 1937, and three were tested under operational conditions by the Legion Condor during the Spanish Civil War. At the beginning of World War II the Luftwaffe had 336 **Ju 87B** aircraft on strength, and others were supplied to Italy (which named them **Picchiatello**), Bulgaria, Hungary and Romania.

Ju 87s were deployed extensively on the Eastern Front, initially with great success, but by 1943 they were suffering such severe losses by daylight that they were switched to a night assault role. When production ended more than 5,700 had been built, the majority after 1940 when their vulnerability without adequate fighter cover had been highlighted in the Battle of Britain, and one can only assume that production continued because no better replacement

was available. A redesigned and improved **Ju 187** was projected in 1943, but following consideration of the design no examples were built.

Variants

Ju 87A-2: production version with supercharged 507-kW (680-hp) Jumo 210Da engine
Ju 87 V-7: prototype for Ju 87B series with 746-kW (1,000-hp) Jumo 211A engine
Ju 87B-0: pre-production batch for Ju 87B series
Ju 87B-1: production version with redesigned fuselage, streamlined wheel spats, 895-kW (1,200-hp) Jumo 211Da engine and maximum bombload of 500 kg (1,102 lb)
Ju 87B-2: improved production version with maximum bombload of 1000 kg (2,200 lb)
Ju 87C-1: intended production version with jettisonable landing gear, folding wings and arrester hook for service with aircraft-carrier *Graf Zeppelin*; the carrier was never completed and aircraft on the production line were finished instead as Ju 87B-2s

Ju 87D-1: generally improved production version with 1051-kW (1,410-hp) Jumo 211J-1 engine and increased armour protection for the crew
Ju 87D-2: strengthened Ju 87D-1 with glider-tow hook
Ju 87D-3: ground-attack version of Ju 87D-1 with increased armour
Ju 87D-4: proposed torpedo-bomber version
Ju 87D-5: dedicated close-support version with jettisonable landing gear and no dive brakes
Ju 87D-7: night ground-attack model converted from Ju 87D-3s and Ju 87D-5s; 1119-kW (1,500-hp) Jumo 211P engine; wing-mounted machine-guns replaced by 20-mm MG 151/20 cannon
Ju 87D-8: day version of Ju 87D-7 without night-flying equipment and flame-dampers
Ju 87F: projected version with extensively revised airframe, increased-span wing and more powerful engine; the considerable changes eventually brought redesignation as **Ju 187**, but this remained a project only
Ju 87G-1: final operational version, a tank-busting conversion of the Ju

87D-5 with a 37-mm cannon beneath each wing
Ju 87H series: dual-control trainer conversions of Ju 87D airframes
Ju 87R series: long-range anti-shipping versions of the Ju 87B with extra fuel and provision for one 250-kg (551-lb) bomb

Specification
Junkers Ju 87D-1
Type: two-seat dive-bomber/assault aircraft
Powerplant: one 1051-kW (1,410-hp) Junkers Jumo 211J-1 12-cylinder inverted-Vee piston engine
Performance: maximum speed 410 km/h (255 mph) at 3840 m (12,600 ft); service ceiling 7290 m (23,915 ft); maximum range 1535 km (954 miles)
Weights: empty equipped 3900 kg (8,598 lb); maximum take-off 6600 kg (14,550 lb)
Dimensions: span 13.80 m (45 ft 3½ in); length 11.50 m (37 ft 8¾ in); height 3.90 m (12 ft 9½ in); wing area 31.90 m² (343.38 sq ft)
Armament: 7.92-mm (0.31-in) MG 17 machine-guns in wings and two similar-calibre MG 81Z guns in rear cockpit, plus up to 1800 kg (3,968 lb) of bombs beneath fuselage, or various alternative underfuselage/underwing loads

---

Junkers Ju 88

Certainly the most versatile German warplane of World War II, the **Junkers Ju 88** in progressively improved versions continued in production throughout the war. It was originated to meet a requirement for a three-seat high-speed bomber and the first prototype, powered by two 746-kW (1,000-hp) Daimler-Benz DB 600Aa engines, made its initial flight on 21 December 1936. Further proto-

types followed, the third with 746-kW (1,000-hp) Junkers Jumo engines and this, during evaluation, attained a speed of 520 km/h (323 mph). Such high performance encouraged record-breaking attempts, and in March 1939 the fifth prototype set a 1,000-km (621-mile) closed-circuit record of 517 km/h (321.25 mph) carrying a 2000-kg (4,409-lb) payload. A total of 10 prototypes was completed, and the first of the pre-production **Ju 88A-0** bombers flew in early 1939, the initial **Ju 88A-1** production

version entering service in September 1939.

Early operational deployment showed that despite good performance and a worthwhile bombload, defensive armament was totally inadequate, leading to the **Ju 88A-4** with increased span wings, structural strengthening to carry greater loads and gunpower increased substantially. This formed the basis for further diverse development of the type, ultimately in so many versions that a detailed listing of them is not possible:

for example, the Ju 88A series extended over Ju 88A-1 to Ju 88A-17 sub-variants. While the Ju 88A was in production an improved **Ju 88B** was planned, with a more extensively glazed nose and power provided by two 1193-kW (1,600-hp) B.M.W. 801MA radials, but flight testing showed only marginal performance improvement and only 10 pre-production **Ju 88B-0** aircraft were built.

The Ju 88 was almost as fast as contemporary fighters, and such performance coupled with excellent manoeuvr-

ability brought development of the **Ju 88C** series. The planned **Ju 88C-1** with B.M.W. 801MA engines was abandoned because the new Focke-Wulf Fw 190 fighter had priority for this powerplant. As a result the first production version was the **Ju 88C-2**, this being the Ju 88A-1 converted on the production line to have a solid nose mounting three 7.92-mm (0.31-in) MG 17 machine-guns and a 20-mm MG FF cannon. Defensive armament comprised two additional 7.92-mm (0.31-in) MG 15 machine-guns. The **Ju 88C-4** was a heavy fighter/reconnaissance model, the **Ju 88C-5** an improved heavy fighter, the **Ju 88C-6a** an improved Ju 88C-5, the **Ju 88C-6b** and **Ju 88C-6c** night-fighters, the **Ju 88C-7a** and **Ju 88-C7b** intruders, and the **Ju 88C-7c**, a heavy fighter. Alphabetically out of sequence were the **Ju 88R-1** and **Ju 88R-2** night-fighters, which were developed and powered by B.M.W. 801MA engines when the supply position of this powerplant eased.

The **Ju 88D** series was long-range reconnaissance aircraft based on the Ju 88A-4, in **Ju 88D-1** to **Ju 88D-5** variants that differed in engines and detail. The **Ju 88G** series represented definitive night-fighter versions that from the early summer of 1944 replaced the earlier Ju 88C and Ju 88R aircraft. Equipped with airborne interception radar and bristling with weapons, the Ju 88Gs were extremely formidable night-fighters, taking a heavy toll of Allied night bombers. They were followed by small numbers of **Ju 88H** aircraft which had a lengthened fuselage to provide in-creased internal fuel capacity, providing extra long-range **Ju 88H-1** reconnaissance and **Ju 88H-2** fighter aircraft. The tank-busting **Ju 88P** was developed from the Ju 88A-4, the **Ju 88P-1** with a 75-mm PaK 40 cannon and the ensuing **Ju 88P-2** to **Ju 88P-4** with different combinations of heavy anti-tank weapons.

The increasing capability of Allied fighters meant that losses began to rise, leading to the higher-performance **Ju 88S** bomber and **Ju 88T** photo-reconnaissance aircraft that represented the final production versions. When production ended almost 15,000 had been built, this total emphasising the significant role that the Ju 88 had played in Luftwaffe operations.

Specification
Junkers Ju 88A-4
Type: four-seat bomber/dive-bomber
Powerplant: two 1007-kW (1,350-hp) Junkers Jumo 211J-1 12-cylinder inverted-Vee piston engines
Performance: maximum speed 470 km/h (292 mph) at 5300 m

Junkers Ju 88G-7a of IV/NJG 6 during winter 1944-45, with the tail painted to resemble a Ju 88C for deception purposes.

(17,390 ft); service ceiling 8200 m (26,900 ft); maximum range 2730 km (1,696 miles)
Weights: empty equipped 9860 kg (21,737 lb); maximum take-off 1400 kg (30,865 lb)
Dimensions: span 20.00 m (65 ft 7½ in); length 14.40 m (47 ft 2¾ in); height 4.85 m (15 ft 11 in); wing area 54.50 m² (586.65 sq ft)
Armament: one forward-firing 13-mm (0.51-in) MG 131 or two 7.92-mm (0.31-in) MG 81 machine-guns, two similar guns in rear of cockpit firing aft and two firing aft below the fuselage, plus up to 2000 kg (4,409 lb) of bombs carried internally and externally

Possibly the single most valuable type operated by the Luftwaffe during World War II, the Ju 88 appeared in a host of forms, but is here represented in its most basic form, the Ju 88A-4 bomber.

Junkers Ju 88 Mistel composites

In 1943 a proposal was made that time-expired Ju 88 airframes could be converted as pilotless missiles, with an attached Messerschmitt Bf 109 whose pilot would control the Ju 88 in flight to a point of release, where he would aim it at its target before detaching his fighter. Known as **Mistel** (mistletoe) composites or, more popularly as *Vater und Sohn* (father and son), a prototype combination was first flown in July 1943 and found to be practicable. The weakness in the concept was that the warhead-carrying Ju 88 was not guided from the moment that the piloted aircraft separated from it, merely continuing in steady flight under the control of its onboard autopilot. Plans for remote-guidance systems were frustrated by an end of the war in Europe.

Several designations resulted from different combinations of fighter and bomber. They include the **Mistel 1** (and **S 1** training version) that combined the Ju 88A-4 and Bf 109F, the **Mistel 2** (and **S 2**) the Ju 88G-1 and Focke-Wulf Fw 190A-8, and **Mistel 3A** (and **S 3A**) the Ju 88A-6 and Fw 190A-6. Extra long-range **Mistel 3B** and **Mistel 3C** resulted from the combination of Ju 88G-10 or Ju 88H-4 bombers with Fw 190A-8s that carried overwing auxiliary fuel tanks. These were intended as pathfinders, the lower component carrying a three-man crew and having the benefit of its own Fw 190 escort, for launch only in emergency.

The only version of the Mistel composite to see service was the Mistel 1, which combined a Ju 88A-4 airframe with a Bf 109F.

Junkers Ju 188

The design of a **Junkers Ju 188** successor to the Ju 88 was well advanced at the outbreak of World War II, but by 1942 it was clear that this would be late in entering service and a stop-gap design was needed urgently to update the Ju 88. Junkers had flown during 1940 the prototype of the Ju 88B, which incorporated a new enlarged forward fuselage and increased-span wings. Although this version did not enter production, only 10 pre-production Ju 88B-0 aircraft being built, it was the later Ju 88E-0 development of this version which was used as the basis for the new bomber/reconnaissance aircraft designated **Ju 188**.

The **Ju 188 V1** and **Ju 188 V2** prototypes were flown in early 1942 and 1943 respectively, and following successful testing the type was ordered into pro-duction. A stipulation of the contract was that the airframe must be suitable, without modification, for the installation of either B.M.W. 801 or Junkers Jumo 213 engines to ensure continuity of production. The initial production version was the **Ju 188E-1**, with 1193-kW (1,600-hp) B.M.W. 801ML engines, which entered service in February 1943; 283 of this version had been delivered by the end of the year. The first Junkers-engined version was the **Ju 188A-2**, with two Jumo 213A-1 engines that each developed 1670 kW (2,240 hp) for take-off with water/methanol injection.

Total production of all Ju 188 variants exceeded 1,000 aircraft, more than half of them being for use in a reconnaissance role. Variants included the Ju 188A-2 bomber and **Ju 188A-3** tor-pedo-bomber; **Ju 188D-1** and **Ju 188D-2** reconnaissance aircraft; **Ju 188E-1** bomber and **Ju 188E-2** torpedo-bomber; **Ju 188F-2** reconnaissance aircraft; and **Ju 188S-1** high-altitude intruder and **Ju 188T-1**

The Junkers Ju 288 V14 was the final prototype of the proposed Ju 288B medium bomber, but it flew only after the Ju 288 series had been abandoned.

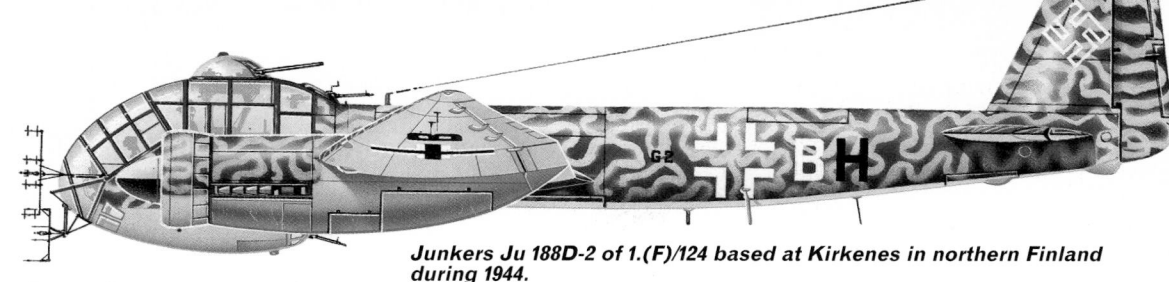

high-altitude reconnaissance versions, both without defensive armament.

Specification
Junkers Ju 188E-1
Type: four-seat medium bomber
Powerplant: two 1268-kW (1,700-hp) B.M.W. 801D-2 radial piston engines
Performance: maximum speed 500 km/h (310 mph) at 6000 m (19,685 ft); service ceiling 9345 m (30,660 ft); range 1945 km (1,209 miles)
Weights: empty equipped 9860 kg (21,737 lb); maximum take-off 9750 kg (31,989 lb)

Junkers Ju 188D-2 of 1.(F)/124 based at Kirkenes in northern Finland during 1944.

Dimensions: span 22.00 m (72 ft 2 in); length 14.95 m (49 ft 0½ in); height 4.44 m (14 ft 7 in); wing area 56.00 m² (602.80 sq ft)
Armament: one forward-firing

20-mm MG 151 cannon in nose, a single 13-mm (0.51-in) MG 131 in dorsal turret and at rear of cockpit canopy, and one 7.92-mm (0.31-in) MG 18

machine-gun in lower front fuselage firing aft, plus a maximum bombload of 3000 kg (6,614 lb)

Junkers Ju 290

In 1936 Junkers had under construction three prototypes of the **Junkers Ju 89** four-engined bomber, but the programme was cancelled during 1937 after the first prototype had flown. With no military interest in the design Junkers developed a civil version designated **Ju 90** of which four prototypes were built, followed by 10 pre-production **Ju 90B-1** aircraft equipped as 38/40-seat airliners. Eight of these entered service with Deutsche Luft-Hansa, the remaining two being ordered by South African Airways but never delivered. Design of an improved **Ju 90S** version was initiated in 1937, this incorporating a new wing and a ventral loading ramp; it was intended to power the type with B.M.W. 139 engines. When these failed to materialise, the B.M.W. 801 was used instead, and the designation was changed to **Ju 290**.

Production of these large aircraft totalled between 60 and 70. Two pre-production **Ju 290A-0** machines were followed by **Ju 290A-1** armed transports, and the designations **Ju 290A-2** to **Ju 290A-9** covered various reconnaissance and maritime reconnaissance roles, except for the **Ju 290A-6** which was a 50-passenger transport. The **Ju 290A-1** (about 12 built) was a reconnaissance/bomber version able to deploy early missiles.

The **Ju 290B-1** was the last of the line to be built, a single prototype of this long-range high-altitude heavy bomber being flown during 1944. The ultimate development was the **Ju 390**, a scaled-up Ju 290 of 55.35 m (181 ft 7¼ in) wing span, powered by six

1268-kW (1,700-hp) B.M.W. 801D engines. Two prototypes were built and tested in 1943; during the evaluation programme the second of these was flown from an airfield near Bordeaux to within about 19 km (12 miles) of the US coast north of New York before returning to France, proof that the specification for a bomber being able to attack New York from European bases could have been met, but the scheme progressed no further.

Specification
Junkers Ju 290A-7
Type: long-range maritime reconnaissance/bomber
Powerplant: four 1268-kW (1,700-hp) B.M.W. 801D radial piston engines
Performance: maximum speed 440 km/h (273 mph) at 5800 m (19,030 ft); service ceiling 6000 m (19,685 ft); range 6090 km (3,784 miles)
Weights: empty 33005 kg (72,764 lb); maximum take-off 46000 kg (101,413 lb)
Dimensions: span 42.00 m (137 ft 9½ in); length 29.15 m (95 ft 7¾ in); height 6.83 m (22 ft 4¾ in); wing area 203.60 m² (2,191.60 sq ft)
Armament: seven 20-mm MG 151 cannon and one 13-mm (0.51-in) MG 131 machine-gun, plus a bombload of up to 3000 kg (6,614 lb), or three Henschel Hs 293, or Hs 294 or FX-1400 Fritz-X missiles

D-AALU was the Junkers Ju 90 V1, with the wings, tail unit, landing gear and engines of the Ju 89 V3 plus a new fuselage.

The Junkers Ju 390 very long-range maritime reconnaissance bomber only reached the second prototype stage. The Ju 390 V1 (illustrated) flew unarmed while the Ju 390 V2 carried four 20-mm cannon, three 13-mm machine-guns and the FuG 200 'Hohentwiel' radar. The third unbuilt Ju 390 was intended as a Hs 293 and Fritz-X missile carrier.

Junkers Ju 388

The failure of the Junkers Ju 288, brought about primarily by technical problems and continual requests by the RLM for design changes, left a gap in the programme for a high-speed long-range bomber. Fortunately, Junkers had initiated development of high-altitude versions of the Ju 188 and three of these designated **Ju 188J**, **Ju 188K** and **Ju 188L** became respectively the **Ju 388J** all-weather fighter, **Ju 388K** bomber and **Ju 388L** photo-reconnaissance aircraft.

High-altitude reconnaissance had the highest priority, and the first prototype was a Ju 388L converted from a Ju 188T; the pre-production batch which followed was converted from Ju 88S airframes, the first of them being handed over to the Luftwaffe in August 1944. By the time production was terminated in December 1944, 47 Ju 388Ls had been built, but the other variants were less fortunate; only three Ju 388J fighter prototypes were completed, and bomber con-

struction totalled 10 pre-production **Ju 388K-0** and five production **Ju 388K-1** aircraft.

A final attempt was made to develop a heavy strategic bomber, and the construction of major sections of a **Junkers Ju 488** hybrid that would have combined assemblies of the Ju 88, Ju 188, Ju 288 and Ju 388 was started in France at the former factory of Latécoère at Toulouse. The two fuselages and wing centre-sections were ready for delivery to Germany for final assembly in July 1944, but were damaged beyond repair by sabotage on the night of 16/17 July. Work on development prototypes of a redesigned **Ju 488A** was started but cancelled in November 1944.

Specification
Junkers Ju 388L-1
Type: three-seat high-altitude photo-reconnaissance aircraft
Powerplant: two 1409-kW (1,890-hp) B.M.W. 801TJ radial piston engines

A high-altitude development of the Ju 88, the Ju 388 was armed solely by a tail barbette of two 13-mm machine-guns.

Performance: maximum speed 615 km/h (382 mph) at 12285 m (40,305 ft), or 655 km/h (407 mph) at 9080 m (29,790 ft) with water/methanol boost; service ceiling 13440 m (44,095 ft); maximum range with auxiliary fuel 3475 km (2,159 miles)
Weights: empty 10252 kg (22,601 lb); maximum take-off 14675 kg (32,353 lb)
Dimensions: span 22.00 m (72 ft

2 in); length 15.20 m (49 ft 10½ in); height 4.35 m (14 ft 3¼ in); wing area 56.00 m² (602.80 sq ft)
Armament: one remotely-controlled tail barbette with 13-mm (0.51-in) MG 131 machine-guns

Junkers W 33 and W 34

The **Junkers W 33** transport aircraft of 1926 was a cantilever low-wing monoplane, derived from the Junkers F 13 of 1919, and an F 13 airframe served as the prototype. Intended for use as a cargo mail transport, the W 33 could also have six seats installed in the cabin if required for use as an airliner. The pilot, and pilot-navigator, were seated side-by-side in a separate cockpit. The designation W 33 applied to the aircraft as powered by an inline engine, usually the Junkers L-5, but the designation changed to **W 34** with the installation of a radial engine. The type was available with wheel or float landing gear. A total of 199 W 33s was built, and both W 33s and W 34s were used in considerable numbers for civil purposes. W 34s saw extensive service with the Luftwaffe from its formation until the end of World War II, being

Like all of Junkers' designs with corrugated skinning, the W 34 was short on aerodynamic elegance and external refinement but was an immensely sturdy and capacious aircraft.

used primarily as navigation trainers and transports. Principal versions in Luftwaffe service were the **W 34hi** with a 492-kW (660-hp) B.M.W. 132A radial, or **W 34hau** with the 485-kW (650-hp) Bramo 322 engine. A three-seat bomber/reconnaissance version of the W 34 was developed by the Swedish factory under the designation **K 43**, examples being exported to Colombia and Finland. A combined total of nearly 1,800 W 34 and K 43 aircraft was produced by the German and Swedish factories.

Specification
Junkers W 34h
Type: transport and communications aircraft
Powerplant: one 492-kW (660-hp) B.M.W. 132 radial piston engine
Performance: maximum speed 265 km/h (165 mph); service ceiling 6300 m (20,670 ft); normal range 900 km (560 miles)
Weights: empty 1700 kg (3,748 lb); maximum take-off 3200 kg (7,055 lb)
Dimensions: span 17.75 m (58 ft 2¾ in); length 10.27 m (33 ft 8⅓ in); height 3.53 m (11 ft 7 in); wing area 43.0 m² (462.85 sq ft)

Kalinin aircraft

One of the most successful of the early Soviet designers, Konstantin Alexeivich Kalinin built his first transport monoplane in 1925. Designated **Kalinin K-1**, this was a strut-braced monoplane with a high-set wing of elliptical planform, a feature which became typical of Kalinin designs. Powered by a 119-kW (160-hp) Salmson RB-9 engine, the K-1 had a maximum speed of 161 km/h (100 mph) and accommodated a pilot in an open cockpit forward of the wing, with an enclosed cabin behind him for three passengers.

The **K-2** which also appeared in 1925 was similar to the K-1 except that it had a 179-kW (240-hp) B.M.W. IV engine and accommodated four passengers. The **K-3**, developed from the K-2, had provision for three stretcher cases. The six-passenger **K-4** was produced in 1928 and 22 were built at Kharkov, entering service on the routes operated by the Soviet Dobrolet and Ukrainian Ukrvozdukhput. The prototype (R-RUAX) and most of the production aircraft retained the B.M.W. IV engine, but alternative powerplants included the Junkers L-5 and the 224-kW (300-hp) Soviet M-6. An ambulance variant had the latter engine

With a colour scheme that fully justified its nickname of 'Zhar-Pitsa' (Firebird), the Kalinin K-12 had nose and 'tail' turrets despite not actually having any tail.

and accommodated two stretcher cases with access via a rectangular door in the starboard side of the aircraft, aft of the cabin.

The **K-5**, which was Kalinin's outstanding design, had an enclosed two-seat crew cabin forward of the wing leading edge and an eight-seat passenger cabin. Production was an impressive 260, terminating in 1934, and installed powerplants included the 335-kW (450-hp) M-15 (Bristol Jupiter built under licence), 358-kW (480-hp) M-22 introduced in 1931, and the M-17F of 544 kW (730 hp) in final series aircraft. Widely used on passenger services within the Soviet Union, some K-5s were still flying in 1940. Wing span was 20.50 m (67 ft 3 in), and with the M-17F engine maximum take-off weight was 4030 kg (8,884 lb) and maximum speed 209 km/h (130 mph).

Kalinin's most remarkable design was

the K-7, a super-heavy bomber with a crew of 11, which flew for the first time on 11 August 1933. Powered by six 559-kW (750-hp) M-34F engines, it had a huge elliptical wing from which projected the crew nacelle, with pilots' and navigator's cabin, a nose gunner's cockpit, and bomb aimer's post below. The twin fin and rudder tail assembly was carried on two tailbooms, at the extremities of which were additional gunners' positions, and two gondolas suspended from the wings housed the multi-wheeled landing gear, bomb-bays and two more gunners' cockpits. Armament was six 7.62-mm (0.3-in) ShKAS machine-guns and up to 9000 kg (19,841 lb) of bombs. On 21 November 1933 one tailboom collapsed in flight and

the K-7 crashed; plans to build two further bombers and a 120-passenger transport were abandoned.

Kalinin reverted to two-seat light sportplane/trainer types with his next two designs, the **K-9** parasol-wing monoplane, and the **K-10** low-wing monoplane.

The **K-12**, known alternatively as the **BS-2** or **'Zhar Ptitsa'**, was a reduced-scale aerodynamic prototype for a full-sized bomber. Powered by two 358-kW (480-hp) M-22 radial engines, the K-12 flew quite well but construction of a full-scale version of the K-12 and of a new bomber, the twin-engined **K-13**, was abandoned when Kalinin was arrested and shot in the 1938 purge in the Soviet Union and his bureau was dissolved.

Kaman H-2 Seasprite

During 1956 the US Navy held a design competition to finalise the details of its requirement for a high-performance all-weather utility helicopter. Kaman was adjudged the winner and in late 1957 received a contract for four prototype and 12 production **Kaman HU2K-1** helicopters; this designation was changed later to **UH-2A** and the name **Seasprite** allocated. Of conventional helicopter configuration with four-bladed main and tail rotors, the type is powered in current versions by two 1007-kW (1,350-shp) General Electric T58-GE-8F turboshaft engines. The Seasprite has been built in many versions, and these are enumerated below.

Variants
UH-2A: initial production version powered by one 932-kW (1,250-hp) General Electric T58-GE-8B turboshaft engine; equipped for IFR operation; 88 built
UH-2B: production version, generally similar to UH-2A, but equipped only for VFR operation; 102 built
UH-2C: redesignation of UH-2A/UH-2B aircraft following installation of two T58-GE-8B turboshaft engines

NUH-2C: redesignation of one UH-2C after being equipped to carry and launch Sidewinder and Sparrow III missiles for evaluation
NUH-2D: redesignation of NUH-2C when re-equipped for use to study operation of helicopters from small non-aviation ships
HH-2C: search and rescue version of UH-2C with chin-mounted Minigun turret, waist machine-gun positions and extensive armour protection. First version to introduce four-bladed tail rotor; six conversions from UH-2C
HH-2D: search and rescue version similar to HH-2C, but without armament and armour; 67 conversions from earlier single-engined Seasprites
SH-2D: ASW anti-ship missile defence version to meet US Navy's LAMPS (Light Airborne Multi-Purpose System) requirement; 20 conversions from HH-2Ds
YSH-2E: two evaluation conversions of HH-2Ds with advanced radar and LAMPS equipment
SH-2F: developed LAMPS version of which deliveries began in 1973; many early versions converted to this configuration and initial deliveries of

new-production SH-2Fs began in 1984; all US Navy SH-2Fs, new or converted, are expected to remain in first-line service throughout the 1990s

Specification
Kaman SH-2F
Type: ASW, ASMD and SAR helicopter
Powerplant: two 1007-kW (1,350-shp) General Electric T58-GE-8F turboshafts
Performance: maximum speed 265 km/h (165 mph) at sea level; service ceiling 6860 m (22,500 ft); range with maximum fuel 679 km (422 miles)
Weights: empty 3193 kg (7,050 lb); normal take-off 5805 kg (12,800 lb)
Dimensions: main rotor diameter 13.41 m (44 ft 0 in); length, rotors turning 16.03 m (52 ft 7 in); height, rotors turning 4.72 m (15 ft 6 in); main rotor disc area 141.25 m² (1,520.5 sq ft)
Armament: can include air-to-surface missiles, torpedoes, rockets or guns

Kaman SH-2F Seasprite

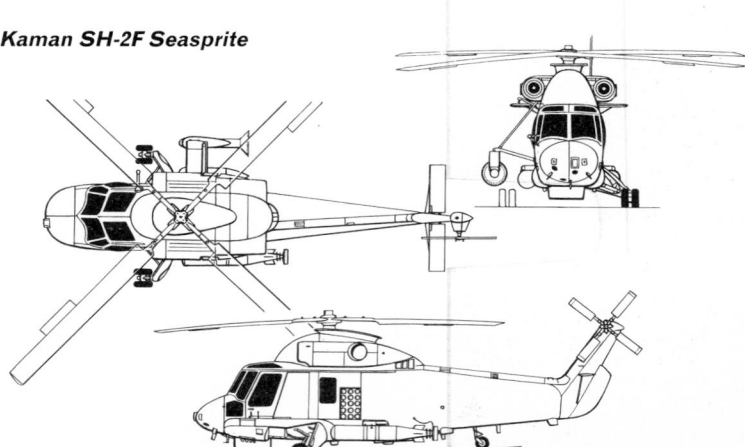

Kaman H-43 Huskie
to
Kawasaki Ki-32

Kaman H-43 Huskie

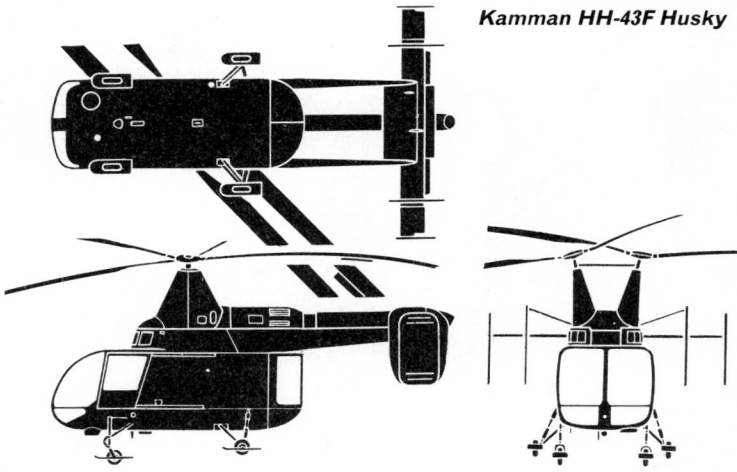

Kamman HH-43F Husky

Charles H. Kaman established the Kaman Aircraft Corporation in December 1945 to manufacture a new helicopter rotor and control system of his own design. Development of the basic intermeshing rotor system and its servo flap control was completed in late 1946 and the first experimental **Kaman K-125A** helicopter was flown on 15 January 1947. From it was evolved first the **K-190**, flown in 1948, and then the **K-225** three-seat utility helicopter; two examples of the K-225 were acquired by the US Navy in 1950. Used for evaluation purposes, they led to an initial contract for 29 **HTK-1** trainers which, in 1962, were redesignated **TH-43E**. Contemporary with production of the HTK-1, Kaman developed the **K-600**, ordered for service with the US Marine Corps and US Navy under the respective designations **HOK-1** and **HUK-1**; these were redesignated **UH-43C** and **OH-43D** in 1962. Eighteen aircraft similar to the US Navy's HUK-1s were also acquired by the US Air Force under the designation **H-43A Huskie**.

One HOK-1 was flown as a testbed aircraft with an Avco Lycoming XT53 turboshaft engine, and service testing confirmed the considerable performance improvement offered by this powerplant. This led to the **H-43B**, first flown on 13 December 1958, which became the major production version of the Huskie with a total of 193 built; of this number 31 were supplied under the US Military Assistance Program to Burma (12), Colombia (6), Morocco (4), Pakistan (6) and Thailand (3). Slightly larger than the earlier H-43A (later **HH-43A**), the H-43B (later **HH-43B**) had a cabin seating up to eight passengers and was powered by a 615-kW (825-shp) Avco Lycoming T53-L-1B turboshaft engine. Final production version was the **HH-43F** (40 built for the USAF and 17 for Iran). Generally similar to the HH-43B airframe, except for internal rearrangement to seat 11 passengers, this last version of the Huskie had an 858-kW (1,150-shp) Lycoming T53-L-11A derated to 615 kW (825 shp) for improved performance in 'hot-and-high'

conditions.

An interesting variant of the Huskie family derived from a conversion of one of the original K-225s. Under US Navy contract, Kaman installed in this aircraft a 130-kW (175-shp) Boeing YT50 (Model

502-2) gas-turbine engine. When first flown with this powerplant on 10 December 1951, this was the first helicopter in the world to have its rotors powered by a turbine engine.

Kamov Ka-8 and Ka-10

Nikolai I. Kamov began the study of rotating-wing design in the late 1920s, and in conjunction with N. K. Skrzhinskii was responsible for two of the earliest successful Soviet rotorcraft, the **KaSkr-I** and **KaSkr-II**. Kamov's first helicopter design was the ultralight **Kamov Ka-8** of 1945, comprising a very basic steel-

tube uncovered structure mounted on two pontoons and having an exposed seat for the pilot. Powered by a 20-kW (27-hp) engine, it introduced the co-axial contra-rotating rotors that have since been a 'trademark' of Kamov design, enabling the aircraft to dispense with the complication of an anti-torque tail rotor.

The Kamov Ka-10M was built in small numbers, mainly to test the designer's twin rotor configuration.

The slightly larger **Ka-10** (NATO reporting name **'Hat'**) followed in 1948, introducing a 41-kW (55-hp) Ivchenko AI-4V engine. Built in small numbers for test and evaluation, it was followed by an improved **Ka-10M** which introduced

twin tail fins and rudders.

Kamov Ka-15 and Ka-18

With experience gained from the Ka-8 and Ka-10, Kamov designed the far more practical **Kamov Ka-15** two-seat general-purpose helicopter. This had an enclosed cabin with fixed four-wheel landing gear beneath it, and was intended for use as a spotter aircraft by ice-breakers, merchant ships, and by the Soviet navy. Retaining the contra-rotating co-axial twin rotors and twin fins and

rudders that had proved successful on the Ka-10, the Ka-15 was powered initially by a 168-kW (225-hp) Ivchenko AI-14V engine, but a 209-kW (280-hp) supercharged AI-14VF was introduced at a later date. In addition to production for the navy, the Ka-15 (NATO reporting name **'Hen'**) has been produced as the **Ka-15M** for civil use, available in agricultural, ambulance and in mail/passenger-

carrying versions.

A four-seat development of the Ka-15, which differed basically by having a lengthened fuselage to accommodate four passengers, had the designation **Ka-18** (NATO reporting name **'Hog'**). It was powered by the supercharged Ivchenko AI-14VF as standard, and also introduced more advanced avionics and instrumentation. Like its predecessor it was built for use by the navy, and also in a variety of civil versions, primarily for use by Aeroflot.

Kamov helicopters, epitomised by the Ka-18, have always been notable for their compact, if tall, twin rotor arrangement.

Kamov Ka-20 and Ka-25 'Hormone'

The **Kamov Ka-20** (NATO reporting name **'Harp'**) was seen by Western observers for the first time at the 1961 Soviet Aviation Day celebrations. Although larger and with twin turbine powerplant, it was clearly derived from the Ka-15 and Ka-18, and judging by a search radar housing beneath the forward fuselage was considered to be a new anti-submarine helicopter. It has since come to be regarded as the prototype of the **Ka-25** (NATO reporting name **'Hormone'**), of which three versions are known to be in service. These comprise the basic ship-based **'Hor-**

A standard Kamov Ka-25 'Hormone-A' operated from a carrier deck of the former AV-MF (Soviet naval air force).

mone-A' ASW aircraft, the 'Hormone-B' target-seeking electronics variant which uses its radar to provide targeting and guidance data for ship-launched cruise missiles, and the 'Hormone-C' SAR and general-utility helicopter. Most of these Ka-25s are fitted with emergency flotation 'boots' on each of the four landing gear legs, which inflate automatically in the event of a ditching. Late production versions are believed to be powered by two 738-kW (990-shp) Glushenkov GTD-3BM turboshaft engines. A civil variant, the Ka-25K, is also in service, used as a fly-ing-crane or as a passenger-carrier with tip-up seats for 12 people arranged around the walls of the cabin, so that it can be used alternatively as a cargo carrier.

Kamov Ka-22 Vintokryl

Forsaking for once the co-axial contra-rotating rotors that are a feature of his designs, Kamov produced the **Kamov Ka-22,** a contemporary of the Ka-20 and also seen for the first time at the Soviet Aviation display in 1961. This was a large twin-rotor/twin-turboprop converti-plane: it was a fairly conventional trans-port aircraft with fixed wings spanning 28.00 m (91 ft 10¼ in) and non-retractable tricycle landing gear, it had a 4192-kW (5,622-shp) TV-2 turboprop mounted at each wingtip, each driving a conventional propeller or large-diameter four-bladed rotor. Named **Vintokryl** (NATO reporting-name **'Hoop'**), it established a number of convertiplane class records, but only the one example appears to have been built.

Featuring an early attempt at combining the advantages of a fixed wing with rotary technology, the Kamov Ka-22 set several records, but ultimately proved impossible as a civil or military transport.

Kamov Ka-26 'Hoodlum'

First announced in early 1964, the general-purpose **Kamov Ka-26** helicopter (NATO reporting name **'Hoodlum'**) is of typical Kamov helicopter design and incorporates a conventional tail unit with twin endplate fins and rudders, with tailplane and elevators between. The aircraft is carried on four-wheel fixed landing gear, and power is provided by two 242-kW (325-hp) Vedeneev M-14V-26 radial piston engines. These are each housed in a pod, one mounted at each tip of short-span stub wings on top of the fuselage. The cabin is fully enclosed and as standard is equipped for one-man operation; the remainder of the cabin can be used for a variety of purposes, including agricultural spraying and dusting, air ambulance, cargo- or passenger-carrying, geophysical survey, and search and rescue. More than 850 **'Hoodlum-As'** have been built to date, and these have served with civil operators in some 15 countries, as well as with the air forces of Hungary, Bulgaria and Sri Lanka. A modified Ka-26 featuring the jet control system destined for the projected Ka-118 (similar to the MDC NOTAR system) is currently under test. The **'Hoodlum-B'**, (designated the **Ka-126**) is a utility version powered by twin Vedenyev M14 turboshaft engines, and is used as a flying crane to which can be added a cabin seating seven passengers. The type is also usable as an ambulance, or with detachable agricultural equipment for roles such as crop-spraying, forestry patrol, powerline or oilpipe inspection, cargo hauling, etc. First flown in 1988, Ka-126 development and production is the responsibility of the Romanian IAR company.

The **Ka-226** Westernised version of the Ka-26 is currently under development. Re-engined with Allison 250-C20B turboshaft engines, plus Western avionics and other equipment, the first aircraft is due to fly during the first quarter of 1992.

Aeroflot uses several hundred Ka-26s on light duties, including crop-spraying, air ambulance and survey work.

Kamov Ka-27/28/29/32 'Helix'

Design of a general-purpose military helicopter to replace the 'Hoodlum' began in 1969 and the first prototype flew in December 1974. Designated **'Helix'** by NATO, the first operational versions were seen in 1981 aboard 'Sovremenny'-class destroyers of the Soviet navy. All versions are powered by two Klimov/Isotov TV3-117V turboshaft engines driving foldable contra-rotating rotors and equipped with a typical Kamov four-wheel landing gear. The **Ka-27PL 'Helix-A'** is the basic ASW version, mainly used in pairs, one tracking and one attacking submarines. The export version, sold to India and Yugoslavia, is designated **Ka-28.** The **'Helix-B'** comes in two versions, the **Ka-29TB** assault transport plus an undesignated variant for electronic warfare. The Ka-32 **'Helix-C'** civil helicopter first flew in December 1974 and is available as the **Ka-32T** utility transport and flying crane, the radar-carrying **Ka-32S** maritime utility version equipped for adverse weather operations such as SAR or vertical replenishment in remote areas, and the **Ka-32K** flying crane version with a retractable gondola for a second pilot. **'Helix-D'** is the **Ka-27PS** search and rescue and plane guard version in wide use with the Soviet navy since 1983.

The civilian version of the 'Helix', the Ka-32, has proved itself to be a significantly better 'heavy-lifter' than comparable Western-developed helicopters.

Specification
Kamov Ka-29TB 'Helix-B'
Type: twin-engined assault transport and electronic warfare helicopter
Powerplant: two 1660-kW (2,225-shp) Klimov/Isotov TV3-117VK turboshafts
Performance: maximum speed 250 km/h (155 mph); service ceiling 5000 m (16,400 ft); endurance or range 800 km (497 miles)
Weights: empty 5520 kg (12,170 lb); maximum take-off 12600 kg (27,775 lb)
Dimensions: rotor diameter 15.9 m (52 ft 2 in); length 11.6 m (38 ft); height 5.4 m (17 ft 8 in); main rotor area 198.5 m² (2,138 sq ft)
Armament: four pylons mounted on outriggers can carry four-round clusters of AT-6 'Spiral' air-to-surface missiles or 57/80-mm rocket packs; a single 7.62-mm four-barrelled machine-gun can fire through door behind pilot on starboard side

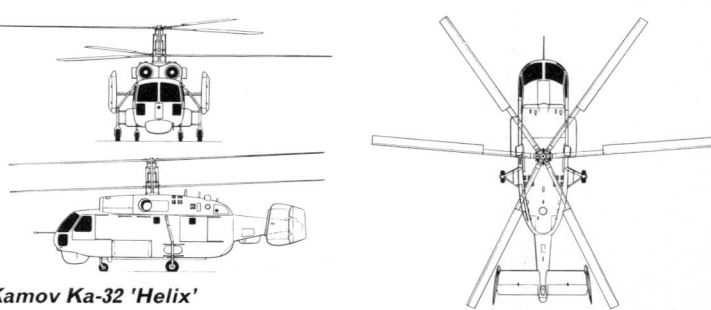

Kamov Ka-32 'Helix'

Kamov Ka-136 'Hokum'

The **Ka-136** twin turbine combat helicopter is believed to have flown for the first time during the summer of 1984, and early operational examples were scheduled to enter service in 1991. Roughly similar to the AH-64 Apache gunship, the **'Hokum'** mainly differs in having the traditional Kamov contra-rotating rotor. Although at least one of the prototypes was reported to have side-by-side seating for the pilots, production aircraft feature tandem seating. Western analysts offer the opinion that 'Hokum' is designed as a fast (350 km/h; 217 mph) adverse-weather low-level anti-helicopter helicopter, and is also intended as an escort for Soviet navy

'Helix' assault helicopters. Powered by two 1640-kW (2,200-shp) Klimov TV3-117VK turboshafts, and with a maximum take-off weight of 7500 kg (16,500 lb), the compact 'Hokum' rotor has a diameter of 14.0 m (45 ft 10 in). Offensive armament is hung from pylons under stub wings, and can include unguided rocket packs and air-to-air missiles, plus a single rapid-fire gun mounted under the nose.

Intended as the Soviet armed forces new attack helicopter, the future of the Kamov 'Hokum' is now less certain. The type will enter production, however.

Kawanishi E7K

In 1932 the Imperial Japanese Navy sought a replacement for the Navy Type 90-3 Reconnaissance Seaplane which had been built as the Kawanishi E5K. The resulting three-seat **Kawanishi E7K1** was an equal-span biplane of conventional design, powered by a 462-kW (620-hp) Hiro Type 91 engine. First flown on 6 February 1933, the prototype was handed over to the Japanese navy three months later for service trials, being flown in competition against the Aichi AB-6 developed to meet the same requirement. The E7K1 was ordered into production as the **Navy Type 94 Reconnaissance Seaplane** in May 1934, entering service in early 1935, and quickly proving popular for its ease of handling. However, its Hiro engine was unreliable, and although late production E7K1s had a more powerful version of the Hiro 91, this offered no improvement. During 1938 Kawanishi built an **E7K2** prototype which, generally similar to the E7K1, replaced the Hiro engine with a Mitsubishi Zuisei 11 radial. Flown

for the first time in August 1938, the E7K2 was ordered into production three months later under the designation **Navy Type 94 Reconnaissance Seaplane Model 2**, the original version then becoming the **Navy Type 94 Reconnaissance Seaplane Model 1**. Production of the E7K1 totalled 183 (57 built by Nippon), and of the E7K2 about 350 (some 60 built by Nippon).

As a type the E7Ks saw extensive use from 1935 until the beginning of the Pacific war, when the E7K1s were relegated to second-line duties. The E7K2s, however, continued in first-line service until 1943, and both versions were used in *kamikaze* operations in the closing stages of the war. When, in the second half of 1942, Allied codenames were allocated to Japanese aircraft, the E7K2 became known as **'Alf'**.

Specification
Kawanishi E7K2
Type: three-seat reconnaissance floatplane

Powerplant: one 649-kW (870-hp) Mitsubishi Zuisei 11 radial piston engine
Performance: maximum speed 275 km/h (171 mph) at 2000 m (6,560 ft); service ceiling 7060 m (23,165 ft); endurance 11 hours 30 minutes
Weights: empty 2100 kg (4,630 lb); maximum take-off 3300 kg (7,275 lb)
Dimensions: span 14.00 m (45 ft 11¼ in); length 10.50 m (34 ft 5½ in);

Possessing excellent endurance, the E7K2 remained in front-line service with the Imperial Japanese Navy until 1943.

height 4.85 m (15 ft 10½ in); wing area 43.60 m² (469.31 sq ft)
Armament: one fixed and two trainable 7.7-mm (0.303-in) Type 92 machine-guns, plus 120 kg (265 lb) of bombs

Kawanishi H6K

To meet a requirement of the Imperial Japanese Navy for a high-performance flying-boat, the **Kawanishi Type S** or **H6K** was proposed to provide the 220-km/h (137-mph) cruising speed and 4500-km (2,795-mile) range specified. Of parasol-wing configuration with a slender two-step hull, the resulting prototype was powered by four 626-kW (840-hp) Nakajima Hikari radial engines mounted at the wing leading edge. First flown on 14 July 1936, the prototype in early tests showed a need for hull modification to improve water performance; subsequent service trials following changes to the hull showed that both water and flight handling were satisfactory, but the aircraft was considered to be underpowered. Three more prototypes followed, two of these and the original 'boat being equipped with more powerful engines, and these were the first to enter service, in January 1938, under the designation **Navy Type 97 Flying-Boat Model 1**. Simultaneously, the type was ordered into production and eventually a total of 217 of all versions was built. Following early operational deployment in the Sino-Japanese war, they were used extensively from the outbreak of the Pacific war. By late 1942, when the type was allocated the Allied codename **'Mavis'**, they were becoming vulnerable to fighter aircraft and were relegated to roles in areas where little fighter opposition was expected, many remaining in service until the end of the war.

Variants
H6K1: designation of the three prototypes following installation of 746-kW (1,000-hp) Mitsubishi Kinsei 43 engines
H6K2: initial production version; similar to H6K1 but with minor equipment changes
H6K3: designation of two H6K2s completed as VIP transports
H6K4: major production version with increased fuel capacity, revised armament and, from August 1941, with 798-kW (1,070-hp) Kinsei 46 engines
H6K2-L: unarmed transport version, basically as early H6K4s; Japan Air Lines received 18 of these aircraft, each equipped as 18-passenger transports
H6K4-L: unarmed transport version as above, but with Kinsei 46 engines and more cabin windows
H6K5: final production version with Kinsei 51 or 53 engines and revised armament

Kawanishi H6K5 of the Imperial Japanese Navy air force.

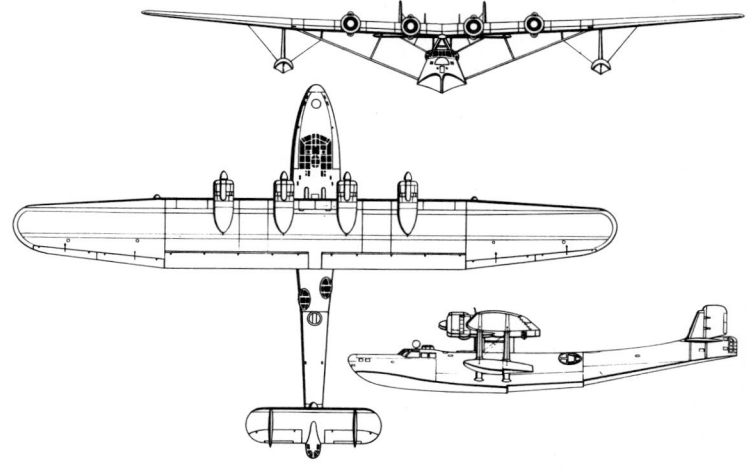

Specification
Kawanishi H6K5
Type: long-range maritime
reconnaissance/bomber flying-boat
Powerplant: four 969-kW (1,300-hp)
Mitsubishi Kinsei 51 or 53 engines

Performance: maximum speed
385 km/h (239 mph) at 6000 m
(19,685 ft); service ceiling 9560 m
(31,365 ft); maximum range 6775 km
(4,210 miles)
Weights: empty 12380 kg (27,293 lb);

maximum take-off 23000 kg (50,706 lb)
Dimensions: span 40.00 m (131 ft
2¾ in); length 25.63 m (84 ft 1 in);
height 6.27 m (20 ft 6¾ in); wing area
170.00 m² (1,829.92 sq ft)
Armament: four 7.7-mm (0.303-in)

Type 92 machine-guns (in a forward
turret, two beam blisters and an open
dorsal position) and one 20-mm cannon
in tail turret, plus two 800-kg (1,764-lb)
torpedoes or up to 1000 kg (2,205 lb) of
bombs

Kawanishi H8K

Realising that the development of a flying-boat larger than the Kawanishi H6K would take some two or three years, the Imperial Japanese Navy gave the Kawanishi company a development contract for such an aircraft as soon as the H6K entered service in 1938. The resulting **Kawanishi H8K1** prototype, flown for the first time on 31 December 1940, was of high-wing monoplane configuration with a large conventional hull and powered by four 1141-kW (1,530-hp) Mitsubishi MK4A engines. Accommodating a crew of 10, the H8K1 was well armed, had good protective armour, and bulk fuel tanks within the hull that were partially self-sealing and incorporated a carbon dioxide fire-extinguishing system. Early tests showed the new flying-boat to be dangerously unstable on the water, leading to extensive hull modifications before the H8K1 was ordered into production in late 1941 under the designation **Navy Type 2 Flying-Boat Model 11**, which was later allocated the Allied codename **'Emily'**. Early production aircraft were soon in service, the type's operational debut being made on the night of 4/5 March 1942. Used for

Fast and heavily armed with five 20-mm cannon, the Kawanishi H8K2 was one of the best flying-boats of the war.

bombing, reconnaissance and transport missions, 167 H8Ks were built and the type remained in service until the end of the war, being considered one of the finest military flying-boats ever produced.

Variants

H8K1: designation of the three prototypes and first 14 production aircraft, all with MK4A engines; late

production examples had MK4B engines of the same power
H8K1-L: redesignation of first prototype following conversion for use in a transport role, powered by higher-rated MK4Q engines
H8K2: major production version, with MK4Q engines, increased armament, fully-protected fuel tanks and ASV radar; 112 built as **Navy Type 2 Flying-Boat Model 12**
H8K2-L: production transport developed from H8K1-L; accommodation for 29 to 64

passengers and armament reduced; ordered into production as **Navy Type 2 Transport Flying-Boat Seiku** (clear sky) **Model 32;** 36 built
H8K3: designation of two prototypes with retractable wingtip stabilising floats and retractable dorsal turret; otherwise as production H8K2s, but not placed in production
H8K4: redesignation of H8K3 prototypes following installation of 1361-kW (1,825-hp) Mitsubishi MK4T-B Kasei 25b engines; not placed in production

Kawanishi N1K1 Kyofu

Foreseeing a need for close air support during amphibious landings in areas where there was no adjacent airfield for land-based fighters, the Imperial Japanese Navy initiated in 1940 the development of floatplane fighters. The **Kawanishi N1K1** to meet this requirement was a comparatively heavy mid-wing monoplane with a central main float and two underwing stabilising floats, and was powered by a single 1089-kW (1,460-hp) Mitsubishi MK4D Kasei radial engine. This, initially, was equipped with contra-rotating propellers to minimise the on-water torque effect of the powerful engine, but problems with these propellers led to use of a conventional engine/single-propeller powerplant.
Following satisfactory service trials

the N1K1 was ordered into production as the **Navy Fighter Seaplane Kyofu** (mighty wind), but when these aircraft began to enter service in early 1943 the changing war situation meant they were no longer needed in a close air support role. As a result production ended in 1944 after 97 had been built and the N1K1, allocated the Allied codename **'Rex'**, was used only in a defensive role. The designation **N1K2** was issued for a proposed version with a more powerful engine, but none was built.

Another ambitious Japanese design that failed to live up to expectations, the Kawanishi N1K1 float-plane fighter was originally intended to have contra-rotating propellers.

Kawanishi N1K1-J/N1K2-J Shiden

During 1942 Kawanishi began development of a land-based version of the N1K1 under the designation **Kawanishi N1K1-J**. Basically the same airframe was used, but the decision to power the new type with the newly-developed Nakajima NK9H Homare engine brought a series of problems, those relating to the engine persisting through the type's service career. In order to use the full output of this engine a large-diameter propeller was needed, requiring the development of telescopic main landing gear units, and this resulted in another major source of headaches for the design team. When the N1K1-J prototype

was first flown, on 27 December 1942, its superb performance and manoeuvrability brought concentrated efforts to develop it for service, rewarded at the end of 1943 by an order for production as the **Navy Interceptor Fighter Shiden** (violet lightning), which was allocated subsequently the Allied codename **'George'**. Although N1K1-Js began to enter service in early 1944, the type represented an interim measure, for development of an improved version, the **N1K2-J**, had been initiated in mid-1943. This introduced major redesign, including a change from mid-wing to low-wing configuration, a new length-

ened fuselage, revised tail surfaces and new, less complicated, main landing gear units. Despite its unreliability, the Nakajima NK9H engine was retained. The N1K2-J prototype was flown for the first time on 31 December 1943, being ordered into production almost immediately as the **Navy Interceptor Fighter Shiden KAI**. This aircraft continued in production and development until the end of the war, being used extensively in Formosa, Honshu, Okinawa and the Philippines; and in the closing stages of the war a number were expended in *kamikaze* attacks.

Variants

N1K1-J: designation of prototypes and initial production version, prototypes being powered by the 1357-kW (1,820-hp) Homare 11 engine; production aircraft had Homare 21 engines, and armament of two 7.7-mm (0.303-in) machine-guns and four wing-mounted 20-mm cannon; production, including prototypes, totalled 1,007
N1K1-Ja: variant of N1K1-J with armament of only four 20-mm cannon
N1K1-Jb: variant of N1K1-J with wing modification to allow the four 20-mm cannon to be mounted within the wings, and to carry two 250-kg (551-lb) bombs on underwing racks; some late-production aircraft carried six air-to-ground rockets under the fuselage.

N1K1-Jc: fighter-bomber variant of N1K1-Jb, with underwing racks for four 250-kg (551-lb) bombs
N1K2-J: production version, 423 built, including 22 by other manufacturers and an unknown number of N1K2-Ks (below); armament as N1K1-Jb
N1K2-K: two-seat trainer conversion of N1K2-J; armament of four 20-mm cannon only
N1K3-J: designation of two prototypes with engine moved forwards to improve longitudinal stability; armament as N1K2-K plus two fuselage-mounted 13.2-mm (0.52-in) machine-guns
N1K3-A: proposed carrier-based variant of N1K3-J; not built
N1K4-J: designation of two prototypes with improved 1491-kW (2,000-hp) Homare 23 engine; armament as N1K3-J
N1K4-A: single prototype of carrier-based variant of N1K4-J
N1K5-J: single prototype, to be powered by a 1641-kW (2,200-hp) Mitsubishi MK9A engine, destroyed before completion during USAAF air raid

Specification
Kawanishi N1K2-J
Type: single-seat land-based interceptor fighter
Powerplant: one 1484-kW (1,990-hp) Nakajima NK9H Homare 21 radial piston engine
Performance: maximum speed 595 km/h (370 mph) at 5600 m

A late-production Kawanishi N1K2-J Shiden KAI 'George' fighter of the 343rd Kokutai (naval air corps), Imperial Japanese Navy air force assigned to the defence of the Japanese mainland during 1945.

(18,370 ft); service ceiling 10760 m (35,300 ft); maximum range with drop-tank 2335 km (1,451 miles)
Weights: empty 2657 kg (5,858 lb); maximum take-off 4860 kg (10,714 lb)
Dimensions: span 12.00 m (39 ft 4½ in); length 9.35 m (30 ft 8 in); height 3.96 m (13 ft 0 in); wing area 23.50 m² (252.96 sq ft)
Armament: as detailed under Variants

Kawanishi N1K1-J Shinden

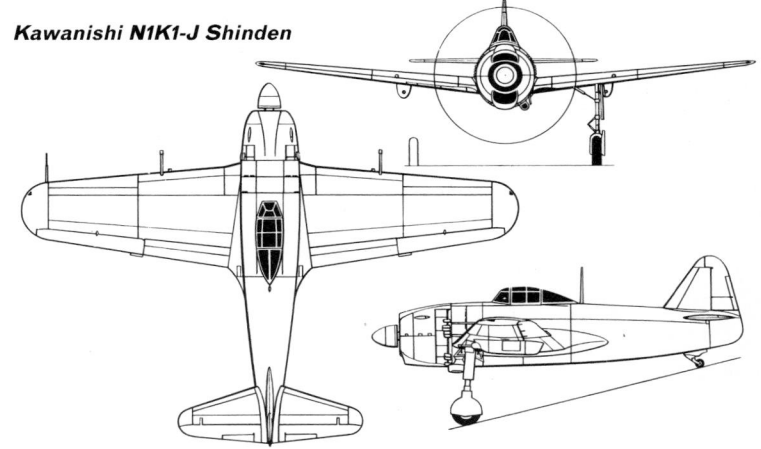

Kawasaki C-1

To meet a requirement of the Japanese Air Self-Defense Force for a new transport aircraft to replace in-service Curtiss C-46s, Nihon Aeroplane Manufacturing Company initiated design of the new transport aircraft during 1966. Following the award of a contract for two prototypes in early 1968, a full-scale mock-up was completed later in the year. The first of the **XC-1** prototypes, both assembled at the Gifu factory of Kawasaki Heavy Industries, was flown for the first time on 12 November 1970. Evaluation of this aircraft and the second prototype led to a contract for two pre-production prototypes and following further satisfactory evaluation the initial production order for 11 **Kawasaki C-1** transports was placed in 1972. The C-1 is a high-wing monoplane, this configuration ensuring that the cabin volume is not compromised by wing structure, has a high T-tail, retractable tricycle landing gear,

and is powered by two Mitsubishi-built Pratt & Whitney JT8D-9 turbofan engines, each of 6577-kg (14,500-lb) thrust, which are installed in pylon-mounted underwing pods. Operated by a crew of five, the C-1 has a flight deck and cabin/cargo hold which are both air-conditioned and pressurised, and the fuselage structure includes a rear-loading ramp-door. The cabin can accommodate typically 60 troops, 45 paratroops, 36 stretchers and medical attendants, or a variety of heavy equipment or palletised cargo. C-1 components were produced under sub-contract by Fuji (outer wing panels), Mitsubishi (centre/aft fuselage sections and tail surfaces), Nihon (flight control surfaces and engine pods), Kawasaki being responsible for the forward fuselage, wing centre-section and final assembly and testing. A total of 31 was built for the JASDF, the last being delivered on 21 October 1981.

Tailored to the short-range transport requirements of the Japanese Air Self Defence Force, the Kawasaki C-1A has been constantly updated.

Specification
Kawasaki C-1
Type: twin-engined medium-range military transport
Powerplant: two 64.5-kN (14,500-lb) Mitsubishi (Pratt & Whitney) JT-8D-M-9 turbofans

Performance: maximum speed 435 kt (806 km/h; 501 mph); service ceiling 11580 m (38,000 ft)
Weights: maximum take-off weight 45000 kg (99,120 lb)
Dimensions: span 3.60 m (100 ft 4 in); length 29 m (95 ft 1 in)

Kawasaki Ki-32

Designed in 1936 to meet an Imperial Japanese Army requirement for a single-engined light bomber, the **Kawasaki Ki-32** was a mid/low-wing monoplane with fixed tailwheel landing gear and accommodation for a crew of two. Power was provided by a 634-kW (850-hp) Kawasaki Ha-9-II V-12 engine, but this proved to be so temperamental that the Ki-32 proved unsuccessful in competitive trials against the Mitsubishi Ki-30 that had been developed against the same requirement. However, the desperate need for aircraft following the start of full-scale war with China in 1937 resulted in the Ki-32 being ordered into production in July 1938 under the official designation **Army Type 98 Single-Engine Light Bomber**. A total of 854

A first-generation monoplane trainer, the Kawasaki Ki-32 was an interim type with fixed and spatted main gear and a small bomb bay.

Ki-32s was built before production ended in May 1940, and the type was used operationally at the beginning of the Pacific war and later allocated the Allied codename **'Mary'**. However, during 1942 the type was withdrawn from front-line service and then given employment in training units.

Specification
Type: two-seat light bomber
Powerplant: one 634-kW (850-hp) Kawasaki Ha-9-IIb V-12 piston engine

Performance: maximum speed 423 km/h (263 mph) at 3490 m (12,925 ft); service ceiling 8920 m (29,265 ft); range 1960 km (1,218 miles)
Weights: empty 2349 kg (5,179 lb); maximum take-off 3762 kg (8,294 lb)
Dimensions: span 15.00 m (49 ft

2½ in); length 11.64 m (38 ft 2¼ in); height 2.90 m (9 ft 6¼ in); wing area 34.00 m² (365.97 sq ft)
Armament: one fixed and one trainable 7.7-mm (0.303-in) Type 89 machine-gun, plus up to 450 kg (992 lb) of bombs

Kawasaki Ki-45 Toryu
to
L.F.G. Roland C.II

Kawasaki Ki-45 Toryu

In early 1937 Kawasaki was instructed by the Imperial Japanese Army to initiate the design and development of a twin-engined fighter that would be suitable for long-range operations over the Pacific. This was initiated under the designation Kawasaki **Ki-38**, but extensive design changes brought redesignation as the **Ki-45** and it was not until January 1939 that the first prototype was flown, a cantilever mid-wing monoplane with retractable tailwheel landing gear, the fuselage accommodating its two-man crew in tandem enclosed cockpits. The originally installed 611-kW (820-hp) Nakajima Ha-20B radials failed to develop their rated power, resulting in the first **Ki-45-I** prototype with 746-kW (1,000-hp) Nakajima Ha-25s not being flown until July 1940. Development problems with this powerplant delayed the initial production order until September 1941, when manufacture of the **Ki-45-KAI** began under the official designation **Army Type 2 Two-Seat Fighter Model A Toryu** (dragon slayer). Entering service in August 1942, the type was first used in combat during October 1942, being allocated the Allied codename **'Nick'** shortly afterwards. It was soon found to be effective against the USAAF's Consolidated B-24 Liberators, and when B-24s were used more extensively for night operations the Ki-45 was adapted to attack them. In this way the night fighting capability of the type was discovered, leading to a specially-developed night-fighter variant which proved to be one of the most successful Japanese aircraft in this category. A total of 1,698 Ki-45s was built, used for the defence of Tokyo and in the Burma, Manchuria and Sumatra theatres of operation. On 28 May 1944 four Ki-45s pioneered the use of aircraft for *kamikaze* attacks against Allied shipping.

Variants
Ki-45: designation of three prototypes, with Nakajima Ha-20B engines and armament of three 7.7-mm (0.303-in) machine-guns and one 20-mm cannon

Kawasaki Ki-45 KAIc of the 53rd Sentai (air group), Imperial Japanese Army air force based at Matsudo in Chiba Prefecture for defence of the home islands during late 1944 and 1945.

Ki-45-I: designation of prototypes with Nakajima Ha-25 engines and armament as Ki-45
Ki-45-KAI: designation of 12 pre-production aircraft with Ha-25 engines
Ki-45-KAIa: initial production version with Ha-25 engines; armament of two 12.7-mm (0.5-in) machine-guns in fuselage nose, one 7.92-mm (0.31-in) rear-firing gun on trainable mount, and one forward-firing 20-mm cannon
Ki-45 KAIb: ground-attack/anti-shipping version; early production with Ha-25 engines, late production with developed Mitsubishi Ha-102; armament of one 20-mm cannon in nose, one forward-firing 37-mm cannon in fuselage, and one rear-firing 7.92-mm (0.31-in) machine-gun
Ki-45 KAIc: night-fighter version, 477 built; Ha-102 engines and armament comprising one forward-firing 37-mm cannon, two obliquely-mounted upward-firing 20-mm cannon, and one 7.92-mm (0.31-in) aft-firing machine-gun
Ki-45 KAId: anti-shipping version; Ha-102 engines and armament of two forward-firing 20-mm cannon, one forward-firing 37-mm cannon and one 7.92-mm (0.31-in) aft-firing machine-gun
Ki-45-II: designation of version to be

Kawasaki Ki-45 KAIs.

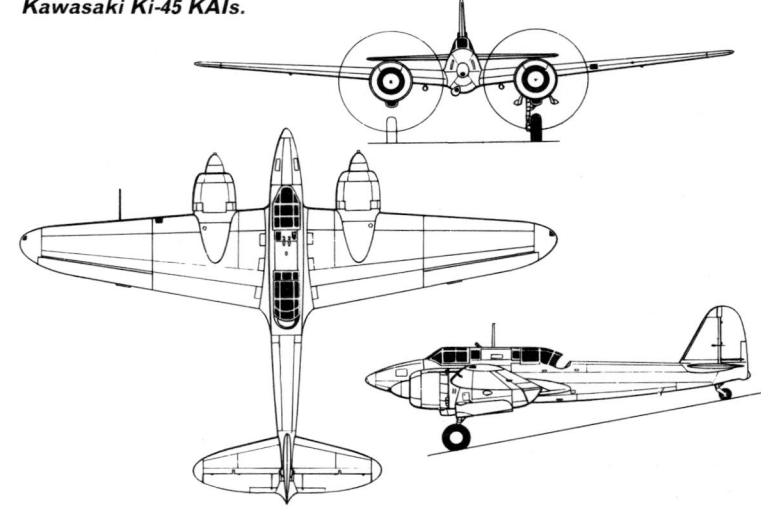

powered by two 1119-kW (1,500-hp) Mitsubishi Ha-112-II radials; developed instead as **Kawasaki Ki-96** single-seat fighter, but built only as a prototype

Specification
Kawasaki Ki-45 KAIc
Type: two-seat night-fighter
Powerplant: two 805-kW (1,080-hp) Mitsubishi Ha-102 engines
Performance: maximum speed 545 km/h (339 mph) at 7000 m

(22,965 ft); service ceiling 10000 m (32,810 ft); range 2000 km (1,243 miles)
Weights: empty 4000 kg (8,818 lb); maximum take-off 5500 kg (12,125 lb)
Dimensions: span 15.05 m (49 ft 4½ in); length 11.00 m (36 ft 1 in); height 3.70 m (12 ft 1½ in); wing area 32.00 m² (344.46 sq ft)
Armament: cannon and machine-guns as listed under Variants, plus (all versions) provision for two drop-tanks or two 250-kg (551-lb) bombs on underwing racks

Kawasaki Ki-48

An Imperial Japanese Army requirement of 1937 for a high-performance twin-engined light bomber led to design and development of the **Kawasaki Ki-48**, a cantilever mid-wing monoplane with retractable tailwheel landing gear, and power provided initially by two 708-kW (950-hp) Nakajima Ha-25 radial engines. The fuselage accommodated a crew of four and incorporated an internal bomb bay. It was not until July 1939 that the first of four prototypes was flown, and following the resolution of initial problems the type was ordered into production in late 1939 under the designation **Army Type 99 Twin-Engine Light Bomber Model 1A**. Ki-48s used operationally in China during the autumn of 1940 proved fast enough to be virtually immune from enemy defences, but their deployment at the beginning of the Pacific war, when they were allocated

the Allied codename **'Lily'**, showed that this speed was not good enough to provide protection against USAAF fighters. By then an improved **Ki-48-II** was already under development, with protected fuel tanks, armour protection for the crew and more-powerful Nakajima Ha-115 engines, and this entered production in the spring of 1942 under the designation **Army Type 99 Twin-Engine Light Bomber Model 2A**. Even this had little chance of survival against improving Allied fighters, and by October 1944 it had been declared obsolescent, most Ki-48s ending their days in *kamikaze* attacks.

Variants
Ki-48: designation of four prototypes and five pre-production aircraft
Ki-48-Ia: initial production version with armament of three 7.7-mm

(0.303-in) machine-guns on pivoted mounts in nose, dorsal and ventral positions, plus a maximum bombload of 400 kg (882 lb)
Ki-48-Ib: version of Ki-48-Ia with minor equipment changes and detail refinement; production of Ki-48-Ia and Ki-48-Ib versions totalled 557
Ki-48-II: designation of three prototypes built in early 1942
Ki-48-IIa: initial production version of Ki-48-II; defensive armament as Ki-48-Ia, but maximum bombload

The Kawasaki Ki-48-IIa was the direct product of combat experience with the Ki-48-I series. It had self-sealing fuel tanks, extra armour and extra power.

increased to 800 kg (1,764 lb)
Ki-48-IIb: production version generally as Ki-48-IIa, but with dive-brakes in the undersurface of each outer wing panel
Ki-48-IIc: production version

generally as Ki-48-IIa, but revised armament incorporating an extra machine-gun of 12.7-mm (0.5-in) calibre; production of all Ki-48-II versions totalled 1,408
Ki-81: projected heavily armed and armoured version of Ki-48; not built
Ki-174: single-seat special attack version of Ki-48; not built

Specification
Kawasaki Ki-48-IIb
Type: four-seat light bomber/dive-bomber
Powerplant: two 858-kW (1,150-hp)

Nakajima Ha-115 engines
Performance: maximum speed 505 km/h (314 mph); service ceiling 10100 m (33,135 ft); maximum range 2400 km (1,491 miles)
Weights: empty 4550 kg (10,031 lb); maximum take-off 6750 kg (14,881 lb)

Dimensions: span 17.45 m (57 ft 3 in); length 12.75 m (41 ft 10 in); height 3.80 m (12 ft 5½ in); wing area 40.00 m² (430.57 sq ft)
Armament: as detailed under Variants

Kawasaki Ki-61 Hien

Designed around the Kawasaki Ha-40 engine, a licence-built version of the German Daimler-Benz DB 601A, the **Kawasaki Ki-60** prototype proved disappointing and was soon abandoned. Efforts were then concentrated on an alternative design, the **Kawasaki Ki-61**, the first of 12 prototypes being flown during December 1941. This, like the Bf 109, had a liquid-cooled engine and was at one time erroneously considered by the Allies to be a licence-built version of that famous fighter. Service tests proved so satisfactory that the Imperial Japanese Army quickly accepted the type for production under the designation **Army Type 3 Fighter Model 1 Hien** (swallow), this subsequently being allocated the Allied codename **'Tony'**. The initial **Ki-61-I** production version began to enter combat operations from New Guinea in April 1943, soon proving that it was well able to hold its own against Allied fighters, and with increasing production the type was soon found in all theatres in which the Japanese Army was operating. When production ended in January 1945, a total of 2,666 had been built. The development of an improved **Ki-61-II** began in the autumn of 1942, but only 99 had been delivered when, in January 1945, manufacture of its Kawasaki Ha-140 engine was brought to an end as the result of USAAF air attacks.

Variants
Ki-61: designation of the 12 original prototypes
Ki-61-I: initial production version; armament comprised two fuselage-mounted 7.7-mm (0.303-in) machine-guns and two wing-mounted 12.7-mm (0.5-in) guns
Ki-61-Ia: as Ki-61-I, but with the wing-mounted machine-guns replaced by two imported 20-mm Mauser MG 151 cannon
Ki-61-Ib: as Ki-61-I, but with the fuselage-mounted machine-guns replaced by guns of 12.7-mm (0.5-in) calibre
Ki-61-Ic: revised version to simplify maintenance; armament of two fuselage-mounted 12.7-mm (0.5-in) machine-guns and two wing-mounted 20-mm Ho-5 cannon of Japanese design and manufacture

Ki-61-Id: as Ki-61-Ic, but with the 20-mm cannon replaced by 30-mm Ho-105 cannon
Ki-61-II: designation of eight prototypes with increased-area wing and Kawasaki Ha-140 engine
Ki-61-II KAI: designation of 30 prototype/pre-production aircraft, with reversion to Ki-61-I wing and redesigned tail surfaces
Ki-61-IIa: initial production version with armament as Ki-61-Ic
Ki-61-IIb: as Ki-61-IIa, but with armament of four 20-mm Ho-5 cannon
Ki-61-III: single prototype of proposed improved version

Specification
Kawasaki Ki-61-Ic
Type: single-seat fighter
Powerplant: one 876-kW (1,175-hp)

Kawasaki Ki-61-KAIc of the 23rd Dokuritsu Dai Shijugo Chutai (independant squadron) Imperial Japanese Army air force, based at Yontan on Okinawa during April 1945.

Kawasaki Ha-40 V-12 piston engine
Performance: maximum speed 560 km/h (348 mph); service ceiling 10000 m (32,810 ft); maximum range 1900 km (1,181 miles)
Weights: empty 2630 kg (5,798 lb); maximum take-off 3470 kg (7,650 lb)
Dimensions: span 12.00 m (39 ft 4½ in); length 8.95 m (29 ft 4¼ in); height 3.70 m (12 ft 1¾ in); wing area 20.00 m² (215.29 sq ft)
Armament: as detailed under Variants, plus provision for two drop-tanks or two 250-kg (551-lb) bombs

Kawasaki Ki-100

The Kawasaki Ki-61-II was regarded as a worthwhile high-altitude interceptor to tackle the USAAF's Boeing B-29s at their cruising altitude of some 9145 m (30,000 ft), but plans to deploy the aircraft in this role came to an end when production of the Kawasaki Ha-140 engine was terminated by USAAF air attacks. Kawasaki by then had 275 completed Ki-61-II airframes without powerplants, and it was decided to bring these into service with an alternative engine. With no inline engine available, it meant the airframe had to be adapted for the installation of a large-diameter radial, the Mitsubishi Ha-112-II which had the same power output as the Ha-140. First flown with this new engine on 1 February 1945 as the **Kawasaki Ki-100**, the aircraft was immediately revealed to be an exceptional interceptor, one regarded by some as Japan's outstanding fighter aircraft of the Pacific war. Three prototypes were completed and enthusiastic service trials resulted in an immediate order

for the remaining 272 airframes to be similarly powered under the designation **Army Type 5 Fighter Model 1A**, these having the company designation **Ki-100-1a**. Simultaneously, the army requested Kawasaki to initiate new production, and the airframe that had been designed for the Ki-61-III, with a cut-down rear fuselage and all-round-view bubble canopy, was adopted for the **Ki-100-1b**. A total of 99 of this version was built before production was halted by the growing intensity of USAAF air attacks.

Variant
Ki-100-II: designation of three prototypes with the Mitsubishi Ha-112-IIru turbocharged engine to improve high-altitude performance; no production examples built

Specification
Kawasaki Ki-100-1a/b
Type: single-seat interceptor fighter

Powerplant: one 1119-kW (1,500-hp) Mitsubishi Ha-112-II engine
Performance: maximum speed 590 km/h (367 mph) at 10000 m (32,810 ft); service ceiling 10670 m (35,005 ft); range 2000 km (1,243 miles)
Weights: empty 2700 kg (5,952 lb); maximum take-off 3670 kg (8,091 lb)
Dimensions: span 12.00 m (39 ft 4½ in); length 8.80 m (28 ft 10½ in); height 3.75 m (12 ft 3½ in); wing area

A classic example of a stopgap design that exceeded all expectations, the Ki-100 proved to be one of the finest Japanese fighters of World War II.

20.00 m² (215.29 sq ft)
Armament: two fuselage-mounted 12.7-mm (0.5-in) Ho-103 (Type 1) machine-guns and two wing-mounted 20-mm Ho-5 cannon, plus two drop-tanks or two 250-kg (551-lb) bombs

Kawasaki Ki-102

Derived from the Ki-96 twin-engined single-seat fighter, development of which from the Ki-45 was abandoned after three prototypes had been completed, the **Kawasaki Ki-102** was intended as a two-seat attack fighter for primary deployment in a close-support role. Some assemblies of the Ki-96 prototypes were incorporated in the three

Ki-102 prototypes, the first completed in March 1944. A cantilever mid-wing monoplane, with retractable tailwheel landing gear and powered by two Mitsubishi Ha-112-II radials, the two-man crew was accommodated in separate enclosed cockpits. Twenty pre-production aircraft were built before production was ordered under the official designa-

tion **Army Type 4 Assault Plane,** Kawasaki designation **Ki-102b**. Allocated the Allied codename **'Randy'**, these aircraft saw little service, being used over Okinawa while the majority was held in reserve in Japan.

The urgent need for interceptors to attack the USAAF's bomber fleets brought the modification of six pre-production Ki-102s as the prototypes of a twin-engined high-altitude fighter. These differed primarily from the Ki-102b

by having a revised tail unit and turbo-charged Mitsubishi Ha-112-IIru engines. However, problems with this engine installation resulted in only about 15 being completed before the war ended.

Variants
Ki-102: designation of prototypes and pre-production aircraft
Ki-102a: high-altitude fighter version; armament of one 37-mm Ho-203 cannon and two 20-mm Ho-5 cannon

Ki-102b: ground-attack version; armament of one 57-mm Ho-401 cannon, two 20-mm Ho-5 cannon, and one rear-firing 12.7-mm (0.5-in) Ho-103 (Type 1) machine-gun
Ki-102c: proposed night-fighter version with increased wing span, lengthened fuselage, revised tail surfaces, primitive AI radar and armament of two 30-mm Ho-105 and

two 20-mm Ho-5 cannon; only two completed
Ki-108: two prototypes of high-altitude fighter with pressurised cabin; both conversions of Ki-102b airframes with structural improvements of Ki-102c; these were still being tested at the end of the war

Specification
Kawasaki Ki-102b
Type: twin-engined close-support aircraft
Powerplant: two 1119-kW (1,500-hp) Mitsubishi Ha-112-II engines
Performance: maximum speed 580 km/h (360 mph) at 6000 m (19,685 ft); service ceiling 11000 m (36,090 ft); range 2000 km

Weights: empty 4950 kg (10,913 lb); maximum take-off 7300 kg (16,094 lb)
Dimensions: span 15.57 m (51 ft 1 in); length 11.45 m (37 ft 6¾ in); height 3.70 m (12 ft 1¾ in); wing area 34.00 m² (365.98 sq ft)
Armament: as listed under Variants, plus (all versions) provision for two drop-tanks or two 250-kg (551-lb) bombs

Kawasaki T-4

Designed to replace the Lockheed T-33 and Fuji T-1 jet trainers in service with the JASDF, the **Ka-851** project was selected in September 1981. Designated the **XT-4** during development, 91 production **T-4s** are on order and about 40 had been delivered by mid-1990. The first of four prototypes flew on 29 July 1985 and the first production aircraft was delivered to the JASDF in September 1988. Kawasaki is the prime contractor for the programme, with Fuji and Mitsubishi sharing in the production of major components. The high-wing tandem-seat jet, powered by two IHI-30 turbofan engines, is used to bridge the gap between the T-5 turboprop basic trainer and the T-2 advanced jet trainer.

Specification
Type: two-seat intermediate jet trainer
Powerplant: two 1670-kg (3,680-lb) thrust Ishikawajima-Harima Industries F3-IHI-30 turbofan engines
Performance: maximum speed 1038 km/h (645 mph); service ceiling 15240 m (50,000 ft); range on internal fuel 1297 km (806 miles)
Weights: empty 3700 kg (8,157 lb); maximum take-off 5500 kg (12,125 lb)
Dimensions: span 9.9 m (32 ft 7 in); length 13.0 m (42 ft 8 in); height 4.6 m (15 ft 1 in); wing area 21.0 m² (226.0 sq ft)

The Kawasaki T-4 is one of the best jet trainers available today and is an illustration of how far the Japanese aviation industry has progressed.

Kellett KD-1 series

The **Kellett KD-1** autogyro of 1934 was of similar overall configuration to the contemporary British Cierva C.30, with two open cockpits in tandem, and was powered by a 168-kW (225-hp) Jacobs L-4 radial engine. Extensive testing of this machine by the company led to the decision to put into production a commercial version designated **KD-1A**, which incorporated a three-bladed rotor with folding blades, a mechanical system to spin-up the rotor, a rotor brake, lightweight tailwheel landing gear, and a number of detail refinements; the Jacobs L-4 radial engine was retained for this model. A generally-similar KD-1A, but with a single-seat open cockpit, was used on 19 May 1939 for a first demonstration of the capability of the type to provide feeder air-mail services, carrying a cargo of mail from the centre of Washington to the city's Hoover Airport. A little less than two

The Kellett KD-1A autogyro was an advanced design with a rotor that could be clutched to the engine for pre-flight spin up.

months later, on 6 July, Eastern Airlines inaugurated the first scheduled air-mail service with a rotary-wing aircraft, a **KD-1B**, which differed from the KD-1A only by having an enclosed cockpit for the pilot.

At an earlier date, in 1935, the US Army decided to evaluate the capability of the Kellett machine, acquiring a single KD-1 which it designated **YG-1**. It was followed in 1936 by a second example equipped with radio which was designated **YG-1A** and in 1937 by seven **YG-1B** aircraft with equipment changes. In 1942 seven more were obtained for use in an observation role, as **XO-60**, the designation of six of them changing to **YO-60** after their 168-kW

(225-hp) Jacobs R-775 engines had been replaced by 224-kW (300-hp) Jacobs R-915-3s, some revision had been made to the cabin enclosure and additional observation windows had been provided. One YG-1B gained a constant-speed rotor, being redesignated **YG-1C**, and, when its powerplant was changed subsequently from the Jacobs R-775 to the more powerful R-915, the new designation **XR-2** was applied. After this aircraft was destroyed by rotor ground resonance problems, one other YG-1B was similarly converted for continued evaluation under the designation **XR-3**. These aircraft were the first practical rotary-wing aircraft used by the US Army, but after their construction had been completed Kellett discontinued the production of autogyros.

Keystone bombers

The Huff-Daland company designed a large single-engined biplane bomber, the prototype (serial no. 23-1250) being acquired by the US Army in 1923. Designated **Huff-Daland XLB-1**, this was powered by a 597-kW (800-hp) Packard 1A-2540 engine which, mounted in the nose, meant that the bomb aimer's position was in the centre fuselage. This prototype was followed by 10 generally-similar **LB-1** pre-production aircraft, which differed by accommodating an extra crew member and by the installation of an improved Packard 2A-2540 engine. More, extensive, service trials led to a conclusion that the single-engine powerplant was unsatisfactory, and Huff-Daland began development of a twin-engined version of the LB-1 with two 313-kW (420-hp) Liberty V-1410-1 engines mounted on the lower wing, one on each side of the fuselage. Testing of this single **XLB-3** led to replacement of the Liberty V-1410s by two 306-kW (410-hp) Pratt & Whitney

R-1340-1 Wasp engines, this revised version being designated **XLB-3A** and accommodating a crew of five. Just before delivery of the XLB-3A for service testing, the company name was changed to Keystone Aircraft Corporation, with the result that all of these prototype/pre-production aircraft, together with subsequent production aircraft, are known usually as Keystone bombers. However, a reversion to Liberty engines produced the **XLB-5** prototype and it, and 10 production **LB-5** aircraft delivered before the XLB-3A, entered service as Huff-Daland aircraft; 25 **LB-5A** bombers with tail unit changes were Keystones. The **XLB-6** of 1927, a conversion of an LB-5 airframe, introduced new wings and a revised engine installation, one 391-kW (525-hp) Wright R-1750-1 Cyclone being strut-mounted between the wings on each side of the fuselage. It was followed by 17 production **LB-6** aircraft with detail improvements, and these LB-5/-5A and LB-6 air-

craft represented the first in-service production examples of a series of Keystone biplane bombers that were to serve with the US Army Air Corps into the early 1930s. Entering service initially with squadrons of the USAAC 2nd Bomb Group, they later equipped squadrons of the 7th and 19th Bomb Groups, representing the backbone of the US Army's

A cornerstone of US military aviation in the 1920s, the Keystone LB-6 was modelled closely on the XLB-6 prototype apart from internal improvements and vertical tail surfaces of a more angular outline. It could carry a 2000-lb bomb load.

heavy offensive force, and also served with overseas units in Hawaii, the Panama Canal Zone and the Philippines.

Variants

LB-7: identical to LB-6s except for installation of 391-kW (525-hp) Pratt & Whitney R-1690-3 Hornet engines; 18 built

LB-8: designation of one LB-7 following installation of 410-kW (550-hp) Pratt & Whitney R-1860-3 engines for evaluation

LB-9: designation of one LB-7 following installation of 429-kW (575-hp) Wright GR-1750 Cyclone engines for evaluation

LB-10: designation of one LB-6 following installation of 391-kW (525-hp) Wright R-1750-1 engines for evaluation

LB-10A: production version of LB-10 but with 391-kW (525-hp) Pratt & Whitney R-1690-3 engines; 63 built, but all delivered as **B-3A** aircraft following introduction of 'B' designations for all USAAC bomber types

LB-11: designation of one LB-6 following installation of 391-kW (525-hp) Wright R-1750-3 engines for evaluation

LB-11A: redesignation of LB-11 following installation of 391-kW (525-hp) Wright GR-1750 engines for evaluation

LB-12: designation of aircraft generally similar to LB-7 except for installation of 429-kW (575-hp) Pratt & Whitney R-1860-1 direct-drive engines for

LB-13: seven aircraft ordered under this designation were delivered as five **Y1B-4** pre-production aircraft with 429-kW (575-hp) Pratt & Whitney R-1860-7 engines, and two **Y1B-6** pre-production aircraft with 429-kW (575-hp) Wright R-1820-1 engines

LB-14: three production aircraft ordered with 429-kW (575-hp) Pratt & Whitney GR-1860 engines, but delivered as **Y1B-5** aircraft with 391-kW (525-hp) Wright R-1750-3 engines

B-4A: production version of Y1B-4; 25 built

B-5A: production version of Y1B-5; 27 built

B-6A: production version of Y1B-6; 39 built

Specification

Keystone B-4A
Type: five-seat light bomber
Powerplant: two 429-kW (575-hp) Pratt & Whitney R-1860-7 radial engines
Performance: maximum speed 195 km/h (121 mph); service ceiling 4265 m (14,000 ft); range 1376 km (855 miles)
Weights: empty 3607 kg (7,951 lb); maximum take-off 5992 kg (13,209 lb)
Dimensions: span 22.76 m (74 ft 8 in); length 14.88 m (48 ft 10 in); height 4.80 m (15 ft 9 in); wing area 106.37 m² (1,145.0 sq ft)
Armament: three 7.62-mm (0.3-in) Browning machine-guns, plus up to 1134 kg (2,500 lb) of bombs

Klemm lightplanes

Dr Ing. Hans Klemm began his career as a highly successful designer of lightplanes soon after World War I, when he was working for Daimler at Stuttgart. In 1926 he established his own company, Klemm Leichtflugzeugbau GmbH, at Böblingen, near Stuttgart, the first product of this new organisation being the **Klemm L 25** of which, over the years, more than 600 were produced. A two-seat cantilever low-wing monoplane, in its initial form as the L 25 the aircraft was powered by a 15-kW (20-hp) Mercedes-Benz two-cylinder engine, but subsequent versions included the **L 25 1a** with a 30-kW (40-hp) Salmson AD-9 engine, a seaplane version of this aircraft designated **WL 25 1a**, and a three-seat **L 25 1b** with the forward cockpit enlarged to seat two. Following the same lines Klemm produced the lengthened and strengthened **L 26a**, the **L 27** with an enlarged forward cockpit, the aerobatic **L 28** powered by a 112-kW (150-hp) Siemens Sh 14a engine, and the **L 30** similar to the L 25/L 26 series but intended for assembly by flying clubs.

In 1933 the **KI 31** and **KI 32** were introduced, four- and three-seat cabin monoplanes respectively and both powered by the Siemens Sh 14a radial. They were followed by a considerable change in design with the **KI 33**, a single-seat ultralight of high-wing monoplane configuration powered by a 30-kW (40-hp) Argus engine. Next came the important **KI 35** two-seat low-wing monoplane which, in the original **KI 35a** prototype as flown in 1935, was powered by a 60-kW (80-hp) Hirth HM 60R engine. The second prototype, the **KI 35b**, had a 78-kW (105-hp) Hirth HM 504A-2, which also powered the initial **KI 35B** production version. This became available with wood or metal floats as the **KI 35BW** and, in addition to production for the home market, KI 35s of different versions were exported to Czechoslovakia, Hungary, Romania and Sweden, the last country also building the type under licence for use by her air force. In 1938 the improved **KI 35D** was developed for use as a primary trainer by the Luftwaffe, resulting in large-scale production. This

version had strengthened landing gear, available with floats, skis or wheels as required, and reverted to use of the lower-powered Hirth HM 60R engine.

Before that, however, lightplane design and manufacture had continued with the **KI 36** four-seat cabin monoplane which was developed especially to compete in the 1934 Challenge de Tourisme Internationale; it was available as the **KI 36A** with the 164-kW (220-hp) Hirth HM 508F engine, or **KI 36B** with the 112-kW (150-hp) Bramo Sh 14A radial. Final versions to be produced before the

The KI 35 was the company's best-selling design, surviving examples being highly prized.

beginning of World War II were the **KI 105** two-seat light monoplane powered by a 37-kW (50-hp) Z.9-92 engine, an enclosed cabin version of the same aircraft with a 78-kW (105-hp) Hirth HM 500A-1 engine under the designation **KI 107**, and the **KI 106**, a developed version of the KI 35D powered by a 75-kW (100-hp) Hirth HM 500.

Koolhoven FK 41

Following a number of less successful one-off designs, including the **FK 32** two-seat sesquiplane trainer, the **FK 33** nine-passenger three-engined transport (which served with both Lufthansa and the German Aero company), the **FK 34** three-seat reconnaissance floatplane and the **FK 30 Toerist** ultra-light two-seater, Koolhoven, who had by then formed his own company, produced the **Koolhoven FK 41.**

This was a three-seat high-wing cabin monoplane intended for sport or touring use, the first aircraft (H-NAER) making its initial flight during July 1928. A batch of FK 41s was built in the Netherlands, in

two versions, the **FK 41 Mk I** with a 78-kW (105-hp) Cirrus Hermes engine and the **FK 41 Mk II** with a 97-kW (130-hp) de Havilland Gipsy. Both versions were built under licence in the UK by the Desoutter Aircraft Company, British production of both versions totalling 41.

Later FK 41s had simplified tail assemblies, and both Dutch and British-built aircraft made a name for themselves in many countries during the period up to World War II.

Specification

Type: three-seat sport/touring cabin monoplane

Powerplant: one 97-kW (130-hp) de Havilland Gipsy Major I engine
Performance: maximum speed 195 km/h (121 mph)
Weight: maximum take-off 900 kg (1,984 lb)
Dimensions: span 10.50 m (34 ft

The Koolhoven FK 41 was a moderately successful touring aircraft, and was notable for the three struts bracing the wing on either side of the fuselage.

5½ in); length 7.80 m (25 ft 7 in)

Koolhoven FK 43

Before the advent of the successful **Koolhoven FK 43**, the designer had produced as one-off types in 1929 the **FK 40**, a high-wing cabin monoplane with a 78-kW (105-hp) Cirrus engine, and the **FK 42** parasol-wing light two-seat sport monoplane powered by a 172-kW (230-hp) Gnome-Rhône Titan radial. The FK 42 was a four-passenger transport (PH-AES) which began its career with KLM and ended up as an air ambulance, flown by the Nationalists in the Spanish Civil War.

The prototype FK 43 (PH-AFW) was flown for the first time in 1931, and was a high-wing cabin monoplane for three passengers. It was built for private owners and as an air taxi. KLM bought six which were operated for several years out of Schiphol on taxi routes. The FK 43 proved a rugged aircraft with its fixed wide-track landing gear, and its design was refined progressively, the tailplane in particular being subjected to considerable modification. Powered by a 97-kW (130-hp) Gipsy Major engine, the

The Koolhoven FK 43 enjoyed limited sales success and was gainfully employed by the Dutch airline KLM as an air taxi.

FK 43 attained a maximum speed of 190 km/h (118 mph), spanned 10.90 m (35 ft 9¼ in), had a length of 8.30 m (27 ft 2¾ in), and a maximum take-off weight of 1140 kg (2,513 lb).

Three FK 43s were taken over by the Dutch air arm (the LVA) in 1939 and one example was requisitioned by the RAF in 1940. Post-war, in 1947, the Fokker factory built eight improved FK 43s with 123-kW (165-hp) Genet Major engines as air taxis.

Other single-engined monoplanes built by the Koolhoven company included the **FK 53 Junior**, a two-seat cabin monoplane with a low-set inverted gull-type wing and powered by a 46-kW (62-hp) Walter Mikron engine; the prototype (PH-FKJ) flew in 1936, a second example in 1938. The **FK 54** was a three-seat braced high-wing cabin monoplane, powered by a 104-kW (140-hp) Gipsy Major engine, but no production examples were built.

Koolhoven FK 51

The prototype of the **Koolhoven FK 51** biplane basic trainer made its first flight on 25 May 1935 from Waalhaven. It bore the provisional designator Z-1, later replaced by the civil registration PH-AJV when the machine was used as a demonstrator. An equal-span biplane of mixed construction, the FK 51 was designed for engines in the 186-kW (250-hp) to 373-kW (500-hp) range. Its divided landing gear was of wide track to cater for the rough handling it would receive from trainee pilots.

The Royal Dutch air force (LVA) ordered a total of 25 FK 51s in 1936-37, these being powered by the 201-kW (270-hp) Armstrong Siddeley Cheetah V radial. Later, a further 29 aircraft were acquired with 261-kW (350-hp) Cheetah IXs. Army serials were from 1 to 25 for the first batches and 400 to 428 for the final batch. The Dutch Naval air arm (MLD) obtained 24 FK 51s, serialled E-1 to E-24, each powered by a 335-kW (450-hp) Pratt & Whitney radial. The Dutch East Indies army (LA) procured between 1936 and 1938 28 FK 51s with 313-kW (420-hp) Wright Whirlwinds. At

This aircraft was the third of 24 Koolhoven FK 51s operated in the basic training role by the Dutch naval air arm in the late 1930s.

least seven other FK 51s went to the East Indies with serials from K-102 upwards; the original batch bore numbers K-2 to K-29.

The Republican government in Spain, engaged in civil war with the Franco insurgents, was sufficiently impressed by the demonstration given by prototype PH-AJV to order 28 FK 51s. With serials EK-001 to EK-028, they were delivered in two versions, 11 of them powered by 298-kW (400-hp) Armstrong Siddeley Jaguar IVa radials and 17 **FK 51bis** aircraft fitted with the 335-kW (450-hp) Wright Whirlwind R-975E radials. Some of the Spanish FK 51s were used as night flying trainers, based at Carmoli airfield. Others were operational as night-fighters or reconnaissance aircraft, in which role they were armed with two fixed 7.7-mm (0.303-in) Vickers machine-guns in the leading edge of the upper wing, with a single Lewis gun of

the same calibre on a pivot mounting for operation by the observer.

With production totalling at least 142, the FK 51 was Frits Koolhoven's most successful design after his return to the Netherlands.

Specification
Type: two-seat basic trainer biplane
Powerplant: one 313-kW (420-hp) Wright Whirlwind radial engine

Performance: maximum speed 253 km/h (157 mph); service ceiling 6500 m (21,325 ft); range 825 km (513 miles)
Weights: empty equipped 980 kg (2,160 lb); maximum take-off 1450 kg (3,197 lb)
Dimensions: span 9.00 m (29 ft 6¼ in); length 7.85 m (25 ft 9 in); height 2.85 m (9 ft 4¼ in); wing area 27.00 m² (290.64 sq ft)

Koolhoven FK 52

The prototype of the **Koolhoven FK 52** two-seat fighter-reconnaissance aircraft was first flown on 9 February 1937, an equal-span biplane with fixed landing gear, a glazed canopy over the tandem crew cockpits, and with power provided by an 619-kW (830-hp) Bristol Mercury VIII radial engine. Five series aircraft followed, the prototype crashing on 11 August 1937 before these aircraft were completed. Three were scrapped during 1940, but two were obtained by the Swedish Count von Rosen and sent to

Finland where they went into service with the air arm (the Lentolaivue) for reconnaissance and light-bombing missions in the Winter War and the Continuation War against the Soviet Union.

The FK 52 spanned 9.80 m (32 ft 1¾ in), had a maximum take-off weight of 2500 kg (5,511 lb) and a maximum speed of 370 km/h (230 mph) at 4000 m (13,125 ft). Armament comprised two fixed and one trainable 7.5-mm (0.295-in) machine-guns, plus 100 kg (220 lb) of bombs.

Finland used a pair of Koolhoven FK 52 reconnaissance aircraft to good effect in both its wars against the Soviet Union.

Koolhoven FK 58

Designed by Eric Schatzki, formerly of the Fokker company, the **Koolhoven FK 58** was a single-seat low/mid-wing monoplane of mixed construction. Designed in great haste to meet a French requirement for a fighter to operate in Indo-China, the prototype (PH-ATO) flew for the first time on 17 July 1938, only three months after the first drawings had been made. A robust, unattractive aircraft, the FK 58 had an enclosed cockpit with rearward sliding canopy, inward-retracting main landing gear units and a strut-braced tailplane.

The French authorities eventually ordered 50 aircraft and later the Dutch LVA decided to acquire 36 machines. In the event, a second prototype and 17 production aircraft for France were completed at Waalhaven, but to overcome various production problems the remaining 23 aircraft at Waalhaven were transferred to Nevers in France for final assembly. The 17 Dutch-built aircraft were flown to Buc airfield and were eventually issued, along with one or two machines from Nevers, to the Polish training division at Lyons and to a hastily

formed *escadrille de regroupement* formed at Salon-de-Provence. The remainder were kept in reserve until the French surrender in June 1940, but soon afterwards they were all scrapped.

The Dutch order was based on availability of the Bristol Taurus III radial engine, which was never delivered. Production went ahead with the intention of using the less powerful Bristol Mercury VIII engine, which would give inferior performance, but the production line was destroyed during a Luftwaffe air attack on Wallhaven, on 10 May 1940, before any aircraft of the Dutch order had been completed.

Specification
Type: single-seat fighter
Powerplant: one 768-kW (1,030-hp) Gnome-Rhône 14N-39 piston engine
Performance: maximum speed 475 km/h (295 mph) at 5000 m (16,405 ft); service ceiling 10000 m (32,810 ft); range 750 km (466 miles)
Weights: empty equipped 1930 kg (4,255 lb); maximum take-off 2750 kg (6,030 lb)
Dimensions: span 10.97 m (35 ft 11¾ in); length 8.68 m (28 ft 5¾ in); height 2.99 m (9 ft 9¾ in); wing area 17.30 m² (186.21 sq ft)
Armament: four 7.5-mm (0.295-in) FN Browning machine-guns

Kyushu J7W Shinden

The first flight of the unique **Kyushu J7W Shinden** (magnificent lightning), a canard-configuration single-seat fighter, was made on 3 August 1945, but the end of World War II later that month brought an end to development and production plans. Designed by a team under the leadership of Captain Masaoki Tsuruno of the Imperial Japanese Navy, the configuration of this aircraft had been

effectively confirmed by the flight testing of three specially designed and built **MXY6** gliders. The construction of two **J7W1** prototypes followed, these each having a slender fuselage and mounting in a mid-position on the nose a short-span foreplane incorporating elevators at the trailing edge. The rear-mounted cantilever monoplane wing was set low on the fuselage, had moderately swept

The Kyushu J7W1 was one of the most strikingly different aircraft designs to emerge from Japan's aircraft factories during World War II. It was intended as a high-performance interceptor of canard configuration. This would have enabled it to mount a heavy armament of 30-mm cannon in its nose.

leading edges and conventional ailerons with, just inboard of these on each wing,

a fin and rudder extending above and below the trailing edge. The landing gear

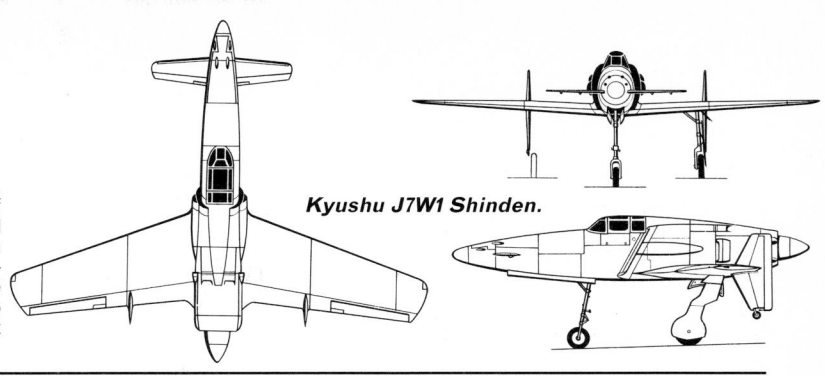

Kyushu J7W1 Shinden.

was of retractable tricycle type; the pilot was accommodated in an enclosed cockpit, directly above the leading edge of the wing; and power was provided by a 1588-kW (2,130-hp) Mitsubishi MK9D radial engine, mounted in the rear fuselage to drive a six-blade pusher propeller. By the end of the war the second prototype had been completed but not flown.

The J7W1 spanned 11.11 m (36 ft 5½ in), had a maximum take-off weight of 5288 kg (11,526 lb), and was estimated to have a maximum speed of 750 km/h (466 mph). Armament was four nose-mounted 30-mm Type 5 cannon. In the planning stage was the **J7W2** version to be powered by a 900-kg (1,984-lb) thrust Ne-130 turbojet.

Kyushu K11W Shiragiku

The **Kyushu K11W** was designed by Watanabe to meet an Imperial Japanese Navy requirement for a crew trainer. A mid-wing cantilever monoplane with retractable tailwheel landing gear, the K11W accommodated a pilot and radio operator/gunner in a canopied cockpit above the wing, with the instructor, bomb-aimer and navigator in a cabin below the wing. Power was provided by a 384-kW (515-hp) Hitachi GK2B Amakaze 21 radial engine. First flown in prototype form during November 1942, the K11W was soon ordered into production as the **Navy Operations Trainer Shiragiku** (white chrysanthemum), these

Seen in its 'surrender' markings of white with green crosses, this Kyushu K11W1 crew trainer was photographed in Shanghai in 1945.

aircraft having the company designation **K11W1**. Almost 800 were built by Kyushu from 1943 to 1945, being used extensively by the navy. In the closing stages of the Pacific war many K11W1s were used in *kamikaze* attacks. In addition to this standard version, a small number were built of all-wooden construction under the designation **K11W2** and equipped for use in ASW and trans-

port roles. The K11W1 spanned 14.98 m (49 ft 1¾ in), had a maximum take-off weight of 2640 kg (5,820 lb) and had a maximum speed of 230 km/h (143 mph).

The same basic design was used for a dedicated anti-submarine aircraft, the **Kyushu Q3W1 Nankai** (south sea), which reached only prototype form.

Kyushu Q1W Tokai

During 1942 Watanabe designed an ASW aircraft to meet an Imperial Japanese Navy requirement for a specialized aircraft in this category. Designated **Kyushu Q1W**, this was a cantilever mid/low-wing monoplane with retractable tailwheel landing gear, and powered by two Hitachi GK2C Amakaze 31 radial engines. Operated by a crew of three, the Q1W was planned to use an advanced search radar, but this failed to materialize and instead the Q1W had to make do with an earlier and somewhat ineffective radar complemented by MAD (magnetic anamaly detection) equipment. First flown in September 1943, the **Q1W1** was ordered into production in early 1944 as the **Navy Patrol Plane Tokai** (eastern sea), later allocated the Allied codename

'Lorna'. It proved to be unsuccessful in operational service, too slow and too vulnerable to attack by Allied fighters, and only about 150 had been built by the time the Pacific war ended.

Variants
Q1W1-K: four-seat trainer prototype of all-wooden construction, intended as a flying classroom for electronic equipment operators
Q1W2: designation of a small number of aircraft with the rear fuselage structure of wood

Specification
Kyushu Q1W1
Type: anti-submarine patrol aircraft
Powerplant: two 459-kW (610-hp) Hitachi Gk2C Amakaze 31 engines

Performance: maximum speed 230 km/h (199 mph) at 1340 m (4,395 ft); service ceiling 4500 m (14,765 ft); range 1340 km (833 miles)
Weights: empty 3100 kg (6,834 lb); maximum take-off 5315 kg (11,718 lb)
Dimensions: span 16.00 m (52 ft 6 in); length 12.09 m (39 ft 8 in); height 4.12 m (13 ft 6 in); wing area 38.20 m^2 (411.19 sq ft)
Armament: one rear-firing 7.7-mm

A dedicated anti-submarine aircraft, the Kyushu Q1W1 was a simple aircraft of relatively low performance, designed to dive-bomb its targets.

(0.303-in) Type 92 machine-gun and two 250-kg (551-lb) depth charges or bombs; one or two 20-mm cannon in fuselage nose optional

L.F.G. Roland C.II

The airship-building Motorluftschiff Studiengesellschaft, which had been formed in Berlin in 1960, was later superseded by Flugmaschine Wright GmbH with a factory at Adlershof for the construction of Wright biplanes. When the company failed in 1912, Krupp and other financiers used the premises to found Luftfahrzeug Gesellschaft (L.F.G.). However, with the well-known Luftverkehrs GmbH (L.V.G.) also established in Berlin, it was decided that the close similarity of the commonly-used L.F.G. and L.V.G. abbreviations could cause confusion, leading to the L.F.G. company registering the trade name 'Roland' which was adopted as part of the title.

Activities at the beginning of World War I were confined to licence-production of Albatros two-seat reconnaissance aircraft, but the company's design engineer, Dipl. Ing. Tantzen, evolved a new aircraft in this category with which he hoped to achieve much higher performance standards. This was the **L.F.g. Roland C.II**, nicknamed *Walfisch* (whale) at a later date, the name undoubtedly derived from the deep fuselage adopted by Tantzen, with the upper

biplane wing mounted to the top of the fuselage and so removing the need for centre-section struts. Thus Tantzen intended to eliminate one source of drag and, at the same time, he replaced the conventional interplane struts by a single wide-chord I-section strut for the same reason. The pilot and observer/gunner, seated in open cockpits, had an excellent field of view over the upper wing, but despite large cut-outs in the roots of both wings the forward/downward view was restricted. Landing gear was of fixed tailskid type.

The prototype was flown for the first time in October 1915, and modified production aircraft began to enter service in early 1916. A total of about 300 was built, some by Linke-Hoffman Werke under licence.

Variants
C.IIa: designation of generally similar aircraft with revised and reinforced wingtips
C.III: single prototype of developed version with a 149-kW (200-hp) Benz Bz.IV engine and conventional interplane struts

C.VIII: single prototype developed from C.III with revised fuselage and 194-kW (260-hp) Mercedes D.IVa engine

Specification
L.F.G Roland C.II
Type: two-seat reconnaissance/escort fighter
Powerplant: one 119-kW (160-hp) Mercedes D.III inline piston engine
Performance: maximum speed 165 km/h (103 mph); endurance 4 hours
Weights: empty 764 kg (1,684 lb);

Its rotund fuselage earned the L.F.G. Roland C.II the nickname 'Walfisch', meaning Whale.

maximum take-off 1284 kg (2,831 lb)
Dimensions: span 10.30 m (33 ft 9½ in); length 7.70 m (25 ft 3¼ in); height 2.90 m (9 ft 6¼ in); wing area 26.00 m^2 (279.87 sq ft)
Armament: one 7.92-mm (0.31-in) Parabellum machine-gun in the rear cockpit and (later production aircraft) one 7.92-mm (0.31-in) LMG 08/15 forward-firing gun

L.F.G. Roland D.II and D.IIa
to
Lavochkin La-9 and La-11

L.F.G. Roland D.II and D.IIa

With the C.II in production, Dipl. Ing. Tantzen concentrated on developing a single-seat version for use as a fighter/scout. Thus resulted the **L.F.G. Roland D.I** with a fuselage that was not so deep, its less ponderous lines duly bringing the nickname *Haifisch* (shark). By comparison with the C.II, however, there was considerable change in wing configuration, the two wings being unstaggered and with a small amount of sweepback on the leading edge, and conventional interplane struts replacing the I-struts. The D.I was first flown in July 1916, being followed shortly afterwards by an improved **D.II** incorporating a revised tail unit and additional improvements to reduce drag. Both the D.I and D.II were powered by the 119-kW (160-hp) Mercedes D.III engine, and the generally similar **D.IIa** resulted from installation of the more powerful Argus As.III engine. These aircraft began to enter service from early 1917 and more

The L.F.G. Roland D.III prototype used the fuselage of the D.II, but the few production aircraft had a shallower fuselage.

of all versions are believed to have been built, the majority of them by the Pfalz Flugzeug-Werke. The D.I/II/IIa aircraft were not particularly popular with the pilots to whom they were allocated, heavy controls and an inferior field of view being the main complaints.

Variants
L.F.G. D.III: in an attempt to improve the forward view the D.III introduced a conventional fuselage and wing centre-section struts; although representing an improvement over the D.II/IIa, it was inferior to the equivalent Albatros type and, in consequence, was built in only small numbers
L.F.G. D.V: single prototype, basically similar to D.III but with refined fuselage

Specification
L.F.G. Roland D.IIa
Type: single-seat fighter/scout
Powerplant: one 134-kW (180-hp) Argus As.III inline piston engine
Performance: maximum speed 170 km/h (106 mph); endurance 2 hours
Weights: empty 635 kg (1,400 lb);

maximum take-off 795 kg (1,753 lb)
Dimensions: span 8.90 m (29 ft 2½ in); length 6.95 m (22 ft 9½ in); height 2.95 m (9 ft 8¼ in); wing area 22.00 m² (236.81 sq ft)
Armament: two forward-firing 7.92-mm (0.31-in) LMG 08/15 machine-guns

L.V.G. B.I, B.II and B.III

Established at Johannisthal airfield, Berlin, some years before World War I, Luftverkehrs GmbH (L.V.G.) was involved with the operation of dirigibles before turning to the construction of heavier-than-air craft, then building Farman types under licence. The company's first original design was started in 1912, an unequal-span two-seat biplane with fixed tailskid landing gear, which was powered originally by a Mercedes D.I inline engine. Designated **L.V.G. B.I**, the type was built in small numbers, but with the outbreak of World War I, it soon entered production for the German military aviation service. Operational use showed the desirability of some improvements, these including the provision of a cut-out in the upper wing to improve the view of the pilot, seated in the

rear cockpit, and introduction of an 89-kW (120-hp) Mercedes D.II engine. Then designated **B.II**, this version was built by the parent company and under sub-contract by Otto-Werke GmbH and Luftfahrzeugbau Schütte-Lanz. Entering service in 1915 the B.II was used primarily for training, but was also deployed in unarmed reconnaissance and scouting roles. Final variant was the **B.III**, intended specifically for training, and incorporating some structural strengthening for this purpose.

Specification
L.V.G. B.I
Type: two-seat reconnaissance/scout/training aircraft
Powerplant: one 75-kW (100-hp) Mercedes D.I inline piston engine

Performance: maximum speed 105 km/h (65 mph); endurance 4 hours
Weights: empty 726 kg (1,600 lb); maximum take-off 1075 kg (2,370 lb)
Dimensions: span 12.12 m (39 ft 9¼ in); length 8.30 m (27 ft 2¾ in);

This L.V.G. B.II was one of those licence-built by Luftfahrzeugbau Schütte-Lanz.

height 2.95 m (9 ft 8¼ in); wing area 35.40 m² (381.05 sq ft)

L.V.G. C.I and C.II

When the German air force needed an armed reconnaissance aircraft in 1915, L.V.G. responded with the **L.V.G. C.I.** This was basically a strengthened version of the B.I/II, with the pilot's and observer's positions reversed, so that the rear cockpit could be given a ring mounting for a machine-gun. Because of the increase in weight the more powerful 112-kW (150-hp) Benz Bz.III engine was installed, but only a small number of C.Is was built before introduction of the **C.II,** the major production version. This differed by introducing structural refinements and the more powerful Mercedes D.III engine, the first of the type entering service in late 1915. It is believed that about 300 C.I/C.II aircraft were built for use in a variety of roles, including light bombing operations.

Variants
L.V.G. C.III: single experimental aircraft, which was basically a C.II with the observer and his machine-gun accommodated in the forward cockpit

C.IIs were the first aircraft to bomb London, when six bombs were dropped near Victoria station on 28 November 1915.

L.V.G. C.IV: basically a slightly enlarged version of the C.II powered by a 164-kW (220-hp) Mercedes D.IV engine; believed produced in small numbers

Specification
L.V.G. C.II
Type: two-seat reconnaissance/light bombing aircraft
Powerplant: one 119-kW (160-hp) Mercedes D.III inline piston engine
Performance: maximum speed 130 km/h (81 mph); service ceiling 4000 m (13,125 ft); endurance 4 hours
Weights: empty 845 kg (1,863 lb); maximum take-off 1405 kg (3,097 lb)
Dimensions: span 12.85 m (42 ft 2 in); length 8.10 m (26 ft 7 in); height 2.93 m (9 ft 7¼ in); wing area 37.60 m² (404.74 sq ft)

Armament: one 7.92-mm (0.31-in) Parabellum machine-gun and (late production aircraft) one forward-firing 7.92-mm (0.31-in) LMG 08/15 machine-gun plus up to 60 kg (132 lb) of light bombs

L.W.D. Junak

A primary trainer aircraft intended for military rather than flying club use, the **L.W.D. Junak-1** (cadet-1) was also of low-wing monoplane configuration, but accommodated instructor and pupil in separate tandem cockpits covered by a single continuous transparent canopy. First flown on 22 February 1948, the Junak-1 was powered by a 93-kW (125-hp) M11D engine, a licence-built version of the Russian Shvetsov M11 powerplant. The subsequent **Junak-2**, which was regarded as the production form of this trainer, had a 119-kW (160-hp) Polish-built M11FR engine, and the final **Junak-3** was generally similar except that it had tricycle landing gear instead of the tailwheel landing gear of the Junak-1 and Junak-2.

When fitted with a tricycle undercarriage the Junak 2 became the Junak 3.

L.W.S. 3 Mewa

Following proposals from Zbyslaw Ciolkosz, the L.W.S. team began in early 1936 detail design work on a two-seat reconnaissance aircraft. Only slightly larger in size than the earlier L.W.S. 2, it had a similar wing configuration, but a tail unit and landing gear of new design. Designated **L.W.S. 3 Mewa** (gull), this aircraft had been tailored to accept the Gnome-Rhône Mars radial engine for which licence construction rights were being negotiated by the Polish government. Three prototypes were built, the **L.W.S. 3/I** being the first to fly in the autumn of 1937. It was powered, as were all the prototypes, by a 533-kW (715-hp) Gnome-Rhône 14M-01 Mars engine. Most interesting of these was **L.W.S. 3/II**, which introduced vertical tail surfaces that could be lowered in flight to give the observer a clear field of fire for his machine-gun over the rear fuselage and tailplane. The **L.W.S. 3/III** was, in effect, the pre-production prototype, incorporating features to speed quantity manufacture. However, as a result of collective delays, and the need to import engines until Polish production of the powerplant was under way, it was not until the morning of 2 September 1939 that the first unarmed production **L.W.S. 3A Mewa A** was flown and, so far as is known, only two other examples became airborne.

Variants
Mewa B: proposed production version for the Bulgarian air force, identical to the Mewa A, except that it would have been powered by the 641-kW (860-hp) Fiat A.74RC radial engine
L.W.S. 7 Mewa 2: proposed advanced version of the Mewa for service with the Bulgarian air force; this would have had an increased-span wing of advanced design and was intended to be powered by the indigenous Polish 671-kW (900-hp) P.Z.L. Legwan radial engine

Specification
L.W.S. 3A Mewa A
Type: two-seat reconnaissance aircraft
Powerplant: one 544-kW (730-hp)

Gnome-Rhône 14M-05 Mars 5 radial engine
Performance: cruising speed 310 km/h (193 mph) at 3600 m (11,810 ft); service ceiling 8500 m (27,885 ft)
Weights: empty 1748 kg (3,854 lb); maximum take-off 2420 kg (5,335 lb)
Dimensions: span 13.45 m (44 ft

The Mewa was an agile design intended for reconnaissance and army co-operation.

1½ in); length 9.50 m (31 ft 2 in); height 2.65 m (8 ft 8¼ in); wing area 27.00 m² (290.64 sq ft)
Armament: (proposed) twin rear-firing machine-guns

Lake Buccaneer

In 1946 ex-Grumman employee David B. Thurston established the Colonial Aircraft Corporation at Sanford, Maine, to build a 2/3-seat amphibian inspired by the 1944 G-65 Tadpole design abandoned earlier by Grumman. The prototype, designated **Colonial XC-1**, and powered by a 93-kW (125-hp) Lycoming O-290-D engine, carried three passengers and flew for the first time on 17 July 1948. A cantilever shoulder-wing monoplane with a single-step all-metal hull housing a retractable tricycle landing gear, the design featured its single engine mounted on a pylon above the hull, driving a pusher propeller. The production version, the **C-1 Skimmer** (24 built), was fitted with a 112-kW (150-hp) O-320 engine, followed by eighteen 134-kW (180-hp) four-seat **C-2 Skimmer IV**s before the company was declared bankrupt in 1959. The **LA-4P** was a modified C-2 with a bigger wing and other improvements and the prototype (N261B), which flew in November 1959, was followed by two **LA-4A**s.
The Lake Aircraft Corporation, formed to acquire the assets in 1960, was itself taken over by Consolidated Aeronautics in 1962, and after changing hands several times more the company was acquired by Armand Rivard in September 1979. Since then the Lake LA-4 four-seat amphibian has progressed from the 134-kW (180-hp) LA-4-180 through the Rajay-turbosupercharged **LA-4T** to the 149-kW (200-hp) LA-4-200 Buccaneer, and sales of the LA-4 basic design had reached over 900 by 1982, when the stretched fuselage five/six-seat **LA-250 Renegade** was launched. Powered by a 186-kW (250-hp) Lycoming IO-540 engine, more than 100 have been built, including a single radar-equipped **Seawolf** military version able to carry bombs, rocket or machine-gun pods on underwing hardpoints. Also currently available are the **Turbo 270 Renegade** fitted with a turbocharged TIO-540 engine, and the **Special Edition Seafury** version which is extra corrosion-proofed for sea operation.

Specification
Lake LA-4-200 Buccaneer
Type: four-seat light amphibian
Powerplant: one 149-kW (200-hp) Avco Lycoming IO-360-B1A engine
Performance: maximum cruising speed 241 km/h (150 mph) at 2440 m

(8,000 ft); service ceiling 4480 m (14,700 ft); maximum range with reserves 1328 km (825 miles)
Weights: empty equipped 705 kg (1,555 lb); maximum take-off 1220 kg (2,690 lb)
Dimensions: span 11.58 m (38 ft 0 in); length 7.59 m (24 ft 11 in); height 2.84 m (9 ft 4 in); wing area 15.79 m² (170.0 sq ft)

Despite a totally different name the Lake Buccaneer is unmistakably an improved Skimmer, with more modern avionics and a bigger engine.

In prototype form, the Colonial Skimmer was an advanced three-seat amphibian that filled a niche in the market which went uncontested for 40 years.

Latécoère 15

In 1917 Pierre Latécoère established Forges et Ateliers de Construction Latécoère with an aircraft works at Toulouse-Montaudran. His experimental **Latécoère 1** two-seat fighter of 1918 was unsuccessful and the company concentrated for a period on licence manufacture of the Salmson 2 reconnaissance biplane, over 800 of which were built. In 1919 there appeared the **Laté 3** postal aircraft, followed by two examples of the **Laté 4**, a 10-passenger three-engined transport biplane. In 1922, the year in which the company name was changed to the Société Industrielle d'Aviation Latécoère, two prototypes were flown; these comprised the **Laté 8**, an ungainly six-passenger biplane with a single 224-kW (300-hp) Renault 12Fe engine, and the twin-engined **Laté 13**, also a transport. The **Laté 5** of 1924, a biplane powered by three 280-kW (375-hp) Lorraine 12Da engines was intended either as a four-man bomber or a 24-passenger transport, but was unsuccessful. The same year saw the test flight of the **Laté 6**, an advanced bomber escort fighter in the *multiplace de combat* category. An all-metal sesquiplane with considerable sweepback and powered by four 194-kW (260-hp) Salmson Z-9 engines, it also failed to gain a production contract.
The first successful Latécoère design was the **Laté 15**, the prototype being flown in 1924 and being followed by nine series aircraft. The Laté 15 had a parasol

wing spanning 18.00 m (59 ft 0¾ in) and a lower stub wing, landing gear with twin-wheel main units, and power provided by two 194-kW (260-hp) Lorraine 8-B1 engines. Accommodation comprised an open cockpit for the pilot, just forward of the wing leading edge, with a cabin for six passengers to the rear. The Laté 15s were operated on the Casablanca-Oran stage of the air routes flown by the Latécoère airline subsidiary. One Laté 15 was temporarily redesignated **Laté 15H** after float landing gear had been installed, but was soon restored to

its original landplane configuration. The initial success of the Laté 15 was short-lived as the aircraft was soon found to be underpowered. From the basic design was developed the **Laté 19** twin-engined two-seat night-bomber, which dispensed with the lower stub wings and had open defensive machine-gun positions situated in the nose and amidships. Two were built in 1926 for the Armée de l'Air, as was the sole **Laté 20**, an ambulance variant.

The Latécoère 15 abandoned its floats as unsuccessful and readopted a more conventional undercarriage.

Latécoère 21 and 32

The first flying-boat produced by Latécoère was the **Laté 21**, intended for Mediterranean postal and passenger routes. The prototype (F-ESDH), first flown in 1926, had a parasol wing with lower stub wings which acted as stabilising sponsons. Two 313-kW (420-hp) Gnome-Rhône Jupiter 9Ab radials were mounted in tandem on the wing, and the single-step hull terminated in a large single fin and rudder. Open side-by-side pilots' cockpits were located in line with the wing leading edge and there was cabin accommodation for seven passengers. Successful tests with the Laté 21 led to the construction in 1927 of five slightly modified **Laté 21bis** and a single **Laté 21ter**, with Farman 12We engines. The Laté 21bis spanned 22.00 m (72 ft 2¼ in), had a maximum take-off weight of 5730 kg (12,632 lb) and possessed a maximum speed of 172 km/h (107 mph). The **Laté 23** was an enlarged version of the Laté 21,

Seven Latécoère 21s were used by Aéropostale on its Marseilles-Algiers route, later replaced by the Laté 3.

powered by Farman engines and spanning 28.00 m (91 ft 10¼ in). With accommodation for eight passengers it had a maximum take-off weight of 7503 kg (16,541 lb), but the sole prototype broke up on take-off on 31 December 1927, killing its crew of four.

A strengthened and remodelled version of the Laté 23 was built as the **Laté 32**, the prototype (F-AILN) appearing in 1928 and being followed by seven production examples. They were flown mostly on the Marseilles-Algiers route, but were unreliable in service and involved in several accidents. At the end of 1931 all surviving Laté 32s were re-engined with the Hispano-Suiza 12Hbxr.

The **Laté 34.0** was a three-engined development which appeared in 1930,

the single example (F-AKDI) being powered by three 298-kW (400-hp) Hispano-Suiza 12Jb engines, two mounted as tractors and the third as a pusher. It was lost in a fatal crash caused by structural failure on 2 April 1930. These unfortunate and ill-fated early Latécoère machines often flew short of passengers and insufficient freight to make their use economical. The last of them to be designed for the Mediterranean service was the **Laté 501**. Flown for the first time from Biscarrosse base on 24 February 1932, it had three engines arranged as on the Laté 34.0. Intended for eight passengers as against 10 for the Laté 34.0, it was far stronger than its predecessors and mainly of metal construction. Despite improved flying qualities and performance of the Laté 501, no further examples were ordered by the French authorities.

Latécoère 28

Developed from the Latécoère 26, the **Latécoère 28.0** was a braced high-wing monoplane powered by a Renault 12Jbr engine. The enclosed cockpit accommodated a pilot and co-pilot/engineer, and the cabin was furnished for eight passengers. Seventeen Laté 28.0s were followed by 29 **Laté 28.1** aircraft with a 373-kW (500-hp) Hispano-Suiza 12Hbxr engine. A number of Laté 28.0s were converted subsequently to Laté 28.1 standard.

The sole **Laté 28.2** was a mail carrier and established several payload/speed world records in 1931. The first of five **Laté 28.3** mail carriers was flown by the celebrated Jean Mermoz on 11/12 April 1930 to achieve a world closed-circuit distance record for seaplanes of 4308.34 km (2,677.085 miles).

The Latécoère 28 was a successful aircraft, holding several records and performing reliably as a mail carrier. This Latécoère 28.1 has a Hispano-Suiza engine.

The remaining Laté 28.3s were used on Mediterranean routes and charter services. The **Laté 28.1/H** was a wheel landing gear version of the Laté 28.3. Two one-off aircraft were the **Laté 28.3-I**, a passenger version of the Laté 28.3, and the **Laté 28.4-I**, also developed from the Laté 28.3 but powered by a Gnome-Rhône 14Kbr radial engine of 522 kW (700 hp). In 1930 there appeared the **Laté 28.5**, structurally strengthened and powered by a 485-kW (650-hp) Hispano-Suiza 12Nbr, followed by three **Laté 28.6** aircraft, also Hispano-powered and built for Venezuela, which had already purchased two Laté 28.1s.

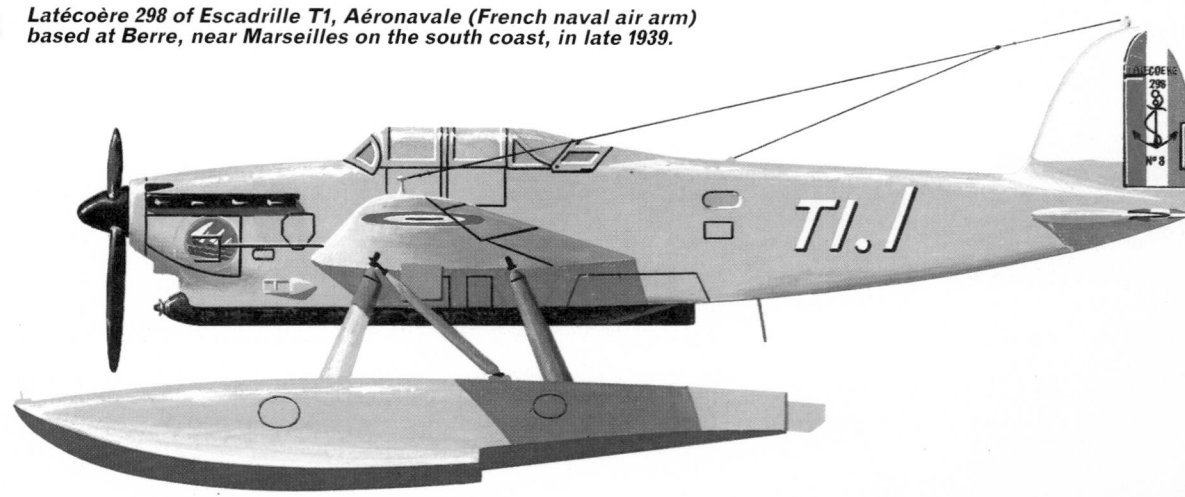

Specification
Latécoère 28.0
Type: eight-passenger monoplane
Powerplant: one 373-kW (500-hp) Renault 12Jb V-12 piston engine
Performance: maximum speed 223 km/h (139 mph); service ceiling 5200 m (17,060 ft); range 950 km (590

miles)
Weights: empty equipped 2173 kg (4,790 lb); maximum take-off 3856 kg (8,501 lb)
Dimensions: span 19.25 m (63 ft 1¾ in); length 13.64 m (44 ft 9 in); height 3.58 m (11 ft 9 in); wing area 48.60 m² (523.14 sq ft)

Latécoère 298

The **Latécoère 298.01** was flown for the first time on 8 May 1936. An all-metal single-engined mid-wing monoplane with a crew of three, it had sharply tapering wings and twin floats. The torpedo was carried semi-recessed in the underside of the fuselage and mounted on a ventral crutch. Service testing resulted in production orders for a total of 177 Laté 298s. They differed mainly in having a crew canopy of entirely new design and comprised 29 **Laté 298A** aircraft delivered from October 1938 onwards, followed by 42 **Laté 298B** aircraft with dual controls and folding wings, and finally 106 **Laté 298D** machines with dual controls and fixed wings. One Laté 298D was converted with a ventral

Latécoère 298 of Escadrille T1, Aéronavale (French naval air arm) based at Berre, near Marseilles on the south coast, in late 1939.

observation gondola, under the designation **Laté 298E**, but was considered unsatisfactory.

Four French navy *escadrilles* were equipped with the Laté 298 in September 1939, namely HB1 and HB2 (Laté 298Bs with folding wings) aboard the seaplane-carrier *Commandant Teste*, T1 at Berre and T2 at Cherbourg. Engaged initially on coastal patrols, the Laté 298s were pressed into service for ground-attack and dive-bombing missions when

the Germans launched their *Blitzkrieg* on France. Many of the type remained in service with the Vichy regime, which ordered 30 **Laté 298F** aircraft from the Breguet company for use in the overseas empire; these aircraft were basically similar to the Laté 298D but without dual controls. Under Free French control, Laté 298 Escadrille 3.S operated on Lake Constance in Germany on policing duties until disbanded at the end of January 1946.

Specification
Latécoère 298D
Type: three-seat torpedo-bomber reconnaissance seaplane
Powerplant: one 656-kW (880-hp) Hispano-Suiza 12Ycrs-1 V-12 piston engine
Performance: maximum speed 287 km/h (178 mph); service ceiling 5100 m (16,730 ft); range 1000 km (621 miles)
Weights: empty equipped 3070 kg

(6,768 lb); maximum take-off 4600 kg (10,141 lb)
Dimensions: span 15.50 m (50 ft 10¼ in); length 12.56 m (41 ft 2½ in); height 5.25 m (17 ft 2¾ in); wing area 31.60 m² (340.15 sq ft)
Armament: two fixed forward-firing and one manually-aimed 7.5-mm (0.295-in) Darne machine-guns, plus one 670-kg (1,477-lb) Type DA torpedo, or up to 500 kg (1,102 lb) of bombs, or three depth charges, or nine flares

Latécoère 521, 522 and 523

The giant **Latécoère 521** flying-boat (F-NORD), named *Lieutenant de Vaisseau Paris*, was built to order as a North Atlantic passenger carrier. It superseded the **Laté 520** four-engined project and was powered by six 485-kW (650-hp) Hispano-Suiza 12Ybrs-2 V-12 engines nacelle-mounted beneath the parasol monoplane wing. Short span stub wings were carried on each side of the hull, being strut-braced to the upper wing and incorporating a stabilising float at each tip. On the high-mounted wing the outboard engines were mounted singly and the inner units in tandem pairs driving tractor and pusher propellers.

The lower section of the two-step hull had a bow mooring station, behind which were the radio-navigation compartment, a 20-passenger saloon, six de luxe cabins, a further passenger compartment seating 26, a kitchen, and finally a baggage hold. The upper deck contained the control cabin, engineer's compartment, a cabin for 18 passengers and a second baggage hold.

After its initial flight on 10 January 1935, the Laté 521 made a number of demonstration flights before setting out in December 1935 for Dakar, West Africa, then Natal, Brazil, and finally the French West Indies. It reached Pensacola in Florida on 13 January 1936, where, caught in a hurricane, it was sunk

Built expressly for the proposed passenger routes over the North Atlantic, the Latécoère 521 was a monster of its time, with three decks of accommodation.

at its moorings. Salvaged and returned to France, the 'boat was rebuilt for the Air France Transatlantique company, flying again in June 1937. It later made a nonstop flight to Brazil, and then a staged flight across the North Atlantic, the return flight in September 1937 being made non-stop. With more powerful engines, four staged flights to New York and back were made between May and July 1939. Then taken over by the French navy and attached to Escadrille E.6, the Laté 521 was used for patrols over the North Atlantic. Stranded at Port Lyautey on the Atlantic coast of Morocco in June 1940, it was returned eventually to Berre in southern France, where it was broken up in August 1944. The Laté 521 spanned 49.31 m (161 ft 9¼ in), had a maximum take-off weight of 32180 kg (70,945 lb) and could attain a maximum speed of 255 km/h (158 mph).

The success of the Laté 521 led to orders for three civil **Laté 522** and three navalised **Laté 523** aircraft. In the event only one Laté 522 (*Ville de Saint Pierre*) was built. Tested in April 1939, it differed considerably from the Laté 521, with its

accommodation re-arranged, the upper hull redesigned, maximum take-off weight increased, and with 686-kW (920-hp) Hispano-Suiza 12Y-36/37s engines. Before the outbreak of war, two double North Atlantic crossings were achieved and then the aircraft was militarised and allocated to patrol Escadrille E.6 at Lanvéoc-Poulmic, near Brest. Damaged on a liaison flight to French Somaliland in February 1941, the Laté 522 eventually returned to France, where it was demolished in August 1944.

The three Laté 523s were delivered to the Escadrille E.6 (later 6.E), the first example (*Altair*) having flown initially on 21 October 1938. Resembling the Laté 522, each carried a crew of 14 and was armed with five 7.5-mm (0.295-in) Darne machine-guns and up to 1350 kg (2,976 lb) of bombs. Used on Atlantic patrol, only one of the Laté 523s survived the German invasion of June 1940 and after repairs in Vichy France was sent to scadrille 4.E at Dakar, where it was abandoned for lack of spares in August 1942.

Latécoère 631

A remarkable design for its time, the **Latécoère 631** was intended to carry 46 passengers on services across the South Atlantic. Like the Laté 521 it had six engines, but all were mounted individually at the leading edge of the highset monoplane wing. The two-step hull had excellent lines with no more excrescences, the stabilising floats retracted into the outer engine nacelles, and the tail unit incorporated twin fins and rudders. Due to wartime conditions, construction of the **Laté 631.01** prototype took four years, the aircraft being flown for the first time on 4 November 1942, and three more aircraft ordered in 1942 were not flown until March 1945, late

1946 and May 1947 respectively. Of seven additional Laté 631s ordered in 1944 by the Vichy regime, six were completed between September 1947 and October 1949.

Laté 631.01 flight tests were interrupted by the German occupation of southern France in 1943. After they were resumed, the machine was confiscated and flown to Friedrichshafen in Germany on 20 January 1944, where it was destroyed in an air attack the following day, along with the other French giants, the Potez-CAMS 141 and Sud-Est SE.200.

The other Laté 631s went into service with Air France from 1947 and then were sold to various lesser companies, with which they operated mainly as freight carriers. The second machine remained

The Latécoère 631 was truly a remarkable design for 1937, but its development was halted by the outbreak of war. It entered service only after the end of hostilities, by which time the era of the large flying-boat was rapidly drawing to a close. The second prototype (illustrated) flew in March 1945 but, sadly, it was broken up in 1956.

in use until broken up in 1956, while the third, sixth, seventh and eighth were lost in accidents between March 1950 and

September 1955. After the loss of the eighth aircraft, surviving aircraft were scrapped.

Lavochkin LaGG-3

LaGG-3 of an unidentified V-VS (Soviet air force) unit on the Ukranian front during 1942.

Involved in aviation design from his student days, S. A. Lavochkin joined the Soviet Union's TsKB (Central Design Bureau) and gained valuable experience as a member of several design teams before joining with V. P. Gorbunov and M. I. Gudkov in 1938 to start the design of a new single-seat fighter. Designated initially **I-22** but later redesignated **LaGG-1** (Lavochkin, Gorbunov and Gudkov), the prototype was flown for the first time on 30 March 1940. Early flight tests proved somewhat disappointing, and modifications included the installa-

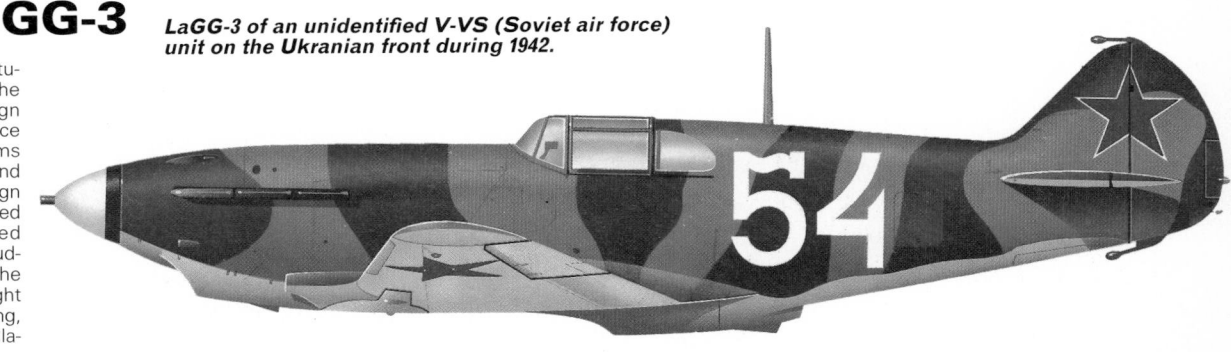

tion of a higher-rated and supercharged version of the Klimov M-105 engine that powered this prototype. Simultaneously, the fuel capacity was increased, and a three-bladed propeller and wing leading-edge slats introduced. In this form the I-22 was redesignated **I-301** and was ordered into production as the **LaGG-3**. A cantilever low-wing monoplane of clean lines, with retractable tailwheel landing gear, it was unique among fighter aircraft of its period by being of all-wood construction, except for metal-frame fabric-covered control surfaces; the fuselage, tail unit and wings had a wooden basic structure to which diagonal strips of plywood were bonded by phenol-formaldehyde resin.

Used extensively in the early stages of fighting against the invading Germans, the LaGG-3 acquitted itself reasonably well, primarily because the form of structure that had been adopted proved to be robust in service use and resistant to combat damage, and the type was also used in action in Finland. More than 6,500 LaGG-3s are believed to have been built, late versions with a retractable tailwheel and provision to carry drop-tanks. Armament varied considerably, but a typical installation comprised a 20-mm cannon firing through the propeller hub, two 12.7-mm (0.5-in) machine-guns, and underwing racks for rockets or light bombs.

Specification
Lavochkin LaGG-3
Type: single-seat fighter
Powerplant: one 925-kW (1,240-hp) Klimov M-105PF V-12 piston engine
Performance: maximum speed 560 km/h (348 mph) at 5000 m (16,405 ft); service ceiling 9600 m (31,495 ft); range 650 km (404 miles)
Weights: empty 2620 kg (5,776 lb); maximum take-off 3280 kg (7,231 lb)
Dimensions: span 9.80 m (32 ft 1¾ in); length 8.90 m (29 ft 2½ in); wing area 17.50 m² (188.37 sq ft)
Armament: see text

Lavochkin La-5 and La-7

The LaGG-3 had proved a good stop-gap fighter, considered to be valuable particularly because it was constructed from plentiful wood rather than more scarce light alloys. There was no doubt, however, that it was the poorest performer of its contemporary generation of fighters. In 1941 Lavochkin's design team began urgent development of the LaGG-3 to provide improved performance, and the first step was the installation of a Shvetsov M-82 radial engine. This was found to give not only an increase of some 6 per cent in maximum speed, but also improved performance at higher altitudes. In May 1942 production was switched to this engine installation as an interim stage of development, the resulting aircraft designated **Lavochkin LaGG-5**. Within only a few weeks it was superseded by the **La-5**, with a cut-down rear fuselage to allow installation of a cockpit canopy giving an all-round view, but still bad inadequate performance to meet the Messerschmitt Bf 109G-2 on equal terms. Efforts were then made to reduce weight and drag, and to provide still more power, leading to the **La-5FN**. This introduced metal wing spars and reduced fuel capacity for weight saving, a higher-rated version of the Shvetsov engine, and wing leading-edge slats to improve combat manoeuvrability.

Built in numbers approximating 10,000, the La-5FN was first seen in action during the Battle of Stalingrad in late 1942. Refined progressively, the type remained in service for the remainder of World War II, being used primarily as a fighter/fighter-bomber; a two-seat trainer version was also built under the designation **La-5UTI**. Further development to provide a high-altitude interceptor (and trainer) variant resulted in the **La-7** (and **La-7UTI**) retaining the same powerplant, but with improved performance achieved by further aerodynamic refinement and weight saving. La-7/-7UTI production exceeded 5,500 and these were the last of the Lavochkin series-built aircraft to see operational service in World War II.

La-5FN of a Czech operational training unit, based at Malacky in Slovakia, during 1945-46.

Variants
La-7R: two conversions of La-7s with booster rocket in the rear fuselage; experimental only
La-7TK: conversion of one La-7 with two TK-3 turbochargers installed to give improved high-altitude performance; experimental only
La-126: experimental version with revised wings and a PVRD-430 auxiliary ramjet engine mounted beneath each wing

Specification
Lavochkin La-7
Type: interceptor fighter
Powerplant: one 1380-kW (1,850-hp) Shvetsov M-82FN (ASh-82FN) radial piston engine
Performance: maximum speed 665 km/h (413 mph); service ceiling 10800 m (35,435 ft); range 635 km (395 miles)
Weights: empty 2638 kg (5,816 lb); maximum take-off 3400 kg (7,496 lb)
Dimensions: span 9.80 m (32 ft 1¾ in); length 8.60 m (28 ft 2½ in); wing area 17.50 m² (188.37 sq ft)
Armament: two or three Beresin B-20 20-mm cannon, plus provision for up to 200 kg (441 lb) of bombs on underwing racks

Lavochkin La-9 and La-11

Continuing development and refinement of the LaGG-3/La-5/La-7 family brought a revised version of the La-7 which differed sufficiently to be allocated the designation **Lavochkin La-9**. Retaining a Shvetsov radial engine powerplant, the La-9 benefitted from further weight reduction (effected by increasing proportions of light alloy in relation to wood in the structure) while the wings and tailplane gained square-cut tips, and the vertical tail surfaces were increased in height. The fuselage incorporated an improved cockpit, but a deeper aft fuselage somewhat restricted the pilot's rear view. The La-9's heavy armament comprised four 23-mm forward-firing cannon. In addition to the basic La-9, an **La-9UTI** two-seat trainer was built, and these aircraft first entered service in late 1944. Although not used operationally during World War II, La-9s served with most Soviet first-line fighter units in the immediate post-war years and many were supplied to the nation's allies, including China. A long-range escort version of the La-9 was also developed under the designation **La-11**, and this differed by being of all-metal construction, and having increased fuel capacity and only three 23-mm cannon. It could be identified easily, as the underfuselage intake for the oil cooler on the La-9 had been replaced by an intake duct within the engine cowling. Used extensively by the North Korean air force during the Korean War, the La-11 was the last piston-engined fighter to be designed by Lavochkin, and continued in service with Communist forces into the 1960s.

Specification
Lavochkin La-11
Type: single-seat escort fighter
Powerplant: one 1394-kW (1,870-hp) Shvetsov ASh-82FNV radial piston
Performance: maximum speed 690 km/h (429 mph) at 6200 m (20,340 ft); service ceiling 10250 m (33,630 ft); range 750 km (466 miles)
Weight: maximum take-off 3995 kg (8,807 lb)
Dimensions: span 9.95 m (32 ft 7¾ in); length 8.60 m (28 ft 2½ in); wing area 17.70 m² (190.53 sq ft)
Armament: three 23-mm cannon

A long-range version of the La-9, the Lavovchkin La-11 was relatively lightly armed with only three 23-mm cannon to permit the carriage of an additional 275 litres (50 Imp gal) of fuel.

The Lavochkin La-9 embodied all the lessons learned with the La series, featuring improved armament, avionics and aerodynamics.

Let L-200 Morava
to
Lioré-et-Olivier 20

Let L-200 Morava

On 8 April 1957 Let flew the prototype of a twin-engined four/five-seat business aircraft designed by Ladislav Smrcek. Designated **Let L-200 Morava**, the machine was a cantilever low-wing monoplane with permanently-attached wingtip fuel tanks and had a tail unit incorporating twin endplate fins and rudders. Landing gear was of retractable tricycle type, and power for the prototype and L-200 series aircraft was provided by two 119-kW (160-hp) Walter Minor 6-III inline engines. The original production model was superseded first by the generally similar **L-200A**, with more powerful Walter M 337 engines and, subsequently, by the final production version, the **L-200D**, which was introduced in mid-1962. This differed by in-

Built in significant numbers, the Morava was also exported in quantity, which was unusual for an Eastern Bloc light aircraft.

corporating improved systems, strengthened landing gear, and three-bladed constant-speed propellers. When production ended in 1968 more than 1,000 had been built, many being supplied to Aeroflot for this airline's operations in the Moscow, North and Ukrainian Directorate areas. The type was also built under licence in Yugoslavia.

Variant
L-300: a turboprop-powered version of the Morava was planned under this designation but was not manufactured

Specification
Let L-200D Morava
Type: twin-engined light business aircraft
Powerplant: two 157-kW (210-hp) Walter M337 inline piston engines
Performance: maximum cruising speed 285 km/h (177 mph); service

ceiling 6200 m (20,340 ft); range 1800 km (1,118 miles)
Weights: empty 1360 kg (2,998 lb); maximum take-off 2000 kg (4,409 lb)
Dimensions: span 12.30 m (40 ft 4¼ in); length 8.60 m (28 ft 2½ in); height 2.25 m (7 ft 4½ in); wing area 17.30 m² (186.22 sq ft)

Let L-410 Turbolet

The **Let L-410 Turbolet** twin-engined light transport was designed for use on local service and feeder operations, including those from grass airfields. The first prototype (OK-YKE) made its maiden flight on 16 April 1969, powered by two 533-ekW (715-eshp) United (later Pratt & Whitney) Aircraft of Canada PT6A-27 turboprops driving three-bladed propellers. Excessive airframe vibration and cabin noise levels were overcome with the third prototype (of four) which introduced four-bladed propellers. The Canadian engine was retained for the 27 **L-410A** aircraft built during 1971-74, and for the **L-410AF**, an aerial survey version with a glazed nose, one example of which was supplied to Hungary during 1974. The prototype **L-410M**, powered by 548-ekW (735-eshp) Walter M 601A turboprops, was flown during 1973 and the first of 109 production aircraft was delivered in 1976.

The improved **L-410UVP** first flew in November 1977. This featured a stretched fuselage, longer span wings, increased area fin and rudder, and a larger door. Powered by M-601B engines, and able to carry 15 passengers, production ended in 1985 after 495

Let L-410UVP of Aeroflot, which served in large numbers on the Soviet carrier's short-haul routes.

had been built, and it was replaced on the production lines by the further improved and current **L-410UVP-E**. With a revised interior capable of accommodating 19 passengers and two crew, deliveries began in 1986 and around 370 had been built by mid-1991. Customers include Aeroflot, together with the air forces of Czechoslovakia, Bulgaria, Hungary, Poland and former East Germany, and civil sales have been claimed in Sweden and Denmark. The Walter

M-601E-powered L-410UVP-E has a strengthened wing fitted with 200-litre (44-Imp gal) tiptanks giving increased range. Total production of the L-410 series reached 1,000 by the end of 1990, of which 300 were for military use.

Specification
Let L-410UVP
Type: utility light transport
Powerplant: two 544-ekW (730-eshp) Walter M 601B turboprops

Performance: maximum cruising speed 365 km/h (227 mph) at 3000 m (9,845 ft); altitude 6000 m (19,685 ft); range with maximum payload and reserves 390 km (242 miles)
Weights: empty equipped 3800 kg (8,378 lb); maximum take-off 5800 kg (12,787 lb)
Dimensions: span 19.48 m (63 ft 10¾ in); length 14.47 m (47 ft 5¾ in); height 5.83 m (19 ft 1½ in); wing area 35.18 m² (378.69 sq ft)

Let L-610

Studies began in 1983 of a 40-seat pressurised development of the L-410 feederliner powered by two newly developed Walter M-602 turboprop engines driving five-bladed 'quiet' propellers. Prototype construction of this **L-610** began early in 1988 and the first of three flying prototypes (OK-130) was rolled out in November. The first flight took place on 28 December 1988, and the type was exhibited at the Paris air show in June 1989. The first of 600 aircraft for Aeroflot was shown at the Paris air show in June 1991, and others are on order for CSA. Current activities centre around the completion of the flight test programme and achieving certification. To improve sales prospects to the West, one of the prototypes (re-designated **L-610G**) is being re-engined with 1305-kW (1,750-

With the Let 610 commuter aircraft, the Czech manufacturer hoped to win large numbers of orders from Aeroflot, which failed to materialise.

shp) General Electric CT7-9Ds, and was due to fly before the end of 1991, with certification and first deliveries targetted for the end of 1992. Let has also announced plans to stretch the L-610 into a 50-55 seater, probably using GE CT7 or PW100 engines.

Specification
Let L-610
Type: 40-seat turboprop regional airliner
Powerplant: two 1358-ekW (1,822-eshp) Walter M-602 turboprops
Performance: cruising speed 408 km/h (253 mph); maximum speed 490 km/h (304 mph); ceiling 10250 m

(33,630 ft); range with maximum payload 870 km (540 miles)
Weights: empty 9000 kg (19,841 lb); maximum take-off 14500 kg (31,970 lb)

Dimensions: span 25.60 m (84 ft); length 21.41 m (70 ft 3 in); height 7.60 m (24 ft 11 in); wing area 56.0 m² (602.8 sq ft)

Let M1D Sokol, M2 Skaut and M3 Bonzo

Let became responsible for continued production of these three aircraft types which had been developed initially under the overall control of Ceskoslovenske Zavody Letecke. The **M1D Sokol** was a three-seat utility cabin monoplane which, with the addition of optional dual controls, was suitable for use as a trainer. A cantilever low-wing monoplane with fixed tailwheel landing gear, it was available optionally with floats as the **M1E**, and power for both versions was provided by a 78-kW (105-hp) Walter Minor 4-III inline engine. The **M2 Skaut** was a lighter-weight side-by-side two-seat trainer with dual controls as standard. It, too, was of low-wing monoplane configuration, but had fixed tricycle landing gear and was powered by a

Designed during the German occupation of Czechoslovakia, the Let M1 Sokol (Falcon) was produced after the war in several versions, including the M1A two-seater, the M1C three-seater (illustrated) and the M1E twin-float seaplane.

56-kW (75-hp) Praga D flat-four engine. Largest of the trio was the four-seat **M3 Bonzo**, of similar configuration to the M1 Sokol but introducing a more powerful Walter Minor 6-III inline engine and retractable tricycle landing gear.

Specification
Let M3 Bonzo
Type: four-seat cabin monoplane

Powerplant: one 119-kW (160-hp) Walter Minor 6-III inline piston engine **Performance:** cruising speed 240 km/h (149 mph); service ceiling 5000 m (16,405 ft); range 1000 km (621 miles)

Weights: empty 580 kg (1,279 lb); maximum take-off 1100 kg (2,425 lb) **Dimensions:** span 10.60 m (34 ft 9¼ in); length 7.75 m (25 ft 5 in); height 2.25 m (7 ft 4½ in); wing area 15.90 m² (171.15 sq ft)

Let Z-37 Čmelák

Design of the **Let Z-37 Čmelák** (bumblebee) agricultural aircraft began in Czechoslovakia in 1961, and the **XZ-37** prototype flew for the first time on 29 March 1963. A cantilever low-wing monoplane of basically metal construction, but with some fabric covering, it had a fixed tailwheel landing gear and accommodated the pilot in an enclosed cockpit forward of the chemical hopper. Behind the hopper was a rudimentary seat used to ferry a loader or mechanic, and the Čmelák could be used during the winter months for mail or cargo transport using optional ski landing gear. The aircraft could also be equipped for glider towing. Production aircraft had the 235-kW (315-hp) Avia M 462RF radial engine, but at least one aircraft was flown in 1968 with a 224-kW (300-hp) Continental engine. The production Čmelák, designated **Z-37A**, introduced a number of refinements, including structural strengthening and more extensive use of non-corrosive materials, together with some stainless steel in the most critical areas.
When production of the Z-37A ended

in the mid-1970s, around 700 of all versions had been built, including 27 **Z-37A-2 Sparka** two-seat agricultural pilot trainers. In addition to national use, Čmeláks were exported to Bulgaria, Finland, East Germany, Hungary, India, Iraq, Poland, Yugoslavia and the UK.
A turbine-engined version, the **XZ-37T Agro-Turbo** (OK-146), powered by a 515-kW (691-shp) Walter M-601B turboprop, made its first flight on 6 September 1981. Development of a lower-powered model fitted with a 365-kW (490-shp) M-601Z engine began in 1982, this variant entering production as the single-seat **Z-37T** (first flight by OK-072 on 12 July 1983) and the two-seat **Z-37T-2** ag-pilot trainer. Early aircraft were delivered to Slov-Air in 1985 and by 1989 estimates claimed that about 30 aircraft had been built. Current versions (produced by Zlin) are designated **Z-137T**.

Specification
Let Z-37T Agro-Turbo
Type: two-seat agricultural aircraft

Let Z-37 Čmelák

Powerplant: one 365-kW (490-shp) thrust Walter M-601Z turboprop **Performance:** working speed 145 km/h (90 mph); cruising speed 190 km/h (118 mph); maximum speed 218 km/h (135 mph); range 350 km (217 miles)

Weights: empty 1250 kg (2,756 lb); maximum payload 1000 kg (1,984 lb); maximum take-off 2525 kg (5,566 lb) **Dimensions:** span 13.63 m (44 ft 8 in); length 10.46 m (34 ft 4 in); height 3.50 m (11 ft 6 in); wing area 26.69 m² (287.3 sq ft)

Letov Š 1 and Š 2

Alois Šmolik, who had formerly designed for the Austrian government, was established in 1919 at the newly formed Czechoslovak Military Air Arsenal, whose design and manufacturing facilities were taken over by Vojenská továrna na letadla Letov in 1920.
Šmolik's first design was the **Letov ŠH 1** two-seat unequal-span reconnaissance biplane. In total, 28 ŠH 1 with 172-kW (230-hp) Hiero L engines and 64 **ŠM 1** aircraft with 194-kW (260-hp) Maybach Mb.IVa engines were built from 1920 onwards for the Czech air arm. At

A wholly unexceptional biplane, the Letov Š 1 was remarkable only as the first aircraft to be completely designed and built in Czechoslovakia.

some stage the ŠH 1 was redesignated **Š1** and the ŠM 1 became the **Š 2**. Armament comprised three 7.7-mm (0.303-in) machine-guns and up to 120 kg (265 lb) of bombs. The Š1 spanned 13.23 m (43 ft 4¾ in), and the Š2 slightly less. Maximum take-off weight of the Š1 was 1375 kg (3,031 lb) and maximum speed

194 km/h (120 mph). The **Šm A 1** was a commercial adaptation with a glazed canopy over the rear cockpit for one or two passengers.

Letov Š 18, Š 118, Š 218

The prototype **Letov Š 18** appeared in 1925, a lightly-built two-seat trainer biplane intended as a replacement for the variety of foreign types still in Czech service at that time. Powered by a 45-kW (60-hp) Walter NZ 60 radial engine, the Š 18 could attain a maximum speed of 140 km/h (87 mph), had a maximum take-off weight of 550 kg (1,213 lb), and a wing span of 10.00 m (32 ft 9¾ in). Proving manoeuvrable and easy to maintain, the Š18 was built in some numbers for the air arm, and 10 were exported to Bulgaria.
In 1926 the **Š 118** was produced with a 63-kW (85-hp) Walter NZ 85 engine. It

Of conventional structure and layout and powered by a five-cylinder radial engine, the Š 18 was a popular sports plane.

proved very popular, with sales to private owners and civil aero clubs following on a large scale. Others were used by the Military Central Flying School (the VLU). Soon afterwards Letov developed the **Š 218**, which had a metal-tube fuselage instead of the previous wooden structure and was powered by an 89-kW (120-hp) Walter NZ 120 engine. Ten were exported to Finland in 1930-31, where 29 were sub-

sequently built under licence. Other Š 218s went to civil aero clubs and the Czech air arm. Most of the Finnish-built aircraft had a 112-kW (150-hp) Bramo 14 radial engine, giving a maximum speed of 154 km/h (96 mph).

Letov Š 231

In 1933 Letov tested two prototypes of the **Š 231** single-seat fighter, an unequal-span biplane with a basic structure of metal with fabric covering. They were much refined by comparison with the earlier Š 31 and Š 131 fighters, with a fuselage that was of almost circular cross-section, and the 418-kW (560-hp) Bristol Mercury IV S2 radial engine was enclosed in a Townend ring. The first prototype had four CZ Model 28 7.92-mm (0.31-in) machine-guns mounted in pairs in the upper wing, while the second had them in the lower wing. Wing span was 10.06 m (33 ft 0 in), maximum take-off weight 1770 kg (3,902 lb) and maximum speed 348 km/h (216 mph).

Unusually for a fighter of the early 1930s, the Letov Š 231 had an armament of four fixed machine-guns. In the second prototype (illustrated) they were located in pairs in the lower wings with the muzzles projecting ahead of the leading edge.

A production series of 25 aircraft followed, and in late 1936 seven of these aircraft were delivered to Bilbao where they operated with Spanish Republican forces in the Spanish Civil War. They were not assembled accurately so that although two were destroyed by enemy action, the remainder were lost in accidents. Twelve more Š 231s arrived at Cartagena in the south of Spain, equipping Escuadrilla 2, Grupo 71, of the Republican air arm, but little is known of their exploits. Most survived until February 1939, when they were destroyed to prevent them from falling into Nationalist hands.

Letov Š 328

Developed from the Š 228, the **Letov Š 328** was intended for Finland, but when the order was lost this aircraft attracted the interest of the Czech authorities. So, although the prototype had flown in 1932, series production for the Czechoslovak air arm did not begin until 1934. An unequal-span biplane basically of metal construction and, but for sheet metal fuselage decking, entirely fabric-covered, the Š 328 had its two-man crew in tandem open cockpits, the observer occupying an unusually roomy position with lateral and floor observation panels. By 1935 Š 328s were entering service with the Czech air regiments as observation/reconnaissance aircraft, with light bombing as a secondary role. In addition, four twin-float **Š 328V** aircraft were built for service at the Czechoslovak seaplane school on Yugoslavia's Adriatic coast.

Continuing orders kept the Š 328 in production at the Letov Letňany factory for five years, some aircraft being constructed during the German occupation. The total built is recorded as 412, but there may have been more. The German occupying power used some of the type in flying training schools, and from 1942 onwards as night intruders on the Eastern Front. Other examples were passed in 1939 to the puppet Slovak regime, which employed them in the Polish campaign in September 1939, and in the

Letov Š 328 operated by the Slovak Insurgent Air Force from Tri Duby airfield in September 1944.

Ukraine during the invasion of the Soviet Union, largely against partisan units. Bulgaria received 62 Š 328s, deploying a number of them on patrols over the Black Sea. Finally, three Slovak Š 328s flew with the patriots engaged in the National Uprising, used on reconnaissance patrols from Tri Druby airfield, in the foothills of the Carpathians, during August-October 1944.

The **Š 428** was a version of the S 328 with a V-12 485-kW (650-hp) Avia Vr-36 engine and fixed armament increased to four machine-guns, but only one prototype was built. The **Š 528** of 1935 was powered by a 597-kW (800-hp) Walter Krsd radial engine, the Gnome-Rhône Mistral Major built under licence, providing a maximum speed of 330 km/h (205 mph). Six Š 528s were built for the Czech air police.

Specification
Letov Š 328
Type: two-seat reconnaissance/observation aircraft
Powerplant: one Walter-built 474-kW (635-hp) Bristol Pegasus II-M2 radial piston engine
Performance: maximum speed 280 km/h (174 mph); service ceiling 7200 m (23,620 ft); range 700 km (435 miles)
Weights: empty equipped 1680 kg (3,704 lb); maximum take-off 2640 kg (5,820 lb)
Dimensions: span 13.71 m (44 ft 11¾ in); length 10.36 m (33 ft 11¾ in); height 3.40 m (11 ft 2 in); wing area 39.40 m² (424.11 sq ft)
Armament: two fixed wing-mounted 7.92-mm (0.31-in) machine-guns and two similar guns on a Skoda pivot mounting over observer's cockpit, plus up to 500 kg (1,102 lb) of bombs

Levasseur PL 2

Pierre Levasseur was just 20 years of age in 1910 when he opened his first factory in Paris. He concentrated on the development of aircraft propellers before building in 1913 two revolutionary prototypes, the Landeroin-Robert monoplane and the Pouche and Primard 'Tubavion'.

His first original design was the **Levasseur PL 1**, a three-seat tourer (TO.3) biplane with the fuselage strut-mounted between the wings; this flew in April 1921, but no production examples resulted. The **PL 2.01** single-seat torpedo-bomber (AT.1) followed, the first of a series of Levasseur designs for naval aviation. An equal-span biplane inspired by Blackburn aircraft, it was flown for the first time in November 1922. The **PL 2.02** introduced a four-bladed propeller and other powerplant improvements, being followed by nine series aircraft in 1923; these had inflatable ballonets and jettisonable landing gear for use in an emergency put-down at sea. In 1926 these aircraft, forming Escadrille 7B2, entered service aboard the French carrier *Béarn*, and the last PL 2s were scrapped in 1932. Series aircraft, which spanned 15.15 m (49 ft 8½ in), were powered by the 433-kW (580-hp) Renault 12Ma engine. Maximum take-off weight was 3653 kg (8,053 lb) and maximum speed 180 km/h (112 mph). Armament comprised a 450-kg (992-lb) torpedo, or an equivalent weight in bombs, plus a single 7.7-mm (0.303-in) machine-gun.

Levasseur PL 7

After the unsuccessful **PL 6** two-seat fighter biplane, Levasseur's only design for the French army, the company turned to the task of providing a replacement torpedo-bomber for the PL 2. The prototype **Levasseur PL 7** which followed was a development of the PL 4, a two-seat sesquiplane spanning 18.00 m (59 ft 0¾ in) which was burdened by a complexity of wing bracing struts. Powered initially by a 410-kW (550-hp) Farman 12We engine, the **PL 7.01** was flown subsequently with both Hispano-Suiza and Renault powerplants; the wing struts were redesigned, the structure simplified, and the fin modified. Test flying in this revised form was resumed in 1928, two years after the prototype had first flown.

A series of 15 aircraft was ordered in 1929. Nine were delivered with the 18-m wing but the French admiralty, uncertain

The PL 7 torpedo-bomber had all the ungainliness of a typical French aircraft of the time.

of the more effective wing design, ordered five of the remaining aircraft to be delivered with 16.50 m (54 ft 1½ in) span wings of varying areas, the final machine having a span of 17.25 m (56 ft 7¼ in). The various PL 7s went into service with Escadrille 7B1 on the carrier *Béarn* from July 1930, and after comparative tests the 16.50 m (54 ft 1½ in) span wing with square-cut tips was selected for the definitive **PL 7 T2B2b**,

the tips of the upper wing being hinged to fold downwards to fit the lifts aboard the *Béarn*. Ten of the original PL 7s were modified to this new configuration and 30 new aircraft were ordered. When vibration problems resulted in the disintegration of two PL 7s in flight the type was grounded from June 1931. With strengthened wing bracing, reinforced engine bearers and three-bladed propellers they were returned to service from

September 1932 onwards. In this final modified version the PL 7 had a maximum speed of 170 km/h (106 mph) and maximum take-off weight of 3950 kg (8,708 lb). Armament comprised two 7.5-mm (0.295-in) machine-guns on a ring mounting operated by the observer, plus either a 670-kg (1,477-lb) Type 400 torpedo or up to 510 kg (1,124 lb) of bombs. Although totally obsolete, the PL 7 was still in first-line service aboard the

Béarn when war broke out in September 1939.

A **PL 7T** transport displayed at the 1926 Salon de l'Aéronautique was in fact a PL 4 with a Gnome-Rhône Jupiter 9ab radial and a deepened fuselage accommodating pilot and mechanic in side-by-side open cockpits, and with an enclosed cabin for six passengers. The PL 7T never flew and was scrapped when the salon closed.

Levasseur PL 10 and PL 101

The prototype of the **Levasseur PL 10** three-seat carrier reconnaissance (R.3b) biplane flew for the first time in the spring of 1929. The PL 10 had equal-span folding wings, and the deep slab-sided fuselage had a hull-shaped undersurface. Armament comprised a single 7.5-mm (0.295-in) machine-gun operated by the pilot, plus twin 7.5-mm (0.295-in) guns operated by a gunner, whose cockpit was immediately behind that of the pilot. The observer, in the rear cockpit, had a Cayère-Montagne bombsight, and six 10-kg (22-lb) bombs could be carried on underwing racks. Production of the PL 10 totalled 30 aircraft, and these began to enter service with carrier Escadrille 7S1 in 1931. Power was provided by a 447-kW (600-hp) Hispano-Suiza 12Lb engine and maximum speed was 198 km/h (123 mph). The PL 10 spanned 14.20 m (46 ft 7in) and had a

Wearing the colours of Escadrille 781, this PL 10 displays its unusual three-seat layout with the gunner in the middle.

maximum take-off weight of 2880 kg (6,349 lb).

The **PL 101.01** made its first flight in March 1933 differing from the PL 10 in having wide-track landing gear and limited sweepback on the wings. Thirty production aircraft followed, these weighing 270 kg (595 lb) more than the PL 10s in overload condition, but being credited with a maximum speed of 220 km/h (136 mph). PL 101s replaced the PL 10s on the *Béarn* during 1935, and five were still in service at the outbreak of World War II.

Several projects were developed from the PL 101, the only ones built being the **PL 107** (two prototypes) and the **PL**

108. They introduced a fuselage of improved aerodynamic shape, had wheel fairings for the fixed landing gear and a glazed crew canopy. Powered by a 552-kW (740-hp) Gnome-Rhône 9Kfr, the PL 107 had a maximum speed of 235 km/h (146 mph), and the PL 108 with a 537-kW (720-hp) Hispano-Suiza 9Vbrs radial could attain 266 km/h (165 mph).

Final product of the company was the

PL 400, built to an Armée de l'Air requirement, inspired by the German Fiesler Fi 156 Storch, for a STOL observation machine. A high-wing cabin monoplane powered by a Potez 9C radial of 164 kW (220 hp), the PL 400 flew for the first time on 19 December 1939, but German occupation put an end to construction of the **PL 401** development with a Renault 6Q-09 engine of similar power.

Levasseur PL 15

The prototype **Levasseur PL 15** twin-float biplane flew for the first time with temporary wheel landing gear in October 1932. A production order for 16 aircraft as **PL 15 T2B2b** followed, these entering service from 1934 onwards with navy Escadrille 7B2 aboard the seaplane-carrier *Commandant Teste*. By comparison with the earlier PL 14, the PL 15 had a redesigned slender fuselage without the 'avion marin' type hull. Power was provided by a 485-kW (650-hp) Hispano-Suiza 12Nbr engine, and the wings folded for storage aboard ship. Surviving PL 15s, taken out of service at the end of 1938, formed Escadrille 3S6 for anti-submarine patrol along the Atlantic coast from September 1939 onwards. The PL 15 was armed with two 7.5-mm (0.295-in) machine-guns, and a torpedo or up to 450 kg

Developed from earlier Levasseur designs, the PL 15 had a more conventional fuselage and a mass of typical Levasseur inter-wing strutting.

(992 lb) of bombs.

The PL 15 was developed into the **PL 151**, a mid-wing monoplane with a small stabilising plane mounted over the fuselage. A full-scale mock-up was built, but no further development was undertaken. The **PL 154,** converted from the fourth PL 15, was a three-seat landplane torpedo-carrier which was abandoned after limited test flying. Later designs included the unusual **PL 200** monoplane, intended as an advanced reconnaissance seaplane, with a shoulder-wing mounted on a short nacelle for the three crew members, at the front of which

was the 537-kW (720-hp) Hispano-Suiza 9Vbrs radial engine. Test-flown in February 1935, the PL 200 achieved a maximum speed of 225 km/h (140 mph) by comparison with the 208 km/h

(129 mph) of the production PL 15. It was re-engined with a 552-kW (740-hp) Gnome-Rhône 9Kfr engine in October 1935 as the **PL 201**, but development was abandoned soon afterwards.

Lioré-et-Olivier 20

A three-seat version of the LeO 122 prototype, the **Lioré-et-Olivier 20** won the 1926 French ministry of war competition for a new night-bomber, and in September of that year the prototype established world distance records with a 2000-kg (4,409-lb) payload.

The first order for 50 aircraft, for the French Aéronautique Militaire, was received at the end of 1926, the first LeO 20s being flight-tested at Villacoublay in 1927. Further orders followed, and the last of the 311 machines taken on charge by the French air arm was accepted in December 1932. The LeO 20s equipped the 12 escadrilles of the 21e and 22e Régiments d'Aviation based at Nancy and Chartres respectively. A considerable number went to the multi-engined training school of the Aéronautique Militaire at Etampes. LeO 20s were supplied later to the 12e Régiment d'Aviation at Reims

Backbone of the French air force for 10 years, the LeO 20 was a clumsy yet magnificent design.

and to the 34e Régiment d'Aviation at Le Bourget. The type remained the backbone of the French night-bomber force for a decade.

Nine LeO 20s were exported in 1928-29, seven to Romania and two to Brazil, as a result of demonstration flights abroad by a LeO 20 registered F-AIFI, which was later delivered to the Armée de l'Air. At the beginning of 1937 224 LeO 20s were still in French service, although by that time its relatively low speed meant that the type was obsolete. On the eve of World War II, 92 LeO 20s were still in flying condition, many as target tugs or trainers with flying schools in France and North Africa, and a further 23 were in storage. Earlier, a number had

been re-designated **LeO 201** when adapted for parachute training.

Specification
LeO 20
Type: three-seat night-bomber
Powerplant: two 313-kW (420-hp) Gnome-Rhône 9Ady (Jupiter) radial piston engines
Performance: maximum speed 198 km/h (123 mph); service ceiling 5760 m (18,900 ft); range 1000 km (621

miles)
Weights: empty equipped 2725 kg (6,008 lb); maximum take-off 5460 kg (12,037 lb)
Dimensions: span 22.25 m (73 ft 0 in); length 13.81 m (45 ft 3¾ in); height 4.26 m (13 ft 11¾ in); wing area 105.00 m² (1,130.25 sq ft)
Armament: five 7.7-mm (0.303-in) machine-guns, plus up to 1000 kg (2,205 lb) of bombs

Lioré-et-Olivier 203, 204 and 206
to
Lockheed 14 Super Electra

Lioré-et-Olivier 203, 204 and 206

In search of a more powerful night-bomber, the Lioré-et-Olivier design team developed a large four-engined machine, the **Lioré-et-Olivier LeO 203.** This was first flown in May 1930, and was powered by four 224-kW (300-hp) Gnome-Rhône 7Kb radials mounted in pairs on the lower wings. Soon afterwards a floatplane version was flown under the designation **LeO 204.**

A 1931 order for 40 LeO 203s was transferred to the **LeO 206**, the first of which made its maiden flight in June 1932. This had a redesigned nose, a ventral balcony which housed the bomb-bay and, at the rear, a defensive gun position, and was powered by four 261-kW (350-hp) Gnome-Rhône 7Kd radials. The LeO 206 equipped Groupe de Bombardement III/12 at Reims and then GB I/22

at Chartres. Three aircraft of the original order for 40 were completed as **LeO 207** machines with a nose section similar to that of the LeO 203 and a smaller ventral balcony than that of the LeO 206. Performance was improved by the installation of Gnome-Rhône Titan Kds supercharged engines.

The ability of the LeO 206 to remain aloft on only three or even two engines gave it an extended life. Nicknamed *Caravelle*, 29 were still in flying condition in September 1939, the majority of them stationed in Morocco.

Specification
LeO 206
Type: four-seat night-bomber
Powerplant: four 261-kW (350-hp) Gnome-Rhône 7Kd Titan radial piston

engines
Performance: maximum speed 215 km/h (133 mph); service ceiling 7250 m (23,780 ft); range 2000 km (1,243 miles)
Weights: empty equipped 4230 kg (9,236 lb); maximum take-off 8450 kg (18,629 lb)
Dimensions: span 24.54 m (80 ft 6¼ in); length 14.77 m (48 ft 5½ in); height 6.28 m (20 ft 7¼ in); wing area 118.00 m² (1,270.18 sq ft)
Armament: six 7.7-mm (0.303-in) machine-guns (in nose, tail and ventral positions), plus up to 1500 kg (3,307 lb) of bombs

The LeO 206 was distinguishable by its ventral 'balcony', a long extension housing the bomb bay and defensive guns.

Lioré-et-Olivier 451

Laying claim to being one of the most aesthetically attractive twin-engined aircraft of World War II, the **Lioré-et-Olivier 451** originated from a French official specification of 1934 calling for a B.4-category four-seat day-bomber. Designed by Jean Mercier, the **LeO 45.01** prototype flew on 16 January 1937. The aircraft showed great promise, but control problems on take-off led to revision of the tail assembly, and the Hispano-Suiza 14AA radial engines also caused development delays. In September 1938 Gnome-Rhône 14N engines were installed and the aircraft redesignated **LeO 451.01.** Meanwhile series production had begun at the SNCASE plants at Clichy and Levallois, Lioré-et-Olivier having been nationalised in February 1937. The first series LeO 451 was flown on 24 March 1939 but, of a total of 1,783 LeO 451s and variants ordered, only 452 had flown by 25 June 1940.

The excellence of the LeO 451 design resulted in the Vichy authorities, with German approval, ordering 225 machines in August 1941, all contracts outstanding at the time of the 1940 surrender having been regarded as void. LeO 451 no. 453, the first product of the SNCASE Ambérieu factory, flew on 30 April 1942.

Variants included the **LeO 455.01** with 1025-kW (1,375-hp) Gnome-Rhône 14R engines, which flew on 3 December 1939. Five other LeO 451s were converted as similarly powered **LeO 455Ph** civil aircraft in 1948, and were used by the Institut Géographique National for topographic work. In 1946 40 North African-based LeO 451s were converted to **LeO 453** standard with Pratt & Whitney R-1830-67 radials. Some equipped navy Escadrille 11.S, while others were used for liaison or air-sea rescue. Four civil aircraft were used for glider towing.

The service history of the LeO 451 began in December 1939, when the conversion of operational *escadres* was started. The first war mission was on 11 May 1940, when aircraft of Groupes de Bombardement I/12 and II/12 attacked the Maastricht bridges in the Netherlands in an attempt to slow up the Ger-

man *Blitzkrieg*. From then until the Armistice in June more and more LeO 451s went into service, equipping several *escadres*. Their losses in daylight raids were heavy and in June long-range attacks at night were made on German and Italian targets. Orders had included the **LeO 451M**, modified for naval use, and one of this version was delivered at the end of May 1940.

Vichy Armée de l'Air and Aéronavale units in North Africa converted to the LeO 451 in 1940 and 1941. They took part in actions in the Levant in 1941 and against the Allies landing in North Africa at the end of 1942, suffering considerable losses, mostly on the ground. From July 1944 surviving LeO 451s in North Africa were switched to communications duties; 12 redesignated **LeO 451E2**'s were used for a variety of tasks, including glider towing. When the German forces took over unoccupied France in November 1942, they seized all available LeO 451s. Some were passed to the Regia Aeronautica for use as bomber trainers, but about 50 machines were converted as **LeO 451T** transports for the Luftwaffe. Twelve aircraft, redesignated **LeO 451C**, were used as mail carriers for Air France.

Several surviving LeO 451s which were not converted as LeO 453s remained in service in a variety of roles for several years post-war.

Specification
LeO 451 B.4
Type: four-seat medium bomber

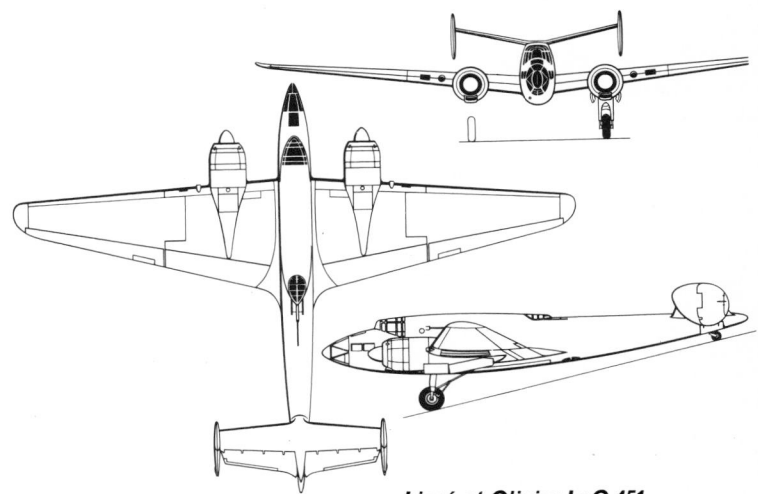

Lioré-et-Olivier LeO 451

Powerplant: two 850-kW (1,140-hp) Gnome-Rhône 14N 48/49 radial piston engines
Performance: maximum speed 495 km/h (308 mph); service ceiling 9000 m (29,530 ft); range 2300 km (1,429 miles)
Weights: empty equipped 7815 kg (17,229 lb); maximum take-off 11400 kg (25,133 lb)

Dimensions: span 22.50 m (73 ft 9¾ in); length 17.17 m (56 ft 4 in); height 5.24 m (17 ft 2¼ in); wing area 68.00 m² (731.97 sq ft)
Armament: two 7.5-mm (0.295-in) MAC machine-guns (one fixed forward-firing and one in a retractable ventral turret) and one 20-mm HS 404 cannon (in a retractable dorsal turret) plus up to 1500 kg (3,307 lb) of bombs

Lioré-et-Olivier LeO 451 of the 1ʳ Escadrille Groupe de Bombardment 1/11, l'Armée de l'Air, based at Oran-La Sénia airfield (Morocco) in mid-1941.

Lioré-et-Olivier H-24, H-24-2 and H-24-2/1

The result of prolonged design work by Benoit and his design team, the **Lioré-et-Olivier H-24.01** made its first flight in November 1929. A cantilever high-wing monoplane flying-boat, the H-24 had an enclosed pilot's cockpit, cabin accommodation for 10 passengers and a distinctive tall single fin and rudder, and was powered by two 373-kW (500-hp) Renault 12Jb V-12 engines mounted in tandem on a pylon over the hull. This single aircraft was used purely for development, making a number of test and demonstration flights before being scrapped at Antibes in 1934.

Developed from the H-24 was the **H-24-2**, of similar configuration but powered by four Gnome-Rhône radial engines mounted in tandem pairs over the thick-section wing. The first two of 14 production aircraft for Air France were H-24-2s, and the remaining 12 were **H-24-2/1** aircraft with a revised engine installation. The first H-24-2 had flown for the initial time in March 1933, and

One of the company's most successful aircraft, the H-24-2 was notable for its immensely thick wing and the tandem pairs of radial engines strut-mounted above the centre-section. It was widely used on Air France's Mediterranean services.

before long all the machines were employed on Air France routes linking Marseilles with Athens, Tunis and Beirut. Ten aircraft were still operational in September 1939, and were flown under Italian supervision after the German occupation of southern France in November 1942. It is understood that most were scrapped shortly afterwards.

The H-24-2 and H-24-2/1 had an enclosed crew cabin with side-by-side pilots' seats and a navigation and radio compartment; 15 passengers could be accommodated in a cabin beneath the wings, and there was a sizeable luggage and mail hold at the rear.

Specification
LeO H-24-2/1
Type: twin-engined passenger flying-boat
Powerplant: four 261-kW (350-hp) Gnome-Rhône 7Kd Titan Major radial piston engines
Performance: maximum speed 240 km/h (149 mph); service ceiling 4500 m (14,765 ft); range 1100 km (684 miles)
Weights: empty equipped 5868 kg (12,937 lb); maximum take-off 8700 kg (19,180 lb)
Dimensions: span 28.00 m (91 ft 10¼ in); length 18.45 m (60 ft 6½ in); height 6.33 m (20 ft 9¼ in); wing area 116.25 m² (1,251.35 sq ft)

Lioré-et-Olivier H-25

Powered by two 429-kW (575-hp) Hispano-Suiza 12Hb engines, the **Lioré-et-Olivier LeO 25** prototype four-seat night-bomber was delivered in 1928 as part of the second series batch of LeO 20s. It showed little improvement over the LeO 20, from which it could be distinguished by its redesigned fin. The next year it was redesignated **LeO 252.01** after being re-engined with Hispano 12Mbr engines, and in 1931 it was fitted with two large wooden floats for evaluation by the French navy. The second LeO 252, slightly modified, appeared in 1932 and was bought by Romania.

Three landplane developments of the LeO 252 were delivered to Brazil as **LeO 253** aircraft in 1931, but were not assembled until the following year when they took part in the civil war in that country. The LeO 253 had a maximum speed of 215 km/h (136 mph). The **LeO H-254** flew for the first time in the summer of 1932, and was a refined version of the H-252 intended for production, but only two examples were built and these were used at Berre to familiarise Farman F.168 crews with the more advanced aircraft to come. The **LeO H-255** was a version of the H-254 with 515-kW (690-hp) Hispano-Suiza 12Xbrs engines. Flown first as a landplane, then as a seaplane, it gained several world height-

with-load records for seaplanes. The **LeO H-256** appeared in late 1932, introducing increased wing area.

The **LeO H-257** was a considerable advance over the previous prototypes, powered by the Gnome-Rhône 14Kbrs Mistral Major radial engines preferred by the French navy, and with an enclosed cabin for the pilot. It first flew in March 1933 and was sufficiently impressive to earn an order for 60 **LeO H-257bis** series seaplanes with more powerful Gnome-Rhône 14Kirs/Kjrs engines, a strengthened structure, and the nose gun position enclosed in a glazed rotating cupola. In fact, the **LeO H-258** was delivered before the H-257bis, 26 going into service, initially with Escadrilles 3B1 and 3B2, from June 1935 onwards. The H-258 had two 484-kW (650-hp) Hispano-Suiza 12Nbr engines and attained a maximum speed of 240 km/h (149 mph). The H-257bis went into service from June 1936, equipping seaplane Escadrilles 3B1, 3B2, then B-1, B-2, B-3 and finally E.7 and 3S4. The Armée de l'Air used the landplane version with fixed independent mainwheels in Groupe de Bombardement II/25.

After neutrality patrols during the Spanish Civil War, the LeO floatplanes were used as convoy escorts and for submarine patrols from September 1939, seeing action in the English Chan-

nel, and on the Atlantic and Mediterranean coasts. Some were flung into action on bombing raids against the German *Blitzkrieg* in the summer of 1940, suffering heavy losses. At the outbreak of war 19 landplane LeO H-257bis aircraft were still in service in North Africa, and in August 1940 the Vichy regime had 53 floatplanes on strength. The last examples were withdrawn from training and target towing duties at the end of 1944.

The solitary **H-259**, the last of the H-25 series, had 641-kW (860-hp) Hispano-Suiza 12Ydrs/Yfrs engines and disappointing performance, and, after test flights in 1935, no orders were received.

Specification
Lioré-et-Olivier H-257bis
(floatplane)
Type: five-seat torpedo-bomber-reconnaissance float biplane

Despite its stalky appearance the H-257bis was an effective seaplane and was ordered in large numbers.

Powerplant: two 649-kW (870-hp) Gnome-Rhône 14Knrs/Kors radial piston engines
Performance: maximum speed 230 km/h (143 mph); service ceiling 8000 m (26,245 ft); range 1500 km (932 miles)
Weights: empty equipped 5300 kg (11,684 lb); maximum take-off 9560 kg (21,076 lb)
Dimensions: span 25.50 m (83 ft 8 in); length 17.54 m (57 ft 6½ in); height 6.80 m (22 ft 3¾ in); wing area 133.50 m² (1,437.03 sq ft)
Armament: three 7.5-mm (0.295-in) Darne machine-guns, plus one 670-kg (1,477-lb) DA torpedo or up to 600 kg (1,323 lb) of bombs

Lioré-et-Olivier H-246

Designed to an official requirement of 1935, the **Lioré-et-Olivier LeO H-246.01** flying-boat prototype flew on 30 September 1937. A graceful parasol-wing monoplane, its metal hull incorporated a flight deck for the four-man crew and a main cabin for 26 passengers.

In January 1938, Air France ordered six **H-246.1** aircraft in addition to the prototype, and two aircraft were about to enter service on the Marignane–Algiers route when war broke out. The French navy intended to impress all six series aircraft for maritime reconnaissance, but in the event only one was converted. This was the third series aircraft, which flew in June 1940, and then went into service with Escadrille 9.E with a modified extended glazed nose section. It was armed with four 7.5-mm (0.295-in) Darne machine-guns and 600 kg (1,323 lb) of bombs.

From October 1939 to November 1942 the civil LeO boats operated the route to Algiers for Air France. After that they were seized by the Luftwaffe, converted to carry 21 troops or 14 stretcher cases, and armed with five 7.92-mm (0.31-in) MG 15 machine-guns, one in a bow turret, two in lateral positions and two more firing through windows at the rear of the flight deck. They were used on a variety of tasks, including brief operations in Finland. Post-war, two surviving LeO H-246.1s were used for a time on the Air France Marignane–Algiers route.

Specification
LeO H-246.1
Type: transport flying-boat
Powerplant: four 537-kW (720-hp) Hispano-Suiza 12Xgrs/Xhrs V-12 piston engines
Performance: maximum speed

The Lioré-et-Olivier H-246 was a product of the 'Golden Age' of flying-boats of the inter-war years, but its career was cut short by the outbreak of hostilities in 1939. Flying for a time between Algiers, Algeria, and Vichy, France, the aircraft were eventually pressed into Luftwaffe service. Only one, the third production H-246 (illustrated), ever wore French military marks before the occupation.

330 km/h (205 mph); service ceiling 7000 m (22,965 ft); range 2000 km (1,243 miles)
Weights: empty equipped 9800 kg (21,605 lb); maximum take-off 15000 kg

(33,069 lb)
Dimensions: span 31.72 m (104 ft 0¾ in); length 21.17 m (69 ft 5½ in); height 7.15 m (23 ft 5½ in); wing area 131.00 m² (1,410.12 sq ft)

Lockheed 1, 2 and 5 Vega

First becoming keenly interested in aviation during 1910, the brothers Allan and Malcolm Loughead (pronounced Lockheed) founded in early 1916 the first company to bear their name, Loughead Aircraft Manufacturing Company, at Santa Barbara, California. This organisation ran into financial difficulties and was wound up in 1921, and it was not until late 1926 that there was formed a new company, the Lockheed Aircraft Company. This company title lasted for less than three years, but in that time a remarkable aircraft was developed and put into production, the **Lockheed Vega** which was designed by John K. ('Jack') Northrop with assistance from Gerard F. ('Gerry') Vultee, both later to found significant American aircraft companies. A cantilever high-wing monoplane of wooden construction, it had a beautifully streamlined monocoque fuselage built up from two half-shells of plywood that had been pressure-formed to shape in a concrete mould. Low-drag landing gear was of fixed tailwheel type (but Vegas were used frequently with floats or skis), enclosed accommodation was provided for a pilot and four passengers, and powerplant for the initial version of the Vega, later identified as the **Vega 1**, was a 168-kW (225-hp) Wright J-5 Whirlwind radial engine. The initial aircraft (2788, later registered NX913) was flown for the first time on 4 July 1927 and was acquired by newspaper-owner George Hearst to compete in the Oakland to Hawaii Dole Race, sponsored by James D. Dole, which began on 16 August 1927. The Vega, by then named **Golden Eagle** and flown by Jack Forst and Gordon Scott, disappeared without a

NC513E was a Lockheed Vega 5, construction number 52, built to the order of the Schlee-Brock company. It was powered by an uncowled Pratt & Whitney Wasp.

trace en route but, fortunately for Lockheed, the unexplained loss of this aircraft did not prohibit further sales; within the short space of six years the capability of the Vega was world renowned. A host of achievements brought this fame, but there is space here to mention only three of the highlights. These included the first trans-Arctic flight and the first exploratory flight over Antarctica (Wilkins and Eielson in the Vega 1 X3903); the first solo transatlantic flight by a woman from Newfoundland to Ireland (Amelia Earhart in the Vega 5B NC7952); and the first solo round-the-world flight (Wiley Post in the Vega 5B *The Winnie Mae*). When production ended a total of 128 Vegas had been built: 115 by Lockheed, nine by Detroit Aircraft Corporation (of which Lockheed was a division from 1929-31) and four by others.

Variants
Vega 1: original production version, powered as built by a 168-kW (225-hp) Wright J-5, J-5A, J-5AB, J-5B or J-5C Whirlwind engine
Vega 2: production version which differed primarily by having the 224-kW (300-hp) Wright J-6 Whirlwind engine
Vega 2A: redesignation of one Vega 2 for operation at a higher gross weight
Vega 2D: redesignation of two Vega 1s and one Vega 2 following installation

of a 224-kW (300-hp) Pratt & Whitney Wasp Junior engine
Vega 5: major production version (35 built) with engines that included the 306-kW (410-hp) Pratt & Whitney Wasp A, 336-kW (450-hp) Wasp B or 313-kW (420-hp) Wasp C1, most installed with a NACA low-drag cowling
Vega 5A Executive: basically as Vega 5, but with executive interior
Vega 5B: basically as Vega 5, but intended for operation as seven-seat aircraft at a higher gross weight
Vega 5C: basically as Vega 5 but with revised tail surfaces and operating at higher gross weight
DL-1: version of Vega 5C with light alloy fuselage produced during ownership by Detroit Aircraft Corporation
DL-1B: similar to DL-1 but equipped as six-passenger transports for airline use
DL-1 Special: one aircraft exported to the UK for record-breaking and racing use
Y1C-12: designation of one DL-1

aircraft acquired by the US Army Air Corps for evaluation
Y1C-17: designation of one DL-1B aircraft acquired by the US Army Air Corps for high speed and record-breaking flights
UC-101: US Army Air Force designation of one Vega 5C impressed for service in 1942

Specification
Lockheed Vega 5C (landplane)
Type: seven-seat cabin monoplane
Powerplant: one 336-kW (450-hp) Pratt & Whitney Wasp SC-1 radial piston engine
Performance: maximum speed 298 km/h (185 mph); service ceiling 5485 m (18,000 ft); standard range 885 km (550 miles)
Weights: empty 1163 kg (2,565 lb); maximum take-off 2155 kg (4,750 lb)
Dimensions: span 12.50 m (41 ft 0 in); length 8.38 m (27 ft 6 in); height 2.59 m (8 ft 6 in); wing area 25.55 m² (275.0 sq ft)

Lockheed 3 Air Express

The very considerable success and proven reliability of the Vega made this aircraft of interest to many airlines, but Western Air Express required some of its own ideas incorporated, the association bringing the name **Lockheed 3 Air Express**. With a fuselage, landing gear and tail unit generally similar to the Vega, this aircraft differed primarily by having an increased-span parasol wing, a cabin seating four passengers or carrying 2.83 m³ (100 cu ft) of mail, with the pilot's open cockpit moved to the rear of the cabin. Power was provided as standard by a 306-kW (410-hp) Pratt & Whitney Wasp, but at least one was flown with a Wasp engine of 391 kW (525 hp), and some of these engines were enclosed by the NACA-developed low-drag cowling. A total of seven of these aircraft was built, plus one **Air Ex-**

press Special with which Laura Ingalls intended to make a non-stop transatlantic flight in 1931. Western Air Express, which had inspired this development of the Vega, acquired only a single example. The basic Air Express spanned 12.95 m (42 ft 6 in), had a maximum take-off weight of 1984 kg (4,375 lb) and possessed a maximum speed of 269 km/h (167 mph) at sea level.

Variants
Lockheed 4 Explorer: derivative of the Air Express/Vega series with low-set monoplane wing, fixed landing gear and 336-kW (450-hp) Pratt & Whitney Wasp; span was 14.78 m (48 ft 6 in) and maximum take-off weight 4086 kg (9,008 lb); designed for a non-stop trans-Pacific flight to Japan; two aircraft only: first crashed during take-

NC514E was the second Lockheed Air Express and was powered by a Wasp C radial engine. First used as a company demonstrator, it was sold in January 1930 to the New York, Rio & Buenos Aires Line for services to South America, where it acquired twin-float landing gear.

off for the record attempt in July 1929, and the replacement aircraft with jettisonable landing gear crashed during trials in September 1929; theoretical range was 8850 km (5,500 miles)

Lockheed 7 Explorer: improved version of Model 4 with 336-kW (450-hp) Wasp C; first aircraft crashed during trials in May 1930, and second made some moderately successful flights before being written off

Lockheed 8 Sirius

Developed originally to meet a requirement of Charles Lindbergh for a low-wing monoplane of high performance, the **Lockheed 8 Sirius** combined what was basically a Vega wooden fuselage with a new low-set cantilever wing. First flown in November 1929, and then powered by a 336-kW (450-hp) Pratt & Whitney Wasp radial engine, the Sirius had non-retractable tailwheel landing gear and two open cockpits in tandem. Before accepting this aircraft, Lindbergh had a sliding canopy installed to enclose the two cockpits. In the following year, before Lindbergh set out on a survey flight for Pan American Airways, a 429-kW (575-hp) Wright Cyclone engine and twin-float landing gear were in-

NR211 was the first Lockheed Sirius and it was built expressly to the orders of Charles Lindbergh. The sliding cockpit canopy was the suggestion of Mrs Lindbergh and the Sirius went on to complete several long-range survey flights. The aircraft still survives today as part of the National Air and Space Museum.

stalled. For its final survey flight in 1933 it was powered by a 529-kW (710-hp) Wright Cyclone engine.

The success of Lindbergh's aircraft led to the construction of 13 more by Lockheed, comprising four similar **Sirius 8**, eight **Sirius 8A** with enlarged tail surfaces, and a single four-seat **Sirius 8C** aircraft which had an enclosed cabin for two between the engine and pilot's cockpit. One Sirius built by the Detroit Aircraft Corporation, with a metal fuselage and Lockheed wooden

wing, had the designation **DL-2**. Lindbergh's Sirius spanned 13.04 m (42 ft 9¼ in), weighed a maximum of 3220 kg (7,099 lb), was capable of a maximum of 298 km/h (185 mph), and had a range of 1570 km (975 miles), all in landplane configuration.

Lockheed 8 Altair

When acquiring his Sirius, Charles Lindbergh had intimated that he might be interested in having retractable landing gear, with a result that the company designed an alternative wing to accept inward-retracting main landing gear units. Although this feature was not adopted by Lindbergh, it became available as a retrofit for Sirius aircraft, first flown on a company-owned Sirius 8A during September 1930. Redesignated **Lockheed Altair 8D** in this form, the aircraft was loaned to the US Army Air Corps during 1931 and in November of that year, with a new 336-kW (450-hp) Pratt & Whitney R-1340-17 engine installed, was acquired by the USAAC under the designation **Y1C-25**. Four more aircraft were con-

The 1930 Altair was the first of Lockheed's aircraft designs to be built with a retractable undercarriage.

verted, two Sirius 8As becoming **Altair 8D** aircraft, the Detroit Aircraft DL-2 being redesignated **Altair DL-2A** and, most famous of all, one Sirius receiving the designation **Sirius 8 Special**. This last aircraft was later acquired by Sir Charles Kingsford Smith and, modified to **Altair 8D** configuration and named *Lady Southern Cross*, was used by this pilot, with P. G. Taylor as his navigator, to make the first crossing of the Pacific Ocean from Australia to the United States between 20 October and 4

November 1934.
　In addition to the conversions, six Altairs were built as new, one of them an **Altair DL-2A** built by Detroit Aircraft and powered by a 481-kW (645-hp) Wright R-1820E Cyclone which was

acquired by the US Navy under the designation **XRO-1**. Typical data includes a span of 13.03 m (42 ft 9 in), a maximum take-off weight of 2220 kg (4,895 lb) and a maximum speed of 333 km/h (207 mph) at 2135 m (7,000 ft).

Lockheed 9 Orion

Seeing, in the latter part of 1930, a potential market for a light transport aircraft, Lockheed began development of the six-passenger **Lockheed 9 Orion**. This combined a Vega fuselage with the low-wing and landing gear of the Altair, and the NACA cowling introduced on the Air Express, the first such Orion being flown in early 1931. Orion production totalled 35, and the single Altair DL-2A was also converted to Orion configuration.
　The first Orion (NC960Y) entered service with Bowen Air Lines at Fort Worth, Texas, in May 1931, and the type found use with 12 other American airlines. At least 13 of these aircraft, from various sources, were supplied to the Spanish Republican air force in late 1936, soon after the beginning of the Spanish Civil War.

Variants
Orion 9: original production version with a 306-kW (410-hp) Pratt & Whitney Wasp A or 313-kW (420-hp) Wasp C radial engine; 14 built
Orion 9A Special: one aircraft with

a 336-kW (450-hp) Wasp SC engine and some minor airframe revisions
Orion 9B: two aircraft with 429-kW (575-hp) Wright R-1820-E Cyclone engines; supplied to Swissair
Orion 9C: redesignation of the single Altair DL-2A following conversion to Orion configuration
Orion 9D: production version with some minor airframe revisions and powered originally by the Pratt & Whitney Wasp S1D1 engine; 13 built
Orion 9E: three aircraft, generally similar to Orion 9, but powered by the 336-kW (450-hp) Wasp SC1 engine
Orion 9F: one executive aircraft with 481-kW (645-hp) Wright R-1820-F2 Cyclone engine
Orion 9F-1: one executive aircraft with a 485-kW (650-hp) Wright SR-1820-F2 Cyclone engine
UC-85: US Army Air Force designation allocated to one Orion 9D impressed for service in June 1942
Orion-Explorer: designation allocated to one Orion 9E following replacement of a damaged wing with

that of the crashed second Explorer 7, installation of fixed landing gear and a 482-kW (600-hp) Wasp S3H1 engine; later fitted with floats, it was used by Wiley Post and Will Rogers for a round-the-world flight attempt, but both men died when the aircraft crashed in Alaska on 15 August 1935

Specification
Lockheed Orion 9D
Type: light transport aircraft
Powerplant: one 410-kW (550-hp) Pratt & Whitney Wasp S1D1 radial piston engine

Built for Varney Air Service, this Lockheed Orion eventually found its way to Spain for the Civil War and was destroyed there.

Performance: cruising speed 330 km/h (205 mph); service ceiling 6705 m (22,000 ft); range 1159 km (720 miles)
Weights: empty 1651 kg (3,640 lb); maximum take-off 2359 kg (5,200 lb)
Dimensions: span 13.04 m (42 ft 9¼ in); length 8.64 m (28 ft 4 in); height 2.95 m (9 ft 8 in); wing area 27.32 m² (294.10 sq ft)

Lockheed 10 Electra

Lockheed's first major move towards becoming a significant manufacturer of transport aircraft came with design of the **Lockheed 10 Electra**. Providing accommodation for 10 passengers, the Electra was a cantilever low-wing monoplane of all-metal construction, with retractable tailwheel landing gear and a tail unit incorporating twin fins and rudders. Powered by two Pratt & Whitney Wasp Junior SBs, the prototype was flown for the first time on 23 February 1934, and was followed by 148 production aircraft. The Electra entered service during 1934, initially with Northwest Airlines, and in the late 1930s was used by eight American operators. By the time that the USA became involved in World War II, however, few remained in national airline service for the rapid growth in air travel had already shown these small-capacity aircraft to be uneconomical. In addition to those built for the home market, Electras were exported to Argentina, Australia, Canada, Chile, Colombia, Japan, New Zealand, Poland, Romania, USSR, UK, Venezuela and Yugoslavia. Small numbers also saw service in the Spanish Civil War and with the outbreak of World War II the type was impressed for service with the Royal Air Force and Royal Canadian Air Force. Use of the Electra by small civil operators continued after the war, as it was cheap to buy and operate, but few remained in service after the late 1960s.

Variants
Electra 10-A: major production version with Pratt & Whitney Wasp Junior SBs; 101 built
Electra 10-B: generally similar to Electra 10-A, but powered by 328-kW (440-hp) Wright R-975-E3 Whirlwind engines; 18 built
Electra 10-C: version for Pan American Airways with 336-kW (450-hp) Wasp SC1 engines; 8 built
Electra 10-D: projected military variant; none built
Electra 10-E: generally similar to Electra 10-A but powered by 447-kW (600-hp) Wasp S3H1 engines; 15 built; most famous of these was NR16020 in which, during a round-the-world flight attempt, Amelia Earhart and her navigator Fred Noonan disappeared without trace on 2 July 1937
XR2O-1: designation of single staff transport for the US Navy, powered by 336-kW (450-hp) Pratt & Whitney R-985-48 engines
XR3O-1: designation of single convertible ambulance/transport aircraft for US Coast Guard, powered by 328-kW (440-hp) Wright R-975-E3 engines
XC-35: designation of single research aircraft developed from standard Electra with pressurised cabin, powered by 410-kW (550-hp) Pratt & Whitney XR-1340-43 turbocharged engines; used by the US Army Air

Corps to gain valuable experience of pressurisation and the use of turbocharged engines
Y1C-36: US Army Air Corps designation of three Electra 10-As, with 336-kW (450-hp) Pratt & Whitney R-985-13 engines, for use as transports
C-36A (later **UC-36A**): designation of 15 Electra 10-As impressed for service with the US Army Air Force in World War II
C-36B (later **UC-36B**): designation of five Electra 10-Es impressed for USAAF service
C-36C (later **UC-36C**): designation of seven Electra 10-Bs impressed for USAAF service
Y1C-37: designation of one aircraft, generally similar to the Y1C-36s, acquired for service with the US National Guard Bureau

G-AEPN was one of the Electras ordered by British Airways fitted with variable-pitch propellers and electric flaps.

Specification
Lockheed Electra 10-A
Type: short-range light transport
Powerplant: two 336-kW (450-hp) Pratt & Whitney Wasp Junior SB radial piston engines
Performance: maximum speed 325 km/h (202 mph) at 1525 m (5,000 ft); service ceiling 5915 m (19,400 ft); range 1305 km (810 miles)
Weights: empty 2927 kg (6,454 lb); maximum take-off 4672 kg (10,300 lb)
Dimensions: span 16.76 m (55 ft 0 in); length 11.76 m (38 ft 7 in); height 3.07 m (10 ft 1 in); wing area 42.59 m² (458.50 sq ft)

Lockheed 12 Electra Junior

When the Lockheed 10 Electra first entered service, its 10-passenger capacity was considered to be too small for airline operators, but too large for operators of feederline services. To satisfy the latter demand, Lockheed decided to produce a reduced-scale version which would accommodate six passengers and a crew of two, and, by retaining the powerplant of its larger sister, offer enhanced performance. The resulting aircraft, designated **Lockheed 12 Electra Junior**, was flown for the first time on 27 June 1936 and, perhaps much to the surprise of the company, its sales success almost equalled that of the Lockheed 10, with a total of 130 built. The majority of production aircraft were designated **Lockheed 12-A**, but many of the total entered military service. The US Army Air Corps acquired three seven-seat **C-40** (later **UC-40**), 10 five-seat **C-40A** (later **UC-40A**) and one experimental **C-40B** aircraft with fixed tricycle landing gear; the designation **C-40D** (later **UC-40D**) was allocated to 10 Lockheed 12-As impressed for wartime service. The US Navy received one seven-seat **JO-1**, five six-seat **JO-2** aircraft (one of which was allocated for US Marine Corps use), and a single **XJO-3** with fixed tricycle landing gear which was used for carrier deck-landing trials.

The type was used also by the air arms of Argentina, Canada, Cuba and the UK, as well as by the Netherlands East Indies army, this last service being the major military user with a total of 36. Of this number, 16 were specially-developed **Model 212** crew trainers, with a forward-firing 7.7-mm (0.303-in) machine-gun, a similar weapon in a dorsal turret, and underfuselage racks for up to 363 kg (800 lb) of bombs.

One of the most interesting aircraft was that acquired by NACA, predecessor of NASA, which was used to evaluate a wing de-icing system that utilised hot gases from the engine exhaust. One of the most unusual applications of the Lockheed 12-A was by Australian Sidney Cotton who, under the cover of his position as an executive of the Dufaycolour Company, used his specially modified camera-carrying Lockheed 12-A to take clandestine reconnaissance photographs of German military installations in the three months leading up to the beginning of World War II.

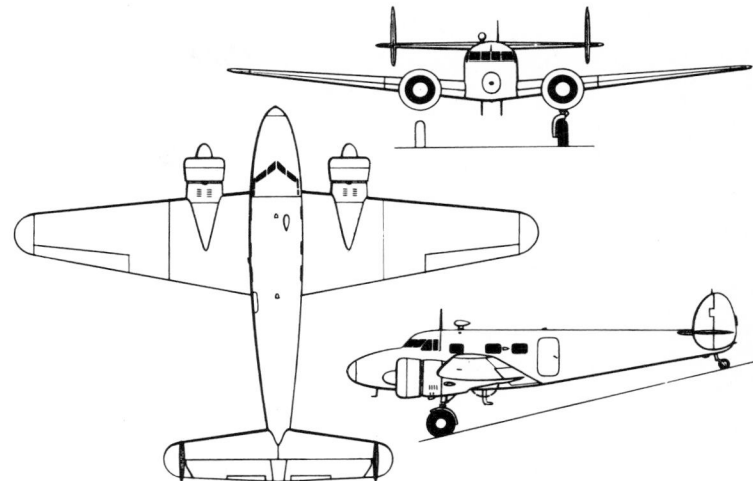

Lockheed 12 Electra Junior

Specification
Lockheed 12-A
Type: six-passenger light transport
Powerplant: two 336-kW (450-hp) Pratt & Whitney Wasp Junior SB radial piston engines

Performance: maximum speed 362 km/h (225 mph) at 1525 m (5,000 ft); service ceiling 6980 m (22,900 ft); range 1287 km (800 miles)
Weights: empty 2615 kg (5,765 lb);

maximum take-off 3924 kg (8,650 lb)
Dimensions: span 15.09 m (49 ft 6 in); length 10.97 m (36 ft 4 in); height 2.97 m (9 ft 9 in); wing area 32.70 m² (352.0 sq ft)

Lockheed 14 Super Electra

Designed to compete against the DST/DC-2/DC-3 series being developed by the Douglas company, the **Lockheed 14 Super Electra** failed, by reason of its smaller capacity, to present any significant competition. Of the same general configuration as the earlier Lockheed 10 Electra, it differed primarily by having a much deeper fuselage accommodating a maximum of 14 passengers, a mid-set wing, and introduced such advanced features as integral fuel tanks in the wing, Fowler-type trailing-edge flaps, fully-feathering propellers and, at a later stage of production, fixed wing slats. These improvements, combined with powerful engines and high wing loading, gave the Super Electra excellent performance but, by comparison with the important and larger-capacity Douglas DC-3, it was less efficient in operation, with the result that only 112 were built by Lockheed. First flown in prototype form on 29 July 1937 and certificated on 15 November 1937, initial deliveries were made shortly afterwards. By far the majority of the Super Electras were exported and, in addition, a total of 119 was licence-built in Japan for use by the Imperial Japanese Army. These, powered by 671-kW (900-hp) Mitsubishi Ha-26-I radial engines, were designated **Army Type LO Transport** and were later allocated the Allied code name **'Thelma'**.

Variants
Lockheed 14-H and **14-H2:** initial production version powered by Pratt & Whitney Hornet S1E-G or S1E2-G radial engines respectively
Lockheed C-14H-1: redesignation of one 14-H following conversion as the prototype of an all-cargo version; later reconverted to 14-H configuration
Lockheed 14-08: redesignation of Trans-Canada Air Lines 14-H2s after

replacement of standard engines by 895-kW (1,200-hp) Twin Wasp S1C3-Gs
Lockheed 14-WF62 or **14-F62:** export production version with 671-kW (900-hp) Wright SGR-1820-F62 Cyclone engines
Lockheed 14-WG3B: export production version with 671-kW (900-hp) Wright GR-1820-G3B engines
Lockheed 14-N: designation of four aircraft built to the requirements of individual private customers
C-111: US Army Air Force designation of three 14-F62s impressed for service in Australia
XR4O-1: US Navy designation of a single 14-H2 acquired as a staff transport

Specification
Lockheed 14-H Super Electra
Type: short/medium-range civil transport
Powerplant: two 652-kW (875-hp) Pratt & Whitney Hornet S1E-G radial piston engines
Performance: maximum speed

A Super Electra with a non-standard window arrangement. Howard Hughes completed his around-the-world flight in a this aircraft.

398 km/h (247 mph) at 2135 m (7,000 ft); service ceiling 7405 m (24,300 ft); maximum range 3315 km (2,060 miles)
Weights: empty 4672 kg (10,300 lb);

maximum take-off 7938 kg (17,500 lb)
Dimensions: span 19.96 m (65 ft 6 in); length 13.51 m (44 ft 4 in); height 3.48 m (11 ft 5 in); wing area 51.19 m² (551.0 sq ft)

This was one of three Lockheed 14-H2s bought by Air Afrique, which greatly appreciated the type's speed, range and good handling.

Lockheed 18 Lodestar
to
Lockheed C-141 StarLifter

Lockheed 18 Lodestar

Design and development of the **Lockheed 18 Lodestar** began as a result of the poor sales achievement of the Lockheed 14 Super Electra, the prototype being flown for the first time on 21 September 1939. Converted from a Super Electra, it differed primarily by having the fuselage lengthened by 1.68 m (5 ft 6 in) to provide accommodation for 15 to 18 passengers, depending upon the other facilities provided; some were produced with high-density bench seating for a maximum of 26 passengers, and were available with a variety of engines by Pratt & Whitney and Wright. Despite the improved economy demonstrated by the Lodestar, Lockheed failed again to achieve worthwhile sales in the United States as most operators were committed to purchase DC-3s from the Douglas Company. Fortunately, the type appealed more to export customers, with airlines or government agencies in Africa, Brazil, Canada, France, the Netherlands, Norway, South Africa, the UK and Venezuela ordering a total of 96 aircraft. There was only limited military interest before the beginning of World War II, but later procurement, particularly by the US Army Air Force, raised the total of Lodestars built by Lockheed to 625 before production ended. Unlike the Hudson, the Lodestar has no record of stirring action but, nevertheless, the type was able to fulfil an important medium-range transport role. Only small numbers saw post-war service, mostly with small operators, but a number of interesting conversions as executive transports were carried out in the USA by companies like Howard Aero and Lear Inc.

Variants
XR5O-1: single aircraft with 895-kW (1,200-hp) Wright R-1820 Cyclone engines, acquired for evaluation by US Coast Guard
R5O-1: designation of three aircraft as staff transports, two US Navy and one US Coast Guard, powered by 895-kW (1,200-hp) Wright R-1820-97 Cyclone engines
R5O-2: single US Navy aircraft, equivalent to impressed USAAF C-59, with 634-kW (850-hp) Pratt & Whitney R-1690-25 Hornet engines
R5O-3: three aircraft acquired by the US Navy as VIP transports, powered by 895-kW (1,200-hp) Pratt & Whitney R-1830-34A engines
R5O-4: designation of 12 seven-passenger transports, under construction for civil customers, impressed for US Navy service and powered by 895-kW (1,200-hp) Wright R-1820-40 engines
R5O-5: designation of 41 aircraft, generally as USAAF C-60, but equipped as 14-seat passenger transports for US Navy service
R5O-6: designation of 35 aircraft, generally as USAAF C-60A, but equipped as 18-seat paratroop transports for USN and USMC
C-56 to **C-56E:** under this series of designations, 36 commercial Lodestars were impressed for US Army Air Force service
C-57 and **C-57B:** designation of 20 commercial Lodestars impressed for USAAF service
C-57C: designation of three C-60As after being re-engined with 895-kW (1,200-hp) Pratt & Whitney R-1830-43 engines
C-57D: redesignation of one C-57A after being re-engined for a second time
C-59: designation of 10 impressed civil Lodestars; seven were transferred to the RAF under Lend-Lease, being designated **Lodestar Mk IA**
C-60: designation of 36 impressed civil Lodestars; 16 were transferred to the RAF under Lend-Lease, being designated **Lodestar Mk II**
C-60A: under this designation 324 new aircraft were built for the USAAF, equipped as 18-seat paratroop transports and powered by 895-kW (1,200-hp) Wright R-1820-87 engines
XC-60B: single experimental aircraft acquired by USAAF for evaluation of hot-air de-icing system
C-60C: proposed 21-seat troop transport; not built
C-66: single aircraft equipped as VIP transport for the President of Brazil

Specification
Lockheed Lodestar Model 18-07
Type: civil transport
Powerplant: two 652-kW (875-hp) Pratt & Whitney Hornet S1E2-G radial piston engines
Performance: maximum speed 351 km/h (218 mph) at 2440 m (8,000 ft); service ceiling 6220 m (20,400 ft); standard range 2897 km (1,800 miles)
Weights: empty 5103 kg (11,250 lb); maximum take-off 8709 kg (19,200 lb)
Dimensions: span 19.96 m (65 ft 6 in); length 15.19 m (49 ft 10 in); height 3.61 m (11 ft 10 in); wing area 51.19 m^2 (551.0 sq ft)

The quality of the Lodestar's design is highlighted by the fact that, as late as 1957, Swedish operator Linjeflyg flew four Lockheed 18s as profitable short-range transports.

Lockheed 37 Ventura and Harpoon

The success of the Hudson in RAF service led Lockheed to propose a military version of the larger Lockheed 18 Lodestar and resulting British interest led to development of the **Lockheed 37.** During 1940 a total of 675 of these aircraft was contracted for the RAF, which named the type the **Ventura,** and the company lost little time initiating production in the Vega factory. By comparison with the Hudson, the Ventura had far more effective armament, a heavier bomb load and more powerful engines, and appeared to have considerable potential. First used operationally by the RAF on 3 November 1942, the type was soon found to be unsuited to daylight operations and was transferred to Coastal Command. Nevertheless, the Ventura was procured in large numbers under Lend-Lease, and was built for the US Army Air Force and US Navy, this last service designating it as the **PV-1 Ventura.** Venturas served with all the Commonwealth nations, the Free French and

with the Brazilian air force. A long-range version, the **PV-2,** had been ordered by the US Navy in June 1943 and, differing in several respects from the Ventura, was named the **Harpoon;** Ventura and Harpoon production totalled 3,028 in September 1945. Post-war surplus PV-2 aircraft were supplied to Italy, Japan, the Netherlands, Peru and Portugal.

Variants
Ventura Mk I: initial production version to British contract, powered by 1380-kW (1,850-hp) Pratt & Whitney Double Wasp S1A4-G engines; a number were modified subsequently in the UK for service with Coastal Command, being redesignated **Ventura GR.Mk I**
Ventura Mk II: similar to Ventura Mk I, but with larger-capacity bomb bay and 1491-kW (2,000-hp) Pratt & Whitney R-2800-31 engines
Ventura Mk IIA: similar to Ventura Mk II, but with revised armament

Even the addition of equipment such as the .50-calibre machine-guns in the dorsal turret cannot detract from the sleek lines of the Lockheed 18. With armament, a bomb bay and a coat of blue paint the Lodestar became the PV-1 maritime reconnaissance bomber.

Ventura GR.Mk V: RAF designation of version of US Navy PV-1 for service with Coastal Command; some modified subsequently to transport configuration as **Ventura C.Mk V**

B-34 (later **RB-34**): under this designation about 20 aircraft, similar to Ventura Mk IIA, were impressed by the USAAF from Lend-Lease production; some later had ASV radar installed

B-34A (later **RB-34A**): 101 aircraft taken from Lend-Lease procurement and used by the USAAF in training roles

B-34B (later **RB-34B**): 13 aircraft from Lend-Lease procurement, used by the USAAF as navigation trainers

B-37: version with 1268-kW (1,700-hp) Wright R-2600-13 engines and revised armament for USAAF, but only 18 of order for 550 built

PV-1: first version for US Navy, generally as Ventura Mk II, but with reduced defensive armament, modified bomb bay to carry bombs, depth charges or one torpedo, and with search radar; late production had provision for HVAR rockets on underwing launchers, and a few were modified for US Marine Corps use as night-fighters, equipped with

British air interception radar

PV-1P: redesignation of some PV-1s following conversion for use in the photo-reconnaissance role

PV-2: improved version for US Navy with new larger-span outer wing panels to increase fuel capacity, revised tail unit and armament; leaking integral fuel tanks and skin wrinkling led to wing re-design, applied to 31st and remaining 469 production aircraft; wing span 22.86 m (75 ft), wing area 63.73 m² (686 sq ft)

PV-2C: redesignation of first 30 PV-2s, used in a training role after the integral fuel tanks in the outer wing panels had been sealed off

PV-2D: similar to PV-2, with armament revisions, but only 35 delivered before VJ-Day brought contract cancellation

PV-2T: redesignation of PV-2s used in small numbers as unarmed trainers

PV-3: designation applied by US Navy to 27 Ventura Mk IIs taken over from British contract

Specification
Lockheed PV-1 Ventura
Type: maritime patrol aircraft

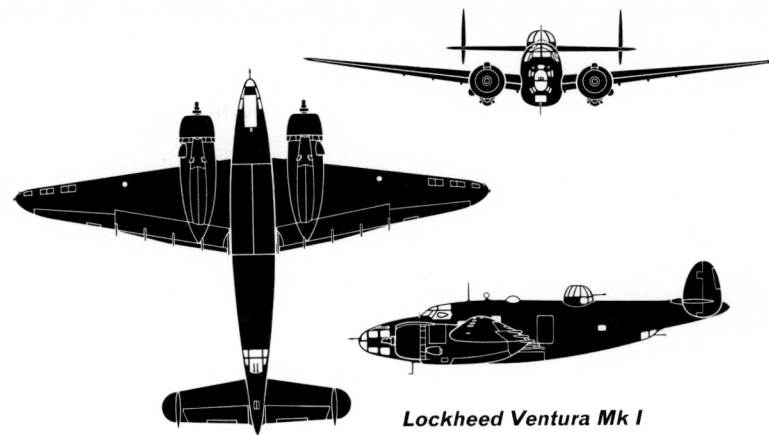

Lockheed Ventura Mk I

Powerplant: two 1491-kW (2,000-hp) Pratt & Whitney R-2800-31 radial piston engines
Performance: maximum speed 518 km/h (322 mph) at 4205 m (13,800 ft); service ceiling 8015 m (26,300 ft); normal range 2189 km (1,360 miles)
Weights: empty 9161 kg (20,197 lb); maximum take-off 14096 kg (31,077 lb)
Dimensions: span 19.96 m (65 ft

6 in); length 15.77 m (51 ft 9 in); height 3.63 m (11 ft 11 in); wing area 51.19 m² (551.0 sq ft)
Armament: two 12.7-mm (0.5-in) forward-firing machine-guns, two similar guns in dorsal turret and two 7.72-mm (0.3-in) machine-guns in ventral position, plus up to 1361 kg (3,000 lb) of bombs, or six 147-kg (325-lb) depth charges, or one torpedo

Lockheed 89 Constitution

Although two prototypes of the **Lockheed 89 Constellation** were built for the US Navy, under the designation **XR60-1,** no production examples of this large transport aircraft resulted because development of the 4101-kW (5,500-shp) Wright Typhoon turboprop engines intended to power production aircraft was abandoned. As it was, the Constitutions were flown with engines of only 2610 kW (3,500 hp) for test purposes. As

military transports, the 57.63 m (189 ft 1 in) span Constitutions would have carried a crew of 12 and 168 service personnel on two decks.

The Constitution evolved to meet a Pan Am requirement for a high-capacity, long-range airliner, but the only two examples ever completed were built against an order from the US Navy.

Lockheed 188 Electra

The design of the **Lockheed L-188 Electra** began in 1954, and in the following year the company received a launching order from American Airlines. The prototype, first flown on 6 December 1957, was a low-wing monoplane of conventional configuration with retractable tricycle landing gear and powered by four Allison 501D-13, 501D-13A or 501D-15 turboprop engines. Standard accommodation was for 66 to 80 passengers, but a high-density arrangement was available optionally to seat 98. Built initially as the **L-188A**, the Electra became available also as the longer-range **L-188C** with increased fuel capacity and operating at a higher gross weight. A total of 170 had been built when production ended unexpectedly early as a result of passenger loss of confidence in the type after two had disintegrated in flight, and by the time remedial modifications

Australia was one of the best export markets for the Lockheed Electra and among the Antipodean orders was one for L-188As placed by Ansett. The first aircraft were delivered in 1959.

had been incorporated customer airlines were interested in turbojet- rather than turboprop-powered aircraft. About half of the total built remained in service in 1992, many of them converted by Lockheed Aircraft Service for convertible passenger/cargo or all-cargo use.

Specification
Lockheed L-188A Electra
Type: short-medium-range transport
Powerplant: four 2796-kW (3,750-shp) Allison 501D-13 or 501D-13A turboprops; optionally four 3020-kW (4,050-shp) 501D-15 turboprops

Performance: maximum cruising speed 652 km/h (405 mph); service ceiling 8655 m (28,400 ft); range 3541 km (2,200 miles)
Weights: empty 26036 kg (57,400 lb);

maximum take-off 51256 kg (113,000 lb)
Dimensions: span 30.18 m (99 ft 0 in); length 31.85 m (104 ft 6 in); height 10.01 m (32 ft 10 in); wing area 120.77 m² (1,300.0 sq ft)

Lockheed AH-56A Cheyenne

In a seemingly strange field of design for Lockheed, the company was one of 12 which submitted proposals to meet a US Army requirement for a heavily armed gunship. Lockheed was eventually selected to develop and build an initial batch of 10 aircraft based on its proposal, under the designation **Lockheed AH-56A Cheyenne**, this being a compound helicopter with a slender fuselage, short-span wings, retractable landing gear and accommodation for a crew of two. It was powered by a General Electric T64-GE-16 turboshaft engine,

The Cheyenne was an ambitious design, but lost out to the rival AH-64 due to project costs and development problems.

finally developing 2927 kW (3,925 shp), this driving four-blade main and tail rotors, plus a three-blade pusher propeller at the tail of the aircraft. Flight trials began on 21 September 1967, and in early 1968 the US Army contracted for an initial batch of 375 production aircraft. Unfortunately, development problems brought cancellation of the production

programme on 19 May 1969 and, although progress had been made, the development contract was also terminated in August 1972. The Cheyenne, which had demonstrated a maximum

speed of 407 km/h (253 mph), would have been armed with a cannon, grenade-launcher or Minigun in a nose turret, with anti-tank missiles or air-to-ground rockets on underwing racks.

Lockheed C-5 Galaxy

To meet a USAF Military Air Transport Service (MATS) requirement for a very large strategic transport to complement the Lockheed C-141, and with the ability to operate from the same airfields, Lockheed's design proposal was selected in October 1965, to be powered by a new General Electric turbofan engine for which a development contract had been placed two months earlier. Construction of the prototype began in August 1966, by which time the aircraft had been designated **Lockheed C-5A Galaxy**, and this flew for the first time on 30 June 1068. The first operational examples was delivered to Military Airlift Command (MAC) on 17 December 1969 and a total of 81 were built to equip four squadrons. Of similar overall configuration to

the C-141 StarLifter, although very much larger and with a lower deck that has an unobstructed length of 36.91 m (121 ft 1 in) and width of 5.79 m (19 ft), it has in addition forward loading capability, via a visor type upward-hinged nose. It also has 28-wheeled retractable landing gear, to cater for operations with heavy loads from unpaved surfaces, each wheel-bogie having a shock-strut that can be shortened on the ground to simplify loading and unloading.

The Galaxy has proved to be an important logistics transport in MAC service, first proving itself on supply missions between the United States and South East Asia.

A major setback suffered by the type was the discovery in the late 1970s of

the early onset of wing structural fatique, forcing the design of a new wing. This was flown on a C-5A and all 77 remaining Galaxies subsequently went through an eight-month rework programme until the last was re-delivered in mid-1987. In 1982 the USAF optioned and ordered a further batch of new aircraft designated **C-5B** powered by 53,000-lb thrust TF39-GE-1C turbofans. The first of these flew for the first time on 10 September 1985 and the 50th and last example rolled off the Lockheed production line in 1989.

Specification
Lockheed C-5A Galaxy
Type: heavy logistics transport
Powerplant: four 18597-kg (41,000-

lb) Allison thrust General Electric TF39-GE-1 turbofans
Performance: average cruising speed 834 km/h (518 mph); range with maximum payload 6033 km (3,749 miles); range with 51075-kg (112,600-lb) payload 10507 km (6,529 miles)
Weights: basic operating 153286 kg (337,937 lb); maximum take-off 348813 kg (769,000 lb)
Dimensions: span 67.88 m (222 ft 8½ in); length 75.54 (247 ft 10 in); height 19.85 m (65 ft 1½ in); wing area 575.98 m² (6,200.0 sq ft)

The familiar shape of the Galaxy will live on, not least in the form of the C-5B, as the USAF's premier strategic transport.

Lockheed C-130 Hercules

Many television viewers will remember the 'continuing story of Peyton Place', and this particular entry could well be entitled 'the continuing story of the **Lockheed Hercules'**, for this remarkable transport aircraft has already been in production for over 35 years. Its origin came in 1951 with a US Air Force decision to acquire a fleet of turboprop transports for use by the Military Air Transport Service (MATS), later Military Airlift Command (MAC), as well as by Tactical Air Command (TAC). Of what is now regarded as typical military transport configuration, the Hercules has a high-set wing to maximize cabin space and a hydraulically-actuated loading ramp which, when closed, forms the under-surface of the upswept rear fuselage. The first of two **YC-130** prototypes was flown on 23 August 1954. These two aircraft, like early **C-130A** aircraft, were powered by four 2796-kW (3,750-shp) Allison T56-A-1A turboprop engines. The first production C-130A was flown on 7 April 1955, and initial deliveries to TAC units began in December 1956.

Since that time more than 2,000 Hercules have entered service with military forces and civil operators around the world and owing to sustained demand, the 1992 planned production rate remains around 35-37 every year. The most recent military version is the C-130J Advanced Hercules proposed by Lockheed in 1989. Intended to replace the large USAF C-130E fleet, the C-130J features a two-pilot 'glass' cockpit, advanced avionics including a HUD, and uprated T56 Series IV turboprop engines. Well named Hercules, Lockheed's medium lifter has found deployment in far more than the 12 legendary tasks.

Variants

AC-130A: redesignation of C-130As converted as gunships for use in South East Asia

Lockheed Hercules C.Mk 1 of the Lynham Transport Wing, Royal Air Force.

C-130A-II: redesignation of C-130As modified for an electronic reconnaissance role
DC-130A (earlier and briefly **GC-130A**): redesignation of C-130A converted to serve as drone launch and control aircraft
JC-130A: redesignation of C-130As modified to serve as missile trackers over the Atlantic test range
NC-130A: designation of C-130As used for special tests
RC-130A: designation of C-130A equipped for photo-reconnaissance role
TC-130A: designation of a C-130A converted as the prototype of a proposed crew trainer; later converted to RC-130A
C-130B: second production version with increased fuel capacity and gross weight
C-130B-II (later **RC-130B**): redesignation of C-130Bs modified for electronic reconnaissance; reverted subsequently to C-130Bs
HC-130B: designation of 12 search and rescue aircraft for US Coast Guard
JC-130B: designation of C-130Bs

converted for aerial recovery of satellite data capsules; most later reconverted to C-130B standard
KC-130B: designation of two inflight-refuelling tanker conversions of C-130Bs
VC-130B: temporary redesignation of one JC-130B when used as a staff transport
WC-130B: designation of new-build aircraft and C-130Bs converted for weather reconnaissance
C-130D: designation of ski-equipped version for Arctic service
C-130E: third production version with increased internal and external fuel, and powered by 3020-kW (4,050-shp) Allison T56-A-7 turboprops
AC-130E: redesignation of C-130Es following conversion as gunships
DC-130E: redesignation of C-130Es following conversion as drone launch and control aircraft
HC-130E: redesignation of C-130Es converted for crew recovery with the Aerospace Rescue and Recovery Service
JC-130E: temporary designation of

one C-130E used for test purposes
MC-130E: redesignation of HC-130Es when later converted for clandestine use
NC-130E: temporary designation of one C-130Es used for test purposes
WC-130E: redesignation of C-130Es converted for a weather reconnaissance role
C-130F: US Navy utility transport, similar to C-130B, procured initially as **GV-1U**
KC-130F: US Marine Corps tanker version, procured as **GV-1**, and powered by 3661-kW (4,910 shp) Allison T56-A-16 turboprops
LC-130F: four ski-equipped aircraft with T56-A-16 engines for use in Antarctica, procured by the US Navy as **UV-1L**
C-130G: four transport aircraft for the US Navy; as C-130Es but with T56-A-16 engines
EC-130G: redesignation of the four C-130Gs following conversion as VLF communications relay stations
C-130H: production version, similar to C-130E, but with airframe and system

improvements and T56-A-15 engines flat-rated to 3362 kW (4,508 shp)

C-130H(CT): redesignation of MC-130Es following installation of T56-A-15 engines and improved avionics

C-130H-MP: (later **PC-130H**): maritime patrol/SAR version of C-130H

C-130H(S): military production version, basically the C-130H with the longer fuselage of the L-100-30

AC-130H: redesignation of AC-130Es following installation of T56-A-15 engines and provision of inflight-refuelling capability

DC-130H: redesignation of one C-130H following conversion as drone launch and control aircraft

EC-130H: redesignation of EC-130Es following installation of T56-A-15 engines

HC-130H: rescue and recovery aircraft with re-entry tracking radar and Fulton aircrew recovery system

KC-130H: inflight-refuelling tankers

JHC-130H: redesignation of two HC-130Hs after conversion for aerial recovery of satellite data capsules

VC-130H: redesignation of two HC-130Hs converted as VIP transports

WC-130H: redesignation of 15 HC-130Hs following conversion for weather reconnaissance

C-130J: USAF C-130E replacement proposed by Lockheed in 1989, incorporating some features of the HTTB, including uprated T56 Series IV engines, two-man EFIS-equipped cockpit, and advanced avionics

C-130K: version with Allison T56-A-15 engines for Royal Air Force as **Hercules C.Mk 1**; version with stretched fuselage designated **Hercules C.Mk 3**

HC-130N: designation of 15 SAR aircraft for recovery of aircrew and space data capsules

HC-130P: aircrew recovery aircraft similar to HC-130H, but equipped for inflight-refuelling of rescue helicopters

EC-130Q: advanced version of the US Navy's EC-130G VLF communications relay station, based on the C-130H

KC-130R: tanker version for US Marine Corps, similar to KC-130H

LC-130R: designation of six examples for US Navy of C-130H with ski landing gear

RC-130S: redesignation of two JC-130As equipped with high intensity lighting for night SAR missions

KC-130T: tanker for US Marine Corps

Reserve. Similar to KC-130R but with improved avionics including INS, Omega, Tacan, and colour radar plus new autopilot and flight director. 16 delivered to Squadron VMGR-234 and VMGR-452 from November 1983.

KC-130T-30H: KC-130T for the USAMC but with 4.5 m (15 ft) stretched fuselage of C-130H-30 allowing increased internal fuel capacity. Two delivered late in 1991

AC-130U: new gunship version of MC-130H for 16th Special Operations Squadron, USAF based at Hurlburt Field, with armament reduced to one 25-mm and one 40-mm cannon plus a 105-mm howitzer, but much improved survivability. Twelve ordered from Rockwell International with the first flying on 20 December 1990

EC-130V: conversion (by General Dynamics at Fort Worth) of the US Coast Guard's last HC-130H airframe to take the Hawkeye's AN/APS-145 radar and associated rotordome mounted above the fuselage, to enable longer endurance interception missions against drug runners. The aircraft first flew at the end of July 1991 and trials were completed by October the same year.

L-100: civil transport version of the C-130, first flown on 20 April 1964, and powered by 3020-kW (4,050-shp)

Allison 501-D22 turboprop engines

L-100-20: lengthened fuselage version of L-100, by 2.54 m (8 ft 4 in), with Allison 501-D22 turboprop engines, or 3362-kW (4,508-shp) 501-D22A engines optional

L-100-30: basically as L-100-20, but with fuselage extended an additional 2.03 m (6 ft 8 in)

L-100F Super Hercules: 1992 Lockheed proposal for civil variant re-engined with Allison GMA 2100 turboprops driving 6-blade composite propellers, giving reduced fuel burn (17 per cent) and higher cruising speed (15 per cent), allowing L-100F to carry up to 21000 kg (46,300 lb) of freight over 3200 km (1,990 miles)

HTTB: Lockheed proposed the High Technology Test Bed version of the L-100-20 Hercules in the early 1980s and flew the prototype (N130X) on 19 June 1984. Powered by 3915 kW (5,250-shp) Allison 501D Series IV engines, the HTTB is intended for research and development in STOL flight. Equipped with advanced computer controlled flight controls, sophisticated avionics and navigation systems and improved cockpit displays, external differences include a longer dorsal fin, reprofiled nose, horizontal tailplane leading root

The US Coast Guard uses HC-130Hs as long-range MarPat and SAR aircraft. Originally fitted with Fulton STAR recovery gear, this has been removed and the familiar nose regained.

extensions ('horsals'), greatly enlarged flaps, and a reinforced undercarriage to allow high sink landings at heavier weights, demonstrated by a 365 m (1,198 ft) landing run at 59000 kg (130,073 lb) achieved in November 1989

Specification
Lockheed C-130H Hercules
Type: medium/long-range combat transport
Powerplant: four 3362-kW (4,508-hp) Allison T56-A-15 turboprops
Performance: maximum cruising speed 602 km/h (374 mph); service ceiling 10060 m (33,000 ft); range with maximum payload 4002 km (2,487 miles)
Weights: empty operating 34356 kg (75,743 lb); maximum take-off 79379 kg (175,000 lb)
Dimensions: span 40.41 m (132 ft 7 in); length 29.79 m (97 ft 9 in); height 11.66 m (38 ft 3 in); wing area 162.11 m^2 (1,745 sq ft)

Lockheed C-141 StarLifter

Designed to meet a USAF requirement for a large turbofan-powered freighter/troop-carrier, able to provide global-range airlift for Military Airlift Command and strategic deployment capabilities for Strategic Air Command, Lockheed's submission was the winner from four proposals. Designated **Lockheed C-141A StarLifter**, the aircraft had a swept wing mounted high on the fuselage to minimize cabin obstruction, a distinctive tail T-tail, and was powered by four turbofan engines pylon-mounted beneath the wing. The large cabin could accommodate 154 troops, 123 fully-equipped paratroops, or 80 stretches with seats for up to 16 walking casualties or attendants. Two paratroop doors were provided at the rear of the cabin, and straight-in cargo loading was catered for in the upswept rear fuselage, incorporating clamshell doors and a loading ramp. A total of 284 was built for the US Air Force.

The StarLifter began squadron opera-

The USAF's fleet of C-141 StarLifters began life wearing a white and grey colour scheme. Today, they are being repainted in an overall grey scheme.

tions with MAC in April 1965, the type's capability being amply demonstrated during operations in Vietnam, but it was soon realized that inflight refuelling capability was essential, and that in most cases the C-141As had load capability greater than their physical capacity. Thus, in mid-1976 Lockheed received a contract for a prototype conversion of a C-141A, with the fuselage lengthened by 7.11 m (23 ft 4 in) and inflight-refuelling capability added. Designated **YC-141B**, the prototype was first flown on 24 March 1977, and since that time 270 surviving C-141As have been converted to **C-141B** configuration, the last of them being redelivered on 29 June 1982. The volume of the cargo compartment has been increased by 61.48 m^3

(2,171.0 cu ft), making it possible to load 13 instead of 10 463L cargo pallets and, in effect, increasing the fleet by some 87 aircraft.

Specification
Lockheed C-141B StarLifter
Type: long-range logistics jet transport
Powerplant: four 9525-kg (21,000-lb) thrust Pratt & Whitney TF33-P-7 turbofans

Performance: maximum cruising speed 910 km/h (566 mph); unrefuelled range with maximum payload 4723 km (2,935 miles)
Weights: operating empty 67186 kg (148,120 lb); maximum take-off 155582 kg (343,000 lb)
Dimensions: span 48.74 m (159 ft 11 in); length 51.29 m (168 ft 3½ in); height 11.96 m (39 ft 3 in); wing area 299.88 m^2 (3,228.0 sq ft)

Lockheed Constellation, Super Constellation and Starliner

Design of the **Lockheed L-49** began in 1939 to meet the requirement of Pan American Airways and Transcontinental & Western Air (now Trans World Airlines), for a 40-passenger airliner for use on domestic routes. Manufacture was initiated but with the outbreak of World War II aircraft on the production line were commandeered for service with the USAAF as transports under the designation **C-69**, the first being flown on 9 January 1943. A total of 22 entered USAAF service before the contract cancellations following VJ-Day. Production of civil aircraft then began under the company designation **L-049 Constellation**, using components that had been intended for C-69s, but with the interiors completed to airline standard and with basic accommodation for 43 to 48 passengers, or a maximum of 60 in a high-density layout. The first Constellation was certificated for civil operations on 11 December 1945, the type entering service first with Pan Am and TWA, the latter inaugurating a regular US-Paris service on 6 February 1946.

The first true civil Constellations were **Lockheed L-649** aircraft with 1864-kW (2,500-hp) Wright 749C-18BD-1 engines and far more luxurious interiors seating 48 to 64 passengers as standard, or 81 in a high-density arrangement. This version was replaced in production during 1947 by the longer-range **L-749** with additional fuel yet able to carry the same payload, but by the end of 1949 the demand for air travel was increasing and operators were then looking for aircraft of greater capacity. This brought development of the **L-1049 Super Constellation**, with the fuselage lengthened by 5.59 m (18 ft 4 in), and Super 'Connies' entered service during their production life with a variety of interior layouts that could seat a maximum of 109 passengers. Last of the civil Constellation-derived airliners was the **L-1649A Starliner**, with a completely new wing of increased span and with far greater fuel capacity, providing a range considerably in excess of any of its predecessors. When production ended in the late 1950s a total of 856 aircraft of all versions, both civil and military, had been built, and brief details of the different marks are given under variants.

Variants

L-049: designation of original civil Constellations, produced from components stockpiled for military C-69 transports
L-649: designation of the first post-war Constellations built and furnished entirely as civil airliners
L-649A: generally similar to L-649 but with increased fuel capacity
L-749: long-range version of Constellation, generally similar to L-649A but with strengthened landing gear
L-749A: generally similar to L-749, but with strengthened structure for operation at higher gross weight
L-1049: initial version of Super Constellation, with standard accommodation for 69 to 92 passengers and 1864-kW (2,500-hp) Wright 749C-18BD-1 engines

Their days with the major airlines done, many Constellations soldiered on with small cargo carriers 'south of the border'.

L-1049C: improved version of Super Constellation with 2424-kW (3,250-hp) Wright 87TC-18DA-1 Turbo-Compound engines
L-1049D: generally similar to L-1049C, but intended for convertible passenger/cargo operations with cargo doors in the port rear fuselage and strengthened flooring
L-1049E: generally similar to L-1049C, but certificated for operation at a higher gross weight
L-1049G: high gross weight version with 2535-kW(3,400-hp) Wright 972TC-18DA-3 Turbo-Compound engines and provision for wingtip fuel tanks
L-1049H: final production version of Super Constellation, combining L-1049D and L-1049G configurations
L-1649: prototype of the Starliner, basically a Super Constellation airframe, with a redesigned, more efficient wing containing additional fuel, and powered by 2535-kW (3,400-hp) Wright 988TC-18EA-2 Turbo-Cyclone engines
L-1649A: production version of the Starliner, of which 43 were built
C-69: designation of original military transport version
C-69C-1 (later ZC-69C-1): one-off VIP military transport
XC-69E: redesignation of one C-69 used as engine test-bed
C-121A: designation of cargo/personnel transport versions of L-749 for USAF, with strengthened floors and port rear fuselage cargo door; those converted in service as VIP transports were redesignated **VC-121A**
VC-121B: one VIP aircraft, similar to standard L-749, equipped for possible Presidential use
PO-1W: two examples of an airborne early-warning (AEW) aircraft for US Navy, derived from L-749 airframe
R7O-1 (later R7V-1 then C-121J): USN version of L-1049D, powered by 2424-kW (3,250-hp) Wright R-3350-91 Turbo-Compound engines
R7V-1P: temporary designation of one R7V-1 equipped for polar ice-pack reconnaissance
R7V-2: four experimental aircraft with L-1049 airframes, powered by 5,550-shp (4139-kW) Pratt & Whitney YT34-P-12A turboprop engines for USN evaluation
VW-2 Warning Star (later

EC-121K): US Navy AEW aircraft, 222 built, with L-1049 airframe, avionics equipment developed for PO-1W, 3,400-hp (2535-kW) Wright R-3350-34 or R-3350-42 Turbo-Compound engines, and wingtip auxiliary fuel tanks
WV-2E (later **EC-121L**); one experimental conversion of WV-2 as avionics test-bed; first aircraft to carry a large rotating radome above the fuselage
WV-2Q (later **EC-121M**): redesignation of WV-2s re-equipped for electronic countermeasures (ECM) role
WV-3 (later **WQC-121N**): eight aircraft, similar to WV-2 but without tiptanks, for weather reconnaissance duties
C-121C: US Air Force version of USN R7V-1, but with R-3350-34 engines
JC-121C: redesignation of two C-121Cs and one TC-121C converted for avionics and systems research
RC-121C: USAF AEW aircraft, similar to USN WV-2; later redesignated **TC-121C** and used for AEW training
VC-121C: redesignation of C-121Cs converted for use as VIP transports
RC-121D (later EC-121D): USAF version of USN WV-2, differed by having wingtip tanks and revisions of interior layout and equipment
VC-121E: VIP aircraft equipped for Presidential use, based on R7V-1 airframe
YC-121F: two experimental aircraft as R7V-1s, but with 4474-kW (6,000-shp) Pratt & Whitney T34-P-6 turboprop engines for USAF evaluation
C-121G: redesignation of 32 R7V-1s transferred from USN to USAF use
EC-121H: redesignation of 42 EC-121Ds following installation of specialized avionics equipment
EC-121J: redesignation of two

The Starliner was the ultimate expression of the Constellation design. With its longer wings and fuselage and new engines, it was unquestionably the definitive piston-powered airliner.

EC-121Ds with additional avionics
JC-121K: redesignation of one EC-121K used for avionics experiments
NC-121K: redesignation of EC-121Ks used by the USN for various tests
EC-121P: redesignation of EC-121Ks with updated ASW equipment
EC-121Q: redesignation of EC-121Ds with advanced avionics equipment
EC-121R: redesignation of EC-121K and EC-121P aircraft equipped to process relayed data from air-delivered ground seismic devices along major jungle routes in Vietnam
NC-121S: ECM and electronic reconnaissance aircraft converted from C-121Cs
EC-121T: redesignation of earlier AEW aircraft following conversion to enhance AEW capability

Specification
Lockheed L-1649A Starliner
Type: long-range civil transport
Powerplant: four 2535-kW (3,400-hp) Wright 988TC-18EA-2 Turbo-Compound radial piston engines
Performance: maximum speed 606 km/h (377 mph) at 5670 m (18,600 ft); service ceiling 7225 m (23,700 ft); range with maximum payload 7950 km (4,940 miles)
Weights: empty 41569 kg (91,645 lb); maximum take-off 72575 kg (160,000 lb)
Dimensions: span 45.72 m (150 ft 0 in); length 35.41 m (116 ft 2 in); height 7.54 m (24 ft 9 in); wing area 171.87 m² (1,850.0 sq ft)

Lockheed F-22 Rapier

In April 1991 the **Lockheed F-22** was declared the winner of the USAF Advanced Tactical Fighter competition initiated in 1981 to find a replacement for the F-15 Eagle, and a $12-billion engineering development programme began to develop an agile, fly-by-wire, stealthy, radar-equipped fighter. The US Navy joined the programme in April 1986 with a requirement to find a follow-on to the F-14D Tomcat. In October the same year the DoD announced the selection of Lockheed and Northrop to each develop and build two prototypes of the YF-22 and YF-23 respectively. At that point Lockheed teamed with Boeing and General Dynamics to develop an ATF under an agreement that the winning company would become the prime contractor. The first prototype YF-22, 87-3997/N22YF, powered by specially-developed General Electric YF120 engines, took to the air for the first time on 29 September 1990 when Lockheed test pilot Dave Ferguson flew the aircraft from the Palmdale factory to Edwards Air Force Base. This was swiftly followed by 87-3998/N22YX on 30 October 1990, powered by alternative Pratt & Whitney YF119 engines. After a full evaluation against the competing Northrop/McDonnell Douglas YF-23 design, the YF119/YF-22 combination was declared the winner.

Design of the definitive F-22A was frozen in March 1992, and differences from the prototypes include an increase in the span of the diamond-shaped wing to 13.59 m (44 ft 6 in) but without increasing the area. Leading-edge sweep has been reduced to 42° (from 48°), wing root thickness reduced and camber and twist reduced to improve supersonic manoeuvrability; area of the twin vertical tail surfaces has been reduced to 27.12 m² (89 sq ft), but no change made to the horizontal tails; the cockpit moved forward to increase visibility and the engine inlet lip moved aft by 0.45 m (1 ft 6 in). The F-22A fuselage length has been shortened by 63 cm (25 in). A primary requirement was the ability to reach Mach 1 without the use of an after-burner (dubbed 'supercruise' by the USAF) and thus fly the segment of any mission spent over hostile territory supersonically.

The first production aircraft is due to fly in March 1995, and the USAF expect the initial F-22A squadron to become operational in 2002, following a four-year flight test programme. Planned USAF buy is 648 aircraft, and the first batch of 11 aircraft will comprise nine F-22A single-seat and two F-22B two-seat prototypes. Projected cost of the F-22 was quoted in 1991 as $59.4 million each. On 25 April 1992, by which time the aircraft had been successively named Lightning II, Super Star and, finally, Rapier, the programme received a setback when N22YX was damaged while making a practice approach to Edwards AFB, by which time the first prototype had been grounded at Marietta, partially dismantled and allocated to ground-based development tests.

Specification
Lockheed YF-22
Type: single-seat supersonic air superiority fighter
Powerplant: two 157-kN (35,000-lb) thrust Pratt & Whitney F119 augmented turbofans
Performance: maximum speed Mach 2.2 or 2335 km/h (1,451 mph); service ceiling 19812 m (65,000 ft); combat radius 1285 km (800 miles)

Weights: empty equipped 14061 kg (31,000 lb); normal take-off 26308 kg (58,000 lb)
Dimensions: span 13.1 m (43 ft); length 19.55 m (64 ft 2 in); height 5.39 m (17 ft 8 in); wing area 77.1 m² (830 sq ft)
Armament: both prototypes were unarmed but production F-22s will have either a 20-mm or 25-mm built-in cannon plus AIM-9 and AIM-120 air-to-air missiles housed in the internal weapons bay

Winner of the 1991 ATF competition, the F-22 will replace the F-15 Eagle as the USAF's premier air combat fighter.

Lockheed F-94 Starfire

Within six months of its formation, in the autumn of 1947, the United States Air Force advised Lockheed of an urgent requirement for a two-seat all-weather fighter. Successful use of the Lockheed P-80 Shooting Star, and the T-33 trainer derived from it, led to the suggestion that a fighter could be based on the T-33 to meet the US Air Force request. The close relationship can be gauged by the fact that a modified F-80 served as the prototype for the T-33, and the same aircraft then became one of the two Lockheed **YF-94** prototypes. It differed by having the fuselage lengthened to house fire-control radar, and modified to accept the more powerful Allison J33-A-33 turbojet with an afterburning thrust of 2722 kg (6,000 lb). Flown on 16 April 1949, approximately 12 months from initiation of the idea, the two YF-94s were troubled initially by powerplant problems, delaying entry into service until 29 December 1949. Even then, the USAF acquired its first turbojet-powered all-weather fighter far quicker than would have been possible in any other way. Production was a total 854 aircraft in three main versions, and these gave a decade of valuable service, serving first with the US Air Force in Korea, and remaining in use with Air National Guard units until 1959.

Variants
F-94A: initial production version, early aircraft conversions of T-33 airframes taken from the production line; basically similar to YF-94 prototypes, but carrying full equipment and four 0.5-in (12.7-mm) guns
YF-94B: prototype for second production version, with improved avionics and utility systems
F-94B: second production version, generally similar to YF-94B prototype, with Allison J33-A-33 or -33A engine, and large wingtip fuel tanks
YF-94C (ex-YF-97A): designation of two prototypes of improved higher-performance version, introduced a new wing, all-rocket armament, new tailplane, and a more powerful Pratt & Whitney J48 turbojet, a licence-built version of the Rolls-Royce Tay
F-94C Starfire (ex-F-97A): final production version, generally as with the YF-94C prototypes, but with refinements; entering service in July 1951, the F-94Cs were improved progressively throughout their operational life

Specification
Lockheed F-94C Starfire
Type: two-seat all-weather fighter
Powerplant: one Pratt & Whitney J48-P-5 turbojet with standard thrust of 2880 kg (6,350 lb) and 3969 kg (8,750 lb) with afterburning
Performance: maximum speed 1030 km/h (640 mph) at sea level; service ceiling 15665 m (51,400 ft); standard range 1296 km (805 miles)
Weights: empty 5764 kg (12,708 lb); maximum take-off 10970 kg (24,184 lb)
Dimensions: span 11.38 m (37 ft 4 in); length 13.56 m (44 ft 6 in); height 4.55 m (14 ft 11 in); wing area 21.63 m² (232.80 sq ft)
Armament: 24 folding-fin rockets in nose, plus 24 similar rockets in two wing pods

In the fashion of most fighters of the day, the F-94 needed a drag-chute to reduce its landing roll. This Starfire is seen arriving at Philadelphia in 1955.

Lockheed F-104 Starfighter

In 1952 Lockheed's Chief Engineer, C. L. 'Kelly' Johnson, was faced with the daunting task of designing and developing a single-seat fighter that would be far superior to anything that the Communists were using over Korea. He opted for small size, so that on the power of a single engine it would have high speed and excellent manoeuvrability, and he aimed to cut complexity to a minimum so that this factor would combine with small size to keep unit costs as low as possible. Johnson designed a wide-chord short-span unswept wing with a maximum thickness of only 10.16 cm (4 in), and this had a leading edge so sharp that it needed protective covering on the ground to prevent injury. The tail unit had its tailplane set almost at the tip of the fin, and the fuselage, tailored around the General Electric J79 engine that had been selected to power this **Lockheed F-104 Starfighter**, meant there was little room for equipment and, for example, no airborne interception radar was carried. The first of two **XF-104** prototypes, each powered by a 3538-kg (7,800-lb) thrust Wright XJ65-W-6 turbojet engine (4627 kg/10,200 lb afterburning thrust) was flown on 4 March 1954, but almost four years of development followed before the USAF gave clearance for squadron use of the Starfighter in January 1958. By then the USAF had lost interest in this class of fighter and accepted only 296 for its own use. However, a group of NATO countries, under the leadership of West Germany, decided to manufacture an improved version to equip their air forces, leading to a major international production programme in which the Starfighter was built in Belgium, Italy, the Netherlands and West Germany for NATO forces, and also in Canada and Japan. As a result, production ended an additional 2,282 F-104s had been built, and a large number of these remain in service.

The final Starfighter development was carried out by Aeritalia/Alenia who upgraded 150 Italian air force F-104 aircraft between 1986 and 1990, and these are still in front-line service. Designated **F-104S-ASA** (Aggiornamento Sistemi d'Arma), they were reworked to accept more advanced equipment such as the FIAR Setter airborne radar, improved ECM and IFF, and more up-to-date electrical and weapons delivery systems plus extra pylons fitted outboard of the wing tanks to allow the carriage of the Aspide or AIM-9L Sidewinder AAMs. The first conversion flew in March 1985

Lockheed F-104G Starfighter of Marinefliegergeschwader 1, Marineflieger (West German naval air arm), based at Schleswig. This aircraft is wearing the unit markings and camouflage of the late 1960s.

and the initial definitive F-104S-ASA was delivered to the AMI in November 1986. All 150 were in service by the end of 1990.

Variants
YF-104A: 17 pre-production aircraft with fuselage lengthened by 1.68 m (5 ft 6 in), increased fuel and powered initially by the General Electric XJ79-GE-3 of 6713 kg (14,800 lb) afterburning thrust; during extended testing the improved J79-GE-3A of similar thrust became standard
F-104A: first production version, initially with J79-GE-3A engine, but later retrofitted with J79-GE-3B; ventral fin and blown flaps; 153 built
NF-104A: redesignation of three F-104As modified for use in USAF astronaut training
QF-104A: redesignation of YF-104A/F-104A aircraft converted as radio-controlled target drones
F-104B: two-seat combat trainer version of the F-104A with revised fuel system and armament; 26 built
F-104C: tactical strike version for USAF Tactical Air Command; with J79-GE-7 engine of 7167 kg (15,800 lb) afterburning thrust, and armed with Sidewinder missiles, or with bombs or rocket pods for conventional or nuclear strike; inflight-refuelling probe; 77 built
F-104D: combat trainer version of F-104C; 21 built for USAF, plus 20
F-104DJ aircraft for Japan
F-104F: refined version, similar to F-104D, for Luftwaffe; 30 built
F-104G: major production version, built in Canada, Europe and the United States; by comparison with F-104C had strengthened structure, aerodynamic improvements, advanced avionics and equipment, and J79-GE-11A engine of 7076 kg (15,600 lb) afterburning thrust, or licence-built version of this engine in European production aircraft; 1,127 built
RF-104G: tactical reconnaissance

version of F-104G; 189 built
TF-104G: two-seat trainer version of F-104G with full combat capability; 220 built
F-104J: version of F-104G for Japan, but equipped as an all-weather interceptor; three sample aircraft built by Lockheed; Mitsubishi assembled 29 from Lockheed components and then built 178; Japanese-assembled/built aircraft have licence-free version of J79-GE-11A engine
F-104N: designation of the aircraft similar to F-104G built for NASA as supersonic chase aircraft
F-104S: Aeritalia multi-role version developed from F-104G; 254 built in Italy for the Italian and Turkish air forces, powered by J79-GE-19 with 8364 kg (17,900 lb) afterburning thrust
F-104S-ASA: Aeritalia/Alenia upgrade of 150 Italian air force F-104S with improved radar, ECM, IFF and weapon delivery systems, plus ability to carry more advanced AAMs; first flown in March 1985
CF-104: Canadian-built version of F-104G (by Canadair) powered by the licence-built J79-OEL-7 engine of 7167 kg (15,800 lb) afterburning thrust and fitted with removable inflight-refuelling probe; 200 built

CF-104D: two-seat trainer version of CF-104, built by Lockheed for the Canadian air force, powered by the licence-built J79-OEL-7 engine; 38 built

Specification
Lockheed F-104G Starfighter
Type: single-seat multi-mission fighter
Powerplant: one General Electric J79-GE-11A turbojet of 7076 kg (15,600 lb) afterburning thrust
Performance: maximum speed 1845 km/h (1,146 mph) at 15240 m (50,000 ft); service ceiling 15240 m (50,000 ft); range 1740 km (1,081 miles)
Weights: empty 6348 kg (13,995 lb); maximum take-off 13170 kg (29,035 lb)
Dimensions: span (excluding missiles) 6.36 m (21 ft 9 in); length 16.66 m (54 ft 8 in); height 4.09 m (13 ft 5 in); wing area 18.22 m² (196.10 sq ft)
Armament: one 20-mm General Electric six-barrelled cannon, wingtip-mounted Sidewinder air-to-air missiles and up to 1814 kg (4,000 lb) of stores

Turkey now ranks as one of the chief surviving Starfighter operators, especially since it became a repository for cast-off NATO F-104s. These F-104Gs are all ex-Italian aircraft.

Lockheed F-117

Successfully kept secret for nearly 15 years, the Lockheed **F-117A** was the winning submission for the 'black' XST (Experimental Stealth Technology) competition of 1975-76 sponsored by the US Defense Advanced Research Projects Agency. Both Northrop and Lockheed were contenders for the programme, but in 1976 Lockheed was awarded the contract and built two technology demonstrator prototypes under a programme codenamed 'Have Blue'. Powered by General Electric CJ610 turbojet engines, the first XST made its initial flight in December 1977 from Groom Lake, Nevada, piloted by William C. Park, but both prototypes ultimately crashed, one in May 1978 and the other in 1980.

Promising test results led to the development of two scaled-up YF-117A-LO prototypes which were followed by 57

production F-117As ordered in batches during the fiscal years 1980 to 1986 plus 1988. The first pre-production aircraft flew for the first time on 18 June 1981, and the first F-117A was handed over to the USAF in August 1982. Despite much worldwide speculation, the air force resisted confirming the existence of the programme until November 1988 when they released a rudimentary and misleading photograph of the aircraft, and confirmed the designation. The next logical 'F number' should have been the F-19, and many agencies used this for some time when identifying the spectral aircraft. The USAF had allocated F-112 to F-116 to Soviet fighters acquired clandestinely for evaluation, and the designation F-117 was thought to be in use for the same purposes and consequently attracted less attention.

The F-117A was declared operational

in 1983, but the aircraft flew only at night from its secret base at Tonopah, 140 miles north-west of Las Vegas, Nevada, to preserve programme secrecy, until late in 1989 when daytime flying began. Two aircraft were lost in accidents in July 1986 and October 1987 and these were attributed to pilot disorientation associated with fatigue.

F-117As, reportedly nicknamed 'Wobblin Goblin', but more usually referred to by its pilot as the 'Black Jet' and officially named **Night Hawk**, first went into action in December 1989 as part of Operation Just Cause mounted by the US to remove from office General Manuel Noriega of Panama. The aircraft's performance in placing ordnance onto specific targets with absolute precision was considered a vindication of the whole programme. Further action came in January 1991 with the Gulf conflict and a major proportion of the USAF fleet (42 out of the surviving 54) were eventually based in Saudi Arabia with 415th Tactical

Fighter Squadron 'Nightstalkers', the 416th TFS 'Ghostriders' and the 417th Tactical Fighter Training Squadron 'Bandits', all comprising the 37th Tactical Fighter Wing, one of whose aircraft dropped the very first bomb of Operation Desert Storm on 17 January 1991.

The result of a radical design philosophy which seeks to minimise the radar signature of an aircraft, the F-117A features angular multi-faceted air frame panels designed to deflect and in some cases absorb radar energy. The heavily-swept wing of just over 67° illustrates highly-complex aerodynamics and the intakes, doors and access panel shapes are all optimised to reflect radar signals. Wing and fuselage are aerodynamically blended and made of conventional aluminium but specially coated with radar absorbent materials. Tail surfaces, or 'ruddervators', are made of composites, and the whole aircraft is controlled by a quadruplex fly-by-wire system. The comprehensive avionics fit includes forward- and downward-looking infra-red systems; head-up and head-down displays; a retractable laser designator; multi-function CRTs; a mission computer and flight control comuputer/navigation system interface, plus a global positioning system. Powerplants are non-afterburning variants of the General Electric F404 engine used in the F-18 Hornet.

Specification (estimated)
Type: single-seat stealth strike fighter
Powerplant: two 4900-kg (10,800-lb) thrust General Electric F404-GE-F102 turbofans
Performance: maximum speed Mach 1; normal operating speed Mach 0.9
Weights: empty operating 13609 kg

(30,000 lb); maximum take-off 23814 kg (52,500 lb)
Dimensions: span 13.20 m (43 ft 4 in); length 20.08 m (65 ft 11 in); height 3.78 m (12 ft 5 in); wing area 105.9 m² (1,140 sq ft)
Armament: underfuselage internal weapons by can accommodate full range of USAF tactical fighter ordnance but principally two 907-kg (2,000-lb) bombs of GBU-10/GBU-27 laser-guided type, or AGM-65 Maverick or AGM-89 HARM air-to-surface missiles

The 'Stealth Fighter' comes from a long line of successful 'Skunk Works' designs. Its replacement, or something akin to that, may already be flying.

Lockheed Hudson

The first American-built aircraft to be used operationally by the RAF during World War II, the **Lockheed Hudson** stemmed from urgent British requirements in early 1938 for a maritime patrol/navigational trainer aircraft. Faced with the problem of producing these aircraft as quickly as possible, Lockheed proposed a militarised version of the Lockheed 14 Super Electra. As then envisaged, the new aircraft was generally similar to the Lockheed 14-WF62, except for the introduction of a modified fuselage that incorporated nose and dorsal gun turrets, a bomb bay in the centre fuselage, and a navigator's position within the fuselage, to the rear of the wing trailing edge. However, as the British Purchasing Commission was seeking a maritime reconnaissance aircraft rather than a bomber, this configuration was not acceptable. The BPC suggested, instead, that the navigator should be accommodated nearer to the pilot, and on the following day Lockheed produced a new mock-up accommodating him in a glazed nose position. This proved good enough for contract negotiations to begin, leading to an order in late June 1938 for 200 **B14L** aircraft, as the type was then designated by Lockheed; there was a provision in the contract that 250 would be accepted provided that the total was delivered before the end of December 1939. The first B14L, unarmed and with a mock dorsal turret, was flown for the first time on 10 December 1938; the 250th production aircraft came off the assembly line during the first week of November 1939. When production ended in May 1943 a total of 2,941 had been built, comprising 1,338 aircraft purchased directly from Lockheed, 1,302 under US Department of the Army contracts for supply under Lend-Lease, 300 as trainers for the US Army Air Force, plus a single civil **B14S** which was supplied to Sperry. Thus the **Hudson**, as the B14L was named by the RAF, elevated Lockheed into the ranks of major aircraft manufacturers.

Despite its derivation from a peaceful airliner, the Hudson achieved some surprising 'firsts'. A Hudson of No. 224 Squadron, for example, shot down a Dornier Do 18 flying-boat on 8 October 1939, the first RAF victory to be recorded in World War II by an American-built aircraft; a Hudson of No. 220 Squadron located and directed British naval forces to the German prison ship *Altmark* in February 1940; a Hudson from No. 269 Squadron damaged, and then accepted the surrender of the German submarine *U-570* in the Atlantic on 27 August 1941; No. 280 Squadron was the first to be equipped with airborne lifeboats and

Lockheed Hudson Mk III of No. 279 Sqn Royal Air Force, based at Sturgate, in Britain, in 1942.

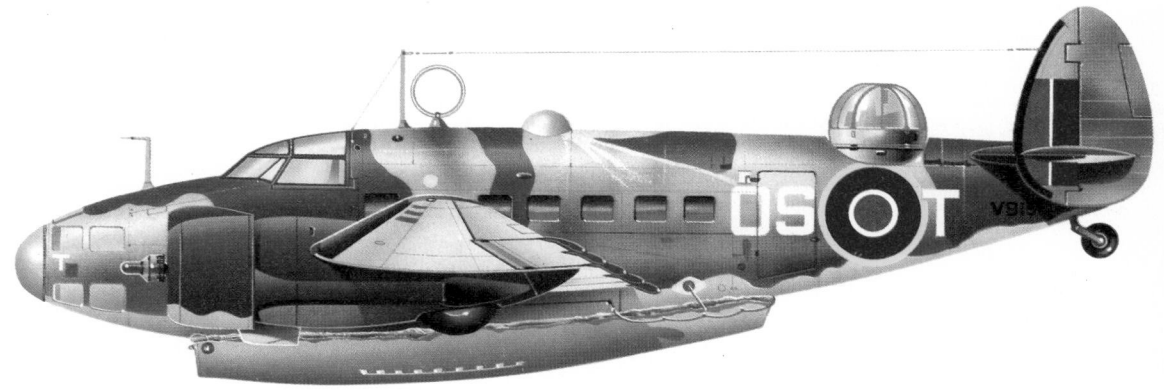

Lockheed A-29 bomber of the United States Army Air Corps in pre-war markings and camouflage.

deployed the first in the North Sea in early May 1943; and in the same month a Hudson of No. 608 Squadron became the first aircraft in RAF service to sink a German U-boat by rocket fire. The first sinking of a U-boat (*U-701*) by an aircraft of the US Army Air Force was recorded by a **Lockheed A-29** on 7 July 1942; and US Navy **PBO-1** aircraft (USN designation of the A-29) sank the first two U-boats to be credited to that service in World War II on 1 and 15 March 1942. In addition to being used by British and Commonwealth air forces and by the USAAF and USN, the type served also in small numbers with British Overseas Airways Corporation, the Chinese air force, and the Portuguese naval air arm.

Variants
Hudson Mk I: original direct-purchase version for the RAF with 820-kW (1,100-hp) Wright GR-1820-G102A engines; 351 built
Hudson Mk II: direct-purchase version, generally as Mk I, but with airframe strengthening and constant-speed propellers; 20 built
Hudson Mk III: version combining Hudson Mk II airframe with 895-kW (1,200-hp) Wright GR-1820-G205A engines; 428 direct-purchase aircraft for British/Comonwealth air forces before the introduction of Lend-Lease
Hudson Mk IIIA: British and Commonwealth designation of Lend-Lease version similar to Hudson III, but

with 895-kW (1,200-hp) Wright R-1820-87 engines; procured by the USAAF as **A-29** and by the US Navy as **PBO-1**; Hudson Mk IIIA production totalled 800, including 384 with convertible interiors for troop transport, procured as A-29A
Hudson Mk IV: RAAF redesignation of 50 Hudson Mk Is, but powered by 783-kW (1,050-hp) Pratt & Whitney Twin Wasp S3C-G engines; RAAF redesignation also of improved version acquired originally as Hudson Mk II
Hudson Mk IVA: RAAF designation of Lend-Lease version procured by the USAAF as **A-28**; 52 built
Hudson Mk V: direct purchase version, similar to Hudson Mk III, but

with 895-kW (1,200-hp) Twin Wasp S3C4-G engines; 409 built

Hudson Mk VI: Lend-Lease version procured by the USAAF as **A-29A:** generally similar to Hudson Mks III/V but with 895-kW (1,200-hp) Chevrolet-built Pratt & Whitney R-1830-67 engines; 450 built

Hudson C.Mk VI: redesignation of a number of RAF Hudson Mk VIs following the removal of armament for use in a transport role

A-29B: redesignation of 24 USAAF A-29As following conversion for photo-reconnaissance

AT-18: designation of 217 aircraft with 895-kW (1,200-hp) Wright R-1820-87 engines procured by the USAAF as gunnery trainers

AT-18A: 83 aircraft, generally similar to AT-18, procured by the USAAF as un-

The Lockheed AT-18, 300 of which were built, was a dedicated gunnery trainer version of the Hudson series, which was fitted with a Martin dorsal turret (two 0.5-in/12.7-mm machine-guns) similar to those found on most American bombers.

armed navigational trainers

B14S: designation of a single aircraft for the Sperry Gyroscope Company for use as an instrument test aircraft

Specification
Lockheed Hudson Mk I
Type: maritime patrol-bomber
Powerplant: two 820-kW (1,100-hp) Wright GR-1820-G-102A radial piston engines
Performance: maximum speed

396 km/h (246 mph); at 1980 m (6,500 ft); service ceiling 7620 m (25,000 ft); range 3154 km (1,960 miles)
Weights: empty 5276 kg (11,630 lb); maximum take-off 7938 kg (17,500 lb)
Dimensions: span 19.96 m (65 ft 0 in); length 13.51 m (44 ft 4 in); height

3.61 m (11 ft 10 in); wing area 51.19 m² (551.0 sq ft)
Armament: two 7.7-mm (0.303-in) forward-firing machine-guns, and two similar weapons in a dorsal turret, plus up to 635 kg (1,400 lb) of bombs or depth charges in internal bomb bay

Lockheed L-1011 TriStar

Lockheed's wide-body airliner, designated **Lockheed L-1011 TriStar**, originated to meet the requirements of American Airlines for a large-capacity short/medium-range transport. Construction of the first aircraft began in early 1968, and this was flown initially on 17 November 1970, a cantilever low-wing monoplane with 35° of wing sweep, powered by three 19051-kg (42,000-lb) thrust Rolls-Royce RB.211 turbofans, and with accommodation for a crew of two to four and from 256 to 400 passengers. At this stage of development Lockheed and Rolls-Royce each ran into financial difficulties, both requiring aid from their respective governments before the programme could be resumed and, as a result, certification was not gained until 14 April 1972, with the first revenue flight made by Eastern Air Lines on 26 April 1972. Some teething troubles were experienced, primarily with the engines, but in a very short time the Tristar was proving popular with operators and passengers alike.

This TriStar 1 of Pacific South West (with the airline's famous smile under its nose) was later converted to -100 standard like many early model aircraft.

The original production version, designated **L-1011-1**, was followed into service by the longer-range **L-1011-100** carrying additional fuel and certificated for operation at a higher gross weight. To provide better performance from 'hot-and-high' airfields the **L-1011-200** was developed with 21772-kg (48,000-lb) thrust RB.211-524 engines, but in other respects this model is similar to the L-1011-1. It was available optionally with the increased fuel tankage of the L-1011-

100, the improved performance of the RB-211-524 engine giving it a slight increase in range, and it is certificated for operation at a high gross weight. Final member of the family is the long-range **L-1011-500**, introducing many features tested and incorporated in the original aircraft (N1011) which has since become designated as the **Advanced TriStar**. The L-1011-500 has RB.211-524B or RB.211-524B4 engines, the fuselage reduced in length by 4.11 m (13 ft 6 in), in-

The initial production TriStar was L-1011-1, like this example operated by Gulf Air.

creased fuel tankage, revised interior layout and accommodation for 246 to a maximum 330 passengers.

At the end of 1981 Lockheed, disappointed by lack of sales, announced that with the end of TriStar production it would withdraw from the civil jet airliners market, and the 250th and final air-

craft (TriStar 500 CS-TEE of TAP-Air Portugal) rolled off the Burbank line in August 1983, not flying until January 1984. The last two aircraft to be delivered were the Series 500s JY-AGI and AGJ handed over to Royal Jordanian in June 1985. Contemplating the time when the TriStar would be replaced by more advanced types, in 1986 Monarch Aviation of Miami designed a conversion to modify an aircraft into a dedicated freighter by installing an upward-opening 4.38 m (14 ft 4 in) × 2.71 m (8 ft 9 in)

cargo door on the port side upper fuselage forward of the wing and deleting all passenger-related equipment. The first conversion was carried out in May 1987 by Pemco Aeroplex (then Hayes) using an early aircraft, and both Royal Jordanian and Saudia are thought to be interested in converting their fleet to freighters in due course. Lockheed and the British company Marshall of Cambridge have also engineered cargo conversions of the TriStar, the latter having modified six TriStar 500s acquired from

British Airways in 1983 into tanker/transporter (K.Mk 1/KC.Mk 1s) for the Royal Air Force. Three more were acquired from Pan American in 1984/85 and subsequently used as C.Mk 2 transports, and are also scheduled to be converted to K.Mk 2 tankers.

Specification
Lockheed L-1011-500 TriStar
Type: long-range transport
Powerplant: three 22680-kg (50,000-lb) thrust Rolls-Royce RB.211-524B or

RB.211-524B4 turbofans
Performance: maximum cruising speed 974 km/h (605 mph) at 9145 m (30,000 ft); service ceiling 12800 m (42,000 ft); range with maximum payload 9653 km (5,998 miles)
Weights: empty operating 109299 kg (240,963 lb); maximum take-off 224982 kg (496,000 lb)
Dimensions: span 47.35 m (155 ft 4 in); length 50.05 m (164 ft 2½ in); height 16.87 m (55 ft 4 in); wing area 321.06 m² (3,456.0 sq ft)

Lockheed Model 1329 JetStar I/II

To meet a US Air Force requirement for an 'off-the-shelf' high-performance light transport, Lockheed developed the **Lockheed 1329 JetStar**. A clean low-wing monoplane with swept wings and swept tail surfaces, the JetStar was powered in prototype form by two 2200-kg (4,850-lb) thrust Bristol Orpheus 1/5 turbojet engines. The first of two prototypes was flown on 4 September 1957, with flight testing proving satisfactory, but when planned licence-production of the Orpheus engine could not be finalised, Lockheed chose instead to power the initial production version by four 1361-kg (3,000-lb) thrust Pratt & Whitney JT12A-6 engines, mounted in pairs on each side of the rear fuselage. The anticipated military demand failed to materialise in any significant numbers, with the result that the majority of the 204 JetStars that were built, before production ended in 1980, were sold as business/executive aircraft.

Variants
JetStar I: original production version, differing from the first prototype by having increased fuel capacity provided by a permanently attached streamlined fuel tank at mid-span of each wing, de-icing of wing and tail unit leading edges and Pratt & Whitney JT12A-6 engines; a slightly lengthened fuselage provided executive standard accommodation for a crew of two and 10 passengers; late production aircraft had 1497-kg (3,300-lb) thrust JT12A-8 turbojet engines
JetStar 731: conversion developed by AirResearch, replacing the Pratt & Whitney powerplants of Jet Star I aircraft with more fuel-efficient Garret TFE731-1 turbofan engines; about 60 JetStar Is were converted to this standard

Lockheed L-1329 JetStar II in Iraqi Airways colours. The line between civilian and military operation of these aircraft, as with many of Iraqi Airways aircraft, was always indistinct.

الخطوط الجوية العراقية
YI-AKC

JetStar II: new production version incorporating Garrett TFE731-3 engines as standard and a number of refinements
C-140A: five aircraft for USAF, basically similar to early production JetStar Is and equipped for calibration of navigation beacons
C-140B: convertible cargo/passenger version for USAF, five built; otherwise generally similar to C-140A
VC-140B: designation of six additional production aircraft, generally similar to C-140A, except equipped as VIP transports; the five C-140Bs were also converted to this configuration

Specification
Lockheed JetStar II
Type: light transport
Powerplant: four 1678-kg (3,700-lb) thrust Garrett TFE731-3 turbofans
Performance: maximum cruising speed 880 km/h (547 mph) at 9145 m (30,000 ft); service ceiling 13105 m (43,000 ft); range with maximum payload 4820 km (2,995 miles)

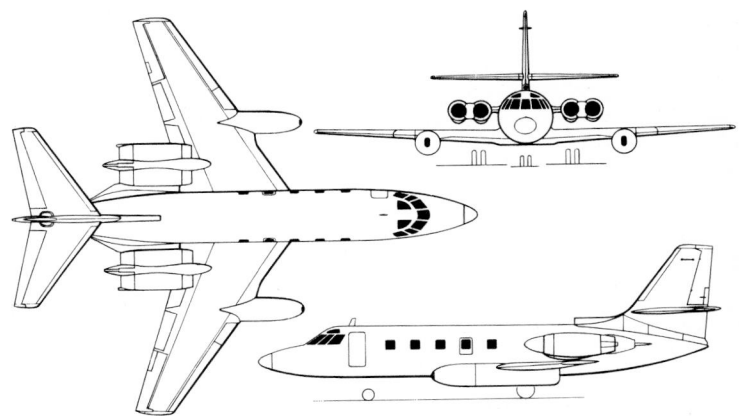
Lockheed L-1329-25 JetStar II

Weights: empty operating 11294 kg (24,900 lb); maximum take-off 20185 kg (44,500 lb)
Dimensions: span 16.59 m (54 ft

5 in); length 18.41 m (60 ft 5 in); height 6.22 m (20 ft 5 in); wing area 50.40 m² (542.5 sq ft)

Lockheed XFV-1 Salmon

Under the designation **Lockheed XFV-1**, the company completed and flew the first of two prototypes (138657/58) of a single-seat VTOL research aircraft. Powered by a 4362-kW (5,850-shp) Allison XT40-pA-6 turboprop engine, the **Salmon** was one of a number of tail-sitter designs originated in the early 1950s. Basically, the aircraft was a conventional mid-wing monoplane without normal landing gear. The tail had equal-span cruciform surfaces each incorporating a shock-strut and castoring wheel, and the aircraft was intended to

stand vertically on its tail unit for take-off and landing. However, as the 5294-kW (7,100-shp) T54-A-3 engine intended for the proposed XFV-2 VTOL fighter derivative did not materialise, the XFV-1 was fitted with a temporary conventional undercarriage and operated from this until the whole programme was cancelled in June 1955 and construction of the second prototype abandoned. Span was 9.40 m (30 ft 10 in), maximum take-off weight 7358 kg (16,221 lb) and maximum speed estimated at 933 km/h (580 mph).

Before any attempt was made at VTO (vertical take-off), the Lockheed XFV-1 was flown using an improvised 'conventional' landing gear. This was due primarily to the initial engine's lack of power for sustained vertical flight. The aircraft's unusual name 'Salmon' was derived from the name of the programme's chief test pilot.

The Lockheed XFV-1 in its vertical position, as first intended by its designers.

Lockheed P-3 Orion
to
Lockheed P2V Neptune

Lockheed P-3 Orion

When in August 1957 the US Navy needed an advanced ASW/maritime patrol aircraft, the urgency was highlighted by the fact that they were prepared to accept a development of an off-the-shelf civil aircraft to meet the requirement. Lockheed proposed a developed version of the L-188 Electra, gaining an initial research and development contract on 8 May 1958. The third Electra airframe was modified as an aerodynamic prototype for early evaluation by the US Navy, flying from Burbank in August 1958. This was followed by the **Lockheed YP3V-1** operational prototype, late named **Orion**, which first flew on 25 November 1959. The first production **P3V-1** was flown on 15 April 1961, with initial deliveries being made to US Navy Patrol Squadrons VP-8 and VP-44 on 13 August 1962, by which time the type had been redesignated the **P-3**. Retaining the basic airframe structure of the Electra, the new aircraft differed by having a fuselage shortened by 2.24 m (7 ft 4 in) and modified to incorporate a large weapons bay together with new avionics and utility systems. Mines, depth-bombs, torpedoes or nuclear devices can be accommodated in the weapons bay, and there are 10 underwing pylons for a variety of stores. The major changes in the 30 years since the Orion entered service have been in avionics equipment and capability, and more than 640 have been built to date, with the type continuing in production (now at Marietta, Georgia) until 1995/56 for South Korea, who ordered eight **P-3C Update IIIs** in December 1990. Other Orions are in service in Australia, Iran, the Netherlands, New Zealand, Norway, Pakistan, Portugal, Spain and in the USA with the Navy, the Customs Service, NASA and NOAA. Potential operators, probably of surplus USN aircraft, remain Thailand and Greece. Following the assembly in Japan of four P-3C aircraft from Lockheed-built components, over 100 of the type is being licence-built by Kawasaki for the Japanese Maritime Self-Defence Force. In addition, 21 examples of a derived version known as the **CP-140/140A** were delivered to the Canadian Forces.

Variants

P-3A: original production version for the US Navy, with 3356-kW (4,500-shp) Allison T56-A-10W turboprop engines; original submarine detection equipment superseded by advanced 'Deltic' system from 109th production aircraft, but most early P-3s retrofitted to this standard; 157 built

P-3A (CS): four Navy aircraft modified with enhanced radar for US Customs pending delivery of P-3 AEW&Cs

EP-3A: seven P-3As modified for electronic reconnaissance test and evaluation

NP-3A: three P-3As used for special test purposes with US Naval Research Laboratory at Patuxent River, Maryland

RP-3A: two P-3As modified for scientific use by Oceanographic Development Squadron VXN-8, based at NAS Patuxent River

TP-3A: 12 P-3As modified for pilot training duties with all ASW gear removed. Operated by Fleet Replacement Squadrons VP-30 and VP-31

UP-3A: 38 P-3As with ASW gear deleted for use as utility transports

VP-3A: three WP-3As and two P-3As converted to VIP and staff transports

WP-3A: four P-3As converted in 1971 for weather reconnaissance to replace WC-121 Super Constellations. One later became an NP-3A and three others VP-3As

P-3B: production version from and including 158th Orion, powered by 3361-kW (4,910-shp) Allison T56-A-14s and with 'Deltic' ASW detection equipment; ASW capability progressively upgraded

EP-3B: two P-3As converted for ELINT duties with US Navy Squadron VQ-1 based at Da Nang AB, South Vietnam

NP-3B: one P-3B converted to testbed with US Naval Research Laboratory

P-3C: production version with A-NEW system. First flew 18 September 1968, and entered service 1969; 267 built

P-3C Update I: new and improved avionics — 31 built from January 1975 onwards

P-3C: Update II: 44 aircraft built from August 1977 with infra-red detection and sonobuoy reference systems plus Harpoon ASM capability

P-3C Update II.5: 24 P-3Cs produced in 1981, given more reliable navigation and communication systems, plus IACS submarine communications link and standardised wing pylons

P-3C Update III: last 50 of US Navy given new acoustic processor, sonobuoy receiver, and improved APU. Deliveries began in May 1984

P-3C Update IV: installation of equipment originally destined for cancelled P-7 LRAACA and currently in full-scale development by Boeing. All P-3C Update II and II.5 aircraft to be equipped with first funding from FY1994 onwards. Improved ESM system plus addition of AN/APS-137(V) radar and new sensors to detect quieter submarines

EP-3C: Elint version of P-3C for JMSDF developed by Kawasaki. Three

funded

NP-3C: one P-3C converted to testbed for US Naval Research Laboratory

RP-3C: the YP-3C modified to replace the RP-3A with Squadron VXN-8

UP-3C: two utility-configured Orion aircraft for JMSDF from Kawasaki production line

RP-3D: one P-3C modified to collect atmospheric data for operation by US Naval Squadron VXN-8

WP-3D: two P-3C conversions for Department of Commerce for operation by National Oceanographic and Atmospheric Administration (NOAA)

EP-3E Aries: conversion of 10 P-3As and two EP-3Bs for Elint. Carries radars in large fairings above and below fuselage plus ventral radome forward of wing

EP-3E Aries II: 12 low-houred P-3Cs fitted with equipment transferred from EP-3E, first conversion (by Lockheed AS, Greenville, S. Carolina) delivered November 1988 and all in service by 1991 with special reconnaissance Squadrons VQ-1 and VQ-2 of US Navy

NP-3E: various aircraft relegated to permanent test status by US military. One new build aircraft ordered by Japanese Defence Agency from Kawasaki

P-3F: six P-3Cs delivered to Imperial Iranian Air Force in late-1970s fitted with flight refuelling equipment compatible with Boeing 707 tankers

P-3G: original designation of Lockheed LRAACA selected in October 1988 to replace the Orion but redesignated P-7A in 1989. Two prototypes followed by 123 production aircraft were planned

P-3H: proposed P-3C upgrade designed to replace the P-7A LRAACA cancelled in July 1990. Update IV avionics proposed together with redesigned cockpit, new wings and engines, FY1992 funding requested

P-3K: five for New Zealand. Planned upgrade cancelled 1990

P-3N: designation of two P-3Bs operated by Norwegian Coast Guard on EEZ surveillance, SAR and training. Some ASW equipment deleted

Like many of the Orions built as P-3Bs, this aircraft was to become a P-3C under the update programme.

P-3P: six ex-RAAF P-3Bs for Esquadra 601 of Portuguese air force based at Montijo. One converted to approximate Update II standard by Lockheed with others carried out by OGMA

P-3W: 20 P-3C-IIs for RAAF but with AQS-901 processors plus Barra sonobuoy system installed in place of USN items

P-3AEW&C: rotodome-equipped Airborne Early Warning and Control version of ex-RAAF P-3Bs for US Customs anti-narcotics patrol duties. Two delivered June 1988 and June 1989, with third on order. Prototype (N91LC) first flew 14 June 1984, followed by first for US Customs on 8 April 1989

CP-140 Aurora: 18 modifed P-3Cs fitted with S-3 Viking ASW systems selected in July 1976 for the Canadian Forces Long Range Patrol Aircraft (LRPA) Argus replacement programme

CP-140A Arcturus: three further CP-140s fitted with role equipment suitable for environmental and fishery patrol ordered to replace Trackers used previously. ASW equipment deleted. All delivered by September 1991

Specification
Lockheed P-3C Orion
Type: ASW patrol aircraft
Powerplant: four 3661-kW (4,910 shp) Allison T56-A-14 turboprops
Performance: maximum speed 761 mph/h (473 mph); patrol speed 381 km/h (237 mph); maximum mission radius 3853 km (2,383 miles)
Weights: empty 27892 kg (61,491 lb); maximum take-off 64410 kg (142,000 lb)
Dimensions: span 30.38 m (99 ft 8 in); length 35.61 m (116 ft 10 in); height 10.27 m (33 ft 8½ in); wing area 120.77 m² (1,300.0 sq ft)
Armament: mines, depth-bombs, torpedoes and rockets in internal weapons bay or on underwing pylons to 9072 kg (20,000 lb)

Lockheed P-38 Lightning

The unusual configuration adopted for the **Lockheed P-38 Lightning** stemmed from a US Army Air Corps requirement of 1937 for a high-performance fighter. It demanded a maximum speed, rate of climb and range that could

not then be met in a conventional single-engine layout, and to achieve the desired performance the Lockheed design team adopted twin engines. A mid-wing monoplane with the pilot's nacelle mounted on the wing centre-section,

the P-38 had twin booms extending aft from the extremities of this assembly, mounting the two engines forward and twin fins and rudders aft, with the booms linked by the tailplane/elevator assembly. The nose unit of the tricycle landing gear retracted into the central nacelle, and the main units into the twin booms. The **XP-33** prototype, powered

by two 716-kW (960-hp) Allison V-1710-11/15 counter-rotating engines, was flown for the first time on 27 January 1939, and was lost as the result of an undershoot after accumulating less than 12 hours flight time. Fortunately, in that time there was sufficient indication of an ability to meet USAAC requirements, and an order for 13 **YP-38** prototypes

followed on 27 April 1939. Production aircraft began to enter service in late 1941, and a first (shared) combat victory was recorded on 14 August 1942, with the destruction of a Focke-Wulf Fw200C-3 Condor over the North Atlantic, but the type's first regular combat operations began in North Africa on 19 November 1942. Built to a total of 10,037 aircraft, including 113 produced under sub-contract by Consolidated-Vultee, the Lightning was used by the USAAF in every theatre of action. In the Pacific, Lightnings were credited with the destruction of more Japanese aircraft than any other fighter in USAAF service, and they are well recorded in air force history for a string of memorable actions, including the interception and destruction, some 885 km (500 miles) from their base on Guadalcanal, of the Mitsubishi G4M carrying Japan's Admiral Isoroku Yamamoto. And, of course, the USAAF's 'ace of aces' of World War II, Major Richard I. Bong, scored all of his 40 confirmed victories while flying P-38s in the Pacific zone. In Europe, P-38s served mainly with the 9th Air Force, being used extensively on long-range fighter escort duties in support of 8th Air Force daylight bombing missions against German targets. But with the end of war, and the inevitable contract cancellations that followed VJ-Day, most of the USAAF's Lightnings disappeared very quickly, with only a few late models remaining in service until 1949.

Variants

YP-38: designation of pre-production aircraft, generally similar to prototype but with 858-kW (1,150-hp) Allison V-1710-27/-29 engines giving opposite propeller rotation

P-38 (later **RP-38**): initial production version, generally as YP-38 and with armament of four 12.7-mm (0.5-in) machine-guns and one 37-mm cannon, and addition of armour protection and bullet-proof glass

P-38E (later **RP-38E**): production version, generally as P-38 but with system revisions; 36 built

P-38E (laterf **RP-38E**): production version with further system revisions and 37-mm cannon replaced by onew 20-mm cannon; 210 built

P-38J-5 Lightning of the 70th Fighter Squadron, 20th Fighter Group, US 6th Air Force based at Kings Cliffe (UK) in spring 1944.

P-38F: production version, the first regarded as combat-ready; 527 built, including 150 ordered originally under British (as **Lightning Mk I**) and French contracts; the French order would have been transferred to the UK, but after testing initial examples the RAF refused to accept any more aircraft; powered by 988-kW (1,325-hp) Allison V-1710-49/-53 engine, there were several sub-variants, the most important being the **P-38F-15** which introduced manoeuvring flaps

P-38G: production version, generally similar to P-38F-15, but incorporated a number of revisions and improvements during the production run; 1,082 built

P-37H: production version, similar to P-38G, but with 1063-kW (1,425-hp) Allison V-1710-89/-91 engines; 601 built

P-38J (later **F-38J**): generally similar to P-38H but with many detail changes throughout the 2,970-aircraft production run; for use in a light bomber role some were modified to have a glazed nose to the centre nacelle for use by a bomb aimer, or were equipped with bombing radar

P-38K: single prototype, with 1063-kW (1,425-hp) Allison V-1710-75/-77 engines in a P-38G airframe

P-38L (later **F-38L**): final Lockheed production version with 1100-kW (1,475-hp) Allison V-1710-111/113 engines, but otherwise generally similar to P-38J; 3,810 built

P-38L-5: version generally similar to P-38L produced by Consolidated-Vultee; 2,000 contracted but only 113 completed by VJ-Day

P-38M: redesignation of P-38F, P-38K and P-38L aircraft, totalling about 80, modified by the USAAF and by Lockheed for service as two-seat night-fighters, which were just entering

service as the war ended

TP-38L: designation of small number of aircraft modified by the USAAF as two-seat trainers; similar P-38J conversions were unofficially known as **TP-38J**

F-4-1 (later **RF-4-1**): unarmed photo-reconnaissance version of P-38E carrying four cameras; 99 built

F-4A-1: unarmed reconnaissance version of P-38F carrying four cameras; 20 built

F-5A: unarmed reconnaissance version with five cameras, one similar to P-38E but remainder similar to P-38G; 181 built

F-5B: unarmed reconnaissance version of P-38J; 200 built

F-5C: redesignation of about 123 P-38Js converted by Lockheed to F-5B configuration but with improved camera installations

F-5E: redesignation of 205 P-38J and 500 P-38L aircraft converted by Lockheed to F-5C configuration

F-5F: redesignation of one F-5B following revision of camera installation

F-5F-3: redesignation of P-38L aircraft with F-5F camera installation

F-5G-6: final photo-reconnaissance conversion from P-38L-5 airframes

FO-1: US Navy redesignation of four F-5Bs acquired from the USAAF

XF-5D: single example of experimental two-seat reconnaissance aircraft

XP-38A: single example of P-38 used during 1942 for experiments in cockpit pressurisation

XP-49: single prototype developed from P-38 with, initially, 1148-kW (1,540-hp) Continental XIV-1430-9/11 engines, strengthened landing gear and pressurised cockpit; no production aircraft resulted

A radical development of the P-38 was the XP-58 Chain Lightning, a two-seat heavy fighter design. Powered by a pair of 1939-kW (2,600-hp) Allison V-3420 engines, the sole prototype was intended to have an armament of four 37-mm or one 75-mm cannon plus machine-guns.

XP-58 Chain Lightning: totally new and much larger aircraft, prototype flown eventually, on 6 June 1944, with two 19329-kW (2,600-hp) Allison V-3420-11/-13 engines, but no production followed

Specification
Lockheed P-38L Lightning
Type: single-seat fighter
Powerplant: two 1100-kW (1,475-hp) Allison V-1710-111/-113 V-12 piston engines
Performance: maximum speed 666 km/h (414 mph) at 7620 m (25,000 ft); service ceiling 13410 m (44,000 ft); normal range 724 km (450 miles)
Weights: empty 5806 kg (12,800 lb); maximum take-off 9798 kg (21,600 lb)
Dimensions: span 15.85 m (52 ft 0 in); length 11.53 m (37 ft 10 in); height 3.91 m (12 ft 10 in); wing area 30.47 m² (328.0 sq ft)
Armament: four 12.7-mm (0.5-in) machine-guns and one 20-mm cannon, plus up to 1451 kg (3,200 lb) of bombs

Lockheed P-80 Shooting Star

Lockheed F-80A Shooting Star of the 61st Fighter Squadron, 56th Fighter Group, based at Selfridge Field, Michigan, in 1948.

The design of what was to become the first operational jet fighter of the US Army Air Force began in June 1934, tailored around the 1361-kg (3,000-lb) thrust British Halford H.1B turbojet. The first **Lockheed XP-80** prototype with this powerplant was flown initially on 8 January 1944, but the second and third **XP-80A** prototypes each had a 2983-kg (4,000-lb) thrust Genertal Electric I-40, as did the pre-production **YP-80A** aircraft. A sleek, low-wing monoplane with retractable tricycle landing gear, the **P-80 Shooting Star** began to enter USAAF service in early 1945, and a total of 45 had been delivered by the time World War II ended. Two of these had been flown to Italy for operational evaluation, but were carefully kept away from any combat situation. The very good performance of this first Lockheed jet fighter had resulted in plans to produce 5,000 but these were curtailed drastically after VJ-Day. However, the aircraft was selected to re-equip front-line pursuit groups of the USAAF, and those serving with the US Far East Air Force in June 1950 went into action when the Korean War started. When production

ended, Lockheed had built a total of 1,732 P-80 (later **F-80**) variants, but far more successful was the **T-33A** two-seat trainer development. Basically an F-80 with a lengthened fuselage to accommodate a second seat in tandem, T-33A has served with more than 30 air forces. Lockheed built 5,691, a further 210 were assembled by Kawasaki in Japan. Canadair built 656 which, powered by locally-built Rolls-Royce Nenes, were known under the designation **CL-30 Silver Star**. Considerable numbers of aircraft remain in service.

Variants

P-80A (later **F-80A**): initial production version, powered by the 1746-kg (3,850-lb) thrust General Electric J33-GE-11 turbojet engine; armament of six 12.7-mm (0.5-in) machine-guns; 917 built

XP-80B: prototype of an improved version, with revised wing section and

a 1814-kg (4,000-lb) thrust Allison J33-A-17 turbojet

P-80B (later **F-80B**): production version with many improvements, and introducing an ejection seat and provision for jet-assisted take-off (JATO) equipment; 240 built

P-80C (later **F-80C**): final production version, initially with 2087-kg (4,600-lb) thrust J33-A-23 engines, and late production aircraft with 2449-kg (5,400-lb) thrust J33-A-35 engines

XFP-80A: single prototype of a photo-reconnaissance version, later **XF-14**
ERF-80A: redesignation of one F-80A used to test camera equipment
F-14A (later **FP-80A** then **RF-80A**): production photo-reconnaissance version, the first 38 conversions of new-production P-80As, and the remaining 114 new-build aircraft
RF-80C: redesignation of 70 F-80As following conversion for the reconnaissance role
DF-80A: redesignation of F-80As following conversion as drone directors
QF-80A/QF-80C/QF-80F: redesignation of aircraft converted as radio-controlled drones

TO-1 (later **TV-1**): US Navy designation of 50 P-80Cs acquired as jet-powered advanced trainers for the US Marine Corps
TP-80C (later **TF-80C** then **T-33A**): following successful testing of the first TP-80C two'-seat trainer, flown initially on 22 March 1948, the type entered production for the USAF; 128 built
AT-33A: version of T-33A for service with smaller air forces, had armament revision making it suitable for weapon training or COIN operations
DT-33A: redesignation of T-33As following conversion as drone directors
NT-33A: redesignation of T-33As following conversion for special tests
QT-33A: redesignation of T-33As

following conversion as radio-controlled drones
RT-33A: reconnaissance versiopn of the AT-33A for smaller air forces; 85 conversions
TO-2 (later **TV-2**): US Navy version of T-33A
TV-2D: redesignation of TO-2/TV-2s after conversion as drone directors
TV-2KD: redesignation of TO-2/TV-2s after conversion as radio-controlled drones
T2V-1 SeaStar (later **T-1A**): development of TV-2 with humped cockpit, leading and trailing-edge flaps, boundary layer control and 27677-kg (6,100-lb) thrust Allison J33-A-24 turbojet

Specification
Lockheed F-80C Shooting Star
Type: single-seat fighter
Powerplant: one 2449-kg (5,400-lb) thrust Allison J33-A-35 turbojet
Performance: maximum speed 966 km/h (594 mph) at sea level; service ceiling 14265 m (46,800 ft); range 1328 km (825 miles)
Weights: empty 3819 kg (8,420 lb); maximum take-off 7646 kg (16,856 lb)
Dimensions: span 11.81 m (38 ft 9 in); length 10.49 m (34 ft 5 in); height 3.43 m (11 ft 3 in); wing area 22.07 m^2 (237.6 sq ft)
Armament: six 12.7-mm (0.5-in) machine-guns, plus two 454-kg (1,000-lb) bombs and eight rockets

Lockheed P2V Neptune

Initial studies on a land-based patrol air-craft for service with the US Navy were made by Lockheed's Vega subsidiary in 1941. However, in the urgency of aircraft production before and during the early years of World War II, no further de-velopment of this design followed until 1944. By then the US Navy had an urgent requirement for such an aircraft, and Lockheed discovered that the Vega de-sign proposal of 1941 could meet this need with little modification. A contract for two **Lockheed XP2V-1** prototypes and 14 **P2V-12** production aircraft was received, and the first prototype was flown on 17 May 1945. A fairly large mid-/high-wing monoplane with retractable tricycle landing gear, the type was powered initially by two 1715-kW (2,300-hp) Wright R-3350-8 Duplex Cyclone engines. Carrying a crew of seven, it had a weapons bay for two torpedoes or 12 depth charges, plus six defensive machine-guns. The generally-similar P2V-1 production aircraft differed by having underwing mountings for up to 16 rockets.

P2V-1s began to enter service in March 1947 and proved effective in their role. The Korean War expanded the re-quirement for such aircraft, and the later involvement of the United States in South East Asia, plus need to provide similar capability for the Western allies, kept Lockheed busy producing P2Vs in a multiplicity of versions, with the final production figure totalling 1,181.

Variants
XP2V-2: single prototype for imnproved version, with 2088-kW (2,800-hp) Wright R-3350-24W engines, first flown 7 January 1947
P2V-2: generally similar to XP2V-2, but able to carry sonobuoys and with extensive armament revisions; 80 built
P2V-2N: designation of two P2V-2s equipped especially for polar exploration
P2V-2S: the prototype of an AEW version carrying search radar
P2V-3: similar to P2V-2, but with 2386-kW (3,200-hp) Wright R-3350-26W engines; 53 built
P2V-3B: designation of five aircraft modified for close-support evaluation
P2V-3C: designation of 12 aircraft modified to serve as carrier-based nuclear-weapon carriers
P2V-3W: production AEW version of Neptune; 30 built
P2V-3Z: designation of two P2V-3s modified to serve as combat transport aircraft for VIPs
P2V-4 (later **P-2D**): AEW version, equipped as P2V-2S prototype, with engine variations and wingtip auxiliary fuel tanks; 52 built

P2V-5: major production version; an ASW aircraft in many sub-variants; differed basically from P2V-4 by having 2424-kW (3,250-hp) R-3350-30WA engines and larger-capacity wingtip tanks; it was retrofitted with a glazed nose and MAD (magnetic anomaly detection) equipment; 424 built
P2V-5F (later **P-2E**): generally as P2V-5, but with 2610-kW (3,500-hp) R-3350-32W engines and two underwing mounted 1474-kg (3,250-lb) thrust auxiliary turbojets; post-1962 variants were one **EP-2E** permanent test aircraft and several **OP-2E/AP-2E** US Navy/US Army special-sensor aircraft
P2V-5FD (later **DP-2E**): drone launch and control vehicles modified from P2V-5Fs
P2V-5FE (later **EP-2E**): designation of P2V-5Fs carrying extra avionics equipment
P2V-5FS: (later **SP-2E**): designatioh of P2V-5Fs with Jezebel/Julie acoustic search equipment
P2V-6 (later **P-2F**): multi-role version with R-3350-WA engines, increased capacity wingtip tanks, and lengthened bomb bay; 67 built
P2V-6B (later **P2V-6M** and **MP-2F**): anti-shipping version armed with Petrel missiles; 16 built
P2V-6F (later **P-2G**): redesignation of P2V-6s following installation of two 1542-kg (3,400-lb) thrust Westinghouse J34-WE-36 auxiliary turbojets
P2V-6T (later **TP-2F**): redesignation of P2V-6s converted to serve as crew trainers
P2V-7 (later **P-2H**): final production version of Neptune with 2610-kW (3,500-hp) R-3350-32W piston engines and 1542-kg (3,400-lb) thrust Westinghouse K34-WE-36 auxiliary turbojets; 287 built; post-1962 variants included several **AP-2H** special-sensor conversions, **DP-2H** drone-controllers,

one **EP-2H** special reconnaissance aircraft, and one **NP-2H** special-test aircraft
P2V-7B: designation of 15 aircraft for Netherlands naval air arm with hardened nose incorporating four 20-mm cannon
P2V-7LP (later **LP-2J**): designation of four P2V-7s with retractable ski landing gear for use in Antarctica
P2V-7S (later **SP-2H**): redesignation of P-2Vs following installation of Jezebel/Julie acoustic search equipment
P2V-7U (later **RB-69A**): electronic surveillance version for the USAF; 5 built and 2 converted from P2V-7s
P2V-7KAI: following assembly in Japan by Kawasaki of 48 P2V-7s from components built in the USA by Lockheed, Kawasaki produced a developed version of which the P2V-7KAI was the prototype; designated **P-2J**, this had a lengthened fuselage to house additional avionics and two 2125-kW (2,850-shp) General Electric T64-IHI-10 turboprop engines, plus two 1400-kg (3,086-lb) thrust Ishikawajima-Harima J3-IHI-7C auxiliary turbojets; some were later converted to **UP-2J** target tugs

Specification
Lockheed P2V-7 (later P-2H

This cleaned-up P2V-1 named 'The Turtle' set a world piston-engined distance record in 1946.

Neptune)
Type: long-range maritime patrol aircraft
Powerplant: two 2610-kW (3,500-hp) Wright R-3350-32W Turbo-Compound radial piston engines, plus two 1542-kg (3,400-lb) thrust Westinghouse J34-WE-36 auxiliary turbojets
Performance: maximum speed 649 km/h (403 mph) at 4265 m (14,000 ft); service ceiling 6705 m (22,000 ft); maximum range 5930 km (3,685 miles)
Weights: empty 22650 kg (49,935 lb); maximum take-off 36240 kg (79,895 lb)
Dimensions: span 31.65 m (103 ft 10 in); length 27.94 m (91 ft 8 in); height 8.94 m (29 ft 4 in); wing area 92.90 m^2 (1,000.0 sq ft)
Armament: twin 12.7-mm (0.5-in) machine-guns in dorsal turret, plus provision for underwing rockets and up to 3629 kg (8,000 lb) of bombs, depth charges or torpedoes

Japan's Kawasaki-built P-2Js had a host of engine and equipment improvements.

Lockheed QT-2, Q-Star and YO-3A

to

Loire 43, 45 and 46

Lockheed QT-2, Q-Star and YO-3A

The detection of Viet Cong guerrillas operating in Vietnam presented difficult problems, small units being able to attack from and merge back into the jungle with comparative ease. Although sensors were developed to keep track of such units, their short detection range meant that they were useless unless they could be carried low over the jungle by a vehicle that would be difficult for the enemy to locate. Thus Lockheed Missiles and Space Company proposed the development of a slow-flying powered aircraft with a silenced engine, leading to two two-seat **Lockheed QT-2** prototypes which combined the airframe of the Schweizer SGS 2-32 sailplane with a specially silenced 75-kW (100-hp) Continental O-200-A engine driving a four-bladed propeller. Tested in Vietnam, complete with sensor packages, they

Most successful of Lockheed's quiet sensor platforms was the YO-3A. Thirteen such aircraft were acquired by the 1st Army Security Agency Company and operated from Long Binh between 1970 and 1972. After their retirement from army service the aircraft were used for a number of purposes, including the detection of poachers.

proved to be most effective. A third airframe was more extensively modified and used to test a variety of propellers, this aircraft being designated **Q-Star**. During its evaluation programme, the Q-Star was flown with a Wankel-type rotary combustion engine. Final development of this idea came in the form of the far more refined **YO-3A** with retractable

landing gear and a 157-kW (210-hp) Continental IO-360-D engine. A total of 14 was built, 13 of them being operated

successfully in Vietnam for almost two years before the operating unit was deactivated in early 1972.

Lockheed S-3 Viking

With the evolution of quiet deep-diving nuclear-powered submarines, the US Navy considered that high priority should be afforded to the development of a new generation of hunter-killer ASW aircraft. Lockheed was the winner of a US Navy competitive contract, awarded in August 1969, for development of such an aircraft designated **Lockheed S-3A** and later named **Viking**. Working in partnership with Vought Aeronautics which designed and built the wings, tail unit, landing gear and engine pods, and with Univac Federal Systems which designed and developed the advanced digital computer to provide high-speed data-processing, Lockheed designed and built the fuselage, integrated the avionics system, and carried out final assembly and systems integration. Of fairly conventional configuration for carrier operation, the S-3A is a high-wing monoplane with hydraulically-folding wings, retractable tricycle landing gear, and air-conditioned and pressurised accommodation for its crew of four. The first prototype was flown initially on 21 January 1972, the type entering US Navy service with squadron VS-41 on 20 February 1974. Since that time a total of 187 has been built and delivered, these serving with 14 US Navy squadrons. The **US-3A** COD version applies to the conversion of a handful of early S-3A RDT&E examples to carry cargo and/or mail following the deletion of all ASW role equipment. These serve with squadron

A flight of two Lockheed S-3As of anti-submarine squadron 31 (VS-31) deployed aboard the nuclear-powered carrier USS Dwight D. Eisenhower. The Viking is a superb example of how to pack maximum payload and systems into minimum airframe.

VRC-50, operating in the Indian and Pacific oceans. A dedicated tanker version of the Viking, designated **KS-3A** was tested in 1980 but found unsatisfactory and in 1985 the US Navy turned instead to adapting the standard Viking for 'buddy' refuelling from the aircraft's own tanks, thus retaining the primary ASW capability. Another requirement has led to the conversion of other Vikings into **ES-3A** Elint and Sigint versions initially to supplement and ultimately to replace the venerable EA-3B Skywarriors still in use. The first adaption, an aerodynamic test vehicle, flew in 1990 and nine definitive conversions equip two units, squadrons VQ-5 (formed April 1991), and VQ-6 (formed August 1991) based at NAS Agana, Guam, and NAS Cecil Field, Florida, respectively. In 1981, Lockheed received a $14.5-million contract covering a Viking weapons system improvement programme, including the ability to carry the Harpoon ASM, the resulting aircraft to be redesignated **S-3B**. Initially two S-3As were modified and the first of

these flew on 13 September 1984. Flight testing continued until 1985 followed by a full technical and operational evaluation, which led to a full go ahead in April 1986 for the conversion of 22 aircraft. The first of these was delivered to squadron VS-27 in December 1987 and an order for a further 24 conversions awarded in December 1988. All of these were ordered for Atlantic Fleet squadrons and the re-equipment of the Pacific squadrons was under active negotiations in 1991.

Specification
Lockheed S-3A Viking
Type: carrier-based patrol/attack aircraft
Powerplant: two 4207-kg (9,275-lb)

thrust General Electric TF34-GE-2 turbofans
Performance: maximum cruising speed 686 km/h (426 mph); loiter speed 296 km/h (184 mph); combat range more than 3701 km (2,300 miles)
Weights: empty 12088 kg (26,650 lb); normal ASW mission take-off 19278 kg (42,500 lb)
Dimensions: span 20.93 m (68 ft 8 in); length 16.26 m (53 ft 4 in); height 6.93 m (22 ft 9 in); wing area 55.55 m^2 (598.0 sq ft)
Armament: weapons including bombs, depth-bombs, mines or torpedoes up to 907 kg (2,000 lb) in internal weapons bay, plus cluster bombs, flare-launchers or auxiliary fuel tanks on underwing pylons

Lockheed SR-71 Blackbird

On 29 February 1964, President Johnson revealed that the US Air Force possessed a new high-speed high-altitude reconnaissance aircraft which he identified as the **A-12**. He claimed that it had been flown at speeds of more than 3219 km/h (2,000 mph) and to heights in excess of 21335 m (70,000 ft). Even now, almost 20 years later, virtually nothing concrete is known of that aircraft, but there is little doubt that it was the progenitor of the delta-winged Lock-

heed **YF-12A** interceptors that were evaluated by the USAF. Construction of YF-12s amounted to only three YF-12As and one YF-12C, but although they were capable of remarkable (which was in reality an SR-71A) performance no production aircraft were built. However, when the Lockheed U-2 flown by Frank Powers was brought down over Sverdlovsk in the Soviet Union it emphasised the need for faster and higher-flying reconnaissance aircraft for special mis-

sions. The A-12 and ensuing YF-12A formed the basis for the **Lockheed SR-71A 'Blackbird'** used by the USAF's Strategic Air Command. Designed by a team headed by C. L. 'Kelly' Johnson, the two-seat SR-71A was fabricated largely of titanium to maintain the structural integrity of the airframe when subjected to kinetic heating; at speeds in excess of Mach 3, for example, some structural components reached temperatures of 5432°F (3000°C). And because aerodynamic drag increases dramatically with speed, the slimmest possible fuselage and thinnest delta wing were

adopted, together with integral lifting 'chines' for the forward fuselage to prevent the nose from pitching down as speed increased. Two Pratt & Whitney J58 continuous-bleed turbojet engines formed the heart of a complex propulsion system, these engines alone providing all of the low-speed thrust. However, at Mach 3 they produced only 18 per cent of the thrust, the remainder being generated by suction in the intakes (54 per cent) and from special nozzles at the rear of the multiple-flow nacelles (28 per cent). Not surprisingly, fuel consumption was high, and the air-

craft had inflight-refuelling capability.

Ordered to replace the subsonic U-2 in the unarmed reconnaissance role, the SR-71A flew for the first time on 22 December 1964 from Palmdale, California, in the hands of Lockheed test pilot Robert Gilliland. It entered service as the USAF's first Mach 3 aircraft in January 1966 with the 4200th Strategic Reconnaissance Wing at Beale AFB, California. Production is believed to have totalled 32 aircraft, all two-seaters, with two later modified into SR-71B trainers along with a single SR-71C. By 1988 only six SR-71s remained operational and the type was withdrawn from service in November 1989. An official retirement ceremony was held at Beale AFB in January 1990 and during the course of that year the remaining USAF aircraft were distributed as gate guardians with examples going to Edwards AFB, Robins AFB, Castle AFB, Beale AFB and March AFB. Two others went to the Air Force Museum at Wright-Patterson AFB and the Smithsonian Air & Space Museum in Washington, DC. Other SR-71s were placed in 'flyable storage' with Lockheed at Palmdale and NASA received three for undesignated purposes.

Always able to capture world attention with its sizzling performance, the SR-71 held FAI accredition for record flights between New York-Farnborough in September 1974 (a fantastic 1 hour 55 minutes and 42 seconds) plus a few days later the return flight London-Los Angeles (3 hours 47 minutes and 39 seconds). Finally on 6 March 1990, the SR-71 allocated to the Smithsonian Institute captured another record when it flew from Los Angeles, California, to Dulles International Airport, Washington, in a staggering 64 minutes and five seconds at an average speed of 2,153 mph.

The surprise at the sudden withdrawal of the Blackbird fleet has lessened with the rise in reported sightings of a new and as yet unidentified high-speed aircraft which may be the SR-71's successor. The 'black' aircraft, assumed to be a Lockheed design and code-named 'Aurora', has been seen moving at high-supersonic speed, with the resultant sonic 'bangs', over southern California. It is believed to be powered by a revolutionary new engine which leaves a distinctive 'sausage-string' shaped contrail at high altitude coupled with an unmistakable sound.

Specification
Lockheed SR-71A
Type: two-seat reconnaissance aircraft
Powerplant: two 14742-kg (32,500-lb) thrust Pratt & Whitney J58 afterburning bleed turbojets
Performance: maximum speed

Lockheed SR-71A Blackbird of the 9th Strategic Reconnaissance Wing, US Air Force, based at Beale AFB (California) during the 1970s.

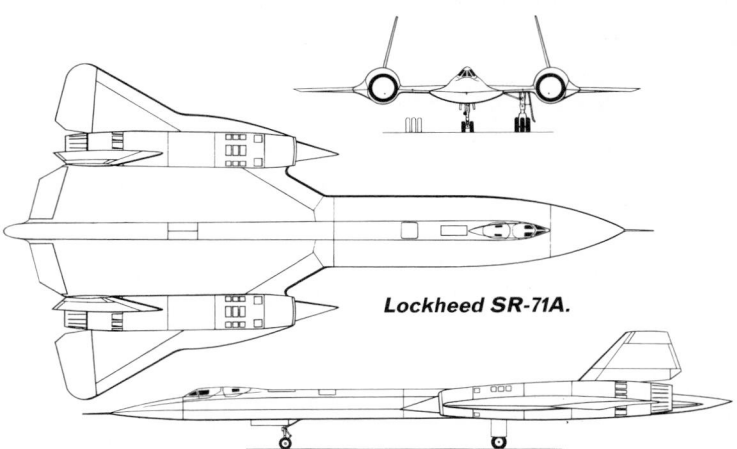

Lockheed SR-71A.

Mach 3 to 3.5 at 24385 m (80,000 ft); maximum sustained cruising speed Mach 3; unrefuelled range 4168 km (2,590 miles)
Weights: estimated maximum take-off 77111 kg (170,000 lb)

Dimension: span 16.94 m (55 ft 7 in); length 32.74 m (107 ft 5 in); height 5.64 m (18 ft 6 in)

Lockheed U-2

Pre-knowledge of the military strength and activities of a potential enemy can play an important role in negotiations that may prevent wars. In the United States President Eisenhower had such thoughts in mind when, in July 1955, he proposed an 'Open Skies' policy under which both US and Soviet reconnaissance aircraft would be free to make unrestricted flights over each other's territory, thus reducing tensions and increasing mutual trust. This was rejected by the Soviet Union, but a month after that Lockheed flew the first example of a remarkable new reconnaissance aircraft, the **Lockheed U-2**, which had been designed and built under conditions of great secrecy in the company's so-called 'Skunk Works'. It had remarkable high-flying and long-range performance that resulted from the powerplant and configuration. The former was a Pratt & Whitney J57 with revised fuel system, and the aircraft's high-aspect ratio glider-like wing allowed range to be extended by shutting down the engine to flight-idle and gliding over long distances. Intended for operation at altitudes where detection and interception were unlikely, the U-2 bristled with data-gathering devices.

That the U-2 was detectable and vulnerable was demonstrated on 1 May 1960 when, during an overflight of the Soviet Union, the aircraft flown by the American Frank Powers was knocked down by a surface-to-air missile. Powers escaped by parachute and was captured, leading to a new temperature-drop in the 'cold war'. The value of the U-2 was demonstrated in 1962 when these aircraft made early discovery of attempts to install ballistic missile sites in Cuba, and provided the foundation for the pressures which eventually ensured their removal.

Specification
U-2A: initial production version, powered by a Pratt & Whitney J57-P-7 or J57-P-57A turbojet, of 4763-kg (10,500-lb) or 5080-kg (11,200-lb) thrust respectively
WU-2A: designation of U-2As used by the USAF for atmospheric research
U-2B: improved production version with strengthened airframe, Pratt & Whitney J57-P-13 or J57-P-13B turbojet of 7167-kg (15,800-lb) or 7711-kg (17,000-lb) thrust respectively, and increased fuel capacity
U-2C: production version with increased fuel capacity, and a lengthened nose accommodating additional equipment for the electronic intelligence (Elint) role

U-2CT: two-seat conversion trainer; two produced with separate stepped cockpits
U-2D: two-seat version of U-2B for high-altitude research
U-2EPX: proposed maritime surveillance for US Navy, two produced as conversions of U-2Rs; tested but not adopted by the US Navy
U-2R: redesigned and improved version of earlier production models, much larger, heavier, and with increased fuel capacity
TR-1A: single-seat developed version of the U-2R with J75-P-13 engine, and introducing more advanced avionics

Intended as a sensor platform for use in a European war, the TR-1A now finds itself to be an aircraft without a mission. All surviving examples have been redesignated as U-2s.

Specification
Lockheed U-2C (in NASA service)
Type: high-altitude reconnaissance aircraft
Powerplant: one 7711-kg (17,000-lb) thrust Pratt & Whitney J75-P-13B turbojet
Performance: cruising speed 740 km/h (460 mph) at 19810 m (65,000 ft); operating altitude 19810 to 21335 m (65,000 to 70,000 ft); range 4635 km (2,880 miles)

Weight: maximum take-off 10225 kg (22,542 lb)
Dimensions: span 24.38 m (80 ft 0 in); length 15.24 m (50 ft 0 in); height 4.57 m (15 ft 0 in); wing area 52.49 m² (565.0 sq ft)

Lockheed Vega 35

North American Aviation Inc, designed during 1937 the prototype of a light-weight primary trainer which it designated **North American NA-35**. Powered by a 93-kW (125-hp) Menasco Pirate inline engine, it was of low-wing monoplane configuration with fixed tail-wheel landing gear, and seated the instructor and pupil in tandem open cockpits. When the NA-35 failed to win a US Army Air Corps contract in 1939, North American sold all rights to Lockheed's Vega subsidiary. Vega built only four of these **Vega 35** aircraft, two with more powerful (119-kW/160-hp) Menasco

Lockheed's Vega 35 was built in only very small numbers, as the company was involved in more adventurous and profitable aircraft designs.

Pirate D-B engines, the first flown in 1941, but by then the company had no manufacturing capacity available and Vega 35 production was abandoned. Span was 9.07 m (29 ft 9 in), maximum weight 875 kg (1,930 lb) and maximum speed 216 km/h (134 mph).

Lockheed Vega Starliner

Designed by Lockheed's subsidiary AiRover Company, which by 1938 became the Vega Airplane Company, the **Vega Starliner** was a five/six-seat low-wing cabin monoplane with retractable landing gear and an unusual powerplant. This comprised two 194-kW (260-hp) Menasco C6S-4 inline engines,

mounted side-by-side, and coupled to drive together, or independently in emergency, a single propeller. First flown on 22 April 1939, the Starliner was abandoned after some 85 flight test hours as there was no demand for an aircraft in this category. Span was 12.50 m (41 ft), maximum weight 2722 kg

Though first tested with single vertical tail surfaces, the Vega Starliner was ultimately flown with twin endplate surfaces, having been so repaired as a consequence of a forced landing after a propeller failure.

(6,000 lb) and maximum speed 338 km/h (210 mph).

Lockheed VZ-10 Hummingbird

Under the company designation **Lockheed VZ-120**, Lockheed designed and developed two prototypes of a VTOL aircraft using turbojet engines to provide direct lift. The centre fuselage formed a giant ejector duct, more than doubling lift. The first of these was flown on 7 July 1962, but it was not until 20 November 1963 that a first successful flight involving transitions from vertical to horizontal flight, and vice versa, were completed. By then redesignated **XV-4A**, the two prototypes were handed over to the US Army for whom they had been built

The serial on this aircraft (62-4503) identifies this Hummingbird as the first of a pair of Lockheed XV-4A research machines. It is seen here in conventional flight.

under contract. In late 1966 Lockheed modified one of the XV-4As to a new **XV-4B** configuration, the major change being repalcement of the XV-4A's two 1361-kg (3,000-lb) thrust engines by four each of 1368-kg (3,015-lb) thrust. Testing began in August 1968, but when the aircraft was destroyed in an accident in early 1969 further development was abandoned. Leading data for the XV-4B include a span of 8.25 m (27 ft 1 in), a maximum weight of 5706 kg (12,580 lb) and a speed of 745 km/h (463 mph).

Loening M series

American pioneer constructor Grover C. Loening, who had designed and built his first flying-boat in 1911, established the Loening Aeronautical Engineering Company at New York in early 1918. The first aircraft designed and developed after formation of the company was a two-seat braced high-wing monoplane that was intended for the fighter role. Landing gear was of fixed tailskid type and power for this aircraft, designated **Loening M-8**, was a 224-kW (300-hp) Hispano-Suiza engine mounted in the nose to drive a tractor propeller. Tandem open cockpits were provided for the pilot and rear gunner, the latter armed with

The M-8-1 offered its crew excellent fields of vision and fire, in addition to some advanced streamlining of the radiator and aerofoil wing-struts.

twin 7.62-mm (0.3-in) Lewis guns. Although tested satisfactorily by the US Army and gaining a contract for 5,000 aircraft, the M-8 was cancelled with the end of World War I and no production examples were completed.

Soon after the war the US Navy acquired a single example of this aircraft under the designation **M-8-0**, and following satisfactory testing the company

received an order for an additional 46 comprising 10 M-8-0 and 36 **M-8-1** aircraft, all for the observation role. A final order covered six **M-8-1S** seaplanes with twin-float landing gear. Data for the M-8-0 include a span of 9.98 m (32 ft 9 in), a maximum weight of 938 kg (2,068 lb) and a maximum speed of 233 km/h (145 mph) on the 224-kW (300-hp) Hispano-Suiza V-8 engine.

Loening OL

The most successful military design of the Loening company was the unusual **Loening OL** amphibian first flown in 1923. In an attempt to produce a high-performance amphibian, its design was in effect a conventional two-seat biplane that was mounted on top of a large single float, and stabilising floats were mounted beneath the tip of each lower wing. The wheeled gear for land operations comprised two mainwheels and a tailskid; when operating from water the mainwheels could be swung up clear of the waterline. Tandem open cockpits were provided for the crew, and the four **XCOA-1** prototypes ordered by the US Army were powered by the 298-kW

(400-hp) Liberty V-1650-1 engine. When production ended a total of 165 additional aircraft had been built for service with the US Army Air Corps and US Navy, and details of the several versions are given below, the USAAC's models being those prefixed OA and XO.

Variants
COA-1: designation of three XCOA-1s

following conversion to COA-1, plus nine additional production aircraft
OA-1A: 15 production aircraft, generally as COA-1, but with redesigned tail surfaces
OA-1B: nine production aircraft generally similar to OA-1A
OA-1C: 10 production aircraft, similar to OA-1B but with redesigned fin and rudder

XOA-1A: designation of a prototype generally as OA-1A, but with a Wright V-1460-1 Tornado engine
OA-2: eight production aircraft, as OA-1C, but powered by the Wright V-1460-1 engine
XO-10: redesignation of XOA-1A following incorporation of experimental amphibian gear
OL-1L: two aircraft generally similar to COA-1, but introducing a third cockpit in tandem and 384-kW (440-hp) Packard 1A-1500 engines; second aircraft incorporated a number of improvements

OL-2: five aircraft virtually identical to COA-1
OL-3: four aircraft identical to the second, improved OL-1
OL-4: six aircraft as OL-3, but with the Liberty V-1650-1 engine
OL-6: 28 aircraft as OL-3, but incorporating the fin and rudder introduced on the OA-1C
XOL-7: designation of one OL-6 after the installation of new experimental wings
XOL-8: designation of one OL-6 after experimental installation of a Pratt & Whitney Wasp radial engine

OL-8: 20 aircraft, basically as OL-3, but with only two cockpits and powered by the Pratt & Whitney Wasp engine
OL-8A: 20 aircraft as OL-8, but with arrester gear for carrier operators
OL-9: 26 aircraft as OL-8, but produced after Loening had merged with Keystone Aircraft Corporation
XHL-1: two aircraft, similar to OL-8, but with the fuselage modified for use in an ambulance role, with a single open cockpit and seating six patients in the fuselage

Specification
Loening/Keystone OL-9
Type: amphibious observation aircraft
Powerplant: one 336-kW (450-hp) Pratt & Whitney R-1340-4 Wasp radial piston engine
Performance: maximum speed 196 km/h (122 mph) at sea level; service ceiling 4360 m (14,300 ft); range 1006 km (625 miles)
Weights: empty 1655 kg (3,649 lb); maximum take-off 2451 kg (5,404 lb)
Dimensions: span 13.72 m (45 ft 0 in); length 10.59 m (34 ft 9 in); height 3.89 m (12 ft 9 in); wing area 46.82 m² (504.0 sq ft)

Lohner aircraft

The Austro-Hungarian company Jacob Lohner Werke und Co., which was established in Vienna before World War I, began construction of a two-seat biplane intended for service as an unarmed reconnaissance aircraft. Built in a series of improving **Lohner B** types until 1917, they were powered by engines in the 63- to 119-kW (85- to 160-hp) range produced primarily by Austro-Daimler, but also by other manufacturers. An armed version was developed as the **Lohner C.I** and this, powered by a 119-kW (160-hp) Austro-Daimler, had a single machine-gun for operation by the observer in the rear cockpit. Far more important, however, were the flying-boats developed by the company for maritime patrol and reconnaissance, for although not built in very large numbers, they had an important influence on the development of Italian flying-boats. The Macchi L.1 of 1915, of which about 140 were built, was based on a captured **Lohner L**, and progressive refinement of this design can been seen in the Macchi 'boats of World War I. Lohner's first flying-boat to enter pro-

duction was the **Lohner E**, with biplane wings, a single-step wooden hull, and the tail unit carried on struts well above the level of the rear hull. It was powered by an 63-kW (85-hp) Hiero engine in pusher configuration, and about 40 were built. Major production version, with something over 100 built, was the Lohner L of generally similar configuration but with a more powerful engine by Austro-Daimler. Other variants of this design included the photo-reconnaissance **Lohner R** and the **Type S** unarmed trainer.

Specification
Lohner L
Powerplant: one 119-kW (160-hp) Austro-Daimler inline piston engine
Performance: maximum speed 105 km/h (65 mph); endurance 4 hours
Weight: maximum take-off 1700 kg (3,748 lb)
Dimensions: span 16.20 m (53 ft 1¾ in); length 10.25 m (33 ft 7½ in)
Armament: one 8-mm (0.315-in) Schwarzlose machine-gun, plus up to 200 kg (441 lb) of bombs

The Lohner C.1 was the only two-seater of Lohners' to be designated as an armed aircraft, although some of the earlier B series did have a machine-gun for the observer.

An experimental type of 1917, the Lohner triplane fighter was powered by a 138-kW (185-hp) Austro-Daimler inline and featured a built-up rear decking/dorsal fin.

The most successful flying-boat used by the Austro-Hungarian navy was the Lohner L, a three-seater that was not infrequently used for the bombing of inland targets on the Italian front.

Loire 43, 45 and 46

The prototype **Loire 43** single-seat fighter flew on 17 October 1932. Of all-metal construction with stressed skinning and a high gull wing, the Loire 43 used the Hispano-Suiza 12Xbrs V-12 engine of 515 kW (690 hp) specified by the French air ministry for all 10 competitors in the then-current single-seat fighter competition. The **Loire 43.01** first prototype was lost in a crash on 14 January 1933, but by then a development, the **Loire 45.01**, had been completed. It differed by having a 552-kW (740-hp) Gnome-Rhône 14Kds engine, as well as some structural refinement, and was first flown on 20 February 1933. Later re-engined with a 671-kW (900-hp) Gnome-Rhône 14Kfs radial, the Loire 45.01 then demonstrated a speed of 370 km/h (230 mph). Subsequent modifications included raising the wing at the root and lowering the engine slightly to improve visibility for the pilot. Further redesign of the wing, landing gear and tailplane led to the **Loire 46.01**, flown for the first time on 1 September 1934. An order for 60 series aircraft was received in spring 1935, and these incorporated further improvements and introduced a radio transmitter/receiver.

Loire 46 series aircraft numbers 2 to 6 inclusive were delivered clandestinely to the Spanish Republican government in September 1936 and fought briefly against the Franco forces, but within a few months two were lost in accidents and two were shot down. Deliveries to the Armée de l'Air began in November

1936, and by 1937 the 6e Escadre based at Chartres had converted all its four *escadrilles* to the type. However, in March 1939 all surviving Loire 46s were transferred for use by the Cazaux gunnery school and other flying schools.

Specification
Loire 46
Type: single-seat fighter
Powerplant: one 671-kW (900-hp) Gnome-Rhône 14Kfs radial piston engine
Performance: maximum speed 390 km/h (242 mph); service ceiling 11750 m (38,550 ft); range 750 km (466 miles)
Weights: empty equipped 1360 kg

(2,998 lb); maximum take-off 2100 kg (4,630 lb)
Dimensions: span 11.83 m (38 ft 9¾ in); length 7.88 m (25 ft 10¼ in); height 4.13 m (13 ft 6½ in); wing area 19.50 m² (209.90 sq ft)
Armament: four 7.5-mm (0.295-in) MAC machine-guns in the wings, plus provision for underfuselage bomb racks

Loire 46 of the Aerial Gunnery School, l'Armée de l'Air, based at Cazaux (France) in 1939 and early 1940.

Loire 50 and 51
to
Macchi M.24

Loire 50 and 51

A three-seat parasol-wing flying-boat for liaison or training duties, the **Loire 50.01** prototype first flew on 7 September 1931. After being sunk in an accident it was recovered and on 24 March 1932 was flown as an amphibian, the two main wheels retracting to a horizontal position clear of the water. In summer 1933 its 172-kW (230-hp) Salmson 9Ab radial was replaced by a 261-kW (350-hp) Hispano-Suiza 9Qd radial, and it was then redesignated **Loire 50bis**. Six series **Loire 501** amphibians, closely resembling the Loire 50bis and retaining its crew arrangement, were delivered in 1935 to various *sections de servitude* (general-duty flights) at French naval air

The oddest feature of the Loire 51 was the 'retractable' landing gear, whose main units lifted only to the horizontal position to permit water operations.

stations, the last surviving Loire 501 reported at Karouba (Bizerta, Tunisia) in August 1941.

Specification
Loire 501
Type: communication flying-boat
Powerplant: one 261-kW (350-hp) Hispano-Suiza 9Qd radial piston engine
Performance: maximum speed 195 km/h (121 mph) at 1000 m

(3,280 ft); service ceiling 4850 m (15,910 ft); range 1100 km (683 miles)
Weights: empty 1385 kg (3,053 lb); maximum take-off 2150 kg (4,740 lb)

Dimensions: span 16.00 m (52 ft 6 in); length 11.10 m (36 ft 4½ in); height 4.47 m (14 ft 8 in); wing area 39.40 m² (424.1 sq ft)

Loire 70

An eight-man long-range maritime reconnaissance and bombing flying-boat designed to a 1932 French navy requirement, the prototype **Loire 70** made its maiden flight on 28 December 1933. During prolonged tests the original three 373-kW (500-hp) Gnome-Rhône 9Kbr radials were replaced by more powerful 9Kfr engines, and other changes included supplementing the large single fin and rudder with a pair of small auxiliary fins, elimination of the bow gun position, and relocation of the bomb-aimer/navigator in the extreme nose. Seven production aircraft were delivered to Escadrille E.7 at Karouba to join the prototype in a 12-month period from June 1937. From the beginning of hostilities, in September 1939, the Loire 70s patrolled the Mediterranean until three

Among the defensive arrangements of the Loire 70 were several machine-gun positions, including a manually operated turret just forward of the raised flight deck. Another was behind the trailing edge at the rear of the cockpit, and a third was in a watertight hatch just above the rear step of the hull. The maximum bombload was 600 kg (1323 lb).

of four surviving machines were destroyed in an Italian air raid on their base on 12 June 1940. Nothing was heard subsequently of the surviving flying-boat.

Specification
Type: long-range maritime reconnaissance flying-boat
Powerplant: three 552-kW (740-hp) Gnome-Rhône 9Kfr radial piston

engines
Performance: maximum speed 235 km/h (146 mph); service ceiling 4000 m (13,125 ft); range 3000 km (1,864 miles)
Weights: empty equipped 6500 kg (14,330 lb); maximum take-off 11500 kg (25,353 lb)

Dimensions: span 30.00 m (98 ft 5¼ in); length 19.50 m (63 ft 11¾ in); height 6.75 m (22 ft 1¾ in); wing area 136.00 m² (1,463.94 sq ft)
Armament: six 7.5-mm (0.295-in) machine-guns, plus up to 600 kg (1,323 lb) of bombs, or four 75-kg (165-lb) anti-submarine grenades

Loire 102

Designed for the South Atlantic mail route between West Africa and Brazil, the **Loire 101** Bretagne (Brittany) flew for the first time on 12 May 1936. A large superstructure, on the lines of the naval vessels for which the firm was famous, was set on top of the two-step hull and contained the control cabin and various crew compartments. Forward in the hull was a comfortable cabin for four passengers, to the rear of which were holds for mail, baggage and freight. Set on top

The 1936-vintage Loire 102 is seen here in its originally intended shape; that is, fitted with twin vertical tail surfaces. Later on in life a third fin was added, on the centreline, between the first pair. The final arrangement saw the flying-boat fitted with a single large fin-and-rudder assembly, was aided by two smaller auxiliary surfaces outboard.

of the high braced wing were four 537-kW (720-hp) Hispano-Suiza 12Kbrs-1 liquid-cooled engines in tandem pairs.

Vibration problems of the Loire 102 (F-AOVV) were never resolved and the flying-boat was finally scrapped in 1938.

The 'boat had a wing span of 34.00 m (111 ft 6½ in) and a maximum take-off weight of 19100 kg (42,107 lb).

Loire 130

Built to meet a 1933 requirement of the French navy for an all-purpose shipboard catapult-launched three-seat seaplane, the prototype **Loire 130** high-wing monoplane flying-boat flew for the first time on 19 November 1934. Persistent stability problems delayed development and it was not until August 1936 that an initial production order was placed for two versions, the **Loire 130M** (Metropole) and **Loire 130C** (Colonie), the latter being strengthened and equipped for use in tropical climates. Power was provided by a Hispano-Suiza engine mounted on struts over the hull.

The Loire 130 did not reach French

navy *escadrilles* until 1938. By 1939 it equipped Escadrille 7S2 aboard the seaplane carrier Commandant Teste and 7S3 and 7S4 embarked on various capital ships and cruisers. Overseas the Loire 130 was with 8S2 at Fort-de-France, French Antilles, 8S3 in West Africa, and 8S4 in the Levant (now Lebanon). In 1939-40 the type went on to equip several newly formed shore-based and shipborne units and also equipped Armée de l'Air units, including 1/CBS in French Indo-China (now Vietnam).

Not all the Loire 130s on order had been completed by the time of the June 1940 armistice with the Germans, but permission was given for 30 more of the type to be built under the auspices of the

Intended for shipboard operations, the Loire 130 had detachable wingtips and elevators and a complex wing folding mechanism.

Vichy regime. It is believed that overall nearly 150 examples of this efficient aircraft were delivered, performing a range of duties which included reconnaissance, observing and ranging for naval guns, coastal patrol and convoy escort, as well as liaison work. In this last capacity the Loire 130 could carry up to three passengers.

From November 1942 all catapults were removed from French ships, the Loire 130s thenceforth being shore-based. The last Loire 130 in flying condition, with Escadrille 8.S in Indo-China, was withdrawn and scrapped in late 1949.

Specification
Type: three-seat general-purpose flying-boat

Powerplant: one 537-kW (720-hp) Hispano-Suiza 12Xbrs V-12 piston engine
Performance: maximum speed 226 km/h (149 mph) at 2800 m (9,185 ft); service ceiling 6000 m (19,685 ft); range 1100 km (684 miles)
Weights: empty equipped 2090 kg (4,608 lb); maximum take-off 3396 kg (7,487 lb)

Dimensions: span 16.00 m (52 ft 6 in); length 11.30 m (37 ft 1 in); height 3.85 m (12 ft 7½ in); wing area 40.10 m² (431.65 sq ft)
Armament: two 7.5-mm (0.295-in) Darne machine-guns, plus two 75-kg (165-lb) SM anti-submarine grenades or two G-2 bombs of the same weight attached to bomb racks on the sides of the forward hull

Loire 210

In 1933 the French navy issued a requirement for a single-seat catapult-launched fighter seaplane to serve with the fleet. Loire's entry for this competition, the **Loire 210.01**, flew for the first time on 21 March 1935. It combined a Loire 46 fuselage with a new low wing, the outer sections of which could be folded for shipboard stowage. The pilot was accommodated in an open cockpit just aft of the wing, and the landing gear comprised a large central float and two underwing auxiliary floats. Power was provided by a single 730-kW (980-hp) Hispano-Suiza 9Vbs radial engine.

After prolonged trials the rival Bernard

A prolonged gestation period meant that the Loire 210 fighter was obsolete by the time it entered service. Its service career was further blighted by severe structural problems.

110, Potez 453 and Romano R.90 were eliminated, despite superior speed, and 20 series Loire 210s were ordered in March 1937. Production aircraft differed from the prototype by having four rather than two wing-mounted 7.5-mm (0.295-in) Darne machine-guns, and the Loire 210s were allocated to new navy Escadrilles HC.1 and HC.2 in August 1939, but the loss of five machines as a result of wing structural failure led to grounding of the remainder some three months

later. Wing span was 11.79 m (38 ft 8¼ in), maximum take-off 2100 kg (4,629 lb) and maximum speed 315 km/h (196 mph).

Loire 250

The **Loire 250**, all-metal single-seat fighter prototype first flown on 27 September 1935, was a low-wing monoplane with retractable tailwheel type landing gear. Powered by a 746-kW (1,000-hp) Hispano-Suiza 14Ha-7a radial engine, the Loire 250 accommodated its pilot in a cockpit enclosed by a long fully-glazed canopy. The **Loire 250** was in competition with the Dewoitine D.513 and Morane-Saulnier MS.405, and before the fly-off against these aircraft underwent a number of modifications to improve performance. However, these obviously proved inadequate for although the prototype had a maximum speed of 480 km/h (298 mph), following tests its development was abandoned and the projected armament of two 20-mm cannon and two 7.5-mm (0.295-in) machine-guns was never installed.

Loire-Nieuport 40 series

The single-seat **Loire-Nieuport 40** prototype dive-bomber made its first flight in June 1938. An inverted gull-wing monoplane developed from the Nieuport 140, it was intended for shipboard use and had folding wings. The main landing gear units retracted into underwing nacelles, and the lower half of the rudder divided vertically so that it opened in two sections which acted as dive brakes. The 225-kg (496-lb) bomb was carried beneath the fuselage on a crutch which swung forward to ensure the weapon cleared the propeller when released in a dive. Official tests brought tail unit modifications, and elimination of the tail dive-brakes in favour of using the extended landing gear as a braking device. Six more L.N.40s were ordered, but by the time of delivery a further 36 had been requested by the French navy and the production version been redesignated **L.N.401**. In the same year, 1939, the Armée de l'Air ordered 40 **L.N.411** aircraft, which differed only by deletion of the wing folding and other specialised naval equipment.

Four pre-production L.N.401s flew with Escadrille AC.1 of the Aéronavale for training in mid-1939, and production aircraft entered service with Escadrilles AB.2 and AB.4. The Armée de l'Air relinquished its L.N.411s in favour of the navy, and aircraft of this type re-equipped Escadrille AB.4 in April 1940. Between 10 May and 4 June virtually all available dive-bombers of this type were expended in attacks on the advancing German armies in northern France. The remnants were transferred to Hyères in the south where, issued with some replacement aircraft from reserves, they carried out reconnaissance and naval escort duties against the Italians, making a night attack on 18 June on naval vessels in Imperia harbour. Surviving aircraft were flown to North Africa on 25 June,

Loire-Nieuport L.N.401 of Escadrille AB.2 Aéronavale, based at Berck (France) in May 1940.

where they were subsequently put into store.

A total of 24 L.N.401s and 411s was assembled from components by SNCASO at Chateauroux by March 1942. The aircraft were then flown to Hyères, where 12 were seized by Axis forces in November 1942. The remainder had been taken to Bizerta-Karouba, where they were subsequently lost, along with earlier stored machines, in Allied air raids. Total production of both versions is believed to have slightly exceeded 100.

The **L.N.402** was a one-off variant with a more powerful Hispano-Suiza 12Y-31 engine, and the **L.N.42** had a new wing of shorter span and a 820-kW (1,100-hp) Hispano-Suiza 12Y-51 engine. It had not made a proper test flight before being hidden from the occupying German forces, and finally flew at Toussus-le-Noble on 24 August 1945, only to be scrapped in 1947.

Specification
Loire-Nieuport L.N.401

Type: single-seat shipboard dive-bomber
Powerplant: one 515-kW (690-hp) Hispano-Suiza 12Xcrs V-12 piston engine
Performance: maximum speed 380 km/h (236 mph); service ceiling 9500 m (31,170 ft); range 1200 km (746 miles)
Weights: empty equipped 2135 kg

(4,707 lb); maximum take-off 2823 kg (6,224 lb)
Dimensions: span 14.00 m (45 ft 11¼ in); length 9.75 m (31 ft 11¾ in); height 3.50 m (11 ft 5¾ in); wing area 24.75 m²2 (266.42 sq ft)
Armament: one engine-mounted 20-mm cannon and two wing-mounted 7.5-mm (0.295-in) machine-guns, plus a maximum bombload of 225 kg (496 lb)

In the face of intense anti-aircraft fire, the Aéronavale's L.N.40 dive bombers suffered almost 100 per cent casualties trying to stem the German invasion of France during 1940.

Macchi M.67

Work on the new Castoldi design for the 1929 Schneider Trophy contest at Calshot began at the end of 1928. Three **Macchi M.67** aircraft (serials MM.103-105) were built, first flights being made in early August 1929. By comparison with the M.52, the new design had a straight wing, a slimmer fuselage, and a remarkably powerful engine, the 1342-kW (1,800-hp) Isotta-Fraschini 2-800 designed by Giustino Cattaneo. To resolve attendant cooling problems the wing surface cooling radiators were augmented by additional coolant and oil radiators mounted flush in the lower nose surface and at each side of the rear fuselage. Subsequently, additional cooling surfaces were mounted on the float

struts and on the upper surfaces of the floats.

On 22 August Giuseppe Motta, flying an M.67, stalled and crashed into Lake Garda, thus only two of these aircraft were available to take part in the Trophy race on 7 September. One was forced to retire to resolve fumes in the cockpit, and the other when the pilot was scalded by boiling water from a fractured pipe in the complex cooling system, thus ending the racing career of the type.

The M.67 had the same wing span as the M.52, was slightly longer at 7.77 m (25 ft 6 in), and the heavy engine increased maximum take-off weight to 2180 kg (4,806 lb). Estimated maximum speed was 584 km/h (363 mph).

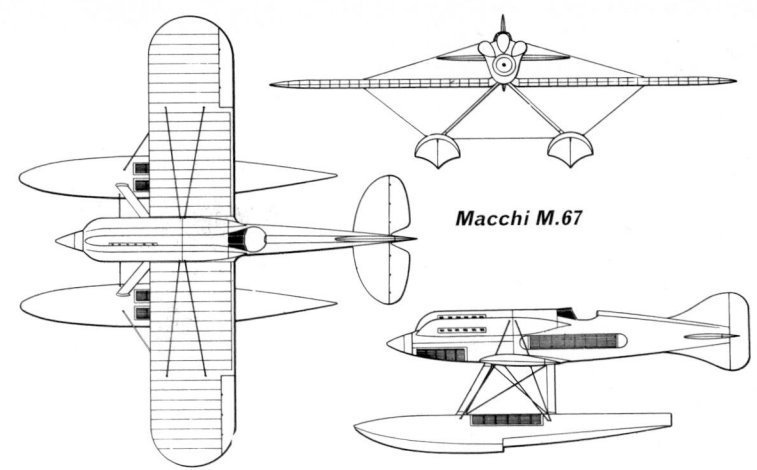

Macchi M.67

Macchi M.C.72

With the **Macchi M.C.72** Mario Castoldi reached the pinnacle of his design career. Intended for the 1931 Schneider Trophy contest, the M.C.72 was tailored around the new Fiat A.S.6 engine, designed by Tranquillo Zerbi, which comprised two 1119-kW (1,500-hp) A.S.5 engines mounted in tandem on a common crankcase. In effect, each A.S.5 drove one of the contra-rotating propellers via a co-axial shaft, counter-rotating propellers eliminating the on-water torque problems which had plagued high-powered seaplanes.

Compared with earlier Macchi floatplanes the fuselage shape of the M.C.72 was different, but the tail and wings attached to this slim fuselage were clearly a development of previous designs by Castoldi. The long twin metal floats were carried on four broad-chord struts which were covered with coolant radiators, the wing was covered with flat-tube surface radiators, there were additional radiators on the upper surface of the floats, and an oil cooler was fitted around the sides and undersurface of the rear fuselage, aft of the pilot's open cockpit.

The first of five M.C.72s (serialled MM.177-181) flew from Desenzano on Lake Garda in June 1931. Troubles were experienced with the engine's carburetion system, but considering the remarkably short development period significant progress had been made by 2 August, when Giovanni met with disaster and was killed when his machine crashed into the lake. The problems with the M.C.72s could not be resolved in time for the 1931 Schneider contest and Italy did not participate. Nevertheless, development of the M.C.72 continued, despite the loss of a second machine during a record attempt, and finally the carburetion problems were overcome with the use of a specially blended fuel. On 10 April 1933 Warrant Officer Agello established a world speed record over a 3-km (1.86-mile) course at an average of 682.078 km/h (423.825 mph), and the M.C.72 later established a world speed record over a 100-km (62.14-mile) course and gained the Coupe Louis Blériot in October 1933. Finally, the absolute speed record was raised to 709.209 km/h (440.683 mph) by Agello on 23 October 1934. This successful

M.C.72 is preserved at the Aeronautica Militare Italiana museum at Vigna di Valle, some 35 km (22 miles) from Rome.

Specification
Type: single-seat racing seaplane
Powerplant: one 2125-kW (2,850-hp) Fiat A.S.6 24-cylinder double V.12 piston engine
Performance: maximum speed 708 km/h (440 mph)
Weights: empty equipped 2500 kg (5,512 lb); maximum take-off 3025 kg (6,669 lb)

The Macchi M.C.72 may be regarded as the ultimate float plane racer, and still holds the world speed record for a piston-engined float plane. The mighty A.S.6 double V-12 engine had enormous cooling requirements, so much of the wing surface, float legs and floats themselves were flush radiators.

Dimensions: span 9.48 m (31 ft 1¼ in); length 8.32 m (27 ft 3½ in); height 3.30 m (10 ft 10 in); wing area 15.00 m² (161.46 sq ft)

Macchi M.C.94

Designed by Castoldi purely as a flying-boat, the prototype **Macchi M.C.94** passenger transport was given retractable landing-gear at an early stage, but remained the only amphibian in the M.C.94 series, the 11 production machines being flying-boats. Construction was mainly of wood, with a cantilever high wing and two-step hull with single fin and rudder, and power was provided by two 574-kW (770-hp) Wright Cyclone SGR-1820-F52 radial engines. On the seventh production machine these engines were replaced by 559-kW (750-hp) Alfa Romeo 126 RC 10s. The en-

Given Italy's extensive coastline, the use of commercial flying-boats blossomed during the 1920s and 1930s. The Macchi M.C.94's high wing provided its passengers with an unobstructed view.

closed cabin for the three-man crew was set well forward, and the comfortable main cabin accommodated 12 passengers.

The M.C.94 went into service on the Adriatic routes of the Ala Littoria airline from 1936 and a number continued in operation during World War II. Three ex-

Ala Littoria M.C.94s were sold to a Buenos Aires-based airline in 1939. Wing span was 22.79 m (74 ft 9¼ in) and maximum take-off weight 8200 kg

(18,077 lb), maximum speed with the Alfa Romeo engines 292 km/h (181 mph), and range 1490 km (926 miles).

Macchi M.C.200 Saetta

Following the end of Italy's military campaigns in East Africa a programme was initiated to re-equip the Regia Aeronautica, the **Macchi M.C.200 Saetta** (lightning) being designed by Mario Casoldi to meet the requirement for a single-seat fighter. First flown as a prototype (MM.336) on 24 December 1937, this was a cantilever low-wing monoplane mainly of metal construction, with retractable tailwheel landing gear, an enclosed cockpit, and power provided by a Fiat A.74 RC 38 radial engine. Flight test-

Initial examples of the M.C.200 were notable for their neat cockpit canopies, which offered their pilots a good all-round view while protecting them from the elements. However, for some reason Italian pilots preferred open cockpits and this feature was later built into the design.

ing proved highly successful and the M.C.200 won the fighter contest held during 1938, being ordered into produc-

tion with an initial contract for 99 aircraft. First production deliveries were made in October 1939, and by the time that Italy became involved in World War II in June 1940 about 150 had been accepted by the Regia Aeronautica; production eventually totalled 1,153, some 400 being built by Macchi and the remainder by Breda and SAI-Ambrosinia. First used operationally as escort fighters in attacks on Malta in autumn 1940, Saettas saw service in Greece, North Africa and Yugoslavia. A number were involved in operations on the Eastern Front during 1941-42, and after the Italian armistice of September 1943, 23 Saettas were flown to Allied airfields in southern Italy, being used subsequently by pilots of the Italian Co-Belligerent Air Force.

Variants
M.C.200 (prototypes): two aircraft with the 626-kW (840-hp) Fiat A.74 RC 38 engine
M.C.200: production version with uprated A.74 RD engines; early, intermediate and late production had, respectively, enclosed, open and semi-enclosed cockpits
M.C.200AS: tropicalised version
M.C.200CB: fighter-bomber version with provisions for a maximum 320-kg (705-lb) bomb load or two underwing auxiliary tanks
M.C.201: single prototype of developed version with revised fuselage and a 746-kW (1,000-hp) Fiat A.76 RC 40 engine; flown only with A.74 RC 38 engine and development abandoned in favour of M.C.202

Specification
Type: single-seat interceptor fighter/fighter-bomber
Powerplant: one 649-kW (870-hp) Fiat A.74 RC 38 radial piston engine
Performance: maximum speed 502 km/h (312 mph) at 4500 m (14,765 ft); service ceiling 8900 m (29,200 ft); range with auxiliary fuel 870 km (540 miles)
Weights: empty 1895 kg (4,178 lb); maximum take-off 2590 kg (5,710 lb)
Dimensions: span 10.58 m (34 ft 8½ in); length 8.19 m (26 ft 10¼ in); height 3.50 m (11 ft 5¾ in); wing area 16.80 m² (180.84 sq ft)
Armament: two 12.7-mm (0.5-in) forward-firing machine-guns in engine cowling; some late production examples had two additional 7.7-mm (0.303-in) wing-mounted guns

Macchi M.C.202 Folgore

Mario Castoldi was convinced that full potential of the M.C.200 design could be achieved only with greater horsepower, and this was confirmed when the **Macchi M.C.202 Folgore** (thunderbolt) prototype flew for the first time on 10 August 1940, powered by an imported Daimler-Benz DB 601A engine. Ordered into production without delay, the M.C.202 had a new fuselage (incorporating an enclosed cockpit) to accept the larger engine, but retained tail unit, landing gear, and wings generally similar to the M.C.200. Produced by Macchi Breda and SAI-Ambrosini alongside the M.C.200, early production aircraft were powered by imported DB 601A-1 engines until Alfa Romeo had a licence-built version available. Limited manufacture of this engine restricted the number of M.C.202s to about 1,500, 393 built by Macchi, which explains continued production of the M.C.200. Initial deliveries of production M.C.202s went to units in Libya from November 1941, and in Sep-

Combining the aerodynamic flair of designer Mario Castoldi with the fruits of German aero engineering, the Macchi M.C.202 Folgore was one of the best Italian fighters to appear during World War II.

tember of the following year their deployment began on the Eastern Front.

Variants
M.C.202 (prototype): one only, basically a re-engined M.C.200 airframe which also introduced a retractable tailwheel
M.C.202AS: tropicalised version
M.C.202CB: fighter-bomber version with provision for up to 320-kg (705-lb) bomb load or two auxiliary fuel tanks
M.C.202D: single experimental aircraft with revised radiator

Specification
Type: single-seat interceptor fighter/

fighter-bomber
Powerplant: one 876-kW (1,175-hp) Alfa Romeo RA.1000 RC 41-I Monsone inverted V-12 piston engine
Performance: maximum speed 595 km/h (370 mph) at 5000 m (16,405 ft); service ceiling 11500 m (37,730 ft); range 765 km (475 miles)
Weights: empty 2350 kg (5,181 lb); maximum take-off 3010 kg (6,636 lb)

Dimensions: span 10.58 m (34 ft 8½ in); length 8.85 m (29 ft 0½ in); height 3.04 m (9 ft 11½ in); wing area 16.80 m² (180.84 sq ft)
Armament: initially two 12.7-mm (0.5-in) machine-guns in engine cowling; later series added two 7.7-mm (0.303-in) wing-mounted guns; one batch had a 20-mm cannon beneath each wing

Macchi M.C.205V Veltro

Fundamentally a developed version of the M.C.202, the **Macchi M.C.205V Veltro** (greyhound) prototype comprised a production M.C.202 airframe with an imported Daimler-Benz DB 605A engine of 1100 kW (1,475 hp). Flown for the first time on 19 April 1942, it was put into production immediately, but some delay resulted before Fiat's licence-built version of the Daimler-Benz engine, the RA.1050 RC 58 Tifone (typhoon), became available in significant numbers. As a result, the production M.C.205V Veltro did not become operational until mid-1943, its first known action occurring in early July when the type was deployed in support of torpedo-bombers attacking Allied naval forces off Sicily. Just two months later, when the Italian government headed by Marshal Badoglio made peace with the Allies, the Regia Aeronautica had a total of 66 Veltros. Of this total only six gained Allied airfields to serve with the Italian Co-Belligerent Air Force, the remainder being used by the Republican Socialist Italian air force.

Production continued on a limited scale after the Armistice, and ultimately a total of 262 had been built; of this total a small number were used by the Luftwaffe, equipping one *Gruppe*. Regarded as the best Italian fighter aircraft of World War II, the Veltro was capable of meeting such renowned fighters as the North American P-51D Mustang on equal terms.

Variants
M.C.205: single prototype with

Macchi M.C.205V Veltro of the 1ª Squadriglia, 1° Gruppo of the Aeronautica Nazionale Repubblicana, based in northern Italy during late 1943.

standard armament of late production M.C.202s, comprising two 12.7-mm (0.5-in) and two 7.7-mm (0.303-in) machine-guns
M.C.205V: production version, generally as prototype; late production had two 20-mm cannon in place of German MG 151 wing machine-guns; 262 built
M.C.205N-1: prototype of high-altitude interceptor version with increased-span wing and armament comprising one engine-mounted 20-mm cannon and four fuselage-mounted 12.7-mm (0.5-in) machine-guns
M.C.205N-2: alternative prototype of high-altitude version, differing only by

having armament comprising three 20-mm cannon and two 12.7-mm (0.5-in) machine-guns
M.C.206: prototype of further developed version, not completed; would have had a further increase in wing span
M.C.207: prototype of further developed version, not completed; generally as M.C.206 but with armament of four wing-mounted 20-mm cannon

Specification
Macchi M.C.205V Veltro
Type: single-seat interceptor fighter/fighter-bomber
Powerplant: one 1100-kW (1,475-hp)

Fiat RA.1050 RC 58 Tifone engine
Performance: maximum speed 642 km/h (399 mph) at 7200 m (23,620 ft); service ceiling 16370 m (37,090 ft); range 1040 km (646 miles)
Weights: empty 2581 kg (5,691 lb); maximum take-off 3408 kg (7,154 lb)
Dimensions: span 10.58 m (34 ft 8½ in); length 8.85 m (29 ft 0½ in); height 3.04 m (9 ft 11½ in); wing area 16.80 m² (180.84 sq ft)
Armament: two 12.7-mm (0.5-in) and two 7.7-mm (0.303-in) machine-guns; later production had two 20-mm cannon replacing 7.7-mm (0.303-in) guns

Macchi M.B.308

Designed by Ermanno Bazzochi, the **Macchi M.B.308** cantilever high-wing cabin monoplane first appeared in 1946. It accommodated pilot and co-pilot side by side and had fixed tricycle landing gear. Built in quantity, it achieved considerable success at post-war sporting meetings and contests, but as well as its use by private owners for sport flying and touring, it was flown as a trainer by Italian aero clubs and by the Aeronautica Militare. For some 15 years it was one of the most widely used Italian aircraft.

Variants built included two-seaters

This is the three-seat version of the basic Macchi M.B.308, the M.B.308G, with its distinctive extra cabin window.

with 63-kW (85-hp) Continental C85s, or 67-kW (90-hp) C90s, the M.B.308 three-seater, and the **M.B.308 Idro** twin-float seaplane. The original version, with 48-kW (65-hp) Continental C65 engine, had a maximum speed of 175 km/h (109 mph).

Malmo Flygindustri MFI-9

A. B. Malmö Flygindustri began the production of aircraft with the **Malmo MFI-9 Junior**, which had originated as the **Andreasson BA-7** designed by Bjorn Andreasson before he joined the company. The BA-7 prototype, powered by a 48-kW (65-hp) Continental A65 engine, had flown first on 10 October 1958, but the production prototypes and production aircraft built by MFI incorporated redesigned tail surfaces, the first of the production aircraft flying on 9 August 1962, by which time MFI had become a subsidiary of the Swedish Saab company. A braced shoulder-wing monoplane with fixed tricycle landing gear, the MFI-9 had an enclosed cabin with side-by-side seating for two and was powered by a more powerful Rolls-Royce Continental O-200 engine. This version was also produced under licence in Germany by Messerschmitt-Bölkow-Blohm, which designated the aircraft

MBB 208 C Junior and built about 200. MFI built 25 examples of the MFI-9 Junior, following it in production by the more developed **MFI-9B Trainer** (43 built) which had a further revision of tail surfaces, an enlarged cabin, and incorporated a number of refinements. Both MFI versions were available with optional float or ski landing gear. Final variant was the **MFI-9 Mili-trainer**, of which two prototypes were evaluated by the Swedish air force, and these differed primarily by having underwing attachment points for a variety of missiles or rockets. The prototypes of an enlarged development of the MFI-9 were flown in 1969-70 under the designations **Saab MFI-15** and **MFI-15B**.

Specification
MFI-9B Trainer (landplane)
Type: two-seat sport/trainer aircraft
Powerplant: one 75-kW (100-hp)

Rolls-Royce Continental O-200A flat-four piston engine
Performance: maximum speed 240 km/h (149 mph) at sea level; service ceiling 4570 m (15,000 ft); range with maximum payload 800 km (497 miles)
Weights: empty 340 kg (750 lb); maximum take-off 575 kg (1,268 lb)

With a new tail and bigger cockpit the MFI-9 Junior became the MFI-9B trainer for the Swedish air force.

Dimensions: span 7.43 m (24 ft 4½ in); length 5.85 m (19 ft 2¼ in); height 2.00 m (6 ft 6¾ in); wing area 8.70 m (93.65 sq ft)

Martin 4-0-4

A Martin 4-0-4 of Caribbean operator Marco Island Airways.

Attempting to gain a share of the post-World War II demand for civil airliners, the Glenn L. Martin Company flew on 22 November 1946 the prototype of a twin-engine 36/40-seat transport designated **Martin 2-0-2**. The first of these entered service in October 1947, but the loss of a 2-0-2 in 1948 as a result of wing structural failure led to modification of other in-service aircraft and production of this version was brought to an end. The prototype of an improved **Martin 3-0-3** had been flown on 20 June 1947, but with a need to redesign the wing structure it was decided instead to develop a new **Martin 4-0-4**. This incorporated the wing structural revisions and introduced a pressurised and slightly lengthened fuselage, accommodating as standard a crew of three or four and 40 passengers. When production ended in early 1953 a total of 103 had been built, this number including two supplied to the Coast Guard as staff transports under the designation **RM-1G** (later **RM-1Z** and finally **VC-3A**); they were subsequently transferred to the US Navy.

Specification
Martin 4-0-4
Type: short/medium-range transport
Powerplant: two 1790-kW (2,400-hp)

Pratt & Whitney R-2800-CB16 radial piston engines
Performance: maximum speed 502 km/h (312 mph) at 4420 m (14,500 ft); service ceiling 8840 m (29,000 ft); range with maximum payload 1738 km (1,080 miles)
Weights: empty equipped 13211 kg (29,126 lb); maximum take-off 20366 kg (44,900 lb)
Dimensions: span 28.42 m (93 ft 3 in); length 22.73 m (74 ft 7 in); height 8.66 m (28 ft 5 in); wing area 80.27 m² (864.0 sq ft)

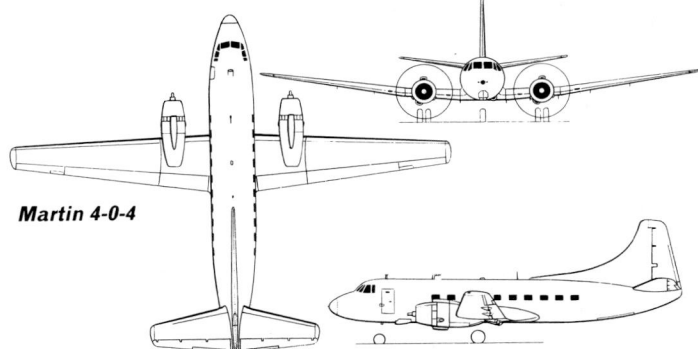

Martin 4-0-4

597

Martin 167 Maryland

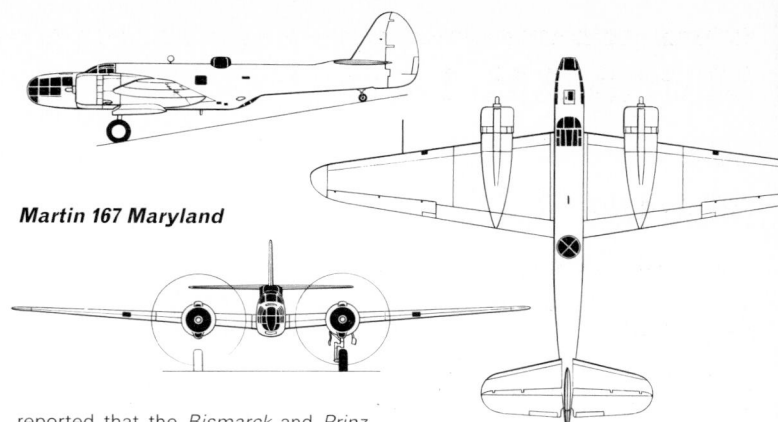

Martin 167 Maryland

Designed to meet a US Army Air Corps specification for an attack bomber, the **Martin XA-22** prototype was a twin-engine cantilever low/mid-wing monoplane with retractable tailwheel landing gear and accommodation for a crew of three. It was flown for the first time on 14 March 1939, but following official tests was rejected by the USAAC. However, the company had received a first production order for 115 aircraft from France even before the prototype had flown, but the start of delivery was delayed until the US arms embargo was lifted in October 1939; by that time France had contracted for an additional 100 aircraft. Only 140 of these **Model 167F** aircraft were delivered before the French armistice in June 1940, having the French designation **Martin 167A-3** and seeing action against Axis forces until June 1940 and subsequently, with Vichy forces in West Africa and the Middle East, against the Allies.

With the collapse of French resistance in Europe, the outstanding 75 aircraft on order were diverted to the UK for service with the RAF and these, together with an additional 75 ordered by the RAF,

were designated as **Maryland Mk 1**. All were powered by 783-kW (1,050-hp) R-1830-SC3G Twin Wasp radial engines with single-stage superchargers. Further British orders followed for an improved **Maryland Mk II** with more powerful engines and two-stage superchargers, a total of 150 of this version being delivered to the RAF. Marylands were deployed initially for target towing and long-range reconnaissance, proving to be particularly valuable in this latter role, and were also used as light bombers. The first operational unit to receive the Maryland, in September 1940, was No. 431 Flight (later No. 69 Squadron) formed at Malta, and the type saw service in the Western Desert with Nos 39 and 223 Squadrons. Some 72 of the RAF's Marylands were re-allocated to serve with Nos 12, 20, 21 and 24 Squadrons of the South African Air Force. Marylands also saw service with the Fleet Air Arm. Among the notable operations of the type were the reconnaissance sorties that preceded the successful Fleet Air Arm attack in November 1940 on the Italian fleet in harbour at Taranto. Another FAA Maryland

reported that the *Bismarck* and *Prinz Eugen* were at sea in May 1941.

Specification
Martin Maryland Mk II
Type: three-seat reconnaissance/bomber aircraft
Powerplant: two 895-kW (1,200-hp) Pratt & Whitney R-1830-S3C4G Twin Wasp radial piston engines
Performance: maximum speed 447 km/h (278 mph) at 3595 m (11,800 ft); service ceiling 7925 m (26,000 ft); range with maximum bombload 1738 km (1,080 miles)

Weights: empty 5086 kg (11,213 lb); maximum take-off 7624 kg (16,809 lb)
Dimensions: span 18.69 m (61 ft 4 in); length 14.22 m (46 ft 8 in); height 4.57 m (14 ft 11¾ in); wing area 50.03 m² (538.50 sq ft)
Armament: four 7.7-mm (0.303-in) wing-mounted Browning machine-guns, one 7.7-mm (0.303-in) Vickers 'K' gun each in dorsal and ventral positions, plus a bombload of up to 907 kg (2,000 lb)

Martin 170 Mars

On 23 August 1938 the US Navy ordered from Martin a single prototype of the **Martin 170** design for a patrol bomber of flying-boat configuration. Designated **XPB2M-1**, it was the world's largest flying-boat when flown for the first time on 3 July 1942, but by then the United States had become involved in World War II and it was decided not to proceed with procurement of the type as a patrol bomber. Instead, the 'boat was modified for use in a transport role, becoming redesignated **XPB2M-1R** and entering service in December 1943. It remains the largest flying-boat to have been operated by the US Navy and an early demonstration of its capability came in 1944, when a 9299-kg (20,500-lb) cargo was

The Martin JRM-2 was a unique aircraft, being a version of the JRM-1 cleaned up for operations at a maximum take-off weight 20,000 lb higher than the JRM-1s MTOW of 145,000 lb. The aircraft had an impressive span of 200 ft.

delivered to Hawaii in a 7564-km (4,700-mile) round trip completed in only 27 hours 36 minutes, resulting in a US Navy order for a production version under the designation **JRM-1 Mars**. This covered 20 aircraft to be completed specially for the transport role, but the end of World War II brought contract cancellations and only five were built, plus a single **JRM-2** for operation at a higher gross

weight. When the five JRM-1s were later modified to this latter standard they became redesignated **JRM-3**. These 60.96 m (200 ft) span aircraft were powered by four 1715-kW (2,300-hp)

Wright R-3350-8 engines, and an appreciation of their capacity can be gained from the fact that on 19 May one of them, *Marshall Mars*, carried a total of 301 passengers, plus its crew of seven.

Martin 187 Baltimore

Whereas the Martin Maryland had been designed to meet a US Army Air Corps specification, the **Martin 187** was developed from the Maryland to specific British requirements. It differed primarily by having more powerful engines and a deeper fuselage to allow direct communication between crew members; however, like aircraft such as the Maryland, Douglas Boston and Handley Page Hampden, its narrow-section fuselage made it virtually impossible for injured crew members to change positions in flight. An order of 400 of these aircraft, named **Baltimaore** by the RAF, was placed in May 1940, and following introduction of the US Lend-Lease Act two batches, of 575 and 600, were ordered in June and July 1941 respectively, and the full total of 1,575 aircraft was duly produced for the RAF. It should be noted, however, that this full total was not received, for some Mk III and Mk IIIA aircraft were lost during transatlantic delivery when two cargo ships carrying them were sunk. Initial deliveries of Baltimore Mk 1s were made in late 1941, being issued first to Operational Training Units, and were followed by deliveries of Mk IIs in 1942 to Nos 55 and 223 Squadrons operating in the Middle East. All Baltimores were used operationally entirely in the Mediterranean theatre, proving to be effective day and night bombers. In

addition to those used by the RAF, Baltimores were allocated by the RAF for service with the Royal Australian Air Force, Free French Air Force, Greek No. 13 (Hellenic) Squadron, Italian Co-Belligerent Air Force, and the South African and Turkish air forces.

Variants
Baltimore Mk I: original production version to UK order with 1193-kW (1,600-hp) Wright GR-2600-A5B Cyclone engines; the dorsal turret had only a single hand-operated Vickers 'K' gun; 50 built
Baltimore Mk II: generally similar to Mk I, with twin hand-operated Vickers guns in the dorsal turret; 100 built
Baltimore Mk III: improved version to UK order, introducing more powerful Wright R-2600-19 engines and a Boulton Paul hydraulically-powered dorsal turret containing four 7.7-mm (0.303-in) Browning machine-guns; 250 built
Baltimore Mk IIIA: first Lend-Lease version, procured by the USAAF under the designation **A-30**; generally similar to the Mk III but with Martin-built electrically-actuated dorsal turret containing two 12.7-mm (0.5-in) Browning machine-guns; 281 built
Baltimore Mk IVA: basically similar to Mk IIIA but with detail changes;

procured by the USAAF under the designation **A-30A**; 294 built
Baltimore Mk V: final and major production version, basically as Mk IV but for the introduction of 1268-kW (1,700-hp) R-2600-29 engines; procured by the USAAF under the designation A-30A; 600 built

Specification
Martin Baltimore Mk IV
Type: four-seat light bomber
Powerplant: two 1238-kW (1,660-hp) Wright R-2600-10 Cyclone 14 radial piston engines
Performance: maximum speed 491 km/h (305 mph) at 3505 m (11,500 ft); service ceiling 7100 m (23,300 ft); range with 454-kg (1,000-lb) bombload 1741 km (1,082 miles)

Martin Baltimore Vs saw action in North Africa with the RAF's Desert Air Force.

Weights: empty 7013 kg (15,460 lb); maximum take-off 10251 kg (22,600 lb)
Dimensions: span 18.69 m (61 ft 4 in); length 14.80 m (48 ft 5¾ in); height 5.41 m (17 ft 9 in); wing area 50.03 m² (538.50 sq ft)
Armament: four 7.7-mm (0.303-in) wing-mounted machine-guns, two or four similar guns in dorsal turret, two 7.62-mm (0.3-in) machine-guns in ventral position, and provision for four similar guns in fixed rear-firing position, plus a bomb load of up to 970 kg (2,000 lb)

Martin AM-1 Mauler

Benefitting from early combat experience in World War II, the US Navy drew up its specification for a new single-seat carrier-based attack aircraft. The **Martin Model 210** design proposal gained a contract for two **XBTM-1** prototypes, the first being flown initially on 26 August 1944. A cantilever low-wing monoplane with retractable tail-wheel landing gear, powered by a 2237-kW (3,000-hp) Pratt & Whitney XR-4360-4 radial engine, the XBTM-1 was tested successfully and gained a contract for 750 **BTM-1** series aircraft. By the time that the first of these was flown, on 16 December 1946, the designation had been changed to **AM-1** and the name **Mauler** selected. World War II had also ended, and instead of the planned procurement only 149 AM-1s (excluding prototypes) had been completed when production ended in October 1949. Initial deliveries to an active unit went to Attack Squadron VA-17A on 1 March 1948, but these aircraft saw little first-line service, being transferred to US Navy Reserve squadrons when production ended. The total of 149 built included 17 **AM-1Q** aircraft completed as ECM (electronic countermeasures) aircraft.

Specification
Martin AM-1 Mauler
Type: single-seat carrier-based attack aircraft

Powerplant: one 2218-kW (2,975-hp) Wright R-3350-4 Cyclone 18 radial piston engines
Performance: maximum speed 591 km/h (367 mph); service ceiling 9295 m (30,500 ft); range 2897 km (1,800 miles)
Weights: empty 6577 kg (14,500 lb); maximum take-off 10608 kg (23,386 lb)
Dimensions: span 15.24 m (50 ft 0 in); length 12.55 m (41 ft 2 in); height 5.13 m (16 ft 10 in); wing area 46.08 m² (496.0 sq ft)
Armament: four forward-firing 20-mm cannon, plus up to 2041 kg (4,500 lb) of assorted bombs and rocket projectiles

The prototype Mauler was designated XBTM-1, indicating its intended role as a torpedo bomber. Its large trailing-edge flaps made it ideal for carrier operations.

Martin B-10, B-12 and B-14

Under the company designation **Martin Model 123,** Martin began in the early 1930s the design of a dramatically advanced conception of a bomber aircraft which it hoped would prove of interest to the US Army. A cantilever mid-wing monoplane with retractable tail-wheel landing gear, and powered by two 448-kW (600-hp) Wright SR-1820-E Cyclone engines, it accommodated a three-man crew. When tested officially in July 1932, under the experimental designation **XB-907,** it was found to have a maximum speed of 317 km/h (197 mph) at 1830 m (6,000 ft), which was superior to that of fighter aircraft then in US Army Air Corps use. Before being ordered into production some changes were introduced, these including an increase in wing span, the provision of a nose turret to mount a 7.62-mm (0.3-in) machine-gun, and the installation of 503-kW (675-hp) Wright R-1829-19 engines. Then redesignated **XB-907A,** official tests proved entirely satisfactory with the maximum speed increased by 16 km/h (10 mph), and the type was ordered into production on 17 January 1933. The XB-907A prototype was acquired by the US Army and given the designation **XB-10.**

Production aircraft began to enter service in June 1934, and in addition to conventional duties in a bomber role a number were operated for a time on large twin floats for coastal patrol. The type remained in US Army Air Corps service until the late 1930s and, in addition, was exported by Martin for use by the air arms of Argentina (35), China (nine), the Netherlands (118), Siam (now Thailand) (23), Soviet Union (one), and Turkey (20). Those flown by Dutch crews in the Netherlands East Indies were among the first US bombers to see operational use during World War II.

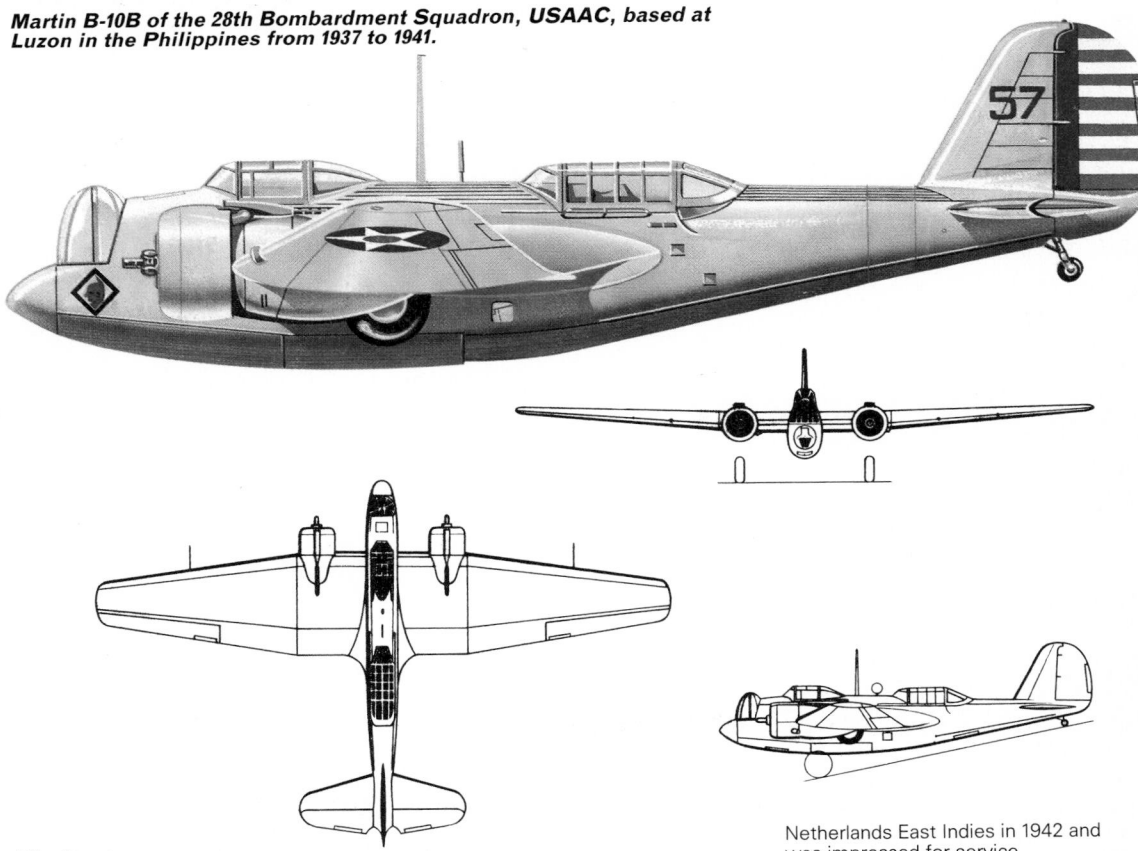

Martin B-10B of the 28th Bombardment Squadron, USAAC, based at Luzon in the Philippines from 1937 to 1941.

Variants
YB-10: initial production version with 503-kW (675-hp) R-1820-25 engines and separate enclosed canopies for the pilot's and gunner/radio operator's cockpit; 14 built
B-10: designation of two additional production aircraft, as YB-10

YB-10A: designation of single prototype with two 503-kW (675-hp) R-1820-25 turbocharged engines
RB-10MA: USAAF designation of one export aircraft which escaped from the Netherlands East Indies in 1942 and was impressed for service
B-10B: major production version as YB-10, but with more powerful R-1820-33 engines; 103 built
B-10M: redesignation of some B-10Bs converted for use as target tugs
YB-12: production version, as YB-10,

but powered by 578-kW (775-hp) Pratt & Whitney R-1690-11 engines; 7 built

B-12A: production version as YB-12, but with provision to carry an auxiliary fuel tank in the bomb bay for long-range ferry flights; 25 built

B-12AM: redesignation of some B-12As converted for use as target tugs

YB-13: designation of planned version of YB-10 with 522-kW (700-hp) Pratt & Whitney R-1860-17 Hornet engines; not built

XB-14: designation of single aircraft, similar to YB-10, but powered by two 708-kW (950-hp) Pratt & Whitney R-1830-9 Twin Wasp engines

YO-45: temporary designation of one YB-10 with 503-kW (675-hp) R-1820-17 engines for evaluation in a high-speed reconnaissance role

Model 139: designation of basic export model

Model 139WH-1/2: initial export models for Dutch East Indies; two separate canopies

Model 139WH-3/3A: follow-up export models for Dutch East Indies; one long 'glasshouse' canopy and otherwise known as **Model 166**

Specification
Martin B-10B
Type: three-seat medium bomber
Powerplant: two 578-kW (775-hp) Wright R-1820-33 Cyclone radial piston engines
Performance: maximum speed 343 km/h (213 mph) at optimum

altitude; service ceiling 7375 m (24,200 ft); maximum range 1996 km (1,240 miles)
Weights: empty 4391 kg (9,681 lb); maximum take-off 7439 kg (16,400 lb)
Dimensions: span 21.49 m (70 ft 6 in); length 13.64 m (44 ft 9 in); height 4.70 m (15 ft 5 in); wing area 62.99 m² (678.0 sq ft)
Armament: three 7.62-mm (0.3-in) machine-guns in nose and rear turrets and a ventral position, plus up to 1025 kg (2,260) lb of bombs

Martin M-26 Marauder

Designed to meet a demanding US Army Air Corps specification of 1939 for a high-speed medium bomber, the **Martin Model 179** proposal was considered to be so far in advance of competing submissions that in September 1939 the company was awarded an 'off the drawing board' contract for 201 of these aircraft. This action, unprecedented in USAAC history, required no prototype or preproduction aircraft, and the first production **B-26**, as the type was designated, was flown initially on 25 November 1940. Subsequently named **Marauder**, the aircraft was a cantilever shoulder-wing monoplane with a roomy fuselage of circular cross-section accommodating a crew of five (later seven), and with retractable tricycle landing gear; it was powered by two 1380-kW (1,850-hp) Pratt & Whitney R-2800-5 Double Wasp radial engines. Official testing confirmed that the B-26 more than met the official specification, but this performance had been achieved at the expense of good low-speed handling characteristics. The B-26A which followed introduced improvements considered to be desirable from early squadron experience, but the resulting increase in gross weight only aggravated the low-speed handling problem. Training accidents multiplied and a board of investigation was set up to consider whether to end production; it decided, wisely as it proved, to introduce modifications to improve low-speed performance and to revise handling techniques. As a result the Marauder went on to record the lowest attrition rate of any American aircraft operated by the US 9th Air Force in Europe.

Early deployment of the B-26 by the USAAF was confined to the Pacific theatre, but in November 1942 B-26B and B-26Cs began to appear in North Africa, equipping 12 squadrons of the 17th, 319th and 320th Bombardment Groups of the US 12th Air Force. They provided admirable ground support to Allied ground forces in Corsica, Italy, Sardinia, Sicily and southern France, and Marauders used in a tactical role went from strength to strength in operations with the US 9th Air Force. Under Lend-Lease the RAF received a total of 522 Marauders, used by the RAF's Nos 14, 39, 326, 327 and 454 Squadrons and the South African Air Force's Nos 12, 21, 24, 25 and 30 Squadrons, these being deployed most successfully alongside the B-26s of the US 12th Air Force, after initial failure in a torpedo-carrying role.

Variants
B-26: initial production version; 201 built

B-26A: generally as B-26, with 1380-kW (1,850-hp) R-2800-9 04 -39 engines, provisions for increased fuel capacity and an externally-mounted torpedo, system revisions and heavier armament; 139 built

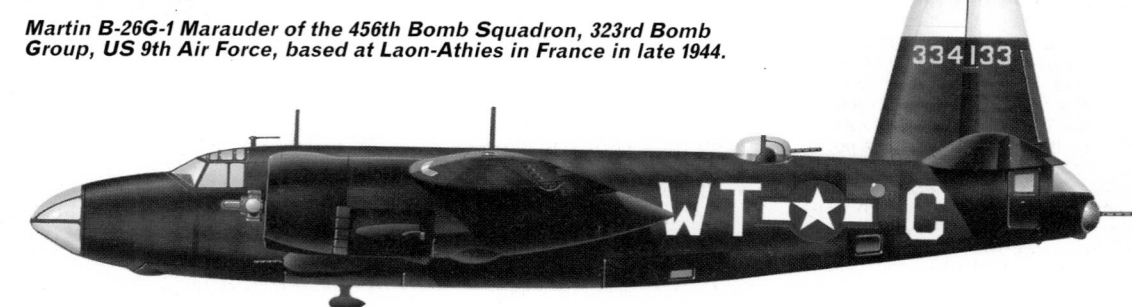

Martin B-26G-1 Marauder of the 456th Bomb Squadron, 323rd Bomb Group, US 9th Air Force, based at Laon-Athies in France in late 1944.

B-26B: improved and major production version, with 1491-kW (2,000-hp) R-2800-41 engines; armament revisions and increased armour protection; the 642nd and subsequent aircraft had a 1.83-m (6-ft) increase in wing span, taller vertical tail surfaces and additional armament; 1,883 built

AT-23A (later **TB-26B**): redesignation of 208 B-26Bs following conversion in 1943 for use a target tugs/gunnery trainers

CB-26B: redesignation of a few B-26Bs following conversion for a transport role

B-26C: production version from separate production line at Omaha, Nebraska, generally as sub-variants of B-26B and with R-2800-43 engines; 1,210 built

AT-23B (later **TB-26C**): redesignation of 375 B-26Cs following conversion in 1943 for use as target tugs/gunnery

This wartime photograph shows to good effect the sleek aerodynamics and slender wing, which, coupled with its Double Wasp engines, gave the Marauder such outstanding performance.

trainers

XB-26D: designation of a single experimental conversion of one B-26 to evaluate hot air de-icing of wing and tail unit leading edges

XB-26E: one-off experimental lighter-weight version, with the dorsal turret moved forward to a position just aft of the wing trailing edge

B-26F: production version, introducing 3° 30' increase in wing incidence to improve take-off performance, and equipment changes; 300 built

B-26G: production version generally as B-26F but with detail changes; 893 built

TB-26G: final production version of the B-26G for use in a crew training or target towing role; 57 built, of which 47 were transferred to the US Navy under the designation JM-2

XB-26H: redesignation of one B-26G after conversion to test landing gear configuration proposed for the Boeing B-47

JM-1: redesignation of 225 AT-23Bs following transfer to the US Navy

JM-1P: redesignation of small number of JM-1s following conversion for use in a photo-reconnaissance role

JM-2: see TB-26G above

Marauder Mk I: RAF designation of Lend-Lease B-26As

Marauder Mk IA: RAF designation of Lend-Lease B-26Bs

Marauder Mk II: RAF designation of Lend-Lease B-26Cs

Marauder Mk III: RAF designation of Lend-Lease B-26Fs and B-26Gs

Specification
Martin B-26G Marauder
Type: seven-seat medium bomber
Powerplant: two 1491-kW (2,000-hp) Pratt & Whitney R-2800-43 Double Wasp radial piston engines
Performance: maximum speed 455 km/h (283 mph) at 1525 m (19,800 ft); service ceiling 6035 m (19,800 ft); range 1770 km (1,100 miles)
Weights: empty 11476 kg (25,300 lb); maximum take-off 17327 kg (38,200 lb)
Dimensions: span 21.64 m (71 ft 0 in); length 17.09 m (56 ft 1 in); height 6.20 m (20 ft 4 in); wing area 61.13 m² (658.0 sq ft)
Armament: 11 12.7-mm (0.5-in) machine-guns (in fixed forward-firing, trainable nose and waist mounts, and in power-operated dorsal and tail turrets), plus up to 1814 kg (4,000 lb) of bombs

Martin XB-48

During 1944 the US Army Air Force issued its first specification for a large jet bomber, the **Martin Model 223** being one of the contenders to meet this requirement. Two **XB-48** prototypes were ordered, the first of them flying on 14 June 1947 as a large shoulder-wing monoplane with the capability of carrying up to 9072 kg (20,000 lb) of bombs. Power was provided by six 1701-kg (3,750-lb) thrust Allison J35-A-5 turbojets, three mounted beneath each wing. The landing gear was of the new bicycle form with main units ahead of and behind the bomb bay. The 33.02 m (108 ft 4 in) span Model 223 failed to win a production contract.

In 1947 Martin rolled out its prototype XB-48 bomber, which was based on specifications issued during 1944. However, the pace of aircraft design was so rapid at that time that the enormously heavy machine with its conventional straight wing was obsolete before it ever took to the air.

Martin XB-51

The **Martin Model 234** was designed originally to meet a US Army Air Force requirement for a close-support bomber, being allocated the designation **XA-45**. However, it was developed instead as a medium bomber with turbojet powerplant and two prototypes were ordered under the designation **XB-51**. A cantilever mid-wing monoplane with swept wings and tail surfaces, it was powered by three 2640-kg (5,820-lb) thrust General Electric J47-GE-7 or -13 turbojets, one pylon-mounted low on each side of the forward fuselage and the third within the rear fuselage. Other features included pressurised accommodation for the two-man crew, provisions for JATO (jet-assisted take-off) units, and a braking parachute. The first was flown in 1949, but no production order resulted, despite outstanding reliability and handling.

Originally designated A-45, only a pair of Martin's XB-51 jet bombers was built. The design was more advanced than the XB-48, but failed to gain a production contract.

Martin B-57

Martin was selected in 1950 to undertake licence production of the English Electric Canberra, the first aircraft of foreign design to enter operational deployment with the US Air Force after World War II. The initial Martin version, built to establish the production line, was the B-57A, first flown on 20 July 1953. Only eight were constructed before manufacture was switched to the RB-57A. RB-57As entered service in 1954, and the extensively-built B-57B night intruder joined Tactical Air Command's 461st Bombardment Wing in early 1955. The USAF's B-57 saw little serious employment until the outbreak of war in Vietnam, when B-57Bs then serving with Air National Guard units were recalled for first-line use as strike bombers. Also notable in that conflict was the reconnaissance RB-57D, developed by Martin.

Specification
Martin B-57B
Type: night intruder
Powerplant: two 3266-kg (7,200-lb) thrust Wright J65-W5 turbojets
Performance: maximum speed 937 km/h (582 mph) at 12190 m (40,000 ft); service ceiling 14630 m (48,000 ft); range 3701 km (2,300 miles)
Weights: empty 11793 kg (26,000 lb); maximum take-off 24948 kg (55,000 lb)
Dimensions: span 19.51 m (64 ft 0 in); length 19.96 m (66 ft 6 in); height 4.75 m (15 ft 7 in); wing area 89.18 m² (960 sq ft)
Armament: eight 12.7-mm (0.5-in) machine-guns, or four 20-mm cannon; 16 underwing rockets and up to 2722 kg (6,000 lb) of bombs in internal bomb bay

A gloss black finish and bright red markings was the standard appearance of the B-57B night intruder.

Martin MB-1 and MB-2

Withdrawing from his association with the Wright-Martin Aircraft Corporation, American pioneer Glenn Martin established the Glenn L. Martin Company at Cleveland, Ohio, in late 1917. Requested by the US Army to develop a bomber aircraft that would be superior to the Handley Page O/400, the designer's **Martin MB-1** design proposal was rewarded with a production order for 10 aircraft on 17 January 1918, the first of these aircraft flying on 17 August 1918. Of conventional biplane configuration, with twin fins and rudders mounted above the tailplane and with four-wheel main landing gear, the MB-1 was powered by two 298-kW (400-hp) Liberty 12A engines strut-mounted between the wings, one on each side of the fuselage, and accommodated a crew of three in open cockpits. Delivery to the US Army Air Service began in October 1918, the first seven being designated officially **GMB** (Glenn Martin Bomber), although four of them were equipped for use in an observation role. The remaining three aircraft on this order were completed as one long-range **GMT** (Glenn Martin Transcontinental), one with a nose-mounted 37-mm cannon designated **GMC** (Glenn Martin Cannon), and a third as a 10-passenger transport designated originally **GMP** (Glenn Martin Passenger), later **T-1**. In addition six MB-1s modified for use as mail carriers were built subsequently for the US Postal Service, but some were later transferred to the US Army.

From the MB-1 Martin developed an improved **MB-2** for use as a night bomber, which differed by having increased-span strengthened wings that could be folded outboard of the engines, revised two-wheel main landing gear, and more powerful Liberty engines. The US Army contracted for 20 of the aircraft in 1920, adopting initially the company's MB-2 as the official designation, but the sixth and subsequent aircraft were designated **NBS-1** (Night Bomber Short-range) upon receipt. Government policy in the immediate post-war depressed state of the US aircraft industry was to share production orders between manufacturers, and as a result NBS-1s were built also by Aeromarine (25); Curtiss (50), the last 20 of them equipped with turbochargers for the engines; and L.W.F. (Lowe, Willard and Fowler) (35), of which four were completed as dual-control trainers.

The US Navy also showed some interest in the MB-1/MB-2, acquiring two MB-1s under the designation **MBT** (Martin Bomber-Torpedo), plus eight improved **MT** (Martin Torpedo) aircraft, which were basically MB-1s incorporating the increased span wing of the MB-2. The MTs were designated subsequently **TM-1**.

Specification
Martin MB-2/NBS-1
Type: four-seat night bomber

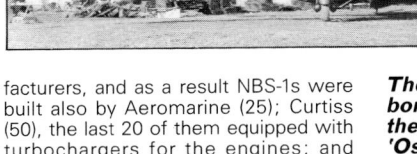

The MB-2 became the first bomber to sink a battleship with the destruction of the German 'Ostfriesland' in a 1921 test.

Powerplant: two 313-kW (420-hp) Liberty 12 V-12 piston engines
Performance: maximum speed 159 km/h (99 mph) at sea level; service ceiling 2590 m (8,500 ft); range 898 km (558 miles)
Weights: empty 3297 kg (7,269 lb); maximum take-off 5472 kg (12,064 lb)
Dimensions: span 22.61 m (74 ft 2 in); length 13.00 m (42 ft 8 in); height 4.47 m (14 ft 8 in); wing area 104.14 m² (1,121.0 sq ft)
Armament: five 7.62-mm (0.3-in) machine-guns, plus up to 816 kg (1,800 lb) of bombs carried internally

Martin Model 130 China Clipper and Model 156

Intended for long-range transoceanic services, the **Martin Model 130 China Clipper** was a large four-engined monoplane flying-boat, the airframe incorporating a two-step hull of advanced design. Three were built for Pan American Airways during 1935, each accommodating a crew of four and a maximum of 48 passengers for daytime operations; optionally, the cabin could be equipped to cater for 18 passengers with sleeping bunks for night operations. Power was provided by four 597-kW (800-hp) Pratt & Whitney R-1830 Twin Wasp engines, mounted in nacelles at the leading edge of the wing. Operating experience with the Model 130 led to the design and development of an improved **Model 156** which differed in a number of ways, but retained the basic hull and

When it was introduced in 1937 the Martin Model 156 'Soviet Clipper' was the largest flying boat in existence and was derived closely from the Model 130. This impressive machine was later sold to the Soviet Union.

wing of the Model 130. It introduced a braced tail unit incorporating twin fins and rudders, powerplant comprising four 746-kW (1,000-hp) Wright GR-1820-G2 Cyclone radial engines, and had accommodation for a crew of five and a maximum of 46 passengers. Testing of the Model 156 proved successful, but the outbreak of World War II and the company's involvement in production of aircraft ordered by the UK and France prevented any further development or

production. Pan American's Model 130 Clippers entered service on 21 October 1936, and were used on the airline's routes from San Francisco to Manila in the Philippine Islands. Two were impressed by the US Navy in 1942, and used on general transport duties without redesignation.

Martin P4M Mercator

The US Navy made several attempts to gain the benefit of high over-target performance combined with long range by introducing mixed powerplant. The **Martin Model 219** patrol bomber represented one of the results of such a specification, two **XP4M-1** prototypes being ordered on 6 July 1944. The first was flown on 20 September 1946 as a cantilever shoulder-wing monoplane with retractable tricycle landing gear. Its powerplant comprised two 2218-kW (2,975-hp) Pratt & Whitney R-4360-4 Wasp Major radial engines, but each nacelle also incorporated a 17350-kg (3,825-lb) thrust Allison J33-A-17 turbojet. After a protracted development programme 19 **P4M-1** production aircraft were built, the first being delivered to US Navy Squadron VP-21 on 28 June 1950,

The Mercator was in fact a four-engined aircraft, with a pair of turbojets in the rear of each piston-engine nacelle.

and all served with this unit. Most of them were converted into P4M-1Q Elint aircraft, one being shot down.

Specification
Martin P4M-1 Mercator
Type: patrol bomber
Powerplant: two 2424-kW (3,250-hp) Pratt & Whitney R-4360-20A radial piston engines and two 2087-kg (4,600-lb) thrust Allison J33-A-10A or -23 turbojets
Performance: maximum speed 660 km/h (410 mph) at 6125 m (20,100 ft); service ceiling 10545 m

(34,600 ft); range 4570 km (2,840 miles)
Weights: maximum take-off 40088 kg (88,378 lb)
Dimensions: span 34.75 m (114 ft 0 in); length 25.60 m (84 ft 0 in); height 7.95 m (26 ft 1 in); wing area 121.79 m²

(1,311.0 sq ft)
Armament: four 20-mm cannon (two each in nose and tail turrets) and four 12.7-mm (0.5-in) machine-guns (two in dorsal turret and one each side of the fuselage), plus up to 2722 kg (6,000 lb) of bombs

Martin P5M Marlin

With the US Navy requiring a new patrol flying-boat, Martin decided to develop the successful PBM Mariner, the resulting **Martin Model 237** design combining the wing and upper hull of the Mariner with the new lower hull structure. The close relationship between the two types is emphasised by the fact that a PBM-5 Mariner served as the prototype **XP5M-1** which, when ordered into production, was given the name **Marlin**. The modified hull of the XP5M-1 incorporated radar-directed nose and tail turrets, as well as a power-operated dorsal turret, and power was provided by two 2424-kW (3,250-hp) Wright R-3350 radial engines. This prototype flew for the first time on 30 May 1948, but it was not until two years later that the **P5M-1** was ordered into production, the first of these series aircraft being flown on 22 June 1951. Initial deliveries, to US Navy Squadron VP-44, began on 23 April 1952 and the type remained in service until the mid-1960s. In addition to those operated by the US Navy, 10 of the later **P5M-2** version were supplied to France under the American MAP for use by the Aéronavale.

Variants
P5M-1 (later **P-5A**): initial production version; differed from prototype by having the nose turret replaced by a radome for APS-80 search radar, raised flight deck, dorsal turret deleted, and introduced uprated 2535-kW (3,400-hp) R-3350-30WA engines; 160 built
P5M-1G: redesignation of seven P5M-1s for use by the US Coast Guard
P5M-1S (later **SP-5A**): redesignation

of P5M-1 following installation of MAD (magnetic anomaly detection) and echo-sounding and sonobuoy detection equipment for use in the ASW role
P5M-1T (later **TP-5A**): redesignation of US Coast Guard P5M-1Gs when taken into US Navy service as crew trainers
P5M-2 (later **P-5B**): second production version, with modified hull, a T-tail, retractable MAD gear, equipment changes and uprated R-3350-32WA engines; 115 built
P5M-2G: designation of four P5M-2s built for use by US Coast Guard; became P5M-2s when later accepted for use by the US Navy
P5M-2S (later **SP-5B**): redesignation of most P5M-2s after being equipped

with advanced avionics and detection equipment for use in ASW role

Specification
Martin P5M-2
Type: patrol flying-boat with 11-man crew
Powerplant: two 2573-kW (3,450-hp) Wright R-3350-32WA Turbo-Compound radial piston engines
Performance: maximum speed 404 km/h (251 mph) at sea level; service ceiling 7315 m (24,000 ft); range 3299 km (2,050 miles)
Weights: empty 22900 kg (50,485 lb); maximum take-off 38555 kg (85,000 lb)
Dimensions: span 36.02 m (118 ft 2 in); length 30.66 m (100 ft 7 in); height 9.97 m (32 ft 8½ in); wing area

The Martin Model 237 was the first twin-engined flying-boat to be developed for the US Navy for ASW duties after the war, and was the last flying-boat to serve with the Navy, lasting until 1966. The later P5M-2 introduced the distinctive 'T-tail', as shown here on an SP-5B of VR-40.

130.62 m² (1,406.0 sq ft)
Armament: four torpedoes, four 907-kg (2,000-lb) bombs or mines, or smaller weapons up to 3629 kg (8,000 lb) total carried internally, and up to eight 454 kg (1,000 lb) of bombs or mines carried externally

Martin P6M SeaMaster
to
Maule aircraft

Martin P6M SeaMaster

To meet a US Navy requirement for a high-performance multi-role flying-boat, the company offered its very advanced **Martin Model 275** design. This had an all-metal hull of high length/beam ratio, mounting a cantilever high-set sharply-swept wing incorporating so much anhedral that the stabilising floats at the wing-tips could be attached permanently; the tail unit was of T-tail configuration with all-swept surfaces. Above the wing, to minimise spray ingestion, were mounted four Allison turbojet engines, and pressurised accommodation was provided for a crew of five. The first **XP6M-1** prototype was flown on 14 July 1955, the second following on 18 May 1956, and Martin received orders

The Martin XP6M-1 made its first flight from Chesapeake Bay on 14 July 1955. The dark blue aircraft were ambitious designs and during the flight test programme two were destroyed in the air. One broke the sound barrier in a dive.

for six pre-production **YP6M-1** 'boats powered by Allison J71 turbojets each developing a maximum 5897 kg (13,000 lb) afterburning thrust. Successful flight testing led to an order for 24 production **P6M-2** aircraft named **SeaMaster**, which differed primarily by having 7711-kg (17,00-lb) thrust non-afterburning Pratt & Whitney J75-P-2 turbojet engines. However, the contract was cancelled on 21 August 1959 after only three had been built and these, together with the YP6M-1s, were scrapped at a later date. They were the fastest flying-boats ever built.

Martin PBM Mariner

The **Martin Model 162** was designed in 1937 to meet a US Navy requirement for a new patrol flying-boat, the company building first a quarter-scale single-seat **Martin 162A** to evaluate the flight characteristics of the design, and following satisfactory tests the US Navy ordered initially a single **XPBM-1** development prototype, flown first on 18 February 1939. This was powered by two 1193-kW (1,600-hp) Wright R-2600-6 Cyclone radial engines, mounted in large nacelles which incorporated weapons bays to accommodate a combined total of 907 kg (2,000 lb) of bombs or depth charges. Produced in considerable numbers and several versions, details of which are given under Variants, the **PBM Mariner**, as the type became named, was to see service primarily in air-sea rescue, ASW and transport roles. The PBM-3B Mariner was supplied under Lend-Lease for service with the RAF, which designated the variant **Mariner GR.Mk I**, the first arriving at Beaumaris, Anglesey, in August 1943. However, after only a short period of evaluation it was decided that the type would not be used operationally by the RAF, and the aircraft were placed in storage pending their return to the United States. The other wartime user was the Royal Australian Air Force, which received 12 from 1943, these serving with No. 41 Squadron. Post-war, deliveries of small numbers were made from US Navy stocks to Argentina, the Netherlands and Uruguay.

Martin PBM Mariner of the Aviacion Naval Uruguaya (Uruguayan naval air service) based at Punta del Este from 1956 to 1963.

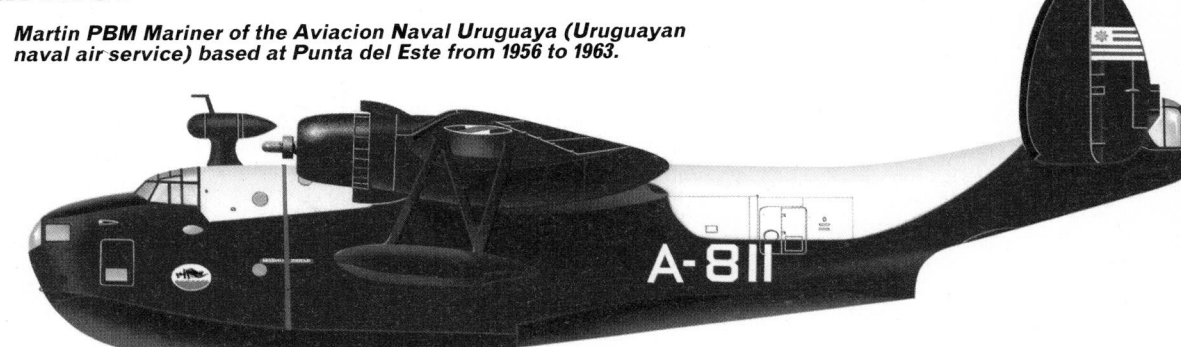

A-811

Variants
XPBM-1: initial prototype with cantilever gull-wing incorporating retractable stabilizing floats beneath the wings
PBM-1: initial production version introducing distinctive dihedral tailplane with inward canted twin fins and rudders; 20 built
XPBM-1A: redesignation of XPBM-1 following modification for armament tests
XPBM-2: single prototype, generally as PBM-1, but with increased fuel capacity and provisions for catapult launching
PBM-3B: designation of version of PBM-3 supplied under Lend-Lease to

RAF; it was the first PBM-3 production version, and the first to introduce larger non-retractable stabilizing floats; the PBM-3B had 1268-kW (1,700-hp) R-2600-12 engines in lengthened nacelles; 32 built
PBM-3C: production version, generally as PBM-3B, but introducing armour protection, bombload of up to 1814 kg (4,000 lb) and revised armament; 274 built, of which four were supplied to US Coast Guard
PBM-3D: production version as PBM-3C, but introducing more powerful R-2600-22 engines, search radar, self-sealing fuel tanks, provisions for up to 3628 kg (8,000 lb) of bombs, two torpedoes on underwing racks, and further revision of defensive armament; 201 built
XPBM-3E: redesignation of one PBM-3 after conversion for use as a radar development aircraft
PBM-3R: transport version of the PBM-3 without armament, and introducing cargo loading doors, strengthened flooring, and provisions to seat 20 passengers; 50 built
PBM-3S: ASW version of the PBM-3C with extra fuel, defensive armament reduced to four machine-guns, and able to carry four 147-kg (325-lb) depth charges; 156 built
XPMB-5: designation of two prototypes, generally as PBM-3D, but with 1566-kW (2,100-hp) Pratt & Whitney R-2800-34 Double Wasp

From the PBM-3 series onwards, Mariners were fitted with fixed underwing floats.

engines
PBM-5: major production version, generally as XPBM-5, but with R-2800-22 or -34 engines; 631 built
XPBM-5A: single prototype as PBM-5, but introducing retractable tricycle landing gear to provide amphibious capability
PBM-5A: production version of XPBM-5A, used mainly by the US Coast Guard for air-sea rescue; 36 built
PBM-5E: designation of PBM-5s when equipped with AN/APS-15 radar
PBM-5G: redesignation of four PBM-5s which were supplied to the US Coast Guard for air-sea rescue duties
PBM-5M: redesignation of one PBM-5E after conversion for use in missile tests
PBM-5S: redesignation of a small number of PBM-5s following installation of special ASW equipment

Specification
Martin PBM-3D Mariner

Type: seven/eight-seat patrol flying-boat
Powerplant: two 1417-kW (1,900-hp) Wright R-2600-22 Cyclone radial piston engines
Performance: maximum speed 340 km/h (211 mph) at 455 m (1,500 ft); service ceiling 6035 m (19,800 ft); range 3605 km (2,240 miles)
Weights: empty 15048 kg (33,175 lb); maximum take-off 26308 kg (58,000 lb)
Dimensions: span 35.97 m (118 ft 0 in); length 24.33 m (79 ft 10 in); height 8.38 m (27 ft 6 in); wing area 130.80 m² (1,408.0 sq ft)
Armament: eight 12.7-mm (0.5-in) machine-guns in nose and dorsal turrets and in waist and tail positions, plus up to 3628 kg (8,000 lb) of bombs or depth charges

Martin SC-1/SC-2/T3M and T4M

The first torpedo-bomber to be designed and built by the Curtiss Aeroplane and Motor Company was a three-seat biplane which could be provided with alternative float or wheel landing gear, and powered by a 391-kW (525-hp) Wright T-2 engine (Curtiss CS-1), or 436-kW (585-hp) Wright T-3 (Curtiss CS-2). After delivery of six CS-1s and two CS-2s to the US Navy, the production of an additional 35 aircraft was put out to tender, Martin being awarded the contract and building an aircraft generally similar to the CS-1 under the designation **SC-1**. Martin also received a follow-on order for 40 aircraft equivalent to the CS-2, these being built and delivered as **SC-2** machines. The SC-2 also had a US Navy designation **T2M**, and when the Martin company developed an improved version this was allocated the designation **T3M**; it differed primarily by having a basic fuselage structure of steel tube, with the pilot and torpedo-man located further forward. The delivery of 24 **T3M-1** aircraft powered by the 429-kW (575-hp) Wright T-3B engine began in late 1926, and was followed by an order for 100 **T3M-2** machines with equal-span wings and 529-kW (710-hp)

Known to the company as the Model 74, the Martin T4M-1 was a development of the T3M series with a Pratt & Whitney radial replacing the original Wright engine. This is a VT-28 aircraft seen over the USS Saratoga.

Packard 3A-2500 engines. Final Martin production version was the **T4M-1** with Pratt & Whitney R-1690-24 Hornet radial engine, 102 being delivered during 1927-28 before the Martin company's Cleveland factory was sold to Great Lakes Aircraft Corporation, when Great Lakes was given the opportunity of continuing production of the T4M-1; a total of 18 with R-1690-28 engines and 32 with Wright R-1820-56 Cyclones were designated **TG-1** and **TG-3** respectively. Wheeled versions of the T3M-2 and T4M-1 served aboard the carriers USS *Lexington* and USS *Saratoga*, and T4M-1s in service with Reserve units remained in use until the mid-1930s.

Variants

XT3M-3: redesignation of the first T3M-2 after being re-engined with a Pratt & Whitney R-1690 Hornet radial

engine
XT3M-4: redesignation of XT3M-3 following installation of a Wright R-1750 Cyclone engine
XT4M-1: prototype of the T4M-1 version, powered by an R-1690 engine

Specification
Martin T4M-1
Type: three-seat torpedo-bomber/scout
Powerplant: one 391-kW (525-hp) Pratt & Whitney R-1690-24 Hornet radial piston engine

Performance: maximum speed 183 km/h (114 mph) at sea level; service ceiling 3085 m (10,150 ft); range 584 km (363 miles)
Weights: empty 1783 kg (3,931 lb); maximum take-off 3661 kg (8,071 lb)
Dimensions: span 16.15 m (53 ft 0 in); length 10.85 m (35 ft 7 in); height 4.50 m (14 ft 9 in); wing area 60.94 m^2 (656.0 sq ft)
Armament: one 7.62-mm (0.3-in) machine-gun on Scarff ring mount in rear cockpit, plus one torpedo carried externally

Martin-Baker aircraft

James Martin established the Martin-Baker Aircraft Company in 1934 to build aircraft based on an unusual lattice-like steel-tube construction that he had evolved. It was claimed that this construction provided a lightweight and robust structure that was cheap and easy to assemble and repair. Designed as the first practical aircraft to adopt this structure, the **Martin-Baker M.B.1** cantilever low-wing monoplane had enclosed accommodation for two and, powered by a 119-kW (160-hp) Napier Javelin IIIA engine, was flown for the first time during March 1965. Only one experimental aircraft was built and this was destroyed by fire in early 1938. Mar-

tin-Baker then turned to the design of a single-seat fighter to meet the requirements of Air Ministry Specification F.5/34, the **M.B.2** prototype built as a private venture. A clean cantilever low-wing monoplane powered by a 746-kW (1,000-hp) Napier Dagger III 'H' engine, it was flown for the first time on 3 August 1938. Although incorporating many advanced ideas and demonstrating a maximum speed of 563 km/h (350 mph) during official trials, no production order followed and the aircraft was eventually scrapped.

An even more potent fighter prototype followed with the **M.B.3**, designed to satisfy Specification F.18/39 for a

single-seat fighter to supersede the Hawker Hurricane and Supermarine Spitfire. A well-proportioned low-wing monoplane powered by a 1506-kW (2,020-hp) Napier Sabre II engine, the M.B.3 was flown for the first time on 31 August 1942 and during testing attained a top speed of 668 km/h (415 mph) at optimum altitude. Armed with six 20-mm cannon, this aircraft clearly had potential, but no further development followed after it crashed on 12 September 1942. The designation **M.B.4** was allocated to a new fighter but this remained only a project, one that would have united the M.B.3 airframe and a Rolls-Royce Griffon engine, but Martin-Baker continued development of this idea in the one-off **M.B.5**. A single-seat

fighter powered by a 1745-kW (2,340-hp) Griffon 83 engine driving three-bladed contra-rotating propellers, it was flown for the first time on 23 May 1944 but although having superb handling qualities and a top speed of 740 km/h (460 mph) at 6095 m (20,000 ft) the M.B.5 failed to gain a production contract. Martin-Baker's **M.B.6**, the company's final aircraft design, was for a turbojet-powered delta-wing tailless fighter, but this remained a project only. However, James (later Sir James) Martin's innovative design capability went on to produce the equipment for which he became world famous, the Martin-Baker ejection seat, which has saved over 6,000 lives to date.

Designed around the powerful but temperamental Napier Sabre engine, the M.B.3 had good performance and a potent fixed armament of six 20-mm cannon, but it crashed, killing Captain Baker.

Perhaps the best fighter to be developed in Britain during the war, the Martin-Baker M.B.5 combined performance, agility and firepower in a neat package that was simple to produce, easy to maintain and a delight to fly. The prototype was later broken up by the manufacturer.

Martinsyde F series fighters

This series began with the **Martinsyde F.1**, a large two-seat biplane with the crew accommodated in tandem open cockpits and, curiously for an aircraft that was intended as a fighter, the pilot occupied the rear seat. Thus, the observer would have had a seriously restricted field of fire for his trainable machine-gun and would have been unable to direct the aim of fixed forward-firing machine-guns. Only two examples of the F.1 were built, each of them powered by a 186-kW

(250-hp) Rolls-Royce engine, but as these aircraft did not progress beyond official testing and were flown without weapons, it is difficult to appreciate what armament the F.1 would have carried. Only a single example of the ensuing **F.2** was built, a more compact tandem two-seat biplane powered by a 149-kW (200-hp) Hispano-Suiza engine. Although tested officially it really had little chance for success for, although by comparison with the F.1 crew positions

were reversed, the pilot's field of view was limited severely by the biplane wing centre-sections above and below him.

The **Martinsyde F.3** single-seat fighter was basically a smaller version of the F.2, its pilot in an open cockpit just aft of the wing, which incorporated a fairly large cut-out in the centre-section trailing edge. Aerodynamically refined and powered by a 213-kW (285-hp) Rolls-Royce Falcon experimental engine, it was shown in official tests to have extremely good performance; armament consisted of two synchronised forward-firing machine-guns. Six F.3s, each

powered by a 205-kW (275-hp) Rolls-Royce Falcon III engine, were ordered and should, presumably, be regarded as pre-production aircraft for the generally similar **F.4 Buzzard**, which differed primarily by siting the pilot's cockpit further aft and by introducing a more powerful Hispano-Suiza engine. Although ordered in large numbers, only about 60 had been delivered to the RAF by the end of World War II. Martinsyde was left with a stock of about 200 F.4s. Numbers of these were sold for service with foreign air forces, and some formed the basis of a number of civil variants.

Variants

Martinsyde F.4A: two-seat tourer conversion of F.4
Martinsyde Type A.Mk I: two-seat long-range conversion of F.4
Martinsyde Type AS.Mk I: version of above with float landing gear
Martinsyde Type A.Mk II: conversion of F.4 with enclosed four-seat cabin forward of the pilot's open cockpit
Martinsyde F.6: two-seat conversion of F.4 with wing and landing gear revisions
Martinsyde A.D.C.1: designation of version developed by the Aircraft Disposal Company, after Martinsyde had gone into liquidation in 1921, which differed mainly by having as powerplant a 295-kW (395-hp) Armstrong Siddeley Jaguar radial engine
Nimbus Martinsyde: one aircraft converted by A.D.C. to be powered by a 224-kW (300-hp) A.D.C. Nimbus

Martinsyde F.4 Buzzard of the Esquadrilha Independente de Aviacao de Caca, Portuguese air force, based at Tancos in 1923.

engine
Martinsyde A.V.1: one aircraft, basically as F.4A, for engine designer Amherst Villiers

Specification
Martinsyde F.4
Type: single-seat fighter

Powerplant: one 224-kW (300-hp) Hispano-Suiza V-8 piston engine
Performance: maximum speed 108 km/h (145 mph) at sea level; service ceiling 7620 m (25,000 ft); endurance 2 hours 30 minutes
Weights: empty 776 kg (1,710 lb); maximum take-off 1038 kg (2,289 lb)

Dimensions: span 9.99 m (32 ft 9½ in); length 7.77 m (25 ft 5¾ in); height 3.15 m (10 ft 4 in); wing area 29.73 m² (320.0 sq ft)
Armament: two forward-firing synchronised 7.7-mm (0.303-in) Vickers machine-guns

---

Martinsyde G.100 Elephant and G.102

An improved and considerably larger single-seat scout biplane, in comparison with the S.1, was designed by Martinsyde during the summer of 1915, designated **Martinsyde G.100**, and the prototype was flown for the first time during September of that year. Its larger size resulted from the requirement that it should be capable of some five hours' endurance for use as an escort for two-seat observation/reconnaissance aircraft. Powered by the 89-kW (120-hp) Beardmore engine, G.100s began to enter service on the western front in early 1916, distributed to squadrons in small numbers. They gained the nickname **Elephant** in France, presumably because of their large size for a single-seat scout, and the name has endured. The only squadron to be equipped with the type was No. 27, and the squadron's association with this aircraft is recognised by the fact that this unofficial name is perpetuated by the incorporation of an elephant in the squadron badge. The G.100 was followed in late 1916 by the improved **G.102** which had a more

powerful Beardmore engine, enabling it to lift a greater load at the expense of endurance, with the result that this version saw more use in a bombing role. A total of about 300 G.100/102 Elephants was built, of which 133 were delivered to squadrons on the western front, 64 to units in the Middle East, and most of the remainder to training units. Derived from the G.101/102 design was a further improved single-seat fighter of biplane configuration known as the **Martinsyde RG**. First tested officially in early 1917, and powered by a 142-kW (190-hp) Rolls-Royce Falcon engine, the RG demonstrated excellent performance but failed to gain a production contract because of a shortage of the Falcon engine, this having a priority allocation for the Bristol Fighter.

Specification
Martinsyde G-102
Type: single-seat scout
Powerplant: one 119-kW (160-hp) Beardmore inline piston engine
Performance: maximum speed

167 km/h (104 mph) at 610 m (2,000 ft); service ceiling 4875 m (16,000 ft); endurance 4 hours 30 minutes
Weights: empty 813 kg (1,793 lb); maximum take-off 1115 kg (2,458 lb)
Dimensions: span 11.58 m (38 ft

0 in); length 8.23 m (27 ft 0 in); height 2.95 m (9 ft 8 in); wing area 38.09 m² (410.0 sq ft)
Armament: two 7.7-mm (0.303-in) Lewis guns (one forward-firing above the upper wing and one rear-firing on a mounting behind the cockpit), plus a maximum of 118 kg (260 lb) of bombs on underwing or underfuselage racks

Too large to be an effective single-seat fighter, the Martinsyde F.100 had a good operational ceiling and range and thus became a reconnaissance and light bomber aircraft in the form of the G.102.

Maule aircraft

Belford Maule began the design of an enclosed-cabin four-seat light aircraft in 1956, designating it the **Maule M-4**, and establishing the Maule Aircraft Corporation at Jackson, Michigan, to develop and manufacture the type. First flown on 8 September 1961, the M-4 is a braced-wing monoplane with fixed tail-wheel landing gear and, in its original M-4 version, was powered by a 108-kW (145-hp) Continental O-300-A flat-six engine. Production began in 1963, and since that time more than 1,100 examples of the M-4 and its subsequent versions have been sold. The M-4 became known subsequently as the **M-4 Jetasen**, being followed in late 1964 by the **M-4 Rocket** introducing a 157-kW (210-hp) Continental IO-360-A engine. Later versions included a de luxe version of the Jetasen, the **M-4 Astro-Rocket** with a 134-kW (180-hp) 6A-335-B1A engine, and the **M-4 Strata-Rocket** which was basically an M-4 Rocket with a 164-kW (220-hp) Franklin 6A-350-C1 engine.

In 1968 the company moved to better

facilities in Moultrie, Georgia, and began development of an improved **M-5** based on the M-4 Strata Rocket. It differed in having a 30 per cent increase in flap area and enlarged tail surfaces to give improved STOL performance. Two prototypes, flown in 1971, kicked off the Lunar Rocket Line. These were the **M-5-210C** (marketed as the Strata Rocket) and the Franklin-powered **M-5-220C** with engines of 157 and 164 kW (210 and 220 hp) respectively and both entered production early in 1974. Later versions comprised the four-door unnamed **M-5-180C** powered by a 134 kW (180 hp) O-360-C1F, the turbocharged **M-5-210TC** and the **M-5-235C** with an Avco Lycoming O-540-J1A5D. This was developed into the **M-6-235 Super Rocket** with wing span increased 0.71 m (2 ft 4 in), larger flaps, higher gross weight and carrying more fuel. The **Maule Patroller** was a derivative of the latter. Maule Aircraft went into Chapter 11 bankruptcy in 1984 and a new company, Maule Air Inc., was formed to continue production of a new variant, the **M-7**. The M7-235 Super Rocket has a bigger cabin with extra windows, plus other refinements, and a tricycle under-

carriage version (the **MX-7-180 Star Rocket**) and a turboprop version (the **MX-7-250 Starcraft** with an Allison 250 powerplant) are currently under development. The MX-7-180 four-seat Star Rocket is a M-7 with short wings as fitted to the M-5, and the **MX-7-235 Star Rocket** has a 235-hp fuel injection engine. By 1991 production of the Maule family of designs had reached around 1,700 aircraft, including the best selling M-5-235C with sales of 380.

Specification
Maule M-5-235C Lunar Rocket
Type: four-seat light aircraft
Powerplant: one 175-kW (235-hp)

The M.5 Lunar Rocket series combines high performance with dramatic STOL capability.

Avco Lycoming O-540-J1A5D flat-six piston engine
Performance: maximum speed 277 km/h (172 mph) at optimum altitude; service ceiling 6095 m (20,000 ft); range with standard fuel 885 km (550 miles)
Weights: empty 635 kg (1,400 lb); maximum take-off 1043 kg (2,300 lb)
Dimensions: span 9.40 m (30 ft 10 in); length 7.16 m (23 ft 6 in); height 1.89 m (6 ft 2½ in); wing area 14.67 m² (157.90 sq ft)

Max Holste M.H.152 and M.H.1521 Broussard
to
McDonnell Douglas A-4 Skyhawk

Max Holste M.H.152 and M.H.1521 Broussard

Differing considerably from the company's first product, the **Max Holste M.H.152** was designed to meet a French army requirement for a light-weight liaison/observation aircraft. Of braced high-wing monoplane configuration, it had fixed tailwheel landing gear, a tail unit similar to that of the M.H.52, and accommodated a pilot and four passengers. The prototype, first flown on 12 June 1951, was powered by a 164-kW (220-hp) Salmson 8AS Argus engine, but by the time that it had flown the French army had changed its ideas and was no longer interested in the low-powered M.H. 152. While hoping to market this aircraft for civil use in agricultural, ambulance, light transport or photographic roles, the company decided to develop a slightly larger and considerably more powerful version. Designated **M.H.1521** and later named **Broussard**, this generally similar aircraft seated a pilot and five passengers and had a Pratt & Whitney engine more than double the power of the Salmson Argus;

an alternative ambulance interior was available to accommodate two stretchers and two sitting casualties or medical attendants. Flown initially in prototype form on 17 November 1952, the first civil production aircraft was flown on 16 June 1954, followed eight days later by the first specially equipped military aircraft. Built in considerable numbers for both civil and military use, very few M.H.1521 Broussards remain in use.

Variants
M.H.1521A: designation of version of M.H.1521 which was equipped specifically for agricultural use
M.H.1522: designation of prototype conversion, first flown on 11 February 1958, with a wing incorporating full span leading-edge slots and double-slotted trailing edge flaps to improve STOL performance

Specification
Max Holste M.H.1521 Broussard
Type: six-seat utility aircraft

Powerplant: one 336-kW (450-hp) Pratt & Whitney R-985-AN-1 radial piston engine
Performance: maximum speed 270 km/h (168 mph) at 1000 m (3,280 ft); service ceiling 5500 m (18,045 ft)
Weights: empty 1530 kg (3,373 lb);

maximum take-off 2500 kg (5,512 lb)
Dimensions: span 13.75 m (45 ft 1¼ in); length 8.65 m (28 ft 4½ in); height 3.65 m (12 ft 0 in); wing area 25.20 m² (271.26 sq ft)

A rugged STOL transport, the Max Holste M.H. 1521 Brussard survives in military service only with the Chad Air Force, France having retired its examples.

McDonnell F-4 Phantom II

McDonnell RF-4B Phantom II of VMCJ-2, US Marine Corps, based at NAS Jacksonville, Florida, in 1970.

When production of the **McDonnell F-4 Phantom II** ended in October 1979, a total of 5,057 had been built for the US Air Force (2,597), US Navy/Marine Corps (1,264) and export customers (1,196). In addition, 11 in kit form had been supplied to Japan, where Mitsubishi built an additional 127 under licence to bring the final figure for Phantom II production to 5,195. This remarkable total far outstrips that of any other post-1960 jet aircraft built in the Western world, and is challenged only by the Mikoyan-Gurevich MiG-21. The Phantom II's history began 26 years earlier when, in September 1953, the company began studies for a twin-engined all-weather fighter to supersede the McDonnell F3H Demon in US Navy service. However, the Chance Vought F8U Crusader promised to fulfil the fighter role, and McDonnell was encouraged to develop instead an attack aircraft. Then requirement changes led to a large-scale redesign for the aircraft to undertake an all-weather attack/fighter role, and in July 1955 the company received a contract covering two **XF4H-1** prototypes and five pre-production aircraft; these were given the name Phantom II, the Roman numerical suffix being used to avoid confusion with the earlier McDonnell Phantom.

First flown on 27 May 1958, the Phantom II soon proved that it offered completely new capability, able to operate over a 467-km (290-mile) radius of action with a loiter for up to two hours, and it was the first aircraft which could detect, intercept and destroy any target within its radar range without assistance from surface-based radar. Such capability meant that the US Navy lost little time in ordering the initial **F4H-1** production version, redesignated **F-4A** in September 1962. Additionally, the type proved attractive to the US Air Force which, almost by tradition, did not normally order US Navy aircraft. Phantoms saw

extensive use in South East Asia, and since that time Phantoms have played (and continue to play in the 1990s) a significant first-line role in service with the armed forces of Egypt, Greece, Iran, Israel, Japan, South Korea, Spain, Turkey, the UK, the United States and West Germany; the type also served temporarily with the Royal Australian Air Force pending the delivery of General Dynamics F-111s. In addition to their service use, F-4s have held world absolute records in their time, an altitude record of 30040 m (98,556 ft) set on 6 December 1959 and a speed record of 2585.43 km/h (1,606.51 mph) on 22 November 1961. These have since been beaten, but with other distinctions gained at various times, and a world low-altitude speed record of 1452 km/h (902 mph) which stood for 16 years, they distinguish the Phantom as one of the world's finest all-round military combat aircraft.

Variants
XF4H-1: two original all-weather fighter prototypes with two 6713-kg (14,800-lb) afterburning thrust General Electric J79-GE-3A-turbojets
F-4A (originally **F4H-1F**): pre-production version with basic armament of four Sparrow III guided

missiles; as the intended powerplant was not available, all were powered by 7326-kg (16,150-lb) afterburning thrust J79-GE-2/-2A engines, the F suffix to the original designation indicating a non-standard engine; 45 built
F-4B (originally **F4H-1**): production version generally similar to late F-4As, but powered by the intended 7711-kg (17,000-lb) afterburning thrust J79-GE-8 turbojets; equipped for fighter/strike role, F-4Bs had APQ-72 fire-control radar and could carry the basic Sparrow missiles plus four AIM-9 Sidewinders, or up to 7257 kg (16,000 lb) of assorted weapons; 649 built
EF-4B: redesignation of one F-4B following conversion for ECM training
NF-4B: redesignation of one F-4B used for development testing
QF-4B: designation of F-4Bs converted to drone configuration as supersonic targets for new missile development
RF-4B: production version of unarmed day/night reconnaissance aircraft generally as F-4B but with lengthened nose; standard radar/mission avionics of F-4B replaced by cameras, plus radar and infra-red sensors; 46 built for US Marine Corps
F-4C (originally **F-110A**): fighter/attack version for US Air Force, generally as

F-4B, but with dual controls, 7711-kg (17,000-lb) afterburning thrust J79-GE-15 engines, and numerous system changes; 635 built
EF-4C: redesignation of a number of F-4Cs following conversion to 'Wild Weasel' configuration for ECM role
YRF-4C (originally **YRF-110A**): designation of two F-4Bs following conversion to serve as prototypes of tactical reconnaissance version for USAF
RF-4C: production version of tactical reconnaissance aircraft for USAF, basically an F-4C airframe in RF-4B configuration; 499 built
F-4D: USAF production version, generally as F-4C, but with avionics tailored to USAF missions; 773 built, of which 68 transferred to Iran (32) and South Korea (36)
EF-4D: redesignation of F-4Ds converted to 'Wild Weasel' configuration
YF-4E: redesignation of first YRF-4C following conversion to serve as prototype for F-4E version
F-4E: major production version, introducing more powerful J79-GE-17 turbojets, increased fuel, redesigned nose with smaller APQ-120 radar, leading-edge slats to improve manoeuvrability, and 20-mm multi-

barrelled cannon; 1,405 built, from which aircraft were supplied to Australia, Greece, Iran, Israel, Turkey, South Korea and West Germany

F-4E(J): air-defence version of F-4E for Japanese Air Self-Defence Force with reduced fuel capacity; 13 built by MDC, plus 126 built under licence by Mitsubishi with Kawasaki as sub-contractor; last delivered in May 1981; initial batch of 45 currently under revision to **F-4EJ** Kai model with improved weapon and avionic systems including digital displays, a new HUD, fire control system, RWR and nose-mounted Texas Instruments AN/APQ-172 radar; improved missile fit gives lookdown/shootdown capability to Sparrow and Sidewinder AAMs; first trials aircraft was flown in July 1984 and up to 100 airframes available for conversion

RF-4E: export version of F-4E for tactical reconnaissance; 130 built

RF-4E(J): unarmed reconnaissance version of F-4EJ for JASDF; 14 built and currently under conversion to **RF-4EJ** Kai standard (see F-4EJ above) together with further 17 F-4EJs to be converted into RF-4EJ Kai

F-4F: 175 air-superiority versions of F-4E for Luftwaffe; introduced leading-edge manoeuvring slats of late production F-4E but with air-to-ground weapons system and related avionics deleted; 110, mostly in service with JG71 and JG74, are being upgraded by DASA/MBB under the German MOD's ICE (improved combat effectiveness) programme; the first two aircraft were reflown in 1991 and improvements include installation of the Hughes/Telefunken AN/APG-65 radar, ability to carry four AIM-120 AMRAAMs on Frazer-Nash launchers, new cockpit displays, fire control computer, laser inertial platform, IFF system and enhanced resistance to electronic jamming and other countermeasures

F-4G: designation used initially for 12

F-4Bs operated in Vietnam with ASW-21 datalink system; reverted subsequently to F-4B configuration

F-4G: used later as redesignation of F-4Es converted to 'Wild Weasel' configuration

YF-4J: redesignation of three F-4Bs following conversion to serve as prototypes of proposed fighter version for US Navy

F-4J: production fighter for US Navy, with 8119-kg (17,900-lb) afterburning thrust J79-GE-10 turbojets, enlarged wing and tail revisions to improve take-off/landing, and advanced avionics including automatic carrier landing system; 12 built

F-4K: revised version of F-4J for use by Royal Navy, and powered by 9305-kg (20,515-lb) afterburning thrust Rolls-Royce Spey RB.168-25R Mk 202/203 turbofan engines; two **YF-4K** prototypes followed by 50 production aircraft; RN designation **Phantom FG.Mk 1**

F-4M: version of F-4K for use by Royal Air Force; same powerplant but with slight variations from F-4K, and retaining Sky Flash missile and external weapon capability; two **YF-4M** prototypes and 116 production aircraft; RAF designation **Phantom FGR.Mk 2** for ground attack/tactical reconnaissance

F-4N: redesignation of 228 USN F-4Bs following updating with advanced avionics and strengthening of structure under 1971 Service Life Extension Program; some later converted to **QF-4N** pilotless target drones to replace veteran QF-86s used by Pacific Missile Test Center at Point Mugu, California, and likely to be last use of F-4 by US Navy

F-4S: redesignation of F-4Js following updating with strengthened structure and introduction of leading-edge slats

Specification
McDonnell F-4E Phantom II
Type: two-seat multi-role fighter/strike aircraft
Powerplant: two 8119-kg (17,900-lb) afterburning thrust General Electric

After a long career with both the Navy and the Royal Air Force the last two remaining RAF squadrons, No. 56 and 74 Sqns, retired their aircraft in 1992.

J79-GE-17 turbojets
Performance: maximum speed 2390 km/h (1,485 mph) or Mach 2.25 at 12190 m (40,000 ft); service ceiling 18975 m (62,250 ft); combat radius 958 km (595 miles)
Weights: empty 13397 kg (29,535 lb); maximum take-off 27964 kg (61,651 lb)
Dimensions: span 11.71 m (38 ft 5 in); length 19.20 m (63 ft 0 in); height 5.03 m (16 ft 6 in); wing area 49.24 m² (530.0 sq ft)
Armament: one 20-mm M61A1 rotary cannon and four AIM-7 Sparrow missiles semi-recessed beneath fuselage, or up to 1370 kg (3,020 lb) of weapons on centre pylon, and up to 5888 kg (12,980 lb) on underwing weapons

McDonnell XF-85 Goblin

Designed to meet a USAAF requirement for a single-seat 'parasite' escort fighter that could be carried within a large bomber, the **McDonnell XF-85 Goblin** was ordered in March 1947 to the extent of the development of two prototypes. Features of the design included low/mid-set foldable swept wings of 6.44 m (21 ft 1½ in) span, a short rotund fuselage, no landing gear except for emergency skids, a retractable hook to engage a trapeze on the parent aircraft, six tail surfaces spaced around the rear fuselage, and power provided by a 1361-kg (3,000-lb) thrust Westinghouse J34-WE-7 turbojet mounted in the rear fuselage. A first free flight was made on 23 August 1948 after launch from a Boeing EB-29B 'mother-

The McDonnell XF-85 owed its unique proportions entirely to the design constraints imposed upon it. It was the first of a series of American attempts to produce a 'parasite-fighter' that could be carried and launched by bombers to defend them once in hostile airspace. Its small size and poor manoeuvrability mitigated against it but the concept was later attempted with a larger B-36 and an F-84 with much better results.

plane', but little more than two hours of flight tests were sufficient to show that turbulence around the bomber created difficult control problems. When this fac-

tor was coupled with the realisation that so small and specialised an aircraft would not have the speed and manoeuvrability of fighters that it would be expected to intercept, further development was abandoned.

McDonnell F-101 Voodoo

To meet a USAF requirement of 1946 for a long-range turbojet-powered fighter that could be used in a penetration or escort role, McDonnell made design proposals which resulted in the award of a contract of two **McDonnell XF-88** prototypes in February 1947. The first of these was flown initially on 20 October 1948, a low/mid-wing monoplane with swept wings and tail surfaces, a lengthy fuselage to house fuel for the long-range requirement, and two 1361-kg (3,000-lb)

thrust Westinghouse XJ34-WE-13 turbojets mounted in the lower centre-fuselage. Testing showed that the type was disappointingly slow, a factor attributed to inadequate power, and the **XF-88A** second prototype differed by having XJ34-WE-22 turbojets with afterburners. These engines increased fuel consumption but, though Mach 1 was exceeded in dives, as the USAF was short of funds the programme was terminated.

With the outbreak of war in Korea the US Air Force was faced with an urgent requirement for a more capable escort fighter, for it was discovered very quickly that available aircraft with adequate range did not have the capability to take on the Mikoyan-Gurevich MiG-15s of the North Korean and Chinese air forces, and those that could 'mix it' with the MiGs did not have the range. An improved version of the XF-88 was ordered as the **F-101 Voodoo**, to give Strategic Air Command the long-range escorts that it needed for its Convair B-36 bombers, and although the potential range of the

F-101 was quite inadequate for the task, it seemed almost as if the USAF hoped this was a problem that would resolve itself. When it was realised that this was wishful thinking, the F-101s for SAC were cancelled. Then it was decided that, subject to satisfactory evaluation, the type would be ordered into production for service with Tactical Air Command. The first **F-101A** was flown initially on 29 September 1954, demonstrating supersonic capability during its first flight, and the type began to enter service in early 1957, being delivered first to the USAF's 27th Tactical Fighter

Wing. Like the F3H Demon, the Voodoo was too late for service in the Korean War, and the tactical fighter versions had only a short period of first-line use. Reconnaissance versions, however, proved to be of great value in operations over North Vietnam and, after being replaced by McDonnell Douglas RF-4Cs, continued to serve with the Air National Guard into the mid-1970s. **RF-101A** and **RF-101C** aircraft transferred to the Chinese Nationalist air force remained in use for some years, and **CF-101B** and **CF-101F** fighter entered service with the Royal Canadian Air Force in late 1961. Ten years later the surviving Canadian Voodoos were exchanged for a number of refurbished aircraft, and four Canadian Armed Forces squadrons continued to operate until they were replaced by McDonnell Douglas CF-18s.

Variants
F-101A: initial production version with two Pratt & Whitney J57-P-13 turbojets, each rated at 4627-kg (10,200-lb) thrust, or 6804-kg (15,000-lb) thrust with afterburning; armed with four 20-mm cannon and equipped to carry a 735-kg (1,620-lb) or 1688-kg (3,721-lb) nuclear weapon; 77 built
NF-101A: redesignation of one F-101A when used by General Electric for the flight testing of J79-GE-1 turbojet engines
YRF-101A: redesignation of two F-101As used as prototypes for a reconnaissance version; generally as F-101A, but armed and with a lengthened nose to house four of a total six cameras
RF-101A: production reconnaissance version, generally similar to the prototypes; 35 built
F-101B: production version of a two-seat all-weather long-range interceptor with a revised forward fuselage

incorporating tandem two-seat cockpit for pilot and radar operator (aft), inflight-refuelling probe, and an advanced fire-control system for the all-missile armament of two MB-1 Genie nuclear missiles and four Falcon homing missiles, or six Falcon missiles; 407 built
CF-101B: Royal Canadian Air Force designation of 56 F-101Bs received from July 1961
RF-101B: USAF redesignation of ex-Canadian CF-101Bs following modification to serve as two-seat reconnaissance aircraft
TF-101B: dual-control conversion and operational trainer version of F-101B with limited combat capability; 72 built
F-101C: single-seat fighter version, generally as F-101A, with strengthened structure for use by TAC in a nuclear strike role; 47 built
RF-101C: reconnaissance version of the F-101C, otherwise generally as RF-101A; 166 built
F-101D: projected version with General Electric J79 engines; not built
F-101E: projected version with General Electric J79 engines; not built
F-101F: redesignation of 153 F-101Bs following deletion of inflight-refuelling probe and installation of an infra-red detection system and improved fire-control system
CF-101F: RCAF designation of 10 TF-101Bs received in 1961-62
TF-101F: redesignation of TF-101Bs after conversion to F-101F detection/fire-control standard
RF-101G: redesignation of F-101As after withdrawal from first-line service and conversion for use by Air National Guard unit in a reconnaissance role
RF-101H: redesignation of F-101Cs converted, as were the RF-101Gs, for ANG use

McDonnell F-101B Voodoo

Specification
McDonnell F-101B Voodoo
Type: two-seat long-range all-weather interceptor
Powerplant: two 6749-kg (14,880-lb) thrust afterburning Pratt & Whitney J57-P-55 turbojets
Performance: maximum speed 1965 km/h (1,221 mph) or Mach 1.85 at 12190 m (40,000 ft); service ceiling 16705 m (54,800 ft); range 2494 km (1,550 miles)
Weights: empty 13141 kg (28,970 lb); maximum take-off 23768 kg (52,400 lb)

Compared with the initial F-101, the F-101B had superior range, inflight-refuelling capability, better performance and an improved fire-control system.

Dimensions: span 12.09 m (39 ft 8 in); length 20.54 m (67 ft 4¾ in); height 5.49 m (18 ft 0 in); wing area 34.19 m² (368.0 sq ft)
Armament: two MB-1 Genie missiles with nuclear warhead and four AIM-4C, -4D or -4G Falcon missiles, or six Falcon missiles

McDonnell F2H Banshee

Following the success of the FH-1 Phantom in US Navy and US Marine service, McDonnell was requested to submit its design for a new and improved jet fighter to supersede the FH-1. The company's design submission led to the receipt of a contract in early 1945 for three **McDonnell XF2D-1** prototypes, these later gaining the name **Banshee**. McDonnell's design covered an improved version of the Phantom of increased size, incorporating folding wings, and with a lengthened fuselage to house more fuel, and with similarly-mounted and more powerful Westinghouse turbojet engines. The first prototype was flown on 11 January 1947, by then redesignated **XF2H-1**, and successful testing and evaluation led to contracts that were to call eventually for a total of 892 production aircraft of which details are given under Variants. Initial deliveries of production F2H-1s, to US Navy Squadron VF-171, began in August 1948, and the type proved of great value as an escort fighter during the Korean War. By the end of that conflict the F2Hs had been superseded by more advanced fighters, but continued in use in a reconnaissance role for a number of years and, in service with US Navy Reserve units, were flown until the mid-1960s. In November 1955 a total of 39 ex-US Navy F2H-3s was transferred to the Royal Canadian Navy, these being that service's first operational jet fighters; when the last were retired, in September 1962, they also proved to be the last carrier-based fighters in Canadian service.

McDonnell F2H-2 Banshee of the US Navy in typical 1950s midnight blue scheme.

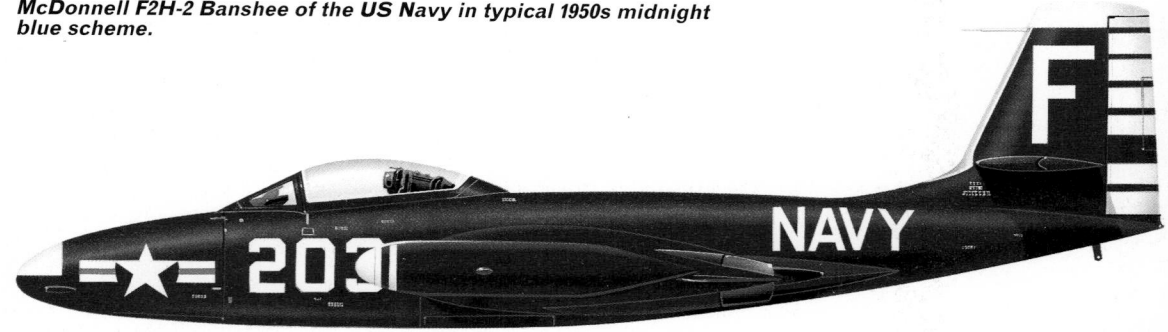

Variants
F2H-1: initial production version, generally similar to prototype with two 1361-kg (3,000-lb) thrust Westinghouse J34-GE-22 turbojets; 56 built
F2H-2: second production version, introducing slightly lengthened fuselage with increased fuel capacity, wingtip fuel tanks, and 1474-kg (3,250-lb) thrust Westinghouse J34-WE-34 turbojets; 308 built
F2H-2B: fighter-bomber version, with underwing racks for two 227-kg (500-lb) bombs; 25 built
F2H-2N: night-fighter version, with slightly lengthened nose to house AI radar; 14 built
F2H-2P: reconnaissance version,

without armament and with lengthened nose for up to six cameras; 89 built
F2H-3 (later **F-2C**): all-weather fighter with lengthened fuselage for increased fuel capacity, APQ-41 radar installed in the nose, and underwing bomb racks as F2H-2B; 250 built
F2H-3P: proposed reconnaissance version of F2H-3; not built
F2H-4 (later **F-2D**): final production version of Banshee, with 1633-kg (3,600-lb) thrust Westinghouse J34-WE-38 engines, and APG-37 radar to give improved all-weather capability; 150 built

Specification
McDonnell F2H-3 Banshee

Type: single-seat all-weather carrier-based fighter
Powerplant: two 1474-kg (3,250-lb) thrust Westinghouse J34-WE-34 turbojets
Performance: maximum speed 933 km/h (580 mph) at sea level; service ceiling 14205 m (46,600 ft); range 1883 km (1,170 miles)
Weights: empty 5980 kg (13,183 lb); maximum take-off 11437 kg (25,214 lb)
Dimensions: span 12.73 m (41 ft 9 in); length 14.68 m (48 ft 2 in); height 4.42 m (14 ft 6 in); wing area 27.31 m² (294.0 sq ft)
Armament: four 20-mm cannon, plus underwing racks for two 227-kg (500-lb) or four 113-kg (250-lb) bombs

McDonnell F3H Demon

Experience gained by the US Navy with the McDonnell FD-1 Phantom and F2H Banshee brought an appreciation that there was no valid reason why carrier-based turbojet-powered fighters need be inferior in any way to their land-based counterparts. The two **McDonnell XF3H-1** prototypes ordered from McDonnell on 30 September 1949 were expected to prove this belief, but for a variety of reasons it was to prove a costly exercise. Planned as a high-performance day fighter, the F3H had a basic configuration that included swept wings and tail surfaces, with lateral fuselage intakes for the single turbojet engine mounted in the rear fuselage. Powerplant selected for the XF3H-1 was the new Westinghouse XJ40, but failure to develop this engine to the design power output and reliability was largely responsible for enormous costs and delays suffered by the **F3H** programme. It was complicated also by the US Navy's requirement for redesign so that production aircraft, of which 150 had been contracted before the prototypes had flown, could be completed as all-weather night-fighters. The first XF3H-1 made its maiden flight on 7 August 1951, but it was not until 24 December 1953 that the first production **F3H-1N Demon** was flown, differing from the prototype by having APG-51 radar and armament comprising four 20-mm cannon and underwing racks for other weapons. These early F3H-1Ns were powered by the Westinghouse J40-WE-22 turbojet (developing 3266-kg/7,200-lb thrust, or 4944-kg/10,900-lb thrust with afterburning) as a result of the failure of the intended J40 engine to develop its design

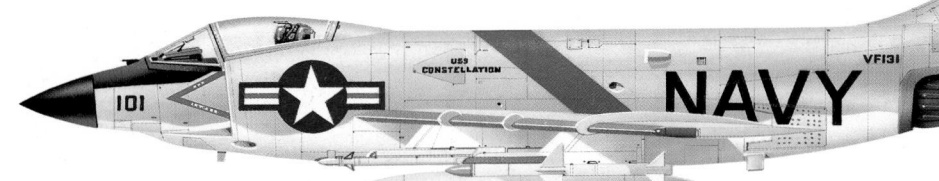

McDonnell F3H-2 Demon of VF-131, US Navy, based on board the USS Constellation *in the early 1960s.*

thrust. The aircraft were as a consequence seriously underpowered and, after 11 accidents in which two pilots lost their lives, production was halted. The situation was resolved finally by installation of the Allison J71 turbojet in production **F3H-2s**, and a total of 519 of all versions had been built when production ended in late 1959. Initial deliveries, to US Navy Squadron VF-14, were made in March 1956, and the type equipped 11 squadrons before being withdrawn from first-line service in September 1964. The Demon saw few combat operations, being too late for use in Korea and retired before the US became involved in Vietnam, its service career having been cut short by a newer generation of more capable fighters evolved during the long development period of the Demon.

Variants
F3H-1N: initial production version; some were used for ground instruction purposes, the remainder scrapped; 58 built

F3H-1P: planned reconnaissance version of the F3H-1N with the Westinghouse J40 engine; not built

F3H-2N (later **F-3C**): two F3H-1N airframes were taken from the production line to serve as F3H-2N development aircraft; differed by having almost 18 per cent increase in wing area, Allison J71-A-2 engines, basic armament of the F3H-1N, but equipped to deploy four AIM-9 Sidewinder missiles; 140 built

F3H-2M (later **MF-3B**): generally similar to F3H-2N, but equipped to carry four AIM-7 Sparrow I radar-guided missiles instead of Sidewinders; 80 built

F3H-2 (later **F-3B**): definitive production version retaining provision to deploy Sparrow missiles, but basically a strike fighter carrying up to 2722 kg (6,000 lb) of bombs and/or rockets; 239 built

F3H-2P: planned reconnaissance version of the F3H-2; not built

F3H-3: projected production version

with General Electric J73-GE-3 engines; not built

Specification
McDonnell F3H-2/F-3B Demon
Type: single-seat carrier-based strike fighter
Powerplant: one 4400-kg (9,700-lb) thrust Allison J71-A-2E turbojet with afterburning rating of 6350-kg (14,000-lb) thrust
Performance: maximum speed 1041 km/h (647 mph) at 9145 m (30,000 ft); service ceiling 13000 m (42,650 ft); maximum range 2205 km (1,370 miles)
Weights: empty 10039 kg (22,133 lb); maximum take-off 15377 kg (33,900 lb)
Dimensions: span 10.77 m (35 ft 4 in); length 17.96 m (58 ft 11 in); height 4.44 m (14 ft 7 in); wing area 48.22 m² (519.0 sq ft)
Armament: four 20-mm cannon plus up to 2722 kg (6,000 lb) of bombs or rockets; retained provision to carry Sparrow III missiles

McDonnell FH-1 Phantom

Because in 1942 the established sources of supply for US Navy aircraft were then overwhelmed by the demands of wartime, the Bureau of Aeronautics entrusted the new and comparatively inexperienced McDonnell Aircraft Corporation with the task of designing and building two prototypes of what was to become the US Navy's first carrier-based turbojet-powered single-seat fighter. Designated **McDonnell XFD-1**, the resulting prototypes were of low-wing monoplane configuration, had retractable tricycle landing gear, and accommodated the pilot in an enclosed cockpit well forward of the wing. The powerplant comprised two Westinghouse turbojets, one mounted in each wing root, but the first flight on 26 January 1945 was made on the power of only one of these engines, as the second had not been delivered. Successful trials and US Navy evaluation, during which the XFD-1 became the first US jet aircraft to be flown onto and from an aircraft carrier, the USS *Franklin D. Roosevelt*, brought a contract for 100 **FD-1**

McDonnell FH-1 Phantom of the US Navy

Phantom fighters, the designation being changed to **FH-1** before delivery began in January 1947. End-of-war contract cancellations meant that only 60 FH-1s were built, equipping initially US Navy Squadron VF-17A which, in May 1948, gained the distinction of being the world's first carrier-based jet fighter squadron. Subsequent operators were Marine Squadrons VMF-122 and

VMF-311, but within little more than two years these early jet fighters had been withdrawn from service.

Specification
McDonnell FH-1 Phantom
Type: single-seat carrier-based jet fighter
Powerplant: two 726-kg (1,600-lb) thrust Westinghouse J30-WE-20

turbojets
Performance: maximum speed 771 km/h (479 mph) at sea level; service ceiling 12525 m (41,100 ft); standard range 1118 km (695 miles)
Weights: empty 3031 kg (6,683 lb); maximum take-off 5459 kg (12,035 lb)
Dimensions: span 12.42 m (40 ft 9 in); length 11.35 m (37 ft 3 in); height 4.32 m (14 ft 2 in); wing area 24.64 m² (276.0 sq ft)
Armament: four 12.7-mm (0.5-in) machine-guns mounted in the nose

McDonnell XP-67

The McDonnell Aircraft Corporation was formed at St Louis, Missouri, during July 1939, its primary occupation throughout World War II being the sub-contract production of aircraft and components for other manufacturers. However, during those years the company was active in aircraft design, its first US Army Air Force contract being for two prototypes of an experimental single-seat high-altitude fighter designated **McDonnell XP-67**. The design attempted to gain

A superb example of the designers' art, the XP-67 was to carry six 37-mm cannon.

additional lift from the airframe by blending the centre fuselage and engine nacelles into the wings to create a larger area of true aerofoil section. Powered by two 1007-kW (1,350-hp) Continental XI-1430-17/-19 engines, driving counter-rotating propellers, the prototype was flown for the first time on 6 January

1944. Considerable trouble was experienced with the engines, and after the first prototype was lost on 6 September

ber, as a result of an engine fire, the programme was abandoned before the second prototype had been completed.

McDonnell XV-1 and Model 120

Primarily as a research vehicle, McDonnell designed and built two prototypes of a somewhat complicated convertiplane under the designation **McDonnell XV-1**. The fuselage, mounted on skid landing gear, had a 391-kW (525-hp) Continental R-975 piston engine at the rear to drive a pusher propeller; the mid/high-set wings mounted twin tailbooms with twin vertical surfaces, inter-connected by tailplane and elevator; and above the fuselage was a three-bladed rotor with blade-tip pressure jets. Extended testing as part of a combined US Army/US Air Force programme began with tethered flights, followed by a first free flight on 14

July 1954 and a first conversion from vertical to horizontal flight on 29 April 1955. Although demonstrating a maximum speed of 322 km/h (200 mph), the XV-1 was too complex for the small advantages gained over a conventional helicopter. Subsequently, on 13 November 1957, McDonnell flew the first of two prototypes of a small crane helicopter, designated **Model 120**, which had been developed as a private venture. This used the rotor developed for the XV-1, but although tested successfully it found no market and further development was abandoned.

A far-sighted convertiplane project, the XFV-1 had a torqueless main rotor driven by tip-mounted jets, wings to off-load the rotor in forward flight and a two-bladed propeller.

McDonnell Douglas A-4 Skyhawk

One of the most successful post-World War II aircraft to serve with the US Navy, the **McDonnell Douglas A-4 Skyhawk** originated as a private-venture design under a team headed by Ed Heinemann. Thus, when the US Navy began the search for a turbine-powered successor to the Douglas AD-1 (A-1) Skyraider, the company was able to propose a new attack aircraft with a gross weight of about half that of the official specification and one which was considerably faster. Of monoplane configuration, with a low-set delta wing incorporating integral fuel tanks, the design had a fuselage which accommodated avionics in the nose, additional fuel aft of the pilot's cockpit, and the Wright J65 turbojet (a licence-built Armstrong Siddeley Sapphire) in the centre fuselage. Ordered during the Korean War, the prototype was flown on 22 June 1954 and the first preproduction aircraft on 14 August 1954, with initial deliveries to US Navy Attack Squadron VA-72 beginning on 26 October 1956. Three months later, in January 1957, VMA-224 became the first US Marine Corps squadron to receive Skyhawks. It was a fortunate period in which to introduce this sparkling new attack aircraft, for by the time the US Navy and US Marines became involved in operations in Vietnam, both of these services were able to deploy the Skyhawk with the greatest confidence in its capability; indeed, such was its effectiveness that steadily improving A-4s remained in production until February 1979, built to a total of 2,960 aircraft including trainers, and exported to the armed forces of several nations. The Skyhawk continues in service with the US Navy and US Marine Corps in a training role, and other nations whose armed forces are equipped with the type include Argentina, Indonesia, Israel, Kuwait, Malaysia, New Zealand and Singapore.

Variants

XA4D-1: designation of one prototype, powered by a 3266-kg (7,200-lb) thrust Wright J65-W-2 turbojet
YA4D-1 (later **YA-4A** and then **A-4A**): designation of 19 pre-production aircraft generally similar to XA4D-1; introduced the 3493-kg (7,700-lb) thrust J65-W-4 or J65-W-4B turbojet and armament of two 20-mm cannon and up to 2268 kg (5,000 lb) of weapons on an underfuselage and two

underwing hardpoints
A4D-1 (later **A-4A**): production aircraft, as YA4D-1; 146 built
A4D-2 (later **A-4B**): production version with strengthened rear fuselage, inflight-refuelling equipment, and the 3538-kg (7,800-lb) thrust J65-W-16A turbojet; 542 built
A4D-2N (later **A-4C**): production version introducing terrain-following radar, autopilot and a number of other improvements; J65-W-16A engines, later uprated to 3856-kg (8,500-lb) thrust with designation change to J65-W-16C; 638 built
A4D-3: proposed all-weather version with Pratt & Whitney turbojet; not built
A4D-5 (later **A-4E**): improved production version, introducing the 3856-kg (8,500-lb) thrust Pratt & Whitney J52-P-6A turbojet and two additional underwing hardpoints to allow maximum weapon load of 3719 kg (8,200 lb); 494 built
A4D-6: proposed development with 5216-kg (11,500-lb) thrust Pratt & Whitney TF30 turbofan installed in an enlarged airframe; not built
TA-4E: designation of two production prototypes of a two-seat trainer version; generally as A4D-5, but with fuselage lengthened 0.76 m (2 ft 6 in) and reduced internal fuel
TA-4F: production version of TA-4E with the 4218-kg (9,300-lb) thrust Pratt & Whitney J52-P-8A turbojet; 240 built
A-4F: final attack production version for US Navy; introduced the J52-P-8A engine, and additional avionics in a hump-back fairing on the rear fuselage; 146 built
A-4G: version similar to A4D-5 but with J52-P-8A engine; eight built for Royal Australian Navy; sold to RNZAF in 1984
TA-4G: two two-seat trainers for the RAN; generally similar to the TA-4F; sold to RNZAF in 1984
A-4H: production version for the Israeli air force; generally similar to A4D-5 but with J52-P-8A engine; introduced a braking parachute, and replaced 20-mm guns by two of 30-mm calibre; 90 built
TA-4H: two-seat trainer version of the A-4H for Israel; 10 built
TA-4J: two-seat trainer for the US Navy, similar to TA-4F, but with reduced tactical systems, and armament of only one 20-mm cannon (not always fitted), and powered by 3856-kg (8,500-lb) thrust J52-P-6

McDonnell Douglas A-4M Skyhawk II

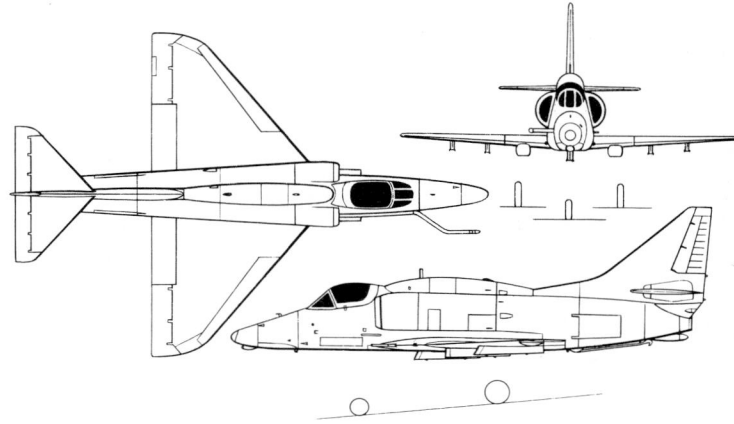

engine; 291 built
A-4K: version generally similar to A-4F for Royal New Zealand Air Force, but incorporating a braking parachute; 10 built
TA-4K: two-seat version of A-4K for RNZAF; four built
A-4KU: production version for Kuwait government, generally similar to A-4M below; 30 built
TA-4KU: two-seat trainer version of A-4KU for Kuwait; six built
A-4L: redesignation of A-4Cs after withdrawal from first-line use and updated for use by reserve squadrons; all with J65-W-16C engines
A-4M: production version for the US Marine Corps, introducing a number of improvements, equipped with braking parachute and the more powerful J52-P-408A engine; 162 built
A-4N: production version for Israeli air force; generally similar to A-4M but with advanced avionics and systems, and 30-mm cannon; 117 built
A-4P: redesignation of ex-US Navy A-4Bs refurbished for servicve with the air force of Argentina
A-4PTM: designation given to 40 Malaysian A-4Cs and A-4Ls reworked in US by Grumman into Peculiar to Malaysia (PTM) versions; these incorporate new radios, Ferranti gunsights, Hughes ARBS, Lear Siegler AHARS and braking chute; missile

capability enhanced by ability to carry Sidewinders and Mavericks on extra wing pylons
A-4Q: redesignation of ex-US Navy A-4Bs refurbished for service with Argentina's naval air arm
A-4S: redesignation of ex-US Navy A-4Bs overhauled and updated for service with the Republic of Singapore Air Force
TA-4S: two-seat trainer version of A-4S for Republic of Singapore Air Force (two separate canopies)

Specification
McDonnell Douglas A-4M Skyhawk
Type: single-seat carrier-based attack-bomber
Powerplant: one 5080-kg (11,200-lb) thrust Pratt & Whitney J52-P-408A turbojet
Performance: maximum speed 1078 km/h (670 mph) at sea level; tactical radius with 1814 kg (4,000 lb) bombload 547 km (340 miles)
Weights: empty 4747 kg (10,465 lb); maximum take-off 11113 kg (24,500 lb)
Dimensions: span 8.38 m (27 ft 6 in); length 12.29 m (40 ft 3¾ in); height 4.57 m (15 ft 0 in); wing area 24.15 m² (260.0 sq ft)
Armament: two 20-mm cannon, plus up to 4153 kg (9,155 lb) of weapons on five external hardpoints

McDonnell Douglas YC-15
to
McDonnell Douglas DC-10

McDonnell Douglas YC-15

In the early 1970s the US Air Force issued a requirement for a C-130 Hercules replacement. This was designated the Advanced Medium STOL Transport (AMST) and McDonnell Douglas was one of five US companies selected to submit proposals. In November 1972 the company, together with Boeing, was awarded a contract to each design, build and test two prototypes for a fly-off and evaluation. The McDonnell Douglas entry was the YC-15A and the prototype (72-1875) flew for the first time on 26 August 1975. Following a 600-hour test programme, AMST funding was discontinued in 1979, and no further development of either company's design took place. However, the first prototype YC-15A was used to take the CFM56

Key to the remarkable performance of the YC-15 was the use of wide-span double-slotted flaps, blown by the efflux from the underwing engines.

turbofan engine aloft for the first time, installed in the port outer position. Later MDC, planning a civil version, made modifications to the wings and powerplants but little commerical interest was generated and both prototypes were later distributed to Davis-Monthan and Wright-Patterson AFBs. The YC-15A featured a typical transport fuselage with rear loading doors/ramps, heavy duty retractable landing gear and a tall T-tail. Its STOL capability centred on a partnership between wing and power-

plant, the supercritical wing incorporating wide-chord double-slotted flaps over 75 per cent of the span. These, when fully deflected, were blown by the efflux

from four wing-mounted Pratt & Whitney JT8D-17 turbofans each of 71-kN (16,000-lb) thrust, providing so-called 'powered lift'.

McDonnell Douglas C-17A

Following evaluation of US industry design submissions under the US Air Force's C-X programme of October 1980, McDonnell Douglas was chosen in August 1981 as prime contractor to develop a long-range cargo transport under the designation C-17A. The new aircraft was designed to combine the load-carrying capacity of the C-5 Galaxy with the STOL performance of the C-130 Hercules. Full-scale development was cancelled in January 1982 and replaced in July 1982 with a slower-paced programme which called for the design of three prototypes, one to fly and the others ground test specimens. All three were formally ordered in December 1985, and construction of the flying prototype (87-0025) began in November 1987. This was completed in December 1990 and flew for the first time on 15 September 1991, taking off from Long Beach and landing back at Edwards AFB, California. The first batch of production aircraft was ordered in January 1988, followed by another four in 1991, bringing the number of airframes ordered to date to 10. The first production aircraft joined the flight test programme on 18 May 1992. In 1991 the USAF requirement was reduced from 210 to 120 aircraft, by which time the original target unit price of $125 million had escalated to $294 million. Development is planned to be complete by 1993 and first service deliveries are scheduled for 1994 to the 17th AS at Charleston, South Carolina. Feasibility studies of a future tanker ver-

sion are under way at MDC. Configured similarly to the Galaxy and StarLifter, and about the same size as the latter, the four-engined high-wing T-tailed military jet transport features the blown flap system developed for the aborted YC-15, with flaps extending into the exhaust flow from the podded engines for landing and take-off. Fitted with a GEC fly-by-wire system and the inevitable NACA winglets, the C-17A is expected to operate from 915-m (3,000-ft) airstrips and is capable of being refuelled in flight.

With a three-man flight deck crew comprising the pilot, co-pilot and loadmaster, the C-17A can carry up to 102 paratroopers, while the main hold can accommodate AH-64 Apache attack helicopters, M1 Abrams main battle tanks or five-ton expanding vehicles. Access is via the hydraulically-powered rear ramp stressed to take loads of up to 18150 kg (40,000 lb).

Specification
Type: long-range heavy cargo jet transport
Powerplant: four 185-kN (41,700-lb) thrust Pratt & Whitney F117-PW-100

turbofan engines
Performance: maximum cruising speed at low altitude 648 km/h (403 mph); maximum cruising speed at altitude Mach 0.77; range on internal fuel with 75750-kg (167,000-lb) payload 4445 km (2,765 miles); ferry range on internal fuel 8710 km (5,412 miles)
Weights: empty equipped 22000 kg (269,000 lb); maximum payload 78100 kg (172,000 lb); maximum take-off 263100 kg (580,000 lb)
Dimensions: span 52.20 m (171 ft 3 in); length 53.04 m (174 ft); height 16.79 m (55 ft 1 in); wing area 353 m² (3,800 sq ft)

The first C-17 (known as aircraft T-1) was rolled out in the familiar 'lizard' camouflage scheme. The six initial production aircraft (P-1 to P-6) will wear the new overall grey scheme, and T-1 has been repainted to match.

McDonnell Douglas DC-9

Although facing a considerable degree of competition, Douglas initiated the design of a completely new short-range twin-jet transport at the beginning of the 1960s. With confidence in the design, construction of this aircraft began on 26 July 1963 and the first **Douglas DC-9**, as the type was designated, made its maiden flight on 25 February 1965. At that time Douglas had received orders for only 58 DC-9s, and an anxious period ensued before the company began to feel that its investment might be re-

couped. It is unlikely that it could have then believed the DC-9 would prove to be the company's greatest success to date, with orders for civil and military versions, and the **MD-80** (formerly **DC-9 Super 80**) totalling well over 2,000 by March 1992, of which 1,865 had been delivered. A cantilever low-wing monoplane with swept wings and a T-tail with all swept surfaces, the initial **DC-9 Series 10 Model 11** production aircraft accommodated a flight crew of two, cabin attendants, and between 80 and

90 passengers according to layout. Power was provided by two 55-kN (12,250-lb) thrust Pratt & Whitney JT8D-5 turbofans, pod-mounted one on each side of the rear fuselage, and it was this version that first entered service with Delta Airlines on 8 December 1965. It was the company's intention from the outset to produce and market the DC-9 in several versions, to meet the differing requirements of civil operators, and the use was extended by special conversions for military use; brief details of all these aircraft are given under Variants. DC-9 Series 30 and subsequent versions were made available in specialised sub-

variants comprising freight (**F**), convertible (**CF**), and passenger/freight (**RC**) configurations.

Variants
DC-9 Series 10 Model 15: as Series 10 Model 11, except for installation of 62-kN (14,000-lb) thrust JT8D-1 turbofan engines for operation at a higher gross weight
DC-9 Series 20: version for hot/high use with 1.22-m (4-ft) increase in wing span, two 65-kN (14,500-lb) thrust JT8D-9 turbofans and accommodation for up to 90 passengers
DC-9 Series 30: developed version

with fuselage lengthened by 4.54 m (14 ft 10¾ in) to accommodate 105 to 119 passengers, wing span as Series 20, and initially with 62-kN (14,000-lb) thrust JT8D-7 turbofans; later available with engines of 65- to 72-kN (14,500- to 16,000-lb) thrust

DC-9 Series 40: lengthened fuselage (by 1.92 m; 6 ft 3¾ in) version of Series 30 seating up to 132 passengers; produced only with engines of 65- to 72-kN (14,500- to 16,000-lb) thrust

DC-9 Series 50: short/medium-range development of Series 30, with fuselage lengthened by an additional 2.44 m (8 ft 0 in) to seat a maximum 139 passengers; redesigned cabin interior and produced with 69- to 72-kN (15,500- to 16,000-lb) thrust turbofans only

C-9A Nightingale: aeromedical transport version of DC-9 Series 30 in

McDonnell Douglas DC-9-50 of Hawaiian Air

service with the US Air Force; 21 built

C-9B Skytrain II: fleet logistic transport combining features of the DC-9 Series 30 and 40; in service with the US Navy and Marines (15 built) and Kuwait (2 built)

VC-9C: VIP transport, based on the DC-9 Series 30, in service with the USAF's Special Air Missions Wing; 3 built

Specification
McDonnell Douglas DC-9 Series 50
Type: short/medium-range airliner
Powerplant: two 72 kN (16,000 lb) thrust Pratt & Whitney JT8D-17 turbofans
Performance: maximum cruising speed 898 km/h (558 mph); long range cruising speed 821 km/h (510 mph);

maximum range with 97 passengers 3327 km (2,067 miles)
Weights: empty 28068 kg (61,880 lb); maximum take-off 54885 kg (121,000 lb)
Dimensions: span 28.47 m (93 ft 5 in); length 40.72 m (133 ft 7¼ in); height 8.53 m (28 ft 0 in); wing area 92.97 m² (1,000.7 sq ft)

McDonnell Douglas DC-10

Design of the **McDonnell Douglas DC-10** began in 1966, to meet a requirement of American Airlines for a large-capacity civil transport. With the receipt of an order for 25 plus 25 options from American Airlines and 30 plus 30 options from United Airlines, the DC-10 was put into production in April 1968. Of low-set swept-wing monoplane configuration, and with all-swept tail surfaces, the DC-10 adopted 'conventional' three-engine configuration with one engine pylon-mounted beneath each wing and the third engine installed at the base of the fin. The initial production **DC-10 Series 10** was flown first on 29 August 1970, and following receipt of certification, on 29 July 1971, American Airlines introduced the type into revenue service one week later, on 5 August. The company ultimately received 446 orders for civil DC-10s, the last of which was delivered to Nigeria Airways in 1989, but the production line continued to manufacture the generally similar **KC-10A Extender** inflight-refuelling/cargo aircraft for the US Air Force until the beginning of 1990.

Variants
DC-10 Series 10: initial production version, seating a maximum 380 passengers, and powered by General Electric CF6-6D or CF6-6D1 turbofan engines of 178 kN (40,000 lb) or 182 kN (41,000 lb) thrust respectively; 122 built
DC-10 Series 10CF: convertible passenger/cargo version of the Series 10; 9 built
DC-10 Series 15: basically similar to Series 10, but with General Electric CF6-50C2F engines, each of 207 kN (46,500 lb) thrust, permitting higher gross weight; 7 built
DC-10 Series 30: extended-range intercontinental version; has wing span increased by 3.05 m (10 ft), increased fuel capacity, standard landing gear supplemented by a two-wheel main gear unit beneath the fuselage, and power provided by General Electric CF6-50A or CF6-50C turbofan engines, each of 218-kN (49,000-lb) or 227-kN (51,000-lb) thrust respectively; 161 built, including unspecified number of Series 30ER aircraft (probably 3 or 4)
DC-10 Series 30CF: convertible passenger/cargo version of Series 30, late production with 234-kN (52,500-lb) thrust General Electric CF6-50C1 engines; 26 built
DC-10 Series 30ER: extended-range version of Series 30, with additional fuel and 240-kN (54,000-lb) thrust

McDonnell Douglas KC-10A of Strategic Air Command, USAF, in the early 1980s.

General Electric CF6-50C2B engines
DC-10 Series 40: intercontinental-range version, similar to Series 30, but first 22 aircraft with 220-kN (49,400-lb) thrust Pratt & Whitney JT9D-20 turbofans and subsequent aircraft with JT9D-59A engines each of 235 kN (53,000 lb) thrust; 42 built
KC-10A Extender: under this designation the US Air Force selected to DC-10 in late 1977 to meet its Advanced Tanker/Cargo Aircraft requirement; basically a conversion of the DC-10 Series 30CF, the KC-10A has additional fuel cells in the lower fuselage, an inflight-refuelling boom, boom operator's station, inflight-refuelling receptacle and an improved cargo-handling system; multi-year contracts covered the supply of 60 KC-10As, the first of them being test flown (from Long Beach to Yuma) on 12 July 1980; initial deliveries to the USAF began on 17 March 1981 and the last was accepted in April 1990 and delivered to Seymour Johnson AFB, North Carolina; following the loss of one aircraft on the ground, 59 KC-10As remain in USAF service

Specification
McDonnell Douglas DC-10 Series 30
Type: commercial transport
Powerplant: three 226-kN (51,000-lb) thrust General Electric CF6-50C turbofans
Performance: maximum cruising speed 908 km/h (564 mph) at 9145 m (30,000 ft); service ceiling at average cruise weight 10180 m (33,400 ft); range with maximum payload 7411 km (4,605 miles)
Weights: empty 121199 kg (267,197 lb); maximum take-off 263084 kg (580,000 lb)

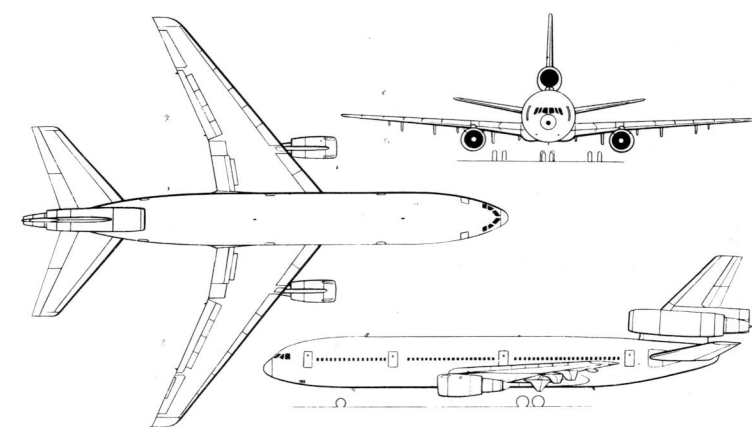

McDonnell Douglas DC-10-30

Dimensions: span 50.41 m (165 ft 4½ in); length 55.50 m (182 ft 1 in); height 17.70 m (58 ft 1 in); wing area 367.70 m² (3,958.7 sq ft)

Nigeria Airways is notable as the operator of the last DC-10 to roll off the production line at Long Beach.

McDonnell Douglas F-15 Eagle

Following more than three years of design studies for the 1968 F-X advanced air-superiority fighter, some sponsored by the US Air Force and others company-funded, McDonnell Douglas was selected as the prime contractor in December 1969 and received an initial contract covering the manufacture of 20 **F-15** aircraft (by then named **Eagle**) for development and test purposes, comprising 18 **F-15A** single-seat fighters and two **TF-15A** two-seat trainers (later re-designated **F-15B**). The first to fly was the F-15A (71-0280) on 27 July 1972, followed by the prototype two-seat TF-15A on 7 July 1973. Under subsequent production contracts and multi-year procurement programmes, the USAF is scheduled to receive a total of 1,488 F-15s by the mid-1990s, and of this total 1,250 had been delivered by September 1990, and are in widespread operational service.

Forty F-15A/B Eagles were also delivered to the Israeli air force between 1976 and 1982, and Saudi Arabia received 96 **F-15C**s and **F-15D**s between 1981 and 1991. Negotiations for a further 72 late production models for Saudi Arabia have been under way for some time but without a resolution to date. The Japanese Air Self-Defence Force ordered 100 Eagles in the late 1970s, comprising 88 single-seat **F-15J** and 12 two-seat **F-15DJ** aircraft, 86 of this total to be licence-built by Mitsubishi. The first of these flew in June 1980, and most have since been delivered and equip the Central, Northern and Western air defence forces of the JASDF, operating from bases at Chitose, Komatsu, Hyakuri and Tsuiki. Early in 1992 the planned Japanese purchase was revised upwards to 191 aircraft.

In mid-1979, production F-15As and Bs were superseded on the production lines by the improved single-seat F-15C and its equivalent two-seat F-15C versions, with increased internal fuel, totally updated mission avionics and (Fuel and Sensor) FAST packs, the latter low-drag conformal pallets which attach to the sides of the engine air intake trunk. In addition to fuel, FAST packs can contain avionics and reconnaissance cameras, with missiles and air-to-ground weapons mounted externally.

To fulfil the USAF Enhanced Tactical Fighter (ETF) requirement, the **F-15E Strike Eagle** was developed by McDonnell Douglas and Hughes. This dual-role, two-seater fighter intended for long-range interdiction missions in all weathers, day or night, retains full air-to-air combat capability. The prototype, converted from the second F-15B, flew for the first time in August 1981 and, following a fly-off against the F-16XL, the Strike Eagle was declared the winner in 1984. Full scale development began immediately. The first new-build F-15E flew in December 1986 and the type went into service at Luke AFB, Arizona, in August 1987. Featuring redesigned controls, the F-15E has multi-purpose CRT displays monitoring navigation, weapons aiming and delivery systems, a wide-angle HUD, AN/APG-70 synthetic aperture radar plus the ability to carry the Martin Marietta LANTIRN weapons and

targeting pods, one containing FLIR and the other terrain following radar. Maximum weapon load is 11100 kg (24,500 lb) and combat range around 1270 km (790 miles). The Strike Eagle went into service at Luke AFB, Arizona, in August 1987 and, with several squadrons operational, production of this version continues for the USAF.

The Eagle is a highly efficient combat aircraft, its capability endorsed by the USAF plan to acquire almost 1,500 of them. It has a maximum speed of well over Mach 2 and a thrust-to-weight ratio that provides a rocket-like rate of climb. Such capability is essential for an interceptor operating from ground standby, rather than constant air patrol, which means the pilot of such an aircraft needs as much help as possible from advanced avionics and systems. The Eagle's head-up display provides such capability, enabling the pilot to concentrate on the real world outside his aircraft, while glowing symbols and figures visible on the HUD presents all the information required to intercept and destroy enemy aircraft without removing his eyes from the target.

Variants

F-15 STOL/MTD Agile Eagle: under a USAF contract, F-15B 71-0290 was modified in 1987/88 to become the short take-off and landing/manoeuvre technology demonstrator; the three-year, 150-hour flight test programme called for research into four areas comprising two-dimensional thrust vectoring and thrust reversing engine nozzles, integrated flight/propulsion system, rough field landing gear, and

Latest model of the F-15 to appear is the F-15E. This example carries a LANTIRN (Low-Altitude Targeting and Navigation Infra-Red for Night) pod.

advanced pilot/vehicle interface; the STOL/MTD first flew on 7 September 1988 and the programme was completed on 12 August 1991
F-15/HARM: currently the USAF's favoured F-4G 'Wild Weasel' replacement, the F-15/HARM airframe/missile combination can carry the AGM-88 HARM (High speed Anti-Radiation Missile) under development for use in the late 1990s

Specification
McDonnell Douglas F-15C Eagle
Type: single-seat air-superiority fighter
Powerplant: two 106-kN (23,930-lb) afterburning thrust Pratt & Whitney F100-PW-100 turbofans
Performance: maximum speed (high, clean) Mach 2.5; zoom ceiling 30480 m (100,000 ft); unrefuelled flight endurance 5 hours 15 minutes

The F-15C is arguably the world's greatest air superiority fighter, with its combination of radar, weapons and manoeuvrability seemingly vindicated in the Gulf War. This colourful pair of fully-armed Eagles wears the markings of the 5th FIS.

Weight: maximum take-off 30844 kg (68,000 lb)
Dimensions: span 13.05 m (42 ft 9¾ in); length 19.43 m (63 ft 9 in); height 5.63 m (18 ft 5½ in); wing area 56.48 m² (608.0 sq ft)
Armament: one M61A1 20-mm six-barrelled cannon and four AIM-9 Sidewinder, four AIM-7 Sparrow or eight AMRAAM air-to-air missiles; in the secondary attack role up to 7300 kg (16,000 lb) of weapons can be carried externally

McDonnell Douglas F/A-18 Hornet

Under the programme identification VFAX, the study of a lightweight multi-mission fighter for the US Navy was initiated in early 1974. Later in the year, however, funds for the study were withdrawn and the US Navy was instructed instead to look closely at the General Dynamics YF-16 and Northrop YF-17 lightweight fighter prototypes which had been built for competitive evaluation by the US Air Force. Learning of this, McDonnell Douglas evaluated both designs, concluding that Northrop's YF-17 most nearly met the US Navy's original requirement, and teamed with Northrop to submit a design proposal. Then identified as the **Navy Air Combat Fighter (NACF)**, it had considerable appeal to the US Navy and, following further design refinement it was announced on 22 January 1976 that full scale development was to be initiated of two single-seat versions, the **McDonnell Douglas F-18** and **A-18** for fighter and attack roles respectively. Later named **Hornet**, the aircraft is a cantilever mid-wing monoplane with folding wings; a tail unit incorporating outward canted twin fins and rudders and all-moving tailplanes, one on each side of the fuselage, movable collectively or differentially; retractable tricycle landing gear with a nose unit suitable for catapult launching; an arrester hook for carrier landings; and a powerplant of two 71-kN (16,000-lb) thrust General Electric F404-GE-400 turbofan engines.

The first of 11 development aircraft (160775) was flown by MDC test pilot Jack Krings at Lambert-St Louis on 18 November 1978. All 11 had flown within 12 months, plus two **TF/A-18A** two-seat trainers (later redesignated **F-18B**). The first production **F/A-18A** was delivered to the US Navy in May 1980 and the first operational unit was squadron VFA-125 at NAS Lemoore. Operational improvements were initiated in the mid-1980s and led to the **F/A-18C** single-seater with improved night attack capability through an avionics upgrade and improved flight instruments, plus increased missile capability from its nine hardpoints which allowed the carriage of the AIM-120 and the AGM-65F Maverick. Re-engined with a more powerful F404-GE-402 turbofan, the first F/A-18C flew on 3 September 1986 and was delivered later the same month to the Naval Warfare Center. Following acceptance, the type ultimately replaced the A-7 Corsair with the USN. The two-seat **F/A-18D** dedicated night-attack version equipped with FLIR flew in May 1988 and went into service on 1 November 1989, replacing the A-6 Intruder with the USMC. Further development has resulted in the longer-range stretched-fuselage **F/A-18E** and **F/A-18F** versions of the F/A-18C and D fitted with improved APG-73 radar and 11 hardpoints. Full scale development of the E/F is due to begin later in 1992, and the US Marine Corps is to receive 300. In the export market the Hornet was also chosen by Kuwait, who is scheduled to receive 32 F-18Cs and eight F-18Ds between August 1991 and September 1993. In 1988, the F/A-18 was selected by the Swiss air force as its New Fighter Aircraft, and the purchase of 34 aircraft to equip three squadrons received government approval in June 1992. South Korea selected the F-18 for its Korean Fighter Programme in 1989 and ordered 120, but the decision was suspended in October 1990 and overturned in March 1991 in favour of the F-16. Early in 1992, the Finnish government signed an agreement to buy 64 F/A-18s for its air force.

By the middle of 1992, McDonnell Douglas had delivered more than 1,100 Hornets, and the truly versatile combat jet seems likely to attract more significant orders in the future.

The F/A-18C offers much improved avionics and weapons capability over earlier models, and all US Navy and Marine Corps Hornets are to be upgraded to that level. The remaining Spanish EF-18s will also be radically modified.

Variants

F/A-18A: initial production version; both fighter and attack variants carry this designation, differing only in a small amount of operational equipment and armament; 75 ordered by Australia in October 1981 for operation by RAAF, comprising 57 F/A-18As and 18 F/A-18Bs; first two deliveries made from MDC in October 1984 with remainder built in Australia by ASTA; last aircraft completed and delivered in May 1990
CF-18: designation of Hornet for Canadian Armed Forces, fitted with ILS and special survival pack; 148 ordered but cut back to 114 single-seat **CF-18A**s and 24 two-seat **CF-18F**s; first delivered in October 1982 and the last in September 1988
EF-18: designation of 72 carrier-capable Hornets for the Spanish air force ordered in May 1983; 60 single-seat **EF-18A**s and 12 **EF-18B**s (locally designated **C-15** and **CE-15** respectively), delivered between the spring of 1986 and July 1990
F-18D(CR): projected two-seat dedicated all-weather reconnaissance F-18D variant proposed to replace USMC RF-4B Phantoms
RF-18: designation of reconnaissance version of the F/A-18A; configuration tested on first prototype (160775) in February 1984, but airframe since transferred to NASA, and the only RF-18 flying is 161214 at Patuxent River
TF/A-18A: initial tandem two-seat trainer version of the **F/A-18A** retaining combat capability, but with small reduction in fuel capacity; later redesignated **F/A-18B**
Hornet 2000: proposed by McDonnell Douglas for co-development in the mid-1980s, the advanced Hornet 2000 would have larger wing and horizontal tail surfaces, two fuselage plugs enabling extra fuel, more powerful engines and an improved cockpit; estimated cost in 1987 was $26.5 million each

Specification
McDonnell Douglas F/A-18A Hornet

Type: carrier-based naval strike fighter
Powerplant: two 71-kN (16,000-lb) thrust General Electric F404-GE-400 turbofans
Performance: maximum speed (high, clean) Mach 1.8; combat ceiling 15240 m (50,000 ft); combat radius on fighter mission more than 740 km (460 miles)
Weight: maximum take-off for attack mission 22317 kg (49,200 lb)
Dimensions: span 11.43 m (37 ft 6 in); length 17.07 m (56 ft 0 in); height 4.66 m (15 ft 3½ in); wing area 37.16 m² (400.0 sq ft)
Armament: one M61 20-mm six-barrelled cannon mounted in the nose, plus nine external hardpoints with a maximum capacity of 7700 kg (17,000 lb) of mixed stores, including AIM-7 Sparrow and AIM-9 Sidewinder air-to-air missiles

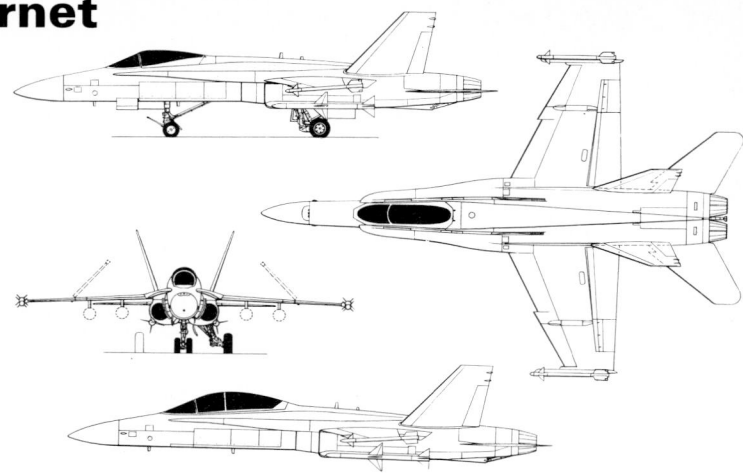

McDonnell Douglas F/A-18A Hornet with F/A-18B lower side view.

McDonnell Douglas MD-11

MDC began studies in 1978 of an aircraft to replace the DC-10 on the Long Beach production line. These progressed through the DC-10 Series 60 stretches of 1979, the MD-100 tri-jet of 1982, the three-engined MD-XXX of 1984, to the wide-body **MD-11** tri-jet of 1985. This is essentially a stretched DC-10, but with a new outer wing incorporating winglets, a new tail, a two-pilot EFIS flight deck and the choice of either General Electric CF6-80C, Pratt & Whitney PW4460 or Rolls-Royce Trent 650 turbofan engines, although the latter installation was shelved following the demise of sole customer Air Europe in 1991. Four versions of the MD-11 are produced and have been bought by airlines. These are all-passenger, combi, all-cargo and passenger/cargo convertible aircraft (see Variants), and a further developed version (the MD-12) awaits a formal launch. By 1986 MDC held 92 'commitments' from 12 airlines, and a full go-ahead was given in December that year. Construction of the first of five prototypes started in 1987, and assembly began in March 1988. After many delays, the first aircraft, powered by CF6-80 engines, flew on 10 January 1990 and after a four-plane, 2,000-hour test programme, FAA certification was achieved in November 1990. Deliveries to airlines began the same month when Finnair received its first aircraft. The total number of MD-11s sold at one time reached 180, but after airline mergers (BCAL and Minerve) and failures (Air Europe) plus some cancellations (Singapore, JAT and SAS), the current figure for firm orders stands at 127, with around 50 delivered to date.

The MD-11 has been born into a troubled air transport world and early problems in its flight test programme were of little help.

Variants

MD-11P: all-passenger version able to carry 293 people over 11000 km (7,000 miles), or 405 passengers in single economy-class seating; launch customer British Caledonian in 1986
MD-11 Combi: passenger/freight combination version typically able to carry 176 passengers and six cargo pallets (in aft cabin) on main deck plus more freight in underfloor compartments; Combi has 4 by 3 m (160 by 102 in) upward-opening cargo door on rear port fuselage side; launch customer Alitalia in April 1987
MD-11F: all-freight version fitted with 3.5 by 3 m (140 by 102 in) cargo door forward of wing on port side, with passenger doors and windows deleted; able to carry up to 102 tons of cargo on main and lower decks; launch customer Federal Express in May 1987
MD-11CF: convertible passenger/freight version under development for certification in 1994; passenger doors and windows retained; launch customer Martinair in August 1991

Specification
McDonnell Douglas MD-11P
Type: long-range jet airliner
Powerplant: either three 273-kN (61,500-lb) thrust General Electric CF6-80C2D1F turbofans or three 267-kN (60,000-lb) thrust Pratt & Whitney PW4460 turbofans
Performance: economical cruising speed at 10670 m (35,000 ft) 876 km/h (544 mph); maximum level speed at 8230 m (27,000 ft) 962 km/h (597 mph); service ceiling 9935 m (32,600 ft); range with maximum payload 9270 km (5,760 miles)
Weights: empty 125870 kg (277,500 lb); maximum payload 55655 kg (122,700 lb); maximum take-off 273300 kg (602,500 lb)
Dimensions: span 51.6 m (169 ft 6 in); length 61.2 m (200 ft 10 in); height 17.6 m (57 ft 9 in); wing area 338.9 m² (3,648 sq ft)

McDonnell Douglas MD-80

For operators of the DC-9 who sought to offset rising fuel costs of the mid-1970s, McDonnell Douglas proposed new versions of the DC-9-50. These appeared at different times as the Series 50RSS (Refanned Super-Stretch), the Series 55, and the Series 60. The definitive **DC-9 Super 80** was launched in October 1977, by which time MDC had secured 27 orders and nine options. These comprised 15 for launch customer Swissair, eight for Austrian Airlines and four for Southern Airways (later merged into Republic). By comparison with the DC-9-50, the wing span was increased by 4.39 m (14 ft 5 in) and fuselage length by 5.34 m (14 ft 2 in), allowing up to 172 passengers to be carried. Other improvements included aerodynamic refinements, updated systems, the introduction of a performance management system and more fuel-efficient Series 200 Pratt & Whitney JT8D turbofan engines.

In June 1983 the company adopted a new system of MD designations, breaking away from the old Douglas Commercial system. The Super 80 thus became the generic **MD-80**, with variants identifying the exact model. The first of three prototypes made its first flight on 19 October 1979 from Long Beach and, following a 1,000-hour flight test programme, the basic **MD-81** received FAA certification in August 1980, with first delivery to Swissair following swiftly in September. By April 1992, when McDonnell Douglas delivered the 1,000th aircraft to American Airlines (its 253rd), the MD-80 series order book was quoted as 1,137.

Variants
MD-81 (formerly the **Super 81**): basic version with two 82-kN (18,500-lb) thrust JT8D-209 turbofan engines; maximum take-off weight of 29200 kg (64,410 lb); typically carries 125 to 146 passengers
MD-82 (formerly the **Super 82**): powered by uprated Dash 217 engines

Already a confirmed DC-9 operator, Swissair was the launch customer for the MD-81, or DC-9 Super 81 as it was then known. The '81' referred to the year of the aircraft's design.

giving 89-kN (20,000-lb) thrust bestowing improved 'hot-and-high' performance; maximum take-off weight 67800 kg (149,500 lb); first flew on 8 January 1981 and went into service with Republic Airlines the following August; typical passenger load between 137 and 146; also built in China since 1986 under licence by the Shanghai Aviation Industrial Corporation, first locally-built aircraft flying for the first time on 2 July 1987
MD-83: fitted with extra fuel tanks, the heavier (MTOW 72600 kg; 16,000 lb) but longer-ranged MD-83 first flew on 17 December 1984; powered by slightly more powerful 93-kN (21,000-lb) thrust Dash 219 turbofans; fitted with a 'beefed-up' landing gear and brakes; Series 83 went into service with Alaska Airlines in February 1985.

Smallest of the current 'MD-family', the MD-87 is selling well to carriers who need an aircraft smaller than the 140-seat MD-80.

MD-87: in 1985 MDC announced a scaled-down version of the MD-80, fuselage shortened by 5.3 m (17 ft 4 in); capable of seating between 109 and 130 passengers, but fitted with the same engines, systems and flight deck; first flight took place on 4 December 1986 and first deliveries made to Finnair and Swissair after certification in November 1987

MD-88: launched in January 1986 in response to a requirement from Delta Airlines; basically standard MD-82 fitted with an advanced EFIS cockpit, plus windshear warning system; first flew on 15 August 1987 and first example delivered to Delta in January 1988; other carriers have ordered MD-88s including Aerolineas Argentinas and Aviaco

Specification
McDonnell Douglas MD-82
Type: medium-range twin-jet airliner
Powerplant: two 89-kN (20,000 lb) thrust Pratt & Whitney JT8D-217 turbofans
Performance: maximum cruising speed Mach 0.80; maximum level speed 925 km/h (575 mph); range with

McDonnell Douglas has used an MD-80 airframe as a high-tech engine testbed. Here it carries a PW-Allison 578-DX propfan.

155 passengers 3800 km (2,360 miles)
Weights: empty 35629 kg (78,549 lb); maximum payload 19709 kg (43,451 lb); maximum take-off 67900 kg (149,500 lb)
Dimensions: span 32.8 m (107 ft

10 in); length 45.0 m (147 ft 10 in); height 9.0 m (29 ft 8 in); wing area 118 m² (1,270 sq ft)

McDonnell Douglas MD-87
Type: medium-range twin-jet airliner
Powerplant: two 89-kN (20,000 lb) thrust Pratt & Whitney JT8D-217C turbofans
Performance: cruising speed Mach

0.80; maximum level speed 925 km/h (575 mph); range with 130 passengers 4395 km (2,731 miles)
Weights: empty 33183 kg (73,157 lb); maximum payload 17619 kg (38,843 lb); maximum take-off 65500 kg (140,000 lb)
Dimensions: span 32.8 m (107 ft 10 in); length 39.7 m (130 ft 5 in); height 9.3 m (30 ft 6 in); wing area 118 m² (1,270 sq ft)

McDonnell Douglas MD-90

Basically a re-engined and updated MD-80, and identified originally as the **DC-9 Super 90**, the type became the **MD-90** when formally launched in November 1989 on the back of 115 options taken by Delta Airlines. Intended to supplement the MD-80 on the Long Beach production line from the mid-1990s, three major versions have been announced to date, but only the Series 30 ordered. Delta became the launch customer when it converted 26 of its options into firm orders in January 1990, alongside Alaska Airlines (20), Japan Air Systems (six later increased to 10), and ILFC (15, subsequently cancelled). Construction of the prototype began in 1990 and first flight is scheduled for February 1993, with the second following in September. Certification is planned for August 1994, followed by first deliveries in October, simultaneously to Delta and Alaska Airlines.

The MD-90 has an identical fuselage cross-section, the advanced high-lift wing and EFIS cockpit of the MD-80, and variants defined by using selected modular components. The Pratt & Whitney JT8D-200 series engines have been replaced by advanced V2500 quiet low-emission turbofans.

In June 1992, after a protracted contest, mainly between Boeing and MDC, CATIC (China National Aero-Technology Import/Export Corporation) ordered a first batch of 20 **MD-90-30T**s (in kit form) to be assembled by the Shanghai Aviation Industrial Corporation, and took options on another 20. Ultimate Chinese requirement is for 170 **Trunkliners** (originally 150) to be delivered over 10 years, with the first due in 1997. Shortly

afterwards, in July 1992, SAS switched an outstanding order for seven MD-80s to the MD-90, bringing the total of firm orders to 83. The airline also optioned six more.

Variants
MD90-10: basic version powered by two 97-kN (22,000-lb) thrust V2522-D5 engines and intended to replace the MD-87; typical passenger configuration will be between 111 and 116

MD90-30: fuselage stretched by 1.45 m (4 ft 9 in) and powered by two 111-kN (25,000-lb) thrust V2525-D5 engines; intended to replace the MD-83; typical configuration 158 seats

MD90-30T Trunkliner: special 147-seat version developed to Chinese requirements with modified four-wheel tandem undercarriage to enable operations from poor runways

MD90-40: further stretched version (to 52.3 m; 171 ft 6 in), powered by two 124-kN (28,000-lb) thrust V2528-D5 engines; typical seating arrangements for 181 passengers; MDC estimate Series 40 first flight date to be the second quarter of 1994 with first delivery in mid-1995; projected **MD90-40EC** with increased fuel and payload intended for European use

MD90-50: projected version also with V2528-D5 engines announced by MDC in June 1992

Specification
McDonnell Douglas MD90-30
Type: medium-range twin-jet airliner
Powerplant: two 111-kN (25,000-lb) thrust International Aero Engines V2525-D5 advanced turbofans
Performance: cruising speed at 10670 m (35,000 ft) Mach 0.76; range 4329 km (2,690 miles)
Weight: empty 39275 kg (86,588 lb); maximum take-off 70760 kg (156,000 lb)
Dimensions: span 32.8 m (107 ft 8 in); length 46.5 m (152 ft 6 in); height 9.42 m (30 ft 11 in); wing area 112.3 m² (1,209 sq ft)

FAA certification for the MD-90 was granted in November 1994.

McDonnell Douglas MD-95

At the 1991 Paris air show, McDonnell Douglas announced an agreement with CATIC, Northwest Airlines and Pratt & Whitney to study the joint development of a new 105-125 seat jet airliner to replace the DC-9-30. Designated the **MD-95**, and fitted with the advanced EFIS cockpit of the MD-88 and a Cat IIIA

autoland system, the MD-95 would be offered with new quiet, clean, fuel-efficient versions of the P&W JT80, or the advanced Rolls-Royce Tay turbofan. Given a go-ahead before the end of 1992, the aircraft could be available for commercial service by late 1996 or early 1997. One proposal is that the Chengdu

Aircraft Corporation, already involved in the MD-82 programme, would build the aircraft for CATIC, which MDC would then market around the world. For its part, Northwest is looking for a replacement for its fleet of 142 DC-9-30s.

Specification (provisional)
McDonnell Douglas MD-95
Type: medium-range twin-jet airliner

Powerplant: two 74.0-kN (16,500-lb) thrust Pratt & Whitney JT8D-216 or two 79.5-kN (18,000-lb) thrust Rolls-Royce Tay 670 turbofans
Performance: cruising speed Mach 0.76; range 3240 km (2,014 miles)
Weight: maximum take-off 53700 kg (118,400 lb)
Dimensions: span 32.6 m (107 ft 10 in); length 37.3 m (122 ft 6 in); height 9.4 m (30 ft 9 in)

McDonnell Douglas/British Aerospace Harrier II

US Marine Corps experience with, and enthusiasm for, the Hawker Siddeley (HSA) **AV-8A Harrier** vertical take-off strike fighter led to proposals by McDonnell Douglas (MDC) and HSA to jointly develop an improved version for service with the USMC. However, the British government opted out of these plans in 1975, after which the two companies continued independent development. The **Harrier II** introduced much lighter composite materials into the structure, and these, together wirh advanced high-lift features such as supercritical wing and leading edge root extensions (LERX), were developed by the UK company to enhance a combat manoeuvrability. Another design objective was to increase available lift and thrust for short and vertical take-off operations without resort to a higher-powered engine. Other improvements included a strengthened landing gear, and extra weapon pylons.

Following a successful flight test programme using two **YAV-8B** testbeds modified from **AV-8A** airframes, four full-scale development aircraft were ordered in April 1979 and all were flying by June 1982. In August 1981 the definitive **AV-8B Harrier II** was ordered into full production, with the British company (by then part of British Aerospace) and MDC nominated as prime industrial partners, sharing the workload roughly 40 and 60 per cent respectively. The original USMC requirement for 257 Harrier IIs later stabilised at 328 aircraft, including 24 two-seaters, while the Royal Air Force ordered 60 single-seaters, designated Harrier **GR.Mk 5**. First deliveries from the twin Harrier II production lines were made to the USMC in October 1983 and initial operational capability achieved in mid-1985. Deliveries of Harrier GR.Mk 5s to the RAF began in May 1987. Shortly afterwards the USMC took delivery of the first Harrier II specially equipped for night attack missions. This allows round-the-clock close air support for ground troops and the new equipment – which includes a forward looking infra-red sensor, a digital moving map in colour, and night vision goggles for the pilot – was built into all USMC AV-8Bs completed after mid-1989.

In September 1990 Italy, Spain and the USA signed a joint Memorandum of Understanding to proceed with the further improved **Harrier II Plus**, a maritime strike version of the AV-8B equipped with a nose-mounted Hughes AN/APG-65 search radar, and a formal agreement covering full development was signed in February 1992. Twenty-four aircraft still to be built for the Marine Corps will be delivered as Harrier II Plus versions and a further six were ordered in June 1992 for delivery in 1993/94. The Spanish and Italian navies have optioned 30 more. The first aircraft is due to fly in October 1992.

Harrier II export orders have been received from the Spanish Navy (Armada/Marina) which ordered 12 **EAV-8Bs** in March 1983 to supplement their single- and two-seat **AV-8S Matadors** already in service with 8 Squadron on the carrier *Principe de Asturias*, and these

McDonnell Douglas AV-8B Harrier II of the United States Marine Corps

The AV-8 has made several significant naval sales, most recently to Italy. This Spanish AV-8B Matador serves with Nova Escuadrilla (nine squadron) of the Arma Aérea de la Armada (Spanish naval air arm) aboard the carrier Principé de Asturias. The unit was formed in September 1987.

were delivered to 9 Squadron between 1987 and September 1988. The Italian Navy ordered two **TAV-8Bs** in May 1989 to start training pilots for 16 Harrier Plus VTOL jets scheduled to operate from the aircraft-carrier *Guiseppi Garibaldi* in 1994. The TAV-8Bs were delivered in September 1991, and the Italians have since announced their intention of raising the single-seat Harrier fleet to 24 aircraft. The RAF has also ordered 13 two-seat TAV-8B trainers, compatible with its fleet of night attack Harrier GR.Mk 5/7s, to equip No. 233 OCU at Wittering, and these will be designated **T.Mk 10**.

Variants

AV-8B Harrier II: basic close air support version acquired by the US Marine Corps (300) and the Spanish Navy (12); first of two YAV-8Bs, converted from AV-8As, flew on 19 November 1978 at Lambert St Louis airport, Missouri; first production AV-8B delivered to USMC October 1983; original powerplant was the 92-kN (21,450-lb) thrust F402-RR-406A (Pegasus 11-21) but aircraft delivered from December 1990 are fitted with the F402-RR-408 (Pegasus 11-61)

AV-8B Night Attack Harrier II: the 167th and subsequent AV-8Bs were

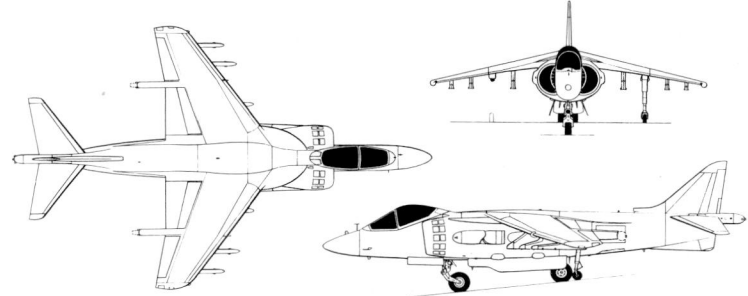

McDonnell Douglas/BAe AV-8B Harrier II

equipped with a GEC FLIR and the pilot equipped with night vision goggles to give full night attack capability; first aircraft was a converted AV-8B and flew on 26 June 1987; production deliveries to the US Marine Corps began in September 1989

AV-8B Harrier II Plus: first publicised in June 1987, the radar-equipped night attack version will also be used for anti-shipping strike using Sea Eagle and Harpoon missiles; fitted with the F402-RR-408 engine, enlarged LERXs, and enhanced air-to-air missile capability allowing the carriage of Sparrow and AMRAAM

EAV-8B: designation of 12 standard single-seat AV-8Bs for Spanish Navy

TAV-8B: designation of Harrier II two-seat trainer in service with USMC (24), and Italian Navy (two); first flew on 21 October 1986 with initial delivery to USMC in March 1987

Harrier GR.Mk 5: variant of AV-8B for RAF but with some equipment changes, including Pegasus 105 engine

of 95-kN (21,500-lb) thrust, and two 25-mm ADEN cannon; fitted with nine weapon stations under the fuselage and wings, the extra two wing points being intended for self-defence Sidewinder AAMs; two development prototypes plus 60 production aircraft ordered in 1982; 40 built to GR.Mk 5 standard, while the following 22 completed to interim **GR.Mk 5A** standard (without FLIR); contract awarded to BAe in 1990 calls for 58 GR.Mk 5/5As to be updated to **GR.Mk 7s**, and the conversion programme is currently underway with about 12 completed to date

Harrier GR.Mk 7: 34 ordered as GR.Mk 5s in April 1988 but delivered to GR.Mk 7 standard from 1990; very similar to the Night Attack AV-8B, the aircraft is basically a GR.Mk 5 with night attack capability provided by nose-mounted FLIR sensor, digital moving map and cockpit compatible with night vision goggles; last new-build aircraft delivered in June 1992,

but conversion of GR.Mk 5s continues
Harrier GR.Mk 9: variant of GR.Mk 5 proposed for RAF with Pegasus 11-61 engine and AIM-120 missile capability; not adopted
Harrier T.Mk 10: RAF version of TAV-8B two-seat trainer but with night attack capability; contract for 13 placed in August 1992

Specification
MDC/BAe AV-8B Harrier II Plus
Type: short take-off and vertical landing jet fighter/attack aircraft
Powerplant: one 105.8 kN (23,800 lb) thrust Rolls-Royce F402-RR-408 Pegasus 11-61 turbofan
Performance: maximum speed at sea level 1065 km/h (661 mph); maximum speed at altitude Mach 0.92;

combat radius with two Harpoons, two Sidewinders and two 1136-litre (250-Imp gal) drop tanks 1128 km (701 miles)
Weights: empty 6344 kg (13,968 lb); maximum external warload 6003 kg (13,235 lb); maximum take-off 14061 kg (31,000 lb); maximum VTO 9342 kg (20,595 lb)
Dimensions: span 9.25 m (30 ft 4 in); length 14.5 m (47 ft 9 in); height 3.5 m

(11 ft 8 in); wing area 21.3 m² (230 sq ft)
Armament: one 25-mm cannon mounted in an underfuselage pod with ammunition in the other, plus eight wing pylons capable of carrying six AIM-9 Sidewinder air-to-air missiles, or four Maverick laser guided air-to-surface missiles, six Mk 83 or 15 Mk 82 bombs, or 12 rocket pods, or four 1136-litre (250-Imp gal) drop tanks

McDonnell Douglas AH-64 Apache

Originally designed by Hughes Helicopters to meet a US Army requirement for an Advanced Attack Helicopter (AAH) for day or night adverse weather missions against armoured vehicles, the Model 77 was selected for production as the **AH-64** in December 1976 following competitive evaluation (as the **YAH-64**) against the YAH-63 submitted by Bell. The first two YAH-64 prototypes were flown on 30 September and 22 November 1975, and named **Apache** in 1981. The first production Apache flew in January 1984 from Mesa, Arizona, and first deliveries were made to Fort Rucker, Alabama, in January 1985.

This remarkably agile helicopter has four-bladed main and tail rotors, is powered by two General Electric T700 turboshaft engines, has stub wings incorporating trailing-edge flaps and an all-moving tailplane to enhance conventional helicopter controllability. Its crew of two are seated in tandem in an armour-protected cockpit, the pilot to the rear on an elevated seat, and the co-pilot/gunner forward. Keys to the capability of the Apache are the co-pilot/gunner's Target Acquisition and Designation System (TADS) and the Pilot's Night Vision Sensor (PNVS) systems. TADS is a complex device incorporating a laser designator/range-finder and tracker, and forward-looking infra-red, which is backed by direct-view optics and a TV system. The PNVS is effectively an advanced FLIR system which provides the pilot with data allowing nap-of-the-earth flight in a combat area, and at altitudes that will prevent or delay detection by the enemy.

The US Army plans to procure 807 AH-64s and deliveries started in January

1985. By December 1991 700 had been delivered and the last is scheduled to join the US Army in December 1993. Known export customers for the so-called **International Apache** are Israel, which received 18 Petans (Cobra) between September 1990 and October 1991; Saudi Arabia, which ordered 12 for delivery beginning later in 1992; Egypt (24), with first deliveries in 1994; Greece (12); and the United Arab Emirates (20). Others are reported to be on order for Bahrain (eight), South Korea and Kuwait.

Apaches were used in Operation Just Cause in Panama in 1989 and during Desert Storm in 1991, 15 US Army battalions equipped with 228 AH-64s wrought havoc among Iraqi armour.

At the end of 1990 full-scale development was authorised of a new version incorporating a mast-mounted Martin/Westinghouse Longbow millimetre-wave fire control radar system in combination with the 'fire and forget' Rockwell AGM-114 Hellfire anti-tank missile. An aerodynamic mock-up of the **AH-64D** flew for the first time on 11 March 1991. Production versions will also have the more powerful Dash 701C engine. A more modest update without the Longbow radar and uprated engine is designated **AH-64C**. The first of four AH-64D prototypes being built to undertake the 2,000-hour test programme flew for the first time on 15 April 1992. The first of 535 AH-64C/D conversions are scheduled to enter service in 1996.

Variants
AH-64B: conversion of 254 AH-64As with minimal improvements derived from Desert Storm experience
AH-64C: interim updated AH-64A but

without Longbow radar and Dash 701C engine
AH-64D Longbow Apache: full update of AH-64A including Longbow/Hellfire integration and T700-GE-701C engine; 227 to be converted
International Apache: export version of AH-64A

Entering US Army service in 1985, the high point of the AH-64's career so far has been its performance in Operation Desert Storm where it fired the first shots. The latest version is the Longbow Apache, with its millimetric-band radar.

Specification
McDonnell Douglas AH-64D Longbow
Type: advanced attack helicopter
Powerplant: two 1417-kW (1900-shp) General Electric T700-GE-701C turboshafts
Performance: maximum speed 309 km/h (192 mph); service ceiling 6250 m (20,500 ft); maximum range on internal fuel 611 km (380 miles)
Weights: empty 4657 kg (10,268 lb); maximum warload 771 kg (1,700 lb); maximum take-off 8006 kg (17,650 lb)

Dimensions: main rotor diameter 14.6 m (48 ft 0 in); length, rotor turning 17.3 m (57 ft); height 4.2 m (13 ft 10 in); main rotor disc area 168.1 m² (1,809 sq ft)
Armament: Hughes XM230E1 30-mm automatic cannon in underfuselage turret, plus four hardpoints under stub wings for up to 16 Hellfire anti-tank missiles or 76 70-mm folding-fin rockets, or combinations of the two

McDonnell Douglas Explorer

The MDX McDonnell Douglas Experimental helicopter programme was revealed in February 1988 and a decision to develop a production vehicle announced in January 1989. Final go-ahead was approved by the MDH board in April 1992. Formally named the **Explorer** in March 1992, the MDX was evolved to embody the NOTAR (NO TAil Rotor) and HARP all-composite five-bladed main rotor technologies into a new eight to 10-seat light commercial helicopter. Risk-sharing partners are Hawker de Havilland of Australia, responsible for the de-

sign and manufacture of the fuselage for delivery to the MDH factory at Mesa for completion, and Kawasaki Heavy Industries which manufacture the transmission. Dual engine selection, one from Pratt & Whitney and the other from Turboméca, is being offered to customers, and current plans call for the first 100 aircraft to have PW206A engines. First flight is planned for December 1992, certification for early 1994 and initial customer deliveries later that year. By March 1992 MDH were claiming 257 'certificates of interest' (paid deposits)

for the Explorer. Target price in 1990 was $2.3 million each (now $2.73 m). The company is also studying the possible submission of the Explorer for the US Army Light Utility Helicopter (LUH) programme.

Specification (provisional)
McDonnell Douglas Explorer
Type: eight-seat twin-engined turbine-powered helicopter
Powerplants: two 450-kW (638-shp) Pratt & Whitney Canada PW206A or similar rated Turboméca TM319-2C

Arrius turboshafts
Performance: cruising speed 278 km/h (172 mph); maximum speed 322 km/h (200 mph); range with full payload 584 km (316 miles)
Weights: empty 1260 kg (2,780 lb); internal payload 1150 kg (2,550 lb); on external cargo hook 1360 kg (3,000 lb); maximum take-off 2540 kg (5,800 lb)
Dimensions: main rotor diameter; 10.3 m (33 ft 9 in); rotors turning 11.6 m (38 ft 2 in); height to top of rotor head 3.74 m (12 ft 4 in); main rotor disc area 11.1 m² (120 sq ft)

McDonnell Douglas MD520/530 Series

In January 1984, when Hughes Helicopters became a subsidiary of McDonnell Douglas, development continued of military and civil versions of the **Model 500** and these remain in production as the **MD500E** and the **MD530 Lifter** (optimised for load carrying). Following the development, construction and flight testing (on 17 December 1981) of a

NOTAR (NO TAil Rotor) testbed based on a Hughes 500 airframe, certificated versions went into volume production as the **MD520N** (a NOTAR version of the MD500) and the **MD530N** (a NOTAR version of the MD530F). Output from the Mesa, Arizona, line is already sold out to 1994. The definitive MD530N prototype flew on 29 December 1989, fol-

lowed by the MD520N on 1 May 1990. A production MD520N flew in June 1991 and certification followed on 17 September the same year.

First customer to put the MD520N into service was the Phoenix City Police Department in October 1991, when they received the first of seven ordered earlier. By July 1992 20 had been de-

livered to customers in the US, South Korea, Switzerland, France, Venezuela, Guatemala and Canada. In 1991 the US Army awarded MDH a contract to convert two standard AH/MH-6E 'Little Bird' stealthy light attack helicopters to the NOTAR configuration. These were delivered to the elite 160th Special Operations Aviation Regiment based at Fort Campbell, Kentucky, in July 1992 for further evaluation.

Specification
McDonnell Douglas MD530N
Type: five-seat light utility helicopter
Powerplant: one 485-kW (650-shp) Allison 250-C30 turboshaft
Performance: maximum cruising speed at sea level 249 km/h (155 mph); normal range at sea level 354 km (220 miles)
Weights: empty 742 kg (1,636 lb); maximum take-off 1519 kg (3,350 lb)
Dimensions: main rotor diameter 8.33 m (24 ft 6 in); rotor turning 8.69 m (28 ft 6 in); height to top of rotor head (standard skids) 2.74 m (9 ft 0 in); main rotor disc area 5.45 m² (586.8 sq ft)

McDonnell Douglas has pioneered NOTAR (NO TAil Rotor) technology and is the first manufacturer to offer it on a production helicopter. US Army special operations MH-6s are also being modified to this standard.

Mercury aircraft

Mercury Aircraft Inc. of Hammondsport, New York, produced its first original design, a three-seat enclosed cabin monoplane known as the **Mercury Kitten**, in 1928. This failed to gain any commercial interest and the company then concentrated on the development of a two-seat primary trainer, designated **Mercury Chic T-2**. A lightweight parasol-wing monoplane with a basic structure of welded steel tube, entirely fabric-covered, the Chic T-2 had fixed tailskid landing gear and accommodated pilot and pupil passenger in tandem open cockpits. As first flown in late 1928 it was underpowered by a 48-kW (65-hp) Velie radial engine, and was quickly modified to accept a 67-kW (90-hp) LeBlond 7D radial. This became the standard powerplant, providing the 10.87 m (35 ft 8 in) span trainer with a maximum speed of 185 km/h (115 mph). The company hoped to gain worthwhile orders, but it was the wrong time for such an aircraft, and although about 15 were sold before the economic depression of the early 1930s, almost as many remained unsold and were eventually scrapped.

Meridionali helicopters

Elicotteri Meridionali SpA was formed with assistance from Costruzioni Aeronautica Giovanni Agusta primarily to service Italian armed forces helicopters, and operations began in October 1967. In 1968 the company acquired rights to produce, market and maintain Boeing CH-47C Chinooks in service in Italy and certain other countries, this operation being centred at the Sesto Calende works. Despite sweeping recent industry mergers, EM remains an independent entity affiliated to Agusta. The company was responsible for the EMA 124 three-seat light helicopter derived from the Bell 47 built under licence by Agusta in the 1950s.

The Meridionali EMA 124 bears more than a passing resemblance to the Bell Model 47 on which it was based. However, the Italian aircraft had considerably more aerodynamic refinement than its American counterpart.

Messerschmitt Bf 108 Taifun

Until the outbreak of World War II, Willy Messerschmitt's M.35 proved to be one of the world's outstanding aerobatic aircraft; from it was developed the revolutionary **Messerschmitt M.37**, which was later designated **Bf 108 Taifun** (typhoon). This originated from an order for aircraft to compete in the 4th Challenge de Tourisme Internationale of 1934, six aircraft being built to fulfil this contract. The prototype (D-ILIT) began flight tests in the spring of 1934, and was a cantilever low-wing monoplane with retractable main landing gear and tailskid, an enclosed cabin seating four, and powered by a 186-kW (250-hp) Hirth HM 8U engine; the type was tested also with the 164-kW (220-hp) Argus As 17 engine. The production **Bf 108A** aircraft were unsuccessful in the Tourisme Internationale, the handicapping system favouring lighter and less advanced designs, but the Bf 108A's high performance meant that in the late 1930s the type was used to make a number of record flights and also gained some competition success. The Bf 108 was adopted by the Luftwaffe in the communications role, was used by the Luftdienst for tasks such as supply and target towing, and was also exported in some numbers to Bulgaria, Hungary, Japan, Romania, the Soviet Union, Switzerland and Yugoslavia. With the outbreak of war, two German embassy Bf 108s were impressed for RAF service, named Messerschmitt Aldons; several others served with the RAF for a short time after the war. Manufactured in Germany until 1942, when production was transferred to the SNCAN factory at Les Mureaux, near Paris, a total of 885 had been built by the end of the war. SNCAN (Nord) continued development of the type after the war, building both the Bf 108 (as the **Nord 1002 Pingouin**) and **Me 208** in several versions to a total of about 285 aircraft. A few original Bf 108s and a number of Nord-built examples are still flying.

Variants
Bf 108B: major production version with a number of improvements, including a tailwheel replacing the tailskid, and powered by the 201-kW (270-hp) Argus As 10c engine
Bf 108C: proposed high-speed version with a 298-kW (400-hp) Hirth HM 512 engine; not built
Me 208: improved version with retractable tricycle landing gear; two prototypes built by SNCAN during the war, one of which was destroyed in an air raid

In its definitive form, the Taifun became known as Messerschmitt Bf 108B. Apart from being fitted with a more powerful engine, it differed from the Bf 108A in having an aerodynamically-balanced rudder and elevators. The Bf 108 series marked the beginning of a new era for the company by the introduction of low-wing cantilever monoplanes of stressed-skin construction. The wings had a patented single spar, trailing-edge flaps and automatic leading-edge slats.

Specification
Messerschmitt Bf 108B
Type: four-seat cabin monoplane
Powerplant: one 179-kW (240-hp) Argus As 10C engine
Performance: maximum speed 300 km/h (186 mph); service ceiling 5000 m (16,405 ft); maximum range 1000 km (621 miles)
Weights: empty 880 kg (1,940 lb); maximum take-off 1385 kg (3,053 lb)
Dimensions: span 10.50 m (34 ft 5½ in); length 8.30 m (27 ft 2¾ in); height 2.30 m (7 ft 6½ in); wing area 16.40 m² (176.53 sq ft)

Messerschmitt Bf 109
to
Messerschmitt Me 309

Messerschmitt Bf 109

In the mid-1930s the build-up of the Luftwaffe provided the impetus for considerable updating of both fighter and bomber concepts. Willy Messerschmitt was then well advanced with design of the Bf 108 and, before it flew, had already started work on a single-seat fighter, the **Messerschmitt Bf 109**. It was to fly in competition against Arado Ar 80, Focke-Wulf Fw 159 and Heinkel He 112 prototypes, the Bf 109 and He 112 then being selected for further development with an order for 10 examples of each. The original Bf 109 prototype, first flown on 28 May 1935, was powered by a 518-kW (695-hp) Rolls-Royce Kestrel engine, but the second had the 455-kW (610-hp) Junkers Jumo 210A for which the aircraft had been designed. The preproduction protypes had various combinations of armament, the first three becoming **Bf 109A** aircraft, while later examples served as prototypes of the **Bf 109B**. Early sub-variants included the **Bf 109B-1** with a 474-kW (635-hp) Jumo 210D engine and the **Bf 109B-2** with a 477-kW (640-hp) Jumo 210E, the latter soon replaced by the 500-kW (670-hp) Jumo 210G.

Production 109B-1s were delivered first in early 1937 to the Luftwaffe's top fighter unit, JG 132 'Richthofen', and like several other German types the Bf 109 was blooded first in the Spanish Civil War, serving with the Legion Condor from the summer of 1937. Just before that, five non-standard Bf 109s took part in an international flying meeting in Zurich, two of them with 708-kW (950-hp) Daimler-Benz engines which conferred higher performance. The team won the Circuit of the Alps contest, plus a team race, a speed event, and a climb and dive competition. This success was crowned on 11 November 1937 when a Bf 109, flown by Dr-Ing. Hermann Wurster, raised the landplane world speed record to 610.55 km/h (379.38 mph), using a boosted DB 601 engine of 1230 kW (1,650 hp).

Meanwhile, production deliveries were continuing with the Bf 109B, supplanted gradually by the **Bf 109C-1** with the 522-kW (700-hp) Jumo 210Ga engine. Output was then being stepped up, with the fighters being built also by Arado, Erla, Focke-Wulf and Feiseler, and by September 1938 almost 600 had been produced. A year later, when World War II began, the Luftwaffe had more than 1,000 Bf 109s in service, but following the collapse of France no serious effort was made to increase production, then averaging about 156 aircraft per month. By 1941 only Messerschmitt, Erla and WNF (Austria) were building Bf 109s, but in 1942 production by Messerschmitt reached almost 2,700, and was supplemented during 1943 by production in Hungary, where around 600 were built. In spite of heavy Allied bombing, Bf 109 manufacture in Germany during 1944 reached almost 14,000, and although no accurate overall production figures exist it is estimated that some 35,000 were built, a figure second only to the Ilyushin Il-2/Il-10 series, of which 42,330 are reported to have been produced.

Messerschmitt Bf 109 of 1./JG 1, based at Seerapen (Germany) in August 1939.

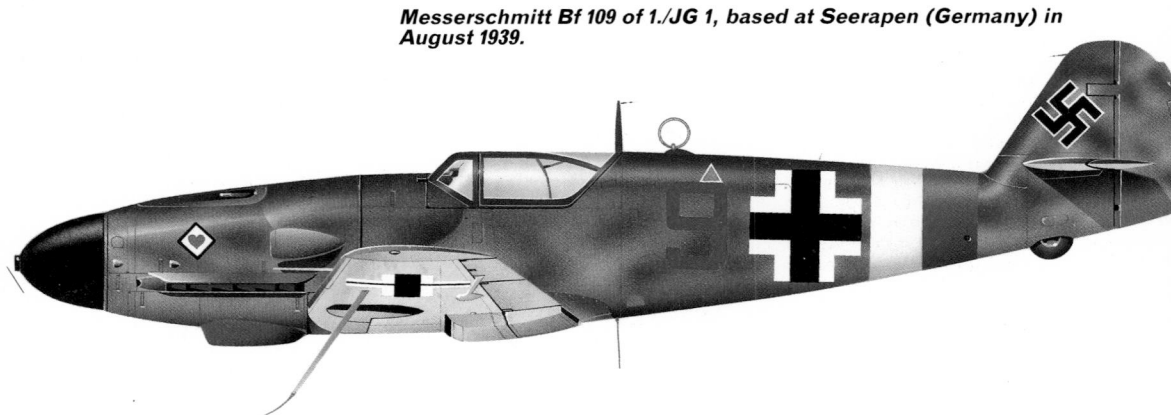

Bf 109s had taken part in the attack on Poland which had marked the beginning of World War II and had played a significant role in all subsequent Luftwaffe fighter operations, making their last major sortie, involving 120 aircraft, on 7 April 1945. In addition to production for the Luftwaffe, Messerschmitt had exported Bf 109s to Bulgaria, Finland, Hungary, Japan, Romania, Slovakia, Spain, Switzerland, the USSR and Yugoslavia. Hispano, in Spain, produced the Bf 109 for the Spanish air force under a licence negotiated in 1942, the first **Ha-1109-J1L**, combining Messerschmitt-built sample airframes and early Hispano-Suiza engines, being flown from early March 1945. Subsequent production included the **HA-1109-K1L** with the French Hispano-Suiza HS-12Z-89 engine of 969 kW (1,300 hp), **HA-1109-M1L** with the Rolls-Royce Merlin 500-45 engine of 1044 kW (1,400 hp), and the generally similar **HA-1112** with revised armament. Corresponding two-seat trainer versions were the **HA-1110-K1L** and **HA-1110-K1L** with Hispano-Suiza engines, and the **HA-1110-M1L** with the Merlin engine. One other source of production was in Czechoslovakia which, post-war, equipped its air force with the **Avia S-99** (with DB 605A engines) and a far larger number of **S-199** aircraft with Jumo 211F engines; they remained in service until 1957, being used for the last five years in a training role.

Only the major variants and sub-variants of the Bf 109 in German service are listed below.

Variants
Bf 109A: initial prototypes with Rolls-Royce Kestrel and Junkers Jumo engines

Messerschmitt Bf 109K-4 of II./JG 77 based at Bönningheim (Germany), in December 1944.

Bf 109B: the preproduction **Bf 109B-0** had the 455-kW (610-hp) Jumo 210B engine; the production **Bf 109B-1** and **Bf 109B-2** had Jumo 210D and Jumo 210E engines of 474 kW (635 hp) and 477 kW (640 hp) respectively
Bf 109C: built as **Bf 109C-0** and sub-variants **Bf 109C-1** to **Bf 109C-3**, all powered by the 477-kW (640-hp) Jumo 210G, but with differing armament
Bf 109D: the **Bf 109D-0** aircraft, converted from Bf 109B airframes, plus a small number of production **Bf 109D-1** aircraft, were the first (except for prototypes) to introduce the 716-kW (960-hp) Daimler-Benz DB 600A engine
Bf 109E: first large-scale production

version, introducing the 820-kW (1,100-hp) Daimler-Benz DB 601A engine with direct fuel injection and improved super-chargers; sub-variants were designated **Bf 109E-0** to **Bf 109E-9**, with 895-kW (1,200-hp) DB 601N or 969-kW (1,300-hp) DB 601E engines and variations in armament
Bf-109F: production version, in sub-variants from **Bf 109F-0** to **Bf 109F-6**, with DB 601N or DB 601E engines and variations of armament; introduced a number of airframe refinements resulting in improved performance at altitude
Bf 109G: major production version with provision for cockpit

Messerschmitt Bf 109G-14

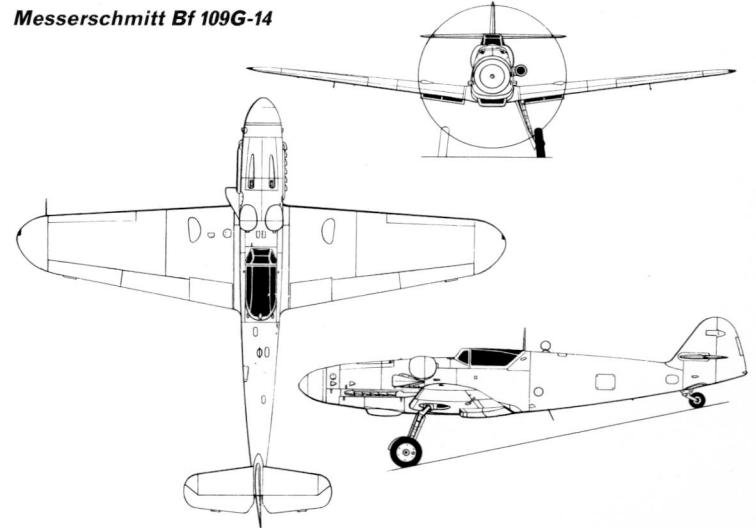

pressurisation, in sub-variants from **Bf 109G-0** to **Bf 109G-16**; proving to be of no significant value, pressurisation provision was deleted from Bf 109G-6 and subsequent sub-variants; Bf 109G-0s retained the DB 601E engine, but the Bf 109G-1 was the first to introduce the new DB 605A engine of higher compression ratio, developing a maximum 1100 kW (1,475 hp); later versions of this engine, the DB 605DC for example, produced a maximum of 1491 kW (2,000 hp) with water/methanol injection; the Bf 109G-12 differed by being a tandem two-seat trainer

Bf 109H: high-altitude development of the Bf 109F with a 2.00 m (6 ft 6¾ in) increase in wing span, built in small numbers; **Bf 109H-0** aircraft had DB 601E engines, and **Bf 109H-1** aircraft the DB 605A
Bf 109K: production version built as **Bf 109K-0** with DB 605D engine; **Bf 109K-2** and **Bf 109K-4** with 1119-kW (1,500-hp) DB 605ASCM/DCM; **Bf 109K-6** similar to the Bf 109K-2 but with different armament; and **Bf 109K-14** with the DB 605L engine
Bf 109T: initially 10 conversions of the Bf 109E as **Bf 109T-0**, with increased wing span, foldable outer wing panels,

wing spoilers, arrester hook and catapult spools for service aboard the aircraft-carrier *Graf Zeppelin*; followed by 60 generally similar **Bf 109T-1** production aircraft with the DB 601N engine; however, when work on the aircraft-carrier ended, these aircraft had the arrester hooks and catapult spools removed, becoming redesignated **Bf 109T-2**

Specification
Messerschmitt Bf 109G-6
Type: single-seat fighter
Powerplant: one Daimler-Benz DB 605AM inverted V-12 piston engine

developing 1342 kW (1,800 hp) with water/methanol injection
Performance: maximum speed 621 km/h (386 mph) at 7000 m (22,965 ft); service ceiling 11750 m (38,550 ft); range 720 km (447 miles)
Weights: empty equipped 2673 kg (5,893 lb); maximum take-off 3150 kg (6,945 lb)
Dimensions: span 9.92 m (32 ft 6½ in); length 9.02 m (29 ft 7 in); height 3.40 m (11 ft 2 in); wing area 16.05 m^2 (127.77 sq ft)
Armament: two 13-mm (0.51-in) MG 131 machine-guns and three 20-mm MG 151 cannon

Messerschmitt Bf 110

The **Messerschmitt Bf 110** was the company's submission to a Luftwaffe requirement for a twin-engine fighter, for which Focke-Wulf and Henschel also prepared designs. Primary role was that of a heavy fighter, but the capability of being deployed as a high-speed bomber was also stipulated. Changes in requirements for the fighter resulted in Messerschmitt being the only candidate, and the first of three prototypes was flown on 12 May 1936. The two 679-kW (910-hp) Daimler-Benz DB 600A engines proved very unreliable, but a speed of 505 km/h (314 mph) was recorded during tests and the general performance was considered reasonable. Engine unreliability plagued the three prototypes, but the pre-production batch of **Bf 110A-0** aircraft had reliable 507-kW (680-hp) Junkers Jumo 210Da engines which resulted in a considerable performance penalty. The long wait for the new fuel-injection DB 601A seriously delayed the Bf 110 programme; after the fourth preproduction aircraft had been completed in March 1938, the company switched to the **Bf 110B**, a cleaned-up version with provision for two 20-mm cannon to supplement the four machine-guns of the Bf 110A-0, a total of 45 being built with Jumo engines. They comprised the **Bf 110B-1**, the camera-carrying **Bf 110B-2**, and a few Bf 110B-1s that were modified subsequently for use as two-seat trainers under the designation **Bf 110B-3**.

Availability of DB 601A engines led to the introduction of the **Bf 110C**, initially in the form of 10 preproduction **Bf 110C-0** aircraft delivered for evaluation in January 1939, and followed closely by the first **Bf 110C-1** series fighters. As production built up, Focke-Wulf and Gotha joined the programme. The new fighter first proved its capabilities during the Polish campaign, and in December 1939 confirmed its value as a bomber destroyer by shooting down nine out of 22 Vickers Wellingtons on a mission over the Heligoland Bight. Early use had shown the importance of the Bf 110, production priority ensuring that 315 had been delivered by the end of 1939 and a production rate averaging 102 per month throughout 1940.

However, in 1940 the Bf 110 began to encounter opposition from modern single-engine fighters for the first time and was found unable to match the manoeuvrability of the Hawker Hurricane and Supermarine Spitfire; with only a single rear-firing gun the Bf 110 was unable to defend itself adequately, and from the beginning of the Battle of Britain Bf 110 units suffered very heavy losses. The type was deployed temporarily on bombing and reconnaissance missions, but in the winter of 1940-4 found its most suitable role as a night-fighter.

Initially the Bf 110 night-fighter had no specialised equipment, crews relying upon keen eyesight for the interception of enemy bombers. An early airborne aid was an infra-red sensor carried by the **Bf 110D-1/U-1**, which proved to be a failure, but in mid-1941 ground-controlled interception was becoming established and very soon the Bf 110 night-fighter units were achieving important success. Twelve months later they were being equipped with *Lichtenstein* air-interception radar, and by the autumn of 1942 most Luftwaffe night-fighters carried a version of this airborne aid. In mid-1943 the RAF countered this capability by introducing the radar-jamming bundles of aluminium foil strips known as 'Window', gaining an ascendancy that lasted for some six months before the Bf 110s were equipped with more advanced radar that could be effective despite 'Window' jamming. In early 1944 the German night-fighter force was at the peak of its capability, and at this time some 320 Bf 110s were deployed in this role, representing about 60 per cent of the total night-fighters available for defence of the German homeland. A year later more advanced night-fighters had entered service, only 150 Bf 110s then being operational with the night-fighter groups, and all became rapidly less and less effective as German fuel supplies dried up.

Produced in many variants, about 6,050 Bf 110s had been built when production ended in March 1945. Minor variants were legion, and only the more important versions are listed below.

Variants
Bf 110A-0: designation of four preproduction aircraft with Junkers Jumo 210B engines
Bf 110B: initial production version, produced in sub-variants **Bf 110B-0** to **Bf 110B-2**, the **Bf 110B-3** being a conversion of earlier aircraft
Bf 110C: production version introducing two 820-kW (1,100-hp) Daimler-Benz DB 601A fuel-injection engines; built in sub-variants **Bf 110C-0** to **Bf 110C-7**, the **Bf 110C-4** showing its capability as a fighter-bomber and the **Bf 110C-5** as a reconnaissance aircraft
Bf 110D: production version, built in sub-variants **Bf 110D-0** to **Bf 110D-3**, and including the **Bf 110D-2** long-range fighter-bomber and **Bf 110D-3** convoy escort
Bf 110E: production version, built in sub-variants **Bf 110E-0** to **Bf 110E-3**, the **Bf 110E-1** and **Bf 110E-2** being fighter-bombers or night-fighters, and the **Bf 110E-3** a long-range reconnaissance version
Bf 110F: production version, generally as Bf 110E, but introducing 1007-kW

(1,350-hp) DB 601F engines; built in sub-variants up to **Bf 110F-4**
Bf 110G: production version, introducing 1100-kW (1,475-hp) DB 601B-1 engines; built in sub-variants up to **Bf 110G-4**
Bf 110H: final production version, basically similar to Bf 110G; built in sub-variants up to **Bf 110H-4**

Specification
Messerschmitt Bf 110G/R3
Type: three-seat night-fighter
Powerplant: two 1100-kW (1,475-hp) Daimler-Benz DB 601B-1 inverted V-12 piston engines
Performance: maximum speed 550 km/h (342 mph) at 6980 m (22,900 ft); service ceiling 8000 m (26,245 ft); maximum range with drop tanks 2100 km (1,305 miles)
Weights: empty 5090 kg (11,222 lb); maximum take-off 9890 kg (21,804 lb)
Dimensions: span 16.25 m (53 ft 3¾ in); length 13.05 m (42 ft 9¾ in);

A Messerschmitt Bf 110E-2 fighter-bomber shows off features such as the extended tail (which housed a dingy) and external bomb racks (paired ETC 50 racks under the wings and two ETC 500 racks under the fuselage). These permitted the carriage of up to 1200 kg (2,645 lb) of bombs. The Bf 110E succeeded the Bf 110D, which itself was a longer-range version of the Bf 110C. Powered by a pair of Daimler-Benz 601E engines, the E series also formed the nucleus of the Luftwaffe's initial night-fighter units.

height 4.18 m (13 ft 8½ in); wing area 39.40 m^2 (413.35 sq ft)
Armament: two 30-mm MK 108 cannon and two 20-mm MG 151 cannon in nose, and two 7.92-mm (0.31-in) MG 81 machine-guns on trainable mount in rear cockpit

Messerschmitt Bf 110C-3

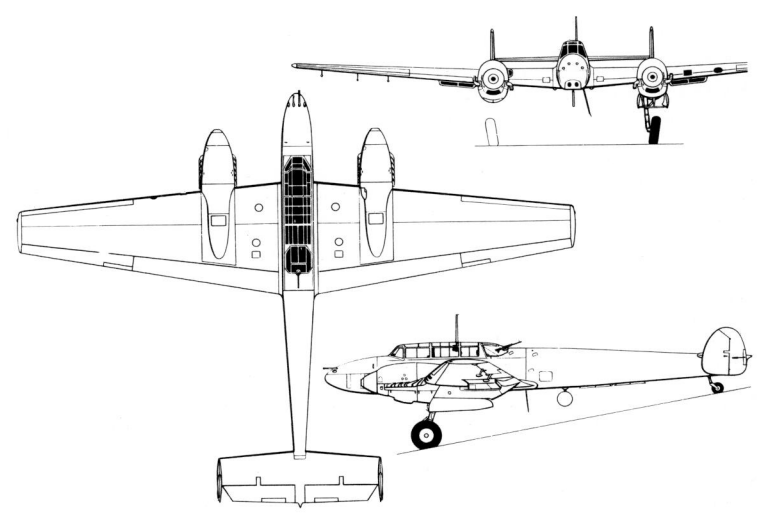

Messerschmitt Bf 161

After early testing of the Messerschmitt Bf 110, the company was contracted to proceed with development of similar specialised reconnaissance and bomber aircraft designated **Messerschmitt Bf 161** and **Bf 162** respectively. Of generally similar appearance and configuration to the Bf 110 they were, however, quite new aircraft with few components in common. First to fly, in the spring of 1937, was the **Bf 162 V1** (D-AIXA) followed by two more prototypes, but it was then decided that Messerschmitt should concentrate on fighter/reconnaissance types and development of

D-AOBE was a Bf 162 V2, and was the aircraft which Messerschmitt entered for the Luftwaffe's Schnellbomber competition in the late 1930s. It was beaten by the Junkers offering, the superlative Ju 88.

the Bf 162 was halted; the three prototypes were used for sundry research and development tasks. Two prototypes of

the Bf 161 were flown, but their fate was the same as that of the Bf 162s when it

was realised that versions of the Bf 110 could well fulfil the reconnaissance role.

Messerschmitt Me 163 Komet

The remarkable **Messerschmitt Me 163 Komet** (comet) rocket-powered fighter was developed from the designs of Dr Alexander Lippisch who, for many years, had been working on tailless sailplane designs. In January 1939 he and his design team joined the Messerschmitt company and began work to adapt the **DFS 194** tailless research glider to be powered by a 400-kg (882-lb) thrust Walter rocket motor. Successful testing of this aircraft, during which a speed of 550 km/h (342 mph) was attained, resulted in Messerschmitt receiving an order for six **Me 163A** prototypes.

The first prototype was tested initially as a glider, towed by a Messerschmitt Bf 110. Prototypes were tested at Peenemünde in the summer of 1941 powered by the Walter HWK RII-203b rocket motor of 750-kg (1,653-lb) thrust, and demonstrated speeds of up to 885 km/h (550 mph). Flown by Heini Dittmar, an Me 163A, towed to a height of 4000 m (13,125 ft) before the engine was fired, attained 1003.9 km/h (623.85 mph) before losing stability as a result of compressibility effects. Dittmar succeeded in regaining control, and the wing was redesigned to alleviate this problem. There were many development problems, those posed by the highly unstable liquid fuel for the rocket motor and by the jettisonable wheeled dolly/retractable skid landing gear being the most difficult to resolve. Following the Me 163A prototypes, a preproduction series of 10 **Me 163A-0** aircraft was built by Wolf Hirth and used as training gliders. Considerable redesign preceded the order for six prototype and 70 production **Me 163B Komet** point interceptors, the preproduction protypes having the designation **Me 163Ba-1**, and the first production deliveries of **Me 163B-1a** interceptors began in May 1944. The type saw action for the first time on 28 July of that year when five Me 163s from 1./JG 400, the

first operational unit, attacked a formation of Boeing B-17s. This proved ineffective, for the closing speed of about 1300 km/h (808 mph) meant that the slow-firing MK 108 cannon could be fired for only three seconds before the pilot had to break off his attack. At this stage of the war the provision of an effective weapon was to prove an insoluble prob-

Under the temporary designation Ju 248 V1, the Me 263 V1 featured a bubble canopy, larger flaps and automatic wing slats.

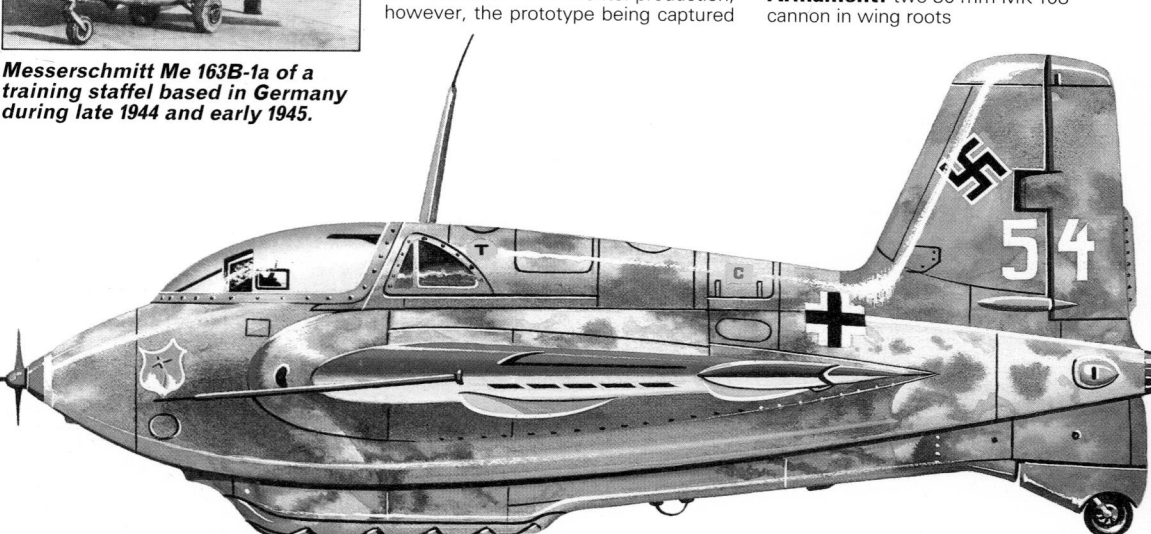

Messerschmitt Me 163B-1a of a training staffel based in Germany during late 1944 and early 1945.

lem, and production of the Me 163B-1a ended in February 1945 after nearly 400 of all variants had been built. They included a few examples of the **Me 163S** tandem two-seat trainer which, with ammunition and fuel tanks removed to provide space for a second seat, had to be flown as a glider, and the **Me 163C-1a** of which three were built but only one flown. This was an improved version of the Me 163B, with a revised airframe and a modified powerplant to increase powered endurance.

Projected developments included the **Me 163D** with further refinement and retractable tricycle landing gear; one prototype was built, and because Junkers would have developed and produced this version it gained the temporary designation **Junkers 248** before reverting to a Messerschmitt designation as the **Me 263**. It did not enter production, however, the prototype being captured

by the Soviets, who modified wings and tail surfaces before flying it in 1946 as the **I-270(ZH)**, but its development was soon abandoned. Plans were made for production of a licence-built version in Japan, designated **Mitsubishi Ki-200**.

Specification
Messerschmitt Me 163B-1a
Type: single-seat interceptor fighter
Powerplant: one 1700-kg (3,750-lb) thrust Walter HWK 509A-2 rocket motor
Performance: maximum speed 960 km/h (596 mph) at 10000 m (32,810 ft); service ceiling 12100 m (39,700 ft); maximum powered endurance 7 minutes 30 seconds
Weights: empty 1905 kg (4,200 lb); maximum take-off 4110 kg (9,061 lb)
Dimensions: span 9.32 m (30 ft 7 in); length 5.84 m (19 ft 2 in); height 2.77 m (9 ft 1 in); wing area 18.50 m² (199.14 sq ft)
Armament: two 30-mm MK 108 cannon in wing roots

Messerschmitt Me 209

In the years between 1935, when Germany first revealed formation of the Luftwaffe, and the outbreak of World War II, Adolf Hitler was most anxious to impress upon the world the capability of the fighter aircraft that equipped his new air force. This resulted in design of the **Messerschmitt Me 209** to be used to establish a new absolute world speed record. With only superficial resemblance to the Bf 109, the Me 209 was tailored around a specially-built Daimler-Benz DB 601ARJ engine with a take-off rating of 1342 kW (1,800 hp), which could be boosted to a peak of 1715 kW (2,300 hp) for very short periods. This capability proved sufficient for the Me 209 to set a

The Me 209 was intended from the outset as a record breaker, but the basic fuselage was used in the otherwise totally different Me 209 V4 in the effort to build a Bf 109 succesor. The snake was added as a bit of propaganda.

new record, Flugkapitän Fritz Wendel flying the first specially-prepared prototype on 26 April 1939 at an average speed of 755.136 km/h (469.22 mph). At this point the German propaganda ministry stepped in, details for ratification submitted to the FAI identifying the record-breaking aircraft as the **Messerschmitt Me 109R** in an attempt to

convince other nations that the record had been gained by a variant of the Luftwaffe's new fighter. Nevertheless, the record stood for just over 30 years, but although attempts were made by the

Messerschmitt company to develop a new fighter based on the Me 209 design, **Me 209A** prototypes flying later in the war, the programme was later abandoned.

Messerschmitt-Bölkow-Blohm Flamingo Trainer

Designed in 1958 by SIAT (Siebelwerke-Allgemeine-Transportanlagen) of West Germany, reformed in 1952, the prototype **SIAT-222** (D-EKYT) four-seat all-metal touring aircraft flew for the first time on 15 May 1961, powered by a 134-kW (180-hp) Lycoming O-360 piston engine. To overcome some shortcomings the aircraft was redesigned into the **SIAT-223** with a shorter fuselage, re-profiled wing and bigger fin and rudder, and the first of these (D-ECRO) made its maiden flight on 1 March 1967.

In May 1969, SIAT was merged into MBB, and two further prototypes, now designated the **MBB Flamingo**, were flown. Production aircraft, powered by 149-kW (200-hp) Lycoming IO-360-C1A, were exported to military customers including Turkey (15) and Syria for use as trainers. The aircraft was too sophisticated for use with flying clubs, although a few were sold to civil operators including Swissair, which bought 10 series A-1s for its pilot training school in Zurich. Flamingo sub-types were the **Model 223A-1** trainer seating two plus two, and the **Model 223K-1** single-seat aerobatic version.

MBB, after building 35, plus another 17 sub-contracted out to Farner, transferred the whole Flamingo programme to Hispano Aviacion of Spain just before the company was merged into CASA, which then built a batch of 50 including

30 more military trainers for Syria. The first CASA-built aircraft flew on 14 February 1972. Production of the Flamingo by CASA ended in the mid-1970s and the Model 223 project was handed back to a MBB subsidiary, Flugzeug-Union-Sud (FUS), who converted one aircraft (D-EFWC) into the restyled **MBB Flamingo Trainer T1**. This flew on 25 April 1979 and was later fitted with a Porsche PFM 3200 engine, and designated **Model 223-M4**. However, no further sales of the Flamingo Trainer materialised and series production never began.

A Flamingo basic trainer operated by the Syrian air force.

Variants
Flamingo Trainer A1: standard trainer version powered by a 149-kW (200-hp) Avco Lycoming IO-360 engine driving two-bladed Hartzell propeller
Flamingo Trainer K1: aerobatic version powered by a 149-kW (200-hp) AIO-360 engine driving two-bladed Hartzell propeller
Flamingo Trainer T1: trainer version with a turbocharged 157-kW (210-hp) TO-360-C1A6D engine driving two-bladed Hartzell or three-bladed constant-speed propeller

Specification
Type: three/four-seat basic or aerobatic trainer
Powerplant: one 149-kW (200-shp) Avco Lycoming IO-360 piston engine
Performance: cruising speed 241 km/h (150 mph); maximum speed 278 km/h (173 mph); service ceiling 6690 m (22,000 ft); range 893 km (555 miles)
Weights: empty 700 kg (1,543 lb); maximum payload 227.6 kg (502 lb); maximum take-off 1050 kg (2,315 lb)
Dimensions: span 8.28m (27 ft 2 in); length 7.6 m (24 ft 11 in); height 2.7 m (8 ft 10 in); wing area 11.5 m² (123.8 sq ft)

Messerschmitt-Bölkow-Blohm HFB 320 Hansa

Designed by Hamburger Flugzeugbau GmbH before its merger with Messerschmitt-Bölkow, the **HFB 320 Hansa** twin-jet executive transport/feederliner is of distinctive configuration. To avoid compromising cabin volume, its cantilever mid-set wings have 15° of forward sweep, which means that the main spar passes through the fuselage to the rear of the passenger cabin. Other features of its configuration include wingtip fuel tanks, a T-tail unit with all-swept surfaces, retractable tricycle landing gear, and two podded turbojet engines, mounted one on each side of the rear fuselage. The prototype (D-CHFB) was flown for the first time on 21 April 1964, and the first production Hansa on 2 February 1966. The first 15 Hansas had 12.7-kN (2, 850-lb) thrust General Electric CJ610-1 engines, the next 20 the 13.1-kN (2,950-lb) thrust CJ610-5, and subsequent aircraft the more powerful CJ610-9. Finding itself in a highly competitive market, MBB endeavoured to attract military sales in such roles as casualty evacuation, liaison, light freighting, navigation training, radio and radar reconnaissance, and VIP transportation; it attracted only one military customer, the West German Luftwaffe. This service received 14 out of 45 Hansas that were built, and they continue in use in an ECM training role and for VIP transport.

Specification
Type: twin-jet transport

The main operator of the Hansa jet today is the Luftwaffe. Much-modified aircraft are flown by JBG 32 as ECM trainers.

Powerplant: two 13.7-kN (3,100-lb) thrust General Electric CJ610-9 turbojets
Performance: maximum cruising speed 825 km/h (513 mph) at 7620 m (25,000 ft); service ceiling 12190 m (40,000 ft); range with 544-kg (1,200-lb) payload and reserves 2370 km (1,473 miles)
Weights: empty 5425 kg (11,960 lb); maximum take-off 9200 kg (20,283 lb)
Dimensions: span 14.49 m (47 ft 6½ in); length 16.61 m (54 ft 6 in); height 4.94 m (16 ft 2½ in); wing area 30.14 m² (324.43 sq ft)

Messerschmitt-Bölkow-Blohm/Kawasaki BK 117

Following the signature of an agreement in February 1977, MBB and Kawasaki in Japan initiated the joint development of a new twin-turbine utility helicopter, suitable for both civil and military use, designated **MBB/Kawasaki BK 117**. With an airframe structure very similar to that of the MBB 105, the BK 117 com-bines the MBB BO 105's rigid rotor with a transmission developed by Kawasaki and introduces as powerplant two Avco Lycoming LTS 101-650B-1 turboshaft engines. It provides accommodation for a pilot and seven passengers as standard, or a pilot and up to six passengers in an executive layout. The BK 117 can be equipped for use in roles such as cargo transport, firefighting, law enforcement, medical evacuation (with pilot, one or two stretchers and two medical attendants/sitting casualties), offshore support, and SAR. German and Japanese prototypes flew for the first time on 13 June 1979 (D-HBKA) and 10 August 1979 (JQ0003) respectively. Kawasaki was first to fly a production aircraft (JQ1001) on 24 December 1981; MBB followed with D-HBKC on 23 April 1982, this machine being the first production aircraft to be delivered to a customer, in early 1983.

In addition to being built in Germany

(at Donauworth) and Japan (Gifu), an agreement was concluded in 1982 for the type to be built in Indonesia under licence by IPT Nurtanio as the NBK-117. By January 1990 more than 250 BK 117s had been delivered worldwide, including 36 by Kawasaki, the standard aircraft now being the BK 117B-1. Since April 1990 a BK 117 engine testbed has been flying equipped with Turboméca Arriel turboshafts in an effort to offer customers an alternative engine, and certification was scheduled for 1992. On 1 September 1991, MBB transferred its Helicopter Division to Eurocopter Hubschrauber GmbH. This was later integrated with Aérospatiale's helicopter interests into the Paris-based Franco-German Eurocopter Holdings, placing the NH-90, BO 105, BO 108 and BK 117 into a world class helicopter grouping.

Variants
BK 117A-1: initial production version with LTS 101-650B-1 engines
BK 117A-3: certificated in March 1985 with larger tail rotor fitted with twisted blades and take-off weight increased to 3200 kg (7,055 lb)
BK 117A-4: certificated in July 1986 with increased transmission limits at take-off power, improved tail rotorhead, and extra internal fuel (on German aircraft), all giving enhanced performance
BK 117 B-1: fitted with more-powerful LTS 101-750B-1 engines to provide further increased performance and 140 kg (309 lb) more payload; certificated in 1987
BK 117M: military version of A-1 proposed by MBB in 1985, and flying since 1988; fitted with taller skids, a

Lucas turret mounted under the fuselage houses a Browning 12.7-mm automatic machine-gun and 450 rounds of ammunition, controlled by a helmet-mounted sight; outrigger pylons can carry up to eight HOT II or TOW anti-tank missiles, air-to-air missiles, rocket-pods, or forward-firing cannons; a doorway gunners position with a 0.50-in gun can also be installed, or 11 troops can be carried

Specification
Type: twin-turbine utility

Powerplant: two Avco Lycoming LTS 101-650B-1 turboshaft engines, each with a take-off rating of 410 kW (550 shp)
Performance: maximum cruising speed 250 km/h (155 mph) at sea level; maximum operating height 4570 m (15,000 ft); range with maximum payload and no reserves 500 km (311 miles)
Weights: empty equipped 1650 kg (3,637 lb); maximum take-off 2850 kg (6,283 lb)
Dimensions: main rotor diameter

The majority of sales for the BK 117 have so far been to civilian customers, despite the availability of several capable military versions. Many aircraft are operated as air ambulances, as the BK 117's capacious interior and smooth flying characteristics make it ideal for patients.

11.00 m (36 ft 1 in); length, rotors turning 13.00 m (42 ft 8 in); height 3.83 m (12 ft 7 in); main rotor disc area 95.03 m² (1,022.93 sq ft)

Meyers OTW

The Meyers Aircraft Company was formed at Tecumseh, Michigan during 1936 to manufacture a two-seat training biplane designed by Allen Meyers. The design was prompted by the anticipated demand for trainer aircraft that would be triggered by introduction of the CAA War Training scheme, under which civil flying schools would provide primary flying training for potential military pilots. The prototype **Meyers OTW** was flown initially on 10 May 1936, a conventional lightweight training biplane with tandem seating for two in open cockpits. A total of 102 was built before production ended in 1944, but many have since been re-

Of the total of 102 Meyers OTW biplanes built, no fewer than 16 are preserved and in use as sport aircraft or aerobatic trainers. This example has been restored at Fond du Lac, in Wisconsin.

stored and are in current use in the United States.

Variants
OTW-125: original production version with a 930kW (125-hp) Warner Scarab radial engine
OTW-145: production version, generally as above, but with a 108-kW (145-hp) Warner Scarab engine
OTW-160: final production version

with a 119-kW (160-hp) Kinner R5
OTW-KR: single aircraft, generally as

other production aircraft, but with a 89-kW (120-hp) Ken-Royce 7G engine

---

Microjet 200

The **Microjet 200** lightweight jet trainer was unusual because its design was initiated in the late 1970s by the French company Microturbo SA to find a new market for its products, which includes the design and manufacture of small gas turbines. The all-wood prototype (F-WZJF) first flew on 24 June 1980, followed by the first of three improved pre-production **Microjet 200B**s (F-WDMT) on 19 May 1983, by which time the project was in the hands of the specially-formed marketing subsidiary Microjet SA. A fourth airframe underwent static testing at the CEAT Toulouse. A cantilever low-wing monoplane of mixed construction, fitted with a V-tail, retractable tricycle landing gear, and powered by two Microturbo TRS-18 turbojets, the **MJ200** provided enclosed but unpressurised two-seat side-

The Microjet 200 was one of several small jet designs aimed at reducing the cost of primary training for air forces.

by-side accommodation for an instructor and pupil, and was intended as a low-cost high-performance turbine-powered aircraft suitable for military pilot training. Two more pre-production examples flew in January 1985 and November 1986 (offset by the loss of F-WDMT in March 1985) and these featured improvements such as a longer fuselage, additional V-tail sweep, reprofiled canopy, uprated TRS-18 engines and, on the last aircraft, weapon hardpoints under the wing. Initially MJ200 components were fabricated by Marmande Aéronautique and assembled by Microturbo, but the last two aircraft were built entirely by Marmande. Although the Microjet 200B attracted a lot of attention by its diminutive size and sprightly per-

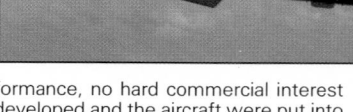

formance, no hard commercial interest developed and the aircraft were put into store in the late 1980s.

Specification
Microjet 200
Type: two-seat light jet trainer
Powerplant: two 1.30-kN (293-lb) Microturbo TRS-18-1 turbojet engines
Performance: cruising speed 389

km/h (241 mph); maximum speed 555 km/h (345 mph); service ceiling 9150 m (30,000 ft); range on internal fuel 741 km (461 miles)
Weights: empty 780 kg (1,719 lb); maximum take-off 1300 kg (2,866 lb)
Dimensions: span 7.56 m (24 ft 9 in); length 6.6 m (21 ft 10 in); height 2.76 m (9 ft 0 in); wing area 6.28 m² (67 ft 7 in)

Mikoyan-Gurevich MiG-23 and MiG-27
to
Mil Mi-6

Mikoyan-Gurevich MiG-23 and MiG-27

One of the most important tactical warplanes of the Soviet Union, the **Mikoyan-Gurevich MiG-23** (NATO reporting name **'Flogger'**) was first flown in prototype form during 1966, entering service for evaluation some four years later. This air comabt fighter, and its ground-attack **MiG-27** derivative, was in large-scale production between 1969 and 1984.

Designed to provide Frontal Aviation with a tactical fighter offering secondary ground-attack capability, and capable of meeting contemporary Western fighters on more than equal terms, the MiG-23 was designed around the primary aim of an aircraft that could operate effectively without being tied to massive concrete runways. The Mikoyan bureau is known to have adopted two approaches to this requirement: first was the **Ye-23** (or **Ye-230**) prototype, which was of tailed-delta configuration and incorporated high-lift devices to give STOL capability, powered by a single turbofan engine supplemented by a battery of Kolseov lift-jets amidships for VTOL operations; the alternative prototype was the **Ye-231**, which deleted the lift-jets and replaced the delta wing by a variable-geometry wing very similar to that of the General Dynamics F-111. The prototypes were evaluated during 1966-67, with a decision to develop the swing-wing Ye-231 finalised probably during 1968, resulting in the pre-production **MiG-23S 'Flogger-A'** which, powered by a Tumansky R-27 turbojet with an afterburning thrust of 10200 kg (22,485 lb), first entered service for operational evaluation in 1970-71. At about this time it must have been decided to optmise the MiG-23 as an air-combat fighter, and to develop a dedicated ground-attack parallel version, which was allocated the designation MiG-27. In consequence, aerodynamic changes were made to the MiG-23, the fuselage structure being lightened and more advanced avionics being introduced by the time the initial **MiG-23M** version entered service in 1973. More or less simultaneously the dedicated attack variant was developed and, while having much in common with the MiG-23, this was sufficiently different to warrant the allocation of the separate designation **MiG-27**. This differs primarily by having a completely redesigned forward fuselage, providing a better field of view for the pilot, increased armour protection, terrain-avoidance radar and provision to deploy a wide variety of air-to-surface weapons. There appear to be only two versions of the MiG-27, differing in the shape of the nose, avionics and aerodynamics, and these have the NATO reporting names **'Flogger-D'** and **'Flogger-J'**.

Both the MiG-23 and MiG-27 are in large-scale use with the former Soviet air force, an estimated 3,000 reported being operational. They served with the Warsaw Pact air forces, and were exported to the air arms of Algeria, Angola, Bulgaria, Cuba, Czechoslovakia, East Germany, Egypt, Ethiopia, Hungary, India, Iraq, Libya, North Korea, Poland, South Yemen, Syria and Vietnam. The MiG-23M/K 'Flogger J' is also currently in production in India.

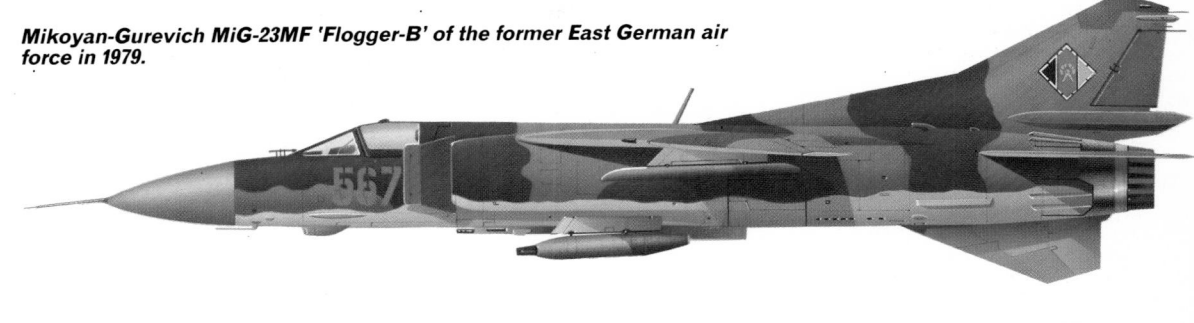

Mikoyan-Gurevich MiG-23MF 'Flogger-B' of the former East German air force in 1979.

Mikoyan-Gurevich MiG-23BN 'Flogger-F' of the Czechoslovakian air force in the late 1970s and early 1980s.

Variants
MiG-23S 'Flogger-A': pre-production version used for operational evaluation
MiG-23SM 'Flogger-A': generally as MiG-23S, but with four weapon pylons beneath engine intakes and fixed inboard wing panels
MiG-23M 'Flogger-B': initial production version, introducing redesigned airframe housing the more powerful Tumanskii R-29 turbojet
MiG-23MF 'Flogger-B': major production version since 1978, introducing improved radar and an IR sensor pod
MiG-23U 'Flogger-C': tandem two-seat trainer version of MiG-23MF, retaining operational capability
MiG-23 'Flogger-E': export version, similar to MiG-23MF, but with a more austere standard of equipment and small radar

MiG-23BN 'Flogger-F': export version for use as fighter-bomber, basically as MiG-23MF but introducing revised forward fuselage and increased armour of the MiG-27 'Flogger-D'
MiG-23MF 'Flogger-G': sub-variant of MiG-23MF with lighter-weight radar and new fin
MiG-23BN 'Flogger-H': sub-variant of MiG-23BN with avionics revisions
MiG-23MLD 'Flogger K': current multi-role tactical fighter version with modified leading-edge devices and 'Kaira' weapon control system

Specification
Mikoyan-Gurevich MiG-23MF
Type: single-seat air-combat fighter
Powerplant: one Tumanskii R-29 turbojet engine with afterburning thrust of 12500 kg (27,550 lb)
Performance: maximum speed 2500 km/h (1,550 mph) or Mach 2.35 at optimum altitude; service ceiling 18600 m (61,025 ft); maximum combat radius 1300 km (808 miles)
Weights: maximum take-off 20100 kg (44,315 lb)
Dimensions: span spread 14.25 m (46 ft 9 in) and swept 8.17 m (26 ft 9½); length 16.8 m (55 ft 1½ in); height 4.35 m (14 ft 4 in); wing area 28.00 m² (301.40 sq ft)
Armament: one 23-mm GSh-23 cannon in fuselage belly pod, plus five pylons for a variety of rockets or air-to-air missiles

The latest model of the 'Flogger' is the MiG-27M 'Flogger J-2'. It is easily identifiable by its relocated pitot tubes below the nose, which is also fitted with a new marked target seeker.

Mikoyan-Gurevich MiG-25

Knowing that the US Air Force had named North American Aviation as prime contractor to develop the B-70 strategic bomber, with Mach 3 capability, the Soviet Union planned an advanced interceptor that could offset this threat. This led to the design and development of the **Mikoyan-Gurevich MiG-25**, later allocated the NATO reporting name **'Foxbat'**, but when news came that the North American B-70 programme had been cancelled, emphasis of MiG-25 development was shifted to high-speed reconnaissance rather than interception. The first initimation in the West that this aircraft, identified by the MiG design bureau as the **Ye-266**, had flown came in April 1965 with a Soviet claim that the aircraft had established a new speed record in a 1000-km (621-mile) closed circuit. Since that time, further records have been set by the Ye-266 and developed **Ye-266M**, the latter holding the current absolute world altitude record of 37650 m (123,524 ft). A cantilever high-wing monoplane with swept leading edges, a slender fuselage blended into the engine air inlets, twin outward-canted vertical tail surfaces and all-moving horizontal tail surfaces, the MiG-25 is constructed primarily of steel, with titanium used for the leading edges of wing and tail unit to maintain structural integrity despite the high temperatures resulting from kinetic heating.

The reconnaissance capability of the MiG-25 first became apparent in early 1971, when four were deployed by VVS units operating in Egypt. Used for the reconnaissance of Israeli operations during 1971-72, they proved to be completely immune from interception by Israeli air force McDonnell Douglas Phantoms. Since that time MiG-25s have become more extensively used by the VVS, and versions have been exported also to Algeria, India, Iraq, Libya and Syria. Production terminated in 1984 in favour of the MiG-31.

Variants

MiG-25 'Foxbat-A': basic interceptor production version, with up to four air-to-air missiles carried underwing; 200 rebuilt into 'Foxbat-E'
MiG-25R 'Foxbat-B': basic reconnaissance production version, carrying cameras, sensors and ECCM equipment; this version has a maximum speed of Mach 3.2

MiG-25U 'Foxbat-C': two-seat trainer version, introducing a new nose section with a separate pupil cockpit
Ye-133: designation of aircraft used by Svetlana Savitskaya to establish a number of women's height and speed records, including a women's world speed record of 2683.44 km/h (1,667.412 mph) set on 22 June 1975
MiG-25R 'Foxbat-D': reconnaissance version, basically similar to 'Foxbat-B' but with additional electronic sensors and no cameras; more than 160 'Foxbat-B/D' reconnaissance aircraft believed to be in use by the VVS
MiG-25PD 'Foxbat-E': conversion for interception at lower altitudes

Specification
Mikoyan-Gurevich MiG-25
Type: single-seat interceptor
Powerplant: two Tumanskii R-31 turbojets each with an afterburning thrust of 12250-kg (27,006-lb)
Performance: (estimated) maximum combat speed 2975 km/h (1,849 mph) or Mach 2.8; service ceiling 24395 m (80,000 ft); maximum combat radius 1450 km (901 miles)
Weights: (estimated) empty 20000 kg (44,092 lb); maximum take-off 36200 kg (79,807 lb)
Dimensions: span 13.95 m (45 ft 9¼ in); length 23.82 m (78 ft 1¾ in); height 6.10 m (20 ft 1¼ in); wing area 56.83 m² (611.73 sq ft)
Armament: underwing pylons for the carriage of up to four air-to-air missiles

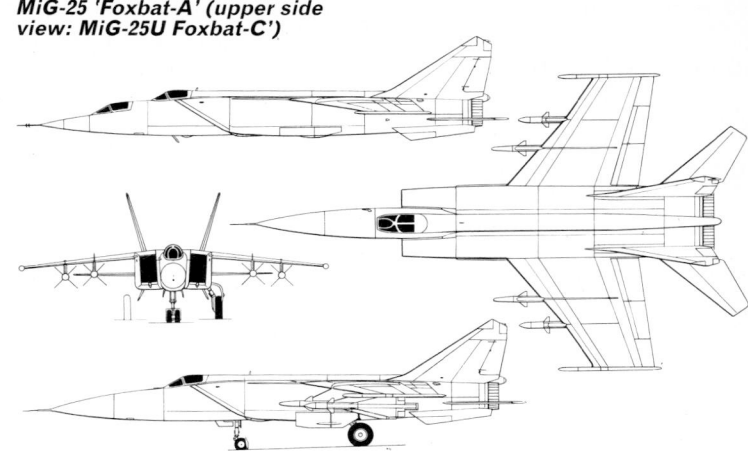
MiG-25 'Foxbat-A' (upper side view: MiG-25U Foxbat-C')

Despite the impressive array of air-to-air missiles posed in front of it, this is a reconnaissance 'Foxbat-D'. This aircraft, the MiG-26R, carries no cameras but relies on electronics such as its nose-mounted SLAR (Side-Looking Airborne Radar).

Mikoyan-Gurevich MiG-29

Designed to a 1972 requirement intended to replace the MiG-21, MiG-23, Su-15 and Su-17 with the Soviet air force, the **MiG-29,** originally revealed in a US satellite photograph and designated 'Ram-L', made its first flight on 6 October 1977. After many design changes the first deliveries of **'Fulcrum As'** were made to Soviet Frontal Aviation in 1983 and the type was declared operational early in 1985.

The first hard information became available when the aircraft was examined by Western authorities during an exchange visit to Finland by a MiG-29 unit in 1986. Configured similarly to its F/A-18 Hornet rival, the supersonic and extremely agile MiG-29 has a highly swept (45°) low-mounted wing above twin reheated turbofan engines buried in the fuselage but under the wing. The tailplane has two vertical and two horizontal stabilisers. A conventional landing gear has twin steerable nosewheels and large single low-pressure mainwheels.

More than 600 MiG-29s are now in service with the former Soviet forces, and the type has been exported to Cuba, Czechoslovakia, East Germany (now serving with the Luftwaffe), Iran, Iraq, North Korea, Poland, Romania, Syria, Yugoslavia and India, where the type is licence-built by Hindustan Aeronautics for the air force as the **Baez** (Eagle).

The latest version, sometimes referred to as the **MiG-33 'Fulcrum Plus'**, is reported to be under development at the Zhukovsky test centre. Featuring thrust vectoring engine nozzles, it could be in service by 1995.

Variants
MiG-29: standard land-based single-seat fighter version dubbed by NATO 'Fulcrum-A'
MiG-29UB: two-seat trainer version, designated **'Fulcrum-B'**, with second seat added ahead of normal cockpit, and periscope provided for rear crew member; underwing hardpoints retained but nose radar replaced by radar rangefinder
MiG-29: 'Fulcrum-C' variant of 'Fulcrum-A' but with enlarged fuselage behind cockpit containing avionics

The Czech and Slovak air force has a single MiG-29 'Fulcrum-A' squadron based at Zatec. The unit is affiliated with the NATO 'Tiger Squadrons', and its aircraft wear a tiger fin stripe.

relocated from lower fuselage; in service with Soviet air force units alongside examples of 'Fulcrum-A'

MiG-29K: 'Fulcrum-D' designation given to two prototypes of maritime version converted from early 'Fulcrum As'; intended for operation from ski-jump of Soviet aircraft-carriers, the hooked MiG-29K (K for *korabelnyy*, or ship-based) underwent trials aboard *Tbilisi* (since renamed *Admiral Kuznetsov*) in November 1989; modifications include upward-folding outer wing panels, each with eight underwing hardpoints, deletion of intake doors, addition of inflight-refuelling capability, strengthened landing gear and extra fuel tanks in fuselage; fitted with 98-kN (22,000-lb) RD-33K powerplants

MiG-29M 'Improved Fulcrum': developed version, first flown in 1989 with uprated RD-33K engines, quadruplex fly-by-wire system, EFIS cockpit in a longer canopy, eight wing hardpoints; modified tail surfaces and marginally changed wing position, nose radome reprofiled and lengthened by 20 cm (7 in), and a wider and longer dorsal spine; shown at Minsk in February 1992 carrying two TV-guided AS-14 'Kedge' anti-shipping missiles

Features of note on the navalised MiG-29K include the additional outboard weapons pylons on the folding section of the wing.

plus 'AMRAAMSKIs' on outboard pylons

MiG-33 'Fulcrum Plus': reported to be a canard-equipped 'Fulcrum' with thrust vectoring nozzles, currently under development for service in the mid-1990s

Specification
MiG-29 'Fulcrum-A'
Type: single-seat supersonic air superiority jet fighter and ground attack aircraft
Powerplant: two 81-kN (18,300-lb) thrust reheated Sarkisov RD-33 turbofan engines
Performance: maximum speed at sea level Mach 1.06 or 1,300 km/h (805 mph); at altitude Mach 2.35 or 2,465 km/h (1,530 mph); maximum rate of climb 19800 m/min (65,000 ft); service ceiling 18500 m (60,700 ft); range on internal fuel 1500 km (932 miles); with external tanks 2495 km (1,550 miles)
Weights: empty 10900 kg (24,030 lb);

maximum take-off 18480 kg (40,740 lb)
Dimensions: span 11.3 m (37 ft 3 in); length 17.3 m (56 ft 10 in); height 4.7 m (15 ft 6 in); wing area 35.2 m² (379 sq ft)
Armament: six underwing hardpoints capable of carrying six AA-10 'Alamo' or AA-11 'Archer' radar or infra-red guided

air-to-air missiles, also provision for earlier AA-8 or AA-9 missiles or bombs, 50-mm, 80-mm or 240-mm rocket pods or submunition dispensers; single 30-mm GSh-30 cannon and 130 rounds of ammunition are installed in the port wing root leading edge extension

Mikoyan-Gurevich MiG-31

Developed during the early 1970s from the 'Foxbat' interceptor to counter the threat of low-flying cruise missiles and bombers, the agile two-seat **MiG-31 'Foxhound'** first flew on 17 September 1975 and went into service in 1983. Fitted with a sophisticated 'look down/ shoot down' radar capable of simultaneously tracking 10 targets and engaging four, the 'Foxhound' remains in production at the Gorky/Nizhny Novograd factory and more than 200 have been delivered to date, with about 24 going to China.

The fifth **MiG-31M 'Improved Foxhound'**, shown to CIS leaders at Minsk in February 1992, was carrying four belly-mounted variants of the AA-9 'Amos'/R-33 missile, together with four so-called 'AMRAAMSKIs' under the wings. With airframe refinements such as a longer dorsal spine, cut-away fin roots, enlarged fin root fillets, smaller wing fences, bigger leading edge root extensions, larger brake parachute fairing, a redesigned nosewheel landing gear and cockpit transparencies, plus the addition of wingtip ESM/ECM pods and a retractable inflight-refuelling probe on the starboard side, the new version should bring significant improvements over earlier models, but MiG-31M development beyond flying prototypes may be affected by cut-backs in expenditure.

Specification
MiG-31 'Foxhound'
Type: two-seat jet interceptor
Powerplant: two 152-kN (34,170-lb) thrust Soloviev D30F-6 turbofan engines
Performance: level speed at 17500 m (57,400 ft) 3000 km/h (1,865 mph); maximum speed Mach 2.83; service ceiling 20600 m (67,600 ft); range on

internal fuel at supersonic speed 720 km (447 miles); subsonically with external tanks 1400 km (870 miles)
Weights: empty 21825 kg (48,115 lb); maximum take-off 46200 kg (101,850 lb)
Dimensions: span 13.4 m (44 ft 2 in); length 22.6 m (74 ft 5 in); height 6.1 m (20 ft 2 in); wing area 61.6 m² (663 sq ft)
Armament: four semi-recessed hardpoints under fuselage can carry AA-9 AAMs, while wing hardpoints can carry AA-5, AA-6 or AA-8 missiles

inboard and fuel tanks outboard; a single GSh-6-23 23-mm cannon plus 260 rounds of ammunition is mounted in the starboard underside fuselage, but believed deleted on the MiG-31M

Though it bears a distinct family resemblance to the MiG-25 'Foxbat', the MiG-31 is a very different aircraft. This is a standard 'Foxhound', though it is fitted with pods resembling the prominent finned pods fitted to the wingtips of the later MiG-31M.

Mil Mi-1 and Mi-2

After being given responsibility for his own design bureau in 1947, Mikhail Mil went on to design the **Mil-1**, originally known as the **GM-1**, the first conventional helicopter of single main rotor and anti-torque tail rotor configuration to enter series production in the Soviet Union. First flown in September 1948, the type entered service with the Soviet air force in 1951. Built for both civil and military use, and codenamed **'Hare'** by NATO, construction of the Mi-1 tailed off in the Soviet Union in 1956-57, after manufacture of the airframe and engine

Mi-1s are no longer in service with the Finnish air force.

was initiated in Poland as the **SM-1**, and substantial numbers were exported from both lines. Total production of the Mi-1 was estimated at between 2,500 and 3,00. In 1961 Mil announced the **Mi-2** turbine-powered development of the 'Hare' with the single piston engine replaced by two Isotov GTD-350 turboshafts mounted above the cabin roof, and the prototype (**V-2**) flew for the first time in September of that year. Following completion of its development programme in the Soviet Union, the Mi-2, by then codenamed **'Hoplite'** by NATO, was handed over to the WSK-PZL Swidnik factory in Poland for pro-

duction and further development, and this has continued through the **SM-2** and Allison-engined **Kania/Kitty Hawk** to the **Sokol** (Falcon) current production version.

Variants

Mi-1: initial standard version seating a pilot and three passengers

Mi-1 Moskvich: a refined version initially built for Aeroflot with better soundproofing and equipment and all-metal rotor; improvements later became standard and the name was dropped

Mi-1NKh: general-purpose version for use in agricultural, ambulance, freight and mail-carrying roles

Mi-1P: float-equipped version of Mi-1

Mi-1T: subsequent standard production version of Mi-1 seating a pilot and two passengers

Mi-1U: dual control trainer version of Mi-1

Specification
Mil Mi-1 'Hare'

Type: general-purpose light utility helicopter

Powerplant: one 429-kW (575-hp) Ivchenko AI-26V piston engine

Performance: cruising speed 140 km/h (85 mph); maximum speed 205 km/h (125 mph); hovering ceiling 2000 m (6,500 ft); range 590 km (370 miles)

Weights: empty 1760 kg (3,900 lb); maximum take-off 2550 kg (5,650 lb)

Dimensions: main rotor diameter 14.3 m (47 ft 1 in); length 12.0 m (39 ft 4 in); height 3.3 m (10 ft 10 in); main rotor disc area 161.5 m² (1,739 sq ft)

Mil Mi-4

Design of the **Mil Mi-4**, a conventional helicopter with about four times the capacity of the Mi-1, was initiated in 1951 and the first example was flown during May 1952. Produced initially for use by the Soviet armed forces in assault and troop transport roles, the **Mi-4 'Hound-A'** has clamshell rear doors to simplify the loading of vehicles and freight; alternatively, the cabin can accommodate up to 14 troops. Military Mi-4s are recognisable easily by having a ventral gondola which was intended originally for a navigator or observer, but can also house avionics equipment. Produced in large numbers for Soviet military use, the Mi-4 was also exported for service with more than 20 foreign air arms. A number remain in current use, and in more recent years conversions have been reported in Soviet use for ASW (**'Hound-B'**) armed close support and ECM (**'Hound-C'**). From 1964 production of civil versions was initiated and combined civil/military production by Mil was estimated at 3,500 when production terminated in 1969. All versions can be equipped with inflatable pontoons which, mounted so that the landing wheels project below them, can be used for amphibious operations. The Mi-4 was also manufactured under licence in

China, a total of about 1,000 built when production ended in 1979, and of which approximately two-thirds were for civil use.

Variants

Mi-4: basic military production version with clamshell rear doors; this configuration adopted also for civil cargo versions

Mi-4P: civil transport version used extensively by Aeroflot and seating eight to 11 passengers in furnished cabin; current major use in ambulance configuration carrying up to eight stretchers and a medical attendant

Mi-4S: basically an agricultural version with a large chemical container in the main cabin, but used also for fire-fighting operations

Z-5: Chinese military version of the Mi-4, this being in service with both the army and navy

Xuanfeng: Chinese name for civil version of the Mi-4, at least one of which is flying with the PT6T-6 twin turbine engine

Specification
Mil Mi-4P

Type: civil transport helicopter

Powerplant: one 1268-kW (1,700-hp) Shvetsov ASh-82V radial piston engine

Performance: maximum speed 210 km/h (130 mph) at 1500 m (4,920 ft); service ceiling 5500 m (18,045 ft); range with 11 passengers 250 km (155 miles)

Weights: empty 5390 kg (11,883 lb); maximum take-off 7800 kg (17,196 lb)

Dimensions: main rotor diameter

The obsolete Mi-4 still soldiers on with air forces which have not the means to replace them.

21.0 m (68 ft 10¾ in); length rotors turning 25.02 m (82 ft 1 in); height 5.18 m (17 ft 0 in); main rotor disc area 346.00 m² (3,724.43 sq ft)

Mil Mi-6

When first announced, following its maiden flight in September 1957, the **Mil Mi-6** (NATO reporting name **'Hook'**) was by far the world's largest helicopter. Its maximum payload exceeds the total weight of the Sikorsky S-64A, which on its appearance a decade later was the largest helicopter outside the USSR. Developed to meet both VVS and Aeroflot requirements, the Mi-6 was also the first turbine-powered helicopter to enter production in the USSR. Five aircraft were involved in the development programme, which was completed very quickly for such a revolutionary aircraft, with production beginning in 1960. Of conventional helicopter configuration, the Mi-6 introduced two readily-detachable short-span shoulder wings which offload the rotor by some 20 per cent in cruising flight; for heavy-lift operations the stub wings are removed to give greater payload capability. The Mi-6 was used in 1962 to set up no

fewer than 14 speed and height-with-payload records that were ratified by the FAI; four of these remained unbeaten in 1983. Major production version was the **Mi-6A**, of which more than 800 had been delivered when manufacture ended in 1981. The 'Hook' was exported to Algeria, Egypt, Ethiopia, Iraq, Syria, Vietnam and Peru, where it is used by both the air force and army. Flown by a crew of five, the Mi-6 has also seen extensive use with Aeroflot in civil engineering support work on projects such as bridge-laying, and as a versatile heavy transport in areas inaccessible to other vehicles. Another version, developed into the **Mil-10 'Harke'**, is optimised as a flying crane.

Variants

'Hook A': basic military transport version able to carry 70 combat-equipped troops or 65-90 civil passengers; also used in the air ambulance role, it can accommodate 41 stretcher cases and two medical attendants; can also be fitted for fire-fighting role with spraying or water bombing equipment; in the freight role the Mi-6 can carry an internal cargo payload of 12000 kg (26,455 lb)

'Hook-B': military command support version

'Hook-C': further developed command support version, designated **Mi-22**, and identified by additional antennas

Specification
Mil Mi-6A

Type: heavy transport helicopter

Powerplant: two 4101-kW (5,500-shp) Soloviev D-25V turboshafts

Performance: maximum speed 300 km/h (186 mph); service ceiling 4500 m (14,765 ft); range with 8000-kg (17,637-lb) payload 620 km (385 miles)

Weights: empty 27240 kg (60,054 lb); maximum vertical take-off 42500 kg (93,696 lb)

Dimensions: main rotor diameter 35.00 m (114 ft 10 in); length, rotors turning 41.74 m (136 ft 11¼ in); height 9.86 m (32 ft 4¼ in); main rotor disc area 962.11 m² (10,356.4 sq ft)

A Mil Mi-6 'Hook-A' of the Egyptian air force during the 1970s.

Mil Mi-8
to
Mil Mi-24

Mil Mi-8

A Mil-8T 'Hip' of Polish operator Instal.

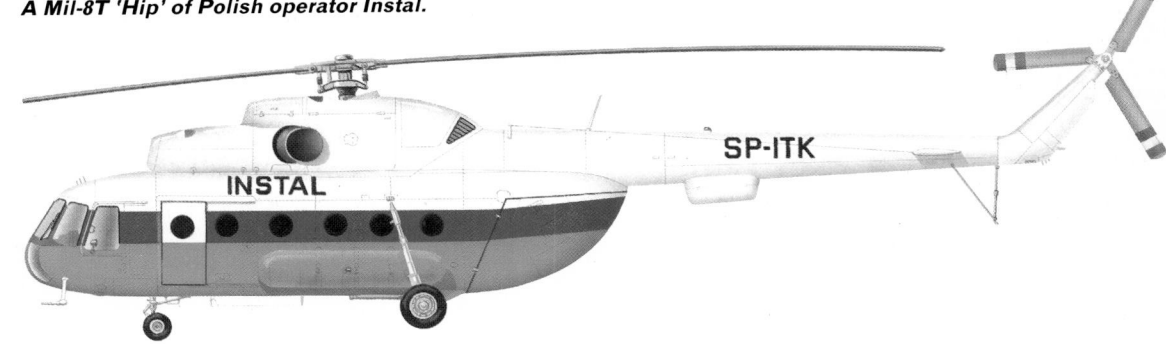

Designed originally in 1960, the **V-8 'Hip-A'** prototype helicopter was basically a turbine-powered version of the Mi-4, retaining initially its rotor, transmission and a number of other components. Intended powerplant was two Isotov turboshaft engines, but as these were not fully developed when the V-8 was nearing completion, it was powered instead by a single large Soloviev turboshaft derated to the 2013-kW (2,700-shp) limit of the transmission, for its first flight in June 1960. However, the second machine (flown for the first time on 17 September 1962) introduced the Isotov engines, each then rated at 1119 kW (1,500 shp), and this became the standard installation on early production aircraft, designated **Mil Mi-8** (NATO reporting name **'Hip'**). The only other major change to be introduced since that time resulted from problems with the main rotor inherited from the Mi-4, replaced in 1964 by a five-bladed rotor of more advanced design in the **'Hip-B'** prototype. The availability of so much engine power, by comparison with the 1268 kW (1,700 hp) of the Mi-4, meant the new helicopter had a larger cabin, providing accommodation for a crew of two or three and up to 28 passengers in a standard airline configuration. Since series construction began, a total of 10,000 Mi-8s have been built, for both civil and military use. Some components are built in China.

Large numbers of Mi-8s are used by Aeroflot in the transport role, being deployed also for ice reconnaissance, rescue operations and logistic support, but even greater numbers are operated by the Soviet Union's Frontal and Naval Aviation and, in addition, these helicopters have been supplied to the armed forces of about 40 other nations. The military versions are identified usually by their NATO reporting names.

Variants
Mi-8: standard production passenger version, accommodating 28 to 32 passengers
Mi-8T: utility civil transport, intended primarily for the carriage of internal or

external freight, but able to accommodate 24 passengers on sidewall tip-up seats
Mi-8 Salon: de luxe civil transport with optional nine- and 11-seat interiors
'Hip-C': military assault transport with external stores racks on each side of cabin for 128 rockets or other weapons; some uprated to Mi-17 standard as **Mi-8T** and **Mi-8TB,** with port-side tail rotor
'Hip-D': airborne communications version
'Hip-E': heavily-armed attack helicopter, with 12.7-mm (0.5-in) machine-gun in nose, external racks for up to 192 rockets and four AT-2 'Swatter' anti-tank missiles

'Hip-F': export version generally similar to 'Hip-E' but with six AT-3 'Sagger' ATMs
'Hip-G': communications-relay model
'Hip-H': updated Mi-8 with uprated engines giving improved performance; redesignated **Mi-17**
'Hip-J': ECM version
'Hip-K': ECM jammer version with antenna array on each side of boom; some uprated to Mi-17 standard, with port-side tail rotor

Specification
Mil Mi-8
Type: civil transport helicopter
Powerplant: two 1268-kW (1,700-

An unarmed Mi-8T 'Hip-C' transport helicopter serving with the Soviet Group of Forces in Germany.

shp) Isotov TV2-117A turboshafts
Performance: maximum speed 260 km/h (162 mph) at 1000 m (3,280 ft); service ceiling 4500 m (14,765 ft); range with 28 passengers 500 km (311 miles)
Weights: empty 6799 kg (14,989 lb); maximum take-off 12000 kg (26,455 lb)
Dimensions: main rotor diameter 21.29 m (69 ft 10¼ in); length, rotors turning 25.24 m (82 ft 9¾ in); height 5.65 m (18 ft 6½ in); main rotor disc area 356.00 m² (3,832 sq ft)

Mil Mi-10

The **V-10** prototype was a development of the Mi-6 heavylift helicopter, but optimised for the flying-crane role. Retaining basically the same rotor, transmission and powerplant, the V-10 had a slender fuselage more like that of a fixed-wing aircraft and, since it dispensed with the pod-and-boom configuration, appears (falsely) to be much greater in length. Wide-track stalky quadricycle landing gear is provided, so that the helicopter can taxi over a bulky load that is to be carried externally, and because it is intended to be used more extensively in the heavylift role than the Mi-6, it dispenses with the stub wings of this earlier helicopter. First flown during 1960, the V-10 entered production as the **Mil Mi-10**, then gaining the NATO reporting name **'Harke'**, and being super-

The Mil Mi-10's unique external cargo platform allows it to carry a payload of up to 1500 kg (33,069 lb).

seded in 1964 by a developed version designated **Mi-10K** which was designed specifically for the carriage of slung loads. The Mi-10K differs from the Mi-10 by having landing gear that is 2.00 m (6 ft 6¾ in) shorter, and has a flight deck for one (instead of two) pilots, the second pilot being accommodated in a gondola beneath the nose with an aft-facing seat and with full controls for both helicopter and the load. The main cabin can be used for freight and/or passengers, the latter totalling 28 on somewhat austere tip-up seats. Construction of both versions totalled 55 when production ended in 1971; manufacture was resumed briefly in 1977, but no new production figures have been quoted.

Specification
Mil Mi-10K
Type: heavy flying-crane helicopter
Powerplant: two 4101-kW (5,500-shp) Soloviev D25V turboshafts
Performance: maximum cruising speed with slung load 202 km/h (125 mph); service ceiling 3000 m (9,840 ft); range with typical load 250 km (155

miles)
Weights: empty 24680 kg (54,410 lb); maximum take-off with slung cargo 38000 kg (83,776 lb)
Dimensions: main rotor diameter 35.00 m (114 ft 10 in); length, rotor turning 41.89 m (137 ft 5¼ in); height 7.80 m (25 ft 7 in); main rotor disc area 962.11 m² (10,356 sq ft)

Mil Mi-12 (V-12)

Although only two examples of the **Mil Mi-12** were built, both being V-12 prototypes, this giant machine is worthy of mention as the world's largest helicopter to have flown to date. To economise in effort and development cost, the Mil design team adopted the main rotor, transmission and powerplant of the Mi-6, using them in duplicate, one such unit being located at the tip of each of the extensively-braced fixed wings. The use of twin counter-rotating main rotors eliminated the requirement for a tail rotor, the tail unit consisting instead of conventional surfaces, plus endplate fins at the tips of the tailplane. The four Soloviev D-25 VF turboshaft engines had a combined output of 19388 kW (26,000 shp), enabling the V-12, first flown on 10 July 1968, to establish a series of records

A true aerial giant, the Mi-12 astounded the West when it first appeared at the Paris air show. While it could lift enormous weights, 'Homer' proved to have several failings, and limited demand made further development uneconomic.

in February 1969 which, when submitted for ratification, was the first intimation received in the West of the existence of this giant helicopter, then allocated the NATO reporting name **'Homer'**. Later in the year, on 6 August 1969, the V-12 lifted a payload of 40204.5 kg (88,636 lb) to a height of 2255 m (7,398 ft), establishing a record that remains unbeaten. The first prototype was destroyed in a non-fatal landing accident during 1969,

but although the second prototype was used for a large number of demonstration flights, no further development or production ensued.

Mil Mi-14

The **Mi-14**, allocated the NATO reporting name **'Haze'**, is an amphibious version of the Mi-8 intended to replace the Mi-4 in the ASW and mine countermeasure roles with the Soviet navy. The prototype, designated **V-14**, was first flown in September 1969 with a redesign watertight hull and sponsons containing fuel and a retractable undercarriage to confer water stability. Using the twin powerplants and rotor system of the Mi-17, the 'Haze' went into service in 1977 and has become the basic shore-based helicopter with the Soviet navy for use in three distinct roles. Although amphibious, the Mi-14 is, like its Sea King counterpart, only intended for occasional operations from water. By 1991, about 230 had been delivered, with exports to Bulgaria, Cuba, East Germany, North Korea, Libya, Poland, Romania, Syria and Yugoslavia.

Variants
Mi-14PL 'Haze-A': basic ASW version equipped with dunking sonar and search radar
Mi-14PW: Polish designation of 'Haze-A'

Mil Mi-14 'Haze-A' of the AV-MF (Soviet Naval Aviation) in the early 1980s.

Mi-14BT 'Haze-B': mine countermeasures version
Mi-14PS 'Haze-C': search and rescue version fitted with two searchlights in nose, a sliding double door on the port side alongside a retractable hoist capable of lifting three persons in a basket

Specification
Mil Mi-14
Type: shore-based twin-engined maritime helicopter
Powerplant: two 1454-kW (1,950-shp) Isotov TV3-117MT turboshafts
Performance: cruising speed 215

km/h (133 mph); maximum speed 230 km/h (143 mph); range with maximum fuel 1135 km (705 miles)
Weights: empty (estimated) 9000 kg (17,650 lb); maximum take-off 14000 kg (30,865 lb)
Dimensions: main rotor diameter 21.20 m (69 ft 10 in); length 25.3 m (83 ft); main rotor disc area 356 m² (3,832 sq ft)
Armament: internal bomb bay accommodating homing torpedoes, bombs or depth charges

Mil Mi-17

The **Mi-17** retains the codename **'Hip-H'**, denoting its derivation from the Mi-8 design. First identified in 1980-81, the Mi-17 is virtually a revision of the Mi-8 design using a combination of the 'Hip' airframe but with the port-side tail rotor, and fitted with the more powerful powerplants of the Mi-14. These result in an overall improvement in performance, particularly the hovering ceiling. The type remains in current production for both civil and military use as a cargo-carrying helicopter, with secondary capability as a passenger transport capable of carrying up to 24 passengers, or 12 stretcher cases when used as an ambulace. The first export examples were delivered to Cuba in 1983, and Mi-17s are now in service in Angola, Hungary, India, North Korea, Nicaragua, Papua New Guinea, Peru and Poland, as well as the CIS.

Variants
Mi-17PPA 'Hip-K derivative': extensively-modified ECM communications-jamming version, fitted with many additional aerials and antennas, first seen in 1990 and known to be in service with the Hungarian air force

Mi-17-1VA 'Hip-H': flying hospital version first seen at 1989 Paris air show equipped with more powerful 1678-kW (2,250-shp) TV-3-117VM engines

Specification
Mil Mi-17 'Hip-H'
Type: twin turboshaft multi-role helicopter
Powerplant: two 1454-kW (1,950-shp) Isotov TV3-117MT turboshafts
Performance: cruising speed

240 km/h (149 mph); maximum speed 250 km/h (155 mph); ceiling 5000 m (16,400 ft); hovering ceiling 1760 m (5,775 ft); range on internal fuel 495 km (307 miles)
Weights: empty 7100 kg (15,653 lb); internal payload 4000 kg (8,820 lb); external sling load 3000 kg (6,614 lb); maximum take-off 13000 kg (28,660 lb)
Dimensions: main rotor diameter 21.2 m (69 ft 10 in); length overall, rotors turning 25.3 m (83 ft 2 in); height to top of rotor head 4.7 m (15 ft 7 in);

The most obvious difference between the Mi-17 and Mi-8 is the former's tail rotor, which has been relocated to the port side of the tail. In addition, Mi-17s are almost invariably fitted with engine intake guards.

main rotor disc area 365 m² (3,832 sq ft)
Armament: as for Mi-8, plus capability to fit GSh-23 23-mm gun packs

Mil Mi-24

The **Mi-24,** which has the NATO reporting name **'Hind'**, was developed during the mid-1960s to provide a multi-role military helicopter of formidable capability. It appears to be evolved from the Mil Mi-8/Mi-14 family, but a combination of reduced size and increased power gives this aircraft improved manoeuvrability and performance. While of the same basic configuration as its predecessors, and with a dynamic system based on that of the Mi-8, the Mi-24 has a more slender fuselage suitable for the gunship role, but with sufficient capability to accommodate a crew of four and a maximum of eight armed troops. The tricycle landing gear has retractable main units and a semi-retractable nose unit. Short-span cantilever shoulder wings with considerable anhedral are a distinguishing feature, and each provides mountings for a variety of weapons. Entering service in 1973-74 and deployed initially in East Germany, the Mi-24 has developed during military exercises into variants for armed assault, for anti-armour use, and for use as a helicopter escort, well able to oppose enemy helicopters in air-to-air combat. About 1,500 'Hinds', in production since the early 1970s, are currently in service with CIS forces. The type saw much action in Afghanistan, used as the proving ground for many operational improvements to the 'Hind'. The type was also used in the Iraq/Iran war of the early 1980s. The Mi-24 has been widely exported and a number are in service on most continents, with examples delivered to, or operating in, Afghanistan, Algeria, Angola, Bulgaria, Chad, Cuba, Czechoslovakia, Germany, Hungary, India, Iraq, Libya, Mozambique, Nicaragua, North Korea, Peru, Poland, Sri Lanka, Syria, Vietnam and Yemen. Production continues at a low rate and by 1991 more than 2,300 had been built. FAI records set by the **A-10** experimental variant of the 'Hind' gave some indication of the type's capabilities, as when on 2 September 1978 over a 15/25-km (9.3/15.5-mile) course it achieved a speed of 368.4 km/h (228.9 mph).

Variants

Mi-24 'Hind': early production version, reported in 1972 but not seen until 1973; introduced into Soviet service in 1973/74

Mi-24 'Hind-A': second production model, with tail rotor moved from the starboard to port side of the tailfin; used as armed assault helicopter, carrying eight troops and three crew members

Mi-24 'Hind-B': initial production model with tail rotor on starboard side, wings without anhedral, no wingtip stations and only four underwing hardpoints; test use only

Mi-24 'Hind-C': dedicated training helicopter similar to 'Hind-A', but without nose-gun installation and wingtip stations

Mi-24D 'Hind-D': initial dedicated gunship variant; first reported around 1977, Mi-24D is basically a late production 'Hind-A' with revised forward fuselage containing separate cockpits for pilot and gunner, the latter controlling a single 12.7-mm (9.50in) turret-mounted machine-gun and pylon-mounted AT-2 'Swatter' wire-guided ATMs; some versions had 23-mm cannon in turret

'Hind-G1', an aircraft with no Western parallel, has had its outboard missile rails replaced with a 'clutching hand' apparatus which appears to be used for gathering samples in a contaminated environment.

A Mil Mi-24 'Hind-D' of the 6th Pomeranian Airborne Assault Brigade, Polish air force, based in Inwrocklow in the late 1980s.

Mi-24W 'Hind-E': improved version of 'Hind-D' gunship first reported in early 1980s; equipped with 12 AT-6 'Spiral' radio-guided ATMs mounted on stub wings together with AA-8 'Aphid' air-to-air missiles for self-defence

Mi-24P 'Hind-F': Mi-24P (P for pushka, cannon) version of gunship, appeared in 1982 fitted with 30-mm GSh-30-2 cannon in starboard uderfuselage nose pack which includes 750 rounds of ammunition

Mi-24R 'Hind-G 1': fitted with wingtip 'grapplers' or 'clutching hands' apparently used in connection with NBC technology, the Mi-24R was first reported in 1986 after the Chernobyl disaster

Mi-24K 'Hind-G 2': similar to Mi-24R but with large camera installed in cabin with lens on starboard side

Mi-25: export version of 'Hind-D'

Mi-35: export version of 'Hind-E'

Mi-35P: export version of 'Hind-F'

Specification
Mil Mi-24D 'Hind-E'

Type: twin-engined assault/gunship helicopter

Powerplant: two 1640-kW (2,200-shp) Isotov TV3-117 turboshafts

Performance: cruising speed 270 km/h (168 mph); maximum speed 335 km/h (208 mph); service ceiling 4500 m (14,750 ft); hovering ceiling

1500 m (4,920 ft); range on internal fuel 500 km (310 miles)

Weights: empty 8200 kg (18,078 lb); external payload 2400 kg (5,290 lb); maximum take-off 12000 kg (26,455 lb)

Dimensions: main rotor diameter 17.3 m (56 ft 9 in); length overall, rotors turning 21.5 m (70 ft 6 in); height to top of rotor head 3.9 m (13 ft 0 in); main rotor disc area 235 m² (2,530 sq ft)

Armament: one 12.7-mm machine-gun in remotely-controlled turret under nose; wingtip pylons for four AT-2

'Hind-E' is an improved version of the initial 'Hind-D' gunship, which carries an improved sensor fit under the nose.

'Swatter' anti-tank missiles; four underwing hardpoints able to carry pods containing either 32 57-mm or 20-mm rockets; pods containing 23-mm GSh-23 cannon; or up to 1500 kg (3,300 lb) of bombs or mines; AK-47 guns can be fired from the cabin windows

'Hind-G1', an aircraft with no Western parallel, has had its outboard missile rails replaced with a 'clutching hand' apparatus which appears to be used for gathering samples in a contaminated environment.

Mil Mi-26

Except for the V-12 prototypes that preceded it, the **Mil Mi-26 'Halo'** is the heaviest helicopter to have flown to date. Designed to provide Aeroflot with a heavylift helicopter to assist in the exploitation of undeveloped regions, this aircraft began life in the early 1970s, as soon as it became clear that the V-12 was not going to fulfil this role. It required the costly and time-consuming design and development of a completely new rotor and transmission system, which was precisely why the Mil bureau had arrived at the configuration of the V-12. As a result the design, development and testing of a suitable dynamic system, plus the need to meet an official requirement that the aircraft's empty weight should be only half that of its maximum take-off weight, meant that it was not until 14 December 1977 that the **V-26** prototype achieved its first hovering flight. Of similar overall configuration to the Mil Mi-6 heavylift helicopter, and with a fuselage of similar dimensions, the Mi-26 has a smaller-diameter (but eight-bladed) main rotor and powerplant of almost double the output, enabling it to carry 66 per cent more payload than the Mi-6. This was demonstrated effectively on 3 February 1982 when, as just one of a string of new records established by the Mi-26, this new helicopter lifted a total mass (helicopter plus payload) of 56768.8 kg (121,153.8 lb) to a height of 2000 m (6,560 ft).

Development of the 'Halo' was completed in 1983 and the type was in civil and military service by 1985, since when about 70 have been built. The production model carries a crew of five, and up to 85 combat-equipped troops, or two airborne infantry combat vehicles. A new version is reported to be under development to replace the 'Hook' in the command support role, with uprated engines, composite rotor blades and maximum payload increased to 22000 kg (48,500 lb).

Specification
Type: heavylift helicopter
Powerplant: two 8380-kW (11,240-

'Big' numbers are the Mi-26's forte. With a maximum take-off weight of 56000 kg, it is the first helicopter ever to operate with an eight-bladed main rotor.

In service with both Aeroflot and the former Soviet air force, some Russian-operated 'Halos' now carry the Russian Republic's new civilian registration prefix.

shp) Lotarev D-136 turboshafts
Performance: maximum speed 295 km/h (183 mph); service ceiling 4600 m (15,100 ft); range with maximum fuel 800 km (487 mph)
Weights: empty 28200 kg (62,170 lb); maximum take-off 56000 kg (123,450 lb)
Dimensions: main rotor diameter 32 m (106 ft); length with rotors turning 40.0 m (131 ft 4 in); height to top of rotor head 8.1 m (26 ft 8 in); main rotor disc area 804.2 m^2 (8,657 sq ft)

Mil Mi-28

First flown in November 1982, and designed to fulfil the same role as the American AH-64 Apache which it generally resembles, the agile **Mi-28 'Havoc'** military helicopter was scheduled to enter full service with the CIS forces in 1992, but lost out to the Kamov Ka-50. The three prototypes had a conventional three-bladed tail rotor but this has since been replaced by a 'delta 3' x-configured rotor comprising two independent two-bladed propellers mounted on the same shaft. The gunner, seated in a heavily-armoured front cockpit ahead of the pilot, controls a 30-mm cannon normally used on ground vehicles. This is mounted under the nose, which contains a low light level TV and FLIR night control systems. Stub wings, each fitted with two hardpoints, can carry AT-6 'Spiral' radio-guided ATMs,

UV-20 pods, or fuel tanks. Infra-red suppressors and decoy dispensers are also fitted to the 'Havoc', which is designed to offer high survivability in battle.

Specification
Type: twin-engined helicopter gunship
Powerplant: two 1640-kW (2,200-shp) Isotov TV3-117 turboshafts
Performance: cruising speed 265 km/h (165 mph); maximum speed 305 km/h (189 mph); service ceiling 5800 m (19,025 ft); range with maximum fuel 470 km (292 mph)
Weights: empty 7000 kg (15,430 lb); maximum take-off 11400 kg (25,130 lb)
Dimensions: main rotor diameter 17.2 m (56 ft 5 in); length (excluding rotor) 16.8 m (55 ft 3 in); height 4.8 m (15 ft 9 in)
Armament: one 30-mm Type 2A42 cannon mounted in a turret under the nose plus 300 rounds of ammunition; stub wing pylons can each carry 480 kg

(1,058 lb) of weapons including up to 16 AT-6 anti-tank missiles, UV-20 rocket pods containing 57- or 80-mm rockets, or external fuel tanks

The Mi-28 lost out to the Kamov Ka-50 in its bid to enter service with the Red Army, but Mil plans to build the aircraft for export.

Mil Mi-34

Codenamed **'Hermit'** by NATO, the **Mi-34** is a two/four-seat light helicopter in the same class as the Gazelle and Ecureuil, but powered by a piston engine. The first of two prototypes flew for the first time in 1986, and the type was revealed to the West for the first time at the Paris air show in June 1987. The Mi-34 is competing against the Polish turbine-powered Swidnik SW-4 as a replacement for the fleet of obsolete training helicopters, such as the Mi-1, used in large numbers. However, no decision has yet been made regarding series production of the 'Hermit'. A development is also under way to re-engine the Mi-34 with two 164-kW (220-hp) VAZ-430 rotary engines normally used to power VAZ cars, and which run on Mogas. First flight of the prototype, designated **Mi-34V**, is scheduled for 1993.

Specification
Type: light utility helicopter
Powerplant: one 242-kW (325-hp)

The Mi-34 'Hermit' is fitted with a nine-cylinder M-14 radial piston engine, virtually the same engine as that fitted to the Su-26 and -29 aerobatic aircraft. Intended as a light utility and training aircraft (primarily for the former quasi-military state flying organisation, the DOSAAF) the Mi-34 is also extremely agile.

Vedeneyev M-14V-126 nine-cylinder radial piston engine
Performance: cruising speed 160 km/h (99 mph); maximum speed 210 km/h (130 mph); service ceiling 4500 m (14,765 ft); hovering ceiling 1500 m (4,920 ft); range with 90-kg (198-lb) payload 450 km (280 miles)
Weights: normal 1260 kg (2,777 lb); maximum take-off 1350 kg (2,976 lb)
Dimensions: rotor diameter 10.0 m (32 ft 9 in); length 8.71 m (28 ft 7 in); rotor disc area 78.5 m² (845 sq ft)

Mil Mi-38

Revealed in model form at the 1989 Paris air show, the **Mi-38** medium-range turbine-powered multi-role helicopter is in the same class, and bears a strong resemblance to the EH.101, with the exception of the 'delta 3' double-propeller tail rotor. Primarily designed to replace the Mi-8 and Mi-17 series of helicopters, the prototype is scheduled to fly by 1993 and the type to enter production in 1996. Designed from inception to be certificated (to FAA Part 29) and sold in Western markets, the Mi-38 incorporates many advanced features such as a two-pilot 'glass cockpit' and fly-by-wire flight control system, and uses many composite components together with a composite main and tail rotors. Initial powerplants are two 1753-kW (2,350-shp) Klimov TV-7-117V turboshafts, but suitable Western engine installations will be optional. As with the EH.101, a number of variants are under development including military utility and special role versions, a passenger version seating 32 passengers, and specialised cargo hauling, ambulance and air survey versions.

Miles M.2 Hawk series

In 1932 F. G. Miles had flown a small single-seat biplane known as the **Miles M.1 Satyr**. Only one was built but it flew well, but was written off in 1936. Miles' previous experience with the Southern Martlet and Metal Martlet biplanes led to the desire to build a two-seat monoplane replacement for biplanes which had virtually cornered the market. The result was the **M.2 Hawk**, flown in March 1933 and the forerunner of a brilliant series of Miles monoplanes. Powered originally by the 71-kW (95-hp) Cirrus IIIA engine, later **M.2c** aircraft offered the 89-kW (120-hp) de Havilland Gipsy III. Other variants included the **M.2a** with an enclosed cabin, **M.2b** single-seat long-range version with an 89-kW (120-hp) Hermes IV engine, and the three-seat **M.2d**. Hawk production totalled 55.

Further development of the basic type led to the **Hawk Major** series (64 built), beginning with the **M.2F** with the 970-kW (130-hp) de Havilland Gipsy Major engine and encompassing a whole range of variants up to the **M.2T**. Single-seat racing models were known as the **Hawk Speed Six**; three were built with 149-kW (200-hp) Gipsy Six engines, and another somewhat smaller racing variant was the **M.5 Sparrowhawk**, of which five were built. The prototype survived the war and in 1953 was modified considerably by the installation of two 150-kg (330-lb) thrust Turboméca Palas jet engines to become the **M.77 Sparrowjet** with a speed of 370 km/h (230 mph). The final pre-war development was the **Hawk Trainer**, of which 25 were built, and the basic design was later developed into the M.14 Magister.

G-AEEL was the last of nine Miles M.2X Hawk Trainer aircraft, the type being a version of the M.2W Hawk Trainer with a balanced rudder of greater area. The M.2W was itself a development of the Hawk Major and entered service with the Royal Air Force's No. 8 Elementary and Reserve Flying School from 1935 onwards.

The 1953 prototype of the M.5 Sparrowhawk was converted to turbojet power as the M.77 Sparrowjet, flying in its revised form on 14 December. It was destroyed in a hangar fire in 1964.

Miles M.3 Falcon

The first true cabin aircraft designed by F. G. Miles, the **Miles M.3 Falcon** prototype (G-ACTM) was flown first on 12 October 1934. This prototoype was a three-seat cabin monoplane, but the first production example seated four in a wider cabin. A number of variants of the basic aircraft were flown under the names **M.3A Falcon Major** and **M.3B Falcon Six**, total production amounting to 36, of which six were impressed for service with the RAF at the outbreak of World War II. Powered by a 149-kW (200-hp) de Havilland Gipsy Six inline engine, the 10.67 m (35 ft 0 in) span Falcon had a maximum speed of 290 km/h (180 mph) and normal range of 901 km (560 miles).

Most of the production run of the F. G. Miles-designed M.3 Falcon cabin monoplane were powered by an inverted 130-hp (97-kW) Gypsy major piston engine. This aircraft was delivered from Britain to Sweden in 1936.

Miles M.4 to M.8

Basically an enlarged version of the M.3A Falcon Major, the **Miles M.4 Merlin** was a five-seat touring monoplane flown in 1935 with a 149-kW (200-hp) de Havilland Gipsy Six engine. Four were built, two seeing service in India and one in Australia. The one-off **M.6 Hawcon** combined parts of the Hawk and Falcon, used the same engine as the M.4, and was designed for thick-wing research by the Royal Aircraft Establishment at Farnborough. Four sets of wings were used for this work, these being of varying thickness.

Developed from the M.3B Falcon Six, the **M.77 Nighthawk,** of which five civil examples were built, was intended for use as a trainer and three-seat communications aircraft, and was eventually ordered by the RAF as the M.16 Mentor. The **M.8 Peregrine** of 1936 was Miles' first twin-engined aircraft, with 153-kW (205-hp) de Havilland Gipsy Queen engines and seats for six passengers plus two crew. Although its performance was good, manufacture could not be undertaken because the company was then busy with Magister production, and only one more Peregrine, with 216-kW (290-hp) Menasco Buccaneer engines, was built as a flying laboratory for the RAE.

With its forward raked windscreen (a distinctive Miles feature), the Peregrine was the first twin-engined aircraft to be built by the company.

Miles Master (M.9, M.19, M.24 and M.27)

The growing capability of high-performance monoplanes entering RAF service from the late 1930s highlighted the need for an advanced trainer with similar performance, and Miles designed a low-wing monoplane trainer to be powered by the 556-kW (745-hp) Rolls-Royce Kestrel XVI used in the Hawker Fury and Hart biplanes. When the design was submitted to the Air Ministry it was considered premature, but the company continued with construction of the prototype as a private venture, and this, named **Kestrel**, was flown for the first time on 3 June 1937. It was very soon demonstrating a maximum speed only about 24 km/h (15 mph) below that of the Hurricane, and had handling characteristics similar to those of the Hurricane and Spitfire. With no alternative in prospect, the Air Ministry ordered the Miles trainer on 11 June 1939 under the designation **Miles M.9 Master**, but requested changes, including use of the de-rated 533-kW (715-hp) Kestrel XXX, which reduced the maximum speed to 113 km/h (70 mph) below that of the Kestrel prototype. Even then, it was still the best training aircraft of its day, and the first of 900 examples of the **M.9A Master Mk I** was flown on 31 March 1939. Eight months later Miles flew the first **M.19 Master Mk II**, differing by having a 649-kW (870-hp) Bristol Mercury XX radial engine, which had been substituted at Air Ministry request because the supply of Kestrel engines was dwindling. The Ministry then discovered it had no stocks of Mercury engines and the 615-kW (825-hp) Pratt & Whitney Wasp Junior was installed in a modified airframe to produce the **M.27 Master Mk III**. However, both Mercury and Twin Wasp Junior engines were used in production aircraft, the eventual number built totalling 1,747 Master Mk IIs and 602 Master Mk IIIs. To these figures can be added 26 **M.24 Master Fighter** aircraft, each armed with six 7.7-mm (0.303-in) machine-guns. These last

Miles M.9A Master Mk 1 of a Royal Air Force Flying Training School in the 1940s.

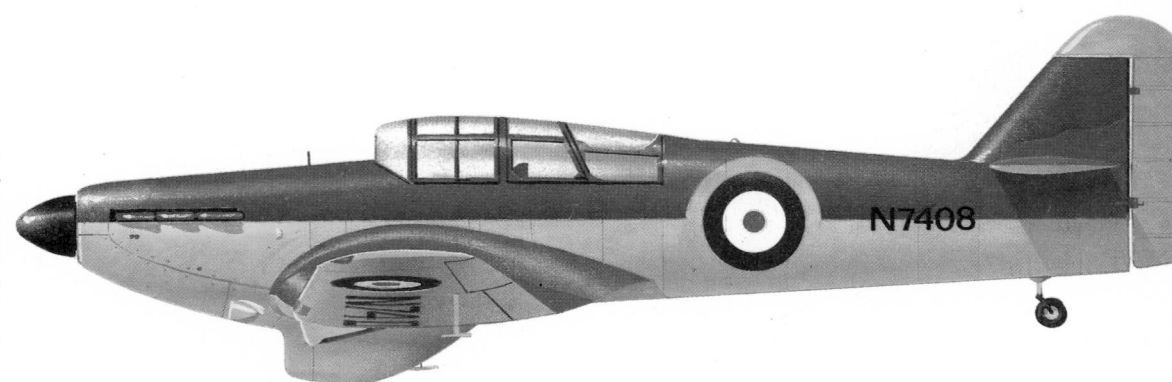

were produced during the Battle of Britain for emergency use. In addition to use by the RAF a number of Master Mk IIs were supplied to Egypt (26), Portugal (one), South Africa (450) and Turkey (18). One was transferred to the US Army Air Force and one Master Mk III went to the Irish Air Corps. When production ended a total of 3,227 had been built, the Miles Master proving to be the most significant trainer of indigenous design to serve with the RAF during World War II.

Specification
Miles M.19 Master Mk II
Type: two-seat advanced trainer
Powerplant: one 649-kW (870-hp) Bristol Mercury XX nine-cylinder radial piston engine
Performance: maximum speed 389 km/h (242 mph) at 1830 m (6,000 ft); service ceiling 7650 m (25,100 ft); range 632 km (393 miles)
Weights: empty 1947 kg (4,293 lb);

maximum take-off 2528 kg (5,573 lb)
Dimensions: span 11.89 m (39 ft 0 in) (from 1941, 10.85 m/35 ft 7 in); length 8.99 m (29 ft 6 in); height 2.82 m (9 ft 3 in); wing area 21.83 m² (235.0 sq ft)
Armament: provision for one fixed forward machine-gun and practice bombs

Production of the Master numbered approximately 1,800 aircraft. Based on the 1939 Master I, the second aircraft first flew after the outbreak of war. Master IIs were exported to Egypt, Portugal and Turkey.

Miles M.11A Whitney Straight and M.17 Monarch

In the mid-1930s wealthy aviation enthusiast Whitney Straight approached F. G. Miles to design a new lightplane for flying club use, the result being the **Miles M.11 Whitney Straight** two-seat cabin monoplane of low-wing configuration. The prototype (G-AECT) was flown for the first time on 14 May 1936, and its all-round good qualities resulted in the production of 50 **M.11A, M.11B** and **M.11C** aircraft over the next two years. A number of these were used for experimental purposes, including the testing of various engines and, on the

prototype, of auxiliary aerofoil flaps, the data gained proving beneficial to later Miles aircraft. No new M.11 aircraft were supplied for military use, but a number were impressed for service as communications aircraft during World War II, their number including 23 for the RAF (21 in the UK and two in India), and three for the Royal New Zealand Air Force. An improved model of the M.11 was developed with three-seat accommodation and flown as the **M.17 Monarch** on 21 February 1938. Although this proved satisfactory, the company's involvement with Master and Magister production meant that it was possible to complete only 11 before the outbreak of World War II, five of these being impressed into RAF service.

Specification
Miles M.11
Type: two-seat cabin monoplane
Powerplant: one 97-kW (130-hp) de Havilland Gipsy Major inline piston engine
Performance: maximum speed 233 km/h (145 mph); range 917 km (570 miles)

Weights: empty 578 kg (1,275 lb); maximum take-off 860 kg (1,896 lb)
Dimensions: span 10.87 m (35 ft 8 in); length 7.62 m (25 ft 0 in); height 1.98 m (6 ft 6 in); wing area 17.37 m² (187.0 sq ft)

G-AFLW was the fifth Miles M.17 Monarch and was built in 1938. The type was three-seat development of the successful M.11 Whitney Straight series. In total, only 11 aircraft were built.

Miles M.12 to M.18

Built to the specification of Charles Lindbergh, the only **Miles M.12 Mohawk** was a tandem two-seat cabin monoplane with a 149-kW (200-hp) Menasco Buccaneer engine. The one-off **M.13 Hobby**, a tiny single-seater built for the

Built to the requirements of Charles Lindbergh, the M.12 was a beautifully-finished low-wing monoplane. Only one was built.

1937 King's Cup race, had a 104-kW (140-hp) de Havilland Gipsy Major II engine. Trouble with the retractable landing gear prevented it from competing and it was sold eventually to the RAE for full-scale wind tunnel tests, its 6.53 m (21 ft 5 in) span being easily accommodated in the 7.32 m (24 ft) tunnel.

Miles made two attempts to build further trainers for the RAF, the first being the **M.15**, of which two prototypes were built in 1939 to specification

T.1/37 with 149-kW (200-hp) de Havilland Gipsy Six engines. However, they could not meet the specification, but neither could competing designs from four other companies.

In an attempt to provide a replacement for the Magister, Miles flew the **M.18** with a 97-kW (130-hp) de Havilland Gipsy Major engine in December 1938. While the fuselage was similar to that of the Magister, the square cut thick wing and tail surfaces were new. After much

vacillating, a decision against production was reached by the Air Ministry, but a further three M.18s were built, the second having a 112-kW (150-hp) Blackburn Cirrus Major III engine.

HM545 was the second prototype of the M.18, otherwise known as the M.18 Mk II, generally similar to the first machine apart from its engine and having its tail moved forward.

Miles M.14 Magister

Following the success of the civil M.2 Hawk Trainer series in the EFTS role, the Air Ministry drew up Specification T.40/36 for a development of the Hawk Trainer as an elementary trainer for the RAF, reversing an earlier decision to buy only metal aircraft. Design changes included the provision of enlarged cockpits and blind flying equipment. Following its first flight on 20 March 1937, production of the **Miles M.14** to a revised specification (T.37/37) was authorised, and initial deliveries were made to the RAF on their first monoplane trainers in the following May. But the **Magister**, as it was then named, was soon found to have a spinning problem; this was promptly rectified and modified airframes and subsequent production aircraft received the designation **M.14A**. At the peak of RAF use, Magisters equipped 16 Elementary Flying Training Schools and the Central Flying School, and were in use with various commands, the last example being retired in 1948. In addition, a number saw service with the British army and the Fleet Air Arm. Built from 1937 to 1941, total construction by Miles amounted to 1,293, and an additional 100 were built under licence in Turkey following the evaluation of four received directly from the

Miles M.14 Magister of an RAF Elementary Flying Training School in the 1940s.

manufacturer. RAF contracts covered 1,229 aircraft and other countries acquiring Magisters for military use included Ireland (15), Egypt (42) and New Zealand (two), in addition to a number supplied to civil customers. After World War II many RAF Magisters came onto the civil market under the designation **Hawk Trainer III**, and equipped numerous flying clubs.

Specification
Type: two-seat elementary trainer
Powerplant: one 97-kW (130-hp) de Havilland Gipsy Major 1 inline piston engine
Performance: cruising speed 199.5 km/h (124 mph); maximum speed 228.5 km/h (142 mph); service ceiling

5486 m (18,000 ft); range 612 km (380 miles)
Weights: empty 571 kg (1260 lb); maximum take-off 836.8 kg (1,845 lb)
Dimensions: span 10.3 m (33 ft 10 in); length 7.5 m (24 ft 7 in); height 2.0 m (6 ft 8 in); wing area 16.3 m² (176 sq ft)

Miles M.16 Mentor

Developed from the M.7 Nighthawk, the **Miles M.16 Mentor** was designed to meet the requirements of Air Ministry Specification 38/37 for a three-seat cabin monoplane for use in a communications role; it was required to be suitable also for instrument or radio training by day or night. The prototype (L4932) was flown on 5 January 1938, service testing resulting in an order for 45 aircraft including prototypes. This 10.85 m (35 ft 7 in) span aircraft was powered by a 149-kW (200-hp) de Havilland Gipsy Six I inline engine, providing a maximum speed of 251 km/h (156 mph) at sea level. Used by the RAF for communications and training, only one of them survived the war.

Miles M.25 Martinet

Before the issue of Air Ministry Specification 12/41, it had been standard RAF practice to use out-dated aircraft, however unsuitable, for the task of target towing. The outbreak of World War II had highlighted this short-sighted policy, leading to the procurement of an aircraft designed specifically for such a role. The **Miles M.25** prototype (LR241) was flown for the first time on 24 April 1942, the aircraft being based on the Miles Master Mk II but with a lengthened nose to compensate for the weight of target-towing equipment. Incorporated within a modified cockpit was the drogue cable winch, which could be powered by an electric motor or wind-driven propeller, and there was comfortable space for the operator and stowage of the drogue targets. The type entered service as the **Miles Martinet** and between 1942 and 1945 a total of 1,724 was built; the type was complemented in 1946 by the **M.50 Queen Martinet** which had been developed to Specification Q.10/43. This was a radio-controlled pilotless target version of the Martinet, 11 being built as new and the remaining 54 being conversions of M.25s. Planned variants included a glider-tug version of the Martinet, similar to the Master GT Mk II, and the **M.37** two-seat trainer of which two prototypes were built. Six surplus Martinets received civil registrations after the war, four of them sold to Sweden and operated by the civil target-towing company Svensk Flygjärst.

Specification
Miles Martinet
Type: two-seat target tug
Powerplant: one 649-kW (870-hp) Bristol Mercury XX/XXX 9-cylinder radial piston engine
Performance: maximum speed 386 km/h (240 mph) at 1770 m (5,800 ft); range 1117 km (694 miles)
Weights: empty 2105 kg (4,640 lb); maximum take-off 3062 kg (6,750 lb)
Dimensions: span 11.89 m (39 ft 0 in); length 9.42 m (30 ft 11 in); height 3.53 m (11 ft 7 in); wing area 22.48 m² (242.0 sq ft)

The RAF's first purpose-designed target-towing aircraft was the M.25 Martinet, of which more than 1,700 were built. It proved far more satisfactory than previous aircraft, which had merely been conversions of existing types such as the Henley, Battle or Defiant.

Miles M.33 Monitor

Designed to Air Ministry Specification Q.9/42 for a high-speed target tug, the **Miles M.33 Monitor** was a clean-looking cantilever high-wing monoplane with retractable landing gear and power provided by two wing-mounted engines. The Miles proposal was at first rejected as it was considered there were no suitable engines available, but with agreement to use the 1268-kW (1,700-hp) Wright Cyclone R-2600-31 Miles received a contract for 600 aircraft. The prototype (NF900) was flown for the first time on 5 April 1944 and handled well, but the end of the war was approaching before development was completed and the contract was reduced first to 200 and then to 50, and was finally cancelled after 20 had been delivered. Even these were not used by the RAF as intended, only 10 Monitors entering service with the Royal Navy for operation briefly as the **Monitor TT.Mk II** before replacement by de Havilland Mosquito TT.Mk 39s. With a wing span of 17.15 m (56 ft 3 in), the M.33 Monitor had a maximum speed of 579 km/h (360 mph) and service ceiling of 8840 m (29,000 ft).

As well as being an outstanding target-tug, the first to be fitted with a hydraulic winch, the Monitor was also used to simulate dive-bombing attacks on ships at speeds of up to 400 mph (664 km/h).

Miles M.35 and M.39B Libellula

Among the collection of projects which emerged from Miles during World War II, two of the strangest were the **Miles M.35** and **M.39** tandem-wing aircraft, and while most of the projects did not materialise these two were built and flown.

The M.35 was conceived as a layout practicable for a carrier-based fighter, the pilot being in the extreme nose with

Intended as an aerodynamic test-vehicle for a proposed tandem-wing naval fighter, the Miles M.35 proved the concept but then fell foul of the authorities.

the pusher engine mounted behind the rear wing. With lift provided by two wings, span could be short and there would be no need for wing-folding. The M.35 was completed and flown in six weeks but proved to be unstable. Wind tunnel tests showed the problems to be curable and George Miles conceived a heavy bomber, the M.39, to be powered by three turbojet engines, or in its initial form with two high-altitude Rolls-Royce Merlin 60s or Bristol Hercules VIIIs.

A five-eighths scale model of the bomber was built and designated **M.39B**, flying for the first time on 22 July 1943 and proving to be aerodynamically stable. Flight trials were initially on a private basis, but in 1944 the M.39B went to the Royal Aircraft Establishment

at Farnborough, where it suffered two accidents. After extensive repairs the work ended.

Specification
Miles M.39B Libellula
Type: two-seat tandem-wing research aircraft
Powerplant: two 104-kW (140-hp) de Havilland Gipsy Major 1C inline piston engines
Performance: maximum speed 264 km/h (164 mph)
Weights: empty 1091 kg (2,405 lb); maximum take-off 1270 kg (2,800 lb)
Dimensions: span 11.43 m (37 ft 6 in); length 6.76 m (22 ft 2 in); height 2.82 m (9 ft 3 in); wing area 23.15 m² (249.2 sq ft)

Miles hoped to do for the bomber what the M.35 had nearly done for the fighter, this time with the twin-engined Miles M.39B as the test aircraft.

Miles M.38 Messenger

At the private request of certain army officers in June 1942, George Miles designed and built the prototype of an air observation post (AOP) aircraft. It was required to carry a crew of two, radio, armour protection and other military equipment, and to be able to operate out of and into small tree-surrounded fields in all weathers. The resulting **Miles M.38** prototype (U-0223) was a cantilever low-wing monoplane with fixed tailwheel landing gear, powered by a 104-kW (140-hp) de Havilland Gipsy Major inline engine. The wing incorporated fixed aerofoil trailing-edge flaps and when flown on 12 September 1942 it was found that these provided the requisite STOL performance. Great enthusiasm for its capability was shown by an AOP squadron which Miles allowed to

flight test the aircraft, but shocked by the design, construction and testing of a military aeroplane without its knowledge, the Ministry of Aircraft Production refused to order this prototype into production for the AOP role. In late 1943 a small order was placed for the aircraft for use in a VIP transport role under the designation **M.38 Messenger** and eventually a total of 21 was built. Among VIP operators allocated personal Messengers were Field Marshal Sir Bernard Montgomery and Marshal of the RAF Lord Tedder. An additional 71 were built post-war for civil use, bringing total production to 92. One aircraft was modified in 1944 by introducing conventional trailing-edge flaps and installing a 112-kW (150-hp) Blackburn Cirrus Major engine. When tested this machine, designated

M.48 Messenger 3, was found to offer so little improvement in performance over the standard M.38 that no production followed. In its role as a VIP transport the 11.02 m (36 ft 2 in) span Messenger had a maximum speed of 187 km/h (116 mph) and range of 418 km (260 miles).

With his M.38, Miles was again in trouble, as the design had not been cleared with the Ministry of Aircraft Production. Thus, the type was not built for the AOP role for which it was originally intended, being built instead in small numbers as a VIP transport.

Miles M.57 Aerovan

Miles was a prolific designer, and a mass of projects passed through the drawing office, though many of these came to nothing. One unusual looking design which did make the grade was the **Miles M.57 Aerovan**, a twin-engine light freighter which flew first in January 1945. In appearance the wings and tail unit were similar to those of the Messenger, but somewhat larger, while the fuselage was of pod and boom layout.

A number of UK and overseas orders were placed and the Aerovan entered production with a longer pod than the prototype, which was designated **Aerovan Mk I**, and the second prototype the **Aerovan Mk II**. The first **Aerovan Mk III** production model was similar to the Mk II, and seven were built with 112-kW (150-hp) Blackburn Cirrus Major III

G-AILC was the fifth Aerovan Mk IV, a variant very similar to the Mk III, apart from having four circular rather than rectangular windows along the fuselage.

engines, the standard Aerovan powerplant. The next version, the **Aerovan Mk IV**, differed in detail and 40 were built. One **Aerovan Mk V** with 108-kW (145-hp) de Havilland Gipsy Major 10 engines and two **Aerovan Mk VI** aircraft with 145-kW (195-hp) Avco Lycoming O-435-4A engines were built; one of the latter was fitted with an experimental Hurel-Dubois high aspect ratio wing in 1957 when it became known as the **HDM.105**. The last known surviving Aerovan was the first Mk VI, operating in

Italy in 1968, although a pair of uncompleted airframes were around for some years.

At very low cost, Aerovans carried loads up to the size and weight of a family car.

Miles M.60 Marathon

With the **Miles M.60 Marathon**, the company broke new ground, for it was the company's first all-metal aircraft and the first with four engines. Flown in 1946 with Gipsy Queen 71 engines, the Marathon was the winner in a competitive bid to Air Ministry Specification 18/44, and the Ministry ordered three prototypes for BOAC.

Miles was frustrated severely by the vacillations of the Ministry of Aircraft Production, which gave orders and counter orders throughout the pre-pro-

duction stages, but when the prototype flew test pilots soon found it was a very pleasant aircraft to handle. Loss of the prototype in a fatal crash during trials at Boscombe Down was attributed to pilot error. The second prototype flew in

One of the interesting projects jeopardised by the financial crash of Miles was the Marathon. With the take-over of the company by Handley-Page, it became the H.P.R.1 and served with the RAF.

February 1947, but before a production contract could be signed the Miles company suffered financial collapse and its aircraft assets were eventually acquired by Handley Page.

The company became Handley Page (Reading) Ltd. and the M.60 Marathon was redesignated **Handley Page H.P.R.1 Marathon I**. A production order for 50 was placed, 30 for BEA and 20 for BOAC's associated companies. In the event the BEA order was reduced to 25 and later seven, then cancelled com-

pletely, and 28 of the Marathons were modified for use by the RAF as navigation trainers as the **Marathon T.Mk 11**, serving for six years before being replaced by Vickers Varsities. Handley Page built only 40. The remaining aircraft operated in a number of overseas countries including West Germany, Jordan, Nigeria, Canada, Japan and Burma. Some were used experimentally, including use as engine test-beds, and the last survivors were scrapped around the mid-1960s.

Variant
M.69 Marathon II: designation of single prototype, flown by the Handley Page company, initially with two 753-kW (1,010-hp) Armstrong Siddeley Mamba turboprop engines; later used to test two Alvis Leonides Major radial engines

Specification
Miles M.60 Marathon
Type: light transport (18-22 passengers)

Powerplant: four 246-kW (330-hp) de Havilland Gipsy Queen 71 inline piston engines
Performance: maximum speed 322 km/h (200 mph) at 1890 m (6,200 ft); service ceiling 5030 m (16,500 ft); range 1368 km (850 miles)
Weights: empty 5198 kg (11,460 lb); maximum take-off 7484 kg (16,500 lb)
Dimensions: span 19.81 m (65 ft 0 in); length 15.93 m (52 ft 3 in); height 4.27 m (14 ft 0 in); wing area 46.45 m² (500.0 sq ft)

Miles M.65 Gemini and M.75 Aries

Conceived as a twin-engine retractable landing gear version of the Messenger, the **Miles M.65 Gemini** flew first on 26 October 1945 and was an immediate success. It was the last Miles aircraft to enter quantity production and in its **Gemini Mk 1A** initial form was powered by 75-kW (100-hp) Blackburn Cirrus engines, and had non-retractable auxiliary trailing-edge flaps; one **Gemini Mk 1B** was built with retractable flaps. The single **Gemini Mk 2** was created by installing 93-kW (125-hp) Continental engines, while production **Gemini Mk 3A** aircraft had 108-kW (145-hp) de Havilland Gipsy Major 10s. There were several sub-variants with detail differences, but the most power-

ful version with two 116-kW (155-hp) Blackburn Cirrus Major III engines, a strengthened structure and larger fins and rudders, was deemed sufficiently different to be designated **M.75 Aries**.

A total of 170 Geminis and two Aries was built, around two-thirds of them

One of Miles' most successful designs ever was the M.65 Gemini, seen here in the form of a Gemini 1A. Developed from the Messenger, it used a similar wing and fuselage but had a twin-finned tail. The prototype flew with fixed landing gear but all 170 production aircraft had retractable units.

being exported, before the company collapsed in 1947, and the type could be

considered as Miles' most popular postwar aeroplane.

Miles M.68 Boxcar, M.71 Merchantman and M.100 Student

In the midst of a mass of projects, Miles flew three prototypes which deserve brief mention. The **Miles M.68 Boxcar**, flown on 22 August 1947, had four 75-kW (100-hp) Blackburn Cirrus Minor II engines and was basically of Aerovan layout, except that the centre section of the fuselage was designed to mount a detachable container 1.37 m (4 ft 6 in) square and 3.05 m (10 ft) long, the idea being that freight containers could be pre-loaded and the aircraft could be flown with or without the container attached.

In the same month Miles flew the **M.71 Merchantman** with four 186-kW (250-hp) de Havilland Gipsy Queen 30 engines and a modified Marathon wing. Configuration was

otherwise similar to that of the Aerovan, but the aircraft was of metal construction. Neither of these promising designs was able to proceed because of the firm's collapse.

The **M.100 Student** is outside the basic Miles Aircraft history, since it was a private venture by F. G. and George Miles started in 1953. A two-seat side-by-side all-metal jet trainer, the Student was powered by a 400-kg (882-lb) thrust Turboméca Marboré turbojet and flew on 15 May 1957. Miles had hoped to secure an RAF order, which in the event went to the Jet Provost, and the Student did not go into production. The Student was subsequently proposed for several training orders, but without success.

The Miles M.71 Merchantman was the ultimate development of the Aerovan design philosophy, and could carry 5,000 lb (2268 kg) of freight or 20 passengers over 850 miles (1367 km).

Mitsubishi 1MF

The **Mitsubishi 1MF** was among the first designs produced for the Mitsubishi Internal Combustion Engine Co. Ltd, set up by the Mitsubishi industrial concern in 1920. One of three types designed by Herbert Smith, formerly of the British Sopwith company, to meet requirements issued by the Imperial Japanese Navy for aircraft to equip its first aircraft-carrier (the *Hosho*), the **1MF1** initial version was an unequal-span single-seat carrier-based fighter biplane, powered by a 223-kW (300-hp) Hispano-Suiza 8

engine, which entered production in 1921 as the **Navy Type 10-1 Carrier Fighter**. It was followed by the **1MF2**, an experimental variant with modified upper-wing ailerons. The series **Type 10-2** or **1MF3** had twin Lamblin radiators fitted between the landing gear legs, the **Type 10-3 (1MF4)** had the pilot's cockpit relocated farther forward and a redesigned tailplane, while **1MF5A** was a version of the 1MF4 with experimental flotation gear.

Production of the 1MF series ended in

Powered by a Hispano Suiza 8 engine, the Mitsubishi IMF clearly shows the Sopwith influence brought to the company's designs by Herbert Smith.

1928 with the 138th example. The Type 10 proved a tough, reliable fighter and remained in service for a number of years, latterly as an advanced trainer. Maximum speed (Type 10-2) was 205 km/h (127 mph), wing span was 8.50 m (27 ft 10¾ in) and maximum take-off weight

was 1280 kg (2,822 lb). Armament comprised two fixed synchronised 7.7-mm (0.303-in) Vickers machine-guns.

Mitsubishi 1MT1N

A Herbert Smith design intended for service aboard the Japanese aircraft-carrier *Hosho*, the **Mitsubishi 1MT1N** flew for the first time in August 1922. A

single-seat triplane torpedo-bomber, it entered service as the **Navy Type 10 Torpedo Bomber**, powered by a 336-kW (450-hp) Napier Lion engine

which gave it a maximum speed of 205 km/h (127 mph) and a service ceiling of 6000 m (19,680 ft). Production totalled 20, but the Type proved difficult

to fly and impossible to operate from an aircraft-carrier when carrying its offensive load, an 800-kg (1,764-lb) torpedo, and the type was soon scrapped.

Mitsubishi 2MB1
to
Mitsubishi G4M

Mitusbishi 2MB1

After building 57 Nieuport 81 trainers for the Imperial Japanese Army as the **Mitsubishi Ko-1**, followed by 145 Hanriot HD-14s under the designation **Mitsubishi Ki-1**, Mitsubishi submitted the experimental **2MB2 Washi** two-seat light bomber biplane designed by Alexander Baumann in 1925. This was rejected for production, the Imperial Army preferring Herbert Smith's more conventional **2MB1**, a large two-seat biplane with wide-track divided landing gear. This entered service in 1927 as the **Army**

The Mitisubishi 2MB2 Washi was a relatively advanced sesquiplane design with neat interplane bracing and wide-track landing gear, but it was ultimately rejected.

Type 87 Light Bomber, 48 being built, and each was powered by a 336-kW (450-hp) Hispano-Suiza engine which gave a maximum speed of 185 km/h (115 mph); the 2MB1 had a maximum take-off weight of 3300 kg

(7,275 lb) and wing span of 14.80 m (48 ft 6¾ in). Armament comprised one fixed forward-firing 7.7-mm (0.303-in) machine-gun, twin guns of the same

calibre on a ring mounting for the observer, and provision for a fourth gun firing through a ventral trap; maximum bomb load was 500 kg (1,102 lb).

Mitsubishi 2MR

Another Herbert Smith design, the first example of the **Mitsubishi 2MR** two-seat carried-based reconnaissance biplane flew in January 1922. The type entered service as the **Type 10 Carrier Reconnaissance Biplane** and was built in a number of versions. The **2MR1** had a frontal radiator for its 224-kW (300-hp) Hispano-Suiza 8 engine, while the **2MR2** had twin underslung Lamblin radiators and redesigned tail surfaces. The **2MR4**, which was the main production version, had some further revisions of the wing and tail unit, and other variants with minor changes were the **2MRT1, 2MRT2, 2MRT2A, 2MRT3** and **2MRT3A**. Total production of all

versions was 159, the last machine leaving the workshops in 1930. After long carrier service, the 2MR was used as a trainer in the late 1930s.

The 2MR4 version spanned 12.04 m (39 ft 6 in), had a maximum take-off weight of 1320 kg (2,910 lb), and was armed with two fixed forward-firing 7.7-mm (0.303-in) machine-guns, with twin guns of the same calibre mounted over the observer's cockpit, and could carry three 30-kg (66-lb) bombs.

The **R-2.2** and **R-4** civil conversions had an enclosed cabin for two passengers replacing the rear cockpit, and a number of ex-army surplus 2MRs were sold on the civil market in the 1930s.

Visible in silhouette under the fuselage are the two Lamblin radiators of this Mitsubishi 2MR carrier-based reconnaissance aircraft.

Mitsubishi 2MB8

In 1927 Mitubishi enlisted the help of German designer Baumann to meet an Imperial Japanese Army requirement for a new reconnaissance aircraft. The resulting Mitsubishi **2MR1 Tobi** two-seat sesquiplane was a grotesque aircraft, which performed only slightly worse than Baumann's next design, the **1MF2 Hayabusa** parasol-wing single-seat fighter of a year later. A third unsuccessful type was the **2MR7** short-range reconnaissance biplane of 1928.

In 1930, however, three **2MR8** parasol-wing reconnaissance monoplanes were built and tested successfully. Of mixed construction, they had fixed wide-track divided landing gear and were powered by a 354-kW (475-hp) Mitsub-

The wide track undercarriage of the Mitsubishi 2MRS was an obvious advantage for rough field operations. The mount for a machine-gun is visible just above the centre-section.

ishi Type 92 radial engine. Accepted by the army, the 2MR8 went into service in 1932 as the **Type 92 Reconnaissance Aircraft**. Production terminated in 1933 with the 230th machine. Maximum speed was 220 km/h (137 mph), wing span 12.75 m (41 ft 10 in), and maximum take-off weight 1770 kg (3,902 lb). The Type 92 was normally armed with a fixed forward-firing 7.7-mm (0.303-in) machine-gun

mounted above the wing centre-section, with single or twin guns of the same calibre on a ring mounting over the observer's cockpit.

The Type 92 saw active service in Manchuria with the air battalions (later air wings) of the army's Kanto Command Air Corps between 1933 and 1936. A civil

version of the Type 92 was used as a survey aircraft by Japanese National Railways. Powered by a 298-kW (400-hp) Mitsubishi A-5 engine, it was registered J-AARA and differed externally from the military aircraft in having a glazed canopy over the crew cockpits and spat-type main wheel fairings.

Mitsubishi A5M

An Imperial Japanese Navy specification of 1934 for a single-seat fighter with a maximum speed of 350 km/h (217 mph) then seemed an almost unattainable target. However, Mitsubishi's **Ka-14** prototype designed to this requirement, and flown for the first time on 4 February 1935, demonstrated a top speed of 450 km/h (280 mph) in early trials. Unfortunately it had some aerodynamic shortcomings, and the inverted gull-wing of this aircraft was replaced by a conventional low-set monoplane wing in the second prototype which, with a 436-kW (585-hp) Nakajima Kotobuki

2-KAI-1 radial engine, was ordered into production as the **Navy Type 96 Carrier Fighter Model 1 (Mitsubishi A5M1)**. The generally similar **A5N2a** which followed, powered by the 455-kW (610-hp) Kotobuki 2-KAI-3 engine, and the **A5M2b** with the 477-kW (640-hp) Kotobuki 3 engine, were regarded as the Japanese navy's most important fighter aircraft during the Sino-Japanese War. Two experimental **A5M3** aircraft were flown with the Hispano-Suiza 12Xcrs engine, but the final and major production version was the **A5M4**, built also as the **A5M4-K** tandem two-seat trainer.

All versions of the A5M were allocated the Allied codename **'Claude'**, and when production ended a total of 788 had been built by Mitsubishi, including prototypes; a further 303 were built by Watanabe (39) and the Omura Naval Air Arsenal (264). The Japanese army also shown interest in the A5M, resulting in the evaluation of a **Ki-18** prototype generally similar to the Ka-14, but although fast this was considered to be lacking in manoeuvrability. Mitsubishi produced two re-engined and improved **Ki-33** prototypes but they, too, were considered insufficiently manoeuvrable and no army production contract resulted.

At the beginning of the Pacific war the

A5M4 was in first-line use, but its performance was found inadequate to confront Allied fighters and by the summer of 1942 all had been transferred to second-line duties, many surviving A5M4 and A5M4-Ks being used in *kamikaze* attacks in the closing months of the war.

Specification
Mitsubishi A5M4
Type: single-seat carrier-based fighter
Powerplant: one 529-kW (710-hp) Nakajima Kotobuki 41 (Bristol Jupiter) radial piston engine
Performance: maximum speed 440 km/h (273 mph) at 3000 m (9,840 ft); service ceiling 9800 m

(32,150 ft); maximum range 1200 km
(746 miles)
Weights: empty 1216 kg (2,681 lb);
maximum take-off 1705 kg (3,759 lb)
Dimensions: span 11.00 m (36 ft
1 in); length 7.55 m (24 ft 9¼ in); height
3.20 m (10 ft 6 in); wing area 17.80 m²
(191.60 sq ft)
Armament: two forward-firing
7.7-mm (0.303-in) machine-guns, plus
two 30-kg (66-lb) bombs

*Mitsubishi A5M4 of Lieutenant Tamotsu Yokoyama, leader of the
fighter element of the carrier* Soryu *on blockade duty in the East China
Sea during November 1939.*

Mitsubishi A6M Zero-Sen

Without doubt the most famous
Japanese single-seat fighter aircraft of
all time, the **Mitsubishi Zero-Sen
(Type 0 Fighter)** was designed to
meet an Imperial Japanese Navy requirement for an A5M replacement. A
cantilever low-wing monoplane,
powered in **A6M1** prototype form by a
582-kW (780-hp) Mitsubishi MK2 Zuisei
radial engine, the type was flown for the
first time on 1 April 1939. Testing
showed excellent performance, except
that maximum speed was below navy
specification, leading to an **A6M2** prototype with a 690-kW (925-hp) Nakajima
NK1C Sakae engine which flew on 18
January 1940. This was so successful
that in July 1940 Mitsubishi was
contracted to build 15 pre-production
A6M2s for evaluation in China, and at the
end of that month the type was ordered
into production as the **Navy Type 0
Carrier Fighter Model 11 (A6M2
Model 11)**. This version was built also
as the **A6M2 Model 21** with manually
folded wingtips, and as the **A6M2-K**
two-seat trainer. A floatplane version of
the Zero-Sen was built by Nakajima (to a
total of 327) under the designation
A6M2-N. Revised versions of the
A6M2 included the **A6M3 Model 22**
with the Nakajima NK1F Sakae 21 engine
and the similarly-powered A6M3 with
clipped wings instead of folding wingtips. Major production version was the
A6M5 Model 52, introduced in 1943 to
counter the growing capability of Allied
fighters, built also in sub-variants
A6M5a, A6M5b and **A6M5c** which
differed primarily in armament, the
A6M5d-S night-fighter with a 20-mm
cannon mounted obliquely in the rear
fuselage, and the **A6M5-K** two-seat
trainer. By then the A6M had really
attained its optimum state of development, but Japan's desperate position led
to a re-engined version of the A6M5c
which entered production as the
A6M6c Model 53c in late 1944, and
the fighter/dive-bomber **A6M7 Model
63** with an underfuselage rack for one
250-kg (551-lb) bomb built from
mid-1945. Final variant was the **A6M8c
Model 64c**, of which two prototypes
were built with 1119-kW (1,500-hp) Mitsubishi MK8K engines, but no series aircraft were produced before the end of
the war.

Unbelievably successful when introduced into the Sino-Japanese War, this
amazing fighter, allocated the Allied
codename **'Zeke'**, seemed to fill the
skies over the Pacific during 1941 and
early 1942. However, after the Battle of
Midway in June 1942, Allied fighters
began to gain the initiative and the A6M
never again held wide-scale air superiority. But despite shortcomings the type
remained in service until the end of the
war, built to a total of approximately
10,450 by Mitsubishi (3,880) and Nakajima (6,570). In addition, 515 A6M2-K and
A6M5-K trainers were built by Hitachi
(279) and the 21st Naval Air Arsenal at
Omura (236). Large numbers of early
versions were used in *kamikaze* attacks
during the closing months of the war.

Specification
Mitsubishi A6M6c Model 53c
Type: single-seat interceptor fighter/
fighter-bomber
Powerplant: one 843-kW (1,130-hp)
Nakajima Sakae 31 radial piston engine
Performance: maximum speed
557 km/h (346 mph) at 6000 m
(19,685 ft); service ceiling 10700 m
(35,105 ft); maximum range 1800 km
(1,118 miles)
Weights: empty 1895 kg (4,178 lb);
maximum take-off 2950 kg (6,504 lb)
Dimensions: span 11.00 m (36 ft
1 in); length 9.07 m (29 ft 9 in); height
3.50 m (11 ft 5¾ in); wing area 21.30
m² (229.28 sq ft)
Armament: two 20-mm cannon (in
wings) and three 13.2-mm (0.52-in)
machine-guns (two in wings and one in
fuselage), plus underwing launch rails
for eight 10-kg (22-lb) or two 60-kg
(132-lb) air-to-air rockets

Mitsubishi A6M2

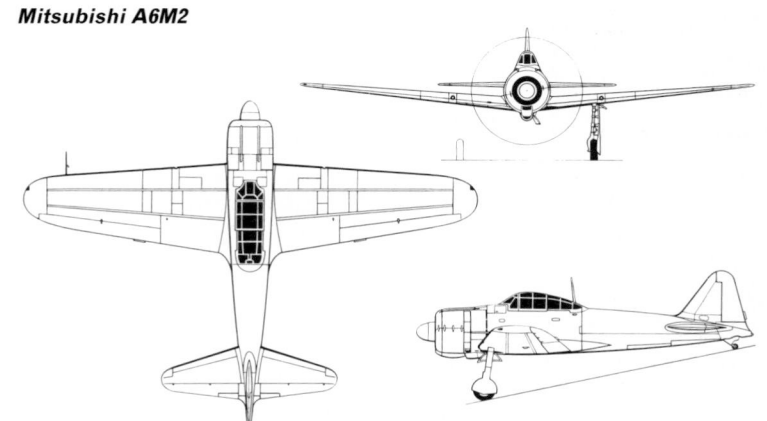

*With a 330-litre drop tank and sophisticated propeller/engine
management techniques, the Zero had phenomenal range.*

Mitsubishi A7M

The design by Mitsubishi of a carrier-based fighter to supersede the A6M Zero-Sen had been planned by the Japanese navy as early as 1940, but was frustrated by the company's involvement in urgent development and production programmes. It was not until 1942 that design of the **M-50 Reppu** (hurricane) began, but the continuing pressure on Mitsubishi for developments of the A6M meant that it was not until 6 May 1944 that the first prototype, which by then had the company designation **Mitsubishi A7M1**, was flown for the first time. A cantilever low-wing monoplane with retractable tailwheel landing gear, the A7M1 soon revealed excellent flight characteristics, but as predicted by Mitsubishi the type's maximum speed on the power of the in-

To produce the A7M2 from the A7M1, the company had to redesign the entire forward fuselage of the Reppu to accommodate the more powerful MK9A radial engine.

stalled Nakajima NK9K Homare 22 engine was below specification. Further testing was abandoned until availability of the 1641-kW (2,200-hp) Mitsubishi MK9A radial engine made it possible to build seven **A7M2** prototype and service trials aircraft, the first prototype being flown on 13 October 1944. Clearly a potent fighter that could meet Allied opposition on equal terms, the Reppu had a maximum speed of 630 km/h (391 mph) at optimum altitude and was ordered into production as the **Navy**

Carrier Fighter Reppu Model 22. Unfortunately, by then it was too late for the Japanese navy, Allied air attacks and an earthquake limiting production to only one aircraft, allocated the Allied code-

name **'Sam'**. Development of similar land-based fighters was planned under the designations **A7M3** and **A7M3-J**, but neither was built before the war ended.

Mitsubishi B1M

Most successful of Herbert Smith's designs for Mitsubishi was undoubtedly the **Mitsubishi 2MT,** a two-seat biplane topedo-bomber. The **2MT1** prototype flew in January 1923 and as the **B1M1** entered production for the Imperial Japanese Navy as the **Type 13 Carrier Attacker**. The basic design was subject to continuing modifications and the final **B1M3** production version was a three-seater.

When the Shanghai Incident broke out in January 1932 the carriers *Kaga* and *Hosho* were in Chinese waters and the Imperial Japanese Navy 1st Air Wing deployed 32 Type 13 Attackers from the *Kaga* and nine from the *Hosho* against targets in and around Shanghai. They also carried out attacks in co-operation with Japanese ground forces. On 5 February 1932 two Type 13s escorted by three Nakajima Type 3 Carrier Fighters were engaged in aerial combat with some Chinese Vought Corsairs, while on 22 February three Type 13s with fighter escort from the *Kaga* were attacked by American volunteer pilot Robert Short in a Boeing Model 218 biplane (export version of P-12E). The fighter escort commander destroyed Short's aircraft, but the Type 13 of formation commander

Lieutenant Susumi Kotani had already been shot down by the American.

As a result of the failure of the Yokosho B3Y1 attack aircraft, a number of B1M3s remained in first-line service past obsolescence into the mid-1930s.

Variants
2MT1: prototype and initial production version
2MT2 and 2MT3: slightly modified versions of 2MT1 which, together with 2MT1s, carried the naval designation **B1M1** or **Type 13-1 Carrier-Attacker**; 196 built
2MT4 Otori: twin-float reconnaissance version of 2MT2; three tested but did not enter production
2MT5: version powered by 373-kW (500-hp) Hispano-Suiza Vee-12 engine; 116 built
3MT2: three-seat version with 447-kW (600-hp) Hispano-Suiza; Mitsubishi built 88 1929-30 and Hiro Arsenal later completed an additional 40; naval designation **B1M3** or **Type 13-2-2 Carrier Attacker**; one instead of two fixed forward-firing machine-guns
T-1.2: designation for civil conversions with enclosed passenger cabin for two

The B1M was Herbert Smith's most successful design for Mitsubishi and it remained in large-scale service well into the 1930s.

or three behind pilot's cockpit; each arrangement was different; other Type 13s used as naval or civil trainers at end of active service

Specification
Mitsubishi 2MT2
Type: two-seat carrier-based torpedo-bomber
Powerplant: one 373-kW (500-hp) Napier Lion engine
Performance: maximum speed

210 km/h (130 mph); service ceiling 4500 m (14,765 ft)
Weights: empty 1442 kg (3,179 lb); maximum take-off 2697 kg (5,946 lb)
Dimensions: span 14.77 m (48 ft 5½ in); length 9.77 m (32 ft 0¾ in); height 3.50 m (11 ft 5¾ in); wing area 59.00 m² (645.09 sq ft)
Armament: two fixed and two pivoted 7.7-mm (0.303-in) machine-guns; one 18-in torpedo, or two 240-kg (529-lb) bombs

Mitsubishi B2M

In 1928 Mitsubishi presented to the Imperial Japanese Navy three new types: the **Mitsubishi 1MF9 Taka** carrier fighter biplane, which featured a French-type *avion marin* keel; the **Type R** experimental twin-engine monoplane flying-boat, built also in a civil transport version, both of them based on Rohrbach designs; and the **3MR4** carrier reconnaissance biplane. This last was in reality designed by G. E. Petty, chief designer of the British Blackburn Aeroplane Company, and had been built in the UK. Three development prototypes were constructed subsequently· by Mitsubishi, and it was decided that the aircraft would be used primarily as a carrier-based torpedo-bomber. Prolonged difficulties prevented naval adoption of the 3MR4 until March 1932, when it went

Powered by the distinctive Hispano Suiza 12 piston engine, the Mitsubishi B2M1 was designed from the outset as a carrier-based torpedo bomber; bomb racks were later fitted.

into service as the **Navy Type 89-1 Carrier Attacker** or **Mitsubishi B2M1**.

Powered by a 485-kW (650-hp) Hispano-Suiza 12Lb engine, the B2M1 had a maximum speed of 213 km/h (132 mph), and was an equal-span biplane with wide-track landing gear, its crew of three carried in tandem cockpits. Defensive armament comprised one fixed and one movably-mounted 7.7-mm (0.303-in) machine-gun; and for offensive purposes an 800-kg (1,746-lb) torpedo car-

ried between the main landing gear legs could be supplemented by six light bombs on underwing racks.

An improved **B2M2** or **Type 89-2** appeared in 1934, this having a wing span of 14.98 m (49 ft 1¾ in) and a maximum take-off weight of 3600 kg

(7,936 lb), but its overall performance showed little advantage over the B2M1. Production of both versions totalled 204, and they were used extensively for medium- and low-level bombing attacks against Chinese troops during the Shanghai Incident.

Mitsubishi B5M

Bearing the company designation **Mitsubishi Ka-16**, this cantilever low-wing monoplane, carrier-based torpedo-bomber flew in prototype form as the **Navy 10-Shi Experimental**

Attacker in 1936. A three-seater, it had a long glazed crew canopy and was distinguished easily from its Nakajima B5N rival by having fixed cantilever landing gear with spat-type wheel fairings. The

wings outboard of the landing gear could be folded upwards for carrier stowage.

As a precaution against problems with the B5N, this **Mitsubishi B5M1** design was placed in production and went into service as the **Navy Type 97 Carrier Attack Bomber Model 2**, gaining initially the Allied codename **'Mabel'**,

later changed to **'Kate 61'**. At least 125 had been delivered when the obvious success of its rival brought production to a halt. The B5M1 saw some action from land bases in the South Pacific before being relegated to training and liaison duties.

Powered by a 746-kW (1,000-hp) Mitsubishi Kinsei 43 radial, the B5M1 had a maximum speed of 380 km/h (236 mph). Armament comprised one 7.7-mm (0.303-in) trainable machine-gun, plus an 800-kg (1,764-lb) torpedo or an equivalent weight of bombs.

Known to the manufacturer as the Ka-16, Mitsubishi's B5M1 was a three-seat cantilever-wing torpedo bomber intended for carrier operations. It was denied wider-scale production and service only by the excellence of the competing Nakajima B5N, which entered service as the Type 97 Torpedo Bomber. The Mitsubishi aircraft was designated the Type 97-2 Carrier Attacker, mainly as a back-up for the Nakajima design. One hundred and twenty-five B5M1s were built and the type saw combat, but operated only from land bases.

Mitsubishi F-1

The development of a close air-support fighter from the Mitsubishi T-2 supersonic trainer was first planned in 1972, two production T-2 trainers being taken to serve as prototypes, initially under the designation **FS-T2-Kai**. The airframe is basically similar to that of the T-2, differing primarily by the rear cockpit area being adapted to serve as a compartment for the more advanced avionics and equipment which is carried to fulfil the close-support role. Both modified aircraft were first flown in June 1975 and completed a year of service trials with the JASDF Air Proving Wing before the type was ordered into production in 1976 under the designation **Mitsubishi F-1**.

Generally similar in dimensions and performance to the T-2, the F-1 has a maximum take-off weight of 13700 kg

The F-1 serves primarily in the anti-ship role, though this is described officially as 'anti-landing craft' to conform with the constitutionally enshrined self-defence ethos of the JASDF.

(30,203 lb) and its more sophisticated weapons system allows for the carriage and use of weapons that include a Vulcan multi-barrel cannon, a variety of rockets and bombs, Mitsubishi ASM-1 air-to-surface missiles, AIM-9 Sidewinder air-to-air missiles, or auxiliary fuel tanks for long-range missions.

A total of 77 F-1s was ordered and the initial production aircraft flew for the first time on 17 Jun 1977. Deliveries to the 3rd Squadron of the 3rd Air Wing at Misawa began in September 1977 and later to the two squadrons of the 8th Air Wing at Tsuiki, with the final aircraft being received on 9 March 1987.

Mitsubishi F-1 of the 3rd Air Squadron, Japan Air Self-Defence Force, based at Misawa (Japan) in the early 1980s.

Mitsubishi F1M

In 1935 Mitsubishi designed for the Japanese navy under the designation **Ka-17** a two-seat observation floatplane suitable for catapult launching. Flown first during June 1936, this biplane was powered by a 611-kW (820-hp) Nakajima Hikari engine but had disappointing performance, leading to four modified **F1M1** prototypes with the more powerful Mitsubishi Zuisei 13 radial engine. Subsequent testing and service trials proved satisfactory, and the type was ordered into production as the **Navy Type 0 Observation Seaplane Model 11 (Mitsubishi F1M2)**, later allocated the Allied codename **'Pete'**. Production totalled 1,118, built by Mitsubishi (528) and the 21st Naval Air Arsenal (590); a small number of this total were converted for use as two-seat trainers under the designation **F1M2-K**.

Used extensively from ships and

shore bases for coastal patrol, convoy escort and reconnaissance, the F1M was also deployed successfully in the unexpected roles of fighter and dive-bomber.

Specification
Mitsubishi F1M2
Type: two-seat patrol/reconnaissance floatplane
Powerplant: one 652-kW (875-hp) Mitsubishi Zuisei 13 radial piston engine
Performance: maximum speed 370 km/h (230 mph) at 3440 m (11,285 ft); service ceiling 9440 m

Despite its technical obsolescence, the F1M2 emerged as a true maid-of-all-work as a first-line aircraft serving in secondary theatres.

(30,970 ft); range 740 km (460 miles)
Weights: empty 1928 kg (4,251 lb); maximum take-off 2550 kg (5,662 lb)
Dimensions: span 11.00 m (36 ft 1 in); length 9.50 m (31 ft 2 in); height 4.00 m (13 ft 1½ in); wing area

29.54 m² (317.98 sq ft)
Armament: two forward-firing 7.7-mm (0.303-in) machine-guns and one gun of similar calibre on pivoted mounting in rear cockpit, plus two 60-kg (132-lb) bombs

Mitsubishi FS-X/TFS-X

The requirement for a Mitsubishi F-1 replacement was designated the **FS-X** and issued to the Japanese industry in the mid-1980s. Mitsubishi was named prime contractor in November 1988 and Kawasaki and Fuji will participate in the programme, which calls for the development and production of 130 close support fighters based on the General

Dynamics F-16C airframe, with the American company taking a 40 per cent share in the project. Delays over US technology transfer philosophy have retarded the programme by about two years, and in 1991 cost of the project was estimated to have risen by 70 per cent to over $2 billion. Four prototypes (two single-seat and two **TFS-X** two-seaters)

are under construction, with the first FS-X scheduled to fly in mid-1995, and a decision to begin production planned for 1996. First deliveries of the developed FS-X are required by 1999. Construction is taking place at the Nagoya plant.

Bearing a strong resemblance to the F-16, differences include a 1.0 m (3 ft 3 in) longer fuselage, wing span increased by 1.0 m (3 ft 3 in), resulting in a 25 per cent increase in wing area, and a bigger diameter nose radome to house

the advanced radar antenna. Large ventral canards mounted on the engine intakes will increase agility via a full advanced fly-by-wire system. The 129-kN (29,000-lb) thrust General Electric F110-GE-129 turbofan engine was selected as the FS-X powerplant in December 1990 and will be partly built in Japan. Armament is expected to include the AAM-3 air-to-air missile and XASM-2 anti-shipping missile, both developed and built by Mitsubishi.

Mitsubishi G3M

In 1934 Mitsubishi designed a twin-engine bomber/transport under the initial designation **Ka-15**, a cantilever mid-wing monoplane with retractable tailwheel landing gear. Powered by two 559-kW (750-hp) Hiro Type 91 engines, the prototype made its first flight during July 1935. Twenty more Ka-15 prototypes followed to evaluate several engine/propeller combinations, service trials resulting in a production order in June 1936 under the designation **Navy Type 96 Attack Bomber Model 11 (Mitsubishi G3M1)**. The first 34 production aircraft had 679-kW (910-hp) Mitsubishi Kinsei 3 engines, and these were followed by the **G3M2 Model 21** with increased fuel capacity and 802-kW (1,075-hp) Kinsei 41 or 42 radials. Subsequent production included the **G3M2 Model 22** with improved armament and the **G3M3 Model 23** with further uprated engine. A number were converted for transport duties from G3M1 aircraft under the designations **G3M1-L** and **L3Y1 Model 11**, and from the G3M2 Model 21 as the **L3Y2 Model 12**. Production totalled 1,048, including prototypes, built by Mitsubishi (636) and Nakajima (412), the bomber and transport aircraft being allocated the Allied codenames **'Nell'** and **'Tina'** respectively.

G3M2s first demonstrated their long-range capability on 14 August 1937, when a squadron based at Taipei, Taiwan, attacked targets 2010 km (1,249 miles) distant in China. The type is perhaps best known for its part in the sinking of the British battleship HMS *Prince of Wales* and battle-carrier HMS *Repulse* on 10 December 1941, just three days after the initial attack on Pearl Harbor. The type served through the Pacific war, but by 1943 most were being deployed in second-line roles.

Mitsubishi G3M3 of the Takao Kokutai, 21st Koku Sentai, operating from Hanoi, Indo-China, during March 1941.

Specification
Mitsubishi G3M3 Model 23
Type: seven-crew long-range bomber
Powerplant: two 969-kW (1,300-hp) Mitsubishi Zuisei 51 radial piston engines
Performance: maximum speed 415 km/h (258 mph) at 5900 m (19,360 ft); service ceiling 10280 m (33,725 ft); maximum range 6230 km (3,871 miles)

Weights: empty 5240 kg (11,552 lb); maximum take-off 8000 kg (17,637 lb)
Dimensions: span 25.00 m (82 ft 0¼ in); length 16.45 m (53 ft 11¾ in); height 3.69 m (12 ft 1¼ in); wing area 84.30 m² (907.32 sq ft)
Armament: one 20-mm cannon and four 7.7-mm (0.303-in) machine-guns, plus one 800-kg (1,764-lb) torpedo or an equivalent weight of bombs carried beneath the fuselage

Mitsubishi G4M

To an Imperial Japanese Navy requirement of 1937 for a land-based bomber to supersede the G3M, the company designed the extensively-built **Mitsubishi G4M**, a roomy mid-wing monoplane whose prototype, powered by two 1141-kW (1,530-hp) Mitsubishi Kasei 11 radial engines, was flown for the first time on 23 October 1939. Service trials proving satisfactory, the type was ordered into production in 1940 as the **Navy Type 1 Attack Bomber Model 11 (G4M1 Model 11)**, the first series aircraft entering operational service in the summer of 1941. Subsequent production versions included the generally similar **G4M1 Model 12**; the **G4M2 Model 22** with 1342-kW (1,800-hp) Mitsubishi MK4P Kasei 21 engines and a number of revisions, followed by the similar **G4M2 Model 22A** and **G4M2 Model 22B** with armament variations. These were followed by the **G4M2a Model 24**, introducing 1361-kW (1,825-hp) MK4T Kasei 25 engines and bulged bomb bay doors, and **G4M2a Model 24A/24B** sub-variants with armament changes. Final production version was the **G4M3 Model 34** which, too late in the war, attempted to reduce the shortcomings of its predecessors by introducing self-sealing fuel tanks and adequate armour protection. Experimental variants to evaluate various engines included one **G4M2b Model 25**, two **G4M2c Model 26**, one **G4M2d Model 27**, and two **G4M3 Model 36** aircraft; and in addition a considerable number of G4M2a Model 24B and 24C aircraft were modified to carry the navy's MXY7 piloted missile for suicide attacks, becoming redesignated **G4M2e Model 24J** in this role. Just before production of the G4M the navy had a very urgent requirement for a long-range escort fighter for use in the Sino-Japanese War, and 30 of these aircraft were built for this specific role under the designation **G6M1**. When they proved unsuccessful, some were converted later as **G6M1-K** trainers or **G6M1-L2**

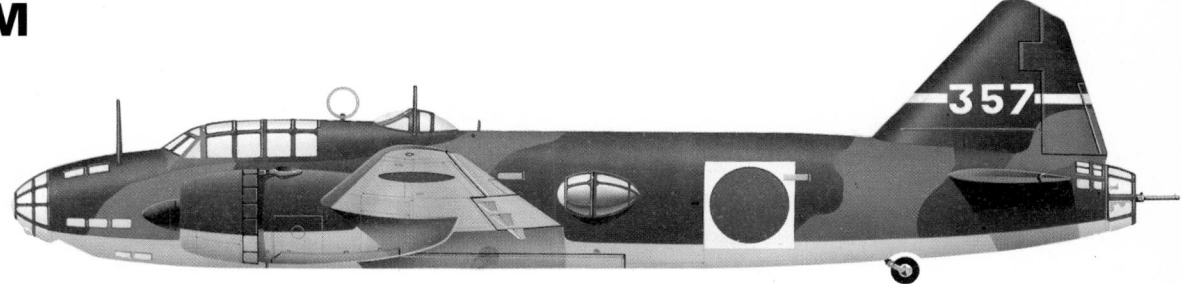

Mitsubishi G4M1 of the 705th Kokutai, Imperial Japanese Navy air service, operating from Rabaul (New Britain) in 1943.

transports. When production ended, Mitsubishi had built a total of 2,446 of all versions, this number including prototypes and the 30 G6M1s.

Allocated the Allied codename **'Betty'**, the G4Ms have become recorded in aviation history for a number of events. These include participation in the sinking of HMS *Prince of Wales* and *Repulse;* involvement in the first air raid on Darwin, Australia; service as MXY7 missile-carriers; and on 19 August 1945, the carriage of the Japanese surrender delegation to Ie-Shima in two G4M1s. Considerably more success might have been attributed to these bombers if they had incorporated adequate armour and self-sealing fuel tanks at an early date; as it was, of the total built only the 60 G4M3 production aircraft had this essential protection. Throughout, the designers were crippled by the demands for very long range, which really called for four engines.

Specification
Mitsubishi G4M3 Model 34
Type: seven-crew long-range bomber

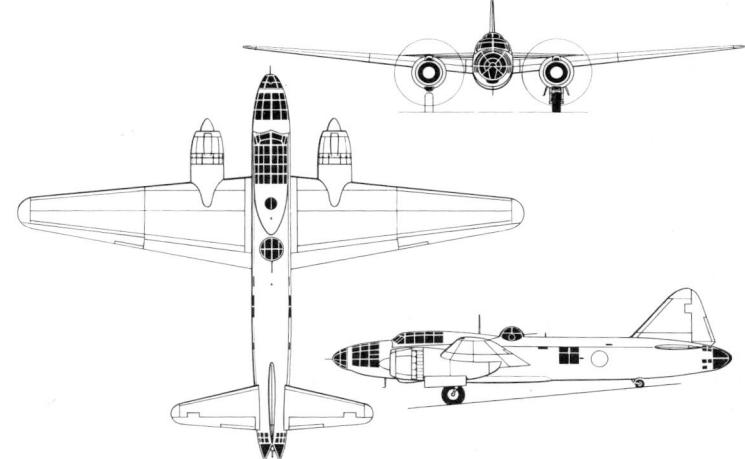

Mitsubishi G4M2a Model 24.

Powerplant: two 1361-kW (1,825-hp) Mitsubishi MK4T Kasei 25 radial piston engines
Performance: maximum speed 470 km/h (292 mph) at 5150 m (16,895 ft); service ceiling 9220 m (30,250 ft); maximum range 4335 km (2,694 miles)
Weights: empty 8350 kg (18,049 lb);

maximum take-off 12500 kg (27,558 lb)
Dimensions: span 25.00 m (82 ft 0¼ in); length 19.50 m (63 ft 11¾ in); height 6.00 m (19 ft 8¼ in); wing area 78.13 m² (841.01 sq ft)
Armament: four 20-mm cannon and two 7.7-mm (0.303-in) machine-guns, plus one 800-kg (1,764-lb) torpedo or 1000 kg (2,205 lb) of bombs

Mitsubishi J2M Raiden
to
Mitsubishi Ki-51

Mitsubishi J2M Raiden

An Imperial Japanese Navy requirement of 1938 for a single-seat interceptor led to the design and construction of three **Mitsubishi J2M1** prototypes, the first being flown initially on 20 March 1942. A cantilever low-wing monoplane with retractable tailwheel landing gear, the type suffered a protracted development because the demands on engine production had limited severely the choice of a suitable powerplant. It resulted in the installation of a 1066-kW (1,430-hp) Mitsubishi Kasei 13 radial of large diameter, an extension shaft being provided between the engine and reduction gear to ensure the nose entry was of minimum diameter. Early tests revealed that the J2M1 could not meet the navy's specification for maximum speed and rate of climb, installation of the more powerful MK4R-A Kasei 23a engine being necessitated and leading to redesignation as **J2M2**, and it was this version that was ordered into production in October 1942 as the **Navy Interceptor Fighter Raiden Model 11**. Continuing teething problems with the J2M2 meant that the type did not enter service until December 1943, by which time the major production version, the **J2M3**, which differed primarily in its armament, was being built. Variants included the similar **J2M3a** with revised armament, the final production **J2M5** with the 1357-kW (1,820-hp) Mitsubishi MK4U-4 engine, produced as the J2M5 and **J2M5a** with differing armament, plus two **J2M4** prototypes with turbocharged engines and single **J2M6** with a revised cockpit, a conversion of a J2M3. When production ended Mitsubishi had built a total of 476 aircraft of all versions, this number including prototypes.

Allocated the Allied codename **'Jack'**, the J2M Raiden (thunderbolt) first saw operational service during 1944, but enjoyed little success until the closing stages of the war, then playing a more vital role as Japan's defensive perimeter was gradually closing around the home islands.

A captured Imperial Navy air service J2 Raiden in the company of Allied fighters.

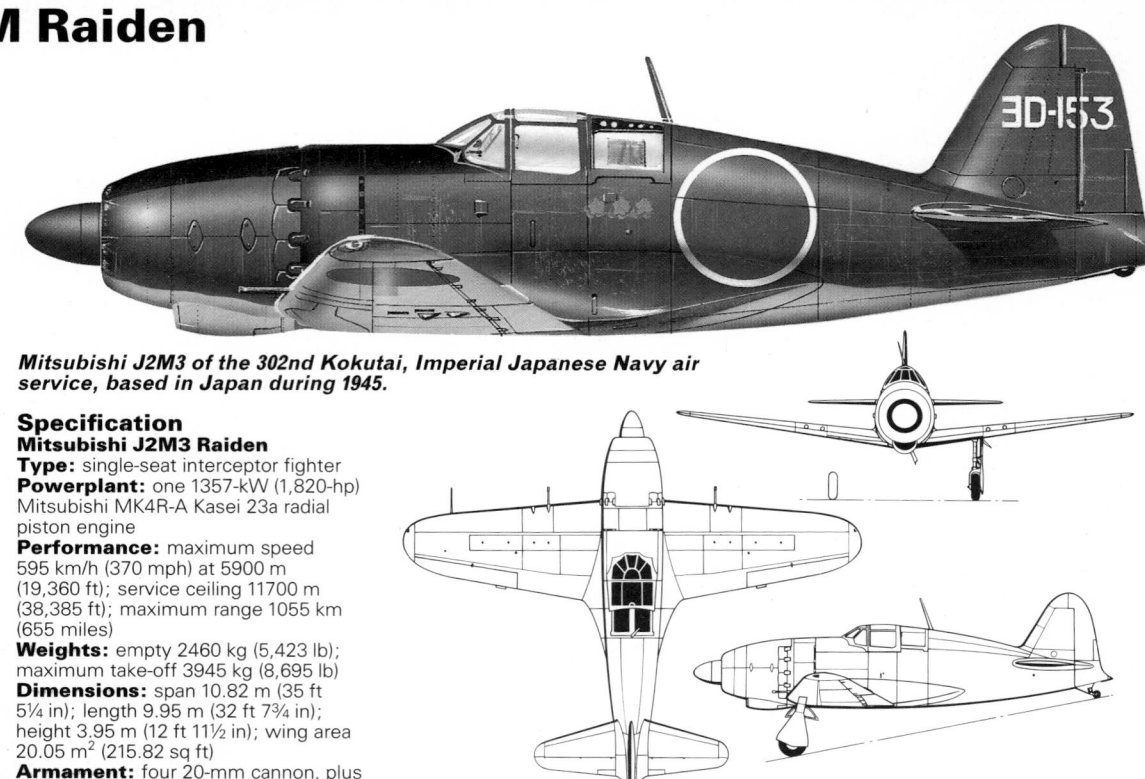

Mitsubishi J2M3 of the 302nd Kokutai, Imperial Japanese Navy air service, based in Japan during 1945.

Specification
Mitsubishi J2M3 Raiden
Type: single-seat interceptor fighter
Powerplant: one 1357-kW (1,820-hp) Mitsubishi MK4R-A Kasei 23a radial piston engine
Performance: maximum speed 595 km/h (370 mph) at 5900 m (19,360 ft); service ceiling 11700 m (38,385 ft); maximum range 1055 km (655 miles)
Weights: empty 2460 kg (5,423 lb); maximum take-off 3945 kg (8,695 lb)
Dimensions: span 10.82 m (35 ft 5¼ in); length 9.95 m (32 ft 7¾ in); height 3.95 m (12 ft 11½ in); wing area 20.05 m² (215.82 sq ft)
Armament: four 20-mm cannon, plus two 60-kg (132-lb) bombs on external racks

Mitsubishi J2M3

Mitsubishi J8M Shusui

Development of the Messerschmitt Me 163B rocket-powered fighter in Germany prompted Japan to acquire rights to build this aircraft and its Walter rocket engine. Because of losses in transit only one sample engine and an instruction manual for the Me 163 survived, and Mitsubishi was tasked with design of the interceptor which had the army and navy designations **Mitsubishi Ki-200** and **J8M** respectively. With **J8M1** prototype design finalised, the 1st Naval Air Arsenal began construction of a full-scale training glider version under the designation **MXY8 Akigusa** (autumn grass), and this was towed into the air and flown for the first time in December 1944. A heavier glider, with ballast tanks to approximate the weight of the oper-

The J8M was by any standard a remarkable achievement for, within a few months, designers completed an aerodynamic copy of the Messerschmitt Me 163B using only a simple instruction manual.

ational aircraft, was also built under the designation **Ku-13 Shusui** (sword stroke). Design of the rocket engine was a combined project of Mitsubishi together with the army and navy, resulting in the 1500-kg (3,307-lb) thrust Toko Ro.2, and this powerplant was installed in the first of the **J8M1 Navy Experimental Rocket-Powered Interceptor Fighter Shusui** prototypes com-

pleted by Mitsubishi. On 7 July 1945 the prototype J8M1 was flown for the first time, crashing soon after take-off as a result of engine failure, and no further examples were flown before the end of the war.

Mitsubishi K3M

Designed by Herbert Smith, the Sopwith designer working in Japan, the **Mitsubishi 4MS1** prototype crew trainer made its maiden flight in 1930. Production continued until 1941, and examples pressed into service as liaison aircraft in the postwar period were to be found in a variety of national markings. A strut-braced high-wing cabin monoplane with fixed wide-track landing gear, the 4MS1 was powered by a single engine. The first **K3M2** production version entered naval service in 1932 as the **Type 90 Crew Trainer**, in which configuration pilot and gunner were located in separate open cockpits, with instructor and two pupils in the enclosed cabin. Later liaison/passenger variants accommodated five passengers in the cabin. Total production of all versions amounted to 625.

Variants

K3M1: service designation of 4MS1 prototype and three test aircraft built in

Unlovely and of lowly performance, the K3M was nevertheless an important aircraft in the inventory of the Japanese naval air arm. Seen here is a Mitsubishi K3M2 'Pine'; over 600 examples were provided.

1930-31; powered by 254-kW (340-hp) Hispano-Suiza 8 V-8 engine
K3M2: company designation 4MS2, built in 1932-35; powered by 254-kW (340-hp) Hitachi Amakaze 11 radial engine; Mitsubishi built 70, balance of 247 constructed later by Aichi
3K3M3: in 1939 Watanabe took over production from Aichi and built this new version which incorporated an enlarged fin and rudder and was powered by a Nakajima Kotobuki 2 radial; some aircraft were modified as **K3M3-L** light transports for up to five passengers or an equivalent weight in freight; total Watanabe production 301
Ki-7: designation of two aircraft tested

by Imperial Japanese Army in 1932; basic K3M structure, one with a Mitsubishi 92 radial and the other a Nakajima Kotobuki
MS-1: a single civil transport (J-BABQ) with a 343-kW (460-hp) Jupiter VI radial

Specification
Mitsubishi/Watanabe K3M3
Type: five-seat crew trainer
Powerplant: one 433-kW (580-hp) Nakajima Kotobuki 2 Kai 2 radial piston engine

Performance: maximum speed 235 km/h (146 mph); service ceiling 6390 m (20,965 ft); range 800 km (497 miles)
Weights: empty 1360 kg (2,998 lb); maximum take-off 2200 kg (4,850 lb)
Dimensions: span 15.78 m (51 ft 9¼ in); length 9.54 m (31 ft 3½ in); height 3.82 m (12 ft 6½ in); wing area 34.50 m² (371.37 sq ft)
Armament: one trainably-mounted 7.7-mm (0.303-in) machine-gun, plus 120 kg (265 lb) of bombs

Mitsubishi K7M

The **Mitsubishi Ka-18** or **11-Shi Experimental Crew Trainer** was a cantilever high-wing cabin monoplane powered by two 254-kW (340-hp) Ha-9 radials. Two prototypes were built, but the Imperial Japanese Navy decided against developing a relatively costly twin-engine type to replace the single-engined K3M then in service. Nevertheless, the two prototypes were used for training by the Japanese navy and received the designation **K7M1**. Each could accommodate a trainee crew of five plus one or two instructors, and carried radio, navigational and camera equipment, two 7.7-mm (0.303-in) machine-guns, plus up to 90 kg (198 lb) of bombs.

Mitsubishi Ki-1

Showing strong signs of Junkers influence, the **Mitsubishi Ki-1-I** heavy bomber flew for the first time in 1933. An angular cantilever low-wing monoplane with a crew of four, it had fixed landing gear, a tail unit incorporating twin fins and rudders, and was powered by two 701-kW (940-hp) Ha-2-2 radial engines, giving a maximum speed of 220 km/h (137 mph). Pilot and co-pilot were seated in tandem under an enclosed canopy, while there were semi-enclosed nose and dorsal turrets and a retractable ventral 'dustbin', each armed with a single

Though of limited performance, the Ki-1 had a useful bomb-load. This aircraft is the Ki-1-II.

7.7-mm (0.303-in) machine-gun; offensive load was up to 1500 kg (3,307 lb) of bombs. The **Ki-1-II** development had 723-kW (970-hp) Ha-2-3 engines and airframe improvements which increased maximum speed to 230 km/h (143 mph).

The two versions went into service as the **Army Type 93-1** and **Army Type 93-2** respectively, and saw limited use in the fighting against China. Total pro-

duction of both versions was 118. Wing span was 26.50 m (86 ft 11¼ in), and the maximum take-off weight of the Ki-1-I 8100 kg (17,857 lb).

Mitsubishi Ki-2

A most successful design, although built only in limited numbers, the **Mitsubishi Ki-2** light bomber was developed from the Junkers K 37, an example of which had been imported from Germany in 1931 and donated by public subscription to the Japanese army. It bore the distinction of being 'Aikoku 1', the first of many such patriotic gifts, sparked off by the fighting in Manchuria.

A three-seat cantilever low-wing monoplane, powered by two 425-kW (570-hp) Nakajima Kotobuki radials, the Ki-2 prototype flew for the first time in the spring of 1933. It was distinguished easily by its corrugated metal alloy decking and twin fins and rudders, and had fixed divided landing gear, with spat-type main wheel fairings often discarded on service aircraft.

Production of the initial version totalled 113, and the type went into operation against the Chinese with great suc-

cess under the designation **Ki-2-I** or **Army Type 93 Twin-engined Light Bomber.** Maximum speed was 225 km/h (140 mph), normal range 900 km (559 miles) and maximum take-off weight 4550 kg (10,031 lb). Single 7.7-mm (0.303-in) machine-guns were mounted in a semi-enclosed nose cockpit and a dorsal position, and maximum bombload was 500 kg (1,102 lb).

The achievements of the Ki-2-I led to the development of the **Ki-2-II**, or **Army Type 93-2 Twin-engined Light Bomber,** the Type 93 then being redesignated retrospectively as the **Type 93-1**. The Type 93-2 retained the same general configuration, but had a fully-enclosed manually-operated nose turret, an enclosed cockpit for the pilot, and main landing gear legs which semi-retracted forward into the engine nacelles. The Ki-2-II had two 559-kW (750-hp) Ha-8 radials giving much im-

proved overall performance with maximum speed increased to 283 km/h (176 mph). In total 61 Ki-2-IIs were built, and these joined the Ki-2-Is in operations against the Japanese. Both versions ended their flying careers in the training role.

A civilianised version of the Ki-2-II named *Otori* (phoenix) was bought by the *Asahi Shimbun* newspaper and made a number of long-range record-breaking and 'goodwill' flights from 1936 to 1939. Registered J-BAAE, it covered

The modernisation begun with the Ki-1 went a step further with Mitubishi's version of the Junkers K 37, the Ki-2. Later versions had enclosed crew positions and retractable gear.

the 4930 km (3,063 miles) from Tachikawa military air base to Bangkok in 21 hours 36 minutes flying time in December 1936, and in early 1939 achieved a round-China flight of some 9300 km (5,780 miles).

Mitsubishi Ki-15

The **Mitsubishi Ki-15** was designed to meet an Imperial Japanese Army requirement of 1935 for a two-seat reconnaissance aircraft. Two prototypes were built, one civil and one military, the latter flying for the first time during May 1936.

Service testing proceeded smoothly and the type was ordered into production as the **Army Type 97 Command Reconnaissance Plane Model 1 (Ki-15-I)**, initial deliveries to the army being made in May 1937. Just before

that the civil prototype (J-BAAI), named *Kamikaze* (divine wind), was flown from Tachikawa to London to collect photographs and films of the coronation of HM King George VI. Following the achievement of *Kamikaze*, a small number of civil aircraft were acquired under the designation **Karigane I** for use by civil operators in Japan.

Deployed in the war against China, the army's Ki-15-I aircraft had virtual freedom of the skies until China introduced the Soviet Polikarpov I-16. Performance of the Ki-15-I was then upgraded by installation of the 671-kW (900-hp) Mitsubishi Ha-26-I engine, the improved **Ki-15-II** entering service in 1939. The same treatment was tried when still higher performance was required at a later date, two **Ki-15-III** prototypes being tested with the 783-kW (1,050-hp) Mitsubishi 102 radial, but no production resulted as more advanced aircraft were then under development. The Imperial Japanese Navy acquired 20 Ki-15-II aircraft under the designation **Navy Type 98 Reconnaissance Plane Model 1 (C5M1)**, plus 30 more with the 708-kW (950-hp) Nakajima Sakae 12 engine as the **C5M2**. Allocated the Allied codename **'Babs'**, the Ki-15/CSM was built to a total of 489 of all versions, being relegated to second-line duties in 1943. Many survived to be used in *kamikaze* attacks.

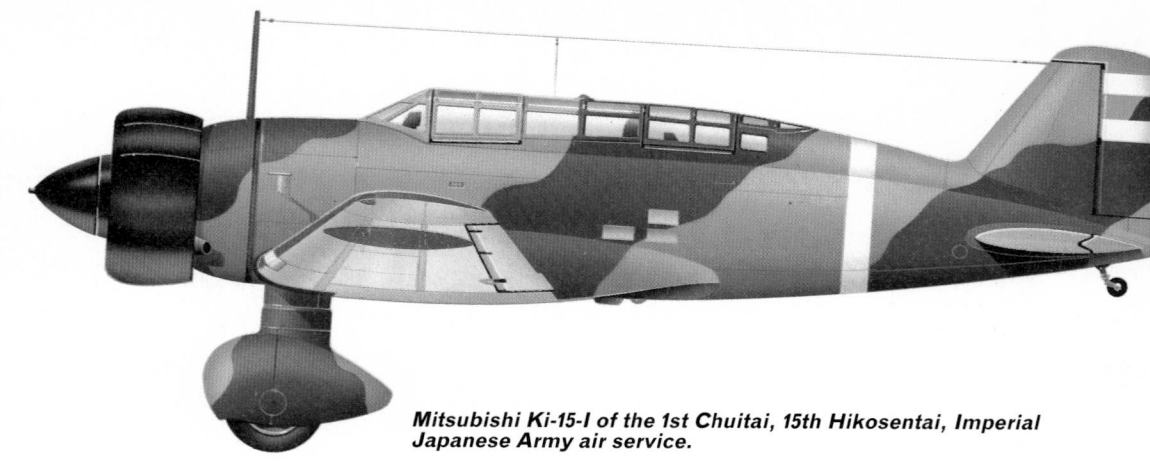

Mitsubishi Ki-15-I of the 1st Chuitai, 15th Hikosentai, Imperial Japanese Army air service.

Specification
Mitsubishi Ki-15-I
Type: two-seat reconnaissance aircraft
Powerplant: one 477-kW (640-hp) Nakajima Ha-8 radial piston engine

Performance: maximum speed 480 km/h (298 mph) at 4000 m (13,125 ft); service ceiling 11400 m (37,400 ft); range 2400 km (1,491 miles)

Weights: empty 1400 kg (3,086 lb); maximum take-off 2300 kg (5,071 lb)
Dimensions: span 12.00 m (39 ft 4¼ in); length 8.70 m (28 ft 6½ in);

height 3.35 m (11 ft 0 in); wing area 20.36 m² (219.16 sq ft)
Armament: one 7.7-mm (0.303-in) machine-gun on a trainable mount in rear cockpit

Mitsubishi Ki-20

Six examples of the **Mitsubishi Ki-20**, a bomber version of the Junkers G 38 giant airliner, were built in secret between 1931 and 1936. By the Imperial Japanese Army they were designated **Type 92 Super Heavy Bomber**, but never flew operationally. Powered by four 597-kW (800-hp) Junkers Jumo engines in slim nacelles, the Ki-20 had a top speed of only 200 km/h (124 mph). Maximum take-off weight was 25488 kg (56,191 lb) and wing span 44.00 m (144 ft 4¼ in). A crew of ten was carried and defensive armament comprised eight 7.7-in (0.303-in) machine-guns and one 20-mm cannon. Maximum bombload over short ranges was 5000 kg (11,023 lb).

Mitsubishi Ki-21

Mitsubishi Ki-21-IIb of the Imperial Japanese Army air service in 1944.

Designed for an Imperial Japanese Army requirement of 1936 for a four-seat bomber, the twin-engine **Mitsubishi Ki-21-I** prototype, as powered by the Nakajima Ha-5 engine, demonstrated performance equal to any of the world's contemporary bombers in the same category. It was ordered into production as the **Army Type 97 Heavy Bomber Model 1A** (Mitsubishi **Ki-21-Ia**), entering service in the summer of 1938. Operational experience in China showed the type to be deficient in armament, leading to the improved **Ki-21-Ib** with five instead of three machine-guns and an enlarged bomb bay, followed by the **Ki-21-Ic** with increased fuel capacity and one extra machine-gun. Continuing development brought four **Ki-21-II** prototypes, introducing more powerful Mitsubishi Ha-101 engines. With the same armament as the Ki-21-Ic this model entered production as the **Ki-21-IIa**. Final production version was the generally-similar **Ki-21-IIb** which incorporated some refinements. In addition to the military Ki-21s, a number of Ki-21-Ia aircraft were later converted for use as unarmed civil freighter/transports.

Ki-21s, which were allocated the Allied codename **'Sally'**, played a significant role in the early stages of the Pacific war, but the increasing numbers and capability of Allied fighters meant that during the last year of the war these bombers were relegated to second-line duties. A total of 2,064 Ki-21s was built, 1,713 by Mitsubishi and an additional 351 by Nakajima.

Specification
Mitsubishi Ki-21-IIb
Type: five/seven-seat heavy bomber
Powerplant: two 1119-kW (1,500-hp) Mitsubishi Ha-101 radial piston engines
Performance: maximum speed 485 km/h (301 mph) at 4720 m (15,485 ft); service ceiling 10000 m (32,810 ft); range 2700 km (1,678 miles)
Weights: empty 6070 kg (13,382 lb); maximum take-off 10610 kg (23,391 lb)
Dimensions: span 22.50 m (73 ft 9¾ in); length 16.00 m (52 ft 6 in); height 4.85 m (15 ft 11 in); wing area

69.60 m² (749.19 sq ft)
Armament: six 7.7-mm (0.303-in)

Mitsubishi Ki-21-IIa

machine-gun, plus a bombload of up to 1000 kg (2,205 lb) according to range

Mitsubishi Ki-30

The **Mitsubishi Ki-30** prototype, powered by a 615-kW (824-hp) Mitsubishi Ha-6 radial engine, was flown for the first time on 28 February 1937. It had been designed and built to meet an Imperial Japanese Army requirement for a light bomber, the company building two prototypes, and the second was flown shortly after with a more powerful Nakajima Ha-5 KAI engine. This latter aircraft not only showed an improvement in performance, but as it exceeded the army's specification the company was given an immediate order for 16 trials aircraft. There were delivered in January 1938 and, two months later, the Ki-30 was ordered into production as the **Army Type 97 Light Bomber**. When used in China in 1938, and at the beginning of the Pacific war, they proved very

The Mitsubishi Ki-30 'Ann' was the penultimate light bomber design in the series that began with the Karigane. Despite early success in Manchuria it quickly became outmoded with Japan's entry into World War II.

Mooney aircraft

Al W. Mooney began his career as a designer of lightplanes during the mid-1920s, later joining the Mono Aircraft Corporation, where he made a significant contribution to the success of the Monocoupe line of aircraft. When Mono closed its doors, Mooney had temporary associations with at least two other companies before joining with K. K. Culver to form the Culver Aircraft Corporation, with which Mooney was associated until the end of World War II. In 1946 Mooney designed an exciting single-seat sporting aircraft known as the **Mooney M-18 Mite**, a low-wing cabin monoplane of 8.20 m (26 ft 11 in) span, powered by a 48-kW (65-hp) Avco Lycoming O-145-B2 engine, had a maximum speed of 222 km/h (138 mph). The designer formed Mooney Aircraft Inc. to build the type, to a total of about 300, produced initially at Wichita, Kansas, and finally at Kerrville, Texas, and the Mite eventually became available in kit form in the early 1970s for construction by amateurs. Mooney moved into the four-seat market with design of the **M-20**, a four-seat cabin monoplane flown in August 1953, which introduced retractable tricycle landing gear and was powered by a 112-kW (150-hp) Avco Lycoming O-320 engine. The M-20 was followed first by the improved **M-20A**, before being superseded by the **Mark 21(M-20C)** of all-metal construction and powered by a 134-kW (180-hp) Avco Lycoming O-360-A1A engine. In 1963 expansion of the Mark 21 range introduced the **Master (M-20D)** without retractable landing gear and the **Super 21 (M-20E)** with a 149-kW (200-hp) IO-360-A1A engine. In 1967 Mooney acquired Alon Inc., continuing to build the famous Alon Aircoupe as the **Mooney A-2A Cadet** and, in the same year, deliveries began of a five-seat pressurised light aircraft known as the **Mustang (M-22)**, powered by a 231-kW (310-hp) Avco Lycoming TIO-540-A1A engine. In the following year the Mark 21 became known as the **Mooney Ranger**, and new extensions of the range included the **Executive 21 (M-20F)** and **Statesman (M-20G)** both with a slightly lengthened fuselage to increase leg room. By then the company was running into financial difficulties, trading briefly as Aerostar Aircraft

A hallmark of all Al Mooney's great modern American lightplane designs was the unique forward-raked tail-fin as illustrated by this basic model four-seat Mooney M-20.

Corporation before being renamed Mooney Aircraft Corporation as a subsidiary of the Republic Steel Corporation. The Ranger then continued in production until 1979, by which time more than 2,000 had been built, being complemented until that time by the **Chaparral**, an updated version of the Super 21, and the **Executive** which was a version of the Ranger with a 149-kW (200-hp) engine.

In 1976 the **Mooney 201 (M20J)** superseded the Executive. The current version is the **Model 201SE**, and just over 1,700 have been built to date. The **Mooney 205** variant was discontinued in the late 1980s after 77 had been built. The **Turbo Mooney 231 (M20K)**, a turbocharged version of the M20J, of which 880 were built, has been replaced on the production line by the **Model 252TSE Turbo Special Edition**. The stretched-fuselage **Model 252 PFM (M20L)** fitted with a 162-kW (217-hp) Porsche PFM-3200 engine flew in May 1987 and the **Model 257TLS (M20M)** TIO-540-AFIA-powered 'Turbo Lycoming Sabre' version of the M20L, with increased fuel capacity, higher maximum take-off weight and extra windows, followed in 1989. On 21 April 1983 Mooney flew the prototype (N301MX) of the **M30 Model 301** (originally called the **MX**), a new pressurised six-seat cabin monoplane powered by a 270-kW (360-hp) Lycoming TIO-540-X27 engine, but further development of the type was suspended in 1987 when Mooney joined with Socata (to form TBM International of France) to develop the similarly-configured **TBM-700** turboprop.

Specification
Mooney M20M Model 257TLS
Powerplant: one 201-kW (270-hp) Textron Lycoming TIO-540-AFIA turbocharged piston engine
Performance: cruising speed at 3960 m (13,000 ft) 371 km/h (230 mph); maximum speed at 7620 m (25,000 ft) 413 km/h (257 mph); service ceiling

7620 m (25,000 ft); range with maximum fuel 1983 km (1,232 miles)
Weights: empty 913 kg (2,012 lb); maximum take-off 1451 kg (3,200 lb)
Dimensions: span 11 m (36 ft 1 in); length 8.2 m (27 ft); height 2.5 m (8 ft 3 in); wing area 16.24 m² (174.8 sq ft)

A step up from the M-20 series was the pressurised Mooney M-22 Mustang with its characteristic short landing gear.

The TBM-700, while now being built solely by SOCATA (the general aviation subsidiary of France's Aérospatiale) includes a lot of the work done by Mooney on the M30 Model 201, not only internally but in the aircraft's general outward appearance.

Morane-Saulnier early monoplanes

Pioneer French aviators Léon Morane and Raymond Saulnier formed the Société Anonyme des Aéroplanes Morane-Saulnier in October 1911, having been associated previously with Borel. A whole family of adventurous shoulder-wing wire-braced monoplanes appeared during 1911-12. Virtually every aircraft

was different, but the most important included the 45-kW (60-hp) Gnome-powered monoplane flown by company pilot Roland Garros from Tunis to Marsala, Sicily, on 18 December 1912, and the 60-kW (80-hp) Gnome-powered twin-float seaplane which participated in the 1913 Schneider Trophy contest. On 23 September 1913 Garros, flying a new monoplane, accomplished a remarkable flight of 730 km (454 miles) from St Raphaël to Bizerta, the whole of this distance being over the Mediterranean.

The success of the new company attracted official interest at home and abroad. A 37-kW (50-hp) Gnome-

powered single-seat monoplane known as the **Morane-Saulnier Type A** was ordered by the French war ministry for the training role, 13 being delivered in 1912. Five 60-kW (80-hp) Gnome-powered **Type C** monoplanes were sold to Russia and two **F** monoplanes to Romania. As with many later designs by Morane-Saulnier, lateral control was by means of wing warping.

Morane-Saulnier Type AC

Developed from the **Type V** via the experimental **Type U**, the **Morane-Saulnier Type AC** was a single-seat shoulder-wing monoplane fighter which appeared in the autumn of 1916. Its major innovation was rigid wing bracing, a truss of steel-tube struts supporting each wing from below. A similar concept was employed on the two-seat parasol-wing **Type AE bis** which was built purely experimentally. The wings incorporated ailerons for lateral control, the fuselage being faired to a circular cross-section and terminating in an angular tail unit. The single Vickers 7.7-mm (0.303-

For its period a singularly advanced aircraft, the Morane-Saulnier Type AC was aerodynamically clean except for the steel truss used to support the wings.

in) machine-gun was partially enclosed in a humped fairing on the forward decking of the fuselage. The Aéronautique Militaire ordered 30 examples of the Type AC, a number being distributed to operational *escadrilles* on the Western Front, but two examples bought for the RFC were never flown operationally.

The Type AC had a maximum speed of 178 km/h (111 mph) and was powered by an 82-kW (110-hp) Le Rhône 9J or 89-kW (120-hp) Le Rhône 9Jb rotary. Span was 9.80 m (32 ft 1¾ in) and maximum take-off weight 658 kg (1,450 lb).

Morane-Saulnier Type AF
to
Morane-Saulnier Type S

Morane-Saulnier Type AF

Flown for the first time on 23 June 1917, the **Morane-Saulnier Type AF** was a businesslike single-seat fighter biplane with unequal-span biplane wings incorporating ailerons, a conventional cross-axle landing gear, and a tail unit with a long fin, divided rudder and a small additional ventral fin. Its single synchronised Vickers 7.7-mm (0.303-in) machine-gun was partly enclosed in a distinctive humped fairing. With its 112-kW (150-hp) Gnome Monosoupape rotary engine, the Type AF (or **MoS.28** under the official designation scheme) had a maxi-

mum speed of 207 km/h (129 mph). Despite its good flying qualities, the Type AF was not produced in quantity, as the SPAD XIII was already well advanced on the production lines. The **Type AFH** variant was intended as an amphibian for shipboard use, being equipped with a large wide main float and a tail float combined with normal landing gear.

With four ailerons and a 112-kW (150-hp) engine, the Type AF was a good fighter aircraft.

Morane-Saulnier Type AI

Test-flown in the early summer of 1917, the **Morane-Saulnier Type AI** was a parasol-wing single-seat fighter monoplane contemporary with the Type AF biplane. It had a sweptback wing braced by parallel struts, a circular-section fuselage of which the forward part was of metal construction, and its 112-kW (150-hp) Gnome Monosoupape 9NI rotary engine had a beautifully contoured metal cowl which helped to give the little fighter a workman-like appearance.

First version to enter production had the service designation **MoS.27** and was armed with a 7.7-mm (0.303-in) Vickers with interrupter gear; a version with twin Vickers guns was designated **MoS.29**. Total production of these C.1 category (single-seat fighter) aircraft was 1,210 machines. The type equipped newly-formed French *escadrilles* MS 156, MS 158 and MS 161 in early 1918, but by mid-May all had been withdrawn as a result of structural and engine problems which had caused a number of accidents.

A version with the 112-kW (150-hp) Gnome engine and modified wing bracing was produced, but production was concentrated mainly on the **MoS.30**, an E.1 (single-seat advanced trainer) version with either an 89-kW (120-hp) Le Rhône 9Jb or a 101-kW (135-hp) Le

Rhône 9Jby rotary engine; a version with a derated 9Jby of 67 kW (90 hp) was designated **MoS.30bis**. Armament was removed and fuel capacity was reduced. The US Army Air Service in France produced 51 MoS.30 trainers, and post-war Belgium bought three, and evaluation aircraft were sold to Japan, the Soviet Union and Switzerland.

A number of French army machines were converted along with a number of other types such as the M.S.35 and M.S.138 as **'Penguins'**. These were a form of ground trainer much favoured by French flying schools in the 1920s. The aircraft in question had much of the fabric wing covering removed, so that the pilot could handle the controls and taxi around the airfield, thus gaining considerable confidence without being able to take off!

Other Type AIs in several versions were sold to civil pilots. Among renowned aviators who demonstrated their skill with the type at air shows in this period were Nungesser, whose aircraft (F-NUNG) sported his personal wartime insignia; and Alfred Fronval who, in his orange and blue Morane (F-ABAO), looped 1,111 times in four hours 56 minutes over Villacoublay aerodrome on 25 February 1928. Three examples of the Type AI are still flown by the Jean Salis

organisation based at Le Ferté-Alais aerodrome.

Variants
1917 experimental: version with all-wood monocoque fuselage and an integral fin and tailplane
1918 experimental: version with 127-kW (170-hp) Le Rhône rotary; not successful

Specification
MoS.27
Type: single-seat parasol monoplane fighter
Powerplant: one 112-kW (150-hp) Gnome Monosoupape 9N rotary engine
Performance: maximum speed 225 km/h (140 mph); service ceiling

7000 m (22,965 ft); endurance 1 hour 45 minutes
Weights: empty equipped 421 kg (928 lb); maximum take-off 649 kg (1,431 lb)
Dimensions: span 8.51 m (27 ft 11 in); length 5.65 m (18 ft 6½ in); height 2.40 m (7 ft 10½ in); wing area 13.39 m² (144.13 sq ft)
Armament: one forward firing synchronised 7.7-mm (0.303-in) Vickers machine-gun

The MoS.30 was a single-seat advanced trainer derivative of the Type AI, this example having a Le Rhône rotary and an extra set of lift wires (between the attachment points for the two steel struts).

Morane-Saulnier Type AN

Designed around the 336-kW (450-hp) Bugatti water-cooled engine, the **Morane-Saulnier Type AN** two-seat fighter was flown in the autumn of 1918, and was a two-bay biplane with equal-span wings. The ungainly engine and twin externally-mounted Lamblin radiators gave the machine an ugly appearance, only partially offset by the beautifully tapered fuselage rear section and elegant tailplane. Variants built included the **Type ANL** with 298-kW (400-hp) Liberty tested late in 1918, and

the 336-kW (450-hp) Renault-powered **Type ANR** and 395-kW (530-hp) Salmson-powered **Type ANS** both flown in 1919. There was no significant post-war interest in the type and development was halted. Official designation of the C.2 (two-seat fighter) category Type AN was **MoS.31**. Armament comprised one fixed Vickers and two trainably-mounted Lewis 7.7-mm (0.303-in) machine-guns. Maximum speed of the original Type AN was 225 km/h (140 mph).

The Type AN owed its extremely ugly front end to the pipes, exhaust stacks and external radiators of a Bugatti water-cooled engine.

Morane-Saulnier Type AR (M.S.35)

Developed from the Type LA and featuring the same wire-braced parasol-wing configuration, the **Morane-Saulnier Type AR** two-seat primary trainer appeared in prototype form as early as

1915. It had a new fin and rudder, tandem open cockpits and dual controls, conventional cross-axle landing gear and a slim, well-designed fuselage. The type went into large-scale production post-war as

the **M.S.35** E.P.2 category two-seater, the principal version being the **M.S.35R** powered by an 60-kW (80-hp) Le Rhône 9C rotary. Others included the **M.S.35A** with an Anzani engine and

M.S.35C powered by a 60-kW (80-hp) Clerget 9C.

Over 400 were built, most flying with the Ecoles de Pilotage of the Aéronautique Militaire, from which they were retired in 1929, some being passed to civil flying clubs and private owners and flown throughout the 1930s. Other operators included the French navy and several foreign air arms, notably Poland (70), the Soviet Union (30), Argentina, Belgium, Brazil, Guatemala, Romania and Turkey. Maximum speed of the M.S.35R was 125 km/h (78 mph) and service ceiling 4600 m (15,090 ft). Wing span was 10.57 m (34 ft 8¼ in) and maximum take-off weight 764 kg (1,684 lb).

Known by two names, like many of the early designs of Morane-Saulnier, the Type AR or M.S.35 demonstrates the attributes of all World War I-era aircraft of the French manufacturer. It had a rotary engine, a braced parasol wing and an elegantly constructed tail. During the war it was known to the French forces as the M.S.35, and afterwards over 400 were built for a wide variety of customers, both civilian and military.

Morane-Saulnier Type BB and Type BH

Built in 1915 to a British order, the **Morane-Saulnier Type BB** was a compact equal-span reconnaissance biplane, with pilot and observer seated close together in tandem beneath a large cut-out in the trailing edge of the upper wing. Total original order was for 150 aircraft to be powered by the 82-kW (110-hp) Le Rhône rotary engine. In the event, as a result of a shortage of the specified engine, most of the 94 aircraft built were powered by the 60-kW (80-hp) Le Rhône. The **Type BH** variant was distinguished by the large streamlined spinner fitted to its two-bladed propeller.

The 60-kW (80-hp) Type BH equipped No. 60 Squadron, RFC and No. 4 Squadron, RNAS in northern France. Some of the No. 60 Squadron aircraft were flown as fighters, the normal trainably-

mounted 7.7-mm (0.303-in) Lewis gun being supplemented by another Lewis fixed above the top wing. The 82-kW (110-hp) version of the Type BB was operated by No. 1 and No. 3 Squadrons, RFC.

The Morane-Saulnier Type 8B of 1915 was a two-seat short-winged biplane which could be powered by a variety of Le Rhône rotary piston engines. This was housed in a large, smooth cowling and fitted with a very outsize spinner for the propeller. It carried several machine-guns: a 0.303-in calibre drum-fed Lewis gun mounted on a spigot for the rear-gunner and a main forward armament of a pair of machine-guns mounted above the wing and firing over the prop.

The type was only a limited success. Wing span was 8.65 m (28 ft 4½ in), maximum take-off weight 750 kg (1,653 lb) and maximum speed 147 km/h (91 mph).

Morane-Saulnier Type G

Developed from the earlier Morane-Saulnier monoplanes, the **Morane-Saulnier Type G** was a two-seat shoulder-wing wire-braced monoplane. Pilot and passenger were seated close together in a single cockpit. The type was built under licence by Grahame-White at Hendon and flown by many renowned pre-war British and French pilots. An order for 94 Type G monoplanes was received from the French war ministry, and the RFC obtained a number of British-built machines. However, when war broke out in August 1914 it was soon found that the Type G had little military application, and surviving aircraft were mostly employed as train-

Steady evolution among the initial series of MoS shoulder-wing monoplanes resulted in the definitive Type G of 1912 with a fully covered fuselage. Seen here is a further development, which incorporated a parasol wing giving the crew a better view.

ers. Wing span was 9.63 m (31 ft 7¼ in) and with a 60-kW (80-hp) Gnome rotary engine maximum speed was 135 km/h (84 mph).

Variants
Morane-Saulnier Type WR: built for the Russian government, this

version had an unusual 'glasshouse' built on to the sides of the fuselage forward of the wing
Morane-Saulnier Type G (1915): although bearing the same designation, this type was a single-seat fighter with

a fixed 8-mm (0.315-in) Hotchkiss machine-gun fitted with deflector gear; only a few were built for the French Aéronautique Militaire, these being powered by the 60-kW (80-hp) Le Rhône rotary engine

Morane-Saulnier Type H

Developed in parallel with the Type G, the **Morane-Saulnier Type H** was a single-seater which flew for the first time in 1913 and soon found favour with a number of outstanding French pilots of the period. Slightly smaller than the Type G, spanning 9.12 m (29 ft 11 in), it had similar raked wing tips and there were a number of other detail design refinements. It is believed that the French war ministry ordered 26 Type Hs and a number served in the first year of World War I, several taking part in the defence of Paris in autumn of 1914, armament being limited to revolvers or carbines carried by the pilots. Several of the type also

The Type H was essentially similar to the Type G but had room for the pilot alone. Evident in this rear view are the prominent wires from the kingpost to the upper surfaces: the forward set was used as landing wires and the others for wing-warping lateral control.

served with the RFC, most of them of British manufacture. Most Type Hs were powered by 60-kW (80-hp) Gnome or Le Rhône rotaries and maximum speed was marginally higher than that of the Type G.

Variant
Morane-Saulnier Type O: this monoplane appeared in 1914, designed for Roland Garros to fly in that year's Monaco aviation rally; one other

example was built; constructed as lightly as possible for competition purposes, its primitive landing gear caused very rough landings and one was later given a new wing and modified landing gear

Morane-Saulnier Type L and Type LA

In August 1913 Morane-Saulnier modified a Type G by fitting a new wire-braced parasol wing. This was the prototype of the **Morane-Saulnier Type L** which appeared in 1914, a frail-looking

two-seat reconnaissance or observation aircraft. The Type L had a slab-sided fuselage, a conventional cross-axle landing gear, and a tail unit comprising only a small rudder and an elevator; some late

production aircraft introduced a fixed fin. The Type L went into production at the Morane-Saulnier Puteaux works to meet an order for 50 machines from Turkey. At the outbreak of war in August 1914 the

Turkish aircraft were requisitioned by the French government. Powered by 60-kW (80-hp) Gnome or Le Rhône rotaries, the Type Ls equipped two newly formed *escadrilles*, MS 23 and MS 26, the latter including the famous Roland Garros among its pilots. In 1914-15 the Type L was often flown as a single-seater, the only armament being a pistol or carbine. Garros conducted experiments with a machine-gun and deflector gear on his Type L, shooting down an enemy aircraft with the aid of this device on 1 April 1915. On 7 June 1915 while flying a Type L single-seater, Flight Sub-Lieutenant Warneford of No. 1 Wing RNAS destroyed the Germany Army Zeppelin *LZ.37* by dropping small bombs on the envelope and setting it on fire. Most of the 600 plus Type Ls were, however, flown by the French, Russians, and British RFC and RNAS as two-seat reconnaissance aircraft, usually unarmed.

The **Morane-Saulnier Type LA** parasol was a much improved aircraft resulting from a number of refinements, but was essentially an interim design awaiting introduction of the more advanced Type P. Only isolated aircraft were used by the French, but the RFC

The Morane-Saulnier Type LA was a 'product improved' version of the Type L, fitted with ailerons instead of wing-warping wires. Illustrated is the ski-equipped version as flown by the Imperial Russian air service.

purchased 24. Similarly powered to the Type L, the **Type LA** had slightly improved performance and was normally armed by a single 7.7-mm (0.303-in) machine-gun on a spigot mounting.

Specification
Type: two-seat reconnaissance aircraft
Powerplant: one 60-kW (80-hp) Gnome or Rhône rotary engine
Performance: maximum speed 115 km/h (71 mph); endurance 2 hours
Weights: empty equipped 385 kg

(849 lb); maximum take-off 655 kg (1,444 lb)
Dimensions: span 11.20 m (36 ft

9 in); length 6.88 m (22 ft 6¾ in); height 3.93 m (12 ft 10¾ in); wing area 18.30 m² (196.99 sq ft)

Morane-Saulnier Type N

The first **Morane-Saulnier Type N** was flown by Garros at the Aspern, Austria, aviation meeting in July 1914. It had the basic Morane-Saulnier shoulder-wing configuration of the period, but the fuselage was faired to a circular section, and the tail unit incorporated a fixed fin as introduced on late Type Ls. Roland Garros had been captured after being forced down in his Type L during April 1915, and the first military Type N to be seen over the Western Front, flown by Eugène Gilbert of Escadrille MS 23, had the name *Le Vengeur* (the avenger). Other specially developed aircraft, designated **Type Nm**, followed, but only a small batch went into service.

They introduced a revised rear fuselage shape and a modified tail unit. Among successful French exponents of the Type N were Jean Navarre of Escadrille MS 12 and pre-war aerobatic pilot Adolphe Pégoud of MS 49.

The Type N was known to the French erroneously as the **Morane Monocoque** and to the British as the **Morane Bullet**. The RFC received 24 of the type after the first French examples had entered service, the type being distributed to several squadrons, the principal operator being No. 6 Squadron. A number also flew with the Imperial Russian Air Service.

Variants
Morane-Saulnier Type I: this had only one major change from the Type Nm, the installation of an 82-kW (110-hp) Le Rhône 9J rotary engine; a few flew briefly with No. 60 Squadron, but the major user was Russia, with a considerable number in service; most successful Russian unit was the XIX Fighter Detachment based at Lusk
Morane-Saulnier Type V: also having the 110-hp Le Rhône engine, this version was modified extensively, with increased wing span and a deeper forward fuselage to accommodate an additional belly fuel tank to provide increased range; 12 were supplied to

the RFC and others to Russia

Specification
Morane-Saulnier Type Nm
Type: single-seat fighter
Powerplant: one 60-kW (80-hp) Le Rhône 9C rotary piston engine
Performance: maximum speed 145 km/h (90 mph)
Weights: empty 288 kg (635 lb); maximum take-off 444 kg (979 lb)
Dimensions: span 8.15 m (26 ft 8¾ in); length 5.83 m (19 ft 1½ in); height 2.50 m (8 ft 2½ in); wing area 11.00 m² (118.41 sq ft)
Armament: one fixed 8-mm (0.315-in) Hotchkiss, or 7.7-mm (0.303-in) Vickers or Lewis machine-gun

Morane-Saulnier Type P

The two-seat **Morane-Saulnier Type P** parasol-wing monoplane reconnaissance aircraft of early 1916 introduced a new fully-faired circular-section fuselage and a wing incorporating ailerons and raked wingtips. The 82-kW (110-hp) Le Rhône 9J rotary engine had a contoured horseshoe cowling in early aircraft, but later machines had a full circular cowling. Production of the Type P totalled 565, but although the type was used quite widely by the French Aéronautique Militaire, no French unit was fully equipped with the type. A considerable number went to the RFC, some equipping Nos 1 and 3 Squadrons in 1916-17. Some RFC aircraft had 60-kW (80-hp) Le Rhône engines.

Armament varied, the observer being armed initially with a Lewis gun on a spi-

The Type P, or Morane-Saulnier 21, was a useful reconnaissance type but was not widely produced. Most were used by the French from 1917, though a number were supplied to the RFC. Above is just such an example, which appears to have had its armament reduced to a single Lewis gun.

got mounting, but this was replaced later by a ring mounting. Some aircraft had a fixed Lewis gun above the wing firing forward, while others had a synchronised Vickers machine-gun, but all were of 7.7-mm (0.303-in) calibre. Two single-seat fighter conversions were tested briefly, one with the wing lowered so that it was braced just above the fuse-

lage. The standard two-seat Type P had a wing span of 11.20 m (36 ft 9 in), had a maximum take-off weight of 732 kg

(1,614 lb) and reached a maximum speed of 156 km/h (97 mph) with the 82-kW (110-hp) engine.

Morane-Saulnier Type S

The **Morane-Saulnier Type S** biplane was a three/four-seat heavy bomber built in 1915; its two 186-kW (250-hp) Renault V-12 engines giving it a maximum speed of 155 km/h (96 mph). Considerably larger than the Type T flown in 1914, the Type S had a wing which spanned 26.00 m (85 ft 3¾ in). Its landing gear was of similar design to that of the Type T, but with twin nose wheels, and gunners' cockpits were located in the nose and amidships. The Type S was successful in official competitions, but no record of the number built is available.

The Morane-Saulnier Type S twin-engined heavy bomber was a very large design for its time. It was based on the Type T unequal-span biplane which, although large, was considerably smaller than the subsequent Type S. It featured the Morane-Saulnier trademark of a finely-tapering rear fuselage and was powered by a pair of Le Rhône rotary piston engines. The two gunners were provided with a single machine-gun each.

Morane-Saulnier Type T
to
Morane-Saulnier M.S.450

Morane-Saulnier Type T

Flown for the first time in July 1914, the **Morane-Saulnier Type T** was a large biplane, powered by two 60-kW (80-hp) Le Rhône rotary engines in streamlined cowlings between the wings. It had a large single fin and rudder, and the landing gear comprised twin main units with four main wheels, an auxiliary nose wheel and a tail skid. The original nose section, with numerous observation portholes, was soon eliminated in favour

In an attempt to reduce drag, the Type T's engines had large spinners fitted. Maximum speed was still only 140 km/h (87 mph).

of a more conventional gunners' cockpit. The pilot and second gunner were seated in tandem, beneath a cut-out in the upper wing trailing edge.

The Type T had a maximum speed of 140 km/h (87 mph) and a wing span of

17.65 m (57 ft 11 in). Intended originally as a bomber, it was ordered into production in 1916 as a three-seat bomber

escort, but the 100-aircraft order is thought to have been cancelled after only a few examples had been built.

Morane-Saulnier Type TRK

Little is known of the **Morane-Saulnier Type TRK**, an unequal-span biplane bomber of 1915. It had two 164-kW (220-hp) Canton-Unné engines mounted in the sides of the forward fuselage, driving large two-bladed wing-mounted propellers by means of inclined shafts. Landing gear layout was similar to that of the Type T biplane and the pilot and co-pilot were seated side-by-side in

The Morane-Saulnier Type TRK had many unusual features. An unusually large triplane, with unequal-span wings, it had fuselage-mounted engines.

the pointed nose section. A third crew member was located in a midships cockpit to operate twin 7.7-mm (0.303-in) machine-guns.

Morane-Saulnier M.S.43

Winner of the 1924 French War Ministry competition for an ET.2 category two-seat intermediate trainer, the **Morane-Saulnier M.S.43** was developed from the **M.S.42** prototype. Whereas the earlier aircraft had been an equal-span biplane, the upper wing of the M.S.43 had considerably more span than the lower and, in addition, incorporated over-

all structural strengthening to cope with the rough surface of contemporary training airfields. Fitted with dual controls in the tandem cockpits, the M.S.43 was built in some numbers, production ending with the 79th machine. The type was in military service until 1929, when a number of surviving aircraft were sold to private owners, and one had been used

This M.S.43 was sold after its military days were over. The undercarriage, designed for student landings, had considerable strength which made it ideal for rough field operations.

by the US military attaché in France. The 134-kW (180-hp) Hispano-Suiza 8Ab V-8 engine gave a maximum speed of 162 km/h (101 mph). Wing span was

10.88 m (35 ft 8¼ in) and maximum take-off weight 1120 kg (2,469 lb).

Morane-Saulnier M.S.50, M.S.51 and M.S.53

A neat parasol-wing monoplane, the **Morane-Saulnier M.S.50C** primary trainer made its appearance in 1924. Powered by an 89-kW (120-hp) Salmson 9Ac radial engine, it had a maximum speed of 168 km/h (104 mph). Six examples were sold to Finland in 1925, where they remained in service until 1932. Finnish serials were 2G6 to 2G11, and later M.S.51 to M.S.56.

Two **M.S.51** aircraft appeared in 1925, one a conversion from an M.S.50, the primary difference being the installation of a 134-kW (180-hp) Hispano-Suiza 8Ab V-8 engine. The **M.S.53** also flew for the first time in 1925. A trainer, like

Introducing rounded tips to the distinctive Morane-Saulnier parasol wing, the Salmson radial engined M.S.50 of 1924 was a neat trainer which found a market in Finland.

the others, it had revised wing bracing and a sweptback parasol wing. Of a limited number built, five were sold to the Turkish air arm. Wing span was 10.70 m (35 ft 1¼ in) compared with 11.70 m (38 ft 4¾ in) for the M.S.50 and M.S.51.

Although built in comparatively small numbers, these trainers represented a

big advance in Morane-Saulnier design, introducing an entirely new wing with

improved aerodynamic profile and rounded tips.

Morane-Saulnier M.S.121, 221, 222, 223 and M.S.224

Built in 1927, the **Morane-Saulnier M.S.121** single-seat light fighter was intended to fulfil a 1926 French official requirement for a lightly built and moderately powered fighter with a good rate of climb, capable of intercepting enemy bombers as they crossed the frontier. Of the seven prototypes built for this so-called 'Jockey' programme, none went into production.

Powered by a 298-kW (400-hp) Hispano-Suiza 12Jb V-8 engine, the M.S.121 had a modest maximum speed of

248 km/h (154 mph). The general configuration, a strut-braced parasol-wing monoplane with cross-axle landing gear, was retained in the next development, the **M.S.221**, which had a reduced maximum take-off weight and a Gnome-Rhône 9Ag radial engine of 358 kW (480 hp). Test flown by Fronval in 1928, the M.S.221 attained 268 km/h (166 mph). Yet more changes in the programme requirements led to the **M.S.222** with a supercharged 9Asb Jupiter, which flew for the first time in

March 1929. Famous aviatrix Maryse Hilz established a height record for women with this machine in 1932. A second example (F-AJZT) flew in October 1930, its engine enclosed by a Townend ring, and this aircraft was used for demonstrations abroad.

The **M.S.223.01** of 1930 was identical with the M.S.222 except that it had new divided landing gear with oleo-pneumatic shock absorbers. Soon after its appearance the French air ministry abandoned the entire 'Jockey' pro-

gramme, but the very similar **M.S.224** was then almost completed. Demonstrated at the 1930 Salon de l'Aéronautique, it had increased wing span and area, and was of all-metal construction, except for wooden ribs. Maximum speed was increased to 299 km/h (185 mph). The next stage of development was the M.S. 225.

Armament for all the Morane-Saulnier 'Jockey' fighters comprised two synchronised fuselage-mounted 7.7-mm (0.303-in) machine-guns.

Morane-Saulnier M.S.129 and M.S.130

The **Morane-Saulnier M.S.129** of 1925 and **M.S.130** of 1926 shared many new design features, and both were developed from the M.S.53. Only relatively few M.S.129s were built, some for the Romanian air arm and some for civil use, but production of the successful M.S.130 totalled 145.

Design features included a new sweptback 'autostable' parasol wing, and the M.S.129 was powered by a 134-kW (180-hp) Hispano-Suiza 8Ab V-8 engine, while the M.S.130 had a more carefully contoured fuselage and an uncrowded 172-kW (230-hp) Salmson 9Ab radial.

Most of the M.S.130s were bought by the French navy, and they served at naval air training centres from 1927 to 1935. Private owners and flying clubs bought 26 of the type and others were exported, 15 to Brazil, two going to Belgium and others to China, Guatemala and Turkey. Only a small batch was used by French military aviation.

The second M.S.130 prototype was modified in 1929 to take new design landing gear (later fitted to the M.S.230), and was entered in that year's Coupe Michelin air race. Two M.S.130s were later converted to M.S.230s.

The M.S.130 spanned 10.70 m (35 ft

1¼ in), had a maximum take-off weight of 1149 kg (2,533 lb) and attained a maximum speed of 208 km/h (129 mph).

Variants
M.S.131: one M.S.130 converted to take a 172-kW (230-hp) Lorraine engine; flown by the US military attaché in Paris
M.S.132: conversion with 89-kW (120-hp) Salmson 7Ac radial
M.S.133: four conversions, one from M.S.130 and three from M.S.129; most powerful variant with 201-kW (270-hp) Gnome-Rhône 5Kc radial
M.S.134: conversion of M.S.130 with

The M.S.130 featured sweptback wings, which produced a measure of inherent stability and were retained as standard.

60-kW (80-hp) Clerget 9B rotary
M.S.136: conversion of M.S.130 with 89-kW (120-hp) Salmson 9Ac radial

Morane-Saulnier M.S.138

First flown in 1927, the **Morane-Saulnier M.S.138** was an EP.2 category two-seat primary trainer developed from the M.S.35, from which it differed in having sweepback on the parasol wing, a revised tail unit and a more rounded fuselage. Most of the 178 aircraft built were used by the Aéronautique Militaire, then remained in service with the Armée de l'Air from its formation until 1935. Others were used by the French Aéronavale and by civil aero clubs, 33 aircraft appearing on the French civil register. In addition Greece bought a small batch. The M.S.138 was powered by a 60-kW (80-hp) Le Rhône 9C rotary engine which

Many M.S.138s were built for the French air force and others went to Greece. This aircraft was rebuilt by RAF personnel in France in 1939-40.

gave it a maximum speed of 135 km/h (84 mph). Wing span was 10.90 m (35 ft 9¼ in) and maximum take-off weight 772 kg (1,702 lb). M.S.138 variants included the **M.S.137** with an 89-kW (120-hp) Salmson 9Ac radial, the **M.S.139** with a 97-kW (130-hp) Clerget 9B rotary, and the **M.S.191** with slightly reduced span, which had subvariants with Clerget 9Bs and Salmson 9Ncs.

Morane-Saulnier M.S.140S and M.S.141S

The **Morane-Saulnier M.S.140S** light ambulance was built to an official French requirement, being a single-bay biplane with staggered swept-back wings and wide-track divided landing gear. The pilot was seated in an open cockpit forward, with behind him a long hinged panel in the starboard side of the

fuselage to permit the loading of a stretcher patient into an enclosed section. Neither the M.S.140S, powered by a 60-kW (80-hp) Le Rhône 9C rotary engine, nor the improved **M.S.141S** development with an 89-kW (120-hp) Salmson 9Ac radial, was accepted for production.

The prototype M.S.141S was intended as a purpose-built flying air ambulance. In the rear fuselage was provision for a single stretcher case and an attendant. The glass panel in the port side was a window fitted for the patient's benefit.

Morane-Saulnier M.S.147, M.S.148 and M.S.149

The series originating with the **Morane-Saulnier M.S.147** monoplane married the fuselage and landing gear of the M.S.130 to the wire-braced parasol wing of the M.S.138. The M.S.147 prototype (F-AIXA) made its initial flight in 1928. Powered by an 89-kW (120-hp) Salmson 9Ac radial, it could attain a maximum 145 km/h (90 mph) and a total of 109 was built. Three **M.S.147P** aircraft were used by the Aéropostale company on its air mail routes, and exports included 30 aircraft to Brazil, five to Greece; other foreign purchasers included Guatemala and Turkey.

The sole **M.S.148**, powered by a 71-kW (95-hp) Salmson 7Ac, appeared in

The majority of the 109 Morane-Saulnier M.S.149 trainers built had disappeared from French service by the mid-1930s. However, this Armée de l'Air aircraft is pictured in action alongside French troops after the outbreak of war in 1939.

1928, and in the following year the first of 56 **M.S.149** aircraft was flown. These were all purchased by the French navy as basic trainers which, powered by the 75-kW (100-hp) Lorraine 5Pa radial engine, reached a maximum 140 km/h (87 mph); the aircraft equipped naval flying schools up to 1935.

Morane-Saulnier M.S.152

The braced parasol-wing two-seat fighter-reconnaissance **Morane-**

Saulnier M.S.152 flew in 1928. It had a ring mounting for twin 7.7-mm (0.303-

in) machine-guns over the observer's cockpit, glazed observation panels in the fuselage sides and a ventral trap for an additional machine-gun or the operation of a camera, and there was provision for

a fixed forward-firing machine-gun. The M.S.152 spanned 12.80 m (42 ft 0 in) and had a maximum speed of only 183 km/h (114 mph) as powered by a 172-kW (230-hp) Salmson 9Ab radial.

Morane-Saulnier M.S.180, M.S.181 and M.S.185

The **Morane-Saulnier M.S.180**, first flown in 1928, was a small single-seat parasol-wing monoplane intended for sport flying and aerobatics, and was powered by a 30-kW (40-hp) Salmson 9Ad engine. The **M.S.181** which

appeared in the next year closely resembled the earlier machine, but had a 45-kW (60-hp) Salmson 5Ac radial engine. Other improvements included an enlarged rudder and a slimmer fuselage. To achieve greater economy, the

company developed the **M.S.185** with wings of increased span and rounded tips. This relied on reduced power, having a 34-kW (46-hp) Salmson radial engine, and was as successful as the M.S.181. Both the M.S.181 and M.S.185

were built in quantity, over 100 being sold to private owners and civil flying clubs. Two M.S.181s, one with an American Franklin engine and the other with the rounded wingtips of the M.S.185, were flying in France in 1983.

Morane-Saulnier M.S.225

Essentially a stop-gap fighter, to bolster the Armée de l'Air's flagging *escadrilles de chasse* pending the arrival of new types under development, the **Morane-Saulnier M.S.225** was exhibited in mock-up form at the 1932 Paris Salon de l'Aéronautique. Flight testing of the prototype proved successful and a production order followed.

The **M.S.225** C.1 category single-seat fighter had an all-metal structure, and wide-track divided landing gear with faired struts and wheel 'spats', and was powered by a Gnome-Rhône 9Krsd radial engine. It had a more rounded fuselage and was generally more robust and heavy than its immediate predecessor, the **M.S.224.01**, and incorporated the sweptback parasol wing which was a feature of so many Morane-Saulnier types of the period.

In total 75 M.S.225s were built by the Puteaux factory. The last of 55 examples for the Armée de l'Air was delivered in November 1933, and the French Aéronautique Maritime accepted the first of 16 machines in February 1934. Three aircraft were delivered to China and the famous pilot Detroyat had one M.S.225 as his personal mount, which was flown in numerous air shows and competitions.

The Armée de l'Air M.S.225 fighters re-equipped two *escadrilles* of the 7ème Escadre at Dijon and two *escadrilles* of the 42ème Escadre at Reims from 1933, being phased out of service with these units during 1936-37. The type also equipped the renowned Escadrille 3C1

of the Aéronavale, based at Marignane, but 3C1 was dissolved at the beginning of 1936 and became the 1ère Escadrille of Armée de l'Air Groupe de Chasse II/8, finally giving up its M.S.225s in July 1938.

Meanwhile the 'Patrouille Acrobatique' (based at Etampes training school) flew five M.S.225s from 1934 to 1938, and the last Armée de l'Air unit to use the M.S.225 was the 'Patrouille' of the Ecole de l'Air situated at Salon de Provence, which received 15 aircraft given up by other units. All were modified for aerobatics, the external difference being the increased height of the vertical tail surfaces. The last great performance of this famous aerobatic team was at Evère, Belgium in 1939. At the outbreak of war 21 aircraft were still in flying condition, but by the summer of 1940 all had been scrapped.

Variants

M.S.226: carrier version of late 1933 with deck landing hook under rear fuselage; remained land-based at Hyères

M.S.226bis: sub-type of M.S.226 with folding wings, flown in 1934

M.S.227: flew in 1933 as flying test-bed for the Hispano-Suiza 12Xcrs engine of 515 kW (690 hp), driving a four-bladed propeller

M.S.275: flown in 1934, this version had modified wings and tail unit, and was powered by a 515-kW (690-hp) Gnome-Rhône 9Krse engine which

gave a maximum speed of 348 km/h (216 mph) at 4000 m (13,125 ft); not adopted for production

M.S.278: conversion of M.S.225 no. 2 for a 388-kW (520-hp) Clerget 14Fos diesel engine powerplant; not successful

Specification

Type: single-seat fighter
Powerplant: one 373-kW (500-hp) Gnome-Rhône 9Kbrs radial piston engine
Performance: maximum speed 333 km/h (207 mph) at 4000 m (13,125 ft); service ceiling 9500 m (31,170 ft); range 700 km (435 miles)

Produced as a stop-gap measure, the M.S.225 had the distinction (alongside the Nieuport-Delage 629) of being one of the first French service fighters with a supercharged engine.

Weights: empty equipped 1217 kg (2,683 lb); maximum take-off 1580 kg (3,483 lb)
Dimensions: span 10.56 m (34 ft 7¾ in); length 7.24 m (23 ft 9 in); height 3.29 m (10 ft 9½ in); wing area 17.20 m² (185.15 sq ft)
Armament: two fixed synchronised fuselage-mounted Vickers 7.7-mm (0.303-in) machine-guns

Morane-Saulnier M.S.230 series

The **Morane-Saulnier M.S.230** Et. 2 category two-seat intermediate trainer was the most important French aircraft of this class during the inter-war years. Flown for the first time in prototype form during February 1929, this robust, strut-braced high parasol-wing monoplane with a circular-section fuselage and wide-track divided landing gear was the result of continuing design development stemming from the Type AR monoplane of World War I. The pupil was seated in an open cockpit below a cut-out in the trailing edge of the wing, with the instructor's cockpit immediately behind him.

An initial French Aéronautique Militaire order for 500 M.S.230s was followed by more military contracts plus others for the French navy, civil flying schools and private owners. Other examples were exported. Morane-Saulnier production was augmented by orders received by SFAN (59) and Levasseur (80), 18 aircraft of the Levasseur 1939 contract being completed post-war. **M.S.233** and **M.S.236** export versions were built by OGMA (Portugal) and SABCA (Belgium) respectively.

The type was used for a wide variety of tasks in addition to training, these including liaison, observation, gunnery instruction, target and glider towing, and aerobatics. In this last role, flown by members of the famous French Armée de l'Air central flying school at Etampes, the olive green and white painted wings

of the team's three M.S.230s became a familiar sight at pre-war French aviation meetings.

Variants

M.S.229: two examples built for Swiss Fliegertruppen in 1931; similar to M.S.230, but with V-8 Hispano-Suiza 8Ac engines; one converted in 1932 to take Wright 9Qa radial

M.S.230: over 1,100 built; Romania bought 20 in 1930 and Greece 25 in 1931; Belgium and Brazil purchased nine each; as well as being the main Armée de l'Air trainer for many years, the type was used by the French navy and a number of well-known private pilots including Louis Dollfus; examples were used for tests with Handley Page slats and with skis; one machine was flown with a Lorraine 9Nb Algol Junior engine

M.S.231: six built with 179-kW (240-hp) Lorraine 7Mb engine in 1930

M.S.232: experimental version with 149-kW (200-hp) Clerget 9Ca diesel engine, flown briefly during November 1930

M.S.233: powered by 172-kW (230-hp) Gnome-Rhône 5Ba or 5Bc radial engine, six built in France and 16 under licence in Portugal for that nation's air arm

M.S.234: 186-kW (250-hp) Hispano-Suiza 9Qa engine; two built, one bought for US ambassador in Paris

M.S.234/2: converted from racing version of M.S.130, participated in 1931

Coupe Michelin air race; had a 172-kW (230-hp) Hispano-Suiza 9Qb with NACA cowling; in 1933, with 9Qa engine, became redesignated **M.S.234 No. 2** and was flown by Michael Detroyat at aerobatic exhibitions in France and the USA up to 1938

M.S.235: one built and flown in 1930 with a 224-kW (300-hp) Gnome-Rhône 7Kb engine

M.S.235H: twin-float version of M.S.235; flown from Lake Berre 1931

M.S.236: Belgian SABCA built 19 examples for the nation's air arm; powered by 160-kW (215-hp) Armstrong-Siddeley Lynx 4C engine; first aircraft flew July 1932

M.S.237: five built for private owners; powered by 209-kW (280-hp) Salmson 9Aba engine; first appeared 1934

Specification
Morane-Saulnier M.S.230

Type: two-seat intermediate trainer
Powerplant: one 172-kW (230-hp) Salmson 9Ab radial piston engine
Performance: maximum speed 205 km/h (127 mph); service ceiling 5000 m (16,405 ft)
Weights: empty equipped 829 kg (1,828 lb); maximum take-off 1150 kg (2,535 lb)
Dimensions: span 10.70 m (35 ft 1¼ in); length 6.98 m (22 ft 10¾ in); height 2.80 mm (9 ft 2¼ in); wing area 19.70 m² (212.06 sq ft)

The Morane-Saulnier M.S.230 was in every way a superb training aircraft with positive handling. It had a robust structure, a reliable Salmson engine and a stable, wide-track landing gear.

Morane-Saulnier M.S.250

With a family resemblance to the M.S.230, but with revised tail surfaces, the **Morane-Saulnier M.S.250** was fully equipped for the advanced training of observers. The rear cockpit was provided with a gun ring and protected by a substantial framed windscreen. Powered by a 172-kW (230-hp) Salmson 9Ab radial, the M.S.250 had a maximum speed of 189 km/h (117 mph). The

This view of the prototype M.S.250 shows the departure in design of the tail surfaces. Both gunner and pilot had windshields.

M.S.251 development was powered by a 179-kW (240-hp) Lorraine 7Mc radial engine.

Morane-Saulnier M.S.315

Developed from the **M.S.300** primary trainer prototype of 1930, and its **M.S.301** and **M.S.302** variants, the **Morane-Saulnier M.S.315** flew for the first time in October 1932. Of typically robust parasol high-wing configuration, it was of mixed construction with divided main landing gear. Four prototypes were followed by 346 series aircraft, 33 of them built post-war. In addition, five higher-powered **M.S.315/2** aircraft were built for civil use, plus a single **M.S.316** with a Regnier inverted-vee engine. The type became the workhorse of the French Armée de l'Air and served also with the Aéronavale and various civil flying schools. It was a favourite at many pre-war airshows flown by such notables as Thoret, Fleurquin and Detroyat.

Between 1960 and 1962, 40 M.S.315s then in use as civil glider tugs were re-

With less power and a greater wing area than the M.S.230, the Morane-Saulnier M.S.315 was an ideal primary trainer and by the standards of the days was built in sizeable numbers. Some survived after the war as target tugs.

engined with the 164-kW (220-hp) war-surplus Continental W-670K radial, being redesignated **M.S.317**.

Specification
Morane-Saulnier M.S.315
Type: two-seat primary trainer
Powerplant: one 101-kW (135-hp) Salmson 9Nc radial piston engine
Performance: maximum speed 170 km/h (106 mph); service ceiling 5500 m (18,045 ft)
Weights: empty equipped 548 kg

(1,208 lb); maximum take-off 860 kg (1,896 lb)
Dimensions: span 12.00 m (39 ft

4½ in); length 7.60 m (24 ft 11¼ in); height 2.80 m (9 ft 2¼ in); wing area 21.60 m² (232.51 sq ft)

Morane-Saulnier M.S.325

An unsuccessful competitor in a French Air Ministry single-seat fighter programme which led eventually to the Dewoitine D.500 and Blériot-SPAD D.510, the **Morane-Saulnier M.S.325** prototype was flown for the first time in early 1933. An all-metal low-wing monoplane with a semi-elliptical

wing braced to the fuselage by two Y-struts, the M.S.325 accommodated its pilot in an open cockpit above the wing trailing edge, protected by an anti-turn-over pylon. The 484-kW (650-hp) Hispano-Suiza 12Xbrs engine provided a maximum speed of 365 km/h (227 mph). Span was 11.80 m (38 ft 8½ in) and maxi-

The M.S.325 displayed many of the characteristics of the first-generation monoplanes such as fixed and faired landing gear and a braced wing. The open cockpit, then preferred by pilots, had a large headrest/anti-roll bar.

mum take-off weight 1789 kg (3,944 lb). The M.S.325 had a number of innova-

tions, but was clearly obsolescent when development was abandoned in 1934.

Morane-Saulnier M.S.340 to M.S.345

The prototype **Morane-Saulnier M.S.340**, flown during April 1933, was designed as a touring or training aircraft. It retained the company's usual parasol-wing monoplane configuration, but introduced 18° of wing sweepback. Of mixed construction, the M.S.340 was fabric-covered with the exception of the metal engine panels. Principal production version was the **M.S.341** and some 40 aircraft of all versions were built up to 1937. Two were flown as liaison aircraft by government (anti-Franco) forces in the Spanish Civil War.

Variants
M.S.340: prototype (F-AMOP) powered by an 89-kW (120-hp) de Havilland Gipsy III engine
M.S.341: first aircraft was converted from M.S.340; powered by 89-kW (120-hp) Renault 4Pdi engine

M.S.341/2 reinforced wing bracing and revised tail unit; four built
M.S.341/3: powered by 104-kW (140-hp) Renault 4Pei engine; as well as civil machines, 12 M.S.341/3s bought by Armée de l'Air for use as elementary trainers; maximum speed 200 km/h (124 mph), wing span 10.20 m (33 ft 5½ in) and maximum take-off weight 920 kg (2,028 lb); one of this type bought by Ethiopia
M.S.342: version with 89-kW (120-hp) de Havilland Gipsy Major engine; second aircraft, with glazed cockpit canopy and wheel fairings, built specially for millionaire Louis Gazaniol of Sidi-bel-Abbès, Algeria
M.S.343: single example (F-APIA) built for famed woman flier Maryse Hilz; had a 130-kw (175-hp) Salmson 9Nd radial engine
M.S.343/2: as M.S.343, but with

101-kW (135-hp) Salmson 9Nc radial engine
M.S.345: appeared in June 1935; one only (F-ANVR) with single profiled wing struts and fully faired landing gear; powered by a 104-kW (140-hp) Renault

4Pei, it was owned by a series of wealthy amateur pilots, but no series production was undertaken

Two of the features that marked the M.S.340 from its predecessors were the greater degree of sweep on its wings and the use of an inverted inline engine.

Morane-Saulnier M.S.350

Flown for the first time on 8 February 1936, the **Morane-Saulnier M.S.350** was a small single-seat open-cockpit aerobatic biplane with equal-span wings, the independent main legs of the fixed landing gear being fully faired and fitted with streamlined wheel 'spats'. Powered initially by a Renault 453/01 engine, the prototype was soon fitted with a Renault 478/01 6 Q/01 of 164 kW (220 hp). Despite lack of service orders for the type, the M.S.350 gained a remarkable reputation thanks to a series of breathtaking demonstrations by

Detroyat at air shows in France and Switzerland in the period up to September 1939. The aircraft was then much modified and fitted with a new Zenith carburettor to permit prolonged inflight flight. Recovered from storage post-war and registered F-BDYL, the M.S.350 saw a limited amount of use until on 8 December 1964 it was damaged beyond repair in Italy and subsequently scrapped. Maximum speed was 255 km/h (158 mph), wing span 8.40 m (27 ft 6¾ in) and maximum take-off weight 990 kg (2,182 lb).

After World War II the Morane-Saulnier M.S.350 aerobatic aircraft was brought back up to flight standard and was used on a sporadic basis until 1964.

Morane-Saulnier M.S.406C-1

To meet a French Air Ministry requirement of 1934 for a new single-seat fighter, the company designed the **Morane-Saulnier M.S.405** low-wing monoplane. First flown on 8 August

1935, the M.S.405 had a basic all-metal structure and retractable main units for its tailskid landing gear, and was powered by a 641-kW (860-hp) Hispano-Suiza 12Ygrs V-12 engine. The

M.S.405-01 and **M.S.405-02** prototypes were used for official tests, the latter having revised wing planform and an Hispano-Suiza 12Ycrs engine, and in early 1937 the company received an order for 15 pre-production M.S.405s and one different **M.S.406**. A subsequent order for 50 M.S.405s was

changed later to cover the same number of the M.S.406, and total production of the M.S.405 was therefore 17, including the prototypes, about half of which were used for experimental purposes. Modifications introduced as the rest of continued official tests resulted in the designation M.S.406C-1 being applied to the production version, of which 1,000 were ordered in March 1938. The manufacture of this number being beyond the capability of Morane-Saulnier, it was arranged for the type to be built by three divisions of the nationalised industry, and the first production aircraft was flown on 29 January 1939. Generally similar to the M.S.405 prototype, the M.S.406 differed primarily by having a lightweight wing structure, the Hispano-Suiza 12Y-31 engine as standard, and detail refinements and changes in equipment.

Meanwhile, Morane-Saulnier was busy with development of the M.S.406 and involved with orders for the export market. They included 12 for China, seized by French colonial authorities en route to their destination; 30 which equipped No. 28 Squadron of the Finnish air force; 13 for Lithuania, undelivered because of the outbreak of World War II; 45 for Turkey; and 20 for Yugoslavia, ordered in early 1940 but not delivered. Poland had ordered 160, but although 50 were despatched to Gdynia none was delivered before the collapse of Polish resistance. Switzerland acquired two early production M.S.406 aircraft as patterns for the licence-construction of 82 **EFW D-3800** fighters by Eidgenössisches Flugzeugwerk. In conjunction with Dornier-Werke AG at Altenrhein, this government factory built 207 examples of a Swiss-developed **D-3801**. Last of the foreign versions were a number of M.S.406s which, after the German occupation of Vichy, France, were distributed between the Croatian and Finnish air forces. Most of the Finnish aircraft were re-engined subsequently with 820-kW (1,100-hp) Klimov M-105P engines captured from the Soviets, the resulting improved per-

formance fighters being known as **Mörkö Moraani**.

Supply problems with the Hispano-Suiza 12Y engine meant that at the outbreak of war only 572 of the planned 1,000 M.S.406s had been delivered to the Armée de l'Air, and it was discovered very quickly that the type was completely outmatched by the German Messerschmitt Bf 109E. During a brief operational period M.S.406 squadrons were credited with the destruction of 175 enemy aircraft, but this had been achieved for the loss of more than 400 of their own number. By the time of the French collapse, 1,081 had been delivered, some for service with the French navy, and the type equipped Groupes III/1, II/2, III/2, II/3, III/3, III/4, III/5, I/6, II/6. III/6, I/7, II/7, III/7, I/9, II/9 and I/10 at home, as well as II/595, II/596, EC 565 and GAM 550. After the Franco-German armistice, however, only one Vichy French air force *groupe* operated these aircraft.

Specification
Morane-Saulnier M.S.406C-1

Morane-Saulnier M.S.406C-1 of the Escadron d'Entraînement, Vichy French air force, based at Toulouse in 1941.

Type: single-seat fighter
Powerplant: one 641-kW (860-hp) Hispano-Suiza 12Y-31 V-12 piston engine
Performance: maximum speed 485 km/h (302 mph) at 5000 m (16,400 ft); service ceiling 9400 m (30,840 ft); range 800 km (497 miles)
Weights: empty 1900 kg (4,189 lb);

maximum take-off 2470 kg (5,445 lb)
Dimensions: span 10.60 m (34 ft 9¼ in); length 8.15 m (26 ft 9 in); height 2.80 m (9 ft 2¼ in); wing area 16.00 m² (172.23 sq ft)
Armament: one engine-mounted 20-mm cannon firing through propeller hub and two wing-mounted 7.5-mm (0.295-in) machine-guns

The M.S.406 was underpowered and retained such obsolete features as a braced tailplane and a measure of fabric covering.

Morane-Saulnier M.S.430 to M.S.435

Drawing heavily on components of the M.S.405 fighter, the Morane-Saulnier design team put forward an advanced trainer under the designation **Morane-Saulnier M.S.430**, the prototype flying for the first time on 3 March 1937. A cantilever low-wing monoplane with inward-retracting landing gear, the M.S.430 located its pupil and instructor in tandem cockpits beneath a continuous glazed canopy, and power was provided by a 291-kW (390-hp) Salmson 9Ag radial engine. Tests continued into 1939, and a single-seat version was evaluated with the designation **M.S.408**. A version with a Gnome-Rhône 7Kfs radial,

designated **M.S.433**, was never completed.

The **M.S.435.01** took off for the first time on 6 December 1939. Powered by a 410-kW (550-hp) Gnome-Rhône 9Kdrs engine, it had a redesigned fuselage of increased cross-section. An order for 60 series machines had been received from the French air ministry six months earlier, but priority in production went to

An advanced trainer suitable for use in the weapons training role, the Morane-Saulnier M.S.435 was based on the M.S.405, but appeared too late.

the M.S.406 fighter, with the result that no series M.S.435 P.2 category (two-

seat advanced trainer) aircraft were delivered before the French collapse in June 1940. The M.S.435.01 spanned 10.71 m (35 ft 1¾ in) and had a maximum speed of 395 km/h (245 mph).

Morane-Saulnier M.S.450

With the issue of a French air ministry requirement of 1937 for a single-seat fighter to supersede the Morane-Saulnier M.S.406, the company found itself in competition with divisions of the nationalised industry. The resulting **Morane-Saulnier M.S.450**, of which three prototypes were built and the first flown on 14 April 1939, differed little from the M.S.406 except for refined lines and the installation of a more powerful Hispano-Suiza engine. The type failed to gain a French production order, losing out to the Dewoitine D.520. However, 12 were licence-built subsequently in Switzerland under the designation **D-3802**, and in this version the wing-mounted machine-guns were replaced by two 20-mm cannon.

The Morane-Saulnier M.S.450 was a far more refined development of the M.S.406 but failed to win a French order, losing out to the superior Dewoitine D.520.

Specification
Morane-Saulnier M.S.450
Type: single-seat fighter
Powerplant: one 820-kW (1,100-hp) Hispano-Suiza 12Y-51 piston engine
Performance: maximum speed 560 km/h (348 mph); service ceiling 10000 m (32,800 ft); range 750 km (466 miles)
Weights: maximum take-off 2500 kg (5,512 lb)
Dimensions: span 10.60 m (34 ft 9¼ in); length 8.80 m (28 ft 10½ in);

height 2.75 m (9 ft 0¼ in); wing area 16.00 m² (172.23 sq ft)
Armament: one 20-mm cannon firing

through the propeller hub and two 7.5-mm (0.295-in) wing-mounted machine-guns

Morane-Saulnier M.S.470 Vanneau
to
Mudry aircraft

Morane-Saulnier M.S.470 Vanneau

Developed under the Vichy regime by Morane-Saulnier chief designer Gauthier, the **Morane-Saulnier M.S.470.01 Vanneau** two-seat advanced trainer prototype made its first flight on 22 December 1944. Successful tests led to a decision by the Armée de l'Air to buy the Vanneau (plover) to train its new generation of pilots, and three prototypes of the revised **M.S.472** were ordered, M.S.372.01 flying on 12 December 1945. In configuration the M.S.470 was an all-metal low-wing cantilever monoplane with pupil and instructor housed under a long glazed canopy. The main landing gear legs retracted inwards to lie partially exposed in the fuselage underside, a feature which was intended to reduce damage in the event of 'wheels-up' landings. The M.S.472 replaced the 515-kW (690-hp) Hispano-Suiza 12X engine of the M.S.470 with a 522-kW (700-hp) Gnome-Rhône 14M radial.

Series M.S.472s were delivered from December 1946 onwards, and series **M.S.474** aircraft, modified for carrier operations, were delivered to the Aéronavale from December 1947, an M.S.472 having been temporarily converted to serve as the prototype M.S.474 in February of that year. Total production of the **M.S.472 Vanneau II**

was 230 and of the **M.S.474 Vanneau IV** 70. Another series version was the **M.S.475 Vanneau V**, the prototype making its maiden flight on 8 August 1947. Production deliveries of the 200 series aircraft to the Armée de l'Air began in March 1950, the M.S.475 differed only in detail from its predecessors except for installation of a 634-kW (850-hp) Hispano-Suiza 12Y-45 V-12 engine.

The M.S.475 proved superior to its predecessors in manoeuvrability, speed and rate of turn, incorporating a wing of improved design, but a more radical modification with an increase in wing surface area was incorporated in one production machine, which was then redesignated **M.S.476.01**. Another M.S.475 was re-engined with an SNECMA Renault 12S-02 of 433-kW (580-hp) and became the **M.S.477.01**, flown in November 1950. The **M.S.478.01** project, to be powered by an Italian Isotta Fraschini Delta engine, was not built, and the last experimental

Designed during the German occupation and first flying in December 1944, the Morane-Saulnier M.S.470 served the Armée de l'Air as an advanced trainer from 1946. Five hundred production aircraft were built.

development of the Vanneau was M.S.472 no. 295 modified as the **M.S.479.01** to take an SNECMA 14X Super Mars engine of 611 kW (820 hp). It began its flight test programme in March 1952, but development was soon abandoned. The Vanneau II, IV and V remained in service at training bases of the Armée de l'Air and Aéronavale into the late 1960s.

Specification
Morane-Saulnier M.S.475 Vanneau V
Type: two-seat basic trainer

Powerplant: one 641-kW (860-hp) Hispano-Suiza 12Y 45 V-2 piston engine
Performance: maximum speed 445 km/h (277 mph); service ceiling 8500 m (27,885 ft); range 1500 km (932 miles)
Weights: empty equipped 2351 kg (5,183 lb); maximum take-off 3125 kg (6,889 lb)
Dimensions: span 10.65 m (34 ft 11 in); length 9.05 m (29 ft 8 in); height 3.62 m (11 ft 10 in); wing area 17.30 m² (186.22 sq ft)
Armament: two MAC 1934 7.5-mm (0.295-in) wing-mounted machine-guns, plus two Alkan racks for light bombs

Morane-Saulnier M.S.560 and M.S.570 series

The prototype **Morane-Saulnier M.S.560** single-seat low-wing aerobatic monoplane (F-WBBB) was built in 1946. It had retractable landing gear, a rearward-sliding cockpit canopy and its powerplant, comprising a 56-kW (75-hp) Train 6D-01 engine, gave a maximum speed of 235 km/h (146 mph). Three variants followed, namely the **M.S.561** and the **M.S.563** (F-BBGC) of 1947 each with a 75-kW (100-hp) Mathis G.4

engine, and the **M.S.562** with a 75-kW (100-hp) Cirrus Minor.

Late in 1946 the **M.S.570** prototype (F-BBBC) was flown, a two-seat tourer-trainer development of the M.S.560. It had a widened forward fuselage, side-by-side seats, and a 104-kW (140-hp) Renault 4Pei engine giving a maximum speed of 265 km/h (165 mph). The three-seat **M.S.571** followed, powered by a Renault 4P-01 of the same power, the

Intended solely as an aerobatic aircraft, the M.S.560 was a small and aerodynamically very clean aircraft which had retractable gear and provided the pilot with a large cockpit canopy.

prototype (F-BBGB) being followed by five more machines. Maximum speed was 240 km/h (149 mph). The **M.S.572** was similar to the basic design, but had

four seats and a 104-kW (140-hp) Potez 4D engine.

Morane-Saulnier M.S.700 series

First twin-engine design by this company since World War I, the **Morane-Saulnier M.S.700** of 1948 was a sleek, cantilever low-wing monoplane with retractable tricycle landing gear, the cabin accommodating five in either an executive transport or air taxi role. Powered by two Potez 4D-33 inline engines, each of 119 kW (160 hp), the M.S.700 had a maximum speed of 290 km/h (180 mph). It was followed by the **M.S.701** with two 134-kW (180-hp) Mathis 8G-20s, the larger, six-seat

M.S.703 with two 179-kW (240-hp) Argus As 10Cs, and the **M.S.704**, simi-

The Morane-Saulnier M.S.700 was a brave attempt at breaking into the market for twin-engined lightplanes/executive aircraft that the Americans captured at the end of the war and have held ever since. The aircraft shown is the Argus-engined M.S.703 which was intended as a dedicated air ambulance.

lar to the M.S.703 but with two 164-kW (220-hp) Potez 4D-31s. The M.S.703 had

a maximum speed of 300 km/h (186 mph), being flown for the first time in 1951. None of the variants was built in quantity, only four being entered on the French civil register.

Morane-Saulnier M.S.733 Alcyon

Development of the **Morane-Saulnier M.S.733 Alcyon** (kingfisher) basic trainer began with the **M.S.730.01** prototype, which flew for the first time on 11 August 1949. With the original 134-kW (180-hp) Mathis 8G.20 inverted V-8 engine replaced by a 179-kW (240-hp) Argus As 10, the prototype (F-WFOB)

flew again in November that year as the **M.S.731**. Two **M.S.732** prototypes (F-WFOD and F-BFDQ) were flight tested in early 1951, each of them powered by a Potez 6D.30 engine and having the previous cantilever fixed landing gear replaced by a new design in which the main units retracted. The first example

of the definitive version flew on 16 April 1951 as the **M.S.733.01**; five pre-production aircraft followed and series aircraft totalled 200; 40 for the French navy, 15 for Cambodia, and the balance for service with the Armée de l'Air as the Alcyon, 70 of them being fitted with machine-gun armament for use as gun-

nery trainers. In 1956 some of the gunnery trainers were converted to counter-insurgency duties, with machine-gun and anti-personnel bomb armament, for use against the nationalist rebels in Algeria. These aircraft were redesignated **M.S.733A**, of which a number were sold later to Morocco.

Specification
Morane-Saulnier M.S.733

Type: two/three-seat basic trainer
Powerplant: one 179-kW (240-hp) Potez 6D.30 inverted inline piston engine
Performance: maximum speed 260 km/h (162 mph); service ceiling 4800 m (15,750 ft); range 920 km (572 miles)
Weights: empty equipped 1260 kg (2,778 lb); maximum take-off 1670 kg (3,682 lb)

Dimensions: span 11.28 m (37 ft 0 in); length 9.32 m (30 ft 7 in); height 2.42 m (7 ft 11 in); wing area 21.90 m² (235.74 sq ft)

The M.S.733 continued Morane-Saulnier's tradition for building quality training aircraft. It served with both the air force and navy and later armed versions saw combat in Algeria.

Morane-Saulnier M.S.760 Paris

In January 1953 Morane-Saulnier flew the prototype **M.S.755 Fleuret**, a two-seat jet trainer which competed with the Fouga Magister for an air force order. The Fleuret lost the competition, but its design formed the basis of the **Morane-Saulnier M.S.760 Paris** which, designed primarily as a high-speed liaison aircraft, can be considered as a forerunner of the executive jet. The first prototype was flown on 29 July 1954, and interest shown by the French military authorities resulted in orders for the air force and navy, the initial production example designated M.S.760A, flying on 27 February 1958. Orders were received for 109 civil and military use, 36 sets of components being supplied to Argentina for assembly at the government factory in Cordoba, with Brazil acquiring 30 for liaison, photographic survey and training. The initial production version was superseded in 1961 by the **M.S.760B Paris II** with 480-kg (1,058-lb) thrust Marboré VI turbojets, and when production ended in 1964 a total of 156 aircraft of the two series had been built, including those assembled in Argentina. The final version was the 1963 Marboré VI-

powered **M.S.760C Paris III**, with an enlarged wing but without tip tanks, plus increased fuel in a redesigned fuselage accommodating five or six 'sat-down' passengers. The sole prototype (F-WLKL) flew for the first time on 28 February 1964 but the variant did not find favour as a business jet and proceeded no further. With the youngest airframe now nearly 30 years old, the Paris is due for replacement. Argentina, with 40 plus aircraft still in service, has selected the FMA Pampa jet trainer, while France, currently operating more than 50, has chosen the TBM700 turboprop.

Specification
Morane-Saulnier M.S.760 Paris I
Type: twin-turbojet liaison aircraft
Powerplant: two 400-kg (882-lb)

thrust Turboméca Marboré II turbojets
Performance: maximum speed 650 km/h (405 mph) at sea level; service ceiling 10000 m (32,800 ft);

range 1500 km (930 miles)
Weights: empty 1945 kg (4,280 lb); maximum take-off 3470 kg (7,650 lb)
Dimensions: span 10.15 m (33 ft 3 in); length 10.05 m (33 ft 0 in); height 2.60 m (8 ft 6 in); wing area 18.00 m² (193.69 sq ft)

Virtually no civilian M.S.760s are to be found today. The last great stronghold of the type is in France with the Armée de l'Air and the Aéronavale. Both services between them maintain a sizeable Paris fleet.

Morane-Saulnier M.S.1500

Flown for the first time on 12 May 1958, the prototype **Morane-Saulnier M.S.1500.01 Epervier** (sparrow-hawk) was a two-seat cantilever low-wing monoplane, with a high glazed canopy for its two-man crew set close behind the single 522-kW (700-hp) Turboméca Bastan IV turboprop; its fixed conventional landing gear had cantilever main legs. the M.S.1500 was intended to meet an official Armée de l'Air requirement for a tactical reconnaissance and counter-insurgency aircraft for service in Algeria against the national-

ist forces. A second prototype was built and tested, but no production orders were received. The M.S.1500 spanned 13.06 m (42 ft 10 in), had a maximum take-off weight of 2850 kg (6,283 lb) and reached a maximum 315 km/h (196 mph).

Owing its unusual nose shape to a Bastan turboprop engine, the M.S.1500 could carry an array of six 50-kg anti-personnel bombs or six 68-mm rocket pods.

Morrisey aircraft

William Morrisey, one-time chief test pilot of the Douglas Company, designed and built a lightweight trainer which he designated the **Morrisey Model 1000C Nifty**. A cantilever low-wing monoplane with fixed tricycle landing gear, it had tandem seating for two beneath a continuous transparent canopy. As first flown during 1948 on the power of a 48-kW (65-hp) Continental A65 flat-four engine, it was intended to be built by amateur constructors. However, the Morrisey Aircraft Company of Santa Ana, California was formed in 1949 to produce and market two certificated versions of the Nifty, the **Model 2000C** and the all-metal **Model 2150** with 67-kW (90-hp) and 112-kW (150-hp) engines respectively. Production and sales rights for the Model 2150 were later acquired by Shinn Engineering Inc., which manufactured and marketed a

small number under the designation **Shinn Model 2150**. In 1967 Shinn sold the type certificate to the Varga Aircraft Corporation of Chandler, Arizona who produced the Model 2150A Kachina, and also certificated the 134-kW (180-hp) Model 2180 in 1981, both also being offered with conventional tail-wheel undercarriages as the Model 2150TG and 2180TG. Production of the Kachina ceased in 1982 when 139 aircraft had been built, and the type certificate reacquired by Bill Morrisey who later announced plans to re-enter the market with an updated Model 2000C.

Specification
Varga Model 2150A Kachina
Type: two-seat tourer/trainer aircraft
Powerplant: one 112-kW (150-hp) Avco Lycoming O-320-A2C flat-four piston engine

Performance: maximum speed 238 km/h (148 mph) at sea level; service ceiling 6705 m (22,000 ft); range with maximum fuel 845 km (525 miles)
Weights: empty 510 kg (1,125 lb); maximum take-off 824 kg (1,817 lb)

The Morrissey Model 2150 has had a long life with many names.

Dimensions: span 9.14 m (30 ft 0 in); length 6.45 m (21 ft 2 in); height 2.79 m (9 ft 2 in); wing area 13.38 m² (144.0 sq ft)

Moskalyev SAM-5

The work of the Russian designer Aleksandr Moskalyev was too much in advance of contemporary ideas and, as a result, the majority of his many designs were built only as prototypes. His most successful design was the **Moskalyev SAM-5**, a light transport of cantilever high-wing monoplane configuration with accommodation for a pilot and four or five passengers. The original prototype was of stressed-skin light alloy construction, but with a works team that had no experience of fabrication in this material Moskalyev was dissatisfied with the standard of workmanship and immediately redsigned the aircraft for an all-wood basic structure. The resulting second prototype, designated **SAM-5bis**, was of generally similar

configuration but introduced wing bracing, had a more slender fuselage and was of mixed ply and fabric covering. Following the completion of official testing the production of 37 aircraft was authorised, the majority being completed for use in an air ambulance role and accommodating three patients and an attendant. Delivered during 1937-38 they remained in service into World War II.

With the SAM-5bis in production, Moskalyev began development of an improved **SAM-5-2bis** with many refinements to reduce drag. Tested subsequently with the MG-21 and a supercharged M-11FN engine, each rated at 149 kW (200 hp), this aircraft not only had impressive performance but

The SAM-5 featured spatted undercarriage to reduce drag. Later designs were exceptionally clean. Here the designer poses with the original prototype.

established distance and height records. Official testing led to an order for 200 SAM-5-2bis in ambulance configuration but, because of the animosity of commissar Kaganovich none were delivered.

Specification
Moskalyev SAM-5bis
Type: lightweight air ambulance
Powerplant: one 75-kW (100-hp) M-11 five-cylinder radial piston engine
Performance: maximum speed

173 km/h (107 mph); service ceiling 2800 m (9,185 ft); range 900 km (559 miles)
Weights: empty 710 kg (1,565 lb); maximum take-off 1219 kg (2,687 lb)
Dimensions: span 12.50 m (41 ft 0 in); length about 8.00 m (26 ft 3 in); wing area 24.00 m² (258.34 sq ft)

Mudry aircraft

Auguste Mudry established Avions Mudry et Cie at Bernay in 1958, initially operating this company as an extension of his Cooperative des Ateliers Aéronautiques de la Région Parisienne (CAARP). All the activities of these two companies were subsequently combined under the title Avions Mudry, which accounts for the occasional use of CAARP/Mudry designations. The company's first (and so far most successful) aircraft is the **Mudry CAP 10 B**, a two-seat lightplane with aerobatic capability which is suitable for sporting or training use. A cantilever low-wing monoplane with a basic structure of wood, and with mixed wood and fabric covering, it is powered in its production version by an Avco Lycoming AEIO-360-B2F flat-four engine. First flown in **CAP 10** prototype form during August 1968 (the CAP 10 B differs by having revised tail surfaces), a total of 260 had been built by early 1992. Almost half of this number have been for military operators, including the French air force (56) and navy (6), and the air arms of Mexico (20). Developed in parallel with the CAP 10 was a single-seat aerobatic version designated **CAP 20**, which was followed by a lighter-weight version **CAP 20L** and available in **CAP 20L-180** and **CAP 20LS-200** variants with Avco Lycoming engines of 134 kW (180 hp) and 149 kW (200 hp) respectively. Construction of the CAP 20L ended in mid-1980 after 12 had been built, the type being superseded by the current production **CAP 21**, which retains the configuration of the earlier design and its 149-kW (200-hp) powerplant, but introduces a wing of advanced aerofoil section. The CAP 21 prototype (F-WZCH) was flown first on 23 June 1980 and initial deliveries of the first batch of 10 production aircraft began in May 1982.

This was followed by a new two-seat basic trainer incorporating some composite materials in its construction, and fitted with a tricycle landing gear. When first flown on 10 September 1982, the CAP-X prototype (F-WZCJ) was powered by an 60-kW (80-hp) Mudry-Buchoux MB4-80 flat-four engine, but in 1983 was re-engined with a 80-kW (108-hp) Lycoming powerplant, intended for the proposed production version to be designated the CAP-X Super. However, only three were built, and although a fourth prototype was planned with a tailwheel undercarriage, further development appears to be unlikely. An agree-

CAP 20Ls were for a long time the mount of the 'Equip de Voltige' display team of 312 Groupement d'Instruction.

Designed for aerobatics as well as for touring, the CAP 10 two-seater is stressed to load factors of +6g and −4.5g.

ment, signed in January 1991 for Sukhoi to build CAP-X4 fuselages, was suspended early in 1992. In 1985 Mudry announced the CAP-230, a CAP-21 re-engined with a 223.8-kW (300-hp) Lycoming powerplant and fitted with a more angular tail. The prototype CAP-21, F-WZCH was rebuilt to this configuration and flew for the first time on 8 October 1985. The production standard aerobatic version became the CAP-231, and the first aircraft (F-WZCI) flew in April 1990 with certification following in July. Customers for the CAP-231 include the Moroccan Air Force 'Marche Verte' aerobatic team. A further improved model, designated CAP-231 EX and intended for competition aerobatics, took to the air on 18 December 1991, initially fitted with a 164-kW (260-hp) Barrett engine, but later replaced with a 227-kW (300-hp) Lycoming AEIO-540 powerplant.

Specification
Mudry CAP 10B
Type: two-seat aerobatic lightplane
Powerplant: one 134-kW (180-hp) Avco Lycoming AEIO-360-B2F flat-four piston engine
Performance: maximum speed

250 km/h (155 mph) at sea level; service ceiling 5000 m (16,405 ft); range with maximum fuel 1200 km (746 miles)
Weights: empty equipped 540 kg (1,900 lb); maximum take-off 760 kg (1,675 lb)
Dimensions: span 8.06 m (26 ft 5 in);

The CAP 20 series was developed in parallel with the CAP 10 as a single-seat aerobatic machine. This is a CAP 20LS-200.

length 7.16 m (23 ft 6 in); height 2.55 m (8 ft 4 in); wing area 10.85 m² (116.79 sq ft)

Myasishchev M-4

Vladimir M. Myasishchev was responsible for contributions to a number of Soviet aircraft designs from 1924, but is best known for the **Myasishchev M-4** which was the nation's first four-engine turbojet-powered strategic bomber to become operational. Following its maiden flight in late 1953, the type was first displayed in a fly-past over Moscow on 1 May 1954. A mid-wing cantilever monoplane with a deep section swept wing, the M-4 has a tail unit with all-swept surfaces, and retractable landing gear comprising two main units in tandem on the fuselage centreline, each with a four-wheel bogie, plus twin-wheel outrigger balancing units which retract into the wingtips. The circular-section fuselage incorporates a pressurised nose compartment and tail turret for the crew, and a large internal weapons bay in the lower fuselage between the main landing gear units. The powerplant comprises four turbojets buried in the wing roots, these being initially Mikulin AM-3Ds each of 8700-kg (19,180-lb) thrust. Designed to carry thermonuclear weapons over intercontinental ranges, the initial bomber version, which has the NATO codename **'Bison-A'**, is believed to have entered service initially in early 1956, and production probably totalled about 200 aircraft. Subsequent modified versions have included the maritime reconnaissance **'Bison-B'**, first identified during 1964, which had a radome in a solid nose replacing the glazed nose of 'Bison-A', and the even later **'Bison-C'**, which was also for maritime reconnais-

Myasishchev M-4 'Bison-C' of the AVMF (Aviatsiya Voyenno-Morskoyo Flota – Naval Aviation).

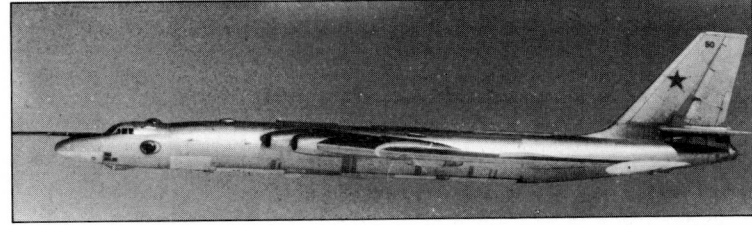

Built as a long-range maritime reconnaissance platform, the 'Bison-B' version of the Myasishchev M-4 was the first Soviet aircraft known to have been produced with an air-to-air refuelling probe.

sance and introduced a larger radar installation in a lengthened nose. One other version is known, a test-bed aircraft powered by four D-15 turbojet engines each of 13000-kg (28,660-lb) thrust and designated **201-M**. This was used in September 1959 to establish a number of payload-to-height records. About 40 tanker/transport versions of the M-4 were estimated to remain in service in 1992. These are to be replaced by Il-78 'Midas' tankers. Basic M-4 airframes were used in the conversion of two **VM-T 'Atlant'** outsize cargo carriers.

These were used to ferry the Buran orbiting space shuttle or Energiya rocket vehicles to and from launch stations in the USSR, until replaced in 1989 by the An-225 'Mriya'. The VM-T used the fuselage and wings of the M-4, but the standard tail surfaces were replaced by large twin endplate fins to allow the 40-tonne payload to sit atop the fuselage.

Specification
Myasishchev M-4 'Bison-A'
Type: four-turbojet strategic bomber/tanker

Powerplant: four 9500-kg (20,943-lb) thrust Mikulin AM-3D turbojets
Performance: (estimated) maximum speed 1000 km/h (621 mph) at optimum altitude; range 10700 km (6,648 miles)
Weights: normal take-off 160000 kg (352,740 lb)
Dimensions: span 50.48 m (165 ft 7½ in); length 47.20 m (154 ft 10¼ in); height 14.10 m (46 ft 3 in); wing area 309.00 m² (3,326.16 sq ft)
Armament: up to 10 23-mm cannon, plus a bombload of up to 9000 kg (19,842 lb) of free-fall weapons

Myasishchev M-17/M-55 Geofizika

Originally identified in 1982 by US reconnaissance satellites as the 'Ram-M' single-seat high-altitude reconnaissance aircraft, and later codenamed 'Mystic' by NATO, the twin-boom straight-wing jet, currently publicised as a high-altitude research aircraft able to carry around 1500 kg (3,305 lb) of sensors, is now known to exist in two versions. The first of two prototype aircraft, designated **M-17 Stratosfera ('Mystic-A')**, first flew in 1988 and are powered by a single 68.6 kN (15,430 lb) thrust Rybinsk RD-36-51V turbojet developed from the Tu-144 SST powerplant. The **M-55 Geofizika ('Mystic-B')**, has two 49 kN (11,025 hp) thrust Perm/Soloviev PS-30-V12 turbojets mounted side-by-side behind a raised cockpit installed in a longer nose, together with a reduced span wing. The role of the 'Mystic-B' is described as environmental sampling missions or high-altitude research and endurance in this role is claimed as over 4 hours loiter capability at 20000 m (65,600 ft). A further variant of the M-55 is reported to be under development with wingroot mounted engines in-

stalled in a conventional fuselage carrying a sweptback tail unit. Two 'Mystic-A' prototypes, followed by two 'Mystic-B' and two pre-production 'Mystic-Bs' were flying by 1992.

Specification
Myasishchev M-55 Geofizika
Type: single-seat high-altitude research jet aircraft
Powerplant: two 49 kN (11,025 lb)

Perm/Soloviev PS-30-V12 turbojets
Performance: maximum level speed 750 km/h (466 mph); endurance at 17000 m (55,775 ft) 7 hours
Dimensions: span 40.7 m (123 ft 6 in); length 24.0 m (78 ft 9 in); height 4.8 m (15 ft 9 in)

The M-55 'Mystic-B' differs from the first M-17 Stratosfera in having a longer jetpipe, shorter engine intakes, a reprofiled nose and an undernose FLIR turret. A subsequent version of the Geofizika is twin-engined.

Myasishchev M-50/M-52

Although built only in prototype form, this design by Myasishchev was an extremely advanced turbojet-powered bomber with supersonic flight capability. In configuration, the Myasishchev M-50, codenamed 'Bounder' by NATO, had a shoulder-mounted cropped delta-wing, a conventional tail unit with all-swept surfaces, and landing gear comprising retractable tandem main units mounted on the fuselage centre line, each with a four-wheel bogie; while retractable outrigger balancing struts, each with two wheels, were mounted near the wingtips. The slender area-ruled fuselage provided pressurised accommodation for a crew of three and incorporated a large weapons bay. Power was provided by

The M-50 probably had all four afterburning turbojets in undering pods at first, but was later revised with the two outermost units mounted on the wingtips. A surviving 'Bounder' can be found in the Monino aviation museum in Moscow.

four wing-mounted Soloviev D-15 turbojets of 13000 kg (28,860 lb) thrust in underwing pods. First flight of the M-50 is thought to have taken place in 1957, and the last of several prototypes, redesignated M-52, took part in the Soviet Aviation Day fly-past in 1961. With the two re-heated outer engines relocated to the wing tips, the M-52 was powered

by four Koliesov ND-7F or VD-7F turbojets, with an afterburning thrust of 18145 kg (40,000 lb). Considered formidable by the West, the M-52 was estimated to be capable of Mach 1.83 or 1950 km/h (1,212 mph) at optimum altitude.

NAMC YS-11

NAMC YS-11 of TOA Domestic Airlines

Design of the **NAMC YS-11** medium-range transport began in 1957, following the receipt of a Japanese government subsidy to assist development of the aircraft by six of the nation's manufacturers, comprising Fuji, Japan Aircraft Manufacturing Co, Kawasaki, Mitsubishi, Shin Meiwa and Showa. Combined initially under the title Transport Aircraft Development Association, this grouping was later renamed the Nihon Aeroplane Manufacturing Company (NAMC), founded jointly by the government and the six member companies. A conventional cantilever low-wing monoplane with retractable tricycle landing gear and a pressurized (and, optionally, air-conditioned), circular-section fuselage, the NAMC YS-11 is powered by two Rolls-Royce Dart turboprop engines. The first of two prototypes was flown initially on 30 August 1962 and, following receipt of type certification, the first production examples were delivered in March 1965. A total of 182 had been built when production ended in 1972, these comprising the basic **YS-11-100** with accommodation for 60 passengers (49 built), the **YS-11A-200** operating at a higher gross weight (92 built); the **YS-11A-300** for mixed traffic, with 46 passengers, 15.3 m³ (540 cu ft) of cargo space and a cargo door (16 built); the all-cargo **YS-11A-400** (nine built); and higher gross weight versions of the YS-11A-200 and YS-11A-300 under the respective designations **YS-11A-500** (four built) and **YS-11A-600** (five built).

Of the total built about 120 remain in service in 1992, with 23 used by the JASDF and JMSDF. JASDF versions include **YS-11-103/105** VIP transports, **YS-11A-218** personnel transports, **YS-11A-305** personnel/cargo transports, **YS-11A-402** all-cargo transports, and **YS-11E** ECM trainers. JMSDF versions include **YS-11-112** cargo transports, **YS-11A-206** ASW trainers, and YS-11A-400 all-cargo transports.

Specification
NAMC YS-11A-200
Type: medium-range transport
Powerplant: two 2457-ekW (3,060-ehp) Rolls-Royce Dart Mk 542-10K turboprops
Performance: maximum cruising speed 470 km/h (292 mph) at 4570 m (15,000 ft); service ceiling 7000 m (22,965 ft); range with maximum

payload 1090 km (677 miles)
Weights: empty operating 15419 kg (33,993 lb); maximum take-off 24500 kg (54,013 lb)

Dimensions: span 32.00 m (104 ft 11¾ in); length 26.30 m (86 ft 3½ in); height 8.98 m (29 ft 5½ in); wing area 94.80 m² (1,020.45 sq ft)

NASA/Rockwell Shuttle spacecraft

This A-Z of Aircraft consists basically of heavier-than-air craft with air-breathing engines, and as such has no place for orbiting spacecraft. However, the **NASA/Rockwell Shuttle** spacecraft merits inclusion, for although it takes off from Earth as a rocket and manoeuvres in orbit as a spacecraft, after re-entry into Earth's atmosphere it is controlled and brought in to an unpowered landing in the mode of a conventional fixed-wing aircraft. In configuration it is a cantilever low-wing monoplane of double-delta wing planform, with a large-volume fuselage of conventional construction, vertical tail surfaces only, and retractable tricycle landing gear. The Shuttle takes off vertically under the power of three

Seen landing back at Edwards AFB after its first flight is the Shuttle Columbia. Despite cheaper alternatives, the Space Shuttle is still the only re-usable space vehicle in service.

Rocketdyne main propulsion engines, each developing 170097-kg (375,000-lb) thrust, plus two Thiokol solid-propellant booster rockets each producing 1315418-kg (2,900,000-lb) thrust, the combined thrust being 3141 tonnes

(3,091.5 tons). The booster rockets are attached to the external liquid propellant tanks, these combined units being jettisoned after take-off for recovery and re-use. In Earth orbit the Shuttle spacecraft is manoeuvred and controlled by means

of two Aerojet orbit manoeuvring engines, plus 38 reaction control engines and six vernier thrusters produced by Marquardt. All of these 'in orbit' power units are bi-propellant liquid rocket engines.

The kinetic heating induced at the time of re-entry into Earth's atmosphere can create localised temperatures of up to 1,648°C (3,000°F) at the spacecraft's nose and on the wing leading edges, and to control the outer skin temperature at a maximum 176°C (350°F) during re-entry, the Shuttle has a thermal protection system consisting of mainly externally-applied insulation tiles. Once within Earth's atmosphere the Shuttle is flown as a conventional winged aircraft, the elevons at the trailing edge of the wing providing pitch and roll control, and the rudder controlling yaw. There is, in addition, a speed brake to give further assistance in achieving accurate unpowered landings. As would be expected, each Shuttle spacecraft has highly sophisticated navigational equipment to ensure accurate positioning for re-entry and location of the landing area. The first orbital flight began when the Shuttle *Columbia* took off on 12 April 1981, completing 36 Earth orbits before landing at Edwards AFB, California, 55 hours later on 14 April.

Since then four more Shuttles have flown. *Challenger* in April 1983, *Discovery* in August 1984 and *Atlanta* in October 1985. *Challenger* was dramtically destroyed by a post-launch explosion in January 1986, killing all six astronauts on board, and the programme was suspended until September 1989 to allow a redesign of the booster system.

A fifth Shuttle, *Endeavor*, was ordered in July 1987 to replace *Challenger*.

Specification
Performance: orbital speed 28325 km/h (17,600 mph); landing speed 341 km/h (212 mph)
Dimensions: span 23.7 m (78 ft); length 37.2 m (122 ft 2 in); height 17.2 m (56 ft 8 in); wing area 249.91 m² (2,690.45 sq ft)
Weights: empty 77354 kg (171,419 lb); landing 104328 kg (230,000 lb)

NDN Aircraft

Nigel Desmond Norman, one of the founders of the Britten-Norman Aircraft Company, builders of more than 1,000 Islander, Defender and Trislander light twins, established NDN Aircraft Ltd early in 1976 to develop a new two-seat basic military trainer designated the **NDN 1 Firecracker**. The prototype (G-NDNI), first flown on 26 May 1977, was of cantilever low-wing monoplane configuration, had a retractable tricycle landing gear, and accomodated instructor and pupil in tandem enclosed cockpits. A turboprop powered version (G-SFTR) was flown on 1 September 1983 under the designation **NDN 1T Turbo Firecracker**, and three were built for the only customer, Specialist Flying Training Ltd of Hamble and later Hurn. In 1981 NDN Aircraft launched a new turboprop agricultural aircraft under the designation **NDN 6 Fieldmaster**, and the prototype (G-NRDC) flew for the first time on 17 December 1981 at Sandown. A braced low-wing monoplane incorporating a titanium chemical hopper as an integral unit of the fuselage structure, the NDN 6 has a non-retractable tricycle landing gear. In 1985 NDN Aircraft ran into difficulties and Desmond Norman formed the Norman Aeroplane Company to operate from a new factory in Cardiff, Wales. A production batch of five NAC-6 aircraft was laid down and the first of these (G-NACL) flew on 29 March 1987 powered by a Pratt & Whitney Canada PT6A-34 and the type was certificated as a cropsprayer in April 1987. Unfortunately NAC went into receivership in October 1988, but not before other examples had been completed and operated in France on fire patrol and waterbombing duties. In April 1989 the NAC 6 programme was revived by the Irish company Croplease Plc and the prototype re-worked into the more powerful **Firemaster-65** waterbomber which flew on 28 October 1989 at Sandown piloted by Neville Duke. Both the Fieldmaster cropsprayer and the Firemaster waterbomber are currently available with either a 750-shp (559-kW) PT6A-34AG engine driving a 3-blade propeller or 1,250-shp (917-kW) PT6A-65AG driving a five-blade prop, adopting the engine dash number to denote the exact model.

Capable of lifting a 4,500-lb (2040-kg) payload, the NAC 6 also carries a second seat with dual controls for a mechanic/loadmaster, or for possible use as a specialised trainer. A 1991 plan for the Yugoslavian aircraft company UTVA to manufacture components and assemble NAC 6 airframes has been delayed by events taking place in that country.

The **NAC 1 Freelance** single-engined four-seat light utility aircraft (G-NACI), powered by a 180 hp (134 kW) piston engine, made its first flight on 29 September 1984 and another (G-NACA) was completed. The Freelance programme was later taken over by Aeronortec Ltd of Sandown on the Isle of Wight.

Specification
1T Turbo Firecracker
Powerplant: one 715-ehp (533-ekW) Pratt & Whitney Aircraft of Canada PT6A-25A turboprop
Performance: maximum speed 420 km/h (261 mph) at 8,000 ft (2440 m); service ceiling 27,700 ft (8445 m); range with standard fuel 1231 km (765 miles)
Weights: empty 1043 kg (2,300 lb); maximum take-off 1928 kg (4,250 lb)
Dimensions: span 7.92 m (26 ft 0in); length 8.33 m (27 ft 4 in); height 3.25 m (10 ft 8 in); wing area 11.89 m² (128.0 sq ft)
Armament: four underwing hardpoints with a combined capacity of 726 kg (1,600 lb) of weapons, including gun pods, GP or fragmentation bombs, and rocket launchers

The Firecracker (illustrated) and Turbo Firecracker found 'newness' to be their own worst enemy. Their qualities were obscured by NDN's lack of track record.

The Fieldmaster has had a slightly happier time. A crop-spraying and a dedicated fire-fighting version , the Firemaster 65, are now available from Croplease and Brooklands Avn.

Nakajima early aircraft

Founded on 6 December 1917 by navy Lieutenant Chikuhei Nakajima as the Nihon Hikoki Seiskusho K.K. (Japan Aeroplane Manufacturing Co. Ltd), this company was reorganised in December 1919 as the Nakajima Hikoki K.K. (Nakajima Aeroplane Co. Ltd), and rapidly became one of the two major Japanese aircraft manufacturers.

During 1919 single examples of the two-seat **Nakajima Type 1, Type 2** and **Type 3** training biplanes were built, but these were followed by the **Type 5** trainer which was a great success, 118 being produced for the Japanese army between 1919 and 1921. Powered by a 112-kW (150-hp) Hall-Scott engine, the Type 5 had a maximum speed of 130 km/h (81 mph). An unequal-span biplane with dual controls, it remained only briefly in army service, a number being sold to civil owners in the early 1920s. Other Nakajima types included the one-off **Type 6** mailplane, the **Type**

Although built as the Nakajima A1N1 this aircraft is obviously a copied Gloster Gambet. Such imported designs gave the fledgling Japanese aircraft industry valuable experience.

7 tourer and the **B-6,** developed from the Breguet 14.

A number of foreign designs were manufactured by Nakajima, including the Nieuport 24 single-seat fighter, 77 being built during 1921-22 as the **Ko-3** fighter trainer, the Nieuport 83 two-seat trainer; 40 being built in 1922 as the **Ko-2;** and the Avro 504K trainer, of which 250 were completed in 1922-24. More important, however, were the Nieuport-Delage NiD-29 single-seat fighter, of which 600 were built under licence between 1924-32, and used in first-line service by the Japanese army in Manchuria and China into the mid-1930s under the designation **Ko-4;** the Hansa-

Brandenburg W 33 twin-float reconnaissance seaplane, of which 160 were built in 1922-25; and the **Nakajima A1N1** and its **A1N2** development, licence-built versions of the Gloster Gambet, of which 150 were completed for the navy during 1929-30 as the **Type 3 Carrier Fighter** and flown during the Shanghai Incident, remaining in first-line service until 1935.

Nakajima A2N

Intended to supersede the A1N1 and A1N2 in service, the **NY** prototype first flew in 1930. It was an unequal-span single-seat fighter of biplane configuration, with divided fixed landing gear which had spatted wheel fairings discarded in later production aircraft. Accepted for service in late 1930 as the **Navy Type 90 Carrier Fighter** the Nakajima A2N was built in several versions. The **A2N1** and **A2N2** had lower wing dihedral only, whereas the **A2N3** had dihedral on both wings. The twin-gun armament was installed in blast troughs on the lower sides of the fuselage in the A2N1, while later versions had them installed in the forward decking. Production totalled 106, built between 1930 and 1935, and later 66 examples of the **A3N1** two-seat training variant appeared, most being conver-

Compared with the A2N1, the Nakajima A2N2 had its two machine-guns moved to a position high on the fuselage. This made them easier for the pilot to clear in the event of them jamming while firing.

sions of the single-seater. A2Ns from the carrier *Kaga* (2nd Carrier Division) flew on operations in the Shanghai area during the 1937 Sino-Japanese Incident.

Specification
Nakajima A2N1
Type: single-seat carrier fighter
Powerplant: one 433-kW (580-hp) Nakajima Kotobuki 2 radial piston engine
Performance: maximum speed 292 km/h (181 mph); service ceiling

9000 m (29,530 ft); range 500 km (311 miles)
Weights: empty 1045 kg (2,304 lb); maximum take-off 1500 kg (3,307 lb)
Dimensions: span 9.37 m (30 ft 9 in);

length 6.18 m (20 ft 3¼ in); height 3.03 m (9 ft 11¼ in); wing area 19.74 m² (212.49 sq ft)
Armament: two 7.7-mm (0.303-in) machine-guns

Nakajima Army Type 91 Fighter

A Japanese army requirement of 1927 for a new single-seat fighter was contested by Nakajima, Kawasaki and Mitsubishi. All the designs were parasol-wing monoplanes developed in Japan by teams wholly or partly led by Europeans, in the case of Nakajima the French engineers Mary and Robin. Structural failure of the Mitsubishi prototype led to severe testing of the survivors, which were then also eliminated. The Nakajima prototype, company designation **NC,** had a slim tapering monocoque fuselage, an uncowled Jupiter radial engine, and elaborate strut bracing connecting wings, fuselage and the wide-track landing gear. Nakajima persevered with the design and built six more prototypes, the last of the series being tested extensively by the Japanese army and accepted for production as the **Army Type 91 Fighter Model 1.** Retaining the same basic configuration as the NC prototype, this was virtually a redesign which resulted in a considerably refined airframe. Production of the Type 91 ter-

minated in 1934 with the 450th aircraft; of these 22 were **Army Type 91 Fighter Model 2** aircraft with modified engine cowlings. A Type 91 was converted for carrier operations and with spatted wheel fairings was submitted for the navy 7-Shi experimental fighter competition, but was rejected. The only other modification from standard army configuration was the use of a three-bladed propeller.

Introduced from 1932 onwards, the Type 91s were deployed in action with the four squadrons of the 11th Air Battalion operating with the army Kanto Command in Manchuria against the Chinese. In 1933 the Type 91 was the principal army fighter and constituted the standard equipment for the newly formed air wings (or Hiko Rentai).

The Type 91 Army Fighter displayed the French influence of its two designers. It was the Japanese army's basic fighter through the early 1930s.

Specification
Type: single-seat air-superiority fighter
Powerplant: one 433-kW (580-hp) Nakajima Kotobuki 2 radial piston engine
Performance: maximum speed 300 km/h (186 mph); service ceiling

9000 m (29,530 ft); range 500 km (311 miles)
Weights: empty 1075 kg (2,370 lb); maximum take-off 1500 kg (3,307 lb)
Dimensions: span 11.00 m (36 ft 1 in); length 7.30 m (23 ft 11½ in); height 3.00 m (9 ft 10 in); wing area 20.00 m² (215.29 sq ft)
Armament: two 7.7-mm (0.303-in) machine-guns

Nakajima A4N1

The 1930s were a busy time for the Nakajima company. A whole series of experimental types appeared, including the **Ki-8** low-wing monoplane two-seat fighter; the **PA** or **Ki-11** low-wing monoplane single-seat fighter, reminiscent of the Boeing P-26, and of which four were built between 1935 and 1937; the **Ki-12** low-wing monoplane with retractable landing gear; the **Ki-19** mid-wing twin-engine bomber; the **NAF-1** and **NAF-2** two-seat carrier fighter biplanes; the **Y3B** 7-Shi carrier torpedo-bomber biplane and the **LB-2** private-venture twin-engine long-range navy bomber.

Yet, even in the middle of this innovative period, Nakajima set to work to build a conventional single-seat biplane fighter, the resulting **YM** prototype being an unequal-span biplane of mixed construction and clearly owing much to

Essentially a stop-gap design pending the arrival of new monoplanes, the A4N1 was agile but slow and poorly armed.

the obsolescent A2N. Nevertheless, it was considered essential by the navy until more modern types could be perfected and Nakajima was accordingly authorized to proceed with development of the biplane concept. The resulting **Navy Type 95 Carrier Fighter (Nakajima A4N1)** had new divided landing gear designed to cope with carrier landings, a tailwheel instead of a tail-skid, and other minor changes which only marginally affected performance by comparison with the earlier fighter, the increase in speed being due entirely to the more powerful Hikari engine. Production totalled 221 between 1935 and 1937.

Specification
Type: single-seat carrier fighter
Powerplant: one 544-kW (730-hp) Nakajima Hikari radial piston engine
Performance: maximum speed 350 km/h (217 mph); service ceiling 7740 m (25,395 ft); range 845 km (525 miles)
Weights: empty equipped 1276 kg

(2,813 lb); maximum take-off 1760 kg (3,880 lb)
Dimensions: span 10.00 m (32 ft 9¾ in); length 6.64 m (21 ft 9½ in); height 3.07 m (10 ft 0¾ in); wing area 22.89 m² (246.39 sq ft)
Armament: two 7.7-mm (0.303-in) machine-guns, plus provision for up to 120 kg (265 lb) of bombs

Nakajima B5N

To meet an Imperial Japanese Navy requirement of 1935 for a carrier-based attack bomber to supersede the Yokosuka B4Y1, Nakajima submitted its **Type K** prototype. A cantilever low-wing monoplane with retractable tailwheel landing gear and powered by a

574-kW (770-hp) Nakajima Hikari 3 engine, it was tested in two versions: with Fowler-type flaps and hydraulic flaps and hydraulic wing folding, and plain flaps and manual wing folding. It was the latter that was ordered into production as the **Navy Type 97 Carrier Attack Bomber Model 1 (Nakajima B5N1).** This proved effective in the Sino-Japanese War until receipt by

the Chinese of more advanced Soviet fighters, then leading to the improved **B5N2** of 1939 with a more powerful engine. As B5N2s replaced B5N1s in service, many of the earlier aircraft were converted for use as advanced trainers under the designation **B5N1-K.** The force of 144 B5N2 bombers included in the initial attack on Pearl Harbor made it clear that the type was better than any

comparable aircraft then in service with the Allies; allocated the Allied codename **'Kate',** the type was also responsible for eliminating the carriers USS *Hornet, Lexington* and *Yorktown.* However, by 1944 the growing capability of Allied fighters resulted in these bombers being withdrawn from first-line service, although they continued to serve effectively in ASW and maritime reconnais-

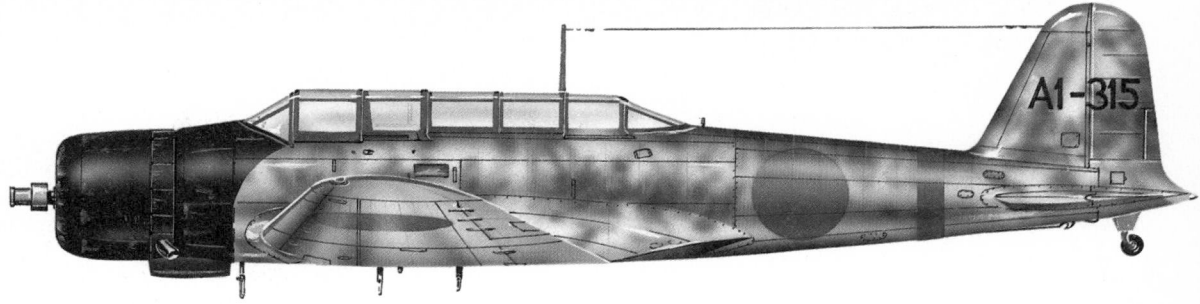

sance roles. Production totalled 1,149, buit by Aichi (200), Nakajima (669) and the navy's Hiro Air Arsenal (280).

Specification
Nakajima B5N2
Type: three-seat carrier-based torpedo-bomber
Powerplant: one 746-kW (1,000-hp) Nakajima NK1B Sakae radial piston engine
Performance: maximum speed 378 km/h (235 mph); service ceiling 8260 m (27,100 ft); maximum range 1990 km (1,237 miles)
Weights: empty 2279 kg (5,024 lb); maximum take-off 4100 kg (9,039 lb)

Nakajima B5N2 of the Imperial Japanese Navy air force, based on the carrier Akagi in 1941-1942.

Dimensions: span 15.52 m (50 ft 11 in); length 10.30 m (33 ft 9½ in); height 3.70 m (12 ft 1½ in); wing area 37.70 m² (405.81 sq ft)
Armament: one 7.7-mm (0.303-in) machine-gun on a trainable mount in rear cockpit, plus a bombload of up to 800 kg (1,764 lb), or one torpedo of equivalent weight

Nakajima B6N Tenzan

To meet an Imperial Japanese Navy requirement of late 1939 for a carrier-based torpedo-bomber to supersede the Nakajima B5N, the company used a similar airframe with revised tail surfaces and introduced its own 1647-kW (1,800-hp) NK7A Mamoru 11 radial engine. The first of two prototypes flew in early 1941 and, following some modifications, the type entered production in 1943 as the **Navy Carrier Attack Bomber Tenzan Model 11 (Nakajima B6N1).** However, after only 135 Tenzan (heavenly cloud) aircraft had been built, Nakajima was ordered to end production of the Mamoru engine and to substitute the Mitsubishi Kasei, bringing redesignation as the **B6N2.** The **B6N2a** variant differed only by having a rear-firing machine-gun of 13-mm (0.51-in) calibre, and two conversions of this variant produced **B6N3** prototypes with 1380-kW (1,850-hp) Mitsubishi MK4T-C Kasei 25C engines for evaluation as land-based bombers. Nakajima production of B6N2s totalled 1,133, all versions being allocated the Allied codename **'Jill'**, and these aircraft were used extensively in the last two years of the war, many expended in *kamikaze* operations.

Nakajima B6N2 Tenzan (Heavenly Mountain) of the Imperial Japanese Navy air force during 1944.

Specification
Nakajima B6N2
Type: three-seat carrier-based torpedo-bomber
Powerplant: one 1380-kW (1,850-hp) Mitsubishi MK4T Kasei 25 radial piston engine

Performance: maximum speed 480 km/h (298 mph); service ceiling 9040 m (29,660 ft); maximum range 3045 km (1,892 miles)
Weights: empty 3010 kg (6,636 lb); maximum take-off 5650 kg (12,456 lb)
Dimensions: span 14.90 m (48 ft 10½ in); length 10.87 m (35 ft 8 in); height 3.80 m (12 ft 5½ in); wing area 37.20 m² (400.43 sq ft)
Armament: two 7.7-mm (0.303-in) machine-guns, one rear-firing and one firing through a ventral tunnel, plus a bombload of 800 kg (1,764 lb), or a torpedo of equivalent weight

Nakajima C6N Saiun

Early experience in the Pacific war showing the need for a long-range carried-based reconnaissance aircraft, Nakajima was instructed in early 1942 to develop an aircraft to meet this Imperial Japanese Navy requirement. It resulted in an airframe similar to that of the company's B6N, the fuselage incorporating camera ports and observation windows, with power provided by a 1358-kW (1,820-hp) Nakajima Homare 11 radial engine. The first prototype flew on 15 May 1943, its performance being disappointing with the Homare 11 engine, and 18 more prototype/pre-series aircraft followed, some with the more powerful Homare 21 engine, before the type was ordered into production in early 1944 as the **Navy Carrier Reconnaissance Plane Saiun (Nakajima C6N1).** Allocated the Allied codename **'Myrt'** when it entered service in the summer of 1944,

The Nakajima C6N1 Saiun (Painted Cloud) proved an admirable 'recce' type with good speed and excellent range characteristics. In that role the cameras were mounted in the centre cockpit, and armament was limited to a single 7.9mm machine-gun in the rear cockpit. It was also used as a torpedo-bomber with the crew reduced to two instead of three. The Saiun made an unexpectedly good nightfighter, carrying a pair of upwardly-firing 20-mm cannon.

the Saiun (painted cloud) was fast enough to enjoy almost complete immunity from interception by Allied fighters. A total of 463 had been built when production ended in August 1945, the total including a small number of

C6N1-S two-seat night-fighter conversions from C6N1 aircraft, and one **C6N2** prototype with a 1476-kW (1,980-hp) Homare turbocharged engine.

Specification
Nakajima C6N1
Type: three-seat carrier-based reconnaissance aircraft
Powerplant: one 1484-kW (1,990-hp) Nakajima NK9H Homare 21 radial piston engine
Performance: maximum speed

610 km/h (379 mph) at 6100 m (20,015 ft); service ceiling 10740 m (35,235 ft); maximum range 5310 km (3,299 miles)
Weights: empty 2968 kg (6,543 lb); maximum take-off 5260 kg (11,596 lb)
Dimensions: span 12.50 m (41 ft 0 in); length 11.00 m (36 ft 1 in); height 3.95 m (12 ft 11½ in); wing area 25.50 m² (274.49 sq ft)
Armament: one rear-firing 7.92-mm (0.31-in) machine-gun on a trainable mount

Nakajima E2N

Built between 1927 and 1929, this two-seat twin-float sesquiplane was powered by a 224-kW (300-hp) Hispano-Suiza engine and could attain a maximum speed of 166 km/h (103 mph). It was intended for shipboard reconnaissance and served with the Japanese navy as the **Type 15 Reconnaissance Floatplane (Nakajima E2N1 and E2N2).** A total of 80 was built, many being relegated to training or sold to civil users during the 1930s. Two machines were bought at the outset for civil fishery patrol duties.

The Nakajima E2N reconnaissance sesquiplane was typical of such floatplanes in service with many naval air arms all around the world at that time.

Nakajima E4N
to
Nakajima Ki-49 Donryu

Nakajima E4N

The first prototype of this equal-span biplane reconnaissance aircraft appeared in 1930 as the **Type 90-2 Reconnaissance Floatplane,** company designation **NZ.** Intended for navy service as the **Nakajima E4N1,** it had twin floats and an uncowled Kotobuki radial engine. This first prototype, however, was rejected in favour of the **NJ** or **Navy Type 90-2-2 Reconnaissance Floatplane.** This was a complete redesign, with a single main float and twin wingtip stabilising floats. It closely resembles the US Vought O3U-1 Corsair biplane and, like it, was intended for shipboard use and catapult launching.

The Nakajima E4N2 was a redesign of the earlier E4N, involving the fitting of a single main float with small stabilising floats at the wingips. Eighty-five of these aircraft served with the navy in the coastal patrol role.

Powered by a 336-kW (450-hp) Nakajima Kotobuki radial engine, the Type 90-2-2 had a maximum speed of 222 km/h (138 mph) and 85 went into service with the Japanese navy as the **E4N2** between 1931 and 1933, a version with fixed wheel landing gear going into service as the **E4N2-C;** 67 of the latter were completed. In 1933 nine of the E4N2-C landplanes were converted as night mail carriers, for use between the

main islands of Japan. Designated **P-1,** the mail carrier was a single-seater with

the pilot accommodated in an enclosed cockpit.

Nakajima E8N

Designed to replace the company's E4N2 in navy service, Nakajima's **MS** submission was basically an updated version of the E4N2. Of similar biplane configuration, with a central float and underwing stabilising floats, it was powered by a 433-kW (580-hp) Kotobuki 2 KAI 1 radial engine, and differed from its predecessor primarily by having revised wings and tail unit. Seven prototypes were tested from March 1934 and, following evaluation against competing aircraft from Aichi and Kawanishi, the MS was ordered into production in October 1935 as the **Navy Type 95 Reconnaissance Seaplane Model 1 (Nakajima E8N1).** An **E8N2** with improved equipment and a more powerful engine was introduced before production ended in 1940, when a combined

The E8N2 is here exemplified by an aircraft operating from the battleship Kirishima. Performance was wholly inadaquate for wartime and the type was soon retired to secondary duties.

total of 755 had been built by Nakajima (707) and Kawanishi (48). Used successfully during the Sino-Japanese War in roles which included artillery spotting and dive-bombing as well as reconnaissance, some were still operating from navy vessels at the beginning of the Pacific war, gaining the Allied codename 'Dave'. They were soon diverted to secondline duties such as communications, liaison and training.

Specification
Nakajima E8N2
Type: two-seat reconnaissance

floatplane
Powerplant: one 470-kW (630-hp) Nakajima Kotobuki 2 KAI 2 radial piston engine
Performance: maximum speed 300 km/h (186 mph) at 3000 m (9,845 ft); service ceiling 7270 m (23,860 ft); range 900 km (559 miles)
Weights: empty 1320 kg (2,910 lb);

maximum take-off 1900 kg (4,189 lb)
Dimensions: span 10.98 m (36 ft 0¼ in); length 8.81 m (28 ft 10¾ in); height 3.84 m (12 ft 7¼ in); wing area 26.50 m² (285.25 sq ft)
Armament: two 7.7-mm (0.303-in) machine-guns, one forward- and one rear-firing, plus two 30-kg (66-lb) bombs

Nakajima G8N Renzan

Developed as the **Experimental 18-Shi Heavy Bomber Renzan (Nakajima G8N1),** this was a very advanced long-range bomber powered by four 1491-kW (2,000-hp) Nakajima Homare 24 radials which gave it a maximum speed of 592 km/h (368 mph) at 8000 m (26,245 ft). Maximum range was 7465 km (4,639 miles). Armament consisted of six 20-mm cannon in twin power-operated dorsal, ventral and tail turrets, two 13-mm (0.51-in) machine-guns in a power-operated nose turret,

Had it enterd service sooner, the G8N1 would have been the Japanese navy's first four-engined bomber.

and single machine-guns of similar calibre in port and starboard beam positions. A maximum bombload of 4000 kg (8,818 lb) could be carried over short ranges.

Four prototypes were built up to June 1945, but the proposed production programme was disrupted by Allied bomb-

ing and was abandoned when the navy's role became defensive rather than offen-

sive. These prototypes were allocated the Allied codename **'Rita'.**

Nakajima J1N Gekko

An Imperial Japanese Navy requirement for a long-range escort fighter, to accompany bombers making attacks deep in Chinese territory, led to the **Nakajima J1N1** prototype, first flown during May 1941. A cantilever low-wing monoplane with retractable tailwheel landing gear, it was powered by two wing-mounted Nakajima Sakae 21 and 22 counter-rotating engines and accommodated a crew of three. Armament comprised a 20-mm cannon and six 7.7-mm (0.303-in) machine-guns. Early tests showed that the J1N1 was suited to the escort fighter role, and the type was developed instead for long-range reconnaissance

under the designation **J1N1-C.** This version differed by having two Sakae 21 engines, armament comprising a single rear-firing machine-gun of 13-mm (0.51-in) calibre, and reduced internal fuel capacity, but with provision for external drop tanks. Following the completion of service trials by seven prototypes, this version was ordered into production as the **Navy Type 2 Reconnaissance Plane,** the designation being changed subsequently to **J1N1-R.** Some of these aircraft later had the rear-firing machine-gun replaced by a 20-mm cannon, and were redesignated **J1N1-F.** In early 1943 it was suggested that the aircraft

might have potential as a night-fighter, one being converted to two-seat configuration for operational evaluation and armed with four 20-mm cannon mounted obliquely in pairs in dorsal and ventral positions. Following the destruction of Consolidated B-24 Liberators by this aircraft, further conversions were made under the designation **J1N1-C KAI** and a production version was ordered as the **J1N1-S Gekko** (moonlight); some of them carried a small searchlight in the nose and late production aircraft had an early form of AI radar. The designation **J1N1-Sa** applied to night-fighters with the downward-firing and ineffective cannon deleted; some, without searchlight or radar, had an extra nose-mounted cannon.

Production of all versions of the J1N by Nakajima totalled 479, and in early operations when confronting the comparatively slow B-24s, the Gekko night-fighter proved an effective weapon; against the faster and more-heavily armed Boeing B-29 Superfortress it was far less conclusive. All versions had the Allied codename **'Irving',** and many were used in *kamikaze* operations during the closing stage of the war.

Specification
Nakajima J1N1-S
Type: two-seat night-fighter
Powerplant: two 843-kW (1,130-hp) Nakajima Sakae 21 radial piston engines
Performance: maximum speed

507 km/h (315 mph) at 5800 m (19,030 ft); service ceiling 9320 m (30,580 ft); maximum range 3780 km (2,348 miles)
Weights: empty 4850 kg (10,692 lb); maximum take-off 8185 kg (18,045 lb)
Dimensions: span 16.98 m (55 ft 8¼ in); length 12.77 m (41 ft 10¾ in); height 3.99 m (13 ft 1½ in); wing area 40.00 m² (430.57 sq ft)
Armament: four 20-mm cannon, in obliquely-mounted upward- and downward-firing pairs

The clean lines of the Nakajima J1N1 inherited from its fighter origins were soon spoiled by the protrusion of armament required for night fighter missions.

Nakajima J5N Tenrai

Designed by Katsuji Nakamura and Kazuo Ohno and built to an 18-Shi specification for a high-speed single-seat interceptor fighter, the **Nakajima J5N1 Tenrai** (heavenly thunder) began flight tests in July 1944. A mid-wing mono-plane with a raised canopy over the pilot's cockpit, it was powered by two 1484-kW (1,990-hp) Nakajima NK9H Homare 21 radials and had a maximum speed of 597 km/h (371 mph). Armament comprised two 30-mm and two

The Nakajima J5N was intended to be a high-performance high-altitude interceptor for use against the B-29 raids. In the event it failed to reach any of its design goals.

20-mm cannon. Six aircraft were built, but as performance was disappointingly below specification no production resulted.

Nakajima Ki-4

Extensively test-flown in 1934, the **Nakajima Ki-4** sesquiplane had divided landing gear with streamlined wheel spats, and accommodated pilot and observer in tandem open cockpits, the pilot just below a cut-out in the trailing edge of the upper wing. The Ki-4 went into production and service in 1935 as the **Army Type 94 Reconnaissance Aircraft Model 2** which dispensed with the wheel fairings and had a redesigned tail unit. Production continued for several years, some aircraft being licence-built by Tachikawa among the total of 516.

The Type 94 was used widely in China by the Japanese army on direct co-operation duties, in close support of the ground forces. It was armed with up to four 7.7-mm (0.303-in) machine-guns and could carry 50 kg (110 lb) of light bombs. A number were still in service in the supply and liaison role in 1941. The Japanese army tested two Ki-4s as seaplanes, one with twin floats and the other with one main and two stabilising floats. A landplane was used for flotation bag tests to check buoyancy in the event of an emergency put-down on water.

Powered by a 477-kW (640-hp) Ha-8 radial engine, the Type 94 could attain a speed of 300 km/h (186 mph). Wing span was 12.00 m (39 ft 4½ in) and maximum take-off weight 2500 kg (5,511 lb)

An attractive feature of the Nakajima Ki-4 was the attempt to provide the rear gunner with a more hospitable cockpit through the provision of a substantial windshield.

Nakajima Ki-27

Nakajima had initiated as a private venture the design of an advanced single-seat low-wing monoplane fighter which it identified as the **PE**. When, in mid-1935, the Imperial Japanese Army instructed Nakajima to design an aircraft of this class for competitive evaluation, the resulting **Nakajima Ki-27** prototype was generally similar to the company's own PE prototype, but incorporated some improvements that resulted from early tests. Two prototypes and 10 pre-production aircraft were used for service evaluation, the pre-production Ki-27s having increased wing span and the cockpit enclosed by a sliding canopy. In this latter form the type was ordered into production in late 1937 as the **Army Type 97 Fighter Model A (Nakajima Ki-27a).** When production ended in 1942 a total of 3,399 had been built, 2,020 by Nakajima and 1,379 by Mansyu, the only variants being the slightly improved late production **Ki-27b,** and two lighter-weight experimental **Ki-27 KAI** aircraft, from which no series construction resulted. These fighters proved effective and reliable in service, and were deployed initially over northern China in March 1938. Here they were able to maintain air superiority until introduction of the Soviet Polikarpov I-16.

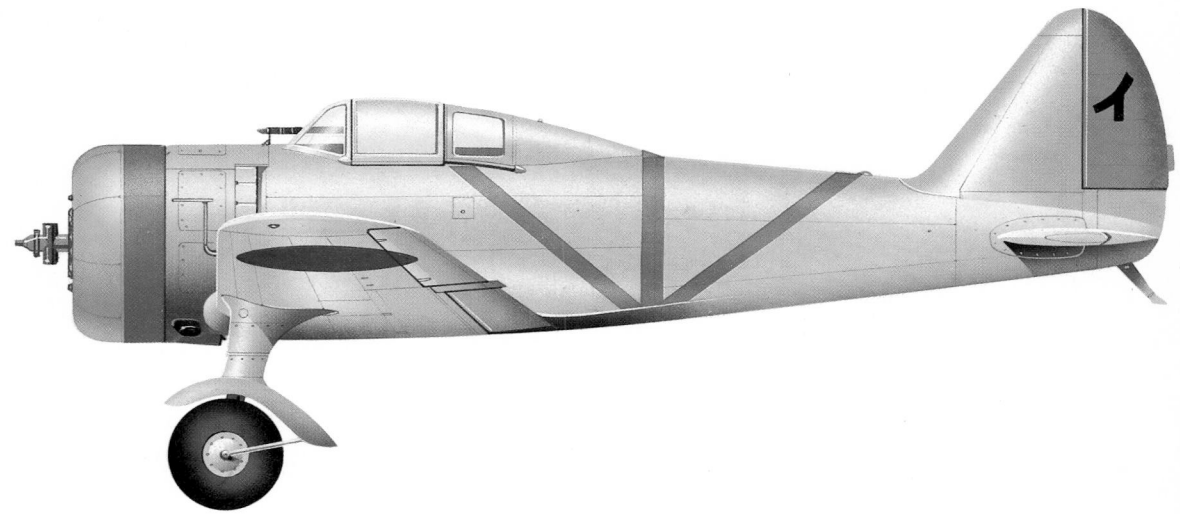

Nakajima Ki-27b of Lieutenant Colonel Toshio Katoh, commander of the 1st Sentai, Imperial Japanese Army air force, based at Kagamigahara in June 1939.

677

Ki-27s took part in the invasion of Burma, Malaya, the Netherlands East Indies and the Philippines, being allocated the Allied codename **'Nate'** (initially **'Abdul'** in the China-Burma-India theatre). They were most effective against the Allies in the early stages of the war, until confronted by more modern fighters, when they were transferred for air defence of the home islands until 1943, and then used increasingly as advanced trainers, with *kamikaze* operations their final role.

Specification
Nakajima Ki-27a
Type: single-seat fighter
Powerplant: one 529-kW (710-hp) Nakajima Ha-1b radial piston engine
Performance: maximum speed 470 km/h (292 mph) at 3500 m (11,485 ft); service ceiling 12250 m (40,190 ft); maximum range 625 km (389 miles)
Weights: empty 1110 kg (2,447 lb); maximum take-off 1790 kg (3,946 lb)
Dimensions: span 11.31 m (37 ft 1½ in); length 7.53 m (24 ft 8½ in); height 3.25 m (10 ft 8 in); wing area 18.55 m² (199.68 sq ft)
Armament: two 7.7-mm (0.303-in) forward-firing machine-guns

Nakajima Ki-34

Nakajima acquired from Douglas Aircraft in the USA licence-construction rights for the DC-2 civil transport. In 1935 a smaller twin-engine light transport, based on the configuration of the DC-2, was designed by Nakajima under the designation **AT-1**; this was not built, but redesign resulted in an improved **AT-2** with two 433-kW (580-hp) Nakajima Kotobuki 2-1 radial engines, and this was flown in prototype form on 12 September 1936. Extensive tests were followed by an order for 32 production AT-2s to equip Greater Japan Airlines and Manchurian Airlines, and in early 1937 the type was adopted also by the Imperial Japanese Army under the designation

Army Type 97 Transport (Nakajima Ki-34). Production of these three crew/eight passenger military transports totalled 318, 19 being built by Nakajima and 299 by Tachikawa. Some of this total were transferred by the army for navy use, and were redesignated **Navy Type AT-2 Transport (Nakajima L1N1).** Both civil and military versions were allocated the Allied codename **'Thora'**, and were in use throughout the Pacific war.

Specification
Nakajima Ki-34/L1N1 and production AT-2
Type: short-range light transport
Powerplant: two 529-kW (710-hp) Kotobuki 41 radial piston engines
Performance: maximum speed 360 km/h (224 mph) at 3360 m (11,025 ft); service ceiling 7000 m (22,965 ft); maximum range 1200 km (746 miles)
Weights: empty 3500 kg (7,716 lb); maximum take-off 5,250 kg (11,574 lb)
Dimensions: span 19.81 m (65 ft 0 in); length 15.30 m (59 ft 2¼ in); height 4.15 m (13 ft 7½ in); wing area 49.20 m² (529.60 sq ft)

The AT-2 was inspired by the DC-2 and, despite problems with engine cooling and landing gear retraction, and some other equipment, it proved popular.

Nakajima Ki-43 Hayabusa

Design and development of a more advanced fighter to supersede the Nakajima Ki-27 was started by the company in December 1937, the first of three **Nakajima Ki-43** prototypes flying during January 1939. A cantilever low-wing monoplane with retractable tailwheel landing gear, the Ki-43 seated its pilot in an enclosed cockpit, and power was provided by a 727-kW (975-hp) Nakajima Sakae Ha-25 supercharged radial engine. Testing of the prototypes revealed poor manoeuvrability, and the 10 pre-production aircraft that followed were of lower basic weight and introduced a wing of increased area that incorporated manoeuvring or 'combat' flaps. This configuration proved good enough for the type to be ordered into production as the **Army Type 1 Fighter Model 1A Hayabusa** (Ki-43-1a), the type enjoying considerable success in the early stages of the Pacific war. With the advent of more effective Allied fighters, improved Ki-43-II prototypes were flown with the higher powered Nakajima Ha-115 engine; introducing armour and self-sealing tanks, and with wing span reduced, this version duly entered production as the Ki-43-IIa. Final variant of the Hayabusa (peregrine falcon) series was the Ki-43-III, but only prototypes had been built before the Pacific war ended. By then production totalled 5,919, these being built by Nakajima (3,239), Tachikawa (2,631), and the 1st Army Air Arsenal (49), all receiving the Allied codename **'Oscar'**. The Hayabusa saw operational service throughout the entire Pacific war, its final deployment being for the defence of Tokyo or in *kamikaze* attacks on the approaching Allies.

Also known as the Ki-43-II Otsu, the Ki-43-IIb had repositioned hardpoints under the wing as earlier versions had lost their propellers while dropping bombs.

Variants
Ki-43-Ia: initial production version, armed with two forward-firing 7.7-mm (0.303-in) machine-guns and with two 15-kg (33-lb) bombs carried externally
Ki-43-Ib: as Ki-43-Ia but with one machine-gun replaced by one of 12.7-mm (0.5-in) calibre

Ki-43-Ic: as Ki-43-Ia but with both machine-guns of 12.7-mm (0.5-in) calibre
Ki-43-II: five prototypes of improved version with armour, self-sealing tanks and the Nakajima Ha-115 engine
Ki-43-IIa: initial Ki-43-II production version with machine-guns as Ki-43-Ic and two underwing racks each to carry a 250-kg (551-lb) bomb
Ki-43-IIb: generally as Ki-43-IIa but

with minor equipment changes
Ki-43-II KAI: version combining progressive modifications of Ki-43-IIa and Ki-43-IIb
Ki-43-IIIa: 10 prototypes, generally as Ki-43-II KAI, but with a Nakajima Ha-115-II engine developing greater power at altitude
Ki-43-IIIb: two interceptor fighter prototypes, with the 932-kW (1,250-hp) Mitsubishi Ha-112 engine, forward-

firing armament of two 20-mm cannon, and underwing racks as for the Ki-43-IIa

Specification
Nakajima Ki-43-IIb
Type: single-seat fighter/fighter-bomber
Powerplant: one 858-kW (1,150-hp) Nakajima Ha-115 radial piston engine
Performance: maximum speed 530 km/h (329 mph) at 4000 m (13,125 ft); service ceiling 11200 m (36,745 ft); maximum range 3200 km (1,988 miles)
Weights: empty 1910 kg (4,211 lb); maximum take-off 2590 kg (5,710 lb)
Dimensions: span 10.84 m (35 ft 6¾ in); length 8.92 m (29 ft 3¼ in);

Nakajima Ki-43IIb of the 3rd Chutai, 25th Sentai, Imperial Japanese Army air force, based at Hankow (China) in January 1944.

height 3.27 m (10 ft 8¾ in); wing area 21.40 m² (230.36 sq ft)

Armament: two 12.5-mm (0.5-in) forward-firing machine-guns, plus two

underwing racks each able to carry a 250-kg (551-lb) bomb

Nakajima Ki-44 Shoki

Nakajima designed and developed at much the same time as the Ki-43 a high-performance interceptor which, with maximum speed and rate of climb having specification priority, was powered by a 932-kW (1,250-hp) Nakajima Ha-41 radial engine. Otherwise of similar configuration to the Ki-43, the new **Ki-44** prototype was flown for the first time during August 1940 and with a satisfactory conclusion to service testing was ordered into production as the **Army Type 2 Single-seat Fighter Model 1A 'Shoki'** (Nakajima Ki-44-Ia). High landing speeds and limited manoeuvrability of the Shoki (demon), which had a comparatively high wing loading for its day, made it unpopular initially with service pilots. However, increased experience in handling the aircraft and its undoubted capabilities as an interceptor ensured that unpopularity turned eventually to respect. When production ended in late 1944 a total of 1,225 of all versions had been built by Nakajima, including prototypes, and they were deployed primarily in defence of the home islands against Allied air attack. All versions had the Allied codename **'Tojo'**.

Variants
Ki-44: prototype and pre-production

Nakajima Ki-44-IIb of the 23rd Sentai, Imperial Japanese army air force based in Japan in 1944.

aircraft with armament of two 7.7-mm (0.303-in) and two 12.7-mm (0.5-in) machine-guns
Ki-44-Ia: initial production version, generally similar to Ki-44
Ki-44-Ib: as Ki-44-Ia except for armament of four 12.7-mm (0.5-in) guns
Ki-44-Ic: as Ki-44-Ib but with modified mainwheel fairings
Ki-44-II: prototype and pre-production aircraft with the more powerful Ha-109 engine
Ki-44-IIa: initial Ki-44-II production version; armament as Ki-44-Ia

Ki-44-IIb: major production version; armament as Ki-44-Ib
Ki-44-IIc: Ki-44-II production version; armament of four 20-mm cannon, or two 40-mm cannon and two 12.7-mm (0.5-in) machine-guns
Ki-44-IIIa: production version with 1491-kW (2,000-hp) Nakajima Ha-145 radial engine and armament of four 20-mm cannon
Ki-44-IIIb: final production version, as Ki-44-IIIa, but with two 20-mm and two 37-mm cannon

Specification
Nakajima Ki-44-IIb

Type: single-seat interceptor fighter
Powerplant: one 1133-kW (1,520-hp) Nakajima Ha-109 radial piston engine
Performance: maximum speed 605 km/h (376 mph) at 5200 m (17,060 ft); service ceiling 11200 m (36,745 ft); maximum range 1700 km (1,056 miles)
Weights: empty 2105 kg (4,641 lb); maximum take-off 2995 kg (6,603 lb)
Dimensions: span 9.45 m (31 ft 0 in); length 8.80 m (28 ft 10½ in); height 3.25 m (10 ft 8 in); wing area 15.00 m² (161.46 sq ft)
Armament: four forward-firing 12.7-mm (0.5-in) machine-guns

Nakajima Ki-49 Donryu

Designed to supersede the Mitsubishi Ki-21 bomber which had entered service in 1938, the **Nakajima Ki-49** was required to have the performance capability to operate without a need for fighter escort. A cantilever mid-wing monoplane powered initially by two 708-kW (950-hp) Nakajima Ha-5 KAI radial engines, the eight-crew Ki-49 prototype was flown for the first time during August 1939. The second and third prototypes and seven pre-production aircraft had 932-kW (1,250-hp) Nakajima Ha-41 engines, which were used to power the initial production **Army Type 100 Heavy Bomber Model I Donryu (Ki-49-I)**, which was ordered into production in March 1941. The first of these aircraft entered operational service in the autumn of that year and, following initial deployment in China, became involved in the Pacific war in the New Guinea area and in attacks on Australia. Such utilisation made it clear that the Donryu (storm dragon) was underpowered, either bombload or speed suffering as a result, and in the spring of 1942 two **Ki-49-II** prototypes were flown with more powerful Nakajima Ha-109 engines, improved armour and

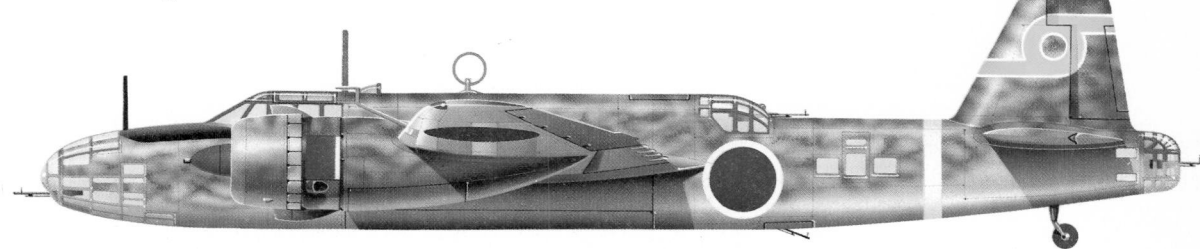

Nakajima Ki-49-IIa of the 3rd Chutai, 62nd Sentai, Imperial Japanese army air force.

self-sealing fuel tanks. This entered production as the **Ki-49-IIa**, which carried the same armament as the production Ki-49-I and was produced also in **Ki-49-IIb** form with a change in armament, three 7.7-mm (0.303-in) machine-guns being replaced by three of 12.7-mm (0.5-in) calibre. Even then performance was inadequate when the Ki-49 was confronted by more advanced Allied fighters, leading to the **Ki-49-III** with the 1805-kW (2,420-hp) Nakajima Ha-117 engine, but only six prototypes had been built when production was terminated in

December 1944. The inability of the Ki-49 to fulfil its intended role meant that in the later stages of the Pacific war the type was deployed on such duties as anti-submarine patrol, troop transport and, in the closing phase, for *kamikaze* attacks. The number built by Nakajima was 769, plus 50 by Tachikawa, Nakajima's total including three **Ki-58** prototypes of an intended escort fighter version with Ha-109 engines, and two **Ki-80** prototypes, a variant intended to serve as a lead aircraft, or pathfinder. All versions of the Ki-49 were allocated the Allied codename **'Helen'**.

Specification
Nakajima Ki-49-IIa

Type: heavy bomber
Powerplant: two 1119-kW (1,500-hp) Nakajima Ha-109 radial engines
Performance: maximum speed 492 km/h (306 mph) at 5000 m (16,405 ft); service ceiling 9300 m (30,150 ft); maximum range 2950 km (1,833 miles)
Weights: empty 6530 kg (14,396 lb); maximum take-off 11400 kg (25,133 lb)
Dimensions: span 20.42 m (67 ft 0 in); length 16.50 m (54 ft 1½ in); height 4.25 m (13 ft 11¼ in); wing area 69.05 m² (743.27 sq ft)
Armament: one 20-mm cannon and five 7.7-mm (0.303-in) machine-guns, plus a maximum bombload of 1000 kg (2,205 lb)

Nakajima Ki-84 Hayate

Introduced into service, during the summer of 1944, of the **Nakajima Ki-84 Hayate** (gale) single-seat interceptor fighter/fighter-bomber came too late for the Imperial Japanese Army. Had it been available earlier and in larger numbers this excellent fighter might well have posed serious problems for the Allies, for it had a higher rate of climb and better manoeuvrability than the North American P-51H Mustang or the Republic P-47N Thunderbolt operating in the Pacific zone. Its design had started in early 1942, successful testing of the two Ki-84 prototypes leading to 83 service trials and 42 pre-production aircraft. High-priority full-scale production began in late 1943 under the official designation **Army Type 4 Fighter Model 1A Hayate (Ki-84-Ia),** sharing with the trials/pre-production aircraft an armament of two 12.7-mm (0.5-in) machine-guns and two wing-mounted 20-mm cannon. Subsequent production versions included the **Ki-84-Ib** with the machine-guns replaced by two 20-mm cannon, the **Ki-84-Ic** with an armament of two 20-mm and two 30-mm cannon, and the **Ki-84-II** which introduced wood into the airframe structure to conserve light alloys and which was in service with either Ki-84-Ib or Ki-84-Ic armament. Allocated the Allied codename **'Frank'**, the Ki-84 was deployed extensively from the end of 1944, and when production ended a total of 3,514 had been built, including 94 by Mansyu. The grand total included also three **Ki-106** prototypes of all-wood construction, built by the 1st Army Air Arsenal at Tachikawa, and a single **Ki-113** with a maximum content of steel in its structure, these four prototypes being built to show significant savings in light alloys. The final variant was the single **Ki-116**, a conversion by Mansyu from a standard Ki-84-Ia, introducing a lighter-weight powerplant, the 1119-kW (1,500-hp) Mitsubishi Ha-33 radial.

Nakajima Ki-84-Ia of the 58th Shimbu-tai in August 1944.

Nakajima Ki-84-Ia

Specification
Nakajima Ki-84-Ia
Type: single-seat interceptor fighter/fighter-bomber
Powerplant: one 1416-kW (1,900-hp) Nakajima Ha-45 radial piston engine
Performance: maximum speed 631 km/h (392 mph) at 6120 m (20,080 ft); service ceiling 10500 m (34,350 ft); maximum range 2168 km (1,347 miles)
Weights: empty 2660 kg (5,864 lb); maximum take-off 3890 kg (8,576 lb)
Dimensions: span 11.24 m (36 ft 10½ in); length 9.92 m (32 ft 6½ in); height 3.39 m (11 ft 1½ in); wing area 21.00 m² (226.05 sq ft)
Armament: two 12·7-mm (0.5-in) · machine-guns and two 20-mm cannon, plus underwing racks for two 250-kg (551-lb) bombs

Nakajima Ki-115 Tsurugi

In January 1945 Nakajima was ordered by the Imperial Japanese Army to design and develop, as quickly as possible, a basic aircraft that could carry a bomb of up to 800-kg (1,746-lb) weight for use in *kamikaze* attacks. The resulting **Nakajima Ki-115** low-wing monoplane prototype was of mixed construction, powered by a Nakajima Ha-35 radial engine and had welded steel-tube main landing gear units, without any form of shock absorption, which were intended to be jettisoned after take-off on a *kamikaze* mission. Flight tests showed that ground handling was unacceptable in this configuration, leading to the introduction of main landing gear units with simple shock absorbers. In this form, and incorporating some minor modifications, the aircraft entered production as the **Ki-115a Tsurugi** (sabre). However, Nakajima had built only 104 production aircraft by the time the war ended, and none of these was used operationally.

Specification
Type: single-seat suicide attack aircraft
Powerplant: one 843-kW (1,130-hp) Nakajima Ha-35 radial engine
Performance: maximum speed 550 km/h (342 mph) at 2800 m (9,185 ft); range 1200 km (746 miles)
Weights: empty 1640 kg (3,616 lb); maximum take-off 2880 kg (6,439 lb)
Dimensions: span 8.60 m (28 ft

Designed from the outset simply as a flying bomb for Kamikaze attacks on American warships, the Nakajima Ki-115 rightly eschewed all frills. The two protrusions visible in front of the cockpit on the upper fuselge are the open fuel filler lids.

2½ in); length 8.55 m (28 ft 0½ in); height 3.30 m (10 ft 10 in); wing area 12.40 m² (133.48 sq ft)

Armament: one bomb of up to 800 kg (1,746 lb) carried semi-recessed beneath the fuselage

Nanchang A-5 Fantan

The A-5, designated Qiangjiji-5 (Attack aircraft 5) in China, originated in 1958 as a Shenyang factory derivative of the J-6 fighter, itself developed from the licence-built MiG-19 'Farmer'. The programme was cancelled in 1961, restarted in 1963 and the prototype flew for the first time on 4 June 1965. After a protracted development phase, the first of two further prototypes was flown in October 1969 and full production authorised at the end of 1969. Changes from the J-6 include stretching the fuselage by 25 per cent to accommodate a large internal weapons bay and fuel cells; splitting the engine intake to each side of the cockpit, and the installation of a search radar in the solid nose. Main wing structure is unchanged but spoilers are deleted and flaps redesigned. By 1992 nearly 1,000 had been built and the type is in squadron service with the Chinese air force and Naval air arm. Others have been exported to Bangladesh (20), North Korea (40), and Pakistan (52), the latter operating three Fantan units, these being Nos. 7, 16 and 26 Squadrons. The A-5K and A-5M improved export versions of the Q-5 II have been developed in conjunction with western companies, but neither has found orders in the market place. The A-5K was produced in conjunction with Thomson-CSF of France and the upgrading included a laser rangefinder, inertial navigation system and head-up display. The first of two development aircraft flew on 17 September 1988, but no sales have been announced to date. The A-5M, developed in parallel with Alenia of Italy, incorporated the navigation/attack system developed for the AMX; the addition of two further underwing stations and the installation of more powerful WP-6A turbojet engines each giving 6,614 lb (29.4 kN) dry thrust. Two prototypes have flown, the first on 30 August 1988 (but lost in crash on 17 October), and the second on 8 March 1989. The A-5M programme was completed in February 1991, but again no orders have materialised.

Variants
Q-5: initial production version for the Chinese armed forces.
Q-5 I: developed version with increased payload and range. Internal bomb bay blanked off allowing main fuel tank to be extended and further tank added. Improved engine, modified landing gear, brake chute relocated and some hardpoints moved to underfuselage position.
Q-5 IA: improved Q-5 I with extra hardpoint under each wing increasing bombload by 1,100 lb (500 kg); new weapon aiming system, and pressure refuelling facility added.
Q-5 II: similar to Q-5 IA but with radar warning system.
A-5C: Export version for Pakistan and later the Bangladesh air forces. Modified from Q-5 I to have upgraded avionics, Martin-Baker Mk.10 ejection seats, and capability to carry and fire Sidewinders and other weapons in PAF inventory.
A-5K Kong Yun (cloud): upgraded export version developed with Thomson-CSF and fitted with laser rangefinder, INS and HUD systems.

Two development aircraft flown, the first in September 1988.
A-5M: alternative upgraded export version of Q-5 II. Two prototypes flown to date, first on 30 August 1988 (but lost in crash on 17 October), and second on 8 March 1989.

Specification
Nanchang A-5C Fantan
Type: single-seat strike fighter
Powerplant: two 25.5 kN (5,732 lb) dry thrust Shenyang WP-6 turbojets
Performance: maximum level speed at 11000 m (36,000 ft) 1190 km/h (740 mph); at sea level 1210 km/h (752 mph); service ceiling 15850 m (52,000 ft); maximum range with full internal and external fuel 2000 km (1,243 miles)
Weights: empty 6494 kg (14,317 lb); maximum take-off with external stores 12000 kg (26,455 lb);
Dimensions: 9.7 m (31 ft 10 in); length 16.2 m (53 ft 4 in); height 4.5 m (14 ft 9 in); wing area 27.9 m^2 (300.8 sq ft)
Armament: one Norinco 23-mm

The A-5's greatest asset is its simplicity and low purchase price. The fact that it is based on obsolete technology is irrelevant.

cannon installed in each wingroot along with 100 rounds of ammunition. Ten hardpoints, two pairs in tandem under centre fuselage, plus three under each wing. Fuselage stations can carry bombs up to 250 kg (500 lb). Wingpoints can carry bombs, rocket or ECM pods, external fuel tanks or anti-shipping missiles.

Nardi F.N.305

Founded in Milan by the brothers Euste, Elio and Luigi Nardi, the partnership Fratelli Nardi built its first aircraft in 1934-5. The prototype **Nardi F.N.305**, serial MM277, made its maiden flight on 19 February 1935, piloted by Arturo Ferrarin. A cantilever low-wing monoplane of mixed construction, with inward-retracting main landing gear legs, it was intended for intermediate training, sport or touring, and was to become available in both single- and two-seat versions. Prototype MM277 was a two-seater with an enclosed canopy over the cockpit and, powered by a 149-kW (200-hp) Fiat A.70S radial engine, attained a maximum speed of 340 km/h (211 mph). Two more prototypes followed, also powered by the Fiat radial, comprising a single-seat fighter trainer and a two-seat basic trainer, both with open cockpits. Two long-range **F.N.305D** variants were built, each powered by a 149-kW (200-hp) Walter Bora radial. The first (I-UEBI) was a two-seater which made a remarkable non-stop flight from Rome to Addis Ababa, Ethiopia, in March 1939, gaining a record for aircraft in its class and covering 4463.80 km (2,773.68 miles) at an average speed of 240 km/h (149 mph). The second machine, the **F.N.305D II**, was a single-seat aircraft bought by Yugoslavia for an abortive non-stop North Atlantic flight. Finally, a prototype was tested

with an Alfa-Romeo 115 engine, and it was this **F.N.305A** version which was put into production at the Piaggio works, the Nardi workshops not being large enough for the task.

To meet Italian air ministry orders a total of 258 series F.N.305s was built by Piaggio, nearly all of them two-seat F.N.305A aircraft which were used as fighter trainers and for liaison by the Regia Aeronautica. Small numbers of the single-seat **F.N.305B** and **F.N.305C** were included in the total, the former having an open cockpit and the latter an enclosed canopy. Production was concentrated largely between 1937 and 1943, although eight partly-built machines were completed by the Piaggio works in 1948. F.N.305A series aircraft resembled the Alfa-Romeo powered prototype except for a redesigned canopy.

In the period 1937-1940 F.N.305s took part in many contests and rallies for sport and touring aircraft, frequently carrying off the prizes and gaining for the Nardi company much favourable publicity; as a result, considerable export orders were received. In 1938 Chile acquired nine machines and Romania 31, the latter country then following this up with licence-manufacture by the IAR company at Brasov, which built a total of 124 F.N.305s, the type becoming the standard Romanian basic/intermediate trainer. Romanian-built aircraft were powered by the IAR 6G-1 engine, a licence-built version of the de Havilland

Gipsy Six engine. Romania subsequently obtained 21 F.N.305s from the sixth production series, acquired in lieu of a planned purchase of SIAI S.83 transports which had been rejected by the Romanian government. The largest export order, for 300 aircraft, was received from the French authorities, but only 41 had been delivered to the Armée de l'Air when Italy declared war on France in June 1940. Final foreign purchaser was Hungary with a 50-aircraft order.

Specification
Nardi F.N.305A
Type: two-seat fighter trainer and liaison aircraft
Powerplant: one 138-kW (185-hp) Alfa Romeo 115 inline piston engine
Performance: maximum speed 300 km/h (186 mph); service ceiling 6000 m (19,685 ft); range 620 km (385 miles)

At first glance the angular fuselage of the conventional-looking Nardi F.N.305A seemed to indicate a type with only moderate performance. Its retractable landing gear, which folded inwards, actually meant that the aircraft had a respectable turn of speed, especially as it was powered by a relatively low-powered engine. A number were ordered by the Italian air force.

Weights: empty equipped 704 kg (1,552 lb); maximum take-off 984 kg (2,169 lb)
Dimensions: span 8.47 m (27 ft 9½ in); length 6.98 m (22 ft 10¾ in); height 2.10 m (6 ft 10¾ in); wing area 12.00 m^2 (129.17 sq ft)
Armament: (when fitted) one or two synchronised 7.7-mm (0.303-in) machine-guns

Nardi F.N.310

Designed by Luigi and Euste Nardi, the **Nardi F.N.310** of 1936 was powered by a 149-kW (200-hp) Fiat A.70S radial, enabling the prototype to attain a maximum speed of 300 km/h (186 mph). A four-seat tourer, with two pairs of side-by-side seats, it was similar to but larger than the F.N.305, with a span of 10.0 m (32 ft 9¾ in) and a maximum take-off weight of 1150 kg (2,535 lb). The main section of the cockpit canopy was divided down the centre and each section hinged forward for access. An ambulance variant had provision for a stretcher case in the rear cabin with the aft pair of seats eliminated.

Nardi F.N.315

Flown for the first time by Giovanni Zappetta on 10 July 1938, the **Nardi F.N.315** was evolved from the F.N. 305, but differed by having a completely new tail unit, a revised and relocated crew canopy, and a wing incorporating increased dihedral and conventional flaps. The first prototype had an Alfa-Romeo 115-I bis engine of 153 kW (205 hp), but other prototypes were tested with a 149-kW (200-hp) Argus As 10E and a 172-kW (230-hp) Hirth HM.508. At the completion of testing Nardi went on to build six Hirth-powered F.N.315s, two of them for the Swiss air arm, followed by 25 Alfa-Romeo-powered aircraft for the Regia Aeronautica, which used them in an intermediate trainer role.

The standard F.N.315 with Alfa-Romeo powerplant had a wing span of 8.47 m (27 ft 9½ in) and a maximum take-off weight of 1045 kg (2,304 lb). Maximum speed was 315 km/h (196 mph), service ceiling 6200 m (20,340 ft) and range 740 km (466 miles).

The Nardi F.N.315 was an up-engined F.N.305 fitted with a new Hirth powerplant. It could be equipped as a two-seat touring or advanced training aircraft, with extra glazing for the passenger. Flown by the Italian air force it was also exported to several nations including Switzerland.

Nardi F.N.316

Ultimate development of the F.N. 305, the prototype of the **Nardi F.N.316** advanced fighter trainer made its initial flight in the autumn of 1941. The selected powerplant, the Isotta-Fraschini Beta RC 10 IZ of 210 kW (270 hp), was beset by continual cooling problems and an initial order for 50 aircraft was not followed by any mass production as had been anticipated originally. In fact, only 49 aircraft were completed, 30 **F.N.316M** single-seater and 19 **F.N.316B** two-seaters. By comparison, with the prototype, both versions had considerable aerodynamic refinement, and redesigned wings and tail unit; the single-seat F.N.316M had an enclosed cockpit. These aircraft served with Regia Aeronautica flying schools from January 1942 (F.N.316M) and June 1943 (F.N.316B), and after the armistice with the Allies a number remained in service with the Luftwaffe in northern Italy, seven being on charge in April 1944.

The F.N.316M had a maximum speed of 330 km/h (205 mph), service ceiling of 6500 m (21,325 ft) and range of 740 km (460 miles). Armament consisted of one or two 7.7-mm (0.303-in) machine-guns.

Nardi F.N.333 Riviera

The **Nardi F.N.333** amphibian flying-boat prototype appeared in September 1952, a luxury tourer of cantilever high-wing monoplane configuration with the cabin mounted on the forward part of a single-step hull. Stabilisation on the water was provided by a pair of floats which retracted into the wing-tips, and two slender booms extended aft from the wings to mount a tail unit with twin vertical surfaces. Of all-metal construction, the F.N.333 prototype was powered by a 108-kW (145-hp) Continental engine mounted behind the cabin and driving a pusher propeller.

Three development aircraft were built by Nardi, the last being the **F.N.333S Riviera** definitive production prototype, but as Nardi did not have the space for

The Riviera, known as the North Star in the US, was Nardi's first post-war aircraft. It had unusual folding wings which kept the floats in the water throughout the folding process. The main units of the landing gear retracted into the fuselage aft of the cabin.

quantity production a series of 30 F.N.333S amphibians was built by SIAI Savoia-Marchetti at Somma Lombardo and Vergiate. The first production aircraft was test flown from Lake Maggiore in 1960, this version differing from the prototype in having a revised tail unit, a more commodious four-seat cabin, and water-proof doors for all three units of the wheel landing gear. The standard 186-kW (250-hp) Continental IO-470-P engine enabled the Riviera to attain a maximum speed of 285 km/h (177 mph). Wing span was 10.40 m (34 ft 1½ in) and maximum take-off weight 1485 m (3,274 lb). Most of the 30 series aircraft that had been built when production ended were sold in the United States.

Naval Aircraft Factory N3N Canary

Designed by the US Navy's Bureau of Aeronautics, this two-seat primary trainer was the NAF's most extensively built aircraft, and was also the last biplane to serve in the US armed forces when the last of the type was retired in 1961. A conventional equal-span biplane with wheeled or central float/stabilising float landing gear, and a basic structure of metal with fabric covering, the type began with the **NAF XN3N-1** prototype first flown during August 1935. Successful testing led to the production of 179 **N3N-1** aircraft, 158 of them powered by the 164-kW (220-hp) Wright J-5 radial engine which the US Navy had held in store. An additional prototype was ordered as **XN3N-2** and one production aircraft was converted to **XN3N-3** prototype configuration, both of them powered by the 179-kW (240-hp) US Navy-built version of the Wright R-760-96 radial engine. This action was taken because the J-5 engine was obsolescent and the last 20 production N3N-1s had the US Navy-built R-760 engine when testing showed them to be suitable. At a later date all remaining N3N-1s had their J-5 engines replaced by R-760-2s, which powered also the 816 **N3N-3** production aircraft built from 1938; these also had revised tail units and landing gear. Except for four aircraft transferred to the US Coast Guard in

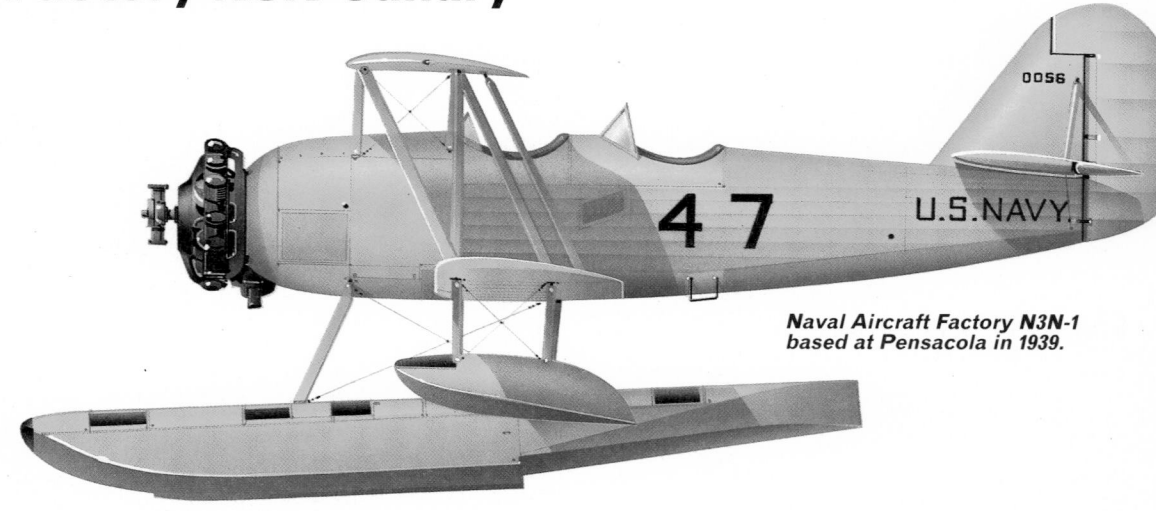

Naval Aircraft Factory N3N-1 based at Pensacola in 1939.

1941, these primary trainers were used extensively by the US Navy throughout World War II, the majority of them becoming surplus soon after the war ended. The exception was a small number of floatplanes which remained in service with the US Naval Academy until 1961.

Specification
NAF N3N-3
Type: two-seat primary trainer
Powerplant: one 175-kW (235-hp) Wright R-760-2 Whirlwind 7 radial piston engine
Performance: maximum speed 203 km/h (126 mph); service ceiling 4635 m (15,200 ft); range 756 km (470 miles)
Weights: empty 948 kg (2,090 lb); maximum take-off 1266 kg (2,792 lb)
Dimensions: span 10.36 m (34 ft 0 in); length 7.77 m (25 ft 6 in); height 3.30 m (10 ft 10 in); wing area 28.33 m² (305.0 sq ft)

Naval Aircraft Factory PN

One of the most successful patrol flying-boats of World War I was the Felixstowe F.5, developed by Squadron Commander John Porte in the UK from a Curtiss design. The NAF built 138 of these for the US Navy under the designation F-5L, the 'L' suffix denoting the Liberty-engined powerplant which replaced the Rolls-Royce Eagle engines of the British version. With a change in designation system in 1922, the F-5L was redesignated **PN-5**, and was followed by a series of models developed by the NAF increasing progressively the capability of this flying-boat. They comprised two with redesigned vertical tail surfaces, originally with the designation **F-6L**, later **PN-6**, followed by two **PN-7** 'boats which combined redesigned wings and 391-kW (525-hp) Wright T2 engines with the existing F-5L hull. The **PN-8**, of which two were built, was generally similar to the PN-7 but introduced a hull of metal construction and 354-kW (475-hp) Packard 1A-2500 engines; one of these was subsequently given modified tail surfaces and engine nacelles, and then redesignated **PN-9**, and two generally similar aircraft with only detail changes had the designation **PN-10**. A far more radical change came with the three **PN-11** aircraft, which introduced completely redesigned and wider metal hull, and one similar

XPN-11 with added twin vertical tail surfaces. The final NAF development was the **PN-12** of which two were built; generally similar to the PN-9, one had a pair of 391-kW (525-hp) R-1750-D Wright Cyclone radial engines, the other two Pratt & Whitney R-1850-A Hornets of similar output. They confirmed the combination of metal hull and radial engines providing optimum performance and, because of the NAF's restricted manufacturing capacity, series production was contracted out to Douglas, Martin and Keystone. Douglas built 25 **PD-1** aircraft with 429-kW (575-hp) Wright engines in revised nacelles; Martin built 30 **PM-1** aircraft with R-1750-D engines, and 25 **PM-2** 'boats which introduced 429-kW (575-hp) Wright R-1820-64 Cyclone engines and the twin vertical tail surfaces tested on the XPN-11; Keystone built 18 **PK-1** machines, all of them virtually identical to the Martin PM-2. Final development of the NAF PN series came when the Hall Aluminium Aircraft Corporation received a US Navy contract to build a version based on the PN-11. A single **XPH-1** prototype differed little from the PN-11 except for having a larger fin and rudder and two 400-kW (537-hp) Wright GR-1750 engines; it was followed by nine **PH-1** aircraft with 462-kW (620-hp) Wright R-1820-86 engines, these aircraft intro-

ducing also a somewhat basic enclosure for the pilots' cockpit. A further 14 aircraft were built for the US Coast Guard for use in the air-sea rescue role, these comprising seven **PH-2** 'boats with 559-kW (750-hp) Wright R-1820F-51 engines, and seven **PH-3** 'boats which differed primarily by having a more refined enclosure for the pilots. Some of the PH-3s soldiered on into World War II, being used briefly on anti-submarine patrols, but these aircraft represented the end of development of the Curtiss flying-boat which had played an important role during World War I.

Specification
NAF PN-12
Type: five-crew patrol flying-boat
Powerplant: two 391-kW (525-hp)

The NAF PN-7 had an elderly hull design characteristic of World War I flying-boats.

Wright R-1750-D Cyclone radial piston engines
Performance: maximum speed 183 km/h (114 mph) at sea level; service ceiling 3320 m (10,900 ft); range 2108 km (1,310 miles)
Weights: empty 3479 kg (7,669 lb); maximum take-off 6406 kg (14,122 lb)
Dimensions: span 22.20 m (72 ft 10 in); length 14.99 m (49 ft 2 in); height 5.11 m (16 ft 9 in); wing area 113.06 m² (1,217.0 sq ft)
Armament: bow and midship positions each with a single 7.62-mm (0.3-in) machine-gun, plus four 104-kg (230-lb) bombs

Naval Aircraft Factory TG

The US Naval Aircraft Factory (NAF), established at Philadelphia, Pennsylvania, in 1918, was created to provide the US Navy with its own manufacturing and test organization. The US Navy then had an urgent requirement for aircraft, with a result that the NAF was involved immediately in what, for the size of its facility, was quite large-scale production. This phase continued until 1922, the NAF then continuing as planned originally until US entry into World War II resulted in new involvement in design and construction on a large scale.

The **NAF TG** of 1922 was a seaplane gunnery trainer of which single examples of five variants were built for evaluation. In basic configuration the TG

With the single-float configuration that became increasingly popular during the 1920s, the TG-2 was intended for gunnery training.

was an equal-span biplane with open cockpits in tandem, a large central float being strut mounted beneath the fuselage and complemented by a small stabilising float beneath each wingtip. Designated **TG-1** and **TG-2**, the first two were powered by the 149-kW (200-hp) Liberty engine, the **TG-3** and **TG-4** by the 149-kW (200-hp) Aeromarine T-6 engine, and the final **TG-5** by a 134-kW (180-hp) Wright-Hispano E-4. All five aircraft built by the NAF were generally

similar externally, but the TG-1, TG-3 and TG-4 had fuselage fuel tanks, while fuel for the other two aircraft was carried in the central float. All had a wing span of

10.97 m (36 ft 0 in) and length of 9.14 m (30 ft 0 in). The TG-2 with a maximum take-off weight of 1359 kg (2,996 lb) had a top speed of 156 km/h (97 mph).

Naval Aircraft Factory TS

The US Navy's Bureau of Aeronautics, which had been established on 10 August 1921, was responsible for the design of the **NAF TS** biplane fighter, the first US Navy aircraft designed specifically for operation from an aircraft-carrier. A single-seat open cockpit biplane, it had landing gear attachments suitable both for wheels or twin floats and was powered initially by a 149-kW (200-hp) Lawrence J-1 radial engine. In accordance with US government policy at this period, tenders were requested for series manufacture, which resulted in the Curtiss Aeroplane and Motor Company receiving a contract to build 34 **TS-1** production aircraft, the first of these entering service aboard the carrier

A6301 was the second NAF TS-1 built and is seen here in floatplane configuration. Note the starter handle on the starboard side of the nose just aft of the engine.

USS *Langley* in December 1922. Operated from US Navy battleships, cruisers and destroyers, floatplane versions of the TS-1 remained in service for some years, being deployed on to the water by crane and recovered in the same way. Curtiss later received a contract for two additional TS-1s of all-metal construction, and these entered service for evaluation under the designation **F4C-1**.

One of the NAF's responsibilities was

to manufacture token numbers of contracted-out designs to keep a check on costings and contract prices, and five

TS-1s were built by NAF for this purpose. In addition, the NAF built four improved aircraft with different powerplant for comparative testing, two with the 179-kW (240-hp) Aeromarine engine, and two with the 134-kW (180-hp) Wright-Hispano E, these having the designations **TS-2** and **TS-3** respectively. One TS-3 was modified subsequently for use in air races, being redesignated **TR-2** and later, with more extensive changes, was used as a trainer by the US Navy team preparing for the 1923 Schneider Trophy contest. The standard TS-1 had a wing span of 7.62 m (25 ft 0 in), maximum take-off weight of 968 kg (2,133 lb), and could attain a maximum speed of 198 km/h (123 mph) at sea level.

Neiva Paulistinha 56 and Campeiro

The Brazilian company Sociedade Aeronáutica Neiva began its activities soon after the end of World War II by building, under sponsorship from the Brazilian government, single- and two-seat sailplanes for supply to the nation's flying clubs. In the late 1950s Neiva began construction of a two-seat lightweight cabin monoplane, designated the **Neiva Paulistinha 56**, which had a braced high-set wing and fixed tailwheel landing gear, and was powered by a Continental C90 flat-four engine. This remained in production until November 1964, by which time a total of 238 had been built, mostly in tourer/trainer versions, but some were equipped also for agricultural use. Final production version was the **Paulistinha 56-C**, but the prototoype (PP-ZTG) of a **Paulistinha 56-D** with an Avco Lycoming O-320-A1A was flown. This aircraft was acquired subsequently by the Brazilian air force which, designating it **L-6A**, used it in a

general purpose role. Although the Paulistinha 56-D was not built as such, it led directly to the generally similar **Campeiro** which differed primarily by having a redesigned structure. A contract for 20 of this version was received from the Brazilian air force in 1962, which operated them under the designation **L-7** for roles such as liaison, observation, rescue and training.

Specification
Neiva Campeiro
Type: two-seat utility aircraft
Powerplant: one 112-kW (150-hp) Avco Lycoming O-320-A flat-four piston engine
Performance: maximum speed

There was little of note about the Nieva Paulistina 56, which provided the Brazilian market with a lightplane comparable to American designs.

215 km/h (134 mph); service ceiling 5200 m (17,060 ft); range with maximum payload 955 km (593 miles)

Weights: empty 491 kg (1,082 lb); maximum take-off 790 kg (1,741 lb)
Dimensions: span 10.70 m (35 ft 1¼ in); length 6.90 m (22 ft 7¾ in); height 2.65 m (8 ft 8¼ in); wing area 16.80 m² (180.84 sq ft)

Neiva Regente and Lanceiro

In 1959 Neiva began the design of a four-seat cabin monoplane with a high-set braced wing, fixed tricycle landing gear, and with power provided initially by a 108-kW (145-hp) Continental O-300 engine. First flown on 7 September 1961 as the **Neiva Regente 360C**, the type was ordered into production for the Brazilian air force with a 134-kW (180-hp) Continental O-360-A1D engine under the initial designation **U-42**, changed later to **C-42**. A total of 80 was built, and these aircraft are used in the utility role. Neiva then developed a three-seat AOP version for the air force, identified by the company as the **Regente 420L**, which differed by having a stepped-down rear fuselage to improve the field of view, and a more powerful Continental engine. Flown first in **YL-42** prototype form during January 1967, 40 were built for

American design influence, chiefly that of Cessna, was evident in the Lanceiro. It was abandoned in the mid-1970s in the light of a growing involvement with EMBRAER projects.

the Brazilian air force under the designation **L-42**. The majority of these military C-42/L-42s remain in service. Neiva also developed a four-seat civil version of the L-42 under the name **Lanceiro**. A prototype (PP-ZAH) flown in 1970 was followed by the first production aircraft, flown in 1973, but by then the company's growing involvement with EMBRAER resulted in the Lanceiro programme being abandoned.

Specification
Neiva L-42

Type: three-seat AOP aircraft
Powerplant: one 157-kW (210-hp) Continental IO-360-D flat-six piston engine
Performance: maximum speed 245 km/h (152 mph) at sea level; service ceiling 4820 m (15,815 ft); range 925 km (575 miles)
Weights: empty equipped 745 kg

(1,642 lb); maximum take-off 1120 kg (2,469 lb)
Dimensions: span 9.13 m (29 ft 11½ in); length 7.21 m (23 ft 7¼ in); height 2.93 m (9 ft 7¼ in); wing area 13.45 m² (144.78 sq ft)
Armament: provision to carry light bombs or rockets on underwing hardpoints

Neiva Universal

Designed in 1963 to provide the Brazilian air force with a new primary trainer, the prototype of the **Neiva Universal** (PP-ZTW) was flown for the first time on 29 April 1966. A cantilever low-wing monoplane of all-metal construction with retractable tricycle landing gear, it has enclosed side-by-side accommodation for instructor and pupil with sufficient space in the cabin for an optional third seat behind them. Power was provided initially by a 216-kW (290-hp) Avco Lycoming IO-540-G1A5 flat-six engine, but later production aircraft have a more powerful version of this engine. A first Brazilian air force contract covered 150 Universals, designated **T-25**, an additional 28 being ordered in 1978. About 160 of this total remain in service, being used as basic, advanced and weapon trainers, the last with two underwing gun pods. A **YT-25B Universal II** prototype was flown for the first time on 22 October 1978, and though it was thought that the Brazilian air force would have a requirement for about 80 examples of this aircraft, which was powered by a

298-kW (400-hp) Avco Lycoming IO-720 engine, none have been produced. In addition to the Brazilian air force T-25s, 10 generally similar aircraft were supplied to the Chilean army; these were later transferred to the Chilean air force, where they remain in service.

Specification
Neiva T-25 Universal
Type: two-seat basic trainer
Powerplant: one 224-kW (300-hp) Avco Lycoming IO-540-K1D5 flat-six piston engine
Performance: maximum speed 300 km/h (186 mph) at sea level; service ceiling 6095 m (20,000 ft); range 1000 km (621 miles)

Weights: empty equipped 1150 kg (2,535 lb); maximum take-off 1500 kg (3,307 lb)
Dimensions: span 11.00 m (36 ft 1 in); length 8.60 m (28 ft 2¼ in); height 3.00 m (9 ft 10 in); wing area 17.20 m² (185.15 sq ft)

A Neiva T-25 Universal in Brazilian air force markings.

Nieuport early monoplanes

Established in 1910 by Edouard de Nié-port, who subsequently changed his name, the Société Anonyme des Etablissements Nieuport had its headquarters at Issy-les-Moulineaux in south west Paris, with a flying school at Villacoublay.

Unfortunately for the historian, most of the early series of monoplanes built by the company do not appear to have carried designations. The very first, a single-seater which flew in 1908, was based on the Blériot formula with an open framework fuselage. Said to be capable of 72 km/h (45 mph) with a 21-kW (28-hp) Darracq engine, it was followed in 1910 by a version with a more streamlined fuselage and a 37-kW (50-hp) Gnome engine. *Jane's All the World's Aircraft* illustrated a version with a 37-kW (50-hp) Gnome engine which was flying in 1911; this was probably the aircraft in which Nieuport himself established a speed record of 133.14 km/h (82.73 mph) at Chalons during 1911. A single-seater with a 22-kW (30-hp) engine of Nieu-

Right from the beginning of the line, Nieuports such as this 1912 monoplane were characterised by a cleanliness of design and an economy of line. Note the extensive wing bracing/warping, and the small rudder.

port's own design was designated **Nieuport Type 2-N**, and this had a maximum speed of 109 km/h (68 mph).

As a result of France's first military aircraft competition, held in 1911 to select aircraft for the armed forces, some 110 prototypes were entered. These were soon narrowed down to 32, and the three winning companies were Deperdussin, Breguet and Nieuport, the last receiving an order for 10 two-seaters; in 1912 one of these became the first aircraft to be fitted with a permanently installed machine-gun.

In 1913 a Nieuport **Type IV** monoplane was looped at Kiev by the Russian pilot Nesterov, and several such aircraft

served with the Russian air service. The British army took five Nieuports on charge, one of which had a 75-kW (100-hp) 14-cylinder Gnome rotary engine.

At the outbreak of war in 1914 Nieuport **Type 6M** aircraft were serving with a few French, Italian and Russian squadrons, but soon became obsolete. It is worth recording that two of the four aircraft competing in the first Schneider Trophy contest at Monaco in 1913 were Nieuports, with 75-kW (100-hp) Gnome engines, and two of the six contestants the following year flew 119-kW (160-hp) Gnome-powered Nieuports. All four aircraft failed to complete the course.

Nieuport Types 10 and 12

In 1914 Gustave Delage joined the Nieuport company and began work on a small two-seat reconnaissance and fighter biplane of advanced design. There were two variants; the **Nieuport Type 10AV** had an observer/gunner's position in the front cockpit and the pilot in the rear, while the **Type 10AR** reversed the positions. With only a 60-kW (80-hp) Gnome or Le Rhône engine, the Type 10 was underpowered as a two-seater and

some were converted to single-seaters, principally by the Royal Naval Air Service in the Aegean and by French squadrons on the Western Front.

In an effort to improve performance, a larger version with an 82- or 97-kW (110- or 130-hp) Clerget engine was introduced as the **Nieuport Type 12**, enabling the Type 10s to be relegated to training duties. The observer in the Type 12 had a Lewis gun in the rear cockpit

The Nieuport 12 sesquiplane was basically an enlarged and up-engined Nieuport 10.

while the pilot had a fixed Vickers gun with interrupter gear firing through the propeller. About 170 Type 10s and Type 12s served with RFC and RNAS squadrons, including some examples licence-built by the Beardmore Company in Scotland; as they were withdrawn to be replaced by Nieuport Type 11s, the earlier aircraft with Le Rhône engines were converted to trainers by the addi-

tion of extra struts and four-wheel landing gear to prevent nosing over; in this form they were designated **80E.2, 81D.2** and **83E.2**. The Type 12 had a wing span of 9.03 m (29 ft 7½ in) and a maximum speed of 125 km/h (78 mph).

Nieuport Types 11 and 16

Nieuport's decision to build an aircraft to compete in the 1914 Gordon-Bennett Trophy contest led to a line of dainty single-seat fighters, the first of which was the **Nieuport Type 11**, built in only four months. On the outbreak of war the contest was cancelled, but the new aircraft's potential was quickly realised and orders were placed by the British and French. The engine was the 60-kW (80-hp) Le Rhône rotary, and a single Lewis gun was mounted on the upper wing. The lower wing had only half the area of the upper, a feature which was to become famous on these aircraft, known also as the **Nieuport Bébé** (baby), because of its small size, or **Nieuport Scout,** which was its primary role.

The high rate of climb and manoeuvrability of the new aircraft, deliveries of which began to French squadrons in 1915, helped the Allies to gain temporary air superiority. Several hundred were built by Macchi in Italy (as the **Nieuport 11000**) and the Type 11 served also with the Belgian Aviation Militaire and the British RFC and RNAS.

An improved version, the **Nieuport 16**, had an 82-kW (110-hp) Le Rhône rotary engine and appeared in 1916. Flown by British, Belgian and French pilots, the Type 16 was the type on which the French ace Georges Guy-

nemer began to make his name. It also pioneered the use of Le Prieur rockets for attacks against balloons and airships, being able to carry eight rockets. These

Nieuport 11 of the 3rd Fighter Squadron at Ciora attached to the 1st Romanian Army in September 1917.

were attached to the wing struts, inclined upwards, and were fired electrically.

Specification
Nieuport Type 11
Type: single-seat fighter
Powerplant: one 60-kW (80-hp) Le Rhône rotary piston engine
Performance: maximum speed

155 km/h (97 mph) at sea level; service ceiling 4500 m (14,765 ft); endurance 2 hours 30 minutes
Weights: empty 350 kg (772 lb); maximum take-off 480 kg (1,058 lb)
Dimensions: span 7.55 m (24 ft 9 in); length 5.80 m (19 ft 0¾ in); height 2.45 m (8 ft 0½ in); wing area 13.00 m² (139.94 sq ft)
Armament: one fixed forward-firing 7.7-mm (0.303-in) Lewis gun

Nieuport Types 14, 15, 18, 20 and 26

In the summer of 1916 Nieuport produced the **Nieuport Type 14**, a two-seat day bomber with a 112-kW (150-hp) Hispano-Suiza inline engine, armed with a Lewis gun mounted in the rear cockpit; three French *escadrilles* received the

type to replace ancient Voisins. The Nieuport 14 obviously made little contribution to the war effort, as the French units were re-equipped only 18 days later with Nieuport Type 17s, becoming fighter squadrons. The **Type 15** two-

seat trainer and the **Type 26** were versions of the Type 14, neither of which entered service. An order from the RNAS for 40 Type 15s with 172-kW (230-hp) Renault engines was cancelled. The **Type 18** single-seat fighter of 1917 also

had a 112-kW (150-hp) Hispano-Suiza, but this engine was of radial configuration. The Type 18 did not enter large-scale production, the same fate befalling the 82-kW (110-hp) Le Rhône-powered **Type 20** two-seater of 1917, although a few of the latter can be traced to the RFC.

Nieuport Types 17, 21 and 23

Experience with the earlier models led in March 1916 to the Nieuport which was destined to become the best known of all, the **Nieuport Type 17**. Stronger than its predecessors, and with an 82-kW (110-hp) Le Rhône or 97-kW (130-hp) Clerget (**Nieuport 17-bis**), the new model was very manoeuvrable and had a high performance with a particularly good rate of climb. A Lewis gun was mounted on the top wing to fire above the propeller, and a sliding mounting enabled it to be pulled down by the pilot and aimed upwards, thereby permitting an attack on enemy aircraft in their blind spot, from below. Later in the aircraft's service life, when a synchronising gear had been perfected to allow the gun to fire through the propeller, a Vickers gun was substituted.

A number of French squadrons re-equipped with the Type 17, together with Belgian, Italian, Russian and RFC units, and the type rapidly made a name for itself with aces who included Nungesser, Ball and Bishop.

The **Type 21** was a variant of the Type 17 with a 60-kW (80-hp) Le Rhône and enlarged ailerons. Russia and the USA received a number of Type 21s, the latter

totalling just under 200. The last batch of US aircraft, delivered in January 1918, had 82-kW (110-hp) Le Rhône engines. Several Type 21s were used post-war by sporting pilots.

A slightly heavier version, the **Type 23**, could be powered by a 60-kW (80-hp) or 89-kW (120-hp) Le Rhône. It was supplied to the air forces of Belgium, France, Italy, the UK and the USA.

Specification
Nieuport Type 17
Type: single-seat fighter
Powerplant: one 89-kW (120-hp) Le Rhône rotary piston engine
Performance: maximum speed 170 km/h (106 mph) at 1980 m 6,500 ft); climb to 4000 m (13,125 ft) in 19 minutes 30 seconds; service ceiling 5350 m (17,550 ft); maximum range 250 km (155 miles)
Weights: empty 374 kg (825 lb); maximum take-off 560 kg (1,235 lb)
Dimensions: span 8.20 m (26 ft 10¾ in); length 5.96 m (19 ft 7 in); height 2.44 m (8 ft 0 in); wing area 14.75 m² (158.77 sq ft)
Armament: one fixed forward-firing 7.7-mm (0.303-in) Vickers or Lewis gun

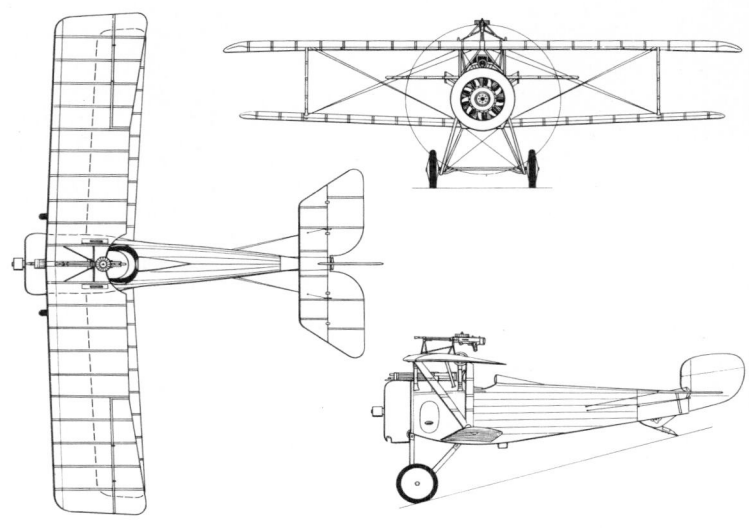

Nieuport 17-bis

Nieuport Types 24, 25 and 27

Nungesser's Nieuport 17-bis had been converted to a Type 23, and later became the prototype for the **Nieuport Type 24**, a more streamlined model with an 89-kW (120-hp) Le Rhône, a fixed and a circular section fuselage. The USA bought 121 Type 24s in November 1917, while others served with Belgian and Italian units, and a few were built under licence in Japan by Nakajima. A further variant, which reverted to the Type 17 tail unit and rectangular wing tips, was the **Type 24-bis**, a trainer used by the French, the American Expeditionary Force which received 140, and the RNAS for which the type was built in England by the British Nieuport and General Aircraft Co. Ltd. The redesignation **Type 25** was applied to the prototype Type 24 after it had been modified to incorporate a tailplane and skid of the type to be used on the **Type 27**.

Basically similar to the Type 24, the Type 27 had a 89-kW (120-hp) Le Rhône engine and served with the air forces of Sweden, the UK and USA, the last buying 287 in November 1917. Macchi also built a number under licence in Italy, but by this time Nieuport realised that a more radical redesign was necessary to match the performance of enemy aircraft on the Western Front.

Specification
Nieuport Type 27
Type: single-seat fighter
Powerplant: one 89-kW (120-hp) Le Rhône rotary piston engine
Performance: maximum speed 185 km/h (115 mph) at sea level; service ceiling 5550 m (18,210 ft); maximum range 250 km (155 miles)
Weights: empty 380 kg (838 lb);

maximum take-off 585 kg (1,289 lb)
Dimensions: span 8.20 m (26 ft 10¾ in); length 5.85 m (19 ft 2⅓ in); height 2.42 m (7 ft 11¼ in); wing area 14.75 m² (158.77 sq ft)
Armament: one fixed forward-firing 7.7-mm (0.303-in) Lewis gun and/or one 7.7-mm (0.303-in) Vickers gun

The Nieuport 27 was the ultimate development of the company's sesquiplane formula. It subsequently built standard biplanes.

Nieuport 27 of No. 1 Squadron, Royal Flying Corps, wearing French three-tone camouflage.

Nieuport Type 28

First flown in prototype form in June 1917, the **Nieuport Type 28** was markedly different to the earlier models. The familiar narrow lower wing and square-cut wing tips gave way to rounded wings of almost equal size and the familiar V-struts were replaced by parallel struts; and the rectangular-section fuselage was superseded by one of circular section. The new nine-cylinder Gnome rotary engine of around 119 kW (160 hp) was fitted to production aircraft and the Type 28 went into large-scale production for France and the USA, ironically as it happened, since by the time it appeared it had been eclipsed in per-

formance by the SPAD. However, the American Expeditionary Force had a desperate requirement for fighters and all SPADs were at that time being delivered to the French, so Nieuport supplied the American squadrons with 297 Type 28s. Probably the most famous unit to be so equipped was the 94th Aero Squadron with its 'hat-in-ring' insignia; Eddie Rickenbacker, who was to become the top US ace, flew a Type 28 with the squad-

ron. Engine problems and a tendency to shed upper-wing fabric in long dives did not endear the Type 28 to its pilots, who were relieved to re-equip with SPAD 13s in July 1918, a relief which was short-lived when they discovered troubles with the Hispano-Suiza engines that powered them.

Post-war, four civil aircraft flew mail between Paris and London in 1920 during a French postal strike, and 12

Type 28s were used by the US Navy in experiments, flying from platforms built over battleship gun turrets.

Specification
Nieuport Type 28
Type: single-seat fighter
Powerplant: one 119-kW (160-hp) Gnome 9N rotary piston engine
Performance: maximum speed 195 km/h (121 mph) at 1981 m (6,500 ft); climb to 5000 m (16,405 ft) in 21 minutes 15 seconds; service ceiling 5200 m (17,060 ft); maximum range 400 km (248 miles)
Weights: empty 532 kg (1,172 lb); maximum take-off 740 kg (1,631 lb)
Dimensions: span 8.00 m (26 ft 3 in); length 6.20 m (20 ft 4 in); height 2.48 m (8 ft 1¾ in); wing area 20.00 m² (215.29 sq ft)
Armament: two fixed forward-firing 7.7-mm (0.303-in) Vickers machine-guns

Nieuport 28 of the 94th Aero Squadron, American Expeditionary Force, based in France during May 1918.

Nieuport-Delage Ni-D 29

An equal-span biplane with ailerons on both upper and lower wings, the first prototype of the **Nieuport-Delage Ni-D 29** single-seat fighter (C.1 category) made its initial official test flight on 21 August 1918. It performed well and achieved the performance required with the exception of ceiling. The second prototype retained the Hispano-Suiza 8Fb engine and the slim circular-section fuselage of its predecessor, but the wing span increased slightly. Then achieving the required ceiling, the Ni-D 29 was ordered into quantity production at the beginning of 1920. Series aircraft had detailed improvements, the principal external difference being the elimination of the upper-wing ailerons and the enlargement of those on the lower surfaces.

Initial deliveries to the French Aviation Militaire were made in 1922, the type equipping Escadrilles SPA 37, 81 and 91 (later renumbered 101, 102 and 103 respectively) stationed in Germany. The type proved popular, although pilots remarked on its tendency to get into a flat spin. Some 250 Ni-D 29 fighters were built for French military aviation by Nieuport and seven other firms, a total of 18 orders being received between 1922 and 1924. By 1925 the Ni-D 29 equipped *escadrilles* of the 1ᵉʳ and 3ᵉ Régiments de Chasse based at Thionville and Chateauroux.

The Ni-D 29 was soon the most important fighter of the 1920s. Spain purchased 30 aircraft, 10 of which were licence-built in that country; Belgium had 108, 87 of them built by SABCA under licence; Japan imported a pattern aircraft, and subsequently Nakajima built no less than 608 under licence, supplying them to the Imperial Japanese Army as the **Ko-4**; Italy bought six French machines and then the Regia Aeronautica obtained 175 series aircraft, 95 built by Macchi as the **Macchi-Nieuport 29** and 80 by Caproni, the type equipping six Italian fighter *sqadriglie* between 1925 and 1928. Finally, Sweden bought nine aircraft, operating them under the designation **J 2**, and Argentina also used a small number.

French Ni-D 29s used operationally against the Rif insurgents in Morocco included a small number of Ni-D 29s, converted to B.1 standard with the ability to carry small bombs, and the Spanish Nieuports also participated in the operations against these North African rebels.

In Japan the Ko-4 licence-built version formed the main equipment of army

Nieuport-Delage Ni-D 29 of the French air force in the 1920s.

fighter units until 1933, playing a major part in air support for the Japanese occupation of Manchuria and in the 1932 Shanghai Incident.

A number of racing versions of the NiD 29 were developed, gaining no fewer than eight world speed records.

Variants
Ni-D 29 B.1: an experimental assault version of the fighter, armed with six 10-kg (22-lb) bombs; exploits with NiD 29 B.1 won renowned pilot Sadi Lecointe three citations and promotion; only small batch converted to B.1 configuration
Ni-D 29bis: shown at 1922 Paris Salon; reduced wing area and steerable tailskid; prototype only
Ni-D 29G: version built in parallel with Hispano-Suiza prototypes; had Gnome 9N rotary engine; first of two built converted to take Hispano engine and fitted with twin main floats and auxiliary tail float, and took part in Grand Prix de Monaco seaplane meeting in 1920; second aircraft tested with the Gnome engine as possible carrierborne fighter, then being converted in 1920 to **Ni-D 32RH** with a 134-kW (180-hp) Le Rhône 9R **Ni-D**

29D: a conversion to attempt altitude record; had Rateau supercharger, enabling it to attain an altitude of 7000 m (22,965 ft)
Ni-D 29 E.1: trainer variant built for French Aviation Militaire; powered by a 134-kW (180-hp) Hispano-Suiza and armed with single synchronised Vickers gun
Ni-D 29 SHV: seaplane variant for 1919 Schneider Trophy contest; wing span reduced to 8.00 m (26 ft 3 in) and airframe stripped of military equipment and given improved external finish; two aircraft built, one also entered in 1921, but no Ni-D 29 actually took part in either contest
Ni-D 29V: developed in 1919 by designer Mary in collaboration with company engineer Gustave Delage, the Ni-D 29V was a lightweight racer, with wing span reduced to a mere 6.00 m (19 ft 8¼ in) and its HS 8Fb engine boosted to give 239 kW (320 hp), maximum take-off weight was reduced to 936 kg (2,063 lb); the three racers built were subjected to numerous modifications and the type swept the board in many events, Sadi Lecointe winning the 1919 Coupe Deutsche and the 1920 Gordon Bennett Trophy races

flying Ni-D 29Vs; the **Ni-D 29V bis** was a one-off conversion intended to produce a higher maximum speed by eliminating the open cockpit with its windscreen and headrest. The pilot had to crouch within the fuselage, relying on tiny teardrop windows on each side for his only external visibility; it was, not surprisingly, lost in a landing accident in April 1921

Specification
Nieuport-Delage Ni-D 29
Type: single-seat fighter
Powerplant: one 224-kW (300-hp) Hispano-Suiza 8Fb V-8 piston engine
Performance: maximum speed 235 km/h (146 mph); service ceiling 8500 m (27,885 ft); range 580 km (360 miles)
Weights: empty equipped 760 kg (1,675 lb); maximum take-off 1150 kg (2,535 lb)
Dimensions: span 9.70 m (31 ft 10 in); length 6.49 m (21 ft 3½ in); height 2.56 m (8 ft 4¾ in); wing area 26.70 m² (287.41 sq ft)
Armament: two fixed forward-firing 7.7-mm (0.303-in) Vickers machine-guns

Nieuport-Delage Ni-D 30T
to
Nieuport-Delage Sesquiplan

Nieuport-Delage Ni-D 30T

The **Nieuport-Delage Ni-D 30T1** biplane transport entered service on the Paris-London route in early 1920 operated by the Nieuport-owned Compagnie Générale Transaérienne. The pilot was seated in an open cockpit behind the single 261-kW (350-hp) Sunbeam Matabele engine, while to his rear was a cabin accommodating four passengers. In

total seven Ni-D 30T1s were built, and they provided twice-daily return services until one (F-CGTY) was lost in the Channel on 27 April 1920 in thick fog. As a result the remaining machines were fitted with a primitive audible frequency guidance sustem developed by A. W. Loth. A single **Ni-D 30T2**, a sesquiplane development of the Ni-D 30T1

One of the earliest of London-to-Paris airliners, the Nieuport-Delage Ni-D 30T carried four passengers in an enclosed cabin.

powered by a 313-kW (420-hp) Darracq 12A engine, made its first flight on 23 March 1921. However, tests revealed several problems and the type's development was abandoned. Maximum speed of the Ni-D 30T1 was 172 km/h (107 mph) and the Ni-D 30T2, which

accommodated up to seven passengers, was only marginally slower.

Nieuport-Delage Ni-D 33

This classic-primary trainer first appeared in 1921 in the **Nieuport-Del-**

age Ni-D 33 SAL version which, powered by a 194-kW (260-hp) Salmson

9Z engine, was built for the French navy. The following year the **Ni-D 33 HS** with a 224-kW (300-hp) Hispano-Suiza 8Fb engine went into production, five

examples being supplied to Japan. It had a maximum take-off weight of 1280 kg (2,822 lb) and a maximum speed of 220 km/h (137 mph).

Nieuport-Delage Ni-D 38

The **Nieuport-Delage Ni-D 38** three-seat tourer biplane was designed to take a range of engines in the 134-kW (180-hp) to 164-kW (220-hp) class, with the

two passengers accommodated in a small cabin located just behind the pilot's open cockpit. The first example was exhibited at the Paris Salon de l'Aé-

ronautique of 1924, being registered subsequently F-AGFK and flying with a war-surplus 134-kW (180-hp) Hispano-Suiza 8Ab engine. In all four Ni-D 38s were completed, the first two having a mail hold in place of the passenger cabin and being operated for a period on a

regular night mail service between Geneva and Bordeaux. The last to be built was flown first with a Renault 8Gd engine, and then with a Hispano 8Ad to become redesignated **Ni-D 381**. It was not scrapped until 1938.

Nieuport-Delage Ni-D 40R

The **Nieuport-Delage Ni-D 40** single-seat high-altitude biplane fighter prototype failed to interest the French authorities, and the company modified it into

the **Ni-D 40R** for an attempt on the world altiitude record. It had a wing span of 14.00 m (45 ft 11¼ in), wing area of 34.00 m² (365.98 sq ft), and power

was supplied by a 298-kW (400-hp) Hispano-Suiza 8Fb supercharged engine. The new version flew for the first time on 1 July 1923, piloted by Sadi Lecointe, who was accommodated in an enclosed pressurised compartment. On 5 September 1923 an altitude of 10741 m

(35,239 ft) was attained, breaking the world record, but Sadi Lecointe improved this to 11145 m (36,565 ft) on 30 October 1923, a record which remained unbroken for the next four years. In 1924 the Ni-D 40R was tested as a floatplane, with a twin float installation.

Nieuport-Delage Ni-D 41 and Ni-D 42S

Built for the 1922 Coupe Deutsche de la Meurthe race, but singularly unsuccessful, the **Nieuport-Delage Ni-D 41** resembled the earlier Sesquiplan, but had a fuselage of greater cross-section and a 298-kW (400-hp) Hispano-Suiza engine. It had a cantilever wing, being developed

from the abortive **Ni-D 37** single-seat fighter prototype, but on the day of the race the Ni-D 41 was unable to take off and nothing more was heard of it.

The **Ni-D 42S** was also developed from the Sesquiplan, but was a more substantial design, with maximum take-

off weight raised from 980 kg (2,160 lb) to 1440 kg (3,175 lb), and was powered by a 447-kW (600-hp) Hispano-Suiza 12Hb engine. After development delays two Ni-D 42S machines were entered for the June 1924 Coupe Beaumont contest. That piloted by Sadi Lecointe won,

when no other machine finished the course, and he continued flying to establish a world record over 500 km (310.69 miles) of 306.696 km/h (190.572 mph). The winning aircraft was displayed triumphantly at the 1924 Paris Salon de l'Aéronautique, marking a high point for Nieuport-Delage, but the company subsequently gave up racing.

Nieuport-Delage Ni-D 42C

On the Nieuport stand at the 1924 Paris Salon de l'Aéronautique were displayed three new designs, each bearing the type number 42. One was the Ni-D 42S racer referred to elsewhere; the other two were sesquiplanes, the **Nieuport-Delage Ni-D 42 C.1** single-seat and the **Ni-D 42 C.1** two-seat fighters. There was little interest in the two-seat aircraft, but the C.1 machine was the first of a successful family of fighters built over the next decade, including the Ni-D 52 and Ni-D 62 series.

The original design had been for a parasol monplane, but this was modified to have a small lower plane in order to achieve a more rigid and reliable wing structure. The prototype flew for the first time in its definitive form at the beginning of 1924, incorporating also a feature taken from the earlier Nieuport racers, namely an auxiliary aerofoil surface

attached to the cross axle of the main leading gear units. The new fighter soon attracted official attention, an order for 25 aircraft for the French Aviation Militaire being received in January 1927, and the type went into service with the 2ᵉ, 3ᵉ and 38ᵉ Régiments d'Aviation in 1928. Powered by a 373-kW (500-hp) Hispano-Suiza 12Hb V-12 engine, the Ni-D 42 attained a maximum speed of 265 km/h (165 mph) and was armed with two wing-mounted 7.7-mm (0.303-in) machine-guns, plus a third gun on the engine cowling synchronised to fire through the propeller disc. Operating with the French *escadrilles de chasse*, the Ni-D 42 was most impressive when compared with other types in service at home and abroad, encouraging Nieuport engineers to set about creating improved developments.

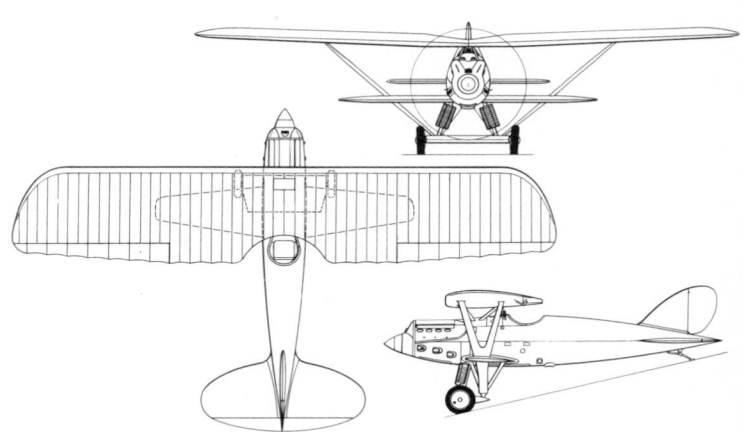

Nieuport-Delage Ni-D 42 with engine radiators on landing gear.

Nieuport-Delage Ni-D 43

The **Nieuport-Delage Ni-D 43** was an *avion marin* aircraft which could take

off and land on the ground or an aircraft-carrier and, if necessary, come down on

the sea in an emergency and remain afloat. A large single-engine biplane, it had normal wheel landing gear, but the wheels projected from a pair of floats only for use in an emergency put-down

at sea. A two-seat fighter armed with four 7.7-mm (0.303-in) machine-guns, and powered by a 336-kW (450-hp) Hispano-Suiza 12 Ha engine, it demonstrated a maximum speed of 200 km/h.

Nieuport-Delage Ni-D 48

Built in 1926 to meet the requirements of the French official 'Jockey' programme for a lightweight, economical single-seat fighter, the **Nieuport-Delage Ni-D 48** had a parasol wing braced on each side to the cross-axle landing gear by means of large Y-type struts, and was powered by a 298-kW (400-hp) Hispano-Suiza 12Jb engine. The Ni-D 48 was displayed at the 1926 Paris Salon de l'Aéronautique and then extensively test-flown, attaining a maximum speed of 275 km/h (171 mph), but it was lost when abandoned in flight during July 1929. The ensuing **Ni-D 48bis** had a Hispano-Suiza 12Hb engine and an enlarged tailplane, but after a few flights further de-

velopment was terminated. However, in 1930 a 224-kW (300-hp) Lorraine Algol radial engine with Townend ring was installed and the aircraft was prepared to be flown in that year's Coupe Michelin air race by René Paulhan. An accident prevented it from taking part but, redesignated **Ni-D 481**, the aircraft gave aerobatic displays at a number of French air shows until scrapped in 1936.

The Nieuport-Delage Ni-D 48 followed company practice of large 'Y-struts' supporting the wings and undercarriage. These struts were made from a pair of sheet-metal pressings.

Nieuport-Delage Ni-D 52

Closely resembling the Ni-D 42 but constructed largely of metal instead of wood, the **Nieuport-Delage Ni-D 52** single-seat fighter prototype appeared in 1927, and in the following year won a competition sponsored by the Spanish government. Nieuport supplied Spain with 34 aircraft and the first of 91 machines built under licence by Hispano Aviacion was flight tested at Getafe airfield in 1930. The last Hispano-built aircraft was delivered in 1936 and the type formed the backbone of the Aviacion Militar for some seven years. At the outbreak of the Spanish Civil War six squadrons still flew the type which, by then, was obsolete. Most fell into Republican hands, only a dozen or so being seized by the Franco forces. The Republican aircraft did not go into action for some time, and when they did were soon surpassed by the Nationalist Fiat C.R.32s, most of the Ni-D 52s then being relegated to coast patrol duties or training. Early in the war the government's Guadalajara workshops assembled some 20 Ni-D 52s from available spare parts, but by 1938 the type had no further value and all surviving aircraft were scrapped.

Variants
Ni-D 72: version of the Ni-D 52 with all-metal skinning; prototype flew 23 January 1928; three series aircraft delivered to Belgium in 1929 and four, somewhat modified, to Brazil in 1931

Nieuport-Delage Ni-D 52 of the Spanish Republican air force in 1936.

Ni-D 82: prototype only of 1930 with revised upper wing planform; flown first with 447-kW (600-hp) Hispano-Suiza 12Lb engine, then changed to 373-kW (500-hp) Lorraine 12Ha Petrel and new vertical tail surfaces fitted; maximum speed 275 km/h (171 mph); in August 1931 lower wing eliminated to turn aircraft into parasol monoplane, and later sold to Spain

Specification
Nieuport-Delage Ni-D 52
Type: single-seat fighter
Powerplant: one 433-kW (580-hp) Hispano-Suiza 12Hb V-12 piston engine
Performance: maximum speed 255 km/h (158 mph); service ceiling 7000 m (22,965 ft); range 400 km (249 miles)
Weights: empty equipped 1368 kg

(3,016 lb); maximum take-off 1837 kg (4,050 lb)
Dimensions: span 12.00 m (39 ft 4½ in); length 7.50 m (24 ft 7¼ in); height 3.00 m (9 ft 10 in); wing area 30.90 m² (332.62 sq ft)
Armament: two forward-firing synchronised 7.62-mm (0.3-in) Vickers machine-guns

Nieuport-Delage Ni-D 62 series

Appearing in 1927, the same year as the Ni-D 52, the **Nieuport-Delage Ni-D 62** retained the wooden structure of the earlier Ni-D 42. It was a refined version of the earlier type with some structural strengthening and a wing of increased chord with smaller ailerons, but the most noticeable external change was a larger tailplane. Between 1928 and 1931 the French Aviation Militaire took delivery of 265 Ni-D 62 single-seat fighters, while the Aéronautique Maritime acquired 50. The **Ni-D 621** was a specialised trainer, three of the type being built, and three Ni-D 62s had twin float installations for use in training French Schneider Trophy pilots.

At the time the **Ni-D 622** development was being built in 1931, the basic design was obsolescent. The Ni-D 622 had the lightweight supercharged Hispano-Suiza 12Md engine, and full-span ailerons were fitted. Production totalled 248 for the Aviation Militaire and 62 for the French navy. By 1933 the main strength of French fighter aviation lay in the little Nieuports, but their shortcomings became evident when Ni-D 622s

attempting to escort General Italo Balbo's renowned formation of Savoia-Marchetti S.55s over Strasbourg found it almost impossible to keep up with the large twin-hulled Italian flying-boats! Variants of the Ni-D 622 included three conversions, the **Ni-D 623** for speed record attempts, the **Ni-D 624** monoplane racer and the **Ni-D 625** for parachute experiments. Twelve of the **Ni-D 626** export version were sold to Peru in 1933. The **Ni-D 629** of 1932 had a Hispano-Suiza 12Mdsh engine of 373 kW (500 hp) with a supercharger for improved altitude performance, and oleopneumatic landing gear, but by the time deliveries of 50 machines to the French *escadrilles de chasse* had been completed in 1935 the design was totally obsolete. Aircraft of the Ni-D 62 series still equipped French reserve units in September 1939, and when the German *Blitzkrieg* was launched in May 1940, 143 aircraft of all versions were still on charge with the Armée de l'Air.

Specification
Nieuport-Delage Ni-D 629

Type: single-seat fighter
Powerplant: one 373-kW (500-hp) Hispano-Suiza 12Mdsh V-12 piston engine
Performance: maximum speed 260 km/h (162 mph); service ceiling 8850 m (29,035 ft); range 900 km (559 miles)
Weights: empty equipped 1385 kg (3,053 lb); maximum take-off 1880 kg

(4,145 lb)
Dimensions: span 12.00 m (39 ft 4½ in); length 7.64 m (25 ft 0¾ in); height 3.00 m (9 ft 10 in); wing area 28.95 m² (311.63 sq ft)
Armament: two fixed forward-firing synchronised 7.62-mm (0.3-in) Vickers machine-guns

Derived from the Ni-D 42, the Ni-D 62 would be the final model to feature the giant 'Y-struts' and cross-axle landing-gear.

Nieuport-Delage Ni-D 121 to Ni-D 125

Developed from the **Nieuport-Delage Ni-D 120** project, the **Ni-D 122** was a single-seat fighter, with fixed landing gear incorporating streamlined wheel fairings. It featured a wing of elliptical planform with reduced thickness in the centre section and, because of its proximity to the fuselage, a large cut-out for the pilot and his windscreen. The **Ni-D 121**, flown during November 1932, differed principally by having a 485-kW (650-hp) Lorraine 12Hars Petrel engine instead of the 515-kW (690-hp) Hispano-Suiza 12Xbrs of the Ni-D 122. Loss of the Ni-D 122 during an official demonstration flight, on 13 April 1933, merely accelerated development, the **Ni-D 123** appearing in February 1934. It could operate on wheels or twin floats, and introduced balances on the movable control surfaces, an innovation later adopted widely by other aircraft manufacturers.

The Ni-D 121 and the **Ni-D 124** (the rebuilt Ni-D 122) were also fitted with the new device. Two examples of the **Ni-D 125** flew in April and June 1934, introducing a number of modifications including an enlarged wing cut-out for the pilot, increased wing dihedral and reinforced landing gear. The engine was a Hispano-Suiza 12Ycrs *moteur-canon* of 641 kW (860 hp), armament thus being increased from twin machine-guns to include a 20-mm cannon firing through the propeller hub. Maximum speed of the Ni-D 125 was 400 km/h (249 mph), compared with 370 km/h (230 mph) for the Ni-D 121, but all aircraft in the series showed a good turn of speed and an excellent rate of climb. In 1935 a batch of six **Ni-D 123H** seaplane fighters was delivered to Peru; these had twin-float landing gear and could attain a maximum speed of 320 km/h (199 mph).

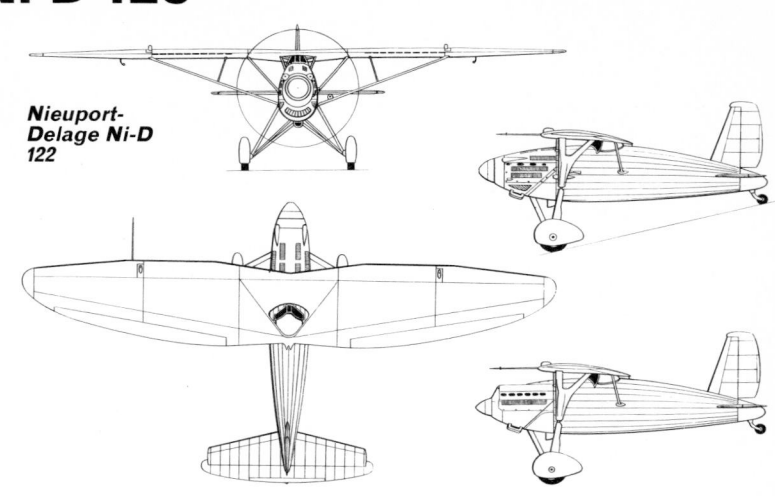

Nieuport-Delage Ni-D 122

Nieuport Ni-140

With the departure of Gustave Delage from the company the designator Ni-D was abandoned by Nieuport in 1934, the year that the **Nieuport Ni-140.01** two-seat dive-bomber appeared. It was this aircraft and its developments, with their superficial resemblance to the Ju 87 Stuka, that led to German accusations during World War II that France had stolen German aircraft blueprints during the 1930s, along with similar claims relating the Potez 63 to the Messerschmitt Bf 110.

Flying for the first time on 12 March 1935, the Ni-140 had been designed to meet a French navy requirement for a carrierborne aircraft. Of metal construc-

The Ni-140.01 bore a passing resemblance to the Ju 87 and was also a dive-bomber.

tion, the Ni-140 was a low-wing monoplane with an inverted gull wing, a glazed crew canopy, large angular single fin and rudder, and fixed landing gear, the main units of which were enclosed in trouser-type fairings. Powered by a 515-kW (690-hp) Hispano-Suiza 12Xbrs V-12 engine, the first prototype attained a maximum speed of 336 km/h (209 mph) but was lost in a forced landing in July 1935. In the following November the **Ni-140.02** made its maiden flight, differing in having increased tailplane surface area

and smaller landing gear fairings. Although the Ni-140.02 came to grief during dive-bombing trials on 15 May 1936, a single-seat **Ni-141** project was developed as the Loire-Neiuport 40, which entered production as the Loire-Nieuport 401 and 411 (see Loire-Nieuport).

Nieuport Ni-160 and Ni-161

Built to an official French requirement finalised in 1935, the **Nieuport Ni-160.01** single-seat fighter was of cantilever low-wing monoplane configuration with wide-track retractable landing gear, and powered by a 515-kW (690-hp) Hispano-Suiza 12 Xcrs *moteur-canon,* driving initially a two-bladed wooden propeller. Armament comprised the engine-mounted 20-mm cannon, plus two wing-mounted 7.5-mm (0.295-in) machine-guns. Ni-160.01 flew for the first time on 5 October 1935, being tested later with a three-bladed metal propeller and dihe-

dral on the previously flat wing. With the installation of a 641-kW (860-hp) Hispano-Suiza 12Ycrs engine and the introduction of cockpit canopy and tailplane revisions the aircraft was redesignated **Ni-161.01**. Flight trials began in April

1936, but this prototype was written off in a crash in September. As a result a full-size mock-up was exhibited at that year's Salon de l'Aéronautique. Two more prototypes were built. The **Ni-161.02** flown in October 1936 later achieved a maximum speed of 478 km/h (297 mph) at 4000 m (13,125 ft), proving faster than any rivals built to the same

official requirement. The **Ni.161.03** of March 1938 introduced a variable-pitch propeller and later acquired two auxiliary vertical tail surfaces, but official attention switched to later designs and hopes for production orders faded. The Ni-161.03 was converted for parachute development work, and **Ni-161.04** was scrapped before completion.

Designed initially as a fighter aircraft, the Nieuport Ni-160 spent all its flying days as a testbed, being fitted with various combinations of engines, guns and other weapons.

Nieuport-Delage Ni-D 390 and Ni-D 391

Developed to the requirements of the Compagnie Aérienne Francaise, the first **Nieuport-Delage Ni-D 390** (F-AIMP) made its initial flight at the end of 1927, being followed by seven more production machines. All were powered by the

134-kW (180-hp) Hispano-Suiza 8Ac engine and accommodated two or three passengers in the cabin. The company also used 20 **Ni-D 391** aircraft, 18 built from scratch and two converted from Ni-D 390s, the Ni-D 391 differing from its

predecessor in having a 149-kW (200-hp) Armstrong Siddeley Lynx radial engine. The **Ni-D 391/2** of 1931 retained the Lynx engine, but had a lengthened fuselage and maximum take-off weight increased by 100 kg (220 lb) to 1500 kg

(3,307 lb); one Ni-D 391 was converted as an air ambulance and flown for a brief period as the **Ni-D 391/3** during 1932. Little was heard of the sole **Ni-D 393**, also of 1931, which was powered by a 179-kW (240-hp) Lorraine 7Ma Mizar engine. The Ni-D 391 had a wing span of 10.60 m (34 ft 9¼ in), and a maximum speed of 175 km/h (109 mph).

Nieuport-Delage Ni-D 450 and Ni-D 650

Two examples of the **Nieuport-Delage Ni-D 450,** a twin-float low-wing monoplane powered by a new and untried 1253-kW (1,680-hp) Hispano-Suiza

18R engine, were built for the 1929 Schneider Trophy contest. In 1928 a full-scale mock-up had been built and the airframes were completed in July 1929, but

problems with the powerplant and the elaborate wing-mounted system of radiators caused delays, and Nieuport-Delage was forced to withdraw from the

Schneider contest in that autumn. The **Nieuport Ni-D 450.01** prototype was launched on 8 April 1930, but overturned during a take-off run in July. The second machine was used as a trainer for French pilots entered for the 1931 Schneider Trophy contest. Redesignated **Ni-D**

650, its external appearance was little changed, and it was lost in an emergency landing on the Seine in July 1931. It was then replaced by the **Ni-D 650.02**, which had a smaller wing and was later fitted with twin-step floats and an enlarged rudder; but this did not fly for the first time until November 1931 and was then scrapped after only two short flights.

The definitive aircraft for the 1931 Schneider Trophy event were to be **Ni-D 651** with a 1491-kW (2,000-hp) Lorraine 12Rcr Radium engine and the **Ni-D 652** with the Renault 12Ncr of similar power. Neither powerplant was

beyond the early testing stage by the time of the contest, although the airframe of the Ni-D 651 had been completed. As a result there were no French entries, and the 1931 contest was a British walkover.

The Nieuport-Delage 459s were built solely as Schneider Trophy contestants in 1929. As such they were naturally seaplanes and were of similar appearance to their contemporary British and Italian rivals. They were powered by Hispano-Suiza engines with an impressive 18 cylinders.

Nieuport-Delage Ni-D 580

The first example of the **Nieuport-Delage Ni-D 580** all-metal parasol-wing monoplane flew in early 1931. In the R.2 (two-seat reconnaissance) category, and intended for the French Aviation Militaire, it was followed by a second version which retained the original 485-kW (650-hp) Hispano-Suiza 12Nb engine, but introduced several improvements. Armed with four machine-guns, the Ni-D

580 had a maximum speed of 265 km/h (165 mph).

The Nieuport-Dealge Ni-D 580 was an armed battlefield reconnaissance aircraft which bore all the trademarks of the role, with tandem open cockpits and slow yet very manoeuvrable flying characteristics.

Nieuport-Delage Ni-D 590

The **Nieuport-Delage Ni-D 590** was a cantilever high-wing cabin monoplane in the Col.3 category, a three-seat aircraft intended for general-purpose duties in French overseas possessions. Flown for the first time in July 1932, it

was powered by three 224-kW (300-hp) Lorraine 9Na Algol radials with Townend rings and, unusually, had a machine-gun position in the fuselage with a good downward field of fire. A second example was built and flown in 1933, this

The Ni-D 590 was a multi-role aircraft built for use in French overseas colonies. Its three engines provided the power for operations in such climates.

Ni-D 690 being a direct development of the Ni-D 590, but powered by a single 224-kW (300-hp) Algol radial. Much

smaller and lighter than its predecessor, it was not successful.

Nieuport-Delage Ni-D 640, 641 and 642

After the unsuccessful **Nieuport-Delage Ni-D 540** of 1931, a high-wing monoplane transport accommodating eight passengers plus 800 kg (1,764 lb) of freight, the company developed the smaller and more compact **Ni-D 640**. Powered by a 164-kW (220-hp) Wright J-5C radial engine, it was an all-wood high-wing cantilever design with a two-seat enclosed cockpit for pilot and co-

pilot forward of the wing, with a cabin for four passengers aft. The next 12 aircraft were completed as **Ni-D 641** machines, differing in having the 179-kW (240-hp) Lorraine 7M Mizar radial engine. Seven were flown by STAR (the Société des Transports Aériens Rapides) on its cargo/passenger services from Paris. Ni-D 641 F-AJRE was owned by Suzanne Deutsch de la Meurthe and

named *Icare II*; she later acquired a second example, F-ILEV. The original Ni-D 640 had been converted into an air ambulance for two stretcher patients, but was then fitted with a Mizar engine to become the thirteenth Ni-D 641. The sole **Ni-D 642**, powered by an Armstrong Siddeley Lynx Major engine, did not find a buyer and was soon scrapped. An experimental **Ni-D 740**, a logical de-

velopment of the Ni-641, was built in 1930 to an official requirement for a two-seat night mail monoplane. Larger than the Ni-D 641, and powered by three 71-kW (95-hp) Salmson 7Ac radials, the two examples built could each carry 300 kg (661 lb) of mail, but had unsatisfactory performance and did not enter service.

The Ni-D 641 spanned 15.40 m (50 ft 6¼ in), had a maximum take-off weight of 1900 kg (4,189 lb) and a maximum speed of 205 km/h (127 mph).

Nieuport-Delage Ni-D 941

Displayed at the 1932 Paris Salon de l'Aéronautique, the **Nieuport-Delage Ni-D 941** was a tailless low-wing cabin monoplane reminiscent of the Lippisch

designs which appeared in Germany. Mounted on fixed tricycle gear the aircraft, intended as a tourer, was powered by an 89-kW (120-hp) Lorraine engine

mounted at the rear of the fuselage nacelle as a pusher. Flown for the first time in February 1934, the sole example was then modified to overcome stability

problems and re-engined with a 101-kW (135-hp) Salmson. In this form it was flown at Villacoublay test centre from September 1935, under the new designation **Ni-D 942**, but no further development was undertaken.

Nieuport-Delage Sesquiplan

The **Nieuport-Delage Sesquiplan** racer which appeared in 1921, designed by Nieuport-Delage engineer Mary, was a sleek shoulder-wing single-seat monoplane powered by a supercharged 224-kW (300-hp) Hispano-Suiza 8Fb engine. Its name came from the auxiliary aerofoil surface attached to the axle of the fixed landing gear. The two examples built were entered for the October 1921 Coupe Deutsche de la Meurthe speed event, and on 26 September Sadi Lecointe flew his aircraft at a speed of 330.275 km/h (205.223 mph), but his aircraft came to grief during the race with a smashed propeller. It was Kirsch in the second Sesquiplan who

won, completing the course at an average 278.360 km/h (172.965 mph).

The surviving aircraft later had revised

The Nieuport-Delage Sesquiplan (sometimes referred to as the model 29) was their most successful racing aircraft. Always in the hands of pilot Sadi Lecointe, the aircraft held the FAI-ratified absolute world speed record no less than seven times between 1920 and 1923. Successive modifications increased its speed from 275.22km/h (171.01 mph) to 374.95 km/h (233.096 mph).

vertical tail surfaces and a 298-kW (400-hp) Wright H.3 installed. Then named

Eugène Gilbert, this aircraft was flown by Sadi Lecointe to establish a world speed record of 375.132 km/h (233.096 mph) on 13 October 1923.

Noorduyn Norseman

Noorduyn Aircraft Ltd, a name soon changed to Noorduyn Aviation Ltd, was established in Canada during 1935, occupying the former Curtiss-Reid factory near Montreal. Work had started in 1934, before formation of the company, on the design of a medium-size versatile transport aircraft that would appeal to a wide civil and/or military market, be suitable for operation in the severe climatic conditions of the Canadian winter, and have optional float, ski or wheel landing gear to give it go-anywhere capability. Named **Noorduyn Norseman I**, the prototype (CF-AYO) was flown first on 14 November 1935, a braced high-wing monoplane with fixed tailwheel landing gear and powered by a Canadian-built 313-kW (420-hp) Wright R-975-E3 radial engine. An enclosed and heated cockpit with side-by-side seating for two was located forward of the wing centre-section, with behind and below it a roomy cabin for eight passengers, seated on easily removable bench seats so that little time was needed to convert the interior for cargo operations. An additional 0.57 m³ (20.0 cu ft) of baggage/cargo space was provided beneath the cabin floor. Initial production version was the **Norseman II** with only minor changes from the prototype, but it was soon discovered that the Norseman was underpowered with the Wright engine, leading first to the **Norseman III** with a 336-kW (450-hp) Pratt & Whitney Wasp

SC (only three built), and the **Norseman IV** with the 410-kW (550-hp) Pratt & Whitney S3H1 or R-1340-AN-1 Wasp engine. The same powerplant was used in the **Norseman V** and **Norseman VI**, the latter designation being used for the aircraft produced during World War II for the RCAF and USAAF, with the designation Norseman V reserved by patriotic Bob Noorduyn for the first postwar civil version with the V signifying victory. In early 1946 the Canadian Car & Foundry (CCF) company acquired manufacturing and sales rights for the Norseman. It then developed a single **Norseman VII** prototype with wing and tailplane of all-metal construction and a lengthened cabin, but although this was flown in 1951, no production examples were built. In May 1953 CCF sold all rights in the Norseman to a specially formed company, Noorduyn Norseman Aircraft Ltd, which has since continued to provide product support to the total of about 50 aircraft which are still in use. Total production by Noorduyn and CCF numbered about 900 aircraft, the majority of them being supplied initially for military use during World War II. RCAF acquisitions began in 1938 with four Norseman IV aircraft, which it operated as wireless trainers under the designation **Norseman Mk IVW**, with additional purchases made after the outbreak of war. Major buyer was the US Army Air Force which, after testing a single Nor-

seman IV, acquired it and six other examples under the designation **YC-64**. Subsequent contracts for Norseman Vs reached a total of 749, designated initially **C-64A** and later **UC-64A**. Three of this total were transferred to the US Navy, which designated them **JA-1**, and under the designation **UC-64B** six with twin floats were used by the US Army Corps of Engineers. Other military operators of the Norseman during or post-World War II included the air forces of Australia, Brazil, Honduras, Indonesia, Netherlands East Indies, Norway and Sweden.

Specification
Noorduyn Norseman V
(landplane)
Type: utility transport
Powerplant: one 410-kW (550-hp)

Extremely reliable and structurally sound, the Noorduyn Norseman had landing gear stubs to which could be attached wheels, floats or skis, making this classic design a true 'bush' aircraft expressly designed for harsh northern environments.

Pratt & Whitney R-1340-AN-1 Wasp radial piston engine
Performance: maximum speed 249 km/h (155 mph); service ceiling 5180 m (17,000 ft); range 1851 km (1,150 miles)
Weights: empty 2123 kg (4,680 lb); maximum take-off 3357 kg (7,400 lb)
Dimensions: span 15.70 m (51 ft 6 in); length 9.75 m (32 ft 0 in); height 3.12 m (10 ft 3 in); wing area 30.19 m² (325.0 sq ft)

Nord 1000 Pingouin and 1100 Noralpha

In early 1942, production of the Messerschmitt Bf 108 Taifun was transferred to the Société Nationale de Constructions Aéronautiques du Nord, known usually as Nord or SNCAN, at Les Mureaux in France. The production line established there built 170 Bf 108s for Germany before the liberation of France in 1944. Nord then continued production of this aircraft under the designation **Nord 1000**, replacing the standard Argus engine in 1945 with the 174-kW (233-hp) Renault 6Q 11 which brought a designation change for this three-seat aircraft to **Nord 1001 Pingouin I**. The **Nord 1002 Pingouin II** which followed, powered by a Renault 6Q 10 of similar power, differed by providing four-seat accommodation. Combined production of Pingouin I and II aircraft was 250, the majority of them finding use in communications and liaison roles with the French armed services.

During 1943-44 Nord built two prototypes of the Messerschmitt Me 208,

which differed from the Bf 108 by introducing retractable tricycle landing gear. Only one survived until the liberation, being designated **Nord 1100 Noralpha**, and this was developed by the company as the **Nord 1101** and **Nord 1102** with Renault 6Q 10 and 6Q 11 engines respectively. The respective designations **Ramier I** and **Ramier II** were allocated by the French armed services. Combined Nord 1101/1102 production was 200 aircraft. Under the designation **N 1104 Noralpha**, Nord used one aircraft to flight-test a 179-kW (240-hp) Potez 6Dba engine, and two N 1101

The Nord N.1100 Noralpha four-seat cabin monoplane was basically a tricycle landing gear version of the pre-war Messerschmitt Bf 108. The version shown is a Nord N.1101, known as the Ramier 1 in French military service. Over 200 Noralphas were built.

Ramier Is were converted for similar tests with the Turboméca Astazou turboshaft engine under the designation **N 1110 Nord-Astazou**, the first (F-WJDQ) being flown on 15 October 1959.

Specification
Nord 1101 Noralpha
Type: four-seat cabin monoplane

Powerplant: one 174-kW (233-hp) Renault 6Q 10 inline piston engine
Performance: maximum speed 305 km/h (189 mph); service ceiling 5900 m (19,355 ft); range 1200 km (745 miles)
Weights: empty 948 kg (2,090 lb); maximum take-off 1645 kg (3,627 lb)
Dimensions: span 11.48 m (37 ft 8 in); length 8.53 m (28 ft 0 in); height 3.25 m (10 ft 8 in); wing area 17.37 m² (187.0 sq ft)

Nord 1200 Norécrin

To participate in a design contest for a two/three-seat cabin monoplane sponsored by the French ministry of transport, Nord built the **Nord 1200 Norécrin** prototype (F-BBBJ) which had the same general configuration as the Nord 1100 series. As first flown on 15 December 1945 it was powered by a 75-kW (100-hp) Mathis G4R engine, but the

initial **N 1201 Norécrin I** production version differed by having a 104-kW (140-hp) Renault 4P01 engine and three-seat accommodation, being redesignated **N 1203 Norécrin II** when powered by the 101-kW (135-hp) Regnier 4L00 engine. A four-seat **N 1202 Norécrin** was tested in 1946 with a 119-kW (160-hp) Potez 4D-1 engine, leading to the

four-seat **N 1203/Norécrin II** with the Regnier 4L00 engine, introduced in 1948, which was followed in 1949 by the **N 1203/III Norécrin III** with modified landing gear. The **N 1203/IV Norécrin IV** introduced the 127-kW (170-hp) Regnier 4L02 engine, and the **N 1203/V Norécrin V** was a similarly-powered two-seat military version armed with machine-guns and rockets. Production was suspended in 1953, being resumed in 1955 with the **N 1203/VI Norécrin**

VI which introduced the 108-kW (145-hp) Regnier 4L14 engine, and the final variants of 1959 were the **N 1204 Norécrin** and **N 1204/II Norécrin** with 93-kW (125-hp) Continental C125 and 108-kW (145-hp) Continental C145 flat-four engine respectively. A total of approximately 470 Norécrins of all versions had been built when production ended.

Specification
Nord 1203/II Norécrin II
Type: four-seat cabin monoplane
Powerplant: one 101-kW (135-hp) Regnier 4L00 inline piston engine
Performance: maximum speed 280 km/h (174 mph); service ceiling 5000 m (16,405 ft); range 900 km (559 miles)
Weights: empty 652 kg (1,437 lb);

maximum take-off 1050 kg (2,315 lb)
Dimensions: span 10.22 m (33 ft 6¼ in); length 7.21 m (23 ft 8 in); height 2.90 m (9 ft 6 in); wing area 13.00 m² (139.93 sq ft)

The Norécrin series was one of France's most successful aircraft designs in the years following World War II.

Nord 1220

The design of a three-seat light trainer was initiated in 1948 under the designation **Nord 1220**, this having retractable tricycle landing gear and being of similar overall configuration to the early-production Norécrin. However, fixed tailwheel landing gear was finalised for the **N 1221 Norélan** prototype (F-WFAU), first flown on 30 June 1948 on the power of a 134-kW (180-hp) Mathis 8G20 inverted Vee engine. Re-engined with a 134-kW (180-hp) 4LO4 inline engine the

The most obvious distinguishing feature of the Nord N.1221 Norélan is the pronounced dihedral angle of the wings. This feature is usually intended to make a design aerodynamically stable.

machine was redesignated **N 1222 Norélan**, and this aircraft plus one other example (both powered by a 179-kW/240-hp Argus AL 10C inverted Vee engine and in two-seat configuration) were flown under the designation **N 1223 Norélan**. No production orders resulted, and only one other two-seat

version was flown as a testbed for the 179-kW (240-hp) Potez 6D0 inline engine

under the designation **N 1226 Norélan**.

Nord 1400 Noroit

Under the designation **Nord 1400**, Nord designed a maritime reconnaissance and air-sea rescue amphibian flying-boat for service with the French navy. A cantilever gullwing monoplane with a two-step all-metal hull, the aircraft had accommodation for a crew of seven, plus a roomy rear cabin with a large sliding door on the port side for rescue operations. It was first flown as a flying-boat on 6 January 1949, as the **N 1400-01 Noroit** (F-WFDL), then powered by two 1193-kW (1,600-hp) Gnome-Rhône 14R radial engines; retractable tailwheel landing gear to provide amphibious capability was installed initially on the **N 1400-02** and on the N 1400-01 at a later date. The **N 1401 Noroit** (F-WFKU) was flown on 6 August 1949 with two 1342-kW (1,800-

The N.1402 was one of the West's last production flying-boats. A formidably-armed reconnaissance and rescue type, the prototype had no weapons.

hp) SNECMA-built Junkers Jumo engines, the second example (F-SFKN) being flown later with similar powerplant, and both were tested in 1950 with two Bristol Hercules radial engines. These pre-production aircraft, plus 21 other examples, were all completed to **N 1402 Noroit** standard for the French navy's Escadrille 5F, the last of them being delivered in 1956.

Specification
Nord 1402 Noroit
Type: reconnaissance and air-sea

rescue flying-boat
Powerplant: two 1566-kW (2,100-hp) SNECMA 12H00 (Jumo 213A) inverted V-12 piston engines
Performance: maximum speed 270 km/h (230 mph) at 2650 m (8,695 ft); maximum range 3450 km (2,144 miles)
Weights: not known

Dimensions: span 31.60 m (103 ft 8 in); length 22.05 m (72 ft 4 in); height 6.85 m (22 ft 5½ in); wing area 100.00 m² (1,076.43 sq ft)
Armament: six 20-mm cannon, in pairs in nose, dorsal and tail turrets, plus provision for bombs in engine nacelles and eight rocket projectiles mounted on brackets on the hull

Nord 1402/1405 Gerfaut

Designed originally by Arsenal, which became SFECMAS after the post-war rationalisation of the French aircraft industry and which in turn was merged into Nord, the **1402A Gerfaut 1A** was a delta-wing research aircraft. Its configuration featured thin delta wings with 58° of sweepback on the leading edge, swept vertical tail surfaces with a high-set delta tailplane, a retractable tricycle landing gear, and engine mounted within the fuselage. When flown for the first time on 15 January 1954 it was powered by a 27-kN (6,173-lb) thrust SNECMA Atar 101C turbojet, and on 3 August 1954 the Gerfaut became the

After a very successful high-speed research programme, the Nord N.1405 Gerfaut II was used for airborne radar development.

first European aircraft to exceed Mach 1 in level flight without any form of power augmentation. The **N1402B Gerfaut 1B** had larger wings, an Atar 101D1 engine of similar thrust, plus some other improvements, and flew for the first time on 9 February 1955. Finally came the **Nord 1405 Gerfaut II** of basically the same configuration, but with a re-

fined structure and fitted with a 37-kN (8,378-lb) thrust Atar 101F. The Gerfaut II made its first flight on 17 April 1956 but was subsequently re-engined with an Atar G21 developing 39 kN (8,818 lb)

thrust with afterburning. On completion of its research programme, the aircraft was used to test the Aladin intercept radar then under development, at high altitudes and speeds.

Nord 1500 Griffon I and II

After early tests of the Gerfaut la, Nord designed and built the **Nord 1500-01 Griffon I** research aircraft, which was intended to flight-test a combined turbojet-ramjet power unit. A delta wing aircraft with 60° of sweepback on the leading edge, the N 1500 had wings with elevons for control in pitch and roll. Thus the tail unit comprised only swept vertical surfaces, and fixed foreplanes were mounted on each side of the forward fuselage. The Griffon I was flown for the first time on 20 September 1955. Initially

The Griffon II was both turbojet and ramjet powered.

powered by a 4,100-kg (9,039-lb) thrust SNECMA Atar 101G21 turbojet, it was flown later with a 3800-kg (8,378-lb) thrust Atar 101F. At the completion of initial testing the airframe was modified to accept a 3500-kg (7,716-lb) thrust Atar 101E3 turbojet within the ducting of an integral ramjet of Nord design, the turbojet being located just forward of the ramjet burners. Then redesignated **N**

1500-02 Griffon II, it was flown first on 23 January 1957, completing more

than 200 test flights before the Nord research programme ended in 1959.

Nord 1601

Under the designation **Nord 1601,** Nord designed a single-seat twin turbojet-powered aircraft to investigate the aerodynamic capability and efficiency of swept wings and related high-lift devices. A cantilever mid-wing monoplane with 33° of sweepback on the wing leading edges, the N 1601 had a wing incorporating ailerons, spoilers, leading-edge slats and trailing-edge flaps. The configuration included swept

tail surfaces, and there were retractable tricycle landing gear and two 1814-kg (4,000-lb) thrust Rolls-Royce Derwent 5 turbojet engines in underslung wing-mounted nacelles on each side of the fuselage. The pilot was accommodated on a Martin-Baker ejector seat in a cockpit enclosed by a jettisonable canopy. The aircraft was first flown on 24 January 1950, and the research programme of the 12.46 m (40 ft 10½ in) span N 1601, which had a maximum speed of 1000 km/h (621 mph) and a ceiling of 12000 m (39,370 ft), provided

valuable design information. An all-weather fighter version of this aircraft was allocated the project number **N 1600** but was not built.

The quirky appearance of the Nord 1601 is explained by the fact that it was intended as a pure research vehicle. Its field of investigation was that of swept-wing flying characteristics and associated high-speed handling. Later it was fitted with experimental high-lift flaps.

Nord 1700 and 1750 Norelfe

A three-seat helicopter of very clean configuration, the **Nord 1750 Norelfe** could be identified easily by its single main rotor and absence of an anti-torque tail rotor. The design had been initiated under the designation **N 1700 Norelfe**, but the two experimental aircraft built were given the designation N 1750 Norelfe, each of them being powered by a Turboméca Artouste turboshaft engine. For torque control the efflux of the Artouste was carried through the tailboom and ejected from a movable duct under pedal control. At forward speeds in excess of 80 km/h (50 mph) this

Powered by a 194-ekW (260-hp) turboshaft, the Nord Norelfe stemmed from the MATRA Cantineau M.C. 101A. The N 1750 is significant as an early NOTAR (NO TAil Rotor) design; instead of a conventional tail rotor it used engine efflux for lateral control.

system was disconnected and transferred automatically to twin vertical tail surfaces which, at such speeds, were adequate to counter torque and could be moved by the same foot pedals for directional control. Both N 1750s and produc-

tion rights were sold to the Spanish company Aerotécnica SA in 1954, this

organisation then redesignating the type the **Aerotécnica AC-13A**.

Nord 2500 Noratlas

Designed as a military transport for service with the French air force, the **Nord 2500 Noratlas** prototype (F-WFKL) was flown for the first time on 10 September 1949. Of similar twin-boom configuration to the Fairchild C-82 and C-119 Flying Boxcar, the prototype was powered by two 1212-kW (1625-hp) SNECMA-built Gnome-Rhône 14R radial engines. This was followed by two **N 2501** prototypes which introduced the powerplant intended for production aircraft, comprising two 1521-kW (2,040-hp) SNECMA-built Bristol Hercules 739 radial engines, and the first of these (F-WFRG) was flown on 28 November 1950. Satisfactory testing led to the initiation of production, and the Noratlas became standard equipment in the air forces of France, West Germany and Israel, providing valuable long-term service. Operated normally by a crew of four or five, the Noratlas has the capacity for 7.88 tonnes (7.5 tons) of cargo, or can accommodate 45 troops (or passengers in civil use), 36 fully-equipped paratroopers, or 18 stretchers and medical attendants when used for casualty evacuation. The German Luftwaffe received a total of 186 of these transports, 25 built by Nord and the balance produced under licence in Germany by the Flugzeugbau Nord. When production ended in October 1961, French and German sources had built a total of 425 Noratlas aircraft in several versions, detailed under Variants, and the type remained in service until the late 1980s.

Nord N 2501 Noratlas of Luftwaffe Luftransportgeschwader (LTG) 61, based at Neubiberg during the 1960s.

Variants
N 2501: standard production version with SNECMA Hercules 739 engines
N 2501IS: version built for Israeli air force, generally as N 2501 above

N 2501A: civil transport version, with two 1230-kW (1,650-hp) SNECMA 758/759 Hercules engines, for Union Aéromaritime de Transport (UAT)
N 2501E: redesignation of standard N 2501 for flight testing of auxiliary powerplant comprising two 400-kg (882-lb) thrust Turboméca Marboré II turbojets mounted in wingtip pods to improve 'hot-and-high' performance
N 2502: civil version for Air Algérie and UAT, with powerplant comprising two SNECMA Hercules 758/759 engines and two Marboré IIE turbojets
N 2502A: civil version as N 2502 for UAT
N 2502B: cargo version with SNECMA Hercules 758/759 engines
N 2502C: cargo version as N 2502B
N 2503: redesignation of original production prototype (F-WRFG) following installation of two 1864-kW (2,500-hp) Pratt & Whitney R-2800-CB17 radial engines for evaluation; first flown January 1956
N 2504: version for use by French

navy as a flying classroom for ASW crews, powerplant as in N 2501E prototype
N 2505: projected ASW version, not built
N 2506: assault transport version with powerplant as N 2504
N 2507: rescue version, powerplant as N 2504
N 2508: cargo version with

The Noratlas served the French air force as a transport from 1951. The final specialist ECM versions were not withdrawn for almost another 40 years.

powerplant comprising two Pratt & Whitney R-2800-CB17 radial engines plus two Turboméca Marboré IIE turbojets

N 2508B: cargo version, generally as above, and with identical powerplant
N 2509: project only, not built
N 2510: project for ASW version of Noratlas, not built

Specification
Nord 2501
Type: twin-engine cargo transport
Powerplant: two 1521-kW (2,040-hp) SNECMA-built Hercules 739 sleeve-valve radial piston engines

Performance: maximum speed 440 km/h (273 mph); service ceiling 7500 m (24,605 ft); range 3000 km (1,864 miles)
Weights: empty equipped 13075 kg (28,825 lb); maximum take-off

21000 kg (46,297 lb)
Dimensions: span 32.50 m (106 ft 7½ in); length 21.95 m (72 ft 0 in); height 6.00 m (19 ft 8¼ in); wing area 101.20 m² (1,089.34 sq ft)

Nord 3200

To meet a requirement of the French army air force for a two seat primary trainer, Nord flew on 17 April 1957 the first (F-MAJD) of 50 **Nord 3202** production aircraft, derived from the **N 3200** and **N 3201** with a 179-kW (240-hp) Salmson 8AS04 and 127-kW (170-hp) Regnier 4L22 engine respectively. A cantilever low-wing monoplane with fixed tailwheel landing gear, the N 3202 pro-

vided tandem two-seat enclosed accommodation for the instructor (rear seat) and pupil, and the production N 3202 was powered by the 179-kW (240-hp) Potez 4D32 inline engine. A second production batch of 50 had the designation **N 3202B**, differing by having the 4D32 engine replaced by a Potez 4D34. N 3202 aircraft with a radio compass and equipped for instrument flight training became redesignated **N 3212**.

Specification

Nord 3202B
Type: two-seat primary trainer
Powerplant: one 194-kW (260-hp) Potez 4D34 inline piston engine
Performance: maximum speed 260 km/h (162 mph) at sea level; range 1000 km (621 miles)
Weights: empty 860 kg (1,896 lb); maximum take-off 1220 kg (2,690 lb)
Dimensions: span 9.50 m (31 ft 2 in); length 8.12 m (26 ft 7¾ in); height 2.82 m (9 ft 3 in); wing area 16.25 m² (174.92 sq ft)

Possessing no special features, the N 3202 was an unexceptional but useful trainer for the Armée de l'Air in the early 1960s.

Nord 3400

Designed as Nord's submission to meet a French army air force requirement for a two-seat observation aircraft, suitable for use also in a secondary casualty evacuation role, the **Nord 3400** prototype (F-MBTD) was flown for the first time on 20 January 1958. A braced high-wing monoplane with fixed tailwheel landing gear, the aircraft had an enclosed cabin providing an excellent field of view, and two-section doors on each

side of the fuselage simplified the task of loading or unloading a casualty and stretcher. The first prototype, powered by a 179-kW (240-hp) Potez 4D30 engine, was followed by a second prototype later in the year. This differed by having a wing of increased area and a more powerful 4D34 engine. In this latter configuration the N 3400 was ordered into production, the first of the series aircraft being delivered on 9 July 1959, and the last of 150 during March 1961.

The N 3400 spotter plane was a direct result of experience in World War II and Indo-China.

Specification
Nord 3400 (production version)
Type: two-seat observation/casualty-evacuation aircraft
Powerplant: one 194-kW (260-hp) Potez 4D34 inline piston engine
Performance: maximum speed 235 km/h (146 mph) at sea level; range 1000 km (621 miles)
Weights: empty 920 kg (2,028 lb);

maximum take-off 1350 kg (2,976 lb)
Dimensions: span 13.00 m (42 ft 7¾ in); length 8.42 m (27 ft 8 in); height 2.20 m (7 ft 3 in); wing area 20.82 m² (224.10 sq ft)

Norman Thompson aircraft

In 1909 Norman Thompson entered partnership with Douglas White to form an aircraft design and construction company known as White & Thompson Ltd at Middleton-on-Sea near Bognor Regis, Sussex. By October 1915 the name had been changed to Norman Thompson Flight Company Ltd, and the first product to emerge from this new organisation was an attractive twin-engine biplane flying-boat which was designated **Norman Thompson N.T.4**. Of the same general configuration as the Curtiss H-4 (Model 6), it differed by being somewhat larger, with a redesigned hull, and a powerplant of two 112-kW•(150-hp) Hispano-Suiza engines mounted between the wings, each driving a pusher propeller. Satisfactory testing led to Admiralty orders for 50 N.T.4s for service with the RNAS, but after the initial batch of six had been delivered, the installation of 149-kW (200-hp) Hispano-Suiza engines brought the redesignation **N.T.4A**. Two prototypes of an improved version, which had the designation **N.2C**, were built and flown in 1918, but were too late to see operational service and no production examples followed. They differed from the N.T.4s by having a hull similar to the Felixstowe F

'boats, a revised tail unit, and power provided by two 149-kW (200-hp) Sunbeam Arab engines.

Most extensively built of the Norman Thompson designs was the **N.T.2B**, a two-seat unequal-span biplane flying-boat. Its enclosed cabin, with side-by-side seating and dual controls, made it ideal for use as a trainer, and its value to the RNAS is well illustrated by the construction of more than 200. As flown originally the N.T.2B was powered by a 119-kW (160-hp) Beardmore engine, and the first 50 production aircraft had either this engine or a 112-kW (150-hp) Beardmore. In late 1917 the 149-kW (200-hp) Sunbeam Arab was introduced, to be replaced later by the more reliable Hispano-Suiza engine of similar power. The N.T.2B was the standard flying-boat trainer in service with the RNAS/RAF until the end of World War I, required in numbers that were beyond the manufacturing capability of the Norman Thompson company, and resulting in subcontract construction by S. E. Saunders Ltd and the Supermarine Aviation Works. Last of the Norman Thompson 'boats was the two-seat **N.1B** biplane prototype, intended for armed patrol, but its performance did not meet official re-

quirements and no further examples were built.

Specification
Norman Thompson N.T.2B
Type: two-seat flying-boat trainer
Powerplant: one 149-kW (200-hp) Sunbeam Arab V-8 piston engine
Performance: maximum speed 137 km/h (85 mph) at 610 m (2,000 ft); service ceiling 3475 m (11,400 ft)
Weights: empty 1053 kg (2,321 lb);

The Norman-Thompson N.T.2B was a useful flying-boat trainer and is seen here in the form of an aircraft with a Sunbeam Arab engine, though a Beardmore had been fitted earlier.

maximum take-off 1437 kg (3,169 lb)
Dimensions: span 14.75 m (48 ft 4¾ in); length 8.34 m (27 ft 4½ in); height 3.25 m (10 ft 8 in); wing area 42.08 m² (453.0 sq ft)

North American A-5 Vigilante

Designed to meet a US Navy requirement for a high-performance all-weather attack aircraft, the **North American NA-247**, known at first as the NAG-PAW (North American General Purpose Attack Weapon), won an order for two **YA3J-1** prototypes on 29 June 1956. The name **Vigilante** was allocated soon after this, and the A3J designation was changed subsequently to **A-5.** The design's cantilever monoplane swept wing incorporated no ailerons, roll control being by the use of spoilers in con-

juction with differential use of an all-moving tailplane on each side of the fuselage and, when it entered service, the Vigilante was the first US production aircraft to introduce variable-geometry intakes for its two General Electric J79 engines. The first of the prototypes, then powered by two YJ79-GE-2 engines each developing 6804-kg (15,000-lb) afterburning thrust, was flown for the first time on 31 August 1958 and carrier trials were completed aboard the USS Saratoga in July 1960. Initial production

version was the **A3J-1 (A-5A)**, US Navy Squadron VAH-7 becoming the first operational unit in June 1961. The primary weapon of the A3J-1 was a free-fall nuclear bomb ejected rearwards from a bomb bay between the tailpipes of the two turbojet engines. A3J-1 production totalled 57 aircraft. This version was followed by an interim long-range bomber version designated **A3J-2 (A-5B)**, incorporating greater fuel capacity and aerodynamic improvements, but because of changes in US Navy

policy only six were built and then converted to serve as a long-range unarmed reconnaissance version designated **A3J-3P (RA-5C)**, equipped with side-looking airborne radar, cameras and electronic counter-measures equipment. The first RA-5C was flown on 30 June 1962, being followed by 55 new production aircraft and the conversion to reconnaissance configuration of 53 A3J-1s. The first squadron equipped with the RA-5C Vigilante was RVAH-5 which, in June 1964, was operating from the USS Ranger, and other Vigilante squadrons included RVAH-1, RVAH-7, RVAH-9 and RVAH-11.

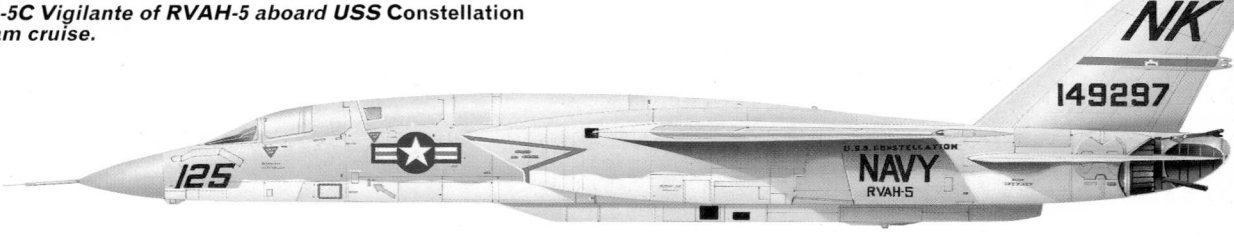

North American RA-5C Vigilante of RVAH-5 aboard USS Constellation during a 1968 Vietnam cruise.

Specification
North American RA-5C
Type: carrier-based long-range reconnaissance aircraft
Powerplant: two 8101-kg (17,860-lb) afterburning thrust General Electric J79-GE-10 turbojets
Performance: maximum speed Mach 2.1; operational ceiling 14750 m (48,400 ft); range 4828 km (3,000 miles)
Weights: empty 17009 kg (37,498 lb); maximum take-off 29937 kg (66,000 lb)
Dimensions: span 16.15 m (53 ft 0 in); length 23.32 m (76 ft 6 in); height 5.91 m (19 ft 4¾ in); wing area 70.05 m² (754.0 sq ft)

The first A-5 Vigilante operational cruise was aboard the USS Enterprise in February 1962. As a Mach 2 strike aircraft the Vigilante had a relatively short career, but in its RA-5C reconnaissance form it was an unparalleled asset. Originally designated A3J-3P, the RA-5C flew in prototype form in June 1962. It integrated all the improvements in range and aerodynamic design that had been developed for the abandoned A-5B project and utilised them to equally good effect.

North American AJ-2 Savage

Developed to a US Navy specification for a high-performance carrier-based bomber, with cruise power provided by two 1790-kW (2,400-hp) Pratt & Whitney R-2800 radials, boosted for the attack phase by a 2087-kg (4,600-lb) thrust Allison J33-A-19 turbojet engine, three **North American NA-146 (XAJ-1)** prototypes were ordered on 24 June 1946. The first flew on 3 July 1948, and 40 production **AJ-1 Savage** (later **A-2A**) aircraft were built, with deliveries to US Navy Squadron VC-5 beginning in September 1949. Modified tail surfaces, additional fuel capacity and more powerful engines were features of 70 **AJ-2** (later **A-2B**) aircraft, the first of which flew on 19 February 1953, while 30 **AJ-2P** reconnaissance aircraft were built with modified noses to house cameras, the first AJ-2P being flown on 6 March 1952. A number of AJ-1s and AJ-2s were later converted for use as tankers.

The AJ-2 Savage was a 'strategic' type purely because it was designed to deliver a nuclear weapon. Its curious mixed jet and propeller configuration was due to the lack of performance of early jet engines and the weight of early nuclear bombs. After a military career many Savages, like these, were converted to civilian water bombers.

North American XA2J-1

In 1948 North American began work on the **NA-163** turboprop-powered derivative of the AJ-1 Savage, two prototypes being ordered in September of that year. The US Navy specified major changes, including deletion of the Allison J33 booster engine, and the first prototype **North American XA2J-1** did not fly until 4 January 1952. Development was hampered by problems with the Allison XT40-A-6 engines, each of which comprised two T38 engines driving contra-rotating propellers through a gearbox, allowing either T38 in each unit to be shut down for long-range cruise. The three-man crew was provided with a pressurised cabin and defensive armament comprised two 20-mm guns in a remotely-controlled barbette. Maximum offensive load was 4911 kg (10,500 lb) of bombs. The completed second prototype was never flown.

The XA2J-1 had a folding vertical tail, similar to that of the AJ-2 Savage.

North American XB-21

Similar in appearance to the Douglas B-18 Bolo, but intended to achieve significantly improved performance, the **North American NA-21** bomber was developed at the company's Inglewood, California plant during 1935-3, the prototype being completed in March 1937. Powered by two 895-kW (1,200-hp) Pratt & Whitney R-2180 Twin Hornet engines with F-10 turbo-superchargers, the **XB-21** carried a six-man crew and armament comprised single 7.62-mm (0.3-in) machine-guns in nose and dorsal turrets, plus a similar weapon in each of the ventral and two waist positions. Short-range bomb load was 4536 kg (10,000 lb), re-

Though displaying the characteristic portly fuselage of US bombers of the 1930s, the XB-21 was notable for the strength of its rearward defences.

ducing to 998 kg (2,200 lb) over 3058 km (1,900 miles).

Only the prototype was built, this having a span of 28.96 m (95 ft), a maximum take-off weight of 18144 kg (40,000 lb) and a maximum speed of 354 km/h (220 mph).

North American B-25 Mitchell
to
North American OV-10 Bronco

North American B-25 Mitchell

Designed to meet a US Army Air Corps requirement for a twin-engined attack bomber, the **North American NA-40** prototype was a shoulder-wing monoplane with retractable tricycle landing gear, accommodating a crew of three and, as first flown in January 1939, was powered by two 820-kW (1,100-hp) Pratt & Whitney R-1830-S6C3-G engines. These were soon replaced by 969-kW (1,300-hp) Wright GR-2600-A71 Cyclone engines, the resulting **NA-40B** being delivered for USAAC testing in March, but within two weeks it had crashed as a result of pilot error. Early tests had been impressive, and North American was requested to continue its development, the **NA-62** design completed in September 1939 having the wing configuration changed from a shoulder to mid position, the fuselage widened to provide side-by-side seating for pilot and co-pilot/navigator in an improved enclosed cockpit, and 1268-kW (1,700-hp) Wright R-2600-9 Cyclones to cater for an increased gross weight and bombload. The NA-62 was ordered into production under the designation **B-25** and named **Mitchell** after the controversial champion of US air power, William 'Billy' Mitchell. The first B-25 was flown on August 1940, the designation changing after 24 had been completed to **B-25A**, this version (40 built) introducing armour and self-sealing fuel tanks, and the balance of the initial contract (120) was built to **B-25B** configuration, which introduced power-operated dorsal and ventral two-gun turrets. **B-25C** production totalled 1,619, this version introducing an autopilot, R-2600-13 engines and additional underwing bomb racks, and was followed by 2,290 examples of the generally similar **B-25D**. Two aircraft taken from the B-25C line were used for experiments in wing de-icing as the **XB-25E** and **XB-25F**, with hot-air and electrical heating respectively. One experimental **XB-25G**, with a 75-mm US Army field gun in the nose, served as prototype for the anti-shipping **B-25G** (405 built) with an M4 75-mm cannon and six machine-guns, used against Japanese targets by the US air forces in the Far East. More heavily armed was the **B-25H** (1,000 built) with a 75-mm cannon and 14 (or in late versions 18) 12.7-mm (0.5-in) machine-guns. Most extensively built was the final production **B-25J** (4,390 built from a contract for 4,805), with Wright R-2600-92 engines

and 12 12.7-mm (0.5-in) machine-guns. Ten examples of an **F-10** reconnaissance version were converted from B-25Ds, and during 1943-44 60 B-25D, B-25G, B-25C and B-25J aircraft were modified as advanced trainers with the respective designations **AT-25A**, **AT-25B**, **AT-25C** and **AT-25D**, redesignated subsequently **TB-25D**, **TB-25G**, **TB-25C** and **TB-25J**; more than 600 of the last model were converted after the war, and between 1951 and 1954 157 Mitchells were modified to **TB-25K** (117) and **TB-25M** (40) flying classrooms for teaching the Hughes E-1 and E-5 fire control radar. Other post-war modifications included **TB-25L** and **TB-25N** multi-engine conversion trainers, with 90 and 47 produced respectively by Hayes Aircraft Corporation, as well as a number of **ZB-25C**, **ZB-25D**, **ZXB-25E**, **CB-25J** and **VB-25J** utility and staff transport.

A total of 706 aircraft, similar to the B-25J, were acquired for use by the US Navy and US Marine Corps under the designations **PBJ-1C** (50), **PBJ-1D** (152), **PBJ-1G** (1), **PBJ-1H** (248), and **PBJ-1J** (255). The RAF received 23 B-25Bs which it designated **Mitchell Mk I**, followed by 432 B-26Cs and 113 B-25Ds as the **Mitchell Mk II**, and 296 B-25Js as the **Mitchell Mk III**. Other nations to use Mitchells have included Australia, Bolivia, Brazil, Canada, Chile, Colombia, Cuba, France, Indonesia, Mexico, Netherlands East Indies, Peru, Uruguay, USSR, and Venezuela.

North American Mitchell Mk II of No. 26 Sqn, Royal Air Force, based in southern England during mid-1944.

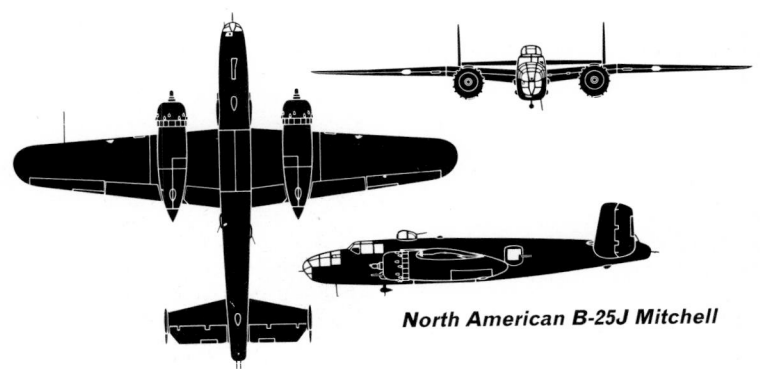

North American B-25J Mitchell

Initial deliveries to the USAAC were made in the spring of 1941, to the 17th Bombardment Group (Medium), and it was an aircraft of this unit that was the first to sink a Japanese submarine on 24 December 1941. Sixteen specially-prepared B-25s from this same group made the historic attack on the Japanese mainland on 18 April 1942, led by Lieutenant Colonel James H. Doolittle, these aircraft were flown off the carrier USS *Hornet*, then the heaviest aircraft operated from an aircraft carrier, to attack targets some 1287 km (800 miles) distant at Kobe, Nagoya, Tokyo and Yokohama, afterwards flying on to China where most of them force-landed. Mitchells served throughout World War II and continued in use for many years after the

war, particularly in the air arms of smaller nations. The USAF's last B-25 staff transport was retired on 21 May 1960.

Specification
North American B-25J
Type: five-seat medium bomber
Powerplant: two 1268-kW (1,700-hp) Wright R-2600-92 Cyclone radial piston engines
Performance: maximum speed 438 km/h (272 mph) at 3960 m (13,000 ft); service ceiling 7375 m (24,200 ft); range 2173 km (1,350 miles)
Weights: empty 8836 kg (19,480 lb); maximum take-off 15876 kg (35,000 lb)
Dimensions: span 20.60 m (67 ft 7 in); length 16.13 m (52 ft 11 in); height 4.98 m (16 ft 4 in); wing area 56.67 m² (610.0 sq ft)

North American XB-28

Envisaged originally as a high-altitude version of the B-25 Mitchell, the **North American NA-63 (XB-28)** emerged finally as an almost entirely different aircraft. With single vertical tail surfaces and a circular-section fuselage with a pressure cabin for the five-man crew, the XB-28 was powered by two 1491-kW (2,000-hp) Pratt & Whitney R-2800 radials and bomb bay capacity was 1814 kg (4,000 lb). Dorsal, ventral and tail turrets, each containing two 12.7-mm (0.5) machine-guns, were remotely controlled from the cockpit; three similar

An advanced derivative of the B-25, the XB-28 offered a pressurised cabin and remotely-controlled gun turrets. It failed to gain a production order.

forward-firing weapons were also fitted. Of three prototypes ordered in February 1940, the first flew in April 1942, the second was cancelled and the third, with a reconnaissance camera installation, crashed during the test programme. Although the XB-28 achieved a maximum speed of 599 km/h (372 mph) at

7620 m (25,000 ft) and could carry a 272 kg (600 lb) bomb load for 3283 km

(2,040 miles), production orders were not placed.

North American B-45 Tornado

The first American four-jet bomber to achieve flight-test status, the **North American NA-130** was evolved from studies which began in late 1944. Aimed at the application of the then-new turbojet propulsion system to existing heavy bomber practice and techniques, other than for the installation of two pairs of 1814-kg (4,000-lb) Allison-built General Electric J-35-A-4 engines in their underslung nacelles, the **XB-45 Tornado** did not represent a major advance. Three prototypes were ordered in 1945 and the first of these was flown by test pilot George Krebs at Muroc Dry Lake (Edwards AFB) on 17 March 1947. A shoulder-wing monoplane, the XB-45 provided accommodation for two pilots under a clear-view fighter-type canopy, and the bombardier sat in the glazed nose. The rear gunner, in a tail turret, operated the aircraft's sole defensive armament, a pair of 12.7-mm (0.5-in) Browning M7 guns.

Variants
B-45A: 96 production B-45As were procured by the US Air Force, first entering service with the 47th Bombardment Group at Barksdale Air Force Base, Louisiana in November 1948, this unit moving to British bases in 1952; only the first 22 retained the J35 engines, later aircraft having 2434-kg (4,000-lb) thrust General Electric J47s; the last B-45As were retired in 1958; 14 **TB-45A** aircraft were modified from bomber airframes for use as target tugs, with bomb bay-mounted reel and cable equipment to which could be attached a Chance Vought target glider; one **JB-45A** was used by Westinghouse as an engine test-bed
B-45B: projected version with revised radar and fire-control systems
B-45C: 10 B-45Cs were manufactured, deliveries beginning in 1949; with uprated 2359-kg (5,200-lb) thrust J47 engines and intended for close-support duties, they had a strengthened airframe to permit operation at a higher maximum take-off weight, increased from 40823 kg (90,000 lb) to 49895 kg (110,000 lb); an additional and externally-evident change was the heavily-framed canopy over the pilots' cockpit; up to 9979 kg

(22,000 lb) of bombs could be carried
RB-45C: 33 RB-45Cs were delivered between June 1950 and October 1951, operating in the photographic-reconnaissance role and carrying a total of 12 cameras in four fuselage positions; the bomb bay housed 25 M122 photoflash bombs and additional fuel tanks; to provide additional take-off power water injection was used, a jettisonable water tank being fitted under each nacelle. This version was first operated by the 91st Strategic Reconnaissance Wing and later flew with the 19th Tactical Reconnaissance Squadron, USAFE, and other units, some with British national insignia; one **JB-45C** was converted for use as an engine test-bed by General Electric

Specification
North American RB-45C
Type: photographic-reconnaissance aircraft
Powerplant: four 2722-kg (6,000-lb) thrust (with water injection) General

Electric J47-GE-13/15 turbojets
Performance: maximum speed 917 km/h (570 mph); service ceiling 12270 m (40,250 ft); range 4072 km (2,530 miles)
Weights: empty 22672 kg (49,984 lb); maximum take-off 50222 kg (110,721 lb)
Dimensions: span 29.26 m (96 ft 0 in); length 23.14 m (75 ft 11 in); height 7.67 m (25 ft 2 in); wing area 109.16 m² (1,175.0 sq ft)
Armament: two 12.7-mm (0.5-in) Browning machine-guns

The North American Tornado is seen here in the form of the B-45A initial production version. Most of these aircraft were later upgraded to B-45C standard with more powerful engines, wingtip tanks and a strengthened airframe.

The reconnaissance version was the RB-45C, which was fitted with 12 cameras in the fuselage and saw action in Korea.

North American B-70 Valkyrie

Developed to USAF General Operational Requirement 38 for an intercontinental bomber to replace the Boeing B-52, the Mach 3 **North American XB-70A** was the subject of an order for three prototypes, awarded on 4 October 1961, although the third was later cancelled. A delta-winged canard design, with wing tips which folded down at 65° to the horizontal to provide improved supersonic

stability, and powered by six 13608-kg (30,000-lb) thrust General Electric J93-GE-3 engines, the first prototype was flown by Alvin S. White and Colonel Joseph F. Cotton on 21 September 1964; it first achieved its design speed of Mach 3 on 14 October 1965. The improved second prototype flew on 17 July 1965, but was lost in a mid-air collision on 8 June 1966. The surviving aircraft car-

ried out a number of test programmes, including work in connection with the US supersonic transport programme, but on 4 February 1969 it was flown to retirement at the US Air Force Museum, Wright Patterson AFB, Dayton, Ohio. Spanning 32.00 m (105 ft 0 in) and with a length of 59.75 m (196 ft 0 in), the XB-70A had a maximum take-off weight of 249476 kg (550,000 lb), or 249.4 tonnes (245.5 tons).

On its fateful last flight on June 8 1966, the No. 2 Valkyrie was operating a photo sortie for General Electric. It was escorted by an F-4, F-5, T-38 and an F-104. Flown by NASA test pilot Joe Walker, the F-104 was caught in the XB-70's turbulent wake. Instantly flipped on its back it collided with the Valkyrie. For a few seconds the new bomber flew on before it, too, fell to the Earth.

North American F-86 Sabre

To meet a US Army Air Force requirement for a day fighter that could be used also as an escort fighter or dive-bomber, North American submitted a design known as the **NA-140**.

Two **XP-86** prototypes of the NA-140 design were contracted in late 1944, but when German research data on the characteristics of swept wings became available soon after the end of the war, North American sought USAAF agreement to redesign the XP-86 to incorporate swept wings and tail surfaces. This cost a year's delay, and it was not until 1 October 1947 that the first prototype was flown, then powered by a Chevrolet-built General Electric TG-180 (or J35-C-3) turbojet of 1701-kg (3,750-lb) thrust; on 25 April 1948, by then re-engined with a General Electric J47 turbojet as the **YP-86A**, this aircraft exceeded a speed of Mach 1 in a shallow dive. The first production version was the **P-86A**, powered initially by a 2200-kg (4,850-lb) thrust General Electric J47-GE-1 turbojet and flown first on 20 May 1948. A month later USAF redesignation resulted in the P-86A becoming the **F-86A** and in 1949, by which time it had gained the name **Sabre**, the new fighter began to enter service with the USAF's 1st, 4th and 81st Fighter Groups, the 94th Squadron of the 1st Fighter Group receiving the first in February 1949. F-86A production totalled 554, the majority having 2359-kg (5,200-lb) thrust J47-GE-3, -7, -9, or -13 turbojets. Subsequent production, arranged chronologically, included the **F-86E** with an all-moving tailplane, and the **F-86F** (1,539) with a modified wing. Most extensively built was the ensuing **F-86D** (2,054), a redesigned all-weather/night fighter, followed by the **F-86H** fighter-bomber (477) with powerful J73 engine, and the **F-86K** (120) which was a simplified version of the F-86D. Under the designation **TF-86** two dual-control trainers were produced as conversions of F-86Fs, and the designation **F-86L** was applied to rebuilds (827) from F-86Ds, which introduced an increased span wing and updated avionics. The **F-86B** (deeper fuselage and larger tyres) and **F-86C** (redesigned fuselage) did not enter production. In addition to aircraft built by North American, Canadair Ltd in Montreal built 60 F-86Es for the USAF, followed by 290 generally similar **Sabre Mk 2** fighters, comprising 230 for the RCAF and 60 for the Mutual Defense Assistance Program. Canadian production continued with one **Sabre Mk 3** to flight test the indigenous Orenda engine, 438 **Sabre Mk 4** for the RAF with General Electric engines, 370 **Sabre Mk 5** aircraft with the 2883-kg (6,355-lb) thrust Orenda 10 turbojet, and 655 **Sabre Mk 6** aircraft with the 3300-kg (7,275-lb) thrust Orenda 14. The Commonwealth Aircraft Corporation in Australia also became involved in Sabre production, modifying the airframe for

North American FJ-3M Fury of VF-142, US Navy, based on USS Hornet in 1957.

two 30-mm Adens and the 3402-kg (7,500-lb) thrust Rolls-Royce Avon 26 engine, and built for the RAAF 21 **Sabre Mk 30** and 20 **Sabre Mk 31** aircraft, plus 69 **Sabre Mk 32** fighters with Australian-built engines. Fiat in Italy assembled 221 F-86Ks from North American-built kits of components, and production in Japan began in the same way, with Mitsubishi leading a group of Japanese companies which first assembled, then increasingly constructed, a total of 300 similar to the F-86F and RF-86F.

A requirement for fighter-bombers to equip the US Navy and Marine Corps, superseding the FJ-1 Fury resulted in a contract for three **XFJ-2 Fury** prototypes for evaluation. These were basically similar to the USAF's F-86E, but with arrester hooks, extending nose gears and catapult hitches. They were followed by 200 **FJ-2** fighters which introduced folding wings, 538 **FJ-3** aircraft with a deeper fuselage and the more powerful Wright J65-W-2 or J65-W-4 turbojet of 3648-kg (7,800-lb), or 3470-kg (7,650-lb) thrust respectively, 152 of the **FJ-4** (later **F-1E**), a completely redesigned attack variant with a 3493-kg (7,700-lb) thrust Wright J65-W-16A engine, and 222 **FJ-4B** (later **AF-1E**) improved attack aircraft, which incorporated a totally new airframe. Two examples of an unusual sub-variant of the FJ-4B had the designation **FJ-4F**; used for evaluation purposes, these each had an auxiliary rocket motor and supplementary fuel tank.

The F-86 saw considerable service in the Korean War where, despite marginally inferior performance to the much vaunted Mikoyan-Gurevich MiG-15, they were able to gain superiority over these aircraft thanks to the superior training and experience of their pilots. Subsequently, in addition to serving with the air arms of NATO and British Commonwealth countries, the F-86 Sabre was supplied to many other countries throughout the world.

Specification
North American F-86D Sabre
Type: single-seat all-weather/night interceptor
Powerplant: one 3402-kg (7,500-lb) thrust afterburning General Electric J47-GE-17B or -33 turbojet
Performance: maximum speed 1138 km/h (707 mph) at sea level; service ceiling 16640 m (54,600 ft); range 1344 km (835 miles)
Weights: empty 5656 kg (12,470 lb); maximum take-off 7756 kg (17,100 lb)
Dimensions: span 11.30 m (37 ft 1 in); length 12.29 m (40 ft 4 in); height 4.57 m (15 ft 0 in); wing area 27.76 m² (288.0 sq ft)
Armament: 24 69.9-mm (2.75-in) air-to-air rocket projectiles

Two examples of the F-86F were modified to TF-86 standard by the addition of another cockpit and the lengthening of the fuselage by 160 cm (63 in). The wing was also moved forward.

The North American F-86K was a simplified version of the F-86D 'Sabre Dog', retaining the radar in its distinctive nose radome, but with an armament of four 20-mm cannon.

North American F-100 Super Sabre

In 1949 North American initiated private-venture development of the F-86 Sabre, the design being known initially as the **Sabre 45** because its wings were swept at 45°. It was intended that this aircraft should be capable of supersonic performance in level flight, and the culmination of two years of design and development was the receipt on 1 November 1951 of a US Air Force contract for two **YF-100** (later **TF-100A**) prototypes and 110 **F-100A Super Sabre** production aircraft. The first of the proto-

types was flown on 24 April 1953, exceeding Mach 1 during this initial flight, and 29 October 1953 was a 'red letter day', when the first production aircraft was flown and the first prototype established a new world speed record of 1215.04 km/h (754.99 mph). When the type became operational with the USAF's 479th Fighter Day Wing, on 29 September 1954, it was the world's first operational fighter capable of supersonic performance in level flight. Early production F-100A Super Sabres were powered

by the Pratt & Whitney J57-P-7 turbojet, developing 6804-kg (15,000-lb) afterburning thrust, but the last 36 of the total of 203 that were built had the 7257-kg (16,000-lb) afterburning thrust J57-P-39 engine. An improved tactical fighter-bomber version was planned as the **F-100B**, but this was revised into the YF-107A, only three of which flew with the J75 engine. With two USAF wings largely equipped, accidents caused by inertia roll-yaw coupling caused a crisis, and major F-100A redesign with tall fins

and extended wings.

Development of the Super Sabre continued with the **F-100C** fighter-bomber, of which 476 were built, this version having inflight-refuelling capability, a Pratt & Whitney J57-P-21 engine and eight underwing weapon pylons. Most extensively built was the **F-100D** attack version with many changes, including a flapped wing, provisions for internal ECM equipment and introduction of the LABS (low-altitude bombing system) for so-called toss delivery of nuclear weapons. A total of 1,274 F-100Ds was built, followed by 339 of the final production version, the **F-100F** tandem two-seat trainer. Sub-variants include a small number of **RF-100A** photo-reconnaissance conversions from F-100As; a single **TF-100C** conversion from an F-100C, which served as a prototype for the tandem two-seat F-100F; and some **DF-100F** drone director conversions from F-100Fs. Under the designation **NF-100F** three F-100Fs were used for

The F-100C was the fighter-bomber development of the pure interceptor F-100A. The version had eight hardpoints under the wings and could be distinguished from the later F-100D by having smaller tail surfaces.

test purposes, and six F-100Fs delivered to the Danish air force from USAF stocks were given the temporary designation **TF-100F**.

Foreign operators have included Taiwan (F-100A), Denmark and France (F-100D and F-100F); and the Turkish air force also operated large numbers of secondhand F-100s. With the US Air Force the Super Sabre saw extensive use in Vietnam, some aircraft being especially modified for use in EW (electronic warfare) and FAC (forward air control) operations; and even when replaced by more advanced aircraft F-100s remained in use with Air National Guard units until 1980.

Specification
North American F-100D Super Sabre
Type: single-seat fighter-bomber
Powerplant: one 7711-kg (17,000-lb) afterburning thrust Pratt & Whitney J57-P-21A turbojet
Performance: maximum speed 1390 km/h (864 mph) or Mach 1.3 at 10670 m (35,000 ft); service ceiling 14020 m (46,000 ft); standard range 966 km (600 miles)
Weights: empty 9525 kg (21,000 lb); maximum take-off 15800 kg (34,832 lb)
Dimensions: span 11.82 m (38 ft 9½ in); length excluding probe 14.36 m (47 ft 1¼ in); height 4.95 m (16 ft 3 in);

wing area 35.77 m² (385.0 sq ft)
Armament: four 20-mm cannon, plus weapon load of up to 3402 kg (7,500 lb) on underwing pylons including bombs, missiles and rockets

Initially designated F-100B, the YF-107A advanced fighter-bomber was powered by a Pratt & Whitney J75 turbojet with a bifurcated variable-wedge dorsal intake behind the cockpit. Three prototypes were built, the first flying on 10 September 1956. Despite demonstrating speeds in excess of Mach 2, the project was cancelled in favour of the F-105.

North American FJ-1 Fury

Ordered on 1 January 1945, and one of three turbojet-powered aircraft for US Navy evaluation (the others being the McDonnell FD Phantom and the Vought F6U Pirate), the first of three **North American NA-134** (US Navy **FJ-1**) prototypes flew on 27 November 1946, powered by a 1733-kg (3,820-lb) thrust General Electric J35-GE-2 engine. One hundred production FJ-1s were ordered on 28 May 1945, but reduced subsequently to 30 aircraft, each armed with six 12.7-mm (0.5-in) machine-guns at the sides of the intake, and having the 1814-kg (4,000-lb) thrust J35-A-2 engine. Production deliveries began in March 1948, the Fury equipping Squadron VF-5A (later VF-51) aboard USS *Boxer*. First carrier landings were made on 10 March 1948 and the Fury, which was the first jet fighter to go to sea under operational conditions, had a maximum speed of 880 km/h (547 mph).

Specification
North American FJ-1 Fury
Type: single-seat carrier-borne fighter
Powerplant: one 17.8-kN (4,000-lb) Allison J35-A-2 turbojet
Performance: maximum speed 880 km/h (547 mph) at 2743 m

Progenitor of the F-86, the FJ-1 did not share the former's sleek lines. Instead, its portly shape was dictated by the need to house all its fuel tanks in the fuselage and the restrictions imposed by the adoption of a technically uncomplicated nose-mounted intake. The Fury was the final Navy fighter to be armed with 0.50-in machine-guns. For a brief period it could also claim to be that service's fastest aircraft, when an FJ-1 reached a speed of Mach 0.87 in 1947.

(9,000 ft); initial climb rate 1005 m/min (3,300 ft/min); service ceiling 9754 m (32,000 ft); ferry range 2414 km (1,500 miles)
Dimensions: span 9.8 m (38 ft 2 in);

length 10.5 m (34 ft 5 in); height 4.5 m (14 ft 10 in); wing area 20.5 m² (221 sq ft)
Weights: empty 4011 kg (8,843 lt); gross 7076 kg (15,600 lb)

Armament: six fixed forward-firing 0.50-in machine-guns

North American O-47

Developed by General Aviation (the precursor of North American Aviation) to meet a US Army specification for an observation aircraft, the **GA-15** represented a radical change in design for such a role in that, unlike its predecessors, it was a low-wing monoplane with an enclosed cockpit, seating a three-man crew. Powered by a 634-kW (850-hp) Wright Cyclone engine, the prototype flew in mid-1935 and to provide an acceptable field of view for the observer a glazed nose position was located under the fuselage. North American put

Designed as an observation aircraft, the North American O-47 was fitted with a large belly with glazed panels. In the event, the aircraft served mainly as a trainer and target tug. The O-47 was the forerunner of the hugely successful T-6 Texan.

the type into production to meet a USAAC contract for 109 **North American O-47A** aircraft ordered in February 1937, later increased to 164. They were powered by 727-kW (975-hp)

Cyclones, while 74 **O-47B** aircraft had 790-kW (1,060-hp) engines and additional fuel capacity. During World War II they served as trainers and target tugs.

North American OV-10 Bronco

A US Marine Corps requirement of the early 1960s for a Light Armed Reconnaissance Airplane (LARA) was met by the **North American NA-300** design submission, and a contract for seven **YOV-10A** prototypes was placed in 1964, the first of them flying on 16 July 1965. With a slender two-seat fuselage nacelle mounting a high-set monoplane wing, the aircraft had twin tailbooms extending aft from the nacelles of the two turboprop engines, each with a fin and rudder, and interconnected by a tailplane/elevator assembly; the main units of the tricycle landing gear retracted into the engine nacelles. Six of the prototypes were powered by 447-kW (600-hp) Garrett T76-G-6/8 engines, but had one Pratt & Whitney YT74-CP-8/10 turboprops for comparative evaluation. The **OV-10A** Bronco production version

had a 3.05 m (10 ft) increase in wing span and more powerful T76-G-10/12 engines, the first flown on 6 August 1967, and 114 were built for the US Marine Corps. These were followed by 157 similar OV-10As for the US Air Force, these entering operational service in Vietnam in 1968. Under the US 'Pave Nail' programme, 15 were provided with special equipment for the location and illumination of targets by night. Other versions have included six **OV-10B** aircraft supplied to Germany as target tugs, followed by 18 turbojet-boosted **OV-10B(Z)** aircraft for the same role. Versions similar to the OV-10A have been supplied to Indonesia (16), Thailand (40) and Venezuela (16), under the respective designations **OV-10F, OV-10C** and **OV-10E**, and six US OV-10As have been transferred to the

Royal Moroccan air force. Two OV-10As were modified under a US Navy contract of 1970 to **YOV-10D NOGS** (Night Observation/Gunship System) aircraft to provide the US Marines with advanced night operational capability. Since evaluation of these aircraft, 17 US Marine Corps OV-10As have been converted to **OV-10D NOS** (Night Observation Surveillance) configuration, now equipped with FLIR (forward-looking infra-red) and a laser target illuminator.

Specification
North American (Rockwell) OV-10D
Type: COIN and night surveillance aircraft
Powerplant: two 776-kW (1,040-shp) Garrett T76-G-420/421 turboprops
Performance: maximum speed

463 km/h (288 mph) at sea level; service ceiling 9145 m (30,000 ft); combat radius with full weapon load 367 km (228 miles)
Weights: empty 3127 kg (6,893 lb); maximum take-off 6552 kg (14,444 lb)
Dimensions: span 12.19 m (40 ft 0 in); length 13.41 m (44 ft 0 in); height 4.62 m (15 ft 2 in); wing area 27.03 m^2 (291.0 sq ft)
Armament: five fuselage/sponson weapon attachment points with combined capacity of 1633 kg (3,600 lb), for a variety of bombs, cannon, machine-guns and missiles, plus two underwing pylons, each with a capacity of 272 kg (600 lb) and suitable for bombs, fuel tanks or Sidewinder missiles

North American OV-10A Bronco of the 601st Tactical Control Squadron, US Air Force, based at Sembach, West Germany, during the 1970s.

Below: The latest Bronco is the OV-10D NOS (Night Observation Surveillance) model. Its extended nose cone is fitted with an underslung turret housing a FLIR (Forward Looking Infra-Red) and laser illuminator. An earlier plan to fit the OV-10D with a gun turret under the fuselage through the NOGS (Night Observation Gunship System) was not proceeded with. Instead, about 20 OV-10s have been upgraded to the less complicated NOS standard. More conversions for the US Marine Corps will follow. The aircraft below serves with VMO-2 at Camp Pendleton. Note the underwing pylons which can be fitted with AIM-9 Sidewinder launch rails.

One of the major users of the Bronco is the Royal Thai Air Force. Thirty-two OV-10Cs were delivered between 1971 and 1974, with four surviving today. 411 Sqn, 41 Wing, based at Chiang Mai and 711 Sqn, 71 Wing, based at Surat Thani, are the two units equipped with the type. The Broncos have been heavily involved in FAC and COIN operations along Thailand's disputed border with Laos and Kampuchea.

North American P-51 Mustang
to
North American T-39 Sabreliner

North American P-51 Mustang

One of the most effective fighter aircraft of World War II, the **North American P-51 Mustang** began life as the **NA-73X** to meet a British requirement of April 1940. Needed desperately because of the grave situation in Europe, it was completed ahead of the 120-day schedule set by the UK, but the 820-kW (1,100-hp) Allison V-1710-F3R engine to power it was delayed and the prototype was not flown for the first time until 26 October 1940. The NA-73X completed a remarkably trouble-free test programme, the first production example of a contract for 320 **NA-73** aircraft being flown on 1 May 1941; the second series aircraft, for RAF evaluation, arrived in the UK in November 1941. Designated **Mustang Mk I**, this aircraft was soon shown in extensive testing to have remarkable performance at low altitudes, declining rapidly as the power output of the Allison engine fell off rapidly above 3660 m (12,000 ft). This meant that the type was of little use for combat or interception roles in Europe. It was clearly well suited for tactical reconnaissance, and its standard armament of four 12.7-mm (0.5-in) and four 7.62-mm (0.3-in) machine-guns meant that it also had potential for ground attack. Equipped with an obliquely-mounted camera, the RAF's Mustang Mk Is began to enter service with No. 2 Squadron of Army Co-operation Command in April 1942, eventually equipping no fewer than 23 squadrons of this command and resulting in a follow-on contract for an additional 300 generally similar aircraft. A condition of US government approval of NA-73 development and production had been the supply of two evaluation aircraft to the US Army Air Corps, which designated them **XP-51**. Just before this, however, the USAAC had ordered 150 **P-51** aircraft for supply to the UK under Lend-Lease, these differing from the initial production aircraft by having self-sealing fuel tanks and four 20-mm cannon replacing the armament of eight machine-guns. The RAF received 93 of this version, designating the variant **Mustang Mk IA**, and 55 camera-equipped **F-6A** aircraft went to the US Army Air Force for tactical reconnaissance; the balance of two aircraft had 1066-kW (1,430-hp) Packard-built Merlin V-1650-3 engines installed for evaluation, then becoming redesignated **XP-78**, later **XP-51B**. This had resulted because testing by the USAAF of its XP-51 prototypes had confirmed RAF findings of the deficiency in high-altitude performance, a weakness explored in the UK by the experimental installation of Rolls-Royce Merlin 61 and 65 engines. With adoption of the same course in the

USA the XP-51Bs demonstrated a maximum speed of 710 km/h (441 mph) at 9085 m (29,800 ft), resulting in large-scale orders for Merlin-engined P-51s. Before that, RAF adoption of the Mustang for use in a ground-attack role brought USAAF procurement of 500 **A-36A** aircraft named initially **Apache** but later adopting the British name Mustang, which incorporated dive brakes and underwing bomb racks. A single A-36A was supplied to the RAF.

Almost simultaneously with procurement of the A-36As, the USAAF ordered 310 **P-51A** fighters with the 895-kW (1,200-hp) V-1710-81 engine, plus armament of four 12.7-mm (0.5-in) machine-guns and underwing racks; of the total 50 were allocated to the RAF, which designated them **Mustang Mk II**, and 35 were converted as tactical reconnaissance **F-6B** aircraft for the USAAF. Production of the Merlin-engined versions began in 1943 with the **P-51B**, of which 1,988 were built at North American's Inglewood, California factory, and with the generally similar **P-51C**, of which 1,750 were built in a new factory at Dallas, Texas. Both differed from the earlier versions by having a strengthened fuselage, redesigned ailerons and armament of four 12.7-mm (0.5-in) machine-guns. Lend-Lease allocations of these versions for the RAF comprised 274 and 636 respectively, all designated **Mustang Mk III**. Some 71 of the P-51Bs and P-51Cs received by the USAAF were modified as **F-6C** tactical reconnaissance aircraft. Major production version was the **P-51D**, with a total of 7,956 built, introducing a bubble canopy to improve the field of view, a

modified rear fuselage, and six 12.7-mm (0.5-in) machine-guns; from this total 136 were modified as tactical reconnaissance **F-6D** aircraft, and 281 were allocated to the RAF which designated them **Mustang Mk IV**. A total of 1,500 generally similar **P-51K** fighters followed, 163 being completed as tactical reconnaissance **F-6K** aircraft and 594 being allocated to the RAF, which designated them Mustang Mk IV also. The testing of **XP-51F**, **XP-51G** and **XP-51J** lightweight prototypes, with a variety of engines, led to the **P-51H** final production version, of which 555 were built before VJ-Day brought cancellation of the balance of 2,000 ordered. Also cancelled were 1,700 similar V-1650-11 powered **P-51L** aircraft and 1,628 **P-51M** fighters; the M was to be the Dallas-built version of the P-51H, of which only a single example was built. On the grand total of 15,386 Mustangs production ended in the USA, but one other minor source of supply was Australia, where Commonwealth Aircraft Corporation began by assembling 80 P-51Ds from imported components, these serving with the RAAF under the designation **Mustang Mk 20**. Licence construction followed for the RAAF, comprising 26 **Mustang Mk 21** aircraft with V-1650-7 engines, 14 of them later converted to **Mustang Mk 22** configuration, 67 **Mustang Mk 23** aircraft with Merlin 66 or 70 engines, and 13 Mustang Mk 22s for tactical reconnaissace; none of these RAAF aircraft saw service before VJ-Day. Under Lend-Lease 50 P-51Ds were supplied to China and 40 to Netherlands forces in the Pacific theatre, and some USAAF P-51s

were supplied to the AVG in China. In the immediate post-war years the type remained in US service with Strategic Air Command until 1949 and for several more years with US Air Reserve and Air National Guard units, being among the first USAF fighters to see action in the Korean War. In the RAF some remained in use with Fighter Command until 1946, and war surplus P-51s continued to have some years of post-war service with over 50 air forces.

P-51s with various modifications have since appeared as civilian racing aircraft, one powered by a 2834-kW (3,800-hp) Rolls-Royce Griffon engine capturing the world speed record for piston-engine aircraft at 803.139 km/h (499.048 mph).

In the 1950s Trans-Florida Aviation marketed a two-seat executive conversion, later offered (in the 1960s as the **Cavalier 2000**) by the Cavalier Aircraft Corporation of Sarasota. These led to a contract from the USAF for a number of new-built **Mustangs** for counter-insurgency and forward air control duties for distribution to MAP recipients. The improved **Mustang II** was followed by versions of the **Turbo Mustang III** powered by Rolls-Royce Dart or Lycoming T55 turboprop engines. At this point the programme was taken over by the Piper Aircraft Corporation, which flew the T55-engined Mustang in April 1971. It was not until September 1981 that Piper received a contract covering the design, development and testing of a lightweight turboprop-powered close-support aircraft based on the P-51. Desig-

Distinguishable from Merlin-powered Mustangs by the carburettor inlet above the engine, the Mustang Mk 1 was Allison-powered.

P-51B of the 364th Fighter Squadron, 357th Fighter Group, US 8th Air Force at Leiston, in 1944.

North American Mustang Mk IV (P-51K) of 19 Sqn, 2nd Tactical Air Force, RAF, in 1945.

nated the **PA-48 Enforcer**, two T55-powered prototypes were built and the first of these flew on 9 April 1983. Following the completion in August 1984 of an extensive evaluation, the USAF lost interest and the project did not proceed further, and the two prototypes went into storage at Davis-Monthan AFB.

Specification
North American P-51D Mustang
Type: single-seat interceptor/long-range escort fighter
Powerplant: one 1264-kW (1,695-hp) Packard Merlin V-1650-7 V-12 piston engine
Performance: maximum speed 703 km/h (437 mph) at 7620 m (25,000 ft); service ceiling 12770 m (41,900 ft); maximum range 3347 km (2,080 miles)
Weights: empty 3232 kg (7,125 lb); maximum take-off 5488 kg (12,100 lb)
Dimensions: span 11.28 m (37 ft 0¼ in); length 9.83 m (32 ft 3 in); height 2.64 m (8 ft 8 in); wing area 21.65 m² (233.0 sq ft)
Armament: six 12.7-mm (0.5-in) machine-guns, plus up to two 454-kg (1,000-lb) bombs or six 127-mm (5-in) rocket projectiles

North American P-64

A single-seat fighter variant of the AT-6 Texan/Harvard was developed by North American for export, with armament comprising two 7.62-mm (0.3-in) machine-guns and two 20-mm cannon, plus provision for up to 181 kg (400 lb) of bombs carried on underfuselage racks. Seven aircraft with the company designation **North American NA-50A** were built for Peru, all delivered by May 1939, and six **NA-68** aircraft were then built for the Royal Thai air force. These were on their way to Thailand by sea when Japan invaded that nation in December 1941 and, seized by US

authorities at Hawaii, they were returned to the USA. Taken into USAAF service, they had all armament removed and were operated as advanced trainers under the designation **P-64**. Powered by a 649-kW (870-hp) Wright R-1820-77 Cyclone radial engine, the P-64 had a maximum speed of 435 km/h (270 mph).

Designed as an export fighter, the NA-68 was built for Thailand but impressed for USAAF service under the designation P-64, despite the fact that it was used solely as a trainer.

North American P-82 Twin Mustang

Although the P-51 had demonstrated exceptional range for a fighter, being able to escort from England bomber squadrons operating to the farthest targets in the Third Reich and over Czechoslovakia, northern Italy and Poland, even greater range capability was required in the Pacific theatre. This led to development of the **North American XP-82 Twin Mustang** prototype, which joined two P-51 fighters by eliminating one port and one starboard wing and both tailplanes, uniting the two remnants with a parallel-chord wing section and a new tailplane with elevator; the revised main landing gear comprised a single unit on each fuselage. Testing of three prototypes led to a USAAF order for 500 **P-82B** fighters, but only 20 had been built when the war ended. Two of this number were converted as night-fighters designated **P-82C** and **P-82D**, with SCR-720 and APS-4 radar respec-

tively. In 1946 the USAAF placed a new order for 250 P-82s, comprising 100 **P-82E** escort fighters, and 150 night-fighters as **P-82F** (100 with APS-4 radar) and **P-82G** (50 with SCR-20 radar). All production B to G variants were redesignated **F-82** in 1948, and the last version to enter service was the **F-82H**, a winterised variant of the F-82/-82G for service in Alaska. Twin Mustangs operated by the US 5th Air Force were among the first US aircraft to operate over Korea. One, flown by a pilot of the 68th Fighter (All-Weather) Squadron, destroyed the first enemy aircraft in the Korean War.

Specification
North American F-82G Twin Mustang
Powerplant: two 1193-kW (1,600-hp) Allison V-1710-143/145 V-12 piston engines

Performance: maximum speed 742 km/h (461 mph) at 6400 m (21,000 ft); service ceiling 11855 m (38,900 ft); maximum range 3605 km (2,240 miles)
Weights: empty 7256 kg (15,997 lb); maximum take-off 11608 kg (25,951 lb)
Dimensions: span 15.62 m (51 ft 3 in); length 12.93 m (42 ft 5 in); height 4.22 m (13 ft 10 in); wing area 37.90 m² (408.0 sq ft)
Armament: six wing-mounted 12.7-mm (0.5-in) machine-guns, plus up to four 454-kg (1,000-lb) bombs, or four auxiliary fuel tanks on underwing racks

Usually flown from the left-hand seat, the North American F-82F Twin Mustang night-fighter carried its radar in a giant centreline pod.

North American T-2 Buckeye

With a requirement in 1956 for a multi-role jet trainer, the US Navy awarded North American a contract to build its **North American NA-241** design, which combined proven components and equipment from earlier aircraft manufactured by the company. Ordered as the **T2J-1** (later **T-2A**), this trainer combined a wing derived from the FJ-1 Fury and the control system of the T-28C Trojan with a single 1542-kg (3,400-lb) thrust Westinghouse J34-WE-36 turbojet, and accommodated the instructor and pupil in tandem, seated (eventually) on zero-zero ejection seats. The first of six initial production T-2As was flown on 31 January 1958 and deliveries to the US

Navy began in July 1959, by which time the name **Buckeye** had been allocated to this trainer. Equipping US Navy Training Squadrons VT-4, -7, -9 and -19, a total of 217 T-2As was built. Two were modified to serve as **YT-2B** prototypes, in which the single J34 turbojet was replaced by two 1361-kg (3,000-lb) thrust Pratt & Whitney J60-P-6 turbojets. The

Until the eventual arrival of the T-45A Goshawk, the veteran Buckeye will continue to be the US Navy's primary jet trainer. Seven squadrons and the Navy Test Pilots School continue to operate T-2Cs.

first was flown on 30 August 1962, being followed by 97 similar **T-2B** aircraft. Final production version was the **T-2C** which introduced General Electric J85 turbojets, preceded by a single **YT-2C** prototype conversion from a T-2B. A total of 273 was built under US Navy contracts, comprising 231 T-2Cs for navy use, plus 12 **T-2D** and 30 **T-2E** aircraft procured for Venezuela and Greece respectively.

Specification
North American (Rockwell) T-2C
Type: two-seat multi-role jet trainer
Powerplant: one 1338-kg (2,950-lb) thrust General Electric J85-GE-4 turbojets
Performance: maximum speed 838 km/h (521 mph) at 7620 m (25,000 ft); service ceiling 13535 m (44,400 ft); range 1465 km (910 miles)
Weights: empty 3681 kg (8,115 lb); maximum take-off 5978 kg (13,180 lb)
Dimensions: span 11.63 m (38 ft 2 in); length 11.79 m (38 ft 8 in); height 4.51 m (14 ft 9½ in); wing area 23.70 m² (255.0 sq ft)

North American T-28 Trojan

The T-28B was the US Navy's initial version of the Trojan. This aircraft flew from NAS Point Mugu, California.

With the requirement for a trainer to replace the North American T-6 Texan in service, the **North American NA-159** design proposal was successful in gaining a contract for two **XT-28** prototypes, the first of them being flown on 26 September 1949. Following satisfactory evaluation of these prototypes, the type was ordered into production for the USAF under the designation **T-28A** and allocated the name **Trojan**. A cantilever low-wing monoplane with retractable tricycle landing gear and a 597-kW (800-hp) Wright R-1300 radial engine, the T-28 provided tandem two-seat accommodation for the instructor and pupil in an enclosed cockpit. The initial 1950 production contract covered 266 **T-28A** aircraft, the first deliveries to Air Training Command being made during the same year, and the number built eventually totalled 1,194. In 1952 it became US policy to standardise trainers for the nation's armed forces, so following evaluation of two USAF T-28As, the US Navy ordered a **T-28B** version which differed primarily by having a 1063-kW (1,425-hp) Wright R-1820-86 engine. Production for the US Navy totalled 489 T-28Bs, followed by 299 **T-28C** aircraft which differed only by having arrester gear for deck landing training. In 1962 North American began the conversion of T-28As for use in a counter-insurgency role; redesignated **T-28D**, these had the Wright R-1820 engine and were given six underwing hardpoints to accept a variety of stores and weapons. North American completed 321 conversions, and Fairchild Hiller another 72. A number were also completed as attack trainers under the designation **AT-28D**. Many T-28Ds were operated in the Congo and Vietnam, and were supplied to the air forces of several nations. In 1958 North American produced the one-off NA-260, a converted T-28A fitted with a Wright R-1820-56S derated to 969.8-kW (1,300-hp). Production was to be by Pacific Airmotive as the PacAero Nomad, but the project did not go any further. Other conversions were the Hamilton T-28R Nomair general purpose aircraft, and the Thompson Aircraft Sales of Phoenix aerial photography version, but only single copies of these were completed. Then in the early 1960s the USAF became interested in a turboprop version of the T-28D with enhanced performance, and three prototypes of the 1822.7-kW (2,450-shp) Lycoming T55 powered YAT-28E were produced. This had 12 hardpoints able to carry a 1814 kg (4,000 lb) warload which could include wingtip mounted Sidewinder AAMs. The first aircraft flew on 15 February 1963 but crashed in March following structural failure. Two more prototypes continued the test programme but the type was not adopted. In France Sud-Aviation converted 245 T-28Ds into Fennecs for the French air force to replace T-6s used in Algeria for close-support, patrol and reconnaissance, and a number of these later served with the Argentine Navy.

Specification
North American T-28B Trojan
Type: two-seat basic trainer
Powerplant: one 1063-kW (1,425-hp) Wright Cyclone R-1820-86 radial piston engine
Performance: maximum speed 552 km/h (343 mph); service ceiling 10820 m (35,500 ft); range 1706 km (1,060 miles)
Weights: empty 2914 kg (6,424 lb); maximum take-off 3856 kg (8,500 lb)
Dimensions: span 12.22 m (40 ft 1 in); length 10.06 m (33 ft 0 in); height 3.86 m (12 ft 8 in); wing area 24.90 m² (268.0 sq ft)

North American T-39 Sabreliner

Successful in both civil and military markets, the **North American NA-246 Sabreliner** was developed originally as a private venture although the programme launch, announced on 27 August 1956, was in response to the US Air Force UTX (Utility Trainer Experimental) specification issued ealier in that month. Laid out with a six-seat interior and to be flown by a two-man crew, the civil-registered prototype was completed in May 1958, although the lack of suitable engines delayed the first flight, which took place at Los Angeles, until 16 September. The initial powerplant comprised two 1134-kg (2,500-lb) thrust General Electric YJ85 turbojets and, thus powered, the prototype completed its military evaluation programme at Edwards Air Force Base in December 1958. A month later the Sabreliner won its first order, for seven **NA-265** or **T-39A** aircraft with 1361-kg (3,000-lb) thrust Pratt & Whitney J60 engines. Military production eventually totalled 213 aircraft. All military models of the T-39 series were certificated to civil airworthiness standards, beginning with the T-39A on 23 March 1962. North American then launched the commercial version, which was type approved as the **NA-265-40 Sabreliner 40** on 17 April 1963. Since then civil production of all models, including the final model, the Sabreliner 65A, totalled well over 600 aircraft when the last aircraft came off the line in 1981. Rockwell International's Sabreliner Division was acquired in 1983 by the specially formed Sabreliner Corporation of St Louis, Missouri, to continue product support. At the end of 1990 the company completed the design of a new version of the Sabreliner designated the Model 85. This has a super-critical wing incorporating winglets, a fuselage stretch of 1.5 m (5 ft), and more powerful TFE731-5 turbofan engines, but further development will require a risk-sharing partner.

Variants
T-39A: 143 aircraft for the US Air Force, the first of which was flown on 30 June 1960 and delivered in October; the production version featured a lengthened nose and additional equipment; initial users were Air Training Command, Strategic Air Command, Systems Command and USAF Headquarters, mainly as communications aircraft
T-39B: six early production aircraft fitted with R-14 NASARR search and ranging radar and APN-131 Doppler navigation equipment to facilitate use as trainers for Republic F-105 pilots, initially at Nellis AFB and later at McConnell AFB
T-39D: USN radar operator trainer, designated originally **T3J-1**; similar to the T-39B but with Magnavox APQ-94 interceptor radar; used to train F-8 Crusader and F-4 Phantom crews, 42 were built and deliveries to NAS Pensacola began in August 1963
CT-39E: seven USN VIP transport and communications aircraft; similar to civil Sabreliner 40 with 1361-kg (3,000-lb) thrust Pratt & Whitney JT12A-8 engines
T-39F: three T-39As were converted to this standard for use by the USAF Fighter Weapons School, Nellis AFB, to train pilots and electronic warfare officers for 'Wild Weasel'-equipped Republic F-105G two-seaters
CT-39G: 12 built for USN fleet tactical transport
T-39N: 17 civil-registered Sabreliner 40s operated since June 1991 under contract by Squadron VT-86 of Training Wing 6 at Penscola to give Naval Flight Officers advanced flight training.
Sabreliner 40: nine-passenger business aircraft with a third window on each side of the fuselage
Sabreliner 50: one aircraft only, similar to Series 40, which was a North American Autonetics Division electronics test-bed
Sabreliner 60: with a 0.97 m (3 ft 2 in) fuselage stretch and five cabin windows on each side, this 10-passenger model has 1497-kg (3,300-lb) thrust JT12A-8 engines and was certificated in April 1967
Sabreliner 65: in production until end of 1981, with supercritical wing and Garrett TFE731-3-1D turbofan engines; prototype flown on 29 June 1977 and type-approved on 28 November 1979
Sabreliner 75: prototype flown on 4 December 1969 as Sabreliner 70, with deeper fuselage and square cabin windows. Certificated in June 1970 but superseded on production line in 1973 by CF700-powered Model 75A first flown on 18 October 1972
Sabreliner 80A: Model 75A with Raisbeck modifications to improve performance. First flown in April 1978
Sabreliner 85: projected re-engined version with stretched fuselage. Design completed in 1990

Specification
North American (Rockwell) Sabreliner 65
Type: business transport aircraft
Powerplant: two 1678-kg (3,700-lb) thrust Garrett TFE731-3-1D turbofans
Performance: maximum cruising speed Mach 0.81; service ceiling 13715 m (45,000 ft); range 4447 km (2,763 miles)
Weights: empty 6420 kg (14,154 lb); maximum take-off 10886 kg (24,000 lb)
Dimensions: span 15.37 m (50 ft 5¼ in); length 14.30 m (46 ft 11 in); height 4.88 m (16 ft 0 in); wing area 35.30 m² (380.0 sq ft)

The first customer for the Sabreliner was the USAF, which bought the T-39A transport. It was used extensively in South-East Asia.

North American Texan/SNJ/Harvard

Almost certainly the most extensively used trainer of all time, with more than 17,000 built by North American, the **Harvard** was derived from the **North American NA-16** prototype first flown in April 1935. A cantilever low-wing monoplane with fixed tailwheel landing gear, open cockpits in tandem and power provided by a 298-kW (400-hp) Wright R-975 Whirlwind radial engine, the type after official testing received a production order under the designation **BT-9**. Modifications were specified in the contract, the most important being enclosed cockpits, and the resulting pre-production **NA-18** incorporated the changes and was powered by a 447-kW (600-hp) Pratt & Whitney R-1340 Wasp engine. However, the Wright R-975 engine was retained for production aircraft, the BT-9 (42 built) being followed by the **BT-9A** (40) which introduced two 7.62-mm (0.3-in) machine-guns, by the **BT-9B** (117) with detail improvements, and by the similar **BT-9C** (67) with some equipment changes. A single **BT-9D**, with revisions of the outer wing panels and rudder, led to the improved **BT-14** (251 built) which introduced a metal-covered fuselage and the 336-kW (450-hp) Pratt & Whitney R-985-25 Wasp Junior engine; in 1941 27 were re-engined with 298-kW (400-hp) R-985-11 engines, and were redesignated **BT-14A**. The US Navy also operated 40 examples of the BT-9 under the designation **NJ-1**, these having the R-1340 Wasp engine. Export orders for these fixed landing gear versions included one for Australia, which served as a pattern aircraft for production by Commonwealth Aircraft Corporation, China (85), Honduras (3), and licence-holding Japan and Sweden (two pattern aircraft each). France received 230 aircraft similar to the BT-9, for service with the air force (200) and navy (30), but only 111 of a similar order for BT-14s had been delivered at the time of the French collapse; the balance of 119 was acquired by the UK, then being supplied to the RCAF, which designated them **Yale Mk I**.

The requirement for a basic combat trainer led to development of the **NA-26**, a version of the NA-16 introducing retractable tailwheel landing gear, the 447-kW (600-hp) R-1340 engine, and equipment representative of contemporary operational types. Production versions included the **BC-1** (177), of which 30 were modified as **BC-1I** instrument trainers; the **BC-1A** (93) with airframe revisions; and a single **BC-1B** with a modified wing centre-section. A change of role to advanced trainer brought new designations, first as the **AT-6 Texan** (94) which differed little from the BC-1A. Subsequent versions included the **AT-6A** (1,847) with the R-1340-49 engine and revised fuel tanks, the **AT-6B** (400) gunnery trainer, the **AT-6C** (2,970) and **AT-6D** (4,388) which had revised structure to economise on light alloys, and the **AT-6F** (956) with strengthened airframe. The US Navy also used the type extensively, following the NJ-1 with the **SNJ-1** (16 similar to the BC-1 but with metal-covered fuselage), **SNJ-2** (61) with R-1340-56 engine, **SNJ-4** (2,400) and **SNJ-5**

North American SNJ-2 of the US Navy

(1,357) equivalent to AT-6C and AT-6D, and **SNJ-6** comprising 931 of the US Army's 956 AT-6Fs which had been procured for the US Navy. The designation **SNJ-5C** applied to SNJ-5s equipped with arrester hooks for deck-landing training.

In June 1938 the UK ordered 200 BC-1s, designating them **Harvard Mk I**, these representing the first of more than 5,000 delivered, mostly under Lend-Lease, to Commonwealth air forces. Most of the first 200 Harvard Mk Is were shipped to Southern Rhodesia for inception of the Commonwealth Air Training Plan, but the RAF retained almost all of a second batch of 200. After 30 similar aircraft were acquired for the RCAF, 600 equivalent to the AT-6 were procured as **Harvard Mk II** and distributed to the RAF (20) and **RNZAF** (67), the remainder being allocated to Canada for use in its contribution to the Air Training Plan. In addition to the Harvard Mk I and II, **Harvard Mk III** aircraft were acquired, equivalent respectively to the AT-6C and AT-6D; the designation **Harvard Mk IIB** applied to 2,610 built as **AT-16** aircraft by Noorduyn Aviation Ltd in Montreal, for use by the RAF and RCAF, and corresponding to the AT-6A. In 1946 this company was taken over by Canadian Car and Foundry, which built for the RCAF 270 **Harvard Mk 4** trainers to T-6G standard and 285 similar aircraft with the designation **T-6J** for the USAF Mutual Aid Program.

From 1949, 2,068 T-6 aircraft of different versions were rebuilt under the designation **T-6G**, introducing the R-1340-AN-1 engine, increased fuel capacity, improved cockpit layout, a steerable tailwheel and other improvements. These entered service with the US Air Force and US Navy, and during the Korean War 97 were modified to **LT-6G** configuration for deployment in battlefield surveillance and FAC roles. In addition to Texans exported to Brazil, China and Venezuela, many other air arms received surplus aircraft from RAF, RCAF and USAAF stocks.

Specification
North American SNJ-5
Type: two-seat advanced trainer
Powerplant: one 410-kW (550-hp) Pratt & Whitney R-1340-AN-1 radial

North American T-6G Texan of the Pakistan air force.

One of the earlier numbers of the great North American T-6 trainer family was the AT-6A, used by the United States Army Air Corps as a gunnery trainer from 1941 onwards. It was fitted with a single 0.3-in (7.62-mm) machine-gun on a pintle mounted in the rear cockpit.

piston engine
Performance: maximum speed 330 km/h (205 mph) at 1525 m (5,000 ft); service ceiling 6555 m (21,500 ft); range 1207 km (750 miles)
Weights: empty 1886 kg (4,158 lb); maximum take-off 2404 kg (5,300 lb)
Dimensions: span 12.81 m (42 ft 0¼ in); length 8.99 m (29 ft 6 in); height 3.58 m (11 ft 9 in); wing area 23.57 m² (253.70 sq ft)

North American X-15

Without doubt the most remarkable and most valuable research vehicle to have been developed within the X-series of USAF/USN-sponsored experimental aircraft, the **North American X-15** was required to meet performance parameters of a maximum altitude of 76200 m (250,000 ft) and a maximum speed of Mach 6, well in excess of 6437 km/h (4,000 mph)! The X-15 programme was funded jointly by the US Air Force and the US Navy, the former overseeing design and construction, although the National Advisory Committee for Aeronautics (NACA) provided overall technical direction. The official Request for Proposals was issued to 12 airframe companies on 30 December 1954, and on 4 February 1955 four engine manufacturers were invited to bid for the rocket motor contract. North American was awarded the airframe contract for its **NA-240** design in November 1955, and the XLR-99 engine contract went to Reaction Motors Inc. in September 1956.

It had always been the intention that the X-15 would be air-launched, and two Boeing B-52s were modified to carry the type under the starboard wing, between the fuselage and the inboard engine, then being redesignated NB-52A and NB-52B. Features of the X-15 were the long cylindrical fuselage with lateral fairings to house control systems and fuel tanks, and the thick wedge-shaped dor-

The X-15A-2 featured two external fuel tanks for greater endurance by this incalculably important high-speed research aircraft.

sal and ventral fins, the lower section of the latter being jettisoned before landing to give clearance for the retractable skids which formed the main landing gear.

The first two **X-15A** airframes were each powered initially by two 3629-kg (8,000-lb) thrust XLR-11 engines, the first aircraft becoming airborne under its mother ship on 10 March 1959. Test pilot Scott Crossfield made the first unpowered release on 8 June, and the same pilot also made the first powered flight, in the second X-15A, on 17 September. The latter machine was the first to be flown with the definitive XLR-99 engine, flying in this form on 15 November 1960. But for a ground-running accident before first flight, the third airframe would have been the first XLR-99-powered machine to fly. However, the accident damage was repaired and, the first X-15A having been re-engined, all three aircraft entered the performance evaluation phase of the programme. Almost 200 flights were made, including a series with the second aircraft which was rebuilt following a landing accident on 9 November 1962. In its rebuilt form it had a fuselage extension of 0.74 m (2 ft 5 in), external auxiliary fuel tanks, and

was given a heat-resistant surface treatment. As the **X-15A-2**, it made its maiden flight on 28 June 1964, and later achieved a maximum altitude of 107960 m (354,200 ft) and a maximum speed of 7297 km/h (4,534 mph).

Specification
North American X-15A
Type: high-speed high-altitude research aircraft
Powerplant: one Reaction Motors

XLR-99 rocket motor with a thrust rating of 25855-kg (57,000-lb) at sea level and approximately 31751-kg (70,000-lb) at peak altitude
Performance: maximum speed 6693 km/h (4,159 mph)
Weights: maximum take-off 15422 kg (34,000 lb)
Dimensions: span 6.71 m (22 ft 0 in); length 15.24 m (50 ft 0 in); height 4.12 m (13 ft 6 in); wing area 18.58 m² (200.0 sq ft)

Northrop Alpha and Beta

In 1928 John K. Northrop and Ken Jay formed the Avion Corporation at Burbank, California. Northrop had in the previous year designed Lockheed's first aircraft, the Vega, and had begun his aviation career with the Loughead Company, designing the wings for the **Loughead F-1** flying-boat in 1916. In 1919 he designed the very clean **Loughead S-1** sporting biplane but the ready availability of surplus military aircraft killed the S-1 and Loughead, which had built the prototype, collapsed in 1920. The company reappeared in 1927 as the Lockheed Aircraft Company.

Northrop's first aircraft for his new company was known as the Flying Wing (see Northrop Flying Wings) but of more immediate consequence was the next design, the **Northrop Alpha**, an all-metal seven-seat single-engine low-wing monoplane. In 1929 Avion Corporation became the Northrop Aircraft Corporation, a division of United Aircraft and Transport Corporation of which Boeing was also a part. Trans Continental and Western Air Inc., (later to become Trans World Airlines) ordered five Alphas with 313-kW (420-hp) Pratt & Whitney Wasp engines and began services on 20 April 1931 from San Francisco to New York, with 13 intermediate stops, the journey taking just over 23 hours. The Alphas were configured for three passengers and 211 kg (465 lb) of mail and cargo, for mail flying was a plum contract at that

time, but regularity and reliability was required. To achieve all-weather and night-flying capability, the Alphas had the most modern radio and navigation equipment, and for winter operations became the first commercial type to be fitted with Goodrich rubber de-icer boots on wing and tail surface leading edges. Thirteen of the 17 Alphas built saw service with TWA, and three were supplied for evaluation to the US Army Air Corps where, had production orders been given, they would have been designated **C-19**.

Various configurations carried the designations **Alpha 2, Alpha 3, Alpha 4** and **Alpha 4-A,** and a number of changes were made between individual aircraft as late modifications were made retrospectively to earlier aircraft, including fitting of streamlined 'trousers' over the original rather utilitarian landing gear. The last conversion was the **Gamma 4-A**, an all-cargo aircraft which could carry 567 kg (1,250 lb); the Gamma 4 and Gamma 4-A had a 336-kW (450-hp) Wasp engine and most of the earlier aircraft were similarly retrofitted.

The last surviving Alpha, the third built, served with the US Assistant Secretary of Commerce for Aeronautics, the Ford Motor Company, National Air Transport (part of United Airlines) and TWA; it was re-acquired by the airline in 1975 and

superbly restored before being placed in Washington's Smithsonian Institution National Air and Space Museum.

In 1931 Northrop built the prototype of an all-metal low-wing sporting monoplane, the **Beta**, a two-seater with a 119-kW (160-hp) Menasco Buccaneer in-line engine. It was converted later to single-seat configuration and fitted with a 224-kW (300-hp) Wright Whirlwind radial engine, in which form it became the first aircraft of such power to exceed 322 km/h (200 mph).

Despite its ungainly appearance and fixed landing gear, the 1930 Alpha may truly be regarded as the first 'modern' airliner.

Northrop YA-9A

Under the designation **Northrop YA-9A**, the company built two prototypes of a single-seat close-support aircraft as the company's submission for the competitive development phase of the USAF's A-X close-support aircraft competition. A cantilever high-wing monoplane, powered by two 2722-kg (6,000-lb) thrust Avco Lycoming ALF 502

turbofan engines, the first of the prototypes made its maiden flight on 30 May 1972. In competitive evaluation the YA-9A lost out to the YA-10A by Fairchild Republic.

The first prototype of the A-9A illustrates its different approach to the competing A-10.

Northrop A-13, A-16, A-17 and A-33

Northrop used the Gamma transport as the basis of a private-venture design for a light attack bomber, identifying this as the **Northrop Gamma 2C** which, powered by a 548-kW (735-hp) Wright SR-1820F radial engine, was acquired for evaluation by the US Army Air Corps in June 1934 under the designation **YA-13**. Subsequently re-engined with a 708-kW (950-hp) Pratt & Whitney R-1830 Twin Wasp, this aircraft was redesignated **XA-16 (Northrop Gamma 2F)**. Following tests of the YA-13 and XA-16, Northrop received a $2 million contract for 110 attack bombers designated **A-17**, but because testing of the XA-16 had shown that the aircraft was over-powered, the Gamma 2F was re-engined with a 559-kW (750-hp) Pratt & Whitney R-1535 Twin Wasp Junior, serving as the prototype for the A-17. Following the incorporation of several other modifications, the first of 109 production A-17 aircraft was delivered in December 1935. A contract was received in the same month for an improved **A-17A**, introducing retractable tailwheel landing gear and the 615-kW (825-hp) Pratt & Whitney R-1535-13 engine. Some 129 were built, initially by Northrop, but in 1937 Douglas acquired the remaining 49 per cent of Northrop Corporation's

Douglas 8A of the Iraqi air force in 1941.

stock, and it was the Douglas Company which completed production of these aircraft. Of the total, 93 served with the USAAC for only 18 months, then being returned to Douglas for sale to the UK and France. The Royal Air Force received 60, designating them **Nomad Mk I**, and all were transferred to the South African Air Force. Douglas also built this aircraft for export under the designation **Douglas Model 8A**, supplying them to Argentina, Iraq, the Netherlands and Norway. A batch of 34 Model **8A-5** aircraft was also built for Peru, 31 of them

being commandeered by the US Army Air Force in early 1942 for use in an attack role. Armed with six 7.62-mm (0.3-in) machine-guns and able to carry up to 816 kg (1,800 lb) of bombs, all were used in a training role under the designation **A-33**.

Specification
Northrop A-17A
Type: two-seat attack aircraft
Powerplant: one 615-kW (825-hp) Pratt & Whitney R-1535-13 radial piston engine

Performance: maximum speed 354 km/h (220 mph); service ceiling 5915 m (19,400 ft); range 1175 km (730 miles)
Weights: empty 2316 kg (5,106 lb); maximum take-off 3421 kg (7,543 lb)
Dimensions: span 14.55 m (47 ft 9 in); length 9.65 m (31 ft 8 in); height 3.66 m (12 ft 0 in); wing area 33.63 m² (362.0 sq ft)
Armament: five 7.62-mm (0.3-in) machine-guns (four forward-firing and one on a trainable mount in rear cockpit), plus four 45-kg (100-lb) bombs

Northrop BT-1 and BT-2

While Northrop was working on the YA-13/XA-16 developments of the Gamma, the company was also testing a scaled-down version for the US Navy under the designation **Northrop XFT-1**. This was one of two Northrop prototypes which failed to attract production orders, the other being the Type 3-A of 1935. Both were all-metal fighters, the XFT-1 with fixed landing gear being intended for the US Navy. Powered originally by a 466-kW (625-hp) Wright XR-1510 radial, it was later re-engined, as the **XFT-2**, with a 485-kW (650-hp) Pratt & Whitney R-1535, but crashed three months later, in July 1936. The **Northrop 3-A** was a similar design for the US Army, but differed from the navy aircraft in having retractable landing gear and a modified canopy. Developed alongside these prototypes was the **XBT-1**, which had semi-retractable landing gear, and this entered production as the **BT-1** torpedo-bomber, the first of 54 being delivered in April 1938. The BT-1 had a 615-kW (825-hp) Pratt & Whitney R-1535

Northrop BT-1 of the US Navy.

Twin Wasp Junior radial engine, but one aircraft was modified as the **BT-2** to have revised landing gear and a 597-kW

(800-hp) Wright XR-1820 Cyclone. With other modifications this was to become the Douglas SBD Dauntless as the

original Northrop Corporation had by then become the El Segundo Division of Douglas.

Northrop B-2A

Following Northrop's earlier experience with flying wings, the company was well placed to develop an **Advanced Technology Bomber (ATB)** required by the US Air Force to replace its elderly B-52s still used in the strategic role since its entry into service in 1955. The original requirement for 133 aircraft was cut back to 76 by 1991, but ultra-high costs (by 1992 $1,020 million each) may cause further reductions in the programme. Preliminary design began in 1978 and a formal contract was placed by the USAF in October 1981 for entry into service in 1995. The airframe is mostly built of composite radar absorbent honeycomb structure using graphite/epoxy materials although some high aluminium and titanium is included. Six aircraft (82-1066 to 1071) were ordered for the 3,500 hour test programme and the existence of the flying wing low-observable or 'Stealth Bomber' revealed to the world in 1987

and the first aircraft unveiled in November 1988. The **B-2** took to the air for the first time on 17 July 1989 from Palmdale piloted by Northrop test pilot Bruce Hinds and USAF Colonel Richard S. Cough. The crew/payload section of the aircraft, which is as close as the B-2 comes to having a fuselage, starts aft of the apex of the wing, ends short of the wing trailing edge, and is smoothly blended into the upper surfaces of the wing. The cockpit provides side-by-side seating for two crew members, both of whom will be pilots (not navigator or radar navigator/bombardier in opera-

After years of debate and outright opposition it now appears as if B-2 production will cease at 20 aircraft. The small 'Silver Bullet' force to enter service will consist of 19 'Stealth Bombers' with one permanent test vehicle.

tional aircraft) seated on ACES II ejection seats. However, a jump seat is provided for an instructor/observer. By April 1992 four aircraft were flying with the 6510th Test Squadron of Air Force Material Command based at Edwards AFB, California. Construction of nine further B-2A airframes has begun but not all of these are fully funded. First unit scheduled to receive the **B-2A** is the 509th Bomb Wing at Whiteman AFB, Missouri.

Specification (Estimated)
Northrop B-2A
Type: low-observable strategic bomber
Powerplant: four 8620-kg (19,000-lb) thrust General Electric F118-GE-100 non-afterburning turbofans
Performance: maximum speed 1010 km/h (545 mph) above 12200 m (40,000 ft) and 917 km/h (569 mph) at sea level; service ceiling over 16765 m (55,000 ft); range on internal fuel with

16920-kg (37,300-lb) warload 9815 km (5,300 nautical miles); range at high altitude on internal fuel with 10890 kg (24,000 lb) warload 12225 km (6,600 miles)
Weights: empty 45360 kg (100,000 lb); maximum warload 22680 kg (50,000 lb); maximum take-off 181437 kg (400,000 lb)
Dimensions: span 52.43 m (172 ft 0 in); length 21.03 m (69 ft 0 in); height 5.18 m (17 ft 0 in); wing area 465.5 m²

(5,000 sq ft)
Armament: two weapons bays located side-by-side under the fuselage centre-section, each fitted with a Boeing Rotary Launcher capable of carrying eight AGM-69 SRAM II or AGM-129A ACM or AGM-137 Tri-Service Standoff Attack Missiles; alternative loads can include eight B61 tactical/strategic or B83 strategic free-fall nuclear bombs, 454 kg (1,000 lb) Mk 36 sea mines

Northrop Delta

While the Gamma was being developed, Northrop was working on a nine-seat transport, which was basically a new fuselage married to Gamma wings. Unfortunately for Northrop, the US 1926 Air Commerce Act was amended to prohibit the use of single-engine aircraft for carrying passengers by night, or over rough terrain where emergency landings could not be made. Consequently, airline use for its intended role was nonexistent in the USA, although three had been sold before the new regulation was announced. Eight others were used as executive transports, and one was bought by Swedish AB Aero-transport, which subsequently acquired a second, and the US Coast Guard operated a Delta

The Northrop RT-01 was the United States Coast Guard version of the Delta airliner. Powered by the 529-kW (710-hp) Wright SR-1820-F3 Cyclone engine, its wingspan was 14.57 m (47 ft 9½ in), maximum take-off weight 3334 kg (7,350 lb) and speed 359 km/h (223 mph).

under the designation **RT-1**, as the Secretary of the Treasury's personal aircraft. The last Delta was supplied to Canada as a pattern aircraft for assembly in that country by Canadian Vickers, who built 20 of various marks with both wheel and float landing gear. Deltas were flown with various engines, includ-

ing the 529-kW (710-hp) and 548-kW (735-hp) Wright SR-1820, 485-kW (650-

hp), 492-kW (660-hp) and 522-kW (700-hp) Pratt & Whitney Hornets.

Northrop F-5 family

In the mid-1950s Northrop began design of its private-venture **Northrop N-156** lightweight fighter with which it hoped to meet a US government requirement for a comparatively inexpensive combat aircraft for supply to friendly nations under the Military Assistance Program. This led first to the **T-38 Talon** trainer for the US Air Force, and it was not until 23 April 1962 that the US Secretary of Defense received USAF approval of Northrop's **N-156F** single-seat fighter prototype. This had a lightweight airframe and advanced aerodynamic features, and was powered by two small turbojets. The prototype had a USAF tail number (59-4987) but no US markings, and it first flew on 30 July 1959. Ordered into production as the **Northrop F-5A Freedom Fighter**, it was preceded into service by the two-seat **F-5B** trainer. F-5Bs entered service with the USAF's 4441st Combat Crew Training Squadron at Williams AFB, on 30 April 1964, the first F-5As being delivered to the same unit four months later. To evaluate the combat potential of the F-5A, a 12-aircraft unit was deployed to South East Asia in October 1965, flying more than 2,500 hours in four months of operations on close-support, interdiction and reconnaissance sorties. In early 1966 the unit was based in Vietnam, then deployed for armed reconnaissance, interdiction and combat air patrols against enemy MiG fighters. Subsequently increased to 18 aircraft, the F-5As of this unit were transferred to the South Vietnamese air force in 1967.

While production of the Northrop F-5A/B was in progress, the company used an F-5A airframe to serve as the prototype of an improved version, powered by two General Electric J85-GE-21 turbojets providing some 23 per cent more thrust than the engines of the F-5A. However, it was not until 20 November 1970 that the revised type was selected for production to fulfil a new requirement for an International Fighter Aircraft. As finalised this **F-5E**,

later named **Tiger II**, had a number of modifications to improve manoeuvrability and short-field performance, greater fuel capacity, and an integrated fire-control (though without radar). The first production F-5E was flown on 11 August 1972 and accepted into USAF service on 4 April 1973. A measure of the capability of the F-5E may be gained by the fact that the top air combat training schools in the USA, the US Navy's Fighter Weapon School and the US Air Force's Aggressor Squadron, both used F-5Es as 'enemy' aircraft in combat training against US squadrons of first-line operational tactical fighters. An **F-5F** lengthened-fuselage tandem two-seat trainer version of the F-5E was also developed, this retaining the integrated fire-control system so that it can be deployed for training or combat.

Northrop also developed an advanced version of the F-5 fitted with a single F404 turbofan engine and other significant improvements as a private venture. Originally designated **F-5G**, it later became the **F-20A Tigershark**. When F-5 Freedom Fighter production finally ended in 1987 with further deliveries to the Singapore air force, no less than 2,622 had been built in Canada by Canadair, in Spain by CASA and by Northrop in the USA. Others were also assembled in the Netherlands and South Korea. Different versions of the type have served with air arms in Bahrain, Brazil, Canada, Chile, Ethiopia, Greece, Honduras, Indonesia, Iran, Jordan, Kenya, Libya, Malaysia, Mexico, Morocco, the Netherlands, Norway, Philippines, Saudi Arabia, Singapore, South Korea, Spain, Sudan, Switzerland, Taiwan, Thailand, Tunisia, Turkey, USA, Venezuela and North Yemen. With vast numbers of F-5s still in service, a number of companies are offering update programmes, the most successful to date being Bristol Aerospace Ltd of Winnipeg, Canada, who received in 1987 a contract to upgrade and extend the life of 56 CF-5A/Ds for the Canadian Forces

Northrop F-5E Tiger II

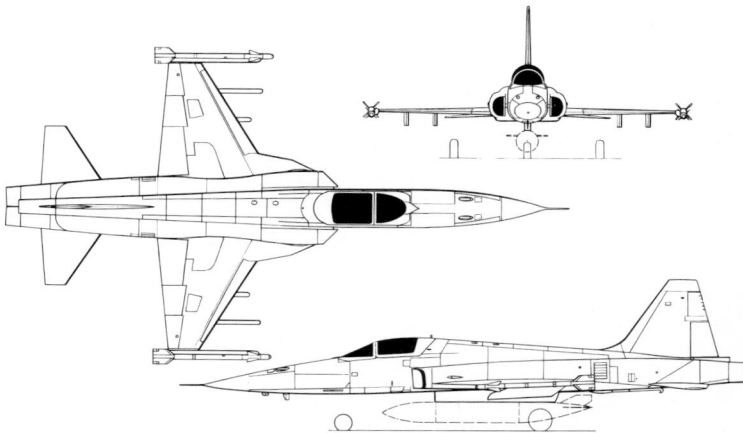

for further use as lead-in trainers. With airframe fatigue life extended by another 4,000 hours, the installation of advanced avionics, and incorporation of aerodynamic improvements the Bristol refurbished F-5A/B becomes the F5-2000, indicating continuation of service beyond the year 2000, and with enhanced performance. Cost of the first modified aircraft, returned to service in 1991, was quoted as $4 million. Fokker and IAI of Israel are also currently offering F-5 upgrades.

Variants
CF-5A/CF-5D: Canadair-built versions of the F-5A/F-5B respectively, for the Canadian Armed Forces, with Orenda-built 1950-kg (4,300-lb) thrust J85-CAN-15 engines
NF-5A/NF-5B: Canadair-built single- and two-seat versions for the Netherlands
RF-5A: reconnaissance variant of the F-5A with four cameras in the nose
RF-5E Tigereye: reconnaissance version of the F-5E with modified forward fuselage to accommodate a wide variety of equipment for this role

SR-5A/SR-5B: CASA-built single- and two-seat versions for the Spanish air force
SRF-5A: CASA-built version of the RF-5A for the Spanish air force

Specification
Northrop F-5E
Type: tactical fighter
Powerplant: two 2268-kg (5,000-lb) afterburning thrust General Electric J85-GE-21 turbojets
Performance: maximum speed Mach 1.64 or 1743 km/h (1,083 mph) at 10975 m (36,000 ft); service ceiling 15790 m (51,800 ft); maximum range with fuel drop tanks, jettisoned after use 2483 km (1,543 miles)
Weights: empty 4410 kg (9,723 lb); maximum take-off 11214 kg (24,722 lb)
Dimensions: span 8.13 m (26 ft 8 in); length 14.45 m (47 ft 4¾ in); height 4.06 m (13 ft 4 in); wing area 17.28 m² (186.0 sq ft)
Armament: two 20-mm M-39 cannon in fuselage nose and two AIM-9 Sidewinder missiles on wingtip launchers, plus up to 3175 kg (7,000 lb) of mixed stores

Northrop YF-17A

Under the designation **Northrop P-530 Cobra**, the company designed as a private venture an advanced tactical combat aircraft. When the US Air Force gave details of its Lightweight Fighter Prototype Program, Northrop adopted for its **P-600** submission many of the aerodynamic innovations and the powerplant that it had intended to use in the P-530. From the four submissions received for this competition, the USAF selected General Dynamics and Northrop each to build two prototypes of their designs under the respective designations YF-16A and **YF-17A**. Northrop's two YF-17A prototypes were flown on 9 June and 21 August 1974, but in the ensuing evaluation the General Dynamics F-16 was selected for production. Subsequent testing of the YF-17As by the US Navy has led to development of this aircraft by McDonnell Douglas and

Northrop to meet the US Navy's requirement for a combat/strike fighter. The resulting aircraft is currently in production for the Navy by these two companies under the designation McDonnell Douglas F/A-18 Hornet.

Key features of the trim and attractive Northrop YF-17A were the outward-canted twin vertical tail surfaces and the leading-edge root extensions blended into the forward fuselage. Powered by a pair of General Electric YJ101 continuous-bleed turbojets, the YF-17A spanned 10.67 m (35 ft), had a normal take-off weight of 9525 kg (21,000 lb) and could attain Mach 2 with ease.

Northrop F-20A Tigershark

In 1979 Northrop developed an advanced version of the F-5 as a private venture supersonic fighter intended primarily for export markets or licence-build, although the company equally pushed the design as a possible replacement for USAF F-4s and F-106s in the Air Defence Fighter role. Originally designated F-5G, the updated design was equipped with a single General Electric F-404-GE-100 advanced turbofan engine and an EFIS or 'glass' cockpit. Later redesignated the F-20A Tigershark to enhance the impression that it was a new aircraft and thus intended for volume production, the Tigershark subsequently bettered all its design goals and demonstrated a reliability record better than 97 per cent. Three aircraft were completed, the first flying in August 1982 and the second one year later while the third flew in May 1984. Following the loss of the first and second aircraft in October 1984 and May 1985 respectively, construction of a fourth airframe was started but abandoned in 1986 when the entire F-20A programme was terminated, fol-

lowing USAF selection of the F-16 for the ADF requirement. A number of countries expressed a strong interest in the F-20A programme including Germany, but more particularly South Korea and India, who were offered the whole project as a package (including drawings, the stored third and uncompleted fourth aircraft) in 1987 by Northrop. However, nothing came of the proposals and the company gave up all hope of sales.

Specification
Type: single-seat tactical fighter
Powerplant: one 8164-kg (18,000-lb) thrust General Electric F404-GE-100 turbofan
Performance: maximum level speed at 13100 m (43,000 ft); service ceiling 17315 m (56,800 ft); combat radius (hi-lo-hi) with two 1249-litre (330-US gal) drop tanks, two Sidewinder AAMs and five Mk. 82 bombs 1019 km (633 miles); ferry range with three 1249-litre (330-US gal) drop tanks 3984 km (2,165 miles)
Weights: empty 5965 kg (13,150 lb);

warload 4080 kg (9,000 lb); maximum take-off 1270 kg (28,000 lb)
Dimensions: span (with missiles) 8.53 m (27 ft 11 in); length 14.4 m (47 ft 3 in); height 4.2 m (13 ft 10 in); wing area 18.6 m² (200 sq ft)
Armament: two 20-mm M39 cannon with 225 rounds per gun located in upper forward fuselage. Centreline, four underwing and two wingtip hardpoints carrying a mix of weapons

Armed with a pair of AIM-7F Sparrows, this is one of the three F-20s which chalked up 1,500 test-flying hours.

such as a General Electric GPU-5/A 30-mm gun pod; two AIM-7F Sparrow or six AIM-9 Sidewinder AAMs; four Maverick air-to-surface missiles; nine Mk. 82 227-kg (500-lb) bombs or four Paveway laser guided bombs.

Northrop F-89 Scorpion

The **Northrop F-89 Scorpion** was designed as a jet replacement for the P-61 Black Widow, and following the placing of a development contract in May 1946, Northrop received an order for two prototypes in December 1946. With the Northrop designation **N-24**, the first **XF-89** flew in August 1948 and demonstrated a sufficiently good performance to attract a production contract for 48 **F-89A** fighters in January 1949. The second prototype, the **XF-89A (N-49)**, was completed in early 1950, but the first aircraft was lost in a fatal crash in February 1950, this being attributed to structural failure caused by flutter in the horizontal tail surfaces. Modifications were made and incorporated in production aircraft and F-89A deliveries began in July 1950; the

Northrop designation was **N-35** and early aircraft had Allison J33-A-21 engines, later changed to 2313-kg (5,100-lb) thrust J33-A-21As which, with afterburners, developed 3084-kg (6,800-lb) thrust. Internal equipment changes from the 19th aircraft led to the **F-89B** which had a Lear autopilot and ILS. Thirty of this variant were built before the **F-89C** appeared with a new tailplane and a number of equipment changes. During the production run of 164 F-89Cs several variants of the Allison turbojet were installed.

Next model to enter service in 1953 was the **F-89D (N-68)** which featured a new Hughes fire-control system, removal of the standard six 20-mm cannon from the nose cone, installation of underwing fuel tanks, and provision for

wingtip pods each carrying 52 folding-fin air rockets. Total production of the F-89D reached 682. The **YF-89E (N-71)** was a one-off test-bed for the Allison YJ71, an engine in the 3175-kg (7,000-lb) thrust class without afterburner. A proposed production version was the **F-89F**, but this and the **F-89G** with revised armament and fire-control were cancelled.

Final production model was the **F-89H (N-138)** of 1956, which was similar to the F-89D but had uprated engines and wingtip pods which had been modified to carry three Hughes Falcon guided air-to-air missiles in addition to 21 rockets. An additional six rockets could be carried beneath the wings; total F-89H production reached 156 but another model, the **F-89J (N-160)**, was a conversion from the F-89D equipped to carry a Douglas MB-1 Genie unguided nuclear-tipped rocket on pylons beneath each wing in addition to four underwing

Falcon GAR-2 guided missiles. The wingtip rocket pods were replaced by fuel tanks.

As the F-89s were replaced in 1957 by Convair F-102s, they were passed to Air Force Reserve squadrons and Air National Guard units, and some were converted as missile- and drone-control aircraft with the designations **DF-89A** and **DF-89B**.

Specification
Northrop F-89D Scorpion
Type: two-seat all-weather interceptor
Powerplant: two 3266-kg (7,200-lb) afterburning thrust Allison J35-A-35, -33A, -41 or -47 turbojets
Performance: maximum speed 1024 km/h (636 mph) at 3230 m (10,600 ft); service ceiling 14995 m (49,200 ft); range 4184 km (2,600 miles)
Weights: empty 11428 kg (25,194 lb);

maximum take-off 19160 kg (42,241 lb)
Dimensions: span 59.97 m (59 ft 8 in); length 16.41 m (53 ft 10 in); height 5.36 m (17 ft 7 in); wing area 52.21 m² (562.0 sq ft)
Armament: 104 70-mm (2.75-in) rockets in wingtip pods, or 27 rockets plus three Falcon missiles

Built as a Northrop F-89D, this Scorpion served as an F-89H prototype and was further developed as an F-89J with provision for Douglas MB-1 Genie nuclear-tipped rockets and Hughes Falcon missiles. Two of the latter are visible here, as are the larger unguided Genies. Developed as Project Ding Dong, a Genie was live-tested over the trials range at Yucca Flats in July 1957. Detonated by ground command, the airburst was monitored by USAF observers located under the explosion.

Northrop Flying Wings

In 1929 John Northrop designed and developed a two-seat single-engine aircraft which was basically a flying wing with two slim booms supporting the tail unit. The aircraft, built by Northrop's newly formed Avion Corporation (later the Northrop Aircraft Corporation) was powered by a 67-kW (90-hp) Menasco engine, initially driving a pusher propeller but modified later to tractor configuration.

Experience with this early aircraft was stored away for a decade until Northrop could pursue his all-wing concept, but in 1940 the **Northrop N-1M** flew with two 48-kW (65-hp) Lycoming engines buried in a thick wing driving pusher propellers. The N-1M was a true all-wing design and its low drag gave improved acceleration in both dive and glide; it also enabled the aircraft to use significantly less power on take-off than conventional aircraft of similar size and weight. Early tests found few problems, the main one being engine cooling, but this was solved by the installation of 89-kW (120-hp) Franklin engines with three-bladed propellers and improved baffles. The N-1M has survived in the US National Air and Space Museum.

Experience with the N-1M convinced Northrop that an all-wing bomber was feasible, and following evaluation by USAAF engineers a design contract was awarded under the designation **XB-35**. Four 18.29-m (60-ft) span **N-9M** scale models were built to provide flight data but the first, flown in December 1942, was lost in a fatal crash early the following year. The first three N-9Ms had two 205-kW (275-hp) Menasco air-cooled engines, but the fourth, the **N-9MB**, had 224-kW (300-hp) Franklins; all drove pusher propellers. A three-year test programme was flown from Muroc Army Air Base, providing much data and giving pilots experience in the handling and performance of flying wings, and the autopilot for the XB-35 was developed in an N-9M. All N-9Ms had retractable landing gear and varying colour schemes; the first two were all yellow, the third (**N-9MA**) was blue on top and yellow underneath, while the fourth (N-9MB) had the colour reversed. The colours identified the top or bottom of the aircraft during observations of the flight programme.

In November 1941 the USAAF ordered two prototype XB-35 flying wing bombers, powered by four 2237-kW (3,000-hp) Pratt & Whitney R-4360 Wasp Major piston engines driving eight-bladed counter-rotating pusher propellers. A further 13 aircraft, designated **YB-35**, were ordered in early 1943. There were many problems with the propellers and gearboxes, but the first XB-35 made its maiden flight on 25 June 1946, followed by the second in the following year.

The end of World War II, together with orders placed for the competing Convair B-36, sealed the fate of the piston-engine B-35, but foreseeing this possibility Northrop received approval from the USAF to modify two of the YB-35s to jet power. Redesignated **YB-49**, the first of these flew on 21 October 1947 with eight 1814-kg (4,000-lb) thrust Allison J35 engines; the second had six 2540-kW (5,600-lb) thrust Allison engines, four buried in the wings and two in underslung pods. Many complimentary reports on the YB-49 were filed by air force officers, and the service was convinced of the advantages of the all-wing configuration, but in June 1948 the second YB-49 was destroyed with the loss of its five man crew in a crash attributed to structural failure.

In spite of this the US Air Force ordered 30 modified **RB-49A** aircraft, one of which was to be built by Northrop and, because of that company's other commitments, 29 by Consolidated Vultee, but this order was later cancelled to provide extra funds for the B-36. The YB-35 programme continued for a while with various test airframes, but in October 1949 the whole programme was cancelled and the aircraft were scrapped. Sole survivor was the six-jet YB-49A, but just four years later this was broken up.

The **XP-56** was the first all-magnesium all-welded airframe and was intended to be an advanced fighter. Powered by a 1491-kW (2,000-hp) Pratt & Whitney R-2800 Double Wasp radial engine submerged in the rear fuselage, driving two three-blade counter-rotating propellers, the first XP-56 flew at Muroc Dry Lake on 6 September 1943 but was destroyed shortly afterwards when a

The YB-49 bomber was cancelled in favour of the Convair B-36 despite being a superior design in almost every respect.

The first XP-56 had only short upper tail surfaces and was lost after a tyre blew out as the aircraft was taxiing. It spanned 12.95 m (42 ft 6 in) and estimated maximum speed was 748 km/h (465 mph).

tyre blew and the aircraft turned over. The second XP-56, flown in March 1944, had an enlarged vertical tail and other modifications, but although flight characteristics were improved the advent of the jet engine curtailed further development.

A Northrop feasibility study in September 1942 for a rocket-powered military interceptor brought the company a contract for design and construction of three **MX-324** gliders to test the aerodynamics of the proposed 9.75-m (32-ft) span flying wing with a prone pilot cockpit. The third glider was converted before completion to the **MX-334** with a 91-kg (200-lb) thrust Aerojet XCAL-200 rocket motor, and following tests with the gliders being towed by a Lockheed P-38 the MX-334 flew under power for 3 minutes 30 seconds on 22 June 1944.

In 1943 Northrop was contracted to

The XP-79 was designed to ram enemy aircraft, cutting them up in mid-air. The airframe was intended to survive 10 such interceptions.

build two **JB-1 (MX-543)** flying wing aircraft; the first was a glider to test characteristics while the second, the **JB-1A**, had two 181-kg (400-lb) General Electric turbojets in place of the pilot, becoming a ground-launched flying bomb with a pre-programmed guidance system. It carried 1814-kg (4,000-lb) thrust rockets to drive the sled on which the JB-1A was mounted along a 122-m (400-ft) track to reach its 257 km/h (160 mph) take-off speed. A change of emphasis to pulsejet designs killed the programme in favour of the **JB-10 (MX-544) Jet Bomb**, an 8.84-m (29-ft) span flying wing with a 363-kg (800-lb)

thrust Ford pulsejet engine. Two 828-kg (1,825-lb) warheads were built as part of the inner wing and the Jet Bomb was launched on a sled from a short 15.24-m (50-ft) track with the assistance of four solid rockets. Northrop delivered over 1,000 sleds and 24 JB-10s to the US Army before the end of World War II.

US Army requirements for an advanced flying wing fighter led in January 1943 to Northrop receiving a design and construction contract for three **XP-79 Flying Ram** aircraft, each to be powered by a 907-kg (2,000-lb) thrust Aerojet rocket engine, but continued problems with design of the latter led to cancellation of the contract and its sub-

stitution by a new contract for one **XP-79B** with two 635-kg (1,400-lb) thrust Westinghouse Model B turbojets. The XP-79B was built of heavy magnesium and steel armour plate, the intention being that it would literally dive on enemy bombers and ram them, slicing off their tails. In case this failed an armament of four 12.7-mm (0.5-in) machineguns was planned, and a prone pilot position was incorporated. On 12 September 1945 the aircraft made its only flight, at Muroc Dry Lake, which ended in a fatal crash following a spin.

The final Northrop flying wing design, although it could more accurately be described as a tailless aircraft, was the

XS-4 Skylancer, a transonic research vehicle with two 726-kg (1,600-lb) thrust Westinghouse turbojets. Later redesignated **X-4**, the first of two aircraft flew at Muroc on 15 December 1948, followed by the second on 7 June 1949. With a span of only 8.18 m (26 ft 10 in) and weight of 3175 kg (7,000 lb), the two X-4s completed their research programme in April 1954 and both survive as museum exhibits.

Specification
Northrop XB-35
Type: seven-crew heavy bomber prototype
Powerplant: four 2237-kW (3,000-

hp) Pratt & Whitney R-4360 radial piston engines
Performance: maximum speed 629 km/h (391 mph) at 10670 m (35,000 ft); service ceiling 12190 m (40,000 ft); range 1159 km (720 miles) with full bombload
Weights: empty 40624 kg (89,560 lb); maximum take-off 94801 kg (209,000 lb)
Dimensions: span 52.43 m (172 ft 0 in); length 16.18 m (53 ft 1 in); height 6.12 m (20 ft 1 in); wing area 371.60 m² (4,000.0 sq ft)
Armament: (proposed) 20 12.7-mm (0.5-in) machine-guns in seven turrets, plus up to 4536 kg (10,000 lb) of bombs

Northrop Gamma

In January 1932 John Northrop and Donald Douglas formed the Northrop Corporation as a partly-owned subsidiary of the Douglas Aircraft Co. The first aircraft from the new corporation was the **Northrop Gamma**, several of which were built to special order for record-breaking flights and research work. The first two aircraft, a **Gamma 2A** and a **Gamma 2B**, were powered respectively by a 585-kW (785-hp) Wright and 373-kW (500-hp) Pratt & Whitney Wasp radial; both were delivered at the end of 1932, the first to Texaco who loaned it to Frank Hawks for record-breaking flights and the second to Lincoln Ellsworth, who eventually used it for a transantarc-

tic flight. TWA bought three **Gamma 2D** aircraft with 529-kW (710-hp) Wright Cyclone engines as single-seat mailplanes in 1934. The second was later re-engined with a 578-kW (775-hp) Wright and was used by Texaco to test oil temperatures and flows before being sold to the US Army Air Corps, which designated it **UC-100**.

A number of Gammas were delivered to individual customers, including two to the UK, a 2E (K5053) for the Aeroplane & Armament Experimental Establishment and a **Gamma 2L** (G-AFBT) the last to be built, was used by the Bristol Aeroplane Co. as a test-bed for its Hercules engines. The Chinese government

ordered 24 **Gamma 2E** aircraft as light bombers, with 529-kW (710-hp) Wright engines; they could carry a 726-kg (1,600-lb) bombload and had four 7.62-mm (0.3-in) forward-firing machineguns in the wings, and one rearward-firing in the rear cockpit. A further 25 Gamma 2Es were assembled in China

The Northrop Gamma 2D was a high-speed mailplane. This aircraft was later modified for high-altitude experiments, paving the way for commercial flying 'above the weather'.

from components provided by Northrop.

Northrop lifting bodies

In mid-1964 Northrop was contracted by the US National Aeronautics and Space Administration (NASA) to produce two all-metal wingless lifting-body re-entry research vehicles, based on experience gained with the **Northrop M2-F1** wooden glider, which made more than 500 flights in 1963-64. The two new vehicles were designated **M2-F2** and **HL-10** and differed in under- and upper-surface fuselage shapes. First flight of the M2-F2 as a glider was made on 12 July 1966 when it was dropped from beneath the wing of a Boeing B-52 at 14235 m (45,000 ft) to make a successful 306 km/h (190 mph) landing four minutes later. Thr HL-10 made a similar

Along with Northrop's HL-10 aircraft, the M2-F2, in all its forms, was used to investigate vital re-entry qualities during the 1960s and 1970s for the later Space Shuttle programme.

flight on 22 December 1966. First powered flight using rockets was made by the HL-10 from a B-52 on 13 November 1968; the M2-F2 was badly damaged on landing in May 1967 and, subsequently rebuilt as the **M2-F3**, made its first powered flight on 2 June 1970, attaining Mach 0.8 at 16155 m (53,000 ft) on three of its four XLR11 rocket chambers. Later in the programme it

recorded a height of nearly 27430 m (90,000 ft) and speed of Mach 1.7, while the HL-10 attained Mach 1.9 and a height in excess of 27430 m (90,000 ft). When

testing ended in 1973 these aircraft had provided much information which was to prove invaluable for NASA's Space Shuttle programme.

Northrop N-3PB

In 1940 Northrop received an order from a Norwegian Buying Commission for the design and construction of a single-engine monoplane patrol bomber with twin floats. The Norwegian order covered 24 aircraft, and in less than eight months the **Northrop N-3PB** prototype flew, on 1 November 1940, powered by an 895-kW (1,200-hp) Wright Cyclone GR-1820 radial engine. It attained a speed of 414 km/h (257 mph) and was then claimed to be the world's fastest military seaplane.

Norway was invaded by the Germans shortly after the contract had been awarded, and the N-3PBs were therefore delivered to a unit of the Royal Norwegian Naval Air Service, operating as an RAF unit from unimproved coastal sites in Iceland on anti-submarine patrol and convoy escort duties. All maintenance had to be performaced in the open, often under extremely harsh environmental conditions, and during 19 months of 1941-42 several were lost

Northrop NP-3B of No. 330 Sqn, RAF Coastal Command based in Iceland during 1941-42.

during water landings in severe arctic weather, but there were no losses due to enemy action. An aircraft was destroyed as late as 1965, in the collapse of a snow-laden hangar, but in the early 1980s an N-3PB was located and re-

stored in Norwegian colours by the manufacturers.

Northrop N-23 Pioneer
to
P.Z.L. P.23 and P.43 Karaś

Northrop N-23 Pioneer

Powered by three 596-kW (800-hp) Wright Cyclone 744BA2 radial engines, the Pioneer could carry up to 36 passengers or five tons of cargo; quick-change fittings enabled seats to be removed easily and cargo restraint rings fitted. At sea level the Pioneer took off at 10433 kg (23,000 lb) gross weight in less than 122 m (400 ft), but in spite of its good performance the ready availability of war-surplus transports doomed the project and it got no further than the prototype stage. The aircraft was lost in a fatal crash about a year after its first flight.

Northrop's experience with the Pioneer was not wasted, however, for in

The ungainly N-23 Pioneer offered excellent STOL performance but failed to find a niche in the post-war market.

March 1948 the company received a $5.5 million contract for 23 aircraft of similar configuration, the **N-32 Raider**. The USAF order covered 13 assault transports for troop training (designated **C-125A**) and 10 for Arctic rescue work (**C-125B**). The first C-125 flew on 1 August 1949, powered by three 895-kW (1,200-hp) Wright Cyclone R-1820-99 radial engine. For short-field operation six 454-kg (1,000-lb) thrust JATO units could be fitted, enabling the aircraft to

take off in less than 152 m (500 ft). It could carry up to 32 troops or 5443 kg (12,000 lb) of cargo or mixed loads. Entry was by an underfuselage ramp and the tailwheel strut served also as a jack to lift

the rear fuselage higher for the loading of bulky equipment. Deliveries to the USAF had been completed by the end of 1950, the C-125s remaining in service until declared surplus in 1955.

Northrop P-61 Black Widow

The first US aircraft to be designed as a radar-equipped night-fighter, Northrop's three-seat twin-engine twin-boom design gained a US Army Air Corps contract for two **Northrop XP-61** prototypes on 11 January 1941, the first of them being flown initially on 21 May 1942. They were followed by 13 service-test **YP-61** aircraft, and the development problems of this aircraft were matched by those to create a new-air-interception radar based on the British cavity magnetron. Nevertheless, the first examples of the **P-61A Black Widow** production version began to appear towards the end of 1943. It was soon discovered that its four-gun remotely-controlled dorsal turret caused severe buffeting when slewed to a beam position, and the turret was deleted after the first 37 aircraft had been built. P-61As began to enter service with fighter groups in the South Pacific in the first half of 1944, the first 'kill' being made on 7 July, and production of this version totalled 200. Deliveries of the ensuing **P-61B** also began in July 1944. This was built to a total of 450, and incorporated as standard provision to carry four 726-kg (1,600-lb) bombs or 1136-litre (300-US gal) drop tanks on underwing racks. The final 250 of these P-61Bs also had the four-gun dorsal turret restored. The last production batch comprised 41 **P-61C** aircraft, 476 being cancelled at the war's end, and bringing the total built to 706. Black Widows were in service in Europe by July 1944, shooting down four German bombers in their first engagement, the type subsequently destroying a number of German flying bombs during the V-1 offensive against Antwerp, and the use of the P-61 for deep in-

Only the first 37 P-61A Black Widows were fitted with the four-gun dorsal turret; this is the 23rd production aircraft.

truder missions in the European theatre emphasises the versatility of this heavy fighter.

Variants
XP-61D: redesignation of two P-61As following installation of R-2800-77 turbocharged engines for evaluation
XP-61E: redesignation of two P-61Bs with dorsal turret and nose radar deleted, increased fuel capacity, and four 12.7-mm (0.5-in) machine-guns installed in nose, four 20-mm being retained
XP-61F: designation allocated to P-61C to be converted to XP-61E configuration; not completed
XF-15 Reporter: redesignation of first XP-61E following conversion as prototype of unarmed reconnaissance aircraft with six cameras in modified nose
XF-15A: designation of prototype conversion of P-61C to XF-15 Reporter configuration
F-15A Reporter: 36 production reconnaissance aircraft, built from part-completed P-61C airframes
F2T-1N : designation applied by US Navy to 12 ex-USAAF P-61As received in late 1945 for use as night-fighter trainers

Specification
Northrop P-61B Black Widow
Type: three-seat night-fighter
Powerplant: two 1491-kW (2,000-hp) Pratt & Whitney R-2800-65 Double

Wasp radial piston engines
Performance: maximum speed 589 km/h (366 mph) at 6095 m (20,000 ft); service ceiling 10090 m (33,100 ft); maximum range 2173 km (1,350 miles)
Weights: empty 10637 kg (23,450 lb); maximum take-off 16420 kg (36,200 lb)
Dimensions: span 20.12 m (66 ft 0 in); length 15.11 m (49 ft 7 in); height 4.47 m (14 ft 8 in); wing area 61.53 m^2 (662.36 sq ft)
Armament: four 20-mm cannon in

USAF serial number 43-8335 was built as a Northrop P-61C Black Widow night-fighter, but was converted to the sole XF-15A reconnaissance aircraft by the installation of a new cockpit and camera equipment.

lower forward fuselage and four 12.7-mm (0.5-in) machine-guns in dorsal barbette, plus up to 2903 kg (6,400 lb) of bombs or other stores on four underwing hardpoints

Northrop T-38 Talon

To meet a US government requirement for a high-performance lightweight fighter that would be suitable for supply to and operation by friendly nations via the Military Assistance Program, Northrop began the private-venture design of such an aircraft in the mid-1950s, identifying it as the **Northrop N-156**. This initial design concept was to form the basis of a family of aircraft, including a

supersonic trainer which had the company designation **N-156T**. Three **YT-38** prototypes were ordered in December 1956, this number being increased to six in June 1958, and the first of them was flown on 10 April 1959. Cantilever low-wing monoplanes with slender area-ruled fuselages, the first two prototypes were each powered by two 953-kg (2,100-lb) thrust non-afterburning

General Electric YJ85-GE-1 turbojets, but the remainder of this first batch had YJ85-GE-5 engines with an afterburning thrust of 1633-kg (3,600-lb). Testing with these latter engines resulted in an initial contract for the **T-38A Talon**, the first of them entering service with the USAF's 3510th Flying Training Wing, at Randolph AFB, on 17 March 1961. The Talon, which seats instructor and pupil in tandem on ejection seats and has a fully powered control system, has gained one of the best safety records of any super-

sonic aircraft in USAF service. As a result, when production ended in early 1972 a total of 1,187 T-38s had been built for the USAF. The US Navy acquired five from the USAF, and three of these remain in service with the Test Pilots School at Patuxent River. Also supplied through the USAF and operated by the German Luftwaffe were 46 used for pilot training in the US. Only export customer was Portugal who received two batches of six Sidewinder-equipped ex-USAF aircraft in 1977 and 1981 to replace F-86

Sabres used in the dedicated air defence role but doubling as advanced pilot trainers. NASA also acquired a number from Northrop, using them as flight-readiness trainers for astronauts. The designations **AT-38A** and **NT-38A** were allocated to two T-38As following their conversion for evaluation as an attack trainer and research/development aircraft respectively. Four of the US Navy's T-38s converted to serve as drone directors were redesignated **DT-38A**. The **AT 38B** is a lightly armed version serving in the Lead-in Fighter Training role at Holloman AFB, New Mexico. Some 700 of these aircraft remain in service in 1992.

Specification
Type: two-seat supersonic basic

One of the few supersonic trainers currently in use, the Northrop T-38A Talon has proved remarkably trouble-free in service and has also built up an unexpectedly good reputation for safety.

trainer
Powerplant: two 1746-kg (3,850-lb) afterburning thrust General Electric J85-GE-5A turbojets
Performance: maximum speed Mach 1.3 or 1381 km/h (858 mph) at 10975 m (36,000 ft); service ceiling 16335 m (53,600 ft); range with maximum fuel 1759 km (1,093 miles)
Weights: empty 3250 kg (7,164 lb); maximum take-off 5485 kg (12,093 lb)

Dimensions: span 7.70 m (25 ft 3 in); length 14.14 m (46 ft 4½ in); height

3.92 m (12 ft 10½ in); wing area 15.79 m² (170.0 sq ft)

Northrop/McDonnell Douglas YF-23A

The **YF-23A** was the unsuccessful candidate for the US Air Force's Advanced Tactical Fighter (ATF) competition of the mid-1980s, held primarily to find a stealthy single-seat replacement for the F-15 Eagle. Two consortia entered the competition, one led by Lockheed and including Boeing and General Dynamics, while the other was led by Northrop in association with McDonnell Douglas. Following the issue of a USAF Request For Proposals in September 1985, Northrop teamed with McDonnell Douglas on the understanding that whichever design was favoured by the USAF, the losing company would participate in the industrial programme associated with the winner. Two YF-23 Prototype Air Vehicles (PAVs) were funded, the first (87-800) powered by a Pratt & Whitney YF119 augmented turbofan, and the other (87-801) with a similar General Electric YF120. The first aircraft, unofficially dubbed the 'Gray Ghost', flew from Edwards AFB, California, on 27 August 1990, followed by the second on 26 October 1990. The flight test programme called for 65 hours to be flown in 50 sorties and this was completed by the second prototype on 18 December

1990. Following the evaluation flight trials, the Lockheed YF-22 was declared the winner on 23 April 1991 (but powered by the F119 engine), and ordered into production. The two Northrop PAVs were subsequently put into secure storage at Edwards AFB, California.

Specification
Northrop YF-23 Prototype Air Vehicle
Type: single-seat tactical fighter
Powerplant: one aircraft with two 155.7 kN (35,000 lb) thrust Pratt & Whitney YF119-PW-100 augmented turbofans, and one with similar thrust General Electric YF120-GE-100 augmented turbofans
Performance: maximum speed Mach 2; supercruise (supersonic speed without afterburner) Mach 1.6; service ceiling 19812 m (65,000 ft); range on internal fuel 1200 km (750 miles)
Weights: operational empty 16783 kg (37,000 lb); internal fuel 952 kg (21,000 lb) combat take-off 29,030 kg (64,000 lb)
Dimensions: span 13.2 m (43 ft 7 in); length 20.5 m (67 ft 4 in); height 4.2 m (13 ft 10 in); wing area 87.8 m²

(945 sq ft)
Armament: (planned) one internal long-barrel M61 20-mm cannon, together with internal bays capable of housing AIM-9 Sidewinders (eight), AIM-120 AMRAAMS, 'Have Dash 2'

AAMs and 'Have Slick' air-to-surface missiles currently under development

Sometimes referred to as the 'Black Widow II', the YF-23 prototypes were officially designated PAV-1 and 2. The second wears the light grey scheme.

Nyeman KhAI-1 and KhAI-5

Under the leadership of Iosif Grigorevich Nyeman, a team at the Kharkov Aviation Institute produced a series of designs between 1930 and 1941. The two most successful were the **KhAI-1** and **KhAI-5**. The first was a cantilever low-wing monoplane of all-wood construction and of similar configuration to the Lockheed Orion. The KhAI-1 had manually-retractable main landing gear units, was powered by a 358-kW (480-hp) M-22 radial engine and accommodated the pilot in an open cockpit and his passengers in an enclosed cabin. Following the first flight of the prototype on 8 October 1932, authorisation for production followed successful testing, and 43 were delivered for use on domestic routes. Series aircraft differed from the prototype by providing a sliding cockpit

enclosure for the pilot. Two examples of a two-seat bomber trainer, designated **KhAI-1B**, resulted from conversions of production KhAI-1 passenger transports. The 14.85 m (48 ft 8¾ in) span civil KhAI-1 had a maximum speed of 324 km/h (201 mph) and range of 1130 km (702 miles).

More extensively built was the KhAI-5 two-seat light attack/reconnaissance aircraft, a cantilever low-wing monoplane of wooden construction with retractable tailwheel landing gear. Pilot and radio operator/gunner were in separate cockpits, the pilot controlling two forward-firing 7.62-mm (0.3-in) ShKAS machine-guns and the gunner being armed wih a single ShKAS mounted in a power-operated turret. An internal bomb bay could accommodate a total 300-kg (661-lb)

bombload. Power for the prototype was provided by a 529-kW (710-hp) Wright Cyclone, but when ordered into production as the **R-10**, the first 180 were powered by the 544-kW (730-hp) M-25B radial, and the remaining 310 with the 619-kW (830-hp) M-62, both of these Soviet engines being derived from the Wright Cyclone. Built during 1938-40, some saw action on skis during the

The Nyeman R-10 bomber was handicapped by its lack of speed and defensive firepower.

Winter War, and at least 60 were transferred to Aeroflot which used them under the designation **PS-5** in a light utility transport role. Maximum speed of the R-10 was 388 km/h (241 mph) at optimum altitude.

P.W.S. 10

The abbreviation P.W.S. identifies the Polish company Podlaska Wytwórnia Samolotów (Podlasian Aeroplane Plant) which was established in 1923 near the town of Biala Podlaska. For the first three years of its existence the company gained a wealth of experience from the

licence construction of Avia and Potez aircraft, and in 1926 began to create original designs. None progressed beyond prototype form until, in 1927, P.W.S. designed a single-seat fighter to meet a requirement of the Polish Department of Aeronautics. A braced monoplane of parasol-wing configuration, with fixed tailskid landing gear and power provided by a Skoda-built Lorraine-Dietrich

engine, it initially had the desingnation **P.W.S. 10M**. It was not until 1929 that the company received a contract for two prototypes, the first being flown in May 1930, and testing of these showed acceptable, but disappointing, performance. In the absence of anything better, the type was ordered into production as the **P.W.S.10**, the company receiving a contract for 80 aircraft. These served

with the 3rd and 4th Air Regiments of the Polish air force from early 1932 and, later, the 5th Air Regiment. But the P.W.S. 10s saw only limited first-line use before being relegated for training duties; some were still being used in this role at the outbreak of World War II. In 1936 15 ex-Polish army P.W.S. 10s were sold in a secret transaction to the Spanish Republican forces, but it was

713

soon discovered that they were unsuitable for operational use in a fighter role and were transferred to training units. As powered by the 336-kW (450-hp) Skoda-built Lorraine-Dietrich engine, the 11.00 m (36 ft 1 in) span P.W.S.10 had a maximum speed of 245 km/h (152 mph) at sea level and a range of only 300 km (186 miles). Armament comprised two forward-firing machine-guns.

Though early designs for the P.W.S. 10 fighter featured a frontal radiator, the production model was fitted with an underslung type, developed indigenously from a Lamblin concept. Armed with twin forward-firing machine-guns, only 65 production aircraft were ever completed. These served with the Polish air force until they were replaced by P.Z.L. P.7 fighters between 1932 and 1933.

P.W.S. 12 and 14

Production P.W.S. 12s had a revised engine cowling.

Contemporary with the P.W.S.10, a less complicated version with a 179-kW (240-hp) Gnome-Rhône Titan engine was designed specifically for use as a single-seat fighter trainer. Designated **P.W.S.11**, this did not progress beyond the prototype stage, but a two-seat intermediate-trainer project designated

P.W.S.12 was developed from it, its biplane configuration resulting from little more than the addition of a new lower wing to the existing airframe. However, the first two P.W.S.12 prototypes, flown in November 1929, had reduced-span staggered biplane wings and introduced a 164-kW (220-hp) Skoda-built version of

the Wright J-5 Whirlwind radial engine. Successful testing led to an order for production P.W.S.12s, but a requested change from wooden to steel-tube fuselage structure, plus the incorporation of some improvements, resulted in this aircraft being redesignated **P.W.S.14** at a later stage. The 9.00 m (29 ft 6¼ in) span

P.W.S.14 had a maximum speed at sea level of 190 km/h (118 mph) and a take-off weight of 1100 kg (2,425 lb).

P.W.S. 16 and 26

A development of the P.W.S.12/14, the generally similar **P.W.S.16** incorporated a number of refinements, including the provision of more efficient ailerons, and the ensuing **P.W.S.16bis** differed primarily by having a revised fuel system to permit inverted flight. Production totalled 20 of each, and the excellent performance of these aircraft resulted in large-scale production of an armed trainer version, the **P.W.S.26**, which also had structural strengthening for use as a dive-bomber. The P.W.S.16/16bis aircraft entered service with Polish air force training units during 1934-35, being relegated to secondary roles when the P.W.S.26 became available in 1937. When production of this last version ended in 1938 a total of 250 had been built and some of these were seized by

The P.W.S. 26 was externally indistinguishable from the P.W.S. 16 apart from its armament installation and the fairing of the inner Vees of the landing gear units into single streamlined legs.

German forces in September 1939. A number were operated by the Luftwaffe, and Germany disposed of 28 refurbished aircraft to Romania. However, the majority of the P.W.S.26s were captured by the Soviets, and many of these entered service with the VVS.

Specification
P.W.S.26
Type: two-seat advanced trainer
Powerplant: one 164-kW (220-hp)

licence-built Wright J-5 Whirlwind radial piston engine
Performance: maximum speed 215 km/h (134 mph) at sea level; service ceiling 4620 m (15,155 ft); range 460 km (286 miles)
Weights: empty 850 kg (1,874 lb);

maximum take-off 1162 kg (2,562 lb)
Dimensions: span 9.00 m (29 ft 6¼ in); length 7.03 m (23 ft 0¾ in); height 2.75 m (9 ft 0¼ in); wing area 24.00 m² (258.34 sq ft)
Armament: one 7.7-mm (0.303-in) machine-gun

P.Z.L. I-22 Iryda

Configured in the classic high-wing twin-jet tandem two-seat monoplane layout, the **I-22** most closely resembles the Franco-German Alpha Jet. The **Iryda** (Iridium) was designed by a team led by Dr Eng Alfred Baron to replace the TS-11 Iskra and Lim-6 aircraft currently serving with the Polish air force. Two prototypes were built, the first flying on 5 March 1985, while the second is used as a static test specimen. The first aircraft was lost in a crash on 31 January 1987, but four

more pre-production examples were flying by September 1991, when an initial order for 12 aircraft was placed by the Polish air force for delivery in 1992/93. The first two aircraft were handed over to the Deblin Aviation Academy on 24 October 1992. A further order for another 30 is pending. P.Z.L. is developing a single-seat combat version of the Iryda designated **I-22MS**, and are also studying a Westernised version. Powerplants under consideration include versions of

the Larzac, Viper and JT15D, along with the K-15 and D-18A Polish engines.

Specification
Type: two-seat advanced jet trainer/light-strike aircraft
Powerplant: two 10.7 kN (2,425 lb) thrust PZL-5 SO-3W22 turbojet engines
Performance: cruising speed 570 km/h (354 mph); maximum level speed at 5000 m (16,400 ft) 840 km/h (522 mph); ceiling 11000 m (36,100 ft); range with maximum payload 420 km

(261 miles); range with maximum fuel 4000 km (2,485 miles)
Weights: empty 4700 kg (10,361 lb); maximum take-off 6900 kg (15,211 lb)
Dimensions: span 9.6 m (31 ft 6 in); length 13.2 m (43 ft 4 in); height 4.3 m (14 ft 1 in); wing area 19.9 m² (214.4 sq ft)
Armament: one 23-mm GSz-23 twin-barrel cannon with up to 200 rounds of ammunition in underfuselage pack. Four underwing hardpoints each capable of carrying 500 kg (1,102 lb) loads can carry bombs, rocket pods or drop tanks (inboard pylons only)

P.Z.L. P.6 and P.7

The company's initial **P.Z.L. P.1** fighter did not progress beyond the prototype stage, but a significant feature of its design was the then unique wing designed by Zygmunt Pulawski. Selecting a high-wing monoplane configuration for his fighter, he wanted to provide the pilot with a better-than-average forward view and designed a gull-type structure, later known internationally as the 'Pulawski wing', which tapered both in chord and thickness and incorporated thin-section sloping inboard panels giving the pilot a clear view between them. Another feature of the P.1 was the so-called scissor-type main landing gear units with oleo-pneumatic shock absorber struts. Two prototypes were built and flown

with Hispano-Suiza engines, but no production order resulted. At this time negotiations were in progress with Bristol in England for licence manufacture of that company's Jupiter radial engine, and P.Z.L. was instructed to adapt the P.1 to accept this powerplant, leading to the construction of four prototypes. These comprised the **P.6/I** with a 336-kW (450-hp) low-altitude Jupiter VI, and **P.7/I** with the 363-kW (485-hp) high-altitude Jupiter VII, flown in August and October 1930 respectively; they were followed in early 1931 by the **P.6/II** which differed mainly by having a revised exhaust system, and the **P.7/II** with revised rear fuselage structure and other refinements. It was the last of

The P.Z.L. P.6/I was powered by a Jupiter VI, whose narrow cowling was punctuated by the twin exhausts for each of the nine cylinders.

these four prototypes that was ordered into production for the Polish air force, which acquired a total of 150 including the prototype. These began to enter service under the designation **P.7a** in late 1932, equipping initially No. 111 Squadron (Eskadra Kościuszkowska) of the 1st Air Regiment, and by the autumn of 1933 Poland had become the first nation in the world to have a first-line force of all-metal monoplane fighters. Just before the outbreak of World War II about 100 of these aircraft remained in service; some 50 of them were flown to Romania in late September 1939 and about the same number were captured by the Germans and these, after refurbishing, were used by the Luftwaffe in a training role.

Specification
P.Z.L. P.7a
Type: single-seat fighter
Powerplant: one 362-kW (485-hp) Skoda-built Bristol Jupiter VII radial piston engine
Performance: maximum speed 320 km/h (199 mph) at 4000 m (13,125 ft); service ceiling 8275 m (27,150 ft); range 560 km (348 miles)
Weights: empty 1010 kg (2,227 lb); maximum take-off 1410 kg (3,109 lb)
Dimensions: span 10.30 m (33 ft 9½ in); length 7.15 m (23 ft 5½ in); height 2.75 m (9 ft 0¼ in); wing area 17.20 m² (185.15 sq ft)
Armament: two 7.7-mm (0.303-in) Vickers Type E machine-guns

P.Z.L. P.11

The installation of a radial engine in the P.Z.L. P.7 diminished the excellent forward view for the pilot that was achieved in the P.Z.L. P.1 with its narrower V-12 engine, and it was proposed to improve this situation by the introduction of a Bristol Mercury radial engine, which was of smaller diameter than the Jupiter that powered the P.Z.L. P.7a. This version of the fighter was designated P.Z.L. **P.11**, but delay in delivery of a Mercury engine from Bristol resulted in the **P.11/I** prototype being flown initially, in August 1931, with a 384-kW (515-hp) Jupiter IX.ASb engine licence-built by Gnome-Rhône. It was not until December 1931 that the **P.11/II** was flown with a 395-kW (530-hp) Bristol Mercury IV.A enclosed in a long-chord Townend ring. This prototype was later re-engined with a 373-kW (500-hp) Gnome-Rhône 9K Mistral engine, with which powerplant it was exhibited at the 1932 Paris Salon de l'Aéronautique. A third aircraft with a Mercury engine, the **P.11/III**, served as a pre-production prototype and, following satisfactory official testing, was approved for production for the Polish air force as the **P.11a**. However, it was preceded on the production line by 50 Mistral-powered **P.11b** aircraft for Romania, all of them delivered by the summer of 1934. Production of the P.11a began with a batch of 30, these being similar to late-production P.11b aircraft, but differed by having the 386-kW (517-hp) Skoda-built Mercury IV.S2 engine. The major production variant, however, was the **P.11c** which adopted more radical measures to improve the pilot's field of view, lowering the engine and resitting the pilot farther to the rear on a raised seat, and a number of other improvements were incorporated at the same time. Production of this version totalled 175, the first batch being powered by the 418-kW (560-hp) Skoda-built Mercury V.S2, but the remainder by the P.Z.L.-built Mercury VI.S2. A version of the P.11c, powered by a licence-built 9K Mistral engine, was built under licence in Romania by I.A.R. under the designation **P.11f**, about 80 being produced during 1936-38.

Deliveries of the P.11c to Polish fighter squadrons were completed by the end of 1936, and at the outbreak of World War II 12 squadrons were equipped with the type, claiming the destruction of 126 Luftwaffe aircraft for the loss of 114 of their own number. When, in early 1939, it became clear that the planned **P.Z.L. P.50 Jastrzab** fighter was unlikely to

materialise, efforts were made to provide the P.11c with greater capability by the installation of a 626-kW (840-hp) licence-built Mercury VIIIa engine and four-gun armament. A prototype was flown as the **P.11g Kobuz** and quantity production was initiated, but the German invasion of Poland had started before any of these aircraft were delivered.

Specification
P.Z.L. P.11c
Type: single-seat fighter
Powerplant: one 481-kW (645-hp) P.Z.L.-built Bristol Mercury VI.S2 radial piston engine
Performance: maximum speed

Restored to pristine condition, this P.Z.L. P.11C of the National Air and Space Museum at Krackow is finished in the markings of No. 122 Sqn.

390 km/h (242 mph) at 5500 m (18,045 ft); service ceiling 8000 m (26,245 ft); range 700 km (435 miles)
Weights: empty 1147 kg (2,529 lb); maximum take-off 1630 kg (3,594 lb)
Dimensions: span 10.72 m (35 ft 2 in); length 7.55 m (24 ft 9¼ in); height 2.85 m (9 ft 4¼ in); wing area 17.90 m² (192.68 sq ft)
Armament: two 7.7-mm (0.303-in) machine-guns, plus underwing racks for lightweight bombs

P.Z.L. P.23 and P.43 Karaś

During 1931 P.Z.L. had designed a six-passenger single-engine light transport, the **P.Z.L. P.13,** for service with LOT, but as it had no appeal to the airline its development was abandoned. It was decided subsequently to use this aircraft as the basis for an army co-operation aircraft accommodating a crew of three, and using as powerplant a licence-built version of the Bristol Pegasus radial engine. Following evaluation of the design by the Department of Aeronautics, P.Z.L. was instructed to build three prototypes and the first, powered by a 440-kW (590-hp) Bristol Pegasus IIM2, was flown for the first time in August 1934. This aircraft had the designation **P.23/I** and name **Karaś** (crucian carp), but testing soon revealed a number of shortcomings. The two following prototypes, **P.23/II** and **P.23/III,** had the engine mounting lowered to improve the forward view, the bomb bay was deleted to provide more room within the fuselage, and improved glazed canopies were introduced, together with a number of other improvements. The P.23/II crashed during flight trials, but the P.23/III performed well and during development flying was modified progressively to what was to be production standard. In 1935 production orders were placed for 40 examples of the **P.23 Karaś A** with the 433-kW (580-hp) P.Z.L.-built Pegasus II, and 210 of the **P.23 Karaś B** with the 507-kW (680-hp) P.Z.L.-built Pegasus VIII. The first P.23A Karaś A flew in June 1936, but development problems with the Pegasus II engine resulted in these aircraft being relegated to the training role. However, the P.23B Karaś B began to enter service in

P.Z.L. P.23B Karaś of No. 42 Sqn, Polish Air Force attached to the Pomorze Army in September 1939.

mid-1937 and when production ended the type equipped 14 first-line squadrons. One Karaś B was modified under the designation **P.42** to serve as a development aircraft for the improved **P.46 Sum**, with a twin fin/rudder tail unit and a retractable ventral gondola. However, the P.46 did not materialise beyond the prototype stage and the P.42 was subsequently converted back to Karaś B standard. One other version similar to the Karaś B entered production, however, as the **P.43A Karaś,** of which 12 were built for the Bulgarian air force and delivered in 1937. This model differed by having a 694-kW (930-hp) Gnome-Rhône radial engine, improved crew accommodation, and armament increased by the addition of a second forward-firing machine-gun. The excellent performance of the P.43A Karaś led to repeat orders, totalling 42, for a further improved **P.43B Karaś** with the 731-kW (980-hp) Gnome-Rhône N.1. Of this total 33 were despatched and delivered by August 1939; of the balance, eight had been packed for despatch and the ninth was in final assembly. With the outbreak of World War II, these aircraft were seized for service with the Polish air force, but only five survived the initial German bombing attacks on the P.Z.L. factory and were flown off to serve with No. 41 Squadron, one of the 12 first-line squadrons then equipped with P.23B Karaś B aircraft. These squadrons were responsible for the bulk of the bombing and reconnaissance operations of the Polish air force during the first 16 days of September 1939, but their aircraft were terribly vulnerable to German opposition and virtually 95 per cent of them were destroyed in action.

Specification
P.Z.L. P.23B Karaś B
Powerplant: one 507-kW (680-hp) P.Z.L.-built Bristol Pegasus VIII radial piston engine
Performance: maximum speed 320 km/h (199 mph) at 3650 m (11,975 ft); service ceiling 7300 m (23,950 ft); range 1260 km (783 miles)
Weights: empty equipped 1928 kg (4,251 lb); maximum take-off 3525 kg (7,771 lb)
Dimensions: span 13.95 m (45 ft 9¼ in); length 9.70 m (31 ft 9¾ in); height 3.30 m (10 ft 10 in); wing area 26.80 m² (288.48 sq ft)
Armament: one 7.7-mm (0.303-in) forward-firing machine-gun, and two single Vickers guns of similar calibre in rear dorsal and ventral positions, plus up to 700 kg (1,543 lb) of bombs on external racks

P.Z.L. P.24
to
P.Z.L. Swidnik Mi-2

P.Z.L. P.24

Because of the terms of licence agreements for the manufacture in Poland of Bristol engines, it was difficult to market export aircraft with P.Z.L.-built versions of these engines. To overcome this difficulty it was decided in February 1932 to develop a new fighter with different powerplant, the airframe of the P.Z.L. P.11 being redesigned to accept a new Gnome-Rhône engine designated 14Kds Mistral Major and rated at 567 kW (760 hp). Availability of the first of these engines delayed until May 1933 the initial flight of the resulting **P.Z.L. P.24/I** prototype, a flight which ended in a forced landing when the propeller disintegrated. The P.24/I did not fly again until October 1933, showing a need for many modifications which were introduced in the **P.24/II** second prototype, this aircraft also being known as the **Super P.24**. On 28 June 1934 the aircraft established an FAI-accredited class speed record of 414 km/h (257.25 mph). A third prototype flown in 1934, the **P.24/III** or **Super P.24bis**, was powered by a 694-kW (930-hp) Gnome-Rhône 14Kfs and armed with two 20-mm cannon and two machine-guns. Exhibited at the 1934 Salon de l'Aéronautique in Paris, this aircraft caused considerable interest and led ultimately to valuable export orders. The first came from Turkey, which not only negotiated a licence for the manufacture of the P.24, but also ordered 40 **P.24A** fighters generally similar to that shown at Paris, 26 **P.24C** aircraft with four wing-mounted machine-guns, and components plus raw materials for the assembly of 20 more P.24As. Next came an order from Bulgaria for 14 **P.24B** aircraft which were similar to the P.24C apart from installed equipment and were delivered from early 1938, followed by 24 P.24Cs and 26 examples of the **P.24F**, the final development of the type, which introduced a 723-kW (970-hp) Gnome-Rhône 14N.07 engine of smaller diameter and had twin cannon and twin machine-gun armament. The **P.24E**, developed to meet a Romanian requirement, was generally similar to

Compared with the P.Z.L. P.24/I, the P.24/II featured a longer chord cowling, a three-bladed metal propeller and several drag-reducing features.

P.Z.L. P.24C of the 4th Regiment, Turkish air force, based at Kütaha in 1939.

the P.24C: six built by P.Z.L. had 671-kW (900-hp) Romanian-built Gnome-Rhône 14KIIc32 engines, but later examples of the 40 or so P.24Es built by I.A.R. in Romania had the 701-kW (940-hp) I.A.R.-built 14KMc36 engine. In late 1939 I.A.R.

developed a low-wing version of the P.24E under the designation I.A.R.80. The four machine-gun equivalent of the P.24F had the designation **P.24G**, and 30 and six respectively were acquired by Greece for service with the Royal Hellenic air force. They comprised almost the entire fighter strength of this last air force and were deployed with considerable success against both the Luftwaffe and Regia Aeronautica.

Specification
P.Z.L. P.24F
Powerplant: one 723-kW (970-hp)

Gnome-Rhône 14N.07 14-cylinder two-row radial piston engine
Performance: maximum speed 430 km/h (267 mph) at 4500 m (14,765 ft); service ceiling 10500 m (34,450 ft); range 700 km (435 miles)
Weights: empty equipped 1332 kg (2,937 lb); maximum take-off 2000 kg (4,409 lb)
Dimensions: span 10.70 m (35 ft 1¼ in); length 7.60 m (24 ft 11¼ in); height 2.70 m (8 ft 10¼ in); wing area 17.90 m² (192.68 sq ft)
Armament: two 20-mm Oerlikon FF cannon and two 7.7-mm (0.303-in) machine-guns

P.Z.L. P.37 Loś

At the outbreak of World War II the **P.Z.L. P.37 Loś** (elk) was not only one of the most advanced bombers produced by the Polish aircraft industry to that date, but was also the only aircraft in service with the Polish air force that could be regarded as being of modern design. P.Z.L. had proposed the **P.Z.L.3** advanced bomber to meet a Department of Aeronautics requirement for an aircraft in this class, but the financial stringencies of 1930 prevented the P.Z.L.3's progress beyond the design stage. P.Z.L.'s next proposal was for a bomber version of the **P.Z.L.30** civil transport which, having failed to attract a buyer,

was converted as a bomber prototype by P.Z.L.; it was later developed and put into production by the L.W.S. company as the L.W.S.4 Zubr. P.Z.L. then produced the design for a twin-engine bomber of monoplane configuration, gaining a contract for three prototypes in 1935; the first of them, the **P.Z.L. P.31/I**, was flown initially in late June 1936. Successful testing of this aircraft, which was powered by two 651-kW (873-hp) Bristol Pegasus XII radial engines, led to a contract for 30 under the designation **P.37A Loś A**. Production was completed in 1938, the first 10 having a single fin and rudder, but the

last 20 sporting the twin fins and rudders which had been introduced and tested on the **P.37/II** prototype. This latter prototype had also been used for development testing of engines in the 746-kW (1,000-hp) class by manufacturers that included Fiat, Gnome-Rhône and Renault. Demonstrated at an exhibition in Belgrade during 1938 and at the Paris Salon in the same year, the P.37A created enormous interest, resulting in export orders for a total of 35 **P.37C** bombers powered by 723-kW (970-hp) Gnome-Rhône 14N.07 engines for Bulgaria (15) and Yugoslavia (20), and 40 **P.37D** bombers with 783-kW (1,050-hp) Gnome-Rhône 14N.20/21 engines for Romania (30) and Turkey (10). In addition, Turkey ordered components for 15

more aircraft and signed a licence to manufacture. Planned delivery for these export aircraft was from June 1940 and, as a result, none of them was completed. The delivery of Loś A aircraft to the Polish air force began in early 1938, and all of these were equipped subsequently with dual controls for use as conversion trainers. Delivery of the ensuing **P.37B Loś B** (which introduced a revised cockpit canopy, twin-wheel main landing gear units, and Pegasus XX engines) began in late 1938. A total of 150 had been ordered, but policy changes that favoured fighters rather than bombers reduced the number to 100, and only about 70 of these had been delivered by the outbreak of war. Even more disastrous for Poland was the fact that of the Loś B aircraft in service only 36 were fully equipped for operational use, though these were supplemented quickly by nine more replacement aircraft. Some 26 of this number were lost in action, and on 17 September 1939 the survivors, plus about 20 other P.37s, were flown to Romania, where they were used subsequently by the Romanian air force. A developed version of the P.37 had been planned under the designation **P.49 Miś** (teddy bear), intended to be powered by engines of up to 1193 kW (1,600 hp). A prototype was under construction, but with the German advance on Warsaw it was destroyed to prevent it from falling into enemy hands.

P.Z.L. P.37B Loś B of the Bomber Brigade, Dispositional Air Force, Polish air force, in September 1939.

Specification
P.Z.L. P.37B Loś B
Type: four-crew medium bomber
Powerplant: two 690-kW (925-hp) P.Z.L.-built Bristol Pegasus XX radial piston engines
Performance: maximum speed 445 km/h (277 mph) at 3400 m (11,155 ft); service ceiling without bombload 9145 m (30,000 ft); range with 2200-kg (4,850-lb) bombload 1500 km (932 miles)
Weights: empty 4280 kg (9,436 lb); maximum take-off 8900 kg (19,621 lb)
Dimensions: span 17.95 m (58 ft 10¾ in); length 12.92 m (42 ft 4¾ in); height 5.09 m (16 ft 8¼ in); wing area 53.50 m² (575.89 sq ft)
Armament: three 7.7-mm (0.303-in) machine-guns in nose, dorsal and ventral positions, plus a bombload of up to 2580 kg (5,688 lb) carried internally

P.Z.L. 102B

On 23 May 1958 P.Z.L. flew the prototype of a two-seat semi-aerobatic light monoplane to which it allocated the designation **P.Z.L. 102**, later giving it the name **Kos** (blackbird). Of all-metal construction, except for fabric-covered tail control surfaces, this had fixed tailwheel landing gear, seated two side-by-side in an enclosed cockpit and, as first flown, was powered by a 48-kW (65-hp) Narkiewicz WN-1 flat-four engine. Further prototypes preceded the production **P.Z.L. 102B** flown first in October 1959, which was powered by a Conti-

The P.Z.L. 102B was blessed with clean lines and good performance from a small engine.

nental C90-12F engine, and the type was built in moderate numbers before production ended in 1964.

Specification
P.Z.L. 102.B
Type: two-seat training/touring monoplane
Powerplant: one 71-kW (95-hp) Continental C90-12F flat-four piston engine
Performance: maximum speed 190 km/h (118 mph); service ceiling

4600 m (15,090 ft); range with maximum payload 640 km (398 miles)
Weights: empty 418 kg (922 lb); maximum take-off 655 kg (1,444 lb)
Dimensions: span 8.50 m (27 ft 10½ in); length 6.95 m (22 ft 9½ in); height 1.90 m (6 ft 2¾ in); wing area 11.00 m² (118.41 sq ft)

P.Z.L. 104 Wilga

Designed as a successor to the Polish-built Yak-12 and the **P.Z.L. 101** developed from it, the original **P.Z.L. 104 Wilga** (thrush) prototype, powered by a 134-kW (180-hp) Narkiewicz WN-6 flat-six engine, was flown for the first time on 24 April 1962. A cantilever high-wing monoplane with fixed tailwheel landing gear and an enclosed cabin, it was followed by prototypes of the **Wilga 2P** and **Wilga CP**, powered by the 138-kW (185-hp) Narkiewicz WN-6RB2 and 168-kW (225-hp) Continental O-470-13A or O-470-L flat-six engines respectively. Intended as a general-purpose aircraft, the P.Z.L. 104 was offered initially in versions equipped for use as a four-seat passenger-carrying or liaison aircraft; for club flying, glider towing or parachuting; for agricultural use with a 500-litre (110-Imp-gal) hopper for dust or liquid application; and as an air ambulance carrying pilot, doctor, two stretcher patients and medical equipment. Following construction of a number of prototypes, the type entered production initially as the **Wilga 3A** club aircraft and the **Wilga 3S** air ambulance. In 1967 the design was revised to give better cabin accommodation and with improved landing gear, pro-

duction beginning in 1968 of the **Wilga 35** which, powered by a 194-kW (260-hp) Ivchenko AI-14R engine, had flown for the first time on 28 July 1967, and of the **Wilga 32** with a 172-kW (230-hp) Continental O-470-K flown on 12 September 1967. This last version was built under licence in Indonesia as the **Lipnur Gelatik 32** (rice bird) with a Continental O-470-R engine of similar output.

Developments of the Wilga 35 have included the **Wilga 35A** intended for aero-club use; the **Wilga 35H** floatplane fitted with Airtech (Canada) LAP-3000 floats; the multi-purpose **Wilga 35M** fitted with a 260.5-kW (360-hp) M-14P radial engine, flown in prototype form in 1990; the **Wilga 35P** tourer or air-taxi version; and the **Wilga 35R** agricultural variant. A version generally similar to the Wilga 35, but meeting US FAR Part 23 requirements, is designated **Wilga 80**. The first of these flew on 30 May 1979, and is available in three versions, the **80A**, for aero-club use, the **80H** floatplane, and as the **80R** for agricultural use. A more radical redesign, originally identified as the **Wilga 88**, has become the **P.Z.L. 105 Flamingo**. The Wilga 35 and 80 remain

in production in 1993, by which time P.Z.L. had sold around 900 variants to countries around the world.

Specification
P.Z.L. 104 Wilga 35A
Type: multi-role lightplane
Powerplant: one 194-kW (260-hp) P.Z.L.-built Ivchenko AI-14RA radial piston engine
Performance: maximum speed 195 km/h (121 mph); service ceiling 4040 m (13,255 ft); range with maximum fuel 670 km (416 miles)
Weights: empty equipped 900 kg

Though distinctly inelegant in appearance, the P.Z.L. 104 Wilga 35 is a thoroughly utilitarian design that combines low cost, strength and reliability with a capacious cabin and a high-set cantilever wing for unobstrcted fields of vision.

(1,984 lb); maximum take-off 1300 kg (2,866 lb)
Dimensions: span 11.12 m (36 ft 5¾ in); length 8.10 m (26 ft 6¾ in); height 2.96 m (9 ft 8½ in); wing area 15.50 m² (166.85 sq ft)

P.Z.L. 105 Flamingo

Designed as a successor to the Wilga 35/80 series, and originally designated the **Wilga 88**, the first of three **P.Z.L. 105** flying prototypes (SP-PRC) took to the air for the first time on 19 December 1989, powered by a 268.5-kW (360-hp) VMKB M-14P powerplant. Production versions will be known as the **P.Z.L. 105M**. The second aircraft, fitted with a

298-kW (400-hp) Textron Lycoming IO-720-A1B powerplant, flew in mid-1991, and is designated the **P.Z.L. 105L**. Certification to US standards was planned for the end of 1992, with customer deliveries due to follow in 1993. Following the same general configuration as the Wilga, but of entirely new design, and offering improved per-

formance, the Flamingo is a six-seat passenger or cargo light aircraft, suitable for a very wide range of uses.

Specification
P.Z.L. 105M Flamingo
Type: six-seat single-engine utility lightplane
Powerplant: one 268.5-kW (360-hp) VMKB M-14P nine-cylinder air-cooled radial engine driving a two-blade propeller or one 298-kW (400-hp)

Textron Lycoming flat-eight engine fitted with a three-blade propeller
Performance: cruising speed 205 km/h (127 mph); maximum speed 306 km/h (190 mph); service ceiling 4140 m (13,575 ft); range with maximum fuel 1085 km (674 miles)
Weights: empty 1130 kg (2,491 lb); maximum take-off 1850 kg (4,078 lb)
Dimensions: span 12.9 m (42 ft 6 in); length 8.70 m (28 ft 6 in); height 2.87 m (9 ft 5 in)

P.Z.L. 106 Kruk

In early 1972 design was initiated of a new agricultural aircraft of braced low-wing monoplane configuration with fixed tailwheel landing gear, a T-tail, and enclosed accommodation for the pilot. First flown in **P.Z.L. 106** prototype (SP-PAS) form on 17 April 1973, then powered by a 298-kW (400-hp) Avco Lycoming IO-720 engine, it was followed by five more prototypes, one of which was similarly powered, but four each had a P.Z.L. 3S radial that was the chosen powerplant for production aircraft, the first version being the **P.Z.L. 106A Kruk** (raven) of which series construction began in 1976. Generally similar to the prototypes, it differed primarily by adopting a conventional tail unit and a larger-capacity chemical hopper, features adopted as standard on all production aircraft. Subsequent P.Z.L. 106A variants have included the **P.Z.L. 106AR** which introduced a geared P.Z.L. 3SR engine and a larger-diameter propeller; the **P.Z.L. 106AS** prototype with a 746-kW (1,000-hp) P.Z.L.-built Shvetsov ASz-62IR radial engine and, following satisfactory tests, 60 P.Z.L. 106A aircraft operated overseas by Pezetel were converted to this powerplant; and the initial version of the Turbo-Kruk,

the **P.Z.L. 106 AT**, which, powered by a 567-kW (760-hp) Pratt & Whitney of Canada PT6A-34AG turboprop engine, flew for the first time on 22 June 1981. The prototype (SP-PKW) of an improved version of the P.Z.L. 106A was flown on 15 May 1981. Designated **P.Z.L. 106B**, this introduced a redesigned wing of increased span and area, and the 106B, **106BR** and **106BS** production variants superseded the corresponding A-series aircraft during 1982. These were followed by the **P.Z.L. 106BT Turbo-Kruk** which first flew on 18 September 1985. Powered by a 538.2-kW (730-shp) Czech-built Motorlet M601D turboprop engine, improvements included increased sweep back on the wing, a taller fin and improved chemical payload. Production of all versions of the Kruk had totalled some 250 aircraft by 1990, including 54 exported to East Germany, and 60 plus Kruks used by the Pezetel agricultural air service organisation operating in Egypt. By 1992, however, production was reported to be at a standstill.

Specification
P.Z.L. 106B
Type: agricultural aircraft

Powerplant: one 441-kW (592-hp) P.Z.L. 3S radial piston engine
Performance: maximum speed with agricultural equipment 137 km/h (220 mph); service ceiling 4600 m (15,090 ft); range with maximum fuel 1100 km (684 miles)
Weights: empty equipped 1670 kg (3,682 lb); take-off 3000 kg (6,614 lb)

The P.Z.L. 106 was designed specifically for the agricultural role, with emphasis placed on first-class handling at low level and low airspeeds. Features on the initial production model Kruk (seen here) are the conventional tail, leading-edge slats and spray bars behind the trailing edge.

P.Z.L. 110 Koliber

The **P.Z.L. 110** is the licence-built and upgraded version of the French SOCATA Rallye 100ST single-engined two/four-seat lightplane. The first aircraft, modified to take an 86.5-kW (116-hp) P.Z.L.-F (for Franklin) piston engine, was first flown on 18 April 1978. Ten Series Is were subsequently built, followed by 25 Series IIs and 45 Series IIIs. In 1987 P.Z.L. launched the Lycoming-powered

Koliber 150, and the prototype (SP-PHA) flew on 27 September 1988, since when examples have been exported to Belgium, Denmark, Germany, Norway, South Africa, Sweden and the UK. In 1991 P.Z.L. announced that they were to offer a 175.3-kW (235-hp) version designated **Koliber 235**, powered by a Textron Lycoming 0-540-B4B5 flat-six engine, and two prototypes were reported to be under construction.

Specification
P.Z.L. Koliber 150
Type: single-engine two/four-seat club tourer or glider tug
Powerplant: one 112-kW (150-hp) Textron Lycoming O-320-E2A flat-four piston engine
Performance: cruising speed 170 km/h (106 mph); maximum speed 270 km/h (167 mph); service ceiling 370 m (12,140 ft); range at 500 m

(1,640 ft) with maximum fuel 600 km (373 miles)
Weights: empty equipped 548 kg (1,208 lb); maximum take-off 850 kg (1,874 lb)
Dimensions: span 9.75 m (31 ft 11 in); length 7.37 m (24 ft 2 in); height 2.80 m (9 ft 2 in); wing area 12.6 m² (136.5 sq ft)

P.Z.L. 130 Orlik/Turbo-Orlik

Design of the **P.Z.L. 130 Orlik** (spotted eaglet) piston-engined two-seat primary and basic trainer began in 1981. Construction of four airframes, one for static test plus three flying prototypes, began in 1982, and the first aircraft (SP-PCA) flew on 12 October 1983, followed quickly by the second. However, the third aircraft did not fly until January 1985, and the two pre-production machines which followed did not take to the air until February 1988, owing to serious delays in deliveries of the 246-kW (330-hp) Vedeneyev M14Pm nine-cylinder Russian powerplant. By that time P.Z.L. was seriously looking for another engine, and one contender was the company-produced but less powerful Kalisz K8-AA, which took the underpowered second pre-production aircraft ('006') into the air in March 1988. Although testing continued over the next two years, and included an evaluation by the Polish air force, the piston-engined Orlik was abandoned in 1990.

In 1985, while waiting for supplies of M14Pm powerplants, P.Z.L. re-engined the third prototype (SP-PCC) with a Pratt & Whitney Canada PT6A-25A turbopro-

pand and this flew (as SP-RCC) on 13 July 1986, was provisionally certificated in January 1987 but crashed later the same month. Three more pre-production aircraft were built, all with different powerplants and ratings. These were the 560-kW (750-shp) Motorlet M601D **(P.Z.L. 130TM)**, the 410-kW (550-shp) PT6A-25A **(P.Z.L. 130T)**, and the 708-kW (950-shp) PT6A-62 **(P.Z.L. 130TP)**, and all flew in 1989/90. In 1991, following the powerplant tests, the Polish air force placed an order for 48 **P.Z.L. 130TB**s powered by the Czech M601E engine and the first production Turbo-Orlik was delivered at the end of 1992. Export sales are now being sought for the PT6A-62-engined **P.Z.L. 130TC**, the PT6A-25C-equipped **P.Z.L. 130TD**, and the PT6A-25A-engined **P.Z.L. 130TE** 'economy' version, with a limited equipment fit and minus ejection seats.

Specification
P.Z.L. 130TB Turbo-Orlik
Type: two-seat tandem basic and advanced trainer
Powerplant: one 560-kW (750-shp)

Motorlet M601E turboprop engine
Performance: maximum level speed at sea level 454 km/h (282 mph); maximum level speed at 6000 m (19,685 ft) 501 km/h (311 mph); range with maximum fuel 970 km (602 miles)
Weights: empty equipped 1600 kg (3,527 lb); external payload 800 kg (1,764 lb); maximum take-off 2000 kg (4,409 lb)

The addition of a turboprop to the original Orlik has improved its looks and performance. The Turbo-Orlik is now entering service with the Polish air force.

Dimensions: span 9.0 m (29 ft 6 in); length 9.0 m (29 ft 6 in); height 3.5 m (11 ft 7 in); wing area 13.0 m² (139.9 sq ft)

P.Z.L. Mielec MD-12

Poland's largest aircraft factory, at Mielec, established in the year before the outbreak of World War II, is known now as P.Z.L. Mielec. One of its early postwar projects was the **P.Z.L. Mielec MD-12** short-range light transport, the

first of several prototypes flying initially during August 1959. A cantilever low-wing monoplane of all-metal construction, it had retractable tricycle landing gear and was powered by four Narkiewicz WN-3 radial engines in wing-

mounted nacelles. Accommodation was provided for a flight crew of two on a separate flightdeck, and the main cabin could accommodate 20 passengers or, when cleared of its easily-removed seating, up to 1900 kg (4,189 lb) of cargo. The MD-12 did not progress beyond the prototype stage, but a photographic survey version was produced in small numbers.

Designated **MD-12F**, and first flown in prototype form on 21 July 1962, this had its internal accommodation arranged for a crew of up to seven, providing four camera positions and a darkroom at the rear of the cabin.

Specification
P.Z.L. Mielec MD-12F

Parnall aircraft

The World War I woodworking company of Parnall & Sons built a number of aircraft to other companies' designs, including Avro 504s and Fairey Hamble Babies. Its first indigenous designs, the **Parnall Scout** Zeppelin chaser and the **Puffin** single-float amphibian, were both unsuccessful, but in 1917 Harold Bolas joined the company as chief designer and during the following year a contract was secured for 300 two-seat fleet reconnaissance and spotting biplanes under the name **Panther**. Shortly after the contract was awarded the Armistice was signed and the Air Ministry reduced the required number to 150. By this time W. T. Avery had obtained ownership of Parnall and refused the revised terms, so the contract was passed to the British & Colonial Aeroplane Co., which built 150 between 1919 and 1920, Parnall having produced only six prototypes. The Panther was not a particularly successful aircraft, but it was one of the first British types designed for carrier operations. Two were supplied to the USA in 1920 and 12 to Japan in 1921-22. The last Fleet Air Arm Panthers were retired in 1926, being replaced by Fairey IIIDs.

With the loss of the Panther contract Avery closed down Parnall & Sons and left the aircraft-manufacturing business. Thereupon George Parnall established a new company, George Parnall & Co., retaining Bolas as chief designer. The first aircraft from the new company was the **Plover**, a single-seat carrier-based biplane fighter which was a competitor to the Fairey Flycatcher as a replacement for the Nieuport Nightjar. Three prototpyes were built, one with a 287-kW (385-hp) Jaguar engine and the others with the 325-kW (436-hp) Bristol Jupiter IV selected for production aircraft. Available as a landplane or twin-float amphibian, the Plover proved inferior to the Flycatcher and only 10 production models were built.

An oddity of 1923 was the **Possum**, a three-seat single-engine triplane with a Napier Lion engine in the fuselage driving propellers on the centre wings through a bevel transmission. Two prototypes were ordered; one is known to have flown in June 1923 but there were problems with the transmission and the second may not have been completed.

In the same year Bolas designed the **Pixie**, a single-seat wooden ultra-light monoplane, for the Lympne Light Aeroplane Trials. The prototype had a 500-cc (30.5-cu in) Douglas engine, but was re-engined with a 736-cc (44.9-cu in)

Douglas and managed to win the speed prize at 122.5 km/h (76.1 mph). The Air Ministry ordered two Pixies with 696-cc (42.5-cu in) Blackburne Tomtit engines and these later became civil aircraft.

Two further Pixies were built for the 1924 trials, and these were two-seat biplanes with a detachable top wing; one had a 24-kW (32-hp) Bristol Cherub III engine and the other a 26-kW (35-hp) Blackburne Thrush, the latter having installed subsequently a 1100-cc (67.1-cu in) Anzani. Both were converted permanently to monoplanes in 1926 with Cherub III engines. Parts of one Pixie had been preserved in the Midlands.

The year 1926 spawned several more oddities from Parnall, including two prototypes of the **Pike**, a Napier Lion-powered biplane capable of wheel or float operation and designed to specification 1/24 as a three-seat reconnaissance aircraft to replace the Fairey IIID; the **Perch** to specification 5/24 as a two-seat wheel/float deck landing trainer and built only as a prototype; and the **Peto** to the most unusual requirement. This small two-seat floatplane to specification 16/24 was required to have folding wings and to fit into a 2.44 m (8 ft) wide hangar on the deck of the submarine M.2. The exacting specification was met by Parnall in most respects and two prototypes were built, the first with a 101-kW (135-hp) Armstrong Siddeley Mongoose engine and the second with a 101-kW (135-hp) Bristol Lucifer. Six production aircraft were reported to have been ordered but only the first can be traced. Unfortunately, the submarine was lost with all hands in an accident attributed to the opening of the hangar doors while submerging.

In July 1927 the Air Ministry ordered two prototypes of the **Pipit**, a metal-framed fleet fighter with the new Rolls-Royce F.XI engine. Designed to specification 21/26, in competition with the Hawker Hoopoe and Gloster Gnatsnapper, none of the three types was adopted.

A single example of the **Imp** two-seat sporting biplane was awarded its certificate of airworthiness in May 1928. Powered originally by a 60-kW (80-hp) Armstrong Siddeley Genet II engine, the Imp was used later to flight test the 48-kW (65-hp) Pobjoy P radial, but was scrapped in December 1933. Among the new aircraft displayed in London's Seventh International Aero Exhibition at Olympia in July 1929 was the newest Bolas design, the **Elf**, a two-seat biplane with folding wings. Powered by a 78-kW

(105-hp) A.D.C. Hermes I engine, the Elf was Parnall's answer to the Moth, but it was an ineffective answer. Only two more were built, and the first of these with an 89-kW (120-hp) Hermes II engine is still preserved by the Shuttleworth Trust in flying condition.

The last Parnall design by Bolas before he emigrated to the USA was the 1930 **Prawn**, a single-seat monoplane flying-boat built to an Air Ministry order. The 48-kW (65-hp) A.C.-Ricardo-Burt engine driving a tractor propeller in the nose could be raised 15° to clear the propeller from spray on take-off and landing, but in practice the engine gave insufficient power for the aircraft to leave the water. The Prawn was the smallest British flying-boat, with a span of only 8.66 m (28 ft 5 in).

Bolas was succeeded by Henry B. Clarke, who submitted a design against specification G.4/31 for a general-purpose military aircraft. The Parnall entry was a biplane powered by a Bristol Pegasus III engine, but it was unsuccessful in a mixed field of monoplane and biplane entries from Armstrong Whitworth, Blackburn, Bristol, Fairey, Handley Page, Westland and Vickers. The last-named won the eventual order but transferred it

The Parnall Possum was odd, insofar as its engine was mounted in the fuselage driving twin propellers on the wings.

from its entry, the Vickers 253, to the more advanced Wellesley.

Specification
Parnall Panther

Type: two-seat carrier-based reconnaissance biplane
Powerplant: one 172-kW (230-hp) Bentley B.R.2 rotary piston engine
Performance: maximum speed 175 km/h (109 mph) at 3050 m (10,000 ft); service ceiling 4420 m (14,500 ft); endurance 4¼ hours
Weights: empty 602 kg (1,328 lb); maximum take-off 1177 kg (2,595 lb)
Dimensions: span 8.99 m (29 ft 6 in); length 7.59 m (24 ft 11 in); height 3.20 m (10 ft 6 in); wing area 31.21 m² (336.0 sq ft)
Armament: one movable 7.7-mm (0.303-in) Lewis gun in rear cockpit

An unsuccessful rival to the de Havilland Moth, only two Elfs were built, one now surviving with the Shuttleworth Trust.

Parnall Heck

In May 1936 George Parnall & Company, the Hendy Aircraft Company and Nash & Thompson Ltd amalgamated to form Parnall Aircraft Ltd. The first aircraft to emerge under the new name was the **Parnall 3308 Heck**, which had first flown in July 1934 as the Hendy Heck. The prototype, built by Westland at Yeovil, was a tandem two-seat cabin monoplane with retractable landing gear and a 149-kW (200-hp) de Havilland Gipsy Six engine.

Troubles with the landing gear led to it being locked down and faired, and a pro-

Despite good performance, the Heck could not break into the market dominated by de Havilland, Miles and Percival. They were sold only to the RAF.

duction batch of six **Heck 1C** aircraft was built at Parnall's Yate, Gloucestershire factory. These were three-seaters with 149-kW (200-hp) de Havilland Gipsy Queen engines and spatted main wheels. No sales resulted and four aircraft were used by the makers on communications, while the other two carried out trials on armaments, gun sights and propellers for the RAF. The last surviving Heck was the second production air-

craft, damaged beyond repair in a taxiing accident in June 1950. One further aircraft was built as the **Parnall 382**

primary trainer, basically an open cockpit Heck, but there was no production order.

Partenavia P.48-B Astore/P.52 Tigrotto

Partenavia Construcioni Aeronautiche was established in Naples at the beginning of the 1950s, building a series of light aircraft designed by Ing. Luigi Pascale. The earliest of these was the **Partenavia P.48-B Astore**, a high-wing two-seater powered by a 48-kW (65-hp) Continental A65 engine. Produced in 1952, it had a maximum speed of 185 km/h (115 mph). It was followed in 1953 by the **P.52 Tigrotto**, a low-wing, two-seat cabin monoplane powered by a 63-kW (85-hp) Continental C85-12F engine, which enabled it to cruise at 200 km/h (124 mph).

Partenavia P.53 Aeroscooter

Mario de Bernadi, who won the 1926 Schneider Trophy contest for Italy in a Macchi M.39 seaplane, drew up the specification for the **Partenavia P.53** **Aeroscooter**, the design being entrusted to Luigi Pascale and construction to Partenavia. The single-seat cockpit incorporated a crash pylon which was intended to mount an optional undriven two-blade rotor, thus reducing stalling speed and engine-off rate of descent. The prototype made its first flight with a 16.4-kW (22-hp) Ambrosini P-25 engine installed and without the rotor, although it was intended that a 28-kW (38-hp) CNA-C2 engine would be fitted later.

Partenavia P.55 Tornado

A 1950s high-performance competition and touring two-seater, the all-wood **Partenavia P.55 Tornado** achieved a maximum speed of 348 km/h (216 mph) on its 112-kW (150-hp) Avco Lycoming O-320 engine. This diminutive aircraft, with a wing span of 7.20 m (23 ft 7½ in), length of 6.02 m (19 ft 8 in) and retractable landing gear, twice won the Giro di Sicilia competition.

Partenavia P.57 Fachiro

Intended as an inexpensive touring four-seater, the prototype **Partenavia P.57 Fachiro I**, powered by a 112-kW (150-hp) Avco Lycoming O-320 engine, flew on 7 November 1958. It was later produced as the **Fachiro II**, first flown on 3 January 1959 and fitted with the 125-kW (168-hp) Avco Lycoming O-360-B2A. The 134-kW (180-hp) Avco Lycoming O-320-A2A was installed in the **Fachiro II-f**, which also introduced a swept fin and rudder. The 9.14 m (30 ft 0 in) span Fachiro II, at a maximum take-off weight of 1050 kg (2,315 lb), had a maximum speed of 240 km/h (149 mph) at sea level.

Partenavia P.59 Jolly

Bearing a family resemblance to the P.57 Fachiro, the **Partenavia P.59 Jolly** had tailwheel landing gear and was a two-seater developed in competition with the winning Aviamilano P.19 Scricciolo under the auspices of the Aero Club d'Italia, for possible selection as the standard trainer for the national flying clubs. The prototype, powered by a 71-kW (95-hp) Continental engine, flew on 2 February 1960. A 75-kW (100-hp) Continental O-200 was fitted later, and the wings were increased in span by 1.02 m (3 ft 4 in) to a total of 10.21 m (33 ft 6 in), the resulting aircraft having a maximum speed of 195 km/h (121 mph).

The Partenavia P.69 Jolly was developed for a light aircraft competition in the late 1950s. It was unsuccessful and only one was completed before the company moved on to other, more lucrative, projects.

The Partenavia P.59 Jolly was developed for a light aeroplane competition held during the late 1950s. It was unsuccessful and only two aircraft were completed before Partenavia moved on to further projects.

Partenavia P.64 Oscar/P.66 100/Charlie/Delta

Work on the **Partenavia P.64 Oscar** began in 1964, this being a four-seat development of the P.57 Fachiro II-f incorporating an all-metal structure, and all versions have been powered by Avco Lycoming engines. The prototype P.64 (I-LRAS) powered by a 134-kW (180-hp) O-360-A was flown on 2 April 1965, but work on an improved **P.64B Oscar B** was initiated in November 1966 and this, first flown early in 1967, had a cut-down rear fuselage and a panoramic rear window to improve the all-round field of view. The Oscar B was also built in moderate numbers under licence in South Africa by AFIC (Pty) Ltd as the **AFIC RSA 200 Falcon**. The Oscar B was subsequently renamed the **Oscar-180**, being complemented later by nine **Oscar-200** with a 149-kW (200-hp) IO-360-A engine, 80 two-seat **P.66B Oscar-100**, powered by an 86-kW (115-hp) O-235-C engine, and 50 three-seat O-320-E-powered **Oscar-150**.

In January 1976 Partenavia flew the prototype of the two/four-seat **P.66C Charlie**, powered by a 119-kW (160-hp) O-320-H. Certificated to US FAR Pt 23 Utility category and cleared for positive g aerobatics and six-turn spins, a total of 97 production Charlies was built between 1977 and 1980, the type having been selected by the Aero Club d'Italia as the standard basic trainer for Italian flying clubs. A subsequent order for 11 aircraft resulted in a resumption of production in 1981. In 1976 Partenavia also developed the **P.66T Charlie** two-seater, powered by an 82-kW (110-hp) O-235-N engine, but only the prototype (I-TRAY) was built. One further development was the **P.66D Delta**, essentially an Oscar-100 with minor modifications. Again only one (I-AVLT) was built, by the Aviolight company of Milan, which in February 1988 assumed the design rights and product support for the Partenavia line of single-engined lightplanes. The Delta flew in September 1988, but further development was subsequently abandoned.

Specification
Partenavia P.66C-160 Charlie
Type: two/four-seater cabin monoplane
Powerplant: one 119-kW (160-hp) Avco Lycoming O-320-H2AD flat-four piston engine
Performance: maximum speed 240 km/h (149 mph); service ceiling 4570 m (15,000 ft); maximum range 780 km (485 miles)
Weights: empty 600 kg (1,323 lb); maximum take-off 990 kg (2,183 lb)
Dimensions: span 10.00 m (32 ft 9¾ in); length 7.24 m (23 ft 9 in);

A mildly successful aircraft in sales terms, the Partenavia P.64 is one of many types which never quite managed to break the American stranglehold on the light aircraft market.

height 2.77 m (9 ft 1 in); wing area 13.40 m² (144.20 sq ft)

Partenavia P.68 Victor/Observer/Spartacus/Viator

The prototype of Luigi Pascale's **Partenavia P.68 Victor** six/seven-seat light twin flew for the first time on 25 May 1970, powered by two 149-kW (200-hp) Avco Lycoming IO-360-A engines. Fourteen pre-production aircraft were followed by the improved **P.68B**, with the fuselage lengthened by 15 cm (6 in) forward of the wing to improve accommodation in the cockpit area of the cabin. It entered production in early 1974 and 190 P.68Bs were built. It was superceded on the production line by the further improved **P.68C**, which introduced a lengthened nose (to accommodate weather radar), increased fuel capacity and several internal changes. A specialised patrol and observation version, the **P.68 Observer**, was developed in 1975/76 in conjunction with Sportavia-Putzer of Germany, with a new forward fuselage incorporating a Plexiglas nose providing a downward and forward view that is claimed to equal that of a helicopter. The prototype (D-GERD) flew in February 1976 but series production was undertaken by Partenavia, which has delivered around 20 to date. The **P.68R** retractable gear version (I-VICR) of the P.68B flew in December 1976, but did not enter production. The **P.68C-TC** with 157-kW (210-hp) TIO-360-C turbocharged engines was certificated in June 1980, since when 36 have been sold. Later, in conjunction with Aeritalia, Partenavia began development of a turboprop version originally called the **P.68 Turbo**. This became the nine-seat **AP.68TP**, and the prototype flew for the first time on 11 September 1978.

Powered by two 245-kW (328-shp) Allison 250-B17C engines, this had a retractable tricycle undercarriage, but the second prototype, designated **AP.68TP Series 100**, reverted to a fixed landing gear, the fuselage stretched by 36 cm (14 in) and an extra window installed. Both had all-moving tailplanes and both were lost during flight tests. Further development produced the fixed-gear eight-passenger **Series 300 Spartacus** with a conventional tailplane and elevators, and the first of these flew on 1 April 1983. This was followed in July 1984 by the **Spartacus RG** (I-RAIZ) with a retractable undercarriage. The RG was in turn developed into the **Spartacus-10** with a longer nose and fuselage stretched by a further 64 cm (25 in) to allow the carriage of 10 passengers, and incorporated a further window. The prototype (I-RAIL) was flown on 29 March 1985 and later designated **ATP.68TP Series 600 Viator**. By 1989 the company was claiming sales of 12 Viators. A pressurised version, designated the **Pulsar**, is reported to be currently under development. Around 400 P.68 variants had been built by 1992.

Specification
Partenavia P.68C Victor
Type: six/seven-seat light transport
Powerplant: two 149-kW (200-hp) Avco Lycoming IO-360-A1B6 flat-four piston engines
Performance: maximum speed 320 km/h (199 mph) at sea level; service ceiling 5850 m (19,200 ft);

The propotype Victor flew in 1970 from the company's airfield at Arzano, but the line was soon moved to the newly-built facility at Casoria. After 14 basic P.68s had been built production was switched to the improved P.68B model. This version seated six in a cabin that had undergone a 15-cm (6-in) stretch. Nearly 200 were sold before Partenavia introduced the version shown opposite, the P.68C.

range with reserves 2100 km (1,305 miles)
Weights: empty 1230 kg (2,711 lb); maximum take-off 1990 kg (4,387 lb)
Dimensions: span 12.00 m (39 ft 4½ in); length 9.55 m (31 ft 4 in); height 3.40 m (11 ft 1¾ in); wing area 18.60 m² (200.22 sq ft)

Partenavia P.70 Alpha

Work on the design of the **Partenavia P.70 Alpha** light aerobatic trainer was begun by Luigi Pascale in August 1970. Construction of the prototype (I-GIOY) began in January 1971 and this flew for the first time on 27 May 1972. The Alpha featured mixed stressed-skin and glass-reinforced plastic construction, the latter material being used for the wing leading edges, the fuselage top decking and tail cone. Power was supplied by a 75-kW (100-hp) Rolls-Royce/Continental O-200-A engine although a version with the 119-kW (160-hp) Avco Lycoming O-320-B was planned. Development was adversely affected by the company's preoccupation with the twin-engined P.68, and the P.70 did not proceed any further.

This is the sole Partenavia P.70 Alpha fixed-undercarriage aerobatic trainer, which first flew in May 1972.

Pasped Skylark

Formed at Glendale, California in the mid-1930s, Pasped Aircraft Company designed and built a two-seat cabin monoplane which it named the **Pasped Skylark**, and this was built in small numbers before the outbreak of World War II. Of mixed construction, the Skylark was of braced low-wing monoplance configuration with fixed tailwheel landing gear that had wire-braced main units, and an enclosed cabin equipped wih side-by-side seating and dual controls. Powered by a 93-kW (125-hp)

Notable for its tall, elegant tail surfaces, the 1930s vintage Pasped Skylark had wooden wings mated with a fuselage constructed from welded steel. Its maximum take-off weight was 855 kg (1,885 lb) and it had a range of 1046 km (650 miles). It sold in small numbers in the US.

Warner Scarab radial engine, the 10.92 m (35 ft 10 in) span Skylark had a maximum speed of 224 km/h (139 mph), but this standard of performance was being equalled or exceeded in the USA by many two-seat monoplanes with less powerful engines, which helps to account for the limited sales success of the Skylark.

Paulista aircraft

The Brazilian Companhia Aeronáutica Paulista was established at Sao Paulo during the mid-1940s to build and repair aircraft. The company's first aircraft of original design to enter production had the designation **Paulista CAP.1 Planalto**, this being a two-seat advanced trainer of cantilever low-wing monoplane configuration. Of all-wood basic structure with fabric and plywood covering, the Planalto had fixed tailskid landing gear, accommodated instructor and pupil in tandem open cockpits and was powered by a 67-kW (90-hp) Franklin flat-four engine.

The next design to enter production was the **CAP.4 Paulistinha** two-seat trainer/tourer monoplane, with high-set braced wings that simplified the provision of an enclosed cabin, seating two in tandem. Of mixed construction, its configuration was completed by a conventional wire-braced tailplane and fixed tailskid landing gear, and power was provided by a Franklin flat-four engine. Limited sales success of the CAP.4 led to development of the basically similar **CAP.4B Ambulancia**, which differed by having the rear seat removed to give increased cabin space for a single stretcher patient, loaded/unloaded via hinged fuselage decking that extended between the wing trailing edge and the fin leading edge. Final variant was the **CAP.4C Paulistinha Radio**, an observation or liaison aircraft for military use; this had a modified cabin and rear fuselage to give the observer, seated back-to-back with the pilot, an excellent rear view and to each side, and provided him with radio equipment for communication.

Specification
Paulista CAP.4 Paulistinha
Type: two-seat trainer/tourer
Powerplant: one 48-kW (65-hp) Franklin flat-four piston engine
Performance: maximum speed 155 km/h (96 mph); service ceiling 4000 m (13,125 ft); range 500 km (311 miles)
Weights: empty 320 kg (705 lb); maximum take-off 540 kg (1,190 lb)
Dimensions: span 10.10 m (33 ft 1¾ in); length 6.65 m (21 ft 9¾ in); height 1.95 m (6 ft 4¾ in); wing area 17.00 m² (182.99 sq ft)

Payen aircraft

French designer Roland Payen began research and development into the delta wing before the outbreak of World War II, building two aircraft to test his theories on the practical form of such a wing. In 1952 he began construction of a small research aircraft which he designated **Payen Pa.49**, comprising a delta wing blended into a simple fuselage structure that contained enclosed single-seat accommodation for the pilot,

The Payen Pa.22 was an aerodynamic test vehicle to validate the concept of the Pa.112 racing aircraft, which also had a proposed fighter derivative.

was supported on the ground by fixed tricycle landing gear, and powered by a 150-kg (331-lb) Turboméca Palas turbojet. With a span of 5.15 m (16 ft 10¾ in) and length of 5.10 m (16 ft 8¾ in) the Pa.49, which was first flown on 22 January 1954, had a maximum speed of 400 km/h (249 mph) on the very modest

thrust of the Palas turbine. This was sufficiently promising for Payen to proceed with design and construction of the improved two-seat **Pa.16B Arbalète I** (crossbow) of 1964, which had a revised wing and fuselage structure and was powered by a 78-kW (105-hp) Hirth engine mounted in the rear fuselage to drive a pusher propeller. Subsequent research aircraft based on this design included the **Pa.61F Arbalète II** with a 134-kW (180-hp) Avco Lycoming flat-four engine; the similar **Pa.61G** which substituted retractable foreplanes for the airbrakes and wing-root strakes of the Pa.61F; and the proposed **Pa.61H** which, similar to the Pa.61G, was to be powered by two 160-kg (353-lb) thrust Turboméca turbojets mounted side-by-side in the rear fuselage. Also projected, but not built, was the four-seat **Pa.610 Arbalète III** intended as a four-seat executive aircraft to be powered by a 149-kW (200-hp) piston engine in a pusher configuration.

Subsequent designs were intended for construction by amateurs, both of them developments of the Pa.49 which had been Payen's first post-war aircraft. These comprised the single-seat **Pa.71**, with a 75-kW (100-hp) Rolls-Royce Continental O-200 engine, intended as a Formula 1 racer, and the two-seat **Pa.149** sporting aircraft designed to be powered by two Turboméca Palas turbojet engines each of 150-kg (331-lb) thrust.

Pazmany aircraft

Ladislao Pazmany designed a two-seat light aircraft for construction by amateurs and formed Pazmany Aircraft Corporation at San Diego, California, to market sets of plans. This first aircraft, which has the designation **Pazmany PL-1 Laminar**, was flown as a prototype on 23 March 1962. Plans were acquired by the Chinese Nationalist air force in Taiwan, which built a single example of the PL-1 for evaluation as a potential basic trainer and, following testing that began with a first flight on 26 October 1968, decided to build this aircraft. Under the designation **PL-1B**, a total of 58 more aircraft were constructed in Taiwan for use by the air force, all of them completed by 1974.

A cantilever low-wing monoplane of all-metal construction, with fixed tricycle landing gear and an enclosed cockpit with side-by-side seating for two, the PL-1 prototype was powered by a 71-kW (95-hp) Continental C90-12F flat-four engine, but the PL-1Bs built in Taiwan were powered by the 112-kW (150-hp) Avco Lycoming O-320 engine.

Shortly after the first PL-1 had flown, Ladislao Pazmany completed the design of an improved **PL-2** of similar external configuration which had a slight increase in cockpit width and extensive changes in the structure to make it easier for amateurs to build.

The first PL-2 to fly (on 4 April 1969) was built by Mr. H. Pio of Ramona, California. Several examples of this version were built for evaluation by the air forces of Indonesia (which designated it the LT-200), Republic of Korea, Sri Lanka, Thailand and Vietnam. On 12 July 1972 the prototype of the PL-4 flew. This single-seat ultra-light low-wing T-tailed sportplane was designed from the outset for home construction, and many hundreds of plansets were sold around the world.

Specification
Pazmany/Lipnur LT-200
Type: two-seat trainer
Powerplant: one 112-kW (150-hp) Avco Lycoming O-320-E2A flat-four piston engine
Performance: maximum speed 245 km/h (152 mph); service ceiling 4570 m (14,995 ft); endurance at economic cruising speed 5 hours 30 minutes
Weights: empty 410 kg (904 lb); maximum take-off 730 kg (1,609 lb)
Dimensions: span 8.53 m (28 ft 0 in); length 5.88 m (19 ft 3½ in); height 2.31 m (7 ft 7 in); wing area 10.78 m² (116.0 sq ft)

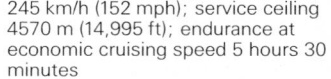

Pazmany PL-1B of the Chinese Nationalist air force.

Pemberton-Billing aircraft

Noel Pemberton-Billing, British designer, constructor and pioneer airman is, perhaps, best known for the company which he founded at Woolston, Southampton, known initially as Pemberton-Billing Ltd but which, in 1916, adopted the later famous name Supermarine Aviation Works Ltd. Before that, however, Pemberton-Billing had initiated the design of a single-seat scout aircraft, the **Pemberton-Billing P.B.9**, whose pilot was seated beneath a large cut-out in the trailing edge of the upper of the equal-span biplane wings. The fixed landing gear incorporated a tailskid, and power was provided by a 37-kW (50-hp) Gnome rotary engine. The performance of the aircraft was found to be satisfactory but only the single example was built and flown, being acquired later by the RNAS for use as a trainer.

The P.B.9 was followed by the **P.B.23**, designed in 1915 as a single-seat scout that had straight biplane wings with considerable gap, so that a fuselage nacelle could be strut-mounted between them. This provided an open cockpit for the pilot and mounted in its rear a 60-kW (80-hp) Le Rhône engine driving a pusher propeller. Twin fins and rudders were mounted on a wide-span tailplane to which the elevator was attached, and the entire tail unit was mounted to four tailbooms extending aft from the wing structure. First flown in early September 1915, the P.B.23 as such failed to win an order, but derived from it was the **P.B.25** which differed by having swept-back wings, modified landing gear and a revised fuselage nacelle, and introduced the 82-kW (110-hp) Clerget rotary engine. However, standard powerplant for the 20 P.B.25 scouts built for the RNAS was the Gnome Monosoupape. The P.B.25s do not appear to have been used operationally, but were stationed at the RNAS stations at Eastchurch and Hendon where they were probably used for training.

To counter German airship attacks on British targets, Pemberton-Billing designed the **P.B.29** quadruplane which was intended to be capable of flight at approximately 56 km/h (35 mph), enabling it to stay on patrol for long periods. The fuselage, with two open cockpits in tandem, was mounted to the second wing, as were the two 67-kW (90-hp) Austro-Daimler engines, each driving a four-blade pusher propeller. The most unusual feature of the P.B.29 was the provision of a third crew position, a gunner accommodated in a streamline fairing mounted between the third and fourth wings, with a machine-gun mounted on top of the wing to give an excellent field of fire. The configuration of this aircraft was completed by a biplane tail unit incorporating three fins and rudders. Only a single P.B.29 was built, and this was soon lost in a flying accident. However, before it had been written off, the P.B.29 had created a great deal of official interest, and Pemberton-Billing was requested to continue development of the design. The resulting **P.B.31 Night Hawk**, powered by two 75-kW (100-hp) Anzani radial engines, had a number of unusual features, including two gun positions above the cabin, the forward gunner having a Davis gun firing a 0.68-kg (1½-lb) shell; a small searchlight was mounted at the fuselage nose with control by Bowden cable so that it could be used for target location, or to assist landing. Power for the searchlight was generated by an onboard auxiliary power unit, this being possibly the first use of an APU on an aircraft. Two P.B.31s had been ordered, but only the first was completed.

Specification
Pemberton-Billing P.B.25
Type: single-seat scout
Powerplant: one 75-kW (100-hp) Gnome Monosoupape rotary piston engine
Performance: maximum speed 159 km/h (99 mph); climb to 4665 m (15,300 ft) in 40 minutes 30 seconds; endurance 3 hours
Weights: empty 490 kg (1,080 lb);

The 1914 P.B.1 was an elegant flying-boat which failed to fly due to excessive water-drag.

maximum take-off 715 kg (1,576 lb)
Dimensions: span 10.06 m (33 ft 0 in); length 7.34 m (24 ft 1 in); height 3.17 m (10 ft 5 in); wing area 25.73 m² (277.0 sq ft)
Armament: one forward-firing 7.7-mm (0.303-in) Lewis gun mounted on top of fuselage nacelle forward of the cockpit

The P.B.31 Night Hawk could remain aloft for 18 hours and was fitted with a single bunk to remedy crew fatigue.

Percival Gull series
to
Piaggio P.16

Percival Gull series

Edgar W. Percival built the prototype of his **Percival Type D.1 Gull** three-seat touring monoplane at Maidstone in 1932, and it flew in that year's King's Cup Race, averaging 229.7 km/h (142.73 mph). The clean design attracted immediate attention and the newly-formed Percival Aircraft Co. sub-contracted construction of a batch of 24 **Type D.2 Gull** aircraft to George Parnall & Co. at Yate. Engines installed included the 97-kW (130-hp) Cirrus Hermes IV and DH Gipsy Major, and the 119-kW (160-hp) Napier Javelin III; these aircraft were more commonly designated **Gull Four**.

Percival Aircraft opened its own factory at Gravesend in 1934 and a revised version, the **Type D.3 Gull Six** with the 149-kW (200-hp) de Havilland Gipsy Six engine, entered production; it had a neater single-strut spatted landing gear and detail cabin improvements, but retained the folding wings of the Gull Four. In 1936 the company moved to a new factory at Luton, where Gull Six production was completed with the 48th Gull, delivered to Shell in South Africa in October 1937.

Percival had been working on a four-seat development of the Gull Six at

The Percival D.3 Gull Six was a classic touring aircraft in its day and several, such as this one, survived the war.

Gravesend, and flew the prototype **Type K.1 Vega Gull** in November 1935. It had dual controls, trailing edge flaps and the same engine as the Gull Six, although later aircraft had the 153-kW (205-hp) Gipsy Six Series II. Vega Gulls achieved a number of successes in racing and long-distance flights, and a total of 90 was built before the last aircraft was delivered in July 1939. Customers were as far afield as Australia, Canada, India, Iraq, Japan and Kenya. Demonstrations by Percival to the services resulted in the supply of Vega Gulls for communications, and the type was developed into the Proctor.

Mention should be made also of the

The Mew Gull saw many changes. Shown here is its most recent incarnation.

Mew Gull, a single-seat racing aircraft which flew at Gravesend in March 1934 with a 123-kW (165-hp) Napier Javelin Ia engine, but by July's King Cup Air Race it was powered by a 149-kW (200-hp) Gipsy Six and achieved 307 km/h (191 mph). This first aircraft was classed as a **Type E.1** and was followed by a completely redesigned model, the **Type E.2**, of which four were built. They achieved a number of racing and long distance records, including one set by Alex Henshaw who flew the third aircraft to the Cape of Good Hope and back in 4 days 10 hours 16 minutes. This Mew Gull survived the war and several accidents and in 1992 was being rebuilt to flying condition. The last aircraft, designated **E.3H**, was again a redesign with a smaller wing and tail and narrower fuselage.

Percival P.28 Proctor series

Developed from the Vega Gull, the **Percival Proctor** was designed to Specification 20/38 for a communications/radio trainer. Successful evaluation of the prototype, first flown on 8 October 1939, led to the initial series **P.28 Proctor Mk I** three-seat communications aircraft (247 built), followed by the **P.30 Proctor Mk II** (175) and **P.34 Proctor Mk III** (437), both of them radio trainers. Designed to Specification T.9/41 and named originally **Preceptor**, the **Proctor Mk IV** radio trainer (258 built) had a longer, deeper fuselage to accommodate four; the increased capacity made it an effective communications aircraft and many later had dual controls installed. Most Proctors built during the war were produced under sub-contract by F. Hills & Sons in Manchester, this company's output comprising 25 Mk I,

100 Mk II, 437 Mk III and 250 Mk IV aircraft. At the end of World War II some 200 Proctor Mk I, Mk II and Mk III aircraft were declared surplus, but some Mk IVs remained in service with communications squadrons until 1955, when surviving aircraft were, similarly, sold on the civil market. In 1945, however, three Proctor IVs had been furnished to civil standards, leading to introduction of the **Proctor 5** (150 built) of which four were supplied to the RAF for use by air attachés under the designation **Proctor C Mk 5**. A single **Proctor 6** floatplane was built in 1946 for the Hudson's Bay Company in Canada.

Specification
Percival Proctor Mk IV
Type: three/four-seat radio trainer/communications aircraft

A rare wartime picture of a Proctor shows its spatted undercarriage and wing-mounted landing light. The aircraft served with the RAF in the communications and radio/navigation training roles.

Powerplant: one 157-kW (210-hp) de Havilland Gipsy Queen II inline piston engine
Performance: maximum speed 257 km/h (160 mph); service ceiling

4265 m (14,000 ft); range 805 km (500 miles)
Weights: empty 1075 kg (2,370 lb); maximum take-off 1588 kg (3,500 lb)

Percival P.40 Prentice

The RAF ended World War II using the same basic trainer that had been in service at the outbreak of war, the de Havilland Tiger Moth, and there was an urgent need for a more modern approach. The **Percival P.40 Prentice** was designed to meet Specification T.23/43 and was an all-metal monoplane with many new features and an all-up weight more than twice that of the Tiger. Since its power was considerably less than twice that of the Tiger its performance was hardly sparkling and, in fact, the old biplane's initial rate of climb of 229 m (750 ft) per minute compared well with the Prentice's 198 m (650 ft) per minute. An unnecessary complication which added to

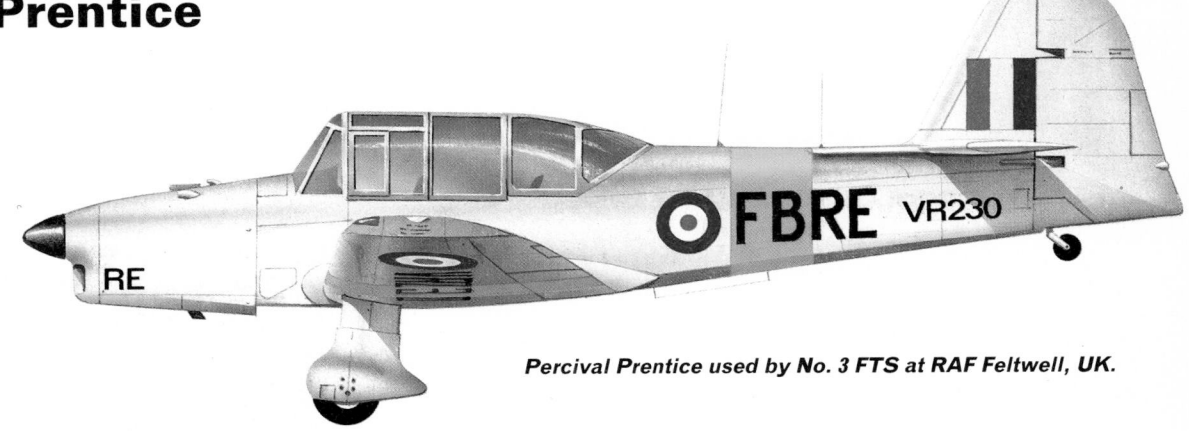

Percival Prentice used by No. 3 FTS at RAF Feltwell, UK.

the weight was an original requirement for a third seat that, in practice, was never used, but the Prentice was the RAF's first side-by-side trainer, a configuration retained until the Tucano entered service in 1988.

The prototype flew in March 1946, and after modifications to the tail surfaces and wing tips an initial batch was supplied for service trials. The Prentice then entered full production on two lines, Percival's Luton factory building 230 for the

RAF, and Blackburn at Brough another 125. Percival additionally built two Prentices for the Lebanon and 200 were reported sold to Argentina. Hindustan Aircraft built 65 for the Indian Air Force with 257-kW (345-hp) de Havilland Gipsy Queen engines, and these served between 1948 and 1959.

Replacement of RAF Prentices by Provosts began in 1953, and in 1955 Aviation Traders at Southend bought 252 surplus Prentices for possible civil conversion,

two others being bought privately. In practice only a few were converted for civil use since they proved expensive to operate. One was configured as a seven seater, but the vast majority were broken up. Several survive in the UK and elsewhere.

Specification
Percival Prentice
Type: two/three-seat military trainer
Powerplant: one 187-kW (251-hp) de

Havilland Gipsy Queen 32 inline piston engine
Performance: maximum speed 230 km/h (143 mph) at 1525 m (5,000 ft); service ceiling 5485 m (18,000 ft); endurance 3½ hours
Weights: empty 1461 kg (3,232 lb); maximum take-off 1905 kg (4,200 lb)
Dimensions: span 14.02 m (46 ft 0 in); length 9.53 m (31 ft 3 in); height 3.92 m (12 ft 10½ in); wing area 28.33 m² (305.0 sq ft)

Percival P.50/P.54 Prince

Shortly after the end of World War II, Percival Aircraft produced the prototype of the five-seat **P.48 Merganser**, first flown on 9 May 1947. A cantilever highwing monoplane with retractable tricycle landing gear, it was powered by two 221-kW (269-hp) Gipsy Queen 51 engines in wing-mounted nacelles, but production of these engines was not continued and lack of a suitable alternative led to development of the larger **Percival P.50 Prince** powered by Alvis nine-cylinder radial engines. Following the first flight of the Prince prototype, on 13 May 1948, 24 production aircraft were built with many detail differences and with engines of 388 to 418 kW (520 to 560 hp), variations re-

The Percival P.50 Prince commercial aircraft was built in small numbers but many versions. The design eventually led to the military Pembroke and Sea Price designs.

flected by the designations **Prince 1, 2, 3, 3A, 3B, 3D, 3E, 4, 4B, 4D, 4E** and **6B**. The planned **Prince 5** was developed instead as the **President**, and details of this aircraft and the related **Pembroke** and **Sea Prince** will be found under the Hunting (Percival) entry. Six special versions fitted with a longer nose and camera hatches were built as P.54 Survey Princes and the first of these (G-ALRY) flew in the early 1950s.

Specification
Percival Prince 2
Type: 10-passenger transport
Powerplant: two 388-kW (520-hp) Alvis Leonides 501/4 radial piston engines
Performance: maximum speed 348 km/h (216 mph); service ceiling

7160 m (23,500 ft); range 1513 km (940 miles)
Weights: empty 3340 kg (7,364 lb); maximum take-off 4990 kg (11,000 lb)
Dimensions: span 17.07 m (56 ft 0 in); length 13.06 m (42 ft 10 in); height 4.90 m (16 ft 1 in); wing area 33.91 m² (365.0 sq ft)

Percival Q.6 Petrel

Edgar Percival's first twin-engine aircraft was the **Percival Type Q**, planned as the **Q.4** four-seat light transport with de Havilland Gipsy Major engines, and as the six-seat **Q.6** feederliner with Gipsy Six engines. Only the latter version was built, the Q.6 prototype first being flown on 14 September 1937. A cantilever low-wing monoplane with fixed tailwheel landing gear, the type entered production in 1938 and 27 were completed, four with retractable landing gear. Government operators included Egypt (2) and the RAF which had seven serving under the designation **Q.6 Petrel** in a communications role. By May 1940 nine British-registered Q.6s were impressed

A Q.6 impressed by the British forces during World War II. Virtually all Q.6s acted as squadron liaison aircraft.

for RAF/Royal Navy use, and two aircraft were also impressed at Heliopolis. Postwar, surviving impressed aircraft and three of the RAF's Q.6 Petrels found their way on to the British civil register, and one (G-AFFD) was being rebuilt on the Isle of Man.

Specification
Type: six-seat communications aircraft
Powerplant: two 153-kW (205-hp) de

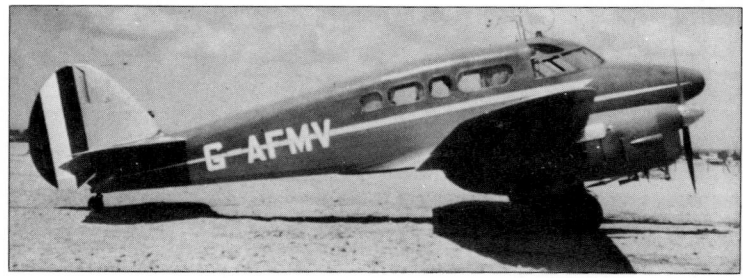

Havilland Gipsy Six inline piston engines
Performance: maximum speed 314 km/h (195 mph); service ceiling 6400 m (21,000 ft); range 1207 km (750 miles)

Weights: empty 1588 kg (3,500 lb); maximum take-off 2495 kg (5,500 lb)
Dimensions: span 14.22 m (46 ft 8 in); length 9.83 m (32 ft 3 in); height 2.97 m (9 ft 9 in); wing area 25.83 m² (278.0 sq ft)

Petlyakov Pe-2

Soviet designer Vladimir M. Petlyakov, who had gained considerable early experience working on the projects of Andrei N. Tupolev, was given the task while imprisoned of designing a new high-altitude fighter which was designated **VI-100**. A cantilever low-wing monoplane with a circular-section fuselage, retractable tailwheel landing gear, and a tail unit incorporating twin fins and rudders, it was powered by two 783-kW (1,050-hp) M-105 V-12 engines with TK-3 turbochargers in wing-mounted nacelles. A pressure cabin had been planned for this aircraft, but this was not available when the VI-100 was nearing completion and, instead, the accommodation was rearranged so that the pilot was seated in an enclosed cockpit well forward of the wing leading edge, the observer/rear gunner being similarly accommodated near the wing trailing edge. Flown for the first time during 1939-40, the VI-100 was found to have problems with the shock-struts of its landing gear and to have some directional instability. The latter was resolved by introducing fins of increased area, but the problems with the shock-struts were

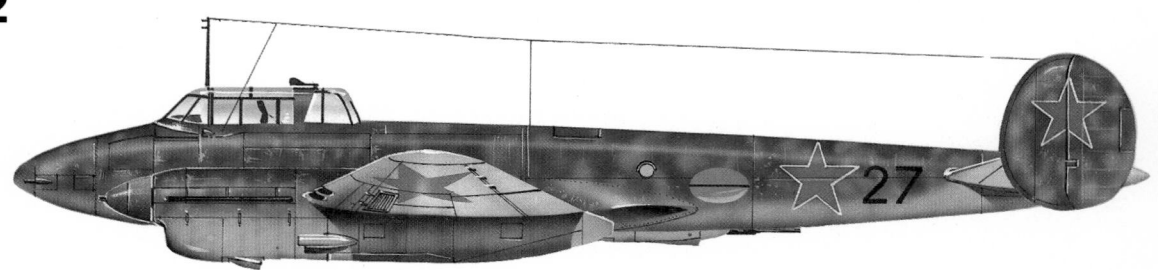

Petlyakov Pe-2FT of an unknown bomber regiment, Soviet air force, operating over the Eastern Front in the latter part of World War II.

less easily solved, and indeed were never completely cured. However, in late May 1940 it was decided to change the role from high-altitude fighter to that of a three-seat dive-bomber, designated **PB-100**, and at this point the pressure cabin was abandoned and the accommodation revised for a crew of three; the pilot's seating was little changed, but a prone position for the navigator/bomb-aimer was provided forward of and below the pilot. One PB-100 was completed as a conversion of a VI-100 and,

following early tests, the type was ordered into production under the designation **Petlyakov Pe-2**.

The Pe-2 proved an outstanding tactical bomber. Its airframe was little changed from that of the PB-100 except for further revision of the accommodation, with the pilot on the port side of an enlarged cockpit, and the navigator/bomb-aimer on a swivel seat behind and to his right, giving him access to a machine-gun, but able to transfer easily to his prone bomb-aiming position on

approach to the target. Third crew member was a radio operator/air gunner, in a separate compartment to the rear of the fuselage fuel tank, with a roof hatch, two side windows and a ventral gun position.

The first production Pe-2 was flown on 18 November 1940, and by 22 June 1941 a total of 458 had been delivered, of which almost 65 per cent were then operational. From late April 1941 the Pe-2 became the standard tactical bomber of the Soviet air force, with a result that when production ended in early 1945 a total of 11,427 had been built. Post-war Pe-2s were supplied to Czechoslovakia (with the designation **B-32**), Poland and Yugoslavia.

Variants

Pe-27(*): first flown in October 1941; equipped with VK-105TK engines and an internal bomb bay for up to four 500-kg (1,102-lb) bombs; later series introduced automatic leading-edge slats, but these were soon dropped

Pe-2Sh: designation of conversion of PB-100 prototype with two 20-mm ShVAK cannon and one 12.7-mm (0.5-in) UBS machine-gun beneath fuselage for ground attack

Pe-3: designation of small number of aircraft produced as bomber interceptors with dive brakes removed and armament of two 20-mm ShVAK cannon, two 12.7-mm (0.5-in) and two 7.92-mm (0.31-in) machine-guns in nose, and one 12.7-mm (0.5-in) machine-gun in dorsal turret

Pe-3bis: night-fighter of which some 300 built, with armament of one 20-mm ShVAK cannon, one 12.7-mm (0.5-in) and three 7.92-mm (0.31-in) machine-guns in nose; late production with two 20-mm ShVAK cannon, and three 12.7-mm (0.5-in) and two 7.92-mm (0.31-in) machine-guns; most with internal bay for three 100-kg (220-lb) bombs and underwing launch rails for eight RS-82 rockets

Pe-3R: fighter/reconnaissance version with vertical/oblique cameras installed

Pe-2MV: version armed with two 20-mm ShVAK cannon and two 12.7-mm (0.5-in) machine-guns in an underfuselage gondola, no bomb bay, and one 7.62-mm (0.3-in) machine-gun in dorsal turret

Pe-2FT: standard production version from spring 1942; similar to Pe-2MV but with reduced nose glazing, dive brakes deleted and a second 7.62-mm (0.3-in) machine-gun for the radio operator/gunner

Pe-2 Paravan: version with barrage balloon deflecting cables linking short boom on fuselage nose and each wingtip

Pe-2FZ: produced in small numbers during 1943, had redesigned cockpit with navigator in a turret with two 12.7-mm (0.5-in) machine-guns; no nose accommodation

Pe-2VI: high-altitude fighter conversion with a pressure cabin and special engine superchargers; used as basis for further development

Pe-2I: two-seat bomber version with redesigned fuselage, increased wing span, deeper bomb bay with capacity of 1000 kg (2,205 lb), two 12.7-mm (0.5-in) machine-guns, one in nose and one in tailcone, and 1230-kW (1,650-hp) VK-107A engines; production intended but abandoned in early 1945

Pe-3M: two-seat fighter version of 1943 with VK-105PF engines, and armament of two 20-mm ShVAK cannon, three 12.7-mm (0.5-in) machine-guns and bombload of up to 700 kg (1,543 lb)

Pe-2S/Pe-2UT/U Pe-2: two-seat trainer versions retaining full bombload, some with four forward-firing machine-guns, two 12.7-mm (0.5-in) and two 7.62-mm (0.3-in); Czech designation was **CB-32**

Pe-6B: standard production bomber from 1944; many structural and systems improvements, armament of three 12.7-mm (0.5-in) and one 7.62-mm (0.3-in) machine-gun

Pe-2R(*): three-seat day reconnaissance version; equipped with three/four cameras, carried armament of three 12.7-mm (0.5-in) machine-guns, and powered by VK-105PF engines

Pe-2R(**): three-seat day reconnaissance version of 1944; as Pe-2R(*) but armed with three 20-mm ShVAK cannon and powered by

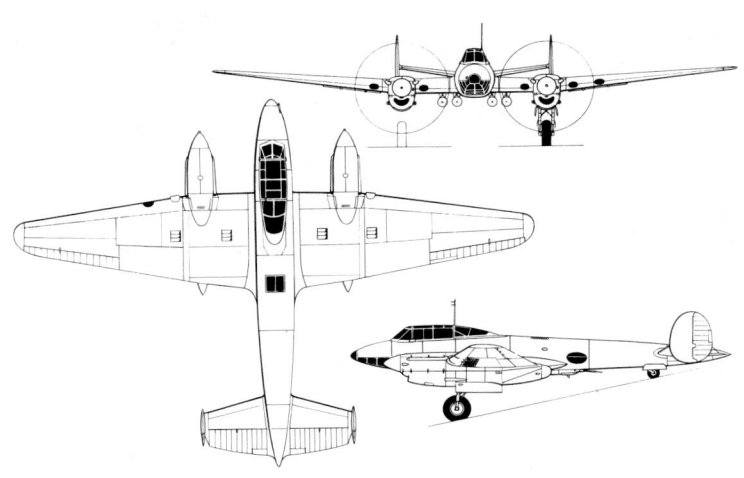

Petlyakov Pe-2 (early production aircraft)

VK-107A engines

Pe-2K: version which introduced wings, nacelles and landing gear designed for the Pe-2I and VK-105PF-1 engines

Pe-2RD: single conversion from Pe-2 with a 300-kg (661-lb) Glushko RD-1 liquid-rocket engine installed in the tail to give improved performance for take-off and combat; tested during 1943-45

Pe-2D: three-seat bomber version of September 1944 with VK-107A engines

Pe-27(**): bomber version of September 1944 with VK-107A engines, bombload of up to 2000 kg (4,409 lb) and armament of three 20-mm ShVAK cannon

Specification
Petlyakov Pe-FT

Type: three-seat bomber

Powerplant: two 940-kW (1,260-hp) Klimov VK-105PF inline piston engines

Performance: maximum speed 580 km/h (360 mph) at 4000 km (13,125 ft); service ceiling 9000 m (29,525 ft); range 1770 km (1,100 miles)

Weights: empty 6200 kg (13,669 lb); maximum take-off 8520 kg (18,783 lb)

Dimensions: span 17.11 m (56 ft 1½ in); length 12.78 m (41 ft 11¼ in); height 3.42 m (11 ft 2¾ in); wing area 40.50 m^2 (435.95 sq ft)

Armament: machine-guns and/or cannon as detailed under variants, plus up to 1000 kg (2,205 lb) of bombs

Petlyakov Pe-8

The **Petlyakov Pe-8** was the Soviet Union's only modern four-engine bomber of World War II, the original design concept being outlined by A. N. Tupolev to meet a mid-1934 requirement for an aircraft of this class. A cantilever mid-wing monoplane of all-metal construction, except for fabric-covered control surfaces, the **ANT-42** as it was then known had retractable tailwheel landing gear with only the main units retracting. Planned powerplant was four wing-mounted engines with a central supercharger installation in the fuselage, but when first flown on 27 December 1936 the ATsN supercharger installation was not available and the ANT-42 was powered by four 820-kW (1,100-hp) Mikulin M-100 Vee engines. Although the aircraft was damaged subsequently in a heavy landing, official testing was completed during 1937, following which the ATsN supercharger, driven by a single M-100 engine, became available. The second prototype ANT-42 was flown on 26 July 1938, this having many improvements including an ATsN-2 supercharger driven by an M-100A engine. There was accommodation for a crew of 11 and the aircraft had full armament comprising electrically-actuated

dorsal and tail turrets, each with a 7.62-mm (0.3-in) ShKAS machine-gun; a nose turret with a single (later twin) ShKAS machine-gun, plus a position in the rear of each inboard engine nacelle, accessible to the gunner through a wing crawlway, each provided with a single 12.7-mm (0.5-in) machine-gun. Standard bombload was six 100-kg (220-lb) or four 250-kg (551-lb) bombs, but over suitable short ranges a maximum overload of 4000 kg (8,818 lb) of bombs could be carried.

The manufacture of five pre-production aircraft was authorised in April 1937, but there was a subsequent attempt to

end the programme. However, production was finally approved in 1939 under the designation **TB-7** and these five pre-series aircraft differed from the ANT-42 by having the ATsN central supercharger installation deleted and the main engines replaced by supercharged AM-35s. At the same time several airframe improvements were introduced and deliveries of these pre-production aircraft began in May 1940. Performance with the AM-35 powerplant was disappointing, leading to the evaluation of several different engines, but in October 1940 the 1044-kW (1,400-hp) ACh-40 diesel was selected as standard powerplant. This proved unreliable, bringing continued use of the 1007-kW (1,350-hp) AM-35A, until those in service were re-

engined with the 1119-kW (1,500-hp) ACh-30B diesel. On the night of 7/8 August 1941 18 of these aircraft made an attack on Berlin, but with one crashing on take-off from engine failure and eight others making forced landings for the same reason, it was finally decided to discontinue the use of diesel engines. By that time the designation TB-7 had been dropped in favour of Pe-8, and when production ended in October 1941 a total of 79 had been built; by the end of 1942 about 48 of this total had been re-engined with the ASh-82FN. One aircraft with AM-35A engines made a remarkable staged flight from Moscow to Washington and back during the period 19 May to 13 June 1942. Surviving aircraft were used extensively during

Just visible on this Soviet air force Petlyakov Pe-8 are the defensive gun positions sited in the rear of the two inboard engine nacelles.

1942-43 for close-support bombing and, from February 1943, were used to deploy the FAB-5000NG 5000-kg (11,023-lb) bomb for point attacks on special targets.

Post-war about 30 Pe-8s survived and were used for a variety of purposes, including employment as engine testbeds, and in 1952 two of them played a key role in establishing an Arctic station before returning the expedition to Moscow in a non-stop flight of 5000 km (3,107 miles).

Specification
Petlyakov Pe-8
Type: long-range heavy bomber
Powerplant: four 1268-kW (1,700-hp) Shvetsov ASh-82FN 14-cylinder radial piston engines
Performance: maximum speed 450 km/h (280 mph) at 9000 m (29,525 ft); range with maximum bombload about 4700 km (2,920 miles)
Weights: empty 18420 kg (40,609 lb); maximum take-off 36000 kg (79,366 lb)
Dimensions: span 39.10 m (128 ft 3¼ in); length 23.59 m (77 ft 4¾ in); height 6.20 m (20 ft 4 in); wing area 188.68 m² (2,031.00 sq ft)
Armament: two 7.62-mm (0.3-in) machine-guns in nose turret, one 20-mm ShVAK cannon in each of dorsal and tail turrets, and one 12.7-mm (0.5-in) machine-gun at the rear of each inboard engine nacelle, plus a maximum bombload of 4000 kg (8,818 lb) all carried internally

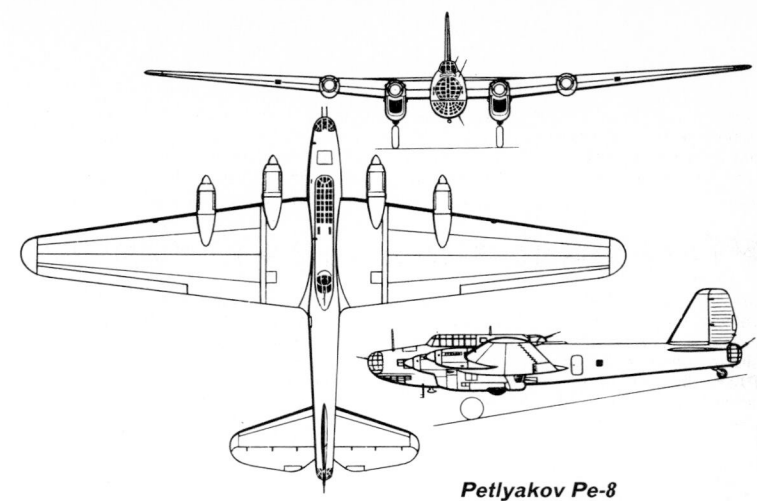

Petlyakov Pe-8

Pfalz A.I/A.II, E.I/E.II/E.III/E.IV and E.V

The Pfalz Flugzeug-Werke GmbH was established at Speyer-am-Rhein during 1913 to design and manufacture aircraft but, like many other European companies, began by building under licence from other nations aircraft that had already proved to be practical and reliable. Thus, Pfalz was soon constructing the Morane-Saulnier Type H shoulder-wing monoplane and Type L parasol-wing monoplane, and from the latter developed a slightly different version powered by a 60-kW (80-hp) Oberursel U.O rotary engine, this being designated **Pfalz A.I**; distinguishing feature of the single **A.II** was the installation of the 75-kW (100-hp) Oberursel U.I. The A.I was deployed during 1914 in the photographic and reconnaissance role.

From the Morane-Saulnier Type H came a separate line of development, for only slightly modified and with the 60-kW (80-hp) Oberursel engine installed it was operated as an unarmed single-seat scout. However, when in 1915 the Fokker synchronising gear was found to be effective, the Pfalz monoplane was equipped with this gear and a single forward-firing LMG 08/15 machine-gun, the type then becoming designated **Pfalz E.I**, of which about 60 were produced; a generally similar airframe with the 75-kW (100-hp) Oberursel engine installed had the designation **E.II**. The single A.II (above) was given Fokker synchronising gear and one machine-gun, and was redesignated **E.III**; it was built in small numbers. The generally similar **E.IV** had structural strengthening and modifications to permit installation of the 119-kW (160-hp) Oberursel U.III rotary engine, but only about 24 had been built when unreliability of this powerplant resulted in introduction of the **E.V**, which combined the E.II airframe with a 75-kW (100-hp) Mercedes D.I engine. This was probably the best of the Pfalz E-series but, appearing too late in the war, was built in only very small numbers.

Specification
Pfalz E.IV
Type: single-seat fighting scout
Powerplant: one 119-kW (160-hp) Oberursel U.III 14-cylinder rotary piston engine
Performance: maximum speed 160 km/h (99 mph); climb to 2000 m (6,560 ft) in 8 minutes 30 seconds; duration 1 hour
Weights: empty 471 kg (1,038 lb); maximum take-off 695 kg (1,532 lb)
Dimensions: span 10.20 m (33 ft 5½ in); length 6.60 m (21 ft 7¾ in); height 2.55 m (8 ft 4½ in); wing area 16.00 m² (172.23 sq ft)
Armament: two synchronised forward-firing 7.92-mm (0.31-in) LMG 08/15 machine-guns

Compared with the E.IV, the Pfalz E.I spanned 9.26 m (30 ft 4¾ in) and weighed a maximum of 535 kg (1,177 lb). It was powered by an Oberursel VO.I.

Pfalz D.III and D.IIIa

On completion of outstanding contracts for the construction of single-seat scouts, Pfalz production continued initially with the L.F.G. Roland D.I, which was built under licence during 1916 and, in early 1917, followed by the L.F.G. Roland D.II. In the summer of 1917 Pfalz finalised the design of a single-seat fighter of its own, leaning heavily upon constructional methods gained from the L.F.G. Roland D.I and D.II fighters. The resulting **Pfalz D.III**, first flown in the summer of 1917, was an unequal span biplane with fixed tailskid landing gear, powered by a 119-kW (160-hp) Mercedes D.III engine and having an open cockpit for the pilot beneath a cut-out in the trailing edge of the upper wing. The Pfalz D.III entered service on the Western Front in late 1917, being followed in early 1918 by the improved **D.IIIa** which introduced the more powerful Mercedes D.IIIa engine. When production ended it was estimated that more than 600 had been delivered. A single example of an experimental triplane version of the D.III was built by mounting a third wing of reduced chord between the existing biplane wings, but it is not known whether this aircraft was ever flown.

The Pfalz D.III of 1916 was a much underrated biplane fighter which combined adequate performance and firepower with good fields of vision and aerial agility.

Specification
Pfalz D.IIIa
Type: single-seat fighter
Powerplant: one 134-kW (180-hp) Mercedes D.IIIa inline piston engine
Performance: maximum speed 165 km/h (103 mph) at 3050 m (10,000 ft); service ceiling 5180 m (17,000 ft); endurance about 2 hours 30 minutes

Weights: empty 695 kg (1,532 lb); maximum take-off 935 kg (2,061 lb)
Dimensions: span 9.40 m (30 ft 10 in); length 6.95 m (22 ft 9½ in); height 2.67 m (8 ft 9 in); wing area 22.10 m² (237.89 sq ft)
Armament: two fixed forward-firing 7.92-mm (0.31-in) LMG 08/15 machine-guns

Pfalz D.XII

Pfalz had achieved little success in the design and production of military aircraft other than with the D.III/IIIa series, which had then been followed by a number of single-seat fighter prototpyes; of these only the D.VIII and Dr.I had been built as series aircraft, to a total of about 40 and 10 respectively. The last Pfalz design to be produced in significant numbers was the **Pfalz D.XII** single-seat fighter, a two-bay biplane with horn-balanced ailerons, a considerably revised tail unit and fixed tailskid landing gear, and power provided by the Mercedes D.IIIa inline engine. First flown during the spring of 1918, versions of the D.XII with both Mercedes D.IIIa and B.M.W.III engines took part in the German fighter trials held at Adlershof in June 1918. Leading pilots agreed that in some respects the D.XII was superior in performance to the Fokker D.VII, but when delivered to combat units it did not at first meet with approval. In fact, it has been suggested that the D.XII would have been deployed more extensively and far more successfully if it had not also had to fight against the reputation of the Fokker D.VII. At the end of the war there were almost 200 Pfalz D.XIIs in service with 10 *Jastas* on the Western Front and, in addition, the type was operational with a number of home-defence fighter units.

Specification
Type: single-seat fighter
Powerplant: one 134-kW (180-hp) Mercedes D.IIIa inline piston engine
Performance: maximum speed 170 km/h (106 mph); service ceiling 5640 m (18,500 ft); endurance 2 hours 30 minutes
Weights: empty 716 kg (1,579 lb); maximum take-off 900 kg (1,984 lb)
Dimensions: span 9.00 m (29 ft 6¼ in); length 6.35 m (20 ft 10 in); height 2.70 m (8 ft 10¼ in); wing area 21.70 m² (233.58 sq ft)
Armament: two fixed forward-firing 7.92-mm (0.31-in) LMG 08/15 machine-guns

Pfalz D.XIV and D.XV

Under the designation **Pfalz D.XIV**, the company built an experimental single-seat fighter which was very similar to the D.XII. It differed primarily by having increased wing span, of 10.00 m (32 ft 9¾ in), and the more powerful 149-kW (200-hp) Benz Bz.IV inline engine which was installed also made it necessary to increase the area of the fin. Maximum speed of the D.XIV was 180 km/h (112 mph), but this was exceeded by the last Pfalz single-seat fighter, the **D.XV**, of which a small number were produced before the end of the war. The major change in this last design resulted from the fuselage being strut-mounted between the biplane wings and, at the same time, all wire bracing was removed from the wing structure. Built in two versions, with powerplant comprising either the 134-kW (180-hp) Mercedes D.IIIa or 138-kW (185-hp) B.M.W. IIIa, the D.XV powered with this latter engine was able to demonstrate a maximum speed of about 200 km/h (124 mph). Span was 8.60 m (28 ft 2½ in).

Pfalz miscellaneous D types

Simultaneously with design and development of the D.III, Pfalz was working on a refined and slightly smaller single-seat fighter which it designated **Pfalz D.VI**. It retained similar wings, landing gear and fuselage to the D.III, but the fuselage was modified to accept an 82-kW (110-hp) Oberursel U.II rotary engine. This was installed with a large spinner in a neat radial cowling, giving the D.VI extremely good lines, completed by the introduction of a redesigned and more workmanlike tail unit. However neat in appearance, the D.VI had an extremely poor rate of climb, and was followed by the generally similar but somewhat larger **D.VII**, of which two versions were built and differing only in the installed powerplant, the 119-kW (160-hp) Oberursel U.III or the Siemens-Halske Sh.III of the same power output, both being rotary engines. Neither the

Powered by the 119-kW (160-hp) Siemens-Halske Sh.III, the Pfalz Dr.I was built in small numbers. Armed with two machine-guns, the Dr.I spanned 8.55 m (28 ft ½ in) with a maximum weight of 705 kg (1,554 lb).

D.VI nor the D.VII entered production, but a smaller number of **Pfalz Dr.I** triplanes were built, this being basically a version of the D.VII which introduced a third wing, of reduced chord and span, between the existing biplane wings. The **D.VIII** biplane of 1918 was also built in small numbers with the 119-kW (160-hp) Siemens-Halske Sh.III rotary engine before production was terminated. Similar in overall appearance to the D.VII, the D.VIII differed primarily by having a two-bay wing and was flown in two other versions: one of them with the 119-kW (160-

hp) Oberursel U.III and the other, which also introduced horn-balanced ailerons, with a 104-kW (140-hp) Goebel Goe.III powerplant.

Phönix C.I

The Austro-Hungarian aircraft manufacturer Phönix Flugzeug-Werke began with licence-manufacture of Albatros and Brandenburg aircraft, turning to aircraft of its own design. The first of these was the **Phönix C.I** two-seat armed reconnaissance and general-purpose biplane, which the company developed from the Hansa-Brandenburg C.II (designed originally by Ernst Heinkel), which it had built under licence. An ugly but practical aircraft, the C.I had fixed tailskid landing gear, was powered by a Hiero inline engine, and accommodated pilot and observer/gunner in tandem open cockpits. Phönix built 110 C.Is and these entered service in the spring of 1918, remaining operational until the end

With a characteristic Heinkel-designed fuselage/tail configuration, the C.I offered its gunner a good field of fire.

of the war. Shortly after the war the Swedish army's engineering department built 30 under licence which were powered by 164-kW (220-hp) Benz inline engines, these remaining in service until the late 1920s.

Specification
Type: two-seat reconnaissance/general-purpose aircraft
Powerplant: one 172-kW (230-hp) Hiero 6-cylinder inline piston engine
Performance: maximum speed 180 km/h (112 mph) at sea level; service ceiling 5400 m (17,715 ft); endurance 3 hours 30 minutes

Weights: maximum take-off 1105 kg (2,436 lb)
Dimensions: span 11.00 m (36 ft 1 in); length 7.52 m (24 ft 8 in); height 2.95 m (9 ft 8¼ in)

Armament: two 8-mm (0.315-in) Schwarzlose machine-guns, one synchronised forward-firing and one on trainable mount in rear cockpit, plus up to 50 kg (110 lb) of bombs

Phönix D.I, D.II and D.III

As mentioned in the entry for the Phönix C.I, the company had built Hansa-Brandenburg designs under licence before turning to the design of its own aircraft. Thus the **Phönix D.I** single-seat fighter, of which a prototype was built in mid-1917, was basically a more developed version of the Hansa-Brandenburg D.I biplane, differing primarily by having more efficient wings, structural improvements and a more powerful engine. Official testing showed it to be fast, but too stable and somewhat difficult to handle. However, given the urgent need for fighters the Phönix D.I was ordered into production, attempts being made later to improve manoeuvrability and performance; thus the **D.II** introduced balanced elevators and

balanced ailerons on the upper wings, and the final production version, the **D.III**, had balanced ailerons on both wings and a more powerful 172-kW (230-hp) Hiero inline engine. The Phönix D-series was built to a total of 158, the last being delivered on 4 November 1918, and these were used both by the air arm and the navy. A number were converted for use in a photo-reconnaissance role, and a number of D.IIIs were transferred to Sweden after the war.

Specification
Phönix D.I
Type: single-seat fighter
Powerplant: one 149-kW (200-hp) Hiero 6-cylinder inline piston engine
Performance: maximum speed

180 km/h (112 mph); service ceiling 6000 m (19,685 ft); endurance 2 hours
Weights: maximum take-off 805 kg (1,775 lb)
Dimensions: span 9.75 m (31 ft 11¾ in); length 6.65 m (21 ft 9¾ in); height 2.80 m (9 ft 2¼ in)
Armament: two synchronised fixed

The D.III was the final development of this distinctive Austro-Hungarian design. It was fast but too stable to make a great fighter.

forward-firing 8-mm (0.315-in) Schwarzlose machine-guns

Piaggio P.2

Genoese industrialist and politician Rinaldo Piaggio started aircraft manufacture at his Finale Ligure factory during World War I, building Caproni bombers, and F.B.A. and Macchi flying-boats under licence. The **Piaggio P.2** was the first original design for the company by Giovanni Pegna. Constructed at the

Sestri Ponente (Genoa) works in 1923, it was a cantilever low-wing monoplane single-seat fighter with a semi-monocoque fuselage and fixed, divided landing gear. Twin radiators for the 224-kW (300-hp) Hispano-Suiza engine were mounted on the fuselage sides just forward of the pilot's open cockpit, and armament comprised twin synchronised Vickers 7.62-mm (0.3-in) machine-guns. The P.2 spanned 10.50 m (34 ft 5½ in).

A clean design for 1923, the Piaggio P.2 had its lines marred only by the protruding radiators on either side of the engine.

Piaggio P.3

The **Piaggio P.3** Pegna-designed night bomber of 1923 was a two-bay biplane with the lower wing of greater span than the upper. The biplane tail unit incorporated triple fins and rudders, and four 149-kW (200-hp) S.P.A. 6A engines were mounted in tandem pairs on the lower wing, driving two tractor and two pusher propellers. Pilot and co-pilot were seated side-by-side in an open cockpit ahead of the wings, and there were gunner's cockpits in the nose and amidships, the rear gunner also operating a tunnel gun for ventral defence. At a later stage two 306-kW (410-hp) Fiat A.20V engines were installed but the P.3 was not accepted by the Regia Aeronautica for quantity production. Wing span was

The four S.P.A. 6A engines of the Piaggio P.3 bomber were mounted in tandem pairs between the wings. The aircraft displayed only moderate performance, and in the event was not accepted for production.

24.00 m (78 ft 9 in) and maximum speed 185 km/h (115 mph).

Piaggio P.6

In 1927 two parallel designs were developed to meet an Italian naval requirement for a two-seat catapult-launched seaplane. One was a small flying-boat, the **Piaggio P.6bis** powered by a single 194-kW (260-hp) Isotta Fraschini V.6 engine mounted between the wings and driving a pusher propeller; the other was the **P.6** floatplane with a large central float, two wing-tip stabilising floats, and a 288-kW (380-hp) A.20 engine in the nose. The two aircraft had identical wing structure, with rigid strut bracing, and each mounted a single defensive machine-gun, that of the fly-ing-boat in the bow, and the floatplane's in the rear cockpit.

The **P.6ter** of 1928 was similar to the P.6, but had an engine boosted to 306 kW (410 hp) to provide a maximum speed of 195 km/h (121 mph). Wing span was 13.50 m (44 ft 3½ in) and maximum take-off weight 2360 kg (5,203 lb). A batch of 15 P.6ter floatplanes was built, and the type was used for a period aboard several Italian capital ships and cruisers.

Intended for use from the catapults of battleships and cruisers, the Piaggio P.6ter was a spotter floatplane built in small numbers.

Piaggio P.7

A truly remarkable design, the **Piaggio P.7** or **Piaggio-Pegna P.c. 7** was built for the 1929 Schneider Trophy contest. A cantilever high-wing monoplane with long slender fuselage, it had twin hydrofoils instead of floats and was intended to float with the wing resting on the surface of the water. While water-borne it was to be driven by an ordinary marine propeller connected by a shaft and clutch to the rear of the 723-kW (970-hp) Isotta Fraschini Special V.6 engine. Once sufficient speed had been attained to lift the aircraft on to the hydrofoils and the normal tractor propeller was clear of the water, this latter propeller would be clutched-in, the marine propeller disengaged, and a conventional take-off would follow.

In practice, problems with the respective clutches prevented the P.c.7 from ever taking off, and although water trials were conducted on Lake Garda by Dal Molin of the Italian Schneider team, the construction of a second aircraft was abandoned.

Sitting on the water before being attached to a hoist, the P.7 was an ingenious attempt to overcome the problems encountered during the Schneider Trophy contests.

Wing span was 6.76 m (22 ft 2¼ in), maximum take-off weight 1738 kg (3,832 lb), and estimated maximum speed 580 km/h (360 mph).

Piaggio P.8

A parasol-wing single-seat floatplane, the small **Piaggio P.8** reconnaissance aircraft of 1928 was intended, like its rival the Macchi M.53, to be stored in a cylindrical container aboard submarines of the large 'Ettore Fieramosca' class. It was designed to be assembled rapidly for deployment at sea on patrol or reconnaissance; after being recovered it could as easily be dismantled and re-stowed in its container. Powered by a 56-kW (75-hp) Blackburn Cirrus II engine, it had a maximum speed of 135 km/h (84 mph).

Another interesting concept was the P.8. This floatplane was designed to fit the cylindrical container of the 'Ettore Fiermosca'-class submarines. When required, the aircraft could be easily assembled and flown on its reconnaissance mission.

Piaggio P.10

In 1932 Piaggio produced the robust three-seat **Piaggio P.10**, a single-bay biplane floatplane with a single main float and two wingtip stabilising floats. Intended for catapult reconnaissance duties from battleships and cruisers of the Regia Marina, the P.10 was of mixed construction and powered by a single 328-kW (440-hp) Piaggio-built Bristol Jupiter VI radial engine in a long-chord cowling. The pilot's cockpit was located just forward of the wings, while the observer was placed in another open cockpit forward of the tailplane. The gunner, with a single 7.62-mm (0.3-in) machine-gun on a ring mounting, was located just in front of the observer in a third cockpit. The P.10 had a span of 13.80 m (45 ft 3¼ in), and maximum speed of 195 km/h (121 mph).

The **P.10bis** was a landplane version with fixed landing gear which appeared in 1933. In the same year there appeared the **P.11** two-seat aerobatic trainer, a licence-built version of the Blackburn

The Piaggio P.11 of 1932 was specifically built as a two-seat aerobatic trainer. In fact, it was little more than a licence-built copy of the Blackburn Lincock and saw limited service in Italian hands. It was followed by the Piaggio P.12, a licence-built Blackburn Segrave.

Lincock biplane, and the **P.12**, none other than the Blackburn Segrave four-seat twin-engine low-wing touring monoplane, also built under licence.

Piaggio P.16

The **Piaggio P.16** three-engine heavy bomber of 1934 was distinguished by a thick-section semi-elliptical wing set at shoulder height, and of inverted gull configuration. Defensive armament comprised four 7.62-mm (0.3-in) machine-guns located in the wing leading edge, in a retractable dorsal turret and in the rear fuselage beneath the high-positioned single fin and rudder. Largely of metal construction, the P.16 had retractable main landing gear units and a non-retractable tailwheel with a spat-type fairing. The bomb-aimer's compartment was located in the underside of the fuselage, just behind the central engine.

The P.16 had a gunner's position under the overhanging tail.

Piaggio P.23
to
Piel Emeraude and Super Emeraude

Piaggio P.23

Built to fly the North Atlantic, with potential for development as a commercial transport, the **Piaggio P.23** had inverted-gull shoulder-mounted wings and was powered by four 671-kW (900-hp) Isotta Fraschini Asso XI R V-12 engines mounted in tandem pairs and driving two tractor and two pusher propellers. It had retractable main landing gear units and twin fins and rudders. A distinctive feature was the 'avion marin' boat-type hull underside to the fuselage, intended to assist in an emergency if the aircraft had to alight on the sea.

Maximum take-off weight was 18400 kg (40,566 lb) and maximum speed a claimed 400 km/h (248 mph); at a cruising speed of 300 km/h (186 mph) its range was estimated to be 5100 km (3,169 miles). However, no transatlantic flight was made and the aircraft was dismantled soon after its appearance in 1935.

The Piaggio P.23 was similar in many ways to the P.16, though the centre-section bracing used six struts and it had four engines.

Piaggio P.23R

An entirely new design, bearing little resemblance to the original P.23, the **Piaggio P.23R** of 1936 had a pencil-shaped fuselage, a cantilever low-set wing with straight taper, and was powered by three 671-kW (900-hp) Isotta Fraschini Asso XI R V-12 engines in sleek cowlings. Intended purely as a record-breaker, the P.23R had a crew of two seated side-by-side in individual cockpits, each with its own windscreen. Later modified by the installation of three 746-kW (1,000-hp) Piaggio P.XI

A beautifully streamlined tri-motor record-breaker, the otherwise impractical Piaggio P.23R was dubbed P.123 by the Italian propaganda apparatus to persuade the UK and France that it was also in production as a bomber.

RC.40 radials, and with an enclosed canopy over each cockpit and revised main landing gear, the P.23R was used on 30 December 1938 to establish new world records, carrying a payload of 5000 kg (11,023 lb) over distances of 1000 km (621 miles) and 2000 km (1,242

miles) at an average speed of 404 km/h (251 mph).

Although the P.23R appeared in Allied wartime recognition manuals as a potential bomber, development of the type had already been abandoned in 1939.

Piaggio P.32

The prototype of the **Piaggio P.32** twin-engine bomber flew in early 1936 powered by two Isotta Fraschini Asso XI V-12 engines. Of mixed construction, the P.32 had a stubby fuselage with a low/mid-set wing incorporating Handley-Page leading-edge slats and double trailing-edge flaps, and a tail unit with twin fins and rudders. The V-12 engines were later replaced by 746-kW (1,000-hp) Piaggio P.XI RC.40 radials. Armament comprised a single 7.7-mm (0.303-in) Breda machine-gun in a nose turret, and twin guns of the same type and calibre in retractable dorsal and ventral turrets.

The radial-engined P.32 had a French-style 'balcony' nose, allowing the fitting of a nose gun turret.

A production series of 16 P.32s with Isotta Fraschini engines went into service with the 47ª and 48ª Squadriglie B.T. of the Regia Aeronautica during 1937, only to be withdrawn and scrapped the following year after a crash which indicated irremediable control problems. Twelve radial-engined aircraft under construction were never completed.

Variants
P.32bis: built by Reggiane; redesigned slimmer fuselage and

retained Isotta Fraschini engines; registered maximum 420 km/h (261 mph) when test-flown February 1937; second radial-engined prototype suffered engine fire in flight and series of 22 P.32bis cancelled

Ca.405: Caproni-Reggiane 'Procellaria' was a slim-fuselage long-range record version of the P.32bis, intended to participate in Istres-Damascus race of August 1937, but was not ready in time

Piaggio P.50

The **Piaggio P.50** four-engine heavy bomber was the first aircraft to be designed for the company by Giovanni Casiraghi, following project outline by Giovanni Pegna. The **P.50-I** (MM 369) prototype, test flown in 1937, was a shoulder-wing monoplane with a large single fin and rudder and four 544-kW (730-hp) Isotta Fraschini XI RC V-12 engines wing-mounted in tandem pairs and driving two tractor and two pusher propellers. Three defensive gun positions included a nose turret, and offensive load was a maximum of 2500 kg

Though it had the appearance of a twin-engined aircraft, the Piaggio P.50 was a four-engined bomber, with each wing carrying a pair of tandem-mounted engines.

(5,512 lb). A second prototype (MM 370) was damaged in a landing accident at Malpensa airfield in 1938. During that year the **P.50-II** (MM 371) appeared with a conventional four-engine layout, the 746-kW (1,000-hp) Piaggio P.XI RC.40 radials driving four three-bladed tractor propellers. Defensive armament was increased to five 12.7-mm (0.5-in) machine-guns. Although no production

ensued, the P.50 was the progenitor of the P.108 of World War II.

The span of the P.50 was 25.76 m (84 ft 6¼ in) and length 19.80 m (64 ft 11½ in). Maximum speed of P.50-I was 435 km/h (270 mph), which rose to 450 km/h (280 mph) in the case of the P.50-II.

Piaggio P.108

The only four-engine heavy bomber to be used operationally by Italy during World War II, the **Piaggio P.108** was developed from the earlier P.50-II. A cantilever low-wing monoplane with retractable tailwheel landing gear, and powered by four Piaggio P.XII RC.35 radial engines, it was first flown in proto-

The P.108B was Italy's only wartime four-engined bomber. This is an aircraft of 274ª Squadrigila which adopted the name of Mussolini's son Bruno.

type form during 1939. Four versions were planned, but only the **P.108B Bombardiere** was built in any quantity. First deployed in night attacks on Gibraltar during early 1942, P.108Bs saw ser-

vice also in the Mediterranean, North African and Soviet theatres of operation. A total of 163 was built, but heavy losses meant that less than five per cent survived to serve with the Aeronautica Nazionale Repubblicana after the armistice with the Allies. The single P.108 prototype was converted subsequently as an anti-shipping aircraft under the designation **P.108A Artiglieri**, its standard armament being supplemented by the installation of a 102-mm (4-in) cannon; it was later captured by

German forces and impressed for service with the Luftwaffe. One prototype and 15 production aircraft were built as 32-passenger civil transports under the designation **P.108C Civile**, but were later modified, as were 24 P.108Bs, for service as military transports accommodating 56 troops; one of the modified P.108Cs was completed as the prototype of a military cargo transport with side loading doors and a ventral hatch, but no further examples were produced. Mention should be made also of the pro-

posed **P.133**, an advanced version of the P.108B with more powerful engines, but the changing fortunes of war meant that the type was never built.

Specification
Piaggio P.108B
Type: heavy bomber
Powerplant: four 1119-kW (1,500-hp) Piaggio P.XII RC.35 18-cylinder radial piston engines
Performance: maximum speed 30 km/h (4267 mph) at 4200 m

(13,780 ft); service ceiling 8500 m (27,885 ft); maximum range 3520 km (2,187 miles)
Weights: empty 17325 kg (38,195 lb); maximum take-off 29885 kg (65-885 lb)
Dimensions: span 32.00 m (104 ft 11¾ in); length 22.30 m (73 ft 2 in); height 6.00 m (19 ft 8¼ in); wing area 135.00 m² (1,453.18 sq ft)
Armament: eight 12.7-mm (0.5-in) machine-guns, plus a bombload of up to 3500 kg (7,716 lb)

Piaggio P.119

Flown for the first time on 19 December 1942 from the company's Villanova d'Albegna airfield, the **Piaggio P.119** was an all-metal low-wing monoplane single-seat fighter with a remarkably slim fuselage. This was made possible by enclosing the 1230-kW (1,650-hp) Piaggio P.XV RC.60 radial engine in the fuselage behind the pilot's fully enclosed cockpit, the three-blade propeller being driven by an extension shaft. The clean lines were broken only by the engine air intake located beneath the fuselage, forward of the wing. Proposed armament was four

In common with most aircraft powered by an engine buried deep within the fuselage, for aerodynamic and weight-distribution reasons, the Piaggio P.119 used a long transmission shaft to drive the tractor propeller, and suffered from the inevitable vibration problems.

nose-mounted 12.7-mm (0.5-in) machine-guns and one 20-mm cannon firing through the propeller hub.

Test flights indicated a maximum speed of 640 km/h (398 mph), but the aircraft was plagued by engine vibration problems and after relatively slight

damage suffered during a landing accident, on 2 August 1943, further development was abandoned and no attempt made to repair it.

Piaggio P.136-L

Under the designation **Piaggio P.136-L**, the company designed an amphibian flying-boat with a two-step all-metal hull, cantilever high-set gull-wing with a strut-mounted stabilising float beneath each outer wing panel, retractable tailwheel landing gear, and power provided by two 194-kW (260-hp) Avco Lycoming GO-435-C2 flat-six engines nacelle-mounted above each wing and driving pusher propellers. The enclosed cabin accommodated five, two seated side-by-side forward and three on a bench seat aft. The prototype was flown first in late 1948, and following the completion of certification tests in the spring of 1949 one example was acquired by the Italian air force for extensive testing, leading to a contract for 14 more P.136 amphibians (awarded in late 1950) for use in coastal patrol and air/sea rescue roles. These were completed

in two versions, as the **P.136-L-1** with 201-kW (270-hp) GO-480-B geared engines, and the **P.136-L-2** with more powerful GSO-480 geared and super-charged engines. In addition to construction for the Italian air force, both versions were marketed in the USA as the **Royal Gull** by Tracker Aircraft Corporation which received three assembled aircraft from Piaggio, plus components for a further 29 aircraft. In addition to assembling these, Tracker also built a small number under licence.

Specification
Piaggio P.136-L-2
Type: five-seat amphibian
Powerplant: two 254-kW (340-hp) Avco Lycoming GSO-480 flat-six piston engines
Performance: maximum speed 335 km/h (208 mph) at sea level;

service ceiling 7800 m (25,590 ft); range 1450 km (900 miles) at 4300 m (14,110 ft)
Weights: empty 2110 kg (4,652 lb); maximum take-off 2995 kg (6,603 lb)
Dimensions: span 13.53 m (44 ft 4¾ in); length 10.80 m (35 ft 5¼ in); height 3.83 m (12 ft 6¾ in); wing area 25.10 m² (270.18 sq ft)

In no way exceptional apart from its pusher powerplant, the Piaggio P.136 amphibian proved to be most useful in Italian service for coastal patrol and search and rescue duties. One of the company's first post-war designs, 23 of the 80 built were delivered to the Italian air force.

Piaggio P.148

Under the designation **Piaggio P.148**, the company designed a lightweight trainer suitable for both primary and aerobatic use. The prototype, first flown on 12 February 1951, was a cantilever low-wing monoplane of all-metal construction, with fixed tailwheel landing gear, and was powered by an Avco Lycoming O-435 flat-six engine. Basically a side-by-side two-seater, there was adequate space in the enclosed cabin for an optional third seat. Official testing resulted in the type being selected by the Aeronautica Militaire Italiana as standard equipment for its primary training schools and a total of 100 were delivered for this purpose.

However, they were later withdrawn from service when the Italian air force adopted all-through jet training but, like many other air forces which followed a similar pattern, they were re-introduced in 1970 when it was appreciated that a piston-engined trainer still had a valuable part to play in the earliest stage of selection for further flight training. In 1962 a small number of Italian air force P.148s

were handed over to the Somalian Aeronautical Corps. The Somalian aircraft weathered years of civil war, their numbers steadily decreasing. A straightforward type to maintain, several survived into the 1980s. One aircraft stood on a plinth as a 'gate guard' over the military side of Mogadishu airport. By 1993, along with the bulk of the Somalian air force, none remained in service.

Specification
Type: two-seat primary/aerobatic trainer
Powerplant: one 142-kW (190-hp) Avco Lycoming O-435-A flat-six piston engine
Performance: maximum speed 234 km/h (145 mph) at sea level; service ceiling 5000 m (16,405 ft); range with allowances 925 km (575 miles)
Weights: empty 876 kg (1,931 lb); maximum take-off 1280 kg (2,822 lb)
Dimensions: span 11.12 m (36 ft 5¾ in); length 8.44 m (27 ft 8¼ in); height 2.40 m (7 ft 10½ in); wing area 18.85 m² (202.91 sq ft)

Piaggio P.148

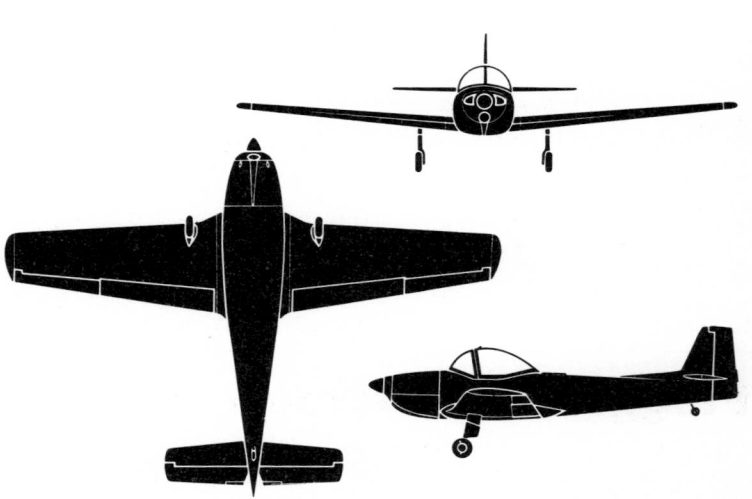

Piaggio P.149

Success of the P.148 led Piaggio to initiate a four-seat tourer development under the designation **Piaggio P.149**, this differing from the P.148 primarily by having retractable tricycle landing gear and a more powerful engine which, when the aircraft was flown in prototype form on 19 June 1953, was a 194-kW (260-hp) Avco Lycoming GO-435. It was only marginally successful until West Germany decided to adopt the type as a standard basic trainer/liaison aircraft for the Luftwaffe, Piaggio delivering the first of a contract for 72 **P.149D** aircraft in May 1957. An additional 190 were built under licence in Germany by Focke-Wulf, the first of them being delivered in November 1957. The type was used also by the air forces of Nigeria, Tanzania and Uganda, but only the last of these three may have a small number still in use.

Piaggio built a total of 88 P.149Ds from 1953 onwards. An enlarged and more versatile version of the P.148, the P.149D differed largely in the addition of a retractable tricycle undercarriage for better performance. Focke-Wulf-built aircraft became the Luftwaffe's primary trainer and a handful were also produced for civil customers. Five P.149Es were acquired by Swissair for pilot training.

Specification
Piaggio P.149D
Type: four/five-seat utility/liaison aircraft or two-seat trainer
Powerplant: one 201-kW (270-hp) Avco Lycoming GO-480 flat-six piston engine
Performance: maximum speed 305 km/h (190 mph) at sea level; service ceiling 6050 m (19,850 ft); range with allowances 1090 km (677 miles)
Weights: empty 1160 kg (2,557 lb); maximum take-off 1680 kg (3,704 lb)
Dimensions: span 11.12 m (36 ft 5¾ in); length 8.80 m (28 ft 10½ in); height 2.90 m (9 ft 6¼ in); wing area 18.85 m² (202.91 sq ft)

Piaggio P.150

Built to compete against the Fiat G.49 and Macchi M.B.323 as a replacement for the North American T-6 used widely by the Aeronautica Militare Italiana, the **Piaggio P.150** made its first flight in November 1952. An all-metal cantilever low-wing monoplane with square cut wingtips and tailplane, the P.150 had wide-track inward-retracting main landing gear legs. Pupil and instructor were housed in tandem with dual controls, under a long glazed canopy. The original powerplant was a 447-kW (600-hp) Pratt & Whitney Wasp R-1340-S3H1 radial engine, which gave a maximum speed of 380 km/h (236 mph). A later version was fitted with a geared Alvis Leonides engine, but the type was not considered suitable to be built in quantity for the Italian air arm.

Intended as a more modern piston-engined replacement for the Italian air force's North American T-6 trainers, the Piaggio P.150 did not achieve production status.

Piaggio P.166

Piaggio P.166-DL3 of Alitalia.

The prototype **Piaggio P.166** flew for the first time on 26 November 1957. Intended originally as a civil light transport, it retained the wings and engines of the P.136-L amphibian and, like the earlier type, the P.166 had its 254-kW (340-hp) Avco Lycoming GSO-480 engines mounted as pushers on the cantilever high-set gull-wing. It also had retractable tricycle landing gear and a single angular fin and rudder with an additional dorsal fin.

The type has good short field operating characteristics, and range can be increased by the use of detachable wingtip fuel tanks. The first 32 P.166s went to civil operators, and later civil versions had increased passenger capacity.

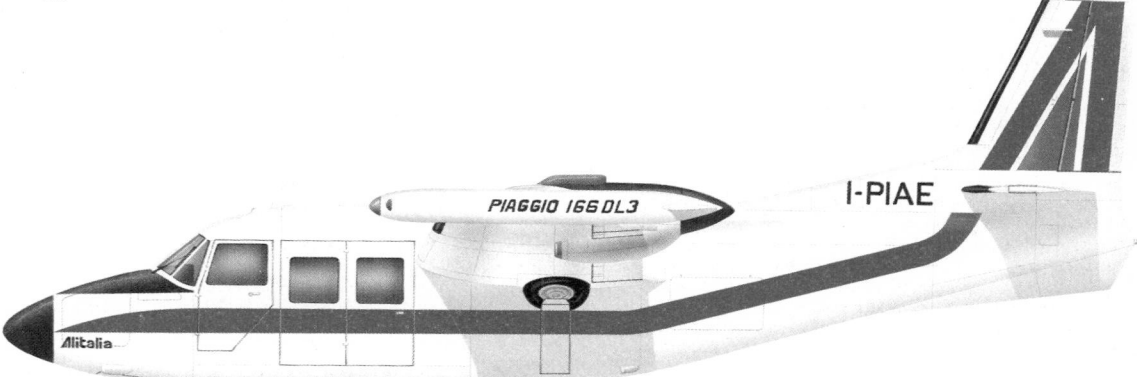

Variants
P.166: first production version; sold widely and used in Australia, New Guinea and distributed in USA by Tracker Corporation; accommodates two pilots and up to six passengers
P.166B: appeared in 1962 and named Portofino; direct-injection 283-kW (380-hp) Avco Lycoming IGSO-480s; six built, most for export
P.166C: redesigned central fuselage section with additional cabin for five passengers and new landing gear main units retracting into streamlined blisters on fuselage sides; in production from 1964
P.166M: militarised version, 51 built

for Aeronautica Militare Italiana; used at the Scuola Plurimotori at Latina and examples attached to military air regions in Italy for liaison and battlefield transport duties; has a strengthened floor for heavy freight and an enlarged freight door
P.166S Albatross: version bought by South Africa and deployed for coastal patrol and search and rescue; 20 built
P.166BL2: powered by 283-kW (380-hp) Avco Lycoming IGSO-540-A1H engines and with increased fuel capacity
P.166-DL3: last production version; first flown in prototype form on 3 July

i976 with powerplant of two Avco Lycoming LTP 101 turboprop engines; can be configured and equipped to order for use in a wide variety of roles; two are used by Alitalia as trainers, and two until recently by Somalian Aeronautical Corps as military transports
P.166-DLR-MAR: currently available specially-configured maritime surveillance version of P.166-DL3; suitable for all-weather day or night use from unprepared strips, it is equipped with an integrated system for search, detection and identification of suspect targets

Specification
Piaggio P.166-DL3
Type: utility light transport
Powerplant: two 447-kW (599-shp) Avco Lycoming LTP 101-600 turboprops
Performance: maximum speed 400 km/h (248 mph) at 3050 m (10,000 ft); service ceiling 8840 m (29,000 ft); range with reserves 2035 km (1,264 miles)
Weights: empty equipped 2650 kg (5,842 lb); maximum take-off 4300 kg (9,480 lb)
Dimensions: span with tiptanks 14.69 m (48 ft 2½ in); length 11.88 m (39 ft 0 in); height 5.00 m (16 ft 5 in); wing area 26.56 m² (285.90 sq ft)

Piaggio P.180 Avanti

At the 1983 NBAA convention in Dallas, Texas, Piaggio announced the birth of a new twin turbo-powered business aircraft. Design work on the **P.180 Avanti** had begun at Piaggio's Genoa headquarters in 1979. Seating six to 10 passengers it was a radical departure from anything the company had previously produced, while utilising the experience gained from building other pusher-types such as the P.166.

The major design feature of the aircraft is its use of three lifting surfaces. The main wing is fitted above the mid-set position in the fuselage, with the main spar running behind the passenger cabin. Its straight leading edge is broken only by the engine nacelle inlets and the wing has a slight dihedral of 2°. The T-tail and elevator act as the second lifting surface, in addition to being orthodox control surfaces. The foreplane, however, is not a simple canard, but provides a positive lift component in addition to that produced by the wing. This in turn allows the wing to be reduced in size, thus decreasing overall weight and drag. The engines were originally specified as Pratt & Whitney Canada PT6A-66A turboprops, but these were later changed in favour of more powerful PT6A-61s. Each drives a five-bladed Hartzell fully-feathering reversible-pitch propeller with spinner. The engines are mounted in composite-material nacelles. The Avanti makes considerable use of composites, if not to the same degree as the rival Beech Starship, for example. Carbonfibre and a Graphite/Epoxy mix represent about 10% of the aircraft's weight, and all of these components are built by Sikorsky and Edo. Wings and tail sections are produced by Piaggio at Genoa, while the forward fuselage is the responsibility of Piaggio Aviation in Wichita. Final assembly is completed in Italy. Aircraft intended for the American market are flown 'green' to the US to a specialist outfitters and there are plans to eventually assemble all aircraft in the United States.

The cockpit is fitted with a Collins EFIS system, comprising three CRTs and Collins navigation and weather radar systems are standard. The aircraft is certified for single pilot operations. The main cabin is pressurised and air conditioned, is fitted with a galley and folda-way tables. An emergency exit is situated at the front on the starboard side with the airstairs on the port side. In 1983 Gates Learjet became a partner in the

project, but withdrew for economic reasons in January 1986. All the tooling and the forward fuselages of the three pre-production Avantis which were on the line at Wichita, were then transferred to Italy. Assembly of the first P.180 began on Piaggio's Finale Ligne plant in 1986 and the first flight was made on 23 September 1986 (I-PJAV). This was followed by the second aircraft (I-PJAR) on 14 May 1987. The Avanti was certified by the Italian authorities in March 1990, and in May of that year the first production aircraft was rolled out. The final hurdle of US certification was passed in October 1990 and the first customer delivery took place the following September. By early 1993, despite or perhaps because of its radical appearance and advanced design, only 20 Avantis had been delivered.

Specification
Piaggio P.180 Avanti
Type: twin-turboprop high-speed corporate aircraft
Powerplant: two 1107-kW (1,485-shp) Pratt & Whitney PT6A-66 turboprops
Performance: maximum operating Mach number Mach 0.67; maximum level speed 482 km/h (455 mph);

service ceiling 12500 m (41,000 ft); maximum range 3187 km (1,980 miles)
Weights: empty, stripped 3384 kg (7,460 lb); max take-off 5080 kg (11,200 lb)
Dimensions: span 14.03 m (46 ft ½ in); length 14.41 m (47 ft 3½ in); height 3.94 m (12 ft 11 in)

Piaggio has backed the P.180 Avanti with a vigorous sales campaign, taking the aircraft on tour around the world and concentrating chiefly on the United States market. Their efforts are, as yet, unrewarded.

Piaggio PD-808

During 1957 the Douglas Aircraft Company in the USA began a design study of a six/ten-seat executive jet aircraft with which it hoped to gain a foothold in the non-commercial civil market. This proved to be unsuccessful, and in 1961 Piaggio acquired design rights with the two companies continuing jointly the development of this light transport. Douglas continued to help in an advisory capacity, but Piaggio was responsible for detail design, manufacture and test. A cantilever low-wing monoplane of all metal construction with a circular-section fuselage, conventional tail unit and retractable tricycle landing gear, the aircraft was powered in prototype form by two 1361-kg (3,000-lb) thrust Rolls-Royce Bristol Viper turbojets pod-mounted one on each side of the rear fuselage. The first of two **Piaggio PD-808** prototypes was flown on 29 August 1964 and the second, flown on 14 June 1966, differed by having larger-

Six Piaggio PD-808ECM electronic warfare trainers serve with the Italian air force's 71° Stormo at Pratica de Mare. The Italian air force is now by far the largest operator of the type.

capacity wingtip fuel tanks and a dorsal fin of greater area; both were later re-engined by more powerful Viper 526s built under licence by Piaggio.

Production was eventually to total only 29 PD-808s including the prototypes, this comprising two seven-seat civil executive transports, plus 25 aircraft for the Aeronautica Militare Italiana. These consisted of 12 **PD-808RM** navigation aid calibration aircraft, three of a **PD-808ECM** electronic countermeasures version carrying two pilots and three ECM operators, six were **PD-808TA** nine-seat communications and navigation trainers and, finally, four **PD-808VIP** six-seat VIP transports. Of

the total, 22 remained in service with the Italian air force in 1984. A turbofan-powered **PD-808TF** was the subject of a design study, but no examples were built.

Specification
Piaggio PD-808
Type: light utility transport
Powerplant: two 1524-kg (3,360-lb) thrust Piaggio (licence-built) Viper Mk 526 turbojet engines

Performance: maximum speed 850 km/h (528 mph) at 6000 m (19,685 ft); service ceiling 13700 m (44,950 ft); range with maximum fuel 2100 km (1,305 miles)
Weights: empty equipped 4830 kg (10,648 lb); maximum take-off 8165 kg (18,001 lb)
Dimensions: span over tiptanks 13.20 m (43 ft 3¾ in); length 12.85 m (42 ft 2 in); height 4.80 m (15 ft 9 in); wing area 20.90 m² (224.97 sq ft)

Piasecki H-21

Developed from the US Navy's HRP-2, the **Piasecki PD-22** tandem-rotor helicopter prototype (US Air Force designation **XH-21**) was first flown on 11 April 1952. Eighteen **YH-21** helicopters had been ordered in 1949 for USAF evaluation, these being followed by an initial production batch of 32 **H-21A** helicopters, named **Workhorse** in USAF service. For use by the Military Air Transport Service Air Rescue Service, the H-21As were each powered by a derated 932-kW (1,250-hp) Wright R-1820-103 engine; the first flew in October 1953. Six more were built to USAF contract but supplied to Canada under the Military Assistance Program.

The second production variant was the **H-21B**, which used the full power of the 1063-kW (1,425-hp) R-1820-103 to cover an increase in maximum take-off weight from 5216 kg (11,500 lb) to 6804 kg (15,000 lb). Some 163 were built, mainly for Troop Carrier Command, and these had autopilots, could carry ex-

The H-21C was the ultimate version of the Piasecki workhorse, and could carry 14 troops or 12 litters in its long cabin.

ternal auxiliary fuel tanks, and were provided with some protective armour. They could carry 20 troops in the assault role.

The US Army's equivalent was the **H-21C Shawnee**, of which 334 were built. This total included 98 for the French army, 10 for the French navy and six for Canada; 32 Shawnees were supplied to West Germany, serving with the army's Heeresfliegerbataillon 300. The H-21C, redesignated CH-21C in July 1962, had an underfuselage sling hook for loads of up to 1814 kg (4,000 lb). Production deliveries were made between September 1954 and March 1959, later helicopters acquiring the company designation **Model 43** when the Piasecki Helicopter Corporation became the Vertol Aircraft Corporation in 1956. The H-21A and H-21B retrospectively became the **Model 42**.

Two turboshaft conversions of H-21C airframes were the **Model 71** (H-21D), with two General Electric T58 engines first flown in September 1957, and the **Model 105** which had two Avco Lycoming T53s. From the latter was designed the Vertol 107 (Boeing Vertol H-46 series).

Specification
Piasecki H-21C Shawnee
Type: troop-cargo transport
Powerplant: one 1063-kW (1,425-hp)

Wright R-1820-103 Cyclone radial piston engine
Performance: maximum speed 211 km/h (131 mph) at sea level; service ceiling 2360 m (7,750 ft); range 644 km (400 miles)
Weights: empty 3629 kg (8,000 lb); maximum take-off 6668 kg (14,700 lb)
Dimensions: rotor diameter, each 13.41 m (44 ft 0 in); length, rotors turning 26.31 m (86 ft 4 in); height 4.70 m (15 ft 5 in); rotor disc area, total 282.52 m² (3,041.07 sq ft)

Piasecki HUP Retriever

The 'flying banana' shape of the HRP-1 was discarded in the **Piasecki Model PV-14**, of which two **XHJP-1** prototypes were ordered for evaluation in the rescue and aircraft-carrier plane-guard roles. This model was developed into the **PV-18**, US Navy designation **HUP-1**, which featured angled endplate fins on the horizontal tail surfaces mounted on the rear rotor pylon. Some 32 HUP-1s, each powered by a single 391-kW (525-hp) Continental R-975-34 engine, were built for the US Navy between February 1949 and 1952; the first squadron, HU-2, took delivery of its initial aircraft in February 1951.

Successful Sperry autopilot trials in an XHJP-1 led to development of the **HUP-2**, whose improved directional ability allowed the endplate fins to be deleted, and the more powerful 410-kW (550-hp) R-975-46 engine was fitted. A total of 339 was built, including 193 for the US Navy. A number of these were designated **HUP-2S** when fitted with dunking sonar equipment for anti-submarine operations. Some 15 HUP-2s were also supplied to the French navy. The US Army ordered an initial batch of

an improved version in 1951, this being known as the **H-25A Army Mule**. Powered by the R-975-46A engine, the H-25A introduced power-boosted controls, strengthened floors and enlarged cargo doors. Fifty similar machines were transferred to the US Navy under the designation **HUP-3**, three serving with the Royal Canadian Navy's Squadron VH-21. Under the unified designation system introduced in September 1962, the HUP-2 and HUP-3 were redesignated **UH-25B** and **UH-25C** respectively.

Specification
Piasecki HUP-3
Type: utility/cargo helicopter
Powerplant: one 410-kW (550-hp) Continental R-975-46A radial engine
Performance: maximum speed 169 km/h (105 mph); service ceiling 3050 m (10,000 ft); maximum range 547 km (340 miles)
Weights: empty 1782 kg (3,928 lb); maximum take-off 2767 kg (6,100 lb)
Dimensions: rotor diameter, each 10.67 m (35 ft 0 in); length, rotors turning 17.35 m (56 ft 11 in); height 3.81 m (12 ft 6 in)

A Piasecki HUP-1 touches down on the fantail of the 'Baltimore'-class heavy cruiser, USS Helena.

Piasecki PV-2, PV-3 and PV-17

Frank N. Piasecki was the holder of the first US helicopter pilot's licence and he formed the P V Engineering Forum in 1943 to develop practical rotorcraft. His first successdul design was the experimental **Piasecki PV-2** single-seater with a 67-kW (90-hp) Franklin flat-four engine driving a three-blade main rotor. Piasecki himself was the pilot for the first flight, made on 11 April 1943.

The next design was the **PV-3**, a development aircraft for the US Navy's **HRP Rescuer** transport and rescue helicopter. Ordered by the US Navy on 1 February 1944 and powered by a Wright R-975 piston engine, the tandem-rotor PV-3 first flew at Morton, Pennsylvania in March 1945. It was followed by two **XHRP-1** airframes, one of which was used for static tests while the other undertook the flight development programme, during the course of which the company changed its name to Piasecki Helicopter Corporation, in June 1946 re-

ceiving an initial order for 10 production **HRP-1** helicopters. The first flew on 15 August 1947, powered by a 447-kW (600-hp) Pratt & Whitney R-1340-AN-1 engine; 20 were built eventually, with a metal-skinned rear fuselage and fabric covering over the main cabin section, although they were often flown with the fabric removed. Service evaluation was undertaken by US Navy Squadron VX-3 and US Marine Corps Squadron HMX-1, while three were delivered to the US Coast Guard with the designation **HRP-1G**. Five improved **PV-17** helicopters, with all-metal fuselage skinning, were ordered in June 1948 as the **HRP-2**, and these also served with the US Coast Guard.

Specification
Piasecki HRP-2
Type: tandem-rotor transport/rescue helicopter
Powerplant: one 447-kW (600-hp)

Pratt & Whitney R-1340-AN-1 radial engine
Performance: maximum speed 169 km/h (105 mph); cruising speed 148 km/h (92 mph); range 483 km (300 miles)
Weights: empty 2404 kg (5,301 lb); maximum take-off 3277 kg (7,225 lb)

Dimensions: rotor diameter, each 12.50 m (41 ft 0 in); length 16.46 m (54 ft 0 in); height 4.52 m (14 ft 10 in); rotor disc area, total 245.30 m² (2,640.51 sq ft)

The PV-3 was the development model for the HRP-1 and may be regarded as the world's first successful tandem helicopter.

Piel Emeraude and Super Emeraude

Known internationally for the design of lightplanes for amateur construction, Claude Piel established Avions Claude Piel in the early 1950s to market plans of his designs. The first of these to receive considerable interest was the **Piel C.P.30 Emeraude**, a two-seat tourer/trainer of cantilever low-wing monoplane configuration with fixed tailwheel landing gear, and providing side-by-side enclosed accommodation with dual controls as standard. The prototype C.P.30, powered by a 48-kW (65-hp) Continental A65 flat-four engine, was flown for the first time in 1952, and report of its performance and flight characteristics resulted in the company receiving many enquiries for ready-built aircraft. Accordingly, Claude Piel granted a number of licences to manufacturers in France, and abroad, and eventually about 250 were built and sold as complete aircraft.

These series-built Emeraudes included the C.P.30 built in 1953, followed by the improved **C.P.301A** which introduced spring shock-absorption for the main landing gear units, clipped wingtips and a more powerful Continental engine.

The **C.P.301B** had a strengthened airframe and a number of refinements, and the **C.P.301C** introduced lengthened main landing gear shock struts, a sliding cockpit canopy and a 71-kW (95-hp) Continental C90 engine. Under the designation **C.P.301S**, Binder Aviatik in Germany built a developed version of the CP.301A which introduced a number of refinements; and a single **C.P.315** with a 78-kW (105-hp) Potez engine, but otherwise a C.P.301C standard, was built by Scintex-Aviation.

Scintex was the major manufacturer of C.P.30/301 aircraft, to a total of about 200, and in collaboration with Claude Piel this company developed an improved **Super Emeraude** incorporating many refinements and, following experience with the C.P.315, a more powerful engine. The Super Emeraude was built in two forms, as the **C.P.1310** which, powered by a 75-kW (100-hp) Rolls-Royce Continental, was first flown on 20 April 1962, followed just over a week later by the **C.P.1315** with a 78-kW (105-hp) Potez 4 E-20 engine. A total of 31 Super Emeraudes was built, 11 of this

number produced by the Co-opérative des Ateliers Aéronautiques de la Région Parisienne (CAARP).

Specification
Piel C.P.301A Emeraude
Type: two-seat tourer/trainer
Powerplant: one 67-kW (90-hp) Continental C90 flat-four piston engine
Performance: maximum speed 220 km/h (137 mph); service ceiling 4500 m (14,765 ft); range 950 km (590 miles)
Weights: empty 380 kg (838 lb); maximum take-off 640 kg (1,411 lb)
Dimensions: span 8.30 m (27 ft 2¾ in); length 6.03 m (19 ft 9½ in); wing area 10.85 m² (116.79 sq ft)

The feature that readily marks the Piel C.P.301A Emeraude from the later C.P.301 models is the use of a hinged door rather than a sliding canopy. One hundred and eighteen of this initial version were produced.

Pilatus P-2

Work on the SB-2 Pelican was followed by design of the **Pilatus P-2** advanced trainer, a cantilever low-wing monoplane of mixed construction with fabric-covered control surfaces. Hydraulically-actuated retractable tailwheel landing gear was standard, and to ensure good take-off performance from high altitude airfields an Argus As 410 A-2 12-cylinder inverted Vee engine was installed. Instructor and pupil were seated in tandem beneath a long jettisonable 'greenhouse' canopy, and were provided with full night-flying instrumentation, radio and oxygen equipment. When required for combat training, there was provision for a machine-gun, gyro-stabilised gunsight and camera gun, with underwing racks for light bombs or rockets; if an observer was under training he could be

Powered by Czech-built Argus engines, the Pilatus P-2 trainers of the Swiss air force were designed for (and gave) intensive service from high-altitude mountain airfields for well over 30 years.

accommodated in the rear cockpit with suitable equipment, including a reconnaissance camera. Built in quantity for the Swiss air force during the late 1940s, the P-2 remained in service until finally withdrawn from a valuable career in 1982.

Specification
Type: two-seat advanced trainer
Powerplant: one 347-kW (465-hp) Argus As 410 A-2 inverted Vee air-cooled engine
Performance: maximum speed 340 km/h (211 mph) at 2500 m

(8,200 ft); economic cruising speed 305 km/h (190 mph) at 4500 m (14,765 ft); range with maximum fuel 865 km (537 miles)
Weights: empty 1520 kg (3,351 lb);

maximum take-off 1970 kg (4,343 lb)
Dimensions: span 11.00 m (36 ft 1 in); length 9.07 m (29 ft 9 in); height 2.70 m (8 ft 10½ in); wing area 17.00 m² (182.99 sq ft)

Pilatus P-3

The undoubted success of the P-2 led to development of a new general-purpose trainer under the designation **Pilatus P-3**, the prototype of which was flown for the first time on 3 September 1953. Intended for use as both a primary and advanced trainer, the P-3 is of cantilever low-wing monoplane configuration and differs from its predecessor by being of all-metal construction. It has retractable tricycle landing gear, but as the P-3 was required by the Swiss air force for 'all-through' training, from the primary stage to the point of passing on to the de Havilland Vampire jet trainer, a lower-powered engine was adopted, the Avco

Though lower powered than the P-2, the Pilatus P-3 was an able basic and advanced trainer.

Lycoming GO-435-C2A. Like the P-2 that preceded it into service, the P-3 has similar standards of equipment or weapons for comprehensive pilot training by day or night. A total of 72 P-3s was built for the Swiss air force, and in 1993 a handful of these remain in service; a small number was also supplied to Brazil, but these have since been superseded by trainers of indigenous design and construction.

Specification
Pilatus P-3
Type: two-seat primary/advanced trainer

Powerplant: one 194-kW (260-hp) Avco Lycoming GO-435-C2A flat-six piston engine
Performance: maximum speed 310 km/h (193 mph) from sea level to 2000 m (6,560 ft); service ceiling 5500 m (18,045 ft); maximum range 750 km (466 miles)

Weights: empty equipped 1110 kg (2,447 lb); maximum take-off 1500 kg (3,307 lb)
Dimensions: span 10.40 m (34 ft 1½ in); length 8.75 m (28 ft 8½ in); height 3.05 m (10 ft 0 in); wing area 16.50 m² (177.61 sq ft)

Pilatus P-4

The **Pilatus P-4** represented another attempt by the company to get into the market for civil aircraft, but this five-seat

cabin monoplane had little more success than its SB-2 predecessor. Of braced high-wing monoplane configuration, with fixed tailwheel landing gear, a braced tail unit and a 142-kW (190-hp) Avco Lycoming O-435 engine, the P-4

had accommodation for a pilot and four passengers. All passenger seats were removable easily so that the P-4 could be used as a cargo carrier, or as an air ambulance accommodating two stretchers and two medical attendants. With a wing

span of 11.85 m (38 ft 10½ in) and maximum take-off weight of 1500 kg (3,307 lb), the P-4 had a maximum speed of 245 km/h (152 mph).

Pilatus PC-6 Porter and Turbo-Porter

With the maiden flight of the first of five prototype **Pilatus PC-6 Porter** general utility transport aircraft on 4 May 1959, the company began a success story that is still continuing; approximately 450 PC-6 aircraft of all versions had been delivered to customers in more than 50 countries by the end of 1993. A braced high-wing monoplane of all-metal construction, with a wing configured for STOL operation, a conventional tail unit and fixed tailwheel landing gear, the PC-6 is powered by a single engine which, in the case of the prototypes and initial production aircraft, was a 254-kW (340-hp) Avco Lycoming GSO-480-B1A6 flat-six engine. Essential go-anywhere capability is provided by landing gear that is suitable for wheels, wheel-skis or floats; and the PC-6 has a cabin which is equipped with a pilot's and one passenger seat as standard, leaving a clear level floor space measuring 2.30 m (7ft 6½ in) by 1.16 m (3 ft 9½ in) which can be used for a variety of purposes.

The initial production PC-6 Porter was followed by the **PC-6/350 Porter** which introduced the 261-kW (350-hp) Avco Lycoming IGO-540-A1A engine, and this was certificated in September 1962. Since that time the Porter has been improved progressively by the introduction of alternative powerplants, gradual refinement of the entire structure, and the introduction of new equipment to enhance the versatility of this very useful aircraft which can be used for a wide variety of roles including ambulance, air survey, cargo carrying, crop dusting or spraying, glider or target towing, parachuting, passenger transport, search and rescue, supply dropping and water bombing. In addition to those supplied for civil use, military operators include the air arms of Angola, Argentina, Australia, Austria, Bolivia, Burma, Chad,

The light weight of its turboprop engine is responsible for the long nose necessary to maintain the PC-6's centre of gravity.

Ecuador, Oman, Peru, Sudan, Switzerland, and Thailand. Under the designation **UV-20A Chiricahua** the US Army also has two Turbo-Porters which were based in Berlin.

Brief details of the resulting variants are given below.

Variants
PC-6/A Turbo-Porter: initial turboprop-powered version with a 390-kW (523-shp) Turboméca Astazou

IIE or IIG engine; first flown on 2 May 1961
PC-6/A1 Turbo-Porter: 1968 version with a 427-kW (573-shp) Turboméca Astazou XII turboprop
PC-6/A2 Turbo-Porter: 1971 version with a 427-kW (573-shp) Turboméca Astazou XIVE turboprop
PC-6/B Turbo-Porter: version with a 410-kW (550-shp) Pratt & Whitney Aircraft of Canada PT6A-6A turboprop; first flown on 1 May 1964
PC-6/B1 Turbo-Porter: generally as PC-6/B, but with a 410-kW (550-shp) PT6A-20 turboprop

PC-6/B2-H2 Turbo-Porter: current production version with a 507-kW (680-shp) Pratt & Whitney Aircraft of Canada PT6A-27 turboprop engine, flat-rated to 410 kW (550 shp) at sea level
PC-6/C Turbo-Porter: version with 429-kW (575-shp) Garrett TPE 331-25D turboprop engine; prototype built by Fairchild Industries in the USA and first flown during October 1965
PC-6/C1 Turbo-Porter: generally similar to PC-6/C, but with a 429-kW (575-shp) Garrett TPE 331-1-100 engine

PC-6/C2-H2 Porter: version developed by Fairchild Industries with a 485-ekW (650-ehp) Garrett TPE 331-101F turboprop, serving as prototype for a militarised version, known as the **Fairchild Peacemaker**, which was equipped for COIN and general-purpose operations; 15 built for USAF under designation **AU-23A**, of which 14 were supplied to the Royal Thai air force; this air force acquired later an additional 20 AU-23As through the USAF military sales programme; several of the total re-

main in service with the RTAF in 1993
PC-6/D-H3 Porter: single prototype only with a 373-kW (500-hp) Avco Lycoming turbocharged engine, modified wingtips and tail surfaces

Specification
Pilatus PC-6/B2-H2 Turbo-Porter
Type: utility transport
Powerplant: one 507-kW (680-shp) Pratt & Whitney Aircraft of Canada PT6A-27 turboprop flat-rated to 410 kW (550 shp)

Performance: maximum cruising speed 260 km/h (161 mph) at 3050 m (10,000 ft); service ceiling 8535 m (28,000 ft); range with internal fuel 1050 km (652 miles)
Weights: empty equipped 1218 kg (2,685 lb); maximum take-off 2770 kg (6,107 lb)
Dimensions: span 15.13 m (49 ft 8 in); length 10.90 m (35 ft 9 in); height 3.20 m (10 ft 6 in); wing area 28.80 m² (310.01 sq ft)

Pilatus PC-7 Turbo-Trainer

Adopting the same technique that had converted the Porter into the Turbo-Porter, as a private venture Pilatus built a turboprop-powered prototype of the P-3 advanced trainer. A P-3 airframe was used for this conversion and the original designation applied to this aircraft was **P-3B**, changed subsequently to **Pilatus PC-7 Turbo-Trainer**. This prototype was flown for the first time on 12 April 1966 but initially it had no appeal to military operators, with a result that the first production PC-7 was not flown until 18 August 1978. In current production form the PC-7 is, like its predecessor, a cantilever low-wing monoplane of all-metal construction and with retractable tricycle landing gear. The cockpit, with a rearward-sliding jettisonable canopy, accommodates two in tandem, and power is provided by a Pratt & Whitney Aircraft of Canada PT6A-25 turboprop

The Pilatus PC-7 Turbo-Trainer is a more than worthy successor to the P-3 and, after an initial delay, began to 'come through' with an impressive string of orders during the late 1970s and into the 1980s.

engine. Six underwing hardpoints are standard to carry a variety of stores/weapons, the two inboard stations suitable for the attachment of auxiliary fuel tanks; total external load on the hardpoints is 1040 kg (2,293 lb).

By early 1993 deliveries had exceeded 400 aircraft. Customers include the air forces and navies of Abu Dhabi, Angola, Austria, Bolivia, Chad, Chile, France, Guatemala, Iran, Iraq, Malaysia, Mexico,

Myanmar, Netherlands, Switzerland and three officially undisclosed customers. Those in service with the Swiss air force are known as **PC-7/CH**. In addition, a small number of paramilitary and even private users have bought the type. The French 'Patrouille Martini' aerobatic team is unique in operating four PC-7s as air show display mounts since 1987.

Specification
PC-7/CH
Type: single/two-seat trainer

Powerplant: one 485-kW (650-shp) Pratt & Whitney Aircraft of Canada PT6A-25A turboprop
Performance: maximum cruising speed 412 km/h (256 mph) at 6095 m (20,000 ft); service ceiling 9755 m (32,000 ft); maximum range 2260 km (1,634 miles)
Weights: empty equipped 1330 kg (2,932 lb); maximum take-off 2700 kg (5,952 lb)
Dimensions: span 10.40 m (34 ft 1½ in); length 9.78 m (32 ft 0¾ in); height 3.21 m (10 ft 6½ in)

Pilatus PC-9

Design of the **Pilatus PC-9** began in May 1982 as a successor to the PC-7 in the basic and advanced training roles. Though it bears a distinct resemblance to preceeding designs, the PC-9 shares only 10 per cent airframe commonality with the PC-7. The main differences include the more powerful engine, redesigned canopy, 'stepped' cockpit with Martin-Baker Mk CH 11A ejection seats, ventral air brake, modified wing and fin and larger wheels with high pressure tyres.

The initial modifications were flight tested on a converted PC-7 and the first of two pre-production PC-9s (HB-HPA) first flew on 7 May 1984. This aircraft was fitted with a Hartzell three-bladed propeller but the second aircraft (HB-HPB) was built to a more representative standard. This included the installation of the Collins 'glass cockpit'. The type received its aerobatic certification from the Swiss authorities on 19 September 1985, ahead of schedule. The PC-9 also complies with US Federal Aviation Authority FAR Part 23 regulations and several US military specifications.

First customer was the Union of Burma Air Force (Myanmar), already a PC-7 operator. This was followed by the Royal Saudi Air Force in 1985, which obtained their aircraft from British Aerospace. BAe had begun offering the PC-9 in 1984 as a prospective replacement for the RAF's Jet Provost fleet. This order was won, in the event, by the Shorts Tucano. After its bid failed, BAe retained

the right to equip Swiss-built aircraft at its Brough factory and offer them as a lead-in type for the Hawk jet trainer. Saudi PC-9s were supplied under the terms of the Al Yamamah agreement. A licensing deal was also struck with Australia's Hawker de Havilland, in 1986, covering 67 aircraft for the Royal Australian Air Force. Two complete aircraft were delivered from Switzerland, followed by six in component form, with the remainder being built in Australia.

Total sales exceed 140 in early 1993. Other military customers have included the US Army (which withdrew their aircraft in 1992) and the Royal Thai Air Force. Pilatus is offering the PC-9 as a JPATS candidate, in conjunction with Beechcraft. This version features a 70 per cent redesign, strengthening the fuselage and canopy and re-equipping the cockpit. The first of these **PC-9 Mk 2**s flew in 1992 and is to be joined by a second demonstration aircraft.

Variants
PC-9/A: Australian version, built under licence by Hawker de Havilland and ASTA; first delivery in December 1987
PC-9B: target-towing version produced for Germany's Luftwaffe and operated by a civilian contractor; fitted with two Southwest RM-24 winches on inboard pylons with targets stowed aft; extra fuel tankage and acoustic scoring system also carried
PC-9 Mk 2: modified PC-9 offered by Pilatus in conjunction with Beech for the USAF/USN Joint Primary Training System (JPATS) competition; the prototype aircraft (N8284M) first flew

in December 1992; an engineering testbed (N26BA) has already chalked up nearly 300 flying hours, and the second Beech production aircraft is nearing completion

Specification
Pilatus PC-9
Type: two-seat high-performance turbo-prop trainer
Powerplant: one 857-kW (1,150-shp) Pratt & Whitney Canada PT6A-62 turboprop with a Hartzell four-bladed HC-D4N-ZA/09512A propeller
Performance: maximum level speed 556 km/h (345 mph); maximum

Hawker de Havilland is undertaking construction of the bulk of the 67 PC-9s destined for use by the Royal Australian Air Force.

permissible diving speed 667 km/h (414 mph); maximum operating altitude 7620 m (25,000 ft); service ceiling 11580 m (38,000 ft); maximum range 1642 km (1020 miles)
Weights: empty 1620 kg (3,571 lb); maximum take-off 3200 kg (7,055 lb)
Dimensions: span 10.12 m (33 ft 2½ in); height 3.26 m (10 ft 8½ in); length 10.05 m (32 ft 11¾ in)

Pilatus PC-12

Referred to by the company as the **Pilatus PC-XII**, the PC-12 is a unique attempt at combining a single powerful turboprop engine with a large and capacious airframe of advanced design, resulting in a aircraft capable of a diverse range of tasks. Announced at the 1989 NBAA show, development of a prototype was rapid and the first flight of P.01 (HB-FOA) took place on 31 May 1991. The second aircraft flew in mid-1992 and Swiss and US certification is expected in 1993. A second production line, possibly in the United States, is planned.

From the outset the aircraft was intended to be a fast and long-ranged type. Pilatus claims it to be 185 km/h (115 mph) faster than the Cessna Caravan and to have longer legs than the Beech King Air, both potential rivals. Pilatus have had a long and successful relationship with the PT6 engine so it was no surprise that they chose it to power their latest venture. Special consideration was given towards making the **PC-12F** a versatile freighter and the 'T-tail' configuration was chosen to avoid potential damage from cargo loading equipment. The fuselage is fitted with a large upward-opening freight door on the port side, while passenger entry is via an integral stairs behind the cockpit. Cabin volume is

9.34 m³ (330 cu ft). Up to nine airline-standard seats can be fitted in the **PC-12P** version. A VIP aircraft, seating six, is available, as is a combi layout for four passengers and 5.94 m³ (210 cu ft) of cargo. A military version for trooping and parachuting is under consideration.

The cockpit is equipped with a Bendix/King EFIS with optional weather radar. The flight deck seats two, but is undergoing certification for single pilot operations. The manufacturer estimates a potential market for over 800 PC-12s. By early 1993 roughly 30 orders had been received. Pilatus has recieved funding for 35 aircraft from its parent company Oerlikon-Buhrle.

Specification
Pilatus PC-12
Type: pressurised single turboprop utility aircraft
Powerplant: one 1327-kW (1,780-shp) Pratt & Whitney PT6A-67B turboprop, driving a four-bladed Hartzell composite propeller
Performance: maximum cruising speed 497 km/h (309 mph); maximum operating altitude 7620 m (25000 ft); maximum IFR range 2965 km (1842 miles)
Weights: (PC-12P) empty 2386 kg

(5260 lb); maximum payload 1150 kg (2535 lb); maximum take-off 4000 kg (8,818 lb)
Dimensions: span 13.78 m (45 ft 2½ in); height 4.14 m (13 ft 7 in); length 13.96 m (45 ft 9½ in)

Its investment in the PC-12 is the largest the manufacturer has ever made in one of its aircraft projects. The future of Pilatus is in its hands, and the company is working hard to sell the type.

Pilatus SB-2 Pelican

Pilatus Flugzeugwerke AG, which is part of the Oerlikon-Buhrle organisation, was established at Stans, Switzerland, in December 1939. First product of the company was a four/six-seat light transport designated **Pilatus SB.2 Pelican**, a braced high-wing monoplane with fixed tricycle landing gear,

powered by a 336-kW (450-hp) Pratt & Whitney Wasp Junior radial engine. The pilot and co-pilot/navigator were seated in a separate compartment forward of the wing leading edge, with a main cabin below the wing which could be arranged to accommodate two to four passengers according to layout. The Pelican, which

The early 1940s Pilatus SB-2 Pelican failed to win any production orders, but set the pattern for future Pilatus designs with STOL performance offered by the full-span slotted-flap/drooping-aileron combination.

was first flown during 1944 and failed to gain any commercial interest, spanned

15.50 m (50 ft 10¼ in) and had a maximum speed of 250 km/h (155 mph).

Piper J-3 Cub, O-59 and L-4 Grasshopper series

C. Gilbert Taylor and his brother had first established the Taylor Brothers Aviation Corporation in 1929 to market the Taylor Chummy lightplane; in 1931 the company was reorganised as the Taylor Aircraft Company, W. T. Piper Sr then being its secretary and treasurer. When the company ran into financial difficulties, manufacturing and marketing rights for the **Taylor Cub**, which had first flown in September 1930, were acquired by W. T. Piper who, in 1937, formed Piper Aircraft Corporation to continue production of this aircraft. A braced high-wing monoplane of mixed basic construction with fabric covering, the Cub had a conventional tail unit, fixed tailskid landing gear (the main units with wheels or optional floats) and an enclosed cabin seating two in tandem.

When first produced by Piper, the **Piper J-3 Cub** was powered by a 30-kW (40-hp) Continental A40-4 flat-four engine, but it was not long before the 37-kW (50-hp) A50-4 or alternative A50-5 with dual ignition system was introduced on the **J-3C-50 Cub**. The re-

sulting improvement in performance made this already attractive lightplane an extremely marketable commodity and during 1938, which was the new company's first full year of production, no fewer than 737 Cubs were built. The Continental A50 was a new engine, early experience proving that it was reliable and had development potential, and it was later re-rated at 48-kW (65-hp) at a higher engine speed. Its introduction by competitors meant that Piper had to follow suit, and in 1940 the **J-3C-65 Cub** appeared with the Continental A65 engine. With alternative Franklin flat-four engines, the 37-kW (50-hp) 4AC-150 or 48-kW (65-hp) 4AC-176, the Cub was designated **J-3F-50** and **J-3F-65** respectively and, similarly, with the Avco Lycoming 37-kW (50-hp) O-145-A1 or 48-kW (65-hp) O-145-B the Cub had the

The NE-1 was the US Navy's equivalent of the Army L-4. Though intended as a trainer, this aircraft was attached to Airship Squadron 32.

respective designations **J-3L-50** and **J-3L-65**. Also built in comparatively small numbers was a version designated **J-3P-50**, powered by a 37-kW (50-hp) Lenape Papoose 3-cylinder radial engine. Sales began to soar, and then in 1941 the US Army selected this aircraft for evaluation in artillery spotting/direction roles, and shortly afterwards ordered 40 similar aircraft under the designation **O-59**. These aircraft were used by the US Army under virtually operational conditions during annual manoeuvres at the end of 1941, and it was very soon discovered that the little Cub had far wider applications than at first anticipated.

This practical experience enabled the US Army to obtain an improved **O-59A** which, powered by a 48-kW (65-hp) Continental O-170-3 flat-four engine, had

The Piper J-3 Cub was a landmark design in aviation history, and many treasured and much-loved aircraft are still airworthy today.

better accommodation for the pilot and observer with an enhanced all-round view. Orders for O-59As totalled 948, but as a result of designation changes they entered service as **L-4A** aircraft, the earlier **YO-59** and O-59 aircraft then being redesignated **L-4**, and the type later received the name **Grasshopper.** Subsequent procurements covered 980 of the **L-4B** version with reduced radio equipment, 1,801 of the **L-4H** variant with only detail changes, and 1,680 of the **L-4J** model which introduced a variable-pitch propeller. Civil Cubs impressed for Army service at the beginning of World War II included eight J-3C-65s and five J-3F-65s which were designated **L-4C** and **L-4D** respectively. Piper was then requested to develop a training glider from the L-4 design and this, with powerplant removed and the forward fuselage redesigned to accommodate an instructor and two pupils, was built to a total of 250 for the US Army under the designation **TG-8**. Three of these gliders were acquired for evaluation by the US Navy under the de-

signation **XLNP-1** and this service also procured 230 **NE-1** aircraft which, basically similar to the US Army's L-4s, were used as primary trainers; 20 similar aircraft procured at a later date were designated **NE-2**. When, post-war, production was switched to the further improved Cub J-4 Coupe, Piper had built a total of 14,125 civil and 5,703 military.

Specification
Piper J-3C-65 Cub
Type: two-seat lightplane
Powerplant: one 48-kW (65-hp) Continental A65 flat-four piston engine
Performance: maximum speed 148 km/h (92 mph); service ceiling 3660 m (12,000 ft); range 402 km (250 miles)
Weights: empty 290 kg (640 lb); maximum take-off 499 kg (1,100 lb)
Dimensions: span 10.73 m (35 ft 2½ in); length 6.78 m (22 ft 3 in); height 2.03 m (6 ft 8 in)

Piper J-4 Cub Coupe

To compete with the expanding range of lightplanes offered by other aircraft manufacturers, Piper produced in 1938 the **Piper J-4 Cub Coupe**. Retaining basically the same airframe as the J-3 Cub, this had a small increase in wing span and introduced improved landing gear with a fully-castoring tailwheel, hydraulic brakes and speed fairings for the wheels. As powered initially by a 37-kW (50-hp) Continental A50-1 it had the designation J-4, but introduction of the 48-kW (65-hp) Continental A65-1 or -8 engine in 1940 brought redesignation as the **J-4A**, and later of the 56-kW (75-hp) Continental A75-9 as the **J-4E**. In 1939 Piper introduced the **J-4B**, differing only in powerplant which initially, was a 45-kW (60-hp) Franklin 4AC-171, but that was soon replaced by the 48-kW

A J-3 development, the Piper J-4 Cub Coupe featured a fully cowled Avco Lycoming engine, spatted undercarriage and even brakes. The type sold in good numbers in the United Staes and several were impressed for wartime military duties.

(65-hp) Franklin 4AC-176-B2 without any change in designation. Last of the J-4s was the version powered by Avco Lycoming engines, the 41-kW (55-hp) O-145-A1 or -A2, or 48-kW (65-hp) O-145-B1, both of these Cub Coupes having the designation **J-4F**. Production of J-4s reached 1,250, and during World War II 17 J-4Es were impressed for service with the USAAF under the designation **L-4E**.

Specification
Piper J-4F Cub Coupe
Type: two-seat lightplane
Powerplant: one 48-kW (65-hp) Avco Lycoming O-145-B1 flat-four piston engine
Performance: maximum speed 161 km/h (100 mph); service ceiling 3660 m (12,000 ft); range 547 km (340 miles)
Weights: empty 336 kg (740 lb); maximum take-off 590 kg (1,300 lb)
Dimensions: span 10.82 m (36 ft 2 in); length 6.86 m (22 ft 6 in); height 2.08 m (6 ft 10 in); wing area 17.00 m² (183.0 sq ft)

Piper J-5 Cruiser

A modest expansion in the capabilities of the J-3 and J-4 range was achieved with the **Piper J-5 Cruiser** which, although basically similar to the J-3, had a minimal increase in fuselage width to provide three-seat accommodation. First seen in early 1940 as the **J-5A Cruiser** with a 56-kW (75-hp) Continental A75-8 engine, it became available subsequently as the **J-5B** with a similarly powered Avco Lycoming GO-145-C2 engine, then being designated **J-5C** with the installation of a 75-kW (100-hp) Avco Lycoming O-235-C. Civil J-5A and J-5B aircraft were impressed for service with the US Army during World War II under the designations **L-4F** and **L-4G** respectively, and the US Navy procured 100 aircraft similar to the J-5C under the designation **HE-1**. These had the 75-kW (100-hp) Avco Lycoming O-235-2, and a hinged

The three-seat Piper J-5 series was one of several modest variations on the J-3 Cub theme that Piper built at Lock Haven because of the overwhelming demand for the airplane.

top decking to the rear fuselage to allow the loading and unloading of a stretcher; when, in 1943, the designation letter H was allocated to identify helicopters, the HE-1s were redesignated **AE-1**. When production ended a total of 1,404 J-5 Cruisers had been built.

Specification
Piper J-5C Cruiser
Type: three-seat lightplane
Powerplant: one 75-kW (100-hp) Avco Lycoming O-235-C flat-four piston engine

Performance: maximum speed 177 km/h (110 mph); service ceiling 4570 m (15,000 ft); range 620 km (385 miles)
Weights: empty 388 kg (855 lb); maximum take-off 703 kg (1,550 lb)
Dimensions: span 10.82 m (35 ft 6 in); length 6.86 m (22 ft 6 in); height 2.08 m (6 ft 10 in); wing area 16.63 m² (179.0 sq ft)

Piper PA-11 Cub Special

After the end of World War II the demand for civil lightplanes seemed for a time to be insatiable, but when low-price government war-surplus aircraft came on the market the situation was changed overnight. One of Piper's plans to meet this challenge was to make available an austerity civil version of the extensively built L-4 Grasshopper. Designated **Piper PA-11 Cub Special**, and powered by a 48-kW (65-hp) Continental A65-8 flat-four engine, it proved to be an attractive proposition, and its price of only $2,495 in 1947 meant that many preferred a slightly dearer new aircraft to a war-surplus model of uncertain history. Before the company ended production of the Cub Special a total of 1,323 civil examples had been built, these aircraft having a maximum speed of 161 km/h (100 mph) and range of 483 km (300 miles). The type appealed also to the US Army for supply to other nations under the Military Aid Program, and 105 aircraft with the 71-kW (95-hp) Continental C90-8F engine were acquired under the designation **L-18B** and delivered to Turkey.

Piper PA-12 Super Cruiser

With the end of World War II in sight, Piper made preparations for large-scale production of lightplanes for civil use, and began by developing an improved version of the J-5C Cruiser of which production had ended during 1942. Although technically a three-seat aircraft, the **Piper PA-12 Super Cruiser** was more usually used and regarded as a de luxe two-seater, and differed from the J-5C only in a number of cosmetic refinements to make it an attractive purchase. The prototype was flown in December 1945 and attracted so much attention that the company soon had an enormous backlog of orders, and when production of this version ended no fewer than 3,758 had been built. Dimen-

sionally little had changed from the J-5C, and having the same 75-kW (100-hp) Avco Lycoming O-235-C engine, the PA-12 had a maximum speed of 183-km/h (114 mph) at sea level.

The Piper PA-12 Super Cruiser was little more than an aerodynamically refined version of the J-5 Cruiser series. Fitted with a Lycoming powerplant in a lengthened and more shapely nose, it was Piper's first post-war aircraft. Still only a three-seater, nearly 4,000 were built from 1945 to 1949 and it is no surprise that many are still airworthy today.

Piper PA-14 Family Cruiser

Despite the fact that Piper had developed the PA-12 Super Cruiser as a three-seat aircraft, the accommodation for three adults was far from generous and the company soon discovered that it was beginning to lose sales to the lightweight four-seaters being marketed by its competitors. In an attempt to provide an aircraft of four-seat capacity without a resulting large price increase, the company revised the fuselage of the PA-12 to give additional width for four seats and installed an Avco Lycoming O-235-C1 engine. Although the resulting **PA-14 Family Cruiser** was offered at a keen price it failed to gain any real interest, and when production ended during 1949 a total of only 232 had been built.

Bearing the same basic relationship to the PA-12 as the J-5 did to the J-3, the Piper PA-14 Family Cruiser finally provided its customers with a genuine four-seat cabin layout.

Specification

Type: four-seat lightplane
Powerplant: one 86-kW (115-hp) Avco Lycoming O-235-C1 flat-four piston engine
Performance: maximum speed 198 km/h (123 mph); service ceiling 3660 m (12,000 ft); range 805 km (500 miles)
Weights: empty 454 kg (1,000 lb); maximum take-off 839 kg (1,850 lb)

Dimensions: span 10.82 m (35 ft 6 in); length 7.06 m (23 ft 2 in); height 1.96 m (6 ft 5 in); wing area 16.66 m² (179.30 sq ft)

Piper PA-15, PA-16 Clipper and PA-17 Vagabond

The first flush of sales success which followed the end of World War II was followed by a period of near disaster when the US government unloaded its accumulation of war surplus-aircraft on to an active market. This sudden influx of some 31,000 aircraft at highly attractive prices almost paralysed the activities of companies like Beech, Cessna and Piper that were building general-aviation aircraft for the popular market. The introduction of Piper's PA-14 Family Cruiser was one of the steps taken to offset this situation, the other being the design and development of a low-cost utility aircraft as a crash programme. Of the same general configuration as the Piper Cub, it reintroduced a shorter-span wing and a low-powered Avco Lycoming O-145-B2 engine, and there were no 'frills' as standard. Which meant, of course, that the basic practical flying machine could be obtained at low cost, and the more de luxe accessories could be added later, as and when they could be afforded. Designated **Piper PA-15**, the prototype was flown for the first time on 29 October 1947 and this new machine was

Offering slightly more power and interior refinement, the stylish Piper PA-17 Vagabond was an indication of the renaissance of the US lightplane industry after World War II.

soon winning orders. By the autumn of 1948, when the market was showing signs of recovery, Piper introduced the **PA-17 Vagabond** which was powered by a 48-kW (65-hp) Continental A65-8 engine and again equipped with the 'frills' as standard. When production ended, Piper had built a combined total of 585 of these two versions, but the company had earlier added to this success by introducing a four-seat version of the PA-15; designated **PA-16 Clipper**, and powered by an 86-kW (115-hp) Avco Lycoming O-235-C1 engine, this utility four-seater was built to a total of 726 from 1949.

Specification
Piper PA-15
Type: two-seat lightplane
Powerplant: one 48-kW (65-hp) Avco

Lycoming O-145-B2 flat-four piston engine
Performance: maximum speed 164 km/h (102 mph) at sea level; service ceiling 3810 m (12,500 ft); range 410 km (255 miles)

Weights: empty 281 kg (620 lb); maximum take-off 499 kg (1,100 lb)
Dimensions: span 8.92 m (29 ft 3 in); length 5.69 m (18 ft 8 in); height 1.83 m (6 ft 0 in); wing area 13.70 m² (147.50 sq ft)

Piper PA-18 Super Cub and L-18/L-21/U-7 series

Certainly the most famous product of the Piper Company, the original version of the **Piper PA-18 Super Cub**, powered by a 67-kW (90-hp) Continental C90-12F flat-four engine, first came on the market in late 1949 after gaining type certification on 18 November 1949. It continued in production with Piper until 1981, when the company disposed of all rights in this aircraft to WTA Inc. of Lubbock, Texas. In the intervening period the PA-18 had appeared in progressively improving form, and had been powered by a variety of engines rated between 67 to 112 kW (90 and 150 hp). In its final Piper production form, as the **PA-18-150**, its basic configuration was that of the earliest two-seat Cubs with braced high-set wings, wire-braced tail unit, and fixed tailwheel landing gear, but powered by a 112-kW (150-hp) Avco Lycoming O-320 flat-four engine. This powerplant had been used also for a specialised agricultural duster/sprayer version designated **PA-18A** which had been introduced in 1952; it incorporated as standard a chemical hopper and spray/dusting gear, but was easily convertible for general-purpose use, and when production ended a total of 2,650 had been built. In addition to civil construction, Piper built 838 PA-18s with the 71-kW (95-hp) Continental C90-8F engine for the US Army under the designation **L-18C**, 108 of this total being

One of the lower-powered Super Cub versions was the PA-18-95 offering modern performance without loss of comfort.

supplied to foreign nations under the Military Aid Program, and the army then ordered 150 examples of the generally similar **L-21A** which differed by having the 92-kW (125-hp) Avco Lycoming O-290-11 engine; at a later date a number of these aircraft were converted for use as trainers, then being redesignated **TL-21A**. Under the designation **YL-21** the US Army evaluated two examples of a version of the PA-18 Cub powered by a 101-kW (135-hp) Avco Lycoming O-290-D2 engine, later acquiring a total of 584 under the designation **L-21B**, a number of them being supplied to foreign nations under MAP. In 1962 in-service L-21Bs were redesignated **U-7A**.

Specification
Piper PA-18-150 Super Cub
Type: two-seat 12-kW (150-hp) Avco Lycoming O-320 flat-four piston engine.
Performance: maximum speed 209 km/h (130 mph); service ceiling 5790 m (19,000 ft); range with maximum payload (740 km (460 miles)
Weights: empty 446 kg (983 lb); maximum take-off 794 kg (1,750 lb)

Dimensions: span 10.73 m (35 ft 2½ in); length 6.88 m (22 ft 7 in); height 2.04 m (6 ft 8½ in); wing area 16.58 m² (178.50 sq ft)

Below: This military L-21B version of the PA-18 is fitted with tandem wheels for use on soft runways near the front line.

Piper PA-20 Pacer

Under the designation **Piper PA-20 Pacer**, the company began production in 1950 of an updated version of the four-seat PA-16 Clipper. It introduced a number of improvements, including a larger area tailplane with balanced elevators, increased fuel capacity, redesigned landing gear and several interior refinements. As at first powered by a 81-kW (108-hp) Avco Lycoming O-235-C1 engine, it had the designation **PA-20 Pacer 115**, but subsequent versions included the **Pacer 125** with a 93-kW (125-hp) O-290-D engine, and the generally similar **Pacer 135** which introduced a variable-pitch propeller. When production ended in 1955 a total of 1,119 had been built, and the PA-20 Pacer 135 could demonstrate a maximum speed of 225 km/h (140 mph) and had a range of 933 km (580 miles).

Piper PA-22 Tri-Pacer

In 1951 Piper introduced its **Piper PA-22 Tri-Pacer**, basically a version of the PA-20 Pacer with tricycle landing gear that incorporated a steerable nosewheel. It also differed from the PA-20 by having initially a 112-kW (150-hp) Avco Lycoming O-320 flat-four engine, and introduced an interconnected aileron and rudder pedal control system, enabling the Tri-Pacer to be flown entirely by the control column without the need to have an input from the rudder pedals during turns. This system was easily disconnected, however, to permit independent use of the ailerons, elevator and rudder. The Tri-Pacer proved a very popular model, and late series aircraft were powered by the slightly more powerful

One of the most successful Piper aircraft of the 1950s, the PA-22 offered new pilots the benefits of tricycle landing gear.

O-320-B engine. When production ended in the early 1960s a total of 7,668 had been built. This figure included a number of a slightly more austere version with the 112-kW (150-hp) engine which were marketed for airport operator and flying club use under the name **Piper Caribbean**.

Specification
Piper PA-22 Tri-Pacer
Type: four-seat cabin monoplane
Powerplant: one 119-kW (160-hp)

Avco Lycoming O-320-B flat-four piston engine
Performance: maximum speed 227 km/h (141 mph); service ceiling 5030 m (16,500 ft); range with maximum fuel (1054 km (655 miles)

Weights: empty 503 kg (1,110 lb); maximum take-off 907 kg (2,000 lb)
Dimensions: span 8.92 m (29 ft 3¼ in); length 6.28 m (20 ft 7¼ in); height 2.54 m (8 ft 4 in); wing area 13.70 m² (147.50 sq ft)

Piper PA-22 Colt 108

On 1 November 1960 Piper announced the introduction of a low cost two-seater which it named **Piper PA-22 Colt 108**. This designation explained to the initiated that its airframe was basically the same as that of the PA-22 Tri-Pacer, but it had a two-seat interior and incorporated in its Standard version a minimum of frills. It was available in optional Custom and Super Custom models with higher standards of installed equipment and instrumentation. Powerplant was the 81-kW (108-hp) Avco Lycoming O-23-C1B flat-four engine, providing this version with a maximum speed of 193 km/h (120 mph) at sea level and a range with maximum fuel of 1110 km/h (690 miles) at 2135 m (7,000 ft). A total of 1,827 was built during the three years that the Colt was in production.

Piper PA-23 Apache and Aztec

On 2 March 1952 Piper flew the prototype of a new twin-engine aircraft which it then identified as the **Piper PA-23 Twin-Stinson**. A cantilever low-wing monoplane of all-metal construction, it had a tailplane set high on the fuselage and mounting endplate fins and rudders, retractable tricycle landing gear and an enclosed cabin seating four in two pairs, and was powered by two 112-kW (150-hp) Avco Lycoming O-320 flat-four engines in wing-mounted nacelles. The tail unit was very soon replaced by a conventional tailplane with centrally mounted single fin and rudder, and it was in this form that it entered production in early 1954 as the **PA-23 Apache**, later designated **PA-23 Apache 150**. The type continued in production as the Apache until 1965, by which time 2,166 had been built, including 1,231 examples of the first production version. The original model was followed in 1958 by the **PA-23 Apache 160** with 119-kW (160-hp) O-320-B engines, and with some interior revisions so that it was classed as a four/five-seat aircraft (816 built), and in 1962 by the similar **PA-23 Apache 235**, which introduced swept tail surfaces and 175-kW (235-hp) Avco Lycoming O-540-B1A5 flat-six engines (119 built).

With sales of the Apache 235 declining, Piper developed an improved version of this aircraft which introduced a 186-kW (250-hp) O-540 engine and provided six-seat capacity. This entered production under the designation **PA-23-250 Aztec** in 1959-60, the US Navy acquiring 20 of these aircraft for use in a utility role, designating them **UO-1**, changed to **U-11A** in 1962. The Aztec was built until early 1982 when production was suspended. In final production form the type had the designation **PA-23-250 Aztec F**, and was available also as the generally similar **PA-23T-250 Turbo Aztec F** which differed by having Avco Lycoming TIO-540 engines with a Garrett turbocharging system.

The entire appearance of the PA-23 series was modernised by the addition of a swept tail on the Aztec 250 and its successors.

Specification
PA-23T-250 Turbo Aztec F
Type: six-seat light transport
Powerplant: two 186-kW (250-hp) Avco Lycoming TIO-540-C1A turbocharged flat-six piston engines
Performance: maximum speed 407 km/h (254 mph) at 5640 m (18,500 ft); service ceiling 7315 m (24,000 ft); maximum range with maximum fuel 2120 km (1,317 miles)
Weights: empty 1507 kg (3,323 lb); maximum take-off 2359 kg (5,200 lb)
Dimensions: span 11.37 m (37 ft 3¾ in); length 9.52 m (31 ft 2¾ in); height 3.07 m (10 ft 1 in); wing area 19.23 m² (207.0 sq ft)

Early PA-23 Apaches had an unswept, rounded tail with a short fuselage seating four.

Piper PA-24 Comanche

On 24 May 1956 Piper flew the prototype of a new single-engine four-seat cabin monoplane that it designated initially **Piper PA-24 Comanche**, but which later became known as the **PA-24-180 Comanche**. A cantilever low-wing monoplane of all-metal construction, this very clean looking aircraft had such features as retractable tricycle landing gear, an all-moving tailplane and a 134-kW (180-hp) Avco Lycoming O-360-A1A engine. The first production aircraft was flown on 21 October 1957, and from the outset was available in four versions, the Standard with basic essential equipment, the Custom, Super Custom and AutoFlite having progressively more sophisticated equipment, the last of them introducing a two-axis autopilot.

The very convincing capability of the PA-24-180 Comanche was demonstrated at an early date by American pilot Max Conrad in establishing FAI-accred-

ited world class distance records of 11211.83 km (6,966.71 miles) in a straight line and 11138.72 km (6,921.28 miles) in a closed circuit during 1959 and 1960 respectively, and in flying a PA-24-250 Comanche in 1959 over a straight-line distance of 12341.26 km (7,668.5 miles); these records remained unbroken in 1983. Mentioned in these records is the **PA-24-250 Comanche** which soon supplemented the PA-24-180 (1,143 built) and while basically similar differed by having the 186-kW (250-hp) O-540-A1A engine; this variant was built to a total of 2,537. This was followed in 1964 by the **PA-24-260** Comanche with a 194-kW (260-hp) version of the O-540 engine, and this model was used by the UK's Sheila Scott between 18 May and 20 June 1966 to establish a new round-the-world class speed record, covering a distance of 46759 km (29,055 miles).

Last of the single-engine Comanches was the **PA-24T-260 Turbo**

Comanche which introduced an IO-540 engine with a Rayjay turbocharger to give considerably improved performance, and when production of the PA-24-260s ended in 1973 a total of 1,028 had been built, giving a Comanche grand total of 4,708.

Specification
PA-24T-260 Turbo Comanche
Type: four-seat cabin monoplane
Powerplant: one 194-kW (260-hp) Avco Lycoming IO-540 flat-six turbocharged piston engine
Performance: maximum speed

A classic among private aircraft, the Comanche offered a low purchase price with high performance and comfort.

389 km/h (242 mph) at optimum altitude; service ceiling 7620 m (25,000 ft); maximum range with maximum fuel 2398 km (1,490 miles)
Weights: empty 859 kg (1,894 lb); maximum take-off 1451 kg (3,200 lb)
Dimensions: span 10.97 m (36 ft 0 in); length 7.62 m (25 ft 0 in); height 2.29 m (7 ft 6 in); wing area 16.54 m² (178.0 sq ft)

Piper PA-25 Pawnee

The rapid expansion of Piper's operations in the 1950s meant that new facilities were soon required, and in 1957 the company opened a new aircraft development centre at Vero Beach, Florida, to be responsible for design, development and testing of new projects. The Vero Beach facility began its operations on a new specialised agricultural aircraft, designated **Piper PA-25 Pawnee**, for experience with the PA-18A configured for agricultural use had shown the active market for this category of aeroplane. A braced low-wing monoplane with fixed tailwheel landing gear, the PA-25 was powered initially by a 112-kW (150-hp) Avco Lycoming O-320 flat-four engine, and this version was later redesignated **PA-25-150 Pawnee**. It had a glass-fibre chemical hopper installed forward of the cockpit, this having a volume of

The Pawnee was markedly different to other Piper products.

0.57 m³ (20 cu ft), and the dust/spray distribution system was the same as that which had been proven on the PA-18A. Advanced design features were intended to reduce the likelihood of an accident and to give the pilot a far better chance of survival in a crash; thus he was given a high sitting position to ensure an excellent all-round view, above average strength seat restraints, and a specially designed structure that was installed to leave the cockpit substantially undamaged in the usual type of low-speed crash associated with agricultural dusting/spraying oprations. Such attention to detail resulted in good sales figures, the PA-25-150 soon followed by the improved **PA-25-235** with structu-

ral strengthening, a larger chemical hopper and a 175-kW (235-hp) Avco Lycoming O-540-B2B5 engine, or optional 194-kW (260-hp) O-540-E. When production of the Pawnee ended in early 1982 approximately 5,000 had been built.

Specification
Piper PA-25-235 Pawnee
Type: single-seat agricultural aircraft
Powerplant: one 175-kW (235-hp) Avco Lycoming O-540-B flat-six piston engine

Performance: maximum cruising speed, duster 161 km/h (100 mph) or sprayer 169 km/h (105 mph); range with maximum fuel, duster 410 km (255 miles) or sprayer 435 km (270 miles)
Weights: empty basic 725 kg (1,598 lb); maximum take-off 1315 kg (2,900 lb)
Dimensions: span 11.02 m (36 ft 2 in); length 7.73 m (24 ft 8½ in); height 2.21 m (7 ft 3 in); wing area 17.00 m² (183.0 sq ft)

Piper PA-28 Cherokee and derivatives

It is unlikely that when Piper first flew the prototype of the four-seat **Piper PA-28-150 Cherokee** sporting/training monoplane on 14 January 1960 that the company could have anticipated the almost infinite variety of this basic design that was to result, or that its production would still be continuing in 1990s. The type started life as a cantilever low-wing monoplane of all-metal construc-

tion with fixed tricycle landing gear and four-seat accommodation in an enclosed cabin, and with power provided by a 112-kW (150-hp) Avco Lycoming O-320, or 119-kW (160-hp) O-320-B2B flat-four engine in the **PA-28-160 Cherokee**. The first production Cherokee was flown on 10 February 1961, and the type was available from the beginning in the same Standard, Custom, Super Custom and

AutoFlite models as mentioned for the PA-24 Cherokee entry, and a similar scheme of optional models with different standards of equipment continues to this day. The **PA-28-180 Cherokee** was introduced for 1962 with a 134-kW (180-hp) O-320-A2A engine, and in 1963 it was followed by the **PA-28-235** which had structural strengthening and installation of a 175-kW (235-hp)

Avco Lycoming O-540-B2B5 flat-six engine for operation at a higher gross weight. In the following year the range was expanded in the opposite direction when the two-seat **PA-28-140 Cherokee** became available with the 104-kW (140-hp) O-320-A2B flat-four engine, but with introduction of the **PA-28-180R Cherokee Arrow** on 19 June 1967 came a significant change, with retractable tricycle landing gear, fuel-injection engine and a constant-speed propeller as standard; at this time production of the PA-28-150 and PA-28-160 versions came to an end. In 1969 Piper made available an optional **PA-28-200R Cherokee Arrow** with a 149-kW (200-hp) IO-360-C1C engine, and in 1971 new models of the PA-28-140 appeared as the **Cherokee Flite Liner**, a two-seat trainer for use by Piper-sponsored training schools, and the **Cherokee Cruiser 2 Plus 2**, which was a de luxe two/four-seat version which in the following year became the standard production model. For 1973 the long-standing PA-28-180 was renamed as the **Cherokee Challenger**, with slight increases in wing span and fuselage length, and improved interior and standards of equipment; at the same time similar changes were introduced on the PA-28-235 which was renamed as the **Cherokee Charger**. In 1974 there came a number of changes in the Cherokee line, the Cherokee 2 Plus 2 being renamed **Cherokee Cruiser**, the Cherokee Challenger the **Cherokee Archer**, and the PA-28-235 the **Cherokee Pathfinder**. At the same time a new member of the family was introduced, the **PA-28-151 Cherokee Warrior** which, powered by a 112-kW (150-hp) O-320-E3D engine, was basically similar to the Archer except for having a completely new wing of increased span. In 1977 Piper ended production of the Cherokee Cruiser and Cherokee Pathfinder, but introduced at the same time the **PA-28-236 Dakota** which, generally similar to the Archer, was powered by the 175-kW (235-hp) O-540-J3A5D flat-six engine and had the new wing of increased span; in 1978 a version of this aircraft with a 149-kW (200-hp) Continental TSIO-360-FB turbocharged engine

Development of the basic PA-28 airframe resulted in the Piper PA-28R Arrow IV with upgraded powerplant and retractable landing gear.

became available as the **PA-28-201T Turbo Dakota**, but only limited demand meant that its production ended in 1980. In this same year, Piper developed to meet the requirements of the Chilean air force a tandem two-seat trainer based on the Cherokee series. Designated **PA-28R-300 Pillan** (devil) in prototype form, this has retractable tricycle landing gear and is powered by the 224-kW (300-hp) Avco Lycoming AEIO-540-H1K5 engine. Following initial construction by assembly, Industria Aeronáutica de Chile was expected to be manufacturing some 80 per cent of this aircraft, designated **T-35** by the Chilean air force, by the end of 1983.

Production of the Cherokee family continued in the 1980s with the introduction of the **PA-28-161 Warrior II** with a 119-kW (160-hp) Avco Lycoming O-320-D3G engine, alongside the **CPA-28-181 Archer II** with a 134-kW (180-hp) Avco Lycoming O-360-A4M. At the higher performance end of the scale the **PA-28RT-201T Turbo Arrow IV** incorporated the same powerplant as used in the Turbo Dakota. EMBRAER also continued to build aircraft under licence in Brazil. Financial problems and the crisis of product liability acted as a severe brake on sales, but a trickle of late model aircraft continue to be built. By January 1991 2,985 PA-28-161s had been sold along with 9,894 Cherokee 180/Archers IIs, and small numbers of Arrows and Turbo Arrows.

Specification
Piper PA-28RT-201T Turbo Arrow IV
Powerplant: one 149-kW (200-hp) Teledyne Continental TSIO-360-FB flat-six turbocharged piston engine

The Cherokee family was one of the greatest light planes of all time, combining good performance with many options.

Performance: maximum speed 330 km/h (205 mph); operational ceiling 6095 m (20,000 ft); maximum range 1665 km (1,035 miles)
Weights: empty 767 kg (1,692 lb); maximum take-off 1315 kg (2,900 lb)
Dimensions: span 10.80 m (35 ft 5 in); length 8.33 m (27 ft 3¾ in); height 2.52 m (8 ft 3¼ in); wing area 15.79 m² (170.0 sq ft)

The ultimate development of the Cherokee is Chile's ENAER T-35 Pillan military trainer, which is now offered in both piston- (as shown below) and turboprop-powered versions.

Piper PA-30 Twin Comanche

When the decision was made to end production of the Piper PA-23 Apache, the company introduced a new twin-engine four-seat cabin monoplane under the designation **Piper PA-30 Twin Comanche**, a cantilver low-wing monoplane with retractable tricycle landing gear and powered by two 119-kW (160-hp) Avco Lycoming IO-320-B flat-four engines. First flown in production form on 3 May 1963, one of these aircraft was used by Max Conrad to establish a new world class distance record when he flew non-stop from Cape Town, South Africa, to St Petersburg, Florida, during 24-26 December 1964. The distance of 12,678.83 km (7,878.26 miles) remained a record in its class in 1993. The PA-30 was superseded in 1965 by an improved four/six-seat **PA-30B-160 Twin Comanche**, and made available also at the same time was the **PA-30B**

Turbo Twin Comanche with Rayjay-turbocharged IO-320-C1A engines, but both were replaced in 1970 by generally similar versions which introduced a powerplant with counter-rotating propellers. Designated **PA-39 Twin Comanche C/R** and **PA-39 Turbo Twin Comanche C/R**, manufacture of these two models ended in 1972, when total production of all versions amounted to 2,142.

Specification
Piper PA-39 Twin Comanche C/R
Type: four/six-seat cabin monoplane
Powerplant: two 119-kW (160-hp) Avco Lycoming IO-320-B1A flat-four piston engines with counter-rotating propellers
Performance: maximum speed 330 km/h (205 mph) at sea level; service ceiling 6095 m (20,000 ft);

maximum range 1931 km (1,200 miles)
Weights: empty 1030 kg (2,270 lb); maximum take-off 1690 kg (3,725 lb)
Dimensions: span over tiptanks 11.21 m (36 ft 9½ in); length 7.67 m (25 ft 2 in); height 2.51 m (8 ft 3 in)

Following on from the Apache, the Piper Twin Comanche, in its several forms, offered useful accommodation, good performance and the reliability of a twin-engined layout.

Piper PA-31 Navajo and derivatives

On 30 September 1964 Piper flew the prototype of a new twin-engine executive aircraft which was then the largest built by the company. Identified at first as the **Piper PA-31 Inca**, the aircraft had been redesignated as the **PA-31 Navajo** when deliveries began on 17 April 1967. A six/eight-seat corporate/commuter transport of cantilever low-wing monoplane configuration with retractable tricycle landing gear, it was powered by two 224-kW (300-hp) Avco Lycoming IO-540-K flat-six engines, and was available in optional Standard, Commuter and Executive versions with differing interior layouts. Made available at the same time was the optional **PA-31T Turbo Navajo**, which differed only by having two 231-kW (310-hp) TIO-540-A turbocharged engines, and the range was extended in 1970 by introduction of the **PA-PA-31P Pressurized Navajo** with a fail-safe fuselage structure in the pressurised section and two 317-kW (425-hp) Avco Lycoming TIGO-541-E1A engines. Production of the PA-31 Navajo ended during 1972 and at the same time the company introduced for 1973 the **PA-31-350 Navajo Chieftain** which, by comparison with its predecessor, had the fuselage lengthened by 0.61 m (2 ft 0 in) and was powered by two 261-kW (350-hp) TIO-540-J2BD turbocharged engines driving counter-rotating propellers. A significant advance in the Navajo family came on 22 October 1973 when Piper flew the first production example of the **PA-31T Cheyenne**, which combined an airframe generally similar to that of the Pressurized Navajo with two 462-ekW (620-ehp) Pratt & Whitney Aircraft of Canada PT6A-28 turboprop engines. In the following year an additional model of the Turbo Navajo was made available, the **PA-31-325 Turbo Navajo C/R**, which introduced a 242-kW (325-hp) version of the counter-

rotating engines installed in the Chieftain. Production of the PA-31P Pressurized Navajo ended during 1977, at which time a total of 248 had been built, but at the same time the company introduced a new version of the Cheyenne, the **PA-31T-1 Cheyenne I**, the original Cheyenne then becoming redesignated **PA-31T Cheyenne II**. Deliveries of the new Cheyenne I, which differed primarily from its predecessor by having 373-kW (500-shp) Pratt & Whitney Aircraft of Canada PT6A-11 turboprop engines, began towards the end of April 1978. The Cheyenne range was extended for 1981 by introduction of the **PA-31T-Cheyenne IIXL**, with the fuselage lengthened by 0.61 m (2 ft) and 559-kW (750-shp) Pratt & Whitney Aircraft of Canada PT6A-135 engines flat-rated to 462 kW (620 shp). In 1982 production of the PA-31 Navajo terminated after 1,317 had been built. Later production versions of the Navajo family include the **PA-31-325 Navajo C/R, PA-31-350 Chieftain** and the PA-31T-1 Cheyenne I, PA-31T Cheyenne II and PA-31T-2 Cheyenne IIXL. However, the loss of the Navajo was compensated for in 1983 by introduction of the

Piper PA-31-350 Najavo Chieftain of Chaparral Airlines, USA.

PA-31P-350 Mojave, which basically combined the airframe of the Cheyenne II with the powerplant of the PA-315-350 Chieftain.

Specification
Piper PA-31-350 Chieftain
Type: six/eight-seat corporate/commuter transport
Powerplant: two 261-kW (350-hp) Avco Lycoming TIO-540-J2BD turbocharged and counter-rotating flat-six piston engines
Performance: maximum speed

The PA-31 Najavo C/R is basically similar to the standard Navajo apart from using counter-rotating engines.

428 km/h (266 mph); certificated altitude 7315 m (24,000 ft); maximum range 2388 km (1,484 miles)
Weights: empty 1915 kg (4,221 lb); maximum take-off 3175 kg (7,000 lb)
Dimensions: span 12.40 m (40 ft 8 in); length 10.55 m (34 ft 7½ in); height 3.96 m (13 ft 0 in); wing area 21.27 m² (229.0 sq ft)

Piper PA-32-260-6 Cherokee Six and derivatives

On 6 December 1963 Piper flew the prototype of a six-seat version of the PA-28 Cherokee, retaining the same general configuration but differing primarily by having a slight increase in wing span, the fuselage lengthened by 1.35 m (4 ft 5 in), and the installation of the 194-kW (260-hp) Avco Lycoming O-540-E4B5 flat-six engine. Designated **Piper PA-32-260-6 Cherokee Six**, it was available initially in Standard, Custom, Executive and Sportsman versions with differing standards of installed equipment. By 1966 the company designation had changed to **PA-32-260** and the Cherokee Six was then available as an optional six/seven-seat aircraft and, as the **PA-32-300**, with an optional 224-kW (300-hp) IO-540-K engine. In 1971 Piper restyled the name to **Cherokee SIX**, but apart from annual product improvement, there were no changes until 1975 when a new version designated **PA-32R-300 Cherokee Lance** entered production to complement the Cherokee SIX, differing by introduction of a new fuselage structure and retractable tricycle landing gear. The 1978 version of the Lance had the conventional tail unit replaced by a T-tail, the designation then changing to **PA-32RT-300 Lance II** and, at the same time, a model with 224-kW (300-hp) TIO-540-S1AD turbocharged engines became available under the designation **PA-32RT-300T Turbo Lance II**. Production of PA-32-260 Cherokee SIX ended in late 1978, the remaining version then being redesignated **PA-32-300 SIX 300**, but in

the following year this also disappeared, together with the Lance II and Turbo Lance II. These aircraft were superseded by the six/seven-seat **PA-32-301 Saratoga** (the basic member of the new related family) which had an increased-span wing, reversion to a conventional tail unit, fixed tricycle landing gear, and a 224-kW (300-hp) IO-540-K1G5D engine driving a constant-speed propeller. Made available simultaneously was the generally similar **PA-32-301T Turbo Saratoga**, which had a turbocharged version of the same engine, and the corresponding **PA-32R-301 Saratoga SP** and **PA-32R-301T Turbo Saratoga SP** which differed by having retractable tricycle landing gear. Only very low volume production continued into the early 1990s.

Specification
Piper PA-32-301T Turbo Saratoga
Type: six/seven-seat cabin monoplane
Powerplant: one 224-kW (300-hp) Avco Lycoming TIO-540-S1AD turbocharged flat-six piston engine
Performance: maximum speed 330 km/h (205 mph); certificated ceiling 6095 m (20,000 ft); maximum range 1593 km (990 miles)
Weights: empty 906 kg (1,998 lb); maximum take-off 1097 kg (3,600 lb)
Dimensions: span 11.02 m (36 ft 2 in); length 8.59 m (28 ft 2 in); height 2.49 m (8 ft 2 in); wing area 16.56 m² (178.30 sq ft)

Piper PA-32RT Turbo Lance II.

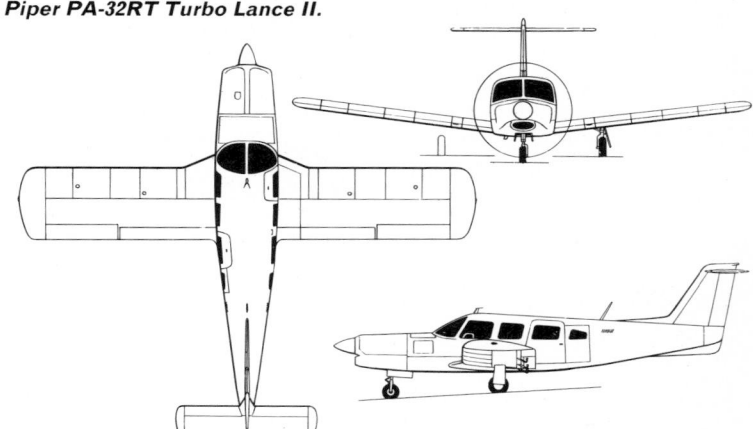

The PA-32 series has undergone a bewildering series of designation changes over the years. This is an early PA-32 Cherokee Six.

Piper PA-34 Seneca

For 1972 Piper introduced the six/seven-seat **Piper PA-34 Seneca** which, basically, was a twin-engine version of the Cherokee SIX with retractable tricycle landing gear, a new fuselage structure and power provided by two 149-kW (200-hp) Avco Lycoming IO-360 flat-four engines. For 1975 149-kW (200-hp) Continental TSIO-360-E turbocharged and counter-rotating engines were introduced and the landing gear was strengthened for operation at higher gross weight, the designation then changing to **PA-34-200T Seneca II**. In 1982 the Seneca II was superseded by an improved **PA-34-220T Seneca III**, and this remains the current production version in 1984. It differs from its immediate predecessor by having more powerful Continental TSIO-360-KB turbocharged and counter-rotating flat-six piston engines. During 1976-77 Piper signed an agreement with the Polish foreign trade association Pezetel under which P.Z.L. Mielec will assemble/manufacture the Seneca for sale in eastern Europe. Designated in Poland as the **P.Z.L. Mielec M-20 Mewa** (gull), the first Polish-built prototype was flown on 25 July 1979. Current production version is the M-20 03 one of the very few light-twins on the market. A total of 4,464 Seneca were delivered by 1 January 1991.

Specification
Piper PA-34-220T Seneca III
Type: six/seven-seat cabin monoplane
Powerplant: two 164-kW (220-hp) Continental TSIO-360-KB
Performance: maximum speed at optimum altitude 364 km/h (226 mph); certificated ceiling 7620 m (25,000 ft);

maximum range 1667 km (1,036 miles)
Weights: empty 1294 kg (2,852 lb); maximum take-off 2155 kg (4,750 lb)
Dimensions: span 11.86 m (38 ft 10¾ in); length 8.72 m (28 ft 7½ in); height 3.02 m (9 ft 10¾ in)

Showing a similarity to the PA-32 series, the Piper Seneca offered seven-seat accommodation, and is seen here in the form of the Seneca III. The type is now licence-built by P.Z.L. and is still an affordable modern light-twin aircraft.

Piper PA-36 Pawnee Brave

Piper announced in 1972 a completely new version of the PA-25 Pawnee agricultural aircraft which introduced a more powerful Continental Tiara 6-285 flat-six engine of 213 kW (285 hp), a new cantilever wing, new safety features, filtration of the air entering the pilot's ventilated and heated cockpit, and a larger standard chemical hopper of 0.85-m³ (30-cu ft) or, optionally, 1.08-m³ (38-cu ft) capacity. Designated **Piper PA-36 Pawnee Brave**, the new model began to enter service in 1973, and in 1977 an additional version with a 224-kW (300-hp) Avco Lycoming IO-540-K1G5 engine became available, the designations of these two aircraft then becoming **PA-36 Pawnee Brave 285** and **PA-36 Pawnee Brave 300**. In 1978 this latter aircraft became the standard model, a new **PA-36 Pawnee Brave 375** being introduced with a 280-kW (375-hp) Avco Lycoming IO-720-D1CD

flat-eight engine, and equipped with the larger of the two chemical hoppers as standard. These were to remain in production with Piper until rights for both versions of the PA-36 were acquired by WTA Inc. in 1981. This latter company was marketing this agricultural aircraft in two versions, the version with the 280-kW (375-hp) engine now being the basic model and redesignated **PA-36 New Brave 375**. It was available optionally with a 298-kW (400-hp) IO-720-D1C engine under the designation **PA-36 New Brave 400**.

Specification
PA-36 Pawnee Brave 300
Type: single-seat agricultural aircraft
Powerplant: one 224-kW (300-hp) Avco Lycoming IO-540-K1G5 flat-six piston engine
Performance: maximum cruising speed 229 km/h (142 mph); service

Piper PA-36 Pawnee Brave

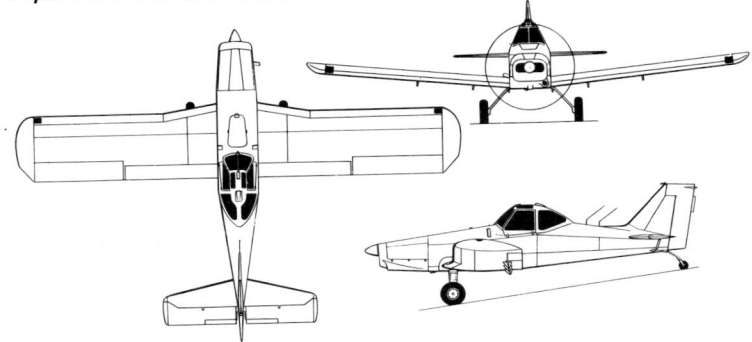

ceiling 1950 m (6,400 ft): range 740 km (460 miles)
Weights: empty equipped 989 kg (2,180 lb); maximum take-off 1996 kg (4,400 lb)

Dimensions: span 11.89 m (39 ft 0 in); length 8.34 m (27 ft 4¼ in); height 2.29 m (7 ft 6 in); wing area 20.96 m² (225.65 sq ft)

Piper PA-38-112 Tomahawk

Following certification on 20 December 1977, Piper introduced for 1978 a completely new two-seat trainer/utility aircraft which it designated **Piper PA-38-112 Tomahawk**. A cantilever low-wing monoplane with fixed tricycle landing gear, a T-tail, and side-by-side enclosed accommodation, it was powered by an Avco Lycoming O-235-L2C engine. Improvements introduced as standard in 1982 resulted in redesignation as the **PA-38-112 Tomahawk II**, but because of economic conditions production was suspended at the end of 1982, at which time 2,497 had been built. Piper hoped that it would be possible to

resume production during 1984. This was not the case as the Tomahawk was one of the types most affected by the product liability laws and was already struggling to find a market.

Specification
Piper PA-38-112 Tomahawk II
Type: two-seat trainer/utility aircraft
Powerplant: one 84-kW (112-hp) Avco Lycoming flat-four piston engine
Performance: maximum speed 203 km/h (126 mph) at sea level; service ceiling 3960 m (13,000 ft);

maximum range 867 km (539 miles)
Weights: empty 512 kg (1,128 lb); maximum take-off 757 kg (1,670 lb)
Dimensions: span 10.36 m (34 ft 0 in); length 7.04 m (23 ft 1½ in); height 2.76 m (9 ft 0¾ in); wing area 11.58 m² (124.70 sq ft)

Designed specifically for pilot training, the Piper PA-38 Tomahawk is a safe yet tractable side-by-side two-seater and was widely sold to both Piper's and other flying schools.

Piper PA-42 Cheyenne III

On 30 June 1980 Piper began production deliveries of a new version of the Cheyenne range of twin turboprop aircraft. Intended for use as a six/11-seat corporate or commuter transport, this **Cheyenne III** differs considerably from its predecessors, a fact reflected in the changed company designation **Piper PA-42**. It has a wing of increased span, lengthened fuselage, a T-tail, and more powerful Pratt & Whitney Aircraft of Canada PT6A turboprop engines installed in lengthened nacelles. The Cheyenne III remains as a current production model, being complemented by the **Cheyenne IIIA** which differs primarily by having 634-kW (850-hp) PT6A-61 turboprop engines flat-rated at 537 kW (720 hp) and offering performance improvements. In addition to the Cheyenne III, Piper was involved in the certification programme of a new **Cheyenne IV** during 1983, with two 1,227-kW (1,645-shp) Garrett TPE331-14A/14B counter-rotating turboprop engines, each of them flat-rated at 746 kW (1,000 shp). Deliveries of the Cheyenne IV began in the early summer of 1984. It was one of the fastest pro-

Piper PA-42 Cheyenne III

peller light twins, at over 644 km/h (400 mph).

The Cheyenne is one of the very few Piper products to remain in volume production after the company's financial reorganisation in 1991/92. Current versions on offer include the Cheyenne IIIA of which 59 had been delivered by early 1993. Nine Cheyenne IIIs delivered to the US Drug Enforcement Administration, fitted with AN/APG-66 radar and a ventral FLIR, are used for day- and night-time surveillance missions. They are

known as **Customs High Endurance Tracker (CHET)** aircraft. Cheyenne IIIs are joined at the Lock Haven production line by the **PA-42-1000 Cheyenne 400**. Originally the Cheyenne IV, it later became the Cheyenne 400LS. Deliveries total 43.

Specification
Piper PA-42-Cheyenne III
Type: six/11-seat corporate/commuter transport
Powerplant: two 537-kW (720-shp) Pratt & Whitney Aircraft of Canada PT6A-41 turboprops
Performance: maximum speed 549 km/h (341 mph); service ceiling 9755 m (32,000 ft); maximum range 4150 km (2,579 miles)
Weights: empty 2898 kg (6,389 lb); maximum take-off 5080 kg (11,200 lb)
Dimensions: span over tiptanks 14.53 m (47 ft 8 in); length 13.23 m (43 ft 4¾ in); height 4.50 m (14 ft 9 in); wing area 27.22 m² (293.0 sq ft)

Piper PA-44-180 Seminole

On 21 February 1978 Piper announced a new low-cost twin-engined four-seat cabin monoplane designated **Piper PA-44-180 Seminole**. A cantilever low-wing monoplane with a T-Tail, retractable tricycle landing gear and power provided by two Avco Lycoming O-360-E1AD counter-rotating engines, the Seminole was complemented on 24 April 1980 by a turbocharged version designated **PA-44-180T Turbo Seminole** with TO-360-E1AD engines. However, production of both versions was terminated at the end of 1982, when a combined total of 431 had been built. Production was restarted in 1988 and 29 were delivered over the next three years.

Combining low costs and modern looks, the PA-44 Seminole was produced in normally aspirated and turbocharged versions.

Specification
Piper PA-44-180T Turbo Seminole
Type: four-seat cabin monoplane
Powerplant: two 134-kW (180-hp) Avco Lycoming TO-360-E1AD turbocharged and counter-rotating flat-four piston engines
Performance: maximum speed at optimum altitude 364 km/h (226 mph); certificated ceiling 6095 m (20,000 ft); maximum range 1519 km (944 miles)
Weights: empty 1116 kg (2,461 lb); maximum take-off 1780 kg (3,925 lb)
Dimensions: span 11.77 m (38 ft 7¼ in); length 8.41 m (27 ft 7¼ in); height 2.59 m (8 ft 6 in)

Piper PA-46 Malibu

Piper announced in late 1982 the intention to introduce in late 1983 a new aircraft which it claimed to be the world's first cabin-class pressurised aircraft with a single piston engine. Designated **Piper PA-46-310P Malibu**, the aircraft is of cantilever low-wing monoplane configuration with retractable tricycle landing gear and powerplant comprising a Teledyne Continental TSIO-520-BE turbocharged engine, the pressurised cabin providing accommodation for a pilot and five passengers.

Certification of the original PA-46-310P was achieved in September 1983 and deliveries commenced the following November. Four hundred and two of this version were built before it was superseded by the **PA-46-350P Malibu**

The Malibu opened up the market for privately owned pressurised singles and has been followed by the TBM 700 and others.

Mirage. By spring 1991 Piper had orders for over 100 of this version but, after several aircraft broke up in adverse weather conditions, the FAA revoked its IMC certification and began a Special Certification Review. Piper worked hard to clear the design's reputation and by February 1992 the Malibu was returned to full operations.

Specification
Piper PA-46-350P Malibu Mirage
Powerplant: one 261-kW (350-hp) Textron Lycoming TIO-540-AE2A

turbocharged and intercooled flat-six engine
Performance: maximum cruising speed 417 km/h (259 mph); service ceiling 7625 m (25,000 ft); range with maximum fuel 2687 km (1,669 miles)
Weights: empty 1265 kg (2,790 lb); maximum take-off weight 1950 kg (4,300 lb)
Dimensions: span 13.11 m (43 ft); length 8.66 m (28 ft 4¾ in); height 3.44 m (11 ft 3½ in)

Piper T-1020 and T-1040

In mid-1981 Piper announced the formation of an Airline Division to provide support to commuter airlines using the Piper PA-31-350 Chieftain on its services and to make available to them specially configured commuter versions of the Chieftain and the PA-31 Cheyenne. Work on the first of these, the **Piper T-1040**, began on 25 March 1980, its alternative **PA-31T-3** designation showing its direct relationship to the Cheyenne. To speed the availability of such an aircraft it combined the wings and landing gear of

the Cheyenne IIXL, fuselage of the Chieftain and the tail unit and powerplant of the Cheyenne I. The first pre-production example was flown on 17 July 1981 and deliveries to commuter airlines began in May 1982. Brief details were released in 1983 of a projected **T-1050** with a fuselage lengthened by 3.51 m (11 ft 6 in) to provide an aircraft suitable for use as a cargo carrier.

The **T-1020 (PA-31-350)**, on which work began in April 1981, is basically a version of the Chieftain which has been

modified specifically for a commuter role, having such items as the doors and landing gear redesigned to withstand the heavy usage of such operation. The prototype was flown for the first time on 25 September 1981, and deliveries to airlines began soon after the receipt of certification. Production ended after 21 T-1020s had been delivered.

Specification
Piper (PA-31T-3) T-1040
Type: 11-seat commuter transport

Powerplant: two 373-kW (500-shp) Pratt & Whitney Aircraft of Canada PT6A-11 turboprops
Performance: maximum speed 451 km/h (280 mph); service ceiling 7315 m (24,000 ft); range with maximum payload 1093 km (679 miles)
Weights: empty 2177 kg (4,800 lb); maximum take-off weight 4082 kg (9,000 lb)
Dimensions: span 12.52 m (41 ft 1 in); length 11.18 m (36 ft 8 in); height 3.96 m (13 ft 0 in)

Pitcairn biplanes

Before turning to the development and production of autogyros, Pitcairn Aircraft Inc., founded in Pennsylvania by Harold Pitcairn, built a series of biplanes designed by Agnew Larsen. First of the family was the **Pitcairn PA-1 Fleetwing**, an unequal span biplane powered by a 119-kW (160-hp) Curtiss C-6 engine which provided accommodation for five in three separate cockpits. Introduced in late 1925, the Fleetwing was followed by the three-seat **PA-2 Arrow** sesquiplane which, with optional 67-kW (90-hp) OX-5 or the Curtiss C-6 engine, was intended for participation in different classes of air races. The **PA-3 Orowing** was also a three-seater with similar engines, but reverted to biplane configuration, being followed in 1927 by the three-seat **PA-4 Fleetwing 2** biplane with an OX-5 engine. In the same year Pitcairn introduced the **PA-5 Mailwing** which, intended as a single-seat cargo or mail carrier, had a cargo/mail hold with a capacity of 227 kg (500 lb) instead of a conventional forward cockpit, the pilot being aft. Powered by a 164-kW (220-hp) Wright J-5 radial, standard Mailwings were complemented by a small number of a generally similar **Sport Mailwing** model, which had conventional three-seat accommodation. The two versions

were built to a combined total of about 18 before introduction of the generally similar **PA-6 Super Mailwing** in 1928, which differed by having an increased capacity cargo/mail hold, and which was available also in a three-seat **PA-6 Super Sport Mailwing** version for the private pilot. Following development via a **PA-6B** prototype, which introduced a refined fuselage and engine cowling to reduce drag, Pitcairn introduced the mail/cargo-carrying **PA-7M Super Mailwing** and three-seat **PA-7S Super Sport Mailwing** in 1929. These production aircraft, of which more than 20 were built, differed by not having the low-drag cowling, but introduced a new Wright seven-cylinder radial engine. Last of the series, introduced in late 1930 before Pitcairn became involved in the development of autogyros, was the **PA-8M Super Mailwing** which, powered by a 224-kW (300-hp) Wright R-975 nine-cylinder radial, had a cargo/mail hold almost double the capacity of the original Mailwing. The prototype PA-8M was later converted to serve as the prototype of a **PA-8S Super Sport Mailwing**, but no production examples were built and, in fact, only about six PA-8Ms were manufactured, sales being adversely

affected by the growing economic depression of the early 1930s.

Specification
Pitcairn PA-7M Super Mailwing
Type: light cargo/mail transport
Powerplant: one 168-kW (225-hp) Wright J-6 radial piston engine
Performance: maximum speed 217 km/h (135 mph); service ceiling 4875 m (16,000 ft); range 837 km (520 miles)
Weights: empty 826 kg (1,821 lb); maximum take-off 1384 kg (3,050 lb)

Fitted with underwing landing light, the Pitcairn Mailwing series was widely used for nocturnal mail flights within the lighted airway system. Keys to its first-rate serviceability were the wide-track landing gear with large tyres, and also the reliable Wright radial engine.

Dimensions: span 10.06 m (33 ft 0 in); length 7.24 m (23 ft 9 in); height 2.90 m (9 ft 6 in); wing area 22.62 m² (243.50 sq ft)

Pitcairn (Cierva) autogyros

US aircraft manufacturer Harold Pitcairn acquired from the British Cierva Autogiro Company in late 1928 a single example of the Cierva C.8L Mk IV and a manufacturing licence. This aircraft, designated C.8W, made the first flight in the USA of an aircraft in this category during January 1929, and Harold Pitcairn formed the Pitcairn-Cierva Autogiro Company in Pennsylvania to continue manufacture and development.

The first Pitcairn development C.8W was a preliminary **Pitcairn PCA-1**, which was followed by the three-seat **PCA-2**, its fixed wings having upturned tips to enhance stability, and power being provided by a 224-kW (300-hp) Wright R-975 radial engine mounted conventionally in the nose to drive a tractor propeller. Its 13.72-m (45-ft) diameter four-blade rotor was mounted on a pylon above the forward fuselage. The interest created in the USA by this first autogyro brought some sales to companies who used the type as an advertising medium, the fuselage emblazoned with the company's name, and among the first to use a PCA-2 to establish new records was the renowned Amelia Earhart, setting a height record of 5615 m (18,415 ft) on 8 April 1931. Three were acquired for evaluation by the US Navy under the designation **XOP-1**. About 20 PCA-2s were built, the type being followed by the two-seat **PAA-1** which was somewhat smaller, was powered by a 93-kW

The Pitcairn PA-39 was a pure autogyro with a direct control three-bladed rotor and without auxiliary wings.

(125-hp) Kinner B5 radial engine, and was of lighter weight construction than the PCA-2 as it was intended more specifically for the private owner. Generally similar to the PAA-1 and with the same powerplant, the **PA-20** gained a slight performance improvement by structural refinement. Related autogyros in this lightweight two-seat category included the **PC-2-30** with an 82-kW (110-hp) Warner Scarab radial, and the **PAA-2** with an 89-kW (120-hp) Martin-Chevrolair inline engine.

Experience with these lower-powered autogyros showed that they presented more handling difficulties for a pilot of only limited experience, and this resulted in development of the **PA-18** with structural refinements and a 119-kW (160-hp) Kinner R5 radial engine. The additional power gave considerably better handling characteristics in the low-speed sector of the flight envelope but, of course, there was only a limited demand for these unconventional aircraft and PA-18 production totalled about 20. However, experience with the PA-18 suggested that earlier versions would benefit by use of this powerplant, leading to an airframe basically the same as that of the PAA-1 which, modified to

accept the Kinner R5 engine, was designated **PA-24**. This modification to PA-24 standard could be made to PAA-1 and PA-20 autogyros.

Developments of the higher-powered PCA-2 included the similar PCA-3, which differed by having a 224-kW (300-hp) Pratt & Whitney Wasp Junior engine, the **PA-21** with a 313-kW (420-hp) Wright engine, and the more developed **PA-34** with a direct-control three-blade rotor, making it possible to dispense with the fixed wing. A similar rotor system was used in the experimental two-seat enclosed cabin **PA-22**, powered by a 56-kW (75-hp) Pobjoy engine, which was also without a fixed wing. However, a redesigned fixed wing with considerable dihedral was used in conjunction with the original four-blade rotor in the **PA-19**, a four/five-seat cabin autogyro powered by a 313-kW (420-hp)

Wright R-975-E2 engine. Four or five of these aircraft were built before, in 1934, economic conditions forced the Pitcairn company to suspend the production of autogyros.

Specification
Pitcairn PAA-1
Type: two-seat autogyro
Powerplant: one 93-kW (125-hp) Kinner B5 radial piston engine
Performance: maximum speed 145 km/h (90 mph); service ceiling 3050 m (10,000 ft); range 402 km (250 miles)
Weights: empty 534 kg (1,178 lb); maximum take-off 794 kg (1,750 lb)
Dimensions: rotor diameter 11.28 m (37 ft 0 in); fixed-wing span 6.93 m (22 ft 9 in); fuselage length 5.66 m (18 ft 7 in); height 3.35 m (11 ft 0 in); rotor disc area 99.89 m² (1,075 sq ft)

Pitts S-1 and S-2

There can be few aviation enthusiasts unaware of the superb aerobatic qualities of the single- and two-seat biplanes designed by Curtis Pitts in the USA. The first **Pitts 190 Special** was built in 1947 for US aerobatic display pilot Betty Skelton, but after manufacturing a comparatively small number of aircraft Curtis Pitts made plans available to amateurs who had the ability, patience and time to construct an aircraft for their own requirements. In late 1976 he sold all sales and production rights and in early 1977 a new company, Pitts Aerobatics, was formed at Afton, Wyoming to continue the provision of plans and kits to amateur constructors, but also to manufacture these aircraft for individuals who wished to acquire a factory-built aircraft.

Current production versions include the **Pitts S-1S Special**, a single-seat biplane with fixed tailwheel landing gear which is powered by a 134-kW (180-hp) Avco Lycoming IO-360-B4A flat-four

Tricky to fly but ultimately rewarding for the skilled pilot, the Pitts S-2S Special is one of the finest aerobatic mounts ever built.

engine, and which has inverted fuel and oil systems incorporated as standard. It has been complemented since 1981 by the single-seat **S-1T Special** which is powered by a 149-kW (200-hp) Avco Lycoming AEIO-360-A1E engine driving a constant-speed propeller. A slightly larger two-seat version with an engine of similar power is available as the **S-2A Special**, and also the two-seat **S-2B** which, with an Avco Lycoming AEIO-540 flat-six engine of 194 kW (260 hp) is capable of unlimited aerobatics with two up. Last of the current versions is the **Pitts S-2S** which, generally similar to the S-2A, combines a slightly shortened single-seat fuselage with the powerplant of the S-2B.

Specification
Pitts S-2A Special
Type: two-seat aerobatic aircraft
Powerplant: one 149-kW (200-hp) Avco Lycoming IO-360-A1A flat-four piston engine
Performance: maximum speed 253 km/h (157 mph); service ceiling 6125 m (20,100 ft); range with maximum fuel 552 km (343 miles)
Weights: empty 454 kg (1,000 lb); maximum take-off 680 kg (1,500 lb)
Dimensions: span 6.10 m (20 ft 0 in); length 5.41 m (17 ft 9 in); height 1.94 m (6 ft 4½ in); wing area 11.61 m² (125.0 sq ft)

Plage & Laskiewicz R-VIII

The Polish company Zaklady Mechaniczne E. Plage and T. Laskiewicz was formed at Lublin in 1864, and the keen interest of the Plage family in early aircraft resulted in the formation of an aviation division which began work in early 1920. With a name that is not too easy to pronounce, the products of this company are frequently associated with the place of manufacture, thus the correctly designated **Plage & Laskiewicz R-VIII** is frequently listed as the **Lublin R-VIII**. The company's early activities were concerned with the licence construction of the Ansaldo A-1 Balilla and A.300, about 70 of each being produced. These were not particularly successful as a result of the company's lack of experience, but the total of some 200 licence-built Potez XV and 25s which followed were of a far higher standard. Licence construction activities ended with a batch of 11 Fokker F.VIIB-3m civil transports. The company then developed a bomber based on the F.VIIB-3m and powered by three Skoda engines. A total of 21 were built, equipping three squadrons of the Polish air force from early 1930, and these were later re-engined with 313-kW (420-hp) Wright radial engines.

The Plage & Laskiewicz R-VIIIbis was the floatplane version, employed on coastal reconnaissance duties.

Early attempts to produce original designs were unsuccessful, and the first aircraft of indigenous design to be built in small quantity was the R-VIII, a reconnaissance/bomber aircraft designed to meet an official requirement and configured as an unequal-span biplane of all-wood construction. There were two open cockpits in tandem, and the rear cockpit could be equipped to accommodate one or two crew members. The first prototype, powered by a 410-kW (550-hp) Farman 12W engine, was flown initially during March 1928. It was followed three months later by a second prototype powered by a 567-kW (760-hp) Lorraine-Dietrich engine. Satisfactory testing of the R-VIII led to a contract for five pre-production aircraft, but after being used in competition during 1930 by the Polish national team, these were returned to the company. Three were subsequently converted to floatplane configuration for service with the Polish navy under the designation

R-VIIIbis, two of them surviving in an operational role until the outbreak of World War 2. Both the R-VIII and R-VIII-bis had a wing span of 17.00 m (55 ft 9¼ in), the R-VIII having a maximum speed of 230 km/h (143 mph) and the floatplane R-VIIIbis of 220 km/h (137 mph).

The company also designed and built the **R-IX**, an eight-seat civil transport development of the R-VIII powered by a 358-kW (480-hp) Gnome-Rhône Jupiter, which accommodated the crew of two in an open cockpit and had the passenger cabin below and forward of their position. However, this model failed to gain any interest when flown in April 1929 and only the one example was built. Final derivative of the R-VIII design was a three-seat coastal patrol floatplane that could be used also as a torpedo-bomber; this had the designation **R-XXII**, but after a lengthy evaluation of the design proposal the project was abandoned.

Plage & Laskiewicz R-XIII

To meet an official requirement of 1927 for a two-seat observation liaison aircraft, the company designed its **Plage & Laskiewicz R-X** braced high-wing monoplane, gaining for this proposal a contract for three prototypes (one for static test) and five pre-production examples. Although it performed well, the R-X failed to gain a production contract, but the same basic design formed the basis of the company's tender for a two-seat trainer designated **R-XIV**, and for an **R-XV** armed reconnaissance/liaison version. The R-XV was rejected, but a contract for 15 trainers was awarded with the provision that the last of the batch should be completed for evaluation in the reconnaissance/liaison role. Because of design similarity to the R-X no prototype was built, the first production R-XIV being flown during July 1930, and the type began to enter service with the Polish air force during the following month.

The last R-XIV was duly completed in the reconnaissance/liaison configuration during July 1931 and, although performing well, was lost during tests. The company was then requested to produce another aircraft with a Scarff ring mount for the observer's defensive gun, and modified tail surfaces to improve his field of fire. Defying superstition this was given the unused designation **R-XIII** and was to prove the most successful of all Plage & Laskiewicz aircraft, built for the Polish army and navy to respective totals of 200 and 20 in several variants. The first R-XIII prototype was flown during August

Plage & Laskiewicz (Lublin) R-XIIID of the Polish air force in 1939.

1931, the first production aircraft entering service in mid-1932. Although obsolete by the outbreak of war in 1939 the type equipped seven observation squadrons, with others in use for liaison, but suffered horrific losses, by far the largest

from the I-180-3 was ordered, with improved fuselage lines, an enclosed cockpit and a redesigned wing of higher aspect ratio. The first three aircraft had been completed by December 1939, taking part in the 1940 May Day flypast. The I-180S spanned 10.10 m (33 ft 1¾ in), had a maximum take-off weight of 2675 kg (5,897 lb) and maximum speed of 585 km/h (364 mph) at 7100 m (23,295 ft).

The I-180S was then refined into the **I-185** with a new wing of NACA 230 profile incorporating split trailing-edge flaps and leading-edge slats, and with tailwheel landing gear of which all units retracted. The **I-185R(02)**, known alternatively as the **I-188** or **I-185M-90**, flew on 10 February 1942 powered by a 1491-kW (2,000-hp) M-71 radial, its maximum speed at 6100 m (20,015 ft) being an impressive 680 km/h (423 mph). Problems with the M-71 engine led to the **I-185RM(03)** or **I-187** prototype, flown with the less powerful M-82A engine of 992 kW (1,330 hp) while the I-185R(02) was grounded. It performed quite well, attaining a maximum 615 km/h (382 mph) during trials which started on 15 April 1942. It was later joined by the I-185R(02) with a new M-71 engine installed, both then armed with three nose-mounted 20-mm ShVAK cannon and used by the 728th Fighter Air Regiment (IAP) for operational trials. The **I-185R (04)** production prototype with an M-71 engine joined the test programme in November 1942, when plans were made to mass-produce the I-185 and the M-71 engine. However, the M-71 powerplant was still in trouble, a successful forced landing being made with I-185R(04) on 16 December 1942; but on 5 April 1943 test pilot V. A. Stepanchenko was killed when the engine of the **I-185E** pre-production prototype failed yet again and development and production plans were terminated.

Polikarpov P-2

A single-bay biplane with considerable stagger, the **Polikarpov P-2** intermediate trainer prototype was test flown successfully at the end of 1927, and this two-seat dual-control aircraft entered production with an initial order for 55 aircraft. The P-2 had a retractable radiator for its 224-kW (300-hp) M-6 in-line engine, and a ring mounting over the rear cockpit for a single DA machine-gun. The original wing bracing (based on teardrop-section diagonal struts), caused considerable problems on the series aircraft, which appeared between 1928 and 1930, and as a result many were modified with conventional bracing wires.

The P-2 trainer filled the gap between the Polikarpov U-2 and the more advanced R-5.

Polikarpov PM-1

A large single-engine passenger aircraft, the prototype **Polikarpov PM-1** flew for the first time on 10 June 1925. It was an unequal-span biplane with the upper wing connected directly to the upper decking of the fuselage. The pilot had an open cockpit just forward of the wing leading edge and the enclosed cabin accommodated five passengers. The 'M' in the designation arose from the single 194-kW (260-hp) Maybach IVa in-line engine which gave a maximum speed of 170 km/h (106 mph).

Successful flight testing brought an order for 10 aircraft to operate on the routes of the German-Soviet airline Deruluft, but as the result of a crash in Germany it is believed that most of the series aircraft were cancelled. The PM-1 (sometimes known as the **P-2**) spanned 15.50 m (50 ft 10¼ in) and had a maximum take-off weight of 2360 kg (5,203 lb).

Polikarpov prototypes

Under this heading are collected together a series of Polikarpov designs which, for one reason or another, failed to enter production. Taken in chronological order, and extending over a period of 18 years, they began with the **Polikarpov DI-1** or **2I-N1** two-seat fighter biplane which was first flown on 12 January 1926. The letter N in its designation signified the powerplant, a 336-kW (450-hp) Napier Lion engine which gave the aircraft a maximum speed of 268 km/h (167 mph). In spite of good performance and excellent lines, poor workmanship led to a loss of wing fabric at low level, and the resulting fatal crash in March 1926 brought an end to development of the DI-1. A similar fate was in store for the **DI-2** (or **D-2**) two-seat fighter, a slightly larger development of the I-3 powered by a BMW VI engine, giving it a maximum speed of 272 km/h (169 mph). However, development came to an end after the prototype crashed during flight testing in 1929.

Design began at the OSS in 1927 of a twin-engine heavy bomber under the project reference **L-2**. Designed in collaboration with Kolpakov, the eventual **TB-2** was of sesquiplane configuration, accommodated a crew of five and was powered by two 507-kW (680-hp) BMW VI engines, which were mounted in nacelles directly on top of the lower wing. When test flown in 1930 the TB-2 had a maximum speed of only 216 km/h (134 mph), and its development was abandoned in favour of the Tupolev TB-3. Very different was the **I-17** lightweight single-seat fighter, a cantilever low-wing monoplane of mixed construction which had been developed under the design bureau designation **TsKB-15**. Powered by a 567-kW (760-hp) Hispano-Suiza 12 Ybrs engine, it was first flown on 1 September 1934, demonstrating a maximum speed of 455 km/h (283 mph). It was followed by the **TsKB-19** with a Soviet M-100 engine and revised landing gear, and it was this latter version that was exhibited at the 1936 Salon de l'Aéronautique in Paris. A **TsKB-33** third prototype had reduced armament to save weight and introduced a surface-evaporation cooling system for the engine, but development was abandoned in 1936. Unbuilt projects included the **I-17Z** parasite fighter, the **TsKB-25** with an M-34RNF engine, and the **TsKB-43** with a more powerful Hispano-Suiza. In the summer of the following year the **TsKB-44** close-support aircraft was flown in prototype form, a twin-engine low-wing monoplane powered by two 716-kW (960-hp) M-103 engines which gave it a maximum speed of 450 km/h (280 mph). Proposed versions included the **MPI** multi-role cannon fighter, **SVB** combat fighter and the **VIT-1** anti-tank aircraft. Only the last was built in prototype form, the VIT-1 being heavily armed with four 37-mm cannon in the wings, a 20-mm cannon in the nose and a dorsal turret with a single 7.62-mm (0.3-in) machine-gun. An improved **TsKB-48**, incorporating a number of revisions and powered by two 783-kW (1,050-hp) M-105 engines, was flown on 11 May 1938 and demonstrated a maximum speed of 513 km/h (319 mph). Designated **VIT-2**, this machine gained official approval, resulting in an order for 50 production aircraft, but no series aircraft were in fact built.

In February 1938 the prototype **Ivanov** was flown, the name by which the aircraft was known being also the name of the competition in which it was participating to find a new reconnaissance/ground attack aircraft for the Soviet air force. A cantilever low-wing monoplane with a crew of two, heavily armed and powered by a 619-kW (830-hp) M-62 radial engine, the Ivanov had a maximum speed of 425 km/h (264 mph). Despite its outstanding qualities, only two prototypes were built. In the spring of 1940 Polikarpov flew the first prototype of its three-seat **SPB(D)**, which resembled a scaled-down version of the VIT-2. Five prototypes of this twin-engine low-wing monoplane were flown, standard armament comprising four machine-guns and a bombload of 1500 kg (3,307 lb). Powerplant consisted of two 783-kW (1,050-hp) M-105 engines, providing a maximum speed of 520 km/h (323 mph), but after two of the prototypes had been involved in fatal accidents development came to an end.

The second I-17 was improved over the first aircraft by way of its inward-retracting wide-track gear.

On 30 July 1944 Nikolai Polikarpov died and his bureau was soon disbanded; several almost completed aircraft were abandoned and all his prototype test programmes were cancelled. Included among these was the **TIS**, a heavy escort fighter in the mould of the Messerschmitt Bf 110 with, in the first **TIS(A)**, a powerplant of two 1044-kW (1,400-hp) AM-37 V-12 engines. These provided a maximum speed of 535 km/h (332 mph) and range of 1720 km (1,070 miles). A second **TIS(MA)** prototype had two 1268-kW (1,700-hp) AM-39 engines and was flown in early July 1944, shortly before all development came to an end. The **ITP** heavy cannon fighter suffered a similar fate, and was a cantilever low-wing monoplane of mixed construction. The first **ITP(M1)** prototype was flown in October 1942, powered by a 1230-kW (1,650-hp) M-107PA engine and armed with one 37-mm and two 20-mm cannon, plus 400 kg (882 lb) of externally-carried bombs or eight RS-82 rockets. The second **ITP(M2)** prototype had a 1342-kW (1,800-hp) AM-39 engine and had the 37-mm cannon replaced by one of 20-mm. The last of these abandoned prototypes was the Polikarpov **NB**, a twin-engine night bomber with a shoulder-mounted cantilever monoplane wing, twin-fin-and-rudder tail unit and powerplant of two 1268-kW (1,700-hp) ASh-82FNV radial engines. The five-crew NB could carry a maximum internal bombload of 5000 kg (11,023 lb) over short ranges and had a maximum speed of 515 km/h (320 mph).

The Polikarpov Ivanov was designed as a fast reconnaissance type.

Polikarpov R-1
to
Polikarpov U-2/Po-2

Polikarpov R-1

In 1918 Nikolai Nikolayevich Polikarpov, then aged 26, was put in charge of the Duks aircraft factory in Moscow, known subsequently as GAZ-1. After producing 20 Fiat-engined versions of the de Havilland D.H.4, the factory built 130 examples of the D.H.9 powered by an Armstrong-Siddeley Puma and over 100 D.H.9s with captured German Mercedes-Benz engines. The **Polikarpov R-1**, a modified development of the D.H.9A with a 298-kW (400-hp) M-5 engine (a licence-built version of the American Liberty), appeared in 1923. Mass-produced until 1931, the R-1 was armed with a fixed 7.7-mm (0.303-in) PV-1 and twin DA machine-guns of the same calibre on a ring mounting. Mikhail M. Gromov, piloting an R-1, led a Soviet flight to the Far East in the summer of 1925, reaching Peking on 13 July.

Variants
R-1 BMW: 20 built with 179-kW (240-hp) BMW IVa engine
R-2: alternatively designated **R-II**, this was a version of the R-1 with the 164-kW (220-hp) Siddeley Puma; 130 built
MR-1: twin-float seaplane version; 124 built 1927-28 at GAZ-10 in Taganrog
PM-2: prototype floatplane with metal floats instead of the MR-1's wooden floats; built in 1927

Specification
Type: two-seat reconnaissance/light bomber aircraft
Powerplant: one 298-kW (400-hp) M-5 Vee engine
Performance: maximum speed 185 km/h (115 mph); service ceiling 5000 m (16,405 ft); range 700 km (435 miles)
Weights: empty equipped 1450 kg (3,197 lb); maximum take-off 2200 kg (4,850 lb)
Dimensions: span 14.02 m (46 ft 0 in); length 9.24 m (30 ft 3¾ in); wing area 44.54 m² (479.44 sq ft)
Armament: three 7.7-mm (0.303-in) machine-guns, plus bombload of up to 400 kg (882 lb)

The R.1 was a licence-built D.H.9A. The skis were a winter necessity.

Polikarpov R-5

Developed over a three year period, the prototype **Polikarpov R-5** two-seat light-bomber/reconnaissance biplane flew for the first time in autumn 1928, proving to be a classic design of which some 7,000 in numerous versions were built by 1937. An unequal span biplane of mixed construction, it had a slim, carefully contoured fuselage and was powered by a 507-kW (680-hp) V-12 engine.

Delivery of the initial production series, with 507-kW (680-hp) M-17B engines, began from GAZ-1 factory in 1931, and the Soviet air arm equipped almost all of its light bomber and reconnaissance units with the type during the 1930s; series aircraft appearing from 1933 had the more powerful M-17F engine. R-5s saw active service in the Far East during border fighting with the Japanese during 1938-39, in the Spanish Civil War on the Republican side, and in the Winter War with Finland (1939-40). The R-5 was still in service in large numbers suring the war against Germany 1941-45, when the type operated on intruder, light bombing and reconnaissance missions, mainly at night, and was also deployed in the liaison role. Many variants were built, as well as a number of experimental versions, and the type was used by Aeroflot during the 1930s, some of them built as or converted to limousines with glazed canopies for pilot and passengers. The basic design compared favourably with the British Hawker Hart family and the US Curtiss Falcon series.

Variants
ARK-5: at least two conversions for Arctic operations in 1935, with streamlined containers for stores faired into fuselage sides and into lower wing; enclosed, heated cockpits and revised vertical tail
P-5: civil passenger version built for the Civil Aviation Authority from 1931 onwards with military equipment removed; by 1940 over 1,000 were in service, most with Aeroflot or Arctic Aviation; majority used to carry payload of freight up to 400 kg (882 lb), but many had an enlarged rear cockpit to accommodate two passengers seated in wicker-type chairs; others were rebuilt with enclosed rear section for two or three passengers; some had the lower wing strengthened to carry beneath them two G-61 containers, each able to accommodate up to seven people lying face down; similar containers used by P-5s involved in rescuing crew from doomed *Chelyushkin* arctic research vessel
Pa-5: twin float version of P-5, built in small numbers
P-5L: 1933 limousine version with two passengers in cabin; small numbers built
PR-5: ultimate transport version of 1936, with redesigned fuselage of greater cross-section and incorporating a pilot's enclosed cockpit and a cabin to seat four passengers, who entered via an airstair door; a centre of gravity problem occurred which was eliminated by slight repositioning of upper wing, modified aircraft being redesignated **PR-5bis**
R-5a: twin-float reconnaissance seaplane version; prototype flown during April 1931 and small quantity built; alternative designations were **MR-5** (often **MR-5bis** to avoid confusion with Chetverikov MR-5) and **Samolet 10**
R-5D: long-range one-off version for record-breaking use
R-5 Jumo: experimental test-bed engine, with the rear cockpit enlarged to accommodate two observers; alternative designation **ED-1**
R-5L: first factory-built limousine version with cabin for two passengers
R-5M-34: experimental version with M-34 engine flown successfully in 1934
R-5Sh: tested during 1931, a Shturmovik ground-attack version with originally four additional PV-1 machine-guns in pairs in faired containers above the lower wings; also had underfuselage container for a load of light bombs with a total weight of up to 500 kg (1,102 lb); 1933 production version had M-17B engine and eight machine-guns in sets of four
R-5SSS: otherwise known simply as **SSS**, this was a redesign to attain improved performance; landing gear with streamlined strut fairings and wheel spats, M-17F engine in redesigned cowling, and fixed armament increased to two ShKAS machine-guns; a ground-attack variant had four more ShKAS machine-guns on lower wings; over 100 of SSS version built during 1935-36; maximum speed raised to 269 km/h (167 mph) and service ceiling to 8000 m (26,245 ft)
R-5T: batch of 50 torpedo-bombers with divided landing gear to permit the underfuselage carriage of an air-launched torpedo
Miscellaneous variants: other experiments with R-5s included testing with Rudlicki 'butterfly' tailplane, replacing landing gear wheels with caterpillar tracks, fitting of inward-retracting main wheels, installing of pivoting front interplane struts for experiments with spin recovery, and fitting of slotted wings

The Polikarpov R-5 was a classic inter-war general-purpose type.

Specification
Type: two-seat light bomber/reconnaissance biplane
Powerplant: one 533-kW (715-hp) M-17F V-12 piston engine
Performance: maximum speed 245 km/h (152 mph); service ceiling 5940 m (19,490 ft); range 1000 km (621 miles)
Weights: empty equipped 1969 kg (4,341 lb); maximum take-off 2997 kg (6,607 lb)
Dimensions: span 15.50 m (50 ft 10¼ in); length 10.55 m (34 ft 7½ in); wing area 50.20 m² (540.37 sq ft)
Armament: one fixed synchronised 7.62-mm (0.3-in) PV-1 machine-gun on forward fuselage decking and twin 7.62-mm (0.3-in) DA machine-guns on ring mounting over rear cockpit, plus a maximum bombload of 400 kg (882 lb)

Polikarpov R-Z (Zet)

Known also as the **R-Zet**, the **Polikarpov R-Z** was the final member of the R-5 family, with a new fuselage of deeper section and entirely revised crew accommodation. The pilot's cockpit was semi-enclosed with folding glazed side panels and, except when operating his single 7.62-mm (0.3-in) ShKAS machine-gun, the observer was seated beneath a canopy comprising one fixed and one sliding section. The landing gear, vertical tail surfaces and upper wing were redesigned, and the more powerful M-34N engine was installed.

Design had been initiated in 1933 and the prototype flew for the first time in January 1935. Production ended in the spring of 1937 after the production of 1,031 aircraft.

The R-Z had a workmanlike appearance, and performed creditably in action against the Japanese in the Far East during 1939 and on the Republican side in the Spanish Civil War. A total of 62 R-Z aircraft was sent to Spain, equipping three groups and seeing a great deal of action. The type flew at low level in tight formation and defensive fire from the ShKAS machine guns proved effective against enemy interceptors. After dropping their bombload of up to 400 kg (882 lb), the aircraft made their return to base individually and at low level. At the end of hostilities 36 R-Zs fell into Nationalist hands. The R-Z was known as the 'Natasha' in Spain, where little use was made of the second ShKAS machine-gun, which was fixed in the forward fuselage.

Although outmoded, the R-Z was still in service with a number of light bomber regiments when the Germans attacked the Soviet Union in June 1941. The first three regiments to be equipped with the Ilyushin Il-2 single-seat ground-attack monoplane converted from the R-Z.

Variants
PT: transport prototype which was not further developed as it had poor flying qualities

P-Z: first in service with Aeroflot in 1936, a mail carrier with provision for two passengers seated face to face, some with underwing containers for additional freight or mail; powered by 611-kW (820-hp) M-34NB engine and a number were in operation until end of war; some were conversions and others built as new

R-ZR: single-seat conversion for record purposes; established a height record of 11100 m (36,417 ft) on 8 May 1937

R-ZSh: one-off Shturmovik prototype with four additional ShKAS machine-guns mounted on lower wing

Specification
Type: two-seat light bomber
Powerplant: one 634-kW (850-hp) M-34N V-12 piston engine
Performance: maximum speed 315 km/h (196 mph); service ceiling 8700 m (28,545 ft); range 1000 km (621 miles)
Weights: empty equipped 2230 kg (4,916 lb); maximum take-off 3500 kg (7,716 lb)
Dimensions: span 15.50 m (50 ft

The Polikarpov R-Z was widely used during the Spanish Civil War in the hands of Republican forces on low-level bombing and harassment missions.

10¼ in); length 9.72 m (31 ft 10¾ in); height 3.60 m (11 ft 9¾ in); wing area 42.52 m² (457.70 sq ft)
Armament: two or three 7.62-mm (0.3-in) ShKAS machine-guns, plus up to 400 kg (882 lb) of bombs

Polikarpov U-2/Po-2

Occupying a unique position in Soviet aviation history, the **Polikarpov U-2** primary trainer biplane had an inauspicious start. The **U-2TPK** prototype, which appeared in early 1927, had been built to achieve economy in repair and maintenance, the wings comprising four identical thick-section interchangeable rectangular panels with square tips. Similarly, a common control surface was used for ailerons, elevators and rudder. The result was a biplane with very poor flight characteristics. It had thus to be re-designed, appearing as a neat, manoeuvrable biplane having staggered single-bay wings with rounded tips, conventional cross-axle landing gear, and tandem open cockpits for instruction and pupil. Powered by a 74-kW (100-hp) radial engine, the new prototype made its first flight on 7 January 1928. An immediate success, it was placed in quantity production, deliveries starting in 1928, and by the time of the German invasion of the Soviet Union in mid-1941 over 13,000 had been completed.

Though its principal role was primary training, the U-2 was soon modified as a light passenger transport, air ambulance and agricultural aircraft. Production continued on a massive scale during World War II, and the U-2 took on an even wider range of duties, including liaison, light attack, night nuisance raider and propaganda aircraft complete with microphone and loud-speaker.

After Polikarpov's death, on 30 July 1944, the U-2 was redesignated **Po-2** in his honour, and post-war it continued in production in the Soviet Union for several years. Trainer and ambulance variants were built on a large scale in Poland from 1948 to 1953. Po-2s served with many Soviet allies and a small number still remain in flying condition in the Soviet Union and several other countries. The total built is credibly reported to be in excess of 33,000.

Variants
U-2A: single-seat agricultural duster aircraft, built in sub-types **U-2AP** and **U-2AO** from 1930, with 250-kg (551-lb) chemical hopper in rear fuselage; post-1944 continued in production and use as **Po-2A** powered by 86-kW (115-hp) M-11K; total production 9,000

U-2G: one-off experimental model with all controls linked to control column

U-2KL: two special aircraft with rear cabin having bulged canopy; appeared in 1932

U-2LSh: light Shturmovik; large number of pre-war aircraft converted for close-support military role from 1941 onwards, plus new production; armed with one 7.7-mm (0.303-in) ShKAS machine-gun on ring mounting over rear cockpit, and racks for 120 kg (264 lb) of bombs, plus rails for four RS-82 rockets; had high reputation among Soviet troops and earned nickname *Kukuruznik* or corn-cutter, resulting from its successful low-level operations; alternative designation was **U-2VOM-1**

U-2LNB: wartime production 1941 on; offensive load raised to 200 kg (441 lb); designation translates as light night bomber, and the type often carried flares or searchlight; usually had silencer attachment for engine exhaust

U-2LPL: prone-pilot research development of 1935

U-2M: alternative designation **MU-2** tested in 1931; the first of several floatplane versions with large central float and two wingtip stabilising floats; no version built in large numbers

U-2NAK: light artillery observation and reconnaissance variant; observer provided with army radio

U-2S: limited series built from 1934, the rear cockpit being replaced by enclosed cubicle for medical attendant and compartment for stretcher case, with hinged top decking over patient; later had windows installed; other versions known as **U-2S-1** and **U-2SS** (*Sanitarnyi Samolyet*, or ambulance aircraft)

U-2SP: third open cockpit installed with other cockpits relocated; total of 861 built 1934-39, mostly for Aeroflot; survivors impressed in wartime for liaison duties

U-2SPL: limousine model with rear cabin for two passengers in place of rear cockpit

U-2UT: built in limited numbers from 1941, mainly for training and powered by 86-kW (115-hp) M-11D engine

U-2VS: basic Soviet air force aircraft, large numbers used by senior personnel for wartime liaison flights; over 9,000 in service for liaison in 1945, by then redesignated **Po-2VS**

U-3: development by N. G. Mikhelson and A. I. Morshchikhin in 1934 as a better flying training model with 149-kW (200-hp) M-48 engine; in no way superior to basic U-2

U-4: cleaned-up model of U-2 with slimmer fuselage; developed by Mikhelson and not built in quantity

Po-2GN: 'voice from the sky' propaganda aircraft with loud-speaker for addressing enemy ground troops; built from 1944

Po-2L: limousine version with enclosed passenger cabin; access door on port side

Po-2P: wartime floatplane, built in limited numbers only

Po-2S: wartime ambulance aircraft, **Po-2S-1** similar to pre-war ambulance aircraft; **Po-2S-2** had M-11D engine, and **Po-2S-3** carried two underwing containers each with stretcher patient; alternative designation for this last variant was **Po-2SKF**

Po-2ShS: staff liaison machine built from 1943; new fuselage with enclosed cabin for pilot and two or three passengers

Po-2SP: specialised post-war version, used for geographic survey and air photography

RV-23: Mikhelson float derivative of U-2 for seaplane altitude record attempts; built in small numbers with 529-kW (710-hp) R-1820-F3 Cyclone radial

CSS-13: designation for Polish version, some with glazed cabin over crew cockpits

CSS-S-13: Polish ambulance version, with canopy over cockpits for pilot and medical attendant and enclosed section for stretcher patient to rear

E-23: research version of 1935 for inverted flight

Miscellaneous variants: many experimental versions were also built, including one to test the Rudlicki 'butterfly' tail and another re-engined with a Siemens Sh 14 engine

Specification
Type U-2VS: trainer and multi-purpose aircraft
Powerplant: one 75-kW (100-hp) M-11 radial piston engine
Performance: maximum speed 156 km/h (97 mph); service ceiling 4000 m (13,125 ft); range 400 km (249 miles)
Weights: empty equipped 635 kg (1,400 lb); maximum take-off 890 kg (1,962 lb)
Dimensions: span 11.40 m (37 ft 4¾ in); length 8.17 m (26 ft 9¾ in); height 3.10 m (10 ft 2 in); wing area 33.15 m² (356.86 sq ft)

The U-2/Po-2 family was probably built in greater numbers than any other aircraft in history. It is not surprising that many examples, such as this CSS-13, are still airworthy.

Pomilio aircraft

Established in Turin during 1916, the Italian company Fabbrica Aeroplani Ing. O. Pomilio & Compagnia was soon in production with an equal-span biplane intended for use as an armed reconnaissance aircraft. Of mixed construction and with fixed tailskid landing gear, the initial version was designated **Pomilio PC** and had two open cockpits in tandem, and was powered by a 194-kW (260-hp) Fiat A.12 engine. Armament consisted of two Revelli machine-guns, one mounted above the upper wing to fire clear of the propeller disc, the other on a trainable mount in the rear cockpit. Early experience with the PC, which began to enter service in March 1917, showed it to have dangerous instability and this led very quickly to the improved **PD** with revised engine cowling and, most importantly, the addition of a ventral fin. Combined production of the PC and PD amounted to 545 aircraft, by far the majority PDs, but the types were superseded in late 1917 by the major production version, the **PE**, built to a total of 1,071. It differed from the earlier aircraft in having a redesigned tail unit incorporating increased area for both the fin and

tailplane, and benefited also from the use of a slightly more powerful version of the Fiat A.12 engine. Detail improvements were introduced throughout the production run, and late series examples had a synchronised forward-firing machine-gun and one or two Lewis guns for the observer.

At the end of the war the Pomilio brothers disposed of their factory to the Ansaldo company and emigrated to the United States where, during 1917-18, Ottorino Pomilio had been sent by the Allies to assist the US government's aviation programme. At the request of the US Army Air Service Engineering Division, he designed a single-seat fighter and a two-seat bomber, the **FVL-8** and **BVL-12**, powered by the 209-kW (280-hp) Liberty 8 and 298-kW (400-hp) Liberty 12 engines respectively. Both were equal-span biplanes with fixed tailskid landing gear, and were then unique in the USA by having the fuselage strut-mounted between the wings, rather than following the usual practice of having the lower wing attached directly to the fuselage. Six examples of each were built, the 8.13 m (26 ft 8 in)

span FVL-8 fighter having a maximum speed of 214 km/h (133 mph), but the 13.79 m (45 ft 3 in) span BVL-12 attained only 179 km/h (111 mph), and no further examples of either design were built.

Specification
Pomilio PE
Type: two-seat armed reconnaissance aircraft
Powerplant: one 224-kW (300-hp) Fiat A.12bis V-12 engine
Performance: maximum speed 195 km/h (121 mph) at sea level; service ceiling 5000 m (16,405 ft); endurance 3 hours 30 minutes
Weights: maximum take-off 1535 kg

Developed from the PC and the PD, the Pomilio PE was used by the Regia Aeronautica for armed reconnaissance from late 1917 onwards. This example has a machine-gun on the centre section and in the rear cockpit.

(3,384 lb)
Dimensions: span 11.80 m (38 ft 8½ in); length 8.95 m (29 ft 4¼ in); height 3.35 m (11 ft 0 in)
Armament: one synchronised forward-firing 8-mm (0.315-in) Revelli machine-gun, and one or two 7.7-mm (0.303-in) Lewis guns on a Scarff ring in rear cockpit

Porokhovshchikov aircraft

Aleksandr Porokhovshchikov was one of the earliest aircraft builders in Russia, dating back to World War I, when he manufacturered aircraft that were mainly similar in overall configuration to those of the Caudron Frères in France. They were, therefore, unequal-span biplanes with fixed tailskid landing gear, a central nacelle to mount the engine and accommodate the crew, and a tail unit carried at the rear on four braced booms extending from the wing structure. Unusually, this configuration was adopted whether the engine was

mounted for operation with a pusher or tractor propeller. Most important was the basic **Porokhovshchikov P-IV**, first flown in February 1917, which entered production some three months later, and which was powered most frequently by a 37-kW (50-hp) Gnome or 60-kW (80-hp) Le Rhône rotary. This first P-IV had the engine in pusher configuration, with the nacelle seating two in tandem open cockpits, but the **P-IVbis** which followed had a tractor engine and side-by-side seating. The later **P-IV 2bis** retained the tractor engine but re-

verted to tandem seating. The post-war **P-VI**, in production from 1921, was basically similar but had a strengthened structure to cater for the more powerful 82-kW (110-hp) Le Rhône engine which was its most usual powerplant. This version had its upper wing centre-section free of ribs and wing covering to give the pilot an improved upward view, but the **P-VIbis** of 1923 had a conventional covered centre-section. In addition to the P-IV family, Porokhovshchikov had also produced a number of **P-V** two-seat advanced trainers, powered by the 60-kW (80-hp) Le Rhône rotary, which was based on the Nieuport IV.

Specification
Porokhovshchikov P-IVbis
Type: two-seat trainer
Powerplant: one 60-kW (80-hp) Le Rhône rotary piston engine
Performance: maximum speed 112 km/h (70 mph); service ceiling 3000 m (9,840 ft); endurance 4 hours 36 minutes
Weights: empty 398 kg (877 lb); maximum take-off 660 kg (1,455 lb)
Dimensions: span 10.21 m (33 ft 5½ in); length 7.30 m (23 ft 11½ in); wing area 33.10 m² (356.30 sq ft)

Porterfield Flyabout

Originating as the **Wyandotte Pup**, designed by Noel Hockaday and built as a project by students at the Wyandotte High School in Kansas City, this lightplane appeared to be such a promising design that Porterfield Aircraft Corporation, also of Kansas City, acquired the design and the services of Hockaday as works manager and designer. The Pup was developed as the **Porterfield Model 35 Flyabout**, a braced high-wing monoplane with two-seat cabin accommodation and fixed tailskid landing gear. As first available in 1935, the Flyabout was powered by a 45-kW (60-hp) LeBlond 5D radial engine. In 1937 the 52-kW (70-hp) LeBlond 5DE engine was installed, the designation then being

changed to **Model 35-70 Flyabout**.
Later versions of this popular aircraft included the **Model 35-V** with a 48-kW (65-hp) Velie M-5 and, top of the range, the **Model 35-W**, known also as the **De Luxe Sport** or **Model 90**, which was powered by a 67-kW (90-hp) Warner Scarab Junior radial engine. Production of all versions combined totalled about 250, some of them being exported, and a number are still airworthy.

Specification
Porterfield 35-70 Flyabout
Type: two-seat cabin monoplane
Powerplant: one 52-kW (70-hp) LeBlond 5DE radial piston engine
Performance: maximum speed

185 km/h (115 mph); service ceiling 4570 m (15,000 ft); range 579 km (360 miles)
Weights: empty 366 kg (806 lb); maximum take-off 594 kg (1,310 lb)
Dimensions: span 9.75 m (32 ft 0 in);

The Model 35 Flyabout was built with several engine options.

length 6.17 m (20 ft 3 in); height 2.01 m (6 ft 7 in); wing area 13.66 m² (147.0 sq ft)

Porterfield Zephyr and Collegiate

In 1936 a lighter-weight version of the Flyabout was developed by the Porterfield Aircraft Corporation as the **Porter-field Zephyr**, later redesignated **Porterfield CP-40**. Generally similar in configuration to the Flyabout, it had a

revised tail unit and was powered by a 30-kW (40-hp) engine, but the limited performance of this version and the

growing demand for pilot training led to its development instead as the **CP-50 Collegiate** with, originally, a 37-kW (50-hp) Continental A50-4 engine. It proved to have more appeal than the Flyabout, being built to a total of about

400 aircraft in versions which included the **CP-55** with a revised engine cowling, **CP-65** (48-kW/65-hp Continental A65-8/-9), **FP-60** (45-kW/60-hp Franklin 4AC-171-A1), **FP-65** (48-kW/65-hp 4AC-176-B29), **LP-50** (37-kW/50-hp Avco Lycoming O-145-A1), **LP-55** (41-kW/55-hp O-145-A3) and **LP-65** (48-kW/65-hp O-145-B1/B2). Final examples were built in 1941, and the manufacture of civil aircraft ceased entirely just before the USA became involved in World War II.

As with the Flyabout, the designations applied to the more successful Collegiate indicated the type and power of the engine. The CP-55 opposite had a 55-hp Continental flat-four.

Specification
Porterfield CP-65 Collegiate
Type: two-seat trainer
Powerplant: one 48-kW (65-hp) Continental A65-8-9 flat-four piston engine
Performance: maximum speed 174 km/h (108 mph); service ceiling

4570 m (15,000 ft); range 438 km (300 miles)
Weights: empty 304 kg (671 lb); maximum take-off 526 kg (1,160 lb)

Dimensions: span 10.59 m (34 ft 9 in); length 6.91 m (22 ft 8 in); height 2.11 m (6 ft 11 in); wing area 15.68 m² (168.80 sq ft)

Potez VIII

The prototype **Potez VIII** two-seat tourer/elementary trainer was first flown on 9 April 1920, powered by a specially designed Potez engine, the 37-kW (50-hp) Potez A 4. A light unequal-span biplane, the Potez VIII had four-wheel landing gear, the tailskid being used for landings only. The unusual A 4 engine was a complete failure and plans were made to produce 100 series aircraft

powered by the 52-kW (70-hp) Anzani 6Ab radial.
Versions built included the **Potez VIII A** of 1922 with the 60-kW (80-hp) Anzani 6 A3 engine and two-wheel conventional landing gear; five were built, two of them later being converted to Potez VIII configuration and one as the **Potez VIII H** central-float seaplane, built especially for a wealthy Marseilles businessman.

Specification
Potez VIII

Type: two-seat tourer or primary trainer
Powerplant: one 52-kW (70-hp) Anzani 6Ab radial piston engine
Performance: maximum speed 142 km/h (88 mph); service ceiling 4000 m (13,125 ft)
Weights: empty equipped 240 kg (529 lb); maximum take-off 470 kg (1,036 lb)
Dimensions: span 8.00 m (26 ft 3 in); length 5.72 m (18 ft 9¼ in); wing area 20.00 m² (215.28 sq ft)

The Potez VIII was the winner of the 1924 Grand Prix de Tourisme, with a team of five.

Potez IX

The **Potez IX** biplane had a deep care-

fully contoured fuselage of entirely new design, was powered by a Lorraine-Dietrich 12Da engine and had an enclosed cabin for four passengers; behind

the cabin was an open cockpit for the pilot. The prototype flew for the first time in 1921 and was followed by 30 series machines which differed in having

vertical tail surfaces of increased area. A one-off **Potez IX S** with wings of increased area was tested in 1921.

Potez X

A three-engined and enlarged version of the Potez IX, the **Potez X A** of 1922 was intended as a general-purpose colonial transport. Powered by three 104-kW

(140-hp) Hispano-Suiza 8Aa engines, one in the nose and one strut-mounted between the wings on each side, the Potez X A seated 10 passengers in the forward fuselage cabin, with the pilot's open cockpit behind. The independent main

landing gear legs were supplemented by side-by-side nose-wheels and a tailskid. Later, more powerful Hispano-Suiza 8Ab engines were substituted for the original units.
The **Potez X B** was a fully militarised version with 209-kW (280-hp) Hispano-

Suiza 8Bec engines, while the **Potez X C** was another civil transport with the same powerplant as the Potez X B.
Wing span was 18.40 m (60 ft 4½ in) and maximum take-off weight 3090 kg (6,812 lb).

Potez XV

A successful private venture design by Louis Coroller, the **Potez XV** two-seat observation biplane was displayed at the Paris Salon de l'Aéronautique in 1921. Powered by a 276-kW (370-hp) Lorraine 12D engine, later replaced by a 224-kW (300-hp) Renault 12Fe, the Potez XV pro-

totype performed well and gained official approval in the H.2 (two-seat observation) category. Large orders were received from the Aéronautique Militaire and first deliveries began towards the end of 1923. Series aircraft had the Lorraine 12Db engine and retained the configuration of the original machine, with conventional cross-axle landing gear, and were largely of wooden construc-

tion with metal panelling covering the forward fuselage and fabric over the remainder.
The Potez XV was exported widely, eight going to Denmark, 12 to Spain, 120 to Romania and 30 of a slightly modified version, designated **Potez XVII**, to Bulgaria. In addition, a sample batch exported to Poland was followed by 135 aircraft licence-built in that country.

The Potez XV was yet another prizewinner, capturing the 1924 Coupe Zenith.

Potez XXVII

Representing an intermediate stage between the Potez XV and Potez 25, despite its later type number, the **Potez XXVII** appeared in 1924. It was a two-seat biplane in the A.2 observation category and combined the engine, fuselage, fin, rudder and cross-axle landing gear of

the Potez XV with a tailplane, balanced elevator and unequal-span wings similar to those of the Potez 25.
The type was built for export only, Poland obtaining 20 machines in 1925 and subsequently building 155 under licence at the P.W.S. works; some were still serving as trainers in 1936. Romania also procured 30 Potez XXVII aircraft in 1926.

This is one of 155 Potez XXVIIs built under licence by P.W.S. for the Polish air force.

Armament was one fixed synchronised and two trainable 7.7-mm (0.303-in) machine-guns and up to 200 kg (441 lb) of bombs. Powered by the 298-kW (400-hp) Lorraine 12Db engine, the 12.89 m (42 ft 3½ in) span Potez

XXVII had a maximum speed of 212 km/h (132 mph).

Potez 25

One of the most famous military aircraft of the inter-war period, the **Potez 25** was developed from the **Potez 24** A.2-category prototype, which had been designed by Louis Coroller and flown in 1924. The refined Potez 25 prototype was built at the new Potez factory at Méaulte and flew for the first time in early 1925. An unequal-span biplane, the Potez 25 had an engine mounting capable of taking a wide variety of powerplants in the 298-kW (400-hp) to 447-kW (600-hp) range. The carefully contoured fuselage accommodated pilot and observer/gunner close together in tandem cockpits beneath a cut-out in the trailing edge of the upper wing centre

The Potez 25 was like its British, French, Dutch and Soviet counterparts, being built in many forms. These are two-seat A.2s.

section. The new cross-axle landing gear had specially designed Potez shock absorbers.
In all, 87 variants of the type were developed for military and civil use, and over 3,500 examples were built in France, most at the Potez factory, but others under licence by A.N.F. Les Mureaux and Hanriot. Abroad, 300 Potez 25s were licence-built in Poland, 200 in Yugoslavia, 70 in Romania and 27 in Portugal. Other countries which used French-built aircraft included China, where the type was used against the Japanese; Paraguay, where it operated

against the Bolivian air arm; Uruguay; Greece; Ethiopia, which flew a small number against the invading Italian troops in 1935; Switzerland, which retained the type in service until 1940; and Estonia. In addition test examples were

sold to the Soviet Union and some dozen other countries. Many of the exported and licence-built Potez 25s were of the B.2 two-seat light bomber version.
Civil Potez 25s with Lorraine engines were used by Aéropostale and its asso-

ciated companies in South America for regular mail flights over the Andes, and also by the Caudron and Hanriot flying schools. The Compagnie Française d'Aviation used Salmson-powered Potez 25s for training.

Variants
Potez 25 1925 experimental: prototype with 336-kW (450-hp) Hispano-Suiza 12Ga engine
Potez 25 A.2: two-seat observation version powered by either the 388-kW (520-hp) Salmson 18Cmb radial or Lorraine 12Eb engine
Potez 25 ET.2: two-seat intermediate trainer; used by Aéronautique Militaire and C.F.A., with 373-kW (500-hp) Salmson 18Ab radial
Potez 25 'Jupiter': licence-built by Ikarus (Yugoslavia) and OSGA (Portugal); French-built aircraft sold to Estonia and Switzerland; powered by 313-kW (420-hp) Gnome-Rhône 9Ac Jupiter radial
Potez 25/5: production version (100 built) in A.2 and CN.2 variants; 373-kW (500-hp) Renault 12Jb V-12 engine and increased rudder area
Potez 25 TOE: major production version, 2,270 built of which 297 exported, 25 used for civil air mail routes and remainder used by French air arm
Potez 25GR: adaptation of standard Lorraine-powered version with increased fuel tankage for long-distance flights
Potez 25M: parasol-wing monoplane conversion of Hispano-Suiza-powered biplane for Romania 1927; no quantity production
Potez 25 Hispano-Suiza:

Potez 25 A.2 of the 2do Escadron de Reconocimiento y Bombardio, Paraguayan air force, operating from Isla Poi in June 1933.

Ministerial VIP transport version with 447-kW (600-hp) Hispano-Suiza 12Lb V-12 engine; this engine also powered the light-bomber/reconnaissance version exported to Greece
Potez 25 Farman (or **Potez 25/4**): reconnaissance version, 12 built with 373-kW (500-hp) Farman 12We engine; used by Armée de l'Air
Potez 25/35: Lorraine-powered variant used for target towing; Aéronavale had 12
Potez 25/55: another Lorraine-powered variant with dual controls; 40 built and used mostly by Aéropostale, the Caudron flying school and the Hanriot airline
Potez 25-O: the letter suffix stood for Océan, in this specially strengthened and modified version for non-stop

North Atlantic crossing; powered by Jupiter radial and with jettisonable landing gear and strengthened landing skid attached to underside of fuselage, but crashed on closed-circuit record attempt in September 1925 and Atlantic flight never attempted; a second transatlantic Potez 25 built 1927, but abandoned for lack of interest
Potez 25H: at least two floatplane versions of Gnome-Rhône Jupiter powered Potez 25 were tested, one with large main float and underwing stabilised floats and the other with twin floats; a version of the Lorraine-powered Potez 25 TOE was flown in Indo-China with twin floats

Specification
Potez 25 TOE
Type: two-seat general-purpose

military aircraft
Powerplant: one 335-kW (450-hp) Lorraine 12Eb broad-arrow piston engine
Performance: maximum speed 208 km/h (129 mph); service ceiling 5800 m (19,030 ft); range 1260 km (783 miles)
Weights: empty equipped 1510 kg (3,329 lb); maximum take-off 2500 kg (5,512 lb)
Dimensions: span 14.14 m (46 ft 4¾ in); length 9.10 m (29 ft 10¼ in); height 3.67 m (12 ft 0¼ in); wing area 47.00 m² (505.92 sq ft)
Armament: one fixed synchronised 7.7-mm (0.303-in) Vickers machine-gun in engine cowling and two 7.7-mm Lewis machine-guns on a TO 7 ring mounting over observer's cockpit, plus a maximum bombload of 200 kg (441 lb)

Potez 29

The prototype **Potez 29** (F-AIQD), test-flown in 1927, was developed as a passenger-carrying version of the Potez 25. It had the same powerplant as the Potez 25 TOE and wings and landing gear of similar design, but introduced a new fuselage with an enclosed cockpit for the two-man crew and a cabin that seated five passengers as standard; the fuselage was deep and filled the entire gap between the upper and lower wings.

The Potez 29 was an immediate success and 29 entered service with civil air lines, principally the CIDNA company and the Yugoslav Aeroput; a number of variants appeared, differing mainly in their powerplant. A large number of the type went to the French Aéronautique Militaire.

Variants
Potez 29: prototype and first six series aircraft; all civil transports with the Lorraine 12Eb engine; four supplied to Yugoslavian airline Aeroput
Potez 29/2: 123 built, engine as

With emphasis more on payload than performance, the Potez 29 biplane was based on a box-like fuselage for maximum passenger or casualty accommodation. The example illustrated is a Potez 29/2 impressed into British service in the Middle East in 1940.

above, 120 for French Aéronautique Militaire; in 1932 each French Colonial *escadrille* had a section of three Potez 29/2 ambulances; two civil machines went to Yugoslavia
Potez 29/4: civil version with 358-kW

(480-hp) Gnome-Rhône Jupiter 9Ady radial; of 15 built, 13 went to CIDNA airline and two to Romania
Potez 29/11: long-range version used by Pelletier d'Oisy, with increased fuel capacity and same engine as Potez 29/5

Potez 32 and 33

Derived from the Potez 29, the **Potez 32** five-passenger transport or mail-plane retained the fuselage, tail unit and landing gear of its predecessor, but was a strut-braced high-wing monoplane. First flown in 1928, the prototype (F-AIKZ) was followed by 54 production aircraft. An initial difference in comparison with the Potez 29 was the employment of a lower-powered, and thus cheaper and more economical, Salmson radial engine; later aircraft had the higher-powered Jupiter. The type was operated by CIDNA, Air Orient and Aéropostale, and 12 were exported to Canada.

The **Potez 33** prototype, tested in March 1928, was a militarised version of the Potez 32 intended for liaison and observation, or as a trainer for pilots and observers. It had dual controls as standard, introduced large observation windows, and had a dorsal machine-gun position; light bombs could be carried.

Variants
Potez 32: civil prototype plus 31

series aircraft; Salmson 9Ab engine
Potez 32/2: one only with 171-kW (230-hp) Lorraine 7Ma engine
Potez 32/3: seven built and all exported to Canada; 164-kW (220-hp) Wright J-5 radial engine
Potez 32/4: powered by 283-kW (380-hp) Gnome-Rhône Jupiter 9Aa and with small increase in wing area; nine built as new and five conversions of Potez 32s
Potez 32/5: experimental version with Hispano-Suiza 9Qd engine
Potez 33/1: prototype and one other machine with 172-kW (230-hp) Lorraine 7Me engine; both purchased by Portugal as military transports
Potez 33/2: version with Salmson 9Ab engine, 40 built; small batch for Brazilian air force, remainder for Aéronautique Militaire; nine aircraft formed main equipment of colonial Escadrille de Madagascar from March 1931
Potez 33/3: built 1931 with 224-kW (300-hp) Gnome-Rhône 7Kdrs radial;

four for Belgium
Potez 33/4: built 1931 with 224-kW (300-hp) Lorraine 9Na; eight for Belgium

Specification
Potez 33/2
Type: general-purpose military aircraft
Powerplant: one 171-kW (230-hp) Salmson 9Ab radial piston engine
Performance: maximum speed 190 km/h (118 mph); service ceiling 4500 m (14,765 ft); range 700 km (435 miles)
Weights: empty equipped 950 kg

This particular Potez 32 wears the colours of the French Compagnie Internationale de Navigation Aérienne, otherwise known as CIDNA.

(2,094 lb); maximum take-off 1750 kg (3,858 lb)
Dimensions: span 14.50 m (47 ft 6¾ in); length 10.15 m (33 ft 3½ in); wing area 35.00 m² (376.75 sq ft)
Armament: one 7.7-mm (0.303-in) Vickers machine-gun on ring mounting, plus light bombs on underfuselage racks

Potez 36

A braced high-wing monoplane, the Potez 36 had wide-track divided landing gear, and its pilot and passenger were seated side-by-side in a fully enclosed cabin. Potez-designed leading-edge slats produced a high safety factor, much appreciated by those with sufficient finance to own the Potez 36 for weekend and holiday flying. Its design also included folding wings, making it suitable for garage storage and easy to tow behind a car.

Potez 36s proved a great success and some 300 were built for private owners and clubs between 1929 and 1933. Some were used by l'Armée de l'Air as scout/liaison aircraft during the 1930s.

Variants
Potez 36/3: prototype and six Potez 36/3 series aircraft; the latter had no slats

Potez 36/5: version with 71-kW (95-hp) Salmson 7Ac engine and no slats; first of five aircraft flown during August 1929
Potez 36/13: production version, powerplant as Potez 36/5 and with leading-edge slats; first 96 examples flown June 1931
Potez 36/14: major production version, 103 built, with 71-kW (95-hp) Renault 4Pb engine, leading-edge slats and wheel brakes
Potez 36/15: first version to have Potez engine, the 75-kW (100-hp) Potez 6Ab; 18 built 1931-32
Potez 36/17: two built in September 1931 with 78-kW (104-hp) Cirrus Hermes IIB engine
Potez 36/19: two with 75-kW (100-hp) Renault 4Pci engine; built November 1932
Potez 36/21: production version with 75-kW (100-hp) Potez 6Ac engine and wheels with balloon tyres; 29 built from November 1932

Specification
Potez 36/3
Type: two-seat sport/touring aircraft
Powerplant: one 45-kW (60-hp) Salmson 5Ac radial piston engine
Performance: maximum speed 150 km/h (93 mph); service ceiling 3600 m (11,810 ft); range 500 km (311 miles)

The leading-edge slats of the Potez 35 bestowed good handling.

Weights: empty equipped 427 kg (941 lb); maximum take-off 650 kg (1,433 lb)
Dimensions: span 10.45 m (34 ft 3½ in); length 7.50 m (24 ft 7¼ in); height 2.45 m (8 ft 0½ in)

Potez 37 and 39

The **Potez 37** and **Potez 39** appeared in 1930. Both were two-seat braced parasol-wing monoplanes of all-metal construction, the former being intended for the fighter-reconnaissance role and having a rear fuselage which tapered into little more than a boom to give the gunner an improved field of fire. The prototype Potez 39 (F-ALRL) was designed for A.2 category observation role, and had a conventional fuselage and redesigned wings with elliptical tips.

The Potez 37 was rejected for production, only two examples being built, but the Potez 39 showed great promise and was adopted by the Armée de l'Air. Series **Potez 390** and **Potez 391** aircraft were subjected to various modifications during production and service, notably the introduction of a rudder with increased area, but they retained the basic features of the design, which included a divided fixed wide-track landing gear with wheel spats; streamlined Vee-struts supporting the wings; and glazed panels in the fuselage sides between the cockpits.

The Armée de l'Air received 232 P-390s and P-391s, the first unit to re-equip in early 1934 being the 34e Escadre, where they replaced Potez 25s.

Variants
Potez 39: prototype; Hispano-Suiza 12Hb engine with larger intake than production aircraft
Potez 390: main series version, powerplant as prototype; total of 244 Potez 390 and 391 aircraft built
Potez 391: built in quantity with 388-kW (520-hp) Lorraine 12Hdr engine; Peru bought 12 equipped as light bombers/night-fighters; had larger air intake than standard French machines
Potez 39/10: in R.2 two-seat reconnaissance category with more powerful 641-kW (860-hp) Hispano-Suiza 12Ybrs engine; flown in January 1934 then demonstrated at Villacoublay before Soviet mission; no production
Potez 49 TOE: general-purpose (colonial) sesquiplane conversion of

Potez 392, the small lower wing braced to the upper by two struts; flown in 1932 with 433-kW (580-hp) Hispano-Suiza 12Hb, but no further development

Specification
Potez 390 A.2
Type: two-seat observation aircraft
Powerplant: one 433-kW (580-hp) Hispano-Suiza 12Hb Vee piston engine
Performance: maximum speed 240 km/h (149 mph); service ceiling 7000 m (22,965 ft); range 700 km (435 miles)
Weights: empty equipped 1492 kg (3,289 lb); maximum take-off 2650 kg (5,842 lb)

The boom-like rear fuselage of the Potez 37 was designed to provide its gunner with a good field of fire. The engine was a 485-kW (650-hp) Hispano-Suiza.

Dimensions: span 16.00 m (52 ft 6 in); length 10.00 m (32 ft 9¾ in); height 3.40 m (11 ft 1¾ in); wing area 35.00 m² (376.75 sq ft)
Armament: one nose-mounted synchronised 7.5-mm (0.295-in) Darne machine-gun, and twin 7.7-mm (0.303-in) Lewis machine-guns on a ring mounting over the observer's cockpit, plus up to 120 kg (265 lb) of bombs on underfuselage racks

Potez 43 series

The success of the Potez 36 tourer led to development of the refined **Potez 43**, the prototype making its first flight in June 1932. It retained the strut-braced high wing which had characterised the P.36, but the span of the leading-edge slats was reduced to equal that of the ailerons and a refined fuselage was introduced with cabin accommodation for three. There was provision for wheel spats and the tail unit was revised.

The prototype and early production aircraft were powered by the Potez 6Ac engine, but later variants relied mainly on the Renault 4. Total production was 161, including a number built specifically for the Armée de l'Air for liaison and training.

Variants
Potez 430: prototype and first 24 series aircraft with Potez 6Ac engine
Potez 431: production version, 60

The Potez 430 lightplane was fitted with short-span leading-edge slats forward of the ailerons.

built from June 1933; leading-edge slats were modified and fin of increased area fitted
Potez 432: three aircraft with 75-kW (100-hp) Renault 4Pei engine
Potez 434: nine aircraft with 89-kW (120-hp) de Havilland Gipsy Major I engine; first example flew on 2 November 1933
Potez 435: 11 aircraft with 89-kW (120-hp) Renault 4Pdi engine
Potez 438: production version with 89-kW (120-hp) Renault 4Pdi engine, and introduced tailwheel; 33 delivered to Armée de l'Air from May 1934 onwards for liaison, observation and training; served with the Centres Aériens Régionaux training reservist

pilots, and also attached to observation units, taking part in army manoeuvres from 1934; equipment included wireless and camera; 17 reconditioned and sold for private use in 1937; others built as new for private owners

Specification
Potez 438
Type: three-seat liaison, observation and training aircraft
Powerplant: one 89-kW (120-hp)

Renault 4Pdi inline piston engine
Performance: maximum speed 170 km/h (106 mph); service ceiling 5000 m (16,405 ft); range 700 km (435 miles)
Weights: empty equipped 560 kg (1,235 lb); maximum take-off 840 kg (1,852 lb)
Dimensions: span 11.30 m (37 ft 1 in); length 7.65 m (25 ft 1¼ in); height 2.36 m (7 ft 9 in); wing area 18.00 m² (193.76 sq ft)

Potez 54

Built as a private venture, the **Potez 54** M.4 category prototype flew for the first time on 14 November 1933. A *multiplace de combat* design by Louis Coroller, it was intended as a four-seater capable of performing duties as escort fighter, bomber or long-range reconnaissance aircraft. Largely of wood construction, the Potez 54 was a high-wing monoplane with twin fins and rudders, powered by two 515-kW (690-hp) Hispano-Suiza 12Xbrs V-12 engines in streamlined nacelles which were connected to the fuselage by stub wings. The main landing gear units retracted into the nacelles, and bomb racks were mounted beneath the stub wings. During development the original tail-

Potez 540

plane was replaced by a single fin and rudder, and in this form the type was redesignated **Potez 540 No. 1** and delivered to the Armée de l'Air on 25 November 1934. Parallel with the Potez

540 were developed the **Potez 541** prototype, powered by Gnome-Rhône 14Kdrs radials, and the **Potez 542** with 537-kW (720-hp) Lorraine Petrel engines.

All versions had defensive armament of manually-operated nose and dorsal turrets and a semi-retractable ventral 'dustbin' position; radio, oxygen, night and blind flying equipment were standard, and reconnaissance cameras could be carried.

Specification
Potez 540
Powerplant: two 515-kW (690-hp) Hispano-Suiza 12Xirs Vee piston engines
Performance: maximum speed 310 km/h (193 mph); service ceiling

5182 m (17,000 ft); range with maximum bombload 1250 km (777 miles)
Weights: empty equipped 3785 kg (8,344 lb); maximum take-off 5950 kg (13,118 lb)
Dimensions: span 22.10 m (72 ft 6 in); length 16.20 m (53 ft 1¾ in); height 3.88 m (12 ft 8¾ in); wing area 76.00 m² (818.08 sq ft)
Armament: three 7.5-mm (0.295-in) Darne machine-guns, plus a bombload of either four 225-kg (496-lb) bombs on external racks, or 10 55-kg (121-lb) bombs in bomb bay

The Potez 54 retained the typically angular lines of French bombers of the 1930s. This 540 is seen at Middle Wallop in 1940.

Potez 56 series

Designed by Louis Coroller as an executive transport, the prototype **Potez 56** (F-ANSU) made its first flight on 18 June 1934. Largely of wood construction, the Potez 56 was a cantilever low-wing monoplane with a wing section based on that of the Potez 53 racer, and with a single fin and rudder. It had exceptionally clean lines, the main landing gear units retracting backwards into the nacelles of the two Potez 9Ab radial engines. There was accommodation for a crew of two in an enclosed cockpit, with a cabin for six passengers. Early tests confirmed that the Potez 56 had good flight qualities and was remarkably stable.

Series production included at least three **Potez 561** aircraft, with variable-pitch propellers to improve take-off, aerodynamically refined engine nacelles and revised cockpit windows.

Military versions followed, for use in the carrierborne liaison, general utility, target tug, and twin-engine pilot training roles. Total production of all versions, military and civil, was 72, the final examples being two Potez 568 P.3 aircraft, the last of a batch that was completed at the time of the June 1940 armistice with Germany.

Variants
Potez 56: prototype and 16 series passenger transports; sometimes known as **Potez 560**
Potez 561: modified version with improved performance; three built
Potez 565: original designation
Potez 56E: one-off aircraft with more streamlined fuselage flown in January 1936; intended for use on carrier *Béarn* and fitted with arrester hook, it ended its career as liaiason aircraft at naval air station Orly, where it was coded OR-31
Potez 566: first of three was flown as **Potez 566 T.3** on 2 July 1937; a three-seater the T in designation stood for Travail, a category of general-purpose aircraft; had fuselage similar to that of the Potez 56E, but with manually-operated dorsal turret for single 7.5-mm (0.295-in) Darne machine-gun and a ventral nacelle with extensive glazing for observer; two Potez 9Eo engines of 179 kW (240 hp) gave a maximum speed of 310 km/h (193 mph)
Potez 567: version for French navy (22 built) and delivered between October 1939 and March 1940; flown by *sections d'entrainement* at various

training stations, its basic function was towing sleeve targets for air-firing exercises
Potez 568: the Armée de l'Air ordered 26 **Potez 568 P.3** aircraft in 1938, which were equipped to train pilots to fly twin-engine aircraft by day or night; the cabin had pilots' seats side-by-side, with the instructor located to the rear behind a large raised windscreen

Specification
Potez 560
Type: eight-seat executive transport
Powerplant: two 138-kW (185-hp) Potez 9Ab radial piston engines
Performance: maximum speed

In general configuration the twin-piston powered Potez 560 bears a remarkable resemblance to the Airspeed Envoy, and was one of the first aircraft ever to be designed from the outset as an executive transport.

270 km/h (168 mph); service ceiling 6000 m (19,685 ft); range 650 m (404 miles)
Weights: empty equipped 1910 kg (4,211 lb); maximum take-off 2980 kg (6,570 lb)
Dimensions: span 16.00 m (52 ft 6 in); length 11.84 m (38 ft 10¼ in); height 4.60 m (15 ft 1¼ in); wing area 33.00 m² (355.22 sq ft)

Potez 58 series

Ultimate development in the series of high-wing monoplane tourers which began with the Potez 36, the **Potez 58** prototype first flew in September 1934. Like its immediate predecessor, the Potez 43, it had accommodation for a pilot and two passengers. The wing retained its Vee-strut bracing, leading-edge slats and folding capability, but the wing root was enlarged, the fuselage and tail unit design further refined, and the divided landing gear strengthened and equipped with spatted wheel fairings as standard.

Variants
Potez 580: first production version, 80 built from autumn 1934 and powered by 89-kW (120-hp) Potez 6B engine; ambulance version was tested,

with provision for stretcher case and attendant
Potez 584: four built in 1935 with 89-kW (120-hp) de Havilland Gipsy Major I engine and tailwheel replacing tailskid
Potez 585: 108 examples built from 1935, 99 of which had military equipment and were delivered against Armée de l'Air orders which had originally called for 120 aircraft; final deliveries in 1938
Potez 586: similar to Potez 585, but cabin redesigned to accommodate pilot and three passengers; 10 built 1936-37

Specification
Potez 585
Type: three-seat liaison and observation aircraft

Powerplant: one 97-kW (130-hp) Potez 6Ba radial piston engine
Performance: maximum speed 190 km/h (118 mph); cruising speed 160 km/h (99 mph); range 750 km (466 miles)
Weights: empty equipped 515 kg (1,135 lb); maximum take-off 906 kg (1,997 lb)

The Potez 595 was distinguished from its Potez 58 relatives largely by its radial powerplant enclosed by a Townend ring.

Dimensions: span 11.30 m (37 ft 0¾ in); length 7.44 m (24 ft 5 in); height 2.36 m (7 ft 9 in); wing area 19.00 m² (204.52 sq ft)

Potez 62 and 65
to
Potez (CAMS) 141, 160 and 161

Potez 62 and 65

The prototype **Potez 62** civil airliner, based on the military Potez 54, made its maiden flight on 28 January 1935. It retained the strut-braced high-set wing of the Potez 54, which was married to a re-designed fuselage of excellent aero-dynamic form. Pilot and co-pilot were seated side-by-side in a control cabin with, to their rear, two cabins accommodating up to 16 passengers. The **Potez 621**, flown later in 1935, introduced 537-kW (720-hp) Hispano-Suiza 12Xrs Vee engines and 2° sweepback on the wings. Production totalled 23, four of the 14 machines built as Potez 62s later being converted to Potez 621 standard, and in 1937 nine Potez 62s were re-engined with 671-kW (900-hp) Gnome-Rhône 14N16/17 radials.

The type interested the Armée de l'Air, which ordered a troop transport version, the **Potez 65** or **Potez 650 TT**, which had accommodation for a crew of three plus 14 fully-equipped troops or, if equipped as an ambulance, with provision for six stretchers, four seated patients and one medical attendant. Two orders totalling 15 aircraft were received by Potez, the first of them being delivered in late 1935. Powered by 537-kW (720-hp) Hispano-Suiza 12 Xirs I or HS 12Xbrs I/grs I engines, and with a maximum take-off weight higher than that of the Potez 62, the military version had maximum speed reduced to 300 km/h (186 mph).

Specification
Potez 62 or 620
Type: civil transport
Powerplant: two 649-kW (870-hp) Gnome-Rhône 14Kirs Mistral radial

piston engines
Performance: maximum speed 325 km/h (202 mph); service ceiling 7500 m (24,605 ft); range 1000 km (621 miles)
Weights: empty equipped 4895 kg (10,791 lb); maximum take-off 7500 kg (16,535 lb)
Dimensions: span 22.45 m (73 ft

Combining the general configuration and stub-mounted powerplant of the Potez 54 with an elegant fuselage, Potez 621s served with Air France in Europe.

7¾ in); length 17.32 m (56 ft 10 in); height 3.90 m (12 ft 9½ in); wing area 76.00 m² (818.08 sq ft)

Potez 63 series

Built in response to a complex French air ministry requirement of 1934, the proto-type **Potez 63.01**, designed by Louis Coroller and his team, first flew on 25 April 1936. Powered by two Hispano-Suiza 14 Hbs radials, it was intended for three major functions: as a C.2 category two-seat interceptor or escort fighter, as a CN.2 category two-seat night-fighter, and as a C.3 category three-seat fighter which would direct by radio the operations of a single-seat fighter unit over the scene of battle.

Of modern appearance, the Potez 63 was the first of the classic twin-engine 'strategic' fighters, an all-metal low-wing monoplane with retractable landing gear, twin fins and rudders, and the crew beneath a long glazed canopy. After a crash landing, the repaired first proto-type was redesignated **Potez 630.01,** emerging with HS 14Ab engines and a redesigned tail unit. A second prototype, the **Potez 631.01,** flew on 15 March 1937 powered by two Gnome-Rhône 14Mars radials, but was otherwise similar to the earlier machine. In June 1937 the Potez Méaulte factory was taken over by the nationalised SNCAN, which soon received orders for a total of 80 Potez 630s and 90 Potez 631s.

The **Potez 633.01,** a B.2 category two-seat day-bomber prototype, flew in late 1937, and although a large series order for the Armée de l'Air was sub-sequently cancelled several export contracts were signed. The bomber retained the glazed panelling seen under the nose of the early prototypes (deleted on series Potez 630s and Potez 631s) and had an internal bomb-bay for eight 50-kg (110-lb) bombs. Romania ultimately received 21 Potez 633s, which were used in support of the German offensive in the Ukraine during 1941; Greece obtained 10 machines, an eleventh aircraft crashing on its delivery flight, and these flew against the invading Italians in October 1940. The balance of the Romanian and Greek orders, 19 and 13 respectively, were seized by the French, as were eight aircraft ordered by China. The type was used by Groupe de Bombarde-

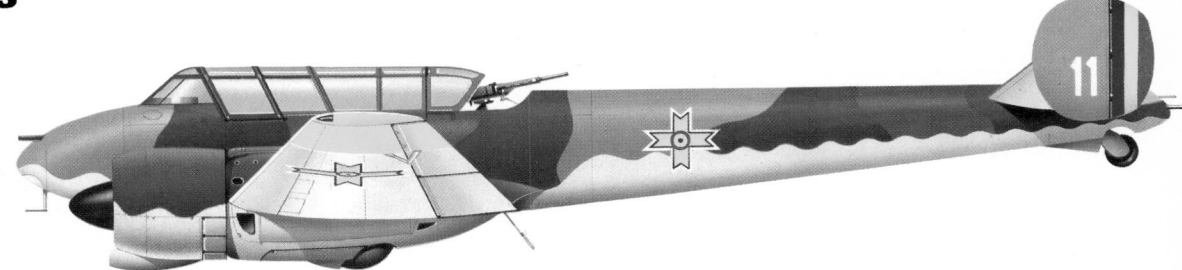

Potez 633 of the Romanian air force in 1940-41.

Potez 63.11 of an Armée de l'Air army co-operation squadron in 1940.

ment d'Assaut II/52, but after one oper-ational mission in May 1940 the aircraft were all used as operational trainers for the Breguet 693.

The relatively poor performance of the Potez 630 led to its early diversion to training duties, but additional orders were received for the Potez 631, and this was allocated in three-aircraft batches to 20 *sections de commandement* of single-seat fighter *escadrilles*. The C.3 concept outlined above was soon dis-carded, and by the time of the Battle of France the Potez 631 was flying with day-fighter Groupe de Chasse II/8 and

night-fighter ECN I/13 and II/13, as well as with the land-based navy Escadrilles AC 1 and AC 2.

The **Potez 637** was intended as a stop-gap A.3 category three-seat army co-operation and reconnaissance air-craft. The prototype flew in the summer of 1938, and all 60 series machines had been delivered by September 1939. The Potez 637 resembled the Potez 631, but had a ventral gondola (for the observer) which also accommodated a machine-gun for defence beneath the tail, and there was provision for a camera in the rear fuselage. The Potez 637 replaced

the Potez 542 in the 33ᵉ and 52ᵉ Escadres de Reconnaissance, the type performing the first reconnaissance mis-sion over the German lines on 4 Septem-ber 1939; frequently unescorted, it suffered heavy losses during the ensu-ing nine months. Potez 637 no. 52 was the first Allied aircraft shot down on the Western Front on 8 September 1939.

The prototype **Potez 63.11 A.3 No. 01**, flown initially on 31 December 1938, had a redesigned nose section, fully glazed and rounded, and the crew canopy had been revised. Further modi-fications had been incorporated in the nose of the first production aircraft which flew on 10 July 1939, and by 31 May 1940 702 series tactical reconnaissance and army co-operation machines had been built.

The Potez 63.11 suffered even more heavily than the other Potez types and by June 1940 over 200 had been lost in action.

Production continued after the German occupation of the Méaulte and Les Mureaux factories, and at least 850 Potez 63.11s were completed in total. The Luftwaffe used over 100 for training and liaison, the Regia Aeronautica 15 and the Romanian air arm 53.

Variants
Potez 63.01 and 630.01: designations of first two prototypes
Potez 631.01: first Gnome-Rhône 14Mars-powered prototype
Potez 630: production fighter with Hispano-Suiza 14Ab engines; 82 built, of which one sold to Yugoslavia and two to Switzerland
Potez 631: production fighter with Gnome-Rhône 14Mars engines; 207 built
Potez 632: originally the **Potez 630 CN2 No.01** prototype night-fighter; intended as **Potez 632 Bp.2** dive-bomber prototype for Aéronavale, but completed as a conventional light bomber with Hispano-Suiza 14Ab engines
Potez 633: production aircraft;

French order for 125 of this B.2 light bomber cancelled, but export orders of 21 delivered to Romania and 10 to Greece; 40 seized by Armée de l'Air
Potez 637: series of 60 reconnaissance aircraft for Armée de l'Air
Potez 63.11 No.01 and **No.02:** prototypes of redesigned three-seat reconnaissance aircraft with new nose section and crew canopy
Potez 63.11: major production version, over 850 built

Specification
Potez 63.11
Type: three-seat tactical

reconnaissance and army co-operation aircraft
Powerplant: two 522-kW (700-hp) Gnome-Rhône 14 M04/05 or 06/07 radial piston engine
Performance: maximum speed 425 km/h (264 mph); service ceiling 8500 m (27,885 ft); range 1500 km (932 miles)
Dimensions: span 16.00 m (52 ft 6 in); length 10.93 m (35 ft 10½ in); height 3.08 m (10 ft 1¼ in); wing area 32.70 m² (351.99 sq ft)
Armament: initially, one fixed forward-firing and one underfuselage fixed rear-firing 7.5-mm (0.295-in) MAC 1934 machine-gun, plus similar gun on

The Potez 63.II was the major production version of the Potez 63 series, seen here in its ground attack form with four 7.5-mm (0.295-in) MAC 1934 machine-guns in underwing fairings.

trainable mounting in rear cockpit; early 1940 supplemented by two additional fixed forward-firing and two additional ventral rear-firing 7.5-mm (0.295-in) MAC machine-guns; most aircraft also had four fixed forward-firing 7.5-mm (0.295-in) MAC 1934 weapons under outboard wing panels; provision for four 50-kg (110-lb) bombs on underwing racks

Potez 670 and 671

Developed from the Potez 631, the **Potez 670.01** three-seat long-range fighter had a fuselage similar to that of its predecessor married to a wing of new design, and main landing gear units that retracted fully into the nacelles of the two 522-kW (700-hp) Gnome-Rhône 14Mars radial engines; the prototype made its maiden flight on 30 March 1939. Re-engined with 596-kW (800-hp) Hispano-Suiza 14Ab 12/13 radials, but retaining the original proposed armament of two forward-firing 20-mm HS-404 cannon and two forward-firing 7.5-mm (0.295-in) MAC 1934 machine-guns plus one aft firing trainably-mounted HS-404 cannon, it was redesignated **Potez 671.01**. When test flown from July 1939 this demonstrated a maximum speed of 500 km/h (311 mph). The specification was revised to two-seat configuration and the first production orders were received, an initial batch of 40 **Potez 671** fighters being under construction at the Potez Méaulte factory when it was overrun by German forces.

Potez 840

The first prototype (F-WJSH) of the **Potez 840** executive transport made its initial flight on 29 April 1961. An all-metal low-wing cantilever monoplane, it was powered by four 328-kW (440-shp) Turboméca Astazou II turboprops, had fully retractable tricycle landing gear, and carried a crew of three with cabin accommodation for up to 18 passengers. A second prototype, flown in June 1962, had Astazou XII engines of 447 kW (600 shp) each.

After a sales tour in North America by the **P-840.02**, plans were made for a production batch of 25 Potez 840s, but in fact only two more prototypes were

The Potez 840 failed to find a niche in an already crowded market despite the additional safety of a four-engined layout when most competitors used only two.

built, one of these being reserved for static testing. Two **Potez 841** aircraft followed, powered by 417-kW (560-shp) Pratt & Whitney Aircraft of Canada PT6A-6 turboprops. Finally, the modified **Potez 842** appeared in 1965, a second aircraft, also powerd by Astazou XIIs following two years later.

These eight light transports were the last aircraft of the Potez marque to be built; one is now exhibited at the Musée de l'Air, Paris, and a second has been re-

stored and is flown under the auspices of the French Association Aéromedicale. The Potez 840 spanned 19.33 m (63 ft 5 in), had a maximum take-off weight of 7800 kg (17,196 lb) and maximum speed of 540 km/h (336 mph).

Potez (CAMS) 141, 160 and 161

The acquisition by Potez in 1933 of Chantiers Aéro-Maritimes de la Seine (CAMS) brought increased interest in the development of maritime aircraft, and the **Potez (CAMS) 141** was designed to meet an official requirement for a maritime reconnaissance flying-boat. A large-span monoplane wing was carried on a faired superstructure above the hull, to which it was braced on each side by large N-struts. A stabilising float was strut-mounted beneath each wing, and the two-step all-metal hull carried at the rear a twin fin-and-rudder tail unit. Carrying a crew of nine to 12, the 41.00 m (134 ft 6¼ in) span Potez 141 was powered by four 694-kW (930-hp) Hispano-Suiza 12Y-26/27 Vee engines in wing-mounted nacelles. First flown on 21 January 1938, successful testing led to large orders, but changing policies and the development of World War II meant that no production aircraft were built.

To meet a French air ministry requirement for a 20-passenger transatlantic flying-boat, which was required to have a cruising speed of 250 km/h (155 mph) and range of 6000 km (3,728 miles), the **Potez (CAMS) 161** was designed and was to have been powered by six 890-hp Hispano-Suiza 12Ydrs Vee engines. To evaluate the design of this 45.72 m (150 ft 10 in) span flying-boat, the company designed and built the **Potez (CAMS) 160** which was a scale replica just over one-third the size of the Potez 161. Powered by six 30-kW (40-hp) Train inline engines and with a crew of two, it demonstrated a maximum speed of 222 km/h (138 mph) at 950 m (3,115 ft), but preparations for war eventually brought development to an end.

The Potez (CAMS) 141 weighed in at 25900 kg (57,096 lb) and had a top speed of 320 km/h (199 mph). Its bomb load totalled 1500 kg (3,308 lb).

Praga aircraft

The Czech aero engine manufacturing company Ceskomoravska-Kolben-Danek, established in 1915, adopted the name Praga for some of its power units. When, in 1931, the company became involved in the design and construction of aircraft the name CKD-Praga was adopted, though the firm was known more usually as Praga. The Praga company acquired the services of engineers Benes and Hajn, formerly with Avia, and their initials were used as part of the designation of some of the early aircraft built by the company. These initial designs included the **Praga E.36** two-seat open cockpit military biplane for multi-role use which, powered by a 447-kW (600-hp) Hispano-Suiza 12 Nbr or Praga ESVR Vee engine, could be armed with two fixed forward-firing synchronised machine-guns, plus an additional gun on a trainable mount in the rear cockpit, and up to some 800 kg (1,764 lb) of bombs. The **B.H.39NZ** biplane of 1931 was a two-seat open cockpit primary trainer powered by an 89-kW (120-hp) Walter NZ radial engine, being followed by the **B.H. 39G** of 1936 with 112-kW (150-hp) Walter Gemma and, in the next year, by the **B.H.39AG** with a 112-kW (150-hp) Armstrong Siddeley Genet Major engine. A refined and

slightly larger version of the B.H.39 for use as an advanced trainer, with a 224-kW (300-hp) Hispano-Suiza Vee engine, had the designation **B.H.41**. Between them, numerically, was a lighter-weight biplane trainer designated **E.40**, which was powered by a 71-kW (95-hp) Walter Minor engine. The **E.44**, of very clean biplane configuration, was designed as a single-seat fighter and, powered by a 410-kW (550-hp) Praga ES Vee engine, had an armament of two synchronised forward-firing machine-guns. A further attempt to produce an attractive single-seat fighter of biplane configuration resulted in the **E.45**, flown with both the Rolls-Royce Kestrel V and Hispano-Suiza 12Ybrs. Each of the powerplants developed some 447 kW (600 hp), and if the reported maximum speed of approximately 400 km/h (249 mph) was in fact attained (a speed superior to that of the contemporary Hawker Fury and Hart), it seems strange that the E.45 was not built in large numbers.

However, Praga gained more success with its civil designs, especially the **E.114 Air Baby** which was also built in small numbers after World War II had ended. A side-by-side two-seat cabin monoplane of high-wing configuration, it was powered initially by a 30-kW (40-hp) Praga B flat-two engine, but was later made available as the **E.115**, with a

48-kW (65-hp) Praga D flat-four engine. Praga then moved up to a four-seat cabin monoplane of high-wing configuration, the **E.210**, which had a twin fin-and-rudder tail unit and was powered by two 71-kW (95-hp) Walter Minor engines in wing-mounted nacelles, arranged to drive pusher propellers. The subsequent **E.214** was also a four-seat cabin monoplane, but of more conventional configuration with a fuselage similar to that of the E.114 and powered by a single 56-kW (75-hp) Pobjoy R radial engine. The last of the company's pre-war designs was the **E.241**, an advanced trainer of biplane configuration which, powered by a 254-kW (340-hp) Walter Pollux engine, had a maximum speed of 240 km/h (143 mph).

The Praga E.114 was built in low numbers, its performance on its small engine when 'two up' being severely limited.

Specification
Praga E.114 Air Baby
Type: two-seat light cabin monoplane
Powerplant: one 30-kW (40-hp) Praga B flat-two piston engine
Performance: maximum speed 150 km/h (93 mph); service ceiling 3300 m (10,825 ft); range 510 km (317 miles)
Weights: empty 265 kg (584 lb); maximum take-off 465 kg (1,025 lb)
Dimensions: span 10.90 m (35 ft 9 in); length 6.58 m (21 ft 7 in); height 1.65 m (5 ft 5 in); wing area 15.20 m² (163.62 sq ft)

Pratt-Read LNE-1

A single civil-registered example of the Pratt-Read all-wood two-seat side-by-side glider was evaluated by the US Navy in 1942. Proving satisfactory this

was acquired and an order placed for 100 additional examples, the first of these production aircraft being used for test and evaluation under the designation

Pratt-Read XLNE-1, the remaining being designated **LNE-1**. In 1943 some 73 were transferred to the USAAF which redesignated the type **TG-32**, but these saw comparatively little use and were

sold as surplus well before VJ-Day. Of cantilever high-wing configuration with monowheel plus skid landing gear, the 16.61 m (54 ft 6 in) span LNE-1 had a maximum launch weight of 522 kg (1,150 lb).

Procaer F15 Picchio

The Italian company, Procaer, known in full as Progetti Costruzioni Aeronautiche SpA, had been involved in development and production of the **Procaer F15 Picchio** four-seat lightplane since the prototype flew for the first time on 7 May 1959. It featured a cantilever low-wing monoplane with a basic structure of wood, covered by plywood with an outer skin of light alloy. Its configuration included permanently attached wingtip tanks, tricycle landing gear, and a fully enclosed four-seat cabin. Initial production version was the F15 with a 119-kW (160-hp) Avco Lycoming engine, followed in 1960 by the **F15A** with 134-kW (180-hp) Avco Lycoming O-360-A1A, the **F15B** certificated in 1962 with greater wing area and larger wing fuel tanks, and the **F15C** which, with a 194-kW (260-hp) Continental IO-470-E engine, was introduced in 1964. Development was then concentrated on the **F15D** with a 186-kW (250-hp) Franklin 6AS-350 turbocharged engine, and the **F15E** with an

all-metal fuselage and a 224-kW (300-hp) Continental IO-520-F. However, production of the F15D was suspended and the F15E was acquired by Societa Aeronautica Italiana Ing A. Ambrosini & C., which redesignated the aircraft **Ambrosini NF 15** and continued its development for a time. But when the NF 15 failed to gain an anticipated Italian air force contract, it did not enter production.

General Avia then developed by arrangement with Procaer an improved version of the F15E Picchio and this, designated **F15F**, had a moulded canopy instead of a conventional cabin to enclose the four seats, and is powered by a 149-kW (200-hp) Avco Lycoming IO-360-A1B1 engine. A prototye (I-PROL) was built by General Avia and flown on 20 October 1977. Both companies sought a third party to begin licence production with in Europe. The sole prototype crashed in 1984 and the F15F never entered production.

Specification
Procaer F15C Picchio
Type: four-seat cabin monoplane
Powerplant: one 194-kW (260-hp) Continental IO-470-E flat-six piston engine
Performance: maximum speed 340 km/h (211 mph); service ceiling 6000 m (19,685 ft); range with maximum payload 1600 km (994 miles)
Weights: empty 800 kg (1,764 lb);

The Picchio is typical of the designs of Stelio Frati: simple construction, clean lines, roomy cabin and excellent performance on a moderate engine.

maximum take-off 1300 kg (2,866 lb)
Dimensions: span 10.10 m (33 ft 1½ in); length 7.52 m (24 ft 8 in); height 2.81 m (9 ft 2½ in); wing area 13.30 m² (143.16 sq ft)

Procter (Nash) Petrel

Procter Aircraft Associates in the UK acquired design rights for the **Mitchell-Procter Kittiwake I** single-seat lightweight aircraft which was intended for amateur construction. From it was de-

veloped the two-seat **Proctor Petrel** which also was designed for amateur construction, but in 1978 controlling interest in the company was acquired by Alan Nash and in 1980 the name of this

company was changed to Nash Aircraft Ltd. The company is continuing development of the Petrel as a production aircraft, which is a cantilever low-wing monoplane with fixed tricycle landing gear. Standard powerplant is a 134-kW (180-hp) Avco Lycoming piston engine.

Side-by-side two-seat accommodation is provided beneath a bubble canopy that gives an excellent all-round view, and the Petrel is considered ideal for glider towing and training. A pre-production batch of five aircraft was under construction in 1983 but the company failed to win any orders.

Promavia Jet Squalus

Italian designer Stello Frati was behind many well known light aircraft. His distinctive style resulted in several shapely designs such as the SIAI-Marchetti SF-260 and Procaer F-15. He established the General Avia company in Italy in 1970 to develop prototypes of his own design which would then be offered to other manufacturers for production. In conjunction with the Belgian Government-backed firm Promavia he began work on the **F.1300 Squalo** primary jet trainer, intended as a low-cost aircraft primarily for the military market. Construction of the prototype began in March 1985 which involved limited use of composites in an all-metal airframe. It was intended to be powered by the Williams WJ-44 or Garrett F199 turbofan. The F.1300 was a conventional side-by-side trainer with a fared-in one piece canopy. The tail and low-set tailplane were mounted on a boom empennage above the engine. Engine intakes protruded from either side of the fuselage above the wing, which itself had 5° of dihedral, and only 1° of leading edge sweep at the root. It was most reminiscent of a T-2 Buckeye without the tip tanks.

By the time the prototype (OO-SQA) was rolled out, both its name and appearance had changed. As the **Jet Squalus F1300 NGT** (Squalus is latin for Shark) it was a far sleeker design. A lengthened, more pointed nose was complemented by a marked increase in tail sweep. The intakes were also redesigned and positioned at the wing roots. On either side of the intakes were small strakes, referred to by Promavia as 'spinners', to smooth the airflow over the wing and reduce stalling speeds. The rear section was deepened and fitted with a ventral airbrake.

Two prototypes were built and the type made its first public appearance in the static display at the Farnborough International air show in 1986. The second aircraft was fitted with the more powerful Garrett TFE109-1 engine as developed for the Fairchild T-46A. Four underwing hardpoints were now available and ejection seats were optional. First flight came on 30 April 1987 and the aircraft has slowly built up over 250 test

flying hours over the intervening years. Customer interest has been slow. In 1991 the Jet Squalus was demonstrated to the Canadian Armed Forces as a potential T-33 replacement. In the event of an order it was planned to transfer production to Saskatoon, Saskatchewan under the auspices of the Promavia International Corporation, but no order was forthcoming. The second prototype (OO-JET) was then configured to airline-standard for pilot training, but by late 1992 had still not flown. If built, the third aircraft is planned to have a pressurised cabin. Promavia are now responsible for the entire Jet Squalus programme and currently have a developmental version on offer for the USAF/USN JPATS competition. Russia's Mikoyan has been touted as a possible, if unlikely, manufacturer for the type not least because of the CIS's pressing need for a new jet trainer.

Variants
AWS (Air Ward System): Four

proposed dedicated versions for maritime patrol/SAR, photographic reconnaissance, weapons training and target towing
ATTA 3000 (Advanced Tactical Training Aircraft): Tandem-seat version proposed for USAF/USN Joint Primary Training System (JPATS) competition. Equipped with staggered ejection-seats, EFIS cockpit, increased weapons capability and one of two engines. No US industry partner announced as yet
ARA 3600 (Attack Reconnaissance Aircraft): projected single-seat light attack and reconnaissance version, announced in 1989 similar to ATTA 300 with revised wing, TFE109-3 engine and up to 1000 kg (2,205 lb) of external stores

Specification
Promavia Jet Squalus F1300 NGT (first prototype only)
Type: two-seat primary and advanced military jet trainer

The Promavia Jet Squalus trainer has suffered a convoluted evolution with little to show for it in the end. Today, it seems increasingly likely that the type will finally be built in Russia, where it will benefit from low production costs.

Powerplant: one 5.92 kN (1,330 lb) Garrett TFE109-1 turbofan
Performance: maximum level speed at 4265 m (14,000 ft) 519 km/h (322 mph); maximum rate of climb 762 m per min (2500 ft per min); service ceiling 11275 m (37,000 ft); ferry range 1850 km (1150 miles)
Weights: empty 1300 kg (2,866 lb); maximum take-off 2000 kg (4,409 lb)
Dimensions: span 9.04 m (29 ft 8 in); height 3.60 m (11 ft 9¾ in); length 9.36 m (30 ft 8½ in)
Armament: four underwing pylons each stressed to 150 kg (331 lb) can carry a variety of bombs, rockets, gun pods and other stores

RFB aircraft

The West German company Rhein-Flugzeugbau GmbH (RFB) was established in 1956, the company's early work being involved with the development of aircraft fuselage and wing structures of glass-fibre-reinforced resins. The renowned late Dr Alexander Lippisch originated the concept of an aircraft that would fly economically in ground effect at low speed and low altitude, and have the capability to overfly ground obstacles. The first research craft based on this idea was the **Collins X-112 Aerofoil Boat** built and flown in the USA in 19634, and development of this concept was continued by RFB in the late 1960s, the **RFB X-113 Am Aerofoil Boat** flying from Lake Constance in late 1970. It was followed by the improved **X-114**, an amphibious aircraft of six/seven-seat capacity, combining the typical reversed delta-wing (providing the ground-effect air cushion) and a ducted-fan power unit. The machine was used as a research aircraft from spring 1977, and the considerable experience gained with this powerplant led to the adoption of the basic type by RFB in more conventional aircraft.

First of these was the **Fanliner**, a two-seat lightweight aircraft developed jointly by RFB and Grumman American

in the USA, which had the wings and tail unit of the Grumman American AA-5A/Cheetah, and an entirely new fuselage incorporating a ducted-fan powerplant. Two prototypes were flown successfully but there was no commercial interest. Development was then concentrated on an earlier proposal for a tandem two-seat trainer with retractable tricycle landing gear and based yet again on ducted-fan propulsion. In March 1975 RFB was awarded a contract for two prototypes by the Federal German defence ministry, and the first of these prototypes, designated **AWI-2**, was powered by two 112-kW (150-hp) Wankel rotating combustion engines driving a variable-pitch fan. The **ATI-2** second prototype differed primarily by having a 313-kW (420-shp) Allison 250-C20B turboshaft engine, and these aircraft flew respectively on 27 October 1977 and 31 May 1978. The AWI-2 was later re-engined with the Allison 250-C20B and brought up to production military standard under the designation **Fantrainer 400**; when given a more powerful Allison 250-C30 engine the aircraft was redesignated **Fantrainer 600**. RFB received an order for 47 Fantrainers from the Royal Thai Air Force, comprising 31 Fantrainer 400s and a further 16 Fantrainer 600s. Two were delivered direct from Germany with the remainer supplied in com-

ponent form, for assembly by the RTAF. The Fantrainer 400 has metal wings while those of the 600 version are composite structures. Assembly of all versions was completed by 1991.

In 1990 Rockwell and MBB announced a turbofan-powered aircraft which they were developing for the USAF/USN JPATS (Joint Primary Aircraft Training System) competitiion. Based on the Fantrainer the **Fan Ranger** has been redesigned to accommodate a Pratt & Whitney JT15D-4 turbofan, and a Collins 'glass' cockpit. The Fan Ranger will be assembled by RFB and the prototype first flew in January 1993.

Specification
RFB Fantrainer 600
Type: basic/IFR trainer
Powerplant: one 485-kW (650-shp) Allison 250-C30 turboshaft engine

Cheap to buy and operate, simple to maintain, the Fantrainer 400 offers a good combination of jet handling and performance.

derated to 447 kW (600 shp)
Performance: maximum speed 430 km/h (267 mph) at 5500 m (18,045 ft); service ceiling 7600 m (24,935 ft); range with maximum fuel 1390 km (864 miles)
Weights: empty 1060 kg (2,337 lb); maximum take-off 2300 kg (5,071 lb)
Dimensions: span 9.70 m (31 ft 10 in); length 9.23 m (30 ft 3½ in); height 3.00 m (9 ft 10 in); wing area 13.90 m² (149.62 sq ft)

R.W.D. 1/2/3/4/7

Intended originally to provide workshops for the students of Warsaw Technical University, premises built at Warsaw-Okecie and known initially as the Warsztaty Lotnicze were renamed Doświadczalne Warsztaty Lotnicze (experimental aviation workshops) in 1931. They were leased to three promising light aircraft designers, Stanislaw Rogalski, Stanislaw Wigura and Jerzy Drzewiecki, the R.W.D. initials of their surnames becoming part of the designation of the aircraft developed by them. First aircraft to emanate from this team before gaining the above workshops was the **R.W.D.1**, a very basic light two-seater of cantilever high-wing monoplane configuration powered by a 25-kW (34-hp) A.B.C. Scorpion flat-two engine. Flown first in September 1928, it was sufficiently successful to bring development of an improved

R.W.D.2 with a 30-kW (40-hp) Salmson AD.9 radial engine. The prototype, first flown in May 1929, proved good enough to complete a tour of Poland and a tour of Europe before establishing a class altitude record of 4004 m (13,136 ft) on 16 October 1929. This capability brought an order for three R.W.D.2s and three similar **R.W.D.4** aircraft with more powerful engines. Used by a Polish national team, these six aircraft had considerable competition success during 1930-31. A single light-weight and refined **R.W.D.7** was developed from the R.W.D.2 for record-breaking purposes and this, powered by a 60-kW (80-hp) Armstrong Siddeley Genet II radial engine, set FAI-ratified world class speed and altitude records of 178.75 km/h (111.06 mph) and 6023 m (19,760 ft) on 12 August 1931 and 30 September 1932 respectively.

The R.W.D.2 featured a Salmson radial piston engine of 30 kW (40 hp). The aircraft seen here was the prototype of 1929.

An **R.W.D.3** liaison aircraft based on the R.W.D.2 was built but proved unsuccessful, and in addition to the three R.W.D.4s built for competition use an additional seven were produced for clubs/private oweners. Spanning 10.50 m (34 ft 5½ in), the standard R.W.D.4 with an 86-kW (115-hp) Cirrus Hermes II engine had a maximum speed of 205 km/h (127 mph) at sea level.

R.W.D.5

The prototype (SP-AGJ) of a much refined version of the earlier R.W.D. two-seaters was flown on 7 August 1931, and in appearance this was a conventional high-wing monoplane typical of the period. Successful testing of the **R.W.D.5** prototype led to the construction of 20 production aircraft by D.W.L. in two batches, these being used extensively in sporting/touring activities and enjoying a good share of competition success. However, the most outstanding performance of the R.W.D.5 was that achieved by SP-AJU converted as the **R.W.D.5bis** for an attempted nonstop flight over the South Atlantic. With a reduced-span reinforced wing, increased fuel capacity and powered by a 97-kW (130-hp) de Havilland Gipsy Major engine, it was flown successfully by Captain Stanislaw Skarzyński to achieve a remarkable nonstop crossing from St Louis-de-Sénégal to Maceió, Brazil during 7/8 May 1933. It remains, to this day, the lightest aircraft to complete a nonstop flight across the South Atlantic, an achievement that brought great respect for the capability of the R.W.D. design team.

Specification
R.W.D.5 (initial production)
Type: light tourer
Powerplant: one 86-kW (115-shp) Hermes IIB inline piston engine
Performance: maximum speed 200 km/h (124 mph) at sea level;

service ceiling 4700 m (15,420 ft); range 1080 km (671 miles)
Weights: empty 445 kg (981 lb); maximum take-off 760 kg (1,676 lb)
Dimensions: span 10.50 m (34 ft 5½ in); length 7.20 m (23 ft 7½ in);

The thick-section cantilever wing of the R.W.D.5 offered its pilot high lift at low speeds.

height 2.70 m (8 ft 10¼ in); wing area 15.00 m² (161.46 sq ft)

R.W.D.8

Most extensively built of all R.W.D. designs, the two-seat parasol-wing **R.W.D.8** was first flown in prototype-form in late 1932. Its design incorporated a braced monoplane wing which had 12° of sweepback on its outer panels, fixed tailskid landing gear and open cockpits in tandem. Powerplant of the prototype was a 86-kW (115-hp) Cirrus Hermes II, but the R.W.D.8 later appeared with a variety of engines in the 75/112-kW (100/150-hp) range before production ended. Early testing showed that the aircraft had excellent performance, and about 100 were built by D.W.L. from early 1934 to 1938. However, the R.W.D.8 was also selected for use as the standard primary trainer of the Polish air force, and with demands far exceeding the capability of the R.W.D. plant a manufacturing licence was granted to Podlaska Wytwórnia Samolotów (P.W.S.). This company's aircraft differed slightly from the civil version, incorporating modifications requested by the Polish air force, and a total of about 500 was eventually built by P.W.S. Licences to build the R.W.D.8 were acquired also by Czechoslovakia, Estonia and Yugoslavia, but only the last country is known to have produced the type in some numbers.

In addition to full participation in sporting events during the mid- to late 1930s, the R.W.D.8 had a stirring finale to its military career in the days that followed the German invasion, even being used to harass enemy troops by dropping grenades upon them. About 60 aircraft escaped to Romania in the closing stage of the battle, many surviving the war, and others captured by German and Soviet forces also found employment in the training role.

Built by D.W.L., this is a standard production R.W.D.8 powered by a 82-kW (110-hp) Walter Junior.

Specification
R.W.D.8 (early production)
Type: sport/tourer aircraft
Powerplant: one 89-kW (120-shp) Walter Major inline piston engine
Performance: maximum speed 175 km/h (109 mph) at sea level;

service ceiling 5000 m (16,405 ft); range 435 km (270 miles)
Weights: empty 480 kg (1,058 lb); maximum take-off 750 kg (1,653 lb)
Dimensions: span 11.00 m (36 ft 1 in); length 8.00 m (26 ft 3 in); height 2.30 m (7 ft 6½ in); wing area 20.00 m² (215.29 sq ft)

R.W.D.9 and R.W.D.20

To compete in the Challenge de Tourisme International of 1932, a new braced high-wing monoplane designated **R.W.D.6** was designed and three examples were built. One of them was lost in an accident during early tests, but the other two took part in the Challenge and one was declared the winner. From this aircraft was developed an improved **R.W.D.9** to take part in the 1934 Challenge, an initial batch of 10 being laid down and the first of these flying in early 1934. Planned powerplant was a new Polish radial engine, the 209-kW (280-hp) Skoda GR.760. but delay in its development meant the prototype was

flown initially with a 198-kW (265-hp) Menasco B-6S Buccaneer. The R.W.D.9 differed primarily from its predecessor by being of four- rather than two-seat configuration, and four of the eight production aircraft (one airframe having been used for static tests) had the

With slats and wing slots fully deployed, this dramatically posed R.W.D.9, named 'Dar Tytoniowcow', flown by Tadeuz Karpinski, climbs steeply to clear the take-off obstacle at the 1934 IV Challenge de Tourisme International in Warsaw.

GR.760 engine, the other four having the 164-kW (220-hp) Walter Bora radial engine. Six of the R.W.D.9s took part in the 1934 Challenge, all of them finishing in the top 10 places and sweeping the board by being first, second and third; almost unbelieveably this performance was repeated in the Circuit of Europe in September of that year, the first three places falling to the R.W.D.9. As powered by the GR.760, the 11.64-m (38-ft 2¼-in) span R.W.D.9 had a maximum speed of 280 km/h (174 mph) at sea level.

For evaluation of fixed tricycle landing gear for lightplanes, the original R.W.D.9 prototype was so equipped; powered by a 97-kW (130-hp) Walter Major inline engine it was tested successfully in late 1938 under the designation R.W.D.20.

R.W.D.10

To provide Polish flying clubs with an aerobatic trainer, the R.W.D. team developed yet another braced high-wing monoplane, the single-seat R.W.D.10, of which the prototype flew for the first time in April 1933. Development of this aircraft to certification stage proved difficult, certification not being gained until 1936, but eventually about 30 aircraft were built. Production aircraft were somewhat refined by comparison with the prototype and these 7.50-m (24-ft 7½-in) span aircraft, powered as standard by a 82-kW (110-hp) P.Z. Inz Junior inline engine, had a maximum speed of 230 km/h (143 mph).

R.W.D.13

The strength of the R.W.D. design team was undoubtedly in aircraft of monoplane high-wing layout: an attempt to develop a twin-engine six-passenger feederliner of low-wing monoplane configuration, the R.W.D.11, failed to progress beyond the prototype stage. The following R.W.D.13 was, in effect, a lower-powered three-seat development of the R.W.D.6, of which two examples had taken part in the Challenge de Tourisme International of 1932. A braced high-wing monoplane of composite construction, with a wing that was foldable and incorporated wide-span leading-edge slats, the three-seat R.W.D.13 was otherwise conventional and powered in prototype form by an engine of 97 kW (130 hp). An initial order for 10 aircraft was followed by a series of repeat orders, and when production ended in September 1939 a total of about 100 had been built. The total included 15 R.W.D.13S ambulances, equipped for

For its day an extremely successful high-braced-wing touring aircraft, the R.W.D.13 possessed only moderate performance, courtesy of its Gypsy Major or Walter Major engine. However, it displayed excellent handling.

a pilot, stretcher case and medical attendant. Some 20 were exported, one of them being given to the Shah of Iran as a wedding present from the Polish government, and four were used as liaison aircraft by the Nationalist forces in the Spanish Civil War. Both the R.W.D.13 tourer and R.W.D.13S ambulance were built under licence in Yugoslavia, seeing extensive service for both civil and military use.

With the outbreak of World War II in September 1939 a number of R.W.D.13s were impressed for service with the Polish air force, and before the country fell to the German forces about 40 were flown to Romania, where most were used by that country's air force through-

out the war; when peace was restored some were returned to Poland.

Specification
R.W.D.13
Type: sport/tourer aircraft
Powerplant: one 97-kW (130-hp) de Havilland Gipsy Major I, or P.Z.Inz Major or Walter Major inline piston engine

Performance: maximum speed 210 km/h (130 mph) at sea level; service ceiling 4200 m (13,780 ft); range 900 km (559 miles)
Weights: empty 530 kg (1,166 lb); maximum take-off 930 kg (2,050 lb)
Dimensions: span 11.50 m (37 ft 8¾ in); length 7.85 m (25 ft 9 in); height 2.05 m (6 ft 8¾ in); wing area 16.00 m² (172.23 sq ft)

R.W.D.14

Under the designation R.W.D.12 a design study for a reconnaissance/observation aircraft derived from the R.W.D.8 was drawn up to meet an official request. However, this failed to gain solid interest and led to a new specification which became the subject of a design contest. The R.W.D. design team proposed a development of the R.W.D.12 powered by an engine of almost double the power, gaining a contract for three R.W.D.14 prototypes, one for static testing. The first, powered by a 313-kW (420-hp) Pratt & Whitney Wasp Junior engine, was flown in 1935 but performance fell below estimates and the improved R.W.D.14a that followed had a P.Z.L.G.1620A Mors radial engine of similar power. Flown in 1936, the aircraft was lost during the same year as a result of structural failure of the tail unit, and this was also the fate of a second R.W.D.14a when tested with a modified tail unit in 1937. Final prototype built by D.W.L. was the R.W.D.14b with

further revisions to the tail unit and the more powerful P.Z.L. G.1620B Mors engine; after satisfactory completion of tests the design was sold to the Polish government, which contracted with the Polish L.W.S. company to build 65 generally similar aircraft under the designation R.W.D.14b Czapla (heron). The type equipped observation squadrons Nos 13, 23, 33, 53 and 63 at the outbreak of war, but the type's speed was such that the squadrons suffered severe losses from ground fire, mostly Polish, and only about 10 escaped to Romania in the closing days of Polish resistance.

Specification
Type: two-seat reconnaissance/observation aircraft
Powerplant: one 350-kW (470-hp) P.Z.L.G.1620B Mors B radial piston engine
Performance: maximum speed 245 km/h (152 mph) at sea level; service ceiling 5000 m (16,405 ft); range 580 km (360 miles)
Weights: empty 1153 kg (2,542 lb); maximum take-off 1700 kg (3,748 lb)

The extensive slotting along the R.W.D.14b Czapla's high-set wing is evident in this fading photograph of the fourth production prototype, built by L.W.S. and powered by the 313-kW (420-hp) P.Z.L. Mors radial piston engine. The R.W.D.14 saw extensive squadron service in the Polish air force but was badly outclassed by 1939.

Dimensions: span 11.90 m (39 ft 0½ in); length 9.00 m (29 ft 6¼ in); height 3.00 m (9 ft 10 in); wing area 22.00 m² (236.81 sq ft)

R.W.D.15

Continuing the braced high-wing monoplane configuration, the R.W.D.15 four/five-seat light tourer was designed to provide a more economic and saleable aircraft in this category than the high-performance R.W.D.9. Of simple lightweight construction and powered by a 153-kW (205-hp) de Havilland Gipsy Six Series II engine, the prototype was flown for the first time in the summer of 1937. Testing showed the aircraft to have excellent performance, and orders for a total of 15 were received, but only four or five of these had been completed by the outbreak of war. Two brand new aircraft were flown from the D.W.L. factory to Romania in the closing stages of the war, carrying D.W.L. designers and technical staff who were seeking to reach France or the UK to carry on the battle against the Germans. The 12.4-m (40-ft 8¼-in) span R.W.D.15 was powered by the de Havilland Gipsy Six Series I engine and had a maximum speed of 240 km/h (149 mph).

R.W.D.16 and R.W.D.21

The R.W.D. design team in combination with D.W.L. had failed to develop a light-plane cheap enough for large-scale sale in Poland, and the R.W.D.16 was intended to redress this situation. A cantilever low-wing and low-powered monoplane of simple design, the prototype (SP-AXY) was flown first in late 1936, and was at that time powered by a 37-kW (50-hp) Walter Mikron I engine. It was modified further before a production batch of R.W.D.16bis aircraft was started in the winter of 1938-39, together with a batch of 10 R.W.D.21 aircraft that differed only by having a 67-kW (90-hp) Cirrus Minor. However, the Avia 3 proposed as powerplant for the R.W.D.16bis did not enter production and the 45-kW (60-hp) Walter Mikron II engine was selected as an alternative. Many airframes were nearing completion at the end of August 1938 but it is doubtful if any were flown. The R.W.D.21 prototypes eventually reached Romania, one being returned to Poland after the war. As powered by the Avia 3 engine, the 11.00-m (36-ft 1-in) span R.W.D.16bis had a maximum speed of 172 km/h (107 mph) at sea level.

R.W.D.17/18/19/22/23 and 25

Germany's invasion of Poland on 1 September 1939, which marked the beginning of World War II, meant that D.W.L. built only a small number of one more production aircraft, the **R.W.D.17**. However, the R.W.D. lightplanes of this company had earlier gained such remarkable competition and record success that brief mention of the last designs is worthwhile. The R.W.D.17 was a parasol-wing two-seat aerobatic trainer and the prototype flown in July 1937, was powered by a 97-kW (130-hp) P.Z.Inz Major engine. Although the type

had been ordered by both the Polish army and navy, only a few civil R.W.D.17s had been completed before the outbreak of war. The **R.W.D.18** was a twin-engine four/five-seat cabin monoplane intended as a business or utility aircraft; with a high mounted wing incorporating STOL features, it was to be powered by two 112-kW (150-hp) Cirrus Major engines, but the incomplete prototype was destroyed in an early air attack. The **R.W.D.19** two-seat cabin monoplane, powered by a 97-kW (130-hp) de Havilland Gipsy Major I, was

flown in early 1939, but was considered to be too expensive to build and operate and was not put into production. Work began in the summer of 1939 on the construction of two **R.W.D.22** prototypes, a three-seat coastal-reconnaissance/torpedo-bomber for the Polish navy. A cantilever low-wing monoplane with twin-float landing gear, it was to be powered by two 350-kW (470-hp) P.Z.L.G.1620B Mors B radial engines, but neither of these aircraft was completed. The final prototype completed by D.W.L. before the outbreak of war was of the

R.W.D.23, a one/two-seat tandem open cockpit monoplane flown in spring 1939 with a 45-kW (60-hp) Walter Mikron II engine. The final design, of which no construction had begun at the outbreak of war, was for a single-seat fighter of cantilever low-wing monoplane configuration. Designated **R.W.D.25**, this would have been powered by a 597-kW (800-hp) Gnome-Rhône Mars radial engine and armed with four wing-mounted machine-guns.

Rawdon T-1

Despite its good performance and modern appearance, the Rawdon T-1 was built only in small numbers as a result of the massive availability of low-cost US military surplus aircraft soon after World War II.

Designed and flown in the USA during the early 1940s, the **Rawdon T-1** was intended to serve primarily as a two-seat trainer, but US involvement in World War II meant that its development was not resumed until after VJ-Day. A semi-cantilever low-wing monoplane with a single bracing strut each side, fixed tailwheel landing gear and powered by a 112-kW (150-hp) Avco Lycoming O-320 flat-four engine, the T-1 accommodated instructor and pupil in tandem beneath a transparent canopy. It was to be de-

veloped also as the agricultural **T-1S** with an underfuselage chemical tank and spray gear, and as the **T-1SD** in which the rear seat was replaced by a chemical hopper and dusting/spraying equipment installed. With competition from established lightplane manufacturers and vast numbers of war surplus aircraft coming on the market there was little demand for the T-1 and only about 35 were built. At a maximum take-

off weight of 862 kg (1,900 lb), the 10.16-m (33-ft 4-in) span T-1 had a top speed of 222 km/h (138 mph).

Rearwin aircraft

Interested in mid-1928 by the possibilities of the growing enthusiasm for sports aviation in the USA, boosted by Charles Lindbergh's solo-flight across the North Atlantic, Ray Rearwin engaged Fred Landgraf as his designer/engineer and began an initial foray into aircraft manufacture. First product was the **Rearwin Ken-Royce 2000C** (the name Ken-Royce derived from his two sons), a conventional unequal-span biplane seating three in tandem open cockpits and powered by a 127-kW (170-hp) Curtiss Challenger radial engine. In spite of good performance only three were built, followed by two or three examples of the **Ken-Royce 2000CO** which differed primarily by having the 123-kW (165-hp) Continental A70 radial engine. Although only five or six Ken-Royce biplanes were built, their success in competition gave the infant company valuable experience and a realisation that its best chance to compete against established manufacturers was in the field of lightplanes. Designed by new chief engineer Douglas H. Webber and Noel Hockaday, the **Rearwin Junior 3000** was a tandem two-seat parasol-wing monoplane with construction and equipment geared to the lowest possible sale price. Powered by a 34-kW (45-hp) Szekely three-cylinder radial engine, it was flown for the first time in mid-1931 but, as the type was launched at a bad economic moment, only 17 were built. It was followed in 1932 by the **Junior 4000** (eight built), which differed by having a 37-kW (50-hp) Aeromarine AR-3 radial, and the even less successful **Junior 3100** (two built) with a 37-kW (50-hp) Szekely, which meant that Rearwin had not yet found a formula for success. It was not to be ever thus, but perhaps it was improving economics rather than originality of design that brought a change for the better with introduction of the **Sportster 7000**, a two-seat cabin monoplane of braced high-wing configuration flown on 30 April 1935. About 75 were built, all powered by the 52-kW (70-hp) Le Blond 5DE or 5E radial engine, before being followed by de luxe and more powerful versions designated

Sportster 8500, 9000-L and **9000-KR** with respectively the 63-kW (85-hp) Le Blond 5DF, 67-kW (90-hp) Le Blond 5F and similarly powered Ken-Royce engine. Though fixed tailskid landing gear was standard, the type was available optionally with skis or floats, and of the total of about 260 built it is estimated some 10 per cent were exported. In 1937 an additional version of the Sportster became available, the **Sportster 9000-W** with a 67-kW (90-hp) Warner Scarab radial, but by then the earlier models had already satisfied the demand and only eight Sportster 9000-Ws were built.

At the height of the economic depression Rearwin had suspended production for a short period, and in design at that time was a two-seat cabin monoplane with a braced high wing that represented an interim stage in development of the Sportster. As first flown in the summer of 1934, powered by a 71-kW (95-hp) ACE Cirrus H-Drive inline engine, the aircraft was designated **Speedster 6000**. Two examples were built and used for development, but by the time certification was gained in late 1937 this engine was out of production. Introduc-

tion of a 93-kW (125-hp) Menasco C-4 inline powerplant converted this aircraft into a true 'speedster', but only about 12 examples of the resulting **Speedster 6000-M** were built. A side-by-side seating development of the Sportster 9000-KR, certificated as the **Cloudster 8090**, proved far more successful. The Cloudster 8090 was powered by a 76-kW (90-hp) Ken-Royce 5F, but demands for higher performance resulted in introduction of the two-seat **Cloudster 8125** with an 89-kW (120-hp) Ken-Royce 7-F, or three-seat **Cloudster 8135** with a similarly-powered Ken-Royce 7-G engine. Production totalled about 125, including 20 **Cloudster 8135-T** trainers for Pan American Airways, which were modified to have two seats in tandem, and 25 Cloudsters were also exported to Iran for use as utility trainers.

Final Rearwin design was the side-by-side two-seat **Ranger 165**, of the same high-wing configuration as its predecessors. This was powered by a 48-kW (65-hp) engine and first flown in April 1940. In initial production form the Ranger had a 56-kW (75-hp) Continental A75-8 flat-four engine, the designation changing to **Skyranger 175**, being followed by the **Skyranger 180, 180-F** and **190-F** with respectively the 60-kW (80-hp) Con-

tinental A80-8, similarly-powered Franklin 4AC-176-F3, or 67-kW (90-hp) Franklin 4AC-199-E3 engine. Rearwin Sportster production totalled more than 80 aircraft before US involvement in World War 2 brought an end to the construction of civil aircraft. At that time Rearwin sold out to Commonwealth Aircraft Corporation which, post-war, built about 275 **Skyranger 185** aircraft with the 63-kW (85-hp) Continental C85-12.

Specification
Rearwin Sportster 8500
Type: sporting/touring aircraft
Powerplant: one 63-kW (85-hp) Le Blond 5DF radial piston engine
Performance: maximum speed 187 km/h (116 mph); service ceiling 4635 m (15,200 ft); range 772 km (480 miles)
Weights: empty 376 kg (830 lb); maximum take-off 640 kg (1,410 lb)
Dimensions: span 10.67 m (35 ft 0 in); length 6.78 m (22 ft 3 in); height 2.06 m (6 ft 9 in); wing area 15.42 m² (166.0 sq ft)

Another type produced only in modest numbers was the Rearwin high-wing series, seen here in the shape of a Le Blond-powered Sportster 9000-KR.

Reggiane Re.2000 series
to
Republic F-84

Reggiane Re.2000 series

Officine Meccaniche Reggiane SA, a subsidiary of the Caproni company, began development in 1937 of a single-seat fighter designed by Antonio Alessio and Roberto Longhi; the latter had about two years earlier returned from working in the USA. The resulting **Reggiane Re.2000 Falco I** prototype was very different from contemporary Italian designs for combat aircraft and was influenced, no doubt, by the stubby aircraft with large-diameter radial engines then being built in North America. A cantilever low-wing monoplane with retractable tailwheel landing gear, the prototype was powered by a 649-kW (870-hp) Piaggio P.XI RC.40 radial engine. Competitive evaluation that followed a first flight during 1938 brought no interest from the Italian air force, but Reggiane built for the Italian navy 12 **Re.2000 Serie II** fighters especially strengthened for catapult launching, and 24 **Re.2000 Serie III** long-range fighters with increased fuel capacity. The company then manufactured several for Hungary, which also built a small number under licence, all of these being operated by the Hungarian air force under the designation **Hejja** (Hawk). Additional Re.2000s were built to a Swedish order for 60, these being operated by the Swedish air force until 1945 under the designation **J 20.**

Conviction that performance of the Re.2000 would benefit from a more powerful engine led to the **Re.2001 Falco II**, powered initially by the Daimler-Benz DB 601A-1, but with Luftwaffe priorities on this powerplant the Re.2001 had to have instead an Alfa-Romeo licence-built version, the RA.1000 RC.41-la Monsonie. Even then, the MC.202 had first call on these engines and, as a result, production of the Re.2001 was limited to only 252. This number included 100 **Re.2001 Serie I, II and III** fighters (with armament variations) and the **Re.2001 Serie IV** fighter-bombers, and 150 **Re.2001 CN** night-fighters. Two new aircraft were built for catapult trials, and a number of conversions were made to evaluate the aircraft as a tandem two-seat trainer, tank-buster and torpedo-fighter; one was used to test an Isotta Fraschini Delta engine.

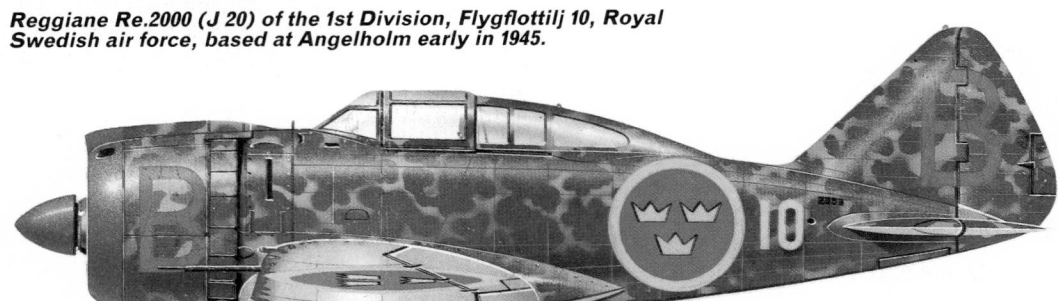

Reggiane Re.2000 (J 20) of the 1st Division, Flygflottilj 10, Royal Swedish air force, based at Angelholm early in 1945.

Reggiane Re.2001 of the 150ª Squadriglia, 2º Gruppo 'Golletto', Regia Aeronautica, based at Pantellaria in August 1942.

The necessity to revert to radial powerplant led to the **Reggiane Re.2002 Ariete** (ram) fighter-bomber (about 50 built), which combined the improved airframe of the Re.2001 with an 876-kW (1,175-hp) Piaggio P.XIX RC.45 engine; these saw service in 1942, suffering heavy losses during the Allied landings on Sicily. The last of this related family was the **Reggiane Re.2005 Sagittario** (archer), probably the best fighter produced in Italy during World War II, which had structural refinements and reverted to the use of an inline engine. The prototype, powered by a Daimler-Benz DB 605A-1, was flown during September 1942, but the produc-

tion version of the Re.2005 had the Fiat RA.1050 RC.58 Tifone, which was a licence-built version of the Daimler-Benz. Only 48 Sagittarios had been delivered before an armistice was signed with the Allies, but these aircraft saw extensive use in the defence of Naples, Rome and Sicily, the survivors battling finally above the crumbling ruins of Berlin.

Specification
Reggiane Re.2005 Sagittario
Type: single-seat fighter/fighter-bomber
Powerplant: one 1100-kW (1,475-hp)

Fiat RA.1050 RC.58 Tifone Vee piston engine
Performance: maximum speed 630 km/h (391 mph) at 7000 m (22,965 ft); service ceiling 12000 m (39,370 ft); range 1250 km (777 miles)
Weights: empty 2600 kg (5,732 lb); maximum take-off 3560 kg (7,848 lb)
Dimensions: span 11.00 m (36 ft 1 in); length 8.73 m (28 ft 7¾ in); height 3.15 m (10 ft 4 in); wing area 20.40 m² (219.59 sq ft)
Armament: three 20-mm cannon and two 12.7-mm (0.5-in) machine-guns, all forward-firing, plus up to 630 kg (1,390 lb) of bombs when deployed as a fighter-bomber

Reims Aviation

In early 1960 the Cessna Aircraft Company acquired a 49 per cent holding in the French company Société Nouvelle des Avions Max Holste, the name then being changed to Reims Aviation SA. This company then had rights to manufacture selected Cessna designs for sale in Europe and Africa, and from that time until early 1983 had assembled no fewer than 6,135 examples of Cessna aircraft. They have included the Cessna Model 150 as the **F 150** and **FA 150 Aérobat;** Cessna Model 152 as the **F 152 Aerobat;** Cessna Skyhawk II as the **F 172 Skyhawk/100** and **F 172 Skyhawk/100 II;** Cessna Hawk XP and Hawk XP/II as the **FR 172K Hawk XP** and **FR 172K Hawk XP/II;** Cessna Car-

dinal RG as the **F 177RG;** Cessna Skylane and Skylane RG as the **F 182** and **F 182RG;** and versions of the Cessna 337 Skymaster as the **F 337**. In addition, Reims developed a version of the Cessna Skyhawk as the **FR 172 Reims-Rocket** with a 157-kW (210-hp) Rolls-Royce/Continental IO-360-D flat-six engine. Details of the original Cessna aircraft can be found under that company's entries, and under Cessna Model 336/337 Skymaster are given brief details of the related F 337 and **F 337P**, and the Reims-developed **FTB 337** and **Milirole.**

The sole indigenous Reims product is the **F406 Caravan II**. Announced in 1982 and based on the Cessna Titan

family, it first flew in September 1983. Since then nearly 100 of the Pratt & Whitney Canada PT6A-112-powered utility aircraft have been ordered in military and civilian versions.

The French Customs Service operates four F406 Caravan IIs fitted with a Bendix/King 1500 surveillance radar under the fuselage.

Renard Epervier

In 1927 Georges and Alfred Renard, who had designed previously for the firm of Stampe & Vertongen, established the Société Anonyme des Avions et Moteurs Renard at Evere, near Brussels, but soon gave up their original intention to design and build aero engines, concentrating instead on aircraft.

The **Renard Epervier** (sparrow hawk) was the company's first design, a parasol-wing single-seat fighter which won a Belgian government design competition in 1927. Of all-metal construction, the Epervier had a narrow circular-section fuselage and fixed landing gear, and was powered by a 358-kW (480-hp) Gnome-Rhône Jupiter VI radial engine.

Two examples were built, neither by Renard. The first was completed by

The Renard Epervier featured a narrow-section fuselage and large spatted undercarriage. Its metal construction gave a crude and angular appearance.

Stamp & Vertongen at Antwerp; its test programme began in 1928, but in October that year test pilot Charles Wouters was forced to abandon the Epervier by parachute when the aircraft was in an uncontrollable flat spin. The second example (OO-AKN), built by SABCA, completed a satisfactory flying programme before being demonstrated in early 1930 by air force Capitaine Vanderlinden in a contest against various French prototypes at Evere. Although

the Epervier did well and was finally purchased by the Belgian air force, no production examples were built. With a wing span of 10.20 m (33 ft 5½ in), this second example had a maximum speed of 273 km/h (170 mph).

Renard R.31

The prototype **Renard R.31** reconnaissance aircraft, designed by Alfred Renard, was flown for the first time on 16 October 1932. A two-seat braced parasol-wing monoplane, largely of metal with fabric covering, it had an unusual faired cabane pylon in place of the normal open strut arrangement, but the pilot could obtain a good field of view above and below the wing by means of an adjustable seat. The fixed landing gear had independent main units and powerplant was a Rolls-Royce Kestrel II.

A total of 32 R.31s was ordered for the Belgian Aéronautique Militaire in 1934, to be built by SABCA and Renard, and from 1935 these replaced the elderly Breguet 19 in the 9ᵉ and 11ᵉ Escadrilles d'Observation. The R.31 in service proved sturdy but lacking in manoeuvrability. During the short campaign in defence of Belgium in May 1940 the aircraft moved from their home base of Liège-Bierset to Duras, but after flying 54 war missions all surviving aircraft were destroyed on 28 May 1940.

Variants
R.31 Lorraine: the second R.31 was tested briefly with a 485-kW (650-hp) Lorraine Petrel engine
R.32: two examples built of this development of the R.31 with redesigned fuselage and a glazed canopy for the crew filling the gap between wing and fuselage; the first R.32 was flown in August 1936, powered by a Gnome-Rhône 14 N01 radial engine; the second R.32 was soon lost, abandoned by its service pilot when he was overcome by cockpit fumes from its 619-kW (830-hp) Hispano-Suiza 12Ybrs engine, which provided a maximum speed of 350 km/h (217 mph)

Specification
Renard R.31
Type: reconnaissance aircraft
Powerplant: one 365-kW (490-hp) Rolls-Royce Kestrel II Vee piston engine
Performance: maximum speed 290 km/h (180 mph); service ceiling 8650 m (28,380 ft); range 650 km (404 miles)

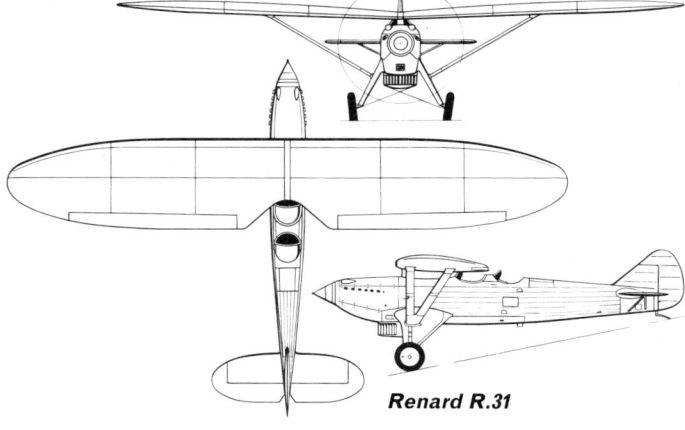

Renard R.31

Weights: empty equipped 1400 kg (3,086 lb); maximum take-off 2150 kg (4,740 lb)
Dimensions: span 14.40 m (47 ft 3 in); length 9.24 m (30 ft 3¾ in); height 2.92 m (9 ft 7 in); wing area 32.00 m² (344.45 sq ft)
Armament: one 7.92-mm (0.31-in) synchronised FN Browning machine-gun in cowling and a similar weapon on ring mounting in observer's cockpit, plus up to 80 kg (176 lb) of bombs

Renard R.36

Designed by Alfred Renard, the impressive **Renard R.36** single-seat fighter was first flown by company pilot Georges Van Damme on 5 November 1937. A clean cantilever low-wing monoplane of light alloy construction, the R.36 had a raised aft-sliding cockpit canopy, inward-retracting main landing gear legs and a wide-chord wing with hydraulically-operated split flaps in four sections. Powered by an Hispano-Suiza 12Ycrs Type 2 *moteur canon*, the R.36 attracted considerable attention, but completion of a six-aircraft evaluation batch was halted when the prototype crashed on 17 January 1939.

Variants
R.37: one R.36 evaluation airframe was completed with an 823-kW (1,100-hp) Gnome-Rhône 14 N21 radial engine in a revolutionary close cowling; exhibited at the Brussels Salon in July 1939, the R.37 was taken by German forces in May 1940; projected **R.37B**

two-seat torpedo-bomber or ground assault aircraft was never built
R.38: a second R.36 airframe completed with a 771-kW (1,030-hp) Rolls-Royce Merlin II and first flown on 4 August 1939, demonstrating a maximum speed of 525 km/h (326 mph); proposed armament was four wing-mounted machine-guns plus 80 kg (176 lb) of bombs; evacuated to France where seized by Luftwaffe
R.40: a third **R.36** airframe, with Merlin engine, developed for France with a unique pressurised cell for pilot which could be jettisoned by means of explosive cartridge; during evacuation in May 1940 components captured by Germans while still in transit on Belgian territory, and ultimate fate unknown

Specification
Renard R.36
Type: single-seat fighter
Powerplant: one 679-kW (910-hp) Hispano-Suiza 12 Ycrs *moteur canon* engine
Performance: maximum speed 515 km/h (320 mph) at 4000 m

(13,125 ft); service ceiling 12000 m (39,370 ft)
Weights: empty equipped 1700 kg (3,748 lb); maximum take-off 2400 kg (5,291 lb)
Dimensions: span 11.64 m (38 ft 2¼ in); length 8.54 m (28 ft 0¼ in); height 2.90 m (9 ft 6¼ in); wing area 20.00 m² (215.29 sq ft)
Armament: one 20-mm engine-mounted cannon and four wing-

Close attention to aerodynamic detail by its designer Alfred Renard provided the Renard R.37 with exceptionally fine nose contours, despite the disadvantage of using a bulky Hispano-Suiza radial piston.

mounted 7.7-mm (0.303-in) Browning machine-guns, plus eight 10-kg (22-lb) bombs

Republic lesser types

Republic P-72: under the designation **XP-72**, Republic designed and built two prototypes of a developed version of the P-47 Thunderbolt which, with higher performance resulting from installation of the 2573-kW (3,450-hp) Pratt & Whitney

R-4360-13 Wasp Major radial engine, was required to serve as an interceptor for the German V-1 flying-bomb. First flown on 2 February 1944, the XP-72 was shown in tests to have a maximum speed of 789 km/h (490 mph), and

although 100 production P-72s were ordered, they were later cancelled.
Republic F-12: under the designation **XF-12** (later **XR-12**), Republic designed and built two prototypes of a large four-engine photo-reconnaissance aircraft of monoplane configuration. Powered by four 2479-kW (3,000-hp) Pratt & Whitney R-4360-31 Wasp Major radial

engines, the first aircraft flew on 2 July 1946, and though tested by the USAAF, no production order resulted. A proposal to develop the design as a 46-passenger for Pan American Airways under the designation **RC-2 Rainbow** also failed to materialise. Spanning 39.37 m (129 ft 2 in) and with a maximum take-off weight of 50530 kg (111,400 lb), the

XF-12 had a maximum speed in excess of 684 km/h (425 mph).

Republic F-91: under the designation **XF-91** and with the tentative name **Thunderceptor**, Republic built to a USAAF contract of March 1946 two prototypes of an experimental high-speed interceptor. This introduced some unusual features: the incidence of the swept and inverse-taper wings was variable; the main units of the tricycle landing gear, each with two small wheels in tandem, retracted outwards into the wingtips; and there was provision for the General Electric J47-GE-3 turbojet to be augmented by up to four rocket engines. The first of the prototypes was flown on 9 May 1949, demonstrating a maximum speed of 1192 km/h (740 mph), but no production examples were built and the prototypes ended their days as research aircraft.

Among the many remarkable features of the Republic XF-91 was its inverse taper wing, with greater chord at the tip than at the root. Visible under the tail is the fairing for the Reaction Motors rocket thruster.

Republic F-84

Republic F-84G Thunderjet of the Fotoflight, Royal Danish air force, in 1956.

Continuing the 'Thunder' prefix that brought fame to Republic with the P-47, the company chose the name **Republic Thunderjet** for the turbojet day fighter that was designed to supersede the P-47 in service. Designed as a single-seat low/mid-wing monoplane of all-metal construction with retractable tricycle landing gear, the type received an initial contract in March 1945 for three **XP-84** prototypes. However, development was bedevilled by a series of problems, in particular those of growing structural weight and low engine thrust, but when the first two prototypes were flown, on 28 February and in August 1946, it was soon discovered that Republic had created another high-performance aircraft, soon confirmed in September 1946 when one of the prototypes established a new US national speed record of 983 km/h (611 mph).

These two aircraft were each powered by a 7.6-kN (3,750-lb) thrust General Electric J35-GE-7 turbojet, specified also for the **YP-84** pre-production batch of 25 aircraft, but this was changed to the 8-kN (4,000-lb) thrust Allison J35-A-15 in a revised contract for 15 **YP-84A** service trials aircraft, these having been preceded by the third prototype completed in similar configuration as the **XP-84A**. They were followed by the **P-84B**, the initial production version (226 built) which introduced an ejection seat, provision for rocket armament and an Allison J35-A-15C of the same thrust as the J35-A-15. The **P-84C** (later **F-84C**; 191 built) had a revised electrical system and the J35-A-13C engine, still of 8-kN (4,000-lb) thrust. More extensive changes were made on the **F-84D** (154 built), including wings and ailerons with heavier-gauge skins, winterised fuel system for the 10-kN (5,000-lb) thrust J35-A-17D engine and revised landing gear structure. The entry of this version into operational service in the Korean War resulted in early introduction of the **F-84E** (843 built) with a slightly lengthened fuselage to improve cockpit accommodation, revised wingtip tanks, and provision of a radar gunsight, and 100 F-84Es were supplied to NATO forces. Last of the so-called straight-wing F-84s was the **F-84G** (3,025 built), of which 1,936 were supplied to NATO forces, and this was the first single-seat fighter to have the capability of deploying nuclear weapons. Powered by the 11-kN (5,600-lb) thrust J35-A-29 turbojet, the F-84G could carry 1814 kg (4,000 lb) of stores externally, had provision for inflight refuelling and, because this made long-range missions possible, was equipped with an autopilot. The type was subsequently equipped with a low-altitude bombing system for the deployment of its nuclear weapons, and the tactically limited flying boom inflight-refuelling system was superseded by the probe and drogue method developed by Flight Refuelling Ltd in the UK. The first two prototypes were two **EF-84E** aircraft converted in the UK, and using inflight refuelling techniques they became on 22 September 1950 the first turbojet-powered single-seat fighters to record a nonstop crossing of the North Atlantic.

Introduction of a swept wing was made first on an F-84E fuselage and this, powered by a 10.5-kN (5,200-lb) thrust Allison XJ35-A-25 engine, made its first flight on 3 June 1950 under the designation **YF-84F**. Performance was disappointing, greater engine thrust being essential, and a second prototype was flown with an Armstrong Siddeley Sapphire turbojet imported from the UK. A licence-built version of this engine, the Wright J65, suffered early development problems, but eventually all but 375 of the 2,713 **F-84F Thunderstreak** aircraft that were built had the 14.6-kN (7,220-lb) thrust Wright J65-W-3, the remainder having earlier and lower-powered J65-W-1 or J65-W-1A turbojets. Of the total built, 1,301 were supplied to NATO air forces.

A final development of the basic design produced a reconnaissance version, the **RF-84F Thunderflash**, which differed primarily by having a 15.7-kN (7,800-lb) thrust J65-W-7 turbojet with wing-root air intakes and cameras mounted in the nose. Production totalled 715, of which 386 were supplied to NATO air forces. To provide long-range reconnaissance capability, 25 F-84Fs were modified under the USAF's FICON (fighter conveyor) project to hook on to a trapeze in a version of the giant Convair B-36 bomber, the GRB-36F. Designated initially **GRF-84F**, later changed to **RF-84K**, after hooking on to their long-range mission these aircraft were carried by it to the designated reconnaissance area. After launch and completion of its reconnaissance task the RF-84K would again hook on for transport back to its base. Such interim ideas have since been superseded by the efficient development of inflight-refuelling to provide these, and other categories of aircraft, with long range capability. F-84F and RF-84F aircraft were the last to remain in USAF serivce, many then being transferred to Air National Guard units before the type was eventually withdrawn from service in 1971.

Variants

EF-84B: two conversions of F-84Bs for 'tip-tow' parasite trials with a Boeing ETB-29 'motherplane'

XF-84H: two F-84Fs were converted under this designation with a 4362-kW (5,850-shp) Allison XT40-A-1 turboprop powerplant driving supersonic propellers under a joint USAF/USN programme

YF-84J: two conversions of F-84Fs with deepened fuselages and enlarged nose intakes, one tested with a 29-kN (8,750-lb) thrust General Electric XJ73-GE-5 and the other with a 29.6-kN (8,920-lb) thrust YJ73-GE-7 turbojet

F-84KX: designation allocated to 80 ex-USAF F-84Bs following conversion to target drone configuration for the US Navy

Specification
Republic F-84F Thunderstreak

Type: single-seat fighter-bomber

Powerplant: one 15.7-kN (7,220-lb) thrust Wright J65-W-3 turbojet

Performance: maximum speed 1118 km/h (695 mph) at sea level; service ceiling 14020 m (46,000 ft); combat radius with drop tanks 1304 km (810 miles)

Weights: empty 6273 kg (13,830 lb); maximum take-off 12701 kg (28,000 lb)

Dimensions: span 10.24 m (33 ft 7¼ in); length 13.23 m (43 ft 4¾ in); height 4.39 m (14 ft 4¾ in); wing area 30.19 m² (325.0 sq ft)

Armament: six 12.7-mm (0.5-in) Browning M3 machine-guns, plus up to 2722 kg (6,000 lb) of external stores

Republic F-84F Thunderstreak of the 1ᵉ Escadrille, 2ᵉ Escadre, Royal Belgian air force, based at Florennes during 1969.

Republic F-105 Thunderchief
to
Republic RC-3 Seabee

Republic F-105 Thunderchief

When the F-84F Thunderstreak entered service in 1954, Republic had already spent some years studying the design of a higher-performance fighter-bomber which the company hoped would be an acceptable successor to the Thunderstreak. Following submission to the USAF of the **AP-63** design proposal, a contract for two **Republic YF-105A** prototypes was awarded, the first of them making its initial flight on 22 October 1965 on the power of a 6804-kg (15,000-lb) thrust Pratt & Whitney J57-P-25 turbojet. This doubling of power by comparison with the F-84F emphasises the increase in size and weight of the YF-105A, the changing role of the 'fighter' also being recognised by the capability to carry up to 5443 kg (12,000 lb) of mixed weapons, of which up to 3629 kg (8,000 lb) of nuclear or other weapons could be carried in an internal bomb bay. No **F-105A** production aircraft were built because of the availability of a more powerful Pratt & Whitney J75 afterburning turbojet, thus there followed four **YF-105B** prototypes that were of similar overall configuration, but with an area-ruled fuselage, swept-forward air intakes and the 7484-kg (16,500-lb) thrust YJ75-P-3 engine. The production **F-105B** (71 built) was basically similar, and began to enter service in August 1958, three years later than planned, with the USAF's 335th Tactical Fighter Squadron; it was not until mid-1959 that the USAF had its first complete squadron of F-105B aircraft.

Major production version was the **F-105D** (610 built) which, powered by the 7802-kg (17,200-lb) thrust J75-P-19W turbojet, had all-weather capability, much improved avionics and detail refinements. Final production version was the **F-105F** (143 built), with a lengthened fuselage to provide tandem two-seat capacity and intended originally for combat proficiency evaluation and transition training. But with US involvement in Vietnam creating an urgent re-

quirement for high-performance fighter-bombers, the F-105F was frequently used in an operational role. Some 86 F-105Fs were later converted for 'Wild Weasel' missions against North Vietnam, equipped with RHAW (Radar Homing And Warning), jamming pods, a missile-launch warning receiver, and other specialised avionics to locate and identify the threat from SA-2 'Guideline' surface-to-air missiles. Of the total of 86, 60 were the subject of more comprehensive modification and became designated initially **EF-105F**, subsequently **F-105G**.

Introduction of 'Wild Weasel'-configured F-105Fs to combat occurred in 1966, and these Thunderchiefs constituted the backbone of the anti-SAM forces until 1973. Surviving F-105Gs served with the 35th TFW at George AFB, California until the late 1970s, when 25 were transferred to the Air National Guard. These have since been retired. F-105Ds also fought in Vietnam, but well over half of the 610 that were built were destroyed, and following their withdrawal in 1969-70 the survivors were passed on to second-line elements of the Air National Guard and USAF Reserve. Progressive updating of these forces in turn brought about a gradual phase-out of the surviving aircraft by 1984.

Variants
RF-105B: proposed reconnaissance version; not built
JF-105B: three system-test aircraft,

built from airframes laid down originally as RF-105B prototypes
F-105C: projected tandem two-seat operational trainer; not built
RF-105D: projected reconnaissance variant of F-105D; not built
F-105E: projected tandem two-seat operational trainer variant of F-105D; not built

Specification
Type: single-seat fighter-bomber
Powerplant: one 7802-kg (17,200-lb) thrust Pratt & Whitney J75-P-19W turbojet, developing 11113-kg (24,500-lb) thrust with afterburning, or 12020-kg (26,500-lb) thrust for 60 seconds with afterburning and water injection
Performance: maximum speed 2237 km/h (1,390 mph) or Mach 2.1 at

Republic F-105D Thunderchief of the 192nd FG, Virginia ANG.

The F-105D Thunderchief was widely used by the USAF in the Vietnam War as an all-weather fighter-bomber capable of carrying a wide range of stores.

10975 m (36,000 ft); service ceiling 12560 m (41,200 ft); ferry range with maximum external fuel 3846 km (2,390 miles)
Weights: empty 12474 kg (27,500 lb); maximum take-off 23967 kg (52,838 lb)
Dimensions: span 10.59 m (34 ft 9 in); length 19.61 m (64 ft 4 in); height 5.97 m (19 ft 7 in); wing area 35.77 m² (385.0 sq ft)
Armament: one M61 Vulcan 20-mm cannon, plus more than 6350 kg (14,000 lb) of mixed stores carried internally and externally

Republic P-43 Lancer

Republic P-43 Lancer

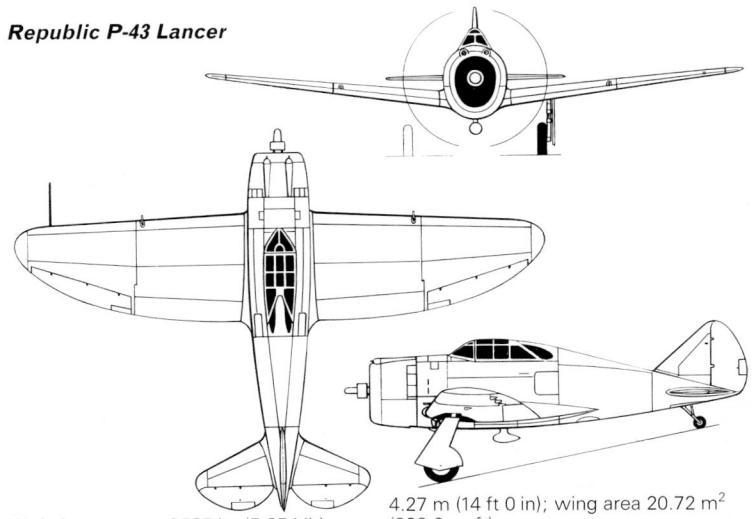

The last example of the Seversky P-35 was completed as an improved version with a turbocharged engine under the designation **XP-41** and this, in effect, served as the prototype of the **Republic P-43 Lancer**. After extensive testing of the XP-41, the company developed a further improved version and, as a result, received a USAAC order for an evaluation batch of 13 aircraft under the designation **YP-43**. This model differed primarily from the P-35 by having a revised wing centre-section, landing gear that retracted inwards instead of aft and, of course, installation of the turbocharged Pratt & Whitney R-1830-35 engine. Testing showed improvements in both maximum speed and high altitude performance, leading to an order in 1940 for 54 production P-43 fighters with the R-1830-47 engine. A projected higher-performance development (the **P-44**) failed to materialise, and the USAAC ordered instead 80 **P-43A** aircraft with the R-1830-49 engine. Final

version was the **P-43A-1**, of which 125 were contracted in 1941 with a further improved engine variant, the R-1830-57. In 1942 the survivors of these 272 aircraft were converted for use in a reconnaissance role, P-43, P-43A and P-43A-1 aircraft being redesignated respectively **RP-43, RP-43A** and **RP-43A-1**, and of this total 152 were converted with different camera installations under the designations **P-43B** (150) and **P-43C** (2). Some of these aircraft were transferred for use by the Chinese and Royal Australian air forces.

Specification
Republic P-43
Type: single-seat fighter
Powerplant: one 1167-kW (1,200-hp) Pratt & Whitney R-1830-47 radial piston engine
Performance: maximum speed 562 km/h (349 mph) at 7620 m (25,000 ft); service ceiling 11580 m (38,000 ft); range 1287 km (800 miles)

Weights: empty 2565 kg (5,654 lb); maximum take-off 3599 kg (7,935 lb)
Dimensions: span 10.97 m (36 ft 0 in); length 8.69 m (28 ft 6 in); height

4.27 m (14 ft 0 in); wing area 20.72 m² (223.0 sq ft)
Armament: two 12.7-mm (0.5-in) and two 7.62-mm (0.3-in) forward-firing machine-guns

Republic P-47 Thunderbolt

Most famous of all Republic aircraft, the **Republic P-47 Thunderbolt** designed by Alexander Kartveli had a significant role to play in World War II, and was built to an astonishing total of 15,677 before production came to an end with cancellation of outstanding contracts after VJ-Day. Like many other major combat aircraft, the P-47 acquired two nicknames bestowed affectionately by its pilots to a friend that had been tried and trusted in battle: 'Jug', a diminutive of Juggernaut that described its ample proportions, and 'T-bolt' derived from its officially-given name. A continuation of the family that had started with Alexander Seversky's P-35 and further developed through the P-43 Lancer and projected higher-performance P-44, the P-47 began by highlighting the indecision of the USAAC in 1940 about whether to procure lightweight or heavyweight fighters. Original plans to order the **Republic AP-4** and **AP-10** projects for lightweight fighters under the designations **XP-47** and **XP-47A** respectively were cancelled when early reports of combat experience in Europe were received. Kartveli then outlined his proposals for a heavy fighter that would meet the new requirement, basing his concept on use of the turbocharged Pratt & Whitney R-2800 Double Wasp, and winning an order for an XP-47B prototype based on this design. A cantilever low-wing monoplane, of conventional all-metal construction except for fabric-covered control surfaces, the new model had retractable tailwheel landing gear and accommodated its pilot beneath an upward-hinged canopy. When flown for the first time, on 6 May 1941, the XP-47B gave an immediate hint of the aircraft's potential, but there were a number of serious problems that had to be remedied. Orders from the US Army were soon received, initially for 171 production P-47B fighters, which began to come off the production line in March 1942 and to equip squadrons of the USAAF's 56th Fighter Group three months later. By January 1943 this group had joined the 8th Air Force in the UK, shortly reinforced by the 78th Fighter Group, and these units became operational in April 1943. Initial encounters with German fighters showed that the Thunderbolt was lacking in performance and manoeuvrability at low and medium altitudes, and had inadequate range to operate as an escort fighter. These shortcomings were met by ensuing variants, which progressively increased the capability of this remarkable aircraft, then regarded as a giant or juggernaut but which, by today's standards, was really quite small. It was, nevertheless, a

giant in achievement, robust, reliable and able to absorb an enormous amount of punishment from enemy weapons, with the exceptionally low loss rate of only 0.7 per cent per mission. The P-47 is credited with the destruction of 4.6 enemy aircraft for the loss of each one of its own number, with some 546,000 combat sorties during which 1,934,000 operational flight hours were accumulated, and with the destruction in Europe (excluding the Italian front) of 3,752 enemy aircraft in the air and 3,315 on the ground. It is little wonder therefore that the P-47 is well remembered in the aviation history of World War II.

In addition to service with the USAAF in the war, P-47s had been used also during this period by Brazil, the Free French air force, Mexico, the RAF, and the Soviet Union. The P-47D and P-47N remained in USAF service for a number of years after the war, passing to Air National Guard units before being phased out of service in 1954, by which time they had been redesignated F-47D and F-47N respectively. Even then, the Thunderbolt had many more years of useful service to offer, operating with the air forces of Bolivia, Brazil, Chile, Colombia, Dominica, Ecuador, France, Guatemala, Honduras, Iran, Italy, Mexico, Nationalist China, Peru, Turkey and Yugoslavia.

Variants

XP-47B: prototype, powered by 1380-kW (1,850-hp), later 1491-kW (2,000-hp) XR-2800 engine (total 1)
P-47B: initial production version with 1491-kW (2,000-hp) R-2800-21, sliding canopy and metal-skinned control surfaces (total 171)
P-47C: revised production version, initially with engine as P-47B but later with 1715-kW (2,300-hp) R-2800-59; longer forward fuselage and provision for belly bomb/drop-tank (total 602)
P-47D: major production version with 1715-kW (2,300-hp) R-2800-21W or 1890-kW (2,535-hp) R-2800-59W engine with water injection; numerous modifications through progressive blocks (total 12,602)
XP-47D: single experimental conversion (1943) of P-47D with

pressurised cockpit
XP-47F: single experimental conversion (1943) of P-47B with laminar-flow wings
P-47G: designation of early version of P-47D built by Curtiss-Wright (total 354)
XP-47H: redesignation of two P-47Ds used as engine test-beds for the 1715-kW (2,300-hp) Chrysler XIV-2220-1 inverted Vee engine
XP-47J: single experimental aircraft based on the P-47D with lightened structure and special 2088-kW (2,800-hp) R-2800-57(C) with turbocharger; attained a level speed of 811 km/h (504 mph) on 2 August 1944, the highest by a piston-engine aircraft
XP-47K: conversion of P-47D with a clearview teardrop canopy from a Hawker Typhoon and cut-down rear fuselage, a modification then introduced on P-47D production line
XP-47L: conversion of P-47D with increased-capacity fuselage fuel tankage
YP-47M: three prototype conversions of P-47Ds to produce high-speed 'sprint' version, with powerplant as used on XP-47J
P-47M: production version of YP-47M (total 130)
XP-47N: conversion from YP-47M with increased-span strengthened wing containing fuel tanks, strengthened landing gear and other modification to provide long-range capability for use in the Pacific theatre

Republic P-47D Thunderbolt of 2.Staffel/Versuchsverband Oberbefehlshaber der Luftwaffe, in September 1944.

P-47N: production version of XP-47N, late production aircraft with 2088-kW (2,800-hp) R-2800-77 (total 1,816)

Specification
Republic P-47D Thunderbolt
Type: single-seat fighter-bomber
Powerplant: one 1890-kW (2,535-hp) Pratt & Whitney R-2800-59W Double Wasp radial piston engine
Performance: maximum speed, clean 697 km/h (433 mph); service ceiling 12495 m (41,000 ft); range with drop-tanks 3058 km (1,900 miles)
Weights: empty 4513 kg (9,950 lb); maximum take-off 7938 kg (17,500 lb)
Dimensions: span 12.43 m (40 ft 9¼ in); length 11.02 m (36 ft 1¾ in); height 4.47 m (14 ft 8 in); wing area 27.87 m² (300.0 sq ft)
Armament: eight 12.7-mm (0.5-in) machine-guns, plus external load of up to 1134 kg (2,500 lb) of bombs, napalm or rockets

Used en masse, P-47D Thunderbolts such as these from the 8th Air Force's 78th Fighter Group were truly formidable aircraft. On 16 April 1945 the group claimed 145 German aircraft destroyed on the ground by strafing attacks.

Republic RC-3 Seabee

Keen to enter the market with a lightweight sporting amphibian, Republic acquired the design of an aircraft in this category from P. H. Spencer, a well-

known designer of single-engine amphibians. The resulting **Republic RC-1** prototype, first flown during 1945, was a cantilever high-wing monoplane of all-

metal construction, except for fabric-covered control surfaces, with stabilising floats beneath the wings, a single-step hull providing three-seat enclosed accommodation, retractable tailwheel landing gear, and the powerplant nacelle-mounted over the wing centre-section to drive a pusher propeller. In production form, as the **RC-3 Seabee**, it had four-seat accommodation and was powered by a Franklin flat-six engine. Demand for the Seabee was enormous, primarily because the company had underpriced it, and when production was brought to an end in late 1947 a total of more than 1,000 had been built. The company's order book was then far from

satisfied, but Republic could not afford to sell each unit at a considerable loss and, in any event, the buyers would soon have disappeared had the Seabee been given a realistic price tag.

Specification
Republic RC-3 Seabee
Type: four-seat amphibian
Powerplant: one 160-kW (215-hp) Franklin 6A-215-B8F or -B9F flat-six engine
Performance: maximum speed 193 km/h (120 mph) at 760 m (2,500 ft); service ceiling 3660 m (12,000 ft); range 579 km (360 miles)
Weights: empty 953 kg (2,100 lb); maximum take-off 1429 kg (3,150 lb)
Dimensions: span 11.48 m (37 ft 8 in); length 8.53 m (28 ft 0 in); height 2.92 m (9 ft 7 in); wing area 18.21 m² (196.0 sq ft)

Seen here in the form of a pre-production prototype, the Seabee remains one of the most distinctive aircraft built.

Rey R.I

An unusual research aircraft designed by Société des Avions F. J. Rey, the **Rey R.I** was a cantilever low-wing monoplane powered by two 161-kW (216-hp) Renault 6QR inline engines. The outer panel of each wing, outboard of the engine, was of variable incidence and linked for limited automatic rotation about their axes to offset the effects of turbulence or wind gusts. An aircraft built to test the system was destroyed during World War II, being followed by two aircraft flown in 1949 and 1951.

Rieseler aircraft

Sportsflugzeugbau Riesler was established at Berlin/Johannisthal airfield in the early 1920s, designing and building the prototype of a single-seat light-weight sporting aircraft of parasol-wing monoplane configuration which was powered by a Haacke flat-two engine. Designated **Rieseler R.III**, it was followed later by a two-seat version designated **R.IV**, and small numbers of production aircraft were built by Mark Abteilung Flugzeugbau at Breslau.

Robin ATL

Work by Avions Pierre Robin on the design of a lightweight two-seater intended to be economical both in terms of cost and operation (potentially available in kit form) began in 1981. Known as the **ATL** (Avions Trés Léger), which translates as 'very light aircraft', it was to be powered by a new 35-kW (47-hp) engine developed in conjunction with Jacques Buchoux of Ateliers ATX (JPX). Extensive use was made of composite materials and the fuselage was built entirely from glass-reinforced plastic. The mid-set wings were wooden and the tail was a distinctive 'V' shape. Its slender shape sat upon a fixed tricycle undercarriage, with side-by-side seating for the pilots. The prototype (F-WFNA) was exhibited at the 1983 Paris Salon, although the first flight did not take place until June 17. To speed certification the ATL was soon fitted with an ATX-converted Volkswagen powerplant and an uprated version of this became the standard production engine. Its increased size entailed a re-modelling of the wing to rebalance the aircraft's centre of gravity.

Initial orders came from the French National Aeronautical Federation (30) and deliveries of 'lassiez-passer', or pre-

Designed to promote the sales of very light, and thus low-powered and affordable, aircraft for the general aviation market, sales of the Robin ATL fell far short of expectations and the company was forced to halt production.

certification, ATLs commenced in 1985. Robin were dogged with certification problems however, and despite being approved by the French authorities in 1986, all ATLs had to be returned to the Dijon factory for further modification. Export sales were hampered by these problems, which stemmed in the main from the powerplant, and only a very small number of ATLs appeared outside France. For the German market a version powered by a four-cylinder 52.5-kW (70-hp) Limbach engine was developed, which was certified in 1989. It was intended that this should become the standard ATL engine, but production ceased after only 10 were built. Several aircraft later had the new engine retrofitted. When the line closed in 1991, 132 Robin ATLs had been delivered.

Variants
ATL Club: initial production version, known as the **Bijou** in the UK
ATL Club Model 88: fitted with a

smaller propeller for increased ground clearance. Also featured improvements to the cabin and increased fuel capacity extending the range to a maximum of 1100 km (683 miles)
ATL Club Model 89: Limbach-powered aircraft

Specification
Robin ATL Club/Bijou
Type: two-seat very-light training and touring aircraft
Powerplant: one JPX 4T 60A 48-kW (65-hp) air-cooled flat-four engine

(converted Volkswagen 2,050 cc automobile engine)
Performance: (Model 89 with Limbach engine) maximum cruising speed 90 kt (167 km/h, 104 mph); service ceiling 4267 m (14,000 ft); range with maximum fuel 1004 km (624 miles)
Weights: empty 360 kg (794 lb); maximum take-off 580 kg (1,278 lb)
Dimensions: span 10.25 m (33 ft 7½ in); length 6.72 m (22 ft 0½ in); height 2 m (6 ft 6¾ in); wing area 12.15 m² (130.8 sq ft)

Robin DR.100/1050 Ambassadeur

Pierre Robin's first light aircraft designs of 1957 were inspired by those of fellow French manufacturer Jodel. The Jodel title itself derived from a contraction of the names of the two principal movers behind the company, pilot Edouard Joly and designer Jean Delemontez. Delemontez joined Robin's Dijon-based team in the late 1950s and began to work on the three-to-four seat **DR.100** series which was eventually produced in parallel with SAN (Jodel). Named the **Ambassadeur**, only 10 of this initial Continental C90-engined version were built before Robin moved on to the more powerful **DR.1050 Ambassadeur**, with a 75-kW (100-hp) Continental 0-200-A powerplant. The design for these aircraft was inspired by Robin's success in the 1961 Tour of Sicily in a modified DR.100, the **DR.100A**. The DR.1050 was fitted with an improved fuel and electrical system, while the **'Scilie'** model benefited from undercarriage spats and a more refined engine cowling. In total 114 were built. Other versions followed, beginning in 1964, including the **DR.1000M Sicile Record** and the **DR.1051 Ambassadeur/1051M Sicile Record** of which over 200 were built mostly with Potez 4E engines.

Robin DR.220, DR.221, DR.250 and DR.253

The success of the DR.1050 series led Robin to develop a stretched version with a new strengthened wing. Two initial prototypes (designated **DR.200**) were developed into the four-seat Robin **DR.250 Capitaine** which first flew on 2 April 1964 (F-WLKZ). Powered by a 119-kW (160-hp) Lycoming O-360-A engine, it was popular with aero clubs and proved to be a capable glider tug. One hundred were sold. A lower-powered two-seat version was launched next, the **DR.220** which was soon improved by the addition of extra cabin space to become the **DR.220 2+2**. This had a child's seat, which was more akin to a small bench, and 83 were built. Next came 62 **DR.221 Dauphin**s with a full four-seat interior, all flying tailplane and an 86-kW (115-hp) Lycoming O-235C engine. At this time Robin was still building aircraft largely of traditional wood and fabric construction.

The advent of the **DR.253 Regent** in March 1967 marked a major development in Robin's history, as it was the first of the fixed tricycle undercarriage light aircraft that would become the company's forte in years to come. Seating four, the DR.253 had a comfortable passenger cabin and was powered by a 134-kW (180-hp) Lycoming O-360-D2A piston engine delivering a maximum take-off weight of (2,440 lb). Robin, now trading as Centre Est Aeronautique, soon developed a tricycle version of the DR.221, the **DR.315 Petit Prince** which first flew in 1968. Available with a range of engines it went on to amass 388 sales, more than the rest of the family combined.

Specification
Robin DR.221 Dauphin
Type: light cabin monoplane
Powerplant: one 86-kW (115-hp) Avco Lycoming O-235-C2A flat-four piston engine
Performance: maximum cruising speed 205 km/h (127 mph) at sea level; service ceiling 3900 m (12,795 ft); range 910 km (565 miles)
Weights: empty equipped 475 kg (1,047 lb); maximum take-off 840 kg (1,852 lb)
Dimensions: span 8.72 m (28 ft 7¼ in); length 7.00 m (22 ft 11½ in);

Exactly 100 DR.250 Capitanes were built, differing chiefly from the earlier DR.200 by the addition of an all-flying tailplane and extended wing leading edges on the inboard sections. Powered by a 119-kW (160-hp) Lycoming O-320-E, it found a market with French aero clubs who found it to be a versatile performer.

height 1.85 m (6 ft 0¾ in); wing area 13.60 m² (146.39 sq ft)

Robin DR.300 and 400

In 1969 Centre Est returned to its roots and changed its name again to Société des Avions Pierre Robin. From its Dijon-Darois factory the company launched a new series of aircraft to build on the success of the four-seat DR.253 and DR.315. The DR.300-series was the result, with individual model designations, such as the **DR.300-108**, DR.300-120 and DR.300-180, reflecting the power of their engines (108-, 120-, and 180-hp respectively). These were complemented by the **DR.340 Major**: a DR.250 with a clear canopy and 104-112-kW (140/150-hp) Lycoming O-320-E engine, the **DR.360 Chevalier**: a DR.340 with a solid cabin roof and 119-kW (160-hp) Lycoming O-320-D engine. A fire at the plant badly damaged the production line in 1972, but in April of that year Robin launched the first of the rejuvenated DR.300s.

First of the new series to fly was the **DR.400/125 Petit Prince** with a 93-kW (125-hp) Avco Lycoming O-235-F2B, a three/four-seater certificated in December 1972. In the same month, the **DR.400/180 Regent** was flown; this was the most powerful of the series, with a 134-kW (180-hp) Avco Lycoming O-360-A, and was a replacement for the DR.253 and DR.380. In June the **DR.400/160 Chevalier** flew, its 119-kW (160-hp) Avco Lycoming O-320-D making it a DR.360 replacement. The remaining three new models also appeared in 1972; the **DR.400/140 Major** with a 104-kW (140-hp) Avco

Lycoming O-320-E in October, the **DR.400/180R Remorquer** glider tug with a 134-kW (180-hp) Avco Lycoming O-360-A in November, and the smallest of the range, the **DR.400/2+2** with a 75-kW (100-hp) Avco Lycoming O-235-C20 in December. This was a two-seater with two small seats for children. All six of the new series featured a canopy which slid forward over the engine cowling to give access to the cabin, replacing the hinged canopies of earlier versions. Lower cabin walls gave easier access and also improved visibility. By 1980 production of the DR.400/2+2 had ended, and the **DR.400/120 Dauphin 80**

with an 84-kW (112-hp) Avco Lycoming O-235-L2A engine had replaced the DR.400/120 Petit Prince, itself introduced in 1975. The remainder of the range still in production comprise the DR.400/160 Major 80, DR.400/180 Regent and DR.400/180R Remorqueur.

Specification
Robin DR.400/180 Regent
Type: four-seat light aircraft
Powerplant: one 134-kW (180-hp) Avco Lycoming O-360-A flat-four piston engine
Performance: maximum speed 278 km/h (173 mph) at sea level;

Typical of the four-seaters available in the current Robin range, the DR.400/120 Dauphin was, in essence, a two-seater with somewhat cramped accommodation for another two passengers in the rear cockpit.

service ceiling 4715 m (15,470 ft); range 1450 km (900 miles)
Weights: empty 600 kg (1,323 lb); maximum take-off 1100 kg (2,425 lb)
Dimensions: span 9.08 m (29 ft 9½ in); length 7.59 m (24 ft 10¾ in); height 2.23 m (7 ft 3¾ in); wing area 14.20 m² (152.85 sq ft)

Robin HR.100

Avions Pierre Robin's first use of metal construction in its light aircraft range was in the prototype DR.253 Regent which was rebuilt with metal wings. Powered by a 134-kW (180-hp) Avco Lycoming O-360 it first flew in this form, as the **Robin HR.100/180**, on 3 April 1969. Three pre-production aircraft flew in 1970 and the first definitive version, the **HR.100/200** with a 149-kW (200-hp) Avco Lycoming IO-360 engine, appeared in 1971. One trials aircraft was completed as the **HR.100/320/4+2**, to seat four adults and two children. First flown in April 1971, the **HR.100/210** had a 157-kW (210-hp) engine and 75 were built before production ended in

February 1976. A higher-powered version with retractable landing gear and substantial airframe modifications was flown in November 1972. This was the **HR.100/285**, powered by a 239-kW (320-hp) Teledyne Continental Tiara engine. The production version, certificated in July 1974, had the 213-kW (285-hp) Tiara 6-285B engine; from 1975 the **HR.100/250TR** was also offered, with the 186-kW (250-hp) Avco Lycoming IO-540 engine.

Specification
Robin HR.100/285
Type: four-seat light monoplane
Powerplant: one 213-kW (285-hp) Teledyne Continental Tiara 6-285 flat-six piston engine
Performance: maximum speed

The final production variant of the Robin HR.100 series was the HR.100/250 with the Avco Lycoming IO-549 flat-six engine.

325 km/h (202 mph) at sea level; service ceiling 5700 m (18,700 ft); range 2130 km (1,323 miles)
Weights: empty 840 kg (1,852 lb);

maximum take-off 1400 kg (3,086 lb)
Dimensions: span 9.08 m (24 ft 10¾ in); height 2.71 m (8 ft 10¾ in); wing area 15.20 m² (163.62 sq ft)

Robin HR.200

The requirement for a two-seat all-metal aircraft for flying clubs and training schools prompted the Robin company to introduce the **Robin HR.200** series the prototype of which flew on 29 July 1971. The basic version was the **HR.200/100 Club** with an 81-kW (108-hp) Avco Lycoming O-235-H2C engine, but also

offered were the **HR.200/120** with a 93-kW (125-hp) Avco Lycoming O-235-J2A, the **HR.200/140** with a 104-kW (140-hp) Avco Lycoming O-320-E, and the **HR.200/160** with a 119-kW (160-hp) Avco Lycoming IO-320-D. Deliveries began towards the end of 1973. As the design progressed a basic low-cost variant was introduced, as the **HR.200/100S**. This was generally similar to the HR.200/100 but had less equipment and

no wheel fairings. The HR.200/120 was phased out in favour of the **HR.200/120B** with an 88-kW (118-hp) Avco Lycoming O-235-L2A. Production of the HR.200 series ended in 1976 after 107 had been built.

Specification
Robin HR.200/160
Type: two-seat light monoplane
Powerplant: one 119-kW (160-hp)

Avco Lycoming IO-320-D flat-four piston engine
Performance: maximum speed 260 km/h (161 mph) at sea level; service ceiling 5000 m (16,405 ft); range 935 km (581 miles)
Weights: empty 530 kg (1,168 lb); maximum take-off 800 kg (1,763 lb)
Dimensions: span 8.33 m (27 ft 4 in); length 6.64 m (21 ft 9½ in); height 1.94 m (6 ft 4½ in)

Robin R.1180 Aiglon

The development of the **Robin R.1180 Aiglon** marked a departure from the company's practice of using a cranked wing as in all earlier derivatives of the original Jodel. Of all-metal construction, with non-retractable landing gear and powered by a 134-kW (180-hp) Avco Lycoming O-360-A3AD engine, the prototype flew for the first time in late 1976. The production version, which introduced a number of improvements, including an enlarged tinted cockpit canopy, was certificated on 19 Septem-

ber 1978. Eighteen **R.1180TD** aircraft ordered by SFACT, for use at the French civil aviation training schools at Carcassonne, Grenoble and Muret, had control columns which were adjustable for height, improved cockpit soundproofing, altered instrument panel layout and increased fuel capacity.

Specification
Robin R.1180 Aiglon
Type: four-seat light monoplane
Powerplant: one 134-kW (180-hp)

The R.1180 Aiglon's most marked characteristic is its use of a straight dihedral wing, in place of Robin's earlier flat wing.

Avco Lycoming O-360-A3AD flat-four piston engine
Performance: maximum speed 251 km/h (156 mph) at sea level; service ceiling 5030 m (16,505 ft); range 1625 km (1,009 miles)

Weights: empty 650 kg (1,433 lb); maximum take-off 1150 kg (2,535 lb)
Dimensions: span 9.08 m (29 ft 9½ in); length 7.26 m (23 ft 9¾ in); height 2.38 m (7 ft 9¾ in); wing area 15.10 m² (162.54 sq ft)

Robin R.2112/R.2160

The **Robin R.2000** series of aerobatic two-seaters was introduced to replace the HR.200, retaining that aircraft's fuselage and fin but introducing a new wing of increased chord and modified section, a rudder of increased area, and an elongated ventral fin to aid spin recovery. The prototype, flown in September 1976, was an **R.2160** with a 119-kW (160-hp) Avco Lycoming O-320-D2A engine, manufactured originally as the **Acrobin** and produced currently as the **Alpha Sport**. A lower-powered trainer, the **R.2100A**, had an 81-kW (108-hp) Avco Lycoming O-235-H engine and 34 were built before the type was superseded in 1979 by the similar **R.2112 Alpha**. Robin has established a Canadian subsidiary, Avions Pierre Robin Inc. based at Lachute in Quebec, which is responsible for local assembly of French-manufac-

A feature of the R.2000 series is the addition of a long ventral fin to aid spin recovery, as seen on the R.2160 in the background.

tured basic components into finished R.2160s. The first of these was completed in 1980, following Canadian certification in October 1979; US certification was obtained in November 1982. Production ceased in 1984 after less than 100 had been built.

Specification
Robin R.2160
Type: two-seat aerobatic monoplane
Powerplant: one 119-kW (160-hp) Avco Lycoming O-320-D flat-four piston engine
Performance: maximum speed 257 km/h (160 mph) at sea level;

service ceiling 4570 m (14,995 ft); range 795 km (494 miles)
Weights: empty 550 kg (1,213 lb); maximum take-off 800 kg (1,764 lb)

Dimensions: span 8.33 m (27 ft 4 in); length 7.10 m (23 ft 3½ in); height 2.13 m (7 ft 0 in); wing area 13.00 m² (139.94 sq ft)

Robin R.3000

In 1978 Robin began development of a new series of all-metal touring and training aircraft, bearing the family designation **Robin R.3000**. Two **R.3140** prototypes were flown, the first on 8 December 1980. This had constant-chord wings whereas the second, which flew on 2 June 1981, introduced the production standard wing, not cranked but of typical Jodel planform; upturned tips were fitted later. Initial production versions are the **R.3120**, a three-seater (or two adults and two children) with an 88-kW (118-hp) Avco Lycoming O-235 engine, and the **R.3140E** which is intended as a low-cost four-seater with a 104-kW (140-hp) Avco Lycoming O-320-D2A and with an opaque canopy top. Other planned models include the **R.3100L** two-seat trainer with an 80-kW (108-hp) Avco Lycoming O-235-L engine, bubble canopy and unfaired wheels. With an improved interior, a 112-kW (150-hp) engine and variable-pitch propeller, the R.3140E becomes

the **R.3150** four-seat tourer, while the substitution of a 119-kW (160-hp) O-360 engine makes this the **R.3160GT**. The most powerful model is likely to be the **R.3180** glider tug, with a 134-kW (180-hp) engine and retractable landing gear. An R.3140 has been fitted with a modified PRV (Peugeot-Renault-Volvo) car engine, adapted for aircraft use by the Ecole National des Ingenieurs de St-Etienne (ENISE), and this was flown on 2 August 1983. The gestation period for this version has been prolonged in the extreme and certification was not achieved until 1993.

A sharp downturn in orders hit the company, forcing the closure of the R.2000 line in 1981. At this time close ties were established with SOCATA and between 1983 and 1988 the Aérospatiale subsidiary were responsible for marketing the R.3000 family. Development continued courtesy of French governmental assistance. The R.3000/120 was phased out in 1987. Current versions on offer include the **R.3000/140** (formerly the **R.3140E**) and the **R.3000/160**, which took the place of the R.3000/120

on the production line. At the Paris air show of 1989 Robin revealed an aircraft fitted with an Aérospatiale ATAL TV camera system, able to transmit real-time images to ground stations. A retractable gear version powered by a 149-kW (200-hp) Textron Lycoming IO-360 engine is under development.

Specification
Robin R.3140E
Type: four-seat light monoplane
Powerplant: one 104-kW (140-hp) Avco Lycoming O-320-D2A flat-four piston engine

This Robin R.3140 displays the upturned wingtips which were added as standard from the second prototype onwards.

Performance: maximum speed 260 km/h (161 mph) at sea level; service ceiling 4420 m (14,500 ft); range 890 km (553 miles)
Weights: empty 575 kg (1,268 lb); maximum take-off 1000 kg (2,205 lb)
Dimensions: span 9.81 m (32 ft 2¼ in); length 7.51 m (24 ft 7¾ in); height 2.66 m (8 ft 8¾ in); wing area 14.47 m² (155.75 sq ft)

Robin X4

The **X4** four-seat experimental light aircraft first flew on 25 February 1991, and appeared at that year's Paris air show. The aircraft is essentially an aerodynamic testbed built on a one-to-one scale to evaluate wind tunnel data and compare the results to the existing DR.400. Fitted with a laminar-sectioned wing of wooden construction, the X4 marks Avions Pierre Robin's first foray

The X4 exists in its present form as proof-of-concept aircraft only for use in the development of future Robin designs.

into the world of composite materials. This is hardly an unexpected move as Robin's aircraft have traditionally been 'light' designs. The view from the extensively glazed cockpit is superior even to that of the R.3000-series. The X4 is powered by a surprisingly small 86.5-kW (116-hp) Textron Lycoming engine.

Robinson Redwing

A two-seat biplane with side-by-side accommodation in a cockpit beneath the trailing edge of the upper wing, the prototype of what was to become known as the **Robinson Redwing** was built by Robinson Aircraft Company Ltd at Croydon, Surrey, later named Redwing Aircraft Ltd. The first prototype, which was retrospectively redesignated **Redwing I**, was first flown in 1930 and powered by a 56-kW (75-hp) A.B.C. Hornet flat-four engine. The **Redwing II** prototype,

The Robinson Redwing II was a pleasant aircraft to fly, but never broke into a market dominated by de Havilland and Avro.

flown in October 1930, was powered by the Armstrong Siddeley Genet IIA radial engine, and was followed by nine production aircraft. The final variant, of which only a single example was built as the **Redwing III**, differed by having reduced-span wings and main landing gear

units incorporating speed fairings, but it was subsequently converted to Redwing II standard. The 9.30-m (30-ft 6-in)

span Redwing II, as powered by the 0-kW (80-hp) Genet IIA, had a maximum speed of 153 km/h (95 mph).

Robinson Model R22

From the time that helicopters became practical aircraft their unit costs have always been high in comparison with those of fixed-wing aircraft of similar capacity. In the United States Franklin D. Robinson formed the Robinson Helicopter Company to design and market a lightweight civil helicopter which would be competitive in price with two-seat fixed-wing aircraft then on the market. His **Robinson Model R22** prototype flew for the first time on 28 August 1975, followed by a second in early 1977, and these two aircraft were used to gain FAA and CAA certification in 1979 and 1981 respectively. This basic model, which became known as the **R22 Alpha**, was replaced from the 501st aircraft onwards, in 1985, by the upengined **R22 Beta.** The R22 family has sold in huge numbers around the world, representing the first affordable helicopter for private use, with 402 produced in 1991 alone. There have also been military customers, such as Turkey, who ordered 10 for basic pilot training. Over 2300 R22s of all versions had been delivered by early 1993, with a healthy order book also.

Variants

R22 Mariner: fitted with floats and wheels, first delivered for offshore work in Mexico and Venezuela
R22 Police: version with special communications fit and optional port-side controls. Uprated electrical generator for searchlight, loudspeaker, siren and ATC transponder
R22 IFR: training version with improved flight instruments and radio for Instrument Flying Rules operations
External load R22: additional cargo hook certified to carry 181-kg (400-lb) underslung load. When fitted aircraft has a VNE (never exceed speed) limit of 75 kt (139 km/h, 86 mph). Conversions undertaken by Classic Helicopter Corp. of Boeing Field, Seattle, Wa.
R22 Agricultural: equipped with low-profile belly hopper and spray-bar system

Specification
Robinson R22 Beta
Type: two-seat light helicopter
Powerplant: one 119-kW (160-hp)

Textron Lycoming O-320-B2C flat-four piston engine
Performance: maximum level speed 180 km/h (112 mph); service ceiling 4265 m (14,000 ft); range with maximum payload 592 km (368 miles)
Weights: empty 379 kg (835 lb); maximum take-off 621 kg (1,370 lb)

The best-selling Robinson R22 is now in service in over 25 countries and certified in 30.

Dimensions: main rotor diameter 7.67 m (25 ft 2 in); length 6.3 m (20 ft 8 in); height 2.67 m (8 ft 9 in); main rotor disk area 46.21 m^2 (497.4 sq ft)

Robinson Model R44 Astro

Having defined the market for a light two-seat helicopter, the Robinson Helicopter Company decided to take the next logical step forward. In the summer of 1986 it announced it was developing a four-seat helicopter based on the R22 design. Designated **R44**, this new aircraft closely resembled its smaller sibling and retained the two-blade main rotor layout. The prototype (N44RH) first flew on 31 March 1990 and two aircraft were engaged on the flight test programme. A third aircraft flew in March 1992, and the type was certificated later that year. A new production site at Santa Maria, California, has been prepared for the R44, though the first 25 aircraft will be built at Torrance alongside the R22. This first batch of helicopters is only being released to customers in the south-western USA, in case they need to be recalled for modifications. Export deliveries will commence in 1993. So far the R44 has displayed all the qualities necessary to rival the R22. In March 1992 36 deposits of $15,000 were taken on the first day of sales alone. By mid-1993 orders were approaching 150.

Fuel consumption is less than 68 litres (15 gal) per hour, and the patented Robinson tri-hinge rotor is fitted with a rotor brake. Flyaway cost of a fully equipped R44 is listed at $235,000.

Specification
Robinson R44
Type: four-seat utility helicopter
Powerplant: one 194-kW (260-hp) Textron Lycoming O-540 flat-six engine, derated to 165 kW (225 hp)

Performance: cruising speed at 75 per cent power 209 km/h (130 mph); service ceiling 4270 m (14,000 ft); maximum range without reserves 643 km (400 miles)
Weights: empty 635 kg (1,400 lb); maximum take-off 1088 kg (2,400 lb)
Dimensions: main rotor diameter 10.06 m (33 ft); height 3.28 m (10 ft 9 in)

The R44 Astro offers a four-seat helicopter with a 110-kt cruise speed, powered by an affordable piston engine. The manufacturer estimates the Astro's hourly operating cost (including maintenance and inspection) at a mere $36 per hour. The prototype R44 is shown here with Frank Robinson himself at the controls.

Rockwell agricultural aircraft

Rockwell-Standard's association with agricultural aircraft began in 1965 with acquisition of the Snow Aeronautical Corporation. This had been established by Leland Snow in 1955 to manufacture an agricultural aircraft of his own design, a single-seat cantilever low-wing monoplane with fixed tailwheel landing gear, powered as the original production **Snow S-2B** by a 336-kW (450-hp) Pratt & Whitney R-985 radial engine. First deliveries were made soon after certification in 1958, the variant being followed by the lower-powered **S-2A** (164-kW/220-hp Continental W670) and improved **450 S-2C**, and **600 S-2C** which introduced a 447-kW (600-hp) Pratt & Whitney R-1340 engine. By the end of 1965 Snow Aeronautical had built 250 S-2s of all versions.

Produced by three manufacturers in a variety of forms, with turboprop or piston engines, the Commander series of 'ag-planes' has wide spray bars and a well situated cockpit.

Rockwell-Standard's Aero Commander division began by concentrating its production activities on a generally similar but refined version of the Snow S-2C which it designated **Rockwell 600 S-2D Snow Commander,** renamed **Ag Commander S-2D** in the following year. By then Rockwell-Commander had acquired rights to the CallAir A-9 and slightly larger B-1 agricultural aircraft, building the A-9 (175-kW/235-hp Avco Lycoming O-540-B2B5) as the **Ag Commander A-9**, a more powerful

version (216-kW/290-hp IO-540) as the **Ag Commander A-9 Super**, and the B-1 (400-hp Avco Lycoming IO-720-A1A) as the **Ag Commander B-1.** For details of subsequent designations and disposal of these CallAir aircraft see

entry for CallAir Model A.

In 1967 the Ag Commander S-2D was replaced by a development designated **Thrush Commander,** retaining the same 447-kW (600-hp) Pratt & Whitney R-1340-AN-1 engine, and in 1974 this was joined by the more powerful but otherwise similar **Thrush Commander S-2R** with a 597-kW (800-hp) Wright Cyclone R-1300-1B radial engine. In 1976 these two aircraft were renamed **Thrush Commander-600** and **Thrush Commander-800** respectively, before being sold to Ayres Corporation of Albany, Georgia, in 1977. Ayres expanded the line and in 1984 was marketing the **Thrush S2R-R1340** with

447-kW (600-hp) Pratt & Whitney powerplant, **Pezetel Thrush S2R-R3S** with a Pezetel PZL-3S engine of identical power, the **Bull Thrush S2R-1820** with 895-kW (1,200-hp) Wright R-1820 Cyclone radial engine with which is claimed to be the world's most powerful agricultural aircraft, and the **Turbo-Thrush S2R-T34, Turbo-Thrush S2R-T15** and **Turbo-Thrush S2R-T11**, with respectively the 559-kW (750-

shp) Pratt & Whitney Aircraft of Canada PT6A-34AG, 507-kW (680-shp), PT6A-15AG and 373-kW (500-shp) PT6A-11AG.

Specification
Rockwell Thrush Commander-800
Type: single-seat agricultural aircraft
Powerplant: one 597-kW (800-hp) Wright R-1300-B1 radial engine

Performance: maximum speed 249 km/h (155 mph); service ceiling 7620 m (25,000 ft); ferry range 531 km (330 miles)
Weights: empty equipped 1860 kg (4,100 lb); maximum take-off, agricultural use 3538 kg (7,800 lb)
Dimensions: span 13.51 m (44 ft 4 in); length 8.89 m (29 ft 2 in); height 2.79 m (9 ft 2 in); wing area 30.34 m² (326.60 sq ft)

Rockwell B-1B

Rockwell B-1B trials aircraft of the US Air Force during 1984.

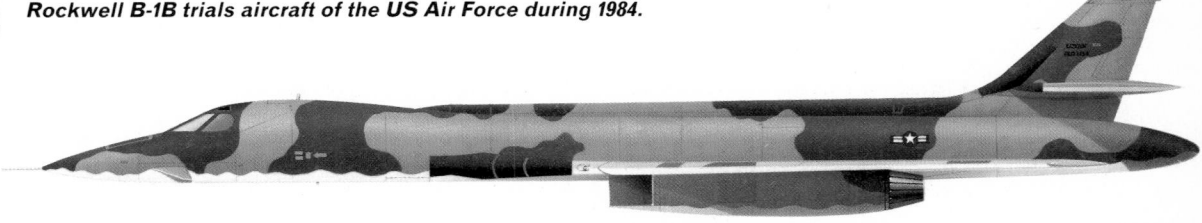

Requests for proposals to meet a USAF requirement for an advanced manned bomber to replace the Strategic Air Command's Boeing B-52s were issued on 3 November 1969, and the successful submissions were received from North American Rockwell for the airframe and from General Electric for the engine. Contracts to cover research, development, test and evaluation were awarded on 5 June 1970, originally for five **Rockwell B-1** flight test aircraft, two structural test airframes and 40 F101 turbofan engines, although these numbers were later reduced. Nevertheless, the first prototype took off on its maiden flight, from Palmdale, California, on 23 December 1974, also the occasion of the first flight of a YF101 engine.

This aircraft undertook a flight test programme involving 79 flights and a total of 403 hours 18 minutes in the air before being stored. The second prototype, flown on 14 June 1976, amassed a total of 282 hours 30 minutes in 60 flights before being similarly deactivated, though not before it had achieved a speed of Mach 2.22 on 5 October 1978. The third prototype, actually the second to fly and used as an avionics testbed, first took to the air on 26 March 1976 and completed 138 flights for a total of 829 hours 24 minutes during the original test programme. Effectively a pre-production aircraft, the fourth B-1 flew on 14 February 1979 and its 70 sorties resulted in 378 hours of flight time.

On 30 June 1977 President Carter cancelled the B-1 production programme in favour of cruise missile development, although testing continued by the incoming Reagan administration eventually resulted in the rehabilitation of the B-1 as America's long-range multi-role strategic bomber. In October 1981 the President announced his intention to order 100 definitive **B-1B** bombers for the US Air Force. Compared with the original B-1, the B-1B has a structurally-strengthened airframe and strengthened landing gear to permit operation at an increased maximum weight. The variable-geometry wing of the B-1 is retained but the variable engine inlets have been replaced by fixed components, together with revised engine nacelles. Weapons bay changes allow a variety of weapons or extra fuel tanks to be carried, and the aircraft has a most advanced defensive and offensive electronics fit, which will enable it to carry out its prime role of high-subsonic low level penetration and attack. This system, designated AN/ALQ-161 has had a troubled development history and been the subject of frequent modifications.

A new flight test programme got underway in March 1983, using the second and fourth prototype B-1As. On 4 September 1985 the first production B-1B was rolled out at Rockwell's Palmdale facility, in California, and made its first flight on 18 October. The first delivery took place on 27 July 1985, to Offutt AFB, and the first operational unit

was the 96th Bomb Wing at Dyess AFB, Texas: 'home of the B-1B'. The fleet is now spread between four wings of Air Combat Command (ACC), and the name **Lancer** has been adopted for the type. Intended as the spearhead of SAC/ACC the B-1B has not had a happy service record. Several aircraft have been lost after catastrophic engine failures and the type has been grounded half a dozen times in the last eight years.

The qualities of the B-1B have been obscured by this unwelcome publicity. It was the USAF's first 'stealthy' bomber, with a radar cross-section one quarter that of the B-52. With the B-2 force now never likely to exceed 20 aircraft, only the B-1B can effectively fulfill the USAF's long-range strategic strike mission. It is designed to penetrate the most hostile airspace at low-level and survive, and is still the nation's principle manned nuclear deterrent. On a more human level the aircraft has two distinct advantages over the B-52, namely a galley and a toilet.

B-1s took no part in the war against Iraq, despite having been qualified to drop a wide range of conventional weapons. Critics claim that this was due to the airframe's 'fragility', but with the B-52s away the B-1B had to shoulder the strategic load at home.

Specification
Type: long-range multi-role strategic bomber

Powerplant: four 64.94-kN (30,000-lb) thrust General Electric 010-GE-102 turbofans
Performance: maximum speed Mach 1.25; low level penetration speed more than 966 km/h (600 mph) at 60 m (200 ft); range unrefuelled 11998 km (7,455 miles)
Weights: maximum take-off 216364 kg (477,000 lb)
Dimensions: span, fully extended 41.67 m (136 ft 8½ in), fully swept 23.84 m (78 ft 2½ in); length 44.81 m (147 ft 0 in); height 10.36 m (34 ft 0 in); wing area 181.16 m² (1,950.0 sq ft)
Armament: there are three internal weapon bays for up to 84 227-kg (500-lb) Mk 82 or 24 907-kg (2,000-lb) Mk 84 conventional bombs; alternatively up to

Though outwardly similar to the B-1A, the B-1B has significant differences in avionics, structural and inlet design.

eight AGM-86B air-launched cruise missiles, 24 AGM-69 short-range attack missiles, 12 B-28 or B-43 free-fall nuclear bombs or 24 B-61 or B-83 bombs can be carried; similar weapons can also be carried on eight external stores stations beneath the fuselage

Seen over the purpose-built hangers of its Ellsworth AFB home, this B-1B is one of the resident 29th Wing's aircraft, formerly part of SAC's 15th Air Force.

Rockwell Commander single-engine series

Formed in December 1944 as the Aero Design and Engineering Company, this organisation (a Division of Rockwell-Standard Corporation) changed its name to Aero Commander in 1960. A merger between Rockwell-Standard Corporation and North American Aviation Inc. during September 1967 brought the new overall company name North American Rockwell Corporation, and in 1973 this was renamed Rockwell International Corporation. Production of the Commander line of single-engine aircraft was terminated by Rockwell in 1980.

The Aero Commander line of single-engine aircraft began in 1965 when Rockwell-Standard acquired Volaircraft Inc. and Meyers Aircraft Company, continuing to produce the Volaire Model 1050 and the Meyers 200B as the **Aero Commander 100** and **Aero Commander 200** respectively. The former was a four-seat braced high-wing monoplane with fixed tricycle landing gear,

The Lark Commander was an upgraded Dart Commander, but failed to break into the light-plane market already dominated by Cessna and Piper.

powered by a 112-kW (150-hp) Avco Lycoming O-320-A flat-four engine, and the latter a high-performance four-seat cantilever low-wing monoplane with retractable landing gear, powered by a 213-kW (285-hp) Continental IO-520-A flat-six engine. In 1968 some minor improvements were incorporated in the Aero Commander 100, which was renamed **Darter Commander**, and production of the Aero Commander 200 was ended. Simultaneously, an improved version of the Darter Commander with a 134-kW (180-hp) engine was introduced as the **Lark Commander**, and in the following year production of the Darter Commander was terminated.

At the end of 1970 North American Rockwell introduced a new four-seat cabin monoplane designated **Aero Commander 111** with fixed landing gear (which in fact was never produced) or **Aero Commander 112** with retractable landing gear; powerplant was the 134-kW (180-hp) Avco Lycoming O-360-A1G6 flat-four engine, and during 1971 production of the Lark Commander was ended. However, the Commander 112 went from strength to strength, with

progressive improvement and introduction of a 149-kW (200-hp) IO-360-C1D6 engine for 1973, and with further improvements becoming redesignated **Aero Commander 112A** in 1974. For 1976 a turbocharged version, with a 157-kW (210-hp) TIO-360-C1A6D engine, was introduced as the **Commander 112TC**, together with a generally similar aircraft which, introducing a more powerful engine and more equipment as standard, was designated **Commander 114**. There was to be yet one more change of designation in 1979, for the final year of production, the turbocharged version of the Commander 112 being marketed as the **Alpine Commander,** and the Commander 114 as the **Gran Turismo Commander**.

The Commander line lay idle for several years as Gulfstream Aerospace, its new owners, attempted to sell it off. Finally, in 1988, a deal was struck with Randall Greene, founder of the Commander Aircraft Company. He bought all rights to support existing aircraft and began production of new Commander 114Bs. The company eventually set up shop in the former Aero Commander factory at Bethany, Oklahoma and de-

livered its first aircraft in mid-1990. In an attempt to circumvent the commercially fatal US product liability laws, aircraft are leased rather than sold. The Commander 114Bs on offer differ in detail from the original 114As, mainly in the realm of aerodynamic refinement. So far nearly 200 orders have been achieved.

Specification
Rockwell Gran Turismo Commander
Type: four-seat cabin monoplane
Powerplant: one 194-kW (260-hp) Avco Lycoming IO-540-T4B5D flat-six piston engine
Performance: maximum speed 307 km/h (191 mph) at sea level; service ceiling 5030 m (16,500 ft); maximum range with maximum fuel 1308 km (813 miles)
Weights: empty 939 kg (2,070 lb); maximum take-off 1479 kg (3,260 lb)
Dimensions: span 10.85 m (25 ft 0½ in); length 7.63 m (25 ft 0½ in); height 2.57 m (8 ft 5 in)

The Gran Tourismo was the ultimate single-engined Commander to be built by Rockwell, but the type has been successfully resurrected by the Commander Aircraft Company.

Rockwell Commander twin-engine series

The starting point of the Rockwell twin-engined Commander line of aircraft began on 5 February 1952 when the first production five/seven-seat **Aero Commander 520** cantilever high-wing monoplane, with retractable tricycle landing gear and powered by two 179-kW (240-hp) Avco Lycoming GO-435-C2 flat-six engines, was delivered by the Aero Design and Engineering Company; three of this version were evaluated by the US Army under the designation **YL-26** (later **YU-9A**). It was superseded in production in 1954 by the improved **Aero Commander 560** which had 201-kW (270-hp) GO-480-B engines, the USAF evaluating a single example under the designation **YL-26A**, then ordering 14 of the later **Commander 560A** with 220-kW (295-hp) GO-480-C1B6 engines. These were designated **L-26B** (later **U-4A**), one

The US Army designation L-26C (later U-9C) was applied to utility military versions of the Aero Commander 680.

serving as the personal transport of President Eisenhower, and the US Army also acquired a single **L-26B** (later **U-9B**).

The Commander 560A was introduced in 1955, together with a new higher performance **Aero Commander 680 Super** which differed primarily by having two 254-kW (340-hp) GSO-480-A1A6 supercharged engines.

The USAF procured two of these for presidential use (**L-26C** later **U-4B**) and the US Army four (**L-26C** later **U-9C**); the US Army also acquired two with SLAR (side-looking airborne radar) as **RL-26D** (later **RU-9D**) and a single **NL-26D** (later **NU-9D**) with special electronics equipment. Growing interest in the Commander series brought introduction in 1958 of the four-seat **Aero**

Commander 500 (two 186-kW/250-hp Avco Lycoming O-540) and a version of the Aero Commander 680 Super with cabin pressurisation designated **Aero Commander 720 Alti-Cruiser**. This last aircraft gained little interest and its production ended in 1960, but in the following year the company began work on the 5/9-seat **Aero Commander Grand Commander**, with two 283-kW (380-hp) Avco Lycoming IGSO-540-B1A engines. Production deliveries began in 1963. In 1964 there was further expansion of the line with introduction of the **Aero Commander Turbo Commander**, which was a turboprop-powered (two 429-kW/575-shp Garrett AiResearch TPE 331) version of the Grand Commander, and in 1965 came delivery of the first example of the **Aero Commander Jet Commander** of which design had been initiated in 1961. This differed from the earlier aircraft by being of mid-wing configuration with all-swept tail surfaces, and had its two 1293-kg (2,850-lb) thrust General Electric CJ610-1 turbojets pod-mounted one on each side of the rear fuselage. Production of the Commander 560 and Commander 680 ended in 1965 and further changes came in 1967, the Commander 500 and Grand Commander being renamed **Shrike Commander** and **Courser Commander** respectively. By 1968 production of the Jet Commander had been terminated, leaving in production the Shrike Commander, Courser Commander and **Hawk Commander**, the last representing a new name for the Turbo Commander, plus the **Courser-Liner** which was a convertible cargo/passenger version of the Courser Commander. By 1970 only the Hawk Commander (by then renamed **Turbo Commander 681**) and Shrike Commander remained in production, the latter in standard and de luxe **Shrike Commander Esquire** versions, but in the following year the line began to grow again, the Turbo Commander 681 being complemented by a similar **Turbo Commander 690** (two 535-kW/717-eshp Garrett AiResearch TPE 331-5-251K turboprops) and **Commander 685** with piston-engine

The Commander 685 was essentially a piston-engined version of the TPE-331-powered Turbo Commander series, with the same high standards of comfort and avionics. A total of 66 was built until 1979.

powerplant (two 324-kW/435-hp Continental GTSIO-520-F). By 1975 only one standard version of the Shrike Commander was available; the Turbo Commander 681 had been dropped, and this was the fate of the Turbo Commander 685 in 1976. For 1980 the Turbo Commander 690 was replaced by a similar **Jetprop 840** and more powerful **Jetprop Commander 980**, but by the end of 1980 Rockwell's entire Commander line had gone, the Jetprop Commanders being acquired by Gulfstream American Corporation. For details of these aircraft and developments see Gulfstream American Commander Jetprop 840/900/980/1000.

Specification
Rockwell Shrike Commander
Type: four/seven-seat light transport
Powerplant: two 216-kW (290-hp) Avco Lycoming IO-540-E1B5 flat-six piston engines
Performance: maximum cruising speed 346 km/h (215 mph) at sea level; service ceiling 5915 m (19,400 ft);

range with maximum fuel, no reserves 1525 km (948 miles)
Weights: empty equipped 2102 kg (4,635 lb); maximum take-off 3062 kg (6,750 lb)
Dimensions: span 14.95 m (49 ft 0½ in); length 11.22 m (36 ft 9¾ in); height 4.42 m (14 ft 6 in); wing area 23.69 m² (255.0 sq ft)

Rockwell XFV-12

Rockwell became responsible in 1972 for development of the US Navy's **XFV-12A** V/STOL Fighter/Attack Technology Prototype programme. Basically a single-seat all-weather V/STOL fighter/attack aircraft, the XFV-12A made use of an augmentor wing concept in which the efflux of its single Pratt & Whitney F401-PW-400 afterburning turbofan engine could be diverted to nozzles in the wings and foreplanes for V/STOL operations. An ejector-flap system was incorporated

Spanning 8.69 m (28 ft 6¼ in) across its rear-set wing, and weighing in at a maximum of 11000 kg (24,250 lb), the XFV-12A was designed to provide a much more advanced supersonic rival to the Harrier, it never flew.

in the design of each wing and foreplane, in which ambient air was mixed with turbine efflux in a ratio of 7:1 to provide the essential jet-lift for vertical operations

and, when the flaps are raised or lowered progressively, for transition from vertical to horizontal flight and vice

versa. The programme proved a disappointment and failed to provide an alternative to the Harrier.

Rockwell/MBB X-31 EFM

The **X-31 Enhanced Fighter Maneuverability (EFM)** programme grew from a joint initiative in 1987 between the US Department of Defense's Defense Advanced Research Projects Agency (DARPA, now renamed ARPA) and the Ministry of Defence for the then Federal Republic of Germany. Its aim was to develop a technology demonstrator to research aircraft manoeuvrability beyond normal flight parameters. It is so far the only 'X-plane' project to involve a foreign nation and was one of the first NATO collaborations to be instituted under the Nunn-Quayle Research and Development Initiative.

Studies in the early 1980s finally laid to rest any notions that the day of the dogfight was over. While it is still supremely important to kill the enemy when BVR (Beyond Visual Range), future fighter designs must be equipped with the capability to out-fly the opposition at close quarters. The X-31 was intended to research all aspects of this high-*g*, low-speed, post-stall flight envelope using new technology, such as vectored thrust engines. A keystone of the programme was the speed with which it progressed. Funding was approved in 1988 and 22 months later the first of two test aircraft was rolled out.

Rockwell and MBB were selected for their experience with the HIMAT and TKF-90 programmes, respectively. Both had been pursuing similar, but independent, research into highly manoeuvrable combat aircraft design and their efforts were finally merged. To keep on schedule and in budget, extensive use was made of existing systems and parts. The proven General Electric F404 turbofan was chosen as the powerplant. A list of other components includes canard

foreplanes (V-22 tailplanes); canopy, ejection seat and leading edge actuators (F/A-18); emergency air start system (F-20); flight control computers (HTTB C-130); air conditioning (F-5E); main wheel tyres (A-7); and wheels and brakes (Citation III).

The first **X-31A** (BuNo. 164584), assembled by Rockwell, initially flew on 11 October 1990. The second (164585) followed on 19 January 1991. The thrust vectoring system had previously been static-tested on a modified F/A-18 Hornet and was first carried in flight by the X-31A on 14 Februry 1991. Since then both aircraft have flown a consistent and detailed series of tests spurred by the proven capability of the Su-27 and MiG-29. At present a single X-31A remains flying with the second aircraft held in reserve.

Specification
Rockwell/MBB X-31A
Type: single-seat highly manoeuvrable research aircraft
Powerplant: one 71.17-kN (16,000-lb) General Electric F404-GE-400 turbofan
Performance: maximum level speed

Mach 1.3; maximum operating altitude 12200 m (40,000 ft)
Dimensions: span 7.26 m (23 ft 10 in); length overall 14.85 m (48 ft 8½ in); height 4.44 m (14 ft 7 in)

The exhaust for the F404-GE-400 engine of the X-31A is vectored by a three-paddle arrangement surrounding the jet pipe. Thrust can be vectored up to 15°, in any direction, from the normal thrust line. The aircraft is flown by a combination of Rockwell, MBB, USN and USAF test pilots from its NAS Patuxent River home.

Rogozarski lesser types

Rogozarski, in full Prva Srpska Fabrika Aviona Zivojin Rogozarski, was established in Belgrade during 1924 and began by building Brandenburg trainers before participating in production of Zmaj Fizir types.

Reconnaissance biplane: a two-seat unequal-span biplane intended for reconnaissance, this original design was powered by a 179-kW (240-hp) Walter Castor radial engine. It reached a maximum speed of 214 km/h (133 mph). An example appeared in 1932 with the civil registration UN-PAU, but no production appears to have been undertaken.

SIM-II: this first design for the company by Sima Milutinović appeared in 1930, and was a parasol-wing monoplane two-seat trainer. Its 75-kW (100-hp) Siemens radial engine provided a maximum speed of 148 km/h (92 mph). A small batch was built for the Yugoslav air force.

SIM-VI: a two-seat dual-control tourer/trainer low-wing monoplane, the prototype (YU-PDX) was powered by a 37-kW (50-hp) Walter Mikron engine. The **SIM-VIa** of 1937 incorporated minor improvements and had its engine uprated to 45 kW (60 hp), raising maximum speed by 10 km/h (6 mph) to 160 km/h (99 mph).

SIM-VIII: developed specifically as a two-seat tourer from the SIM-II, this aircraft incorporated several design changes. A number were produced for private owners and aero clubs with the Siemens 14 engine of 75 kW (100 hp).

SIM-IX: a single-seat trainer prototype with a 119-kW (160-hp) Bramo Sh 14a.

Rogozarski IK-3

Designed in Yugoslavia by Ljubomir Ilić, Kosta Sivcev and Slobodan Zrnić, the **Rogozarski IK-3** was a projected modern single-seat fighter of mixed construction. A cantilever low-wing monoplane, it had wide-track inward-retracting landing gear and an aft-sliding cockpit canopy, and was powered by a licence-built Hispano-Suiza engine. The IK-3 prototype was test-flown for the first time in May 1938 and performed well, but difficulties were encountered with the transparent cockpit panels. An order for 12 series aircraft was received in November 1938, but on 19 January 1939 the prototype was lost in a fatal accident. Nevertheless, production continued and all 12 series aircraft (with considerable redesign, including a new cockpit canopy and simplified main landing gear fairings) had been delivered to the Yugoslav air arm by July 1939.

The IK-3s equipped the 161 and 162 Eskadrila, which formed part of the 51 Grupa based at Zemun airfield. They were in action against Luftwaffe units from 6 April 1941, the first day of the German invasion, but after claiming 11 enemy aircraft the surviving IK-3s were destroyed on the emergency strip at Veliki Radnici to prevent them falling into enemy hands.

Specification
Rogozarski IK-3
Type: single-seat fighter
Powerplant: one 716-kW (960-hp) Avia-built Hispano-Suiza 12Ycrs *moteur canon* engine
Performance: maximum speed 527 km/h (327 mph); service ceiling 9400 m (30,840 ft); range 785 km (488 miles)
Weights: empty equipped 2068 kg (4,559 lb); maximum take-off 2630 kg (5,798 lb)
Dimensions: span 10.30 m (33 ft 9½ in); length 8.00 m (26 ft 3 in); height 3.25 m (10 ft 8 in); wing area 16.50 m² (177.6 sq ft)
Armament: one engine-mounted 20-mm Oerlikon cannon and two fuselage-mounted and synchronised 7.92-mm (0.31-in) FN Browning machine-guns

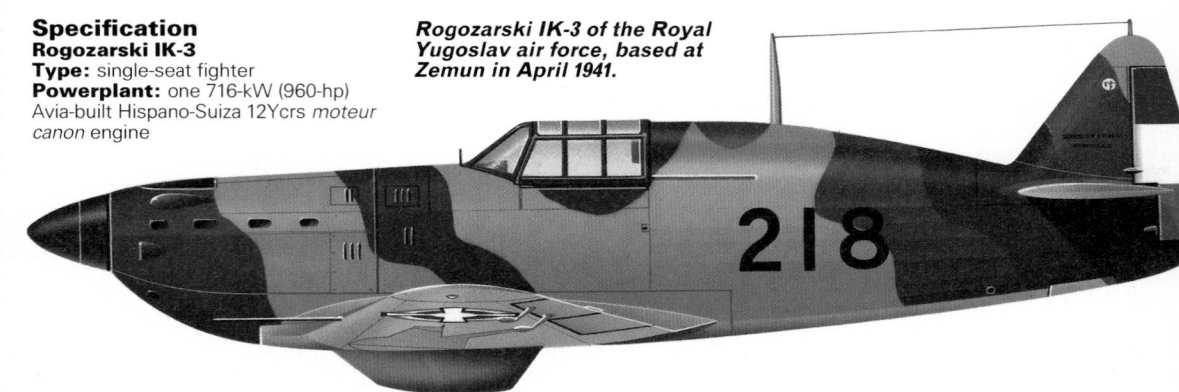

Rogozarski IK-3 of the Royal Yugoslav air force, based at Zemun in April 1941.

Rogozarski PVT

The **Rgozarski PVT** (Prototip Vazduhoplovno Tehcnicki) dual-control advanced trainer flew in prototype form in 1934. Designed by a talented team comprising Ruldolf Fizir, Sima Milutonovic, Kosta Sivcev, Aleksander Biscevic and Ljubomir Ilic, the PVT was a neat braced parasol-wing monoplane largely of wooden construction, with a circular-section fuselage, swept-back wings and robust fixed and divided landing gear.

In production from 1934, and renowned for its excellent handling and aerobatic qualities, the PVT equipped Yugoslav military aviation training schools in large numbers, all fighter pilots receiving their training on the type. Production figures are not known, but 57 were in service at the time of the German invasion of Yugoslavia in April 1941.

Variants
PVT-H: the excellence of the PVT landplane attracted the attention of the Yugoslav navy, and one example was modified to take a pair of Edo light metal floats; successful testing led to a series of production aircraft, used at the navy flying school for advanced training and liaison duties
P-100: a development of the PVT, with more metal in the structure and generally improved lines, the P-100 retained the same Gnome-Rhône K7 radial but introduced a NACA cowling, while the tailplane was redesigned and a tailwheel replaced the tailskid of its predecessor; the P-100 was put into production and 27 had entered service for advanced and aerobatic training by 1941; wing span was reduced compared with the PVT, at 10.20 m (33 ft 5½ in), while maximum take-off weight was down to 1226 kg (2,703 lb) and maximum speed up to 251 km/h (156 mph)

Specification
Rogozarski PVT
Type: two-seat advanced trainer
Powerplant: one 336-kW (450-hp) Gnome-Rhône 7K Titan Major radial piston engine
Performance: maximum speed 240 km/h (149 mph); service ceiling 7000 m (22,965 ft); range 550 km (342 miles)
Weights: empty equipped 965 kg (2,127 lb); maximum take-off 1310 kg (2,888 lb)
Dimensions: span 11.20 m (36 ft 9 in); length 7.38 m (24 ft 2½ in); height 2.10 m (6 ft 10¾ in); wing area 22.10 m² (237.89 sq ft)
Armament: one 7.7-mm (0.303-in) synchronised machine-gun, or one camera gun

The prototype Rogozarski PVT-H proved highly successful and was followed by series of production aircraft.

Rogozarski R-313

Designed by Sima Milutinovic, the **Rogozarski R-313** two-seat light-bomber/reconnaissance aircraft was test flown in early 1940. Largely of wooden construction, it was a cantilever mid-wing monoplane powered by two 373-kW (500-hp) Walter Sagitta I-SR inverted-Vee engines, but even with this low power the R-313 attained a maximum speed of 460 km/h (286 mph) and had considerable development potential. However, on operational test at the time of the German invasion in April 1941, it was lost after a take-off accident

Among the notable features of the R-313 light bomber were the 20-mm cannon in the nose, the raised cockpit for the observer, and the strut mounting for the tail unit just above the rear fuselage.

en route for Greece. Design features of the 13.00-m (42-ft 7¾-in) span R-313 included retractable landing gear, a twin fin-and-rudder tail unit, and armament comprising a 20-mm HS-404 cannon, an 8-mm (0.315-in) FN machine-gun, and an internal bombload of up to 400 kg (882 lb).

Also under development by Rogozarski in 1940 was the **Brucos** (freshman), a two-seat low-wing monoplane primary trainer powered by a 97-kW (130-hp) de Havilland Gipsy Major engine.

Rogozarski SIM-X

Described as a two-seat school aircraft, the **Rogozarski SIM-X** was designed by Sima Milutonovic for Yugoslav military aviation in 1936. Largely of wooden construction, it comprised a circular-section fuselage of new concept, a braced parasol wing and wide-track fixed landing gear of divided type, and was powered by a Walter radial engine. Successful testing of the prototype (YU-PDY) led to the series version being delivered to Yugoslav primary training units from 1937, and a considerable number were completed. At the time of the German invasion of Yugoslavia in spring 1941, some 20 SIM-Xs were still in service at the three principal pilot training schools.

Variants
SIM-XI: a single-seat advanced or aerobatic trainer version of the SIM-X;

powered by a 112-kW (150-hp) Siemens Sh 14a radial, with which maximum speed was 200 km/h (124 mph); dimensions differed somewhat from those of SIM-X

SIM-XII-H: equipped with twin Edo floats, this was a seaplane primary trainer developed from the SIM-X for the Yugoslav navy; powered by a 142-kW (190-hp) Walter Major Six inverted inline engine, it had a more oval-shaped fuselage and increased tail surface area; the prototype flew in February 1937, being followed by four series aircraft in 1939 with specialised instrumentation and used for night flying training

Specification
Rogozarski SIM-X
Type: two-seat primary trainer
Powerplant: one 89-kW (120-hp)

Walter radial piston engine
Performance: maximum speed 192 km/h (119 mph); service ceiling 5000 m (16,405 ft); range 500 km (311 miles)
Weights: empty equipped 548 kg (1,208 lb); maximum take-off 790 kg (1,742 lb)
Dimensions: span 10.00 m (32 ft

Powered by a Czech-built Walter radial piston engine, the Yugoslavian Rogozarski SIM-X floatplane was intended as a military trainer and used mainly for night flying.

9¾ in); length 6.96 m (22 ft 10 in); wing area 18.50 m² (199.14 sq ft)

Rogozarski SIM-XIV-H

The prototype **Rogozarski SIM-XIV-H** flew for the first time on 8 February 1938, demonstrating excellent operating qualities. Built to a January 1937 requirement of the Yugoslav navy for a twin-float coastal reconnaissance seaplane, it was constructed largely of wood and had a low wing braced to the fuselage by parallel struts, and an oval section monocoque fuselage (the glazed fuselage nose being surmounted by a manually operated gun turret) and was powered by two 179-kW (240-hp) Argus 10C engines.

A pre-production batch of six **SIM-XIV-H Series 0** aircraft was ordered, followed by production batches totalling 18 machines. Series 0 aircraft differed from the prototype in having no revolving nose turret, a revised tail unit and a redesigned crew canopy. The first six **SIM-XIV-H Series I** aircraft (ordered in 1939) were delivered in 1940, but the

The little-known Rogozarski SIM-XIV-H was in fact one of the most impressive military floatplanes flown before World War II, but the aircraft was not built in large numbers.

second batch of 12 was still under construction when Germany invaded Yugoslavia in 1941. The Series I machines had engines of higher power, fully cantilevered wings, steel-tube construction for the rear fuselage, and further revisions to the crew canopy and tail unit.

The SIM-XIV-Hs performed well and were comfortable, able to accommodate three passengers in addition to the three-man crew. Following the Axis occupation of Yugoslavia two aircraft reached the Allies in North Africa, and others were taken over by the Italians. Unconfirmed reports refer to as many as eight SIM-XIV-Hs pressed into Italian

service, several of them at the seaplane training school at Orbetello.

Specification
Rogozarski SIM-XIV-H Series I
Type: coastal reconnaissance aircraft
Powerplant: two 201-kW (270-hp) Argus As 10E inverted-Vee piston engines
Performance: maximum speed 243 km/h (151 mph); service ceiling 4500 m (14,765 ft); range 840 km (522

miles)
Weights: empty equipped 2230 kg (4,916 lb); maximum take-off 3350 kg (7,385 lb)
Dimensions: span 15.20 m (49 ft 10½ in); length 11.20 m (36 ft 9 in); height 4.48 m (14 ft 8¼ in); wing area 35.55 m² (382.76 sq ft)
Armament: two 7.5-mm (0.295-in) FN Browning machine-guns (one in nose and one on dorsal mounting), plus up to 200 kg (441 lb) of bombs

Rohrbach aircraft

Dr Ing. Rohrbach, who had been associated with the Zeppelin Werke Staaken GmbH during World War I, formed Rohrbach Metall Flugzeugbau GmbH in 1922 and developed the first production aircraft to have stressed-skin structure of the modern type using non-corrugated skins of aluminium alloy. Construction was carried out at his subsidiary company Rohrbach Metall-Aeroplan A/S in Copenhagen, to evade the terms of the Allied Control Commission which banned the construction of aircraft in Germany; the Danish factory was closed in the late 1920s, when aircraft manufacture in Germany was resumed.

Most of this company's aircraft were developed versions of designs which Rohrbach had created at Zeppelin Werke, the first of them being the **Rohrbach Ro II** flying-boat, which was powered by two 268-kW (360-hp) Rolls-Royce Eagle engines. In October 1923 one of these 'boats, carrying a payload of 250 kg (551 lb), set speed records over

Showing clear signs of Zepplin-Staaken inspiration, the Roland II was built for Deutsche Luft-Hansa and other airlines.

100-, 200-, 500- and 1000-km (61.2-, 124.3-, 310.7- and 621.4-mile) courses, the maximum recorded speed being 159.15 km/h (98.9 mph). About 10 of these Ro IIs were supplied to Japan, where a similarly powered but improved **Ro III** was built in small numbers. A version based on the Ro III design was built by Rohrbach under the designation **Ro IIIa Rodra**, and several of this variant were supplied to Turkey in 1926; they had a strengthened structure and were each powered by two 336-kW (450-hp) Lorraine-Dietrich engines. The designation **Ro IV** applied to a revised version of the Ro III powered by two 336-kW (450-hp) Napier Lion engines, two examples being built for William Beardmore & Co. Ltd in the UK under the name **Beardmore Inverness.**

The **Ro V Rocco** was a 10-passenger flying-boat powered by two 537-kW (720-hp) Rolls-Royce Condor IIIa engines mounted above braced monoplane wings. The only example built was operated by Deutsche Luft-Hansa. The **Ro VII Robbe I**, powered by two 239-kW (320-hp) BMW IV engines, was of similar configuration to the Ro III and IV, but the

designation **Robbe II** was given to a somewhat larger version powered by two 522-kW (700-hp) BMW VI engines. Far more important was the **Ro VIII Roland** landplane, based on the four-engine Zeppelin-Staaken E.4/20 designed by Rohrbach, which had flown successfully in 1920 but was then destroyed by orders of the Allied Control

Commission. The Ro VIII was a semi-cantilever braced monoplane accommodating a crew of two side-by-side in a forward cockpit, with below and behind them an enclosed cabin for 10 passengers, and was powered by three 239- or 268-kW (320- or 360-hp) BMW IV or Va engines respectively; a version designated **Ro VIIIa Roland II** also appeared with three uprated 283-kW (380-hp) BMW Va engines. Between 1927-29 nine of these civil airliners were built for Deutsche Luft-Hansa. The designation **Ro IX Rofix** was applied to a parasol-wing monoplane fighter completed in 1926 which, powered by a 559-kW (750-hp) BMW VIUZ engine, had a maximum speed of 260 km/h (162 mph). A single five-passenger flying-boat, powered by two 336-kW (450-hp) Gnome-Rhône Jupiter VI engines, was flown in 1928 under the name **Rostra**, and the final

production aircraft, before the company was taken over by Weser Flugzeugbau in early 1934, was the **Ro X Romar.** This was a long-range flying-boat accommodating a flight crew of four or five, with two cabins seating as standard a total of 12 passengers, though 16 passengers could be accommodated in the revised **Romar II**. However, only four were built, three of them serving on the Baltic services of Deutsche Luft-Hansa and one with the French navy.

Specification
Rohrbach Ro X Romar
Type: long-range commercial flying-boat
Powerplant: three 485-kW (650-hp) BMW VIUZ Vee piston engines
Performance: maximum speed 210 km/h (130 mph); service ceiling 2800 m (9,185 ft); range with maximum

Only a single Rohrbach Ro V Rocco was ever produced, in 1927, and the aircraft could carry 10 passengers on the strength of its two Rolls-Royce Condor engines. It was used on Luft-Hansa's route from Lübeck to Oslo in May and June 1928, but was then withdrawn.

fuel 4000 km (2,485 miles)
Weights: empty 9900 kg (21,826 lb); maximum take-off 19000 kg (41,888 lb)

Dimensions: span 36.90 m (121 ft 0¾ in); length 22.00 m (72 ft 2¼ in); height 8.50 m (27 ft 10¾ in)

Rollason aircraft

Originally an aircraft sales and service organisation, Rollason Aircraft and Engines Ltd began the construction of lightplanes by acquiring from Roger Druine in France a licence to produce the single-seat Druine Turbulent. Druine's designs were intended for home construction, but the popularity of the Turbulent in the UK (about 25 were built by amateurs) suggested to Rollason that there would be a worthwhile market for a production version. Rollason manufactured 25 as the **Rollason Turbulent**, a simple cantilever low-wing monoplane, standard powerplant being a 25-kW (34-hp) Ardem flat-four engine, but 28- and 30-kW (38- and 40-hp) versions of the Ardem, which was a modification of the

G-ATOH was the fourth D.62B Condor production aircraft, and the first to be fitted with flaps.

Volkswagen motor-car engine, were available optionally. This modest success was followed by the acquisition of a licence to produce the side-by-side two-seat Druine Condor, which Rollason believed it could sell in worthwhile numbers to flying clubs as a trainer/tourer. Of similar general configuration to the Turbulent, the Condor differed primarily by having a wider fuselage and more power. The **Rollason D.62 Condor** prototype was powered by a 56-kW (75-hp) Continental A75 and followed by two **D.62A** aircraft with the 75-kW (100-hp)

Rolls-Royce/Continental O-200-A, which was the powerplant for the slightly modified production **D.62B** of which more than 40 were built. Four examples were also built for a glider-tug **D.62C Con-**

dor, which was powered by the 97-kW (130-hp) Rolls-Royce/Continental O-240-A. The 8.38-m (27-ft 6-in) span D.62B Condor had a cruising speed of 161 km/h (100 mph).

ROMAERO ROMBAC One-Eleven

With the rundown of BAC One-Eleven production by British Aerospace in the early 1980s, an agreement was struck with IAv Bucuresti to transfer the entire production line to Romania. All BAe construction jigs and toolings began to be moved to a newly established production line at Baneasa Airport, Bucharest. At the same time, a corresponding programme for the licence-production of the aircraft's Rolls-Royce Spey 512 powerplants was also established. The One-Eleven had proven to be a reliable and well-liked airliner which, despite its noisy engines, was felt by ROMBAC to have many years of service ahead of it. The initial Romanian version was designated the **One-Eleven 560**, and was based on BAe's final production Series 500, with its stretched fuselage. As a lead in to total Romanian production, a single BAe-built Series 487 freighter and two Series 525 aircraft were delivered between 1981 and 1982.

The first Romanian-built One-Eleven was completed in September 1982 and delivered to TAROM, the national airline. The initial prouction agreement was for 22 aircraft, but work proceeded at a very slow rate. While ROMBAC had all the skilled personnel necessary, in Ceasescu's Romania the aviation industry was starved of the hard currency it needed to buy the materials essential for the One-Eleven. To date only nine aircraft have been delivered, seven of these by 1989. All have been built to a high standard, and achieved CAA certification.

At the same time it was also planned to build a version known as the **One-Eleven 495**. The first orders, for two

aircraft, were received in 1987. This version featured a rough-field undercarraige with low-pressure tyres and was shorter than previous aircraft, utilising the fuselage of the Series 400. ROMBAC intended it to be a convertible passenger/freight aircraft and fitted a side cargo door. This necessitated a complicated redesign which caused many problems, and the first aircraft remains uncompleted on the production line to this day.

Orders for the Spey-engined aircraft dried up and its future was increasingly threatened by the implementation of Stage 3/Chapter 3 noise regulations. A re-engining programme had already been initiated in 1986 by the Dee Howard company of the United States

which, in conjunction with Rolls-Royce, had investigated fitting One-Elevens with Tay 650 engines. While this programme has been shelved, ROMBAC has launched a similar proposal. Offered as the **ROMAERO One-Eleven 2500**, this involves fitting a 95-115 seat One-Eleven 500 with the new engines to comply with demanding noise and pollution restrictions. It was hoped to deliver the first aircraft by 1991, but the project floundered when little airline interest was forthcoming. In 1993 a launch order was recieved for 20 aircraft from newly established American carrier Kiwi Air. At present other orders are rumoured to be in prospect.

Specification
ROMBAC One-Eleven Series 560
Type: twin-engined short/medium-range airliner
Powerplant: two licence-built 55.8-kN (12,550-lb) Rolls-Royce Spey Mk 512-14DW turbofans
Performance: maximum level speed 470 kt (870 km/h; 541 mph); maximum cruising altitude 10670 m (35,000 ft); maximum range 1,989 nm (3515 km/2,184 miles)
Dimensions: span 28.50 m (93 ft 6 in); length overall 32.61 m (107 ft); height 7.47 m (24 ft 6 in)

A TAROM ROMBAC One-Eleven 561RC, One-Eleven 2500 will have Tay engines, a Honeywell EFIS cockpit and may be fitted out by FLS Aerospace in Britain.

Romano lesser types

At the age of 19, Etienne Romano built his **Romano R-1** aircraft, inspired by the Wright biplane, only to see it crash on its first flight. In 1922 he obtained workshops and established Les Chantiers Navals de la Croisette, only then beginning his true career as an aircraft designer

Romano R-2: an observation biplane of seaplane configuration, with a large central float, wingtip stabilising floats and powered by a 60-kW (80-hp) Le Rohône 9C rotary engine

Romano R-3: 1924 development of the R-2 with a 134-kW (180-hp) Hispano-Suiza 8Ab engine; extensively tested by French navy at St Raphaël

Romano R-4: flown in 1927, a more militarised and strengthened development of the R-3, with a 172-kW (230-hp) Salmson 9Ab radial engine and provision for a machine-gun on a mounting in the observer's cockpit

Romano R-5: single-engine patrol/reconnaissance flying-boat flown in September 1932. Of all-metal construction and parasol-wing configuration, it had a two-step hull with stabilising sponsons, accommodated its crew of two in an enclosed cabin, and was powered by a wing-mounted Hispano-Suiza 12Nbr engine of 485 kW (650 hp). Armament was two machine-guns and a 200-kg (441-lb) bombload. In spite of good per-

formance it was not adopted by the French navy for production

Romano R-6: a strut-braced high-wing monoplane powered by three 224-kW (300-hp) Gnome-Rhône 7Kb radials, the R-6 accommodated a crew of two and eight passengers. Flown on 20 December 1932 and acquired by the French air ministry as a VIP transport, it was destroyed in a landing accident during 1934

Romano R-15: flown in 1933, the R-15 was a two-seat cantilever high-wing monoplane amphibian, powered by three 56-kW (75-hp) Salmson 9Aer radials, and accommodating pilot and passenger in an enclosed cabin

Romano R-16: of similar configuration to the R-6 and designed to an official requirement for a three-seat colonial aircraft (Col. 3 category), the R-16 was rejected in favour of the Bloch M.B.120. It was then considered as a ministerial transport under the revised designation **R.160**, but an anticipated order for five production **R-162** aircraft did not materialise. The single R-160, powered by three 224-kW (300-hp) Lorraine 9Na Algol radials, was used in North Africa by Général Paul Armengaud commanding the 5e Région Aérienne

Romano R-110: designed to meet an Armée de l'Air requirement for a three-seat fighter, to serve as a control or aerial command post aircraft for a unit of

single-seat fighters, the R-110 accommodated between the pilot and observer/gunner a *commandant de manoeuvres* to control the single-seat fighters involved in any particular operation. A cantilever low-wing monoplane, largely of metal construction, the R-110 had a twin fin-and-rudder tail unit and retractable tailwheel landing gear, with power provided by two 336-kW (450-hp) Renault 12 Ro2/3 engines. The prototype was flown on 30 March 1938 but no production resulted

Romano R-120: last Romano design, built in prototype form only, the R-120 was designed to meet an official requirement for a B.4 category four-seat medium bomber. A low/mid-wing canti-

The Romano R-110 was an interesting design for an unusual role. It was intended as an aerial command post for other fighters, with an observer and controllers.

lever monoplane of all-metal construction, powered by two 731-kW (980-hp) Hispano-Suiza 14Aa 08/09 radial engines, it was to have been armed by a 20-mm cannon and three machine-guns. Although demonstrating a maximum 520 km/h (323 mph) during trials, it failed to win a production order

Romano R-130: final Romano design for a biplane single-seat fighter with retractable landing gear, but no prototype was built

---

Romano R-80 and R-82

The **Romano R-80.01** first prototype was a private venture by Etienne Romano, and was designed to provide an aerobatic two-seat biplane for company pilot Lemoigne to demonstrate at air shows. Tested in early 1935, it was also flown with great success by Michel Detroyat. Its design features included the provision of ailerons on both wings, robust divided landing gear, and a 179-kW (240-hp) Lorraine 7Me radial engine in a NACA cowling. After testing also by the official STAé, the R80.01 then gave many aerobatic shows with Lemoigne at the controls.

In response to official suggestions, **R-80.02** with the more powerful Salmson 9Aba engine was first flown in March 1936 and exhibited at the Paris Salon de l'Aéronautique of that same year. It incorporated changes already made on the aerobatic prototype, including ailerons on the lower wings only and a fin of increased area. Intended as a two-seat dual-control intermediate trainer, it was soon redesignated **R-82.01**. Two further prototypes were built, both of them being sold to private owners, one of them the well-known aviatrix Lucienne Saby.

A fine aerobatic trainer, the Romano R-82 biplane was built in relatively substantial numbers. The 200 or so production aircraft were all fitted with a long-chord cowling.

Meanwhile, Romano had become part of the nationalised SNCASE and Michel Detroyat became Inspector of Flying Equipment for all the nationalised companies. On the latter's urging, large orders were placed by the state for **R-82** trainers for the Armée de l'Air. In the event, the total of production aircraft was 147, to which was added another 30 ordered in 1937 by the Aéronavale. Series trainers featured a number of refinements and some simplifications, the principal external change being the introduction of a long-chord engine cowling.

By 1 August 1939 70 R-82s had been taken on charge, and all 177 series aircraft had been delivered by May 1940. The R-82 have excellent service with the Armée de l'Air and Aéronavale, largely equipping the Centres d'Instruction and Ecoles de Pilotage.

In February 1938 two R-82s (F-AQJN

and F-AQJP) were purchased by a French intermediary company and ferried to Spain, where they were used for training and liaison duties by the Republican government fighting the Nationalist forces. It is uncertain whether these were new aircraft or machines taken from Armée de l'Air contracts.

Specification
Romano R-82
Type: two-seat intermediate and aerobatic trainer

Powerplant: one 209-kW (280-hp) Salmson 9Aba radial piston engine
Performance: maximum speed 240 km/h (149 mph); service ceiling 6500 m (21,325 ft); range 660 km (410 miles)
Weights: empty equipped 918 kg (2,024 lb); maximum take-off 1328 kg (2,928 lb)
Dimensions: span 9.88 m (32 ft 5 in); length 7.82 m (25 ft 7¾ in); height 3.34 m (10 ft 11½ in); wing area 23.72 m² (255.33 sq ft)

Romano R-90

Built to meet a French navy requirement for a ship-based single-seat fighter seaplane suitable for catapult launching, the **Romano R-90** made its first flight in August 1935. An open-cockpit biplane with the upper-wing gulled into the top of

the fuselage, it had twin floats and was stressed for shipboard operation. Powered initially by a 485-kW (650-hp) Hispano-Suiza 9Vbrs radial, the R-90 was re-engined in October 1935 with a 507-kW (680-hp) Hispano-Suiza 14Hbrs which provided a maximum speed of 380 km/h (236 mph). Against an official request the R-90 was again re-engined in

1937 with a 623-kW (835-hp) Hispano-Suiza 12Ycrs-1 *moteur canon* V-12 engine. This raised maximum speed to an even more impressive 420 km/h (261 mph), but still no production order was received and eventually a small batch of the rival and ill-fated Loire 210 was delivered to the French navy.

Proposed armament for the R-90 was

four 7.5-mm (0.295-in) Darne machine-guns, augmented by a 20-mm cannon in the final version. A landplane fighter development of the R.90, designated **R-92** and powered by the Hispano-Suiza 12Ycrs engine, was rumoured to have been built in prototype form by an unnamed Belgian firm for the Spanish Republican government in 1938.

Rose Parakeet

The Rose Aeroplane and Motor Company designed and put into production in 1936 an attractive single-seat open cockpit biplane suitable for private or club use. Of lightweight construction and powered by a 29-kW (39-hp) Continental

A40 flat-four engine, the 6.10-m (20-ft 0-in) span **Rose Parakeet Model A-1** had a 137 km/h (85 mph) cruising speed and range of 547 km (340 miles). It proved popular, and there were requests for more power, resulting in the **Model A-2** with a 37-kW (50-hp) Menasco M-50 flat-four engine. Production was brought to an end by the outbreak of

World War II, and after the war all rights to the Parakeet were acquired by Foster Hannaford Jr who marketed plans and kits for its construction by amateurs.

The simple yet attractive Rose Parakeet was marketed after the war as the Hannaford Parakeet, with a range of engines.

Rotorcraft RF-1 Pinwheel

The **Rotorcraft RF-1 Pinwheel** one-man helicopter was designed in 1954 to provide military personnel with a simple go-anywhere vehicle. Basically a strap-on device, it relied upon liquid propellants to power a tipjet at the end of each rotor blade, there thus being no rotor torque effect. However, a belt-driven rail rotor was incorporated in the simple and limited structure to provide steering capability. Designed and built under US Navy contract, the RF-1 was extensively tested, leading to development of a similar **Sky Hook** military version. The capability of the Pinwheel can be measured by a maximum speed of 161 km/h (100 mph) and ceiling of 4570 m (15,000 ft).

RotorWay Scorpion 133 and Exec

Brief mention must be made of the **RotorWay Scorpion 133**, known formerly as the **Scorpion Too**, as it is the most successful and attractive of a very small number of helicopters that have been developed for construction by amateurs. Designed by B. J. Schramm, it is of two-blade main/tail rotor configuration, seats two side-by-side in an enclosed cabin and is powered by a 108-kW (145-hp) RotorWay flat-four engine. The de luxe **Exec** is basically similar, but differs by having a much-improved tear drop cabin pod, enclosed tailboom structure and is available optionally with a wider range of equipment.

Royal Aircraft Factory early aircraft

When there was little doubt that balloons and dirigibles would soon be outdated by the growing capability of powered aircraft, His Majesty's Balloon Factory at Farnborough, under the supervision of Mervyn O'Gorman, began the first moves to begin the construction of heavier-than-air craft. The factory had no financial provision for the building of new aircraft, but O'Gorman and his designers, Geoffrey de Havilland and F. M. Green, were anxious to get their hands on an aeroplane of any kind. Their first stroke of luck came in December 1910 when they acquired from the army for 'repair' the wreck of a Blériot monoplane. Of typical Blériot configuration, with tractor powerplant, this re-emerged as the **S.E.1** single-seat biplane with a pusher engine, which certainly went a little beyond the category of a repair. The fact that it crashed within a very short time may have accounted for a reversal of procedure with the Voisin pusher biplane acquired for repair in April 1911; this emerged as the **B.E.1** tractor biplane that still retained its original Wolseley engine, which was shortly after replaced by a 45-kW (60-hp) Renault. It survived until written off following a crash in January 1915, by which time the Balloon Factory had become the Royal Aircraft Factory, following an interim title of Army Aircraft. The B.E.1 had fulfilled a valuable role, helping the team to formulate new ideas, and in the course of its life of almost three years proved a valuable experimental tool. Tractor aircraft from the factory were given the designation Blériot Experimental (B.E.); other designations were Fighting Experimental (F.E.), Reconnaissance Experimental (R.E.).

Royal Aircraft Factory B.E.2

The **Royal Aircraft Factory B.E.2**, which appeared in early 1912, had basically the same fuselage as the B.E.1, but introduced some refinements of structure and a 52-kW (70-hp) Renault engine. Because it had been built at the Royal Aircraft Factory it was ineligible for the 1912 Military Trials but, flown by Geoffrey de Havilland, took part in them for evaluation purposes and was clearly the best all-round aircraft. It was built in some numbers for the RFC, the majority under sub-contract, but it is difficult to determine whether the B.E.2 or the generally similar but slightly improved **B.E.2a** was the first to be used by that service. There is no doubt, however, that a B.E.2a was the first British aircraft to reach France at the outbreak of World War I, and that the type was used in what was probably the first RFC reconnaissance flight. It was followed by the **B.E.2b**, later versions of which introduced ailerons. The more extensively built **B.E.2c** introduced the 66-kW (90-hp) RAF 1a engine and was the first to carry a machine-gun, different arrangements of armament being tried on the **B.E.2d** and the most extensively-built and final version, the **B.E.2e**.

With the B.E.2d/e in service on the Western Front, earlier versions found employment in the UK and other theatres and were, of course, deployed for training. The inherent stability that had seemed such an important feature of the design of the B.E.2, which was intended for use as a reconnaissance aircraft, proved to be the type's downfall, the complete lack of manoeuvrability making the B.E.2 a primary enemy target during the 'Fokker Scourge' of 1915-16 and the 'Bloody April' of 1917. Built to a total of more than 3,200 aircraft of all versions, the type remained in service until 1918, the majority of them then being used as trainers.

Royal Aircraft Factory B.E.2c of the Royal Flying Corps.

Specification
Royal Aircraft Factory B.E.2e
Type: two-seat reconnaissance/light bomber aircraft
Powerplant: one 67-kW (90-hp) RAF 1a inline piston engine
Performance: maximum speed 145 km/h (90 mph) at sea level; service ceiling 2745 m (9,000 ft)
Weights: empty 649 kg (1,431 lb); maximum take-off 953 kg (2,100 lb)
Dimensions: span 12.42 m (40 ft 9 in); length 8.31 m (27 ft 3 in); height 3.66 m (12 ft 0 in); wing area 33.44 m² (360.0 sq ft)
Armament: usually one 7.7-mm (0.303-in) Lewis machine-gun, moved manually from one fixing to another as required, plus (when deployed as a bomber) light bombs on underfuselage racks

Royal Aircraft Factory B.E.8

Under the designation **Royal Aircraft Factory B.E.8** the RAF designed a two-seat scout biplane which was, in fact, the last of the B.E. series to be powered by a rotary engine. Of conventional configuration for the period, the B.E.8 had fixed tailskid landing gear with a pair of skids mounted forward of the main units to reduce the risk of nosing over on rough surfaces. Most unusual feature of the three prototypes built at Farnborough was the provision of a single long cockpit to accommodate both crew members, but production B.E.8s built under sub-contract had minimal structural change to provide two cockpits. The **B.E.8a** introduced in 1915 differed by having new wings which incorporated ailerons for roll control, instead of relying upon the wing warping of the early version, and also had a revised tail unit. No accurate production figures have survived, but about 70 aircraft including prototypes are believed to have been built. A small number of them served briefly in France in a reconnaissance role during 1914-15, but one or two were deployed in early bombing raids; the majority, however, were used to equip training units. Powered by a 60-kW (80-hp) Gnome rotary engine, the 11.49-m (37-ft 8½-in) span B.E.8a had a maximum speed of 113 km/h (70 mph) at sea level.

Royal Aircraft Factory B.E.12

The original concept that military aircraft should be no more than 'eyes in the sky' resulted, inevitably, in the creation of a good and stable observation platform; this was found to be the shortcoming of the B.E.2 when confronted by the more manoeuvrable Fokker monoplane, armed effectively with a forward-firing synchronised machine-gun. However, before the beginning of World War I inherent stability had seemed an essential feature for all military aircraft, which meant the Fokker monoplane represented the *bête noir* of several Allied aircraft. The **Royal Aircraft Factory B.E.12** represented an early and urgent attempt to redress the situation by adoption of the B.E.2c airframe to form the basis of a single-seat fighter. In fact, a little-modified B.E.2c airframe served as the prototype with the standard RAF 1a engine replaced by the considerably more powerful RAF 4a. Although maximum speed was increased by more than 10 per cent, it had apparently been overlooked that the B.E.12 had inherited from its predecessor the same stable flight characteristics and, not surprisingly, it

Built by Daimler, C3113 was an RAF B.E.12b powered by a Hispano-Suiza engine. The type had provision for twin Lewis guns angled obliquely upwards for home defence against Zeppelin raids.

was virtually useless as a fighter aircraft. So urgent was the Allied need for aircraft that the B.E.12 was retained on the Western Front and deployed as a bomber, but its vulnerability to fighter attack meant that from early 1917 only a handful were retained in France for use in a secondary role. An improved **B.E.12a** was in the pipeline, with revised wings and tail unit, but none were sent to France, and combined B.E.12/B.E.12a production amounted to 468. For use in a home defence role about 120 examples of the **B.E.12b** were built, this version differing by the installation of a 149-kW (200-hp) Hispano-Suiza engine and more effective armament: it was supplemented for this task by B.E.12a aircraft and by the B.E.12 machines recalled from France.

Specification
Royal Aircraft Factory B.E.12
Type: single-seat fighter
Powerplant: one 112-kW (150-hp) RAF 4a Vee piston engine
Performance: maximum speed 164 km/h (102 mph); service ceiling 3810 m (12,500 ft); endurance 3 hours
Weights: empty 742 kg (1,635 lb); maximum take-off 1066 kg (2,350 lb)

Dimensions: span 12.42 m (40 ft 9 in); length 8.31 m (27 ft 3 in); height 3.39 m (11 ft 1½ in); wing area 34.47 m² (371.0 sq ft)
Armament: two 7.7-mm (0.303-in) Lewis guns mounted one on each side of the fuselage to fire clear of the propeller disc, or one synchronised Vickers machine-gun, plus two 51-kg (112-lb) or 16 7.3-kg (16-lb) bombs

Royal Aircraft Factory F.E.2

Chronologically, the **Royal Aircraft Factory F.E.2** antedates the B.E.12, and represents an initial solution to the problem of providing effective forward-firing capability before the introduction of interrupter gear: this timed the firing of a fixed forward-aimed machine-gun so that its bullets passed between the blades of the revolving propeller. The F.E.2 was of biplane configuration and had a two-seat fuselage nacelle in which the powerplant was mounted at the rear to drive a pusher propeller. The pilot had the rear position and the forward cockpit was occupied by the observer/gunner, in which position he had an unobstructed field of fire through an arc of just over 180°. Initial version was the **F.E.2a**, powered by a 75-kW (100-hp) Green engine, but disappointing performance resulted in the 89-kW (120-hp) Beardmore engine being installed in the **F.E.2b**, which was entering service in France in small numbers towards the end of 1915. Two **F.E.2c** aircraft were produced by the Factory, these having the pilot seated forward and observer to the rear as it was intended for and used in a night flying role. The designation **F.E.2d** applied to a version with a generally similar airframe, but with a 186-kW (250-hp) Rolls-Royce engine (later named Eagle); this provided considerably improved performance, especially in terms of rate of climb and altitude capability. The remaining designations **F.E.2e**, **F.E.2f**, **F.E.2g** and **F.E.2h** applied to experimental air-

Royal Aircraft Factory F.E.2b of No. 22 Squadron, RFC, based in France during 1917.

craft with alternative engine installations.

In operational service the F.E.2b, working in collaboration with the Airco (de Havilland) D.H.2, gradually restricted the menace of the Fokker monoplane, but was in turn to meet its match when confronted by the more advanced Albatros and Halberstadt scouts that began to equip the German air service in late 1916. However, the suitability of the F.E.2b for night flying meant that it was to be deployed for night bombing operations in Europe and, in small numbers,

for home defence against Zeppelin dirigibles and Gotha bombers, remaining occupied in these roles until the final year of World War I. Production of F.E.2a/F.E.2b aircraft totalled 1,939, and although there is no accurate record of the number of F.E.2ds, it is believed that about 250 were built.

Specification
Royal Aircraft Factory F.E.2b
Type: two-seat fighter
Powerplant: one 89-kW (120-hp) Beardmore inline piston engine
Performance: maximum speed

129 km/h (80 mph) at sea level; service ceiling 2745 m (9,000 ft); endurance 3 hours
Weights: empty 904 kg (1,993 lb); maximum take-off 1347 kg (2,970 lb)
Dimensions: span 14.55 m (47 ft 9 in); length 9.83 m (32 ft 3 in); height 3.85 m (12 ft 7½ in); wing area 45.89 m² (494.0 sq ft)
Armament: initially a single 7.7-mm (0.303-in) Lewis gun, but later a second Lewis gun was added; in a bomber role a maximum of 159 kg (350 lb) of bombs could be carried in various combinations

Royal Aircraft Factory F.E.8

Somewhat similar in configuration to the Airco (de Havilland) D.H.2, the **Royal Aircraft Factory F.E.8** fighter was designed and developed because of the continuing lack in British service of a reliable and efficient interrupter gear for a forward-firing machine-gun. A single-seat pusher biplane, the F.E.8 had to rely upon the very unsatisfactory armament of a single Lewis gun mounted on top of the fuselage nose, where it was accessible to the pilot to reload and clear stoppages. The standard powerplant was a 75-kW (100-hp) Gnome Monosoupape rotary engine, but of the 182 examples of

the F.E.8 accepted by the RFC a small number were powered alternatively by an 82-kW (110-hp) Clerget or Le Rhône rotary.

Introduced into service on the Western Front during August 1916, the F.E.8 proved superior in manoeuvrability to the F.E.2 yet inferior to its contemporary D.H.2. But with the pilot having to concentrate on flying the aircraft in combat and on coping with the vagaries of the Lewis gun it was a far less effective fighter aircraft than the F.E.2. This was highlighted when nine F.E.8s of No. 40 Squadron were eliminated in a single

Designed as a pusher fighter, for lack of adequate interrupter gear, the RAF F.E.8 was a poor fighting aircraft.

action against a formation led by the 'Red Baron' Manfred von Richthofen, when four were shot down in flames and the remaining five were compelled to force-land with damage to the aircraft or injury to the pilot. By the early summer of 1917 all had been withdrawn from front-line use.

Specification
Royal Aircraft Factory F.E.8
Type: single-seat fighter
Powerplant: one 75-kW (100-hp) Gnome Monosoupape rotary piston engine
Performance: maximum speed 151 km/h (94 mph) at sea level; service ceiling 4420 m (14,500 ft); endurance 2 hours 30 minutes
Weights: empty 406 kg (895 lb); maximum take-off 610 kg (1,345 lb)
Dimensions: span 9.60 m (31 ft 6 in); length 7.21 m (23 ft 8 in); height 2.79 m (9 ft 2 in); wing area 20.25 m² (218.0 sq ft)
Armament: one 7.7-mm (0.303-in) Lewis machine-gun mounted immediately forward of the cockpit

Royal Aircraft Factory R.E.5

As mentioned in an earlier RAF entry, inherent stability was regarded as an essential characteristic of a reconnaissance aircraft, and in the two **R.E.1** prototypes designed and built at the Factory in 1913 this aspect of flight had been developed to a remarkable degree. It is recorded that it was possible to fly for quite long periods without touching the controls and if, for example, the aircraft was put into a dive, it could recover unaided. From the R.E.1 was developed the **Royal Aircraft Factory R.E.5**, which in standard form was an equal-span two-seat biplane powered by an 89-kW (120-hp) Austro-Daimler engine, or an equivalent engine produced under licence in the UK by William Beardmore and Co. Only 24 were built, about half of this number serving in France during the summer of 1915 and the remainder being used by training units. Able to carry three 9-kg (20-lb) bombs, the R.E.5 had a maximum speed of 126 km/h (78 mph) at sea level.

The Royal Aircraft Factory R.E.5 was a wholly indifferent aircraft, and is seen here in its standard two-seat form.

Royal Aircraft Factory R.E.7

Developed from the R.E.5, the two-seat **Royal Aircraft Factory R.E.7** was intended to carry heavier loads and was thought to be suitable for escort or reconnaissance duties. An unequal-span biplane powered initially by an 89-kW (120-hp) Beardmore engine, and introduced in France at the beginning of 1916, it was quickly found to be quite unsuitable for use in an escort role as the observer/gunner, accommodated in the forward cockpit, had such a limited field of fire for his single Lewis gun that he was virtually ineffective. However, there was no doubt that the R.E.7 could carry a useful payload, and it was in the capacity of a bomber aircraft that it was found to be most useful, powered by an RAF 4a or 119-kW (160-hp) Beardmore engine. About 25 per cent of the estimated 250 that were built served in France, being used effectively in a bombing role for about three months during the summer of 1916, but their low speed and ceiling when carrying a bombload meant they were extremely vulnerable to enemy attack. After withdrawal from front-line service R.E.7s were used primarily by training units, but also served in a number of experimental roles and particularly as engine testbeds. Some were used as target tugs, trailing a sleeve drogue for air firing practice, and the R.E.7 was probably one of the earliest aircraft to be deployed in such a role.

Specification
Royal Aircraft Factory R.E.7
Type: light bomber
Powerplant: one 112-kW (150-hp) RAF 4a Vee piston engine
Performance: maximum speed 135 km/h (84 mph) at sea level; service ceiling 1980 m (6,500 ft); endurance 6 hours
Weights: empty 1036 kg (2,285 lb); maximum take-off 1565 kg (3,450 lb)
Dimensions: span 17.37 m (57 ft 0 in); length 9.72 m (31 ft 10½ in); height 3.84 m (12 ft 7 in); wing area 50.91 m² (548.0 sq ft)
Armament: no specific defensive armament, but maximum bombload comprised a single 152-kg (336-lb) bomb, or small bombs up to a total of about 147 kg (324 lb)

The R.E.7 was designed as a light bomber, but proved easy meat for fighters thanks to its low speed and ceiling, and indifferent manoeuvrability. It played a more important role as a testbed for engines and other equipment.

Royal Aircraft Factory R.E.8

Looking, in general, rather like a scaled-up version of the B.E.2, the **Royal Aircraft Factory R.E.8** had been designed and developed in early 1916 to meet RFC requirements for an aircraft to perform a reconnaissance/artillery spotting role. It gained the nickname 'Harry Tate', a peculiarly British pun on the official designation which related to a music-hall comedian of the day and, like its predecessor, the R.E.8 was an unequal-span two-seat biplane. Its manufacture to a total of 4,077 examples, of which 22 were supplied to the Belgian air force, would suggest that it was a howling success, but it is a supposition that is far from correct. Early tests of the prototype in mid-1916 showed this new aircraft to have a good maximum speed, rate of climb and a useful operation ceiling, winning produc-

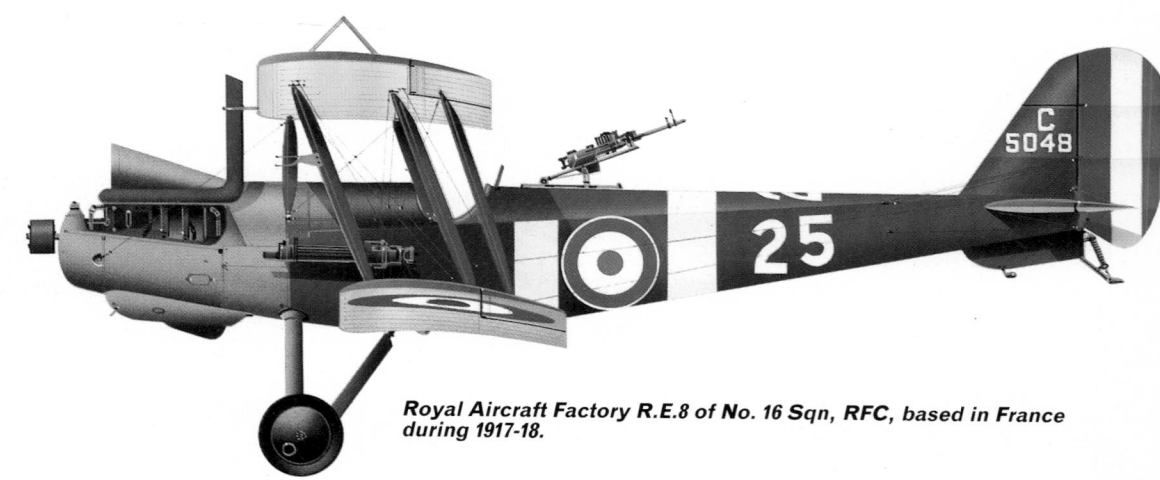

Royal Aircraft Factory R.E.8 of No. 16 Sqn, RFC, based in France during 1917-18.

tion contracts that just went on and on, despite the fact that no one had remembered the lesson of the B.E.2: the R.E.8 was of an inherently stable configuration.

Small numbers of production aircraft began to enter service in France towards the end of 1916, but after several had been lost in accidents the type was temporarily withdrawn while investigation and rectification procedures were carried out. Thus, the R.E.8 gained a revised tail to overcome a tendency to spin and, eventually available in large numbers and despite its short-comings, became accepted by rank and file of the RFC. In the absence of a better vehicle it performed a valuable artillery spotting role, thanks to the courage and dedication of its crews. Deployed extensively from early 1917, and operating in Italy and Palestine as well as on the Western Front, the R.E.8 remained in service until the Armistice.

Specification
Type: reconnaissance/artillery spotting aircraft
Powerplant: one 112-kW (150-hp) RAF 4a V-12 piston engine
Performance: maximum speed 164 km/h (102 mph); service ceiling 4115 m (13,500 ft); endurance 4.25 hours
Weights: empty 717 kg (1,580 lb); maximum take-off 1301 kg (2,869 lb)
Dimensions: span 12.98 m (42 ft 7 in); length 8.50 m (27 ft 10½ in); height 3.47 m (11 ft 4½ in); wing area 35.07 m² (377.50 sq ft)
Armament: one forward-firing synchronised 7.7-mm (0.303-in) Vickers machine-gun and one Lewis gun on a pivoted mounting over the rear cockpit, plus a usual bombload of two 51-kg (112-lb) bombs, or lighter bombs up to an equivalent weight

Royal Aircraft Factory S.E.5 and S.E.5a

With a secure place in aviation history as the mount of ace Allied pilots that include William ('Billy') Bishop, James McCudden and Edward ('Mick') Mannock, the **Royal Aircraft Factory S.E.5** was without doubt the most successful aircraft to emanate from the Factory. A single-seat equal-span biplane designed by a team headed by H. P. Folland, the type benefited from the fact that the designers ensured that it was easy to fly, a factor reflecting the minimal flying training that, because of the pressure of circumstance, was given to trainee pilots before they were posted to their squadrons. This attribute was helped considerably by the adoption of a static engine, the whirling mass of a rotary creating serious torque problems that could be of benefit only to a highly skilled pilot, and recognition of the fact that manoeuvrability must take place over inherent stability. Even then, the S.E.5 was still far less manoeuvrable than its contemporary Sopwith Camel.

The S.E.5 was powered as standard by a newly-developed 112-kW (150-hp) Hispano-Suiza Vee engine and the type first entered operational service in France during April 1917. Development of this engine by Hispano-Suiza later resulted in the availability of a 149-kW (200-hp) version, aircraft with this powerplant and minor modifications being designated **S.E.5a**, and the first of these entered operational service in mid-1917, gradually replacing the S.E.5. Unfortunately, the S.E.5a was plagued by the problems of an inadequately developed engine, as well as by unreliability of the early Constantinesco interrupter gear, but when all went well or, when these shortcomings were gradually eliminated, the S.E.5a proved to be a formidable fighter aircraft. In the closing stages of the war S.E.5a machines were also used extensively in a close-support role,

Royal Aircraft Factory S.E.5a flown by Captain E. Mannock of No. 74 Sqn, RAF, based in France during 1918.

armed with lightweight bombs.

The combined production total for the S.E.5/S.E.5a was 5,205, this figure including a small number of conversions as two-seat trainers. The type served also in Egypt, Mesopotamia, Palestine and Salonika, and S.E.5a fighters were allocated as well for home-defence duties, but their intended use as interceptors was frustrated by the length of time needed for their water-cooled powerplant to reach working temperature. The S.E.5a was also flown by the American Expeditionary Force and plans had been made for the Curtiss Aero-

plane and Motor Company in the USA to build 1,000 for the US Army. The intention was frustrated by contract cancellation following the end of World War I and only a single example was manufactured by Curtiss, but the company subsequently assembled 56 with components supplied from the UK. Post-war a further batch was assembled in the USA by Eberhart Steel Products.

Specification
Royal Aircraft Factory S.E.5a
Type: single-seat fighter
Powerplant: one 149-kW (200-hp) Hispano-Suiza V-8 piston engine
Performance: maximum speed 222 km/h (138 mph); service ceiling 6705 m (22,000 ft); endurance 3 hours
Weights: empty 635 kg (1,400 lb); maximum take-off 887 kg (1,955 lb)
Dimensions: span 8.12 m (26 ft 7½ in); length 6.38 m (20 ft 11 in); height 2.90 m (9 ft 6 in); wing area 22.67 m² (444.0 sq ft)
Armament: one forward-firing synchronised 7.7-mm (0.303-in) Vickers machine-gun and one Lewis gun mounted over the centre-section of the upper wing, plus up to four 18.6-kg (25-lb) bombs

Rumpler early aircraft

In 1909 E. Rumpler and E. Haessner established R. Rumpler Luftfahrzeugbau GmbH in Berlin with the intention of building the Etrich Taube monoplane under licence. The company had soon acquired premises at Berlin/Johannisthal aerodrome and it was reported that in 1912 the company produced no fewer than 60 Taube aircraft. Rumpler also established a civil flying school at the aerodrome, as well as a military flying school at Monchelberg, and between 1912 and the outbreak of war in August 1914 construction and development of the Taube continued, so that the many Rumpler aircraft of this type which were then in military service were considerably improved from the original Etrich Taube. During 1914 Rumpler flew the prototype of two-seat unarmed biplane intended for use in a training and/or re-

Most likely a conversion from a Rumpler B.1 landplane design, this early Rumpler floatplane paved the way for the company's definitive production 4B 11 and 4B 12 military reconnaissance floatplanes. These later aircraft were all fitted with rudders of greater height and increased area for improved handling.

connaissance role and when adopted for military use this had the designation **Rumpler B.I**. An unequal-span biplane with fixed tailskid landing gear, tandem open cockpits and with power provided by a 75-kW (100-hp) Mercedes D.I. inline engine, the B.I proved sufficiently successful for a total of 198 to be built for the military aviation service. Rumpler also produced several alternative versions of

the B.I; these included a twin-float seaplane powered by a 75-kW (100-hp) Benz Bz.I which the company indentified as the **4B 11**, a small number of which were built for use in a reconnaissance role by the German navy. Even more successful was the **Rumpler 4B 12**, a

more developed and workmanlike seaplane powered by a 112-kW (150-hp) Benz Bz.III engine, of which at least 18 were built for the navy. With a wing span of 14.50 m (47 ft 7 in), the Rumpler 4B 12 had a maximum speed of some 135 km/h (84 mph) at sea level.

Rumpler C.I

The early success of the Rumpler B.I, and the seaplanes developed from it for the German navy, encouraged the company, by then renamed Rumpler Flugzeug-Werke, to design a two-seat biplane in the C.I armed category. Bearing a family likeness to the B.I and, like it, retaining a typically Taube tail unit, the **Rumpler C.I** had fixed tailskid landing gear and tandem open cockpits with the observer/gunner at the rear, and was powered by a 119-kW (160-hp) Mercedes D.III inline engine. Early testing left little doubt that the company had produced a successful design, and military evaluation resulted in what were then considered as large-scale orders. No production records have survived, but it was reported that some 250 C.I and improved **C.Ia** aircraft, the latter differing only by having a 134-kW (180-hp) Argus engine, were in service as early as October 1916. It is known that production continued until June 1917. Clearly several hundreds were manufactured, a total beyond the production capability of the Rumpler factory, and the variants were also built under sub-contract by Germania Flugzeug-Werke, Märkische Flugzeug Werke, Hannoversche Waggonfabrik, and Albert Rinne Flugzeug-Werke. In addition, Bayerische Rumpler-Werke developed a dual-control two-seat trainer powered by a 112-kW (150-hp) Benz Bz.III engine.

When the C.I was first introduced on the Western Front in 1915, the single Parabellum machine-gun in the observer's cockpit combined with the C.I's performance was sufficient to give reasonable immunity from attack. Then, when Allied scouts became more capable and aggressive, an LMG 08/15 machine-gun was added for the pilot but, finally, the type was withdrawn from the Western Front and transferred for service in Macedonia and Palestine. Operating in Palestine in early 1917, a small force of C.Is played a vital role in the battle for Gaza. In addition to the C.Is produced for operation on the Western Front, Rumpler also developed a seaplane version for the German navy under the designation **6B 1**. This differed from the C.I only by the installation of twin floats, being followed into production by the very similar **6B 2**, which differed only by introducing the revised tail unit of the C.IV. Combined production of both versions for the German Navy, which used them in a seaplane station defence role, totalled 98 aircraft. Post-war, a number of ex-military C.Is were converted for use in a commercial passenger-carrying role.

Specification
Rumpler C.Ia
Type: two-seat reconnaissance/general purpose aircraft

Powerplant: one 134-kW (180-hp) Argus inline piston engine
Performance: maximum speed 150 km/h (93 mph); service ceiling 5000 m (16,405 ft); endurance 4 hours
Weights: empty 793 kg (1,748 lb); maximum take-off 1300 kg (2,866 lb)
Dimensions: span 12.15 m (39 ft 10¼ in); length 7.85 m (25 ft 9 in); height 3.05 m (10 ft 0 in); wing area 35.70 m² (384.28 sq ft)
Armament: one fixed forward-firing

Seen in the form of the second prototype of 1915, the Rumpler C.1 was one of the best German two-seaters of the war. The pipe projecting above the wing is an exhaust for the engine.

7.92-mm (0.31-in) LMG 08/15 machine-gun and one 7.92-mm (0.31-in) Parabellum gun for use of the observer, plus up to 100 kg (220 lb) of light bombs carried externally

Rumpler C.IV

The undoubted success of the C.I/Ia resulted in further development of the type, Rumpler flying in 1916 the prototype of the **Rumpler C.III**. This differed primarily from the earlier design by being aerodynamically cleaner and introducing balanced ailerons, a revised tail unit and the increased power of a 164-kW (220-hp) Benz Bz.IV engine. However, the promise of early availability of an even more powerful engine meant that the C.III served only as a development aircraft. The production version, designated **C.IV**, differed by having a rede-

signed tail unit, losing the typically Taube appearance, and by having increased surface area to maintain directional stability with the increased power provided by a Mercedes D. IVa inline engine. In spite of excellent performance, reportedly good enough for it to show a clean pair of heels to most Allied scouts at altitudes in excess of 4600 m (15,090 ft), the C.IV was built in comparatively small numbers, a total of less than 100 being produced by Rumpler and sub-contracted by Bayerische Rumpler-Werke. In addition, Pfalz Flugzeug-Werke built a number under licence, these incorporating Pfalz-introduced refinements that included ailerons on all

four wings. Generally similar in other respects, these aircraft served in the German military air service under the designation **Pfalz C.I**.

Because of its combined speed and high-altitude capability, the Rumpler C.IV was used primarily for long-range reconnaissance/photo-reconnaissance, sometimes operating deep behind Allied lines. As in the case of the C.I, several Rumpler C.IVs were converted for use as commercial aircraft in the early post-war period.

Specification
Rumpler C.IV
Type: reconnaissance/photo-

reconnaissance aircraft
Powerplant: one 194-kW (260-hp) Mercedes D.IVa inline piston engine
Performance: maximum speed 170 km/h (106 mph) at 500 m (1,640 ft); service ceiling 6400 m (21,000 ft); endurance 3 hours 30 minutes
Weights: empty 1080 kg (2,381 lb); maximum take-off 1530 kg (3,373 lb)
Dimensions: span 12.65 m (41 ft 6 in); length 8.40 m (27 ft 6¾ in); height 3.25 m (10 ft 8 in); wing area 33.50 m² (360.60 sq ft)
Armament: one fixed forward-firing 7.92-mm (0.31-in) LMG 08/15 machine-gun and one 7.92-mm (0.31-in) Parabellum machine-gun

Rumpler C.VII

Continuing development to improve the high-altitude performance of their C types was carried out by Rumpler, for evaluation of combat reports showed that higher altitude capability could put them beyond the reach of Allied scouts. An interim step was taken with the **Rumpler C.V** development aircraft, in which a 194-kW (260-hp) Mercedes D.IVa engine was installed in a C.III airframe. No significant improvement resulted, leading to a proposal to use a high-compression engine that could maintain its rated performance to a higher altitude. This led to introduction in late 1917 of the **C.VII,** which was basically a C.IV airframe with a Maybach Mb.IV inline engine. Its rated take-off power was some 8 per cent lower than that of the Mercedes D.IVa of the Rumpler C.IV, but this was maintained to an altitude at which the output of the Mer-

The Rumpler C.VII was an effective long-range reconnaissance aircraft.

cedes engine was far lower. The C.VII, virtually identical to the C.IV apart from its powerplant, proved to be a valuable long-range reconnaissance aircraft, but a specialised version was developed subsequently for deployment in a high-altitude photo-reconnaissance role. Known as the **C.VII Rubild**, it differed by dispensing with the standard forward-firing machine-gun, and the elimination of all possible equipment to reduce weight to a minimum, enabling it to operate at an altitude where it was almost immune from interception.

Specification
Rumpler C.VII Rubild
Type: high-altitude photo-reconnaissance aircraft
Powerplant: one 179-kW (240-hp) Maybach Mb.IV inline piston engine

Performance: maximum speed 175 km/h (109 mph) at 1000 m (3,280 ft); service ceiling 7300 m (23,950 ft); endurance 3 hours 30 minutes
Weights: empty 1050 kg (2,315 lb); maximum take-off 1485 kg (3,274 lb)

Dimensions: span 12.55 m (41 ft 2 in); length 8.20 m (26 ft 10¾ in); height 3.40 m (11 ft 1¾ in); wing area 33.60 m² (361.68 sq ft)
Armament: one 7.92-mm (0.31-in) Parabellum machine-gun on a trainable mount in rear cockpit

Rumpler C.VIII

Although carrying the designation of an armed reconnaissance aircraft, the **Rumpler C.VIII** was not intended for deployment in this role, representing instead an aircraft that was designed from

the outset to serve as a two-seat operational trainer. It combined wings similar to those of the C.I, the more developed tail unit of the C.IV, and a 134-kW (180-hp) Argus As.III inline engine which provided adequate performance for the training role. The emphasis of training on this aircraft was to raise the capability of

the observer and, in particular, to give him the opportunity to familiarise himself with operation of the camera, machine-gun and radio under more stressful airborne conditions, which were indeed very different from those of the ground-based classroom. Entering service with flying training units towards

the end of 1917, the Rumper C.VIII proved to be a valuable training tool. Armed similarly to the C.I and C.IV, but without provision for carrying bombs, the 12.18-m (39-ft 11½-in) span C.VIII had a maximum speed of 140 km/h (87 mph) and duration of 4 hours.

Rumpler D.I

Considerable efforts were made by Rumpler to design and develop a successful single-seat fighter in the D category, but these did not meet with very conspicuous success, for by the time the **Rumpler D.I** had been developed to a stage where it was virtually ready for production, taking part in the D types competitions which were held at Adlershof during 1918, the war was virtually over. First of the development prototypes was the **Rumpler 7D 1**, a very clean single-seat biplane incorporating a plywood-skinned circular-section fuselage and fixed tailskid landing gear, and powerplant comprising a 119-kW (160-hp) Mercedes D.III engine. Ensuing development prototypes included the **7D 2**, **7D 4**, and **7D 5**, all powered by the Mercedes D.III and introducing structural refinements that were intended to

The Rumpler D.1 single-seat fighter had a protracted and ultimately none-too-successful development. By the time it was ready for production the war was virtually over for Germany.

save weight and reduce drag. The **7D 7** which followed was generally similar to its immediate predecessors, its main difference being introduction of the more powerful Mercedes D.IIIa engine. The Rumpler D.I which took part in the 1918 fighter competitions appeared in two versions, the first generally similar to the 7D 7 but with further slight structural refinements, the other with a 138-kW (185-hp) BMW engine. This latter aircraft was flown in the competition held in the autumn of 1918 and it seems unlikely that any production aircraft were built, but limited production of the Rumpler D.I without any operational use is quoted in some sources. The D.I as powered by

the 134-kW (180-hp) Mercedes D.IIIa engine had a maximum speed of 180 km/h (112 mph) at 5000 m (16,405 ft)

and was armed with two fixed forward-firing LMG 08/15 'Spandau' machine-guns.

Rumpler G.I, G.II and G.III

In 1915 Rumpler flew the prototype of the first aircraft which it had designed and built in the G (*Grossflugzeuge* or large aeroplane) twin-engine bomber category. Designated **Rumpler 4A 15**, it was a large biplane with fixed landing gear, comprising twin-wheel main units, twin-wheels mounted beneath the fuselage nose and a tailskid. It was powered by two 112-kW (150-hp) Benz Bz.III inline engines. These were mounted on the lower wing, directly over the main landing gear units, each being arranged to drive a pusher propeller. Almost certainly the major production version was the **G.I**, of which about 60 were built, these being powered by either two 112-kW (150-hp) Benz Bz.III or 119-kW (160-hp) Mercedes D.III engines. Defensive armament comprised a single Parabellum machine-gun operated by a gunner in the nose cockpit, but details of the bombload do not appear to have been recorded. It was, presumably, worthwhile for the prototype was reported to have flown in 1915 with a pilot and 15 passengers.

The **G.II** was virtually unchanged, except for the introduction of 164-kW (220-hp) Benz Bz.IV engines and a second Parabellum machine-gun, and the **G.III**, which was the final variant, had revised engine nacelles containing 194-kW (260-hp) Mercedes D.IVa engines and introduced horn-balanced ailerons.

Specification
Rumpler G.I
Type: three-crew heavy bomber
Powerplant: two 119-kW (160-hp) Mercedes D.III inline piston engines
Performance: maximum speed 145 km/h (90 mph); service ceiling 4000 m (13,125 ft); endurance 4 hours
Weights: empty 1998 kg (4,405 lb); maximum take-off 2940 kg (6,482 lb)
Dimensions: span 19.30 m (63 ft 3¾ in); length 11.80 m (38 ft 8½ in); height 4.0 m (13 ft 1½ in); wing area 78.70 m² (847.15 sq ft)
Armament: one 7.92-mm (0.31-in) Parabellum machine-gun on a trainable mount in the nose cockpit, plus an unspecified bombload

The G.1 was designed as a heavy bomber, and was a carefully considered machine. The engines must have hampered crew vision.

Rutan Aircraft/Scaled Composites Incorporated

Mr Elburt L. 'Burt' Rutan first sprang to prominence in the late 1960s with such bold designs as the **Rutan VariViggen, VariEze** and **LongEZ**. Intended for the home-built aircraft market, these radical designs made use of advanced lightweight construction and a distinctive 'pusher' engine layout. To further develop his ideas as production aircraft, Rutan established the Rutan Aircraft Factory (RAF) at Mojave, California, in 1974. The **Model 40 Defiant** was the first aircraft to come off the new production line and was essentially an enlarged and improved VariEze with a four seat cabin and a 119-kW (160-hp) Avco Lycoming engine. The prototype (N78RA) flew on 30 June 1978 and embarked on an extensive test programme. It was planned to build the type as the **Model 74 Defiant** with more powerful 134-kW (180-hp) engines and a

five-seat interior. In the event, the Defiant was made available to home-builders in plan form only, nearly 200 sets of which were sold. Rutan also became heavily involved as a consultant with other agencies under the auspices of Scaled Composites Inc. (SCI), operating from a factory beside the RAF plant at Mojave. SCI was involved in NASA's **AD-1** eliptical swing-wing test aircraft, the **Fairchild/Ames NGT**, and the **Quickie** home-built.

By the early 1980s RAF had several ongoing projects. The **Model 59 Predator** had begun life as a unique joined-wing, strutless biplane. This entailed a sweptback portion of the trailing edge of the wing joining with the forward-swept inverted V tail. The concept was extensively tested and verified by NASA wind-tunnel tests, but in the event the design was much simplified and prototyped by

Advanced Technology Aircraft Company as the **Model 480 Predator**. This was a low-wing monoplane, which made extensive use of composites in its construction and was powered by a 294.5-kW (395-hp) Avco Lycoming IO-720-B1BD flat-eight engine. The main wing had pronounced dog teeth and was fitted with tip-mounted winglets. A canard wing was mounted high on the nose. The aircraft resembled a much modified NDN Fieldmaster. It was hoped to reach a production agreement with SABCA of Belgium but these plans came to nothing.

Rutan also designed the **Model 77-6 Solitaire** single-seat, self-launching sailplane which was sold in plan form. By 1982 his attention had turned to the four-seat **Model 72 Grizzly**, which first flew on 14 January, this was intended as a proof-of-concept aircraft for the STOL potential of a tandem wing, but ended its

days as a tow aircraft for the Solitaire glider and a chase-plane for later Rutan designs.

By June 1985 SCI had been bought by Beechcraft and Burt Rutan was heavily involved in the company's Model 2000 Starship. This canard pusher aircraft bore all the hall marks of his designs, but on a scale far larger than ever before. Intended as an eight/eleven seat business aircraft, an 85 per cent scale version was flown on 29 August 1983 and the first Starship 'proper' (N2000S) followed on 15 February 1986. Rutan was also designing other aircraft for Beechcraft's research and development department including an aircraft resembling a scaled-down Starship and the **Model 81** all-composite five-seat piston-engined lightplane, again making use of Rutan's favoured three-surface layout (that of canard, wing and tail flying surfaces). In 1988 Scaled Composites was sold back to Rutan in partnership with the Wyman-Gordon Company of Worcester, Massachusetts. The sale agreement permitted Rutan the rights to several of the designs he had produced for Beech, and this arrangement saw the Model 81 come to life as the **Rutan Model 81 Catbird**. The sole prototype aircraft (N187RA) won the 1988 California CAFE 400 race, a competition measuring overall airframe efficiency and performance on the grounds of fuel consumption, speed and payload.

Rutan was now branching out into larger potential markets. With the help of a $2.5 million contract from the US DoD's Defence Advanced Research Projects Agency (DARPA) work commenced on the **Scaled Composites Model 133-3, 62 POC Advanced Technology Tactical Transport** or **AT³** for short. This was intended as a short range military transport carrying up to 14 troops, to fill the gap between the Lockheed C-130 and large helicopters such as the Boeing-Vertol CH-47. The proof-of-concept prototype (N133SC) first flew on 29 December 1987, at 62 per cent of the intended finished size. Its STOL performance was due largely to its trimaran layout of a high aspect-wing connected by long engine nacelles to a second 'forward wing', and high T-tail. Powered by a pair of 559-kW (750-shp) Pratt & Whitney Canada PT6A-135A turboprops, it had a retractable tricycle undercarriage. In 1988 it was fitted with a rear loading ramp as originally intended and resumed flight tests with a tail configuration similar to that of the Grumman OV-10. Initial flight tests were completed in July 1989 after 150 hours in the air. The second phase commenced in 1991.

At the same time a new civilian design was taking shape. The **Rutan Model 143 Triumph** was another aircraft originally designed for Beech. Intended to be compatible with a range of powerplants it first flew courtesy of a pair of Williams FJ44 turbofans on 12 July 1988. The Triumph resembles a small jet-powered Starship and was intended to carry up to eight passengers at a cruising speed of 741 km/h (460 mph). The Triumph flew about 110 hours until 1990, chiefly as a chase plane for the ARES project, and was then stored. Its RJ44 engines were returned to Williams, but the design is available to any manufacturer who wishes to take it up. SCI were also involved in the construction of the **Pond Racer** for Mr Robert J. Pond who intended to enter the type in the US unlimited-class air races at Reno and break all existing speed records for piston engined aircraft. Resembling a Lockheed P-38, the twin-boom Pond Racer is powered by two 746-kW (1000-hp) Electromotive/Nissan VG-30 liquid-cooled, turbocharged and intercooled V-6 automobile piston engines.

Rutan's most recent project has also one of the longest histories. In 1981 the United States Army requested studies for a Low Cost Battlefield Attack Aircraft (LCBAA) which Rutan entered. His thoughts on the subject gave birth to the **Model 151 ARES (Armed Response Effective Support)** and design commenced in 1985. The prototype (N151SC) first flew on 19 February 1990 and progressively achieved its design goals of range and speed. Powered by a single 13.12-kN (2,950-lb) Pratt & Whitney JT15D-5 turbojet, ARES has demonstrated a top speed of 750 km/h (466 mph). As its primary function is that of close air support, the ARES is armed with an integral 25-mm GAU-12/U cannon on the starboard side. Fitting the cannon has led to the deliberate situation of the engine intake on the port side only, to avoid the problem of gun gas ingestion. The cannon itself is mounted over the wing and so a concave trough has been built into the forward fuselage, along the path of the shells. The US Navy and Air Force have expressed interest in the ARES, though it remains a private project. Various seating and weapons options could be offered to prospective customers and its purchase price is pegged at around $1 million.

Mention must also be made of the **Rutan Voyager**. At 07.59 on the morning of 14 December 1986, piloted by Dick Rutan and Jeana Yeager, the trimaran Voyager aircraft lifted off from Edwards AFB to begin an epic around the world

flight of some nine days, three minutes and 44 seconds. The 110-ft aircraft, built from Magnamite graphite and Hexcel paper honeycomb flew a distance of 24,986 miles unrefuelled, to return to Edwards at 08.05 on December 23, the first time such a feat has been accomplished.

Showing obvious signs of its VariEze and VariViggen heritage, the Rutan Defiant was a promising design which in the event became available in kit form only, as the designer's attention turned to other projects in the early 1980s.

The Rutan Model 51 is better known as the Scaled Composites ARES (Agile Response Effective Support). The ARES has completed live-firing trials of its GAU-12 cannon, clearly visible in this view of the aircraft. The wing/canard arrangement of the ARES is not dissimilar to that of the Triumph.

Ryan early aircraft

T. Claude Ryan established Ryan Airlines on the US west coast in 1922, and its workshops very soon began the conversion of war surplus aircraft for civil use. Nine Standard open-cockpit biplanes were rebuilt as cabin transports, the **Ryan-Standard** having a four-passenger enclosed cabin immediately behind the engine, with the pilot in an open cockpit to its rear. Ryan had also acquired from two Californian businessmen the long-range Douglas Cloudster, which had been modified by its previous owners to accommodate a pilot and five passengers in three open cockpits. When the upper wing was damaged in a landing accident the opportunity was taken to convert it to accommodate two crew in a forward open cockpit with 10 passengers in an enclosed cabin to their rear, thus producing the one-off **Ryan Cloudster**.

The first original design was the **Ryan M-1**, a braced high-wing monoplane of which the first example was flown on 14 February 1926, accommodating a pilot and mail or two passengers. Most successful of the 16 that were built were nine powered by the 149-kW (200-hp) Wright J-4B radial engine, some being used on the pioneering mail routes of Colorado Airways and Pacific Air Transport. The M-1 was followed by 21 generally similar **M-2** mail/passenger transports, powered by a variety of engines in the 112/149-kW (150/200-hp) range. Successful use of the M-1 and M-2 aircraft led to design of the **B.1 Brougham** which, of basically the same external configuration, had an enclosed cabin for the pilot and four passengers. The prototype B.1 was powered by an Hispano-Suiza Vee engine, but completion of the first production aircraft, to be powered by a 168-kW (225-hp) Wright J-5 Whirlwind radial engine, was delayed by construction of the special one-off **Ryan NYP** (New York Paris) used by Charles Lindbergh for the first and epic solo west to east non-stop flight across the North Atlantic. Derived from the M-1/M-2 design, the NYP differed primarily by having a 177-kW (237-hp) Wright J-5C Whirlwind, and a large-capacity fuel tank in the forward fuselage which eliminated a direct forward view for the pilot. There is no space here to record the pioneering flight of the Ryan NYP, better known by far as the *Spirit of St Louis*, but this historic achievement by Charles Lindbergh initiated new worldwide interest in aviation.

Just before manufacture of the NYP, Claude Ryan had sold his interest in the company to his associate B. F. 'Frank' Mahoney, production of the B.1 Brougham then being continued by the B. F. Mahoney Aircraft Corporation until formation of the Ryan-Mahoney Aircraft Corporation at St Louis in 1928. The New York to Paris flight brought a healthy demand for the similar-looking B.1, built to a total of 150, and this model was followed in 1928 by the slightly enlarged **B.3 Brougham** which provided accommodation for six (nine built), the **B.5**

Brougham of 1929 which introduced some refinements and the 224-kW (300-hp) Wright J-6 engine (61 built), and late in 1929 the last of the line, the **B7 Brougham** (eight built) which was powered by the 313-kW (420-hp) Pratt & Whitney Wasp C-1 engine.

With economic clouds filling the skies, the company adopted the basic configuration of the Brougham for a smaller, lighter weight four-seater which had the designation **C.1 Foursome**. As flown in prototype form in early 1930 it was powered by a 168-kW (225-hp) Wright J-6, but the production version had a 179-kW (240-hp) Wright J-6-7. Its development had come too late to have any effect: the Mahoney-Ryan factory was sold in October 1930 and only three C-1 Foursomes were built.

Specification
Ryan B.1. Brougham
Type: five-seat cabin monoplane
Powerplant: one 168-kW (225-hp) Wright J-5 Whirlwind radial piston engine

Undoubtedly the most famous aircraft produced by Ryan was the NYP, named Spirit of St Louis, flown by Charles Lindbergh in his epic solo flight across the North Atlantic during 1927. Powered by a 177-kW (237-hp) Wright J-5C Whirlwind radial, it spanned 14.02 m (46 ft) and had a maximum take-off weight of 2381 kg (5,250 lb). Theoretical maximum range was 6775 km (4,210 miles).

Performance: maximum speed 201 km/h (125 mph); service ceiling 4875 m (16,000 ft); range 1127 km (700 miles)
Weights: empty 848 kg (1,870 lb);

maximum take-off 1497 kg (3,300 lb)
Dimensions: span 12.80 m (42 ft 0 in); length 8.46 m (27 ft 9 in); height 2.67 m (8 ft 9 in); wing area 25.08 m² (270.0 sq ft)

Ryan FR-1 Fireball

In 1942 the US Navy drew up an unusual specification for a carrier-based fighter-bomber to be powered by one of the new turbojet engines in the rear fuselage, and a piston-engine mounted conventionally in the nose. The latter was seen as the ideal powerplant for landing and long-range cruise, or to supplement the turbojet in high-speed flight. The piston engine was also seen as a useful 'insurance' against failure of the more or less infant turbojet.

Ryan's design proposal was selected as the most realistic submission, gaining an order for three **Ryan XFR-1** prototypes and 100 production **FR-1** aircraft, later named **Fireball**. The first of the prototypes made its initial flight on 25 June 1944 without the turbojet, the first flight with both engines operative being made during the following month. Deliveries of production FR-1s began in March 1945, the type equipping initially US Navy Squadron VF-66. By this time Ryan had received contracts for a total of 1,300 production aircraft. However, VJ-

Converted from an FR-1, the sole Ryan XF2R-1 'Flying Shark' was a radically uprated development of the FR-1 with one 1268-kW (1,700-shp) General Electric TG-100 turboprop and one J31-2 turbojet.

Day cancellations limited total production to only 66 FR-1s, none of which saw operational service in World War II, but the aircraft were used extensively for carrier trials before being phased out of service in late 1947.

Under the designation **XFR2-1** one of the FR-1s was converted to serve as the test-bed for a turboprop powerplant, the General Electric XT31-GE-2, which was the military designation of the General Electric TG-100. This was the first turboprop engine to be designed, built and flown in the USA, initially in a Consolidated Vultee XP-81 on 21 December 1945. it was first flown in the XF2R-1 during November 1946, replacing the Wright Cyclone piston engine, and

during its extended test programme the aircraft attained a maximum speed of about 805 km/h (500 mph) with both engines operating.

Specification
Ryan FR-1 Fireball
Type: single-seat carrier-based fighter-bomber
Powerplant: one 1063-kW (1,425-hp) Wright R-1820-72W Cyclone radial piston engine and one 726-kg (1,600-lb)

thrust General Electric J31 turbojet
Performance: maximum speed on both engines 686 km/h (426 mph) at 5515 m (18,100 ft); service ceiling 13135 m (43,100 ft); range 1658 km (1,030 miles)
Weights: empty 3590 kg (7,915 lb); maximum take-off 4806 kg (10,595 lb)
Dimensions: span 12.19 m (40 ft 0 in); length 9.86 m (32 ft 4 in); height 4.15 m (13 ft 7¼ in); wing area 25.55 m² (275.0 sq ft)

Ryan S-C

Design of a three-seat **Ryan S-C** (Sports-Coupe) enclosed cabin monoplane was initiated as an up-market version of the S-T. It was a considerably refined cantilever low-wing monoplane with fixed tailwheel landing gear, and powered as first flown in the autumn of 1937 by a 112-kW (150-hp) Menasco C4S inline engine. However, the production **S-C-W** had the 108-kW (145-hp) Warner Super Scarab radial engine, this making it look, at first glance, a very different

Ryan's preoccupation with the S-T programme meant that it had little time either to market or build the attractive S-C (Sport-Coupe) lightplane.

aeroplane. However, the company's growing involvement in marketing and production of the S-T meant no serious efforts were made to sell the S-C and only 12 were built, one being exported to Brazil. One example (c/n 211) was impressed for service with the US Army at the outbreak of World War II, being deployed in a liaison role under the de-

signation **L-10**. Spanning 11.43 m (37 ft 6 in), the standard S-C-W had a maximum speed of 241 km/h (150 mph) at 915 m (3,000 ft).

Ryan S-T, ST and PT series

When in 1927, just before construction of the Ryan NYP, Claude Ryan sold his assets in Ryan Air Lines to Frank Mahoney, he continued to operate his flying school, the Ryan School of Aeronautics which he had founded in 1922. With signs of economic recovery in the USA in 1933 he decided the moment had come to re-enter the aircraft manufacturing business, the **Ryan S-T** (Sport-Trainer) being the first product of the new Ryan

Aeronautical Company, established at San Diego, California. A braced low-wing monoplane with fixed tailwheel landing gear and tandem open-cockpit accommodation for the pilot and passenger/pupil, and powered initially by a 71-kW (95-hp) Menasco B-4 Pirate inline engine, the S-T proved an excellent design, although only five examples of this low-powered version were built. It was followed by the **S-T-A** (71 built), **A-T-A**

Special (11 built) and **STM**. This last version was a single-seat fighter development made in small numbers to Bolivia, Ecuador, Guatemala, Honduras, Mexico and Nicaragua; to the Netherlands East Indies as the two-seat **CTM-2** landplane and **STM-S2** seaplane; and to China as the **STM-2E/P**.

This was just the start, however, for in 1939 the US Army Air Corps acquired a single example of the S-T-A for evaluation under the designation **XPT-16**. (This was, incidentally, the first monoplane primary trainer to be procured by

the USAAC.) A further contract for 15 **YPT-16** aircraft for wider service evaluation soon followed, and both of these initial versions were powered by the 93-kW (125-hp) Menasco L-365-1 inline engine. Production for the USAAC was initiated in 1940 with 30 **PT-20** trainers, these being generally similar to the YPT-16s except for minor structural revisions. During the following year Ryan developed a version known as the **ST-3KR** which introduced a Kinner radial engine that the US Army believed would give improved performance, and

The PT-20A was in reality the Ryan PT-20 re-engined with the Kinner R-440 radial. Ryan S-T versions were used widely as trainers by the American forces.

the 100 **PT-21** aircraft contracted in 1941 were powered by the 98-kW (132-hp) Kinner R-440-3. The superiority of this airframe/engine combination resulted in 14 of the YPT-16s and 27 of the PT-20s being given R-440-1 engines of similar power output under the respective designations **PT-16A** and **PT-20A**. Three PT-20s delivered with civil (as opposed to military) Menasco D4 engines were designated **PT-20B**. With a rapid expansion of aircrew training during 1941, Ryan received a contract for 1,023 examples of the most extensively-built version, the **PT-22 Recruit**. This differed from the PT-21 primarily by deletion of the wheel spats and main landing gear fairings, and by introduction of the 119-kW (160-hp) Kinner R-540-1 engine. 25 similar **ST-3** aircraft were ordered by the Netherlands, but by the time they were ready for delivery the country had been overrun by the German advance and they

were accepted instead by the USAAC under the designation **PT-22A**. Following US Army evaluation of the XPT-16/ YPT-16, the US Navy also acquired 100 examples of the ST-3 version, powered by the Kinner R-440-3 engine, and these were given the designation **NR-1 Recruit**. These Ryan trainers remained in USAAC/USAAF service until the end of World War II, and with the US Navy until mid-1944.

Specification
Ryan PT-22 Recruit
Type: primary trainer
Powerplant: one 119-kW (160-hp) Kinner R-540-1 radial piston engine

Performance: maximum speed 211 km/h (131 mph); service ceiling 4725 m (15,500 ft); range 566 km (352 miles)
Weights: empty 596 kg (1,313 lb); maximum take-off 844 kg (1,860 lb)
Dimensions: span 9.17 m (30 ft 1 in); length 6.83 m (22 ft 5 in); height

The STM was a fighter derivative of the S-T series, intended as a low-cost export machine, and was indeed sold to several Latin American air arms.

2.08 m (6 ft 10 in); wing area 12.47 m² (134.25 sq ft)

Ryan YO-51 Dragonfly

Ryan designed especially for the US Army in 1939-40 a braced high-wing army co-operation monoplane with STOL capability. Its crew of two was accommodated in tandem open cockpits, power was provided by a 313-kW (420-hp) Pratt & Whitney Wasp Junior radial engine, and to give the required STOL characteristics the leading and trailing edges of the wing incorporated

full-span slots and Fowler flaps respectively. Three prototypes were ordered under the designation **Ryan YO-51** and name **Dragonfly**, but following evaluation no further examples of this 15.85-m (52-ft 0-in) span aircraft were built.

Full control of the diminutive Ryan Dragonfly could be maintained down to 51.5 km/h.

Ryan research aircraft

During the years 1955-63, Ryan flew a small number of unusual research aircraft, brief details of which follow.
Ryan X-13 Vertijet: first flown on 10 December 1955, this single-seat VTOL (vertical take-off and landing) aircraft was a 'tail-sitter' powered by a 4536-kg (10,000-lb) thrust Rolls-Royce Avon turbojet. Of high-set delta-wing configuration, the X-13 had no landing gear and was designed to take off vertically, being

Derived from the XF3R-1 project for the US Navy, the Ryan X-13 Vertijet proved a highly successful programme, and was at one time hoped to provide the basis for the XF-109 VTOL fighter for the US Air Force. Both aircraft involved in the flight test series have been preserved.

suspended from a mobile ground trailer by a hook beneath for forward fuselage. Two prototypes were built, the initial flight noted above being a conventional take-off on temporary fixed tricycle landing gear, but a first complete transition from vertical take-off to horizontal flight and the reverse procedure to a vertical landing was accomplished on 11 April 1957. Both prototypes completed the full planned test programme.
Ryan VZ-3RY Vertiplane: a V/STOL (vertical/short take-off and landing) research tool, the single-seat VZ-3RY was a simply-constructed proof-of-concept aircraft relying on blown flaps for its V/STOL capability. Of high-wing configuration, it was powered by a single 746-kW (1,000-shp) Avco Lycoming T53-L-1 turboshaft engine mounted within the fuselage, and driving two large-diameter propellers mounted at the wing leading edges. Wide-span double retractable trailing-edge flaps could be extended into the propeller slipstream, enabling the Vertiplane to make a near-vertical take-off at a forward speed of 40 km/h (25 mph) after a 9-m (30-ft) run, and to hover at altitudes up to 1130 m (3,700 ft). Following completion of a 21-flight company test programme the aircraft was handed over to NASA.
Ryan XV-8A Fleep: two of these flexible-wing experimental aircraft were built by Ryan for the US Army, each of them basically a single-seat open-structure autogyro with a Rogallo-type flexible wing. Powered by a 157-kW (210-hp) Continental IO-360A flat-six engine, mounted at the rear of the fuselage structure to drive a pusher propeller, the Fleep had an open platform with 12 inset

cargo tie-down rings, enabling the aircraft to carry a payload (including the pilot) of 454 kg (1,000 lb) at a maximum speed of 105 km/h (65 mph). Simple to fly, it was also quickly erected or dismantled and could be easily transported.
Ryan XV-5A and XV-5B: in general appearance the Ryan XV-5A appeared to be a conventional mid-wing monoplane with retractable tricycle landing gear, with cabin accommodation for a crew of two on side-by-side zero-zero ejection seats. It was, however, a so-called 'fan-in-wing' research aircraft, two large fans being mounted horizontally between the spars of each wing, with a smaller fan in the nose to provide pitch control in vertical flight. It was powered by two 1206-kg (2,658-lb) thrust General Electric J85-GE-5 turbojets, and the efflux of these engines could be used to drive the fans (by peripheral tip-blades) for vertical

Seen here with its stalky but temporary landing gear fitted, the use of a universally-jointed jet-deflection nozzle at the rear of the aircraft gave the pilot of the Ryan VZ-3RY Vertiplane a fair measure of control in hovering flight.

flight, or to be used for conventional jet propulsion in horizontal flight after transition had been completed, which was controlled by deflector vanes above the fans. The first of two prototypes was flown on 25 May 1964, these two aircraft between them accumulating 338 flying hours by October 1966. One was lost in April 1965, and the second damaged in October 1966, but this latter was then rebuilt in modified form during 1967-68 as the XV-5B, being used for continuing research by NASA from mid-1968.

SABCA aircraft

Established in late 1920, and associated with the Belgian national airline SABENA (Société Anonyme Belge d'Exploitation de la Navigation Aérienne), the Belgian aircraft manufacturing company known as SABCA (Société Anonyme Belge de Constructions Aéronautiques) continues its activities in 1984. The major aircraft manufacturer in Belgium, it built some 600 aircraft before World War II, the majority of them under licence. Occupation and subsequent major air raid damage to its factory prevented a return to aircraft manufacture until the early 1950s, the company having operated since then for aircraft assembly, maintenance, manufacture and repair. It currently builds large structures for other companies, and is responsible for assembly and test of the General Dynamics F-16s for service with Belgium and Denmark.

SABCA has built under licence the Avia B.H.21, Avro 504, Breguet XIX, Handley Page W.8., Nieuport 29C.1, Renard R.31 and Savoia-Marchetti S.73,

Designed as a fighter, light bomber, attack and reconnaisance aircraft, the SABCA S.47 could attain some 500 km/h (311 mph).

and in conjunction with the Belgian company Stampe et Vertongen a slightly modified version of that company's RSV.22. SABCA's own designs have included the **SABCA D.P. Monoplane**, an ugly little braced high-wing monoplane powered by a 37-kW (50-hp) Anzani radial engine, which had enclosed accommodation for pilot and passenger. Flown in 1927, it was followed by the **SABCA 2** cantilever high-wing monoplane seating two crew in an open cockpit just forward of the wing, with an enclosed cabin below and to their rear for four passengers; the sole example was used by SABENA. Because of extensive licence-production of other manufacturer's designs it was not until 1935 that SABCA designed and built the **S.20** three-seat cabin monoplane of

braced high-wing configuration which was powered by a 97-kW (130-hp) Walter Major inline engine. The lightweight **S.30** was flown in 1936, with side-by-side accommodation for two in an open cockpit, and power provided by a 30-kW (40-hp) Saroela Aiglon flat-twin engine. Final designs before the outbreak of World War II included the **S.40E** monoplane trainer which, powered by a 104-kW (140-hp) Renault 4Pei inline engine and with tandem two-seat accommodation beneath a transparent canopy, was procured in small numbers for the Belgian air force. It was

followed by a two-seat monoplane fighter, the **S.47**, which was of cantilever low-wing monoplane configuration, powered by an Hispano-Suiza 12 Ycrs Vee-engined *moteur canon*, and armed with a 20-mm cannon and three 7.7-mm (0.303-in) Browning machine-guns, one of them on a trainable mounting for operation by the observer in an enclosed cockpit.

Clearly, from the limited production of its own designs, SABCA had and continues to have the skill to fare better as a producer of aircraft or assemblies from other manufacturers.

Saiman 200

The Società Anonima Industrie Meccaniche Aeronautiche Naval (SAIMAN) began aircraft design in 1937, with Mario Bottini as chief engineer and designer. The **SAIMAN C.4** had won the 1936 Circuito Sahariano, an exacting competition for sporting aircraft, and this had led to an invitation from the Italian air ministry to design a trainer and a more marketable sporting aircraft. This latter became the SAIMAN 202, which was air tested before the **SAIMAN 200** two-seat primary trainer biplane flew in prototype form (aircraft MM364) at the end of 1938. Mainly of wooden construction, it had wide-track divided landing gear and was powered by an Alfa Romeo 115 engine. Two further prototypes were built, followed by three examples of the **SAIMAN 205** which differed only by having a 74-kW (120-hp) Alfa Romeo 110

The SAIMAN 200 was a basic trainer with docile handling and toughness.

engine. Successful tests led to substantial orders, two civil machines purchased by Ala Littoria being followed by three series batches for the Regia Aeronautica. In total 115 aircraft were supplied by Caproni-Vizzola and 25 by SAIMAN between November 1940 and autumn 1941. In early use SAIMAN 200s were involved in several accidents during training flights, resulting in structural strengthening and modifications to the ailerons.

The SAIMAN 200 served at a number of Regia Aeronautica primary training schools, including Siena, Parma, Pistoia, Ferugia, Falconara and Mostar, and others were used for liaison duties. After the September 1943 armistice the air arm of the R.S.I., its German allies, the Italian Co-Belligerent air arm and the

British and Americans used surviving SAIMAN 200s for liaison work; the last flight of one of these aircraft was recorded in 1947.

Specification
Type: two-seat primary trainer
Powerplant: one 138-kW (185-hp) Alfa Romeo 115 inline piston engine
Performance: maximum speed

220 km/h (137 mph); service ceiling 6000 m (19,685 ft); range 475 km (295 miles)
Weights: empty equipped 761 kg (1,678 lb); maximum take-off 1055 kg (2,326 lb)
Dimensions: span 8.78 m (28 ft 9¾ in); length 7.47 m (24 ft 6 in); height 2.50 m (8 ft 2½ in); wing area 22.00 m² (236.81 sq ft)

Saiman 202 and 204

Designed by Mario Bottini in response to an Italian air ministry requirement for a two-seat cabin touring monoplane, the low-wing **SAIMAN 202** prototype (I-BOTT) flew for the first time early in 1938. Mainly of wooden construction the SAIMAN 202 had excellent lines, its fixed landing gear units incorporating wheel spats, and power was provided by a 74-kW (120-hp) de Havilland Gipsy Major engine.

First production of the SAIMAN 202 was for civil use and by 31 December 1939 27 SAIMAN 202 and two **SAIMAN 202bis** aircraft were in private ownership; RUNA, the organisation responsible for training sport fliers with the ultimate objective of military service, had two SAIMAN 202 and four **SAIMAN 202/I** machines, while the company retained two SAIMAN 202s (one being the prototype) and the sole **SAIMAN 204 R**. Nine more civil machines were delivered during 1940. The SAIMAN 202bis had only cabin layout

The SAIMAN 202/M was a simplified 202 RL, and used as an interim trainer.

changes, but the SAIMAN 202/I represented a major redesign and was placed in production in May 1939. The fuselage was improved, the tailplane was repositioned, and improved instrumentation was introduced.

To compete in the prestigious tourer aircraft rally, the IV Avio Raduno del Littorio to be held in the summer of 1939, two aircraft were developed specially, the **SAIMAN 202 RL** having the Alfa Romeo 110 I engine which had been standardised for series civil machines, and a reduced-span wing; the second aircraft was the **SAIMAN 204 R** four-seater with a lengthened cabin and longer nose to accommodate its 137-kW (185-hp) Alfa Romeo 115 engine.

To meet an urgent need for military trainers, the Regia Aeronautica ordered the **SAIMAN 202/M** in October 1939;

this was simplified to cut costs and 215 were built by the parent company, 85 by C.N.A. and 65 by SACA. The type was used widely at flying schools, including those at Siena, Pistoia, Perugia and Orvieto. In addition, several flew with the training sections of the various air commands in Italy, at the blind-flying centre and in the liaison role, some being attached to 'Reparto P' based at Rome. The SAIMAN 202/M was also used as a personal aircraft by several staff officers and by the Italian air attachés at Berlin, Bucharest and Budapest. Many were captured.

Specification
SAIMAN 202/M
Type: two-seat training/liaison aircraft
Powerplant: one 89-kW (120-hp) Alfa Romeo 110 I inline piston engine
Performance: maximum speed 220 km/h (137 mph); service ceiling 5050 m (16,570 ft); range 600 km (373 miles)
Weights: empty equipped 670 kg (1,477 lb); maximum take-off 930 kg (2,050 lb)
Dimensions: span 10.66 m (34 ft 11¾ in); length 7.65 m (25 ft 1¼ in); height 1.91 m (6 ft 3¼ in); wing area 17.66 m² (190.10 sq ft)

SAML S.1 and S.2

The Italian company Società Aeronautica Meccanica Lombarda (SAML) built the German Aviatik B.I under licence until 1915. SAML then developed an improved armed reconnaissance aircraft based on the B.I which, powered by a 194-kW (260-hp) Fiat A.12 inline engine, had the designation **SAML S.1**. This

entered service in 1916 and was joined in the following year by an improved **S.2** which had reduced wing span, a modified rudder and the more powerful Fiat A.12bis engine. Built by SAML and other

Italian sub-contractors to a combined total of some 660 aircraft, the type equipped no fewer than 16 Italian *squadriglie da ricognizione*, serving in Albania, Italy and Macedonia. After World War I many of these aircraft saw continued service in East Africa.

SAN Jodel aircraft

The Société Aéronautique Normande (SAN) was, like Robin, another manufacturer of lightplanes designed by Jodel. The company began with the **SAND D.117 Grand Tourisme**, a two-seat cabin monoplane powered by a 71-kW (95-hp) Continental C90 flat-four engine. SAN then developed a four/five-seat version of this aircraft as the **D.140 Mousquetaire**, powered by the 134-kW (180-hp) Avco Lycoming O-360 engine and flown for the first time on 4 July 1958. Production of the D.117 was terminated by SAN at the end of 1958, after 250 of these aircraft had been built, the company manufacturing instead the three-seat **DR.100 Ambassadeur** which had the same powerplant as the D.117. In 1961 the DR.100 was redesignated **DR.1050 Ambassadeur**, and was joined in the following year by the **D.150 Grand Tourisme** (in 1963 renamed

The D.117 was derived from the D-112 with sleeker lines and a 71-kW (90-hp) engine in place of a 48-kW (65-hp) unit. Maximum speed is 209 km/h (130 mph).

Mascaret), a two-seater combining features of the D.117 and DR.1050. An improved version of the Ambassadeur was introduced in 1963; designated **DR.1052 Excellence**, it was powered by the 75-kW (100-hp) Rolls-Royce/Continental O-200-A, or, optionally, the 78-kW (105-hp) Potez 4 E-20. A glider and banner-towing version of the Mousquetaire was flown in mid-1965, gaining the designation **D.140R Abeille**. By then manufacture of the DR.1052 Excellence had ended, and production was concentrated upon the Mascaret, Mousquetaire and Abeille until the company went into liquidation during 1969.

Specification
SAN D.140E Mousquetaire IV
Type: four/five-seat cabin monoplane
Powerplant: one 134-kW (180-hp) Avco Lycoming O-360-A2A flat-four piston engine
Performance: maximum speed 255 km/h (158 mph) at sea level;

service ceiling 5000 m (16,405 ft); range with maximum fuel 1400 km (870 miles)
Weights: empty 620 kg (1,367 lb); maximum take-off 1200 kg (2,646 lb)
Dimensions: span 10.27 m (33 ft 8¼ in); length 7.82 m (25 ft 8 in); height 2.05 m (6 ft 8¾ in); wing area 18.50 m² (199.14 sq ft)

SCAN 20

The Société de Constructions Aéro-Navales de Port-Neuf (SCAN) designed to the requirements of the French air ministry a lightweight flying-boat suitable to train pilots in the handling of aircraft in this category. Designated **SCAN 20**, it was of cantilever high-wing monoplane configuration, with strut-mounted stabilising floats beneath each wing and a twin-fin-and-rudder tail unit. Power was provided by a single Béarn 6-D inline engine strut-mounted above the hull to drive a pusher propeller, and enclosed cabin accommodation was provided for two pilots, side-by-side, with two passenger seats behind them. Built in

secret during 1941, it was not flown until after the liberation of France, during October 1945. Tests won an order for 30 aircraft, but only 23 were delivered to the French navy from 1951, with a more powerful engine.

Specification
Scan 20
Type: flying-boat trainer
Powerplant: one 208-kW (280-hp) Salmson 8.AS.00 inverted-Vee piston engine
Performance: maximum speed 220 km/h (137 mph) at sea level; service ceiling 5500 m (18,045 ft); range with maximum payload 600 km (373 miles)
Weights: empty 1805 kg (3,979 lb);

maximum take-off 2500 kg (5,512 lb)
Dimensions: span 15.00 m (49 ft 2½ in); length 11.95 m (39 ft 2½ in); height 3.62 m (11 ft 10½ in)

Designed secretly during World War II, the SCAN 20 found limited use in the post-war French navy. Only 23 were built.

SECAN SUC.10 Courlis

The Société d'Etudes et de Constructions Aéro-Navales (SECAN) began, after World War II, to manufacture aircraft accessories and components. In the late 1940s a four-seat lightweight cabin monoplane was designed under the designation **SECAN SUC.10 Courlis** (curlew), comprising a fuselage pod-mounted on fixed tricycle landing gear; above the fuselage was mounted the cantilever wing, from which extended to the rear two tubular booms to carry twin fins and rudders, the booms being united at the rear by the tailplane/elevator assembly. The powerplant was mounted in the rear fuselage to drive a pusher propeller, and the remainder of the cabin had four seats as standard, but was so designed that it could be con-

The large-area door of the SECAN SUC.10 Courlis was designed to facilitate loading and unloading in the type's alternative missions as a light freighter or air ambulance.

verted easily for use as an air ambulance or cargo carrier. SECAN built and delivered 144 of these aircraft, but subsequently reverted to component manufacture and, in particular, specialised in the manufacture of aircraft fuel tanks.

Specification
Type: lightweight cabin monoplane
Powerplant: one 149-kW (200-hp) Mathis 8G40 inverted-Vee piston engine

Performance: maximum speed 210 km/h (130 mph); service ceiling 3500 m (11,475 ft); range with four passengers 1000 km (621 miles)
Weights: empty 1015 kg (2,238 lb);

maximum take-off 1560 kg (3,439 lb)
Dimensions: span 12.35 m (40 ft 6¼ in); length 8.18 m (26 ft 10 in); height 2.68 m (8 ft 9½ in); wing area 19.10 m² (205.60 sq ft)

SEPECAT Jaguar

To meet the joint requirements of the Armée de l'Air and Royal Air Force for a dual-role aircraft, suitable for deployment as an advanced/operational trainer (two seats) or tactical support aircraft, several British and French designs were submitted for consideration. The Breguet Br.121 project was selected for de-

velopment to meet the requirements of the two nations, a go-ahead being given in May 1965, and followed by formation of a Jaguar Management Committee to safeguard each nation's interests. A year later the British Aircraft Corporation (now British Aerospace) and Breguet Aviation (now Avions Marcel Dassault

formed the Société Européenne de Production de l'Avion ECAT (SEPECAT) to design and manufacture the **SEPECAT Jaguar** supersonic strike fighter/trainer. The ECAT of the title relates to the Ecole de Combat et d'Appui Tactique which was the original French requirement.

A cantilever shoulder-wing monoplane, the Jaguar has wings swept at 40°, all-swept tail surfaces, retractable

tricycle landing gear and powerplant of two Rolls-Royce/Turboméca Adour turbofan engines, initially the Adour Mk 102 of 32.5 kN (7,305 lb) afterburning thrust; these engines have since been replaced in the RAF **Jaguar S (GR.Mk 1)** by the uprated Adour Mk 104. The Jaguar has been built in four versions for the British and French air forces, and production for export was designated **Jaguar International**. The initial versions comprise the French single-seat tactical support **Jaguar A** (160 built) which was flown initially on 23 March 1969 and two-seat **Jaguar E** advanced trainer (40 built), first flown on 8 September 1968. The British equivalents are the single-seat tactical support Jaguar S first flown on 12 October 1969 (165 built), which has the RAF designation **Jaguar GR.Mk 1**, and the **Jaguar B** two-seat operational trainer with the RAF designation **Jaguar T.Mk 2** (38 built), first flown on 30 August 1971.

A speed capability of Mach 1.6, and advanced avionics that provide pinpoint navigational accuracy plus the freedom to operate safely at tree-top height, makes the Jaguar an extremely able close-support aircraft. Its ability to carry a heavy weapon load over long range and deliver it with great accuracy makes the Jaguar a formidable adversary. The single-seat Jaguars have a maximum external weapons load of 4536 kg (10,000 lb) on a fuselage centreline and four underwing hardpoints, and stores can include air-to-air and air-to-ground missiles; cluster, free-fall and retarded bombs (including the WE177 nuclear weapon); air-to-surface rockets; reconnaissance pods; and auxiliary fuel tanks.

The versatility of the Jaguar made it an obvious candidate for export, and the Jaguar International for this market was flown for the first time on 19 August 1976. Initial orders were received from Oman (12) and Ecuador (12), these being powered by uprated Adour Mk 804 turbofan engines each rated at 16.23 kN (8,040 lb) afterburning thrust to give improved performance under 'hot-and-high' conditions. Subsequent orders have included an additional 12 aircraft for Oman, these being powered by the Adour Mk 811 of 37.38 kN (8,400 lb) afterburning thrust, and in 1979 an agreement was signed with India covering the manufacture by SEPECAT, at Warton, of 40 aircraft with the Adour Mk 804, to be followed by components for an additional 45 for assembly in India by Hindustan Aeronautics. The first of the Indian aircraft flew on 31 March 1982. Deliveries were made to five squadrons. Eight of these aircraft have been specially modified for the anti-shipping role, equipping 'A' Flight of No. 6 Squadron. These Jaguars feature a distinctive Agave radar nose and BAe Sea Eagle missiles. Plans by the Indian Air Force to up their Jaguar purchase to 160 have so far come to nothing, though the service still hopes to form another Jaguar-equipped squadron. In Indian service the Jaguar is known as the **Shamsher** (which loosely translates as Sword of Justice). The final buyer for the type was Nigeria, long referred to as 'an officially undisclosed customer'. Eighteen aircraft were contracted for, including five train-ers, and the first eight were handed over at Warton in May 1984. They remained in Britain for pilot conversion and training, until delivery to Makurdi in October. The Nigerian Jaguar force of 14 surviving aircraft was withdrawn in 1991, as a cost-cutting measure.

The only other Jaguar variant was a one-off fly-by-wire research aircraft, the **Jaguar ACT (Active Control Technology)**, which was loaned to BAe by the MoD for a series of flight stability trials. Leading-edge root extensions were fitted and the aircraft progressively loaded with weighty ballast to modify its flying characteristics. It was withdrawn from use in November 1984.

From December 1983, 75 surviving RAF Jaguars, with the three squadrons of the Coltishall wing, have been updated to **GR.Mk 1A** standard courtesy of the Ferrant FIN 1064 avionics update. This comprises a new HUD, INS, radar altimeter and moving map display, replacing the already excellent NAV-WASS system. The new fit is both lighter and considerably more compact. The same modification was applied to 14 T.Mk 2s resulting in the **T.Mk 2A**. A further upgrade with higher-powered engines and a night-vision system has been abandoned on cost grounds. Gulf War modifications saw the permanent fitting of AN/ALE-40 flare dispensers under the engine nacelles, an improved IFF and RWR fit, and greater use of external ECM pods. Many Jaguars retain their overwing Sidewinder missile rails, which were previously rarely seen.

Specification
SEPECAT Jaguar S (GR.Mk 1)
Type: single-seat tactical support aircraft
Powerplant: two Rolls-Royce Turboméca Adour Mk 104 turbofans, each rated at 35.78-kN (8,040-lb) afterburning thrust
Performance: maximum speed Mach 1.6, or 1699 km/h (1,056 mph) at 11000 m (36,090 ft); hi-lo-hi attack radius with external fuel 1408 km (875 miles)
Weights: empty 7000 kg (15,432 lb); maximum take-off 15700 kg (34,612 lb)
Dimensions: span 8.69 m (28 ft 6 in); length 16.83 m (55 ft 2½ in); height 4.89 m (16 ft 0½ in); wing area 24.18 m² (260.28 sq ft)
Armament: two 30-mm ADEN cannon, plus up to 4536 kg (10,000 lb) stores carried on five hardpoints; overwing pylons for AAMs

The Jaguar GR.Mk 1A is a potent tactical strike aircraft, notable for the extreme accuracy of its navigation and weapons delivery system. This aircraft carries a Vinten reconnaissance pod.

S.E.T. 3 and S.E.T. 31

Designed by Grigore Zamfirescu, the **S.E.T. 3** of 1929 was a dual-control trainer powered by a 172-kW (230-hp) Salmson 9Ab uncowled radial engine. An equal-span biplane of wood and fabric construction with conventional cross-axle landing gear, the S.E.T. 3 proved to have excellent flying qualities and was ordered into quantity production for the Romanian air force, two batches each of 50 aircraft being delivered. Wing span was 9.80 m (32 ft 1¾ in) and maximum loaded weight 1120 kg (2,469 lb).

The improved **S.E.T. 31** of 1930, which was also built in quantity, was generally similar to the S.E.T. 3, but introduced new divided landing gear and a

Differing from the 1929-built S.E.T. 3 biplane through being fitted with a divided undercarriage, instead of the previous cross-axle arrangement, the S.E.T. 31 saw extensive service with the Romanian air force as a basic trainer.

lower wing of reduced span with considerable dihedral.

S.E.T. 7

Built in quantity for the Romanian air force, the **S.E.T. 7** advanced trainer was largely of fabric-covered wooden construction, and followed the general design of the other low-powered S.E.T. trainer biplanes. Powerplant was a 273-kW (365-hp) Armstrong Siddeley Jaguar radial engine, and maximum speed was 240 km/h (149 mph).

The original S.E.T. 7 appeared in 1930 and was followed during the next year by an experimental twin-float seaplane, but the **S.E.T. 7K** development which appeared in 1934 differed in a number of important respects. The fuselage was an all-metal structure, power was provided by a 283-kW (380-hp) Gnome-Rhône 7Ksd radial engine in a long-chord cowling, the tailplane was redesigned and a mounting was installed in the rear cockpit for a single 7.7-mm (0.303-in) machine-gun. A second machine-gun was mounted inside the engine cowling and synchronised to fire forward through the propeller disc. Equipment included radio, an aerial camera and I.A.R.-Barbieri bomb racks for a maximum load of 144 kg (317 lb) of bombs. Maximum speed was 320 km/h (199 mph). The S.E.T. 7K entered service initially as an observation aircraft and was built in some numbers.

The improved **S.E.T. 7KB** which appeared in 1935 had a more powerful I.A.R.-built version of the Gnome-Rhône 7 and was specialised for tactical reconnaissance and liaison duties. It was followed in production by the **S.E.T. 7KD** of 1939 which differed by having improved equipment and instrumentation and carried an increased bombload.

Grigore Zamfirescu's S.E.T. 7K was widely used for many years by the Romanian air force, being ideally suited to an army co-operation and air observation role. For its military duties the S.E.T. 7K was fitted with a trainable machine-gun for the second crew member, a bulky radio and an additional bombload.

Several S.E.T. 7Ks, KBs and KDs were still in service up to 1944.

Specification
S.E.T. 7KB
Type: two-seat tactical reconnaissance/liaison aircraft
Powerplant: one 313-kW (420-hp) I.A.R.-built Gnome-Rhône 7K radial piston engine
Performance: maximum speed

250 km/h (155 mph); service ceiling 5500 m (18,045 ft); range 580 km (360 miles)
Weights: empty equipped 1115 kg (2,458 lb); maximum take-off 1780 kg (3,924 lb)
Dimensions: span 9.80 m (32 ft 1¾ in); length 7.15 m (23 ft 5½ in); height 3.26 m (10 ft 8¼ in); wing area 26.60 m² (286.33 sq ft)
Armament: two 7.7-mm (0.303-in) machine-guns and 24 12-kg (26-lb) bombs

S.E.T. 10 and S.E.T. X

The **S.E.T. 10** and **S.E.T. X** were, in spite of the designation similarity, two different aircraft. The S.E.T. 10 biplane had a 97-kW (130-hp) de Havilland Gipsy Major inline engine and could attain a maximum speed of 180 km/h (112 mph). Spanning 9.46 m (30 ft 0½ in) and with a maximum take-off weight of just 800 kg (1,764 lb), it was built in limited numbers for the Romanian air force and was used for primary, basic and formation training.

Only two examples of the S.E.T. X equal-span biplane were built. Powered by an uncowled 272-kW (365-hp) Arm-strong Siddeley Jaguar radial engine, the type was a single-seat advanced aerobatic trainer, and equipped with a single synchronised machine-gun.

Only two S.E.T. X advanced aerobatic trainers were built.

SFAN 2 and 4

The Société Française d'Aviation Nouvelle (SFAN) was established in 1935 to construct gliders and light aircraft. To initiate production of the latter, SFAN acquired from Kronfeld Ltd in the UK licence rights to build and market the Kronfeld Drone, modifying the design slightly to meet French requirements and installing a 19-kW (25-hp) Ava flat four-engine. A single-seater, like the Kronfeld Drone, this model was designated **SFAN 2**; a two-seat version with open cockpit, side-by-side seating and a 26-kW (35-hp) Mengin flat-twin engine was produced under the designation **SFAN 4**, this aircraft having a maximum speed of 115 km/h (71 mph).

SFCA aircraft

The French company Société Française de Constructions Aéronautiques (SFCA) was formed in mid-1934 to build light-planes to the design of Maillet. The first to enter production was the **SFCA Maillet 20**, an aircraft of all-wood construction, powered by a 134-kW (180-hp) Régnier inverted inline engine, and seating three in tandem beneath a continuous transparent canopy. The following **SFCA 20 Lignel** was also a cantilever low-wing monoplane of all-wood construction, but introduced retractable main landing gear units. It was designed as a single-seater but could, optionally, be equipped to carry two in tandem beneath a continuous transparent canopy. Powered by a 164-kW

The SFCA Taupin had tandem wings attached to upper longerons and braced to lower longerons. Maximum speed was 135 km/h (84 mph) and the aircraft spanned 8.71 m (28 ft 7 in).

(220-hp) Renault 6Q inverted inline engine, it was a high-performance light-plane able to attain a maximum speed of 385 km/h (239 mph) at sea level.

Some years earlier Frenchman Louis Peyret had designed an unusual tandem monoplane, its tailplane being replaced by a reduced-span wing. SFCA acquired licence rights for this aircraft, developing it as the single-seat **SFCA Taupin** powered by a 22-kW (30-hp) Mengin flat-two engine. Interestingly, both wings were of braced high-set configuration and incorporated full-span trailing-edge

flaps. Those in the forward wing could be used collectively as flaps or differentially as ailerons, while those in the rear wing served as elevators or flaps. A two-seat version known as the **SFCA Tau-pin Cinq-demi**, or **Taupin 5/2**, powered by a 52-kW (70-hp) Régnier inline engine, was under development when French lightplane construction was halted by World War II.

S.I.A. biplanes

In 1917 the Societá Italiana Aviazione produced the **S.I.A.1200**, a large biplane with landing gear comprising four pairs of side-by-side main wheels, a tail skid and two single wheels forward of the main wheels as a precaution against nosing over on landing. The tailplane was of biplane configuration with a six fin-and-rudder arrangement. The S.I.A.1200 was flown over a period from Turin to test theories relating to large aircraft. It was powered by two 447-kW (600-hp) Fiat A.14 engines, and had a maximum speed of 150 km/h (93 mph), wing span of 32.90 m (107 ft 11¼ in) and maximum take-off weight of 8500 kg (18,739 lb).

Also in 1917 appeared the **S.I.A.7B**, a two-seat reconnaissance biplane with equal-span wings; tests showed good

The S.I.A. 7B of 1917 offered good performance and agility, coupled with an excellent field of fire for the rear observer/gunner. The design soon proved to be fundamentally unsound structurally, hastening the development of the S.I.A. 782.

flying qualities and production was started at once. Powered by a 186-kW (250-hp) Fiat A.12 engine, the S.I.A.7B had a maximum speed of 175 km/h (109 mph); wing span was 13.32 m (43 ft 8½ in) and maximum take-off weight was 1650 kg (3,638 lb). Armament comprised two 7.7-mm (0.303-in) machine-guns. When 500 S.I.A.7Bs had been constructed and many had been supplied to front-line *squadriglie*, it was discovered that wing structural weakness was causing accidents. The basic design was strengthened and production re-

started under the designation **S.I.A.7B-2**.

The **S.I.A.9B** was developed specifically as a fast light bomber. Flown in prototype form at the end of 1917, it retained the basic formula of the S.I.A.7, but the structure had been reworked to eliminate the difficulties previously encountered. After a practical bombing raid made in the prototype during February 1918, the S.I.A.9B was placed in production.

The S.I.A.9B had a wing span of 15.50 m (50 ft 10¼ in), maximum take-off weight of 2990 kg (6,592 lb), and powered by a 447-kW (600-hp) Fiat A.14 engine could attain a maximum speed of 215 km/h (134 mph).

SIAI MVT S.50 and S.52

Alessandro Marchetti became the chief designer for SIAI in early 1922, bringing with him his MVT which had been designed at the Vickers-Terni works at La Spezia in 1917. In 1919 it had flown at a speed of over 260 km/h (161 mph) at the Montecelio military testing ground and in 1920 had its SPA 6a engine replaced by the more powerful SPA 6-2a of 213 kW (285 hp). The design was still regarded as competitive for a single-seat fighter in 1922 and was redesignated as the **MVT S.50** in a new number sequence adopted by SIAI after acquiring its new designer.

In 1923 the Commissiriato di Aeronautico initiated a competition for a new Italian fighter powered by a Hispano-Suiza 42 engine of 224 kW (300 hp). Marchetti designed the **S.52**, a reworked version of the S.50 with a similar

In 1922 the young Alessandro Marchetti joined SIAI (Societa Italiana Aeroplani Idrovolanti). The company, established in 1915, would later become Savoia-Marchetti in recognition of the work of its most famous designer. Marchetti's first work for the firm was the S.52, a design inherited from his time spent working on the MVT S.50 at Vickers-Terni. Marchetti's S.52 differed mainly in having a fixed tailplane and elevators, instead of all-moving elevators, with ailerons in place of wing-warping. It was a good design, but failed to secure any orders.

narrow-section fuselage mounted between the upper and lower wings, both

of which were unusually angular and had considerable sweepback. The S.50 had only elevators, whereas the S.52 also had a tailplane, and the rather primitive wing-warping controls of the S.50 were replaced by conventional ailerons on the upper wing. However, the S.52 was defeated by the Fiat CR.1 in the competition, despite its maximum speed of 280 km/h (174 mph).

SIAI S.8
to
SOCATA Rallye series

SIAI S.8

On 12 August 1915 the Societa Idrovolanti Alta Italia (SIAI) was formed in Milan. After licence-production of French F.B.A. flying-boats, the company employed Raffaele Conflenti as chief designer, his **SIAI S.8** flying-boat being test flown by Emilio Taddeoli in 1917. Compared with the F.B.A. 'boats, the S.8 had the lower of its equal-span biplane wings attached directly to the upper surface of a more robust hull, and the tailplane was mounted similarly.

The Italian navy ordered over 800 S.8s, to be built both by SIAI and by sub-

contractors, but production tapered away rapidly at the end of the war, by which time 172 had been delivered. These aircraft equipped the 266ª Squadriglia at San Remo as well as four other Regia Marina *squadriglie*. Total production was at least 214. Early examples were powered initially by an Isotta Fraschini V4B engine, but some later machines had the more powerful 164-kW (220-hp) Hispano-Suiza 44, and a few, fitted with dual controls for training, had the 89-kW (120-hp) Colombo F.150. By 1920 only 63 S.8s survived, most of them in storage.

Specification
Type: two-seat reconnaissance flying-boat
Powerplant: one 134-kW (180-hp) Isotta Fraschini V4B inline piston engine
Performance: maximum speed 144 km/h (89 mph); service ceiling 6000 m (19,685 ft); range 700 km (435 miles)
Weights: empty equipped 900 kg (1,984 lb); maximum take-off 1375 kg (3,031 lb)
Dimensions: span 12.77 m (41 ft 10¾ in); length 9.84 m (32 ft 3½ in); height 3.30 m (10 ft 10 in); wing area 46.00 m² (495.16 sq ft)

The SIAI S.8 saw service as a reconnaissance flying-boat during World War I, but production slowed after the war.

Armament: one 7.7-mm (0.303-in) machine-gun in bow cockpit, plus up to 120 kg (256 lb) of bombs

SIAI S.9

In mid-1918 Conflenti's **SIAI S.9** reconnaissance flying-boat was flown for the first time. It had improved wing and tailplane design by comparison with the S.8, and smoother bow contours. Powered by a 224-kW (300-hp) Fiat A.12bis engine it could attain a maximum speed of 170 km/h (106 mph).

Small numbers were built, but none were bought by the Italian navy and efforts to export military and civil versions, the latter accommodating four passengers in an enclosed cabin, met with only limited success. Single examples of the military aircraft went on to Finland (before the fatal crashes), Sweden and Spain. Belgium obtained a civil version for use in the Congo, and CAMS, founded at St Ouen, France, by the Italian Santoni, built a small number under licence with the designation **CAMS C-9**. Late production aircraft introduced a fin for the first time, and had revised wing structure and a cowling for the engine.

SIAI S.12

The **SIAI S.12** reconnaissance-bomber flying-boat, a refined development of the S.9, appeared at the end of 1918. It introduced the characteristic appearance of SIAI flying-boats over the next decade, with a deep, carefully contoured forward hull, and a slim sharply tapered aft section to the rear of the single step.

The tail unit was more angular than on previous Conflenti designs, and the equal-span wings had sheathed double bracing wires and auxiliary struts to give much greater structural strength.

Despite an excellent maximum speed for its day of 222 km/h (138 mph), recorded officially on 7 January 1921, no Italian navy orders were forthcoming. The S.12 went on to make a name for its parent company by success in sporting

contests, especially in the 1920 Schneider Trophy race.

Although no production was undertaken, the SIAI S.12 set the precedent for the company's future flying-boat designs. The sole example contested the 1920 Schneider Trophy at Venice, which no other nation bar Italy attended, due to post-war stringencies. Piloted by Lt Luigi Bologna, the S.12 flew the course and was declared the winner.

SIAI S.13

Appearing just after the S.12, the **SIAI S.13** was a smaller version of the earlier SIAI S.12 flying-boat, intended for reconnaissance and fighter duties. The crew were seated side-by-side behind a single windscreen and the observer was provided with a single trainably-mounted 7.7-mm (0.303-in) machine-gun, but the bow cockpit featured in the earlier SIAI 'boats was eliminated. Wing bracing was similar to that of the S.12, and with the power of a 187-kW (250-hp) Isotta Fraschini V6 engine the S.13 could attain a maximum speed of 197 km/h (122 mph). Twelve machines were delivered to the Italian navy in 1919.

S.13s were exported to Sweden,

Japan, Norway, Spain and Yugoslavia. CAMS built a French version designated **CAMS C-13**, and the Spanish naval workshops in Barcelona later built seven aircraft under licence. Several Spanish S.13s operating from the seaplane carrier *Dedálo* participated in the campaign against the Riff rebels in Morocco during 1922, and between 1922 and 1924 a further six Spanish S.13s were completed, some as single-seaters.

The S.13 Tip 'S' single-seater also attracted the attention of the Italian navy, but an order for 50 examples was cancelled in favour of developed versions of the Macchi M.7 already in service. Equally unfortunate was the **S.13bis** civil version with stabilising floats of new design and a revised tailplane, which failed to attract any orders.

Piloted by Sgt Guido Janello, the S.13 contested the 1919 Schneider race along with Britain and France, in dense sea fog. It finished the course alone, only to be disqualified for an incomplete circuit.

SIAI S.16

The first flying-boat that Conflenti designed from the outset as a passenger machine was the **SIAI S.16**, which appeared in 1919; it retained the concave hull of its predecessors but was more elegant in appearance.

The S.16 had a most illustrious career and can lay claim to have been the most successful flying-boat of its decade. Military versions were also built and found markets in Italy and abroad, and developed versions made their appearance.

Variants
S.16: original commercial flying-boat with provision for five passengers
S.16bis: this version was also a civil

The SIAI S.16 was a successful military and civil aircraft. This S.16ter, of de Pinedo, is being returned to the water by men of the Royal Australian Air Force after an overhaul at Point Cook in July 1925.

machine, retaining the Fiat A.12bis engine of the S.16, but with a reinforced hull, strengthened wing leading edges, increased fuel capacity and a larger propeller
S.16bis M: this was a militarised version of the S.16bis, with a bow cockpit for an observer-gunner and bomb racks beneath the lower wings; it was very successful throughout the 1920s; the Brazilian navy obtained 15 S.16bis Ms in the mid-1920s; the

Soviet Union ordered two batches, believed to total 80, which served with the Black Sea Fleet aviation until 1931, these aircraft having the Soviet designation **S-1bis**; the Soviet OMOS

workshops modified a number as the **S-1ter** during 1927-28, principal change being the installation of more powerful 336-kW (450-hp) Lorraine-Dietrich engines; a number of the

S.16bis M type, probably 20 machines, were delivered by air to Spain, some of them with 224-kW (300-hp) Hispano-Suiza engines; later a batch of 10 was licence-built at Barcelona, followed by other small orders
S.16ter: this military version was delivered to the Italian navy from 1924, first equipping the 141ª and 145ª Squadriglie (equipped previously with the Macchi M.18) and then replacing the S.16bis M in other units; it was powered by the Isotta Fraschini-built Lorraine-Dietrich 12Db of 298 kW (400 hp)
S.23: simplified training version, only one built

Specification
SIAI S.16ter
Type: two/three-seat bomber-reconnaissance flying-boat
Powerplant: one 298-kW (400-hp) Lorraine-Dietrich 12Db Vee piston engine
Performance: maximum speed 194 km/h (120 mph); service ceiling 4000 m (13,125 ft); range 1000 km (621 miles)
Weights: empty equipped 1852 kg (4,083 lb); maximum take-off 2652 kg (5,847 lb)
Dimensions: span 15.50 m (50 ft 10¼ in); length 9.89 m (32 ft 5¼ in); height 3.67 m (12 ft 0½ in); wing area 52.00 m² (570.51 sq ft)
Armament: one 7.7-mm (0.303-in) machine-gun on ring mounting in bow cockpit, plus up to 220 kg (485 lb) of bombs on underwing racks

SIAI racing seaplanes

The **SIAI S.17** was the company's first specialised seaplane and this, powered by a 2310-kW (310-hp) Ansaldo San Giorgio 4E-14 engine, was flown in the 1920 Monaco Seaplane Meeting. It was damaged beyond repair during take-off for the final event of the meeting and, consequently, was unable to take part in the 1920 Schneider Trophy contest as had been planned. The **SIAI S.19** single-seat seaplane had also been built to take part in the 1920 Schneider Trophy event, its slightly larger and aerodynamically refined airframe to be powered by a 410-kW (500-hp) Ansaldo San Giorgio 4E-29 engine. However, this powerplant was not available in time and the S.19 was withdrawn from the contest. The **SIAI S.21** of 1921, then claimed to be the smallest flying-boat in the world, had inverted sesquiplane wings of only

The SIAI S.19 did not reach the 1920 Schneider Trophy held at Venice due to development difficulties with the powerplant.

7.69 m (25 ft 2¾ in) span and an overall length of 7.62 m (25 ft 0 in). Powered by a 224-kW (300-hp) Ansaldo San Giorgio 4E-14 engine, it took part in the 1921 Monaco Seaplane Meeting, sustaining some damage in the process. It was repaired in time to compete in the 1921 Schneider Trophy contest, but then had to be withdrawn because of the illness of its intended pilot. An even more unusual and very much larger racer was the twin-engined **SIAI S.22** flying-boat which also took part in the 1921 Monaco Seaplane Meeting. With a wing span of 13.50 m (44 ft 3½ in) and maximum take-off weight of 2500 kg (5,512 lb), its two

224-kW (300-hp) Isotta-Fraschini V6bis engines were positioned immediately below the upper-wing centre section, supported by eight struts, and driving one tractor and one pusher propeller. Unfortunately, this aircraft continued along the trail of misfortune that dogged the company's attempts to field a Schneider Trophy winner, for during the tests before the contest it was destroyed in a fatal accident when it crashed into Lake Maggiore.

SIAI-Marchetti S.205 and S.208

The prototype **SIAI-Marchetti S.205** made its initial flight on 4 May 1965 and soon afterwards was displayed at the Paris Salon de l'Aéronautique. A four-seat cabin monoplane tourer of cantilever low-wing configuration, it had tricycle landing gear which, optionally, could be retractable or fixed, the latter with strut fairings and wheel spats. It was intended to be powered by engines in the 134-kW (180-hp) to 224-kW (300-hp) range, but favoured powerplant was the Franklin 6A-350C1 flat-six engine. The need for increased power and capacity led to the **S.208**, the prototype of which was flown on 22 May 1967. This had retractable landing gear, a more powerful 194-kW (260-hp) Avco O-540-E4A5 engine and provision for a fifth seat in the cabin.
Production of all versions of the S.205 and S.208 numbered nearly 400 in four

years, the total including 44 **S.205M** aircraft delivered to the Aeronautica Militare Italiana for liaison and training duties. This variant differs from the civil S.208 in that the starboard-located cabin door can be jettisoned in emergency and that there is also a second door in the port side of the fuselage; full blind-flying and navigation systems are standard on service aircraft. Both civil and military S.208s have two auxiliary wingtip tanks, and maximum speed of this version is 320 km/h (199 mph).

Specification
SIAI-Marchetti S.205
Type: four-seat cabin monoplane
Powerplant: one 164-kW (220-hp) Franklin 6A-350C1 flat-six piston engine
Performance: maximum speed 295 km/h (183 mph); service ceiling 6200 m (20,340 ft); range 1325 km (823 miles)
Weights: empty equipped 750 kg (1,653 lb); maximum take-off 1350 kg (2,976 lb)
Dimensions: span 10.86 m (35 ft 7½ in); length 8.00 m (26 ft 3 in); height 2.89 m (9 ft 5¾ in); wing area 16.09 m² (173.20 sq ft)

Though successful in its own right, the SIAI-Marchetti S.205 is better known as the precursor of the S.208, with all-round vision canopy and more power to carry up to five persons.

SIAI-Marchetti S.210

Adding a second engine transformed the S.205 into the elegant S.210.

Evolved from the S.205 single-engine series, the first of two prototypes of the **SIAI-Marchetti S.210** twin-engine light tourer-executive monoplane flew on 18 February 1970. It was a classic cantilever low-wing all-metal aircraft with re-

tractable tricycle landing gear, powered by two 149-kW (200-hp) Avco Lycoming TIO-360-A1B flat-four engines, giving the 11.63 m (38 ft 1¾ in) span S.210 a maximum speed of 375 km/h (233 mph). Accommodation was provided for a pilot

and five passengers in three pairs of side-by-side seats. A second prototype had staggered cabin entry doors, increased baggage capacity and enlarged rear windows, the ensuing series of 10

production aircraft incorporating the changes made in the second prototype.

SIAI-Marchetti S.211

The first prototype of this turbofan-powered basic trainer was flown on 10 April 1981 at Milan-Malpensa airport, and was exhibited subsequently at the June 1981 Le Bourget Salon de Aéronautique, together with the second prototype. The design was developed as a private venture in the knowledge that orders from the Aeronautica Militare Italiana were unlikely and that success would depend on export orders.
A compact two-seat shoulder-wing

monoplane with retractable tricycle wing landing gear, the S.211 has a secondary light-attack role. The first flight took place on 10 April 1981, with deliveries commencing only in 1984. So far, orders have been slow. Four aircraft supplied to Haiti were returned, leaving the S.211 in service with only two nations. Singapore is the largest operator, with 30 aircraft equipping two squadrons as primary jet trainers. The first six of these were delivered as kits, with the remainder

assembled by Singapore Aerospace. These aircraft will now be moved to Australia as part of Singapore's plan to conduct all its training with the RAAF. In 1988 the Philippines ordered 14 aircraft to be built under licence by the Philippine Aircraft Development Co. (PADCO). The first of these was delivered in knock-down form in 1989 and completed by the end of 1991. Philippine Air Force aircraft were equipped for attack duties, but the type has been grounded after several unexplained losses. The manufacturer's greatest hope for the type is the JPATS version it is offering, with Grumman as

prime US contractor. SIAI-Marchetti's parent company is Italian aerospace conglomerate Agusta, and the S.211 is now formally referred to as the **Agusta S.211**.

Variants
S.211A: fitted with more powerful 14.29-kN (3,190-lb) Pratt & Whitney Canada JT15D-5C engine; two trials aircraft flying in Italy and USA
S.211 JPATS: version entered for USAF/USN Joint Primary Aircraft Training System competition with Grumman Aircraft Systems as US

partner; Grumman was the first to declare an entrant in the competition and is offering, essentially, the improved S.211A; manufacture originally to be split 50-50 with Agusta, but with final assembly in the USA

Specification
Type: two-seat basic trainer
Powerplant: one 11.12-kN (2,500-lb) thrust Pratt & Whitney Canada JT15D-4C turbofan
Performance: maximum cruising speed 665 km/h (413 mph) at 7620 m (25,000 ft); service ceiling 12190 m

The SIAI-Marchetti S.211 combines the classic features of a tandem seat trainer in a small package with an efficient engine.

(40,000 ft); endurance, no reserves 4 hours
Weights: empty equipped 1615 kg (3,560 lb); maximum take-off, clean 2500 kg (5,512 lb)
Dimensions: span 8.43 m (27 ft 8 in); length 9.31 m (30 ft 6½ in); height 3.80 m (12 ft 5½ in); wing area 12.60 m² (135.63 sq ft)
Armament: (secondary role) four

underwing hardpoints for a maximum external load of 600 kg (1,323 lb) of stores that can include machine-gun or

photo-reconnaissance pods, bombs, practice bombs, napalm containers or rockets

---

SIAI-Marchetti SF.260 series

This remarkably successful multi-purpose three-seat low-wing monoplane was designed by Stelio Frati for the Aviamilano company, which designated it the **Aviamilano F.250**, the prototype being first flown on 15 July 1964 on the power of a 186-kW (250-hp) Avco Lycoming engine. SIAI took over the project and redesignated the aircraft **SIAI-Marchetti SF.260**, then installing a more powerful Avco Lycoming O-540 engine.

The initial version, intended for civil use, was designated **SF.260A**, but this proved a rather expensive tourer/taxi aircraft and sales were limited. SIAI-Marchetti then devoted every effort to developing the military potential of the aircraft.

The **SF.260M** prototype first flew on 10 October 1970 and was a three-seat military primary or basic trainer. It introduced a number of structural modifications which were incorporated in all models built subsequently, and its strengthened wings dispensed with the external stiffening which had been a characteristic of the SF.260A.

In May 1972 the **SF.260W Warrior** prototype made it initial flight. Whereas the SF.260M had been marketed with a secondary role of close ground support, the Warrior was intended primarily as a light strike platform and has proved popular with air arms which have limited financial resources. It can perform a wide range of duties, its four underwing pylons carrying a variety of stores which can be used on various army co-operation missions, including low-level

Bearing all the hallmarks of Stello Frati's exemplary design skills, the SF-260M is in world wide service. This is one of 32 delivered to the Belgian air force.

attack and front-line supply drops; additionally, the Warrior can be converted easily for the training role. In 1976 one example was flown of the **SF.260SW Sea Warrior** intended for coast patrol and fishery protection duties. The current civil version, introducing the structural improvements pioneered by the SF.260M, is the **SF.260C** three-seat fully-aerobatic aircraft. The most recently introduced member of the family is the **SF.260TP**, powered by a 261-kW (350-shp) Allison 250-B17C turboprop engine, and this was flown for the first time on 8 April 1981. It has improved performance, including a maximum speed of 420 km/h (261 mph) at 3050 m (10,000 ft); and the company claims that operating costs are much reduced. SIAI-Marchetti proposed kits to convert SF.260 piston-engine aircraft to SF.260TP standard, the range of duties proposed for the latter being the same as for the piston-engine series.

The company had received more than 800 orders for SF.260s of all versions by 1993, of which more than 700 have been delivered, primarily to military customers, in some 20 nations. The largest single order was from Libya (for 240 **SF.260ML**) and they have been supplied to the Italian air force (33 **SF.260AM**). Other SF.260M aircraft

have gone to the air arms of Belgium (36), Bolivia (six), Brunei (two), Burma (10), Burundi (three), the Philippines (32), Singapore (28), Thailand (18), Zaire (20) and Zambia (nine). SF.260Ws serve with the air arms of Burma (10), Comoros (three), Dubai (one), Ireland (11), the Philippines (16), Somalia (16), Tunisia (18) and Zimbabwe (17). SF.260TPs have been ordered by Haiti Airways, and by air arms of Dubai and Zimbabwe and, apart from private use, SF.260C civil versions have served with Air Inter, Maroc, Alitalia and SABENA. Like all SIAI-Marchetti aircraft the SF.260 is now technically the **Agusta SF.260**.

Specification
SIAI-Marchetti SF.260W Warrior
Type: one/three-seat multi-role light military aircraft
Powerplant: one 192-kW (260-hp) Avco Lycoming O-540-E4A5 flat-six

piston engine
Performance: maximum speed 305 km/h (190 mph) at sea level; service ceiling 4480 m (14,700 ft); two-seat ferry range with auxiliary fuel 1715 km (1,066 miles)
Weights: empty equipped 830 kg (1,830 lb); maximum take-off 1300 kg (2,866 lb)
Dimensions: span 8.35 m (27 ft 4¾ in); length 7.10 m (23 ft 3½ in); height 2.41 m (7 ft 11 in); wing area 10.10 m² (108.72 sq ft)
Armament: four underwing hardpoints with a maximum combined capacity of 300 kg (661 lb) when flown as a single-seater; stores can include two SIAI gun pods each with one or two 7.62-mm (0.3-in) FN machine-guns; rockets; anti-personnel, general-purpose or practice bombs; parachute flares; photo-reconnaissance pods; or auxiliary fuel

---

SIAI-Marchetti SF.600TP

Developed from the **SF.600 Canguro** (kangaroo) utility transport powered by two 261-kW (350-hp) Avco Lycoming TIO-540-J piston engines, which was exhibited at the Paris Salon de l'Aéronautique in 1979, the **SIAI-Marchetti SF.600TP** (I-CANG) flew for the first time on 8 April 1981 and was itself exhibited at the Paris Salon of that year.

Intended primarily as a light transport with accommodation for a pilot and 10 passengers, the S.F.600TP was available also as a freighter with a manually-operated swing tail permitting easy loading and unloading of bulky items; as an air ambulance with provision for four stretcher cases and two medical attendants; as a photographic survey aircraft; and as a maritime surveillance aircraft.

Designed by Stelio Frati, the SF.600TP is powered by Allison turboprops and is of robust and straight-forward all-metal construction with fixed tricycle landing gear. It was originally designed as a piston engined aircraft, but SIAI-Marchetti decided to fit turboprops for its produc-

The SIAI-Marchetti SF.600TP is derived from an original piston-engined concept. it entered very limited production and the manufacturer would now like to see it licence-built elsewhere.

tion form. The third prototype (I-KANG) was fitted with a retractable undercarriage and this configuration was made available to interested customers. The SF.600TP was certified by the Italian authorities in 1987 and initial production totalled nine. Three of these entered regular commercial service with Rome-based air taxi operator Sun Line from April 1988 onwards. In 1989 a joint venture was initiated between Gruppo Agusta and the Sammi Corporation of South Korea. It was planned to build the Canguro in Korea under the auspices of Sammi Agusta Aerospace, and sell the aircraft in the Pacific region. A new factory was envisaged with a workforce of 400, but the tooling was never transferred and in recent times the Philippine

Airplane Development Corporation (PADCO) have expressed an interest in building the type. PADCO has previously built parts for several Agusta/SIAI-Marchetti aircraft, including the SF.600.

Variants
S.700 Cormorano: SIAI-Marchetti studied building this amphibious version of the SF.600TP utilising a single-step composite hull to replace the lower fuselage; more powerful Lycoming or Garrett engines were also envisaged; funding was sought from the Italian authorities from 1983 onwards, but never obtained

Specification
Type: utility transport and general-purpose aircraft
Powerplant: two 313-kW (420-hp) Allison 250-B17C turboprops
Performance: maximum speed 305 km/h (190 mph) at 3050 m (10,000 ft); service ceiling 7300 m (23,950 ft); normal range with internal fuel 1580 km (982 miles)
Weights: empty equipped, cargo 1800 kg (3,968 lb); maximum take-off 3300 kg (7,257 lb)
Dimensions: span 15.00 m (49 ft 2½ in); length 12.15 m (39 ft 10¼ in); height 4.60 m (15 ft 1 in)

SIAI-Marchetti S.M.102

On 20 December 1947 SIAI-Marchetti flew the prototype of a six-seat light transport which it designated **SIAI-Marchetti S.M.101**. This was a six-seat cantilever low-wing monoplane with retractable landing gear and powered by a 175-kW (235-hp) Walter Bora radial engine. It was soon discovered that the concept of a single-engine passenger aircraft was unlikely to prove popular, and the company concentrated instead on the twin-engined **S.M.102**, of which the prototype (I-NDIA) flew for the first time at Vergiate airfield on 24 February 1949. A smoothly contoured cantilever low-wing monoplane with a crew of two and having

The SIAI-Marchetti S.M.102 failed to attract any orders from its intended airline market, but did serve in modest numbers with the Italian air force.

cabin accommodation for eight passengers, it was powered by two 373-kW (500-hp) Ranger SGV-770C-1B inverted-Vee engines. The prototype was demonstrated in India and the Middle and Far East without attracting any orders.

The decision was then made to modify the S.M.102 for use by the Aeronautica Militare Italiana. The prototype (MM551) of the new version was first flown on 7 April 1950, and differed

mainly by the installation of two 336-kW (450-hp) Pratt & Whitney R-985 Wasp Junior radial engines, giving a maximum speed of 330 km/h (205 mph); it retained the retractable landing gear and mixed

construction of the original prototype. This version spanned 18.00 m (59 ft 0¾ in) and had a maximum take-off weight of 5050 kg (11,133 lb). A small production run followed.

SIAI-Marchetti S.M.1019

Flown for the first time on 24 May 1969, the **SIAI-Marchetti S.M.1019** prototype was a revision of the Cessna Model 305A/O-1 Bird Dog STOL liaison aircraft to meet an Italian army requirement. Changes were principally the introduction of turboprop powerplant in the form of a 236-kW (317-hp) Allison 250-B15C engine and revision of the tail unit.

The S.M.1019 proved superior to its only competitor, the Macchi AM-3C, and 100 were ordered for the Aviazione Leggera dell'Esercito Italiano, entering service with operational units from summer 1976. The series aircraft are powered by

the uprated 298-kW (400-hp) Allison 250-B17B turboprop and are designated **S.M.1019A** by the manufacturer and **S.M.1019E.I** by the army.

As of early 1993, less than 70 aircraft remained in service with the Aviazione Legerra del'Esercito with seven squadrons and the air arm's training school. They are being progressively withdrawn.

The S.M.1019A spans 10.97 m (35 ft 11¾ in) and has a maximum cruising speed of 280 km/h (174 mph) at sea level. It can carry an underwing stores load of up to 320 kg (705 lb).

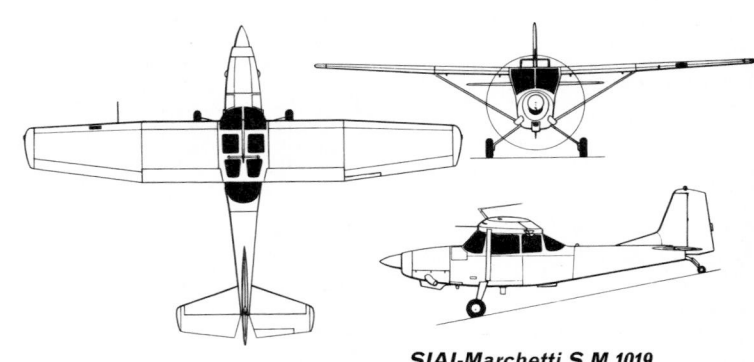

SIAI-Marchetti S.M.1019

SIPA S.10, S.11 and S.12

The Société Industrielle Pour l'Aéronautique (SIPA) was established in France during 1938, initially producing components for other manufacturers under sub-contract. In 1944 the company was given the responsibility of developing the German Arado Ar 396 two-seat advanced trainer, the first of three prototypes being flown on 29 December 1944, after the Liberation. This was put into production for the French air force under the designation **SIPA S.10** (28 built) and was followed by 50 examples of the modified **S.11** which also introduced as powerplant the 433-kW (580-hp) Renault 125 S-12-SO2-3H Vee

The SIPA S.12 advanced trainer spanned 11 m (36 ft 1 in), had a maximum take-off weight of 2325 kg (5,126 lb) and could reach 360 km/h (224 mph).

engine, which was a Renault-built version of the Argus As 411. The designation **S.111** applied to S.11s converted subsequently to an improved standard. Both the SIPA S.10 and S.11 were of mixed construction, but the **S.12** production version (52 built) differed only by introducing an all-metal structure; it was followed by the generally similar **S.121** (58) built with a lighter-weight structure.

A number of S.111 and S.121 aircraft were used by the French air force in Algeria, equipped to carry bombs and rockets for use in a close support role,

and these were redesignated **S.111A** and **S.121A** respectively. The final production figure for all versions built for the French air force totalled 234.

SIPA S.200 Minijet and SIPA 300

Under the designation **SIPA S.200 Minijet**, SIPA flew on 14 January 1952 the prototype of a two-seat lightweight turbo-powered aircraft; this has the distinction of being the world's first all-metal aircraft in this particular category. Intended for use as a basic jet trainer or high-speed liaison aircraft, it was a cantilever mid-wing monoplane with the wing mounted to a fuselage pod, the wing structure carrying twin tubular tailbooms with a twin-fin-and-rudder tail assembly and the booms being united at the rear by a tailplane with elevator. The fuselage pod incorporated an enclosed cabin for two side-by-side seats, and mounted at the rear in the first prototpye a Turboméca Palas I turbojet engine. The second prototype, which differed by being stressed for aerobatics and being provided with wingtip fuel tanks, was powered by the 0.712-kN (353-lb) thrust Palas II turbojet. However, the Minijet was built in only small numbers, four being used for jet conversion training at the St Yan powered flight centre, and two at the Bretigny flight test centre.

Under the designation **SIPA 300**, the

company designed and built the prototype of a more conventional jet trainer that the S.200. The SIPA 300 was a cantilever low-wing monoplane of all-metal construction, with retractable tricycle landing gear, and powered by a 0.712-kN (353-lb) thrust Turboméca Palas II turbojet engine. This was mounted within the fuselage, to the rear of the crew compartment which provided two seats in tandem beneath a continuous transparent canopy, with full dual controls as standard. With a wing span of 8.02 m (26 ft 4 in), the SIPA 300 had a maximum speed of 360 km/h (224 mph).

Specification
SIPA S.200 Minijet
Type: basic jet trainer
Powerplant: one 0.667-kN (331-lb) thrust Turboméca Palas I turbojet
Performance: maximum speed 400 km/h (249 mph) at sea level; service ceiling 8000 m (26,245 ft); range with internal fuel 550 km (343 miles)
Weights: empty 450 kg (992 lb); maximum take-off 780 kg (1,720 lb)

The French SIPA S.200 Minijet was an unusual design in many respects and from the outset was possessed of good performance despite its low-powered engine. The entire cockpit canopy hinged forward for access for the pilots. The first aircraft was exhibited at the Paris air show, Le Bourget, in 1951 and was later used solely as a static testbed. The second aircraft flew on 14 January 1952, a mere 347 days after the design was initiated at SIPA's Suresnes headquarters. Intended as a high-speed trainer or liason type, four aircraft ultimately entered service with the National Powered Flight Centre at St Yan, for jet conversion training.

Dimensions: span 8.00 m (26 ft 3 in); length 5.15 m (16 ft 10¾ in); height 1.78 m (5 ft 10 in); wing area 9.60 m² (103.34 sq ft)

SIPA S.901

In 1947 SIPA designed the **SIPA S.90**, a two-seat light trainer. With a published requirement of the French Service de l'Aviation Légère et Sportive for a two-seat trainer to be used in the organisation's flying schools, SIPA modified the design to conform with the requirement, redesignating the aircraft **S.901**. A cantilever low-wing monoplane of basic wood structure with plywood and fabric covering, it had fixed tailwheel landing gear, two-seat side-by-side enclosed accommodation, and was powered as standard by a Minié 4 DC 30 flat-four

engine. Winning the contest in 1948, the S.901 was built in quantity for the French aero clubs and, in addition, was exported in some numbers. Variants included the **S.902** powered by the 67-kW (90-hp) Continental engine, and the **S.903** tourer with the 69-kW (92-hp) Mathis 4 GB 60 engine, both of these powerplants being of flat-four layout.

Specification
SIPA S.901
Type: two-seat trainer
Powerplant: one 56-kW (75-hp)

There was little remarkable about the SIPA S.901 which nevertheless served most ably as a trainer with French and export customers. One hundred had been built by 1952.

Minié 4 DC 30 flat-four piston engine
Performance: maximum speed 200 km/h (124 mph); service ceiling 4000 m (13,125 ft); range 500 km (311 miles)
Weights: empty 366 kg (807 lb); maximum take-off 600 kg (1,323 lb)

Dimensions: span 8.75 m (28 ft 8½ in); length 5.75 m (18 ft 10½ in); height 1.75 m (5 ft 9 in); wing area 11.20 m² (120.56 sq ft)

SIPA late designs

The final designs of SIPA, before being taken over by an Aérospatiale subsidiary in the late 1960s, included the **SIPA 1000 Coccinelle** two-seat lightplane which was designed for large-scale production. A cantilever low-wing monoplane with fixed tricycle landing gear, it provided enclosed side-by-side seat accommodation and was powered by a 67-kW (90-hp) Continental C90 flat-four engine. The prototype was flown for the first time on 11 June 1955. The ensuing **SIPA 1100** was a multi-role military twin-engined monoplane, suitable for operation from unprepared landing

The installation of a slender turboprop in the nose of the broad SIPA S.2150 Antilope, with its side-by-side cockpit, gave the aircraft an unusual appearance.

strips. A three-seat shoulder-wing monoplane with retractable tailwheel landing gear and powered by two 455-kW (610-hp) Pratt & Whitney R-1340 radial engines, the SIPA 1100 was to have had an armament comprising two 20-mm cannon plus a wide variety of stores carried on external racks. Most interesting was the final design, the

S.2150 Antilope four/five-seat cabin monoplane powered by a 496-ekW (665-eshp) Turboméca Astazou X turboprop engine. First flown on 7 November 1962 and gaining French certification in the spring of 1964, it established six international class records later in that year, and in early 1965 raised the 100-km (62.1-mile) class record to 436 km/h (271 mph). Its planned production was frustrated when SIPA became more closely absorbed into Aérospatiale.

SITAR aircraft

The Société Industrielle de Tolerie pour l'Aéronautique et Matériel Roulant (SITAR) produced some aircraft of the well-known lightplane designer Yves Gardan. These have included the **SITAR GY 100 Bagheera**, suitable for operation as a two-seat trainer or four-seat

light cabin monoplane. A cantilever low-wing monoplane of all-metal construction, with fixed tricycle landing gear, the prototype was flown for the first time on 21 December 1967, powered by an Avco Lycoming O-320 flat-four engine derated to 101 kW (135 hp). An enlarged version of the GY 100 was planned as the **GY 110 Sher Khan** with engine in the 149/224-kW (200/300-hp) range, as well

The SITAR GY 100 Bagheera (named after the black panther in Rudyard Kipling's Jungle Book) bore all the unmistakable characteristics of a design by Yves Gardan.

as a simplified two-seat version designated **GY 90 Mowgli** of which plans

and construction kits were available to amateurs.

SNCAC aircraft

The Société Nationale de Construction Aéronautiques du Centre (SNCAC) was formed with the nationalisation of the French aircraft industry in 1936, combining the well-known organisations of Farman and Hanriot. Often known as Aérocentre or Centre, this new company had of necessity to continue the activities of the former companies, both of which had outstanding civil and military contracts. Thus, SNCAC completed construction of a batch of 11 F.221.1 heavy bombers which had been started by Farman in April 1936, went on to build two batches of the F.222.2, and also completed an Air France contract for four F.224s. Details of these models can be found in the Farman section. In the same way development of the F.223 was continued, but as SNCAC played a more significant role in this aircraft the designation became changed to **SNCAC NC.223**, and details for this

This is the first prototype of the NC.530 with the penultimate tail arrangement of early 1940.

can be found under the entry for Farman NC.223. SNCAC also completed development of the Farman F.470 six-seat crew trainer or coastal reconnaissance floatplane under the designation **NC.470**, producing about 30 for the French navy with the final batch delivered after the beginning of World War II; details can be found under the entry for the Farman NC.470.

When SNCAC was formed, Hanriot was occupied with two basic designs: the H.220/230/232, a two-seat advanced trainer to which SNCAC allocated the designation **NC.600**, and the H.150 three-seat general-purpose military aircraft of which development continued as the **NC.510**. A cantilever shoulder-wing monoplane powered by two wing-

mounted radial engines, the NC.150 displayed a disappointing performance when flown as a prototype in June 1938, leading to extensive redesign under the designation **NC.530**. The first example was flown on 29 June 1939 with the designation **NC.530 Exp**, this being regarded as an experimental rather than prototype aircraft, and it was not until 29 December 1939 that the **NC.530.01** prototype was flown, powered by two 522-kW (700-hp) Gnome-Rhône 14M radial engines. The development pro-

gramme was incomplete by the time of the German invasion in May 1940 and the aircraft was destroyed during the following month. There had been plans to build a version designated **NC.531**, which would have introduced retractable landing gear and 336-kW (450-hp) Renault 12R inverted-Vee engines, as well as an improved **NC.532** of increased span and powered by two 798-kW (1,070-hp) Gnome-Rhône 14N radials, but such plans were frustrated by the events of May 1940.

SNCAC NC.701 and NC.702

Siebel in Germany developed from the Fh 104 Hallore five-seat twin-engined light transport an improved 10-seat development as the Siebel Si 204. Primary wartime production of this latter aircraft was by SNCAC in France, which built it in two versions, as the Si 204A and Si 204D for both French and Luftwaffe service. When the war ended SNCAC continued to build these aircraft as the **SNCAC NC.701** (equivalent to the Si 204D) and the **NC.702** (equivalent to the Si 204A),

The principal external difference between the SNCAC NC.701, as seen here in French military service, and the later NC.702 Martinet was the first aircraft's clean, unstepped cockpit line.

both the with name **Martinet**. They differed by installation of the 440-kW (590-hp) Renault (SNECMA) 12S engine, a French-built version of the German Argus As 411. About 300 were built, a

considerable number of these very useful aircraft being operated by Air France. The 21.83 m (71 ft 7½ in) span NC.702

had a cruising speed of 305 km/h (202 mph) and range of 1400 km (870 miles).

SNCAC FINAL aircraft

Apart from the NC.701/702 Martinet, one of the first post-war products of SNCAC was a production version of the Focke-Wulf Fw 190A which was built under the designation **SNCAC NC.900**. The first NC.900 was flown in March 1945, and of the total of 64 built, 40 were supplied to the French air force and 24 to the French navy. Unsuccessful attempts were made to find a worthwhile market for light planes of indigenous design, these including the **NC.840 Chardonneret** which was an attractive four-seat cabin monoplane of

The SNCAC.854 owed its slightly unusual appearance to its shoulder-mounted wing, a projecting tailplane and small endplate vertical tail surfaces.

braced high-wing configuration. This was followed by the two-seat **NC.853** and **NC.854** with the 56-kW (75-hp) Minié 4DC-32 and the 48-kW (65-hp) Continental A65 engine respectively, the four-seat **NC.856** with a 78-kW (105-hp) Walter engine and (the final development) a twin-engined version of the

NC.856 which had the designation **NC.860**. This was the last aircraft built by SNCAC, and all operations of the company came to an end during 1949.

SNECMA VTOL research aircraft

Primarily an aircraft powerplant design and production organisation, the French company Société National d'Etude et de Construction de Moteurs d'Aviation (SNECMA) became interested, as did Rolls-Royce in the UK, in direct lift from a turbine engine. Having acquired from Professor von Zborowski European rights for his annular wing (or Coléoptère) design, SNECMA initiated in 1952-53 a phase of research and development which led in 1954 to tethered flight tests of a remotely-controlled test vehicle powered by a 0.44-kN (99-lb) thrust SNECMA pulse-jet engine. This led to the full-size pilotless and remotely-controlled **Atar Volant** (flying-star) **C.400 P-1** test vehicle, comprising a

28.44-kN (6,393-lb) thrust SNECMA Atar 101DV turbo-jet engine mounted within a vertical nacelle that was carried on a simple four-wheel landing gear. A first tethered flight on 22 September 1956 was followed by 205 test flights. The first piloted Atar Volant was the **C.400 P-2**, with an ejection seat mounted above the air inlet, first flown untethered on 14 May 1957 and subsequently, completing 123 free and tethered flights by early 1958. Final version of the Atar Volant was the **C.400 P-3**, an improved version of the P-2 which also introduced the more powerful 34.32-kN (7,716-lb) thrust Atar 101E turbo-jet.

These test rigs were followed by the **C.450-01 Coléoptère** prototype re-

search aircraft, which basically combined the C.400 P-3 with an annular wing based on that designed by von Zborowski. The first vertical free flight of the C.450-01 was made on 6 May 1959, but during a transition from vertical to horizontal flight on 25 July the aircraft crashed and was destroyed; the pilot ejected successfully and was uninjured.

The SNECMA C.450 project was one of the most ambitious aeronautical undertakings of the 1950s, with the intention of producing an annular-winged VTOL aircraft capable of high performance in conventional flight.

SOCATA GY 80 Horizon and ST 10 Diplomate

The French company Société de Construction d'Avions de Tourisme et d'Affaires (SOCATA) was formed in 1966, initially as a subsidiary of Sud-Aviation, but subsequent mergers have since made the company a subsidiary of Aérospatiale. SOCATA produced for Sud-Aviation under licence from Yves Gardan a four-seat cantilever low-wing monoplane which was given the designation **SOCATA GY 80 Horizon**. With semi-retractable tricycle landing gear, and power provided by a 134-kW (180-hp) Avco Lycoming O-360-A flat four engine, the 9.70 m (31 ft 9¾ in) span Horizon has a maximum speed of 250 km/h (155 mph) at sea level. SOCATA built more than 250 of these aircraft before production was ended in

1969, and developed from it an improved four-seat cabin monoplane which was named **Super Horizon 2000** and **Provence** before entering production as the **ST 10 Diplomate** in 1969. This differed from the GY 80 by having a slightly lengthened fuselage, a revised tail unit and landing gear, and the more

Despite its good pedigree, the SOCATA ST 10 Diplomate failed to secure any real foothold outside its native France in the highly competitive market for four-seat lightplanes which was so effectively dominated by American designs. Small numbers can still be found in use at airfields around Europe.

powerful 149-kW (200-hp) Avco Lycoming IO-360-C1B flat-four engine. Despite

improved performance, with a maximum speed of 280 km/h (174 mph) at sea level, the Diplomate failed to gain any worthwhile interest and only 56 had been delivered when production was terminated in 1975.

SOCATA Rallye series

SOCATA's association with light aircraft construction began with a tourer designed by Morane-Saulnier, which had become a subsidiary of Sud-Aviation in 1965, the year before SOCATA's formation. SOCATA began its activities as a subsidiary of Sud-Aviation by building versions of these aircraft, retaining the original Rallye names until 1979. All are basically cantilever low-wing monoplanes with fixed tricycle landing gear and variations in powerplant and accommodation. The old Rallye designations were scrapped in 1979 when a new production programme was initiated in that year, new names then being allocated. Most recent production aircraft in the Rallye series, of which SOCATA built approximately 3,300, include the **SOCATA Galopin** (formerly **Rallye 110ST**) two-seat trainer cleared for spins or three/four-seater with spins prohibited, which is powered by a 82-kW (110-hp) Avco Lycoming O-235-L2A engine. This model is also being built

Notable for its bulbous cockpit (a feature of later Morane-Saulnier designs) and distinctive empennage, the SOCATA Ralleye 100T was the baseline model for the highly successful Ralleye family.

under licence in Poland by P.Z.L. Warszawa-Okecie as the **P.Z.L.-110 Koliber** (humming bird), in two/three-seat configuration and powered by a 94-kW (126-hp) P.Z.L. licence-built Franklin 4A-235-B1 engine. The **Galérien (Rallye 180T)** is a special glider-tug or banner-towing versions with a 134-kW (180-hp) Avco Lycoming O-360-A3A, but the **Gabier (Rallye 235GT)** differs by being a high-performance version with STOL capability which has a strengthened airframe and the far more powerful Avco Lycoming O-540 engine. Variants available included one which has tailwheel instead of tricycle landing gear, and the **R 235 Guerrier** (warrior)

military version of the Gabier. The R 235 differs from the earlier machine by having underwing pylons for the carriage of weapons such as rockets and machine-gun pods, as well as practice bombs, flares and a reconnaissance pack.

Specification
SOCATA Gabier
Type: four-seat cabin monoplane
Powerplant: one 175-kW (235-hp)

Avco Lycoming O-540-B4B5 flat-six piston engine
Performance: maximum speed 275 km/h (171 mph) at sea level; service ceiling 4500 m (14,765 ft); range with maximum fuel 1090 km (677 miles)
Weights: empty 694 kg (1,530 lb); maximum take-off 1200 kg (2,646 lb)
Dimensions: span 9.75 m (31 ft 11¾ in); length 7.25 m (23 ft 9½ in); height 2.80 m (9 ft 2½ in)

SOCATA TB 9, TB 10/11, TB 20 and TB 200 XL

Early in 1975 SOCATA initiated the design of a four/five-seat cabin monoplane which it designated **SOCATA TB 10** and later named **Tobago**. First flown on 23 February 1977, and powered by a 119-kW (160-hp) Avco Lycoming O-320-D2A engine, this TB 10 became the founder member of a new series of lightplanes of cantilever low-wing layout with an essentially all-metal structure and fixed tricycle landing gear. A second prototype followed with a 134-kW (180-hp) Avco Lycoming O-360-A1AD engine; the decision to produce both versions resulted in the lower-powered aircraft being regarded as a four-seater and being redesignated **TB 9 Tampico**. The third of the series was flown for the first time on 14 November 1980 and this, the **TB 20 Trinidad**, differs by having retractable tricycle landing gear and a more powerful engine, plus minor airframe changes related to these installations and the increased power. The prototype of an addition to the series was exhibited at the 1983 Paris air show and this, basically similar to the TB 10 and intended for aerobatic flight at training centres for professional pilots, differs mainly by having a Christen inverted flight system for the powerplant. Designated **TB 11**, initial production examples became available in 1984, though the name was never really applied to what was, in effect, a TB 10 with a 134-kW (180-hp) engine. Other proposed, but unbuilt, members of the family included the **TB 15** and **TB 16** which were, respectively, Tobagos and Trinidads fitted with a new Porsche PFM.3200 engine. The family has sold well not least in the United States, starved of modern indigenous lightplanes by its product liability laws. Over 1,100 aircraft had been sold

Though bearing a resemblance to earlier SOCATA lightplanes, the Tobago differs by having a fixed tricycle undercarriage and greater passenger space. It is designed to supplement rather than supplant Rallyes.

by the time a new addition was made in March 1991, with the first flight of the **TB 200 Tobago XL**. This four-to-five seat aircraft is largely similar to the basic TB 10 but is powered by a more powerful 149-kW (200-hp) Textron Lycoming O-230-D2A engine.

Specification
SOCATA TB 20 Trinidad
Type: four/five-seat lightplane
Powerplant: one 186-kW (250-hp) Avco Lycoming IO-540-C4DS5D flat-six piston engine
Performance: maximum speed 310 km/h (193 mph); service ceiling 6095 m (20,000 ft); maximum range with maximum fuel 1785 km (1,109 miles)
Weights: empty 772 kg (1,702 lb); maximum take-off 1335 kg (2,943 lb)
Dimensions: span 9.76 m (32 ft 0¼ in); length 7.71 m (25 ft 3½ in); height 2.85 m (9 ft 4½ in); wing area 11.90 m² (128.09 sq ft)

A cross section of the SOCATA general aviation family features, from the rear, the baseline TB 9 Tampico, a TB 20 Trinidad and, closest to the camera, a TB 21 Trinidad. The TB 20 benefits from a retractable undercarriage, while the TB 21 has a turbocharged Lycoming T10-540-AB1AD engine.

SOCATA TB 31 Omega

In December 1979 Aérospatiale flew the prototype of its two-seat piston-engined **TB 30 Epsilon**, which became the Armée de l'Air's basic training aircraft. Marketing of this aircraft was passed on to the SOCATA general aviation subsidiary, which is now responsible for all Aérospatiale's prop-driven designs. The first Epsilon was later fitted with an experimental turboprop engine and SOCATA decided to develop the design into the privately funded **TB 31 Omega** trainer. Fitted with a Turbomeca TP 319 engine the first Omega (F-WOMG) flew on 30 April 1989. Its appearance has moved away from that of the Epsilon and the two aircraft now share a 60 per cent airframe commonality. The chief difference between the two are the TB 31's extended nose, large unrestricted Poly 76 canopy, swept tail and extended tail fillet. The cockpit is equipped with Martin-Baker 15FC 'through the canopy' ejection seats, effective at zero altitudes and at speeds above 60 kt (111 km/h; 69 mph). A CRT display system for radio and navigation data, which was developed for Portuguese export Epsilons, is fitted as standard to the Omega. The air-

frame has been restressed for greater tolerances and four underwing hardpoints are available. In August 1991 SOCATA signed an agreement with the Sabreliner Corporation to enter the aircraft for the USN/USAF JPATS competition. Sabreliner currently supports all extant civil and military Sabreliners/T-39s and is in charge of the US Navy's Undergraduate Naval Flight Officer training programme, utilising T-39Ns.

Specification
SOCATA TB 31 Omega
Type: basic turboprop trainer
Powerplant: one 364-kW (488-shp) Turbomeca TP 319-1AS Arrius turboprop, derated to 268 kW (360 shp)
Performance: maximum level speed 280 kt; (510 km/h, 322 mph); service ceiling 9145 m (30,000 ft); range at 75 per cent power with reserves 1309 km (813 miles)
Weights: empty equipped 860 kg

(1,896 lb); maximum take-off 1450 kg (3,197 lb)
Dimensions: span 7.92 m (25 ft 11¾ in); height 2.68 m (8 ft 9½ in); length 7.81 m (25 ft 7½ in)

SOCATA's TB 31 Omega is essentially a private venture by Aérospatiale, developed in the hope of breaking into the lucrative, if over-subscribed, advanced trainer market.

SOCATA TBM-700

On 12 June 1987 SOCATA and the Mooney Aircraft Corporation announced their intention to build a six/eight-seat single-engined 'biz-prop'. Mooney had already gone some distance towards developing such an aircraft. At their plant in Columbus, Ohio, Roy LoPresti had designed the Lycoming TIO-540-X27-powered **MX**, known later as the **M.30 Mooney 301**. A prototype (N301MX) was flown in April 1983 but the project was suspended due to funding difficulties, in favour of the new partnership with SOCATA. The French government agreed to meet one third of the new development costs, with SOCATA having design leadership for the project, including construction and certification of the prototypes. The new aircraft would be known as the **TBM 700**.

In June 1988 Valmet of Finland joined the project. Three initial aircraft were built, with Mooney having responsibility for the rear fuselage and wings, SOCATA the forward fuselage and Valmet the tail. Final assembly was at SOCATA's Tarbes-Ossun-Lourdes plant. The first aircraft (F-WTBM) flew on 14 July 1988, the second (F-WKPG) on 3 August 1989, and the third (F-WKDL) on 11 October 1989. By this time Valmet had withdrawn from the programme, leaving the two original partners to continue development.

The TBM 700 interior was revised to seat between four and seven passengers. The cockpit was configured for two pilots, though single pilot certification was one of the prime development goals. The powerplant is a tried and tested PT6A, with a McCauley four-bladed constant-speed fully-featherable metal propeller fitted. The fin is swept, though the wing is essentially straight.

The flaps were designed by ATR and are constructed from Nomex honeycomb composites. Fuel is carried in integral wing tanks.

French DGAC certification was obtained in January 1990, with FAA FAR Pt 23 approval following in August. The first customer delivery was made on 21 December 1990. Mooney finally withdrew from the TBM 700 in May 1991 but, to date, SOCATA has retained the aircraft's previous designation. By early 1993 84 TBM 700s had been built, with production progressing at four a month.

In service in seven countries, the type has also achieved its first military order, as a liaison aircraft with ET 65 of the Armée de l'Air.

Specification
SOCATA TBM 700
Type: four/seven-seat pressurised turboprop transport
Powerplant: one 552-kW (700-shp) Pratt & Whitney Canada PT6A-64 turboprop
Performance: maximum cruising speed 300 kt (555 km/h; 345 mph);

After a protracted development and a slow start, the SOCATA TBM 700 turbo-powered business aircraft is now starting to gather momentum.

service ceiling 9150 m (30,000 ft); maximum range 2985 km (1,855 miles)
Weights: empty equipped 1826 kg (4,025 lb); maximum take-off 2992 kg (6,595 lb)
Dimensions: span 12.16 m (39 ft 10¾ in); height 3.99 m (13 ft 1 in); length 10.43 m (34 ft 2½ in)

SPAD A 1 TO A 5

When the aircraft manufacturing company Société Pour les Appareils Deperdussin (SPAD) became bankrupt, the company was taken over by Louis Blériot who renamed it the Société Pour l'Aviation et ses Dérivés, thus astutely retaining the initials SPAD. This company itself was to build more than 2,000 military aircraft during World War I, but far greater numbers were manufactured by sub-contractors. SPAD military aircraft began with the **SPAD A 1**, which was of unusual configuration. In the UK the Royal Aircraft Factory solved the problem of providing a wide field of fire for a forward firing machine-gun by adopting a pusher layout, with the engine mounted behind the wing at the

The SPAD A 4 was one of those many unfortunate designs that seemed good (or at least adequate) on paper, but which were a positive liability to all concerned once in service.

rear of a fuselage nacelle, and the pilot and gunner in tandem at the front of the nacelle, the gunner and his weapon being accommodated in the forward position. SPAD accepted that this was a good solution to the problem but achieved it in a different way, basically adopting a conventional biplane structure with a rotary engine mounted at the front, but contrived a gunner's position in a structure forward of the propeller.

This arrangement proved unpopular with both pilot and gunner, as the propeller rotated between them at close quarters. Prototypes were built of the A 1 and **A 2**, both with Le Rhône rotary engines; of the **A 3** which was a dual-control trainer

version of the A 2; of the **A 4**, which was an improved version of the A2; and of the **A 5**, which was powered by a Renault 8 engine. Reportedly about 100 A 2s were built, and 12 examples of the A 4 version were sold to Russia.

SPAD S.VII and S.XII

After experience with the SPAD A 1 to A 5, Louis Béchereau adopted a far more conventional layout for the single-seat **S.V** tractor biplane which was flown toward the end of 1915 and this, in effect, served as the prototype for the **SPAD S.VII** which was the company's first really successful military aircraft. With a fabric-covered all-wood structure, except for aluminium panels over the forward fuselage, the S.VII had fixed tail-skid landing gear and a round frontal radiator for its Hispano-Suiza eight-cylinder Vee engine. First flown in April 1916, the S.VII had a beautifully clean airframe for its day and this, combined with the power and reliability of its Hispano-Suiza engine, ensured that it was quickly ordered into production. Delivery of the

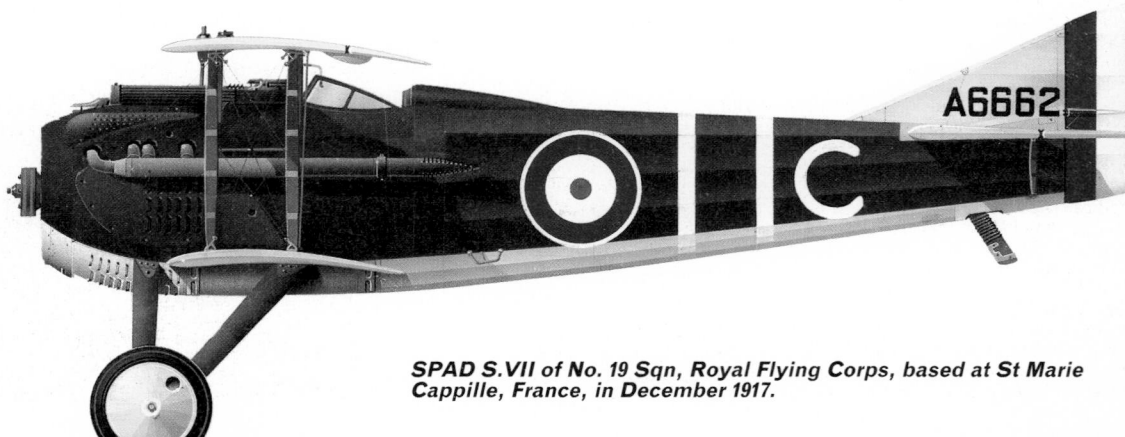

SPAD S.VII of No. 19 Sqn, Royal Flying Corps, based at St Marie Cappille, France, in December 1917.

initial version, powered by a 112-kW (150-hp) Hispano-Suiza 8Aa engine, began in September 1916, and within the first year more than 500 had been built. The second production version, which introduced the more powerful 134-kW (180-hp) 8Ac engine and wings of slightly increased span, was built by SPAD and under sub-contract to a total of about 6,000 aircraft. In addition to the S.VIIs used in large numbers by the French armed services, the types served also with the Royal Flying Corps and Royal Naval Service; the Belgian 5th Squadron; Italy, which had 214 to equip five *squadriglie*; the American Expeditionary Force which took 189 aircraft; and Russia which received 43.

Two development aircraft were flown in 1917, one powered by a Renault 12D engine and the other by a 149-kW (200-hp) Hispano-Suiza 8Bc, and it was this latter aircraft which, when equipped with a 37-mm cannon in addition to its standard Vickers machine-gun, was designated **SPAD XII**. Flown in prototype form on 5 July 1917, the S.XII was built to a total of 300, some with a 164-kW (220-hp) Hispano-Suiza 8Bec engine, and a small number of a floatplane version were used by the Royal Naval Air Service.

Many S.VIIs were in civil use after World War I had ended, being used primarily in a training role, some until 1928. Final derivatives were the **SPAD 62** and **SPAD 72** intended specifically for a training role, which were flown in 1923.

Specification
SPAD S.VII (major production)
Type: single-seat fighter
Powerplant: one 180-kW (134-shp) Hispano-Suiza 8Ac Vee piston engine
Performance: maximum speed 190 km/h (118 mph) at 2000 m (6,560 ft); service ceiling 5485 m

(18,000 ft); endurance 2 hours 15 minutes
Weights: maximum take-off 755 kg (1,664 lb)
Dimensions: span 7.82 m (25 ft 7¾ in); length 6.16 m (20 ft 2½ in); height 2.35 m (7 ft 8½ in)
Armament: one forward-firing

This Italian SPAD S.VII has been immaculately restored by a team of dedicated enthusiasts at FIAR's Baranzate di Bollante plant, in Milan.

synchronised 7.7-mm (0.303-in) Vickers machine-gun

SPAD S.XIII

Not surprisingly, the success of the SPAD S.VII led to developments of the same basic design. Thus, just before introduction of the SPAD S.XII, the company used the S.VII as the basis for a two-seat light bomber/reconnaissance aircraft which differed primarily by having slightly swept and staggered wings to compensate for the altered centre-of-gravity position of the lengthened fuselage. Designated **SPAD S.XI** and introduced into service in late 1917, the model was powered by a new and more powerful (175-kW/235-hp) version of the Hispano-Suiza 8 engine from which the teething problems had not been eliminated. The resulting unreliability of this powerplant, coupled with instability derived from the aircraft's sensitivity to load distribution, made the type unpopular and it was withdrawn from front-line use in mid-1918.

The **SPAD S.XIII** was, however, a very different story, its success considerably exceeding that of the S.VII with a total of 8,472 built. The S.XIII differed from the S.VII by having a slight increase in wing span, improved ailerons and other aerodynamic refinements, plus the increased power from an alternative version of the Hispano-Suiza 8B engine fitted in the S.XII. The prototype was flown for the first time on 4 April 1917 and its considerable improvement in performance ensured an early entry into service, the first examples reaching the Western Front by the end of May 1917. It replaced the S.VII and later Nieuports in the French fighter squadrons, was flown by aces such as Fonck, Guynemer and Nungesser, and served also with the Royal Flying Corps and the air forces of Belgium, Italy and the USA. An almost insatiable demand for this very capable fighter meant that outstanding orders for some 10,000 aircraft were cancelled at the end of World War I, and in the im-

SPAD S.XIII of No. 23 Sqn, Royal Flying Corps, based in France during the second half of 1917, and early 1918.

mediate post-war years the type was exported to Belgium, Czechoslovakia, Japan and Poland.

An improved version of the S.XIII was introduced into service shortly before the end of the war, a single-seat fighter/photo-reconnaissance aircraft which had the designation **SPAD S.XVII**. Equipped with two cameras, but with armament reduced to only a single machine-gun, it had a refined and strengthened structure to cater for installation of a 224-kW (300-hp) Hispano-Suiza 8F engine which gave this version a maximum speed of 240 km/h (149 mph) at optimum altitude. Production totalled only 20 examples, and construction of a projected improved variant designated **SPAD S.XXI** was prevented by an end to the war.

Specification
SPAD S.XIII
Type: single-seat fighter
Powerplant: one 220-kW (164-shp) Hispano-Suiza 8Be Vee piston engine

Performance: maximum speed 224 km/h (139 mph) at 2000 m (6,560 ft); service ceiling 6650 m (21,815 ft); endurance 2 hours
Weights: maximum take-off 845 kg (1,863 lb)
Dimensions: span 8.10 m (26 ft 6¾ in); length 6.30 m (20 ft 8 in); height 2.35 m (7 ft 8½ in)

Armament: two forward-firing synchronised 7.7-mm (0.303-in) Vickers machine-guns

The S.XIIIC-1 was selected by the Bolling Comission for mass production in the US. Two thousand were ordered from Curtiss and then cancelled.

SPCA aircraft

The French company Société Provençale Constructions Aéronautiques (SPCA) was established as an aviation division of the Société Provençale de Constructions Navales and the Messageries Maritimes. It began its activities by building the **SPCA Météore 63** three-engined biplane flying-boat designed by the Compagnie Générale de Constructions Aéronautique, three of these five-passenger aircraft entering service with Air Union in 1926. Subsequently constructed under licence were the **Paulhan-Pillard E.5** three-engined civil flying-boats, which was powered by three 313-kW (420-hp) Gnome-Rhône radial engines, and from the same source the **T3-BN.4** coastal patrol/torpedo-bomber, a large seaplane carried on twin floats which was powered by two 358-kW (480-hp) Gnome-Rhône Jupiter radials.

The company's first original design was the unusual **SPCA 30** five-seat twin-engined fighter, a cantilever low-wing monoplane of 26.50 m (86 ft 11¼ in) span with a central nacelle mounted to the wing centre-section to accommodate a gunner/navigator/observer in the nose and two pilots in separate tandem cockpits above the centre-section. To each side of the nacelle was a conventional fuselage structure, each with a 485-kW (650-hp) Lorraine 18Kd Vee engine mounted conventionally in the nose, a machine-gun-

ner's position to the rear of the wing, and a fin and rudder at the rear, with the two fuselages united by a tailplane with three sections of elevator. All five crew positions were interconnected by crawlways, and the fixed landing gear incorporated a tailskid at the rear of each fuselage.

More practical was the **SPCA 40T** civil transport, a cantilever high-wing monoplane powered by three 101-kW (135-hp) Salmson 9Nc radial engines. This accommodated a crew of two in a cockpit just forward of the wing leading edge, with behind and below them an enclosed cabin suitable for cargo, mail, or four to five passengers. A small number were produced and are reputed to have given reliable service. To meet a French government requirement for a single-engined two-seat colonial transport monoplane, the company designed the cantilever high-wing **SPCA 81** which had fixed tailskid landing gear and, powered by a Gnome-Rhône 7Kb radial engine, had accommodation for a crew of two and four passengers. It was followed in 1933 by the larger three-crew **SPCA 90** of similar overall configuration, but which was powered by three 261-kW (350-hp) Gnome-Rhône 7Kd

The SPCA 81 featured a tall, box-like fuselage capable of carrying four passengers as well as a two-man crew.

radial engines. Required for similar general-purpose transport use and operated by a crew of three, its cabin was large enough for use in an ambulance role carrying two stretcher cases and a medical attendant. Both versions are reported to have seen service in French Morocco, and the last aircraft to be built by SPCA before the company abandoned aircraft design/manufacture in 1935 was a civil transport version of the SPCA 90. Designated **SPCA 91.T**, it differed only by having the cabin area revised to accommodate eight passengers and to provide them with baggage space and a lavatory.

Specification
SPCA 81
Type: colonial transport aircraft
Powerplant: one 224-kW (300-shp) Gnome-Rhône 7Kb radial piston engine
Performance: maximum speed 220 km/h (137 mph); service ceiling 6200 m (20,340 ft); range 700 km (435 miles)
Weights: maximum take-off 2030 kg (4,475 lb)
Dimensions: span 15.00 m (49 ft 2½ in); length 11.00 m (36 ft 1 in); height 3.15 m (10 ft 4 in); wing area 31.50 m² (339.07 sq ft)

Saab-17

The Swedish company Svenska Aeroplan AB was established in 1937, combining AB Svenska Jarnvagsverkstaderna and Svenska Flygmotor AB, to build aircraft and aero-engines for the Swedish government and for export. Early licence production covered the Douglas 8A-1, similar to the US Army Air Corps' A-17; the Junkers Ju 86A twin-engined bomber; and the North American NA-16, from which was developed in the USA the AT-6 Texan. Saab's first original design was for a two-seat reconnaissance aircraft to meet an official requirement, but following the first flight of the **Saab-17** prototype on 18 May 1940 the company made the proposal that its development as a bomber should be given consideration by the Flygvapen. Evaluation of the prototype led to the aircraft being developed for this role as well as for reconnaissance, and 325 were built. A cantilever mid-wing monoplane with retractable tail-wheel landing gear, the Saab-17 had its crew accommodated beneath a long continuous canopy. Powerplant varied, the **B17A** dive-bomber having the 794-kW (1,065-hp) Swedish-built Pratt & Whitney R-1830-SC3G Twin Wasp radial, the **B17B** dive-bomber and similar **S17B** (equipped for the reconnaissance role) the 731-kW (980-hp) Swedish-built Bristol Pegasus XXIV radial, and the **B17C** dive-bomber (which differed from the B17B only in its engine, the Piaggio P.XIbis). Included in the total production were 38 examples of the **S17BS**, a maritime patrol version of the B17B on twin floats. Many of the landplane versions were later given retractable ski landing gear for operation from snow-covered surfaces.

The Saab 17's clean lines meant that it was often mistaken for a fighter by aircraft intruding into Swedish air space. These lines were unaffected by the addition of a retractable ski-undercarriage.

The Saab B17B was the dive-bomber version of the basic Saab B17 series. It was fitted with a bomb-crutch faired into the underside of the fuselage to swing the bomb under the clear of the propeller arc.

Entering service with the Flygvapen in 1941, the Saab-17 was notable for the robust construction that has since been a feature of the company's designs, and the type remained in service until 1948. After World War II 47 were delivered to the Ethiopian air force.

Specification
Saab-17 (B17C)
Type: two-seat dive-bomber
Powerplant: one 761-kW (1,020-hp)

Piaggio P.XIbis RC.40D radial piston engine
Performance: maximum speed 435 km/h (270 mph); cruising speed 370 km/h (230 mph)
Weight: maximum take-off 3865 kg (8,521 lb)
Dimensions: span 13.70 m (44 ft

11¼ in); length 9.80 m (32 ft 1¾ in); height 4.40 m (14 ft 5¼ in); wing area 28.50 m² (306.78 sq ft)
Armament: two 13.2-mm (0.52-in) M/39A machine-guns in wings and one 7.9-mm (0.31-in) M/22 machine-gun on a trainable mount in rear position, plus up to 680 kg (1,499 lb) of bombs

Saab-18

Designed in the late 1930s to meet an official Swedish requirement for a reconnaissance aircraft, the **Saab-18** did not fly in prototype form until 19 June 1942. The delay was the result of changing requirements, the two **Saab-18A** prototypes being redesigned and equipped for the light bomber or dive-bomber role. A cantilever mid-wing monoplane, primarily of metal construction, the Saab-18 had retractable tailwheel landing gear, a twin-fin-and-rudder tail unit, and was powered as first flown by two 794-kW (1,065-hp) Swedish-built Pratt & Whitney R-1830 Twin Wasp radial engines in wing-mounted nacelles. The crew comprised a pilot, navigator/gunner and bomb-aimer, the last having a position in the glazed nose of the fuselage. Early testing of the prototypes revealed that the Saab-18A was underpowered, but with no immediate remedy available the type was ordered into production in **B18A** bomber and **S18A** photo-reconnaissance versions, built to a combined total of 60 aircraft;

late production examples of the S18A also carried radar equipment. The availability in 1944 of a Swedish licence-built version of the much more powerful Daimler-Benz DB 605B powerplant led to the single **Saab-18B** prototype, first flown on 10 June 1944 and followed by 120 **B18B** dive-bomber production aircraft. Final production version was the **T18B** (62 built) which had been developed to serve as a torpedo-bomber but was, instead, completed as an attack aircraft. With a crew of two, this had an armament of two 20-mm cannon plus a 57-mm Bofors gun mounted beneath the nose. The first of the B18A bombers began to enter service with the Flygvapen in June 1944 and production of the last T18B ended in 1948, these 242 production aircraft providing valuable service until the last of them was retired in 1956.

Specification
Saab-18B (B18B)
Type: light bomber/dive-bomber
Powerplant: two 1100-kW (1,475-hp) Daimler-Benz DB 605B inverted Vee piston engines

Performance: maximum speed 575 km/h (357 mph) at optimum altitude; service ceiling 9800 m (32,150 ft); maximum range 2600 km (1,616 miles)
Weight: maximum take-off 8800 kg (19,400 lb)
Dimensions: span 17.00 m (55 ft 9¼ in); length 13.23 m (43 ft 5 in); height 4.35 m (14 ft 3¼ in); wing area 43.75 m^2 (470.94 sq ft)
Armament: one fixed forward-firing 7.9-mm (0.31-in) M/22F machine-gun

The Saab B-18B dive-bomber version of the Saab-18 was distinguishable from its predecessor models by its use of the Daimler-Benz DB 605 inverted-Vee engine, but without the undernose 57-mm Bofors gun of the similar T18B attack aircraft.

and two 13.2-mm (0.52-in) machineguns on trainable mounts, plus an internal bombload of 1500 kg (3,307 lb) and provision to carry air-to-air rockets

Saab-21

In 1941, when the Flygvapen was equipped with a mixture of fighter aircraft of Italian and US origin, it was decided to initiate design and development of an indigenous aircraft in this category that would be suitable for use also in an attack role. The resulting design was of unusual configuration, being a cantilever low-wing monoplane having moderate wing sweep, with central fuselage nacelle to accommodate the pilot on an ejection seat and a rear-mounted powerplant in pusher configuration, twin booms extending aft from the wings with twin fins and rudders united by the tailplane with elevator, and retractable tricycle landing gear. The first of three **Saab-21A** prototypes was flown on 30 July 1943 and these, like a few early production aircraft, were powered by the imported Daimler-Benz DB 605; all subsequent production had a Swedish licence-built version of this engine.

Saab J21A of F12, Flygvapen.

When introduced into service in late 1945 as the **J21A-1** the new type was the only pusher-engined fighter to become operational during World War II, being followed by the generally similar **J21A-2** and, finally, by the **A21A** attack aircraft, these three versions being built to a total of 299 before production ended in 1948. The A21A had the same armament as the J21A fighter, was equipped to carry rockets or light bombs on underwing racks, and had provision for the in-

stallation of a ventral gun pack housing eight 13.2-mm (0.52-in) machine-guns.

Specification
Saab-21A (J21A)
Type: single-seat fighter
Powerplant: one 1100-kW (1,475-hp) Swedish licence-built Daimler-Benz DB 605B inverted Vee piston engine
Performance: maximum speed 640 km/h (398 mph) at optimum altitude; service ceiling 11000 m

(36,090 ft)
Weights: empty 3250 kg (7,165 lb); maximum take-off 4150 kg (9,149 lb)
Dimensions: span 11.60 m (38 ft 0¾ in); length 10.45 m (34 ft 3½ in); height 3.96 m (13 ft 0 in); wing area 22.20 m^2 (238.97 sq ft)
Armament: one nose-mounted 20-mm Hispano cannon and four 13.2-mm (0.52-in) Browning machineguns, two in the nose and two in the wings

Saab-21R

To produce Sweden's first turbo jet-powered fighter, Svenska Aeroplan adapted its Saab-21 design to accept the installation of a de Havilland Goblin gas turbine. This seemed a simple way to gain experience with this form of powerplant and, at the same time, extend the performance capability of the proven Saab-21 design; however, it was to prove rather more difficult a process than had been anticipated. The first requirement was for the aft fuselage nacelle to be widened to accept the new engine and the tailplane moved to the top of the fin to be clear of the jet efflux. It was also decided that because of the higher performance of this aircraft some structural strengthening was essential, and as there was no longer any need to be concerned about propeller ground

Saab A21R of F7, Flygvapen, based at Satenas, with a gun pod.

clearance the landing gear struts were shortened. In this form the first **Saab-21R** prototype was flown initially on 10 March 1947, but almost two years elapsed before all development-problem fixes had been finalised, the first deliveries of production aircraft starting during February 1949. The original Saab-21 production order had been for 120 aircraft, but because of delay in its development a contemporary programme for the specially-designed turbojet-powered

Saab-29 was well advanced, with a result that the Saab-21R order was reduced to only 60 aircraft. These were produced as the **J21RA** with a 1361-kg (3,000-lb) thrust de Havilland Goblin 2 engine, and **J21RB** with a licence-built Goblin turbojet, 30 of each being built.

After comparatively short service in the fighter role, all were converted as attack aircraft, redesignated **A21R** and **A21RB** respectively, and carrying 10 100-mm (3.9-in) or five 180-mm (7.09-in) Bofors rocket projectiles, or 10 80-mm (3.15-in) anti-tank rockets.

Specification
Saab-21RB (J21RB)
Type: single-seat fighter
Powerplant: one 1500-kg (3,307-lb) thrust Swedish licence-built de Havilland Goblin 3 turbojet

Performance: maximum speed 800 km/h (497 mph) at 8000 m (26,245 ft); service ceiling 12000 m (39,370 ft); range 720 km (447 miles)
Weight: maximum take-off 4990 kg (11,001 lb)
Dimensions: span 11.60 m (38 ft 0¾ in); length 10.45 m (34 ft 3½ in); height 2.95 m (9 ft 8 in)
Armament: one nose-mounted 20-mm Hispano cannon and four 13.2-mm (0.52-in) Browning machine-guns, two in the nose and two in the wings

Saab-29

Saab's original project for the **Saab-29** had envisaged it as a conventional monoplane powered by a de Havilland Goblin turbojet, but information on German swept-wing research which became available soon after the end of hostilities in Europe (combined with development of the more powerful de Havilland Ghost turbojet) resulted in redesign to incorporate these features. As the company had no experience of the behaviour of a swept wing it was decided to use a Saab Safir lightplane to test a wing of this configuration, a reduced-scale wing with 25° of sweepback being installed and flown on this aircraft. Negotiations were initiated with de Havilland for licence-production of the Ghost turbojet in Sweden. The first of four Saab-29 prototypes was flown initially on 1 September 1948, but it was not until the spring of 1951 that the aircraft was ordered into production, being the first aircraft in its class to be production-built in Western Europe. Of cantilever shoulder-wing monoplane configuration, the Saab-29 had retractable tricycle landing gear, its powerplant mounted within the rotund fuselage, and with the pilot accommodated on an ejection seat in a pressurised cockpit.

Saab **J 29A** fighters began to enter service with the Flygvapen later in 1951, the type remaining in production until

April 1956, by which time a total of 661 had been built. They remained in service until 1958 when their gradual replacement by the Saab-32 Lansen began, and in 1961-2 30 ex-Flygvapen **J 29F**s were supplied to Austria.

Variants
J 29A: first single-seat fighter production version of which initial deliveries were made in April 1951
J 29B: second improved production version with increased internal tank fuselage, which replaced the J 29A in production during early 1953
A 29B: attack version of the J 29B to which it was generally similar
S 29C: photo-reconnaissance version, similar in construction to J 29B, but equipped with six fully automatic cameras and improved navigational equipment; initial deliveries made in late 1953; equipped retrospectively with outer wing panels introduced on J 29F
J 29D: experimental version, built in small numbers, to evaluate an afterburner of Swedish design
J 29E: first flown on 3 December 1953, introduced outer wing panels incorporating a 'saw-tooth' leading edge to give improved transonic flight characteristic; the afterburner tested in the J 29D was introduced on the J 29E production line
J 29F: final production version, combining all the improvements of

Nicknamed the 'Tunnan' (Barrel) for obvious reasons, the Saab-29 was a considerable achievement for the Swedish aero industry. Seen here are two examples of the ultimate production variant, the J 29F.

earlier versions
A 29F: attack version of the J 29F; in addition to the standard armament of the J 29F was able to carry 24 75-mm (2.95-in) Bofors air-to-air rockets, or up to 500 kg (1,102 lb) of mixed weapons on underwing attachments

Specification
Saab-29F (J 29F)
Type: single-seat fighter
Powerplant: one 2800-kg (6,173-lb) afterburning thrust Flygmotor RM2B (licence-built de Havilland Ghost) turbojet

Performance: maximum speed 1060 km/h (658 mph) at 1550 m (5,085 ft); service ceiling 15500 m (50,855 ft); maximum range 2700 km (1,678 miles)
Weights: empty operating 4300 kg (9,480 lb); maximum take-off 8000 kg (17,637 lb)
Dimensions: span 11.00 m (36 ft 1 in); length 10.13 m (33 ft 2¾ in); height 3.73 m (12 ft 3¾ in); wing area 24.00 m² (258.34 sq ft)
Armament: four 20-mm cannon and two RB24 Sidewinder AAMs

Saab-32 Lansen

First flown as a prototype on 3 November 1952, the **Saab-32** has given the Flygvapen some 28 years of faithful service since deliveries began in 1955, emphasising the capability of this excellent aircraft. Design of this aircraft was initiated in the late 1940s to provide the Swedish air force with an all-weather attack aircraft powered by two de Havilland turbojets, but the promise of an indigenous, and consequently cheaper engine brought cancellation of the original project. Design was drawn up around the new Swedish powerplant, but development delay of this engine threatened Saab's programme and, instead, it was to be given a go-ahead following a decision to power the aircraft by a Rolls-Royce Avon turbojet. Four prototypes of the Saab-32 design were ordered, the type being a two-seat cantilever low-wing monoplane with powered controls, retractable tricycle landing-gear, and the crew of two accommodated in tandem on ejection seats in a pressurised cockpit. Its wing incorporated 35° of sweepback and like that of the Saab-29 before it was evaluated in scaled-down form on a Saab Safir trainer.

Production was started in 1953 of the **A 32A Lansen** (lance), an all-weather attack aircraft powered by a Swedish-built version of the Rolls-Royce Avon Series 100, developing 4500 kg (9,921 lb) afterburning thrust. When production of the A 32A ended in mid-1958, deliveries began almost immediately afterwards of the **J 32B** all-weather/night fighter, of which the first example had flown on 7

January 1957. It introduced the Flygmotor RM6B turbojet, a licence-built version of the Rolls-Royce Avon Series 200 which developed 6900 kg (15,212 lb) afterburning thrust, providing much enhanced performance. Production of the J 32B ended in early 1960. Built almost in parallel with this version was the **S 32C** reconnaissance aircraft with a modified nose to carry advanced cameras as well as radar surveillance equipment. When production ended with delivery of the last J 32B, on 2 May 1960, a total of approximately 450 Saab-32s of all versions had been built for the Flygvapen.

By 1993 only a handful of Lansens remained in military service, chiefly with the Försökscentralen (test and trials unit) of the Flygvapen. Two-seat J 32B and J 32D target tugs are in use along with 14 specially modified **J 32E** electronic warfare 'aggressor' aircraft. These aircraft are operated by F13M, based at Malmslätt, with a permanent detachment at the RFN's Norland missile test range in Videsl, Lapland. Three J 32B target-tugs were formerly operated by civilian contractor Swedair, but they have now reverted to air force control.

Specification
Saab-32B (J 32B)
Type: all-weather/night fighter
Powerplant: one 6900-kg (15,212-lb) afterburning thrust Flygmotor RM6B turbojet
Performance: maximum speed 1145 km/h (711 mph) at optimum altitude; service ceiling 16000 m (52,495 ft); maximum range 3200 km

Saab's excellent Lansen is a little-known aircraft outside Sweden. This is the prototype J 32B, introducing a licence-built Avon engine.

(1,988 miles)
Weights: empty 7000 kg (15,432 lb); maximum take-off 13500 kg (29,762 lb)
Dimensions: span 13.00 m (42 ft 7¾ in); length 14.50 m (47 ft 6¾ in); height 4.65 m (15 ft 3 in); wing area 37.40 m² (402.58 sq ft)
Armament: four 30-mm cannon, plus Sidewinder air-to-air missiles or

unguided air-to-air rockets carried externally

The 1950s-vintage J 32B still remains in limited service with the Flygvapen in the early 1990s as a target-tug.

Saab-35 Draken

Not long after it had given a go-ahead for development and production of the Saab-32, the Swedish air force began to draw up its specification for a new single-seat fighter that would be able to intercept bombers flying in the transonic speed range. The new type was obviously going to need supersonic speed capability (at a time when only the Bell X-1 research aircraft was able to demonstrate such performance), an unprecedented rate of climb, above average range and endurance, and a considerable weapon load. To 'add icing to the cake', it was required to have STOL (short take-off and landing) characteristics to allow for its deployment from a variety of dispersed sites.

Saab began work on this requirement in August 1949, selecting a wing of double-delta configuration that promised great structural integrity with low weight and which, if it performed satisfactorily, would provide the volume needed for the equipment, fuel and weapons demanded by its primary role. The capability of such a wing was confirmed by wind tunnel testing of models and by the **Saab-210** small-scale research aircraft, powered by a 476-kg (1,050-lb) thrust Armstrong Siddeley Adder turbojet. First flown on 21 February 1952, the Saab-210 confirmed that there were no particular problems in the handling of the double-delta wing, and following inspection of a wooden mock-up the company received an order for three **Saab-35** prototypes. Features of the design included fully-powered controls, a combination of bag and integral fuel tanks, and retractable tricycle landing gear complemented by two retractable tail wheels, an arrangement permitting a tail-down landing to gain the full aerodynamic braking effect of the wing. Such a landing, combined with the use of a braking parachute, makes possible a landing run as short as 610 m (2,000 ft).

The first of the prototypes was flown on 25 October 1955, the other two in early 1956, all three of them powered by Rolls-Royce Avon turbojets with afterburners. The type was ordered into production during 1956, and the first series-built **J 35A Draken** (dragon) was flown on 15 February 1958, this being powered by a Flygmotor RM6B turbojet, a licence-built version of the Rolls-Royce Avon. Entry into service began in March 1960,

initially with Flygflottilj 13 at Norrköping, and production for the Flygvapen totalled approximately 525 aircraft in all versions. Sixty **J 35J** and 12 **Sk 35C** two-seat trainers remain in service with F10's four squadrons at Angelholm, in southern Sweden. Serving as pure interceptors, the J 35J 'Johanns' will be retained until 1995 at least.

Saab also developed the Draken for export, under the designation **Saab-35X**, with increased fuel capacity and a higher gross weight to allow the carriage of heavier external loads. The first customer was Denmark, receiving aircraft known as the **A 35XD** (similar to the Swedish J 35F), but becoming the **F-35** once in service with the Kongelige Danske Flyvevabnet (Danish air force). The **RF 35 (Saab S 35XD)** is a variant of the Swedish S 35E photo-reconnaissance Draken, no longer in service. Eventually 11 **Sk 35XD (TF-35)** two-seat trainers were also delivered. Denmark's last Draken squadron, operating all three versions of the aircraft, is slated for disbandment at the end of 1993.

The second export customer was Finland which received 12 **J 35XS** (Swedish J 35F-2) fighters, five **J 35CS** (Swedish Sk 35C) trainers and finally 24 **J 35FS** zero-timed ex-Flygvapnet J 35F single-seaters. A single unit, 'Lapland Wing', flies the aircraft today.

Austria became the fourth Draken operator with the delivery of its aircraft in the mid-1980s. Twenty-three **J 35Ös** (Swedish J 35Ds) serve as the nation's primary air defence fighter.

Now virtually replaced in Swedish service by the Saab 37 Viggen, a total of 606 Drakens was built. Saab achievement in building Europe's first supersonic combat aircraft (and one capable of Mach 2 at that) remains undiminished, with only governmental restrictions impeding wider sales.

Variants

J 35A: first production version with 7000-kg (15,432-lb) afterburning thrust Flygmotor RM6B turbojet, initially with short tailcone but modified retrospectively with longer type
J 35B: improved version with lengthened tailcone, twin retractable tailwheels, and provisions for STRIL-60 datalink for operation with Swedish air-defence control, collision-course radar

and increased external armament
Sk 35C: two-seat operational trainer without combat capability
J 35D: improved production air-defence version with more powerful Flygmotor RM6C turbojet, enlarged air inlets, advanced avionics and a zero-zero ejection seat
S 35E: tactical reconnaissance version with battery of five cameras in a revised nose; a camera or an auxiliary fuel tank can be carried in either or both cannon bays
J 35F: final production version with more advanced avionics and equipped to carry licence-built Hughes Falcon missiles instead of Sidewinders
J 35F-2: upgraded version of basic J 35F (now known as **J 35F-1**) with chin-mounted Ericsson IR scanner
Saab 35H: version offered unsuccessfully to Swiss air force, with Ferranti A.I.23 Airpass radar; single conversion completed only
J 35J: modification of 64 J 35F aircraft for current service; originally designated **J 35F Mod** or **J 35F-Ny** (Ny meaning new), new transponder and ground proximity warning system fitted; radar, IR seeking, IFF, avionics all upgraded; extra weapons pylon fitted inboard of wing

This underside view of a Danish Draken shows to good effect the double-delta planform, and two practice AIM-9 missiles.

Specification
Saab-35A (J 35F)

Type: single-seat interceptor
Powerplant: one 7830-kg (17,262-lb) afterburning thrust Flygmotor RM6C (licence-built Rolls-Royce Avon 300) turbojet
Performance: maximum speed, clean Mach 2 or 2125 km/h (1,320 mph) at 11000 m (36,090 ft); service ceiling 20000 m (65,615 ft); hi-lo-hi radius on internal fuel 560 km (348 miles)
Weights: empty 7425 kg (16,369 lb); maximum take-off 12700 kg (27,998 lb)
Dimensions: span 9.40 m (30 ft 10 in); length 15.35 m (50 ft 4¼ in); height 3.89 m (12 ft 9 in); wing area 49.20 m² (529.60 sq ft)
Armament: one 30-mm ADEN M/55 cannon in starboard wing, two RB 27 and two RB 28 Falcon missiles, plus up to 1000 kg (2,205 lb) of bombs or 12 135-mm (5.3-in) Bofors rockets

Saab managed to achieve Mach 2 performance with the Draken using a single afterburning Avon turbojet. Finland has operated a total of four J 35 variants; this natural metal aircraft is one of the original batch of 12 J 35XSs assembled by Valmet.

Saab-37 Viggen
to
Saab-340

Saab-37 Viggen

Development of the **Saab-37** was initiated to provide the Swedish air force with a completely integrated weapon system based on the concept pioneered in the USA. Prolonged research led to adoption of a then-unique canard configuration for the interceptor that was to form the airborne component of the weapon system. The configuration comprises a large rear-mounted delta wing combined with a delta foreplane incorporating trailing-edge flaps. This was adopted to provide improved STOL performance so that the Saab-37 would be able to operate from short runways and sections of roadway about 500 m (1,640 ft) in length, greatly increasing the flexibility of dispersed operations. This configuration, in combination with a high-power turbofan engine, has provided the essential short take-off capability. The engine also complements short landing capability by introducing thrust reversal, its first use in a combat aircraft. The Saab-37 has been designed for a 'no-flare' approach to landing with a rate of sink of 5 m (16.4 ft) per second, and this has meant the design of special landing gear able to absorb such a high rate of descent. Once on the ground, thrust reversal plus anti-skid brakes ensure the achievement of a minimum landing run. The pilot is accommodated on a zero-zero ejection seat in an air-conditioned, heated and pressurised cockpit, protected by a bird-proof windscreen. Much of the capability of this aircraft results from the incorporation of the latest avionics, including for attack a head-up display linked via an air-data computer to a digital fire-control system; for its own protection ECM (electronic countermeasures) and radar warning equipment; for navigating Doppler radar and radar altimeter; and for landing in all weathers a tactical instrument landing system plus a blind-landing guidance system.

The first of seven prototypes made its maiden flight on 8 February 1967 and the initial **AJ 37 Viggen** (Thunderbolt) single-seater was flown on 23 February 1971, with deliveries being made to Flygflottilj 7 at Satenäs from June 1971 onwards. The AJ designation signifies Attack-Jakt, or attack-fighter, underlining its primary role as an attack aircraft. The next versions to be developed were dedicated reconnaissance Viggens. R&D funding was allocated for a nominal 'S-37' (Spanning, or reconnaissance) aircraft programme in 1971, resulting in the **SF 37 Viggen** (Spanning Foto, or photo-reconnaissance) which was intended to replace the S 35E Drakens and surviving Lansens in their over-land mission. The first prototype flew on 21 May 1973. The SF 37 is fitted with a varied array of seven cameras in a chisel nose, which dispenses with radar of any kind. These systems can also be supplemented by pods, particularly night reconnaissance units, on the Viggen's shoulder pylons.

The second dedicated reconnaissance version is the **SH 37 Viggen** (Spanning Havsövervakning, or sea surveillance) aircraft. The third production Viggen served as the SH 37 prototype, first flying in that configuration on 10

December 1973. A look at any map of Sweden quickly explains why national defence policy places such great emphasis on the threat of seaborne invasion. This goes some way towards explaining the importance of the SH 37's capabilities to the Flygvapen. Fitted with a long-range Ericsson PS-371/A surveillance and attack radar, optimised for over-water operations, the SH 37 also boasts an RKA 40 camera which records radar imagery for analysis. Outwardly, the SH 37 Viggen resembles the AJ 37 aircraft, and if any additional reconnaissance systems are carried they are externally mounted on the shoulder pylons. The usual fit is a night photography pod to port and a LOROP pod to starboard. SH 37 pilots got most of their exercise observing Warsaw Pact naval manoeuvres in the Baltic Sea, but they were no strangers to NATO navy crews either.

Obviously, with the Viggen fulfilling its role as the Flygvapen's primary aircraft system, there was a pressing need for a two-seat trainer version. This role is undertaken by the **Sk 37 Viggen** (Skol, or school), which is somewhat unusual in having two separate cockpits for pilot and instructor.

The Sk 37s have an extended fin and retain the standard Viggen nose, but carry no radar, instead relying on Doppler equipment and DME to find their way around. Based on the AJ, the Sk 37 has reduced fuel capacity as a result of its extra cockpit, and aircraft often operate with external tanks.

The first 27 Viggens were built with weakened spars and early in its career the type gained an unfortunate reputation as a result. The basic integrity of Saab's design was never in doubt, as borne out by the long service of all its post-war military aircraft, so it came as no surprise when the decision was made to proceed with the final and perhaps most radical development of System-37. To replace the J 35 Draken in the air defence role the **JA 37 Viggen** (Jakt, or fighter) was conceived, externally identical to the AJ 37 but underneath a very different aircraft. Design work had been underway at a low rate since 1968, and the first contracts were awarded in 1972. A total of five prototypes were required, the first flying on 4 June 1974. The fuselage was subtly stretched by 7 cm (2.25 in) and the fin gained a distinctive extension (à la Sk 37). The other obvious external difference is a blade VHF aerial, behind the rudder.

An extensive test programme was undertaken to integrate the new Volvo-Flygmotor RM8B engine, Ericsson PS-46 multi-mode radar, and all-new cockpit avionics and displays. While still a relatively small, single-engined aircraft, the JA 37 is phenomenally manoeuvrable and conforms to Sweden's exacting operational requirement for short missions but high sortie rates. Its wing has been restressed to cope with a higher load factor and the aircraft's weight has increased. The first of 149 production JA 37s flew on 4 November 1977, with deliveries commencing in 1980. The final aircraft was

handed over to the Flygvapen on 29 June 1990, bringing to an end the Viggen's production run of 329 aircraft (substantially less than Saab had originally hoped for).

Attempts were made to export the aircraft, first as a Starfighter replacement to NATO nations and Japan, a Mirage III replacement for Australia and, later, as a deep penetration strike aircraft to India. All these efforts came to nought, chiefly because of restrictions imposed on Saab by the national legislature.

A proposal to fund attrition replacements for the Swedish air force was also defeated, and first-generation aircraft will be withdrawn before the new JAS 39 Gripen becomes fully operational. To bridge that gap Saab is undertaking an extensive upgrade programme to modify 115 AJ, SF and SH 37s to **AJS 37** standard. This involves fitting a new digital databus giving each aircraft a true multi-role capability, a terrain-following radar system, and compatibility with some of the armaments being developed for the Saab Gripen (such as the DWS 39 stand-off dispenser weapon).

Variants

AJ 37: initial production version, a single-seat all-weather attack aircraft with a secondary interception capability; powered by 11789-kg (25,990-lb) afterburning thrust Flygmotor RM8A turbofan, a supersonic turbofan developed by Flygmotor from the Pratt & Whitney JT8D turbofan, with Swedish-designed afterburner and thrust reverser
SF 37: single-seat all-weather armed

*Saab AJ 37 Viggen
(lower side view: Sk 37)*

The Saab JA 37 boasts an advanced radar, exceptionally powerful cannons and an effective missile armament. This Viggen wears an early 'low-vis' scheme.

photo-reconnaissance aircraft; basically similar airframe/engine to AJ 37, but with modified nose containing air-data camera to record altitude, course, position and other data, plus seven cameras, an infra-red sensor, and ECM equipment; carries two Sidewinder missiles for self-defence
SH 37: single-seat all-weather armed maritime reconnaissance aircraft; basically similar airframe/engine to AJ 37; equipped with nose-mounted surveillance radar which has a camera to record the radar display and ECM equipment, with data camera and armament as for SF 37
Sk 37: tandem two-seat trainer with secondary attack capability; basically similar airframe/engine to AJ 37,

The SF 37 has a reprofiled nose mounting four vertical/oblique low-level cameras, two long-range vertical cameras and an infra-red camera.

except for deletion of some electronics and forward fuselage fuel tank to permit installation of rear cockpit, and taller fin

JA 37: single-seat interceptor and final production version, with secondary attack capability; improved performance resulting from installation of higher-powered Flygmotor RM8B turbofan and completely revised airframe and avionics

Specification
Saab-37 (JA 37)
Type: single-seat all-weather interceptor/attack aircraft
Powerplant: one 12750-kg (28,109-lb) afterburning thrust Flygmotor RM8B turbofan
Performance: maximum speed more than Mach 2 at optimum altitude; time to 1000 m (32,810 ft) from brake release 1 minute 40 seconds; hi-lo-hi radius with external armament more than 1000 km (621 miles)
Weight: maximum take-off about 17000 kg (37,479 lb)
Dimensions: wing span 10.60 m (34 ft 9¼ in); foreplane span 5.45 m (17 ft 10½ in); length 16.40 m (53 ft 9¾ in); height 5.90 m (19 ft 4¼ in); wing plus foreplane area 52.20 m² (561.89 sq ft)
Armament: one 30-mm Oerlikon KCA cannon, plus three underwing fuselage and four underwing hardpoints to carry weapons that can include two Sky Flash (RB71) and four Sidewinder (RB24) air-to-air missiles; for air-to-ground attack up to 24 135-mm (5.3-in) rockets can be carried

Saab-90 Scandia

An apparently unusual category of aircraft to be designed and built by Svenska Aeroplan, which has concentrated primarily on military aircraft, the **Saab-90 Scandia** represented the company's attempt to join the post-World War II hunt for the legendary 'pot of gold' that would be the reward for the creator of a Douglas DC-3 replacement. Saab was even less successful than some others, producing a total of only 18 Saab-90 aircraft, including the prototype, between 1948 and 1954. A cantilever low-wing monoplane of all-metal construction, with retractable tricycle landing gear and powered by two wing-mounted 1081-kW (1,450-hp) Pratt & Whitney Twin Wasp radial engines, the prototype was flown for the first time on

The Saab-90A Scandia was a conventional and perfectly acceptable short-range airliner, which failed to find a market.

16 November 1946. Accommodation was provided for a flight crew of four or five and 24 to 36 passengers, according to cabin layout. However, only a single order was received for the **Saab-90A** production version, from the Swedish airline AB Aerotransport, but when this was absorbed into SAS (Scandinavian Airlines System) the order was reduced to six. The remaining four aircraft were then sold to Aerovias Brasil (later VASP). Both airlines found them efficient aircraft to operate, resulting in production of two more for SAS and five for VASP,

but that was all. A **Saab-90B** with a pressurised cabin was planned, but with no demand for the type it was not built.

Specification
Saab-90A Scandia
Type: short-range civil transport
Powerplant: two 1342-kW (1,800-hp) Pratt & Whitney R-2180-E1 radial piston engines
Performance: cruising speed 390 km/h (242 mph) at 3050 m (10,000 ft); service ceiling 7500 m (24,605 ft); range 1480 km (920 miles)
Weights: empty 9960 kg (21,858 lb); maximum take-off 16000 kg (35,275 lb)
Dimensions: span 28.00 m (91 ft 10½ in); length 21.30 m (69 ft 10½ in); height 7.10 m (23 ft 3½ in); wing area 85.65 m² (922.0 sq ft)

Saab-91 Safir

Saab flew in 1945 the prototype of the **Saab-91 Safir**, a three-seat cabin monoplane of cantilever low-wing configuration which had retractable tricycle landing gear and was powered by a 97-kW (130-hp) de Havilland Gipsy Major 1C inline engine. Successful testing led to the first production version, the **Saab-91A**, which differed primarily by having the more powerful de Havilland Gipsy Major 10 engine. Swedish air force interest in this aircraft as a primary trainer led to a prototype powered by a 142-kW (190-hp) Avco Lycoming O-435-A flat-six engine, first flown on 18 January 1949. This was adopted by the Flygvapen as a standard trainer under the designation **Sk 50**, built by Saab with the same powerplant as the **Saab-91B**. It could be equipped to carry guns, practice bombs or rockets, and served also with the air forces of Ethiopia and Norway; in a pure training subvariant this version was also adopted by a number of European airlines. The **Saab-91C**, first flown in September

Saab-91D Safir of the Schulgeschwader, Fliegerregiment 2, Österreichische Luftstreikräfte (Austrian air force) during 1969.

1953, differed from its predecessors by having four-seat accommodation. The final production version was the **Saab-91D,** which introduced a number of improvements, including a new Avco Lycoming O-360-A1A engine, disc brakes and other advanced equipment that offered weight saving. When production ended a total of about 320 Safirs

had been built, and examples had been sold to operators in some 20 countries.

Specification
Saab-91D Safir
Type: four-seat cabin monoplane
Powerplant: one 134-kW (180-hp) Avco Lycoming O-360-A1A flat-four piston engine
Performance: maximum speed 266 km/h (165 mph); service ceiling 5000 m (16,405 ft); range 1000 km (621 miles)
Weights: empty 710 kg (1,565 lb); maximum take-off 1205 kg (2,657 lb)
Dimensions: span 10.60 m (34 ft 9¼ in); length 7.95 m (26 ft 1 in); height 2.20 m (7 ft 2½ in); wing area 13.60 m² (146.39 sq ft)

Saab-105

Developed by Saab as a private venture, to add to its product line a lightweight turbojet-powered aircraft able to fulfil a number of civil and military roles, the **Saab-105** entered the design stage in 1959. However, it was not until 29 June 1963 that the first of two prototypes was flown, the long delay being caused by difficulties in finding a suitably small but powerful turbofan engine, eventually found in the 745-kg (1,642-lb) thrust Turboméca Aubisque. A cantilever shoulder-wing monoplane easily recognisable by its marked wing anhedral and high T-tail, it has retractable tricycle landing gear, is powered by two turbofans nacelle-mounted one on each side of the fuselage, and has an enclosed cockpit that accommodates two side-by-side on ejection seats; alternative seating for four can be provided on fixed seats. Fol-

This quartet of Saab-105s comprises Sk 60A aircraft from F21, which used the type for basic training and for liaison with a secondary ground-attack role.

lowing extensive testing of the prototypes the Flygvapen placed an initial order in early 1964 for 130 production aircraft, a figure that was amended later to 150. The first of them was the **Sk 60A** trainer/liaison aircraft, flown initially on 29 August 1965 with deliveries for optional deployment in an attack role. The **Sk 60B** which followed was a dedicated attack version, and the designation **Sk 60C** applied to a number of dual-role attack/reconnaissance aircraft, conversions from Sk 60Bs with a permanent camera installation. In addition to the foregoing, Saab built 40 aircraft for the Austrian air force. Surviving Swedish air force Sk 60s, of which there are four squadrons, have undergone a life exten-

sion programme at Saab. A recently announced re-engining plan, utilising the WilliamsRJ44 turbofan, will see their useful lives extended even further. Saab entered a development of the 105 known as the **Saab 2060**, early in the USAF/USN JPATS competition, but failed to find a US partner for the design.

Variants
Saab-105H: project for the Swiss air force; by comparison with the Saab-105XT it would have had improved performance, increased armament and fuel capacity, and more advanced avionics; not built
Saab-105XT: more developed version of the Sk 60B, with improved performance and increased weapons load resulting from the installation of two more powerful General Electric J85-17B turbojet engines, and with a strengthened wing for the carriage of an external weapon load of up to 2000 kg (4,409 lb)
Saab-105Ö: production version of Saab-105XT for service with the Austrian air force; 40 built, with the first deliveries made in July 1970
Saab-105G: prototype/demonstrator of an improved version of the Saab-105Ö incorporating a number of modifications but, most importantly, advanced avionics and an increase in external weapon load to 2350 kg (5,181 lb); one built

Specification
Saab-105Ö
Type: multi-role light jet aircraft
Powerplant: two 1293-kg (2,850-lb) thrust General Electric J85-17B turbojet engines
Performance: maximum speed 970 km/h (603 mph) at sea level; attack radius hi-lo-hi mission with 1360 kg (2,998 lb) bombload 825 km (513 miles)
Weights: empty 2565 kg (5,655 lb); maximum take-off 6500 kg (14,330 lb)
Dimensions: span 9.50 m (31 ft 2 in); length 10.80 m (35 ft 5¼ in); height 2.70 m (8 ft 10¼ in); wing area 16.30 m² (175.46 sq ft)
Armament: six underwing attachment points for a maximum weapon load of 2000 kg (4,409 lb) and including 30-mm cannon and Minigun pods, high-explosive and napalm bombs, rockets, and air-to-air and air-to-surface missiles

Saab-340

In January 1980 Saab-Scania and Fairchild Industries in the USA announced simultaneously the intention of the two companies to design and develop a new transport aircraft. This unique European/US collaboration in the field of civil aviation led to the maiden flight of the first **Saab-Fairchild 340** prototype (SE-ISF) on 25 January 1983. This, plus a second prototype (SE-ISA) and the first production aircraft (SE-ISB flown on 25 August 1983) participated in the certification programme which saw JAR and FAA approval granted by 29 June 1984. Initial deliveries were made to Crossair, in Switzerland.

A cantilever low-wing monoplane of basic all-metal structure with the selective use of composite materials, the aircraft is of conventional configuration; it has a fail-safe pressurised fuselage structure, retractable tricycle landing gear with twin wheels on each unit, and is powered by two turboprop engines in wing-mounted nacelles.

Fairchild was responsible for design and manufacture of the wings, tail unit and engine nacelles, while Saab, which funded 75 per cent of the development costs, handled the fuselage, systems integration flight-testing and certification. The aircraft itself comprises a round-section fuselage seating up to 35 passengers with a flight attendant and two-person crew. The wing uses NASA-developed low-drag airfoil technology, and two General Electric CT7 turboprops were chosen as powerplants.

Initially two versions were on offer: the basic air transport configuration and an executive version. The first of these 'biz-props' was sold to Pittsburgh's Mellon Bank. The type suffered a setback in 1984 when it was temporarily grounded, after Crossair suffered inflight engine shut downs, but these teething troubles were soon rectified and Saab pressed on with the next stage in the aircraft's development. In 1985, at the Paris air show, Saab launched a 340 with uprated CT7 engines driving larger Dowty propellers. Maximum take-off weight was increased from the original 11793 kg (26,000 lb) to 12872 kg (27,275 lb). Existing SF-340s were offered the improvement as a modification programme.

As a result of an ailing financial position Fairchild withdrew from the SF-340 programme in October 1985, and production was gradually transferred in its entirety to Saab's Linköping home, south of Stockholm. Next version to be offered was the freighter **S340QC** which, as its name suggests, was a quick-change cargo aircraft, the first of which was delivered to Finnaviation in 1987. In that same year, as Saab severed its final links with Fairchild, the family was renamed the **S340**.

1987 also saw the launch of the **Saab 340B**, the current production version, which features higher power output CT7-9B engines, a larger span tailplane, and a further increased maximum take-off weight of 12928 kg (28,500 lb). Crossair was again the launch customer for this version. The arrival of the Saab 340 had a significant effect on sales figures, which had been slowing at that point, having reached 200 aircraft. By mid-1993 Saab 340 orders had exceeded 400, with over 340 delivered, to 28 airlines and four corporate clients.

One of the most recent orders has been for the **Saab 340AEW Erieye** airborne early warning aircraft, the contract for which was signed by the Swedish air force on 3 February 1993. This version features an Ericsson phased array surveillance radar above the fuselage, with three operators in the cabin and a mission endurance of up to seven hours. Six aircraft are anticipated for Swedish service with an initial in-service date of 1995.

The most recently announced improvements to the Saab 340 will enhance the aircraft's hot-and-high performance and short field capability, through a 0.6-m (1.96-ft) wingtip extension referred to as the '1-*g* stall modification'. This increases the Saab 340's take-off weight by 544 kg (1,200 lb), equiva-

Northwest Airlink incorporates Saab 340 operator Express Airlines, based at Memphis and Minneapolis, which feeds its parent company's hub airports in northern and mid-western US.

lent to six/seven passengers. A third-generation cabin interior, common to the Saab 2000, is also being introduced, along with modifications to the APU and optional low-pressure tyres.

Specification
Saab 340B
Type: 35-seat commuter passenger transport
Powerplant: two 1394-kW (1,870-shp) General Electric CT7-9B turboprops
Performance: maximum cruising speed at 4575 m (15,000 ft) 282 kt (522 km/h; 325 mph); service ceiling (standard) 7620 m (25,000 ft); range (with 35 passengers, baggage and reserves) 1807 km (1,123 miles)
Weights: operating empty 8035 kg (17,715 lb); maximum ramp 13063 kg (28,800 lb)
Dimensions: span 21.44 m (70 ft 4 in); height 6.87 m (22 ft 6½ in); length 19.73 m (64 ft 8 in)

Since 1990 a single Saab 240 has been operated by the Flyvapen as a VIP transport, using the callsign 'Swedik 01'.

Saab-2000

Saab's experience with the S340 commuter airliner turned its attention to the future needs of regional and 'feeder' carriers. While the mainstream air transport market was an unpredictable one, Saab felt that the need for smaller, flexible turboprops that could match jet performance over a range of sectors was a clearly defined one whose time had come. Having forged a market with its smaller aircraft, Saab used the S340 as a baseline from which to develop a new 50-seat, high-speed turboprop airliner which was to be called the **Saab 2000**. The go-ahead came with a launch order from Moritz Suter's Crossair, already a firm Saab customer, which signed for 25 aircraft with a further 25 on option, on 15 December 1988.

By late 1989 project definition for the Saab 2000 had been completed, with the contracting out of major portions of the aircraft's construction. CASA of Spain was responsible for the wing design and production, though Saab defined the basic airfoil structure. Valmet of Finland was to build the entire tail unit and elevators, while in England, Westland is responsible for the rear fuselage. For the cockpit, a Collins Proline 4 avionics suite was selected, while a radical reduction in cabin noise levels over existing aircraft was also promised. The concept of 'hub bypass' was central to Saab's sales efforts for the aircraft. To achieve this, Saab planned to build an aircraft capable of 360 kt (665 km/h; 413 mph) over a 1,000-nm (1852-km; 1150-mile) sector, a speed comparable with the BAe 146 (Avro RJ). A jet-like climb performance was also essential, with figures of 0-6096 m (0-20,000 ft) in less than 11 minutes assured. The original choice of engine fell between General Electric's GE38, then under development for the US Navy's projected LRAACA maritime patrol aircraft, and the Pratt & Whitney PW300 turbofan. In the event, and in conjunction with Crossair, Saab opted for the Allison GMA 2100 turboprop, driving six-bladed, low-noise Dowty propellers. As part of the deal Allison was contracted to build the engine nacelles.

First metal was cut at Linköping in February 1990, and the prototype's (SE-001) maiden flight occurred on 26 March 1992. A four-aircraft test programme was established with aircraft No. 2 (SE-002) involved in stability and control certification. Much of the high-temperature and adverse weather flying was undertaken by the No. 2 Saab 2000, which completed two visits to Spain. The first full production-standard aircraft was SE-003, with which all the systems

certification was achieved, only the auto-pilot certification being outstanding in mid-1993. Functional reliability flights were undertaken by aircraft No.4 (SE-004), as part of the ongoing programme which has so far exceeded 1,200 hours across the fleet. All Saab's performance guarantees have been met or exceeded. Take-off and landing distances were bettered by 100-200 m (328-656 ft). Time from brake release to 20,000 ft is less than eight minutes, and in proving this the Saab 2000 easily broke the existing time-to-climb record for an aircraft in its class (previously held by a Grumman E-2 at 10 minutes). Range and weights have all been better than expected on the production standard aircraft, and the promised cruise speed of 360 kt (665 km/h; 413 mph) at 8534 m (28,000 ft) is, on average, 8 kt better. In a dive the Saab 2000 has reached 430 kt (794 km/h; 493 mph) with no ill effects. International noise requirements have been bettered by 9.1 decibels.

Reducing cabin noise was a cornerstone of the Saab 2000 design philosophy and Saab has developed a so-far unique anti-noise system that has been test flown on a Saab 340, ready for inclusion on its larger sibling. This involves a series of microphones, located around the interior, which monitor cabin noise and then re-broadcast an equal opposite wave, thus effectively 'switching off' background noise and vibration.

Saab originally foresaw a market for 1,400 new 40- to 50- seat regional airliners by the end of the century, and sales of 400 Saab 2000s were anticipated. While the manufacturer holds well over 100 paid options, only 36 firm orders had been received by July 1993. First delivery, to Crossair, is scheduled

for the fourth quarter of 1993, while the seventh aircraft and the first for Deutsche BA (formerly Delta Air) flew on 24 June 1993.

Specification
Saab 2000 (pre-production)
Type: 50-seat, high-speed regional airliner
Powerplant: two 3096-kW (4,152-shp) Allison GMA 2100 turboprops
Performance: maximum cruising speed 368 kt (680 km/h; 422 mph); service ceiling 9450 m (31,000 ft); maximum range with 35 passengers, baggage and reserves 1,380 nm (2557 km; 1,589 miles)
Weights: operating empty 13500 kg (29,762 lb); maximum take-off 22000 kg (48,500 lb)
Dimensions: span 24.76 m (81 ft 2¾ in); height 7.73 m (25 ft 4 in); length 27.03 m (88 ft 8¼ in)

Above: The Saab 2000 offers a radical step forward for regional airlines, combining the speed and airfield performance of a jet with the cost benefits of a turboprop. Instead of acting as a feeder-liner, such as the Saab 340, the Saab 2000 has been designed from the outset for 'hub bypass' and is tailored to operate sectors of up to 1,000 nm (1852 km) with a full load of passengers.

Below: Crossair has played a significant part in the entire story of Saab airliners in recent times, having been the launch customer for both the Saab 340 and improved Saab 340B. The Swiss carrier is first in line for the Saab 2000, but the projected delivery date has now slipped into 1994.

Saab JAS 39 Gripen

By early 1980, with Viggen deliveries continuing apace, it was clear that if Sweden was to maintain its status as a military airframe manufacturer, and its policy of operating only indigenous combat aircraft, work on a successor to the Saab Viggen would have to begin soon. Strict government control dictated an aircraft design that would cost only 60-65

per cent more than the Saab 37, and be only half the weight. Its primary role would be as a fighter interceptor, with an important, but secondary, attack mission. It was to be a fully multi-role aircraft, in marked contrast to the mission-specific Viggen family. It was also hoped that this new aircraft would provide a replacement for the ageing Sk 60 (Saab

105) trainer fleet.

The JAS Industry Group was formed by Saab, Volvo Flygmotor, Ericsson and FFV, and their bid to develop the new aircraft was accepted. Preliminary designs were for a single-seat, single-engined, fly-by-wire, delta-winged aircraft, with an all-flying canard. Thirty per cent of its eight-tonne final weight would be of composite materials, and the proven General Electric F404J turbofan was chosen as the powerplant. Volvo Flyg-

motor would share assembly and testing of the engine, designated RM12, with the American manufacturer, while Ericsson was tasked with developing a new multi-mode, pulse-Doppler, X-band PS-046 (later PS-05) radar. FFV was in charge of developing the nav/attack systems. The cockpit would have three CRTs and a wide-angle holographic HUD, and it was planned to integrate a FLIR system with the radar and avionics. New facilities were built by Saab at Linköping to cope with the demand.

Contracts between FMV, the Swedish defence procurement agency and IG JAS for the newly designated **JAS 39** were signed in June 1982. These covered the development of five prototypes and an initial production run of 30 aircraft. Options for a further 110 aircraft were also undertaken. In June 1984 the Riksdag (Swedish parliament) gave the go ahead to this JAS (Jakt, Attak, Spanning: fighter, attack, reconnaissance) project as an affordable answer to the Flygvapen's need for a third-generation combat aircraft. By now the name **JAS 39 Gripen** (Griffin) had been adopted. At the time of its launch only Israel was developing such a totally new fighter design, in the shape of the now-defunct Lavi. The projected requirement was for 350 aircraft, with the first in service by 1992, rather than 1990 as originally hoped.

Engine tests began in 1984, and five test rigs had accumulated over 800 running hours by June 1985. A full-size mock-up was complete by early 1986, and this differed from the initial conceptual drawings by being a more stocky and box-like design, while still retaining its small size and inherent sleekness. The first flight was planned for 1986, but problems with the software for the complex fly-by-wire system (developed by Lear-Siegler, now GEC Astronics) caused this date to be progressively set back. The project was also hit by rising costs, which threatened its cancellation by parliament. Finally, the aircraft was rolled out at Linköping on 26 April 1987. The first JAS 39 (39-1) flew on 9 December 1988, at the hands of Stig Holmström, for a total of 51 minutes. It was its performance from then on that helped the aircraft survive a critical funding review in January of the following year, when the threat of an off-the-shelf purchase, instead of the Gripen, finally subsided.

A real set-back was suffered on the sixth flight, when a failure of the flight control system caused the crash of the first aircraft on 2 February 1989. The pilot, again Stig Holmström, was unhurt. Major software corrections were undertaken in the United States, by Calspan with a modified T-33, and the programme returned to flying status in May. After two investigations the FMV underlined its commitment to the JAS 39, and ultimately the government compensated Saab for its loss. Problems were also encountered with the RM12 which suffered from 'thrust-droop', and cracks in the compressor blades, but these too were soon rectified. The new PS-05/A radar was tested in a modified Viggen (until the end of 1991), and both air and ground tests proved encouraging, if time consuming. A study for a projected two-seat aircraft was begun in 1989, while the single-seat programme continued with the second aircraft (39-2) flying on 4 May 1990. This was followed by 39-4 (the first full avionics fit) on 20 December 1990, 39-3 (first with full radar and

avionics fit) on 25 March 1991 and 39-5 on 23 October 1991.

Flight tests (costed at only $2,500 per hour) soon revealed that aerodynamic drag and induced drag, in clean configuration, were 10 per cent lower than expected. Any engine thrust anomalies had been ironed out, and airfield performance was above the specification. In freeflow, the canards are the primary brakes, deployed from a landing speed of 220 km/h (136 mph). Gripens have repeatedly demonstrated their ability to operate from a standard Base 90 runway, that is to say a hardened road-strip, typically 800 m × 9 m (2600 ft × 30 ft). The JAS 39 has been flown to a load of 9g and the static test air frame has been subjected to 230 per cent of the limit load before failure (design requirement was for 180 per cent only). In October 1991 Saab submitted its costing proposal for the **JAS 39B** trainer and the follow-on Batch 2 order for 110 single-seat aircraft. By January 1992 the flight test programme had reached 300 flights, and that year was joined by the first production aircraft (39-101), allocated after the crash of the prototype. Problems were encountered with the APU and the environmental control systems. A possible replacement APU has been mooted to overcome the current unit's high failure rate.

June 1992 saw the final go-ahead for the Batch 2 aircraft and the JAS 39B. This would feature performance equivalent to that of the JAS 39, but involving a 40 per cent change from that type including a 65.5-cm (25.8-in) fuselage stretch. By mid-1993 90 per cent of the structural design was complete, along with 50 per cent of the actual assembly, and 70 per cent of the subcontracts signed. Ejection seat tests were due to commence in the US in July 1993.

The first aircraft was handed over to the Flygvapen at Linköping on 8 June 1993, being delivered to F7, at Satenäs, the same day. Saab expects to deliver

140 aircraft between 1993 and 2002, in addition to 14 JAS 39Bs. These aircraft will replace eight squadrons of AJ 37 Viggens, but there will then be a need to replace the younger JA 37 aircraft in the air defence role. A total Gripen buy of 300 is likely. The first squadron will be operational by October 1995, and already Saab has a modification programme in hand to recall the initial 30 Batch 1 aircraft and update their software to Batch 2 standard. With a planned production rate of 20 to 30 aircraft a year, Saab is also working hard to sell the Gripen abroad, in a marked reversal of former policy. The JAS 39 was extensively demonstrated to Finland, with Finnish air force pilots flying over 250 sorties in the aircraft, but in the event the order went to the F/A-18. This has not dampened Saab's high hopes for the JAS 39 Gripen.

Specification
Saab JAS 39 Gripen (pre-production)
Type: single-seat, all-weather, multi-role, light fighter
Powerplant: one 80.5-kN (18,100 lb) Volvo Flygmotor RM12 (General

This Gripen, the second prototype, displays a load of Bofors rocket pods, RB 74 Sidewinders and a pair of test cameras for recording weapons releases.

Electric F404-GE-400) turbofan
Performance: no details released, maximum speed quoted as supersonic at all altitudes
Weights: operating empty 6622 kg (14,600 lb); maximum take-off 12473 kg (27,500 lb)
Dimensions: span 8.00 m (26 ft 3 in); height 4.70 m (15 ft 5 in); length 14.10 m (46 ft 3 in)
Armament: internally mounted Mauser BK27 27-mm cannon; five hardpoints for RB71 (Sky Flash), RB74 (AIM-9L Sidewinder) AAMs, RB75 (Maverick ASM), RB15-F AshM, DWS 39 stand-off dispenser weapons system

The second production Gripen was the first to wear the intended two-tone grey air superiority scheme.

Saab-MFI 15 and -MFI 17 Safari-Supporter

On 11 July 1969 Saab flew the prototype (SE-301) of a two/three-seat civil/military trainer or general utility aircraft to which it had allocated the designation **Saab-MFI 15**. As then flown it was powered by a 119-kW (160-hp) Avco Lycoming IO-320-B2 flat-four engine and had a conventional low-set tailplane, but this was modified subsequently to T-tail configuration to minimise damage when oper-

ating from rough airfields. The prototype was flown on 26 February 1971 with a more powerful Avco Lycoming engine, which became the standard powerplant for the production version, which was redesignated **Saab Safari**. A braced shoulder-wing monoplane with fixed tricycle landing gear, available optionally with tailwheel landing gear, it provides side-by-side enclosed accommodation

for two and has dual controls as standard. A military version designated originally **Saab-MFI 17** was flown on 6 July 1972 and differed from the Safari by being equipped more specifically for use as a military trainer, or for such duties as artillery observation, forward air control and liaison; this version was later named **Saab Supporter**. In August 1978 Saab flew a version of the Safari with a

157-kW (210-hp) Continental flat-six turbocharged engine; designated **Safari TS** it did not progress beyond the prototype stage.

Saab built a combined total of about 250 Safari/Supporter aircraft before production ended in the late 1970s. Military Supporters were supplied to the Pakistan air force and army (45), Royal Danish air force (32, which designated it **T-17**) and Zambian air force (20). Licence-production of this aircraft was started in Pakistan during 1976, initially from kits supplied by Saab, but there has been a gradual change to indigenous manufacture from raw materials. Designated **Mushshak** in Pakistan, more than 150 have been built.

Specification
Saab Safari
Type: two/three-seat light aircraft
Powerplant: one 149-kW (200-hp) Avco Lycoming IO-360-A1B6 flat-four piston engine
Performance: maximum speed 235 km/h (146 mph) at sea level; service ceiling 4100 m (13,450 ft); maximum endurance 5 hours 10 minutes
Weights: empty equipped 646 kg (1,424 lb); maximum take-off 1200 kg (2,646 lb)
Dimensions: span 8.85 m (29 ft 0 in); length 7.00 m (22 ft 11½ in); height 2.60 m (8 ft 6½ in); wing area 11.90 m² (128.09 sq ft)

In Danish military service the Saab-MFI 17 Supporter is designated the T-17. Surviving aircraft are used for training and communications duties.

Sablatnig SF series

Austrian Josef Sablatnig established Sablatnig Flugzeugbau GmbH in Berlin during 1915, and the company became well known for a series of floatplanes designed and developed for service with the German navy. The series began with the single **Sablatnig SF 1** two-seater, a fairly basic biplane of conventional wood and fabric construction which was mounted on twin floats and powered by a 119-kW (160-hp) Mercedes D.III inline engine. Its performance must have proved more than adequate, for the SF 1 was followed in German navy service by some 36 examples of an improved but similarly-powered version designated **SF 2**. Deliveries of this aircraft, which was clearly derived from the SF 1, began in August 1916, and 10 of the total were built under sub-contract by L.V.G. Only single examples were built of the **SF 3** two-seat floatplane fighter biplane, **SF 4** single-seat fighter biplane and a triplane variant of the SF 4. The **SF 5** two-seat reconnaissance floatplane, which was a

Josef Sablatnig's SF 3 float-plane was built to the extent of one prototype, being wholly ordinary in every department. This was the spur for a series of Sablatnig designs, built from October 1915 onwards, most of which served with the German forces until the Armistice in 1918.

development of the earlier successful SF 2, was built to a total of 101, the first of them being delivered during March 1917. Probably only a single example was built of the **SF 6**, which was basically an SF 5 airframe with conventional wheel/tail-skid landing gear, this being followed by three examples of the **SF 7** two-seat float-plane fighter which, developed from the SF 3 design, was powered by a 179-kW (240-hp) Maybach engine. Last of the SF series was the **SF 8** dual-control trainer on twin floats, powered by a 112-kW (150-hp) Benz Bz.III engine. The first of 41 on order was delivered in

January 1917, but there is no confirmation that all were delivered.

Specification
Sablatnig SF 5
Type: reconnaissance floatplane
Powerplant: one 112-kW (150-hp) Benz Bz.III inline piston engine
Performance: maximum speed

148 km/h (92 mph)
Weights: empty 1052 kg (2,319 lb); maximum take-off 1605 kg (3,538 lb)
Dimensions: span 17.30 m (56 ft 9 in); length 9.60 m (31 ft 6 in); height 3.55 m (11 ft 7¾ in); wing area 50.50 m² (543.60 sq ft)
Armament: none

Sablatnig miscellaneous aircraft

The only really successful part of the activities of Sablatnig Flugzeugbau was confined to the construction of some 200 SF floatplanes for the German navy. This was perhaps due to the fact that there was less competition in this category of aircraft, for when it came to landplanes the company was virtually a non-starter. Designs during World War I included the **Sablatnig C.I** biplane, a two-seat armed reconnaissance aircraft with a 134-kW (180-hp) Argus As.III engine and fixed tailskid landing gear; the **C.II** biplane of similar configuration with a 179-kW (240-hp) Maybach Mb.IV engine, plus two variants with alternative wing construction; and a **C.III** two-seat monoplane. It is unlikely that more than a single example of each was built, but the **Sablatnig N.I** two-seat night bomber, which would appear to be a development of the C.I., may have been built in small numbers; it was powered by a 164-kW (220-hp) Benz Bz.IV engine and carried full night-flying equipment.

Immediately after the end of World War I a small number of four-seat **P I** civil aircraft were built, these being developed from the N.I, and examples were recorded in service with Danish Air Express and Lloyd-Luftverkehr Sablatnig. It was followed by the more successful **P III**, a solid-looking parasol-wing monoplane that accommodated the pilot in an open cockpit and provided an enclosed cabin for six passengers. Built for service with airlines that included Aeronaut (of Estonia), Danish Air Express, Deutsche Luft-Hansa and Lloyd-Luftverkehr Sablatnig, as well as for the Swiss air force, it represented the final practical Sablatnig design, and by 1921 the company had ceased to exist.

St Louis Cardinal series

The St Louis Aircraft Corporation of St Louis, Missouri, was a subsidiary of the established St Louis Car Company, a builder of what Americans call 'street cars'. During 1928 this organisation designed and developed the **St Louis Cardinal C2-60**, a braced high-wing cabin monoplane with fixed tailskid landing gear that provided side-by-side enclosed accommodation for two. Powered by a 48-kW (65-hp) LeBlond 5-D radial engine, the Cardinal was first flown in 1928 and introduced during 1929, but its limited performance by comparison with the products of established manufacturers meant that only about 10 were built, and the optional **Cardinal C3-90** with a 67-kW (90-hp) LeBlond 7-D engine was even less successful, with six built. The higher-performance **Super Cardinal C2-110**, which was to have been powered by a 82-kW (110-hp) Warner Scarab, appeared in late 1929 with a 75-kW (100-

hp) Kinner K5 engine without a change in designation, and six were built. Only two more attempts were made to gain success, one **Cardinal C2-85** with an 63-kW (85-hp) LeBlond 5-DF radial being produced as a conversion of a C2-90, and one new Cardinal being built in early 1931 with the once-planned 82-kW (110-hp) Warner Scarab; however, this was designated **Cardinal C2-100** to avoid confusion with the Super Cardinal. The company's aircraft-building activities then came to a halt, until resurrected when the US Army Air Corps began to expand in the late 1930s.

Specification
St Louis Cardinal C2-60
Type: two-seat cabin monoplane
Powerplant: one 48-kW (65-hp) LeBlond radial piston engine
Performance: cruising speed 137 km/h (85 mph); service ceiling 2955 m (9,700 ft); range 684 km (425 miles)
Weights: empty 421 kg (929 lb); maximum take-off 658 kg (1,450 lb)
Dimensions: span 9.86 m (32 ft 4 in); length 6.27 m (20 ft 7 in); height 2.13 m (7 ft 0 in); wing area 15.05 m² (162.0 sq ft)

St Louis PT-15

Under the designation **St Louis PT-1W**, the St Louis Aircraft Corporation designed an attractive tandem open-cockpit biplane trainer for the civil market. In 1939 the US Army Air Corps had begun to expand its pilot training programme and thus evaluated a number of civil trainers designed by US manufacturers. A single example of the St Louis PT-1W was procured under the designation **XPT-15**, this being powered by a 168-kW (225-hp) Wright R-760-1 Whirlwind radial engine, and following satisfactory initial tests 13 **YPT-15** aircraft were acquired for wider-scale evaluation. This 10.31-m (33-ft 10-in) span trainer had a maximum speed of 200 km/h (124 mph), but unfortunately for the company no production order resulted. St Louis also designed a two-seat monoplane trainer under the designation **PT-LM-4**, and although this did not enter production the company was soon busy building under sub-contract 200 Fairchild PT-23 trainers for the USAAC, and throughout World War II was kept busy with contracts from the US War Department.

Salmson Cri Cri

With the end of World War I Salmson concentrated upon the manufacture of aero engines and motor cars, and it was not until 1934 that the company again made a foray into aircraft production. Designed by M. Deville, this was the **Salmson Cri Cri** (cricket) two-seat light monoplane of parasol-wing configuration and was intended as a cheap and functional trainer for flying club use. Powered by an uncowled 45-kW (60-hp) Salmson 9ADr radial engine, it had tandem open cockpits with dual controls; this 9.65-m (31-ft 7¾-in) span lightplane had a maximum speed of 150 km/h (93 mph). Following extensive testing it was adopted by the French air ministry for the Aviation Populaire movement, Salmson building 50, but many more were produced under licence. Plans to build a successor with a more powerful engine did not materialise.

Salmson Type 2

In 1912 Emile Salmson established Société des Moteurs Salmson to build and develop the radial water-cooled aero engines which incorporated Canon-Unné design features. With the outbreak of World War I there was a large demand for this powerplant, but once production had been well established the company decided to turn its hand to aircraft manufacture. First came the unsuccessful **Salmson-Moineau S-M.1** reconnaissance biplane, designed by Lieutenant René Moineau and built by Salmson, which was plagued by problems that resulted from its unusual powerplant installation: a 119-kW (160-hp) Salmson Canton-Unné radial was mounted within the fuselage and arranged to drive, via transmission shafts, two tractor propellers mounted between the wings, one on each side of the fuselage. Three or four of these aircraft were used very briefly by the French air force in 1917. In complete contrast was the very successful two-seat **Salmson Type 2** armed reconnaissance biplane designed and built wholly by Salmson; of conventional configuration and of robust construction the

Three of four Salmson-Moineau S-M.1 reconnaissance biplanes saw service during World War I. They were overshadowed by a later design, the Type 2.

type began to enter service in the A.2 two-seat observation/reconnaissance category during 1917 and was built to a total of some 3,200 aircraft. The type is reported to have equipped 24 French reconnaissance squadrons, and 705 of these aircraft were procured by the Americans to equip 11 squadrons. It is interesting to note that the US 12th Aero Squadron recorded in its official history that "... this airplane proved most satisfactory in every respect; no observation airplane used upon the western front up to the conclusion of the armistice gave greater all-round satisfaction."

With the end of World War I many ex-military Salmson Type 2s found continued employment in a variety of civil roles, some being converted by the company with an enclosed cabin for two passengers and thus designated **Salmson Limousine**. Some of these conversions were used by early European airlines, and the Salmson Type 2 was also built under licence in Japan, the army equipping one of its air battalions (three squadrons) with the type.

Specification
Salmson Type 2
Type: armed reconnaissance aircraft
Powerplant: one 194-kW (260-hp) Salmson Canton-Unné radial piston engine
Performance: maximum speed 185 km/h (115 mph); service ceiling 6250 m (20,505 ft); endurance 3 hours
Weight: maximum take-off 1340 kg (2,954 lb)
Dimensions: span 11.80 m (38 ft 8½ in); length 8.50 m (27 ft 10¾ in); height 2.90 m (9 ft 6¼ in)
Armament: one 7.7-mm (0.303-in) forward-firing synchronised Vickers machine-gun, and single or twin 7.7-mm (0.303-in) Lewis guns on trainable mounting in the rear cockpit

Santos-Dumont 14bis and Demoiselle

Alberto Santos-Dumont, a Brazilian domiciled in France, had first hit the Parisian headlines on 19 October 1901 by piloting his No. 6 airship around the Eiffel Tower. The second occasion came on 23 October 1906 when, flying his tail-first boxkite-structure **Santos-Dumont No. 14bis** biplane, he completed the first flight in Europe of more than 25 m (82 ft), covering a distance recorded as almost 60 m (197 ft). This won for him the Archdeacon Prize of 3,000 francs that had been offered for the first pilot to exceed a distance of 25 m (82 ft). It must have seemed unlikely that the incredibly frail and odd-looking No. 14bis, powered by a 37-kW (50-hp) Antoinette engine, could have flown at all. Yet just under three weeks later, on 12 November, Santos-Dumont flew this same aircraft a distance of 220 m (722 ft), recording the first officially recognised sustained flight by a piloted and powered aeroplane in Europe. Having regard to the fact that just over year earlier Wilbur Wright had flown the Flyer III for a distance of 39 km (24 miles), it now seems unbelievable that this 12 November flight by Santos-Dumont was to become also the first internationally-ratified world distance record for aeroplanes.

Mention should be made also of the **Santos-Dumont Demoiselle**, a lightweight aircraft originating from the **Santos-Dumont No. 19**, and the more robust **Santos-Dumont No. 20** (which is preserved in the Musée de l'Air). In late versions the Demoiselle, powered by a flat-twin Darracq engine developing some 22 kW (30 hp), was an attractive aircraft for its day. Because Santos-Dumont allowed any enthusiast to use his design freely to build an example for their own use, the Demoiselle must be regarded as the world's first homebuilt aircraft.

Saro A.7 Severn and A.27

In 1928 a Supermarine Southampton was flown with an experimental weight-saving hull. This was designated **A.14** and had been designed and built by Saunders-Roe. Successful testing of this aircraft encouraged design in 1930 of the **Saro A.7 Severn**, a military flying-boat of sesquiplane configuration that incorporated an almost identical hull and had a powerplant of three 362-kW (485-hp) Bristol Jupiter IX radial engines. Its performance was better than the twin-engine Southamptons and comparable with the three-engined Southampton X but, presumably because the Supermarine aircraft were already in production for the Royal Air Force, no orders were received for the A.7.

With the issue of Air Ministry Specification R.24/32 for a coastal patrol flying-boat Saunders-Roe designed the **A.27 London** which, of similar configuration and only slightly smaller in size than the A.7 from which it was developed, was powered initially by two 652-kW (875-hp) Bristol Pegasus III radial engines. Following official testing an order was placed for 10 aircraft under the designation **London Mk I**, the first of them being delivered in 1936. They were followed by 20 **London Mk II**s, which differed primarily by having more powerful Pegasus engines. All London Mk I aircraft were modified subsequently to London Mk II standard. The type was still in front-line service with RAF Coastal Command at the outbreak of World War II, the last unit to be operational with the type being No. 202 Squadron at Gibraltar, which received American-built Consolidated Catalinas in replacement during 1941.

Specification
Saro A.27 London Mk II
Type: coastal-patrol flying-boat
Powerplant: two 787-kW (1,055-hp) Bristol Pegasus X radial piston engines
Performance: maximum speed 249 km/h (155 mph) at 1905 m (6,250 ft); service ceiling 6065 m (19,900 ft); normal range 1770 km (1,100 miles)
Weights: empty 5035 kg (11,100 lb); maximum take-off 8346 kg (18,400 lb)
Dimensions: span 24.38 m (80 ft 0 in); length 17.31 m (56 ft 9½ in); height 5.72 m (18 ft 9 in); wing area 132.38 m² (1,425 sq ft)
Armament: three 7.7-mm (0.303-in) Lewis guns in bow and mid-ships positions, plus bombs or depth charges to a total load of 907 kg (2,000 lb)

Compared with the original London Mk I, the Mk II had updated engines with four-bladed propellers.

Saro A.17 Cutty Sark

In 1928 A. V. Roe acquired an interest in S. E. Saunders Ltd, the company name then being changed to Saunders-Roe Ltd, whose products were known more usually by the shortenend name Saro. The first design to enter production under the new company name was the **Saro A.17 Cutty Sark**, a lightweight monoplane flying-boat accommodating a pilot and three passengers. As first flown, on 4 July 1929, the prototype (G-AAIP) was powered by two 78-kW (105-hp) ADC Hermes I engines, each strut-mounted above the wing to drive a tractor propeller. The 'boat was later given amphibious capability by the introduction of retractable landing gear, and the satisfactory performance of the type resulted in the construction of 11 more A.17 aircraft. They differed in powerplant, most of them having two 89-kW (120-hp) de Havilland Gipsy II engines,

The sixth production Saro A.17 Cutty Sark was delivered to the Royal Air Force's Seaplane Training Flight at Calshot during December 1930 and served faithfully as a trainer for bigger boats, powered by a pair of de Havilland Gypsy II radial engines.

but the last three to be built had the most powerful standard powerplant of two Armstrong Siddeley Genet Major I engines. The exception was a single aircraft (G-ABVF) built for a San Francisco-Japan flight by a Japanese pilot; this differed from all previous A.17s by having a single 179-kW (240-hp) Armstrong Siddeley Lynx IVC engine, increased fuel capacity and no amphibious capability. Most A.17s had useful lives, especially three operated by Air Service Training at Hamble, Hants, from 1933 to 1938.

Specification
Saro A.17 Cutty Sark
Type: lightweight amphibious flying-boat
Powerplant: two 104-kW (140-hp) Armstrong Siddeley Genet Major I radial piston engines
Performance: maximum speed 172 km/h (107 mph); service ceiling 2745 m (9,000 ft); range 507 km (315 miles)
Weights: empty 1236 kg (2,725 lb); maximum take-off 1769 kg (3,900 lb)
Dimensions: span 13.72 m (45 ft 0 in); length 10.46 m (34 ft 4 in); height 3.40 m (11 ft 2 in); wing area 292.73 m² (320.0 sq ft)

Saro A.19 Cloud, A.21 Windhover and A.33

The success of the Saro A.17 (and in the late 1920s a production series of 11 aircraft was counted a success) led to design and construction of the **Saro A.19 Cloud** prototype, which was little more than an enlarged version of the A.17 Cutty Sark accommodating a crew of two and eight passengers. The twin-engine powerplant installation of the earlier design was retained for the Cloud, for it was appreciated that this allowed great flexibility in the installation of different engines to meet the requirements of individual customers; this was fortunate, for Clouds were eventually powered by five different types of engine. The prototype (G-ABCJ) had initially two 224-kW (300-hp) Wright J-6 Whirlwind radial engines, but after some three years of service in Canada was re-purchased by Saunders-Roe for use a test bed for the 254-kW (340-hp) Napier Rapier IV powerplant, two of these engines being installed together with a small aerofoil surface behind them to minimise slipstream turbulence. One had the unusual installation of three 160-kW (215-hp) Armstrong Siddeley Lynx IVC engines which had been ordered by the purchaser, but problems with this layout resulted in the aircraft being delivered instead with two 317-kW (425-hp) Pratt & Whitney Wasp C radial engines. The fourth and last civil Cloud was powered by two 254-kW (340-hp)

Armstrong Siddeley Serval III engines but, after being sold to a customer in Czechoslovakia during a demonstration tour of Europe, these were subsequently replaced by two 224-kW (300-hp) Walter Pollux engines.

Four A.19 Cloud civil flying-boats could hardly be counted a success, but fortunately for Saunders-Roe the Air Ministry ordered a prototype and 16 production aircraft for pilot and navigator training, these being powered by two Armstrong Siddeley Serval V engines as standard and operated by a crew of two. The cabin accommodation differed from that of the civil Cloud, being equipped with chart tables for the training of six navigators. They served with the School of Air Pilotage at Andover, the Seaplane Training Squadron at Calshot and with No. 48 Squadron, remaining in use 1933-36. One service aircraft, probably the prototype, was later modified to evaluate a Monospar wing as manufactured by General Aircraft Limited. In 1938 Saunders-Roe incorporated a Monospar wing in the one-off **Saro A.33** which, powered by four 619-kW (830-hp) Bristol Perseus XII wing-mounted engines, combined parasol-wing configuration with hull sponsons. Designed to Air Ministry Specification R.2/33 that resulted in the Short Sunderland, the aircraft was damaged severely during taxiing trials and scrapped.

The A.19 Cloud was followed by the somewhat similar **A.21 Windhover** of which only a single example was built. In terms of size it came between the A.17 and A.19 and was designed to accommodate a crew of two and six passengers. Possibly the three-engine powerplant tested on the second Cloud had been shown to have some potential, for three 89-kW (120-hp) de Havilland Gipsy II engines were used to power this aircraft, a distinctive installation that was highlighted by having an auxiliary aerofoil surface carried on struts above the engines. The Windhover remained in use from its first flight in 1931 until being taken out of service in 1938.

Specification
Saro A.19 Cloud (military version)
Type: pilot and navigator trainer
Powerplant: two 254-kW (340-hp) Armstrong Siddeley Serval V I radial piston engines
Performance: maximum speed 190 km/h (118 mph); service ceiling 4265 m (14,000 ft); range 612 km (380 miles)
Weights: empty 3084 kg (6,800 lb); maximum take-off 4309 kg (9,500 lb)
Dimensions: span 19.51 m (64 ft 0 in); length 15.28 m (50 ft 1½ in); height 5.00 m (16 ft 5 in); wing area 60.39 m² (650.0 sq ft)
Armament: provisions for a 7.7-mm (0.303-in) Lewis machine-gun on trainable mountings in bow and rear positions, plus up to four 22.7-kg (50-lb) practice bombs mounted externally

Essentially a scaled-up A.17 Cutty Sark, the Saro A.19 Cloud flying-boat is seen here in the shape of its prototype. This aircraft was used by the manufacturer throughout the mid-1930s for a series of engine trials and other tests.

Saro S.36 Lerwick

Designed to Air Ministry Specification R.1/36 for a reconnaissance flying-boat, the **Saunders-Roe S.36 Lerwick** design was probably the least satisfactory of all the company's efforts, although produced to a total of 21 for service with RAF Coastal Command. A monoplane flying-boat, with a cantilever high-set wing and powered by two 1025-kW (1,375-hp) Bristol Hercules II or IV radial sleeve-valve engines in wing-mounted nacelles, the Lerwick was shown in early tests to have unsatisfactory stability and stalling characteristics. Although modifications were introduced to resolve these problems they were, at best, only

alleviated. The Lerwick began to enter service in late 1940, operated initially by No. 209 Squadron. All 21 aircraft on order had been delivered by November 1940, but following the early loss of two Lerwicks the type was withdrawn from service in May 1941. A few were used for a short time in secondary roles, but most went into storage. The 24.64-m (80-ft 10-in) span Lerwick had a maximum speed of 343 km/h (213 mph), carried a crew of six, and was armed with one Vickers K machine-gun (bow), six Browning machine-guns in dorsal (two) and tail (four) turrets, plus a bombload of 907 kg (2,000 lb).

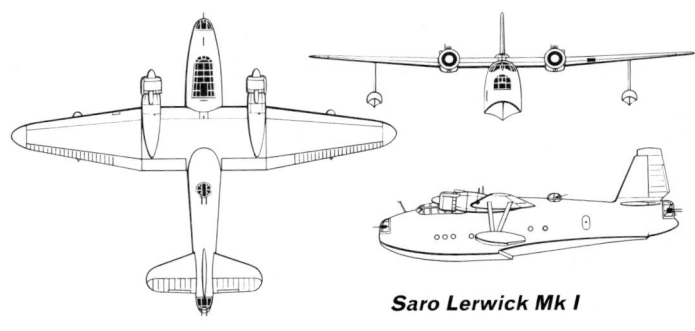

Saro Lerwick Mk I

Saro Skeeter

With the post-World War II lack of interest in flying-boats, Saunders-Roe sought to diversify within the aircraft industry and in January 1951 acquired the Cierva company to gain a foothold in rotary-wing aircraft. Cierva had flown on 8 October 1948 the prototype of an experimental two-seat helicopter which it designated **Cierva W.14 Skeeter I**,

and Saro continued development of this design. Three prototypes of the **Saro Skeeter 6**, powered by the 149-kW (200-hp) Gipsy Major 200, were evaluated by the British Army Air Corps, leading first to an order for four more

evaluation aircraft delivered as three **Skeeter AOP.Mk 10s** and one **Skeeter T.Mk 11** dual-control trainer. The Army Air Corps acquired 64 production **AOP.Mk 12 Skeeter** helicopters which differed by having a 160-kW (215-

hp) Gipsy Major engine, and a small number of similarly-powered **Skeeter T.Mk 13** aircraft were used by the RAF to train army helicopter instructors. In addition, under the designations **Skeeter Mk 50** and **Skeeter Mk 51** the Federal German army and navy acquired six and four helicopters respectively. These helicopters had a main rotor of 9.75 m (32 ft 0 in) diameter and could attain a maximum speed of 267 km/h

(104 mph). A civil variant was planned as the **Skeeter Series 8**, but only a single example was built and no civil orders were received. When production ended, in 1960, the Saunders-Roe rotary-wing activities had been acquired by the Westland group.

The delicate-looking Skeeter AOP.Mk 12 proved a great success in British army service.

Saro lesser types

A half-scale model of a planned maritime reconnaissance aircraft, the **Saro A.37** of 1939 gained the nickname 'Shrimp' because of its comparatively small size. It was of cantilever high-wing monoplane configuration, accommodated a crew of two and was powered by four 67-kW (90-hp) Pobjoy Niagra radial engines in wing-mounted nacelles. Although the A.37 was tested satisfactorily by the Marine Aircraft Experimental Establishment the full-scale prototype was not built, but the 15.24-m (50-ft 0-in) span A.37 fulfilled a useful role in the development by Saunders-Roe and Short Brothers of the Short Shetland flying-boat.

On 16 July 1947 the first of three prototypes of the **Saro SR.A/1** fighter flying-boat was flown, a cantilever low-wing single-seat monoplane that accommodated the pilot on an ejection seat in a pressurised cockpit. The type was powered by two Metropolitan-Vickers F2/4 Beryl turbojet engines, those of the first, second and third prototypes developing 1474 kg (3,250 lb), 1588 kg (3,500 lb) and 1746 kg (3,850 lb) thrust respectively. Although this 14.02 m (46 ft 0

in) span fighter demonstrated excellent performance, with a maximum speed of 824 km/h (512 mph), more considered evaluation by service chiefs of the flying-boat fighter concept brought the conclusion that a land-based turbojet-powered fighter was of greater value, and no more examples of the SR.A/1 were ordered.

Chronologically, the next of the Saunders-Roe lesser types is paradoxically, the giant **Saro SR.45 Princess** flying-boat, of which three prototypes were ordered in May 1946. These were intended for non-stop transatlantic service by BOAC, but early post-war appreciation that landplanes could operate on this route just as safely and more economically killed all interest. Instead, the 'boats were to be completed as long-range military transports for the RAF, but the lack of a suitable powerplant brought even these optimistic hopes to an end. Larger than the Martin Mars and heavier than the Bristol Brabazon I, the Princess prototype was flown for the first time on 22 August 1952 and spanned 66.90 m (219 ft 6 in) with its wingtip floats retracted, weighed 156492 kg (345,000 lb)

on take-off, and could attain a maximum speed of 579 km/h (360 mph) on the power of its 10 2386-kW (3,200-hp) Bristol Proteus 600 turboprop engines. These were mounted in the wings as two single outboard engines and four inboard paired engines, but development problems with the gearboxes of the inboard engines contributed to the decision to end development. The second and third Princesses did not fly and were cocooned.

On 16 May 1957 Saunders-Roe flew a very different aircraft, the first of two supersonic fighter prototypes built to a Ministry of Supply contract to evaluate, for the first time in the UK, the potential of mixed powerplant. This was the **Saro SR.53** landplane fighter with a mid-set delta wing, all-moving delta tailplane, and powerplant consisting of a 794-kg (1,750-lb) thrust Armstrong Siddeley Viper turbojet mounted within the fuselage; this was complemented by a liquid-propellant de Havilland Spectre rocket motor of about 3629 kg (8,000 lb) thrust

TG263 was the first Saro SR.A/1 flying-boat fighter, and was a hefty machine turning the scales at a maximum of 7360 kg (16,225 lb) without overload tanks.

The SR.45 Princess was one of the ultimate flying-boat designs, and with 10 engines (eight in coupled units and two singletons). It has a design maximum take-off weight of 165492 kg (345,000 lb).

in the rear fuselage, mounted below the Viper's tailpipe. An operational SR.53 would have been armed with two wing-tip mounted Firestreak air-to-air missiles. Saunders-Roe had designed more or less in parallel with the SR.53 a slightly larger version designated **SR.177**, which was intended as a multi-role fighter for the RAF. It was the British Admiralty that showed interest in this design, ordering six pre-production prototypes in 1956. There were required to have a strengthened airframe, catapult hitches and an arrester hook, and were to be powered by a 3629-kg (8,000-lb) thrust de Havilland Gyron Junior turbojet plus a de Havilland Spectre 5A liquid-propellant rocket-motor of the same thrust. Although these prototypes were almost complete, they were scrapped as a result of the notorious government White Paper of 1957, which planned to switch from manned interceptors to surface-to-air missiles for UK defence.

Saunders early flying-boats

The boat-building company of S. E. Saunders Ltd, established at Cowes, Isle of Wight, had a reputation for high-speed motorboat hulls that combined light weight and strength due to the company's use of copper-sewn plywood in their construction, a material it named Consuta. This was ideal for aircraft hulls and floats, and as early as 1912 the Sopwith Bat Boat No. 1 combined biplane wings with a Consuta hull. This early association with aviation placed the company in an ideal position to carry out a great deal of sub-contract construction during World War II, and it then began

the design of aircraft in this category soon after the war was over. Its first significant aircraft was the **Saunders Kittiwake**, a two-crew/seven-passenger amphibious flying-boat of biplane configuration which incorporated many advanced ideas, including a detachable hull of Consuta for easy replacement if damaged. Full-span camber-changing surfaces on each wing were provided for good low-speed handling, requiring the provision of interplane ailerons. Designed and built within three months, and completed just too late to take part in the Air Ministry Commercial Amphi-

bian Competition for which it was intended, the Kittiwake flew for the first time on 19 September 1920, powered by two 149-kW (200-hp) ABC Wasp Mk II radial engines, but for lack of commercial interest the Kittiwake was scrapped in 1921. Vickers Ltd acquired an interest in S. E. Saunders in 1918 and requested the company to design and build the prototype of a twin-engine biplane flying-boat which became the **Vickers Valentia**. Powered by two 485-kW (650-hp) Rolls-Royce Condor IA engines, it was flown and tested successfully during 1922, but no further examples were built. It was not until Saunders received an Air Council contract for a two-crew/six-passenger transport flying-boat in 1925 that the

next machine was designed and built as the **Saunders A.4 Medina**. Of unequal-span biplane configuration, with the lower wing of greatest span, it was powered by two 336-kW (450-hp) Bristol Jupiter V radial engines which provided a maximum speed of 185 km/h (115 mph); although in use from 1926 to 1929 no further examples were built. Much larger than either of its predecessors, with a span of 29.57 m (97 ft 0 in), the **Saunders A.3 Valkyrie** of 1927 was designed as a military flying-boat for a crew of five and was powered by three 485-kW (650-hp) Rolls-Royce Condor III engines. Although the Valkyrie's performance was satisfactory, its Consuta hull proved its undoing.

Savoia-Marchetti S.55

One of the most advanced and successful flying-boats to appear anywhere in the world in the period between the world wars, the **Savoia-Marchetti S.55** was designed in response to a request for a new multi-engine torpedo-bomber flying-boat. Its unique features were twin catamaran-type hulls, a thick-section catilever wing of which the centre section accommodated the

pilots' cockpits, and a tail unit incorporating two fins and three rudders supported on twin booms extending from the wings and the rear hulls. The first prototype, powered by two 224-kW (300-hp) Fiat A.12bis engines mounted in tandem over the wing centre-section to drive one tractor and one pusher propeller, was test flown in summer 1924. The aircraft proved to be underpowered, with a

maximum speed of only 160 km/h (99 mph), and a second prototype with two 298-kW (400-hp) Lorraine 12Db engines performed only marginally better; the S.55 still failed to attract the interest of the Italian navy, which was critical of the unconventional design and its limited performance. The company was determined that the new aircraft should be a success and the civil S.55C with accommodation for five passengers in each narrow hull was first flown in summer 1925.

The Ministero dell'Aeronautica belatedly took an interest in the military S.55 and ordered a first batch of 14 Asso-powered machines in 1926, and large numbers were then built to re-equip the Regia Marina's *squadiglie di bombardamento marittimo*. In 1930 an improved version with Fiat A.22R engines and re-designed hulls entered military service, and a second civil version, the S.55P, began operating in Italy, the Soviet Union and the USA.

Variants

S.55: two prototypes and 88 early production military aircraft delivered during 1927-30; all eventually fitted with two 380-kW (510-hp) Isotta-Fraschini Asso 500 engines giving maximum speed of 190 km/h (118 mph)
S.55C: first civil version, of which eight were built and delivered 1925-26; most had Lorraine engines but all were later re-engined with Asso 500s
S.55P: second civil version, 23 delivered 1928-32; had enlarged hulls accommodating 10 passengers and enclosed crew cockpits; believed 14 operated on Società Aerea Mediterranea services linking Rome, Naples, Sardinia and Sicily; powered originally by Asso 500, then Asso 550 Ru and finally 522-kW (700-hp) Fiat A.24R engines; three S.55Ps exported to USA; five sold to Soviet Union in 1932 had 656-kW (800-hp) Asso 750 engines and improved hulls
S.55A: designation of 16 military aircraft (A for Atlantic) delivered with 418-kW (560-hp) Fiat A.22R engines
S.55M: seven built by Piaggio in 1930 with Asso 500 Ri engines; wood structure largely replaced by metal
S.55 Scafo Allargato (enlarged hull): similar to S.55A but with wider and deeper hulls and enclosed crew cockpits; Savoia-Marchetti built 16,

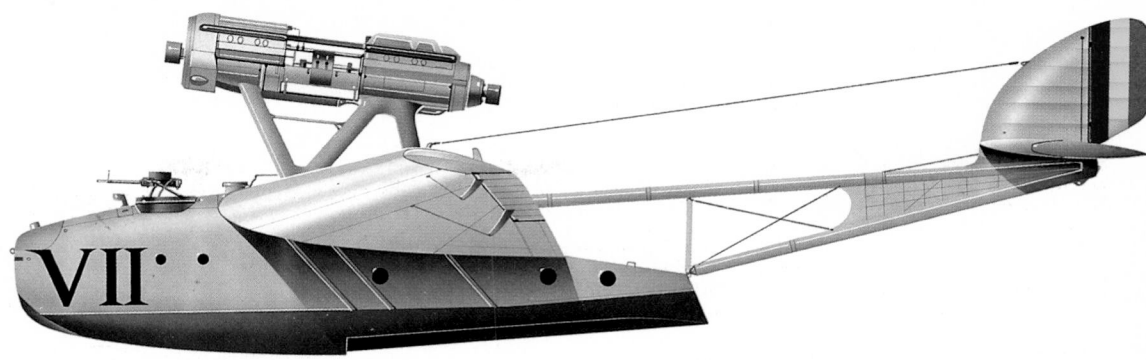

Savoia-Marchetti S.55SA of the 1a Escadrilla Hydro, Romanian air force, based at Constanza during the 1930s.

eight with Asso 500 and eight with Asso 500Ri engines, and CANT also constructed eight of each
S.55 Scafo Allargatissimo (very enlarged hull): hulls further modified and streamlined; Savoia-Marchetti built 20 with Fiat A.22R engines from 1932-33, and in 1933 Macchi completed 16 and CANT six, both lots powered by Isotta-Fraschini Asso 500Ri engines; all delivered to Italian units
S.55X: 25 delivered in 1933 with Asso 750 engines for North Atlantic formation flights; on return to Italy armed and used in flying-boat reconnaissance-bomber units, flying

with 31° and 35° Stormi BM until replaced by CANT Z.506Bs in 1938; three used briefly by Nationalists at beginning of Spanish Civil War, 1937; some military S.55s with differing hulls were also known as S.55Xs when fitted with Asso 750 engines; others of those batches without these later engines were often known by the designation **S.55N**

Specification
Savoia-Marchetti S.55X
Type: long-range bomber-reconnaissance flying-boat
Powerplant: two 656-kW (880-hp)

Isotta-Fraschini Asso 750 Vee piston engines
Performance: maximum speed 279 km/h (173 mph); service ceiling 5000 m (16,405 ft); range 3500 km (2,175 miles)
Weights: empty equipped 5750 kg (12,677 lb); maximum take-off 8260 kg (18,210 lb)
Dimensions: span 24.00 m (78 ft 9 in); length 16.75 m (54 ft 11½ in); height 5.00 m (16 ft 4¾ in); wing area 93.00 m² (1,001.08 sq ft)
Armament: four 7.7-mm (0.303-in) machine-guns; plus one torpedo or 2000 kg (4,409 lb) of bombs

Savoia-Marchetti S.56

The Savoia-Marchetti S.56 proved highly popular in the USA, where the type was built under licence by the American Aeronautical Corporation.

The **Savoia-Marchetti S.56** of 1924, a three-seat trainer/tourer flying-boat, was an unequal-span biplane mainly of wooden construction. Pilot and co-pilot were seated side-by-side in separate cockpits equipped with dual controls, a third cockpit being located just behind them. Power was provided by a 52-kW (70-hp) Anzani engine, but two **S.56A** 'boats built with 60-kW (80-hp) Anzanis had a slight increase in wing span and were given amphibious capability by the introduction of manually-retracted wheel landing gear. At least 12 S.56As were sold to private owners and clubs and four were used by the Regia Aero-

nautica for training; they were powered by a variety of engines, including the 86-kW (115-hp) Fiat A.53, 101-kW (135-hp) Fiat A.54, and Walter Venus radials.

The American Aeronautical Corporation began licence-production of the S.56 in 1929, powered by the 67-kW (90-hp) Kinner K5 engine, and three two-seat machines were followed by at least 40 three-seater. In 1930 the **S.56B**, powered by a 93-kW (125-hp) Kinner B5, was flown in the USA. One was built with an enclosed cockpit canopy and one, coverted to single-seat capacity, with additional fuel tanks and redesignated **S.56C**, was used on a round-the-

world trip by American businessman Zachery Reynolds. An all-metal version of the S.56 was built by the American Edwin Budd Corporation in 1932 and designated **Budd BB-1**.

Specification
American Aeronautical S.56A
Type: three-seat tourer/trainer amphibian flying-boat
Powerplant: one 67-kW (90-hp) Kinner B5 radial piston engine
Performance: maximum speed 138

km/h (86 mph); service ceiling 1670 m (5,480 ft); endurance 3 hours
Weights: empty equipped 658 kg (1,450 lb); maximum take-off 975 kg (2,150 lb)
Dimensions: span 10.72 m (35 ft 2 in); length 7.80 m (25 ft 7 in); height 2.99 m (9 ft 9¾ in); wing area 26.50 m² (285.25 sq ft)

Savoia-Marchetti S.57

Two prototype **Savoia-Marchetti S.57** reconnaissance flying-boats built in 1923 were of wooden construction and had single-step hulls with the pilot

and observer/gunner seated in tandem open cockpits in the bow section. Power was provided by a single 186-kW (250-hp) Isotta-Fraschini V6 engine, and there

was provision for 7.7-mm (0.303-in) Fiat machine-gun on a ring mounting over the observer's cockpit. An experimental **S.57bis** had a 224-kW (300-hp) Hispano-Suiza 42 engine. Span of the S.57 was 11.25 m (36 ft 11 in), maximum take-

off weight 1605 kg (3,538 lb) and maximum speed 215 km/h (134 mph).

In 1925 18 S.57s were delivered to the Italian air arm which used the type as a trainer, allocating examples to first-line *squadriglie* for flight familiarisation.

Savoia-Marchetti S.59

The **Savoia-Marchetti S.59** prototype, flown for the first time in 1925, was a modernised version of the S.16, being a reconnaissance/bomber flying-boat for the Italian maritime reconnaissance *squadriglie*. Its crew was accommodated in two side-by-side cockpits forward of the wings, plus a low cockpit with a Lewis machine-gun on a trainable mount. From the outset it was underpowered, the prototype having a 268-kW (360-hp) Rolls-Royce Eagle engine and series machines the 298-kW (400-hp) Lorraine-Dietrich 12Db. In spite of limited performance with this engine, the first of 40 S.59s for the Regia Aeronautica were delivered in 1926.

The **S.59bis** of 1927 differed only by having the more powerful Isotta-Fraschini Asso 500 engine and was built extensively by the company (82), CANT (50) and Macchi (50), all being delivered

by 1930. Italian *squadriglie* equipped with the type included the 141ª, 142ª, 144ª, 182ª and 184ª. Fifty-one S.59bis flying-boats formed the backbone of the spectacular formation cruise of the western Mediterranean in 1928. During the 1930s many S.59bis aircraft had Handley Page leading-edge slats installed on the upper wing, and after withdrawal from first-line service in 1937 the type continued for many years as a trainer.

S.59bis exports included 10 to Argentina and eight to Romania, and the **S.59P** civil version introduced in 1928 had an enclosed cabin forward of the wings for two crew and four passengers.

Specification
Savoia-Marchetti S.59bis
Type: reconnaissance/bomber flying-

boat
Powerplant: one 380-kW (510-hp) Isotta-Fraschini Asso 500 Vee piston engine
Performance: maximum speed 200 km/h (124 mph); service ceiling 4550 m (14,930 ft); endurance 5 hours
Weights: empty equipped 1950 kg (4,299 lb); maximum take-off 2950 kg (6,504 lb)
Dimensions: span 15.50 m (50 ft 10¼ in); length 10.36 m (33 ft 11¾ in);

height 3.50 m (11 ft 5¾ in); wing area 60.00 m² (645.86 sq ft)
Armament: one Lewis 7.7-mm (0.303-in) machine-gun, plus up to 280 kg (617 lb) of bombs on external racks

Named 'Buenos Aires', this Savoia-Marchetti S.59 made a celebrated flight from New York to Buenos Aires, Brazil, in 1926. The S.59 was intended as a combat type.

Savoia-Marchetti S.62

Of more modern concept than the S.59, the **Savoia-Marchetti S.62** bomber/ reconnaissance flying-boat appeared in prototype form in 1926. It had unequal-span wings, was structurally much tougher than its predecessor, introduced a second gunner's cockpit aft of the wings on a humped section of the hull decking, and was powered by a 380-kW (510-hp) Asso 500 engine.

A limited number of civil **S.62P** flying-boats appeared in 1928, some with an enclosed cabin for crew and four pas-

sengers, and others with open cockpits. A number were used by the Italian SAM airline and single examples were exported to the USA and Spain.

The first example of a developed **S.62bis** was flown in early 1930. This had wings of increased span, a redesigned hull, a more powerful engine, and increased armament and fuel capacity. The Soviet Union ordered 50, the first S.62bis being flown to Sevastopol in March 1930, but only 24 SIAI-built aircraft were supplied to the Soviet Union,

which built 29 more under licence, designating them **MBR-4**. Many were equipped with skis for operation from ice.

Savoia-Marchetti test variants included an S.62bis powered by a geared Asso 500Ri, and a solitary **S.62ter** with a Fiat A.24R engine.

Specification
Savoia-Marchetti S.62
Type: four-seat bomber/ reconnaissance flying-boat
Powerplant: one 634-kW (850-hp) Isotta-Fraschini Asso 750 Vee piston engine

Performance: maximum speed 220 km/h (137 mph); service ceiling 4900 m (16,075 ft); range 2000 km (1,243 miles)
Weights: empty equipped 2630 kg (5,798 lb); maximum take-off 5030 kg (11,089 lb)
Dimensions: span 16.66 m (54 ft 8 in); length 12.26 m (40 ft 2¾ in); height 4.19 m (13 ft 9 in); wing area 69.50 m² (748.12 sq ft)
Armament: four 7.7-mm (0.303-in) machine-guns, plus 600 kg (1,323 lb) of bombs

Savoia-Marchetti S.66

Designed as a replacement for the S.55P, the three-engined **Savoia-Marchetti S.66** passenger flying-boat prototype made its maiden flight in 1931. It had the twin-hull configuration of the S.55, with hulls that were deeper and more elegant in design, similar tail-booms and tail, but power provided by three Fiat A.22R engines mounted above the wing. The pilot and co-pilot were accommodated in an enclosed cockpit in the leading edge of the wing centre-section. Each hull contained initially seven seats and two sleeping couches plus a lavatory, but in the 23 series aircraft the couches were elim-

inated in favour of four more seats in each hull and the engines were replaced by more powerful Fiat A.24Rs.

Specification
Type: passenger flying-boat
Powerplant: three 559-kW (750-hp) Fiat A.24R Vee piston engines
Performance: maximum speed 238 km/h (148 mph); service ceiling 5350 m (17,550 ft); maximum range 1200 km (746 miles)
Weights: empty equipped 7450 kg (16,424 lb); maximum take-off 10950 kg (24,141 lb)

The S.M.66 was in essence a scaled-up version of the S.55 with a powerplant of three instead of two engines. The hull and wings were wooden, while the booms and tail unit were fabric-covered steel.

Dimensions: span 33.00 m (108 ft 3¼ in); length 16.65 m (54 ft 7½ in);
height 4.90 m (16 ft 1 in); wing area 126.70 m² (1,363.83 sq ft)

Savoia-Marchetti S.71

First flown in 1930, the **Savoia-Marchetti S.71** was a three-engine cantilever high-wing cabin monoplane of mixed construction, with fixed tailwheel landing gear, which accommodated a crew of four and eight passengers.

The first four S.71s had Walter Castor radial engines, but the three remaining

aircraft were powered by 276-kW (370-hp) Piaggio P.VIIs.

Specification
Type: eight-passenger light transport
Powerplant: three 179-kW (240-hp) Walter Castor radial piston engines
Performance: maximum speed 235

Though seen here without, the Savoia-Marchetti S.71 was often flown with speed fairings over the landing gear.

km/h (146 mph); service ceiling 6000 m (19,685 ft); range 1600 km (994 miles)
Weights: empty equipped 2900 kg

(6,393 lb); maximum take-off 4600 kg (10,141 lb)
Dimensions: span 21.20 m (69 ft 6¾ in); length 14.00 m (45 ft 11¼ in); height 4.10 m (13 ft 5½ in); wing area 60.00 m² (645.86 sq ft)

Savoia-Marchetti S.72

Resembling an enlarged and strengthened version of the S.71, the **Savoia-Marchetti S.72** was flown as a prototype (MM 219) in 1934 and intended for use as a heavy bomber.

Although not adopted for the Regia Aeronautica, the prototype was first used as a VIP transport linking Italy with the country's colonial empire. In the summer of 1935 it was demonstrated in China before being handed to Generalissimo Chiang Kai-shek as a gift. Six series S.72s were ordered by the Chinese and assembled in China; it is believed that

more were destroyed in Japanese air raids during late 1937.

Specification
Type: bomber/transport aircraft
Powerplant: three 410-kW (550-hp) Alfa Romeo licence-built Bristol Pegasus radial piston engines
Performance: maximum speed 295 km/h (183 mph); service ceiling 8000 m (26,245 ft); normal range 2000 km (1,243 miles)
Weights: empty equipped 6800 kg

(14,991 lb); maximum take-off 12800 kg (28,219 lb)
Dimensions: span 29.68 m (97 ft 4½ in); length 19.95 m (65 ft 5½ in); height 5.50 m (18 ft 0½ in); wing area 118.50 m² (1,275.57 sq ft)
Armament: up to six 7.7-mm (0.303-in) machine-guns and one 20-mm

Designed as a bomber derivative of the S.71, the Savoia-Marchetti S.72 was somewhat larger than its progenitor, but attracted little official Italian interest.

cannon, plus 1000 kg (2,205 lb) of bombs

Savoia-Marchetti S.73

Developed in parallel with the S.81 bomber, the **Savoia-Marchetti S.73** three-engine passenger transport made its maiden flight on 4 July 1934. Of cantilever low-wing monoplane configuration, the S.73 had wings of wooden construction and a roomy welded steel-tube fuselage with plywood and fabric cover-

ing. Pilot and co-pilot were seated side-by-side in an enclosed cockpit, with behind them compartments for the wire-

The S.73 marked the appearance of a three-engined, low-wing layout that would become a trademark.

less operator and mechanic, and a passenger cabin accommodating 18 in two rows of single seats.

Seven Belgian S.73s were flown to England in May 1940, where they were impressed by the RAF; they were sent subsequently to North Africa, where four of them were later taken over by the Regia Aeronautica. Some of the Italian S.73s were impressed into military service in East Africa, while those in Italy were taken over in June 1940 to equip the 605ª and 606ª Squadriglie. After the loss of Italy's East African Empire, three S.73s flew back to Italy by a circuitous route. Making good use of the strength, load-carrying abilities and good serviceability of the type, the Regia Aeronautica used them to carry men and materials, and S.73s of the 247ª Squadriglia flew in support of the Corpo di Spedizione Italiano during its 20-month stay on the Eastern Front from the autumn of 1941. Four S.73s survived the September 1943 armistice, three flying with the Allies and one with the pro-Axis government, all grounded by the end of the war.

Specification
Type: 18-passenger transport
Powerplant: three 597-kW (800-hp) Alfa Romeo 126 RC.10 radial piston
Performance: maximum speed 325 km/h (202 mph); service ceiling 7000 m (22,965 ft); range 1000 km (621 miles)
Weights: empty equipped 7300 kg (16,094 lb); maximum take-off 10800 kg (23,810 lb)
Dimensions: span 24.00 m (78 ft 9 in); length 18.37 m (60 ft 3¼ in); height 4.45 m (14 ft 7¼ in); wing area 92.20 m² (992.46 sq ft)

Savoia-Marchetti S.M.75 and S.M.76

In 1937 the company completed the prototype of its **Savoia-Marchetti S.M.75**, this prototype being flown for the first time on 6 November 1937. It represented a further refinement of the Savoia-Marchetti three-engine cantilever low-wing monoplane formula, with main landing gear units which retracted rearwards into the outer engine nacelles. A 30-passenger airliner, five of an initial batch of six production aircraft were delivered to Ala Littoria, the odd machine being supplied to the Italian air ministry with Regia Aeronautica serial MM 384.

Early experience confirmed the capability and efficiency of the S.M.75 and a total of 90 aircraft was built between 1937 and 1943. The engines were usually Alfa Romeo 126 RC.34s, but 11 aircraft with Alfa Romeo 126 RC.18 radials were designated **S.M.75bis**.

Ala Littoria used a total of 38 S.M.75s on European and African routes, and in 1939 the Italian airline LATI, newly created to operate services to Natal and Rio de Janeiro in Brazil, received its first S.M.75. At the end of 1940 this aircraft was redesignated **S.M.76** after being modified with a longer and wider fuselage, revised wing, increased fuel capacity, and Pratt & Whitney Twin Wasp radial engines.

When Italy declared war in June 1940 all S.M.75s were placed under military control in either the *servizi aerei speciali* or the *nuclei communicazione* run by the airlines.

The Luftwaffe used a number of S.M.75s after 1943, and others were operated by the Italian co-belligerent air force. Post-war, the type remained in service until the last were scrapped in 1949.

Variants
S.M.87: twin-float version of the S.M.75; four built and allocated to the Nucleo Communicazioni 'Ala Littoria' in summer 1940; powered by three 746-kW (1,000-hp) Fiat A.80 radials giving a maximum speed of 365 km/h (227 mph)
S.M.90: one-off prototype powered by three 1044-kW (1,400-hp) Alfa Romeo 135 radials and with a fuselage lengthened to 23.90 m (78 ft 5 in)

Specification
Savoia-Marchetti S.M.75
Type: transport
Powerplant: three 559-kW (750-hp) Alfa Romeo 126 RC.34 radial pistons
Performance: maximum speed 363 km/h (226 mph); service ceiling 6250 m (20,505 ft); range 1720 km (1,069 miles)
Weights: empty equipped 9500 kg (20,944 lb); maximum take-off 13000 kg (28,660 lb)
Dimensions: span 29.68 m (97 ft 1¾ in); length 21.60 m (70 ft 10½ in); height 5.10 m (16 ft 8¾ in); wing area 118.60 m² (1,276.64 sq ft)

The S.75 was the first of the company's aircraft to be fitted with retractable landing gear. This is a military version.

Savoia-Marchetti S.78

Test flown at the end of 1932, the **Savoia-Marchetti S.78** was a bomber/reconnaissance flying-boat developed from the S.62, with power provided by an Isotta-Fraschini Asso 750R engine. The prototype had an enclosed cockpit for the pilots, seated side-by-side, but the total of 49 series aircraft, 32 built by Piaggio and the remainder by SIAI, had open side-by-side pilots' cockpits with individual windscreens.

The last biplane flying-boat used in quantity by the Regia Aeronautica, the S.78 equipped the 144ª ('Leghorn'), 182ª ('Nisida'), 141ª ('La Spezia') and 189ª ('Syracuse') Squadriglie, the first two retaining their machines until 1938. Span was 16.66 m (54 ft 8 in) and maximum take-off weight 5150 kg (11,354 lb), and with its 634-kW (850-hp) Isotta-Fraschini Asso 750R engine the S.78 had a maximum speed of 245 km/h (152 mph). Armament comprised four 7.7-mm (0.303-in) machine-guns and up to 700 kg (1,543 lb) of bombs

Savoia-Marchetti S.M.79 Sparviero

Designed as a three-engine civil transport to accommodate eight passengers, the **Savoia-Marchetti S.M.79 Sparviero** (sparrowhawk) prototype (I-MAGO) was flown for the first time in late 1934. Its capability resulted in early adoption as a bomber/reconnaissance aircraft, producing one of the most successful Italian aircraft in this category of World War II, some 1,300 being built. A cantilever low-wing monoplane of mixed construction, it had retractable tailwheel landing gear, accommodated a crew of four or five and, in prototype form, was powered by three 582-kW (780-hp) Alfa Romeo 126 RC-34 radial engines. Following successful testing, the type was ordered into production as the **S.M.79-I** Sparviero, this version serving with the Aviazione Legionaria during the Spanish Civil War; good reports of its capability led Yugoslavia to order 45 similar aircraft in 1938.

In 1937 the S.M.79 had been tested in a torpedo-bomber role, leading to the **S.M.79-II**, of which most were powered by Piaggio P.XI RC.40 radials. Some 600 S.M.79-I and S.M.79-II aircraft were in service when Italy entered World War II, they and subsequent production versions being deployed in every theatre where Italian forces were operating. Savoia-Marchetti was also successful in gaining export orders, twin-engine **S.M.79B** aircraft being supplied to Brazil (3), Iraq (4) and Romania (24). This last country later acquired an additional 24 **S.M.79JR** aircraft and built 16 more under licence.

In Italian service the S.M.79 was used also for close-support, reconnaissance and transport missions, and its use as a transport continued post-war with the Aeronautica Militare Italiana until the early 1950s. Before that, when the Italians surrendered to the Allies, a small number of S.M.79-I and S.M.79-II aircraft entered service with the Aeronautica Cobelligerante del Sud, and the improved **S.M.79-III** proved of great value to the Aeronautica Nazionale Repubblicana.

Variants
S.M.79-I: bomber prototype and initial production version, differing from first prototype by having revised cockpit and ventral gondola
S.M.79-II: torpedo-bomber equipped to carry two 450-mm (17,7-in) torpedoes; powered by 746-kW (1,000-hp) Piaggio P.XI RC.40 or 768-kW (1,030-hp) Fiat A.80 RC.41 engines
S.M.79-III: improved version of S.M.79-II with ventral gondola deleted and armament revised
S.M.79B: twin-engine export version of S.M.79-I with redesigned nose; powered by 694-kW (930-hp) Alfa Romeo 128 RC.18 engines (Brazil), 768-kW (1,030-hp) Fiat A.80 RC.41 (Iraq) and 746-kW (1,000-hp) Gnome-Rhône Mistral Major K14 (Romania)
S.M.79C: VIP conversion of S.M.79-I with 746-kW (1,000-hp) Piaggio P.XI RC.40 engines and dorsal and ventral gun positions deleted
S.M.79K: version for Yugoslavia, generally similar to S.M.79C
S.M.79JR: export version for Romania, similar to S.M.79B but with two 835-kW (1,120-hp) Junkers Jumo 211 Da engines
S.M.79T: long-range version of S.M.79C with increased fuel capacity and Alfa Romeo 126 RC.34 engines

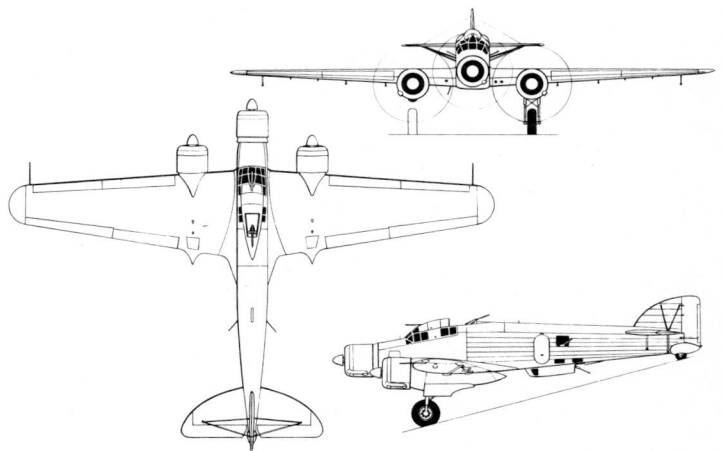

Savoia-Marchetti S.M.79-II

Specification
Savoia-Marchetti S.M.79-I
Type: medium bomber
Powerplant: three 582-kW (780-hp) Alfa Romeo 126 RC.34 radial piston

engines
Performance: maximum speed 430 km/h (267 mph) at 4000 m (13,125 ft); service ceiling 6500 m (21,325 ft); range 1900 km (1,181 miles)

Weights: empty 6800 kg (14,991 lb); maximum take-off 10480 kg (23,104 lb)
Dimensions: span 21.20 m (69 ft 6¾ in); length 15.80 m (51 ft 10 in); height 4.30 m (14 ft 1¼ in); wing area 61.70

m² (664.16 sq ft)
Armament: three 12.7-mm (0.5-in) and one 7.7-mm (0.303-in) machine-guns, plus up to 1250 kg (2,756 lb) of bombs carried internally

Savoia-Marchetti S.M.81 Pipistrello

A development of the S.M.73, the **Savoia-Marchetti S.M.81 Pipistrello** (bat) was a three-engine cantilever low-wing monoplane with fixed tailwheel landing gear. First flown in 1935, it was in service when Italy invaded Abyssinia (Ethiopia) on 3 October 1935 where, in addition to its dedicated bomber role, it was used also for reconnaissance and transport. S.M.81s were among the first aircraft provided to support General Franco in the Spanish Civil War, and others served in Spain later with the Aviazione Legionairia. About 100 were in Regia Aeronautica service when Italy entered World War II, but the type's low speed meant it was used primarily for second-line duties; however, with the cover of darkness many found useful employment as night bombers, particularly in North Africa. Some remained in service at the time of the Italian surrender, then operating with the Aeronautica Cobelligerante del Sud, and a few survived the war to serve for five or six years with the post-war Aeronautica Militare Italiana.

Variants
S.M.81: production version, 535 built,

and powered by a variety of engines including the 485-kW (650-hp) Gnome-Rhône 14K or Alfa Romeo 125 RC.35, 671-kW (900-hp) Alfa Romeo 126 RC.34 and 522-kW (700-hp) Piaggio P.X RC.35
S.M.81B: single experimental twin-engine prototype with 626-kW (840-hp) Isotta-Fraschini Asso XI RC engines

Savoia-Marchetti S.M.81 Pipistrello of the Gruppo Transporti 'Terraciano', air force of the Repubblica Sociale Italiana, operating on the Eastern Front during 1944.

Specification
Savoia-Marchetti S.M.81 Pipistrello
Type: bomber/transport
Powerplant: three 522-kW (700-hp) Piaggio RC.35 radial piston engines
Performance: maximum speed 340 km/h (211 mph) at 1000 m (3,280 ft); service ceiling 7000 m (22,965 ft); range 2000 km (1,243 miles)

Weights: empty 6300 kg (13,889 lb); maximum take-off 9300 kg (20,503 lb)
Dimensions: span 24.00 m (78 ft 9 in); length 17.80 m (58 ft 4¾ in); height 4.45 m (14 ft 7¼ in); wing area 93.00 m² (1,001.08 sq ft)
Armament: usually five 7.7-mm (0.303-in) machine-guns, plus a bombload of up to 1000 kg (2,205 lb) carried internally

Savoia-Marchetti S.M.82 Canguru

Developed from the S.M.75, the **Savoia-Marchetti S.M.82 Canguru** (kangaroo) prototype was flown during 1939. Basically an enlarged version of its predecessor, with a fuselage that was both deeper and longer, it was of the same general configuration. Despite being underpowered, this cargo-troop transport saw widescale service with the Regia Aeronautica and several were used by the Luftwaffe. Equipped specially for the cargo role, it had handling gear for heavy items and sufficient cabin volume to transport a dismantled Fiat CR.42 biplane without difficulty. As a troop transport it had standard accommodation for 40 men and their equipment, but many more could be carried in emergency.

The first of about 400 S.M.82 transports entered service in 1941, and though the type had a secondary bombing capability few were deployed in this role. Following the Italian surrender the type continued to serve in the transport role, some 50 with the Aeronautica

Nazionale Repubblicana and 30 with the Aeronautica Cobelligerante del Sud. Post-war, about 30 remained in service with the Aeronautica Militare Italiana until the early 1950s.

Specification
Type: heavy transport/bomber
Powerplant: three 708-kW (950-hp) Alfa Romeo 128 RC.21 radial piston

engines
Performance: maximum speed 370 km/h (230 mph); service ceiling 6000 m (19,685 ft); range 3000 km (1,864 miles)
Weights: empty equipped 10550 kg (23,259 lb); maximum take-off 18020 kg (39,727 lb)
Dimensions: span 29.68 m (97 ft 4½ in); length 22.90 m (75 ft 1½ in); height

6.00 m (19 ft 8¼ in); wing area 118.60 m² (1,276.64 sq ft)
Armament: (bomber) one 12.7-mm (0.5-in) and four 7.7-mm (0.303-in) machine-guns, plus up to 4000 kg (8,818 lb) of bombs

The Savoia-Marchetti S.M.82 proved a useful transport in World War II, and continued in air force service post-war until replaced by Fairchild C-119G Flying Boxcars, during the 1950s.

Savoia-Marchetti S.M.83

The prototype **Savoia-Marchetti S.M.83** 10-passenger transport flew for the first time on 19 November 1937. It followed closely the design of the S.79 bomber and resembled a refined version of the S.79T long-distance aircraft. Total production was 23, almost all going into service before Italy's entry into World War II. Seven were exported, three for the Romanian air line LARES and four for the Belgian national airline SABENA, which used them on routes to the Congo.

In June 1940 eight LATI S.M.83s were absorbed into the Regia Aeronautica to

form the 615ª Squadriglia, known also as the Nucleo Communicazione LATI. Manned largely by the original airline crews, the S.M.83s were used for passenger flights to East Africa and Libya, as well as maintaining a reduced service to South America.

The S.M.83 was the dedicated transport version of the S.M.79 bomber, and proved very valuable on Itlay's civil routes across the south Atlantic, where the type's good range and great reliability were vital assets.

The S.M.83 spanned 21.20 m (69 ft 6¾ in), had a maximum take-off weight of 11500 kg (25,353 lb), and attained a maximum speed of 444 km/h (276 mph) on the power of three 559-kW (750-hp) Alfra Romeo 126 RC.34 radial engines.

Savoia-Marchetti S.M.84

Designed to succeed the S.79 Sparviero, the **Savoia-Marchetti S.M.84** prototype which flew for the first time on 5 June 1940 had an entirely new fuselage with smooth upper contours. Defensive armament was provided by a Lanciani Delta E dorsal turret that could rotate through a full 360°, this all-round field of fire being blocked only by the twin fins and rudders. Additional armour protection added to overall weight, but the shortcomings of the S.M.84 became apparent only when it first entered service with the 41° Gruppo Bombardmento Terrestre in February 1941 and soon afterwards with the 36° Stormo Aerosiluranti in the torpedo-bombing role. The Piaggio P.XI engines proved unreliable, and a combination of inadequate vertical tail surfaces and high wing loading caused

instability and take-off problems. Nevertheless, production continued and 309 series machines were ordered, although it would appear that only 246 were delivered to the Regia Aeronautica, with a small batch also going to the Slovak air arm.

Specification
Savoia-Marchetti S.M.84
Type: medium bomber/torpedo-bomber
Powerplant: two 746-kW (1,000-hp) Piaggio P.XI radial piston engines
Performance: maximum speed 432 km/h (268 mph); service ceiling 7900 m (25,920 ft); range 1830 km (1,137 miles)
Weights: empty equipped 8846 kg (19,502 lb); maximum take-off 13288

kg (29,295 lb)
Dimensions: span 21.13 m (69 ft 4 in); length 17.93 m (58 ft 10 in); height 4.59 m (15 ft 0¾ in); wing area 61.00 m² (656.62 sq ft)

Armament: four 12.7-mm (0.5-in) Scotti/Isotta-Fraschini machine-guns, plus two torpedoes or up to 1600 kg (3,527 lb) of bombs

An unusual feature of the Savoia-Marchetti S.M.84 bomber was the bomb-aimer's retractable position, visible here under the nose.

Savoia-Marchetti S.M.85 and S.M.86

The prototype **Savoia-Marchetti S.M.86** single-seat dive-bomber was flown for the first time on 19 December 1936. A cantilever shoulder-wing monoplane with a rectangular-section fuselage, it accommodated the pilot well forward under a glazed canopy, and the main landing gear units retracted into the nacelles of the two Piaggio P.VII C.16 radial engines. Despite poor speed and climb characteristics, a second prototype was tested and 32 series aircraft built, introducing some structural refinements, improved combined flaps/air brakes and variable-pitch propellers.

The first prototype of the refined **S.M.86**, powered by two 336-kW (450-hp) Walter Sagitta engines, was flown in mid-1940, attaining a maximum speed of 412 km/h (256 mph). Like the second S.M.86 prototype flown on 7 August

1941 and powered by two experimental Isotta-Fraschini Gamma engines, it did not progress any further.

Specification
Savoia-Marchetti S.M.85
Type: single-seat dive-bomber
Powerplant: two 343-kW (460-hp) Piaggio P.VII C.35 radial piston engines
Performance: maximum speed 368 km/h (229 mph); service ceiling 6500 m (21,325 ft); range 827 km (514 miles)
Weights: empty equipped 2950 kg (6,504 lb); maximum take-off 4190 kg (9,237 lb)
Dimensions: span 14.00 m (45 ft 11½ in); length 10.40 m (34 ft 1½ in); height 3.30 m (10 ft 10 in); wing area 25.80 m² (277.72 sq ft)
Armament: one fixed forward-firing 12.7-mm (0.5-in) or 7.7-mm (0.303-in)

machine-gun, plus one bomb up to a maximum weight of 800 kg (1,763 lb) in internal bay

The pilot of the Savoia-Marchetti S.M.85 was placed well forward in the nose for good visibility, with a clear panel below his feet to acquire targets before beginning the bomb run.

Savoia-Marchetti S.M.95

Developed as a four-engined version of the S.75 transport, the prototype **Savoia-Marchetti S.M.95** was flown for the first time in May 1943. A cantilever low-wing monoplane of mixed construction, with retractable landing gear and powered by Alfa Romeo 128 radial engines, it accommodated a crew of five and 18 passengers.

The third S.M.95 did not fly until after World War II, on 30 July 1945, and was used to inaugurate post-war Alitalia services in Europe. It was followed by 20 production S.M.95s, the last being delivered in November 1949. Several were used by the Aeronautica Militare Italiana as VIP transports, Alitalia acquired six machines and, in July 1949, LATI began a fortnightly service to Venezuela with

three S.M.95s. Four more went to SAIDE, the Egyptian national airline, which flew them for a number of years on routes linking Cairo with Rome and Paris. Most of these transports had been withdrawn from service by 1952.

The earlier S.M.95s retained the Alfa Romeo 128 engines of the prototype, but the LATI machines had Pratt & Whitney Twin Wasps. The later Ala Littoria aircraft, as well as those for Egypt, had 552-kW (740-hp) Bristol Pegasus 48 radials.

Specification
Savoia-Marchetti S.M.85
Type: medium-range transport
Powerplant: four 641-kW (860-hp) Alfa Romeo 128 RC.18 radial pistons

Performance: maximum speed 400 km/h (249 mph); service ceiling 6500 m (21,325 ft); range 2000 km (1,243 miles)
Weights: empty equipped 12800 kg (28,219 lb); maximum take-off 21600

kg (47,620 lb)
Dimensions: span 34.28 m (112 ft 5.5 in); length 24.77 m (81 ft 3.25 in); height 5.70 m (18 ft 8.5 in); wing area 128.30 (1,381.05 sq ft)

A post-war Savoia-Marchetti S.M.95 airliner in use with the Italian air force.

Savoia Pomilio aircraft

The aviation section of the Fiat motor manufacturing company of Turin had built aero engines from 1908. In 1914 the company built the Farman M.F.11 under licence as the **Type 5B**. The **Savoia Pomilio S.P.1** which followed, designed by Major Umberto Savoia and Lieutenant Ottorino Pomilio, was a developed and strengthened version of the Farman; its 186-kW (250-hp) Fiat A.12 engine gave a maximum speed of 135 km/h (84 mph). An aerodynamically refined **S.P.2** followed soon afterwards

and the Fiat aviation section, then reconstituted as the Societá Italiana Aviazione, or S.I.A., built small number of S.P.1s as S.P.2s, in addition to the 300 S.P.2s produced by Pomilio. By spring 1917 S.P.2s equipped 12 *squadriglie* of the Italian Aeronautica Militare operating at the front on reconnaissance, artillery obser-

Aerodynamically an improvement on the S.P.2, the S.P.3 was nevertheless an obsolete design by 1917.

vation and light bombing duties. Armament was normally one machine-gun on a ring mounting, but some dozen aircraft were tested with 25-mm cannon.

The first **S.P.3**, flown in 1917, represented a further development of the basic design which had proved slow and vulnerable. It introduced wings of reduced span and a refined crew nacelle, was lighter in weight, and some aircraft were powered by a 224-kW (300-hp) Fiat A.12bis engine. During the spring and summer of 1917 considerable numbers

of S.P.3s (of which more than 300 were built) joined the front-line *squadriglie*, bringing the total of S.P.-equipped *squadriglie* up to a quarter of all the Italian units engaged in the fighting.

The last aircraft in the series was the **S.P.4**, built by the A.E.R. company. This retained the same general layout, but had machine-guns on trainable mounts in cockpits at the front and rear of the nacelle; power was provided by two 112-kW (150-hp) Isotta-Fraschini V4B engines mounted between the wings.

Production totalled 123 S.P.4s in 1917 and a further 23 in 1918. As well as their use in reconnaissance and light bombing roles, some S.P.4s were used to carry agents and saboteurs behind enemy lines.

Specification
Savoia Pomilia S.P.3
Type: two-seat general-purpose military biplane
Powerplant: one 186-kW (250-hp) Fiat A.12 inline piston engine

Performance: maximum speed 145 km/h (90 mph); service ceiling 5000 m (16,405 ft); range 450 km (280 miles)
Weights: empty equipped 1048 kg (2,310 lb); maximum take-off 1498 kg (3,303 lb)
Dimensions: span 14.70 m (48 ft 2¾ in); length 10.95 m (35 ft 11 in); height 3.55 m (11 ft 7¾ in); wing area 60.00 m² (645.86 sq ft)
Armament: one 7.62-mm (0.3-in) machine-gun, plus light bombs

Schweizer Ag-Cat

The basic design of the **Ag-Cat** agricultural aircraft was originated by the Grumman company, Schweizer building 1,730 of these aircraft under sub-contract for Grumman (later Gulfstream American Corporation) from 1957-79. In 1981 Schweizer acquired all rights to the design and continues to manufacture this aircraft. Of biplane configuration and of robust construction, the Ag-Cat has fixed tail-wheel landing gear and accommodates the pilot in an enclosed cockpit which is pressurised to prevent the ingression of toxic chemicals. The type is available currently in three generally similar versions that differ in powerplant, these being the **Schweizer Ag-Cat B-Plus/600** with a Pratt & Whitney R-1340 radial engine, the **Ag-Cat Turbine (G-164B)** with alternative Pratt & Whitney Canada PT6A turboprop engines ranging from 373 to 559 kW (500 to 750 shp), and to special order the

Ag-Ca B-Plus/450 with a 336-kW (450-hp) Pratt & Whitney R-985 radial engine. There is also a fourth version, the **Ag-Cat Turbine (G-164D),** which differs from the Ag-Cat Turbine (G-164B) by having a larger chemical hopper and alternative PT6A turboprop engines of either 559 or 634 kW (750 or 850 shp).

Specification
Schweizer Ag-Cat B-Plus/600
Type: single-seat agricultural aircraft
Powerplant: one 447-kW (600-hp) Pratt & Whitney R-1340 radial pistons
Performance: working speed 185 km/h (115 mph)
Weights: empty equipped 1656 kg

(3,650 lb); maximum take-off 3184 kg (7,020 lb)
Dimensions: span 12.93 m (42 ft

5 in); length 7.47 m (24 ft 6 in); height 3.51 m (11 ft 6 in); wing area 36.42 m² (392.0 sq ft)

Originating with Grumman, the Ag-Cat is a thoroughly workmanlike agricultural aircraft, with a wind-mill powered spray system.

Schweizer other aircraft

The Schweizer Aircraft Company was founded in 1939 to build gliders and sailplanes, which it still does to this day. This experience in building lightweight aircraft stood it in good stead when the US Army funded development of a new surveillance aircraft in the early 1980s. The requirement was for an ultra-quiet type, capable of long-duration missions, fitted with a wide range of sensors. Flying in 1986, the prototype was modified from an **SGM 2-37A** glider, and an initial batch of three aircraft, known as **RG-8**s, was purchased by the US Army. One of these was lost in a crash and the surviving pair were subsequently transferred to the US Coast Guard for anti-narcotics operations. Based in Miami, and now designated the **RG-8A Condor**, they are used to counter the flow of narcotics into the southern United States.

Flown by a two-man crew, the RG-8s are fitted with a removable equipment pallet in the fuselage that can accommodate a Texas Instruments AAQ-15 FLIR (Forward-Looking Infra-Red), which is fitted to a VHS tape recorder for ease of playback once on the ground. A Low-Light-Level TV (LLLTV) and standard camera fit can also be carried. Communications equipment includes VHF-AM, secure UHF and HF and protected VHF-FM. A satellite navigation system has also been installed. The cockpit instruments are fully compatible with night vision goggles.

Missions are flown by the pilot in the right-hand seat, supported by a surveillance systems Operator (SSO) sitting alongside. RG-8s usually operate singly, supported by a Coast Guard vessel, flying over an 800-km (500-mile) radius. Having detected a target – another surface vessel – the aircraft enters quiet mode, using a low propeller power set-

ting that allows it to descend to low altitude while keeping its noise footprint at a minimum. The target can then be observed and recorded using the systems onboard.

Schweizer's main production type at present is very different. In July 1983 Hughes Helicopters transferred production of its best selling Model 300C helicopters to Schweizer. The first flight of the **Schweizer 300C** took place in June 1984, with responsibility for the whole programme transferred in 1986. Since then the aircraft has been selling steadily, with the total in service approaching 500. Schweizer now offers product support for the entire fleet world-wide, regardless of their original manufacturer. In addition to the basic three-seat civilian version, Schweizer also offers the **Model 300C Sky Night**, a dedicated police version. This model has a strengthened, more crash-worthy cockpit, with armoured seats, a searchlight, PA/siren system, and much improved communications fit. In 1985 the US Army ordered 30 new-build **TH-300C** training aircraft, to supplement its existing Hughes TH-55A Osages. The Royal Thai air force also ordered 24 of the type delivered between 1986 and 1989. An improved version, the **TH-330**, is being offered by Schweizer in conjunction with UNC as a competitor in the US Army's New Trainer Helicopter (NTH) evaluation.

Schweizer's version of the Hughes Model 300 helicopter is outwardly little different from the original. The S.300 has continued selling, however, and a market for both aircraft and spares support is assured for the company for many years to come.

Schweizer's RG-8 surveillance aircraft owes much to the company's experience in sailplane design, its slight shape ideally suited to high-altitude cruising over an extended period. In US Coast Guard service since the mid-1980s, the RG-8A can carry an extensive array of electronic equipment in its 'Q-bay'.

Scottish Aviation Prestwick Pioneer
to
Shin Meiwa D.H.114-TAW

Scottish Aviation Prestwick Pioneer

Known originally as the **Scottish Aviation Prestwick Pioneer**, this four-seat light STOL transport was designed to meet the requirements of Air Ministry Specification A.4/45; it became known more usually as the **Pioneer**. A braced high-wing monoplane with leading-edge slats and large Fowler flaps to give the necessary STOL performance, the prototype was powered by a 179-kW (240-hp) de Havilland Gipsy Queen 32 engine. Disappointing performance with this powerplant resulted in no military order and it was developed by the company as a five-seat civil transport designated **Pioneer 2**, the prototype being powered by a 388-kW (520-hp) Alvis Leonides radial engine and first flown on

During the Malayan conflict the STOL performance of the Pioneer became invaluable to the RAF for jungle operations.

5 May 1950. The remarkable STOL performance of this version resulted in 40 being built for the RAF, which designated them **Pioneer C.C.Mk 1**; entering service in 1953, they saw extensive use in areas such as Aden, Cyprus and Malaya, some remaining operational until the end of the 1960s. Production totalled 59, 13 of this number serving with the Royal Ceylon air force (4) and Royal Malayan air force (9). Spanning 15.16 m (49 ft 9 in), RAF Pioneer C.C.Mk 1s had a maximum speed of 233 km/h (145 mph) at 455 m (1,500 ft).

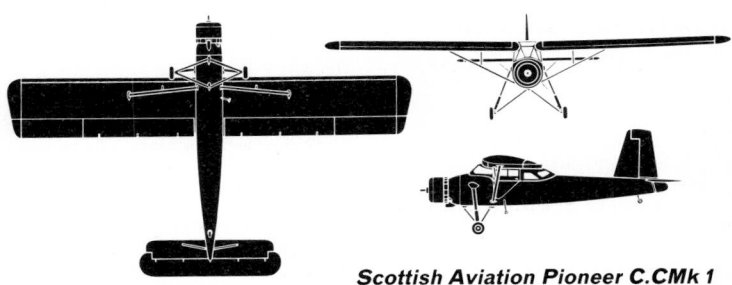

Scottish Aviation Pioneer C.CMk 1

Scottish Aviation Twin Pioneer

Success of the Pioneer led to the design and development of a twin-engine larger-capacity version designated the **Scottish Aviation Twin Pioneer**. This retained several features of the earlier aircraft to ensure good STOL performance, introduced triplicated vertical tail surfaces, revised landing gear and, of course, a much larger fuselage suitable for passenger or cargo carrying that could be equipped alternatively for such roles as air ambulance, executive transport, and geophysical or photographic survey. The prototype, first flown on 25 June 1955, was powered by two 403-kW (540-hp) Alvis Leonides 503/8 radials, but **Twin Pioneer Series 1** production aircraft, the first flown on 28 April 1956, had two 418-kW (560-hp) Leonides 514/8 or 8A engines.

Production totalled 87 aircraft, comprising the Twin Pioneer Series 1, **Twin Pioneer Series 2** with 447-kW (600-hp) Pratt & Whitney R-1340-S1H1-G radials, and **Twin Pioneer Series 3** with Leonides 531 radials. Of this number 29 were exported, 19 saw civil use in the UK, and the balance were supplied to the RAF which designated them **Twin Pioneer C.C.Mk 1** (32) and **Twin**

Pioneer C.C.Mk 2 (7). They were used by the RAF as transports to carry troops (capacity 13), paratroops (capacity 11) and cargo, or for casualty evacuation, light bombing, photographic survey and supply dropping. The last three of the RAF's aircraft were delivered with the more powerful Leonides 531 engines, and during 1961 all of the earlier aircraft were similarly re-engined. Entering service initially in 1958, they served for a decade before being withdrawn from first-line use at the end of 1968.

Specification
Scottish Aviation Twin Pioneer C.C-Mk Type: military utility transport
Powerplant: two 564-kW (640-hp) Alvis Leonides 531 piston engines
Performance: maximum speed 266 km/h (165 mph) at 610 m (2,000 ft); service ceiling 6095 m (20,000 ft);

Scottish Aviation Twin Pioneer C.C.Mk 2

A flight of Twin Pioneers of No. 21 Sqn, RAF, based at RAF Eastleigh, Nairobi, overflies its Kenyan home, in the early 1960s.

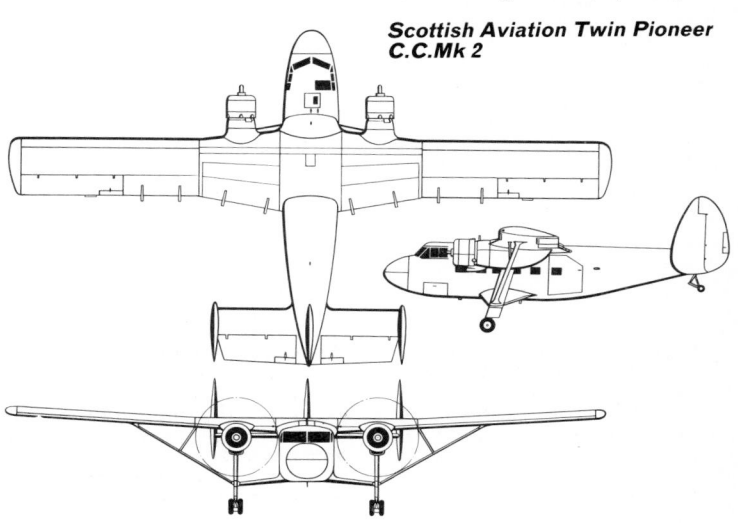

range with maximum payload 338 km (210 miles)

Weights: empty equipped 4627 kg (10,200 lb); maximum take-off 6622 kg (14,600 lb)

Dimensions: span 23.32 m (76 ft 6 in); length 13.79 m (45 ft 3 in); height 3.73 m (12 ft 3 in); wing area 62.24 m² (670.0 sq ft)

Armament: up to 907 kg (2,000 lb) of high-explosive or anti-personnel bombs carried externally

Security Airster S-1-A and S-1-B

In 1933 W. B. ('Bert') Kinner formed Security National Aircraft Corporation at Downey, California, to manufacture a side-by-side two-seat open cockpit monoplane of his own design, designated **Security Airster S-1-A**. Of braced low-wing configuration, it had foldable wings, fixed tailwheel landing gear and was powered as a standard by a 75-kW (100-hp) Kinner K5 radial engine. A separate 'coupe' unit was available as an option to provide enclosed accommodation. It was a bad economic period in which to introduce a new lightplane, first flown in the summer of 1933, and only 15 had been built when production was suspended in January 1935.

In early 1939 Kinner attempted to start again under the title American Aircraft Company, intending to produce in large numbers a generally similar but improved **Airster S-1-B** powered by an own-design 93-kW (125-hp) Security S5-125 radial engine. However, this met with even less success, with only four or five built before the American Aircraft factory and assets were acquired by another company in early 1942. The Airster S-1-B spanned 12.19 m (40 ft 0 in) and had a maximum speed of 180 km/h (112 mph) at sea level.

Seversky AT-12

Under the designation **Seversky 2PA Guardsman**, the company developed from the P-35 a two-seat export version powered by a 746-kW (1,000-hp) Wright R-1820 Cyclone radial engine. Twenty were supplied to Japan and two to the USSR, but of an order received from Sweden for 52 2PAs to be equipped as fighter-bombers only two had been delivered before the balance was impressed for service with the US Army Air Corps. The US Army had no requirement for a two-seat fighter-bomber, but with 783-kW (1,050-hp) Pratt & Whitney R-1830-45 engines installed they entered service as advanced trainers under the designation **AT-12**.

Seversky BT-8

From its SEV-2XP, which had served as the first private-venture prototype of the P-35, Seversky developed for the US Army Air Corps a two-seat basic trainer which had fixed tailwheel landing gear and was powered by a 336-kW (450-hp) Pratt & Whitney R-985-11 Wasp Junior radial engine. Although only 30 were built and supplied to the USAAC under the designation **BT-8**, these aircraft have a place in US Air Force history as its first production monoplane trainer, as well as its first aircraft designed specifically for use in the basic training role. Of the same 10.97-m (36-ft 0-in) span as the P-35, the BT-8 had a maximum speed of 282 km/h (175 mph) at sea level.

The Seversky SEV-2XP was an extremely compact design with a maximum weight of 1837 kg (4,050 lb), and is of great importance as the first United States Army aircraft to be specifically designed for the basic trainer role, as all previous types had been, for the most part, superannuated observation aircraft. Developed from the Seversky 1XP, the BT-8 was modified as a two-seater.

Seversky P-35

Seversky P-35A of the 17th Pursuit Squadron, USAAF, based at Nichols Field (Philippines) during 1941.

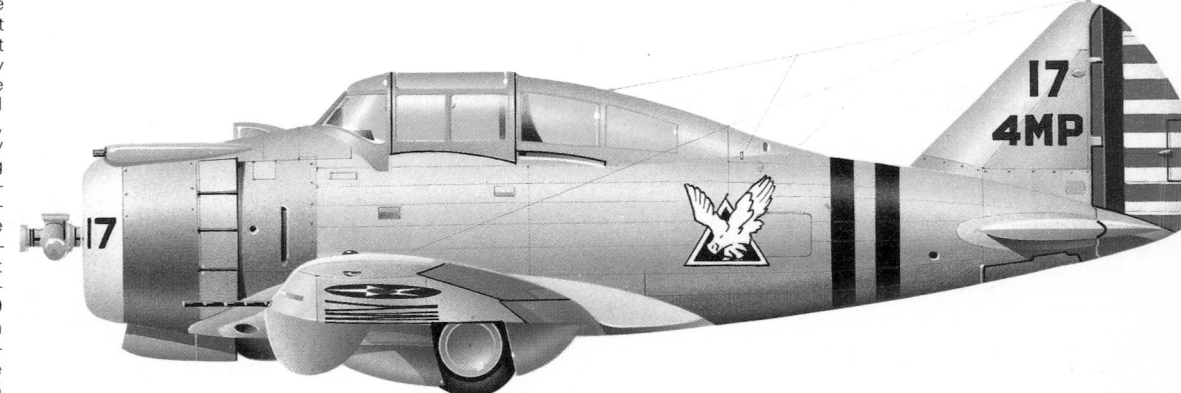

As a private venture, Seversky built the prototype of a two-seat fighter which it designated **Seversky SEV-2XP**, but while being evaluated by the US Army Air Corps in June 1935 this prototype was damaged sufficiently to need factory repair. The company's designer, Alexander Kartveli, took the opportunity to introduce retractable main landing gear and revised the cockpit as a single-seater, the aircraft then being redesignated **SEV-1XP**. When tested by the USAAC it was found to be underpowered, its 634-kW (850-hp) Wright R-1820-G5 Cyclone radial then being replaced by a Pratt & Whitney R-1830-9 Twin Wasp of similar output, resulting in the new designation **SEV-7**. Performance had deteriorated still further, the R-1830-9 delivering little more than 85 per cent of its rated power, resulting in the installation of an R-1830-9 engine with a guaranteed output of 708 kW (950 hp) in the aircraft that was then redesignated **AP-1**. In this form the type was ordered by the USAAC under the designation **P-35**, the first of 77 being delivered in July 1937. The last of the batch was completed as an improved aircraft designated **XP-41**, which flew shortly before the company changed its name to Republic Aircraft Corporation, and this was fundamentally the prototype of the Republic P-43 Lancer.

Under the designation **EP-1** the type was offered for export, the Swedish government ordering the first 15 of a batch of 120 designated **EP-106**, which differed primarily by having a more powerful R-1830-45 engine and heavier armament. Half of these had been delivered by 18 June 1940, being designated **J 9** in Swedish service, but the balance of 60 was requisitioned for the USAAC and delivered under the designation **P-35A**. They were severely mauled by the Japanese when deployed in the Philippines, only eight of 48 remaining airworthy after the first two days of enemy attacks, and this represented the first and last operational use of the type. The remaining 12 P-35As were later supplied to Ecuador.

Specification
Seversky P-35A
Type: single-seat fighter
Powerplant: one 783-kW (1,050-hp) Pratt & Whitney R-1830-45 radial piston engine
Performance: maximum speed 499 km/h (310 mph) at 4360 m (14,300 ft); service ceiling 9570 m (31,400 ft); maximum range 1529 km (950 miles)
Weights: empty 2075 kg (4,575 lb); maximum take-off 3050 kg (6,723 lb)
Dimensions: span 10.97 m (36 ft 0 in); length 8.18 m (26 ft 10 in); height 2.97 m (9 ft 9 in); wing area 20.44 m² (220.0 sq ft)
Armament: two 12.7-mm (0.5-in) and two 7.62-mm (0.3-in) machine-guns, plus up to 159 kg (350 lb) of bombs carried externally

Seversky SEV-3

The **Seversky SEV-3** was the first aircraft to be produced by the Seversky Aircraft Corporation which had been founded by Russian-born Alexander P. Seversky in 1931. A three-seat amphibian of all-metal construction, it was of cantilever low-wing monoplane configuration, powered by a 313-kW (420-hp) Wright J-6 Whirlwind radial engine, and had two cockpits in tandem that could be enclosed by sliding canopies for the pilot (forward) and two passengers (aft). The twin floats were of Seversky design and incorporated main wheels that could be extended and retracted hydraulically; when operating from water with the wheels retracted the floats were locked rigidly in a horizontal position. When the main wheels were extended for land operation the floats became free to pivot upward at the rear, so that as a conventional landing was made small wheels beneath the rear end of each float pushed it upwards until the tail-wheel and extended mainwheels supported the aircraft on the ground.

First flown in June 1933 and built in small numbers for export, the SEV-3 established a world speed record for piston-engined amphibians during that year. Just over two years later (15 September 1935) an **SEV-3M-WW**, then powered by a 529-kW (710-hp) Wright Cyclone engine, set a new record of 370.814 km/h (230.413 mph).

The Seversky SEV-3XAR was the first product of the Seversky Aircraft Corporation, and was designed and initially flight-tested as a floatplane before being converted into a landplane with what, by the standards of the time, were very sleek lines.

Shavrov aircraft

Vladim B. Shavrov had worked as a member of the OMOS design bureau from 1925, and after two years there set out to design and build a light general-purpose amphibian flying-boat, the **Shavrov Sh-1**. A sesquiplane, the Sh-1 had its main wing strut-mounted above the single-step hull and stabilising floats were incorporated into the lower stub-wing. The main wheels of the landing gear were retracted manually. Flown for the first time on 21 June 1929, the Sh-1 performed well, attaining a maximum speed of 126 km/h (78 mph) on its 63-kW (85-hp) Walter radial engine.

The Sh-1 remained a prototype, being developed into the slightly larger and re-fined **Sh-2**, whose first test flight, made from land, was on 11 November 1930. The type later met severe requirements both for operation from water and land and was built in quantity, production being quoted from 300 to 700 according to source. The Sh-2 served throughout the Soviet Union as a utility transport, for liaison, and as a trainer, and for many years was used on fishery protection duties and frontier patrol work. They supported Arctic operations and 16 were built under the designation **Sh-2S** as air ambulances carrying one or two stretcher patients. In 1939 Aeroflot built

additional Sh-2s from available spares and later the type was reinstated in production. As well as use for the civil roles indicated, the Sh-2 was flown by the V-VS as a general-purpose aircraft. A number of later machines had a glazed crew cabin and other refinements, becoming redesignated **Sh-2bis**; most had improved M-11L engines.

The next Shavrov design to be built was the **Sh-5**, first flown on its retractable skis on 19 March 1934. An amphibian flying-boat of high-wing monoplane configuration and intended for aerial photography and survey, it was powered by two 358-kW (480-hp) M-22 radial engines. However, as a result of protracted construction and development no series production was undertaken. This was also the fate of the succeeding **Sh-7**, an amphibian flying-boat of cantilever high-wing monoplane configuration. Intended as a civil utility transport, the Sh-7 had a crew of two and cabin accommodation for four passengers. Its first flight took place on 16 June 1940 and at the end of the year it was decided to produce the Sh-7 in quantity. This was prevented by the outbreak of war in 1941, although the civil prototype was used to carry urgent freight and passengers along the Volga right through the

period of hostilities. The Sh-7 was the last aircraft to be built that was entirely of Shavrov design, although he acted as a consultant to other designers for some years.

Other aircraft from Shavrov were the **Sh-3** light transport amphibian, powered by a 89-kW (120-hp) Cirrus Hermes though the project was under prototype construction in February 1936; and the **MDR-7** long-range reconnaissance flying-boat, whose development was ended in 1937.

Specification
Shavrov Sh-2
Type: general utility amphibian flying-boat

The most unusual feature of the Shavrov Sh-2 amphibian of 1930 was the small cantilever lower wing, with its pair of built-in stabilising floats.

Powerplant: one 75-kW (100-hp) M-11 radial piston engine
Performance: maximum speed 139 km/h (86 mph); service ceiling 3850 m (12,630 ft); range 1300 km (808 miles)
Weights: empty equipped 660 kg (1,455 lb); maximum take-off 937 kg (2,066 lb)
Dimensions: span 13.00 m (42 ft 7¾ in); length 8.20 m (26 ft 10¾ in); wing area 24.70 m² (265.88 sq ft)

Shcherbakov Shche-2

Joining the Kalinin design team in 1926, Aleksai Shcherbakov left in 1935 to specialise in pressure-cabin technology. He later had a major role in development of the Polikarpov I-153 biplane fighter, and although responsible for a number of projects for aircraft and gliders, only one of his designs was built, the **TS-1** transport aircraft.

To meet an urgent need for a light multi-role military transport, Shcherbakov was diverted from his wartime managerial duties to design and develop this semi-cantilever high-wing cabin monoplane which had fixed tailwheel landing gear, twin fin-and-rudder tail unit, and was powered by two radial engines in wing-mounted nacelles. Tested during 1942-43, the largely wooden **Shcherbakov Shche-2**, as the design had by then been designated, entered

production in late 1943 and a reported total of 550 was built before it was phased out in 1946. The Shche-2 proved easy to fly, although it was somewhat underpowered for the roles it fulfilled. These included transport for 16 troops, air ambulance accommodating 11 stretcher cases, assault transport with nine paratroopers, and as a crew and navigation trainer with five inboard. Post-war the Shche-2 survived for a number of years on a variety of civil duties in the Soviet Union and with several of the country's allies.

Specification
Type: general-purpose light transport
Powerplant: two 86-kW (115-hp) M-11d radial piston engines
Performance: maximum speed 155 km/h (96 mph); service ceiling

Though only marginally powered, the Shche-2 proved an immensely useful light transport and commmunications type.

3000 m (9,845 ft); range 980 km (609 miles)
Weights: empty equipped 2235 kg (4,927 lb); maximum take-off 3700 kg

(8,157 lb)
Dimensions: span 20.54 m (67 ft 4¾ in); length 14.27 m (46 ft 9¾ in); wing area 64.00 m² (688.91 sq ft)

Shchetinin aircraft

Under the name Pervoe Rossikoe Tovarishchestvo Vozdukhoplana Vaniya S. S. Shchetinin, the first Russian aviation company was established in St Petersburg during 1909. Deriving this name from its principal founder, S. S. Shchetinin, the company appointed Dmitri P. Grigorovich as its works manager in early 1913. His designs included a long series of aircraft with M for *Morskoi* (marine) designations, and details of these will be found under earlier entries for the Grigorovich M-5, M-9, M-11/M-12, M-15, M-16 and M-24/M-24bis.

Shin Meiwa D.H.114-TAW

Following the end of World War II, the former Kawanishi Aircraft Company resumed its association with the aviation industry in 1949 under the name Shin Meiwa Industry Company Ltd. The company became initially a major overhaul organisation for aircraft of Japanese and US manufacture, and in early 1963 was one of the many companies that finalised a design to re-engine the de Havilland D.H.114 Heron. This small programme, in which five aircraft of Toa Airways were changed from a powerplant of four Gipsy Queen 30s to four 194-kW (260-hp) Continental IO-470-D flat-six engines, also involved the installation of a cabin heating system. Redesignated **DH 114-TAW** following conversion, the first revised aircraft was flown on 12 November 1964.

Shin Meiwa SS-2 and SS-2A

Under a contract awarded in January 1966 Shin Meiwa began design and development of an anti-submarine flying-boat to serve with the Japan Maritime Self-Defense Force. Allocated the company designation Shin Meiwa **SS-2**, the first of two prototypes was flown initially on 5 October 1967 and, following completion of testing by the 51st Flight Test Squadron of the JMSDF, 23 production aircraft were built, entering service under the official designation **PS-1**. A cantilever high-wing monoplane with fixed strut-mounted stabilising floats beneath each outer wing panel, the aircraft has a single-step hull, a T-tail and retractable beaching chassis, and is powered by four 2282-kW (3,060-eshp) Ishikawajima licence-built General Electric T64-IHI-10 turboprop engines. A fifth powerplant, a 1044-kW (1,400-shp) Ishikawajima-built T58-IHI-10 gas turbine mounted within the fuselage, provides compressed air for the aircraft's STOL boundary-layer control system. The first prototype was converted subsequently for evaluation by the National Fire Agency in a water-bombing role.

In 1970 development was initiated of an amphibian version designated **SS-2A**, which differs primarily by having retractable tricycle landing gear.

The first example was flown from water on 16 October 1974 and made its first land take-off on 3 December 1974. This apparently long delay was a result of the difficulties encountered by Dr Kikuhara and his design team in incorporating the landing gear. Eventually, the wheels were carried in fuselage-side fairings, with the tyres left exposed. Apart from the obvious difference, other changes include the removal of all ASW and weapons provision, coupled with an increase in fuel capacity and provision for up to 12 stretcher-cases in the cabin. Canvas seats for 20 are available, and there is also a potential troop-carrying role for up to 100 soldiers. Rescue hatches are provided, with a ramp, and a large door has been cut in in the starboard side for air-dropping rafts and supplies.

The first unit to operate the type, designated **US-1**, was the 71st Kokutai, formed as a dedicated SAR squadron equiped solely with that type. From the seventh aircraft onward a 2603-kW (3,490-hp) T64-IHI-10J engine was fitted, and the type became known as the **US-1A**. The flight deck crew comprises three (two pilots and an engineer), behind whom sit a navigator, radio and radar operators and two observers. Up to five medical staff or rescue divers can be carried as required.

On a typical mission the US-1 has a loiter time of six hours at a radius of 1110 km (690 miles), or two and a half hours at 1850 km (1,150 miles). The US-1 can also be refuelled at sea either by ship or another US-1. Initial production, completed in 1988, amounted to 12 aircraft of which all are still in use. A civil version was mooted after interest in such a venture from Canada and China, and Grumman in the United States. While these plans came to nothing, in a surprise announcement the JMSDF ordered two more US-1As; one in 1992, another the following year. This further bolstering of Japan's SAR assets opens the possibility of continued low-rate production of the US-1.

Compared with the PS-1, the Shin Meiwa SS-2A (US-1) is fully amphibious, a vital asset in search and rescue. An unusual feature is the aircraft's 'fifth' engine, a T58 turboshaft mounted in the rear section which blows air through the flaps and tail section for added lift.

Specification
Shin Meiwa US-1A
Type: air/sea rescue amphibian
Powerplant: four 2602-ekW (3,490-eshp) Ishikawajima/General Electric T64-IHI-10J turboprops
Performance: maximum speed 512 km/h (318 mph); service ceiling 7195 m (23,600 ft); maximum range 3817 km (2,372 miles)
Weights: empty equipped 25500 kg (56,218 lb); maximum take-off 45000 kg (99,208 lb)
Dimensions: span 33.15 m (108 ft 9 in); length 33.46 m (109 ft 9¼ in); height 9.95 m (32 ft 7¾ in)

Short biplanes

The Short brothers - Eustace and Oswald - entered aviation in 1897, buying a coal-gas balloon and teaching themselves to fly. Five years later they flew a balloon of their own manufacture, and in 1905 secured a contract to supply three balloons for the Indian army, followed by other orders from private customers.

In November 1908 Eustace and Oswald were joined by brother Horace, and the name Short Brothers was registered. British rights were obtained for licence production of six Wright Flyers, Short Brothers thus becoming the world's first aircraft constructors; however, they had to make the drawings.

A site at Leysdown on the Isle of Sheppey was chosen, the batch of Flyers being completed there. Work began on the first biplane of Short design, the **Short Biplane No. 1**, flown in the summer of 1909 with a 45-kW (60-hp) Green engine, while the **Biplane No. 2**, for Moore Brabazon, won the Daily Mail prize for the first all-British circular flight on 30 October 1909. The **Biplane No. 3**, a smaller and lighter biplane with a 26-kW (35-hp) Green engine, was unsuccessful, and

was followed by two biplanes designed by J. W. Dunne, one of which was a tailless model for the Blair Atholl Syndicate. For some reason the following construction numbers up to S.25 were not used and the next batch, beginning at **S.26**, were pusher biplanes designed by Horace Short on the basis of the Farman-Sommer type. They were built at Eastchurch, a new factory into which Shorts had moved during May 1910; the first two aircraft had 30-kW (40-hp) Green engines while the third had a 45-kW (60-hp) ENV. **S.27** proved to be the most successful, the type thus becoming known as the S.27, and various engines were fitted to airframes which followed. One of the more famous was the **S.38**, one of two belonging to the Naval Flying School at Eastchurch, which on 10 January 1912 was flown off a wooden platform over the fore gun turret of HMS *Africa*. Two dual-control models, **S.43** and **S.44**, were built for the Central Flying School at Upavon, and the earlier S.33 was flown as a seaplane to test float performance. Further deliveries were made to the CFS, the Naval School and private customers.

In 1914 Frank McClean made a number of flights down the Nile in the **S.80** twin-float seaplane, a two-seater

with a 119-kW (160-hp) Gnome engine, which was presented to the Admiralty in 1914 and re-engined with a 75-kW (100-hp) Gnome. Short's last pusher was the **S.81**, similar to the S.80's original configuration but with added wing floats, which was used for gun trials. Thirty-six dual-control **S.38** type trainers were built for the Royal Navy in 1914-15, 12 by Pemberton-Billing and the remainder by White and Thompson Ltd.

During 1911-13 Short Brothers built several twin-engined biplanes, the first of which was the **S.39 Triple Twin** which had two 37-kW (50-hp) Gnome engines, one at each end of the pilot's nacelle, the forward engine chain-driving two wing-mounted tractor propellers and the rear engine driving a single pusher propeller. The **Tandem Twin**, converted from the S.27, had a

J T C Moore-Brabazon passes low over the airfield at Leydown, in September 1909, in his Vivinus-powered Short Biplane No. 2.

more orthodox arrangement with one tractor and one pusher propeller. The **S.36**, flown on 10 January 1912, represented the first of several single-engined Short tractor biplanes; powered by a 52-kW (70-hp) Gnome engine it was loaned to the Naval Flying School, Admiralty interest resulting in an order for two tractors, the S.41 and S.45. The former had a 75-kW (100-hp) Gnome and was soon converted to a seaplane, as was the smaller S.45 with a 52-kW (70-hp) Gnome. The larger aircraft was the more successful, and another three (S.48-50) were ordered by the Admiralty, being delivered in 1913.

Short Bomber

By 1915 Short Brothers had established a second factory at Rochester, and while the first two Type 184s were taking shape at Rochester the Eastchurch team was working on a modified

landplane version to fill the gap before the new Handley Page O/100s became available. New longer-span wings were introduced, but tests showed that even more area was needed and the span was increased to 25.60 m (84 ft).

Although the resulting Short Bomber had only marginal performance, 110

were ordered. Subsequent cancellations lowered the number to 82, built by Shorts (35), Sunbeam (15), Mann, Egerton (20) and six each by Parnall and Phoenix Dynamo. Apart from the Sunbeam-built aircraft, which had 168-kW (225-hp) Sunbeam engines, all Short Bombers had 186-kW (250-hp)

Rolls-Royce engines. The first aircraft to see service were those of No.7 Wing R.N.A.S., when four of its aircraft, armed with eight 65-lb (29-kg) bombs attacked the submarine pens at Zeebrugge on 15 November 1916. Its service life was cut-short by the arrival of the Handley-Page O/100 bomber.

Short lesser types

Brief mention should be made of a series of varying types which, built throughout the company's history, failed to gain commercial success. They included two **Short N.2A** seaplanes, basically smaller and faster than the Type 184, powered first by the 149-kW (200-hp) Sunbeam Afridi and later by the 194-kW (260-hp) Sunbeam Maori, and two **N.2B** seaplanes also with the Maori engine. They were followed by three aircraft designated **Short Shirl**, built to a requirement for a carrier-based torpedo-bomber, and representing the last of Short's World War I types.

Proposed in 1918 was the **N.3 Cromarty**, an improved version of the Felixstowe F.3/F.5 flying-boats which Shorts Brothers had built under sub-contract (developing also a metal-hulled **S.2** version). Flown in 1921, it was not successful, and the company's attempt to enter the lightplane market in the same year, with three two-seat biplanes which it designated **Short Sporting Type Seaplane**, also failed. The all-metal private-venture **Short Silver Streak** of 1920 interested the Air Ministry, but its order for two prototypes was soon cancelled on economic grounds.

The need for an all-metal aircraft to serve in Iraq resulted in the order being renewed and five were built as the **Short S.3 Springbok I**, three **S.3a Springbok** aircraft with fabric-covered flying surfaces following later. One was rebuilt at a later date for evaluation in an army co-operation role under the designation **Short S.3b Chamois**. In 1924 a tiny single-seat flying-boat powered by two 24-kW (32-hp) Bristol Cherub engines appeared as the **Short S.1 Stellite**; when later re-engined with a single Blackburn engine its name was changed to **Cockle**. Another lightplane of the same year was the **Short S.4 Satellite** which was designed to compete in the Air Ministry competition of 1924 for two-seat lightplanes. Short Brothers then built the **Short S.7 Mussel**, an experimental two-seat monoplane of similar construction to the Cockle. This, and a second Mussel that replaced the first after it was written off in 1928, made a valuable contribution to the

company's knowledge of float design.

When the two **Short S.6 Sturgeon** prototypes failed in competition with the Fairey IIIF, their good performance resulted in the basic design being used for the **Short S.10 Gurnard I** and **Gurnard II**. These had a Bristol Jupiter X and Rolls-Royce Kestrel II engine respectively, and although they performed well in competition the contract went to the superior Hawker Osprey. A very different aircraft was the **Short-Bristol Crusader** racing monoplane seaplane built to compete in the 1927 Schneider Trophy contest; unfortunately, when erected for the contest at Venice the aileron control cables were reversed and the aircraft crashed very soon after becoming airborne. In the same year Short Brothers built the **Short S.11 Valetta** which, with a span of 32.61 m (107 ft), was then the largest floatplane; it was used by Sir Alan Cobham for a survey of the Nile and Central Africa in 1931. Still larger was the **Short S.14 Sarafand** flown on 30 June 1932, a 36.58-m (120-ft) span long-range flying-boat powered by six Rolls-Royce Buzzard engines in tandem pairs; it served purely as a research vehicle before being scrapped in 1936.

To Specification R.24/31 Short Brothers designed and built the **Short S.18** monoplane flying-boat of gull-wing configuration, the two Rolls-Royce Goshawk evaporatively-cooled engines being mounted one at the joint or 'knuckle' of each wing, which brought the unofficial name **Knuckleduster**; the unreliability of this powerplant contributed to the R.24/31 remaining only a prototype.

Shorts and Saunders-Roe combined

The two Short Sperrin bomber prototypes are seen in flight over Aldergrove in Northern Ireland in 1952. Developed in parallel with the V-Bombers, the Sperrin was only ever intended as an 'insurance policy' against the failure of one of the other bombers. However, the S.A.4s did perform valuable work for the V-programme, acting as avionics and radar testbeds.

in design and development of the **Short S.35 Shetland** which, considerably larger than the Sunderland, was intended as a long-range heavily-armed flying-boat. The first of two prototypes flew in late 1944 but was burnt out at its moorings in January 1946; the second, completed as a 40-passenger civil transport, was scrapped when there was no post-World War II demand for such a 'boat. Other post-war developments included the **Short S.A.4 Sperrin** four-jet bomber; the first of two was flown in August 1951 but the more advanced Vickers Valiant gained the production contract. Finally came two research aircraft, first the **Short S.B.1** tailless glider which was a one-third scale model of the company's proposal for a new four-jet bomber; it was rebuilt with

DX166 was the first Short Shetland, a type which arrived too late to replace the classic Sunderland in World War II. Much larger than any previous British flying-boat, the S.35 was also probably the world's first aircraft to employ a three-phase 110-volt AC electrical system. The second 'boat was completed as a civil transport, designated Shetland II seating up to 70 on two decks.

two Turboméca Palas turbojets and first flown as the **S.B.4 Sherpa** in October 1953. The second was the **Short S.B.5**, powered by a Rolls-Royce Derwent turbojet, which was built for low-speed testing of the swept-wing configuration designed for the English Electric P.1 Lightning.

Short Type 184

Urgent demands from the Admiralty for a torpedo-carrying seaplane led Horace Short to design the **Short Type 184**, an aircraft that became the company's most famous product for almost two decades. More than 900 were built by the parent company and nine sub-contractors. The Type 184 first flew with a 168-kW (225-hp) Sunbeam Maori engine, but later models had various engines, including the 169-kW (240-hp) Sunbeam or Renault, and the 194-kW (260-hp) Sunbeam.

In August 1915 one of three Type 184s equipping the seaplane carrier HMS *Ben-My-Chree* in the Aegean became the first aircraft to sink an enemy ship with an 367-kg (810-lb) air-launched torpedo; two others were sunk five days later, but such successes proved to be untypical and the Type 184s were seldom used again in this role. The model continued to serve for other tasks, including

bombing and reconnaissance, and a Westland-built Type 184 was the only aircraft to take part in the Battle of Jutland.

Type 184s served in most theatres of war from the Arctic Circle to the Indian Ocean, and in June 1916 an aircraft with temporary wheels took off from the deck of the seaplane-carrier Campania. In the following year further flights were made from the foredeck of the carrier HMS *Furious*. 184s continued in military service until the early 1920s. Five were civil registered in the UK for pleasure flying, but only four were converted and two were scrapped a year later.

Specification
Short Type 184
Type: two-seat torpedo-bomber/reconnaissance aircraft
Powerplant: one 194-kW (260-hp) Sunbeam Maori Vee engine
Performance: maximum speed 142 km/h (88 mph) at 610 m (2,000 ft); service ceiling 2745 m (9,000 ft);

endurance 2 hours 45 minutes
Weights: empty 1680 kg (3,703 lb); maximum take-off 2433 kg (5,363 lb)
Dimensions: span 19.36 m (63 ft 6¼ in); length 12.38 m (40 ft 7½ in); height 4.11 m (13 ft 6 in); wing area 63.92 m² (688.0 sq ft)
Armament: one 7.7-mm (0.303-in) Lewis gun in rear cockpit, plus one

Serving in virtually all theatres, the Short Type 184 was the major British torpedo seaplane during World War I. It continued in this role for several years after the war's end.

356-mm (14-in) torpedo or up to 236 kg (520 lb) of bombs

Short Type 310

In an effort to improve performance of its Type 184, Short redesigned this aircraft to take the new 231-kW (310-hp) Sunbeam Cossack engine; the resulting aircraft took its designation from the engine power, which was later increased to 239 kW (320 hp). Flown at Rochester in July 1916, the **Short Type 310-A4** could carry the heavier (454-kg/1,000-lb) Mk IX torpedo, although even with the increased power it was not possible to carry both an observer and torpedo.

Production totalled 124 from Short (74) and Sunbeam (50), and 50 remained with the RAF when the war ended. Six were supplied to the Imperial Japanese navy in 1917. The **Short 310-B**, produced only in prototype form, was a patrol seaplane with span decreased from 22.86 m (75 ft) to 20.88 m (68 ft 6 in). Speed was 116 km/h (72 mph), higher in than that of the Short 310-A4.

Short Type 827 and Type 830

By 1913 the tractor engine layout had virtually supplanted the pusher with Short Brothers, and a series of biplane floatplanes came from Eastchurch including nine for the Admiralty, two with 119-kW (160-hp) and seven with 75-kW (100-hp) Gnome engines. Two more 119-kW (160-hp) aircraft followed, plus others too numerous to detail with various engines. One of these seaplanes became the first to drop a torpedo from the air on 27 July 1914.

Seven Short seaplanes, including three **S.74** and two **S.135** types, attacked shipping in the Kiel Canal on Christmas Day 1914, a statement which makes it necessary to explain that two types of numbering system were applied at that time to Short Brothers aircraft: the S number was the constructor's number, while the others were Admiralty serials or designations. Even within this system there was confusion, since the Admiralty tended to designate the type from any one of the serials in the first batch: for example, a batch of six **Short Type 166** seaplanes built by Shorts had the construction numbers S.90 to S.95 and the Admiralty serials 161-166. Westland Aircraft also built 20 of these aircraft. The Type 166 had folding wings and a 149-kW (200-hp) Salmson engine.

The first Short seaplanes to enter quantity production for the RNAS were the **Type 827** and **Type 830**, slightly smaller than the Type 166 and powered respectively by the 112-kW (150-hp) Sunbeam Nubian Vee engine and the 101-kW (135-hp) Salmson radial. Production is believed to have reached 28 Type 830s and 108 Type 827s, with the latter built also by four other companies they served as far afield as East Africa and Mesopotamia.

Specification
Short Type 827
Type: two-seat reconnaissance/bomber floatplane
Powerplant: one 112-kW (150-hp) Sunbeam Nubian Vee engine
Performance: maximum speed 100 km/h (62 mph); endurance 3 hours 30 minutes
Weights: empty 1225 kg (2,700 lb); maximum take-off 1542 kg (3,400 lb)
Dimensions: span 16.43 m (53 ft 11 in); length 10.74 m (35 ft 3 in); height 4.11 m (13 ft 6 in); wing area 47.01 m^2 (506.0 sq ft)
Armament: one Lewis gun in rear cockpit, plus provision for light bombs on underwing racks, rarely fitted operationally

Short S.5, S.12 and S.19 Singapore I, II and III

Short Brothers had great hopes for the **Short S.5 Singapore I** prototype, but its primary claim to fame is that it was used by Alan Cobham for his 37015-km (23,000-mile) survey flight around the African continent. The **S.12 Singapore II** of 1930 was no more successful, but the **S.19 Singapore III** submitted to Air Ministry Specification R.3/33 was rewarded with an order for four development aircraft, the first flown during July 1934. Successful testing led to the construction of 33 more production aircraft, the first of them flown in March 1935. Singapore IIIs served with Nos 203, 205, 209, 210 and 230 Squadrons; 19 of these aircraft remained in service at the outbreak of World War II, continuing in service until replaced by the Short Sunderland.

Specification
Short Singapore III
Type: six-seat general reconnaissance flying-boat
Powerplant: four 418-kW (560-hp) Rolls-Royce Kestrel VIII/IX V-12 piston engines
Performance: maximum speed 233 km/h (145 mph); service ceiling 4570 m (15,000 ft); range 1610 km (1,000 miles)
Weights: empty 8355 kg (18,420 lb); maximum take-off 12475 kg (27,500 lb)
Dimensions: span 27.43 m (90 ft 0 in); length 23.16 m (76 ft 0 in); height

A Short Singapore Mk III of No. 203 Sqn, RAF, based at Aden in 1940.

7.19 m (23 ft 7 in); wing area 170.38 m^2 (1,834.0 sq ft)

Short S.8 Calcutta and S.8/8 Rangoon

In 1926 Imperial Airways ordered two **Short S.8 Calcutta** three-engined biplane flying-boats to be powered by 403-kW (640-hp) Bristol Jupiter XI radial engines. The design of the Calcutta, which accommodated 15 passengers, was based closely on the military Singapore I, and when these aircraft were delivered to Imperial Airways in the late summer of 1928 they were the first stressed-skin metal hull flying-boats to enter commercial service. Production for Imperial Airways totalled five, and Short Brothers built one other for the French government. A manufacturing licence was negotiated with Breguet, this company developing from the Calcutta the very similar Breguet 521 Bizerte.

Short saw the possibility of a military Calcutta in Air Ministry Specification R.18/29, which required a flying-boat for use by No. 203 Squadron at Basra, and eventually built six aircraft which were named **S.8/8 Rangoon**, the last of them handed over in September 1934. Operated by a crew of five, the Rangoon could carry up to 454 kg (1,000 lb) of bombs beneath the wings, and had a single Lewis gun mounted in the nose compartment and one on each side of the fuselage behind the wings. All six aircraft survived, to be flown home in August 1935 when replaced by Singapore IIIs; one civilianised for Imperial Airways was used as a crew trainer for several years.

Short Brothers made one further development of the basic Calcutta design for the Imperial Japanese navy, which required a long-range flying-boat to be licence-built in Japan by Kawanishi, and powered by Rolls-Royce Buzzard engines also licence-built. Short Brothers completed the

S1434 was the RAF's second Short Rangoon, first flown in December 1930, and was used for crew training at Felixstowe. During 1931 this aircraft was flown out to Basra in Iraq as part of No. 203 Squadron.

prototype S.15 K.F.1 at Rochester, and following trials it went by sea to Japan where it was launched in March 1931.

Four were eventually built by flying boat manufacturers Kawanishi, under the designation H3K.

Short S.16 Scion and S.22 Scion Senior

In 1933 Short Brothers entered the field of light transport aircraft with the Short S.16 Scion, a twin-engined high-wing monoplane carrying five or six passengers and powered by two 56-kW (75-hp) Pobjoy R engines. The first Scion flew at Gravesend in August 1933 and received its certificate of airworthiness in February 1934. An initial batch of four production Scion I aircraft was built with 63-kW (85-hp)

Pobjoy Niagara I or II engines, but the fifth Scion 1 and Short Brothers' final batch of 10 Scion II aircraft had 67-kW (90-hp) Pobjoy Niagara IIIs. Because of increasing work on the Empire flying-boats, Short sold production rights of the Scion to Douglas Pobjoy, which built a further six aircraft.

While the Scion was in production Short Brothers built six examples of an enlarged 10-passenger S.22 Scion

Though built with Pobjoy Niagara radial engines as originally intended, this Short Scion II in Australian service was fitted instead with de Havilland Gipsy Minor inlines during 1946.

Senior, each powered by four 67-kW (90-hp) Pobjoy Niagara IIIs. One was used by Short Brothers as a landplane demonstrator, but the last of the

floatplanes was acquired by the Air Ministry, which used it as a test vehicle for flying-boat hull design, its central float being a half-scale version of the Sunderland hull.

Short S.17 Kent and S.17 Scylla

Because of political problems on its route to Cairo, Imperial Airways contracted Short Brothers to build three four-engined flying-boats which would have ample range, good capacity for high-revenue airmail and excellent accommodation for 15 passengers; selected powerplant was the 414-kW (555-hp) Bristol Jupiter XFBM. Designated Short S.17 Kent, the first of these 'boats entered service in May 1931 and the others soon afterwards. The aircraft were kept hard at work, each flying in excess of 6437 km (4,000 miles) per week. One was lost in August 1936 when it made a heavy landing and sank and another was an arson victim at Brindisi in November 1935, but the third survived to be scrapped in June 1938.

A landplane version of the Kent was

Registered G-ACJJ and named Scylla, the first of two Short L.17 landplane transports served magnificently throughout the 1930s with Imperial Airways, and was written off only in April 1940 after being torn from its pickets in a Scotish gale. The aircraft had already been extensively rebuilt after a crash in 1935.

requested by Imperial Airways in early 1933; the resulting two Short L.17 aircraft flown in March and May 1934 were later named Scylla and Syrinx. Powered by four 444-kW (595-hp) Bristol Jupiter XFBM engines, the airliners had accommodation for 39 passengers and were fitted with autopilots. One was used later to test Perseus IIL engines, until it suffered

gale damage, and in the subsequent rebuild 492-kW (660-hp) Pegasus XC

engines were installed. Both aircraft were withdrawn in 1940.

Short S.20 and S.21 Mayo Composite

Carefully-conducted tests had proved that an Imperial Airways' Empire flying-boat could achieve a transatlantic crossing only if its entire payload consisted of fuel. Since it is well known that an aircraft can be flown at a much greater weight than that at which it can take off from the ground, Robert Mayo proposed that a small heavily loaded mailplane be carried to operational altitude above a larger 'mother plane' and then released to complete its long-range task. The proposal was accepted by the Air Ministry and Imperial Airways, which jointly contracted Shorts to design and build such a composite unit. The **Short S.21** *Maia*, the lower component, was a slightly enlarged and modified version of the Empire 'boat; the **Short S.20**

Mercury, the upper long-range unit, was a new high-wing twin-float seaplane with four 254-kW (340-hp) Napier Rapier H engines giving a cruising range of 6116 km (3,800 miles) with 454 kg (1,000 lb) of mail.

The first airborne separation took place on 6 February 1938, and after a number of experimental flights *Mercury* was air-launched over Foynes on 21 July to fly non-stop the 4715 km (2,930 miles) to Montreal in 20 hours 20 minutes with a 272-kg (600-lb)

The Short-Mayo Composite was a fascinating, but ultimately fruitless, attempt to provide a long-range air mail service, but has the distinction of holding a still-unbroken world record.

payload. On 6 October 1938 *Mercury* was launched over Dundee to establish an as-yet unbroken non-stop international seaplane distance record

of 9652 km (5,997.5 miles) to the Orange River, South Africa. However, the outbreak of war ended experimentation, and *Mercury* was eventually broken up at Rochester and *Maia* destroyed by enemy action during May 1941.

Short S.23, S.30 and S.33 Empire flying-boats

By comparison with the company's large and cumbersome biplane flying-boats, the **Short S.23** of 1936 showed a complete change of style. With four 686-kW (920-hp) Bristol Pegasus XC radial engines, a high-set cantilever monoplane wing, and a streamlined hull, and of all-metal construction, the S.23 had a maximum speed of 322 km/h (200 mph), which was 42 km/h (26 mph) faster than the RAF's contemporary Bristol Bulldog fighter. Such was its promise that Imperial Airways placed an order for 28, for airmail had again taken a hand in aircraft procurement when the British government announced that all first-class mail to the Empire would be carried by air, and these machines were to become known also as

G-ADHM 'Caledonia' was the second Short S.23 Empire flying-boat, completed with tankage for a 5310-km (3,300-mile) range. It was scrapped in 1947 after spending 15,143 hours in the air during its fruitful aviation career.

Empire or **'C' class** flying-boats.

The first S.23 (*Canopus*) flew from Rochester in July 1936, entering service at the beginning of September, and as further aircraft became available at the rate of about one aircraft every two weeks they joined the fleet. Operating from the new Imperial Airways flying-boat base at Hythe they were used on services to Australia, Bermuda, Durban, Egypt, Malaya, New

York, and East and South Africa.

Original accommodation was for 1360 kg (3,000 lb) of mail and 24 passengers by day or 16 by night, but an increase of 454 kg (1,000 lb) in mail

load reduced the passenger capacity to 17. Transatlantic trials made in 1937 without payload proved the S.23 could not carry an economic payload over the distance, leading to the Short-Mayo

Composite, and trials were also conducted with inflight refuelling using the Armstrong Whitworth 23 as a tanker. The success of this latter system secured a contract for Flight Refuelling Ltd, which used four Handley Page Harrow tankers to achieve 16 successful flight-refuelled transatlantic crossings before the outbreak of war stopped further development. **Short S.30** aircraft powered by 664-kW (890-hp) Bristol Perseus XIIC engines and with more than double the range of the S.23 were used for the transatlantic trials; last variant was the S.33 with 686-kW (920-hp) Bristol Pegasus XCs. Total production of the Empire flying-boats reached 42, of which 31 were S.23s, nine S.30s and two S.33s, construction of a third S.33 being abandoned.

Several S.23s were impressed for RAF service (two of them being modified to **S.23M** standard with ASV radar and an armament of two four-gun turrets and six depth charges), and a total of 13 Empire 'boats survived the war, by then with 753-kW (1,010-hp) Bristol Pegasus engines; the last, in service with Qantas, was retired in 1941. Shorts also constructed three **Short S.26** 'boats ordered by Imperial Airways for non-stop transatlantic mail services. Larger than the 'C' class and with 1029-kW (1,380-hp) Bristol Hercules engines, the first (*Golden Hind*) launched in June 1939. Known as the **'G' class**, all were impressed for reconnaissance use; one was lost through engine failure but in 1942 the other two were returned to the airline, by then renamed BOAC. One was destroyed in a fatal crash at Lisbon in 1943, and the other survived until it sank during a gale in May 1954

Specification
Short S.23
Type: passenger/mail flying-boat
Powerplant: four 686-kW (920-hp) Bristol Pegasus XC radial piston engines
Performance: maximum speed 322 km/h (200 mph); range 1223 km (760 miles)
Weights: empty 10659 kg (23,500 lb); maximum take-off 18370 kg (40,500 lb)
Dimensions: span 34.75 m (114 ft 0 in); length 26.82 m (88 ft 0 in); height 9.70 m (31 ft 9 ¾ in); wing area 139.35 m² (1,500.0 sq ft)

Short S.25 Sunderland

To meet an Air Ministry requirement for a military general-reconnaissance flying-boat, Short Brothers developed the **Short S.25** design which was ordered into production as the **Sunderland Mk I**. The prototype, flown on 16 October 1937, was the first British flying-boat to have power-operated gun turrets. A total of 90 Sunderland Mk Is was built, 15 of them by the Blackburn Aircraft Company, all powered by four 753-kW (1,010-hp) Bristol Pegasus XXII engines and armed with two 7.7-mm (0.303-in) Vickers 'K' guns in beam positions, two 7.7-mm (0.303-in) Brownings in the nose turret and four similar weapons in the tail turret. They were followed from August 1941 by 43 **Sunderland Mk II** aircraft built by Short Brothers (38) and Blackburn (five); they differed by having 794-kW (1,065-hp/) Pegasus XVIII engines and a power-operated dorsal turret in place of the beam guns.

Most extensively built was the **Sunderland Mk III**, to a total of 456, 170 being produced by Blackburn and the remainder by Short Brothers. These had the same powerplant as the Sunderland Mk II, hull revisions, and were equipped with Air-to-Surface Vessel (ASV) Mk II radar; ASV radar had also been installed retrospectively on earlier versions. A more powerful and heavily armed **Sunderland Mk IV** was developed for use in the Pacific theatre, but the two prototypes were very different from the standard aircraft and were renamed Seaford. Final production version was the **Sunderland Mk V**, introduced in March 1944 and built to a total of 150 by Short (90) and Blackburn (60). It introduced more powerful Pratt & Whitney Twin Wasp radial engines and the ASV Mk IVC radar that equipped late production Sunderland Mk 38 IIIs.

The first operational squadron was No. 230, fully equipped with Sunderland Mk Is by December 1938, and in addition to those used by the RAF the type was operated by the Royal Australian, Royal Canadian and Royal New Zealand air forces. No. 330 Squadron formed at Oban in February 1943 was a Norwegian-manned unit, and No. 343 Squadron which formed at Dakar in November 1943 was manned by former members of the Aéronavale Flottille 7E.

After the end of World War II the RAF's Sunderland force was soon run down and by the beginning of the Berlin Airlift, in June 1948, only Nos 201 and 230 Squadrons and No. 235 Operational Conversion Unit were available to participate. All Britain-based Sunderland operations ended in early 1957, but in the Far East the type remained in service until 1959.

Specification
Short Sunderland Mk V
Type: maritime reconnaissance/bomber flying-boat
Powerplant: four 895-kW (1,200-hp) Pratt & Whitney R-1830-90B Twin Wasp radial piston engines
Performance: maximum speed 343 km/h (213 mph) at 1525 m (5,000 ft); service ceiling 5455 m (17,900 ft); range 4329 km (2,690 miles) with 757-kg (1,668-lb) bomb load
Weights: empty 16738 kg (36,900 lb); maximum take-off 29484 kg (65,000 lb)
Dimensions: span 34.38 m (112 ft 9 ½ in); length 26.00 m (85 ft 3 ½ in); height 10.52 m (34 ft 6 in) wing area 156.72 m2 (1,687.0 sq ft)
Armament: 10 (four fixed, two in bow turret and four in tail turret) 7.7-mm (0.303-in) and two 12.7-mm (0.5-in) machine-guns, plus up to 2250 kg (4,960 lb) of bombs, depth charges or mines

These Sunderland GR.Mk V flying-boats look decidedly war-weary after a period in service with RAF Coastal Command. This version was the definitive development.

Short S.25 Sunderland civil conversions and Solent

In March 1943 BOAC began to operate the first of a fleet of Short Sunderland Mk III flying-boats converted for the civilian transport role. They proved to be a success and in the two years that followed a total of 24 were used by the airline on gradually extending routes that eventually reached as far as Rangoon after VJ-Day. The Royal New Zealand Air Force also received four converted Sunderlands towards the end of 1944.

Lack of long-range transport aircraft in the UK after the war led BOAC to refurbish its fleet to something more approaching airline standards, the resulting version being known as the Short Hythe. A more aesthetically attractive conversion, with the nose and tail turret positions concealed by streamlined fairings, was known as the Short Sandringham, the first appearing in November 1945 with Pegasus engines; subsequent conversions had 895-kW (1,200-hp) Pratt & Whitney Twin Wasp R-1830-92 engines and maximum passenger capacity of 45 on two decks. Around 30 Sandringhams of various types were converted, serving not only with BOAC but in Argentina, Australia, New Zealand, Norway and Uruguay. The straight Sunderland conversions also served in a number of countries, and several of both types have survived.

Following evaluation of a Seaford in 1946, and the cancellation of RAF orders for the type, BOAC received 12 civil versions under the designation Short Solent 2. These had a crew of seven and carried 34 day passengers on two decks in luxury accommodation that included a dining saloon, cocktail bar and promenade. They proved to be popular and BOAC leased the six RAF Seafords which had been declared surplus, and had them converted to 39-passenger Solent 3 configuration. Four new Solents built for Tasman Empire Airways were 44-seaters with a 4828-km (3,000-mile) range.

When BOAC ended flying-boat operations in November 1950 their Solent fleet was dispersed to various operators, including Aquila Airways, and these aircraft lingered on for some years. Two survive, one in Auckland and the other in California.

Specification
Short Solent 3
Type: long-range commercial flying-boat
Powerplant: four 1260-kW (1,690-hp) Bristol Hercules 637 radial piston engines
Performance: maximum speed 430 km/h (267 mph); service ceiling 4725 m (15,500 ft); range 3540 km (2,200 miles)
Dimensions: span 34.38 m (112 ft 9 ½ in); length 26.72 m (87 ft 8 in); height 10.45 m (34 ft 3 ¼ in); wing area 156.72 m2 (1,687.0 sq ft)
Weights: empty 21868 kg (48,210 lb); maximum take-off weight 35652 kg (78,600 lb)

Though ordered as a Solent I, with five cabins each able to accommodate six, or four night passengers, G-AHIY was completed as a Solent II, roughly equivalent to the Sandringham.

Short S.29 Stirling
to
Short S.C.1

Short S.29 Stirling

On 19 September 1938 the **Short S.31** research aircraft, powered by four 90-hp (67-kW) Pobjoy Niagara engines, was flown for the first time. The uninitiated might well have puzzled over its role, but it was in fact a half-scale version of the **Short S.29 Stirling** that had been designed to meet Air Ministry Specification B.12/36 for a seven/eight-crew heavy bomber. The Stirling prototype, first flown on 14 May 1939, was powered by four 1025-kW (1,375-hp) Bristol Hercules II engines, but the first production Stirling, which flew on 7 May 1940, had 1189-kW (1,595-hp) Hercules XIs.

Initial deliveries began in August 1940 and the Stirling was used operationally for the first time on the night of 10/11 February 1941, when three aircraft of No. 7 Squadron attacked oil storage tanks at Rotterdam. The Stirling was thus the RAF's first four-engined monoplane bomber into service, the first to be used operationally in World War II, and also the first to be withdrawn from the bomber role after a final operational sortie on 8 September 1944. This occurred when there were adequate supplies of the Avro Lancaster and Handley Page Halifax bombers for Bomber Command requirements, for the Stirling had an inadequate operational ceiling and could not carry the larger high-explosive bombs that had been introduced by that time. Total production of bomber versions then amounted to 1,759, comprising the **Stirling Mk I** (712) and **Stirling Mk III** (1,047) aircraft; the designation **Stirling Mk II** was allocated to a planned production version to be built in Canada with Wright Cyclone R-2600s, but this was cancelled.

From early 1944 the Stirling's primary role changed to that of glider tug and transport. For the former role two Stirling Mk IIIs were converted as prototypes, losing their nose and dorsal gun turrets, retaining the tail turret and gaining glider towing equipment to become designated **Stirling Mk IV**. They proved efficient in this new role, towing one General Aircraft Hamilcar or two Airspeed Horsas for assault and up to five General Aircraft Hotspurs on a ferry flight or for training. They took part in the D-Day operations in Normandy, in the airborne operations at

Short Stirling Mk V of No. 196 Sqn, RAF, based at Shepherd's Grove, UK during 1946.

Arnhem and the March 1945 crossing of the Rhine. Production of the Stirling IV totalled 450, being followed by the **Stirling Mk V** transport (150 built) for RAF Transport Command. This was configured to carry 40 troops, or 20 fully equipped paratroops, or 12 stretchers and 14 seated casualties. It could be used also for loads such as two

The Short Stirling Mk III was generally similar to previous versions but was fitted with four Hercules XVI engines instead of the earlier Hercules XIs.

jeeps with trailers, or a jeep with a field gun, trailer and ammunition. Mk Vs were the last Stirlings in service, being gradually replaced by the Avro York, with the last of them withdrawn from use in 1946. During 1947 Airtech Ltd of Thame, Oxon, converted 12 Stirling Mk Vs for use by a Belgian civil operator.

Specification
Short Stirling Mk III
Type: heavy bomber
Powerplant: four 1230-kW (1,650-hp) Bristol Hercules XVI radial piston engines

Performance: maximum speed 435 km/h (270 mph) at 4420 m (14,500 ft); service ceiling 5180 m (17,000 ft); range with maximum bombload 950 km (590 miles)
Weights: empty 19595 kg (43,200 lb); maximum take-off 31751 kg (70,000 lb)
Dimensions: span 30.20 m (99 ft 1 in); length 26.59 m (87 ft 3 in); height 6.93 m (22 ft 9 in); wing area 135.63 m² (1,460.0 sq ft)
Armament: eight 7.7-mm (0.303-in) machine-guns in nose, dorsal and tail turrets, plus up to 6350 kg (14,000 lb) of bombs

Short S.45 Seaford

Originating as a more powerful and heavily armed version of the Sunderland for operation in the Pacific theatre, and with a gross weight increasing to 34019 kg (75,000 lb), this aircraft was designated initially **Sunderland Mk IV**. Structural changes to cater for this increased weight resulted in redesignation as the **Short S.45 Seaford**, and the first of two prototypes, powered by 1253-kW (1,680-hp) Bristol Hercules XVII engines, was flown on 30 August

The prototype Short Sunderland Mk IV is seen here in its definitive Seaford guise, with the new tall fin and tail fillet. The Martin tail turret was never fitted, and the aircraft was scrapped after an engine fire in 1947.

1944. Satisfactory testing led to a contract for 30 production aircraft powered by 1283-kW (1,720-hp) Bristol Hercules XIX radial engines, but only six of them were completed before the

programme was cancelled. These six aircraft were leased subsequently by

BOAC, which had them converted to civil transports under the name **Solent**.

Short S.A.1/2 Sturgeon 1, 2, 3 and S.B.3

The **Short Sturgeon** was designed as a torpedo-bomber/reconnaissance aircraft for use on the Royal Navy's new aircraft-carriers and, when submitted to the Admiralty, gained a contract for three prototypes. The torpedo-carrying requirement was soon cancelled, and when construction of the carriers was suspended at the end of World War II the Sturgeon's intended role no longer existed.

A decision was taken to convert the type as a high-speed target-tug against a new specification, Q.1/46, although the first two aircraft were **S.A.1 Sturgeon S.Mk 1** gunnery trainers with provision for armament. The third became the **S.A.2 Sturgeon TT.Mk 2** prototype, which resulted in an order

The nose of the Sturgeon TT.Mk 2 was considerably lengthened in comparison with that of the Mk 1, and was designed for optimum use of the Vinten gunnery camera carried by this variant.

for 23 production aircraft. An interesting feature was the provision of counter-rotating propellers on the two 1238-kW (1,660-hp) Rolls-Royce Merlin 140 engines; the small-diameter propellers allowed close inboard mounting of the engines which gave a compact form when the wings were folded. The Sturgeon had a maximum speed of 595 km/h (370 mph) and could tow a 9.75-m (32-ft) winged target to an altitude of 10030 m (32,900 ft). Some were later

converted to **Sturgeon TT.Mk 3** standard and used from shore establishments, mostly in Malta.

In a bid to make the Sturgeon suitable for anti-submarine, work the 24th (last) airframe was modified to become the **Short S.B.3**. A deep nose was

added, housing a radar scanner and two operators, and it was powered by two 1100-kW (1,475-shp) Armstrong Siddeley Mamba turboprops. Flown in August 1950, it was not a success, and the requirement was met by the Fairey Gannet AEW.Mk 3.

Short S.A.6 and S.B.7 Sealand

One of the Short Brothers' most attractive designs was the **Short S.A.6 Sealand**, a small twin-engined amphibian first flown in January 1948. Trials were satisfactory, and a pre-production batch of four was begun in 1947, the first of these receiving its certificate of airworthiness in July 1949. Production **Sealand I** and **S.B.7 Sealand II** were built and delivered to operators in Borneo (two), Egypt (one), Indonesia (two), Norway (two), Pakistan (three), Venezuela (one) and Yugoslavia (two) The largest single

customer was the Indian navy, which ordered 10; these were probably the last aircraft in service, Shorts having scrapped the prototype in April 1955. It is thought that two Sealands survive, one in Yugoslavia and the other in the USA. The **Sealand III** variant was reduced 150 kg (330 lb) in weight and increased 1.13 m (2 ft 6 in) in span.

Specification
Short Sealand III
Type: seven-passenger amphibian
Powerplant: two 254-kW (340-hp) de

Havilland Gipsy Queen 70 inline piston engines
Performance: maximum speed 298 km/h (185 mph) at 1525 m (5,000 ft); service ceiling 6340 m (20,800 ft); range 958 km (595 miles)

The Short Sealand was one of the most attractive aircraft produced by the company, and the first production aircraft is seen here. It was lost in a crash in September 1949 while on a sales tour of Scandanavia.

Weights: empty 3205 kg (7,065 lb); maximum take-off 4128 kg (9,100 lb)
Dimensions: span 18.75 m (61 ft 6 in); length 12.85 m (42 ft 2 in); height 4.57 m (15 ft 0 in); wing area 32.79 m^2 (353.0 sq ft)

Short S.B.6 Seamew

An Admiralty requirement of 1951 for a simple anti-submarine aircraft for operation in bad weather from small carriers led to the **Short S.B.6 Seamew**, which flew in August 1953. Powered by a 1186-kW (1,590-shp) Armstrong Siddeley Mamba turboprop, the Seamew was of strictly utilitarian appearance, but the crew of two had a good view from the forward placed cockpit. The aircraft proved difficult to handle, and although a number of modifications were incorporated the problems were never fully resolved. A total of 41 production items, including

S.C.2 Seamew Mk 2 aircraft for the RAF, was ordered, but only 19 were completed and, of these, seven had been accepted by the Royal Navy before the programme was scrapped in the 1957 economy drive. Span was 16.76 m (55 ft), maximum take-off weight 6804 kg (15,000 lb) and maximum speed 378 km/h (235 mph).

XA209 was the prototype Short Seamew whose ungainly appearance was dictated by operational rather than aerodynamic considerations.

Short S.C.1

After testing the direct jet-lift capability of turbojet engines, Rolls-Royce designed the 8.9-kN (2,000-lb) thrust RB.108 for use as a vertical lift engine. Short Brothers was given a Ministry of Supply contract under Specification ER.143 for two examples of the **Short S.C.1** delta-wing research monoplane, powered by four RB.108s for vertical take-off and another for horizontal flight. The first conventional flight was made in April 1957 with only the single RB.108 installed; the second aircraft (with lift engines) made its first tethered hovering flight in May 1958 and its first free flight in the following October, and completed the first transition from vertical to horizontal flight during April 1960. In June 1963

the second S.C.1 was damaged in a fatal accident, but was repaired and flown again before economy cuts prevented further development of the

The Short SC.1 was a true pioneer of VTOL, though only one of the ultimately dead-end designs to have seperate lift and thrust engines. Span was 7.16 m (23 ft 6 in), and maximum VTO weight was 3493 kg (7,700 lb).

concept. More important, the swivelling nozzles of the Harrier's Pegasus engine had proved it unnecessary to carry four engines to be used only for

take-off and landing. Both S.C.1s have survived, one being stored by the Science Museum and the other in the Ulster Folk and Transport Museum.

Short S.C.5 Belfast

When after World War II there was virtually no market for flying-boats, Short Brothers attempted to get a foothold in the utility transport field with its **Short S.C.5/10** large military transport on which design work began in February 1959. Of high-wing monoplane configuration and with a circular-section pressurised fuselage, its cargo hold provided a usable volume of 311.49 m³ (11,000 cu ft). This became the RAF's **Belfast C.Mk 1**, able to carry the largest guided missiles, guns and vehicles of the British army and RAF, and convertible to carry 150 to 250 troops. The first of them was flown on 5 January 1964, and with no civil interest in the type only 10 were built for the RAF. The first Belfast entered service with No. 53 Squadron on 20 January 1966; it was then the largest aircraft to have served with the RAF.

When the RAF's long-range heavy transport commitment ended in the late 1970s, the Belfasts were offered for sale on the commercial market. After several abortive attempts by various companies, five were acquired by the British Carrier TAC HeavyLift (now HeavyLift Cargo Airlines). Three have been converted for commercial use, with two held in reserve, and they have proved to be effective, not least during the Falklands campaign. All three of HeavyLift's Belfasts remained in service in late 1993. Of the remaining five, four were scrapped and one is preserved at the Cosford Air and Space Museum.

This is the third Belfast, seen pre-delivery in 1964. Belfasts would be the largest aircraft in the world equipped with a blind landing system, and this example made the type's first automatic landing in June 1966. It was also one of the three Belfasts involved in the memorable massed landing at the Farnborough show of 1964.

Specification
Type: heavy transport
Powerplant: four 4273-ekW (5,730-ehp) Rolls-Royce Tyne RTy.12 turboprops
Performance: maximum cruising speed 566 km/h (352 mph); service ceiling 9145 m (30,000 ft); range with maximum payload and fuel reserves 1609 km (1,000 km)
Weights: empty operating 57606 kg (127,000 lb; maximum take-off 104326 kg (230,000 lb)
Dimensions: span 48.40 m (158 ft 9 ½ in); length 41.58 m (136 ft 5 in); height 14.33 m (47 ft 0 in); wing area 229.09 m² (2,466 sq ft)

Short Belfast C.Mk 1 of No. 53 Sqn, RAF Transport Command, based at Brize Norton (UK) in the late 1960s.

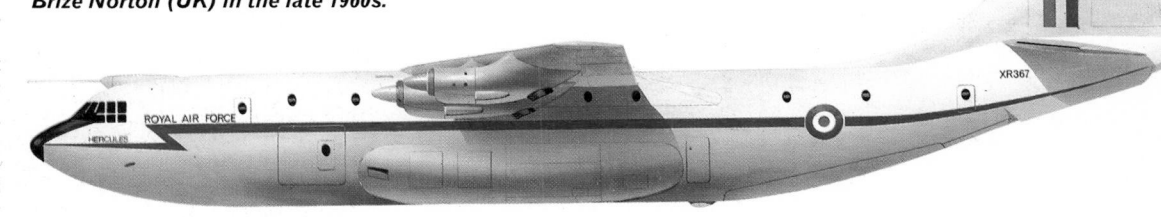

Shorts S.C.7 Skyvan/Skyliner

Design of the **Shorts S.C.7 Skyvan** began as a private venture in 1959, the **Skyvan Series 1** prototype flying for the first time on 17 January 1963. Features of the design were a high aspect ratio wing derived from Hurel-Dubois aircraft and a square-section maximum-volume fuselage, constructed from lightweight double-skin panels, with the undersurface of the rear fuselage formed by a hinged loading door. As first flown the Skyvan was powered by two wing-mounted 291-kW (390-hp) Continental GTSIO-520 piston engines, but it had been intended that it would be powered by Turboméca turboprops; as the **Skyvan Series 1A** it was flown with this powerplant, namely two 388-ekW (520-eshp) Astazou II engines, in May 1963. The first production **Skyvan Series 2** aircraft, with 544-ekW (730-eshp) Astazou XII turboprops, was flown initially on 29 October 1965, and the current production Skyvan Series 3, which superseded the Series 2 in 1968, is powered by Garrett TPE331 turboprops. The **Skyvan Series 3A** introduced in September 1970 was certificated for operation at a higher gross weight.

In a passenger configuration the Skyvan accommodated 19 passengers, as did the deluxe all-passenger version introduced in 1970 as the **Skyliner**. The other production versions were the **Skyvan 3M** military version of the Series 3, and the **Skyvan Series 3M-200** operating at a higher gross weight. One hundred and fifty-three Skyvans of all versions had been delivered by the time production ceased in 1986, the final complete aircraft being handed over to the Amiri Air Wing, Qatar, in February of that year. Another aircraft was on the production line at that time but remained unsold, and was eventually roaded out of the Sydenham factory for scrap. Skyvans served in 47 countries with 15 military air arms and over 70 civilian operators. Surviving aircraft are all almost exclusively freighters, with the type also having found much favour as a parachutist's jump ship.

Specification
Shorts Skyvan Series 3

Short SC.7 Skyvan of Summit Airlines

Type: light utility transport
Powerplant: two 533-kW (715-shp) Garrett TPE331-201 turboprops
Performance: maximum cruising speed 325 km/h (202 mph) at 3050 m (10,000 ft); service ceiling 6860 m (22,500 ft); maximum range with fuel reserves 1117 km (694 miles)
Weights: empty operating 3331 kg (7,344 lb); maximum take-off 5670 kg (12,500 lb)
Dimensions: span 19.79 m (64 ft 11 in); length 12.22 m (40 ft 1 in); height 4.60 m (15 ft 1 in); wing area 34.65 m² (373.0 sq ft)

Shorts 330

Realising that the small capacity of the Skyvan had limited sales, Shorts began design of a refined and larger version which it designated **SD3-30**, changed subsequently to **Shorts 330**. With a 2.97-m (9-ft 9-in) increase in wing span and incorporating a fuselage stretch of 3.78 m (12 ft 5 in), this aircraft provides accommodation for 30 passengers in an interior that can alternatively be configured for mixed passenger/cargo operations. More powerful engines were essential and comprise two 862-kW (1,156-shp) Pratt & Whitney Canada PT6A-45B turboprops, each with a continuous rating of 761 kW (1,020 shp). The first of two prototypes was flown initially on 22 August 1974. Deliveries of the first production aircraft were made in June 1976, and Time Air of Alberta, Canada, initiated the first revenue service on 24 August 1976.

Sales were slow to build, but by the beginning of the 1980s Shorts' intensive marketing effort had begun to pay off, particularly in the United States. Most aircraft would eventually have several owners, as airlines which started out with the 330 outgrew the aircraft and passed it on to newer, smaller carriers to repeat the cycle. Interest in the type dipped as the larger Shorts 360 came on line in 1981, but that year Shorts delivered 18 aircraft, with more orders coming in.

The following year saw the introduction of two new versions, which marked a move away from the thinning civil transport market. The **Shorts 300-UTT** (Utility Tactical Transport) was announced at that year's Farnborough show, and intended was as a multi-purpose transport aircraft for support operations. Maximum payload was increased to 3630 kg (8,000 lb), with a corresponding strengthening of the cabin floor and the provision of tie-down points for securing cargo. Two inward-

opening doors, to facilitate a load of up to 30 paratroops, replaced the Shorts 330's single passenger door on the port side, and the UTT also had a casevac fitting to accommodate up to 15 stretcher cases. As the UTT entered an extended period of certification testing, no orders had been received, and it was not until 1983 that a customer was found. Both the Royal Thai police and army took delivery of a single aircraft each, placing a follow-on order for two more in 1985. A UTT was also delivered to the Amiri Guard Air Wing in 1986.

The second military version met with more success. Originated at the same time as the UTT, the **Sherpa** was intended as both a military freighter and a people mover. Where the Sherpa differs over all previous versions is in its rear cargo door, with ramp, which makes the Sherpa a capable freighter. The strengthened floor can carry up to four standard LD3 containers, seven CO8 containers, or two half-ton vehicles (such as Land Rovers). Seat rails are fitted for rapid configuration changes. In 1983 the United States Air Force in Europe launched a search for the EDS (European Distribution System), to find an existing aircraft that could fulfil the service's need for a small, versatile

cargo aircraft. Against stiff competition, the Sherpa emerged as the winner, and in March 1984 18 Sherpas were ordered as **C-23A**s.

Based with the 10th Military Airlift Squadron at Zweibrücken Air Force Base, in Germany, the C-23A fleet became a common sight at USAF bases around Europe. A further six leased ex-airline aircraft ended up in the hands of the US Army at the United States' missile test range in the Pacific, at Kwajalein Atoll. Procurement of the Sherpa fell under a cloud as a result of the US Senate's dissatisfaction with Shorts' sectarian employment policies in Northern Ireland. The USAF's faith in the aircraft's worth remained seemingly unshaken, but options for a further 48 aircraft were not proceeded with. In 1988, however, an order for a further 10 aircraft was received for the United States Army National Guard, to replace the service's de Havilland Canada C-7 Caribous.

After five years of successful operation, USAFE disbanded EDSA, disestablishing the 10th MAS. Its aircraft were transferred to the Army and the US Forestry Service. A follow-on order for a further 10 Army National Guard Aircraft was placed in January 1992 as **C-23B**s, for delivery that year. Only three C-23As remain in USAF

In its Shorts 330 design, the company extrapolated the Skyvan to a considerable degree, using better streamlining and increasing its capacity without losing the vital minimum field requirements.

service in 1993, stationed at Edwards AFB, California. Theoretically, the Shorts 330 has outlived the Shorts 360, and the line is still open for military customers. In practice, the last orders were those received from the Army National Guard in early 1992. Total Shorts 330, 330-UTT and Sherpa production stands at 179 by mid-1993.

Specification
Shorts 330-200
Type: light transport aircraft
Powerplant: two 893-kW (1,198-shp) Pratt & Whitney Canada PT6A-45R turboprop engines
Performance: maximum cruising speed 351 km/h (218 mph) at 3050 m (10,000 ft); range with maximum passenger payload 875 km (544 miles)
Weights: empty equipped 6680 kg (14,727 lb); maximum take-off 10387 kg (22,900 lb)
Dimensions: span 22.76 m (74 ft 8 in); length 17.69 m (58 ft 0½ in); height 4.95 m (16 ft 3 in); wing area 42.08 m² (453.0 sq ft)

Shorts 360

With sales of the Shorts 330 continuing apace, on 10 July 1980 Shorts announced its intention to launch a new stretched version, the **SD3-60**. To seat an additional six passengers (over the 330's basic layout of 30 seats), the fuselage was lengthened by 0.91 m (3 ft) forward of the wing. The bracing struts and the wing itself were, in turn, restressed to cope with the increased weight. The rear fuselage was re-designed, and tapered towards the aircraft's most obvious difference with the 330, the single swept tail fin.

Intended to operate over short-haul commuter sectors, typically 225 km (140 miles), the resulting **Shorts 360** remained unpressurised, as such a system was deemed too costly and unnecessary for an aircraft with a cruising altitude of only 3050 m (10,000 ft). The restyled fuselage shape not only contributed to the aircraft's improved aerodynamic performance, but increased the baggage space available, remedying the niggling problem of lack of space found in the 330. While Shorts retained the proven Pratt & Whitney PT6 powerplant, the

360 was fitted with the higher powered 861-kW (1156-shp) PT6-45 version. In addition to the good effect these economical engines had on the aircraft's seat-mile costs, they also ensured the 360 bettered FAR Part 36 noise regulations by a significant margin.

The first aircraft (G-ROOM) took to the air six months ahead of schedule on 1 June 1981, and was exhibited publicly at that year's Paris air show. At this time, none of the aircraft which Shorts foresaw as the 360's main competitors – the SF-340, EMB-120, DHC-8 and ATR-42 – had flown, nor

would they for a further two years at best. There then followed a gap of 14 months until the second development aircraft (G-WIDE) appeared, but the manufacturers had been working hard to sign up new customers for the type. Suburban Airlines, of Pennsylvania, became the first to place the Shorts

Aer Lingus founded the operations of its Commuter division with a single Shorts 330, before progressing to a fleet of Shorts 360s. As a customer, Aer Lingus was a prestigious catch for Shorts.

360 in revenue service, taking delivery of their initial 360 on 11 November 1982. By the beginning of 1983 the pace of deliveries had increased, with aircraft rolling off the Sydenham line at the rate of one every two weeks. Increasingly, aircraft were bought by existing Shorts 330 customers, but a notable first was the 1984 order for eight aircraft by China's Civil Aviation Administration (CAAC).

In November 1985 Shorts introduced their second-generation aircraft, the **360 Advanced**. Beginning with construction number 80, this version was fitted with more powerful PT6A-65AR 1062-kW (1,424-shp) engines, and the first delivery was made to Thai Airways, which ordered two. This variant became the new standard production version. The Shorts 360 Advanced ultimately became the **Shorts 360-200**, and as a result all the initial production aircraft are now referred to as **Shorts 360-100**s. By 1988 Shorts had achieved 150 orders for the type with 144 delivered, and another new version had been launched.

From aircraft number 116 onwards (which first flew in February 1987), all aircraft were built to what would become the ultimate production standard as **Shorts 360-300**s. These aircraft were fitted with six-bladed props, redesigned wing struts and engine nacelles, and also featured, for the first time, an auto pilot which was greatly appreciated by the flight crews. A further uprated engine, the PT6A-67R, was fitted, to improve the -300's hot-and-high, and climb performance. The first of these was delivered to Philippine Airlines, and in October 1987 Britain's Capital Airlines took delivery of the first 360-300 certified for 39 passengers, which entered service on their newly founded London-Dublin route. A Shorts 360-300F freighter version was also announced, capable of carrying five LD3 containers, or pallets, up to a maximum weight of 4536 kg (10,000 lb). Launch customer for this version was Germany's Rheinland Air Services, who took delivery of two, beginning in March 1989.

Shorts 360 of Air Ecosse

By the beginning of the 1990s demand for the Shorts 360 had begun to slow, as the aircraft was overtaken by its more modern rivals in the commuter airliner market. By the end of 1989, 160 Shorts 360s of all versions had been sold, but despite having aircraft ready for delivery and on the production line, virtually no further orders were forthcoming. In June 1991 Rheinland Air Service's second and final 360-300F would be the last aircraft delivered; the line closed, having seen a total of 164 aircraft.

Specification
Shorts 360-300
Type: twin-turboprop 36-seat commuter aircraft
Powerplant: two 1062-kW (1424-shp) Pratt & Whitney PT6A-67R turboprops, driving a six-bladed Hartzell constant-speed fully-feathering propeller
Performance: cruising speed 216 kt (400 km/h; 249 mph) at 3050 m (10,000 ft); range at cruising altitude and speed with full load 402 nm (745 km/463 miles)
Weights: operating empty 7870 kg (17,350 lb); maximum take-off 12292 kg (27,100 lb)
Dimensions: span 22.80 m (74 ft 9 ½ in); length 21.58 m (70 ft 9 ⅝ in); height 7.27 m (23 ft 10 ¾ in); wing area 42.18 m² (454 sq ft)

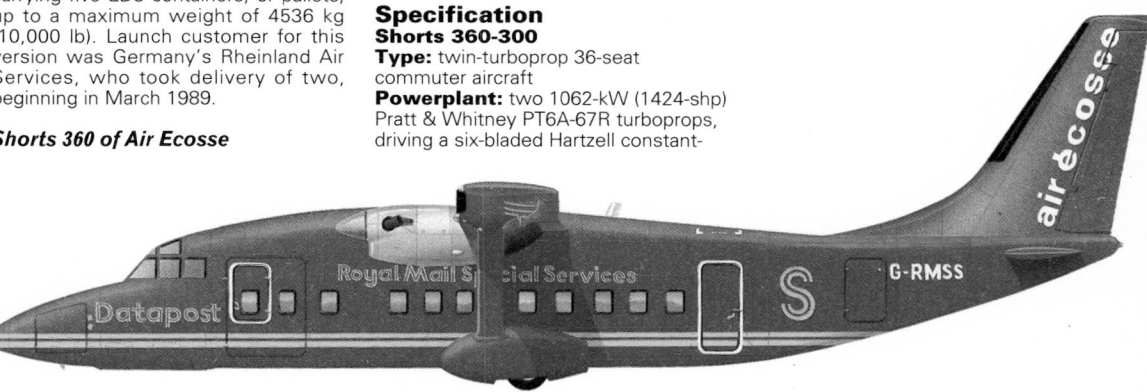

Siebel Fh 104 Hallore and Si 204

The **Siebel Fh 104** and **Si 204** were designed and developed by Siebel in Germany, as noted under the entry for SNCAC NC.701 and NC.702 Martinet. In addition to production of the Si 204 by SNCAC of France, the type was also built by Aero in Czechoslovakia under the military and civil designations of **C.5** and **C.103** respectively.

Siemens-Schuckert D types

Before World War I Siemens-Schuckert Werke had toyed with the development of aircraft, but it was not until the large-scale demand for aeroplanes which resulted from the outbreak of war that serious design and manufacturing efforts were started. In the single-seat fighter category, the **Siemens-Schuckert D.I** of 1916 was based closely on the Nieuport XI, and was of biplane configuration and powered by the 82-kW (110-hp) Siemens-Halske Sh.I rotary engine. Satisfactory testing led to an order for 150, of which only 95 were delivered as completed aircraft, for by mid-1917 the performance of this fighter had been overtaken by new Allied aircraft. A single D.Ia development with greater wing area and a more powerful engine was flown but did not enter production.

Continued development via D.II prototypes led to the **Siemens-Schuckert D.III** of which initial examples were ordered in late 1917. A neat equal-span biplane powered by a 119-kW (160-hp) Siemens-Halske Sh.III rotary engine, the D.III suffered early

About 50 Siemens-Schuckert D.IVs (from an original order for 180 aircraft) reached operational service before the Armistace, and these proved to be outstanding fighters, with an unprecedented rate of climb allied to good agility and adequate speed.

problems from the unreliability of this powerplant. As teething problems were overcome the exceptional rate of climb of the D.III singled it out for use as an interceptor but, unfortunately, its level speed was below that of contemporary fighters. Several D.III prototypes were built to achieve aerodynamic improvement, culminating in the basically similar D.IV production version, which did not become operational until August 1918, and which was some 11 km/h (7 mph) faster than the D.III and had a better rate of climb. A total of 280 D.IVs was ordered but less than half had been delivered by the end of the war. Other D types under development at the war's end included the D.V, which

derived from the D.II/III/IV family, and the D.VI parasol-wing monoplane of which one prototype had demonstrated a maximum speed of 221 km/h (137 mph).

Specification
Siemens-Schuckert D.III
Type: single-seat interceptor
Powerplant: one 119-kW (160-hp) Siemens-Halske Sh.III or IIIa rotary piston engine
Performance: maximum speed 180 km/h (112 mph); service ceiling 8000 m (26,245 ft); endurance 2 hours
Weights: empty 534 kg (1,177 lb); maximum take-off 725 kg (1,598 lb)
Dimensions: span 8.43 m (27 ft 7¾ in); length 6.70 m (18 ft 8½ in); height 2.80 m (9 ft 2¼ in); wing area 18.90 m² (203.44 sq ft)
Armament: two fixed forward-firing 7.92-mm (0.31-in) LMG 08/15 machine-guns

---

Siemens-Schuckert other types

The limited success gained by Siemens-Schuckert with its biplane configured D types was not repeated with the E type (Eindecker) monoplane fighters that followed. First flown in late 1915, the **Siemens-Schuckert E.I** had a then-typical wire-braced monoplane wing, was powered by the 75-kW (100-hp) Siemens-Halske Sh.I rotary engine and armed with a single LMG 08/15 machine-gun.

Following satisfactory eval-uation, 20 production examples were built, and in

Another early development from the Siemens-Schuckert team was the E.1 single-seat fighter, which was completed in 1915. The E.1 was built at the SSW Transformer Works in Nurenburg. It led to the improved E.II and E.IV.

attempts to improve perf-ormance one **E.II** development aircraft, which was similar to the E.I, except for having a 89-kW (120-hp) Argus As.II inline engine, was flown but later destroyed in an accident. The company's ultimate monoplane fighter design was the **E.III** of which only six examples were ever built, and this was little more than an E.I powered by the 75-kW (100-hp) Oberursel U.I piston engine.

Siemens-Schuckert began its wartime construction activities with a series of seven single R (*Riesen-flugzeug*, or giant) bombers. All were of biplane configuration and had a distinctive fork-tailed rear fuselage; power was provided by three engines within the fuselage nose, these driving two tractor propellers. Designated **R.I** to **R.VII**, all were generally similar except for variations in wing span and powerplant, the largest being the 38.45-m (126-ft 1¾-in) span **R.VII** powered by three 194-kW (260-hp) Mercedes D.IVa engines. All entered service, the R.I to R.III being used as trainers and the remainder becoming operational on the Eastern Front. The company's final bomber version was of even more unusual configuration, the 32.00 m (104 ft 1¾ in) span L.I of 1918 having twin fuselages with an engine mounted conventionally in the nose of each, plus a central nacelle with an engine at the rear to drive a pusher propeller. Three L.Is were built, each of them powered by three 179-kW (240-hp) Maybach Mb.IV engines.

Sikorsky early aircraft

Following his first unsuccessful experiments with rotary-wing aircraft in 1909-10, the Russian Igor Sikorsky concentrated upon design and development of fixed-wing aircraft. His **Sikorsky S-1** to **S-5** were little more than experimental types, but with the **S-2** biplane he achieved a first 12-second hop in 1910. Growing experience and capability gained him an appointment in 1912 as designer and chief engineer of the Russo-Baltic Wagon Works (RBVZ) and he at once became involved in design and construction of the world's first four-engined aircraft, named officially **Russkii Vitiaz** (Russian knight). Its 28.00-m (91-ft 10½-in) wing span earned it the nickname '**Le Grand**'. Four 75-kW (100-hp) Argus inline engines were mounted on the lower wings and it was with this powerplant, and piloted by Sikorsky, that the type was flown for the first time on 13 May 1913. On 2 August 1913 it was airborne for 1 hour 54 minutes with eight people aboard and had recorded 53 almost trouble-free flights before it was dismantled after being damaged on the ground.

It formed a basis for development of the **Ilia Muromets series** of four-engined heavy bombers used by the Imperial Russian army during World War I. The first of between 70 and 80 of these aircraft was flown for the first time in January 1914, and on 12 February 1914 the type established a world height-with-payload record, carrying 16 persons to an altitude of 2000 m (6,562 ft). Few of these production aircraft were identical, improvement and developing being continuous, and short engines meant they were flown with a variety of powerplant which, in some cases, involved a mix of engines on one aircraft.

Other designs to enter production during the war period included the **S-16**, a conventional two-seat reconnaissance biplane which, powered by an 60-kW (80-hp) Gnome rotary engine, could be operated on wheel or ski landing gear. The **S-20**, which entered service in 1917, was a single-seat scout powered by an 82-kW (110-hp) Le Rhone rotary; it was Sikorsky's last design in Russia, for with advent of the revolution in 1917 he emigrated to the USA.

There, after great hardship, he established a small company, built and flew the **Sikorsky S-29A** biplane twin-engine transport. The larger S-30 was also a biplane of twin-engine configuration, with accommodation for 10 passengers, but the company's first commercial success came with the single-engined **S-31** which carried three or four passengers. The ensuing **S-32**, **S-33**, **S-34** and **S-35** were unsuccessful, the first real breakthrough coming with an order from Pan American Airways for the **S-36**, an eight-seat amphibian flying-boat powered by two 149-kW (200-hp) Wright Whirlwind radial engines. It marked the beginning of an association that brought fame to the Sikorsky company and provided Pan American with a superb series of flying-boats in which the airline blazed trails across the Caribbean Sea and Pacific Ocean. Sikorsky supplied one S-36 with a bow gunner's position for evaluation by the US Navy as a patrol aircraft under the designation **XPS-1**.

The first Sikorsky Ilya Muromets is seen here durimg its successful first flight. An earlier triasl five days previously on 11 December 1913 ended in near disaster owing to poor lift.

Sikorsky S-38, S-39 and S-41

During the late 1930s Sikorsky introduced its first fuselage pod and twin-boom sesquiplane amphibian, the S-36. From it was developed the Sikorsky S-38, with two 317-kW (425-hp) Pratt & Whitney R-1340 Wasp engines; an eight-seater, it entered service with Pan American Airways on 31 October 1928. Two S-38A 'boats were ordered by the US Navy in October 1928 under the designation XPS-2, and four S-38B 'boats designated PS-3 were fitted with 336-kW (450-hp) R-1340-7 engines. In 1930,

The Sikorsky S-38 was a useful type, this being Pan American's second aircraft, the first built as an amphibian. It spanned 21.84 m (71 ft 8 in), and weighed a maximum of 4753 kg (10,480 lb).

when three more S-38Bs were ordered, the aircraft were reassigned in the utility category, the XPS-2 becoming XRS-2 and the PS-3 becoming RS-3. The US Army Air Corps acquired 11 S-38As in 1929-30 and used them during 1930-33, designating them C-6 and C-6A. The S-39 was a smaller single-engined version of the S-38 with accommodation for five, and was powered by a Pratt & Whitney Wasp Junior. Three 429-kW (575-hp) Pratt & Whitney Hornets powered the 15-passenger S-41, three of which were supplied to a 1930 US Navy order under the designation RS-1.

Sikorsky S-40

Following Pan American's acquisition of New York, Rio and Buenos Aires Airways and its fleet of Consolidated Commodores, the airline brought into service in November 1931 three Sikorsky S-40 amphibians that had been ordered on 20 December 1929. Based on the earlier S-38 and retaining its fuselage pod and twin-boom layout, the S-40, which could carry up to 40 passengers and a crew of six, was powered by four 429-kW (575-hp) Pratt & Whitney Hornet radials. Spanning 34.74 m (114 ft) and weighing a maximum of 15422 kg (34,000 lb) the Sikorsky S-40 was an advanced all-metal flying boat. The 'lower wing' was a strut arrangement carrying the floats and wing bracing.

The first S-40 was named 'American Clipper' by Mrs Herbert Hoover, in a ceremony held on 12 October 1931 and the first passenger-carrying flight took place on 19 November. Flown by Colonel Charles Lindbergh and Captain Basil Rowe, with Igor Sikorsky among the passengers, the S-40 left Miami en route to the Panama Canal Zone, with stops at Cienfuegos in Cuba, Kingston in Jamaica, and at Barranquilla in Colombia. In 1935 the three aircraft were redesignated S-40A, then powered by 492-kW (660-hp) Hornet T2D1 engines.

Pan American Airways was the prime customer for the Sikorsky S-40, 2which at the time was the largest amphibian in the World. Its 28 passengers were carried in unprecedented luxury, with even a smoking room at their disposal.

Sikorsky S-42
to
Sikorsky S-61

Sikorsky S-42

A Pan American specification for a long-range transatlantic flying-boat, issued on 15 August 1931, called for an aircraft able to carry a crew of four and at least 12 passengers over a range of 4023 km (2,500 miles) at a cruising speed of 233 km/h (145 mph). On 30 November 1932 the airline signed contracts, with Martin for its M-130 design and with Sikorsky for the **Sikorsky S-42**. The latter had a conventional flying-boat hull, with four 522-kW (700-hp) Pratt & Whitney Hornet S5D1G engines installed in the leading edge of the parasol wing. The first was delivered to Pan American's Dinner Key base in August 1934 and its

The S-42 was a logical sequel to the earlier pod-and-boom 'boats, retaining the high-wing monoplane layout combined with all-metal hull. It played a key part in opening up transatlantic routes.

first scheduled service, from Miami to Rio de Janeiro, took place on 16 August. During 1935 S-42s pioneered the route across the Pacific from the West Coast to Manila in the Philippines, and in 1937 an S-42 surveyed a South Pacific route to New Zealand. Ten aircraft were built, including three S-42s and three **S-42A** 'boats with 559-kW (750-hp) Hornet S1EG engines, longer-span wings and a 907-kg (2,000-lb) increase in maximum take-off weight. The final four **S-42B** 'boats

introduced a number of aerodynamic improvements, incorporated Hamilton Standard constant-speed propellers and

were able to take advantage of a further 907-kg (2,000-lb) increase in maximum take-off weight.

Sikorsky S-43

The **Sikorsky S-43**, introduced in 1935, was essentially a scaled-down amphibian version of the S-42. Powered by two 559-kW (750-hp) Pratt

& Whitney Hornet engines, this parasol-wing monoplane could carry up to 18 passengers. The type entered service with Pan American in April 1936, on routes around the Caribbean and in Brazil, replacing Consolidated

Commodores. The type also saw service with operators in China, Hawaii, Norway, the Philippines, the USSR and West Africa. Seven were purchased by the US Navy in 1937 under the designation **JRS-1**, and a further 10 were delivered during 1938-39; two of

these served with the US Marine Corps. Five **Y1OA-8** 'boats were supplied to the United States Army Air Corps in 1937. In addition to this, one civil aircraft was impressed in July 1941 and used as a transport under the designation **OA-11**.

Sikorsky S-52

The first US helicopter with all-metal rotor blades, the **Sikorsky S-52-1** two-seater was first flown on 12 February 1947, powered by a 133-kW (178-hp) Franklin engine. In 1948 it established three international heli-

copter records for speed and altitude and was developed into the **S-52-2**, a three/four-seater with a 183-kW (245-hp) Franklin O-425-1 engine which was ordered by the US Marine Corps as a replacement for the HO3S. Deliveries of the **HO5S-1** began in March 1952, and the type served also with the US Coast Guard as the **HO5S-1G**.

The Sikorsky HOSS-1G had a rotor diameter of 10.06 m (33 ft), a maximum take-off weight of 1225 kg (2,700 lb) and a maximum speed of 117 km/h (110 mph). This aircraft served with the United States Coast Guard. Entering service during 1946, a total of nine was procured.

Sikorsky S-55

In 1948 Sikorsky received a contract for five **Sikorsky S-55** utility helicopters for US Air Force evaluation under the designation **YH-19**. The first of these was powered by a 410-kW (550-hp) Pratt & Whitney R-1340-57 mounted in the nose to drive the main rotor gearbox through a long extension shaft, and flew on 10 November 1949. The 447-kW (600-hp) version of the R-1340-57 powered 50 production **H-19A** helicopters, while the 522-kW (700-hp) Wright R-1300-3 replaced it in 270 **H-19B** helicopters, many of which were fitted with rescue hoists and designated **SH-19**. The US Navy placed its first order on 28 April 1950,

for 10 **HO4S-1** machines (similar to the H-19A), which were followed by 61 **HO4S-3** aircraft based on the H-19B; the **HO4S-3G** was a US Coast Guard rescue version. Initial troop and assault transport versions were designated **HRS-1** and **HRS-2**, similar to the HO4S-1, 151 of which were delivered from April 1952. Eighty-four **HRS-3** helicopters with Wright R-1300-3 engines were also built. The US Army's 72 **H-19C** and 338 **H-19D** helicopters, known as the **Chickasaw**, were equivalent to the H-19A and H-19B respectively. Licence-production was undertaken by SNCA du Sud Est in France and by Westland in the UK, the latter developing versions with the Alvis Leonides Major piston engine and with the Bristol Siddeley Gnome

turboshaft under the family name **Whirlwind**.

In 1964 Orlando Helicopter Airways Inc., of Sanford, Florida, was founded by Fred P. Clark to support, and in some cases, re-start production of Sikorsky helicopters no longer built by the parent company. In addition to a huge spares resource, Orlando Helicopters now holds the FAA type certificates for all H-19 and S-55 models. Several versions of the S-55 have since been developed by the firm. These include the **OHA-S-55 Heli-Camper**, a fully fitted out VIP version seating four passengers. New equipment includes a shower, wash-basin and toilet, air conditioning, carpeting and sound-proofing. An optional hydraulic winch, cargo sling or exterior spot-light can also be fitted. The Heli-Camper is powered by an overhauled and reconditioned 596-kW (800-hp) Wright-Cyclone R-1300-3D engine.

The **OHA-S-55 Nite-Writer** is an unprecedented aerial advertising helicopter fitted with a 12.2-m x 2.4-m (40-ft x 8-ft) array of computer-controlled lights which can display messages and graphics, visible over a

distance of 3.2 km (2 miles). More in demand is the **OHA-S-55 Bearcat**, for which Orlando has developed a quick-change hopper and spray system for crop and fertiliser spraying or seed spreading. Certified in 1991, the Bearcat is powered by a Pratt & Whitney R-1340 engine, which can run on automotive fuel, is fitted with a 'quiet' exhaust, and sells for an affordable $300,000.

In October 1985 the company signed an agreement with China's Guangzhou Machinery Tool Company to licence-build OHA-S-55 Bearcats. Under a 20-year joint venture Guangzhou Orlando Helicopters would first assemble American-built parts before progressing to manufacturing entire units. For carrying heavy external loads, such as logging or construction work, Orlando has developed the **OHA-S-55 Heavy Lift** which can deal with underslung weights of up to 1361 kg (3,000 lb). The company has also moved into a unique military market through modifying its S-55s for the US Army Missile Command. As **QS-55 Aggressors** they have been extensively modified to resemble Mil Mi-24 'Hind-E's as flying targets. The Aggressors can be flown by a pilot or as drones (with dummy pilots in their cockpits) and have a new five-bladed main rotor, extensively redesigned nose, stub wings, and chaff and flare dispensers. A second, more aggressive military version is the armed **OHA-AT-**

The Sikorsky S-55 series is now of venerable vintage. This aircraft is a US Army UH-19, which retired its last examples only in the 1980s. Main rotor diameter is 16.15 m (53 ft) and maximum take-off weight 3583 kg (7,900 lb).

55 Defender, design of which began in 1990. Re-engined with a Garrett TPE331-3 turboshaft or a Wright R-1330-3 radial, the Defender also features a stub wing with pylons capable of carrying up to 500 kg (227 lb) of weapons, and a five-bladed rotor. Capable of carrying up to 10 fully-equipped troops, the Defender can also be fitted out to accommodate six stretchers and two attendants.

A small number of civilian Sikorsky-built S-55s are still in use, chiefly in the United States, but the type has now disappeared from the world's military inventories.

Sikorsky S-56

Developed to meet a US Marine Corps requirement for a large assault helicopter to carry 26 troops or military vehicles, for which clamshell nose-opening doors were provided, the **Sikorsky S-56** was the first Sikorsky twin-engined helicopter. Two 1417-kW (1,900-hp) Pratt & Whitney R-2800-50 Double Wasp engines (1566-kW/2,100-hp R-280054s on late production aircraft) were mounted on stub wings, and the nacelles also housed the main legs of the retractable landing gear, the first application of this feature in a

The Sikorsky S-56/XHR2S was one of the first heavy-lift helicopters, and is seen here in the form of a US Army CH-37B Mojave. Maximum external load was (4536 kg) 10,000 lb.

production helicopter. The prototype **XHR2S-1** flew on 18 December 1953 and 60 production machines were delivered from July 1956. Two **HR2S-1W** helicopters were converted for US Navy early warning operations with AN/APS-20E radar under the nose. US Army evaluation of an **HR2S-1**, under the designation **YH-37**, resulted in orders for 94 **H-37A Mojave**

helicopters which went into service, initially with 4th Medium Helicopter Transportation Company, in February 1958. Modernised H-37As redesignated **H-37B** (later **CH-37B**), were redelivered to the US Army from 1961.

Sikorsky S-58

Designed to overcome the range and offensive payload deficiencies of the anti-submarine HO4S version of the S-55, the **Sikorsky S-58** was developed to a US Navy order for a prototype **XHSS-1**, placed on 30 June 1952. The nose engine position was retained for the 1137-kW (1,525-hp) Wright R-1820 engine, but a completely new fuselage, four-bladed main and tail rotors, and transmission system were introduced, together with main rotor and rear fuselage folding to facilitate shipboard stowage. The prototype flew on 8 March 1954, followed by the first production **HSS-1 Seabat** (later **SH-34G**) on 20 September, and the type began to reach anti-submarine squadrons in August 1955. The **HSS-1N** (**SH-34J**) was developed for night operations, equipped with Doppler for navigation, automatic stabilisation and automatic hover coupler, while a single **HSS-1F** (**SH-34H**) flown on 30 January 1957, was powered by two General Electric T58 turboshafts. In 1960 five **HSS-1Z** (**VH-34D**) helicopters joined the Executive Flight Detachment for Presidential and VIP transport duties. Seabats stripped of ASW equipment for utility duties were designated **UH-34G** and **UH-34J**.

The US Marine Corps ordered the **HUS-1 Seahorse** (**UH-34D**) version on 15 October 1954; able to carry 12 Marines, this variant entered service in February 1957. Four **HUS-1L** (**LH-34D**)

helicopters were modified for operation in the Arctic, while inflatable flotation gear identified the US Marines' **HUS-1A** (**UH-34E**) and the US Coast Guard's **HUS-1G** (**HH-34F**). The US Army ordered several hundred **H-34A**, **H-34B** and **H-34C Choctaw** helicopters powered by 1063-kW (1,425-hp) R-1820-84 engines and each carrying 16 troops or eight stretchers in the medevac role, the first unit being equipped in September 1955. The type was exported widely and built under licence in France and the UK, the turbine-powered Westland product known as the **Wessex**. In April 1971 Sikorsky received FAA approval for the **S-58T** PT6A Twin Pac-powered turbine conversion for H-34 airframes. One hundred and forty-six conversions,

or conversion kits, were produced until, in 1981, the rights were sold to California Helicopter International. Since then customers for the **California Helicopter (Sikorsky) S-58T** included New York Airways, the Indonesian and South Korean air forces (now retired) and the government and air force of Thailand. The S-58T is also in service in Argentina with the Presidential Aircraft Squadron.

Small numbers were built of **S-58B** and **S-58D** civil passenger and cargo transport helicopters, a 12-seat airline version being operated by Chicago Helicopter Airways, New York Airways and SABENA. When production was terminated in January 1970, Sikorsky had manufactured a total 1,820 S-58s of all versions.

With its S-58 series, Sikorsky moved away from the pod-and-boom layout with great success. This is a US Army H-34A Choctaw, the third aircraft to be delivered to the service.

In addition to the California Helicopters version, Orlando Helicopters also offers S-58 conversions. An **S-58 Heli-Camper**, similar in fit to the OHA-S-55 Heli-Camper (see Sikorsky S-55 entry) is available, powered by a Wright Cyclone R-1820-84 engine. A further Orlando S-58T conversion is the Orlando Airliner, an 18-seat all-passenger version with nine additional tinted windows fitted on each side of the cabin. Thus far, nearly 30 conversions have been completed.

Sikorsky S-60 and S-64

Sikorsky's first 'flying crane' helicopter was the **Sikorsky S-60**, developed from the S-56 and retaining that machine's powerplant, transmission and rotor system. Work began in May 1958 and the prototype was flown on 2 March 1969; it was capable of lifting a 5443-kg (12,000-lb) payload beneath the fuselage boom, and the co-pilot could turn his seat to face aft to control loading and unloading. The prototype S-60 crashed in April 1961, but by then Sikorsky had begun construction of an enlarged version, with a six-bladed main rotor driven by two 3020-kW (4,050-shp) JFTD-12A turboshaft engines. Designated **S-64**, the proto-

Sikorsky CH-54B Tarhe of the 291st Aviation Company, US Army, during the early 1970s.

Sikorsky's first 'flying crane' helicopter was the **Sikorsky S-60**, developed from the S-56 and retaining that machine's powerplant, transmission and rotor system. Work began in May 1958 and the prototype was flown on 2 March 1969; it was capable of lifting a 5443-kg (12,000-lb) payload beneath the fuselage boom, and the co-pilot could turn his seat to face aft to control loading and unloading. The prototype S-60 crashed in April 1961, but by then Sikorsky had begun construction of an enlarged version, with a six-bladed main rotor driven by two 3020-kW (4,050-shp) JFTD-12A turboshaft engines. Designated **S-64**, the prototype flew on 9 May 1962 and was followed by two further machines for evaluation by the Federal German armed forces. This did not result in German orders, but the US Army placed an order for six **S-64A** helicopters in June 1963, under the designation **CH-54A Tarhe**. This version was powered by 3356-kW (4,500-shp) Pratt & Whitney T73-P-1 engines, and production eventually totalled approximately 60; 10 **CH-54B** helicopters were built with 3579-kW (4,800-shp) T73P-700 engines. The Tarhe served in a heavy-lift role in Vietnam, with the 478th and the 291st Aviation Companies.

Only 97 Tarhes were built for the United States Army between 1964 and 1972. In the later years of its life, the type was largely relegated to Army National Guard units, seven of which were still equipped with it by the beginning of the 1990s. Progressively replaced by the (less-capable) CH-47D, the last unit to give up its CH-54s was D Company, 113th Aviation, of the Nevada Army National Guard, based in Reno, in 1993. On 1 February 1992 Sikorsky sold the rights for the S-64 to Erickson Air-Crane Co., of Central Point, Oregon, who have so far undertaken no production.

Specification
Sikorsky CH-54B
Type: crane helicopter
Powerplant: two 3579-kW (4,800-shp) Pratt & Whitney T73-700

Sikorsky S-61

Designed to combine the hunter/ killer functions in one airframe, the **Sikorsky HSS-2** was the subject of a US Navy contract awarded on 23 September 1957. This called for an all-weather anti-submarine helicopter with 'dunking sonar' equipment and able to carry up to 381 kg (840 lb) of offensive weapons. The **S-61** design had watertight, hull-retractable landing gear in the stabilising floats, and was powered by two General Electric T58 turboshaft engines driving a five-bladed main rotor. The prototype flew on 11 March 1959 and seven **YHSS-2** trials aircraft followed; the type was redesignated **SH-3** in September 1959. The initial production version, the **SH-3A Sea King**, began to reach fleet squadrons in September 1961 and later conversions included the **HH-3A** VIP transport flown by the Executive Flight Detachment, Washington. The essentially similar **CH-124**, assembled by United Aircraft of Canada, was supplied to the Canadian navy. The Royal Norwegian air force acquired **S-61A** helicopters without ASW equipment for rescue duties, and the Royal Malaysian air force acquired **S-61A-4 Nuri** helicopters equipped to carry 31 troops or operate in the SAR role. One hundred and sixty-seven **HSS-2** (now withdrawn), **HSS-2A** (**SH-3D**), **HSS-2Bs** (**SH-3H**) and a further 18 SAR-configured S-61As were built under licence by Mitsubishi, in a programme which was completed in 1990.

More fuel and the replacement of the original 932-kW (1,250-shp) T58-GE-8B engines by 1044-kW (1,400-shp) T58-GE-10s led to redesignation as the SH-3D, first delivered in June 1966 and ordered by Argentina, Brazil and Spain, as well as by the US Navy. Since 1969 Agusta has been building SH-3Ds under licence in Italy as the **Agusta-Sikorsky ASH-3D**. Some 105 **ASH-3A**s with ASW equipment removed were redesignated **SH-3G** for utility duties, while further conversions which have been made since 1971 are of the SH-3H version, with updated ASW and electronic surveillance equipment. While production of the **AS-61** and ASH-3D, **ASH-3TS** (Transporto Special, a VIP version) and **ASH-3H** have now ceased, Agusta claims it could re-open the line in 36 months. The Italian firm did recommence building **AS-61R** (**HH-3F**) search and rescue helicopters to meet an order for

British Airways Helicopters can trace its lineage back to 1947, though today the company has been renamed British International Helicopters. It currently operates a fleet of 15 twin-engined S-61Ns.

two from the national civil protection service and 13 for the air force. These will have upgraded radar, LORAN, FLIR and navigation systems, modifications that will be retrofitted to the air force's existing 19 AS-61Rs. Agusta is also the exclusive overhaul and repair agent for Europe and the Mediterranean.

The SH-3H is the standard version now in service with the US Navy, with approximately 150 earlier aircraft modified to this standard. Supplemented by small numbers of the surviving SH-3G utility version, which has had all the SH-3H's anti-submarine equipment removed, SH-3Hs serve regularly on board the Navy's carriers and at shore bases, but are being steadily replaced by the SH-60 Seahawk and Ocean Hawk. Eight of the SH-3s supplied to Spain have been modified to SH-3H standard, and three of these are now equipped with a Thorn-EMI Searchwater radar in an external inflatable radome (similar to that fitted to Royal Navy Sea King AEW.Mk 3s) for shipboard airborne early warning duties.

Acquired originally for re-supply of its radar stations, the US Air Force **CH-3B** was essentially a de-navalised SH-3, but the **CH-3C** that was ordered in November 1962 introduced a number of major changes, including a rear loading ramp. Allocated the company designation **S-61R**, the prototype flew on 17 June 1963 and the first CH-3C delivery was made on 30 December 1963. An engine change from 969-kW (1,300-shp) T58-GE-1s to 1119-kW (1,500-shp) T58-GE-5s produced the **CH-3E** in February 1966. Some were later converted to **HH-3E** standard for the USAF Aerospace Rescue and Recovery Service, being provided with armour, self-sealing fuel tanks, retractable inflight-refuelling

probe, rescue hoist and 0.5-in (12.7-mm) machine-guns for defensive purposes; this was the 'Jolly Green Giant' as used in Vietnam. These aircraft have now all been retired, replaced by the HH-60. The US Coast Guard operated the **HH-3F Pelican**, which had advanced electronic equipment for SAR duties, but lacked the self-sealing tanks, armour and armament of the HH-3E. These have now virtually given way to the HH-60J Jayhawk.

Civil versions for passenger operations were developed initially as the non-amphibious **S-61L** which, with a lengthened fuselage to seat up to 30 passengers, was first flown on 6 December 1960 and was FAA-approved on 2 November 1961. It was followed by the essentially similar **S-61N** that was, however, an amphibious version with a sealed hull and stabilising floats that housed retractable landing gear; it was first flown on 7 August 1962 and is still in widespread civil use. Westland built versions, still in low-rate production, are

discussed separately, in their own entry.

Orlando Helicopters now provides extensive spares support for the S-61 and is investigating ways to re-engine existing aircraft to run on alternative petrol, propane and alcohol fuels.

Specification
Sikorsky SH-3D
Type: ASW helicopter
Powerplant: two 1044-kW (1,400-shp) General Electric T58-10 turboshafts
Performance: maximum speed 267 km/h (166 mph); range with maximum fuel and 10 per cent reserves 1005 km (625 miles)
Weights: empty 5382 kg (11,865 lb); maximum take-off 9752 kg (21,500 lb)
Dimensions: main rotor diameter 18.9 m (62 ft 0 in); fuselage length 16.69 m (54 ft 9 in); height 5.13 m (16 ft 10 in); main rotor disc area 280.5 m^2 (3,019.1 sq ft)
Armament: external hardpoints for total of 381 kg (840 lb) of weapons, normally comprising two Mk 46 torpedoes

The Sikorsky HH-3E 'Jolly Green Giant' fully proved itself in Vietnam, this example being on the strength of the 48th Aerospace Rescue and Recovery Squadron, USAF, based at Eglin AFB, in Florida.

Sikorsky S-62

The amphibious **Sikorsky S-62** was derived from the piston-engined S-55 and used that helicopter's main and tail rotor system and other components mounted in a new sealed hull. The prototype S-62 flew on 22 May 1958 and was followed by the S-62A production version which, powered by a single General Electric CT58-110-1 turboshaft engine, provided accommodation for up to 11 passengers. One **S-62B** was built with an S-58 main

Combining the rotor system of the S-55 with a turboshaft engine and the amphibious-type hull developed for the S-61, the moderately successful S-62 had a main rotor diameter of 16.15 m (53 ft).

rotor system. The **S-62C** was chosen by the US Coast Guard as a replacement for the HH-34 rescue helicopter and initial deliveries, under the designation **HH-52A** and named **Seaguard**, were made in January 1963. This version powered by a 932-kW (1,250-hp) CT58-GE-8 engine was

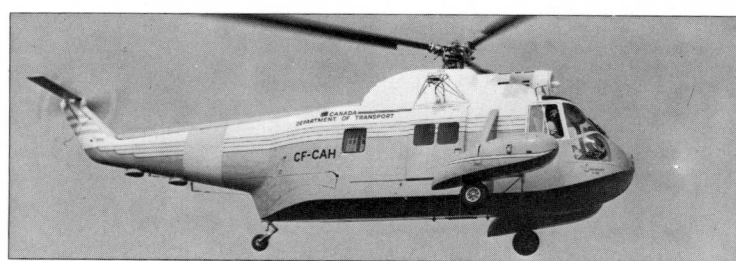

replaced by the HH-3 Pelican. The S-62 was also exported to Japan. By mid-

1993, no military, and only a very small number of civilian, S-62s remain in use.

Sikorsky S-65

For US Marine Corps use Sikorsky developed the **Sikorsky S-65** heavy assault transport helicopter as the **CH-53 Sea Stallion**, first flown on 14 October 1964. It incorporated some components used in the S-64 Skycrane but had a watertight hull and was powered by two 2125-kW (2,850-shp) General Electric T64-GE6 engines. It had rear-loading doors, and among the specified loads were a 105-mm (4.13-in) howitzer or 38 combat-equipped troops. The initial production version was the **CH-53A**, delivered from September 1966, but the **CH-53D** introduced in March 1969 had 2927-kW (3,925-shp) T64-GE-413 engines. A specialised minesweeping version, the **RH-53D**, was first flown on 27 October 1972. **HH-53B** and **HH-53C** SAR variants were built for the US Air Force, the former equipped to a standard similar to that of the HH-3E and powered by 2297-kW (3,080-shp) T64-GE-3 engines; it was first flown on 15 March 1967. More powerful 3,925-kW (5,260-hp) T64-GE-7 engines powered the improved **HH-53C**, the same powerplant being installed in the **CH-53G** produced for the German army. Two **S-65Oe** rescue helicopters were delivered to the Austrian air force in 1970.
Work began in 1971 on an enlarged version with a lengthened fuselage, a new rotor system and three 3266-kW (4380-shp) T64-GE-416 engines. The US Navy contract covering two prototypes and subsequent flight test was awarded in 1973, and the **YCH-53E** flew for the first time on 1 March 1974; the first **CH-53E Super Stallion** delivery to the US Marine Corps took place on 16 June 1981. Since 1982 Sikorsky has been developing the **MH-53E** mine countermeasures variant. It incorporates major equipment changes and has much enlarged sponsons and can carry an additional 3785 litres (1,000 US gal) of fuel.

Variants
YCH-53A: winner of the HH(X) competition, two prototype CH-53As were completed for US Navy evaluation, by March 1966; first flight made by second aircraft (BuNo. 151614) on 14 October 1964, powered by two T64-GE-6 turboshafts
CH-53A: initial production version for US Marine Corps, deliveries

commencing in September 1965; accelerated deployment to South East Asia made after improvements to engine intake filters, defensive armament, crew armour and external lifting capability; selected T64-GE-1 engines retrofitted for extended running at maximum power output when necessary; fitted with hardpoints for towing mine-sweeping gear from 34th aircraft onwards; used by USAF for crew training and later for covert operations in Vietnam and Laos (seven aircraft borrowed from and returned to Navy); 139 built
RH-53A: 15 dedicated mine-countermeasures versions delivered to the Navy via the Marine Corps; re-engined with T64-GE-413 turboshafts; rectangular frame mounted on rear ramp to tow mine clearing sled and rear view mirrors fitted on either side of the nose; used to clear North Vietnamese mines during Operation Endsweep in 1973; RH-53As replaced by RH-53Ds in Navy service and aircraft returned to Marines
TH-53A: former USMC CH-53As used by USAF from 1989 onwards to train MH-53 crews at Kirtland AFB, NM; at least three aircraft in use, stripped of most equipment and camouflaged
HH-53B: eight aircraft similar to CH-53A but delivered to USAF Aerospace Rescue and Recovery Service to supplement HH-3s in South East Asia; refuelling probe relocated to starboard side of nose, pylons fitted to allow carriage of external fuel tanks; armed with three pintle-mounted GAU-2A/B 7.62-mm Miniguns powered by T64-GE-3s, later replaced by T64-GE-7s; quickly supplemented by HH-53Cs and re-assigned to CONUS, the last four HH-53Bs were modified to MH-53J standard in the late 1980s
CH-53C: 22 aircraft built for heavy-lift duties with the USAF; fitted with sponsons and external tanks as developed for HH-53C, it was similar in most respects to this version but lacked a refuelling probe; replaced CH-53As on loan from USMC for covert operations in Laos; later operated by TAC and USAFE; seven surviving CH-53Cs brought up to MH-53J standard in late 1980s
HH-53C: refined version of HH-53B, 44 of which were built for USAF ARRS

The HH-53B was a highly capable combat rescue variant, with armour protection, armament and an inflight refuelling capability via the nose-mounted probe, which is telescopic.

for combat rescue; dubbed 'Super Jolly Green Giant'; dispensed with bracing struts fore the external pylons, and included additional crew armour, and better radio fit to facilitate operations with HC-130 tankers; RHAW and IR jamming systems introduced as a result of experience in North Vietnam during 1972; HH-53Cs used in support of Apollo space missions for emergency capsule rescue; HH-53Cs remained in USAF service until late 1980s when all were converted to MH-53J standard
S-65C-2 (S-65Ö): export version of CH-53C, two of which were delivered to the Austrian air force in 1970; later retired from use due to operating costs and passed on to Israel in 1981
S-65-C3: only other export version of H-53, delivered to Israel from 1969; corresponding to HH-53C, 33 aircraft supplemented by two additional S-65s from Austria in 1981; surviving aircraft now being upgraded by IAI subsidiary

The most powerful member of the Sikorsky S-65 family is the US Marine Corps' three-engined CH-53E Super Stallion. This is the prototype YCH-53E of 1974.

MATA Helicopters
CH-53D: improved version of CH-53A fitted with new transmission increasing hot-and-high performance, first flown on 27 January 1969; 124 built
RH-53D: first flown 27 October 1972; 30 aircraft (named Sea Stallion) specifically developed for anti-mine warfare in the light of positive experience with RH-53A; fitted with an initial powerplant of two T64-GE-415s, RH-53D also differs from RH-53A by inclusion of refuelling probe, automatic flight control system, more powerful cargo hook, and rescue winch; armed with two swivel-mounted 0.5-in machine-guns; six delivered to Imperial Iranian navy before the fall of the Shah

VH-53D: two CH-53Ds delivered to USMC for VIP transport

CH-53G: aircraft built under licence by VFW for a German army order for 135 examples, later reduced to 110; 20 assembled by VFW-Fokker entirely from US-supplied components, then progressively increasing indigenous sources; total includes two US-built CH-53Gs; first German-assembled aircraft deliv-ered on 11 October 1971, entered service in 1973

YHH-53H: first aircraft to be fitted with 'Pave Low I', in trials for a projected night/all-weather combat rescue/ infil-tration mission; fitted with early low-light TV system which proved inadequate, though the first successful night rescue was made with an improved system in December 1972, in Laos; aircraft later modified to 'Pave Low II' standard, with external sponsons and tanks

HH-53H: eight HH-53Cs and YHH-53H modified to definitive 'Pave Low III' standard; delivered between 1979 and 1980 and fitted with FLIR, TF radar, INS, computer generated moving map display, RHAW and chaff/flare dispensers; later re-designated MH-53H

MH-53H: redesignation and modification of HH-53H under the Constant Green programme; all 'Pave Low III' aircraft now being modified to MH-53J standard

MH-53J: modification of 31 HH-53Bs, CH-53Cs and HH-53Cs and modernisation of MH-53Hs to produce 'Pave Low III Enhanced'; fitted with digital databus, improved transmission, T64-GE-415 engines and 453 kg (1,000 lb) of titanium armour; MTOW increased from 19050 to 22680 kg (42,000 to 50,000 lb); those modified from HH-53Bs retain braced external tank pylons of first Super Jollys

YCH-53E: two prototype aircraft fitted

with a third T64-GE-415 increasing total installed power to 9789 kW (13,140-shp); flown on 1 March 1974, first aircraft crashed in September of that year

CH-53E: current production three-engined transport version with 162 orders placed by USMC and USN; features gull-wing tailplane and canted rear rotor; first production aircraft accepted by USMC on 13 December 1980

MH-53E: named **Sea Dragon**, combines airframe and powerplant of CH-53E with mine-sweeping capability of RH-53D; internal fuel capacity increased, and fitted with two swivel-mounted 0.5-in machine-guns; identifiable by outsize sponsons and rear-view mirrors

VH-53F: six VIP aircraft intended for USAF use, allocated USN serials but never delivered

S-80M-1: mine-sweeping version delivered to Japanese Maritime Self-

Defence Force; first of 11 aircraft delivered on 13 January 1989

Specification
Sikorsky CH-53E
Type: heavy transport helicopter
Powerplant: three 3266-ekW (4,380-shp) General Electric T64-416 turboshafts
Performance: maximum speed 315 km/h (196 mph); range with maximum payload 2075 km (1,290 miles)
Weights: empty 15071 kg (33,226 lb); maximum take-off 33339 kg (73,500 lb)
Dimensions: main rotor diameter 24.08 m (79 ft 0 in); fuselage length 22.35 m (73 ft 4 in); height 8.66 m (28 ft 5 in); main rotor disc area 455.4 m² (4,902.0 sq ft)
Accommodation: cargo payload 13608 kg (30,000 lb) internally or 1415 kg (32,000 lb) externally, with seating for 55 troops

Sikorsky S-67, S-69 and S-72

Sikorsky designed and developed the **Sikorsky S-67 Blackhawk** high-speed attack helicopter as a private venture. This combined two 1119-kW (1,500-shp) General Electric T58-GE-5 engines and five-bladed main and tail rotors with a slender gunship fuselage, short-span 8.33-m (27-ft 4-in) fixed wings, a cruciform tail unit with an all-moving horizontal surface, and retractable tailwheel landing gear. Highly manoeuvrable, the S-67 established on 14 December 1970 a new world-class speed record over a 3-km (1.86-mile) course of 348.971 km/h (216.841 mph). Its development was abandoned after an accident in 1974.

In 1972 Sikorsky designed the **S-69** for the US Army. gaining a contract for two **XH-59A** prototypes to evaluate an Advancing Blade Concept (ABC) rotor system comprising two counter-rotating three-bladed rigid main rotors, with a 1361-kW (1,825-shp) Pratt & Whitney Canada PT6T-3 Turbo Twin Pac to power them; the S-69 requires no tail rotor and has a conventional

horizontal tail surface with endplate fins and rudders. Additional power is provided by two pod-mounted 1361-kg (3,000-lb) thrust Pratt & Whitney J60-P-3A turbojets, one on each side of the fuselage, and the S-69 has demonstrated a speed of 488 km/h (303 mph). In 1982 these aircraft were developed into a new **XH-59B** config-uration with advanced rotors, new powerplant, and a ducted pusher propeller at the tail. This approach was seen as a possible solution to the Army's search for a new light attack helicopter (LHX), and further funding was recommended. The S-69/XH-59 programme was abandoned, however, and the need for LHX was only ans-wered in the 1990s with the selection of the RAH-66 Commanche.

Under contract to NASA and the US Army Sikorsky also built two **S-72 Rotor Systems Research Aircraft (RSRA)** designed to serve as test vehicles for a variety of rotors/rotor systems. The configuration included wings of 13.74-m (45-ft 1-in) span, a

tail unit with conventional control surfaces, two 1044-kW (1,400-shp) General Electric T58-GE-5 turboshaft engines to power the rotors and auxiliary powerplant of two 4207-kg (9,275-lb) thrust General Electric TF34-GE-400A turbofan engines. The wings and auxiliary turbofans, which were attachable/detachable on each side of the fuselage, made it possible to test rotors that would be too small to lift and support the S-72 in flight. This then progressed into trials involving an X-wing in place of the main rotor. Using a compressed air system this airfoil could be blown to affect cyclic and collective

The Sikorsky S-69, which was under military evaluation as the XH-59A, was a test bed for the ABC concept in which only the advancing blades of the contra-rotating rotors generate lift, thus reducing drag.

pitch. The wing could be stopped in flight and Sikorsky believed the design had potential for future use as a high-speed 'convertiplane'. First flight took place on 2 December 1987, but after three further flights all funding was suspended and the **S-72X1** was placed in storage at Edwards AFB.

Sikorsky S-70

Designed for the US Army's UTTAS (Utility Tactical Transport Aircraft System) programme, the **Sikorsky S-70** was intended as a replacement for the Bell UH-1 and as such had to be capable of carrying an 11-man infantry squad and its equipment. The first example was flown in **YUH-60A** prototype form on 17 October 1974 and was selected as the winner of the design competition, trumping the Bell 240 and Boeing Vertol 179, on 23 December 1976. This victory was vital to the continued financial well-being of Sikorsky, as the projected order of 1,107 UTTAS helicopters, beginning in 1978, would revive its falling order book. The first production contract covered 15 **UH-60A Black Hawk** helicopters; a further 353 were the subject of a fixed-price option, and an April 1982 contract covered the acquisition of 294 more for delivery up to 1985.

Powered by two 1163-kW (1,560-shp) General Electric T700-GE-700 turboshaft engines, the first production UH-60A flew on 17 October 1978, and entered service with the 101st Airborne Division (Air Assault) in June

the following year. It soon proved far superior to the UH-1H, able to carry loads of up to 20 and to cope with external loads of up to 2000 kg (4,400 lb). With the addition of External Stores Support System (ESSS) pylons the UH-60A can carry stores such as Hellfire missiles and long-range fuel tanks on pylons, and M60 machine-guns in the forward area of the cabin. The US Army has introduced a plethora of versions into service for assault, Medevac, electronic warfare and special operations, all of which are detailed in the variants list below.

When the US Navy's LAMPS (Light Airborne Multi-Purpose System) programme required a helicopter with a capability superior to that of the Kaman Seasprite that won the LAMPS Mk I contract, substantial commonality with the UH-60A meant that significant economies could result from selection of the navalised **S-70L**, the **SH-60B Seahawk**. This version has chin-mounted surveillance radar, ESM

The Sikorsky SH-60B Seahawk is the United States Navy's LAMPS Mk III helicopter, and is steadily repacing both the H-3 Sea King and the H-2 Seasprite on Navy vessels of all sizes.

(electronic support measures) equipment, a starboard-side pylon for MAD (magnetic anomaly detection) equipment, a sonobuoy launcher, automatic rotor folding, tail pylon folding and modified landing gear. The first of five prototypes flew on 12 December 1979, followed by the first production aircraft on 11 February 1983; initial deliveries were made on 24 March. The first US Navy unit to deploy operationally was HSL-41 at North Island, San Diego, California. The SH-60B will operate from frigates and

destroyers, while the **SH-60F** derivative now entering service is an SH-3H Sea King replacement. By 1993 a total of 1,816 H-60/S-70s had been built for customers in 20 nations.

Variants
YUH-60A: three prototypes entered for UTTAS competition with a further three built after Sikorsky had won; extensively modified during test flights resulting in new tail shape, upper fuselage fairing, cabin windows, and rotor shaft

UH-60A: initial production version of Black Hawk assault transport for US Army; manually folding tail boom for C-130 transport; steadily improved over the years through the addition of a rescue hoist, ESSS provision from the 431st production aircraft (retrofitted), M60D machine-guns replaced by M134 Miniguns, infra-red suppressers fitted to exhausts, wire strike protection above cockpit, accident data recorder, Tracor AN/ARN-148 Omega navigation system, satellite communications transceiver and GPS also added; in use with US Customs service as UH-60A 'Pot Hawk' for anti-drug surveillance; delivered to Bahrain Amiri Air Arm, Fuerza Aérea Colombiana, Philippine air force and Royal Saudi land forces; 'Credible Hawk' UH-60As delivered to USAF in mid-1980s as initial combat rescue version to replace HH-3s with ARRS; detail differences from Army Black Hawks include much of the equipment later added to Army UH-60As; 11 'Credible Hawks' ordered initially, and subsequent procurement and upgrade programme repeatedly cut back
GUH-60A: non-flyable instructional airframes
JUH-60A: aircraft temporarily det-ached for test purposes
EH-60A: as part of the US Army's Special Electronics Mission Aircraft programme, TRW equipped a single **YEH-60A** with Quick Fix IIB emitter location gear and associated antennas; funding allocated for 40 aircraft, later designated EH-60C
HH-60A: single development aircraft for USAF HH-60D
MH-60A: 30 UH-60As modified for special operations use pending the delivery of the dedicated MH-60A; nicknamed 'Velcro Hawk' due to the haphazard addition of equipment; now withdrawn from all active-duty units, bar the Oklahoma Air National Guard, and replaced by MH-60L
VH-60A: initial designation for nine USMC VIP aircraft, later allocated VH-60N designation
UH-60B: Sikorsky designation for an improved Army transport version of the Black Hawk with a CRT cockpit, improved engines and other new features; most of these elements were included in the UH-60L
YEH-60B: UH-60A modified for a proposed Stand-Off Target Acquisition System with an underslung rotating sensor in a canoe faring; first flown on

6 February 1981, but proposed acquisition of 78 aircraft abandoned to provide funding for J-STARS
YSH-60B: five Seahawk prototypes for US Navy to fulfil LAMPS Mk III requirement
SH-60B: production ASW Seahawk for US Navy; fitted with RAST probe, 25-tube sonobuoy launcher, towed MAD bird on stub wing to port, AN/APS-142 radar, ALQ-142 ESM system under nose, single-piece pilot's windscreen, folding tailboom; primary armament two Mk 46 torpedoes; aircraft subject to phased upgrade programme involving addition of new weapons capability and avionics
EH-60C: production Quick Fix II-equipped aircraft designed to locate and jam enemy radio transmissions; fitted with antenna array on tailboom and folding whip aerial under fuselage; plans to acquire 130 EH-60Cs later cut to 66
CH-60E: proposed Marine Corps troop-carrying version; not proceeded with as Corps squad size too great for cabin
HH-60D: 'Night Hawk' combat rescue version for USAF, fitted with NVG-compatible cockpit, refuelling probe, ESSS provision, IR jammer, HIRSS exhaust suppressor, rotor de-icing, colour weather radar; subsequently fell victim to procurement cuts and only one development aircraft completed, later used in HH-60A development
HH-60E: proposed reduced specification HH-60D for USAF; not proceeded with in favour of HH-60A
HH-60G: initially designated MH-60G, HH-60G aircraft at first not fitted with full MH-60G special operations equipment but optimised for SAR instead; subject to upgrade when funds allow
SH-60F: dubbed 'Ocean Hawk', the SH-60F provides inner ASW screening for US carrier battle groups; less heavily equipped than SH-60B
MH-60G: 'Pave Hawk' full-specification combat rescue/special operations aircraft for USAF, converted from existing aircraft; fitted with Bendix colour weather radar, Doppler navig-ation, GPS, INS, moving map display, new HF, VHF and satellite comms, IR jammer, threat-warning system, chaff/flare dispensers, FLIR, refuelling probe, IR strobes, ESSS, HUD, digital databus and additional guns; first MH-60Gs delivered to 55th SOS in December 1987 and all aircraft subject to a rolling modification

programme to reach full capability
HH-60H: 'Rescue Hawk' combat rescue/special operations version for US Navy
HH-60J: Jayhawk, ordered by USCG as a replacement for HH-3F on SAR duties
UH-60J: replaced KV-107s in Japan Air Self-Defence Force service and S-61As of the Japan Maritime Self-Defence Force; essentially a Sikorsky S-70A-12 (UH-60L), they differ from US aircraft in being optimised for rescue missions; equipped with rescue winch to starboard, external fuel tanks, Japanese avionics and weather radar, turret-mounted FLIR; first aircraft built by Sikorsky, two more assembled by Mitsubishi which will build the remaining 26 on order entirely in Japan; operational from March 1992
MH-60K: Army special operations version similar to Air Force MH-60G but equipped to a higher standard from the outset; fitted with Texas Instruments FLIR, night vision imaging system, moving map display, OBOGS, T700-GE-701C engines, main rotor brake, and a comprehensive self-defence suite including missile plume detector, radar warning receiver, chaff and flare dispenser, IR jammer, radio jammer and laser warning receiver; prototype flew on 10 August 1990 and the first of 22 currently funded aircraft was delivered in spring 1992; 38 further MH-60Ks are required for Army and ANG units
UH-60L: improvements to UH-60As saw the basic weight of the aircraft increased by 25 per cent; to remedy this situation Sikorsky developed the T700-210C-powered UH-60L which became the standard production transport version for the US Army from October 1989; 190 aircraft ordered, with modifications being retrofitted to UH-60As
MH-60L: UH-60Ls temporarily modified for special operations duties with US Army; replaced stop-gap MH-60As, and referred to as 'Velcro Hawks'; transferred to Reserve units after their replacement by MH-60Ks
VH-60N: 'Presidential Hawk' VIP transports delivered to HMX-1 at MCAS Quantico, originally as VH-60A; fitted with weather radar, extra sound-proofing and VIP cabin, shrouded exhausts, and extensive avionics and communications improvements
UH-60P: 100 UH-60Ls ordered by the Republic of Korea Army, with improved gearbox and main rotor brake; first Sikorsky-built aircraft handed over on

10 December 1990; the next 19 assembled from CKDs, with a further 80 to be built by Korean Air
UH-60Q: 'Dustoff Hawk', Medevac version utilising UH-60L airframe, with purpose-designed medical interior
S-70A: bulk of export Black Hawks delivered using civilian designation with numerical suffix allocated to each customer; deliveries made to Saudi Arabia, Philippines, Thailand, Australia, Jordan, Japan, Brunei, Turkey, Korea, Egypt, Mexico, Hong Kong, Morocco, and Rolls-Royce/Westland in the UK; Royal Saudi land forces received 21 **S-70A-1** Desert Hawks and a further eight **S-70A-L1** Medevac versions, all optimised for desert operations; 39 **S-70A-9**s were delivered to the Royal Australian Air Force, with a further 38 assembled by Hawker de Havilland in Bankstown, NSW
S-70B-6: ASW version for Greece, to be delivered commencing in 1995
S-70C: designation allocated to civilian versions of Black Hawk; applied to VIP-configured Brunei aircraft and also to Black Hawks and Seahawks for Republic of China, to circumvent restrictions on 'military' exports
S-70C(M)-1: Thunderhawk, essentially SH-60F standard aircraft delivered to Republic of China navy from 1993 onwards
WS-70: S-70/UH-60 built under-licence by Westland Helicopters in UK; offered in anticipation of RAF requirement to replace Wessex and Puma transport helicopters

Specification
Sikorsky SH-60B
Type: ASW/ASST shipboard helicopter
Powerplant: two 1261-kW (1,690-shp) General Electric T700-401 turboshafts
Performance: maximum cruising speed 249 km/h (155 mph); normal range about 966 km (600 miles)
Weights: empty 6191 kg (13,648 lb); maximum take-off 9926 kg (21,584 lb)
Dimensions: main rotor diameter 16.36 m (53 ft 8 in); fuselage length 15.26 m (50 ft 1/2 in), height 5.23 m (17 ft 2 in); main rotor disc area 210.1 m² (2,262.0 sq ft)
Armament: crew of three and complete range of ASW sensors, plus basic armament of two Mk 46 torpedoes

Sikorsky UH-60A Black Hawk of the US Army in the early 1980s.

Sikorsky S-76 Spirit

Growing demands for transport helicopters in support of offshore energy operations led Sikorsky to initiate worldwide market research to establish the requirements of such operators. An important consideration was seating capacity, and in 1975 Sikorsky began

the development of a 14-seat commercial helicopter designated **Sikorsky S-76** and later named **Spirit**. The first of four prototypes (N762SA) was flown on 13 March 1977, and the first fully certificated IFR production aircraft was delivered to Air Logistics of Lafayette,

Louisiana, on 27 February 1979.

This two-year certification prog-ramme resulted from the use of an advanced dynamic systems/powerplant combination evolved for military requirements, but further development continued from the time that production began, leading to an improved **S-76 Mk II** from 1 March 1982. This differs by having improved

cabin ventilation, dynamic system refinements, more access panels to simplify maintenance, and an advanced version of the Allison 250 turboshaft engine that gives an increase in guaranteed power output. In 1983 Sikorsky flew the first **S-76B**, to replace the Mk II on the production line. Powered by two 771-kW (1,033-shp) Pratt & Whitney PT6B-36As, the

S-76B incorporates aerodynamic refinements developed for the UH-60. S-76B meets FAR Pt 29 category A IFR requirements. As a follow-on to the S-76B the **S-76C** was announced in June 1989, and flew in May 1990. Powered by Turboméca Arriel 1S1 engines, the 12-seat S-76C has attracted military orders from Hong Kong and Spain, and is also in use with several off-shore operators.

Military sales of the S-76 had been few until the introduction of a dedicated, armed version, the **H-76 Eagle**, in 1985. Featuring armed seats, floor and fuel tanks, the Eagle can be armed with a combination of gun pods, rocket pods and even AAMs on its stub pylons. It can be used in gunship, Medevac, troop-transport, or combat SAR roles and has provision for a chin- or mast-mounted sight. It was selected by South Korea as its new light utility helicopter and an order for up 175 is anticipated. Aircraft are being built in the United States initially, with assembly being gradually transferred to Daewoo-Sikorsky Aerospace Ltd.

The S-76 has also served as a technology demonstrator for several projects. A one-off modification, the **SHADOW** (Sikorsky Helicopter Advanced Demonstrator and Operator Workload) programme saw an S-76 fitted with an add-on cockpit at the nose to test fly-by-wire, voice-actuated and side-stick control methods, together with helmet-mounted sights, FLIR and HUD combinations and an

Sikorsky S-76 Spirit of Petroleum Helicopters Incorporated.

NVG cockpit. It was used extensively by Boeing/Sikorsky in their First Team submission for the US Army's LHX competition to test a night vision system. A second S-76 was fitted with an anti-torque tail-rotor system, as the **Fantail Demonstrator**, playing an important part in the selection of the First Team's design by the US Army as the RAH-66 Commanche.

Sales of the Spirit in all its civil forms were approaching the 500 mark by 1993.

Variants
S-76: original production version, this designation applicable to aircraft delivered before 1 March 1982
S-76A+: unsold S-76s re-engined with Turboméca Arriel turboshafts on demand; produced to special orders only such as SAR aircraft for Royal

Hong Kong Auxiliary Air Force with undernose GEC MRTS FLIR turret and searchlight
S-76 Mk II: production all-weather transport from 1 March 1982, superseded by S-76B
S-76 Utility: simplified version of S-76 Mk II with sliding doors, and optional fixed landing gear; available in civil or military versions
AUH-76: armed utility helicopter version, airframe basically as S-76 Utility, but with avionics and armament to permit deployment in various military roles
S-76B: current production version powered by Pratt & Whitney PT6B-36 turboshafts
S-76C: alternative current production version, powered by Turboméca Arriel 1S1 turboshafts.
S-76D: projected version available from 1994, to be powered by uprated

Turboméca 2S1s
H-76 Eagle: armed version of S-76B
H-76N: projected naval version announced in 1984; no orders received

Specification
Sikorsky S-76 Mk II
Type: all-weather transport helicopter
Powerplant: two 509-kW (682-shp) Allison 250-C30S turboshafts
Performance: maximum cruising speed 269 km/h (167 mph); service ceiling 4570 m (15,000 ft); range with 12 passengers and fuel reserves 748 km (465 miles)
Weights: empty 2540 kg (5,600 lb); maximum take-off 4672 kg (10,300 lb)
Dimensions: main rotor diameter 13.41 m (44 ft 0 in); length, rotors turning 16.00 m (52 ft 6 in), height 4.41 m (14 ft 54 in); main rotor disc area 116.78 m² (1,257.0 sq ft)

Sikorsky S-92

Developed as a competitor to aircraft like the Aérospatiale/Eurocopter Super Puma on the civil market, the **Sikorsky S-92** is a derivative of the S-70 family. The S-70's low-height cabin, inherited from the military Black Hawk, was a major drawback for potential civil customers, so the new design combined the proven transmission, rotor system and power train from various military S-70 sub-types with an all new fuselage.

The fuselage is of conventional construction, but with a 1.83 m (6 ft) square cross-section and a length of 5.89 m (19 ft 4 in) and provision for an optional rear loading ramp. Up to 19 passengers can be seated. The undercarriage is retractable, with aft-retracting twin nosewheels and with twin mainwheels retracting into huge sponsons, which accommodate crash-resistant fuel tanks. The rotor

head is derived from that fitted to the UH-60L, while the transmission system is the 2500-kW (3,350-shp) unit from the SH-60B. The rotor itself is redesigned with graphite spars, broader-chord blades and anhedral tips. Also new is the cockpit, which features colour multi-function flight and engine displays, cockpit voice recorders and extensive monitoring systems. General Electric CT-7 and Rolls-Royce RTM 322 turboshafts have been proposed for the new aircraft.

A military derivative, the **S-92M**, has also reached mock-up form, this featuring automatic main rotor and tailboom folding, semi-retractable inflight-refuelling probe, and a rear loading ramp and floor-mounted freight rollers. Sponsons are further enlarged to house larger fuel tanks. With a cabin volume more than double that of an MH-60G, able to accommodate up to 24 troops or 16 litter patients, the S-92M has been proposed as a replacement for USAF Special Operations MH-53s

and Marine Corps CH-46s. It is proposed to fit General Electric T701-GE-401X engines, which should give a cruising speed of 150 kt (276 km/h; 171 mph) and a range in excess of 400 nm (740 km/460 miles).

Both the S-92 and S-92M have been shelved because market research has

The S-92 has been built in both military and civil mock-up (non-flying) forms but due to lack of current customer interest Sikorsky have shelved the design for now.

shown an insufficiently large market to justify a full-scale launch.

Sikorsky VS-300, R-4, R-5 and R-6

Igor Sikorsky became interested in the design and construction of helicopters during the first decade of the 20th century, building his first rotary-wing aircraft in 1909. Powered by an 18-kW (25-hp) Anzani engine, this failed to lift itself from the ground but his second machine, built in 1910, was just able to claw its way into the air if it did not have to carry a pilot. Sikorsky realised he then had insufficient knowledge to solve the problems and gain success, turning instead to the design and construction of fixed-wing aircraft. It was not until 1939, when he was engineering manager of Vought-Sikorsky in the USA, that Sikorsky began construction

of a new helicopter. It, too, was unsuccessful at first, but his introduction of an anti-torque rotor overcame the last major control problem, following months of trials with various auxiliary rotors fitted to the Sikorsky **VS-300** prototype that had made its first tethered flight on 14 September 1939.

By the spring of 1941 the US

The Sikorsky VS-361A may be regarded as the world's first true production helicopter, with the same basic configuration and control formula as used today. It was powered by a single Warner R-550 radial engine.

government had given Vought-Sikorsky a contract for the development of the

VS-316A two-seat version as the **XR-4**. This aircraft had a fabric-covered fuselage and was powered by a 123-kW (165-hp) Warner R-500 engine; it made its first flight on 14 January 1942.

Thirty pre-production **YR-4** helicopters were ordered, comprising three **YR-4A** and 27 **YR-4B** aircraft, all of which were powered by the more powerful Warner R-550 of 134 kW (180 hp) which drove an enlarged rotor. Uprated 149-kW (200-hp) R550-3 engines were fitted in the main production batch of 100 **R-4B** helicopters. The US Navy received its first helicopter in 1942, a YR-4B on loan from the USAAF and designated **HNS-1**; 24 HNS-1s were later flown by US Navy and US Coast Guard units, the latter operating in the air-sea rescue role. Royal Air Force and Fleet Air Arm units set up in 1945 to evaluate helicopters for service use flew seven YR-4Bs and 45 R-4Bs as the **Hoverfly Mk I**.

The R-4's rotor and transmission system was installed in a new streamlined fuselage with an all-metal semi-monocoque tail boom to become the **VS-316B** or **XR-6**, powered by a 168-kW (225-hp) Avco Lycoming O-435 engine. Some 193 production helicopters were built for the USAAF as the R-6A, for the US Navy as the HOS-

Sikorsky HO3S-1 of the US Navy in the mid-1950s.

1 and for the British as the Hoverfly Mk II. Concurrently, Sikorsky had been working on a completely new helicopter, the VS-337 tandem two-seater with a 14.63-m (48-ft) diameter rotor and powered by a 336-kW (450-hp) Pratt & Whitney R-985-AN-5 radial. The first of these, designated XR-5, flew at Bridgeport on 18 August 1943, and the total subsequent production of 64 machines included four more **XR-5s**, 26 **YR-5A** helicopters and 34 **R-5A** helicopters, the last with litter carriers on each side of the fuselage and used by the Air Rescue Service.

The 21 **R-5D** helicopters modified from R-5A airframes had nosewheel landing gear, a rescue hoist and an external auxiliary fuel tank, while five YR-5As with dual controls were redesignated **YR-5E**. The four-seat civil **S-51** was first flown on 16 February 1946 and initial deliveries were made in August. Los Angeles Airways opened the first scheduled helicopter mail service on 1 October 1947, flying S-51s. A total of 379 S-51s was built, including 66 **H-5**, **H-5G** and **H-5H** models for the USAAF's Air Rescue Service, **HO3S-1** helicopters for the US Navy and **HO3S-1G** helicopters for the US Coast Guard. Westland also built the S-51 under licence in the UK as the **Westland Dragonfly**.

Sikorsky XPBS-1 and VS-44 Excalibur

The US Navy continued its sponsorship of ever-larger flying-boats throughout the 1930s, and on 29 June 1935 ordered a prototype of a Sikorsky design to which the designation **XPBS-1** was given. Powered by four 783-kW (1,050-hp) Pratt & Whitney XR-1830-68 engines and first flown on 13 August 1937, the XPBS-1 patrol bomber had a tail turret with a 0.5-in (12.7-mm) machine-gun, the first such turret to be incorporated in an American military aircraft; similar weapons were installed in the nose turret and in waist positions.

Although the XPBS-1 was not adopted for production, it was the basis for the **Sikorsky VS-44 Excalibur** civil transport, powered by four 895-kW (1,200-hp) Pratt & Whitney R-1830-S1C3-G engines and having a max-

imum range of 6116 km (3,800 miles) when carrying a payload of 2268 kg (5,000 lb). American Export Airlines (AEA) ordered three for a planned transatlantic route to the UK and France, although there were delays in obtaining CAB approval. On 12 January 1942, the US Navy's Naval Air Transport Service gave AEA a contract to operate a wartime route across the Atlantic. The airline's temporary civil certificate, to cover a non-stop New York-Foynes (Ireland) service, was granted on 10 February 1942 and, inaugurated on 20 June, continued

The Sikorsky VS-44A Excalibur was the ultimate expression of the company's commercial flying-boat philosophy. It spanned 37.79 m (124 ft).

throughout the war. One VS-44, used post-war by Antilles Air Boats, survives to this day in the museum at Windsor Locks, Connecticut.

Silvercraft SH-4

Silvercraft SpA, formed in Italy in 1962, designed and built the prototype of a three-seat light helicopter which it flew for the first time in October 1963. Its development was continued with financial and technical assistance from SIAI-Marchetti, the resulting **Silvercraft SH-4** being the first helicopter

of all-Italian design and construction to gain Italian and FAA certification. Of conventional configuration, with two-bladed main and tail rotors, and powered by optional 149- or 175-kW (200- or 235-hp) Franklin 6A-350 series engines that in both cases were flat-rated at 127 kW (170 hp), the type was

The Silvercraft SH-200 was produced in prototype form only, and was a refined version of the earlier SH-4 series with the same rotor but a new Lycoming engine.

available in SH-4 utility and **SH-4A** agricultural versions. A total of about 50 is believed to have been completed, plus prototypes of an improved two-seat **SH-200**, before the company

terminated aircraft production in the late 1970s.

Skandinavisk aircraft

Skandinavisk Aero-Industri A/S was established at Kastrup Airport, Copenhagen, in 1937 to take over the lightplane design and construction activities of Krame and Zeuthen, which had built a single-seat monoplane designated **Krame & Zeuthen KZ-1**. Skandinavisk retained the KZ prefix for its designations, beginning with the **Skandinavisk KZ-2 Sport** two-seat open cockpit trainer/tourer low-wing monoplane powered by a 78-kW (105-hp) Hirth H.M.504A engine; it was followed by the similar **KZ-2 Kupe** that had a wider fuselage with an enclosed side-by-side seating for two and a 67-kW (90-hp) Cirrus Minor engine.

A trainer version of the KZ-2 was supplied in small numbers to the Royal Danish air force. German occupation of Denmark brought an end to activities but, in a brief post-war resumption, before the company gave up aircraft production in the mid-1950s, a few more designs were built. They included the **KZ-3** two-seat lightplane, followed by the **KZ-7 Lark** four-seat high-wing cabin monoplane with a 93-kW (125-hp) Continental C125 engine. The **KZ-8** single-seat advanced trainer brought a

Only 12 Aero-Industri KZ-10s were built, these serving as AOP aircraft with the Danish army for a short time during the early 1950s.

return to low-wing configuration and was powered by the 108-kW (145-hp) Gipsy Major 10 inline engine. Final design to be built was the **KZ-10** two-seat light observation aircraft based on the KZ-7, which introduced a 108-kW (145-hp) Continental C145-2 engine to give this 9.40 m (30 ft 6 in) span aircraft a maximum speed of 215 km/h (134 mph) at sea level.

SOKO G2 Galeb and J-1 Jastreb

to

Sparmann S-1

SOKO G2 Galeb and J-1 Jastreb

All the Yugoslav aircraft factories that had existed before World War II were destroyed during the German occupation, and it was some two or three years after 1945 before it was possible to resume design and construction. Established as Preduzece SOKO in 1951, and now named SOKO Vazduhoplovna Industrija, Ro Vazduhoplovstvo, SOKO began licence construction of various foreign aircraft before it began design of its own first aircraft in 1957. This was the **SOKO G2-A Galeb** (seagull) two-seat trainer. Similar in configuration to the Aer-macchi M.B.326, the first of two prototypes was flown during May 1961 and production was started in 1963. Powered by a 1134-kg (2,500-lb) thrust Rolls-Royce Viper 22-6 turbojet, the G2-A was the standard version for the Yugoslav air force. A **G2-AE** export variant became available from late 1974 and was built for Libya and Zambia.

The Galeb was complemented by a generally similar but higher performance single-seat light attack/tactical reconnaissance version designated **J-1 Jastreb** (hawk), which had a strengthened airframe and was powered by the improved Rolls-Royce Viper 531 turbojet. This was built as the J-1 attack and **RJ-1** tactical reconnaissance aircraft for the Yugoslav air force, with corresponding **J-1E** and **RJ-1E** versions for export. For operational conversion a two-seat TJ-1 was developed. Production of all versions of the Jastreb ended during 1978, and of the G-2A

Soko J-1 Jastreb (second prototype) in Yugoslav air force markings.

Galeb in 1983. It is unlikely that any Jastrebs or Galebs remain in use in Yugoslavia, and the status of the Libyan and Zambian aircraft is uncertain.

Specification
SOKO J-1 Jastreb
Type: single-seat attack/reconnaissance aircraft
Powerplant: one 1361-kg (3,000-lb) thrust Rolls-Royce Viper 531 turbojet
Performance: maximum speed 820 km/h (510 mph) at 6000 m (19,685 ft); service ceiling 12000 m (39,370 ft); range with maximum fuel 1520 km (944 miles)
Weights: empty equipped 2820 kg (6,217 lb); maximum take-off 5100 kg (11,244 lb)
Dimensions: span over tip tanks 11.68 m (38 ft 4 in); length 10.88 m (35 ft 8 in); height 3.64 m (11 ft 11¼ in); wing area 19.43 m² (209.15 sq ft)
Armament: three 12.7-mm (0.5-in) Colt-Browning machine-guns in nose, plus eight underwing attachments for a variety of bombs and rockets, plus napalm tanks

SOKO G-4 Super Galeb

Although designated as the **SOKO G4 Super Galeb**, this two-seat basic trainer/light strike aircraft, which has been designed by SOKO to replace the G2-A Galeb in basic and advanced training units of the Yugoslav air force, differs considerably in design from its near-namesake. Most conspicuously, it has swept wings and all-swept tail surfaces, the tailplane having pronounced anhedral, and its performance is considerably improved by the introduction of a more powerful version of the Rolls-Royce Viper turbojet. The first of two prototypes was flown on 17 July 1978 and the first of six pre-production aircraft on 17 December 1980. These and the first prototype were designated **G-4 PPP**, and had fixed tailplanes with inset elevators and no anhedral.

Production examples (and the second prototype) were designated G-4 and featured an all-moving anhedral tailplane and comprehensive avionics improvements. The G-4 first flew in 1983 and has been ordered in large numbers for the Yugoslav air force. They have already been delivered to the Air Academy at Zemunik (now relocated at Udbina) and to advanced flying schools at Pula and Totograd. The academy fleet includes the 'Letece Zvezde' (Flying Stars) formation display team, whose aircraft are painted in a striking red, white and blue colour scheme. Twelve G-4s, in two batches of six, were delivered to Myanmar in 1991 and 1992.

A developed ground-attack trainer, with advanced avionics, an upgraded nav/attack system, and wingtip missile launch rails has been developed under the designation **G-4M**, but no prototype has flown. A similar single-seat derivative designated **G-5** is also under development.

Specification
Type: basic trainer/light strike aircraft
Powerplant: one 1814-kg (4,000-lb) thrust Rolls-Royce Viper Mk 632 turbojet
Performance: maximum speed 910

km/h (565 mph) at 6000 m (19,685 ft); absolute ceiling 15000 m (49,210 ft); lo-lo-lo combat radius with ventral gun pod and 32 57-mm rockets 300 km (186 miles)
Weights: empty equipped 3250 kg (7,165 lb); maximum take-off 6330 kg (13,955 lb)
Dimensions: span 9.88 m (32 ft 5 in); length 11.86 m (38 ft 11 in); height 4.28 m (14 ft 0½ in); wing area 19.50 m² (209.90 sq ft)
Armament: one 23-mm GSh-23L

The SOKO G-4 Galeb, in its original form, was of wholly Yugoslavian design, but relied heavily on imported components.

cannon in removable ventral pod, plus four underwing attachments for a maximum 1200 kg (2,646 lb) of stores including bombs, cluster bombs, anti-personnel or anti-tank bomblets, napalm tanks, a variety of rockets, and a reconnaissance pod incorporating night illumination capability

SOKO P-2 Kraguj

SOKO designed and developed the P-2 Kraguj as a single-seat modestly-powered lightweight aircraft equipped for use in a counter-insurgency (COIN) role. A cantilever low-wing monoplane of all-metal construction, with a fixed tailwheel landing gear, it was powered as standard by a 254-kW (340-hp) Avco Lycoming GSO-480B1A6 flat-six engine. The prototype is believed to have flown during 1966, and a total of about 30 was built for the Yugoslav air force. They were withdrawn from front-line use during the late 1980s, some being sold on the civil market, and

others going to the territorial defence forces of the various Yugoslav states. Many of these were seized back by the Serbian rump of the Federal Yugoslav air force as Yugoslavia disintegrated, and were put back into service. The 10.64 m (34 ft 11 in) span P-2 had a maximum speed of 295 km/h (183 mph) at 1500 m (4,920 ft), was armed with one 7.7-mm (0.303-in) machine-

gun in each wing, and had two underwing attachments that could each carry a 100-kg (220-lb) bomb, a napalm

Only a small number of Kragujs were built after the air force came to the conclusion that better performance was necessary.

tank or 12-round rocket pod, and four underwing hardpoints that could each carry a 57-mm or 127-mm rocket.

SOKO/CNIAR Orao and IAR-93

The joint international programme known as Jurom was initiated in 1970 to meet the joint requirement of the air forces of neutral Yugoslavia and then-Warsaw Pact member Romania for a single-seat close support/ground-attack aircraft. This partnership was hardly surprising, since then Romanian President Nikolai Ceasescu was a committed isolationist who strove to weaken Soviet influence by forging links with nations outside the Warsaw Pact, and to build up Romania's aircraft industry through international co-operation. This had led to the licence-manufacture of the BAC One-Eleven and Aérospatiale Alouette and Puma helicopters.

In the interests of national pride it was important that the project seemed to be completely collaborative, with neither nation appearing to have project leadership. Thus the aircraft was jointly designed by engineers from Yugoslavia's Vazduhoplovno Technicki Institut and Romania's Institutal de Macanica Fluidelor si Constructii Aerospatiale, while manufacture was entrusted to SOKO and Centrul National al Industriei Aeronautice Romane (CNIAR). Each company constructed prototypes which were flown simultaneously in the two countries on 31 October 1974. These were powered by non-afterburning Viper Mk 622-41R turbojets and were followed by a pair of two-seat trainer prototypes, again flown simultaneously on 29 January 1977. Both versions have the same designation in their respective countries, with no separate designation for two-seaters: **J-22 Orao** (eagle) in Yugoslavia and **IAR-93** in Romania. Following the flight of the two-seat prototypes both companies

began the construction of 15-aircraft pre-production batches, and the first examples were flown during 1978.

Series production of the IAR-93 began in 1979, and of the J-22 in 1980. The initial batch of 20 aircraft in each country lacked afterburners but introduced some changes by comparison with the prototypes. In Yugoslavia the lack of power led to allocation to the reconnaissance role, under the revised designation **IJ-22**, and there are persistent but unconfirmed reports that a handful of the batch were **NJ-22** two-seat trainers. In Romania the initial batch of aircraft was designated **IAR-93A**, and again there were reports that the total included some two-seat trainers.

The definitive production aircraft featured the afterburning Viper Mk 633-41 engine, and was designated **J-22(M)** or **Orao 2** in Yugoslavia, and **IAR-93B** in Romania. The Orao 2 prototype first flew on 20 October 1983, and the type entered production in 1984, although deliveries were delayed until 1986 by the non-arrival of afterburning engines. The variant introduced extended wing leading-edge roots, increased internal fuel capacity and the inboard overwing fences were deleted. Underwing hardpoints were uprated to carry loads of up to 500 kg (1,102-lb) each, and the centreline was cleared for 800 kg (1,763 lb). Finally the aircraft received new avionics, including a Thomson-CSF VE-120T HUD. The prototype and some early aircraft were fitted with prominent vortex generators on each side of the nose, but these have since been deleted.

The equivalent Romanian IAR-93B first flew in 1985, and differed from the

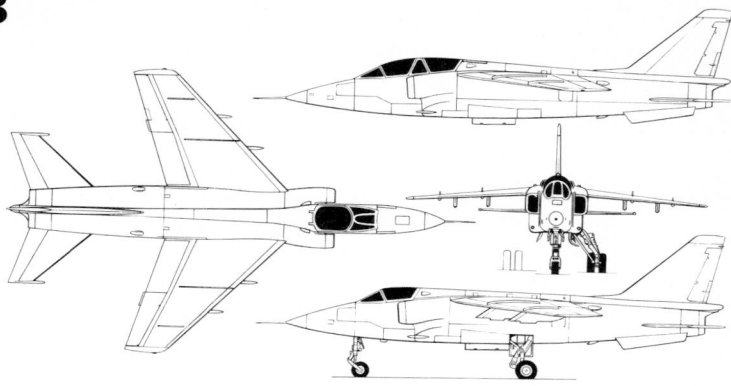

SOKO/CNIAR Orao/IAR-93A (upper side view: two-seat model).

Orao 2 in lacking ventral fins and tailplane anti-flutter weights, and in having a new ranging radar in the nose and a relocated Doppler antenna. The canopy is also redesigned, and now opens sideways, instead of upwards.

There are two-seat versions of both the IAR-93B and the J-22(M), the Yugoslav aircraft having the new designation **Orao 2B** or **NJ-22(M)**. Some of these two-seaters may have been produced by the conversion of early IAR-93A and NJ-22 trainers, since some retain the original four-fence wing. Whether the original trainers had the extended wingroot remains uncertain.

Specification
SOKO/CNIAR IAR-93B

Type: single-seat close-support/ground attack aircraft
Powerplant: two 2268-kg (5,000-lb) afterburning thrust Turbomecanica licence-built Rolls-Royce Viper Mk 633-

47 turbojets
Performance: maximum speed 1160 km/h (721 mph) at sea level; service ceiling 12500 m (41,010 ft); mission radius with four 250-kg (551-lb) bombs and auxiliary fuel 530 km (329 miles)
Weights: empty equipped 5900 kg (13,007 lb); maximum take-off 10100 kg (22,267 lb)
Dimensions: span 9.62 m (31 ft 6¾ in); length 14.90 m (48 ft 10¾ in); height 4.45 m (14 ft 7¼ in); wing area 26.00 m² (279.87 sq ft)
Armament: two 23-mm GSh-23L cannon in lower forward fuselage, plus five external hardpoints; total maximum load of 1500 kg (3,307 lb); stores can include bombs, rockets, cannon pods, reconnaissance pod, night illumination pod, and auxiliary fuel tanks

SOKO/CNIAR-93A of the Romanian air force.

Sopwith early aircraft

British pioneer sportsman/pilot T. O. M. ('Tom') Sopwith first became associated with aircraft construction by rebuilding and modifying several aircraft before the outbreak of World War I. One of the first significant aircraft was the **Sopwith Bat Boat** of 1913, which had an S. E. Saunders 'Consuta' (sewn-plywood) hull and biplane wings, and was powered originally by a 67-kW (90-hp) Austro-Daimler engine driving a pusher propeller.

The first flying-boat to be built in the UK, the Bat Boat served with the Royal Naval Air Service at the outbreak of World War I. Other early Sopwith aircraft in military service were the **Sopwith Three Seater**, a tandem-cockpit biplane carrying two passengers in the forward cockpit and the pilot aft; the **Sopwith Sociable**, a two-seat side-by-side biplane;

Sopwith Anzani Seaplane, with 75-kW (100-hp) Anzani engine; and the **Sopwith Gun Bus** of which six examples, intended for use by the Greek naval air service as seaplane trainers, were impressed by the Admiralty and converted to landplanes; further examples were built under sub-contract by Robey & Company of Lincoln.

More famous was the **Sopwith Tabloid**, a 'high-performance' open-cockpit biplane intended initially for competition purposes, one example of which in floatplane configuration was flown by Howard Pixton to win the 1914 Schneider Trophy contest at Monaco. It clearly had military potential, and three operated by the RNAS at the beginning of World War I were used for attacks on German targets; that flown by Flight Lieutenant R. L. G. Marix on 8 October 1914

destroyed the Zeppelin Z.IX in its shed at Dusseldorf. A further 36 Tabloids were built for the RFC and RNAS and these were followed by 160 examples of a floatplane version, little changed from that flown by Howard Pixton, which entered service as the **Sopwith Schneider**.

Developed from the Schneider was the higher performance **Sopwith Baby**, of which 286 were built for the RNAS by Sopwith (100) and the remainder by Blackburn. These were

The Sopwith Three Seater first appeared at the Olympia Aero Show of 1913, and was one of the most important machines of its day. It is seen here with T. O. M. Sopwith in the rear cockpit.

powered by the 75-kW (100-hp) Gnome, or the 82-kW (110-hp) or 97-kW (130-hp) Clerget engines. With this last engine the 7.82-m (25-ft 8-in) span Baby had a maximum speed of 161 km/h (100 mph) at sea level.

Sopwith 1½-Strutter

Best-known as the **Sopwith 1½-Strutter**, a name believed to derive from the arrangement of the inter plane struts of this single-seat bomber/two-seat fighter biplane, this aircraft had the official Admiralty and RFC designations of **Sopwith Type 9700** and **Sopwith Two-Seater** respectively. The two-seat prototype, flown in late 1915 on the power of an 82-kW (110-hp) Clerget rotary engine, introduced airbrakes and a variable-incidence tailplane, and when production examples entered service with the RNAS in early 1916 it was the first British aircraft to be equipped with synchronising gear to allow the forward machine-gun to fire through the propeller disc. Both single- and two-seat versions were built with 82- and 97-kW (110- and 130-hp) Clerget rotaries, but some two-seaters were also powered by the 82-kW (110-hp) Le Rhone rotary engine.

When first introduced into service on the Western Front the 1½-Strutter had the edge in combat with German fighters, but it was surpassed in performance in a few months by the Albatros and Halberstadt scouts introduced by the enemy. RNAS 1½-

Sopwith 1½-Strutter of No.70 Sqn, RFC, based in France during the latter half of 1916.

Strutters had a longer operational life and towards the end of the war were in service as ship-based aircraft with both skid and wheel landing gear. On 4 April 1918 one took off from a platform mounted over a gun turret of HMAS *Australia*, the first two-seat aircraft to take off from a British warship.

A total believed to be 1,513 Sopwith 1½-Strutters was built for the RFC and RNAS, and the type was also produced in France to a total of two to three times this number. In addition to their use by British forces, this remarkable aeroplane saw service in and/or after World War I with the air arms of Belgium, France, Japan, Latvia, Romania, Russia and with the American Expeditionary Force.

Specification
Sopwith 1½-Strutter

Type: single-seat bomber version
Powerplant: one 97-kW (130-hp) Clerget rotary engine
Performance: maximum speed 164 km/h (102 mph) at 1980 m (6,500 ft); service ceiling 3960 m (13,000 ft)
Weights: empty 597 kg (1,316 lb); maximum take-off 1062 kg (2,342 lb)
Dimensions: span 10.21 m (33 ft 6 in); length 7.97 m (25 ft 3 in); height 3.12 m (10 ft 3 in); wing area 32.14 m² (346.0 sq ft)
Armament: one fixed forward-firing 7.7-mm (0.303-in) Vickers machine-gun, plus up to four 25-kg (56-lb) bombs or an equivalent weight of smaller bombs

Sopwith 5F.1 Dolphin

Designed to give its pilot the best possible field of view, the **Sopwith 5F.1 Dolphin** was an unusual single-seat fighter biplane based on a deep-section fuselage with the upper wing mounted close to it, so that the pilot's head projected through a gap in the centre-section. He thus had a superb upward and all-round view, although at a cost of some restriction in the view below. Powered by a 149-kW (200-hp) Hispano-Suiza engine, the prototype was flown for the first time in May 1917 and, following satisfactory tests, began to enter service as the **Dolphin Mk I** towards the end of the year. Two versions with alternative engines were numbered among the 1,532 Dolphins produced, only 621 of this total entering service before the war ended, the remainder being in storage. They comprised Dolphin Mk Is with the same geared engine as the prototype, but failure of the drive gears led to introduction of the **Dolphin Mk III** with a similarly powered direct-drive version of the Hispano-Suiza engine.

The designation **Dolphin Mk II** was allocated to a version with a 224-kW (300-hp) Hispano-Suiza direct-drive engine that was being built in France, but only small numbers were completed before the war ended.

The Dolphin was not particularly popular with pilots, for its back-staggered wing induced unusual stall characteristics, and the pilot's exposed position could prove fatal in a nose-over following a bad landing. In consequence, some aircraft used by training units were given crash pylons above the centre-section, and Dolphins adopted for a night-flying role had similar pylons above the wing. In addition to their use by the RFC and RAF, No. 1 Squadron of the Canadian Air Force trained with the type but the war ended before they became operational. Five were acquired by the American Expeditionary Force for evaluation.

Specification
Sopwith Dolphin Mk I

Type: single-seat fighter
Powerplant: one 149-kW (200-hp) Hispano-Suiza Vee piston engine
Performance: maximum speed 180 km/h (112 mph) at 3050 m (10,000 ft); service ceiling 6095 m (20,000 ft)
Weight: maximum take-off 911 kg (2,008 lb)
Dimensions: span 9.91 m (32 ft 6 in); length 6.78 m (22 ft 3 in); height 2.59 m (8 ft 6 in), wing area 24.46 m² (263.25 sq ft)

This Sopwith 5F.1 Dolphin shows the type's full production standard, with lateral radiators, shallow top decking and guns.

Armament: two forward-firing synchronised 7.7-mm (0.3003-in) Vickers machine-guns and one or two Lewis guns usually mounted to fire forward and upward over the propeller disc, plus up to four 11.3-kg (25-lb) bombs on external racks

Sopwith F.1 and 2F.1 Camel

The **Sopwith F.1 Camel** fighter, which superseded the Pup in service on the Western Front and was regarded as the finest British fighter of World War I, was basically a further development of the Pup. Somewhat heavier and with a more powerful engine as standard, the Camel had armament, fuel, pilot and powerplant concentrated within a short distance, resulting in outstanding manoeuvrability. This was enhanced by the torque of the large engine, making possible snap turns to starboard which were so fast that some pilots would make a three-quarter right instead of one-quarter left turn; not only did they believe this to be faster in combat, it was tactically confusing to an enemy pilot. This combination of capability made the Camel the most successful Allied fighter of World War I. Remarkably, for more than 70 years, its

official tally of victims was universally accepted as 1,294. Research by Chaz Bowyer, a, British writer, subsequently showed that the unit histories of the RFC, RAF and RNAS alone showed a total of over 2,800, the overall total exceeding 3,000. The type was also used as a day or night fighter by British Home Defence units, and the Camel is considered to have played a significant role in the defeat of the German Gotha bombers in their 'strategic' raids on Britain.

Like the Pup, the type gained a nickname which has long survived the official **Sopwith Biplane F.1** designation of the initial production version. The standard powerplant comprised engines of 75 to 112 kW (100 to 150 hp) by Bentley, Clerget, Gnome and Le Rhône, and the Camel was flown experimentally with a 112-

Sopwith F.1 Camel.

kW (150-hp) Le Rhône and a 134-kW (180-hp) Gnome Monosoupape. Developments included the **F.1/1** with tapered wings, and the **T.F.1** (Trench

Fighter) with a pair of Lewis guns firing downward through the cockpit floor, but neither of these entered production. Some F.1 Camels were operated from ships, but the final production **Sopwith 2F.1 Camel** was designed purposely for shipboard use and some remained in service after the end of World War I. Final production totalled 5,490 aircraft; and in addition to their use by the RFC and RNAC they served with the air forces of Belgium, Canada and Greece, with the American Expeditionary Force, and with the Slavo-British Aviation Group operating in Russia in 1918.

Specification
Sopwith F.1 Camel
Type: single-seat fighter

Powerplant: one 97-kW (130-hp) Clerget rotary piston engine
Performance: maximum speed 185 km/h (115 mph) at 1980 m (6,500 ft); service ceiling 5790 m (19,000 ft); endurance 2 hours 30 minutes
Weights: empty 421 kg (929 lb); maximum take-off 659 kg (1,453 lb)

Dimensions: span 8.53m (28 ft 0 in); length 5.72 m (18 ft 9 in); height 2.59 m (8 ft 6 in); wing area 21.46 m² (231.0 sq ft)
Armament: two forward-firing synchronised 7.7-mm (0.303-in) Vickers machine-guns, plus up to four 11.3-kg (25-lb) bombs carried externally

Sopwith Gnu

The last effort of the Sopwith company to find a market for civil aircraft resulted in the Sopwith Gnu, introduced in May 1919. But the severe economic crisis that followed closely on the end of the war was soon to bring this modest success, and the company's activities, to an end. A conventional equal-span biplane, the Gnu provided open-cockpit seating for a pilot (forward) with two passengers

The Sopwith Gnu spanned 11.6 m (38 ft 1 in), and was 7.8 m (25 ft 10 in) in length. Standard powerplant was a Le Rhône rotary engine.

side-by-side in the rear cockpit, which was enclosed by a glazed roof; however, this proved very cramped accommodation for the passengers and most of the series aircraft had an open rear cockpit. The prototype and nearly all of the 12 production Gnus were powered by a Le Rhône rotary engine, but examples were flown with a 149-

kW (200-hp) Bentley B.R.2 rotary and a 224-kW (300-hp) Wright J-5 Whirlwind radial engine. Only five of the aircraft found buyers, three of them going to Australia. It was a sad end to a remarkable and innovative company.

Sopwith Pup

An elegant little equal-span biplane, the Sopwith Admiralty Type 9901 retained the same form of interplane struts adopted for the 1½-Strutter, but with 20 per cent less wing span it is not surprising that it became regarded as a 'pup' of the earlier aircraft. The nickname Pup, given by air and ground crews, has long outlived the official designation, and the name **Sopwith Pup** is well endorsed in British aviation history. As first flown, this single-seat fighter was powered by an 60-kW (80-hp) Le Rhône rotary engine, and the fact that with this low-powered unit it was a highly manoeuvrable and effective fighter speaks volumes for its design and construction.

The Pup entered service with both the RAF and RNAS in 1916, and its reputation was quickly established, either as a gem to fly or a fighter to be avoided, according to whether one was an Allied or enemy pilot. In fact, it was more than a gem, for with its effective forward-firing synchronised machine-gun, and the ability to remain manoeuvrable and responsive at a greater height than any contemporary fighter at the time of its introduction, it was also a killer. It was in great demand, and production totalled 1,770, the type being used also for home defence, many in this latter category

Sopwith Pup of No.46 Sqn, RFC, based at Izel-le-Hameau (France) during 1917.

with 75-kW (100-hp) Gnome Monosoupape rotary engines, the resulting increase in rate of climb and overall performance making the Pup a most effective interceptor. In RNAS service the type played a significant pioneering role in the operation of

aircraft from ships; one Pup flown by Squadron Commander E. H. Dunning achieved the first landing on a ship under way at sea when he touched down on the deck of the aircraft-carrier HMS *Furious* on 2 August 1917.

An attempt to capitalise on the superb flying qualities of the Pup was made in 1919 with the development of the civil two-seat **Dove**, but its Le Rhône rotary engine was far from suitable for operation by a private pilot and this, more than any other factor, limited production to only 10 aircraft.

Specification
Sopwith Pup

Type: single-seat fighter
Powerplant: one 60-kW (80-hp) Le Rhône rotary piston engine
Performance: maximum speed 180 km/h (112 mph) at sea level; service ceiling 5335 m (17,500 ft); endurance 3 hours
Weights: empty 357 kg (787 lb); maximum take-off 556 kg (1,225 lb)
Dimensions: span 8.08 m (26 ft 6 in); length 6.04 m (19 ft 9 ¾ in); height 2.87 m (9 ft 5 in); wing area 23.60 m2 (254.0 sq ft)
Armament: one forward-firing synchronised 7.7-mm (0.303-in) Vickers machine-gun, plus up to four 11.3-kg (25-lb) bombs on external racks

Sopwith Snipe, Salamander and Dragon

Designed around a newly-developed Bentley B.R.2 rotary engine, the **Sopwith 7F.1 Snipe** was intended as a successor to the Sopwith Camel. The airframe of the first prototype was ready for testing before an example of the B.R.2 engine was available and was, consequently, flown with a 112-kW (150-hp) B.R.1 engine. This was one of the alternative powerplants of the Camel and in this form the Snipe looked very similar to its famous predecessor. Its appearance began to alter with installation of the bigger engine, and the large increase of power brought other structural changes. Satisfactory testing resulted in the type being ordered into production as the Snipe Mk I, deliveries beginning in the summer of 1918, but only about 100 of these aircraft were in service with the RAF in France at the

end of the war, and a total of 497 had been built when production ended in 1919. In its brief operational career the Snipe had proved an exceptional fighter and the type remained in post-war service with first-line squadrons until withdrawn in 1926, it was in use with training schools for some time after that date.

For use in a ground-attack role against enemy trenches, the **Salamander T.F.2** was developed from the Snipe, but had some 295 kg (650 lb) of armour plate beneath the forward fuselage to protect the pilot and fuel tanks from ground-fired weapons. The standard armament of two Vickers machine-guns was

This Snipe was restored to flyable condition by Mr Jack Canary at Wright-Patterson AFB in 1961.

retained, and a variety of experimental installations of downward-firing

weapons was tested. Although 82 had been built when production ended in 1919, only a small number reached France before the Armistice; none was used operationally and the type did not continue in post-war service with the Royal Air Force.

In early 1918 the Snipe prototype had been flown experimentally with a 239-kW (320-hp) A.B.C. Dragonfly I engine. Excellent performance with a maximum speed of 150 mph (241 km/h) won it a production order, and some 76 Sopwith Dragon aircraft were completed with the more powerful 268-kW (360-hp) Dragonfly IA engine as standard. None was used operationally in World War I and the type did not survive because of the unreliability of the Dragonfly powerplant.

Specification
Sopwith Snipe Mk I

Type: single-seat fighter
Powerplant: one 172-kW (230-hp) Bentley B.R.2 rotary piston engine
Performance: maximum speed 195 km/h (121 mph) at 3050 m (10,000 ft); service ceiling 5945 m (19,500 ft); endurance 3 hours
Weights: empty 595 kg (1,312 lb); maximum take-off 916 kg (2,020 lb)

Dimensions: span 9.17 m (30 ft 1 in); length 6.02 m (19 ft 9 in); height 2.67 m (8 ft 9 in); wing area 25.08 m² (270.0 sq ft)
Armament: two forward-firing synchronised 7.7-mm (0.303-in) Vickers machine-guns, plus up to four 11.3-kg (25-lb) bombs on external racks

Sopwith T.1 Cuckoo and B.1

Designed as a torpedo-carrying landplane for operation from aircraft-carriers, the **Sopwith T.1 Cuckoo** was a single-seat equal-span biplane with folding wings. Powered by a 149-kW (200-hp) Hispano-Suiza engine, the aircraft was first flown in mid-1917. Successful testing led to orders for 350 production aircraft, but only 90 had been delivered by the end of World War I, when the balance was cancelled; designated **Cuckoo Mk I**, these aircraft differed from the prototype by having a Sunbeam Arab engine because of the priority held by the Royal Aircraft Factory S.E.6a for the Hispano-Suiza powerplant. The first operational squadron equipped with the Cuckoo was embarked on HMS

This late-production T.1 Cuckoo was built by Blackburn and fitted with a 149-kW (200-hp) Sunbeam Arab engine, an enlarged rudder and tailskid. Span was 14.25 m (46 ft 9 in), maximum take-off weight was 1761 kg (3,883 lb) and top speed 166 km/h (103 mph). Blackburn's torpedo sling is also visible, between the landing gear. Intened for ship board use during World War I the fgirst squadron was not deployed until after the Armistance.

Argus on 19 October 1918 and, in consequence, was not deployed operationally before the Armistice. Aircraft built by the Fairfield

Shipbuilding & Engineering Company of Glasgow with the 149-kW (200-hp) Wolseley Viper engine were designated **Cuckoo Mk II**, and the type was also tested with the 205-kW (275-hp) Rolls-Royce Falcon III. Post-war, six Cuckoo IIs were taken to Japan by the British Air Mission.

Designed and built at about the

same time as the Cuckoo were two examples of a generally similar single-seat bomber designated **Sopwith B.1**, the two prototypes being powered by the 149-kW (200-hp) Hispano-Suiza engine and designed to carry a 254-kg (560-lb) bombload internally. Following official testing during 1917, the B.1 was not ordered into production.

Sopwith Triplane

A fuselage and tail unit similar to those of the Pup, a more powerful engine and the addition of an extra wing were the basic components of the remarkable little fighter known as the **Sopwith Triplane**. Retaining the manoeuvrability of the Pup, the Triplane was faster and had a better rate of climb thanks to the extra wing and 82-kW (110-hp) Clerget rotary that was its standard powerplant. Some late aircraft with the 97-kW (130-hp) Clerget had further performance improvement.

Entering service in early 1917, the Triplane was the first aircraft of its configuration to be used on the Western Front and, in retrospect, it seems almost unbelievable that this diminutive fighter, of which only about 140 were built and flown exclusively by the RNAS, gained almost complete ascendancy over enemy fighters for a period of about seven months, until superseded by the Sopwith Camel in November 1917. The measure of its capability may be gauged from the fact that German pilots would, if possible, avoid combat with a formation of these Triplanes, and from the frenetic efforts of the German aircraft industry to develop a triplane that was equal in capability.

Sopwith Triplane of Flight Lieutenant R. A. Little, No.8 (Naval) Sqn, RNAS, based in northern England during the spring of 1917.

Shortly after development of the standard Triplane, Sopwith flew two examples of another triplane, each with an Hispano-Suiza Vee engine.

Often regarded as re-engined standard Triplanes, these two aircraft, one with a 112-kW (150-hp) and the other with a 149-kW (200-hp) engine, had, in fact, an airframe that was considerably different. Although both had enhanced performance by comparison with the earlier Triplane, no production followed because of a shortage of Hispano-Suiza engines.

Specification
Sopwith Triplane
Type: single-seat fighter
Powerplant: one 97-kW (130-hp)

Clerget rotary piston engine
Performance: maximum speed 188 km/h (117 mph) at 1525 m (5,000 ft); service ceiling 6250 m (20,500 ft); endurance 2 hours 45 minutes
Weights: empty 499 kg (1,101 lb); maximum take-off 699 kg (1,541 lb)
Dimensions: span 8.08 m (26 ft 6 in); length 5.74 m (18 ft 10 in); height 3.20 m (10 ft 6 in); wing area 21.46 m2 (231.0 sq ft)
Armament: one or two forward-firing synchronised 7.7-mm (0.303-in) Vickers machine-guns

Southern Martlet

Having acquired a two-seat Avro Baby airframe from the former Avro factory, together with other aircraft components, F. G. Miles flew the **Southern Martlet** at Shoreham, Sussex, after installing a 45-kW (60-hp) Cirrus I engine. Its inspiring performance brought Southern Aircraft an order for a similar single-seat aerobatic aircraft, and the resulting prototype, powered by a 63-kW (85-hp) A.B.C. Hornet flat-four engine, was flown first in August 1929. It was re-engined subsequently with a 60-kW (80-hp) Genet II radial. Named the Southern Martlet, this small bi-plane was followed by five production aircraft, which varied in detail and/or powerplant. It was followed in 1931 by a single Metal Martlet, which had a steel-tube fuselage and a 78-kW (105-hp) A.D.C. Hermes I engine, but a second example under construction was not completed and was later scrapped.

Sparmann S-1

Edmund Sparmann was an aerobatic pilot, who had worked for Phoenix-Werke in Austria before coming to Sweden in 1919. Naturalised in 1926, he worked as a test-pilot at the Malmslätt works of ASJA. Sparmann was also an inventor and received payments fro the US Government for copyright infringements he suffered during the war.

Established at Stockholm, Sweden, in 1935, Sparmann's Flyplanverkstad designed and produced a single-seat lightplane suitable for advanced civil or military training. A braced low-wing monoplane of 8.00-m (26-ft 3-in) span, with fixed tailskid landing gear and powered by a 97-kW (130-hp) de Havilland Gipsy Major engine, the Sparmann S-1 was built in small numbers for the Swedish air force. Despite support from the air force Sparmann refused to collaborate with other companies and in 1937 his company was bought up by Saab.

Spartan aircraft (UK)

In 1928 Oliver Simmonds designed and built the prototype **Simmonds Spartan**, an aircraft that had a high proportion of interchangeable components to simplify maintenance and spares holding. Of conventional two-seat biplane configuration, the prototype was powered by a 71-kW (95-hp) Cirrus III engine, but some 50 production aircraft, of which about half went to overseas customers, were flown with a variety of engines of 63 to 89 kW (85 to 120 hp). These aircraft were built by Simmonds Aircraft Ltd, but success of the Spartan resulted in this name being adopted in 1930 for a reconstituted Spartan Aircraft Ltd.

Its first product was the **Spartan Arrow**, a slightly larger two-seat biplane of which 28 were built, with engines of 71 to 119 kW (95 to 160 hp). This was followed by a three-seat open-cockpit biplane named **Spartan Three Seater**, of which 19 were built

G-ABWP was the last Spartan Arrow, and was powered by a 78-kW (105-hp) Cirrus Hermes II engine. Span was 9.32 m (30 ft 7 in), and maximum speed 171 km/h (106 mph)

and used extensively in the UK for joy riding. They were redesignated **Three Seater I** after introduction of an improved **Three Seater II** (seven built) in June 1932; both versions had engines of 86 or 89 kW (115 or 120 hp). Spartan Aircraft's final product was the **Spartan Cruiser**, a three-engine light transport developed from the one-off **Saro-Percival Mailplane** designed by Edgar Percival. Saro transferred development of the Mailplane to Spartan, but with no demand for an aircraft of this class Spartan revised the interior to accommodate a crew of two and six passengers, naming the aircraft **Spartan Cruiser I** and retaining the three 89-kW (120-hp) de Havilland

Gipsy III engines of the Mailplane. The production **Cruiser II** (12 built) had more powerful engines, and three examples were built of a refined version designated **Cruiser III** before aircraft construction ceased in May 1935.

Specification
Spartan Cruiser II
Type: light transport
Powerplant: three 97-kW (130-hp) de

Havilland Gipsy Major, Cirrus Hermes IV or Walter Major 4 inverted inline piston engines
Performance: maximum speed 214 km/h (133 mph); service ceiling 4570 m (15,000 ft); range 499 km (310 miles)
Weights: empty 1656 kg (3,650 lb); maximum take-off 2812 kg (6,200 lb)
Dimensions: span 16.46 m (54 ft 0 in); length 11.94 m (39 ft 2 in); height 3.05 m (10 ft 0 in);

Spartan aircraft (USA)

The **Spartan** three-seat open cockpit biplane designed by Willis Brown was first flown on 25 October 1926. It led to formation of the Mid-Continent Aircraft Company at Tulsa, Oklahoma, to produce this aircraft, but within a year Mid-Continent's assets had been acquired by a group of investors and the company was reconstituted as the Spartan Aircraft Company in early 1928. A fabric-covered biplane with an airframe of mixed wood and steel-tube construction. the initial production **Spartan C3-1** was powered by a 93-kW (125-hp) German Siemens-Halske radial engine. Difficulties in engine supply after about 15 had been built led to the **Spartan C3-2**, introduced in late 1928 with a 89-kW (120-hp) Walter radial engine. Production of this version totalled about 35 before introduction of the **Spartan C3-165** in mid-1929 with the 123-kW (165-hp) Wright J-6 radial engine; approximately 40 were built before development of the improved **Spartan C3-225** in 1930. This had performance improvement from its 168-kW (225-hp) Wright J-6 and, built to a total of 14 aircraft, was the penultimate version, the one-off **Spartan C3-166** of 1930, with a 123-kW (165-hp) Comet 7-E radial, being the last of the family.

The American-built Spartan 7W Executive featured not only a retractable undercarriage, but was also notable for its unusual diagonal wingtips.

Growing interest in cabin monoplanes, rather than open-cockpit biplanes, brought the design of the **Spartan C4-225,** this four-seat braced high-wing monoplane being powered by the 168-kW (225-hp) version of the Wright J-6 engine and introduced in early 1930. Five examples were built and followed by two one-offs, the **C4-300** with a 224-kW (300-hp) Wright R-975 engine and the **Spartan C4-301** with a Pratt & Whitney Wasp Junior engine of the same output. The final and unsuccessful attempt to market this design was the five-seat **Spartan C5-301** with Wasp Junior engine, but only about four were sold.

The last of Spartan's lightplanes was the **Spartan C2-60** sport/training aircraft, a braced low-wing monoplane with an open cockpit seating two side-by-side. Powered by a 41-kW (55-hp) Jacobs L-3 radial engine, this was introduced in early 1931. Only 16 had been built before the growing depression in the USA brought a run-down in produc-

tion. In this quiet period the company designed and, in 1936, flew the prototype of a very attractive four-seat cantilever low-wing monoplane with retractable main landing gear units. Of all-metal construction, except for fabric-covered control surfaces, this **Spartan 7-X** prototype became the five-seat **Spartan 7-W Executive** with a 298-kW (400-hp) Wasp Junior engine. A total of 34 was built before production was suspended in 1940, and during World War II 16 of these aircraft were impressed for service with the US Army Air Force under the designation **UC-71**. Although attempts were made to reintroduce the Executive post-war as the Spartan 12-W, none was built.

Gathering war clouds brought development of a two-seat general purpose military aircraft based on the Executive

airframe, adapted to accept the 410-kW (550-hp) Pratt & Whitney Wasp S3H-1 radial engine and carrying light armament, but although four or five examples were built there was no real interest in this aircraft, which had the company designation **FBW-1 Zeus**. Then, out of the blue, came the biggest order of the company's existence when, on 10 July 1940, Spartan received a US Navy contract for 201 two-seat primary trainers based on the Spartan C3 three-seat biplane. Powered by the 164-kW (220-hp) R-680-8 Avco Lycoming radial engine, this variant had the company designation **NS-1**. Duly delivered for service with the US Navy under the official designation **Spartan NP-1**, these 10.29-m (33-ft 9-in) span trainers had a maximum speed of 174 km/h (108 mph).

Sperry/Engineering Division Messenger

Designed in 1921 by the Engineering Division, US Army Air Service, the **Messenger** single-seat biplane was intended to serve literally as a messenger between army commanders in the field and their headquarters. Of conventional biplane configuration and only 6.10 m (20 ft) in span, the Messenger was powered by a 45-kW (60-hp) Lawrance L-4 radial engine giving a maximum speed of 156 km/h (97 mph). Built by Sperry Aircraft Company of Farmingdale, New York, formed by

Elmer Sperry's son, Lawrence, the Messenger was built to a total of 42, including prototypes. In addition to their intended role, the Messengers were used for several experimental purposes; for example, eight of the first 12 were completed as radio-controlled aerial torpedoes. In 1924 they were allocated designations, having been previously referred to simply as Sperry messengers. Eighteen of the first 26 aircraft became **M-1s**, the eight radio-controlled aircraft were designated

MAT (Messenger Aerial Torpedo –to avoid clashing with the AT advanced trainer designation), and the last 16, which had increased fuel capacity, **M-1A**. This led to an official directive being issued to the effect that the aircract were no longer to be referred to as 'Sperry'. One civil example was brought to England by Lawrence Sperry, but it force-landed in the English Channel; Sperry was drowned and very soon after this his company closed down.

The Sperry messenger was used in trials to develop a system whereby an aircraft could hook on to an airship in flight, as evidenced by the overwing hook arrangement.

Stampe aircraft

Established in 1922, the Belgian company Stampe et Vertongen had as its chief designer Alfred Renard and early type designations were prefixed RSV, indicating Renard, Stampe and Vertongen. The company specialised in the design and construction of primary trainer/tourer and advanced trainer aircraft, and early products of the company included the **Stampe et Vertongen RSV.18-100** and **RSV. 26-100** two-seat trainer/tourers which were almost identical, although the first was of monoplane and the second of biplane configuration, each powered by the 75-kW (100-hp) Renard radial engine. Then came the **RSV.20-100**, a two-seat braced parasol-wing monoplane powered by an 82-kW (110-hp) Renard radial engine, and the **RSV.22-180**, which was a two-seat tandem open cockpit advanced trainer of biplane configuration with a 134-kW (180-hp) Hispano-Suiza Vee engine; this last aircraft was available optionally as the RSV.22-200 with a 200-hp (149kW) Renard radial engine. The **RSV. 28-180 Type III** was an advanced trainer with the 134-kW (180-hp) Hispano-Suiza Vee engine, and was equipped specially to train military pilots in blind-flying techniques. The compact **RSV.22-Lynx** advanced trainer of 1932 was so named because of its 160-kW (215-hp) Armstrong Siddeley Lynx radial engine, the same powerplant being employed in the **RSV.26-Lynx** which was equipped for blind-flying training. Several of these early types served with the Belgian air force, in particular the RSV.26-Lynx and RSV.28-180 Type III. The **RSV.32** trainer/liaison aircraft was built to a total of 57 by 1932 in versions which included

G-ASHS was a Stampe et Vertongen SV.4B of the British Tiger Club, converted by Rollason to take a de Havilland Gipsy Major Mk 10-1 engine. Like all SV.4s it has four ailerons.

the **RSV.32-90** (67-kW/90-hp Anzani 10C), **RSV.32-100** (75-kW/100-hp Renard), **RSV.32-105** (78-kW/105-hp Hermes), **RSV.32-110** (82-kW/110-hp Lorraine-Dietrich) and **RSV.32-120** (89-kW/120-hp Gipsy III), the majority serving with the Belgian air force.

Company designations changed to SV after Renard left to work wholly with the Société Anonyme des Avions et Moteurs Renard founded by Georges and Alfred Renard a few years earlier. The **SV.4** of 1933 proved to be Stampe et Vertongen's most successful aircraft, a light tourer/trainer of biplane configuration powered in prototype form by the 89-kW (120-hp) de Havilland Gipsy III engine. It was available initially as the advanced aerobatic **SV.4A** with a 104-kW (140-hp) Renault 4-PO5 engine, but the improved **SV.4B** had redesigned wings, introduced the 97-kW (130-hp) Gipsy Major I engine and was of reduced dimensions. Only about 35 were built before World War II, although after the war another 65 were built by Stampe et Renard, the company formed by a merger of Stampe et Vertongen with SA Avions et Moteurs Renard.

In addition, the SV.4 was licence-built extensively post-war as the **SV.4C** (powered by the 104-kW/140-hp Renault 4-Pei engine), being manufactured in France by SNCAN and in Algeria by Atelier Industriel de

l'Aéronautique d'Alger to a combined total of about 940. The SV.4 was followed by the larger and heavier **SV.5** military training biplane which was powered by the 265-kW (355-hp) Armstrong Siddeley Serval radial engine and could be equipped for both bombing and gunnery training; about 30 were built, 10 of them going to Latvia and the balance to the Belgian air force. Final designs, before the company's activities were brought to an end by the German invasion of 10 May 1940, included a lightweight parasol-wing monoplane designated **SV.18**, powered by an 89-k-W (120-hp) Gipsy III engine. Intended for use as a two-seat tourer under the designation **SV.18M**, it was also offered as a single-seat fighter trainer as the **SV.18MA**.

The post-war activities of Stampe et Renard met with little success after the completion of SV.4Bs; a single **SV.4D** with 130-kW (175-hp) Mathis engine failed to gain any interest, which was also the fate of the **SR.7B Monitor IV** trainer. This was a two-seat cantilever low-wing monoplane powered by a 134-kW (180-hp) Blackburn Cirrus Bombardier 702 inline engine and with its tandem cockpits enclosed by a continuous canopy.

Specification
Stampe et Vertongen SV.4B
Type: aerobatic tourer/trainer
Powerplant: one 97-kW (130-hp) de Havilland Gipsy Major I inverted inline piston engine
Performance: maximum speed 200 km/h (124 mph); service ceiling 5500 m (18,045 ft)
Weights: empty 480 kg (1,058 lb); maximum take-off 780 kg (1,720 lb)
Dimensions: span 8.40 m (27 ft 6¾ in); length 6.50 m (21 ft 4 in); height 2.60 m (8 ft 6¼ in); wing area 19.00 m² (204.52 sq ft)

Standard aircraft

Standard Aircraft Corporation was established at Plainfield, New Jersey, during 1916 in the belief that, despite the nation's isolationist policy, the USA would become involved in World War I. Only the fifth or sixth supplier of aircraft to the US Army Signal Corps, the company's first order was gained in 1916, for the supply of three **Standard H-2** biplanes. Based on the Sloane H-2 biplane, these open-cockpit three-seaters, powered by a 93-kW (125-hp) Hall-Scott A-5 engine, were for use in a reconnaissance role. A US Army order for nine similarly-powered and improved H-3 biplanes was received soon after this, and three similar aircraft equipped as twin-float trainers were supplied to the US Navy under the designation **H-4H**.

More important was the company's J series, very similar in appearance to the Curtiss JN-4 which it was intended to complement in the training role. The initial version was the **SJ** powered by a

The E-1 was built in quite small numbers for flying and gunnery training. After World War I three E-1s were converted by into radio-controlled 'aerial torpedoes'.

75-kW (100-hp) Hall-Scott A-7 inline engine, and the **J-1** or **SJ-I** major production version, which differed only in detail, was built by Standard to a total of approximately 800. The major shortcoming of these aircraft was the Hall-Scott engine, which was unreliable, and the company's attempts to develop a more effective aircraft were not particularly successful. They included the **JR**, similar to the SJ but with a 112-kW (150-hp) Wright-Hispano engine (of which only six were acquired by the US Army as advanced trainers), followed by six more with a number of revisions including equal-span wings, new tail surfaces and 130-kW (175-hp) Hall-Scott A-5 engines. Designated **JR-1B**, a number were also supplied to the

US Post Office Department.

In 1917 Standard developed the smaller **E-1** equal-span biplane, of which two were evaluated by the US Army in the fighter role. Although unsatisfactory as such, the E-1 was ordered as an advanced trainer, being built to a total of more than 100. About half of this number were completed as E-1s with the 75-kW (100-hp) Gnome or 60-kW (80-hp) Le Rhône rotary engine, while the remainder, designated **M-Defense**, differed by having provision for armament.

State Aircraft Factories, People's Republic of China

Following the establishment of the Communist regime in 1949, the new Chinese government reorganised the infant aviation industry along nationalised, state-owned lines. Major State Aircraft Factories were established at Beijing, Chengdu, Hanzhong, Harbin, Nanchang, Shanxii, Shanghai, Shenyang, Tianjin and Xian, most of which have only ever built licensed (or sometimes unlicensed) copies of foreign, usually Soviet, aircraft types.

Details of most of these aircraft are given under their original manufacturer. There follows a table of the major aerospace projects undertaken by the Chinese industry since the Revolution, involving the licence-built (and illicit) production of Soviet types. The Chinese designation comes first followed by followed by the original Soviet designation.

Harbin H-5	Ilyushin Il-28
Xian H-6	Tupolev Tu-16
Shenyang J-5	Mikoyan MiG-17
Shenyang J-6	Mikoyan MiG-19
Chengdu/Shenyang/	
Guizhou J-7	Mikoyan MiG-21
Xian Y-5	Antonov An-2
Harbin Y-7	Antonov An-24
Shanxi Y-8	Antonov An-12
Harbin Z-5	Mil Mi-4
Harbin Z-9	Aérospatiale
	Dauphin

Completely indigenous aircraft include the Harbin Y-12 and SH-5 and the Nanchang A-5 (described under Harbin and Nanchang because they were originated after the factories ceased using their State Aircraft Factory tags). Other important indigenous types are detailed below.

State Aircraft Factory Chengdu JJ-5/FT-5

The **Shenyang J-5** was China's first indigenously built fighter. It was produced with close Soviet collaboration and production followed a carefully planned, four-phase programme under which local workers started with mere assembly of Soviet-built sub-assemblies and ended with manufacture of about 48 per cent of each aircraft. The J-5 made its maiden flight on 19 July 1956, and in September was cleared for mass production. A total of 767 was built.

Later derivatives were developed and constructed by Chengdu. The first of these was the **J-5A**, which was basically a Chinese-built MiG-17PF with indigenous AI radar in a larger, longer, forward fuselage. Small numbers were produced. The prototype made its maiden flight on 11 November 1964. More successful was the **JJ-5**, a two seat trainer derivative of the J-5. This had a slightly lengthened fuselage, and the nose intake and jetpipe were refined. Development began in 1965, when it was becoming clear that the MiG-15UTI then in use had some unacceptable handling characteristics. The crescent wing of the MiG-17, with its reduced sweep on the outer wings, solved many of these problems.

The JJ-5 first flew on 8 May 1966, and 1,061 had been built by 1986, when production ceased. The JJ-5 has been exported (as the FT-5) to a number of customers including Albania, Bangladesh, Pakistan, Sri Lanka and Zimbabwe. Mikoyan themselves never designed a two-seat MiG-17 variant.

State Aircraft Factory Harbin Y-11/Y-12

The **Harbin Y-11** was developed as a general utility aircraft to replace the Antonov An-2/Xian/Shijiazhuang Y-5. The initial aircraft were powered by indigenous Quzhou Huosai-6A 213-kW (285-hp) nine-cylinder radial piston engines based on the Ivchenko A1-14RF. These allowed the aircraft to carry a payload of 940 kg (2,072 lb), which was raised to 1250 kg (2,755 lb) when HS6D engines were fitted. Eight passengers could be carried in addition to the two crew, as opposed to at least 12 in an An-2.

In order to give better single-engine performance the **Y-11B** was developed, with 261-kW (350-hp) Continental TSIO-550-B flat six engines. The prototype first flew on 25 December 1990 and deliveries began in 1992. The **Y-11BI** is similar, with further upgraded Chinese avionics.

The **Y-12I** shares the same configuration as the Y-11, but is of larger overall size, with a bigger fuselage cross-section and a fuselage 'plug' ahead of the wings. It was originally to have been designated Y-11T1, but the Y-12 designation was adopted before the first flight. Y-12 variants are described separately under Harbin.

State Aircraft Factory Nanchang CJ-5 and CJ-6

The basic Yak-18 was built under licence in China as the **Nanchang CJ-5**. The closely related **CJ-6** piston-engined basic trainer was developed at Shenyang in 1956-58 as a successor for the CJ-5. Retaining the latter's overall configuration, it introduced a fully retractable undercarriage, with the main legs folding inwards into the wing centre-section and the nosewheel retracting aft into the forward fuselage. The outer wing panels introduced marked dihedral. The first prototype, flown on 27 August 1958, was fitted with a 108-kW (145-hp) Mikulin M-11ER engine, with which its proved underpowered. It was later modified with an Ivchenko AI-14R engine, flying in this form on 18 July 1960. The CJ-6A was the standard production version from 1965 and introduced an uprated Quzhou Huosai-6A HS6A engine, developed from the more powerful AI-14RF. Production of the **CJ-6A** has totalled more than 1,800 and batches have been exported to friendly nations such as Albania, Bangladesh, Cambodia, Korea, Tanzania and Zambia.

State Aircraft Factory Nanchang J-12

Designed to meet a Chinese requirement for a lightweight STOL fighter, the **J-12** was of broadly similar configuration to the MiG-21. Six prototypes were constructed, the first making its maiden flight on 26 December 1970. Agile, fast and with good STOL characteristics, the J-12 was handicapped by inadequate firepower, ruggedness and engine thrust, and was abandoned in 1977 as the flight test programme was dogged by structural failures.

State Aircraft Factory Shanghai Y-10

The **Shanghai Y-10** was a turbofan-powered four-jet airliner developed for use by CAAC and initiated in 1970. Designed to meet US FAA Regulations, the project provided useful experience of modern commercial airliner manufacturing and flight testing processes and procedures. These were applied during the later co-production of the McDonnell Douglas MD82. Of similar size and configuration to the Boeing 707, the Y-10 prototype represented China's largest aircraft design, and was actually powered by Pratt & Whitney JT3D-7 turbofans taken from CAAC

The Shanghai Y-10 bore a marked resemblance to the Boeing 707, and originally China planned to develop the type into a more advanced twin-turbofan-powered airliner.

Boeing 707s. The cabin could accommodate up to 178 passengers in economy class, 149 in tourist class, or 124 in a mixed configuration. The flight deck carried a crew of five, comprising pilot, co-pilot, navigator, radio operator and flight engineer. The first of two flying prototypes made its maiden flight on

26 September 1980. Development was abandoned because there seemed to be too small a market for the rather expensive indigenous jetliner.

State Aircraft Factory Shenyang JJ-1

The **JJ-1** was the first indigenous Communist Chinese aircraft to reach flight status. A clumsy-looking design, the JJ-1 was of similar configuration to the British Jet Provost, albeit with tandem seating and a canopy which looked as though it had been taken from a MiG-15UTI. It flew for the first time on 26 July 1958 but was abandoned when a CJ-6 and MiG-15UTI training system was adopted, with no basic jet trainer stage.

State Aircraft Factory Shenyang J-6/F-6 and JJ-6/FT-6

The MiG-19 was selected for production under the second Five Year Plan. Drawings were supplied to the Shenyang Aircraft Factory, which produced production tooling and documentation for a copy of the basic MiG-19P under the designation **J-6**. The first Chinese-assembled aircraft made its maiden flight on 17 December 1958. Licence-production of the MiG-19P and MiG-19PM was also assigned to the Nanchang Aircraft Factory. After the programme was halted due to poor quality control, production of the basic MiG-19S 'Farmer-C' day fighter restarted. The aircraft was recertificated in December 1963, and began to enter service in 1964-65.

A number of totally new indigenous variants were produced The most important of these was the **JJ-6** two-seat trainer, which first flew on 6 November 1970. A two-seat MiG-19UTI was built in small numbers by Mikoyan, but the type never entered service, conversion from the MiG-15UTI being judged not to be a problem.

China felt that a trainer with handling characteristics similar to the J-6 was essential, this view being reinforced by significant export orders. The Chinese two-seat trainer owes little to the Russian original. The fuselage is stretched by some 84 cm (33 in) ahead of the wing, and the NR-23 cannon in the wingroots are deleted to make room for extra fuel, restoring fuel capacity to within 150 litres (33 Imp gal) of the single-seater. A single cannon is usually retained below the fuselage. Two ventral fins are added below the rear fuselage to maintain directional stability.

Production of the JJ-6 totalled 634, and many were exported under the designation **FT-6** to serve as conversion and continuation trainers for the F-6 and A-5. The type remains in service in Bangladesh, China, Pakistan and North Korea.

Other indigenous MiG-19 derivatives include the **JZ-6** reconnaissance aircraft. Sub-variants were produced for high- and low-level recce, and a later sub-type was built with optical and infra-red sensors for day and night reconnaissance.Misidentified as the **J-6Xin,** and attributed to have an indigenous all-weather radar in a 'needle-nose radome' intake centrebody, the **J-6III** was actually a high-speed day fighter, whose sharp, conical, needle nose was a variable shock-cone. The prototype flew on 6 August 1969. The J-6III was a very different looking aircraft, with short-span cropped wings and increased-chord ailerons and flaps. The J-6III proved quicker, faster-climbing and tighter-turning than the basic J-6, but was plagued by handling and quality control problems. The more modest **J-6C** was more successful, differing from the basic J-6/MiG-19S in having a relocated brake-chute fairing at the base of the trailing edge of the tailfin, tubeless tyres and disc brakes on the main undercarriage units. Pakistani F-6s

Several versions of the MiG-19 were built in China as the J-6. Most were highly derivative but one, the two-seat JJ-6 conversion trainer has a lengthened fuselage and no Soviet counterpart.

have been further improved, gaining AIM-9 Sidewinder compatibility, Martin-Baker ejection seats and various new avionics systems. They are also configured to carry a huge semi-conformal 'bath-tub' external fuel tank below the belly.

Guizhou was responsible for the final variant, the all-weather **J-6A,** (or **J-6IV**). This was based on the J-6C but with all-weather radar and PL-2 missiles. By comparison with the original all-weather J-6s (based on the MiG-19P and MiG-19PM), it had slightly recontoured radomes, with a larger and more bulbous 'upper lip' and a more pointed

and conical centrebody. It is unknown whether the aircraft retains cannon in the wingroots or under the fuselage. The 1950s-vintage J-6 was produced into the 1980s, by which time approximately 3,000 were built. It was exported to Albania, Bangladesh, Egypt, Iran, Iraq, North Korea, Pakistan, Somalia,

Tanzania, Vietnam and Zambia, most of which continue to operate the aircraft in small numbers. It remains in service in larger numbers with the air force of the People's Liberation Army, with which service it is still numerically the most important type, fulfilling both attack and fighter roles.

State Aircraft Factory Shenyang J-8

The **J-8** originated from a PLA requirement for a fighter with performance and combat capability superior to that of the MiG-21. Shenyang's decision to use twin engines, and the company's long association with the 'tailed delta' MiG-21-type configuration, ensured that the new aircraft looked like a scaled-up MiG-21 similar to Mikoyan's Ye-152A 'Flipper'. Two prototypes were completed in July 1968, the first J-8 making its maiden flight on 5 July 1969. The original J-8 had a small ranging radar in the intake centrebody, and retained the single-piece forward-hinging canopy of the original J-7. The aircraft was armed with a single 30-mm cannon and up to four underwing PL-2 AAMs. Any production was very limited.

The **J-8I** was designed as an all-weather fighter derivative of the basic J-8, and featured a new Type 204 Sichuan SR-4 radar in an enlarged intake centrebody. The 30-mm cannon was replaced by a twin-barrelled 23-mm 23-III cannon, and provision was made for four rocket pods as an optional alternative to the PL-2 missiles. The J-8I retained the same 59-kN (13,450-lb st) WP-7B engines as the basic J-8 but introduced some aerodynamic refinements, with small fences above the wing, revised wingtips and relocated airbrakes. The aircraft also introduced a two-piece canopy, with an upward-hinging rear transparency and a fixed windscreen. Prototype assembly was completed in May 1980, but the aircraft

burned out during its first engine run. The second prototype was hurriedly completed and made the type's maiden flight on 24 April 1981. J-8 and J-8I production totalled about 100 aircraft, and some of the original J-8s are said to have been converted to the later standard.

Although the J-8I marked a great improvement over the original 'Finback', there was clearly scope for a more radical redesign. This led to the development of the **J-8II 'Finback-B'**, which was given the go-ahead in May 1981. The new variant had relocated lateral air intakes to feed its 69-kN (15,430-lb st) WP-13B turbojets, these leaving the nose free for a radar antenna of the largest possible diameter. The engine intakes bear a striking similarity to those of the MiG-23 'Flogger', and the original twin ventral strakes were replaced by a MiG-23-style folding fin. Seventy per cent of the airframe was changed by comparison with the original J-8, as were 30 per cent of the contractor-supplied parts.

The first of four prototypes flew on 12 June 1984. There has been small-scale batch production of the J-8II, but the type may not have entered service. An export version, designated **F-8B**, is powered by a pair of WP-13B turbojets and introduces a pulse-Doppler lookdown radar and digital avionics, with a HUD and two HDDs. It has not won any orders.

On 5 August 1987 Grumman received a $501.8 million contract to

design, develop and test an avionics upgrade for the J-8II under the Foreign Military Sales Program. The massacre in Tienanmen Square led to an immediate

halt on work on the project, and the expulsion of many of the Chinese engineers. Development restarted, but flight test and kit delivery would have required a change in State Department policy; with deliveries unlikely, China pulled out of the project.

Above: The bulk of the original Shenyang J-8Os (initial prototypes) and J-8Is were used solely for trials and testing.

Below: Under the 'Peace Pearl' programme two J-8IIs were sent to Edwards AFB for testing by Grumman.

Stearman aircraft

The Stearman Aircraft Company, established initially at Venice, California in 1927, but soon moving to Wichita, Kansas, combined Lloyd Stearman's design genius with the backing of the Lyle-Hoyt Aircraft Corporation, in 1934 this company became a subsidiary of the Boeing Airplane Company, and in 1939 its Wichita Division.

First design to be built by the new company was the classic **Stearman C3B**, its configuration forming the basis of all subsequent biplanes of Stearman design. In standard form this was an unequal-span biplane with fixed tailskid landing gear, tandem open cockpits for a pilot and two passengers, and a 220-hp (164-kW) Wright J-5 Whirlwind radi-

al engine. Alternative powerplants resulted in the **C3C** (with 150- or 180-hp/112- or 134-kW Hispano-Suiza), **C3K** (128-hp/95kW Siemens-Halske Sh.12), **C3L** (130-hp/97-kW Comet) and **C3R** (225hp/168-kW Wright J-6).

Initial development led to the **Stearman C3MB**, which differed from the C3B only by having the forward (passenger) cockpit adapted to carry cargo or mail, and many C3Bs were later converted to this configuration. It set the pattern for the much larger **Stearman M-2 Speedmail** of 1929 which, powered by a 525-hp (391-kW) Wright Cyclone, could carry a 1,000-lb (454kg) load of cargo/mail. The Speedmail was, in turn, developed as

the **Stearman LT-1**, which replaced the cargo compartment of the M-2 by an enclosed cabin to seat four passengers or carry a 1,200-lb (544kg) payload. The prototype retained the Cyclone engine of the M-2, but production aircraft had the similarly powered Pratt & Whitney Hornet. The **Stearman 4E Junior Speedmail**, introduced in 1930 and powered by the 420-hp (313-kW) Pratt & Whitney Wasp C1 engine, came between the C3 and M-2 in terms of size and capability. Like the C3 it was basically a three-seater, but the forward cockpit was convertible easily to carry cargo/ mail. Built in small numbers, the Stearman 4E was followed by the **Stearman 4C** with 300-hp (224-kW) Wright J-6, **Stearman 4D** with 300hp (224-kW) Pratt & Whitney Wasp Junior, **Stearman 4EM Senior**

Speedmail with the forward cockpit specifically for cargo/mail and a 450-hp (336-kW) Pratt & Whitney Wasp, **Stearman 4CM-1 Senior Speedmail** cargo/mail version of the Stearman 4C with a 300-hp (224-kW) Wright R-975 engine, and a similar adaptation of the Stearman 4D designated **Stearman 4DM-1 Senior Speedmail**. By the time that this last aircraft was certificated, on 27 May 1930, the US economic depression was at its height; only two Stearman 4DM-Is were sold and the company had to look around for a different category of market.

Thus was developed the **Stearman 6A Cloudboy** of 1931 2, a two-seat biplane with tandem open cockpits that was designed specifically as a commercial or military trainer. Powered by the 165-hp (123-kW) Wright J-6 engine, the

Cloudboy had only limited success because of the economic situation, just three civil examples being built. Hopes were raised with a US Army Air Corps order for four similarly powered aircraft, which it designated **YPT-9** but there was no production order to follow. Later USAAC conversions of these aircraft resulted in the designations **YPT-9A** (165-hp/123-kW Continental A70), **YPT-9B** (200-hp/149-kW Lycoming), **YPT-9C** (170-hp/127-kW Kinner), **YBT-3** (300-hp/224-kW Wright J-6-9 Whirlwind) and **YBT-5** (300hp/224-kW Pratt & Whitney Wasp Jr). Subsequent civil developments followed the USAAC pattern, the **Stearman 6F Cloudboy** having Continental, the **Stearman 6D** the Wasp Junior, the

The two-seat Stearman Model 81 was one of the company's later designs, produced just prior to its absorption by Boeing. It was a one-off type which was redesigned over its career by having its forward cockpit blanked off, as seen here.

Stearman 6H the Kinner, and the **Stearman 6L** the Lycoming, but only two or three of each were built.

Although the Stearman company was only just ticking over, energetic efforts found maintenance and repair work to bolster the very small income from sales, and in 1933 the company found time to build a one-off **Model 80** open cockpit two-seat biplane and a

similar **Model 81** which had the cockpits enclosed by a streamlined canopy. It was at this same period that design

began of the **Model 73** which, together with the **Model 75**, was to bring the company undying fame.

Stearman-Hammond Y-1

The Stearman-Hammond Aircraft Corporation was formed in 1936 linked the design capabilities of Lioyd Stearman and Dean Hammond to develop the **Hammond Model Y** for production. Intended as an easy-to-fly aircraft, the resulting **Stearman-Hammond Y-1** (**Y-125**) low-wing monoplane had a fuselage pod with two side-by-side seats, a 125-hp (93-kW) Menasco C-4 engine mounted in the rear of the pod to drive a pusher propeller, twin booms carrying the tail

unit, and landing gear of fixed tricycle configuration. Built in small numbers, the Y-1 had a performance that was rather sluggish with this engine, resulting in the **Y-1S** with 150-hp (112-kW) Menasco C-4S engine which provided this 40 ft (12.19 m) span aircraft with a maximum speed of 130 mph (209 km/h) at 3,000 ft (915 m). Though endowed with the easy-to-fly characteristics that had been sought, overall production was limited to about 20 aircraft, probably by size and price.

R2676 was a Stearman-Hammond Model Y bought from Dutch airline KLM by the Royal Air Force, and scrapped in 1942 after evaluation.

Stinson Detroiter

Initially named the Stinson Aircraft Syndicate, this company was formed in 1926 by pioneer pilot Eddie Stinson to build the Stinson Detroiter four-seat cabin biplane which had been designed jointly by Stinson and the well-known designer Alfred Verville. Designated **SB-1 Detroiter** this initial version incorporated such features as cabin heating, individual wheel brakes and an electric starter for its 164-kW (220-hp) Wright

J-5 Whirlwind engine. Later that same year the company's name was changed to Stinson Aircraft Corporation and at about that time work began on the design and construction of a braced high-wing monoplane version of the Detroiter, the **SM-1D** which had the same powerplant as the **SB-1** but with the cabin laid out as a six-seater. This was to prove the most popular configuration, being followed by the **SM-1DA**

and **SM-1DB** which introduced minor improvements, and the **SM-1DC** and **SM-1DD** one-offs, both two-seaters with a cargo-carrying interior. The SM-1DD was the last of the J-5-powered Detroiters, and about 75 SM-1Ds of all versions had then been built. The conclusion that this aircraft would benefit from more power resulted in the last of the original Detroiter line, the **SM-1F** of 1929 with the 224-kW (300-hp) Wright J-6, this 14.22 m (46 ft 8 in) span version of the SM series having a maximum speed of 212 km/h (132 mph),

many SM-1Ds were later re-engined with this powerplant and redesignated **SM-1D300**. The SM-1F was also available with Edo floats under the designation **SM-1FS**, and production of the SM-1F and SM-1FS totalled about 30.

Two examples of a larger-capacity seven-seat **SM-6B Detroiter** were built in 1928, followed by seven or eight more with eight-seat interiors, and these largest members of the Stinson single-engine aircraft line were powered by the 336-kW (450-hp) Pratt & Whitney Wasp C-1 radial.

Stinson Junior

In 1928 Stinson began to widen the sales net by introducing a scaled-down version of the Detroiter; designated **Stinson SM-2**, this three/four-seat high-wing cabin monoplane was also of lighter construction and, powered initially by a 82-kW (110-hp) Warner Scarab radial engine, was known at first as the **Detroiter Junior**. The Detroiter portion of the name was dropped with production of the **SM-2AA Junior** in 1929, which introduced a new Wright radial engine of 165 hp (123 kW), and after about 24 had been built a demand for even higher performance was met by the **SM-2AB**. Powered by a 164-kW (220-hp) Wright J-5 radial, this 12.6 m (41 ft 6-in) span aircraft had a maximum speed of 209 km/h (130 mph) and production totalled more than 30. Last of the SM-2 family was the **SM-2AC** with a 168-kW (225-

hp) version of the Wright J-6 engine, available optionally with twin floats as the **SM-2ACS**, and total production of the SM-2AC/SM-2ACS was about 20 aircraft.

Continuation of the Stinson Junior series then diverged into two lines. The high-powered **SM-7A Junior** of 1930 with a de luxe interior and 224-kW (300-hp) Wright J-6 (R-975) engine was complemented later in the year by the **SM-7B**, which differed only by having the 224-kW (300-hp) Pratt & Whitney Wasp Junior engine. The alternative line was the **SM-8A** and **SM-8B**, introduced at the same time with a 160-kW (215-hp) Lycoming R-680 radial and the 168-kW (225-hp) Wright J-6 (R-760) radial respectively. Only about six SM-8Bs were sold, but the much lower priced JM-8A proved to be an unexpected success and was sold in hun-

dreds. This 12.70-m (41 ft 8-in) span model of the Junior possessed a maximum speed of 201 km/h (125 mph) and range of 805 km (500 miles). However, the **SM-8D** introduced a little later in the year with a new 168-kW (225-hp) Packard diesel engine was regarded with some suspicion and only two examples were sold. The Junior line then continued without the name Junior, a title which the company feared might suggest an inferior product; thus the **Stinson Model S** of 1931 (over 100 built) differed only from the SM-8A by the addition of some refinements. The alternative **Model W** introduced in the same year was basically similar to the SM-7B and retained its Pratt & Whitney Wasp Junior powerplant but its higher price limited sales to five. The improved **Model R** of 1932 (over 30 built), was a development of the Model S with the same powerplant and had a revised fuselage structure to provide better accommodation. The

The Lycoming-engined Stinson SM-8A was a considerable commercial success.

Model R-2 (two or three built) introduced the 240-hp (179-kW) Lycoming R-680-BA engine, and **Model R-3** (three or four built) was identical except that it had retractable main landing gear units; an **R-3-S** variant had the 245-hp (183kW) R-680-6 engine and a variable pitch propeller. These R-series aircraft marked the end of the true Junior line, but were followed by later related aircraft that still leaned heavily on the basic Detroiter/ Junior classic configuration.

Stinson Trimotors

In 1930 Stinson Aircraft Corporation decided that the moment had arrived to get a toehold in the market for airliners, its first offering being the **Stinson SM-6000 Airliner** introduced in July of

that year. Of braced high-wing monoplane configuration and with accommodation for a pilot and 10 passengers, the SM-6000 was powered by three 160-kW (215-hp) Lycoming R-680

engines, one in the nose and one strut-mounted on each side directly over the main landing gear units. The SM-6000 was complemented later in 1930 by the **SM-6000-A** which differed only by being available with a variety of alternative interior arrangements; the **SM-6000-B** of 1931 was generally similar

but for better interior equipment , and was available as standard in **SM-6000-B1** (all passenger) and **SM-6000-B2** (mail/passenger) versions. In 1932 production was initiated of the **Model U Airliner** which, of the same capacity as its predecessors, had 179-kW (240-hp) Lycoming R-680-BA engines and differed primarily by introducing low-set stub wings mounting an engine at each wingtip. Production of these SM-6000 series tri-motors totalled about 80 aircraft.

The company's next and final three-engine airliner was of very different configuration, the **Model A** being a braced low-wing monoplane that introduced retractable tailwheel landing gear, was powered by three 194-kW (260-hp) Lycoming R-680-5 engines (one in the nose and two in wing-mounted nacelles), and provided accommodation for a pilot, co-pilot, stewardess and 10 passengers. About 35 of this version were built, and two of four supplied to Airlines of Australia were converted subsequently to twin-engine configuration with two 336-kW (450-hp) Pratt & Whitney Wasps.

Stinson L-1 Vigilant

In response to a US Army Air Corps requirement of 1940 for a two-seat light observation aircraft, Stinson submitted its **Stinson Model 74** design proposal to receive a contract or three examples under the desigation **YO-49** for evaluation against submissions from Bellanca (YO-50) nd Ryan (YO-51). Stinson was awarded a contract for 142 **O-49** production aircraft, these often beng listed under the Vultee name, for by 1940 Stinson had become a division of Vultee Aircraft Inc. To provide essential low-speed and high-lift performance, the braced monoplane wing incorporated leading- and trailing-edge high-lift devices, and power was provided by a Lycoming R-680-9 radial engine. A follow-on contract was received for 182 **O-49A** aircraft which had a slightly longer fuselage, some refinements and equipment changes. In 1942 the O-49 and O-49A were redesignated **L-1** and **L-1A** respectively and eight L-1 and 100 L-1A aircraft allocated to the RAF under Lend-Lease became **Vigilant Mk I** and **Vigilant Mk II** respectively, with many of the latter used under joint Anglo-American control. Conversions of O-49 and O-49A aircraft for use in other roles resulted in three **O-49B** (later **L-1B**) ambulances accommodating a single stretcher, a single **L-1C** ambulance with revised interior, 21 **L-1D** aircraft modified from L-1As for pilot training in glider pick-up techniques, seven L-1 conversions as **L-1E** ambulances with amphibious float landing gear, plus five similar conversions from L-1A aircraft, which were redesignated **L-1F**. No additional production aircraft were built, the Vigilant being superseded by the more effective Grasshopper family. The 50 ft 11 in (15.52 m) span L-1A was powered by

The air ambulance role of this USAAC Stinson O-49B is indicated by the cross on the fuselage side. Respectable STOL performance was bestowed by the flaps and slats.

the 220-kW (295-hp) R-680-9 had a maximum speed of 196 km/h (122 mph).

Stinson Model O

Most untypical of all the Stinson urcraft was the **Stinson Model O** of 1933 which, derived from the basic SR Reliant, was a parasol wing monoplane powered by a 164-kW (220-hp) Lycoming R-680-4 radial engine. Intended as a military pilot trainer it had tandem open cockpits for instructor and pupil and provision for the installation of two forward-firing machine-guns, a trainable machine-gun in the rear cockpit, and a light underfuselage bomb rack. Production totalled 10, including the prototype which went later to a US civil flying school, the balance being delivered to Brazil (one), China (three) and Honduras (five). Spanning 12.17 m (39 ft 11 in), the Model O had a maximum speed of 219 km/h (136 mph).

Stinson Model 108 Voyager

The Stinson Model 108 appeared in several forms, this being a Franklin-powered Voyager 150

Throughout World War 2 the Stinson Division of Vultee Aircraft Inc. (later Consolidated Vultee Aircraft Corporation) concentrated upon building military aircraft, but was preparing for peace by the design of an improved **Stinson Model 108 Voyager**. It had far better and cleaner lines than the pre-war Voyager, benefiting from the wealth of experience gained from military aircraft production. First introduced in August 1945 as the **Voyager 125** powered by a 93-kW (125-hp) Avco Lycoming engine, it first entered the post-war market for civil aircraft as the **Voyager 150** with a 112-kW (150-hp) Franklin 6A4-150 engine. Orders flooded in, and by the end of 1946 the company had built more than 1,400. It was followed by an improved Voyager 150 and an alternative utility version named **Station Wagon**; both were available with alternative wheel, float or ski landing gear. Final version was the **Voyager 165** and complementary Station Wagon with the 123-kW (165-hp) Franklin 6A4-165-B3 engine, and by July 1948 Stinson had delivered more than 5,000 Model 108s of all versions. There was then a post-war slump in the market, resulting from thousands of war surplus lightplanes becoming available at knockdown prices; by the end of November 1948 Consolidated Vultee had disposed of its Stinson Division to Piper Aircraft Corporation. However, only desultory efforts were made by Piper to continue sales of the aircraft they called the **Piper-Stinson Voyager** and by the end of 1949 it was no longer available. The 10.36 m (34 ft) span Voyager 165 had a maximum speed of 217 km/h (135 mph) and range of 789 km (490 miles).

Stinson Reliant

The **Stinson Model R** and **Model S** formed the basis of the extensively-built **Stinson Reliant**, the initial **Stinson SR Reliant** introduced in the summer of 1933 being of the same basic configuration. Available alternatively as a twin-float seaplane, the Reliant was built in a long series that differed primarily in powerplant. The SR was powered by a 160-kW (215-hp) Lycoming R-680; the **SR-1** had the R-680-2 and the **SR-2** the R-680-7 engine, each of 179-kW (240-hp) output; and the **SR-3** was basically similar to the SR-1 but for minor structural changes. The **SR-4** introduced the 186-kW (250-hp) Wright R-760-E radial, but the improved **SR-5** of 1934 was available in three versions, the SR-5 having the 168-kW (225-hp) Lycoming R-680-4, and **SR-5B** and **SR-5C** having the 179kW (240-hp) R-680-2 and 194-kW (260-hp) R-680-5 respectively. However, the most extensively built (about 75) civil Reliants were the well-equipped **SR-5A** powered by the 183-kW (245-hp) R-680-6 engine and a very basic (with plenty of options available) **SR-5E** with 168-kW (225-hp) R-680-4.

Most expensive Reliant was was the **SR-5F** with optional Wright R-760-E or R-760-E1 engines of 186-kW (250 hp) or 213 kW (285 hp) respectively. In 1935 Stinson introduced a refined **Reliant SR-6** model. The SR-6 and **SR-6B** with the higher-powered R-680-6 and R-680-5 engines respectively were five-seaters, but the **SR-6A** with the 168-kW (225-hp) R-680-4 was limited to four seats. The **SR-7 Reliant** of 1936 looked a very different aeroplane as a result of the introduction of a double-tapered wing, and was available as the four-seat **SR-7A** with R-680-4 engine, and as the five-seat **SR-7B** or **SR-7C** with R-680-6 and R-680-5 engines respectively. The **SR-8 Reliant** of the same year was generally similar to the SR-7 but available in five variants. The **SR-8A**, **SR-8B** and **SR-8C** corresponded in powerplant to the SR-7A, SR-7B and SR-7C but were all completed as four-seaters, and the **SR-8D** and **SR-8E** were both five-seaters with 213-kW

FK818 was the fifth of a batch of 250 Stinson Reliant Mk Is supplied to the UK for the FAA.

Two Stinson SR-5 Reliants were bought by the US Navy in the mid-1930s, this being the example passed on to the Coast Guard under the designation RQ-1.

(285-hp) and 239-kW (320-hp) Wright R-760-E1 and R-760-E2 engines respectively. Both of the Wright-engined versions were offered optionally for use in utility roles under the designation SR-8DM and SR-8EM. Still further structural refinement was noticeable on the **SR-9** introduced for 1937, available as the **SR-9A**, **SR-9B**, **SR-9C** and **SR-9E** with the same powerplant as the corresponding SR-8 variants. They were supplied to the same standard as all of the earlier aircraft, but de luxe or utility inte-

riors were optional. An addition to the range for 1937 was the **SR-9F** with 298-kW (400-hp) Pratt & Whitney Wasp Junior engine and with the same optional interior finishes. Last of the civil Reliants was the **SR-10** model of 1938 introducing more refinements and available with a still wider range of powerplants of 183 to 336 kW (245 to 450 hp). Most extensively built were the **SR-10B**, **SR-10C**, **SR-10D**, **SR-10E** and **SR-10F** to a total of about 90 of all versions. Production of civil Reliants ended when the USA became

involved in World War 2, and although none were built for service with the USAAF the army operated a total of 46 impressed civil aircraft under **UC-81A** to **UC-81N** designations, covering different SR-8, SR-9 and SR-10 variants, plus one SR-10F which was designated **XC-81D** and used to develop glider pick-up techniques. Two SR-5A and two SR-7B versions of the Reliant were also impressed under the respective designations **L-12** and **L-12A**, and single examples of the Reliant were procured for evaluation by the US Coast

Guard and US Navy under the designations **RQ1** and **XR3Q-1** respectively. During the war 500 new-production Reliants were procured under the designation **AT-19** for Lend-Lease supply to the Royal Navy; basically similar to the **SR-10G** with a Lycoming R-680-E1 engine, a lengthened fuselage and special equipment, they served with 12 squadrons. In addition, 15 UK civil registered Reliants were also impressed for military service.

Specification
Stinson Reliant SR-5A
Type: four-seat cabin monoplane
Powerplant: one 183-kW (245-hp) Lycoming R-680-6 radial piston engine
Performance: maximum speed 217 km/h (135 mph); service ceiling 4725 m (15,500 ft); maximum range 1038 km (645 miles)
Weights: empty 1055 kg (2,325 lb) maximum take-off 1576 kg (3,475 lb)
Dimensions: span 12.50 m (41 ft 0 in); length 8.31 m (27 ft 3 in); height 2.57 m (8 ft 5 in)

Stinson Voyager and Sentinel

In 1939 Stinson entered the lightplane market with introduction of the **Stinson Model 105** which, looking very like a small-scale Junior, was a three-seat braced high-wing monoplane powered by a 56kW (75-hp) Continental A75-3 or 60-kW (80-hp) A80 6 flat-four engine. About 530 of these two civil versions were built in roughly equal numbers, their success resulting during 1941 in the introduction of an improved **Model 10 Voyager** that differed primarily in standards of interior finish and equipment. The basic version with the 90-hp (67-kW) Franklin 4AC-199-E3 engine was designated **Model 10-A** and about 750 were built before production was suspended in 1942, but a few examples with the 56-kW (75-hp) Lycoming GO-145-E3 engine were also built under the designation **Model 10-B**. Six examples of the Model 10-A with the 60-kW (80-hp) Continental O-170-1 engine were procured by the US Army Air Force in 1941 for evaluation under the designation **YO-54**. Successful testing led to an initial order for 275 slightly larger and heavier aircraft with the Lycoming O-435-1 flat four engine under the designation **O-62**. The following order covered 1,456 similar aircraft which were designated **L-5** and

given the name Sentinel when deliveries began in 1942, the O-62s then being redesignated L-5. They were followed by the **L-5A** (688 converted from L-5s) with revised electrical system, the **L-5B** (679) with modified rear fuselage to permit loading of a stretcher, and the **L-5C** (200) with provision for a reconnaissance camera. The **L-5D** designation was not used and the **L-5E** (558) introduced ailerons that drooped with flap extension; the one-off **XL-5** evaluated minor changes and an O-435-2 engine and the final production **L-5G** (115) was simiilar to the **L-5E** except for introduction of the 142-kW (190-hp) O-435-11 engine. In addition to the foregoing, eight Stinson 105s and 12 Model 10-A Voyagers were impressed for USAAF service under the respective designations **AT-19A** (later **L-9A**) and **AT-19B** (later **L-9B**). A total of 306 L-5s of various designations were transferred to the US Marine Corps plus 152 to the US Navy, all 458 receiving the USN designation **OY-1**; of this total 30 later had minor equipment changes to become redesignated **OY-2**. Under Lend-Lease 40 L-5 and 60 L-5B aircraft were supplied to the RAF which designated them **Sentinel Mk I** and **Sentinel Mk II** respectively.

Used extensively by the USAAF throughout World War 2, Sentinels also proved valuable during the Korean War; the RAF deployed its Sentinel Mk Is and Mk IIs in Burma, and those of the USMC and USN served primarily in the Pacific. In 1962 surviving L-6s were redesignated **U-19A** by the USAF and one used as a glider tug by the USAF Academy had the designation **U-19B**.

Specification
Stinson L-5 Sentinel
Type: liaison/spotter aircraft
Powerplant: one 138-kW (185-hp) Lycoming O-435-1 flat-six piston engine
Performance: maximum speed 209 km/h (130 mph), service ceiling 4815 m (15,800 ft); range 676 km (420 miles)
Weights: empty 703 kg (1,550 lb); maximum take-off 916 kg (2,020 lb)
Dimensions: span 10.36 m (34 ft 0 in); length 7.34 m (24 ft 1 in) height 2.41 m (7 ft 11 in)

A Stinson L-5B Sentinel air ambulence lifts off Cub Field No.7 on the island of Okinawa during 1945, demonstrating just the type of operation in which the Stinson Sentinel excelled.

Stout aircraft

The Stout Metal Airplane Company was established in 1922 by W. B. Stout, who was also the chief designer. Early success came with the **Stout 2-AT**

Pullman of 1924, an eight-seat airliner of high-wing monoplane configuration powered normally by a 298-kW (400-hp) Liberty engine. The Stout 2-AT entered service with both Florida Airways and Ford Air Transport Services, the latter operating the type

on its Detroit Chicago and Detroit Cleveland air mail routes from 1926. From this design was developed the one-off 8-passenger **Stout 3-AT** trimotor of 1925; powered by three 149-kW (200-hp) Wright Whirlwind radials it was little more than an ugly adaptation

of the Pullman to mount three engines. However uninspiring this was, the aircraft must have had potential, for the Stout company (after the departure of W. B. Stout) continued development of what eventually became the highly successful Ford Tri-Motor.

Sud-Est (SNCASE) early types

With the nationalisation of the French aircraft industry in 1936 the Société Nationale de Constructions Aéronautiques de Sud-Est (SNCASE) combined the activities of Chantiers Aéro-Maritime de la Seine (CAMS), Lioré-et-Olivier, Potez, Romano, and Société Provençale des Constructions Aéronautiques (SPCA). Some of the programmes that had been initiated by the individual members were continued by the new company, known usually as Sud-Est. These included the **Lioré-et-Olivier LeO 50** design for an unusual three-seat fighter to be powered by two Gnome-Rhône radial engines. Two prototypes were built under the designation **Sud-Est S.E.100**, their unique feature being retractable tricycle landing gear with a steerable nosewheel and small main units that retracted into the fins of the twin fin-and-rudder tail unit. The first prototype was flown on 29 March

The Sud-Est S.E.100 was rolled out 13 months before the German invasion of France as a replacement for Potez 631 escort fighters.

1939, being lost in an accident in April 1940, but the second prototype was not flown and planned production was not started because of the German occupation of France. The designation **S.E.101** was allocated to a version to be powered by two Pratt & Whitney radial engines.

Development of the **Lioré-et-Olivier H.49** six-engine flying-boat, designed to meet a requirement of the French air Ministry for a transatlantic passenger and mail carrier, was continued under the designation **S.E.200**. The construction of four prototypes was initiated, but the two that were completed early in World War II were destroyed by Allied bombing. The other two which were completed and flown

post-war, were equipped to carry up to 80 passengers by day, but they

belonged to an age that no longer had any future for flying-boats.

Sud-Est Vampire, Mistral and Aquilon
to
Sukhoi Su-17, Su-20 and Su-22

Sud-Est Vampire, Mistral and Aquilon

After World War II the French aircraft industry was faced with the task of re-building itself and making up for five lost years in which great strides had been made, not least in the design of jet aircraft. Sud-Est (Société Nationale de Constructions Aéronautiques de Sud-Est –SNCASE) signed an agreement with de Havilland to licence-build the Goblin-powered **Vampire FB.Mk 5**, to gain experience in jet construction and as a prelude to a definitive French version powered by a Hispano-Suiza-built Nene engine. A production line was soon established at Marignane, near Marseilles, and by 1951 100 had been completed for service with the Armée de l'Aire.

The French requirement was for 450 Vampires of all types and work soon began on the **Sud-Est Mistral** (Vampire Mk 53), with its 22.5-kN (5,070-lb) Nene 102 engine. The Mistral employed the wing, fuselage etc. from the Vampire Mk 5, but featured a pressurised cockpit, modified air intakes for its new powerplant and a SNCASO-built ejection seat. Maximum speed increased to 925 km/h (575 mph) as opposed to the FB 5's 852 km/h (530 mph). The first Mistral flew on 2 April 1951 and an initial order for 2,500 was mooted. This number was later sharply revised downwards.

On 31 October 1952 the first French-built de Havilland Sea Venom FAW.Mk 20 took to the air. Powered by a de Havilland Ghost 103 engine, four preceding aircraft had been assembled from UK-supplied parts. This version became known as the **Aquilon 20** and led to the French-assembled **Aquilon 201** of 1954 (Aquilon meaning 'North Wind'). Twenty-five Aquilon 201s were built, followed by a similar number of **Aquilon 202**s (built entirely in France) with upward-hinging, jettisonable, clear-view clam-shell canopies. Every aircraft was fitted with an ejection seat, but the origin of the powerplant varied as some were built in Italy, by Fiat. Four Hispano-Suiza HS404 20-mm cannon were fitted in place of the British Hispano Mk Vs. The next version completed was the all-weather single-seat **Aquilon 203** fighter. Forty aircraft were completed with French APQ-65 radar, and a rear-sliding canopy. The Aquilon 203 had the pilot seating slightly to port and the radar to starboard in addition to a forward fuselage stretch of some 67 cm (6 in). The final Aquilon was the two-seat **Aquilon 204**, which closely resembled the 202. Six aircraft were built, all unarmed and with short-stroke undercarriage. Aquilons served with Flotilles 11 and 16 of the Aéronavale, and training squadrons 2S, 4S, 54S and 59S. Like the Vampires and Mistrals the Aquilon saw action in the fighting for Algeria.

One of the last Aquilon 202s built rolls off the wire aboard the aircraft carrier Clémenceau, after another successful recovery.

Sud-Est helicopters

Sud-Est work on helicopters began with the **Sud-Est S.E.3000**, which was a development of the Focke-Achgelis Fa 223, and Professor Heinrich Focke assisted the company in attempts to refine the design. After gaining initial experience with rotary-wing aircraft, Sud-Est initiated first the design for an experimental single-rotor purely functional helicopter designated **S.E.3101**. Powered by an 82-kW (110-hp) Mathis 4 GB 20 flat-four engine, it had a completely uncovered steel tube structure, with the pilot having only a windscreen to protect him from the elements. The open-work tailboom terminated in a 'butterfly' tail unit, with an anti-torque rotor mounted on each 'wing', and the helicopter was designed purely to test this rotor system. It must have been considered reasonably successful, for a two-seat enclosed-cabin lightweight helicopter using basically the same rotor system (comprising one main and two anti-torque tail rotors) was designed as the **S.E.3110**. However, the design underwent further revision before the first prototype was built. This was of typical pod-and-boom configuration, but the two-seat fuselage pod was only semi-enclosed, with simple twin-skid landing gear, and the tailboom was an open triangular lattice structure. The rotor system included a three-blade main rotor and two-blade anti-torque tail rotor both powered by a Salmson 9NH radial engine. Designated **S.E.3120 Alouette**, this helicopter was flown for the first time on 31 July 1952. Just less than a year later, on 2 July 1953, it was used to establish a new international closed-circuit duration record of 13 hours 56 minutes.

The name survives to this day, for the S.E.3120 marks the starting point of the highly-successful series of Alouette helicopters produced by Aérospatiale.

The S.E.3120 was the precursor of the classic Alouette light helicopter family, though unlike later models it was piston-powered.

Sud-Est military prototypes

The first of several prototypes to emerge from SNCASE was the **Sud-Est S.E.2410 Grognard**, a single-seat attack monoplane to be powered by two turbojets mounted one above the other within the rear fuselage. Before the start of construction a 58 per cent scale model was wind tunnel-tested and satisfactory results signalled a go-ahead. The **S.E.2410 Grognard I** was a mid-wing monoplane with swept wings and tail, its powerplant comprising two Rolls-Royce Nene turbojets licence-built by Hispano-Suiza. First flown on 30 April 1950, it was followed by the **S.E.2415 Grognard II** which differed by having an extended forward fuselage to house radar equipment, and it was planned that in production form this should include a second cockpit. Also projected was an **S.E.2421** all-weather fighter.

The slightly later **S.E.5000 Baroudeur** was a single-seat turbojet fighter that was independent of long runways, taking off from a trolley that could operate from grass fields, and landing on three retractable skids; these could also be used for take-off from snow- or ice-covered surfaces, and the trolley had provision for up to six rockets for rough ground assistance. The prototype was powered by a 27.46-kN (6,173-lb) thrust SNECMA Atar 101C turbojet and flew for the first time on 1 August 1953. It was followed by a generally similar second prototype on 12 May 1954, and just over two months later this aircraft exceeded Mach 1 in a shallow dive. Development continued with three **S.E.5003** pre-production prototypes powered by the 29.4-kN (6,614-lb) thrust Atar 101D, but no production of the Baroudeur followed.

The last of these interesting Sud-Est prototypes was the single-seat **S.E.212 Durandal**, a lightweight delta-wing interceptor with a 44-kN (9,921 lb) thrust SNECMA Atar G-3 turbojet, supplemented by a 8.09-kN (1,819-lb) thrust SEPR.65 rocket motor. The Durandal prototype was flown for the first time on 20 April 1956 and completed its test programme during 1957. A **Durandal IV** with a more powerful Atar turbojet was projected, but development of this aircraft was discontinued when Sud-Est (SNCASE) and Sud-Ouest (SNCASO) were merged on 1 March 1957 to form Sud-Aviation.

The S.E.5003 pre-production Baroudeur is seen here in landing configuration with skids down and brake parachute deployed.

Sud-Est S.E.2010 Armagnac

Developed from the **S.E.2000** project for a large-capacity long-range airliner, the **Sud-Est S.E.2010 Armagnac** prototype was flown for the first time on 2 April 1949. Although it did not prove successful in service, this large airliner represented a considerable forward step for the French aircraft industry with a circular-section pressurised fuselage that had a maximum diameter of 4.70 m (15 ft 5 in). A cantilever mid-wing monoplane with retractable tricycle landing gear, the main units having twin wheels, it was equipped as standard for a crew of six and 84 passengers but had the capacity to accommodate up to 160 in high-density seating. Production of 15 aircraft was planned for service with Air France, but after careful evaluation of prototype test results the airline declined to accept any. Instead, four went to Transports Aériens

Intercontinentaux (TAI), which inaugurated service with the type on 8 December 1952. This operator soon discovered the reason why Air France had declined to accept the Armagnac: it was uneconomical to operate and in less than eight months they had been withdrawn from service. They later carried out an important task for France, then deeply involved with problems in Indo-China, seven Armagnacs serving with the specially formed SAGETA airline to ferry cargo, mail and troops over a staged route from Toulouse to Saigon from late 1953 onwards. In spite of their value in this capacity no more were built.

Specification
Sud-Est S.E.2010 Armagnac
Type: long-range civil transport
Powerplant: four 2610-kW (3,500-hp)

Pratt & Whitney R-4360-B13 Wasp Major radial piston engines
Performance: maximum speed 495 km/h (308 mph) at 4500 m (14,765 ft); service ceiling 6800 m (22,310 ft); range 5120 km (3,181 miles)
Weights: empty 37813 kg (83,363 lb); maximum take-off 77500 kg (170,858 lb)
Dimensions: span 48.95 m (160 ft 7¼ in);

The S.E.2010 Armagnac was the production version of the Sud-Est S.E.2000 project, and the sole experimental development was the S.O.2060 engine test bed.

length 39.63 m (130 ft 0¼ in; height 13.50 m (44 ft 3½ in); wing area 235.60 m² (2,536.06 sq ft)

Sud-Ouest experimental and other aircraft

An interesting series of experimental aircraft designed and flown in prototype form by SNCASO included the **Sud-Ouest S.O.6000 Triton**, of which design and development began in secret during 1943. A mid-wing monoplane with thin-section, short-span wings, a tubby fuselage and retractable tricycle landing gear, this two-seat side-by-side trainer was the first turbojet-engined aircraft of indigenous design to fly in France. The first prototype was built during 1945 and flown for the first time on 11 November 1946, then powered by a Junkers Jumo 004 B2 turbojet. Four more prototypes were ordered with Rolls-Royce Derwent engines, but were in fact all powered by the Hispano-Suiza licence-built Rolls-Royce Nene, the first of them being flown on 19 March 1948.

Designed to meet requirements specified in the first French post-World War II military aircraft programme, the **S.O.6020 Espadon** (swordfish) single-seat interceptor was flown for the first time on 12 November 1948. This was the first **S.O.6020.01** prototype, a cantilever mid-wing monoplane with swept wings, powered by a Hispano-Suiza-built Nene and without armament. The **S.O.6020.02**, with revised air inlets and fin, and carrying an armament of six cannon, was flown on 30 December 1949. The first prototype was modified subsequently to this configuration and from 1952 served as a research aircraft with two wingtip-mounted Turboméca Marboré turbojet

engines; it was later converted to have a supplementary rocket engine installed in the rear fuselage beneath the jetpipe, then becoming redesignated **S.O.6026**. The third of the original prototypes ordered, the **S.O.6020.03**, was not built as such but modified to carry an auxiliary liquid-fuel rocket and jettisonable propellant tanks beneath the fuselage, becoming redesignated **S.O.6025**. Nearest to a production version was the **S.O.6021**, developed from the basic **S.O.6020.02**, but of lighter-weight structure and with powered controls, a smaller pressurised and air-conditioned cockpit equipped with ejection seat, and armed with either six 20-mm or four 30-mm cannon.

Experience gained with the wingtip-mounted turbojets on the S.O.6020.02 Espadon led to initial adoption of this powerplant for the **S.O.9000 Trident** mixed-powerplant research aircraft, flown first on 2 March 1953 and then powered by two Turboméca Marboré II turbojets. In the following year the planned SEPR.481 rocket motor was installed, the Trident first flew with this engine operative on 4 September 1954 and soon after this the Marboré turbojets were replaced by two Dassault M.D.30 Viper ASV.5 turbojets; with the use of its mixed powerplant a speed in excess of Mach 1.5 was recorded. A second prototype was lost during its first flight, but the capability of the first prototype led to a contract for two structurally-refined **S.O.9050 Trident II** prototypes and six pre-production air-

craft were ordered later. The first of the pre-production aircraft was flown on 3 May 1957, its powerplant comprising two Dassault M.D.30s plus an SEPR.631 rocket motor. One of the pre-production aircraft set a world altitude record of 24217 m (79,452 ft) on 2 May 1958, but soon afterwards the production programme was abandoned in favour of the Mirage III.

Of a very different nature and speed range was the **S.O.1310 Farfadet**, an experimental convertiplane combining a three-blade main rotor driven by compressed air with conventional tractor-propeller powerplant and fixed wings. The rotor enabled the Farfadet to take off vertically, hover and land vertically, and the normal powerplant meant it could fly normally in horizontal flight, the rotor then autorotating and partially off-loading the wings. Its powerplant comprised a 268-kW (360-hp) Turboméca Arrius II turbo-compressor to provide compressed air, plus a 268-kW (360-hp) Turboméca Artouste II turboprop engine. The first full transitional flight,

from vertical take-off to horizontal flight and reverse was achieved on 1 July 1953, and its cruising speed in horizontal flight was approximately 240 km/h (149 mph).

One aircraft flown in 1949 and of far less interesting configuration was the **S.O.7010 Pégase** eight-seat light transport. It had an unusual powerplant comprising two 172-kW (230-hp) Mathis 8GB 22 engines mounted back-to-back to form an X-engine and driving through a common gearbox a variable-pitch propeller. A freewheeling interconnection within the gearbox permitted choice of engines to power the propeller, providing for continued safe flight in the event of an engine failure. The last of these Sud-Ouest aircraft was the S.O.7060 Deauville two/three-seat lightplane, a cantilever low-wing monoplane of all-metal construction which, powered by a 78-kW (105-hp) Walter Minor 4-III inline engine, had a maximum speed of 205 km/h (127 mph).

The Espadon was produced in several versions, the one illustrated being the S.O.6025 fitted with liquid-propellant rockets.

Sud-Ouest S.O.30P Bretagne

Following the invasion of France in 1940, a group of Sud-Ouest designers and engineers from factories in the occupied zone became established in Cannes during May 1941 as the Groupe Technique de Cannes, designing and building the prototypes of several aircraft, two of which entered production after the end of war in Europe. The first of these was for a medium-capacity civil transport designated originally **Sud-Ouest S.O.30N**, a cantilever mid-wing all-metal monoplane with retractable tricycle gear, and powered, as flown for the first time on 26 February 1945, by two 1193-kW (1,600-hp) Gnome-Rhône 14R radial engines. Initial production version was the **S.O.30P** which became available as

the **S.O.30P-1** with two 1342-kW (1,800-hp) Pratt & Whitney R-2800-B43 engines, or as the **S.O.30P-2** with the 1790-kW (2,400-hp) R-2800-CA18 and other refinements, the type being named **Bretagne**. Standard accommodation was for a crew of five including stewardess and 30 to 43 passengers. Also available was a cargo version designated **S.O.30C**, with a revised interior incorporating a lowered and strengthened cargo floor, large loading doors in the undersurface of the rear fuselage, and power provided by two Gnome-

The S.O.30P-2 Bretagne was designed, during wartime, for civil operations and then later adapted for air force and naval use.

Rhône 14R.81 engines developing 1380 kW (1,850 hp) with water injection. Production was to total only 45, these serving with Air France, Air Algérie, smaller airlines in the French colonies and with the Armée de l'Air and Aéronavale. Some of the S.O.30P-1

aircraft had auxiliary power provided by two underwing Turboméca Pallas turbojet engines, and powerplants flown experimentally in the Bretagne included the SNECMA Atar 101 and Hispano-Suiza licence-built Rolls-Royce Nene turbojet engines.

Sud-Ouest S.O.95 Corse II

The second of the Groupe Technique de Cannes prototypes to enter production after the war was the **Sud-Ouest S.O.95 Corse II** light mail/passenger transport, which had originated as the **S.O.90**. Carrying nine passengers this had made a dramatic first flight from France to Algiers during the war, despite continual vigilance by the German-Italian armistice control commission. Post-war it was to be developed via **S.O.93** and **S.O.94** prototypes to the series-built S.O.95 Corse II, which flew for the first time on 17 July 1947. A cantilever mid-wing monoplane with retractable tail-wheel landing gear, powered by two wing-mounted

This Sud-Ouest S.O.95 Corse II served with Escadrille de Servitude 50 for transport and training duties.

Renault 12S engines, it accommodated a crew of two with 10 to 13 passengers according to interior layout. The seating could be removed easily for deployment in cargo- or mail-carrying roles. The Corse II had been intended for service on the domestic routes of Air France, but failing to meet the airline's requirements was built instead to a total of 60 aircraft for the Aéronavale, plus a very small number which were used by minor overseas airlines.

Specification
Sud-Ouest S.O.95 Corse II
Type: light mail/passenger transport
Powerplant: two 440-kW (590-hp) Renault 12S-02-201 inverted-Vee piston engines
Performance: maximum cruising speed 350 km/h (217 mph) at 2700 m (8,860 ft); range 1300 km (808 miles) **Weights:** empty 4024 kg (8,871 lb); maximum take-off 5605 kg (12,357 lb) **Dimensions:** span 17.90 m (58 ft 8¾ in); length 12.35m (40 ft 6¼ in); height 4.30 m (14 ft 1¼ in)

Sud-Ouest S.O.1100 Ariel

Early company interest in the development of rotary wing aircraft led to design and construction of the **Sud-Ouest S.O.1100 Ariel I**, an all-metal helicopter with an enclosed cabin for two. The company had sought simplicity by the use of a single three-blade torqueless rotor, driven by tip jets. Thus' its powerplant comprised a 164-kW (220-hp) Mathis G8 engine driving a Turboméca compressor, providing low-pressure air which was fed through the hollow rotor blades to the combustion

chambers of the tip jets, where the air was mixed with fuel and ignited electrically. In its original form as the **Ariel I**, first flown in 1947, the helicopter had a stubby tail boom incorporating twin vertical surfaces. The improved **S.O. 1110 Ariel II**, flown on 23 March 1949, was of generally similar configuration but had revised twin tail surfaces. However, the two-unit powerplant of these first two prototypes was heavy, and in the improved **S.O.1120 Ariel III** it was replaced by a much

An experimental design with tip-jet propulsion, the S.O.1110 Ariel II was powered by a 164-kW (220-hp) Mathis G8 piston engine.

lighter weight 205-kW (275-shp) Turboméca Arrius turbine-compressor unit, the weight saving making it possible to accommodate an additional passenger. The **Ariel III** also differed from its predecessor by having a tail unit that was basically a single fin and rudder, but supplemented in its steering capability by the efflux from the turbine. This was ducted to the tail and could be discharged on either side under the

control of deflector vanes coupled to the conventional rudder. The Ariel was not to be built as a production helicopter, but the data gained from this powered rotor system was to be of value in development of the S.O.1220 Djinn.

Sud-Ouest S.O.1221 Djinn

Experience with the experimental Ariel helicopters brought conviction that it should be possible to drive a helicopter rotor by compressed air jets at the blade tips, avoiding the added weight of fuel and ignition systems that had been required by the tip jets of the Ariel aircraft. Thus, on 2 January 1953 SNCASO flew the **Sud-Ouest S.O.1220** test vehicle, a simple uncovered structure of welded steel tube carrying a two-blade rotor above it, and with a single exposed seat for its pilot. Its powerplant was a Turboméca Palouste turbo-compressor producing a large volume of compressed air which, using a similar distribution method to that of the Ariel, was discharged at the blade tips. Testing showed the system to be an improvement upon the tip jets, leading to the

construction of five two-seat **S.O.1221** prototypes with a fully enclosed cabin, the first of them making its initial flight on 16 December 1953. Just 13 days later this aircraft established a new class altitude record of 4789 m (15,712 ft).

French army interest speeded the construction of 22 pre-production aircraft, most of them for service evaluation, and the first of these was flown on 23 September 1954. Somewhat later, three aircraft from this pre-production batch were acquired by the US Army for evaluation under the designation **YHO-1**. The French army was enthusiastic about the capability and simplicity of the **S.O.1221 Djinn**, ordering 100, and these were used for casualty evacuation (with a pilot and two external litters), liaison, observa-

tion and training. Another military user was the Federal German army which acquired six. The first production aircraft was flown on 5 January 1956, and French and US certification was gained in April 1958. When production ended in the mid-1960s a total of 178 had been built, exported to about 10 countries. Many were used in an agricultural role, equipped with two tanks to contain liquid chemicals and spray bars for its distribution. By the time that production ended Sud-Ouest had twice changed its name, to Ouest-Aviation on 1 September 1956 and Sud-Aviation on 1 March 1957 when it merged with Sud-Est Aviation; this explains why the Djinn is sometimes recorded as the **Ouest S.O.1221** or **Sud-Aviation S.O.1221**.

Specification
Sud-Ouest S.O.1221 Djinn
Type: two-seat light helicopter

The turbine-powered S.O.1221 Djinn was built in modest numbers, but soon overtaken in performance and capability by the Alouette II and III series.

Powerplant: one 179-kW (240-hp) Turboméca Palouste IV turbo-compressor **Performance:** maximum speed 130 km/h (81 mph); endurance with standard fuel 2 hours 15 minutes **Weights:** empty 360 kg (794 lb); maximum take-off, military 800 kg (1,764 lb) **Dimensions:** rotor diameter 11.00 m (36 ft 1 in); length of fuselage 5.30 m (17 ft 4½ in); height 2.60 m (8 ft 6¼ in)

Sud-Ouest S.O.4050 Vautour

As stages in the development of an advanced high-performance experimental twin-jet bomber, Sud-Ouest designed and built two half-scale models. The first of these was the **Sud-Ouest S.O.M.1**, which was a pure glider, launched from a Languedoc 161 'mother-plane' for the first time on 26 September 1949. It was followed by the second model, the **S.O.M.2** powered by a single Rolls-Royce Derwent turbojet engine, and first flown on 13 April 1949. Experience gained with these two aircraft led to the **S.O.4000** prototype, a cantilever mid-wing monoplane of all-metal construction with extremely clean lines. Its retractable landing gear differed from that of the M.2 in having a single nosewheel and four main-wheels, in tandem pairs. Accommodation was provided for two, in tandem, in the nose of the aircraft and the powerplant consisted of two Hispano-Suiza licence-built Rolls-Royce

Sud-Ouest S.O.4050 Vatour of EB 2/92 'Aquitaine', Armée de l'Air, based at Bordeaux in the early 1970s.

Nene turbojets mounted in the rear fuselage. The S.O.4000 was flown for the first time on 15 March 1951.

Subsequently the **S.O.4050 Vautour** was developed, and was to be ordered in quantity for the Armée de l'Air. The S.O.4050 differed considerably from its predecessor, but bene-

fited from the experience with systems and controls that had been evaluated with the half-scale models and the prototype. Of similar mid-wing configuration, it had swept wings and tail surfaces, retractable landing gear comprising two twin-wheel main units in tandem with single small outriggers

retracting into the nacelles of the engines which, in the S.O.4050, were mounted beneath the wing. Sud-Ouest received an order for three prototypes, the first of them being flown on 16 October 1952. These comprised the **S.O.4050-01**, completed as a two-seat all-weather fighter and powered initially by two 23.5-kN (5,291-lb) thrust SNECMA Atar 101B turbojets; the **S.O.4050-02** single-seat ground-attack aircraft with two 27.6-kN (6,217-lb) thrust Atar 101D turbojets, first flown on 16 December 1953; and the **S.O.4050-3** two-seat bomber with two Armstrong Siddeley Sapphire turbojets, flown on 5 December 1954. Testing of these aircraft led to an order for six pre-production aircraft, the last of them a two-seat all-weather fighter which powered by two 44.5-kN (10,000-lb) thrust Rolls-Royce Avon R.A.14 turbojets, made its first flight on 18 October 1955. Full service evaluation of these aircraft led to production

orders for the Vautour in all three versions, and when production ended a total of 140 had been built for the Armée de l'Air with the Atar 101E as the standard powerplant. They comprised 30 **Vautour II-A** single-seat tactical fighters, the first flown on 30 April 1956; 40 Vautour II-B two-seat bombers the first flown on 31 July 1957, and 70 **Vautour II-N** two-seat all-weather fighters, the first flown on 10 October 1956. Eighteen were supplied subsequently to the Israeli air force. Accommodation varied according to role, all crew positions being pressurised and provided with ejection seats, and armament differed consid-

erably, although that of the bomber was similar to that of the tactical support version, described below, except that it did not have the nose-mounted cannon. The all-weather Vautour II-N had the DEFA 30-mm cannon and was armed with rockets and missiles, but also had radar. The designation was changed to **Vautour II-1N** after the later fitting of slab tailplanes.

Specification
Sud-Ouest S.O.4050 Vautour II-A
Type: single-seat tactical fighter
Powerplant: two 34.3-kN (7,716-lb) thrust SNECMA Atar 101E-3 turbojets
Performance: maximum speed 1105

km/h (687 mph); maximum rate of climb 3600 m (11,810 ft) per minute; service ceiling more than 15000 m (49,210 ft)
Weights: empty 10000 kg (22,046 lb); maximum take-off 20000 kg (44,092 lb)
Dimensions: span 15.09 m (49 ft 6⁄ in); length 15.57 m (51 ft 1 in); height 4.50 m (14 ft 9⁄ in)
Armament: four 30-mm DEFA cannon in fuselage nose, up to 240 rockets or 10 bombs in the fuselage bomb bay, and underwing pylons suitable for a total of 76 MATRA M.116E rockets, or 24 120-mm rockets, or two bombs of up to 450 kg (992 lb); or two fuel drop tanks

Sukhoi aircraft 1939-49

After working for A. N. Tupolev, supervising the design of several successful Tupolev aircraft (including the I-4 fighter, and the ANT-25), Pavel Sukhoi was finally invited to open his own OKB (design bureau) in December 1938. Apart from development and production of the ANT-51 under the designation Su-2, the Sukhoi OKB enjoyed little success before it was closed down on Stalin's orders in 1949, producing only a succession of prototypes. It was not until after Stalin's death in 1953 that the disgraced Sukhoi (who had been reassigned as an assistant to Tupolev) was given permission to resurrect his OKB, leading to a new and more successful generation of aircraft. Brief details of the designs built up to 1949 follow.

The **Sukhoi Su-1** (OKB number 330) was a high-altitude single-seat fighter prototype of low-wing monoplane configuration, with retractable tail-wheel landing gear. First flown in October 1940, it was powered by a 820-kW (1,100-hp) M-105P engine with twin TK turbochargers, giving a maximum speed of 640 km/h (398 mph) at 10000 m (32,810 ft). However, unreliability of the turbochargers ended development. A development of the Su-1 was flown briefly in 1943 before its development was abandoned; this was the I-360 or **Su-3**, with reduced wing span and minor design revisions. The **Su-6** prototype was flown in the spring of 1941 and was a single-seat

low-wing monoplane with retractable landing gear intended for use in the Shturmovik role it had armour protection for the pilot, self-sealing main fuel tank, fixed armament of two cannon and four machine-guns and a disposable load of bombs carried internally and rockets borne externally. The second **Su-6(A)** prototype had a 1491-kW (2,000-hp) M-71 radial engine. The **Su-6(2A)** had two-seat accommodation for pilot and gunner with revised armament and a 1641-kW (2,200-hp) ASh-71F engine. The final prototype was the **Su-6 (2A-AM-42)** with 1491-kW (2,000-hp) AM-42 V-12 engine. A derived single seater was the **Su-7,** a mixed-power experimental high-altitude fighter prototype based on the airframe of the Su-6(A) and powered by a turbocharged radial engine, though in its final design form the aircraft was powered by a 1380-kW (1,850-hp) ASh-82FN radial with two TK-3 turbochargers and a 2.94-kN (661-lb) thrust RD-1-KhZ rocket; development was abandoned in 1945.

In the same year the first of two **Su-8** prototypes was flown, a two-seat twin-engine Shturmovik of mid-wing monoplane configuration, with endplate fins on the tailplane. Powered by two 1641-kW (2,200-hp) ASh-71F radials and heavily armed, it did not enter production as it was not required. The larger **ER-2OH** was of similar configuration, but with a cranked wing, and was a bomber/transport design, as was the UTB bomber. An interim step towards jet propulsion

was introduced in the I-107 or **Su-5** first flown in early 1945. This was a conventional single-seat low-wing monoplane, but its powerplant comprised a modified 1230-kW (1,650-hp) VK-1 7A V-12 engine with propeller that, could also be clutched in to drive a VRDK compressor. This had several fuel-burning combustion chambers that with a 10-minute limitation, could provide the thrust equivalent to an additional 671 kW (900 hp). Development was abandoned in summer 1945 when the superiority of the turbojet was recognised.

Sukhoi's first jet-powered interceptor, known as **aircraft K** or **Su-9** was similar in configuration to the Messerschmitt Me 262, albeit with straight, unswept wings, and powered by two 8.8-kN (1,984-lb) thrust RD-10 turbojets. The first of two prototypes was flown on 18 August 1946 but, despite good performance with a maximum speed of 900 km/h (559 mph) at 8000 m (26,245 ft), there were no series-built aircraft as, reportedly, no production capacity was available. An improved **LK** or **Su-11** aircraft was flown in October 1947 with 12.7-kN (2,866-lb) thrust TR-1 turbojets, but the unreliability of these engines led to development being abandoned in 1948, the larger **Su-13 (aircraft KD)** being cancelled at the same time. This had massive engine nacelles housing RD-500 engines and was fitted with swept, variable-incidence tailplanes, and did not fly. The **Su-12** closely resembled the Fw 189 in its configuration, and first flew in December 1947. This saw a reversion to piston engines, being

powered by two wing-mounted 1380-kW (1,850-hp) ASh-82FN radials. It was well armed and armoured and had a speed of 530 km/h (329 mph) at 5300 m (17,390 ft), but was not ordered into production as, by then, it was regarded as outdated. Under construction at the same time as the Su-12, **aircraft E** or the **Su-10** four-jet day bomber was to have been powered by four 14.7-kN (3,307-lb) thrust TR-1A turbojets mounted in staggered pairs, one above the other, at the wing leading edges. Although completed the aircraft was never flown, ending its days as a taxiing trainer. Now seen to be the forerunners of Sukhoi's modern generation of highly successful combat aircraft were **aircraft P** (**Su-15**) flown on 11 January 1949 and **aircraft R** (**Su-17**), which was incomplete when Sukhoi's OKB was closed down in late 1949. The cumbersome-looking Su-15 was a single-seat all-weather interceptor with swept wing and tail surfaces, retractable tricycle landing gear, and a deep fuselage, with nose radome and underslung 'chin' intake. It was powered by two 21.6-kN (4,850-lb) afterburning thrust RD-45F turbojets, installed (staggered) one above the other in the fuselage, but with loss of the prototype on 3 June 1949 further development was abandoned. The **Su-17**, which was designed as a supersonic day fighter and would have been powered by a TR-3 turbojet without afterburner, was incomplete when the Sukhoi OKB activities ended on 1 November 1949. It looked rather like a stretched Lavochkin La-15.

Sukhoi Su-2

Sukhoi Su-2 of a Red Air Force operational training unit in the winter of 1941-42.

Pavel O. Sukhoi began his design career as a member of Tupolev's team at AGOS in 1924. He then participated in a series of Tupolev designs, eventually supervising a virtually independant 'brigade' within the OKB. His designs included the ANT-37A bomber/record-breaker, and the ANT-51. This was a low-wing monoplane intended for tactical reconnaissance and ground attack. The first prototype, flown on 25 August 1937, was powered by an 611-kW (820-hp) M-62 radial engine, but further prototypes with retractable landing gear and more powerful M-87A and M-87B engines were developed. After further redesign and the successful completion of state trials in autumn 1940, the aircraft was ordered into production as the **Su-2** (Sukhoi's brigade having gained OKB status) and allocated the military designation **BB-1** (BB signifying short-range bomber). A cantilever low-wing monoplane with fully retractable tail-wheel landing gear, early

production aircraft were powered by the 708-kW (950-hp) M-88 radial. Pilot and observer/gunner were housed under a long glazed canopy, terminating in a manually-operated gun turret, and both crew had 0.35-in (9-mm) armour protection.

The later production version of the Su-2, powered by a 746-kW (1,000-hp) M-88B engine, was highly regarded by air regiments, until its many shortcom-

ings were revealed by war. The Su-2 was comparable with similar light bombers built in other countries, but the German invasion of June 1941 dramatically demonstrated that light bombers operating at low and medium altitudes were unacceptably vulnerable to enemy fighters unless provided with powerful fighter cover. Nevertheless, production and development continued until the type was phased out of pro-

duction in late 1942, the final version having the M-82 engine. Some Su-2s had been fitted with a second machine-gun in the gun turret and others had a ventral gun on a retractable mounting, but in early 1941 M-88B-powered aircraft were flying with only two wing guns and maximum bombload restricted to 400 kg (882 lb), in a desparate bid to improve performance. From 1942, when most Su-2 regiments had re-equipped with Ilyushin Il-2s, two or three Su-2s were attached to each Shturmovik unit to act as formation leaders and fly reconnaissance, target towing, training and liaison missions.

Variants
ShB: single prototype of improved ground-attack version flown early in 1940 with revised landing gear, more armour, increased bombload of 600 kg (1,323 lb) and 746-kW (1,000-hp) M-88A
Su-4: improved version of Su-2 with 1566-kW (2,100-hp) Shvetsov M-90 engine, armament of two wing-mounted 0.5-in (12.7-mm) BS machine-guns and two 0.3-in (7.62-mm) ShKAS guns in turret, but no underwing racks for offensive stores as Su-4 classed as light bomber; flown December 1941, but production confirmation was the subject of conflicting and confused reports; if built at all probably only in small numbers

Specification
Sukhoi Su-2 (late production)
Type: light bomber/reconnaissance aircraft
Powerplant: one 1044-kW (1,400-hp) Shvetsov M-82 radial piston engine
Performance: maximum speed 486 km/h (302 mph) at 5800 m (19,030 ft); service ceiling 9000 m (29,530 ft); range 1100 km (684 miles)
Weights: empty 3273 kg (7,216 lb); maximum take-off 4700 kg (10,362 lb)
Dimensions: span 14.30 m (46 ft 11 in); length 10.46 m (34 ft 3¼ in); wing area 29.00 m (312.16 sq ft)
Armament: up to nine 0.3-in (7.62-mm) ShKAS machine-guns and up to 400 kg (882lb) of bombs and RS-82/RS-130 rockets on underwing racks

Sukhoi Su-7

After the closure of the Sukhoi OKB in November 1949, Pavel Sukhoi continued his design work under Tupolev. With Stalin's death in 1953, he was given permission to re-establish his design bureau. His first task was to initiate the construction of prototypes of the **S-1**, a low/mid-wing monoplane with swept wings and all-swept tail surfaces which, although derived from the S-17 of 1949, had no commonality of components. Powered by the 63.7-kN (14,330-lb) thrust Lyulka AL-7 turbojet, or afterburning versions of this engine rated at 78.5-kN (17,637-lb) thrust, the S-1 prototypes were used to evaluate various aerodynamic features and armament-configurations. One S 1 with a special AL-7F engine established a national air record of 2170 km/h (1,348 mph) in 1957.

Continuing development led to the **S-2** prototypes which introduced an all-moving tailplane, followed by **S-22** pre-production aircraft incorporating a bulged rear fuselage (effectively area-ruling it). This led to the **Sukhoi Su-7B** (NATO **'Fitter-A'**) which was ordered into production in 1958. Planned as a fighter to intercept the F-100 and F-101, it became, in its various versions, the standard tactical fighter-bomber of the Soviet air forces and was also supplied to Afghanistan, Algeria, Czechoslovakia, Egypt, India, Iraq, North Korea, Poland, Syria, and South Yemen.

Variants
Su-7B: initial production version with AL-7F engine of 88.2-kN (19,842-lb) afterburning thrust
Su-7BM: improved version of Su-7B introducing AL-7F-1 engine, fuselage duct fairings, relocated instrument boom and, progressively during production, JATO (jet-assisted take-off) attachments, tail-warning radar, twin braking parachutes and zero-altitude ejection seat, and lacking the retractable rocket box of the Su-7B
Su-7BKL: production version for operation from unprepared airfields, with redesigned landing gear and flaps, with low-pressure tyres and a steel skid outboard of each main wheel; twin brake chutes in enlarged fairing at base of rudder
Su-7BMK: production version, with upgraded undercarriage of Su-7BKL

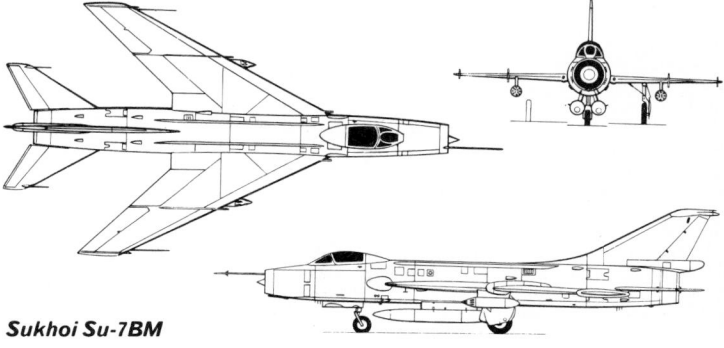

Sukhoi Su-7BM

and new RWR, ILS and rocket-powered KM-1 ejection seat
Su-7U and **Su-7UM:** two-seat trainer versions of Su-7BM and Su-7BMK respectively, all with NATO reporting name **'Moujik'**

Specification
Sukhoi Su-7BMK
Type: ground-attack fighter
Powerplant: one 98-kN (22,046-lb) afterburning thrust Lyulka AL-7F-1 turbojet
Performance: maximum speed clean 1700 km/h (1,056 mph) or Mach 1.6 at 11000 m (36,090 ft) service ceiling, clean 15150 m (49,700 ft); typical combat radius 320 km (199 miles)
Weights: empty 8636 kg (19,040 lb); maximum take-off 14800 kg (32,628 lb)
Dimensions: span 8.93 m (29 ft 3⅜ in); length 17.37 m (57 ft 0 in) height 4.57 m (15 ft 0 in)
Armament: two 30-mm NR-30 cannon in wing roots, plus underwing pylons for two 750-kg (1,653-lb) and two 500-kg (1,102-lb) bombs, but limited to weapon load of 1000 kg (2,204 lb) when two drop tanks are carried

Sukhoi Su-9 and Su-11 and related prototypes

In parallel with work on the swept-wing S-1, Sukhoi produced a family of single-engined delta-winged prototypes which used a basically similar fuselage, tail unit and undercarriage. The first of these was the **T-3** which first flew in early 1956, and which featured a radome in the top of the intake lip. The T-3 was developed through a series of research prototypes (including the **PT-7** with centrebody and lip radomes, and the long-nosed **PT-8**) to the **T-40** which is regarded as the prototype of the **Sukhoi Su-9** (NATO **'Fishpot-B'**) single-seat all-weather fighter. Of low/mid-wing configuration with retractable tricycle landing gear, the Su-9 was powered by the 88.2-kN (19,842-lb) afterburning thrust Lyulka AL-7F turbojet and had underwing pylons to carry its sole armament of four AA-1 (NATO **'Alkali'**) semi-active radar homing missiles. Development continued and the **T-43** flown in the Tushino Aviation Day display in 1961 was the prototype of an improved version which had the designation **Su-11** (NATO **'Fishpot-C'**).

The Sukhoi Su-9 spanned 8.43 m (27 ft 8 in), had an MTOW of 12000 kg (26,450 lb) and could reach 1915 km/h (1,100 mph) at low level.

Basically similar to the Su-9, it differed primarily by having a lengthened and bulged forward fuselage to house more powerful Uragan 5B radar, was armed as standard with two AA-3 (NATO 'Anab') infra-red or semi-active radar homing missiles, and introduced the more powerful Lyulka AL-7F-1 engine. A tandem two-seat trainer **Su-9U** was also built, with the NATO reporting name **'Maiden'**.

The Su-9 entered service during 1959 and was superseded in production by the Su-11 in about 1966. Combined production has been estimated at about 2,000 aircraft. None entered service with Warsaw Pact countries or have been exported. It has been reported that from the early 1970s many were converted for use as radio-controlled targets and most had been retired by 1980.

Specification
Sukhoi Su-11
Type: all-weather fighter
Powerplant: one 98-kN (22,046-lb) afterburning thrust Lyulka AL-7F-1 turbojet
Performance: maximum speed clean 1915 km/h (1,190 mph) or Mach 1.8 at 11000 m (36,090 ft); service ceiling 17000 m (55,775 ft); combat radius with weapons 460 km (286 miles)
Weights: empty 9100 kg (20,062 lb); maximum take-off 14000 kg (30,865 lb)
Dimensions: span 8.43m (27 ft 8 in); length 17.40 m (57 ft 1 in); wing area 26.20 m (282.02 sq ft)
Armament: standard weapons two AA-3 air-to-air homing missiles on underwing pylons

Sukhoi Su-15 and related prototypes

Developed to meet a requirement for a higher-performance interceptor to supersede the Su-11, the **Sukhoi Su-15** was first seen at the 1967 Aviation Day display. The Su-15 originally bore the internal bureau designation **T-58**, and was derived from the one-off T-5 prototype. This was basically a scaled-up version of the Su-9/Su-11 family powered by two turbojet engines, with the same pitot nose intake. The T-58 introduced a solid radar nose and variable F-4-type intakes on the fuselage sides building on experience gained with the single-engined **T-49** and **P-1** prototypes. First entering service with Soviet home defence units in 1967, some 1,500 Su-15s in all versions are estimated to have been built. None have served with Warsaw Pact nations or have been exported, and only a handful remain in operational service in 1993, with an estimated two PVO regiments, although replacement by Su-27s and MiG-31s is proceeding apace.

Variants
Sukhoi T-58: internal OKB designation for Su-15 prototypes (based on eighth version of basic T-5 configuration); first flew 30 May 1962; delivered to air force for service use as **Su-15-98** pending availability of production aircraft.
Su-15 'Flagon-A': initial production version with short-span (8.616 m) wing

and Oriol-D radar; armed with two R-8M (early AA-3 'Anab') missiles and provision for two UPK-23 cannon pods; powered by two R11F2S-300 turbojets.

Sukhoi T-58L (T-58VD) 'Flagon-B': experimental V/STOL aircraft, also erroneously known as Su-15DPD, which introduced three Kolesov lift-jet engines in a centre-fuselage bay; possibly engine testbed for V/STOL T-6-1 forerunner of Su-24

Sukhoi Su-15 'Flagon-D': first large-scale production version, similar to earlier 'Flagon-A' but with increased-span wings (9.34 m) and with two R-98 (AA-3 'Anab') missiles and provision for gun pods.

Sukhoi Su-15T 'Flagon-E': generally similar to 'Flagon-D' but introduced 'Typhoon' radar (still in straight conical radome) and more powerful engines, Tumanskii R-13-300s each of afterburning thrust; strengthened undercarriage to cope with higher all-up weight, including twin nosewheels; production curtailed by failure of original Typhoon radar; some sources suggest production as low as 10

Sukhoi Su-15UT 'Flagon-C': two-seat trainer version of Su-15T, with individual canopy over each seat; periscope provided for rear cockpit to enhance forward view; retains armament and, thus, may retain combat capability; noted before single-seat Su-15T (and Su-15 'Flagon-D') and therefore allocated earlier NATO reporting name

Su-15TM 'Flagon-F': most recent production version, believed to have been designed in 1971 and to have entered service in 1975; generally similar to 'Flagon-E' but introduced ogival nose radome covering scanner for modified 'Typhoon M' radar and more powerful engines; introduced improved R-98M version of AA-3 missile; an Su-15TM armed with AA-3s and underfuselage gun pods was used to shoot down a Korean Air Lines 747 in 1983; erroneously reported to be Su-21 for some years.

Su-15UM 'Flagon-G': two-seat trainer version of Su-15TM.

Specification
Sukhoi Su-15TM 'Flagon-F'
Type: single-seat, all-weather interceptor
Powerplant: two 70-kN (15,730-lb)

afterburning thrust Tumanskii R-13-300 turbojets

Performance: maximum speed, clean at optimum altitude 2230 km/h (1,385 mph); service ceiling 18,500 m (60,700 ft); combat range with weapons 1780 km (1,100 miles)
Weights: (estimated) maximum take-off combat 17200 kg (37,918 lb)
Dimensions: span 9.34 m (30 ft 8 in); length 21.41 m (70 ft 3 in); wing area 36.60 m (394 sq ft)
Armament: four underwing pylons

carry an R-98M (NATO AA-3 'Anab') on each outboard position (one infra-red, one semi-active radar homing) and a close-range R-60 (NATO AA-8 'Aphid') on each inboard position, while two underbelly pylons can be used for UPK-23 gun pods or fuel tanks

This Sukhoi Su-15TM 'Flagon-F' is fitted with twin gun pods. and has a limited look-down/shoot-down capability courtesy of its radar and AA-3 'Anab' missiles.

Sukhoi Su-17, Su-20 and Su-22

Development of the Sukhoi Su-7 had ended with testing of the **S-22I** or **Su-7IG**. This was a variable-geometry aerodynamic testbed in which about 13 ft (3.96 m) of each outer wing panel pivoted; in other respects it was identical to the Su-7. A more powerful engine was introduced, and when tested in 1966 the **Su-7IG** (NATO **'Fitter-B'**) was found to have far superior performance to the standard Su-7 'Fitter-A' family, especially for short-field operations. Entering service in 1971 under the designation **Su-17**, this ground-attack fighter has since been produced in several versions and is in widespread service with the Russian air forces, other former Soviet air forces, and a wide range of export customers. Frontal Aviation have operated all versions, with the possible exception of the Tumanskii-engined **'Fitter-F'**, and similar **'Fitter-J'**.

Variants
Su-17M 'Fitter-C': initial production version for Soviet air forces with extra fuel, advanced avionics and Lyulka AL-21F-3 turbojet; the initial batch (Soviet designation Su-17, NATO possibly **'Fitter-B Mod'**) had less powerful AL7F-1 engines and retained the external cable ducts of late 'Fitter-As' but all had a dorsal spine and upward-hingeing canopy, in place of the original rear-sliding unit; later production aircraft (**Su-17M**) had new inboard wing fences, a new broader-chord three spar tailfin, a single brake chute in a smaller fairing, and twin pitots on the nose; Poland was the only export customer for the full-standard 'Fitter-C'

Su-20 'Fitter-C': export version of 'Fitter-C' but with reduced standard of equipment, supplied to Afghanistan, Algeria, Egypt, Iraq, North Korea and Vietnam

Su-17M-2 'Fitter-D': similar to above but introduced lengthened, drooping forward fuselage, with terrain-avoidance radar and Doppler in an undernose fairing, and with a laser rangefinder in the inlet centrebody

Su-17UM and UM-2D 'Fitter-E': trainer version of 'Fitter-C' with drooped nose to improve forward view

and starboard cannon only; some aircraft (**Su-17UM-2D**) have a dorsal fin fillet, and the Su-17M-style undernose sensor package.

Su-22 'Fitter-F': export version of 'Fitter-D' with similar undernose fairing and 112.8-kN (25,353-lb) afterburning thrust Tumanskii R-29B turbojet in an increased-diameter rear fuselage, able to deploy K-13A (NATO 'Atoll') air-to-air infra-red homing missile; dorsal fin fillet.

Su-17M-3 'Fitter-G': developed version of 'Fitter-E' which retains combat capability and introduced deep dorsal spine, increased fuel capacity, taller squared-off tailfin and sometimes with a small (detachable?) ventral fin; the reporting name of the Tumansky R-29B-powered **Su-22UM-3K** export two-seater remains unknown, although this was first seen in 1980; it may share the 'Fitter-G' appellation.

Su-17UM-3 'Fitter-H': single-seat version of 'Fitter-C' incorporating improvements introduced in 'Fitter-G', with similar bulged spine, ventral fin, and tall tail; enhanced avionics including compatability with anti radar missiles; some used in recce role with large external multi-sensor pod

Su-17M-3 'Fitter-H': externally almost identical to the Su-17M-1, the new variant introduces a new dedicated AAM pylon underwing, between the existing pylons; the aircraft have significantly improved avionics; hungary is the only export customer.

Su-22M-3K 'Fitter-J': generally similar to 'Fitter-H', but with Tumanskii R-29B turbojet and equipped to deploy K-13A 'Atoll' missiles; exported to Angola, Libya, Peru, Syria, and North and South Yemen.

Su-17M-4 'Fitter-K': the latest version, incorporating advanced avionics and with an uprated cooling system which provides the type's only external distinguishing feature – an airscoop on the leading edge of the tailfin root; the ventral fin is always fitted, and the aircraft is compatible with the same recce pod and anti-radar weapons as the 'Fitter-H'; the current Frontal Aviation variant, it has also been exported to Afghanistan, Czechoslovakia, East Germany, Poland, and Vietnam (as the **Su-22M-4K**?); blocks of chaff/flare dispensers can be scabbed onto the rear fuselage, this installation also having been retrofitted to some earlier variants

Specification
Sukhoi Su-17 'Fitter-C'
Type: attack fighter
Powerplant: one 109.8-kN (24,692-lb) afterburning thrust Lyulka AL-21F-3 turbojet
Performance: maximum speed at optimum altitude Mach 2.17; service ceiling 18000 m (59,055 ft); combat radius (hi-lo-hi) 630 km (391 miles)
Weights: empty 10000 kg (22,046 lb), maximum take-off 14000 kg (30,865 lb)
Dimensions: span, unswept 14.00 m (45 ft 11¾ in); swept 10.60 m (34 ft 9¼ in); length 18.75 m (61 ft 6¾ in); height 4.75 m (15 ft 7 in); wing area, unswept 40.10 m (431.65 sq ft)
Armament: two 30-mm cannon in wing roots, plus eight external pylons for up to 4000 kg (8,818 lb) of mixed stores that can include air-to-surface missiles such as AS-7 (NATO 'Kerry'), bombs, nuclear weapons and rockets

The front-line 'Fitter' units stationed in East Germany with the Group of Soviet Forces (16th Air Army) were equipped with the Su-17M-4 'Fitter-K'. In those nations to which this version was exported, such as Czechoslovakia and Poland, it was referred to as the SU-22M-4K.

Sukhoi Su-24

The increasing efficiency of defences led aircraft designers all over the world to the same conclusion: to penetrate, one would have to fly 'under the radar' at very low altitude, using terrain masking. The Sukhoi OKB was entrusted with the task of developing such a bomber as a replacement for the Ilyushin Il-28 and Yak-28.

The requirement was ambitious, calling for supersonic performance (even at low level), day and night, all-weather operation, and the ability to attack fixed and mobile targets with a secondary photographic reconnaissance capability. The requirement also specified that the aircraft should be able to operate from unpaved airstrips of limited size.

The latter part of the requirement led Sukhoi to develop a delta-winged VTOL bomber, with separate cruise and lift engines. This was built as the **T-6-1** and first flew in June 1967. The wing was of compound leading-edge sweep, and was based on the planform used by the **T-58VD**. Planned participation at Domodyedovo was cancelled because of the aircraft's atrocious handling characteristics and the aircraft was converted to STOL configuration, with the lift jets removed, and with downturned wingtips and prominent ventral fins and enormous new slotted flaps. The large size of the wing gave a poor low-level ride.

The success of the Su-17 and Mikoyan 23-11 pointed the way forward, which was to adopt a variable-geometry wing. This was applied to a second T-6 prototype (the **T-6-2IG**), retaining the same basic fuselage. The removal of the heavy lift jets from the centre fuselage left space for extra fuel or weapons. The wing, like that of the broadly contemporary F-111, incorporated similar full-span leading-edge slats and double-slotted flaps. The wing can be swept forward to 16° for take-off and landing, giving a low approach speed and good STOL capability. The wing can be swept back to 69° with intermediate settings of 35° and 45°. The aircraft made its maiden flight during May 1970, powered by a pair of AL-7F-1 turbojets. It was given the cover designation **Su-15M**, and mistranslation of this led to initial Western reports referring to the aircraft as the 'Su-19'.

The production **Su-24 'Fencer-A'** was powered by a pair of Perm/Soloviev AL-21F-3 turbofans. These were originally fed by intakes with variable ramps, which allowed Mach 2.18 performance at high level. The actuators have since been removed to save weight. This restricts top speed to about Mach 1.35, but has virtually no effect on low-level perfor-

The Su-24M 'Fencer-D' is a nuclear-capable strike aircraft, that has been exported to several nations. This Soviet example carries conventional FAB 250 bombs and AS 14 laser-guided ASMs.

mance where very high Mach numbers cannot be attained.

The Su-24 was designed around the Soviet Union's first integrated avionics system, with a bombsight, weapons control system and navigation complex linked by computer. The Su-24 was also the first Soviet aircraft to be equipped with the zero-zero K-36D ejection seat, and also featured a command ejection system which could be actuated by either crew member.

Relatively minor changes in equipment fit resulted in the allocation of new NATO reporting names, although the Soviet designation remained the same, and NATO's different variants were probably regarded in the USSR as a single sub-type, albeit with minor differences in equipment. **'Fencer-B'** had a rear fuselage more closely following the jet pipes, by comparison with the 'boxed-in', slab-sided rear fuselage of the prototypes and 'Fencer-A'. It also introduced a brake chute fairing below the base of the rudder. The **'Fencer-C'** is similar but with triangular RWR fairings on the sides of the fin tip and on the engine intakes extending ahead of the wing leading edge. Apart from a handful of early '-As' all three sub-types have a small air intake at the base of the fin leading edge and the same kink in the tailfin leading edge. Because a control column can easily be fitted in front of the WSO, no dedicated dual controlled trainer variant of the Su-24 has been developed.

The Su-24 entered squadron service during 1974, and began to be deployed outside the USSR in 1979 when a regiment deployed to East Germany for operational evaluation. In 1984 a regiment began operations over Afghanistan, participating in air strikes against rebel targets in the Panjshir Valley.

Work on improving the Su-24's combat effectiveness began in 1975, eventually resulting in the **Su-24M 'Fencer-D'**, which entered service in 1986. This introduced a retractable inflight-refuelling probe above the nose, immediately ahead of the windscreen, and the ability to carry a UPAZ-A buddy refuelling pod on the centreline. The avionics suite was upgraded to allow the aircraft to carry a new generation of TV- and laser-guided weapons, to improve navigational and bombing accuracy, and to enhance survivability.

Most noticeably, the Su-24M received a new radar in a shortened, reshaped radome tipped by a single simple pitot in place of the multiple fittings of the earlier variants. The Kaira

laser and TV designator/tracker gives compatability with the newest Soviet ASMs, and is housed behind a glazed fairing on the centreline ahead of the gun and ammunition fairings. Survivability is enhanced by the improved defensive aids, which include RHAWS, a missile launch warning system, an active ECM, and chaff/flare dispensers.

Some 'Fencer-Ds' lack the large combined fences/underwing pylons, and this may indicate that they have been converted from 'Fencer-C' airframes, or that this fitting is a removeable extra. A handful of Su-24Ms in Soviet colours have been seen in this configuration, along with some (but definitely not all) export aircraft. Aircraft with these fences may qualify for the revised reporting name **'Fencer-D (Mod)'**. Export 'Fencer-Es' are designated **Su-24MK**, and presumably have a downgraded avionics system. Su-24s have been delivered to Libya, Iran, Iraq and Syria. The bomber 'Fencers' are armed with a single GSh-6-23M cannon in the starboard side of the lower fuselage, with the muzzle covered by an eyelid shutter. Ammunition is housed in the port underfuselage fairing. There are hardpoints for a centreline and two underfuselage pylons, with further pylons under the fixed inboard sections of the wing, and with swivelling pylons under the outboard panels. The aircraft can carry the free-fall TN-1000 and TN-1200 nuclear bombs, and a variety of conventional free fall bombs and ASMs.

The Su-24 airframe was a natural choice when it came to looking for a replacement for the Yak-28 'Brewer' in the tactical and maritime reconnaissance and tactical electronic warfare roles, since it combined long range and excellent performance with the ability to carry a reasonable payload. The resulting **Su-24MR 'Fencer-E'** was designed for the primary role of tactical reconnaissance using internal and podded sensors of various types, able to transmit reconnaissance data from some sensors to a ground station in real time. The aircraft also has secondary civilian roles of ecological, environmental, agricultural and forestry

monitoring, and can be used in emergency situations.

'Fencer-Es' have been seen with and without the distinctive combined fences/underwing pylons, and aft of the windscreen are externally almost indistinguishable from the 'Fencer-D' bomber. The most obvious external change is the provision of a larger-capacity, bulged heat exchanger to give increased cooling for the reconnaissance aircraft's many new black boxes.

The **Su-24MP 'Fencer-F'** is a similar-looking aircraft, and like the Su-24MR often has its nose painted white to resemble a standard Su-24M bomber. It can be distinguished from the earlier aircraft by a prominent fairing below the nose, behind the radome, and by the provision of swept-back 'hockey stick' antennas outboard of long shallow strakes on the bottom corners of the intakes, immediately ahead of the mainwheel bays. The pattern of flush dielectric antennas on the sides of the nose is also different, and the smaller 'Fencer-C/-D' heat exchanger is mounted above the fuselage.

The Su-24MP is believed to have a primary electronic intelligence-gathering role. It is believed that only 12 of these aircraft were built, and eight were retained by the Ukraine.

Specification
Sukhoi Su-24 'Fencer-C'
Type: low-level strike aircraft
Powerplant: two NPO Saturn (Lyul'ka) AL-21F-3A turbojets each rated at 76.49 kN (17,196 lb st) dry, 110.32 kN (24,802 lb st) with afterburner
Performance: maximum level speed 'clean' at 11000 m (36,090 ft) 1,251 kt (2320 km/h ; 1,441 mph) and 793 kt (1470 km/h; 913 mph) at sea level ; combat radius 565 nm (1050 km/ 650 miles) on a hi-lo-hi attack mission with a 3000-kg (6,614-lb) warload and two drop tanks
Weights: maximum take-off 39700 kg (87,522 lb)
Dimensions: span 17.63 m (57 ft 10 in) spread and 10.36 m (34 ft 0 in) swept; length 24.53 m (80 ft 5¾ in) including probe; wing area 42.00 m² (452.10 sq ft)

Sukhoi Su-25 and derivatives

The **Su-25 'Frogfoot'** was developed as a 'jet Shturmovik' paralleling the US YA-9 and YA-10 AX contenders. Sukhoi chose a different emphasis to the US companies, producing a relatively

lightly armoured, turbojet-powered aircraft for maximum speed over the battlefield. Designated **T-8**, and allocated the initial reporting name **'Ram-J'**, the new aircraft was initially powered by a

pair of RD-9 turbojets (as used by the MiG-19) and made its first flight on 22 February 1975. The production aircraft was powered by a pair of R-95Sh turbojets (non-afterburning versions of the R-13-300 used by the MiG-21) which were capable of running on a variety of fuels. Service trials included combat

operations in Afghanistan, and resulted in some changes, including dihedral tailplanes, a new internally mounted AO-17 twin-barrelled 30-mm cannon, heavier armour and improved control rods and foam-filled fuel tanks. Further improvements were added during the course of production, including bolt-on chaff/flare dispensers, IR signature suppressors, a freon gas fire extinguishing system and an armoured keel between the engines. The wingtip speed brakes were also refined and twin brake chutes were added. A handful were produced or converted for the target towing role under the designation **Su-25BM**. For operational and conversion training, Sukhoi developed the **Su-25UB**, with tandem cockpits, and the similar **Su-25UT** (redesignated **Su-28**) for advanced training with the DOSAAF and air force flying schools. The **Su-25UTG** was developed from the basic two-seater for carrier training, and had a strengthened undercarriage and an arrester hook below the rear fuselage. Ten were produced, before

production switched to the improved **Su-25UBP**. The Su-25 has been exported to Bulgaria, Czechoslovakia, Iraq and North Korea under the designation **Su-25K/Su-25UBK**.

A second-generation Su-25 was developed as a result of experience during the war in Afghanistan. The **T-8M** was based on the airframe of the Su-25UB, with the internal cannon removed and with the gun bay and the rear cockpit faired over to house new avionics and fuel tanks. First flown in

The Sukhoi Su-25 'Frogfoot' has been steadily improved since its combat debut in Afghanistan. The Su-25T features a much-improved self-defence capability.

August 1984, the **Su-25T** (as it was redesignated) featured an external cannon, and a 192-round chaff/flare dispenser in the trailing edge of the fin. The new avionics suite includes an

INAS, a FLIR, and a collimated TV camera and laser designator/spot tracker/rangefinder. Changes to the FLIR and incorporation of Kinzhal radar led to the new designation **Su-25TM**.

Sukhoi Su-27 and derivatives

The **Sukhoi Su-27** was developed as a long-range interceptor and escort fighter for the IA-PVO, to replace Su-15s and MiG-23s which lacked range, lookdown/shoot-down capability and the ability to operate independently of GCI control. As the **T-10** the aircraft made its maiden flight on 20 May 1971 and was allocated the provisional reporting name **'Ram-K'** and then the full NATO reporting name **'Flanker-A'**. Unfortunately, the aircraft suffered many problems, including excessive drag, inadequate structural strength, flutter and excess weight. It had to be totally redesigned (as the **T-10S**) before it could be put into production. The redesigned aircraft received the reporting name **'Flanker-B'**. The aircraft's large size gives it a massive internal fuel capacity, and a correspondingly long range. It can also carry up to 10 air-to-air missiles (six long-range AA-10 'Alamo' and four short-range AA-11 'Archer'), in addition to its built-in 30-mm cannon. For training Su-27 pilots, a tandem two seat training version was developed under the designation **Su-27UB**. China is so far the only export customer for the Su-27, although the break-up of the USSR has meant that it serves with several former Soviet States, including Russia and the Ukraine. There have been a host of experimental versions of the basic Su-27, including the **P-42**, which smashed many of the time-to-climb records set by the F-15 'Streak Eagle'.

Sukhoi were awarded a contract to develop a long-range interceptor based

on the Su-27 for service on board the USSR's new generation of aircraft-carriers, while Mikoyan were given responsibility for developing a smaller multi-role strike-fighter based on their MiG-29. The resulting **Su-27K** was in many respects a minimum-change version of the basic series production Su-27, with the same avionics and intercept-optimised weapons system. It was fitted with canard foreplanes, was structurally strengthened, and had folding wings and tailplanes, an arrester hook and corrosion protection. The end of the Cold War and the break-up of the Soviet Union left Russia with only one of the planned four carriers, and it was decided to equip this ship with a single aircraft type. Inexplicably, the Su-27K was selected as that type, despite its large size (limiting the number that can be carried), high cost and lack of versatility. It has since been re designated **Su-33**.

To fulfill the very long-range, long-endurance intercept role, Sukhoi developed the **Su-27PU**, a two-seater based on the Su-27UB with provision for inflight refuelling, systems proved for extended operation, and with provision to carry an intercept controller in the rear cockpit to enable the aircraft to act as a mini-AWACS. The aircraft has since been re designated **Su-30**. The derived **Su-30M** (**Su-30MK** for export) adds ground attack capability, and compatability with a wide range of guided air-to-surface weapons. The related single-seat **Su-27P** has the same retractable inflight-refuelling probe, but its intended role is

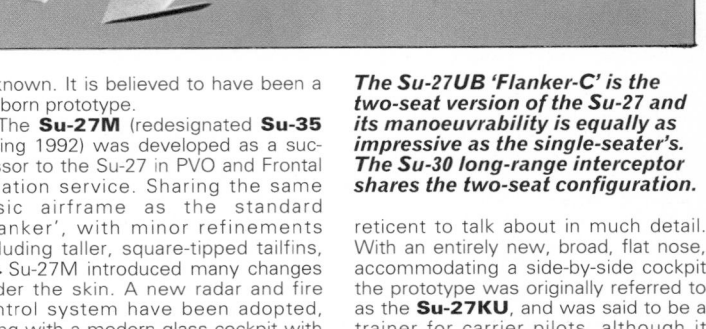

unknown. It is believed to have been a stillborn prototype.

The **Su-27M** (redesignated **Su-35** during 1992) was developed as a successor to the Su-27 in PVO and Frontal Aviation service. Sharing the same basic airframe as the standard 'Flanker', with minor refinements including taller, square-tipped tailfins, the Su-27M introduced many changes under the skin. A new radar and fire control system have been adopted, along with a modern glass cockpit with three multi-function CRT displays. The fly-by-wire control system has also been redesigned. Critical economic problems led to the abandonment of the Su-27M's intended shorter-range, lower-cost, and more versatile counterpart, the MiG-29M, leaving it as the sole Russian tactical fighter programme for the 1990s.

The latest Su-27 variant is something of an enigma, which the OKB are

The Su-27UB 'Flanker-C' is the two-seat version of the Su-27 and its manoeuvrability is equally as impressive as the single-seater's. The Su-30 long-range interceptor shares the two-seat configuration.

reticent to talk about in much detail. With an entirely new, broad, flat nose, accommodating a side-by-side cockpit the prototype was originally referred to as the **Su-27KU**, and was said to be a trainer for carrier pilots, although it lacked the Su-27K's flaps, wing folding and arrester hook. It later emerged that the **Su-27IB** designation had also been applied to the aircraft, signifying that it was a fighter-bomber (Istrebeitel Bombardirovschik), presumably the long-awaited Su-24 replacement, although it lacked radar and any night-attack avionics that would enable it to conduct such a role. It is believed to have now been re designated **Su-32**.

Sukhoi Su-26 and derivatives

Sukhoi's interest in aerobatic aircraft reportedly began when the OKB was involved in fatigue investigation of another company's aerobatic aircraft, which was suffering major problems. Spare capacity at the bureau, coupled with a belief that they could produce a world-beater, led to construction of the **Su-26** prototype which made its maiden flight in June 1984. Four were completed to the original standard, with two-bladed propellors, before production switched to the **Su-26M**, with refined tail surfaces and a three-bladed Hoffman prop. From the sixth aircraft (Su-26M No. 2, side number 06) they had less glazing on the fuselage sides. A team of three Su-26Ms swept the board of men's and women's team prizes at the 1986 World championships, and has continued to dominate the sport ever since.

The Sukhoi Su-29T was a follow-on from the Su-26 and has now been re designated Su-31T. In the hands of experienced pilots, such as Jurgis Kairis, its performances have staggered Western observers.

Further refinements were added to the aircraft which appeared at the 1989 Paris Air Salon, and also in the **Su-26MX** which was developed specifically for export and which was launched at Farnborough the following year. A prototype of the **Su-29** two-seater made its maiden flight during 1991 with a continuous rearward-hingeing canopy over the tandem seats. This aircraft also introduced a new semi-monocoque composite rear fuselage.

Originally known as the **Su-29T**, a single-seat derivative using the same

composite rear fuselage was developed, later being re-designated the **Su-31T**. The **Su-31U** will be a further refined single-seater, reportedly with retractable undercarriage. Related to the Su-26/-29/-30 is a family of heavier tandem two-seat trainers which has

been described as **Su-32**s although this designation has also been applied to the Su-27IB. These have tricycle undercarriages and some also have Western flat-four or flat-six engines. They exist only on paper and in model form at the moment.

Supermarine Attacker

Conceived originally for service with the RAF, the **Supermarine Attacker** was designed with a view to the rapid production of a single-seat fighter to be powered by the Rolls-Royce Nene turbojet engine. It thus combined the wings and landing gear of the Spiteful with a new fuselage and tail unit in the first prototype (TS409), flown initially on 27 July 1946. Two more prototypes with long-stroke landing gear were completed to naval requirements and the first of these (TS413) was flown on 17 June 1947.

Following the conclusion of satisfactory carrier trials aboard HMS *Illustrious*, the Attacker was ordered for the Royal Navy and the Pakistan air force. Production for the Fleet Air Arm totalled 145 and comprised 52 **Attacker F.Mk 1** interceptors, eight **Attacker FB.Mk 1** fighter-bombers and 85 **Attacker FB.Mk 2** fighter-bombers. Attacker F.Mk 1 and FB.Mk 1 aircraft were powered by the Nene 3,

The portly fuselage lines of the Attacker series, here epitomised by this trio of Attacker F.Mk 1s, were necessitated by the considerable diameter of the Nene turbojet, a centrifugal-flow engine.

and the Attacker FB.Mk 2 by the Nene 2. Entering service initially with No. 800 Squadron on 17 August 1951, the Attacker served only briefly with the FAA before being replaced by Hawker Sea Hawks and de Havilland Sea Venoms in 1954, but continued in use with RNVR air squadrons until the latter were disbanded in 1957.

The 36 aircraft supplied to the Pakistan air force were similar to the FAA's Attacker F.Mk 1 but without folding wings and naval equipment.

Specification
Supermarine Attacker F.Mk 1
Type: single-seat carrier-based fighter
Powerplant: one 22.24-kN (5,000-lb)

thrust Rolls-Royce Nene 3 turbojet
Performance: maximum speed 950 km/h (590 mph) at sea level service ceiling 13715 m (45,000 ft); range with standard fuel 950 km (590 miles)
Weights: empty 3826 kg (8,434 lb);

maximum take-off 5339 kg (12,211 lb)
Dimensions: span 11.25 m (36 ft 11 in); length 11.43 m (37 ft 6 in); height 3.02 m (9 ft 11 in)
Armament: four 20-mm cannon in wings

Supermarine Scapa and Stranraer

The **Supermarine Southampton Mk IV** was a considerably revised version of the earlier Southampton which had given the RAF such valuable service. It differed in a number of ways, the most important being the far cleaner installation of its two 391-kW (525-hp) Rolls-Royce Kestrel IIIMS engines in nacelles directly beneath the upper wing. The other noticeable external changes included replacement of the tandem open cockpits by an enclosed cockpit with side-by-side seating for the two pilots, and a change from triple to twin fins and rudders. One other important difference was not externally visible, namely a change to an all-metal basic structure, with all aerodynamic surfaces fabric-covered.

Before the prototype was completed the type was renamed **Supermarine Scapa**, and 14 production aircraft were delivered to the RAF,

the first examples equipping No. 202 Squadron at Malta in May 1935. Other squadrons later equipped were Nos 204, 228 and 240, and the Scapa had a short active life, being withdrawn from front-line use during 1938. Operated by a crew of five, the 22.86-m (75-ft) span Scapa had a maximum speed of 227 km/h (141 mph) at 1000 m (3,280 ft), was armed with three Lewis guns and carried a 454-kg (1,000-lb) bombload.

The closely related **Supermarine Stranraer**, designated originally **Southampton Mk V**, was the last biplane flying-boat designed by R. J. Mitchell. By comparison with the Scapa it was a larger aircraft, of 25.91-m (85-ft) span, introduced a gun turret

A Supermarine Stranraer of No. 240 Squadron, RAF, departs on a wartime patrol in camouflage and with anti-submarine bombs.

in the tail, and in production form was powered by the 652-kW (875-hp) Bristol Pegasus X radial engine. A total of 17 was built for the RAF and these began to enter service with No. 228 Squadron in 1936, eventually equipping

also Nos 201, 209 and 240 Squadrons. Of this number, 15 remained in service at the outbreak of war, but were withdrawn from front-line use during 1940. In addition to those built for the RAF, Canadian Vickers at Montreal produced 40 for the Royal Canadian Air Force and post-war 14 of these were acquired for civil use in Canada.

Supermarine Schneider contestants

Supermarine's first Schneider Trophy contender was the **Supermarine Sea Lion I**, developed from the one-off **Supermarine N.1B Baby** built to Admiralty Air Department Specification N.1B of 1917 for a single-seat fighter of flying-boat configuration. The Sea Lion was thus a small biplane, and its name was derived from its 336-kW (450-hp) Napier Lion engine, strut-mounted between the wings to drive a pusher propeller. Competing in the foggy contest at Bournemouth in 1919, the Sea Lion was retired after one lap and it was not until 1922, in the contest at Naples, that Supermarine again had a contender in the form of the **Sea Lion II**. Developed from the company's one-off **Sea King II** single-seat fighter flying-boat, and again powered by the Napier Lion engine, it was flown to victory by Henri Biard at an average speed of 234.48 km/h (145.7 mph).

For the 1923 contest at Cowes the Sea Lion II was revised and with a 410-kW (550-hp) version of the Napier Lion engine was redesignated **Sea Lion III**; in the contest it was pushed into third place by the US Navy's superb Curtiss CR-3 seaplanes. The next contest was at Baltimore in 1925, where R. J. Mitchell's streamlined all-wood

Supermarine S.4 seaplane, powered by a 522-kW (700-hp) Napier Lion engine, crashed during trials. It was not until 1927 at Venice that the new all-metal **Supermarine S.5** monoplane seaplanes were ready to take part in the contest, one with a 671-kW (900-hp) Napier Lion VIIA and the other with an 652-kW (875-hp) Napier Lion VIIB. They were to take 1st and 2nd places respectively, the winner being flown by Flight Lieutenant S. N. Webster at an average speed of 453.28 km/h (281.66 mph).

In the penultimate contest, held at Calshot in 1929, the improved **Supermarine S.6** powered by a 1417-kW (1,900-hp) Rolls-Royce 'R' engine came first piloted by Flying Officer H. R. Waghorn at a record 528.87 km/h (328.63 mph), but with lack of government support it seemed certain that the UK would be unable to contend in 1931. National-spirited sponsorship by Lady Houston made entry possible, but with insufficient time to design a new aircraft Supermarine could do little more than modify the S.6 to accept a 1752-kW (2,350-hp) version of the Rolls-Royce 'R' engine. The resulting **Supermarine S.6B** flew over the course at Calshot

uncontested to record a speed of 547.305 km/h (340.08 mph) piloted by Flight Lieutenant J. N. Boothman, to win the trophy permanently for the UK. On the same day, 13 September 1931, Flight Lieutenant G.H. Stainforth used the reserve S.6B to establish a new world absoulute speed record of 610.02 km/h (379.05 mph). The combination of Supermarine, R. J. Mitchell, Rolls-Royce and fuel technician F. Rodwell Banks had given the UK a remarkable success.

S1596 was the Supermarine S.6B in which Flight Lieutenant George Stainforth raised the world absolute speed record to 610 km/h (379 mph) on the same day that S1595 captured the Schneider trophy outright for Britain in 1931. R. J. Mitchell's winning design was made possible only through a donation by Lady Houston of £100,000 towards its development costs as the government had refused any further backing. Spanning 9.14 m (30 ft) and taking off at a maximum weight of 2760 kg (6,086 lb), the S.6B later raised the speed record to 655.8 km/h (407 mph).

Supermarine Scimitar

Supermarine's design to meet the requirements of Naval Specification N.113D was at first known as the **Supermarine N.113**, but the aircraft finally selected for production as the Scimitar was derived through the **Supermarine Type 508** and **Type 529** prototypes with straight wings and a butterfly tail unit, and the **Type 525** which introduced swept wings and a cruciform tail unit. The final **Type 544** design differed from the Type 525 by having a fuselage that incorporated area ruling and, importantly, blown flaps that reduced minimum control speed to simplify catapult launch and carrier landing for this heavy aircraft. The first of three Type 544 prototypes (WT854) was flown on 19 January 1956, and initial deliveries of production aircraft were made in August 1957 to No. 700X Trials Flight. The first operational squadron (No. 803) was formed in June 1958 the **Scimitar F.Mk 1** then providing the FAA with a low-level

A Scimitar F.Mk 1 catches the wire as it lands aboard HMS Centaur in April 1961. Note the cannon ports in the starboard inlet trunk

supersonic attacker able to deploy tactical nuclear weapons, a high-level interceptor using air-to-air guided missiles, and a vehicle that could be used in a fighter/reconnaissance role at extreme ranges. A total of 76 was built to equip Nos 800, 804 and 807 Squadrons until superseded by the Blackburn Buccaneer from 1969.

Specification
Supermarine Scimitar F.Mk 1
Type: single-seat carrier-based multi-role aircraft
Powerplant: two 50.04-kN (11,250-lb) thrust Rolls-Royce Avon 202 turbojets
Performance: maximum speed 1143 km/h (710 mph) at sea level service ceiling 14020 m (46,000 ft); range 2288 km (1,422 miles)

Weights: empty 10869 kg (23,962 lb); maximum take-off 15513 kg (34,200 lb)
Dimensions: span 11.33 m (37 ft 2 in); length 16.87 m (55 ft 4 in); height 5.28 m (17 ft 4 in); wing area 45.06 m² (485.0 sq ft)

Armament: four 30-mm ADEN cannon and four 454-kg (1,000-lb) bombs or four Bullpup air-to-ground missiles or four Sidewinder air-to-air missiles, or other optional stores including drop tanks and nuclear weapons

Supermarine Sea Otter

Basically an improved version of the Walrus, which it superseded in Fleet Air Arm service from 1944 for reconnaissance and air/sea rescue duties, the **Supermarine Sea Otter** (at first named **Stingray**) was the last biplane amphibian to be designed by the company, and also the last aircraft of biplane configuration in squadron service with the FAA. Of all-metal basic construction with fabric-covered aerofoil surfaces and incorporating a more refined structure than that of the Walrus, the Sea Otter differed primarily by having its 638-kW (855-hp) Bristol Mercury XXX radial engine mounted in tractor configuration.

Essentially a tractor-engined and updated version of the company's Walrus, the Supermarine Sea Otter was the last biplane in Fleet Air Arm squadron service.

Armament comprised three Vickers 'K' guns, and up to 454 kg (1,000 lb) of bombs could be carried. The prototype was first flown in September 1938, but it was not until November 1944 that the Sea Otter entered operational service, initially with No. 1700 Squadron. Production totalled 292 aircraft including prototypes and included 250 **Sea Otter Mk I** reconnaissance/communi-

cations aircraft and 40 **Sea Otter Mk II** air/sea rescue aircraft. In addition to serving with No. 1700 Squadron the type equipped Nos 730, 742, 753, 778, 781, 799, 1701, 1702 and 1703 Squadrons. Post-war disposals resulted in examples serving with the Danish air force, Dutch navy and French customs

administration in Indo-China, and a number were acquired for civil use including two operated by Qantas Empire Airways. Spanning 14.02 m (46 ft), the Sea Otter Mk II had a maximum speed of 248 km/h (154 mph) at 1525 m (5,000 ft) and maximum range of 1344 km (835 miles).

Supermarine Seagull and Walrus

The **Supermarine Seal II** of 1921, a three-crew deck-landing amphibian for RAF use as a fleet spotter from Royal Navy aircraft-carriers, was converted as the prototype **Seagull** during the following year. Of biplane foldable-wing configuration with retractable wheel landing gear to give amphibious capability, the Seagull was powered by a 358-kW (480-hp) Napier Lion II engine strut-mounted between the wings to drive a tractor-propeller. The production **Seagull Mk II** had minor improvements and the 367-kW (492-hp) Napier Lion IIB engine, being built to a total of 26 that included one for Japan and three civil aircraft. Production was brought up to a total of 32 by six **Seagull Mk III** aircraft for the Royal Australian Air Force and these, generally similar to the RAF Seagull Mk IIs, differed primarily by having a similarly-rated Napier Lion V.

The experimental installation of a Bristol Jupiter IX radial engine in pusher configuration led to the prototype **Seagull Mk V** powered by a 462-kW (620-hp) Bristol Pegasus IIM2 radial engine, of which 24 were ordered by the Australian government. Evaluation of this aircraft led to the type being adopted for service with the Fleet Air Arm under the name **Walrus Mk I** and these, built by Supermarine, had metal hulls. Production eventually totalled 746, of which 461 were built by Saunders-Roe, this number including 191 **Walrus Mk II** aircraft with Saro wooden hulls and the Bristol Pegasus

VI engine. Entering service with the FAA in 1936, the Walrus was stressed for catapult-launching-equipped battleships and cruisers of the Australian British and New Zealand navies, and throughout most of World War II was operational in practically every theatre of war. The type also played a significant air/sea rescue role in RAF service, large numbers of rescued aircrew having a special place in their memory for the Walrus, better known to wartime servicemen as the 'Shagbat'. Pre-war, six Seagull Mk Vs were exported to Turkey, and post-war eight Walrus aircraft were supplied to Argentina.

Specification
Supermarine Walrus Mk I
Type: four-crew spotter-reconnaissance amphibian
Powerplant: one 559-kW (750-hp) Bristol Pegasus VI radial piston engine
Performance: maximum speed 217

km/h (135 mph) at 1450 m (4,750 ft); service ceiling 5210 m (17,100 ft); range 966 km (600 miles)
Weights: empty 2223 kg (4,900 lb); maximum take-off 3266 kg (7,200 lb)
Dimensions: span 13.97 m (45 ft 10 in); length 11.35 m (37 ft 3 in); height 4.65 m (15 ft 3 in); wing area 56.67 m² (610.0 sq ft)
Armament: one 7.7-mm (0.303-in) Vickers 'K' gun in bow and one or two similar weapons amidships, plus up to 272 kg (600 lb) of bombs carried beneath the wings, or two Mk VIII depth charges

Supermarine Walrus Mk I of No. 700 Sqn, Fleet Air Arm, based on HMS Belfast in the early 1940s.

Supermarine Southampton

The **Supermarine Southampton** was developed from the 10-passenger **Supermarine Swan** which, operated by Imperial Airways on loan from the Air Ministry, complemented the activities of the Sea Eagles on the Southampton Channel Islands route during 1926-27. In finalising the design of the Southampton the later-renowned R. J. Mitchell achieved his first great success, for no fewer than 68 of these elegant five-crew flying-boats were built for the RAF. Of biplane configuration and with underwing stabilising floats, the sleek hull was upswept at the rear to mount the tailplane which carried above it triple fins and rudders; powerplant comprised two Napier Lion engines strut-mounted between the wings. The first of six **Southampton Mk I** 'boats with wooden hulls was flown for the first time on 10 March 1925, and initial deliveries to the RAF's No. 480 Coastal Reconnaissance Flight began a few months later.

The major production **Southampton Mk II** introduced a duralumin hull that gave significant performance increase, for not only was it of light structural

weight but it also eliminated the weight penalty of some 400 lb (181 kg) of water soaked up by the wooden hull.

The Southampton equipped the RAF's Nos 201, 203, 204, 205 and 210 Squadrons, serving the RAF faithfully for more than a decade. Examples were built also for the Royal Australian Air Force, Argentina, Japan and Turkey.

Supermarine Southampton Mk I of No. 480 (Coastal Reconnaissance) Flight, RAF, based at Calshot during the mid-1920s.

Specification
Supermarine Southampton Mk II
Type: general reconnaissance flying-boat
Powerplant: two 373-kW (500-hp) Napier Lion VA W-12 piston engines
Performance: maximum speed 174 km/h (108 mph) at sea level; service ceiling 4265 m (14,000 ft); maximum range 1497 km (930 miles)
Weights: empty 4082 kg (9,000 lb); maximum take-off 6895 kg (15,200 lb)
Dimensions: span 22.86 m (75 ft 0 in); length 15.58 m (51 ft 11 in); height 6.82 m (22 ft 42 in); wing area 134.61 m² (1,449.0 sq ft)
Armament: three 7.7mm (0.303-in) Lewis guns (one each in bow and two midships positions), plus up to 499 kg (1,100 lb) of bombs

Supermarine Spiteful and Seafang

The **Supermarine Spiteful** and **Seafang** were intended respectively to supersede the Spitfire and Seafire in service. Superficially the Spiteful closely resembled the Spitfire, but was virtually a completely new design with square-cut laminar-flow wings that, as they were of thin section, demanded wider-track inward-retracting main landing gear units. Three prototypes were ordered in three versions and, flown from June 1944, comprised the **Spiteful F.Mk 14** (Griffon 65/five-bladed propeller), **Spiteful F.Mk 15** (Griffon 89 or 901 contra-rotating propellers), and **Spiteful F.Mk 16** (three-stage Griffon 101 and five-bladed propeller). A contract for 67 Spiteful F.Mk 14s was cancelled after the 17th

had been completed on 17 January 1947. Only three of this total were used by the RAF, delivered to test establishments.

The Seafang, which differed from the Spiteful in having full carrier gear, had no more success, only 18 being completed from an order for two prototype and 150 production aircraft. They comprised eight **Seafang F.Mk 31** fighters with the Griffon 61 engine and 10 Seafang F.Mk 32 fighters with the Griffon 89, contra-rotating propellers and folding wings. The Spiteful F.Mk 16 spanned 10.82 m (35 ft 6 in) and was powered by a 1771-kW (2,375-hp) Rolls-Royce Griffon 101, giving a maximum speed of 795 km/h (494 mph) at optimum altitude.

VB895 was the second Seafang prototype, and was the first of the Seafang F.Mk 32 series with the 1752-kW (2350-hp) Griffon 89 engine.

Supermarine Spitfire and Seafire

Without doubt the best known British aircraft of World War II, the **Supermarine Spitfire** originated from the **Type 224** designed by R. J. Mitchell to meet the requirements of Specification F.7/30. A cantilever low-wing monoplane of all-metal construction, it had an inverted-gull wing and 'trousered' fixed main landing gear, and was powered by a 447-kW (600-hp) Rolls-Royce Goshawk II Vee engine. When the Type 224 was tested its performance proved disappointing, and it was no more successful than any of the other submissions to this specification; none of them gained an Air Ministry contract.

Given a free hand to design a new single-seat fighter unfettered by official specifications, Mitchell outlined on his drawing board the delightful **Type 300**. Smaller, sleeker and with drag-reducing retractable landing gear, it was tailored around the new Rolls-Royce P.V.12 (Merlin) engine; the wings were not only of distinctive elliptical shape, but they housed eight machine-guns, all of them firing outside the propeller disc. Air Ministry Specification F.36134 was drawn up around the Type 300 and a prototype was ordered. This (K5054) was powered by a 738-kW (900-hp)

Supermarine Spitfire LF Mk XVI of No. 74 Sqn, RAF, during 1945.

Rolls-Royce Merlin 'C' and flew for the first time on 5 March 1936. Comparatively little flight testing was needed to confirm it as a winner, and its superb handling qualities and performance resulted in a first contract (for 310 **Spitfire Mk I** aircraft) being awarded on 3 June 1936. However, planned mass production was slow to gain momentum and it was not until July 1938 that the first Spitfire Mk I reached No. 19 Squadron at Duxford; only five had been delivered by the time of the Munich crisis in September of that year, but the trickle was eventually to become a flood that totalled 20,334 Spitfires and 2,556 related new-build **Seafire** naval fighters. A degree of multi-role capability was to result from the development of low-altitude clipped wings (prefix LF), and high-altitude increased-span wings (HF), the standard wing being identified as F, and with variations of armament within these wings comprising eight machine-guns (suffix A), two cannon and four machine-guns (B), four cannon (C) and two cannon, two 12.7-mm (0.5-in) machine-guns and up to 454 kg (1,000 lb) of bombs (E).

By the outbreak of war on 3 September 1939, the RAF had nine

operational Spitfire squadrons, and on 16 October 1939 a Spitfire of No. 603 Squadron claimed the first German aircraft to be destroyed over the UK in World War II, a Heinkel He 111. By August 1940, shortly before the Battle of Britain reached its climax, RAF Fighter Command could call upon 19 Spitfire Mk I squadrons. By December 1940 Spitfire Mk IIs were carrying out 'Rhubarb' sweeps over occupied Europe, and the first to serve overseas were Spitfire Mk VBs flown to Malta from HMS *Eagle* on 7 March 1942.

Soon after that date the same mark was operational in the Middle East, and by early 1943 the first Spitfire Mk Vs were arriving in the Pacific theatre. In growing numbers and with increasing capability the Spitfire served throughout World War II, not only with the RAF but with the nation's allies, including US and Soviet squadrons. It also had the distinction of remaining in production throughout the entire war and was operational post-war, the last mission flown by a photo-reconnaissance Spitfire PR.Mk 19 of No. 81 Squadron in Malaya on 1 April 1954.

The success of the Hawker Sea Hurricane as operated by the Fleet Air Arm from Royal Navy aircraft-carriers resulted in development of the Supermarine Seafire, the first conversions from Spitfire Mk VBs being carried out by Air Service Training at Hamble, Hampshire. Initial deliveries of the resulting Seafire Mk IB began in January 1942, and the type was used in growing numbers of different marks throughout the war. Seafire Mk 47s of No. 800 Squadron served with distinction in the Korean War, and when Seafires were withdrawn from frontline service, the type remained operational with training squadrons and RNVR air squadrons until 1967.

Variants

Spitfire Mk I: initial production with 768-kW (1,030-hp) Merlin II; eight 7.7-mm (0.303-in) Browning guns (at first four because of supply shortages) or, **Spitfire Mk IB,** four 7.7-mm (0.303-in) guns and two 20-mm cannon; 1,566 built
Spitfire Mk II: built at Castle Bromwich; 876-kW (1,175-hp) Merlin XII; 750 **Spitfire Mk IIA** and 170 **Spitfire Mk IIB** built
Spitfire Mk III: one-off experimental prototype with 954-kW (1,280-hp) Merlin XX
Spitfire Mk IV: Griffon-engined prototypes (2), same mark number used for 229 PR versions of Spitfire Mk V
Spitfire Mk V: with strengthened fuselage for 1074-kW (1,440-hp) Merlin 45 or 1096-kW (1,470-hp) Merlin 50,

drop tank and bomb provision, F or LF wing and A, B or C armament; 94 **Spitfire Mk VA,** 3,923 **SpitfireMk VB** and 2,447 **Spitfire Mk VC** built
Spitfire Mk VI: high-altitude interceptor with 1055-kW (1,415-hp) Merlin 47, pressurised cockpit and HF wing; 100 built
Spitfire Mk VII: high-altitude interceptor with two-stage Merlin 61, 64 or 71, pressurised cockpit, retractable tailwheel and, often, broad pointed rudder; 140 built
Spitfire Mk VIII: definitive fighter with two-stage Merlin 61, 63 or 70, unpressurised cockpit and LF, F or HF wings; 1,658 built
Spitfire Mk IX: union of two-stage Merlin 61, 63 or 70 with Spitfire Mk V airframe; LF, F or HF wings and B, C or E armament; 5,665 built
Spitfire Mk X: pressurised version of Spitfire PR.Mk XI Merlin 77, one with HF wing; 16 built
Spitfire Mk XI: unarmed long-range PR version with Merlin 61, 63 or 70; 471 built
Spitfire Mk XII: low-level interceptor with single-stage Griffon II or IV of 1294-kW (1,735-hp), LF wing, B armament; 100 built
Spitfire Mk XIII: low-level PR aircraft based on Spitfire Mk V with Merlin 32 and only four 0.303-in (7.7-mm) machine-guns; 18 built
Spitfire Mk XIV: redesigned and strengthened airframe for 1529-kW (2,050-hp) Griffon 65 or 66 with five-bladed propeller, broad tail and, often, teardrop canopy; F or LF wings, C or E armament; 957 built
Spitfire Mk XVI: as Spitfire Mk IX with Packard Merlin 226, F or LF wing, usually C or E armament, many with teardrop canopy; 1,054 built
Spitfire Mk XVIII: definitive fighter

with two-stage Griffon, teardrop canopy and extra wing fuel, F wings and E armament
Spitfire FR.Mk XVIII (post-war) Spitfire FR.Mk 18: rear fuselage reconnaissance camera; 300 built
Spitfire Mk XIX (post-war PR.Mk 19): unarmed PR version, most pressurised; two-stage Griffon; 225 built
Spitfire Mk XX: one-off prototype rebuilt from Spitfire Mk IV and prototype Spitfire Mk XII
Spitfire Mk 21: redesigned airframe, mainly Griffon 61 or 64 with five-bladed propeller, C armament; 122 built
Spitfire Mk 22: minor changes from Spitfire Mk 21, some with 1771-kW (2,373-hp) Griffon 85 and contra-rotating propellers; 278 built
Spitfire Mk 24: minor changes, Spiteful tail, short-barrel Mk V cannon; 54 built
Seafire Mk IB: navalised Spitfire Mk VB; 166 built
Seafire Mk IIC: catapult hooks and strengthened landing gear Merlin 32 with four-bladed propeller; 372 built
Seafire Mk III: double-folding wing and 1182-kW (1,585-hp) Merlin 55M; 1,220 built
Seafire Mk XV: single-stage 1380-kW (1,850-hp) Griffon VI most with sting hooks and late production with teardrop canopy; 390 built
Seafire Mk XVII or Mk 17: as

Seafire Mk XV with teardrop canopy and, often, strengthened landing gear, some (Seafire FR.Mk 17) with camera in place of rear tank; 232 built
Seafire Mk 45: airframe as Spitfire Mk 21, non-folding wing, Griffon 61/five-bladed propeller or 85/contraprops; 50 built
Seafire Mk 46: as Seafire Mk 45 with teardrop canopy, Seafire FR.Mk 46 with rear-fuselage camera late production with Spiteful tail; 24 built
Seafire Mk 47: with folding wing, 1771-kW (2,375-hp) Griffon 87 or 88 with chin inlet and contraprops, increased fuel, late production all FR type with camera; 140 built

Specification
Supermarine Spitfire Mk VA
Type: single-seat interceptor fighter
Powerplant: one 1102-kW (1,478-hp) Rolls-Royce Merlin 45 Vee engine
Performance: maximum speed 594 km/h (369 mph) at 5945 m (19,500 ft); service ceiling 11125 m (36,500 ft); maximum range 1827 km (1,135 miles)
Weights: empty 2267 kg (4,998 lb); maximum take-off 2911 kg (6,417 lb)
Dimensions: span 11.23 m (36 ft 10 in); length 9.12 m (29 ft 11 in); height 3.02 m (9 ft 11 in); wing area 22.48 m² (242.0 sq ft)
Armament: eight 7.7-mm (0.303-in) Browning machine-guns

The Supermarine Seafire FR.Mk 47, seen here in the form of an aircraft picking up the wire aboard a Royal Navy carrier, was the naval equivalent of the Spitfire F.Mk 22, but with the necessary addition of hydraulic wing folding.

Supermarine Swift

Development of the **Supermarine Swift** started in 1946 when the Air Ministry began the process of procuring a replacement for the Gloster Meteor. Two prototypes of the **Type 510** were ordered, which was basically a development of the Nene 2-powered Supermarine Attacker, but provided with wings and tailplane swept at an angle of 40°. First flown on 29 December 1948, this was developed progressively via the **Type 517** which had a variable-incidence tailplane, and the **Type 535** which introduced tricycle landing gear, a modified fuselage to accept a Rolls-Royce Nene with afterburning capability, plus other revisions and refinements. The first of 193 production aircraft was flown on 25 August 1952, this being a **Swift F.Mk 1** with twin 30-mm ADEN cannon, Avon RA.7 engine without reheat and a fixed-incidence tailplane. Subsequent versions included the **Swift F.Mk 2** with four ADEN cannon and a new wing incorporating a compound-taper leading edge; the Swift F.Mk 3 with an afterburning Avon RA.7R engine; and the **Swift F.Mk 4** with a variable-incidence tailplane.

After only a short time in service the unsuitability of the Swift for deployment in an interceptor role led to the deci-

sion to concentrate on its development as a tactical reconnaissance aircraft. This brought production of 58 **Swift FR.Mk 5** aircraft, plus four converted from Swift F.Mk 4s, the first of which entered service with No. 2 Squadron in Germany in early 1956. They differed from the Swift F.Mk 4 by having the nose lengthened to accommodate three cameras, a frameless canopy and a new wing with increased chord forward of the ailerons to give a 'saw-tooth' leading edge. At one period Swift FR.Mk 5s equipped both No. 2

and No. 79 Squadrons, the type remaining operational with No. 2 Sqn in Germany until summer of 1961.

A subsequent development built to a total of two prototypes and 12 production aircraft had the designation Swift F.Mk 7. These had a lengthened nose to accommodate radar and an increased-span wing to carry four Blue Sky air-to-air missiles in addition to the standard four ADEN cannon. They were used for weapons trials at RAF Valley before being withdrawn for use in a variety of experimental roles.

Specification
Supermarine Swift FR.Mk 5

Type: single-seat tactical reconnaissance aircraft
Powerplant: one 42.04-kN (9,450-lb) afterburning thrust Rolls-Royce Avon 114 turbojet
Performance: maximum speed 1102 km/h (685 mph) at sea level; service ceiling 13960 m (45,800 ft); range 1014 km (630 miles)
Weights: empty 6094 kg (13,435 lb); maximum take-off 9707 kg (21,400 lb)
Dimensions: span 9.86 m (32 ft 4 in); length 12.88 m (42 ft 3 in); height 4.11 m (13 ft 6 in)
Armament: two 30-mm ADEN cannon, plus provision for underwing bombs or rockets

Supermarine Swift FR.Mk 5 of No. 2 Sqn, RAF, based at Jever, West Germany during the late 1950s.

Svenska aircraft

In 1921 Carl Bucker established Svenska Aero Aktiebolaget at Lidingo, near Stockholm, to build aircraft of Heinkel design. Early products of this company were the **Svenska S.1** and **S.11** twin-float seaplanes, **HD 14** torpedo-bomber and **HD 17** fighter reconnaissance aircraft. Indigenous designs began with the Pirat two-seat multi-purpose biplane, available with wheel or float landing gear; for use as a trainer it was powered by a 149-kW (200-hp) Armstrong Siddeley Lynx, or for operational use by the 317-kW (425-hp) Armstrong Siddeley Jaguar. It was followed by the two-seat **Falken**, a lightweight tandem open-cockpit biplane intended for both primary and advanced training when powered by Armstrong Siddeley Mongoose and Lynx engines of 101 kW (135 hp) and 149 kW (200 hp) respectively. The company's most significant aircraft was the

The Svenska J6 Jaktfalk (seen here) was an unremarkable fighter, which in its definitive J6B form with the Jaguar radial had a maximum speed of 310 km/h (193 mph).

Jaktfalk (gerfalcon), a 9.00-m (29-ft 6¼-in) span single-seat biplane fighter powered by a 373-kW (500-hp) Armstrong Siddeley radial engine. The prototype was acquired by the Flygvapen for evaluation under the designation **J5**, and this resulted in an order for two more prototypes which, powered by the 388-kW (520-hp) Bristol Jupiter VIIF supercharged engine, were given the designation **J6**. Five J6 production aircraft were built by Svenska Aero before the company ran into financial difficulties, the assets of the company then being acquired by AB Svenska Jarnvagsverkstaderna, which built three more **J6A** aircraft in

1931 and seven **J6B** aircraft in 1934 with Jupiter and Jaguar engines respectively; the J6B had a maximum speed of 310 km/h (193 mph) at 4500 m (14,765 ft). The last of these aircraft remained in Flygvapen service until 1941. AB Svenska designed and built

subsequently a three-seat light cabin monoplane with a 108-kW (145-hp) Walter Mars radial engine designated **Viking I**, and the **Viking II** four-seat development with a 149-kW (200-hp) Gipsy Six inline engine; both were available with wheel or float landing gear.

Swallow aircraft

Established at Wichita, Kansas, the Swallow Aircraft Company Inc. produced in the late 1920s a three-seat open cockpit biplane which, deriving from earlier Laird designs, was known as the **Swallow New Swallow** or **Commercial Three-Seater**. About 100 with the 67-kW (90-hp) Curtiss OX-5 were produced, and small numbers were also built with Hispano-Suiza and Wright Whirlwind engines. Pioneering Varney Air Lines began its CAM.5 air mail route with five Swallows that each had the forward passenger cockpit adapted to carry mail and was powered by the 149-kW (200-hp) Wright J4 Whirlwind. A lightweight development followed with introduction of the

Swallow TP two-seat trainer in 1929, powered initially by the Curtiss OX-5, and about 200 were built before a shortage of this powerplant brought the introduction of the **Swallow TP-K** with 75-kW (100-hp) Kinner K5 (13 built) and **Swallow TP-W** with the 110-hp (82-kW) Warner Scarab (three built). An attempt to revitalise sales brought the introduction of the **Swallow Sport** in 1930, available in **HA**, **HC** and **HW** versions with Axelson, Continental and Wright engines respectively, but because of the growing economic depression this model was a complete failure. Attempts were made in the late 1930s to recapture past successes, bringing

the introduction of the lightweight **Coupe** two-seat cabin monoplane and a two-seat braced low-wing monoplane designated **LT-65**, but by then the USA was on the brink of war and time had run out for the Swallow company.

Known as the 'J-4 Swallow', this open-cockpit aircraft has been restored to its former glory, to fly in the colours of one-time American operator, mail carrier Varney Air Lines.

Tachikawa Ki-9

Designed for use as a primary or intermediate trainer (role change being achieved by the use of a different engine in the same airframe) the **Tachikawa Ki-9** unequal-span two-seat biplane appeared in late 1934. The first of three prototypes was flown on 7 January 1935, powered by a 261-kW (350-hp) Hitachi Ha-13a radial. A similarly-powered second prototype was followed by the third with a 112-kW (150-hp) Nakajima NZ seven-cylinder radial. Tests indicated centre of gravity problems for the proposed primary trainer and the Ki-9 was developed in the higher-powered intermediate training role only.

Production deliveries began in 1935. Designated the **Army Type 95-I Medium Grade Trainer Model A** and later given the Allied codename **'Spruce'**, the Tachikawa biplane had

complex split-axle landing gear with fairings over the top of the wheels. In 1939 this was modified and simplified, the fuselage slightly shortened and all-up weight reduced. The resulting **Army Type 95-I Model B or Ki-9 Kai** had improved manoeuvrability and flight characteristics. Both versions were used widely for blind-flying training with a folding hood over the rear cockpit, and at least one was modified with a glazed canopy over the rear cockpit for use as a staff officer transport.

Production by Tachikawa totalled 2,395, ending in 1942. At least another 220 Ki-9s were constructed by Tokyo Gasu Denki in the last two years of the war. The Japanese army's standard basic trainer, the Ki-9 was also flown in wartime by Japanese satellite countries and postwar by Indonesia.

This Ki-9 Kai was on the strength of the Kumagaya Army Flying School as indicated by the insignia (red and white) on the rudder.

Specification
Tachikawa Ki-9 Model A
Type: basic trainer
Powerplant: one 261-kW (350-hp) Hitachi Ha-13a radial piston engine
Performance: maximum speed 149 mph (240 km/h); service ceiling 19,030 ft

(5800 m); endurance 3 hours 30 minutes
Weights: empty equipped 1120 kg (2,469 lb); maximum take-off 1580 kg (3,483 lb)
Dimensions: span 10.32 m (33 ft 10¼ in); length 7.90 m (25 ft 11 in); height 3.10 m (10 ft 2 in)

Tachikawa Ki-17

Developed after the failure of the low-powered variant of the Ki-9 prototype, the **Tachikawa Ki-17** biplane had a slimmer fuselage, more square-cut equal-span wings and a redesigned tailplane. The first of two prototypes was flown in July 1935. Trials were successful and the only major change made to subsequent production aircraft was the deletion of the upperwing ailerons to eliminate oversensitive control inputs.

Between 1936 and 1943 Tachikawa completed 658 series Ki-17s and the type was used at four major flying schools and the Army Air Academy. The Ki-17 bore the official designation **Army Type 95 III Primary Trainer**, Allied codename **'Cedar'**.

Specification
Tachikawa Ki-17
Type: two-seat primary trainer
Powerplant: one 112-kW (150-hp)

In production form the Tachikawa Ki-17 was fitted with ailerons only on the lower wings, the provision of such controls on all four wings having made the prototype decidedly skittish in the air.

Hitachi Ha-12 radial piston engine
Performance: maximum speed 170 km/h (106 mph), service ceiling 5300 m (17,390 ft); endurance 3 hours 45 minutes
Weights: empty equipped 639 kg (1,409 lb); maximum take-off 914 kg (2,015 lb)
Dimensions: span 9.82 m (32 ft 21 in);

length 7.85 m (25 ft 9 in); height 2.95 m (9 ft 84 in); wing area 26.20 m² (282.02 sq ft)

Tachikawa Ki-36 and Ki-55

The **Tachikawa Ki-36** two-seat army co-operation aircraft was first flown in prototype form on 20 April 1938. A cantilever low-wing monoplane with fixed tailwheel landing gear, powered by a 336-kW (450-hp) Hitachi Ha-13 radial engine, the Ki-36 accommodated its crew beneath a long 'greenhouse' canopy. Following tests it was ordered into production with a more powerful engine as the Army Type 98 Direct Co-operation Plane. When construction ended in January 1944, a total of 1,334 had been built.

Army use of the Ki-36 suggested it would be suitable as an advanced trainer, resulting in development of the **Ki-55** for this role. After prototype testing in September 1939, the type was ordered as the **Army Type 99 Advanced Trainer**, and when pro-

duction ended in December 1943 a total of 1,389 had been built. The Ki-36 was deployed initially in China with considerable success; when confronted by Allied fighters at the beginning of World War 2 it was found to be extremely vulnerable and withdrawn to the Chinese fronts. Both versions, allocated the Allied codename **'Ida'**, were used in a *kamikaze* role in the closing stages of the war. An advanced version of the Ki-36 with retractable landing gear and a more powerful engine had been planned as the **Ki-72,** but was not built.

Specification
Tachikawa Ki-36
Type: army co-operation aircraft
Powerplant: one 380-kW (510-hp) Hitachi Ha-13a radial piston engine
Performance: maximum speed 348

km/h (216 mph) at 1800 m (5,905 ft), service ceiling 8150 m (26,740 ft); range 1235 km (767 miles)
Weights: empty 1247 kg (2,749 lb); maximum take-off 1660 kg (3,660 lb)
Dimensions: span 11.80 m (38 ft 8½ in); length 8.00 m (26 ft 3 in); height 3.64 m (11 ft 11¼ in); wing area 20.00 m² (215.29 sq ft)
Armament: one forward-firing and

Developed from an obsolescent army co-operation aircraft, the Tachikawa Ki-55 advanced trainer served with four army flying schools, and was also delivered to satellite air arms such as Siam.

one rear-firing 7.7-mm (0.303-in) machine-gun, plus an external bombload of up to 150 kg (331 lb)

Tachikawa Ki-54

Designed as an advanced trainer/crew trainer, the **Tachikawa Ki-54** was flown in prototype form during the summer of 1940. A cantilever low-wing monoplane with retractable tailwheel landing gear, it was powered by two wing-mounted Hitachi Ha-13a radial engines. Successful testing led to the initial version intended primarily for pilot training, ordered during 1941 as the **Army Type 1 Advanced Trainer Model A (Tachikawa Ki-54a)**. It was built in several versions to a total of 1,368, and allocated the Allied codename **'Hickory'**.

Variants
Ki-54b: major production version completed as crew trainer

The eight-seat Tachikawa Y-59 was the civil airliner version of the military Ki-54 Type 1 Transport of 1940, and was built in small numbers for Japanese domestic customers.

Ki-54c: transport/communications version with seats for eight passengers; a number built for civil use had the designation **Y-59**
Ki-54d: designation of small number equipped as ASW aircraft carrying eight 60 kg (132-lb) depth charges
Ki-110: prototype of all-wood version of Ki-54c; destroyed before completion
Ki-111: project for fuel tanker version
Ki-114: project for advanced all wood version of Ki-110

Specification
Tachikawa Ki-54b
Type: crew trainer
Powerplant: two 5 Hitachi Ha-13a radial piston engines
Performance: maximum speed 375 km/h (233 mph) at 2000 m (6,560 ft); service ceiling 7180 m (23,555 ft); range 960 km (597 miles)

Weights: empty 2954 kg (6,512 lb); maximum take-off 3897 kg (8,591 lb)
Dimensions: span 17.90 m (58 ft 8¾ in); length 11.94 m (39 ft 2 in); height 3.58 m (11 ft 9 in); wing area 40.00 m² (430.57 sq ft)
Armament: four 7.7-mm (0.303-in) machine-guns, plus practice bombs

Tachikawa Ki-74

From 1937 Tachikawa produced a number of interesting designs which did not go into series production. These included the **TS-1** single-seat ultra-light low-wing cabin monoplane; the **R-38** two-seat parasol-wing monoplane primary trainer; the **SS-1** twin-engined low-wing monoplane developed from the Lockheed 14 and intended for high-altitude research; the **Ki-70** twin-engined high-speed reconnaissance monoplane; and the **A-26**, later redesignated **Ki-77**, a long-distance record aircraft with a remarkably slim fuselage and finely tapered wide-span monoplane wings. However, it was the **Tachikawa Ki-74** monoplane which attracted the greatest official support.

By 1941 the project had been confirmed as a long-range high-altitude bomber reconnaissance aircraft, and the first of the prototypes, powered by 1641-kW (2,200-hp) turbocharged Ha-211-Ru radials, flew in March 1944. Thirteen pre-production machines followed, powered by more reliable 1491-kW (2,000-hp) Ha-104 Ru engines, giving a maximum speed of 570 km/h (354 mph) at 8500 m (27,885 ft). They carried 1000 kg (2,205 lb) of bombs and were defended by a single remotely-controlled 12.7-mm (0.5-in) machine-gun in the tail. Although not used operationally, the Ki-74 received the Allied codename **'Patsy'**.

The **Ki-94-II** pressurised single-seat

fighter, with a 1790-kW (2,400-hp) Nakajima Ha-44 radial engine, was completed in August 1945, but the end of the war prevented it being test flown. Flight trials began in July 1945 of three **Ki-106** all-wood fighter prototypes, based on the Nakajima Ki-84 and powered by the 1484-kW (1,990-hp) Nakajima Ha-45 engine.

Visible under this Tachikawa Ki-74 high-altitude bomber are the bomb bay and ventral hatch leading to the interior of the aircraft. Spanning 27.00 m (88 ft 7 in), the Ki-74 was designed for a maximum range of 80000 km (4,971 miles) at a service ceiling of 12000 m (39,370 ft).

Tachikawa KKY Ambulance

Established in December 1924 and known originally as the Ishikawajima Aircraft Manufacturing Company, this firm built a series of two-seat biplanes between 1927 and 1933. These included the **T-2** and **T-3** reconnaissance aircraft and the **R1(CM-1)**, **R-2**,

R-3 and **R-5** trainers. Only one or two examples of each were tested except for the R-3, five of which were delivered to the Japanese army between 1929 and 1931.

The **Tachikawa KKY Army Small-type Light Ambulance** was

test flown in 1933. An unequal-span cabin biplane powered by a 89-kW (120-hp) Cirrus Hermes IV in-line engine, it carried pilot, attendant and two stretcher cases. Series production terminated in 1939 with the 23rd aircraft. Many had been donated to the

army as **'Aikoku'** aircraft. Wing span was 10.00 m (32 ft 9¾ in) and maximum speed 180 km/h (112 mph). A version with a 112-kW (150-hp) Kamikaze radial engine appeared in 1939; the two examples built received the designation **KS-I** and were used for air survey work.

Taylor Chummy and Cub

The Taylor Brothers Aircraft Corporation began its productive activities with the **Taylor Chummy**, a two-seat lightplane of braced high-wing monoplane configuration with enclosed side-by-side accommodation. Powered by either Kinner K5 or Brownback Tiger radial engines, both of 67-kW (90-hp) output, the Chummy proved a popular lightplane when introduced in 1928, but lack of finance and poor trading limited sales. The company then moved to Bradford, Pennsylvania, and was renamed the Taylor Aircraft Company; additional finance was gained, but the slow slide towards recession brought Chummy production to an end. President, designer and chief engineer C. Gilbert Taylor developed an improved but similar two-seater certifi-

Though successful in its own right, the Taylor J-2 Cub is more important as the immediate precursor to the seemingly immortal Piper Cub series of high-wing lightplanes.

cated as the **Cub E-2** when powered by a 28-kW (37-hp) Continental A40 engine. Marketed aggressively and competitively, it was built to a total of more than 300 and carried the company through the depression. It was followed by the **Cub F-2** with 30-kW (40-hp) Aeromarine AR3-40 engine (about 30), **Cub H-2** with 26-kW (35-hp) Szekely SR-3-35 (about four) and, finally, the highly successful and improved **Cub J-2** with alternative Continental A40 engines of 28 or 30 kW (37 or 40 hp). More than 1,200 were sold before the

production line was destroyed by fire in early 1937, Taylor then leaving the company. While attempts were being made to resolve the situation 63 aircraft were assembled and marketed by

Aircraft Associates Inc. at Long Beach, California before all rights to the Cub were acquired from Taylor Aircraft by William T. Piper, who continued its production as the enduring Piper Cub.

Taylorcraft (USA) aircraft

After leaving the Taylor Aircraft Company, C. Gilbert Taylor established the Taylorcraft Aviation Company at Alliance, Ohio, in 1936; later that year the name was changed to the Taylor-Young Airplane Company, and in 1940 this became the Taylorcraft Aviation Corporation. Although Gilbert Taylor had developed a sales-winning aeroplane in the Cub, with the start of his new company in 1936 he looked closely at the basic Cub configuration and concluded that it would be even more popular with a wider fuselage to provide side-by-side seating. This was the fundamental change introduced in the **Taylor-Young Model A** of 1937, a braced high-wing monoplane with fixed tailwheel landing gear and an enclosed side-by-side cabin for two, and powered by a 30-kW (40-hp) Continental A40-4 flat-four engine. The Model A proved an immediate winner and more than 600 were sold before production was switched to the **Model BC**, specifically the **Model BC-50** with 37-kW (50-hp) Continental A50. Subsequent variations on this theme included the **Model BC-65** and refined **BC-12-65** (48-kW/65-hp Continental A65), **Models BF-50, BF-60, BF-65** and **BF-12-65** with Franklin engines of a horsepower indicated by the final figure, and **Models BL-50, BL-55, BL-65** and **BL-12-65** with Lycoming engines.

These aircraft sold in hundreds, and the company's primary problem was to build them fast enough. Nevertheless, time was found to accede to requests for a tandem two-seat version of the family, leading to introduction of the **Tandem DC-65** in late 1941. This,

powered by the 48-kW (65-hp) Continental A65 and Franklin or Lycoming engines of similar output in the **Tandem DF-65** and **DL-65**, led to the extensively-built Taylorcraft L-2 Grasshopper. Production of the Grasshopper and training gliders represented a major portion of the company's wartime activities but time was found to design the **Model 15 Foursome**, basically an enlarged version of the Model BC providing four-seat accommodation and with a 112-kW (150-hp) Franklin 6A4-150-B3 engine. Only one was built before the company went bankrupt in 1946, Taylor reforming it yet again in 1949 as Taylorcraft Inc. Production of the **Model 15** was then started as the **Model 15A Tourist**, but only about 20 were built.

Like most manufacturers of light-planes Taylorcraft enjoyed an early post-war boom, marketing variants of the pre-war and wartime developments under a variety of names. They differed mainly in detail and powerplant and in most cases were difficult to externally distinguish one from another. Two-seat versions included the **Ace** (Continental A65 engine), **De Luxe 65** and **De Luxe 85** (Continental A65 and A85), **Model 19 Sportsman** (Continental C8512F), **Special De Luxe** (Continental A65) and **Traveler** (Continental A65). An alternative version of the four-seat Model 15A Tourist became available with Continental C145-2 engine, and the company's final four-seat developments before closing down finally in 1958 were based on the Model 15. This was the new **Model 20** that differed mainly by introducing

extensive use of glass-fibre skins and had as powerplant the 168-kW (225-hp) Continental O-470-J engine. It was available in versions that included the tourer **Model 20 Zephyr 400**, utility **Ranch Wagon**, agricultural **Topper** and floatplane **Seabird**.

In 1968 an entirely new Taylorcraft Aviation Corporation was formed to provide product support to the very large number of Taylorcraft aircraft in use worldwide. In 1973 this company began production of a side-by-side two-seater **Model F-I9 Sportsman** 100 which is based on the pre-war Model B. It was superseded in 1980 by the **Model F-21** which is powered by a 88-kW (118-hp) Lycoming O-235-L26 flat four engine, and was joined in 1983 by the **Model F-21A** with a revised and increased capacity fuel system. Typical of its long line of predecessors, the 10.97-m (36-ft) span Model F-21 had a maximum speed of 201 km/h (125 mph) at sea level and a range of 644 km (400 miles).

In 1986 the company was bought by a group of former Piper Aircraft Company employees and operations moved to Piper's home town of Lock Haven, Pennsylvania, which ironically

Inheriting the classic lines of previous Taylorcraft designs, the F-22B Ranger Patrol was introduced in 1990. Promoted as a rugged STOL aircraft for a wide range of duties, it was offered with a range of Lycoming piston engines.

was also what C. G. Taylor had done in 1936. The new company was less successful however, with only 16 aircraft completed before it was forced to seek Chapter 11 bankruptcy protection in August 1986. Sold in 1989, the Taylorcraft was bought by Aircraft Acquisition Corp. of Morgantown, West Virginia. The line was re-opened at Lock Haven in November of that year, producing the **Model F-21B Classic'** and the **Model 180GT**, though at the time six new models were announced. In 1990 the F-21B matured into the **F-22 'Classic'** which was available in several forms, including tricycle (**F22A Tractor** and **F-22C Trooper**), tailwheel (**F-22B Ranger**) and floatplane (**F-22S**) configurations. In 1992 Taylorcraft Aircraft became independent of AAC, but production was halted again in October of that year.

Taylorcraft L-2 Grasshopper

In 1941 the US Army evaluated four examples of the Taylorcraft Model D under the designation **YO-57**, these being powered by the 48-kW (65-hp) Continental YO-170-3 engine. Successful evaluation for use in artillery spotting/liaison roles brought an order for the basically similar **O-57 Grasshopper** (70 built), followed by the **O-57A** that was modified to improve all-round view and had radio installed (336). These were redesignated **L-2** and **L-2A** respectively in 1942, when an additional 140 L-2As were built. The next production version was the **L-2B** (490) which had revised equipment, and the final, most exten-

The designation L-2A covered some 330 surviving O-57As when the observation category was replaced by the liaison category during 1942.

sively built **L-2M** (900) introduced a fully cowled engine and wing spoilers. Taylorcraft civil versions were also impressed for use in the training of glider pilots; they included the **L-2C** (nine DC-65), **L-2D** (one DL-65), **L-2E** (seven DF-65), **L-2F** (seven BL-65), **L-2G** (two BF-65), **L-2H** (nine BC-12-65), **L-2J** (four BL-1265), **L-2K** (three BF-12-65) and **L-2L** (one BF-50). As powered by the 48-kW (65-hp) Continental O-170-3, the 10.79-m (35-ft

5-in) span L-2 had a maximum speed of 142 km/h (88 mph).

From the same basic Model D was developed the **Taylorcraft ST-100** training glider, a new lengthened fuselage being devised after removal of the engine to provide three-seat capacity. A

total of 250 was built for the US Army Air Force under the designation **TG-6**, plus three for US Navy evaluation as the **XLNT-1**. After testing was completed, the US Navy acquired 10 more from the USAAF as XLNT-1, followed by 25 more which it designated **LNT-1**.

Ted Smith Aerostar series

In October 1967 Ted Smith Aircraft Company flew prototypes of the **Aerostar 600** and **Aerostar 601**, both cantilever mid-wing monoplanes with retractable tricycle landing gear; they provided luxury air-conditioned cabin accommodation for six and differed only in powerplant, the 600 having two 216-kW (290-hp) Avco Lycoming I-540 flat-six engines, and the 601 the TIO-540 turbocharged version of the same engine. In the following year the **Aerostar 601P** was introduced, differing from the Aerostar 601 by having TIO-540 engines with higher flow-rate turbochargers so that bleed air could be used for cabin pressurisation. In 1978 Piper Aircraft Corporation acquired what had then become Ted Smith Aerostar Corporation and, initially, continued to manufacture all three versions. All were out of produc-

Piper's great plans for the Aerostar were thwarted by economic downturn despite new models such as the Aerostar 700P.

tion in 1982, by which time a total of 874 had been built by the two companies. Piper replaced the 601P, which they built initially as the **Sequoia**, with an improved **Piper Aerostar 602P**, which differed primarily in having TIO-540-A1A5 engines for improved performance: It was joined in mid-1983 by the **Piper PA-60 Aerostar 700P**. Generally similar to the earlier aircraft, it had two 261-kW (350-hp) Avco Lycoming TIO-540U2A flat-six counter-rotating engines which gave further performance improvements. With a wing span of 11.18 m (36 ft 8 in), the 700P had a maximum speed of 507 km/h (315 mph) at 5485 m (18,000 ft)

and a maximum payload range (with reserves) of 1001 km (622 miles). Having discontinued production of the non-pressurised models, Piper moved production to their main plant at Vero Beach, where the last Aerostar was built in 1984. Production for all versions (including prototypes) totalled 1089.

Temco TE-1 Buckaroo and Model 51 Pinto

Temco, known in full as the Texas Engineering & Manufacturing Company Inc., of Dallas, in 1947 acquired manufacturing rights for the Globe Swift Model GC-1, which it had built under sub-contract for Globe, and then continued production of this aircraft as the **Temco Swift Model GC-1B**. Temco also developed from it a two-seat primary trainer designated **TE-1 Buckaroo**, available initially in **TE-1A** (108-kW/145-hp Continental C145-2H) and **TE-1B** (123-kW/165-hp Franklin 6A4-165-B3) versions. Three TE-1As were evaluated by the USAF under the designation **YT-35**, while Israel and Italy also had one each for evaluation. No production resulted but the USAF subsequently acquired 10 TE-1Bs under the designation **T-35A**, and these were supplied to the Saudi Arabian air force. Temco produced a civil variant, the **Model 33 Plebe**, of which a single example was tested by the US Navy but no civil or military production followed. The 8.94-m (29-ft 4-in)

span **TE-1B Buckaroo** had a maximum speed of 251 km/h (156 mph) at sea level.

In the early 1950s Temco initiated design of a lightweight primary jet trainer which it designated **Model 51 Pinto**. A cantilever mid-wing monoplane with retractable tricycle landing gear, accommodating the instructor and pupil in tandem in an enclosed cockpit, it was powered by a Continental J69-T-9 turbojet.

The prototype, first flown on 26 March 1956, was later tested by the US Navy, which then ordered 14 production aircraft under the designation **TT-1**. The first jet trainer in service with any of the US air arms, it was

operated by the US Navy to study the feasibility of using jet aircraft for primary training. No further production followed, and plans for a Super Pinto attack trainer also failed.

Specification
Temco TT-1 Pinto
Type: jet primary trainer

Powerplant: one 4.1-kN (920-lb) thrust Continental J69-T-9 turbojet
Performance: maximum speed 555 km/h (345 mph) at 4570 m (15,000 ft); service ceiling 9815 m (32,200 ft); endurance at sea level 1 hour 30 minutes
Weight: maximum take-off 1996 kg (4,400 lb)
Dimensions: span 9.09 m (29 ft 10 in); length 9.32 m (30 ft 7 in); height 3.30 m (10 ft 10 in); wing area 13.94 m² (150.0 sq ft)

The Pinto's sleek lines would not look out of date on an air base ramp today, and belie its age. TT-1 was the United States Navy designation for the Temco Model 51, of which a small evaluation batch was ordered in the mid-1950s.

Thomas Brothers and Thomas-Morse aircraft

The Thomas Brothers Aeroplane Company was founded at Bath, New York, in 1912, and in 1915 built for the Royal Naval Air Service 24 **Thomas T-2** biplanes; powered by the 67-kW (90-hp) Curtiss OX-5 engine, these were delivered to the UK in two batches. A very similar aircraft, with floats instead of wheeled landing gear and powered by the 75-kW (100-hp) Thomas engine, was produced for the US Navy to a total of 15 under the designation **SH-4**. The company then built for evaluation by the US Army Signal Corps under a contract of 1916 two two-seat open-cockpit biplanes which, powered by the 101-kW (135-hp) Thomas Model 8 engine, were given the designation **D-5**.

In January 1917 Thomas Brothers combined with the Morse Chain Company to found the Thomas-Morse Aircraft Corporation. The new company made a more serious attempt to meet US military training requirements, resulting in the compact **Thomas Morse S-4** single-seat advanced trainer prototype, which was of equal-span biplane configuration and powered by a licence-built 75-kW (100-hp) Gnome rotary. Following evaluation it was produced as the **S-4B** with the Gnome engine (100 built), followed by an

improved **S-4C** of which 498 were built (51 with Gnome engines and the balance with the more reliable 60-kW/80-hp Le Rhône rotary). Of this total the US Navy received 10 S-4B and four S-4C aircraft which it used as trainers, plus six more S-4Bs that, converted as floatplanes, were designated **S.5**. A single **S.4E** prototype was built as an aerobatic trainer, differing mainly by having revised tail surfaces and an 82-kW (110-hp) Le Rhône engine.

Thomas-Morse then initiated the design of fighter aircraft, two each of three different prototypes being built for evaluation as the **MB-1**, **MB-2** and **MB-3**. The last, powered by a 224-kW (300-hp) Wright-Hispano engine, was considered the most capable. Following official evaluation of two more MB-3 biplane prototypes, the company built 50 production aircraft; 11 of these were transferred to the US Marine Corps for use as advanced trainers. The improved **MB-3A** was built to a total of 200 by Boeing under sub-contract, some of which were converted later as advanced trainers under the designation **MB-3M**. One MB-3 was converted for use as a racing aircraft under the designation **MB-6**, and a similar MB-3A conversion was desig-

nated **MB-7**. Unsuccessful designs included the **MB-9** parasol-wing fighter and the **MB-10** primary trainer.

The final Thomas-Morse design to enter quantity production before the company was acquired by Consolidated Aircraft Corporation in 1929 was the **O-19**, built in several **XO-6**, **O-6** and **XO-6B** prototypes. Early evaluation aircraft included the **XO-19** (Pratt & Whitney Wasp), **YO-20** (Pratt & Whitney Hornet), **XO-21** (Curtiss Chieftain), **XO-21A** (Wright Cyclone), O-19 and **O-19A** (Pratt & Whitney Wasp) and **O-23** (Curtiss Conqueror). Two late variants included the **Y1O-33** conversion from an **O-19B** (Curtiss Conqueror) and **Y1O-41** (geared Curtiss Conqueror). A

conventional two-seat biplane, mainly of metal construction except for fabric-covered wings and fixed tail surfaces, the initial production O-19B (70 built) differed from the O-19A by having modified cockpits; the **O-19C** (71) introduced a tailwheel and detail changes; the one-off **O-19D** VIP transport was converted from an O-19C; and the final **O-19E** (30) differed from the O-19C by having an increased-span upper wing and the 429-kW (575-hp) Pratt & Whitney R-1340-15 Wasp.

The Thomas-Morse O-19C was distinguished mainly by the Townend ring cowling for its Pratt & Whitney R-1340 radial engine.

Thurston aircraft

David B. Thurston established Thurston Aircraft Corporation at Sandford, Maine, in 1966 to produce a lightweight amphibian of his own design which had the designation **Thurston TSC-1A Teal**. With a monoplane wing set high on all-metal hull structure, the Teal seated two or three in an enclosed cabin and was powered by a 112-kW (150-hp) Avco Lycoming O-320-A3B flat-four engine mounted above the hull; manually-retractable tailwheel landing gear was provided for amphibious operations. Production began after certification was gained in August 1969, the 16th and subsequent aircraft, which introduced some refinements, being designated **TSC-1A1 Teal**. In 1972 David Thurston joined the

Schweizer Aircraft Corporation, which continued to build the Teal in the form of an improved **TSC-1A2 Teal II** before selling the production rights to the Teal Aircraft Corporation of Markham, Ontario, in early 1976. This last company built a developed **TSC-1A3 Marlin** before running out of financial steam in early 1979.

Before the Schweizer acquisition Thurston had designed in conjunction with an aviation magazine a landplane version designated **TSC-2 Explorer**. Marvin Patchen Inc., which financed this development, acquired the production rights for this aircraft, planning to build civil and law-enforcement versions as the Explorer and Observer respectively. Subsequently, Dr Maitland

Reed's National Dynamics (Pty) Ltd of Durban, South Africa, acquired this project from Patchen but later decided not to build either version of this aircraft.

The original TSC-1A Teal (illustrated) was a two-seater, while the improved TSC-1A1 introduced an optional third seat.

Transall C.160

The C.160NG is a uniquely French version of the Franco-German Transall family. A new production version, it is fitted with an air-to-air refuelling probe.

The original Transall (Transporter Allianz) group was formed in January 1959 to comprise Aérospatiale in France with Messerschmitt-Bölkow-Blohm and Vereinigte Flugtechnische Werke in Germany. This group built the **Transall C.160** twin-turboprop transport for the air forces of France (50 **C.160F**), West Germany (90 **C.160D**), Turkey (20 **C.160T**) and South Africa (nine **C.160Z**) before production ended in 1972. In addition, four C.160Fs were converted for use by Air France in night mail operations with the revised designation **C.160P**.

A high-wing monoplane with a pressurised interior, the C.160 incorporates a door/ramp in the upswept rear fuselage and paratroop deployment doors on each side of the fuselage. The programme was relaunched in 1977, initially to provide the French air force with additional aircraft. France ordered a total of 29 (increased from 25 in 1982) of these second-series C.160s, the **C.160NG** (Nouvelle Génération), four of which were intended to serve as communications relay aircraft. In addition, three of these new aircraft

have also been supplied to Indonesia (and are flown by Pelita Air Service) for use in moving the nation's people to less populated islands. Ten of the French aircraft were equipped from the outset with hose-and-drogue air-to-air refuelling equipment, while five others have provision for easy conversion to tanker status. In a transport role they can accommodate 93 troops, or 61-88 fully-equipped paratroops, or 62 stretchers with four attendants, or vehicles and/or cargo to a maximum weight of 16000 kg (35,274 lb). First deliveries were made to ET 64 at Evreux in 1981. Four C.160NGs were later fitted out as **Astarté** (Avion-Station-relais de Transmission exceptionelles) to provide wartime communications with France's ballistic missile submarine fleet, in much the same way as the US Navy's EC-130Q TACAMO Hercules were. Production of the C-160NG ceased in 1985. Modular kits were developed to make possible their deployment in **C.160S** maritime

surveillance, **C.160SE** electronic surveillance and proposed **C.160AAA** airborne early warning configurations. Two aircraft were more dramatically modified to **Gabriel** standard, with several fuselage fairings, wingtip pods, and a large, retractable, domed fairing beneath the forward fuselage. Operated as Elint platforms by EET 11/54 at Metz, one aircraft was deployed to the Gulf during Operation Desert Shield/Desert Storm.

Specification
Transall C.160
Type: multi-role transport

Powerplant: two 4549-ekW (6,100-eshp) Rolls-Royce Tyne RTy.20 Mk 22 turboprops
Performance: maximum speed 513 km/h (319 mph) at 4875 m (16,000 ft); service ceiling 8230 m (27,000 ft) at 45000 kg (99,208 lb) AUW; range with maximum payload 1850 km (1,150 miles)
Weights: empty operating 29000 kg (63,934 lb); maximum take-off 51000 kg (112,436 lb)
Dimensions: span 40.00 m (131 ft 2¾ in); length 32.40 m (106 ft 3½ in); height 11.65 m (38 ft 2¾ in); wing area 160.00 m² (1,722.28 sq ft)

Transavia PL-12 Airtruk and Skyfarmer

Designed by Luigi Pellarini, the **Transavia PL-12 Airtruk** is a multi-role aircraft of unusual configuration, comprising strut-braced sesquiplane wings; a fuselage pod to accommodate the pilot and passengers/cargo and to mount in the nose the powerplant; twin booms extending aft from the wings and each carrying a fin and rudder plus a T-tailplane; and landing gear of fixed tricycle type. The prototype was first flown on 22 April 1965, and since then 118 have been built and sold for service in Australia, Denmark, Malaysia, New Zealand, South Africa, Taiwan Thailand and Yugoslavia. In 1981 the Airtruk name was changed to **Skyfarmer** and Transavia went on to consider a turboprop version the **T-550**, and completed a mockup of the military **M.300** support aircraft. Versions offered since then for more

peaceful roles include the **PL-12-U** utility aircraft that can be equipped for aerial survey, ambulance, cargo, or passenger-carrying (five) roles; the dedicated agricultural **Skyfarmer T-300** which also differs by having a 224-kW (300-hp) Avco Lycoming IO-540-KIA5 engine; and the improved **Skyfarmer T-300A** with a more roomy cabin and some aerodynamic refinements. The T-300A became the standard production model in 1981 and remains in very low-volume production (built chiefly to order) at Transavia's Seven Hills factory in New South Wales.

Specification
Transavia PL-12-U Airtruk
Type: multi-purpose aircraft
Powerplant: one 224-kW (300-hp) Teledyne Continental IO-520-D flat-six piston engine

Performance: maximum speed 196 km/h (122 mph) at 915 m (3,000ft); service ceiling 3810 m (12,500 ft)

Weights: empty 1017 kg (2,242 lb); maximum take-off 1925 kg (4,244 lb)
Dimensions: span 11.98 m (39 ft 3½ in); length 6.35 m (20 ft 10 in); height 2.79 m (9 ft 2 in); wing area 24.53 m² (264.0 sq ft)

Specific single-role requirements frequently led to some very odd aircraft, and Australia's Transavia Airtruk is a classic example of this tendency.

Travel Air aircraft

The Travel Air Manufacturing Company was established at Wichita, Kansas, in late 1924 by founder members that included such well-known aviation names as Walter Beech, Clyde Cessna

and Lloyd Stearman. With the genius of such men available it would have been surprising if the new company had not produced some remarkable aircraft. But of course they did, the

Travel Air 1000 marking the beginning of a success story that lasted until 1930 when the company sought security from the growing recession by accepting a take-over bid from Curtiss-Wright Corporation. Introduced in 1925, the Travel Air 1000 was a conventional biplane powered by a 67-kW

(90-hp) Curtiss OX-5 engine and seating three in tandem open cockpits (pilot at the rear), but it was the subtle relationship between aerofoil sections, wing gap and stagger and the configuration of the tail unit that elevated the Travel Air above the category of 'just another biplane'.

The **Travel Air 2000** that followed differed only in minor detail, but the extensive range of variants built until 1930 included the **SC-2000** (119-kW/160-hp Curtiss C-6), **Travel Air 3000** (112- or 134-kW/150- or 180-hp Hispano-Suiza Model A or Model E), **Travel Air A-4000** (112-kW/150-hp Axelson), **B-4000** (164-kW/220-hp Wright J-5), **BC-4000**, **SBC-4000** floatplane and **C-4000** (127-kW/170-hp Challenger), **E-4000** (123-kW/165-hp Wright J-6), **K-4000** (75-kW/100-hp Kinner K5), **W-4000** (82-kW/110-hp Warner Scarab), **B9-4000** (224-kW/300-hp Wright J-6-9), **Travel Air 8000** (89-kW/120-hp Fairchild-Caminez), **Travel Air 9000** (93-kW/125-hp Ryan-Siemens), **Model 4D** (168- or 179-kW/225- or 240-hp Wright J-6) and, the last to be certificated before Curtiss-Wright took over, the **Model 4P** (104-kW/140-hp ACE La.1).

In different vein was the **Travel Air 5000**, a light transport of braced high wing monoplane configuration seating five and with a 164-kW (220-hp) Wright J-5 engine; it was basically a development prototype for the improved six-

The Travel Air 4000 series was akin to the Model 3000 series, but introduced a radial engine in place of the lower-powered inline type, providing the type with far more 'sporty' performance.

seat **Travel Air 6000** with the same powerplant. Later variants included the **A-6000A** (336-kW/450-hp Pratt & Whitney Wasp), available also as the **SA-6000-A** floatplane, and followed by the **Travel Air 6000-B** and floatplane **S-6000-B** with 224-kW (300-hp) Wright J-6-9 radial engine. The final Travel Air design was also a braced high-wing monoplane, but a lighter-weight four-seat aircraft; it entered production with the 168-kW (225-hp) Wright J-6 engine as the **Travel Air Model 10-D** following certification in early December 1929. Versions with engines ranging from 137 to 224 kW (185 to 300 hp) were intended by Travel Air (one **Model 10-B** was flown with a 224-kW/300-hp Wright J-6), but the take-over by Curtiss-Wright brought such plans to an end. Brief details of the subsequent development of Travel

Air designs can be found under the entry for Curtiss-Wright miscellaneous types.

Specification
Travel Air E-4000
Type: three-seat biplane
Powerplant: one 123-kW (165-hp) Wright J-6 radial piston engine

Performance: maximum speed 193 km/h (120 mph); service ceiling 3960 m (13,000 ft); range 1046 km (650 miles)
Weights: empty 769 kg (1,695 lb); maximum take-off 1226 kg (2,702 lb)
Dimensions: span 10.06 m (33 ft 0 in); length 7.34 m (24 ft 1 in); height 2.72 m (8 ft 11 in); wing area 26.85 m² (289.0 sq ft)

Tupolev early aircraft

Co-founder with Zhukovskii of TsAGI, Tupolev formed his own design bureau during 1925, having previously been head of the state committee examining the uses of metal in aircraft construction. Influenced by the pioneering techniques of Junkers, Tupolev instigated the use of Kolchug (dural-type) aluminium alloy in the single-seat **ANT-1** technology demonstrator with many alloy components and the **ANT-2** light transport with an all-

Kolchug airframe with corrugated skin. The single aircraft proved the practicality of the construction technique, but was not put into production. Its success was, however, enough to persuade the air force to consider procuring aircraft built in this way, the **ANT-3** being the first such aircraft to be selected. The prototype flew for the first time in August 1925. An unequal-span biplane, intended for reconnaissance duties, it was of all-metal construction with cor-

rugated sheet covering. The original 298-kW (400-hp) Liberty engine was replaced by a 336-kW (450-hp) Napier Lion, the aircraft then being redesignated **R-3NL**. The first 12 series aircraft had Liberty engines but the next 18 had the Soviet development of this powerplant, which was designated M-5. The final 79 aircraft with the 336-kW (450-hp) Lorraine Dietrich engine were designated **R-3LD**, and one ANT-3 was tested with a 507-kW (680-hp) BMW VI. Most R-3s saw military service, but a few retaining the ANT-3 designation

were flown as mailplanes or used for liaison and for propaganda flights. The **R-3LD** version had a maximum speed of 205 km/h (127 mph), was armed with three 0.303-in (7.7-mm) machine-guns and could carry 10 10-kg (22-lb) bombs on external racks. Plans for a Shturmovik version with 400 kg (880 lb) of armour protection came to nothing. The **ANT-10 (R-7)** was a refined development powered by a BMW VI engine, but when tested in 1930 it was found to be inferior to the Polikarpov R-5 and was abandoned.

Tupolev ANT-4 (TB-1)

A cantilever low-wing monoplane powered by two 336-kW (450-hp) Napier Lion engines, the prototype **TB-1** or **Tupolev ANT-4** made its maiden flight on ski landing gear on 26 November 1925. Intended mainly for the heavy bomber role, the ANT-4 was of all-metal construction with corrugated metal sheet covering and a glazed nose section. The aircraft was heavily influenced by Junkers, the German company that was unsuccessfully trying to sue Tupolev for patent infringements. The second aircraft was the true TB-1 bomber prototype; flown initially in July 1928 it had a redesigned nose section with 'balcony'-type gunner's cockpit and a crew of five including three gunners, and was powered by two 544-kW (730-hp) BMW VI engines. A third prototype, designated **ANT-4bis**, had revised engine nacelles and increased armament.

The first series machine was completed as a propaganda aircraft; named *Strana Sovietov* (Land of the Soviets) it

was equipped for a staged flight across Siberia and on to New York but was soon damaged severely in a forced landing. A second aircraft was prepared and completed the journey, using wheels or floats as appropriate, and this second *Strana Sovietov* covered 21242 km (13,199 miles) between leaving Moscow on 23 August 1929 and arriving in New York on 1 November.

Production of the TB-1 continued until August 1932, a total of 152 being delivered plus 66 **TB-1P** twin-float bomber/torpedo seaplanes. These were built at the Fili works, where Junkers production was terminated to make way for the new indigenous aircraft. The ANT-4s were front-line equipment for a number of years before being relegated to the transport role with the revised designation **G-1**. Many were used as freighters by Aeroflot and by the Soviet Arctic Aviation Authority (Aviaarktika), final examples of the type being grounded in 1945. The TB-1 was also used in a

number of experiments, including autopilot and drone trials, inflight refuelling of other aircraft, rocket-assisted take-offs, cargo parachute drops, and Zveno trials with parasite fighters.

It was the first twin-engined all-metal cantilever monoplane to enter production in the world.

Specification
Tupolev TB-1
Type: heavy bomber
Powerplant: two 507-kW (680-hp) M-17 Vee piston engines
Performance: maximum speed 178 km/h (111 mph); service ceiling 4830 m

The G-1 designation was applied to some 90 time-expired TB-1 bombers converted to the freight role. Stripped of military equipment they were operated by Aeroflot.

(15,850 ft); range 1000 km (621 miles)
Weights: empty equipped 4520 kg (9,965 lb); maximum take-off 6810 kg (15,013 lb)
Dimensions: span 28.70 m (94 ft 2 in); length 18.01 m (59 ft 1 in); wing area 120.00 m² (1,291.71 sq ft)
Armament: six 0.3-in (7.62-mm) DA machine-guns, plus an internal bombload of 1000 kg (2,205 lb)

Tupolev ANT-5 (I-4)

The first prototype of the **Tupolev ANT-5** all-metal sesquiplane single-seat fighter was flown in July 1927, powered by a Jupiter IV engine. A second example had a Jupiter VI engine. Delivery of **I-4** series aircraft began in October 1928. These incorporated a number of revisions, including enlarged

tail surfaces with a balanced rudder, and introduced the M-22 radial engine which was the Soviet-built version of the Jupiter VI. Production ended in January 1934 after 371 had been built. As well as equipping Soviet fighter eskadrilii for a number of years, I-4s were used in experiments with rockets

and in the parasite fighter trials (**I-4Z**) conducted by Vakhmistrov. Variants included the I-4bis monoplane and the I-4P floatplane.

Specification
Type: single-seat fighter
Powerplant: one 358-kW (480-hp) M-22 radial engine
Performance: maximum speed 231 km/h (144 mph); service ceiling 7000 m

(22,960 ft); range 840 km (522 miles)
Weights: empty equipped 978 kg (2,156 lb); maximum take-off 1430 kg (3,153 lb)
Dimensions: span 11.40 m (37 ft 4¾ in); length 7.28 m (23 ft 10½ in); wing area 23.80 m² (256.19 sq ft)
Armament: two 0.303-in (7.7-mm) PV-1 synchronised machine-guns, plus four 50-kg (110-lb) bombs

Tupolev ANT-6 (TB-3)

The **Tupolev TB-3** all-metal cantilever monoplane was the most advanced four-engined heavy bomber in service in the world in the early 1930s. The prototype was flown first on 22 December 1930 and production began at the end of 1931, continuing through many modifications until early 1937 when a total of 818 had been built. For many years the TB-3 was the backbone of the VVS (Soviet air forces) heavy bomber units. A number retained the bureau designation **ANT-6** and were used for transport, particularly in the Arctic. In 1938-39 TB-3s were used operationally against the Japanese, but by the time Germany invaded the Soviet Union in 1941 most had been converted as paratroop or freight transports under the designation **G-2**. Other uses then consisted of night bombing and transport work of all kinds, including the carriage of vehicles or tanks between landing gear legs, and glider towing. Use in parasite fighter experiments led in 1941 to Black Sea Fleet TB-3s being used to launch two Polikarpov SPB dive-bomber versions of the I-16 fighter, for raids on pinpoint targets in the Ukraine and Romania.

Variants

Prototypes: first prototype with 447-kW (600-hp) Curtiss Conqueror

Five examples of the ANT-6 were built to support the Soviet bases in the Arctic, with fully enclosed flight-decks, extensive de-icing and heating equipment, interchangeable wheels and skis and a 14-m (46-ft) wide brake chute.

engines; this aircraft modified in 1931 as production prototype; two other prototypes flown with 544-kW (730-hp) BMW VI engines
TB-3/M-17: some 400 built to end of 1933; introduced revised landing gear with independent fixed tandem main units and large tail skid, and corrugated KA dural sheet covering for wings and fuselage
TB-3/M-34: less than 100 built; had 619-kW (830-hp) M-34 engines and introduced bomb-aimer's gondola under nose
TB-3/M-34R: introduced improved M-34R engine, some airframe revisions, and a tail gunner's position; nine 'civilianised' TB-3/M-34RDs made tour of European capitals 1934
TB-3/AM-34RN: introduced in 1935; had 723-kW (970-hp) AM-34RN engines to improve performance at altitude, and revised defensive gun positions with 0.303-in (7.7-mm) ShKAS machine-guns
TB-3/AM-34FRN: tested September 1936; introduced revised landing gear

with large single main wheels, redesigned nose with enclosed manually-operated turret, smooth instead of corrugated sheet covering and 671-kW (900-hp) AM-34FRN engines; about 100 built
TB-3/AM-34FRNV: final version, similar to TB-3/AM-34FRN but with enclosed dorsal gun turret and 895-kW (1,200-hp) AM-34FRNV engines; about 100 built
TB-3D: one aircraft tested with Charomsky AN-1 diesel engines
ANT-6A: batch of five TB-3/AM-34Rs with enclosed flight deck, special equipment and skis for Aviaarktika (Soviet Arctic Aviation Authority); used for many special operations 1937-44

Specification
Tupolev TB-3 M-17
Type: four-engined heavy bomber
Powerplant: four 533-kW (715-hp) M-17F Vee piston engines
Performance: maximum speed 197 km/h (122 mph); service ceiling 3800 m (12,470 ft); range 1350 km (839 miles)
Weights: empty equipped 10967 kg (24,178 lb); maximum take-off 17200 kg (37,920 lb)
Dimensions: span 39.50 m (129 ft 7 in); length 24.40 m (80 ft 0¾ in); wing area 230.00 m² (2,475.78 sq ft)
Armament: eight 7.7-mm (0.303-in) DA machine-guns in nose, dorsal positions and underwing 'dustbins'; up to 2000 kg (4,409 lb) of bombs

Tupolev ANT-7 (R-6)

The **Tupolev ANT-7** prototype was a scaled-down version of the ANT-4. First flown on 11 September 1929, it was powered by two 544-kW (730-hp) BMW VI engines. Production began in summer 1930 as the multi-purpose **R-6** for the air force, with a total of 435 built by June 1934. The **KR-6** version was a long-range reconnaissance aircraft with increased fuel capacity and no bombload, and the **MR-6** was a naval floatplane variant. Many late production aircraft were delivered for civil use under the designation **PS-7** or **P-6**; modifications were minimal, including a strengthened freight floor and elimination of gunners' positions. The **MP-6**

After its retirement from front-line duties, the ANT-7(R-6) was widely used for civil tasks, this example being allocated to Arctic flying, in the hands of Aviaartika.

was the civil floatplane version, and many P-/MP-6s and PS-7s had enclosed cockpits for Arctic use. The specially built **R-6L** was a one-off 'limousine' version incorporating a nine-passenger cabin.

Specification
Tupolev R-6
Type: reconnaissance-bomber and escort fighter

Powerplant: two 533-kW (715-hp) M-17F Vee engines
Performance: maximum speed 230 km/h (143 mph); service ceiling 5620 m (18,440 ft); range 800 km (497 miles)
Weights: empty equipped 3856 kg (8,500 lb); maximum take-off 6472 kg

(14,268 lb)
Dimensions: span 23.20 m (76 ft 1¼ in); length 15.06 m (49 ft 5 in); wing area 80.00 m² (861.14 sq ft)
Armament: five 0.303-in (7.7-mm) DA machine-guns, plus a bombload of up to 500 kg (1,102 lb)

Tupolev ANT-9

The prototype of the **Tupolev ANT-9** high-wing monoplane transport made its first flight in May 1929. Of all-metal construction with corrugated alloy skinning, it had enclosed accommodation for two pilots and nine passengers. Its three 172-kW (230-hp) Gnome-Rhône Titan radials were replaced in series machines by domestic M-26s, which

proved to be underpowered and were in turn replaced by imported Wright Whirlwinds of 224 kW (300 hp) each. After the first batch of some 12 aircraft the design was revised to twin-engined configuration, with two 507-kW (680-hp) M-17 engines raising maximum speed from 205 km/h (127 mph) to 215 km/h (134 mph); this version was known usually as the **PS-9**, and about 70 were built.

The ANT-9 prototype, registered

URSS-309, made a tour of European cities in the summer of 1929, and the three-engined ANT-9s served with the Soviet-German airline Deruluft on the Moscow Berlin service. Some were also operated by the VVS as troop or VIP transports. The PS-9 was flown widely on passenger services, the most famous being the propaganda aircraft Krokodil, with a suitably decorated plywood nose complete with a set of sharp teeth.

The one-off **ANT-14 Pravda**, which served as flagship of the propaganda squadron, was an enlargement of the ANT-9, powered by five 358-kW (480-hp) Jupiter radials and capable of carrying a crew of five and 36 passengers at a maximum 236 km/h (147 mph). It spanned 40.40 m (132 ft 61/2 in) as against the 23.80 m (78 ft 1 in) of the ANT-9. Pravda carried over 40,000 passengers before being grounded in 1941.

Tupolev ANT-25

The first **Tupolev ANT-25 (RD)** special long-range aircraft was flown initially on 22 June 1933, powered by a single M-34 engine, but the second example flown three months later had a 671-kW (900-hp) geared M-34R. In configuration the ANT-25 was an all-metal cantilever low-wing monoplane of 34.00-m (111-ft 61/2-in) span, with enclosed accommodation for a three-man crew.

With a crew led by Chkalov, the M-34R-powered ANT-25, registered N-025-1, made a remarkable flight. Taking off from Moscow on 18 June 1937, after accelerating down a spe-

The ANT-25 was a singularly advanced design, built around an extraordinary cantilever wing.

cially prepared concrete ramp so that it could become airborne with an overload of fuel, it reached the west coast of the USA where a forced landing was made after it had been flown a distance of 9130 km (5,673 miles) nonstop in 63 hours 25 minutes. A considerably modified aircraft made a second spectacular flight with a crew under Gromov. Leaving Moscow on 12 July 1937 it landed safely at San Jacinto,

California, after a non-stop journey of 11500 km (7,146 miles) completed in 62 hours 17 minutes.

An improved version of the ANT-25 was ordered into production for long-range bombing research, some 20

examples being reported as delivered by spring 1936 when the balance of the 50-aircraft order was cancelled. They were flown with various engines and in revised configurations in a wide variety of tests and experiments.

Tupolev ANT-23 (I-12) and ANT-31 (I-14)
to
Tupolev Tu-154

Tupolev ANT-23 (I-12) and ANT-31 (I-14)

The **Tupolev ANT-23** or **I-12** experimental single-seat fighter was flown in 1931. It had twin tailbooms each containing a heavy-calibre Kurchevsky cannon and was powered by two 391-kW (525-hp) Gnome-Rhône Jupiter VI engines, one at each end of the pilot's nacelle. When it proved unsuccessful the Tupolev bureau took up the

concept of a cannon-fighter once again with the **ANT-31** or **I-14**, which made its first flight in May 1933.

The I-14 was an all-metal cantilever low-wing monoplane with retractable landing gear. Armament comprised one 0.303-in (7.7-mm) PV1 machine-gun and two 37-mm APK-37 cannon. The much modified **I-14bis** with two

ShKAS machine-guns and two APK-11 cannon was placed in production in 1935, but of the 55 ordered only 18 were delivered, the last in December 1936, due to availability of the superior Polikarpov I-16. Powered by a 537-kW (720-hp) M-25A radial, series I-14bis fighters had a maximum speed of 375 km/h (233 mph).

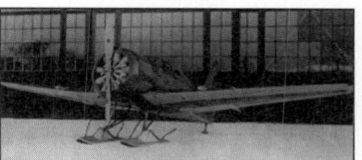

For its period the ANT-31 was a very advanced concept, its major drawback being the continued use of corrugated skinning.

Tupolev ANT-35

The **Tupolev ANT-35** all-metal light passenger transport prototype was based on the SB-2 bomber, and was flown initially on 20 August 1936. Of low-wing configuration with retractable main landing gear units, it was powered by two 597-kW (800-hp) Gnome-Rhône 14K radials, later replaced by

Soviet M-85s; its near circular-section fuselage accommodated a crew of two or three and 10 passengers. The improved **ANT-35bis** prototype was followed by nine series aircraft powered by 746-kW (1,000-hp) M-62IR engines, and the type entered service with Aeroflot as the **PS-35**, delivered

from 1937 to 1939. After June 1941 several were used for liaison and VIP transport, this 20.80-m (68-ft 3-in) span aircraft having a maximum speed of 372 km/h (231 mph) and a range of 1640 km (1,019 miles).

The Tupolev ANT-35, seen here in a heavily retouched photograph, may be regarded as the civilian counterpart to the SB-2 bomber.

Tupolev ANT-37 (DB-2)

Developed from the uncompleted **Tupolev ANT-36 (DB-1)**, a single-engined long-range bomber based on the ANT-25, the **Tupolev ANT-37 (DB-2)** long-range bomber was developed by Sukhoi's design brigade under Tupolev's overall control. Powered by two 597-kW (800-hp) Gnome-Rhône 14K radial engines, the prototype flew on 16 June 1935 but crashed in the following month. The **DB-2D** was a redesign with particular attention paid to rectifying faults in the tail unit. It was

followed in turn by the **DB-2B** or **ANT-37bis,** of which only three were built as record breakers/research aircraft after rejection of the design in favour of the Ilyushin DB-3.

The first DB-2B, named *Rodina* (motherland) was flown to a long-distance women's record by an all-female crew, covering 5908 km (3,671 miles) on 24/25 September 1938 before making an emergency landing. Examples survived well into the wartime period, flying for Aeroflot or on research projects.

Possessing high-aspect ratio wings inspired by those of the ANT-25, the Tupolev ANT-37 featured a stressed-skin construction of dural. It had a wing span of 31.00 m (101 ft 10½ in) and a speed of 342 km/h (213 mph).

Tupolev ANT-40

Tupolev SB-2bis of the Red air force, captured by the Germans late in 1941.

Owing something to the earlier experimental twin-engined **Tupolev ANT-21 (MI-3)** multi-seat fighter of 1933 and the **Tupolev ANT-29 (DIP)** cannon fighter, the initial prototype of the **Tupolev ANT-40 (SB)** -'SB' indicating fast bomber - was first flown on 25 April 1934, powered by two Wright Cyclone radial engines. Re-engined with Soviet M-87s, it was rebuilt after a landing accident and considerably modified. The second and third prototypes had Hispano-Suiza engines, increased chord, a taller fin and rudder assembly, and revised ailerons. These aircraft were flown in October 1934 and September 1935 respectively, and further changes led to the definitive design which entered production in 1935.

The SB was an all-metal mid-wing monoplane with a crew of three or four, initial production aircraft being powered by 559-kW (750-hp) M-100 engines. These were superseded first by 641-kW (860-hp) M100As, while the final production **SB-2bis**, first flown in October 1936, had more powerful M-103 engines. Total production was 6,656 aircraft, the last machines appearing in late 1940. Built in greater numbers than any comparable light twin-engined bomber of its time, the SB-2 initially gave a good account of itself on the Republican side in the

Spanish Civil War. It was later involved in frontier skirmishes in the Far East with the Japanese, but by the time it took part in the Winter War with Finland in 1939-40 was obsolescent .

Foreign operators of the type included Czechoslovakia, which imported 53 M-100A-powered SBs and then placed the type under licence production as the **B-71**, powered by Czech-built Hispano-Suiza engines. A total of 111 out of a 161-aircraft order were delivered, most of them being operated by the Luftwaffe as trainers and glider tugs after the fall of Czechoslovakia. Finland used 24 SB and SB-2bis bombers operationally, most of them captured originally by the Germans. China obtained some 200 SBs in late 1937, but most were lost during

Japanese bombing attacks.

When the German invasion of the Soviet Union began in June 1941, the SB and SB-2bis equipped a large number of Soviet front-line light bomber *eskadrilii*. Many were lost. Surviving machines soldiered on into 1943, although by that time they were used chiefly in night operations.

Developments of the SB included the **PS-40** civil transport delivered to Aeroflot in some numbers in 1938; **USB** or **SB-3** crew trainer with an instructor's open cockpit in a new solid nose section (used also as glider tugs); **PS-41** and **PS-41bis** transports built in 1939 and 1940 respectively; **ANT-41 (T-1)** torpedo-bomber (1936) and the **ANT-46 (DI-8)** two-seat cannon fighter.

Tupolev's principal assistant was responsible for a development of the SB-2bis known as the Archangelskii Ar-2.

Specification
Tupolev SB-2bis
Type: light bomber
Powerplant: two 716-kW (960-hp) M-103 Vee piston engines
Performance: maximum speed 450 km/h (280 mph); service ceiling 7800 m (25,590 ft); range 2300 km (1,429 miles)
Weights: empty equipped 4768 kg (10,511 lb); maximum take-off 7880 kg (17,372 lb)
Dimensions: span 20.33 m (66 ft 8½ in); length 12.57 m (41 ft 2¾ in)
Armament: up to six 0.3-in (7.62-mm) ShKAS machine-guns, plus a bombload of 600 kg (1,323 lb)

Tupolev giant aircraft

The **Tupolev ANT-16** or **TB-4** was a super-heavy bomber powered by six 619-kW (900-hp) M-34 engines, two of them mounted in tandem above the fuselage. Armament comprised two 20-mm cannon and 10 machine-guns, plus a maximum bombload of 10000 kg (22,046 lb). First flown on 3 July 1933, the TB-4 spanned 54.00 m (177 ft 2 in) and attained a maximum speed of 200 km/h (124 mph).

The renowned and tragic **Tupolev ANT-20** *Maxim Gorky* was an eight-engined passenger-cum-propaganda monoplane. Six 671-kW (900-hp) AM-34FRN engines were mounted in the wing leading edge and two more over the fuselage. Equipped with printing press, cinema, film laboratory and many other features unique at the time, the ANT-20 carried a crew of 20. Test flown for the first time on 17 June 1934, it was destroyed in a mid-air collision on 18 May 1935 with a stunting I-5 fighter which had been acting as escort. The *Maxim Gorky* spanned 63.00 m (206 ft 8¼ in), had a maximum

take-off weight of 42000 kg (92,594 lb) and was capable of a maximum speed of 245 km/h (152 mph).

Public reaction to the loss of the *Maxim Gorky* led to a fund to build 16 more giant aircraft. In the event only one **ANT-20bis** was built, this also being known as the **PS-124** or **L-760**. Flown for the first time in late 1939, it differed considerably from the ANT-20, having a redesigned wing, fuselage and tailplane. Power was provided by six 895-kW (1,200-hp) AM-34FRNV engines set in the wing leading edge. Completed as a passenger transport with accommodation for 64 plus a crew of nine, the ANT-20bis was similar in size to the ANT-20 but was slightly heavier, and had a maximum speed of 275 km/h (171 mph).

The **Tupolev ANT-22** or **MK-1** with six 619-kW (830-hp) M-34R engines was a long-range bomber reconnaissance flying-boat, its twin-hull design clearly inspired by the Italian Savoia-Marchetti S.55. Test flown for the first time on 8 August 1934, it

An enormous achievement for its time, the Tupolev ANT-20bis used considerably more powerful engines than the ANT-20, permitting the elimination of the two overwing engines.

established several weight-to-height world records in December 1936, but was abandoned soon afterwards. Armament comprised eight 7.7-mm (0.303-in) ShKAS machine-guns, one 20-mm cannon and a bombload of up

to 6000 kg (13,228 lb). The MK-1 spanned 51.00 m (167 ft 33/4 in) and had a maximum speed of 223 km/h (145 mph).

The colossal **ANT-26** heavy bomber was stopped in 1936 before completion.

Tupolev Tu-2

Designed by Andrei Tupolev while in detention, the first prototype of this powerful bomber was known as **Aircraft 103**, using the number assigned to his design team. Development was protracted and the prototype, known otherwise as the **Tupolev ANT-58** flew initially on 29 January 1941; an improved version, the **103U** or **ANT-59**, flew on 18 May the same year. During tests the original 1044-kW (1,400-hp) AM-37 V-12 engines were replaced by ASh-82 radials. Efforts to simplify the design for quantity production led to the **103V** or **ANT-60** and series aircraft designated **Aircraft 103S** or **ANT-61** entered service from November 1942 onwards, being redesignated **Tu-2** early in 1943. They had heavy-calibre machine-guns, more powerful ASh-82FNV engines and dispensed with the divebrakes of the original prototypes. As production got under way the refined **Tu-2S** was introduced, but difficulties at the factories resulted in only some 1,100 Tu-2s and Tu-2S bombers being delivered before the end of the war. However post-war production brought the total built to 2,527. The Soviet Tu-2s performed well and had flying qualities close to those of a single-seat fighter. Tu-2S bombers fought in the Korean conflict with the North Korean forces, and equipped a number of the Soviet Union's allies including China, Poland and Yugoslavia. Post-war a large number of developments were built, some

Tupolev Tu-2S of a Soviet bomber regiment operating on the Eastern Front in 1945.

in quantity. The NATO reporting name for the series was **'Bat'**.

Variants

ANT-62T: torpedo bomber, flown and entered production in 1947; earlier test aircraft known as **Tu-2T**
ANT-67: long-range bomber with ACh-39 diesels and crew of five
Tu-1 (ANT-63P): long-range three-seat escort fighter based on Tu-10; appeared end 1946
Tu-2D (ANT-62): long-range version; redesigned forward fuselage, new long-span wings and side-by-side seating for two pilots
Tu-2DB (ANT-65): long-range bomber development, 1641-kW (2,200-hp) AM-44TK engines
Tu-2F (ANT-64): special photo reconnaissance version
Tu-2G: modified high-speed cargo transport; carried light vehicles externally
Tu-2M (ANT-61M): believed designation

of production version with 1417-kW (1,900-hp) ASh-83 radials
Tu-2N: testbed for Rolls-Royce Nene turbojet
Tu-2R: specialised reconnaissance aircraft
Tu-2RShR: prototype with 57-mm RShR cannon in forward fuselage
Tu-2K: two examples used for ejection seat tests
Tu-2Sh: 1944 *Shturmovik* ground attack version
Tu-2 Paravan: two aircraft used for tests of barrage balloon cable deflectors/cutters
Tu-2/104: radar-equipped all-weather interceptor tested in 1944
Tu-6: reconnaissance aircraft conversions
Tu-8 (ANT-69): final long-range bomber of late 1946; armed with five B-20 cannon, some aimed indirectly from sighting stations
Tu-10 (ANT-68): 1945 prototype for

general-purpose bomber, had 1380-kW (1,850-hp) AM-39FN engines; post-war production totalled at least 50 with 1491-kW (2,000-hp) AM-42 engines

Specification
Tupolev Tu-2S
Type: four-crew medium bomber
Powerplant: two 1380-kW (1,850-hp) ASh-82FNV radial piston engines
Performance: maximum speed 550 km/h (342 mph); service ceiling 9500 m (31,170 ft); range 1400 km (870 miles)
Weights: empty equipped 7474 kg (16,477 lb); maximum take-off 11360 kg (25,045 lb)
Dimensions: span 18.86 m (61 ft 10½ in); length 13.80 m (45 ft 3½ in); height 4.55 m (14 ft 11 in); wing area 48.80 m² (525.30 sq ft)
Armament: two 20-mm ShVAK cannon, three 12.7-mm (0.5-in) UBT machine-guns, plus maximum bombload of 4000 kg (8,818 lb)

Tupolev Tu-4 and family

Based on the Boeing B-29 Superfortress (examples of which had made emergency landings in Russia during 1944 in the course of operations against Japan), the **Tupolev Tu-4** differed in its armament and powerplant. It was a heavier aircraft and did not possess either the pressurised tunnel linking the forward to midships crew locations or the integral fuel tankage of the B-29. The first of a 20-aircraft pre-production batch flew on 3 July 1947. Series production terminated after over 400 aircraft had been delivered in 1952, by which time the Tu-4 was in large scale service with the Soviet DA (Long-

Range Aviation), being accorded the NATO reporting name **'Bull'**. Some were used as wingtip-to-wingtip inflight-refuelling tankers, others as conventional HDU-equipped tankers. The type was exported to China where some were re-engined with Ivchenko AI-20 turboprops and were sporadically used into the 1990s as AEW and drone launching platforms.

Specification
Type: long-range heavy bomber
Powerplant: four 1790-kW (2,400-hp) Shvetsov ASh-73TK radial piston engines

Performance: maximum speed 558 km/h (347 mph); service ceiling 11200 m (36,745 ft); range 5100 km (3,169 miles)
Weights: empty equipped 35270 kg (77,757 lb); maximum take-off 66000 kg (145,505 lb)
Dimensions: span 43.08 m (141 ft 4 in); length 30.19 m (99 ft 01/2 in); wing area 161.70 m² (1,740.58 sq ft)

Externally the Tu-4 was virtually indistinguishable from the B-29 with only the modified nacelles and revised armament as clues.

Armament: either five twin 12.7-mm (0.5-in) UBT machine-guns or five B-20E 20-mm or NS-23 23-mm cannon, plus a max bombload of 8000 kg (17,637) lb

Tupolev post-war aircraft

While continuing to dominate heavy bomber design, the Tupolev bureau was less successful in its efforts to produce light and medium bombers for the VVS, producing a string of unsuccessful prototypes. Even in the heavy bomber and transport fields, though, there were false starts and projects which led nowhere.

Tu-70: one-off passenger transport developed in parallel with Tu-4; flown on 27 November 1946; new nose with conventional cockpit/flight deck instead of low-drag Superfort-style nose; designed for crew of eight and 48 VIP passengers, but used with crew of six and 72 passengers as staff transport for air force

Tu-72: designation of unflown three-engined bomber project; formed basis of Tu-73

Tu-73: first flown on 29 December 1947; intended as a competitor to the Il-28; second (unbuilt) aircraft intended as **Tu-73R** or **Tu-74** tactical recce aircraft

Tu-75: one-off transport derivative of Tu-4 to carry 10000 kg (22,046 lb) of freight or 100 troops

Tu-77: jet-propelled five-seat medium bomber, development began in mid-1946; wing and tailplane developed from those of the Tu-2S but considerably strengthened, while the fuselage was a new design with a longer fully-glazed nose; tricycle landing gear was adopted for the first time in a Soviet bomber of this size; powered by two 2268-kg (5,000-lb) thrust Rolls-Royce Nene I turbojets; first two aircraft built flown at the Tushino display on 3 August 1947, the first aircraft having made its initial flight on 27 June; followed by a small evaluation batch believed to be of no more than 50 aircraft; service designation **Tu-12**

Tu-78: derivative of Tu-73, first

The Tu-70 72-seat airliner failed to disguise its debt to the B-29. While Tuploev revamped the fuselage design, the familiar Boeing tail was retained along with the original bomb-aimer's nose.

example actually converted from incomplete second Tu-73; first flew 17 April 1948; new nose glazing and intake for rear fuselage engine in extended dorsal fin fillet

Tu-79: unbuilt derivative of Tu-78 eventually with no rear fuselage engine, reconfigured tail surfaces etc.

Tu-80: both Tupolev and Myasishchev (with DVB-202 prototype) undertook extensive development of basic Tu-4 design; Tu-80 prototype flown November 1949 had redesigned nose section, large vertical fin/rudder and retained tricycle landing gear layout; rearranged armament of five twin 23-mm NS-23 cannon; powered by four 1790-kW (2,400-hp) ASh-73FN radials, maximum speed of 650 km/h (404 mph); no production

Tu-81: twin-engined tactical bomber based on Tu-78/Tu-79 with removal of third engine compensated for by installation of powered tail turret housing twin 23-mm cannon; first flew 1949 and ordered into production as **Tu-14** retaining VK-1 powerplant; 200 ordered for the Soviet navy, deliveries to *eskadrilii* beginning in 1950; specialised versions included in the overall production were the **Tu-14R (Tu-81R)** photo-reconnaissance aircraft and the **Tu-14T (Tu-89)** which carried two Type 45-36-A torpedoes in weapons bay; production terminated after about 100 to allow factory to tool up for Tu-16 production

Tu-82: experimental swept-wing project based on Tu-73 fuselage; test flown in February 1949; second

prototype with tail turret, first with two turrets above and below fuselage

Tu-85: two examples built for flight testing and third for static tests, first example flown late 1949; extensive refinement of Tu-80 design with crew of 16; bombload 20000 kg (44,092 lb); defensive armament in five positions with total of 10 NS-23 cannon; powered by four 3207-kW (4,300-hp) VD-4K piston engines giving maximum speed of 665 km/h (413 mph) at 10000 m (32,810 ft) and maximum range of 13000 km (8,078 miles); advent of turboprops and turbojets, and adoption of swept wings led to abrupt termination of development in favour of Tu-95 'Bear'; allocated reporting name **'Barge'** by NATO

Tu-86: swept-wing bomber project based on Tu-14 fuselage with wing scaled up from Tu-82

Tu-91: contender for a VVS

requirement for a jet Shturmovik; **'Boot'** was an extraordinarily ugly machine somewhat akin to the Fairey Gannet; abandoned in 1957 after at least one prototype had flown

Tu-98: codenamed **'Backfin'** by NATO; initially misidentified as an Ilyushin and subsequently as Yakovlev Yak-42; nose section similar to that of aircraft like the Yak-28, Il-28 and Tu-14, but mated to unusual transonic airframe with shoulder intakes and mid-set swept wing; prototype mischievously 'shown' to Western delegation visiting Kubinka after project abandoned

The Tupolev Tu-89 (service designation Tu-14T) was a dedicated torpedo-bomber version of the Tu-14, with a modified turret and rudder.

Tupolev Tu-16

The **Tupolev Tu-88** (Aircraft N) which served as the prototype of the **Tu-16 'Badger'** was flown for the first time in the winter of 1952. It had a fuselage, structure, systems and defensive armament based on those of the Tu-4, combined with a new swept wing, retractable landing gear of tricycle configuration, and new indigenous AM-3 turbojets designed and developed by the Mikulin bureau. Production of the Tu-16 began in 1953 and it began to enter service with Long-Range Aviation in 1955. Later production aircraft, including many 'Badger-As', were powered with the uprated Mikulin AM-3M, providing improvements in both maximum range and speed. Total Soviet production is believed to be about 2,000, of which many remain in service to this day. Variants are listed below under their Soviet designations and NATO reporting names. The type has been supplied to Egypt, Iraq and Indonesia. It continues in production in the People's Republic of China under the designation Xian H-6 (B-6 for export) and this nation is believed to have about 120 in service.

Variants

Tu-16 'Badger-A': basic strategic bomber deploying conventional or nuclear free-fall weapons; Chinese production version (Xian **H-6**) is based on this variant; 'Badger-A' also applies to **Tu-16A** nuclear bomber (Chinese **H-6A** nuclear bomber similar), **Tu-16T**

The 'Badger-F' is a dedicated electronic intelligence gathering variant of the Tu-16 family, with passive multi-band receivers in the two underwing pods.

torpedo bomber, **Tu-16K** airborne lifeboat carrier, **Tu-16N** wingtip-to-wingtip tanker and an undesignated probe-and-drogue tanker; some converted as **Tu-16G** (**Tu-104G**) for training Aeroflot crews and for fast mail services

Tu-16KS-1 'Badger-B': similar to 'Badger-A' but equipped initially to carry KS-1 Komet III (AS-1 'Kennel') anti-shipping missiles, with retractable dustbin radome aft of bomb bay; many reconverted as free-fall bombers

Tu-16K-10 'Badger-C': anti-shipping version carrying K-10 (AS-2 'Kipper') ASM beneath fuselage with 'Puff Ball' radar in broad flat nose radome

Tu-16K-26 'Badger-C Mod': conversion of Tu-16K-10 with provision for smaller K-26 (AS-6 'Kingfish') ASMs under wings instead of, or in addition to, centreline K-10

Tu-16R 'Badger-D': conversion of 'Badger-C' for maritime reconnaissance, Elint and mid-course missile guidance; chin radome enlarged, new radomes projecting from bomb bay

Tu-16R 'Badger-E': similar to 'Badger-A' but provision for photo-reconnaissance pallet in bomb bay and passive Elint capability

Tu-16R 'Badger-F': similar to 'Badger-E' with underwing ESM pods

Tu-16K-? 'Badger-G': similar to

'Badger-A' but equipped to carry also AS-5 ('Kelt') ASMs beneath wings; 'Short Horn' radar beneath nose; AS-6 sometimes carried; Chinese **H-6-IV** (**B-6D**) similar, with drum-like chin radome, and C-601 Silkworm missiles underwing

Tu-16K-26 'Badger-G Mod': version equipped specially to carry AS-6 'Kingfish' ASMs with new missile guidance radar in ventral radome between engine intakes

Tu-16PP 'Badger-H': ECM aircraft for use in an escort or stand-off role equipped with chaff dispensers in the bomb bay and array of Elint receivers

Tu-16PP 'Badger-J': ECM version equipped to jam enemy emitters, with flat plate antennas at wingtips and ventral canoe radome; various ram air inlets, heat exchangers etc.

Tu-16R 'Badger-K': recce version carrying different equipment

Tu-16R 'Badger-L': maritime version

with thimble nose radome in centre of transparent nosecone, underwing pods and ECM tailcone

Specification
Tupolev Tu-16 'Badger-A' (late production)
Type: medium bomber with many subsidiary roles

Powerplant: two 9500-kg (20,944-lb) thrust Mikulin AM-3M turbojets

Performance: maximum speed 960 km/h (597 mph); service ceiling 15000 m (49,200 ft); range with maximum weapon load 4800 km (2,983 miles)

Weights: empty 40300 kg (88,846 lb); maximum take-off 75800 kg (167,110 lb)

Dimensions: span 32.93 m (108 ft 0½ in); length 34.80 m (114 ft 2 in); height 10.82 m (35 ft 6 in); wing area 164.65 m² (1,772.34 sq ft)

Armament: seven 23-mm NR-23 cannon, plus a maximum weapon load of 9000 kg (19,842 lb)

Tupolev Tu-22

Development of the **Tupolev Tu-22 'Blinder'** supersonic bomber/maritime patrol aircraft began in 1955, under the Tupolev bureau designations **Aircraft Yu** and **Aircraft 105**. The rapidly growing capability of Western air defence systems at that period threatened the continued viability of the subsonic Tu-16, and the Tu-22 was designed to make possible the penetration of enemy air space at higher altitude and supersonic speed. Features of the design included a 52°sweep wing with small LERXes, area ruling and the use of rear-mounted Dobrynin engines that avoided the drag and weight penalties of long inlet ducts. The landing gear retracts into typical Tupolev-style trailing-edge pods. First seen publicly in 1961, the Tu-22 has since been built to an estimated total of about 250, of which some 180 were believed to be in service in 1983 with the DA (140) and AV-MF (40). The type has also been supplied in small numbers for service with the Iraqi and Libyan air forces. Five versions were built and these are listed below under VVS designations and NATO reporting names.

Tupolev Tu-22 'Blinder-A' of the Libyan Arab Republic air force, during the early 1980s.

Variants
Tu-22 'Blinder-A': initial version, basic bomber/reconnaissance aircraft with internal weapon bays for up to 12,000 kg of free-fall weapons, including the FAB-9000 9000-kg bomb; inflight-refuelling probe not fitted to initial production batches; RBP-4 ('Short Horn') radar; post-1968 production batches fitted with 16500-kg (36,375-lb) VD-7M engines
Tu-22K 'Blinder-B': generally similar to 'Blinder-A', but with recess in weapons bay to allow carriage of AS-4 ('Kitchen') stand-off missile, larger Rubin 'Down Beat' radar, and inflight-refuelling probe

Tu-22R 'Blinder-C': maritime reconnaissance version of 'Blinder-A' with cameras or sensors in weapons bay; RBP-4 Initsiativa radar
TU-22U 'Blinder-D': trainer version with instructor accommodated in raised and enclosed cockpit aft of standard flight deck
TU-22P 'Blinder-E': EW version developed from Tu-22R with RBP-4 radar, ECM tailcone replacing tail turret, underfuselage Elint pod, and many antennas for EW equipment

Specification (estimated)
Tupolev Tu-22
Type: supersonic bomber

Powerplant: probably two Dobrynin VD-7M turbojets
Performance: maximum speed 1610 km/h (1,000 mph) or Mach 1.5 at 12190 m (40,000 ft); service ceiling 18290 m (60,000 ft); combat radius 2200 km (1,367 miles)
Weight: maximum take-off 92000 kg (202,821 lb)
Dimensions: span 23.50 m (77 ft 1¼ in); length 42.6 m (139 ft 9 1/4 in); height 10 m (32 ft 9½ in); wing area 162.00 m² (1,722.282 sq ft)
Armament: one 23-mm NR-23 cannon in tail barbette, plus up to some 12000 kg (26,455 lb) of stores in weapons bay, or AS-4 'Kitchen'

Tupolev Tu-22M

At one time believed to have been designated **Tupolev Tu-26,** the aircraft known to NATO as 'Backfire' was identified by the Soviet Union in SALT-2 documents as the **Tu-22M.** It began life as a comparatively simple swing-wing derivative of the Tu-22. The sharply swept wing of the Tu-22 was optimised for high performance and, clearly, a variable-geometry wing offered a far better solution. Development began about 1966, but Western reports that Tu-22 airframes were converted to produce the **Tu-136** prototype and early production aircraft were incorrect. These aircraft, which were identified by NATO as **'Backfire-A',** and which were never photographed until one appeared in the Monino museum, were in fact built to a completely new design, although they did retain the wing trailing-edge undercarriage fairings of the 'Blinder', and differed in many respects to the later production versions. The ensuing **Tu-22M-2 'Backfire-B'** was a developed version which introduced increased-span outer wing panels, revised vertical tail surfaces, redesigned landing gear to eliminate

Tupolev Tu-22M 'Backfire-A' of the Soviet naval air force in the early 1980s.

the large landing gear fairing pods of the Tu-22, and inflight-refuelling capability. The tail turret houses two GSh-23L twin-barrelled cannons. 'Backfire-B' is powered by a pair of Kuznetsov NK-22 afterburning turbofan engines rated at 215 kN (48,315 lb) afterburning thrust. The later **Tu-22M-3** with NK-25 engines and revised ramp-type engine intakes has been allocated the NATO reporting name **'Backfire-C'.** It has a new 'Down Beat' radar in a distinctive upturned nosecone, and a new tail turret and a rotary launcher in bomb bay. About 350 are estimated to be in service with the DA (240) and AVMF (110).

Specification (estimated)
Tupolev Tu-22M-3 'Backfire-C'
Type: medium bomber and maritime reconnaissance/attack aircraft
Powerplant: two Kuznetsov NK-25 afterburning turbofan engines each rated at 245.2 kN (55,100 lb) afterburning thrust
Performance: maximum speed at optimum altitude 2000 km/h (1,242 mph) or Mach 1.88; combat radius with typical weapon load 1187 km (1,365 miles)
Weight: maximum take-off 126400 kg (278,660 lb)
Dimensions: span, unswept 34.28 m

(112 ft 5½ in) and swept 23.30 m (76 ft 5½ in); length 42.46 m (139 ft 3¾ in); unswept wing area, 183.58 m² (1,892 sq ft)
Armament: single GSh-23L twin-barrelled 23-mm cannon in tail barbette, plus two Kh-22 (AS-4 'Kitchen') or four Kh-15P (AS-16 'Kickback') on pylons beneath each inboard wing panel, plus six KH-15Ps on rotary launcher in weapons bay, or, reportedly, up to 24000 kg (52,910 lb) of bombs carried both internally and on racks under intakes; normal load is single KH-22 or 12000 kg (26,455 lb) of bombs

Tupolev Tu-28P

In the late 1950s, the Soviet Union was faced with the problem of being able to intercept Western missile-carrying subsonic aircraft before they were able to launch their long-range missiles. The requirement demanded an aircraft of considerable size and, in fact, the **Tupolev Tu-28P** developed to fulfil this role is the world's largest all-weather interceptor. Descended from the **Tu-98** prototype of the mid-1950s, this new supersonic aircraft was allocated the Tupolev bureau designation **Tu-102.** The two prototypes first seen publicly in 1961 were identified by the NATO reporting name **'Fiddler-A'.** The Tu-102 was not adopted for production but was used instead, under the bureau designation **Tu-128,** as the basis of the long-range interceptor which entered production in the early

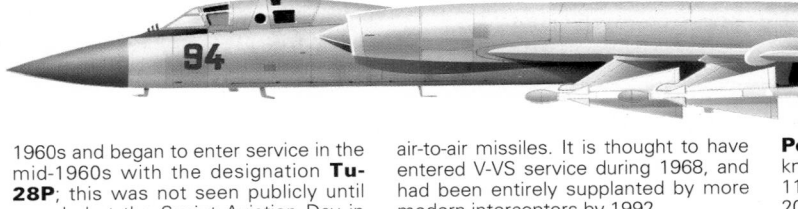

Tupolev Tu-28P 'Fiddler-A' of the IA-PVO (Soviet air defence forces), based in the USSR during the 1970s.

1960s and began to enter service in the mid-1960s with the designation **Tu-28P**; this was not seen publicly until revealed at the Soviet Aviation Day in 1967, and was then allocated the NATO name **'Fiddler-B'.** A mid-wing monoplane with swept wings and tail surfaces. the Tu-28P is powered by two afterburning turbojet engines, accommodates a crew of two in tandem and carries four large AA-5 ('Ash')

air-to-air missiles. It is thought to have entered V-VS service during 1968, and had been entirely supplanted by more modern interceptors by 1992.

Specification (estimated)
Tupolev Tu-28P
Type: long-range interceptor
Powerplant: two 11200-kg (24,690-lb) afterburning thrust Lyulka AL-21F turbojets

Performance: maximum speed 1850 km/h (1,150 mph) or Mach 1.74 at 11000 m (36,090 ft); service ceiling 20000 m (65,615 ft); range 5000 km (3,105 miles)
Weight: maximum take-off 40000 kg (88,185 lb)
Dimensions: span 18.10 m (59 ft 4½ in); length 27.20 m (89 ft 3 in)
Armament: four AA-5 'Ash' air-to-air missiles

Tupolev Tu-95 and -142

Descended indirectly from the American Boeing B-29 via the Tupolev Tu-4, refined Tu-80 and larger Tu-85, the **Tu-95** was developed for use by the Soviet Union's DA (Long-Range Aviation) as an intercontinental strategic bomber - a role in which the latest variants still serve. Design of the Tu-95 version began before 1952, its overall configuration being similar to that of the Tu-16 although of much larger size and powered by four Kuznetsov NK-12 turboprop engines, the bench-testing of which started in 1953. First flown in prototype form during 1954, the aircraft was allocated the service designation **Tu-20**, but this soon lapsed into disuse. Tu-20s began to enter service with the DA bomber force in 1955. In an age when turbojets and turbofans are the major power source for first-line military aircraft, it seems almost unbelievable that the Tu-95, allocated the reporting name **'Bear'** by NATO, has remained in operational use for almost 40 years. Nevertheless, its turboprop powerplant gives remarkably high speed and, at the same time, long range and endurance.

Additionally, the large size of the Tu-95 has permitted the carriage of extensive radar equipment and the largest Soviet air-to-surface missiles and bombs. The designation Tu-142 is applied to new-build maritime recce versions for the AV-MF. Production was suspended by President Yeltsin as a unilateral arms limitation measure. Variants are listed below, with NATO reporting names where appropriate.

Variants

Tu-95/1: prototype with 8,950-kW (12,000-ehp) Kuznetsov 2TV-2F turboprops; flew 1952, destroyed
Tu-95/2: prototype with TV-12 turboprops of same rating; flew 1955
Tu-95M 'Bear-A': original strategic bomber version with internal bomb bay for conventional or nuclear free-fall weapons
Tu-95U 'Bear-A': conversion of basic bomber for training; often identified by broad red stripe around rear fuselage

The Tu-95 'Bear-D' is a rebuilt 'Bear-A'. A notable feature common to all 'Bears' is the twin trailing-edge fairings aft of the inboard engines, for the undercarriage.

for SALT verification
Tu-95K: experimental conversion airdropping MiG-19 SM-20 in trials connected with K-20 missile system
Tu-95K-20 'Bear-B': first seen 1961; generally as 'Bear-A' but with large, flat nose radar replacing transparent nose cone and recessed (AS-3 'Kangaroo') air-to-surface missile, later versions with supersonic (AS-6 'Kingfish') ASM known as **Tu-95M-5;** nose-mounted inflight-refuelling probe; designation **Tu-95KD** applied
Tu-95KM 'Bear-C': first seen 1964; generally as 'Bear-B'
Tu-95RT 'Bear-D': maritime reconnaissance/Elint version with comprehensive multi-sensor installations and refuelling probe; glazed nose with chin and belly radomes
Tu-95MR 'Bear-E': maritime reconnaissance version, probably converted from Tu-95M; seven-camera installation in pallet in weapons bay; inflight-refuelling probe
Tu-95 K-22 'Bear-G': rebuilds of 'Bear-B' and 'Bear-C' to carry AS-4 updated avionics
Tu-95M-55: unidentified missile-carrier; may not have entered service
Tu-95MS 'Bear-H': new-build platform carrying 3000-km (1,860-mile) range AS-X-15 cruise missile; variants known to NATO as 'Bear-H' are not conversions but new aircraft from the reopened production line at Taganrog; Tu-95MS-6 has provision for six missiles on internal rotary launcher; Tu-95MS-16 has same internal launcher and underwing pylons for two more missiles between fuselage and inboard engines, and for three more between the inner and outer engines
Tu-95MR 'Bear-J': new-build (or conversion from Tu-142M?) with fin spike projecting forward from leading

edge of tip, and with underfuselage winch package for VLF trailing wire antenna; assumed to be TACAMO-style communications relay aircraft
Tu-96: unflown high-speed bomber development with NK-16 turboprops
Tu-119: unflown but converted Tu-95M intended as testbed for nuclear engine
Tu-142 'Bear-F' and 'F Mod 1': advanced ASW version with lengthened fuselage (aprox 2 m) accommodating avionics and sonobuoy stowage; glazed nose and radomes similar to Tu-95RT; increased fuel capacity
Tu-142M 'Bear-F Mods 2-4': Further refined ASW versions based on new fuselage, with further fuselage stretch (aprox 25 cm), redesigned increased-height cockpit and drooping refuelling probe; **Mod 3** has rearward-projecting MAD spike at trailing edge of fin-tip, cleaned-up rear fuselage; **Mod 4** similar with thimble radome in centre of nose glazing, new multi-sensor antenna group under nose and new EW antennas below tail; exported to India;

Tu-142M variants not conversions but new aircraft from the reopened production line at Taganrog
Tu-142LL: conversion of 'Bear-F Mod 3' as engine testbed; test engine housed in nacelle below centre fuselage

Specification
Tupolev Tu-95MS 'Bear-H'
Type: long-range bomber
Powerplant: four 11033-ekW (14,795-ehp) Kuznetsov NK-12M turboprops
Performance: (estimated) maximum speed 815 km/h (506 mph) at 12495 m (41,000 ft); service ceiling 12000 m (39,370 ft); maximum range with typical bombload 12550 km (7,800 miles)
Weight: maximum take-off 188000 kg (414,470 lb)
Dimensions: 51.10 m (167 ft 7¾ in); length (excluding probe) 48.50 m (159 ft 11 in); height 12.12 m (39 ft 9 in); wing area 310.50 m² (3,342.30 sq ft)
Armament: two 23-mm NR-23 cannon in tail turret, plus a maximum bombload of 11340 kg (25,000 lb)

Tupolev Tu-104

With an urgent Aeroflot need in the early 1950s for a modern airliner of greater capacity, range and speed than in-service aircraft, the Tupolev design bureau developed as the **Tupolev Tu-104** a minimum-change civil version of the Tu-16 bomber, basically by introducing a new pressurised fuselage. The prototype made its first flight on 17 June 1955 and the type entered Aeroflot service during the following summer. Introduced first on the Moscow-Irkutsk route, the 50-passenger Tu-104 was powered by two 6750-kg (14,881-lb) thrust Mikulin AM-3 turbojets and immediately reduced flight times by more than half, bringing transformation to the airline's medium-range routes. The powerplant was later uprated to the 8700-kg (19,180-lb) thrust Mikulin AM-3M, which also powered the improved **Tu-104A** featuring a revised cabin for 70 passengers. Continuing development of the Mikulin engine encouraged development of the lengthened-fuselage (by 1.21 m/3 ft 11½ in) **Tu-104B**, with standard seating for 100 passengers. This entered service on 15 April 1959.

When production ended the following year about 200 Tu-104s of all versions had been built, these serving Aeroflot reliably until 1981. The designations **Tu-104D** and **Tu-104V** were applied to Tu-104As with in-service modifications to accommodate 100 and 85 passengers respectively, without the fuselage stretch. Six aircraft supplied to the Czechoslovakian airline CSA were basically Tu-104As seating 81 passengers, and small numbers of Tu-104s have been used by the VVS for cosmonaut training and as personnel transports. One, with a pointed nose, served as a weather research aircraft.

The **Tu-104E** was used to set a 2000-km (4,410-lb) closed circuit record while carrying a 15-tonne payload. The NATO reporting codename for the Tu-104 was **'Camel'**. At least one aircraft was converted on the production line to serve as the **Tu-110** prototype, with four engines in the wingroots. It was assigned to the VVS after rejection by Aeroflot despite superior economy, field length requirements, performance and handling.

Specification
Tupolev Tu-104B
Type: medium-range transport
Powerplant: two 9700-kg (21,385-lb) thrust Mikulin AM-3M-500 turbojets
Performance: maximum speed 950 km/h (590 mph) at 10000 m (32,810 ft); service ceiling 11500 m (37,730 ft); range with maximum payload 2650 km (1,647 miles)
Weights: empty 41600 kg (91,711 lb); maximum take-off 76000 kg (167,551 lb)
Dimensions: span 34.54 m (113 ft 4 in); length 40.05 m (131 ft 4¾ in); height 11.90 m (39 ft 0½ in); wing area 183.50 m² (1,975.24 sq ft)

The Tu-104B was an improved version of the Tu-104 with uprated engines, but also with three small raised windows above each wing.

Tupolev Tu-114 and Tu-126

Just as a successful redesign of the military Tu-16 provided for Aeroflot the medium-range Tu-104, a similar adaptation of the Tu-95 was made to fill the requirement for a long-range transport with intercontinental capability. Chronologically, the first to fly was the Tupolev **Tu-116** (late 1956); this was basically a demilitarised Tu-20 with the weapons bay/tail turret eliminated and the rear fuselage equipped as a 24/30-seat passenger cabin. It was used to test the powerplant in civil operation and evaluate airfields on proposed routes, being followed by two similar aircraft; all three were accepted by Aeroflot under the designation **Tu-114D** and used for route-proving and publicity purposes. The true Tu-114 (NATO reporting name **'Cleat'**) had configuration changes and introduced a new circular-section fuselage with seating arrangements including 220 passengers (high-density), 170 seats (typical) and 120 (long-range non-stop). The first Tu-114 was flown on 3 October 1957, and 25-30 entered service with Aeroflot from 1961. During 1960, the Tu-114 had demonstrated that it was the fastest propeller-driven aircraft in the world when, on 9 April, one carrying a 25000-kg (55,115-lb) payload over a 5000-km (3,107-mile) circuit set an as-yet-unbroken speed record of 877.212 km/h (545.07 mph). In addition to use on long-range domestic routes, the Tu-114 operated to Canada, India and Japan, but from 1971 was gradually

Like its half brother the Tu-20, the Tu-114 airliner was a striking aircraft, distinguishable by its tailplane lowered into the fuselage.

withdrawn from service.

A military derivation of the Tu-114 has the designation **Tu-126** and NATO reporting name **'Moss'**; believed to be conversions of ex-Aeroflot civil airliners, these aircraft have been modified for use as airborne warning and control aircraft with a rotating radome pylon-mounted over the rear fuselage. The aircraft also has an inflight-refuelling probe and a number of blisters and fairings covering operational equipment. The former passenger cabin provides ample space for extensive communications, radar and signal processing equipment, and consoles for specialist operators.

Specification
Tupolev Tu-114
Type: long-range civil transport
Powerplant: four 11033-ekW (14,795-eshp) Kuznetsov NK-12MV turboprops
Performance: maximum cruising speed 770 km/h (478 mph); service ceiling 12000 m (39,370 ft); range with maximum payload 6200 km (3,853 miles)

Now out of service, the Tu-126 AWACS probably possessed greater military ability than admitted by the United States.

Weights: empty 91000 kg (200,620 lb); maximum take-off 171000 kg (376,990 lb)
Dimensions: span 51.10 m (167 ft 7¾ in); length 54.10 m (177 ft 6 in); height 15.50 m (50 ft 10¼ in); wing area 311.10 m² (3,348.76 sq ft)

Tupolev Tu-124

Aeroflot's requirement for a short/medium-range airliner to replace the Ilyushin Il-14 led to the design of what was basically a reduced-scale version of the Tu-104. The prototype **Tupolev Tu-124** was first flown in June 1960, five years after the Tu-104, and introduced aerodynamic and system refinements, plus newly developed and much more efficient turbofan engines. In fact, the Soloviev D-20P twin-spool turbofans installed in these aircraft were the first such engines to equip any of the world's short/medium-range airliners. Tu-124 had seats for 44 passengers and entered service with Aeroflot on 2 October 1962, but the major production version was the 56-seat **Tu-124V**. Variants included the **Tu-124K** and **Tu-124K2** with de luxe seating for 36 and 22 passengers respectively. About 100 were built, this number including three for CSA in Czechoslovakia and two for Interflug in East Germany, but Aeroflot has now retired its Tu-124s. A small number entered military service, and it is

believed that some are still used for research and test purposes. The NATO reporting name is **'Cookpot'**.

Specification
Tupolev Tu-124V
Type: short/medium-range transport

Powerplant: two 5400-kg (11,905-lb) thrust Soloviev D-20P turbofans
Performance: maximum speed 970 km/h (603 mph) at 8000 m (26,245 ft); service ceiling 11700 m (38,385 ft); range with maximum payload 1220 km (758 miles)
Weights: empty 22500 kg (49,604 lb); maximum take-off 38000 kg (83,776 lb)
Dimensions: span 25.55 m (83 ft 9¾ in); length 30.58 m (100 ft 4 in); height 8.08 m (26 ft 6 in); wing area 119.00 m² (1,280.95 sq ft)

The Tupolev Tu-124 was a scaled-down Tu-104, with more economical turbofans rather than turbojet engines. This is one of three adopted by the Czech flag-carrier CSA.

Tupolev Tu-134

Codenamed **'Crusty'** by NATO, the **Tu-134** was essentially a derivative of the Tu-124, with a modern T-tail. It had a rear-engined layout to improve aerodynamic and engine efficiency and to reduce cabin noise. Originally designated **Tu-124A**, the new aircraft differed in having an increased-span wing, increased travel flaps, two-section ailerons, and a slightly lengthened fuselage that was redesigned so that the wing box passed through it below floor level. The first two prototypes were produced by conversion of two incomplete Tu-124s, and the first of these

made its maiden flight during 1962, by which time the Tu-134 designation had been adopted.

Originally configured to seat 64 passengers (16 first class, 20 tourist and 28 economy in front, mid and rear cabins) with four crew (two pilots, navigator and steward) accommodation was soon increased to 72 (44 and 28) in a two-cabin layout.

The improved **Tu-134A** introduced an APU, a strengthened wing, and a fuselage stretched by 2.7 m (8 ft 8 in). Various cabin layouts, all with 28-seat rear cabin, accommodated a maximum

Flying a typically 'flat' approach favoured by Eastern European pilots, this early model Aeroflot Tu-134 wears its Tupolev badge proudly.

of 84. The **Tu-134A2** replaced the traditional bomber-style glazed nose, while the **Tu-134A3** introduced lightweight seats raising capacity to 96, and more powerful Soloviev D-30 Series III engines. The **Tu-134B** removed the navigator from the flight deck but retained the flight engineer, and had spoilers for direct lift control. Many examples were converted for trials, research and miscellaneous duties, including the **Tu-134UBL** for training Tu-160 aircrew (the aircraft had a Tu-160 radome grafted onto its nose), and the **Tu-134BSh** nav trainer which had Tu-22M radar in nose.

Specification
Tupolev Tu-134A
Type: short/medium-range transport
Powerplant: two 30.26-kN (6,800-lb) Soloviev D-30-II turbofans

Performance: maximum cruising speed 885 km/h (550 mph); service ceiling 11890 m (39,010 ft; range with maximum payload 1890 km (1,174 miles

Weights: empty 29050 kg (64,044 lb); maximum take-off 47000 kg (103,617 lb)
Dimensions: span 29 m (95 ft 1¾ in); length 37.05 m (121 ft 6¾ in)

The Tupolev Tu-134 found favour as a VIP transport with Warsaw Pact nations including Poland, Czechoslovakia and Hungary.

Tupolev Tu-144

The **Tupolev Tu-144** began design in the early 1960s, the prototype (SSSR-68001) being flown on 31 December 1968. Of like configuration, and with similar performance to the Aérospatiale/British Aerospace Concorde, the aircraft has a matching ogival delta wing with the powerplants grouped at the rear of the wing and a drooping nose to improve the pilot's view in low-speed regimes. The production version had a flight crew of three and 140 passengers as standard, and began proving flights with cargo between Moscow and Alma Ata on 26 December 1975. This variant also had retractable but non-moving canard foreplanes, lengthened fuselage, redesigned intakes, increased span and removal of pilots' ejection seats. From 22 February 1977, the Tu-144 was used in a series of 50 proving flights between Moscow and Khabarovsk, and the first passengers services, between Moscow and Alma Ata, began on 1 November 1977. These were terminated on 1 June 1978 after a fatal accident. Reports were received in 1979 of a developed **Tu-144D** with more eco-

nomical Kolesov turbofan engines but, since that time, there has been no evidence of any renewed airline activity with these supersonic aircraft, though several have been used as testbeds and trials aircraft at Zhukovskii. Two remain active. The NATO reporting name is **'Charger'**.

Specification
Tupolev Tu-144 (production)
Type: supersonic transport
Powerplant: four Kuznetsov NK-144 turbofans each of 20000-kg (44,092-lb) afterburning thrust
Performance: maximum cruising speed 2500 km/h (1,553 mph) or Mach 2.35; operating ceiling 18000 m (59,055 ft); range with maximum payload 6500 km (4,040 miles)
Weights: empty 85000 kg (187,393 lb);

maximum take-off 180000 kg (396,832 lb)
Dimensions: span 28.80 m (94 ft 5¾ in); length 65.70 m (215 ft 6½ in); wing area 438.00 m² (4,714.75 sq ft)

Though it has long been withdrawn from airline service as a result of aerodynamic and system problems, the Tupolev Tu-144 'Charger' was nevertheless the first supersonic passenger transport to fly.

Tupolev Tu-154

The **Tupolev Tu-154** (NATO reporting name **'Careless'**) was designed as a replacement for aircraft like the An-10, Tu-104 and Il-18. It resembles the Boeing 727 in configuration but is larger and has more powerful engines. The Tu-154 has retractable tricycle landing gear incorporating a six-wheel bogie on each main unit, these retracting into characteristic trailing-edge fairings. Initial examples flown in 1971 were powered by 9500-kg (20,944-lb) thrust Kuznetsov NK-8-T turbofans. Aeroflot began service with the Tu-154 on 8 February 1972, and improved versions introduced since that time include the **Tu-154A** and **Tupolev Tu-154B**, both with more powerful engines, greater fuel capacity and performance/reliability refinements; the **Tu-154B-2** incorporating more advanced operating equipment and uprated engines; a **Tu-154C** all-cargo version; and the **Tu-154M** (initially designated **Tu-164**) with Soloviev D-30KU-154II turbofans each flat-rated at 10600-kg (23,369-lb) thrust, a redesigned tailplane and other refine-

Tupolev TU-154B-2 of Hungarian state airline, Malev.

ments. More recent versions include the **Tu-154S**, a dedicated freighter offered as a conversion of the Tu-154B, or theoretically as a new-build aircraft, the hydrogen-fuelled **Tu-155** testbed, and the **Tu-154M2** with two Perm/Soloviev PS-90A turbofans. The latter is scheduled to fly in 1995. Operated by a crew of three or four,

the Tu-154 provides accommodation for between 140 and 180 passengers according to cabin layout.

Specification
Tupolev Tu-154A
Type: medium-range passenger transport
Powerplant: three 10500-kg (23,149-lb)

thrust Kuznetsov NK-8-2U turbofans
Performance: cruising speed 900 km/h (559 mph) at 12000 m (39,370 ft); range with maximum payload 2750 km (1,709 miles)
Weights: empty 50775 kg (111,940 lb); maximum take-off 94000 kg (207,235 lb)
Dimensions: span 37.55 m (123 ft 2¼ in); length 47.90 m (157 ft 1¾ in)

Tupolev Tu-160

Designed under the designation **Aircraft 70**, the aircraft later designated **Tu-160** (NATO codename **'Blackjack'**) is the world's largest combat aircraft, and is the Soviet equivalent to the US B-1. The Tu-160 closely resembles the latter in basic configuration, but features high-level penetration role as well as low-level, terrain-following capability. Production was stopped as a unilateral arms limitation move, but may be restarted. Eighteen aircraft are operational with a regiment based at what should have been a temporary base in the Ukraine. Independent Ukraine has kept these aircraft. About four more are based at a definitive Russian base, with further trials aircraft at Zhukhovskii.

Specification
Tupolev Tu-160 'Blackjack'

With an array of other Tupolev aircraft visible in the background this unpainted Russian air force Tu-160 blasts off the runway at the Zhukovskii aerospace test centre, outside Moscow.

Type: heavy bomber
Powerplant: four Samara Trud NK-321 afterburning turbofan engines each rated at 245.2 kN (55,100 lb) afterburning thrust
Performance: maximum speed at optimum altitude 2000 km/h (1,242 mph) or Mach 1.88; combat radius with typical weapon load 12000 km (7,455 miles)
Weight: maximum take-off 275000 kg (606,261 lb)
Dimensions: span, unswept 55.70 m (182 ft 9 in) and swept 35.6 m (116 ft 9 ½ in); length 54.1 m (177 ft 6 in)

Armament: internal tandem weapons bays with rotary launchers for 12 Kh-15P (AS-16 'Kickback') SRAMs or six RK-55 (AS-15 'Kent') ALCMs; alternatively can carry 16330 kg (36,000 lb) of free-fall bombs

Tupolev Tu-204

Designed as a replacement for the Tu-154 as a short-to-medium range jetliner, the **Tu-204** was originally intended to retain a T-tail (interestingly enough, so too did the Boeing 757, which clearly influenced the Tupolev OKB). From the start, Tupolev envisaged extensive use of composite materials (most notably in the tail unit), and intended the new aircraft to be built around a new supercritical wing with generous high-lift devices, powered by underwing turbofans, fitted with a triplex fly-by-wire control system (with analog fly-by-wire and not mechanical back-up) and a modern glass cockpit, and with a lowered cabin floor, giving more room at shoulder level.

Powered by a pair of Perm/Soloviev PS-90AT turbofans each rated at 157 kN (35,000 lb st), the prototype made its maiden flight on 2 January 1989, delayed by late delivery of its engines. The engines performed well in early tests and gave remarkable fuel efficiency, albeit with a specific fuel consumption three to four per cent higher than had been predicted. This was not low enough to compete with the Boeing 757-200, the larger Soviet engines (a compromise between the requirements of the Il-96 which needs larger engines, and the Tu-204 which needs smaller ones) burning fuel 27 per cent faster per passenger carried, due in part to the Tu-204's lower permitted maximum take-off weight. Capable of two-crew operation, the Tu-204 does

The Rolls-Royce RB-211-powered Tu-204-220 is being marketed by the joint UK-Russian company Bravia, which has placed an order for 30 aircraft with a view to leasing them out to other airlines..

have provision for a flight engineer on the flight deck. Initial production aircraft are designated **Tu-204-100**.

The flight deck is designed for two-pilot operation, but Aeroflot demanded provision for a flight engineer, and for a fourth seat for an instructor or supernumerary. Aft of the flight deck is a galley and toilet, with another galley and more toilets at the back of the passenger accommodation. There are three basic passenger configurations, all single aisle. One hundred and ninety can be accommodated in the first layout, with 12 four-abreast first-class seats, 35 six-abreast business-class seats and 143 six-abreast tourist-class seats. The second layout accommodates 196 with 12 first-class and 184 tourist-class, while the third option is for 214, all tourist .

A long-range, heavier-weight version, originally designed to be powered by Progress D-18T turbofans, Western engines like the PW4000 or shrouded UHB (Ultra High Bypass) engines, was postponed, while another project matured into the **Tu-204-200** which benefited from being offered with non-Soviet powerplants. The first of these was the 193-kN (43,000-lb) Rolls-Royce RB.211-535, a mock-up of which was

supplied in December 1990 for installation checks. The Rolls-Royce-engined **Tu-204-220** prototype made its maiden flight on 14 August 1992. Rolls-Royce-engined aircraft are equipped with avionics supplied and integrated by Sextant Avionique. A second Western engine option is the 185.5-kN (41,700-lb) Pratt & Whitney PW2037, the **Tu-204-230** with these engines being proposed with avionics by Honeywell. General Electric and SNECMA have proposed a new fan for the existing PS-90 engine, which would be a fourth option for the Tu-204-200, the basic 200 series aircraft being powered by the Perm PS-90AT.

Users of the Tu-204 include Aeroflot, Orel Avia (a new Russian airline), while Bravia have ordered a batch for resale. The Tu-204 design has been scaled

down to produce the as-yet unflown T-tailed and rear-engined Tu-334.

Specification
Tupolev Tu-204
Type: medium-range passenger transport
Powerplant: two Perm/Soloviev PS-90AT turbofans each rated at 157 kN (35,000 lb st)
Performance: cruising speed 810-850 km/h (503-528 mph) at 12000 m (39,370 ft); range with maximum payload 3850 km (2,392 miles)
Weights: empty 59,000 kg (130,070 lb); maximum take-off 110,755 kg (244,170 lb)
Dimensions: span 42.00 m (137 ft 9½ in); length 46.22 m (151 ft 7¾ in); height 13.88 m (45 ft 6½ in), wing area 182.4 m² (1,963.4 sq ft)

Utva aircraft

The Yugoslavian company Fabrica Aviona Utva flew in 1956 the prototype of a four-seat braced high-wing cabin monoplane designated **UTVA-56**. Powered by a 194-kW (260-hp) Lycoming GO-435-C2B2 engine, this served as prototype for the more developed **UTVA-60**, which introduced the 201-kW (270-hp) GO-480-B1A6 engine.

It was built in versions which included the basic **U-60-AT1** four-seat utility aircraft, the similar **U-60-AT2** with dual controls, the agricultural **U-60-AG**, the **U-60-AM** ambulance accommodating two stretchers and attendant, and the **U-60H** floatplane version of the U-60-AT1. In 1965 Utva flew the prototype of a specialised agricultural aircraft, the **UTVA-65 Privrednik**, which combined the wings, tail unit and landing gear of the UTVA-60 with a

new fuselage. This UTVA-65 was available as the **UTVA-65 Privrednik-GO** or **UTVA-65 Privrednik-IO** with 220-kW (295-hp) GO480-G1A6 or 224-kW (300-hp) IO-540K1A5 Lycoming engines respectively, and was superseded in 1973 by the **UTVA-65 Super Privrednik-350** powered by the 261-kW (350-hp) Lycoming IGO-540-A1C engine.

At the end of the 1960s Utva introduced a developed version of the

UTVA-60 under the designation **UTVA-66**, introducing several refinements and the supercharged GSO-480-B1J6 engine for improved performance. It was available in basic UTVA-66 form, as the **UTVA-66-AM** ambulance, the **UTVA-66H** floatplane and, from 1974, as the **UTVA-66V** armed military utility aircraft. Current production of this company is concentrated on the **UTVA-75** low-wing monoplane two-seat trainer/utility aircraft which provided side-by-side enclosed cabin accommodation. Well over 200 of these aircraft had been built by early 1993, and the type was available also with a four-seat interior under the designation **UTVA-75A**. The most recent production UTVA-75, which is powered by the 134-kW (180-hp) Avco Lycoming IO-360-BIF flat-four engine, has a wing span of 9.73 m (31 ft 11 in) and a maximum speed of 215 km/h (134 mph). There is a hardpoint incorporated in each wing so that a light underwing

weapon load can be carried for military training. The UTVA-75 is suitable also for the role of glider tug. The strife in the former-Yugoslavia has ended any civil aircraft production by the firm for the foreseeable future.

Among the basic statistics for the UTVA-60 were a span of 11.40 m (37 ft 5 in), a MTOW of 1815 kg (4,001 lb) and a maximum cruising speed of 230 km/h (143 mph) over a range of 750 km (466 miles).

VFW-Fokker aircraft

The West German company Vereinigte Flugtechnische Werke GmbH and Fokker in the Netherlands became equal partners in 1969 in Zentralgesellschaft VFW-Fokker mbH. The companies continued to trade independently as VFW-Fokker in Germany and Fokker-VFW in the Netherlands respectively. On 10 September 1971 VFW-Fokker flew the first of three prototypes of a single-seat V/STOL (vertical/short take-off and landing) experimental strike/reconnaissance aircraft designated **VFW-Fokker VAK 191B**. Of fairly conventional swept-wing monoplane configuration, the VAK 191B had a powerplant comprising two Rolls-Royce RB.162-81 lift jets for VTOL flight, and a Rolls-Royce/MTU RB.193-12 vectored-thrust turbofan for forward propulsion. This programme was terminated in the mid-1970s.

With financial backing from the West German government, VFW-Fokker initiated construction and development of

The VFW-Fokker VAK 191B V/STOL fighter project was one of the most ambitious undertaken in West Germany after World War II. Lift jets were located in the forward and rear portions of the long fuselage, with a vectored thrust engine in the mid-section. Span was 6.16 m (20 ft) and maximum vertical take-off weight 8000 kg (17,625 lb). Its small wing hindered its STOL performance.

three prototypes of a short-range twin-turbofan civil transport designated **VFW 614**. The first of these prototypes was flown on 14 July 1971, certification was gained on 23 August 1974 and the first of the production aircraft was flown on 28 April 1975. A cantilever low-wing monoplane with moderately swept wings and tail surfaces, this 40/44-passenger aircraft had an unusual design feature: the installation of its two 32-kN (7,280-lb) thrust Rolls-Royce/SNECMA M45H Mk 501 turbofan engines, one pylon-mounted above each wing. With only limited orders for 16 aircraft from Air Alsace (three), Cimber Air (two), Touraine Air Transport (eight) and the Luftwaffe (three), the VFW 614 was uneconomic to build, and production ended in early 1978 after the completion of these air-

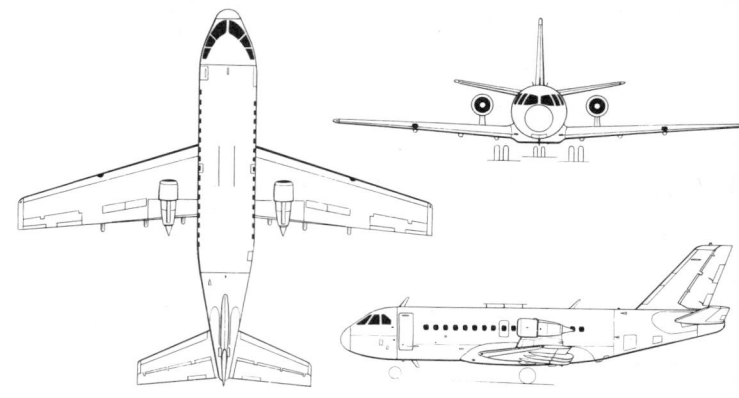

VFW-Fokker 614

craft. With a wing span of 21.50 m (70 ft 6½ in) and a cruising speed of 705 km/h (438 mph) at 7620 m (25,000 ft),

the VFW 614 had a range of 1205 km (749 miles) with 40 passengers and fuel reserves.

VL aircraft

The Finnish aircraft company Valtion Lentokonetehdas (VL) was formed in 1928 from the earlier IVL (Ilmailuvoimen Lentokonetehdas). Its early activities included production for Osakeyhtio Sääski of the **Sääski II** open-cockpit biplane (about 10 built) and slightly improved **Sääski IIA** (about 24 built). VL's first design to enter production was the **VL Kotka II** (six built) following testing of the **Kotka I** prototype. A two-crew maritime reconnaissance biplane powered by a 429-kW (575-hp) Wright R-1820-E Cyclone radial engine, the type remained in service until 1944. Then came a series of three trainers. The first of these was the **Tuisku** advanced armed trainer biplane, whose prototype of 1933 was followed by the initial production **Tuisku I** (13 built) and final improved **Tuisku II** (16 built), which was powered by the 160-kW (215-hp) Armstrong Siddeley Lynx radial engine. The **Viima I** (one prototype and one production) of 1935 was a two-seat elementary trainer or liaison aircraft, the production **Viima II** (22 built) powered by the 112-kW (150-hp)

Siemens-Halske Sh.14A radial engine. More important was the **Pyry** (thunderstorm) low-wing monoplane advanced trainer, the prototype **Pyry I** of 1939 being followed by the production **Pyry II** (40 built) with a 313-kW (420-hp) Wright R-975-E3 radial.

VL designed and produced only a single combat type, the **Myrsky** (storm) prototype of 1942, which was a single-seat low-wing monoplane fighter with retractable landing gear, followed by

the pre-production **Myrsky I** (three built) and improved production **Myrsky II** (47 built). Powerplant was the licence-built 794-kW (1,065-hp) Pratt & Whitney R-1830-S1C3-G Twin Wasp radial engine, and armament comprised four 12.7-mm (0.5-in) Browning machine-guns. Spanning 11.00 m (36 ft 1 in), the Myrsky II had a maximum speed of 530 km/h (329 mph) at optimum altitude. They were operated mostly during the closing

stages of World War II in a close-support role to drive German forces from Finnish territory. Ten improved **Myrsky III** aircraft were not completed, but VL flew a single similar **Pyörremyrsky** (whirlwind) prototype with a 100-kW (1,475-hp) Daimler-Benz DB 605 Vee engine.

The Tuisku (blizzard) was the first in a series of military trainers built by VL in the early 1930s.

Vakhmistrov parasite fighter-schemes

One of the earliest protagonists of parasite fighters, to be carried by bomber aircraft for defence over enemy territory, Vladimir S. Vakhmistrov gained Soviet air force approval in 1931 to carry out experiments. The first aircraft, designated **Z-1**, combined a Tupolev TB-1 equipped to carry a Tupolev I-4 fighter above each wing. This combination was first flown on 3 December 1931 and tested successfully on several occasions. Development continued with the **Z-1a** that comprised a TB-I carrying two Tupolev I-5s, and the **Z-2** combining a Tupolev TB-3 with an I-5 above each wing and a third over the fuselage. A significant advance was made with the **Z-5,** in which the TB-3 had a trapeze beneath the fuselage to which a suitably-equipped Grigorovich I-Z fighter could hook-on in flight; such a

The prototype Z-6 is seen here with two Polikarpov I-5s, two I-16s and a Grigorovich I-Z.

hook-on during 23 March 1935 was the world's first beneath a fixed-wing aircraft. It suggested that a bomber might be able to carry a fighter for defence in a far distant target area, the fighter being recovered after a successful action for transport back to base. Later and more serious consideration of such a scheme, not only in the USSR, brought realisation of its impracticality.

Vakhmistrov's experiments continued with the **Z-6,** which comprised a TB-3 carrying a Polikarpov I-16 beneath each wing, and a similar **Z-7** combina-

tion in which a third I-16 hooked on to an underfuselage trapeze in the air. Most amazing of all the experiments was that made with the *Aviamatka* motherplane, a TB-3/AM-34 flown during 1935 and carrying an I-16 above and an I-5 below each wing and which, during flight, lowered its underfuselage trapeze to which an I-Z fighter hooked

on; all five fighters were then released simultaneously in the air. The culmination of Vakhmistrov's work was the formation of an operational unit, equipped with six TB-31AM-34 carriers and 12 I-16 aircraft modified to carry a 250-kg (551-lb) bomb beneath each wing, then becoming designated **SPB**.

Valmet aircraft

Soon after World War II had ended, Valtion Lentokonetehdas (VL) became integrated into the large state-owned Valtion Metallitehaat Lentokonetehdas, known in short since 1958 as Valmet Oy. The company's first post-war product was the **Valmet VH-1** prototype of a two-seat advanced monoplane trainer with retractable landing gear and a 537-kW (720-hp) Bristol Mercury VIII radial engine. First flown on 6 February 1951, the type was built for the Finnish air force initially as the **VH-2 Vihuri** (squall), and followed by the improved **VH-3**, all delivered by late 1956. Since that time Valmet has built for the air force the Aérospatiale CM.170 Magister under licence, assembled 12 Saab 35XS Drakens, and was most recently involved in the licence-manufacture of 46 of a total of 50 British Aerospace Hawk Mk 51s.

Following receipt of a Finnish air force contract in early 1973, Valmet designed, developed and produced the **Valmet L-70 Miltrainer**, which is designated **Vinka** by the air force. A cantilever low-wing monoplane with fixed tricycle landing gear, it accommodates instructor and pupil in side-by-side enclosed accommodation; power is provided by a 149-kW (200-hp) Avco Lycoming AEIO-360-A1B6 flat-four engine. Following successful testing of the first prototype, flown initially on 1 July 1975, 30 production Vinkas were built for the air force, all of them delivered by the end of 1982.

The Vinka led, in 1983, to the **L-80TP Turbo Trainer**, essentially an L-70 with retractable gear and a

Seen here in its prototype form (then christened the Leko-70) the Valmet L-70 spans 9.85 m (32 ft 3¾ in), with a MTOW of 1200 kg (2645 lb) and a maximum speed of 240 km/h (149 mph) at sea level.

268-kW (360-shp) Allison 250B-17D turboprop engine. By the time the L-80TP flew it had been rechristened the **L-90TP Redigo**. The first aircraft (OH-VTP) flew on 1 July 1986 with the original Allison engine, but the second Redigo was fitted with a more powerful Turboméca TP 319 turboprop (although it had been derated to 313 kW/420 shp). This aircraft was lost in an accident in August 1988, but the type was finally certified by the Finnish authorities in September 1991. The definitive production engine became a higher-powered Allison 250-B17F. The first orders had come from the Ilmavoimat (Finnish air force) for 10 aircraft in 1989 to act as lead-ins for the air force Hawk jet trainers. This was followed by a further 18 deliveries to customers abroad, including 10 for the Mexican air force.

Specification
Valmet L-90TP Redigo
Type: two-seat side-by-side turboprop military trainer
Powerplant: one flat-rated 313-kW

(420-shp) Allison 250-B17F turboprop
Performance: maximum level speed 224 kt (415 km/h; 218 mph); service ceiling 7620 m (25,000 ft); range with max fuel at 6000m (19,685 ft) 755 nm (1400 km/870 miles)
Weights: empty, equipped 950 kg (2,094 lb); maximum take-off (with stores) 1900 kg (4,189 lb)
Dimensions: span 10.60 m (34 ft 9¼ in);

length overall 8.53 m (27 ft 11¾ in); height overall 3.20 in (10 ft 6 in)
Armament: six underwing hardpoints with a total capacity for 1100 kg (2,425 lb) of gun, rocket or reconnaissance pods

The L-90TP Redigo is stressed to withstand up to +7 and -3.5 g. A zero-zero ejection system is available, as an option, for the crew.

Vertol Model 42 and Model 44

Vertol Aircraft Company (Canada) Ltd was formed in 1954, primarily to carry out servicing and overhaul of the Piasecki (later Vertol) H-21 helicopters in service with the Royal Canadian Air Force. The company carried out an exclusive conversion of eight RCAF H-21s for civil use and these **Vertol Model 42A** helicopters, each powered by the 1063-kW (1,425-hp) Wright R-1820-103 engine, were equipped to

carry 19 passengers, or 1279 kg (2,820 lb) of internal cargo, or a 2268-kg (5,000-lb) slung load. They were used by Spartan Air Services for supply and transport in support of the mid-Canada early-warning radar chain.

When the Piasecki Helicopter Corporation became Vertol Aircraft Corporation in 1956, development was initiated of civil versions of the Piasecki H-21 under the company designation

Vertol Model 44. Powerplant consisted of the 1063-kW (1,425-hp) Wright 977C9 HD1 Cyclone radial engine, and the helicopter was available in three versions. These comprised the **Model 44A** utility cargo/passenger transport able to carry 19 civilian passengers or 20 troops, or 12 stretchers with two medical attendants, or a 2500-kg (5,512-lb) external cargo load; the **Model 44B** was the

standard passenger transport with an airliner cabin for a maximum 15 passengers; and the **Model 44C** was a VIP transport with custom-designed interior. Model 44Bs supplied to New York Airways and the Swedish navy had a sealed lower fuselage and rubberised floats above the standard landing gear to permit emergency operation from water. Three Model 44Bs were also built for Canada's Spartan Air Services, complementing its Model 42As in support of the mid-Canada early-warning radar chain.

Vickers F.B.5

The large and well-known armament, engineering and shipbuilding group known as Vickers Ltd established an aviation department in early 1911, building first eight differing shoulder-wing monoplanes derived from the French R.E.P. designs of Esnault-Pelterie. As armament manufacturers with an aviation department it is not surprising that the company received a contract from the Admiralty for an experimental armed fighter biplane. Thus was designed the **Vickers E.F.B.1** (experimental fighting biplane) that marks the beginning of the company's military designs. An unequal-span biplane, it had a central nacelle with two open cockpits in tandem and at the rear a 60-kW (80-hp) Wolseley engine driving a pusher propeller. Its fixed tailskid landing gear incorporated a skid projecting well forward of the wheels to reduce the danger of nosing over when landing, and the tail unit was carried on wire-braced uncovered tubular steel tailbooms. When exhibited at the 1913 Aero Show at Olympia it caused something of a stir because of its armament, comprising a movable Vickers machine-gun in the forward cockpit; it must have been an anticli-

max when subsequently the aircraft crashed during its first take-off.

Similar but improved **E.F.B.2** and **E.F.B.3** aircraft were flown successfully under the power of the 75-kW (100-hp) Gnome rotary engine, leading to an Admiralty order for six aircraft designated **E.F.B.4**. Before they were completed the War Office took over the order, an **E.F.B.5** prototype preceding production of the company's first military aircraft, the **F.B.5 Gunbus** of which more than 200 were built. The type was used mainly by the RFC, only about 15 being delivered to the RNAS. Detail improvements were introduced during production, and the unwieldy belt-fed Vickers machine-gun of early aircraft was replaced later by the lighter drum-fed Lewis gun on a pivot mounting. As powered by the 75-kW (100-hp) Gnome Monosoupape rotary engine, the 11.13-m (36-ft 6-in) span Gunbus had a maximum speed of 113 km/h (70 mph) at optimum altitude and an endurance of about 4 hours 30 minutes. Experimental variants of the F.B.5 were flown during 1915, these including one powered by an 82-kW (110-hp) Clerget rotary engine, and two with the 112-kW (150-hp) Smith radial

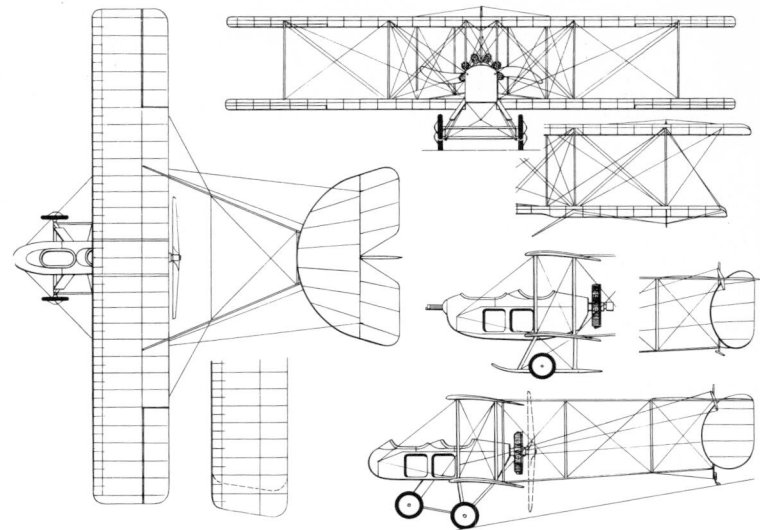

Vickers E.F.B.2 (scrap views; gun-carrying model)

engine; no further examples were built. In addition to production by Vickers, the F.B.5 was built under licence by S.A.

Darracq et Cie at Suresnes, France, and by A/S Nielson and Winthers at Copenhagen, Denmark.

Vickers F.B.14

A two-seat fighter/reconnaissance aircraft of conventional biplane configuration, with tandem open cockpits and fixed tailskid landing gear, the **Vickers F.B.14** was designed around a new 172-kW (230-hp) BHP (Beardmore, Halford and Pullinger) inline engine. The prototype airframe, which like that of the F.B.5 had a basic steel-tube structure, was awaiting its engine in mid-1916, but development of the BHP engine seemed protracted and it was flown instead with a 119-kW (160-hp) Beardmore. Not surprisingly, its performance was far below estimates, and when Vickers had difficulty with reliability of the Beardmore the majority of the 50 or so production aircraft were deliv-

ered to the RFC without engines. Vickers had tested one with the older and reliable 89-kW (120-hp) Beardmore engine but performance was far below an acceptable figure. Subsequent attempts to resolve the powerplant problems resulted in the **F.B.14A** (112-kW/150-hp Lorraine-Dietrich Vee engine), **F.B.14D** (186-kW/250-hp Rolls-Royce Mk IV Vee engine) and **F.B.14F** (112-kW/150-hp RAF 4a engine). Performance with the Rolls-Royce engine was by far the best, with a maximum speed of 180 km/h (112 mph) at optimum altitude, but as this was quite inferior to the contemporary Bristol F.2B there was no further development of the F.B.14.

Though in itself unsuccessful, the Vickers F.B.14 (seen here in a modified form with straight-edged fin, pilot's headrest and curved top-decking), provided the company with the structural basis for most of its tractor biplanes in the 1920s. The fuselage was built of steel tube.

Vickers F.B.19

Derived from the **E.S.1** and **E.S.2** experimental scout aircraft, the **Vickers F.B.19 Mk I** was a neat but tubby single-seat fighter with equal-span unstaggered biplane wings, and was powered by a 75-kW (100-hp) Gnome Monosoupape or 82-kW (110-hp) Le Rhône rotary engine. It was complemented by the **F.B.19 Mk II** with staggered wings, powered by either Clerget or Le Rhône rotaries, each of 82 kW (110 hp). Both Mk I and Mk II aircraft were armed with a single Vickers machine-gun synchronised to fire forward through the propeller disc by means of Vickers-Challenger interrupter gear. About 50 F.B.19 Mk I and 12 F.B.19 Mk II aircraft were built for the RFC, but the types saw only brief

service on the Western Front and in the Middle East because performance was inferior to that of most of the opposing fighters; a few were used for Home Defence but the majority ended their days in training units. Following evaluation of a Mk I aircraft in Russia, a further 12 Mk II aircraft were built for this nation, but it is doubtful if they ever saw service use. Spanning only 7.32 m (24 ft) and with a length of 5.54 m (18 ft 2 in), the diminutive F.B.19 Mk I with Monosoupape engine was the faster, attaining 164 km/h (102 mph) at 3050 m (10,000 ft).

The Vickers F.B.19 Mk II could be distinguished from the similar Mk I by its staggered wing cellule.

Vickers F.B.27 Vimy, Vimy Commercial and Vernon

The **Vickers F.B.27 Vimy** bomber prototype (B9952) was flown for the first time on 30 November 1917. Like the de Havilland D.H.10 Amiens and Handley Page V/1500, it was designed to provide the RAF with a strategic bomber that could attack industrial tar-

gets in Germany. Although token numbers of each arrived in France before the Armistice of 11 November 1918, none of them saw operational service in World War I. Of biplane configuration, with a biplane tail unit and accommodating a crew of three, the first

Vimy prototype was powered by two 154-kW (207-hp) Hispano-Suiza engines, the second by 194-kW (260-hp) Sunbeam Maoris, the third by 224-kW (300-hp) Fiat A-12s and the fourth by the 268-kW (360-hp) Rolls-Royce Eagle VIII which became standard. The

F.B.27A Vimy Mk II was ordered into large-scale production, but contract cancellations at the war's end limited the total built to about 230. It was not until July 1919 that the Vimy was in full RAF service, equipping first No. 58 Squadron in Egypt, then other squadrons in the Middle East and in the UK. It remained in first-line service until replaced by the Vickers Virginia during 1924-25, but No. 502 Squadron in Northern Ireland was operational with the type until 1929. Apart from aircraft with No. 502 Squadron, some 80 Vimys were re-engined with Armstrong Siddeley Jaguar or Bristol Jupiter radial engines from 1925 and used by training schools and as parachute trainers at RAF Henlow.

The Vimy is, of course, remembered in aviation history for its pioneering flights, including the first non-stop west-east crossing of the North Atlantic by John Alcock and Arthur Whitten Brown, the first England-Australia flight by Ross and Keith Smith and their crew, and the attempted first England-South Africa flight by Pierre van Ryneveld and Christopher Q. Brand, of which the final leg, Bulawayo to Cape Town, was completed in a D.H.9.

In January 1919 Vickers began development of the Vimy for civil use, introducing in the **Vimy Commercial** a new larger-diameter fuselage to provide a cabin for 10 passengers and retaining the powerplant of two Rolls-Royce Eagle VIII engines. The prototype, first flown on 13 April 1919, was followed by 43 production aircraft for

Vickers Vimy Ambulance of the RAF based in the Middle East during the early 1920s.

China (40) and one each for the Instone Air Line, Grands Express Aériens and the USSR. Five generally similar aircraft, incorporating a nose loading door, were completed as **Vimy Ambulance** aircraft for the RAF and equipped to accommodate four stretchers or eight sitting patients, plus two medical attendants.

Final derivative of the Vimy/Vimy Commercial was the **Vickers Vernon** bomber/transport used by the RAF during its policing of Iraq from 1921. Serving with Nos 45 and 70 Squadrons at Hinaidi, they not only carried out their basic task, but were used as air

ambulances and played a significant role in establishing the Cairo-Baghdad airmail route. **Vernon Mk I** aircraft (20 built) differed little from the Vimy Commercial, but the **Vernon Mk II** (25) introduced 336-kW (450-hp) Napier Lion II engines and the **Vernon Mk III** (10) had Lion III engines, increased fuel tankage and oleo-pneumatic landing gear. The Vernon was superseded by the Victoria from 1927.

Specification
Vickers Vimy Mk II
Type: heavy bomber
Powerplant: two 268-kW (360-hp)

Rolls-Royce Eagle VIII Vee piston engines
Performance: maximum speed 166 km/h (103 mph) at sea level; service ceiling 2135 m (7,000 ft); maximum range 1448 km (900 miles)
Weights: empty 3222 kg (7,104 lb); maximum take-off 4937 kg (10,884 lb)
Dimensions: span 20.75 m (68 ft 1 in); length 13.27 m (43 ft 6½ in); height 4.76 m (15 ft 7½ in); wing area 122.44 m² (1,318.0 sq ft)
Armament: one 7.7-mm (0.303-in) Lewis machine-gun on a Scarff ring mounting in both nose and mid positions, plus up to 1123 kg (2,476 lb) of bombs on external racks

Vickers Type 54 Viking, Type 78 Vulture and Type 83 Vanellus

During 1918 Vickers designed a light amphibian with biplane wings and tail unit, its Consuta plywood hull being built by the company's S. E. Saunders subsidiary and incorporating an enclosed cabin seating four passengers. Its powerplant, a 205-kW (275-hp) Rolls-Royce Falcon, was strut-mounted below the upper wing to drive a pusher propeller. Designated **Vickers Viking**, it was flown for the first time in late 1919. It was in a forced landing with this aircraft, on 18 December 1919, that the company's famous chief pilot, Sir John Alcock, was killed. From this **Viking I** was developed a series of aircraft with progressive improvements, especially to the hull (some of

which had open cockpits), and differing powerplant. They comprised the one-off **Viking II** (268-kW/360-hp Rolls-Royce Eagle VIII) and **Viking III** (336-kW/450-hp Napier Lion), followed by the production **Type 54 Viking IV**. Of the 26 that were sold, examples in several type numbers went to the armed services of Argentina, Canada, France, Japan and the Netherlands, and for civil use in Argentina, Canada, the Soviet Union and the USA. Ironically, Sir Ross Smith, knighted like Sir John Alcock for a Vickers Vimy pioneering flight, was killed in an accident with a Viking IV on 13 April 1922. The final version was the **Viking V** with Napier Lion engine, two built for service with

the RAF in Iraq.

The aircraft that was to have been the **Viking VI**, with redesigned wing structure and Napier Lion engine, was designated **Type 78 Vulture I**; a second example with a 268-kW (360-hp) Rolls-Royce Eagle IX had the designation **Type 95 Vulture II** but was later re-engined with a Napier Lion. These two aircraft were used during 1924 in an unsuccessful round-the-world flight attempt, at first designated **Viking VII** but later named **Type 83 Vanellus**, was a single aircraft for evaluation by the RAF as a three-seat (pilot, observer/gunner and gunner) open-cockpit fleet-spotter; it differed primarily from its predecessors

by having a monoplane tail unit. The 15.24-m (50-ft 0-in) span Viking IV with Napier Lion powerplant had a maximum speed of 182 km/h (113 mph) at sea level.

Seen at Hinaidi is the Vickers Viking VI (Vulture II) in which Squadron Leader A. S. C. McLean and a crew of two attempted to fly around the world in 1924, until crashing in Burma.

Vickers Type 56 Victoria, Type 264 Valentia and Type 72 Vanguard

Derived from the Virginia bomber, the **Vickers Victoria** military transport has a significant place in RAF history, playing a conspicuous role in the evacuation of 586 people from Kabul to Peshawar during 1928-29. Two Victoria prototypes were ordered in April 1921, the first of them (J6860) being designated **Type 56 Victoria Mk I** and first flown on 22 August 1922. A large equal-span biplane with a biplane tail unit, its powerplant comprised two 336-kW (450-hp) Napier Lion IXA engines, and the large-capacity fuselage accommodated two crew in an open cockpit in the nose, with up to 23 fully-equipped troops in the enclosed cabin. The second prototype **Type 81 Victoria Mk II** was flown in January 1923 and the initial production **Type 117 Victoria Mk III** introduced slightly swept outer wing panels incorporating some dihedral and, initially, 336-kW (450-hp) Lion II engines. The designation **Type 145 Victoria Mk IV** applied to a prototype introducing a basic wing structure of metal. This was followed by the last large-scale production version, the **Type 169 Victoria**

Closely resembling the Victoria, only one Vickers Vanguard civil transport was built for use by Imperial Airways.

Mk V, which had this wing structure, 425-kW (570-hp) Napier Lion VIIB engines and was without fixed vertical tail surfaces. Final production version was the **Type 262 Victoria Mk VI** with the 464-kW (622-hp) Bristol Pegasus IIL3 radial engine, and when Victoria construction ended a total of 97 had been built including prototypes.

The success of the Victoria Mk VI led to orders for new production aircraft (28 built) with this powerplant. these being designated **Type 264 Valentia**; in addition, 54 Victorias were converted subsequently to Valentia standard. A small number with 474-kW (635-hp) Pegasus IIM3 engines had the same designation. At the outbreak of World War II the RAF had 60 Valentias on strength, many of them remaining in service until 1941, and in Iraq two continued in use until May 1944.

A one-off civil variant designated

Type 72 Vanguard, accommodating 23 passengers and powered by two Napier Lion engines (later 485-kW/650-hp Rolls-Royce Condor III engines as the **Type 103 Vanguard**) entered service with Imperial Airways in May 1928. It was destroyed in an accident in late 1928 when being tested after modification of the tail unit as the **Type 170 Vanguard**.

Specification
Vickers Valentia
Type: troop transport

Powerplant: two 464-kW (622-hp) Bristol Pegasus IIL3 radial engines
Performance: maximum speed 193 km/h (120 mph) at 1525 m (5,000 ft); service ceiling 4955 m (16,250 ft); range 1287 km (800 miles)
Weights: empty 4964 kg (10,944 lb); maximum take-off 8845 kg (19,500 lb)
Dimensions: span 26.62 m (87 ft 4 in); length 18.14 m (59 ft 6 in); height 5.41 m (17 ft 9 in)
Armament: underwing racks could be attached to carry a maximum bombload of 998 kg (2,200 lb)

Vickers Type 57 Virginia

A large biplane, which in construction differed little from the Vickers Vimy designed and developed in the closing stages of World War I, the **Vickers Type 57 Virginia** was flown in prototype (J6856) form on 24 November 1922. The type became the backbone of the RAF's heavy night-bomber squadrons in the years between the two world wars, remaining in first-line service from 1924 until the mid-1930s, and then continuing in use for parachute training at RAF Henlow. When production ended a total of 124 had been built for the RAF. First of the 10 variants was the initial prototype, the **Virginia Mk I** powered by two 336-kW (450-hp) Napier Lion engines, later replaced by two 485-kW (650-hp) Rolls-Royce Condor III engines as the **Type 96 Virginia Mk I**; subsequently it was given a lengthened fuselage, a new forward fuselage and gun positions known as fighting-tops at the wing trailing edges, resulting in a new prototype designated **Type 115 Virginia Mk VIII**. It was converted to **Type 129 Virginia Mk VII** and finally **Virginia Mk X** standards.

The second prototype, the **Type 76 Virginia Mk II**, differed in the installation of its Napier Lion engines and had a lengthened nose to improve the bomb-aimer's efficiency. After tests and use in service trials it was converted, like the original prototype, to

Virginia Mk VII and finally Virginia Mk X standard. The **Type 79 Virginia Mk III**, built to an Air Ministry contract of late 1922, was similar to the Virginia Mk II in original form but differed mainly by having dual controls, provision for underwing bombs and 349-kW (468-hp) Napier Lion II engines. Almost identical to the Mk III, the **Type 99 Virginia Mk IV** had additional equipment and an increase in underwing bombload; one was used to test the installation of a third (central) rudder in the biplane tail unit, a feature which distinguished the first major production version, the **Type 100 Virginia Mk V** (22 built). The **Type 108 Virginia Mk VI** (25) introduced revisions in wing folding and rigging, and six Virginia Mk Vs were updated to this configuration. The second Virginia Mk III was returned to Vickers for installa-

Vickers Virginia Mk VII of No. 7 Sqn, RAF, based at Worthy Down in the late 1920s.

tion of a redesigned nose to improve the pilot's field of view and, simultaneously, acquired the accumulated improvements of the Mk VI plus a lengthened rear fuselage and wing sweepback to improve stability; in this form it served as the **Type 112 Virginia Mk VII** prototype, followed by 11 production aircraft and 38 conversions of earlier marks to this standard. The **Type 128 Virginia Mk IX** (eight built and 27 conversions) introduced automatic slats, wheel brakes and a tail gunner's position, and the final **Type 139 Virginia Mk X** (50 built and 53 conversions) incorporated an all-metal basic structure. Apart from playing a vital role in the operational development of what was to become RAF Bomber Command, many Virginias continued to be used for a variety of test purposes as late as 1941.

Specification
Vickers Virginia Mk X
Type: heavy night-bomber
Powerplant: two 433-kW (580-hp) Napier Lion VB W-12 piston engines
Performance: maximum speed 174 km/h (108 mph) at 1525 m (5,000 ft); service ceiling 4725 m (15,500 ft); range 1585 km (985 miles)
Weights: empty 4377 kg (9,650 lb); maximum take-off 7983 kg (17,600 lb)
Dimensions: span 26.72 m (87 ft 8 in); length 18.97 m (62 ft 3 in); height 5.54 m (18 ft 2 in); wing area 202.34 m² (2,178.0 sq ft)
Armament: single 0.303-in (7.7-mm) Lewis gun in nose and twin Lewis guns in tail, plus up to 1361 kg (3,000 lb) of bombs

Vickers Type 61 Vulcan

In early 1921 design was initiated of the **Vickers Vulcan** transport, a biplane of 14.94 m (49 ft 0 in) span with a deep oval-section fuselage completely filling the space between the equal-span wings. It accommodated the pilot in an open cockpit forward of the upper wing, with below and behind him a roomy enclosed cabin for six to eight passengers. To limit selling price to the minimum, the low-cost war-surplus 268-kW (360-hp) Rolls-Royce Eagle VIII engine was installed in the first six aircraft (Type 61) to be completed, but as a number of perfor-

mance problems were encountered the last two examples (Type 74) had the 336-kW (450-hp) Napier Lion. One of the early production aircraft was completed as a cargo carrier (Type 63) for Air Ministry evaluation, but was subsequently reconverted as a passenger carrier and used with one other Eagle-powered and the two Napier Lion-powered aircraft by Imperial Airways on European service. Their very limited reliability meant the Vulcan had a short useful life, only one or two surviving in service beyond the mid-1920s.

G-EBFC was a Vulcan ordered by Imperial Airways. The Type 74 had a MTOW of 3062 kg (6,750 lb) and a maximum speed of 180 km/h (112 mph).

Vickers Type 71 Vixen series

In 1922 Vickers began as a private venture the design and development of a two-seat military biplane which could be adapted for use in a number of roles. Designated **Vickers Type 71 Vixen Mk I**, the prototype flown in early 1923 was powered by a 336-kW (450-hp) Napier Lion I engine. Following official testing it was suggested that the aircraft be converted to make it suitable for use as a day bomber, the Vixen I then being given a lengthened fuselage and specialised equipment for evaluation under the new designation **Type 87 Vixen Mk II**. Although testing was satisfactory, the type was then considered more suitable for use as an armed reconnaissance aircraft, the Air Ministry ordering six such aircraft under the designation **Vickers Type 94 Venture**. These aircraft were not accepted for use as such, being distributed to various RAF units for experimental purposes. Continued development of the Vixen led to the **Type 91 Vixen Mk III**, basically a version of the Venture with increased wing area and a higher compression Lion II engine to give

The Vixen was descended from the F.B.14 and paved the way for most of Vickers' inter-war, single-engined, tractor biplanes.

improved performance at altitude; it was evaluated both as a landplane and seaplane. In 1924 the Vixen Mk III had its fuselage lengthened and a 485-kW (650-hp) Rolls-Royce Condor III engine installed to become the **Type 105 Vixen Mk IV;** later that year, with the same powerplant and further airframe revisions, it was redesignated **Type 126 Vixen Mk VI**.

Vickers' success with the Vixen came from overseas, 10 Vixen Mk Is with Napier Lion engines being built for Portugal under the designation **Type 93 Valparaiso Mk I,** plus four with Rolls-Royce Eagle engines as the **Type 92 Valparaiso Mk II**. One of these aircraft was returned to the company in 1929 for installation of a Gnome-Rhône Jupiter VIa engine, and following its return and testing by the Portuguese air force at least 13 more were licence-built in Portugal with this powerplant, all of them being designated **Type**

168 Valparaiso Mk III. Chile acquired a single Valparaiso Mk I for service evaluation, ordering in 1925 18 of these aircraft which, with minor changes and installation of the 373-kW (500-hp) Lion V engine, were designated **Type 116 Vixen Mk V**. The Vixens used overseas were having problems with their wings and tail units, which had a basic structure of wood, and development of an all-metal basic structure was planned under the

designation **Vixen Mk VII**. However, this was given the designation **Type 130 Vivid** and, in parallel, another version with a metal airframe was built under the name **Type 131 Valiant**. Both remained one-offs, the Vivid having a 373-kW (500-hp) Lion VA high-compression engine and the Valiant having a 339-kW (455-hp) Bristol Jupiter VI. The Vivid was flown subsequently as a floatplane powered by a 403-kW (540-hp) Napier Lion XI engine.

Vickers Type 113 Vespa
to
Vought F-8 Crusader

Vickers Type 113 Vespa

The **Vickers Type 113 Vespa Mk I** first flown in September 1925 was built as a private venture to the requirements of Air Ministry Specification 30/24 for an army co-operation aircraft. An unequal-span well-staggered biplane with tandem open cockpits, it was powered as first flown by a Bristol Jupiter IV radial; the Vespa was under-powered with this engine, which was then replaced by a 339-kW (455-hp) Jupiter VI. After being damaged in an accident during June 1926 it was rebuilt with wings of metal basic structure and redesignated **Type 119 Vespa Mk II** but, although tested successfully, it was not ordered for the RAF. However, six **Type 149 Vespa Mk III** aircraft with a number of airframe refinements were supplied to

Bolivia during 1929, in which year four aircraft with 365-kW (490-hp) Armstrong Siddeley Jaguar VIC engines were ordered for the Irish Army Air Corps and designated **Type 193 Vespa Mk IV**, four more aircraft with some improvements subsequently being built for Ireland as the **Type 208 Vespa Mk V**. During 1930 the Vespa Mk II was modified to a standard similar to the Irish Vespa Mk IVs and, powered by a 395-kW (530-hp) Bristol Jupiter VIIF engine, became designated **Type 210 Vespa Mk VI**.

Seen at Brooklands before hand-over to the Irish Air Corps at Casement Aerodrome, Baldonnel, is this Vickers Vespa IV. This version had metal wings and struts.

It was used for demonstrations in China, but on return to the UK was modified yet again, and with a Bristol Pegasus 'S' supercharged engine installed was redesignated **Type 250 Vespa Mk VII**, being used on 16

September 1932 to establish a new world altitude record of 13404 m (43,976 ft). Following that it was acquired by the Air Ministry and used by the RAE for high-altitude research.

Vickers Type 120 Vendace

Built to the requirements of Air Ministry Specification 5A/24 for a floatplane trainer, the single **Vickers Type 120 Vendace Mk I** was a fairly conventional folding wing equal-span biplane with tandem open cockpits, and was powered by a 205-kW (275-hp) Rolls-Royce Falcon III engine. Tested officially in both landplane and floatplane form, it was retained for experimental purposes but no production order followed. One **Type 133 Vendace Mk II** with a 224-kW (300-hp) ADC Nimbus engine was built in 1928 as a private venture

The unusual landing gear layout of the Vendace I was the result of Vickers' ultimate objective of using the type on floats. The entire fuel supply was held in two streamlined overwing tanks.

and sold for aerial survey use in South America. The unusual landing gear layout of the Vickers Vendace I was the result of the ultimate objective of using the type on floats. The entire fuel supply was contained in the two streamlined tanks above the upper-wing centre-section. In landplane form

the Vendace I spanned 13.59 m (44 ft 7 in), weighed a maximum of

1576 kg (3,475 lb) and had a top speed of 188 km/h (117 mph).

Vickers Type 121 Wibault series

French designer Michel Wibault became associated with Vickers as a consulting engineer, resulting in the patented Vickers-Wibault light alloy construction, the main feature of which was the use of corrugated skins that could, if necessary, be removed easily for maintenance or repair. Wibault was founder of Avions Michel Wibault, and Vickers ordered from this company a single example of the Wibault 7 for use as a demonstrator. It differed from the standard French version by having Vickers landing gear and a 336-kW (450-hp) Bristol Jupiter VI radial engine. During 1926 Vickers built 26 generally similar aircraft designated **Vickers Type 121 Wibault Scout** for the Chilean air force. Similar construction was used for the **Vickers Type 125 Vireo** prototype, a single-seat fighter for shipboard use with wheel or float landing gear. First flown in March 1928, the Vireo was powered by a 172-kW (230-hp) Armstrong Siddeley Lynx IV but, although tested officially, no orders resulted. Only slightly more successful was the **Vickers Viastra** braced high-wing monoplane transport, which used the same form of construction. The **Type 160 Viastra I** prototype, powered by three 201-kW (270-hp) Armstrong Siddeley Lynx Major

engines, was flown on 1 October 1930, and an order was received for three examples for West Australian Airways. These were 12-seat aircraft, the first two, designated **Type 198 Viastra II**, being powered by two 391-kW (525-hp) Bristol Jupiter XIF engines and a single **Type 203 Viastra VI** having just one Jupiter XIF engine; however, as the Viastra IIs were unable to maintain height on one engine, the Viastra VI was later cancelled although completed. The designation **Type 199 Viastra III** applied to the original prototype when re-engined with two Armstrong Siddeley Jaguar VIC engines, becoming **Type 220 Viastra VIII** when flown later with three Jupiter VIFM engines. Final version was the one-off **Type 259 Viastra X**, with two Bristol Pegasus engines, built as a VIP transport for HRH The Prince of Wales. First flown in April 1933, it was little used in its intended role, being employed from

1935 by the Air Ministry for radio experiments until withdrawn from service in 1937.

The Vickers Vireo monoplane fighter spanned 10.67 m (35 ft), had a maximum speed of 193 km/h (120 mph) and was armed with a pair of 7.7-mm (0.303-in) machine-guns.

G-ACCC was the sole Vickers Viastra X, another aircraft built using Wibault's construction methods. Its 21.34-m (70-ft) wings had large slats, and it served as a VIP transport for HRH The Prince of Wales.

Vickers Type 123 Scout

Developed as a private-venture single-seat fighter, the one-off **Vickers Type 123 Scout** biplane, powered by a 298-kW (400-hp) Hispano-Suiza T52 Vee engine, was flown for the first time on 9 November 1926. Its performance was considered to be inadequate and the airframe was converted to be powered by a new Rolls-Royce engine designated F.XIS, developing about 373 kW (500 hp), and was redesignated **Type 141 Scout**. Submitted to compete in the Air Ministry F.21/26 single-seat fighter

competition during 1928 it failed to gain any home interest, but in 1929 Bolivia ordered for its air force six aircraft generally similar to the Type 141 but which, with 336-kW (450-hp) Bristol Jupiter VIA radial engines, revised landing gear and some other small

During the 1920s and 1930s Vickers' military aircraft were relatively widely sold abroad, this line-up in Bolivia comprising four Bolivian Scouts (right) with three Vickers Vespas.

modifications, were designated **Type 143 Bolivian Scout**. Delivered from January 1930, they were considered by that air force to be highly satisfactory.

Vickers Type 132 Vildebeest and Type 266 Vincent

Designed to replace the Hawker Horsley day/torpedo-bomber in RAF service, the **Vickers Vildebeest** was a conventional equal-span biplane with fixed tailwheel landing gear and single-engine powerplant. As first flown in **Type 132** prototype form in April 1928, it was powered by a 343-kW (460-hp) Bristol Jupiter VIII radial engine, but a variety of powerplants was tested (**Types 192**, **194** and **209**) before an overheating problem was resolved in the **Type 214** by installation of a new Bristol engine designated XFBM, later developed into the Pegasus. Production for the RAF included four basic models, the initial production **Type 244 Vildebeest Mk I** having the Pegasus I engine. It was followed by the **Type 258 Vildebeest Mk II** which introduced the 492-kW (660-hp) Pegasus IIM3 engine, and then by the **Type 277 Vildebeest Mk III** with a revised rear cockpit giving this version three-seat capacity. The final production version, of which 18 were built, was the **Type 286 Vildebeest Mk IV** which had the 615-kW (825-hp) Bristol Perseus VIII, making it the world's first aircraft with a sleeve-valve engine. Vildebeest Mk Is entered service with the RAF in 1933; about 100 remained in service at the outbreak of World War II and the type was last used operationally against Japanese forces at Singapore in 1942. Of the 183 built by Vickers, 39 were supplied to the RNZAF and, in addition, 26 **Type 245** aircraft with Hispano V-12 engines were built under licence in Spain.

Vickers Vincent of the Royal New Zealand Air Force in 1940.

With a requirement for a three-seat general-purpose aircraft to supersede the Fairey IIIF and Westland Wapiti in RAF service, the Air Ministry selected a modified version of the Vildebeest which gained the designation **Vickers Type 266 Vincent**. Derived directly from the Vildebeest Mk III, a converted Vildebeest Mk I serving as the prototype, the Vincent differed by carrying an auxiliary fuel tank instead of a torpedo, and by having specialised equipment and message pick-up hook for use in an army co-operation role. Entering service with the RAF in late

1934, the Vincent found employment in Aden, Egypt, India, Iraq, Kenya and the Sudan, built to a total of 197; about half remained in RAF service at the outbreak of World War II and continued to serve in Iraq until 1941. The Vincent was also supplied in small numbers to Iraq and the RNZAF.

Specification
Vickers Vildebeest Mk IV
Type: two-seat torpedo-bomber
Powerplant: one 615-kW (825-hp) Bristol Perseus VIII sleeve radial piston engine

Performance: maximum speed 251 km/h (156 mph) at 1525 m (5,000 ft); service ceiling 5180 m (17,000 ft); range with maximum payload 1014 km (630 miles)
Weights: empty 2143 kg (4,724 lb); maximum take-off 3856 kg (8,500 lb)
Dimensions: span 14.94 m (49 ft 0 in); length 11.48 m (37 ft 8 in); height 4.47 m (14 ft 8 in); wing area 67.63 m² (728.0 sq ft)
Armament: one forward-firing 7.7-mm (0.303-in) Vickers machine-gun and one 7.7-mm (0.303-in) Lewis gun on trainable mount in rear cockpit, plus one 457-mm (18-in) torpedo or 454 kg (1,000 lb) of bombs

Vickers Type 134 Vellore and Type 212 Vellox

The **Vickers Type 134 Vellore Mk I** was a large equal-span biplane intended as a freight carrier. Powered by a 391-kW (525-hp) Bristol Jupiter IX radial engine, it had an open cockpit forward of the wings seating two side-by-side, with behind and below them a large cargo hold. It was then re-engined with the Armstrong Siddeley Jaguar VI in an England-Australia flight in 1929 that terminated in the aircraft being written off in a crash landing. The designation Vellore Mk II was not used, but two twin-engined versions were built as the **Type 172 Vellore Mk III** and **Type 173 Vellore Mk IV** with 391-kW (525-hp) Bristol Jupiter XIF radials. Final deriva-

tion of the design was the single **Type 212 Vellox** intended as a civil transport with cabin accommodation for a steward and 10 passengers. Powered by two 447-kW (600-hp) Bristol Pegasus IM3 radial engines and first flown on 23 January 1934, it was acquired by Imperial Airways but used only as a freighter.

The Vickers Vellore I is seen here in its original form with a neatly installed Bristol Jupiter radial engine. In this form the Vellore I spanned 23.16 m (76 ft), had an all-up weight 4309 kg (9,500 lb) and could attain a maximum speed of 183 km/h (114 mph).

Vickers Type 246 Wellesley

In 1933 Vickers began construction of a prototype biplane to Air Ministry Specification G.4/31 for a general-purpose torpedo-bomber. Simul-

taneously, as a private venture, the company built to the same specification an alternative design of monoplane configuration based on extensive use of light alloy geodetic construction

developed by Barnes N. Wallis. When tested by the RAF, the **Type 246** monoplane proved far superior to the **Type 253** biplane and, as a result, in September 1935 an initial order was placed for 96 of these monoplanes with the name **Vickers Type 281 Wellesley**. When production of the definitive **Type 287 Wellesley Mk I** ended in May 1938 a total of 176 had been built, and the type first entered RAF service with No. 76 Squadron in April 1937. The Wellesley became well known in 1938 when, used by the RAF Long-Range Development Flight, two of three **Type 292** aircraft (Pegasus XXII) led by Squadron Leader R. Kellett completed successfully a non-stop 11520.4-km (7,158.4-mile) flight from Ismailia, Egypt, to Darwin, Australia; this established a world absolute distance record that remained unbroken until 1945.

By the outbreak of World War II some 100 Wellesleys remained in RAF service in the Middle East, being used operationally against Italian forces at a later stage and remaining in use for maritime patrol until 1941. Other Wellesley models were the **Type 289**

Vickers Wellesley Mk I of No. 76 Sqn, RAF, based at Finningley in 1938.

testbed for the Hercules HE15 radial, the **Type 291** blind-flying model, the **Type 294** with strengthened wing and **Type 402** experimental three-seater.

Specification
Vickers Wellesley Mk I
Type: two-seat medium bomber
Powerplant: one 690-kW (925-hp)

Bristol Pegasus XX radial piston engine
Performance: maximum speed 367 km/h (228 mph) at 6005 m (19,700 ft); service ceiling 10060 m (33,000 ft); range with maximum payload 1786 km (1,110 miles)
Weights: empty 2889 kg (6,369 lb); maximum take-off 5035 kg (11,100 lb)
Dimensions: span 22.73 m (74 ft 7 in);

length 11.96 m (39 ft 3 in); height 3.76 m (12 ft 4 in); wing area 58.53 m² (630.0 sq ft)
Armament: one forward-firing 7.7-mm (0.303-in) Vickers machine-gun and one Vickers 'K' gun on trainable mount in rear position, plus up to 907 kg (2,000 lb) of bombs in underwing panniers

Vickers Type 271 Wellington

Initial experience gained with geodetic construction in the Wellesley was of great value when Vickers tendered to Air Ministry Specification B.9/32 for a medium day bomber. A contract was awarded for a B.9/32 prototype, a mid-wing monoplane with retractable tail-wheel landing gear powered by two 682-kW (915-hp) Bristol Pegasus X radial engines. This **Vickers Wellington** was first flown on 15 June 1936, and satisfactory early tests led on 15 August 1936 to an initial order for 180 **Wellington Mk I** production aircraft. These were the first of many and in October 1938 began to equip No. 9 Squadron; at the outbreak of World War II in the following September eight squadrons were fully equipped and others had token numbers. When production ended in October 1945, a total of 11,461 Wellingtons of all versions had been built. Nicknamed 'Wimpey' after a cigar-smoking American cartoon character named J. Wellington Wimpey, this aircraft formed the mainstay of RAF Bomber Command's operations over Europe during the first half of World War II, played a vital role in the Battle of the Atlantic, and was still fulfilling an important training role at the beginning of the 1950s. In the interim period Wellingtons had taken part in the first attack on Germany in World War II, but after suffering unacceptable losses as a day bomber were switched to night operations from 18 December 1939. They formed the major component of the first '1,000-bomber raid', were used to destroy enemy magnetic mines, to lay mines in enemy waters and to test a large variety of different powerplants and an even wider range of weapons that included models of the 'skip bomb' designed by Barnes Wallis.

Variants
Prototypes
Type 271: initial prototype flown on 15 June 1936
Type 285 Wellington Mk I: pre-production prototype with Pegasus X engines flown 23 December 1937

Armourers fuse bombs before loading. After suffering considerable losses in daylight bombing, the Wellington came of age as a nocturnal bomber.

Type 290 Wellington Mk I: initial production version (183 built) with 746-kW (1,000-hp) Pegasus XVIII engines, Vickers turrets and 'dustbin'
Type 408 Wellington Mk IA: production version (187 built) with Pegasus XVIII engines, Nash & Thompson turrets and 'dustbin'
Type 416 Wellington Mk IC: production version, 2,685 built
Type 423 covered conversion of all bombers to carry 1814-kg (4,000-lb) bomb; beam guns and no 'dustbin'
Type 298 Wellington Mk II: prototype with 854-kW (1,145-hp) Merlin X engines, first flown 3 March 1939
Type 406 Wellington B.Mk II: production version with Merlin X engines; 400 built
Type 299 Wellington Mk III: two prototypes, one with Hercules HE1.SM and one with Hercules III engines
Type 417 Wellington B.Mk III: production versions (1,517 built) with 1119-kW (1,500-hp) Hercules XI engines
Type 410 Wellington Mk IV: prototype with Pratt & Whitney Twin Wasp radials
Type 424 Wellington B.Mk IV: production version; 220 built with Twin Wasps
Type 421 Wellington Mk V: high-altitude prototype with Hercules III engines

Type 407 Wellington Mk V: high-altitude prototype with Hercules VIII engines
Type 432 Wellington Mk VI: prototype with various Rolls-Royce Merlins
Type 442 Wellington B.Mk VI: production version (63 built) with Sperry bomb sight; **Type 449** covered two production **Wellington Mk VIG**
Type 429 Wellington GR.Mk VIII: production version (397 built) with Pegasus XVIII engines; 58 with Leigh Light; provision for AS weapons, some with provision for torpedoes
Type 437 Wellington IX: single transport prototype, conversion of Mk IA with Hercules XVI engines
Type 440 Wellington B.Mk X: production version (3,803 built) with Hercules VI or XVI engines; **Type 619** covered post-war conversion to **Wellington T.Mk 10;** some sold to France and six to Royal Hellenic air force in 1946
Type 454 Wellington Mk IX: prototype with ASV.Mk II radar and

The Vickers Wellington Mk I was quite lightly armed in comparison with its successors, with only five rifle calibre machine-guns in nose, tail and ventral positions.

Hercules VI/XVI engines; **Type 459** with ASV.Mk III radar
Type 458 Wellington GR.Mk XI: production version (180 built) with ASV.Mk III and Hercules VI/XVI engines
Type 455 Wellington GR.Mk XII: production version (58 built) with Leigh Light, ASV.Mk III and Hercules XVI engines; some sold to France in 1946
Type 466 Wellington GR.Mk XIII: production version (844 built) with Hercules XVI engines
Type 467 Wellington GR.Mk XIV: production version (841 built) Hercules XVI engines; many supplied to France during 1944 5, and some sold to France in 1946

Conversions
Wellington C.Mk XV: service conversions of Wellington Mk IAs as transports for 18 troops

Wellington C.Mk XVI: service conversions of Wellington Mk ICs as transports for 18 troops
Type 487 Wellington T.Mk XVII: service conversions to trainers using Vickers kits, Mosquito-type AI radar and Hercules XVII engines
Type 490 Wellington T.Mk XVIII: production version (80 built) plus some conversions of Wellington Mk XIs; Hercules XVI engines
Wellington T.Mk XIX: service conversions of Wellington Mk X to trainer

Experimental
Type 416 Wellington (II): experimental installation of 40-mm

Vickers gun in dorsal position applied to original Wellington Mk II prototype and modified with twin fins
Type 418 Wellington DWI.Mk I: conversion of one aircraft for mine detonation; Ford auxiliary power unit
Type 419 Wellington DWI.Mk II: conversion of one aircraft for mine detonation; Gipsy Six auxiliary power unit
Type 435 Wellington Mk IC: conversion of one aircraft to evaluate Turbinlite
Type 439 Wellington Mk II: experimental installation in Wellington Mk II of Vickers 40-mm gun in nose
Type 443 Wellington Mk V: one aircraft converted to Hercules VIII testbed

Type 445 Wellington (II): testbed for Whittle W2B/23 turbojet in tail
Type 470 and **Type 486** covered Wellington Mk II with Whittle W2B and W2/700 respectively
Type 478 Wellington Mk X: one aircraft with trial installation of Hercules 100
Type 602 Wellington Mk X: one aircraft as testbed with Rolls-Royce Dart turboprops
Wellington Mk III: one aircraft with glider-towing clearance for Hadrian, Hotspur and Horsa

Specification
Vickers Wellington B.Mk III
Type: six-crew medium bomber

Powerplant: two 1119-kW (1,500-hp) Bristol Hercules XI radial piston engines
Performance: maximum speed 410 km/h (255 mph) at 3810 m (12,500 ft); service ceiling 5790 m (19,000 ft); range 2478 km (1,540 miles) with 2041 kg (4,500 lb) of bombs
Weights: empty 8417 kg (18,556 lb); maximum take-off 13381 kg (29,500 lb)
Dimensions: span 26.26 m (86 ft 2 in); length 18.54 m (60 ft 10 in); height 5.31 m (17 ft 5 in)
Armament: eight 7.7-mm (0.303-in) machine-guns (two in nose and four in tail turret and one on each beam), plus a maximum bombload of 2041 kg (4,500 lb) or one 1814-kg (4,000-lb) bomb

Vickers Type 284 Warwick

Designed to Specification B.1/35 for a heavy bomber, the **Vickers Type 284 Warwick** was intended to complement the Wellington in service. However, the lack of suitable high-power engines for this larger and heavier version of the Wellington delayed its first flight until 13 August 1939, powered by two Rolls-Royce Vultures. Performance with this powerplant was disappointing and the **Type 401** second prototype was flown on 5 April 1940 with Bristol Centaurus engines. Although performance was improved, a decision to install Pratt & Whitney Double Wasps added to the delay and more than a year elapsed before a Double Wasp prototype was flown. By then the original requirement no longer existed, for the Handley Page Halifax and Short Stirling were already in service, with the Avro Lancaster following not far behind. In consequence, the Warwick was developed for air/sea rescue, meteorological reconnaissance, transport and for ASW (anti-submarine warfare), but was not used in this last role until World War II had ended. Despite the slow start, 845 Warwicks of all versions were built, including prototypes, and they provided valuable service, especially in the air/sea rescue and transport roles.

PN811, one of the last Warwicks built, was delivered as a GR.Mk V for service with 179 Sqn, RAF Coastal Command. Similar to the GR.Mk II, it had ASV radar.

Variants
Warwick B.Mk I: intended original production bomber version; only 16 of 150 on order were built and used for a variety of test purposes
Warwick C.Mk I: 14 **Type 456** transport aircraft, conversions of Warwick B.Mk Is, for use by BOAC on North African and Mediterranean routes; later transferred to No. 167 Squadron
Warwick ASR: 40 conversions from Warwick B.Mk Is for air/sea rescue, carrying two sets of Lindholme life-saving equipment; retained bomber capability
Warwick ASR (Stage A): 10 conversions from Warwick B.Mk Is for air/sea rescue, carrying one airborne lifeboat Mk I and two sets of Lindholme gear
Warwick ASR (Stage B): 20 conversions from Warwick B.Mk Is for air/sea rescue, carrying equipment as

above plus ASV radar and tail turret
Warwick ASR.Mk I (Type 462): finalised air/sea rescue version as above, deploying Mk I or Mk II airborne lifeboats; 205 built with 1380-kW (1,850-hp) Pratt & Whitney Double Wasp R-2800-S1A4G engines
Warwick ASR.Mk VI (Type 485): last air/sea rescue production version, 94 built; as Warwick ASR.Mk I but with Double Wasp R-2800-2SBG engines
Warwick B.Mk II: single prototype of **Type 413** bomber version with Bristol Centaurus engines; conversion from Warwick B.Mk I
Warwick GR.Mk II (Type 469): general-reconnaissance production version; 118 built, with powerplant of two Bristol Centaurus VI engines
Warwick GR.Mk II Met: meteorological reconnaissance version of Warwick GR.Mk II; 14 built
Warwick C.Mk III (Type 460): transport/freighter version; 100 built: carrying eight to 10 passengers in VIP version, 24 fully-equipped troops, or freight

Warwick GR.Mk V (Type 474): final production version; 210 built, plus 1 experimental; modified nose incorporating ASV radar, and equipped with Leigh Light and ASW equipment

Specification
Vickers Warwick GR.Mk II
Type: six-crew general reconnaissance aircraft
Powerplant: two 1864-kW (2,500-hp) Bristol Centaurus VI sleeve radial piston engines
Performance: maximum speed 422 km/h (262 mph) at 610 m (2,000 ft); service ceiling 5790 m (19,000 ft); range 3460 km (2,150 miles)
Weights: empty 14118 kg (31,125 lb); maximum take-off 23247 kg (51,250 lb)
Dimensions: span 29.48 m (96 ft 8½ in); length 20.88 m (68 ft 6 in), height 5.64 m (18 ft 6 in),
Armament: eight 0.303-in (7.7-mm) machine-guns in nose and dorsal twin-gun turrets and four-gun tail turret, plus a maximum weapon load of 6917 kg (15,250 lb)

Vickers Type 491 Viking, Type 607 Valetta, Type 648 Varsity

The Brabazon Committee made proposals for British transport aircraft to be built after World War II; however, no provision was made for interim transports until these new aircraft became available. Among government selections of aircraft to fill this temporary gap was a civil version of the Vickers Wellington, identified initially as the **Vickers Type 491 VC1 (Vickers Commercial 1)**, later named **Viking**. This combined the fabric-covered outer wing panels of the Wellington, its engine nacelles and landing gear, with 1249-kW (1,675-hp) Bristol Hercules 130 engines and a new stressed-skin fuselage to accommodate a flight crew of three, a stewardess and 21 passengers. The prototype (G-AGOK) was flown for the first time on 22 June 1945, the type gained certification on 24 April 1946, and BEA operated its first Viking service from London to

Copenhagen on 1 September 1946.
The initial production version (19 built) was the **Viking IA** with 1260-kW (1,690-hp) Hercules 630 radials, followed by the **Viking I** (31) which introduced stressed-skin wings and tail unit, and the major production **Viking IB** (113) which had the forward fuselage lengthened by 0.71 m (2 ft 4 in) to seat a total 24 passengers (later with a maximum of 36) and introduced Hercules 634 engines of similar power output. When all of the Vikings had eventually been withdrawn from service in 1974, the type had served with operators in Africa, Argentina, Denmark, Ireland,

The Varsity T.Mk I was the RAF's crew training version, with tricycle landing gear instead of the tailwheel unit of the Viking and Valetta. The underfuselage gondola held 24 practice bombs.

France, West Germany, India, Iraq, Southern Rhodesia, Trinidad and the UK. Mention should be made of one Viking (G-AJPH) used as a Rolls-Royce Nene engine testbed, the world's first transport aircraft to fly solely on turbojet power.
A military variant of the Viking entered RAF service under the designa-

tion **Type 607 Valetta**, and differed primarily from the civil transport by having a strengthened floor, large loading doors and 1473-kW (1,975-hp) Hercules 230 engines. More than 250 Valettas were built, their number including the **Valetta C.Mk 1** for ambulance, freight, glider-tug, troop-carrying and supply-dropping roles; the **Valetta**

C.Mk 2 VIP transport for nine to 15 passengers; and the **Valetta T.Mk 3** used as a flying classroom for trainee navigators. The second military version was the **Type 648 Varsity T.Mk 1** crew trainer which replaced the Wellington T.Mk 10 crew trainer in RAF service. It differed from the standard Viking by having increased wing span, retractable tricycle landing gear and an underfuselage pannier to accommodate a bomb-aimer and stowage for 24 practice bombs. A total of 160 Varsity T.Mk 1s had been built for the RAF when production ended in 1954, many of them remaining in service into the 1970s.

Vickers Valetta C.Mk 1 of No. 242 Operational Conversion Unit, RAF Transport Command, in the late 1940s.

Specification
Vickers Viking IB
Type: civil transport
Powerplant: two 1260-kW (1,690-hp) Bristol Hercules 634 sleeve radial piston engines
Performance: maximum cruising speed 338 km/h (210 mph) at 1830 m (6,000 ft); service ceiling 7240 m (23,750 ft); range with maximum payload 837 km (520 miles)
Weights: empty 10546 kg (23,250 lb); maximum take-off 15354 kg (34,000 lb)
Dimensions: span 27.20 m (89 ft 3 in); length 19.86 m (65 ft 2 in); height 5.94 m (19 ft 6 in); wing area 81.94 m² (882.0 sq ft)

Vickers Type 630 Viscount

Originating from the UK Brabazon Committee proposals for post World War II civil transports, the **Vickers VC.2 Viscount** was designed originally to the Brabazon IIB specification for a 24-seat short/medium-range transport with turboprop powerplant. This resulted in the **Type 630** 32-seat prototype, powered by four 738-kW (990-ehp) Rolls-Royce Dart RDa.I Mk 502 engines and first flown on 16 July 1948, but it gained no commercial interest, BEA having just bought the Ambassador. Discussions with BEA led to the **Type 700 Viscount** with pressurised accommodation for 40-59 passengers, powered by four 1044-kW (1,400-shp) Dart Mk 506 engines, or **Type 700D** with the 1193-kW (1,600-shp) Dart Mk 510. The latter engines powered the lengthened-fuselage 65/71-seat capacity **Type 800**, but the final **Type 810** had Dart Mk 525 engines and structural strengthening for operation at a higher gross weight.

On 29 July 1950 the Type 630 prototype inaugurated the world's first scheduled commercial passenger service by a turbine-powered aircraft, this being a two-week operation only between London and Paris. The Type 700, certificated on 17 April 1953, inaugurated services between London and Cyprus on the following day, and the combined operator/passenger reaction to their comfort and performance resulted in large orders. At one time it seemed the Viscount had broken into the US civil transport market in a big way, but these were premature hopes. Nevertheless, with a total of 444 built when production ended in 1964, the Viscount gained the record of the UK's most extensively built airliner of all time. Despite its seeming obsolescence in the face of overwhelming jet proliferation the Viscount remained in airline service in significant numbers throughout the 1970s and 1980s. Its Rolls-Royce dart turboprops were reliable and easy to maintain and it offered a quite respectable level of passenger comfort. By 1993 levels had declined to approximately 50 in regular passenger and freight-carrying use.

Specification
Vickers Type 810 Viscount
Type: short/medium-range transport
Powerplant: four 1566-ekW (2,100-ehp) Rolls-Royce Dart RDa.7/1 Mk 525 turboprops
Performance: maximum cruising speed 563 km/h (350 mph) at 6095 m (20,000 ft); service ceiling 7620 m (25,000 ft); range with maximum payload, no reserves 2776 km (1,725 miles)
Weights: empty operating 18854 kg (41,565 lb); maximum take-off 32885 kg (72,500 lb)
Dimensions: span 28.56 m (93 ft 8½ in); length 26.11 m (85 ft 8 in); height 8.15 m (26 ft 9 in)

PK-MVG of Merpati Nusantara Airlines was a Vickers Viscount 828, one of the last aircraft built, originally to an order from All Nippon Airways.

Vickers Type 667 Valiant

The technological developments of World War II, and in particular the deployment of nuclear weapons over Hiroshima and Nagasaki, brought the realisation in the UK that a new generation of long-range bomber aircraft would be required by the RAF if the nation was to maintain a viable nuclear bomber force. Thus came development of the RAF's V-bomber force, of which the **Vickers Type 667 Valiant** was the first to enter service in 1955. Designed to meet Specification B.9/48, the Valiant was a cantilever monoplane with a high-set wing incorporating compound sweep; it had a pressurised cabin for its five-man crew, and was powered by turbojet engines. The Valiant prototype (WB210) first flown on 18 May 1951 had four 28.9-kN (6,500-lb) thrust Rolls-Royce RA.3 Avon turbojets, but this aircraft caught fire uncontrollably on 12 January 1952. Development was then continued by the second prototype which, with 33.3-kN (7,500-lb) RA.7 Avons, flew for the first time on 11 April 1952.

The first of five pre-production **Type 674 Valiant B.Mk 1** long-range bombers was flown on 22 December 1953, and the type made an impressive appearance at the Farnborough air show of September 1955 when a fly-past was made by 12 aircraft of No. 138 Squadron. The Valiant was used operationally to deploy high-explosive bombs during the Suez Campaign of late 1956, dropped the UK's first atomic bomb over Maralinga, South Australia, on 11 October 1956, and released the nation's first thermonuclear weapon over the Pacific Ocean on 15 May 1957. When Valiant production ended in August 1957 a total of 107 had been built, including prototypes, of which 104 were delivered to the RAF. The development of surface-to-air anti-aircraft missiles switched the V-force from its intended high-altitude strategic role to low-level penetration of enemy air space which, in the case of the Valiant force, accelerated the wing spar metal fatigue that caused them to be withdrawn from service in January 1965.

Variants
Valiant B.Mk 1 (Type 706): initial production version, long-range bomber; 36 built including five pre-production aircraft, one used as testbed for Pegasus engine
Valiant B(PR).Mk 1 (Type 710): long-range strategic reconnaissance version; 11 built
Valiant B(PR)K.Mk 1 (Type 733): multi-role version for use as a bomber, reconnaissance aircraft or inflight-refuelling tanker; 13 built
Valiant BK.Mk 1 (Type 758): bomber/tanker version; 44 built
Valiant B.Mk 2: single prototype of Type 667; extensively redesigned version with lengthened nose, strengthened wings and revised landing gear; demonstrated speed of 891 km/h (552 mph) at sea level compared with Valiant B.Mk I's sea level speed of 666 km/h (414 mph)

Specification
Vickers Valiant B.Mk 1
Type: long-range bomber
Powerplant: four 44.7-kN (10,050-lb) thrust Rolls-Royce RA.28 Avon 204/205 turbojets
Performance: maximum speed 912 km/h (567 mph) at 9145 m (30,000 ft); service ceiling 54,000 16460 m (ft); maximum range 7242 km (4,500 miles)
Weights: empty 34419 kg (75,881 lb); maximum take-off 63503 kg (140,000 lb)
Dimensions: span 34.85 m (114 ft 4 in); length 32.99 m (108 ft 3 in); height 9.80 m (32 ft 2 in); wing area 219.43 m² (2,362.0 sq ft)
Armament: no defensive weapons, conventional or nuclear weapons carried internally, to maximum bombload of 9525 kg (21,000 lb)

XD827 was delivered to the Royal Air Force as one of 44 Vickers Valiant BK.Mk I air-to-air tankers built, but is seen here without the underwing tanks associated with this role.

Vickers Type 950 Vanguard

To provide BEA with a 100-seat-class airliner to supersede the Vickers Viscount, a new design was started by Vickers as the **Type 870**. Both BEA and Trans-Canada Air Lines were simultaneously in the market for an aircraft in this category and the final **Type 950** was designed to meet the needs of both. Although an attractive aircraft, there is little doubt that its commercial success was compromised by the selection of turboprop rather than turbojet powerplant, for at that time turboprops were yielding to jets; their fuel economy became important only in the late 1970s. Just two orders were finalised for 43 aircraft: the first was that of BEA for 20 **Type 951 Vanguard** aircraft to accommodate a flight crew of three, two cabin crew and 126 passengers. BEA's order was later amended and only six Type 951s were built, the remaining 14 being **Type 953** aircraft with the same operating crew but with seating for 135 passengers; all 20 had the same powerplant, comprising four 3717-ekW (4,985-ehp) Rolls-Royce Tyne RTy.1 Mk 506 turboprops. The second order came from Trans-Canada, which acquired a total of 23, these being **Type 952 Vanguard** aircraft with a more powerful version of the Tyne,

structural strengthening for operation at a higher gross weight and accommodation for five crew and 139 passengers. The Type 950 prototype was flown first on 20 January 1959, and both BEA and Trans-Canada introduced the Vanguard into service in early 1961. One of Trans-Canada's aircraft was converted later for all-cargo operation under the name **Cargoliner**, and BEA Vanguards with similar conversions were renamed Merchantman; the latter are the only type still in service with three flying for Hunting Cargo Airlines (formerly Air Bridge carriers) in 1993.

Specification
Vickers Type 952 Vanguard
Type: short/medium-range transport
Powerplant: four 4135-ekW (5,545-ehp) Rolls-Royce Tyne RTy.11 Mk 512 turboprops
Performance: maximum cruising speed 684 km/h (425 mph) at 6095 m (20,000 ft); service ceiling 9145 m (30,000 ft); range with maximum payload, no reserves 2945 km (1,830 miles)
Weights: empty equipped 37421 kg (82,500 lb); maximum take-off 63977 kg (141,000 lb)

G-APES was a former British European Airways Vanguard Type 953 which was converted to all-cargo configuration as a Type 953C Merchantman. It was flown from East Midlands, by Air Bridge, specially equipped to transport racehorses around Europe. Sadly, it has been replaced in this task by a Lockheed L.188 Electra.

Dimensions: span 36.14 m (118 ft 7 in); length 37.45 m (122 ft 101/2 in); height 10.64 m (34 ft 11 in); wing area 141.86 m² (1,527.0 sq ft)

Vickers Type 1100 VC10 and Type 1150 Super VC10

The **Vickers Type 1100 VC10** was developed in response to a BOAC requirement in 1957 for an airliner able to carry a 15422-kg (34,000-lb) payload over a range of up to 6437 km (4,000 miles) on its Commonwealth routes. BOAC served 'hot-and-high' airfields with relatively short runways, and the aircraft was tailored for such operations, thus making it impossible to compete economically with Boeing's 707. This was despite the VC10's large-capacity circular-section pressurised fuselage with six-abreast seating, the rear-engine layout pioneered by Sud-Aviation with the Caravelle, the clean and efficient swept wing that incorporated high-lift devices and was free from interference drag from the powerplant and its mountings, and an all-swept tail unit which, incorporating a T-tail, remained well clear of the jet engine efflux. The prototype (G-ARTA) was flown for the first time on 29 June 1962, certification was gained on 23 April 1964, and BOAC introduced the **Type 1101 VC10** into service on its London-Lagos route six days later. VC10 production comprised the Type 1101 (12) for BOAC with four 93.5-kN (21,000-lb) thrust Rolls-Royce Conway RCo 42, an operating crew of 10 and 115 mixed-class or 135 economy-class passengers; the similar **Type 1102** (two) for Ghana Airways, the second with a large cargo door; the **Type 1103** (three) for British United Airways, similar to the second Type 1102; the **Type 1106** (14) for RAF

Vickers VC10 C.Mk 1 of No. 10 Sqn, RAF, based at Brize Norton in the early 1980s.

Support Command as multi-role aircraft, RAF designation **VC10 C.Mk 1**, with a revised wing, more powerful Conway RCo 43 powerplant and increased fuel capacity; and the single **Type 1109**, which was the redesignation of the Type 1100 prototype following conversion with a Type 1106 wing for sale to Laker Airways.

Development of the type came with the **Type 1150 Super VC10** which introduced a fuselage lengthened by 3.96 m (13 ft 0 in), increased fuel capacity and Rolls-Royce Conway RCo 43 engines. Two versions were built, the **Type 1151** (17) for BOAC accommodating 16 first-class and 123 economy-class passengers, and the similar **Type 1154** (five) for East African Airways incorporating a large cargo door and configured for mixed cargo/passenger traffic. BOAC introduced the Super VC10 on its London-New York route on 1 April 1965. When British Airways, the successor to BOAC, operated its final service with the type on 29 March 1981, its small

VC10/Super VC10 fleet had carried over 13 million passengers without accident.

With the final withdrawal of the type from service a number were acquired by the British government for conversion as inflight-refuelling tankers to expand the RAF's capability in this area. The initial programme covered nine conversions, comprising five Type 1101 VC10s and four Type 1154 Super VC10s, which as tankers have the RAF designations **VC10 K.Mk 2** and **VC10 K.Mk 3** respectively. The first VC10 K.Mk 2 conversion was flown on 22 June 1983. All RAF VC-10s have standardised on the Conway Mk 550B engine (equivalent to the military Mk 301) and deleted outboard thrust-reversers. All are also capable of carrying the nose-mounted refuelling boom. No.101 Sqn's aircraft saw intensive action during operation Desert Storm refuelling RAF and US Navy aircraft over 381 sorties. Five aircraft formerly stored at RAF Abingdon are now being converted to **VC10 K.Mk.4** standard, similar to the K Mk 3 but without fuse-

lage tanks, and thus will comparatively short-ranged. First delivery was made early in 1993. By 1995 All 13 Brize-Norton-based 10 Sqn VC10 C.Mk 1s will be converted by F R Aviation to **C.Mk 1(K)** tanker standard with removable underwing Mk 17 refuelling pods.

Specification
Vickers Type 1151 Super VC10
Type: long-range civil transport
Powerplant: four 97-kN (21,800-lb) thrust Rolls-Royce Conway RCo 43D Mk 550 turbofans
Performance: maximum cruising speed 935 km/h (581 mph) at 9450 m (31,000 ft); economic cruising speed 885 km/h (550 mph) at 11580 m (38,000 ft); range with maximum payload 7596 km (4,720 miles)
Weights: empty operating 71937 kg (158,594 lb); maximum take-off 151953 kg (335,000 lb)
Dimensions: span 44.55 m (146 ft 2 in); length 52.32 m (171 ft 8 in); height 12.04 m (39 ft 6 in)

Victa Airtourer

Designed by Henry Millicer, the **Victa Airtourer** was a light monoplane seating two side-by-side in an enclosed cabin, and the prototype, powered by a 48-kW (65-hp) Continental A65 engine, was flown for the first time on 31 March 1959. The initial production versions were the **Airtourer 100** (75-kW/

100-hp Continental O-200-A) and **Airtourer T2** (86-kW/115-hp Avco

This Victa Airtourer T3 was built in the UK, by Glos-Air at Staverton, in 1965-66. It spans 7.92 m (26 ft), has an all-up weight of 862 kg (1,900 lb) and cruises at 222 km/h (138 mph).

Lycoming O-235-C2A), of which a combined total of 170 had been built by the Australian company Victa Consolidated Industries Pty Ltd before it disposed of world manufacturing rights to Aero Engine Services Ltd (AESL) of New Zealand in 1966. AESL later amalgamated with Air Parts (NZ) Ltd to form New Zealand Aerospace Industries Ltd, and manufacture of the Airtourer continued until 1974, by which time an additional 80 had been built. They included versions designated **Airtourer T3** (97-kW/130-hp Rolls-Royce Continental), **Airtourer T4** (112-kW/150-hp Avco Lycoming O-320-E2A) and similar **Airtourer T5**. From the Aerospace Airtrainer CT/4, a four-seat civil version designated **Aircruiser CT/2** was developed but failed to find a worthwhile market.

The **CT-4 Airtrainer** was a military version of the Airtourer, 96 of which were built between 1972 and 1977. AESL was bought out by Pacific Aerospace and in mid-1990 the line was re-opened after an order for eight **CT-4B**s. A retractable **CT-4R** is planned.

Voisin aircraft

The French brothers Charles and Gabriel Voisin began kite-building experiments in the last year or so of the 19th century, incorporating modified Hargrave-type box-kite structures in the two-float gliders designed and built in 1905 in association with Ernest Archdeacon and Louis Blériot. In the following year they established the company Les Frères Voisin at Billancourt where they designed and built two basically similar aircraft. Of biplane configuration and with a boxkite tail structure incorporating a rudder, both aircraft had their powerplant in pusher configuration, and progressive development of this basic concept represented the company's main activity

The Voisin Icare, seen here poised inelegantly on a land chassis, was designed as a flying-boat for a pilot and six passengers. Span was 22 m (72 ft 2 in) and it was powered by a 149-kW (200-hp) Clerget engine.

before World War I. Neither of these first aircraft was successful, the first not being flown and the second for Léon Delagrange achieving only a series of hop flights during 1907. Major progress was made with the aircraft built for Henry Farman, the **Voisin-Farman I** powered by a 37-kW (50-hp) Antoinette engine progressing from a 771-m (2,530-ft) flight in October 1907, via an unofficial 1030-m (3,379-ft) circular flight in November, to a circular flight of 1 km (0.62 miles) on 13 January 1908. Having gained these and

other successes, the Voisin brothers appear to have become complacent, continuing to build and develop the same basic aircraft. It was not until the approach of World War I that more active design began.

Voisin aircraft 1914-18

All the Voisin biplanes that entered service during World War I had a characteristic layout, comprising a short nacelle for the two-man crew, a pusher engine at the rear and a tall slim rudder hinged to a vertical rod that in turn was connected to the upper and lower wings by two pairs of long tubular booms; landing gear comprised two pairs of wheels attached to the nacelle.

The **Voisin Type 1913** or **13.5 Mètres** (so called from the wing span) was in service briefly with Escadrilles V.14 and V.21 of the Aéronautique Militaire at the outbreak of hostilities. Known as the **Type L**, it was powered by either an 60-kW (80-hp) Le Rhône 9C or a 52-kW (70-hp) Gnome 7A rotary engine. Maximum speed in either case was 94 km/h (58 mph). These two versions were designated retrospectively **Type I** and **Type II** by the French army, which had about 70 in service; others were supplied to Russia.

The prototype **Type LA** or **Type III** flew in February 1914. Powered by an 89-kW (120-hp) Salmson (Canton-Unné) M9 engine, it was heavier than its predecessors and armed with a single machine-gun operated by the pilot. The French claimed the first victory in combat on 5 October 1914, when the Type LA of Escadrille V.24 crewed by Franz and Quenault shot down a German Aviatik B.I. A version of the Type LA fitted with three floats was operated by the French navy. In April 1915 the **Type LAS** version with airframe revisions went into production.

Nearly 1,000 French Type IIIs were built. The British Savage company built 50 under licence, while large numbers were constructed in Russia by the Duks company. Later aircraft had chutes to launch bombs up to a weight of 60 kg (132 lb); before that light bombs or *fléchettes* (darts) were carried in the cockpit and thrown over the side. Type IIIs equipped the 1er Groupe de Bombardement established in September 1914 under Capitaine de Goys. Mass daytime attacks were made on targets behind the German lines, including railway junctions, troop concentrations and industrial sites.

The **Type IV Ca.2**, equipped with a 37-mm Hotchkiss gun, was built in **Type LB** and **Type LBS** versions corresponding to the LA and LAS variants of the Type III. The **Type V** and **Type VI** of 1916 were powered by 112-kW (150-hp) Salmsons and shared the factory LAS designation of Type III; some 450 were completed. They were used largely for night bombing, excessive losses having brought mass daylight raids by Voisins to a close in autumn 1915. Versions of the Voisin were built in Italy by S.I.T. of Turin to a total of 112; they included one powered by a 119-kW (160-hp) Isotta-Fraschini V.4B engine.

In mid-1916 Voisin began production of 103 **Type VII** A.2-category two-seat observation aircraft with 134-kW (180-hp) Renault 8G engines, these being for use in a reconnaissance role. The **Type VIII** of autumn 1916 was

built in two versions, most of the 1,100 or so being **Type LAP** two-seat night bombers carrying a 180-kg (397-lb) offensive load, while a small number of **Type LBP** aircraft were *avions canons* with 37-mm Hotchkiss guns. The Type VIII had a larger redesigned rectangular crew nacelle and was powered by the 164-kW (220-hp) Peugeot 8Aa engine, giving a maximum speed of 118 km/h (73 mph). The **Type LAR** version of September 1917 was a two-seat night bomber with a bombload of 300 kg (661 lb); the 37-mm cannon variant was the **Type LBR**.

The nacelle was again revised, the overall structure was strengthened and power was provided by a 209-kW (280-hp) Renault 12Fe which raised maximum speed marginally to 130 km/h (81 mph). Until the end of the war in November 1918, virtually all French night bomber units were equipped with Voisin biplanes. The **Type X** was an

The obsolete configuration of Voisin aircraft right through World War I is illustrated by this Type LAS of No. 2 Wing RNAS, over Imbros in the Aegean during 1915. Max speed was 105 km/h (65 mph).

air ambulance version which appeared post-war, and was also built in quantity, some 900 being completed.

Experimental types tested during this period included the single-engined **Type M** with a conventional fuselage and engine carried just below the upper wing; the **Type O** with two engines fore and aft of the nacelle; and a four-engined triplane with a slim fuselage. The last **Voisin** type, built in 1920, was a development of the earlier triplane and intended as a night bomber or transport aircraft, its four 164-kW (220-hp) Hispano-Suiza 8Bc engines producing a maximum speed of 130 km/h (81 mph).

Vought A-7 Corsair II

This highly successful subsonic attack aircraft originated from a US Navy requirement for an aircraft to replace the Douglas A-4 Skyhawk. On 19 March 1964 Vought was awarded a contract for three prototypes under the navy designation **A-7**, the company reviving the name of its most famous wartime fighter in designating this new aircraft **Vought Corsair II**. One of the requirements of the specification had been that the new aircraft should be based on an existing design, to keep costs low and to speed delivery. While the A-7 was of basically similar configuration to the F-8 Crusader (though dispensing with its variable-incidence wing), it was, in fact, a completely new design with no large-scale commonality of structural assemblies. The first prototype was flown on 27 September 1965, almost four weeks ahead of

schedule, and initial deliveries to the navy began on 14 October 1966. Less than four months later, on 1 February 1967, US Navy Squadron VA-147 became the first to be commissioned with the Corsair II. Long before then, in December 1965, the US Air Force had also decided to adopt a denavalised version of the A-7 to serve as a subsonic tactical fighter. Primary change was selection of the Allison-built Rolls-Royce Spey to power it instead of the Pratt & Whitney TF30 turbofan of the Navy's A-7.

US Navy Corsair IIs equipped 27 squadrons during the Vietnam War, flying more than 90,000 combat missions, and the type was also used by the USAF in that theatre, although to a far lesser extent. By 1993 the last A7D and A-7Ks had been retired from UNited States Air National Guard service. The US Navy too, had relinquished the type, but its last two squadrons saw intensive use during operation Desert Storm. They were disbanded on their return home The Corsair II has been exported to Greece and Portugal. While the Portuguese aircraft are being supplemented with refurbished F-16As, Greece has taken delivery of significant numbers of additional former USN aircraft, replacing Mirage F1s with some squadrons.

Variants
A-7A: initial USN production version with 5148-kg (11,350-lb) thrust TF30-P-6 turbofan, 199 built
A-7B: second USN production version, initially with TF30-P-8, later modified to TF30-P-408; 196 built
A-7C: third USN production version with TF-30-P-408 engine and avionics of later A-7E; 67 built
A-7D: USAF production version with TF41-A-1 (Spey) engine, M61 cannon, inflight-refuelling capability and advanced nav/attack system, later provided with auto manoeuvring flaps and Pave Penny laser tracker; 459 built
A-7E: major USN production version based on A-7D, but with uprated TF41-A-2 (Spey) engine; later equipped with FLIR (forward-looking infra-red)
A-7H: aircraft for Hellenic air force, land-based version of A-7E; 60 built

A-7K: two-seat trainer version of A-7D for US Air National Guard; one conversion from A-7D plus 31 new production aircraft
A-7P: refurbished A-7A with TF30-P-408 engine for export to Portugal, initially 20 aircraft; subsequent contract covered 30 more refurbished aircraft, to include six two-seat trainers
TA-7C: redesignation of A-7B and A-7C aircraft converted as two-seat trainers
TA-7H: two-seat trainer version of A-7H for Greece; five built
YA-7E or **YA-7H:** designations applied to **V-159** two-seat prototype designed and built as a private venture by Vought

Specification
Vought A-7E Corsair II
Type: carrier-based attack bomber
Powerplant: one 6577-kg (14,500-lb) thrust TF30-P-408 (derived from Rolls-Royce Spey) turbofan
Performance: maximum speed clean, 1123 km/h (698 mph) at sea level; tactical radius with typical weapon load 1127 kg (700 miles)

Related conceptually to the Vought F-8 Crusader, but a completely redesigned aircraft, the A-7 Corsair II was a valuable light attack aircraft in both USAF and USN service. It constantly underlined its reputation as one of the most accurate strike aircraft ever built in numerous bombing and gunnery competitions.

Weights: empty 19,490 lb (8841 kg); maximum take-off 19051 kg (42,000 lb)
Dimensions: span 11.81 m (38 ft 9 in); length 14.06 m (46 ft 1½ in); height 16 ft 0¾ in (4.90 m); wing area 34.84 m²

(375.0 sq ft)
Armament: one 20-mm M61A1 multi-barrelled cannon, plus up to 6804 kg (15,000 lb) of mixed stores carried externally

Vought F-8 Crusader

A US Navy requirement of 1952 for a supersonic air-superiority fighter resulted in eight design submissions, and in May 1953 the Vought design was selected for prototype construction with a contract for two **Vought XF8U-1** prototypes. The design's high-mounted foldable wing incorporated an unusual design feature in being of variable incidence, the increased angle of attack being used to keep the fuselage more nearly level during low-speed operations and thus enhance the pilot's view during, for example, carrier landing. The first of the prototypes was flown on 25 March 1955 and deliveries of the initial production F8U-1 began to US Navy Squadron VF-32 in March 1957. Representing a development of just less than four years from receipt of the original prototype contract, this was no mean achievement for a new carrier-based fighter of high supersonic capability. The Crusader remained in production over a period of eight years, the final series of 48 F-8E (FN) aircraft for the French navy being delivered in January 1965. The Crusader provided the US Navy and US Marine Corps with a valuable aircraft that saw service in US involvement in Vietnam, and the last USMC RF 8 reconnaissance aircraft were retired only in the late 1980s. Aircraft delivered to the Phillipines were also withdrawn then, and remain stored. The French navy is upgrading 17 aircraft to bridge the gap before it takes delivery of Rafale M.

Variants
XF8U-1 (later **XF-8A**): two original unarmed prototypes with the 6713-kg (14,800-lb) thrust Pratt & Whitney J57-P-11 turbojet
F8U-1 (later **F-8A**): initial production version, most with 7348-kg (16,200-lb) thrust J57-P-4A engine; armament of four 20-mm cannon, plus rockets in fuselage packs; later retrofitted to carry Sidewinder missiles 318 built
YF8U-1 (later **YF-8A**): redesignation of one F8U-1 used for development testing
YF8U-1E (later **YF-8B**): redesignation of one F8U-1 converted as prototype of F8U-1E

F8U-1E (later **F-8B**): production version of F8U-1 with limited all-weather capability; 130 built
F8U-1D (later **DF-8A**): designation of F8U-1s after conversion as drone directors
F8U-1KD (later **QF-8A**): target drone conversions of the F8U-1
YF8U-1P (later **YRF-8A**): development versions of F8U-1 for photo-reconnaissance
F8U-1P (later **RF-8A**): photo-reconnaissance version of F8U-1 with camera bay in forward fuselage and weapons deleted
XF8U-1T: conversion from XF8U-2NE (below) for evaluation as two-seat operational trainer prototype; 72-kN (16,200-lb) thrust J57-P-20 turbojet and only two 20-mm cannon, when used as trainer was redesignated **F8U-1T** (later **TF-8A**)
YF8U-2 (later **YF-8C**): redesignation of two F8U-1s used for flight testing of 75.2-kN (16,900-lb) thrust J57-P-16 turbojet F8U-2 (later **F-8C**): production version with J57-P-16 engine and twin ventral fins, 187 built
F8U-2N (later **F-8D**): production version with 80.1-kN (18,000-lb) thrust J57-P-20 turbojet additional fuel and provision for four Sidewinder missiles,

152 built
YF8U-2N (later **YF-8D**): designation of aircraft used for development testing for F8U-2N version
XF8U-2NE: conversion from F8U-1 to serve as F8U-2NE prototype; later converted as XF8U-1T prototype (above)
F8U-2NE (later **F-8E**): improved production version, 80.1-kN (18000-lb) thrust J57-P-20A turbojet, advanced radar and underwing pylons for two AGM-12 Bullpup missiles or up to 1814 kg (4,000 lb) bombs; 286 built
F8U-3: redesigned version of which five were built but only three flown for evaluation against F4H Phantom II; Sidewinder or Sparrow III missiles and 109-kN (24,500-lb) or 115.7-kN (26,000-lb) thrust J75-P-5A or J75-P-6 engines respectively; redesigned nose air intake and ventral fins for high-altitude longitudinal stability which cycle into horizontal position for landings and take-off
F-8E (FN): version of F-8E for French navy with blown flaps and other high-lift improvements 48 built
DF-8F: drone director conversions from F-8A
RF-8G: redesignation of 73 RF-8A after refurbishing; strengthened airframe, addition of ventral fins, and installation of J57-P-20A engine
F-8H: 89 rebuilds from F-8D

introduced strengthened airframe and blown flaps
F-8J, F-8K and **F-8L:** rebuilds as above, respectively of F-8E (136) F-8C (87) and F-8B (61)

Specification
Vought F-8E Crusader
Type: carrier-based fighter
Powerplant: one 80.1-kN (18,000-lb) thrust Pratt & Whitney J57-P-20A turbojet
Performance: maximum speed approximately Mach 1.8, or 1802 km/h (1120 mph) at 12190 m (40,000 ft); service ceiling 17680 m (58,000 ft); range 1609 km (1,000 miles)
Weight: maximum take-off 15422 kg (34,000 lb)
Dimensions: span 10.72 m (35 ft 2 in); length 16.61 m (54 ft 6 in); height 4.80 m (15 ft 9 in)
Armament: four 20-mm Colt-Browning cannon, two Sidewinder missiles and underfuselage rocket pack, or four Sidewinder missiles, plus underwing racks for two 907-kg (2,000-lb) bombs, or two Bullpup missiles, or 24 Zuni air-to-surface rockets

The Vought F-8 Crusader was a truely great carrierborne fighter, offering range coupled with sustained supersonic performance. The variable incidence wing is clearly visible in this photograph.

Vought O2U and O3U/SU Corsair

First aircraft to bear the famous company name **Vought Corsair**, the initial **O2U** was little more than a developed version of the UO/FU series that incorporated an all-steel tube fuselage structure and introduced the Pratt & Whitney Wasp radial engine. Deliveries to the US Navy began in 1927 and production totalled 291 in several versions.

From 1930 the O2U began to be superseded in US Navy service by the **O3U Corsair**, which was basically similar to the O2U-4, one of which was fitted experimentally with the Grumman amphibious float. O3U aircraft, later allocated **SU** designations, were built to a total of 289 for the US Navy. By the time the USA became involved in World War II these Corsair biplanes had been withdrawn from first-line use, although 141 remained in service in secondary roles. A few O3U-6s were converted by the Naval Aircraft Factory to radio-controlled pilotless configuration for experimental use, and these were provided with fixed tricycle landing gear to simplify take-off and landing operations. Export versions included the **Corsair V-65F** for the Argentine navy, the **V-80P** for the Peruvian air force and the **V-85G** for Germany.

Variants
O2U-1: two prototypes followed by 130 production aircraft with interchangeable wheel/float landing gear, 336-kW (450-hp) Pratt & Whitney R-1340-88 Wasp engine and armament of one forward-firing and two 7.62-mm (0.3-in) machine-guns on trainable mount in rear cockpit
O2U-2: version with increased-span upper wing and wing refinements, larger rudder and R-1340-B engine; 37 built for US Navy
O2U-3: as O2U-2 with revised wing rigging, redesigned tail surfaces and R-1340-C engine; 80 built
O2U-4: as O2U-3 but with changes of equipment; 42 built
O3U-1: generally as O2U-4 and incorporating Grumman amphibious float tested on one aircraft; 87 built
O3U-2: improved version introducing strengthened airframe; several airframe revisions, redesigned tail unit and Pratt & Whitney R-1690 Hornet engine; 29 built; redesignated **SU-1** soon after entering service
O3U-3: as O3U-2 but with 410-kW (550-hp) R-1340-12 engine; 76 built
O3U-4: generally as O3U-3, but with R-1690-42 engine; 65 ordered and delivered as **SU-2** (45 built) and **SU-3** with low-pressure tyres (20 built)
XO3U-5: SU-2 tested with Pratt & Whitney GR-1535 radial engine
XO3U-6: prototype of O3U-6 version converted from O3U-3
O3U-6: production version of XO3U-6 with NACA engine cowl and enclosed cockpits; 32 built, 16 with R-1340-12 and 16 with R-1340-18 engines
SU-1: redesignation of O3U-2
SU-2: redesignation of O3U-4
SU-3: redesignation of O3U-4 with low-pressure tyres
SU-4: production version of SU-2; 20 built

Specification
Vought SU-4 Corsair
Type: two-seat scout
Powerplant: one 447-kW (600-hp) Pratt & Whitney R-1690-42 Hornet radial piston engine
Performance: maximum speed 269 km/h (167 mph) at sea level; service ceiling 5670 m (18,600 ft); range 1094 km (680 miles)
Weights: empty 1502 kg (3,312 lb); maximum take-off 2161 kg (4,765 lb)
Dimensions: span 10.97 m (36 ft 0 in); length 8.37 m (27 ft 5½ in); height 3.45 m (11 ft 4 in); wing area 31.31 m² (337.0 sq ft)
Armament: three 7.62-mm (0.3-in) machine-guns, one forward-firing and two on trainable mount in rear cockpit

The O3U-3 was widely deployed on major US warships; this one was allocated to the USS Colorado.

Vought OS2U Kingfisher

Designed to replace the O3U Corsair biplanes that Vought had built earlier for the US Navy, the **Vought VS-310 Kingfisher** incorporated new construction features, including the use of spot welding. Evaluation of the design proposal led to a US Navy contract for a prototype which was powered by a 336-kW (450-hp) Pratt & Whitney R-985-4 engine; it was flown for the first time in landplane configuration in March 1938 and in its intended floatplane version on 19 May 1938. A successful conclusion to official testing brought the first production order for the **OS2U-1** Kingfisher, and when these aircraft began to enter service from August 1940 they were the first catapult-launched monoplane observation aircraft to serve with the US Navy. Built quite extensively, the Kingfisher was not only valuable in the scout/observation role when operated from onboard ship but, in service with US Navy inshore patrol squadrons, proved very successful in the ASW and air/sea rescue roles. The type was used also by the Royal Navy, which received 100 under Lend-Lease, these being operated under the designation **Kingfisher Mk I**, serving as catapult-launched reconnaissance aircraft and as trainers. Others were supplied to Argentina (nine), Chile (15), the Dominican Republic (three), Mexico (six) and Uruguay (six); 24 en route to the Netherlands East Indies were docked in Australia when these islands were overrun by the Japanese, and 18 of them served with the RAAF.

Variants
XOS2U-1: original prototype with Pratt & Whitney R-985-4 engine
OS2U-1: first production version with 336-kW (450-hp) R-985-48 engine; 54 built
OS2U-2: production version introducing equipment changes and R-985-50 engine of the same power output; 158 built
OS2U-3: major production version introducing self-sealing fuel tanks, armour protection, and the R-985-AN-2 engine of the same output; 1,006 built
OS2N-1: version built by Naval Aircraft Factory, as OS2U-3, but some with the R-985-AN-8 engine; 300 built
XOS2U-4: prototype conversion from one OS2U-2 with narrow-chord wings and other aerofoil revisions; production OS2U-4 not built

The follow-on to the same company's Corsair for the US Navy, the Vought OS2U Kingfisher could be operated with wheeled landing gear and a fixed tailwheel. It was generally found flying from floats for observation and air sea rescue duties.

Specification
Vought OS2U-3 Kingfisher
Type: two-seat observation aircraft
Powerplant: one 336-kW (450-hp) Pratt & Whitney R-985-AN-2 radial piston engine
Performance: maximum speed 264 km/h (164 mph) at 1675 m (5,500 ft); service ceiling 3960 m (13,000 ft); range 1296 km (805 miles)
Weights: empty 1870 kg (4,123 lb); maximum take-off 2722 kg (6,000 lb)
Dimensions: span 10.95 m (35 ft 11 in); length 10.31 m (33 ft 10 in); height 4.61 m (15 ft 1½in)
Armament: two 7.62-mm (0.3-in) machine-guns (one forward-firing and one on trainable mount in rear cockpit), plus two 45-kg (100-lb) or 147-kg (325-lb) bombs on underwing racks

Vought SBU

First flown in May 1933, the **Vought XF3U-1** prototype was designed and built to meet a US Navy requirement for a two-seat fighter biplane, and was powered by a 522-kW (700-hp) Pratt & Whitney R-1535-80 engine. However, after completion of testing, the company was requested to modify this conventional aircraft into a scout-bomber under the designation **XSBU-1**, which differed from the XF3U-1 by having strengthened wings of increased area, greater internal fuel capacity and provision to carry a 227-kg (500-lb) bomb beneath the fuselage. Following further tests from June 1934, an order was placed for 84 production **SBU-1** aircraft, and deliveries began on 20 November 1935. Generally similar to the prototype, these were followed by the **SBU-2** (40 built) which differed by introducing the 559-kW (750-hp) R-1535-98 engine. The XSBU-1 prototype was converted for use as an engine testbed, and under the company designation **V-142A** a small number were built for export to Argentina. The last biplane to be designed and built by Vought for the US Navy, the type was still in service with the US Navy Reserve in 1941. Spanning 10.13 m (33 ft 3 in), the SBU-1 had a maximum speed of 330 km/h (205 mph) at 2715 m (8,900 ft), and both versions were

armed with 7.62-mm (two 0.3-in) Browning machine-guns, one forward-firing and one on a trainable mount over the rear cockpit, and could carry a 227-kg (500-lb) bomb.

Identified by its serial number as the first Vought SBU-1, this aircraft shows the neat installation of the Pratt & Whitney R-1535 radial in a long-chord cowling. The two-seat SBU of 1932 was to be Vought's last biplane design for the US Navy and though it was intended as a fighter it only ever served in the scout-bomber role.

Vought SB2U Vindicator

In late 1934-35 Vought received a US Navy order for two prototypes – the **Vought XSB2U-1** monoplane and, for competitive evaluation, the **XSB3U-1** biplane – to satisfy the requirement for a new carrier-based scout-bomber. Both machines were tested in the early summer of 1936, and there was no doubt of the superiority of the monoplane: an initial order for 54 production **SB2U-1** aircraft was placed on 26 October 1936. The close relationship of this aircraft to the Vought SBU is confirmed by the fact that the XSB3U-1 prototype was basically an SBU-1 with retractable main landing gear units, but the SB2U-1 differed by having an all-metal basic structure with part-fabric and part-metal covering, outer wing panels that folded for carrier stowage, an arrester hook in the rear fuselage, and powerplant comprising an 615-kW (825-hp) Pratt & Whitney R-1535-96 Twin Wasp Junior engine. Subsequent orders for the US Navy included the generally similar **SB2U-2** (58 built), and the **SB2U-3** (57 built) which introduced armour protection, increased fuel, the R-1535-02 engine and heavier armament; these were the first models to be named **Vindicator**. One SB2U-2 tested on twin floats was given the

designation **XSB2U-3**. US Navy squadrons equipped with SB2Us saw action in the Pacific during 1942, including participation in the Battle of Midway, but were soon retired from first-line service because of their vulnerability to fighters such as the Mitsubishi A6M.

Under the company designation **V-156B,** Vought built and delivered 24 of 40 ordered for the French navy, some of these falling into German hands when the French capitulated. Similarly, 50 with the designation

Vought SB2U-2 of the 5th Section leader of Bombing Squadron VB-2 deployed the USS **Lexington** *in July 1939.*

V-156B-1 were built for the British Fleet Air Arm which designated them **Chesapeake Mk I** following combat evaluation; all were used in an operational training role by Nos 728 and 811 Squadrons.

Specification
Vought SB2U-3 Vindicator
Type: carrier-based scout/bomber
Powerplant: one 615-kW (825-hp) Pratt & Whitney R-1535-02 Twin Wasp Junior radial piston engine
Performance: maximum speed 391

km/h (243 mph) at 2895 m (9,500 ft); service ceiling 7195 m (23,600 ft), range 1802 km (1,120 miles)
Weights: empty 2556 kg (5,634 lb); maximum take-off 4273 kg (9,421 lb)
Dimensions: span 12.80 m (42 ft 0 in); length 10.36 m (34 ft 0 in); height 3.12 m (10 ft 3 in); wing area 28.33 m² (305.0 sq ft)
Armament: two 12.7-mm (0.5-in) machine-guns (one forward-firing and one on trainable mount in rear cockpit), plus up to 454 kg (1,000 lb) of bombs

Vought VE-7/VE-9 and VO/FU

The American company Lewis & Vought of Long Island, New York, designed and flew in the summer of 1918 the **Lewis & Vought VE-7** biplane trainer that had tandem open cockpits and was powered by the 112-kW (150-hp) Wright-Hispano engine. Although the type was tested satisfactorily, no immediate production followed, but soon after World War I the US Navy procured a total of 128 in several variants built by Vought and the Naval Aircraft Factory (NAF). These had the 134-kW (180-hp) Wright-Hispano E-2 engine, and were followed by the improved **VE-9** of which 42 were built for the US Army (25) and US Navy (21). Subsequent development resulted in the **UO** which had an airframe basically similar to that of the VE series but with some refinements (the most noticeable being the revised vertical tail surfaces) and which was powered initially by the 149-kW (200-hp) Lawrence J-1 or J-3, later by Wright J-1 or J-3 radial engine, and from 1927 many were re-engined with the 164-kW (220-hp) Wright J-5. Final development brought an order for 20 U0-3 single-seat

catapult-launched floatplane fighters, but before delivery these were redesignated **FU-1**. Apart from their single-seat rather than two-seat configuration, they differed by incorporating some structural refinements, a smaller fin, a supercharger to improve performance, and an armament of 7.62-mm (0.3-in) forward-firing machine-guns. Despite the fact that they emanated from a World War I design, many of these excellent and well-built aircraft were serving in secondary roles into the early 1930s.

Variants
VE-7: initial production version standard two-seat trainer, of which the US Navy received 20 from Vought and 16 from the NAF
VE-7G: gunnery trainer with a synchronised Vickers machine-gun forward and a 7.62-mm (0.3-in) Lewis gun on a trainable mount in rear cockpit; 19 built by NAF
VE-7GF: designation of one VE-7G with flotation gear
VE-7H: single-float seaplane version, nine built by NAF
VE-7S: redesignation of one VE-7

following conversion to single-seat fighter
VE-7SF: single-seat fighter version with flotation gear; built by Vought (40) and NAF (24)
VE-7SH: single floatplane conversion of VE-7SF
VE-8: single VE-7 variant for testing
VE-9: improved version with 134-kW (180-hp) Wright-Hispano E-3 engine; 42 built by Vought and one conversion from VE-7
VE-9H: single-float observation version of VE-9; four built by Vought
UO-1: production two-seat observation aircraft developed from VE-9, optional wheel or twinfloat landing gear; 141 built by Vought

UO-2: redesignation of one UO-1 following conversion for racing use
UO-3: original designation allocated to FU-1
UO-4: two aircraft for US Coast Guard; similar to UO-1, but with 168-kW (225-hp) Wright J-5 engine and revised wing of UO-3/FU-1
UO-5: redesignation of 15 UO-1 conversions with Wright J-5 engine and revised wing of UO-3/FU-I
FU-1: single-seat catapult-launched floatplane fighter, ordered initially as

Wearing the markings of the USS Tennessee's catapult flight, the UO-1 could operate from floats or wheeled landing gear.

UO-3 but redesignated FU-1 before delivery began in 1927; improved wings, revised vertical tail surface and supercharger for the Wright J-5 engine
FU-2: redesignation of FU-1s following conversion to two-seat trainers when withdrawn from first-line service in 1928

Specification
Vought UO-1 (landplane)
Type: observation aircraft

Powerplant: one 149-kW (200-hp) Wright J-3 radial engine
Performance: maximum speed 200 km/h (124 mph) at sea level; service ceiling 5730 m (18,800 ft); range 626 km (395 miles)

Weights: empty 678 kg (1,494 lb); maximum take-off 1046 kg (2,305 lb)
Dimensions: span 10.45 m (34 ft 3½ in); length 7.45 m (24 ft 5½ in); height 2.67 m (8 ft 9 in); wing area 26.92 m² (289.80 sq ft)

Vultee V-1A

The **Vultee V-1** prototype designed by Gerard F. Vultee and built by the Airplane Development Corporation was an all-metal stressed-skin monocoque monoplane seating a pilot and six passengers. It incorporated inward-retracting main landing gear units and created a considerable impression when test flown for the first time on 19 February 1933. The production **V-1A** introduced a wider and lengthened fuselage to accommodate two crew and eight passengers, had other structural revisions and a 559-kW (750-hp) Wright SR-1820-F2 Cyclone engine. In total, 24 V-1As were built before production ended in early 1936.

The V-1 prototype (modified to take a second pilot) and eight V-1As were bought by American Airlines during 1934, but two years later all were sold off as the company switched to twin-engined airliners. Nevertheless, most

The Vultee V-1A was very typical of the advanced aircraft of the day, featuring stressed-skin construction and a fully retractable landing gear. Maximum take-off weight was 3856 kg (8,500 lb).

V-1As were purchased and used by private companies and wealthy individuals. One V-1A with twin floats was bought by the Soviet Union, and another was used in an attempt to make the first New York-London-New York flight; it was used later by the

Vultee V-1A

Nationalist forces in Spain. Seven ex-American Airlines V-1As were also used in the Spanish Civil War by the Republican air arm, these being armed with four or five machine-guns and underfuselage racks for light bombs;

they saw little action and four of them fell into Nationalist hands at the end of the war. The 15.24-m (50-ft 0-in) span V-1A had a maximum speed of 362 km/h (225 mph) and a range of 1609 km (1,000 miles).

Vultee V-11 and V-12

The prototype **Vultee V-11** attack bomber flew in the summer of 1935 and was lost in a crash during that September. It had retained the wing and landing gear of the V-1A, but introduced a modified tailplane and a new elliptical cross-section fuselage with a long raised canopy covering tandem crew cockpits. Shortly afterwards the **V-11G** prototype was flown, the main change being replacement of the original Cyclone engine by a new 746-kW (1,000-hp) SGR-1820-G2 Cyclone. Another prototype, the three-seat **V-11GB**, was also offered to customers.

The Chinese Nationalist government ordered 30 **V-11G**s, which saw some action against the invading Japanese, and the Soviet Union ordered one pattern V-11GB and arranged to build the type under licence as the **BSh**, but production ended after only 31 aircraft had been built. This was due to the fact that performance with the 686-kW (920-hp) M-62 engine was regarded as inadequate, especially as it was considered essential to introduce protective armour. As a result, the Soviet aircraft were redesignated **PS-43** and used for high-speed mail transport; those surviving into World

War II were used in a military liaison role. Turkey ordered 40 V-11GBs, which were delivered to the 2nd Regiment of the nation's air arm in 1937. Finally, Brazil purchased 18 standard V-11GBs, plus eight examples of a twin-float seaplane version equipped for torpedo bombing.

Impressed by the export orders, the US Army Air Corps bought seven V-11GBs for evaluation, designating them **YA-19**. They were delivered in 1939, two then being converted as engine testbeds, the **XA-19A** being flown with an experimental Avco Lycoming O-1230-1 of 951 kW (1,275 hp) and the **XA-19B** with the 1342-kW (1,800-hp) Pratt & Whitney R-2800-1 Double Wasp.

The **V-12** development flown in 1939 had aerodynamic refinements and a more powerful Pratt & Whitney Twin Wasp engine. The Chinese Nationalists ordered one example, modified to take a Wright Cyclone 9 engine of 783 kW (1,050 hp), and this was redesignated **V-12C**; it was armed with two 12.7-mm (0.5-in) and four 7.62-mm (0.3-in) machine-guns and had an internal bombload of 490 kg (1,080 lb). The Chinese then built 25 V-12Cs under licence at the CAMCO

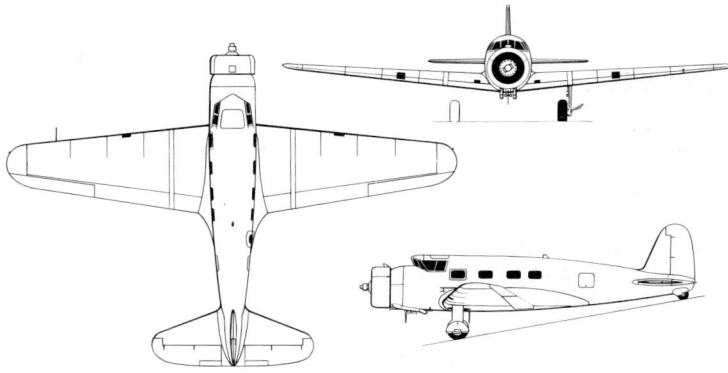

The Vultee V-11GB was modelled closely on the V-11G, but had a neat, retractable, ventral machine-gun position.

factory at Loiwing before the more powerful **V-12D** attracted their attention; this had a redesigned fuselage, the Wright GR-2600-A5B engine of 1193 kW (1,600 hp), and armament that was the same as that of the V-12C. Two pattern aircraft were sent to China and licence-manufacture of 50 was begun. After damage to the CAMCO factory in a Japanese bombing raid, all salvaged items from incomplete V-12Ds were sent to Bangalore, India, where some were assembled by Hindustan Aircraft and sent back to China.

Specification
Vultee V-11GB
Type: three-seat attack aircraft
Powerplant: one 746-kW (1,000-hp) Wright SGR-1820-G2 Cyclone radial piston engine
Performance: maximum speed 369 km/h (229 mph); service ceiling 7010 m (23,000 ft); range 1971 km (1,225 miles)
Weights: empty equipped 2801 kg (6,176 lb); maximum take-off 5188 kg (11,437 lb)
Dimensions: span 15.24 m (50 ft 0 in); length 11.42 m (37 ft 5½ in); height 3.05 m (10 ft 0 in); wing area 35.67 m² (384.0 sq ft)
Armament: six 7.62-mm (0.3-in) Browning machine-guns, plus a maximum internal bombload of 272 kg (600 lb)

Vultee V-48 (P-66 Vanguard)

The **Vultee V-48** was a fighter development of the BT-13, retaining the same basic configuration, but with retractable tailwheel landing gear, single-seat accommodation and with its 895-kW (1,200-hp) Pratt & Whitney R-1830-S4C4-G engine initially close-cowled to minimise drag, requiring an extension drive shaft for the propeller. Named **Vanguard**, it first flew in September 1939 and was found to have engine overheating problems, but with only minimal drag reduction it was decided to revert to a conventional

engine installation, with which the second **V-48X** prototype was flown on 11 February 1940. Five days earlier the company had received an order from Sweden for 144 of these aircraft, and a **V-48C** production prototype was flown on 6 September 1940. A US

The late-production standard of the Vultee Model 48C fighter, originally flown in 1939, was distinguished by the reduced glazing aft of the sliding cockpit canopy section.

advanced trainers by the USAAF, which designated them **P-66**.

Specification
Vultee P-66 Vanguard
Type: single-seat fighter
Powerplant: one 895-kW (1,200-hp)

Pratt & Whitney R-1830-33 Twin Wasp radial piston engine
Performance: maximum speed 547 km/h (340 mph) at 4600 m (15,100 ft); service ceiling 8595 m (28,200 ft); range 1529 km (950 miles)
Weights: empty 2375 kg (5,235 lb);

maximum take-off 3349 kg (7,384 lb)
Dimensions: span 10.97 m (36 ft 0 in); length 8.66 m (28 ft 5 in); height 2.87 m (9 ft 5 in); wing area 18.30 m² (197.0 sq ft)
Armament: four 7.62-mm (0.3-in) and two 12.7-mm (0.5-in) machine-guns

Vultee V-72 (A-31/A-35 Vengeance)

The **Vultee V-72** represented continuing improvement of the basic V-11/ V-12 design, and with knowledge of the successful application of dive-bombing techniques in the Spanish Civil War the V-72 was designed to incorporate such capability. This development came at the right moment for a British purchasing mission of 1940 which, with even more comprehensive knowledge of the potential of dive-bombing, placed an order for 700. Built by Northrop and Vultee, the latter having inadequate production capacity, these aircraft were designated **Vengeance Mk I** and **Vengeance Mk IIB,** respectively, by the RAF. Following the introduction of Lend-Lease in 1941 the USAAF ordered 300 more aircraft for the UK, allocating the designation **A-31**, and Northrop- and Vultee-built examples of these aircraft had the respective RAF designations **Vengeance Mk IA** and **Vengeance Mk III**. With experience of the vulnerability of the Junkers Ju 87 to its own fighters in the Battle of Britain, the RAF realised that the Vengeance was unsuitable for deployment in Europe and used them to equip Nos 45, 82 84 and 110 Squadrons in Burma where they had considerable success.

Vultee A-35B Vengeance of GB1/32, Free French Air Force, based in North Africa during 1943.

When the USA became involved in World War II, the USAAF commandeered 243 of the aircraft in production for the UK and these entered service as V-72s. Vultee then built 99 aircraft designated **A-35A**B, which differed in armament and equipment, followed by 831 **A-35B** aircraft with increased armament and the Wright R-2600-13 engine. Of this total, 29 were supplied to Brazil, plus 562 to the UK which designated them **Vengeance Mk IV**. The RAF transferred a small number to the Royal Australian Air Force and also converted some as **Vengeance TT.Mk IV** target tugs; almost all of the USAAF's aircraft were used in this latter role. Variants included the **XA-31A** static test airframe, becoming **XA-31B** when used to test a 2237-kW (3,000-hp) Pratt & Whitney XR-4360-1 Wasp Major engine, plus five **XA-31C** conversions from A-31s as testbeds for the 1640-kW (2,200-hp) Wright R-3350-13/-17 Cyclone engine.

Specification
Vultee A-35B Vengeance
Type: two-seat dive-bomber
Powerplant: one 1268-kW (1,700-hp)

Wright R-2600-13 Cyclone radial piston engine
Performance: maximum speed 449 km/h (279 mph) at 4115 m (13,500 ft); service ceiling 6795 m (22,300 ft); range 3701 km (2,300 miles)
Weights: empty 4672 kg (10,300 lb); maximum take-off 7439 kg (16,400 lb)
Dimensions: span 14.63 m (48 ft 0 in); length 12.12 m (39 ft 9 in); height 4.67 m (15 ft 4 in); wing area 30.84 m2 (332.0 sq ft)
Armament: six 12.7-mm (0.5-in) machine-guns, plus up to 907 kg (2,000 lb) of bombs

Vultee V-74

In 1938 the US Army Air Corps tested the **Vultee V-54** basic combat trainer, but although considered operationally ideal for the task the aircraft was regarded as being unnecessarily complicated and overpowered. Vultee then developed the **V-74** to meet this requirement, a cantilever low-wing monoplane with fixed tailwheel landing gear which accommodated two in tandem beneath a continuous canopy and was equipped with dual controls and blind-flying instrumentation as standard. Satisfactory testing brought an order for 300 aircraft in September 1939, at that time the largest order placed by the US Army for basic trainers. Subsequent production raised the total to 11,537 aircraft, making this one of the USA's most prolific trainers of World War II. The initial version, which

Though little known today, the Vultee Valiant was of primary importance to the United States during World War II, and is seen here in the form of a BT-13, the most widely used of this basic trainer version.

had the USAAC designation **BT-13** and name **Valiant**, was followed by the **BT-13A** (6,407 built), differing only in detail and in having a variant of the R-985 Wasp Junior engine. Then came the **BT-13B** (1,125 built) with revised electrical system and, because of a shortage of the R-985 Wasp Junior, by the **BT-15** (1,693 built) with the 336-kW (450-hp) Wright R-975-11 Whirl-wind engine. Of this total 1,350 BT-13A and 650 BT-13B aircraft were transferred to the US Navy, which designated them **SNV-1** and **SNV-2B,** respectively. Under the designation **XBT-16B,** one BT-13A was rebuilt

with a plastic fuselage for evaluation, but all versions were retired from USAAF and US Navy service as soon as World War II ended.

Specification
Vultee BT-13A Valiant
Type: basic trainer
Powerplant: one 336-kW (450-hp) Pratt & Whitney R-985-AN-1 Wasp

Junior radial piston engine
Performance: maximum speed 290 km/h (180 mph); service ceiling 6600 m (21,650 ft); range 1167 km (725 miles)
Weights: empty 1531 kg (3,375 lb); maximum take-off 2039 kg (4,496 lb)
Dimensions: span 12.80 m (42 ft 0 in); length 28 ft 10 in (8.79 m); height 11 ft 6 in (3.51 m); wing area 239.0 sq ft (22.20 m2)

Vultee V-84 (XP-54)

As the **XP-54**, Vultee built two prototypes of its **Vultee V-84** monoplane twin-boom single-seat fighter with retractable tricycle landing gear. The central nacelle housed the pilot in a pressurised cabin, and mounted at the rear in pusher configuration was a 1715-kW (2,300-hp) Avco Lycoming XH-2470-1 H-type engine driving a four-bladed pusher propeller. The XP-54 was first flown on 15 January 1943 and demonstrated a maximum speed of 649 km/h (403 mph), but no production followed.

The XP-54 was built as a result of the wartime R-40C fighter competition which saw its unconstrained design requirements answered by some unorthodox, yet brilliant, aircraft. The 'Swoose Goose', as it was strangely nicknamed, beat the competing Curtiss XP-55, and two aircraft were completed . It failed to enter production due to its rising weight and falling performance, coupled with an unreliable Lycoming engine.

Waco biplanes
to
Westland Scout and Wasp

Waco biplanes

At the beginning of the 1920s a group of enthusiasts in the USA formed Weaver Aircraft Co., the trade name Waco being formed from its initials; although the company's name was changed subsequently to Advance Aircraft Company and again in 1929 to become Waco, the aircraft were always called Wacos.

The first aircraft of consequence was the 1922 three-seat **Waco Model 6**, with a 67-kW (90-hp) Curtiss OX-5 engine, followed in 1923 by the improved **Model 7**. The **Model 8** cabin biplane of 1924 was an eight-seater with a 149-kW (200-hp) Hall-Scott Liberty Six engine, but the first Waco to make its mark was the 1925 **Model 9**, of which the company built 47 in 1925 and 164 the following year. In 1927 the **Model 10** supplanted the Model 9, and in that year alone around 370 were built with various engines up to the 224-kW (300-hp) Wright Whirlwind. One Whirlwind-powered aircraft won the 1928 USA National Air Tour, a 10140-km (6,300-mile) reliability and efficiency competition, and by then Waco had become the USA's largest producer of commercial aircraft. Modification of the Model 10 to the **Model 10-T** by the use of redesigned, tapered wings transformed performance, and the type was much in evidence as an aerobatic and racing aircraft; of 50 built five were supplied to China as trainers in 1929.

Since Waco biplanes ran to more than 110 variants, it is impossible to list them all; three-letter designations were adopted from 1930, the first letter indicating engine type, the second the basic airframe type and the third the series; suffix letters or numbers were applied in some cases to further identify a variant. In 1931 Waco moved into the cabin biplane market with the **Model QDC**, a four-seater with a 123-kW (165-hp) Continental engine. It proved to be a wise move, although the company continued with a lengthening range of open-cockpit biplanes for general and sport flying. The **Model UBF** three-seater of 1932 had a 157-kW (210-hp) Continental engine and is noteworthy mainly because in 1934 the US Navy procured two under the designation **XJW-1** as conversion trainers for parasite fighter experiments with the airship USS *Macon*. While Waco production continued with a variety of models, including a long line of cabin biplanes built over the following years, the vast range of designations was probably logical, but externally many of the aircraft were difficult to distinguish from each other.

Between 1934 and 1937 Waco developed the **Model D** series aircraft for military use, offering versions with engines between 186 and 366 kW (250 and 450 hp) as trainers, fighters, bombers, etc. The **Model WHD** company demonstrator, with racks beneath the fuselage able to carry a bomb of 113 kg (250 lb), with a forward-firing fixed gun on the lower wing and a trainable gun in the rear cockpit, was

sold to Nicaragua. A number of others went to small air forces with limited budgets (such as Cuba), and India used the **Model F** series in the trainer role. The **Model UMF** of mid-1934, with a 157-kW (210-hp) Continental or 168-kW (225-hp) Jacob L-4, was a three-seat open-cockpit biplane built in small numbers mainly for military use; four were delivered to Guatemala in 1934 for military pilot training and three to Cuba in 1937 to train naval pilots.

Certificated in April 1934, the **Model YKC** soon became the company's best seller, powered with the new 168-kW (225-hp) Jacobs L-4 engine. It was developed into the **Model ZKS-6** with the 213-kW (285-hp) Jacobs L-5 and continued in production until 1937.

A new series of four/five-seat **Custom Cabin** models introduced in 1935 were somewhat larger and more internally luxurious than their predecessors, but in spite of higher prices they sold well; most popular was the **Model YOC**, available initially with a 168-kW (225-hp) Jacobs L-4, but the later **Model YOC-1** aircraft had the 213-kW (285-hp) Jacobs L-5. The **Model CPF** of 1935 was chosen by the Brazilian government for training purposes and, of the 41 aircraft built, all but one went to Brazil. These had 186-kW (250-hp) Wright R-760-E engines and were two-seat open cockpit models; 30 were delivered in crates to the Brazilian army and 10 to the navy, the latter fitted with Edo floats. The **Model YQC-6** was another Custom Cabin four/five-seat biplane offered with a choice of seven different engines, largest of which was the 246-kW (330-hp) Jacobs L-6. Several examples were exported to Canada, mostly **Model ZQC-6** variants with 213-kW (285-hp) Jacobs engines; some had extra doors and were used as freighters carrying up to 363 kg (800 lb) of cargo. Other models included **Model YQC-6** aircraft for India with the 168-kW (225-hp) Jacobs. By the end of 1936 there were more than 1,140 Waco aircraft in active operation, some more than 10 years old.

The 1937 **Model YKS-7/ZKS-7** was introduced with, respectively, the 168- and 213-kW (225- and 285-hp) Jacobs engines, the former proving more popular in production that continued until 1941. Four aircraft served with the USAAF, two Model YKS-7s being designated **UC-72K** and two Model ZKS-7s as **UC-72M**. The **Model EGC-7** of 1937, with a 239-kW (320-hp) Wright R-760-E2, was ordered by the Brazilian army, which received 30 in 1938-39, the Brazilian government acquiring the manufacturing rights during the following year. Introduction of the **Model UPF-7** open-cockpit trainer in 1937 proved a money-spinner for Waco. Offered initially as a two/three-seat sporting aircraft with a 164-kW (220-hp) Continental W-670K engine, it came at a time when such types were being superseded, but six were bought for the Guatemala army air corps as **Model VPF-7** aircraft with 179-kW (240-hp) Continental engines. It says much for the reliability of the type that all six returned to the USA in 1959. A

number of Model UPF-7s were bought by civilian flying schools, including the Boeing School of Aeronautics, and the USAAF evaluated one under the designation **XPT-14** and then acquired 13 **YPT-14** (later **PT-14**) aircraft; in 1942 an impressed UPF-7 was designated **PT-14A**. The US government's Civilian Pilot Training Program (CPTP) of 1939 authorised vast sums for the training of civilian pilots in case of war, and the programme was implemented at various educational institutions. Requirement for a standard trainer led to orders for 600 Model UPF-7s for the CPTP and the Civil Aeronautics Authority ordered 31 for their own private flying unit. The CPTP also bought 20 Model VKS-7F cabin four-seaters with 179-kW (240-hp) Continental W-670 engines. A surviving UPF-7 is still flying in the USA with a 373-kW (500-hp) engine, providing a spectacular rival to Stearmans in aerobatic displays. Mention of the **Model EGC-8** of 1937 should be made if only to record that one of the seven aircraft built became a testbed for the six-cylinder in-line Menasco engine later being purchased by Howard Hughes and presented to one of his associates. It was later restored to standard Model EGC-8 configuration with a 239-kW (320-hp) Wright R-760 radial engine, and won the Contemporary Age, Outstanding Closed Cockpit award at the 1980 EAA Fly-In at Oshkosh, Wisconsin.

The **Model JHD** of 1937, designed for small air forces, was a two-seat closed-cockpit biplane that could carry a variety of military equipment. It had a 272-kW (365-hp) Wright R-975 engine and attracted only one order, six for the government of Uruguay delivered in January 1938. With the **Model ZVN**

The CUC-2 was typical of the 'Custom' biplanes, with its elegant fin and short-span lower wing.

experimental four-seater cabin biplane, Waco broke with tradition and introduced tricycle landing gear which proved easier to fly and was able to operate into smaller airfields than the taildraggers. It entered production as the **Model ZVN-8** (213-kW/285-hp Jacobs L-5) and **Model AVN-8** (224-kW/300-hp Jacobs L-6). Production amounted to about 20, and a few served with the USAAF (three Model AVN-8s as **UC-72J** and a Model ZVN-8 as **UC-72L**). One Model ZVN-8 was acquired by the British Air Ministry for tricycle landing gear tests.

The last Waco cabin biplane was the **Model E**, flown in 1939. By this time much of the company's production facilities were given over to the Model UPF-7, but nearly 30 Model Es were built between 1939 and 1942 in three versions, the **Model ARE** (224-kW/300-hp Jacobs L-6MB), **Model HRE** (213-kW/285-hp Lycoming R-680) and **Model SRE** (298-kW/400hp Pratt & Whitney Wasp Junior). The last was the most popular and was named **Aristocrat**. The end of the Waco biplane line was mourned by many, but large numbers survived the war and have been lovingly restored to flying condition. A total of 44 Wacos of 16 different models, some with tricycle landing gear, were impressed for military use, receiving designations up to **UC-72Q**, and were used throughout the war.

Flown by the civil training schools during the war, the Waco UPF-7 was a sturdy reliable aircraft, well suited to rough treatment.

Waco aircraft, post World War II

Waco intended to enter the post-war light aircraft market and flew the prototype four-seat **Waco Aristocraft** in March 1947. A four-seat all-metal high-wing monoplane with twin fins and rudders, and retractable landing gear, it had a 160-kW (215-hp) Franklin engine driving a pusher propeller mounted at the rear of the fuselage. The company received around 300 orders but early tests showed a need for large development costs and this, plus the obvious impending slump in the private aircraft market, caused the programme to be cancelled. Waco withdrew from aircraft manufacturing and concentrated on utility products. An attempt was made to re-enter the aviation scene in the late 1960s with plans to market licence-built versions of the French SOCATA Rallye and the Italian SIAI-Marchetti SA.202 and SF.260. These plans did not mature, presumably because of the extensive competition from indigenous lightplanes in this class.

This was not the end for Waco designs, however, as in 1983 the YMF-3 biplane was resurrected at the hands of the Classic Aircraft Corporation, Lansing, Michigan. Finding that all Waco type certificates had passed to the FAA, Classic began building the **Waco Classic F-5**, flying the prototype in November 1986. This has since been joined by the **YMF Super**, with an enlarged front cockpit, and by late 1993 over 50 aircraft of both types had been delivered. Classic is offering the YMF Super at a flyaway price of $196,000.

Wassmer aircraft

The French Société des Etablissements Benjamin Wassmer set up an aviation department which began its activities by building the Jodel D.112 under licence. Wassmer then developed a de-luxe version as the **Jodel-Wassmer D.120 Paris-Nice**, which was powered by a 71-kW (95-hp) Continental C90-12F flat-four engine. The company's first indigenous design was the **Wassmer WA-40 Super IV**, a four-seat cabin monoplane powered by a 134-kW (180-hp) Avco Lycoming O-360-A1A engine. The prototype was first flown on 8 June 1959 and it became available in three variants with different standards of equipment; a version with non-retractable landing gear was introduced in 1965 as the **WA-41 Baladou**. In the following year a new four-seat light cabin monoplane was flown in prototype form as the **WA-50**; this made extensive use of glass-fibre in its construction and had retractable landing gear, but the production versions developed from it had fixed tricycle landing gear. They comprised the **WA-51 Pacific** (112-kW/150-hp Avco Lycoming O-320-E2A), **WA-52 Europa** (119-kW/160-hp IO320-B1A) and **WA-54 Atlantic** (134-kW/180-hp Avco Lycoming O-360-A and other refinements). Final Wassmer design was for a two-seat trainer with side-by-side seats in an enclosed cabin; first flown in November 1975 and designated **WA-80 Piranha**, this was powered by a 75-kW (100-hp) Rolls-Royce Continental O-200-A flat-four engine. In March 1967 Wassmer had flown the **WA-4/21** prototype, a development of the WA-40/-41, and in 1971 formed a joint company with Siren SA to build an all metal derivative. This became the **Cerva CE.43 Guépard**, of which 43 had been built before Wassmer went into liquidation in 1977. On 1 February 1978 a new company, Issoire Aviation was set up by Société Siren, which acquired Wassmer's remaining assets and began building E-75 and D-77 gliders in addition to providing spares support for existing Wassmers.

Though developed from the WA-40, the Wassmer WA-51 Pacific has a totally different look, as a result of its revised glassfibre construction.

Watanabe E9W

The Watanabe Ironworks company began aircraft production in 1931. The first aircraft of its own design to be built was the **Watanabe E9W1**, a small reconnaissance seaplane for submarine-borne operations. It was capable of being easily dismantled for stowage in a small hangar on the submarine's deck and easily assembled for launching. An unequal-span twin-float biplane, the E9W1 had provision for a crew of two and was armed with a single 7.7-mm (0.303-in) machine-gun operated by the observer. The prototype, test-flown in 1934-35, was followed by 32 series aircraft which went into service as the **Navy Type 96**

Small Reconnaissance Seaplane, the last being delivered in 1940. The E9W1 served with several fleet submarines until replaced by the E14Y1 monoplane. It received the Allied codename **'Slim'** in 1942. Powered by a 224-kW (300-hp) Hitachi Tempu II radial engine, the 10.00-m (32-ft 9**3/4**-in) span E9W1 had a maximum speed of 232 km/h (144 mph).

Other Watanabe designs of that period included the **WS-103S** reconnaissance seaplane, seven of which were sold to Siam (Thailand) in 1938, and the **K6W1** and **K8W1** trainer floatplanes; three of each were supplied to the Japanese Navy for test in 1937 and 1938, respectively. In 1943 Watanabe was succeeded by Kyushu Hikoki K.K.

Designed to fit into a small hangar on large submarines, the E9W was one of the better such designs.

Weiss aircraft

The Manfred Weiss company began aircraft manufacture in 1928, first building the Fokker C.V biplane for the LüH (clandestine Hungarian air arm) and then continuing with the Udet U.12 Flamingo trainer plus 80 examples of the **Hungária**, a U.12 development, in five versions.

The **Weiss WM-10 Olyv** (buzzard) used the company's own 75-kW (100-hp) MW Sport I engine, the prototype first flying during September 1931. In November it was modified to take the 89-kW (120-hp) Sport II engine and given improved landing gear. A single-bay two-seat primary training biplane, the WM-10 was adopted officially, eight **WM-10a** machines being delivered in 1933. The last airframe, modified to take a 97-kW (130-hp) Sport III engine, became the **WM-13**, and the limited range of the WM-10 was overcome by providing increased fuel capacity. Most WM-10s were later upgraded to WM-13 standard. Maximum speed of the 9.50-m (31-ft 2-in) span WM-13 was 190 km/h (118 mph).

Five new airframes with the Siemens Sh.12 engine served with combat units as aerobatic trainers under the designation **EM-10**. In 1938 surviving WM-10 aircraft had the Siemens engine fitted, all then being known as WM-10s. They served as primary trainers until 1941, when the three remaining aircraft were handed over to the para-military Hungarian flying organisation for glider towing.

The **WM-16A Budapest** light bomber/reconnaissance biplane was evolved from the Fokker C.V. Powered by a 410-kW (550-hp) Gnome-Rhône K-9 radial, nine were delivered in 1935, followed by nine **WM-16B** aircraft during the next year with the Weiss-built 641-kW (860-hp) Gnome-Rhône K-14 engine that gave this latter version a maximum speed of 310 km/h (193 mph). The one-off **WM-20** basic trainer of 1937, powered by a 239-kW (320-hp) K-7 radial, was followed by the prototype **WM-21 Sólyom** (falcon), in reality a modified WM-16B. The basic design was simplified for service use, a tailskid replacing the Budapest's tailwheel to shorten landing runs on grass airfields. The structure was also strengthened and refined, and instrumentation was improved. Powered by the 649-kW (870-hp) WM-14A radial (developed from the Gnome-Rhône K14), the 12.90-m (42-ft 3¾in) span WM-21 had a maximum speed of 320 km/h (199 mph). Armament comprised three 0.31-in (7.9-mm) Gebauer machine-guns plus

The WM-21 Sólyom was an unremarkable biplane which served first as a front-line type and later as a trainer.

12 10-kg (22-lb) anti-personnel bombs and 120 1-kg (2.2-lb) incendiary bombs. In all, 128 series Sólyom biplanes were built, 25 by Manfred Weiss, 43 by MAVAG and 60 by MWG. They were operated by short-range recon- naissance squadrons from 1939 until the last two units were re-equipped in the spring of 1944; by then some 80 Sólyoms were flying as advanced trainers, a role in which the type continued until 1945.

WM-21s patrolled the Romanian border during the 1940 Transylvanian dispute, but first operational use was in April 1941 during the Axis invasion of Yugoslavia, by which time six squadrons and two independent flights were equipped with the type. They were heavily involved from June 1941, supporting Hungarian army units in the Ukraine, but during 1942-43 WM-21s were deployed mainly in oper- ations against Soviet partisans.

Welch OW

It is perhaps unkind to describe the **Welch OW** as an ugly little monoplane, for Orin Welch had set out to design and produce a cheap and functional lightplane for the 'man in the street'. The resulting aircraft was of braced high-wing configuration with an enclosed cabin for two and pow- ered by a variety of engines. Those certificated included the **OW-5M**, mainly with a 30-kW (40-hp) Continental A-40-4 flat-four; **OW-6M** with 28-kW (37-hp) Aeronca

E-113-B, and **OW-7M** with a 36-kW (45-hp) O-2 engine designed by Orin Welch. Total production in the late 1930s amounted to about 20 aircraft, most of them OW-5Ms with the Continental engine, and this version had a wing span of 10.49 m (34 ft 5 in) and maximum speed of 145 km/h (90 mph).

Bearing a certain resemblance to the Aeronca C-3 lightplane series, the Welch OW-5M of the early 1930s was designed for ease of operation and simplicity of maintenance.

Westland 30

Under the designation **Westland 30** (initially **WG 30**), the company developed an enlarged, twin-engined transport version of the Lynx, begin- ning in 1976. Westland foresaw a market for the type in VIP, passenger and cargo transport, and off-shore support operations. The first aircraft (G-BGHF) flew on 10 April 1979. CAA and FAA type certification of the basic production version, the **Series 100**, powered by a pair of 846-kW (1,135-shp) Rolls-Royce Gem Mk 41-1 turboshafts, was granted in 1982. Compared to the Lynx, the Westland 30 featured a greatly increased cabin coupled with a larger rotor, increased fuel capacity and a new flight control system. In January 1984 the **Series 100-60** appeared, powered by two 940-kW (1,260-shp) Gem 60-3 engines. Rolls-Royce was replaced by General Electric in the **Series 200**, which was powered by a pair of 1277-kW (1,712-shp) CT7-2B engines. This version first flew in 1983. The **Series 300** of 1986 offered a General

Westland 30 of Airspur

Electric CT7 or Rolls-Royce Turboméca RTM 322 powerplant, and also had an increased maximum take-off weight, composite BERP rotor blades, consid- erably reduced noise and vibration levels and an optional EFIS cockpit. Two military tactical transport versions were also developed, the **TT30** and the **TT300**, but these met with even less success than the civilian versions.

British Airways ordered two heli- copters, for delivery in 1982, and obtained a third the following year. Sixteen further aircraft were spread among several operators in the United States, such as PanAm/Omniflight (for services between John F. Kennedy, Newark and downtown New York) and Airspur. These aircraft were largely Series 100s and 100-60s, operated on lease. By early 1984 only 19 orders had been received. In 1986

the Westland 30 received its last, and largest, order for 21 Series 100- 60s from the Helicopter Corp- oration of India, financed largely by UK government assistance. Production ended in January 1988 with the com- pletion of the 38th airframe. The Helicopter Corporation of India became Pawan Hans and its 19 surviving Westland 30-160s are stored at Delhi and Bombay, the company hav- ing failed to sell them on several recent occasions.

Westland IV and Wessex

The six-seat **Westland IV** light trans- port of 1928 was a braced high-wing monoplane, powered originally by three 71-kW (95-hp) ADC Cirrus Mk III inline engines and accommodating a crew of two in an enclosed flight deck, with a separate four-seat cabin. First flown on 22 February 1929, it was followed by a second aircraft with 78-kW (105-hp) ADC Cirrus Hermes I engines. The

construction of two more aircraft had started, but these were completed instead with three 78-kW (105-hp) Armstrong Siddeley Genet Major I radi- al engines and given the name **Wessex**, the two Westland IVs then being converted to this standard. Six more examples of the Wessex were built, the last four each having a metal- skinned forward fuselage and more-

powerful Genet Major IA engines: one of them, for service with Portsmouth, Southsea and Isle of Wight Aviation, had baggage space reduced to allow for the carriage of six passengers. These aircraft proved reliable and most were in service for a number of years; the last two, operated by Air Pilots Training at Hamble, were finally with- drawn from use in 1940. With a wing span of 17.53 m (57 ft 6 in), late ver- sions of the Wessex had a maximum speed of 196 km/h (122 mph).

Powered by three Genet Major I radials, the Westland Wessex had an all-up weight of 2608 kg (5,750-lb) and cruised at 161 km/h (100 mph).

Westland Dragonfly, Widgeon

Negotiations in 1946 between Westland Aircraft of Yeovil, Somerset, and Sikorsky in the USA led to a licence for construction of the Sikorsky S-51 in the UK. Basically similar to the US-built aircraft, the type was assembled from British-built compo- nents and in all but one variant was powered by the Alvis Leonides engine. The first civil **Westland/ Sikorsky WS-51** was flown on 5 October 1948 and on 24 July 1951 the type became the first British-built helicopter to gain a certificate of air-

worthiness. Before that, in 1950, a ver- sion designated **Dragonfly HR.Mk 1** equipped the Royal Navy's first heli- copter squadron, No. 705 formed at RNAS Gosport. Built to a total of 133, the Dragonfly was followed by a developed version, the **Westland**

Essentially a development of the S-51A, the Widgeon was powered by a 388-kW (520-hp) Alvis Leonides 521/2 radial, had a main rotor diameter of 14.99 m (49 ft 2 in) and cruised at 142 km/h (88 mph).

Widgeon, the prototype of which was a conversion of a Dragonfly to provide five-seat capacity and which benefited from the introduction of the improved rotor of the Sikorsky S-55. Widgeon production totalled 14, several of them conversions of Dragonflies.

Variants
Dragonfly HR.Mk 1: initial air/sea rescue (ASR) version for Royal Navy with the Alvis Leonides 50 radial engine
Dragonfly HC.Mk 2: similar to

Dragonfly HR.Mk 1 but equipped as casualty evacuation aircraft for the RAF
Dragonfly HR.Mk 3: major production ASR version for Royal Navy (58 built); generally as Dragonfly HR.Mk 1 but introduced all-metal rotor
Dragonfly HC.Mk 4: casualty evacuation version for RAF, similar to Dragonfly HR.Mk 3
Dragonfly HR.Mk 5: final ASR version for Royal Navy, similar to Dragonfly HR.Mk 3
Westland/Sikorsky Mk 1A: civil

version with 388-kW (520-hp) Alvis Leonides 521/1 engine; most used as civil transports. but small numbers to Japan for rescue, and to Italian and Thai air forces
Westland/Sikorsky Mk 1B: civil version similar to Mk 1A but with 336-kW (450-hp) Pratt & Whitney R-985-B4 Wasp Junior engine

Specification
Westland Dragonfly HR.Mk 1
Type: naval ASR helicopter

Powerplant: one 403-kW (540-hp) Alvis Leonides 50 radial piston engine
Performance: maximum speed 153 km/h (95 mph) at sea level; service ceiling 3780 m (12,400 ft); range 483 km (300 miles)
Weights: empty 1987 kg (4,380 lb); maximum take-off 2663 kg (5,870 lb)
Dimensions: main rotor diameter 14.63 m (48 ft 0 in); length, rotors turning 17.54 m (57 ft 6½ in); height 3.95 m (12 ft 11½ in); main rotor disc area 168.11 m² (1,809.56 sq ft)

Westland Limousine

With the end of World War I and a prospect for expanding civil aviation services, Westland Aircraft designed a biplane light transport to accommodate three passengers in an enclosed cabin, the pilot seated at the rear with his head projecting through the cabin roof. Designated **Westland Limousine I**, the first aircraft was flown in July 1919. It was powered by a Rolls-Royce Falcon III engine, which was regarded as standard powerplant, and ultimately equipped two of the subsequent four

Limousine II aircraft after one had first been tested with a 306-kW (410-hp) Cosmos Jupiter radial engine, the remaining two having 224-kW (300-hp) Hispano-Suiza Vee engines. To compete in the Air Ministry's 1920 Commercial Aeroplane Competition, a scaled-up version to accommodate a pilot and five passengers was built as the **Limousine III** and was powered by a 336-kW (450-hp) Napier Lion engine. This won the Air Ministry prize in its class but, despite this, only one other

Limousine III was built. The 11.51-m (37-ft 9-in) span Limousine II as powered by the 205-kW (275-hp) Rolls-Royce Falcon III had a maximum speed of 161 km/h (100 mph) and range of 644 km (400 miles).

The Westland Limousine III of 1920 was scaled up from preceeding Limousine designs, to a span of 16.46 m (54 ft 0 in), and had a maximum speed of 190 km/h (118 mph).

Westland Lynx

One of the three helicopters included in the Aérospatiale/Westland co-production agreement of 1968, the **Westland Lynx** was designed initially for naval and civil roles, but early appreciation of its suitability for a wide range of military operations has led to an expanded development programme under the titles Army and Navy Lynx. Production was shared 70 per cent by Westland and 30 per cent by Aérospatiale. The first of six prototypes was flown on 21 March 1971, being followed by seven pre-production prototypes to speed development. Service trials began first in 1976 with No. 700L Naval Air Squadron at RNAS Yeovilton, Somerset, this being a joint Royal Navy and Royal Netherlands navy operational evaluation unit; similarly, an Army Aviation trials unit was established at Middle Wallop, Hampshire, in mid-1977. Deliveries of production aircraft to operational units began following completion of the latter trials in December 1977, the Lynx entering service first with Army Aviation squadrons in West Germany. The first Royal Navy unit (No. 702 Sqn) became operational in December 1977. Westland's current production aircraft are improved versions of the Army and Navy Lynx known as the **Battlefield Lynx** and **Super Lynx**, respectively, with all versions detailed more closely below. By 1993, 380 Army and Navy versions had been completed for customers in 17 nations.

Variants
Lynx AH.Mk 1: general-purpose/ utility version for the British army with skid landing gear, able to operate in roles that include anti-tank, strike, armed escort, casualty evacuation, command post, logistic support, reconnaissance, tactical transport and SAR; 113 built; **AH.Mk 1GT** is interim version before AH.Mk 7 conversion
Lynx HAS.Mk 2: Royal Navy general-purpose version with non-retractable tricycle landing gear and foldable tail rotor pylon, suitable for roles that

include ASV, search and strike, ASW classification and strike communications, fire support, liaison, reconnaissance, SAR, troop transport and vertical replenishment
Lynx Mk 2 (FN): version for French navy, generally similar to HAS.Mk 2
Lynx HAS.Mk 3: second anti-submarine version for Royal Navy with uprated powerplant and transmission; equipped with two 835-kW (1,120-hp) Rolls-Royce Gem 41-1 turboshaft engines, and GEC-Marconi Seaspray radar in modified nose; 23 delivered between March 1982 to April 1985; 53 surviving HAS.Mk 2s converted to HAS Mk 3 standard by 1989; further improved version designated
HAS.Mk 3S
Lynx HAS.Mk 3 ICE: two aircraft converted for Arctic use by Royal Navy
Lynx HAS.Mk 3 GM: unofficial designation for 19 Gulf Modification aircraft originally delivered for use by Armada patrol, involving secure comms, tactical navigation and ESM fit
Lynx HAS.Mk ACTS: phase two of current upgrade programme featuring addition of RAMS 4000 central tactical system
Lynx HAS.Mk 4 (FN): version for French navy with powerplant of Lynx HAS.Mk 3
Lynx AH.Mk 5: version similar to Lynx AH.Mk 1, three for MoD (PE) with uprated Gem engines
Lynx AH.Mk 7: currently in service; improved British Army version featuring box-like exhaust shrouds, composite main rotor and reversed tail

rotors; all surviving AH. Mk 1s converted to AH.Mk 7 standard by RN at Fleetlands from March 1988
Lynx HAS.Mk 8: latest version for Royal Navy featuring 15 new-build and 45 converted airframes featuring increased weights, internal MAD, improved rotors, avionics and ESM systems; Seaspray radar relocated to chin position and GEC-Marconi Sea Owl thermal imager fitted to nose instead; initial deliveries scheduled for early 1994; export version designated **Super Lynx**
Lynx AH.Mk 9: latest battlefield version for British army; fitted with tricycle undercarriage which precludes carriage of TOW missiles; 16 new aircraft on order plus eight AH.Mk 7 conversions; export version designated **Battlefield Lynx**
Lynx Mk 21: version for Brazilian navy similar to Lynx HAS.Mk 2
Lynx Mk 22: unbuilt version for Egyptian navy
Lynx Mk 23: version for Argentine navy similar to Lynx HAS.Mk 2
Lynx Mk 24: unbuilt version for Iraqi army
Lynx Mk 25: version for Royal Netherlands navy, which designated them **UH-14A;** similar to Lynx HAS.Mk 2
Lynx Mk 26: unbuilt, unarmed version for Iraqi army
Lynx Mk 27: version for Royal Netherlands navy which designated them **SH-14B;** uprated Gem engines and equipped for ASW role with sonar; nine delivered

The Lynx AH.Mk 1 was the initial production version delivered to the British army, later upgraded to AH.Mk 7 standard.

Lynx Mk 28: version for State of Qatar police; generally as Lynx AH.Mk 1 but with uprated Gem 47-1 turboshafts and special equipment, including flotation gear
Lynx Mk 80: version for Royal Danish navy, similar to Lynx HAS.Mk 2; eight built
Lynx Mk 81: version for Royal Netherlands navy which designated them **SH-14C;** uprated Gem engines and magnetic anomaly detection (MAD) gear, some converted to SH-14B standard through deletion of MAD and addition of sonar; eight built
SH-14D: conversion of five Dutch navy UH-14As and eight SH-14Cs with Alcatel dipping sonar, UHF radios, RWR, FLIR, GPS, radar altimeter, composite blades and Gem Mk 42 engines
Lynx Mk 82: unbuilt version for Egyptian army
Lynx Mk 83: unbuilt version for Saudi army
Lynx Mk 84: unbuilt version for Qatari army
Lynx Mk 85: unbuilt version for UAE army
Lynx Mk 86: version for Royal Norwegian air force coast guard; similar to Lynx HAS.Mk 2, but with uprated Gem engines and non-folding tail rotor pylon; six built
Lynx Mk 87: embargoed version for Argentine navy, similar to Lynx Mk 23

but with uprated engines
Lynx Mk 88: version for the Federal German navy similar to Lynx Mk 86; equipped with sonar; 19 built
Lynx Mk 89: version for Nigerian navy; equipped for ASW/SAR roles; three built
Lynx Mk 90: single follow-on aircraft for Danish navy assembled in Denmark; delivered in 1988

Super Lynx Mk 95: five aircraft for Portuguese navy; equivalent to HAS. Mk 8; deliveries commenced in 1993
Super Lynx Mk 99: 12 aircraft for South Korean navy; delivered between 1989 and 1991; equivalent to HAS.Mk 8
Battlefield Lynx 800: AH.Mk 9 re-engined with LHTEC T800 turboshafts; development project

terminated in 1992

Specification
Westland Lynx HAS.Mk 2
Type: general-purpose naval helicopter
Powerplant: two 671-kW (900-shp) Rolls-Royce Gem 2 turboshafts
Performance: maximum cruising speed 232 km/h (144 mph); maximum standard range 593 km (368 miles)

Weights: empty 2740 kg (6,040 lb); maximum take-off 4763 kg (10,500 lb)
Dimensions: main rotor diameter 12.80 m (42 ft 0 in); length, rotors turning 15.16 m (49 ft 9 in); height 3.59 m (11 ft 9 in); main rotor disc area 128.71 m² (1,385.45 sq ft)
Armament: can include (according to role) cannon, depth charges, Minigun pods, missiles, rockets and torpedoes

Westland Lysander

With a name that is perhaps the best-known among Westland products, the **Westland Lysander** originated as the company's design to meet the requirements of Air Ministry Specification A.39/34 for an army co-operation aircraft. With a distinctive high-set wing and small stub-wings attached to the main wheel struts to carry weapons/stores, it was easily recognisable. The crew of two had enclosed accommodation and power was provided by a Bristol Mercury radial engine. The first of two proto-types was flown initially on 15 June 1936, successful testing resulting in a contract for 144 aircraft. The type began to enter service with No. 16 Squadron RAF in June 1938, and when production ended a total of 1,652 had been built. They were the first British aircraft to be based in France at the beginning of World War II and the last to see action in France during the evacuation from Dunkirk. They also saw service in Burma, Egypt, Greece, India and Palestine, and following withdrawal from first-line use played an important role in clandestine operations and fulfilled valuable ASR and target-towing roles.

Variants
Lysander Mk I: original production version with 664-kW (890-hp) Bristol Mercury XII radial engine; 169 built
Lysander Mk II: similar to Lysander Mk I but powered by 675-kW (905-hp) Bristol Perseus XII; supplied to

France (one), Ireland (six) and Turkey (36); about 20 RAF aircraft were later transferred to Free French air force; one supplied to National Steel Car Corporation (later Victory Aircraft) of Malton, Ontario, as pattern for licence-construction of 75 with Perseus XII engines
Lysander Mk III: similar to Lysander Mk I but with Bristol Mercury XX radial engine; Westland built 367 and 150 licence-built in Canada
Lysander Mk IIIA: similar to Lysander Mk III but with Mercury 30 engine and additional machine-gun in rear cockpit; 347 built, of which 11 supplied to Free French (one),

Westland Lysander Mk II of the Turkish air force, based at Yesilköy in 1940.

Portugal (eight) and US Army Air Force (two)
Lysander Mk IIISCW: conversions of Lysander Mk III and Mk IIIA for clandestine operations carrying agents or VIPs to and from enemy territory; extra fuel and access ladder to rear cockpit on left side
Lysander TT.Mk 1: designation of Lysander Mk I after conversion for target towing
Lysander TT.Mk 2: designation of Lysander Mk II after conversion for target towing
Lysander TT.Mk III: designation of Lysander Mks I/II/III converted for target towing
Lysander TT.Mk IIIA: 100 new production target tugs with Mercury 30 engines

Specification
Westland Lysander Mk III
Type: army co-operation aircraft
Powerplant: one 649-kW (870-hp) Bristol Mercury XX radial piston engine
Performance: maximum speed 341 km/h (212 mph) at 1525 m (5,000 ft); service ceiling 6555 m (21,500 ft); range 966 km (600 miles)
Weights: empty 1980 kg (4,365 lb); maximum take-off 2866 kg (6,318 lb)
Dimensions: span 15.24 m (50 ft 0 in); length 9.30 m (30 ft 6 in); height 4.42 m (14 ft 6 in); wing area 14.15 m² (260.0 sq ft)
Armament: four 7.7-mm (0.303-in) Browning machine-guns (one in each wheel spat and two on trainable mount in rear cockpit), plus up to 227 kg (500 lb) of bombs

Westland Scout and Wasp

Strengthening its grip on the British rotary-wing aircraft market, Westland acquired Saunders-Roe Ltd in August 1959. Saro itself had taken over the Cierva Autogiro Company in January 1951 and continued development of the Cierva Skeeter light helicopter. Experience with production of this aircraft led to the **Saunders-Roe P.531** prototypes, the first of them flown on 20 July 1958, and was followed in 1959 by an Army Air Corps order for pre-production **P.531-2 Mk 1** aircraft. Following extensive evaluation, this five-seat utility light helicopter was ordered into production as the **Scout AH.Mk 1**, which began to enter service in early 1963, a total of 150 being built. In addition, small numbers were built for the Royal Australian Navy, Royal Jordanian air force, and the police departments of Bahrain and Uganda. Parallel development of the P.531 resulted in production of the **Wasp HAS.Mk 1** for the Royal Navy (originally designated **Sea Scout HAS.Mk 1**). This differed from the army Scout by having quadricycle landing gear instead of skids, and folding rotor blades and tail section to facilitate

The Scout's anti-tank capability came courtesy first of the SS.11, then SS.12 wire-guided missile.

shipboard stowage. A total of 98 Wasps was built for the Royal Navy, these first entering service in the summer of 1963. Wasps were also supplied to the navies of Brazil, the Netherlands, New Zealand and South Africa. As powered by a 783-kW (1,050-hp) de-rated Rolls-Royce/Bristol Nimbus 103 or 104 turboshaft engine, the Westland Wasp had a maximum speed of 193 km/h (120 mph) at sea level. Ten former Dutch aircraft were supplied to the Indonesian navy, after refurbishment by Westland, and are still in use along with those of the Royal New Zealand Navy. The only surviving Scout operator in 1993 is the British army. Thirty-eight active AH.Mk Is, with more in storage, remain in use with Nos 658 Sqn at Netheravon, 660 Sqn at Hong Kong and Brunei, and 666 Sqn (TA) at Middle Wallop.

An early Wasp undertakes the type's deck landing sea trials aboard HMS Nubian.

Westland Sea King and Commando
to
Yakovlev Yak-1

Westland Sea King and Commando

A licence agreement finalised with Sikorsky in 1959 allowed Westland to use the airframe and rotor system of the Sikorsky SH-3 Sea King as the basis for a new ASW helicopter for the Royal Navy. Following test and evaluation of prototype and pre-production aircraft assembled from Sikorsky-built components, the first production **Westland Sea King HAS.Mk 1** for the navy was flown on 7 May 1969, the type entering service the same year. At that time, the Sea King HAS.Mk 1 was similar to the Sikorsky Sea King, but powerplant comprised two Rolls-Royce Gnome H.1400 turboshaft engines. More significantly, Westland had adapted the large cabin as a tactical compartment for ASW operations, this meaning that the British Sea King was able to operate as an independent unit in an ASW role. Subsequent development has changed this helicopter very considerably.

Westland also built a tactical version known as the **Commando**, which is suitable for such roles as cargo transport, casualty evacuation, logistic support and troop transport (28 men can be carried). Further variants are detailed in the table below. Deliveries for the Sea King and Commando totalled 326 by the end of 1993.

Variants
Sea King HAS.Mk 1: initial ASW version for Royal Navy; since updated to Sea King HAS.Mk 2 by Royal Navy; 56 completed
Sea King HAS.Mk 2: ASW/SAR version for Royal Navy with uprated Gnome H.1400-1 turboshafts; 21 completed
Sea King HAR.Mk 3: SAR version for Royal Air Force with Gnome H.1400-1 turboshafts; 16 delivered in 1979 plus three in 1985; upgraded to **HAR.Mk 3A** standard through addition of greatly improved avionics, navigation and communications gear
Sea King HC.Mk 4: version of Commando Mk 2 for Royal Navy; combines folding rotor and tail of Sea King, non-retractable landing gear of Commando and Gnome H.1400-1 turboshafts; last aircraft delivered in 1990, total production 89; some aircraft

modified with RWR, missile approach warning system, chaff/flare dispensers, tactical navigation equipment, and NVG cockpit for Gulf War operations
Sea King Mk 4X: two aircraft, basically as HC.Mk 4; for development use by RAE Farnborough
Sea King HAS.Mk 5: developed ASW/SAR version for Royal Navy with Gnome H.1400-1 engines and advanced avionics; all Sea King HAS.Mk 2 aircraft upgraded to this standard along with 30 new-build aircraft delivered between 1980 and 1986
Sea King HAS.Mk 6: substantially improved anti-submarine warfare version for Royal Navy comprising five conversions from Mk 5 standard and 25 new aircraft
Sea King Mk 41: SAR version for Federal German navy with H.1400 turboshafts
Sea King Mk 42: ASW version for Indian navy with H.1400 turboshafts
Sea King Mk 42A: ASW version for Indian navy with H.1400-1 turboshafts
Sea King Mk 42B: anti-ship version for Indian navy, H 1400-1 turboshafts and equipped to carry Sea Eagle missiles
Sea King Mk 43: SAR version for Norwegian air force with H.1400 turboshafts
Sea King Mk 43A: SAR version for Norwegian air force with H.1400-1 turboshafts
Sea King Mk 45: ASW version for Pakistan navy with H.1400 turboshafts
Sea King Mk 47: ASW version with

Westland Sea King HAR.Mk 3 of No. 202 Sqn, RAF, deployed to the South Atlantic during the Falklands campaign of 1982.

H.1400-1 turboshafts, ordered by Saudi Arabia for Egyptian navy
Sea King Mk 48: SAR version for Belgian air force with H.1400-1 turboshafts
Sea King Mk 50: multi-role version for Royal Australian Navy; developed from Sea King HAS.Mk 1 but with H.1400-1 turboshafts; two additional but similar aircraft ordered in 1983 were allocated designation **Sea King Mk 50A**
Commando Mk 1: version with H.1400 turboshafts ordered by Saudi Arabia for Egyptian air force
Commando Mk 2: version with H.1400-1 turboshafts for Egyptian air force
Commando Mk 2A: version as Commando Mk 2 for Qatar Emiri air force
Commando Mk 2B: version as Commando Mk 2 with VIP interiors for Egyptian air force
Commando Mk 2C: version as Commando Mk 2B for Qatar Emiri air force

Specification
Westland Sea King HAS.Mk 5
Type: ASW helicopter
Powerplant: two 1238-kW (1,660-shp) Rolls-Royce Gnome H.1400-1 turboshaft engines
Performance: cruising speed 208 km/h (129 mph) at sea level; range with maximum standard fuel 1230 km (764 miles)
Weights: empty equipped 6202 kg (13,672 lb); maximum take-off 9525 kg (21,000 lb)
Dimensions: main rotor diameter 18.90 m (62 ft 0 in); length, rotors turning 22.15 m (72 ft 8 in); height 4.72 m (15 ft 6 in); main rotor disc area 280.47 m² (3,019.08 sq ft)
Armament: four Mk 46 torpedoes or four Mk 11 depth charges

Unlike its American counterparts, the Westland Sea King is designed to fly and operate as an autonomous hunter and killer, its advanced onboard sensors and analysis to potent weapons.

Westland Walrus

When the Royal Navy considered in 1919 that its need for a three-seat spotter/reconnaissance aircraft had become urgent, the best solution offered was a conversion of the de Havilland D.H.9A. The prototype was

produced as the Armstrong Whitworth Tadpole, which differed from the D.H.9A by losing its clean fuselage line to accommodate a third crew member, resulting in a bulge above and below to give the increased internal volume.

However, it was Westland that won the contract for 36 **Westland Walrus** aircraft; these differed by the introduction of a number of changes, including a 336-kW (450-hp) Napier Lion II engine, jettisonable main landing, flotation bags, arrester gear for the fore and aft arrester wires then standard, easily detachable wings for

shipboard stowage and armament of one 7.7-mm (0.303-in) synchronised Vickers III gun and one or two Lewis guns in the rear Scarff mounting. In other respects the Walrus was basically similar to the earlier de Havilland D.H.9A, but its Lion engine gave a maximum speed of 200 km/h (124 mph).

Westland Wapiti

Air Ministry Specification 26/27 for a general-purpose aircraft marked a modest beginning to post-World War I re-equipment of the RAF. Because funding was equally modest, a require-

ment was that the new design should use a high proportion of de Havilland D.H.9A components. Westland had developed for Airco the prototype D.H 9A (and was prime contractor for

this version of the D.H.9) and the company thus had a head start, winning the initial contract for 25 production **Westland Wapiti** aircraft. The prototype first flew in March 1927 and the type entered service with No. 84 Squadron in Iraq. A conventional biplane with tandem open cockpits, the

Wapiti was built in a number of versions for the RAF to a total of 517, and about 80 of these were still in service in India at the outbreak of World War II.

Variants
Wapiti Mk I: initial production version

with 313-kW (420-hp) Bristol Jupiter VI radial engine

Wapiti Mk IA: improved version with 358-kW (480-hp) Jupiter VIIIF engine and Handley Page leading-edge slats; in addition to construction for the RAF, 38 were built for the Royal Australian Air Force

Wapiti Mk IB: similar to Wapiti Mk IA but introduced divided main landing gear; in RAF use the Jupiter VIIIF engines were later replaced by the 410-kW (550-hp) Armstrong Siddeley Panther; four supplied to South Africa

Wapiti Mk II: developed version introducing all-metal basic structure

Wapiti Mk IIA: major production version with revised wing construction; suitable for use with wheel or float landing gear

Wapiti Mk III: version of which 27 were licence-built in South Africa; similar to Wapiti Mk IIA and with the 365-kW (490-hp) Armstrong Siddeley Jaguar VI engine

Wapiti Mk V: version developed from projected **Wapiti Mk IV** with lengthened fuselage and several refinements; powered by 410-kW (550-hp) Bristol Jupiter VIIIF

Wapiti Mk VI: dual-control trainer version, 16 built

Westland Wapiti Mk 1A of the Royal Australian Air Force, in service as a glider-tug during the 1940s.

Wapiti Mk VII: initially a Wapiti Mk V, used under designation **Houston-Wallace** or **P.V.6** before conversion to Wapiti VII as experimental aircraft

Wapiti Mk VIII: version developed from projected Wapiti Mk IV with 382-kW (512-hp) Armstrong Siddeley Jaguar VI; four built for Central Chinese government

Specification
Westland Wapiti Mk IIA
Type: general-purpose military aircraft
Powerplant: one 358-kW (480-hp) Bristol Jupiter VIII or VIIIF radial piston engine
Performance: maximum speed 225 km/h (140 mph) at 1525 m (5,000 ft); service ceiling 6280 m (20,600 ft); range 853 km (530 miles)

Weights: empty 1728 kg (3,810 lb); maximum take-off 2449 kg (5,400 lb)
Dimensions: span 14.15 m (46 ft 5 in); length 9.65 m (31 ft 8 in); height 3.61 m (11 ft 10 in); wing area 43.48 m² (468.0 sq ft)
Armament: one 7.7-mm (0.303-in) Vickers synchronised machine-gun and one 7.7-mm (0.303-in) Lewis gun on Scarff ring over rear cockpit, plus up to 263 kg (580 lb) of bombs

Westland Welkin

Designed to meet an Air Ministry requirement of 1940 for a high-altitude fighter, the **Westland P.14** design won an order for **Welkin** evaluation prototypes to be flown in competition against the Vickers Type 432. The Welkin was a cantilever mid-wing monoplane with retractable tailwheel landing gear, powered by two Rolls-Royce Merlin engines and accommodating its pilot in a pressurised cabin. The first of Westland's prototypes was flown on 1 November 1942. Tests made during 1943, with the Welkin flown in mock combat against a de Havilland Mosquito Mk IX at 10670 m (35,000 ft) and against

another Welkin at heights up to 12190 m (40,000 ft), resulted in a production order for 100 **Welkin Mk I** aircraft. About 80 were built before the contract was cancelled, as the anticipated high-altitude attacks by the Germans failed to materialise. None of the aircraft were issued to squadrons, being used instead for high-altitude research. A single **Welkin NF.Mk II** prototype was produced as a conversion of a Welkin Mk I, having a lengthened nose to accommodate an AI radar installation. The 21.34-m (70-ft 0-in) span Welkin Mk I as powered by two 932-kW (1,250-hp) Rolls-Royce Merlin 72/73 or

76/77 Vee engines had a maximum speed of 663 km/h (387 mph) at 7925 m (26,000 ft), and a service ceiling of 13410 m (44,000 ft).

Welkins never entered service, as a high-altitude bomber threat never materialised, and flight tests proved it was not as agile as had been hoped against other fighters.

Westland Wessex

The company's success with the Whirlwind led to licence negotiations with Sikorsky to build the S-58, for Westland considered that this somewhat larger helicopter had excellent development potential with the introduction of turbine powerplant. A single example was imported and modified initially by the installation of an 820-kW (1,100-shp) Napier Gazelle NGa.11 turboshaft engine, but the prototype and pre-production examples of the **Westland Wessex** had as powerplant the 1081-kW (1,450-shp) Napier Gazelle Mk 161. The initial production version for the Royal Navy began to enter service on 4 July 1961, and the type was subsequently built in several variants. In 1993 the Wessex is in service only with No. 22 Sqn, RAF, on SAR duties, and The Queens' Flight at RAF Benson.

Variants
Wessex HAS.Mk 1: Royal Navy ASW version with Napier Gazelle Mk 161 powerplant
Wessex HC.Mk 2: high-performance development of Wessex HAS.Mk 1 for the RAF with two coupled Bristol Siddeley Gnome Mk 110/Mk 111 turboshafts, each rated at 1007 kW

(1,350 shp); used primarily as transports (16 troops) or air ambulance (eight stretchers)
Wessex HAS.Mk 3: advanced Royal Navy ASW version with 1193-kW (1,600-hp) Napier Gazelle Mk 165 and a comprehensive automatic flight-control system
Wessex HC.Mk 4: two aircraft as Wessex HC.Mk 2 but with VIP interiors for service with The Queen's Flight
Wessex HU.Mk 5: troop-carrying assault helicopter for the Royal Marine Commandos; similar to Wessex HC.Mk 2
Wessex HAS.Mk 31: 27 built for Royal Australian Navy, similar to Wessex HAS.Mk 1 but with 1174-kW (1,575-hp) Napier Gazelle Mk 162 flat-rated to 1148 kW (1,540 shp); delivery began in August 1962 and when later given updated ASW systems became redesignated
Wessex HAS.Mk 31B
Wessex Mk 52: 12 similar to Wessex HC.Mk 2 for Iraqi air force
Wessex Mk 53: three similar to Wessex HC.Mk 2 for Ghana air force
Wessex Mk 54: one similar to Wessex HC.Mk 2 for service in Brunei
Wessex Mk 60: civil version seating

10 to 16 passengers according to role, 15 survivors in rescue operations, or as an air ambulance can carry eight stretchers, two sitting casualties and a medical attendant

Specification
Westland Wessex HC.Mk 2
Type: tactical transport/ground assault helicopter
Powerplant: two coupled 1007-kW (1,350-shp) Bristol Siddeley Gnome Mk 110 and Mk 111 turboshafts
Performance: maximum speed 212 km/h (132 mph) at sea level; range with maximum fuel 769 km

(478 miles)
Weights: empty 3767 kg (8,304 lb); maximum take-off 6123 kg (13,500 lb)
Dimensions: main rotor diameter 17.07 m (56 ft 0 in); length, rotors turning 20.04 m (65 ft 9 in); height 4.93 m (16 ft 2 in); main rotor disc area 228.81 m² (2,463.0 sq ft)
Armament: in anti-tank role equipped with Nord SS.11 air-to-surface missiles

In its HU.Mk 5 assault transport version the Wessex was a regular mount for the Royal Marines, as on this Norwegian exercise.

Westland Whirlwind

Easily recognisable, with two large engine nacelles that seemed to dominate this fighter and with a cruciform tail unit that helped to confirm recognition, the **Westland Whirlwind I** was designed to the requirements of Air Ministry Spec-ification F.37/35. The first of two proto-types was flown on 11 October 1938, but because of development problems with the Rolls-Royce Peregrine engine it was not until June 1940 that the type entered service with No. 263 Squadron, and later with No. 137 Squadron. The Whirlwind was the first single-seat twin-engined fighter in RAF service, and combined excellent manoeuvrability, high speed at low altitude and the heavy fire power of four nose-mounted 20-mm cannon that marked it out as a valuable addition to Fighter Command. The Whirlwind's low-level speed and fire power, plus a

Westland Whirlwind Mk 1, of No. 263 Sqn, RAF.

standard-fuel range of some 1287 km (800 miles), meant the type was ideal as an escort fighter for light bombers, and in 1942 when equipped with external bomb racks (as the **Whirlwind Mk IA**) saw extensive use on Rhubarb operations against cross-Channel installations. Unfor-tunately, the Whirlwind had problems which limited the number produced to 112: it had trouble with its tempra-mental Peregrine engines, which equipped no other type, and had a high landing speed that meant it was lim-ited severely in the number of air-fields into which it could operate. By 1943 it had been withdrawn from first-line service.

Westland Whirlwind

Westland's continued progress in the rotary-wing market was expanded considerably following the conclusion of a new licence agreement with Sikorsky in November 1950: this covered manufacture of the Sikorsky S-55 for the British forces and certain approved nations. Before Westland production got under way, the Royal Navy received from the USA under the Mutual Defense Assistance Program 25 Sikorsky S-55s. They comprised 10 with the 447-kW (600-hp) Pratt & Whitney Wasp R-1340-40 engines and 15 with the 522-kW (700-hp) Wright R-1300-3 engines, designated **Whirl-wind HAR.Mk 21** and **Whirlwind HAS. Mk 22** respectively.

Variants
Whirlwind Srs 1: initial civil production version with 447-kW (600-hp) R-1340-40 Wasp or 522-kW (700-hp) R-1300-3 Cyclone engine
Whirlwind Srs 2: civil version similar to Srs 1 but with 582-kW (780-hp) Alvis Leonides Major Mk 155 or Mk 755 engine derated to 559 kW (750 hp)

Whirlwind Srs 3: civil version similar to Srs 1 and 2, but introducing turboshaft powerplant of 783-kW (1,050-shp) General Electric T58 in the prototype; production aircraft had the licence-built version designated Bristol Siddeley Gnome H.1000
Whirlwind HAR.Mk 1: Royal Navy version with R-1340-40 engine
Whirlwind HAR.Mk2: RAF version, similar to Whirlwind HAR.Mk 1
Whirlwind HAR.Mk 3: Royal Navy version, similar to Whirlwind HAR.Mk 1 but with R-1300-3 engine
Whirlwind HAR.Mk4: RAF version for troop transport/ rescue operations in Malaya; powered by 447-kW (600-hp) R-1340-57 engine suitable for 'hot-and-high' use
Whirlwind HAR.Mk 5: version with powerplant of the civil Whirlwind Srs 2; three built for the Royal Navy and four for Austria
Whirlwind HAS.Mk 7: Royal Navy ASW version with the same powerplant as the civil Whirlwind Srs 2; first British helicopter equipped for use in an ASW role
Whirlwind HCC.Mk 8: two with

552-kW (740-hp) Alvis Leonides Major Mk 160 and VIP interiors for The Queen's Flight
Whirlwind HAR.Mk 9: turbine-engined (Gnome H.1000) conversions of Whirlwind HAS.Mk 7s for use in SAR and ice-patrol duties
Whirlwind HAR.Mk 10: version for RAF, new production with Gnome H.1000 engines, plus some conversions of Whirlwind HAR. Mk 2 and Whirlwind HAR.Mk 4 to same powerplant
Whirlwind HCC.Mk 12: two aircraft with Gnome H.1400 turboshafts and VIP interiors for The Queen's Flight

Specification
Westland Whirlwind HAR.Mk 10
Type: three-crew/eight-passenger

transport/SAR helicopter
Powerplant: one 783-kW (1,050-shp) Bristol Siddeley Gnome H.1400 turboshaft
Performance: cruising speed 167 km/h (104 mph); hovering ceiling 4815 m (15,800 ft)
Weight: maximum take-off 3629 kg (8,000 lb)
Dimensions: main rotor diameter 16.15 m (53 ft 0 in); length, rotors turning 18.94 m (63 ft 1½in); height 4.04 m (13 ft 3 in), main rotor disc area 204.95 m² (2,206.19 sq ft)

The Westland Whirlwind series was a precursor to the Wessex, with a little help from Sikorsky on both counts. Illustrated is a Whirlwind HAR.Mk 10.

Westland Widgeon

From 1924 Westland gained modest success with the **Westland Widgeon** two-seat lightplane that was des-igned and built initially as the **Widgeon Mk I** to compete in the Air Ministry's Two-Seat Light Aeroplane Trials of 1924. A braced high-wing monoplane with tandem open cockpits, it was powered initially by a 26-kW (35-hp) Blackburne Thrush radial piston engine. Damaged during trials, it was rebuilt as the **Widgeon Mk II**, then powered by a 45-kW (60-hp) Armstrong Siddeley Genet radial, and as a result of successful testing it was put into production as the **Widgeon Mk III**. A total of about 30 was built, these including a number designated **Widgeon Mk IIIA** by the manufacturer, which dif-fered in construction. They were pow-ered by a wide variety of piston engines as selected by individual owners, ranging from the 56-kW (75-hp) Armstrong Siddeley Genet II to the 89-kW (120-hp) Cirrus Hermes II. As powered by the 75-kW (100-hp) de Havilland Gipsy I, the Westland Widgeon Mk III had a maximum speed of 174 km/h (108 mph).

Westland Wyvern

The last fixed-wing military aircraft to be produced by the company, the **Westland W34** design was finalised to meet the requirements of Spec-ification N.11/44 for a single-seat ship-based strike aircraft. It was a demanding specification, the problems being compounded by selection of the new Rolls-Royce Eagle 24-cylinder sleeve valve engine to power it, but it was also required that the airframe should be suitable for easy installation of turboprop engines when these became available. A cantilever low-wing monoplane of all-metal stressed-skin construction with retractable tail-wheel landing gear, the first of six

VW867 was delivered as a Wyvern TF.Mk 2 and is seen in flight in its original form before the fitting of auxiliary tail fins.

Wyvern prototypes was flown on 12 December 1946. These were followed by 10 pre-production **Wyvern TF.Mk 1** aircraft, also with the Eagle engine, but this new engine had teething problems and development flying was so protracted that turboprop engines became available before any prod-uction decision was made. From the turboprops that were evaluated, the Armstrong Siddeley Python was selected for the 20 pre-production

Wyvern TF.Mk 2 aircraft, 13 deliv-ered being as such and the balance being completed to **Wyvern TF.Mk 4** (later **Wyvern S.Mk 4**) production

standard before delivery. The same engine was used to power the 90 production Wyvern S.Mk 4s, the first of which entered operational service with No. 813 Squadron in May 1953, some six and a half years after the first flight of the prototype. The type later equipped Nos 827, 830 and 831 Squadrons, No. 830 being the only squadron to use the Wyvern operationally, during the Suez crisis of late 1956. The Wyvern then continued in service until March 1958 when No. 813 Squadron was disbanded. A one-off variant was the **Wyvern T.Mk 3** two-seat trainer prototype.

Wibault 7

Michel Wibault's first aircraft was the **Wibault Wib.1** C.1 category single-seat fighter biplane powered by a 164-kW (220-hp) Hispano-Suiza 8Be engine. Tested in November 1918, the Wib.1 was too late for World War I and not built in quantity. The Société des Avions Michel Wibault was formed in late 1919 and two prototypes followed, the **Wib.2** of 1921 being a large two-seat biplane night bomber in the Bu.2 category and the **Wib.3** of 1923 being a C.1 parasol-wing fighter.

The **Wib.7** C.1. category prototype of 1924 was similar in configuration to the Wib.3, but powered by a 358-kW (480-hp) Gnome-Rhône 9Ad radial engine. The principal innovation was the all-metal system of construction which became a Wibault patent. Quantity production followed, 60 **Wib.72** fighters with strengthened wing bracing going to the French Aéronautique Militaire and entering service in 1929 with the 32ᵉ and 35ᵉ Régiments d'Aviation at Dijon and Lyons, respectively. Meanwhile, Wibault became a consultant to Vickers in the UK, which produced 26 Wib.7s under the designation **Vickers Type 121** for Chile.

The prototype **Wib.73** of 1927 was a C.1 fighter powered by a 336-kW (450-hp) Lorraine 12Eb engine. Plans to build the type in Poland were scrapped, although the P.Z.L. company eventually delivered three Wibault 7s with Wright radial engines and 25 Wibault 72s to the Polish military aviation in 1929-30. The Wib.73 was sold only to Paraguay, which acquired seven. A variant with strengthened fuselage and arrester hook, the **Wib.74**, was delivered to the French navy for operation from the carrier *Béarn*. Eighteen Wib.74 were followed by 18 examples of the camera-equipped **Wib.75**. These naval aircraft flew with Escadrilles 7C1 and 7C2 until the end of 1937.

Although it was hardly noticeable for its performance, Michel Wibault's post-war Wibault 7 of 1924 was an admirable fighter possessing great strength, considerable agility and a good field of view for the pilot, despite the position of the wing.

Wibault 280 series

The first flight of the 10-passenger **Wibault-Penhoët 280** prototype took place at Villacoublay in November 1930. Backed by money from the Penhoët shipyards at St Nazaire, Wibault produced the all-metal cantilever low-wing monoplane that performed well on the power of three 224-kW (300-hp) Hispano-Wright 9Qa radials. These were soon replaced by Gnome-Rhône 7Kb engines of the same power, the re-engined prototype then designated **Wib.281**. A second aircraft of the same type was built and then converted to **Wib.282** standard as the first of eight to be powered by three 261-kW (350-hp) Gnome-Rhône 7Kd radials. Similar to the Wib.281, these differed by having engine cowlings. Accommodating 12 passengers, one aircraft flew with the CIDNA company and several were flown on the Air Union Paris-London *Voile d 'Or* (Golden Clipper) service in 1933. Air France took delivery of the first of 10 **Wibault 283** aircraft in early 1934; these had the same power and passenger capacity as their predecessor type but had increased fuel capacity.

The Wibault 280 series was vitally important to the development of French commercial aviation during the 1930s. This aircraft is an Air Union Golden Clipper Wib.282T.

Wideroe C.5 Polar

Wideroe's Flyveselskap og Polarfly A/S, Norway's oldest air service operator, built in its workshops a single-engined general-purpose monoplane for its own use. Designated **Wideroe C.5 Polar**, it was a braced high-wing monoplane suitable for operation on floats, skis or wheels, and had an enclosed cabin able to accommodate a pilot and five passengers. The passenger seats were easily removable so that the interior could be used as an air ambulance or for cargo. Powered by a 261-kW (350-hp) Wright R-760-E2 radial, which gave this 13.72-m (45-ft 0-in) span aircraft a maximum speed of 240 km/h (149 mph) in landplane configuration, the C.5 was completed in 1948 and entered service, although built in only small numbers.

Designed by Birger Hönningstad, the Wideroe Polar was equally at home on wheels or floats.

Windecker Eagle

The **Windecker AC-7 Eagle 1** was a conventional low-wing monoplane accommodating four in an enclosed cabin. In its early prototype form, first flown on 7 October 1967, it had the distinction of being one of the earliest all-plastics aircraft, with an airframe constructed entirely of glass-fibre-reinforced material. The production prototype, incorporating retractable tricycle landing gear and powered by a 209-kW (280-hp) Continental IO-520-C flat-six engine, was flown in May 1970, and the first production aircraft was delivered on 7 October 1970. Only a small number were built, including one aircraft acquired by the USAF under the designation **YE-5B** which, with a three-bladed propeller of composite construction, was used to evaluate the radar signature of all-plastics aircraft. The 9.77-m (32-ft 0-in) span Eagle has a maximum speed of 340 km/h (211 mph).

The Eagle 1, built from Fibaloy, emerged coloured from the mould.

Wright Aeronautical aircraft

Wright aircraft of a different vintage to the Flyer and its derivatives included four biplanes developed in conjunction with the US Navy for air racing activities. These comprised the unequal-span **Navy Wright NW-1** landplane of 1922 and the equal-span **NW-2** floatplane of 1923, both powered by the 485-kW (650-hp) Wright T-2 Vee engine. They were followed by the equal-span **F2W-1** landplane and **F2W-2** floatplane of 1923 and 1924, respectively, both with the 582-kW (780-hp) Wright T-3 Tornado Vee engine. Mention should be made also of the **XF3W-1 Apache** single-seat fighter prototype acquired by the US Navy in 1926. Of biplane configuration and powered by a 336-kW (450-hp) Wright P-1 radial piston engine, this was used by the United States Navy as a testbed for the 313-kW (420-hp) Pratt & Whitney Wasp radial engine, and was flown experimentally both with wheel and float landing gear.

Wright brothers aircraft

Aviation enthusiasts, and many people with only casual interest in aircraft, are aware that the Wright Flyer built by the brothers Orville and Wilbur Wright has the distinction of being recognised officially as the world's first heavier-than-air craft to be flown in powered, manned, controlled and sustained flight. This was achieved at Kill Devil Hill, Kitty Hawk, North Carolina, on 17 December 1903, when, in the first of four flights made on that day, and piloted by Orville, the Flyer was airborne for 12 seconds and covered a distance of 36.6 m (120 ft); in the fourth and final flight, with Wilbur as pilot, a distance of 260 m (852 ft) was covered in 59 seconds. Few people are aware of the range of Wright aircraft pre- and post-Flyer, and for brevity and ease of reference they are listed below under the Variants section. Wright companies were formed in France, Germany and the UK in 1908, 1909 and 1913, respectively; the first American Wright Company was established in 1909. In 1916 the Wright Company merged with the Glenn L. Martin company to form the Wright-Martin Aircraft Corporation; a year later Martin withdrew from the association and the company was renamed the Wright Aeronautical Corporation.

Variants
Wright gliders: No. 1 (5.18-m/ 17-ft 0-in span) was flown during 1900

both as a kite and glider, followed by **No. 2** (6.71-m/22-ft 0-in span) which introduced controllable wing warping; **No. 3** (9.78-m/32-ft 1-in span), the first to embody the results of their own research was used for almost 1,000 gliding flights, modified as experience was gained, No. 3 led directly to the Flyer

Flyer: initial version with 9-kW (12-hp) engine of Wright design

Flyer II: similar to Flyer but with modified wing and engine tuned to deliver some 11 kW (15 hp); not considered successful

Flyer III: the first really practical and controllable model, using the engine and propellers of Flyer II; on 5 October 1905 made a flight of 39 minutes 23 seconds covering a distance of 38.9 km (24.2 miles)

Model A: first so-called standard biplane seating pilot and passenger; powered by 22.4-kW (30-hp) Wright engine and spanning 12.50 m (41 ft 0 in); maximum speed of 64 km/h

(40 mph); one procured by US Army

Model B: similar to Model A but introducing 26-kW (35-hp) Wright engine, wheel and skid landing gear, and rear- instead of forward-mounted elevators; two procured by US Army

Model C: improved version with 37-kW (50-hp) Wright engine and dual controls; seven procured by US Army and three by the US Navy, the latter with 45-kW (60-hp) Wright engine and twin floats designated **Model C-H** (hydro)

Model D: single-seat version of Model C; two procured by US Army which called them **Model D Scout**

Model Ex: smaller-size single-seat version of Model B for exhibition flying

Model F: the first Wright of modern appearance, this two-seater introduced a 67-kW (90-hp) Austro-Daimler engine and a conventional fuselage and tail unit; one procured by US Army

Model G Aeroboat: single aircraft acquired by US Navy; similar to Model F but with hull replacing fuselage

Model H-S: reduced-span version of the Model F with Wright 45-kW (60-hp) engine

Model K: floatplane version of the Model F; one procured by US Navy

Model L: single-seat version of Model F with 52-kW (70-hp) engine

Model R: known also as **Wright-Martin Model R**; featured configuration then conventional for

The Model C was confusingly designated Model B by the USN.

1916 period with unequal-span biplane wings, tandem open cockpits, fixed tailskid landing gear and powerplant of one 93-kW (125-hp) Hall-Scott engine with tractor propeller; 12 acquired by US Army, nine as landplanes and three as floatplanes

Yakovlev early aircraft

While working for the Moscow Air Force Engineering Academy, Aleksandr Sergeyevich Yakovlev designed his first aircraft in his spare time. Designated **AIR-1**, this was a compact biplane two-seat trainer powered by a 45-kW (60-hp) ADC Cirrus engine. An improved version, the **AIR-2**, introduced interchangeable floats, while the **AIR-3** was a monoplane version with braced parasol wing. Further development with extra fuel tankage resulted in the **AIR-4**; a military liaison variant was known as the **AIR-8**.

In 1931, Yakovlev designed the **AIR-5**, a braced high-wing cabin monoplane powered by a Wright Whirlwind engine. When licence-production of this engine fell through, the aircraft was redesigned to accept the indige-

nously designed M-11 radial and, as the **AIR-6**, 20 such aircraft were built for civil transport and ambulance duties.

Under the design bureau designation **AIR-14**, the **UT-1** was a cantilever low-wing monoplane aerobatic trainer used by the Soviet air force (V-VS). A total of 1,241 was built and several were used in 1942 with machine-guns and rocket launchers. Deriving from the **AIR-10** cantilever low-wing monoplane, the **Ya-20** was intended as a military trainer. Under the V-VS designation **UT-2**, the type was built in considerable numbers (7,243) and continued in service long after 1945. Yakovlev's first twin-engined design was the **AIR-17** (**UT-3** in V-VS service), a low-wing monoplane military crew trainer which featured a glazed

nose for the bomb-aimer. Only 30 were built, powered by 164-kW (220-hp) MV-6 engines and carrying two 7.7-mm (0.303-in) ShKAS machine-guns. A five-passenger civil version, the **Ya-19**, was abandoned in 1938 because of the worsening international situation.

Specification
Yakovlev UT-2
Type: primary trainer
Powerplant: one 75-kW (100-hp) M-11 radial piston engine

The UT-2 was of vital importance to the USSR during World War II, serving as the standard trainer.

Performance: maximum speed 210 km/h (130 mph); service ceiling 3500 m (11,485 ft); range 500 km (311 miles)
Weights: empty equipped 616 kg (1,358 lb); maximum take-off 856 kg (1,887 lb)
Dimensions: span 10.20 m (33 ft 5½ in); length 7.00 m (22 ft 11½ in); wing area 17.12 m² (184.28 sq ft)

Yakovlev Yak-1

Yakovlev Yak-1M of the 1st 'Warszawa' Fighter Regiment, Soviet air force, operating in the Warsaw area of Poland in late 1944.

Design of the **Yakovlev Yak-1** medium-altitude interceptor/fighter began in November 1938, and from it evolved a series of remarkable aircraft (produced in vast numbers) which made an important mark in the history of aviation. Known initially as the **I-26**, the type had a wooden wing combined with a fuselage of mixed construction and main landing gear units retracting inwards into the underside of the wing. The I-26 looked a thoroughbred and was dubbed 'Beauty' by its design team. Flown initially on 13 January 1940, the first prototype was soon lost in a fatal accident, but the development programme was continued without any break by the second prototype which incorporated some improvements. A pre-production batch of Yak-1s was flying by the end of the year and 64 initial series machines had also been completed by then. Changes were introduced during the course of production, and many aircraft of the main variants were completed from early 1942 with all increased span more pointed wing. A new pilot's canopy and cut-down rear fuselage were introduced on the **Yak-1B** and reduction of overall weight was achieved with the **Yak-1M**. The mount of many leading Soviet fighter pilots, Yak-1s

equipped a high proportion of fighter *eskadrilli* from 1942 onwards, when the type was phased out of production in mid-1943 a total of 8,721 series aircraft of all versions had been completed.

Variants
I-26: designation of two prototypes
Yak-1: in product version; from October 1941 had M-105PA engine
Yak-1B: originated as field modification with all-round vision cockpit canopy and cut-down rear fuselage decking, accepted officially in July 1942 and in full production early 1943; many Yak-1Bs and some Yak-1s and Yak-1Ms had a new, more-pointed wing
Yak-1M: many structural changes to reduce weight, revised aircraft introduced on production lines in late

1942; incorporated pilot's canopy introduced on Yak-1B and powered by 940-kW (1,260-hp) M-105PF engine; maximum speed increased to 585 km/h (364 mph) at 3800 m (12,465 ft)
I-28: three experimental aircraft with new wing of reduced span, two-stage supercharger and intended for high-altitude operation; during tests in June 1942 these aircraft attained 665 km/h (413 mph) at 10000 m (32,810 ft)
I-30: two prototypes introducing improved all-metal version of I-28 wing and heavier armament; one had retractable tailwheel
I-33: small batch reported as built in 1943 with the 1007-kW (1,350-hp) M-106 engine; maximum speed 610 km (379 mph) at 3600 m (11,810 ft) but soon withdrawn as engine unreliable

Specification
Yakovlev Yak-1 (early production)
Type: single-seat interceptor/fighter
Powerplant: one 783-kW (1,050-hp) M-105P Vee piston engine
Performance: maximum speed 540 km/h (336 mph) at sea level; service ceiling 10000 m (32,810 ft); range 700 km (435 miles)
Weights: empty equipped 2347 kg (5,174 lb); maximum take-off 2847 kg (6,276 lb)
Dimensions: span 10.00 m (32 ft 9¾ in); length 8.47 m (27 ft 9½ in); height 2.64 m (8 ft 8 in); wing area 17.15 m² (184.61 sq ft)
Armament: one engine-mounted 20-mm ShVAK cannon and one 12.7-mm (0.5-in) UBS machine-gun in fuselage, plus two 100-kg (220-lb) bombs on underwing racks

Yakovlev Yak-2 and Yak-4
to
Yakovlev Yak-42

Yakovlev Yak-2 and Yak-4

Intended originally as a high-speed reconnaissance aircraft, the **Yakovlev Ya-22** prototype was powered by two M-103 engines and made its maiden flight on 22 February 1939. A two-seat low-wing monoplane with wooden wings and a fuselage of mixed construction, the Yak-22 had retractable tailwheel landing gear and a tail unit incorporating a twin fin-and-rudder assembly. Yakovlev was then instructed to modify the design to serve as a bomber, the aircraft being redesignated **BB-22** (*blizhnii bombardirovshchik* or short-range bomber). This resulted in major revisions of accommodation, armament and fuel storage, plus the provision of an internal bomb bay. The first series BB-22 was completed on 31 December 1939 and flown on skis on 20 February 1940. By that time two factories were in production and experimental variants – the **R-12** photographic reconnaissance aircraft and **I-29** (or **BB-22 IS**) long-range escort fighter – were being prepared for test flights. The BB-22 was redesignated **Yak-2** at the end of 1940, and as powered by two 716-kW (960-hp)

M-103 Vee engines had a maximum speed of 530 km/h (329 mph) at sea level service ceiling of 8800 m (28,870 ft) and range of 800 km (497 miles).

In 1940 the basic design was further refined to improve the crew positions, field of view and armour protection; the M-105 engine was introduced with better protection for the fuel system, and provisions were made for external bomb racks. Then redesignated **Yak-4**, the aircraft entered production in the autumn of 1940 and about 600 of both versions were built, the majority of them Yak-4s. They were not particularly successful in service, many of them being lost in the early days of the German invasion.

Specification
Yakovlev Yak-4
Type: light bomber
Powerplant: two 783-kW (1,050-hp) Klimov M-105 Vee piston engines
Performance: maximum speed 545 km/h (339 mph); service ceiling 9500 m (31,170 ft); range 1200 km (746 miles)

Weights: empty equipped 4000 kg (8,818 lb); maximum take-off 5200 kg (11,464 lb)
Dimensions: span 14.00 m (45 ft 11¾ in); length 9.34 m (30 ft 7¾ in); wing area 29.70 m² (319.70 sq ft)
Armament: two 7.7-mm (0.303-in) ShKAS machine-guns, plus a maximum bomb load of 800 kg (1,764 lb)

Better known for his fighters during World War II, Yakovlev also produced the excellent Yak-2 light bomber, seen here in the form of its BB-22 prototype.

Yakovlev Yak-3

Design began at the end of 1941 of a single-seat fighter using the new VK-107 engine, requiring the least-possible drag, smallest dimensions and weight consistent with a manoeuvrable and tough machine. Due to delays with the new engine and pressure to build the maximum number of aircraft already on the production lines, this new **Yak-3** programme was shelved. A new small wing was developed and tested along with other changes on a Yak-1M in late 1942, and the first Yak-3 prototype was flown in late 1943. Although evaluation aircraft flew in combat, the first series Yak-3s did not enter operation with the 91st IAP until July 1944. The Yak-3 was found to be an exceptional dogfighter at altitudes up to 4000 m (13,125 ft). Its improved performance was remarkable, particularly as the initial non-availability of the VK-107 engine forced reliance to be placed on the VK-105PF-2 that had powered earlier Yaks. Built to a total of 4,848, the Yak-3 achieved fame and a very high score rate against German aircraft in 1944-45. The Yak-3 equipped the famous Free French 'Normandie-Niemen' unit, and achieved its peak of perfection when the VK-107A engine of 1268 kW (1,700 hp) became available in limited numbers from August 1944, the type's maximum speed then improving to 720 km/h (447 mph) at 6000 m (19,685 ft).

Yakovlev Yak-3 of Major General G. N. Zakharove, commander of the 303rd Fighter Aviation Division, Soviet air force, during 1944.

Variants
Yak-3: initial production version; deliveries to V-VS began in July 1944
Yak-3/VK-107A: about 100 built; in operation 1945
Yak-3/VK-108: experimental and fastest Yak-3 aircraft with VK-108 engine; first flown 19 December 1944, demonstrated a maximum speed of 745 km/h (463 mph) at 6000 m (19,685 ft)
Yak-3T: anti-tank version built in small numbers with 37-mm N-37 cannon and two 20-mm B-20S cannon
Yak-3T-57: one-off Yak-3T with a 57-mm OKB-16-57 cannon
Yak-3P: small quantity with three 20-mm B-20 cannon and two 12.7-mm (0.5-in) UBS machine-guns
Yak-3RD (or **Yak-3D**): experimental

adaptation of series aircraft to take Glushko RD-1 rocket unit in tail
Yak-3V: high-altitude variant
Yak-3PD: flown in 1944 with supercharged VK-106 engine; intended to have pressurised cabin
Yak-3U: rebuilt aircraft with ASh-82FN radial engine and twin B-20 cannon; despite heavy engine overall weight, weighed less than standard Yak-3; during series of test flights started on 12 May 1945 demonstrated a maximum speed of 710 km/h (441 mph) at 6100 m (20,015 ft)
Yak-3TK: VK-107A-powered version tested in 1945 with turbocharger
Yak-3UTI; developed as conversion trainer in late 1945 with ASh-21 radial engine; became eventually Yak-11

Specification
Type: short-range interceptor fighter
Powerplant: one 969-kW (1,300-hp) Klimov VK-105PF-2 Vee piston engine
Performance: maximum speed 655 km/h (407 mph) at 3100 m (10,170 ft); service ceiling 10700 m (35,105 ft); range 900 km (559 miles)
Weights: empty equipped 2105 kg (4,641 lb); maximum take-off 2660 kg (5,864 lb)
Dimensions: span 9.20 m (30 ft 2¼ in); length 8.49 m (27 ft 10¼ in); height 2.42 m (7 ft 11¼ in); wing area 14.83 m² (159.53 sq ft)
Armament: one engine-mounted 20-mm ShVAK cannon and two synchronised 12.7-mm (0.5-in) UBS machine-guns

Yakovlev Yak-6 and Yak-8

Conceived as a light utility transport, the twin-engined low-wing **Yakovlev Yak-6** was largely of wooden construction and flown for the first time in June 1942; it had retractable tailwheel landing gear and accommodated two crew and four passengers. An NBB (or short-range night bomber) version had external racks for five 100-kg (220-lb) bombs under the fuselage and provi-

sion for a single 7.7-mm (0.303-in) ShKAS machine-gun, but the Yak-6 could also be equipped to carry stores or freight (including a 500-kg/1,102-lb external load) or for use as an ambulance aircraft, glider tug or close-support aircraft carrying 10 RS-82 rockets. Often flown with the main landing gear

units locked down, the Yak-6 was also used to supply partisans, and by 1944 most operational units had one of these aircraft to ferry personnel between bases. Production totalled about 1,000.

The **Yak-6M** was an improved version which finally led to the somewhat larger **Yak-8**, the prototype of which was first flown at the beginning of 1944. This was to have been a dedicated transport, essentially for military use, with accommodation for up to six passengers, but in the absence of anticipated higher-power engines its performance was disappointing and no series production ever took place.

Specification
Yakovlev Yak-6
Type: multi-role light military transport
Powerplant: two 104-kW (140-hp) M-11F radial piston engines
Performance: maximum speed 230 km/h (143 mph); service ceiling 3380 m (11,090 ft); range 580 km (360 miles)
Weights: empty equipped 1433 kg

(3,159 lb); maximum take-off 2500 kg (5,512 lb)
Dimensions: span 14.00 m (45 ft 11¼ in); length 10.35 m (33 ft 11½ in); wing area 29.60 m² (318.62 sq ft)

The Yak-6 was built in quite large numbers as a cheap but nonetheless capable transport.

Yakovlev Yak-7

In parallel with the I-26 (or Ya-26), the Yakovlev design bureau developed a two-seat version under the designation **Yakovlev Ya-27**. One pre-production I-26 was completed to this configuration. It was intended to serve not only as a dual-control fighter trainer, but also as a liaison and unit support aircraft. Compared with the I-26, the Ya-27 was simplified and of reduced weight, the tandem cockpits being enclosed by an extended glazed canopy. The resulting **Yak-7** aircraft entered production in May 1941 and was soon found to have better flying qualities than those displayed by series Yak-1s. This performance, combined with the urgent need for more fighters, led to production of a single-seat version of which the first was flown in June 1941; in the following month the fighter was officially designated **Yak-7A** and the two-seater **Yak-7V**. By the end of 1941 a new single-seater, the **Yak-7B**, had replaced the Yak-7A. Total delivery of all versions of the Yak-7 was 6,399 aircraft, production terminating in early 1943; of this number, some 1,500 were Yakovlev Yak-7Vs.

Yakovlev Yak-7, of an unidentified fighter regiment, Soviet air force, during 1942.

Variants
Ya-27: prototype two-seater converted from early pre-production I-26
Yak-7: original designation for two-seat liaison/trainer and also for first single-seat conversion
Yak-7A: series version of single-seat fighter with 783-kW (1,050-hp) M-105P engine; rear cockpit deleted and faired over, pointed wing with span of 10.25 m (33 ft 7½ in)
Yak-7V: definitive designation for two-seater which by July 1941 was in large-scale production; same wing span as Yak-7A; some Yak-7Vs had fixed

landing gear and could operate with wheels or skis
Yak-7B: wing span reduced to 10.00 m (32 ft 9¾ in) but with same wing area as Yak-7A and Yak-7V; landing gear simplified and equipment improved; very important type in V-VS inventory that performed well against enemy fighters; some 5,000 of this version built
Yak-7D: experimental version with wooden wing incorporating metal spars and increased fuel capacity
Yak-7/M-82: version with redesigned forward fuselage to mount an M-82 radial engine and tested in 1941; armed

with one fuselage-mounted 12.7-mm (0.5-in) UBS machine-gun and two 20-mm ShVAK cannon
Yak-7T: two aircraft tested with engine-mounted heavy cannon for anti-tank duties; one had 37-mm NS-37 and the other 45-mm NS-45
Yak-7K: field conversion of 1944 for use as VIP transport with very comfortable rear cockpit; several conversions completed
Yak-7PVRD: two series aircraft tested with two DM-4C ramjets on pylons under wings; maximum speed enhanced by 90 km/h (56 mph)

Yakovlev Yak-9

A development of the experimental Yak-7DI fighter, the original **Yakovlev Yak-9** differed in having a revised rudder and wooden wings incorporating metal spars; the series version, which entered production in the summer of 1942, also introduced a retractable tailwheel. Deliveries to V-VS IAPs (fighter regiments) began in October 1942 and the type was soon engaged in the Battle of Stalingrad. By February 1943 production aircraft were being built with reduced-span wings that incorporated duralumin ribs and with the initial powerplant (an M105PF or M-105PF-1 being replaced by the 925-kW (1,240-hp) M-105PF-3. The Yak-9 operated with a wide variety of armament, including all types of aircraft cannon then in production in the Soviet Union, and during 1943 there appeared variants which developed the full potential of the Yak-9 for use in anti-tank, light bomber and long-range escort roles.

The second generation of Yak-9s began with the **Yak-9U** prototype of late 1943, which introduced a redesigned airframe, a new wing of increased span and area, and the more-powerful VK-107 engine; to overcome resulting centre of gravity problems the wing was moved slightly forward. Production of the Yak-9 ended in 1946 after a record 16,769 aircraft had been delivered. Main post-war operators, apart from the Soviet Union, were Bulgaria, Poland and Yugoslavia.

Variants
Yak-9: prototype developed from Yak-7DI, and initial series in production from mid-1942; armament of one 20-mm

Yakovlev Yak-9 of René Schall, commander of the 4ᵉ Escadrille, GC3 'Normandie-Niemen', Free French air force, based at Dubrovka near Smolensk during June 1944.

ShVAK cannon and one 12.7-mm (0.5-in) UBS machine-gun, plus six RS-82 rockets or two 100-kg (220-lb) FAB-100 bombs
Yak-9M: standard version with cannon and two 12.7-mm (0.5-in) UBS machine-guns
Yak-9D: long-range escort version with additional fuel extending range up to 1330 km (826 miles) and introducing M-105PF-3 engine; in operation from summer 1943
Yak-9T: tested December 1942 with 11P-37 anti-armour cannon and wing racks for 2.5-kg (5.5-lb) B hollow-charge bombs in special containers; other Yak-9Ts had MP-20, VYa-23 or MP-23VV cannon; entered service in early 1943
Yak-9K: saw limited service from 1943; armed with 45-mm cannon
Yak-9B: special bomber version built in limited numbers; internal bay behind cockpit containing four 100-kg (220-lb) FAB-100 bombs or containers with 128 PTAB light bombs
Yak-9MPVO: limited number for use in night-fighter role and equipped with searchlight and RPK-10 radio compass

Yak-9DD: ultra-long-range escort fighter; like Yak-9D but with additional fuel capacity bringing maximum range to 2200 km (1,367 miles); used to escort US heavy bombers on shuttle raids against Romanian oil wells; also equipped 236th IAD (fighter division) based at Bari in southern Italy, and operated for a time over Yugoslavia in support of partisans
Yak-9U: prototype flew December 1943 with wing of all-metal basic structure; initially had M-105PF-2 but more-powerful VK-107A engine phased into production line from late 1944
Yak-9UT: version of Yak-9U with light alloy stressed skinning over entire airframe; entered service early 1945
Yak-9UV: tandem two-seat conversion trainer
Yak-9P: in addition to engine-mounted cannon had one or two fuselage-mounted synchronised 20-mm cannon
Yak-9R: tactical or photo-reconnaissance version with specialised equipment
Yak-9PD: high-altitude experimental

version with M-105PD engine incorporating two-stage gear-driven supercharger and armed with single 20-mm cannon; believed small batch saw limited actions against high-flying German reconnaissance aircraft late in World War II

Specification
Yakovlev Yak-9U
Type: single-seat interceptor/ fighter
Powerplant: one 1230-kW (1,650-hp) Klimov VK-107A Vee piston engine
Performance: maximum speed 698 km/h (434 mph) at 5000 m (16,405 ft); service ceiling 11900 m (39,040 ft); range 870 km (541 miles)
Weights: empty equipped 2716 kg (5,988 lb); maximum take-off 3098 kg (6,830 lb)
Dimensions: span 9.77 m (32 ft 0¾ in); length 8.55 m (28 ft 0½ in); height 2.96 m (9 ft 8½ in)
Armament: one 20-mm MP-20 cannon and two 12.7-mm (0.5-in) UBS machine-guns plus provision for two 100-kg (220-lb) bombs on racks underwing

Yakovlev Yak-10 and Yak-13

A four-seat strut-braced high-wing cabin monoplane, the **Yakovlev Yak-10** was of simple design and of mixed construction. First flown in late 1944 under the provisional designation **Yak-14**, the aircraft did not perform well and was redesigned. Official testing was finally concluded in June 1945 and 40 aircraft, then redesignated Yak-10, were built for military liaison duties. Subsequent variants included the **Yak-10V** with dual controls and the **Yak-10S** ambulance. The **Yak-10G** twin-float seaplane did not go into production, and a single example of the Yak-10 was flown with skis. The standard Yak-10 with the 108-kW (145-hp)

The Yak-13 was built for direct comparison with the high-wing Yak-10, and spanned 11.50 m (37 ft 8½ in) with a maximum speed of 250 km/h (155 mph) at sea level.

M-11FM engine had a maximum speed of 200 km/h (124 mph).

The **Yak-13**, known originally as the **Yak-12**, was a cantilever low-wing monoplane prototype built for comparison with the Yak-10. The engine cabin, rear fuselage and tailplane were almost identical with those of the Yak-10 and were combined with the new wing. Although found to perform well when tested in 1945, the Yak-13 was more

expensive to build than the high-winged Yak-10 (this feature was

retained in the later Yak-12 series), and no Yak-13 production was undertaken.

Yakovlev Yak-11

The prototype of the **Yakovlev Yak-11** two-seat advanced trainer was first flown in 1945 and known originally as the **Yak-3UTI**. Testing continued with the ASh-21 radial engine and a further refined prototype appeared in 1946, official tests being completed satisfactorily in October 1946. Then designated Yak-11, the aircraft had metal wings, a fuselage of mixed construction and fully retractable tailwheel landing gear, with the instructor and pupil seated beneath a continuous glazed canopy. Ordered into production for the V-VS, series Yak-11s were delivered from the summer of 1947. Total production in the Soviet Union was 3,859, and an additional 707 were built in Czechoslovakia from October 1953

The Yak-11 (seen here in the form of the Czech-built C-11) was derived from the Yak-3 fighter, but had the exceptional load factor of 15.4, and was powered by a neatly cowled engine.

under the designation **C-11**. In 1958 the **Yak-11U** version appeared with retractable tricycle landing gear; it was built in small numbers in both the Soviet Union and Czechoslovakia, the latter model being designated **C-11U**.

The Yak-11 proved a very successful aircraft and saw widespread service with Warsaw Pact countries, as well as in the Middle East and China, and established a number of world class records for speed over distance.

Specification
Yakovlev Yak-11
Type: advanced trainer/liaison aircraft
Powerplant: one 425-kW (570-hp) Shvetsov ASh-21 radial piston engine
Performance: maximum speed 465 km/h (289 mph); service ceiling 7100 m (23,295 ft); range 1280 km (795 miles)

Weights: empty equipped 1900 kg (4,189 lb); maximum take-off 2440 kg (5,379 lb)
Dimensions: span 9.40 m (30 ft 10 in); length 8.50 m (27 ft 10½in)
Armament: one synchronised 12.7-mm (0.5-in) UBS or 7.7-mm (0.303-in) ShKAS machine-gun

Yakovlev Yak-12

The prototype **Yak-12** made its maiden flight late in 1947. Although of similar configuration to the earlier Yak-10, it was a totally new design with a wing of different aerofoil section, a more extensively glazed fuselage seating two as standard but with provision for a third (rear) seat, revised tail unit, landing gear suitable for wheels or skis, and power provided by a 119-kW (160-hp) M-11FR radial engine.

Series production started almost immediately, deliveries being made to the V-VS for artillery spotting and liaison duties. Specialised versions of the original production model followed, and availability of the more-powerful AI-14R engine in 1950 led to the **Yak-12R** prototype, flown in June that year, and to a new generation of aircraft, with the final, extensively-built four-seat Yak-12A entering service in 1957. Production was established in parallel and then exclusively in Poland, as the **PZL 101 Gawron,** while various Chinese copies were developed and mass-produced in that country. Large numbers of this adaptable aircraft

The Yak-12 was built extensively in the USSR, Poland and China.

remain in service, many having been passed to flying schools or being used by Aeroflot and the Soviet civil aviation authority.

Variants
Yak-12: original prototype and initial series aircraft; at least 300 built, mostly for military use
Yak-12A: production version introduced with new wing and redesigned tailplane; some 1,500 built in Soviet Union, used mainly for civil purposes including local short-range passenger services and for agricultural work; operated by V-VS for liaison
Yak-12B: experimental STOL variant of biplane configuration and with 224-kW (300-hp) AI-14RF engine
Yak-12GR: twin-float seaplane version of original series aircraft with M-IIFR engine
Yak-12M: introduced in 1955 and had extended rear fuselage, greatly enlarged tail surfaces and

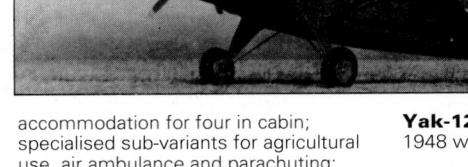

accommodation for four in cabin; specialised sub-variants for agricultural use, air ambulance and parachuting; production exceeded 1,000 and was also licence-built in Poland
Yak-12R: first version with AI-12R introduced increased-span wing with all-metal basic structure; standard accommodation for a pilot and two passengers; some 2,000 built; used by V-VS and Soviet civil aviation authority; specialised agricultural, light freight and ambulance versions; several versions licence-built in Poland
Yak-12S: M-11FR-engined ambulance version first flown 1948; accommodated single stretcher and medical attendant with stowage for medical kit

Yak-12SKh: agricultural variant of 1948 with chemical hopper

Specification
Yakovlev Yak-I2A
Type: liaison and general-purpose aircraft
Powerplant: one 194-kW (260-hp) Ivchenko AI-14R radial piston engine
Performance: maximum speed 230 km/h (143 mph); service ceiling 4550 m (14,930 ft); range 1070 km (665 miles)
Weights: empty equipped 1059 kg (2,335 lb); maximum take-off 1588 kg (3,501 lb)
Dimensions: span 12.60 m (41 ft 4 in); length 9.00 m (29 ft 6¼ in); height 2.44 m (8 ft 0 in); wing area 22.66 m² (243.92 sq ft)

Yakovlev Yak-15

The first successful Soviet jet-propelled fighter and the first to enter squadron service, the single-seat **Yakovlev Yak-15** was a straightforward conversion from the piston-engined Yak-3. A new deep forward fuselage accommodated the RD-10 turbojet, and many special features included a frameless windscreen with aft-sliding blown canopy and heavier sheet metal skin beneath the rear fuselage as protection

against the heat of the exhaust efflux. Development began in February 1945 and although there were previous trial 'lift-offs', the first flight was delayed until 24 April 1946. It was shown publicly at Tushino, in August .On that day it took to the air at the hands of pilot Ivanov, along with the first MiG-9 Twelve pre-production aircraft were completed in the autumn of that year, these being followed by 280 series air-

craft delivered to the V-VS during 1947. Variants included the **Yak-21** two-seat dual-control trainer and the experimental **Yak-15U** with tricycle landing gear.

Specification
Yakovlev Yak-15
Type: single-seat fighter
Powerplant: one 8.83-kN (1,984-lb) thrust RD-10 turbojet
Performance: maximum speed 786

km/h (488 mph) at 5000 m (16,405 ft); service ceiling 13350 m (43,800 ft); range 510 km (317 miles)
Weights: empty equipped 2350 kg (5,181 lb); maximum take-off 2635 kg (5,809 lb)
Dimensions: span 9.20 m (30 ft 2¼ in); length 8.78 m (28 ft 9¾ in); wing area 14.85 m² (159.85 sq ft)
Armament: two nose-mounted 23-mm NS-23 cannon

Yakovlev Yak-17

First flown in early 1947, the **Yakovlev Yak-17** prototype differed from the Yak-15 mainly in having retractable tricycle landing gear; other improvements included the more powerful RD-10A turbojet, a degree of internal and external redesign, and structural strengthening. The problem of short range was tackled by the provision of jettisonable fuel tanks beneath the wingtips. Series production ended in 1948 with the 430th aircraft, and examples of the Yak-17 were presented to the Czech and Polish air arms. The **Yak-17UTI** was a tandem two-seat dual-control trainer variant, the prototype flying in mid-1947 and entering production almost immediately. As well as serving with the Soviet air arm, Yak-17UTI trainers were supplied in small numbers to China and Poland.

Specification
Yakovlev Yak-17
Type: single-seat fighter
Powerplant: one 9.81-kN (2,205-lb) thrust RD-IOA turbojet
Performance: maximum speed 750 km/h (466 mph) at 6000 m (19,685 ft); service ceiling 12750 m (41,830 ft); range with tip tanks 717 km (446 miles)
Weights: empty equipped 2430 kg (5,357 lb); maximum take-off with external fuel 3323 kg (7,326 lb)
Dimensions and Armament: as for Yak-15

Superficially a redesign of the Yak-15, with retractable tricycle undercarriage, the Yak-17 also benefited from an internal redesign.

Yakovlev Yak-18

In 1943 the basic Yakovlev UT-2M trainer was given a number of improvements, including enclosed cockpits and modified landing gear with tailwheel. This revised aircraft was designated UT-2MV and from it was developed the **Yakovlev Yak-18** prototype, flown in 1945, which had a basic all-metal structure with mixed fabric and metal covering. After extensive testing, the Yak-18 was accepted for production in early 1947, and several thousand of the basic design were built for military and civil use as a primary trainer, both in the Soviet Union and in many other countries inside and outside the Communist Bloc. Many developments followed, a number of them being built in quantity. The last version, the **Yak-18T**, was almost a new aircraft which was produced extensively from 1974 and is still in production. In total, over 9,000 of all versions have been built to date and the type is now being increasingly exported to the West..

Variants
Yak-18: prototype and first production series; used widely by military and civil flying schools in former Soviet Union, by DOSAAF clubs, in former Soviet Bloc and by number of third-world countries; Soviet civil Yak-18s gained a number of FAI-recognised records

The Yak-18 was the standard basic trainer in the Soviet Union and its 'friendly' nations for over 30 years. Still in production, it is now appearing in the West.

between 1949 and 1954
Yak-18U: prototype flown in 1954; series production in small numbers began in the following year; entirely new retractable tricycle landing gear
Yak-18A: prototype tested in 1957 as Yak-20 with 194-kW (260-hp) AI-14R engine, structural strengthening, increased wing span (10.60 m/34 ft 9¼ in), redesigned tail unit, greater fuel capacity and many refinements; built in large numbers and total of this and earlier versions when production ceased at the end of 1967 was 6,760
Yak-18P: specialised single-seat aerobatic aircraft developed from 1959, with the ability to fly inverted for up to five minutes; built in two variants with different cockpit arrangements; Yak-18Ps took part with fair success in many international aerobatic contests
Yak-18PM: 1965 aerobatic development with 224-kW (300-hp) AI-14RF engine, cockpit further aft and other improvements; won 1966 international championships at Tushino aerodrome (Moscow)
Yak-18PS: like Yak-18PM but with

retractable tailwheel landing gear; first flown during 1969
Yak-18T: totally reworked light passenger transport (for Soviet civil aviation authority, or GVF) of which design began in 1964; principal version carries three passengers plus baggage transport, but four other variants comprise trainer, advanced trainer, mail or cargo aircraft with 250-kg (551-lb) payload, and air ambulance; prototype flown in 1967 and pre-production aircraft used for a variety of trials until 1973; series aircraft available from 1974; more than the original five versions are now planned; by 1993 over 2,000 have been built and production is continuing, series aircraft

have the 268-kW (360-hp) M-14P engine, giving a maximum speed of 295 km/h (183 mph)

Specification
Yak-18 (first series)
Type: primary trainer
Powerplant: one 119-kW (160-hp) M-11FR radial piston engine
Performance: maximum speed 248 km/h (154 mph); service ceiling 4000 m (13,125 ft); range 1050 km (652 miles)
Weights: empty equipped 816 kg (1,799 lb); maximum take-off 1120 kg (2,469 lb)
Dimensions: span 10.30 m (33 ft 9½ in); length 8.07 m (26 ft 5¼ in); wing area 17.00 m² (182.99 sq ft)

Yakovlev Yak-23

Although the Yakovlev bureau tested a number of barrel-fuselage jet fighter prototypes in the period up to 1951, the main emphasis was on developing the Yak-15 concept to the ultimate as a back-up to the more sophisticated MiG-15. Experimental fighters developed to achieve this aim included the Yakovlev Yak-19 powered by an RD-10F and test flown early in 1947; the Yak-25 with the more powerful RD-500 turbojet which flew in October 1947; the swept-wing **Yak-30** whose maiden flight took place in September 1948; and the **Yak-50** with a VK-1 engine, flown on 15 July 1949. All of these remained experimental fighters, but the Yak-23 was developed for series production. The Yak-23 retained the well-tried fuselage layout of the Yak-15 and Yak-17, was of stressed-skin construction and designed for ease of maintenance, the entire forward fuselage being easily removable. The type differed externally from the Yak-17 in having much enlarged vertical tail surfaces, the horizontal surfaces being mounted some way up the fin, and the

The Yakovlev Yak-23 may be regarded as the culmination of the Yak-15 basic design with underslung engines, though in this refined development the tricycle landing gear was fully retractable into internal bays.

main landing gear units were set much further inboard with the undercarriage retracting into the lower fuselage.

First flight of the prototype was on 17 June 1947, and with minor changes the Yak-23 went into production at the beginning of 1948. A total of 310 was built, many of them serving with the Soviet Union's East European allies, including Bulgaria, Czechoslovakia (designation **S-101**), Poland and Romania. The **Yak-23UTI** trainer was tested in 1949 and the Romanians rebuilt one single-seater as a dual-control trainer in 1956.

Specification
Yakovlev Yak-23
Type: single-seat fighter

Powerplant: one 15.59-kN (3,505-lb) thrust RD-500 turbojet
Performance: maximum speed 975 km/h (606 mph) at optimum altitude; service ceiling 14800 m (48,555 ft);

range 1200 km (745 miles) with external fuel
Weights: empty equipped 2000 kg (4,409 lb); maximum take-off 3036 kg (6,693 lb)

Yakovlev Yak-24

When development of the large **Yakovlev Yak-24** transport helicopter began at the end of 1951, the design team had little experience of rotary-wing aircraft, such experience being limited to the co-axial **EG** of 1947 and **Yak-100** of 1949, neither of which progressed beyond the experimental stage. Considerable difficulties were encountered by the large design team, but after extensive ground testing, tethered flights were achieved by the fourth prototype from 3 July 1952. With official tests completed on later prototypes, production began in April 1955, and only four months later evaluation aircraft were demonstrated at Tushino airport during the Soviet Aviation Day display. At least 100 of these twin-rotor helicopters were built, the large fuselage accommodating a crew of three and up to 30 armed troops or 18 stretchers cases, or 3000 kg (6,614 lb) of freight/vehicles with access by rear ramp. The structure

This Yak-24 is of the definitive production standard, with dihedral endplate fins. The type was never truly successful, but over 100 were built.

included horizontal braced tail surfaces with endplate fins, and the fuselage was supported on the ground by fixed quadricycle landing gear.

The **Yak-24UB,** flown in December 1957, included many design improvements and was placed in production from 1959, about 50 being delivered; this version could carry 40 fully equipped troops or up to 3500 kg (7,716 lb) of cargo. The civil **Yak-24A** of 1960 accommodated 30 passengers, and the Yak-24 was a VIP transport with a shorter fuselage and provision for nine passengers.

Specification
Yakovlev Yak-24
Type: military heavy-duty helicopter

Powerplant: two 1268-kW (1,700-hp) Shvetsov ASh-82V radial piston engines **Performance:** maximum speed 175 km/h (109 mph); service ceiling 4200 m (13,780 ft); range 266 km (165 miles) **Weights:** empty equipped 10607 kg (23,384 lb); maximum take-off 14270 kg (31,460 lb) **Dimensions:** rotor diameter, each 20.00 m (65 ft 7½ in); length of fuselage 21.34 m (70 ft 0 in); rotor disc area, total 314.15 m² (3,381.60 sq ft)

Yakovlev Yak-25

First seen at the Soviet Aviation Day display at Tushino in July 1955, the **Yakovlev Yak-25** twin-jet all-weather and night interceptor marked a new phase in the design of Yakovlev fighters. It was in configuration a mid-wing monoplane of all-metal construction with swept wings and tail surfaces, had retractable bicycle landing gear with small wingtip outriggers, and was powered in prototype and early production form by two 2200-kg (4,850-lb) thrust AM-5 turbojets, a new slim axial-flow turbine mounted in low-drag underwing nacelles. The first prototype is believed to have flown during 1953 and the type was in production by late 1954, an estimated figure of no more than 1,000 being built before production was terminated in the late 1950s. The original production version was allocated the NATO reporting name **'Flashlight-A'** and accommo-

Seen in immaculate pre-delivery metal finish is a Yak-25, whose most striking features are the use of two wing-mounted turbojets to leave the nose free for the large interception radar.

dated a crew of two (pilot and radar operator). There are unresolved problems of designation regarding subsequent developments, which include: **'Flashlight-B'** (Yak-25R ?), a prototype fighter/reconnaissance aircraft with the second crew member in the nose; an improved **'Flashlight-C'** (Yak-27P ?), a tactical reconnaissance version with increased wing span and, like later production 'Flashlight-As', powered by an improved RD-9 turbojet in longer nacelles. A high-altitude reconnaissance version with unswept extended-span wings (21.50 m/70 ft 6 in) and known to NATO as **'Mandrake'**

was probably designated **Yak-25RD** or **Yak-26.** None of these aircraft remain in service.

Specification
Yakovlev Yak-25 'Flashlight-A' (late production)
Type: all-weather/night interceptor
Powerplant: two 27.46-kN (6,173-lb) thrust RD-9 turbojets

Performance: maximum speed 1090 km/h (677 mph) at optimum altitude **Weight:** maximum take-off 11350 kg (25,022 lb) **Dimensions:** span 11.00 m (36 ft 1 in); length 15.67 m (51 ft 5 in); wing area 31.50 m² (339.07 sq ft) **Armament:** two forward-firing 37-mm N-37 cannon in underfuselage fairing

Yakovlev Yak-28

Although of the same general configuration as the earlier Yak-25 and its associated aircraft, the **Yakovlev Yak-28** first seen during the 1961 Aviation Day display was a shoulder-wing monoplane with the leading edge extended further forward. The other externally noticeable changes included the adoption of the bicycle landing gear (the rear unit being moved farther aft to permit the incorporation of a weapons bay in the lower fuselage), the introduction of a taller fin and rudder, and changed powerplant in revised nacelles. The delivery of production aircraft began in 1962 with the **Yak-28P** all-weather interceptor which has the NATO reporting name **'Firebar'.** Remaining in service in substantial numbers into the 19890s, no examples are now in use. A strike **Yak-28I** (NATO **'Brewer-C'**), which is believed

'Brewer-D' was a multi-sensor reconnaissance aircraft. The bay, used for weapons in other variants, could be occupied by one of three mission pallets.

to have entered production during 1963, introduced a lengthened forward fuselage navigator/bomb-aimer's position, being followed by the multi-sensor reconnaissance **Yak-28R** (**'Brewer-D'**) and an ECM escort version known as **'Brewer-E'** (**Yak-28E** ?). The remaining variant, the **Yak-28U** (**'Maestro'**), is a tandem dual-control trainer, and may be conversions of earlier Yak-28s.

Specification
Yakovlev Yak-28P 'Firebar' (late production)
Type: all-weather interceptor

Powerplant: two 60.8-kN (13,669-lb) afterburning thrust Tumanskii R-11 turbojets **Performance:** maximum speed 1180 km/h (733 mph), service ceiling 16000 m (52,495 ft) **Weights:** maximum take-off 19000 kg (41,890 lb) **Dimensions:** span 12.95 m (42 ft 6 in); length 23.00 m (75 ft 5 in); wing area 37.60 m² (404.74 sq ft) **Armament:** two AA-2 (NATO 'Atoll'), AA-2-2 ('Advanced Atoll') or AA-3 ('Anab') air-to-air missiles

Yakovlev Yak-38

Development of a V/STOL fighter for the Soviet navy's new 'Kiev' class of aircraft-carriers began during the early 1960s. Intensive studies bore fruit in the shape of a number of Yakovlev

Yak-36 'Freehand' research aircraft, with a bicycle undercarriage under the fuselage augmented by wingtip outriggers. The aircraft is believed to have been powered by a pair of 36.78-kN

(8,267-lb) Koliesov engines, each with a rotating nozzle. These gave a tremendous thrust margin, and powerful autostabilisers gave a rock-steady hover, using reaction control 'puffer jets' in the tail, wingtips and at the tip of a long nose-probe. The Yak-36 was not an operational aircraft, although it

did lead directly to the **Yak-38**. This first flew during 1971 (reportedly as the **Yak-36MP**), and was first seen during trials of the *Kiev* in the Black Sea during 1975. Required by international treaty to declare details of the vessel's complement, the USSR described the new fighters as 'Yak-36s', leading to some confusion among Western analysts until 1984, when East European magazines began to use the type's correct Yak-38 designation.

Powered by a single 68-kN (15,300-lb) Soyuz/Tumanskii R27V-300 turbojet with twin rotating nozzles, the Yak-38 also has a pair of 30-kN (6,725-lb) Koliesov/Rybinsk RD-36-35FVR lift jets mounted in tandem immediately aft of the cockpit. Initially capable of VTOL operation only, the perfection of an automatic landing system allowed rolling take-offs, with the lift jets being activated and the rear nozzles being rotated automatically at 'the optimum point in the take-off run'. If the aircraft's height, rate of descent or attitude go outside prescribed limits, the pilot is automatically ejected.

The latest estimates suggest that the Yak-38 is marginally supersonic at altitude, and in the ground attack role has a lo-lo-lo combat radius of about 100 nm (185 km/115 miles) or a hi-lo-hi radius of about 185 nm (335 km/208 miles). For reconnaissance, a maximum range of about 250 nm (460 km/286 miles) is possible, while in the air defence role a one-hour CAP can be mounted 100 nm

In operational terms, the Russian navy's Yakovlev Yak-38 'Forger' suffered from being limited exclusively to vertical take-offs and landings, and from having to drag about two unused and heavy lift engines during conventional forward flight.

(185 km/115 miles) out from the ship. Up to four pylons can be fitted under the inboard sections of the wing, able to carry a theoretical maximum weapon load of about 2000 kg (4,409 lb), although two pylons are normally left empty. Yak-38s have been seen carrying UB-16-57 and UB-32-57 rocket pods, R60 (AA-8 'Aphid') AAMs, bombs of up to 500 kg (1,102 lb), and various cannon pods. Auxiliary fuel tanks can be carried by some modernised and late production aircraft, which bear the designation **Yak-38M**.

The Yak-38's unique operating and handling characteristics made the construction of a two-seat trainer essential. The resulting **Yak-38U** has tandem cockpits under separate sideways-hinging canopies, with the longer nose having a pronounced 'droop'. Improve-

ments during service included the provision of auxiliary blow-in doors in the sides of the main intakes, and fore-and-aft fences on each side of the upper fuselage intake for the lift jets. The basic colour scheme worn by these aircraft is also changing. The dark green anti-corrosion paint used on the undersides is retained, but the dark blue topsides are giving way to grey upper surfaces. Production of the **'Forger'** was limited to about 90 aircraft, and of these 37 are known to have been lost,

resulting in 32 ejections (19 automatic), all of which were successful. When deployed, each carrier had a squadron with 12 single-seaters and two twin-stickers. Reports that the Yak-38 has been retired from service or permanently withdrawn from deck operations are almost certainly premature since, although *Minsk* and *Novorossiysk* are being mothballed, another of the 'Kiev'-class carriers (*Gorshkov*, formerly *Baku*) remains in service and *Kiev* itself is under repair.

Yakovlev Yak-40

Designed in the early 1960s as a feederliner to replace Lisunov Li-2s (Soviet-built DC-3s), the **Yakovlev Yak-40** was required to operate from grass airfields or semi-prepared strips. The resulting aircraft has high-lift lightly-loaded wings and, for added safety, three- rather than two-engined powerplant. In configuration, the Yak-40 is a cantilever low-wing monoplane with retractable tricycle landing gear, rear-mounted engines and with accommodation for a flight crew of two or three and up to 32 passengers. The provision of a ventral rear door with airstair makes it possible to operate the Yak-40 from airfields with minimum facilities, and an onboard auxiliary power unit makes the type independent of ground equipment for engine starting and the maintenance of cabin heating and air-conditioning. The first flight of

the prototype was made on 21 October 1966, the type entering revenue service with Aeroflot on 30 September 1968. When production ended in 1976 over 800 had been built. The majority of these are still in service in 1993, with both military and civilian operators The type has the NATO reporting name **'Codling'**. In conjunction with Skorost, Yakovlev is now offering the **Yak-40TL** conversion. This entails replacing the three existing Ivchenko AI-25engines, with two 31.14-kN (7,000-lb) Textron-Lycoming LF 507-1N turbofans. This results in an improved cruising sped, better hot-and-high performance and a substantial lowering of operating costs.

Specification
Type: short-range transport
Powerplant: three 14.7-kN (3,300-lb)

The diminutively-engined Yak-40 entered service with Aeroflot in 1968 and since then has been widely exported, for a Soviet-built type.

thrust Ivchenko AI-25 turbofans
Performance: maximum cruising speed 550 km/h (342 mph) at 7000 m (22,965 ft); range with maximum payload 1450 km (901 miles)
Weights: empty 9400 kg (20,723 lb);

maximum take-off 16000 kg (35,274 lb)
Dimensions: span 25.00 m (82 ft 0¼ in); length 20.36 m (66 ft 9½ in); height 6.50 m (21 ft 3¾ in); wing area 70.00 m² (753.50 sq ft)

Yakovlev Yak-42

With an Aeroflot requirement for a medium-range transport to replace Ilyushin Il-18s and Tupolev Tu-134s in service, Yakovlev sought to reduce the development time-scale by evolving a larger-capacity version of the Yak-40. Three prototypes were built, the first with 11° wing sweep and the other two with 23° sweep, this latter angle being chosen for production aircraft that became designated **Yakovlev Yak-42**. This type also differs from the Yak-40 by having all-swept tail surfaces, twin wheels on each landing gear unit and, of course, more-powerful engines. Early production aircraft entered Aeroflot service in late 1980, these having a single passenger cabin seating a maximum of 120 passengers. An alternative 100-passenger local-service layout is available, and certification of a 'stretched' 140-passenger version is believed to be imminent. The entire accommodation is pressurised, and there is provision for convertible passenger/cargo interiors. The type has the NATO reporting name **'Clobber'**.

Built at Smolensk, the Yak-42

entered Aeroflot service on the Moscow-Krasnodor route in late 1980 as a Tu-134 replacement. By early 1993 almost 100 had been delivered, largely to Aeroflot. Subsequent versions include the **Yak-42D**, with an increased fuel load. The **Yak-42E-LL** engine testbed was exhibited at the 1991 Paris air show, fitted with a ZMKB Progress D-236 propfan in place of its starboard engine. A survey version, the **Yak-42F**, carries two large pods

underwing, believed to house electro-optical sensors. Currently, Yakovlev is working on the **Yak-42M**; based on the existing design, it features a lengthened fuselage, supercritical wings with 'winglets', three engines (mounted in the style of the DC-10), and an EFIS cockpit. Prototype construction began in 1991, with serious production slated to commence in 1995.

Specification
Type: medium-range transport
Powerplant: three 63.74-kN (14,330-lb) thrust Lotarev D-36 turbofans

Performance: maximum cruising speed 810 km/h (503 mph); range with maximum payload 900 km (559 miles)
Weights: empty 28960 kg (63,845 lb); maximum take-off 53500 kg (117,947 lb)
Dimensions: span 34.20 m (112 ft 2 in); length 36.38 m (119 ft 4¼ in); height 9.80 m (32 ft 1 in); wing area 150.00 m² (1,614.64 sq ft)

A scaled-up and swept-wing Yak-40, the Yakovlev Yak-42 took a considerable period to develop, but is still an important part of the company's future plans.

Yakovlev Yak-41 'Freestyle'
to
Zmaj aircraft

Yakovlev Yak-41 'Freestyle'

The **Yak-41** was developed as a supersonic replacement for the Yak-38 for service aboard the Soviet navy's 'Kiev'-class carriers. Development began during 1975. Spotted by a Western satellite at Zhukhovsky during the mid-1980s, the new (and still unflown) aircraft was assigned the reporting name **'Ram-T'** before the standard reporting name **'Freestyle'** was revealed in 1988. The first of two flying prototypes (in addition to two static test airframes) made its maiden flight in March 1989, in the hands of Chief Test Pilot Andrei Sinitsin, under the bureau designation **Yak-141**. If it enters service, the designation Yak-41 will be used.

As funding problems worsened Yakovlev attempted to demonstrate their aircraft's performance, and OKB Designer General, A. N. Dondukov, announced that the aircraft would attempt to set a series of FAI records for V/STOL types. Twelve such records (all previously held by the Harrier or AV-8B) were seized during 1991, including maximum altitudes of 13100 m (42,979 ft) with a 1000-kg (2,204-lb) payload and a 2000-kg (4,409-lb) payload, various times to height with the same loads and a peak vertical climb rate record of 15000 m (49,213 ft) per minute.

The flight test programme progressed smoothly (apart from some early recirculation problems) until October 1991, when the second prototype, coded '77', was badly damaged in a landing accident on board the *Gorshkov*. The rear fuselage suffered damage from an engine fire, and the forward fuselage was reportedly damaged when the pilot ejected. It was at one time suggested that it would be rebuilt as the prototype **Yak-41M**, but this was not funded. At the same time, funding was cut back, and the Soviet navy expressed its reservations about the aircraft's 'technical and tactical characteristics'. Yakovlev bravely vowed to continue development, but was forced to abandon completion of the first two-seater. The first prototype ('48') was put into storage until shortly before the September 1992 Farnborough SBAC show, where it emerged with the new code '141'.

The **Yak-141** is powered by a single 152-kN (34,150-lb st) Koptychenko

In the Yak-141, the Yakovlev bureau have developed the world's first supersonic V/STOL combat aircraft, but the practical operational problems involved in the project call any further serious development into question.

R-79V-300 lift-cruise engine. The engine produces about 20 per cent less thrust in the hover mode. The main nozzle can be rotated through 95° to give some forward thrust for braking or to move backwards in the hover. The main engine is augmented by a pair of 39-kN (8,767-lb) Rybinsk/Kuznetsov RD-41 (also quoted as RD-36) lift jets mounted in tandem, inclined about 15° aft. To help in the transition to forward flight the nozzles can be vectored further aft to about 24°, and to give thrust braking can be angled forward to 2°. Retractable intake and exhaust doors are located above and below the fuselage immediately behind the cockpit.

To minimise recirculation of exhaust gases (which dramatically reduces thrust) twin strakes are fitted under the fuselage, along with retractable airdams. Longitudinal control in the hover is achieved entirely by differential thrust, and the usual 'puffer jets' are not fitted. Directional (yaw) control is achieved using sideways-looking air bleed ejectors in the tailcones, while roll control relies on 'puffer jets' in the wingtips. The location of the main nozzle between the deep, titanium-shrouded tailbooms allows the nozzle to be located closer to the aircraft's centre of gravity (without the thrust losses inherent in a bifurcated exhaust) and also reduces the aircraft's IR signature from most aspects.

A short take-off is achieved by rotating the nozzle of the main engine to 65° during the take-off roll, simultaneously increasing the thrust of the lift jets. An even shorter take-off roll (a claimed 5 m/16.4 ft) can be achieved by rotating the nozzle to 65° before take-off. Because afterburner is used during such short take-offs, runway surfaces can suffer heat damage. For this reason steel matting is usually used in preference to a concrete runway.

The 'Freestyle's' controls are actuated by a triplex full-authority digital FBW control system with mechanical backup. Yakovlev claims that this gives a level

of agility broadly comparable with that enjoyed by the MiG-29 but, in fact, manoeuvrability is considerably less impressive, although the main engine can be vectored in forward flight (VIFFed) to reduce turn radius or make an unpredictable change in the plane of flight. Harrier operators have found VIFFing to be a valuable combat technique, although it does have the disadvantage of killing energy at an alarming rate, and must be used with caution.

The Yak-141 is claimed to have 'the same radar as the MiG-29', but whether this means the elderly NO-19 of the basic 'Fulcrum' or the NO-10 of the MiG-29M is uncertain. The aircraft also features a laser/TV target designator, a helmet-mounted sighting system, and avionics systems similar to the MiG-29 and Su-27. Four underwing weapons pylons are provided, all of them inboard of the wing fold, and a fifth pylon is provided under the centre fuselage. This can carry a 2000-litre (440-Imp gal) conformal fuel tank. The second prototype flew with AA-10 'Alamo' and AA-11 'Archer' missiles underwing during its ill fated carrier trials, but other weapons can be carried, including the Vympel AAM-AE 'Amraamski' and a variety of guided ASMs, free-fall bombs and rocket pods, up to a limit of 2600 kg (5,732 lb). Provision is made under the port side of the fuselage for a single GSh-30-1 30-mm cannon, with 120-rounds of ammunition.

The Yak-141 is equipped with a lightweight version of the Zvezda K-36V ejection seat, which can be actuated by the pilot or by an auto-eject system similar to that used by the Yak-38. This incorporates a variable nozzle on the second stage rocket for use in low altitude or unusual attitude escapes.

Following Operation Desert Storm, Yakovlev began studies of a redesigned

Yak-141, hoping to produce a land-based STOL fighter of the kind which might have been able to operate from Iraqi airfields even after coalition air attacks. This, it was hoped, would appeal to the Russian air force. The new version would have a new, more powerful version of the R-79 engine, a strengthened undercarriage and uprated brakes (to allow a shorter 120-m/394-ft landing run), and increased internal fuel capacity. The wing is redesigned to be trapezoidal in shape, like that of the YF-22, and the LERXes are extended forward to the intake lips. A wraparound windscreen and bubble canopy would also be added.

Funding difficulties have led Yakovlev to seek international partners for further development of all variants of the aircraft, discussing the project with Indian and South African aerospace companies, and perhaps with China and Abu Dhabi.

Specification
Yakovlev Yak-141 'Freestyle'
Type: V/STOL fighter
Powerplant: one MNPK 'Soyuz' R-79V-300 rated at 107.67 kN (24,206 lb st) dry and 152.00 kN (34,171 lb st) with afterburning, and two RKBM RD-41 each rated at 41.78 kN (9,392 lb st) dry
Performance: maximum level speed: 'clean' at 11000 m (36,090 ft) 1800 km/h (971 kt; 1,118 mph); range: 1,133 nm (2100 km/ 1,305 miles) after STO with drop tanks or 755 nm (1400 km/ 870 miles) after VTO with internal fuel; service ceiling: more than 15000 m (49,215 ft)
Weights: maximum take-off 19500 kg (42,989 lb) for STO
Dimensions: span 10.10 m (33 ft 1¾ in); width folded 5.90 m (19 ft 4¼ in); length 18.30 m (60 ft 0 in); height 5.00 m (16 ft 5 in)

Yatsenko I-28

Vladimir Yatsenko designed in 1938 a single-seat fighter, and authorisation for the construction of two prototypes under the designation **I-28** was given in August of that year. A cantilever low-wing monoplane of mixed construction, the I-28 had a wing of inverted-gull configuration to keep the retractable main landing gear units as short as possible, enclosed accommodation for the pilot beneath a rear-sliding canopy, and a 708-kW (950-hp) M-87 radial engine. Flown in the spring of 1939, this prototype was lost during

official testing in mid-year. An order was issued for 30 production aircraft plus a single prototype of an attack version designated **I-28Sh**, but only five of the production I-28s were completed before the programme was cancelled in early 1940. As powered by an 820-kW (1,100-hp) M-87B engine, the second I-28 prototype had a maximum speed of 421 km/h (262 mph) at sea level.

Though not readily apparent in this illustration of the first aircraft, the Yatsenko I-28 had a very long-chord cowling that covered the M-87 radial engine.

Yermolayev Yer-2

Designed by V. G. Yermolayev, previously a member of the design team concerned with the STAL series of aircraft, the **DB-240** long-range bomber prototype was flown for the first time in June 1940. A second prototype followed in September, by which time preparations for mass production at Voronezh were in hand, but the German invasion led to evacuation of the factory in July 1941, by which time 128 examples of the DB-240 had been delivered under the designation **Yermolayev Yer-2**. An all-metal mid-wing monoplane of inverted gull-wing configuration and with a twin fin-and-rudder tail unit, the Yer-2 had tailwheel landing gear, the main units retracting into the nacelles of its two M-105 engines; accommodation was provided for a crew of four.

By the autumn of 1941 the Yer-2 was in action with two air regiments, making attacks as far distant as Berlin and Konigsberg, but the need for increased

The chief problem with the promising Yermolyayev Yer-2 design was the choice of the main powerplant, this being an example with AM-35 engines.

range led to experiments with AM-35 engines (April 1942) and a modified wing. Following tests with Charomsky diesels, a new version with ACh-30B engines was approved for production in December 1943 at the Yer-2 factory, which was then established in Siberia. Some 300 examples of the **Yer-2/ACh-30B** were built, forming the backbone of the Soviet long-range bombing force; they also incorporated some improvements, including a revised cockpit, a larger-calibre machine-gun in the ventral position and an enlarged bomb bay accommodating three 1000-kg (2,204-lb) bombs. Maximum speed of this version was 446 km/h (277 mph) and its range 5000 km (3,107 miles), but despite this capa-

bility most Yer-2 operations were of necessity carried out at short range on targets behind the front line.

Specification
Yer-2 (first series)
Type: long-range bomber
Powerplant: two 783-kW (1,050-hp) Klimov M-105 Vee piston engines
Performance: maximum speed 491 km/h (305 mph); service ceiling 7000 m

(22,965 ft); range 4000 km (2,485 miles)
Weights: empty equipped 6500 kg (14,330 lb); maximum take-off 11920 kg (26,279 lb)
Dimensions: span 23.00 m (75 ft 5½ in); length 16.34 m (53 ft 7¼ in); wing area 72.00 m² (775.03 sq ft)
Armament: one 12.7-mm (0.5-in) UBT and two 7.7-mm (0.303-in) ShKAS machine-guns, plus a bombload of up to 1000 kg (2,204 lb)

Yokosuka aircraft

The Imperial Japanese Navy's First Naval Air Technical Arsenal at Yokosuka was concerned primarily with research and the design of aircraft for the navy. It also constructed prototypes of its designs, but in the majority of cases production versions of these aircraft were built by established manufacturers. After the construction of several experimental floatplanes, Yokosuka developed the **Rogo-Ko**, a two-seat reconnaissance biplane on floats powered by a 149-kW (200-hp) Hispano-Suiza engine; between 1917-20 218 were built, the majority by Aichi and Nakajima. Development of the **Igo-Ko** training biplane resulted in the construction of 70 during 192-22. There followed the **Yokosuka K1Y1** biplane, which entered service in 1924 as the **Navy Type 13 Training Seaplane**, being complemented by the slightly improved **K1Y2** in 1928. Resembling the Avro 504, the **Yokosuka K2Y** was flown in 1929 and adopted as the **Navy Type 3 Primary Trainer**, built to a total of 360 in **K2Y1** and **K2Y2** versions by 1940. The following trainer was the **Yokosuka K4Y** tested in 1930 and which, as the **Navy Type 90 Primary Trainer Seaplane**, was built to a total of 209 by 1940. The last, and by far the most important of the Yokosuka-designed trainers, was the **Yokosuka K5Y1**, first flown during December 1933. Adopted in January 1934 as the Navy Type 93 Intermediate

An indifferent aircraft, the B4Y1 was a three-seat carrier attack bomber which saw service during the 1930s, and provided weapons training during World War II.

This is the prototype of the E14Y series. Trials revealed that the tail area was wholly insufficient, and production aircraft thus had a revised vertical tail with a detachable upper portion.

Trainer, it was built to a total of 5,770 by the end of the Pacific war, being allocated the Allied codename **'Willow'**. Built in three versions, with float and wheel landing gear, the 11.00-m (36-ft 1-in) span K5Y1 with a 254-kW (340-hp) Hitachi Amakaze radial engine had a maximum speed of 212 km/h (132 mph).

In the reconnaissance aircraft category, Yokosuka designed in the mid-1920s a twin-float seaplane of biplane configuration which, powered by a 298-kW (400-hp) Lorraine engine, was adopted for production as the **Navy Type 14 Reconnaissance Seaplane (Yokosuka E1Y1)**. Built to a total of 320 from 1925 to 1934, this number included several variants, including the **E1Y2-C** developed into the **Yokosuka E5Y1**, a three-seat reconnaissance floatplane of which 20 were built as the **Navy Type 90-3 Reconnaissance Seaplane**. In 1929 Yokosuka designed and built a prototype plus minor production **Yokosuka E6Y1** light twin-float seaplanes which had the official designation **Navy Type 91 Light Reconnaissance Seaplane**. Of biplane configuration, the E6Y1 was designed for easy stowage in a deck hangar aboard navy submarines, but more significant in this last category was the **Yokosuka E14Y1**, built to a total of 126 as the **Navy Type 0 Small Reconnaissance Seaplane**. Used aboard ocean-going submarines

of the Japanese fleet, these aircraft made some notable flights: one from the submarine *I-7* made a post-attack assessment of damage at Pearl Harbor, and that carried by *I-25* was the only heavier-than-air craft to drop bombs on the USA during World War II. In 1934 the staff of the Yokosuka Navy Arsenal turned their hand to the design of a twin-engined flying-boat, the **Yokosuka H5Y** powered by two 895-kW (1,200-hp) Mitsubishi Shinten 21 radial engines. Although built to a total of 20 during 1936-40 as the **Navy Type 99 Flying-Boat**, its performance was disappointing and, consequently, was deployed only on second-line duties.

Yokosuka designers had rather more success in the attack bomber and medium bomber class, beginning with the rather indifferent **Yokosuka B3Y1**, of which 129 were built during 1933-34 as the **Navy Type 92 Carrier Attack Bomber**. The **Yokosuka B4Y1** three-seat carrier attack bomber was designed to meet a

requirement of 1934, the evaluation of five prototypes with different powerplant being followed by 205 production aircraft built during 1937-38. Designated officially as the **Navy Type 96 Carrier Attacker**, these aircraft were used as advanced trainers after Pearl Harbor but, as the Allies believed they were still in first-line service, the type was allocated the codename **'Jean'**. The last aircraft in this bomber category was the **Yokosuka D3Y** two-seat bomber trainer powered by a 1163-kW (1,560-hp) Mitsubishi Kinsei 62 radial engine. Basically of all-wood construction to save strategic materials, only two prototypes and three production aircraft were built under the official designation **Navy Type 99 Bomber Trainer Myojo** (Venus).

The Yokosuka H5Y was intended to complement the four-engined Kawanishi H6K, but proved radically underpowered with only two 895-kW (1,200-hp) engines.

Yokosuka D4Y Suisei

In late 1938 the First Naval Air Technical Arsenal at Yokosuka was instructed to design a single-engined carrier-based bomber, an aircraft in this category being required urgently by the Imperial Japanese Navy. The resulting **D4Y1** prototype was a low/mid-wing cantilever monoplane of all-metal construction with retractable tailwheel landing gear, accommodating a crew of two in tandem beneath a continuous transparent canopy; it was equipped for carrier operations and an internal bomb bay was incorporated in the fuselage structure, this having the volume to accommodate a single bomb of up to 500-kg (1,102-lb) weight. Intended powerplant was a licence-built version of the Daimler-Benz DB601A, but as this Japanese-built Aichi Atsuta was not available in time an imported DB600G of 716 kW (960 hp) was installed in each of the early prototypes. Although the DB600G had an output some 20 per cent below the expected rating of the Atsuta, performance exceeded all expectations until service trials revealed weakness in the wing structure. As a result the first production version, **the Navy Type 2 Carrier Reconnaissance Plane Model 11 Suisei** (comet) (**Yokosuka D4Y1-C**), had structural requirements far less demanding than a dive-bomber, and initial production deliveries were made in the autumn of 1942.

Wing reinforcement and improved dive brakes led to production of the **Navy Suisei Carrier Bomber Model 11 (D4Y1)** in March 1943 and within a year some 500 had entered service. Deployed in June 1944 against Allied amphibious attacks on the Mariana group of islands, the Suiseis

The Yokosuka D4Y Suisei was a useful reconnaissance/bomber type, but suffered from inadequate armour protection.

operating from Japanese carriers were mauled severely by Allied fighters, lack of armour protection and self-sealing fuel tanks making them vulnerable even to small-calibre weapons. Built in many versions to a total of 2,038, the majority by Aichi, all were allocated the Allied codename 'Judy'.

Variants
D4Y1 prototypes: five, powered by imported 716-kW (960-hp) Daimler-Benz DB600G engines; armament of two forward-firing 7.7-mm (0.303-in) and one rear-firing 7.92-mm (0.31-in) machine-guns
D4Y1 pre-production: generally as prototypes but with a 895-kW (1,200-hp) Aichi AEIA Atsuta 32 engine
D4Y1-C: reconnaissance version of D4Y1 with camera in rear fuselage and armament as prototypes
D4Y1 Suisei: initial dive-bomber production version, similar to prototypes but with strengthened structure and improved dive brakes
D4Y1 Kai: as D4Y1 Suisei but equipped for catapult launching
D4Y2: improved version introducing AEIP Atsuta 32 engine; armament as prototypes
D4Y2a: as D4Y2, but rear-mounted 7.92-mm (0.31-in) machine-gun replaced by one of 13-mm (0.51-in) calibre
D4Y2-C: reconnaissance version of D4Y2
D4Y2a-C: reconnaissance version of D4Y2a

D4Y2 Kai: designation of D4Y2 with catapult launch points
D4Y2a Kai: designation of D4Y2a with catapult launch points
D4Y2-S: night-fighter conversion of D4Y2, bomb racks, rear firing and carrier equipment removed; bomb bay sealed; single 20-mm cannon mounted obliquely in fuselage to fire upwards and forwards, and some equipped also with air-to-air rockets
D4Y3: generally as D4Y2 but powered by 1163-kW (1,560-hp) Mitsubishi MK8P Kinsei radial engine
D4Y3a: as above, but with armament of D4Y2a
D4Y4: single-seat *kamikaze* attack version of D4Y3; standard forward-firing guns and one 800-kg (1,764-lb) bomb

Specification
Yokosuka D4Y2
Type: single-seat carrier-based dive-bomber
Powerplant: one 1044-kW (1,400-hp) Aichi Atsuta 32 inverted-Vee piston engine
Performance: maximum speed 550 km/h (342 mph) at 4750 m (15,585 ft); service ceiling 10700 m (35,105 ft); range 1465 km (910 miles)
Weights: empty 2440 kg (5,379 lb); maximum take-off 4250 kg (9,370 lb)
Dimensions: span 11.50 m (37 ft 8¾ in); length 10.22 m (33 ft 6 in); height 3.74 m (12 ft 3 in); wing area 23.60 m² (254.04 sq ft)
Armament: two 7.7-mm (0.303-in) forward-firing and one 7.92-mm (0.31-in) rear-firing machine-guns, plus a bomb load of up to 800 kg (1,765 lb)

Yokosuka MXY7 Ohka

The **Yokosuka MXY7 Ohka** (cherry blossom) epitomises the desperate measures taken by Japan in an attempt to defend its homeland, being envisaged as a rocket-propelled piloted aircraft with a 1200-kg (2,646-lb) high-explosive warhead in the nose. To be carried and launched from a 'mother' aircraft, the Ohka was designed to glide as far as possible before making a final high-speed approach under rocket power to impact on its target. Design emphasis was to make the aircraft simple to build, using non-strategic materials, and very easy to fly.

Early unpowered prototypes were tested in October 1944, the first powered flight being made during the following month, but even before these trials had been made the MXY7 had entered production as the **Navy Suicide Attacker Ohka Model 11**. A total of 755 was built by March 1945, and this version was the only one to see operational service. The type's ini-

tial deployment, carried into action by 16 Mitsubishi G4M2e aircraft, was little short of disastrous, all the 'mother' planes being destroyed by Allied fighters and the Ohkas being released uselessly short of their intended targets. Limited success came later when, for example, the American destroyer USS *Mannert L. Abele* was sunk by a direct hit on 12 April 1945. By then, however, production of the Ohka Model 11 had been terminated for it was realised that the launch vehicle was too slow and vulnerable. An unpowered water-ballasted version known as the **Ohka K-1** (45 built) was developed for training purposes, the water being jettisoned to reduce landing speed.

Subsequent attempts to give the weapon greater capability resulted in the **Ohka Model 22** with reduced span and a lighter warhead, necessitated by the intention to launch it from the much-faster Yokosuka P1Y1 Ginga. The Ohka Model 22 dispensed with the

rocket, which was replaced by a TSU-11 jet engine with a 75-kW (100-hp) four-cylinder piston-engine compressor, but tests showed it to be underpowered. Only one other version was built, the **Ohka Model 43 K-1 Kai** two-seat trainer, which had flaps and extendable skids for landing and a single rocket to give some experience under power.

Specification
Yokosuka MXY7 Model 11
Type: single-seat suicide attack aircraft
Powerplant: three Type 4 Mk 1 solid-propellant rockets with a combined thrust of 800 kg (1,765 lb)
Performance: maximum speed 650

A design borne of utter but faithful desperation was the Yokosuka MXY7 Ohka kamikaze aircraft, which could have proved totally devastating had the type's motherplanes been able to approach undisturbed to within launch range of their targets. This is a turbojet-powered Model 22.

km/h (404 mph); range 37 km (23 miles)
Weights: empty 440 kg (970 lb); maximum launch 2140 kg (4,718 lb)
Dimensions: span 5.12 m (16 ft 9½ in); length 6.07 m (19 ft 11 in); height 1.16 m (3 ft 9¾ in); wing area 6.00 m² (64.59 sq ft)

Yokosuka P1Y Ginga

Requiring a fast medium bomber for dive-bombing, low-altitude bombing or torpedo attack, the Imperial Japanese Navy instructed the Yokosuka First Naval Air Technical Arsenal in 1940 to begin design of such an aircraft. The resulting **Yokosuka P1Y** prototype flown in August 1943 was a mid-wing, all-metal monoplane, powered by two Nakajima NK9B Homare 11 radial engines. Its performance was satisfac-

tory, but the P1Y suffered from maintenance problems that plagued its service life. All remedial attempts failed, delaying until early 1945 the entry into service of the **Navy Bomber Ginga Model 11**. Production totalled 1,098, built by Kawanishi (96) and Nakajima (1,002), and if there had been adequate manpower to service these aircraft before each operational sortie they would have proved formidable adver-

saries. This was not possible and as a result the Ginga (Milky Way), allocated the Allied codename **'Francis'**, was tried unsuccessfully in a variety of alternative roles; its brief operational life of only six months was terminated by the end of the Pacific war.

Variants
P1Y (prototypes): six, with Nakajima NK9B Homare 11 engines; armament of one 7.7-mm (0.303-in) forward-firing machine-gun and one rear-firing 20-mm cannon

P1Y1 Ginga: initial production version; as P1Y but forward-firing machine-gun replaced by 20-mm cannon
P1Y1a: production version with 1361-kW (1,825-hp) Nakajima NK9C Homare 12 engines, 20-mm cannon in nose and one 13-mm (0.51-in) rear-firing machine-gun
P1Y1b: production version as P1Y1a, but with two 13-mm (0.51in) rear-firing machine-guns
P1Y1c: production version as P1Y1b, but nose cannon replaced by third 13-mm (0.51-in) machine-gun

P1Y1-S: night-fighter conversions of P1Y1; four obliquely-mounted 20-mm cannon firing forward and upward, plus one rear-firing 13-mm (0.51-in) gun
P1Y2-S: production night-fighter with two 1380-kW (1,850-hp) Mitsubishi MK4T-A Kasei 25a radials; armament of three 20-mm cannon, two obliquely-mounted and one rear-firing
P1Y2: production bomber; powerplant as P1Y2-S, armament as P1Y1
P1Y2a: production bomber as P1Y2 but with armament of P1Y1A
P1Y2b: production bomber as P1Y2 but with armament of P1Y1b
P1Y2c: production bomber as P1Y2 but with armament of P1Y1c

In common with other Japanese aircraft designed hurriedly during the run-up to Japan's entry into World War II, the P1Y Ginga was potentially formidable, but plagued by development and maintenance problems. This seriously delayed its debut.

Specification
Yokosuka P1Y1 Ginga
Type: medium-bomber
Powerplant: two 1357-kW (1,820-hp) Nakajima Homare 11 radial piston engines
Performance: maximum speed 547 km/h (340 mph) at 5900 m (19,355 ft); service ceiling 9400 m (30,840 ft); maximum range 5370 km (3,337 miles)
Weights: empty 7265 kg (16,017 lb); maximum take-off 13500 kg (29,762 lb)
Dimensions: span 20.00 m (65 ft 7½ in); length 15.00 m (49 ft 2 in); height 4.30 m (14 ft 1 in); wing area 55.00 m² (592.03 sq ft)
Armament: two 20-mm cannon (one forward- and one rear-firing), plus a bomb load of up to 1000 kg (2,205 lb), or one 800-kg (1,764-lb) torpedo

Zeppelin-Staaken R series

Soon after the beginning of World War I, Count von Zeppelin initiated the development of heavy bombers which he could foresee would be of great importance to the nation's war effort. The design of landplane versions began under the leadership of Professor Baumann, the first of them being the Zeppelin-Staaken **V.G.O.I** which established a basic layout and size for the remainder of these giant aircraft. With biplane wings, a slab-sided fuselage and biplane tail unit, the V.G.O.I was supported on the ground by fixed tailskid-type landing gear whose main units had multiple wheels, plus two more wheels beneath the nose. Initial powerplant of the V.G.O.I comprised three 179-kW (240-hp) Maybach Mb.IV engines, one in a nacelle between the wings and one on each side of the fuselage and one in the nose. First flown on 11 April 1915, the V.G.O.I was found to be underpowered and was re-engined subsequently with five similar Maybach engines, each nacelle containing two engines in tandem, but crashed under test.

A series of one-offs followed, the **V.G.O.II** with three engines being similar to the V.G.O.I. The **V.G.O.III** introduced six 119-kW (160-hp) Mercedes D.III engines, two in each nacelle and two side-by-side in the nose. The fourth aircraft, of the same six-engined layout but with 164-kW (220-hp) Benz Bz.IV engines in the nacelles and Mercedes D.IIIs in the nose, was identified as the **R.IV**, the first of the series to have the R (*Riesenflugzeug*, or giant aircraft) designation. The **R.V** reverted to use of the 179-kW (240-hp) Maybach Mb.IV

The Zeppelin-Staaken R.IV spanned 42.20 m (138 ft 5½ in), had an all-up weight of 13035 kg (28,737 lb) and possessed a maximum speed of 125 km/h (78 mph). Defensive armament was six or seven 7.92-mm (0.31-in) parabellum machine-guns.

engine (five of them being installed), but the production **R.VI**, of which the first was delivered in June 1917, had four more-powerful engines and eliminated the powerplant from the fuselage nose. R.VI production totalled 18, one being built by the company and the remainder under sub-contract by Aviatik (six), Ostdeutsche Albatros Werke (four) and Schutte-Lanz (seven). They were followed into production in 1918 by the similar **R.XIV** (three aircraft) and **R.XV** (three aircraft), both versions having five Maybach Mb.IV engines. An advanced four-engined version developed by Aviatik, with one 164-kW (220-hp) Bz.IVa and engine in each nacelle, was allocated the designation **R.XVI (Av)**; three were to have been built but only one was completed before the end of the war. Variants included the single **R.VII** which differed from the R.IV by having two Mercedes D.IIIs in the nose and four Benz Bz.IVs in the nacelles; the **Type**

The R.XV was the ultimate development of the Zeppelin-Staaken R series, and had the standard span of 42.20 m (138 ft 5 ½ in), a maximum take-off weight of 14450 kg (31,856 lb) and a top speed of 130 km/h (81 mph). Armament was six machine-guns.

L twin-float seaplane with four 194-kW (260-hp) Mercedes D.IVa engines; and three **Type 8301** twin-float seaplanes which had the same powerplant but introduced an entirely new fuselage. Post-war one more 'giant' was completed, the **E.4/20** designed by Dipl. Ing. Adolf Rohrbach. This differed considerably from the wartime series, being a high-wing monoplane powered by four 183-kW (245-hp) Maybach engines. It accommodated a crew of two in an open cockpit and the cabin, to which access was gained through a hinged nose section, seated 18 passengers. Tested in the autumn of 1920, it was banned by the Allied Control Commission and was scrapped two years later.

Specification
Zeppelin-Staaken R.VI
Type: seven-crew heavy bomber
Powerplant: four 183-kW (245-hp) Maybach Mb.IV or 194-kW (260-hp) Mercedes D.IVa inline piston engines
Performance: maximum speed 135 km/h (84 mph); service ceiling 4320 m (14,175 ft); maximum duration 10 hours
Weights: empty 7921 kg (17,463 lb); maximum take-off 11848 kg (26,120 lb)
Dimensions: span 42.20 m (138 ft 5½ in); length 22.10 m (72 ft 6 in); height 6.30 m (20 ft 8 in); wing area 332.00 m² (3,573.74 sq ft)
Armament: four 7.92-mm (0.31-in) Parabellum machine-guns, plus a maximum short-range bomb load of 2000 kg (4,409 lb)

Zlin aircraft

Developed from the Zlin 381, the Zlin 22 introduced side-by-side seating in a large cockpit.

Founded in 1935, the Czech Zlinska Letecka Akciova Spolecnost was a subsidiary of the well-known Bata Shoe Company. Its first product was the wooden **Zlin XII** two-seater, a low-wing monoplane powered by a 34-kW (45-hp) Persy II engine and available in both open and cabin versions. The following **Zlin XIII** was also a two-seater of similar configuration, but with an enclosed cabin and a 97-kW (130-hp) Walter Minor engine. The **Zlin XV** of 1939 had a 78-kW (105-hp) Zlin Toma 4 engine and was available in open or closed cockpit variants. The **Zlin 212**, adopting a new designation, was a cabin trainer development of the Zlin XII with a Walter Mikron engine.

During the closing stages of World War II, the Zlin factory at Otrokovice

opened a production line for the Bucker Bu 181 Bestmann and its Hirth engine, with manufacture continuing post-war as the **Zlin 181**. Around 180 were built, most of which went to the Czechoslovakian air force as trainers under the designation **C-6**. The factory changed its name to Moravan postwar, but the name Zlin was retained as part of the aircraft designation.

The next development was the **Zlin 281**, with the 78-kW (105-hp) Toma 4 engine, of which about 100 were built for the civil market. Production was switched in 1948 to the **Zlin 381** with the 78-kW (105-hp) Walter Minor III engine; 184 were built, many for the Czech air force as the **C-106**, and 45 went to the Hungarian air force.

Several variants were available, including a tourer, a semi-aerobatic trainer and a fully-aerobatic version, with one Zlin 381 being used to test the 112-kW (150-hp) Praga E engine. Licence-production was undertaken in Egypt as the **Gomhouria Mk 1** with the Walter Minor engine, followed by the **Gomhouria Mk 2** with the 108-kW (145-hp) Continental C-145. Several Egyptian variants followed, production ending in that country in early 1979

after more than 300 had been built, but a programme of refurbishment has been undertaken.

In 1947 Zlin broke away from the tandem-seating layout with the **Zlin 22 Junak**, a wooden monocoque two-seat side-by-side cabin monoplane. The prototype was powered by a 43-kW (57-hp) Persy III, but this engine was discontinued and production aircraft had the 56-kW (75-hp) Praga D, being redesignated **Zlin 22D**. Some 200

Junaks were built before production ended in 1950. A three-seat version, the **Zlin 22M**, had a 78-kW (105-hp) Walter Minor 4-III. Two prototypes were built of the **Zlin 122**, a three/four-seater with a 78-kW (105-hp) Toma 4 engine.

A Czech air force specification for a primary trainer attracted two entrants, the Praga E.112 and **Zlin 26 Trener**; when evaluated in 1948 the Zlin 26 gained the production contract. Of mixed wood and metal construction, it had a 78-kW (105-hp) Walter Minor 4-III engine and was the forerunner of a series of aerobatic monoplanes which brought the company to the forefront in world aerobatic competitions. The Zlin 26, which had the Czech air force designation **C-5**, was superseded in 1953 by the all-metal **Zlin 126 Trener II** with the same engine. It was produced for both home and export markets and was designated **C-105** in air force service. The **Zlin 226** of 1955 had the 119-kW (160-hp) Walter Minor 6-III engine, and was produced initially as the **Z.2226B** glider tug and in the following year as the **Z.226T Trener-6 (C-205)**. Total production reached 252, and this version was supplied to 19 countries. A fully aerobatic single-seat model, the **Z.226A Akrobat**, was built in several versions for home and export markets. Logical development continued with the similarly powered **Z.326 Trener-Master**, flown in prototype form in 1957 and basically a version of the Zlin 226 with retractable landing gear, plus a single-seat aerobatic derivative, the **Z.326A Akrobat**; both models had provision for wingtip fuel tanks. The **Zlin 526**, first flown in 1966, introduced a constant-speed propeller and transferred the main pilot's position to the rear cockpit. There was also a single-seat aerobatic version, the **Z.526A Akrobat**, and a further development of the two-seater was the **Z.526F**, flown in 1968 and certificated in the following year. It had a 134-kW (180-hp) Avia M137A engine as standard but was available with optional powerplant to customer requirement. Final version in the series was the **Zlin 726**, flown in March 1973 and differing in detail, mainly shorter-span wings with a metal-covered rudder and elevators. The **Z.726K** was a more-power-

The Zlin 526 introduced a constant-speed propeller to the successful Trener series.

ful model with a 157-kW (210-hp) Avia M337AK supercharged engine. When production of the Z.26/726 series ended in 1977, a total of 1,452 of all versions had been built.

The series secured a mass of successes in aerobatic competitions between 1957 and 1969, including first placings in the Lockheed Trophy competition held in the UK in 1957, 1958, 1961, 1963, 1964 and 1965, and first in the Leon Biancotto Trophee aerobatic competitions held in France in 1965, 1967 and 1969.

While the Z.26 family concentrated on aerobatic capability, the need for a side-by-side trainer and light tourer led to the **Zlin 42**, flown in prototype form in October 1967. Powered by a 134-kW (180-hp) Avia M137A engine, the Zlin 42 met FAR Pt 23 airworthiness specifications in the aerobatic category and could be used also as a glider tug. A four-seat development, the **Zlin 43**, flew in December 1968 with a 157-kW (210-hp) Avia M337 engine; the two types had an 80 per cent commonality of structural components and both entered production. The series version of the Z.42 was designated **Zlin 42M**, and around 250 were built; the German Democratic Republic was a major customer and others are known to have been supplied to Hungary. A development was the **Zlin 142**, with the same engine as the Zlin 43, construction of this type beginning in 1981 and 350 being delivered by 1993. The type has now been certified in to FAR Pt 23 standard, and by the Canadian Department of Transport. Production of the Zlin 43 began in 1972, but only 80 had been built by early 1977, in which year production seems to have ended. Most recently Zlin, has developed the

Zlin 242, a Lycoming AEIO-360-AIB6-powered version of the 142, intended for the US market.

While the Zlin 26/726 series had been the supreme aerobatic types for some years, it became obvious that a smaller, more-nimble aircraft was needed to challenge new competition, and in 1973 Zlin began design of the **Zlin 50L**, a fully-aerobatic single-seater with a 194-kW (260-hp) Avco Lycoming AEIO540-D4B5 engine. The prototype flew in July 1975 and by the following March two more prototypes and seven production aircraft were flying. In the 1976 World Aerobatic Championships at Kiev, Zlin 50s gained second place in the team event and third in the men's individual competition. Around 80 Z.50Ls were built, including several for export, and a developed version - the **Z.50LS** - was subsequently flown in 1981. Aircraft of this type won the European Aerobatic Championships in 1983, and the World Championships in

Although mainly intended as a light tourer, the Zlin 42 has an aerobatic capability and can also be used for glider towing.

1984 and 1986.The most recent development is the **Z50M**, fitted with an Avia M 137 AZ inline engine and a constant-speed propeller. Production commenced, at a slow rate, in 1989.

Zlin also produces a turbine-engined version of the LET Z-37 Cmelak agricultural aircraft. A previous turboprop version, the XZ37T, was flown by LET with a 515-kW (691-shp) Walter M601B engine in September 1981, but the new Zlin version, to be known as the **Z.137T Agro-Turbo**, has a 362-kW (485-shp) Motorlet M601Z turboprop. Forty-four have been produced so far.

From its introduction in the mid-1970s, the Zlin 50 swept all before it in aerobatic competitions around the world.

Zmaj aircraft

Fabrika Aeroplana I Hidroplana Zmaj was established at Zemun, Yugoslavia, in 1927 and first built Dewoitine D.1 fighters, Gourdou-Leseurre fighter-trainers and Hanriot H.32 landplane and H.41 seaplane trainers under licence. The company's leading designer was Rudolf Fizir, most of his early designs being known by the make of powerplant selected. Among types built between 1927 and 1932 were the **Zmaj Fizir-Maybach**, a basic biplane trainer with a 194-kW (260-hp) Maybach engine; the **Fizir-Wright**, a reconnaissance biplane of which Zmaj built nine during 1929 with the 172-kW (230-hp) Wright Whirlwind radial, and the **Fizir-Lorraine** of 1932 with the 298-kW (400-hp) Lorraine engine and intended for reconnaissance. Also built in 1932 were the **Fizir-Mars** biplane primary trainer twin-float seaplane, powered by the 104-kW (140-hp) Walter Mars radial, and the **Fizir-Jupiter** observation seaplane with a 283-kW (380-hp) Gnome-Rhône Jupiter

engine. Other Fizir designs built by Zmaj during that period included the **Nebojsa** (brave fellow) of 1930, a cabin tourer monoplane with a 119-kW (160-hp) radial engine, and the **A.F.2** light amphibian with a 63-kW (85-hp) Walter Vega radial.

Produced in greater numbers was the **F.P.2**, developed from the earlier **F.P.1** prototype, a biplane trainer powered by a 313-kW (420-hp) Rakovica licence-built Gnome-Rhône K-7 radial. Of all-wooden construction, the F.P.2 entered large-scale production as a basic trainer for Yugoslav military aviation; although the number built by Zmaj is not known, at the time of the German invasion in April 1941 66 were still serviceable at pilot training schools. Several were used subsequently by the Regia Aeronautica and the satellite Croat air arm. The F.P.2 had a wing span of 10.80 m (35 ft 5 in) and a maxi-

Built in large numbers, the Zmaj FN served with Yugoslavian training schools. This example is seen after capture, during World War I, by the Italians.

mum speed of 238 km/h (148 mph). Another important type was the **Zmaj F.N.** light primary trainer biplane, the prototype of which was flown in 1929. It went into quantity production with both Zmaj and Rogozarski, initially with an 89-kW (120-hp) Maybach engine, but the powerplant used in greater numbers was the Walter NZ radial of the same horsepower; an improved F.N., built from 1937, introduced several refinements. Records show that

when Yugoslavia was invaded by Axis forces in 1941, some 140 F.N. biplanes were still in service at Nos 1, 2 and 3 Pilot Training Schools of the army air arm. Some were used later by Croat forces and one is believed to have served later in the war with Yugoslav partisans; one is preserved at the National Air Museum. With a wing span of 10.80 m (35 ft 5 in), the F.N. had a maximum speed of 148 km/h (92 mph).

Index of aircraft by type

927